NRW CASE 24.3   Finance/Management

FUNDS TRANSFERS

The firm is currently concluding negotiations for a very large sale with a retail store that has locations throughout the southwest. The resulting contract should be for an amount in the high six figures. Carlos is willing to let the retailer pay for the orde... check. Helen would prefer that the customer ... either a cashier's check or a certified check. Ma... pointed out that, given the "time value" of mo... the sooner the firm receives the funds, the bett... will be. She thinks that the firm should insist ... wire transfer of the funds as soon as the retaile... ceives the goods. They all agree that the time v... of money is import... ...hey like ...ai's id...

NRW CASE 10.2   Sales/Manufacturing

REVOKING AN OFFER

NRW made a written offer to Joe Daily, one of its suppliers, in which the firm offered to buy Joe's entire supply of microchips at list price. NRW's letter promised to keep the offer open for four weeks. Two weeks after mailing the letter, NRW received an offer from another firm to sell virtually identical microchips to NRW for 20 percent less than Joe's list price. Carlos wants to accept this offer and has asked you whether NRW can revoke the offer to Joe. What will you tell him?

...S CONSIDERATIONS What factors should ...s consider... ...kes a w...en p...

NRW CASE 19.1   Marketing and Sales

ADVERTISING THE PRODUCT

Helen wants to advertise the StuffTrakR extensively on television, with ads showing the product in use and suggesting the benefits and time to be saved through its use. Mai and Carlos agree with Helen in principle, but they suggest that the product should be enhanced somewhat in order to "grab" the viewers and, hopefully, really spur sales. They have suggested some exaggerated examples that could be use... cluding having a StuffTrakR on the family dog. ... scenario, the dog runs off, but the family is a... track it down thanks to the StuffTrakR. The ... mercial ends with the ...ppy family reunited w... pet, and a voic... ...omet...g lik...

NRW CASE 25.1   Management/Finance

SOURCES OF FINANCING

The firm needs a quick infusion of capital, and Mai and Helen would like to have the firm borrow some money for the operation of the business. However, they expect that the bank will want some sort of collateral before making any loan to the firm. Neither Mai nor Helen wants to use her personal assets as security for any credit they receive, but they are not sure that NRW has any assets that can be used to secure the loan. They ask you what assets NRW has that might be useful as collateral for any loans they seek. What will you tell them?

EIGHTH EDITION

Business Law

Principles and Cases in the Legal Environment

Daniel V. Davidson
Radford University

Brenda E. Knowles
Indiana University South Bend

Lynn M. Forsythe
California State University, Fresno

THOMSON
™
SOUTH-WESTERN
WEST

Australia · Canada · Mexico · Singapore · Spain · United Kingdom · United States

THOMSON

SOUTH-WESTERN

WEST

Business Law: Principles and Cases in the Legal Environment, 8th Edition
Daniel V. Davidson, Brenda E. Knowles, and Lynn M. Forsythe

VP/Editorial Director:
Jack W. Calhoun

VP/Editor-in-Chief:
Michael P. Roche

Publisher:
Rob Dewey

Developmental Editor:
Bob Sandman

Marketing Manager:
Steven Silverstein, Esq.

Production Editor:
Emily S. Gross

Manufacturing Coordinator:
Rhonda Utley

Compositor:
Trejo Production

Printer:
Quebecor World Taunton
Taunton, MA

Design Project Manager:
Chris Miller

Internal Designer:
Chris Miller

Cover Designer:
Beckmeyer Design

Cover Photograph:
Getty Images

To my wife and best friend, Dee, and to our children, Jaime and Tara. Thanks to each of you for your love and support.

Daniel V. Davidson

For Paul, Mark, and Vicki, who steadfastly supported me during my numerous travails; and for my four miraculous grandchildren (Kyle, Madelyn, Matt, and Beth), who unfailingly rekindle my sense of wonderment and bring me unbridled joy.

Brenda E. Knowles

In loving memory of my father-in-law, John Poptanich (1921–2000).

To my family for all their love and support, especially Jim, Mike, and Mary Helen Poptanich; and Aileen and Robert Zollweg. And to our colleagues and students, thanks for your ideas and suggestions.

Lynn M. Forsythe

Brief Contents

How to find cases: P. 102

Contents

Preface

A Business-Oriented Business Law Text

Business Law: Principles and Cases in the Legal Environment, Eighth Edition, offers students a business-oriented introduction to the legal and ethical topics that affect business. This perspective may seem obvious. After all, isn't a business law textbook by its very nature oriented toward the practice of business? While it might seem that they should, not all business law textbooks adopt such an orientation. Textbooks that typically teach the law, often clearly and in great detail, can fail to show students how the law will affect their future careers in the business world. Our goal as business law and legal environment instructors is not to train lawyers, but rather to train future businesspeople to anticipate and avoid legal problems. If legal problems arise, it is critical to know how to recognize the nature of these problems and work with a lawyer to achieve solutions. Legal problems, even lawsuits, are business problems that can be managed.

Our strategy in revising this, our eighth, edition is threefold:

• To present, in an accessible style, a current and comprehensive introduction to the legal topics relevant to business

• To demonstrate how these topics apply to the practice of business

• To provide an approach to legal analysis—often termed *critical thinking*—for addressing legal problems encountered in the practice of business

We also support more fully the teaching and learning process associated with using the text. Our association with West Legal Studies in Business allows us to offer a wide array of supplementary materials for instructors and students.

NRW Business Cases

We have included an integrated, continuous business case or scenario. As the NRW case threads throughout the text, the individual features profile the experiences of a hypothetical business, NRW, owned and operated by a "local" group of entrepreneurs known to the students. Each chapter begins with an Agenda that highlights the major legal issues from the chapter that are likely to be relevant to NRW. Within each chapter there are three NRW Application Boxes that address particular legal issues and call for students to offer guidance to the firm. Each application box is categorized by the relevant functional area of business—management, manufacturing, finance and accounting, sales, marketing, international business, and personal law. Finally, application boxes include questions involving Business Considerations, Ethical Considerations, and International Considerations. These questions ask the students to go beyond NRW's problem and to decide how the type of problem faced might affect other business concerns. See page xx for an Overview to the NRW business case.

New Coverage in the Eighth Edition

As we mentioned, our first goal is to present, in an accessible style, a current and comprehensive introduction to the legal topics relevant to business. Toward this goal, the book is divided into 10 parts based on traditional topical areas of undergraduate business law. We have made the following content changes and updates to the eighth edition.

Part 1 Foundations of Law Part 1 presents an overview of law and the legal system. The eighth edition provides extended coverage of ethics and international law topics. In particular, Chapter 1, "Introduction to Law," provides a more detailed discussion of theories of jurisprudence and a new exhibit outlining these theories. Chapter 2, "Business Ethics," has an increased focus on the application of ethical theories in the practice of business, including the introduction and discussion of some additional ethical theories and an exhibit comparing a number of these theories.

Part 2 The American Legal System Part 2 examines the court system and the legal system used in the United States. We have placed the coverage of constitutional regulation of business in this section. This encourages a discussion of fundamental constitutional law principles while maintaining the focus on business and the application of the legal system to business problems and concerns. The material on dispute resolution has been organized into one chapter that is designed to show the similarities and the differences in the various types of dispute resolution. We examine a civil trial and then look at a number of Alternative Dispute Resolution (ADR) approaches to the same problem, including some new material dealing with on-line dispute resolution (ODR). This section concludes with an examination of torts and business crimes, respectively. The criminal law coverage includes computer crimes.

Part 3 Contracts Part 3 examines the primary importance of contract law to business. The chapters contained here have been substantially updated, and there is significant attention paid to e-commerce and its growing importance in the area of contract law. Chapter 9 is an introduction to contracts, discussing contract theories and the various areas included in contract law. Chapter 10 covers offer and acceptance, and Chapter 11 discusses consideration. Chapter 12 deals with voidable contract areas, "Contractual Capacity" and "Reality of Consent," while Chapter 13, "Legality of Subject Matter and Proper Form of Contracts," examines void agreements and unenforceable contracts, respectively. Chapter 14 discusses the rights of third persons and contract interpretation. The contract section ends with Chapter 15, "Contractual Discharge and Remedies."

Part 4 Sales and Leases Part 4, which addresses the law of sales and leases, has been significantly revised. Each of the first three chapters examines aspects of Article 2, the Law of Sales. Each chapter then has some coverage of Article 2A, the Law of Leases, that is compared to the coverage of Article 2. Finally, each of these chapters then compares international sale of goods law, as embodied in the CISG, to the coverage provided by the UCC. "Warranties and Product Liability" has been moved to the final chapter in this part. This relocation is intended to emphasize the potential impact that breach of warranty cases can have on a business, and to highlight the fact that many times breach of warranty cases do not fit into the more traditional areas of business concerns. Rather than reflect a "mere" breach of contract, a breach of warranty may well result in substantial damages, thus making it logical for a businessperson to give separate treatment to this area of law. Part 4 also examines incoterms and ISO 9000, and how each of these areas can affect contracts for the sale of goods in an international setting. There is also a brief discussion of several proposed United Nations conventions that may soon be ratified and that will also affect international sales and other international business transactions.

Part 5 Negotiables Part 5 discusses UCC Articles 3 (Revised), 4 (Revised), 4A, and 7. In addition, it includes a discussion of electronic funds transfers. This new coverage reflects the changes in negotiable instrument law with the revision of Articles 3 and 4 of the UCC.

Part 6 Debtor-Creditor Relations Part 6 examines debtor-creditor relations by looking at three related areas. The first area of coverage involves secured transactions under the newly revised Article 9 of the UCC. The revisions to Article 9 are substantial, and the coverage of this topic is significantly changed to reflect this new, "simplified" treatment. Next is a chapter dealing with "Other Credit Transactions," which looks at the various types of credit that a business may extend to its customers or use in acquiring those assets needed to conduct the business. Included here is a brief look at "payday loans," a relatively new and controversial type of consumer loan. Finally, Part 6 examines the federal protections available under the Bankruptcy Reform Act of 1994. The bankruptcy material has been condensed into one chapter that compares the relief available under Chapters 7, 11, and 13 of the Bankruptcy Reform Act. There is also a short discussion of the proposed new Bankruptcy Reform Act and the possible ramifications if it is enacted by Congress.

Part 7 Agency Part 7 explains the agency relationship and its importance in conducting a business enterprise. Special emphasis is given to the liability of both the principal and the agent for contracts entered into by the agent and to the liability of both the employer and the employee for torts and crimes committed by the employee. Policy reasons for the rules are addressed. Protection of the employer's confidential information and covenants not to compete are also discussed.

Part 8 Business Organizations Part 8 treats the various types of business organizations in a unique manner. Rather than have separate chapters dealing with the various organizations, the text treats the organizations in a compare-and-contrast fashion within the chapters. The emphasis is no longer on how the various types of business organizations should be implemented, but rather on why a particular form should be chosen. The coverage includes an examination of the limited liability company (LLC) and the limited liability partnership (LLP), as well as the traditional business organizations: proprietorship, partnership, limited partnership, and corporation. Coverage of the Revised Uniform Partnership Act is increased, since it has been adopted by more states. We also include thorough discussions of franchising in Chapter 35 and securities regulation in Chapter 36.

Part 9 Government Regulation of Business Part 9 addresses the regulatory issues regularly faced by businesses, including coverage of antitrust law, consumer protection, environmental protection, and labor and fair employment law. Chapter 38, "Consumer Protection," is devoted entirely to consumer law and stresses concepts that relate back to Chapter 27, "Other Credit Transactions," from Part 6. There is also one chapter devoted to environmental law—Chapter 39, "Environmental Protection"—that addresses most of the major environmental statutes. This coverage includes a discussion of some of the policy reasons behind the statutes and the penalties to be faced for violations. The final chapter in this section is "Labor and Fair Employment Practices," a detailed examination of the rights and responsibilities of management and its employees.

Part 10 Property Protection Part 10 examines real and personal property law and "wealth protection." Part 10 also offers updated coverage on intellectual property law. The first chapter in this part discusses real property, government regulation of real property, and the types of joint ownership. Transfer on death ownership is also included in this edition. The second chapter examines personal property and bailments. The third chapter addresses intellectual property, including a discussion of copyright law and of computers and the law. The part and the text conclude with a consideration of techniques for transferring wealth, including wills, estates, and trusts. Recent changes in transfer tax laws are included.

New and Improved Applications

Our second goal for this revision is to demonstrate how the legal topics presented here apply to the practice of business. Toward this goal, *Business Law* offers the following features, many of them unique to this text.

Court Cases

Each chapter contains three court cases primarily in the language of the court. Cases are organized into the following parts:

- Facts—the facts of the case
- Issue(s)—the issues, in the form of questions, on which the decision hinges
- Holding—the court's answer to the issue(s)
- Reasoning—the reasoning the court used in reaching its decision, in the language of the court

We have made an effort in this edition to include more judicial language in the cases. Our selection of cases includes both classic, landmark opinions and current, cutting-edge cases. In addition, all of the court cases end with a Business Considerations question and an Ethical Considerations question. These questions illustrate the impact of court cases on business and how business decisions may lead to litigation. Ethical considerations show how ethics constantly affects decision making. Limiting ethical concerns to a cursory examination in an obligatory ethics chapter profits no one; rather, an emphasis on ethics should be an integral part of business decision making.

Resources for Business Law Students

Web sites have been included throughout the text, pointing those students who want to "dig deeper" into particular areas to a starting point for additional information on a variety of topics. There is also a Web site related to the text, available at http://davidson.westbuslaw.com.

Discussion Questions, Case Problems and Writing Assignments

Each chapter concludes with 10 discussion questions, four legal case problems, and some "specialized" case problems. Each chapter contains one *business* application case, one *ethics* application case, one *critical thinking* case, and one *You Be the Judge* case problem. The legal case problems ask students to test their understanding of principles and terms covered in the chapter, and the business application, ethics application, and critical thinking problems ask students to apply these concepts to business situations. The You Be the Judge case problem asks the student to prepare an opinion that applies the facts learned to the issues presented in the case. By so doing, the student will gain a greater appreciation for the difficulties involved in drafting an opinion and will (hopefully) consider the alternatives more carefully in his or her role as "judge" of the case. All the end-of-chapter materials can be used as study tools in reviewing the material, as class or small-group discussion material, or as writing assignments.

Supplemental Resources

The eighth edition of *Business Law* now has a site on the World Wide Web devoted to teaching and learning resources for the text (http://davidson.westbuslaw.com). Come visit to see for yourself.

The following supplemental resources are also available with the eighth edition. For more information about any of these supplements, contact your Thomson Learning/West Legal Studies Sales Representative for more details, or visit the textbook's Web site.

- *Study Guide* (0-324-15368-6)

- *Telecourse Study Guide* (0-324-20310-1)

- *Instructor's Manual* (0-324-15369-4)

- *Test Bank* (0-324-15365-1)

- ExamView testing software (0-324-15366-X)

- Microsoft PowerPoint Lecture Review Slides (download at http://davidson.westbuslaw.com)

- Telecourse Videos—30 half-hour telecourse videos, developed by INTELECOM in conjunction with the third edition of *Business Law,* provide coverage for key topics in business law. Contact your local Thomson Learning/West Legal Studies Sales Representative for more details.

- Videos. Qualified adopters using this text have access to the entire library of West videos, a vast selection covering most business law issues. There are some restrictions, and if you have questions, please contact your local Thomson Learning/West Legal Studies Sales Representative or visit http://www.westbuslaw.com/video_library.html.

A Note on AACSB Curricular Standards

The AACSB curricular standards relevant to business law and the legal environment of business state that curricula should include ethical and global issues; the influence of political, social, legal and regulatory, environmental, and technology issues; and the impact of demographic diversity on organizations. We believe *Business Law: Principles and Cases in the Legal Environment* uniquely satisfies these standards.

First, global issues are treated in depth in several areas, beginning with Chapter 3, "International Law." The "International Sales of Goods: CISG" is covered in Chapters 16 through 19 (more than in any other current business law text), and letters of credit are addressed in Chapters 3 and 27. We also have included an "International Applications" question in each of the NRW boxes "threaded" throughout the text.

We have revised Chapter 2, "Business Ethics," to reflect more of the application of ethical theories than the theories themselves. Ethics questions also appear following court cases, NRW business application boxes, and at the ends of chapters.

Second, we have revised the text with the intent of creating a book that is intuitive, engaging, and oriented toward providing the legal skills students will need in the business world. Hence, the contents of the book stretch beyond the mere presentation of "legal topics" to encompass the spectrum of "political, social, legal, regulatory, environmental, and technological issues." The pedagogical features are designed to augment this content.

Finally, the attention to applications, evidenced in the Agenda, and the NRW business application thread case, uniquely contributes to showing how demographic diversity affects organizations. In the NRW case, the principals must understand the cultural and political challenges that a larger domestic and international market (and workforce) pose for them. These include issues ranging from employee privacy to labor law, from employee use of NRW computers to sexual harassment. By following the case, students are immersed in these problems and are asked to offer advice as questions arise. This encourages sensitivity and an understanding of other points of view.

On another level, the principals (and, vicariously, the students) learn that successful businesses today are often cross-functional. In this case, Mai, Carlos, and Helen need to recognize how the law applies to marketing, sales, management, finance and accounting, and manufacturing, and they must be able to act on this knowledge. The students, by assuming an advisory role with NRW, have a unique glimpse at the cross-functional nature of many business activities today. *Business Law* supports the current trend toward integrating business disciplines.

Acknowledgments

Writing a textbook is always an arduous undertaking, even if the text is "merely" a revision of a previous edition. This edition has been no different, and in many ways it has been more difficult. There have been numerous substantive changes in the law since the last edition, and each of these warranted our attention. There are also several areas that are in a state of upheaval as we go into print, and trying to be as up-to-date as possible while meeting a production deadline can be a problem for the entire production team.

This edition of the book would not have been possible without the help, assistance, and guidance of our developmental editor, Bob Sandman. Bob is always there when we need him. His good humor, his patience, and his support have been invaluable to us. Production Editor Emily Gross has also been tremendous. She has provided advice when needed and has assisted Bob in helping us put together this book.

Each of the authors owes a hearty "thank you" and a sincere "well done" to the other two authors. Each provided feedback, (positive) criticism, and support to the others during the hectic days of reading copyedited pages and page proofs. Each of us brings a unique personality to the process, and we have learned how and when to merge our talents to produce the best book possible. As authors, we have been a team for quite some time, working together through eight editions of the text. We each write about an equal number of chapters, and we each have input into the chapters written by the other authors. We sincerely believe that our group effort has been successful and that the sum of our contributions is greater than the parts. We hope you enjoy using this book as much as we have enjoyed preparing it.

A special thanks to our families. They put up with the late nights and the short deadlines and provide support and suggestions to help us get through the process every time we revise the text. Without their support and encouragement, we would never be able to accomplish our goal.

Finally, a sincere thank you to the following reviewers, whose suggestions, criticism, questions, observations, and keen and insightful commentaries on our work helped us maintain our focus and write a text that preserves content but is user-friendly, readable, and enjoyable:

Bruce E. Brown, *New River Community College*
Philip E. DeMarco, *Mission Community College*
Brian J. McCully, *Fresno City College*
Susan Mitchell, *Des Moines Area Community College*
Robert L. Mitchum, *Arkansas State University Beebe Campus*
Edward L. Welsh Jr., *Mesa Community College*

About the Authors

Daniel V. Davidson

Daniel V. Davidson received both his B.S. in business administration and his J.D. from Indiana University, Bloomington. He is an inactive member of the Connecticut Bar Association. He has taught at Central Connecticut State College in New Britain; St. Cloud State University in Minnesota; the University of Arkansas, Fayetteville; and California State University, Fresno. He recently finished serving as the associate dean of the College of Business and Economics at Radford University in Virginia and is professor of business law.

Professor Davidson has published numerous articles on business law, the teaching of business law, and business ethics. He was named the Outstanding Teacher of the Year at Central Connecticut State College. In 1979 he received the Outstanding Faculty Award from the Arkansas chapter of Beta Alpha Psi, and in 1980 he was named the Razorback Award winner as the Outstanding Business Professor, both at the University of Arkansas. In 1984, Professor Davidson was awarded the Meritorious Performance Award at California State University, Fresno. In 2001, he received the Outstanding Faculty Award from the College of Business and Economics at Radford University.

Professor Davidson is a member of Alpha Kappa Psi, Beta Gamma Sigma, Sigma Iota Epsilon, and Beta Alpha Psi. He is also a member of the Academy of Legal Studies in Business and its Southern Regional. He has held all of the offices in the Southern Regional, including president, and is currently serving as the senior advisory editor for the *Southern Law Journal* and the *Proceedings* of the region's annual meeting.

Brenda E. Knowles

Brenda E. Knowles received a B.A. *magna cum laude* from the University of Evansville, an M.A. from Miami University, and a J.D. from the Indiana University School of Law, Bloomington. She is professor of business law and director of the Honors Program at Indiana University South Bend, where she has been the recipient of two systemwide, all-university teaching awards, the Amoco Foundation Excellence in Teaching Award and the Wilbert Hites Distinguished Teaching Award for Mentorship. She has received numerous other systemwide and school citations for excellent teaching. She also has been active in FACET, the faculty colloquium on excellence in teaching and learning in the academic community. In 1995, Professor Knowles was named director of the Honors Program (a position theretofore always held by liberal arts faculty members). In 1997, the Student Association at Indiana University South Bend chose her as the campus's "Outstanding Educator."

Professor Knowles specializes in research on employment discrimination, pedagogy, and intellectual property law. She publishes her work in professional journals and has won an award for her research. In addition, she has been recognized both nationally and locally for her professional and civic accomplishments, most recently through the W.

George Pinnell Award for outstanding service to Indiana University. Professor Knowles is an active member of the Academy of Legal Studies in Business (ALSB) and of several regionals. More specifically, having held every office, she is a past president of both the ALSB and the Tri-State Academy of Legal Studies in Business. Professor Knowles presently serves as the chair of the ALSB's Research and Teaching Mentorship Programs; and, in 1994, she won the ALSB's Master Teacher Award. In 1998, she received the ALSB's Senior Faculty Excellence Award. Moreover, she is a member of Beta Gamma Sigma. She is licensed to practice law in Indiana and is a member of the American, Indiana State, and St. Joseph County Bar Associations.

Lynn M. Forsythe

Lynn M. Forsythe received her B.A. from The Pennsylvania State University and her J.D. from the University of Pittsburgh School of Law. She passed the bar examinations in the states of California and Pennsylvania. She is professor of business law at the Craig School of Business at California State University, Fresno. Professor Forsythe held administrative positions at the school, including director of graduate business programs, interim department chair, and co-chair of the AACSB Reaccreditation Committee. She is currently the undergraduate assessment coordinator for the school and the assessment coordinator for the legal environment option.

Professor Forsythe is the author of numerous articles on business law and business law pedagogy. She has held the positions of editor-in-chief, staff editor, and reviewer for *The Journal of Legal Studies Education,* and is currently advisory editor for that journal. She received the 1992 School of Business Faculty Award for Educational Innovation and previously was awarded a university Meritorious Performance Award. She has been an estate and gift tax attorney for the Internal Revenue Service and has taught business law, administrative law, government regulation of business, real estate law, business ethics, estate planning, and business and society. She is active in IMPAC, a statewide effort to address topical coverage in the core curriculum. She has recently been appointed to the Intersegmental Business Administration Council, an effort to coordinate the core business curriculum in California and improve the articulation of business courses in the California community colleges, California state universities, and Universities of California.

Professor Forsythe is a member of Beta Gamma Sigma and Alpha Kappa Psi. She was active in the American Bar Association Section of Taxation, for which she chaired subcommittees and panels, including an American Law Institute—American Bar Association advanced program. She is active in the Academy of Legal Studies in Business, for which she served as academic program co-coordinator for the 1983 meeting, liaison to the National Conference of Commissioners on Uniform State Laws, member of the Executive Committee, and chair and vice-chair of its Business Ethics Section. She has held all the offices, including president, in the Western Regional Academy of Legal Studies in Business.

PART 1

Foundations of Law

gnorance of the law is no excuse." The basic truth of this old adage seems simple and obvious. However, the simplicity of this basic truth tends to hide the complexity of the law. Each citizen—and resident—of this country has "constructive notice" of the law. This means that each person is expected to be aware of, and to abide by, all the laws of the land. The enormous scope of "the law" makes this expectation virtually impossible; attempting to know all aspects of the law is likely to be an exercise in futility for most people. No one person can realistically be expected to know *all* that the law entails, yet every person is expected to obey *every* aspect of the law—or to face possible sanctions for failing to do so.

Part 1 of this book will first help you to understand what law is, how it operates, and how it affects business. Each part of this text will offer insights into various aspects of the law, especially the area of business law. A thorough knowledge of the law takes years of specialized study, but this text will begin to open doors of understanding for you, and to provide references to other sources for you to explore and study. We hope it will help to remove the "ignorance of the law [that] is no excuse."

Overview

NRW Needs Your Help!

What Is NRW? Many people dream of owning their own business, of being their own boss, of becoming a successful entrepreneur. Three friends from college, Mai Nguyen, Carlos Rios, and Helen Wainwright, have such a dream—and they believe that they have a product that will let them attain this dream. The three friends are trying to get in on the ground floor of the anticipated Radio Frequency Identification (RFID) chip market through the development of NRW. They have a good idea and they have developed a viable plan, but they know that they will need help and advice as they get their business from the drawing board to the customers.

The RFID technology involves a computer chip that emits a radio frequency that can be picked up by a computer. The computer, in turn, can notify the user as to the location of the chip—and of the item to which the chip is attached. RFID technology has been available since the 1980s, and it is already utilized in a number of areas, including livestock tracking and automated vehicle identification systems. However, the chips can also be used for smaller items, such as car keys, glasses, or the TV remote control, among others, and this is the area NRW first plans to develop. The business will sell a relatively low cost chip embedded in a small plastic disk that can be attached to common household items, especially those that are commonly misplaced. This disk, called a StuffTrakR, will be relatively inexpensive to produce and should sell at a low enough price to attract considerable consumer interest. The customer can then go to his or her computer, open the NRW application, and highlight the "lost" item. The computer will pick up the radio frequency being broadcast by that chip and show the customer where in the house the item is located.

While NRW will initially emphasize the StuffTrakR, its hope for long-term success lies in the development of its second product, a commercial chip used in tracking inventory and sold to commercial outlets, especially retail stores. This product, the InvenTrakR, would also be relatively inexpensive, but the potential market is enormous. Of course, NRW will need a lot of help and a lot of luck to succeed, and that is where *you* come in.

What Is *Your* Role in *NRW*? Mai, Carlos, and Helen are just starting their business. While they will have an attorney to whom they can turn on various legal issues, they do not want to have to use their attorney every time a question arises. Instead, they would like to be able to ask *you* to be their consultant, since you are learning about business law. When a problem does arise that has business law implications, the friends would like to consult with you, asking you for advice and suggestions. Obviously, they do not want you

to "practice law," but they would appreciate your help in determining whether an issue might have serious legal implications, how they might avoid legal problems, and when they should consult their attorney.

NRW is, of course, a fictional company created and operated by three fictional characters. But the use of this fictional business will illustrate how the legal concepts discussed in each chapter might apply in the business environment. Each chapter will begin with an "Agenda," which highlights some of the major issues relevant to a small business that are discussed in that chapter. Within each chapter there are three different scenarios, each of which addresses a particular issue that might arise in a business setting. For each of these scenarios you are asked to provide guidance and advice to the firm about the legal implications raised by the scenario. You are also asked to look at the business, ethical, and international implications involved in the scenarios. You will become a more enlightened consultant as you progress through the text. The problems you confront will involve many different functional areas of business besides law—management, marketing and sales, finance and accounting, international business—and even a few personal issues. This approach is intended to help you to recognize the interrelationship between the various business subjects that is necessary for a business to succeed. Business courses should be viewed not in isolation but as an integrated series of materials that, when properly combined, can help a business to maximize its chances for success.

The People Behind NRW **Mai Nguyen** is a graduate of the local university, with a major in information science and technology. Mai is the computer "guru" of the team, and she has several years of experience after graduation with several computer firms.

Carlos Rios also graduated from the local university. Carlos majored in accounting, with a minor in finance. He is a CPA who worked with a regional accounting firm before agreeing to join NRW with his classmates and friends.

Helen Wainwright was a management major at the local university, with a minor in advertising. She spent two years in human resources for a manufacturing firm in Detroit, but decided to return to the campus area to seek her M.B.A. However, after meeting with Mai and Carlos, Helen has decided to join them in starting NRW and to delay her graduate studies for a while.

Elliot Fuston is married to Helen Wainright. Elliot does not work for the firm, but his actions may affect the firm from time to time. Helen and Elliot have no children.

You are the consultant who will provide advice and guidance on potential legal issues—and other related topics—that the business encounters in its developmental stages. Without your considered input and suggestions the business is much less likely to succeed, despite the dedication and expertise of the three entrepreneurs who have started this enterprise.

CHAPTER 1

Introduction to Law

AGENDA

NRW Mai, Carlos, and Helen need to understand what types of law will influence NRW. Will NRW be subject to federal regulation? To state regulation? To administrative regulation? How will these types of regulations affect NRW? Most of the legal issues in business law involve civil law. Obviously, members of the firm need to concern themselves with numerous civil law topics. Should they also be concerned with criminal law? How does criminal law influence business?

What happens when a party to a lawsuit asks the court for a particular action as the remedy? Why are lawyers and courts so interested in prior court decisions?

These and other questions will arise as you read this chapter. Be prepared! You never know when the firm or one of its members will seek your advice.

What Is the Relationship among Law, Order, and Justice?

Law

This book is about understanding the law of business. Before we begin our study, however, we must answer a basic question: What is *law*? Many definitions exist, ranging from the philosophical to the practical. Plato (427–347? B.C.), a Greek philosopher who studied and wrote in the area of philosophical idealism, said law was *social control*. Sir William Blackstone (1723–1780), an English judge and legal commentator, said law was rules specifying what was right and what was wrong. For our purposes, however, we shall define law as "rules that must be obeyed." People who disobey these rules are subject to sanctions that may result in their being required to do something they would not voluntarily do, such as paying a fine or going to jail. Our society has many kinds of rules, but not all rules can be considered "law." A rule in baseball, for example, says that after three strikes the batter is out. This rule, however, is not law. All laws are rules, but all rules are not laws. What differentiates a law from a rule? Simply stated, *enforceability* separates laws from rules. People who do not follow the rules in baseball are not arrested or taken to court. They are simply ejected from the game. In contrast, people who break laws can be held accountable for their actions through court-imposed sanctions.

Many different types of legal rules exist. One type defines a specific way to create a legal document, for example a contract or a will. A second forbids certain kinds of conduct; criminal law is an excellent example of this kind of legal rule. (*Criminal law* is the body of law dealing with public wrongs called crimes.) A third type of legal rule was created to compensate persons who have been injured because someone else breached a duty. For example, when an automobile manufacturer negligently builds a car, and the manufacturer's negligence is the direct cause of an injury, the manufacturer may have to pay the injured person monetary damages. (*Negligence* is the failure to do something a reasonable person would do, or doing something a reasonable and prudent person would not do.) Rules about creating legal documents, defining crimes, and specifying legal duties are generally rules about substantive law. (*Substantive law* is that part of law that creates and defines legal rights. It is distinct from the law that defines how laws should be enforced in court.) Finally, our legislative bodies and courts establish rules to take care of their everyday business. For example, all states have a rule concerning the maximum number of days defendants have before they must answer a civil lawsuit; this is an example of procedural law. (*Procedural law* is the methods used to enforce rights or obtain compensation for the violation of rights.) The distinction between substantive law and procedural law is important and will be revisited throughout our discussion of business law.

We will view the law as a body of rules that establish a certain level of social conduct, or of *duties*, that members of the society must honor. One way to view these duties is shown in Exhibit 1.1. The party or parties who are injured can seek enforcement of their rights in courts of law. Enforcement consists of one of three legal remedies: (1) paying money as damages or as a fine, (2) equitable relief, such as being subject to an *injunction*, a court order that directs a person to do or not do something, or (3) going to jail or prison.

Order

The law usually considers an *order* as a legal command issued by a judge. But we are not concerned with order in

---

EXHIBIT	1.1 Duties in a Society

Duties

Imposed by law and /or society (involuntary)		Assumed by the individual (voluntary)
Torts	**Crimes**	**Contracts**
(Civil wrongs, harm to an individual)	(Societal wrongs, harm to the society)	
Individual Seeks Remedies	Society Seeks Sanctions (fine and/or imprisonment)	Individual Seeks Remedies

that sense. Another definition of *order* is the absence of chaos. *Chaos* is confusion and total disorganization. If the laws of a society were always followed and never broken, perfect order would result. No crime would exist, and everyone would be safe. History, however, tells us that no society with perfect order has ever existed.

The words *law* and *order* are often linked together. It is natural to link them because, when the law is followed, there will be order. However, precisely because the law is not followed all the time by all the people, perfect order does not exist. Society is always *somewhat* chaotic and disorganized. One of the reasons people do not always obey the law is that they may not be aware of what the law is. However, our legal system *presumes* that everyone *is* aware of the law and what it requires. If the society did not presume that everyone knows the law, society would be more chaotic than it already is. In that case, individuals accused of breaking the law would have an excellent defense: They could argue that they did not know they were breaking the law, and the society would then have to prove the person's knowledge before sanctions could be imposed. The presumption that everyone knows the law, that "ignorance of the law is no excuse," creates an incentive for all citizens to study the law. Our educational system plays an important role in permitting us to learn the law.

Justice

Justice is a difficult term to define. When we speak of *justice*, we normally mean "fairness." Although perfect justice *is* fair, there is more to the concept of justice than merely being fair. Justice, as used in the Anglo-American legal system, refers to both the *process* and the *results* obtained in the process. Courts try to *administer* justice in conformity with the laws of the territory. From a social perspective, justice may be affected as much—or even more—by appearances than by results. Thus, lawyers are required to avoid the *appearance* of impropriety in their dealings. If the public perceives that the system is not just, it will be less likely to accept the results the system provides. This, in turn, might lead to the destruction of the order developed in society through its laws and their enforcement.

The ultimate goal of any legal system should be attaining justice by continually searching for fairness and equity. Fairness is less abstract than justice, and thus it is easier to address on a practical level. Most people have a basic concept of "fairness" that can be applied to any given situation, even though those same people may not have a similar concept of "justice." For example, when you see a bully pick on a victim, you probably believe that this conduct is not fair. In this type of situation, the conduct is clearly unfair, and it also is clearly unjust. In most situations, however, it is difficult to determine what a fair-and-just result would be. For example, suppose that a wealthy individual is accused of committing a crime. That wealthy individual hires the best attorneys he or she can find, and—in a very public trial—is found not guilty by the jury. Many people might question whether this result is *fair*. However, the process followed in the legal system assures—at least to some extent—that the result of the trial is *just*.

Different theories of justice exist, causing additional confusion. In Anglo-American law, there are two primary theories of justice: commutative justice and distributive justice. (In this context, *commutative justice* is the attempt to give all persons identical treatment based on the assumption that equal treatment is appropriate. Individual differences are not considered. *Distributive justice,* on the other hand, is the attempt to allocate justice in a way that considers individual differences.) This distinction originated with Aristotle.[1] In our legal system each theory is followed in some situations and not followed in others. By using both types of justice, the courts try to mete out a form of justice that is perceived as fair to the public that allows for some flexibility by the courts. While reading cases in the text, ask yourself which theory of justice is being applied by the courts.

Commutative justice attempts to give every person that which is due to him or her by placing everyone on an equal footing. Commutative justice ignores personal worth, merit, and social class. In most situations, misdemeanors are punished under the concept of commutative justice; all speeders are treated the same, regardless of factors such as income, profession, type of automobile, and so forth. Much of contract law uses a commutative justice perspective.

Distributive justice attempts to treat each person as that person should be treated, taking into account the differences among people. It does *not* consider all people equally deserving or equally blameworthy. It assigns to a person the rewards that person deserves based on personal merit or services provided. Different types of distributions may be appropriate in various situations; for example, distribution of salary may be based on contribution to the company. Distribution of food stamps may be based on need. Distributive justice also assigns the punishment that the specific crime deserves. In criminal law, felony cases often use distributive justice, especially when the judge has a significant amount of discretion in sentencing. Suppose two people attempt an armed robbery together, and get caught, arrested, tried, and convicted. One may be sentenced to a much longer jail term than the other. Why? Perhaps one person planned the crime, and the other person was persuaded to participate. Perhaps one person is a first-time criminal, and the other has been convicted of five prior armed robberies. Distributive justice might also be used as a philosophical basis for affirmative action programs, which attempt to make up for past unconstitutional discrimination. Some ethicists focus their attention on issues of distributive justice.

The Nexus: Practicability

What we often refer to as "*the Law*" is really a system consisting of law, order, and justice. Combined, they make up the U.S. legal system. All the elements should balance in perfect equilibrium so that one element does not adversely affect any other. If we had total order, we would have very little justice; if we had total justice, we might have very little order. The *nexus* (link between elements) of the two concepts is the point of *practicability*. For example, to achieve perfect justice with respect to traffic violations, we need jury trials with counsel to ascertain precisely whether a driver did in fact violate the speed limit. However, the costs of such a venture are so prohibitive that no municipality or other local jurisdiction can afford to pay for it. As a result, most traffic courts tend to achieve "assembly line" justice rather than perfect justice.

The Law as an Artificial Language System

Many terms used in the law are also used in everyday speech, but often they have totally different meanings in the law. This text will define many of the terms for you in the chapter. There are also numerous law dictionaries available on line. You might want to check—and bookmark—one or more of those on-line sources. A fairly easy-to-use dictionary is available at http://dictionary.law.com/. Another good site is http://www.lectlaw.com/def.htm. The list of terms may seem endless: *offer, acceptance, consideration, guaranty, employee,* and so on. How many times do you use the word "consideration" or "employee" without intending the legal meaning? Because terms may have different connotations within the law, be on guard for subtle shifts in meaning. If you are in doubt, read the passage again or check the definition.[2]

In addition, it is impossible to discuss the law intelligently without reference to some words that are defined only in the law. Examples of this specialized vocabulary include *estoppel, appellee, assignee, bailee, causa mortis, caveat venditor, quid pro quo,* and *codicil.* You make no assumptions when you study a foreign language; therefore, make none about the law. Remember these three rules

about our artificial language system to improve your mastery of this material:

1. Legal terms may appear to be synonyms with everyday words, but they are not.

2. Legal terms may have more than one legal meaning.

3. Some legal terms have no relation to everyday language.

The Origins of the Law of Business

In England, the law of business began as a private system administered outside regular law courts. (We will talk about the English law, because that is the source of most of U.S. law. However, business law had different origins in other countries, like the trading countries of the Mediterranean region and Asia.) In England, the law of business began as rules observed by businesspeople in their dealings with one other. It was called the law merchant because it was administered in courts established in the various merchant guilds, commonly called Merchant Courts. (*Law merchant* is those rules of trade and commerce used by merchants in England beginning in the Middle Ages.) Eventually, it was integrated into the English common law court system. (In this context, *common law* is that unwritten law which is based on custom, usage, and court decisions; it differs from *statutory law*, which consists of laws passed by legislatures.) The law merchant is now recognized and enforced by the courts. We will generally consider the law merchant as part of the common law. Today, the law of business includes contracts, sales, negotiable instruments, secured transactions, agency, partnerships, and corporations, among other topics.

Why Study the Law of Business?

This textbook may be called a primer in "prevention." The focus is on (1) how to recognize legal problems; (2) how to avoid these legal problems if possible; and then (3) how to resolve them as quickly as possible if or when they do arise. The legislatures and the courts act in much the same manner, often attempting to prevent problems, but also providing remedies if the problems cannot be prevented or avoided. *Preventive law* is law designed to prevent harm or wrongdoing before it occurs. Many statutes are intended to prevent certain conduct by providing for sanctions against

NRW CASE 1.1 Management

HEALTH INSURANCE FOR NRW EMPLOYEES

When Mai, Carlos, and Helen first began the firm, they gave virtually no consideration to providing health insurance benefits for NRW's employees. Mai and Carlos purchased their own health insurance and Helen had insurance through her husband Elliot's employer. In addition, the quotes for health insurance for NRW were very expensive. The firm has grown and expanded. Several of the employees have asked Carlos about a benefits package that would include health insurance coverage. They have also asked Carlos to see if any health insurance can be made convertible into private coverage or portable to a new employer if any employee changes jobs. Carlos has asked you whether the firm should provide health insurance for the employees, and what the consequences of providing—or not providing—such coverage would be. What advice will you give him?

BUSINESS CONSIDERATIONS Should NRW provide health insurance as an employee benefit for its employees? What are the business implications—including taxation—if such coverage is provided? What are the business and legal implications if such coverage is not provided?

ETHICAL CONSIDERATIONS Would it be ethical for NRW to provide coverage for Mai, Carlos, and Helen, but not for other employees? What are the ethical implications of withholding insurance coverage for the firm's employees merely to increase its profits?

INTERNATIONAL CONSIDERATIONS Assume that some of NRW's employees work in foreign countries. Would that affect NRW's legal or moral obligation to provide health insurance for those employees?

any persons who violate the statutory provisions. *Remedial law* is also an important aspect of the law. When a particular problem begins to arise, courts or legislatures may anticipate its future development and attempt to resolve the problem. The lawmakers, however, cannot predict or prevent every potential legal problem. Thus, the individual needs to know what he or she can do to prevent as many problems as possible.

You should understand the legal implications of what you are doing in your roles as businessperson and con-

sumer. Otherwise, many actions may have unexpected legal consequences. If you understand the issues raised here and can apply your knowledge to particular business situations, you may save yourself great expense later. It is helpful to understand the legal environment in which a business operates. If business executives "scan" their environment, they can often identify trends. Sometimes a business or industry may impact the direction of the change by being alert to the changing environment. A business taking direct action is called proactive. To be *proactive* means to identify potential problem areas and actively participate in resolving them. For example, industries may decide to self-regulate in order to persuade the legislature that government regulation is unnecessary. The video game industry created a rating system for games at least in part to avoid prospective legislative action. Not all businesses, however, are proactive. Some are *reactive,* waiting to see what develops. They do not initiate change, but make change only when forced to do so. In general, business is a very practical subject. As you will see, the law of business is just as practical.

Another reason to study the law of business is that it will help you develop valuable decision-making skills. Legal style of analysis can be used in business decision making. This study will also sensitize you to particular situations in which you may need the assistance of a lawyer. Legal counsel can be helpful in preventing problems as well as in seeking remedies if a problem exists. For example, in the sale of commercial real estate, you will discover that the buyer or seller needs the assistance of a lawyer *before,* rather than after, an earnest money contract is signed.

What Are the Needs of a Legal System?

The Need to Be Reasonable

A legal system must be reasonable. It should rely on reasonable conclusions based on facts. Speeding laws are reasonable because one can prove that higher speeds on busy streets are related to higher numbers of accidents.

In addition to being reasonable, laws must be applied in a reasonable manner A law stating that Juana, a consumer, will have property taken away from her if she does not pay for the property is certainly reasonable. It would be unreasonably applied if Juana stopped paying for the property and, without notice or warning, Ramiro, the seller, removed the property. Juana should first be informed that the money is due and payable and then receive a chance to say why the money could or should not be paid. Then, if the money still was not paid, Ramiro could possibly repossess the property or seek other remedies through the legal process.

The Need to Be Definite

The law must be definite, not vague. For example, a law stating that all contracts "for a lot of money" must be in writing would not clearly specify when a contract must be in writing, leading to confusion. The Statute of Frauds, however, states that all contracts for the sale of goods costing $500 or more must be in writing, which is very clear. If one has a contract for $499.99, it need not be in writing; but if the contract is for $500 it must be in writing. There is a *definite* point at which a writing is required.

Sometimes the law is unable to state precisely what one must do in all circumstances. In such cases, the law uses the word "reasonable" rather than set precise boundaries. If an automobile driver hits a pedestrian and causes injury, the pedestrian may sue the driver. In this situation, the law does not state that speed in excess of a particular amount is necessary in order to find the driver at fault. If the only information you had was that the speed limit was 55 miles per hour and the car was going 50 miles per hour, could you find the driver at fault? Under these conditions, the law would ask the question: Was the driver's conduct reasonable under the circumstances? If so, it will be considered an accident without civil liability; if not, the driver will be liable for any injury to the pedestrian. In the final analysis, the law provides an answer. Thus, the law is definite.

The Need to Be Flexible

To say that the law must be both definite and flexible seems like a contradiction in terms. The law needs to be definite in order to establish a standard. In other respects, the law must be flexible so that it can be applied in many different *individual* situations. For example, if a drunk driver kills a family wage earner and the family files a wrongful death lawsuit, recovery would be based on the future earning capacity of the wage earner. (*Wrongful death* is unlawful death. It does not necessarily have to involve a crime.) It would not be based on a table of damages. If trees did not bend in the wind, they would break. Our legal system is like those trees: It must bend without breaking. However, because of this flexibility, our legal system loses some of its predictability.

The Need to Be Practical

Because people depend on the law to guide their actions, the law needs to be practical and oriented to action rather than to thought. However, there are thoughtful ideas supporting the legal system. The law must deal with real issues created by real people. For example, most courts will decide only real disputes between the parties; they will not decide hypothetical cases. Courts will also avoid cases where the issue is *moot* (abstract; not properly submitted to the court for a resolution; not capable of resolution) or where there is no real case and controversy. (A *case and controversy* is a case brought before the court where the plaintiff and defendant are really opposed to one another on significant issues.)

The Need to Be Published

If we had the best set of laws imaginable but no one knew about them, they would be virtually useless. In traffic law, for example, if no speed limits were posted, arbitrary enforcement would be the rule and drivers would not know how fast they could legally drive. In general, people cannot voluntarily comply with secret laws and rules. Therefore, all laws must be published. Once a law has been published, we can presume that all people know it. Consequently, ignorance of the law is no excuse.

The Need to Be Final

If a controversy exists and the legal system is used to resolve it, one thing is certain: At some point in time the matter will be resolved. It may not be resolved to the full satisfaction of the person who "won" the case, but it will be resolved. In this sense, the law is like a political election. On election day, someone wins and someone loses. The outcome may be delayed, but eventually it is final. In criminal law, if the defendant wins the case in trial court, the matter ends. In many situations, the prosecutor cannot appeal. A defendant who is convicted in criminal trial court, however, can appeal to the highest court in the state system. If the defendant does not gain a reversal, the matter ends unless the U.S. Supreme Court reviews the case. The official Web site of the U.S. Supreme Court is located at http://www.supremecourtus.gov/. Exhibit 1.2 outlines the needs of a legal system.

What Are the Purposes of a Legal System?

Achieving Justice

As previously discussed, justice is basically equated to fairness. Sometimes we achieve it and sometimes we do

EXHIBIT 1.2 **The Needs of a Legal System**

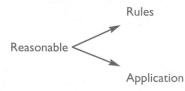

Legal System

Reasonable → Rules

Reasonable → Application

Definite rules and limits

Flexible standards (to keep up with changes in society and technology)

Practical rules based on reality

Published (communicated)

Final—to put an end to a case at a particular time

Anarchy/Chaos

Unreasonable → Arbitrary and/or unreasonable rules

Unreasonable → Uneven and/or biased applications

Vague or unclear rules, no defined standards

Rigid and unbending standards; "Stone-Age" rules in a modern world

Hypothetical or impractical rules based on wishful thinking

Unpublished—"Surprise" rules

Ongoing, continuous—never seeming to end

---

not. In the law of business, we deal more with commutative justice—treating each person equally—than with distributive justice. In a contract, for example, commutative justice gives each person what that person is entitled to under the contract—no more, no less. The rule of *caveat emptor* (let the buyer beware) is an example of how the law allocates risk in a business transaction. If the buyer does not thoroughly examine the goods before they are bought, the buyer cannot seek redress in the courts if what is bought does not conform to the buyer's expectations.

A trend exists, however, to introduce elements of distributive justice into the law of business. The courts, legislatures, and administrative agencies are attempting to reallocate the risks of business transactions by taking into account the status of the parties. For example, in 1976 the Federal Trade Commission established a rule concerning consumer transactions that resulted in more protection for the consumer.

Another limit placed on the doctrine of commutative justice is that of *unconscionability* (the condition of being so unreasonably favorable to one party, or so one-sided, as to shock the conscience). An 18th-century English case provides an excellent definition for this concept: unconscionable contracts are contracts that are so unfair that "no man in his senses and not under delusion would make [them] on the one hand, and no honest and fair man would accept [them] on the other."[3] Our legal system considers that some contracts ought not to be enforced even if they fully comply with all the rules concerning contract formation.

Providing Police Power

Because justice is the ultimate purpose of a legal system, providing police power may be viewed as an intermediate purpose of a legal system. When most students see the term *police power*, they usually envision a uniformed police officer with a badge and gun. That, however, is just one part of what we call police power. Police power is inherent in all governments. This power allows for the creation and enforcement of laws designed to protect the public's health, safety, and general welfare.[4] Laws and ordinances concerning police, fire, sanitation, and social welfare departments in state and local governments stem from police power.

Maintaining Peace and the Status Quo

Ever since the days of ancient England, one of the clearest purposes of the law has been to "keep the King's peace." Most modern torts and crimes can trace their origin to a simple breaching of the King's peace. Today, laws that govern the relationships between private individuals, such as the laws governing assault, battery, trespass, and false imprisonment, are private forms of keeping the peace. Closely associated with keeping the peace is the concept of maintaining the status quo—that is, keeping things the way they are. It is natural for the law to maintain the status quo unless changing things will benefit society. It is possible to obtain a preliminary injunction from a court that will maintain the status quo until the lawsuit is finally resolved. The petitioner must allege and prove irreparable injury to obtain a preliminary injunction.

NRW CASE 1.2   Management

SECURITY ISSUES

Carlos Rios plans to visit Washington, D.C., next week for a conference on "tracking" technology, including sessions at the White House and the Pentagon on possible military uses of the technology. Mai and Helen recognize that this trip is important to NRW, but they are a little concerned because of the "attack" of 9/11/01 and several violent incidents at the White House. For example, two individuals have fired shots at the White House and one individual apparently tried to crash a plane into the building. White House security and the D.C. police have strengthened security around the White House and have applied strict rules about people carrying weapons or acting in a suspicious manner. While Mai and Helen appreciate the extra security, they do not understand why different rules seem to apply to the White House than exist in their hometown. They have asked you to explain how or why this is permitted. What will you tell them?

BUSINESS CONSIDERATIONS Is it reasonable to have different legal rules about carrying weapons near the White House than in other areas? Should the police apply the rules differently in this vicinity? Should there be different rules in airports? Can a business impose different rules concerning the carrying of weapons on or around the workplace? What factors would cause a business to do so?

ETHICAL CONSIDERATIONS Is it ethical for the government to have different rules near the White House than it has in other places? What are the ethical implications of having special rules in certain specified areas or under certain conditions?

INTERNATIONAL CONSIDERATIONS Assume this was an international conference in a foreign country. Would the security issues be any different for Carlos? Why? Are there any concerns about sharing NRW's technology with foreign countries? Why?

Providing Answers

On a philosophical level, the law should be just; but on a practical level, it should provide answers. Sometimes the answers the law provides are not satisfactory. If Melanie sues Troy, a neighbor, because Troy is allegedly creating a nuisance on his property, and Troy wins the case in the trial court, then Melanie can appeal the decision to the next higher court. (*Nuisance* is the title we give to the unreasonable or unlawful use of a person's own property that interferes with another person's use and enjoyment of his or her property.) In most states this higher court is called an *appellate court* (court that has the power to review the decisions of lower courts). If an appellate court rules in favor of Troy, a further appeal may be taken to the state's highest court. In that court, Melanie may win and thereby receive a satisfactory answer. But whether she wins or loses, she and Troy will each be provided with an answer on completion of the appellate process.

Providing Protection

The law protects all kinds of interests. You have already seen that the law concerns itself with protecting individuals. The tort law of assault and battery is a classic example of protection of the individual. The law also protects persons less conspicuously when it protects their civil rights. *Civil rights* are the rights found in the first 10 amendments to the U.S. Constitution (the Bill of Rights) and due process and equal protection under the Fourteenth Amendment. The Constitution, and numerous other documents, can be accessed at the FirstGov Web site's Reference Shelf at http://www.firstgov.gov/Topics/Reference_Shelf.shtml#Laws/ that includes links to Historical Documents, Libraries, Federal Register, and Statistics.

Civil rights laws are extremely important in modern litigation and have their historical background in the first 10 amendments to the U.S. Constitution. (Refer to the Constitution in Appendix A at the end of this book; it is worthwhile for you to refresh your memory about its features.) Persons are protected in the free exercise of their speech, are free to choose or not to choose a religion, can peacefully assemble, and may petition their government for a redress of grievances (a rarely used freedom). The U.S. Constitution contains the right to be protected from unreasonable searches and seizures, the right against compulsory self-incrimination of a crime, the right to a grand jury, the right against *double jeopardy* (a rule of criminal law that states that a person will not be tried in court more than once by the same government for the same criminal offense), the right to a jury trial, and the right to bail. Proponents argue that the Constitution provides a right to bear arms but constitutional experts disagree on whether this is an individual right or a right to form a militia.

The government is also in the business of protecting *itself.* A government's self-protection is an ancient right that goes back to Roman law. It is based on the concept that if the *sovereign* (above or superior to all others; that from which all authority flows) is *truly* sovereign, it cannot be attacked legally. Because the sovereign is, by definition, supreme, it cannot be subject to attack nor can it be held liable to its inferiors. Thus, the rule of *sovereign immunity* was developed, shielding the sovereign from lawsuits against it, but permitting the sovereign to file lawsuits. This rule still stands, to some extent, although the federal government and many states have passed special statutes permitting individuals to sue them for *torts* (civil wrongs—see Chapter 7 for a discussion of torts).

Finally, the law is concerned with the protection of property. All property is characterized as either personal or real property. *Personal property* is all property with the exception of real property. In general, if property is movable, it is personal property. *Real property*, on the other hand, is land and whatever is affixed to land, such as a house. However, personal property can have dual meanings in law. In addition to the meaning above, it may also mean property that is owned by individuals, as opposed to public property that is owned by the government or the community. Our legal system has a variety of laws that protect both types of property.

Enforcing Intent

The law of contracts is based on *freedom of contract*. It is this rule that allows each of us to be our own "legislator" to a limited extent. We make our own "laws" of conduct, as long as the contracts into which we enter do not violate the general principles of contract law. For example, you may wish to enter into a contract with a supplier of goods. You may want to make the contract today so that it will immediately bind the other party. Perhaps you have found a good price and do not think you will find a better one. Your problem, however, is that you do not presently have the money to pay for the goods, but you know that you can easily resell them for an immediate cash profit within 10 days after delivery. You should, therefore, seek a provision in the contract stating that the buyer will pay the seller for the goods 11 days after receipt of the goods. Of course, if you cannot resell the goods within the 10 days as anticipated, you will have a financial problem. This is more a question of business judgment, however, than of law.

Providing Rehabilitation

Both criminal law and civil law are directed toward rehabilitation. Criminal law should, among other things, rehabilitate the criminal. Civil law is also involved in rehabilitation to some extent: Contract law provides rehabilitation for a party harmed by a breach of the contract. Tort law provides for a form of rehabilitation in the assessment of damages for the victim of the tort. The federal bankruptcy law is directed toward the rehabilitation of honest debtors.

Facilitating Commercial Transactions

One of the major characteristics of the U.S. legal system is that it facilitates commercial transactions. For example, very few automobiles would be sold in the United States, if car dealers insisted on cash payment. Our national economy is still very reliant on the automobile industry; the prosperity of the steel, energy, and transportation industries is directly related to that of the automobile. Thus, reducing the number of automobiles sold could harm the national economy. Accordingly, the extension of credit for the purchase of automobiles greatly facilitates trade. The use of checks and credit cards also accelerates commercial transactions. When sellers can retain a security interest in goods, they may be willing to extend credit to persons who might otherwise not be in a financial position to make the purchase. (*Security interest* is a collateral interest taken in the property of another to secure payment of a debt or contract performance.) The U.S. legal system fosters free and open competition and facilitates trade, greatly contributing to the business and financial power of the United States. Exhibit 1.3 outlines the purposes of a legal system.

Jurisprudence

Jurisprudence is the study of the science or philosophy underlying the law. In Latin, jurisprudence means the "wisdom of the law." However, there are really many different "wisdoms" of the law reflected in a number of different philosophical views; these views vary based on the values inherent in the law, the development of the law, and its proper role in society. The law continues to change, and knowledge of the legal philosophies will improve your ability to understand the law and predict future trends. Here is a brief introduction to some of the philosophical approaches. Note that sometimes there is even disagreement among philosophers who basically subscribe to the same theory.

Natural Law Theory

The *natural law* theory believes that the law should be based on what is correct and moral. It is composed of these four concepts:

EXHIBIT   1.3   The Purposes of a Legal System

Purpose	Reason
Achieving justice	To provide "justice" so that the needs of the members of society are addressed.
Providing police power	To provide a social structure so that "wronged" individuals do not have to resort to self-help; to give society control of the system.
Maintaining peace and the status quo	To provide each member of society with a feeling of personal security and a structure on which each individual can rely.
Providing answers	To achieve practical justice; lets the members of society know what is expected of them and what they may reasonably expect from others.
Providing protection	To define and establish social guidelines and protect the entire society if any of these guidelines are not followed and obeyed.
Enforcing intent	To provide some method for permitting private agreements and for ensuring that these agreements are honored or enforced.
Providing rehabilitation	To allow a person who violates the guidelines of the society a second chance; recognizes that anyone can make a mistake.
Facilitating commercial transactions	To support freedom of contract and private ownership of property; each of these concepts encourages and promotes business transactions.

1. There are certain legal values or value judgments.

2. These values are unchanging because their source is absolute. Natural law theorists disagree about the sources. Theorists believe that they are Nature, God, *or* Reason.

3. These values can be determined by human reason.

4. Once they are determined, these values supersede any form of human law. Once the natural law is discovered, it nullifies any contradictory law created by humans.

This theory rests on some significant assumptions—the world is perceived as a rational order with values and purposes built into it; the laws of nature describe how things should be; and humans should use reason to grasp what should be done. Many early Greek philosophers were natural law theorists. In the history of Christian thought, the dominant theory of ethics has been the theory of natural law, best exemplified by St. Thomas Aquinas.[5] Natural law theory is found in the words of the Declaration of Independence, "We hold these Truths to be self-evident, that all Men are created equal, that they are endowed by their Creator with certain unalienable Rights. . . ." The natural law theory focuses on fairness and justice, even though some disorder will result when individuals decide that the written law is not "natural law." Criticisms of natural law include whose values are to be included in the natural law and who determines whether a manmade law is unjust because it violates natural law.

Legal Positivism

Legal positivism is composed of three theoretical parts. (1) "[L]egal validity is ultimately a function of certain kinds of social facts."[6] (2) Social facts give rise to legal validity, which is authoritative due to some kind of social convention. (3) There is *no* overlap between notions of law and morality. This last part is in direct opposition to natural law theory. Legal positivists disagree on the correct interpretation of these three theoretical parts. One alternate statement proposed by some positivists includes these primary beliefs: (1) Law is the expression of the will of the legislator or sovereign, and must be followed. (2) Morals are separate from law and should not be considered in making legal decisions; for example, judges should not consider factors outside the legal system such as contemporary community values. (3) Law is a closed system in which correct legal decisions are reached by reference to statutes and court precedents. (*Precedents* are decided cases that establish legal authority for later cases.) The *legal positivist* approach believes that the law is the result of lawmaking by a legitimate government. In the United States, this is primarily executive orders, legislation, court opinions, and administrative rules and regulations. Under this theory, legality and morality are separated. The positive law approach promotes stability in the law and the supremacy of written laws. Criticisms of legal positivism include that it is too narrow and too literal-minded, and that its refusal to consider social, ethical, and other factors makes it static and unable to serve society well.

Sociological Theory

Under the *sociological* theory the role of prior law in the form of precedents is minimized. The law's source should be contemporary opinion and customs. In creating statutes or court decisions, the lawmaker should record community interests; become familiar with the community standards and mores; and make a decision conforming to these standards. Criticisms of the sociological theory include that following the theory would make the law too unpredictable. Community standards change and thus the law would be changing all the time. In a court decision relying on this theory, the judge may discuss sociological factors and current customs. For example, a court may consider "contemporary community standards" to determine whether a magazine is obscene.

Historical Theory

The *historical* theory holds that the law is primarily a system of customs and social traditions that have developed over time. It is very similar to the sociological school; however, its focus is more historical than contemporary. Each nation develops its own individual consensus about what the law should be. The law is an evolving system, and precedents have a significant role. Legitimacy is obtained from the historical will of a nation's people.

Law and Economics Theory

Law and economics theory applies classical economic theory and empirical methods to explain legal doctrines and to predict judicial decisions. It argues for using economic analysis as both a description about how courts and legislators behave and as a prescription about how courts and legislators *should* behave. The law and economics theory is closely allied with the University of Chicago, where it originated. It is sometimes called The Chicago School. This theory is commonly used in areas such as torts, contracts, and property law. Under the theory, the legal system should be viewed as a system to promote the efficient allocation of resources in society. For example, buyers and sellers in the market exchange goods or services of value. The exchange is maximizing value for both the buyer and seller. Richard A. Posner is currently a leader in law and economics theory. In his words,

[M]any areas of law, especially the great common law fields of property, torts, crimes, and contracts, bear the stamp of economic reasoning. It is not a refutation [of this theory] that few judicial opinions contain explicit references to economic concepts. Often the true grounds of decision are concealed rather than illuminated by the characteristic rhetoric of judicial opinions. Indeed, legal education consists primarily of learning to dig beneath the rhetorical surface to find these grounds, many of which may turn out to have an economic character.[7]

(*Rhetoric* is the art or science of using words.)

The proper goal of statutory and common law is to promote wealth maximization, which can be accomplished by facilitating the mechanisms of the free market. Also, market transactions reflect autonomous judgments about the value of individual preferences. (*Autonomous* refers to the right of the individual to govern himself or herself according to his or her own reason.) Critics contend that this theory tends to be politically conservative and generally rests on only one type of economic philosophy to the exclusion of others. Another criticism is that the theory could be acceptable as a *descriptive theory* (theory that describes how things are and reports what is observed) to explain what the law is, but it is not helpful as a *prescriptive theory* (theory that states what people should do or what should occur).

Feminist Legal Theory

The *feminist legal* theory holds that the law does not treat women equally. The law is structured to promote the interests of white males and to exclude women. As with some of the other theories, there are a wide variety of views under this theory. Many feminist legal theorists are also concerned about persons of color. (There is also a critical race theory, which focuses on how people of color are excluded from the legal system.) Followers of feminist legal theory assert that the current legal system is dominated by men, and that women are often victimized and their perspectives ignored. They argue that the male perspective has shaped many areas of law including property law, contract law, criminal law, constitutional law, and civil rights law. They also contend that the law should consider the female perspective. For example, workplace behavior that may not seem harassing to men may seem harassing to women, and the law should address this accordingly. With the 1991 case of *Ellison v. Brady*,[8] federal courts began using the reasonable woman standard in cases where women were being sexually harassed.

A 1998 Italian case attracted the attention of feminist legal theorists. The case was heard by Italy's highest criminal appeals court, which determined that an 18-year-old girl was not raped, based in part on the fact that she was wearing jeans. For more details see Case Problems and Writing Assignments 2. The ruling said that it is "common knowledge that it's nearly impossible to even partially remove jeans from a person without their co-operation, since this operation is already very difficult for the wearer."[9] It also said that "jeans cannot be removed easily and certainly it is impossible to pull them off if the victim is fighting against her attacker with all her force."[10] The case has been sent back for retrial but Rosa, the victim, says she doesn't think she can go through another trial.[11] The decision sparked protests from Italy to California. On a historical note, rape has been considered a criminal felony in Italy only since 1996. Prior to that time, it was considered a "crime of honor" against the woman's family. A defendant could avoid punishment by agreeing to marry the woman or by proving that she had many sexual experiences.[12]

The feminist legal theory is criticized for being too narrow in focus and for failing to recognize changes taking place as more women enter the workforce, including the legal profession.

Critical Legal Studies Theory

The *critical legal studies* (CLS) movement holds that the content of the law in liberal democracies reflects " 'ideological struggles among social factions in which competing conceptions of justice, goodness, and social and political life get compromised, truncated, vitiated, and adjusted.' The inevitable outcome of such struggles, [in] this view, is a profound inconsistency permeating the deepest layers of the law."[13] The law is not objective and neutral. The current law reflects a cluster of beliefs that convinces people that they are living in a natural hierarchy, but this cluster of beliefs really has been created by those in power. The elite uses these beliefs to rationalize its power. The elite maintains its power, wealth, and privilege using law, economics, mass communication, and religion. In order to accomplish social and political change, the law must be examined and

critiqued. The current law is a combination of legal and nonlegal beliefs that is used to maintain the status quo, especially in the political and economic spheres. This is accomplished by convincing others that those in power should remain in power. The legal system, including legal education, is a deceptive social mechanism for the preservation of power by those who currently have it. People can free themselves of this perspective only by critically examining these beliefs. Generally, people who subscribe to the CLS view wish to overturn the status quo. This theory is criticized as being basically a negative position; it does not have any concrete suggestions about how to change the social, political, and legal systems.

Exhibit 1.4 summarizes the foregoing philosophical approaches to jurisprudence.

Change in the Legal System

A student of the law should note that people do not always comply with the law. When you observe people in your community repeatedly doing something, you might conclude that this behavior is lawful, but this assumption may be unwise. For example, drivers may repeatedly violate posted speed limits. During your study of business law, you should try to distinguish these three distinct questions:

1. What is the law about this topic?

2. How do people and businesses behave?

3. What should the law be on this topic?

Answers to these questions will vary based on the state or region under analysis. The most variance will occur about what the law should be. Individuals will disagree on the

EXHIBIT   1.4   Theories of Jurisprudence

Theory	Primary Characteristic
Natural Law	Source of law is nature, God, or reason.
Legal Positivism	Source of law is the legislature.
Sociological	Source of law is contemporary community standards and customs.
Historical	Law evolves over time based on custom and social traditions.
Law and Economics	Classical economic theory should be applied to all areas of the law.
Feminist Legal	Legal system is dominated by the perspective of white males; women's perspectives are ignored and women are victimized.
Critical Legal Studies	Law is a combination of legal and nonlegal beliefs; it must be critiqued to create social change and political growth.

answer to this question, based on their views about jurisprudence and their values. Proactive businesspeople may suggest answers that will benefit their particular business enterprise or industry.

What Are the Sources of Law in the U.S. Legal System?

The U.S. legal system is based on the Constitution, treaties, statutes, ordinances, administrative regulations, common law, case law, and equity. The elements are separate but interdependent; together they constitute our system. These elements must be thought of as a system—a change in one element should not be considered in isolation. Such a change will affect one or more parts of the system. In a civil rights suit, a person may allege a violation of constitutional rights (Fourteenth Amendment), a statutory right (Civil Rights Act of 1964), an administrative regulation (Equal Employment Opportunity Commission guideline), past decisions of the courts, called *stare decisis* (to abide by, or adhere to, decided cases; policy of courts to stand by decided cases and not to disturb a settled point of law), and *equity* (if all else fails, the person should win because it is fair). The important thing to remember is that all the parts of the legal system are interconnected and that the whole is more than the sum of the parts.

Constitutions

A *constitution* is the fundamental law of a nation. It may be written or unwritten—the British constitution is said to be unwritten. Clearly, the U.S. Constitution is written (see Appendix A of this text). It allocates the powers of government and also sets limits on those powers. Our founding fathers knew that all tyrants had two powers: the power of the purse and the power of the sword. The Constitution places the power of the purse exclusively with Congress and the power of the sword with the Executive branch. The Judiciary, our third branch of government, has neither the power of the purse nor the power of the sword. However, it has the power to interpret the meaning of the U.S. Constitution and to decide the constitutionality of the laws passed by Congress. In the case of *Marbury v. Madison*,[14] the U.S. Supreme Court for the first time applied the doctrine of *judicial review* (the power of the courts to say what the law is). That case held that the Supreme Court has the power to decide whether laws passed by Congress comply with the Constitution. If they do not, they are unconstitutional and

thus of no force or effect. We will discuss the unique nature of the Constitution further in Chapter 5.

Our states also have constitutions, and they are the fundamental laws of those states. The U.S. Constitution, however, is the supreme legal document in the United States and thus will take precedence over state constitutions.

Treaties

Treaties are formal agreements between two or more nations. The United States enters into treaties for various purposes including providing protection, for example, through the North Atlantic Treaty Organization (NATO), and promoting trade, for example, through the North American Free Trade Agreement (NAFTA). Treaties are the only elements of our legal system that do not stem from the Constitution. Treaties are made, not with the authority of the Constitution, but under the authority of the United States. This difference is important because the power to make a treaty is a function of sovereignty and not a function of the constitution. In most cases, treaties require enabling legislation to be passed by Congress. The case of *Missouri v. Holland*[15] established that statutes passed in accordance with a valid treaty cannot be declared unconstitutional. Once made, treaties also become the supreme law of the land.

Statutes

Statutes are the acts of legislative bodies. They prohibit or command the doing of something. The word "statute" is preferred when one is referring to a legislative act to distinguish it from such other "laws" as ordinances, regulations, common law, and case law. The U.S. Congress, via its Web site Thomas (for Thomas Jefferson) provides news and information on Congress, bills before Congress (text, summary, and status), the *Congressional Record*, and committee information. It allows you to track bills at http://thomas.loc.gov/ and includes Information Sources for Legislative Research at http://thomas.loc.gov/home/legbranch/otherleg.html.

The best example of state statutory law is found in the Uniform Commercial Code (UCC) (see Appendix B). All 50 states, the District of Columbia, and the U.S. Virgin Islands have adopted at least portions of the law. The UCC is very important and, accordingly, is the subject of many of the chapters contained in this book. The UCC covers the following subjects: sales, leases, negotiable instruments, bank deposits and collections, fund transfers, letters of credit, bulk transfers, documents of title, investment securities, and secured transactions.

Ordinances

Ordinances are laws passed by municipal bodies. Cities, towns, and villages, if incorporated, have the power to establish laws for the protection of the public's health, safety, and welfare. These entities are to be distinguished from counties, which generally do not have legislative power. Counties usually have the power to enforce state laws within their boundaries.

Administrative Regulations

Administrative regulations are rules promulgated by governmental agencies, most of which are created by the legislative branch of government. Examples of agencies include the Federal Trade Commission (FTC) on the federal level and an insurance commission on the state level. These bodies have unusual powers, which will be discussed in Chapter 5. The rules and regulations of these entities have the full force and effect of law.

Common Law

Common law consists of the unwritten law of a country, based on custom, usage, *and* the decisions of the law courts. The development of the common law is depicted in Exhibit 1.5. Not all nations have a "common law" per se. Most European nations, for example, have code-based legal systems in which "common law" is not followed. Courts lack the authority or power to "make law" through judicial rulings. By contrast, nations following the Anglo-American legal tradition do have common law.

Case Law

Case law derives from the many reported cases being decided by federal and state courts, and it is part of the common law previously discussed. Quite often the judges must interpret statutes in order to apply them to actual cases and controversies. These interpretations place what lawyers call a "judicial gloss" on the statute. You will not fully understand a particular statute until you have read both the statute *and* the cases that have interpreted it. *Case law*, then, is the law as pronounced by judges.

The American Law Institute (ALI) is dedicated to promoting clarification of the law, improving the administration of justice, and drafting the Restatements of the Law. *Restatements* are not actually part of the law; rather they are treatises that summarize the law on a subject. When there are conflicting approaches, the Restatement "recommends" one of the alternatives. Restatements become part of the case law when a court relies on a particular section in reaching its opinion.

Stare decisis is an ancient doctrine that means the question has been decided. For example, if a particular legal point is well settled in a certain jurisdiction, a future case with substantially the same facts will be decided in accordance with the principle that has already been decided. This is one of the reasons that lawyers do a great deal of legal research. The doctrine of *stare decisis* is also called precedents. Even though a legal matter has been settled, it does not mean the legal system must remain static. The Gilder Lehrman Institute of American History maintains a Web site of historic Supreme Court decisions at http://www.gliah.uh.edu/supreme_court/supreme_court.cfm/. Professor Douglas Linder, University of Missouri–Kansas City Law School, maintains a Famous Trials Web site at http://www.law.umkc.edu/faculty/projects/ftrials/ftrials.htm that includes interesting background information and pictures. The trials begin with the Trial of Socrates (399 B.C.).

A precedent remains in effect until it is changed. (Precedents do not play a major role in all legal systems.) Remember that the legal system evolves. Lawyers and petitioners in court are constantly asking to have precedents changed, and sometimes they are successful. Occasionally, the court will change or modify the precedents. When a court changes the precedents, it will generally support its decision with one of these three reasons:

1. The prior rule is out of date; it is not appropriate to present-day society.

2. The prior case is distinguishable because the facts are different in one or more significant details.

EXHIBIT   1.5   Common Law

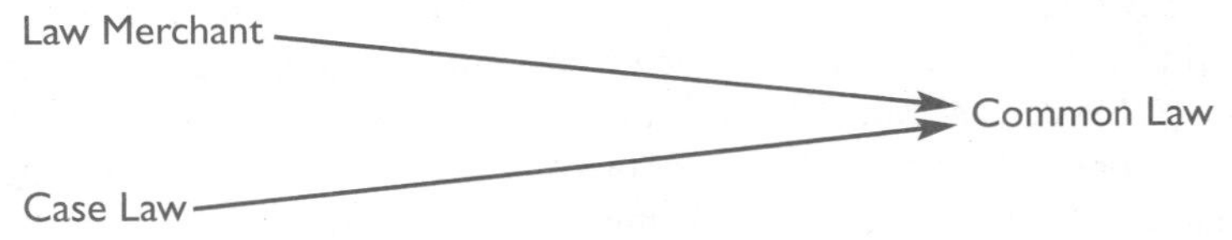

3. The judge or justice who made the prior ruling was incorrect or wrong.

Judges may be reluctant to state that the prior ruling was in error, especially if they participated in making the prior ruling. It is easier to state that someone else made an error. Judges *sometimes* do admit that the rule they fashioned earlier is not the preferred response to a particular legal problem.

When a court follows precedent it is striving to make the law *definite,* satisfying one of the needs of a legal system. However, as times and situations change, courts need to be able to change. The law would not be *flexible,* another need of a legal system, if precedents could never be changed. Courts have a difficult time balancing these two needs—definite and flexible—in deciding whether to apply precedents. *Brown v. Board of Education*[16] is an example of a court overturning precedents. In that case, the U.S. Supreme Court decided, contrary to prior decisions, that providing separate schools for black and white children was unconstitutional.

Dictum is language in a court opinion that is not necessary to the decision before the court. It is an observation or remark by a judge that is not necessarily involved in the case or essential to its resolution. These remarks or asides are not part of the precedents. Dictum can provide valuable clues about how that judge might decide future cases.

An opportunity to "make law," as it is called, occurs when jurisdictions are in conflict over a point of law. For example, many states are divided into various judicial districts, and courts in each of these districts may issue written legal opinions. If two or more districts have published conflicting opinions on a particular point, and the state's supreme court has *not* issued an opinion on the point, the time is ripe for the creation of a new rule, statewide, that will resolve the matter once and for all. Until the statewide rule is created, however, each court creates precedents for itself and for any courts directly under it. When there are no prior court decisions on a point of law, the court may state that the case is one of first impression. *First impression* occurs when an issue is presented to the court for an initial decision; the issue presents a novel question of law for the court's decision and it is not governed by any existing precedent.

Equity

Equity is defined as a body of rules applied to legal controversies when no adequate remedy at law exists. These rules are based on the principles outlined by Justinian during his reign as the Byzantine emperor of Rome (A.D. 527–565): "to live honestly, to harm nobody, [and] to render to every man his due." These rules were developed outside the common law courts in England by an officer of the king

called the chancellor. The primary reasons for development of equity were the unfair decisions made by the law courts and the limited types of remedies available in law courts.

Today, the rules of law and equity are joined into one system of law. The injunction is an equitable remedy, but before U.S. courts will issue an injunction, the person requesting it must show proof that the remedy at law would be inadequate. For example, if your neighbors are burning rubber tires on their property and the prevailing wind carries the obnoxious odor directly across your property, their action will destroy the peaceful use and enjoyment of your land. In general, no amount of monetary damages would be sufficient to allow them to continue to burn rubber tires. In that case, you would not have an adequate remedy at law, and you could request that the court issue an injunction to stop your neighbors from burning those tires. In a larger sense, however, equity may be viewed as a doctrine that results in the legal system's adherence to the principle of fairness. Exhibit 1.6 summarizes some of the differences between law and equity.

How Is the Law Classified?

Federal versus State Law

Our legal system is divided into two branches: federal and state. The FedLaw Web site, intended for federal employees and others engaged in federal legal research, is at http://www.thecre.com/fedlaw/default.htm/. American lawyers must learn not only the law of their states but the law of the federal courts as well. In addition, lawyers should know the majority rule. The *majority rule* is simply the rule that most states have adopted. Quite often there is a *minority rule,* followed by a smaller number of states. Rarely, if ever, do the states agree on all aspects of a law. Washburn University School of Law maintains links to a number of sites including state law sites at http://www.washlaw.edu/; links to state government, legislative information, and information for all states at http://www.washlaw.edu/uslaw/statelaw.html#allstates/; and a searchable state law site at http://www.washlaw.edu/uslaw/search.html. Exhibit 1.7 outlines the sources of the U.S. legal system. Note that there is some overlap between case law and common law.

Common versus Statutory Law

As discussed earlier, the legal system consists of both common and statutory laws. Judges in the United States and the United Kingdom generally have the power to

EXHIBIT　1.6　Distinctions Between Actions in Law and in Equity[a]

Characteristic	In Law	In Equity[b]
Type of relief	Money to compensate plaintiff for his or her losses	Action, either in the form of ordering the defendant to do or not to do something, or in the form of a decree about the status of something[c][d]
Nature of proceeding	More restricted by precedents	More flexible and less restricted by precedents, supposed to create equity (justice)
Time limit for filing lawsuit	Applicable period fixed by the statute of limitations[e]	A reasonable period of time as determined by the judge on a case-by-case basis[f]
Decider of fact	Jury trial, if requested by a party	No jury trial, judge decides the facts[g]
Enforcing a decision	Plaintiff may begin an execution of the judgment[h]	Plaintiff may begin contempt proceedings if the defendant does not perform as directed; defendant may be placed in jail and/or fined[i]

a. Actions at law and those in equity are no longer as distinct as they once were. As a result, many states allow "combined" trials with issues of law and issues of equity being tried together.

b. Traditionally, a court of equity was called court of chancery, and the judge was called a chancellor.

c. Common equitable remedies include injunction, specific performance of a contract, rescission of a contract, and reformation (correction or rewriting of) a contract.

d. Courts would prefer to award monetary damages. Equitable relief is only granted when the plaintiff can show the court that money would be inadequate.

e. The statue of limitations period will depend on the state and the type of lawsuit. It will be a fixed period.

f. If the plaintiff has waited too long to file suit under the circumstances, the judge will apply the doctrine of laches and the suit will be dismissed.

g. Some states permit the use of an advisory jury.

h. In an execution, the clerk of the court issues a formal document and the sheriff seizes the defendant's money and/or other property. If property is seized, the sheriff will sell it and use the proceeds to pay the plaintiff.

i. The court is authorized to place the defendant in jail until he or she complies (or agrees to comply) with the court decree.

"make law" by interpreting statutes or applying precedents, and those interpretations become "common" law. Judges also apply the statutory law. Statutory law refers to legislative enactments, the statutes passed by the legislative bodies of the state. Common law is "unwritten" law, law developed over time by judicial action. Common law fills the gaps where other sources of law do not cover a particular topic. Statutory enactments override common law, filling the gap with a statutory provision and eliminating the need for unwritten coverage.

Civil versus Criminal Law

The U.S. legal system also separates civil and criminal law. *Civil law* is private law wherein one person sues another person. *Criminal law* is public law in which a government entity files charges against a person. For example, assume a person becomes violently abusive and attacks another individual, and thus inflicts bodily harm on the innocent individual, the district attorney, as the representative of a government entity, may prosecute the attacker for assault. If convicted, the attacker may go to jail or prison. In addition, the person who was injured may sue the attacker in court for money damages. The additional suit would not constitute double jeopardy or its civil law equivalent, *res judicata*, since two different theories of action exist: civil and criminal. (*Res judicata* is a rule of civil law that a person will not be sued more than once by the same party for the same civil wrong.)

Substantive versus Procedural Law

Substantive law deals with rights and duties given or imposed by the legal system. *Procedural law* is devoted to how those rights and duties are enforced. For example, the law of contracts is substantive law. The law of pleadings describes the steps used to enforce those rights or duties.

EXHIBIT 1.7   The Sources of Law in the U.S. Legal System

Authority	Source	Definition
F, S	Constitution	Supreme law of the land; fundamental basis of domestic law
F	Treaties	Not based on the Constitution; formal agreements between nations; fundamental basis of international law/relations
F, S	Statutes	Acts of the legislature; control of domestic conduct; subject to limits imposed by the Constitution
S	Ordinances	Laws passed by municipal bodies and designed to control purely local problems, subject to any limits imposed by statutes or by the Constitution
F, S	Administrative Regulations	Acts of administrative agencies; control of specific areas of conduct; subject to any limits imposed by statutes or by the Constitution
S	Common Law	Principles and rules that have developed over time and are based on custom and usage; provide rules when statutes and the Constitution do not
F, S	Case Law	Precedents, established interpretations of areas of law in which the courts define what the law is
F, S	Equity	Special rules and relief when "the law" does not provide a proper and/or adequate remedy

Legend: F = federal; S = state

(*Pleadings* are formal statements filed in court specifying the claims of the parties.) A controversy over the mental ability to form a valid contract is a substantive matter, but how one goes about getting the dispute into a court is a matter of procedure. Where one files the lawsuit, what must be alleged, how one notifies the defendant, and how long the defendant has to answer the allegations are all examples of procedural law. This book is devoted primarily to *substantive* law.

Public versus Private Law

Private law is the body of law that deals with the property and relationships of private persons. It includes the areas of *property law* (ownership and transfer of assets), *contract law* (rights and duties that arise from enforceable agreements), *tort law* (other private wrongs, such as negligence, invasion of privacy, and defamation), and *business relationships* (agency, partnerships, corporations, and similar entities). *Public law* deals with the relations between private individuals and the government. It also deals with the structure and operation of the government itself. *Constitutional law* (law relating to the government and its activities), *criminal law* (law relating to offenses against the government), and *administrative law* (law relating to government agencies) are types of public law. Both private law and public law are very important to business decision making.

An excellent source of information on both private and public law is the Legal Information Institute (LII) maintained by the Cornell Law School. LII provides links to the Homeland Security Act of 2002, Supreme Court decisions, opinions of the New York Court of Appeals, a hypertext version of the full U.S. Code and Uniform Commercial Code (UCC), treaties, statutes, and other legal documents at http://www.law.cornell.edu/.

Legal Systems in Other Countries

Sometimes we assume that all countries have the same or similar legal systems. This ethnocentric view can result in a rude shock when a U.S. citizen traveling in a foreign country continues to act as he or she would act at home. The U.S. citizen may find that behavior that is tolerated in the United States constitutes a crime in a foreign country, and that many of the protections he or she expects in the United States do not apply abroad. Other countries have different historical and sociological backgrounds. Citizens' values and government rules may differ from those of the United States. For example, life insurance isn't accepted under traditional Muslim law.[17]

NRW

LOBBYING THE GOVERNMENT ON BEHALF OF NRW

A number of citizens are concerned that products such as StuffTrakR will lead to the invasion of privacy for many customers who are merely using the product in their own homes. They are concerned that location information could be gathered through the customer's computer or from computers outside the person's home. These citizens have lobbied members of the state legislature demanding a statutory approach to guarantee the privacy of customers who buy StuffTrakR or similar products. Responding to complaints from organized consumer groups and individuals, the state legislature is considering the enactment of a statute that prohibits the marketing of StuffTrakR in the state unless the manufacturer can "guarantee" privacy. NRW does not believe the problem is as serious as these groups contend. However, Mai, Carlos, and Helen don't think they can provide the necessary proof. NRW would obviously like to stop the state legislature from enacting this proposed legislation because it would prevent NRW from selling StuffTrakR in the state. Mai, Carlos, and Helen wonder what they can do and turn to you for advice. What will you tell them?

BUSINESS CONSIDERATIONS What options are available to NRW under these circumstances? What can—or should—a business do when it feels that proposed legislation will have a serious impact on the firm's profitability?

ETHICAL CONSIDERATIONS Would it be ethical for a firm to attempt to influence potential legislation? What ethical considerations would arise should a firm decide to attempt to influence members of the legislature?

INTERNATIONAL CONSIDERATIONS Assume that a foreign government was considering a ban on StuffTrakR because of its concerns about consumer privacy rights. Would NRW have the same options or would its options be different? Why?

With the exception of the United Kingdom, most of Europe, including France, Germany, and Sweden, follows civil law. In this context, *civil law* means that the legal system relies on statutory law. The statutes are grouped into codes, and the judges administer the codes. Judges,

therefore, do not make law to the degree that they do in the United States. The judge relies primarily on the code and secondarily on other statutes passed by the legislative bodies.

Until recently, the former Union of Soviet Socialist Republics (USSR) followed a unique version of civil law. Owing to its socialist philosophy, private ownership of property was limited. The primary goal of this legal system was to preserve state ownership of all means of production. Consequently, the Soviet Union's law primarily consisted of public law such as criminal law. The law of property, contracts, and business organizations did not play a role. Many of the former Soviet republics are now beginning to engage in *privatization* (the process of going from government ownership of business and other property to private individual ownership). A body of private law is being developed as these countries move toward a more traditional civil law system. The new countries often rely on consultants, like attorneys, from the United States in developing their new system of commercial law.

In addition, the U.S. legal system is based on the law of precedents previously discussed in this chapter. However, there are other countries, such as Mexico, where precedent is not important. Each judge does his or her best to fashion a fair result in the particular case before the court. In civil law systems, precedent is not significant. In the European Union (EU), the role of precedents is increasing. Decisions made by the EU Court of Justice become precedents in all the member countries. Although the EU is primarily a code system, it is moving toward the use of precedents and more of a common law approach.

There are a number of legal systems based on religious teachings. The Hindu legal system is one example. Their system is a personal and religious law system that states that Hindus should act in accordance with this law wherever they live. The Hindu system has been recorded in law books called *smitris*. Most Hindu law applies to family matters. Anglo-Hindu law evolved in most Hindu countries while they were British colonies, because judges were applying a combination of English and Hindu laws. When it gained its independence from the United Kingdom, India replaced Anglo-Hindu law with a civil code primarily based on Hindu law.

Muslims believe in Islamic law or *Shari'a,* which is based on the Koran and other religious writings. Saudi Arabia relies almost exclusively on Islamic law. Other countries apply Islamic law in some areas, such as family law, and supplement it with secular law. In 1998, the Pakistani prime minister, Nawaz Sharif, proposed a constitutional amendment to transform their legal system into an Islamic system. (The current legal system is based on British common law.) Their constitution already permits the courts to overturn any statute that is un-Islamic.[18]

A number of other religions also have legal systems, including Catholicism and Judaism. These legal systems generally provide tribunals for resolving disputes.

The Attorney-Client Relationship

Legal issues are critical in all businesses, even though some businesses are subjected to more government regulation than others. Whether the business is faced with litigation or is practicing prevention and attempting to avoid legal problems, attorneys can be important resources in a business. One of the primary purposes of this text is to assist you in speaking intelligently with your attorney and to enable you to more fully understand what he or she says to you.

Hiring an Attorney

Each state has a body of law dealing with the attorney-client relationship. It generally addresses an attorney's obligation to his or her client and the extent of the obligation to keep client confidences. The ALI has written and published the Restatement (Third) of the Law Governing Lawyers on lawyer-client relationships.[19]

Attorneys are generally paid a flat fee (a one-time fee), an hourly fee (based on an hourly rate), or a contingent fee (based on a percentage of the settlement or award.) Contingent fees are not permitted in criminal cases; in some states, they may be disallowed for other types of cases too. The following should be helpful when you need to hire an attorney:

1. Generate a list of potential lawyers by asking personal and business contacts. Try to find friends who have had a similar type of legal difficulty. Use *Martindale-Hubbell Law Directory*, West's Legal Directory (online), or directories maintained by your state bar association to discover additional information about the lawyers on your list. The Web site operated by Law.com has a law dictionary feature and a link to the *Martindale-Hubbell Law Directory* at http://www.law.com/. You can also locate a lawyer by using the West Legal Directory at the FindLaw Web site at http://directory.findlaw.com/.

2. Shop around and interview more than one attorney.

3. When interviewing, ask lawyers about their experience in this particular area of the law. Also ask: What are the probable outcomes of your dispute? How long will the legal matter take?

4. Find out how the attorney is going to charge and what services you, as the client, will receive for the fee. For example, it is common in litigation for a fee to include a trial, but no appellate work. Will a contingent fee be based on the award before or after expenses? If the attorney is going to charge an hourly rate, what is the smallest unit of time that is used for billing? In other words, will you be billed for 10 minutes or 15 minutes for a simple phone call to the lawyer? What is a realistic estimate for the total bill and expenses? You should realize that it is more difficult to make a realistic estimate for some types of cases than others, particularly when the workload may depend on the decisions of the opponent. How often will the attorney send you a bill? Will the attorney put the estimate in writing? Will the attorney enter into a written contract with you?

5. Ask whether the fee will include private investigators, filing fees, expert witnesses, other attorneys, paralegals, photocopies, and so on. Generally, it does not. What other types of fees and expenses does the lawyer anticipate?

6. Find out if you can take steps to reduce the legal fees. For example, you may be able to do some tasks yourself.

7. Ask if the attorney will need additional information from you.

8. Find out the attorney's procedure for handling billing disputes. Will the attorney charge for the additional hours spent on the billing dispute? Will the attorney agree to mandatory arbitration of the fee if the parties cannot resolve the dispute?

9. What are the alternatives to litigation? (See Chapter 6.) Does the attorney recommend any of them for this case? Does the attorney know any mediators or arbitrators who would be appropriate?

10. Try to discern whether client complaints have been filed against this attorney. Often this information is made public and is available from the disciplinary agency for the state. This is generally the state bar association or the state supreme court.

11. Select the approach you plan to take with the case and choose a lawyer whose style is similar to the approach you selected. Do you want someone who is extremely aggressive or more conciliatory?

12. Do *not* hire an attorney who is unable to communicate effectively with you or is unwilling to answer questions.

Clients are sometimes dissatisfied with the services provided by their attorneys. In 1994, Consumer Union surveyed members regarding their experiences with attorneys from 1991 to 1994 and discovered that of the 30,000 respondents, clients involved in adversarial cases were more likely to be displeased with the legal services they received than those involved in nonadversarial matters. For example, 27 percent of the people who had hired an attorney for an adversarial matter were dissatisfied with the work performed by the lawyer. The survey noted that *some* clients were unhappy with an aspect of their case. Common "complaints" included the manner in which the attorney (1) expedited the resolution of the matter; (2) kept them informed; (3) charged fees and expenses; (4) protected their rights and financial interests; (5) informed them about costs early in the process; and (6) did not act in a polite and considerate manner toward them.[20]

Resolving Problems with Legal Counsel

If a problem does arise from the attorney-client relationship, you should first try to resolve the problem with the attorney and/or the law firm. Begin with a clear letter expressing your concern and what you would like the attorney to do. If the problem is not resolved at this stage, you can fire the attorney and hire another. However, it may be costly for the replacement to become familiar with the dispute, and replacing an attorney may postpone the ultimate resolution of the legal matter.

If you believe the attorney breached one of the codes of ethics, you can report him or her to the disciplinary board. The American Bar Association (ABA) has a code of ethics for attorneys, and most states also have their own codes of ethics. Copies are usually available from the library or the state bar association or disciplinary board. Bar associations or disciplinary boards will not provide legal assistance to you but may investigate and take punitive action against the attorney, if appropriate. Most states have established a fund for clients who lose money because the attorney takes it from them and uses it inappropriately (for example, embezzles it). Practicing attorneys in the state are generally required to pay into the fund. As a last resort, you can sue the attorney for malpractice; however, then you will have to hire another attorney and begin a new litigation. In addition, it may be difficult for you to prove your damages, especially if you lost a lawsuit while the first attorney was representing you. Then the defendant will argue that even with another attorney, you still would have lost the suit.

Summary

Law consists of rules that must be obeyed because they are enforceable in courts of law. Order is the absence of chaos, and our legal system strives to create and to maintain order. Justice is fairness. Commutative justice seeks to treat each person the same regardless of circumstances. Distributive justice seeks to vary treatment as appropriate in the situation. Our legal system seeks constantly to balance law, order, and justice. Its ultimate goal is to achieve equilibrium.

The law is an artificial language system that includes everyday words with technical meanings. The law also uses words that are unique to the law. The law of business includes contracts, sales, negotiable instruments, secured transactions, agency relationships, partnerships, and corporations. By studying the law of business, you will learn how to avoid legal problems. If legal problems should develop, however, this knowledge will sensitize you to their ramifications. As a result, you will know when an attorney should be consulted.

A legal system needs to be reasonable, definite, practical, published, and final. A legal system should be directed toward achieving justice. It does so by properly utilizing police power; by keeping the peace or maintaining the status quo when irreparable injury is threatened; by providing answers; by protecting people, property, and government; by enforcing intent; by rehabilitating people; and by facilitating commercial transactions. There are various philosophies about how the law works or how it should work.

Our legal system is like a three-dimensional chess game in which a move in one subsystem can affect other subsystems. The sources of law in the U.S. legal system are constitutions, treaties, statutes, ordinances, administrative regulations, common law, case law, and equity. The law is a multidimensional system, including common and statutory law, civil and criminal law, substantive and procedural law, and public and private law. The legal system is also composed of two branches—federal law and state law. A traveler or businessperson should not assume that foreign law is similar to U.S. law.

Discussion Questions

1. John Locke stated, "Where there is no law, there is no freedom."[21] What do you think he meant by this statement?

2. Noted legal scholar Roscoe Pound said, "Law must be stable and yet it cannot stand still."[22] What do you think he meant? How does this statement relate to the purposes of the legal system? Explain your answer.

3. What are the risks when a business takes a reactive approach to a potential problem arising in the legal system?

4. What are the jurisprudential approaches of the following court opinion discussing whether an obligation to return an engagement ring should be based on fault?

   [T]he fault rule is sexist and archaic, a too-long enduring reminder of the times when even the law discriminated against women. . . . In ancient Rome the rule was fault. When the woman broke the engagement, however, she was required not only to return the ring, but also its value, as a penalty. No penalty attached when the breach was the man's. In England, women were oppressed by the rigidly stratified social order of the day. They worked as servants or, if not of the servant class, were dependent on their relatives. The fact that men were in short supply, marriage above one's station rare[,] and travel difficult abbreviated betrothal prospects for women. Marriages were arranged. Women's lifetime choices were limited to a marriage or a nunnery. . . . Men, because it was a man's world, were much more likely than women to break engagements. When one did, he left behind a woman of tainted reputation and ruined prospects. The law . . . gave her the engagement ring, as a consolation prize. When the man was jilted, a seldom thing, justice required the ring's return to him. Thus, the rule of life was the rule of law—both saw women as inferiors.[23]

5. Which jurisprudential view do you most closely agree with? Why?

6. John Rawls writes about justice and the elements that are necessary for a just society. He describes the "Bargaining Game," a theoretical community of men and women who get together to bargain for a completely new set of moral rules (laws) that they must all obey in the future. Once the rules are selected, the players must adhere to the rules, even if the rules are not in their self-interest in a particular situation. The players choosing the rules do not know their own position in society, talents, or abilities. Rawls calls this the veil of ignorance.[24] Rawls has been interpreted as saying "In effect, the parties choose principles for the design of society as if their places in it were to be determined by their worst enemies."[25] What rules do you think the players would choose and why?

7. When does a business need to be familiar with the laws and legal systems of other countries?

8. Jeremy Bentham (1748–1832), an English lawyer, is best known for his utilitarian philosophy that the object of law should be to achieve the "greatest happiness of the greatest number." Discuss the implications of the following statement based on your knowledge of common versus statutory law:

   Do you know how they make [common law]? Just as a man makes laws for his dog. When your dog does anything you want to break him of, you wait until he does it and then beat him. This is the way you make law for your dog, and this is the way judges make laws for you and me. They won't tell a man beforehand. . . . The French have had enough of this dog-law; they are turning it as fast as they can into statute law, that everybody may have a rule to go by. . . .[26]

9. Explain the role of the Restatements of law.

10. In the United States, the general rule is that each party pays his or her own attorney's fees. There are a few exceptions provided under specific statutes. In the United Kingdom, the general rule is that the loser pays the winner's attorney's fees. Should the United States adopt the British rule? Why or why not?

Case Problems and Writing Assignments

1. The Smithsonian Institution has a collection of nude photographs taken of college freshmen from Ivy League and other elite schools. Schools involved include Harvard, Princeton, Swarthmore, Yale, Vassar, and Wellesley. Many of the universities and colleges involved required all freshmen to pose in the nude for a frontal and a profile picture. This practice began in the early 1900s. At first, the pictures were taken as part of physical education classes to study posture; poise and posture were considered important in health. The pictures were then continued as part of a research project by W. H. Sheldon, who believed that there was a relationship between body shape and other traits such as intelligence. (Scientists generally dismiss his research today.) Schools allowed Sheldon access to take pictures of their students from the 1940s through the 1960s. Many of the schools have destroyed their collections. How the Smithsonian received the collection and who is actually pictured in the Smithsonian collection is unclear. Some prominent people were allegedly photographed during this period, including former president George H. W. Bush and Senator Hillary Rodham Clinton. A number of people have filed suit seeking an injunction against any displays or other uses of these pictures without permission of the subject in the photograph. What should the Smithsonian or other museums or research institutes do when they receive property of this nature? Why? Should a business have a policy for handling sensitive information or photographs about its employees or customers? Who

should have ownership rights in pictures such as these? What should be the Smithsonian's ethical obligation in regard to these pictures? Would the fact that some prominent people may be included affect this ethical obligation? [See Brigette Greenberg, "Smithsonian Blocks Access to Nude Photos," *The Fresno Bee*, January 21, 1995, pp. A1 and A12.]

2. In 1992, Rosa, an 18-year-old woman in Southern Italy went for a driving lesson. Rosa claims that the 45-year-old instructor took her to a remote area and raped her. The instructor argued that the sex was consensual. The all-male panel of judges on the criminal appeals court concluded that Rosa consented, after considering that it is difficult to remove jeans without the cooperation of the wearer, that Rosa waited several hours to tell her parents, and that Rosa returned to the driving school later that day for a driving theory lesson. The appeals court also said, "It should be noted that it is instinctive, especially for a young woman, to oppose with all her strength the person who wants to rape her. And it is illogical to say that a young woman would passively submit to a rape . . . for fear of undergoing other hypothetical and no more serious offenses to her physical safety."[27] The case has been returned for retrial. Do you agree with the appeals court decision? Why or why not? Some information is lacking in the English language press. What additional information is important? [See "Judge Defends Rape-Jeans Ruling: 'We Have Complete Respect for Women,' Says Italian at Centre of Storm," *The Gazette* (Montreal), February 13, 1999, Art & Entertainment, p. D20; Alessandra Stanley, "'Denim Defense': Court Ruling in Italy Rekindles Angry Debate About Rape, Justice/The Judges' Ruling—That a Woman Who Is Wearing Jeans Can't Be the Victim of Rape—Incensed the Nation and Prompted a Protest in Parliament," *Minneapolis Star Tribune*, February 17, 1999, p. 11A; and "The Denim Defense," *Sacramento Bee*, February 19, 1999, Editorials, p. B6.]

3. Margaret Beattie was seriously injured in an automobile accident in Delaware. She incurred medical expenses of nearly $300,000 and was a quadriplegic following the accident. She filed suit against her husband for damages, alleging that his negligence was the cause of her injuries. Because the Beatties had substantial liability insurance, Margaret Beattie would have received a large sum in damages if she were able to establish her case. Unfortunately for her, Delaware follows the precedent of not allowing one spouse to sue the other spouse in tort. Should this precedent prevent Margaret from being allowed to sue her husband for her damages? [See *Beattie v. Beattie*, 630 A.2d 1096 (Del. 1993).]

4. Connecticut enacted a statute that went into effect October 1, 1993. Under the statute, police are permitted to seize a person's car if he or she patronizes prostitutes from the car. Police may arrest the person hiring the prostitute and impound the car. The person can recover his or her car for use prior to trial by posting a bond equal to the vehicle's book value. If the person is found not guilty in court, he or she is entitled to the return of the car and any bond that was posted. If someone else owns the car and the owner did not realize the car would be used to solicit prostitutes, the owner is entitled to have the car returned. Is this Connecticut law fair or just? [See "Police Hope to Drive Away Prostitutes by Confiscating Clients' Cars," *The Fresno Bee*, October 17, 1993, p. A9.]

5. **BUSINESS APPLICATION CASE** Janette Knudson became a quadriplegic in a car accident in June 1992. Eric Knudson was her husband at the time. His employer's health plan (Plan), Earth Systems, Inc., covered $411,157.11 of her medical expenses. Great-West Life & Annuity Insurance Co. paid most of it. The Plan's reimbursement provision gave it "the right to recover from the [beneficiary] any payment for benefits" paid by the Plan that the beneficiary was entitled to recover from a third party. This right was transferred to Great-West in a separate agreement. The Knudsons filed a tort action in California state court seeking to recover from Hyundai Motor Company, the manufacturer of the car in which they were riding, and other alleged wrongdoers. The parties negotiated a $650,000 settlement, most of which was allocated as follows: $256,745.30 to a Special Needs Trust under California statutes to provide for Janette's medical care; $373,426 to attorney's fees and costs; $5,000 to reimburse the California Medicaid program; and $13,828.70 (the portion of the settlement attributable to past medical expenses) to satisfy Great-West's claim under the reimbursement provision of the Plan. The state court approved the settlement. Great-West filed this federal action under § 502(a)(3) of the Employee Retirement Income Security Act of 1974 (ERISA) to enforce the Plan's reimbursement provision by requiring the Knudsons to pay the Plan $411,157.11 of any proceeds recovered from third parties. Section 502(a)(3) of ERISA authorizes a civil action "to enjoin any act or practice which violates . . . the terms of the plan, or . . . to obtain other appropriate equitable relief." Is this an action for equitable relief under § 502(a)(3) of ERISA authorizing Great-West's lawsuit? What advice would you give to businesses in Great-West's position? [See *Great-West Life & Annuity Insurance Company v. Knudson*, 534 U.S. 204, 2002 U.S. LEXIS 399 (2002).]

6. **ETHICAL APPLICATION CASE** Michael Fay, an American teenager, aged 18, was found guilty of spray-painting and throwing eggs at cars and possessing street signs in his room in Singapore. After Fay confessed, he was sentenced to four months in jail, fined $2,215, and subjected to six blows with a cane. This is a standard penalty for this type of behavior. Caning involves blows with a soaked rattan cane that is one-half inch thick. Prisoners often become unconscious during canings; however, a doctor revives them before the flogging continues. Caning causes severe pain and can cause serious bleeding and leave permanent scars. Prior to the caning, President Clinton and the parents (George Fay and Randy Chan) requested clemency from Singapore's president, Ong Teng Cheong. Is Fay's punishment under the Singapore criminal justice system appropriate? Why or why not? Is this a reasonable method to obtain law and order? Should the U.S. president have intervened? Why or why not? [See William Murphy, "Boy's Parents Losing Hope on Flogging," *The Fresno Bee*, April 15, 1994, p. A13; Jim Steinberg, "Fresnans Split on Flogging Penalty," *The Fresno Bee*, April 2, 1994, pp. B1 and B2.]

7. **CRITICAL THINKING CASE** The California legislature passed a state law that makes it a crime for citizens to knowingly lodge false accusations against police officers. After Rodney King's 1991 videotaped beating by police officers, there was a flood of complaints against officers. The California Supreme Court in a unanimous decision upheld the statute, stating that the law does not violate freedom of speech guaranteed by the Constitution. Civil rights groups argued that people would be afraid to make legitimate complaints against police officers, because people thought the officers would encourage prosecutors to file criminal charges against the complainants. In the case before the court, a couple accused an Oxnard police officer of exposing himself to a group of at-risk teenagers. The Oxnard police department investigated the incident and could not corroborate the couple's claim. The couple contends that their allegations are true and that the incident is being covered up. In the opinion, the California Supreme Court said that the legislature could criminalize knowingly making false accusations against peace officers without criminalizing all false accusations. The couple will ask for review by the U.S. Supreme Court. Is this law sound policy? What public policy was the legislature attempting to advance? [See David Kravets, "Calif. Supreme Court Upholds Police Complaint Law," *Sacramento Bee*, December 5, 2002. http://www.sacbee.com/state_wire/v-print/story/5471799p-6455685c.html/.]

8. **YOU BE THE JUDGE** Under federal law, telemarketers must keep "do-not-call lists." If you get a call from a telemarketer, and you don't want any more calls, be clear and direct. Ask them to put you on their "do-not-call list." Write down the name of the company and the date. If the company calls again, hang up and file a complaint with the Federal Trade Commission. The company faces fines of up to $10,000 per violation if it continues to call homes on the list. The Direct Marketing Association, an organization of mail-order companies and other direct marketers, also maintains a list of people who do not wish to be called. It is entitled Telephone Preference Service.[28] In a recent letter to the editor, Charlie Hollomon wrote,

"If a telemarketer has a right to call, the citizen has a greater right to know who is calling. Instead of No-Call Lists, there should be OK to Call Lists, which citizens could use to indicate their willingness to receive solicitations. Telemarketers should then be required by law to be sure a citizen's phone is on such a list before calling."[29]

A number of states have passed or are considering statutes to protect consumers. For example, Louisiana and Pennsylvania recently enacted "Do-Not-Call List" statutes. A proposed statute to strengthen Nebraska's law has not been successful. Telemarketing is a big industry in Nebraska. One of the opponents, State Senator Jon Bruning said, "Philosophically, it was a big government bill. People can simply not answer the phone or hang up the phone if they don't want to talk. I didn't think we needed government to step in and save us from the free market."[30]

Assume that your state has just enacted a tough statute providing for a "No Call" list with penalties for violators. Three telemarketers have filed a class action suit to invalidate the law. (A *class action suit* is a lawsuit involving a group of plaintiffs or defendants who are in substantially the same position as each other.) The case has been brought in *your* court. How will *you* rule? [See Asa Aarons, "Getting Your Name on Do-Not-Call List Can Pull the Plug on Telemarketers," *New York Daily News*, March 23, 1999, p. 18; Ed Anderson, "No-Call List May Quiet Phones; Bill Hangs up on Telemarketers," *Times-Picayune*, May 20, 1999, Orleans Edition, p. A5; Letter from Pennsylvania Attorney General Mike Fisher, Do Not Call List, with links and enrollment information, http://www.nocallsplease.com/; Louisiana Public Service Commission Do Not Call Program Web site, with links and enrollment information, http://host.ntg.com/donotcall/. The Realtor Magazine Online has a chart entitled "States with Established Do-Not-Call Laws" with information about the state lists, fines, and links to the state contact agency on its Web site at http://www.realtor.org/rmomag.NSF/pages/donotcallapr02?OpenDocument=/.]

Notes

1. *Black's Law Dictionary*, 3rd ed. (St. Paul, Minn.: West, 1933), 1050.
2. Lloyd Duhaime of Duhaime & Company publishes a legal dictionary online and links to topical subjects at http://www.duhaime.org/diction.htm. Law.com has a law dictionary on its Web site at http://dictionary.law.com/.
3. *Earl of Chesterfield v. Janssen*, 28 Eng. Rep. 82, 100 (Ch. 1750).
4. *Drysdale v. Prudden*, 195 N.C. 722, 143 S.E. 530, 536 (1928).
5. James Rachels, *The Elements of Moral Philosophy*, 2nd ed. (New York: McGraw-Hill, 1993), 50.
6. "Law, Philosophy of," Section I.2, *The Internet Encyclopedia of Philosophy*, James Fieser, general editor, The University of Tennessee at Martin (1999), http://www.utm.edu/research/iep/.
7. Ibid., Section III.3, quoting Richard Posner, *Economic Analysis of Law*, 4th ed. (Boston: Little, Brown, 1992), 23. Posner currently serves as the chief judge of the U.S. Court of Appeals for the Seventh Circuit.
8. 924 F.2d 872, 878 (9th Cir. 1991).
9. "Judge Defends Rape-Jeans Ruling: 'We Have Complete Respect for Women,' Says Italian at Centre of Storm," *Montreal Gazette*, February 13, 1999, Art & Entertainment, p. D20.
10. Alessandra Stanley, "'Denim Defense': Court Ruling in Italy Rekindles Angry Debate About Rape, Justice/The Judges' Ruling—That a Woman Who Is Wearing Jeans Can't Be the Victim of Rape—Incensed the Nation and Prompted a Protest in Parliament," *Minneapolis Star Tribune*, February 17, 1999, 11A.
11. "Judge Defends Rape-Jeans Ruling," n. 9.
12. "The Denim Defense," *Sacramento Bee*, February 19, 1999, Editorials, p. B6.
13. *The Internet Encyclopedia of Philosophy*, Philosophy of Law, Section III.2, p. 12, quoting Andrew Altman, "Legal Realism, Critical Legal Studies, and Dworkin," *Philosophy and Public Affairs*, 15, no. 2 (1986): 221.
14. 1 Cranch 137, 2 L. Ed. 60 (1803).

15. 252 U.S. 416 (1920).

16. 347 U.S. 483 (1954).

17. "American Phoenix Will Provide Reinsurance to Oman Insurer," *Mealey's Litigation Report: Reinsurance* 9, no. 19 (February 11, 1999).

18. "An Islamic Legal System? Pakistan," *National Law Journal*, September 14, 1998, p. A14; Beena Sarwar Lahore, "Rights—Pakistan: Nawaz Sharif's Use of Religion Fools No One," IAC Newsletter Database, Global Information Network, Inter Press Service (September 16, 1998).

19. This is the first Restatement on this topic. It is labeled Third because it is part of the Third Series of Restatements. Information about this Restatement is available on the ALI Web site at http://www.ali.org/ali/A252.htm (accessed 12/8/02).

20. "When You Need a Lawyer," *Consumer Reports* (February 1996): 34–39.

21. John Locke, *Second Treatise of Government*, Section 57, ed. and introduction by Thomas P. Perdon (New York: Liberal Arts Press, 1952).

22. Roscoe Pound, *Interpretations of Legal History* (New York: Macmillan, 1923), I.

23. *Lindh v. Surman*, 702 A.2d 560, 1997 Pa. Super. LEXIS 3241 (Pa. Super. 1997), citing *Aronow v. Silver*, 538 A.2d 851, 853 (N.J. Super. 1987). The Pennsylvania Supreme Court affirmed the decision of the lower courts to use a strict no-fault rule in *Lindh v. Surman*, 560 Pa. 1, 1999 Pa. LEXIS 3498 (1999) (Case 42.1 in this book).

24. John Rawls, *A Theory of Justice* (Cambridge, Mass.: Harvard University Press, Belknap Press, 1971).

25. Chandran Kukathas and Philip Pettit, *Rawls: A Theory of Justice and its Critics,* (Palo Alto, Calif.: Stanford University Press, 1990), 39.

26. Jeremy Bentham, *The Works of Jeremy Bentham* (New York: Russell and Russell, 1962), 231.

27. Alessandra Stanley, "'Denim Defense'" n. 10.

28. Asa Aarons, "Getting Your Name on Do-Not-Call List Can Pull the Plug on Telemarketers," *New York Daily News*, March 23, 1999, p. 18.

29. Charlie Hollomon, "Letters: In My Opinion; Put Limits on Telemarketers," *Atlanta Journal and Constitution*, March 31, 1999, p. 17A.

30. Robynn Tysver, "'No Call' Phone List Hung Up: A Bill Targeting Unwanted Telemarketing Pitches Fails to Advance to the Next Round," *Omaha World-Herald*, April 8, 1999, Sunrise Edition, News, p. 11.

Business Ethics

AGENDA

NRW Mai, Carlos, and Helen need to understand and appreciate the ethical obligations and expectations under which they will operate NRW. Businesses today are expected to act ethically, even if they do not have any formulated ethical theory that provides guidance in this area, and this expectation is likely to increase. The principals also need to realize that a business must satisfy the *social contract* it has with society, even if they don't realize that they have entered into such a "contract."

They must weigh their decisions, taking into account the potential impact—both beneficial and harmful—on each of the constituent groups of the firm. They may want to decide how they should measure the ethics of any conduct they undertake for the business. They need to consider how a business manager knows what the social contract theory demands of the business. They will also need to know who the constituents of the business are and how their conduct can affect these different constituent groups. These and other questions need to be addressed in covering the material in this chapter. Be prepared! You never know when the firm or one of its members will seek your advice.

For quite some time a significant number of people have viewed the topic of business ethics as an oxymoron, a contradiction in terms. Some of these people have made jokes about the topic, while others have viewed any discussion of ethics for a business as an interesting academic exercise but one without any *real* meaning in the "real world" of commerce. However, the events of 2002 have caused a change in attitude among even the most jaded of observers. The corporate scandals and the resulting loss of trust by the public has once again shown that ethics is important in business, and that a perceived lack of ethics in a firm or in an industry can have devastating effects on the firm, the industry, or even the entire economy. Please try to keep the events, and the resulting economic harm, in mind while covering the material in this chapter.

Ethics and Morality

It is fairly standard for people to equate ethics with morality, and to use the words "ethics" and "morals" interchangeably. In so doing, they find it easier to discuss the topic of ethics. However, such an equation is not altogether accurate. *Ethics* refers to a guiding philosophy—the principles of conduct governing an individual or a group.[1] By contrast, *morals* relate to principles of right and wrong behavior as sanctioned by or operative on one's conscience.[2] From the perspective of an individual, ethics and morals may, and frequently do, have the same meaning. However, from the perspective of a group—including a society—it is more appropriate to speak of ethics. Thus, when we speak of ethics, we are talking about societal values, the accepted conduct within a given society. In contrast, when we speak of morals, we are talking about individual values, the accepted conduct *of* an individual *by* that individual. Different societies may have different ethics, but the morals of any given individual should remain relatively constant no matter which society that person should happen to be in at any point in time. Ethical conduct is conduct that is deemed right—or at least accepted as not wrong—within a societal setting. Moral conduct is conduct that the individual considers right—or at least does not consider wrong—without regard to the attitude of the society.

To further complicate this already complex issue, societies also have standards that go beyond ethics. The ethical standards of a society reflect what is considered "right" and "wrong" within that society in a general manner. Some wrong behavior may be merely a matter of rude conduct, frowned on within the society, but not of sufficient seriousness or severity to merit more than a social dislike of the conduct. Other "wrong" conduct may be considered much

more serious, calling for more than a societal frown; this conduct may be so inappropriate for the society that the person who acts in this "wrongful" manner may be subjected to a fine or even to incarceration. To help ensure that people within a society act in a socially acceptable manner, the society enacts laws and regulations, usually with penalties attached for conduct in violation of the law or regulation in question. These laws enacted by society provide an ethical floor—a minimum standard of behavior that is expected from each member of that society.

Although it is a broad generalization, conduct that violates a law or a regulation of a society is generally deemed unethical by that society. This is not to say that all unethical conduct is also illegal; rather it says that all illegal conduct is also unethical. Of course there are examples where some members of a society will act in a manner that violates a law or a regulation in order to force the society to reconsider its official position, with the aim of changing the law, and thereby changing the official social values the law affects. One such example involves Dr. Martin Luther King Jr., and his encouragement of civil disobedience in the 1950s. His conduct was technically illegal—and thus could be viewed as unethical—at the time. However, the success of the Civil Rights movement ultimately changed the laws regarding equal rights and racial discrimination, thereby changing the social values reflected by the laws governing human rights in this country. Dr. King acted in a *moral* manner, effecting changes that, in turn, made his conduct ethical *in hindsight*.

To take a simple, albeit controversial, example, let us examine the abortion issue in the United States. Since the Supreme Court's opinion in *Roe v. Wade*,[3] doctors in the United States have been able to legally, and therefore ethically, perform abortions in this country. Prior to that opinion, abortions were considered illegal in numerous states, and any doctor who performed an abortion was acting in an unethical—not to mention illegal—manner. The change in the law led to a change in the ethics of the society. In a similar vein, women now may ethically choose to have an abortion when they could not have so chosen prior to the *Roe v. Wade* decision. However, the fact that such a decision is ethical (acceptable to society) does not mean that it will be considered moral by everyone. Many women would not consider having an abortion because they view abortions as immoral. For these women to have an abortion would require them to violate their personal moral values. The fact that *society* considers such a procedure ethical would not affect how these women feel from a *personal* perspective. If these women choose not to have an abortion, they are acting both morally (adhering to their personal values) and ethically (adhering to society's values.) In other words, as long as their personal values—

their morals—do not involve acting in a manner prohibited by society's ethics, there is no problem with their adherence to their values.

If the personal morals of an individual call for conduct prohibited by society's ethics, however, there is a potential problem. For example, suppose a person feels that stealing is moral as long as the victim of the theft is wealthy. This person will encounter problems if he or she acts on the basis of this moral value by stealing from a wealthy victim. If this person decides to steal from the wealthy, he or she may be acting morally (adhering to his or her personal values), but will be deemed to have acted unethically by society (violating the society's values). Our society deems theft to be an illegal and an unethical act even though, purely personally, the conduct may be acceptable, and thus moral, to the individual.

Ethical Theories

Before the topic of business ethics can be addressed, it is imperative to have at least an introductory exposure to some of the more widely cited ethical theories and principles. This section of the chapter introduces several of these ethical theories and principles and compares them to one another. When we study these ethical theories, it is important to remember that there is no single "best" ethical theory everyone should follow. Each individual and each organization must choose the theory that best suits his, her, or its values and morals. The theory followed can be chosen in any fashion, even if that fashion seems entirely arbitrary to other people. The theory chosen can even be a combination of features from several different theories. For example, some people base their ethical beliefs on the Golden Rule (Do unto others as you would have others do unto you) while others select an "ends" approach (the outcome of the conduct determines its ethical nature). The important point is that a theory has been chosen and is being followed.

The study of ethics and of ethical principles is well known in philosophy, but it is relatively new to business. Business students have long been used to "hard-and-fast" rules and theories in their classes. Some of these rules or theories, such as *caveat emptor* and *laissez-faire* economics, were followed for a while and then discarded as society and its values changed. Others are still followed today. For example, "debits equal credits" is a given in accounting classes, and an accounting student can tell at a glance if the debits and the credits are equal. If they are not equal, that same accounting student knows that a problem exists and will then endeavor to find the problem and to solve it. However, the mere fact that debits do, in fact, equal credits does not guarantee that there is not a problem. An error might happen to be exactly offset by one or more other errors. Such errors are not as obvious as the one that exists when the debits and the credits do not match, but they are every bit as real, and they are more difficult to find. Business ethics is somewhat similar to this latter example.

Studying ethical theories and principles is not nearly as "hard and fast" as most other business topics, and the problems are not nearly as obvious in an ethical setting as the problems from the examples here. Yet questions of ethics—particularly questions of business ethics—are among the most important questions the businessperson of the modern era will face in his or her career. The manager may face the dilemma of choosing among bad alternatives; or the decision may entail a trade-off between short-term gains and long-term gains; or the decision may involve short-term gains (or losses) compared to longer-term losses (or gains).

While ethics can be defined as the system, or code, of morals of a particular person, religion, group, or profession,[4] such a definition does not provide much help in the area of business ethics. Business does not fit neatly into any of the categories mentioned in the definition. Although a business may be recognized as a legal person, the business is not a "particular person," nor does any one individual influence business enough to provide moral or ethical modeling for the firm. Even though it is undoubtedly true that some businesspeople worship "the almighty dollar," business does not qualify as a religion in any realistic sense of the term. Likewise, the "group" to which business belongs is too diverse to have a single system or code of morals.

Similarly, "business" is not a single profession like medicine or law, susceptible to the adoption of a single code of professional conduct, or of ethics, if you will. Thus, for most people, the study of business ethics comes down to an analysis of the system or code of morals of a particular person, the specific businessperson whose conduct is being evaluated. Unfortunately, the ethical standard too often applied in this situation is the ethical standard of the observer, and not that of the person being observed. To properly treat the ethical issues of a businessperson, some kind of analytic framework must be established, and some basic understanding of the ethical parameters of business needs to be developed.

Consequential and Nonconsequential Principles

Before a framework for the analysis of business ethics can be developed, some decisions must be made as to what values and standards are being measured, and on what basis the measurement is being made. Two broad categories of ethical theories exist, based on either consequential (teleological) principles or on nonconsequential (deontological) principles.

Consequential principles judge the ethics of a particular action by the consequences of that action. Consequential ethics, therefore, determines the "rightness" or the "wrongness" of any action by determining the ratio of good to evil that a given action will produce. A person practicing consequential ethics needs to evaluate each of his or her possible alternative actions, measuring the good (and the evil) that may result from the alternatives. The "right" action is that action which produces the greatest ratio of good to evil of any of the available alternatives. Among the major theories of ethical behavior under the consequential principles are egoism, utilitarianism, and feminism, also known as the "feminist philosophy." Each of these theories will be examined in more detail later in this section.

Nonconsequential principles tend to focus on the concept of "duty" rather than on any concepts of right and/or wrong. Under the nonconsequential approach, a person acts ethically if that person is faithful to his or her duty, regardless of the consequences that follow from being faithful to that duty. If a person carries out his or her duties, the greatest good must occur because the duty of the individual was carried out. If each individual carries out his or her duty, society knows what to expect from each individual in any and every given situation. This provides for greater long-term continuity than would arise if each individual based every choice he or she made on the anticipated consequences of each particular action for that individual. In addition, society imposes duties to maximize the values society wants, and by meeting that duty the individual is furthering the interests of that society. The "categorical imperative" advanced by Immanuel Kant and the "veil of ignorance" advocated by John Rawls are two of the best-known theories in support of the nonconsequential principles of ethics. Both of these theories will be discussed in detail later in this chapter.

Consequential Ethics

Egoism The doctrine that posits that self-interest is the proper goal of all human action is known as egoism.[5] (Do not confuse an *egoist*, a person who follows the ethical theory of egoism, with an *egotist*, a person who has an exaggerated sense of self-importance.) In the doctrine of egoism each person is expected to act in a manner that will maximize his or her long-term interests. In so doing, society is expected to benefit because when each individual acts in a manner that produces the greatest ratio of good to evil, the sum of all of these individual "good-producing" actions within the society will produce the greatest total good for the society.

One common misconception of egoism is that all egoists are hedonistic seekers of pleasure who emphasize instant gratification. This misconception treats one's pleasure as being equal to one's best interests. In fact, an egoist may well decide to act in a "selfless" manner because doing so will further the long-term self-interest of that person to a greater degree than will any short-term pleasures he or she might be able to enjoy. An egoist may be willing to make a personal sacrifice today to receive some benefit in the future, and doing so is perfectly consistent with the doctrine of egoism. Similarly, an egoist may obtain self-gratification from performing acts that benefit others; such actions may further one's long-term interests by increasing one's satisfaction.

In the same manner that an individual may follow egoism, so may an organization. From an organizational perspective, egoism involves those actions that best promote the long-term interests of the organization. Thus, a corporation may establish a minority hiring program or a college scholarship program, and in so doing the corporation may well be acting in a purely egoistic manner. These programs may advance the long-term interests of the corporation by improving its public image, reducing social tensions, or avoiding legal problems that might otherwise have arisen. The short-term expenses incurred in such programs are more than offset by the benefits to be derived in the future; the programs may appear to be generous and public spirited when in reality they are undertaken for purely "selfish" reasons—as befits the ethical theory of the particular firm.

Utilitarianism The second major consequential approach to ethics is utilitarianism. To a utilitarian, the proper course of conduct to follow in any given setting is the course that will produce the greatest good (or the least harm) for the greatest number.[6] Rather than focus on the interests of the individual (as an egoist would), the utilitarian focuses on the interests of the society. The ethical course of conduct is the one that best serves the interests of the social group as a whole, regardless of the impact on any individuals or any subgroups of the total social system. In theory, someone who is a utilitarian does not care if the "good" is immediately felt or if it is long term in nature. The only concern is whether the "good" to be derived—whenever it is derived—produces the greatest possible quantity of good available among the alternatives from which the choice was made.

There are two primary types of utilitarianism, *act utilitarianism* and *rule utilitarianism*. Act utilitarianism is concerned with individual actions and the effect of those actions on the social group as a whole more than it is concerned with obeying rules. An act utilitarian expects each person to act in a manner that will produce the greatest net benefit for the social group, even if such actions require the breaking of a social "rule." While it is felt that rules should generally be followed, exceptional situations may compel an act utilitarian to break the rules for the greater good of the society. Thus, to an act utilitarian, telling a "little white lie" may be the most ethical course of conduct in a given situation if telling the lie produces more total good than would be obtained by telling the truth, by avoiding the answer, or by any other alternative.

A rule utilitarian believes that strict adherence to the rules of the society will generally produce the greatest good for the greatest number. A rule utilitarian tends to follow all of the rules of the society without exception. This can lead to a problem in some situations. The rules that are followed can cause the rule utilitarian to become inflexible, especially when he or she faces a unique situation for which the rules were not designed. For more information on utilitarian theory, visit http://ethics.acusd.edu/theories/Utilitarianism/, which provides links to many articles on this theory.

Feminism Feminism, or the feminist philosophy (also called the ethics of caring), has gained in popularity recently. This ethical theory emphasizes that particular attention be paid to the effect of decisions on individuals, especially those individuals in a close relationship with the decision maker.[7] This philosophy focuses on character traits such as sympathy, compassion, loyalty, and friendship. While decisions are still based on doing the greatest good, other factors must also be considered. Among these factors are social cooperation and the realization that in many situations the parties are not of equal power or ability. The structure of the society must be protected, and the rights and interests of the less capable person should be protected as well. This philosophy is still developing, but it bears watching in the future. Feminism as an ethical theory is explained in more detail at http://plato.stanford.edu/entries/feminism-ethics/.

Nonconsequential Ethics

Kant and the Categorical Imperative
The nonconsequential principles of ethical theory are best exemplified by the categorical imperative developed by Immanuel Kant, an 18th-century German philosopher. Kant felt that certain universal moral standards exist without regard to

the circumstances of the moment or the values of any particular society.[8] Under Kant's theory, when people follow these universal moral principles, they are acting morally and ethically. When people do not follow these universal principles, they are acting unethically. Individual variations and consequences are irrelevant. The universal moral principles impose a duty on each person, and the performance of that duty is what determines the "rightness" or the "wrongness" of any given action.

Kant also posited perfect duties and imperfect duties. Perfect duties are those things a person must always do or refrain from doing, such as the duty of a merchant never to cheat a customer. Imperfect duties involve things a person should do, but not necessarily things a person must do. For example, a person should contribute to charities, but a person should not necessarily contribute to all charities, nor should a person have to contribute to any particular charity every time that charity solicits contributions.

Based on his theories, Kant developed his categorical imperative. The categorical imperative, simply stated, says that each person should act in such a manner that his or her actions could become the universal law. In a perfectly ethical and moral world, each person is expected to act as every person ought to act. The rules to be followed are unconditional, and adherence to these rules is imperative. If each person carries out his or her duty by following these "universal rules," society will be properly served by each individual.

Kant's approach to ethics is also applicable to organizations. An organization is judged in the same manner as an individual; the organization is expected to obey the categorical imperative, just as an individual is expected to obey it. The organization is to act according to its duty, with its actions being judged against the "universal law" standard—would such conduct be proper if all organizations were to act in the same manner? The organization would be expected to act in a manner that discharges its duty to every aspect of society, which would include recognition of the rights of others and the duty owed to others.

Rawls and the Veil of Ignorance
John Rawls took the works of Locke, Rousseau, and Kant as a starting point to develop his own theory of justice.[9] Rawls viewed these earlier works as the foundation for a "contract theory" of justice, and he presented his conception of justice as a higher level of abstraction from the earlier theories. Rawls felt that a truly just society would be one where the rules governing the society were developed behind a veil of ignorance, behind which no person would know his or her personal characteristics. If people made the rules while wholly ignorant of their unique combination of race, religion, color,

gender, wealth, age, or education, they would enact rules they would be willing to live under regardless of their own combination of factors once they stepped out from behind the veil of ignorance.

In a situation where each member of the society is willing to live under the rules developed behind the veil, true justice can be obtained. The society will adopt a proper constitution, create an appropriate method for legislation based on the constitution, and develop a proper method for dispute resolution; finally, judges and administrators will apply rules to particular cases, and citizens in general will follow the rules.[10] One of the many Web sites that provide more information on Rawls and his theories is http://oak. cats.ohiou.edu/~piccard/entropy/rawls.html.

Exhibit 2.1 summarizes and analyzes these theories as they apply in a business setting.

Other Theories There are other ethical theories that may also influence one's ethical outlook. Two of these will be discussed very briefly.

Relativism. Ethical relativism states that two people or two societies may hold ethical views that are opposed to one another, and yet both may be correct. In other words, this theory posits that ethics and values are relative and may change from one location to another. While it is true that different societies have different values (that is, the death penalty is a socially acceptable punishment in some societies, but not in others), the individual is more commonly governed by his or her *morals*, and personal morals do not change from one location to another. Relativism seems to be of more importance to sociologists and anthropologists than to ethicists.[11]

The Golden Rule. The Golden Rule theory of ethics advises each person to "do onto others as you would have others do onto you." This is a generally accepted principle in Judeo-Christian thought, and an admirable rule for people to follow. However, as an ethical theory it is difficult to measure and it is also difficult to define how to determine if one is following the principle in his or her conduct.

A Synthesis for Ethical Decision Making

Each of these ethical theories provides a possible framework for evaluating the ethics of a business and for evaluating the ethics of the people who operate the business. Remember, there is no one universally accepted theory or

approach to ethics in general, nor is there an accepted and universal approach to business ethics. Each firm in the business environment can select a theory of ethics to follow in developing its own ethical approach to conducting its business, whether it chooses a consequential theory, a nonconsequential theory, or a composite theory. Before choosing a theory, however, the businessperson should also take into account several other factors. These factors should include, but not be limited to, the short-term versus the long-term impact of any decisions, the constituent groups that will be affected by the decision being made (constituent groups are discussed later in the chapter), and the way in which the ethical decision fits within the laws and regulations affecting the business in this area.

Perhaps a business would be best advised to seek a synthesis of these different theories, as tempered by the social contract theory, to develop an approach to ethical issues. This approach would provide a structure for evaluating actions and options regardless of the ethical theory that most closely reflects the values of the business. One such synthesis is suggested by the work of Vincent Ruggerio.[12] Ruggerio suggests that there are three common concerns in ethical decision making: obligations, ideals, and effects. From this foundation we can develop a framework for ethical decision making without regard to whether the theory followed is a consequential or a nonconsequential theory. In making a decision, the following factors should be considered:

• The obligations that arise from organizational relationships

• The ideals involved in any decisions that are made

• The effects or consequences of alternative actions

Any actions that honor obligations while simultaneously advancing ideals and benefiting people can be presumed to be ethical actions. Any actions that fall short in any respect become suspect.[13] This is not to say that these latter actions are necessarily unethical. However, since these actions have a negative impact on one or more of the areas of concern, the actions should be very carefully evaluated, and alternatives should be examined to see if a better alternative has been overlooked.

With this in mind, the firm should follow a two-step process in order to assure that it is making ethical decisions. The first step is to identify the important considerations involved (obligations, ideals, and effects). The second step is to decide where the emphasis should lie among these three considerations. This approach allows the firm to apply its ethical principles to an ethical problem while also taking into account the social contract and the relative positions of each of the constituent groups of the business.

EXHIBIT   **2.1**   **A Comparison of Ethical Theories**

Ethical Theory	**Positive Aspects in a Business Context**	**Negative Aspects in a Business Context**
Egoism (Consequential theory—an act is ethical when it promotes the best long-term interests of the firm.)	1. Provides a basis for formulating and testing policies. 2. Provides flexibility in ethical decision making for business. 3. Allows a business to tailor codes of conduct to suit the complexity of its particular business dealings.	1. May ignore blatant wrongs. 2. Incompatible with the nature and role of business. 3. Cannot resolve conflicts of egoistic interests. 4. Introduces inconsistency into ethical counsel.[14]
Utilitarianism (Consequential theory—the most ethical decision is the one that produces the greatest good, or the least harm, for the greatest number of people.)	1. Provides a basis for formulating and testing policies. 2. Provides an objective manner for resolving conflicts of self-interest. 3. Recognizes the four constituent groups of a business. 4. Provides the latitude in ethical decision making that business seems to need.	1. Utilitarians ignore conduct which appears to be wrong in-and-of itself. 2. The principle of utility may be in conflict with the principle of justice. 3. It is very difficult to formulate satisfactory rules.[15]
Feminism (Consequential theory—the ethics of caring, it recognizes the importance of personal relationships.)	1. Provides a basis for formulating and testing policies. 2. Provides an objective manner for resolving conflicts of self-interest. 3. Recognizes the four constituent groups of a business. 4. Provides flexibility in ethical decision making for business.	1. Places undue emphasis on those closest to the decision maker. 2. May be more concerned with the "community" than with the business. 3. It is very difficult to formulate satisfactory rules.[16]
Categorical Imperative (Nonconsequential theory—only when we act from a sense of duty do actions have ethical worth.)	1. The categorical imperative takes the guesswork out of ethical decision making in business. 2. Introduces a needed humanistic dimension into business ethics decisions. 3. The concept of duty implies the ethical obligation to act from a respect for rights and the recognition of responsibilities.	1. Provides no clear way to resolve conflicts among duties. 2. There is no compelling reason that the prohibition against certain actions should hold without exception.[17]
Veil of Ignorance (Nonconsequential theory—rational agents, unaware of their personal characteristics or places in society, choose the principles they wish to have govern everyone in society.)	1. The veil of ignorance takes the guesswork out of ethical decision making in business. 2. Introduces a needed humanistic dimension into business ethics decisions. 3. Implies the ethical obligation to act from a respect for rights and the recognition of responsibilities.	1. Uses the better-off members of society to assume the welfare of the worst-off. 2. There is no compelling reason for following universal principles that might be agreed to in theory.[18]

The following case was decided in the late 19th century. Although the case has nothing to do with business, it does provide an opportunity to examine some of the problems that can arise in the study of ethics. Compare the ethical stances of the defendants in this case with the ethical theories discussed earlier. This case illustrates how simple it sometimes is for a person to rationalize conduct that would generally be viewed as reprehensible.

The Game Theory of Business

Business as an Amoral Institution

Historically, many viewed business as an amoral institution. Since any given business was inanimate, and since only animate objects could be expected to possess "morality," it stood to reason that a business was not expected to possess "morality." Because it could not be expected to be moral, it also could not be immoral. Morality and immorality were reserved for animate beings, and inanimate objects were amoral. When most businesses were relatively small and local in nature, this did not present much of a problem. The owners and operators of businesses were known in the community, and even though the business was viewed as amoral, the owner or operator was held to community standards. Thus most businesses were operated in an ethical manner in order to keep the local customers satisfied.

However, as businesses grew increasingly larger and more complex, this local flavor was lost. Businesses no longer operated in a restricted geographic market and no longer had to adhere to community standards. Eventually, society began to demand some minimal ethical standards for businesses. Included among these standards were the expectations of fair play and honesty, and the expectation that a business would seek profits for its investors. If a business did not meet these demands voluntarily, society could seek intervention and help from the legislature, which would then, at least on occasion, enact statutes setting minimal business standards of behavior. If the business obeyed these laws, it met the duty of fair play; if the managers did not blatantly lie to the customers, the business met the duty of honesty; if the firm generated profits for its investors, it met this duty.

2.1

REGINA v. DUDLEY AND STEPHENS
14 Q.B.D. 273 (1884)

FACTS In July 1884, four British sailors were cast away in a storm 1,600 miles from the Cape of Good Hope in an open lifeboat. The only food the crew found aboard the lifeboat was two one-pound tins of turnips. They were able to catch a turtle on their fourth day at sea, but had no other food beyond the turnips and the turtle through the 20th day. All four of the seamen were suffering from hunger and thirst by this time, and the youngest was delirious from drinking seawater. At that point, Dudley proposed that the other three should kill the youngest so that they would have food and liquid, and Stephens agreed. The next day, while Brooks was sleeping, Dudley killed the boy. While Brooks did not condone the act, he shared in the "bounty," and for the next four days the three men fed on the body and blood of the boy. They were rescued by a passing ship on the 29th day and taken to England, where they were arrested and charged with murder.

ISSUE Was the killing of the boy an act of murder or an act of self-defense?

HOLDING It was an act of murder.

REASONING Excerpts from the opinion of Lord Coleridge, Chief Justice:

[The court granted] that if the men had not fed upon the body of the boy they would probably not have survived to be so picked up and rescued, but would within the four days have died of famine. [It also agreed] that the boy, being in a much weaker condition, was likely to have died before them . . . [t]hat under these circumstances there appeared to the prisoners every probability that unless they then fed or very soon fed upon the boy or one of themselves they would die of starvation. That there was no appreciable chance of saving life except by killing some one for the others to eat. . . .

[The court addressed the self-defense issue by examining the words of Lord Hale. In the chapter in which he deals with the exemption to murder created by compulsion or necessity, he stated:] "If a man be desperately assaulted and in peril of death, and cannot otherwise escape unless, to satisfy his assailant's fury, he will kill an innocent person then present, the fear and actual force will not acquit him of the crime and punishment of murder, for he ought rather to die himself than kill an innocent; but if he cannot otherwise save his own life the law permits him in his own defence to kill the assailant."

[The court recognized the stress the sailors faced, and acknowledged that the temptations they faced were powerful, but denied that these things created a "necessity" justifying homicide.] Nor is this to be regretted. Though law and morality are not the same, and many things may be immoral which are not necessarily illegal, yet the absolute divorce of law from morality would be of fatal consequence; and such divorce would follow if the temptation to murder in this case were to be held by law an absolute defence of it. It is not so. To preserve one's life is generally speaking a duty, but it may be the plainest and the highest duty to sacrifice it. . . . It is not needful to point out the awful danger of admitting the principle which has been contended for. Who is to be the judge of this sort of necessity? By what measure is the comparative value of lives to be measured? Is it to be strength, or intellect, or what? It is plain that the principle leaves to him who is to profit by it to determine the necessity which will justify him in deliberately taking another's life to save his own. . . . [I]t is quite plain that such a principle once admitted might be made the legal cloak for unbridled passion and atrocious crime. There is no safe path for judges to tread but to ascertain the law to the best of their ability and to declare it according to their judgment; and if in any case the law appears to be too severe for individuals, to leave it to the Sovereign to exercise that prerogative of mercy which the Constitution has intrusted to the hands fittest to dis-

pense it. . . . It is therefore our duty to declare that the prisoners' act in this case was willful murder, that the facts as stated in the verdict are no legal justification of the homicide; and to say that in our unanimous opinion the prisoners are upon this special verdict guilty of murder.

[The court then proceeded to pass a sentence of death on the prisoners. Queen Victoria subsequently commuted the sentences, setting the punishment to be served by Dudley and Stephens at six months imprisonment.]

BUSINESS CONSIDERATIONS Assume that a business is facing serious economic problems. While there are several alternatives available, the easiest method of economic recovery for the business is to "cannibalize" a subsidiary of the firm (to strip away the assets, leaving an empty shell). What should the business do?

ETHICAL CONSIDERATIONS Is it possible to make a (superficially) persuasive ethical argument in support of the defendants on either an egoistic or a utilitarian basis, if one so desires? Can a persuasive argument be made under either the categorical imperative or the veil of ignorance?

As an example, look at the court opinion in *Dodge v. Ford Motor Company,*[19] a 1919 opinion by the Supreme Court of Michigan. Ford Motor Company was an extremely successful enterprise at the time, and it was paying dividends reflecting that success. Between "ordinary dividends" of 5 percent *per month* and special dividends that had averaged more than *400 percent* per annum over the previous five years, the stockholders were receiving substantial returns on their investments. At that time, Henry Ford and the board of directors announced a change. While Ford would continue to pay regular dividends of 5 percent per month, there would be no more special dividends. Instead, the board announced its intention to reduce the price of new cars, and to make substantial investments in socially beneficial programs for the employees and the community. Two of the stockholders, the Dodge brothers, filed suit to prevent this conduct proposed by Mr. Ford. The Michigan Supreme Court ruled that the board of directors of a corporation may *not* place the interests of the public ahead of the interests of the stockholders, and may *not* divert corporate funds to noncorporate purposes. The board was instructed to continue to maximize profits and to leave any charitable or public benefit contributions for individuals who chose to make such contributions from personal funds.

Notice what the court said a corporation is expected to do. Would such conduct by a corporation be considered ethical today? If not, what has changed? Investors still want a return on their investments, and they expect to receive dividends from the corporations with whom they invest. Businesses are still expected to earn a profit, and to return at least a portion of that profit to the shareholders.

The *Dodge v. Ford Motor Company* case is viewed as a landmark opinion, providing guidance for boards of directors in closely held corporations. While this opinion deals directly with the conflict between the desire of the Ford board to provide for the workers, and the challenge by shareholders who wanted dividends, the basic thrust of the opinion is that the board has a duty to the shareholders to maximize the return on their investments.

Many people have argued that the *Dodge* opinion prohibited any charitable contributions by a corporation, unless such contributions were expressly authorized in the corporation's charter or bylaws. However, courts have generally disagreed with this position, finding an implicit authority to make contributions, if such contributions are in the best long-term interests of the firm. The next case is considered to be *the* landmark opinion on this topic.

A.P. SMITH MFG. CO. v. BARLOW
98 A.2d 581 (N.J. 1953)

FACTS The A.P. Smith Manufacturing Company was incorporated in 1896, and was engaged in the manufacture and sale of valves, fire hydrants, and special equipment, mainly for the water and gas industries. The plant was located in East Orange and Bloomfield, New Jersey. Over the years, the firm was a regular contributor to the local community chest, as well as to Upsala College in East Orange and to Newark College (now a part of Rutgers University). In 1951 the board of directors adopted a resolution to join in the Annual Giving to Princeton University, authorizing the payment of $1,500 to the university. The board's resolution stated that the contribution was "in the best interests of the company." Several stockholders questioned the propriety of this contribution, and the corporation instituted a declaratory judgment action in the Chancery Division to determine whether the contribution was **intra vires** (within the powers of the corporation) or **ultra vires** (outside the powers of the corporation).

ISSUE May a corporation legally make charitable contributions from corporate funds, or is such an issue an unlawful "wasting" of corporate assets?

HOLDING Yes, a corporation may—in fact, should—make charitable contributions under certain circumstances.

REASONING Excerpts from the opinion of Judge Jacobs:

[T]he president of the company, testified that he considered the contribution to be a sound investment, that the public expects corporations to aid philanthropic and benevolent institutions, that they obtain good will in the community by so doing, and that their charitable donations create favorable environment for their business operations. In addition, he expressed the thought that in contributing to liberal arts institutions, corporations were furthering their self-interest in assuring the free flow of properly trained personnel for administrative and other corporate employment....

The objecting stockholders have not disputed any of the foregoing testimony nor the showing of great need by Princeton and other private institutions of higher learning and the important public service being rendered by them for democratic government and industry alike. Similarly, they have acknowledged that for over two decades there has been state legislation on our books which expresses a strong public policy in favor of corporate contributions such as that being questioned by them. Nevertheless, they have taken the position that (1) the plaintiff's certificate of incorporation does not expressly authorize the contribution and under common-law principles the company does not possess any implied or incidental power to make it, and (2) the New Jersey statutes which expressly authorize the contribution may not constitutionally be applied to the plaintiff, a corporation created long before their enactment....

When the wealth of the nation was primarily in the hands of individuals they discharged their responsibilities as citizens by donating freely for charitable purposes. With the transfer of most of the wealth to corporate hands and the imposition of heavy burdens of individual taxation, they have been unable to keep pace with increased philanthropic needs. They have therefore, with justification, turned to corporations to assume the modern obligations of good citizenship in the same manner as humans do. Congress and state legislatures have enacted laws which encourage corporate contributions....

In 1930 a statute was enacted in our State which expressly provided that any corporation could cooperate with other corporations and natural persons in the creation and maintenance of community funds and charitable, philanthropic or benevolent instrumentalities conducive to public welfare, and could for such purposes expend such corporate sums as the directors "deem expedient and as in their judgment will contribute to the protection of the corporate interests."...

The appellants contend that the foregoing New Jersey statutes may not be applied to corporations created before their passage. Fifty years before the incorporation of The A. P. Smith Manufacturing Company our Legislature provided that every corporate charter thereafter granted "shall be subject to alteration, suspension and repeal, in the discretion of the legislature."... A similar reserved power was placed into our State Constitution in 1875 ... and is found in our present Constitution....

State legislation adopted in the public interest and applied to preexisting corporations under the reserved power has repeatedly been sustained by the United States Supreme Court above the contention that it impairs the rights of stockholders and violates constitutional guarantees under the Federal Constitution.... It seems clear to us that the public policy supporting the statutory enactments under consideration is far greater and the alteration of preexisting rights of stockholders much lesser than in the cited cases sustaining various exercises of the reserve power.... And since in our view the corporate power to make reasonable charitable contributions exists under modern conditions, even apart from express statutory provision, its enactments simply constitute helpful and confirmatory declarations of such power, accompanied by limiting safeguards.

In light of all of the foregoing we have no hesitancy in sustaining the validity of the donation by the plaintiff. . . . We find that it was a lawful exercise of the corporation's implied and incidental powers under common-law principles and that it came within the express authority of the pertinent state legislation. . . .

The judgment entered in the Chancery Division is in all respects Affirmed.

BUSINESS CONSIDERATIONS How can charitable contributions by a corporation be justified from a business perspective, presuming that the primary purpose of the business is to generate profits for its stockholders?

ETHICAL CONSIDERATIONS If the court's opinion reflects society's values in this case, what happened to social expectations concerning corporate conduct between the *Dodge v. Ford Motor Company* opinion and this opinion? How should this change have affected corporate decision making?

The "Game Theory"

As society and the courts began to recognize the existence of corporate duties, the concept of business as an amoral institution became untenable. If a business had duties, it also had some ethical responsibilities. These responsibilities, however, tended to be based on adherence to "rules" and obeying those rules. If a business obeyed the rules and stayed within the law, it was deemed to be acting in an ethical manner. This approach to business ethics led to the development of the "game theory" as a means of judging the ethical stance of the business.[20] Basically, the game theory equates the operation of a business with playing a game, and the rules from various games are applicable to determine the ethics of the business. If a manager of a firm lied to his or her customers, the manager—and consequently, the business—had acted unethically. However, if the manager bluffed his or her customer, the manager—and the firm—may have acted in an ethical manner, presuming that bluffing is an acceptable part of the game being played. Bluffing is, after all, an accepted part of several games, including poker. Of course, one person's bluffing may well be another person's lying, but such conundra were left for others to solve.

There is a basic flaw in the game theory of business ethics. Game theories and game rules are fair and equitable only if all of the participants in the game are aware a game is being played. If any of the participants do not realize a game is being played, they cannot be aware of the rules of that game and thus will be at a disadvantage. To take advantage of people under such circumstances would not be ethical.

Under the game theory, a number of rules were developed and followed. For example, *caveat emptor* (let the buyer beware) was a "rule" of the business game for a substantial period in U.S. history. Similarly, *laissez faire* economic regulation was a rule of business in the United States. Business and its customers were aware of these rules and played the business game accordingly. Eventually, however, business began to industrialize and to gain an increasing ability to produce for larger and larger markets. The game was no longer quite as fair as it had been before, and as the game became more one-sided in favor of business, the other "players" (the customers) began to seek new rules for the game. When business would not voluntarily change the rules, the customers asked the government to intervene. This led to government regulation of business, and eventually an entirely new playing field on which the game of business was to be conducted. This new playing field is the one on which business must operate today.

The Social Contract Theory

Many business executives today argue that U.S. business is too regulated by the government. These people see domestic business drowning in a sea of bureaucratic red tape while less-regulated foreign firms are assuming control of the economy. They want to be unfettered, set free from the "excessive" regulations imposed by the government and allowed to compete freely with foreign producers. Although this attitude can possibly be justified from a simplistic economic position, it fails to take into account two factors: the spillover costs society must pay when a business fails to act in a responsible and ethical manner, and the "social contract" between business and society. When business became too large for local control, the society sought legislative intervention to force compliance with social demands. This is the gist of the social contract. Business must comply with the demands of the society if it wants to continue to exist and to operate within that society. The social contract defines the permissible scope of business conduct and goes beyond the purely economic issues. If society wants more

NRW

IS BUSINESS A GAME?

One of Helen's classmates from college was visiting Helen recently. The classmate seemed excited to learn that Helen was involved in starting a business. He pointed out that he, too, had formed a business, and that he was now doing quite well for himself. He then offered her some "free advice" for the business. He urged Helen to convince her fellow entrepreneurs to set their prices high for their consumer customers when they first enter the market, before there is much competition. He thinks that the product is distinct enough, and will generate enough demand, that the public will pay dearly for StuffTrakR. He also thinks that InvenTrakR will be a much-desired product, but that commercial customers will be less likely to purchase the product if the price is high. He also urged them to use the cheapest components possible on the StuffTrakR, allowing them to maximize their profits early, before any other firms enter the market. And he advised not cutting corners with InvenTrakR until the firm gains a solid footing in the market. As he pointed out, NRW can always increase its quality and lower its prices later. After all, business is "a game, just like Monopoly, only with real money." This advice bothered Helen, and she has asked your advice. To what extent is business "just a game"? If business is "just a game," what are the rules (if any) of the game?

BUSINESS CONSIDERATIONS What business problems might arise for NRW, or for any other firm, if it adopts an attitude such as this?

ETHICAL CONSIDERATIONS Can the ethical theory the firm follows help the principals in determining whether to listen to the advice of Helen's friend? Explain your reasoning.

INTERNATIONAL CONSIDERATIONS Are ethics deemed more important in other nations or cultures than in the United States? Are there likely to be differences in ethical standards in different nations? What should a business do in order to ensure that it is acting ethically regardless of where it is operating?

from business than profits, business must accept this mandate in order to survive in society. To do otherwise is to breach the social contract.

The social contract theory basically posits that business can exist only because society allows it to exist, that business must satisfy the demands of the society if it is to be allowed to continue. If business does not satisfy the demands of society, society will change the "rules of the game," and in so changing the rules, the permission that business now has may well be revoked. Today, society expects (and demands) more from business than mere profits. Environmental concerns, consumer safety and protection, and quality of life, among other things, must also be provided for in the production process. If these added demands cause costs to rise, so be it. If business as we know it will not meet these demands voluntarily, these demands will be met by regulation—or by society's changing the form of business or the rules of doing business. Not only has the "game theory" of business been rejected by society, but the rules by which business is allowed to exist have also been changed by the social contract theory.

Some of the fraud allegations and reporting problems of 2002 show the potential impact of the social contract theory, and also show how rapidly the government can respond to change the "rules of the game" when a serious problem or crisis arises that causes a public uproar. The 1990s were a period of almost unparalleled growth and prosperity in the United States, and a significant number of people became rich—or richer, in some cases—during this extended period of good financial news. However, when the economy finally began to show signs of slowing, or even of entering into a downward cycle, many people were afraid that the good times were coming to an end. While most businesses sought ways to minimize the harm of the downturn, seeking new markets and new strategies, downsizing, or making adjustments in their business policies and strategies, some businesses—and their executives—took a more "creative" approach to the problem. They elected to cheat! There were misstated financial records and reports, false earnings reports, erroneous listings of expenses and income to make the "bottom line" look better on paper than it was in reality. Enron, Adelphia Communications, WorldCom, and Global Crossing, among others, were eventually exposed for their wrongdoing, and the fallout was tremendous. And the allegations of wrongdoing were not restricted to the corporate world. Arthur Andersen, one of the "Big Five" public accounting firms, was found guilty of Securities Act violations. Martha Stewart was accused of insider trading in violation of the securities laws. The public was appalled, and the effect on the stock market was devastating.

The government reacted promptly, and harshly, to these problems. President George W. Bush condemned the corporate scandals, stating that "America is ushering in a new era of responsibility, and that ethic of responsibility must extend to America's boardrooms."[21] Congress responded quickly, passing the Sarbanes-Oxley Act of 2002, which requires that chief executive officers and chief financial officers certify the accuracy of quarterly financial reports. Knowingly certifying an inaccurate report can result in fines of up to $1 million and incarceration for up to 10 years.[22]

The private sector also became actively involved in addressing some of these issues. The Corporate Accountability and Listing Standards Committee of the New York Stock Exchange initiated a thorough review of its policies and procedures in February 2002 and released its report in June 2002. This report was designed to "enhance the accountability, integrity and transparency of [the NYSE's] 2,800 listed companies and to help restore investor trust and confidence."[23] In the second half of 2002 more than 100 companies hired "ethics officers" to work with the management of companies, including the boards of directors, by conducting training courses dealing with various ethical issues.[24] Each of these responses involves the application of the social contract theory to a perceived problem that had caused a public outcry over misconduct by business.

The Constituents of a Business

In dealing with the social contract theory and in evaluating the ethical stance of any given business, it is important to recognize that each business has a number of constituent groups and that each group of constituents will have different wants, needs, and desires. (How the constituent groups are viewed, and how they are counted, is a matter of interpretation. For simplicity's sake, we have listed the constituents as belonging to one of *four* distinct groups. More members or more groups could easily be used, if so desired.) The business manager must base decisions affecting the business, at least in part, on the impact these decisions will have on the various constituents. Some decisions will affect all of the constituent groups, although not equally. Others will affect only some of the groups. Deciding how each group will be affected, and how much weight to give to each group, is essential in reaching ethical decisions. Exhibit 2.2 shows the constituent groups a corporation must consider.

Businesses owe duties to each of the constituent groups. Businesses also have expectations, knowing that they are owed duties from each of the constituent groups.

As an example of how these duties can affect a business in its decision process, consider the following. A firm has developed a new production method that will lower costs (which will lead to increased profits) while simultaneously making safer products. To adopt this new method will benefit two constituent groups, stakeholders and customers. However, this new method will require relocating the plant, and it may produce a number of pollutants. Relocating the plant will cause harm to current employees who may be unable or unwilling to relocate, and to the current community, which will suffer economic harm from reduced employment. The possible increase in pollutants will harm the community at the site of the new plant, although this harm will be offset to some extent by the increase in employment and the economic "ripple effect" a new plant will cause. Somehow a balancing of these competing interests must be undertaken in reaching a decision that reflects the best short-term and long-term interests of the firm.

The social contract theory can be explored more fully at http://plato.stanford.edu/entries/contractarianism-contemporary/.

EXHIBIT **2.2** Constituents of a Business

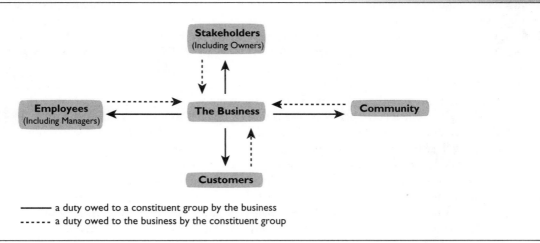

——— a duty owed to a constituent group by the business
- - - - - a duty owed to the business by the constituent group

The Changing Social Environment

Over the years, business has changed, and with it the attitudes of society toward business. The early days of commerce featured primarily local trade, with mainly handcrafted goods produced and sold by local merchants and artisans. Under these circumstances, the rule of *caveat emptor* was followed, and the success of any business was, to a significant extent, dependent on the reputation of its owner-operator.

Eventually, business began to industrialize and to gain an increased capacity for productivity. As businesses began to produce more, they were able to expand their geographic markets from local to regional. This expansion caused some minor changes, although the buyer still had to beware. No longer could the buyer expect to be personally acquainted with the seller. Although the reputation of the seller remained important, much of the spread of that reputation was now by hearsay. The buyer and the seller were becoming separated by distance.

Industrialization continued to expand, and transportation and communication also grew and developed. The advent of the railroads allowed truly national business operations for the first time. With this opportunity to deal on a national scope, manufacturers became aware of "economies of scale." The age of "bigger is better" had arrived. Now *caveat emptor* took on more meaning. No longer could a buyer rely on a seller's reputation. Sellers were combining into trusts, and available substitutes for a seller's goods began to decline. Buyers were being thrust into a "take-it-or-leave-it" position.

For the first time, the public expectation of business made a drastic change. The public began to request government intervention to protect the consumer and the worker from "big business." The government responded with what business must have thought was a vengeance. The Interstate Commerce Commission, the antitrust statutes, the Securities and Exchange Commission, and a myriad of other agencies and acts were created in relatively rapid succession.

Why did these changes occur? Fundamentally, because business was so busy meeting its own perceived needs that it ignored the expectations and the demands of the public. Was business acting illegally? In most cases, no. Was business acting unethically? From our contemporary perspective, probably; from a historic point of view, probably not. The key point to remember is that, in most cases, business was being conducted in a manner that had been socially and legally acceptable up to that time. However, as society changed and as the demands of society changed, business

---

NRW CASE 2.2   Marketing/Management

NRW

SHOULD NRW ADOPT A CODE OF ETHICS?

Mai recently attended a business ethics seminar conducted by one of her friends. After attending this seminar, and after thinking about all of the corporate scandals that had recently been revealed, she believes that NRW should adopt a formal "Code of Ethics" for the firm to follow. She asserts that such a code will help the company not only to respond to ethical dilemmas as they arise, but also to plan ahead in order to avoid ethical problems in the future. She also states that such a code, if properly publicized, can help the firm improve its profits. Carlos disagrees with Mai. He believes that since the business is run by people who are already ethical in their own lives, such a code in unnecessary. He also thinks that advertising any code of ethics is too much like "blowing your own horn," and is more likely to turn people off toward the firm than to attract them to do business with the firm. They have asked for your advice. What will you tell them?

BUSINESS CONSIDERATIONS Why might it be a good idea to adopt a code for the business now, even if it is owned and operated by people who are already ethical? Why might such a code be a bad idea?

ETHICAL CONSIDERATIONS If the firm is to adopt a code of ethics, what ethical theory should be selected as the foundation for the code? Explain your reasons.

INTERNATIONAL CONSIDERATIONS Are there any international standards or codes that a firm can follow that might show a commitment to ethical conduct? Should a firm follow a different ethical theory or code in each country in which it does business, or should it just follow one theory or code regardless of where it does business?

---

failed to respond. Then, when business failed to respond, society sought legislative intervention. The end of the 19th century saw the birth of the social contract as an essential element of conducting business.

One example of the changing social environment is the area of "employment at will." An at-will employee is one who works for the employer only so long as both parties agree to the employment. There is no fixed term of employment, and either party may terminate the employment relationship at any time merely by giving notice to the other party. Historically, courts upheld the right of the employer to discharge an at-will employee "for good cause, for no cause, or even for cause morally wrong. . . ."[25] The employer's unlimited right to discharge an employee was too often abused by the employer, which led to a reevaluation of the traditional "at-will" doctrine. In *Pierce v. Ortho Pharmaceutical Corporation*,[26] the court ruled that, generally speaking, an employer in an employment at will is free to terminate the employment relationship at any time, with or without cause. However, the court also stated that firing an employee for a reason that violates public policy would not be done in good faith and could result in liability for wrongful discharge.

The following case involved an alleged wrongful discharge. After reading the court's opinion, decide whether you would have reached the same result that the court did on these facts.

2.3

WISEHART v. MEGANCK
2002 Colo. App. LEXIS 1426 (Colo. Ct. of App., 1st Div., 2002)

FACTS Wisehart worked for Vectra Bank Colorado, N.A. as a loan officer in an at-will relationship. Bank policy required him to obtain the approval of other bank officers when processing certain loans. While the bank's loan policy required written approval of the officers to be obtained before any closing, in practice the approvals were sometimes obtained afterwards. On the day before the scheduled closing of a particular loan, Wisehart met with a senior loan officer to obtain his approval. That officer told Wisehart that he needed more detailed information regarding the loan and requested Wisehart to provide it. When Wisehart returned with the requested information later that afternoon, the officer had departed and could not be located. Following the meeting with Wisehart, and without receiving the requested information, the officer informed another bank employee that he was not going to approve the loan. In fact, neither the officer nor the bank had any objection to the loan. Wisehart's superiors knew the loan closing date well in advance and specifically were aware on the date of the closing that Wisehart intended to proceed with it. Despite opportunities to do so, no one informed Wisehart that the bank officer did not intend to give his approval, and thus that the loan had not been properly approved.

While Wisehart was attending the closing the next day in another city, the bank issued his final paycheck in anticipation of termination. When Wisehart returned to the bank, Meganck, one of his supervisors, informed him that he was being terminated for failing to obtain the required written approvals before closing.

Wisehart then initiated this action asserting claims for fraudulent misrepresentation and concealment against the bank and Meganck, essentially alleging that defendants had fraudulently set him up to be terminated. Wisehart further alleged that the bank's stated reason for termination masked a plan to replace employees like himself who had been long-term employees of another financial institution that had merged with the bank.

Contending that Colorado does not recognize a claim of fraud in the employment-at-will context, defendants filed a motion for summary judgment. The trial court held that Wisehart's claims, even though couched in terms of fraud, essentially asserted a claim for wrongful termination, and the fact that his termination was achieved through fraud did not change the true nature of the claims. The court concluded that, even though defendants may have created a reason to terminate plaintiff's employment, that action did not give rise to a claim because defendants were free to terminate him without any reason whatsoever since the employment was "at will." As a result, the court dismissed Wisehart's claims, and this appeal followed.

ISSUE Was Wisehart wrongfully terminated from his employment with Vectra Bank?

HOLDING No. This was an employment at will, which allowed the bank to terminate the employment at any time for any reason.

REASONING Excerpts from the opinion of Judge Casebolt:

Plaintiff contends the trial court incorrectly held that he could not pursue his fraud claims because he was an at-will employee. He asserts that employers should be subject to ordinary fraud rules that apply generally in all settings. Defendants assert the trial court correctly held that allowing a fraud claim under these circumstances would improperly undermine the employment at will doctrine. We agree with defendants. . . . In Colorado, an agreement of employment that is for an indefinite term is presumed to be at will. Either the employer or the employee may terminate at-will employment at any time with or without cause, and such termination generally does not give rise to a claim for relief. . . .

The at-will nature of the employment relationship reflects a matter of public policy. . . . The at-will employment doctrine promotes flexibility and discretion for employees to seek the best position to suit their talents and for employers to seek the best employees to suit their needs. By removing encumbrances to quitting a job or firing an employee, the at-will doctrine promotes a free market in employment analogous to the free market in goods and services generally. . . .

At the same time, strict application of the at-will doctrine may invite abuse and lead to injustice. Accordingly, legislation and the common law have restricted application of the at-will doctrine to balance the interests of employers and employees. . . . For example, certain federal and state statutes have created private claims for relief for wrongful discharge based on discrimination with respect to race, color, gender, national origin, ancestry, religious affiliation, disability, and age. State statutes also permit such claims in cases of termination resulting from an employee engaging in lawful activity off premises during nonworking hours, responding to a jury summons, and certain activities of "whistle-blowing." . . .

Colorado also recognizes a claim for relief for wrongful discharge in violation of public policy. This judicially crafted exception restricts an employer's right to terminate when the termination contravenes accepted and substantial public policies as embodied by legislative declarations, professional codes of ethics, or other sources. . . . These exceptions address societal concerns, while honoring the general rule that employment affects private interests, and therefore parties generally are free to bargain for conditions of employment. . . .

Operating from the premise that parties are free to require cause for termination, Colorado also recognizes that an employer's failure to follow termination procedures contained in an employment manual can serve as the basis for a breach of contract or promissory estoppel claim. . . . In addition, Colorado recognizes the viability of certain other tort claims that arise around the employment relationship. . . .

To summarize, employers operating under at-will employment principles are generally free to discharge employees for any reason, even if that reason is wrong or incorrect, as long as the reason asserted does not trigger a recognized exception to the at-will termination doctrine noted above. Employees in such a relationship likewise may leave employment for any reason and at any time. Moreover, the presumption of at-will employment places the burden on the plaintiff to plead and prove circumstances that would authorize application of one of the recognized exceptions to the doctrine. . . .

Here, plaintiff's claims arise out of the termination of his at-will employment relationship under which his employer was free to terminate him any time, with or without any reason. Plaintiff's claims do not fall within any of the recognized exceptions to the doctrine of at-will employment, nor do they allege allowable theories or tort claims surrounding the employment relationship.

Moreover, plaintiff does not assert that the parties agreed to vary the at-will relationship to require cause for termination. Courts in other states have recognized claims for fraudulent misrepresentation resulting in termination when there is evidence of such an agreement in part because the presumption of at-will employment is rebuttable by evidence of a contrary agreement between the parties. . . .

Here, in contrast, plaintiff specifically disavowed any contract or estoppel claim for relief, and he does not assert any agreement varying the at-will employment relationship. Further, he did not plead a claim of wrongful discharge in violation of public policy.

Accordingly, unless there is another basis to allow a fraud claim under these circumstances, plaintiff's claims fail.

Plaintiff asserts that he is entitled to pursue claims that his termination resulted from fraudulent misrepresentation and concealment. He contends that an employer may not assert its right to terminate at will as a defense to a fraud claim. Plaintiff essentially asks us to recognize an exception to the at-will doctrine where the employer commits fraud to justify termination of an at-will employee. We decline to do so.

This is a question of first impression in Colorado. Most other courts that have considered such claims have concluded that the at-will doctrine precludes a claim for relief when fraud is the means used to effect termination. . . .

Here, while we likewise do not condone the bank's conduct, we find no basis to depart from the general rule that either party to an at-will employment contract may terminate the relationship for any reason, even if wrong, without giving rise to liability. . . . Unless the plaintiff pleads and proves a recognized exception to the at-will employment doctrine . . . the doctrine restrains courts from inquiring into the basis for termination and advances the value of a free market in employment for which the parties bargained.

We therefore decline to recognize an exception to the at-will employment doctrine for claims in which a fraud is employed to justify the termination of an at-will employment relationship. Plaintiffs' claims against the bank and Meganck therefore fail as a matter of law. . . .

In light of our disposition, we need not address plaintiff's remaining contentions.

The judgment is affirmed.

BUSINESS CONSIDERATIONS Should a business have a policy regarding employment termination in order to provide protection from lawsuits such as this one?

Should a business formally adopt an employee handbook spelling out the rights and obligations of the employees and of the firm?

ETHICAL CONSIDERATIONS At one point in its opinion the court mentions a restriction on the right of an employer to summarily dismiss an "at-will" employee if such dismissal violates provisions of the employee handbook. Is it ethical for a business to decide *not* to adopt a handbook in order to prevent granting any such rights to its employees?

Problems with Business Ethics

A basic problem faces any business that seeks to act in an "ethical" manner. There are no fixed guidelines to follow, no formal code of ethics to set the standards under which the business should operate. Numerous professional organizations have their own codes of ethics or conduct. For example, the legal profession has the Code of Professional Responsibility; the medical profession has its Hippocratic Oath; the accounting profession has a code of ethics and also has generally accepted auditing standards (GAAS) and generally accepted accounting principles (GAAP); the real estate industry has a code of conduct; and various other groups or organizations have similar codes. However, business has no code, no "road map" of ethical conduct. The closest thing business has to an ethical guideline is the law. If a business is acting within the law, it is acting legally and is arguably meeting its minimum social requirements. However, this forces business into a reactive posture, always responding to legislative demands. It would seem that a proactive position in which business establishes its own path would be preferable.

Given this overriding problem, what can be done to provide a solution? At the present time, probably nothing can be done in the global sense. But it may be possible for each industry to develop a code of ethics for that particular industry, in much the same manner that the real estate industry has developed a code for its members. If such an industry-wide approach does not prove feasible, each individual firm can develop its own personal code of ethics. Although such a microapproach may not be ideal, it at least gets business to embark on the journey toward formalizing its ethical posture.

The Human Factor

As we mentioned earlier, business was frequently viewed as an amoral institution in the past. Workers were expected to leave their personal values at the front gate when they reported to work, and then (presumably) to retrieve them at the close of the working day. At the same time, workers were expected to be loyal agents of the firm. Generally, this was interpreted to mean that if a course of conduct was beneficial to the employer, the employee was to follow that course. If a course of conduct was not beneficial to the employer, the employee was not to follow it. The attitudes and opinions of the employees were ignored.

The "loyal agent" attitude was described—and then rebutted—by Alex C. Micholos in his article "The Loyal Agent's Argument."[27] The loyal agent's argument presumes that the principal follows the ethical theory of egoism, and that the loyal agent must also act egoistically for the principal. The argument runs as follows:

- As a loyal agent of the principal, I ought to serve his interests as he would serve them himself if he possessed my expertise.

- The principal will serve his interests in a thoroughly egoistic manner.

- Therefore, as a loyal agent of this principal, I must operate in a thoroughly egoistic manner on his behalf.

In order to operate in a thoroughly egoistic manner, a person acts in the way that best advances his or her interests, presuming that everyone else is doing the same thing. The gist of the loyal agent's argument is that a truly loyal agent will put the principal first in any decisions between conflicting interests. Thus, the traditional argument posits that a loyal agent is expected to act without regard to ethical considerations as long as the conduct puts the principal first. There is a major flaw in this traditional loyal agent's argument. Too many people feel that a loyal agent, if acting in a truly egoistic manner, has license—if not a duty—to act immorally and unethically if doing so will advance the interests of the principal. Micholos argued that the truly loyal agent must exercise due care and skill in the performance of the agency duties and must act in a socially acceptable manner while furthering the interests of the principal. To do otherwise will have a long-term detrimental impact on the principal and will therefore be disloyal.

The Legal Aspect

The U.S. legal system contains numerous ethical components. For example, a person is presumed to be innocent until proven guilty in criminal law. Each person is entitled to due process of the law and to equal protection under the law. Protections exist against compulsory self-incrimination and cruel and unusual punishment. The Constitution provides for free speech, free exercise of religion, and the right to counsel, among other rights and guarantees.

Business law also attempts to reflect the ethical standards of the society and to promote ethical conduct in the realm of business. The law of sales imposes a duty on each party to a sales contract to act in good faith. Bankruptcy is designed to give an honest debtor a fresh start. Agency law imposes the duties of loyalty and good faith on the agent.

The laws that regulate business have developed, to a significant extent, under the social contract theory. Governmental regulations of business were enacted initially, in many cases, in response to a public demand for protection from the abuses and excesses of "big business." Antitrust laws were intended to control business and to protect the ideal of a free and competitive economy, while the Federal Trade Commission was established to stop unfair and deceptive trade practices.

The apparent success of the antitrust laws encouraged both the public and the government in the use of statutes to force business to meet the demands of the public. The consumer movement of the 1960s led to a number of protective statutes by both the federal and state governments. The federal government was concerned with protecting consumer credit and consumer product safety. State governments tended to be more concerned with safety and with home solicitations. In either case, government became involved only after a perceived problem was identified, public demands for protection were raised, and the business community failed or refused to adequately meet the demands of the public.

The 1960s and 1970s also saw an increased public awareness of and concern about pollution of the environment. Again, a number of protests and a great deal of public action were ignored by the business community in general, and once again governmental intervention was the tool used to address the problem. Governmental environmental protection statutes were intended to clean up the environ-

ment in order to protect the quality of life for our population, for wildlife, and for future generations. Government involvement was triggered once more by the failure of the business community to address environmental issues the public had raised.

Similar steps were followed in other areas such as labor and fair employment. The public expressed a concern over how business was treating a perceived problem. However, the steps business took toward solving the problem were less than the public demanded. Consequently, the legislature was asked to intervene on behalf of the public.

In virtually every circumstance, though, the statutory treatment of the problems is relatively rigid and potentially expensive for business. Similar protections could have—and should have—been developed within the business community, with a great deal less rigidity and a great deal less expense, had business been willing to meet the challenge directly. Instead, by having waited until the government told it what to do, business now has a much stricter regulatory environment in which to operate.

In each of these areas, and in a number of others, the application of the social contract theory is apparent. Society perceived problems and demanded that certain corrective steps be taken to alleviate the problems. Business had an opportunity to take the corrective steps in a manner devised by business, but failed—or refused—to do so. At that point, the government stepped in to resolve the problem in a rigid, statutory manner when no satisfactory solutions were advanced by business. By failing to respond in a proactive manner, which would have permitted a custom-tailored, microfocused solution by each affected business or industry, the business community was left with a reactive, macro-oriented solution that must, by definition, extend across industry lines and that is intended to control all aspects of the business community with one broad regulation.

Multinational Ethics

There is an old adage that states: "When in Rome, do as the Romans do." This adage is very appropriate when considering business ethics in a multinational setting. If business ethics tended to be Kantian in nature, with firms throughout the world seeking—and then following—a categorical imperative, there would not be any problem. Since a categorical imperative is a rule for which any and every exception has been developed, businesses would merely have to follow the resulting rules, and their actions would be ethical by definition. Unfortunately, there is no categorical imperative for business, nor are most businesses Kantian in their ethical perspectives. Thus, problems with business ethics exist, and these problems are compounded in an international environment.

A businessperson tends to follow his or her personal moral and ethical values and to apply these values in judging the ethics of others. While the "loyal agent's" argument stresses that a truly loyal agent will put the interests of the principal ahead of the interests of the agent, that same agent will normally work only for a principal whose interests and values can be reconciled with the interests and the values of the agent. If the demands and requirements of a job consistently conflict with the morals and the ethics of an employee, that employee is likely to give up the job before changing his or her ethical perspective. Similarly, the ethical stance of the firm is likely to be consistent with the ethical values of the society. If the firm does not conform to socially acceptable standards, the "social contract theory" is used to change the permissible scope of the firm's conduct.

Even if a business has a formal, stated objective of acting in a socially responsible and ethical manner, problems may occur. What happens when that firm expands its operations into another country? What happens when a truly loyal and ethical agent of the firm is reassigned to a foreign post within the company? This expansion or reassignment may have serious ethical implications. The social contract between the new location and its businesses may well be different from the social contract between the firm and its domicile state, calling for a reappraisal of what is acceptable—or even desirable—behavior. For instance, a firm may open a new plant in a nation with very lax environmental protection statutes. This same firm, in its domicile state, has been an environmentally concerned business that has taken many pro-environment steps to reduce pollution in its production. If the firm tries to be as environmentally active in its new location, it will be at a short-term competitive disadvantage. If it seeks to be economically competitive, it will be acting in a manner contrary to its stated company policy of environmental concern and protection. What should the firm do?

Although there is no perfect solution, any firm that is considering expansion into another country needs to make every effort to learn about the cultural differences that exist between the two nations, and to take steps to reduce any culture shock or conflict prior to the expansion. The firm may consider hiring citizens of the other nation, or it may consider requiring some form of educational exposure to prepare its employees for the move. The employees should be taught as much as possible about the new country, and they should also be urged to "watch and learn." The firm and its employees should be aware that they are visitors, guests in another nation, and should act as if they were personal guests at the home of a new friend. Above all else, the firm

and its employees should avoid being judgmental. New countries and new cultures may seem strange and exotic, or they may seem merely different, but the new country will provide the social values that drive the social contract under which the firm will now be conducting business. Assimilation and acceptance are essential!

A Recommendation for Business

U.S. businesses need to develop a model or a framework of ethical behavior. It is more than likely that no single model can be developed that will apply equally to every industry within the U.S. economy, but it is possible to suggest a general outline for business. This general outline can then be tailored by each industry to the needs and the demands of that particular industry. For example, business should probably lean toward the consequential ethical theories rather than the nonconsequential theories. Consequential theories are more readily understood and more easily accepted by the public than the more esoteric nonconsequential approaches. Additionally, consequential theories

---

NRW CASE 2.3   **Marketing/Management**

OPERATING NRW ETHICALLY

Mai, Carlos, and Helen have each seen numerous examples of what they consider unethical conduct, both in the workplace and in society at large. Carlos has several friends who are employed in a sales capacity, and a number of his friends believe that it is perfectly legitimate to say virtually anything short of an outright lie in order to close a sale with a customer. They frequently "push the envelope" to the edge, grossly exaggerating qualities of the product being marketed, often to the detriment of the purchasers of that product. Mai knows a few information systems people who would not hesitate to claim credit for the work of others, and she also knows a few who would even assert privileges based on their seniority in order to gain credit for the work of others. (Of course, both know even more people who do not act in this manner, but these others do not disturb them.) Helen has seen people lie on their resumes or job applications, claiming accomplishments that were totally fictitious. She has also seen situations in which a person

continued

who did not meet the criteria set out in the job description was hired because the particular applicant knew someone who was able to influence the hiring decision. All three of the principals believe that such conduct is generally harmful to a business and its reputation, especially with repeat customers. They also know they would like to operate this business ethically, but they don't know how to verbalize this goal. They have asked you for your advice. What will you tell them?

BUSINESS CONSIDERATIONS Where might the principals look for examples of what they should or should not do? As one of the original entrants into this particular field, should NRW attempt to be proactive in establishing an ethical code, or should the firm wait for governmental guidance?

ETHICAL CONSIDERATIONS Should the principals adopt a formal ethics code or policy as they begin the company, or should they be less formal until they see what sorts of ethical issues arise in the operation of the firm? What advantages are there for having a formal written code for a firm? What advantages are there for taking an informal and flexible approach to ethics?

INTERNATIONAL CONSIDERATIONS Should a business look to international rules and regulations in trying to establish its ethical standards, or should it look at the rules and regulations of its home nation? Might the International Chamber of Commerce and its interpretation of the law merchant provide guidance in this area?

especially with respect to its constituents (stakeholders, employees, customers, community, etc.). This approach works well with any ethical principle adopted, takes into account the people to whom the firm must answer, and provides a framework for decision making that is comparable to other types of business decisions regularly made by managers.

Business should also consider its public relations image in deciding how to proceed within the consequential area. A utilitarian approach, one that is most concerned with the greatest good for the greatest number, is more acceptable to society than an egoistic approach. Society already tends to view business as egoistic—perhaps excessively so—without its formal adoption of such a theory as the driving force behind ethical considerations. Also, many people seem incapable of distinguishing between egoistic and egotistic. (Egoists measure their conduct on the basis of self-interest, choosing the course of conduct that will provide the greatest benefit to themselves. Egotists are self-centered, characterized by excessive references to themselves.)

Next, business should avoid rigid rules that force specific actions or reactions, especially with the rapid changes of the modern technological age. This does not mean business should not have rules and standards, but, rather, that the rules and standards should be flexible enough to change as society and the business environment change. Business should also advocate the loyal agent's argument, while emphasizing that a truly loyal agent will act within the law while keeping the best interests of the principal in mind.

Whenever possible, businesses should learn to work with the government in establishing statutory regulations. By taking a proactive role in regulation, business cannot only help to protect its own best interests but also show its concern for society and its various constituents.

The development of a comprehensive business ethic will not be easy, nor will it be greeted with open arms by all businesses or business leaders. The alternative, however, is excessive regulation, public distrust, and a general malaise in the business community. Steps can be taken to benefit both business and society, which can ultimately only be better for business.

are more flexible and thus more responsive to social and technological changes.

Regardless of the overriding theory, business should adopt a "synthesis" approach to resolving ethical issues. The firm should first identify the important considerations involved (obligations, ideals, effects) and then decide where the emphasis should lie among these three considerations,

Summary

It is important to distinguish ethics from morals. "Ethics" refers to either individual or group (including societal) values, whereas "morals" refers to individuals' values and matters of conscience. Throughout this book we use "ethics" to refer to group or social values and "morals" to refer to individual values.

Over the history of this country, the social environment in which business operates has changed drastically. As the social environment has changed, the demands of society on business have also changed. Business, however, has been slow to recognize or to accept these changes.

For a substantial amount of time, business was judged by the "game theory." This theory does not take into account several factors, including the fact that the customers of a business may not be aware that a game is being played. For a substantial part of the 20th century, business has been judged by the social contract theory. The social contract theory says that business must respond to the demands of the society, or the society will be permitted to change the "rules of the game" to ensure that business will comply. If business does not act as society demands, society will have the legislature enact rules to force compliance.

Even if businesses (and businesspeople) want to act ethically, it is difficult for them to do so. There are no clear-cut guidelines for most businesses to follow in adopting a code of ethics, and agreements among competing firms within an industry as to what should be done could be challenged as a conspiracy to restrain trade, a violation of antitrust laws. Still, some effort must be made. Business can make this effort by recognizing the human element—the fact that its employees are humans, with human wants, desires, and values. Business needs to recognize that unless it responds voluntarily, the legislature will often intervene. Business also needs to recognize that the courts are beginning to recognize ethical aspects to corporate conduct.

The corporate scandals of 2002 have also led to a change in the social contract and to statutory and regulatory changes as well. Firms that engage in questionable activities, such as Enron, WorldCom, and Global Crossing, have an impact on firms and stakeholders well beyond the reach of the particular firm accused of wrongdoing. New laws and new rules will have an impact on executives for many years, to a significant extent because of the unethical conduct of a relatively small group of executives for a relatively short period of time.

Finally, business must make changes and develop ethical standards in a more global setting. Multinational trade carries with it multinational responsibilities, including meeting the ethical standards and expectations of other nations. The social contract business must follow will become more confusing and more restrictive as more and more businesses discover the profits of international trade.

Discussion Questions

1. What is the "social contract theory," and how does this theory affect the ethical conduct of business within the society in which that business operates? Does the United States follow the social contract theory?

2. What are the advantages and disadvantages for a business that decides to be "proactive" in the area of ethics? What are the advantages and disadvantages for a business that decides to be "reactive" in this area? Based on your response, which option would better serve a business? Explain your reasoning.

3. Assume that a manager for a national business must make a decision between two alternatives. Alternative A would be very profitable for the company in the short term but might have some long-term negative repercussions. Alternative B would have very positive long-term implications, but would not be profitable in the short term. Alternative A will make the manager look good immediately, while Alternative B will not enhance the manager's reputation in the near future. The manager's employment contract with the firm will expire in the near future, and she would like to negotiate a new contract for a longer time period. Presuming that this manager is to act as a truly "loyal agent," which alternative should be chosen? Explain.

4. Can the "game theory," which allows—and even encourages—bluffing, be reconciled with the basic social obligations and responsibilities a business is expected to perform? Should business follow the game theory in every situation, in only some situations, or in no situations? Explain and give examples where appropriate.

5. It has been established scientifically and medically that cigarette smoking is a health hazard, not only to the smoker but also to those persons subjected to second-hand smoke. As a result, sales and profits for tobacco companies have declined substantially in the United States. Cigarette smoking is increasing in some parts of the world, especially in Asia, with a steadily increasing demand for American-made cigarettes. The sale of American cigarettes to this growing Asian market can generate literally billions of dollars in sales over the next few years. Many of the restrictions the tobacco companies face in the United States do not exist in these Asian nations, nor are there any restrictions on advertising. However, the health hazards posed by consumption of the product are the same as those faced in the United States. From an ethical perspective, what should American cigarette manufacturers do under these circumstances? Justify your answer and explain the theory under which you reached your conclusions.

6. Steven teaches English to a class of immigrants who are studying English as a prelude to seeking citizenship in the United States. Steven and his wife, Helen, had also been expecting their first child, an event they eagerly anticipated. His students were also excited about the pregnancy, even having a baby shower for them after class one evening. Helen gave birth to a healthy baby girl, and Steven shared this news with his students the day after the birth. Much to his surprise, the students did not share in his enthusiasm. In fact, several members of the class expressed their sorrow over the news. To these students it was viewed as bad luck for a couple's first child to be female

rather than male. Steven would like to explain to these students that such a view is not prevalent in the United States. How should Steven approach this situation with his students? How does ethical relativism affect this situation?

7. A business has its headquarters in nation A and has plants in nations B and C. The ethical standards in nation A prohibit a certain business practice as illegal. That same practice is considered ethical in nation B, while nation C views the practice as legal but highly unethical. What position regarding this practice should the business follow? Should the business follow a different practice in each of the three nations, or should it adopt one, uniform policy? Why?

8. Assume that an employee has strong ethical and philosophical problems with a company's policies and practices. As a result, the employee refuses to carry out certain instructions from his supervisor. When questioned about the refusal to follow the instructions, the employee explains why they were not obeyed. What should the company do in this case in order to protect the integrity of the firm and to protect the values of the employee? What should an employee do if he or she finds himself or herself in this type of employment relationship?

9. How does the utilitarian theory of ethics compare with the ethical views expressed in the feminist philosophy? Which do you think is more appropriate for a business to follow? Explain your reasoning.

10. John Rawls proposes that universal rules can be developed, provided that these rules are developed behind a "veil of ignorance." How would such a veil of ignorance enhance or hinder the development of a business code of ethics for an industry?

Case Problems and Writing Assignments

1. The University of Texas Law School is one of the most prestigious law schools in the country, consistently ranking in the top-20 listing of America's top law schools. Admission to the law school is extremely competitive, with many applicants being denied admission each year. In making its admission decision, the law school applied its "Texas Index" (TI), a numerical ranking system based on the applicant's undergraduate grade point average and Law School Admission Test score, to sort applicants into three categories: "presumptive admit," "presumptive deny," and "discretionary zone." The TI category of each applicant determined how extensive a review of the application would be applied by the admissions office.

Candidates in the "presumptive admit" and the "presumptive deny" categories were subjected to little review, while the students in the "discretionary zone" category were subjected to extensive review. All students in this category except blacks and Mexican-Americans were grouped and their files reviewed by a subcommittee from the admissions committee. These subcommittees could vote to extend an admission offer, place the student on the waiting list, or reject the application. Black and Mexican-American candidates were reviewed differently. They were given a lower TI for initial classification (189 for blacks and Mexican-Americans, 199 for other candidates in 1992), and had a much higher admission rate "on the margin" than did "nonminority" candidates. This was done, at least in part, to allow the University of Texas to attain its stated target of 10 percent Mexican-Americans and 5 percent blacks in each law school class year. In addition, the law school maintained segregated waiting lists, using these lists to help ensure that the school met its stated targets for minority membership in the class.

Four white applicants were denied admission to the law school in 1992, even though they had higher TIs than a number of black and/or Mexican-American candidates who were admitted. These students sued the school, alleging a denial of due process and/or equal protection of the law under the Fourteenth Amendment to the U.S. Constitution. The law school relied on the precedent set in *Regents of the University of California v. Bakke*, a 1978 Supreme Court decision upholding this sort of admission program for public universities. Without regard to the legal issues involved, how should this case be resolved ethically? Would the resolution of this case by a utilitarian be different than its resolution under the theories of Kant or Rawls? [See *Hopwood v. State of Texas*, 78 F.3d 932 (1996).]

2. Ibanez is a member of the Florida Bar Association. She is also a Certified Public Accountant (CPA), licensed by the Florida Board of Accountancy, and she is authorized by the Certified Financial Planner Board of Standards to use the designation "Certified Financial Planner" (CFP). Ibanez referred to these credentials in her advertising and other communications with the public concerning her law practice. She included the designations CPA and CFP on her business cards, her law office stationery, and in her Yellow Pages listing. Despite the fact that she had qualified for each of her designations and that there was no question raised as to the truthfulness of these communications, the Florida Department of Business and Professional Regulation, Board of Accountancy issued a reprimand to Ibanez for "false, deceptive, and misleading" advertising. Ibanez challenged this reprimand on the grounds that her advertising qualified as "commercial speech," subject to constitutional protections. Commercial speech can be banned or regulated by the state if it is false, deceptive, or misleading. If it is not false, deceptive, or misleading, the state can regulate such speech only by showing that such regulation directly and materially advances a substantial state interest in a manner no more extensive than is necessary to serve that state interest.

Was the advertising by Ibanez "commercial speech," and therefore entitled to constitutional protections? Was the effort of the Florida Department of Business and Professional Regulation acting within its authority by reprimanding her for her advertisements? How far should a business (including a member of a profession) be allowed to go in advertising goods or services before that business should be subjected to state regulation affecting the right of the business to advertise? [See *Ibanez v. Florida Dep't of Business and Professional Regulation*, 114 S. Ct. 2084 (1994).]

3. Norris was hired as a mechanic by Hawaiian Airlines in 1987. The terms of Norris's employment were governed by a collective bargaining agreement between Hawaiian Airlines and the International Association of Machinists and Aerospace Workers. In 1987, during a routine preflight inspection of an airplane, Norris noticed that one of the tires on the plane was worn. After removing the wheel to replace the tire, Norris noticed that the axle sleeve was scarred and grooved (it should have been "mirror-smooth"), which could cause the landing gear to fail. He recommended that this axle sleeve be replaced, but his supervisor said that it should just be sanded smooth and returned to the plane. The sleeve was sanded and returned, and the plane flew as scheduled. At the end of the shift, Norris refused to sign the maintenance record indicating that the repairs had been performed satisfactorily and that the plane was fit to fly. When Norris refused to sign the maintenance record, he was suspended by his supervisor pending a termination hearing. Norris immediately went home and reported the problem with the sleeve to the Federal Aviation Administration (FAA). Norris then invoked the grievance procedure called for by the collective bargaining agreement. Following the grievance hearing, Norris was discharged for insubordination. Norris then sued the airline in Hawaii's circuit court for wrongful discharge, alleging that his discharge violated both the public policy of the Federal Aviation Act and the Hawaii Whistleblower Protection Act. The airline removed the case to the U.S. District Court and asserted that Norris was not entitled to remedies due to the provisions of the Railway Labor Act (which has also covered airlines since 1936), which provides for mandatory arbitration proceedings to resolve such controversies. How should the court resolve this case? What ethical issues are raised by these facts? Would this case be resolved differently under ethical considerations than under legal considerations? [See *Hawaiian Airlines, Inc. v. Norris*, 114 S. Ct. 2239 (1994).]

4. Haworth was the blood bank supervisor at the Deborah Heart and Lung Center within the Deborah Hospital. Part of the responsibility of the blood bank was to collect blood samples from patients and to test those samples. The blood bank also ensured that there was an adequate supply of the proper blood type for the patient when the patient underwent surgery. Following an argument with his supervisor, Haworth destroyed an entire rack of patient blood samples. Following a leave of absence due to "stress," Haworth was offered a less stressful— but lower-level—job. Haworth refused to accept this reassignment, and the hospital discharged him at that time. Haworth claimed the discharge violated the Conscientious Employee Protection Act. He alleged that the destruction of the blood samples was a communicative act designed to show his objection to an allegedly defective blood identification system, and that the discharge was an illegal retaliatory act by the hospital.

Was Haworth's conduct a communicative act, protected by the CEPA? How should a manager react when an employee takes actions that are contrary to the firm's interests but that may involve a legitimate protest by the employee? What if the manager believes the protest is not legitimate? [See *Haworth v. Deborah Heart and Lung Center*, 638 A.2d 1354 (N.J. Super. 1994)].

5. **BUSINESS APPLICATION CASE** On September 27, 1994, McGarry entered into a one-year employment contract with Saint Anthony's and began serving as its music minister/director of Music in October 1994. St. Anthony's pastor, Father Robert Lynam, who was authorized to hire and fire employees, signed the contract. The contract contained the following provision for termination:

The parties involved shall give notice of termination of employment at least thirty days in advance of the termination. The termination time must be completed by the employee or if the employer does not wish the termination to be completed the employer shall fulfill all contractual financial agreements.

This litigation arose out of the fact that McGarry had been receiving shipments of illegal anabolic steroids at St. Anthony's. He was arrested on February 1, 1995, in the parking lot of St. Anthony's for possession of anabolic steroids. He admitted he was expecting the package and that he knew it contained anabolic steroids. McGarry stated he had been taking steroids to assist him with bodybuilding even though he knew they were illegal. He admitted that he had the steroids delivered to him at St. Anthony's on three prior occasions and that he injected himself with the deca durabolin approximately once a week.

On February 2, 1995, Father Lynam received word of a newspaper article that reported McGarry's arrest at St. Anthony's for receiving anabolic steroids. The same day, McGarry met with Father Lynam and, according to the pastor, agreed to resign and to turn in his keys. The following morning, McGarry called Father Lynam's secretary to arrange removal of his belongings. On February 5, 1995, Father Lynam found that a microphone was missing and faxed a note to McGarry asking him to look for it. On February 7, 1995, McGarry wrote back that he intended to continue his duties at the church unless he was fired. He also wrote that if was not fired, he would show up for choir rehearsal the next day. Father Lynam immediately replied by fax that it was clear that McGarry had resigned on February 2, 1995, by virtue of his returning his keys and equipment and not appearing for mass after his resignation. McGarry responded by fax that he did not resign and intended to continue unless fired. Father Lynam then sent the following fax: "Let me make it perfectly clear that you are not to come on Church property, and you are not to cause any disruption with choir or Masses." McGarry faxed back a message questioning whether he had been fired. On or prior to February 6, 1995, McGarry applied to another parish for similar employment, but was rejected when inquiry was made to Father Lynam regarding McGarry's employment at

St. Anthony's and Father Lynam informed the prospective employer of the incident that had occurred.

On March 30, 1995, McGarry filed a complaint against St. Anthony's alleging breach of employment contract, wrongful discharge, defamation, and interference with a prospective economic advantage. St. Anthony's moved for summary judgment. On December 20, 1996, an order was executed dismissing McGarry's claims with prejudice. Did St. Anthony's breach the employment contract with McGarry? Was McGarry wrongfully discharged? Did St. Anthony's improperly interfere with a prospective economic advantage? What could St. Anthony's have done differently in this situation to avoid the lawsuit? [See *McGarry v. St. Anthony of Padua*, 704 A.2d 1353 (N.J. Super. A.D. 1998).]

6. **ETHICAL APPLICATION CASE** Ruben Escamilla Jr., an 18-year-old, was arrested and convicted in San Antonio, Texas, on a marijuana charge. He was placed on probation for the offense. One condition of his probation was that he had to undergo periodic drug tests to ensure that he was honoring the terms of his probation by not ingesting any other substances. When he showed up for his drug test on June 6, it was discovered that he was using a Wizzinator to circumvent the drug test. (A Wizzinator consists of a phallic device and a pouch containing synthetic urine that can be strapped to the body beneath the wearer's clothing. For the sake of authenticity, the Wizzinator is available in a variety of skin tones.) Escamilla was taken into custody for violating his probation and was also told that he could face additional misdemeanor charges. Texas was one of only three states that prohibit the use or manufacture of any substance or device used to falsify drug test results. The Wizzinator could be purchased over the Internet for $150. Is it ethical for a company to sell a product that has, as its express purpose, allowing people to pass drug tests by falsifying the results of those tests? Should a company be allowed to sell an item in interstate commerce when the express purpose of the product is to allow the product's purchasers to pass drug tests? [See "Wizzinator, a Fake Urine Device, Makes Drug Testers Go the Extra Mile," *Roanoke Times*, June 20, 2002, p. A5. See also http://www.thewhizzinator.com/forms/whiz11.htm.]

7. **CRITICAL THINKING CASE** Rohm & Haas acquired Morton International in 1999. Unfortunately for Rohm & Haas, it had to deal with the change-of-control agreements (often called golden parachutes) that Morton had awarded to its executives prior to the acquisition. Any change of control (a term carefully defined in the contracts) triggered a three-year "employment period" for Morton's senior executives. During this span each manager's position, salary, fringe benefits, and perquisites were protected against erosion. The contract (the "Morton Agreement") provided benefits in the event of death, disability, or discharge without cause; employees could even trigger the discharge benefits by quitting. Rohm & Haas decided to negotiate individually with each of the executives entitled to these benefits.

One of these executives was Stephen Gerow. During the negotiations Rohm & Haas offered Gerow about $1 million more than his existing deal, in exchange for a release of all legal claims and an extension from two years to three of Gerow's noncompetition agreement. Gerow, who had been told that his services were no longer required, took the offer and signed a new contract that replaced the elaborate definition of the "Change of Control Date" in the Morton Agreement. Two side agreements included the release and the establishment of a trust to hold the sums (about $2.3 million) that Gerow was to receive for his promise not to compete with Rohm & Haas. The trust was to hand over these funds, plus investment income, after confirming that Gerow had refrained from competition for the agreed time.

Gerow received more than $4.5 million in severance pay, including payments in lieu of fringe benefits and retirement contributions that the firm would have made had he remained employed, and compensation for the promise not to compete. He was not satisfied and filed suit seeking almost $10 million extra—the amount he said he would have received had he remained employed during the three years after the acquisition, and had his pay and benefits been increased to match those of Morton's very top executives, whose packages (Gerow insisted) were the measure of his protection under the agreement Gerow signed with Rohn & Haas. Gerow's position, in other words, was that he was entitled to *both* the pay he would have received had he stayed, and the severance benefits he actually received on his discharge. He insisted that this was the consequence of the provisions creating a three-year "employment period" with protection of salary and status.

How should the court rule in this case? Is it ethical for a business to establish "golden parachutes" for its executives in the event of a takeover? How does a golden parachute arrangement affect the duties that a business owes to its other constituents? [See *Gerow v. Rohm & Haas Company*, 2002 U.S. App. LEXIS 21535 (7th Cir. 2002).]

8. **YOU BE THE JUDGE** A number of real estate agents in the Atlanta metropolitan area believe that it is easier to sell homes if the homes have a "lived-in" look. This is especially important in upscale neighborhoods with more expensive homes. In line with this philosophy, the Atlanta Showcase of Homes arranges for people with a flair for decorating to rent certain homes for sale. In exchange for their decorating talent and their residence in the homes, these tenants are given very favorable rent and flexible leases. Samuel Rael, an attorney in Atlanta, rented a very nice home in the Marietta area just outside Atlanta from the Atlanta Showcase of Homes. While living in the house, Rael took in a roommate, his friend Michael Wright. Shortly thereafter, the Atlanta Showcase of Homes began eviction proceedings against Rael and his friend. The reason for the eviction notice was quite simple. Wright is awaiting trial on charges of rape, and he is under "house arrest." He must wear an ankle monitor that prevents him from venturing more than

150 feet from the house. Rael and Wright are fighting the eviction efforts of the Atlanta Showcase of Homes, alleging that they have done nothing wrong and have not violated the terms of their rental agreement. Atlanta Showcase of Homes alleges that an accused felon living in the house makes any sale unlikely and that Wright's presence in the house violates at least the spirit of the agreement. If this case were brought to *your* court, how would *you* decide this controversy? Should a real estate agent who rents houses to people in order to make the houses easier to sell be allowed to specify conditions in its rental agreements to prevent "unsavory" characters from living in the houses? [See "Man Won't Leave Posh Digs Without a Fight," *Roanoke Times*, March 10, 1999, p. A8.]

Notes

1. *Merriam Webster's Collegiate Dictionary*, 10th ed. (Springfield, Mass.: Merriam-Webster, 1993), 398.
2. Ibid., 756.
3. 410 U.S. 113, 93 S. Ct. 705 (1973).
4. William H. Shaw and Vincent Berry, *Moral Issues in Business*, 4th ed. (Belmont, Calif.: Wadsworth, 1989), 2.
5. Ibid., 51.
6. Ibid., 55.
7. Rogene A. Buchholz and Sandra B. Rosenthal, *Business Ethics, the Pragmatic Path Beyond Principles to Process* (Upper Saddle River, N.J.: Prentice Hall, 1998), 68–69.
8. Shaw and Berry, n. 4, 63.
9. John Rawls, *A Theory of Justice* (Cambridge, Mass.: Harvard University Press, Belknap Press, 1971).
10. Ibid., 195–201.
11. Shaw and Berry, n. 4, 52–55.
12. Ibid., 58–60.
13. Buchholz and Rosenthal, n. 7, 68–69.
14. Shaw and Berry, n. 4, 66–67.
15. Rawls, n. 9, 195–210.
16. Hugh LaFollette, "The Truth in Ethical Relativism," *Journal of Social Philosophy* (1991): 146–154.
17. Vincent Ryan Ruggerio, *The Moral Imperative* (Port Washington, N.Y.: Knopf, 1973).
18. Shaw and Berry, n. 4, 77.
19. 170 N.W. 668 (Mich. 1919).
20. A. Carr, "Is Business Bluffing Ethical?" *Harvard Business Review* (January–February 1968).
21. "President Condemns Corporate Scandals," *Roanoke Times*, June 30, 2001, A1.
22. "Reform Has Many CEOs Rushing to Comply," *Roanoke Times*, August 9, 2002, A9.
23. "Where We Stand," *Your Market, Straight Talk for Investors*, The New York Stock Exchange (Time, Inc. Custom Publishing: New York Stock Exchange, July 2002), 3.
24. Jonathan D. Salant, "Ethics Officers to Teach the Lost Art of Fair Play," *Roanoke Times*, November 1, 2002, 1.
25. *Payne v. Western & Atl. R.R. Co.*, 81 Tenn. 507, 519–210 (1884).
26. 417 A.2d 505 (N.J. Super. 1980).
27. Tom L. Beauchamp and Norman E. Bowie, *Ethical Theories and Business*, 2nd ed. (Englewood Cliffs, N.J.: Prentice Hall, 1983), 247.

CHAPTER 3

International Law

AGENDA

NRW NRW needs to be aware of the importance of international business, even though the firm currently conducts most of its business in the United States. It is quite possible that the firm will be able to export its products to a number of other countries, especially the StuffTrakR. It is also quite possible that similar firms in other countries will attempt to import their products into the U.S. market, thus possibly competing directly with NRW and potentially reducing the firm's market share and/or profitability.

If NRW decides to export its product, what international markets should it look to initially? Does the North American Free Trade Agreement (NAFTA) make Canada and Mexico attractive markets? Does the European Union (EU) offer enough of an opportunity to make that a more attractive market? Are there any export restrictions that might make it difficult for the firm to export its product due to its technological basis?

These and similar questions are likely to arise in the material in this chapter. Be prepared! You never know when the firm or one of its members will seek your advice.

Any business forecaster of the 1970s who had predicted the end of the Cold War, the political (and economic) collapse of the Soviet Union, the dismantling of apartheid in South Africa, or the possibility that the Czech Republic, Hungary, and Poland would become members in the North Atlantic Treaty Organization (NATO), might have been told to sell his or her story to the supermarket tabloid newspapers. Many people would also have been very dubious about the prospects for a strong, unified European community, a North American free trade zone, or a "war" on terrorism. Yet each of these events has taken place in just over a generation, and these changes represent only some of the massive political and economic shifts that have occurred around the world in recent years. One can add to that list the destruction of the Berlin Wall and the reunification of Germany, the separatist referendum in Quebec, the split of Czechoslovakia into two countries, and the cruel civil wars in such countries as the former Yugoslavia and Somalia. Hong Kong, the Asian economic powerhouse, has reverted to the control of the Chinese government. A number of the economies in Asia have suffered devastating downturns, affecting world trade and international markets. Mexico has been through a recession. Argentina has had political and economic turmoil, and Brazil's economy has faced the threat of collapse. The last quarter of the 20th century was a time of unprecedented political and economic change, and the pace of change is continuing in this century. As a result, a businessperson must develop an international— even global—perspective in order to have the greatest chance for success.

Business in a Global Village

Each of these events has created both opportunities and risks for U.S. businesses. For example, the changes in the former Soviet Union have created new opportunities for companies such as PepsiCo and McDonald's to develop substantial business activities in these former Soviet republics, which are now independent nations. On the other hand, events such as the war in the former Yugoslavia have destroyed many of the factories and offices of foreign businesses, killed employees, and prevented goods from entering and leaving the area. Market fluctuations in Asia and South America have caused concerns and worries in other markets around the world, including the U.S. market. The U.S. economy has also suffered setbacks. The stock market has plunged, unemployment has increased, and corporate scandals have shaken the public's confidence. Yet, despite these problems, when viewed from a long-term perspective, opportunities for U.S. businesses to compete in global markets have never been better.

If U.S. businesses have learned one lesson in the past few years, it is, as Marshall McLuhan once said, that we all live in a "global village." Companies such as Coca-Cola and General Electric employ global advertising strategies. Other companies, including all of the major U.S. auto companies, have joint manufacturing and marketing agreements with their Japanese and/or European competitors. Numerous other firms and industries are also affected by the global market, some for the better and some for the worse. The textile firms of the American Southeast find themselves competing with textiles imported from a number of other nations. Retail outlets across the country carry products manufactured in other nations. State governments are establishing departments to promote international trade by businesses located within the state. "Internationalization" is permeating society at virtually every level.

In 1997 the United States exported $937.6 billion in goods and services and imported $1,047.8 billion. By 2000 that figure had grown to $1,414 billion in exports and $1,797 billion in imports.[1] When measured in goods and merchandise alone, U.S. imports have grown from $244 billion in 1980 to $877 billion in 1997. In that same time, U.S. exports have grown from $220.8 billion to $689 billion.[2] In many cases, typically American companies such as McDonald's, General Motors, and Digital Equipment find most of their revenues or profits coming from overseas operations. Foreign investment in the United States doubled between 1985 and 1990. Marshall McLuhan was right: We are so economically interdependent on one another that we do live in a global village. To succeed in the business world of the next century, every businessperson must be familiar with the basic rules of international business.

Going "Global"

As communications and transportation have improved, buyers and sellers in different markets have been able to find one another more easily, which has made it easier for them to do business together. Technology has opened the global marketplace to businesses of all sizes, allowing them to sell their goods, services, and technology. Future advances in technology will make interactions between buyers and sellers in different markets even easier, increasing the potential for international trade and the likelihood—or even the need—for a business to "go global."

A business has many options once it decides to "go global." For example, as it develops its international customer base, the business may decide to change the way it organizes itself. The business may move from simple selling relationships toward direct investments in major foreign markets. Most businesses start their international operations simply by selling to foreign customers. They may exhibit their products at international trade fairs, or an international buyer may visit a potential seller on a buying trip or be referred to the seller by another satisfied international customer. Like any direct selling relationship, the parties govern their rights and obligations using a contract. Many of the concerns a seller or buyer would have in a local transaction will be the same in an international transaction. Others, however, are special to the international transaction.

Suppose that Acme Novelties, Inc., a company based in Arizona, decides to expand its business from national to international. Acme may be selling a variety of items to its traditional buyers in the United States, another variety of items to a Mexican business, and still other items to a buyer in Ireland. While business would appear to be good for Acme, not too long ago these sorts of contracts could pose serious problems for the firm. By entering into contracts with customers in three different countries, Acme would, at least theoretically, be facing potential legal problems under three entirely different sets of laws. While most of Acme's sales in the United States would be governed by the Uniform Commercial Code (UCC), the sale to the Mexican customer would possibly be influenced by Mexican law, which has a strong European influence and is based on the Napoleonic Code, and the sale to the Irish customer would possibly be influenced by Irish law, which has a strong English common law influence. In addition, the sale to the Irish customer could be affected to some extent by the European Union (EU), of which Ireland is a member, and its rules. The sale to the Mexican customer could be affected by the North American Free Trade Agreement (NAFTA), a treaty to which both Mexico and the United States are signatories.

What happens if the tendered goods are rejected by each of these buyers? Whose law will govern the rights and obligations of the parties? Historically, experienced international traders would specify in their contracts which law would govern the transaction. Thus, the Arizona seller could have negotiated the contract so that the UCC was controlling in all three transactions. Or the parties could have agreed to have any disputes settled by arbitration. International sales contracts would often call for any disputes to be arbitrated, rather than tried, so the parties could avoid using unfamiliar court systems and unfamiliar laws.

In 1988, the United Nations Convention on Contracts for the International Sale of Goods (CISG) went into effect. The CISG provides a law of sales contracts specifically for contracts between businesses in countries that have approved the convention. In the United States, the CISG

NRW CASE 3.1 International Business

NRW

BENEFITS AND COSTS OF "GOING GLOBAL"

Carlos spends a considerable amount of time "surfing the Net," and he believes that NRW should use the Internet to take an international approach to its operations from the beginning. Helen doesn't think that the firm is ready to "go global" yet. She would prefer to approach this venture a bit more cautiously by beginning with a regional perspective. While she would like to see the firm grow to the point where it has a national—or even an international—market, she does not want to overextend now. Mai agrees with Helen. She doesn't think that NRW will be ready to "go global" in the near future, but she also doesn't think that it would hurt the firm if it at least "thinks globally" while it acts regionally. The members ask you for your opinion. What will you tell them?

BUSINESS CONSIDERATIONS Should a newly created business operation be concerned with "going global," or should its emphasis be on survival for the short term in its natural regional location? When should a high-tech firm begin to think about global, or at least international, operations? Should a more traditional manufacturing firm approach this issue differently?

ETHICAL CONSIDERATIONS Should the firm take international considerations into account in setting up its business practices and internal code of ethics, or should it leave such considerations for the future? How might such international considerations affect how the firm conducts its business or establishes its code of ethics?

INTERNATIONAL CONSIDERATIONS Are international considerations or plans necessarily different from domestic considerations or plans? Must a firm choose between "going global" and "staying at home"?

---

replaces the Uniform Commercial Code in any sales transactions between a U.S. firm and a business from another CISG country. Fortunately, the CISG is much like Article 2 (the law of sales) of the Uniform Commercial Code, and provisions of the CISG are often similar to the UCC's provisions, so it should quickly become familiar to American managers. (Article 2 of the UCC, Sales, Article 2A of the UCC, Leases, and the CISG are discussed in detail in Chapters 16–19.)

As of March 2001, the CISG had been ratified by 62 countries, including the United States and other important trading countries, such as China, France, Germany, and several republics of the former Soviet Union. (The complete list of member nations is shown in Exhibit 16.1.) Over the next several years, the CISG is likely to become the law in even more countries. This should reduce the concerns faced by companies like Acme Novelties in the example on page 55.

Doing Business in a Global Market

As a business grows, it may decide that it needs a more systematic effort to find customers in foreign markets. Often, it will turn to individuals or businesses in other major markets to act as go-betweens in attracting foreign buyers to the company's products. The business may seek an agent or it may opt for a distributor. An agent is a person or company who finds buyers on behalf of the seller and usually is paid a commission for the resulting sales. The sales contract is still between the buyer and seller (although in a few cases the agent has the authority to accept orders on the seller's behalf). The buyer gets the goods directly from the seller and looks to the seller to solve any problems with the sale. A distributor, by contrast, buys goods from the seller and resells them directly to customers. The distributor bears the risk that the goods will not sell or that customers will fail to pay for the goods. Generally, customers look to the distributor for service after the sale. Businesses with intellectual property rights—such as patents, copyrights, and trademarks—sometimes find it best to sell to a foreign business the right to make, copy, or market the products covered by those rights. Generally, the buyer of the rights will pay a fee plus a royalty—that is, a percentage of the price or profit—on any products sold.

One very popular method for entering the international business environment is franchising. U.S. fast-food businesses have used franchising as the major method of entering foreign markets. In a franchise, a license is granted by the franchisor to allow the franchisee to conduct business under the name of the franchisor. This license covers primarily the trademarks, for example, brand names such as Big Mac®, Whopper®, or Century 21®. In return for a fee and royalty paid to the franchisor, the franchisee earns the benefit of the reputation of the trademarks, national and international advertising, and a wide customer base. Many U.S.-based franchisors have identified their largest growth opportunities as coming from international franchising. (Franchising is covered in detail in Chapter 35.)

Another method for entering the international marketplace is through a joint venture. *Black's Law Dictionary* defines a joint venture in the United States as "an association of two or more persons to carry out a single business enterprise for profit." In international business, joint ventures are viewed somewhat more broadly than that definition implies. The concept covers businesses such as General Motors and Toyota, which built a plant together in California to manufacture Chevrolets and Toyotas on the same production lines. It also covers groups of companies that cooperate in research and development activities and even those that jointly market products. The joint venture has proven itself a successful way for companies to enter new markets, because they get the benefit of local expertise from their joint venture partners.

In many instances, a growing international business will decide to incorporate an operation separately in another country. If the business controls the new corporation, then it is the parent and the new corporation is the subsidiary. A subsidiary may be wholly owned by the parent company, or the parent company may have partial ownership. (In some countries, foreign businesses must involve local owners in the ownership and management of subsidiaries.)

Cross-Cultural Negotiations

The United States is geographically isolated from most of its trading partners. When the U.S. economy was the benchmark for the rest of the world, such isolation was not much of a problem. In those halcyon days, U.S. international business was frequently able to employ a "take it or leave it" attitude, knowing that the other party had little choice but to "take it," unless the other party was willing to do without. Why? Not many alternative sources existed for many goods beyond the United States.

Such a situation no longer exists. International competition has become heated, and the emergence of alternative sources of goods and services has produced the need for international traders to become aware of cultural differences in dealing with their customers. If a customer can receive satisfactory goods or services from several sources, other factors besides quality or price may enter into the equation. The successful international businessperson needs to learn as much about his or her trading partners and their cultures as possible in order to present the goods and services in the best possible light.

While there are no universal characteristics of any given culture, there are certain guidelines that tend to hold true. Among these guidelines are the following: national negotiating styles; differences in decision-making techniques; proper protocol in the negotiations; the social aspects of negotiating; time, and how it is viewed by various cultures; the importance of developing personal relationships between the negotiators; and social mores and taboos.[3] For example, the American desire to get things done, and preferably to get them done quickly, is at odds with the Chinese approach, to proceed more slowly, operating at a pace that is personally satisfying. Americans frequently make decisions based on a cost-benefit analysis, with little consideration given to face saving. By contrast, the Japanese consider saving face crucial in their social interactions. Many gestures are deemed to be acceptable in some cultures but may be considered rude—or even obscene—in others. The ability of a businessperson to successfully navigate through the cultural differences of his or her trading partners is instrumental to success in the international arena.

Differences in language can also have an impact on cross-cultural negotiations and business dealings. When the parties to a contract speak different languages, the contract that each party *thinks* he or she entered may be significantly different from the contract that his or her trading partner *thinks* the parties entered.

The following case is a classic in the area of international sales. The case involved parties from three different nations, and each party had a different primary language. This language difference may not have been important in the formation of the contract, but it appears that it was very important in its interpretation. Ironically, the central controversy involved the definition of a seemingly simple term used in the contract: chicken.

3.1

FRIGALIMENT IMPORTING CO. v. B.N.S. INT'L SALES CORP.
190 F. Supp. 116 (S.D.N.Y. 1960)

FACTS Stovicek, a representative of the Czechoslovak government, was in New York at the World Trade Fair, where he met Bauer, the secretary of B.N.S. Several days later, Stovicek contacted Bauer to see if B.N.S. would be interested in exporting chicken to Switzerland. Frigaliment, a Swiss firm represented by Stovicek, offered to purchase "25,000 lbs. of chicken 2½-3 lbs. weight, Cryovac packed, grade A government-inspected, at a price up to 33 cents per pound," and stated an interest in further offerings. B.N.S. accepted the offer, and Frigaliment sent a confirmation the following morning. The cables exchanged by the parties were predominantly in German, although the English word "chicken" was used to avoid confusion. (The German word "huhn" includes both broilers and stewing chickens.) B.N.S. sent a total of 175,000 pounds of chicken to Frigaliment under the two contracts the parties entered. Frigaliment objected to the tendered delivery, alleging that the "heavier" chickens (125,000 pounds of 2½-3-pound chickens) were not young chickens suitable for broiling or frying but were older, stewing chickens, or "fowl." Frigaliment sued for breach of warranty, alleging that the goods delivered did not correspond to the description of the goods as established by trade usage. B.N.S. denied a breach, asserting that it delivered goods that corresponded to the contract term "chicken."

ISSUE Did the goods tendered by B.N.S. satisfy the description of the term "chicken" as used in the contract?

HOLDING Yes, Frigaliment failed to persuade the court that the word "chicken" meant only young chickens suitable for broiling and frying.

REASONING Excerpts from the opinion of Judge Friendly:

The issue is, what is chicken? Plaintiff says "chicken" means a young chicken, suitable for broiling and frying. Defendant says "chicken" means any bird of that genus that meets contract specifications on weight and quality, including what it calls "stewing chicken" and plaintiff pejoratively terms "fowl." Dictionaries give both meanings, as well as some others not relevant here. To support its claim, plaintiff sends a number of volleys over the net; defendant essays to return them and adds a few serves of its own. Assuming that both parties were acting in good faith, the case nicely illustrates Holmes's remark "that the making of a contract depends not on the agreement of two minds in one intention, but on the agreement of two sets of external signs—not on the parties' having meant the same thing but on their having said the same thing...." I have concluded that the plaintiff has not sustained its burden of persuasion that the contract used "chicken" in the narrow sense.

The action is for breach of the warranty that goods sold shall correspond to the description. Two contracts are in suit. In the first, dated 2 May 1957, defendant, a New York sales corporation, confirmed the sale to plaintiff, a Swiss corporation, of

> US Fresh Frozen Chicken, Grade A, Government Inspected, Eviscerated 2½–3 lbs. And 1½–2 lbs. Each

> all chicken individually wrapped in Cryovac, packed in secured fiber cartons or wooden boxes, suitable for export

> 75,000 lbs 2½–3 lbs @ $33.00

25,000 lbs 1½–2 lbs @ $36.50

per 100 lbs FAS New York

Scheduled May 10, 1957, pursuant to instructions from Penson & Co., New York.

The second contract, also dated 2 May 1957, was identical save that only 50,000 lbs. of the heavier "chicken" were called for, the price of the smaller birds was $37 per 100 lbs., and shipment was scheduled for 30 May. The initial shipment under the first contract was short but the balance was shipped on 17 May. When the initial shipment arrived in Switzerland, plaintiff found, on 28 May, that the 2½–3-lb. birds were not young chicken suitable for broiling and frying but stewing chicken or "fowl"; indeed many of the cartons and bags plainly so indicated. Protests ensued. Nevertheless, shipment under the second contract was made on 29 May, the 2½–3-lb. birds again being stewing chicken. Defendant stopped the transportation of these at Rotterdam.

This action followed. Plaintiff says that, notwithstanding that its acceptance was in Switzerland, New York law controls. Defendant does not dispute this, and relies on New York decisions. I shall follow the apparent agreement of the parties as to the applicable law. Since the word "chicken" standing alone is ambiguous, I turn first to see whether the contract itself offers any aid to its interpretation. Plaintiff says that 1½–2-lb. birds necessarily had to be young chickens since the older birds do not come in that size, hence the 2½–3-lb. birds must likewise be young. This is unpersuasive—a contract for "apples" of two different sizes could be filled with different kinds of apples even though only one species came in both sizes. Defendant notes that the contract called not simply for "chickens" but for "US Fresh Frozen Chicken, Grade A, Government Inspected." It says the contract thereby incorporated by reference the Department of Agriculture's regulations, which favor its interpretation. . . .

When all the evidence is reviewed, it is clear that defendant believed it could comply with the contracts by delivering stewing chicken in the 2½–3-lb. size. Defendant's subjective intent would not be significant if this did not coincide with an objective meaning of "chicken." Here it did coincide with one of the dictionary meanings, with the definition in the Department of Agriculture's regulations to which the contract made at least oblique reference, with at least some usage in the trade, with the realities of the market, and with what plaintiff's spokesman had said. Plaintiff asserts it to be equally plain that plaintiff's own subjective intent was to obtain broilers and fryers; the only evidence against this is the material as to market prices and this may not have been sufficiently brought home. In any event, it is unnecessary to determine that issue. For plaintiff has the burden of showing that "chicken" was used in the narrower rather than in the broader sense, and this it has not sustained.

This opinion constitutes the Court's findings of fact and conclusions of law. Judgment shall be entered dismissing the complaint with costs.

BUSINESS CONSIDERATIONS One of the potential problems in international trade is the likelihood of misunderstandings when the parties to a contract speak different languages. What should a business do to minimize the risk of misunderstandings due to the fact that the other party to a contract speaks a different language?

ETHICAL CONSIDERATIONS Is it ethical for a U.S. business to insist that any contracts it enters into with firms from other nations be written in English rather than in the language of the other nation? Should the contract be drafted in both languages to ensure that each party is dealing with a contract written in its native tongue?

Extraterritoriality: U.S. Laws, International Applications

American businesses are used to operating under the laws of the United States. However, as more and more businesses expand into foreign nations they will begin to face a dilemma. Obviously they will have to obey the laws of the nations in which they are operating. But will they also have to continue to obey the laws of the United States? Put another way, do the laws of the United States (or of any

other sovereign nation) end at its borders or do they reach across borders into other nations? This question is of major concern to international businesses. In addition, if domestic law does apply internationally, businesses need to know whether all domestic laws apply internationally, or if application is limited to only some laws.

Antitrust Law

The U.S. antitrust laws are intended to ensure that business in the United States is conducted on a level playing field by protecting competition. Various anticompetitive activities are prohibited by these statutes. For example, the Sherman Antitrust Act states in its first section that "every contract, combination . . . or conspiracy in restraint of trade or commerce among the several States, or with foreign nations, is declared to be illegal." Is this statute applicable internationally, or only domestically?

According to the precedent set in several cases, the United States does have antitrust laws with extraterritorial application. However, U.S. courts have not been in full agreement on the meaning of those statutes with respect to international commerce. Among U.S. courts, there has been no consensus on how far the jurisdiction should extend. Some courts use the "direct and substantial effect" test; they examine the effect on U.S. foreign commerce as a prerequisite for proper jurisdiction. Other courts have used a test that looks at whether a conspiracy exists that adversely affects American commerce.

In general, however, most courts prefer to evaluate and balance the relevant considerations in each case. The courts determine whether the contacts and interests of the United States are sufficient to support the exercise of extraterritorial jurisdiction. The U.S. Supreme Court even allowed an alleged violation of the Sherman Act to be decided by Japanese arbitration. In that case, *Mitsubishi Motors Corp. v. Soler Chrysler-Plymouth, Inc.*,[4] a firm in Puerto Rico entered into a contract with a Swiss firm and a Japanese firm. The contract specified that any disputes were to be resolved by submission of the case to the Japanese Arbitration Association. An antitrust issue arose in the case; and the Puerto Rican firm asserted that antitrust issues could not be resolved by arbitration, despite the contract's terms, but rather had to be settled by a U.S. federal court. The U.S. Supreme Court disagreed and compelled arbitration as provided for in the contract to settle the dispute.

In an effort to resolve the issue, Congress passed the Foreign Trade Antitrust Improvement Act[5] in 1982. This amendment to the Sherman Antitrust Act says that the courts need to examine the site of the injury in determining whether the antitrust laws apply. The act is aimed at protecting the U.S. market from antitrust problems caused here, and attempts to exclude pure export activities from antitrust coverage. The language of the Sherman Act, can be found at http://www.usdoj.gov//atr/foia/divisionmanual/ch2.htm. A discussion of the scope of the Sherman Act can be found at http://www.bartleby.com/65/sh/ShermanA.html/ and the various antitrust acts are discussed in more detail in Chapter 37.

The Foreign Corrupt Practices Act

Many businesses that are new to the international marketplace have some trouble understanding the different values of people from other cultures or the way business may be conducted in foreign nations. The differences may be relatively minor, or they may be substantial. One area that has been particularly troublesome involves payments to officials in other countries. If a business makes a payment to a foreign official, is the business giving that official a gift or is the official being bribed?

In an effort to address this problem and to provide guidelines for U.S. firms doing business in other nations, Congress passed the Foreign Corrupt Practices Act[6] (FCPA) in 1977. This act, an amendment to the Securities Exchange Act of 1934, covers foreign corrupt practices and provides accounting standards that firms must follow in reporting payments made to foreign officials. Significant amendments to the FCPA were made in 1988.

The FCPA applies only to firms that have their principal offices in the United States. The act prohibits giving money or anything else of value to foreign officials with the intent to corrupt. This is a very broad standard, but basically the act is intended to prevent the transfer of money or other items of value to any person who is in a position to exercise discretionary authority in order to have that person exercise his or her authority in a manner that gives an advantage to the donor of the "gift."

Interestingly, the act does not prohibit so-called grease payments to foreign officials, although these, too, may look like bribes. A grease payment is a payment to a person in order to have him or her perform a task or render a service that is part of the person's normal job. The "grease" is intended to get the person to do the job more quickly or more efficiently than he or she might have otherwise. By contrast, a payment that is made with the intent to corrupt is one that is designed to have the donee do something he or she might not have been obligated to do or to make a favorable choice among options.

Many businesspeople have claimed that the FCPA places American firms at a competitive disadvantage. These people argue that prohibiting American firms from making bribes means they are not able to compete with foreign firms, thus costing the American firms contracts, profits, and jobs. They argue that "everyone else is doing it, so why shouldn't we?" It is apparent that the U.S. Congress does not agree with them; and the FCPA will continue to regulate payments made or gifts given to foreign officials by representatives of American companies for the foreseeable future.

In the following case there are issues involving violations of the Foreign Corrupt Practices Act, allegations of legal malpractice, and a question of criminal intent in relation to the FCPA.

Employment

As pointed out previously, U.S. antitrust law, at least in some cases, has extraterritorial application. Similar reasoning has led the courts to conclude that some U.S.

STICHTING TER BEHARTIGING VAN DE BELANGEN VAN OUDAANDEELHOUDERS IN HET KAPITAAL VAN SAYBOLT INTERNATIONAL B.V. v. SCHREIBER.
145 F. Supp. 2d 356; 2001 U.S. Dist. LEXIS 7847 (S.D. N.Y. 2001)

FACTS Stichting Ter Behartiging Van de Belangen Van Oudaandeelhouders in Het Kapitaal Van Saybolt International B.V., a Dutch entity, represents the shareholders of Saybolt International B.V., a Dutch company that was the parent of two American entities, Saybolt North American and Saybolt, Inc. (collectively Saybolt) at the time the issues in this case arose. In 1995 officers of Saybolt arranged to pay a bribe to a Panamanian official in order to obtain a lease concession. The bribe was paid through a foreign affiliate rather than through one of the American entities. When evidence of the bribe was uncovered, a grand jury in Massachusetts indicted both Saybolt companies for violation of the Foreign Corrupt Practices Act, and a grand jury in New Jersey indicted David Mead, CEO of Saybolt, Inc. and vice-president of Saybolt North American, and Frerik Pluimers, president of Saybolt International B.V. and chairman of the board of Saybolt North America. The two Saybolt defendants pleaded guilty and Mead was convicted in a jury trial. Pluimers remains a fugitive.

Prior to arranging the bribe, Saybolt received legal advice from Philippe Schreiber, a lawyer who was both Saybolt's legal counsel and a director of Saybolt North America. Schreiber repeatedly advised Saybolt that payment of the Panamanian bribe would be illegal if made by an American company, but he allegedly advised Saybolt that a bribe payment by a foreign affiliate might be legal. He also allegedly failed to advise Saybolt that any involvement by Saybolt or its officers in arranging the affiliate's payment could result in criminal liability. The plaintiffs then claimed that the bribe was arranged by Saybolt on the basis of this misleading legal advice. As a result they have filed suit for legal malpractice against Schreiber and the law firm for which he works.

ISSUE Did Saybolt rely on the allegedly erroneous advice of its legal counsel, thus negating its *mens rea* in this case?

HOLDING No. There is no evidence that Saybolt relied on the advice of its counsel and the required *mens rea* was established in the prior criminal proceedings.

REASONING Excerpts from the opinion of District Judge Jed S. Rakoff:

[The defendants argue that] if Saybolt had in good faith relied on Schreiber's advice, Saybolt would have believed that its arranging the bribe through a foreign affiliate was permissible and thus Saybolt would have lacked the *mens rea* necessary for a criminal conviction of violating the FCPA; whereas it has already been conclusively established in both of the parallel criminal cases that Saybolt knew at the time it authorized the bribe that what it was doing was illegal and corrupt.

The Court entirely agrees with this argument. Indeed, the Court concludes that Saybolt's own guilty plea to criminally violating the FCPA in arranging the bribe is sufficient in itself to grant defendants' motion. To enter such a plea Saybolt had to affirm, as it did, that it undertook the misconduct in question with knowledge of the corruptness of its acts. . . . Since, if it had in fact relied on Schreiber's allegedly erroneous and misleading advice, Saybolt would not have believed at the time that its misconduct was unlawful or corrupt, it could never have made this admission at its allocution or, indeed, entered its guilty plea at all. Conversely, since Saybolt did in fact plead guilty and admit its criminal intent, it is bound by those admissions, and therefore cannot now contend either that it relied on Schreiber's alleged advice or that that advice, even if erroneous, in any way proximately caused whatever damages, if any, were incurred by Saybolt. . . .

While Saybolt's guilty plea is therefore a sufficient basis in itself to grant defendants' motion, an independent and equally sufficient basis is provided by the collateral estoppel effect of the criminal proceedings that resulted in the conviction of Saybolt's former chief executive officer, Mead, whose own criminal *mens rea*, necessarily found by the jury that convicted him, is attributable to Saybolt by virtue of respondeat superior. . . .

Like Saybolt, Mead was convicted of violating the FCPA by arranging the bribe at issue in this case. . . . Not only was Mead's corrupt intent a necessary element of that conviction, but also the very claim on which plaintiff here relies—Schreiber's alleged failure to advise Saybolt and its officers that payment of the bribe would be illegal even if channeled through a foreign corporate affiliate if arranged by Saybolt's U.S.-based officers— was squarely put before, and rejected by, the jury that convicted Mead. Indeed, Mead's counsel, on summation, made this the cornerstone of his defense, repeatedly arguing that Mead lacked criminal intent because he relied on Schreiber's allegedly erroneous and/or inadequate advice. . . . Further still, the Court in Mead's trial specifically instructed the jury not to convict if it found that Mead believed that payment of the bribe was legal. . . . Thus, by convicting Mead the jury necessarily determined that he—and thus Saybolt—acted in knowing violation of the law despite Schreiber's alleged advice.

Like Saybolt's own admissions of criminal intent, the jury's determination of Mead's criminal intent and its rejection of his defense based on Schreiber's alleged advice must be accorded issue-preclusive effect in the instant litigation. For collateral estoppel to apply, the party to be precluded must have been, or been in sufficient privity to, a party to the prior litigation. In addition, "the court must determine that (1) the issues in both proceedings are identical, (2) the issue in the prior proceeding was actually litigated and actually decided, (3) there was full and fair opportunity to litigate in the prior proceeding, and (4) the issue previously litigated was necessary to support a valid and final judgment on the merits." . . . . Since plaintiff here is simply Saybolt's assignee, there is obvious privity with respect to Saybolt's own plea; and even though Saybolt was not a party to the Mead criminal case, Mead was indicted and convicted for criminal activity he undertook for Saybolt's benefit in his capacity as chief executive officer of Saybolt, and his intent is therefore directly imputable to Saybolt. . . .

Regarding the other four elements: first, the issue of criminal intent decided in the two criminal cases is identical to, and dispositive of, a necessary element of plaintiff's instant claim that plaintiff was injured by Schreiber's allegedly erroneous advice, since if Saybolt knew its actions were wrongful, regardless of the advice allegedly given by Schreiber, then Schreiber's advice was neither materially relied upon by Saybolt nor proximately caused any injury to Saybolt. Second, as shown above, the question of Saybolt's knowing illegality was unquestionably actually litigated and decided in both criminal cases. Third, the parties in both of the criminal cases were able to fully and fairly litigate this issue, and had ample incentive to do so. Indeed, Mead, facing incarceration, had the strongest possible incentive to defend against the criminal charges brought against him; and while plaintiff argues that Saybolt, which paid a $1.5 million fine, had no incentive to litigate because by the terms of Saybolt's sale (consummated after the events that precipitated this lawsuit) the fine was paid out of monies that would have reverted to Saybolt's former shareholders had Saybolt escaped monetary penalty, the prospect of a felony conviction (not to mention its collateral civil consequences) was more than ample incentive to defend. . . . Finally, as previously shown, knowing and corrupt intent was absolutely necessary to support both Saybolt's and Mead's convictions.

While the Court has carefully considered, and rejected, plaintiff's other arguments, only one even merits mention. Plaintiff contends that even if all the factors of collateral estoppel are satisfied, application of the doctrine is unfair under these circumstances and thus the Court should exercise its discretion to permit relitigation. . . . Specifically, plaintiff claims that if, notwithstanding Saybolt's corrupt intent, Schreiber had expressly told them that what they were proposing was illegal, they would not have arranged the bribe. Aside from its speculative nature, however, this and other equitable arguments advanced by plaintiff are singularly unappealing and unpersuasive. Saybolt, on any view of the facts, undertook to arrange the bribe of a high-ranking official of Panama, a despicable act of corruption designed to enhance Saybolt's profits at the expense of the most elementary principles of honest government. Saybolt's former shareholders who stood to reap the financial benefits of that corrupt activity can hardly complain of the losses attendant on the exposure of those crimes.

Accordingly, defendants' motion for summary judgment in their favor is hereby granted, and the complaint is dismissed with prejudice. . . .

BUSINESS CONSIDERATIONS Should a business be able to avoid criminal prosecution by showing that it only undertook the challenged conduct after its attorney gave assurances that the conduct was legal? Does this defense seem to be arguing that "ignorance of the law *is* an excuse"?

ETHICAL CONSIDERATIONS Is it ethical for a business to attempt to "pass the buck" by blaming its legal counsel for bad advice when the business is indicted for illegal conduct?

employment laws also apply outside the domestic environment. Of particular concern are the nondiscrimination provisions of domestic employment law.

Congress has amended Title VII of the Civil Rights Act of 1964, extending protection against employment discrimination to Americans working for American companies, even when the employee is working in another nation. Thus, the protections of Title VII extend across national boundaries, at least for U.S. workers employed by U.S. firms, regardless of the location to which the worker is assigned.

Free Trade Zones

At one time, it was necessary to know the laws of each of the countries involved in an international transaction. The complexity that entailed as well as the increased number of countries in the world since the end of World War II impeded international trade. In an effort to alleviate this problem, countries in common geographical areas have banded together to form economic unions to facilitate and expedite trade. The two most significant regional groupings are the European Union (EU), composed of 15 Western European nations, and the North American Free Trade Area, which includes the United States, Canada, and Mexico. Other groups in Asia, Africa, and Latin America are now looking to the examples set by these major regional groups to create a legal foundation for their own free-trade areas.

The European Union

The European Union (EU) was created by the Treaty of Rome in 1957. Currently, the member states are Austria, Belgium, Denmark, Finland, France, Germany, Greece, Ireland, Italy, Luxembourg, the Netherlands, Portugal, Spain, Sweden, and the United Kingdom. In the Treaty of Nice the EU proposed expansion of its membership, subject to approval by all of the current members. On October 21, 2002, Irish voters voted in favor of the proposal, completing the unanimous acceptance of the expansion.[7] The newly approved members are Cyprus, the Czech Republic, Estonia, Hungary, Latvia, Lithuania, Malta, Poland, Slovakia, and Slovenia.[8] The formal invitations for these nations to officially join the EU will probably be issued in December 2002, with membership to begin in 2004. (Romania, Bulgaria, and Turkey have also applied for membership, but their applications have yet to be approved. In addition, Switzerland is preparing for a referendum on joining the EU.) Obviously, the final composition of the EU will not be known for several more years.

The purpose of the European Union is to establish a common customs tariff for outside nations importing goods into the community and to eliminate tariffs among EU members. In furtherance of this purpose, the EU has its own legislative, executive, and judicial branches. The treaty also covers the free movement of workers, goods, and capital within the community. It is aimed at accomplishing international cooperation. The EU is governed by the Council of Ministers, the European Commission, the European Parliament, and the Court of Justice. Exhibit 3.1 depicts the governing structure of the European Union.

The Treaty of Rome established four main objectives for the freedom of movement within the EU: the movement of goods, people, services, and capital. Since the treaty, the EU has developed a large body of law designed to achieve these four objectives.

In 1986, the EU adopted the Single European Act, mandating the creation of a unified market by the end of 1992. In 1991, the heads of state of the EU member countries signed the Maastricht Treaty on European Political and Monetary Union, which strengthened the EU institutions

---

INTERNATIONAL MARKETS AND FREE TRADE ZONES

Mai is excited about the marketing opportunities NAFTA provides for NRW. She believes that a strong potential market exists in Canada right now, and that the Mexican market presents an even stronger potential market within the next few years. Carlos agrees with Mai, but he thinks that South America is the *real* opportunity for NRW. Carlos believes that NAFTA will expand soon, and that any firm ready to capitalize on the opportunities in South America will be extremely successful. While Helen appreciates these sentiments, she believes that the firm's greatest chance for international sales lies with European customers, and she would like the firm to target the EU. They have asked you for your opinion. What will you tell them?

BUSINESS CONSIDERATIONS Should the firm be concerned with an "either-or" position in considering international growth and expansion, or should it be more willing to consider planned expansion into both trade zones? Should the firm look only at these two trade zones (NAFTA and EU), or should it be concerned with expanding into any global markets that seem interested in the product?

ETHICAL CONSIDERATIONS In considering expansion into new markets in other countries, what sorts of ethical issues might cause concern? Are there potential cultural issues the firm should consider? Might these potential cultural issues vary from one nation or free trade zone to another?

INTERNATIONAL CONSIDERATIONS Should a business stress sales within any free trade zone to which its home nation belongs, or should it seek markets without regard to free trade zones? What benefits are present in remaining within a free trade zone?

EXHIBIT **3.1** The European Union

Council of Ministers
Legislative branch of the EU

Issues directives, impelling each member state to put its law into compliance with EU policy

Issues regulations, superior to national laws and that may require national amendments in order to ensure compliance with EU

EUROPEAN COMMUNITY

Austria	Denmark	Finland
Belgium	Germany	France
Greece	Luxembourg	Ireland
Italy	Spain	The Netherlands
Portugal	Sweden	The United Kingdom

European Commission
Advisory body that proposes legislation to the council

Enforces EU law, primarily by means of imposing substantial fines for noncompliance

Creates detailed regulations in the areas of competition and agricultural law (under a delegation from the Council of Ministers)

Assembly
European Parliament

Consults with the council on legislation
Proposes amendments to legislation
Can force the council to resign with a vote of "no confidence"

Court of Justice
Court of last resort within the EU

Court opinions become the domestic law for all member nations of the EU

and called for the establishment of a common currency, the European Currency Unit (ECU), by the close of the decade.

Goods The EU has a customs union that is designed to eliminate customs duties among all member nations. In addition, the union has a common tariff with respect to trade between member nations and nonmember nations. As a result, no burdens are placed on trade between member nations, but a burden is placed on trade with countries outside the EU.

Persons One of the benefits of citizenship in an EU member country is the right to free movement anywhere within the union. EU nationals and their families may reside anywhere in the EU. Students may enroll in vocational programs anywhere in the EU. Workers may work anywhere in the EU without work permits, on the same terms as nationals of that country. One of the more controversial provisions of the Maastricht Agreement allows any EU national to vote in both municipal and European Parliament elections wherever they may live. Thus, an Irish citizen living in Rome could vote in Rome's city elections, as

well as voting for Rome's representative to the European Parliament.

Services As the world moves toward a more service-oriented economy, the free movement of services becomes an increasingly important benefit of EU membership. Banks, insurance companies, and financial services businesses are now entitled to provide their services equally across the EU. Similarly, many kinds of professionals may now practice their professions anywhere in the EU. For example, doctors, dentists, architects, travel agents, and hairdressers—once they meet minimum requirements—all may practice in countries other than their own. The EU also gives people the right to establish businesses anywhere in the EU on the same terms that apply to local entrepreneurs, thus allowing them to operate freely throughout the EU.

Capital The European Monetary System (EMS) was created in 1979. Its purpose is to allow only limited fluctuations in the currencies of various member nations from preset parity prices. This was to be accomplished through a joint credit facility that would lend support to an EMS currency when it needed an infusion of capital. To further stabilize the currencies of member countries, the EU created the European Currency Unit, or ECU. The ECU was actually a "basket" of currencies, based on the exchange rates of the member countries. In 1992, the Maastricht Agreement called for the creation of the ECU as a real currency, designed to replace the pounds, marks, pesos, and francs used in the various member nations. Not all of the member states were willing to join in on the move to the ECU, and the ECU left each member state with its own currency as well as the ECU, providing for some potential for confusion. Subsequently, the European Commission decided to take a significantly different approach. It decided to create a new currency to replace both the ECU and the national currencies of the member states.

This new EU currency, the "euro," was introduced effective January 1, 1999. The euro has been approved as the official currency of 11 of the 15 EU member states. The euro replaced the ECU on January 1, 1999, at a conversion rate of 1:1. To help effectuate and smooth the transition, the European Commission enacted two Council Regulations. The first of these regulations provided for continuity of contracts, precision in conversion rates, and rounding rules to deal with this new currency.[9] The second regulation addressed the issues of substituting the euro for national currencies, the transition period for the changeover to the euro, the currency itself, and some other related issues or topics. Council Regulations were used because these regulations are applicable directly to the member states without the need for any national implementing legislation, debate, or other concerns.[10]

Competition Law To create a truly common market, the EU needs extensive rules on competition. The Treaty of Rome set up the basic structure of EU competition law, and the Council of Ministers has issued a large body of directives and regulations. Further, the European Commission, as the law's main enforcer, has issued regulations and decisions implementing the law. The main concerns under competition law are covered in Article 85, Article 86, the area of negative clearances, and extraterritoriality.

Article 85 Like U.S. antitrust law, Article 85 of the Treaty of Rome prohibits agreements, contracts, cartels, and joint activities that intend to restrict or distort competition within the EU. For example, price fixing, limiting or allocating markets, tying arrangements, and price discrimination are all prohibited under Article 85. However, Article 85 recognizes that some contracts benefit consumers by improving the production or distribution of goods or by promoting product improvements. The European Commission, therefore, can exempt activities from Article 85,

either by issuing an individual exemption for a particular situation or by a block exemption for similarly situated businesses. An example of a block exemption would be the Commission guidelines for franchises; these tell potential franchise businesses which contract provisions are acceptable and which will bring Commission action.

Article 86 The second major EU competition law is Article 86 of the Treaty of Rome. It bars one or more companies from using a dominant market position to restrict or distort trade. Prohibited abuses of dominant positions include tying arrangements, price fixing, price discrimination, and other conduct similar to that prohibited under U.S. antitrust law. Either buyers or sellers can have dominant positions. The Commission and the Court of Justice of the European Union have defined dominance by a practical test: a firm or firms having the power to "act without taking into account their competitors, purchasers or suppliers" possess a dominant position. (See *Europemballage Corp. v. Commission,* E.C.R. 215 [1973].) Thus, no specific market share is required; instead, the Commission looks at the firm's power to control suppliers and customers and its ability to prevent competition.

Negative Clearance A business concerned about its actions violating either Article 85 or Article 86 can apply to the European Commission for permission to engage in activities that appear to violate EU competition laws. This permission is known as a negative clearance. If a negative clearance is granted, this means that the commission has reviewed the proposed conduct, and—if the business does what it has indicated—the commission will not prosecute it under either Article 85 or Article 86.

Extraterritoriality The EU position on the reach of its power to regulate competition has expanded considerably over the last 20 years. It now appears that conduct anywhere can be subject to EU competition rules if it is intended to affect and does affect the EU market. The European Court of Justice has ruled that Article 85 has extraterritorial application if the conduct in question is intended to affect parties or businesses located within the European Union.[11] This should serve as a warning to companies that engage in activities that are lawful in their home country but also affect the European market.

The North American Free Trade Agreement

One powerful alternative to the EU is the free-trade partnership recently formed in North America under the

North American Free Trade Agreement (NAFTA). The first piece of NAFTA went into effect in 1989, with the ratification of the Canada–U.S. Free Trade Agreement. As with its counterpart, the EU, one major purpose of the Canada–U.S. Free Trade Agreement was the elimination of tariffs on sales of goods between the two countries. The agreement called for the elimination of all tariffs between the nations by 1998. (As a practical matter, most such tariffs were already gone.) Goods qualify for tariff-free treatment if they are 50 percent North American in content. Also like the EU, the Canada–U.S. Free Trade Agreement made it easier for Canadian and U.S. citizens to work in each other's countries and for investments to flow across the border. Unlike the EU, however, the Free Trade Agreement did not set up a host of new institutions or require the two countries to give up much of their sovereignty. The only new institutions created by the agreement were binational panels of experts to be convened as needed to resolve trade disputes between the two countries. These expert panels replace the court systems for both countries in eligible cases.

In 1993, Mexico joined its Canadian and U.S. counterparts in the North American Free Trade Agreement. NAFTA creates a free-trade area encompassing all of North America, a market large enough to compete successfully with Asian and European trade groups. There are still some concerns about NAFTA, but there is no concerted effort by any of the governments involved to rescind the agreement. Free trade with Mexico presents different concerns than it did with Canada. U.S. environmental and labor groups object to Mexico's reputation for having a lax legal environment, and Canadians worry about more jobs moving south.

There have been several proposals made over the past few years to increase and to strengthen NAFTA. In 1994, some 34 nations from the Western Hemisphere agreed to negotiate a "Free Trade Area of the Americas" by 2005. Such a free-trade zone would encompass virtually all of the Western Hemisphere, with 34 nations and more than 800 million citizens. This agreement was reemphasized in April 2001 when President Bush made his first speech to the Organization of American States. In this speech the president reiterated the idea of a "Free Trade Area of the Americas" and pledged to lay the groundwork for such a zone.[12]

In July 2002 the "Guayaquil Consensus"[13] was presented as the final document produced following a two-day summit meeting among leaders from 10 South American nations. The document proposed an increase in cooperation between the two major trading blocs in South America (Mersocur, made up of Brazil, Argentina, Uruguay, and Paraguay, with Chile and Bolivia as associate members; and the Andean Pact, made up of Venezuela, Colombia, Ecuador, Peru, and Bolivia), which will, in turn, lead to a better negotiating position with the United States. The ultimate goal is a hemisphere-wide free-trade zone, a "Free Trade Area of the Americas," which is based on a combination of the members of NAFTA, Mersocur, and the Andean Pact into one large trade zone.

Other Free Trade Zones

There are a number of other free-trades zones around the world, although none of the others possesses the economic might of either the European Union or NAFTA. For example, there are at least four free-trade zones in Latin America. The Central American Common Market is composed of Costa Rica, El Salvador, Guatemala, Honduras, Nicaragua, and Panama. The MERCOSUS Common Market is composed of Argentina, Brazil, Paraguay, and Uruguay. The Andean Common Market is made up of Bolivia, Ecuador, Colombia, and Venezuela. And the Caribbean Community includes Barbados, Belize, Dominica, Jamaica, Trinidad-Tobago, Grenada, St. Kitts-Nevus-Anguilla, St. Lucia, and St. Vincent.

There are at least three African free-trade zones as well. These include the Economic Community of West African States, the Economic and Customs Union of Central Africa, and the East African Community. There is also a treaty, the Treaty Establishing the African Economic Community, which has 51 signatories. This treaty is intended to create an African equivalent to the European Union.

Each of these free-trade zones has the potential to influence international trade within its member states and to help—or hinder—the economic growth and development of the member nations.

The General Agreement on Tariffs and Trade

Following World War II, the Western Allies envisioned an international economic organization that would provide leadership and coordination for international trade, like the United Nations in the political environment. A charter was drafted for an International Trade Organization (ITO) in 1948, but the charter was not adopted by enough nations, effectively shelving the ITO.

Prior to the proposed ITO charter, U.S. negotiators proposed a general agreement on tariffs and trades as a stepping-stone to prepare the way for ITO ratification. The Western Allies accepted this American proposal in 1947, creating the first General Agreement on Tariffs and Trade (GATT). When the ITO failed to generate sufficient support for ratification, GATT became the accepted framework for regulating international trade.

GATT promoted free trade by seeking to reduce tariffs and quotas between nations. It promoted fair trade by defining such trade practices as unfair government subsidies of exports and dumping (selling goods below fair value on a foreign market). It also provided panels to resolve trade disputes. GATT worked through "rounds" of discussions, during which countries agreed to reduce tariffs for all GATT members. The final round of GATT, known as the Uruguay Round, also raised non-goods-related issues such as trade-related intellectual property rights, investment protection, services, and agricultural subsidies.

The Uruguay Round was frustrating for many of the participants, and a number of the objectives that were expected were not achieved. One major achievement, however, was the establishment of the World Trade Organization (WTO). The WTO is an international economic organization that is intended to provide leadership and coordination for international trade. Thus, 47 years after the ITO was defeated, a WTO has been created. GATT did, indeed, provide an interim stepping-stone to the international organization, albeit for a much longer period than originally expected.

World Trade Organization

The World Trade Organization was created during the Uruguay Round of GATT discussions and officially established January 1, 1995. However, the WTO is not merely an extension of GATT. The WTO has a completely different character than did GATT, and it has a completely different mission. GATT was a multinational agreement, not an organization, and was intended to regulate trade in merchandise goods. There was no institutional foundation for GATT. By contrast, the WTO is an *organization* headquartered in Geneva, Switzerland, with a formal structure, a permanent staff, and a (sizeable) operating budget. The WTO has expanded coverage not only to include merchandise goods but also to cover some trade in services and to provide protection for intellectual property. As of October 2002 there were 145 member countries in the WTO, with several dozen more nations listed as "observers," most of which had applied for membership but had not yet been admitted to the organization. (Among the nations that have applied but not yet been admitted are Russia, Saudi Arabia, and Vietnam.)[14]

The highest authority within the WTO is the Ministerial Conference, which is composed of representatives from each member nation. The Ministerial Conference must meet at least once every two years and has the authority to make decisions on any matters under any of the multilateral trade agreements recognized by the WTO. While the Ministerial Conference is the highest authority, the day-to-day operations of the WTO are conducted by the General Council. The General Council serves as the Dispute Settlement Body of the WTO, and as the Trade Policy Review Body. It also reports to the Ministerial Conference. The General Council delegates a great deal of its responsibility to three other councils—the Council for Trade in Goods, the Council for Trade in Services, and the Council for Trade-Related Aspects of Intellectual Property Rights. Obviously, the WTO has a much wider responsibility than did GATT, covering areas other than international trade in goods.

Dispute resolution under the WTO is considerably quicker than was the case under GATT and promises to be much more effective. When controversies arise under the WTO, the dispute is submitted to a panel of trade experts. This panel will then have the authority to rule for one or the other of the complainants. When the panel rules for one of the nations, that nation will be given permission to retaliate against the other nation unless or until the losing nation changes the trade practice that was the subject of the dispute. In addition, the other member nations are expected to exert pressure on the losing nation to encourage a change in practice in order to ensure compliance. Since the member nations encompass a significant majority of world trade, such pressure and unofficial sanctions should prove to be very effective.

UNCITRAL

The United Nations Commission on International Trade Law (UNCITRAL) is perhaps the most important organization involved in addressing issues of private international trade. The UN General Assembly established UNCITRAL in 1966. This Commission attempts to provide harmonization of private international law in order to encourage and enhance international trade. UNCITRAL is actively involved in the development and enactment of UN conventions dealing with international trade, such as the CISG and the Convention on the Recognition and Enforcement of Foreign Arbitral Awards. It is also actively involved in creating model laws and legal guides designed to serve as templates for the legislative bodies of any nations that are addressing international trade issues. Information about UNCITRAL can be found at http://www.uncitral. org/. Information on international law, including UNIDROIT and the Hague Conference on Private International Law as well as UNCITRAL can be found at http://www.asil.org/resource/Home.htm.

WTO 1995

The International Organization for Standardization (ISO)

The International Organization for Standardization (ISO) is an international body dedicated to developing uniform standards in a number of different areas, thus enhancing international trade. There are 101 nations and 145 standardizing bodies that belong to the ISO and help to establish the standards that will be followed by all of the member nations. According to the ISO:

standards are documented agreements containing technical specifications or other precise criteria to be used consistently as rules, guidelines, or definitions of characteristics, to ensure that materials, products, processes and services are fit for their purposes.[15]

As an example, the ISO developed the standards used for credit cards, phone cards, and "smart" cards, specifying the optimal thickness for these cards, among other things. Such standards allow the cards to be used worldwide.

The ISO has developed the Agreement on Technical Barriers to Trade (TBT), also known as the "Standards Code," in an effort to reduce any impediments to trade due to differences between national regulations and standards. This Agreement "invites" the signatory nations to help ensure that the standardizing bodies within each nation accept and comply with a "Code of good practice for the preparation, adoption and application of standards" as embodied in the Agreement.[16] The ISO works closely with the World Trade Organization (WTO) in an effort to enhance the development of international trade. In fact, the TBT is also known as the WTO Code of Good Practice.

The ISO has also developed two sets of quality standards for businesses. The first, ISO 9000, deals with "quality management"; the second, ISO 14000, deals with environmental management. Firms may choose to seek ISO certification for their products under either of these plans. Such "certification" is voluntary for the firms seeking it, although the requirements can be quite rigorous. Neither ISO 9000 nor ISO 14000 is a *product* standard. Rather, both are *management system* standards. The *quality* standards of ISO 9000 address those features of a product or service that are required by customers of the firm, and then address the production process that is followed by the firm as it seeks to ensure that these features are present. Similarly, ISO 14000 addresses what the firm does in its efforts to minimize any harmful effects on the environment caused by its activities.[17]

Exports

In order to have truly international trade, some countries must import goods and other countries must export goods. Many students have a simplistic view of importing and exporting, not realizing that there are a significant number of problems to resolve in moving goods from one nation to another. These problems frequently begin with getting goods out of their nation of origin.

All exports leaving the United States must be licensed. For most goods and technology, the licensing process simply involves stamping a general license statement on the export documents. Some goods and technology, however, require validated licenses issued by the Department of Commerce, which maintains a commodity control list that gives the licensing status of thousands of export items. Businesses that export in violation of the export-licensing policy face criminal prosecution and loss of export privileges.

U.S. exports are regulated for three purposes. The first is to protect the nation in time of short supply (for example, Alaskan crude oil may be exported only if it does not adversely affect domestic supply). The second purpose is to protect national security (for example, exporting nuclear material to Iraq is not currently permitted). The third purpose is to further U.S. foreign policy interests (for example, all exports to Libya were banned in 1986 as a response to Libya's support of terrorism).

Imports

Getting the goods out of their home country is only half the battle; next the goods must be moved into the nation of destination. All goods imported into a country must "pass" customs. Passing customs usually means paying a certain sum of money—known as a tariff or duty—at the port of entry, based on the type and value of the goods. For example, when Subaru imported the Brat motor vehicle into this country, the U.S. Customs Service had to determine whether the Brat was a truck or a sports car. This was an important determination, since the duty to be paid differed depending on the category to which it rightfully belonged. If the Brat was a truck, it would require a larger duty than if it were a sports car. Subaru successfully argued that the Brat—despite the fact that it was a two-seat vehicle with a cargo bed—was a sports car. To further this argument, Subaru sold the Brat with two rear-facing plastic seats bolted into the bed of the cargo deck.

Once the type of import is determined, the analysis turns to its valuation. Is the proper valuation its wholesale value at the point of origin or destination, its retail value at the point

NRW CASE 3.3   Manufacturing/Marketing

PRODUCTION AND LICENSE OF NEW PRODUCTS INTERNATIONALLY

A European manufacturer has expressed serious interest in selling both InvenTrakRs and StuffTrakRs in Europe. While this firm would like to sell the NRW products in Europe, it does not want to import them. Instead this firm has suggested that it be allowed to manufacture NRW's products at its European plant and sell them within the EU. The manufacturer has suggested a licensing agreement that would designate it as the sole and exclusive distributor of any NRW products or technology for Europe. This manufacturer claims that by doing this, both his firm and NRW will gain a significant share of the European market, and NRW will avoid any possible import duties or fees for its European sales. Helen is concerned that this could eventually be harmful to the firm, and she is also worried about possible repercussions involving the competition rules of the EU. She has asked for your advice on these matters. What will you tell her?

BUSINESS CONSIDERATIONS What are the potential drawbacks for a domestic business if it allows a foreign firm to have an exclusive distributorship of its products and technology? Should the firm seek some other arrangement to better protect and position itself for sales in other countries?

ETHICAL CONSIDERATIONS Assume that the technology used by a business has substantial national security implications, but that the firm can acquire an export license. Without regard to profits, should the firm export its products despite the potential for compromising national security? What arguments support your response?

INTERNATIONAL CONSIDERATIONS How much of a factor should export fees or import duties play in a firm's decision to expand outside its home nation? What protections exist for a firm if another nation decides that the firm is "dumping" its products or otherwise harming the foreign nation's market position in a given industry?

of origin or destination, or a combination of those factors? In general, the transaction value of the goods is used. The transaction value is the price the importer paid for the goods, plus certain other necessary and related expenses.

The U.S. Customs Court has exclusive jurisdiction over civil actions challenging administrative decisions of the U.S. Customs Service.

One problem that is becoming increasingly serious involves the "dumping" of goods into foreign markets. "Dumping" involves the selling of goods in foreign markets at a price below that charged in the domestic market. Very commonly, a firm that is dumping goods in a foreign market has a protected market at home, so the firm is not concerned about retaliatory pricing in its home market. The firm can then sell its products in other countries at an unfair price, often to the detriment of the domestic firms in that other country. As a result, many nations have antidumping duties that are used to raise the cost of importing the goods, thus offsetting the cost advantage enjoyed by the dumped goods. The WTO has been involved in numerous cases involving allegations of dumping. For example, Mexico recently applied an anti-dumping duty to U.S. imports of high-fructose corn syrup, a sweetener used in soft drinks and food products. The U.S. challenged this duty, and the WTO determined that the duty violated the WTO trading rules. The WTO determined that Mexico had imposed the duty in order to protect its domestic sugar industry and not because U.S. firms were actually dumping the corn syrup in Mexico.[18]

Letters of Credit

International traders also face special problems when paying for goods, services, and technology. In a domestic transaction, a seller can easily check the buyer's creditworthiness. If the buyer wrongfully rejects the goods, the seller is probably familiar enough with the market to know how to resell the goods or can have them returned fairly easily. In an international transaction, however, the seller will find it harder to check the buyer's financial status, harder to collect unpaid amounts from a foreign buyer, and more expensive or difficult to resell or reship rejected goods. To solve these problems posed by the international marketplace, buyers and sellers often use letters of credit to pay for goods, services, or technology.

When a letter of credit is used, the contract between buyer and seller will require the buyer to get a letter from its bank. The letter is the bank's promise that it will pay the contract price upon the seller's presentation of documents specified in the contract. To protect itself, the buyer will carefully specify which documents the seller must present to the bank to get payment. If the seller does not want to collect from a foreign bank, the contract can require the buyer to have a bank convenient to the seller that will confirm the letter of credit.

Suppose that Salesco, Inc., in California, contracts with Buyco, in Australia, for the sale of 5,000 electric motors at a total price of U.S.$5,000,000. The sales contract specifies that Buyco will pay by means of a letter of credit issued by First Australia Bank and confirmed by First San Diego Bank. The sales contract also specifies that payment will be made upon presentation of an invoice, packing list, export declaration, and negotiable on-board bill of lading (indicating the goods had been loaded on the ship). Buyco would go to its bank, First Australia, which would—for a fee—issue a letter stating the terms as specified in the contract. The bank would send that letter to First San Diego Bank, which would then write a letter to Salesco confirming the terms of the original letter of credit. Once Salesco obtained all the documents specified in the letter, it would go to its bank, First San Diego, which would compare the documents with the list in the letter of credit. If the documents were in order, First San Diego would pay Salesco, then forward the documents to First Australia, which would get payment from Buyco, then give Buyco the documents so it could take delivery of the motors. Exhibit 3.2 illustrates how the transaction would work.

As you can see, sellers are pleased to use letters of credit. They are paid for goods even before the buyer receives them, and they are paid even if the goods turn out to be defective. Buyers are less pleased to use letters of credit, but at least they know the goods are present, loaded, and ready for shipment before they pay for them. In order to further protect themselves, buyers can carefully specify which documents are required before the letter is to be paid. In some instances the buyer will also require a third party to inspect the goods as they are loaded for shipment. Buyers are also protected by the legal obligation that the documents the seller presents must strictly comply with the documents required in the letter of credit before the bank can pay the seller.

The importance of letters of credit is further emphasized by the fact that there is a United Nations Convention dealing with them, the *United Nations Convention on Independent Guarantees and Stand-by Letters of Credit,* drafted in New York in 1995. This convention had been signed by only seven nations as of October 2002, although it went into effect January 1, 2000. (The United States is the only major trading nation that signed the convention. Other signatories include Belarus, Ecuador, El Salvador, Kuwait, Panama, and Tunisia.) Letters of credit are dealt with in more detail in Chapter 27.

Information and Technology

Historically, patent, copyright, and trademark protection extended only within the boundaries of each country. An inventor who wanted to protect an invention in any other countries would have to obtain a patent in each country. To complicate matters, some countries did not recognize exclusive patent rights in some kinds of products, such as pharmaceuticals. These countries felt it more important to deliver life-saving drugs to their people than to protect the

---

EXHIBIT 3.2 Using a Letter of Credit in an International Sale of Goods

1. Buyco and Salesco enter a sales agreement, with Buyco agreeing to provide a letter of credit and Salesco agreeing to deliver 5,000 electric motors to Buyco.

2. Buyco goes to its bank, First Australia, to acquire a letter of credit to be paid at First San Diego Bank. The letter of credit specifies that payment is to be made on presentation at First San Diego Bank of an invoice, a packing list, an export declaration, and a negotiable on-board bill of lading.

3. First Australia produces the letter of credit and sends it to First San Diego Bank.

4. First San Diego Bank receives the letter of credit and contacts Salesco confirming the terms of the letter of credit and the documents required in order to receive payment.

5. Salesco arranges for the transportation of the goods, procures the necessary documents, and takes those documents to First San Diego Bank.

6. First San Diego Bank confirms that all required documents are present and in proper order and pays Salesco as per the letter of credit.

7. The paid letter of credit is returned to First Australia, which then pays First San Diego Bank for the letter of credit.

8. First Australia informs Buyco that the letter of credit has been paid and collects the amount of the letter, plus any fees, from Buyco.

profits of the pharmaceutical companies. Today, although no worldwide intellectual property rights exist, a real trend has grown toward international protection of copyrights, patents, and trademarks. In 1988, for example, the United States became the 80th member of the Berne Convention for the Protection of Literary and Artistic Works. A copyright holder who publishes a book in the United States will now receive the same protection in other member countries that local authors do.

Patent law is also moving toward international protection. Under the European Patent Convention, only one filing and one patent examination can obtain protection in 18 countries. Similarly, the Patent Cooperation Treaty allows only one patent application and examination to serve as a basis for patent filings in up to 115 countries, as of 2002.

Trademark law has also moved toward some international recognition, though not as quickly as the other areas of intellectual property protection. The Madrid Agreement—to which 42 countries (but not the United States) belonged as of 1996—allows one application to provide protection in all member countries. The EU has moved toward an EU-wide recognition of trademarks but does not yet have uniformity. U.S. businesses have faced serious problems in recent years with counterfeit goods. Levi Strauss, Apple Computer, and other companies have reported large revenues lost due to imports that counterfeit company trademarks or patents. The United States has toughened its enforcement of the laws designed to oppose these counterfeiters. Section 337 of the Tariff Act of 1930 was amended in 1988 to allow any owner of a registered U.S. intellectual property right, who believes that an import infringes on that right, to apply to the U.S. International Trade Commission for an order banning the goods. This order can also fine the importer up to $100,000 per day or twice the domestic value of the goods. In addition, Congress amended the Trade Act of 1974 with a section called "Special 301," requiring the U.S. trade representative to identify countries that do not protect U.S. intellectual property rights. Once identified, the United States will negotiate improvements with those countries. If no improvements result, the United States must retaliate against those countries. Special 301 has been effective in getting many countries to improve their intellectual property laws.

Nationalization

Nationalization of privately owned business entities is a risk that exists primarily in developing countries. Nationalization is the act of converting privately owned businesses into governmentally owned businesses. In general, international trade can be carried on without fear of nationalization; the exporter merely ensures that payment is guaranteed before shipment of goods. However, international investment is not so simple a matter. To build and operate an aluminum plant or an oil refinery requires a large investment of capital. If, during the time the investment is paying for itself, it is nationalized, the result is usually a loss to the investor. It is for that reason and others that international investment decisions usually require a shorter payback period than national investment decisions.

Is nationalization legal? It depends on your perspective. For the most part, from the viewpoint of the country that nationalizes a private property, some act of the legislature or head of state makes it legal within that country. From the viewpoint of international law, however, it may not be legal. If it does not comply with international law, it is termed a confiscation, not a nationalization. If it does comply with international law, it is called an expropriation. The key element is whether the state has a proper public purpose and, in addition, whether "just compensation" is paid for the property. No matter what it is called, there is little that can be done if it occurs. One means of insuring an investment against the risk of loss is by utilizing the facilities of the Overseas Private Investment Corporation (OPIC). OPIC furnishes low-cost insurance against nationalization, confiscation, lack of convertibility of foreign earnings, and general loss due to insurrection, revolution, or war. OPIC currently insures more than 400 projects in 50 countries.

Act of State Doctrine

One reason for the importance of seeking insurance protection for overseas investments is the act of state doctrine. The doctrine states that every sovereign state is bound to respect the independence of every other sovereign state and the courts of one country will not sit in judgment on the acts of the government of another performed within its own borders. The concept of the act of state doctrine is embedded in the notion of sovereign immunity. Certainly each sovereign state recognizes all other states' sovereignty. But the act of state doctrine is not a specific rule of international law. International law does not require that nations follow this rule, and in the United States, the Constitution does not require it. Judicial decisions of the United States, however, have recognized the doctrine. The doctrine is based on the theory that a nation is not qualified to question the actions of other nations taken on their own soil. In fact, denouncing the public decisions of other nations can have a decidedly adverse effect on the conduct of a nation's foreign policy.

But what about a situation in which a U.S. bank held promissory notes issued by a group of Costa Rican banks payable in the United States in U.S. dollars? Would there be a lack of jurisdiction if the Costa Rican government, after the notes were signed, refused to allow the payments in U.S. dollars? Does the act of state doctrine apply? The Second Circuit said an emphatic no when it held that the situs (location) of the debt was in the United States and not Costa Rica and, therefore, the doctrine did not apply. (See *Allied Bank v. Banco Credito,* 757 F.2d 516 [2d Cir. 1985].)

Sovereign Immunity

In the traditions of international law, all nations are equal and sovereign. Thus, a nation is immune from suit for its actions, either by individuals or by other countries. To be sued, a nation must agree to give up its sovereign immunity. For example, the United States passed the Federal Tort Claims Act to allow individuals to sue the U.S. government for negligent or wrongful acts. On an international level, the doctrine of sovereign immunity causes businesses some trouble, especially because many governments operate businesses such as airlines, banks, auto companies, and even computer firms. The United States has taken actions to limit the effect of sovereign immunity in its courts. In

1976, Congress enacted the Foreign Sovereign Immunities Act, which declared that U.S. courts would not recognize sovereign immunity when the sovereign engaged in commercial, rather than political, activities. So, for example, a state-owned bank could be subject to suit over its failure to pay a letter of credit. The United States has also negotiated many bilateral investment treaties containing provisions for other governments to waive the right to claim sovereign immunity.

The Foreign Sovereign Immunities Act was amended in 1996 with the passage of the Antiterrorism and Effective Death Penalty Act,[19] which permits American citizens to sue those foreign states officially classified as terrorist states for terrorist conduct that results in the death or injury of an American citizen. The Act also provides for punitive damages to be assessed against the terrorist state if it is found guilty of the prohibited conduct. (This provision is commonly referred to as the "Flatow Amendment.") The following case involves a suit filed under the Foreign Sovereign Immunities Act as amended, and an effort by the plaintiff to hold a nationalized bank liable for the debts of its home nation. Follow the court's reasoning and then decide whether you agree with the final decision.

3.3

FLATOW v. ISLAMIC REPUBLIC OF IRAN
2002 U.S. App. LEXIS 22071 (9th Cir. 2002)

FACTS On April 9, 1995, Alisa Flatow, an American college student spending a semester studying in Israel, was killed in an explosion when the bus in which she was traveling collided with a van loaded with explosives. The U.S. Department of State later concluded that the Shaqiqi faction of the Palestine Islamic Jihad committed the bombing. The State Department also determined that the Islamic Republic of Iran provided material support and resources to the Palestine Islamic Jihad.

Shortly after the bombing, Congress amended the Foreign Sovereign Immunities Act (FSIA), as part of the Antiterrorism and Effective Death Penalty Act (AEDPA), effective April 24, 1996. The Act created an exception to the sovereign immunity of those foreign states officially designated by the Department of State as terrorist states if the foreign state commits a terrorist act, or provides material support and resources to an individual or entity that commits such an act, which results in the death or personal injury of a U.S. citizen. Congress also expressly provided that punitive damages be available in actions brought under the state-sponsored terrorism exception to sovereign immunity. Relying

upon these new provisions, Stephen M. Flatow, as Alisa's father and executor of her estate, filed a wrongful death complaint against Iran and its officials on February 26, 1997, in the U.S. District Court for the District of Columbia. On March 11, 1998, the district court entered a default judgment against Iran in favor of Flatow in the amount of $247,513,220.

Flatow registered his judgment with the District Court for the Southern District of California and then obtained a writ of execution for $247,513,220 on property in Carlsbad, California, owned by California Land Holding Company, a wholly owned subsidiary of Bank Saderat Iran (BSI). BSI was an Iranian bank, organized in 1952 and privately owned and operated until it was nationalized by the Iranian government in 1979. Flatow contended that since BSI was owned by the Islamic Republic of Iran, any assets it owned were actually owned by the Islamic Republic of Iran, the judgment debtor. As the California Land Holding Company was about to sell the property, Flatow and BSI agreed that the writ of execution should be released from the property so that escrow could close. Pursuant to a consent order entered on October 1, 1999, the proceeds of the sale were held in an interest-bearing account subject to the lien created by the writ of execution.

BSI filed a motion for the release of the money on November 1, 1999. After extensive briefing by the parties and the U.S. government, as well as oral argument on whether BSI's assets could be used to satisfy a judgment against the Islamic Republic of Iran, the court found that the evidence Flatow presented was not sufficient to overcome the presumption that BSI was a juridical entity separate and apart from the Islamic Republic of Iran and therefore BSI was not subject to execution of the judgment against Iran. The district court granted BSI's motion for the release of the money and terminated the case. Flatow appealed from this decision.

ISSUE Was BSI so tied to the Islamic Republic of Iran that its assets could be treated as belonging to the government, the judgment debtor from the earlier trial?

HOLDING No. The government owned the Bank, but its day-to-day operations were conducted in much the same manner as any other bank. The ownership issue alone was not sufficient to make its assets subject to seizure to satisfy the prior judgment.

REASONING Excerpts from the opinion of Circuit Judge Bright:

[In reaching its decision the District Court] relied upon the Supreme Court's *First Nat'l City Bank v. Banco Para El Comercio Exterior de Cuba* (holding that unless the entity is found to be "so extensively controlled by [the foreign state] that a relationship of principal and agent is created" or recognizing the entity as separate "would work fraud or injustice," the FSIA does not permit execution upon the entity's assets). In *Bancec*, the Supreme Court clearly stated that the FSIA does not govern substantive liability for foreign states or their instrumentalities. *See* 462 U.S. at 620. ("The language and history of the FSIA clearly establish that the Act was not intended to affect the substantive law determining the liability of a foreign state or instrumentality, or the attribution of liability among instrumentalities of a foreign state.") The enumerated exceptions to the FSIA provide the exclusive source of subject matter jurisdiction over civil actions brought against foreign states . . . but the FSIA does not resolve questions of liability. Questions of liability are addressed by *Bancec*, which examines the circumstances under which a foreign entity can be held substantively liable for the foreign government's judgment debt. This distinction between liability and jurisdiction is crucial to our resolution of this case.

In *Bancec*, the government of Cuba expropriated property from First National City Bank (subsequently known as "Citibank"). Citibank asserted a set-off against the plaintiff Bancec based upon the Cuban government's seizure of Citibank's Cuban assets. . . . The Court addressed the issue of whether the acts and liabilities of the foreign sovereign government of Cuba could be attributed to the state-owned banking entity, Bancec.

The Court held that Bancec was not an entity independent from the Cuban government. . . . In making this determination, the Court noted that Bancec had been dissolved and its capital split between a Cuban national bank and the foreign trade enterprises of the Cuban Ministry of Foreign Trade. . . . Furthermore, Bancec was empowered to act as the Cuban government's exclusive agent in foreign trade, the government supplied all of Bancec's capital and owned all of its stock, and all of Bancec's profits were deposited in the General Treasury. Bancec's Governing Board consisted of delegates from Cuban government ministries and the president of Bancec was the Minister of State. . . . The Court explained, "To hold otherwise would permit governments to avoid the requirements of international law simply by creating juridical entities whenever the need arises." . . .

Nonetheless, under *Bancec*, even though an entity or instrumentality is wholly-owned by a foreign state, that entity is accorded the presumption of independent and separate legal status. . . .

The Court indicated that the presumption of separate juridical status may be overcome in two ways. First, where it can be shown that the "corporate entity is so extensively controlled by its owner that a relationship of principal and agent is created, we have held that one may be held liable for the actions of the other." . . . Second, an instrumentality should not be deemed a separate juridical entity where doing so would work "fraud or injustice.". . . Having laid out these two exceptions to the presumption of separate juridical status, the Court declined to provide a "mechanical formula for determining the circumstances under which the normally separate juridical status of a government instrumentality is to be disregarded." . . .

Flatow argues that the district court erred in applying *Bancec* and concluding that BSI is a separate juridical entity, which cannot be held liable for Flatow's judgment against Iran. Flatow rests his argument almost entirely upon the contention that the Iranian Constitution, which nationalized the banking industry after the 1979 Iranian revolution, creates a principal-agent relationship between BSI and the Iranian government. Flatow argues that this fact alone demonstrates the control required by *Bancec* to preclude an entity from separate juridical status.

The district court considered and rejected this argument in a thorough, well-reasoned opinion. Specifically, the court concluded that the facts of this case are different from those in *Bancec.* The court found that Flatow had not shown that BSI operates as an arm of the Iranian government or that BSI's mission is to further the policies of the Iranian government. Additionally, unlike in *Bancec,* BSI is not attempting to use a United States court to recover on a claim while at the same time trying to avoid being the subject of an adversary proceeding. BSI is a nonparty to the underlying case.

In rejecting Flatow's principal-agent argument, the district court also pointed out that BSI is an Iranian corporation, organized under the banking laws of Iran as a banking corporation, but it has its own Articles of Association. BSI was founded in 1952 and until 1979, BSI was a privately owned bank. BSI consists of more than 3,000 branch offices throughout the Middle East, London, Paris, Hamburg, and New York. The New York office is the only office BSI has in the United States. . . .

Flatow argues that Iran's ownership of BSI's capital precludes BSI from being considered a separate juridical entity under *Bancec.* However, Flatow is incorrect in his belief that this fact alone is determinative. As the Supreme Court recognized in *Bancec,* an entity fully owned by a foreign state is still accorded the presumption that it is a separate juridical entity. . . .

We reject Flatow's argument that the Iranian Constitution and the nationalization of Iranian banks are sufficient to overcome the *Bancec* presumption, and accordingly, we affirm the decision of the district court.

We also affirm the district court's determination that Iran's limited supervision, through the role of the General Assembly of Banks and the High Council, does not constitute day-to-day control sufficient to overcome the separate juridical entity presumption. The government involvement must rise to a higher level. . . . The daily affairs of BSI and its 3,000 branch offices are overseen by the Board of Directors, consisting of career bankers, the Managing Director, and other bank officers. On this record, the level of economic control exercised by the Iranian government over BSI appears quite limited, and we agree with the district court that Flatow has not shown that the Iranian government is the real beneficiary of BSI's banking operations.

This panel joins other courts in expressing regret that its holding forestalls the Flatow family's efforts to execute their judgment against Iran. . . . There has, however, been substantial payment of damages through the legislation passed by the United States Congress. . . . The government of Iran should pay its debt to the Flatow family, but BSI cannot be held liable for this debt. We follow the clear path set out by the applicable case law. Thus, we AFFIRM the district court.

BUSINESS CONSIDERATIONS Is a foreign business that is owned in whole or in part by its domestic government less likely to do business in the United States since the enactment of the Foreign Sovereign Immunities Act and its amendments? Would a similar law in another nation reduce the willingness of an American business to expand to that nation?

ETHICAL CONSIDERATIONS Is it ethical for a government to own and operate a business and to then attempt to avoid liability by asserting sovereign immunity? Is it ethical for a nation to deny the protection of sovereign immunity in its courts to other governments or nations?

Dispute Resolution

The best method of resolving an international business dispute is by providing a means for handling that contingency at the time the international transaction is created. Three principal options for settling a dispute are available: the International Court of Justice, national courts, and arbitration.

The International Court of Justice

The International Court of Justice (ICJ) has limited value in solving international business disputes. The ICJ is an agency of the United Nations, and its procedures were established in the United Nations Charter. A private person has no standing before the ICJ; only nations may appear before the court. A private person who has a grievance against a state not his or her own must first secure the agreement of his or her own state to present the claim. The issue then becomes whether the other state will allow the matter to appear before the ICJ for resolution. Each state must agree to be bound by the court's decision; if they do not, there is no jurisdiction to hear the claim. Exhibit 3.3 lists the authorities the ICJ uses in reaching its decisions.

National Courts

A private person can usually resort to settlement of a dispute with a foreign nation by seeking redress through the courts of that state. Private persons can sometimes obtain adequate relief in their native state's judicial system. For example, a favorable judgment from a U.S. court may

EXHIBIT   3.3   Authorities Used by the International Court of Justice

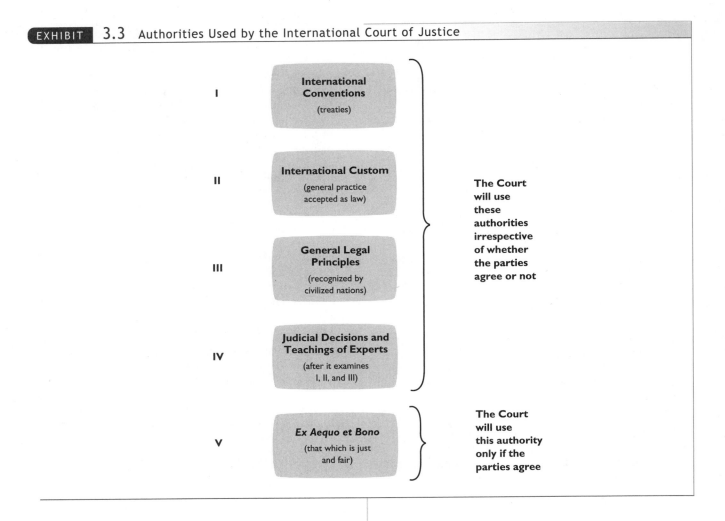

I — **International Conventions** (treaties)

II — **International Custom** (general practice accepted as law)

III — **General Legal Principles** (recognized by civilized nations)

IV — **Judicial Decisions and Teachings of Experts** (after it examines I, II, and III)

The Court will use these authorities irrespective of whether the parties agree or not

V — ***Ex Aequo et Bono*** (that which is just and fair)

The Court will use this authority only if the parties agree

be filed in another country and, under certain conditions, can execute on assets in the foreign country on the basis of the other country's judicial decision. U.S. courts are likely to enforce a judgment obtained in another country following a full and fair trial, before an impartial court, with an opportunity for the defendant to be heard. A biased or corrupt court or a case that did not give a defendant an adequate chance to defend against the claims of the plaintiff would probably lead a U.S. court to require a plaintiff to retry the entire claim in a U.S. court, rather than enforce the prior judgment.

The recognition of foreign judgments is not a matter of international law, but rather a matter of comity. As the U.S. Supreme Court stated in the landmark case of *Hilton v. Guyot*, 159 U.S. 113 (1895), comity is "the recognition which one nation allows within its territory to the . . . acts of another nation, having due regard both to international duty and convenience, and to the rights of its own citizens, or other persons. . . ." Comity is a matter of respect, goodwill,

and courtesy that one nation gives to another, at least partly with the hope that the other nation will return the favor.

Arbitration

For various reasons, a particular international dispute may not be appropriate for resolution in the ICJ or national courts. In that case, international arbitration might be the best course of action. Many international commercial contracts include provisions for using arbitration. One hundred thirty-two countries, including the United States, have signed the 1958 United Nations Convention on the Recognition and Enforcement of Foreign Arbitral Awards (T.I.A.S. No. 6997) as of October 2002. The countries that have signed this convention have agreed to use their court systems to recognize and enforce arbitration decisions. The fact that so many nations have ratified this UN convention provides fairly persuasive evidence that arbitration is becoming the preferred method for resolving disputes in international business.

On-line Dispute Resolution (ODR)

A new form of alternate dispute resolution (ADR) has recently developed. This new form takes advantage of technology to provide a method for resolving disputes online, without requiring either of the parties to travel or to be overly inconvenienced. On-line Dispute Resolution (ODR) is now available in a number of circumstances. NAFTA provides for on-line dispute resolution, especially in a controversy between a consumer and a business, to encourage consumers to assert their rights even though the business from which they purchased the goods in dispute is in another nation. A significant number of e-commerce businesses, which may well have customers in a number of countries, have provided for ODR as a part of the sales contract.

ODR is likely to involve mediation as the preferred method for resolving disputes. Each party submits its position to the on-line mediator, who then suggests settlement options to each party. However, the potential for growth is tremendous. All that is required to utilize this method is access to the Internet and a willingness to use the system. ODR can be synchronous or asynchronous; it can be extremely simple or relatively complex; and while it is now normally used only for mediation, it can also be used for arbitration. While this method of dispute resolution is relatively new, it is likely to become extremely common and widespread in a relatively short time.

Summary

We live in an interdependent world. Consequently, businesspeople should be aware of the international implications of their business dealings. In addition to being familiar with the laws and customs of the countries where they do business, managers must be aware that competition and employment laws, among others, may reach beyond national borders.

Global trade agreements (such as GATT and the WTO) and regional free-trade zones (such as the EU and NAFTA) are becoming much more important in the world economy. They provide businesses with frameworks for trade and, increasingly, with efficient access to large markets. These organizations have substantially changed the rules of the game in international business recently, and familiarity with them is essential if a businessperson desires success in the international arena. These organizations will serve as models for others all over the world in the years to come.

There is an increasing emphasis on private international trade law. Organizations such as UNCITRAL and UNIDROIT are attempting to draft model statutes that will help to increase international trade and to provide uniform coverage for businesses that operate across national borders. The International Organization for Standardization (ISO) encourages businesses to adhere to certain quality standards and encourages its member nations and organizations to look for methods of implementing such standards as broadly as possible. The WTO and the ISO are working together in a few areas to develop uniform standards and to establish codes of good conduct.

Changes in international trade, and in the emphasis placed on global development, have led to a number of "new" business concerns. Although imports and exports, labor, and information and technology have been recognized as important aspects of domestic trade for years, it is only recently that they have gained similar recognition in the international arena. Continuing development of regulation in these areas will shape the global market in the near future.

One risk to international business investment is nationalization, the taking of private property by a national government. If the nationalization complies with international law, it is called an expropriation. If it does not, it is called a confiscation. The act of state doctrine is used to justify the position that one country will not stand in judgment of the actions of other countries carried on within their own territories.

Sovereign immunity is the legal doctrine that a sovereign government cannot be sued unless it allows itself to be sued. International law provides three mechanisms for the resolution of international business disputes. The International Court of Justice (ICJ) is the appropriate forum when one nation sues another, provided that each nation agrees to the suit. Domestic courts are used for the resolution of disputes between citizens of different nations. Last, arbitration is used in international as well as domestic business disputes.

Dispute resolution is also changing as international business continues to grow and to develop. The International Court of Justice and the World Trade Organization have some provisions for dealing with transnational trade disputes. However, both are somewhat formal and require that a nation be involved before either will assert any jurisdiction. Of course, national courts can be used, as they have been used for resolving trade disputes within their respective nations for years. However, this is likely to be expensive, even by lawsuit standards, and at least one of the parties is likely to have a "home court advantage" that may be difficult to overcome. As a result, international trade is more likely to rely on nonjudicial resolution. Arbitration has been a staple of international trade for genera-tions, and it will continue to be used to resolve many dis-putes. A recently introduced method, ODR, has tremen-dous potential as a method of resolving transnational disputes in a relatively quick and inexpensive manner.

Discussion Questions

1. Which recent agreements and enactments have increased the accuracy of the term "global village" in the area of inter-national business? What, if anything, seems to be operating in a manner contrary to the concept of developing a global village?

2. What are the arguments in favor of restricting the application of a nation's laws to its territorial limits? What are the argu-ments in favor of expanding the application of a nation's laws beyond its territorial limits? Which set of arguments is more persuasive ethically?

3. What is the significance of the Treaty of Rome? How does the Treaty of Rome compare with the North American Free Trade Agreement (NAFTA)?

4. What are the main differences between Article 85 and Article 86 of the Treaty of Rome? Suppose that a business fears that conduct it is proposing may be subject to challenge under either of these articles. How can that business be sure in advance that its activities will not be found to violate either section?

5. Two corporations, one organized in Belgium and the other in the United Kingdom, seek to merge. They are both in the computer software business. The Belgian corporation has 15 percent of the EU market, and the British corporation has 30 percent. What problems do these facts raise with respect to the Treaty of Rome? If, instead, these two firms were located in the United States, with one in New York and the other in Illinois, would their prospective merger raise the same problems?

6. Assume that a letter of credit issued for the sale of goods internationally contains a simple typographical error. Is it more appropriate to penalize the seller or the buyer in such a situation? How substantial should an error be before either of the parties is penalized?

7. A U.S. corporation wishes to export a new computer microchip outside the United States. Do you envision any problems in complying with U.S. law in exporting this com-puter microchip? Do you envision any problems in com-plying with European Union (EU) law in importing this computer microchip into the European market? Would problems exist in importing this computer microchip into nations other than NAFTA or EU nations?

8. How do the United Nations Convention on Contracts for the International Sale of Goods (CISG), the General Agreement on Tariffs and Trade (GATT), and the World Trade Organiza-tion (WTO) affect international trade? To which types of international trade contracts do each of these (CISG, GATT, WTO) apply?

9. Three doctrines are often applied to international dealings: comity, act of state, and sovereign immunity. How do each of these doctrines affect international dealings and potential legal controversies?

10. You are a financial adviser to a multinational manufacturing corporation. You have been asked to evaluate a proposal for the firm to invest $500 million in a foreign country. The investment will involve building and staffing a factory in the foreign nation. What factors would influence your decision if the proposed location were in an underdeveloped nation with a relatively unstable government? Would your consider-ation be different if the proposed investment were to take place in a nation in the EU or in Russia? Why should the loca-tion of the investment affect the decision to invest?

Case Problems and Writing Assignments

1. The European Commission charged 41 wood pulp producers with violations of Article 85 in that the producers were accused of taking concerted action to fix prices for the wood pulp sold to EU customers. Each of the wood pulp producers was oper-ating outside the EU, although all of them imported products into the EU market. The producers claimed that the EU had no jurisdiction in this case, since all of the alleged price-fixing activity took place outside the EU and was therefore beyond the jurisdiction of the commission or its sanctions. The commis-sion rejected this claim and fined 36 of the producers. These 36 producers appealed to the Court of Justice of the European Communities. Does Article 85 have extraterritorial application beyond the borders of the EU in a case such as this? Which fac-tors most influenced your decision? [See *Re Wood Pulp Cartel v. Commission,* 4 C.M.L.R. 901 (1988).]

2. On March 3, 1989, Banque de L'Union Haitienne (Union Bank) issued a letter of credit in favor of its customer, Eleck S.A., in the amount of $1,400,000. On the same day, Union Bank contracted with Manufacturers Hanover to act as advising, confirming, and paying bank in the transaction. The parties all agreed that their relationship would be governed by the Uniform Customs and Practices (UCP) for documentary credit. After several amendments to the original document, the letter of credit was assigned an expiration date of April 30,

1989. The original letter was assigned to North American Trading, which subsequently changed its name to International Basic Economic Company (IBEC). On April 19, 1989, IBEC first presented the documents to Manufacturers Hanover, which rejected the initial request due to its (Manufacturers Hanover's) determination that the documents did not conform to the terms and conditions of the letter of credit. Eleck contacted Union Bank to notify it of the rejection. On April 20, Union Bank telexed Manufacturers Hanover, inquiring as to the nature of the discrepancies that caused the rejection of the documents. On April 21, Manufacturers Hanover telexed Union Bank, informing them that IBEC should resubmit the documents on April 24. This telex did not reach Union Bank until April 24, and it did not identify any particular discrepancies contained in the original documents submitted by IBEC. IBEC twice resubmitted its documents to Manufacturers Hanover without success, on April 21 and again on April 24. On the afternoon of April 24, IBEC finally made a successful presentation of the documents to an employee of Manufacturers Hanover who had not been involved in any of the earlier rejections of the documentation. As a result, Manufacturers Hanover transferred $1,473,189 to IBEC's account with Republic National Bank of Miami. The next day, IBEC wire-transferred the funds overseas, and the principals of IBEC disappeared shortly thereafter. Upon notification of the payment, Union Bank transferred the funds to Manufacturers Hanover. The documents presented to Manufacturers Hanover ultimately proved to be fraudulent, and Union Bank sued Manufacturers Hanover for reimbursement of the amount transferred under the letter of credit. Did the presentation of the documents satisfy the conditions as set out in the original letter of credit? What could or should Union Bank have done differently in this case in order to maximize its protections and/or to minimize its risks? What, if anything, did Manufacturers Hanover do improperly in paying the questionable documents? [See *Banque de L'Union Haitienne v. Manufacturers Hanover International Banking Corp.*, 787 F. Supp. 1416 (S.D. Fla. 1991)].

3. Boureslan was a naturalized U.S. citizen who was born in Lebanon. The two defendants were both Delaware corporations. In 1979, Boureslan went to work for Aramco Service Company (ASC), a subsidiary of Arabian American Oil Company (Aramco), in Houston, Texas. (Aramco's principal place of business was Dhahran, Saudi Arabia; ASC's principal place of business was Houston.) In 1980, Boureslan requested, and was granted, a transfer to Saudi Arabia to work for Aramco. He remained in Saudi Arabia until 1984, at which time he was discharged by Aramco. Boureslan filed a complaint of employment discrimination with the Equal Employment Opportunity Commission (EEOC) and also sought relief under both federal and state law, alleging that he was harassed and ultimately discharged because of his race, religion, and national origin in violation of law, including Title VII of the Civil Rights Act of 1964. The respondents filed a motion for summary judgment, alleging that the district court lacked subject matter jurisdiction in the case since Title VII protections do not extend to U.S.

citizens working in other nations, even if working for an American company. The district court dismissed the suit, and this decision was upheld by the Fifth Circuit Court of Appeals. Boureslan and the EEOC petitioned for certiorari, and the Supreme Court granted their petitions in order to resolve the issue. Did Congress intend for the protections of Title VII to apply to U.S. citizens employed by American employers outside the United States? What are the ethical implications when a multinational firm provides different protections and benefits to workers in two or more of its locations, based purely on the happenstance of geographic location and inconsistent national laws? What should the firm do in such a situation? [See *Equal Employment Opportunity Commission v. Arabian American Oil Co.*, 499 U.S. 244 (1991)].

4. Alberto-Culver, an American manufacturer based in Illinois, purchased from Scherk, a German citizen, three enterprises owned by Scherk and organized under the laws of Germany and Liechtenstein, together with all trademark rights of these enterprises. The sales contract, which was negotiated in the United States, England, and Germany, signed in Austria, and closed in Switzerland, contained express warranties by petitioner that the trademarks were unencumbered, and a clause provided that "any controversy or claim [that] shall arise out of this agreement or the breach thereof" would be referred to arbitration before the International Chamber of Commerce in Paris, France, and that Illinois laws would govern the agreement and its interpretation and performance. Subsequently, after allegedly discovering that the trademarks were subject to substantial encumbrances, Alberto-Culver offered to rescind the contract. Scherk refused, and Alberto-Culver filed suit for breach of contract and fraud. Scherk moved to dismiss the action, or, in the alternative, to stay the proceedings pending arbitration of the dispute before the ICC in Paris. The district court denied the motions by Scherk, ruling that the arbitration clause was unenforceable. The court of appeals affirmed, and Scherk appealed to the U.S. Supreme Court. How should the Supreme Court rule in this case? What reasons can you suggest in support of the decision the Supreme Court should reach? If the contract was between two American businesses, would a different result be reached by the courts? [See *Scherk v. Alberto-Culver Co.*, 417 U.S. 506 (1974)].

5. **BUSINESS APPLICATION CASE** Timberlane was a lumber company with a long history in the lumber business. In looking for alternative sources of lumber for delivery to its distribution system on the east coast of the United States, Timberlane decided to expand its operation to Honduras. Accordingly, it formed a local company, acquired tracts of forest land, developed plans for a modern log-processing plant, and acquired equipment to transport to Honduras. Timberlane also learned that a plant once operated by Lima (another lumber company) might be available and began attempts to acquire this plant. According to Timberlane, Lamas and Casanova, both lumber companies, and the Bank of America, which had significant financial interests in Lamas and Casanova, conspired to prevent Timberlane from acquiring the Lima plant. In addition,

Timberlane alleged that its operations were crippled and that its employees were harassed, defamed, and falsely imprisoned at various times in an effort to prevent Timberlane from gaining a position in the lumber industry in Honduras. Timberlane alleged that these actions constituted violations of the Sherman Act and the Wilson Tariff Act and sued the alleged conspirators, claiming more than $5 million in damages. Did the alleged conduct constitute a violation of the Sherman Act? Does the Sherman Act have extraterritorial application so that it applied in this case? [See *Timberlane Lumber Co. v. Bank of America N.T. & S.A.*, 549 F.2d 597 (9th Cir. 1976).]

6. **ETHICAL APPLICATION CASE** In 1981, Harry Carpenter, chairman and chief executive officer of W.S. Kirkpatrick & Co., learned that the Republic of Nigeria was interested in contracting for the construction and equipment of an aeromedical center at Kaduna Air Force Base in Nigeria. Carpenter made arrangements with Benson Akindele, a Nigerian citizen, under which Akindele agreed to secure the contract for W.S. Kirkpatrick. It was further agreed that, provided Akindele did secure the contract for W.S. Kirkpatrick, a "commission" equal to 20 percent of the total contract price would be paid to two Panamanian entities controlled by Akindele. It was understood that this "commission" would be paid to officials of the Nigerian government as a bribe once the contract was awarded to W.S. Kirkpatrick. The contract was awarded to W.S. Kirkpatrick; the "commission" was paid to the Panamanian entities and then distributed to various Nigerian officials. Environmental Tectronics, one of the unsuccessful bidders for the contract, learned of the arrangement between Carpenter and Akindele and brought the matter to the attention of both the Nigerian Air Force and the U.S. Embassy in Lagos, Nigeria. (All parties agreed that it was a violation of Nigerian law to pay or to receive a bribe in connection with the award of a government contract.) If the allegations made by Environmental Tectronics are proven, should Carpenter, Akindele, and W.S. Kirkpatrick be found guilty of violations of the Foreign Corrupt Practices Act? Should Environmental Tectronics be entitled to any remedies in a civil action against any or all of the parties accused of illegal conduct in this case? What ethical issues are raised by the facts in this case? Explain your reasoning. [See *W.S. Kirkpatrick & Co. v. Environmental Tectronics Corp.*, 493 U.S. 400 (1990).]

7. **CRITICAL THINKING CASE** All parties, save Riley and First-Bank, are British citizens or entities. Kingsley Underwriting is a predecessor in interest to Lime Street Underwriting. Both are registered underwriting agencies with Lloyd's. Bankside Syndicate, Ltd. is a registered managing agent with Lloyd's and conducts the day-to-day business of Lime Street. Lloyd's is a British corporation with its principal place of business in London. Lloyd's was incorporated in 1891, but it has functioned as a market for writing insurance policies for some 300 years. Riley was interested in becoming a member of Lloyd's and traveled to England on several occasions to pursue this quest. In January 1980, Riley entered into a General Undertaking with Lloyd's and a Members' Agent's Agreement with the Underwriters. Both of these agreements provided that the

courts of England would have exclusive jurisdiction over any dispute and that the laws of England would apply. Additionally, the Members' Agent's Agreement provided for arbitration in the event of any dispute.

Riley's underwriting began in January 1980 with a premium income limit of 150,000 pounds. He remained a member of Lloyd's through 1990, and each year increased the amount of premium income underwritten. By 1989, Riley was underwriting premium income in excess of a million pounds. In connection with his underwriting, Riley was required to meet Lloyd's deposit requirements. Riley obtained letters of credit from FirstBank. FirstBank in turn issued letters of credit to First National Bank of Boston (Guernsey) Ltd. as security for a letter of credit to be issued by the London branch of the Guernsey Bank in favor of Lloyd's. In the event a member failed or refused to cover his pro rata share of underwriting liability, then Lloyd's could draw on the letter of credit to cover the obligation. In the event the letter of credit was insufficient, Lloyd's would look to a member's assets to satisfy any remaining underwriting liability.

The syndicate in which Riley participated experienced large losses, resulting in calls in excess of 300,000 pounds. Riley was notified that, if he did not satisfy the calls, Lloyd's would draw against the letter of credit issued by Guernsey Bank. Guernsey Bank would then draw on the FirstBank letters of credit. Proceeding apparently on the theory that the best defense is a good offense, Riley filed an action seeking declaratory judgment, rescission, and damages against defendants other than First-Bank. Riley claimed that these defendants engaged in the offer and sale of unregistered securities and made untrue statements of material fact and material omissions in connection with the sale of securities, violating the Securities Act of 1933, the Securities Exchange Act of 1934, and Rule 10b-5. Riley sought a writ of attachment against Lloyd's and an injunction to prevent defendants from drawing on the letters of credit. Prior to a preliminary injunction hearing the parties entered into a court-approved stipulation that the hearing would be limited to the threshold issues of the applicability and effect of the forum selection clause and the arbitration clause.

Were the choice of forum and law provisions in Riley's contract with Lloyd's valid and enforceable? Were the arbitration and choice of law provisions in Riley's contract with the Underwriters, requiring arbitration in England and the application of English law, valid and enforceable? [See *Riley v. Kingsley Underwriting Agencies, Ltd.*, 969 F.2d 953 (10th Cir. 1992).]

8. **YOU BE THE JUDGE** Steel Authority of India, Ltd. (SAIL) was selling steel plate in the United States at a price below that being charged by U.S. steel producers. As a result, the U.S. Steel Group, Bethlehem Steel, and several other U.S. steel producers filed a complaint with the U.S. Department of Commerce, accusing SAIL of "dumping" the plate steel in the U.S. market and seeking the imposition of antidumping duties on SAIL to protect the competition within the U.S. market for plate steel. The Department of Commerce investigated the conduct of

SAIL and determined that SAIL was, in fact, guilty of dumping its steel plate in the U.S. market. Although SAIL provided certain requested information, the Department of Commerce decided that this information was not "usable." Instead the Department of Commerce based its findings on the "facts available" clause of the Tariff Act of 1930. The "facts available" clause allows the Department of Commerce to make findings and to reach conclusions based on the facts that it has available, if it determines that the firm being investigated has refused to provide necessary information or has otherwise failed to present information necessary for a determination. India objected to the imposition of this antidumping duty against SAIL and challenged the conduct of the United States with the WTO. This controversy has been brought before *you*, serving on the dispute settlement panel of the WTO. How will *you* decide the issues? What is the basis of *your* decision? [See *World Trade Organization*, Vol. 8, No. 7 (Transnational Law Associates, LLC, International Law Update, July 2002).]

Notes

1. U.S. Census Bureau, *Statistical Abstract of the U.S. 2001* (121st edition, U.S. Department of Commerce).

2. Report FT900 (97). Bureau of Census, Foreign Trade Division, Final 1997.

3. Paul A. Herbig and Hugh E. Kramer, "Do's and Don't's of Cross-Cultural Negotiations," *Industrial Marketing Management*, 21 (1992): 287.

4. 473 U.S. 614 (1985).

5. 15 U.S.C. § 6a.

6. 15 U.S.C. § 78dd.

7. "EU Glows after Ireland 'Yes' Vote," MSNBCNews.com, October 21, 2001.

8. "European Union Moves Eastward," CNBCNews.com, October 9, 2002.

9. Joint Information Notice by the European Commission and the European Central Bank on the detailed computation of the irrevocable conversion rate for the Euro, http://www.ecb.int/change/ch990311.htm.

10. Institutions of the European Union, http://www.europa.eu.int/inst-en.htm.

11. *Re Wood Pulp Cartel et al. v. Commission*, 4 C.M.L.R. 901 (1988).

12. Ian Christopher McCaleb, "Bush Envisions Western Hemisphere Free-Trade Zone," cnn.com, April 17, 2001.

13. "South American Summit Ends with Free-Trade Agreement," *Roanoke Times*, Sunday, July 28, 2002, p. A16.

14. "World Trade Organization," Microsoft® Encarta® Online Encyclopedia 2002, http://encarta.msn.com/ © 1997–2002.

15. "What Are Standards," ISO Web site (accessed 7/17/02), http://www.iso.ch/iso/en/aboutiso/introduction/index.html.

16. "The Agreement on Technical Barriers to Trade (TBT)," ISO Web site (accessed 7/22/02), http://www.iso.ch.

17. "The Basics," ISO Web site, http://www.iso.ch/iso/en/iso9000-14000/tour/plain.html.

18. "WTO Appellate Body Rules in Favor of U.S. in Challenge to Mexico Antidumping Duties on High Fructose Corn Syrup," World Trade Organization, Vol. 7, No. 11 (Transnational Law Associates, LLC., International Law Updates, Nov. 2001).

19. 28 U.S.C. §§ 1602 et seq.

PART 2

The American Legal System

To successfully handle legal problems that arise in the workplace, and to avoid many of these problems before they arise, a businessperson needs to understand how the U.S. legal system operates. This section of the text addresses this topic in some detail.

Chapter 4 describes the powers and the limitations of the federal government as set forth in the U.S. Constitution. It also describes courts and jurisdiction. Chapter 5 examines the constitutional bases for government regulation of business, paying special attention to the clauses that provide a foundation for government regulation while simultaneously imposing restraints on that foundation: the commerce clause, the equal protection clause, the due process clause, and the takings clause.

Chapter 6 examines several methods for dispute resolution in the legal system. This chapter includes the anatomy of a hypothetical civil suit involving our "resident" business, NRW, and a discussion of alternative dispute resolution choices.

Chapter 7 describes torts and the body of civil law concerned with these "private" wrongs that may arise. In particular, this chapter discusses intentional torts, negligence, and strict liability. Chapter 8 describes crimes and the body of law concerned with "public" wrongs. This chapter focuses on crimes that are more likely to affect business—computer crimes, embezzlement, forgery, and fraud, for example. The chapter also discusses the objectives of criminal law, the bases of criminal responsibility, and the nature of various offenses.

CHAPTER 4

The American Legal System and Court Jurisdiction

AGENDA

NRW Mai, Carlos, and Helen never realized how important it is for owners and operators of a business to understand the complexities of the U.S. legal system until they began NRW. Now a number of questions have arisen. What, for example, do the NRW entrepreneurs need to know about state and federal court systems, or about the different types of jurisdiction? Might they be sued—or be forced to sue—in states other than their state of residence? How does a court obtain authority over business entities? What types of cases might they encounter? For example, Mai, Carlos, and Helen obtained a U.S. patent on StuffTrakR. However, they are not sure how well this patent will protect the technology behind the tracking device. Can NRW test this claim in court before a challenge arises, or will the firm have to wait until the patent is being used without authorization before they can sue? They have also discovered that they will have to use care to distinguish the rules applicable to the federal government and those applicable to the states.

These and other questions will arise as you read this chapter. Be prepared! You never know when the firm or one of its members will seek your advice.

The Federal Constitution

The Constitution of the United States is a unique document for two reasons: it is the oldest written national constitution, and it was the first to include a government based on the concept of a separation of powers. A copy of the Constitution is included as Appendix A of this book. The U.S. Constitution was created in reaction to the tyranny of English rule; it was intended to prevent many of the problems the founding fathers felt were present under the English system. England has an unwritten constitution and a system of government that tends to merge the legislative, executive, and judicial functions. In contrast, our written constitution established a governmental structure which has three separate "divisions" and a series of checks and balances whereby the power of one branch is offset, at least to some extent, by that of the others. The Emory Law School maintains a hypertext and searchable version of the U.S. Constitution at http://www.law.emory.edu/ FEDERAL/usconst.html. This is an excellent starting place for research on the Constitution.

History taught the persons who founded the United States that all tyrants had at least two powers—the power of the purse and the power of the sword. Consequently they separated these powers by placing the power of the purse (fiscal and monetary control) in the legislative branch of government and the power of the sword (control over armed forces) in the executive branch. The third branch of government, the judicial branch, does not have the formal, written power that exists in the other branches of government. It does, however, possess what may be the most important power, at least from a constitutional perspective. The judicial branch has the power to decide where and how the other two branches may properly exercise their powers. This power was "created" by the Supreme Court itself in the landmark case of *Marbury v. Madison,*[1] and is called the power of judicial review. We shall discuss judicial review in greater detail later in this chapter. Doug Linder, professor of law at the Missouri–Kansas City Law School, has an article on judicial review, including information about *Marbury v. Madison* and links to additional information about the case, at http://www.law.umkc.edu/faculty/projects/ftrials/ conlaw/judicialrev.htm.

Allocation of Power

Legislative Power Article I of the Constitution creates a Congress consisting of two houses: the Senate and the House of Representatives. Congress has the power to levy and collect taxes, pay debts, and pass all laws with respect to certain enumerated powers, such as providing for the common defense and general welfare, regulating commerce, borrowing and coining money, establishing post offices and building highways, promoting science and the arts, and creating courts inferior to the U.S. Supreme Court. The Administrative Office of the U.S. Courts maintains a Web site about the federal court system at http:// www.uscourts.gov/.

Executive Power The U.S. Constitution, Article II, creates the executive branch of government by establishing the offices of president and vice-president. The president is the commander-in-chief of the armed forces of the United States. In addition, the president has the power to make treaties and to nominate ambassadors, judges, and other officers of the United States. The Senate must confirm all presidential appointments, as well as ratify all treaties. Without Senate confirmation, the appointee cannot take office, nor will any treaty become effective for the nation. The vice-president is the president of the Senate and also serves for the president when or if the president is unable to serve. An interesting Web site about U.S. presidents entitled History of U.S. Presidents can be accessed at http://www. whitehouse.gov/history/presidents/index.html.

Administrative Agencies, an Additional Executive Power Administrative agencies also wield power under the executive branch of government, even though they are not discussed in the U.S. Constitution. These agencies are sometimes called a fourth branch of government. They are generally created by Congress through the passage of a statute. Often the executive branch requests the creation of an agency. The statute that creates the agency is called the *enabling statute,* and it specifies the power and authority of the agency. Most federal agencies have the power, within their authority, to make rules and regulations that are similar to statutes and to decide controversies involving these rules and regulations. (These controversies are resolved in administrative hearings; they are not cases in the literal sense of the word.) The exact authority and the organization of the agencies vary greatly. Administrative agencies exist on the federal, state, and local levels. See Chapter 5 for a more detailed discussion of administrative agencies.

Judicial Power Article III of the Constitution vests federal judicial power in one Supreme Court and in such other inferior courts as Congress may create. The president nominates all U.S. federal judges; moreover, if they are confirmed by the Senate, they are permitted to serve in office for the rest of their lives, as long as their behavior is "good."

The actual wording of Article III limits rather than expands judicial power. Under Section 2 of Article III, generally the federal courts may hear and decide only cases and controversies (claims brought before the court in regular proceedings to protect or enforce rights or to prevent or punish wrongs). Legally, *cases and controversies* can be defined as matters that are appropriate for judicial determination. For a matter to be appropriate for judicial determination,

The controversy must be definite and concrete, touching the legal relations of parties having adverse legal interests. It must be a real and substantial controversy admitting of specific relief through a decree of a conclusive character, as distinguished from an opinion advising what the law would be upon a hypothetical state of facts.[2]

Constitutional law has evolved through precedents so that, today, the following are not considered to be a case or a controversy:

• *Advisory opinions* (Opinions rendered by a court at the request of the government or of an interested party that indicate how the court would rule on a matter should such litigation develop.[3])

• *Moot cases* (Cases in which a determination is sought on a matter which, when decided, cannot have any practical effect on the controversy; a question is moot when it presents no actual controversy or where the issues have ceased to exist.[4])

• Lack of *standing* (Standing means that the party has a sufficient stake in an otherwise justiciable controversy to obtain judicial resolution;[5] a party who does not have such a sufficient stake lacks standing.)

• *Political questions* (Questions that the court refuses to decide, due to their purely political character or because their determination would encroach on executive or legislative powers.[6])

The doctrine of the separation of powers requires that *federal* courts deal only with judicial matters. An *advisory opinion* is one in which the executive branch or an interested party refers a question to the judicial branch for a nonbinding opinion. However, rendering nonbinding opinions is not the purpose of the federal judicial system. Accordingly, whenever a member of the executive branch requires an advisory opinion, the question is referred to the Justice Department within the executive branch for an opinion from the attorney general. Under the U.S. federal system of government, the attorney general is the appropriate person to issue an advisory opinion. Contrary to the federal rule, some state courts are empowered to give advisory opinions. The International Court of Justice and the courts of a number of other nations also will issue advisory opinions.

The federal courts will hear only cases that are appropriate for a judicial solution. *Moot cases* are those cases in which the matter has already been resolved, or those cases in which any attempt at a resolution would have no practical effect. Sometimes the "resolution" occurs through the passage of time or a change in circumstances. In the case of *DeFunis v. Odegaard,*[7] the Supreme Court stated that the question of whether a student should be admitted to a law school was a moot case because by the time the Court could have issued its opinion, the student would have been on the brink of graduation. The law school informed the Supreme Court that regardless of the outcome of the suit, the law school would award DeFunis a degree if he passed his final quarter of coursework. Accordingly, as an example of judicial efficiency, it chose not to write an opinion on the merits of the suit.

Only persons who can demonstrate that they have actually been harmed or injured have *standing* to sue. Courts will generally define standing as having a direct and immediate personal interest. Courts use standing as part of the Article III limitation of federal judicial power to decide cases and controversies. In addition, statutes may grant standing to sue. For example, if you saw a person punch someone in the nose, you would not have standing to sue the aggressor for *assault* (a threat to touch someone in an undesired manner) or *battery* (the unauthorized touching of another person without either legal justification or that person's consent); only the person who was hit would have standing to sue because he or she was the one who was injured.

Even though many political questions in our society involve real controversies, the doctrine of our courts is that courts will not hear them. Why? While a political question may be considered a very real controversy, it is not considered to be a *judicial question* (a question that is proper for a court to decide). This rule is based on the concept of *judicial restraint,* a judicial policy of refusing to hear and decide certain types of cases. For example, if a citizen asserts that a state is not based on a democratic form of government, that claim will not be heard in a U.S. federal court because it is a political question. Similarly, if a citizen thinks that our nation's foreign policy is incorrect, our courts cannot be used to debate the point because foreign policy is a political question. What constitutes a political question, however, is not always clear. For instance, is *legislative apportionment*—the ratio of legislative representation to constituents—a political question? Historically, the courts have said no.

Now that the four limits that constrain judicial power have been discussed, we will consider the one concept that

NRW

PRODUCT SAFETY LAWS

Carlos read an article in a business publication that predicted which states would pass the strictest product safety laws in the next 12 months. The author of the article thought that a number of the laws being proposed would be more consumer oriented, and hence less "business friendly," than the current statutes in those states. Mai, Carlos, and Helen believe that their products are not likely to be affected by such statutes at this time. However, Carlos is still concerned about the long-term effect on the company that could be caused by the passage of additional consumer-friendly state legislation. He asks what you would advise the company to do. What will you tell him?

BUSINESS CONSIDERATIONS What practical steps can a business take to avoid the impact of a new product safety law proposed in a state? What legal steps can a business take to avoid a proposed product safety law? Can the firm avoid the jurisdiction of the state's courts? How?

ETHICAL CONSIDERATIONS Is it ethical for a business to attempt to avoid product safety laws? Since product safety laws are enacted to protect consumers, would it be ethical for a firm to attempt to discourage state legislation that might harm the firm while helping consumers?

INTERNATIONAL CONSIDERATIONS Assume that the article was discussing foreign legislation instead of legislation in a state. How can NRW attempt to influence foreign legislation? Is it ethical for NRW to try to influence legislators in another country? Why or why not?

has expanded judicial power. When you read the Constitution, you will not find the specific power of judicial review mentioned. That is because it is a court-created power. In 1803 the chief justice of the U.S. Supreme Court, John Marshall, created this doctrine of law in the landmark case of *Marbury v. Madison*.[8] This power is based on an interpretation of the Constitution that states that our courts may examine the actions of the legislative and executive branches of government to ascertain whether those actions conform to the Constitution. If they do not, the courts have the power to declare those actions unconstitutional and, therefore,

unenforceable. Thus, under this doctrine the Supreme Court can declare an act of Congress invalid if the congressional act does not conform to the Constitution. Similarly, the Court can declare conduct by the president, or any other member of the executive branch, invalid if the conduct conflicts with the Constitution. This concept of judicial power does not exist in England, where the Parliament is supreme. Therefore, the branch of government that has neither the power of the purse nor the power of the sword has significant power because it can determine what action by the other branches is legal. Since 1803, the power of U.S. courts to judicially review all actions of the legislative and executive branches of government has gone unchallenged. It has become the cornerstone of our doctrine of the separation of powers. Furthermore, this power of the Supreme Court to invalidate legislation also extends to all state legislation because of the supremacy clause in the federal Constitution.

The Watergate scandal, remembered by many as a low point in American history, may be viewed as a high point with respect to the doctrine of judicial review. In 1974, President Nixon was ordered to produce the now-famous Watergate tapes for use in a federal prosecution. Nixon claimed executive privilege and refused the order to turn over the tapes to the federal prosecutor. The Supreme Court, in a unanimous opinion, denied Nixon's claim and ordered him to release the tapes. President Nixon complied with the order of the Supreme Court, thus ending a constitutional crisis. Subsequently, Nixon became the first—and so far, only—U.S. president to resign from office. See the Web site at http://www.law.umkc.edu/faculty/projects/ftrials/ftrials. htm for interesting background on and discussion of a number of famous trials, including some low points in judicial history. This site was prepared by Doug Linder.

Role of Judges Despite the robes, the title, or the trappings of office, judges are people, too. As a result, the personalities and experiences of individual judges and justices may very well affect their rulings in any given case. The jurisprudential views of the judges impact the rulings in particular cases and the precedents being set for a jurisdiction. (For example, there are numerous articles about how Justice Ruth Bader Ginsburg's work experiences and views affect her decisions.[9] The same is true of other judges and justices. Justice Clarence Thomas made some pointed observations from the bench during a case involving cross burning that reportedly changed the tone of the proceedings.[10]) Judges who favor judicial restraint believe that the judge's role is to make sure that a law is legal and constitutional. These judges believe that if there is something wrong with the legal system, judges should not correct it. Corrections should be left to the legislature. For example, in addressing the asbestos litigation Justice Souter writes, "[T]his litigation defies customary judicial administration and calls for national legislation."[11] Judges who are activists believe that their role is to encourage social change: it is not necessary to wait for the legislature to act. The impact of the U.S. Supreme Court justices is particularly strong. The current justices on the Supreme Court are Chief Justice William H. Rehnquist and Justices Stephen Breyer, Ruth Bader Ginsburg, Anthony M. Kennedy, Sandra Day O'Connor, Antonin Scalia, David H. Souter, John Paul Stevens, and Clarence Thomas. Brief biographies of the current justices are available at the Supreme Court Web site, http://supremecourtus.gov/about/about.html.

Original Constitution

The original Constitution, signed on September 17, 1787, contained a number of rights pertaining to individuals. Among these is the right of habeas corpus. *Habeas corpus* is the name given to a variety of writs issued to bring a party before a court or judge. The original act is the English statute of 31 Car. 2 (1679); it has been amended in England and adopted throughout the United States.[12] In Latin, habeas corpus means, "You have the body."[13] This right may be used by all persons who have been deprived of their liberty. There are special forms of the writ (a *writ* is a writing issued by a court in the form of a letter ordering some designated activity); however, when the words "writ of habeas corpus" are used alone, the writ is addressed to the person who detains an individual. The writ commands that person to produce the individual in a court and to comply with any order by the court issuing the writ. This is probably the most common form of the writ.

Another right established by the Constitution is that Congress may pass no bills of attainder. A *bill of attainder* is a "legislative trial" whereby a person is judged a felon or worse by act of the legislature and not by a court of law.

Congress also may not enact ex post facto laws. An *ex post facto* law is a law passed after an occurrence or act, which retrospectively changes the legal consequences of such act. For example, if a business entered into a perfectly legal transaction in January, Congress cannot declare that transaction illegal in a statute passed after January. (Of course, Congress *can* declare similar transactions illegal in the future.) As used in the Constitution, the prohibition on ex post facto laws applies only to criminal law.[14] This prohibition includes laws that make an act a crime; make a crime into a more serious crime; change the punishment for a crime; or alter the legal rules of evidence for proving a crime.

These are some of the most notable constitutional rights. However, other individual rights, such as trial by

---

NRW CASE 4.2　　Management

HOW TO PROTECT NRW'S PATENT

Helen is very concerned that another firm will "steal" the technology behind StuffTrakR and InvenTrakR, and produce and sell a copy at a price below NRW's costs. Although NRW holds a patent on the key components, Helen knows that patents are not always upheld in court. Consequently, she would like to file a suit with the court to determine if the patent will be upheld *before* a competitor duplicates it. She asks you how she should proceed. What advice will you give her?

BUSINESS CONSIDERATIONS How does uncertainty about the validity of a patent affect a business? What can a business do to reduce the risk? What technique or techniques would be most effective?

ETHICAL CONSIDERATIONS Analyze the ethical perspective of any business that would attempt to "steal" NRW's technology. Is commercial or industrial espionage an ethical method of doing business?

INTERNATIONAL CONSIDERATIONS How can a business protect its technology and patents from competitors in foreign countries? Are international protections available? Is there an international forum for resolving disputes involving technology or patents?

---

jury in most criminal cases, were also written into the original Constitution. Doug Linder's Constitutional Conflicts Web site addresses a number of such issues and topics. This site can be accessed at http://www.law.umkc.edu/faculty/projects/ftrials/conlaw/home.html.

Amendments to the Constitution

Four years after the U.S. Constitution was signed, the first 10 amendments were passed. These amendments, known as the Bill of Rights, were designed to ensure that certain individual rights were protected. For example, the First Amendment provides that "Congress shall make no law respecting an establishment of religion, or prohibiting the free exercise thereof; . . ." The First Amendment provides the basis for the separation of church and state. In all, 27 amendments to the Constitution have been passed—see Appendix A. The amendments to the Constitution reflect the citizens' concerns about particular topics and reflect changes in the society. The Constitution itself serves as the "supreme law of the land" for U.S. society.

In the following case, the court discussed the establishment of religion clause and whether Michael Newdow had standing to sue. Newdow represented himself in these pro-ceedings. The court reversed and remanded the case to the federal district court. Shortly after making its decision, the court granted a *stay* (an order postponing a judgment or proceeding).[15] See Case Problems and Writing Assignments 4 for a discussion of some of the later decisions arising out of this case.

4.1

NEWDOW v. UNITED STATES CONGRESS
292 F.3d 597, 2002 U.S. App. LEXIS 12576 (9th Cir. 2002)

FACTS Michael Newdow is an atheist whose daughter attends public elementary school in the Elk Grove Unified School District (EGUSD). In accordance with state law and a school district rule, EGUSD teachers begin each day by leading their students in a recitation of the Pledge of Allegiance. The California Education Code requires that public schools begin each school day with "appropriate patriotic exercises" and that giving the pledge satisfies this requirement. To implement the statute, the EGUSD has promulgated a policy that states: "Each elementary school class [shall] recite the pledge of allegiance to the flag once each day." Their teacher leads Newdow's daughter's class in reciting the pledge. On June 22, 1942, Congress first codified the pledge as "I pledge allegiance to the flag of the United States of America and to the Republic for which it stands, one Nation indivisible, with liberty and justice for all." On June 14, 1954, Congress amended the pledge to add the words "under God" after the word "Nation." Newdow's daughter does not have to participate in the pledge; however, she has to watch her class.

ISSUES Did Newdow have standing to bring this suit? Does the EGUSD practice violate the Establishment clause of the Constitution?

HOLDINGS Yes, Newdow had standing. Yes, the practice violates the Constitution.

REASONING Excerpts from the opinion of Circuit Judge Alfred T. Goodwin:

[T]he federal courts lack jurisdiction to issue orders directing Congress to enact or amend legislation. Because the words that amended the Pledge were enacted into law by statute, the district court may not direct Congress to delete those words any more than it may order the President to take such action. . . . [I]n determining whether or not the acts of members of Congress are protected by the Speech and Debate Clause, the court looks solely to whether or not the acts fall within the legitimate legislative sphere; if they do, Congress is protected by the absolute prohibition of the Clause against being "questioned in any other Place." . . . [T]he question of the constitutionality of the 1954 Act remains before us. . . .

Article III standing is a jurisdictional issue. . . . To satisfy standing requirements, a plaintiff must prove that "(1) it has suffered an 'injury in fact' that is (a) concrete and particularized and (b) actual or imminent, not conjectural or hypothetical; (2) the injury is fairly traceable to the challenged action of the defendant; and (3) it is likely, as opposed to merely speculative, that the injury will be redressed by a favorable decision." . . . "Parents have a right to direct the religious upbringing of their children and . . . have standing to protect their right." . . . Newdow has standing to challenge the EGUSD's policy and practice regarding the recitation of the Pledge because his daughter is currently enrolled in elementary school in the EGUSD. . . . [T]he standing requirements for an action brought under the Establishment Clause are the same as for any other action. "The requirement of standing focuses on the party seeking to get his complaint before a federal court and not on the issues he wishes to have adjudicated." . . . The "psychological consequence presumably produced by observation of conduct with which one disagrees . . . is not an injury sufficient to confer standing under Art. III, even though the disagreement is phrased in constitutional terms." . . . [T]he Supreme Court . . . has indirectly broadened the notion of Establishment Clause standing in public education cases by holding that the mere enactment of a statute may constitute an Establishment Clause violation. . . . The relevant issue is whether an objective observer, acquainted with the text, legislative history, and implementation of the statute, would perceive it as state endorsement of prayer in public schools." . . .

[T]he legislative history of the 1954 Act shows that the "under God" language was not meant to sit passively in the federal code unbeknownst to the public; rather, the sponsors of the amendment knew about and capitalized on the state laws and school district rules that mandate recitation of the Pledge. The legislation's House sponsor, Representative Louis C. Rabaut, testified at the Congressional hearing that "the children of our land, in the daily recitation of the pledge in school, will be daily impressed with a true understanding of our way of life and its origins," and this statement was incorporated into the report of the House Judiciary Committee. Taken within its context, the 1954 addendum was designed to result in the recitation of the words "under God" in school classrooms throughout the land on a daily basis. . . . The mere enactment of the 1954 Act in its particular context constitutes a religious recitation policy that interferes with Newdow's right to direct the religious education of his daughter. Accordingly, we hold that Newdow has standing. . . .

The Establishment Clause of the First Amendment states that "Congress shall make no law respecting an establishment of religion," a provision that "the Fourteenth Amendment makes applicable with full force to the States and their school districts." . . . [T]he Supreme Court has used three interrelated tests to analyze alleged violations of the Establishment Clause in the realm of public education: the three-prong test . . . ; the "endorsement" test . . . ; and the "coercion" test. . . . [In the Supreme Court's most recent case it applied all three.] We are free to apply any or all of the three tests, and to invalidate any measure that fails any one of them. . . .

[T]he statement that the United States is a nation "under God" is an endorsement of religion. It is a profession of a religious belief, namely, a belief in monotheism. The recitation that ours is a nation "under God" is not a mere acknowledgment that many Americans believe in a deity. Nor is it merely descriptive of the undeniable historical significance of religion in the founding of the Republic. Rather, the phrase "one nation under God" in the context of the Pledge is normative. To recite the Pledge is not to describe the United States; instead, it is to swear allegiance to the values for which the flag stands: unity, indivisibility, liberty, justice, and—since 1954—monotheism. The text of the official Pledge . . . impermissibly takes a position with respect to the purely religious question of the existence and identity of God. . . . "The government must pursue a course of complete neutrality toward religion." . . . The Pledge . . . is an impermissible government endorsement of religion because it sends a message to unbelievers "that they are outsiders, not full members of the political community, and an accompanying message to adherents that they are insiders, favored members of the political community." . . . Consequently, the policy and the Act fail the endorsement test.

Similarly, the policy and the Act fail the coercion test. . . . [T]he policy and the Act place students in the untenable position of choosing between participating in an exercise with religious content or protesting. . . . Although the defendants argue that the religious content of "one nation under God" is minimal, to an atheist or a believer in certain non-Judeo-Christian religions or philosophies, it may reasonably appear to be an attempt to enforce a "religious orthodoxy" of monotheism, and is therefore impermissible. The coercive effect of this policy is particularly pronounced in the school setting given the age and impressionability of schoolchildren, and their understanding that they are required to adhere to the norms set by their school, their teacher and their fellow students. . . . The coercive effect of the Act is apparent from its context and legislative history, which indicate that the Act was designed to result in the daily recitation of the words "under God" in school classrooms. President Eisenhower, during the Act's signing ceremony, stated: "From this day forward, the millions of our school children will daily proclaim in every city and town, every village and rural schoolhouse, the dedication of our Nation and our people to the Almighty." . . .

[T]he legislative history . . . reveals that the Act's sole purpose was to advance religion, in order to differentiate the United States from nations under communist rule. "The First Amendment requires that a statute must be invalidated if it is entirely motivated by a purpose to advance religion." . . .

BUSINESS CONSIDERATIONS Can a business legitimately start the workday with a group pledge? With a prayer?

ETHICAL CONSIDERATIONS Is it ethical for one person to sue seeking to stop a generally accepted practice within a community? Is it ethical for a community to impose allegedly religious standards that violate the beliefs of an individual within that community?

The Courts and Jurisdiction

Jurisdiction is the power of a court to affect legal relationships. We will examine four aspects of jurisdiction:

1. Subject matter jurisdiction (the power of a court to hear certain kinds of legal questions)

2. Jurisdiction over the persons or property

3. Concurrent versus exclusive jurisdiction

4. Venue

Subject Matter Jurisdiction

In our discussion of the Constitution, we said that the Supreme Court was limited to deciding cases and controversies. In addition, Article III of the Constitution defines the Supreme Court's *subject matter jurisdiction* as including all cases in law and equity arising under the Constitution, the statutes of the United States, and all treaties. The subject matter jurisdiction granted to the Supreme Court is extensive. A state juvenile court, on the other hand, is limited solely to hearing matters concerning children, that arose within the state and under its laws. If an adult were brought before a juvenile court, the court would lack subject matter jurisdiction. Because it may decide only matters concerning people under 18 years of age, a juvenile court is an inappropriate court for a case involving an adult. Likewise, a federal bankruptcy court may not decide a criminal matter because its jurisdiction is limited to bankruptcy matters. Subject matter jurisdiction determines which court is the "right" court to hear a particular type of case or controversy. However, more than one court may have subject matter jurisdiction over a case.

Jurisdiction over the Persons or Property

In addition to the appropriate subject matter jurisdiction, a court must also have jurisdiction over the persons or property whose rights, duties, or obligations the court will decide. Basically, three techniques exist for obtaining jurisdiction over persons or property—in personam, in rem, and quasi in rem. First we will discuss *in personam jurisdiction,* the authority of the court over the specific person or corporation. Can the person or the corporation properly be brought within the control of the court?

In Personam Jurisdiction Jurisdictional questions do not arise over the person of the plaintiff, who filed the lawsuit. The plaintiff chooses to file the suit in a particular court and so implicitly consents to the court's jurisdiction. It is inconsistent to allow the plaintiff to file the suit and then complain that the same court lacks jurisdiction over him or her.

The *defendant* (the person who answers a lawsuit), however, does not choose the court. Often, if the defendant were given a choice, he or she would choose not to have any trial. If a trial *must* take place, he or she might well prefer to have it held elsewhere. The question, then, is how to obtain in personam jurisdiction over the defendant. How or why can the court legally compel the defendant to attend, or decide the defendant's rights if he or she refuses to attend the trial?

One technique is if the defendant consents to the court's jurisdiction. Consent can occur by merely responding to a lawsuit that has been filed. It can occur either by express consent or by failure to raise the issue of jurisdiction and, instead, responding to the legal questions. Consent can also be given prior to the lawsuit. This is commonly accomplished by a contract clause or by appointment of an agent to accept *service of process.* (Service of process is the delivery of a legal notice to inform the person served of the nature of the legal dispute.) A corporation is considered to have given consent when it registers with a state as a *foreign corporation* (a corporation that had its articles of incorporation approved in another state) and asks permission to conduct business in the state. Courts have concluded that a corporation that engages in business as a foreign corporation without the required registration has given implied consent. Delaware Intercorp publishes an article entitled "What Other Steps Might You Need to Take?" which deals with the steps in establishing a business. The article includes a discussion of registering as a foreign corporation in another state and in another country. The article is at http://www.delawareintercorp.com/else.htm.

A court will also have jurisdiction over a defendant who is physically present in the state when he or she is served with process. This would include a person who is on a trip to the state or even merely passing through the state on his or her way to another destination. Courts will generally decide that there is no jurisdiction over a defendant who is tricked into entering the state by the plaintiff. A corporation is physically present in a state in which it is *doing business.* (Doing business is also used as the basis of implied consent by some states.) For example, a corporation is doing business in a state in which it has stores, offices, warehouses, and regular employees. The courts have decided numerous cases about what constitutes doing business and have devised various tests for recognizing doing business. Two of these tests are (1) whether the corporation's activities were single, isolated transactions or continuous and substantial activities; or (2) whether the corporation's agents were only soliciting offers in the state or were engaged in additional activities.

In the landmark case of *International Shoe Co. v. Washington,*[16] the U.S. Supreme Court concluded that before a defendant is required to appear in a state court, the defendant must have certain *minimum contacts* with the state. Otherwise, the suit would offend traditional concepts of fair play and substantial justice. This case created a constitutional test for in personam jurisdiction. The defendant in this case was a corporation, but the ruling appears to apply to individuals as well.

In personam jurisdiction also exists in the state of domicile. Domicile is a complicated legal doctrine (and most of its complexity is outside the scope of this text). Human beings have one and only one domicile. A person may choose his or her domicile or the law may assign it. *Domicile* is usually a person's home, the place where he or she is physically present and where he or she intends to remain for the time being. Domicile does *not* require that a person live in a state for a certain minimum period of time. Consequently, domicile contrasts with residency statutes that require, for example, a person to live in a state for a set period of time before voting in the state or being eligible for in-state tuition at its colleges and universities.

Suppose that both the plaintiff and the defendant are domiciliaries of Alaska; Alaska has jurisdiction over them. On the other hand, if the plaintiff is a domiciliary of Alaska but the defendant is a domiciliary of Oregon, Alaska *may* not have proper jurisdiction over the defendant. If the plaintiff wants to sue the defendant in a state court, the plaintiff might need to go to Oregon and sue the defendant there, since a *defendant's* state of domicile is almost always an appropriate forum. (*Forum* is the court that is or will be conducting the trial.) Potential jurisdiction in a federal court will be discussed later in this chapter.

Corporations are domiciled in the state in which they are incorporated. They are also considered to be domiciled in the state where they have their corporate headquarters, if this is a different state. Thus, a corporation may have two domiciles, and it may be sued in either of the states where it is domiciled. A corporation is *also* subject to in personam jurisdiction in all states in which the corporation does business because it is physically present there.

Most states have laws called *long-arm statutes*. The purpose of these statutes is to permit the state to exercise in personam jurisdiction when ordinarily this would not be possible. A common type of long-arm statute permits a state to exercise authority over a person who drives on its roads. This type of long-arm statute is also called a nonresident motorist statute. Suppose a resident of Nebraska drives a car on the roads of Kansas and injures a resident of Kansas. In that situation, the courts of Kansas would have personal jurisdiction over the resident of Nebraska, because it would be unfair to require the resident of Kansas to go to Nebraska to sue. Other states have enacted much broader long-arm statutes. For example, Illinois enacted a statute listing certain acts that would confer jurisdiction if done in the state. California and Texas,[17] on the other hand, enacted long-arm statutes that provide for in personam jurisdiction whenever it complies with the U.S. Constitution.[17] As with other matters under the control of the states, there is great variation among long-arm statutes.

The courts are facing a new problem in resolving whether in personam jurisdiction exists in cases involving the Internet. As Internet usage grows and as e-commerce continues to develop, this area will attract a great deal of the court's attention across the world. For now, U.S. courts are relying on the precedent established by *International Shoe*, applying the concepts from that case to Internet cases by analogy. One of the leading Internet cases is *Zippo Manufacturing Co. v. Zippo Dot Com, Inc.*,[18] which involved a dispute over the ownership of an Internet domain name. The district court applied the criteria set out in *International Shoe* to determine if the defendant had "specific contacts" with Pennsylvania. It reformulated the criteria as follows:

A three-pronged test has emerged for determining whether the exercise of specific personal jurisdiction over a non-resident defendant is appropriate: (1) the defendant must have sufficient "minimum contacts" with the forum state, (2) the claim asserted against the defendant must arise out of those contacts, and (3) the exercise of jurisdiction must be reasonable.[19]

From this the court decided that if a person enters into contracts with residents of another jurisdiction, and those contracts involve the knowing and repeated transmission of computer files over the Internet, personal jurisdiction over the person in that other jurisdiction would be proper. However, if a person simply posts information on an Internet Web site, there are not sufficient contacts with any "foreign" jurisdictions to permit the exercise of personal jurisdiction over the person posting the information. Such passive Web sites only make information available. Between these two extremes lies the troublesome area. In this area a person might be involved with an interactive Web site that allows for the exchange of information between the person and the host computer. In these situations, personal jurisdiction will depend on the level of interaction and also on whether the exchange of information is commercial in nature.[20]

There are still a number of questions to be answered in this area. The ultimate resolution of some of these issues is likely to have a major impact on the future growth and development of e-commerce.

In Rem Jurisdiction If a state court cannot obtain in personam jurisdiction on any of these grounds, another approach—called in rem jurisdiction—can be used. *In rem jurisdiction* exists when the court has authority over the property or status of something belonging to the defendant that is located within the control of the court. In rem jurisdiction allows the state to exercise its authority over something such as land or a marital domicile within its boundaries. The court's judgment will affect everyone's rights in that "thing." It does not impose a personal obligation on the defendant. For example, if an individual or a corporation has real property in one state but resides in another, the state where the property is located can exercise in rem jurisdiction over the property in a *condemnation* proceeding (court proceeding to take property for public use or declare property forfeited).

In the following case, the court discussed in rem jurisdiction under the federal anticybersquatting statute. After

reading the opinion, decide whether you agree with the court's decision and with the scope of this statute.

Quasi in Rem Jurisdiction In this type of jurisdiction, the court determines the rights of particular persons to specific property. (It is distinct from *in rem* jurisdiction, because a court with in rem jurisdiction will determine the rights of all persons in the thing. It differs from *in personam*

4.2

PORSCHE CARS NORTH AMERICA, INC. v. PORSCHE.NET
302 F.3d 248, 2002 U.S. App. LEXIS 17531 (4th Cir. 2002)

FACTS Porsche Cars North America, Inc. and Dr. Ing. h.c.F. Porsche AG, a German company, brought this suit against 128 Internet domain names related to the name "Porsche." Porsche dismissed some defendants and the court entered default judgments against many of the others for failure to appear. Christian Holmgreen, a British citizen, had registered the two involved in this dispute, collectively called "the British domain names." Congress enacted the Anticybersquatting Consumer Protection Act[21] (ACPA or "the anticybersquatting statute"), authorizing in rem actions against domain names in certain circumstances. Three days before trial, the British domain names notified the district court that Holmgreen had decided to submit to personal jurisdiction in the U.S. District Court for the Southern District of California. The British domain names moved to dismiss the in rem claims, arguing that Holmgreen's decision removed the Eastern District of Virginia's in rem jurisdiction.

ISSUE Did the Eastern District of Virginia court have in rem jurisdiction?

HOLDING Yes, the court had in rem jurisdiction over the British domain names under the ACPA.

REASONING Excerpts from the opinion of Circuit Judge Diana Gribbon Motz:

The Internet is . . . a network of computers all around the world through which people communicate. . . . Federal law defines a domain name as "any alphanumeric designation which is registered with or assigned by any domain name registrar, domain name registry, or other domain name registration authority as part of an electronic address on the Internet." . . . A person seeking the right to use a particular domain name may register with one of a number of registrar organizations that assign domain names on a first-come first-served basis. Many consumers look for a given company's Web site by checking to see if the company uses a domain name

made up of the company's name or brand name with the suffix ".com." . . . For this reason, "companies strongly prefer that their domain name be comprised of the company or brand trademark. . . ."

The . . . [ACPA] statute authorizes in rem jurisdiction over a domain name if personal jurisdiction over the registrant of the domain name is unavailable. . . . [T]he structure of the ACPA undoubtedly expresses Congress's preference for in personam suits: the holder of a trademark must convince the court that in personam jurisdiction over a person is unavailable before an ACPA in rem action may proceed. The statute . . . does not require . . . that those conditions continue throughout the litigation. If it did, in rem jurisdiction could be lost even long after a court has made the requisite statutory finding permitting in rem jurisdiction under the ACPA. . . .

Porsche's assertion of substantive claims under federal statutes, the ACPA and the trademark dilution statute, invokes a federal court's subject-matter jurisdiction, while in rem jurisdiction concerns a court's authority over the res—in this case, the domain names Porsche seeks. . . .

[I]t is black-letter law that the conditions that create diversity jurisdiction, one well-known basis for subject-matter jurisdiction, need not survive through the life of the litigation. . . . [A] court determines the existence of diversity jurisdiction "at the time the action is filed," regardless of later changes in originally crucial facts such as the parties' citizenship or the amount in controversy. . . . [P]ersonal jurisdiction . . . seems far more analogous to in rem jurisdiction. . . . [P]ersonal jurisdiction is indubitably waived absent timely objection. . . .

Although at the beginning of a civil forfeiture case the res must be located in the jurisdiction that asserts authority over it, the [Supreme] Court has held that a federal court's . . . jurisdiction over the in rem case survives even if the res is removed from the jurisdiction. . . . [The ACPA does not] suggest any reason to treat ACPA in rem jurisdiction differently. The statute permits "the owner of a mark" to "file" an in rem action against a domain name if "the court finds that the owner . . . is not able to obtain in personam jurisdiction over . . . a civil defendant." . . . It thus calls for a finding early in the case as to whether in rem jurisdiction exists. . . . [T]he statutory requirement that the court make a specific finding reduces defendants' options by designating a finding that must be made, and thus a point at which the court will consider objections to the assertion of in rem jurisdiction. . . . [The ACPA] permits "the owner of a mark" to "file" an in rem action if "the court finds that the owner is not able to obtain in personam jurisdiction over a person who would have been a civil defendant." Because the ACPA refers specifically to filing and a finding, it indicates far more clearly than the diversity statute that once the action is filed and the finding is made, in rem jurisdiction is ordinarily complete. . . .

[T]he policy interests that lead courts to continue to entertain cases even after the end of conditions that originally yielded diversity jurisdiction apply with equal force [here]. . . . [U]nder the British domain names' theory, Holmgreen could have delayed even longer before submitting to personal jurisdiction; perhaps he might even have chosen to wait to see how the trial went, and then submitted to personal jurisdiction to stave off the expected . . . adverse judgment. Nothing in the ACPA or its legislative history suggests that Congress intended to permit such manipulation. . . . [T]he British domain names objected much too late to in rem jurisdiction on the grounds of personal jurisdiction over . . . Holmgreen. . . . Because the British domain names delayed so long and entirely without excuse . . . we need not address subtleties presented by the anticybersquatting law. . . . We decide only that early in an . . . [ACPA]

case, the availability of personal jurisdiction may defeat in rem jurisdiction . . . and that submission three days before trial . . . is far too late.

. . . [T]he British domain names contend that . . . the in rem provisions of the ACPA violate the Due Process Clause. . . . [Their] principal constitutional challenge to the ACPA provisions . . . centers on the "contacts" necessary for in rem jurisdiction. They argue that the Due Process Clause requires that to bring an ACPA in rem action in the Eastern District of Virginia, Porsche must prove that Holmgreen personally has minimum contacts with that jurisdiction. . . . However, . . . [precedents] holds that "property alone is not sufficient 'contact' to support personal jurisdiction over a nonresident as to matters unrelated to the property." . . . Porsche's claims against the British domain names are entirely "related to the property." . . . [I]n "an in rem proceeding in which the property itself is the source of the underlying controversy between plaintiff and defendant, . . . due process is satisfied" by assigning jurisdiction based on the location of the property. . . . In a case that directly concerns possession of the defendant domain names, the registrant's other personal contacts with the forum are constitutionally irrelevant to the assertion of in rem jurisdiction over the domain names he registered. . . . Congress plainly treated domain names as property in the ACPA. . . . Congress may treat a domain name registration as property subject to in rem jurisdiction if it chooses, without violating the Constitution. . . .

BUSINESS CONSIDERATIONS How can a company best protect its name and trademark from cybersquatters?

ETHICAL CONSIDERATIONS Is it ethical to cybersquat on a domain name with the hopes of selling the name to the company for a large price? What is Holmgreen's ethical perspective? Why?

jurisdiction because there is no authority over the person of the defendant.) *Quasi in rem* jurisdiction is authority obtained through property under the control of the court. The court obtains control of the property through one of two methods. In the first, the property is within the jurisdiction of the court and the plaintiff wishes to resolve issues of ownership, possession, or use of the property—for example, to foreclose a mortgage. In the second method, the dispute does not concern the property but is personal to the plaintiff, such as a breach of contract or the commission of a tort. Jurisdiction will exist if the plaintiff can locate the defendant's property within the state and bring it before the court by *attachment* (seizure of the defendant's property) or *garnishment* (a procedure to obtain possession

of the defendant's property when it is in the custody of another person). Limitations exist on when attachment or garnishment is allowed. When the plaintiff's suit is successful, the recovery is limited to the value of the property. Exhibit 4.1 summarizes the techniques for obtaining jurisdiction over the defendant.

Service of Process In cases of either in personam, in rem, or quasi in rem jurisdiction, there must be proper service of process on the defendant to inform him or her of the lawsuit. Proper service of process includes *actual notice,* in which one is personally served by an officer of the court; this can also include service by registered mail. If actual notice cannot be obtained after reasonable attempts to do

EXHIBIT   4.1   Methods to Obtain Jurisdiction over the Defendant

Type of Jurisdiction	Type of Judgment	Differences Between Individual and Corporate Defendants	
		Individual	*Corporation*
In personam Authority over a specific person or corporation within the control of the state. Authority may derive from consent, domicile, physical presence, or long-arm statutes.	Affects the person.	**Consent** Defendant consents to personal jurisdiction; consent can occur before or after a suit has begun.	**Consent** A corporation consents when it registers as a foreign corporation within the state.[c]
		Domicile Defendant has a residence—usually a home—at which he or he is/has been physically present and intends to remain for the time being; individuals have only one domicile.[a]	**Domicile** A corporation is incorporated (articles of incorporation) and/or has its corporate headquarters in the state.
		Physical Presence Defendant is served by hand while he or she is within the geographic boundaries of the state.[b]	**Physical Presence** A corporation is recognized as "doing business" in the state.
In rem Authority over property or status within the control of the state. Settles ownership interests in property or status for all persons.	Affects the property or status.	The rules for individuals and corporations are basically the same.	
Quasi in rem Authority obtained through property under the control of the state. Settles issues of ownership, possession, or use of property; or settles personal disputes unrelated to the property.	Affects the rights of specific people to property.[d]	The rules for individuals and corporations are basically the same.	

a. Some people are not capable of selecting domiciles for themselves; thus, they have domiciles determined for them by legal rules (e.g., minors).
b. Most states will decline to exercise jurisdiction if the defendant is brought into the state by force or enticed into the state by fraud.
c. If the corporation fails to register, the court may imply consent from the act of doing business in the state. Generally, implied consent is limited to cases arising from the actual doing of business in the state.
d. A successful plaintiff is limited to the value of the property.

so, notice may be served publicly by a posting on the property or in a newspaper. This is called *constructive service.* Proper notice may also include service at the office of the

state's secretary of state. For example, when an out-of-state corporation registers in Delaware, the state may specify that process may be served on Delaware's secretary of state.

Concurrent versus Exclusive Jurisdiction

In certain cases, more than one court may exercise jurisdiction. If so, it is called *concurrent jurisdiction*. On the other hand, some subjects can be heard only by a particular court; this is called *exclusive jurisdiction*. Examples of exclusive jurisdiction in the federal courts are suits in which the United States is a party or suits that involve some areas of admiralty law, bankruptcy, copyright, federal crimes, and patent cases. Exhibit 4.2 illustrates the jurisdictional domains of federal and state courts.

Venue

Once a court establishes that it has proper jurisdiction over the subject matter and the person, it must then ascertain whether proper venue exists. *Venue* literally means "neighborhood." In a legal sense, however, it means the proper geographical area or district where a suit can be brought. In state practice, it is usually a question of which county is appropriate. In federal practice, the question of venue is which federal judicial district is the appropriate one. In state practice, if both the plaintiff and the defendant are residents of the same state, in personam jurisdiction exists in that state's courts. But which of the state courts is best situated to hear the case? For example, venue could be proper in the area where an incident, such as an automobile accident, occurred.

The residence of the defendant also may be considered in determining the proper venue. More than one court may have proper venue. The laws of each state spell out in great detail the appropriate courts that would have venue.

Choice of Laws

Choice of laws is the selection of which jurisdiction's laws should be applied to a particular incident; that is, what laws should govern the subject before the court. Although it is also called "conflict of laws," legal scholars argue that choice of laws is the more appropriate title. Another complication in this area is that the court will use choice of laws rules to determine the *substantive laws* (the laws that create, define, and regulate rights) that should be applied to the dispute; however, the forum court will use its own procedural laws. (*Procedural law* provides the method of enforcing rights or obtaining redress for the violation of rights). The following example provides a hint of the difficulties that may arise in a choice of laws case.

Julia, a domiciliary of Massachusetts, entered into a contract with Karen, a domiciliary of Vermont, while they both were in Connecticut. The contract concerned goods that were located in Maine and were to be shipped to New York. While the goods were in transit, they were stopped and taken by Dawn, a domiciliary of New Hampshire, who was a creditor of Julia. This situation

---

EXHIBIT 4.2 A Comparison of Federal and State Court Jurisdiction

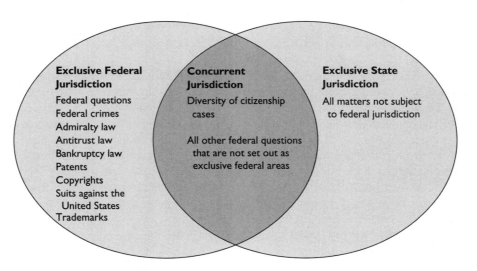

Exclusive Federal Jurisdiction

Federal questions
Federal crimes
Admiralty law
Antitrust law
Bankruptcy law
Patents
Copyrights
Suits against the
  United States
Trademarks

Concurrent Jurisdiction

Diversity of citizenship
  cases

All other federal questions
  that are not set out as
  exclusive federal areas

Exclusive State Jurisdiction

All matters not subject
  to federal jurisdiction

raises many legal questions. What should Karen do to get the goods? In which state should the lawsuit be filed? And, specifically with reference to the choice of laws doctrine: What law should the court apply—the law of Massachusetts, Vermont, Connecticut, Maine, New York, or New Hampshire? It could be that Karen would win if the law of Massachusetts, Connecticut, or New York were applied but would lose if the law of Vermont, Maine, or New Hampshire were applied. Hence, choice of laws issues are quite important.

Choice of laws issues are sometimes resolved by statutes that indicate which law should be applied. In business transactions, these issues may also be resolved by the parties' specifying which state (or national) law should apply. The courts generally will use the parties' selection as long as there is a reasonable relationship between the state selected and the transaction.

We will not attempt to resolve the questions posed in this example because it is clearly too complex for an undergraduate course in the law of business. You need only be aware of the complexity of this matter and the common solution to the problem—that is, stating in the written contract that if there should be any dispute concerning the contract, the laws of a particular state will apply. This is a form of *preventative law*.

Federal Courts

In addition to the general grounds discussed previously with respect to jurisdiction, two specific grounds exist for federal jurisdiction: (1) federal question and (2) diversity of citizenship *plus* amount in controversy.

Federal question jurisdiction derives directly from Article III of the Constitution. *Federal questions* are questions that pertain to the federal Constitution, statutes of the United States, and treaties of the United States. Also included, today, are all regulations of federal administrative agencies. For example, if a person is denied a job because of race, that will raise a federal question, because such discrimination raises concerns about violations of the Constitution, federal statutes, and federal regulations. If a publishing company brings an action asserting that another publishing company has infringed its copyright, it raises a federal question, because copyright is both a constitutional and a statutory question. States do not have the right to issue copyrights, and state courts do not have the subject matter jurisdiction to decide copyright cases.

Federal question jurisdiction is not necessary when diversity of citizenship is present and vice versa. *Diversity of citizenship* exists when the plaintiff is a citizen of one state and the defendant is a citizen of another; it also exists when

---

NRW CASE 4.3   Management/Marketing

NRW

LAWSUIT AGAINST A SUPPLIER

Mai, Carlos, and Helen purchased a license for software from MicroSources, a California firm located in Silicon Valley. Assume that NRW is an Ohio corporation. NRW was unaware that the software was defective and used it in the StuffTrakR units, causing them to malfunction. These units were sold to customers directly and through retail outlets. Customers have been calling NRW and complaining about the StuffTrakR units. This situation has also caused an increase in warranty repair work. Mai, Carlos, and Helen are concerned about the short- and long-term effects on the company's finances and reputation. They ask you what the company should do. What will you tell them?

BUSINESS CONSIDERATIONS What can a business do to reduce the chance of purchasing defective supplies and software? Can NRW sue the software firm? In what court(s) could the suit be filed? What additional information will be necessary and why? Would filing the suit improve or harm NRW's reputation?

ETHICAL CONSIDERATIONS What should NRW do to protect its reputation? Are there any ethical restrictions on what NRW does to protect its reputation?

INTERNATIONAL CONSIDERATIONS If the supplier were in a foreign country instead of Silicon Valley, how would that affect the situation? What would be the effect if the consumers were in a foreign country?

---

one party is a foreign country and the other is a citizen of a state. The primary reason underlying diversity jurisdiction is that if a citizen of Hawaii must file suit in Iowa in order to obtain jurisdiction over the defendant, it is possible that the court of Iowa might favor its citizen over the citizen of Hawaii. In that case, the plaintiff can file suit in federal court. Law.com published an article by Matthew Haggman of the *Miami Daily Business Review*. This article, entitled "Snuffed Out," deals with the issue of diversity jurisdiction in the recent lawsuit filed in Florida courts by foreign governments against the tobacco companies. The article can be accessed at http://www.law.com/jsp/article.jsp?id=1032128879166.

When federal jurisdiction is based on diversity of citizenship, a further requirement exists: a *minimum amount in question*. Title 28, § 1332(a) of the United States Code requires that the amount in question must exceed $75,000 in diversity cases. In contrast, cases in which the federal courts have exclusive jurisdiction generally do not require a minimum amount in controversy. The purpose behind the amount is to prevent federal courts from dealing with trifles and to reduce the caseload in federal courts.

Most federal cases are highly complex, and the precise amount is a matter that is often unknown when the lawsuit is filed. Accordingly, the courts look to the amount the plaintiff, acting in good faith, has determined to be in dispute. This is called the *plaintiff viewpoint rule.*

Another aspect of diversity jurisdiction is called complete diversity. *Complete diversity* requires that no plaintiff

be a citizen of the same state as any of the defendants. This rule, however, poses complex problems when there are multiple plaintiffs and/or defendants. Complete diversity also prohibits having an alien plaintiff and an alien defendant in the same suit, even when the aliens are from different countries. (An *alien* is a person or corporation belonging to another country.) In the following case the Supreme Court addressed issues of personal and subject matter jurisdiction. Note the special treatment of complete diversity when the case involves foreign parties.

Exhibit 4.3 depicts the two grounds for federal jurisdiction.

4.3

RUHRGAS AG v. MARATHON OIL COMPANY
119 S. Ct. 1563, 1999 U.S. LEXIS 3170 (1999)

FACTS The underlying controversy stems from a venture to produce gas in the Heimdal Field of the Norwegian North Sea. In 1976, respondents Marathon Oil Company and Marathon International Oil Company acquired Marathon Petroleum Company (Norway) (MPCN) and respondent Marathon Petroleum Norge (Norge). Ruhrgas is a German corporation; Norge is a Norwegian corporation. Marathon Oil Company, an Ohio corporation, and Marathon International Oil Company, a Delaware corporation, moved their principal places of business from Ohio to Texas while the venture was being formed. Before the acquisition, Norge held a license to produce gas in the Heimdal Field; following the transaction, Norge assigned the license to MPCN. In 1981, MPCN contracted to sell 70 percent of its share of the Heimdal gas production to a group of European buyers, including petitioner Ruhrgas AG. The parties' agreement was incorporated into the Heimdal Gas Sales Agreement, which is "governed by and construed in accordance with Norwegian Law," and disputes thereunder are to be "exclusively and finally settled by arbitration in Stockholm, Sweden, in accordance with" International Chamber of Commerce rules.

Marathon Oil Company, Marathon International Oil Company, and Norge (collectively, Marathon) filed this lawsuit against Ruhrgas in Texas state court on July 6, 1995, asserting state law claims of fraud, tortious interference with prospective business relations, participation in breach of fiduciary duty, and civil conspiracy. Marathon asserted that Ruhrgas had furthered its plans at three meetings in Houston, Texas, and through a stream of correspondence directed to Marathon in Texas. Ruhrgas removed the case to the District Court for the Southern District of Texas. A suit

between "citizens of a State and citizens or subjects of a foreign state" lies within federal diversity jurisdiction under 28 U.S.C. § 1332(a)(2). Section 1332 has been interpreted to require "complete diversity." The foreign citizenship of defendant Ruhrgas, a German corporation, and plaintiff Norge, a Norwegian corporation, rendered diversity incomplete.

The district court dismissed the case for lack of personal jurisdiction. The district court addressed the constitutional question and concluded that Ruhrgas's contacts with Texas were insufficient to support personal jurisdiction. Finding "no evidence that Ruhrgas engaged in any tortious conduct in Texas," the court determined that Marathon's complaint did not present circumstances adequately affiliating Ruhrgas with Texas. The district court concluded that Marathon had not shown that Ruhrgas pursued the alleged pattern of fraud and misrepresentation during the Houston meetings. The court further found that Ruhrgas attended those meetings "due to the [Heimdal Agreement] with MPCN." As the Heimdal Agreement provides for arbitration in Sweden, "Ruhrgas could not have expected to be hailed into Texas courts based on these meetings." The court also determined that Ruhrgas did not have "systematic and continuous contacts with Texas" of the kind that would "subject it to general jurisdiction in Texas."

ISSUE Must a district court resolve issues of subject matter jurisdiction before issues of personal jurisdiction?

HOLDING No. There is no "hierarchy" of jurisdictional review that the court must follow in determining that the court has proper jurisdiction over the case.

REASONING Excerpts from the opinion of Justice Ginsburg:

Jurisdiction to resolve cases on the merits requires both authority over the category of claim in suit (subject-matter jurisdiction) and authority over the parties (personal jurisdiction), so that the court's decision will bind them.... We hold that in cases removed from state court to federal court, as in cases originating in federal court, there is no unyielding jurisdictional hierarchy. Customarily, a federal court first resolves doubts about its jurisdiction over the subject matter, but there are circumstances in which a district court appropriately accords priority to a personal jurisdiction inquiry. The proceeding before us is such a case....

Subject-matter limitations on federal jurisdiction serve institutional interests. They keep the federal courts within the bounds the Constitution and Congress have prescribed.... [S]ubject-matter delineations must be policed by the courts on their own initiative.... Personal jurisdiction . . . "represents a restriction on judicial power . . . as a matter of individual liberty." Therefore, a party may insist that the limitation be observed, or he may forgo that right, effectively consenting to the court's exercise of adjudicatory authority. These distinctions do not mean that subject-matter jurisdiction is ever and always the more "fundamental." Personal jurisdiction, too, is "an essential element of the jurisdiction of a district . . . court," without which the court is "powerless to proceed to an adjudication." In this case, . . . the [proposed] impediment to subject-matter jurisdiction . . . rests on statutory interpretation, not constitutional command. Marathon joined an alien plaintiff (Norge) as well as an alien defendant (Ruhrgas). If the joinder of Norge is legitimate, the complete diversity required by 28 U.S.C. § 1332 . . . is absent....

If a federal court dismisses a removed case for want of personal jurisdiction, that determination may preclude the parties from relitigating the very same personal jurisdiction issue in state court.... [O]ur "dualistic . . . system of federal and state courts" allows federal courts to make issue-preclusive rulings about state law in the exercise of supplemental jurisdiction.... Most essentially, federal and state courts are complementary systems for administering justice in our Nation. Cooperation and comity, not competition and conflict, are essential to the federal design.... If personal jurisdiction raises "difficult questions of [state] law," and subject-matter jurisdiction is resolved . . . easily . . . , a district court will ordinarily conclude that "federalism concerns tip the scales in favor of initially ruling on [subject matter jurisdiction]." . . . The federal design allows leeway for sensitive judgments of this sort.... What the concept does represent is a system in which there is sensitivity to the legitimate interests of both State and National Governments." . . .

BUSINESS CONSIDERATIONS How can a company involved in international transactions protect itself from being drawn into a lawsuit in a foreign county? Would Ruhrgas be surprised by this lawsuit in light of the arbitration agreement?

ETHICAL CONSIDERATIONS Would it be ethical for Marathon to add Norge as a plaintiff to avoid diversity of citizenship?

Specialized Courts

Congress has, from time to time, created courts of *limited* jurisdiction. At present, these courts include the claims court, the court of veteran appeals, the court of international trade, and the tax court. Congress has created *federal district courts* (trial courts in the federal court system) in every state. Each state has at least one; some states have many. Rhode Island, for example, has one district court, and Texas has four. The courts contained in each district constitute the general trial courts of the federal system. Emory Law School maintains a map of the circuits and links to recent court decisions from the 13 U.S. circuit courts of appeals and the Supreme Court at http://www.law.emory.edu/FEDCTS.

All of the district courts are grouped into circuits. Currently there are 13 circuits. Each circuit has a court of appeals, which hears appeals from the trial courts. Courts of appeals do not retry the case; rather, they review the record to determine whether the trial court made errors of law. Generally, a panel of three judges from the circuit hears appeals. Decisions of the court of appeals establish precedents for all district courts in the circuit. For the most part, the decisions of these *circuit courts of appeals* are final. In a very few cases, further appeal may be made to the U.S. Supreme Court. The circuit courts of appeals have their own Web sites, for example, the Ninth Circuit's Web site is at http://www.ce9.uscourts.gov/.

The 13 federal judicial circuits and their seats are: First: Boston, Massachusetts; Second: New York, New York; Third: Philadelphia, Pennsylvania; Fourth: Richmond, Virginia; Fifth: New Orleans, Louisiana; Sixth: Cincinnati, Ohio; Seventh: Chicago, Illinois; Eighth: St. Louis, Missouri; Ninth: San Francisco, California; Tenth: Denver, Colorado; Eleventh: Atlanta, Georgia; Twelfth: District of

EXHIBIT 4.3   The Two Grounds for Federal Jurisdiction

For Federal Jurisdiction the Case Must Involve

Either	*Or*
Federal Question	**Diversity of Citizenship**
The controlling law involves a federal statute, rule, or regulation; an issue of U.S. constitutional law; or a treaty.	Parties on one side of the controversy are citizens of a different state than the parties on the other side.
The case involves a consul or ambassador as a party.	*and*
The case involves maritime or admiralty law.	**A Minimum Amount in Controversy (Excluding Costs and Interest)**
The United States is a party to the action.	The plaintiff must sue for more than $75,000.
The case is between two or more states.	

Columbia, Washington, DC; Thirteenth: Federal Circuit, Washington, DC. For detail on the federal judicial circuits, see Exhibit 4.4.

The *Supreme Court* sits at the apex of the U.S. judicial system and it is the only court created by the Constitution. The Constitution does not specify the number of judges on the Supreme Court. It has a Chief Justice and eight Associate Justices by statute (28 U.S.C. § 1). They are nominated by the president and confirmed by the Senate, and they serve for life. All federal judges—except those appointed to serve on the specialized courts—serve for life.

As mentioned previously, certain cases may be appealed to the Supreme Court. However, the court may affirm a case routinely without permitting oral arguments or giving the case formal consideration. The court is more likely to hear a case under the following conditions:

- Whenever the highest state court declares a federal law invalid

- Whenever the highest state court validates a state law that is challenged based on a federal law

- Whenever a federal court declares a federal statute unconstitutional and the government is a party to the suit

- Whenever a federal appellate court declares a state statute invalid on the grounds that it violates federal law

- Whenever a federal three-judge panel rules in a civil case involving an equitable remedy

Certiorari, which means "to be more fully informed," is used whenever the Supreme Court desires to hear a particular case even though there is no right of appeal. It is through this technique that state court cases can be heard by the Supreme Court. When the Supreme Court decides to grant certiorari, it issues a writ of certiorari that orders the lower court to certify a record of the proceedings and send it to the Supreme Court. A minimum of four justices must agree to hear the case on certiorari. Other than that there are no hard-and-fast rules. Nevertheless, there are certain situations in which the Supreme Court is more likely to grant certiorari:

- Whenever two or more circuit courts of appeals disagree with respect to the same legal issue

- Whenever the highest state court has decided a question in such a manner that it is in conflict with prior decisions of the U.S. Supreme Court

- Whenever the highest state court has decided a question that has not yet been determined by the U.S. Supreme Court

- Whenever a circuit court of appeals has decided a state law question that appears to be in conflict with established state law

- Whenever a circuit court of appeals has decided a federal question that has not yet been decided by the U.S. Supreme Court

The Supreme Court also has original jurisdiction in a number of cases or controversies. When the Supreme Court exercises its original jurisdiction it serves as a trial court. Article III, Section 2 of the Constitution states that the Supreme Court shall have original jurisdiction "In all Cases affecting Ambassadors, other public Ministers and Consuls, and those in which a State shall be a Party."

Exhibit 4.5 describes how the federal courts are related to each other. Federal agencies are not courts. However, they often perform courtlike functions, also called *quasi-judicial* functions. They are shown in Exhibit 4.5 to illustrate the appeal "path" from the agency to the court system.

EXHIBIT 4.4   The Thirteen Federal Judicial Circuits

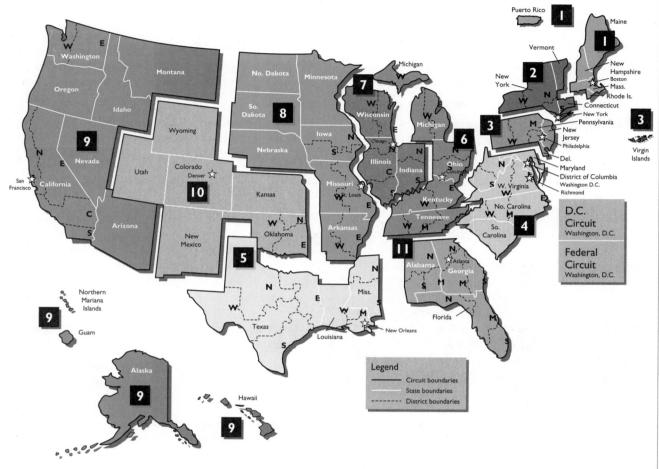

State Courts

All states have *inferior trial* courts. These may include municipal courts, juvenile courts, domestic relations courts, traffic courts, small claims courts, probate courts, and justice courts presided over by justices of the peace. (Historically, justices of the peace were not required to be lawyers. Many states have changed their rules and now require new justices of the peace to be lawyers.) For the most part, inferior trial courts are not *courts of record*—that is, there is no record or transcript made of the trial. In cases of appeals from their decisions, there is a trial de novo, "a new trial," in a court of general jurisdiction.

The more significant cases involving matters of state law originate in *courts of general jurisdiction* (courts having the judicial power to hear all matters with respect to state

law). In a few jurisdictions, two courts exist at this level. One court is charged with resolving all questions of law and the other with resolving all matters of equity. An example of a question of law is a suit seeking money damages. Most business law cases fall into this category. Equity suits, on the other hand, are those where the plaintiff is seeking a special remedy, such as an *injunction* (a writ issued by the court of equity ordering a person to do or not do a specified act), because monetary damages will not make the plaintiff "whole."

Each state has at least one *court of appeals*. It is usually called the supreme court, but there are exceptions. In New York State, for example, the "supreme court" is a court of general trial jurisdiction, whereas the Court of Appeals is the highest court in the state. Sometimes intermediate courts of appeals also exist, as in the federal system. These appellate

EXHIBIT 4.5 The Federal Judicial System

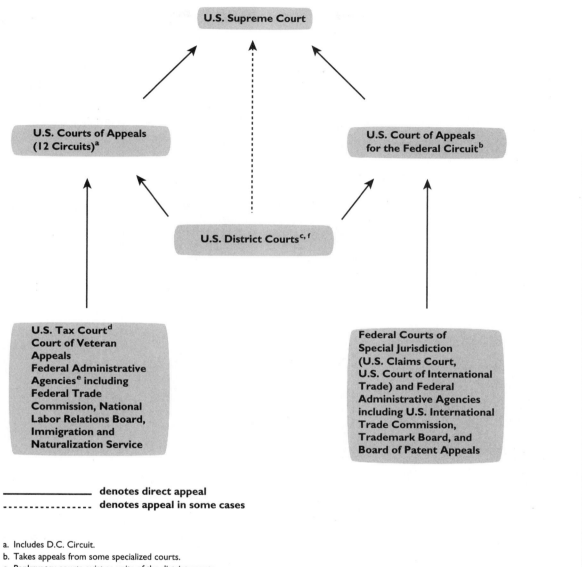

----------- denotes direct appeal
- - - - - - - - - - denotes appeal in some cases

a. Includes D.C. Circuit.
b. Takes appeals from some specialized courts.
c. Bankruptcy courts exist as units of the district courts.
d. In some cases, there is Supreme Court review.
e. Administrative agencies perform courtlike functions; however, they are *not* courts.
f. Appeals from some federal agencies go to the U.S. District Courts.

courts review the trial court record to determine whether the lower court made any errors of law. Appellate courts do not usually review decisions of facts made by the lower court. Trials de novo are exceptions to this general rule.

An example of a case history is *Bennis v. Michigan*. It was originally decided by the Wayne County Circuit Court, then appealed (in this order) to the Michigan Court of Appeals, the Michigan Supreme Court, and then the U.S. Supreme Court.[22]

Exhibit 4.6 describes a typical state system and its interrelationship with the federal system. State agencies, like federal agencies, are not courts; a person can appeal an unfavorable agency decision to the intermediate court of appeals in most states.

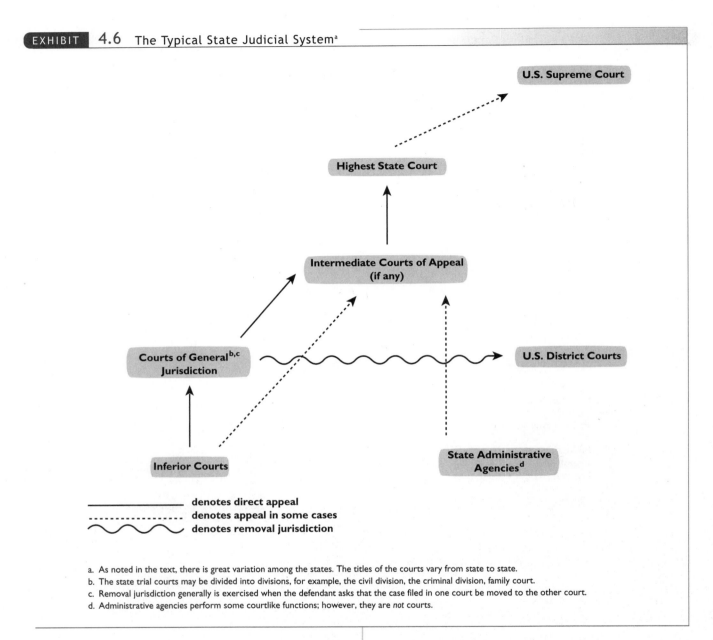

EXHIBIT   4.6   The Typical State Judicial System[a]

a. As noted in the text, there is great variation among the states. The titles of the courts vary from state to state.
b. The state trial courts may be divided into divisions, for example, the civil division, the criminal division, family court.
c. Removal jurisdiction generally is exercised when the defendant asks that the case filed in one court be moved to the other court.
d. Administrative agencies perform some courtlike functions; however, they are *not* courts.

How to Find the Law

We have already referred to some legal cases in this and previous chapters. Other cases will be cited in succeeding chapters. If you want to go to the library and read these or other cases in their entirety, you will need to know how to find the law.

Federal Court Cases

If you are looking for the case of *Mitsubishi Motors Corporation v. Soler Chrysler-Plymouth, Inc.,* 473 U.S. 614, 87 L.

Ed. 2d 444, 105 S. Ct. 3346 (1985), for example, you will find it in any of three different sources. First, the U.S. Government Printing Office publishes the official *United States Reports.* The case will be found on page 614 of volume 473. Alternatively, you can find the case on page 444 of volume 87 of *Lawyer's Edition, Second,* published by the Lawyers Cooperative Publishing Company. Finally, you can find the case in volume 105 of the *Supreme Court Reporter,* which is published by West Publishing Company, at page 3346.

All reported cases decided by the circuit courts of appeals are found in the *Federal Reporter.* If you are looking for the case of *Johnson Controls v. United Association of*

Journeymen, you will find it at 39 F.3d 821 (7th Cir. 1994). In other words, go to volume 39 of the *Federal Reporter, Third Series,* and turn to page 821. The *(7th Cir. 1994)* means the case was decided by the Seventh Circuit Court of Appeals, which sits in Chicago, and hears cases from district courts in Illinois, Indiana, and Wisconsin. The case was decided in 1994.

U.S. district court cases are found in the *Federal Supplement Series.* If you are looking for the case of *Hoeflich v. William S. Merrell Co.,* you will find it at 288 F. Supp. 659 (E.D. Pa. 1968). Following the established format for legal references, look for volume 288 of the *Federal Supplement;* the case will be found on page 659. The *(E.D. Pa. 1968)* means the case was decided in the U.S. District Court for the Eastern District of Pennsylvania in 1968.

State Court Cases

The National Reporter System is published by West Publishing Company and includes the *Supreme Court Reporter,* the *Federal Reporter,* the *Federal Supplement, Federal Rules Decisions,* and the *Bankruptcy Reporter.* The reporter system also contains seven regional reporters for state cases. They are as follows:

1. *Atlantic Reporter*—Connecticut, Delaware, Maine, Maryland, New Hampshire, New Jersey, Pennsylvania, Rhode Island, Vermont, and the District of Columbia Municipal Court of Appeals

2. *Northeastern Reporter*—Illinois, Indiana, Massachusetts, New York, and Ohio

3. *Northwestern Reporter*—Iowa, Michigan, Minnesota, Nebraska, North Dakota, South Dakota, and Wisconsin

4. *Pacific Reporter*—Alaska, Arizona, California, Colorado, Hawaii, Idaho, Kansas, Montana, Nevada, New Mexico, Oklahoma, Oregon, Utah, Washington, and Wyoming

5. *Southeastern Reporter*—Georgia, North Carolina, South Carolina, Virginia, and West Virginia

6. *Southwestern Reporter*—Arkansas, Kentucky, Missouri, Tennessee, and Texas

7. *Southern Reporter*—Alabama, Florida, Louisiana, and Mississippi

These reporters contain most of the reported cases at the state supreme court and appellate court levels. Some significant trial court decisions are also included. Decisions of inferior courts are not included. The National Reporter System also includes the *Military Justice Reporter* and separate state reporters such as the *New York Supplement,* the *California Reporter,* and *Illinois Decisions.*

States generally also have their own system for publishing cases independent of the National Reporter System.

Computerized Legal Research

Legal research has entered the computer age. Two systems devoted to legal research are available—Lexis (part of LexisNexis) and Westlaw. The techniques are similar although the particular computer commands vary. Both systems allow you to indicate what material you wish to search and to enter key words for search terms. If your search terms are not appropriate or are too broad, you may not locate the desired material. Historical cases may not have been added to the data banks, but recent cases and articles generally are available. Manuals and handbooks specify which material can be retrieved from the system, including the years that are in the database.

There are also a number of sites on the World Wide Web that contain articles on statutory law, court cases, and government activity. A few of these sites are highlighted throughout each chapter. Web sites can be established without much restriction on the creator or on content. Some of the sites change addresses or stop operating. Consequently, the Web addresses may become dated. If you have a link that is outdated and no longer connects to the article or case indicated, return to the root Web site and begin your search from that point. Search engines like Google can also be used to locate legal material. When conducting research on the Web, also remember that the information may not be reliable.

Summary

The federal Constitution is unique because it created the doctrine of separation of powers. As a result, our government is divided into three distinct branches: legislative, executive, and judicial. There is also an unofficial "fourth branch" of government, administrative agencies.

Judicial power has limits. For example, courts cannot issue advisory opinions or decide moot cases or political questions. In all cases, the plaintiff must have standing to sue. The doctrine of judicial review was created by Chief Justice John Marshall in the landmark case of *Marbury v.*

Madison. The doctrine represents an expansion of judicial power, because it allows the Supreme Court to determine whether a statute passed by Congress is in compliance with the Constitution or whether the executive branch has acted in accordance with the Constitution.

Our court system is based on the concept of jurisdiction. Jurisdiction means the legal power to decide a case. It can be divided into subject matter jurisdiction, jurisdiction over the dollar amount (which is often considered an aspect of subject matter jurisdiction), and jurisdiction over the persons or property. There are basically three techniques for obtaining jurisdiction over the persons or property—in personam, in rem, and quasi in rem. The type of jurisdiction will affect the type of judgment the court can award.

Jurisdiction can be concurrent, in which more than one court can hear and decide a case, or it may be exclusive, in which only one court can hear the matter. A federal district court's jurisdiction is based on either federal question or diversity of citizenship jurisdiction. In all diversity cases, the jurisdictional amount of over $75,000 must be met. Complete diversity is also required. The federal court system includes specialized courts, district courts, appellate courts, and the Supreme Court.

Discussion Questions

1. Why is the U.S. Constitution considered unique?

2. Where is the constitutional protection of habeas corpus found? What does the term mean?

3. Why is the identity of the individual Supreme Court justices important?

4. What is meant by the term jurisdiction?

5. Describe long-arm statutes. Do they serve a legitimate state purpose? Do they make it easier to sue businesses? Do they make it easier for businesses to file suit?

6. Why do some states have only one court of general jurisdiction, whereas others have two?

7. What are the advantages and disadvantages of specialized courts, such as tax court or family court?

8. The highest court in a state determines that a state law violates the federal Constitution. Can the U.S. Supreme Court review that decision, or is the decision of the state court final?

9. Go to the nearest law library, or Westlaw or Lexis terminal, and determine who were the attorneys for the appellees in *Porsche Cars North America, Inc. v. Porsche.net*, 302 F.3d 248, 2002 U.S. App. LEXIS 17531 (4th Cir. 2002).

10. In light of the attack on 9/11/01 and the recent wave of patriotism, an employer is considering beginning the workday with the pledge of allegiance to the U.S. flag. While most of the managers are in favor of this approach, a few of them are concerned that it might infringe on the rights of some of their employees or cause some employees to feel uncomfortable. What should the employer do and why? Would your answer be different if the plant or office was located outside of the United States? Why?

Case Problems and Writing Assignments

1. International Shoe Co. was a Delaware corporation, having its principal place of business in St. Louis, Missouri. The state of Washington sued International Shoe because it wanted International Shoe to contribute to the state's unemployment compensation fund. International Shoe had no office, manufacturing plant, or warehouse in Washington. International Shoe had local sales representatives in Washington who created a large volume of business. The sales representatives exhibited their samples and solicited orders from customers. The orders were transmitted to the office in St. Louis where the company either rejected or accepted the order. Was there sufficient contact between International Shoe and the state to justify jurisdiction or would it offend traditional notions of fair play and substantial justice? [See *International Shoe Co. v. Washington*, 326 U.S. 310, 66 S. Ct. 154 (1945).]

2. A Republican Senate candidate, Michael Huffington, alleged that 17 deceased citizens "voted" in Fresno County in the 1994 election. Les Kimber, an ousted Fresno city council member, also charged that campaign workers for his opponent, Dan Ronquillo, used voter fraud. In one incident, election materials indicate D. Eddie Ronquillo, Dan Ronquillo's son, registered a 2-year-old boy and his 17-year-old mother. Absentee ballots were requested for these two minors. The absentee ballot requests indicated at the bottom "Paid for by the friends of Dan Ronquillo." (These two individuals did not vote, and the absentee ballots were discarded.) The mother contended that she never registered to vote. Norma Logan, Fresno County elections manager, said that part of the problem was allowing political groups to pay a bounty for registering voters or getting the voters to use absentee ballots. She contended that it was an incentive for some people to file fraudulent documents. Norma would like California to ban bounty payments. Consider the practice of paying a bounty for registering voters. What is the likely consequence of this practice? When bounties are paid in business situations, what are they called? What sometimes happens in businesses when "bounties" are offered

to workers? Analyze the ethics of individuals registering people who are not eligible to vote (for example, minors and people who are deceased). Is whether the individuals are motivated by the bounty, or by political reasons, relevant? [See Jim Boren and Angela Valdivia, "Kimber Lawsuit Against Ronquillo Alleges Voter Fraud," *The Fresno Bee*, December 29, 1994, pp. A1 and A12; and Jim Boren, "Huffington Says 17 Who Voted Were Dead," *The Fresno Bee*, January 5, 1995, pp. A1 and A14.]

3. Zachary Hood attended a first-grade class in a public school in Medford, New Jersey. As a reward, his teacher told Zachary that he could read a story of his choice to the class. He selected one of his favorites, the biblical tale of Jacob and Esau. His teacher decided that a Bible story would not be appropriate and would not allow Zachary to read his story out loud. The version that Zachary wanted to read does not mention God or the Bible. It is simply the story of two brothers who quarrel and then resolve their differences. The other students in the class were permitted to read the stories they chose. "[T]he case underscores the enduring tension between a teacher's right to supervise assignments and a student's right to express individual initiative." The teacher would have allowed Zachary to read the story to her privately. His parents wanted the story read aloud to the class. Eric Treene, an attorney with the Becket Fund for Religious Liberty, is representing the Hoods before the appellate court. He argues, "The government requires the school to be neutral to religion and this is being hostile to religion." How should the school respond? Why? [See Marjorie Coeyman, "First-grader Tests Ban on Religion in Class," *Christian Science Monitor*, June 15, 1999, p. 1.]

4. Michael Newdow had alleged in the district court suit involving the Pledge of Allegiance (Case 4.1 in this chapter) that he was the father and had custody of the minor child. No legal custody question or order was disclosed to the federal courts at that time. In fact, Newdow and Sandra Banning formed a family consisting of an unmarried man, an unmarried woman, and their biological minor child. They lived together part of the time and lived in separate homes in Florida and California from time to time, with informal visiting arrangements. This informal arrangement apparently was not subject to any custody order until February 6, 2002, after Newdow had appealed his case on the Pledge of Allegiance in his daughter's public elementary school. On February 6, the California Superior Court entered an order containing the following language:

The child's mother, Ms. Banning, to have sole legal custody as to the rights and responsibilities to make decisions relating to the health, education and welfare of [the child]. Specifically, both parents shall consult with one another on substantial decisions relating to non-emergency major medical care, dental, optometry, psychological and educational needs of [the child]. If mutual agreement is not reached in the above, then Ms. Banning may exercise legal control of [the child] that is not specifically prohibited or inconsistent with the physical custody order. The father shall have access to all of [the child's] school and medical records.

(Newdow filed a motion in the California Superior Court for a modification of the custody order, seeking joint legal custody of their child.) Does the grant of sole legal custody to Banning deprive Newdow, as a noncustodial parent, of Article III standing to object to unconstitutional government action affecting his child? [See *Newdow v. U.S. Congress*, 313 F. 3d 500, 2002 U.S. App. LEXIS 24513 (9th Cir. 2002).]

5. BUSINESS APPLICATION CASE On January 26, 1996, Michetti Pipe Stringing, Inc. (Michetti), filed a complaint in Alabama state court seeking damages for an alleged breach of contract and fraud by Murphy Bros., Inc. (Murphy). Michetti did not serve Murphy at that time, but three days later it faxed a "courtesy copy" of the file-stamped complaint to one of Murphy's vice-presidents. The parties then engaged in settlement discussions until February 12, 1996, when Michetti officially served Murphy under local law by certified mail. On March 13, 1996 (30 days after service but 44 days after receiving the faxed copy of the complaint), Murphy asked to have the case moved to the U.S. District Court for the Northern District of Alabama under 28 U.S.C. § 1441. (This is called removal.) Murphy invoked the jurisdiction of the federal district court based on diversity of citizenship. Michetti is a Canadian company with its principal place of business in Alberta, Canada; Murphy is an Illinois corporation with its principal place of business in that state. Michetti moved to return the case to the state court, asserting that the removal was untimely under 28 U.S.C. § 1446(b), which provides:

The notice of removal of a civil action or proceeding shall be filed within thirty days after the receipt by the defendant, through service or otherwise, of a copy of the initial pleading setting forth the claim for relief upon which such action or proceeding is based, or within thirty days after the service of summons upon the defendant if such initial pleading has then been filed in court and is not required to be served on the defendant, whichever period is shorter.

What action starts the removal period—delivering the faxed copy or the official process? [See *Murphy Brothers, Inc. v. Michetti Pipe Stringing, Inc.*, 119 S. Ct. 1322, 1999 U.S. LEXIS 2346 (1999).]

6. ETHICAL APPLICATION CASE The Pasadena Crematorium and other funeral service companies allegedly sold human body parts and organs to a biological supply company. The body parts were allegedly removed without permission from the decedents being prepared for cremations or funerals. In the class action lawsuit, the plaintiffs were suing for negligent infliction of emotional distress. The plaintiffs were relatives and friends of the deceased persons. Who has standing to sue in this situation? Would the alleged behavior of the crematorium and funeral homes be ethical? Why or why not? [See *Christensen v. Pasadena Crematorium of Altadena*, 2 Cal. Rptr. 2d 79 (1991).]

7. CRITICAL THINKING CASE The Census Bureau announced a plan to use two forms of statistical sampling in the 2000 decennial census to address a chronic and growing problem of

"undercounting" certain identifiable groups of individuals. Two sets of plaintiffs filed separate suits challenging the legality and constitutionality of the Bureau's plan and the court consolidated the cases. For the last few decades, the Census Bureau has sent census forms to every household, asking residents to complete and return them. The Bureau followed up by sending enumerators to personally visit all households that did not respond by mail. Despite this comprehensive effort, the Bureau has always failed to reach a portion of the population. This shortfall has been labeled the census "undercount." Some identifiable groups—including certain minorities, children, and renters—have historically had substantially higher undercount rates than the population as a whole. The Bureau formulated a plan for the 2000 census that used statistical sampling to supplement data obtained through traditional census methods. Congress passed the 1998 Departments of Commerce, Justice, and State, the Judiciary, and Related Agencies Appropriations Act, which provides that the Bureau's Census 2000 Operational Plan "shall be deemed to constitute final agency action regarding the use of statistical methods in the 2000 decennial census." The act also permits any person aggrieved by the plan for using statistical sampling in the decennial census to bring a legal action in the trial court. It further provides for review by appeal directly to the Supreme Court. The publication of the Bureau's plan for the 2000 census occasioned two separate legal challenges. The first suit was filed by four counties and residents of 13 states who claimed that the Bureau's planned use of statistical sampling to apportion representatives among the states violates the Census Act and the census clause of the Constitution. The U.S. House of Representatives filed the second challenge. Did the counties, individuals, and the House of Representatives have standing to sue the Census Bureau under Article III of the Constitution? [See *Department of Commerce, et al. v. United States House of Representatives et al.;* and *Clinton et al. v. Glavin et al.,* 119 S. Ct. 765, 1999 U.S. LEXIS 902 (1999).]

8. YOU BE THE JUDGE Bob Herbert, a columnist for the *New York Times,* wrote two tough articles accusing Nike Corporation of cruelly exploiting cheap Asian labor. Nike CEO Philip Knight replied in a letter to the editor, which the *Times* published. According to Knight's letter, "Nike has paid, on average, double the minimum wages as defined in countries where its products are produced under contract." He also stated that Nike contractors provide "free" meals and health care; others report that they typically provide only subsidies. (Nike is headquartered in Beaverton, Oregon.) Marc Kasky, a community activist, sued, claiming that Knight's letter was false advertising and violated California law. He also alleged that Nike made numerous false statements about its hiring practices in Asia. This contention was based on a comparison between statements made by Nike representatives and statements by impartial parties. In May 2002, the California Supreme Court, in a 4-3 opinion, ruled that Knight's rebuttal was commercial speech, which enjoys less constitutional protection than regular speech and is more closely regulated by the government. Assume that you are on the U.S. Supreme Court, and this case has been appealed to *you.* How would *you* rule and why? [See Roger Parloff, "Can We Talk?" *Fortune* (September 2, 2002): 102–110.]

Notes

1. 1 Cranch 137, 2 L. Ed. 60 (1803).
2. *Aetna Life Ins. Co. v. Haworth,* 300 U.S. 227, 240 and 241 (1937).
3. *Black's Law Dictionary,* 6th ed. (St. Paul, Minn.: West, 1990), 54.
4. Ibid., 1008.
5. Ibid., 1045.
6. Ibid., 1158.
7. 416 U.S. 312 (1974).
8. 1 Cranch 137, 2 L. Ed. 60 (1803).
9. Sheila M. Smith, "Comment: Justice Ruth Bader Ginsburg and Sexual Harassment Law: Will the Second Female Supreme Court Justice Become the Court's Women's Right Champion?" 63 *U. Cin. L. Rev.* 1893, Summer 1995.
10. Lawrence Hammack, "Supreme Court Takes Closer Look at Virginia Ban on Cross Burning," *Roanoke Times,* December 12, 2002, p. 4.
11. *Ortiz v. Fibreboard Corporation,* 1999 U.S. LEXIS 4373 (1999).
12. *Black's Law Dictionary,* 7th ed. (St. Paul, Minn.: West, 1999), 715–716.
13. Ibid., 601.
14. Ibid., 601.
15. *Newdow v. United States Congress.,* 2002 U.S. App. LEXIS 12826 (9th Cir. 2002). On February 28, 2003 while this text was in production, the Ninth Circuit rejected the Bush administration's request to reconsider its decision in the Newdow case. [See *Newdow v. U.S. Congress,* 2003 U.S. App. LEXIS 3665.] The court refused to hear the case en banc. The majority reaffirmed its opinion that it is unconstitutional to have school children participate in the pledge of allegiance. The court withdrew the opinion in Case 4.1 and issued a revised opinion.
16. 326 U.S. 310 (1945).
17. Tex. Civ. Prac. & Rem. Code Ann. § 17.042 (1997).
18. 952 F. Supp. 1119 (W.D. Pa. 1997).
19. Ibid., 1122–23.
20. Ibid., 1124.
21. 15 U.S.C. § 1125 et. seq.

Constitutional Regulation of Business

AGENDA

NRW In its various activities, NRW probably will face fairly substantial regulation at both the state and the federal level. The firm will want to know *why* the government is able to regulate its efforts and *how* these regulations will affect it. Given its use, the production of the StuffTrakR may raise some privacy questions. If the government does increase its regulation of the product, several due process issues may result from this heightened regulation of a particular industry. Most of this potential governmental oversight will subject the firm to administrative regulation as well.

These and other issues are likely to arise during your study of this chapter. Be prepared! You never know when the firm or one of its members will seek your advice.

Historical Perspective

In the United States today, government heavily regulates business. Local regulations tell a company where it may conduct business. State regulations cover the sale of securities, loan rates, and highway weight limits. Federal regulations address pollution, the safety of employees, consumer protection, and labor negotiations. And these represent only a few of the regulations that a business faces.

Pervasive governmental regulation of business, however, has not always been the case. As is often mentioned in American history texts, the United States was built on a *laissez faire* economy that reflected the belief that business operates best when uninhibited by the government. Business owners ran business and politicians ran government, and the two groups left each other alone. Buyers often were ignored, with *caveat emptor* ("let the buyer beware") being the rule of the land. Workers remained virtually unprotected: If they did not like their jobs, they could quit. If they did not go to work, they were fired. If they joined a union, they also were fired—and they quite often faced criminal conspiracy charges as well.

The 19th century was a great time to be an American entrepreneur, especially a wealthy one. These easy times came to an end, however, when the general populace viewed too many "captains of industry" as "robber barons." Many people moreover resented the abuse and mistreatment workers suffered. And, given the lack of land remaining for westward migration, people increasingly clamored for reform. Present-day governmental regulation emerged from these tumultuous times.

Should Government Regulate Business?

Over the last few decades, people have been asking, "Should government regulate business?" The answer is either *yes* or *no*, depending on which type of business is at issue, what type of regulation is being discussed, and which level of government is involved. The answer also depends to some degree on whether the business consists of international trade, domestic trade, or regional/local trade. In general, such a question consists of a number of factors, and the answers may vary over time as the circumstances of the business change.

History shows that society needs some regulation—or intervention—by government. Governmental regulation typically takes two forms: social regulation (concern for such issues as workplace safety, equal opportunity, environmental protection, and consumer protection) and economic regulation (the behavior of firms, especially the

firms' effects on prices, production, industry conditions for entry or exit, and so on). In 2000, there were 2,708,101 people working in federal agencies.[1] Obviously, had they not been working in the federal bureaucracy, presumably they could have worked at jobs producing other goods and services. Clearly, then, one must compare the costs of regulation—in terms of administration, compliance, and efficiency—with its perceived benefits.

Many people today believe this balance has tipped too far and has resulted in the overregulation of business. Indeed, the pervasiveness of the government's reach over business activities has led to cries for deregulation and a lessening of this glut of laws. Given the complexities of business at the advent of the 21st century, however, no one realistically believes that these laws will magically disappear.

Business's "social contract" requires that it pay heed to the various social and economic issues mentioned above. Somewhere between the extremes of overregulation and underregulation, a happy medium must exist so as to maximize the well-being of business, society, and government. Yet, as we learned in the preceding chapters, in the absence of this balance, laws can become so burdensome on individuals that they may violate the rights guaranteed to individuals by the Constitution. Since the law in many instances views firms as legal, or *juristic*, persons, businesses also can assert various constitutional rights and thus curb what they view as excessive governmental regulation. Hence, just as the Constitution stands as the guardian of individual rights, it in addition represents a significant weapon for businesses to use when they challenge the laws and regulations that affect them.

The Commerce Clause

Perhaps the single most important constitutional provision that affects business is the commerce clause. Article I, Section 8 of the Constitution states that Congress shall have the power "to regulate Commerce with foreign Nations, and among the several States, and with the Indian Tribes." In addition, Article I, Section 8 gives Congress the power to levy taxes. The interplay between these two powers forms the basis for much of the federal government's regulation of business.

The history of the commerce clause has been checkered. The Supreme Court initially had interpreted the clause, next expanded these interpretations, later contracted these interpretations, and then expanded them again. In 1824, the Supreme Court had its first occasion to interpret the commerce clause. Chief Justice Marshall's opinion in *Gibbons v. Ogden* defined commerce as "the commercial intercourse between nations, in all its branches . . . regulated by prescribing rules for carrying on that intercourse."[2] Marshall further noted that the federal government can regulate commerce that *affects* other states, even if that commerce is local in nature.

As a result of this interpretation, for nearly three-quarters of a century, federal power to regulate business was broad. The Interstate Commerce Act of 1887 permitted the Interstate Commerce Commission (ICC) to regulate local railroad rates and local railroad safety because such issues directly affected interstate rates and safety.[3] The federal government also could regulate local grain and live-stock exchanges because they, too, involved transactions that affected the rest of the nation.

Not all the court opinions of the period favored regula-tion by the federal government, however. In the 1873 Supreme Court decision *In re State Freight Tax*, the Court stated that in the commerce clause *among* meant *between*.[4] As a result, this opinion held that the federal government could regulate only interstate commerce (that is, between two or more states; between a point in one state and a point in another state). By limiting the definition of commerce, the Court similarly contracted the federal power to regulate business. In its 1888 *Kidd v. Pearson* decision, the Court ruled that commerce meant transportation.[5] As a result of these two opinions, federal regulation of business suddenly became restricted to actual interstate transportation and did not reach business deals that affected interstate business but that were conducted entirely in one state. Such transactions, defined as intrastate (that is, begun, carried on, and com-pleted wholly within the boundaries of a single state), there-fore remained beyond the scope of federal regulation.

This new, restricted definition of interstate commerce underlay the passage of the Sherman Act in 1890 (see Chapter 37 for a detailed treatment of this act). Indeed, this new defi-nition of the federal authority to regulate business led the Court to narrower interpretations and, consequently, the Court's invalidation of many subsequent federal enactments.

A shift in the Court's restrictive view of the exercise of federal power did not occur until 1937. In *NLRB v. Jones & Laughlin Steel Corp.*, which overturned 50 years of narrow interpretation, Chief Justice Hughes said:

When industries organize themselves on a national scale, making their relation to interstate commerce the dominant factor in their activities, how can it be main-tained that their industrial relations constitute a for-bidden field into which Congress may not enter when it is necessary to protect interstate commerce from the par-alyzing consequences of industrial war?[6]

Thus, the Court had come full circle. As Justice Jackson noted in *United States v. Women's Sportswear Manufacturers Association*, a 1949 case involving a Sherman Act challenge

to a local price-fixing arrangement, "If it is interstate com-merce that feels the pinch, it does not matter how local the operation which applies the squeeze."[7] In upholding the right of the federal government to regulate the conduct in dispute, Justice Jackson provided us with both a pictur-esque definition of interstate commerce and the one most courts presently would accept as controlling.

This expansive definition of the reach of the federal government under the commerce clause also provided the federal government with a vehicle for ridding society of dis-crimination and bigotry, as the *Heart of Atlanta Motel, Inc. v. United States*[8] decision demonstrates. The Heart of Atlanta Motel had a policy of refusing service to blacks. The federal government challenged this policy as a violation of Title II of the Civil Rights Act of 1964, which prohibits discrimination based on race, religion, or national origin by those who offer public accommodations. The government claimed that the motel was involved in interstate commerce and that federal intervention therefore was justifiable. The motel argued that it was a purely intrastate business and hence exempt from federal regulation under Title II. The Supreme Court held that because of its provision of services to interstate travelers, the motel was involved in interstate commerce. In reaching its decision, the Court focused on the following facts: (1) The motel was readily accessible from two interstate highways; (2) it also advertised in national magazines and placed bill-boards on federal highways; and (3) approximately 75 per-cent of its guests came from outside the state of Georgia. In the Court's view, allowing such discrimination would dis-courage travel by the black community. Furthermore, the motel was set up to serve interstate travelers; it drew much of its business from interstate travelers; and it was involved in interstate commerce. Hence, the Court concluded that Title II gave the government authority to prohibit Heart of Atlanta Motel's discriminatory practice of renting rooms only to white people.

The myriad current state and federal laws have rele-gated this function of the commerce clause largely to a legal artifact. Nevertheless, you should remain mindful of the significance of the commerce clause largely in this histor-ical context and its continuing importance as the jurisdic-tional basis for many federal regulatory schemes.

Exclusive Federal Power

Early on, court constructions viewed three areas as exclusive enclaves of federal regulation: commerce with foreign nations, commercial activities involving Indian tribes (that is, Native Americans), and commerce between the states (that is, interstate commerce). Courts generally have recognized that Congress enjoys plenary (that is, full, complete, absolute) power over foreign commerce or trade.

For instance, the state of Washington does not have the authority to sign a treaty regulating tuna-fishing rights with Japan or Canada; only Congress has such power.

Similarly, owing to the unique status that Native Americans have occupied in U.S. history, only Congress has the power to regulate such commerce. Congress's plenary power in this area stems from the quasi-sovereign status that historically has been accorded to Native American tribes. As such, Native American tribes have virtually complete control over their own reservations and land; the states have little say over reservation affairs. Federal law generally preempts even state or local regulation of off-reservation activities.

As we noted earlier, the phrase "among the several states" has spawned a great deal of litigation concerning when federal power over interstate commerce is plenary. Precedents over the years have established two such areas: (1) Congress's power to regulate the channels and facilities of interstate commerce and (2) Congress's power to regulate activities that originate in a single state but have a national economic effect. Under this first prong, Congress can regulate interstate carriers, roads, television and radio stations, and so on. Congress also has the power to exclude from such interstate channels or facilities the goods, persons, or services designated by Congress as harmful to interstate commerce. Congress, then, under this federal police power, can stop the interstate shipment of stolen vehicles, diseased animals, spoiled meat, fungi-ridden fruit, or defective products. Businesses so affected can do little to challenge this exercise of federal power. Besides the channels or facilities of interstate commerce, Congress has plenary power to regulate all commerce or activity that affects more than one state. Note that even intrastate commerce may be subject to such federal control if the intrastate activity has a "substantial effect" on interstate commerce or if Congress rationally could conclude that the activity in question affects interstate commerce.

As the *Heart of Atlanta Motel* case indicates, it takes very little commercial activity to trigger the application of this federal power over commerce. To illustrate, in *Burbank v. Lockheed Air Terminal, Inc.*, the Supreme Court struck down a local ordinance that prohibited jet airplane takeoffs during specified hours (11:00 P.M. to 7:00 A.M. local time).[9] The Court invalidated this ordinance because of the need for national uniformity in airplane flight patterns (having this airport "off limits" for several hours could create clogs in air traffic) and because federal law, in the form of agencies concerned with aeronautical and environmental matters, preempted such local or state initiatives.

Clearly, though, this federal power is not boundless. For example, in *U.S. v. Lopez*, the Supreme Court invalidated a federal law that had made it a federal criminal offense for anyone to possess a firearm in a school zone.[10] The Court held that the act exceeds Congress's authority under the commerce clause. Why? The possession of a gun in a local school zone in no sense constitutes an economic activity that might, through repetition elsewhere, have a substantial effect on interstate commerce. The advocates of the law argued that possession of firearms in a school zone could lead to violent crime, which, in turn, would hurt the national economy by (1) increasing the costs associated with violent crime, (2) reducing people's willingness to travel to areas they deem unsafe, and (3) threatening the learning environment, which would lead to poorly educated citizens. The Court, however, concluded that this argument demonstrated too tenuous a nexus to interstate commerce for the Court to sustain the law. Although not a business case, this decision may affect business in the future; the decision seems to cut back on 60 years of Supreme Court precedents that had shown broad deference to congressional authority to regulate activities that arguably affect interstate commerce.

Concurrent State Power

In our interdependent domestic economy, virtually all businesses vie for market shares with similar firms in other states. Consequently, Congress's sweeping power to regulate commerce seems practically absolute.

Yet the states enjoy concurrent power with the federal government to regulate commerce within the state. Just as the federal government wishes to promote the welfare of its citizens, so does each state. Hence, state regulation of economic matters is permissible as long as the regulation in question passes muster under a so-called balancing test that compares the burdens on interstate commerce caused by the regulation and the importance of the state interest that underlies the regulation.

Therefore, courts generally uphold valid state initiatives in furtherance of local health and safety measures that do not purport merely to protect local economic interests. For example, state regulation of milk products that involves testing or certification of the milk will survive a legal challenge based on the commerce clause unless the state discriminates in favor of in-state producers (that is, "local yokels") to the detriment of out-of-state producers or unless the costs of compliance, when compared with the putative benefits of the law, impose an unreasonable or undue burden on interstate commerce. In the absence of discrimination against out-of-state firms or the imposition of an undue burden, the states have concurrent power to regulate commerce.

The state's concurrent power to regulate commerce ceases, however, if the state regulation conflicts with federal law. As you may remember, the supremacy clause of Article VI of the Constitution invalidates such state legislation. If Congress expressly prohibits state regulation in a given area or if federal law impliedly preempts the regulatory area, federal law supersedes the state's power to regulate as well.

State powers of taxation can pose special problems under the commerce clause because the states' legitimate interest in increasing their revenues by taxing business entities may burden interstate commerce. As we will see later, such discriminatory taxes, in addition to violating the commerce clause, may pose due process and equal protection problems, too. Although Congress, pursuant to the commerce clause, can authorize or prohibit state taxation that affects interstate commerce, in the absence of such federal legislation the states can tax corporations and other business entities.

State tax laws that single out—that is, discriminate against—interstate commerce usually violate the commerce clause. Nondiscriminatory taxation schemes that impose the same type of tax on local business and on interstate entities require courts to employ a "balancing" test in which they weigh the state's need for additional revenue against the burden imposed on interstate commerce by such taxes. Although interstate commerce is not immune from paying state taxes, such businesses need pay only their fair share; taxation that amounts to undue burdens, unfair discrimination, or multiple taxation generally does not survive challenges brought under the commerce clause (and perhaps not under the due process clause, either).

A state tax that is legal under the commerce clause must be applied to an activity that has a substantial *nexus* (or connection) with the taxing state; must be fairly apportioned; must not discriminate against interstate commerce; and must be fairly related to the services provided by the state. Many courts then look at whether certain *minimum contacts* exist between the person, entity, or transaction taxed and the state levying the tax. If such state *jurisdiction* seems lacking, a violation of due process may have occurred.

Most of the precedents in this area involve state legislative schemes that tax goods shipped in interstate commerce; taxes imposed on firms doing business in a given state; and highway, airport, sales, and use taxes. As a businessperson, you therefore should recognize the possible legal issues in such state tax laws.

Exclusive State Power

The state's plenary power to regulate commerce covers purely local activities that only remotely affect other states. Given the interdependent nature of our economy and the Supreme Court precedents we have discussed, the instances in which a state has exclusive power over commerce remain comparatively rare. Exhibit 5.1 provides a useful framework for understanding the analysis courts employ during

---

EXHIBIT 5.1 Commerce Clause Analysis

I. Areas of Exclusive Federal Regulation

  A. Commerce with foreign nations

  B. Commerce involving Indian tribes (i.e., Native Americans)

  C. Commerce involving the channels and facilities of interstate commerce

  D. Commerce that is interstate in nature or that originates in a single state but that has a "substantial effect" on interstate commerce

  E. Commerce where Congress has prohibited state regulation or where federal law impliedly preempts the regulatory area

II. Areas of Concurrent Federal and State Regulation

  A. "Balancing" test employed: the burdens on interstate commerce compared to the importance of the state interest underlying the state regulation

  B. State initiatives in furtherance of the state's "police power" (i.e., the promotion of the general welfare of the state's citizens) generally permissible unless:

   1. The state regulation imposes an undue, or unreasonable, burden on interstate commerce

   2. The state regulation discriminates in favor of in-state firms and against out-of-state firms

   3. The state regulation conflicts with federal law and thus is invalidated by the supremacy clause

III. Areas of Exclusive State Regulation

  A. Purely local activities with remote effects on other states' commerce

their disposition of a challenge based on the commerce clause.

In the following case a person found liable under a California state law challenged the validity of the law, claiming that it interfered with interstate commerce in contravention of the commerce clause. Using the foregoing principles, analyze the court's opinion and decide whether you agree with the court's decision.

"Spam," or the mass mailing of unsolicited commercial e-mail (UCE) for the purpose of facilitating the advertising of various products and services, represents an aspect of e-commerce that has triggered both state and private action. For instance, several states have passed statutes banning spamming. Echoing the result in the *Friendfinders* case, at least one—Washington—has held that the state's "anti-spam" legislation is constitutionally valid under the commerce clause. But the practice of spamming raises other issues as well. Because recipients often view spam as a nuisance and because spamming can put such stress on Internet Service Providers (ISPs) that their systems may

5.1

FERGUSON v. FRIENDFINDERS, INC.
115 Cal. Rptr. 2d 258 (2002)

FACTS Mark Ferguson sued Friendfinders, Inc. for violating California law by sending him unsolicited e-mail advertisements that were allegedly deceptive and misleading. Section 17538.4 of the California Business and Professions Code regulates conduct by persons or entities doing business in California who transmit unsolicited advertising materials. Section 17538.4, which originally applied only to faxed documents, was amended in 1998 to extend to e-mail. The statute defines "unsolicited e-mail documents" as "any e-mailed document or documents consisting of advertising material[s] . . . when the documents (a) are addressed to recipients who do not have existing business or personal relationships with the initiator and (b) were not sent at the request of or with the consent of the recipient." Among other things, Section 17538.4 requires that a "person or entity conducting business in this state" who causes an unsolicited e-mail document to be sent to include in the subject line of each e-mail message ADV: as the first four characters or ADV:ADLT if the advertisement pertains to adult material. Section 17538.4 applies to unsolicited e-mailed documents that are "delivered to a California resident via an electronic mail service provider's service or equipment located in this state." Ferguson alleged that Friendfinders sent him and others unsolicited e-mail advertisements that did not comply with the requirements set forth in Section 17538.4 of the California Business and Professions Code. Among other things, Ferguson alleged that the subject lines of the e-mail messages failed to begin with the characters "ADV:". Citing this same reason, Ferguson asserted a cause of action for unlawful advertising practices. Friendfinders in turn argued that the relief Ferguson sought would constitute an unconstitutional interference with interstate commerce, since the Internet cannot be regulated by individual states because it is a national infrastructure without territorial boundaries. The lower court agreed that the state statutory provision at issue violated the commerce clause of the U.S. Constitution.

ISSUE Does the California statute violate the commerce clause?

HOLDING No. Section 17538.4 does not discriminate against or directly regulate or control interstate commerce. Because it serves a legitimate local public interest and the burden it imposes on interstate commerce is not excessive when viewed in light of its local benefits, Section 17538.4 is valid under the commerce clause.

REASONING Excerpts from the opinion of Judge Haerle:

The Commerce Clause provides that "Congress shall have power . . . to regulate commerce . . . among the several states." . . . "This affirmative grant of authority to Congress also encompasses an implicit or 'dormant' limitation on the authority of the States to enact legislation affecting interstate commerce." . . . In other words, the dormant Commerce Clause precludes state regulation in certain areas "even absent congressional action." . . . "As the volume and complexity of commerce and regulation have grown in this country, the Court has articulated a variety of tests in an attempt to describe the difference between those regulations that the Commerce Clause permits and those regulations that it prohibits." . . . Supreme Court authority establishes two primary lines of inquiry: "first, whether the ordinance discriminates against interstate commerce, . . . and second, whether the ordinance imposes a burden on interstate commerce that is 'clearly excessive in relation to the putative local benefits' . . ." This first level [of] inquiry, which applies a strict scrutiny analysis, has been extended to state regulations that directly regulate interstate commerce. . . . State laws that regulate commerce occurring outside state borders have been found to offend the dormant Commerce Clause. . . . The second inquiry, which is employed to evaluate regulations that do not discriminate against interstate commerce or directly regulate it, is a balancing test which requires that a court uphold a state regulation that serves an important public interest unless the benefits of that regulation are outweighed by the burden imposed on interstate commerce. . . . In the present case, respondents concede that section 17538.4 does not discriminate against out-of-state actors. . . . However, respondents contend that . . . when section 17538.4 is viewed in the context of Internet reality, the statute regulates beyond California's borders and that its extraterritorial reach violates the dormant Commerce Clause. . . . First, respondents argue that the geographic limitations on the scope of section 17538.4 are ineffectual because of the very nature of the Internet. UCE [unsolicited commercial e-mail] is transmitted via the Internet which functions in cyberspace, a place respondents characterize as being "wholly insensitive to geographic distinctions" [quoting *Pataki*, a New York precedent]. . . . The problem with this argument is that section 17538.4 does not regulate the Internet or Internet use per se. It regulates individuals and entities who (1) do business in California, (2) utilize equipment located in California and (3) send UCE to California residents. The equipment used by electronic-mail service providers does have a geographic location. And e-mail recipients are people or businesses who function in the real world and have a geographic residence. . . . These limitations distinguish section 17538.4 from the New York statute at issue in *Pataki* and avoid the problems which most concerned the *Pataki* court. Second, the record does not support respondents' claim that it is impossible to determine the geographic residence of a UCE recipient. [L]ists of e-mail addresses sorted by geographic residence exist already or can be created and utilized by senders of UCE. Respondents have offered no evidence supporting a contrary conclusion. Instead, they argue . . . that "there is no practical way to ascertain which addresses are California residents." That respondents consider section 17538.4's requirements inconvenient and even impractical does not mean that statute violates the Commerce Clause. . . . [The State's regulation of UCE has] developed because UCE, . . . often referred to as "spam," can be and usually is sent to many recipients at one time at little or no cost to the sender. Since the cost of sending unsolicited bulk e-mail is "negligible," spammers "have little incentive to consume resources in an efficient manner." . . . Studies indicate that 10 to 30 percent of all e-mail sent on a given day consists of UCE. . . . In contrast, the costs created by UCE are substantial. Internet Service Providers (ISPs) incur significant business related costs accommodating bulk e-mail advertising and dealing with the problems it creates.

. . . Individuals who receive UCE can experience increased Internet access fees because of the time required to sort, read, discard and attempt to prevent the future sending of UCE. . . . The financial harms caused by the proliferation of UCE have been exacerbated by the use of deceptive tactics . . . to disguise the identity of the UCE sender and the nature of his or her message. Such deceptive tactics increase the already significant costs that UCE imposes on Internet users. . . . States have a substantial interest in preventing the cost-shifting which is inherent in the sending of deceptive UCE. . . . We agree that . . . protecting a state's citizens from the economic damage caused by deceptive UCE constitutes a "legitimate local purpose." . . . In addition, . . . deceptive UCE poses non-economic dangers as well. . . . Studies indicate that UCE often contains offensive subject matter, is a favored method for pursuing questionable if not fraudulent business schemes, and has been successfully used to spread harmful computer viruses. . . . California has a substantial legitimate interest in protecting its citizens from the harmful effects of deceptive UCE and that section 17538.4 furthers that important interest. . . . We must next consider whether the burden that section 17538.4 imposes on interstate commerce outweighs the benefits of that statute. To the extent that section 17538.4 requires truthfulness in advertising, it does not burden interstate commerce at all "but actually 'facilitates it by eliminating fraud and deception.'" . . . Further, . . . "truthfulness requirements . . . make spamming unattractive to many fraudulent spammers, thereby reducing the volume of spam." . . . Nor do the statute's affirmative disclosure requirements impose any appreciable burden on senders of UCE. As the Attorney General has observed, the cost of placing particular letters in the subject line of the e-mail and including a valid return address in the message itself "is appreciably zero in terms of time and expense." . . . We conclude that the burdens imposed on interstate commerce by section 17538.4 are minimal and do not outweigh the statute's benefits. Therefore, respondents have failed to carry their burden of proving that section 17538.4 violates the dormant Commerce Clause.

BUSINESS CONSIDERATIONS Should a business adopt a policy for using electronic means of communication, especially e-mailings and "banners" that appear on Internet pages, to promote its products? If so, what sorts of matters should be addressed in the policy? Should the firm be concerned only with legal issues, or should it also consider ethical issues in drafting its policy?

ETHICAL CONSIDERATIONS Many people are offended when they receive "spam" (unwanted e-mail), especially when that e-mail contains advertising for products. Is it ethical for a business to send spam in its efforts to sell products?

"crash," many ISPs have instituted anti-spamming policies aimed at protecting their respective subscribers. In turn, those firms that initiate spam have challenged such policies on First Amendment grounds. As you will learn, while the First Amendment protects commercial speech, the First Amendment comes into play only through state action (that is, the enactment of a governmental statute, regulation, or rule). Hence, as private actors, ISPs presumably have the right to regulate the use of their own property without offending the First Amendment. Congress, which has had anti-spam bills before it for several years, may eventually enact federal prohibitions on spam as well. Try to keep abreast of the various constitutional challenges that "spammers" may mount if such legislation becomes a reality. (You can report spamming to uce@ftc.gov.)

The Equal Protection Clause

Another constitutional provision that acts as a curb on the government's power to regulate business is the equal protection clause. The Fourteenth Amendment states: "nor shall any State . . . deny to any person within its jurisdiction the equal protection of the laws." Supreme Court precedents have determined that in most situations the Fifth Amendment's due process clause provides that the *federal* government must guarantee equal protection to all persons as well. Basically, this guarantee means that when the government classifies people, it must treat similarly situated people similarly. In recent years, courts have used the equal protection clause to protect a broad panoply of individual rights. Yet this provision also limits the types of regulations government can impose on businesses.

Whether applied to the protection of individuals' civil rights or businesses' rights, the equal protection clause protects individuals and other entities only from invidious discrimination (that is, repugnant discrimination stemming from bigotry or prejudice). What constitutes invidious discrimination? All governmental statutes and regulations classify (or discriminate) among groups. This kind of discrimination—mere differentiation—does not necessarily implicate the equal protection clause, however. For example, when the government says professionals or businesses must secure licenses, the government is differentiating (discriminating) among people who need such licenses as a prerequisite for doing business and those who do not. But such differentiation per se does not constitute the discrimination banned by the equal protection clause. Only when such differentiation stems from prejudice, big-

otry, or stereotyping on racial, ethnic, gender, or similar bases does illegal discrimination result.

The equal protection clause prohibits only discrimination that derives from governmental (that is, so-called state) action; it does not reach actions taken by private individuals. Hence, under this clause, one can challenge only those actions taken by federal and state governments (or by any of their subdivisions or agencies) pursuant to enacted laws or regulations.

Over the years, the Supreme Court has developed various tests for determining the legality of economic regulations challenged under the equal protection clause. As to each of these three possible tests, courts will review the legislative classification at issue with regard to the "fit" that exists between the means the legislative body has used to accomplish a desired end, or objective, and the impact the legislation has on the people affected by the regulation.

Level 1: The Rational Basis Test

Under the traditional, or so-called rational basis, test, the government can distinguish among similarly situated persons if the statutory scheme—or classification—is rationally related to a legitimate state interest (or aim). Courts generally do not second-guess legislators' intent. Courts thus presume that the regulation is valid unless no conceivable justification exists for the law. Simply put, courts allow governmental entities wide latitude when, pursuant to their police power, these regulators enact social and economic regulations; courts only rarely invalidate such measures.

Level 2: The "Compelling State Interest" Test

If a regulatory measure involves invidious discrimination—that is, intentional discrimination against certain racial or ethnic groups—or certain fundamental rights, courts initially will presume such regulations are invalid. Courts will apply strict scrutiny to all such legislation and uphold only those measures necessary to accomplish a compelling state interest. In these instances, the regulating body must show that no alternative, less burdensome ways exist to accomplish the state objective or goal. Regulators only occasionally have successfully justified this type of legislation.

Over the years, the Supreme Court has held that laws that impinge on so-called suspect classifications and thus burden the rights of African-Americans, Hispanics, and Asian-Americans must meet this compelling state interest standard. The Court has protected these groups from the application of such laws because these groups represent discrete, insular (that is, isolated from others) minorities whom other citizens view as unassimilable into American society and whom the government may easily identify because of the groups' immutable physical characteristics.

To justify singling out such disenfranchised groups (those restricted from enjoying certain constitutional or statutory rights owing to systemic prejudice or bigotry), the legislature must satisfy the compelling state interest (level 2) test and the strict scrutiny approach that a court must apply to the law. For example, *Yick Wo v. Hopkins* involved a denial of a permit to operate a laundry business.[11] Since all 199 non-Chinese permit seekers had been granted the permit, the egregious denial of the license to Yick Wo, the only Chinese applicant, violated the Fourteenth Amendment. Given the systemic prejudice against Chinese people at the time because of the widely held view that the Chinese were unworthy of citizenship, Yick Wo was a member of a discrete, insular minority who had suffered historical disenfranchisement. His immutable physical characteristics—the shape of his eyes and his skin color, for example—also made him more easily identified and singled out by the government. The city council could not show that its denial of Yick Wo's permit represented the only means of accomplishing the state interest (avoidance of fire hazards) involved here; hence, the city council had failed to show that its treatment of Yick Wo passed muster under the compelling state interest test.

Citing *Yick Wo v. Hopkins* and upholding its underlying predicates, the Supreme Court recently—in *Romer v. Evans*—held that a referendum-based amendment to the Colorado state constitution violates the equal protection clause. The amendment prohibited all legislative, executive, or judicial action at any level of state or local government designed to protect homosexual persons from discrimination.[12] Finding that the amendment was a status-based enactment divorced from any factual context from which the Court could discern a relationship to a legitimate state interest, the Court concluded that the amendment instead "classifie[d] homosexuals not to further a proper legislative end but to make them unequal to everyone else. This Colorado cannot do. A state [under the equal protection clause] cannot so deem a class of persons a stranger to its laws."[13]

Note that if the facts had been different in the *Yick Wo v. Hopkins* case and 199 Chinese had obtained their permits, a lone unsuccessful white applicant, presumably could sue under the Fourteenth Amendment for "reverse discrimination." The Supreme Court since 1989 has said that "benign" racial classifications used by the government for affirmative action purposes will be judged under the strict scrutiny/compelling state interest test as well.[14] (An example would be a city's decision to award a certain percentage of city con-

tracts to minority-owned businesses because of the city's desire to correct societal discrimination.) *Adarand Constructors, Inc. v. Peña*, which involved a challenge to a federal program that granted preferential treatment to minority subcontractors, reinforces this 1989 holding.[15]

In *Adarand*, the Supreme Court held that reviewing courts must subject all racial classifications, imposed by whatever federal, state, or local governmental entity, to the strict scrutiny standard.[16] This case makes it clear that federal racial classifications, like those set up by a state, must

---

NRW CASE 5.1   Management

CHALLENGING AN APPARENTLY UNCONSTITUTIONAL LAW

The firm has recently learned that the federal government is requiring all new devices that use computer chips to provide auxiliary peripheral devices to users who are disabled. This new law does not apply to any devices that were available on the market last year (the year before NRW was established). In order to comply with the law, NRW will need to substantially enhance the audio and tactile components, which in turn will significantly increase the cost per unit. The firm's members view this law as unconstitutional and wish to challenge it. If they ask you for your advice in this matter, what will you tell them?

BUSINESS CONSIDERATIONS How should a business react to a proposed change in the law that will affect its current business practices? Should the business immediately begin the implementation of methods for complying with the new law, or should the business try to take steps to prevent or delay the effective date of the new law?

ETHICAL CONSIDERATIONS Is it ethical to enact laws that apply to all customers so as to provide benefits or protections for a small number who require special accommodations to use the products covered? Would it be more ethical for the government to refrain from requiring such accommodations, thereby leaving some members of society unable to receive benefits otherwise generally available within society?

INTERNATIONAL CONSIDERATIONS Do all countries approach the regulation of business as the United States does?

serve a compelling governmental interest and must be narrowly tailored to further that interest. Under this standard, only affirmative action plans that respond to specific, provable past discrimination and that are narrowly tailored to eliminate such bias would be legal. Although the Court acknowledged that, practically speaking, it would be hard for the government to meet this test, the Court did not view its decision as dealing a fatal blow to the vast network of federal affirmative action programs that presently exist. Many commentators, however, believe this decision will bring on an avalanche of court challenges to governmental minority preference programs and will fuel the growing political backlash against affirmative action efforts. *Adarand* itself is instructive in this regard, as the case has been before the Supreme Court three times since 1995. In 2002, the Supreme Court dismissed the writ of certiorari it earlier had granted because of significant changes in the posture of the case that had occurred after that grant of certiorari.[17]

Just as the equal protection clause prohibits virtually all legislation that burdens a suspect classification, it also subjects to the compelling state interest test any governmental action that penalizes or unduly burdens a *fundamental right* (one expressly or impliedly guaranteed in the Constitution). Accordingly, the Supreme Court has struck down laws that forbade a drugstore to sell birth control devices and a doctor to discuss birth control issues with his or her patients. The Court believed these laws implicate the right of privacy, interpreted by the Court as encompassing the marital relationship and procreation. Similarly, had Yick Wo been a Presbyterian and the only unsuccessful applicant, he could have argued that the city council's prior, publicly articulated, anti-Presbyterian sentiments had led to the penalizing of his First Amendment right of freedom of religion.

Intermediate Level: The Substantially Important State Interest Test

In the 1970s, the Supreme Court flirted with the idea of placing gender-based laws under level 2 analysis, particularly if the challenged legislative enactment unduly burdened women. At that time, many commentators argued that, first, women represent a discrete, insular minority owing to their belated receipt of the right to vote, the existence of Married Women's Property Acts that denied women the capacity to contract, and so on. Second, women represent a group of individuals who manifest immutable physical characteristics; in other words, women's secondary sex characteristics ordinarily distinguish women from men and vice versa.

While the Court never accepted these arguments—apparently it believed the discrimination caused by gender-based laws failed to rise to the level of invidiousness found in most level 2 cases—the Court carved out an intermediate tier of analysis for decision makers to use in evaluating challenges to gender-based laws. Consequently, although classifications based on gender are not "suspect," they deserve more judicial attention than classifications judged under the level 1, rational basis test. Hence, the Court formulated an intermediate tier of analysis and placed classifications based on gender in this "quasi-suspect" classification.

Statutory schemes that encompass quasi-suspect classifications must be "substantially related to an important state interest." If the enacting body cannot meet this test, courts will invalidate the legislation. Thus, older laws that prohibited women from entering certain occupations (say, becoming a barber) nowadays would be decided under this intermediate tier of analysis. Similarly, if Yick Wo had been a woman and the city council's ordinance had said no woman could obtain a permit, the city council would need to show that its prohibition against women advanced a substantially important governmental objective. Otherwise, the ordinance would violate the equal protection clause. Note that men are protected from burdensome laws as well. In *Craig v. Boren*, the Supreme Court invalidated an Oklahoma law that allowed females to drink beer at age 18 but prohibited males from drinking beer until age 21.[18]

Relying on these precedents, the Supreme Court recently held that the exclusion of women by the Virginia Military Institute (VMI) violated the equal protection clause. VMI argued that the alterations to its "adversative" method of training that would be necessary to accommodate women would be so drastic as to destroy VMI's program and its mission to produce "citizen-soldiers." The Court characterized this argument as falling well short of the showing necessary to justify the classification as "substantially related to an important state interest." The Court therefore concluded that because neither VMI nor the state of Virginia had proffered an "exceedingly persuasive justification" for categorically excluding all women from VMI's programs, the school's policies were unconstitutional.[19]

The Due Process Clause

Besides guaranteeing equal protection, both the Fifth and Fourteenth Amendments protect against deprivations of "life, liberty, or property without due process of law." You probably associate the due process clause with individual rights, and perhaps specifically with the protection of persons accused of crimes, as mentioned in Chapter 8. Hence, the government cannot deprive us of our lives (for example, by subjecting us to capital punishment) without according us due process. Similarly, the government cannot deprive us of liberty—interpreted by the Court to include one's freedom from physical restraints imposed without due process and in noncriminal contexts to involve such issues as involuntary commitments to mental institutions. In the context of business, the term *liberty* also encompasses the right to contract and to engage in gainful employment.

Still, the life and liberty components of the due process clause fade in importance compared to the property dimension of the provision. The Supreme Court has found few interpretive problems inherent in this third prong of the clause, perhaps because most of us more intuitively understand the concept property than we do the intangible concept *liberty*. Thus, the Court not surprisingly has construed the word *property* to include ownership of real estate, personal property, and money; but the Court also has extended the term *property* to entitlements to specific benefits set out under applicable state or federal law. Hence, if state action deprives us of property rights such as public employment, public education, continuing welfare benefits, or continuing public utility services, that deprivation cannot constitutionally occur in the absence of due process. The due process required by notions of fundamental fairness involves two dimensions: procedural protections and substantive considerations.

Procedural Due Process

Before the government can deprive one of life, liberty, or property, one usually must be afforded some kind of hearing. Such hearings generally require notice to the aggrieved party, an opportunity for that person to present his or her side of the story, and an impartial decision maker. The government ordinarily can refrain from providing counsel, because counsel usually is not constitutionally required as is the case with indigent criminal defendants. The applicable rules and regulations, however, often allow counsel to be present. The timing of the hearing—whether it must occur before or after the deprivation of a protected interest—and the extent of the procedural safeguards afforded to the affected individual vary.

Courts generally balance the individual interests involved with the governmental interest in fiscal and administrative efficiency. Prior Supreme Court precedents have held that a hearing must precede, for example, the termination of welfare benefits, the government's seizure and forfeiture of real estate allegedly used in connection with the commission of crimes, termination of public employment, and prejudgment garnishment of wages. Evidentiary hearings prior to the termination of benefits need not occur in situations involving disability benefits, some terminations of parental rights, and some license suspensions (for example, failure to take a Breathalyzer test); but postsuspension hearings may be required in such circumstances.

For example, assume a state passes a law saying women can cut only women's hair and men can cut only men's hair. Patrick McCann, who runs a unisex barbershop, flouts the law and continues to cut women's hair. The state licensing board in response notifies him that it plans to revoke his license (state action has occurred), gives him a hearing in which he has an opportunity to present his side of the dispute, and convenes a panel (probably made up of other licensed barbers) that has no apparent biases against McCann. With these procedural steps taken against him, McCann ordinarily will not be able to use the due process clause to challenge the subsequent revocation of his license; the hearing he has received apparently fulfills the requirements of procedural due process.

Substantive Due Process

The substantive aspects of due process, however, may hold more promise for McCann. The *substantive* dimension of due process focuses not on providing fundamentally fair procedures but on the content, or the subject matter, of the law. One deprived of life, liberty, or property under arbitrary, irrational, and capricious social or economic laws may challenge such losses under the due process clause. In short, under substantive due process principles, a regulation is invalid if it fails to advance a legitimate governmental interest or if it constitutes an unreasonable means of advancing a legitimate governmental interest.

Owing to its overuse in the first 30 years of the 20th century, courts for many years viewed substantive due process as a discredited constitutional doctrine. In that earlier period, judges, by substituting their personal views for those of the legislatures that had enacted the laws, struck down a whole host of social and economic legislation. In the mid-1930s, however, the resurrection of the theory began. Today, courts generally defer to legislators' judgments regarding social and economic matters and thus presume such laws are valid unless the challenger can persuade the courts that the laws actually are demonstrably arbitrary and irrational. Judicial deference normally leads to the courts' upholding such laws, as occurred in *Pacific Mutual Life Insurance Co. v. Haslip*, where the Supreme Court upheld a jury award of punitive damages and the state's postverdict procedures for reviewing such awards as reasonable.[20]

Since the mid-1960s, the Supreme Court has used substantive due process primarily as a vehicle for protecting

NRW CASE 5.2   Management

CHALLENGING LOCAL LAWS

One city in which NRW has opened a retail outlet has announced that a new city ordinance will go into effect in three months. This new ordinance requires all non-automobile-related firms selling interactive tracking systems to register with a particular city official. NRW is the only non-automobile-related firm that is currently selling such systems in that state, and the firm believes that NRW has been singled out for discriminatory treatment by this ordinance. The firm members ask you what they can or should do under these circumstances. What will you tell them?

BUSINESS CONSIDERATIONS Suppose that a city ordinance makes conducting business in a particular city too difficult or too expensive for a particular firm. Should the firm move its operation out of the city, or should it seek a variance or exemption from the city?

ETHICAL CONSIDERATIONS Is it ethical for a business to pick and choose where it will operate based on local laws or regulations? What ethical considerations will such a decision raise?

INTERNATIONAL CONSIDERATIONS Suppose that a business believes it has been singled out for discriminatory treatment by a foreign government rather than a particular city. What can the business do in this situation? What legal recourse might be best for the firm? Is the regulation of a given industry—say, automobiles or pharmaceuticals—common in countries other than the United States?

certain fundamental personal rights that are implied by constitutional wording and phraseology. Hence, beginning in the mid-1960s, the Court has struck down on grounds of irrationality and arbitrariness state laws making the use of contraceptives by anyone, including married persons, illegal. Such laws impermissibly infringe on the so-called zone of marital privacy protected by the Court. In coming to this result, the Court viewed such legislation in a fashion virtually identical to strict scrutiny and applied something very akin to the compelling state interest test. The liberty component of the due process clause also guarantees a competent person, who has clearly made his or her wishes known beforehand, the right to terminate unwanted med-

ical treatment.[21] Laws holding otherwise can be challenged on substantive due process grounds.

As you studied this section, you probably noticed the complementary relationship between substantive due process and guarantees of equal protection under the law. Both constitutional guarantees mandate a rational fit between the objectives of the law and the group of people affected thereby. When all persons are subject to a law that deprives them of a life, liberty, or property interest, due process probably applies. When a law classifies certain people for certain purposes, the equal protection doctrine probably becomes the appropriate vehicle for challenging the law.

Under either theory, the Supreme Court since the mid-1930s has required judges to give great deference to legislative prerogatives when judges are called upon to review social legislation that does not involve personal fundamental rights. The same is true of economic legislation: Judges should uphold all such legislation unless the challenger can show the absence of any rational relationship to any legitimate governmental aim or interest.

To check your understanding of this section, ask yourself whether Pat McCann, from our earlier example, could challenge his license revocation under substantive due process. Consider, too, whether McCann could sue under the equal protection clause.

The Takings Clause

Besides guaranteeing procedural and substantive due process, the Fifth Amendment also provides that "private property [shall not] be taken for public use, without just compensation." This Fifth Amendment restraint on the power of the federal government moreover applies to the states through the Fourteenth Amendment's due process clause. Under this "takings" clause, the government must take the property for "public use" and must pay "just compensation" to the property owner involved.

In litigation, the disagreement between the parties often centers on whether a *taking* has occurred, in which case the Constitution obligates the government to pay just compensation, or whether the governmental action amounts only to *regulation* under the exercise of its police power, in which case no compensation is owed. While the Supreme Court has set out no clear formula for judging when a taking has occurred, any actual appropriation of property will suffice. For example, if the state through formal procedures condemns a business for the purpose of constructing a parking garage on a state college campus, a taking has occurred. The state will have to pay just compensation to the owner of the property that was razed owing to the state's exercise of its power of eminent domain (that is, a state or municipality's power to take private property for public use).

But less-than-complete appropriations of property may suffice as takings as well. For instance, the Court has held that federal dam construction resulting in the repeated flooding of private property, and low, direct flights over private property located contiguous to federal or municipal airports, constitute takings if they destroy the property's present use or unreasonably impair the value of the property and the owners' reasonable expectations regarding it.

As the *Lucas v. South Carolina Coastal Council* case discussed in Chapter 41 demonstrates, a land use regulation that fails to advance substantially legitimate state interests or that denies an owner the economically viable use of his or her land is a taking subject to the Fifth Amendment.[22] In the absence of such factors, zoning ordinances—the most common type of land use regulations—ordinarily pass muster under the takings clause even if the regulations restrict the use of the property and cause a reduction in its value, so long as the ordinances substantially advance legitimate state interests and do not extinguish fundamental attributes of ownership.

During the attempted taking, the government must afford the affected property owner procedural due process. However, the just compensation paid by the governmental regulator need reflect only the fair market value of the property; the price does not have to compensate the owner for the sentimental value of the property, the owner's unique need for the property, or the gain the regulating body realizes by virtue of the taking.

In the following case a city planning commission approved a business's application in exchange for the business owner "giving" some of its land to the city. The commission apparently viewed this exchange as a quid pro quo, but the business owner viewed it as an illegal taking. After reading the case, decide which party you think had the more persuasive argument.

The Supreme Court recently added to its property rights jurisprudence when it decided *Monterey v. Del Monte*

5.2

DOLAN v. CITY OF TIGARD
512 U.S. 374 (1994)

FACTS The Tigard, Oregon, City Planning Commission conditioned approval of Florence Dolan's application to expand her plumbing and electric supply store and pave her parking lot on her agreement to dedicate land (1) for a public greenway so as to minimize the Fanno Creek flooding that would result from the increases in the impervious surfaces associated with her development and (2) for a pedestrian/bicycle pathway intended to relieve traffic congestion in the city's central business district. In appealing the Commission's denial of her request for variances from these standards to the Land Use Board of Appeals (LUBA), Dolan alleged that the land dedication requirements were not related to the proposed development and therefore constituted an uncompensated taking of her property under the Fifth Amendment. The LUBA, the state court of appeals, and the state supreme court affirmed the Commission's decision.

ISSUE Did the land dedication requirements imposed on Dolan constitute an unconstitutional taking of her property under the Fifth Amendment?

HOLDING Yes. The city did not show that it had made an individualized determination that the required dedications related both in nature and extent to the impact of the proposed settlement. The absence of such a connection therefore rendered the city's actions unlawful under the takings clause of the Fifth Amendment.

REASONING Excerpts from the opinion of Chief Justice Rehnquist:

The Takings Clause of the Fifth Amendment made applicable to the states through the Constitution's Fourteenth Amendment . . . provides: "Nor shall private property be taken for public use, without just compensation." One of the principal purposes of the Takings Clause is "to bar Government from forcing some people alone to bear public burdens which, in all fairness and justice, should be borne by the public as a whole." . . . Without question, had the city simply required petitioner to dedicate a strip of land along Fanno Creek for public use, rather than conditioning the grant of her permit to redevelop her property on such a dedication, a taking would have occurred. . . . Such public access would deprive petitioner of the right to exclude others, "one of the most essential sticks in the bundle of rights that are commonly characterized as property." . . . On the other side of the ledger, the authority of state and local governments to engage in land use planning has been sustained against constitutional challenge since 1926. The Supreme Court consistently has held that a land use regulation does not effect a taking if it "substantially advances legitimate state interests" and does not "deny an owner economically viable use of his land." . . . The sort of land use regulations discussed in the cases just cited, however, differ in two relevant particulars from the present case. First, they involved essentially legislative determinations classifying entire areas of the city, whereas here the city made an adjudicative decision to condition petitioner's application for a building permit on an individual parcel. Second, the conditions imposed were not simply a limitation on the use petitioner might make of her own parcel, but a requirement that she deed portions of the property to the city. [Recent Supreme Court precedents under the Fifth and Fourteenth Amendments circumscribe] governmental authority to exact such a condition. . . . Under the well-settled doctrine of "unconstitutional conditions," the government may not require a person to give up a constitutional right—here the right to receive just compensation when property is taken for a public use—in exchange for a discretionary benefit conferred by the government where the benefit sought has little or no relationship to the property. . . . Petitioner contends that the city has forced her to choose between the building permit and her right under the Fifth Amendment to just compensation for the public easements. . . . She argues that the city has identified "no special benefits" conferred on her, and has not identified any "special quantifiable burdens" created by her new store that would justify the particular dedications required from her which are not required from the public at large. In evaluating petitioner's claim, we must first determine whether the "essential nexus" exists between the "legitimate state interest" and the permit condition exacted by the city. If we find that a nexus exists, we must then decide the required degree of connection between the exactions and the projected impact of the proposed development. . . . Undoubtedly, the prevention of flooding along Fanno Creek and the reduction of traffic congestion in the Central Business District qualify as the type of legitimate public purposes we have upheld. . . . The second part of our analysis requires us to determine whether the degree of the exactions demanded by the city's permit conditions bears the required relationship to the projected impact of petitioner's proposed development. . . . "[A] use restriction may constitute a 'taking' if not reasonably necessary to the effectuation of a substantial government purpose."

. . . [The states previously have adopted various tests for determining whether the necessary connection between the required dedication and the proposed development suffices for constitutional purposes. But the Court today enunciates a new test.] We think a term such as "rough proportionality" best encapsulates what we hold to be the requirement of the Fifth Amendment. No precise mathematical calculation is required, but the city must make some sort of individualized determination that the required dedication is related both in nature and extent to the impact of the proposed development. . . . [When one applies this test to the city's findings, it becomes apparent that the city's imposition of] a permanent recreational easement upon petitioner's property that borders Fanno Creek [would cause her to] lose all rights to regulate the time in which the public entered onto the greenway, regardless of any interference it might pose with her retail store. Her right to exclude would not be regulated, it would be eviscerated. . . . We conclude that the findings upon which the city relies do not show the required reasonable relationship between the floodplain easement and petitioner's proposed new building. With respect to the pedestrian/bicycle pathway . . . the city has not met its burden of demonstrating that the additional number of vehicle and bicycle trips generated by petitioner's development reasonably relate to the city's requirement for a dedication of the pedestrian/bicycle pathway easement. . . . No precise mathematical calculation is required, but the city must make some effort to quantify its findings in support of the dedication for the pedestrian/bicycle pathway beyond the conclusory statement that it could offset some of the traffic demand generated. [The city's failure to meet its burden of proof therefore mandates the reversal of the previously rendered judgment of the Supreme Court of Oregon].

BUSINESS CONSIDERATIONS Was it reasonable for Dolan to expect the city to absorb the adverse effects on the city that arguably would result from Dolan's proposed expansion of her business? How should a business react to a situation in which the business is expected to make a community-benefit "contribution" in exchange for permission to expand or move the business activity?

ETHICAL CONSIDERATIONS If the Court had disposed of this case on ethical—rather than legal—grounds, would its decision have been different? What ethical concerns did this case raise?

Dunes at Monterey, Ltd.[23] In this case, a firm sought to develop a condominium project on a parcel of environmentally sensitive land along the California coast. After the planning commission over a period of five years had

rejected several plans and had imposed increasingly stringent demands on the developer, the firm filed a lawsuit under § 1983, which creates a duty to refrain from interfering with the federal rights of others and provides money damages and injunctive relief for violations under color of state law. In a 5-4 decision, the Court held that the developer was entitled to a jury trial on its regulatory taking claim. In doing so, the Court emphasized the narrowness of its ruling on the availability of jury trials in such cases. Indeed, the Court stressed that it was not setting out the precise demarcation of the respective provinces of judges and jury in determining whether a zoning decision substantially advances governmental interests. Nevertheless, the Court concluded that whether a challenged regulation has deprived a landowner of all the economically viable uses of his or her property is a jury question. The Court conceded that whether a land use decision substantially advances legitimate public interests involves a tougher call probably best understood as a mixed question of fact and law. In this case, however, the Court viewed the protracted sequence of the developer's applications and the city's rejections as sufficiently factbound to make the question of liability appropriate for a jury's consideration. The dissenters, in contrast, viewed such inverse condemnation cases as analogous to eminent domain proceedings in which no jury trial ordinarily is available because the compensation required by the Fifth Amendment is the fair market value of the property on the date on which the property is appropriated. (Inverse condemnation is an action brought by a property owner against a governmental entity that has the power of eminent domain; the property owner typically seeks just compensation for land taken for public use in situations in which the governmental entity does not intend to initiate eminent domain proceedings.)

Interestingly, the Court held that the "rough proportionality" standard enunciated in the *Dolan* case applies only in the special context of exactions—land use decisions conditioning approval of development on the dedication of the property to public use. According to the Court, the *Dolan* rule considers whether dedications demanded as conditions of development are proportional to the development's anticipated impacts. *Dolan* is not readily applicable to situations like the *Monterey* case, in which a landowner bases his or her challenge on a denial of development rather than excessive exactions. Hence, the Court concluded that *Dolan* would not apply to the regulatory taking context exemplified by the *Monterey* decision.

Although we have emphasized only the due process and takings clauses of the Fifth Amendment, you have learned from earlier chapters that this provision in the Constitution also prohibits *double jeopardy* (being tried twice for the same offense) and compulsory self-incrimination. Thus, the Fifth Amendment's many facets represent an effective curb on illegitimate governmental action taken against individuals or businesses.

The First Amendment/ Commercial Speech

The First Amendment, as you remember, protects individual freedom of speech. Businesses, however, as legal (or *juristic*) persons, arguably enjoy protected First Amendment rights as well. Indeed, commercial speech—speech that involves commercial transactions, particularly the advertising of business products and services—does qualify

---

NRW CASE 5.3   Management

NRW

CITY OFFICIALS CONFISCATE STUFFTRAKR UNITS

Assume that the proposed ordinance requiring auxiliary peripheral devices has taken effect. NRW has decided to add such a feature to its units as soon as practicable. In the meantime, the firm has decided to suspend any new sales in that community until the reconfigured units are ready. Mai calls the store manager to inform him of this decision and to have him return all the unsold units in the store to the NRW factory for redistribution to areas where the present units can legally be sold. Mai thereupon learns that the city, citing the units' noncompliance with the city ordinance, has already confiscated all the units in the store. Mai asks you if the city can legally do this. What will you tell her?

BUSINESS CONSIDERATIONS What should a business do to protect itself from takings carried out by the government? What sorts of protections are available for the business?

ETHICAL CONSIDERATIONS Is it ethical for the government to take private property for a public purpose? What alternatives might be available that would allow the government to meet its obligation to the public while protecting the property interests of owners?

INTERNATIONAL CONSIDERATIONS What rights can a business assert if its products are "nationalized" by the government in another country where the business has been operating? What legal recourse might the business seek? How does one effect a legal taking under international law? In what circumstances may such a taking occur?

for First Amendment protection. Although the Supreme Court has had difficulty in defining the term "commercial speech" with precision, one thing is clear: The parameters of this protection are not coextensive with the boundaries of protected individual speech.

Clearly, the government can and does regulate private expression. The First Amendment, though a fundamental right, is not an absolute one. In deciding whether to limit speech, the government engages in yet another balancing test in which it compares such factors as the importance of these rights in a democratic society, the nature of the restriction imposed by the law, the type and importance of the governmental interest the law purports to serve, and the narrowness of the means used to effectuate that interest.

Courts ordinarily view laws presumptively invalid that, by punishing some speech and favoring other speech, burden the content of individual speech ("content-based" regulations). Hence, such laws must pass the "strict scrutiny/compelling state interest" test (the "least restrictive alternative") and be narrowly drawn measures designed to achieve such a compelling state interest. Courts in addition can strike down substantially overbroad and vague laws (those that proscribe protected activity and thus "chill" others into refraining from the exercise of constitutionally protected expression). The government, however, may outlaw defamation, advocacy of unlawful action, obscenity, and "fighting words." The government also can subject lawful speech to time, place, and manner regulation (it can require demonstrators to obtain permits, limit the demonstration to a certain venue, and so on).

Thus, because the government can regulate private expression, it comes as no surprise that the government can regulate commercial speech and even ban such speech that is false and misleading. Although the First Amendment protects commercial speech, the greater potential for deception and confusion posed by commercial speech allows the government to regulate even the content of commercial (as opposed to noncommercial) speech so long as the restriction serves and advances a substantial governmental interest in a manner no more extensive than necessary (that is, "sufficiently tailored") to achieve that governmental objective. For example, in 1994 the Supreme Court held in *Turner Broadcasting System, Inc. v. Federal Communications Commission* (*Turner I*) that the federal laws requiring cable television stations to devote a specified portion of their channels to local programming (the "must carry" provisions) were not content-based laws.[24] In 1997, after a remand for more fact-finding, the Court—in *Turner II*—affirmed this holding.[25] Hence, the Court rejected the argument that these "must carry" provisions should be judged under the strict scrutiny/compelling state interest test and instead upheld the challenged provisions because they were sufficiently tailored to serve the important governmental interest relating to the preservation of local broadcasting. The recent challenges to Congress's attempt to regulate "indecent" content on the Internet, specifically the Communications Decency Act of 1996, implicate similar issues. The act outlawed electronic transmission of lewd and indecent materials to anyone under age 18 and criminalized any commercial communication service that allows its system to be used for such transmissions. The Supreme Court's invalidation of this law as illegal content-based blanket restrictions on speech[26] is a harbinger of the types of issues that promise to provide a fertile field for continuing litigation. Try, therefore, to keep abreast of the Supreme Court's disposition of the legal developments relating to the regulation of telecommunications.

The Supreme Court in *Lorillard Tobacco Company v. Reilly* utilized many of the principles of law just discussed. After reading the opinion, decide whether you agree with the Court.

5.3

LORILLARD TOBACCO COMPANY v. REILLY
533 U.S. 525 (2001)

FACTS In 1999, Massachusetts' attorney general promulgated comprehensive regulations governing the advertising and sale of cigarettes, smokeless tobacco, and cigars. These regulations addressed the use of tobacco products by children under legal age and prevented access to such products by underaged consumers. Among other matters, these regulations (1) prohibited any outdoor advertising of such tobacco products within 1,000 feet of schools or playgrounds, (2) provided that tobacco product advertising could not be placed lower than 5 feet from the floor of any retail establishment located within a 1,000-foot radius of any school or playground, (3) barred the use of self-service displays of tobacco products, and (4) required that tobacco products be placed out of the reach of all consumers and in a location accessible only to salespeople. The petitioners, a group of tobacco manufacturers and retailers, in filing suit against the attorney general, asserted that the cigarette advertising regulations were preempted by the Federal Cigarette Labeling and Advertising Act

(FCLAA), which prohibits (a) requiring cigarette packages to bear any statement relating to smoking and health other than a statement required by another FCLAA provision, and (b) any requirement or prohibition based on smoking and health that was imposed under state law with respect to the advertising or promotion of any cigarettes when the packages have been labeled in conformity with § 1333 of the FCLAA. The tobacco manufacturers and retailers also claimed that the regulations violated the First Amendment. The district court held that the FCLAA did not preempt the restrictions and that the outdoor advertising restrictions and the sales practices regulations were valid under the First Amendment. However, the district court struck down the point-of-sale advertising restrictions. The First Circuit Court of Appeals affirmed on the preemption issue but then upheld all the regulations in question as a valid exercise of state power under the First Amendment.

ISSUES Were the regulations in question preempted by the FCLAA? Did the regulations violate the First Amendment?

HOLDINGS Yes, the regulations governing the outdoor and point-of-sale advertising of cigarettes were preempted by the FCLAA. Regarding the second issue, yes and no. Some of the regulations violated the First Amendment, and some represented a valid exercise of state power over the sale and use of tobacco products.

REASONING Excerpts from the opinion of Justice O'Connor:

The FCLAA's pre-emption provision, § 1334, prohibits (a) requiring cigarette packages to bear any "statement relating to smoking and health, other than the statement required by" § 1333, and (b) any "requirement or prohibition based on smoking and health . . . imposed under state law with respect to the advertising or promotion of any cigarettes the packages of which are labeled in conformity with" § 1333. The Court's analysis begins with the statute's language. . . . Congress pre-empted state cigarette advertising regulations like the Attorney General's because they would upset federal legislative choices to require specific warnings and to impose the ban on cigarette advertising in electronic media so as to address concerns about smoking and health. In holding that the FCLAA does not nullify the Massachusetts regulations, the First Circuit concentrated on whether they are "with respect to" advertising and promotion, concluded that the FCLAA only pre-empts regulations of the content of cigarette advertising. The court also reasoned that the regulations are a form of zoning, a traditional area of state power, and therefore a presumption against pre-emption applied. . . . This Court rejects the notion that the regulations are not "with respect to" cigarette advertising and promotion. There is no question about an indirect relationship between the Massachusetts regulations and cigarette advertising; the regulations expressly target such advertising. . . . The Attorney General's argument that the regulations are not "based on smoking and health" since they do not involve health-related content, but instead target youth exposure to cigarette advertising, is unpersuasive because, at bottom, the youth exposure concern is intertwined with the smoking and health concern. Also unavailing is the Attorney General's claim that the regulations are not pre-empted because they govern the location, not the content, of cigarette advertising. The content/location distinction cannot be squared with the pre-emption provision's language, which reaches all "requirements" and "prohibitions . . . imposed under State law." A distinction between advertising content and location in the FCLAA also cannot be reconciled with Congress's own location-based restriction, which bans advertising in electronic media, but not elsewhere. . . . The FCLAA['s] comprehensive warnings, advertising restrictions, and pre-emption provision would make little sense if a State or locality could simply target and ban all cigarette advertising. . . . The FCLAA's pre-emption provision does not restrict States' and localities' ability to enact generally applicable zoning restrictions on the location and size of advertisements that apply to cigarettes on equal terms with other products, . . . or to regulate conduct as it relates to the sale or use of cigarettes, as by prohibiting cigarette sales to minors. . . . Massachusetts' outdoor and point-of-sale advertising regulations relating to smokeless tobacco and cigars violate the First Amendment, but the sales practices regulations relating to all three tobacco products are constitutional. . . . [This result derives from the controlling precedent, *Central Hudson Gas and Electric Company v. Public Service Commission of New York*]. Under *Central Hudson*'s four-part test for analyzing regulations of commercial speech, the Court must determine (1) whether the expression is protected by the First Amendment, (2) whether the asserted governmental interest is substantial, (3) whether the regulation directly advances the governmental interest asserted, and (4) whether it is not more extensive than is necessary to serve that interest. Only the last two steps are at issue here. The Attorney General has assumed . . . that the First Amendment protects the speech of petitioners, none of whom contests the importance of the State's interest in preventing the use of tobacco by minors. The third step of *Central Hudson* requires that the government demonstrate that the harms it recites are real and that its restriction will in fact alleviate them to a material degree. . . . The fourth step of *Central Hudson* requires a reasonable fit between the legislature's ends and the means chosen to accomplish those ends, a means narrowly tailored to achieve the desired objective. . . . The outdoor advertising regulations prohibiting smokeless tobacco or cigar advertising within 1,000 feet of a school or playground violate the First Amendment. Those regulations satisfy *Central Hudson*'s third step by directly advancing the governmental interest asserted to justify them. The Court's . . . record reveals that the Attorney General has provided ample documentation of the problem with underage use of smokeless tobacco and cigars. In addition, the Court disagrees with petitioners' claim that there is no evidence that preventing targeted advertising campaigns and limiting youth exposure to advertising will decrease underage use of those products. . . . Whatever the strength of the Attorney General's evidence to justify the outdoor advertising regulations, however, the regulations do not satisfy *Central Hudson*'s fourth step. Their broad sweep indicates that the Attorney General did not "carefully calculate the costs and benefits associated with the burden on speech imposed." . . . The record indicates that the regulations prohibit advertising in a substantial portion of Massachusetts' major metropolitan areas; in some areas, they would constitute nearly a complete ban on the communication of truthful information. This substantial geographical reach is compounded by other factors. "Outdoor" advertising includes not only advertising located outside an establishment, but also advertising inside a store if visible from outside . . . [, as well as] oral statements. The uniformly broad sweep of the geographical limitation and the range of communications restricted demonstrate a lack of tailoring. The governmental interest in preventing underage tobacco use is substantial, and even compelling, but it is no less true that the sale and use of tobacco products by adults is a legal activity. A speech regulation cannot unduly impinge on the speaker's ability to propose a commercial transaction and the adult listener's opportunity to obtain information about products. The Attorney General has failed to show that the regulations at issue are not more extensive than necessary. . . . The regulations prohibiting indoor, point-of-sale advertising of smokeless tobacco and cigars lower than 5 feet from the floor of a retail establishment located within 1,000 feet of a school or playground fail both the third and fourth steps of the *Central Hudson* analysis. The 5-foot rule does not seem to advance the goals of preventing minors from using tobacco products and curbing demand for that activity by limiting youth exposure to advertising. Not

all children are less than 5 feet tall, and those who are can look up and take in their surroundings. . . . Assuming that petitioners have a cognizable speech interest in a particular means of displaying their products, . . . the regulations requiring retailers to place tobacco products behind counters and requiring customers to have contact with a salesperson before they are able to handle such a product withstand First Amendment scrutiny. The State has demonstrated a substantial interest in preventing access to tobacco products by minors and has adopted an appropriately narrow means of advancing that interest. . . . Because unattended displays of such products present an opportunity for access without the proper age verification required by law, the State prohibits self-service and other displays that would allow an individual to obtain tobacco without direct contact with a salesperson. It is clear that the regulations leave open ample communication channels. They do not significantly impede adult access to tobacco products, and retailers have other means of exercising any cognizable speech interest in the presentation of their products. The Court presumes that vendors may . . . display actual tobacco products so long as that display is only accessible to sales personnel.˙

BUSINESS CONSIDERATIONS The tobacco producers and manufacturers provide a product that has been shown to be harmful to the health of its consumers. Should the business include a warning about the potential harmful effects for its consumers in its advertising? When does the right of the business to advertise become subordinate to the right of the society to protect its members from potential harm?

ETHICAL CONSIDERATIONS Should a business that sells a product that harms its consumers be allowed to advertise? If such a policy were to be adopted by society, where would it end? Since people die in auto accidents, should auto advertising be prohibited?

You can access the *Lorillard* case and other Supreme Court cases at http://www.law.cornell.edu/supct/, Cornell Law School's Legal Information Institute—Decisions of the Supreme Court. The Oyez Project, a site maintained by Jerry Goldman of Northwestern University, at http://oyez.nwu.edu provides digital recordings of selected Supreme Court decisions.

---

* Because the lower courts failed to consider the issue, the Court declines to reach the smokeless tobacco petitioners' argument that, if the outdoor and point-of-sale advertising regulations for cigarettes are pre-empted, then the same regulations for smokeless tobacco must be invalidated because they cannot be severed from the cigarette provisions. The Court also declines to address the cigar petitioners' First Amendment challenge to a regulation prohibiting sampling or promotional giveaways of cigars and little cigars because that claim was not sufficiently briefed and argued before the Court.

Administrative Agencies

Administrative agencies conduct much of the work of regulating business. Most of us are familiar with the three official branches of the federal government—the legislative, executive, and judicial—but we may tend to overlook the unofficial fourth branch. This so-called administrative branch of government has been especially active since the 1930s. The Great Depression and the presidency of Franklin Delano Roosevelt saw a tremendous growth in the use of administrative agencies as a major means of effecting regulation. Because a great deal of government intervention in the business sphere derives from the actions of administrative agencies, some familiarity with administrative law is essential to understanding governmental regulation of business.

Congress sets up administrative agencies; and since Congress "creates" them, Congress can terminate them. Hence, they are not an independent branch of government. They have only as much authority as the legislature delegates to them, and as a result they must answer to Congress for their conduct. Congress establishes a basic policy or standard and then authorizes an agency to carry it out.

Once established, the agency will have certain powers that are quasi-legislative (to enact rules and regulations, but not statutes) and quasi-judicial (to hold hearings, but not trials). The agency is allowed to pass rules and regulations within its area of authority and to hold hearings when it believes violations of its rules and regulations have occurred. In so doing, federal administrative agencies must follow the Administrative Procedures Act (APA), which mandates public participation and sets out the rules and procedures that such agencies must follow as they legislate, adjudicate, and enforce their regulations. The power of Congress to abolish any agency and the power of the courts to review any agency's conduct are considered sufficient control devices. It is believed that the agency will not exceed its authority or abuse its discretion as long as these two *official* branches of government keep a watchful eye on the agency's conduct.

Some of the constitutional provisions discussed earlier in the chapter limit the power of administrative agencies. Remember that an agency, in order to ensure procedural due process, must provide fairness in its proceedings. A person involved in a proceeding that affects his or her individual rights (that is, those involving *adjudicative* facts) ordinarily is entitled to a hearing of some sort. Also remember that due process generally includes the right to present witnesses, the right to cross-examine witnesses, the right to an impartial decision maker, and possibly other rights as well. Agency proceedings involving only rule making or fact-finding concerning principles of general application (that is, those involving *legislative* facts) usually require fewer procedural safeguards. Notice of the time, place, and purpose of the meeting might satisfy procedural due process in this latter context. Moreover, the agency may enact only rules and regulations that bear a rational relationship to the agency's purpose or function. Under substantive due process doctrines, then, litigants may challenge unreasonable, arbitrary, and capricious administrative rules. Such rules also may deny the persons affected the equal protection of the law.

The respective agencies' enabling statutes ordinarily spell out the methods by which one can seek review of agency decisions. Anyone dissatisfied with treatment received at the hands of an administrative agency generally may ask a federal district court or circuit court of appeals to review the administrative proceedings in question. Judicial review ordinarily focuses on four possible areas of agency error:

1. The agency violated procedural due process.

2. The agency violated substantive due process.

3. The agency otherwise violated the Constitution.

4. The agency exceeded its authority.

A court, however, will review the proceedings only from the point of view of their legality. As to *questions of fact* (for example, what actually transpired), a court must follow the *substantial evidence rule*, which states that a court must uphold the agency's findings of fact if such findings are based on substantial evidence. If instead the judicial review involves *questions of law* (for example, jurisdictional or procedural issues), a court remains free to substitute its judgment for those of the agency; courts need not give deference to the agency's determinations regarding these issues.

A court will review *discretionary* acts under the "abuse of discretion" rationale and therefore will invalidate arbitrary, unreasonable, or capricious decisions.

Owing to the restricted nature of judicial review and the pervasive nature of administrative agencies in the business world, this area of regulation has become quite important today. A person who plans to advance very far in business is well advised to study administrative law in further detail. Firms involved in e-commerce in particular need to acquire an understanding of the Federal Trade Commission's recent initiatives and the context in which these enforcement activities have arisen.

Prior to the advent of the Internet, anyone bent on compiling personal information about a given person faced many obstacles. Typically, one would have to search through public records in various places. But the interconnectivity of extensive databases and the emergent technologies that can utilize "cookies" to amass information bearing on a given consumer's spending habits, product preferences, or travel plans, for example, have exponentially expanded the amount of information that firms can gather, analyze, and make available to third parties. (Cookies are software applications that enable a Web site operator to store information in a text file on the consumer's own computer.) Many times consumers are either unaware of cookies or lack the knowledge required to interpret the information stored in these files. Web site tracking services such as DoubleClick use cookies for profiling customers, who then are targeted for specific advertising or promotional activities. In short, accumulating information has in itself become "big business," and no firm can afford to miss out on the opportunities afforded by this information "explosion."

Even though much of this information takes the form of aggregate statistical analyses, technological developments have opened up the possibility of collecting personally identifiable information. The resultant availability of information, which presently is much cheaper to amass than at any previous time in history, has triggered consumer concerns about privacy and electronic security. The emerging consensus is that any firm that collects personal information should have a policy that gives notice to the consumer of the firm's data collection methods. The consumer or subject of the practices in addition should have the choice either to opt in or to opt out with regard to the collection of data. Opting in means that the consumer has expressly consented to the collection and/or use of personally identifiable information. In contrast, opting out indicates the consumer has rejected all such efforts to collect or use this type of information. Furthermore, the consumer should have the ability to access and review the information collected for accuracy and to object to erroneous data. Any on-line firm that collects or uses personally identifiable information must also ensure the security of its data collection methods, including the means to prevent unauthorized access to, or disclosure of, such information. Finally, the on-line firm must afford the consumer avenues for redressing any violations of the Web site's privacy practices, including access to dispute resolution mechanisms. Protecting privacy has always involved balancing individual interests such as what Supreme Court Justice Louis Brandeis over a century ago characterized as "the right to be left alone" with societal interests in order and efficiency. Today's business environment is rife with potential threats to individual privacy. Reconciling the tension between con-

sumers' desires to protect information gathered about them and on-line firms' desires to collect marketing data—and doing so without stunting growth of e-commerce—has occupied scholars, governmental regulators, and the business community, to name but a few groups.

Further complicating this debate is the fact that the United States traditionally has been reluctant to institute comprehensive regulations and policies concerning privacy. Rather, the United States has followed a so-called sectoral approach that mirrors both its historical reliance on laissez-faire economics and the fact-specific, case-by-case common law tradition. Regulation of privacy occurs only in discrete sectors (like public health or telecommunications) and only as a result of abusive activities that have injured the public. On the other hand, the European Union (EU) customarily has embraced a so-called omnibus approach to privacy that comprehensively covers all industries and the government, and oftentimes delegates the protection of privacy to a central governmental official or agency. Obviously, these models differ greatly. Harmonizing these approaches becomes even more crucial in this era of multinational corporations and on-line businesses. With firms doing business all over the globe and the boundary-less dimensions of cyberspace, the issue of how to treat these privacy interests becomes especially significant.

Since 1998, multinational companies and Web site operators have needed to familiarize themselves with the EU's complicated Privacy Directive because of its prohibition on the transfer of personal data outside the EU to countries that do not "adequately" protect such personal data. In covering personally identifiable information about individuals and the processing of such information, the Directive applies to a broad range of commercial and governmental activities. To illustrate, e-commerce businesses that have Web sites in Europe should make sure their systems can obtain the express consent of consumers when personal information is collected. In other words, the Directive endorses the opt-in approach to consent. To overcome the potentially burdensome requirements of the Directive, since 2000 it has been possible for U.S. firms that comply with the "safe harbor" principles agreed to by the EU and the U.S. Department of Commerce to receive personally identifiable data from EU citizens without violating the Directive. Thus far, only a small number of firms have been certified as being in compliance with the safe harbor rules. Still, this program provides an interesting example of workable options for facilitating the international transfer of data.

To learn more about the data protection safe harbor, see http://europa.eu.int/comm/enterprise/ict/policy/standards

/ipse_finalreport.pdf on the EU's Web site. Information about the U.S. safe harbor program is also available on the Department of Commerce's Web site: http://www.export.gov/safeharbor/.

In the United States, the Federal Trade Commission (FTC) is the administrative agency that has taken the lead in shaping e-commerce business practices. Its activities also illustrate the U.S. sectoral approach to privacy. As part of its charge to regulate unfair or deceptive methods of competition that are in, or affect, interstate commerce, the FTC has had a significant impact on the development of the law of cyberspace. In particular, the FTC has focused on consumer protection as it relates to data privacy (including the collection of information from children), advertising, contests/promotions, and on-line fraud (especially with regard to auctions and firms that either never deliver goods purchased on line or deliver goods in an untimely fashion). After much consideration and debate, the FTC has decided not to champion extensive regulation of e-commerce through administrative regulations or enabling statutory enactments. Rather, the FTC has concentrated its efforts on consumer education and the targeting of certain practices—say credit rehabilitation services—through "sweeps" whereby the FTC, in conjunction with other federal or state agencies, attempts to root out deceptive practices. Such enforcement efforts have encouraged self-regulation by on-line businesses.

Still, the FTC has not totally absented itself from the regulatory arena. To illustrate, the 1998 Children's Online Privacy Protection Act (COPPA) grew out of FTC recommendations for congressional action. COPPA in general prohibits on-line service providers from assembling or releasing personally identifiable information collected from a child under the age of 13 without notice to, and the consent of, the child's parents. Such information includes names, addresses, telephone numbers, Social Security numbers, and any other type of information that can facilitate either physical or on-line contact with a child. As the implementing agency for COPPA, the FTC has promulgated rules requiring any Web site operator to provide notice to parents of the site's information practices. Moreover, the operator must employ "reliable" methods to verify that the operator has obtained parental consent prior to the operator's collection, use, or disclosure to third parties or the public (such as through chat rooms) of any personal information about children. Reliable methods for obtaining verifiable parental consent include communications to the parents through postal mail, facsimile, digital signatures, and e-mail linked to a personal identification number (PIN) or password. Put differently, COPPA's rules endorse the opt-in approach to the "choice" dimension of fair information practices. COPPA also requires parental access to any information collected about children. The FTC can bring enforcement actions based on deceptive and unfair trade practices against any on-line firm that fails to disclose fully its information collection practices or to adhere to the policies and practices it has disclosed to consumers. State attorneys general can enforce compliance with the act by filing actions in federal court as well.

COPPA involves an explicit validation of the FTC's recently enunciated mandate: that all Web site operators adopt and publicize privacy policies that ensure effective data management techniques. Put differently, firms that have an Internet presence, including promises to consumers about the security of personal information (for example, credit card and Social Security numbers), will need to have in place reasonable and appropriate procedures designed to ensure the security of any information collected. Unless the policy unquestionably limits its application to on-line activities, the privacy policy will apply to the off-line collection and use of information as well—an area traditionally left unregulated. This apparent shift in focus by the FTC signals the agency's intention to protect consumers from the misuse of personal information regardless of how the information was collected or where it originated. At the very least, on-line firms will need to review their privacy policies and revise any provisions so as to clarify exactly when the policies apply. Some firms may even have to bear the costs of obtaining consent from customers from whom the firms previously have acquired information.

The recent settlements forged by the FTC with Eli Lilly and Company and Microsoft Corporation, respectively, may provide businesses with guidelines for exemplary security policies. The prominence of the FTC's roles takes on added significance given the lack of congressional support for federal on-line privacy legislation. It remains to be seen whether the enforcement of the laws—the FTC's preferred approach—rather than the passage of additional laws to preserve on-line privacy will sufficiently protect consumers so as to enhance consumer confidence in e-commerce. You might find it useful to choose an industry—say pharmaceutical companies—and then go to the Web sites of several firms and compare the privacy policies of the firms. Ask yourself whether the policies would make you hesitant about providing personal information to the companies.

You may also want to check out the Electronic Privacy Information Center's Web site at http://www.epic.org or the FTC's efforts concerning privacy at http://www.ftc.gov/privacy/. You can learn about cookies at http://www.cookiecentral.com/.

Summary

Governmental regulation of business is a fact of life in the modern business environment. Whether regulation takes the form of local zoning ordinances, state income taxation, or federal antitrust regulation, businesses today must address it. And the only way to deal with government regulation is to recognize and understand it. Federal regulation of business is based on both the commerce clause of the U.S. Constitution, which authorizes Congress to "regulate commerce among the several states," and Congress's taxing power, also included in the Constitution.

Most regulation derives from the commerce clause. The commerce clause has been interpreted in such a way that federal regulation is permitted only if interstate commerce is involved. To qualify as interstate, the transaction must directly affect citizens of at least two different states or countries. If an interstate connection is present, federal regulation may be applied. The federal government exclusively regulates many aspects of business, but the states have concurrent power to regulate in certain areas. States, however, can exercise exclusive regulatory power over commerce only rarely.

The equal protection clause protects against invidious discrimination. Over the years, the Supreme Court has developed various tests for determining the legality of regulations challenged under this provision of the Constitution.

The Constitution's guarantee of due process has a distinct procedural dimension and a substantive dimension. These aspects guarantee fundamental fairness and freedom from the application of irrational, unreasonable, and arbitrary laws whenever the government deprives anyone of life, liberty, or property.

Under the takings clause of the Fifth Amendment, the government can take property for public use so long as the government pays just compensation to the affected property owner. In addition, the Fifth Amendment's prohibitions on double jeopardy and compulsory self-incrimination also serve as curbs on illegitimate governmental action.

The First Amendment protects commercial speech but to a lesser degree than it does individual speech. The government can ban false and misleading commercial speech and can even regulate other types of commercial speech as long as the restriction serves and advances a substantial governmental interest and in a manner no more extensive than necessary to achieve that governmental objective.

Much of the actual regulation of business is effectuated by administrative agencies. Administrative agencies are created by Congress, and Congress then delegates to the agencies the authority to carry out certain duties. Agencies are involved in a large number of regulatory areas. In carrying out their responsibilities, these agencies are required to assure due process of law, and they are subject to judicial review to ensure that they conduct themselves properly.

In the United States, the Federal Trade Commission has taken the lead in shaping e-commerce practices, in the area of consumer protection as it relates to data privacy. The European Union's Privacy Directive may cover multinational companies and on-line operators; hence, becoming familiar with the Directive's rules is an important aspect of doing business globally.

Discussion Questions

1. How do you define the phrase "interstate commerce"? Do you accept or reject the Supreme Court's definition of this term? Why?

2. Name and explain the areas of commerce over which the federal government has exclusive jurisdiction. What are the areas of concurrent state and federal regulation? When does the state have exclusive jurisdiction over commerce?

3. Explain in detail the various tests a court must apply when it evaluates a law challenged on equal protection grounds.

4. Discuss the factors courts must take into account in deciding whether a group is a "suspect classification" for purposes of equal protection analysis.

5. Name and explain the various interests protected under the Fifth Amendment.

6. What does substantive due process mean? How does a court determine when a violation of this constitutional right has occurred?

7. How does procedural due process differ from substantive due process? What protections must the government provide to individuals and businesses under this aspect of the Fifth and Fourteenth Amendments?

8. What powers does the government enjoy under the takings clause? What rights does an individual or business have under this clause?

9. How does the protection accorded commercial speech differ from the protection granted to individual speech?

10. What powers are possessed by administrative agencies? From what source or sources do administrative agencies derive these powers?

Case Problems and Writing Assignments

1. The Mushroom Promotion, Research, and Consumer Information Act mandates that fresh mushroom handlers pay assessments used primarily to fund advertising promoting mushroom sales. This federal statute also authorizes the secretary of agriculture to establish a Mushroom Council, which can impose mandatory assessments on handlers of fresh mushrooms in an amount not to exceed one cent per pound of all mushrooms produced or imported. Although the assessments can be used for research, consumer information, and industry information, it is undisputed that the Council spends most of the monies raised by the assessments for generic advertising to promote mushroom sales. United Foods, Inc., a large, Tennessee-based agricultural enterprise, grows and distributes many crops and products, including fresh mushrooms. In 1996, United Foods refused to pay its mandatory assessments under the Act. United Foods wished to convey the message that its brand of mushrooms is superior to those grown by other producers. It therefore objected to being charged for a message favored by a majority of the other producers. The forced subsidy for generic advertising, it contended, violated the First Amendment.

The government argued that *Glickman v. Wileman Brothers & Elliott, Inc.*, a recent precedent, permitted the assessment. This case held that the First Amendment was not violated when agricultural marketing orders, as part of a larger regulatory marketing scheme, required producers of California tree fruit to pay assessments for product advertising. In the *Glickman* case, the California tree fruits were marketed pursuant to detailed marketing orders that had displaced competition to such an extent that the scheme was expressly exempted from the antitrust laws. In short, the market for the tree fruit regulated by the program was characterized by collective action rather than the aggregate consequences of independent competitive choices. The producers of tree fruit who were compelled to contribute funds for use in cooperative advertising did so as a part of a broader collective enterprise in which the regulatory scheme had already constrained their freedom to act independently. To that extent, the growers' mandated participation in an advertising program with a particular message was the logical outgrowth of a valid scheme of economic regulation.

In contrast, the mushroom-growing business is unregulated, except for the enforcement of a regional mushroom advertising program; and the mushroom market has not been collectivized, exempted from antitrust laws, subjected to a uniform price, or otherwise subsidized through price supports or restrictions on supply. In short, mushroom producers are not forced to associate as a group that makes cooperative decisions. Moreover, almost all the funds collected under the mandatory assessments are for one purpose: generic advertising. United Foods therefore claimed that the assessments, by reducing the amount of money available for it to conduct its advertising, violated the First Amendment's guarantees of freedom of speech. The secretary of agriculture, in contrast, argued that the generic advertising was germane to the marketing orders' purposes and consistent with the overall statutory scheme. The secretary further submitted that the assessments were constitutional under Supreme Court commercial speech precedents because the assessments were not used to fund ideological or political views. In these circumstances, whose arguments were more compelling? [See *U.S. v. United Foods, Inc.*, 533 U.S. 405 (2001).]

2. In 1985, the city of Dallas authorized the licensing of "Class E" dance halls to provide a place where younger teenagers could socialize with each other but not be subject to the potentially detrimental influences of older teenagers and young adults. The ordinance restricted admission to Class E dance halls to persons between the ages of 14 and 18. Parents, guardians, law enforcement, and dance hall personnel were excepted from the ordinance's age restriction. The ordinance also limited the hours of operation of Class E dance halls to between 1 P.M. and midnight daily when school was not in session.

Charles M. Stanglin operated the Twilight Skating Rink in Dallas and obtained a license for a Class E dance hall. Using movable plastic cones or pylons, he divided the floor of his roller-skating rink into two sections. On one side of the pylons, persons between the ages of 14 and 18 danced, while on the other side, persons of all ages skated to the same music. No age or hour restrictions applied to the skating rink. Stanglin did not serve alcohol on the premises, and security personnel were present. Stanglin sued in district court to enjoin the enforcement of the age and hour restrictions of the ordinance. He contended that the ordinance violated substantive due process and equal protection under the U.S. and Texas constitutions and that it unconstitutionally infringed the rights of persons between the ages of 14 and 18 to associate with persons outside that age bracket. The trial court, in upholding the ordinance, found that it was rationally related to the city's legitimate interest in ensuring the safety and welfare of children. The Texas court of appeals upheld the ordinance's time restriction, but it struck down the age restriction as violative of minors' First Amendment associational rights. To support a restriction on the fundamental right of "social association," the court said, "the legislative body must show a compelling interest"; and the regulation "must be accomplished by the least restrictive means." The court recognized the city's interest in "protect[ing] minors from detrimental, corrupting influences," but held that the "[c]ity's stated purposes . . . may be achieved in ways that are less intrusive on minors' freedom to associate." The U.S. Supreme Court granted certiorari. Did the Dallas ordinance violate any constitutional right of association? Did a rational relationship exist between the ordinance's age restriction and the city's interests? [See *City of Dallas v. Stanglin*, 490 U.S. 19 (1989).]

3. G & G Fire Sprinklers, Inc. is a fire protection company that installs fire sprinkler systems. G & G served as a subcontractor on several California public works projects. The California Labor Code requires that contractors and subcontractors on such projects pay their workers a prevailing wage that is determined by the State. At the time relevant here, if workers were not paid the prevailing wage, the contractor was required to pay each worker the difference between the prevailing wage and the wages paid, in addition to forfeiting a penalty to the State. The awarding body was required to include a clause to this effect in all contracts. The Code further authorizes the State to order the withholding of payments due a contractor on a public works project if a subcontractor on the project fails to comply with certain Code requirements. The Code permits the contractor, in turn, to withhold similar sums from the subcontractor. On the other hand, the Code permits the contractor, or its assignee, to recover the wages or penalties withheld by bringing suit against the awarding body. The awarding body retains the wages and penalties pending the outcome of the suit.

   In 1995, the state's Division of Labor Standards Enforcement (DLSE) determined that G & G, as a subcontractor on three public works projects, had violated the Code by failing to pay the prevailing wage and by failing to keep and/or furnish payroll records upon request. The DLSE issued notices to the awarding bodies on those projects, directing them to withhold from the contractors an amount equal to the wages and penalties forfeited owing to G & G's violations. The awarding bodies withheld payment from the contractors, who in turn withheld payment from G & G. The total withheld, according to G & G, exceeded $135,000. G & G then sued, claiming that the issuance of the withholding notices without a hearing constituted a deprivation of property without due process of law in violation of the Fourteenth Amendment. Should G & G win? [See *Lujan v. G & G Fire Sprinklers, Inc.*, 532 U.S. 189 (2001).]

4. In order to acquire the waterfront parcel of Rhode Island land at issue, Anthony Palazzolo and some associates formed Shore Gardens, Inc. (SGI) in 1959. Palazzolo eventually became the sole shareholder. Most of the property was then, and is now, salt marsh subject to tidal flooding. The wet ground and permeable soil thus would require considerable fill before significant structures could be built. Over the years, various governmental agencies rejected SGI's intermittent applications to develop the property. After 1966, no further applications were made for over a decade. Two intervening events, however, deserve mention. First, in 1971, the state created the Rhode Island Coastal Resources Management Council (Council) and charged it with protecting the state's coastal properties. The Council's regula-

tions, known as the Rhode Island Coastal Resources Management Program (CRMP), designated salt marshes like those on SGI's property as protected "coastal wetlands" on which development is greatly limited. Second, in 1978, SGI's corporate charter was revoked, and title to the property passed to Palazzolo as the corporation's sole shareholder.

In 1983, Palazzolo applied to the Council for permission to construct a wooden bulkhead and fill the entire marshland area. The Council, in rejecting this application, concluded that it would conflict with the CRMP. In 1985, Palazzolo filed a new application, seeking permission to fill 11 of the property's 18 wetland acres in order to build a private beach club. The Council rejected this application as well, ruling that the proposal did not satisfy the standards for obtaining a "special exception," namely that the proposed activity serve a compelling public purpose. Subsequently, Palazzolo filed a lawsuit asserting that the state's wetlands regulations, as applied by the Council to his parcel, had taken the property without compensation in violation of the Fifth and Fourteenth Amendments. The suit further alleged that the Council's action had deprived him of "all economically beneficial use" of his property, resulting in a total taking that required compensation in the amount of $3,150,000, a figure derived from an appraiser's estimate as to the value of a 74-lot residential subdivision on the property. The lower courts ruled against Palazzolo on grounds that (1) his takings claim was not ripe; (2) he lacked the right to challenge regulations predating 1978, the time when he had succeeded to the legal ownership of the property; (3) he would be unable to assert a takings claim based on the denial of all economic use of his property in light of the undisputed evidence that he had $200,000 in development value remaining on an upland parcel of the property; and (4) because the regulation at issue predated his acquisition of title, he could have had no reasonable investment-backed expectation that he could develop his property and, therefore, lacked any basis for recovery. Who had the stronger arguments—Palazzolo or the state? [See *Palazzolo v. Rhode Island*, 533 U.S. 606 (2001).]

5. BUSINESS APPLICATION CASE The Town of Clarkstown, New York, agreed to allow a private contractor to construct within the town's limits a solid-waste transfer system to separate recyclable from nonrecyclable items and to operate the facility for five years, at which time Clarkstown would buy it for one dollar. To finance the transfer station's cost, the town guaranteed a minimum waste flow to the facility, for which the contractor could charge the hauler a tipping fee, which, at $81 per ton, exceeded the disposal cost of unsorted solid waste on the private market. In order to meet this waste flow guarantee, Clarkstown adopted a flow control ordinance requiring all nonhazardous solid waste within the town to be deposited at the transfer station. While recyclers like C & A Carbone, Inc. (Carbone) might receive solid waste at its own sorting facilities, the ordinance required such recyclers to bring nonrecyclable residue to the transfer station. The ordinance in effect thus forbade such recyclers to ship such waste themselves and required them to pay the tipping fee on trash that already had been

sorted. After discovering that Carbone had shipped nonrecyclable waste to out-of-state destinations, Clarkstown sought a state court injunction requiring that this residue be shipped to the transfer station. Finding the ordinance constitutional, the state court granted summary judgment to Clarkstown; and the appellate division affirmed. On appeal, on what constitutional basis should Carbone focus its arguments? [See *C & A Carbone, Inc. v. Town of Clarkstown*, 511 U.S. 383 (1994).]

6. **ETHICAL APPLICATION CASE** In September 1992, the operators of the Women's Health Center (WHC), an abortion clinic in Melbourne, Florida, sought an injunction against certain antiabortion protestors. At that time, a Florida state court permanently enjoined Madsen and the other protesters from blocking or interfering with public access to the clinic and from physically abusing persons entering or leaving the clinic. Six months later, WHC, complaining that access to the clinic was still impeded by the protesters' activities and that such activities also had discouraged some potential patients from entering the clinic and had had deleterious physical effects on others, sought to broaden the injunction.

In issuing this broader injunction, the trial court found that, despite the initial injunction, protesters congregating on the paved portion of the street leading up to the clinic and marching in front of the clinic's driveways had continued to impede access to the clinic. The trial court found that as vehicles heading toward the clinic slowed to allow the protesters to move out of the way, "sidewalk counselors" would attempt to give the vehicles' occupants antiabortion literature. The number of people congregating varied from a handful to 400, and the noise varied from singing and chanting to the use of loudspeakers and bullhorns. A clinic doctor testified that as a result of having to run such a gauntlet to enter the clinic, the patients, owing to heightened anxiety and hypertension, needed a higher level of sedation before they could undergo surgical procedures and thereby faced increased risks from such procedures. The noise caused stress not only for the patients undergoing surgery but also for those recuperating in the recovery rooms. Doctors and clinic workers in turn were not immune even in their homes. The protesters picketed in front of clinic employees' residences, rang the doorbells of neighbors, provided literature identifying the particular clinic employee as a "baby killer," and occasionally confronted the clinic employees' minor children who were home alone.

Given this and similar testimony, the state court viewed the original injunction as insufficient "to protect the health, safety and rights of women in Brevard and Seminole County, Florida, and surrounding counties seeking access to [medical and counseling] services." The state court therefore amended its prior order and enjoined a broader array of activities. Although the Florida supreme court upheld the injunction, the Court of Appeals for the Eleventh Circuit struck it down. At the U.S. Supreme Court, what constitutional arguments would the parties make? Who should win and why? If you were deciding this case on ethical grounds, with whom would you side—the protesters or the clinic and its personnel? Why? [See

Madsen v. Women's Health Center, Inc., 512 U.S. 753 (1994), modified at *Schenck v. Pro-Choice Network of Western New York*, 519 U.S. 357 (1997).]

7. **CRITICAL THINKING CASE** 44 Liquormart, Inc. (44 Liquormart) and Peoples Super Liquor Stores, Inc. (Peoples) were licensed retailers of alcoholic beverages. 44 Liquormart operated a store in Rhode Island, and Peoples operated several stores in Massachusetts that were patronized by Rhode Island residents. Peoples used alcohol price advertising extensively in Massachusetts, where such advertising is permitted, but Rhode Island newspapers and other media outlets have refused to accept such ads. In 1991, 44 Liquormart placed an advertisement in a Rhode Island newspaper. The advertisement did not state the price of any alcoholic beverages. Indeed, it noted that "State law prohibits advertising liquor prices." The ad did, however, state the low prices at which peanuts, potato chips, and Schweppes mixers were being offered, identify various brands of packaged liquor, and include the word "WOW" in large letters next to pictures of vodka and rum bottles.

Based on the conclusion that the implied reference to bargain prices for liquor violated the statutory ban on price advertising, the Rhode Island Liquor Control Administrator assessed a $400 fine. After paying the fine, 44 Liquormart, joined by Peoples, sought in federal court a declaratory judgment that the two statutes and the administrator's implementing regulations violated the First Amendment and other provisions of federal law. The parties stipulated that the price advertising ban is vigorously enforced, that Rhode Island permits "all advertising of alcoholic beverages excepting references to price outside the licensed premises," and that the proposed ads do not concern an illegal activity and presumably would not be false or misleading. The parties disagreed, however, about the impact of the ban on the promotion of temperance in Rhode Island.

The district court concluded that the price advertising ban was unconstitutional because it did not "directly advance" the state's interest in reducing alcohol consumption and was "more extensive than necessary to serve that interest." The district court reasoned that the party seeking to uphold a restriction on commercial speech carries the burden of justifying it and that the Twenty-first Amendment did not shift or diminish that burden. Acknowledging that it might have been reasonable for the state legislature to "assume a correlation between the price advertising ban and reduced consumption," the court held that more than a rational basis was required to justify the speech restriction and that the state had failed to demonstrate a reasonable fit between its policy objectives and its chosen means. The court of appeals reversed. It found inherent merit in the state's submission that competitive price advertising would lower prices and that lower prices would produce more sales. Moreover, it agreed with the reasoning of the Rhode Island Supreme Court that the Twenty-first Amendment gave the statutes an added presumption of validity. The Supreme Court thereafter granted certiorari. Did Rhode Island's statutory ban on the advertising of liquor prices except at the place of sale violate the First Amendment? Would the Twenty-first Amendment shield this advertising ban from constitutional scrutiny? [See *44 Liquormart, Inc. v. Rhode Island*, 517 U.S. 484 (1996).]

8. YOU BE THE JUDGE The pharmaceutical firm Eli Lilly and Co. (Lilly) has a Web site called http://www.prozac.com/. From March 2000 though June 2001, Lilly offered a service called "Medi-Messenger," whereby the firm would provide individualized e-mail reminders concerning medication. Pursuant to its own privacy policy, Lilly assured all those who signed up for the Medi-Messenger service that "Eli Lilly and Company respects the privacy of visitors to its Web sites." The Lilly policy further specified that its sites "have security measures in place, including the use of industry standard secure socket layer encryption (SSL), to protect the confidentiality of any of Your Information that you volunteer." On June 27, 2001, Lilly sent all 669 subscribers to its Medi-Messenger service an e-mail that inadvertently included every subscriber's e-mail address in the "To" field. This disclosure was unintentional, and Lilly had never before made any inappropriate disclosures.

Prompted by a complaint from the American Civil Liberties Union, the Federal Trade Commission (FTC) sought to hold Lilly legally accountable for this glitch, based on Lilly's own privacy policy. Using as its jurisdictional basis the allegedly false or misleading representation that Lilly had made during the sign-up process for Medi-Messenger, the FTC claimed that Lilly had failed to implement internal measures and policies that protected the privacy and confidentiality of the personal information supplied by its customers. Among other things, the FTC suggested that Lilly should be held accountable not only for ensuring the sensitivity of the information supplied to it by its customers but also for preventing cyberattacks on such data.

Assume that Lilly and the FTC agree to settle this on-line privacy complaint. If you were representing the FTC, what specific provisions (or safeguards) would you require Lilly to include in its internal privacy policies to ensure that Lilly in the future would be able to maintain adequate controls on information security? [See 70 U.S.L.W. 2507–2508 (Feb. 19, 2002).]

Notes

1. *Statistical Abstract of the United States 2001*, 121st ed. (Washington, D.C.: U.S. Department of Commerce), 319.
2. 22 U.S. (9 Wheat.) 1 (1824).
3. 24 Stat. 379 (1887).
4. 82 U.S. (15 Wall.) 232 (1873).
5. 128 U.S. 1 (1888).
6. 301 U.S. 1 (1937).
7. 336 U.S. 460, 464 (1949).
8. 379 U.S. 241 (1964).
9. 411 U.S. 624 (1973).
10. 514 U.S. 549 (1995). See also *U.S. v. Morrison*, 529 U.S. 598 (2000), where, in like vein, the Supreme Court, in holding that Congress had exceeded its authority under the Commerce Clause, invalidated the federal Violence Against Women Act.
11. 118 U.S. 356 (1886).
12. 517 U.S. 620 (1996).
13. Ibid. at 635.
14. *City of Richmond v. J. A. Croson Co.*, 488 U.S. 469 (1989).
15. 515 U.S. 200 (1995).
16. Ibid. at 202.
17. *Adarand Constructors, Inc. v. Mineta*, 534 U.S. 103 (2001).
18. 429 U.S. 190 (1976).
19. *U.S. v. Virginia*, 518 U.S. 515, at 516 and 534 (1996).
20. 499 U.S. 1 (1991).
21. *Cruzan v. Director, Missouri Department of Health*, 497 U.S. 261 (1990).
22. *Lucas v. South Carolina Coastal Council*, 505 U.S. 1003 (1992).
23. 526 U.S. 687 (1999).
24. 512 U.S. 622 (1994).
25. *Turner Broadcasting System, Inc. v. Federal Communications Comm'n*, 520 U.S. 180 (1997).
26. *Reno v. American Civil Liberties Union*, 521 U.S. 844 (1997).

Dispute Resolution

AGENDA

NRW While driving an NRW van, Carlos Rios is involved in an accident with another vehicle, causing property damage to both vehicles and physical injuries to the parties inside the other car. The passengers in the other car are planning to file a lawsuit against Carlos and NRW. Mai, Carlos, and Helen want to know whether NRW is liable for Carlos's actions. They also want to know how NRW should defend itself in this situation. What steps should Mai, Carlos, and Helen take to minimize their involvement or the involvement of NRW in any future traffic accidents?

Mai, Carlos, and Helen do not *plan* to be involved in any legal proceedings while conducting their business. They intend to be careful to minimize the risk of a lawsuit. They hope to select clients, customers, employees, and suppliers who will honor their contracts with NRW, so that NRW will not be forced to seek legal relief. They recognize, however, that inevitably they and/or the firm are likely to have a legal controversy. From discussions with you, and from their experience in the workplace, they realize that lawsuits can be time consuming and expensive. As a result, they would prefer to be able to settle any disputes or controversies in some alternative manner, if possible. Should they include mandatory arbitration provisions in their contracts with suppliers and retailers? Who should be specified as the arbitrator? Would it be better to include a provision for arbitration or a provision for mediation in their employment contracts? When might the firm want to "rent-a-judge" in settling a controversy? When is it better to negotiate than to litigate?

These and other questions will arise as you read this chapter. Be prepared! You never know when the firm or one of its members will seek your advice.

Overview

People in American society have a great many fears and concerns. Some of these fears may seem irrational to other individuals—for example, a fear of the dark or a fear of heights. Others are viewed as much more rational to most members of our society—for example, a fear of catching certain diseases or a fear of losing one's job. One area that causes fear and concern to the average person is involvement in the legal process, for example, as a result of an automobile accident. Someone may be apprehensive about being sued and being required to pay damages or filing suit seeking damages from another person.

This chapter explores the stages of a hypothetical case arising from such a situation. While this material may not alleviate the concern or the fear that you may have, it should help to shed some light on *what* is done, *why* it is done, and *how* it integrates with the workings of our judicial system in a civil suit. Exhibit 6.1 sets out the six stages a *party* (plaintiff or defendant in the lawsuit) is likely to encounter in a civil *suit* (lawsuit, the formal legal proceeding used to resolve a legal dispute). Each of these stages is examined in more detail as we follow the progress of our hypothetical lawsuit through the legal system.

Costs of Litigation

Before an individual or business entity pursues litigation, he or she should consider the costs of the litigation. There are likely to be direct and obvious costs, and indirect, often hidden, costs. The kinds and amounts of fees will vary depending on the type of litigation. In order to make an informed decision about whether to sue or defend a suit, the parties should consider the probable outcomes of litigation. The parties should also consider the likelihood that alternate dispute resolution (ADR) will be effective and its costs. (*Alternate dispute resolution* consists of methods of resolving disputes other than traditional litigation.) Even though some forms of ADR are becoming more formal, time consuming, and expensive, ADR may still reduce overall costs. The Association for Conflict Resolution (ACR) is concerned about conflict resolution, ranging from conflicts between nations to conflicts between family members. It provides information about conflict resolution techniques at http://www.acresolution.org/.

There are a number of factors that a potential party should consider before deciding whether to initiate any lawsuit or agree to otherwise settle a dispute. Some of the more important factors include the following:

- The legal system is unpredictable, and a trial may be very time consuming

- It is difficult to determine the likelihood of winning the suit with any degree of certainty

- The amount of money a party might win (or lose) may determine whether he or she wants to proceed with a trial or seek a settlement

EXHIBIT 6.1 The Six Steps Involved in Most Civil Lawsuits	
Pleadings	The case begins by filing documents identifying the parties (the person suing and the person being sued), explaining what the claim is about, and asking the court to do something—usually to award monetary damages.
Service	The person being sued (the defendant) must be formally notified. Service is usually obtained by preparing a summons and then having the summons and a copy of the complaint personally delivered to the defendant.
Discovery	Both sides have to gather facts and information to prepare for trial. Discovery can involve examining documents, records, and other pieces of physical evidence as well as taking the statements of the parties and other witnesses.
Pretrial motions	Parties request the court to make procedural decisions or other rulings by filing motions with the court. Motions are often in writing.
Trial	The court hears evidence offered by each side and decides issues of both fact and law.
Enforcing the judgment	If a party wins a judgment at trial, he or she still has to collect the money awarded. A judgment can be enforced by putting a lien on property, garnishing wages, or obtaining a court order for the transfer of bank accounts or other property.

- The ability of the other party to pay any judgment might make suing a waste of time and money *or* might make suing the preferred alternative

- The amount that the lawyer(s) would charge, and when the lawyers would bill

- The amount of court costs, including filing fees

- The additional fees that might be incurred, including the fees for expert witnesses (for example, accountants, economists, and doctors), fees for preparing exhibits, fees for medical tests and exams, fees for *depositions* (the formal process of asking a potential witness questions under oath outside the courtroom), and the cost for jury consultants

- The amount of time that the parties, their families and friends, and company employees would spend in preparing for the litigation

- The manner in which this lawsuit and/or additional publicity would affect the reputations of the parties

- The effect on the continuing relationship between parties to the suit

- The stress and emotional toll that the lawsuit will take on those involved

- Personal time and effort (for example, employees may be preparing for the litigation in lieu of working on regular employment tasks)

- Distraction from personal and professional goals (for example, employees may be distracted from the goals of the enterprise)

This is a listing of some of the primary factors to be considered. In addition, there may be some hidden costs associated with the suit.

Litigation is also expensive for the court system. As a result, courts have rules to reduce the costs. For example, a court may permit a class action lawsuit, which is a lawsuit involving a group of plaintiffs or defendants who are in substantially the same situation. This is more efficient than facing the prospects of many individual lawsuits, each of which is likely to involve the same basic facts and issues of law. Of course, combining the plaintiffs or defendants into a class is not always appropriate. Law.com published an article by Shannon P. Duffy of *The Legal Intelligencer* entitled "National Class Action Against Kia Denied" at http://www.law.com/jsp/article.jsp?id=1032128879114. It is an article about the court's decision not to grant nationwide class action status in a case against Kia.

Many courts have established additional procedures to make complex litigation run more efficiently and smoothly.

For example, if there are 300 cases against four insurance companies, with each of the plaintiffs seeking recovery under the insurance policies for injuries allegedly suffered due to exposure to toxic mold, the court may designate an individual judge or panel of judges to handle the suits. In consultation with the legal counsel, the judge(s) may impose additional rules to aid in handling the cases. The judge may require things like electronic filing of complaints and motions. (In civil practice, the *complaint* is the plaintiff's first pleading. It informs the defendant that he or she is being sued.)

The Problem

Nic Grant, a college sophomore, saved some money earned from a part-time job to take his girlfriend, Nancy Griffin, to dinner at a very expensive and sophisticated restaurant on Mount Washington, overlooking the Point in downtown Pittsburgh. Nic called for Nancy at her apartment in Cranberry Township about 6 o'clock on June 6 and was driving through Butler County toward the restaurant when his car was struck by a white van with the NRW logo on it. The accident happened at the intersection of Route 19 (Perry Highway) and Rowan Road in Cranberry Township, Butler County.

Nic spent the next five days in the hospital. As a result, he did not show up for work and consequently lost his job. He was also unable to take his college final examinations or to complete his research projects for several of his classes. In fact, Nic was forced to withdraw from college for the term. Nancy, who did not have a job, also suffered injuries from the impact and sought medical treatment. Nic's roommate, who is taking a course in business law, advised Nic that he and Nancy were likely to have a claim against the other driver and recommended that they consult a lawyer to learn what their potential rights might be.

Carlos Rios, one of the principals and an officer of NRW, was in Pittsburgh to work at a trade show displaying electronic products. He worked at the booth in the Pittsburgh Convention Center from 8:30 A.M. until 5:30 P.M. on June 6, with a half-hour lunch break. None of the other principals of the firm could leave the NRW office for the trade show. Consequently, Carlos had to work the booth by himself.

After a long and tiring day at the trade show, Carlos packed the sample products in the NRW van and left the Convention Center parking lot at 5:45 P.M. on the evening of June 6. Before heading home, he drove toward Butler, to a restaurant recommended by a friend, Trattoria Restaurant on Main Street. Carlos had directions from an Internet map site, but was unfamiliar with the area. While he was trying to negotiate the streets, read the map he had printed, and remember his friend's instructions, he was involved in an accident. The NRW van being driven by Carlos hit the car owned and operated by Nic Grant. (For purposes of this chapter, NRW is an Ohio corporation licensed as a foreign corporation doing business in Pennsylvania.)

Client's Interview with a Lawyer

Nic recognized that he needed legal assistance and consulted the local bar association. The local bar association referred Nic to an attorney, Ms. Lyn Carroll. (FindLaw provides access to West's Legal Directory at http://www. directory.findlaw.com/. The Web site includes information about whether you need a lawyer and how to hire one. Chapter 1 contains additional information about hiring an attorney.) Nic called Ms. Carroll and scheduled an initial interview. At this initial interview, Nic recounted all the facts of that evening, to the best of his recollection. Nic then mentioned that he had not notified either the driver of the other vehicle or NRW. Ms. Carroll agreed to assist Nic in obtaining compensation and offered to help Nancy as well. Ms. Carroll recognized that it might be a conflict of interest for her to represent both Nic and Nancy, especially if Nic was also negligent in causing the accident. (In order for Lyn Carroll to comply with the ethics rules for attorneys, she would need to send each prospective client a letter disclosing the possible conflict of interest and seeking their consent to having her as the attorney for each despite this potential conflict.)

When meeting with Ms. Carroll, Nic asked a number of questions including what payment terms she would require in order to represent him, and whether there were any opportunities to negotiate or arbitrate a settlement rather than go to trial. Nic wanted to know if Ms. Carroll was willing to work toward a negotiated settlement and whether this would affect the amount of attorney's fees that would be owed. Following this initial meeting, Nic and Nancy agreed to meet with Ms. Carroll a few days later to discuss, read, and sign the client-attorney contract. As indicated in the contract, payment was to be based on a contingency fee. (A *contingency fee* is a fee to be paid to an attorney based on some contingency or event. The most common provisions are that the fee is due only if the case is settled or won.) Other bases for attorney's fees are not dependent on results: for example, flat rate and hourly rate fees. Whatever the fee arrangement, it is specified in the contract between the client and the attorney. The contract agreed to in this case appears as Exhibit 6.2. The American Bar Association's (ABA's) Center for Professional Responsi-

bility maintains information on legal ethics, regulation of lawyers, client protection, and links to the 2003 Edition of the Model Rules of Professional Conduct at http://www. abanet.org/cpr/home.html.

Since NRW has insurance, an attorney hired by the insurance company is likely to be the "lead counsel" in this case. However, that attorney will focus on protecting the interests of the insurance company, not the interests of NRW. If NRW loses the case, the insurance company will pay for the damages covered by the insurance policy, and NRW will have to pay for any other damages. Consequently, in many situations the firm would hire its own attorney. The firm's attorney would normally work with the insurer's attorney, and the two of them would agree on the strategy to take. We will assume in this case that NRW has no liability in excess of the policy limits and will not need its own attorney. We will refer to NRW and Carlos as the defendants. The insurance company is not really a defendant. It is providing insurance for NRW's liability. (In practice it is often difficult to decide whether to hire your own attorney in addition to the one hired by the insurer.)

In this case, the insurance company has selected Jefferson Jones of the Pittsburgh law firm of Jones, Murphy, Sabbatino, and Schwartz, which specializes in defending against personal injury suits. The insurer has worked with Mr. Jones numerous times in past cases. Mai and Carlos scheduled an appointment to meet with Mr. Jones to discuss the case.

Even though the accident occurred in Butler County, the defendants can hire an attorney from Pittsburgh, located in Allegheny County. Attorneys are licensed at the state level and not the county level. Once licensed, the attorney can practice law anywhere within the state's jurisdiction. Rules of court and court procedures may vary somewhat from county to county, and the attorney will need to know or learn the rules in Butler County for this trial, as well as knowing the Pennsylvania Rules of Civil Procedure. Each state has its own rules of procedure for both civil and criminal trials, as does the federal court system. Civil trials conducted in federal court are controlled by the Federal Rules of Civil Procedure. Legal Information Institute (LII), maintained by the Cornell Law School, provides the Federal Rules of Civil Procedure in a hypertext and searchable format at http://www.law. cornell.edu/rules/frcp/overview. htm. The rules of procedure in many states are modeled after these rules.

Neither party is required to hire an attorney. Either the plaintiffs, the defendants, or both sides to the case could choose to represent themselves in court. This is called appearing *pro se* (appearing in one's own behalf). This may be very unwise depending on the circumstances. A nonlawyer often mislabels concepts, misses key points, and is not familiar with the rules of civil procedure.[1]

EXHIBIT **6.2** Client-Attorney Contract

AGREEMENT

THIS CONTRACT entered into, by, and between NIC GRANT and NANCY GRIFFIN, hereinafter referred to as CLIENTS, and LYN CARROLL, hereinafter referred to as ATTORNEY, WITNESSETH:

1. Clients hereby retain and employ attorney to represent them in the prosecution of their claim and cause of action for damages sustained by them as a result of an automobile accident occurring 6 June 2003 on Route 19 and Rowan Road, Butler County, Pennsylvania, resulting in injuries and damages to clients.

2. Clients agree to pay attorney for her services rendered pursuant to this employment contract at the rate of twenty-five percent (25%) if the case is settled prior to trial and at the rate of thirty-three and one-third percent (33⅓%) of the net amount recovered if the case goes to trial.

3. All necessary and reasonable costs, expenses, investigation, preparation for trial, and litigation expenses shall be initially paid for by attorney and then deducted from the amount of any settlement or recovery, and the division between the parties shall be made after deduction of said expenses. Furthermore, clients shall reimburse attorney for all such costs and expenses even if no recovery is made or, in the alternative, if the costs and expenses should exceed the amount of the recovery.

4. Attorney agrees to undertake the representation of clients in the prosecution of the above claims and causes of action, using her highest professional skill to further the interest of said clients in all matters in connection with their claims and causes of action, and to diligently pursue said claims and causes of action.

5. No settlement or other disposition of the matter shall be made by attorney without the written approval of clients.

IN WITNESS WHEREOF, the parties hereto have executed this instrument in triplicate originals this 17th day of June 2003.

CLIENT _____
NIC GRANT

CLIENT _____
NANCY GRIFFIN

ATTORNEY _____
LYN CARROLL

Investigation of the Facts

In the interviews with her clients and in subsequent telephone conversations, Ms. Carroll gathered information concerning the accident. On the basis of this preliminary information, she obtained medical releases from both clients in order to review the hospital and medical records of each of them. Nic also gave her copies of the hospital bills and the estimate for the car repair. Finally, Ms. Carroll obtained a copy of the police report filed by José Gonzalez, the officer who responded to the accident scene.

After reviewing the file, Ms. Carroll wrote to the university that Nic and Nancy had been attending for proof that they had withdrawn from classes after June 6, 2003. She also wrote to Nic's former employer for information about Nic's wages, normal work week, and proof that he was fired on June 10, 2003. Once all the material requested was in the file, her preliminary investigation was finished. She concluded that Nic was driving with Nancy in his car on Rowan Road, Cranberry Township, Butler County, when the car was struck by a van operated by Carlos Rios. The van was owned by NRW and was decorated with permanent signs on both doors advertising NRW products. At this point, Ms. Carroll wrote a letter to Mai Nguyen, an officer of NRW. It appears as Exhibit 6.3. It is important for Ms. Carroll to determine that there is basis for a suit, because attorneys and clients who file frivolous lawsuits may be subject to penalties.

Negotiation of a Settlement

Upon receipt of the letter of notice, Mai Nguyen contacted NRW's insurance company to inform them of its contents. The insurance carrier immediately assigned an adjuster to the case. The adjuster contacted Ms. Carroll to ascertain the nature of the injuries. On the basis of this information, the adjuster attempted to negotiate a settlement by offering $17,027 to Mr. Grant and $5,680 to Ms. Griffin. Since the offers covered only out-of-pocket expenses and did not include any allowance for lost wages or for pain and suffering, both Nic and Nancy rejected the offers. When no other offers were made by the insurer, Ms. Carroll filed suit on November 15, 2003. (Note that Nic Grant is claiming at least $16,000 and Nancy Griffin is claiming at least $8,000 in pain and suffering in addition to any other losses either of them will be able to prove.) In many situations, the negotiations would be

---

EXHIBIT   6.3   Letter of Notice

LYN CARROLL J.D.
Attorney at Law
Suite 654
Butler Savings Building
Butler, Pennsylvania 15205

25 June 2003

Ms. Mai Nguyen
President
NRW
9876 Appian Way
Maineville, OH 44444

Mr. Carlos Rios
c/o NRW
9876 Appian Way
Maineville, OH 44444   RE: *Nic Grant and Nancy Griffin v. NRW and Carlos Rios*

Dear Ms. Mai Nguyen and Mr. Carlos Rios:

I have been retained by Mr. Nic Grant and Ms. Nancy Griffin to represent them in a cause of action arising from your van colliding with the car owned and operated by Mr. Grant on 6 June 2003. Ms. Griffin was a passenger in Mr. Grant's car at that time. My preliminary investigation indicates that the accident was caused by inattention and carelessness by your driver, Mr. Carlos Rios, and by improper maintenance of your van.

Should you or your liability carrier wish to discuss this matter with me in order to achieve a just and equitable settlement, please contact me within twelve days from the date of this letter. If I do not hear from you or your representative within that period, I shall file suit against you without further notice.

Sincerely,

Lyn Carroll

LC: rj
cc: Mr. Grant
     Ms. Griffin

more extensive. Ms. Carroll might have a conference with the insurance adjuster, the insurance company's attorney, or NRW's attorney in an effort to resolve the conflict and reach a settlement without resorting to a civil suit.

There is some advantage to waiting to initiate suit. Plaintiffs will want to know that their injuries are completely healed and no new injuries are discovered. In this case, waiting might also be an advantage to NRW, since Nic may obtain replacement employment. In general, a plaintiff must be sure to initiate his or her suit by filing the complaint before the statute of limitations expires. The suit should also commence before the memories of the parties and witnesses begin to fade. Before filing suit the attorney should discuss alternatives to litigation with her clients.

A Civil Suit

Filing the Suit

The complaint should be definite and it should contain sufficient information for the defendant to understand the nature of the litigation so that he or she can begin to prepare his or her defense. Exhibit 6.4 shows the plaintiffs' original complaint, which was filed in the *Court of Common Pleas* (title used in some states for trial courts of general jurisdiction). After it was filed, the prothonotary's office delivered a copy to the sheriff. (*Prothonotary* is the title used in some states to designate the chief clerk of court.) In many states, the clerk of court's office performs the same functions as the prothonotary's office. The sheriff then serves copies of the complaint on all the defendants. Depending on the type of suit and the state, any responsible adult who is not a party to the suit may be able to serve the complaint. In some states, the complaint is accompanied by a *summons* (a writ requiring the sheriff to notify the person named that the person must appear in court to answer a complaint).

Since NRW is registered as a foreign corporation, its complaint was delivered by mail to Mai at the principal office of the corporation. Many states permit service of process on registered foreign corporations by delivery of the complaint to the state's own secretary of state. If either NRW or Carlos Rios planned to claim that the court lacked jurisdiction over them or the lawsuit, they would have done it at this time instead of filing a general answer. (See Chapter 4 for a discussion of jurisdiction.)

Exhibit 6.5 displays a copy of the defendants' answer. Most complaints and answers will be more detailed than these examples and must include individual numbered items specifying the elements that constitute the legal cause of action.

Sometimes the defendant does not answer the complaint. In these cases, the court will generally enter a *default judgment,* a judgment in default of the defendant's appearance. In these cases the court is only "listening" to the plaintiff's side, so the court generally awards the plaintiff what he or she is requesting. Default judgments are valid in civil cases if the court has proper jurisdiction, including jurisdiction over the defendant, and the defendant has been properly served in the case.

At this point in the proceedings, the plaintiffs have sued the defendants in a court of law and the defendants have filed an answer. Before trial, both attorneys may simplify the legal issues, amend their complaints and answers, and attempt to limit the number of expert witnesses, if any. The purpose is to reduce costs and the length of trial.

Pretrial Proceedings

At this point, the discovery process begins. *Discovery* is a general term that applies to a group of specific methods used to "discover" information and to narrow the issues to be decided by the trial. Lawyers use the process to shorten the actual trial, if there is one, or to eliminate the need for a trial if the case can be settled. If one side sees that there is little hope it can win the suit, it is often in that party's best interests to settle the case. The scope of discovery is very broad. Generally, one can discover all information that is relevant even if it cannot be introduced as evidence during the trial. The standard used is whether the discovery request is reasonably calculated to lead to admissible evidence. Exhibit 6.6 on page 142 depicts the five common discovery devices.

Depositions Traditionally, a *deposition* is the reducing to writing of a witness's sworn testimony taken outside of court. The testimony begins with the witness swearing that the testimony will be truthful. If it is not, the witness can be held in contempt, as President Clinton was in Paula Jones's case.[2] Increasingly, attorneys also videotape the deposition. This is permitted in a number of jurisdictions, including federal courts (Federal Rules of Civil Procedure § 30[b][2]) and California courts (California Civil Procedure § 2025[p]). If the deposition is later used at trial, the jury will view the film of the deposition instead of having the deposition read to them. Generally, this is more interesting and the jurors are more likely to pay close attention to the questions and answers. Depositions are used routinely today. They are used to preserve testimony from someone who, for good cause, may not be able to attend the trial. They are also used to impeach the witness when the witness appears at trial and gives evidence that conflicts with what he or she said at the time the deposition was

EXHIBIT   6.4   Plaintiffs' Original Complaint

Plaintiffs' Original Complaint

COURT OF COMMON PLEAS OF BUTLER COUNTY, PENNSYLVANIA

NIC GRANT	:	A.D. No. 23465
and	:	
NANCY GRIFFIN, Plaintiffs	:	
	:	Civil Action Law
	:	
V.	:	A jury trial is demanded.
	:	
NRWᵃ	:	
and	:	
CARLOS RIOSᵇ, Defendants	:	
	:	

NOW COME NIC GRANT and NANCY GRIFFIN, hereinafter called PLAINTIFFS, complaining of NRW, a foreign corporation doing business in the Commonwealth of Pennsylvania, and CARLOS RIOS, hereinafter called DEFENDANTS, who may be served with citation by service, upon NRW's statutory agent and Mr. Rios's place of employment, MAI NGUYEN, 9876 Appian Way, Maineville, Ohio, and for cause of action would respectfully show unto the court that:

On or about 6 June 2003, plaintiffs were driving on Rowan Road, Butler County, Pennsylvania. As a result of defendants' negligence, plaintiffs have incurred, and will continue to incur, various medical expenses; they have suffered, and will continue to suffer, pain; Mr. Grant has been unable to work and has already lost wages in the sum of $10,000.00; Mr. Grant's ability to earn wages in the immediate future has been temporarily impaired; and plaintiffs have suffered a loss of tuition incurred in the course of furthering their education by having to leave school and by having to postpone their graduation date by one semester.

WHEREFORE, plaintiffs demand judgment against defendants, individually, jointly, and/or severally in an amount in excess of $50,000.00ᶜ, their costs, and all other proper relief.

LYN CARROLL
Attorney at Law
Suite 654
Butler Savings Building
Butler, PA 15205
(412) 555-0123

a. If NRW were not a corporation, but the name under which Mai, Carlos, and Helen did business, the complaint would name Mai Nguyen, Carlos Rios, and Helen Wainwright, d/b/a NRW (d/b/a is an abbreviation for "doing business as" that is used when people operate a business under another name).

b. Some states, including California, permit a plaintiff to include "John Doe(s)" as defendant(s), if the plaintiff does not know the true names of all the defendants. Then the plaintiff can add the defendant(s) later, if it would be just to do so.

c. Many courts today require compulsory arbitration for smaller cases. For example, in Butler County, cases under $10,000 will be referred to compulsory arbitration. The arbitrators there consist of a panel of three attorneys who have agreed to serve as arbitrators. A party who is not satisfied with this arbitrators' award could appeal to the Court of Common Pleas.

EXHIBIT **6.5** Defendants' Original Answer

Defendant's Original Answer

COURT OF COMMON PLEAS OF BUTLER COUNTY, PENNSYLVANIA

NIC GRANT	:	A.D. No. 23465
and	:	
NANCY GRIFFIN, Plaintiffs	:	
	:	Civil Action Law
	:	
V.	:	
	:	
NRW	:	
and	:	
CARLOS RIOS, Defendants	:	
	:	

NOW COME NRW and CARLOS RIOS, defendants in the above styled and numbered cause, and for answer to Plaintiffs' Original Complaint would respectfully show unto the court:

Defendants deny each and every material allegation contained in Plaintiffs' Original Complaint. In addition, defendants allege that it was the negligent driving of Nic Grant that caused plaintiffs' injuries and the injuries of the defendants.

WHEREFORE, having fully answered, defendants pray that the complaint be dismissed, for their costs, and for all other proper relief, including damage to the NRW van.

JONES, MURPHY, SABBATINO, and SCHWARTZ
Suite 1010
First National Bank Building
Pittsburgh, PA 15205
(412) 555-0191

By _____

ATTORNEYS FOR DEFENDANTS

ON 12 December 2003 the original of this answer was filed in the Prothonotary's office. A copy of this answer was mailed to Ms. Lyn Carroll, attorney for plaintiffs, Suite 654, Butler Savings Building, Butler, Pennsylvania 15205.

By _____

JEFFERSON JONES

taken. (To *impeach* means to question the truthfulness of a witness by using some evidence.) A deposition may be obtained from *any* party *or* witness.

Interrogatories *Interrogatories* are written questions from one side to the other. Like depositions, interrogatories produce a written record of answers to questions. However, because both the questions and the answers are written, the answers are not as spontaneous as in a deposition. The answer is made under oath, but the respondent has the time to contemplate and carefully phrase the written answers to the questions posed. Often, a person's attorney will review a draft of his or her answers before they are returned. Interrogatories may be sent to any party to the

EXHIBIT 6.6 Discovery

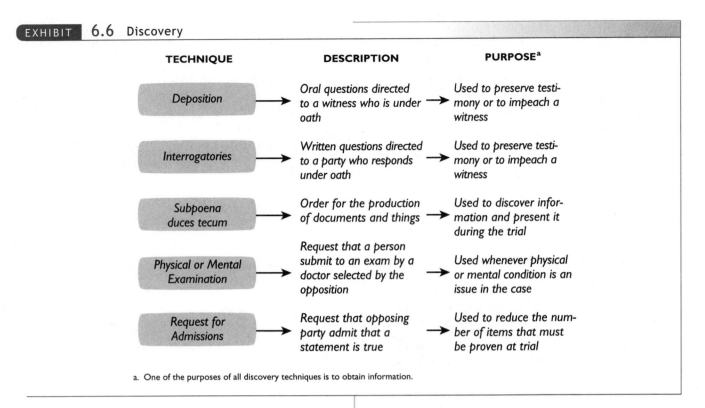

TECHNIQUE	DESCRIPTION	PURPOSE[a]
Deposition	Oral questions directed to a witness who is under oath	Used to preserve testimony or to impeach a witness
Interrogatories	Written questions directed to a party who responds under oath	Used to preserve testimony or to impeach a witness
Subpoena duces tecum	Order for the production of documents and things	Used to discover information and present it during the trial
Physical or Mental Examination	Request that a person submit to an exam by a doctor selected by the opposition	Used whenever physical or mental condition is an issue in the case
Request for Admissions	Request that opposing party admit that a statement is true	Used to reduce the number of items that must be proven at trial

a. One of the purposes of all discovery techniques is to obtain information.

lawsuit, but *not* to other witnesses. That is, if a witness is neither a plaintiff nor a defendant, an interrogatory may not be obtained from that witness.

Production of Documents and Things In many lawsuits, testimony alone is insufficient to win the case. In Nic and Nancy's case, Ms. Carroll also must introduce the records of the two doctors, the hospital, and the police report. Because of the circumstances, Ms. Carroll may also request that NRW produce records it possesses reflecting when and where the van was bought and any internal NRW communications used in tracking repair records and mechanical difficulties. The legal form used to obtain those documents is called a subpoena duces tecum. (A *subpoena duces tecum* is a court order to appear and bring the specified documents or records.)

Physical or Mental Examination Whenever the physical or mental condition of a party to the suit is in question, the court may order that party to submit to an examination by a physician. Here both the present condition of the plaintiffs and their physical condition prior to the accident are in question, so a medical examination may be necessary.

Request for Admission One party can serve on the opponent a written request for an *admission,* which takes

the form of a question asked by one party to which the answer is either yes or no. If the recipient fails to answer in a stated period of time (usually 30 days), the matter is deemed admitted. For example, Ms. Carroll may request an admission that Carlos Rios was driving the van.

The Result of Discovery As a result of the discovery process, the attorneys for the defendants, NRW and Carlos Rios, informed their clients that it appears the accident was primarily caused by Carlos's negligence and his unfamiliarity with the streets. Mr. Jones recommended a settlement offer of $23,000 and Mai, Carlos, and Helen agreed. (A settlement offer is really an offer to negotiate.) Ms. Carroll informed her clients of the offer and recommended rejection. Nic and Nancy rejected the offer, and since the defendants made no additional offers, the case went to trial.

Pretrial Conferences Many courts now utilize pretrial conferences to encourage the parties to settle the dispute themselves. However, not all judicial systems and judges favor these conferences. Often the pretrial conferences result in a settlement. Even if there is no settlement, the conference generally succeeds in further clarifying the legal and factual issues involved in the case. Depending on the situation, participation in settlement conferences may be mandatory or voluntary.

NRW CASE 6.1   Management

PREPARING TO MEET WITH THE ATTORNEY

Mai, Carlos, and Helen are preparing for their first meeting with Mr. Jones, and they are understandably nervous. They would like to know what information they should collect and take to the meeting. They would also like to know what they should expect at the meeting. They ask you to make a list of the information that would be legally relevant to this lawsuit. They also ask you what they should expect at this first meeting. What will you tell them?

BUSINESS CONSIDERATIONS Frequently, a business will have certain items it wishes to treat in a confidential manner, but the business may need to reveal some or all of this information to its attorneys in preparation for a legal proceeding. What procedures should the business follow to maximize its protection while still being as open and honest as necessary with its counsel? What steps should the law firm take to protect the confidentiality of its clients?

ETHICAL CONSIDERATIONS Suppose that the known facts make it relatively obvious that a business is liable for the wrongful conduct of one of its agents. Is it ethical for the business and its attorneys to use expensive and time-consuming delaying tactics in an effort to persuade the injured party to settle out of court? Would it be ethical to seek an alternate form of dispute resolution rather than go to trial?

INTERNATIONAL CONSIDERATIONS If the litigation were going to occur in a foreign country, how would the situation change? When would the foreign court apply its own laws?

Businesspeople need to be aware that *many* courts require the parties to participate in pretrial conferences. Some jurisdictions base the requirement on the amount of damages. In Butler County, for example, during pretrial conferences the attorneys meet with the judge. The parties are requested to be available either outside the courtroom or by telephone. Then, if a settlement offer is made, the attorney can quickly inform his or her client and obtain a prompt response. This procedure is common in many courts. Depending on the jurisdiction and the judge's preferences, the judge *may* take a very active role in attempting

to fashion a compromise that would be acceptable to both parties. Some judges may be harsh with parties who do not accept reasonable settlement offers or who do not participate in pretrial conferences in good faith. In some jurisdictions, nonbinding arbitration may be required in addition to or instead of a settlement conference.

Demurrer The purpose of a demurrer is to challenge the legal sufficiency of the other party's pleading as a pleading. For example, demurrers can be raised to the plaintiff's complaint, the defendant's answer, or the defendant's counterclaim. The grounds for a demurrer are usually limited by statute. Common grounds include failure to state facts sufficient to constitute a legal cause of action (general demurrer), lack of jurisdiction (special demurrer), lack of capacity to sue (special demurrer), and uncertainty or ambiguity (special demurrer).

A general demurrer challenges only defects that appear on the *face* of the pleading. At this point the parties cannot produce additional evidence or sworn statements. Each jurisdiction has different requirements as to what constitutes a sufficient pleading and the amount of detail required. In deciding whether to grant a demurrer, the court must accept as true all the facts that are in the pleading. Assuming all the facts that are pleaded are true, the issue is whether they would entitle the plaintiff to any judicial relief. If the demurrer is denied, the party requesting the demurrer will be given time to answer. If the demurrer is granted, generally the losing party will be given permission to amend the pleading to make it sufficient.

Demurrers have been abolished in federal courts. In federal courts, a party would use a *motion* (request to a judge to take certain action) to dismiss instead of a general demurrer. Motions to dismiss are discussed in the following section.

Motion to Dismiss Depending on the jurisdiction, motions to dismiss can be raised on the same grounds as general or special demurrers. A motion to dismiss can be made after different pleadings. When a court considers a motion to dismiss, it *generally* accepts that the material facts alleged in the complaint are true. The pleading is construed in the light most favorable to the party who filed it. The pleading need only state a claim upon which relief can be granted. The purpose of a motion to dismiss is to avoid the expense of unnecessary trials.

If the motion to dismiss is granted, it may be with or without prejudice. If the motion is granted *without prejudice*, the plaintiff can amend and refile the complaint. The judge will often establish a deadline for amending the complaint. If the motion is granted *with prejudice*, the plaintiff cannot revise the complaint and the trial is terminated. In some jurisdictions, there is an absolute right to amend once. A motion to dismiss is a final decision in the case that can be appealed. Many of the cases in this text were decided on a demurrer or a motion to dismiss.

Motion for a Summary Judgment

A *motion for a summary judgment* is a request to have the judge declare one side the winner because there are no material issues of fact. It is a technique for going beyond the allegations stated in the pleadings and attacking the basic merits of the opponent's case. Traditionally, it was difficult to obtain summary judgment, because most courts believed that its use violated the other party's right to a trial. Other courts indicated that there was no *right* to a trial when there was no genuine dispute about the facts. The modern view is that there is no right to a trial, and courts today are thus more willing to grant summary judgments.

This technique permits the examination of evidentiary material, such as admissions and depositions, without a full-scale trial. The purpose of a motion for a summary judgment is to avoid the expense of unnecessary trials. Consequently, it is usually decided before trial. Either party can file a motion for summary judgment. The party filing the motion must make an initial showing to justify the court's review. The opposing parties are entitled to have time to present their own materials. The length of time depends on the jurisdiction. The standard for granting a summary judgment is that *no genuine issue or no triable issue exists as to any material fact.* If this standard is satisfied, the moving party is entitled to a judgment as a matter of law. In some jurisdictions the court will not consider the pleadings in making its decision. The court can grant a partial summary judgment on some issues or claims and not on others. In most courts, summary judgment is procedurally distinct from *judgment as a matter of law* even though they use essentially the same standard. It is also distinct from motions on the pleadings, which permit the court only to review the pleadings and do *not* permit review of evidence. Many of the court cases in this book were appeals of summary judgments by the party who lost.

On Nic and Nancy's behalf, Ms. Carroll introduced a motion for a summary judgment, claiming that no material facts appear to be in dispute; rather, the case is merely a matter of applying the law.

The Trial

In Nic and Nancy's case, the judge denied the plaintiffs' pretrial motions and the legal process continued. The actual trial proceeding is governed by technical rules of trial practice. Generally, representation in court is best left to the attorneys. A good plaintiff or defendant, however, takes an active role in assisting the lawyer.

Jury Selection

A legal case can be resolved by a trial before a judge, without a jury. The judge then decides questions of fact *and* questions of law. Such a trial is often less expensive and less time consuming. Nic Grant and Nancy Griffin agree with their attorney that a jury will generally favor the plaintiffs and their arguments, and they elect to have a jury trial. A request for a jury trial must be made in a timely manner. This was noted on the plaintiffs' original complaint (Exhibit 6.4).

Members of the jury are referred to as *petit jurors* (ordinary jurors on the panel for the trial of a civil or criminal action). Traditionally, civil juries consisted of 12 jurors. Some jurisdictions have reduced this number in civil trials. Generally, 6 to 12 jurors are used. In federal court, a civil jury also consists of 6 to 12 members.[3]

Alternate jurors may also be selected. Alternate jurors sit with the regular jurors and hear the evidence. If a regular juror becomes ill or has to leave the jury for some reason during the production of evidence, an alternate "joins" the jury and it continues to function. Without alternate jurors, the judge would have to select a new jury and begin the trial again. An alternate juror can substitute for a regular juror even during deliberations in some jurisdictions; the jury will then start its deliberations from the beginning.

Most states select potential jurors from the voter registration list or the list of licensed drivers or both. The prospective jurors may be required to complete a juror information form. The form elicits information on which the respective attorneys may base their questions to the jury in what is called the *voir dire* examination (examination of potential jurors to determine their competence to serve on the jury). Voir dire is an important part of the trial. Questions need to be asked in the proper manner to obtain helpful, accurate answers, without offending potential jurors. The information offered by the prospective jurors is used by the judge and counsel as the basis for challenging jurors as biased and, thus, ineligible to serve. The attorneys for both parties and/or the judge can ask questions. For example, an attorney may request that the judge ask any potentially embarrassing questions so that the attorney can try to maintain good rapport with the potential jurors. Generally, the procedure is that the attorneys submit written questions to the judge prior to voir dire. In some jurisdictions, the judge may control voir dire by asking all the questions of the potential jurors. At the opposite extreme—New York, for example—voir dire is conducted by the attorneys outside the courtroom; the judge is called in only if problems arise. The procedure depends on the rules of court and the judge's preferences in courtroom procedure. In civil disputes in Butler County, the judge usually conducts voir dire of all the prospective jurors at one time. In Nic and Nancy's case, for example, if a potential juror happened to work for NRW, Ms. Carroll would challenge that person and request that the judge excuse the person. On the other hand, if one of the prospective jurors was a member of Nic's fraternity, Mr. Jones would examine the student very carefully to see whether he or she would favor a fellow member.

Businesses are available that specialize in assisting parties in selecting sympathetic jurors. These jury consultants come from varying backgrounds including psychology, sociology, and marketing. They investigate the backgrounds of potential jurors and collect statistics about the reactions of some socioeconomic groups to trials generally and to issues that are expected to arise in the particular trial on which they are consulting. For example, Trial Behavior Consulting, Inc. maintains a Web site at http://www.trialbehavior.com/ with information about preparing for trial including Jury Selection, Voir Dire & Trial Monitoring and ADR Preparation.

Jury consultants sometimes arrange a *shadow jury* consisting of "jurors" with demographic backgrounds similar to the impaneled jurors. The shadow jury sits in the public area of the courtroom and members report their impressions of the evidence. This can be particularly helpful in highly technical cases, where there is a concern that the jurors may be confused by the details. Through this technique, attorneys can have continuous feedback on how their presentation is being perceived.

Another technique is the *mock jury*—the lawyers practice their case before a group of mock jurors with demographic backgrounds similar to those of the actual jurors.

Two methods exist for dismissing prospective jurors. First, a potential juror can be removed *for cause*. When a juror is removed for cause, generally an attorney first suggests to the judge that the juror will probably be biased. Challenges for cause occur if (1) the juror has a financial stake in the case or similar litigation; (2) members of the juror's family have such an interest; or (3) there is reason to believe the juror will be partial. The judge then decides whether he or she agrees; if so, the potential juror is dismissed. The judge can also make this decision on his or her own initiative. (When a judge raises an issue on his or her own, we say that the judge does it *sua sponte,* which means voluntarily, without prompting or suggestion, of his or her own will or motion.) There is no limit on the number of potential jurors who can be removed for cause.

A second technique is to remove a prospective juror by the use of a *peremptory challenge*. Unlike removal for cause,

each side is allotted a limited number of peremptory challenges. The judge decides the number of peremptory challenges prior to beginning the jury selection process. In federal court, for example, each side receives three peremptory challenges.[4] With peremptory challenges, the attorney does not need to discuss his or her reasons for wanting to remove the juror. The purpose of peremptory challenges is to allow each side to act on hints of bias that may not be provable or even rationally explainable. Some attorneys act on their intuition in deciding whom to eliminate from the jury. The attorney intuitively decides which potential jurors he or she trusts and which he or she does not trust. The attorney then uses peremptory challenges to eliminate those potential jurors that he or she distrusts the most. The use of these challenges is discretionary with the attorney. Historically, there have been no limits on the use of this discretion. Recent court decisions, however, have determined that one side may not use peremptory challenges to remove jurors of one gender,[5] religion, race, or color from the jury. (The precedents began with *Batson v. Kentucky,*[6] a criminal case. It is now used in criminal and civil cases.)

In the following case, the court discussed the issue of peremptory challenges, which the court called *Batson* challenges. Notice how the court responded to the pretext advanced by counsel. (*Pretext* is a false or weak reason advanced to hide the actual reason or motive.)

The decision about whether to exclude a person from the petit jury may be reached after that individual juror is questioned. In the alternative, it may be made after an entire set of jurors is sitting in the jury box. For example, the judge may then ask each attorney in turn if the attorney has any objections to the jury sitting in the box. A judge may discuss eliminating jurors at both points. The techniques used for jury selection will depend on the rules of court and the judge's preferences.

Removal of Judges California has a unique procedure that allows each party one peremptory challenge against the judge assigned to the case. This peremptory challenge must be filed before any proceedings begin in front of the judge being challenged.[7] Most jurisdictions do not permit peremptory challenges to a judge; however, they have other procedures to disqualify a judge. A judge is not permitted to preside over any action in which he or she has any bias, has a financial interest, is related to any of the parties or attorneys, or there are any facts that would impair the judge's impartiality. For example, if the plaintiffs have appealed the judge's *gag order* (order to be silent about a pending case) to the state supreme court, the judge may be biased. The judge may raise this issue *sua sponte* or it can be raised by one of the parties.[8]

6.1

DAVEY v. LOCKHEED MARTIN CORPORATION
301 F.3d 1204, 2002 U.S. App. LEXIS 17866 (10th Cir. 2002)

FACTS Susan Davey brought an employment discrimination action against her former employer, Lockheed Martin Corporation (LMC). Davey filed a charge with the Equal Employment Opportunity Commission (EEOC) alleging sex discrimination and retaliation, and the EEOC issued her a notice of right to sue. During trial, LMC's peremptory strikes were made to three women, whereupon Davey challenged them under the precedents set in *Batson*. The district court asked whether counsel for LMC believed Davey had made a prima facie case of gender discrimination. Counsel for LMC replied: "No, I don't. Given the number of females that are still left on the jury. There would still be four." The district court directed LMC to explain its gender-neutral grounds for striking the three potential jurors. Counsel for LMC explained:

> There's a common basis for striking actually all three of those people. And that is none of them work in a workplace setting. This is a case of discrimination, alleged discrimination in the workplace. They need to understand concepts such as performance evaluations, rankings, what supervisors are confronted with on a day-to-day basis is something that would be useful to the jurors' understanding of the case. [Ms. Elder] is not working outside of the home. Miss Whitely is not working outside of the home, and Miss Murley is not working for an employer but works for herself selling Mary Kay cosmetics. So frankly, the major basis for striking each one of them is that they do not have current employers and so they would not have that perspective to bring to their deliberations.

In response, Davey's counsel argued:

> Your Honor, that's clearly pretexual. Let's take [Ms. Elder]. [Ms. Elder] worked for ten years as a nurse. She was a head nurse. Had responsibilities for other individuals whom she was supervising as a nurse. She clearly was someone who was aware of policies and procedures. Nurses have to follow those policies, and clearly she knew about personnel policies because that was her job.

Counsel for LMC argued that Ms. Elder had been out of the workplace for 14 years and the reason she was struck was because she did not have current employment. The district court found:

> Now, it seems to me that [Ms. Elder], if she worked as a nurse in some major hospitals for ten years and supervised up to eight people, would have had an ability to do those things that are the objection—would have had an opportunity to do the very things that [counsel for LMC] said is a primary reason for striking her. . . . So I do find that striking of [Ms. Elder] is based on gender discrimination; and so under the law that I've already cited, I'm going to invalidate that peremptory challenge and will require the defendant to strike another juror.

Counsel for LMC attempted to give additional reasons for striking Ms. Elder, but the district court dismissed the reasons because they had not been stated originally.

ISSUE Did the district court err in granting Davey's challenge to LMC's use of its peremptory challenge to remove Ms. Elder?

HOLDING No. The district court's decision is correct.

REASONING Excerpts from the opinion of Circuit Judge Briscoe:

In *Batson*, the Court held that the Equal Protection Clause of the Fourteenth Amendment forbids a prosecutor to use peremptory challenges to exclude African-Americans from jury service because of their race. The prohibition was later extended to include gender discrimination, and to be applicable in civil cases.

> Our commitment to equal justice under law, carved into stone outside the courthouse, would be mocked by allowing discriminatory peremptory challenges inside. The practice not only causes the silent sting of discrimination, it "mars the integrity of the judicial system and prevents the idea of democratic government from becoming a reality."

. . . [T]he Court set forth a three-part burden-shifting approach . . . :

> Under our *Batson* jurisprudence, once the opponent of a peremptory challenge has made out a prima facie case of [gender] discrimination (step one), the burden of production shifts to the proponent of the strike to come forward with a [gender]-neutral explanation (step two). If a [gender]- neutral explanation is tendered, the trial court must then decide (step three) whether the opponent of the strike has proved purposeful racial discrimination.

. . . The presence of members of the subject gender on the final jury "is a relevant factor in negating an alleged *Batson* violation. . . ." However, at the time the *Batson* challenge was made in this case, LMC had not had the opportunity to strike the other female jurors. Each party was given only three peremptory challenges. After the district court ruled that LMC could not strike Ms. Elder, LMC exercised its remaining peremptory challenge on yet another female. . . . "[T]he issue of whether [Davey] established a prima facie case of discrimination is moot because [LMC] gave [its] explanation of the peremptory challenge of [Ms. Elder] and the district court ruled on the ultimate question of intentional discrimination." "Once a [gender] neutral reason is offered, the trial court's decision on the ultimate question of discriminatory intent represents a finding of fact of the sort accorded great deference on appeal." "We will not disturb the district court's findings of fact unless, following a review of the entire evidence, we are left with a definite and firm conviction that a mistake has been committed."

LMC's reason for striking Ms. Elder was that she did not have current employment. The district court's finding of pretext relied on the fact that Ms. Elder had past employment. . . . [A] district court's ultimate finding of discrimination is based in large part on judging the credibility of the exercising party's counsel at the time the neutral reason for the challenge is made. We cannot say it was clearly erroneous for the district court to determine that LMC's explanation for striking Ms. Elder was pretextual.

BUSINESS CONSIDERATIONS How can a business like LMC reduce lawsuits based on sex discrimination and retaliation? How can a lawyer avoid claims that he or she is using peremptory challenges in a discriminatory manner?

ETHICAL CONSIDERATIONS What is the ethical perspective of *Batson* and the cases that have interpreted it?

Opening Statements After the jury is chosen, each side has an opportunity to tell the jury what it intends to prove during the trial. This serves as an introduction to the party's case and helps the jury integrate the evidence that follows. The attorney for the plaintiff makes an opening statement, followed by the attorney for the defendant.

Direct Examination After a witness has been sworn in, the attorneys question the witness. Witnesses who lie can be held in contempt. The plaintiff's attorney questions his or her witnesses first. The rules of evidence include rules concerning what information an attorney may elicit from the witnesses as well as how an attorney may request the information. (A detailed discussion of these rules, however, is beyond the scope of this book.)

Trial attorneys are reluctant to ask questions when they do not know how a witness will respond. This is the reason for pretrial preparation of witnesses. Failure to adequately prepare can be disastrous.

Expert Witnesses An *expert witness* is a witness possessing special knowledge who offers opinions based on facts that have been produced as evidence. For example, Nic Grant or NRW may call medical experts and accident reconstruction engineers. Expert witnesses are permitted to testify concerning their opinions. They are allowed to state their own conclusions and to discuss hypothetical situations described by the attorneys. In this way, expert witnesses are distinguished from regular witnesses, who are not permitted to present opinions, state conclusions, or respond to hypothetical questions. Courts may accommodate special witnesses, such as experts, by allowing them to testify when it is convenient for the witness's schedule. For more information about expert witnesses, visit the Web site of the National Registry of Experts (NRE) at http://www.expert-registry.com/. The Web site provides information about locating an expert witness for a lawsuit or becoming an expert witness.

Cross-examination After Ms. Carroll questions each of her witnesses, Mr. Jones has an opportunity to question them. Skillful use of cross-examination by competent counsel is the best means to clarify matters brought up in direct examination. After the cross-examination, the party who called the witness (Ms. Carroll) *may* examine the witness again on redirect and the opposing party (Mr. Jones) *may* examine the witness on recross. The process of examination and cross-examination continues until Ms. Carroll has no other witnesses to call. Next, Mr. Jones directly examines his witnesses one at a time, and Ms. Carroll cross-examines each one until the defense has no further witnesses to call. At this point, both sides "rest" their cases.

Motion for a Directed Verdict A motion for a directed verdict is addressed to the judge, usually at the close of the opponent's case. The standard used by the judge is whether the plaintiff has made a *prima facie* case (a case that is obvious on its face, which may be rebutted by evidence to the contrary) on which he or she is entitled to recover. If the plaintiff has *not* presented a prima facie case, the defendant is entitled to a directed verdict. In most jurisdictions, the judge cannot weigh the evidence—the judge

SELECTING JURORS

Ms. Carroll and Mr. Jones are conducting the voir dire examination of a prospective juror, Andy Motz. Andy is a 23-year-old business student at the same university as Nic Grant and Nancy Griffin. His father, Ted Motz, is a senior claims supervisor at State-Wide Insurance Company. Mai, Carlos, and Helen believe that Mr. Jones should exclude this person from the jury. They ask you what additional questions Mr. Jones should ask Andy before making a decision whether to remove him from the jury. What additional information would be helpful in making a rational decision? If cause for removal cannot be established, should Mr. Jones use a peremptory challenge to remove this potential juror? What should Mr. Jones do if he disagrees with his clients on jury selection?

BUSINESS CONSIDERATIONS Should the attorney for a business that sells high-tech, upscale products try to select jurors who have a relatively high income level and a higher-than-average educational level? Would such a firm be better served by waiving its right to a jury trial and letting the judge serve as finder of fact?

ETHICAL CONSIDERATIONS What ethical considerations enter into the jury selection process? Some wealthy parties to lawsuits are able to afford expensive jury consultants and profilers. Does this give them an unethical advantage over people who cannot afford such litigation support?

INTERNATIONAL CONSIDERATIONS Should an attorney remove all people who were born in a foreign country from a jury? Why? If this trial were taking placing outside the United States, is it likely that a jury could be used in the trial?

---

must look solely at the evidence produced by the party against whom the motion is sought, accept any reasonable inference from that evidence, and disregard all challenges to the credibility of that evidence. (A minority of jurisdictions permit the weighing of evidence.) If the motion is granted, the court has determined that the defendant must win as a matter of law.

If the motion is not granted, the trial will continue. After the presentation of the defendant's evidence, the plaintiff may request a directed verdict on the defendant's cross-complaint and/or the defendant can again request a directed verdict. In some states a motion for nonsuit is used in a similar manner.

Closing Arguments After both sides rest, each has an opportunity to persuade the jury by reviewing the testimony, restating the significant facts, and then drawing conclusions from those facts that best support its position. Thus, each attorney takes the same body of evidence and attempts to reach a favorable conclusion by emphasizing the evidence favorable to his or her client and minimizing unfavorable evidence. This stage is called *closing arguments* or *summation*.

The Verdict At the conclusion of closing arguments, the judge discusses the law with the jury and charges them to answer certain questions with respect to the evidence *adduced* (given as proof) at trial. As part of the charge, he or she instructs them in the applicable areas of law and defines any legal concepts. This is called the *charge to the jury* or *jury instructions*. Many states now have published standardized jury instructions so that the judge does not have to write new jury instructions each time.

The jury may be directed to reach a general verdict and/or a special verdict. In a *general verdict,* the jury is asked who should win the lawsuit and how much damage was suffered, if any. In a *special verdict,* the jury is asked specific questions about the relevant factual issues in the case.

After the jury withdraws from the courtroom, they *deliberate* on the evidence in private and attempt to reach a verdict. In many jurisdictions, the jury *may* request that parts of the evidence be "read back" to them during the deliberation process. In a civil case, many rules of court do not require a unanimous decision; some even authorize a decision by a majority vote of the jurors. In Pennsylvania, the verdict is valid if at least five-sixths of the jurors agree to it.[9] In federal court, a unanimous jury must decide a civil case unless the parties agree to the contrary.[10] After the petit jurors reach a verdict, it is announced in open court. The verdict is the stated opinion of the jury. If the judge concurs in the verdict, he or she enters a judgment. This is the most common type of verdict.

In our case, the jury deliberated and held for the plaintiffs, Nic Grant and Nancy Griffin, for $21,026 and $5,498, respectively. The court then entered a judgment in those amounts for the two plaintiffs. The judgment is the court's official decision and appears as Exhibit 6.7.

Judgment In most cases, the judge will agree with the jury's verdict. The judge who disagrees may enter a *judgment*

EXHIBIT   **6.7**   Court's Judgment

COURT'S JUDGMENT
COURT OF COMMON PLEAS OF BUTLER COUNTY, PENNSYLVANIA

NIC GRANT and NANCY GRIFFIN, Plaintiffs	: : :	A.D. No. 23465
	:	Civil Action Law
V.	: :	
NRW and CARLOS RIOS, Defendants	: : : :	

On the 9th day of November 2004 this cause came to be heard, plaintiffs appearing in person and by their attorney, LYN CARROLL, and defendants appearing in person and by their attorneys, JONES, MURPHY, SABBATINO, and SCHWARTZ. All parties announcing ready for trial, a jury composed of Mae Brown and eleven others of the regular panel of the petit jurors of this court was selected and impaneled and sworn according to law to try the issues of fact arising in this cause. After the introduction of all the evidence, the instructions of the court, and the arguments of counsel, said jury retired to consider its verdict, and after deliberating thereon returned unto court the following verdict:

We, the jury, find in favor of the plaintiffs, Nic Grant and Nancy Griffin, and assess their damages at $21,026 and $5,498, respectively.

_____

MAE BROWN, FOREPERSON

IT IS, THEREFORE, BY THE COURT, CONSIDERED, ORDERED, AND ADJUDGED that the plaintiffs, NIC GRANT and NANCY GRIFFIN, are entitled to recover of and from the defendants, NRW and/or CARLOS RIOS, the sums of $21,026 and $5,498, respectively, plus their court costs herein expended. Said judgment shall bear interest from this date until paid at the rate of SIX PERCENT PER ANNUM.[a]

ENTERED this 15th day of November 2004.[b]

_____

JUDGE

APPROVED AS TO FORM:

_____

Attorney for Plaintiffs

_____

Attorneys[c] for Defendants

---

a. The rate of interest allowed depends on the jurisdiction. Butler County allows 6 percent.
b. Notice that this is approximately one year after the lawsuit was initiated.
c. This is plural because the defendants are represented by a law firm—Jones, Murphy, Sabbatino, and Schwartz.

notwithstanding the verdict. Traditionally, this was called a judgment *non obstante veredicto,* hence the abbreviation judgment n.o.v. When a judge declares a judgment n.o.v., he or she substitutes his or her own decision for that of the jury. Either a plaintiff or a defendant may be awarded a judgment n.o.v. A judgment n.o.v. is appropriate only if the jury's verdict is incorrect as a matter of law; that is, there is no substantial evidence to support the jury verdict. Most courts use the same standard as that used for a directed verdict. The court disregards all conflicts in the evidence, does not consider whether the witnesses are credible, and gives face value to the evidence in favor of the party who received the verdict. The party who won the original verdict will likely appeal the judgment n.o.v.

Posttrial Proceedings

Execution and Attachment A party who wins a *judgment* can attach the judgment debtor's property. State laws on execution and attachment vary. For comparison pur-poses, you might want to look at the information about executions in Colorado at the Lawdog.com Web site at http://www.lawdog.com/states/co/judm.htm, and the Maine statute on execution liens at http://janus.state.me.us/legis/statutes/14/title14sec4651-A.html/. Gary Neustadter, Santa Clara University School of Law, posted an article on Enforcement of Judgment on his Web site at http://www.scu.edu/law/FacWebPage/Neustadter/article9/main/commentary/5.html.

In the following case, the court addressed whether the deputy violated the owners' rights when attaching the boat and trailer.

Motion for a New Trial Often the losing party will request the court to either enter a judgment n.o.v. *or* grant a new trial. A *motion for a new trial* is filed with the same judge who originally heard the case, unless that judge is disabled or disqualified. The party making the motion is requesting the court to order a new trial. The party must justify the request and explain why a new trial is proper.

6.2

JOHNSON v. OUTBOARD MARINE CORPORATION
172 F.3d 531, 1999 U.S. App. LEXIS 5444 (8th Cir. 1999)

FACTS Following a default judgment for approximately $650.00 against Starfish Marine, Inc., a Lancaster county court issued a valid writ of execution. The writ instructed the sheriff of Lancaster County to execute, or levy, on "any and all personal property of the judgment debtor located at 1812 W. Arlington, Lincoln, NE." Deputy Pekarek determined that the judgment debtor had been dissolved for nonpayment of taxes. He tried to execute the writ at the above address on September 16, 1996. No one answered the door, so Pekarek left a civil process card with instructions to contact him. Three days later, Deputy Pekarek again attempted to contact the occupants of the W. Arlington address, and left another card. He learned from the Secretary of State that Marvin Rumery had been the secretary of Starfish Marine, and Lawrence Johnson had been the president and treasurer. On September 24, Pekarek phoned the Rumery residence and left a message stating that he was attempting to serve the writ and that he intended to levy on the boat in the driveway. Pekarek received a phone call from an individual claiming to be Rumery's attorney. Pekarek explained his attempts to serve the writ and his intention to levy on the boat.

On September 26, Pekarek failed for a third time to speak with anyone at W. Arlington. He received a report that Rumery was cleaning out the boat. Pekarek went to the W. Arlington address and spoke with Rumery. Rumery stated that the boat was actually owned by his father-in-law, Lawrence Johnson, but could not produce any documentation of ownership for either the boat or the trailer. Pekarek spoke with Rumery's attorney on the phone; the attorney told Pekarek that he could not levy on the boat. Despite this conversation, Pekarek seized the boat and trailer and had them towed away. On October 2, 1996, Rumery and Johnson delivered a Notice of Exemptions to the execution, which was filed with the court. On October 11, the county court ordered the boat and trailer released to Rumery and Johnson.

ISSUE Did the sheriff and deputies violate Rumery and Johnson's rights under the Fourth and Fourteenth Amendments of the Constitution?

HOLDING No. The sheriff and the deputies were acting under a valid writ and did not act in an unreasonable manner in seizing the property.

REASONING Excerpts from the opinion of Circuit Judge Beam:

We review a grant of summary judgment de novo, considering all evidence in a light most favorable to the nonmoving party. A motion for summary judgment should be granted if there is no genuine issue of material fact and the moving party is entitled to judgment as a matter of law. We may uphold a grant of summary judgment for any reason supported by the record, even if different from the reasons given by the district court. . . .

Public servants may be sued under [U.S.C.] section 1983 in either their official capacity, their individual capacity, or both. The amended complaint does not specify in what capacity the law enforcement defendants are being sued. . . . This court has held that, in order to sue a public official in his or her individual capacity, a plaintiff must expressly and unambiguously state so in the pleadings. . . . Absent . . . an express statement, the suit is construed as being against the defendants in their official capacity. A suit against a public employee in his or her official capacity is merely a suit against the public employer. . . . A political subdivision may be held liable for the unconstitutional acts of its officials or employees when those acts implement or execute an unconstitutional policy or custom of the subdivision. . . . Rumery and Johnson have failed to allege facts—or produce evidence—showing that the deprivation of their property was the result of a policy or custom of Lancaster county. . . . [T]he plaintiffs have presented nothing that would indicate liability on the part of the county. Thus, summary judgment was proper. . . .

Even assuming . . . the plaintiffs properly named the deputies and the sheriff in their individual capacities, the plaintiffs' case must fail because there are no alleged facts or evidence that suggest a violation of their rights under the Constitution or statutes of the United States, a prerequisite to section 1983 liability. In section 1983 actions against public officials in their individual capacity, a plaintiff must show that the defendant violated "clearly established statutory or constitutional rights of which a reasonable person would have known." . . .

Plaintiffs allege violations of the Fourth and Fourteenth Amendments. The Fourth Amendment prohibits . . . unreasonable searches and seizures by government actors. In the context of the Fourth Amendment, a seizure of property occurs whenever there is "some meaningful interference with an individual's possessory interest in that property." The boat and trailer were undoubtedly "seized." . . . The question is whether there was anything unreasonable about the seizure which would place it among those [seizures] prohibited by the Fourth Amendment. . . . The deputy was executing a valid writ. . . . Pekarek was informed by a superior that, even if the property was not corporate property, Rumery, as an officer of the dissolved corporation, had no protection from an execution to satisfy the judgment. Rumery was cleaning out the boat, some indication that it was soon to be moved or hidden, and Rumery could not produce any documentation of ownership for either the trailer or the boat. The boat was levied upon in the daylight hours in Rumery's driveway so there were few of the privacy concerns often associated with Fourth Amendment analysis. . . .

The plaintiffs' only argument that the execution was an unreasonable seizure, is that Pekarek was wrong in his belief that he could levy on the boat and trailer, and Rumery's attorney told him so at the time of the levy. This fails for two reasons. . . . [T]he fact that Pekarek was in error does not in itself make the seizure unreasonable. . . . [I]t cannot seriously be suggested that a deputy has an obligation to follow or even believe the legal advice given by a stranger under these facts. Failure to heed the threats or warnings of Rumery's attorney did nothing to make the seizure unreasonable for purposes of the Fourth Amendment. The plaintiffs also claim they were deprived of their property without due process of law in violation of the Fourteenth Amendment. . . . "In general, due process requires that a hearing before an impartial decisionmaker be provided at a meaningful time, and in a meaningful manner." . . . Plaintiffs have not argued that the hearing on October 11 was not meaningful or reasonably prompt. Therefore, . . . due process was satisfied and there was no Fourteenth Amendment violation.

BUSINESS CONSIDERATIONS What could Rumery and his attorney do to prevent the attachment of the property? What type of evidence would have persuaded Pekarek?

ETHICAL CONSIDERATIONS Was it ethical for Pekarek to proceed with the attachment after discussing the matter with Rumery's attorney? Was it ethical for Rumery and Johnson to file this suit?

Common grounds for a motion for a new trial include: the judge committed a prejudicial error in conducting the trial; there were perceived irregularities in the jury's behavior; or the evidence was insufficient to support the verdict. In extremely rare cases, a new trial may be granted based on newly discovered evidence. To obtain a new trial on this basis, the moving party must show that the newly discovered evidence pertains to facts in existence at the time of trial; the evidence is material; and the moving party with reasonable diligence could not have obtained the information prior to trial. The latter requirement is to prevent a party from obtaining a new trial when the party was negligent in failing to obtain the evidence for the original trial. A new trial will *not* be granted because a party's attorney in the original trial was incompetent.

A party who believes that the damage award is excessive *or* too small can also request a new trial. When the motion for new trial is based on the amount of damages, a judge may, for example, grant a new trial unless a plaintiff agrees to accept a reduction in the amount of damages. This is called *remittitur*. Some states also permit granting a new trial unless a defendant agrees to accept an increase in the amount of the award. This is called *additur*. Obviously, conducting a new trial is expensive for the parties *and* the court system.

Appeal After losing the decision, the attorneys for NRW might file a notice of appeal with a higher court. The rules of court specify the time limit for filing an appeal. Appeals, however, are limited to questions of law. In other words, the appellate court will generally not reverse a lower court unless the lower court made an error of law. In this case, the decision is in accordance with the law; consequently, NRW does not appeal. NRW now owes the plaintiffs $21,026 and $5,498.

If a case is appealed, the appellate court can *affirm* the decision, which indicates approval, or *reverse* the decision, which indicates an error of law. Appellate courts can affirm some parts of the decision and reverse others. Sometimes the appellate court reverses and *remands* the case because the lower court made a mistake of law and the case is returned to it for correction. Exhibit 6.8 depicts the stages of a trial.

A Comment on Finality

One of the great virtues of the law is finality. When a cause of action has been litigated and reduced to a judgment and all appeals have been exhausted, the matter comes to an end. In this case, the doctrine of *res judicata* applies. *Res judicata* means that when a court issues a final judgment, the subject matter of that lawsuit is finally decided between the parties to the suit. This doctrine prevents further suits from being brought by the same parties on the same issues. In other words, the matter comes to rest. Remember, however, that *res judicata* does not prevent timely appeals nor does it prevent criminal proceedings based on the same behavior.

The Need for Alternatives to a Civil Suit

Regular lawsuits are often expensive, and they are frequently time consuming. A business that is plagued by frequent lawsuits will suffer financially, and the financial burden for businesses facing large class action lawsuits may be even worse. As a result, many businesses may prefer to seek an alternative form of dispute resolution, such as arbitration. Even the federal government is participating in arbitration. For example, the United States arbitrated the value that was due to the amateur filmmaker Abraham Zapruder for seizing his film of the assassination of President John F. Kennedy.[11] There is normally a significant passage of time between the filing of a lawsuit and the resolution of the case by the court. Even if a plaintiff has what seems to be a good case, there is no guarantee that the plaintiff will prevail at trial.

For a business defendant, the time spent in preparing for the trial and then having officers attend the pretrial and trial proceedings represents a significant cost factor even if the business wins the case. Many businesses prefer to settle the case—the earlier the better—by paying the plaintiff and saving all the time and trouble that a trial requires. If an alternative means of resolving the dispute was available, those businesses would be likely to use it.

Alternatives to litigation do exist and these *alternate* forms of *dispute resolution* are becoming increasingly popular. ADR provides a number of benefits:

• The burden on the court system is reduced.

• An injured party with a legitimate claim is likely to be compensated sooner. When one considers the time-value of money, this can be a significant factor.

• Businesses (and other defendants) are less likely to settle specious claims merely for the sake of expediency and/or because the settlement is less expensive than the expenses of a trial.

• ADR is less adversarial, allowing the parties to reach a more amicable resolution. This, in turn, permits the parties to continue to do business together or to coexist in harmony in the future.

As a result of these—and other—benefits, the use of ADR is becoming more common, especially in the resolution of disputes involving a business. Increasingly, courts are *requiring* parties to attempt alternative methods of dispute resolution first, before allowing them to seek judicial remedies. Because these processes are usually less expensive and faster, they tend to create less tension in the relationship of the parties. This is particularly important in disputes between family members, such as child custody cases, and in business situations where the parties may wish to continue to do business together. For example, difficulties arose when Whoopi Goldberg was filming *T. Rex*. The parties agreed to use arbitration whenever problems occurred so that they could continue to produce the film.[12]

EXHIBIT 6.8 Common Steps of a Trial

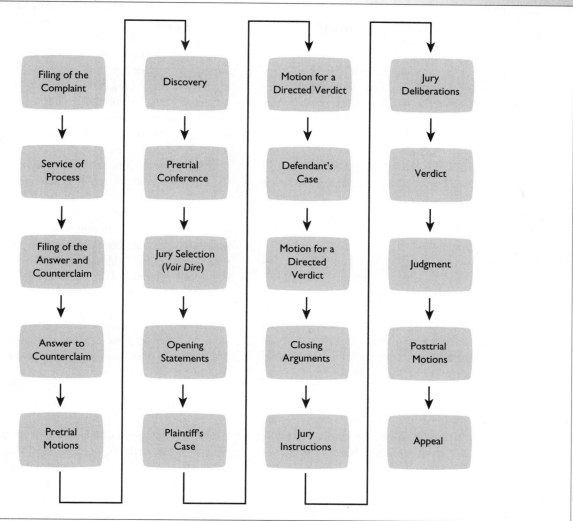

Continuity of relationship is not an issue in Nic Grant and Nancy Griffin's suit against NRW, since the parties do not have an ongoing relationship. ADR can be used with more than two parties. However, for the sake of simplicity we will talk about two-party disputes.

ADR has its limits, and it is not appropriate for resolving every form of legal dispute. ADR cannot be used in criminal matters, for example, and it does not establish legal precedent. In addition, some matters need to be debated in a public forum, which is not provided by ADR. However, when ADR is used within its limits, it usually provides quick and sure resolutions in a manner that is advantageous for all of the parties involved. For an interesting article on the future of ADR, see "Electronic Alternative Dispute Resolution" by Hakim Ben Adjoua, published in the *National Paralegal Reporter On-line 2000* by the National Federation of Paralegal Associations, at their Web site at http://www.paralegals.org/Reporter/On-line00/adr.htm.

Negotiation

Perhaps the earliest, and simplest, form of ADR is *negotiation*. Negotiation involves the discussion and resolution of a controversy by the parties involved. Negotiation is so common that most people do not even consider it as a form of ADR. Instead, they think of it as merely a method for settling disputes or controversies. That is the gist of ADR, however—settling a dispute or a controversy without resorting to the courts.

If the parties to the dispute recognize the wisdom in handling the dispute themselves and are willing and able to negotiate a solution acceptable to the parties, negotiation is an excellent method of dispute resolution. If the parties are able to resolve the matter themselves, with or without consulting their attorneys, they can probably save time and money. However, the parties may not *think* of negotiation as a possible solution, or they may not be *willing* to negotiate a settlement. Since negotiation is handled strictly by the parties, all interested parties must be willing to negotiate before it can serve as an effective method for resolving the dispute. For example, Nic and Nancy could try to negotiate a settlement with NRW's insurance company rather than take the case to trial. In so doing, they may wish to have Ms. Carroll assist them in the negotiation. The insurance adjuster or the attorneys of the insurer may represent NRW in the negotiation.

Mediation

Mediation is similar to negotiation, although there is a significant difference. Mediation involves the use of an impartial third party, a *mediator*, who attempts to help the parties reach a mutually acceptable resolution to their dispute. Usually, just one mediator is used. The mediator does not act as a decision maker; rather, he or she facilitates communication between the parties. The mediator listens to the parties and assists them in resolving their differences, or as many of the aspects of their dispute as possible. There are no formal procedures. The parties may choose to have a lawyer, a family member, or some other adviser present during the mediation. Generally, the mediator should not have any financial or personal interest in the result of the mediation without the written consent of all the parties. A prospective mediator should promptly disclose to the parties any circumstance likely to cause bias or the appearance of bias.

The advantages of mediation are that it is less expensive than litigation, it is quicker, and generally the results are perceived as more satisfactory. Participants are generally more satisfied because they agree to the result. Nic, Nancy, Mai, Carlos, and Helen could use mediation to attempt to resolve their dispute. The insurance company would also need to be represented if they are going to be asked for payment. The parties may use a commercial service to locate an appropriate, unbiased mediator. The International Academy of Mediators provides a directory of members and information about mediation at http://www.iamed.org/index1.cfm. The Uniform Mediation Act[13] of the ABA Section of Dispute Resolution and the National Conference of Commissioners on Uniform State Laws (NCCUSL) is available at the Harvard Law School Web site at http://www.pon.harvard.edu/guests/uma/.

Generally, the mediator does not impose a solution on the parties. Some mediators, however, take a more forceful role in attempting to fashion an agreement; others believe a more passive role is appropriate.

More than one mediation technique can be used in an attempt to resolve the disagreement. One mediation technique is *caucusing*. In this technique, the mediator meets with each party separately. Another mediation technique is *shuttle mediation,* where the mediator physically separates the parties during the mediation session and then runs messages between them.

Mediation sessions are private; usually only the parties, their representatives, and the mediator will be present. Other people generally may attend only with the permission of the parties and the mediator.

In most cases, mediation is successful; however, if it is not, the parties can utilize another ADR technique or submit their dispute for judicial resolution. Consequently, an important principle of mediation is confidentiality; otherwise the parties will not discuss the issues freely. The parties must be confident that what they say or admit in mediation will not be used against them in court. The parties should agree to maintain the confidentiality of the mediation and not to rely on or introduce into evidence at any arbitration, judicial, or other proceeding (1) the views expressed by a party, (2) suggestions made by a party, (3) admissions made by a party, (4) proposals made by the mediator, (5) views expressed by the mediator, and/or (6) the fact that a party was or was not willing to accept a proposal. The mediator should not be required to testify or divulge records in any adversarial proceeding. No stenographic record of the mediation process is prepared. An American Arbitration Association (AAA) Mediation usually follows these steps:

1. When parties request mediation, the AAA appoints a qualified mediator. If the agreement of the parties names a mediator or specifies a method of appointing a mediator, that designation or method is followed.

2. After a mediator has been selected, the first meeting date is arranged.

3. The parties meet with the mediator, who guides their negotiations and helps them to reach a settlement.

4. Private caucuses may be held between the mediator and each party in an attempt to bring disputants closer together.14

To help the parties, the AAA maintains a Web site with biographical information on mediators and current developments in arbitration at http://www.adr.org/index2.1.jsp.

There is a disagreement about whether mediators should undergo some certification process and become "certified."

The proponents of mediator certification believe that standards would encourage the confidence of the courts and the disputing parties. It would also ease the backlog in civil courts. The opponents to certification feel that it would limit the diversity of mediators at a time when this diversity is in demand. Lawyers, judges, psychotherapists, and ministers have entered the field of mediation. In addition, opponents argue that (1) the profession is still developing, (2) it is too early for certification, (3) there are no adequate standards for certification, and (4) certification at this time would be unfair and misleading to the public. In addition, there have been relatively few complaints against mediators.

A mediator should have good problem-solving skills and be fair. Roberta Kerr Parrott, a professional mediator, explains:

The challenge is always, when there's conflict, to create a possibility for both sides, both parties, to win. To make sure that I'm quiet enough long enough to hear what the real issues are so that we're dealing with what people are feeling and thinking at the heart of the issue rather than dealing with the surface.[15]

Knowledge of the law, while important in some cases, is only one possible competency a good mediator needs. Other necessary skills for mediators include:

* patience, persistence, concentration, and focus toward the goal

* the ability to distinguish between stated positions of the disputants and their real interests

* the ability to remain positive and constructive, even with difficult parties

* the ability to maintain confidentiality

* the ability to remain unbiased in the search for the truth of the situation and the solutions that work best for all concerned under the circumstances

* the ability to secure a resolution that is truly satisfactory for the participants: substantively, procedurally, and psychologically[16]

Standards of Conduct

Model standards of conduct for mediators have been drafted. However, these standards are nonbinding. The final draft has been available since September 1995 and has been endorsed by the ABA Section on Dispute Resolution, the ABA Section on Litigation, the AAA , and the Society of Professionals in Dispute Resolution.[17] A summary appears as Exhibit 6.9.

The standards do not choose between the conflicting approaches to mediation; instead, they concentrate on the similarities between the approaches. One particularly difficult issue is how active a mediator should be. Some contend that a mediator should only *facilitate* the settlement of disputes. Others believe that mediators should *evaluate* the proposals and *comment* on the viability of an approach in

---

EXHIBIT 6.9 Model Standards of Conduct for Mediators

A Mediator shall:

1. Recognize that mediation is based on the principles of self-determination by the parties.

2. Conduct the mediation in an impartial manner.

3. Disclose all actual and potential conflicts of interest reasonably known to the mediator.

4. Mediate only when the mediator has the necessary qualifications to satisfy the reasonable expectations of the parties.

5. Maintain the reasonable expectations of the parties with regard to confidentiality.

6. Conduct the mediation fairly and diligently, and in a manner consistent with the principle of self-determination by the parties.

7. Be truthful in advertising and solicitation for mediation.

8. Fully disclose and explain the basis of compensation, fees, and charges to the parties.

9. Have a duty to improve the practice of the profession.

Reprinted by permission of the American Arbitration Association, New York, NY.

court. A number of states (for example, Florida, Texas, and Indiana) have adopted standards of conduct for mediators.[18]

Compensation

There is no hard-and-fast rule regarding the compensation of mediators. In fact, compensation among mediators can vary widely. Many mediators are volunteers who serve as mediators through various community organizations. Others are professional mediators who rely on mediation to provide much of their income. The parties should discuss the compensation issue and how the expenses will be shared before agreeing to submit their disagreement to mediation.

Arbitration

Arbitration is the process of submitting a dispute to the judgment of a person or group of persons called arbitrators for resolution. The final decision of the arbitrator or panel of arbitrators is called an *award*. It is usually binding on the parties. *Advisory arbitration* is similar to traditional arbitration; however, it focuses on specific issues in the dispute and the award is not binding on the parties.

Arbitration begins with an agreement between the parties to arbitrate, usually in the initial agreement. The parties *can* agree to arbitrate: this is usually contained in the original agreement. The terms in an arbitration agreement can vary widely. An agreement to arbitrate is basically a contract or a portion of a contract. Like all contracts, to be valid, it must be based on *mutual assent*, meaning the parties must agree to be bound by exactly the same terms. If a party agrees to an arbitration clause because of *fraud* (when one party enters into a contract relying on a false statement of material fact) or *duress* (when one party enters into a contract due to a wrongful threat of force), the agreement will not be valid. (For a detailed discussion of what constitutes a valid contract, see Chapters 9–15.) Litigation may ensue if a party feels that the arbitration agreement was invalid. A judge would then determine the legality of the arbitration provision. AAA recommends a standard contract clause such as this one:

Any controversy or claim arising out of or relating to this contract, or the breach thereof, shall be settled by arbitration administered by the American Arbitration Association in accordance with its [applicable] rules and judgment on the award rendered by the arbitrator may be entered in any court having jurisdiction thereof.[19]

Exhibit 6.10 illustrates the steps used in an AAA arbitration. The form for submitting a dispute to the AAA appears as Exhibit 6.11.

NRW CASE 6.3   Management

SERVING AS A MEDIATOR

Helen has been asked to serve as a mediator in a dispute between two local firms that are each active in electronic research. Both firms agreed that their controversy should be resolved without taking the issue to court; and both agreed that Helen possessed the necessary qualifications to mediate their dispute. Helen is concerned about the request, and she has asked you whether she is qualified to serve as a mediator in this situation. What advice will you give her?

BUSINESS CONSIDERATIONS Should a business adopt a policy concerning its officers serving as mediators in disputes? What are the possible drawbacks—or benefits—to having officers mediate disputes between other firms?

ETHICAL CONSIDERATIONS Suppose a businessperson learned about certain new techniques or technical developments while serving as a mediator and this information would be of great use to the businessperson's firm. What ethical considerations would enter into any decision as to whether the information should be used? What legal considerations might enter into this situation?

INTERNATIONAL CONSIDERATIONS Would your recommendation to Helen change if the two firms were formed in a foreign country? Why?

In arbitration, a hearing is held before an arbitrator or a panel of arbitrators. There are two types of arbitration—binding and nonbinding or advisory. In nonbinding arbitration, the parties can consider the decision but do not have to follow it. Generally, a party *cannot* appeal the decision in binding arbitration. There are limited grounds for appeal, including problems of mutual assent in the agreement to arbitrate. Some courts will also consider an appeal if the arbitrator refused to admit evidence that would have been admissible in court.

Many states have statutes that provide for arbitration and the enforcement of the arbitrators' awards in the courts of the state. Statutes in Arizona,[20] California,[21] and Michigan[22] expressly authorize arbitration agreements, as does the Federal Arbitration Act.[23] LLI, maintained by Cornell Law School, provides a hypertext and searchable version of 9 U.S.C. § 1, the Federal Arbitration Act, at http://www4.law.cornell.edu/uscode/9/ch1.html. At one time,

EXHIBIT **6.10** Steps in an AAA Arbitration

1. A party files a demand for arbitration with an AAA regional office, and a case administrator is assigned to follow the case through to its conclusion.

2. Other parties named in the demand are notified and replies are requested.

3. The case administrator reviews panel qualifications and lists individuals suitable for the particular case. Information on AAA panelists is maintained on a computer.

4. The list is sent to the parties, each of whom numbers in order of preference the names that it finds acceptable.

5. An arbitrator is selected by the administrator according to the mutual desires of the parties. If the parties are unable to agree, the AAA may appoint an arbitrator.

6. The administrator arranges a hearing date and location convenient to the parties and to the arbitrator.

7. At the hearing, testimony and documents are submitted to the arbitrator, and witnesses are questioned and cross-examined.

8. The arbitrator then issues a binding award, copies of which are sent to the parties by the case administrator.

American Arbitration Association, *Resolving Your Disputes* (November 1995), p. 8. Reprinted with permission of AAA.

courts did not favor arbitration because it was considered an improper means of avoiding the judicial system. Today, that is no longer the attitude of the courts.

Various organizations offer panels of arbitrators. Parties may select their own arbitrator(s) or the arbitrator(s) may be selected by the organization. The AAA, for example, has a specific panel of arbitrators for commercial disputes. It also has panels for other types of disputes. The parties select their arbitrator from the panel members. Nic, Nancy, Mai, Carlos, Helen, and the insurance company could contact the AAA to obtain an arbitrator for their dispute.

Arbitrators charge about $400 to $700 a day.[24] Fees vary depending on the region and the type of case. Despite the expense, one finance company reported a 66 percent reduction in legal expenses by using arbitration.[25]

If both parties comply willingly with the arbitration award, no further action is required. If one side does not, court action to "confirm" the decision is necessary.

Controls on Arbitration

The states have developed their own individual approaches and laws to address arbitration issues. Some state statutes are more pro-arbitration than others; some attempted to restrict the scope of arbitration. For example, some states (such as Alabama) did not permit arbitration clauses in consumer contracts, although they permitted the use of arbitration and arbitration clauses in other types of contracts.[26] The U.S. Supreme Court addressed this issue in *Allied-Bruce Terminix Companies, Inc. v. Dobson.*[27] The

Alabama Supreme Court, relying on state law, had declared that a consumer did not have to go to arbitration as specified in the arbitration agreement signed by the parties. The U.S. Supreme Court heard the case on writ of certiorari to the Alabama Supreme Court and overturned that decision. It ruled that individual states could not regulate or prevent the use of arbitration by their statutes. The Federal Arbitration Act covers all transactions involving interstate commerce. For a more detailed discussion of what constitutes interstate commerce, see Chapter 5.

Statutory Coverage

Arbitration is subject to statutory coverage and provisions at the state, federal, and international levels. The statutory law is clarified by judicial interpretation at all levels. Parties seeking resolution of their disputes through arbitration should ascertain how arbitration is viewed and regulated at the level in which they are involved.

At the state level, the Uniform Arbitration Act (1956) was adopted in 46 states and the District of Columbia, Puerto Rico, and the Virgin Islands.[28] The NCCUSL has enacted the Uniform Arbitration Act (2000) to update and advance the use of arbitration; it has been adopted by 4 states.[29] Alabama, Georgia, Mississippi, and West Virginia have not adopted either act; they each have their own methods for regulating arbitration.[30] However, the 2000 act has been introduced into the West Virginia legislature.[31]

At the federal level, the Federal Arbitration Act (FAA), originally enacted in 1925, provides some federal guide-

EXHIBIT 6.11 American Arbitration Association Submission to Dispute Resolution Form

American Arbitration Association
SUBMISSION TO DISPUTE RESOLUTION

Date: _____

The named parties hereby submit the following dispute for resolution under the _____

_____ Rules* of the American Arbitration Association.

Procedure Selected: ☐ Arbitration   ☐ Mediation Settlement
☐ Other _____
(Describe.)

FOR INSURANCE CASES ONLY:

_____ to _____

Policy Number   Effective Dates   Applicable Policy Limits

Date of Incident _____   Location _____

Insured: _____   Claim Number: _____

Names of Claimants	**Check if a minor.**	**Amounts Claimed**
_____	☐	_____
_____	☐	_____

Nature of Dispute and/or Injuries Alleged (Attach additional sheets if necessary.):

Place of Hearing: _____

We agree that, if binding arbitration is selected, we will abide by and perform any award rendered hereunder and that a judgment may be entered on the award.

To Be Completed by the Parties

Name of Party _____   Name of Party _____

Address _____   Address _____

City, State, and ZIP Code _____   City, State, and ZIP Code _____

( ) _____   ( ) _____

Telephone   Fax   Telephone   Fax

Name of the Party's Attorney or Representative _____   Name of the Party's Attorney or Representative _____

Name of Firm (if Applicable) _____   Name of Firm (if Applicable) _____

Address _____   Address _____

City, State, and ZIP Code _____   City, State, and ZIP Code _____

( ) _____   ( ) _____

Telephone   Fax   Telephone   Fax

Signed† (may be signed by a representative) Title _____   Signed† (may be signed by a representative) Title _____

Please file three copies with the AAA.

* *If you have a question as to which rules apply, please contact the AAA.*
† *Signatures of all parties are required for arbitration.*

Form G1-9/95

lines to be followed in arbitration. It also attempts to ensure that arbitration clauses are given the same protection and enforceability as other contract clauses. Section 2 of the Federal Arbitration Act provides: "Written provision in any maritime transaction or a contract evidencing a transaction involving commerce to settle by arbitration a controversy thereafter arising out of such contract or transaction . . . shall be valid, irrevocable, and enforceable, save upon such grounds as exist at law or in equity for the revocation of any contract."

At the international level, arbitration is most likely to be regulated by the 1958 UN Convention on Recognition and Enforcement of Arbitral Awards, an international treaty dealing with arbitration. This convention has been ratified by more than 80 nations.[32] In this hemisphere, the Inter-American Convention on International Commercial Arbitration also regulates international arbitration.[33] The International Chamber of Commerce also supports and encourages arbitration, and many firms involved in international business seek to resolve their disputes through its arbitration provisions. The federal statute and the international treaties are designed to increase the acceptance and use of arbitration as an alternative method for resolving disputes.

The Supreme Court in the following case discussed whether an Americans with Disabilities Act (ADA) dispute must be arbitrated when an employee has signed an arbitration agreement.

6.3

EQUAL EMPLOYMENT OPPORTUNITY COMMISSION v. WAFFLE HOUSE, INC.
534 U.S. 279, 2002 U.S. LEXIS 489 (2002)

FACTS When Eric Baker applied for employment at the Waffle House, he signed an agreement that "any dispute or claim" concerning his employment would be "settled by binding arbitration." All Waffle House employees were required to sign a similar agreement. Baker began working as a grill operator and 16 days later he suffered a seizure at work. Soon after that he was discharged. Baker did not initiate arbitration proceedings; however, he filed a claim with the Equal Employment Opportunity Commission (EEOC) alleging that his discharge violated the Americans with Disabilities Act (ADA). After an attempt to resolve the issue, the EEOC filed an enforcement action alleging violation of the ADA in federal court. Baker was not a party to the suit. The complaint requested injunctive relief to eradicate the effects of past and present unlawful employment practices, to order specific relief designed to make Baker whole, and to award punitive damages.

ISSUE Does an agreement between an employer and an employee to arbitrate employment-related disputes bar the EEOC from pursuing judicial relief, including relief specific to this employee?

HOLDING No. The arbitration agreement did not prevent the EEOC from pursuing victim-specific relief.

REASONING Excerpts from the opinion of Justice Stevens:

Several Courts of Appeals have considered this issue and reached conflicting conclusions. . . . We granted the EEOC's petition for certiorari to resolve this conflict. . . . When Title VII was enacted in 1964, it authorized private actions by individual employees and public actions by the Attorney General. . . . In 1972, Congress amended Title VII to authorize the EEOC to bring its own enforcement actions. . . . Moreover, the amendments specify the judicial districts in which such actions may be brought. They do not mention arbitration proceedings. In 1991, Congress again amended Title VII to allow the recovery of compensatory and punitive damages by a "complaining party." The term includes both private plaintiffs and the EEOC. . . . [T]hese statutes unambiguously authorize the EEOC to obtain the relief that it seeks . . . if it can prove its case against respondent. . . .

There is no language in the statute or in . . . [precedents] suggesting that the existence of an arbitration agreement between private parties materially changes the EEOC's statutory function or the remedies that are otherwise available.

The FAA was enacted in 1925, and then reenacted and codified in 1947. . . . [I]ts "purpose was to reverse the longstanding judicial hostility to arbitration agreements that had existed at English common law and had been adopted by American courts, and to place arbitration agreements on the same footing as other contracts." The FAA broadly provides that a written provision in "a contract . . . to settle by arbitration a controversy thereafter arising out of such contract . . . shall be valid, irrevocable, and enforceable, save upon such grounds as exist at law or in equity for the revocation of any contract." Employment contracts, except for those covering workers engaged in transportation, are covered by the Act. . . . We have read these provisions to "manifest a 'liberal federal policy favoring arbitration agreements.'" Absent some ambiguity in the agreement, . . . it is the language of the contract that defines the scope of disputes subject to arbitration. . . . For nothing in the statute authorizes a court to compel arbitration of any issues, or by any parties, that are not already covered in the agreement. The FAA does not mention enforcement by public agencies; it ensures the enforceability of private agreements to arbitrate, but otherwise does not purport to place any restriction on a nonparty's choice of a judicial forum. . . .

[O]nce a charge is filed, . . . the EEOC is in command of the process. . . . If . . . the EEOC files suit on its own, the employee has no independent cause of action, although the employee may intervene in the EEOC's suit. . . . The statute clearly makes the EEOC the master of its own case and confers on the agency the authority to evaluate the strength of the public interest at stake. . . .

The FAA directs courts to place arbitration agreements on equal footing with other contracts, but it "does not require parties to arbitrate when they have not agreed to do so." . . . Because the FAA is "at bottom a policy guaranteeing the enforcement of private contractual arrangements," we look first to whether the parties agreed to arbitrate a dispute . . . to determine the scope of the agreement. While ambiguities in the language of the agreement should be resolved in favor of arbitration, we do not override the clear intent of the parties, or reach a result inconsistent with the plain text of the contract, simply because the policy favoring arbitration is implicated. "Arbitration under the [FAA] is a matter of consent, not coercion." Here there is no ambiguity. No one asserts that the EEOC is a party to the contract, or that it agreed to arbitrate its claims. It goes without saying that a contract cannot bind a nonparty. Accordingly, the proarbitration policy goals of the FAA do not require the agency to relinquish its statutory authority if it has not agreed to do so. . . .

[W]e are persuaded that, pursuant to Title VII and the ADA, whenever the EEOC chooses . . . to bring an enforcement action in a particular case, the agency may be seeking to vindicate a public interest, not simply provide make-whole relief for the employee, even when it pursues entirely victim-specific relief. To hold otherwise would undermine the detailed enforcement scheme created by Congress simply to give greater effect to an agreement between private parties that does not even contemplate the EEOC's statutory function. It is true . . . that Baker's conduct may have the effect of limiting the

relief that the EEOC may obtain in court. If, for example, he had failed to mitigate his damages, or had accepted a monetary settlement, any recovery by the EEOC would be limited accordingly. . . . As we have noted, it "goes without saying that the courts can and should preclude double recovery by an individual." . . .

The only issue before this Court is whether the fact that Baker has signed a mandatory arbitration agreement limits the remedies available to the EEOC. The text of the relevant statutes provides a clear answer to that question. They do not authorize the courts to balance the competing policies of the ADA and the FAA or to second-guess the agency's judgment concerning which of the remedies authorized by law that it shall seek in any given case. . . . [I]n this context, the statute specifically grants the EEOC exclusive authority over the choice of forum and the prayer for relief once a charge has been filed. . . .

BUSINESS CONSIDERATIONS Why would an employer want an arbitration clause included in its employment contracts? If such a clause is used, should the clause also specify how arbitrators will be selected?

ETHICAL CONSIDERATIONS Was it ethical for Waffle House to fire Baker in this case? Is it ethical for an employee to seek judicial relief after agreeing to submit any controversies to arbitration?

Organizations

There are a number of organizations that actively support arbitration and provide both the forum in which an arbitration occurs and the arbitrator. Some of these organizations operate exclusively within the United States; others operate internationally. Within the United States, arbitration is supported by the Judicial Arbitration and Mediation Services, Inc. (J.A.M.S.), which employs only former judges as arbitrators; the Federal Mediation and Conciliation Service; and the AAA. Internationally, the AAA (which operates both domestically and internationally); the International Chamber of Commerce, headquartered in Paris; and the London Court of Arbitration (which is *not* a court, despite the title of the organization) support arbitration. The International Chamber of Commerce maintains its arbitration page at http://www.iccwbo.org/home/menu_international_arbitration.asp. It also provides information about ADR and its International Court of Arbitration page at http://www.iccwbo.org/index_court.asp.

The AAA administers more than 60,000 cases in an average year.[34] Its services include arbitration, mediation, minitrial, *fact-finding* (a process where an arbitrator investigates a dispute and issues findings of fact and a nonbinding report), education, and training. When the AAA is involved in an arbitration, it can (1) refer a list of potential arbitrators, (2) serve as an *intermediator* between the parties and the arbitrator in negotiating the arbitrator's compensation, and (3) collect a deposit for arbitrator compensation. The AAA administrator handles the administrative details, so that the parties do not deal directly with the arbitrator. This helps ensure that the parties will not discuss the case privately with the arbitrator prior to the hearing. The AAA requires its arbitrators to issue awards within 30 days after the close of the hearings, unless the contract between the parties specifies another time limit.[35] Except in labor and international cases, the AAA encourages arbitrators to write itemized awards instead of lengthy opinions.[36] It promulgates rules for specific types of arbitration and it also has special procedures for large, complex commercial cases.

Minitrial

In ADR, the term *minitrial* describes a process in which the parties' attorneys present an abbreviated form of their case. The parties are permitted to use expert witnesses to support their case. A *neutral* (unbiased) person acts as chair. Senior executives from the firms involved also attend the presentation. After the presentation, the senior executives meet in an attempt to resolve the dispute. Before the presentation the parties usually specify what will happen if the senior executives are unable to settle the case. For example, if the senior executives *are* unable to settle the case, the neutral may be empowered to mediate or to provide a nonbinding advisory opinion informing the parties of the probable outcome of litigation. A minitrial would not be appropriate to resolve Nic and Nancy's claims.

Note that in court matters, judges use the term "minitrial" to refer to an abbreviated judicial proceeding on a few issues, for example, a minitrial on damages.

Rent-a-Judge Trial

A "rent-a-judge" trial is another alternative method of dispute resolution. When the parties elect to use this method, they pay a fee to a "judge" to settle the dispute. "Judges" in these cases are typically retired judges, people who are well trained in presiding over dispute resolution and who bring the reputation and prestige of their former positions to their current role. Rent-a-judge "cases" occasionally involve a "jury" of hired experts, particularly in technical cases.

The major advantage of the rent-a-judge option is that it is much faster than regular civil litigation. In addition, the proceedings are relatively private and do not become part of the public record. Many time-consuming trial procedures are eliminated in rent-a-judge trials, providing an additional savings of time and money.[37] These "trials" are significantly less formal and are generally conducted in conference rooms.

It is not uncommon for the parties in a civil case to wait four to five years before they can get their case to trial. These same parties can get their case to "trial" with a rent-a-judge in a matter of weeks. As a result, the use of rent-a-judge trials is growing more popular. Because all states accept some form of private resolution of cases, rent-a-judge resolutions are likely to become more common in the future. A number of companies now exist to assist clients in locating rent-a-judges. One company, Judicate, even has its own private courthouse in Los Angeles. In some jurisdictions, the clerk of court's office maintains a list of retired judges who are willing to serve as rent-a-judges. Depending on the jurisdiction, the decisions of rent-a-judges may be appealed to the public court of appeals.[38] Nic and Nancy might agree to having a retired judge from Butler County serve as a rent-a-judge. If they are experiencing financial difficulty, the speed of using a rent-a-judge and the opportunity for a quick payment would be attractive.

Small Claims Court

Another technique to reduce legal expenses is for a party to file the legal dispute in small claims court. Although this *is* litigation, it significantly reduces the costs. This option permits a party to effectively represent himself or herself. Generally, the opponent can also appear without a lawyer. Quick resolution of disputes is usually available. Small claims courts do not utilize legalese and standard rules of evidence. The procedures vary from state to state. The jurisdictional amounts also vary—the upper limit may range from $1,000 (Mississippi and parts of Virginia) to $10,000 (parts of Tennessee).[39] In most states, Nic and Nancy's claims would exceed the jurisdictional limits of small claims court.

Some small claims courts publish booklets to assist parties in small claims actions. There may also be government employees who provide free or low-cost legal services to parties who are filing complaints in small claims courts. Participants do not need to be familiar with legal jargon; however, participants need to be organized and to bring their witnesses and any physical evidence with them to the hearing. Participants should prepare a brief, coherent presentation of the case. It is also helpful to observe a couple of small claims cases in advance of the hearing date.

If the defendant does not show up on the trial date, the court hears only the plaintiff's side. This is called a *default judgment*. If the plaintiff does not appear on the trial date, the case is dismissed.

Execution

Before filing the complaint, consider whether the defendant is likely to be able to pay a judgment. Generally, a successful plaintiff will have to conduct the collection process himself or herself. This is usually accomplished by discovering the defendant's assets and obtaining permission (in a written legal document called a writ) from the court to levy on them. The plaintiff then takes the writ to the court in the locality where the assets are located; completes a form requesting execution; pays a fee; and asks a sheriff, marshal, or constable to collect the described assets. Execution is described briefly in Case 6.2, *Johnson v. Outboard Marine Corporation*.

Summary

Lawsuits are based on factual circumstances. Therefore, it is the client's responsibility to reveal all the facts to his or her attorney. If all the facts are not known, the attorney might draw the wrong legal conclusion. If the facts warrant a lawsuit, one of the first things the attorney should do is to apprise the potential defendant of liability and seek to settle the case without filing a lawsuit. Attorney's fees are an important consideration in deciding whether the client should sue.

Before filing a suit, parties usually have an opportunity to settle the matter, either through a settlement conference or arbitration. After suit is filed, the discovery process takes place. Discovery is designed to narrow the legal issues, thus encouraging pretrial settlement or reducing the duration of the actual trial. During voir dire, the petit jury is selected for the trial. Potential jurors can be dismissed for cause or by use of a peremptory challenge. Consultants may be hired to assist the attorneys in selecting the jury and/or presenting an effective case before the jury.

The doctrine of *res judicata* means that when a court issues a final judgment, the subject matter of the case cannot be relitigated between the same parties. However, it does not prevent appeals from the final judgment.

The time, trouble, and expense associated with trials have led to an increasing emphasis on ADR methods. There are five major ADR methods outside the judicial system, and one that involves a specialized court within the judicial system.

Negotiation is probably the oldest and most common form of ADR. The parties discuss their dispute and reach a mutually agreeable solution to the problem. Negotiation is restricted only by the willingness of the parties to compromise.

Mediation is slightly more formal than negotiation. In mediation, the parties turn to a mediator, a third person who helps the parties to find a mutually acceptable solution. Mediators do not provide a solution; they provide a procedure for helping the parties reach a solution. The mediator facilitates communication rather than acting as a decision maker.

Arbitration involves a third party, the arbitrator, who listens to the arguments of each party and then renders an award to resolve the controversy. The arbitrator is a decision maker. Arbitration is commonly *binding,* meaning that the parties agree to abide by the decision.

Minitrials involve a neutral person chairing a presentation of the evidence before the senior executives of the companies. After this presentation, the senior executives meet and attempt to settle the dispute.

Rent-a-judge trials are a variation on arbitration, using a person in the role of "judge" rather than arbitrator to resolve a controversy. Rent-a-judges, often retired judges, preside over informal "trials" in private "courtrooms" to resolve disputes.

Small claims courts provide relatively informal resolution for small civil claims. The rules and the jurisdictional limits of these specialized courts vary widely among the states.

Discussion Questions

1. Is there any conflict of interest if Lyn Carroll represents both plaintiffs in this case? Why or why not? Is there any conflict of interest if Jefferson Jones represents both defendants in this case? Why or why not?

2. Are contingency fee contracts fair to clients? What are the advantages of contingency fee arrangements for clients? What are the disadvantages for clients?

3. Why are interrogatories limited to a party to a lawsuit and yet depositions can be taken from any witness?

4. In the case of Nic Grant versus Carlos Rios and NRW, suppose a jury is made up almost solely of people on public assistance. In your opinion, is this providing the parties with a fair trial? Why?

5. What is *res judicata*? How does the concept of *res judicata* affect lawsuits?

6. What ethical perspective(s) are reflected in the Model Standards of Conduct for mediators?

7. The Los Angeles County Bar Association sued in federal court to obtain more local judges, primarily due to a backlog of cases in the civil courts.[40] What are the primary causes of the backlog in civil courts? What could be done to alleviate this backlog?

8. What are the advantages and disadvantages of including the following clause in an agreement to arbitrate: "Upon the request of a party, the arbitrator's award shall include findings of fact and conclusions of law"?[41]

9. Parties who submit their claims to resolution with a rent-a-judge may be allowed to appeal the result of their "case" to the court of appeals. Will wealthy parties, who can afford to use rent-a-judge trials, lose interest in reforming the legal system if they can use private judging and still appeal to public appellate courts? Is that a concern? Why or why not?

10. Small claims courts are specialized civil courts within the state court system. Why is small claims court more like ADR than it is like a regular civil court? How is small claims court more like a regular civil court than a category of ADR?

Case Problems and Writing Assignments

1. On January 31, 1997, Judge Fujisaki instructed jurors in the civil trial of O. J. Simpson that they must "insulate themselves from all news media—watch no TV, listen to no radio and read no newspapers." He told them that he wanted to avoid sequestering the jury. A juror had just been removed from the trial for legal cause during deliberations; he was concerned that she might be giving interviews and did not want the jury tainted.

   Jurors were also instructed to "have someone screen their phone calls, mail and faxes." The judge was concerned about reports that two jurors in the Simpson criminal trial were contacting members of the civil jury panel. They were allegedly trying to promote a deal for public appearances after the trial. Brenda Moran and Gina Marie Rosborough, two criminal jurors, announced a book deal shortly after the verdict in the criminal trial. Moran acknowledged writing a letter to the civil jurors recommending Bud Stewart as an agent. Both women stated that it was supposed to be delivered *after* the verdict, not while deliberations were going on. Faxes were sent to news producers offering to arrange interviews with three civil trial jurors in the case. The faxes were signed Bud Stewart, the agent mentioned in the letter from Moran.

   Discuss the interrelationships between fair trials, the public's interest in obtaining information, and the media's business interests. It appears that Bud Stewart was attempting to get ahead of other agents. How could he have solicited business and clients without interfering with the legal process? [See Linda Deutsch and Michael Fleeman, "Simpson Juror Replaced; Talks Start Anew," *The Fresno Bee*, February 1, 1997, pp. A1 and A11; and "Juror Dismissed in Simpson Case," *Merced Sun-Star*, February 1, 1997, pp. A1 and A8.]

2. A woman and her daughter were abducted from Kmart's parking lot. The offenders raped the victim while holding her child at knifepoint. In a jury trial, the woman and her daughter successfully sued Kmart for failure to provide adequate security. Their attorney was Paul Minor. Kmart moved for a new trial and a remittitur and a *stay* (an order suspending a judicial proceeding) pending the decision on these motions. The district court denied these motions and three days later Minor obtained a writ of execution from the clerk of court. Accompanied by newspaper and television reporters, Minor went to the local Kmart establishment with two federal marshals and sought execution on the writ by seizing money assets in the store's registers and safe. The district court discovered Minor's steps to execute the judgment and instructed the Marshals' office to cease and desist pending a telephone conference that afternoon. At the conference, the court directed Kmart to submit a bond so that all matters would be stayed pending appeal. Kmart moved for sanctions against Minor, claiming that it was entitled to an automatic stay of execution. Rule 62(f) of the Federal Rules of Civil Procedure provides in pertinent part:

   in any state in which a judgment is a lien upon the property of the judgment debtor and in which the judgment debtor is entitled to a stay of execution, a judgment debtor is entitled, in the district court therein, to such stay as would be accorded the judgment debtor had the action been maintained in the courts of that state.

   Rule 62(a) of the Mississippi Rules of Civil Procedure provides:

   Automatic Stay: Exceptions. Except as stated herein or as otherwise provided by statute or by order of the court for good cause shown, no execution shall be issued upon a judgment nor shall proceedings be taken for its enforcement until the expiration of ten days after the later of its entry or the disposition of a motion for a new trial. . . .

   Apparently Minor's intention was to embarrass Kmart. Should Minor be sanctioned for his behavior? Why or why not? [*Whitehead v. Food Max of Mississippi, Inc.*; *Kmart Corporation v. Minor*, 277 F.3d 791, 2002 U.S. App. LEXIS 458 (5th Cir. 2002).]

3. Melinda Kay Broemmer was 21 years old, unmarried, and 16 or 17 weeks pregnant. She was a high school graduate earning less than $100.00 a week and had no medical benefits. The father-to-be insisted that Broemmer have an abortion, but her parents advised against it. Broemmer says that the time was one of considerable confusion and emotional and physical turmoil for her. Her mother contacted Abortion Services of Phoenix and made an appointment for Broemmer. During their visit to the clinic, Broemmer and her mother expected to receive information and counseling on alternatives to abortion and the nature of the operation. They did not receive that information. Broemmer was escorted into an adjoining room and asked to complete three forms, one of which was an agreement to arbitrate. The agreement to arbitrate included language that "any dispute aris[ing] between the Parties as a result of the fees and/or services" would be settled by binding arbitration and that "any arbitrators appointed by the American Arbitration Association (AAA) shall be licensed medical doctors who specialize in obstetrics/gynecology." Broemmer completed all three

forms in less than five minutes and returned them to the front desk. Clinic staff made no attempt to explain the agreement to her before or after she signed, and did not provide her with copies of the forms. After she returned the forms to the front desk, she was taken into an examination room where pre-operation procedures were performed. Broemmer returned the following day and Doctor Otto performed the abortion. As a result of the procedure, she suffered a punctured uterus that required medical treatment. Was the arbitration provision binding on Broemmer? [See *Broemmer v. Abortion Services of Phoenix, Ltd.*, 840 P.2d 1013 (Ariz. 1992).]

4. Steven Gwin bought a lifetime "Termite Protection Plan" (Plan) from the local office of Allied-Bruce Terminix Companies, a franchise of Terminix International Company. In the Plan, Allied-Bruce promised "to protect" Gwin's house "against the attack of subterranean termites," to reinspect periodically, to provide any "further treatment found necessary" and to repair, up to $100,000, damage caused by new termite infestations. The Plan's contract provided in writing that "any controversy or claim . . . arising out of or relating to the interpretation, performance or breach of any provision of this agreement shall be settled exclusively by arbitration." In the spring of 1991, Mr. and Mrs. Gwin wished to sell their house to Mr. and Mrs. Dobson. The Gwins had Allied-Bruce reinspect the house, and they were told there was no infestation. But, no sooner had they sold the house and transferred the Termite Protection Plan to Mr. and Mrs. Dobson than the Dobsons found the house swarming with termites. Allied-Bruce attempted to treat and repair the house, but the Dobsons thought that Allied-Bruce's efforts were inadequate. They sued the Gwins, Allied-Bruce, and Terminix. Allied-Bruce and Terminix immediately asked the court for a stay, to allow arbitration to proceed. Was the arbitration clause enforceable against the Dobsons? What is the affect of the Federal Arbitration Act? [See *Allied-Bruce Terminix Companies, Inc. v. Dobson*, 513 U.S. 265 (1995).]

5. **BUSINESS APPLICATION CASE** Annette Phillips worked as a bartender at a Hooters restaurant in Myrtle Beach, South Carolina. She alleged that a Hooters's official grabbed and slapped her buttocks. Phillips asked her manager for help and she was told to "let it go." She quit her job. Phillips's attorney contacted Hooters, claiming that the attack and the restaurant's failure to deal with it violated Phillips's Title VII rights. Hooters responded that Phillips was required to submit her claims to arbitration.

In 1994 Hooters implemented an ADR program. Hooters conditioned eligibility for raises, transfers, and promotions upon an employee signing an agreement to arbitrate employment-related disputes. Phillips signed the agreement, which said that Hooters and the employee agree to arbitrate all disputes arising out of employment, including "any claim of discrimination, sexual harassment, retaliation, or wrongful discharge, whether arising under federal or state law." It further stated "the employee and the company agree to resolve any claims pursuant to the company's rules and procedures for alternative

resolution of employment-related disputes, as promulgated by the company from time to time. Company will make available or provide a copy of the rules upon written request of the employee." No employee was given a copy of Hooters's arbitration rules and procedures. Hooters sent a copy of the rules to Phillips's attorney.

Under these rules the employee must provide the company with a notice of her claim at the outset, including the nature of the claim and the specific acts or omissions on which it is based. Hooters does not have to file a response or a list of its defenses. Simultaneously, the employee must provide the company with a list of all fact witnesses and a brief summary of the facts known by each one. The company does not have to reciprocate. Each party selects an arbitrator and those two arbitrators select a third arbitrator. The third arbitrator must be selected from a list provided by Hooters. There is no input from the employee in the generation of the list. Hooters is free to make a list consisting solely of managers and people with family and/or financial relationships with Hooters. Nothing in the rules prevents Hooters from retaliating against arbitrators who rule against Hooters. Hooters may expand the scope of the arbitration to any matter, but the employee cannot raise any matter not included in the original notice. Hooters can move for summary dismissal of the employee's claims, but the employee cannot move for summary dismissal of Hooters's claims. Hooters may record the arbitration hearing by audio-taping, videotaping, or verbatim transcription. The employee cannot. Hooters can bring suit to cancel or modify an arbitral award, but the employee cannot. Hooters can cancel the agreement to arbitrate upon 30 days' notice, but the employee cannot. Hooters reserves the right to modify the rules "in whole or in part," whenever it wishes and "without notice" to the employee. Hooters could even modify the rules in the middle of an arbitration. Hooters filed suit to compel arbitration. Phillips argues that she should not be required to arbitrate. Assume that you have been hired by Hooters to resolve the problem with Phillips. What would you do? You have also been assigned the responsibility to revise their arbitration program. What changes would you make? [See *Hooters of America, Inc. v. Phillips*, 173 F.3d 933, 1999 U.S. App. LEXIS 6329 (4th Cir. 1999).]

6. **ETHICAL APPLICATION CASE** David Weber was hired by defendant Strippit, Inc. as an international sales manager for various Asian markets. After an initial training period at Strippit's headquarters in Akron, New York, Weber had his office in his home in Minnesota. On February 2, 1993, Weber, then 54 years old, suffered a major heart attack. Following his second hospital stay, Weber was placed on strict physical limitations and was advised by his doctor not to work for nearly two months. Beginning in October 1993, several months after Weber had returned to work following his second hospitalization, defendants required Weber to complete further training and advised him of the possibility that he would be required to relocate to Akron. Strippit reduced Weber's commissions and informed him that his employment could be terminated at any time.

Weber underwent another angioplasty in early 1994. Defendants informed Weber that he must relocate to Akron. Defendants eventually ordered Weber to either relocate to Akron or, if he was unwilling to leave Minnesota, to accept a position as a domestic sales engineer at a much lower salary. Weber told defendants that his doctor advised him to remain in Minnesota for six months prior to relocating for medical reasons. Defendants refused to wait the six months and Weber was either terminated or abandoned his employment. At the conclusion of the trial, the jury returned a unanimous verdict for defendants. During jury selection, defendants exercised all three of their peremptory challenges to remove jurors over the age of 50. At that time, and again as part of his motion for a new trial, Weber alleged that defendants violated his right to a representative jury through this use of their peremptory challenges. Did the defendants violate Weber's rights by using their peremptory challenges to remove older jurors? [See *Weber v. Strippit, Inc.,* 1999 U.S. App. LEXIS 17919 (8th Cir. 1999).]

7. **CRITICAL THINKING CASE** Ceasar Wright began working as a longshoreman in Charleston, South Carolina. He was a member of Local 1422 of the International Longshoremen's Association, AFL-CIO (the Union), which uses a hiring hall to supply workers to several stevedore companies represented by the South Carolina Stevedores Association (SCSA). Clause 15(B) of the Collective Bargaining Agreement (CBA) between the Union and the SCSA provides: "Matters under dispute which cannot be promptly settled between the Local and an individual Employer shall . . . be referred in writing . . . to a Port Grievance Committee. . . ." If the Port Grievance Committee cannot reach an agreement . . . then the dispute must be referred to a District Grievance Committee. If the District Grievance Committee cannot reach a majority decision, then the committee must employ a professional arbitrator.

While Wright was working for Stevens Shipping and Terminal Company, he injured his right heel and his back. He sought compensation from Stevens and ultimately settled the claim for $250,000 and $10,000 in attorney's fees. In January 1995, Wright returned to the Union hiring hall and asked to be referred for work. Between January 2 and January 11, Wright worked for four stevedoring companies, none of which complained about his performance. When the stevedoring companies realized that Wright had previously settled a claim for permanent disability, they informed the Union that they would not accept Wright for employment. The Union suggested that the ADA entitled Wright to return to work if he could perform his duties. Wright hired an attorney and filed charges of discrimination with the Equal Employment Opportunity Commission (EEOC) and the South Carolina State Human Affairs Commission, alleging that the stevedoring companies and the SCSA had violated the ADA by refusing to hire him. Did the general arbitration clause in the CBA require Wright to use the arbitration procedure for an alleged violation of the ADA? [See *Wright v. Universal Maritime Service Corporation,* 119 S. Ct. 391, 1998 U.S. LEXIS 7270 (1998).]

8. **YOU BE THE JUDGE** Justine Maldonado filed a sexual harassment lawsuit against the Ford Motor Company. Maldonado alleged that a supervisor, Daniel P. Bennett, sexually harassed her. Three other women have also sued Ford alleging sexual harassment by Bennett. Bennett was convicted in 1995 of the crime of exposing himself to three young women. This conviction was expunged from his record because he met the good-behavior requirements under Michigan law. There was no gag order in this case. Circuit Court Judge William J. Giovan dismissed Maldonado's suit because she and her lawyer, Miranda Massie, had discussed the case with reporters, including evidence that the court had said was inadmissible. Much of the information was a matter of public record. However, the judge said that it was an attempt to prejudice potential jurors and a violation of a Michigan law that forbids publicizing a conviction that has been expunged. According to the judge, "The behavior in question has been intentional, premeditated and intransigent. . . . It was designed to reach the farthest boundaries of the public consciousness." There has been other conflict between Massie and the judge. Massie had asked the judge to remove himself because a member of Ford's law firm handled a fund-raising event for his reelection. In addition, the judge said that Massie was disrespectful to him because she indicated to the media that it was difficult to get a fair trial against Ford in that town. Assume that the dismissal of the case has been appealed to *your* court. How would *you* rule? Why? [See Danny Hakim, "Sex-Bias Suit Against Ford Is Dismissed on Trial Remarks," *New York Times,* August 27, 2002, Late Edition-Final, p. C1.]

Notes

1. It is generally unwise for a lawyer to represent himself or herself even though he or she may know the rules, since the lawyer is emotionally involved in the case.
2. David A. Lieb, "Clinton Ordered to Pay $90,000 in Penalty Fees in Jones Contempt Case," *The Fresno Bee,* July 30, 1999, pp. A1, A22.
3. Fed. R. Civ. Proc. § 48.
4. 28 U.S.C. § 1870.
5. *J.E.B. v. T.B.,* 114 S. Ct. 1419 (1994).
6. 476 U.S. 79 (1986).
7. Cal. Civ. Proc. Code § 170.6.

8. 28 U.S.C. § 455 and Cal. Civ. Proc. Code § 170.
9. 42 Pa. Con. Stat. Ann. § 5104.
10. Fed. R. Civ. Proc. § 48.
11. Eric Lichtblau, "Zapruder Film Costs U.S. $16 Million," *The Fresno Bee,* August 4, 1999, pp. A1, A5.
12. *Whoop, Inc. v. Dyno Productions, Inc.,* 75 Cal. Rptr. 2d 90 (Cal. App. 2nd Dist. 1998).
13. The primary concern of the Uniform Mediation Act (2001) is to keep mediation communications confidential. It has not yet been adopted by any state; however, in 2002 it was introduced to

the legislatures in Nebraska, New York, Oklahoma, South Carolina, and Vermont. "A Few Facts about the Uniform Mediation Act (2001)," NCCUSL Web site, http://www.nccusl.org/nccusl/uniformact_factsheets/uniformacts-fs-uma2001.asp (accessed 12/15/02) and "Summary Uniform Mediation Act (2001)," NCCUSL Web site, http://www.nccusl.org/nccusl/uniformact_summaries/uniformacts-s-uma2001.asp (accessed 12/15/02).

14. American Arbitration Association, *Resolving Your Disputes* (November 1995), pp. 8–9. Reprinted by permission of AAA.

15. Quoted in Teresa V. Carey, "Credentialing for Mediators—To Be or Not to Be?" *U. San Francisco L. Rev.* 635, at 640, Spring 1996.

16. Ibid., 641.

17. Richard C. Reuben, "Model Ethics Rules Limit Mediator Role: Despite Controversy, Standards Expected to Improve Respect for Profession," *ABA Journal* (January 1996): p. 25.

18. Ibid.

19. American Arbitration Association, *Drafting Dispute Resolution Clauses—A Practical Guide* (June 1994), 5. Reprinted by permission of AAA.

20. Ariz. Rev. Stat. Ann. §§ 12-1501–1518.

21. 9 Cal. Civ. Proc. Code §§ 1280 et seq., at § 1295.

22. Mich. Stat. Ann. §§ 27A.5040–5065.

23. 9 U.S.C. §§ 1 et. seq., at § 2.

24. "When You Need a Lawyer," *Consumer Reports* (February 1996): 39.

25. Curtis D. Brown, "New Law Lets Creditors Cut Court Costs," *Credit World* (July/August 1996): 30–31.

26. Ibid.

27. 513 U.S. 265 (1995).

28. Information on the Uniform Arbitration Act (1956) was provided in an e-mail from Katie Robinson, Communications Officer, NCCUSL, January 7, 2000.

29. It has been adopted by Hawaii, New Mexico, Nevada, and Utah. "A Few Facts about the Uniform Arbitration Act (2000)," NCCUSL Web site, http://www.nccusl.org/nccusl/uniformact_factsheets/uniformacts-fs-aa.asp (accessed 12/15/02).

30. See note 28.

31. See note 29.

32. American Arbitration Association, *Drafting*, 37.

33. Ibid.

34. American Arbitration Association, *Resolving*, 3.

35. American Arbitration Association, *Why Labor and Management Use the Services of the American Arbitration Association* (November 1993), 5.

36. American Arbitration Association, *Drafting*, 30.

37. Deborah Shannon, "Rent-A-Judge," *American Way Magazine* (February 1991): 33–36.

38. Ibid., 34.

39. "Do-It-Yourself Justice—Small Claims Court," *Consumer Reports* (February 1996): 36.

40. Deborah Shannon, "Rent-a-Judge," 33.

41. American Arbitration Association, *Drafting*, 30.

Torts

A
G
E
N
D
A

NRW NRW would also like to avoid committing torts. Gabino, a former NRW employee, is applying for new positions with several different firms; potential employers are calling Mai to inquire about Gabino's employment history with NRW. Mai wants to avoid lawsuits for defamation and invasion of privacy. What should Mai tell them when they call?

A competitor has been advertising the merits of its product in comparison with another tracking device that looks like a StuffTrakR unit. This "other device" is depicted as an inferior unit that does not perform very well. Although NRW is not specifically named in the advertisement, it seems obvious that the "other device" is a StuffTrakR. Can NRW successfully sue this competitor for product disparagement in order to protect NRW's image and reputation? Also, a group of people have banded together to protest—or even prevent—the use of personal item tracking devices, and they have threatened to file invasion-of-privacy lawsuits based on the idea that the units can be used to track people's movement. Mai, Carlos, and Helen think that this argument stretches the invasion of privacy doctrine. Do NRW's products invade people's privacy? Should NRW worry about these legal threats? What legal defenses might be available to them? What would occur if an employee were negligent in operating an NRW vehicle on "official" business? Who would be liable for any damages—NRW, the employee, or both? What can our entrepreneurs do to avoid liability?

These and other questions will arise as you read this chapter. Be prepared! You never know when the firm or one of its members will seek your advice.

Objectives of Tort Law

Tort law is concerned with a body of "private" wrongs, whereas *criminal law,* which we shall study in Chapter 8, is concerned with "public" wrongs. Tort law has evolved over hundreds of years. It supports the protection of an individual's rights with respect to his or her property and person. It is a complicated body of law because of the long period of development and the various exceptions that have evolved in its application. In addition, tort law is based on common law; consequently, the rules vary from state to state. The discussion here, therefore, is fairly general. The Legal Information Institute (LII), maintained by the Cornell Law School, provides an overview of tort law and a link to the Federal Tort Claims Act at http://www.law.cornell.edu/topics/torts.html. The Federal Tort Claims Act permits some suits against the federal government for the torts of its workers. The American Bar Association (ABA) Section on Tort and Insurance (TIPS) maintains its Web site at http://www.abanet.org/tips/home.html. The site contains information about tort and insurance law and section activities.

Tort law provides a mechanism for persons who have been wronged to seek remedies in our court system. In general, the remedy sought is money damages to compensate for the injury. People can avoid committing these wrongs by adhering to various "duties." For example, society recognizes a duty to refrain from physically injuring other persons or their property. Society also recognizes a duty to refrain from injuring the reputation of others.

Because tort law recognizes certain duties, it raises the policy question of exactly which rights society should protect through the imposition of duties. For example, should society recognize as a wrong only behavior intended to be a wrong? Should society also recognize as a wrong an unintended wrong due to someone's negligence? Should society also recognize as a wrong unintended behavior in which the person is *not* negligent? These are the questions discussed in this chapter.

Society has developed the body of tort law to resolve social and economic policy questions. The law takes into consideration a number of factors including the social usefulness of the conduct of a person; the interests asserted by the plaintiff; the justification (if any) for the defendant's conduct; the economic burden placed on the defendant if liability is imposed; and the question of spreading the cost of liability from one to many persons. The law also has the unique problem of respecting past decisions while maintaining flexibility within the legal system in order to provide solutions to modern problems. For instance, tort law has to adjust to technological advances such as defamation and invasion of privacy through the use of the computer. The mission of American Tort Reform Association (ATRA) is legislative reform and public education. It maintains a Web site at http://www.atra.org/atra/, where it discusses some of its proposals and the states that have adopted them.

Theories of Tort Liability

This chapter discusses intentional torts, negligence, and strict liability. Exhibit 7.1 depicts the three theories of tort liability. *Intentional torts* are those wrongs in which the persons being sued acted in a willful or intentional manner; they either wanted the act to occur or knew that the act would probably occur. Suppose that someone said something offensive to you, and you said, "If you don't apologize, I'll punch you in the nose." If that person did not apologize and as a result you punched him in the nose, the law states that *you* are the party "in the wrong." When you punched the other person in the nose you committed the tort of *battery* on that other person. Provocation is not an issue here, since generally the law does not recognize the privilege of striking someone for making offensive remarks. (In this context,

---

EXHIBIT **7.1** The Three Theories of Tort Liability

TORT LIABILITY

Intentional Torts	Negligence	Strict Liability in Tort
The accused acts in a willful or intentional manner.	The conduct of the accused is compared to the "reasonable and prudent" person.	The accused is generally involved in conduct that is deemed abnormally dangerous.
Involves a simple duty to avoid the act or conduct.	Involves a reasonable duty to avoid the act or conduct.	Involves a strict duty to be responsible for the harm caused.
There must be a showing of fault.	There must be a showing of fault.	There is no need to show fault.
The harm must be foreseeable.	The harm must be foreseeable.	The harm must be foreseeable.

privilege is a circumstance excusing liability for an intentional tort.) *Inc. Magazine* has an article entitled "Tort Claims Business Owners Should Watch Out For," which discusses intentional torts, at its Web site at http://www.inc.com/articles/legal/gen_biz_law/defamation/15379.html.

The law of *negligence* is based on a concept of fault in which morality and law have been intermingled. How should society apportion the costs of accidents? Often, society has to make a moral statement when an injury occurs. Suppose a child darts out from behind a parked car an instant before the driver's car reaches that point; the driver immediately brakes in an effort to avoid hitting the child but is unable to stop in time to avoid the accident. In all likelihood, this accident would be considered unavoidable—it occurred without any negligence on the part of the driver. The child, even though injured, would be denied any compensation from the driver for the accident.

On the other hand, if a child is walking across the street in a designated crosswalk and an automobile hits him or her because the driver is drunk or driving too fast, then society says that the driver breached a duty to drive the car in a reasonable manner. Accordingly, the driver will have to pay for damages suffered by the child. The amount of injury is not a factor in determining liability; what is relevant is how the injury occurred.

Under *strict liability,* persons can be held liable to injured parties even if their conduct was neither intentional nor negligent. That is, they can be held liable even if the damage arising from their conduct was not their fault. Some activities are classified as either ultrahazardous or abnormally dangerous, and if injury results from these activities, the actor will be held liable. For example, suppose you have a pet rattlesnake in a sealed glass cage and you place the cage in your backyard with signs on the fence that say: *Danger—Poisonous Snake, Beware.* If the snake somehow gets out and bites someone, you can be held liable for the resulting injuries despite your warnings or your best efforts to protect people. If your rattlesnake causes injury, you will simply have to pay. You will not be permitted to prove that you were careful. Increasingly, legislatures are creating strict liability for parents when their children intentionally cause injury to others.[1]

Duty

We live in a legal system in which we all have a duty to protect other persons from harm. The question the courts must examine is what degree of duty exists under what specific circumstances. With respect to intentional torts, we all have a simple duty to avoid liability-causing behavior. However, with respect to negligence, we all have a "reasonable" duty to avoid this type of behavior. Generally, the law states that reasonable duty is a standard of ordinary skill and care, based on the facts of each individual case. In order to test for a breach of duty in any particular situation, the law has constructed a person against whom the conduct of the defendant is to be compared. This purely hypothetical person is known as the *reasonable and prudent person.* Note that this hypothetical person is not perfect, he or she is merely reasonable and prudent.

Foreseeability

Both intentional torts and negligence are based on the concept of fault. Strict liability, to the contrary, is not. All theories of liability, however, require *foreseeability,* the knowledge or notice that a particular result is likely to follow a certain act.

Foreseeability addresses the likelihood that something will happen in the future. It is easy to see that if you point a loaded gun at someone and pull the trigger, you will cause that person harm. But suppose you get in your car and drive down a dark street, within the speed limit and with your lights on. A child darts out from behind a parked car, and you hit the child. Were you negligent, or was it merely an unavoidable accident? This is a more difficult question. Foreseeability is determined by what a "reasonable and prudent person" would expect. Thus, the foreseeability of a child darting into the street in front of your car would depend on such factors as the degree of darkness, the lateness of the hour, how densely populated the area was (that is, rural or urban, residential or business), other children observed in the area, signs regarding children at play, and so forth. Until these factors are considered, there can be no determination of the foreseeability of the child's action, and consequently of your negligence.

Intentional Torts

Assault

Assault is wrongful, intentional conduct that would put a reasonable person or victim in immediate apprehension *or* fear of offensive, nonconsensual touching. Verbal threats alone are not an assault. Some movement toward the person must accompany the verbal threat. The threats of harm must be immediate: Threats of future harm are not sufficient to constitute an assault. The actor must have the actual or apparent ability to cause immediate harm to the victim. Pointing an unloaded pistol at a person, for example, is an assault if the victim has no way of knowing whether the pistol is loaded. The victim must feel apprehension: Actual fear is not required.

Battery

Some legal authorities have defined *battery* as a consummated assault. It is the wrongful, intentional, offensive, and nonconsensual touching of the victim. Touching an extension of the victim's body, such as a purse or backpack, also constitutes a battery. For example, removing a chair from underneath a person who briefly stood up and began to sit down again is a battery when the person hits the floor instead of being reseated. The key element is that the actor intended the natural consequence of removing the chair—the victim's fall to the ground. As far as the law is concerned, it is the same as pushing the person to the ground. On the other hand, if the removal of the chair was done innocently, and the fall to the ground was unintended, there is no tort of battery.

Defamation

Defamation occurs when an actor intentionally makes an untrue statement concerning a victim to a third person, and the statement injures the victim's reputation. Truth of the statement is a defense. As with other intentional torts, it is sufficient that the actor made the statement willfully. Notice that the defamatory remark must be *published,* which is defined as read or heard by others. Consequently, a negative remark made directly to the victim and not overheard by anyone else is not "published." The statement need not name the victim; however, the statement must be reasonably interpreted as referring to the victim. The statement must reduce the victim's reputation among well-meaning individuals. If the actor curses at the victim, this will not reduce the victim's reputation. It is interpreted more as an indication that the *actor* is extremely angry and is not controlling his or her temper. Some courts apply the *libel-proof plaintiff doctrine* when the fact finder decides that the plaintiff's reputation for a trait is so poor that, with regard to that trait, it could not be further damaged by the statement.[2]

An interesting development in this area of law presents a potential problem for employers and supervisors. Recently, disgruntled employees, especially those who have been discharged, have been suing their former employers for defamation. A number of these suits have been based on remarks made by the employer to coworkers of the employee filing suit. In addition, a number of former employees have sued for defamation due to comments made by the employer or supervisor about the former employee to potential new employers, for example, during a reference or "character check."

Two forms of defamation exist: *slander,* an oral statement that exposes a person to public ridicule or injures a person's reputation; and *libel,* a written or printed statement that exposes a person to public ridicule or injures a person's reputation. The reason for the two forms, each of which has slightly different elements, is that each was developed in a different English court. *Slander,* which is spoken defamation, developed in the *English church courts* (the ecclesiastical courts that had jurisdiction over spiritual matters). *Libel* (written defamation) developed in the *Star Chamber* (an English common law court that had jurisdiction over cases in which the ordinary course of justice was so obstructed by one party that no inferior court could have its process obeyed). The tort of defamation is an important exception to the First Amendment's guarantee of free speech. Accordingly, U.S. courts have modified some of the common law rules.

Slander is spoken communication that causes a person to suffer a loss of reputation. The common law rule distinguished between slander per se and slander per quod. *Slander per se* occurs when a person says that another person is seriously immoral, seriously criminal, has a social disease, or is unfit as a businessperson or professional. In those cases, there is no need to prove actual damages. *Slander per quod* is any other type of oral defamatory statement.

Libel is a written, printed, or other "permanent" communication that causes a person to suffer a loss of reputation. There are also two kinds of libel. *Libel per se* is libelous without having to resort to the context in which the remark appeared. For example, if a newspaper printed a story that referred to a person as a "known assassin for hire," there is no need to show the context of the statement. On the other hand, *libel per quod* requires proof of the context. For example, suppose a television talk show host says that a particular woman just gave birth to a child. In order to prove that it was libel, the woman must prove that she is not married and that she has not made public details of her private life. Many jurisdictions no longer distinguish between libel per se and libel per quod.

With the development of technology, the scope of libel has expanded from its historic basis. It is obvious that a book, a magazine, or a newspaper is written, so that defamatory remarks in any of these constitute a potential libel. Less obviously, films, videos, and television broadcasts that contain defamatory remarks are deemed libelous rather than slanderous. Since the medium containing the remark is relatively permanent, the remark can be "republished" any time the film or video is replayed. Thus, by analogy, these forms of communication are viewed as the equivalent of a written defamation rather than the equivalent of a spoken defamation. Electronic communications have opened up an entirely new "medium" for defamation, as is shown in Case 7.1, *Koch v. ProSTEP, Inc.*

New York Times Co. v. Sullivan[3] is a landmark case in U.S. jurisprudence. The U.S. Supreme Court held that when a public official sues for libel, the public official must also prove that the false statement was made with "actual malice" in addition to the other elements of libel. The court defined *actual malice* as knowledge that the statement was false or was made with reckless disregard of whether it was false or not. Some courts actually call it *New York Times malice* instead of actual malice. Since 1964, the Court extended the definition of a *public official* to include candidates for public office as well as incumbents. The Court has also extended the holding to "public figures" as well as public officials. A *public figure* is a person who has a degree of prominence in society. Thus, a person who chooses to become active in society and who not only receives, but actually solicits, attention in the media will be classified as a public figure.

In the following case, the court addressed whether a summary judgment on the issue of libel was appropriate. The court also treated an e-mail as a "written" communication, so that a defamatory e-mail would constitute libel. Decide whether you agree with the court's opinion.

7.1

KOCH v. PROSTEP, INC.
2002 U.S. Dist. LEXIS 19790 (N.D. Tex. Dallas Div. 2002)

FACTS Sally Koch and Dr. Thomas Klesmit (Plaintiffs) each brought suit against ProSTEP, Inc. and Kevin A. Lehmann (Defendants) on a number of grounds including libel. Lehmann is the founder and president of ProSTEP, an Internet networking and marketing company. ProSTEP is a multilevel marketing company that provides various services to its members including training materials, prospective newsletters, marketing training sessions, communications technology, and business leads. ProSTEP pays commissions for the recruitment of new "downline" members. (*Downline members* refers to individuals who join ProSTEP through existing members. For example, A's downline consists of the people A recruits and all the people that they eventually recruit.) ProSTEP sponsors various Web sites including the Wealth Builders Network (WBN). Koch and Klesmit were members of ProSTEP. Lehmann drafted two e-mails informing all individuals on the ProSTEP listserv of his decision and reasons for terminating Koch and Klesmit. Lehmann pointed out that Koch and Klesmit had received training, solicited assistance, and downplayed their relationship with ProSTEP. He noted they tried to private-label various facets of ProSTEP and that Klesmit had publicly indicated a desire to move the entire WBN organization from ProSTEP onto "SmartNetworker, Inc.," which Klesmit had founded. The e-mail at issue was published to all ProSTEP members, as well as to members of Plaintiffs' Nutrition for Life International (NFLI) and WBN downlines.

ISSUE Are the plaintiffs entitled to a trial on the issue of defamation?

HOLDING Yes. The plaintiffs are entitled to a trial on the issue of defamation.

REASONING Excerpts from the opinion of Magistrate Judge Wm. F. Sanderson:

Texas law defines libel as a "defamation expressed in written . . . form that tends to . . . injure a living person's reputation and thereby expose the person to public hatred, contempt or ridicule, or financial injury or to impeach any person's honesty, integrity, . . . or reputation. . . ." A cause of action for libel arises when one publishes a false and defamatory statement of fact of and concerning another. . . . Publication of defamatory words occurs when such words are communicated either orally or in writing to a third person who is capable of understanding their defamatory import. . . . In order to be libelous, a statement must be capable of having a defamatory meaning. Whether words are capable of a defamatory meaning is a question of law based on how a person of ordinary intelligence would perceive the entire statement in light of the surrounding circumstances. . . . [A] plaintiff must establish that the defendant: 1) published a false statement; 2) that was defamatory; 3) while acting with either actual malice—if the plaintiff was a public figure—or negligence—if the plaintiff was a private individual—regarding the truth of the statement. . . .

[T]he court must determine whether Lehmann's statements were merely statements of opinion or . . . statements of fact, because . . . a defamatory expression is not actionable unless it constitutes a statement of false fact. . . . Falsity "for constitutional purposes [depends upon] the meaning a reasonable person would attribute to a publication, and not on a technical analysis of each individual statement." Whether a publication makes a statement of fact that is false and defamatory depends upon a reasonable person's perception of the entirety of the publication, not merely on individual statements. Texas defamation law embraces the view recognized by the United States Supreme Court . . . that opinions or ideas, which include implied assertions of objective fact, may be actionable. Hence, an opinion may be actionable in a defamation case if the statement contains an implied assertion of fact. . . . [G]enuine issues of fact exist as to the character of the statements contained in Lehmann's e-mails. . . . [A] defendant can defeat a libel claim by establishing the truth of the alleged libelous statements. . . . [The affidavits of witnesses disclose conflicting facts; thus] . . . summary judgment is not appropriate on this issue.

. . . The question of public figure status is one of constitutional law for courts to decide. Public figures fall into two categories: (1) all-purpose, or general-purpose, public figures and (2) limited-purpose public figures. General-purpose public figures are those individuals who have achieved such pervasive fame or notoriety that they become public figures for all purposes and in all contexts. Limited-purpose public figures . . . are only public figures for a limited range of issues surrounding a particular public controversy. To determine whether an individual is a limited-purpose public figure, the Fifth Circuit has adopted a three-part test: (1) the controversy at issue must be public both in the sense that people are discussing it and people other than the immediate participants in the controversy are likely to feel the impact of its resolution; (2) the plaintiff must have more than a trivial or tangential role in the controversy; and (3) the alleged defamation must be germane to the plaintiff's participation in the controversy. . . . [Defendants contend that Koch and Klesmit are limited-purpose public figures because they sought publicity by marketing.] . . . Defendants have wholly failed to show how the instant dispute between an internet marketing business . . . and its members/independent contractors constitutes a public controversy. . . . [T]he court finds that Plaintiffs are private individuals—for defamation purposes. . . .

". . . [A] private individual may recover damages from a publisher . . . of a defamatory falsehood as compensation for actual injury upon a showing that the publisher . . . knew or should have known that the defamatory statement was false." . . . [G]enuine issues of material fact exist regarding whether Lehmann knew or should have known that his statements were false. . . . [S]ummary judgment is likewise not appropriate on this issue.

. . . In . . . [precedents], the court applied the following test for holding a corporate entity guilty of libel for its agent's acts: 1) an agent of the corporation; 2) acting "on behalf of the corporation" (in the course and scope of their duties); 3) communicated a false statement; 4) to a person a) other than a corporate employee or b) to a corporate employee whose course and scope of their [sic] duties for the corporation did not require receipt of the false communication; 5) and that communication proximately caused; 6) damages to plaintiff. Plaintiffs have proffered the following evidence . . . : that Lehmann is the president and CEO of ProSTEP (his emails also bear this out); that Lehmann's e-mails were generated for the purpose of discharging his duties to ProSTEP and its members; that Lehmann's e-mails contained false statements; that persons both within, as well as outside of, ProSTEP [received them]. . . ; and that Lehmann's e-mails caused Plaintiffs financial injuries (some recipients of the e-mails refused to join Plaintiffs' respective downlines). . . . [Defendants have not offered any contradictory evidence, so ProSTEP is not entitled to summary judgment on this issue.]

BUSINESS CONSIDERATIONS Could Lehmann have avoided the defamation lawsuit? How? Would it be important to a businessperson to avoid a lawsuit alleging defamation? Why?

ETHICAL CONSIDERATIONS Did any of the parties—Koch, Klesmit, or Lehmann—act ethically? From an ethical perspective, what should they have done differently?

Disparagement

Disparagement occurs when a business product is defamed. Generally it requires that a person make a false statement about a business's products, services, reputation, honesty, or integrity; the speaker publishes the remark to a third party; and the speaker knows the remark is false *or* the speaker makes the statement maliciously and with intent to injure the victim. It is also called *trade libel,* if the statements are written, or *slander of title,* if the statements are oral. It is also sometimes called *product disparagement.* The

Texas Beef Group's unsuccessful lawsuit against Oprah Winfrey for her statements about beef was based in part on product disparagement.[4]

False Imprisonment

False imprisonment is the detention or restraint of a person without legal justification or consent. This tort protects a person from the wrongful loss of liberty and freedom of movement. For example, if at the end of a college class your professor locks the door and says that no one

NRW CASE 7.1   Marketing

UNFAIR ADVERTISING

Another firm in the electronic tracking industry has been advertising that it has the best tracking device on the market. The firm's ads do not name any competitors, but they do show what appears to be a StuffTrakR unit next to their product. In the ads, the "StuffTrakR" is not operating very well and generally seems to be an inferior product. Carlos wants to sue the other company for defamation, product disparagement, or something similar. Helen is not sure that NRW has grounds to sue, but she is concerned about what these ads will do to NRW's image. Mai, Carlos, and Helen ask you what NRW's rights are in this situation, and what they would need to prove in court if they sue. What will you tell them?

BUSINESS CONSIDERATIONS What practical steps can a business take to bolster its reputation? What could a business do to counteract negative publicity by a competitor?

ETHICAL CONSIDERATIONS Is it ethical to use comparison advertising to create a false impression of a competitor's product? Is it ethical to intentionally create a negative impression of a competitor's product if you believe the impression is reasonably accurate? What moral obligations do you owe to competitors?

INTERNATIONAL CONSIDERATIONS Assume that the other firm was incorporated in a foreign country. How would that affect NRW's rights? What effect would it have if the advertisements were shown on foreign television stations or in foreign magazines rather than in the United States?

can leave the room, this action is false imprisonment. Sometimes standing in a doorway and refusing to let a person pass is also false imprisonment. As with other torts, there are defenses. For example, a privilege exists when a retail store's security officer has just cause to suspect a customer of shoplifting. If the security officer detains the customer, the security officer's acts will be privileged as long as the officer uses reasonable means in the detention. *Loss Prevention & Security Journal* published an article by Audrey J. Aronsohn entitled "Protecting Your Assets: The Privilege to Detain Comes with Risks" that addresses this issue. The article can be found at http://www.losspreventionjournal.com/articles/271legal.html.

Emotional Distress

A growing body of law concerns situations that, for public policy reasons, are being recognized by courts and legislatures as torts. The law protects an individual from suffering *serious indignity* that causes emotional distress. This "protection," however, is balanced against the interest of the state in not opening the courts to frivolous and trivial claims. Many states require a physical injury in addition to emotional distress. In this context, an airline was liable when it unreasonably insulted a passenger on an aircraft. A mortician training school was held liable for mental distress to 23 people who took their loved ones to funeral homes and instructed that the bodies *not* be embalmed. In some of these cases, the deceased was going to be cremated. However, the training school "wrongfully" obtained the bodies and used them for instructional purposes in the embalming clinic.[5] A number of employees are suing their former employers for inflicting emotional distress. Most states recognize causes of action for both intentional and negligent infliction of emotional distress.

In the following case, the court examined whether the store had committed the torts of false imprisonment and/or intentional infliction of emotional distress. After reading the opinion, decide whether the store's security personnel acted appropriately, and whether the situation could have been handled more professionally.

Invasion of Privacy

Under common law, no tort of invasion of privacy existed. However, our courts have begun to recognize that unwarranted invasions of privacy are *actionable*, ruling that these "invasions" furnish grounds for a legal action in some situations. *Privacy* refers to an individual's right to be left alone. Originally, this tort began with someone's peering into a home without permission. A person's privacy is invaded if that person becomes subject to unwarranted intrusions into his or her right to be left alone. These unwarranted intrusions have led to lawsuits and to the awarding of damages to the person whose privacy was invaded. Liability has been found for the public disclosure of private matters, such as playing a tape of a private citizen's telephone call without permission or a valid search warrant. In most states, simple invasion of privacy has been expanded: It now includes (1) intrusion on physical solitude; (2) unauthorized use of the plaintiff's likeness or life story; (3) presenting the plaintiff in a false light; and (4)

JOSEY v. FILENE'S, INC.
187 F. Supp. 2d 9, 2002 U.S. Dist. LEXIS 2592 (D. Conn. 2002)

FACTS Tommy Josey and his friend, Jermaine Jenkins, went to the Filene's store to purchase clothing. The Filene's security guards observed Josey and Jenkins on the store security monitors. According to the security officers, they were suspicious because Josey and Jenkins selected large amounts of merchandise without looking at the price tags and used a sales register in a different department from the one where they chose the clothing. Josey used his Filene's charge card to purchase the clothing. Josey and Jenkins then proceeded to leave the store when store security personnel apprehended them. The security officers said they apprehended the men because they believed that Josey had used his Filene's employee discount to purchase clothing for Jenkins in violation of store policy. The security personnel considered this to be theft of property. After handcuffing Josey and Jenkins, the store security guards brought the two men to a small holding cell. After ascertaining that Josey no longer worked for Filene's and, therefore, could not use his discount, Filene's decided not to pursue the matter. After Josey and Jenkins were detained for approximately 45 minutes to an hour, they were given their merchandise and allowed to leave.

ISSUE Should Josey have a trial on the issues of false imprisonment and/or intentional infliction of emotional distress?

HOLDING Yes, there is a basis for a trial on false imprisonment, but not on intentional infliction of emotional distress.

REASONING Excerpts from the opinion of District Judge Janet C. Hall:

Connecticut General Statutes § 53a-119a provides, in pertinent part:

> (a) Any owner, authorized agent or authorized employee of a retail mercantile establishment, who observes any person concealing or attempting to conceal goods displayed for sale therein, or the ownership of such goods, or transporting such goods from such premises without payment thereof, may question such person as to his name and address and, if such owner, agent or employee has reasonable grounds to believe that the person so questioned was then attempting to commit or was committing larceny of such goods . . . may detain such person for a time sufficient to summon a

police officer to the premises. . . . For the purposes of this subsection, "reasonable grounds" shall include knowledge that a person has concealed unpurchased merchandise . . . or is leaving such premises with such unpurchased or concealed . . . merchandise in his possession.

. . . The statute is clearly aimed at allowing stores to detain individuals suspected of stealing goods, or what is commonly referred to as shoplifting. The case law . . . demonstrates that stores may detain and question someone and then rely on the privilege when they reasonably suspect that person of stealing merchandise. . . . In this case . . . there is no allegation that the security guards saw Josey concealing or attempting to conceal goods. . . . [T]here is no dispute that Josey brought all the merchandise he selected to the register and paid [the] full price of the clothing with his credit card. Nor is there any allegation that he attempted to alter or remove any identifying labels on the clothing.

The defendant . . . [claims] that, by improperly receiving an employee discount, the security guards had reasonable grounds to believe that Josey was committing larceny because he was not paying the full price for the goods. Such abuse of the employee discount is considered theft by the store security guards. . . . [T]he defendant argues that Josey was committing employee discount fraud by unlawfully purchasing goods for his friend in violation of the employee discount policy. While abuse of an employee discount is undoubtedly a serious issue for the store, the court finds reliance on § 53a-119a in this case improper. . . . [A]n employee discount is not immediately applied to a purchase. Instead, an employee gets charged for the full amount of the merchandise. That amount is charged to a Filene's credit card. The employee discount is then applied retroactively to the card when the purchase gets processed through the store's Boston office. Therefore, Josey had payed [sic] full price for the merchandise he bought and had not . . . committed any theft. . . . [W]hen discussing the history behind § 53a-119a, [the court] noted that the purpose of enacting the statute was to give "merchants a qualified privilege to detain and question suspected shoplifters. . . ." In this case, there was no evidence that Josey was committing such a larceny, having paid full price for his goods. Nor was there the type of pressing need to detain . . . given that the store could have prevented the application of the discount by simply not applying it to Josey's account. There remains a disputed issue of fact whether Josey had committed employee discount abuse by paying for his friend's clothing. However, the court finds that § 53a-119a does not provide a privilege for a store who seeks to detain an individual suspected of such abuse. Again, there was no concealment of goods or attempt to conceal goods which is what this statute covers. . . .

In order to assert a claim for intentional infliction of emotional distress, the plaintiff must establish four elements: (1) that the actor intended to inflict emotional distress; or that he knew or should have known that the emotional distress was a likely result of his conduct; (2) that the conduct was extreme or outrageous; (3) that the defendant's conduct was the cause of the plaintiff's distress; and (4) that the distress suffered by the plaintiff was severe. "Liability for intentional infliction of emotional distress requires conduct that is so extreme and outrageous that it goes beyond all possible bounds of decency, is regarded as atrocious, is utterly intolerable in a civilized society, and is of a nature that is especially calculated to cause, and does cause, mental distress of a very serious kind." While the court is certain that the experience of being handcuffed in front of other shoppers and being detained in the mall was not a pleasant experience, the court cannot find that these actions rise to the level of extreme or outrageous behavior. . . . In addition, the court cannot conclude that the distress Josey suffered was severe. While he testified that he was embarrassed by being apprehended in front of other shoppers, he has not sought medical attention for his distress. . . . Josey also testified that he is afraid to go back into the Filene's store and is afraid that people he knew saw him and will think he is [a] thief. However, his fear has not prevented him from frequenting the mall or other Filene's stores in the area. He also testified . . . that he has not had the situation arise that someone saw the apprehension and thought badly of him. . . . [T]he court finds that there is no evidence supporting the assertion that Josey has suffered severe distress. . . .

BUSINESS CONSIDERATIONS Should Filene's change its employee discount practices? Why? What policies and practices should Filene's have for its security guards? Why?

ETHICAL CONSIDERATIONS Is it ethical to use an employee discount to purchase items for friends? Why or why not?

appropriation of plaintiff's name, face or likeness for commercial purposes. For example, the use of a famous person's name, photograph, voice, song, or image in an advertisement without permission is an invasion of privacy. This version of invasion of privacy is often described as an invasion of the famous person's right of publicity, since he or she is deprived of the opportunity to sell his or her name or likeness to some other company. Publication is not required for invasion of privacy. Unlike defamation, truth is not a defense. Under the First Amendment, the courts have created a privilege for the media when it is reporting on newsworthy events. Then the media will be protected even when the news report is inaccurate, unless the error was made deliberately or recklessly.

Trespass

In common law, trespass was one of the most common torts. Today, the general tort of "trespass" has evolved into some of the specific torts already discussed. The traditional tort of *trespass* remains as the tort used to protect property interests against nonconsensual infringements. There are two types of trespass—trespass to land and trespass to personal property. A person who ventures onto the property of another without permission is a trespasser. The following is an example of trespass to personal property. If you return to the parking lot after class, and someone is sleeping in the backseat of your car, that person is trespassing on your car. The only question is one of damages. Even if the person trespassed through mistake and did no harm, there will be nominal *damages* of, say, five dollars. If, on the other hand, the person trespassed before and had been warned, then higher damages likely would be assessed. Of course, the trespasser will be liable for any actual harm caused by the unwarranted invasion of your car.

Conversion

Conversion occurs when a person intentionally exercises exclusive control over the personal property of another without the permission of the owner. In such a case, the converter is liable for damages. If a person obtains possession of the property lawfully but is then told by the owner to return it and refuses to do so, that person is also a converter. When the owner seeks the return of the property in court, the proper action is one for *replevin*, an action to recover possession of goods unlawfully taken. Damages can also be obtained if the owner suffered harm during the conversion. Sometimes the owner does not desire the return of the property, for example, if it is now in damaged condition. In this case, the owner asks for reimbursement for his or her loss.

INVASION OF PRIVACY

Several people have complained that the various types of personal item trackers (PITs), like the StuffTrakR produced by NRW, should be banned. The basic argument put forward by these people is that once a microchip is placed on a personal item such as keys or glasses, computer hackers might be able to discover the frequency of a customer's chip and then track the customer's movements. One militant group of these people have formed an "action team" named "POPPN" (Protect Our Personal Privacy Now) that is threatening to file invasion-of-privacy lawsuits against every personal tracker manufacturer and retailer in the United States. NRW is not yet on solid financial ground, and Mai is concerned that such a lawsuit could bankrupt the firm before it has a chance to succeed. Helen seems less concerned, but she is still worried. She has asked you if Mai's fears are valid. What will you tell her? Why?

BUSINESS CONSIDERATIONS Suppose that a business is facing the prospect of a number of lawsuits over its product. Should the business be proactive on the issue, or would it be better to wait and react to any suits that are filed? Why? If the firm chooses to be proactive, what should it do?

ETHICAL CONSIDERATIONS Assume that a group is attempting to intimidate manufacturers and retailers in a given industry by threatening to file lawsuits unless the demands of the group are met. Is such behavior ethical? From an ethical perspective, how should the firms in the industry react to such threats?

INTERNATIONAL CONSIDERATIONS Should NRW be permitted to sell StuffTrakRs in foreign countries? Why? Do other countries or other cultures have a different perspective on the issue of personal privacy?

Misappropriation of Trade Secrets

Misappropriation of trade secrets occurs when an actor unlawfully acquires and uses the trade secrets of another business enterprise. The victim must prove that a trade secret exists. A *trade secret* is some exclusive knowledge of commercial value that has been generated by the labors of a specific person or group of people. The owner must have implemented reasonable steps to protect the trade secret. The actor must have acquired it by some unlawful or improper means, such as industrial espionage, theft, or bribery. Some states, like Texas, require that the actor acquire the secret as a result of a confidential relationship with the victim.[6] Texas also requires that the actor "use" the trade secret.[7] This tort is also called *theft of trade secrets.* Most states have adopted the Uniform Trade Secrets Act to codify their laws on trade secrets.[8]

Fraud

Fraud is an extremely complex tort. It concerns the misrepresentation of a material fact made with the intent to deceive. If an innocent person reasonably relies on the misrepresentation and is damaged as a result, the injured person may successfully sue for fraud. There are five elements of fraud:

1. A material fact was involved; an opinion usually will not constitute fraud.

2. The fact was misrepresented (a falsehood).

3. The falsehood was made with the intent to deceive (*scienter*).

4. The falsehood was one on which another person justifiably relied (reasonable reliance).

5. That person was injured as a result (damage).

For example, if a jeweler sells a rhinestone as a diamond with the knowledge that it is a rhinestone, the action is fraud. If a bank customer knowingly obtains a loan on the basis of a false financial statement, it is fraud. If a corporation solicits persons to buy stock for the purpose of building a new plant when, in reality, the corporation wants the money to pay off existing liabilities, it is fraud. The list is virtually endless.

Exhibit 7.2 summarizes the intentional torts discussed in this chapter.

Civil RICO Violations

The Racketeer Influenced and Corrupt Organizations Act, commonly referred to by the acronym RICO,[9] is discussed in more detail in Chapter 8; however, it also deserves mention here. RICO is directed at a pattern of racketeering activity. A *pattern* means two or more racketeering acts within a 10-year period. Racketeering acts range from violent acts such as murder to less violent acts such as mail fraud. The RICO statute includes a long list of racketeering acts. Individuals and businesses that are injured can sue those who are violating the statute. For example, on

EXHIBIT 7.2   Intentional Torts

Specific Tort	Definition	Defenses
Assault	Conduct that would put a reasonable person in apprehension of an immediate battery	Conditional privilege Consent Necessity/Justification Self-defense
Battery	Intentional offensive touching	Conditional privilege Consent Necessity/Justification Self-defense
Defamation	Slander (spoken), libel (written) Statements that harm a person's reputation	Truth Absolute privilege (legal or congressional proceeding) Conditional privilege
Disparagement	Defamation of a business product, service, or reputation	
False Imprisonment	The detention of one person by another against his or her will and without just cause	Privilege Consent
Emotional Distress	Causing a serious indignity	
Invasion of Privacy	Unwarranted intrusions on the privacy of another	Privilege
Trespass	Subjecting real or personal property to harm or infringement	Privilege Consent Necessity
Conversion	Intentional exercise of exclusive control over the personal property of another without permission	Necessity Consent
Misappropriation of Trade Secrets	Taking secret business data for unauthorized use	
Fraud	The misrepresentation of a material fact made with the intention to deceive	
RICO	Violation of federal statute by engaging in a pattern of racketeering activity	

September 22, 1999, the U.S. Justice Department filed a civil RICO lawsuit against the tobacco industry.[10] Successful plaintiffs in a civil action may recover treble damages, attorney's fees, and reasonable court costs. (*Treble damages* are three times the amount of actual damages.) A criminal conviction is not a prerequisite to filing a civil RICO suit.

Defenses to Intentional Torts

As is true with the torts themselves, there is a great deal of variation from state to state in how the defenses are actually defined and what constitutes a defense. The following sections contain a brief description of some of the common defenses.

Consent   Even though a tort has been committed, the law may not compensate the injured party if, in fact, that person consented to the tort. Most cases involve issues of implied consent. (*Implied consent* is consent inferred by a person's conduct, such as signs, actions, inaction, or silence.) The law will not infer consent unless it is reasonable under the circumstances. For example, football players obviously batter each other throughout the course of a game. Even though the tort of battery may have been committed, it is not actionable because the law views each player as having consented to the touching. However, if a player intentionally exceeds the implied consent, he or she may be liable for the tort. For example, a professional boxer consents to being punched during the bout. However, most courts would hold that a boxer does not consent to being bitten in the ear during a match, or to being punched by the other fighter after the bell has sounded to end the bout.

Privilege Permission is given voluntarily, whether it is expressed or implied. The law also recognizes a defense that is imposed for public policy reasons, privilege. Because the law seeks to protect certain social interests more than others, it developed the concept of privilege. Privilege may be recognized in a number of situations including these:

- If someone moves to strike you, you have the ancient privilege of self-defense. Most states also recognize the privilege to defend family members.

- Retail businesses have a privilege to detain persons they reasonably believe have committed theft.

- Persons whose property is stolen have the privilege of going onto another person's property in order to retrieve it.

- Judges and legislators have the privilege of saying things that might be defamation under other circumstances, in order to stimulate debate and encourage independence of thought and action.

Necessity Whenever a person enters another's land for self-protection, the law recognizes that action as a necessity and disallows the nominal damages ordinarily awarded for trespass. For example, if you are in a boat on a lake and a storm suddenly develops, you may enter a private cove, tie up to a private dock, and find shelter on the land in order to protect yourself. Due to the necessity, no trespass exists. However, the law permits the landowner to collect actual losses if, for example, you use his or her provisions while tied to the private dock.

Truth Truth is one of the best defenses with respect to the tort of defamation. A defendant will win if he or she can prove that the statement was true. If an individual accuses a businessperson of being a crook and is sued for defamation, the defendant will win if it can be proven that the businessperson is a "fence" for stolen property. Exhibit 7.3 summarizes the defenses available against specific intentional torts.

Negligence

Negligence exists when four conditions are met. First, the defendant must have owed the plaintiff a duty. Second, the defendant must have breached the duty by acting in a particular manner or failing to act as required. Third, the plaintiff must suffer an injury, and that injury must be one that the law recognizes and for which money damages may be recovered. Fourth, the breach of that duty must be the actual as well as the "legal" cause of the plaintiff's injury.

Duty

The reasonable-and-prudent-person rule has been established in negligence law in order to determine the "degree" of duty. With respect to negligence, everyone has a duty to use reasonable care to avoid behavior that does not measure up to the standards of the reasonable and prudent person. This standard is more difficult to explain and apply than is the standard of simple duty generally applied in intentional torts cases. Generally, however, the law states that *reasonable duty* is a standard of ordinary skill and care, based on the facts of each individual case.

If, while you are quietly fishing on the shore of a lake, you see a man 100 feet away fall out of his boat and begin to drown, do you have a duty to help him under common law? The answer is no, you did not create the hazard in the first place. On the other hand, suppose you are in the boat with the man and you push him out of the boat as a joke, not knowing that he cannot swim. Now you will have a duty to help him. Since you have created the hazard, you have a duty to provide help to the person or persons placed at risk by your conduct. Similarly, Chanie, who owns a boatyard and rents boats to the public, does not have a duty to ensure the safety of every person who rents a boat merely because she is in the business of renting boats. However, if she rents a boat to Abel and the boat springs a leak and Abel drowns because it was defective or improperly maintained, Chanie is likely to have breached her duty to rent safe boats and could face liability for negligence.

Foreseeability, in negligence, addresses the likelihood that something will happen in the future. It is determined by what a "reasonable and prudent person" would expect.

To test for a duty in any particular situation, the law has constructed a person against whom the conduct of the defendant is to be compared. This purely hypothetical person is known as the *reasonable and prudent person.* Again, it is important to remember that this "person" is not perfect, he or she is merely reasonable and prudent. Three areas help to define the reasonable and prudent person: knowledge, investigation, and judgment. There is also a statutory standard that is applied in certain situations.

Knowledge As the amount of knowledge existing in the world increases, so does the amount of knowledge that the reasonable and prudent person is expected to possess. In this sense, therefore, the law presumes that everyone has

EXHIBIT 7.3 Effective Defenses Against Intentional Torts

Consent	Privilege	Necessity	Truth
Assault	Assault	Trepass	Defamation
Battery	Battery	Conversion	
False Imprisonment	False Imprisonment		
Trespass	Trespass		
Conversion	Defamation		
Invasion of Privacy	Invasion of Privacy		

complete knowledge of the law. If we have no knowledge of the law, how can we be expected to obey it?

Investigation Investigation is closely related to knowledge. It is our obligation to find out. We assume that a reasonable person knows certain information. We also assume that the reasonable person will do research or tests to discover additional information. Before you drive a car, for example, the law presumes that you will ascertain that the brakes are working properly. If you are a drug manufacturer, the law presumes that you will discover if your drug will cause any harmful side effects. If you have failed to do adequate testing, you will have violated the standard of care of a reasonable and prudent person. Note that a harmful side effect does not necessarily mean that the manufacturer is negligent. Some drugs do have harmful side effects for some or many patients; however, the drug may still be beneficial for the majority to whom it is administered. In this case, distribution of the drug with proper warnings attached is permitted. The adequacy of the warning was an issue in a recent lawsuit against a manufacturer of the oral polio vaccine, when a father alleged that he contracted polio as a result of his daughter receiving the vaccine.[11]

Judgment You have probably heard some people say that one person has "good" judgment or another has "bad" judgment. While this may be true, legally it will not matter. The law measures both persons against the same standard. In a tort case, the defendant must have acted reasonably or else he or she will be found to have breached the duty of reasonable care. We have no hard-and-fast rules here. The outcome always depends on the facts of each case. When a missing fact is discovered, it can change the outcome. Therefore, before beginning any activity, the law expects people to ask questions such as: What is the likelihood that this particular activity will harm someone else? If harm might occur, what is the likely extent of the harm? What must I give up to avoid risk to others?

Assume that you just got a new rifle and want to test it and adjust the sights (or scope) for maximum accuracy for the hunting season. You find an isolated field in the country and set up a target at the base of a bald hill 300 yards away. No one else is present. After firing the first shot, however, you begin to attract a crowd. Assume that with each shot the crowd gets larger. At what point do you stop shooting to avoid injury to an innocent person? The decision to stop involves the exercise of reason. The exercise of reason is *judgment.*

Statutory Standard In some cases, the law solves the problem of limits, like the ones just raised, by providing a standard contained in a statute. For example, most state traffic laws say that when it begins to get dark, all drivers are required to turn on their headlights. While traveling down a road at night without your lights on, you hit and injure a pedestrian. The law will conclude that you breached a standard of reasonableness no matter what your excuse. Most of these statutes provide a criminal penalty, but that penalty is irrelevant in a civil proceeding such as a tort case. In most states, breaching the statutory standard is *negligence per se* (inherent negligence; negligence without a need for further proof). However, the states are not in agreement as to whether this should be treated as a conclusive presumption where evidence to the contrary is not permitted. Some states, such as California,[12] instead treat negligence per se as a rebuttable presumption. The person is allowed to present evidence that, under the circumstances, violating the statutory standard was the most careful behavior.

Breach of Duty

In general, the plaintiff has to prove that the defendant caused injury by not adhering to the reasonable-and-prudent-person standard. In some cases, however, that strict requirement of proof is relaxed because the law has

NRW CASE 7.3   Management

JOB REFERENCES FOR FORMER EMPLOYEES

Recently, NRW expanded by hiring three workers. Unfortunately, Mai, Carlos, and Helen have not had much experience in selecting employees. Two of the workers are excellent and fit in well with the business. The third, Gabino, was not a good fit and was fired after the first three weeks. Mai, Carlos, and Helen also suspect Gabino of falsifying company reports. Since his dismissal, Gabino has been applying for other jobs. Although he did not list NRW as a reference, Gabino did list NRW as his last place of employment. Consequently, four potential employers have been calling NRW and leaving messages for Mai. They are understandably interested in why Gabino's employment lasted only three weeks. Mai knows she cannot avoid the messages from the prospective employers much longer. She calls you to ask what she should do. Specifically, she wants to know what she should say and not say when she returns the calls. What will you tell her?

BUSINESS CONSIDERATIONS Should a business adopt a policy regarding references for former employees? Is a business less likely to face liability if it gives only oral recommendations, or should it put everything in writing? Why?

ETHICAL CONSIDERATIONS Is it ethical to give a good recommendation for a "bad" employee to help that employee obtain other employment? Is it ethical to give a bad recommendation for a good current employee to make it more difficult for him or her to leave?

INTERNATIONAL CONSIDERATIONS Is a former employer more or less likely to be sued on the basis of a reference call or letter in a foreign country? Why? Are the expectations of privacy different in other nations?

developed the doctrine of *res ipsa loquitur*, which means "the thing speaks for itself." To apply *res ipsa loquitur* in a case, the injury must meet the following three tests: (1) this occurrence would ordinarily not happen in the absence of someone's negligence; (2) it must be caused by a device within the exclusive control of the defendant(s); and (3) the plaintiff in no way has contributed to his or her own injury.

For example, if a patient submits to an operation to remove infected tonsils and leaves the operating room with a surgical instrument embedded in her throat, there is no need to require direct testimony on the point. It speaks for itself; someone in the surgery room was negligent. In some states, *res ipsa loquitur* creates a presumption of negligence. Its effect is to shift the burden of proof from the plaintiff to the defendant(s). In this situation, the hospital personnel and the surgeons will each need to show that they were careful. In other states, the burden of proof remains with the plaintiff. *Res ipsa loquitur* creates an inference of negligence, which the jury weighs with the rest of the evidence.

Harm

If the plaintiff is not injured, the defendant will not be held liable in damages. For example, Chad speeding down a city street at 70 miles per hour is clearly breaching the duty to drive in a safe and reasonable manner; but if no one is injured, no one can successfully sue for negligence. If harm is caused, it must be of a type for which the law allows damages to be awarded. For example, hurt feelings may be real, but the law does not award damages for hurt feelings.

Causation

The heart of the law of negligence is causation. Causation has two components: actual cause and "legal" cause, which is also called proximate cause.

Actual Cause The law determines whether X, an act by one party, is the actual cause of Y, a result affecting the other party. The courts examine whether "but for" the occurrence of X would Y have happened. This is called the *but-for test*. For example, a defendant in an automobile accident case may have failed to signal a turn properly. But if the accident would have happened even if he had signaled properly, the failure to signal is not the actual cause of the accident. It fails the "but-for" test.

Proximate Cause *After* actual cause has been established, the focus shifts to what the law calls *policy questions*. Such questions have nothing to do with whether the defendant actually did the act. What is decided here is whether the law should hold the defendant liable. At some point the law will say, "Enough," the legal boundary for liability has been crossed. Beyond this point the defendant will not be held liable. To solve these policy questions, the law has developed a three-pronged test:

1. What is the likelihood that this particular conduct will injure other persons?

2. If injury should occur, what is the degree of seriousness of the injury?

3. What is the interest that the defendant must sacrifice to avoid the risk of causing the injury?

For example, assume that the defendant is negligent with respect to Emilio placing Emilio in danger. Carla tries to rescue Emilio and suffers some injury as a result. The defendant will be held liable for Carla's injuries as well as Emilio's because it is foreseeable that people will try to rescue someone in peril, and the defendant's conduct created the peril.

Defenses to Negligence

Assumption of the Risk Common law developed a doctrine that the defendant will win if it can be proved that the plaintiff voluntarily assumed a known risk. For example, have you ever examined cigarette packages? They bear various warnings, some of which are "Surgeon General's Warning: Smoking by pregnant women may result in fetal injury, premature birth, and low birth weight," or "Quitting smoking now greatly reduces serious risks to your health," or "Cigarette smoke contains carbon monoxide." Historically, a longtime cigarette smoker who contracted lung cancer and sued the cigarette manufacturer has lost because the manufacturer defended on the basis of the plaintiff's voluntary assumption of the risk. (New scientific evidence is allowing the courts to reexamine tobacco company liability in this area.) Courts will generally apply assumption of the risk to a skier who breaks her leg while skiing on a mountain slope.

Contributory Negligence Another defense at common law is *contributory negligence*. Suppose Justin wears a black raincoat at night and jaywalks across a busy street; he is hit by a car. If Justin sues and the defendant can assert and prove Justin actually contributed to the injury, Justin will lose in a state that applies contributory negligence. Contributory negligence bars recovery. (In the legal sense, *bar* means to prevent or to stop.)

Comparative Negligence In a growing number of jurisdictions, the doctrine of contributory negligence has been replaced by the doctrine of *comparative negligence* through legislative acts or judicial precedents. Here, the fact finder (usually the jury) determines to what degree the plaintiff contributed to his or her own injury. Comparative negligence is generally perceived to be more fair; however, it may be difficult for the trier of fact to determine the relative faults. For example, if Jason is injured to the extent of $100,000 in damages but contributed 35 percent to his

injury, he will be awarded $65,000 instead of losing completely, as he would under the doctrine of contributory negligence.

Jurisdictions may select from three variations of comparative negligence. *Pure* comparative negligence would allow the plaintiff to recover no matter how negligent he or she was. (For example, the California Supreme Court adopted pure comparative negligence in *Li v. Yellow Cab Co.*[13]) However, some jurisdictions feel it would be unfair to allow the plaintiff to recover if he or she was the primary cause of the injury, for example, if the plaintiff was 95 percent responsible for causing the accident. Consequently, two other variations of comparative negligence prevent recovery to the party who was mostly to blame. One version permits recovery only if the plaintiff contributed less than 50 percent of the negligence to his or her injury. It is commonly called the "less than" type of comparative negligence. This is probably the most common variety of comparative negligence. Another version allows recovery if the plaintiff contributed 50 percent or less to his or her injury, which is commonly called the "equal to or less than" version. The differences may appear inconsequential, but they are significant to the parties of a lawsuit who may be denied recovery because the jury concluded that they were each 50 percent at fault. The application of comparative negligence becomes more difficult when there are three or more parties. States have different ways of handling multiple-party situations. The effect of comparative negligence laws may be minimal in automobile accidents in "no-fault" states. The National Conference of Commissioners on Uniform State Laws (NCCUSL) has adopted the Uniform Apportionment of Tort Responsibility Act (2002), which contains a modified comparative fault system.[14] Medical groups, insurance groups, and others advocate change in the tort liability system, particularly as it applies to their businesses. For example, the American Medical Association Advocacy Resource Center provides a state-by-state chart of liability reform laws on its Web site at http://www.acc.org/advocacy/statelaws_breakdown.pdf.

Strict Liability

Recall that with respect to intentional torts, everyone has a duty to avoid such behavior. With respect to negligence, we have a duty to use reasonable care. This section examines a situation in which the law states that we have an absolute duty to make something safe, whether we are at fault or not is irrelevant. *Strict liability* is imposed without regard to fault. The law prescribes the situations in which there is strict liability.

Whenever a person undertakes an extremely hazardous activity and it is foreseeable that injury may result, that person can be held "strictly liable" if injury does result, whether or not the person was at fault. For example, if you use explosives on your property and by so doing cause windows to be blown out of an adjoining neighbor's house, you will be held liable no matter how careful you were in handling those explosives. Generally, the areas in which we have strict liability are set out in the applicable statutes and court precedents. *Rylands v. Fletcher*[15] is credited with creating this legal doctrine.

Through the development of the doctrine of strict liability, U.S. courts have shifted emphasis from ultrahazardous activity to dangerous activity, and the doctrine seems to be expanding in scope. Today, the following activities are considered strict liability activities in most states: the keeping of wild animals, the use of explosives, and dangerous activities. Some states have added strict liability for the owner of a motor vehicle if injury occurs when the driver has the owner's permission.[16] California imposes strict liability on parents for the willful misconduct of their minor children; there is a $10,000 limit on parental strict liability.[17] Remember, though, strict liability does not automatically arise. Courts can create new precedents; generally, however, courts look to existing precedents and statutory law. This is another area in which the legal system is making policy decisions about who should justly bear the loss.

Product Liability

Product liability is a growing concern of businesses. Manufacturers *and* distributors of products may be held liable based on these legal theories: (1) fraud in the marketing of the product (which will follow the general rules of fraud), (2) express or implied warranties (warranties will not be discussed in this chapter, since they are based on contract theories), (3) negligence, and (4) strict liability. People who are injured by a product may claim and attempt to prove more than one theory of liability; that is, these theories are not mutually exclusive. The law firm of Ashcraft and Gerel, LLP, has an article entitled "Product Liability Claims—Unsafe, Defective and Unreasonably Dangerous Products" at its Web site at http://www.ashcraftandgerel.com/ddprod. html. For information about the Japanese product liability law see "Guide to the Product Liability Law" at the Web site of United for a Multicultural Japan at http://www.tabunka. org/special/product.html.

Negligence in product liability can include negligence in design, construction, labeling, instructions, packaging, and assembly. When an injured person uses the negligence theory for product liability, there must be a close causal connection between the negligence and the injury. The lawsuit will be subject to the usual defenses for negligence, including contributory negligence, comparative negligence, and assumption of the risk. To establish a negligent failure to warn claim, many states require the plaintiff to prove the following elements: (1) the defendant designed the product; (2) the defendant knew or had reason to know that the product was likely to be unreasonably dangerous; (3) the defendant had no reason to believe that the users would realize the risk; (4) the defendant failed to use ordinary care in warning the user of the risk of harm; and (5) the failure to warn directly caused the injury. In addition, the product must malfunction or fail.[18]

The following case dealt with Swope, an employee who was injured at work through repeated exposure to ozone and through an accident. His wife was also a plaintiff in the suit, so the case referred to them as the Swopes. It is common to sue multiple tortfeasors as Swope did here. He sued his employer under battery law and the manufacturer of the equipment under product liability law for failure to adequately warn. The court discussed the Restatements. Restatement (Second) of Torts, a publication of the American Law Institute (ALI), states the preferred version of the common law of torts. It is used by courts as an authoritative reference, but the Restatement is not binding on them. It becomes precedent in the court only after a judge has relied on a section and referred to it in his or her opinion.

Strict liability for products is clarified by § 402A of the Restatement (Second) of Torts, and has been adopted by most states. Section 402A of the Restatement (Second) of Torts has long been considered the seminal document on product liability. However, ALI has adopted revisions to § 402A and published them in Restatement (Third) of Torts: Product Liability.[19] ALI hopes this new document will shape product liability law in the future.

Section 402A of the Restatement (Second) of Torts establishes the strict liability rule: A seller will be held liable for a product that contains a defect or is unreasonably dangerous to use. (*Unreasonably dangerous* seems vague to both laypersons and lawyers; there have been many court decisions attempting to define and clarify the term.) The defect must be in the product when it leaves the control of the defendant. As with other forms of strict liability, the plaintiff does not need to prove negligence or fraud in order to recover. Generally, the plaintiff must show that strict liability applies to this situation, that the product had a defect when it left the defendant's possession or was unreasonably dangerous, and that the plaintiff was harmed. Since this is a tort cause of action, the seller cannot avoid liability by disclaiming it. Contributory or comparative negligence by the

Product liability- fraud, negligence, warranties, strict liability

7.3

SWOPE v. COLUMBIAN CHEMICALS CO.
281 F.3d 185, 2002 U.S. App. LEXIS 934 (5th Cir. 2002)

FACTS Claude Swope was employed by Columbian from March 1987 until several days after his final exposure to ozone on July 10, 1996. Columbian continually required Swope to breathe ozone without protective respiratory equipment throughout his employment. Columbian repeatedly caused employees to breathe levels of ozone high enough to cause them respiratory discomfort, "choke ups," nausea, headaches, and chest pains. On at least three occasions, other employees had been taken to hospital emergency rooms or given oxygen on the premises. Many times, employees had to flee the immediate vicinity because the ozone level had become intolerable. It appears that the only safety instruction Columbian ever gave to employees was to vacate the area, get some fresh air, and return to work when they felt better. Swope was aware that Columbian continually required him to breathe high levels of ozone, but he was not aware that it was damaging his lungs. Swope's physician declared that Swope suffered injury from frequent exposures of ozone and other toxic substances over a period of years during the course and scope of his employment at Columbian. Columbian refused to monitor ozone levels at the plant. Columbian purchased and used ozone generators manufactured by Emery Industries; Henkel Corporation is the successor to Emery.

ISSUES Is Swope entitled to a trial on the intentional tort of battery against Columbian? Is he entitled to a trial on a product liability claim against Henkel?

HOLDING Yes. Swope is entitled to a trial on the issue of battery and product liability.

REASONING Excerpts from the opinion of Circuit Judge Dennis and District Judge Dowd:

[Swopes is limited to using the Workers' Compensation Act against Columbian unless he can show an intentional tort.] [According to] the Restatement (Second) of Torts concerning the intentional tort of battery:

> A harmful or offensive contact with a person, resulting from an act intended to cause the plaintiff to suffer such a contact, is a battery.

> The intention need not be malicious nor need it be an intention to inflict actual damage. It is sufficient if the actor intends to inflict either a harmful or offensive contact without the other's consent....

> The original purpose of the courts in providing the action for battery undoubtedly was to keep the peace by affording a substitute for private retribution. The element of personal indignity involved always has been given considerable weight. Consequently, the defendant is liable not only for contacts that do actual physical harm, but also for those relatively trivial ones which are merely offensive and insulting.

> The intent with which tort liability is concerned is not necessarily a hostile intent, or a desire to do any harm. Rather it is an intent to bring about a result which will invade the interests of another in a way that the law forbids....

> Bodily harm is generally considered to be any physical impairment of the condition of a person's body, or physical pain or illness. The defendant's liability for the resulting harm extends, as in most other cases of intentional torts, to consequences which the defendant did not intend, and could not reasonably have foreseen, upon the obvious basis that it is better for unexpected losses to fall upon the intentional wrongdoer than upon the innocent victim.

In Louisiana, "battery does not require direct bodily contact between the actor and the victim." "The contact may be with an inanimate object controlled or precipitated by the actor...." Consequently, the Swopes ... stated a valid cause of action in battery against Columbian.... Columbian had been provided Material Safety Data Sheets (MSDS) regarding ozone for at least ten ... years prior to Mr. Swope's disability.... [The data sheets indicated the short term and long term dangers.] Mr. Bobby Jordan, Columbian's general plant manager, and Mr. Richard Bianchi, Columbian's maintenance supervisor ... testified that Columbian knew ... that inhalation of ozone could be fatal to workers and damaging to their lungs.... [Columbian had received numerous reports that the concentrations of ozone were excessive and that employees were being harmed by their exposure.] Mr. Swope testified that Columbian never informed him of the characteristics of ozone, its chemical properties, or the danger of lung damage from excessive ozone exposure. He stated that Columbian gave him no special handling instructions regarding ozone, even though he was constantly exposed to the gas emitted by the generators during his work.... [I]t is clear that a reasonable jury could find that Columbian knew ... that it was continually exposing Mr. Swope to high levels of ozone ... and that his direct inhalations of such large quantities of ozone would do gradual, but definite and repeated, bodily harm. . . . [I]n order to prove a battery, it is not necessary for the plaintiff to show that a tortfeasor desired to do any harm or even that the defendant knew to a substantial certainty the full extent of the bodily harm that would result. Because . . . [there is] conflicting evidence from which a jury could reasonably reach different conclusions . . . [summary judgment should not be granted.] . . .

[In discussing the duty to warn under product liability, the court noted an expert witness reported that Emery's instructions for purging ozone from the generator were inaccurate and untrue. The instructions called for a 30-minute wait. A witness testified that as a practice Columbian adhered to the 30-minute wait. On the day of the accident, Swope and a coworker opened the door and replaced a tube, they shut the door to get some silicon, and when Swope reopened the door, he was struck by a blast of ozone and he could not breathe.] . . . [A] jury could . . . find that Columbian reasonably relied on the safety instructions and representations of Emery and did not discover their inaccuracy and the dangerous characteristic of the generator to retain ozone after purgation until Mr. Swope's final exposure. . . . LPLA § 2800.57(B)(2) explicitly requires that the manufacturer, in order to be relieved of his duty to warn, prove that the user or handler of the product already knew or reasonably should have been expected to know of the product's dangerous characteristic. Once this threshold burden of

proof has been met, it may be plausible to find an implication in the statute that the purchaser becomes a sophisticated intermediary with an exclusive or concurrent duty to warn his employee users and handlers of the danger. . . . [T]hese were the first ozone generators Columbian had ever purchased from Emery and that the vast majority of Columbian's experience had been with other makes and models of generators. . . . [T]here is nothing in the record to suggest why even a highly experienced user or handler of ozone generators should have been expected to know that the particular Emery generators . . . could not be safely and adequately purged in the manner prescribed by Emery. . . . There is nothing in the record to indicate that Columbian had ever made an ozone generator or had any occasion to delve into the intricacies of its internal operation. . . . Columbian had never dismantled or performed major internal maintenance on the Emery generators. . . . [T]here is a genuine dispute as to whether Columbian already knew or reasonably should have known of "the characteristic of the product that may cause damage and the danger of such characteristic." . . .

BUSINESS CONSIDERATIONS **What safety precautions should Columbian implement? What safety precautions should Henkel implement? Why?**

ETHICAL CONSIDERATIONS **Did Columbian treat its employees in an ethical manner? Was Columbian using the employees as a means to its own ends, or was Columbian concerned about the rights of the workers?**

plaintiff cannot be used as a defense. The manufacturer may prove the following defenses depending on the situation—*obviousness of hazard* (the risk in the product is evident, such as a sharp knife), product misuse by the plaintiff, and assumption of the risk. There is also a strict liability failure-to-warn theory. Missouri, for example, uses five elements for a strict liability failure-to-warn claim: (1) the defendant sold the product in the course of its business; (2) when used as reasonably anticipated and without knowledge of its characteristics, the product was unreasonably dangerous at the time of sale; (3) the defendant did not give an adequate warning of the danger; (4) the product was used in a reasonably anticipated manner; and (5) the plaintiff was damaged as a direct result of the product being sold without an adequate warning.[20] The courts often assume that if adequate warnings were given, the user would have heeded them. This is a rebuttable presumption in some states, including Missouri.[21] Another question is whether

adequate information is available absent a warning from the manufacturer.

Tort Liability of Business Entities

Before leaving this introduction to tort law, we should mention that businesses *can* be held liable for the torts of their employees. Initially, courts were reluctant to impose liability. Today, however, liability is more readily assessed. Liability is generally imposed through the doctrine of *respondeat superior*. *Respondeat superior* means that the superior should answer or pay for the torts of employees that occur in the course and scope of employment. *Respondeat superior* does not excuse the employee: The employee will be held liable in addition to his or her employer. *Respondeat superior* is discussed in detail in Chapter 31.

Summary

Tort law is designed to protect an individual's rights with respect to his or her person and property. To do this, the law uses the concept of "duty." Tort law deals with "private" wrongs, whereas criminal law deals with "public" wrongs.

Three theories of tort liability exist: intentional torts, negligence, and strict liability. Intentional torts are those in which a person acted in a willful or intentional manner. Intentional torts to persons are assault, battery, defamation, disparagement, false imprisonment, emotional distress, and invasion of privacy. Invasion of privacy includes intrusion on physical solitude, unauthorized use of the plaintiff's likeness, presenting the plaintiff in a false light, and appropriation of plaintiff's likeness for commercial purposes. Intentional torts to property are trespass, conversion, and misappropriation of trade secrets. Different torts have various defenses. Common defenses include consent, privilege, necessity, and truth.

Negligence is the unintentional causing of harm that could have been prevented if the defendant had acted as a reasonable and prudent person. Defenses to negligence suits include assumption of the risk, contributory negligence, and comparative negligence. Strict liability is a separate basis of tort liability because it is independent of intent or negligence. Our legal system, through the legislatures and/or courts, has declared that if certain activities cause harm, the actor will be strictly liable without regard to fault.

Central to a discussion of all three theories of liability are the concepts of duty and foreseeability. Duty imposes a certain kind of conduct and therefore is action oriented. With intentional torts, one has a duty to avoid committing the tort. With negligence, one has a duty to exercise reasonable care. With strict liability, one has an absolute duty to make something safe; there is automatic liability if harm occurs. Foreseeability concerns the thought process. If the hypothetical reasonable and prudent person would have foreseen harm, liability exists.

Discussion Questions

1. We all have a duty to protect other persons from harm. How does tort law resolve the question of the extent of that duty?

2. Why is it that intentional torts, negligence, and strict liability all involve the issue of foreseeability?

3. It can be scientifically proven that pollution from the smokestacks of a steel plant in Beaumont, Texas, is carried in the clouds over the Gulf of Mexico and deposited on Orlando, Florida. It is also known that the pollutants carry cancer-causing chemicals. On what theory can a person who contracted cancer while living in Orlando successfully sue the steel plant? Discuss your answer with respect to proximate cause.

4. Tony, a waiter in a hotel restaurant, asks a male guest, "Is this woman your wife or your mistress?" Is the hotel liable for Tony's comment? Would your answer be any different if the waiter had asked, "Is this woman your wife or your daughter?"

5. Ramon knocks on your front door; after you admit him, he accuses you of being a stalker and a serial killer. Has he committed a tort against you? Would your answer be any different if he said the same things in the presence of another person?

6. Heather decides to go shopping at the XYZ Department Store. While she is in the sportswear department, the store detective suspects her of stealing a swimsuit. The detective approaches Heather and says, "Excuse me, but would you mind if I asked you a few questions?" She responds, "Well, I'm really in quite a rush. I'm on my lunch hour and I have to get back to work." Nevertheless, she submits to the questioning, which lasts for 20 minutes. Has there been a false imprisonment? Would your answer be any different if the detective had said, "Excuse me, I suspect you of stealing a swimsuit. Would you mind if I asked you a few questions?"

7. When the legislature and the courts make parents civilly liable for their children's acts, what public policy is being advanced? Is this beneficial to society or not? Why?

8. A gorilla escapes from a traveling circus, enters a shopping center, and destroys $347,500 worth of property. The businesses whose property was destroyed decide to sue the circus to recover their damages. The circus can prove that it did not act negligently and that it was not at fault in the escape of the gorilla. Given this situation, will these lawsuits succeed against the circus?

9. A manufacturer of chemical products markets suntan oil without sufficiently investigating the fact that under certain circumstances the vapors of the product become flammable. Suppose Amir uses the product, and as he rubs the oil on his chest, it ignites and burns him. Can Amir successfully sue the manufacturer for negligence? Why?

10. Professor Ortiz has established a listserver for her business law class. She posts procedural announcements on the listserver. She also uses the listserver to inform the class about interesting Web sites and to discuss journal articles and current events with the class. Students can post information to

the listserver. Professor Ortiz also communicates with students individually via e-mail. She will often inform them about their grades and comment on student work.

One day immediately after grading their second set of papers, she prepared an e-mail note to Nora Williamson. It said, "Nora, your last paper was extremely poorly written. It contained five sentence fragments, incorrect usages of words, and numerous misspelled words. In addition, you seem to have misunderstood the assignment. Consequently, your grade on this assignment is a D–. Sincerely, Professor Ortiz." Professor Ortiz intended to send this message only to Nora; however, she accidentally hit the group reply function on her e-mail and sent the message to the entire class. There are two students named Nora in the class.

Assume also that some of the students in Professor Ortiz's class begin discussing the dean of students, Dr. Watts, on the listserver. Many of the comments are critical, since Dr. Watts has taken a strong stand against alcoholic beverages on campus. In addition, Dr. Watts is dating the president of the university. Some typical comments on the listserver include, "She is such a prude."; "Dr. Watts seems to believe in do as I say and not as I do."; and "The quality of student services has declined drastically since she was appointed as dean of students." Analyze the potential torts in this situation.

Case Problems and Writing Assignments

1. G.J.D. and Darwin Thebes were involved in an intimate relationship for approximately five years. During that time Thebes took sexually explicit photographs of G.J.D., which he then kept hidden. G.J.D. did not see the photographs until several years later after she had ended her relationship with Thebes. G.J.D. alleged that Thebes distributed photocopies of the photographs throughout the community when he learned she was ending their relationship. The photocopies included G.J.D.'s address and phone number as well as captions, which implied that she was a prostitute. The distribution of the photocopies was calculated to ensure that they would be found by G.J.D.'s friends and relatives, including her minor children, her mother, her brother, and her employer. Should G.J.D. recover for defamation, intentional infliction of emotional distress, or invasion of privacy? Thebes committed suicide while the lawsuit was pending. Should his estate be liable for actual and punitive damages? [See *G.J.D. v. Johnson*, 552 Pa. 169, 1998 Pa. LEXIS 1275 (Pa. 1998).]

2. Parents of the three high school students who were shot and killed by Michael Carneal, in a Paducah, Kentucky, high school in December 1997 have filed a $100 million wrongful death lawsuit. Eighteen computer and video games companies have been named as defendants in the suit. The producers of the film *The Basketball Diaries* are also named as defendants; it is contended that the film and games influenced Carneal. Carneal was a devotee of violent games. The complaint alleges that Michael was "profoundly influenced" by his exposure to violent media and that "the media's depiction of violence as a means of resolving conflict . . . further condoned his thinking." "In fact, Carneal's sharp shooting may be linked to his video game prowess. He had never shot a pistol before and yet got hits with eight out of nine shots, three of which were kills, according to Mike Breen, lead counsel for the plaintiffs in the case." According to Lt. Col. Dave Grossman, who teaches the psychology of murder for the federal government, "They are murder simulators which over time teach a person how to look another person in the eyes and snuff their life out." The Marine Corps uses the game *Doom* to train soldiers. (Similar lawsuits may also result from the shooting in Littleton, Colorado. The killers in that school were identified as obsessive players of violent games.)

   Game makers made it big in 1998, with revenues of $6.2 million. The action game category accounts for 52 percent of Sony Playstation sales and 36.5 percent of Nintendo 64 sales. The video game industry is "keeping heads down" until the heat cools. Doug Lowenstein, president of the Interactive Digital Software Association, is the only spokesman. He indicates that game manufacturers are making an increased effort to promote the ratings system, including working with retailers to enforce age restrictions when the games are sold. Should the game manufacturers and film producers be held liable? What theories would apply? Why? [See Deborah Claymon, "Game Makers Scramble for Way to Avoid Spotlight over Violence," *The Fresno Bee*, June 13, 1999, pp. C1, C2.]

3. Ronald Reed was driving his pickup truck on E. L. Harris's Ranch, where he had been working as a farmhand for approximately 13 years. As Reed approached a private railroad crossing that had no crossbucks, gates, or warning lights, he slowly rolled up to the crossing and checked both right and left for any approaching trains. He did not, however, look directly in front of him. As Reed crossed over the train tracks, his truck hit a replacement rail that had been left uncovered by Union Pacific. Union Pacific elicited testimony from Reed that, although he did look to both sides when crossing the railroad tracks, he did not look straight in front of him, where the replacement rail was situated. Reed also said there was nothing either outside or on the inside of his truck that obstructed his view of the tracks. He further testified that he did not stop prior to crossing over the tracks. The impact of hitting the rail caused Reed to be thrown and twisted around the inside of the truck. It also jerked the steering wheel to the right, causing the truck to become stuck on the rail. After dislodging his truck, Reed brought his coworker, Ted Vanbuskirk, to the railroad crossing where the accident occurred. They approached the accident scene in the same truck Reed had been driving at the time of the accident. As they neared the track, Vanbuskirk tes-

tified that, although specifically looking for the replacement rail, he could not see it from the truck. Only after stepping out of the truck and walking up to the tracks was he able to see the replacement rail. Harris, Reed's employer, corroborated Reed's story by testifying that he could not see the rail from his truck, and saw it only when he walked up to the tracks to fix a gate. Later that day, Reed began to feel pain and stiffness. That evening, Reed went to the hospital. A few weeks after the initial emergency room visit, Dr. Macareg performed a CT scan that showed that Reed had a mild degenerative disk disease. Dr. Macareg opined that the accident aggravated Reed's pre-existing degenerative disk condition. Was it proper for the trial court to instruct the jury on comparative negligence? [See *Reed v. Union Pacific Railroad Company,* 1999 U.S. App. LEXIS 16008 (7th Cir. 1999).]

4. Douglas R. Tenbarge worked as a drywall installer. His primary duty was to apply drywall compound and tape along the seams of drywall panels with an Ames Auto Taper, known as a Bazooka. The Bazooka is a tube 56 inches in length and 2¼ inches in diameter used to apply joint compound and tape simultaneously to drywall seams in ceilings and walls. It weighs 7 pounds when empty and 20 pounds when filled to capacity with joint compound and a 500-foot roll of tape. The Bazooka is operated by holding it with both hands and applying pressure against the seam as the joint compound and tape are being fed out of the tube. The Bazooka requires repetitive wrist motions and the exertion of considerable pressure to apply the tape and compound. Lacking handholds, "the Bazooka is awkward to support and maneuver, particularly while doing overhead work." In 1991, after experiencing numbness in his hands and fingers, Tenbarge was diagnosed with carpal tunnel syndrome (CTS). In December 1992 and January 1993, Tenbarge underwent surgery on both wrists. He returned to work in April 1993, only to sustain an elbow injury. He underwent a third surgery late in 1993. Tenbarge filed suit against Ames, the manufacturer and lessor of the Bazooka. Should the trial court have permitted the jury to consider whether Ames had a duty to warn Tenbarge? [See *Tenbarge v. Ames Taping Tool Systems, Inc.,* 1999 U.S. App. LEXIS 15028 (8th Cir. 1999).]

5. BUSINESS APPLICATION CASE Mark Sanders was working as a telepsychic in PMG's Los Angeles office, giving "readings" to customers who telephoned PMG's 900 number (for which they were charged a per-minute fee). The psychics' work area consisted of a large room with rows of cubicles, about 100 total, in which the psychics took their calls. Each cubicle was enclosed on three sides by five-foot-high partitions. The facility also included a separate lunchroom and enclosed offices for managers and supervisors. The door to the PMG facility was unlocked during business hours, but PMG, by internal policy, prohibited access to the office by nonemployees without specific permission. An employee testified the front door was visible from the administration desk and a supervisor greeted any nonemployees who entered. Stacy Lescht, a reporter employed by ABC in an investigation of the telepsychic industry, obtained employment as a psychic in PMG's Los Angeles office. When she first entered the PMG office to apply for a position, she was not stopped at the front door or greeted by anyone until she found and approached the administration desk. Once hired, she sat at a cubicle desk, where she gave telephonic readings to customers. Lescht testified that while sitting at her desk she could easily overhear conversations conducted in surrounding cubicles or in the aisles near her cubicle. When not on the phone, she talked with some of the other psychics in the phone room. Lescht secretly videotaped these conversations with a "hat cam," a small camera hidden in her hat. A microphone attached to her brassiere captured sound. Among the conversations Lescht videotaped were two with Sanders, the first at Lescht's cubicle, the second at Sanders's. May a person who lacks a reasonable expectation of complete privacy in a conversation because it could be seen and overheard by coworkers (but not the general public) nevertheless have a claim for invasion of privacy by intrusion based on a television reporter's covert videotaping of that conversation? What can the media legitimately do to obtain a story? How can a business protect its privacy and that of its employees? [See *Sanders v. American Broadcasting Companies, Inc.,* 978 P.2d 67, 1999 Cal. LEXIS 3900 (Cal. 1999).[22]

6. ETHICAL APPLICATION CASE Rose Cipollone smoked cigarettes from 1942 until 1984, when she died. She smoked cigarette brands made by the defendant until 1968. She claimed that she started smoking because she wanted to imitate the "pretty girls and movie stars" in defendant's advertisements. Rose claimed that she believed advertisements that said, "Play Safe, Smoke [Liggett's] Chesterfield" and "Nose, Throat, and Accessory Organs not Adversely Affected by Smoking Chesterfield." In 1981, Rose was diagnosed with lung cancer. Rose filed suit alleging that her cancer was caused by her use of the defendant's products for a 40-year period. Rose died before trial because of complications from the lung cancer. Thomas Cipollone, her son, continued the suit, individually and as a representative of her estate. The lawsuit requested compensation based on the following legal theories: strict liability, negligence, breach of warranty, intentional tort, and conspiracy. Did the cigarette manufacturers breach a duty to warn? Why or why not? What is the effect of the printed warnings imposed by federal statute on cigarette manufacturers beginning in 1969? [See *Cipollone v. Liggett Group, Inc.,* 505 U.S. 504 (1992). Aspects of the case were also considered by the Supreme Court at 502 U.S. 1055 (1992); 502 U.S. 923 (1991); and 499 U.S. 935 (1991). Lower courts considered the case at 893 F.2d 541 (3rd Cir. 1990); 789 F.2d 181 (3rd Cir. 1986); 649 F. Supp. 664 (N.J. 1986); and 593 F. Supp. 1146 (N.J. 1984).]

7. CRITICAL THINKING CASE Consumers Union of United States, Inc. (CU) published a story in its magazine *Consumer Reports,* in which it rated the Suzuki Samurai "Not Acceptable" based on its propensity to roll over during accident avoidance tests. Since that time, CU has publicly referred to the negative Samurai rating in various media. CU is a nonprofit corporation that engages in comparative testing and evaluation of

consumer products and services, the results of which are published in the magazine *Consumer Reports*. In order to provide buying and safety advice to automobile purchasers, CU's Automotive Testing Division (ATD) tests approximately 40 cars and other vehicles each year. CU's negative rating of the Samurai was detailed in an article that described the steps CU took to test the Samurai, Jeep Wrangler, Isuzu Trooper II, and Jeep Cherokee. The article highlighted the results of the short-course tests. There is some evidence that the CU employees at the test site were pleased when the Samurai tipped. CU submitted to the National Highway Traffic Safety Administration (NHTSA) a copy of the article, the videotape from its press conference, and a diagram of its short course in support of a petition to establish a minimum stability standard to protect against unreasonable risk of rollover. (The Web site of NHTSA is at http://www.nhtsa.dot.gov.) NHTSA issued a decision denying the motor vehicle defect petition filed earlier by another group. The NHTSA also stated "the rollover crash involvement of the Samurai appears to be within the range of most other light utility vehicles." NHTSA's opinion also criticized CU's testing protocols, stating as follows:

The existing test procedures for assessing the rollover propensity of vehicles are unsatisfactory because they do not provide for repeatable, reproducible results, and there are no accepted performance criteria. The testing appears to rely on the skill and influence of the driver and the presumption that the vehicle suspension, tire, and road surface characteristics will remain constant throughout the testing.

NHTSA concluded by stating that, although the CU testing results were "cause for some concern,"

the test procedures do not have a scientific basis and cannot be linked to real-world crash avoidance needs, or actual crash data. Using the same procedures, probably any light utility vehicle could be made to roll over under the right conditions and driver input.

CU published a subsequent article criticizing the NHTSA's decision. Between 1988 and 1996, CU republished references to the 1988 Samurai rating on at least 24 separate occasions. CU continued to refer to the rating after this suit was filed. CU states that several events supported its belief in the correctness of its "Not Acceptable" rating including a 1988 England-based Consumers' Association article that buttressed the Samurai rollover claim; a 1988 lawsuit filed by seven state attorneys general charging Suzuki with false and misleading advertising regarding the Samurai's rollover potential; the decision in a court case in which the court suggested that Suzuki knew of the Samurai's rollover propensity and did nothing to correct it; the disclosure of documents from the court cases suggesting that Suzuki knew of the Samurai's rollover propensity; and eight years of further SUV testing by CU during which time only the Samurai and Isuzu Trooper tipped. Suzuki filed this suit alleging that CU's ongoing publication of the negative Samurai rating constituted product disparagement. Suzuki is a public figure, so under applicable law it must show that CU acted with "actual malice" to recover for product disparagement. Is there sufficient evidence of product disparagement for the case to go to trial? [See *Suzuki Motor Corporation v. Consumers Union of United States, Inc.,* 292 F.3d 1192, 2002 U.S. App. LEXIS 12405 (9th Cir. 2002).]

8. **YOU BE THE JUDGE** Caesar Barber, from the Bronx, N.Y., weighs 272 pounds. He filed a lawsuit against McDonald's, Kentucky Fried Chicken, Wendy's, and Burger King for contributing to his weight problem. He has a number of health problems commonly associated with high weight—two heart attacks, diabetes, high blood pressure, and high cholesterol. He claims the fast-food chains deceived him with ads that said "100 percent beef" and that they created a de facto addiction. The case alleges that McDonald's failed to adequately disclose material facts about its high-fat food. "The law of warnings is not designed for the best and brightest of us. . . . It is aimed at helping people who need to be told not to stand on the top step of a ladder or not to use a hair dryer in the bathtub," says John Banzhaf, a legal activism teacher at George Washington University Law School. All of the restaurants have nutritional information in their restaurants and online. Is there actual causation? Is there proximate causation? What other evidence would be helpful? How would you rule if this case were brought in *your* court? [See Sheryl Y. Fred, "Super-Sized Plaintiff Attacks Fast-Food Chains," *Corporate Legal Times* (October 2002); The Insider, 75; Emily Heller, "Weighing Chances of Fast-Food Fat Suits," *Fulton County Daily Report*, December 13, 2002.]

Notes

1. See *Cal. Civ. Code* § 1714.1.
2. *Church of Scientology Int'l. v. Time Warner, Inc.,* 932 F. Supp. 589 (S.D.N.Y. 1996), at 593–594.
3. 376 U.S. 254, 1964 U.S. LEXIS 1655 (1964).
4. Barbara Wartelle Wall, "Following 'Oprah,' An Update on Food-Product Disparagement Laws," published at Gannett News Watch at http://www.gannett.com/go/newswatch/98/june/nw0619-8.htm (accessed 12/17/02), and Paul McMasters, Section IV of Libel Law/Punitive Damages/Tort Actions of the First Amendment and the Media 1999 Online Outline at http://www.mediainstitute.org/ONLINE/FAM99/LPT_A.html (accessed 12/17/02).

5. "Mortician Training Schools' Wrongful Acts Were Not Insured," *Death Care Business Advisor* (September 4, 1997).
6. *Texas Tanks, Inc. v. Owens-Corning Fiberglas Corp.,* 99 F.3d 734 (5th Cir. 1996).
7. Ibid.
8. The Uniform Trade Secrets Act with the 1985 amendments has been adopted in Alabama, Arizona, Colorado, Delaware, District of Columbia, Florida, Georgia, Hawaii, Idaho, Iowa, Kansas, Kentucky, Maine, Maryland, Michigan, Minnesota, Mississippi, Missouri, Montana, Nebraska, Nevada, New Hampshire, New Mexico, North Dakota, Ohio, Oklahoma, Oregon, South Carolina, South Dakota,

Tennessee, Utah, Vermont, Virginia, West Virginia, and Wisconsin. The following states have adopted the 1979 act, but not the 1985 amendments: Alaska, Arkansas, California, Connecticut, Illinois, Indiana, Louisiana, Rhode Island, and Washington. See the National Conference of Commissioners on Uniform State Laws (NCCUSL) Web site, "A Few Facts about the Uniform Trade Secrets Act," http://www.nccusl.org/nccusl/uniformact_factsheets/uniformacts-fs-utsa.asp (accessed 12/16/02).

9. 18 U.S.C. §§ 1961 et seq.

10. Susan B. Garland, "Can a Tough-Guy Law Deck Big Tobacco?" *Business Week* (October 11, 1999): 158, 160.

11. Michael Riccardi, "Drug Manufacturer Must Warn of Risks," *The Legal Intelligencer,* July 15, 1999, p. 4.

12. See Jury Instructions for Negligence Per Se, BAJI 3.45 (1992 Revision), *California Jury Instructions, Civil,* 7th ed. (St. Paul, Minn.: West, 1992). Drafted by the Committee of Standard Jury Instructions, Civil, of the Superior Court of Los Angeles County and used throughout the state of California.

13. 119 Cal. Rptr. 858, 532 P.2d 1226 (1975).

14. NCCUSL Web site, "Press Release: August 5, 2002, New Act on Tort Responsibility Completed," http://www.nccusl.org/nccusl/pressreleases/pr080502_TORT.asp (accessed 9/4/02).

15. L.R. 3 H.L. 330 (1868).

16. For example, Cal. Veh. Code § 17150.

17. Cal. Civ. Code § 1714.1.

18. *Tenbarge v. Ames Taping Tool Systems, Inc.,* 1999 U.S. App. LEXIS 15028 (8th Cir. 1999).

19. ALI Web site at http://www.ali.org/ (accessed 12/19/02).

20. See note 18.

21. Ibid.

22. The California Supreme Court denied a petition to review the decision of the Second Appellate District at 2000 Cal. LEXIS 1892 (2000).

Crimes and Business

AGENDA

NRW NRW has recently been victimized by a series of minor crimes, including theft from its warehouses. This has led Mai, Carlos, and Helen to a general discussion of crimes, and especially of victim's rights when crimes are committed. Throughout this chapter, we will consider what NRW and other businesses can do to deter crime and to reduce the likelihood of becoming victims of criminal conduct.

The entrepreneurs want to know whether, in general, NRW can be held liable for criminal activity perpetrated by its employees on company time or on company property. For example, they want to know if NRW must pay any traffic tickets issued to employees who are driving company vehicles when they are ticketed. They also want to know if the firm can be held liable if any employees make unauthorized copies of computer software. They want to know who will be criminally responsible in these situations—the employee, NRW, or both. To answer these questions you will need to distinguish between criminal law and civil law throughout this chapter.

Suppose that Mai, Carlos, or Helen suspect an employee of selling drugs at work, and also suspect that he is storing these drugs in his locker at NRW. NRW has a zero tolerance policy on drug use and/or possession at work. Can the firm search the locker without permission? Can they ask the police to search the locker? Do they need probable cause in either circumstance? What are the legal restrictions on a private search?

These and other questions will arise as you read this chapter. Be prepared! You never know when the firm or one of its members will seek your advice.

Why Study Criminal Law?

Why should a business law textbook contain a chapter on criminal law? The reason is that businesses are constantly confronted with the *effects* of crimes, such as embezzlement, forgery, and fraud, to name only a few kinds of crimes we will discuss in this chapter. In addition, there are a number of crimes with which a business can be charged. Therefore, to prevent a criminal act, or to deal effectively with a crime once it has occurred, you need to know what constitutes a crime and its legal ramifications.

Criminal law developed through a long history of precedents. However, most states have codified their criminal laws. As you should expect, the exact rules vary from state to state. Begin by referring to Exhibit 8.1, which summarizes the primary distinctions between civil law and criminal law. Try to distinguish between the two areas throughout this chapter. Remember that one action or series of actions may constitute *both* a civil wrong and a criminal wrong. It will also be helpful to look at Exhibit 8.2, which examines the six steps in a typical criminal proceeding. The LII, maintained by the Cornell Law School, provides an overview of criminal law and links to federal and state criminal statutes, organizations, journals, and other resources at http://www.law.cornell.edu/topics/criminal.html.

Objectives of Criminal Law

The objectives of criminal law are the protection of persons and property, the deterrence of criminal behavior, the punishment of criminal activity, and the rehabilitation of the criminal. You can access additional information on criminal law from the U.S. Department of Justice Web site, which provides links to its activities and information about victims, civil rights violations, and prisons at http://www.usdoj.gov/.

Protection of Persons and Property

Someone once said that a lock was designed to keep an honest person honest. It is for the same reason that the government declares certain conduct to be illegal. The government believes that all persons and their property should be protected from harm. In Chapter 7, however, you learned that tort law also protects persons and property. What is the difference? The primary difference between tort law and criminal law is that tort law results in money damages being paid by the actor to the individual victims, whereas criminal law may result in loss of freedom by sending the actor to jail or prison. Private interests are served through the awarding of damages. The public interest, on the other

---

EXHIBIT   8.1   Distinctions Between Civil Law and Criminal Law

Question	Civil Law	Criminal Law
What type of action leads to the lawsuit or case?	Action against a private individual	Action against society
Who initiates the action?	Plaintiff	Government
Who is their attorney?	Private attorney	District Attorney (D.A.) or the U.S. Attorney General
What is the burden of proof in the case?	Preponderance of the evidence	Beyond a reasonable doubt
Who generally has the burden of proof?	Plaintiff	Government
Is there a jury trial?	Yes, except in actions in equity	Yes, except in cases involving certain infractions and misdemeanors
What jury vote is necessary to win the case?	Jury vote depends on jurisdiction or agreement of the parties. Often a simple majority or two-thirds jury vote is sufficient	Unanimous jury vote needed for the government to win a conviction
What type(s) of punishment is imposed?	Monetary damages or equitable remedies	Capital punishment, prison, fines, and/or probation

EXHIBIT 8.2 The Six Steps in a Typical Criminal Proceeding

1. Preliminary Hearing or a Grand Jury Hearing

A preliminary hearing is generally a public hearing where a magistrate considers the evidence against the accused and determines if there is probable cause to hold a criminal trial. The prosecutor need not present all the government's evidence at the preliminary hearing, just sufficient evidence to have the case go to trial. A grand jury, on the other hand, hears the evidence in secret. Generally, the witnesses appear before the grand jury one at a time. The district attorney appears before the grand jury and may lead the questioning of the witnesses. The grand jury determines if a crime has been committed and, if so, which individuals were involved in the crime. If a grand jury issues an indictment against an individual, there will be a trial.

2. Arraignment

The suspect appears before the court and is informed of the criminal charges and asked how he or she pleads. Generally, the amount of bail is set at this stage.

3. Discovery

Both sides have to gather facts and information to prepare for trial. Discovery can involve examining documents, records, and other pieces of physical evidence, as well as taking the depositions (statements) of witnesses or the parties themselves. Discovery is generally more limited in criminal cases than in civil cases. One of the concerns is that if the defendant knows who will testify for the government, the defendant, defendant's relatives, and friends may intimidate the witnesses. Some discovery actually occurs at the preliminary hearing and arraignment.

4. Pretrial Motions

If the parties need the court to make procedural decisions or other rulings as the case moves toward trial, they do so by filing the appropriate motions with the court. In criminal cases, this may include a motion to suppress evidence that was illegally obtained by the police.

5. Trial

The court hears the evidence offered by both sides and decides issues of both fact and law during the process.

6. Sentencing

If the defendant is found guilty beyond a reasonable doubt, the defendant will be sentenced to jail, probation, parole, and/or to pay a fine.

hand, is served by punishing criminal activity. If all persons respected everyone else's person and property, there would be very little reason for criminal law.

Deterrence of Criminal Behavior

One method used to reduce criminal behavior is to present a sufficient *deterrent* (a consideration that stops or prevents a person from acting) to antisocial behavior. The presumption inherent in criminal law is that if we make the punishment sufficiently harsh, people and businesses who contemplate criminal behavior will avoid it because they fear the punishment. If people fear the punishment, they will not commit a criminal act. If a sufficient number of people fear the punishment, there will be a reduction in that crime. The severity of the punishment is often an issue with corporate defendants. What constitutes a substantial penalty for an individual would be a minimal penalty for a corporation such as General Motors or Merrill Lynch, Pierce, Fenner & Smith, Inc.

Criminologists have noted that severity alone is not a sufficient deterrent. Individuals considering criminal behavior must also believe that they are likely to be identified and punished. If criminals believe that they will not be linked to the crime and tried in court or that they will not be found guilty, the deterrent effect will be reduced.

In our society, the Constitution states that there shall be no cruel and unusual punishment. If our laws allowed the death penalty for even minor offenses, there would probably be fewer minor offenses. But is that just? To many people, the loss of one's life for stealing a loaf of bread seems too high a price to pay for fewer loaves of bread being stolen. Similarly, many feel that caning a teenager for vandalism or graffiti or castrating a rapist is too extreme. The problem, therefore, is to decide how much punishment will deter criminal behavior without being deemed excessive, and therefore unconstitutional—at least in the United States.

Punishment of Criminal Activity

Since we most likely cannot deter all criminal activity, our legal system accepts that a certain level of criminal activity will exist in society. Accordingly, we punish criminal activity for punishment's sake. There is no such thing as a

NRW CASE 8.1   Management

PROTECTING AGAINST CRIME

Mai, Carlos, and Helen have become somewhat concerned about crimes in their community, and how those crimes may affect NRW. They have read that the crime rate is rising in their community and across the country, and that crimes against small, closely held companies are particularly devastating. Mai, Carlos, and Helen wonder what they can do to protect their business and themselves without violating legal rules. They ask you for advice. What will you tell them?

BUSINESS CONSIDERATIONS Suppose that a business decided to take aggressive steps to try to reduce crime in its community, especially crimes that affect the business enterprise. Would this be viewed favorably or unfavorably in the community? Why? From a business perspective, is public perception an important factor in making this decision? Why?

ETHICAL CONSIDERATIONS If a business *did* decide to take aggressive steps to try to reduce crime in its community, its conduct would have to be practical as well as legal. Is this feasible? Would such a decision be ethical? What ethical considerations should constrain the firm's decision?

INTERNATIONAL CONSIDERATIONS If a business has factories or offices in foreign countries, what can the business do about crime in those communities? How would a foreign location affect NRW's options?

free lunch: If a criminal takes something without paying for it, the criminal law makes that individual pay for it through deprivation of freedom for a period of time. In addition, the use of criminal forfeiture as a punishment for certain types or classes of crimes is growing. (*Criminal forfeiture* is government confiscation of property as a punishment for criminal activity.) For example, some jurisdictions confiscate the vehicle when the driver solicits a prostitute from the vehicle. The U.S. Sentencing Commission maintains a Web site with information about the federal sentencing guidelines and federal sentencing statistics at http://www.ussc.gov/.

Rehabilitation of the Criminal

Our criminal justice system does not *end* with imprisonment, probation, or a fine. Our government has designed various programs to educate and train criminals in legitimate occupations during the period of incarceration. Theoretically, then, criminals should have no reason to return to a life of crime. Sometimes sentences are suspended; that is, not put into effect. In such cases, the government supervises the individuals' activities to ensure that they have learned from their mistakes.

The Components of Criminal Responsibilities

Generally, an individual is presumed innocent until proven guilty. The government has the burden of proving that the suspect is guilty *beyond a reasonable doubt.* (*Beyond a reasonable doubt* is the degree of proof required in a criminal trial, which is proof to a moral certainty; there is no other reasonable interpretation). The government must prove all the parts of the crime.

There are two components, or elements, in every crime. In order for the defendant to be found guilty of an alleged criminal act, the state must prove that both elements are present to the degree specified in the state's criminal statute. The state must prove beyond a reasonable doubt that the defendant committed the prohibited criminal *act,* and that the defendant possessed the necessary *mental state* at the time the act was committed. The criminal intent is called *mens rea.* If only one element is present or can be proved beyond a reasonable doubt, no crime exists. For example, if you decide to embezzle from your employer and then take no steps to implement your decision, you have not committed a crime. Similarly, if a cigarette you are smoking in a motel ignites the draperies in your room and causes the motel to burn down, you have not committed the crime of arson. In the latter case, you may be liable for negligence, but you have not committed arson.

The Act

The law generally imposes criminal liability only when an individual acts in a manner that is prohibited by law. Ordinarily, the prohibited act must be voluntarily committed by the person before criminal liability will attach. This means that a person who is forced to act illegally against his or her will does not act voluntarily and may not be legally responsible for the act. However, the court *may* decide that the threat used to force the conduct was not sufficient to remove the free will of the actor, and will still impose liability. Also, some situations may *require* an individual to act or respond to the circumstances in a particular way. In these situations, a failure to act may be deemed a criminal "action" sufficient to justify prosecution by the government. This responsibility to act may be imposed by a statute or by judicial precedent.

Mental State

To be held criminally responsible for an illegal act, the actor must intend to do the act. Historically, various terms were used to describe this mental state: *consciously, intentionally, maliciously, unlawfully,* and *willfully.* Today our approach to the problem is more systematic. This current approach involves the use of one of five terms, depending on the specific requirements of the statute; it is more specific than the previous approach. The terms used are as follows:

1. *Purpose*—An actor acts with purpose if it is his or her conscious objective to perform the prohibited act.

2. *Knowledge*—An actor acts with knowledge if he or she is aware of what he or she is doing.

3. *Recklessness*—An actor acts with recklessness if he or she disregards a substantial and unjustifiable risk that criminal harm or injury may result from his or her action.

4. *Negligence*—An actor acts in a criminally negligent manner if he or she should have known that a substantial and unreasonable risk of harm would result from his or her action.

5. *Strict liability*—An actor will be held strictly liable if he or she acts in a manner that our law declares criminal even if none of the preceding four elements is present. This theory is used primarily for crimes that have a light punishment—for example, violating public health laws with respect to the sale of food. This theory is also used in statutory rape cases simply because our society has a vested interest in protecting our youth.

Seriousness of the Offense

Criminal law classifies all offenses into three categories according to their level of seriousness. These categories are, from least to most serious, misdemeanors, felonies, and treason. Some states have an additional category called infractions or violations.

Infractions or Violations

Some states have a separate category for petty offenses called *infractions* or *violations.* They are generally punishable only by fines. Some examples include disturbing the peace and illegal gaming.

Misdemeanors

Misdemeanors are minor offenses that are punishable by confinement of up to one year in a city or county jail, a small fine, or both. Public intoxication, speeding, and vandalism are likely to be classified as misdemeanors.

Felonies

Felonies are major offenses punishable by confinement from one year to life in a state or federal prison, a large fine, or both. In some states, special capital felony statutes provide for the sentence of death. Arson, burglary, grand theft, murder, and rape are normally classified as felonies.

Treason

Treason is the most serious offense against the government. It consists of waging war against the government or of giving aid and comfort to our enemies in time of war.

Crimes versus Torts

It is important to remember that one act can be the legal basis for both a criminal lawsuit and a civil lawsuit. The two separate suits will not be barred by the doctrine of *res judicata,* nor by the rule against double jeopardy. In many situations, a *criminal act* (an act against the rules of society) will also involve an infringement on the social rights and expectations of an individual. If one act is both a crime and a tort, it may be prosecuted by the government in the criminal system and the harmed individual may be able to seek remedies in the civil system.

Selected Crimes

We are unable to list all of the common crimes in this text. We will, however, mention selected crimes that have applications for either detection or prevention in the marketplace. In many situations, it is the business that is the victim, not the perpetrator, of the crime. However, it is possible for a business to be the perpetrator of a crime, and there are a number of criminal statutes aimed primarily at business activities. Some of the federal statutes directed at business activities are discussed in other chapters of the text. In this chapter, we will discuss the federal Counterfeit Access Device and Computer Fraud and Abuse Act of 1984; Racketeer Influenced and Corrupt Organizations Act (RICO); and the Currency and Foreign Transactions Reporting Act, among others.

The Currency and Foreign Transactions Reporting Act is a federal statute passed to prevent money laundering and requires the filing of Currency Transaction Reports (CTRs). A *currency transaction report* is a report businesses must file if a customer brings $10,000 or more in cash to the business. The National Conference of Commissioners on Uniform State Laws (NCCUSL) has written the Uniform Money Services Act (2000) for adoption by state legislatures. It enhances enforcement of existing money laundering laws and provides a framework for dealing with nondepository providers of financial services. *Nondepository providers* are providers of services such as check cashing and currency exchange. While these businesses provide some financial services traditionally related to banking, they do not hold clients' deposits or provide other banking services.[1]

The court in the following case reviewed the defendant's conviction on conspiring to "launder" money. After reading the court's opinion, decide whether you agree with the decision, and also whether you agree with the charges brought against the defendant.

8.1

UNITED STATES v. TOWNSEND
1999 U.S. App. LEXIS 13872 (5th Cir. 1999)

FACTS Braxton Townsend was charged alone in a five-count *indictment* (a written accusation of criminal conduct issued to a court by a grand jury). Count I charged that Townsend possessed with intent to distribute approximately five grams of cocaine base. Count II charged that Townsend possessed with intent to distribute four ounces of cocaine base. Count III charged Townsend with carrying a firearm during and in relation to a drug-trafficking crime. Count IV charged Townsend with conspiring to commit money laundering with drug trafficking proceeds in violation of 18 U.S.C. § 1956(h). (*U.S.C.* is the abbreviation for the United States Code.) Count V charged Townsend with causing a financial institution to fail to file a Currency Transaction Report for a currency transaction in excess of $10,000, in violation of 31 U.S.C. §§ 5313 and 5324(a)(1).

In August 1993, Townsend began building a home in Lena, Mississippi. Prior to the commencement of the building process, Townsend made arrangements with his cousin, Diane Kincaid, to open two accounts at Deposit Guaranty National Bank. Kincaid opened a checking account and a savings account under her name and the name of Townsend's sister, Willie DuPlasser. The purpose of opening the two bank accounts was to permit Kincaid to write checks for expenses related to the construction of Townsend's home in Lena. At the time that the construction began, Townsend lived in Milwaukee, Wisconsin, and Kincaid lived in the Lena, Mississippi, area.

The original arrangement between Townsend and Kincaid encompassed the following: when Townsend wanted Kincaid to make a deposit, he would travel to Mississippi and bring her the cash in a bank bag. Later, once Townsend had moved to Mississippi and before the construction of the home was completed, Kincaid would pick up the money from Townsend. Townsend would often give Kincaid money in excess of $10,000. Townsend instructed Kincaid, however, that when making bank deposits she should keep each deposit under $10,000. Townsend also told Kincaid to make the deposits at different branches of the bank and to vary the deposits between the savings and checking accounts. Due to Townsend's illiteracy, Kincaid handled all of Townsend's legal and financial matters until the completion of his home in September 1994. (Kincaid was not charged in the crime; she testified for the government.)

During the construction process, Townsend would place money in a safe deposit box to pay for the cost of building his home. The contractor testified at trial that he presented receipts for the building materials to Kincaid, who, in turn, would pay him. The contractor explained that the house measured approximately 8,000 square feet and that Townsend spent approximately $380,000 building it.

The Government produced evidence that Townsend had not filed tax returns for the 1990, 1993, and 1994 tax years. In 1991, Townsend failed to report any income and his wife Lora's reported income was $6,077. In 1992, the Townsends reported an income of $7,000.

An agent with the Internal Revenue Service (IRS) testified that as early as 1989, Townsend had been receiving food stamps and other governmental assistance from Illinois, Wisconsin, and Mississippi. The IRS agent stated that it was her professional opinion that the funds used to build the house came from drug activities. The agent explained that in the course of her investigation, she had checked with authorities and determined that there were open investigations on Townsend for criminal activity involving drugs in other states. The agent stated that her investigation allowed her to gather intelligence information that showed that Townsend had been previously involved in drug activities, that he had no legal sources of income, and that he had large sums of money that could not be accounted for legitimately.

Based upon the probable cause resulting from a controlled drug buy, officers obtained a warrant to search Townsend's property. On the morning of November 17, 1996, the search transpired. In the course of the search, a box containing money was discovered in the downstairs master bedroom closet of Townsend's home. During the search, the agents found over $5,000 in cash, four ounces of crack cocaine, and 41 guns. The jury found Townsend guilty on all five counts of the indictment.

ISSUE Did the prosecutor present sufficient evidence at trial to support Townsend's conviction on violation of 18 U.S.C. § 1956(h), conspiracy to launder money?

HOLDING Yes. There was sufficient evidence presented at trial to support the conviction.

REASONING Excerpts from the opinion of Circuit Judge Reynaldo G. Garza:

When the sufficiency of the evidence is challenged on appeal, this Court reviews the evidence and all the reasonable inferences which flow therefrom in the light most favorable to the verdict. The conviction must be affirmed if any rational trier of fact could have found the essential elements of the offense beyond a reasonable doubt.... Townsend contends that the evidence at trial was insufficient to support his conviction for conspiracy to launder money under 18 U.S.C. § 1956(h).

We do not agree with Townsend's assertion. To establish a violation of section 1956 (a)(1), the Government must prove that Townsend: "(1) knowingly conducted a financial transaction (2) that involved the proceeds of an unlawful activity (3) with the intent to promote or further that unlawful activity." Section 1956(h) states: "any person who conspires to commit any offense defined in this section or section 1957 shall be subject to the same penalties as those prescribed for the offense ... which was the object of the conspiracy."

After reviewing the record, the parties' briefs and hearing oral argument, we find that the evidence presented at trial is sufficient to support Townsend's conviction for conspiracy to commit money laundering. The Government showed that Townsend's only legitimate sources of income were food stamps and disability payments. The fact that Townsend routinely provided his cousin with large sums of cash for deposit into bank accounts, that he had purchased a home worth approximately $300,000 without substantial evidence of any legitimate income, that he sold crack cocaine to Jones [Sheila Jones, a confidential informant] on November 14, 1996, and that four ounces more of crack cocaine were discovered on his property, is sufficient to support his conviction....

BUSINESS CONSIDERATIONS What procedures should a bank or other business establish to prevent violating the requirements for Currency Transaction Reports?

ETHICAL CONSIDERATIONS Was it ethical for Townsend to jeopardize Kincaid's welfare by involving her in this scheme? Was it ethical for Kincaid to testify against Townsend during his trial? Did the contractor have an obligation to report Townsend?

Murder/Manslaughter

Homicide is the killing of one human being by another. It is not necessarily a criminal act. It will *not* be a criminal act if the killing was lawful; for example, if there was a justification such as self-defense. *Murder,* however, is the willful, unlawful killing of a human being by another with *malice aforethought* (deliberate purpose or design). *Manslaughter* occurs when the killing is unlawful, but without malice. Manslaughter is usually divided into two categories—*voluntary* (upon a sudden heat of passion) or *involuntary* (in the commission of an unlawful act or in the commission of a lawful act without due caution). It is common for the state to charge a defendant with both murder and manslaughter and to let the decider of fact (the jury, if there is one; the judge if there is no jury) determine which crime was actually committed.

Arson

Arson is the intentional or willful burning of property by fire or explosion. Originally, this crime was restricted to the burning of a house. Today, in most states, the crime has been expanded to include the burning of all types of *real property* (land and items of property permanently attached to land) and many types of *personal property* (property other than land).

Burglary

Burglary is the breaking and entering of a structure with the intent to commit a felony inside the structure. Originally, this crime was restricted to the breaking and entering of a house at night, but, like arson, it has been expanded to include other structures, such as stores and warehouses. The crime also is no longer limited to night-time conduct, but can occur at any time of day or night.

Embezzlement

Embezzlement is the taking of money or other property by an employee who has been entrusted with the money or property by his or her employer. Businesses should establish practices and procedure to reduce the likelihood of being victimized by embezzlement.

In the following case, the court addressed whether there was sufficient evidence to support the trial court conviction of embezzlement, conspiracy, and violation of a federal statute[2] that made it a federal crime to steal property from an organization receiving more than $10,000 in federal

benefits in a one-year period. Do you agree with the court's assessment of the sufficiency of the evidence?

Forgery

Forgery is the making or altering of a negotiable instrument or credit card invoice in order to create or to shift legal liability for the instrument. It generally consists of signing another person's name to a check, promissory note, or credit card invoice or altering an amount on any of those documents. To win any such case, the government must generally prove that the accused acted with the intent to defraud. A business entity should use care in maintaining checks and signature stamps; it should also reconcile bank statements to discover potential forgeries.

8.2

UNITED STATES v. DUBON-OTERO
292 F.3d 1, 2002 U.S. App. LEXIS 10041 (1st Cir. 2002)

FACTS Advanced Community Health Services was incorporated in the Commonwealth of Puerto Rico as a for-profit corporation. (It later became a nonprofit corporation.) Luis Dubon-Otero served as legal advisor and Jorge Garib-Bazain as the medical director. Dr. Yamil Kouri-Perez was a consultant from the Harvard Institute for International Development who, together with Jeanette Sotomayor-Vazquez, the administrative director, and Angel Luis Corcino-Mauras, the comptroller, conducted the day-to-day operations of Health Services. Dubon and Garib were charged with conspiring to use Health Services funds to pay personal expenses and make political payoffs. In January 1988, Health Services contracted with the Municipality of San Juan to provide services for AIDS patients. Under the contract, Health Services became "the exclusive source of AIDS counseling and professional services in San Juan," so federal monies were directed to Health Services.

ISSUE Was there sufficient evidence to convict the defendants of embezzling or stealing funds from Health Services?

HOLDING Yes. The government provided the trial court with sufficient evidence.

REASONING Excerpts from the opinion of Senior Circuit Judge John R. Gibson:

In reviewing a challenge to the sufficiency of the evidence, "the verdict of a jury must be sustained if there is substantial evidence . . . to support it." . . . The Government presented evidence that between 1987 and May

1991 Dubon received $10,000 per month from Health Services as a legal retainer, although Health Services' board of directors had authorized a retainer of only $5,000. Someone had tampered with the original board minutes to show authorization for a monthly retainer of $10,000, allowing Dubon to funnel the additional $5,000 per month to Kouri. Specifically, the director of the word processing center where the minutes were transcribed testified that the original page of the minutes setting forth the retainer as $5,000 was replaced in another set of minutes with a page showing the retainer as $10,000. The page showing the retainer as $10,000 was a different consistency than the rest of the minutes and was not produced at the same word processing center. Corcino testified the additional $5,000 was going to Kouri to pay Kouri's home rent and credit card bills. Corcino further testified that Kouri could not be on Health Services' payroll because Kouri was under contract with the Harvard Institute for International Development, which in turn had a contract directly with the Municipality of San Juan.

The Government also presented evidence that Garib employed a personal housekeeper, as well as a secretary for his private practice, using Health Services' money. Corcino, Health Services' comptroller, testified that for a long time he was not aware that Health Services was paying for a private secretary and personal housekeeper for Garib, and that in his opinion such payments constituted an unauthorized diversion of Health Services funds for personal use. The housekeeper testified that the signature on the timesheets bearing her name was not hers. The secretary testified that while she was paid by Health Services, ninety-nine percent of her time was spent on tasks related to Garib's private practice.

Finally, there was evidence at trial that Appellants also used Health Services assets to purchase political support, which Health Services was dependent upon for its funding. Before the San Juan mayoral election of 1988, Garib allegedly loaned a $19,000 video camera to one of the candidates, Jose Granados-Navedo. The camera had been purchased with a Health Services check. Garib and Kouri later met with Granados to discuss Health Services providing other financial support for his campaign.

To generate more cash, Garib, Sotomayor, and Corcino then met with Antonio Fernandez, the owner of IMA Productions, and presented him a Health Services check made out to IMA in the amount of $60,000 and signed by Garib and Sotomayor. Only some of this money was intended to pay for services performed by IMA. Garib asked Fernandez to endorse the check and cash it—or else write separate IMA checks payable to other persons who had not rendered services—so Garib could recover the excess in cash. Garib explained Health Services had an urgent need of cash to make certain payments that it could not make by company check. When Fernandez refused to participate, Garib stated that he had solved the problem in another way. Garib later met with Granados and gave him a box containing more than $100,000 in cash.

Granados lost the election. After the new administration assumed office, payments on the AIDS contract were delayed. Kouri later told Corcino that he had taken care of the problem by arranging for $5,000 a month to be paid to the candidate who had won the election, Mayor Hector Luis Acevedo, and $5,000 to the Director of the Health Department of the Municipality, Dr. Freddie Borras. Regular payments by the Municipality on the AIDS contract then resumed. The $10,000 monthly payments were raised by cashing Health Services checks issued to persons who had performed no services. Several of these checks were signed by Garib and Dubon. Dubon's law firm was also involved in cashing a series of these Health Services checks at Dubon's direction, with at least one of the checks being issued to Dubon's son, who had performed no services.

Toward the end of 1990 Dubon told Corcino, "I am not going to sign for that [expletive] any longer." He did not, however, object to the continued diversion of the funds.

Viewing this evidence in the light most favorable to the Government, as we must, we conclude that a rational jury could find beyond a reasonable doubt that Dubon and Garib were participants in a conspiracy to use Health Services funds to pay personal expenses and make political payoffs as charged in the indictment. The evidence of informal alterations of the board minutes as a means to funnel funds to Kouri, of the apparent use of a forged signature to divert Health Services' funds to pay for Garib's personal housekeeper, of the use of a Health Services' employee to do work almost exclusively for Garib's private practice, and of the clandestine efforts to turn Health Services checks into cash are all evidence from which a jury could find that defendants "without valid authority" embezzled, stole, or obtained by fraud money or property.

. . . We conclude the district court did not err in its instructions to the jury. The district court instructed that theft involved taking property without authority and that embezzlement involved taking property under one's control belonging to another. Its further instructions that there was a crime if the money or property stolen "was owned by or was under the care, custody, or control of [Health Services]," was proper. . . . The instructions taken as a whole fairly and adequately informed the jury of the applicable law. . . .

The district court . . . tracked the statutory language in instructing the jury. . . . The relevant statutory language states: "The circumstance [that must exist for there to be a federal crime] is that the organization . . . receives, in any one year period, benefits in excess of $10,000 under a Federal program involving a grant, contract, subsidy, loan, guarantee, insurance, or other form of Federal assistance." . . . Accordingly, we affirm.

BUSINESS CONSIDERATIONS What can a business or non-profit organization do to avoid becoming the victim of embezzlement?

ETHICAL CONSIDERATIONS What are the ethics of the conspirators? Why? What are the ethics of the elected officials who received goods and money?

Credit Card and Check Legislation

Today customers make extensive use of credit cards, *debit cards* (cards that transfer funds from a customer's bank account to the merchant's bank account), and checks. This creates a number of difficulties, particularly for mail

order, e-commerce, and other businesses. For instance, criminals may steal an individual's credit card, debit card, or the card number and use it to make substantial purchases. Card numbers may be obtained by (1) accessing home or business computer files, (2) obtaining carbon copies of credit slips, or (3) using small machines that

E-COMMERCE SECURITY

Mai, Carlos, and Helen have been considering creating a Web site to sell StuffTrakR directly to consumers. However, they are concerned about possible security breaches on their Web site, where hackers may "steal" customer information such as credit card numbers, names, addresses, and so forth. How can NRW best protect itself and its customers from such dangers? Should it go forward with its plan? The entrepreneurs have asked you for advice. What will you tell them? Why?

BUSINESS CONSIDERATIONS How can a business provide security at its Web site? Is security important? Why?

ETHICAL CONSIDERATIONS Is there a moral difference between theft of customer information by NRW employees and theft of this same information by others? Why?

INTERNATIONAL CONSIDERATIONS Does the situation change if the thief is in a foreign country? If so, how does it change?

quickly swipe a card and retain the information. Dishonest employees can obtain this information and then sell it to other criminals. Some states have enacted *separate* legislation making it a crime to misuse someone else's credit or debit card without permission. Other states treat this as a type of forgery. Businesses can establish procedures to reduce the likelihood of being victimized by criminals with fraudulent account numbers.

Criminals may steal the checks of an individual or business and forge the signature on the checks. A different type of problem arises when the owner of a bank account writes checks when there are insufficient funds in the account. Most states have enacted statutes that make it a crime to write or transfer (make, draw, or deliver) a check when there are insufficient funds in the account. These are commonly called *bad check statutes*. Some states require the *mens rea* that the suspect acted knowingly or with fraudulent intent.

Identity Theft

Identity theft occurs when a thief steals personal information, such as the name, address, Social Security number, and/or name of a person, and then uses this information to access the victim's credit. The thief can obtain the personal information on the Internet, through public records, stealing from the victim's mailbox,[3] or going through the victim's trash. *Hackers* (outsiders who gain unauthorized access to computers or computer networks) may gain access to personal information through an individual's personal computer, an employer's computer systems, a business's client records, or a credit card company's records. One hacker stole 80,000 credit card numbers.[4] In some cases, the thief may actually work for a credit card company or credit card department of a retailer. In some state or federal prisons, cheap inmate labor is utilized for various enterprises. In one case, the state was using inmates to process credit card applications and some of the inmates were stealing personal information from the applications.

Once the thief has obtained the information, he or she may apply for credit using the victim's name or may access the victim's accounts, such as bank accounts, retirement accounts, or Social Security accounts. For advice on how to prevent identity theft and what to do if you are a victim, see the federal government central Web site on identity theft at http://www.consumer.gov/idtheft/. The state of Nebraska offers a brochure on identity theft at its Web site at http://www.ago.state.ne.us/consumer_protection/.

Criminal Fraud

Fraud is a broad term that covers many specific situations. The English courts were very reluctant to criminalize fraudulent behavior, preferring to allow tort law to handle most situations. Over the years, however, legislation was passed in both England and the United States to overcome the historic view that "[we] are not to indict one for making a fool of another."[5] Today, most states have statutes that cover variations of what is generally called *criminal fraud, false pretense,* or *theft by deception*. Most states require proof of the following elements to convict a person of criminal fraud:

• the speaker (or writer) made a false statement of fact;

• the statement was material, that is, the statement would affect the listener's decision;

• the listener relied on the statement; and

• the speaker intended to mislead the listener.

Note that the fraudulent party can be either the buyer or the seller. For example, suppose that a savings and loan creates the impression through the distribution of false appraisals that certain real estate assets are worth $100,000 in order to induce a person to invest in those assets. In fact, the assets are worth substantially less than the false appraisals show. The savings and loan and its officers could be found guilty of criminal fraud if an investor enters a partnership with the savings and loan involving the purchase, development, or other investment in those assets.

Larceny

Larceny is the wrongful taking and carrying away of the personal property of another without the owner's consent and with the intent to permanently deprive the owner of the property. The most common forms of larceny are shoplifting and picking pockets. The use of force is not needed. Larceny is a serious problem for retail businesses because merchandise is often lost through shoplifting. In addition, if customers feel unsafe because pickpockets operate in an area they will avoid certain stores and shopping centers.

Robbery

Robbery is a form of aggravated theft. It is basically larceny *plus* the threat to use violence or force. In order to be a robbery, the robber must use either violence or the threat of injury sufficient to place the victim in fear, and the robber must then take and carry away something either in the possession or in the immediate presence of the victim. If the same property had been carried away without the use of violence or a threat of injury, the act would be a mere theft.

Espionage

Stealing trade secrets is called economic spying or *espionage*. In 1996, the federal government enacted the Economic Espionage Act, which also assists in prosecuting hackers.[6] The act makes espionage a federal offense punishable by 25 years in prison or a $25,000 fine for an individual. It also provides for fines of up to $10 million for companies found guilty of such conduct.[7] The "victim," however, must have taken reasonable safety precautions to protect its trade secrets.[8] FBI director Louis Freeh told a Senate panel that 23 countries are engaged in economic spying against U.S. businesses.[9]

Computer Crime

"The only secure computer is one that's turned off, locked in a safe, and buried 20 feet down in a secret location—and I'm not completely confident of that one either," said Bruce Schneier, author of a book entitled *E-mail Security*.[10] The legal aspects of computers will be discussed in detail in Chapter 43. Advances in computer technology have led to the development of new activities, some positive and some negative. Some of these negative behaviors are now recognized as crimes. Companies like The Gap, Hitachi America, PeopleSoft, Playboy Enterprises, and Twentieth Century Fox each attract from 1 to 30 hacker attempts per day.[11]

With our increased dependence on computers, computer criminals can create extensive damage. According to a recent article on computer safety, "The going estimates for financial losses from computer crime reach as high as $10 billion a year. But the truth is that nobody really knows. Almost all attacks go undetected—as many as 95% says the FBI."[12] In addition to civil liability for improper use, many states now recognize the following activities as computer crimes:

1. *Unauthorized use of computers or computer-related equipment.* This may include the use of business computers for personal projects, including homework and personal e-mail. It also includes transferring software purchased by a business to a personal computer.

2. *Destruction of a computer or its records.* Computer viruses destroy or alter records, data, and programs. Annually there are numerous virus alerts—some are fakes and some are legitimate. Businesses expend significant resources to protect themselves from viruses and to correct the damage they cause. This includes a virus that "infects" the computers in a college computer lab and subsequently infects students' disks and home computers.

3. *Alteration of legitimate records.* This would include altering a student's grade record in the registrar's office.

4. *Accessing computer records to transfer funds, stocks, or other property.* This would include entering a bank's computer system and transferring funds without authorization. For example, in 1994 Citibank discovered that Russian hackers made $10 million in illegal transfers. Initially the bank called in a private security firm. When Citibank finally spoke to the FBI and the media, it lost some of its top customers. Competitors lured them away by promising customers that the competitors' computer systems were more secure than those of Citibank.[13]

Congress enacted the federal Counterfeit Access Device and Computer Fraud and Abuse Act of 1984 to strengthen state attempts to deal with computer crime. The act criminalized the unauthorized, knowing use or access of computers in the following ways:

1. To obtain classified military or foreign policy information with the intent to injure the United States or to benefit a foreign country. This would include accessing classified Pentagon files. This constitutes a felony under the act.

2. To collect financial or credit information, which is protected under federal privacy law. This would include accessing credit card accounts to obtain credit card numbers and credit limits.

3. To use, modify, destroy, or disclose computer data and to prevent authorized individuals from using the data. This would include intentionally transferring a virus to a computer.

4. To alter or modify data in financial computers that causes a loss of $1,000 or more. (This would include the previously mentioned unlawful transfer of funds from Citibank.)

5. To modify data that impairs an individual's medical treatment.

6. To transfer computer data, including passwords, that could assist individuals in gaining unauthorized access that either affects interstate commerce or allows access to a government computer. This would include the use of a "sniffer" program, which can hide in a computer network and record passwords, and then transferring this information to others.

The first category constitutes a felony and the remaining five categories constitute misdemeanors.

Computer users may engage in some of these new crimes. In addition, computer technology has enabled some individuals to commit more traditional crimes, but with a new, "high-tech" twist due to the use of a computer. For example, one individual is being investigated for a number of computer-linked activities—computer fraud, computer "stalking" under the computer nickname "Vito," harassing and threatening computer users online, transporting a minor for sexual purposes, and sexual molestation.[14]

Corporate Liability for Crimes

Originally, courts held that a corporation was not answerable for crimes because the corporation was not authorized to commit crimes and, therefore, lacked the power to commit them. However, there is a growing trend in many states to hold corporations criminally responsible when their officers and agents commit criminal actions in the execution of their duties. This trend is evidenced by court decisions and statutory law and the Model Penal Code.[15] Corporate directors, officers, and employees are also *personally* liable for crimes they commit while acting for the corporation. The California Corporate Criminal Liability Act enlarged the criminal liability of corporate managers.[16]

Corporate liability is more common when the corporation is accused of violating a statute that is *mala prohibita*

NRW CASE 8.3   Management

NRW

SHOULD NRW USE "OUT-OF-OFFICE" MESSAGES?

Helen read in an article that people who post "out-of-office" messages on their e-mail accounts experience an increase in computer hacking and theft. Helen is about to fly to Detroit to represent NRW at a trade show for a week. She was planning to use an "out-of-office" greeting to let people know that her response would be delayed. Now she is not certain what she should do. She asks you for advice. What advice do you give her?

BUSINESS CONSIDERATIONS Should NRW institute a general policy regarding the use of "out-of-office" messages? Why? Is there a concern about receiving flight itineraries via e-mail and sharing them with co-workers and family members? Why?

ETHICAL CONSIDERATIONS What ethical issues should NRW consider in establishing a policy? What is the ethical perspective of computer hackers? Why?

INTERNATIONAL CONSIDERATIONS Are there any international considerations because e-mail messages easily cross national boundaries? What if a computer hacker from Australia obtains access to Helen's computer?

(wrong because it is prohibited). However, when the criminal act is one requiring a specific mental state, such as battery with intent to kill, the courts generally refuse to hold the corporation liable unless the corporation itself participated in the acts or a high-ranking official participated in the acts with the intent to benefit the corporation.

Corporate liability is sometimes limited to *white-collar crime*. Although this term does not have a precise meaning, it generally means crimes committed in a commercial context by professionals and managers. When liability is imposed against the corporation, punishment is usually in the form of a fine. Often, the officers and agents are tried separately and convicted for their behavior.

There is an active debate over whether, as a matter of policy, corporations *should* be held criminally liable. The following arguments are generally advanced in support of corporate criminal liability:

1. Financial sanctions against the corporation will reduce dividends for the shareholders. The shareholders will then take a more active role to (1) ensure that the corporation will behave legally, (2) express

concern to management when acts or policies appear to be unethical or illegal, and (3) elect directors who will carefully monitor corporate behavior.

2. The shareholders are the ones who benefit when the corporation commits crimes. They receive higher dividends when the crime increases revenue or lowers the cost of doing business. If the corporation is not assessed a fine, the shareholders benefit from the criminal activity. For example, past violation of criminal statutes controlling the disposal of hazardous wastes may have benefited the company and the stockholders by reducing expenses and increasing profits.

3. There are a large number of potential individual suspects in a corporation. Governments lack the resources to build cases against specific individuals; it is less expensive and time consuming to build a case against the corporation as a whole.

4. Many corporate decisions are committee decisions or are decisions that are approved at a number of managerial levels. The responsibility for making decisions and implementing them is often divided between individuals or divisions. In these cases, it is difficult to identify the culpable individuals, so the entire corporation should be held responsible for the decision.

5. When individual wrongdoers can be identified, it is unfair to single them out for punishment. Their actions are probably consistent with the general pattern of conduct throughout the corporation.

6. Corporations are not really harmed by the loss of an individual manager. The manager can take the blame and act as a scapegoat; and the corporation can continue to thrive. The corporation benefits from the illegal act and does not suffer the costs of the crime. The public may forgive the corporation for the crime if an individual wrongdoer is identified and punished.

7. When the sanction is based on a crime of omission (that is, failure to act), the failure often occurs because the duty to perform was not clearly delegated to any specific person or office. If no specific person is held liable and the corporation is not held liable, there is no incentive to comply with the law.

8. When the government takes action against the corporation, the public then identifies the crime with the corporation. Disclosure of full information about businesses is essential in market-oriented societies. Consumers can then make informed decisions about which firms they want to transact business with. For example, Archer Daniels Midland's (ADM's) alleged price-fixing may cause some potential consumers to choose not to do business with ADM.[17]

Some of these arguments are quite compelling. However, there are also some arguments for the other perspective, and some of these are equally compelling. Those opposed to corporate criminal liability advance the following arguments:

• Imposing fines against corporations is a waste of time and effort because the fines are not substantial and do not act as a deterrent. The firm will respond by increasing prices and passing the costs on to consumers. In reality, consumers would be punished and not the corporation.

• Fines themselves are paid from profits and, therefore, reduce shareholders' dividends. It is unjust to pass the costs on to the shareholders because they lack the power to control corporate decision making in most corporations.

• Commonly, criminal prosecutions of corporations are not well publicized. Consequently, they do not harm the corporation's public image. Corporations will use their public relations expertise to overcome any negative publicity.

RICO: Racketeer Influenced and Corrupt Organizations Act

The RICO statute[18] became law in 1970 as part of the Organized Crime Control Act. According to the law's legislative history, it was the intent of Congress to remedy a serious problem: the infiltration of criminals into legitimate businesses, as both a "cover" for their criminal activity and as a means of "laundering" profits derived from their crimes. RICO makes it a federal crime to obtain or maintain an interest in, use income from, or conduct or participate in the affairs of an enterprise through a pattern of racketeering activity. The federal courts interpret the provisions of RICO. The LII, maintained by the Cornell Law School, provides a hypertext and searchable version of 18 U.S.C. § 1961, popularly known as the Racketeer Influenced and Corrupt Organizations (RICO) Act at http://www.law.cornell.edu/uscode/18/1961.html.

Government prosecutors and plaintiffs' attorneys recognized the opportunity to use the statute against commercial enterprises. Plaintiffs' attorneys are involved because the statute permits individuals, whose business or property is injured by a violation of the statute, to file a civil action. Successful plaintiffs in a civil action may recover treble damages, attorney's fees, and reasonable court costs. For example, beneficiaries of group health insurance policies used RICO to sue the insurance company.[19] This is an example of the overlap between criminal and civil law systems. A prior conviction in a criminal suit is not required in order to file a civil RICO suit. Some observers contend that this is leading to unfounded lawsuits and out-of-court settlements by intimidated firms. The government can also file civil RICO actions. When the federal government proceeds with a civil suit, the burden of proof is reduced. High civil penalties can provide a lucrative law enforcement technique.

Since 1970, Congress has amended the law and the courts have interpreted a number of its sections. The definitions of terms used in the statute are found in § 18 U.S.C. 1961. Section 1962 lists the activities that are prohibited. Persons employed or associated with any enterprise are prohibited from engaging in a pattern of racketeering activity. A *pattern* constitutes committing at least two racketeering acts in a 10-year period. These racketeering acts are called *predicate acts* under RICO. Racketeering activity has been broadly defined and includes most criminal actions, such as bribery, antitrust violations, securities violations, fraud, acts of violence, and providing illegal goods or services. Michael Milken was convicted under RICO of scheming to manipulate stock prices and of defrauding customers. Racketeering acts also include acts relating to the Currency and Foreign Transactions Reporting Act previously mentioned. RICO violations are added to other criminal charges when there is a pattern of corrupt behavior, such as bribery. Defendants may raise issues of double jeopardy when they are tried for both the predicate acts and the RICO violation. Courts generally determine that the prohibition against double jeopardy is not violated because the predicate acts and the RICO offenses are separate and distinct crimes.[20]

Criminal and civil penalties are described in U.S.C. § 18 1963, and §§ 1965–1968 cover procedural rules. Individuals convicted of criminal RICO violations can be fined up to $25,000 per violation, imprisoned for up to 20 years, or both. RICO also provides for the criminal forfeiture of any property, including business interests obtained through RICO violations. The property will be forfeited even if the property or business is itself legitimate. The defendant's assets can be temporarily seized before the trial begins to prevent further crimes. Some states have enacted their own state RICO laws.

Since the federal RICO law can be applied to legitimate business activities, it presents a potential concern for all business organizations, public and private. Recently, businesses have been lobbying for legislative amendments to limit the application of RICO.

Selected Defenses

The four classic defenses to criminal liability are duress, insanity, intoxication, and justification.

Duress

Duress exists when the accused is coerced into criminal conduct by threat or use of force that any person of reasonable firmness could not resist. Not all governments permit this defense; those that do vary with respect to the crimes to which it is applicable. Generally, the three essential elements of the defense are:

1. an immediate threat of death or serious bodily harm,

2. a well-grounded fear that the threat will be implemented, *and*

3. no reasonable opportunity to escape the threatened harm.

Insanity

Insanity exists when, as a result of a mental disease or defect, the accused either (1) did not know that what he or she was doing was wrong or (2) could not prevent himself or herself from doing what he or she knew to be wrong. The exact definition varies from state to state. This defense has been attacked for a variety of reasons, but chiefly because the definition is still ambiguous. Although it is raised often, the insanity defense is rejected in many of the cases in which this defense is raised.

Intoxication

Intoxication may be either voluntary or involuntary. Voluntary intoxication is not a defense unless it negates the specific intent required by a statute. For example, the crime of rape is said to require a general intent. Intoxication, therefore, would not be a valid defense. On the other hand, assault with the intent to commit rape is said to require specific intent. In that case, intoxication may be a valid defense. Generally, involuntary intoxication is a good defense. *Involuntary* intoxication, for instance, can occur if one is forced to drink an alcoholic beverage against one's will or without one's knowledge. An example of the latter would be if a host offered a guest a soft drink which the host had spiked with drugs without the guest's knowledge.

The defense of intoxication is summarized in Exhibit 8.3.

Justification

Justification exists when a person believes an act is necessary in order to avoid harm to himself or herself or to another person. The key to this defense is that whatever the person does to avoid harm must be less than the harm to be avoided. For example, sometimes property has to be destroyed to prevent the spread of fire or disease. A

EXHIBIT 8.3 Intoxication as a Defense

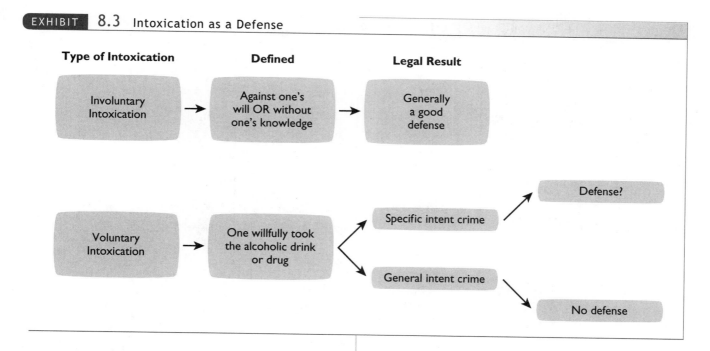

rancher's cows may be destroyed to prevent the spread of mad cow disease. A pharmacist may dispense a drug without a prescription if to do so would save a person's life.

The Law of Criminal Procedure

Criminal procedure is the area of law that addresses the judicial process in a criminal case. It is concerned with ensuring criminal justice without unduly infringing on individual rights. The drafters of the U.S. Constitution were determined to avoid the excesses and abuses that had occurred under English rule. As a result, the area of criminal procedure was very important. There was a desire to protect the rights of the individual to the greatest extent possible without making law enforcement impossible. The LII, maintained by the Cornell Law School, provides an overview of criminal procedure and links to resources at http://www.law.cornell.edu/topics/criminal_procedure.html.

The Constitution contains numerous criminal procedure provisions and protections, among them the guarantees of *due process* (the proper exercise of judicial authority as established by general concepts of law and morality) and *equal protection* (the assurance that any person before the court will be treated the same as every other person before the court). The defendant must be informed of the charges against him or her, must be tried before an impartial tribunal, must be permitted to confront witnesses against him

or her, and cannot be compelled to testify against himself or herself. The defendant is entitled to a speedy trial, may not be held subject to excessive *bail* (the posting of money or property for the release of a criminal defendant while ensuring his or her presence in the court at future hearings), and may not be subjected to cruel and unusual punishment if convicted. No citizen may be subjected to unreasonable searches and seizures; U.S. courts have determined that the only evidence that may be admitted at trial is evidence properly obtained. Exhibit 8.4 depicts the stages of criminal procedure. Note that a criminal trial is similar to a civil trial in many respects. The stages of a civil trial are discussed in Chapter 6. Many of the motions discussed in Chapter 6 can also be used in criminal trials.

The law presumes that the defendant is innocent until he or she is proven guilty. The burden of proof that must be satisfied in a criminal trial is the heaviest such burden in U.S. jurisprudence: The government must convince the jury of the defendant's guilt beyond a reasonable doubt, or the defendant must be acquitted.

Legal disputes may arise between a suspect and the police who search the suspect's business, home, car, or person. Under the Fourth Amendment to the Constitution, people are protected from unreasonable searches and seizures. When is a search and possible seizure reasonable, and therefore legal? A search will be valid if any *one* of the following occurs:

• It is properly conducted under a legal search warrant based on probable cause.

EXHIBIT   8.4   The Common Stages of Criminal Procedure[a]

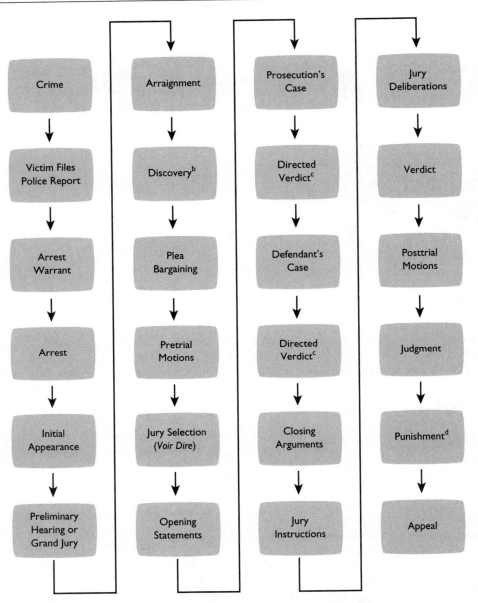

a. The exact order may vary.
b. Discovery is more limited in criminal cases than in civil cases.
c. Directed verdicts are not generally used *against* a criminal defendant.
d. A criminal defendant may be imprisoned beginning at the time of the arrest, if the court determines that bail is not appropriate or if the defendant cannot raise the amount of bail.

- It is conducted without a warrant by officers acting with probable cause. In some situations, courts use a "lower" standard than probable cause. Most common examples of the reduced standards are when an officer "pats down" a suspect because the officer is concerned that the suspect has a concealed weapon, or the evidence is in a motor vehicle that could be driven away.

- It is conducted with the permission of the owner of the property or a person with proper possession of the property, such as a tenant who rents an apartment.

- An emergency or exigent circumstance, such as a fire in the building, requires police to enter onto the premises.

Once police are legally on the property, they may observe and act on any criminal behavior they see.

Sometimes a business is subjected to a search. An example would be if the Occupational Safety and Health Administration (OSHA) wants to search a business for safety violations. On the other hand, sometimes the business wants to search an employee's locker, desk, or computer. The law in this area is very sophisticated and depends in part on (1) who is actually doing the search, (2) the employee's expectation of privacy in the area, and (3) the basis for the employer's suspicion. Numerous Web sites address this issue, which promises to become increasingly important as technological advances enhancing surveillance are developed. One such site is maintained by the Illinois Municipal League, which provides assistance to municipal governments. It published "Investigating and Enforcing Alleged Violations of an Acceptable Use Policy for Internet Access—Workplace Searches," by Roger Huebner and Jerry Zarley. The article deals with public employer searches of employees' computers, particularly for violation of the employer's acceptable use policy (an *acceptable use policy* specifies how employees may use computers), and can be found at http://www.iml.org/legalsection/legal_q&a/2000/11nov.htm. HRhero.com is a Web site for human resource professionals sponsored by M. Lee Smith Publishers, LLC. It published "Employees Beware: Big Brother Is Watching," by Shannon P. Garbette, about monitoring and searching employee computers at http://www.hrhero.com/topics/electronic/watching.shtml.

In England, police who conduct illegal searches are punished by the police force for violating the rules. In the United States, we generally use a different approach. Evidence obtained through an illegal search may not be used in court; this is called *suppression of evidence*.

In the following case, the Fourth Circuit court of appeals reviewed the search of a government employee's computer and office. This is a legal area that is developing rapidly. Be aware that there is a split of authority among the jurisdictions on some of these issues.

A police officer acting with probable cause may arrest and accuse an individual of committing a crime, or the arrest may occur under a warrant issued by a judge. A police officer who has probable cause to believe that a crime has been committed, or is being committed, may take the suspect into custody without obtaining a warrant. If an arrest warrant is used, it must be issued by a judge and be based on probable cause. The judge's finding of probable cause may be based solely on a sworn, written statement that names the person to be arrested or adequately describes him or her.

Once arrested and charged with criminal conduct, the accused should be given a preliminary hearing. Preliminary hearings are not required in most jurisdictions if there has been a grand jury hearing (discussed next). At the preliminary hearing, a magistrate determines whether there is probable cause to proceed to a trial. The charges against the accused will be dropped if the magistrate decides that there is no probable cause, or that there is not enough evidence to proceed to trial, or that there is virtually no chance to obtain a conviction. Then the accused will be released from custody.

A grand jury may also be involved in the pretrial stages of criminal proceedings. A *grand jury* is a jury panel charged with hearing complaints of possible criminal conduct and determining whether there is reason to believe that a crime has been committed and by whom. After hearing the evidence presented by the prosecutor, the grand jury will issue a *bill of indictment* if it believes that a person has committed a crime and a trial should be held. The government will then proceed to trial on the basis of this indictment, and a preliminary hearing is not required.

Once the grand jury has issued an indictment or the magistrate at a preliminary hearing has determined that probable cause exists, the accused is *arraigned* (called before a court to enter a plea on an indictment or criminal complaint). At the arraignment, the accused is informed of the charges against him or her, and, if necessary, the court appoints an attorney to represent the defendant.

A common pretrial motion at this point is a motion for *change of venue*. In criminal cases, change of venue is requested if pretrial publicity was negative to the defendant. The defense counsel argues that the trial location should be moved to ensure the defendant a fair trial.

The defendant enters a plea to the charges. If the plea that is entered is guilty or *nolo contendere* (no contest; a plea in a criminal proceeding that has the same effect as a plea of guilty but that cannot be used as evidence of guilt), the court moves to the sentencing stage. If the plea is not guilty, a trial date is set and it is determined if bail is appropriate.

UNITED STATES v. SIMONS
206 F.3d 392, 2000 U.S. App. LEXIS 2877 (4th Cir. 2000)

FACTS Mark L. Simons was employed as an electronic engineer at the Foreign Bureau of Information Services (FBIS), a division of the Central Intelligence Agency (CIA). FBIS provided Simons with a computer with Internet access and a private office. FBIS instituted a policy regarding Internet usage by employees. The policy stated that employees were to use the Internet for official government business only. Accessing unlawful material was specifically prohibited. The policy explained that FBIS would conduct electronic audits to ensure compliance and that "users shall . . . understand FBIS will periodically audit, inspect, and/or monitor the user's Internet access as deemed appropriate." FBIS contracted with Science Applications International Corporation (SAIC) to monitor the use of computer resources. Clifford Mauck, a manager at SAIC, was testing the system when he entered the keyword "sex" and found a large number of Internet "hits" originating from Simons's computer. It was obvious from the names of the sites that they were not visited for official purposes. Mauck reported this to Katherine Camer (of FBIS). From his own workstation, Robert Harper (of SAIC) examined Simons's computer and found over 1,000 picture files. Several of the pictures were pornographic in nature. It was discovered that some of the pornographic pictures were of minors. Harper physically entered Simons's office, removed the original hard drive, replaced it with a copy, and gave the original to the FBIS area security officer. A number of government employees worked together to prepare an application for a warrant to search Simons's office and computer. The affidavit attached to the warrant expressed a "need" to conduct the search in secret. The warrant was issued on August 6, 1998. It stated that the executing officers were to leave a copy of the warrant and a receipt for any property taken at Simons's office. The warrant mentioned neither permission for, nor prohibition of, secret execution. A team conducted the search during the evening of August 6, 1998, when Simons was not present. Neither a copy of the warrant nor a receipt for the property seized was left in the office or given to Simons. Simons was indicted on one count of knowingly receiving child pornography and one count of knowingly possessing child pornography. Simons moved to suppress the evidence.

ISSUES Was the warrantless search of Simons's office to retrieve the hard drive constitutional? Was the August search pursuant to the warrant constitutional?

HOLDINGS Yes, the warrantless office search was constitutional. Yes, the August search was also constitutional, however, the case was remanded for the district court to consider whether Federal Rule 41(d) was intentionally disregarded when the government failed to leave a copy of the warrant or a receipt for the property that was taken.

REASONING Excerpts from the opinion of Circuit Judge Wilkins:

[T]he record does not indicate which search or searches yielded the four computer picture files used against Simons at trial. Consequently, we . . . [must] review the constitutionality of all of the searches. . . . The Fourth Amendment prohibits "unreasonable searches and seizures" by government agents, including government . . . supervisors. To establish a violation of his rights . . . , Simons must first prove that he had a legitimate expectation of privacy in the place searched or the item seized. . . . Government employees may have a legitimate expectation of privacy in their offices or in parts of their offices such as their desks or file cabinets. . . . However, office practices, procedures, or regulations may reduce legitimate privacy expectations. . . .

We first consider Simons' challenge to the warrantless searches of his computer and office by FBIS. We conclude that the remote searches of Simons' computer did not violate his Fourth Amendment rights because, in light of the Internet policy, Simons lacked a legitimate expectation of privacy in the files downloaded from the Internet. . . . Simons did not have a legitimate expectation of privacy with regard to the record or fruits of his Internet use in light of the FBIS Internet policy. The policy clearly stated that FBIS would "audit, inspect, and/or monitor" employees' use of the Internet, including all file transfers, all websites visited, and all e-mail messages, "as deemed appropriate." This policy placed employees on notice that they could not reasonably expect that their Internet activity would be private. . . . FBIS' actions in remotely searching and seizing the computer files . . . did not violate the Fourth Amendment.

. . . Harper's entry into Simons' office to retrieve the hard drive presents a distinct question. . . . The burden is on Simons to prove that he had a legitimate expectation of privacy in his office. . . . Simons has shown that he had an office that he did not share. . . . [T]here is no evidence in the record of any workplace practices, procedures, or regulations that . . . [would reduce his expectation of privacy.] We . . . conclude that, on this record, Simons possessed a legitimate expectation of privacy in his office. . . .

[W]e must determine whether FBIS' warrantless entry into Simons' office to retrieve the hard drive was reasonable. . . . A search conducted without a warrant . . . is "per se unreasonable" unless it falls within one of the "specifically established and well-delineated exceptions" to the warrant requirement. One exception to the warrant requirement arises when the requirement is rendered impracticable by a "special needs, beyond the normal need for law enforcement." . . . [T]he . . . Court held that when a government employer conducts a search pursuant to an investigation of work-related misconduct, the Fourth Amendment will be satisfied if the search is reasonable in its inception and its scope. A search normally will be reasonable at its inception "when there are reasonable grounds for suspecting that the search will turn up evidence that the employee is guilty of work-related misconduct." "The search will be permissible in its scope when 'the measures adopted are reasonably related to the objectives of the search and not excessively intrusive in light of . . . the nature of the misconduct.'"

The question thus becomes . . . whether the search was carried out for the purpose of obtaining "evidence of suspected work-related employee misfeasance." . . . [Based on FBIS's handling of the hard drive,] we will assume that the dominant purposes of the warrantless search of Simons' office was to acquire evidence of criminal activity, which had been committed at FBIS using FBIS equipment. . . . Simons' violation of FBIS' Internet policy happened also to be a violation of criminal law; this does not mean that FBIS lost the capacity and interests of an employer. . . . We have little trouble concluding that the warrantless entry of Simons' office was reasonable under the Fourth Amendment standard. . . . At the inception of the search FBIS had "reasonable grounds for suspecting" that the hard drive would yield evidence of misconduct because FBIS was already aware

that Simons had misused his Internet access to download over a thousand pornographic images, some of which involved minors. The search was also permissible in scope. The measure adopted, entering Simons' office, was reasonably related to the objective of the search, retrieval of the hard drive. And, the search was not excessively intrusive. Indeed, there has been no suggestion that Harper searched Simons' desk or any other items in the office. . . .

In the final analysis, this case involves an employee's supervisor entering the employee's government office and retrieving a piece of government equipment in which the employee had absolutely no expectation of privacy—equipment that the employer knew contained evidence of crimes committed by the employee in the employee's office. . . . We consider that FBIS' intrusion into Simons' office to retrieve the hard drive is one in which a reasonable employer might engage. . . .

Simons argues that the August search violated the Fourth Amendment and Federal Rule of Criminal Procedure 41(d) because the search team executing the warrant left neither a copy of the warrant nor a receipt for the property taken. . . . There are two categories of Rule 41 violations: those involving constitutional violations, and all others. . . . [W]e conclude that the failure of the team . . . to leave either a copy of the warrant or a receipt for the items taken did not render the search unreasonable under the Fourth Amendment. The Fourth Amendment does not mention notice, and the Supreme Court has stated that the Constitution does not categorically proscribe covert entries. . . . [W]e perceive no basis for concluding that the 45-day delay in notice rendered the search unconstitutional. . . .[21]

BUSINESS CONSIDERATIONS How would this situation be different if Simons worked for a private employer? Should a private employer adopt an Internet use policy? Why? What should it say?

ETHICAL CONSIDERATIONS Was Simons's use of his work computer ethical? Why? Were his employer's secret searches of the computer ethical? Why?

At the trial, the government has the burden of proving its case beyond a reasonable doubt, and it must satisfy this burden within the established rules of evidence. Any violation of the rules of evidence will result in the exclusion of the improper evidence, which often effectively destroys the government's case. When this happens, the defendant will be acquitted.

In criminal cases, we still use 12 jurors plus alternates. An alternate replaces a regular juror who is not able to continue on the jury. A jury may be *sequestered*; that is, the jurors are not permitted to return home during the evenings and weekends. The jurors are kept separate from the rest of society, so that others will not influence their views. Jurors are generally not sequestered in civil cases. For example, in the O. J. Simpson civil trial, Judge Fujisaki rejected the plaintiffs' request that the jury be sequestered, stating that "there was no precedent for sequestering jurors at public expense in a civil trial. . . ."[22]

If the jurors are deadlocked and are unable to reach a decision, it is called a *hung jury*. In 1994 Erik and Lyle Menendez were tried for the murder of their parents. The Menendez brothers admitted to the killing but defended themselves based on self-defense. In the first trial, "twin" juries were used since some of the evidence was only admissable against Erik and other evidence was only admissable against Lyle. The juries that heard the case were unable to reach a verdict, and the Los Angeles County district attorney had the Menendez brothers retried and obtained convictions against both brothers. This does not violate the prohibition against double jeopardy.

If the defendant is found guilty, the court moves to the sentencing stage. Sentencing is governed by legislative guidelines to some extent, but the guidelines are normally very broad and somewhat vague. A great deal of judicial discretion is usually involved in sentencing. Under current federal law, federal judges have much less discretion in sentencing for federal crimes than most state court judges. Federal judges rely heavily on the federal sentencing guidelines.

Summary

Criminal law is designed to protect persons and property from harm. In addition, it is designed to deter criminal behavior. Of course, the best protection is the absence of criminal activity; however, some criminal activity will always exist. Many believe that the law should punish criminals for their wrongful acts and/or try to rehabilitate them while they are incarcerated.

Criminal responsibility is based on two essential elements—a physical act and a mental state. The physical act must be overt. The mental state actually consists of one of the following: purpose, knowledge, recklessness, negligence, or strict liability. A similarity to civil law exists, but the interests protected are different: Civil law protects private interests, whereas criminal law protects public interests. Accordingly, one can be held liable twice for the same act, once in civil law and once in criminal law. This is not double jeopardy because there are two distinct bases of liability.

Most crimes can be classified as misdemeanors, felonies, or treason. Misdemeanors constitute the least serious crimes; felonies are more serious. Treason, the most serious, involves acts to overthrow the government or provide aid or information to another government.

The selected crimes discussed in the chapter are murder/manslaughter, arson, burglary, embezzlement, forgery, credit card and check crimes, identity theft, fraud, larceny, robbery, espionage, computer crimes, and violations of the Currency and Foreign Transactions Reporting Act and the RICO statute. Courts may hold a corporation liable for crimes committed on its behalf. A public policy debate is occurring over the appropriateness of this trend. The criminal defenses mentioned are duress, insanity, intoxication, and justification.

The law of criminal procedure is very technical. An individual suspected of committing a crime can be arrested only upon probable cause. Probable cause is initially determined either by the arresting officer or by a judge issuing an arrest warrant. Once arrested, the accused is generally entitled to a preliminary hearing, which requires a finding that there is sufficient evidence to proceed to a trial. Grand jury hearings can also be used. The grand jury may issue an indictment if it believes the accused has committed a crime.

During a criminal trial, the government must prove its case beyond a reasonable doubt, and it must abide by numerous constitutional guarantees, such as due process and equal protection. Only after a conviction can an accused person be sentenced to a fine or imprisonment. However, temporary criminal forfeiture is permitted for certain crimes. In addition, a criminal defendant can be imprisoned pending trial because the magistrate determines that bail is not appropriate or the defendant is not able to post bail.

Discussion Questions

1. A man coated a carousel at Watkins Park in Indianapolis with skin-dissolving chemicals. Eleven children and one adult were sent to the hospital with irritated skin on their faces, hands, and legs.[23] Has the man committed any crimes? If so, which ones?

2. Nazik's business is losing money. She decides to burn down her place of business, collect the proceeds of her insurance, and start over again. The building burns down, but a homeless person sleeping in the building at the time is burned to death. What is Nazik's criminal liability? Is she liable for arson, homicide, criminal fraud? Why?

3. The Model Penal Code is a proposed criminal code that many states have used to revise and modernize their criminal laws. It consolidates larceny, embezzlement, false pretenses,

extortion, blackmail, fraudulent conversion, receiving stolen property, and all other similar offenses into the one general offense of theft. What advantages and/or disadvantages can you find to this approach?

4. Helen went on her business trip to Detroit. Since she returned, she has noticed a couple of strange charges on her credit card. She suspects that she is a victim of identity theft. What should she do? What can you do to try to prevent identity theft?

5. What crimes are associated with increasing computer usage? What steps can a company take to protect itself from falling victim to these crimes?

6. Crimes are either *mala in se* (morally wrong) or *mala prohibita* (wrong because the law says they are wrong). To which category do each of these belong: arson, cultivation of marijuana, income tax evasion, and the activities covered under the RICO? Why?

7. Some states have enacted "Son of Sam" laws, which prevent criminal defendants from receiving financial gain by publishing books about their crimes. These laws are not applicable to attorneys, the victims, or the victims' families. Are these laws just? Why or why not? Should these laws be applied to defendants who wish to use profits from books for their legal defense? Why or why not?

8. A Justice Department study of 12 cities found that the rate of dissatisfaction with police among blacks is more than twice that among whites. For example, in Chicago, Illinois, 11 percent of the whites and 31 percent of the blacks were dissatisfied with the police.[24] What might explain the difference in satisfaction?

9. Every day people die in police chases. Based on federal studies, about 40 percent of police chases end in crashes.[25] Oftentimes people are injured or killed: It may be the suspect who is running from the police; it can also be the officer or bystanders. How can the legal system balance the need to keep the peace and apprehend suspects with the need for public safety?

10. Mai has a large barn on her property. This barn has been vacant for quite some time, and Mai thinks that, with minor renovations, it would make an excellent warehouse from which to distribute NRW products. Helen points out that the property is not zoned for commercial activities, and that such use might be criminal without the proper zoning. Carlos argues that it cannot be criminal because NRW cannot *intend* to commit a crime (since businesses are inanimate creatures, they cannot have *any* intent), and criminal intent is an essential element in any criminal conviction. Can NRW transform the barn into a distribution center? Why or why not?

Case Problems and Writing Assignments

1. The Michigan state treasurer has filed a lawsuit against Jack Kevorkian, the advocate of assisted suicide. In March 1999, Kevorkian was convicted of second degree murder in the death of Thomas Youk, who had Lou Gehrig's disease. Kevorkian was 71 years old at the time. He was sentenced to 10 to 25 years in prison. The state treasurer wants to charge Kevorkian for the cost of keeping him in prison. The treasurer is asking the court to freeze all of Kevorkian's assets and to appoint the prison warden at the Oaks Correctional Facility as a receiver to control Kevorkian's funds. Does this constitute cruel and unusual punishment? Why? [See "In brief, Kevorkian Sued by State," *The Fresno Bee*, July 11, 1999, p. A4.]

2. Michael Lasch has been arrested and charged with theft by deception, criminal attempt, unlawful use of a computer, criminal trespass, and impersonating an employee. Lasch is a plumber in the Philadelphia area and he called Bell Atlantic and ordered an "ultra call-forwarding" service for telephones of at least five of his competitors. (*Call-forwarding* can be used to transfer phone calls from one phone number to another and is activated by entering code numbers from any phone.) Through this technique, Lasch was able to intercept calls placed to his competitors. Moreover, Lasch knew most of the plumbers whose calls he intercepted.

One competitor, Lucas Ltd., claimed that Lasch took only the better customers and told others that he would not take their service calls. Lucas says he is getting phone calls from angry customers who were not served. The scheme was discovered when a customer called Lucas to compliment him on work that was done over the Christmas holiday. Lucas told her that his plumbers had not been to her home during the holidays. Did Lasch commit a crime? Which one or ones? What could Lasch's competitors have done to protect their telephone calls and customers? Can you suggest any business practices that would have helped the plumbers discover the scheme more quickly? What steps could Bell Atlantic have taken to prevent this from occurring or to discover it more quickly? [See Dinah Wisenberg Brin, "Plumber Flushes His Competitors by Using Call-Forwarding," *The Fresno Bee*, January 29, 1995, p. A10.]

3. *Fortune* magazine published an article about security on company computers. They hired WheelGroup Corp., a computer security firm, to "break into" the computer system of a *Fortune* 500 company. The company agreed to have its security tested as long as its identity was kept secret. A computer expert from Coopers & Lybrand was hired to protect the company, its data, and systems during the experiment. In a companion article, *Fortune* published the steps used by WheelGroup to gain access to the computer system, including the names and functions of software commonly used by hackers to gain access. There are also periodicals, such as *Phrack* and *2600: The Hacker Quarterly*, which specialize in hacker information. Is it

ethical to publish detailed information about how to break into others' computers? Why or why not? [See "How We Invaded a *Fortune* 500 Company," *Fortune* (February 3, 1997): 58–61; and Richard Behar, "Who's Reading Your E-mail?" *Fortune* (February 3, 1997): 57–70.]

4. The attorney general of the United States approved "Operation Gunsmoke," a special national fugitive apprehension program. One of the dangerous fugitives identified as a target of "Operation Gunsmoke" was Dominic Wilson, the son of Charles and Geraldine Wilson. Dominic Wilson had violated his probation on previous felony charges. The police computer listed his address as 909 North StoneStreet Avenue in Rockville, Maryland. Unknown to the police, this was actually the home of Dominic Wilson's parents. The Circuit Court for Montgomery County issued three arrest warrants for Dominic Wilson. The warrants made no mention of media presence or assistance. In the early morning hours of April 16, 1992, a Gunsmoke team of deputy marshals and police officers assembled to execute the Dominic Wilson warrants. A reporter and a photographer from the *Washington Post* accompanied the team. They had been invited by the marshals to accompany them on their mission as part of a Marshal's Service ride-along policy. At around 6:45 A.M., the officers, with media representatives in tow, entered the dwelling at 909 North StoneStreet Avenue in the Lincoln Park neighborhood of Rockville. Charles and Geraldine Wilson were still in bed when they heard the officers enter the home. Charles Wilson, dressed only in a pair of briefs, ran into the living room to investigate. Discovering at least five men in street clothes with guns in his living room, he angrily demanded that they state their business, and repeatedly cursed the officers. Believing him to be an angry Dominic Wilson, the officers quickly subdued him on the floor. Geraldine Wilson next entered the living room wearing only a nightgown. She observed her husband being restrained by the officers. When the officers learned that Dominic Wilson was not in the house, they departed. The *Washington Post* photographer took numerous pictures. The print reporter was also apparently in the living room observing the confrontation between the police and Charles Wilson. At no time were the reporters involved in the execution of the arrest warrant. The *Washington Post* never published its photographs of the incident. The Wilsons sued the law enforcement officials in their personal capacities for money damages. They contended that the officers' actions in bringing members of the media violated their Fourth Amendment rights. Recognizing a split among the Circuits on this issue, the U.S. Supreme Court granted certiorari. When police officers invite the media into a private home to observe the execution of a search warrant, do the officers violate the Fourth Amendment? [See *Wilson v. Layne*, 119 S. Ct. 1692, 1999 U.S. LEXIS 3633 (1999).]

5. BUSINESS APPLICATION CASE Rick Wells complained to the Reno Police Department that Hallman Chevrolet; its owner, John Stanko; and employees appropriated his $600 factory rebate, due on a new car purchase, by forging his signature on a rebate assignment form. Wells recounted his dealings with Hallman Chevrolet to police in a written statement. Wells underwent a polygraph examination at the Reno Police Department and the examiner concluded that Wells was speaking truthfully. The county handwriting analyst determined that the signature in question "exhibits the characteristics of a 'simulated forgery.'" Police forwarded their report to the Washoe County District Attorney's Office. District attorney investigators confronted owner Stanko. Stanko stated that Wells had authorized the dealership to reproduce his signature. In support of his claim, Stanko voluntarily produced two power of attorney forms purportedly signed by Wells and a list of rebates (Rebate Recap Sheet) credited to the dealership. The D.A. investigators submitted the power of attorney forms to the county handwriting analyst, who concluded that there was "no basis for identifying Wells as the writer." Investigators discovered that the forms, even if signed by Wells, did not authorize the dealership to reproduce his signature on other documents. Investigators returned to the dealership to question Stanko, whereupon he angrily refused to cooperate.

D.A. investigators began to contact other customers listed on the Rebate Recap Sheet, including Daniel and Donna Pease. The dealership received a $500 rebate from Chevrolet for the Peases' transaction, but the Peases apparently did not receive credit for the rebate. D.A. investigators decided to seek a search warrant because they believed they had probable cause to suspect Hallman Chevrolet of criminal conduct. D.A. investigators executed the warrant and seized 151 transaction files. One current and two former Hallman Chevrolet employees voluntarily came forward to confirm dealership policies encouraging salesmen to engage in fraudulent and unfair business practices. They stated that it was dealership policy not to tell customers about rebates and to get them unknowingly to assign their rebates to the dealership. Former employee William Dallman stated that he had observed salesmen forging names on rebate assignment documents and that it was common practice to add the cost of an extended warranty to the purchase price without informing the customer. Another former employee, Bobby Atkerson, stated that he once overheard three salesmen discussing the forgery of a customer's signature. When the discussion ended, Atkerson entered the room and observed a piece of paper with 16 versions of customer Rick Wells's signature.

Assistant District Attorney Donald Coppa impaneled a Washoe County grand jury on July 8, 1992. Before presenting the evidence, A.D.A. Coppa told the grand jury that they were investigating the "business practices" of Hallman Chevrolet and its employees. The grand jury returned an 81-count indictment, the largest in the history of the county, charging 17 Hallman Chevrolet employees with 409 felony offenses. Just before trial the deputy district attorney dismissed most of the charges due to an alleged procedural error in the indictments. Nevada judge Whitehead dismissed the remaining charges against Hallman *with prejudice* (a dismissal of a lawsuit that prevents the party from initiating the same lawsuit again) based on what he found to be egregious prosecutorial misconduct. The Washoe prosecutors appealed the decision to the Nevada Supreme Court, but the newly elected D.A. dismissed that appeal before it was heard. Hallman Chevrolet filed this civil rights action. Are the D.A.s liable for violating Hallman's rights in establishing probable cause, seeking search warrants, and convening the grand jury? [See *Herb Hallman Chevrolet, Inc. v. Nash-Holmes*, 169 F.3d 636, 1999 U.S. App. LEXIS 3332 (9th Cir. 1999).]

6. **ETHICAL APPLICATION CASE** Jan Ronne Damant called federal agents and told them the location of Cary Stayner, a murder suspect. (Stayner has subsequently been convicted of four murders.) Shortly after Damant's call, the FBI agents arrested him. Agents praise the way Damant handed Stayner to them. Damant saw a picture of the suspect on a television alert for Joie Armstrong's murder and recognized him as the man camping near her home. At the time, authorities had not connected the Armstrong murder to the Carole Sund, Juli Sund, and Silvina Pelosso murders. Stayner connected himself to the Sund and Pelosso murders after he was caught.

Francis and Carole Carrington, through a foundation they established, had offered $50,000 for the arrest and conviction of the person who kidnapped their daughter (Carole Sund), granddaughter (Juli Sund), and their friend (Silvina Pelosso) in Yosemite. The foundation spokesperson said that Damant did not provide information leading to the arrest and conviction of the person responsible for the Sund and Pelosso murders. Is the foundation legally liable to pay the reward? Why? Should the foundation pay the reward? Why? [See M. S. Enkoji, "Reward for Stayner Goes Unpaid, *The Fresno Bee*, December 11, 2002, p. B5.]

7. **CRITICAL THINKING CASE** José Ignacio Lopez de Arriortua (Lopez) was a high-level General Motors (GM) executive when Volkswagen AG of Germany (VW) hired him as president after a "public and bitter" bidding contest between GM and VW. (VW refers to VW of Germany only.) Much of the bidding war for Lopez's services was reported in newspapers like the *Wall Street Journal.* When Lopez eventually left GM for VW, he took other GM managers with him. Subsequently, GM documents were found in "possession" of these executives and in apartments frequented by them in Germany. GM contended that its proprietary information was taken, including designs for "Plant X," a new factory design that is supposed to improve flexibility.

GM accused Lopez and VW of conspiring to steal company secrets when Lopez left GM in 1993. The VW board tried unsuccessfully to extricate itself from this conflict. German prosecutors filed criminal charges of industrial spying against Lopez in December 1996. In addition, U.S. federal judge Nancy Edmonds in Detroit ruled that GM could proceed with a civil suit against Lopez and all of VW's top management.

Lopez resigned his position with VW on November 29, 1996. This occurred shortly after a federal judge decided that GM was permitted to file RICO charges against VW. Consequently, if GM won the lawsuit it would be eligible for treble damages.[26] Is it likely that VW violated RICO? Is it likely that Lopez and his colleagues who "relocated" to VW violated RICO? What critical evidence must be proven by GM?[27] [See Daniel Howes, "Ex-GM Exec Faces Bribery Investigation: Automaker Isn't Included in Justice Department Probe, Source Says," *Detroit News,* February 19, 1997, p. A1; Daniel Howes and David Shepardson, "U.S.: Lopez Probe 'Still Active': Justice Department Vows to Keep Working on Espionage Case Against Ex-GM Official," *Detroit News,* May 22, 1998, p. F1.]

8. **YOU BE THE JUDGE** Marjorie Knoller and her husband, Robert Noel, were keeping two huge presa canario dogs in their San Francisco apartment. When Knoller took the dogs out one day, the dogs savagely mauled and killed their neighbor, Diane Whipple, outside her apartment door as she returned home with groceries. After the death, Knoller and Noel were cavalier about the death and even blamed the victim. Knoller was convicted of second-degree murder and she and her husband were convicted of involuntary manslaughter and having a mischievous dog that killed someone. Judge James Warren overturned Knoller's conviction of second-degree murder but let the other convictions stand. Assume that Warren's decision has been appealed to *your* court. What would *you* rule and why? [See Kim Curtis, "Judge Throws Out Murder Conviction of Dog-Attack Defendant," Associated Press Wire (June 17, 2002).]

Notes

1. The Uniform Money Services Act (2000) has been adopted by Vermont. NCCUSL Web site, "A Few Facts about the Uniform Money Services Act (2000)" at http://www.nccusl.org/nccusl/uniformact_factsheets/uniformacts-fs-msa.asp (accessed 12/21/02) and "Summary Money Service Act (2000)" at http://www.nccusl.org/nccusl/uniformact_summaries/uniformacts-s-msa.asp (accessed 12/21/02).
2. U.S.C. § 666 et seq.
3. Theft of mail is a felony in the United States.
4. "FBI: Hacker Stole 80,000 Credit Cards," *CNN.com* (December 9, 2002), http://www.cnn.com/2002/TECH/internet/12/09/israel.hacker.ap/index.html (accessed 12/9/02).
5. *Regina v. Jones,* 91 Eng. Rep. 330 (1703).
6. "The Enemy Within: Christian Tyler Reports on How Cold War Spy Tactics Are Being Adapted to Big Business," *Financial Times (London)* April 12, 1997, p. 1.
7. Ibid.
8. Richard Behar, "Who's Reading Your E-mail?" *Fortune* (February 3, 1997): 57–70, at 59.
9. Ibid., 64.
10. Ibid., 58 and 59.
11. Ibid., 70.
12. Ibid., 59.
13. Ibid., 64.
14. Jerry Bier, "Computer Stalker Trial Is Delayed," *The Fresno Bee,* June 5, 1996, pp. B1 and B3.
15. Model Penal Code (1985) § 2.07.

16. California Penal Code § 387.

17. For information about the alleged price fixing, see Mark Whitacre as told to Ronald Henkoff, "My Life as a Corporate Mole for the FBI," *Fortune* (September 4, 1995): 52–62.

18. See 18 U.S.C. §§ 1961 et seq.

19. See *Humana, Inc. v. Forsyth,* 119 S. Ct. 710, 1999 U.S. Lexis 744 (1999).

20. See *U.S. v. Bellomo,* 1997 U.S.Dist. LEXIS 434 (S.D.N.Y. 1997).

21. This case was remanded to the district court, which heard the case at 107 F. Supp. 2d 703 (2000). Further litigation occurred at 246 F.3d 670 (2001), 2001 U.S. App. LEXIS 4091 (2001), and 534 U.S. 930 (2001). None of these decisions affect the issues presented in this case.

22. Linda Deutsch and Michael Fleeman, "Simpson Juror Replaced; Talks Start Anew," *The Fresno Bee,* February 1, 1997, pp. A1 and A11.

23. "Police Say Chemical Coated on Carousel; National Briefs/ Indiana," *The Boston Globe,* June 21, 1999, p. A11; Man Charged in Placing Chemical on Carousel," *The Arizona Republic,* June 21, 1999, p. A8.

24. "What's News—World-Wide" column, "Blacks' dissatisfaction with police is . . .", *Wall Street Journal,* June 4, 1999, p. A1.

25. Mike Madden, "It's Your Average Day in the U.S. and Someone Will Die in a Police Chase," *The Fresno Bee,* July 11, 1999, p. A7.

26. Daniel Howes, "Ex-GM Exec Faces Bribery Investigation: Automaker Isn't Included in Justice Department Probe, Source Says," *Detroit News,* February 19, 1997, p. A1; Daniel Howes and David Shepardson, "U.S.: Lopez Probe 'Still Active:' Justice Department Vows to Keep Working on Espionage Case Against Ex-GM Official," *Detroit News ,* May 22, 1998, p. F1.

27. On January 9, 1997, GM and VW voluntarily settled their legal differences, thus avoiding costly and highly publicized litigation. Both sides officially apologized. The agreement specified that GM would get $100 million in cash and VW promised to purchase $1 billion of GM parts over a seven-year period. German prosecutors have dropped the criminal charges. Brian Coleman, "Lopez Case Is Dropped in Germany," *Wall Street Journal,* July 28, 1998, p. A12.

Contracts

The law of contracts forms the foundation of business law. Virtually every aspect of business involves contracts, as does much of a person's everyday life. When you rent an apartment, you sign—or orally agree to—a contract known as a lease. When you take a job, you enter into a contract of employment. Any purchase of goods, services, or real estate involves some form of contract. Even marriage is a type of contract.

This part of the book will examine the traditional elements of contract law—the common law of contracts. Later parts will consider various special types of contracts, among them sales, negotiable instruments, and secured transactions (that is, credit arrangements, covered by Article 9 of the UCC, in which the creditor retains a security interest in certain assets of the debtor). Increasingly, you will be contracting online, so an understanding of the "rule of engagement" for e-commerce contracts is vital as well. Keep in mind, however, that all these specialized forms are merely variations on the basic form. Thus, to understand these specialized forms of contracts, you first need the thorough understanding of the common law of contracts presented here.

CHAPTER 9

Introduction to Contract Law and Contract Theory

AGENDA

NRW NRW will enter into a large number of contracts as the business develops. NRW will have contracts with suppliers, customers, and employees, with its insurer, and it may well have to enter into leases for rented space. Mai, Carlos, and Helen will need to know how contract formation occurs, what type of contract to enter, and what rights and liabilities they undertake as a result of contract formation. It is quite likely they will turn to you for assistance at many steps along the way. Be prepared! You never know when the firm or one of its members will seek your advice.

The Importance of Contract Law

Of all the aspects of law examined in this text, none is as significant or pervasive in our lives as the law of contracts. Virtually every personal or business activity involves contract law: charging a birthday gift on a credit card, buying and insuring a car, leasing an apartment, writing a check, paying for college, and working at an establishment covered by an employment agreement are some examples. Even filling up our gasoline tanks involves contract law. Not only are we making a contract with the gasoline retailer, but the gasoline companies themselves receive much of their oil as a result of international contracts.

Increasingly, our contracting involves electronic commerce (e-commerce) in which one enters contracts online. These commercial activities will generate revenues in the trillions of dollars in the very near future. Such contracts typically take three different forms: business-to-business, or so-called B2B transactions; business-to-consumer, or B2C transactions; and consumer-to-consumer, or C2C transactions. B2B transactions ordinarily involve manufacturers and suppliers. B2C exchanges typically consist of the sale of goods and services through Web sites such as Amazon.com or the provision of computer services and information through subscription-based services such as America Online (AOL). Consumer-to-consumer (C2C) markets, of which eBay is the most widely recognized example, represent yet another business model for e-commerce. B2B markets oftentimes rely on electronic interchanges (EDI) or systems of interrelated computers used for ordering inventory, invoicing, record keeping, payments, and financing that have few human aspects. In short, this business model may totally bypass the human actors we ordinarily associate with the contracting process. B2C markets, with which most of us are more familiar, may involve such activities as buying CDs, books, clothes, and airplane tickets or reserving hotel rooms or rental cars. They may likewise involve activities in which the parties are not face to face and may indeed be unaware of the geographical location of the other party. C2C exchanges may employ the long-standing auction format, but the bidders can neither see the actual goods nor gauge the body language of their fellow participants—factors that most persons who attend auctions would deem very important.

All of these markets pose issues that traditional contract law did not consider. For centuries, the contracting parties either were face to face during negotiations or communicated signed documents by letter or telegraph. In con-trast, the anonymity of on-line contracting, the virtually instantaneous transmissions that characterize such dealings, and the resultant paperless contracts bring up such concerns as whether electronic communications suffice as offers and acceptances, the validity of electronic signatures, and the like. In short, the Internet, as a far-reaching cultural phenomenon that is reshaping society, involves significant policy questions that center on the Internet's impact on existing institutions, including the law. The emergence of wholly new business models (for example, MP3 technologies) or centuries-old forms of business (for example, auctions) now cast in a new garb (think eBay) highlight the need for strategies that will facilitate the further development of these on-line transactions while ensuring confidence among the domestic and international players in this important area. The last decade has witnessed a great deal of scholarly debate about whether we need to scrap the existing laws as they relate to contracts in favor of wholly new legal models for cyberspace-based commercial activities. But most experts agree that traditional principles of contract can adequately address most of the issues generated by on-line activities. On the other hand, legal bodies in the United States and international entities such as the United Nations continue to promulgate rules that address the special challenges to traditional contract law that the on-line business environment represents. Hence, acquiring an understanding of the broad outlines of these new "rules of engagement" is an important dimension of business education in the 21st century.

Simply put, the law of contracts affects our most mundane activities, as well as some rather sensational ones such as surrogacy contracts (whereby women contract to have babies for infertile couples) and privately forged settlements of international business disputes that courts otherwise would have decided. The law of contracts, especially since the advent of the Internet, also brings up the possible application of various U.S. statutes and international rules, as well as proposed enactments targeted particularly at e-commerce. Though increasingly applied to the electronic commerce setting, contract law still relies largely on settled common law rules. Hence, this chapter will emphasize the broad categories of common law contracts and contractual situations.

Commercial Law Contracts

When most of us think of the word "contract," we envision the mercantile world. Historically, our system of free enterprise has stressed the importance of freedom of contract and a corresponding protection of contractual rights. This was not always so, however. Blackstone's *Commen-*

taries on the Laws of England, first published in 1756, devoted 380 pages to real property law but only 28 pages to contracts. Thus, the law of contracts apparently constituted a subdivision of the law of property rather than the independent branch of law that we know today.[1]

Part of the reason for the 18th century's de-emphasis of contract law stems from the historical roots of this substantive part of the law. Although always broadly a part of the common law, mercantile traditions grew out of the law merchant, which represented the accumulation of commercial customs from as early as Phoenician times. The mercantile courts were separate from courts of law, and the merchants (or guilds) administered their own rules and customs. Hence, the evolution of commercial law remained outside the mainstream of legal development until fairly late in English history, the end of the 17th century. In the late 1800s, after the assimilation of the law merchant into the common law, several acts of Parliament addressed commercial law subjects.

Influenced by these English precedents, various legal bodies in the United States penned a wide variety of statutes, such as the Uniform Negotiable Instruments Law and the Uniform Sales Act, covering American commercial law. By the 1930s, several such model acts existed. But the effectiveness of these acts was limited: Commercial remedies differed from state to state, and the acts quickly became outmoded and thus not reflective of modern commercial practices. For these reasons, and especially to effect an integration of inconsistent statutes, the American Law Institute (ALI) and the National Conference of Commissioners on Uniform State Laws (NCCUSL) in the 1940s began working on what we call today the Uniform Commercial Code.[2]

By viewing commercial transactions as a single subject of the law, the UCC, as the Uniform Commercial Code is commonly known, revolutionized prior approaches to commercial transactions. The drafters saw, for example, that a sale of goods (movable, identifiable, items of personal property) may constitute one facet of such a transaction. They also realized that a buyer may use a check for payment of the purchase price of the goods or that the seller may retain a security interest in the goods (a claim against collateral-personal property or fixtures) to ensure payment of the balance of the debt. The Uniform Commercial Code articles on sales, negotiable instruments (checks, drafts, notes, and certificates of deposit), bank deposits and collections, and secured transactions (credit arrangements in which the vendor retains a security interest in certain assets of the debtor) correspond roughly to the scenarios described above. The UCC has fulfilled its original goals of simplifying, clarifying, and modernizing

the law governing commercial transactions; permitting the continued expansion of commercial practices through custom, usage, and agreement of the parties; and making uniform the law among the various jurisdictions.[3] Most states' commercial statutes, with minor variations, have reproduced the UCC articles in their entirety. Louisiana, while it has incorporated some of the articles of the UCC into its commercial laws, remains unique in that it has not wholly adopted the UCC. The Code appears in the back of the text as Appendix B. You can also access the UCC, including the Official comments, at http://www.law.cornell.edu/ucc/2/overview.html.

International law is also moving toward uniformity to some extent. For example, the United Nations Convention on Contracts for the International Sale of Goods (CISG) provides coverage for international sales of goods that is similar to the coverage provided by Article 2 of the UCC for the sale of goods within the United States. (The CISG is discussed in some detail in the Sales material, Chapters 16–19.)

In addition to the Uniform Commercial Code, the National Conference of Commissioners on Uniform State Laws (NCCUSL) has drafted other statutes for possible adoption by the states. Examples include the Uniform Partnership Act and the Uniform Consumer Credit Code. The most recent draft legislation by this body, the 1999 Uniform Computer Information Transactions Act (UCITA), sets out a comprehensive set of rules for contracts related to computer information. UCITA, in § 102 (10), defines computer information as "information in electronic form obtained from or through use of a computer, or that is in digital or equivalent form capable of being processed by a computer." Thus, the act covers contracts involving the licensing or purchasing of software, computer games, on-line access to databases, on-line books, and the like. Certain exemptions apply; furthermore, UCITA may govern only a part of a given transaction. Like the UCC, UCITA has various parts that cover all aspects of such mass licensing arrangements from the formation of contracts through remedies for breaches of contracts. Only two states—Maryland and Virginia—as of 2002 had enacted UCITA.

Another NCCUSL-proposed law is the Uniform Electronic Transactions Act (UETA). Though both proposed enactments deal with e-commerce, they do so in divergent ways. For example, UETA validates the use of electronic transactions in the business and governmental sectors (for example, electronic contracts, electronic signatures, and the use of electronic agents for electronic contracting) but does so while remaining neutral with regard to the media the parties choose to use. In short, UETA views paper and electronic media as equal—neither is better or worse for business transactions. Moreover, the act applies only to the procedural aspects of the parties' transactions (that is, the parties' use of electronic records and communications). Hence, whether the parties engage in paper or electronically based transactions, the same legal principles govern the parties' relationships. Put differently, UETA applies only to the procedural aspects of the parties' transactions; it does not displace the substantive rules of law that otherwise cover such issues as contract formation, the retention of records, the performance of obligations, and the parties' rights and liabilities. UCITA, in contrast, limits its coverage to contracts involving computer information but does impose rules on such contracts. Likewise, whereas UETA will not apply to the parties' transactions unless they explicitly agree to use electronic commerce in these dealings, UCITA applies to any agreement that falls within its scope. Although 38 states, as well as the District of Columbia, have adopted UETA by late 2002, many more may do so, given Congress's enactment of the Electronic Signatures in Global and National Commerce Act (known as the federal E-SIGN Act) in 2000. This federal law asserts that no contract, record, or signature may be denied legal effect solely because it is in electronic form. For contracting parties who have agreed to use electronic signatures, this statute thus makes electronic contracts and signatures as legally valid as hard copy, paper ones. The law exempts certain transactions, such as court papers, wills, and health insurance terminations; but experts predict that the E-SIGN Act will promote such Internet contracting activities as buying insurance or real estate online, obtaining mortgages online, and paying monthly bills electronically.

These laws have regularized commercial transactions so that transactions from state to state will remain more consistent. Such uniformity fosters predictability of result without necessarily sacrificing the law's capacity to change when commercial practices dictate such adjustments. Just as the UCC makes the uniformity of laws a foremost goal of domestic (that is, U.S.) law, so too are such uniformity and harmonization significant objectives in the global arena. To illustrate, several European Union (EU) directives may cover e-commerce transactions. Moreover, the United Nations Convention on Contracts for the International Sale of Goods (CISG) may apply to the sale of goods unless the parties agree to subject themselves to some other rule of law.

You should check whether your state has adopted these uniform acts and codes or whether instead it relies on its own statutes to cover these areas of the law. You can do so by accessing http://www.nccusl.org, the site of the National Conference of Commissioners on Uniform State Law. You also may find it beneficial to look at http://www.ucitaonline.com/, which will give you information about UCITA, as well as http://www.uetaonline.com/docs/pfry700.html/, which will acquaint you with UETA. To learn about the United Nations Convention on Contracts for the International Sale of Goods, go to http://www.uncitral.org/en-index.htm.

Common Law Contracts

The existence of statutes concerned with commercial contract law should not overshadow the importance of common law contracts. Many doctrines regarding modern-day contracts stem from "judge-made" law, court decisions growing out of contractual disputes from earlier times. Contract disputes decided on a daily basis in jurisdictions around the country significantly add to this body of precedents. The UCC states that common law supplements the UCC in those areas where the Code is silent. It is appropriate, then, that most of the discussion in Chapters 9–15 centers on common law contract principles—that is, principles derived from the judgments and decrees of courts.

Definition of a Contract

Many definitions exist for the word "contract." In general, a contract is a legally binding and legally enforceable promise, or set of promises, between two or more competent parties. Put another way, a contract is "a promise or set of promises for the breach of which the law gives a remedy, or the performance of which the law in some way recognizes as a duty."[4] Most of us intuitively understand what a contract is. Still, situations exist that at first glance may appear to be contracts but are not:

Assume that you are a Rolling Stones fan. The Stones are in the United States for a concert tour. You are extremely eager to attend a concert by these vintage rock and rollers. A friend promises you tickets to the show, and you of course are elated. Two days later, your friend calls to tell you he is taking an old flame instead of you. As you hang up, your anger and disappointment cause you to think about suing your friend. After all, you had an agreement; and he has broken a promise to you. You think you deserve to collect money damages for the harm you have suffered.

Does your agreement give rise to a legally enforceable contract? Will a court protect your expectations and award you damages? The short answer is probably no. Most courts will view this situation as a breached social obligation, not a breached contractual promise. You occasionally may read of people suing in small claims courts for the expenses incurred in making plans for dates that never occurred

NRW

NRW CASE 9.1 Sales/Management

WHAT TYPE OF LAW WILL GOVERN NRW'S CONTRACTS?

NRW will sell its products directly to a number of its initial customers, and the firm also will install many of the InvenTrakR systems so purchased. The sale of both products involves the sale of *goods* (that is, movable, identifiable items of personal property) and thus is governed by the Uniform Commercial Code. However, the installation of the InvenTrakR product is a *service* and as such is governed by common law principles. Helen wants to know whether the contracts the firm enters will be governed in part by one type of law (the UCC) and in part by another type of law (common law of contracts) or whether the court is more likely to determine that one aspect of the transaction "controls," so that the entire contract will be governed by this type of law. What will you tell her?

BUSINESS CONSIDERATIONS If a business provides both goods and services, should it price one higher than the other in order to imply which aspect of law—the UCC or common law—controls? Should the firm specify which aspect controls in the contract? Why?

ETHICAL CONSIDERATIONS The sale of goods carries certain *warranties* if the seller is a merchant. Is it unethical to try to designate the contract as being primarily for services in order to avoid giving these warranty protections to the customers?

INTERNATIONAL CONSIDERATIONS Would your answer differ under the UN Convention on Contracts for the International Sale of Goods?

---

because they were "stood up." If the plaintiffs win these "contract" actions (and sometimes they do), higher courts generally overturn these results on appeal because the more settled rule calls such situations broken social obligations, not breached contracts. Stated differently, you should be aware that a court will not deem all agreements "contracts."

Contrast the earlier situation involving the Rolling Stones with this scenario:

You call a ticket outlet, order two tickets for the Rolling Stones concert, and give your credit card number. When you arrive at the box office days before the concert to pick up your tickets, you learn the outlet has sold them to someone else.

Can you successfully sue this time? Perhaps you can, because this situation seems to involve more than a mere social obligation and to have created binding economic obligations on both sides. Thus, to protect your economic expectations, a court may call this a contract and award you damages (that is, the amount of money it will take to put you back in the position you would have enjoyed had the contract been performed). Hence, the part of the definition that alludes to a "legally enforceable" or "legally binding" agreement takes on significance because it means that not every promise, agreement, or expectation ripens into a contract. In essence, a contract is any agreement between two or more parties that a court will recognize as one that creates legally binding duties and obligations between the parties.

Elements of a Contract

Given the law's emphasis on promises or mutual assent, it is not surprising that the first requirement for a valid contract is an agreement. Basically, an agreement consists of an offer and an acceptance of that offer. The law looks at the agreement from the viewpoint of a reasonable person and asks whether such a person would believe that an offer and an acceptance, respectively, actually had occurred. Second, the parties must support their agreement with consideration, that is, something bargained for and given in exchange for a promise. Third, the parties must have capacity, or the legal ability to contract. Fourth, the contract must reflect the genuine assent of each party. If one party has procured the assent of the other person by fraud or duress, for example, courts may set the contract aside owing to the disadvantaged party's lack of genuine assent to the agreement. Fifth, the subject matter of the contract must be legal. The legality of the bargain is questionable, for instance, if the parties have agreed to do something that violates a statute or public policy. Sixth, in some cases, the law requires that a contract evince certain formalities. Despite the fact that courts ordinarily will enforce oral contracts (even though it is risky to make an oral contract because of the difficulties in trying to prove exactly what each party said), some categories of contracts must be in writing to be legally effective.

In summary, to be valid, a contract must be

- founded on an agreement (that is, an offer and an acceptance),

- supported by consideration,

- made by parties having the capacity to contract,

- based on these parties' genuine assent,

- grounded in a legal undertaking, and

- expressed in proper form, if applicable.

Each of these requirements is discussed in detail in Chapters 9–14. Exhibit 9.1 shows the elements of a contract.

From Status to Freedom of Contract and Back Again

The development of contract law occurred relatively late in English legal history. Why? In part, because of feudalism. Feudal society set social hierarchies that prevailed throughout Europe between the 11th and 13th centuries. In such a rigid, stratified society, each person occupied a specific social position. Social circumstances thus determined one's rights and the conduct expected of that person. For example, feudal lords owed few duties to lowly serfs; but serfs owed their lives to their lords.

Imagine the disruptive effect contract law, which calls for the performance of mutual duties and obligations, would have had on such a social order. It is not surprising, then, that property law assumed foremost importance during these times and that status was more important than contract rights. If a serf was the property of the lord, courts did not need to bother with protecting what the state considered the serf's rather trivial expectations. Accordingly, the development of contract law was unnecessary.

Yet, as England became a commercial center, the law merchant and contracts became more important than status. Furthermore, during the social and political reforms of the late 18th and 19th centuries, the rise of capitalism brought with it demands for freedom of contract. This political emphasis on the importance of the individual and of private property accelerated the growth of what we now call contract law. To a largely agrarian society dedicated to self-reliance and individualism, protection of expectations and enforcement of obligations took on added importance. The demise of a status-oriented society thus ushered in a contract-oriented social order.

Ironically, as an aftermath of the Industrial Revolution, the 20th century witnessed numerous restrictions on the 19th century's adoption of virtually unrestricted freedom of contract. Legislatures and courts have curtailed this freedom of contract and have reinstated—to a limited extent—a tilt back toward status. Labor laws, environmental protection statutes, and consumer enactments represent a few examples of how lawmakers lately have restricted freedom of contract. Similarly, through common law decisions, courts have protected individuals with little bargaining power even after these persons have consummated a contract, thus hampering the continued development of freedom of contract.

The doctrine of unconscionability, mentioned in Chapter 1 and explored in Chapters 11 and 12, provides a perfect example of this protection. Suppose two parties have bargained. If, in the court's opinion, one of them (usually a corporation or business entity) had grossly superior bargaining power, or leverage, over the other (especially a consumer), the court sometimes will set such a contract aside on the grounds of unconscionability—that is, because the contract is shockingly oppressive or grossly unfair to one of the parties. (Do not, however, make the mistake of believing you can rely on this remedy to get out of each and every contract for which you belatedly wish to avoid responsibility!) Such developments have convinced some commentators that this progression shows an interesting circularity: that is, a movement from status to freedom of contract and back to status again.

Classifications of Contracts

The law categorizes or distinguishes contracts in various ways. These categories are not always mutually exclusive, so several different terms may apply to the same contract. For example, suppose a restaurant orders produce and meat from its supplier at set prices, and the supplier promises to deliver on a predetermined schedule. The understanding between these parties invokes several categories of contracts simultaneously: In short, this agreement is an informal, bilateral, valid, express contract.

Formal versus Informal Contracts

The distinction between formal and informal contracts derives from the method used in creating the contract. In early common law times, the contracting parties generally engaged in certain formalities (hence, the term formal). To be valid, for example, a contract had to be under seal; that is, the document had to be closed with wax and imprinted with one's insignia, or distinctive mark. Very few contracts are under seal today because most jurisdictions have abolished the need for certain classes of private contracts or instruments to be under seal. This trend toward eliminating sealed, or formal, contracts demonstrates that the need for ceremonies and formalities to ensure validity has largely passed.

Informal (or simple) contracts are a more common category of contracts today. In these, the emphasis is not on the form or mode of expression but instead on giving effect to the

EXHIBIT 9.1 The Elements of a Contract

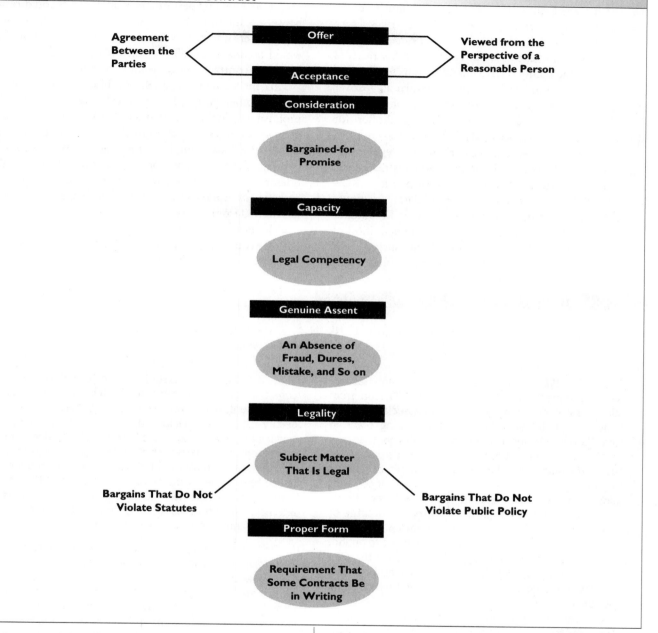

promises of the parties. Informal contracts do not require a seal. Such contracts may be either oral or written and, in fact, may even be implied from the conduct of the parties.

Unilateral versus Bilateral Contracts

Every contract has at least two contracting parties. The person who makes an offer (called the *offeror*) generally promises to do something or to pay a certain amount if the person to whom the offer has been made (called the *offeree*) will comply with the offeror's request. Usually, then, in return for this promise, the offeror demands a certain act or a certain promise of the offeree as acceptance. The form of the acceptance demanded determines whether the contract is a *unilateral* contract (a promise on one side only) or a *bilateral* contract (promises on both sides).

If the offeror promises to pay the offeree $50 for raking the offeror's yard, this contract is unilateral. Only one person, the offeror, has promised to do anything. The offeree accepts the offer by performing the requested act (that is, raking).

The case of *Kuhnhoffer v. Naperville Community School District 203*, 758 F. Supp. 468 (N.D. Ill. 1991), illustrates the nature of unilateral contracts. From 1979 to 1988, Larry Kuhnhoffer worked for the school district as a school bus driver. At the end of each school year, Kuhnhoffer received a letter from the school district thanking him for the previous year's work and inviting him to return as a driver in the fall. However, during the summer of 1988, the Naperville police department arrested Kuhnhoffer for driving under the influence of alcohol. This arrest resulted in the suspension of Kuhnhoffer's driving privileges for six months. When Dr. Michael Kiser, the school district's assistant superintendent, learned of this suspension, Kiser informed Kuhnhoffer that the district could not hire him as a school bus driver in the fall. Consequently, Kuhnhoffer sued for breach of contract. Because of the definition of unilateral contracts, Kuhnhoffer's suit did not succeed. The judge ruled that the school district's offer constituted a uni-lateral contract offer. Because an offer of a unilateral contract is accepted by performance, no contract could result between Kuhnhoffer and the school district until he commenced performance. Without a valid license, Kuhnhoffer would be unable to fully perform his end of the bargain; hence, no contract ever came into existence.

In contrast, if one party (the promisor) makes a promise and the other party (the promisee) accepts the offer by promising to do the requested act, a bilateral contract results because promises exist on both sides of the agreement. To use the previous example, assume the offeror promises to pay the offeree $50 if the offeree will promise to rake the offeror's yard. When the offeree accepts by so promising, an exchange of promises has occurred; and a bilateral contract has derived from the parties' bargaining.

The next case addresses these issues. See if you agree with the court's application of these concepts in *Wells Fargo Bank, N.A., v. United States.*

9.1

WELLS FARGO BANK, N.A. v. UNITED STATES,
88 F.3d 1012 (Fed. Cir. 1996)

FACTS In 1982, the borrower, American Gasohol Refiners (American) sought a $20,000,000 loan from Mid-Kansas Federal Savings and Loan Association (Mid-Kansas) to build an ethanol manufacturing plant in rural Kansas. Farmers use ethanol (an alcohol that may be blended with gasoline) as fuel. Ethanol's price fluctuates depending on changes in the prices of corn or the other grains from which it is made and of oil. Mid-Kansas and American applied to the Farmers Home Administration (the Administration) for a guarantee of 90 percent of this loan. Federal legislation authorizes the Administration to "make and insure loans to public, private, or cooperative organizations . . . for the purpose of improving, developing, or financing business, industry, and employment and improving the economic and environmental climate in rural communities. . . . Such loans, when originated, held, and serviced by other lenders, may be guaranteed by the Secretary [of Agriculture]. . . ." According to one Administration official, "the purpose of the lender program is to get banks to make loans that they ordinarily wouldn't make. They are high risk loans."

Upon receipt of a request for a loan guarantee, the Administration evaluates the application and determines whether it may guarantee the loan. If so, the Administration provides the lender and the applicant with a Conditional Commitment for Guarantee. This form advises the lender that the approval of any guar-antee it has submitted is subject to the completion of all conditions and requirements set forth in the Conditional Commitment, one of which conditions is that the lender certify "that it has no knowledge of any adverse change, financial or otherwise, in the borrower, his business, or any parent, subsidiaries, or affiliates since it requested a loan note guarantee." The Conditional Commitment issued to Mid-Kansas and American in October 1982 also stated that "when these conditions and requirements are met, Farmers Home Administration will issue a loan note guarantee in the amount of ninety percent."

In December 1982, Wells Fargo agreed to finance American's construction of the proposed ethanol plant. Subsequently, the Conditional Commitment to Mid-Kansas and American (which had changed its name to High Plains), and which would have expired in 1983, was extended. The ethanol plant was built and began production in 1984, but because Wells Fargo and High Plains determined that an additional $3.5 million was necessary to bring the plant to full production, Wells Fargo, High Plains, the Administration, and several other interested parties in September 1985 extended the Conditional Commitment through June 1986. This agreement also reaffirmed that upon the applicant's compliance with the conditions of the Commitment, the Administration would issue the guarantee for the benefit of Mid-Kansas or if Wells Fargo became the lead lender, for the benefit of Wells Fargo. A new

Conditional Commitment naming Wells Fargo as the lead lender was executed in October 1986. However, owing to its apprehensions about the economic viability of alcoholic production facilities, the Administration at this time issued a directive under which it identified 15 areas of deficiency with regard to Wells Fargo. Additional correspondence ensued, both between Wells Fargo and the Administration and within the Administration, some of which documents indicated the Administration's satisfaction with the bank's responses to each point and the Administration's intention to issue the guarantee. Based on these discussions, Wells Fargo agreed to provide an additional $5,000,000 in financing for the project.

Nonetheless, in December 1986, the Administration refused to execute a guarantee because of the Administration's belief that the low price of ethanol and the high cost of grain constituted an adverse change in High Plains's financial condition (that is, the company's inability to generate sufficient cash flow to meet its obligations as of October 1986, or in the foreseeable future). After the Administration denied an administrative appeal of the refusal to issue the guarantee, Wells Fargo filed a breach of contract suit against the Administration owing to the Administration's failure to honor its commitment to guarantee a construction loan that Wells Fargo had extended pursuant to the federal ethanol loan guaranty program.

ISSUE Was the Conditional Commitment a unilateral contract, under which the Administration's commitment to issue the guarantee became binding when the bank began performance by making the loan to American?

HOLDING Yes. The Conditional Commitment constituted a unilateral contract by which the government had agreed to guarantee the loan upon Wells Fargo's performance of the conditions specified, and Wells Fargo had accepted the contract through beginning performance (that is, by making the $20,000,000 loan to finance the construction of the ethanol plant).

REASONING Excerpts from the opinion of Judge Friedman:

Although Administration regulations characterize the Conditional Commitment as mere "advice" to the lender, . . . the document itself shows that the government is making a binding promise: . . . Conditional Commitments are signed by the Administration's state director, the lender, and the borrower. The document lists twenty-nine separate conditions that must be satisfied before the Administration issues the loan guarantee. These include such costly endeavors as obtaining insurance, establishing an escrow account, paving a road,

obtaining permits, and providing extensive documentation to the Administration. No lender and borrower would be willing to undertake such steps in reliance on mere "advice" rather than a firm promise. Moreover, in reliance on the Conditional Commitment, Wells Fargo risked the $20,000,000 it furnished to High Plains. That the government's promise to issue the loan guarantee was contingent upon High Plains and Wells Fargo's performance of numerous conditions does not make the promise any less binding. Indeed, the essence of a unilateral contract is that one party's promise is conditional upon the other party's performance of certain acts, and when the other party performs, the first party is bound. . . . The fact that Mid-Kansas was the named lender in the 1982 Conditional Commitment and that Wells Fargo was not substituted as the lead lender until 1986 does not affect the binding nature of the 1982 commitment. The Administration was aware from the outset that Wells Fargo would provide the $20,000,000 financing for the ethanol facility. Furthermore, the 1986 Conditional Commitment that explicitly made Wells Fargo the lead lender stated that "the Conditional Commitment for Guarantee . . . continue in effect. . . . Thus, the 1982 Conditional Commitment was fully applicable to Wells Fargo. The Administration nevertheless refused the guarantee for two reasons. . . . [N]either reason justified the Administration's refusal to issue the guarantee. High Plains's alleged financial problems resulting from low ethanol prices and high grain prices were the very kinds of economic risks that were inherent in the ethanol manufacturing business. It was those risks that underlay the loan guarantee program. Whatever financial difficulty High Plains may have had as a result of these price fluctuations, it was not an "adverse change . . . in the Borrower, [or] his business" within the meaning of the certification clause of the Conditional Commitment. That provision related to changes in High Plains's own internal financial condition, not to changes in the markets in which High Plains operated and did business. . . . We agree that "the evidence offered by the [Administration] . . . does not support a finding that an adverse change had taken place.

BUSINESS CONSIDERATIONS Is the government's guaranteeing high-risk loans an advisable public policy? Why or why not?

ETHICAL CONSIDERATIONS Did the Administration have an ethical obligation to refrain from "changing the rules of the game" four years into the parties' relationship? Or did ethics obligate the Administration to be very conservative with regard to guaranteeing high-risk loans, particularly since the taxpayers ultimately would bear the risk of High Plains's default on its loan?

Valid, Voidable, Void, and Unenforceable Contracts

A *valid* contract is one that is legally binding and enforceable. In contrast, a *voidable* contract is one that may be either affirmed or rejected at the option of one or more of the contracting parties. The agreement is nonetheless valid until it is rejected or disaffirmed. For example, if a person buys a car in the belief that it was driven only 50,000 miles when in actuality it was driven 250,000 miles, that contract may be voidable on the basis of fraud or misrepresentation. However, the contract remains valid and fully enforceable until the buyer disaffirms the agreement.

Void agreements, though they outwardly may appear to be contracts, can never have any legal effect. They are unenforceable and never become contracts because they lack one of the essential elements of a contract. An agreement to murder someone is void; a court will not enforce this agreement because it lacks the element of legality.

On the other hand, it is possible to have a seemingly binding contract that will not be given effect in a court of law. Suppose, for example, that the contract involved is one that must be in writing (such as a contract for a sale of goods priced at $500 or more); if this contract is oral, it will be *unenforceable*. Note that the contract otherwise appears to meet all the criteria of a valid contract.

Express versus Implied Contracts

An *express* contract is one in which the parties set forth their intentions specifically and definitely, either in writing or orally. Most contracts are of this type.

An *implied* contract is one that must be discerned or inferred from the actions or conduct of the parties. Even though the parties should have expressed their intentions more clearly, it still is possible to conclude that a true contract exists. These agreements are often called contracts implied in fact because, the circumstances indicate that, despite the absence of explicit language to this effect, the parties intended to create a contract.

Assume, for example, that two parties have had a well-known, years-long understanding that grain will be accepted when delivered. If one party takes grain to the elevator and the elevator refuses to accept it, the facts of the parties' prior, long-standing relationship and their previous conduct may allow a court to enforce this agreement as a contract implied in fact.

Practically speaking, many agreements have express provisions and also include terms that must be discerned from the actions of the parties. In short, a given contract may not fall neatly into one or the other of these categories, as *Janusaukas v. Fichman* illustrates.

NRW CASE 9.2   Personal Law

COLLECTING DAMAGES FROM A FRIEND

One of Carlos's friends recently purchased a car stereo and a set of speakers for his new car. As a favor for his friend, Carlos installed the stereo and the speakers. In order to complete the installation, Carlos had to purchase some installation hardware and had to cut larger openings in the dash and the rear deck. By the time Carlos had obtained the installation hardware, cut the holes, and installed the stereo system, he had spent about four hours working on his friend's car. Once the installation was complete, the friend complained that, because Carlos had taken too long to complete the job, the friend had missed an appointment. He also complained about the holes Carlos had cut, alleging that they were not needed and that they hurt the aesthetic look of the interior. Carlos was offended by this response to his "good deed" and decided that he should be compensated for his efforts. (He also would like an apology, but realizes that there *are* limits to his legal options.) He asks you whether he can recover for his time and expenses in either contract law or under quasi-contract. What will you tell him?

BUSINESS CONSIDERATIONS If a service business needs to modify or alter the customer's property in order to render the service, should the business obtain permission before making the modification or alteration, or should the business just complete the job? What legal issues might be raised by doing the alteration without prior permission?

ETHICAL CONSIDERATIONS Is it ethical for an employee to use his or her employer's tools and equipment to do favors for friends? What ethical issues arise when an employee does so?

INTERNATIONAL CONSIDERATIONS Are certain ethical values universal? If you answer this question yes, identify the values in question. If you answer this question no, why is it impossible to achieve consensus with regard to ethics?

Executory versus Executed Contracts

An *executory contract* is one in which some condition or promise remains unfulfilled by one or more of the parties. For instance, if a person agrees to buy a king-sized mattress

9.2

JANUSAUKAS v. FICHMAN
793 A.2D 1109 (CONN. APP. 2002)

FACTS In 1993, Albert Janusaukas, who was 50 years old, first consulted Richard A. Fichman, an ophthalmologist. Although Janusaukas's severe myopia had required him to wear glasses since grade school, he hoped that a new procedure, radial keratomy (RK), would correct his nearsightedness so that he no longer would have to wear corrective glasses or contact lenses. Each physician Janusaukas previously had consulted had said that his myopia was so great that he would not benefit from RK surgery. Nevertheless, in 1993, Janusaukas sought out Dr. Fichman because of his advertisements claiming that RK could cure nearsightedness. Janusaukas also had read a brochure stating that Dr. Fichman was one of the nation's leaders in the field of RK. During the initial consultation, Janusaukas mentioned that several other physicians had told him that he could not achieve his goal—the ability to see without the aid of glasses or contact lenses—through RK. However, Dr. Fichman asserted that new procedures allowed him to operate successfully on patients with myopia as severe as Janusaukas's. Dr. Fichman's own training, as well as the prevailing opinion in the medical community at that time, indicated that RK would offer no improvement in Janusaukas's eyesight. Nonetheless, Dr. Fichman told Janusaukas that the RK procedure would result in the attainment of 20/40 or 20/50 vision, uncorrected, in Janusaukas's left eye and 20/20 vision, uncorrected, in the right eye. Dr. Fichman moreover claimed he was "the best in the business." Dr. Fichman performed RK surgery on Janusaukas in May 1993. Following this surgery, Janusaukas's myopia worsened; his vision became subject to glare both day and night, and his near vision became blurred as well. Dr. Fichman performed several enhancement procedures between September 1993 and 1995. In early 1996, Janusaukas sought second and third opinions. Both ophthalmologists told him the chances of achieving his vision goal through the RK surgeries performed by Dr. Fichman were virtually nonexistent. Janusaukas later sued Dr. Fichman for breach of an implied contract, specifically, Dr. Fichman's warranties that RK would lead to an improvement in Janusaukas's vision.

ISSUE Had the parties entered into an implied contract to the effect that the RK surgery would improve Janusaukas's vision?

HOLDING Possibly. Because the plaintiff had introduced sufficient evidence for a jury to have found an implied contract, the trial court had erred in directing a verdict in favor of Dr. Fichman.

REASONING Excerpts from the opinion of Judge Mihalakos:

The plaintiff's first claim is that the court improperly directed a verdict for the defendant, Dr. Fichman, with regard to count four of the . . . complaint, which alleged a contract claim based on the breach of a promise, warranty or guaranty. . . . "A true implied contract can only exist where there is no express one. It is one which is inferred from the conduct of the parties though not expressed in words. . . . It is not fatal to a finding of an implied contract that there were no express manifestations of mutual assent if the parties, by their conduct, recognized the existence of contractual obligations. An "implied" contractual promise cannot be created by plucking phrases out of context; there must be a meeting of the minds between the parties. . . . In order to support contractual liability, the [defendant's] representations must be sufficiently definite to manifest a present intention on the part of the [defendant] to undertake immediate contractual obligations to the plaintiff." . . . There was no express contract between the defendant and the plaintiff. A contract can be inferred, however, from the conduct of the parties. The defendant's representations regarding the plaintiff's vision improvement through RK were definite enough to manifest his intention to immediately undertake to improve the plaintiff's vision through RK. The parties, further, through their actions, inferentially recognized the existence of their contractual obligations. The plaintiff paid the defendant, and the defendant performed the RK procedure on the plaintiff's eyes. The plaintiff then subjected himself to another procedure that the defendant performed to help achieve the result for which the parties originally had contracted. Because the plaintiff introduced at trial sufficient evidence so that the jury, reasonably and legally, could have found there was an implied contract, it was improper for the trial court to direct a verdict for the defendant. The court should have left the issue for the jury to decide.

BUSINESS CONSIDERATIONS How does a firm go about designing an advertising campaign for a new technology, product, or procedure? What factors should a firm keep foremost in mind?

ETHICAL CONSIDERATIONS Assess the ethics of both the plaintiff and the defendant. Can either one in these circumstances definitively lay claim to the moral high ground?

set from Honest John's, the contract is executory: The firm still must deliver the mattresses, and the buyer must pay for the set. If the buyer pays for the mattresses prior to delivery, the contract is also executory, although technically the buyer has executed his or her part of the contract.

An *executed contract* is one in which the parties have fully completed or performed all the conditions or promises set out in the agreement. In the last example, when Honest John's delivers the mattress set, the contract will be executed. Neither party has anything further to do.

Quasi Contracts versus Contracts Implied in Fact

One type of implied contract deserves special attention. This is a contract implied in law, or a *quasi contract*. Lawsuits alleging quasi contract as the basis for recovery also may be called suits for *unjust enrichment*. Under certain circumstances, the law will create a contract between the parties, despite their wishes and intentions, in order to prevent the unjust enrichment of one party. In these situations, even though it may be clear that the parties did not actually contract with each other, the law will treat the parties as if they had.

Like a contract implied in law, a contract implied in fact also is an implied contract. It differs from a contract implied in law in that sufficient facts or evidence of conduct exist for a court to find on equitable grounds that the parties actually meant to contract with each other. Perhaps the language should have been more explicit, but a court can conclude with some certainty that the parties intended to create a binding agreement. Thus, a contract implied in fact is a true contract. In contrast, a contract implied in law is a fiction engineered by a court so as to effect justice between two parties. Unlike a contract implied in fact, this is not a true contract, hence the name quasi contract.

To clarify further the difference between a contract implied in fact and a contract implied in law, consider this example:

Mattie is sitting on her front porch when a painting crew arrives. The painting crew has the wrong address (111 Riverside Drive instead of 1111 Riverside Drive). Mattie nevertheless allows the crew to paint her house and later tries to argue that since she had not asked for the services, she owes zero for them.

To prevent Mattie's unjust enrichment at the painters' expense, most courts will force Mattie to pay the painters, on a restitutionary basis (that is, an equitable basis by which the law restores an injured party to the position he or she would have enjoyed had a loss not occurred), for the

---

CONTRACTUAL CONSIDERATIONS

From your consultation, the firm's members realize that, in any potential contract, NRW must first ascertain whether common law or the Uniform Commercial Code governs the transaction. However, Carlos and Mai still have trouble making this distinction. What law—the UCC or common law—will govern NRW's contracts to buy, for instance, the metals and other alloys that it will use in manufacturing the NRW units? What law will govern NRW's contracts with trucking firms to deliver manufactured NRW units to distributors across the country? Why? If these contracts amount to $10,000 or more, should the contracts be in writing?

Also from your consultation, Carlos and Mai recognize that they must be aware of the requirements for contract formation under both the UCC and the common law. Again, however, both need your assistance. For example, if Mai's friend helps complete the design for the StuffTrakR, should NRW take care to spell out a formal pay arrangement in advance? Why?

Furthermore, because NRW's products involve intellectual property, should the firm have its employees sign restrictive covenants to refrain, for a specified time and in a specified geographic area, from competing with NRW? What law will govern this contract? Should this covenant also specify that employees may not divulge trade secrets and other proprietary, confidential information?

Carlos and Mai have asked for your advice on these matters. What will you tell them?

BUSINESS CONSIDERATIONS Why is it important for business practitioners to become well-versed in contract law? To ensure the general public's understanding of the rudiments of contract law, should high schools make business law a required course?

ETHICAL CONSIDERATIONS Does a family-owned business, or one owned by close friends, face more ethically related issues (for example, the division of responsibility and/or financial accountability) than a business that is not so structured?

INTERNATIONAL CONSIDERATIONS If international law governs the issues involved in Carlos and Mai's questions, would your advice differ?

benefit she has received (a newly painted house) or, put another way, for the detriment suffered by the painters (the cost of their supplies, services, and so on). Mattie will be liable in quasi contract or a contract implied in law only for the reasonable value of the services rendered; the painters cannot "gouge" her by charging, after the fact, an exorbitant price. A contract implied in fact does not exist here because of the lack of any facts suggesting that Mattie and the painting company had dealt with each other before the crew arrived at Mattie's house. Evidence of an intention to contract, however sloppy the execution of the contract, would have made this a true contract, or a contract implied in fact. Given the absence of any such evidence, the court instead creates a contract—a quasi contract or contract implied in law—to prevent Mattie's unjust enrichment.

Do not be misled into believing that every time one person receives a benefit, a quasi-contractual recovery will be possible. Remember that the policy underlying such recoveries is the avoidance of injustice. Mattie has to pay because she knowingly allowed the painters to proceed. Had she not been present, however, the painters probably would be unable to hold Mattie liable because they had conferred the services on her as a result of their negligence

or mistake; they had come to the wrong house. In these circumstances, it is not inequitable to allow Mattie to retain the benefits bestowed on her. By the same token, a person who confers a gift (for example, assume Mattie's brother contracts with a painting company to redo Mattie's dilapidated house as a surprise for her) or one who volunteers a service (a neighbor who decides to paint Mattie's house while Mattie is away for the weekend) will not be able to recover later from Mattie in quasi contract. The same result will apply to a person who buys supplies in a mistaken belief that a contract exists, or who incurs foreseeable difficulties and later tries to make the recipients of the services pay for these extra costs or services on a quasi-contractual basis. Still, remember that courts can, in a given circumstance, create a contract in order to avoid injustice.

Lawrence v. DiBiase addresses several of these issues. Analyze the court's opinion in light of these principles of contract law.

You can check your understanding of the elements of a contract by going to the 'Lectric Law Library's Laypeople's Law Lounge at http://www.lectlaw.com/lay.html/ (use the "contracts" link). Exhibit 9.2 shows the different classifications of contracts.

9.3

LAWRENCE v. DIBIASE
2001 Del. Super. LEXIS 368

FACTS Iran Lawrence specialized in "fiberart," with work on display in several local and regional corporate headquarters, as well as The White House. She held advanced degrees in both interior design and fiber and textile design. Although she had occasionally offered her services as an interior designer, prior to the project at issue in this case she had never been involved with either a major commercial project or the design of a tile floor. Augustine DiBiase, Jr. was one of the owners of DiBiase Brothers, a construction firm that developed both residential and commercial projects, as well as a partner in MSG, a firm created to develop the Main Street Galleria in Newark, Delaware. Serving as the project's general contractor, DiBiase Brothers began the construction of the Galleria in 1995 and completed it in the spring of 1996.

According to Lawrence, DiBiase's wife, Sandy, asked Lawrence to help DiBiase select the colors for a proposed tile floor at the Galleria. Lawrence contended that, during their initial meeting in February 1996, DiBiase asked her to prepare a new, more elaborate, tile design. In order to meet a compressed time

schedule set by DiBiase, Lawrence asserted that she worked about 16-18 hours per day on this task. Although no written contract covered Lawrence's services, she maintained that DiBiase always understood she expected to be paid. She contended that DiBiase, in rejecting her first fee of $50,000-$60,000, asked her to supply him with a more realistic price. On or about March 7, 1996, Lawrence accordingly submitted to DiBiase an invoice reflecting a "design fee" of $27,400. DiBiase refused to pay Lawrence because he and his wife allegedly had earlier informed Lawrence there was no budgetary line for payment to Lawrence. According to DiBiase, Lawrence, as a favor to his wife, agreed to assist him in the selection of the colors for the tiles in the star burst design he and his partners had already selected. He further maintained that Lawrence, after viewing the "star burst," had suggested to him that she could provide a more appealing design; and, with DiBiase's acquiescence, she agreed to do so. As compensation, DiBiase emphasized, Lawrence requested only that DiBiase agree to display prominently in the first floor common area of the Galleria a gold plaque recognizing Lawrence's work. DiBiase alleged that he first became aware that Lawrence expected payment for her services when, on March 7, 1996, she presented him with an invoice for services. By this time, according to DiBiase, most of the tile for the first floor had already been installed per Lawrence's design (with modifications as required by DiBiase to "simplify" the design). DiBiase refused to pay the $27,000 invoice amount; but as an accommodation to his wife's friend, DiBiase did offer to pay Lawrence $2,000, an amount that reflected 40 hours of work at $50 per hour. Lawrence refused to accept this amount; and, after further discussions failed to yield a satisfactory resolution for her, she filed this lawsuit. Lawrence claimed that DiBiase was obliged to pay her, pursuant to either a contract implied in fact or a quasi contract, the reasonable value of her services as recognized in the local interior design community.

ISSUE Could Lawrence recover damages under either a contract implied in fact or a quasi contract?

HOLDING Lawrence could not recover under a contract implied in fact but could receive compensation for her services under a quasi-contractual theory.

REASONING Excerpts from the opinion of Judge Slights:

Lawrence has argued that the court may imply the existence of a contract from the facts surrounding the parties' negotiations. An implied in fact contract is legally equivalent to an express contract; the only difference between the two is the proof by which the contract is established. . . . "An express agreement is arrived at by words, while an implied agreement is arrived at by acts." . . . The inquiry in both instances focuses on whether the parties have "indicated their assent to the contract." . . . In other words, to prevail on a theory of implied in fact contract, the plaintiff must establish that the parties, through their actions, "demonstrated a meeting of the minds on all essential terms of the contract," . . . including price. . . .

Lawrence . . . failed to prove the existence of an implied in fact contract by a preponderance of the evidence. Specifically, Lawrence has not established that she reached a meeting of the minds with DiBiase with respect to the price of her services. Indeed, the Court is not satisfied that Lawrence herself knew what she would charge for her services when she began the design work for DiBiase. Her description of the first conversation with DiBiase regarding fees reveals that she was thinking like an artist, not an interior designer working on a commercial project. When DiBiase summarily rejected this proposal, Lawrence worked backwards from this amount to formulate her subsequent fee proposals utilizing an arbitrary methodology more appropriate for artistic works than commercial design projects. Under

these circumstances, it can hardly be said that the parties mutually assented to Lawrence's fees. And, absent agreement with respect to this critical term, it cannot be said that the parties formed a valid implied in fact contract.

An implied in law contract, or quasi contract, does not depend upon the mutual assent of the parties. "Quasi-contractual relationships are imposed by law in order to work justice and without reference to the actual intention of the parties." . . . Quasi contracts correct unjust enrichment; they are designed to remedy "the unjust retention of a benefit to the loss of another, or the retention of money or property of another against the fundamental principles of justice or equity and good conscience." . . . To prove a quasi contract, Lawrence must establish: (1) that she performed her services with an expectation that she would be paid; (2) that the services were performed under circumstances which should have put DiBiase on notice that she expected to be paid; and (3) that DiBiase retained . . . the benefit of her services. . . .

The Court concludes that Lawrence has carried her burden of proof on each of the three elements. . . . Notwithstanding Lawrence's inapt negotiation style, the Court is able to discern her expectation that she would be paid for her services. . . . The exact form and amount of the compensation was not settled in her mind, as evidenced from her own testimony with respect to the evolving nature of her fee requirements. Nevertheless, based on the extensive preparations and elaborate final product produced by Lawrence, and the history of the relationship as contemporaneously recounted by her in her March 7, 1996, letter to DiBiase, the Court rejects the notion that she intended her work to be performed gratuitously. As stated, she expected some compensation for her services. Lawrence's expectations, while perhaps previously unclear, were unambiguously defined on March 5, 1996, when she presented her invoice to DiBiase. This event is significant to the Court's analysis of the *prima facia* elements of a quasi contract because the presentation of the invoice to DiBiase . . . clearly evidences all three elements of the claim. When the invoice was presented by Lawrence, she expressed her intention to be paid, and DiBiase's acknowledgment of receipt of the invoice evidences his appreciation of Lawrence's expectation for payment.

This exchange then placed DiBiase at a crossroads. The evidence reveals that the installation of the tile floor had not begun in earnest as of March 5. The evidence also reveals that had he chosen to reject Lawrence's fee proposal and return her design work, DiBiase could have exchanged the tiles he had purchased to install Lawrence's design, chosen an alternative design, including the "star burst" he initially was considering, and ordered and received the tiles needed for installation of the newly chosen design, all within a matter of weeks, if not sooner. . . . He did not do so. Instead, he purportedly rejected Lawrence's fee proposal out of hand, but then installed her design in the Galleria and thereby retained the value of her services without payment. Under these circumstances, the Court will impose a quasi contract upon the parties to remedy the unjust enrichment DiBiase has enjoyed since March of 1996. . . .

BUSINESS CONSIDERATIONS **The court noted that Lawrence could have avoided this dispute if she had "employed basic common-sense business precautions."**

Specifically, what should Lawrence have done? What factors should the court use to decide the appropriate measure of damages (that is, the fair value of the services rendered)?

ETHICAL CONSIDERATIONS **DiBiase indicated that he believed he was enlisting the assistance of his wife's friend to provide creative input with regard to the design of the tile floor. If one asks the advice of a professional in such circumstances, is it unethical to assume that one will not be obligated to pay for the expertise provided?**

EXHIBIT **9.2 Classification of Contracts**

Type of Contract	Definition	Example
Formal	One created by certain rituals, ceremonies, or formalities.	A contract that requires notarization, such as the transfer of an automobile title to another person.
Informal	One created through oral or written statements or through the parties' conduct; needs no special rituals.	An oral contract to buy a used compact disc player costing $400.
Unilateral	One created by a promise given in exchange for an act.	A contract in which the borrower agrees to pay back the $400 consumer loan obtained from a bank.
Bilateral	One created by a promise given in exchange for another promise.	A contract in which one person promises to sell her dental equipment and another promises to buy the equipment.
Valid	One that manifests all the essential elements of a contract.	A contract to buy a car from a dealership.
Voidable	One that manifests all the essential elements of a contract and is legally binding unless disaffirmed by one or more of the contracting parties.	A contract to sell a termite-ridden house when the seller has knowledge of the extensive termite damage.
Void	One that lacks the essential elements of a contract.	A contract in which a lender charges the borrower a usurious rate of interest on a loan.
Unenforceable	One that manifests the essential elements of a contract but will not be given effect by a court of law.	An oral contract to guarantee the payment of another person's debts if that person fails to pay.
Express	One created by the parties' setting out their intentions specifically and definitely.	A contract that lists the price, the terms of the sale, the delivery date, and other details regarding the purchase of a car.
Implied	One discerned or inferred from the actions or conduct of the parties.	A person walking into a hair salon and asking for a haircut without discussing price.

EXHIBIT 9.2 *continued*

Type of Contract	Definition	Example
Implied in fact	Despite the absence of explicit language, the parties intended to contract with each other; a true contract.	A contract in which a person has received medical care without discussing the terms. The person will be obligated to pay for the treatment.
Implied in law	Contract created by a court for the parties, despite their wishes and intentions, in order to avoid injustice and/or the unjust enrichment of one party.	A contract to provide landscaping around a home in a development. When the homeowner fails to pay, a court orders the owner of the development to pay the landscaper because of the enhanced value of the development.
Executory	One in which some promise or obligation remains unfulfilled.	A contract to sell a horse, saddle, and bridle. The seller forgets to bring the saddle on the date of delivery.
Executed	One in which all parties have completed their promises or obligations under the terms of the agreement.	A contract to buy a computer for $2,000 with delivery effected by the seller in exchange for the buyer's giving a certified check for $2,000 at the time of delivery.

Summary

The law of contracts affects us more often than any other area of law. Commercial law, especially the Uniform Commercial Code's integration of older statutes and common law rules, has become increasingly important in the United States. For the first time, many statutes attempt to harmonize areas of the law that previously varied from state to state. The development of e-commerce has led to additional proposed statutes—for example, the Uniform Computer Information Transactions Act and Uniform Electronic Transactions Act that the states can enact into law. The federal Electronic Signatures in Global and National Commerce Act (the E-SIGN Act) promotes e-commerce by making electronic documents and signatures as legally valid as those involving paper and written signatures. The common law has also spawned numerous contract principles that affect the legal environment of business. Although the word "contract" has many definitions, it commonly means a legally binding and legally enforceable promise or set of promises between two or more competent parties.

Historically, contracts were of minor importance because a feudal society had little interest in protecting the parties' expectations. With the advent of freedom of contract and rising industrialism, by the 19th century contract law had outstripped property law in significance. Ironically, today the law appears to be swinging back to a concern with status, as evidenced by protective statutes and recent common law decisions.

Six requirements must be met for a contract to be valid: (1) an agreement (that is, an offer and an acceptance), (2) supported by consideration, (3) made by parties having the capacity to contract, (4) based on these parties' genuine assent, (5) grounded in a legal undertaking, and (6) expressed in proper form, if applicable. Contracts may be classified as formal or informal; unilateral or bilateral; valid, voidable, void, or unenforceable; express or implied; and executed or executory. These categories are not necessarily mutually exclusive.

A contract implied in fact consists of evidence of sufficient facts or conduct from which a court can conclude that the parties intended to enter into a binding agreement. A contract implied in fact thus is a true contract. A quasi contract, or contract implied in law, is not a true contract. It is a different type of implied contract in which a court creates a contract for the parties, despite their wishes and intentions, in order that justice may be served. Not every situation in which a benefit has been conferred, however, gives rise to this equitable, restitutionary remedy called a quasi contract.

Discussion Questions

1. Define the term "contract."

2. Distinguish between a contractual obligation and a social obligation.

3. Name and define the six requirements for a valid contract.

4. Why do some commentators claim that the history of contract law has swung from status to freedom of contract and back again?

5. Explain the following categories of contracts: (a) formal, (b) informal, (c) unilateral, (d) bilateral, (e) valid, (f) voidable, (g) void, (h) unenforceable, (i) express, (j) implied, (k) executory, and (l) executed.

6. What are the legal requirements for showing a quasi contract?

7. What is the Uniform Commercial Code, and why is it important?

8. Suppose Joan asks the bank for a loan. What kind of contract will result from the bank's granting her this loan?

9. A contract involving an interest in land (such as a contract for the sale of a house) must be in writing. What is the legal effect of an oral contract in this situation?

10. What is the difference between a contract implied in fact and a contract implied in law?

Case Problems and Writing Assignments

1. Jason Ullmo attended first grade at Gilmour Academy, a private Catholic elementary and secondary school. After Jason was diagnosed with a hearing impairment, his parents transferred him to another school where he was diagnosed as having a learning disability as well. From the second through the sixth grade, Jason's new school provided him with an individualized educational program. Nevertheless, because Jason wished to return to Gilmour, Mrs. Ullmo met with its director of admissions, who allegedly told her "that it didn't make any difference that Jason had learning disabilities," that "Gilmour maintained a very nurturing environment," and that the school "would work with Jason." Jason subsequently returned to Gilmour for the seventh grade and continued his schooling there through the twelfth grade. Each year that Jason attended Gilmour, the Ullmos signed an enrollment agreement that obligated students and their parents to abide by the rules set forth in Gilmour's *Student and Parent Handbook*. Besides containing policies regarding academics, discipline, and related matters, the *Handbook* also included a section entitled "Philosophy," which stated:

   As a premier independent Catholic preparatory school (preschool through high school), Gilmour Academy models itself on the family and takes as its mission the search for excellence in each person. Gilmour teachers mirror the Holy Cross tradition as they work for the full development of their students, in and out of the classroom, respecting pupils' differing abilities and styles of learning.

   After returning to Gilmour, Jason struggled academically. He routinely failed to complete assignments and earned below-average grades. The Ullmos attributed Jason's difficulties to Gilmour's failure to adequately accommodate his learning disability. They were particularly dissatisfied with Gilmour's refusal to adopt the recommendations made by Jason's psychologist, who suggested, among other things, that the school allow Jason to take tests orally and that he be given more time to complete his assignments. Notwithstanding these complaints, the Ullmos had Jason return to Gilmour each year. Despite his consistently poor academic performance, Jason was graduated from Gilmour in 1998. A few months later, the Ullmos, suing on behalf of themselves and Jason, sought damages for breach of contract. They maintained that Gilmour had breached its promise to "work for the development" of its students and to respect students' "differing abilities and styles of learning" as set forth in the *Handbook*. Who should win this case? Why? [See *Ullmo ex rel. Ullmo v. Gilmour Academy*, 273 F.3d 671 (6th Cir. 2001).]

2. Plaintiff Miguel Angel Gonzalez, a citizen of Mexico, was a highly ranked professional boxer. Defendant Don King was the chief executive officer and sole owner of DKP, a boxing promotional firm. This lawsuit involves two contracts. The first contract, dated February 15, 1996, was an exclusive promotional agreement between Gonzalez and DKP. The second contract, dated January 15, 1998, was a bout agreement for a boxing match with Julio Cesar Chavez held on March 7, 1998. The bout agreement incorporated some of the terms of the promotional agreement and also provided for a purse of $750,000 for the Chavez match. DKP paid this purse, a fact not disputed in this litigation. Paragraph 11 of the bout agreement, the focus of the dispute here, gave DKP the option to promote four of Gonzalez's matches following the Chavez match. The relevant portion of Paragraph 11 then provided:

   In the event FIGHTER loses or draws the BOUT, or any option Bout, FIGHTER'S purse for each bout subsequent to such loss or draw shall be negotiated between PROMOTER and FIGHTER but shall not be less than AS PER PROMOTIONAL AGREEMENT unless a different sum is mutually agreed upon. The foregoing options as well as all other terms set forth in this Agreement are valid and enforceable regardless of the outcome of any bout provided for hereunder, i.e., win, lose or draw.

   Moreover, pursuant to the terms of the promotional agreement, Gonzalez and DKP apparently agreed that if Gonzalez won the Chavez match, Gonzalez would receive at least $75,000 for the next fight, unless the parties agreed otherwise. Similarly, if Gonzalez lost the Chavez match, Gonzalez would receive at least $25,000 in subsequent matches, unless the parties agreed otherwise. However, neither the promotional agreement nor the bout agreement explicitly stated the purse for subsequent matches in the event of a draw in the Chavez match. Since the Chavez match ended in a draw, the parties subsequently disputed whether the purse for subsequent matches could be determined with sufficient certainty to enforce the contract. Gonzalez contended that the omission of a purse for fights following a draw rendered the contract so indefinite as to constitute an unenforceable agreement to agree. Should a court accept Gonzalez's contention? Why or why not? [See *Gonzalez v. Don King Productions, Inc.*, 17 F. Supp. 2d. 313 (S.D. N.Y. 1998).]

3. In 1997, the Los Angeles County Metropolitan Transportation Authority (MTA) abolished its police force and entered into a contract with the County of Los Angeles to provide the MTA with law enforcement services through the County sheriff. Jack Herman was a former MTA police officer who did not pass the sheriff's review process. Neither the MTA nor the County offered him an alternative position. On the contrary, representatives of the MTA and the County met and mutually agreed not to place Herman in MTA or County employment. Section 2.1(A) of the contract states in relevant part:

On the transfer date, all MTA [police officers] who elect to transfer to County and who have successfully passed the [sheriff department's] personnel review process shall transfer to County without any change in rank or loss in salary. . . . For sworn personnel who have not passed the [sheriff department's] personnel review process, the parties shall meet and reach mutual agreement on the placement of such personnel. . . .

Herman contended that the latter provision of Section 2.1(A) entitled him to employment with the MTA or a department of the County other than the sheriff's department in a job comparable in pay to his former position as an MTA police officer. The County argued that Section 2.1(A) of the contract would not entitle Herman to employment with the County or the MTA for three reasons. First, the County asserted, the language providing "the parties shall meet and reach mutual agreement" on the placement of former MTA police officers leaves an essential element of the contract undetermined and therefore makes the contract void. Second, the County maintained, this language is also unenforceable because it purports to obligate the County "to employ another in personal service," employment otherwise prohibited by California's civil code. Finally, the County submitted, even if Section 2.1(A) is enforceable, it does not require the MTA or the County to hire former MTA officers who do not meet the sheriff's standards in some other capacity—it only requires the parties to "agree on the placement of such personnel." According to the County, it had satisfied its obligations under the contract by meeting with the MTA and mutually agreeing on Herman's placement—the agreement being that he would not be placed

with either agency. How should the court rule in this case? [See *Herman v. County of Los Angeles*, 119 Cal. Rptr. 2d 691 (Cal. App. 2d Dist. 2002).]

4. Housewright Lumber Company was the general contractor and Frank Millard & Company was a mechanical and electrical subcontractor on a project for the Iowa Army Ammunition Plant in Middletown, Iowa. In November 1993, Housewright contacted Millard concerning a bid on the project. The original bid submitted by Millard for $132,000 included the mechanical portion of the contract but did not include the insulation section involved in the present dispute. Housewright thereupon requested that a Millard official provide a quote on that item because Housewright was relying on Millard to do the insulation work. On March 1, 1994, after Millard had already begun work on the mechanical portion of the contract, Housewright mailed Millard a contract including the insulation work and adding an additional $2,000 to the contract price. Millard refused to sign that contract because neither Housewright nor Millard could ascertain the extent of the insulation work until another subcontractor had completed some asbestos abatement work. On March 24, 1994, the parties signed a second contract, which was identical to the March 1 contract, with one exception. On the second contract, Millard's chairman had added a handwritten addendum that provided: At the end of the project we will review the cost of duct insulation and responsibility. This addition occurred prior to either party's signing the contract. After completing its work, Millard sent Housewright an invoice for $12,009.56, an amount representing a $14,009.56 charge for the insulation work less the $2,000 figure added to the original bid. Refusing to pay this charge, Housewright claimed that the written addendum to the contract was without legal significance. In rebuttal, Millard argued that the addendum required Housewright to pay Millard on a time-and-material basis for all the insulation work actually performed. In these circumstances, who had the more persuasive argument? [See *Frank Millard & Co. v. Housewright Lumber Company*, 588 N.W.2d 440 (Iowa 1999).]

5. **BUSINESS APPLICATION CASE** Morris Winograd had been John Keaton's insurance agent from the time Keaton was a young man. In 1993, Keaton left his job as a mechanic and opened a barbecue business on premises leased to him by George Williams. The lease ran from 1993 to 1999 with a monthly rental of $700. In 1995, Williams, owing to financial troubles, asked whether Keaton would be interested in buying the premises. Keaton was not in a position to do so but suggested Winograd as a prospect for buying the property. Winograd, in fact, eventually purchased the property so as to establish a new, more elaborate restaurant and bar to be known as Wynny's. Winograd consequently wanted to renovate the entire premises, including that portion occupied by Keaton's barbecue restaurant. According to Keaton, on or about September 1995, Winograd raised the question of buying out Keaton's business. Keaton said he responded with a price of $175,000, a figure Winograd agreed to pay. According to Keaton, pursuant to Winograd's requests, Keaton agreed to vacate the premises by December 1995, and to stay on

to help Winograd run Winny's. Around January 1996, Winograd began the renovations and also began paying a weekly salary for Keaton's services with respect to Winograd's new bar and restaurant. Keaton presented three independent witnesses (in addition to his daughter) to corroborate what he described as Winograd's promise to pay him a promissory note of $175,000 for his business. When Keaton sued for breach of contract, Winograd denied ever agreeing to pay Keaton anything for the barbecue business. Winograd further contended that the assets of Keaton's business had little, if any, value; that its earnings were negligible; and that whatever value it may have had did not approach $175,000. Winograd further claimed that Keaton had willingly terminated operation of his business so that he (Keaton) could accept employment as manager of Winograd's new establishment, where he would be paid $800 per week—more than he ever could have earned from his barbecue restaurant.

Had the parties entered into a contract concerning the sale of Keaton's business? If the court were to find the existence of an agreement, should the court nonetheless invalidate it for lack of specificity? [See *Satellite Entertainment v. Keaton*, 789 A.2d 662 (N.J. Super. A.D. 2002).]

6. ETHICAL APPLICATION CASE Alphons Cheloha was a bachelor and retired farmer who lived in rural Nebraska. In late July or August 1988, Alphons was admitted to a nursing home, where he remained until his death on October 10, 1993. Robert Cheloha was Alphons's nephew and lived less than a mile from Alphons's home. During Alphons's lifetime, few people other than Robert paid any attention to Alphons's needs. Robert provided transportation for Alphons's doctor appointments and grocery shopping, made arrangements for Alphons's medical and nursing home care, paid Alphons's bills, and managed Alphons's finances. Robert testified that in April 1986, he had a discussion with Alphons regarding Robert's desire to be compensated for the services that Robert had been providing to Alphons. As corroborated by Robert's mother, Alphons allegedly responded, "I am so glad that you have been helping me . . . , and I want you to be paid." On August 11, 1988, Alphons executed a durable power of attorney, naming Carl (Robert's father and Alphons's brother) and Robert as Alphons's attorneys in fact. The power of attorney instrument did not contain a provision authorizing Robert to compensate himself or to make gifts from Alphons's property.

On September 20, 1995, Sophia Cheloha, as the personal representative of the estate of Alphons, filed a petition in equity that sought an accounting from Carl and Robert as to all the transactions in which they had engaged under the power of attorney. Sophia alleged that sums of money expended by Carl and Robert, in their capacities as Alphons's attorneys in fact, were not solely for the benefit of Alphons and were actually paid to the detriment of Alphons. At the bench trial on the matter, Robert admitted that he had used the power of attorney to convert $33,495.05 in certificates of deposit owned by Alphons to his (Robert's) own use. Robert, however, testified that these monies represented compensation for services rendered by him pursuant to an oral contract with Alphons.

Had Alphons entered into an express oral contract or, alternatively, an implied contract with Robert, by which Alphons had agreed to pay Robert $33,495.05 in certificates of deposit as compensation for services rendered? What could the parties have done differently so as to minimize the chances of subsequent litigation? Do you think Robert acted in an ethically admirable fashion? Why or why not? Should relatives provide services to each other without any expectation of payment? Does your decision depend on the particular circumstances involved? [*Cheloha v. Cheloha*, 582 N.W.2d 291 (Neb. 1998).]

7. CRITICAL THINKING CASE. AmeriPro Search, Inc. was an employment referral firm that placed professional employees with interested employers. In May 1993, Elaine Brauninger, an agent of AmeriPro, contacted Fleming Steel Company and learned that Fleming was seeking an employee with an engineering background. Brauninger then contacted Kohn, the president of Fleming and the person responsible for all decisions relating to employment and salaries. In their initial discussion, Brauninger advised Kohn that the fee for her services would equal 30 percent of the candidate's first year's salary. Kohn rejected this fee as too high. Kohn then told Brauninger that he and AmeriPro would determine the fee only after reaching an agreement to hire a candidate. Brauninger agreed and thereafter sent Kohn resumes of potential candidates and a copy of AmeriPro's fee agreement. One of the candidates referred to Fleming was Dominic Barracchini. Kohn interviewed Barracchini on April 8, 1994, but did not hire Barracchini because Barracchini's salary request was too high. In February 1995, because he was laid off and thus in the market for a job, Barracchini called Brauninger to inquire whether Fleming was still trying to fill the position for which he had previously interviewed. Brauninger never returned Barracchini's call. At Barracchini's initiative, Kohn interviewed and hired Barracchini as an engineer in June 1995. On September 6, 1995, AmeriPro sent Fleming a letter claiming entitlement to $14,400 for the placement of Barracchini with Fleming. When Fleming refused to pay the demanded fee, AmeriPro sued Fleming for the commission fee. Had AmeriPro and Fleming entered into a contract pursuant to which Fleming would pay AmeriPro a commission for placing Barracchini with Fleming? What, if anything, should AmeriPro have done to avoid what happened in this case? [See *AmeriPro Search, Inc. v. Fleming Steel Company*, 787 A.2d 988 (Pa. Super. 2001).]

8. YOU BE THE JUDGE In July 1997, plaintiff Jason Brody and 10 other rejected medical school applicants sued Finch University of Health Sciences/The Chicago Medical School for breach of contract stemming from the plaintiffs' reliance on certain of the defendant medical school's alleged representations. Specifically, the plaintiffs pointed to statements in the school's catalogue to the effect that "[t]hose students who enrolled in defendant's Applied Physiology Program (the Program) and received a grade point average (GPA) of 3.0 or higher would be admitted to the defendant's medical school." The evidence at the trial showed that on July 22, 1996, the first day of orientation, Timothy R. Hansen, the director of the Program, had

issued to the plaintiffs a memorandum stating that the medical school "[did] not expect to accept more than 50 students from the 1996–97 Applied Physiology class into the entering class in 1997." The "School of Graduate and Post Doctoral Studies Catalog" for 1995–96 stated that the school reserved the right to modify programs. However, it also stated that "modification[s] of program requirements will not adversely affect those students already in a program." Eighty students in the 1996–97 Program—including the plaintiffs—achieved a 3.0 GPA or better. On or around June 26, 1997, Michael Booden, general counsel for the defendant, informed the plaintiffs' counsel that the medical school was accepting only the top 50 students from the Program and that the class size of the medical school would consist of approximately 150 students. As of June 26, 1997, 50 applicants from the Program had been offered admission to the medical school.

At the 1997 bench trial of the plaintiffs' lawsuit, Theodore Booden, the dean of the medical school, noted that the Program had been built on the premise that some highly qualified students were being rejected by medical schools. Hence, the defendant wanted to give such students an opportunity to prove that they were capable of handling the curriculum in the hopes they would be accepted into a medical school, either the defendant's or another's. In recent years, however, the defen-

dant had received an abundance of qualified persons applying to the medical school from outside the Program and thus had decided to "raise the bar" and limit acceptance of the Program's graduates to 50 students. At the trial, each of the plaintiffs recounted their communications with the defendant, their employment prior to enrolling in the Program, and their circumstances before and after enrolling in the Program. According to the plaintiffs, the defendant's admissions department routinely informed the plaintiffs that, if they achieved a 3.0 or better GPA, they would have a 90 percent to 95 percent chance of obtaining admission to the defendant's medical school. Some of the plaintiffs visited the campus and spoke with Dr. Hanson and Dean Booden, who also indicated to those plaintiffs that, historically, a GPA of 3.0 was enough to get accepted into its medical school. With the defendant's encouragement, some plaintiffs even telephoned former graduates of the Program who subsequently had been admitted to the defendant's medical school.

Given the evidence offered at the trial, had the plaintiffs shown the existence of an implied contract in fact that the students who successfully completed the Program would be admitted to the defendant's medical school? Discuss the ethics of both the school and the rejected applicants. [See *Brody v. Finch University of Health Sciences*, 698 N.E.2d 257 (Ill. App. 2d Dist. 1998).]

Notes

1. A. G. Guest, *Anson's Law of Contracts*, 26th ed. (Oxford: Clarendon Press, 1984), 1.
2. Bradford Stone, *Uniform Commercial Code in a Nutshell*, 5th ed. (St. Paul, Minn.: West, 2002), ix–x.

3. UCC § 1-102 (2) and Comment 1.
4. *Restatement (Second) of Contracts* § 1 (St. Paul, Minn.: American Law Institute Publishers, 1981).

Contractual Agreement: Mutual Assent

AGENDA

NRW As Mai, Carlos, and Helen work to get NRW "up and running," they will enter into quite a few contracts. They also will buy goods and services from a number of businesses. They therefore need to know *how* to enter contracts, and they will need to know what legal effect different types of communications have on the existence—or lack thereof—of contracts. They moreover will want to know whether any advertising they use constitutes a potential contract offer.

These constitute just a few of the areas where they may have questions. Be prepared! You never know when the firm or one of its members will seek your advice.

The First Step in Contract Formation

Agreement is the essence of a contract. Once there has been a valid offer by the offeror (the person making the offer) and a valid acceptance by the offeree (the person to whom the offer is made), we are well on our way to having a legally binding contract because, generally, few problems exist concerning capacity, genuine assent, legality, and proper form (the remaining requirements for a contract). On the other hand, precisely because these two aspects of contract formation (offer and acceptance) are so important, courts closely examine the words and conduct of the parties to determine whether a bona fide (that is, a good faith) offer and acceptance indeed are present.

From common law times, numerous rules have developed for checking the authenticity of the offer and the acceptance. Under these rules, the threshold for contract formation remains high because courts require rather clearcut statements that the parties are freely and voluntarily entering into a particular agreement. Conversely, under the Uniform Commercial Code (UCC), a court can more easily infer a bona fide offer and acceptance from the conduct of the parties, even if the parties have omitted terms such as price, mode of payment, or mode of delivery. In this chapter, we discuss the reasons for these developments.

Mutual Assent and the Objective Theory of Contracts

The initial phase of contract formation requires the assent of both parties to the agreement. The parties must agree to exactly the same terms. Without this mutual assent, no agreement ever comes into existence.

How do we judge whether the parties have mutually consented to the transaction? If you are in a particularly mischievous mood, you may say to a friend, "Tom, I'll let you buy my mountain bike for $200; that's the offer." Since Tom knows the frame itself sells for $500, he quickly says, "I'll take it." Does this exchange constitute a valid offer and acceptance? Will you have to sell the bike, or will the law permit you to say that you were kidding and did not intend to make an offer?

Common law rules tell us that the offeror has the right to set the terms of the offer (and to control the method by which the offeree accepts the offer). In so doing, the offeror

must exhibit a clear and present intent to offer. You fairly straightforwardly enumerated the terms of the offer. But is it apparent from the content of your statement that you were only kidding?

To determine whether a valid offer exists, the law applies an objective standard (one that is capable of being observed and verified without being distorted by personal feelings and prejudices). Under common law, to decide whether an offer has been made, a court or a jury puts itself in the offeree's place (that is, in Tom's shoes) to ascertain if a reasonable offeree would believe that you, in offering the bike at this price, were serious. Since the law judges your words and conduct by an objective instead of a subjective test (one that is capable of being observed and verified through individual feelings and emotions), your secret intent (you were joking and did not really want to sell the bike) cannot be shown. Hence, in this example, a court may find that you have made a valid offer to Tom.

Obviously, this result depends heavily on the facts. If you clearly are jesting, are excited, or are even visibly angry, details supporting the existence of these facts may lead to a different result. Thus, a word to the wise: Beware of making "offers" you do not mean, since both common law and UCC principles may hold you to these statements.

The following case illustrates these important concepts. After reading the court's opinion, decide whether you agree with the conclusion reached by the court.

Offer

Let us look more closely at this first phase of reaching agreement: the offer. An offer involves an indication (by a promise or another commitment) of one's willingness to do or refrain from doing something in the future. An offer implicitly invites another person, in order to seal the bargain, to assent to the promise or commitment.

Clear Intention to Contract and Definiteness of the Offer

To fulfill the common law's requirements, an offer must show a clear intention to contract and be definite in all respects. An agreement to agree at some future time, for example, lacks these prerequisites of a common law offer. Similarly, statements of opinion, statements of intention, and preliminary negotiations do not result in bona fide offers because they lack definiteness. But reasonable people will differ as to what constitutes a clear, definite offer and what instead involves only preliminary negotiations or dickering.

10.1

D&N PROPERTY MANAGEMENT & DEVELOPMENT CORPORATION, v. THE COPELAND COMPANIES
190 F. Supp. 2d 618 (S.D.N.Y. 2002)

FACTS Nicholas Mattera, an officer, director, and owner of 50 percent of the shares of D&N Property Management & Development Corporation, entered into a consulting arrangement with The Copeland Companies on or about September 19, 1997. The original agreement, which was to expire by its terms at the end of April 1998, set Mattera's daily rate of compensation at $875. During May 1998, Mattera and Winthrop Cody, Copeland's chief information officer, began negotiations aimed at extending the terms of the original agreement. Accordingly, on May 29, 1998, Mattera sent Cody a letter in which Mattera proposed a contract extension through the end of 1999, at a rate of $875/day for the remainder of 1998 and a rate of $945/day during 1999. Between May 29 and June 1, 1998, Cody made handwritten changes to the proposal, namely that Copeland would use D&N only through June 30, 1999, with arrangements for the rest of 1999 to be determined at a later date. Cody also did not countersign the document on the "accepted and agreed" line. Nonetheless, Mattera initialed Cody's handwritten changes to the May 29, 1998, letter and delivered the document to Cody. Cody never signed this letter.

On or about June 10, 1998, Mattera typed and delivered to Cody a new letter that incorporated all the terms of the May 29, 1998, letter, as altered by Cody and initialed by Mattera. Cody then crossed out the typed statement that the term would extend from January 1, 1999, through June 30, 1999, and wrote the following by hand on the document: "okay through 12/31/98, extension to 1999 to be determined at a later date." Mattera never countersigned, initialed, or otherwise indicated his consent to Cody's change to the June 10 letter.

In early December 1998, during the reopening of discussions with Mattera concerning a contract extension, Cody for the first time raised the possibility of Mattera's providing services to Copeland on a "part-time basis" in 1999. Professing to have been "confused" by Cody's comments about the prospect of Mattera's working part-time for Copeland, Mattera asserted that he already had a contract extending through 1999 at the rate of $945/day. In support of this assertion, Mattera enclosed a copy of a June 24, 1998, document that set out the terms Mattera had mentioned. Yet, throughout the November to early December period in which the parties had been discussing a potential extension of the June 10 agreement, Mattera had never raised the exis-

tence of this purported letter. Despite the fact that Cody believed that the document was a fraud, the parties continued to discuss a possible extension of D&N's consulting arrangement. Mattera offered several more proposals, each of which Copeland rejected.

Finally, on or about January 15, 1999, Copeland formally advised Mattera that it no longer needed his consulting services after January 18, 1999. Copeland paid Mattera for the days he had worked for Copeland in January 1999 at the billing rate of $875/day. Several months after the check was sent to him, and in contemplation of the filing of this action, Mattera sent Copeland a letter protesting the amount as too low. Mattera subsequently sued Copeland for breach of contract.

ISSUE Would a reasonable person have viewed the May 29 letter as an offer that Mattera had accepted by initialing the changes Cody had made?

HOLDING No. The circumstances surrounding the May 29 letter—the fact that the parties had just begun negotiations, the fact that Mattera had initiated many other contract negotiations after the execution of this alleged contract, the fact that neither party had relied on this contract, and the fact that Mattera had forged contracts at a later date—all should lead to the conclusion that no reasonable person would have viewed the May 29 letter, as marked up by Cody and initialed by Mattera, as an offer and acceptance that resulted in a binding contract.

REASONING Excerpts from the opinion of Judge McMahon:

Under New Jersey law, the issue of whether an offer has been made becomes "whether the one to whom the proposal was made had reason to believe that it was intended as an offer." . . . Thus, whether Copeland, through Cody, made a counteroffer to Mattera by changing some of the terms on Mattera's May 29 offer, but not signing or initialing the marked-up letter, does not depend on what Cody subjectively intended, or upon what Mattera believed that Cody meant, but rather "upon what meaning the [marked-up letter] should have conveyed to a reasonable person cognizant of the relationship between the parties and all of the antecedent and surrounding facts and circumstances." Under New Jersey contract law, evidence of the circumstances surrounding the alleged contractual transaction is admissible. . . . Likewise, "the conduct of the parties after execution of the contract is entitled to great weight in determining its meaning and significance." . . .

In this case, it is necessary to resort to evidence of the parties' other dealings in order to ascertain whether a reasonable person who was cognizant of all the antecedent and surrounding facts and circumstances would consider the marked-up May 29 letter to be a valid and binding contract. [In this regard, the court concluded] that the marked-up May 29 letter was not a valid and binding contract. The facts that persuade me are as follows: . . . First, Mattera had an unvarying practice of asking Cody to indicate his assent to a contract by signing his name under the words "Accepted and Agreed to." . . . as of the time Mattera initialed Cody's changes to his May 29 letter, Cody had not so signed [it]. . . . Second, Cody's signature on the "Accepted and Agreed to" line was added to the document at an unknown date sometime after June 1 by Mattera and not by Cody, thus suggesting that Mattera did not believe the document in its June 1, 1998 state . . . would be upheld as a valid and binding contract. . . . Third, on June 10, Mattera prepared a freshly typed version of [the May 29 letter], incorporating Cody's suggested changes, and returned it to Cody for signature. I do not accept Mattera's testimony that he did this only to "clean up" the already agreed contract. Mattera begins the "cleaned-up" letter by referring to a June 8 conversation with Cody that he asserts was the basis for the terms that follow. That reference is not consistent with his statement that he only wanted to "clean up" an already-existing agreement whose terms were allegedly agreed well prior to June 8. Moreover, the preparation of the June 10 letter is consistent with the fact that, as of that date, Cody had not signed [the May 29 letter]. I find that Mattera wrote the letter precisely so that Cody would sign something firmly indicating that his contract would be extended at least until June 1999. That did not happen.

I find that the facts of this case, examined objectively, lead to the conclusion that it was not reasonable for Mattera to believe that Cody's unsigned handwritten changes were a binding offer. The handwritten changes were part of an ongoing negotiation over a possible contract extension. . . . Mr. Mattera's subsequent forgery of Cody's signature on [the May 29 letter], and his [Mattera's] completely forged [June 24 letter], further bolster his ineffective and disingenuous claim that [the May 29 letter] constituted a binding contract. The [June 10 letter] as altered by Cody was never agreed to [by] Mattera. The fact that Mattera continued to render services after [June 10] can be explained by the fact that the parties had already agreed (orally) to continue under the terms of the expired September 1997 written contract until they agreed to a new contract. They did not do so on [June 10] and were thus operating on a day to day basis throughout the year 1998 without benefit of any written contract. There are no binding written contracts between D&N and Copeland. Copeland was free at any time to decide that it no longer needed . . . Mattera's services. The rate agreed to in the absence of a written contract was $875 per [day] as set in the September 1997 contract. Thus, Copeland paid D&N everything to which it was entitled.

BUSINESS CONSIDERATIONS What could Copeland have done differently so as to avoid the litigation that occurred here? Should a firm have special rules for contracting with consultants and any other such temporary employees? Are such relationships inherently risky, legally speaking?

ETHICAL CONSIDERATIONS The court, in concluding that Mattera had forged the June 24 letter, found it "neither logical nor credible" that Cody would have changed his mind only a few days after altering the June 10 letter to scale back on the duration of Mattera's employment in 1999 and have offered Mattera employment at an enhanced rate through the entire year 1999. Mattera's alleged conduct contributed to his losing the lawsuit. Ethically speaking, what else did Mattera lose?

Since these are questions of fact that a judge or jury can later decide, be cautious. If you want to make an offer, be specific in all particulars. Haggling or dickering lacks definiteness regarding the details of the transaction and your intentions; hence, such preliminary negotiations ordinarily are too vague to constitute a valid offer. Winning or losing a lawsuit can turn on such minute distinctions as how a court interprets the words expressed by the parties. For example, are the words, "I can send you two trademark logos at $5,000 per logo" identical in intent to "I offer to sell you two trademark logos at $5,000 per logo"? Many people would view these statements as virtually identical, but a strict common law interpretation treats only the second statement as a bona fide offer. The law views the other statement merely as an indication of a willingness to negotiate rather than a bona fide offer.

Despite the common law requirement that an offer be definite in all its material (or essential) terms, you should be aware that the UCC relaxes this common law prerequisite in several significant ways. For instance, UCC § 2-204 states that a contract for sale under the Code will not fail for indefiniteness as long as the parties have intended to form a contract and a reasonably certain basis for giving an appropriate remedy exists, even though one or more of the terms of the agreement may have been left open. In addition, the UCC contains several so-called gap-filling provisions whereby the court can supply the terms—including price, place of delivery, and mode of payment—omitted by the parties.[1] The Code also validates output contracts (calling for the buyer to purchase all the seller's production during the term of the contract) and requirements contracts (in which the seller agrees to provide as much of a product or service as the buyer needs during the contract term), both of which would be too indefinite for common law courts to enforce.[2] Because the Code is predicated on the idea that commercial people (particularly merchants) want to deal with each other, it has eliminated some of the ticklish technicalities that impede contract formation under common law. You will learn more about these and other revolutionary changes in common law brought about by the Uniform Commercial Code when you read Chapters 16 through 19. Like the UCC, the Uniform Computer Information Transactions Act endorses "gap fillers" if the contract is otherwise vague.[3] Similarly, both the UCC and UCITA impose a duty of good faith on the contracting parties; the parties need not refer specifically to this duty.

Still, on-line sellers should take great care in ensuring that any offer is clear and conspicuous. Among other matters, the sellers' Web sites should refer would-be buyers to a link that sets out the entire contract, including terms relating to remedies, payment, refunds and returns, privacy policies, dispute resolution mechanisms, and the like. Moreover, the offer should clearly indicate how to accept the offer. Ordinarily, the Web site includes a box stating "I agree" or "I accept the terms of the offer." In turn, the customer indicates acceptance of the offer by clicking on the box. Courts generally enforce such "click-on" agreements (also called "click-wrap" agreements or "click-on" licenses).

Advertisements and Auctions

The law in general does not treat advertisements as valid offers because they ordinarily lack sufficient specificity to be defined as such. Instead, the law views advertisements as invitations for persons to come in and make offers for the types of goods and at the prices indicated in the advertisements. Notice that this rule demonstrates yet another "pro-offeror" tilt of the common law. A contrary perspective that advertisements constitute offers would presuppose that a merchant has an unlimited supply of merchandise. Thus, the principle that advertisements ordinarily are not offers protects merchants from the hardships such a contrary rule might produce. On occasion, however, an advertisement, catalog, circular, price list, or price quotation shows suffi-

NRW CASE 10.1 Management

UNDERSTANDING CONTRACT FORMATION

One of the firm's salespeople, Chris, has been studying contract law in his Legal Environment of Business class. He explains to Helen that, based on what he has been told in class, contracts are fairly technical and difficult to create, due in part to such things as the "mirror image" rule. He believes that this principle gives NRW a great deal of latitude in discussing its product with potential customers because one can classify much of the conversation as mere "sales talk," and no contract offer will result. Helen is not sure that Chris has a thorough knowledge of contract law. Helen remembers that service contracts and employment contracts are often technical and that courts are likely to examine them very carefully. However, she also has heard that courts are much more likely to "find" contracts in the area of sales even if the courts discern that the traditional common law requirements are lacking. Helen asks you for your advice. What will you tell her?

BUSINESS CONSIDERATIONS What can a business do to protect itself from an overly exuberant sales force when the sales representatives are trying to make contracts with customers?

ETHICAL CONSIDERATIONS Suppose a business finding itself with a questionable deal recognizes a possible escape from that deal owing to a technicality in contract law. Is it ethical for the firm to use this technicality to get out of the deal? Is it ethical to hold another party to a contract he or she does not realize is being formed?

INTERNATIONAL CONSIDERATIONS Contract formation in the United States is heavily influenced by the common law, although the sale of goods is now regulated by Article 2 of the UCC. What law regulates the international sale of goods? How does it compare to the common law or to Article 2 of the UCC?

cient detail for a court to say that a valid offer exists. Such a result, however exceptional, sometimes occurs.

In the following case, the court used many of these common law principles when it determined whether the parties had created a binding contract.

ABBOTT LABORATORIES v. ALPHA THERAPEUTIC CORP.
164 F.3d 385 (7th Cir. 1999)

FACTS In 1978 Abbott Laboratories had sold its scientific products division to Alpha Therapeutic Corporation. The division manufactured and distributed "factor concentrate," a blood product used to treat hemophiliacs. Abbott agreed to indemnify (reimburse) Alpha for any losses arising from the inventory transferred. As it turned out, Abbott chose a good time to get out of the blood products business. In the 1980s, a class of hemophiliacs who claimed to be infected with HIV through the use of factor concentrate brought suit against members of the blood products industry, including Alpha. In the negotiations to create an industry-wide class settlement, Alpha brought up the Abbott indemnification issues. On August 9, 1996, after extensive negotiations, Sharon Jones, Abbott's senior counsel, wrote to Edward Colton, Alpha's general counsel. In this "final settlement offer," Jones named the proposed dollar figure and outlined the "essential terms from Abbott's perspective," including a series of releases that Abbott sought in exchange for its settlement payment. Jones also noted that because "it is Abbott's intention to have no further obligation to Alpha, . . . Abbott will be proposing more precise language in the anticipated settlement agreement in order to accomplish this directive." Finally, in response to a request from Alpha, the letter indicated that Abbott would be willing to defer its payment if the parties could agree on an interest rate. In an August 26 letter, Colton responded, "Alpha has agreed to accept Abbott Laboratories' settlement offer of [the proposed settlement amount]. In general, we agreed with the terms and conditions contained in your 9 August 1996 letter." Colton also requested that the settlement agreement be "resolved with respect to all the terms and conditions and ready for execution before September 12th." He wanted to present the agreement as a "done deal" at Alpha's September 13 board meeting because several executives from Japan who could execute the agreement would be present. Finally, Colton asked Abbott to defer payment until January 15, 1997, and proposed a 7 percent interest rate. In the following months, the parties exchanged and modified several proposed settlement agreements. On December 9, 1996, Jones sent Colton her final version of the settlement agreement and asked that the agreement be executed by December 11. On January 6, 1997, Colton informed Jones that in light of the uncertainty of the blood products class settlement negotiations, Alpha would not be willing to settle unless Abbott significantly increased the settlement amount. Instead,

Abbott sued, seeking to enforce an alleged agreement that required Alpha to indemnify Abbott indefinitely into the future for any defense costs and losses related to factor concentrate.

ISSUE Did the exchange of the two letters in August constitute a binding settlement agreement between Abbott and Alpha?

HOLDING No. The letters failed to show the parties' intentions to be bound to the material terms of the proposed settlement. Hence, the parties lacked the mutual assent necessary for a legally binding agreement.

REASONING Excerpts from the opinion of Judge Evans:

Under Illinois contract law, a binding agreement requires a "meeting of the minds" or mutual assent as to all material terms. . . . Whether the parties had a 'meeting of the minds' is determined not by their actual subjective intent, but by what they expressed to each other in their writings. Thus, the parties decide for themselves whether the results of preliminary negotiations bind them, and they do so through their words. . . . Abbott contends that the August letters between Jones and Colton constitute a legally binding offer and acceptance which show the parties' mutual assent to the terms contained in Ms. Jones's letter. That letter, says Abbott, outlined all the material terms: (1) the settlement amount; (2) a global release by Alpha and Green Cross for all hemophiliac claims; (3) indemnification of defense costs for all such claims; (4) a release of all environmental claims arising from any property sold to Alpha and Green Cross; and (5) a release of any other indemnification claims arising from the 1978 asset sale agreement. Abbott points out that Jones also stated in the letter that this was Abbott's "final settlement offer," expressing her belief that Abbott would be bound by the terms of the offer if Alpha accepted. And, Abbott argues, Colton accepted the offer on behalf of Alpha in his August 26 letter, when he wrote "Alpha has agreed to accept Abbott Laboratories' settlement offer of [the proposed amount]." . . .

There is superficial appeal to Abbott's argument that it was unfair for Alpha to pull a switcheroo in its position on the proposed settlement amount solely because the class action negotiations were going badly. . . . This argument breaks down, however, upon examination of the degree to which the parties decided to bind themselves in August. . . . In this case, the words in the two August letters do not show a clear intent to be bound on behalf of either Abbott or Alpha. . . . Jones wrote in her August 9 letter that she was only reiterating the "general terms" of the proposal currently on the table and attempting to identify the "essential terms from Abbott's perspective." There is a strong implication . . . that Jones expects Alpha to counter with essential terms of its own that will require further negotiation. She also says she will be proposing more precise language regarding the release terms in the "anticipated settlement agreement." As a general rule, anticipation of a more formal future writing does not nullify an otherwise binding agreement. . . . Here, however, Jones explicitly leaves the details of the release provisions open for future negotiation . . . [which] calls into question Abbott's intent to be bound at that time. Similarly, Colton's August 26 letter does not sufficiently express an intent to be bound to Jones's terms. In the sentence immediately following the one where he agreed to the proposed dollar figure, Colton wrote that Alpha agreed to the terms in the August 9 letter "in general." He also wrote that he wanted "the Agreement resolved with respect to all terms and conditions and ready for execution before September 12." . . . All . . . this language strongly implies that Colton did not yet consider the settlement a "done deal." Instead, he understood that certain terms would have to be hammered out before the executives signed off on the deal. Abbott argues that informal writings between parties can constitute a binding settlement agreement unless the parties decide to expressly condition their deal on the signing of a formal document. . . . This is an accu-

rate statement of the rule, but informal writings must still manifest each party's intent to be bound by the material terms proposed. . . . The settlement that Alpha and Abbott were trying to hammer out was a complicated, long-term arrangement involving huge sums of money. Although there is no requirement that an agreement, even a big one, be "signed, sealed, and delivered" to be binding, the magnitude of a deal requires careful scrutiny of any claim that informal letters in the course of freewheeling settlement negotiations constitute a binding agreement. To be binding, such letters must clearly manifest the desire of each party to be bound to the material terms of the proposed deal. Agreement "in general" with a clear contemplation that further negotiations as to material terms will be required is simply not enough to form ties that bind. Therefore, we find that there was no binding settlement agreement between Abbott and Alpha.

BUSINESS CONSIDERATIONS Would it have been advisable for the parties to have sought a mediator, or some other objective third party, to help them arrive at a settlement figure? Or are the determinations of such financial matters best left to the internal management of each firm? Support your position fully.

ETHICAL CONSIDERATIONS Do you agree with Abbott that it was unfair of Alpha to pull a "switcheroo" in Alpha's position on the proposed settlement amount solely because the class action negotiations were going badly? Why or why not?

Normally, courts require a showing that the merchant has placed some limitation on the advertised goods before courts will find that the advertisement constitutes an offer. For example, the merchant may have specified a time limit, such as "for one day only." Or the merchant may have designated a quantity limit, such as "while they last" or "to the first 10 customers," in the advertisement. In such a situation, the courts are somewhat more likely to find that the advertisement is an offer and not an invitation to deal or to negotiate. Again, courts utilize as the deciding factor the objective standard of what a reasonable person would have thought.

Auctions are similar to advertisements in that the seller is not actually the offeror, although he or she may appear to be offering the goods for sale through the auctioneer. In reality, the law treats the bidder as the offeror. For a sale to occur, the seller must accept the bid. The seller can even refuse to sell to the highest bidder unless the auction is publicized as "without reserve." (In an auction without reserve, the seller must let the goods go to the highest bidder; he or she cannot withdraw the goods if the price bid is too low.) Once the auctioneer lets the hammer fall, the

seller has accepted the bid. But until this point, the bidder can withdraw the offer and thus avoid the formation of a contract of sale. Section 2-328 of the UCC covers these points, which are discussed again in Chapter 16.

For a useful illustration of how an e-commerce auction site works, check out eBay's Web site at http://www.ebay.com/. Note the various mechanisms that eBay has instituted to enhance consumer trust and to lower transaction costs (for example, fraud) for its users. Note too the legal boilerplate that is typical of B2C transactions.

Communication of the Offer to the Offeree

Another requirement for a bona fide offer is that the offeror (or his or her agent) must communicate the offer to the offeree. At first glance this rule may seem nonsensical. How can a person accept an offer if he or she does not know it exists? Believe it or not, that sometimes happens. For example, assume that two parties have been haggling over the terms of a real estate transaction. After much correspondence, the would-be buyer (offeree) writes, "Okay, you win. I will pay $80,000 for the land," and mails the letter to the offeror. A day later, before the arrival of the mail, the would-be seller (offeror) coincidentally arrives at the same figure, and writes, "This is my final offer. I will sell you the land for $80,000. Take it or leave it," and mails this letter to the offeree. Later, the offeror wants to sell this land to a third person who is interested in purchasing it; but the original offeree claims that he and the offeror now have a contract for $80,000. Despite the claims of the original offeree, the offeror probably can sell the land to the third party because most courts will hold that the original offeree has not validly accepted the offer. This is true because at the time of the would-be buyer's purported acceptance, no offer to sell the land at a price of $80,000 had been communicated to the original offeree. And, you will recall, an offer has no legal effect until the offeror (or his or her agent) communicates it to the offeree. Courts liken the correspondences in this example to identical offers crossing in the mail, each asking for and necessitating an acceptance before any valid contract ensues, and neither receiving the required acceptance. This result once again underscores the common law offeror's iron-fisted control over the terms of the offer (and the method of acceptance).

This requirement of communicating the offer to the offeree sometimes arises in the context of general offers. Although most offers are made by one person to another, offers made to the general public or a similar class of large numbers of persons are perfectly legal. A reward, such as money for the arrest and conviction of the persons who vandalized an office complex, represents the best example of a general offer. Even though some case results to the contrary exist, most courts require that the party who performs the act contemplated by the reward (here, the identification

of the vandals so as to lead to their prosecution and conviction) must have known of the reward and must have intended the act as acceptance of that offer. Under this view, in order for a valid acceptance to occur, a general offer must be communicated to the offeree. Under the rule followed in a majority of jurisdictions, then, a person who coincidentally identifies the vandals without knowledge of the reward is ineligible to receive the reward. Exhibit 10.1 summarizes the steps needed for reaching an agreement.

Duration of the Offer

Usually, offers satisfy these common law rules and will be legally effective. The next question that often arises concerns the duration of the offer; that is, how long will it remain open? Four methods for terminating an offer exist: (1) lapse, (2) revocation, (3) rejection, and (4) acceptance.

Lapse   Sometimes the offeror will state in the offer when it will terminate and thus set the life span for the offer. This brings about the potential lapse of the offer (that is, the expiration or the loss of an opportunity because of the passage of a time limit within which the opportunity had to be exercised). For instance, an offer may state, among other things, "This offer will remain open for 30 days." If after 30 days the offeree has not responded, the offer automatically lapses. The offeror is under no legal duty to communicate to the offeree the fact that the offer has lapsed. After 30 days, the offeror can make the same offer to anyone else.

In many cases, the offeror neglects to state any time period in the offer. In these situations, how long does the offeree have before he or she must respond? To avoid lapse, the offeree must accept within a reasonable time. Determi-

---

EXHIBIT   10.1   Offer: The First Phase of Reaching an Agreement

A *bona fide* offer by the offeror must:

- Show a clear intention to enter into a contract.
- Be *definite* in all respects.
- Be *communicated* to the offeree or to his or her agent.

Communications by the offeror that do *not* reflect a *bona fide* offer include:

- Any *undisclosed secret* intentions.
- Statements made in *jest* or in *strong excitement.*
- Preliminary negotiations.
- Price quotations, dickering, advertisements, invitations to deal.

nation of what constitutes a reasonable time becomes a question of fact that a judge or jury decides. The trier of fact will consider such things as industry conditions, customs, and usages of trade. In volatile commodities markets, an offer may lapse in a matter of seconds. On the other hand, given a downturn in the real estate market, a period of days or weeks may constitute a reasonable time if the offer involves a sale of real property. To avoid such uncertainties, the offeror should state specifically when the offer lapses.

Lapse also may occur by operation of law. That is, regardless of the wishes of the parties, an offer automatically lapses upon the following occurrences: (1) the death or insanity of the offeror or offeree, (2) the supervening (additional or unexpected) illegality of the subject matter of the offer, or (3) the destruction of the subject matter involved in the offer. In other words, if Joe Olivetti offers to sell some cattle to Joan Hays, but Joe dies before she accepts, the offer automatically lapses. Joe's estate does not have to inform Joan of his death. Similarly, if two days after Joe makes the offer, his cattle are quarantined because it is discovered that they have hoof and mouth disease, Joe's offer will lapse because the sale of such infected cattle is illegal. If lightning strikes the barn, starting a fire that kills the cattle, the offer also lapses. No communication to Joan is necessary in these last instances either.

Revocation Another method of terminating an offer, besides lapse, is revocation. Under common law, the offeror possesses virtually unlimited rights to revoke at any time before acceptance. This is true whether or not the offeror uses the word "revoke," as long as an intention to terminate the offer is clear. In general, revocation does not become effective until it is communicated to (or received by) the offeree. Interestingly, such communication may be effective whether communicated directly or indirectly. Using our earlier example, Joe may state bluntly, "Joan, I revoke my offer to you." Alternatively, Joan may hear that Joe has sold the cattle to Len Hill. In either case, an effective revocation has occurred.

Usually, Joe will be dealing only with Joan or, at most, with a few parties. This is not the case with a general offer to the public. If Joe has lost his prize Dalmatian, Jake, and has offered a reward for the return of or information about the dog, Joe need only revoke his offer in the same manner (or medium) in which he made the original offer. Because it is too burdensome to require Joe to communicate with every possible "taker" of his offer, public revocation suffices. It is even effective against a person who has not seen the advertisement and who later comes forward with information about Jake.

Methods do exist for taming this seemingly unlimited power of revocation by the Joes of the world. For example,

---

NRW CASE 10.2 Sales/Manufacturing

NRW

REVOKING AN OFFER

NRW made a written offer to Joe Daily, one of its suppliers, in which the firm offered to buy Joe's entire supply of microchips at list price. NRW's letter promised to keep the offer open for four weeks. Two weeks after mailing the letter, NRW received an offer from another firm to sell virtually identical microchips to NRW for 20 percent less than Joe's list price. Carlos wants to accept this offer and has asked you whether NRW can revoke the offer to Joe. What will you tell him?

BUSINESS CONSIDERATIONS What factors should a business consider when it makes a written promise to keep an offer for goods open for a specific time? Would the business consider different factors if the offer were for the purchase of services?

ETHICAL CONSIDERATIONS Is the common law rule that generally permits revocation of an offer at any time prior to acceptance an ethical rule? Is the UCC rule regarding merchants and the sale of goods more ethical?

INTERNATIONAL CONSIDERATIONS Suppose that NRW had made an oral promise to keep an offer open to a microchip supplier located in another country, and then decided that it wanted to revoke the promise. Since the promise was oral rather than written, could NRW revoke the offer before the promised time had expired?

---

by forcing Joe to promise to keep the offer open for a stated time, Joan can prohibit Joe's power of revocation. The promise itself does not protect Joan from revocation. But if she takes an option (a contract to keep an offer open for some agreed-on time period) on the cattle, Joe is legally bound to hold the offer open for the agreed-on period of time. Joan will have to pay Joe for the option; but once she does so, he cannot sell the cattle to anyone else during the option period without breaching this option contract. Usually, Joan is under no obligation to exercise the option. If she does not, Joe can keep the money or other consideration paid to him for the option. If Joan does exercise the option, normally the money paid for the option will be subtracted from the purchase price. Depending on the bargaining position of the parties, however, this is not always the case.

Another exception to the rule that an offeror can revoke an offer at any time before acceptance comes from UCC § 2-205, which is also known as the "firm offer" provision:

An offer by a merchant to buy or sell goods which by its terms gives assurance that it will be held open is not revocable, for lack of consideration, during the time stated, or if no time is stated, for a reasonable time, but in no event may such period of irrevocability exceed three months.

The Code demands that merchants, as professionals, keep their word even if they have been given no consideration for their assurances. Simply put, the Code dramatically changes the common law doctrine regarding the offeror's right to revoke when the offeror is a merchant (a person who regularly deals in goods of the kind or has the knowledge or skill peculiar to the practices or goods involved in the transaction) and the other provisions of § 2-205 have been met.

Finally, the equitable doctrine of promissory estoppel prohibits offerors from revoking their offers. Promissory estoppel prohibits a promisor from denying the making of a promise or escaping liability for that promise when the promisee justifiably relied on the promise being kept. Under this theory, offerors are prevented (estopped) from asserting a defense otherwise available to them (generally that they as common law offerors have the right to revoke the offer). For Joan, the offeree in our earlier example, to assert this doctrine, she must show that (1) Joe, the offeror, promised or represented to her that he would hold the offer open; (2) she relied on these promises or representations; (3) she consequently suffered a detriment (maybe she passed up the opportunity to purchase other cattle because she thought she would get Joe's); and (4) injustice can be avoided only by forcing the offeror to leave the offer open. In several cases, successful plaintiffs have used this doctrine to cut off the offeror's power of revocation.

Rejection   Thus far, we have dwelt on the offeror's power to terminate the offer. The offeree, of course, can refuse the offer and thereby terminate it. The law calls the offeree's power of termination rejection. Like revocations, rejections are not effective until communicated to (or received by) the offeror. Hence, as the offeree, Joan can tell Joe that she no longer is interested in the cattle and thereby reject Joe's offer.

The usual rule holds that an offer cannot later be accepted after lapse, revocation, or rejection, because after these events the offer has expired. Yet, if the parties nonetheless still are willing to deal, there may be a valid agreement subsequent to one of these events. However, the parties generally are not obligated to continue the transaction unless they find it advantageous to do so.

Exhibit 10.2 summarizes the various methods for terminating an offer.

Acceptance

Acceptance is the usual mode of "terminating" an offer. This represents a significant moment for the offeror and offeree because they have arrived at an agreement. Barring problems with consideration, capacity, genuineness of assent, legality, or proper form, a binding contract now exists.

Acceptance involves the offeree's assent to all the terms of the offer. Because this is so, the offeree's intention to be bound to the entire offer must be clear. Thus, the offeree's uncommunicated mental reservations will not be binding on the offeror. As with offers, courts apply the objective test to see whether the acceptance is valid. That the acceptance is oral, written, or implied (for example, through an act such as cashing a check) generally does not affect its validity, as long as the offer has been communicated to the offeree (or the offeree's agent), and it is the offeree (or the offeree's agent) who accepts.

Mirror Image Rule

Under common law rules, an acceptance must be not only clear but also unconditional. This concept, called the *mirror image* or *matching ribbons* rule of common law, means that the acceptance must match, term by term, the provisions in the offer. Any deviation from these terms, whether by alteration, addition, or omission, makes the acceptance invalid and tantamount to a rejection of the offer originally made. This result follows from the common law offeror's power to set the terms of the offer and the acceptance.

Any deviation from the terms of the offer brings about a qualified acceptance, known as a *counteroffer*. Counteroffers terminate offers by replacing the prior offer with the new *counter*offer and reversing the status of the parties. There will not be an agreement unless the original offeror is willing to accept the (new) terms of the counteroffer. As you have seen in other contexts, the original offerors are not obligated to do so unless they still want to deal. Therefore, if you desire to enter into a contract with the offeror, you should pay close attention to the language of the acceptance. Mere inquiries, requests, and terms implied by law, if part of the acceptance, do not invalidate it. Thus, if Mustafa offers to sell his car to Juanita for $2,000, and Juanita says, "I'll take the car at $2,000 as you offered, but I'd like you to throw in the snow tires," a valid acceptance probably exists. Juanita's added statement is a request, rather than a demand, and thus would not be treated as a counteroffer. Contrast this with Juanita's saying, "I accept if

EXHIBIT 10.2 Termination of the Offer

Method of Terminating the Offer	General Rule	Exceptions to the General Rule
1. Lapse—the termination of an offer through the passage of time or the occurrence of some condition	1. The offer ends at the time stated in the offer if a time is stated. 2. If no time is stated, the offer lapses after a reasonable time has passed. 3. The offeror does not need to communicate to the offeree the fact that the offer has lapsed. 4. Lapse may occur by operation of law upon: (1) the death or insanity of any of the contracting parties; (2) the supervening illegality of the subject matter; or (3) the destruction of the subject matter when neither party is at fault.	
2. Revocation—the termination of an offer by the offeror	1. Under common law, the offeror has a virtually unlimited right to revoke at any time before acceptance.	1. Options—contracts for which a person has paid money and that allow the person to buy or sell property at an agreed-on price or time period—make an offer irrevocable. 2. The "firm offer" provision of the UCC (§2-205) makes an offer irrevocable. 3. Promissory estoppel, whereby an offeror will be prevented from asserting a defense otherwise available to him or her in order to serve justice, can be applied to cut off the power of revocation.
	2. Revocation is not effective until it is communicated to (or received by) the offeree or the offeree's agent (i.e., the mailbox rule is inapplicable to revocations).	1. In public offers, public revocation is effective even against a person who does not know about it. The offeror need not communicate directly with every possible offeree.
3. Rejection—the termination of an offer by the offeree	1. The offeree rejects the offer by indicating directly or indirectly that he or she will not accept the offer. 2. A counteroffer is tantamount to a rejection of the offer.	1. Inquiries, requests, and terms implied by law that avoid making the acceptance conditional are not counteroffers. 2. The original offeror can deal with the new "offeror" on the new terms if he or she so desires.
	3. Rejection is not effective until it is communicated to (or received by) the offeror or the offeror's agent (i.e., the mailbox rule is inapplicable to rejections).	

EXHIBIT 10.2 continued

Method of Terminating the Offer	General Rule	Exceptions to the General Rule
4. Acceptance—the termination of an offer by the offeree's assenting to all the terms of the offer	1. Acceptance must be clear and unconditional. 2. Silence generally is not tantamount to acceptance.	1. The prior dealing of the parties may validate acceptance based on silence.
	3. Acceptance must match, term by term, the provisions of the original offer.	1. Inquiries, requests, and terms implied by law that avoid making the acceptance conditional have no effect on the validity of the acceptance. 2. Under UCC § 2-207, an acceptance containing additional or different terms may still constitute a valid acceptance unless acceptance is expressly made conditional on assent to such terms.
	4. Qualified, or conditional, acceptances are counteroffers.	1. The original offeror can accept these new terms if he or she wishes.
	5. Acceptance may be oral, written, or implied.	1. Under the UCC, the conduct of the parties alone may establish a contract (see UCC § 2-207).
	6. Acceptance must be accomplished by the offeree or the offeree's agent.	
	7. Acceptance is not effective until it is communicated to (or received by) the offeror or the offeror's agent.	1. In the absence of a stipulated mode, acceptance is effective upon dispatch to the implied agent in jurisdictions that recognize the mailbox rule. 2. The UCC sanctions acceptances in any manner and by any medium reasonable in the circumstances (UCC § 2-206).

you throw in the snow tires." The latter statement sounds more like a proviso or a condition and may constitute a counteroffer, making the purported acceptance legally ineffective unless Mustafa is prepared to let Juanita have the snow tires as part of the deal.

By permitting a contract to arise between the parties even if the offeree adds terms or includes different terms in the purported acceptance, both UCITA and the Uniform Commercial Code continue their respective relaxations of common law rules. To illustrate, § 2-207 of the UCC reflects the drafters' knowledge of commercial realities, specifically the fact that buyers and sellers in commercial settings generally exchange their respective forms (for example, purchase order forms or order acknowledgment forms), which may contain contradictory terms. Rather than hamper commercial dealings by judging the inconsistent terms under the common law rule that any variance in the material terms of the offer and acceptance constitutes a counteroffer and hence a rejection of the original offer, the UCC drafters permit a contract to arise between the parties unless the offeree expressly indicates that his or her acceptance of the offer is conditioned on the offeror's assent to these additional or different terms.

Section 2-207 of the Code furthermore sets out a scheme for determining the operative terms of the contract in these circumstances. For instance, between merchants, the additional terms automatically become part of the contract without the offeror's consent unless the original offer expressly requires the offeree to accept the terms of the offer; the additional terms materially alter the contract (that is, they would unfairly surprise or be unduly oppressive to the offeror); or the offeror has notified the offeree that he or she will not accept the new terms. This same section of the Code also states that conduct by both parties that recognizes the existence of a contract is sufficient to establish a contract for sale even though the writings of the parties otherwise do not establish a contract. In the on-line context, one's conduct in repeatedly accessing a Web site, after one has an opportunity to become aware of the terms of the license, may bind one to the terms set on the Web site.

Recall that e-commerce sellers should have a Web site feature that enables the buyer to indicate his or her acceptance by "clicking" on the box. As noted earlier, courts generally enforce click-on or click-wrap agreements/licenses. The law is not so clear-cut with regard to "shrink-wrap agreements" (or "shrink-wrap licenses"). These terms refer to agreements that are enclosed with the goods—say a computer or software—and a buyer consequently is not aware of these agreements before unwrapping (or opening) the goods. Such shrink-wrap agreements, or licenses, typically obligate the buyer to abide by such terms if he or she accepts whatever is in the box—here a computer or software. If the buyer fails to object to the terms and uses the product after having had an opportunity to become familiar with the terms, the buyer's conduct leads most courts to conclude that an acceptance has occurred. On the other hand, in some circumstances, courts will not enforce the contracts if the courts believe they are unconscionable (shockingly unfair), a point discussed in Chapter 11.

You will learn more about these concepts in succeeding chapters, but for now appreciate the alterations of common law rules embodied in the UCC and the underlying rationales for these changes.

Manner and Time of Acceptance

Besides accepting unconditionally, in order to effect a valid acceptance, the offeree must avoid one other pitfall: The offeree must accept in exactly the mode specified, or *stipulated*, by the offeror in the offer. Thus, if the offeror says that acceptance must occur by telegram, a letter will not constitute an effective acceptance. Similarly, if the offer says, "Acceptance required by return mail," an acceptance placed in the mail two days later is invalid. Finally, when the offer says, "Acceptance effective only when received at our home office," a contract will not arise until the offeror receives the acceptance.

Although the offeror enjoys the right to set out the exact mode of acceptance he or she may choose not to do so. In such cases, the offeree can use any *reasonable* medium of communication, as long as he or she acts within a reasonable time. Usually, the offeree will choose the same medium used by the offeror. By implication, this medium is a reasonable and therefore an authorized mode of communication. Hence, in the absence of a stipulated method of acceptance, if the offeror makes the offer via the mail, the offeree's mailing of an acceptance represents a reasonable (or authorized) mode of acceptance and thus a valid response. Another medium, such as the telephone, may be reasonable, and therefore authorized as well, if the parties have used this medium in their prior dealings or if local or industry custom sanctions it.

Use of an authorized mode of communication in such circumstances takes on particular significance because, in most states, these acceptances become legally effective *at the time of dispatch* (mailing, wiring, etc.). This is called the *mailbox rule*, or *implied-agency rule*, because the post office or telegraph office is deemed to be the agent of the offeror. To illustrate, assume that the offeror has not stipulated the mode of acceptance for an offer that was mailed to the offeree on September 28. The offeror subsequently attempts to revoke the offer on October 1 and then learns that the offeree had mailed an acceptance to the offeror on September 30. A contract exists as of September 30, and thus there is no "mere offer" that the offeror can revoke. The fact that the offeror had not received the acceptance until after he or she attempted to revoke the offer is irrelevant. The law treats the post office as the offeror's agent and thus concludes that the offeror "received" the acceptance on September 30, the date the offeree deposited the letter with the post office. Because some letters never arrive, it is advisable, of course, for the offeree to secure postal or telegraphic receipts in order to prove after the fact the date on which he or she actually dispatched the acceptance.

In contrast, where the offeree has used an unauthorized mode of communication, the strict rule states that the acceptance is ineffective until the offeror actually receives it; the mailbox rule is not applicable. Even so, some courts will enforce the agreement if the acceptance, even though communicated via an unauthorized mode, is timely, especially if the courts can construe the offeror's language about the proper mode as a suggestion rather than a stipulation or condition. UCC § 2-206(1)(a), by sanctioning acceptances "in any manner and by any medium reasonable in the circumstances," lends credence to such decisions.

As you can see, the time of contract formation is crucial. The mailbox rule allows acceptance, and hence a contract, to occur even before the offeror knows of the acceptance. Such acceptances cut off the offeror's otherwise almost unlimited right to revoke, because in order for an attempted revocation to be effective, it must occur prior to acceptance. Offerors can curtail the effect of the mailbox rule if they stipulate that acceptances will not be effective until received by them. Moreover, both the CISG and the technological realities of e-commerce have eroded the importance of the mailbox rule. The CISG, as is true of the rule followed in most civil law nations, makes acceptances effective on receipt. UCITA, while it makes electronic acceptance or performance effective on receipt, does acknowledge that receipt in and of itself will not guarantee that the content sent corresponds with the content received. Because receipt under the Uniform Electronic Transactions Act (UETA) occurs when the electronic record reaches the recipient's designated system (that is, an Internet service provider) rather than upon personal notice to the intended recipient, the transmission of the acceptance and the receipt of it are virtually instantaneous. Hence, as UETA heralds, once electronic messaging and mail/delivery tracking systems become more widespread, common law rules concerning the timing of acceptances (or revocations) will presumably become less significant. Note, too, that in any event, the mailbox rule applies only to acceptances: Revocations and rejections do not take effect until they are communicated to (that is, are received by) the offeree and offeror, respectively. Moreover, revocations and rejections do not become legally binding upon dispatch, as acceptances sometimes do.

Silence

As the foregoing discussion implies, some overt act necessarily accompanies acceptance. For this reason, acceptance requires a clear intent to accept. Thus, the settled weight of authority holds that mere silence by the offeree cannot constitute acceptance. However, in some isolated cases, the prior dealings of the parties may permit acceptance based on silence. The following case illustrates many of the concepts that relate to the manner of acceptance and the time when it occurs.

Bilateral versus Unilateral Contracts

The last major issue regarding acceptance concerns whether the contract, if formed, will be bilateral or unilateral. The weight of authority holds that an offer that contemplates the making of a *bilateral* contract may be accepted by either a direct communication of a promise to the offeror or a counterpromise inferred from the offeree's conduct or other circumstances.

NRW CASE 10.3   Sales/Manufacturing

ACCEPTING OFFERS

Unbeknownst to Carlos and Helen, Mai has been negotiating the purchase of a piece of real estate that she believes will represent an ideal distribution center once the firm has secured a loyal customer base. The would-be seller has the contracts ready and has asked that Mai stop by and sign the papers. Although she has indicated verbally that they probably will sign the agreements (she believes she can convince Carlos and Helen to do so), several weeks have passed without their having done so. Mai is somewhat worried that the would-be seller will bring a breach of contract action against the firm. She thus seeks your advice as to whether her fears are unfounded or legitimate. How will you answer her queries?

BUSINESS CONSIDERATIONS Why is it important for a firm to act diligently as to all its obligations? What does a firm risk if it does not do so?

ETHICAL CONSIDERATIONS Do you condone, on ethical grounds, the fashion in which Mai is acting in these circumstances? Why or why not?

INTERNATIONAL CONSIDERATIONS The "mailbox rule" establishes certain rules regarding acceptance under common law principles. Do these same rules apply in an international setting?

When the offer instead contemplates the formation of a *unilateral* contract, it usually is unnecessary for the offeree to communicate acceptance. The offeree accepts the offer merely by completing the act called for in the offer. Subsequent notice to the offeror would be redundant because the offeror eventually will learn of the acceptance when the offeree requests payment for the services rendered.

Nevertheless, disputes may arise between the parties as to how much time an offeree has for completing the performance mentioned in the purported unilateral contract. If the offeror says, "I'll pay you $50 to chop firewood for me" and the offeree says, "Okay," the offeree may think chopping wood at any time within the next two months will constitute a binding acceptance. On the other hand, the offeror may get nervous when the firewood is not in the wood rack within two weeks and therefore may make the

OKOSA v. HALL
718 A.2d 1223 (N.J. Super. A.D. 1998)

FACTS Obianuju Okosa was involved in an accident with defendant Tawn D. Hall on March 16, 1994. Hall was uninsured. Accordingly, the plaintiffs, Mr. and Mrs. Okosa, seeking Personal Injury Protection (PIP) benefits, brought an action against Hall and the plaintiffs' insurer, New Jersey Citizens United Reciprocal Exchange. The plaintiffs were insured under an automobile insurance policy that required a quarterly premium payment to be made on February 28, 1994. At the close of business on February 28, 1994, the insurer directed a letter to the Okosas. The letter, which was posted on March 1, 1994, advised the Okosas that they had failed to pay the $347.50 installment then due and that their policy would be automatically canceled at 12:01 A.M. on March 16, 1994, unless they made payment by that date. The letter further advised them:

> If we receive payment *on or before the cancellation date*, we will continue your policy with no interruption in the protection it affords. *If you've recently mailed your payment, please disregard this notice.* [emphasis added]

On March 15, 1994, while the policy was still in effect, the plaintiffs mailed, by certified mail, a check for the required payment. The automobile accident with the uninsured defendant occurred the next day. It is not known exactly when the plaintiffs' check was received, but the insurer deposited and cashed the check on March 22, 1994. In response to the Okosas' claims, the insurer subsequently advised them that the company would pay no PIP benefits because of the policy's cancellation prior to the accident. This litigation then ensued.

ISSUE Had the insureds' payment of the premium by certified mail on the day before the expiration of the policy avoided the cancellation of the policy?

HOLDING Yes. The application of the mailbox rule would validate the payment as timely and hence effective in avoiding the cancellation of the policy.

REASONING Excerpts from the opinion of Judge Kimmelman:

Plaintiffs contend that the so-called "Mailbox Rule" applies to the facts of this case and that the installment payment mailed on March 15, 1994 constituted a timely payment made prior to 12:01 A.M. on March 16, 1994.

Generally speaking, the Mailbox Rule sanctions the formation or completion of a contractual undertaking upon the act of mailing where the use of the mail is authorized by the other party as the medium for response. The rule is succinctly set forth as follows:

> Where parties are at distance from one another, and an offer is sent by mail, it is universally held in this country that the reply accepting the offer may be sent through the same medium, and, if it is so sent, the contract will be complete when the acceptance is mailed, . . . and beyond the acceptor's control; the theory being that, when one makes an offer through the mail, he authorizes the acceptance to be made through the same medium, and constitutes that medium his agent to receive his acceptance; that the acceptance, when mailed, is then constructively communicated to the offeror.

There is no question in this case that the carrier addressed plaintiffs by mail concerning their tardy payment. Its letter of February 28, 1994, posted March 1, 1994 invited plaintiffs' response with payment by mail. In so responding, plaintiffs did so by means of certified mail. The use of certified mail by plaintiffs was perspicacious because it insured proof of mailing and its use avoided the thorny issue which would arise from a fraudulent response by them that post-dated the accident. . . . We have completely reviewed the record and are satisfied that by authorizing the use of mail as a means of paying premiums, the carrier constituted the postal authorities as its agent. Accordingly the decision in this matter is controlled by the Mailbox Rule. As a consequence, the entry of summary judgment in favor of the insurer is reversed.

BUSINESS CONSIDERATIONS The mailbox rule imposes the risk of nondelivery on the offeror. Could the insurer have changed the language of the notice sent to those who had not paid installments on time so as to reduce or eliminate bearing this risk? What might such a provision have stated?

ETHICAL CONSIDERATIONS How can the risk of nondelivery of a reply be allocated in a manner that is fair and equitable to both parties? Is the current rule ethical? Was the Okosas' conduct in waiting until the last minute to mail in the overdue installment ethical? Why or why not?

same offer to someone else who completes the job sooner. In such circumstances, the offeror may not want to pay the first offeree for the wood delivered two months later; enough wood already has been supplied.

Because of such timing problems, courts remain somewhat hostile to unilateral contracts and, if possible, construe such alleged contracts as bilateral. More important, the contracting parties can avoid such timing problems by writing down all the pertinent details (delivery date, price, etc.) in advance, whether the offeror proposes a bilateral or a unilateral contract. Good business planning, even in everyday affairs, helps avoid potential legal difficulties.

Section 2-206(1)(b) of the Uniform Commercial Code eliminates many of the the common law distinctions between bilateral and unilateral contracts by specifying that, unless the parties unambiguously indicate otherwise, "an order or other offer to buy goods for prompt or current shipment shall be construed as inviting acceptance either by a prompt promise to ship or by the prompt or current shipment of conforming or nonconforming goods. . . ." In the first instance, a bilateral contract is formed; in the second, a unilateral contract. Acceptance is effective in either case. To check your understanding of the concepts in this chapter, use the resources at the Legal Information Institute, a site maintained by the Cornell Law School at http://www.law.cornell.edu/topics/contracts.html/.

Summary

Agreement represents perhaps the most important aspect of contract formation. To have agreement, there must be an offer and an acceptance. Assent to a contract must be mutual, and the common law offeror can set the terms of both the offer and the acceptance. An offer is an indication (by a promise or another commitment) of one's willingness to do or to refrain from doing something in the future. Courts employ an objective test to assess whether the parties have mutually assented to the terms of the agreement. Such a test asks whether a reasonable offeree would believe that the offeror has made an offer. No secret intent on the offeror's part can be shown.

To be a genuine offer under the common law, the offer must manifest a clear and present intent to contract and must be definite in all respects. Statements of opinion, statements of intention, and preliminary negotiations are too indefinite to constitute offers. The same is true of most advertisements: The law usually construes advertisements as invitations for persons to come in and make offers for the types of goods and at the prices indicated in the advertisements. An offer has no legal effect until the offeror communicates it to the offeree. General offers are perfectly legal; but many jurisdictions require that they, too, be communicated to the offeree in order for a valid acceptance to occur.

The four methods of terminating an offer include (1) lapse, (2) revocation, (3) rejection, and (4) acceptance. Generally, neither a revocation nor a rejection takes legal effect until communicated to or received by the other party. However, if an offeree uses an authorized (or reasonable) mode of communication, an acceptance may be effective on dispatch. The offeror's power of revocation may be limited by options, by the "firm offer" provision of the UCC, or by promissory estoppel. All three doctrines have certain elements that the offeree must prove before the offeree can cut off the offeror's right to revoke. Acceptance is the usual mode of terminating an offer. A bona fide offer and acceptance bring about an agreement, which in most cases will be tantamount to a contract. Acceptance involves the offeree's assent to all the terms of the offer. The acceptance must be clear and must be communicated to the offeror. Under the mirror image rule of common law, an acceptance has to match, term by term, the provisions in the offer. A qualified acceptance—one that deviates from the original terms—is called a counteroffer. A counteroffer terminates the original offer and in effect brings about the rejection of the offer unless the original offeror is willing to deal on the new terms. If the offeror has not stipulated the mode necessary for a valid acceptance, use of any reasonable (or authorized) mode of communication will make the acceptance effective on dispatch. This is called the mailbox rule. If, in contrast, the offeree has used an unauthorized mode, acceptance must be actually received to be effective; the mailbox rule will be inapplicable. The mailbox rule does not apply to revocations or rejections. Silence by the offeree ordinarily does not constitute acceptance under the common law. More widespread use of CISG, UCITA, and UETA principles presumably will weaken the relevance of the mailbox rule.

In bilateral contracts, communication of the acceptance usually is necessary; but this is not true for unilateral contracts. In unilateral contracts, the offeree accepts the offer merely by completing the act called for in the offer. Because of the problems that can arise from disputes concerning how much time the offeree in unilateral contracts has to accept, courts are hostile to this category of contract. The UCC eliminates many of the common law distinctions between bilateral and unilateral contracts.

Discussion Questions

1. What does a court mean by "mutual assent"?

2. Explain the phrase "objective theory of contracts."

3. Briefly state the common law rules surrounding a valid offer.

4. Name and define the ways in which an offer can terminate.

5. Is an advertisement a bona fide offer? Why or why not?

6. In what situations will "lapse" occur by operation of law?

7. Discuss the common law rules of revocation.

8. Name and list the elements for each of the methods available for terminating the offeror's power of revocation.

9. What are "counteroffers," and how do they arise?

10. Explain the term "mailbox rule" and its significance.

Case Problems and Writing Assignments

1. After John Roth made a written offer to buy real property, George E. Malson, the seller, made a written counteroffer on a standard form adopted by the California Association of Realtors. The form had a signature line, entitled "ACCEPTANCE," whereby Roth could accept the counteroffer. Instead of signing the "ACCEPTANCE" portion of the form, however, Roth signed a different portion of the form, entitled "CHANGES/ AMENDMENTS." Roth also wrote in certain terms of the purchase, although it ultimately turned out that these terms did not vary from the terms of Malson's counteroffer. Roth left the line for the expiration date for the counter-counteroffer blank. Roth conveyed the form to Stromer Realty by the November 8 deadline for the expiration of Malson's counteroffer. However, Malson did not accept Roth's counteroffer. Rather, on November 16, 1995, Malson's attorney advised Stromer that Malson had rejected Roth's counter to Malson's counteroffer and was taking the property off the market. On November 17, 1995, Malson memorialized this conversation in a letter sent to Stromer. Arguing that a contract existed between the parties, Roth later sued Malson for breach of contract and specific performance (that is, an equitable remedy granted when monetary damages would be insufficient and the object of the contract is unique and in which the court orders performance of the contract exactly as agreed). Roth contended that his giving an absolute, unqualified acceptance—in substance though not in form—to Malson's counteroffer had formed a binding contract. Should a court agree with Roth's claim? [*Roth v. Malson*, 79 Cal. Rptr. 2d 226 (Cal. App.3d Dist. 1998).]

2. Gregg Gill, a former employee of B&R International, Inc., alleged that B&R had breached an agreement to provide him severance pay. To establish his contention, Gill relied on an unsigned memorandum, dated February 22, 1993, and the response to that memorandum. The memorandum was written by Robbie Reid, B&R's president, chief executive officer, and controlling shareholder. Addressed to Gill and three other employees, the memorandum, which was not written on corporate letterhead, stated: "Attached is a Shareholder's Agreement for your review, and comments. The amounts shown are the final amounts being offered for their respective values. I have reviewed this and feel this agreement to be not only equitable, but very simple. . . . My alternative offer is to give each of you a Promissory Note equal to the dollars I have earlier indicated that would become due and payable upon the sale of the company. If the company [is] never sold, or if you were terminated for cause or left at your own discretion, then there would be no value payment. . . . I would like to have your comments on the Shareholder's Agreement before Wednesday . . . and whether or not you intend to become a shareholder on [the] terms offered." Gill's response stated: "Given my current financial obligations, the appropriate option at this time is the $100,000 promissory note. If the stock option can remain open (Feb. 22 memo), I would like to consider it at a future date." Reid made this handwritten notation on Gill's response: "I *respect* your decision—no problem—It is not fair to leave stock option open for you & not for others—We can discuss stock [at] a future date & a different price—Robbie." No promissory note was ever executed or delivered to Gill by either Reid or B&R. Gill also acknowledged that he was the only B&R employee to accept the lump sum payment option; the other employees elected to buy the stock. Had B&R offered Gill and certain other employees an opportunity either to purchase B&R stock at a favorable price or to receive a lump sum payment of $100,000? Had Gill accepted this offer so as to form an enforceable contract? [See *Gill v. B&R International, Inc.*, 507 S.E.2d 477 (Ga. App. 1998).]

3. A former International Business Machines Corporation (IBM) employee, Dennis Gomer, owned and operated Computer Consulting & Network Design, Inc. (CC&ND). CC&ND helped school districts in Kentucky and Tennessee prepare and submit government grant applications for installing computer networks. Upon the receipt of grant money, IBM typically served as the prime contractor; and CC&ND sought, but was not guaranteed, work as a subcontractor. Because CC&ND was not an IBM-approved subcontractor, it had to submit proposals through Manpower Technical, which was an approved subcontractor.

In 1998, CC&ND assisted Anderson County in obtaining a government grant. IBM was listed as a prospective prime contractor on the grant application and as such was required to submit a proposal to Anderson County that included subcontractor pricing. On November 24, 1999, CC&ND submitted a subcontractor proposal to IBM through Manpower Technical for the Anderson County project. The proposal defined the scope of the work to be done by CC&ND, quoted a total fixed price, and identified line item costs. A series of e-mail messages between Gomer and Terry Eaves, IBM's principal consultant, followed. On November 24, 1999, Eaves replied to Gomer's proposal by stating that several items were unacceptable. Eaves also stated, "I have committed to you that you will be Project Manager at Anderson County." He ended the message by requesting that Gomer resubmit the proposal. On November 26, Gomer replied and expressed appreciation for Eaves's willingness to "negotiate" with him. Gomer stated he would remove the unacceptable items in exchange for certain assurances from IBM. On November 29, Eaves sent a message again requesting that Gomer remove the unacceptable items and noting additional changes. Eaves reiterated, "You have my commitment and support in being the project manager for the Anderson County Project." He closed by reminding Gomer of the need to resubmit the proposal through Manpower Technical. On December 13, Gomer sent Eaves another message stating that the project appeared to be "in a state of flux" and that they would "move-forward" when Eaves got some "solid framework for [the] project." Gomer also referred to his "proposal" several times and requested additional information regarding the project.

On December 26, almost one month after CC&ND claimed it had entered into a contract with IBM, Gomer submitted another "proposal" through Manpower Technical. The second proposal retained one of the unacceptable items Gomer had told Eaves would be removed. It also stated, "this offer is valid until 31 December 1999." On January 3, 2002, IBM submitted to Anderson County a proposal that included the price of CC&ND's proposal to Manpower Technical. Anderson County subsequently refused IBM's proposal because it exceeded the grant amount. Anderson County then met with Gomer and asked that CC&ND's proposal amount be lowered so that he could serve as project manager and keep the project within Anderson County's budget. On his refusal, IBM resubmitted a proposal that excluded CC&ND and the other subcontractors. After Anderson County accepted this proposal, CC&ND filed this action alleging breach of contract. Who should win and why? [See *Computer Consulting & Network Design, Inc. v. International Business Machines Corp.*, 184 F. Supp. 2d 618 (W.D. Ky. 2002).]

4. Alison H. was a minor female who resided with her parents in Belchertown, Massachusetts. The Belchertown public school system was responsible for providing special education to students with learning disabilities. Though it began providing special education services to Alison at the beginning of the fifth grade, these were discontinued halfway through the school year. From then on, Alison's parents, the plaintiffs, had a running dispute with the school as to the special education services Alison should receive and where they would be given. No agreement could ever be reached on an appropriate individualized educational plan (IEP) for Alison.

On January 30, 1996, the plaintiffs retained attorney Claire Thompson to represent them as to the question of an appropriate IEP for Alison. During the subsequent negotiations, the plaintiffs made clear that they thought that White Oak School was the most appropriate placement for Alison and would meet their IEP demands. White Oak School was a private institution specializing in special education for children with learning disabilities. On August 21, 1996, the attorney for the school system faxed Thompson a letter that indicated the school system's belief that it was unlikely that Thompson or her clients would ever be satisfied with the IEP developed by Belchertown or the educational program provided by Belchertown. Therefore, the school officials offered Mr. and Mrs. H. the opportunity for Alison to attend White Oak for the 1996–1997 school year. This letter further stated: "*As a condition of finalizing this agreement, Belchertown would be looking for the withdrawal of the request for hearing, which hearing is scheduled for September 11, 1996, as well as a release of any and all claims arising prior to the execution of the agreement.*" The letter asked for an answer to this offer by August 23, 1996. Within a matter of hours Thompson replied by fax and accepted Belchertown's offer. The school prepared a new IEP for Alison's attendance at White Oak School; the parents accepted the IEP on September 3, 1996; and the scheduled hearing before the Bureau of Special Education Appeals was canceled. For Alison's attendance at White Oak School for the 1996–1997 school year, Belchertown paid a total of $22,295.20 in tuition and transportation costs.

By a letter dated November 6, 1996, Thompson asked that Belchertown School pay her attorney's fees totaling $6,112.40 through August 26, 1996. Taking the position that the plaintiffs had waived any claim for attorney's fees when they had accepted Belchertown's offer to place Alison in White Oak School, the Belchertown school officials rejected the demand for attorney's fees. Had the plaintiffs' acceptance of Belchertown's offer to place Alison in White Oak School subject to the condition that there be "a release of any and all claims arising prior to the execution of the agreement" amounted to a waiver of the plaintiffs' claim for attorney's fees? [See *Alison H. v. Byard*, 163 F.3d 2 (1st Cir. 1998).]

5. BUSINESS APPLICATION CASE Karla Schikore worked at a subsidiary of BankAmerica Corporation (the Bank) from 1978 to March 31, 1998. Pursuant to the federal Employee Retirement Income Security Act (ERISA), the Bank's Plan Administrator has discretionary authority under the Plan to determine employees' eligibility for benefits and to construe the terms of the Plan. The Plan rules, contained in the Plan Description, provided that an employee with at least $10,000 in her account who wished a lump-sum disbursement of benefits following termination of employment must submit a benefit payment election form to the BankAmerica Retirement Plans Service Center (Service Center) at least one year prior to the termination date. If employment was terminated before the one-year anniversary of the filing of the election form, the request for lump-sum disbursement was not honored and benefits instead were paid in five annual installments beginning in the calendar year after the employee reached 65 years of age.

Schikore, who was 51 years old at the time of this litigation, stated that she had completed the election form in December

1996, had mailed it to the Service Center, and had retained a copy for her records. In March 1998, prior to terminating her employment with the Bank, Schikore applied for a lump-sum disbursement of her benefits. At the time, the Plan informed Schikore that she did not have an election form on file at the Service Center. Immediately upon learning this, Schikore faxed a copy of the completed form to the Service Center. The Plan nevertheless denied Schikore's request for lump-sum disbursement on the basis that it did not have her election form on file one year prior to her March 1998 request.

Asserting that the common law mailbox rule creates a presumption of receipt that the Plan had failed to rebut, Schikore appealed the Plan's decision to the Plan Administrator. The Plan Administrator denied Schikore's appeal on the grounds that (1) because ERISA preempts (takes precedence over) common law rules, the mailbox rule was inapplicable to employee benefit plans; (2) even if the mailbox rule would otherwise apply, the Plan's contractual rules expressly required actual receipt as opposed to the mere mailing of the document; and (3) the Plan rules precluded a lump-sum disbursement because the Service Center did not have her election form on file one year prior to her March 1998 request. Schikore filed suit under the relevant ERISA provision that permits a participant "to recover benefits due to [her] under the terms of [her] plan, to enforce [her] rights under the terms of the plan, or to clarify [her] rights to future benefits under the terms of the plan." Given what you know of the mailbox rule, who would prevail in this lawsuit—the Bank or Schikore? [See *Schikore v. BankAmerica Supplemental Retirement Plan*, 269 F.3d 956 (9th Cir. 2001).]

6. **ETHICAL APPLICATION CASE** The Denis F. McKenna Co. (McKenna) sought a declaratory judgment against Mary Ann Smith, David Drew, and Drew Holdings, Inc. (Drew). McKenna filed the lawsuit to enforce an alleged real estate contract between McKenna and Smith and to obtain a preliminary injunction to prevent Smith from selling the property to Drew. Smith owned residential property that she placed up for sale for $459,000. On November 18, 1997, at approximately 10:30 A.M., Denis McKenna, president of The Denis F. McKenna Co., made an offer to buy the property through Peg Spengler, his real estate agent. The offer, for $435,000, expired at noon that day. When Smith saw the offer at about 11:00 or 11:30 A.M., she told Mary Jane Kraus, her real estate agent, that she wanted to consult with her attorney, Eugene Callahan, and her brother before she entered into a contract. Just before noon, although Smith still wanted to speak with Callahan, Smith made a counteroffer of $450,000, subject to Callahan's approval. McKenna responded by offering $442,500 and imposed a deadline of 2:00 P.M. that afternoon. Because she wanted to speak with Callahan before making her decision about the offer, Smith requested that McKenna extend the deadline until 3:00 P.M. When informed of Smith's comments, McKenna raised his offer to $450,000. Kraus informed Spengler that, while Smith likely would accept McKenna's offer, Smith still wanted to speak with Callahan. Spengler then asked Kraus for permission to deliver the offer to Smith personally. Kraus agreed but reiterated that Smith wanted to speak with her attorney before Smith signed any contract. At approximately 1:30 P.M., Spengler took the offer (which expired at 2:00 P.M. and included an attorney approval clause) to Smith's home. While Spengler waited, Smith unsuccessfully continued her attempts to reach Callahan. Callahan's secretary told Smith that as long as the contract included an attorney approval clause, Smith could sign it because Callahan, after reviewing the document, could reject the offer. However, Spengler told Smith that there was "no deal" and McKenna "would walk" if Smith did not sign the contract by 2:00 P.M. As a result, Smith signed the contract even though she had not reached Callahan. Spengler then faxed a copy of the contract to Callahan's office. The contract, a standardized real estate contract widely used in the Chicago area, included a nonnegotiable attorney approval clause that stated:

This contract is contingent upon the approval hereof as to form by the attorneys for Purchaser and Seller within 5 business days after Seller's acceptance of this contract. . . . [Written] notice of disapproval . . . given within the time period specified makes this contract . . . null and void. . . . [The] earnest money shall be returned to Purchasers.

On November 18, 1997, Drew offered to buy Smith's property for $480,000. On November 19, 1997, Callahan sent Spengler written notice (by fax and first-class mail) that Smith was rejecting the McKenna contract pursuant to the attorney approval clause. Furthermore, Coldwell Banker returned the $2,000 earnest money check that McKenna had submitted. Smith accepted the Drew offer on November 25, 1997. Callahan subsequently stated that the Drew contract was not relevant to his rejection of the McKenna contract. Rather, Callahan specifically objected to paragraph one of the contract, which gave Smith only a maximum of three hours in which to accept the contract.

Did Smith's purported acceptance of the contract before her attorney, in accordance with the attorney approval clause, had had the opportunity to review the contract, constitute a valid acceptance? Did Callahan act in bad faith in disapproving the contract? Did Callahan materially breach the agreement when he sent the notice of rejection to Spengler, McKenna's agent, rather than to McKenna? Assess the ethics of all the parties here, especially those of Spengler and Callahan. Would you have acted the same way each did or differently? Why? Does the existence of a standard realty form give an inherent advantage to the seller? If so, does this fact make the use of such forms unethical? Does the arguably excessive verbiage employed in such forms confuse—or enlighten—the would-be purchaser? Would the adoption of a "plain-English" approach to the drafting of these forms affect your assessment of the underlying ethical issues? Why or why not? [*Denis F. McKenna Co. v. Smith*, 704 N.E.2d 826 (Ill. App. 1st Dist. 1998).]

7. **CRITICAL THINKING CASE** Frank Crain Auctioneers, Inc. is a Kentucky real estate auctioneer that conducted an auction sale in Baldwin County, Alabama, on March 27, 1999. Before the sale, Crain sent out brochures describing the properties offered for

sale and mailed postcards to local real estate agents. Randy Delchamps, a licensed real estate broker and the owner of Randy Delchamps Real Estate Development Company in Mobile, received a postcard from Crain that stated:

We welcome the participation of other real estate professionals in this important auction. A fee equal to two percent (2%) top bid price will be paid from the auctioneer's commission to any licensed real estate broker or salesperson whose prospect successfully closes on the property. To qualify for payment of [the] commission, your prospect must be registered with Frank Crain Auctioneers forty-eight (48) hours prior to the auction. The broker or salesperson must attend and register his or her prospect on the day of the auction and must be present at the signing of the sales contract.

Delchamps's administrative assistant, Tracy Castillow, telephoned Crain's office, spoke to someone named "Susan," stated that she (Castillow) was calling on behalf of Randy Delchamps Real Estate, and inquired what she needed to do to register Delchamps for the auction. Susan took Delchamps's name, address, and fax telephone number and told Castillow that she (Susan) "had [Delchamps] registered." Castillow did not mention that Delchamps had a prospective buyer or that he expected to earn a 2 percent sales commission. Moreover, Susan did not ask whether Delchamps wanted to register a prospective buyer. Delchamps attended the auction on March 27, 1999. When he arrived, David Rice, a Crain employee who was conducting the auction, gave him a bid card as well as a brochure on the properties to be auctioned and said, "I have you registered." Delchamps did not tell Rice that he (Delchamps) was expecting a commission from any sale at the auction, nor did Rice tell Delchamps that he might earn such a commission. With a bid of $1,595,000, Delchamps was the highest bidder on one parcel of property. After the auction, he gave Rice a personal check, signed "Randy Delchamps," as a deposit for 10 percent of the bid

and signed a contract to buy the property in the name of "Randy Delchamps and/or assigns." Delchamps explained that he had added the phrase "and/or assigns" because he "was not buying [the property] just for himself" but instead for an as-yet-unnamed entity that would be formed to buy the property. The closing was set for 60 days after the auction. Before the closing, Delchamps and his investors formed a limited liability corporation, "D.M.M.H.K., L.L.C.," to buy the property. Delchamps owned a 25 percent interest and was the managing member of the L.L.C. Sometime during the 60-day interim, Delchamps inquired about a commission. Stating that Delchamps had not complied with the terms of the offer, Crain refused to pay him one. Did a contract entitling Delchamps to a commission exist between Crain and Delchamps? [See *Frank Crain Auctioneers, Inc., v. Delchamps*, 797 So. 2d 470 (Ala. Civ. App. 2000).]

8. **YOU BE THE JUDGE** The TV Corporation International (dotTV) registers Internet domain names for a fee. In April 2000, dotTV auctioned off the domain name "Golf. tv." Je Ho Lim, a resident of South Korea, bid $1,010 for this domain name. On or about May 25, 2000, Lim received an e-mail entitled "E-MAIL INVOICE FOR DOMAIN REGISTRATION." Sent in response to Lim's bid, the e-mail said, "Congratulations! You have won the auction for the following domain name "—golf." Lim thereafter authorized a credit card payment to dotTV. Sometime later, however, dotTV notified Lim that "we have decided to release you from your bid." The company also told Lim to "disregard" the acceptance notification because it was an "e-mail error." Later, dotTV publicly offered the name "Golf. tv" at an opening bid of $1,000,000. Lim subsequently sued dotTV for breach of contract. Using the concepts discussed in this chapter, frame the arguments for Lim and dotTV, respectively. Then decide who has the more compelling arguments. [See *Lim v. The.TV Corporation, International*, 121 Cal. Rptr. 2d 333 (Cal. App. 2d Dist. 2002).]

Notes

1. UCC, §§ 2-305, 2-309, and 2-310.
2. Ibid., § 2-306.
3. UCITA § 305.

Consideration: The Basis of the Bargain

AGENDA

NRW NRW will, hopefully, be entering into a number of contracts for the sale of its products. It will also be entering into a number of other contracts in order to acquire the materials and parts to produce the products. The members of the firm want to be certain NRW is entering into legally binding contracts. One of their concerns centers on whether they are truly giving and/or receiving consideration in their contracts, and whether that consideration is adequate. They also want to avoid making or receiving any illusory promises in any of their contracts. They understand that bargaining, promises, and exchanges figure prominently in any assessment of whether consideration exists. Yet they also have heard that in certain situations courts will enforce agreements despite a lack of consideration.

NRW presently confronts these and other contractual issues. Be prepared! You never know when the firm or one of its members will seek your advice.

As discussed in Chapter 10, contract law addresses the importance of the parties' reaching an agreement. In addition, the law requires some evidence that the parties' agreement is mutual. One way for courts to find this "mutuality" is by determining that the parties have made an *exchange* of value. This exchange of value, the quid pro quo of contract formation, is called *consideration*. This chapter concentrates on this third requisite of contract formation.

The Bargain as a Contract Theory

Despite the rather checkered history that surrounds its principles, no doctrine of common law is as firmly entrenched today as the concept of consideration. Although the meaning of the concept is shrouded in historical traditions, familiarity with the doctrine's tenets remains fundamental to an understanding of modern contract law.

Remember that early in the history of contracts the parties underwent elaborate rituals, such as sealing their contracts with wax and placing their insignia in the wax, in order to demonstrate their willingness to be bound to the terms embodied in the agreement. Although few contracts are under seal nowadays, the idea that the parties actually ought to bargain and exchange something of value rather than merely make empty promises has lingered. Today, this emphasis is evident in the notion that the presence of consideration indicates the parties' exchange of something of value that results in an agreement between the parties. Thus, consideration shows that some obligation or duty worthy of a court's protection genuinely exists. It also establishes that the parties are acting deliberately and intend to bind themselves to the terms of the agreement.

Because it rids contracts of excessive formality while encouraging exchanges between people, the doctrine of consideration initially appears well suited to commercial and economic activity and hence to the study of business law. Nevertheless, some of the legal results under this doctrine seem quite harsh. For this reason, theories have emerged that permit an agreement to be binding in some cases despite a lack of consideration.

Definition of Consideration

Among the many definitions of the term *consideration*, one of the most common states that consideration is a waiver (that is, a voluntary surrender of a legal right), or promised waiver, of rights bargained for and given in exchange for a promise. Consideration always consists of either a benefit to the promisor or a detriment to the promisee, bargained for and given in exchange for a promise. In view of the previous discussion, it is no surprise to see that the words *bargain*, *promise*, and *exchange* play such a prominent role in this definition. Consideration usually takes the form of money; but it may consist of an intangible, noneconomic benefit (or detriment) or anything of value to the parties.

Consideration as an Act or a Forbearance to Act

Implicit in this doctrine is the necessity of the parties' bargaining over some present event or object and exchanging something of value so as to bind themselves to do (or to refrain from doing) something. It is important, then, to check the parties' language closely. Words that sound like promises actually may be illusory (that is, they derive from false appearances or are fallacious) because the parties really have not committed themselves in any manner to the bargain. If one party never actually agrees to do anything (for example, if someone says, "I will sell you my farm for $80,000 if I feel like it"), the promise is illusory and unenforceable because consideration is absent.

In unilateral contracts, consideration manifests itself in an act or a forbearance to act. In the latter situation, the consideration comes from refraining from engaging in a legal act. For example, suppose your parents promise to send you to Europe for the summer if you will earn straight A's in school. If you do, the agreement is supported by consideration and will be enforceable in a court of law, assuming you live in a state where family members can sue each other if they breach (that is, fail to perform) this agreement.

Now apply the definition of consideration to see why this agreement is enforceable. You waived your right to unlimited leisure time in exchange for your parents' promise. You and your parents bargained about the straight A's, so the trip is not a gift to you. You must do something (study more than you might like) or refrain from doing something (watching television or engaging in other leisure activities) to earn it. Furthermore, your parents, the promisors (those who make a promise or commitment) received a benefit (the satisfaction of knowing you are an honor student) while you, the promisee (one to whom a promise or commitment has been made), suffered a detriment (studying hard all year) as a result of this bargain. Your act of making perfect grades therefore has been given in exchange for your parents' promise to pay for your trip abroad. Note that the benefit they receive has no dollars-and-cents economic value, yet the law views the benefit as sufficient consideration to support their side of the bargain. They will receive what they asked of you. Think about these principles as you consider *Herremans v. Carrera Designs, Inc.*

Consideration as a Promise to Act or to Forbear

Both the *Herremans* case and the earlier hypothetical bargain evince the formation of a unilateral contract. The analysis will be the same, however, if you *promise* to earn straight A's in exchange for your parents' *promise* to send you to Europe. In this situation, a bilateral contract is created, with the respective promises constituting the consideration to support the agreement, as long as the promises are genuine and not illusory.

Take this example one step further. For instance, if your parents breach this contract and you want to sue them, they may bargain with you about dropping the lawsuit. If they promise to pay you $1,000 in exchange for your promise to forgo legal action, you will have made another enforceable contract. Why? A promise to act or to forbear from a certain action, bargained for and given in exchange for another promise, constitutes consideration. Therefore, you should be able to convince a court to force your parents to pay, should they refuse to do so.

11.1

HERREMANS v. CARRERA DESIGNS, INC.
157 F.3d 1118 (7th Cir. 1998)

FACTS Carrera Designs, Inc. (Carrera) employed Timothy Herremans as the manager of one of its plants. The failure of a major customer to pay its bills had caused Herremans's annual bonus in 1995 to be lower than usual. Carrera decided that, since the failure was not Herremans's fault, the company would, though not contractually obligated to do so, pay him the additional bonus that he would have earned but for the customer's default. Carrera promised to pay the additional bonus in three equal annual installments, and Herremans promised to continue working for Carrera. However, Carrera fired Herremans 10 months later, in November 1996. Thereupon, Herremans sued Carrera for the unpaid portion of his 1995 and 1996 bonuses. Carrera claimed that because Herremans had intended to work for Carrera until his retirement (which would not have occurred in the next three years), its contract with Herremans lacked consideration.

ISSUE Had Herremans given consideration in exchange for Carrera's promise to pay Herremans's bonus in three additional installments?

HOLDING Yes. As an at-will employee, Herremans was free to quit his employment with Carrera at any time. Hence, his giving up that right in exchange for Carrera's promise of a bonus constituted consideration for that promise.

REASONING Excerpts from the opinion of Judge Posner:

Herremans argues that even if he is not entitled to double damages under the wage payment law, he is entitled to . . . actual . . . damages for breach of a contractual entitlement to the bonuses. His bonus for 1995 was depressed by the failure of a major customer of the plant to pay its bills—thus underscoring [the] point that Herremans's entitlement to bonus did not depend on just his own time and effort and product. Carrera decided that since the failure was not Herremans's fault, the company would, though not contractually obligated to do so, pay him the additional bonus that he would have earned had it not been for the customer's default. It promised to pay him the additional bonus in three equal annual installments and the promise was supported by consideration—Herremans' promise to continue working for Carrera. Carrera argues that since . . . Herremans intended to work for Carrera until his retirement, which was not due within the next three years, he gave up nothing by agreeing to continue working.

But consideration is a formal rather than a substantive requirement of the law of contracts. A promise is supported by consideration if it is formally conditioned on a promise by the promisee, even if the promisor would have carried out the promised undertaking without a reciprocal promise. [As Farnsworth's treatise on contracts notes, if] X promises to go to work for Y, a successful investment advisor, at a salary of $40,000 a year, Y's reciprocal promise of that salary is enforceable without inquiry into whether X, who let us say is independently wealthy, would have agreed to work for Y without any pay at all, perhaps for the experience or because he likes Y. To allow promisors' motives to be dissected would disserve an important purpose of contract law—to minimize the occasions on which parties to contracts must submit themselves to the vagaries of juries. . . . It is not as if Herremans had been contractually obligated to remain in Carrera's employ; in that event, the promise of the bonus in exchange for his agreeing to stay on would have been a modification of the contract unsupported by consideration and so unenforceable. . . . His contract was one of employment at will; he was free to quit at any time; and his giving up that right in exchange for the promise of a bonus was consideration for that promise, . . . even if, as in our earlier example, he would have stayed on anyway.

BUSINESS CONSIDERATIONS Assume Carrera Designs, Inc., has asked you to modify its contractual language so that in the future it can avoid litigation of the type it had with Herremans. What additions, deletions, or modifications will you make?

ETHICAL CONSIDERATIONS Ethically speaking, should Carrera have denied Herremans's bonuses? Should Herremans, as a terminated employee (assuming he had deserved to be fired), have accepted them?

Adequacy of Consideration

Will your parents win in the earlier example if they argue that the $10,000 they will spend on your trip to Europe is too much, or that you really are doing nothing—because becoming an honor student is insufficient to constitute a detriment to you—to secure your side of the bargain? Usually not, because courts generally are unreceptive to such arguments. The classic rule states that courts will not inquire into the adequacy of the consideration. Courts instead will assume that the parties themselves remain the best judges of how much their bargain is worth and whether their performances are substantially equivalent. In other words, courts ordinarily will not second-guess the parties after the fact. *Christian v. Gouldin* illustrates this important principle.

11.2

CHRISTIAN v. GOULDIN
804 A.2d 865 (Conn. App. 2002)

FACTS F. Glenn Christian, Norman H. Gouldin, Angelo L. Miglietta, and James M. Belcher formed Keene Industries Company, a general partnership, in June 1988. The partnership owned Keene Industries, Inc. In May 1989, the partnership restated and amended its partnership agreement. That partnership agreement (the May agreement) stated that upon termination of a partner's employment, the departing partner's interest in the partnership would consist of three components: a pro rata share of the partnership's income, an amount based on the departing partner's capital account; and a guaranteed payment based on the partnership's determined value. The income and capital portions were to be paid within 180 days of termination; and the guaranteed amount was to be paid quarterly over four years in equal installments. However, the May agreement also included a limiting provision that allowed the partnership to defer payments to withdrawing partners on a per capita basis in the event that total payouts to such partners exceeded $650,000 in any given fiscal year. Christian's employment with Keene Industries Company and Keene Industries, Inc., terminated on December 31, 1991, thereby triggering these liquidation provisions. On that date, Christian's income and capital portions of the liquidation payments equaled $94,597.28; and his guaranteed payment was $900,000. On January 1, 1992, after some negotiations, the remaining partners presented him with a proposed new agreement (the letter agreement) expressly referencing his termination and subsequent payout. Christian executed that letter agreement on January 15, 1992. Using the May agreement's method of calculation, the letter agreement specified the exact amounts owed to Christian. The guaranteed payout installments, however, would now be dispersed monthly during a five-year period. Furthermore, any payments 30 days or more overdue would accrue interest at a rate of 10 percent per annum. Additionally, the letter agreement provided that all payments to Christian would be from the partnership's funds without any personal liability on the part of the individual partners. In short, by signing the letter agreement, Christian released and discharged the partnership, its partners, and the corporation from all other claims. On September 29, 1999, Christian sued the individual partners and the partnership for breach of contract owing to the nonpayment of the guaranteed payment portions of the liquidation payout. On July 28, 2000, the remaining individual partners asserted the signed general release and the provisions of the letter agreement as defenses to personal liability. Christian, in turn, argued that the letter agreement was unenforceable because it was not supported by consideration.

ISSUE Was the letter agreement supported by consideration?

HOLDING Yes. The letter agreement, in releasing the individual partners from personal liability for debts arising from the liquidation payments owed to Christian on his withdrawal from the partnership, was supported by consideration and therefore was enforceable.

REASONING Excerpts from the opinion of Judge Foti:

The plaintiff . . . argues that the court improperly determined that he had "received consideration in exchange for his promise to seek payment only from the assets of the partnership without recourse to the individual partners" because a genuine issue of material fact remained as to that issue. We disagree.

Consideration consists of "a benefit to the party promising, or a loss or detriment to the party to whom the promise is made." . . . Although an exchange of promises usually will satisfy the consideration requirement . . . "a promise to do that which one is already bound by his contract to do is not sufficient consideration to support an additional promise by the other party to the contract." . . . "A modification of an agreement must be supported by valid consideration and requires a party to do, or promise to do, something further than, or different from, that which he is already bound to do." . . . Nevertheless, "the doctrine of consideration does not require or imply an equal exchange between the contracting parties. . . . The general rule is that, in the absence of

fraud or other unconscionable circumstances, a contract will not be rendered unenforceable at the behest of one of the contracting parties merely because of an inadequacy of consideration." . . . After reviewing the facts of the present case, we conclude that the court reasonably determined that the provision in the letter agreement to pay interest on late payments was a promise by the defendants to do something they had not agreed to in the May agreement. Additionally, because the letter agreement now is the operative document regarding payout, the plaintiff no longer is subject to a potential reduction in his payouts due to the May agreement's payout cap. Our review of the documents leads us to agree with the court's determination. . . . Either of those changes to the original agreement could potentially benefit the plaintiff, and each falls within the definition of consideration previously set forth. The fact that the plaintiff may have given up substantial rights under the May agreement in exchange for concessions that in hindsight may seem less valuable does not make the consideration inadequate. Further, . . . nothing in the record . . . suggests fraud or unconscionable behavior on the part of the partnership in negotiating the agreement. Therefore, we agree with the court that the letter agreement was supported by proper consideration.

BUSINESS CONSIDERATIONS What provisions should partnership agreements contain? What are the advantages and disadvantages of doing business in the partnership form?

ETHICAL CONSIDERATIONS Was it ethical for Christian to attempt to have the letter agreement set aside once he realized its terms were less advantageous to him? Did the remaining partners behave ethically in seeking a release of personal liability?

Exceptions to the general rule that courts will not inquire into the adequacy of the consideration do exist, however. If a court finds evidence of fraud, duress, undue influence, mistake, or other similar situations at the time of contract formation, adequacy of consideration becomes a much more significant issue. Courts in these situations may permit one or more of the litigants to back out of the deal. Under either the common law or the Uniform Commercial Code (see § 2-302 of the UCC, which holds that a court may refuse to enforce a contract if it is shockingly unfair or oppressive), the doctrine of unconscionability in some circumstances also can form a further basis for overturning bargains when the consideration appears to be grossly inadequate. But remember that courts do not routinely use this rationale to overturn bargaining between parties.

Consideration in Special Contexts

Contracts for the Sale of Goods

As explained in Chapter 9, the "firm offer" provision of the Uniform Commercial Code (§ 2-205) states that an offer to buy or sell goods by a merchant who gives assurance in writing that the offer will be held open may be irrevocable for a period of up to three months even if no consideration has been paid to the offeror. Intended to encourage commercial activity that is free from hagglings about "options," this provision dramatically changes the common law rules concerning consideration. Thus, even in the absence of consideration, courts will enforce a UCC firm offer. The same is true of modifications under the UCC: They, too, are enforceable without consideration under § 2-209(1). In contrast, the common law would require consideration in both situations.

In this context, recall again output and requirements contracts, two types of sales contracts mentioned earlier in Chapter 10. Unless the language of these contracts indicates otherwise, courts ordinarily enforce output and requirements contracts as contracts supported by consideration. These courts reason that consideration is present in the form of the respective detriments suffered by the buyer and seller when they obligate themselves to deal exclusively with the other party in these circumstances. The promises undergirding such contracts, then, are nonillusory and make the bargains enforceable.

Suretyship Contracts

Although the UCC has relaxed the requirement of consideration in some situations, the common law definitely requires consideration in suretyship contracts. Such contracts always involve three parties: a principal debtor, a creditor, and a surety. The *surety* agrees to be liable to the creditor in the event of the principal debtor's default (the debtor's failure to perform a contractual obligation, without legal excuse or justification for the nonperformance). Such arrangements occur frequently in commercial transactions. To illustrate, assume that Chan Wai (the principal debtor) wishes to buy a new car. She may seek financing from a credit union (the creditor), which in turn may require that she bolster her credit (and decrease its risk) by having another person (such as her father or mother) sign the note as a surety. In so doing, the surety agrees to be primarily liable on the debt; the credit union can sue the surety once Chan Wai defaults. The lender does not have to sue Chan Wai first as a prerequisite to seeking payment from the surety.

If the principal debtor and surety simultaneously promise to pay the promissory note, a single consideration (the loan of money to Chan Wai by the credit union) will support these promises. Given the presence of consideration, both promises will be enforceable. If, in contrast, the credit union lends the money for the car to Chan Wai and later asks a surety to promise to pay in the event of her default, this second promise must be supported by new consideration before the surety's promise is legally binding. As discussed in the Past Consideration section of this chapter, Chan Wai's preexisting obligation to the credit union (because the loan has already been made) does not

---

Finance

ACQUIRING FINANCING FOR NRW

The firm members are considering a number of options for acquiring financing for the firm as it grows. Helen recently has discussed acquiring a line of credit for NRW from a local commercial bank. The bank officer with whom Helen has dealt has informed her that NRW at this time does not have a sufficiently adequate history to justify a significant line of credit. The officer does point out, however, that the bank may be willing to grant the firm a line of credit if the firm has a surety who is willing to join the firm in its application. Helen remains uncertain of exactly what a suretyship arrangement entails. She therefore has asked you what a surety is and whether the firm should seek such an arrangement. What will you tell her?

BUSINESS CONSIDERATIONS When should a business be willing to enter into a suretyship arrangement? When should an officer of a business be willing to serve as a surety for the firm?

ETHICAL CONSIDERATIONS Is it ethical for a lender to require the officers of a small business to serve as sureties for the firm? Would your answer be different if the business were a partnership or proprietorship rather than a corporation? Why?

INTERNATIONAL CONSIDERATIONS Are suretyship arrangements common in Europe, Asia, and Africa? Why or why not?

---

constitute consideration for enforcing the surety's subsequent promise to pay the credit union.

Liquidated Debts

If one owes a debt to another person, partial payment of that debt is not consideration for full discharge of the debt. For instance, assume Ravi Singh has his dentist perform a root canal treatment on him. At the outset, the dentist tells Ravi the treatment will cost $390, and Ravi agrees that this is a fair price. If Ravi pays $250, he cannot successfully argue that this part payment is consideration for full discharge of the debt. Put in legal terms, the dentist will be able to argue that Ravi is under a preexisting duty to pay the entire $390. Since neither party has waived any rights nor has either engaged in any bargaining in exchange for this promise to pay $250, there is, by definition, an absence of consideration here. Hence, by the settled rule, Ravi is liable for the entire bill, or $390. It is crucial to note that the debt is *liquidated*; that is, the amount owed is not disputed. Ravi has agreed to pay $390, and he should not, after the fact, be allowed to escape this obligation. Such a legal result would throw commercial dealings into shambles!

Unliquidated Debts

Now let us assume that the debt is not liquidated. Suppose that Ravi initially has agreed to pay $390 for the root canal treatment. However, after the dentist treats him, Ravi continues to have soreness around the gums, and the treated tooth still is sensitive to thermal changes. Although Ravi wants to live up to his obligation to pay his debt, he does not believe he should pay the dentist the entire amount because he remains dissatisfied with the results of the treatment. At the point Ravi expresses these objections to the dentist, the debt is *unliquidated*; that is, the precise amount owed is in dispute. If Ravi in these circumstances sends the dentist a check for $250—particularly if he in some fashion indicates that this amount represents full payment for his entire indebtedness—the dentist should understand that cashing Ravi's check permits Ravi to argue that he owes her nothing more. Her act of cashing the check shows that she impliedly has agreed to accept $250 as full payment of the debt. Thus, she is subject to the common law rule that payment toward an unliquidated debt that is intended as and accepted as full payment is consideration for full discharge of the debt.

Instead, if the dentist wishes both to collect the entire $390 she alleges Ravi owes and to protect her rights fully, she should not cash Ravi's check for $250. Rather, she should return it to Ravi with a note stating that she is not agreeing to accept the tendered amount as full payment of the debt. If she is strapped for cash, she may be able to cash the check and try to preserve her rights against Ravi by endorsing it "with full reservation of all rights." Ideally, to avoid the application of the rule that partial payment of an unliquidated debt that is accepted (expressly or impliedly) as full payment of the debt is consideration for a full discharge of that debt, she should refrain from cashing the check.

Alternatively, Ravi and the dentist may negotiate and ultimately agree that $250 is the amount owed. In this case, each receives a benefit (Ravi, by paying $140 less than he thought he would have to pay; the dentist, by getting most of the $390) and each suffers a detriment (Ravi, by believing $250 is still too much; the dentist, by thinking she has lost $140) as a result of the bargained-for promise to pay. This notion of an exchange of rights is a hallmark of consideration.

One last note is appropriate. When Ravi and the dentist agree on the $250 sum, technically there is a compromise (of the unliquidated debt) that subsequently has led to a satisfaction and an accord. A *compromise* is the settlement of a disputed claim by the mutual agreement of the parties. The agreement as to the amount is an *accord*, and the fulfillment of the agreement (the actual payment of the agreed-upon amount) is a *satisfaction*.

Composition Agreements

Unliquidated debt situations form the basis for a court's enforcement of a composition agreement, or an agreement between a debtor and a group of creditors to accept a smaller percentage of the debt owed in full satisfaction of the claim, as consideration for full discharge of the debt. Even though you will not study bankruptcy, or the federal law proceedings that are designed to give an "honest debtor" a fresh start, until Chapter 28, you probably are aware that the bankruptcy of the debtor poses grave financial risks for the creditor. Put differently, in bankruptcy proceedings a creditor ordinarily realizes only a few cents on every dollar owed; consequently, it often is in the creditor's best interest to give the debtor more time to pay (before the creditor forces the debtor into bankruptcy) or to agree with other creditors to accept smaller sums in full cancellation of larger claims through a composition agreement.

For example, suppose Doug (the debtor) owes Ann, Bill, and Cara (the creditors) $6,000, $4,000, and $2,000, respectively. The creditors each may agree to accept 50 percent of the respective debts as full satisfaction of their claims against Doug. Thus, if Doug pays Ann $3,000, Bill $2,000, and Cara $1,000, none of the three will be able to sue for the remaining amount. Courts analogize the result here to a settlement of an unliquidated debt situation, in which the resultant compromise between the debtor and a creditor represents a satisfaction and accord for the debts. Similarly, in composition agreements, those agreed to by the debtor and a group of creditors, payments accepted by the creditors are supported by consideration and thus constitute full discharge of the debts.

Some courts instead will characterize the sums owed to Ann, Bill, and Cara as liquidated debts and will find insufficient consideration in the subsequent agreement to justify full discharge of the debts. Ironically, these same courts in the next breath may sanction such agreements on public policy grounds (the debtor's avoidance of bankruptcy and the creditors' realization of partial payment). Whatever the rationale, courts clearly favor composition agreements and therefore enforce them.

Absence of Consideration

Under certain circumstances, courts will find a total absence of consideration and will not enforce the agreement that the parties have shaped.

Illusory Promises

You will recall that promises that do not bind the promisor to a commitment are illusory promises. Such promises can be performed without any benefit to the promisor or without any detriment to the promisee and hence are not supported by consideration. A promise "to order such goods as we may wish" or "as we may want from time to time" is not a genuine promise at all; it only appears to set up a binding commitment. Instead, it actually allows the promisor to order nothing. Such "will, wish, or want contracts," as they often are called, are void because they lack consideration.

Contracts that purport to reserve an immediate right of arbitrary cancellation (any action that indicates a desire to terminate the obligations set out in the contract) fall into this category of contracts as well. Because of the potential unfairness of allowing one side, by merely giving notice of cancellation, to free itself from an agreement to which the other side considers itself bound, courts are hostile to attempted exercises of a right of arbitrary cancellation. Courts therefore try to find some actual or implied limitations on the purported immediate right of arbitrary cancellation so as to make it a nonillusory, or binding, promise. Since consideration will exist for such promises, the agreement will be enforceable.

Preexisting Duty

If one performs or refrains from performing an act that one has a preexisting obligation to do or to refrain from doing, settled law holds that such a person has suffered no detriment. Consequently, no consideration is present to support the underlying promise or performance.

This principle often manifests itself in cases involving law enforcement officers. Assume you live next door to a policewoman, and she approaches you with this proposition: For $50 she will undertake extra patrols around your house when you are gone on a trip. Since this sounds like a good deal to you, you agree. But you have second thoughts later and do not pay her. When she sues you in small claims court, she probably will lose because she has a preexisting

---

| NRW CASE 11.2 | Finance/Management |

NRW

ARRANGING CREDIT TERMS

NRW recently made a large sale to a retail establishment. The purchaser arranged credit terms with NRW and agreed to pay for the purchase over the next 24 months. Shortly after making this purchase, the customer encountered some serious short-term financial difficulties. As a result, it has fallen behind in its payments to NRW and now faces the possibility of being forced into bankruptcy. The customer is convinced that it can weather these problems and shortly can become a profitable and viable business entity again, *if* it can find a way to meet its short-term financial problems without resorting to bankruptcy. The customer has asked NRW to agree to accept smaller monthly payments spread over the next 36 months. The company's president states that his company has proposed similar arrangements with several of its other creditors. The firm members ask you what they should do under these circumstances. What will you say? What is the legal significance of agreeing to the customer's proposal?

BUSINESS CONSIDERATIONS Should a business that regularly sells on credit to its customers establish a policy for handling situations in which its customers encounter financial problems, or should a firm handle each case individually as the situation arises? What are the benefits and the drawbacks to each approach?

ETHICAL CONSIDERATIONS Is it ethical for a firm, after granting credit to its customers, to adopt a hard-line approach when any of the customers encounters difficulties? Is it ethical for a credit customer to threaten to resort to bankruptcy relief if the other party (the creditor) balks at allowing the refinancing of the credit arrangement?

INTERNATIONAL CONSIDERATIONS What percentage of countries across the globe recognize the concept of bankruptcy? Do other nations have bankruptcy protections similar to the protections available in the United States? What sort of relief might be offered in other nations?

---

duty (imposed by law) to try to keep your home free from burglaries. In making those extra patrols, she has suffered no detriment; so consideration to support her promise to you is lacking.

Besides obligations or duties imposed by law, pre-existing duties may stem from contractual agreements. Numerous cases address these situations. For example, suppose G & H Painting Service has contracted with you to paint your basement for $900. Halfway through the job, the crew boss tells you he will dismiss the crew unless you agree to pay him $200 more (he has just seen the latest consumer price index and knows inflation is winning against him). Because you are having a party in two days, you grudgingly say yes. On completion of the job, do you have to pay $900 or $1,100? Based on the doctrine of preexisting obligations, you generally will have to pay only $900, since the firm already owes you the duty of finishing the basement. But if you subsequently want G & H to lay a concrete patio for you, your promise to pay $500 in return for G & H's work on the patio is supported by new consideration—G & H has not obligated itself to construct the patio as part of the original agreement—and you must pay $500 more for this additional work.

To return to the earlier example, assume now that in the middle of winter a freakish humid spell causes a paint-resistant mold to grow in your basement. As a result, G & H has to paint the walls three times to cover the mold. If this blight arises after the firm begins the work, most courts will characterize it as an unforeseen or unforeseeable difficulty and will order you to pay the higher price. The same will hold true if you and the firm had canceled the original contract and had started anew with different promises and obligations. In both situations, consideration will support the new promises. Under the common law, strikes, inflation in the prices of raw materials, and lack of access to raw materials do not meet the test of "unforeseen or unforeseeable difficulties." Accordingly, new promises extracted on these bases ordinarily will lack consideration and thus be unenforceable.

Moral Consideration

Remember that harsh outcomes sometimes result from the application of the doctrine of consideration. Promises made from a so-called moral obligation embody one such subcategory of consideration and ordinarily are not enforced. In general, courts adhere strictly to the requirement of consideration in these contexts.

For example, suppose your child is saved without injury from the jaws of a snarling Doberman pinscher because of the efforts of a passerby. The person who saves your child unfortunately suffers deep cuts that eventually require cosmetic surgery. Faced with such generosity, who among us will not promise this person the world? You are only human, so you offer to pay this Good Samaritan's lost

---

NRW CASE 11.3 | Management/Law

NRW

CHANGING THE TERMS OF A CONTRACT

Assume that, in checking the order acknowledgment form it has received from High-Tech, NRW discovers that High-Tech has reserved the right to cancel its resultant contract with NRW for any reason and at any time. What legal problems—if any—does this language potentially present for NRW? Suppose instead that High-Tech informs NRW that it is unilaterally raising its prices to NRW due to a strike at one of High-Tech's plants. Will NRW be legally obligated to pay this higher amount?

BUSINESS CONSIDERATIONS The order acknowledgment form that High-Tech sent to NRW included proposed additional terms to the contract between the parties. Very commonly where businesses conduct their negotiations over long distances, they do so by exchanging forms. Should a business have a policy of always reading the forms sent by the other party and of objecting to any terms in the form that are different from the terms the recipient thought the contract included? Does a firm's use of Electronic Data Interchanges (EDIs) compound such problems?

ETHICAL CONSIDERATIONS Is it ethical to put new terms into a written confirmation of the contractual agreement? Does it matter if the proposed additional terms favor the party who sent the writing, favor the party to whom the writing was sent, or are neutral?

INTERNATIONAL CONSIDERATIONS How does the Convention on Contracts for the International Sale of Goods (CISG) treat such proposed additional terms in international sales contracts?

---

wages while she is in the hospital. As time passes, though, you grow less willing to pay, and finally you cease paying her altogether. If she sues you, you will usually win because a court will conclude that she has bestowed a gift on you—that is, saving your child. Consequently, no consideration was present. Note, too, that prior to the humanitarian gesture, no bargaining in exchange for your promise to pay occurred. You may not think this particular result under this doctrine is harsh. Another disinterested party may take a different view, however, and may question your ethics here as well. Therefore, in a few jurisdictions, courts will reject the settled rule and hold that the passerby is entitled to win. Remember, though, that this is the position taken by a minority of courts.

Past Consideration

Related to this doctrine of moral consideration is the doctrine of past consideration. This issue typically arises when a person retires and the company offers the former employee a small stipend "in consideration of 25 years of faithful service." Since the old services are already executed (completed or finished), they cannot form the basis for a new promise. The same is true of a promise to pay a relative based on the promisor's "love and affection" for the promisee. Notice that, in both cases, neither bargaining nor an exchange of anything of value has occurred. Neither of the promises is supported by consideration, and neither

will be enforceable. In short, as traditional legal authority holds, "Past consideration is no consideration." In disposing of the following case, the court applied many of the concepts covered in this chapter.

Exceptions to the Bargaining Theory of Consideration

As you should now realize, whether or not the parties have bargained with a resulting exchange of value appears crucially important under the common law rules surrounding consideration. Still, in the following four situations,

---

11.3

CARLISLE v. T & R EXCAVATING, INC.
704 N.E. 2d 39 (Ohio App. 9th Dist. 1997)

FACTS Thomas Carlisle owned and operated T&R Excavating, Inc. (T&R). Janis Carlisle was the owner and director of Wishing Well, Inc. Ms. Carlisle and Mr. Carlisle married in 1988. Shortly afterward, she began doing all the bookkeeping for T&R, including organizing and modernizing its bookkeeping system. Mr. Carlisle allegedly offered to pay her for her work, but she refused to accept any salary. During 1992, Ms. Carlisle decided to build a preschool and kindergarten facility. Mr. Carlisle helped her find a location for the preschool and choose a general contractor for the construction of the preschool. In September 1992, Ms. Carlisle signed a proposal in which T&R agreed to do all the excavation work for the facility at no cost, provided the preschool paid T&R's expenses. In December 1992, in anticipation of a divorce, the Carlisles prepared a document in which, to repay Ms. Carlisle for her secretarial and computer services to T&R, Mr. Carlisle agreed to fulfill the terms of the 1992 proposal. Sometime during early 1993, T&R began performing the excavation and site work for the preschool. According to Mr. Carlisle's testimony, Ms. Carlisle stopped providing bookkeeping or secretarial services to T&R after January 1993. The couple separated during March 1993, but T&R continued working on the project until late May or early June 1993. By that time, Wishing Well, Inc. had paid approximately $35,000 for the materials used by T&R for the excavation and site work. However, Ms. Carlisle ultimately hired other workers to finish the excavation and site

work. After the preschool opened for business on August 28, 1993, one week later than originally planned, Ms. Carlisle sued T&R for breach of contract. The lawsuit requested damages equal to the amount it had cost to have others finish the excavation and site work, as well as the amount lost owing to delays allegedly attributable to T&R's failure to work during certain periods prior to T&R's final abandonment of the job. T&R, in turn, claimed that the agreement lacked consideration and that the scope of the work T&R had agreed to do was so uncertain that the meeting of the minds necessary for contract formation had never existed.

ISSUE Was the agreement supported by consideration?

HOLDING No. The absence of any consideration meant no contract between the parties existed.

REASONING Excerpts from the opinion of Judge Dickinson:

A contract consists of an offer, an acceptance, and consideration. . . . Without consideration, there can be no contract. . . . Under Ohio law, consideration consists of either a benefit to the promisor or a detriment to the promisee. . . . To constitute consideration, the benefit or detriment must be "bargained for." . . . Something is bargained for if it is sought by the promisor in exchange for his promise and is given by the promisee in exchange for that promise. . . . The benefit or detriment does not need to be great. In fact, a benefit need not even be actual, as in the nature of a profit, or be as economically valuable as whatever the promisor promises in exchange for the benefit; it need only be something regarded by the promisor as beneficial enough to induce his promise. . . . Generally, therefore, a court will not inquire into the adequacy of consideration once it is found to exist. . . . Whether there is consideration at all, however, is a proper question for a court. . . . Gratuitous promises are not enforceable as contracts, because [of the absence of] consideration. . . . A written gratuitous promise, even if it evidences an intent by the promisor to be bound, is not a contract. . . . Likewise, conditional gratuitous promises, which require the promisee to do something before the promised act or omission will take place, are not enforceable as contracts. . . .

While it is true, therefore, that courts generally do not inquire into the adequacy of consideration once it is found to exist, it must be determined in a contract case whether any "consideration" was really bargained for. If it was not bargained for, [no contract exists]. There is no evidence in the record of any benefit accruing to T & R or any detriment suffered by Ms. Carlisle due to their agreement that could constitute consideration for a contract. . . . Mr. Carlisle testified that he wanted to help Ms. Carlisle with the preschool and that they both agreed the preschool would be a good retirement benefit for them. . . . A desire to help cannot be consideration for a contract; rather, it is merely a motive. . . . Further, the possibility of sharing in the income from a spouse's business, which would be marital income, cannot be consideration for a contract because one is already entitled to share in marital income. . . . No bargaining is necessary to obtain that which one already has. The decision to build the preschool to provide income later was more in the nature of a joint effort by Mr. Carlisle and Ms. Carlisle to obtain a single benefit together, rather than a bargained-for exchange. Finally, the relationship between Mr. Carlisle and Ms. Carlisle could not have been consideration for a contract. . . . Ms. Carlisle testified at trial that she understood the agreement to consist of T & R's promise to do excavation and site work for no charge, and her promise to "pay [T & R] back for the supplies." The promise of reimbursement for out-of-pocket costs, standing alone, was not a benefit or detriment supporting a contract. Money changed hands, but the reimbursement was not a bargained-for benefit to the promisor or detriment to the promisee. No reasonable interpretation of Ms. Carlisle's testimony could support a conclusion that T & R promised to provide the free services in order to induce her to promise to reimburse it for materials only. Rather, the testimony suggested . . . a gratuitous promise by T & R to provide free services on the condition that Ms.

Carlisle agree to reimburse it for the cost of materials that would be used in providing those services. . . .

Consideration was also not shown by Ms. Carlisle's testimony that Mr. Carlisle told her, after she refused payment for her bookkeeping services to T & R, that he would help her with her building. First, Ms. Carlisle did not argue that her secretarial services were consideration for T & R's promise. . . .

Second. . . if Mr. Carlisle made the statement after Ms. Carlisle had done the work for T & R, her services were "past consideration" and could not support a contract. . . . Likewise, the "separation agreement" signed by Mr. Carlisle and Ms. Carlisle during December 1992 suggested a gratuitous promise by Mr. Carlisle. It described his promise to do the work as "repayment to Jan for her secretarial services and computer programming to T & R Excavating, Inc." The word "repayment" suggested that Ms. Carlisle's past services induced Mr. Carlisle's promise. As stated above, past consideration is not legally sufficient to support a contract. . . .

The only way Ms. Carlisle could have properly recovered the value of the services, therefore, is if she had argued and proved, under a theory of promissory estoppel, that she had reasonably relied to her detriment on T & R's promise. . . . She has made no mention of detrimental reliance in her brief to this Court, nor is it clear whether she was trying to argue it at trial. . . .

Nowhere in the record is there a suggestion that she would not have built the preschool, or built it as she did, without relying on the promise of free services by T & R. Moreover, the preschool cost approximately $800,000 to build, and T & R's fulfilled promise would have saved Ms. Carlisle only about $35,000, according to the trial court's decision and award. This amount is less than five percent of the building cost. There is, therefore, no argument, no evidence, and no basis for inferring that Ms. Carlisle relied to her detriment on T & R's promise. Ms. Carlisle failed to establish that there was consideration for T & R's promise to do free excavation and site work for the preschool, or that she relied to her detriment on the promise. The promise, therefore, was not legally enforceable.

BUSINESS CONSIDERATIONS The parties here, though married, tried to separate their business and marital interests—a laudable objective. In hindsight, what additional steps could the parties have undertaken so as to minimize the probability of litigation and thus to fulfill their initial objective?

ETHICAL CONSIDERATIONS Is it ethical for one spouse to expect the other to do work of a business nature for a nominal fee? Fully support whichever position you take.

courts will enforce agreements despite a lack of consideration: (1) promissory estoppel, (2) charitable subscriptions, (3) promises made after the statute of limitations has expired, and (4) promises to repay debts after a discharge in bankruptcy.

Promissory Estoppel

Promissory estoppel was discussed in Chapter 10 in the context of preventing an offeror's revocation of an offer. To recapitulate, courts apply this equitable doctrine in order to avoid injustice. Essentially, the elements are the same for consideration as for offers. In both, the promisor makes a definite promise that he or she expects, or should reasonably expect, will induce the plaintiff-promisee to act (or refrain from acting) in a manner that may be detrimental to the latter person. Accordingly, the law, to avoid injustice, holds the promisor to his or her promise. Simply put, the promisor is prevented from asserting a defense (here, lack of consideration) that is normally available to the promisor.

Though inapplicable in the *Carlisle* decision, promissory estoppel might apply in the case of an employer who offered to pay its employee "in consideration of 25 years of faithful service." The employee might use promissory estoppel as a substitute for consideration so as to enable the employee to win. In other words, if the employer in fact has paid the former employee $400 a month for 10 years, and the employee, owing to an expectation of continued stipends, has given up opportunities for part-time employment, some courts will conclude that the employer must continue the payments despite the absence of bargaining or of an exchange of anything of value.

Charitable Subscriptions

Likewise, promissory estoppel may help promisees win in the category of charitable subscriptions, which is another exception to the requirement of consideration. You probably can guess how this legal issue—the written promise to pay a certain sum to a nonprofit charity—arises.

Typically, a generous person wishes to donate a sizeable amount to a worthy charity and promises to do so. Later, this humanitarian zeal wanes and the person no longer wishes to live up to the written agreement. If you are the donor, what do you argue? In all likelihood, you will try to argue that you intended to bestow a gift. Since by definition a gift lacks consideration (there is neither bargaining nor an exchange of value), you will claim that you therefore can avoid liability for this promise.

Ordinarily, though, a would-be donor will have to live up to the agreement because charitable institutions rely on the belief that the amount pledged in written subscriptions will be forthcoming and because people make pledges based on the knowledge that other people will be making similar pledges. Courts, of course, believe that charitable institutions (like universities, hospitals, agencies, or churches) serve noble purposes. Thus, in addition to resorting to promissory estoppel as a substitute for consideration, courts alternatively may enforce the promise on public policy grounds. Again, the would-be donor needs to examine the ethical dimensions of his or her decision to renege on the promised charitable subscription.

Promises Made after the Expiration of the Statute of Limitations

State statutes of limitations set time limits on when creditors can bring suit against debtors for the sums owed to the creditors. Ordinarily, this period is from two to six years, after which the creditor cannot maintain suit against the debtor. Sometimes the debtor wants to repay the debt even if this time limit has passed. As you already have learned, there seems to be no consideration present in such a circumstance; there is an absence of any bargaining, and the debtor's promise arguably represents moral consideration at best.

Yet under most state statutes and decisions, the law will enforce the debtor's new promise to pay if it is in writing. The public policy of encouraging people to pay their debts generally forms the basis for this exception to the bargaining theory of consideration.

Promises to Pay Debts Covered by Bankruptcy Discharges

The same policy applies and the result is similar when a debtor promises to pay a debt covered by a discharge in bankruptcy. Again, no consideration underlies this new promise; but most states will allow the enforcement of the promise, provided that the debtor makes the promise to pay in full compliance with the reaffirmation provisions of the Bankruptcy Act and with a full understanding of the significance of this promise, as required by the Bankruptcy Code. Exhibit 11.1 offers a summary of many of the principles associated with consideration.[1]

EXHIBIT   11.1   Consideration: A Summary

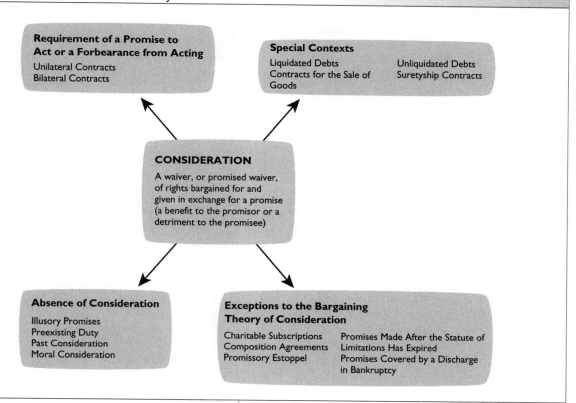

Requirement of a Promise to Act or a Forbearance from Acting
Unilateral Contracts
Bilateral Contracts

Special Contexts
Liquidated Debts   Unliquidated Debts
Contracts for the Sale of Suretyship Contracts
Goods

CONSIDERATION
A waiver, or promised waiver, of rights bargained for and given in exchange for a promise (a benefit to the promisor or a detriment to the promisee)

Absence of Consideration
Illusory Promises
Preexisting Duty
Past Consideration
Moral Consideration

Exceptions to the Bargaining Theory of Consideration
Charitable Subscriptions   Promises Made After the Statute of
Composition Agreements   Limitations Has Expired
Promissory Estoppel   Promises Covered by a Discharge
                            in Bankruptcy

UCITA parallels the UCC's rules regarding consideration in that UCITA § 303 states that an agreement modifying a contract is binding without consideration. UCITA § 111 similarly mirrors the UCC by allowing a court to refuse to enforce any contract that the court deems unconscionable. Although the parties generally can vary the effect of any provision of UCITA, § 113(a)(2) prohibits the parties' freedom to do so if the resultant agreement would contravene § 111 or otherwise violate fundamental public policy (see § 105b).

Summary

Consideration is a firmly entrenched doctrine in modern law. Consideration consists of any waiver or promised waiver of rights bargained for in exchange for a promise. Consideration exists when there is a benefit to the promisor or a detriment to the promisee bargained for and given in exchange for a promise. In unilateral contracts, consideration may take the form of an act or a forbearance to act. In bilateral contracts, the respective promises constitute consideration. In the absence of fraud, duress, undue influence, or unconscionability, courts generally will not inquire into the adequacy of the consideration. Although no consideration is necessary under the UCC provisions relating to firm offers and modifications of sales contracts, consideration is necessary to hold a surety liable.

The doctrine of preexisting obligations mandates that one pay a liquidated debt in full; part payment is not consideration for full discharge of the debt. In contrast, part payment of an unliquidated debt, if accepted as full payment, represents a compromise of the debt and is supported by consideration. Such an accord and satisfaction completely cancels the debt. The same rationale validates composition agreements between the debtor and a group of creditors.

Agreements based on illusory promises or promises grounded in either preexisting legal duties or preexisting contractual relationships lack consideration. The same is true of promises founded on moral obligations and on past consideration. The four exceptions to the bargaining theory of consideration are (1) promissory estoppel, (2) charitable subscriptions, (3) promises to repay made after the statute of limitations has expired, and (4) promises to repay debts covered by discharges in bankruptcy. In these situations, courts will give effect to agreements without consideration.

Discussion Questions

1. Define *consideration*.

2. Can "doing nothing" ever suffice as consideration to support a promise?

3. Why do courts refuse to inquire into the adequacy of consideration?

4. Why does the UCC dispense with requiring consideration in situations involving "firm offers" and modifications?

5. Explain why part payment of a liquidated debt is not consideration for full discharge of the debt, but part payment accepted as full payment for an unliquidated debt is.

6. Define the following: a *compromise*, an *accord*, and a *satisfaction*.

7. Discuss why an illusory promise cannot ever constitute consideration.

8. Why does it make sense to say that performing a preexisting duty does not constitute consideration?

9. Why does the law generally refuse to recognize moral and past "consideration" as sufficient to support an agreement between two or more parties?

10. Explain the four situations in which courts will enforce agreements despite a lack of bargaining (and hence consideration).

Case Problems and Writing Assignments

1. In 1984, Harlan Anderson and James Brooksbank formed a corporation, Total Mix Ration, Inc., for the purpose of developing, producing, and marketing a device for mixing feed for farm animals. Each owned one-half of the outstanding shares. The parties signed two shareholder agreements between 1994 and 1996. On April 30, 1996, Anderson and Brooksbank signed a new shareholder agreement that superseded all prior agreements. This 1996 agreement stated that Anderson would personally guarantee the repayment of 50 percent of the amount of the loans ($173,739.90) incurred in connection with the Phase 1 and Phase 2 loans obtained in 1994 and 1995. In the 1996 agreement, Anderson and Brooksbank also promised to contribute equal amounts of loans to the corporation, but neither guaranteed any of these loans. Moreover, the agreement obligated both men to make an additional loan in the amount of $33,000 each should Phase 3 of the development of the corporation occur. The agreement further obligated each to make other loans from time to time as needed. After signing the 1996 agreement, Anderson and Brooksbank issued a loan to the corporation in the amount of $6,000 each. Nothing in the agreement or on the checks indicated the purpose of these loans, but the letter sent with a later shareholder agreement signed only by Brooksbank and mailed to Anderson described the $6,000 amounts as loans for Phase 3. Less than three months after the execution of the 1996 agreement, Brooksbank notified Anderson that he (Brooksbank) was recalling the $173,739.90 note relating to the loans and that Anderson's share under the note was $86,869.95. Two months later, Brooksbank filed a lawsuit to recover the $86,869.95 allegedly owed under Anderson's personal guarantee. Anderson claimed the guarantee was unenforceable because Brooksbank had given no consideration for the 1996 agreement. Did Brooksbank, by promising in the 1996 agreement to advance an additional $33,000 in unguaranteed loans to the corporation and through his commitment to contribute unguaranteed loans to the corporation in amounts equal to those to be made by Anderson, provide sufficient consideration to make the 1996 agreement enforceable? [See *Brooksbank v. Anderson*, 586 N.W.2d 789 (Minn. App. 1998).]

2. Scott Specialty Gases (Scott) employed Diane Blair from January 1995 through March 1999 as the Plumstead Medical Products Division plant manager. After resigning on March 24, 1999, she filed a federal lawsuit alleging employment discrimination. Scott argued for dismissal of the lawsuit on the grounds that Blair had agreed to submit all employment-related claims to binding arbitration. Scott had placed a mandatory arbitration provision in an updated employee handbook that Scott had distributed to all employees in February 1998. Indeed, Blair had been given the assignment of

making sure that all the Medical Products' employees signed an "Acknowledgment of Receipt and Reading" of the revised handbook. Blair herself had signed such an acknowledgment on February 27, 1998. That acknowledgment stated that she had read the arbitration provision and agreed to submit any disputes arising out of her employment to a final and binding arbitration. The acknowledgment Blair had signed read:

I understand that nothing in this Handbook can be modified or deleted, nor can anything be added in any way by oral statements or practice. Only the Executive Committee of Scott Specialty Gases can change this Handbook, and the change must be in writing. If Scott Specialty Gases makes any material changes, it will give me a copy of them, and by remaining employed by Scott Specialty Gases thereafter I will be deemed to have accepted these changes. . . .

In response to Scott's motion to dismiss based on the arbitration agreement, Blair claimed that the arbitration agreement lacked consideration and was not binding on her. Specifically, she submitted that Scott had not agreed to be bound to the arbitration and that what she viewed as Scott's unilateral ability to alter the agreement had rendered the agreement illusory. How should the court decide this case? [See *Blair v. Scott Specialty Gases*, 283 F.3d 595 (3rd Cir. 2002).]

3. Richard and Janet Oscar entered into a restaurant lease agreement with Chris Simeonidis for a 10-year term beginning January 1, 1990, and ending December 31, 1999. The agreement set the rental rate at $2,500 per month with annual increases tied to the consumer price index, with the annual increase being, at a minimum, 5 percent. The lease agreement also obligated the tenant, Simeonidis, to pay the monthly real estate taxes, including any increases. Although the lease agreement recited that it represented the parties' full agreement that "may not be changed except in writing signed by the landlord and the tenant," from the outset the parties deviated from the terms of the agreement. For example, Simeonidis had assumed the lease (Nick Barrise was the original lessee) in the second year of the lease's term. Yet the Oscars had charged Simeonidis $2,500 inclusive of real estate taxes. According to the Oscars, they did this to help Simeonidis develop his business and also as a favor to their friend, Barrise. Simeonidis contended the Oscars had not increased the rent or made him pay taxes as specified in the lease because the commercial rental market in the area was severely depressed. In any event, over the years, the rent paid by Simeonidis and accepted by the Oscars was below that set forth in the lease agreement. During the final two years of the lease agreement, the Oscars increased the rent to $3,150 a month, inclusive of taxes. Simeonidis paid that amount without challenge.

As the 10-year term was about to expire, the Oscars sent a renewal letter to Simeonidis offering to continue the lease at a new rent of $5,000, inclusive of real estate taxes. When Simeonidis did not respond to that and other letters, the Oscars filed a complaint seeking possession of the premises. During the ensuing litigation, the Oscars' expert witness testified that the fair market rental value of the premises was $5,500, exclusive of

the real estate taxes that Simeonidis was to pay separately. Simeonidis challenged this valuation on the grounds that his utilities cost about $2,000 per month and that the interior repairs to the property for which he was responsible exceeded the expenses normally charged to a tenant. Simeonidis subsequently discovered evidence, specifically an amended agreement between Barrise and the Oscars signed just before Simeonidis had assumed the lease. The clause relating to the extension of the lease that read "Increases based upon fair market value" was to be changed so as to read "Increases based upon [the] terms of the original agreement." The court concluded that this amended agreement lacked consideration and was unenforceable. The court based its conclusion on its view that the Oscars had signed the amendment as a favor to Barrise and in order to ensure their having a tenant who paid the rent more regularly than Barrise had. The court characterized these reasons as preexisting duties that lacked supporting consideration. Simeonidis argued that the depressed commercial market could lead to the Oscars' receiving a benefit if the amended agreement's provisions were followed. The court noted, one could argue that the parties, by adopting a familiar formula (basing increases on the original term of the lease rather than relying on a more ambiguous and indeterminate formula, fair market value), had benefited each other by reducing the uncertainties that otherwise would attend their future dealings. Who had the better argument—the court or Simeonidis? Was the court correct? [See *Oscar v. Simeonidis*, 800 A.2d. 271 (N.J. Super. A.D. 2002).]

4. In the spring of 1991, Coulter & Smith, Ltd. (Coulter) and Dr. Roger Russell entered into a letter agreement whereby Coulter would develop Russell's property in conjunction with adjacent property it owned. Pursuant to their agreement, Coulter had the option to purchase the lots located on Russell's property after Coulter had completed the initial stages of the development of the subdivision. Among other things, Coulter stated in the letter agreement that it "would proceed posthaste to annex and develop our tracts jointly." The letter agreement, signed by Dr. Russell, gave Coulter a 10-year option to purchase lots. At the time of the execution of the letter agreement, Coulter and Russell also entered into a three-way work exchange agreement in which Coulter promised to make improvements in the master drain system for the benefit of Russell's property. Unfortunately, when the development did not proceed as expeditiously as planned, each party blamed the other for the delays. In 1994, after Russell had taken steps to sell the property to someone else, Coulter filed a lawsuit alleging breach of the option contract contained in the letter agreement. Russell claimed the option contract lacked consideration. Would you agree? [See *Coulter & Smith, Ltd. v. Russell*, 966 P.2d 852 (Utah 1998).]

5. **BUSINESS APPLICATION CASE** On January 6, 1991, Giancarlo and Antonio DiMizio entered into a contract with Oswaldo Romo for the sale of Luca Pizza of Anderson, Indiana, for the sum of $150,000.00 at 7 percent per annum. Further, the contract provided that Romo would, "upon complete payment of the $150,000.00 purchase price, . . . initiate payment to Sellers

of a 6 percent fee on the gross receipts less sales tax for the remaining period of the lease and any extensions of the lease as hereinafter provided." The contract also contained a provision allowing for the recovery of attorney's fees and costs by the prevailing party of any dispute arising out of or relating to the contract or its breach. Romo subsequently requested a reduction in the percentage fee collected on the restaurant's gross receipts owing to the fact that he was struggling financially. The DiMizios agreed to reduce their commission and, on September 11, 1996, entered into a written modification of their original contract of sale with Romo. The addendum and modification of the contract provided:

In consideration of the promise of the [s]ellers not to seek enforcement of the terms of the [o]riginal [c]ontract regarding payment of a percentage of the gross receipts, and for other valuable consideration as set forth in the [o]riginal [c]ontract and this [a]ddendum and [m]odification, the [b]uyer shall pay to [s]ellers [t]wo percent (2%) of the gross receipts of the business, for a period of two (2) years; the percentage of gross receipts paid to [s]ellers shall be three percent (3%) for so long as the [b]uyer operates a pizza restaurant in the City of Anderson in the Mounds Mall.

The parties reaffirmed all the terms of the original contract not inconsistent with the modification. In December 1997, without any direct assistance from the DiMizios, Romo renegotiated with the Simon Property Group a new lease that would commence upon the expiration of the previous lease held by the DiMizios. Following his January 24, 1998, payment, Romo consequently discontinued all the remaining payments of the commissions due to the DiMizios. As a result, the DiMizios sued Romo for breach of contract. Romo argued that the modification was not supported by consideration, particularly since he had obtained the new lease without the DiMizios' assistance. He also asserted they had not consulted with him on other matters affecting the pizza business, as they had promised to do pursuant to the modification. Romo alternatively submitted that the modification was unconscionable because of his limited English skills. Who should win? What steps could the parties have taken so as to minimize the possibilities of litigation? [See *DiMizio v. Romo*, 756 N.E.2d 1018 (Ind. App. 2001).]

6. **ETHICAL APPLICATION CASE** Ross-Simons of Warwick, Inc. (Ross-Simons), the plaintiff, is a substantial national retailer of items such as china and crystal. Ross-Simons ordinarily sells at prices below suggested retail prices, with discounts often reaching 50 percent. An important aspect of Ross-Simons's sales strategy is the development of a large bridal registry actively promoted by the firm. Each year the program attracts approximately 15,000 new registrants, business that is important to Ross-Simons because each new registration likely will result in multiple purchases on behalf of the registered couple. Baccarat, Inc. (Baccarat) is the U.S. subsidiary of Companie des Cristalleries de Baccarat and the exclusive U.S. distributor of the world-renowned French lead crystal. Prior to 1992, Baccarat had refused to sell crystal to Ross-Simons because of Baccarat's philosophy that luxury items such as Baccarat crystal were not appropriate for discounting. Furthermore,

when Baccarat had become the exclusive distributor of Haviland Limoges china in 1991, it had terminated Ross-Simons's status as an authorized dealer of the china.

As a result of Baccarat's decisions, Ross-Simons in 1992 filed an antitrust lawsuit against Baccarat. Prior to a court hearing of the antitrust suit on its merits, the parties entered into an "agreement of compromise and settlement." The substance of the 1992 agreement was contained in section three, which enumerated the respective obligations of the parties under the settlement. According to these "mutual covenants," Ross-Simons agreed to dismiss its antitrust suit, that such dismissal would be without prejudice (that is, Ross-Simons had not waived, or given up, its right to sue sometime in the future), and that each party would bear its own costs and legal expenses. In exchange for this dismissal, Baccarat accepted several duties. First, Baccarat agreed to reinstate Ross-Simons as an authorized dealer of Haviland Limoges porcelain dinnerware and to appoint Ross-Simons as an authorized dealer of Baccarat crystal. For each line of goods, Baccarat promised that Ross-Simons would be "entitled to purchase and resell such products at such prices and upon such terms as are available to other authorized dealers." Second, Baccarat promised not to "terminate Ross-Simons's status as an authorized dealer, or otherwise discriminate against Ross-Simons in any manner" because of Ross-Simons's discount pricing policies. Baccarat further agreed not to discriminate against Ross-Simons's applications for authorization to sell at additional stores, but would "consider all applications . . . under the same standards generally applied to other authorized dealers."

Following the execution of the 1992 agreement, the parties cordially maintained a sizeable business relationship. Indeed, during this period, Ross-Simons grossed approximately $1 million annually in Baccarat crystal sales. The dynamics of that relationship changed, however, when Jean-Luc Negre assumed the presidency of Baccarat in 1994. Replacing Francois de Montmorin, the Baccarat president who had executed the 1992 agreement on Baccarat's behalf, Negre told Ross-Simons officials that he viewed discounting as an inappropriate method of selling luxury items like Baccarat crystal. Shortly thereafter, Baccarat refused to grant authorized dealer status to a new Ross-Simons store. In 1995 Baccarat proposed an agreement containing authorized dealership provisions inimical to Ross-Simons's discount pricing strategies; Ross-Simons filed a lawsuit alleging Baccarat's breach of the 1992 agreement. Baccarat countered by arguing that the 1992 agreement lacked consideration. To support its claims, Baccarat pointed out that while the agreement required Baccarat to deal with Ross-Simons without regard to Ross-Simons's discounting policies, the 1992 settlement had not required Ross-Simons to order any amount of products from Baccarat except that which Ross-Simons had chosen to order. Furthermore, Baccarat viewed Ross-Simons's dismissal of the antitrust suit as inadequate consideration because the parties had agreed that the dismissal would be without prejudice. Should a court agree with Baccarat's contentions? Did Negre behave ethically?

Do different nationalities view ethics differently, or are ethics universal in application? [See *Ross-Simons of Warwick, Inc. v. Baccarat, Inc.*, 182 F.R.D. 386 (D.R.I. 1998).]

7. CRITICAL THINKING CASE John P. S. Janda, a physician born in India, sued the Madera Community Hospital for the breach of his employment contract allegedly occasioned by the hospital's decision to close its orthopedic department. Upon the closure of the department, the hospital had awarded an exclusive contract to the only Caucasian orthopedic surgeon on staff. Janda claimed that the closure thus was motivated by a racial animus that contravened the hospital's bylaws, which prohibit the denial of medical staff privileges on the basis of race, color, sex, religion, or national origin. Put differently, Janda argued that the bylaws form a contract between the hospital and its medical staff. In rebuttal, the hospital asserted that the bylaws do not create an enforceable contract because of the absence of a mutual exchange of consideration. Specifically, the hospital submitted that California statutes mandate a hospital's adoption of written bylaws concerning the organization and governance of the hospital and its medical staff and that, by statute, physicians have a legal duty to abide by the written bylaws adopted by the medical staff. Hence, the hospital maintained that because it had a preexisting legal duty to establish the bylaws and Dr. Janda had a preexisting legal duty to comply with the bylaws, no legally recognizable consideration ever passed between the parties. Would you agree that no contract existed between the parties? Why? [See *Janda v. Madera Community Hospital*, 16 F. Supp. 2d 1181 (E.D. Cal. 1998).]

8. YOU BE THE JUDGE Gayle Moore and her husband bought a Suzuki four-wheel all-terrain vehicle (ATV) in May 1993 from Suzuki, Arctic Cat Motor Sports. At the time of the sale, the salesperson offered the Moores a $50 rebate to be issued on completion of an ATV rider safety class. On October 23, 1993, the Moores attended an ATV rider safety class held on the property of Hartley Motors, Inc. James Croak instructed the class using the curriculum of the ATV Safety Institute. Before starting the instruction, Croak requested that all participants sign a consent form and release. Moore did so. The driving portion of the class took place on a course marked with cones on unpaved ground. During the class, Moore drove her ATV through high grass beyond a cone marking the course. Her vehicle rolled up on a rock protruding from the ground in the high grass. Thrown from her vehicle, Moore suffered injuries as a result. When Moore sued the instructor, the ATV Safety Institute, and Hartley Motors, Inc. for negligence, the defendants introduced the consent form and release that Moore had signed. Moore then argued that the release was invalid because she had received no consideration for signing it. Specifically, she contended that the $50 rebate promised by the salesperson upon the completion of the course was to have been the consideration for her release of liability. Because she had not completed the course, she argued, the $50 rebate was unavailable. She therefore submitted that because she had not received any consideration for the release, it was ineffective to protect the defendants from liability. Alternatively, Moore argued that the release was unconscionable and contrary to public policy. How would *you* decide this case? [See *Moore v. Hartley Motors, Inc.*, 36 P.3d 628 (Alaska 2001).]

Notes

1. You can enhance your understanding of the material in this chapter by checking out your campus library's electronic holdings. In doing so, if you find EBSCOhost, a common database, access the LexisNexis Academic Web resource. There you will find cases and law reviews that deal with consideration and associated topics. Emerald Library, another such resource, has law-related articles as well.

CHAPTER 12

Contractual Capacity and Reality of Consent

NRW Carlos has heard that some types of contracts are voidable. He is unclear about what this term means, but he definitely wants to refrain from entering into any contracts that are voidable at the option of the other party. Helen thinks that a large market for StuffTrakR potentially exists among well-to-do teenagers. She therefore thinks the firm should investigate this market. From both a professional and a legal perspective, Mai does not think the firm should target this youth-oriented market.

The firm will have to decide how to advertise and market NRW's products. Should NRW use slick advertising that portrays the products as capable of doing more than they actually do? Will adopting this strategy have any effect on the contracts they enter? Can a firm be held responsible for misleading ads that may constitute misrepresentation and fraud? The firm members also differ as to how "hard-line" an approach the firm should take in securing a contractual agreement.

These and other questions are likely to surface in this chapter. Be prepared! You never know when the firm or one of its members will seek your advice.

Legal Capacity

Capacity, the fourth requirement for a valid contract, mandates that the parties to the contract have the legal ability to bind themselves to the agreement and to enforce any promises made to them. However, incapacity, or the lack of such capacity, is the exception, not the rule. Hence, the burden of proof regarding incapacity falls on the party raising it as a defense to the enforcement of the contract or as a basis for rescission of the contract.

To determine contractual capacity, the law looks at the relative bargaining power of the parties involved. Historically, older persons have taken care of the younger members of society. By allowing children under a certain age to disaffirm (or withdraw from) the contract, the law attempts to protect children, who remain less adept at bargaining, from overreaching by these more experienced bargainers. The same is true of persons who lack mental capacity, such as insane persons: Contracts made by these persons may be absolutely void, voidable (the insane person can disaffirm the contract), or even valid (if, for example, contract formation occurs during a period of lucidity). Thus, the existence or absence of legal capacity and the consequences of proving incapacity depend heavily on the facts and on a given person's status.

Indeed, the law often uses status as a basis for making distinctions that in fact may limit the legal rights of any persons falling within these classifications. For this reason, many jurisdictions restrict the contractual rights of minors, insane persons, intoxicated persons, aliens, and convicts. In earlier times, the common law, through statutes called Married Women's Property Acts, curtailed the contractual rights of married women. Most states have eliminated these legislative restrictions, but some vestiges of these acts remain in a few states. The extent of the legal disability placed on such classes of individuals is the focus of this section of the chapter.

Minors

Most jurisdictions no longer follow the earlier common law rule that any person of either sex under 21 years of age is a minor (or an infant). Most states by statute have changed this rule to allow for achievement of majoritarian status (that is, adult status) as early as age 18 for almost all purposes. (A common exception involves the purchase or consumption of alcoholic beverages.) Some states allow for termination of infancy status upon marriage or emancipation (that is, the attainment of legal independence from one's parents).

Disaffirmance/Rescission

To protect minors in their dealings with adults, the law allows minors to disaffirm (or avoid) their contracts with adults except in certain specialized cases, such as contracts involving necessaries (things that directly foster the minor's well-being). When the minor decides not to perform the legal obligations contemplated in the agreement and thus *disaffirms* the contract, this action results in a voidable contract. Stated differently, the minor has the option of either performing the contract or avoiding it. The converse is untrue: The adult who has contracted with a minor ordinarily will not be able to use the infancy of the minor to avoid the contract unless the minor allows the adult to disaffirm the contract. Simply put, do not contract with minors! Or, if you do, realize that the minor's powers in a given instance may be quite pervasive. Practically speaking, besides refusing to deal with minors, you can curtail their powers of avoidance by insisting that a parent or other adult cosign the contract as well. In this fashion, you effectively will limit the minor's power of *rescission*, or the ability to have the contract set aside. This is true because even if the minor disaffirms the contract, the adult cosigner still will remain liable on it.

Upon disaffirmance, the minor, if possible, must return to the adult the property or other consideration that was the object of the contract. Strong policy reasons exist for this rule, called the *duty of restoration*. It clearly seems unfair to let the minor "have it both ways"—that is, withdraw from the contract and yet retain the consideration. The law therefore says that if the minor wants to avoid a contract, he or she must *totally* avoid it.

Sometimes, however, the minor cannot return the property or other consideration because it has been damaged or destroyed. For example, Ace Used Cars will be very upset if, 18 months into the agreement, Marcie, the 17-year-old with whom Ace has dealt, asks for the money that she already has paid on the car as well as a total release from the contract and in exchange presents Ace with a demolished car. In most states, minors like Marcie will get exactly what they wish because merely giving the car back fulfills the minor's duty of restoration. In some states, however, Ace will be able to set off any payments received from Marcie owing to the damaged condition of the car. Courts in other jurisdictions will impose liability on minors like Marcie for the reasonable value of the benefit the minor received by virtue of Marcie's having use of the car for the period prior to the wreck.

Note how the court in the following case utilizes many of these principles.

12.1

SCHMIDT v. PRINCE GEORGE'S HOSPITAL
784 A.2d 1112 (Md. App. 2001)

FACTS On March 7, 1997, Michelle M. Schmidt, then 16 years old, was involved in a two-vehicle collision. At the time, she was driving a 1997 Ford Escort owned by Lewis Arno Schmidt Sr., her grandfather, and was insured with personal injury protection (PIP) benefits through her father's insurance company, Erie Insurance Group. Schmidt was transported to Prince George's Hospital, where she was initially admitted as "Jane Doe," without an emergency contact person or telephone number, because she was unconscious at the time of arrival. Although the hospital later was able to identify Schmidt's name and address, at that time it could ascertain only that her father was "Mr. Schmidt" and his telephone number. Owing to the severity of Schmidt's injuries, the hospital provided the necessary emergency medical care needed for treating a brain concussion and an open scalp wound. As of her discharge on March 8, 1997, Schmidt had incurred hospital expenses in the amount of $1,756.24. Soon after her release from the hospital, Schmidt filed for benefits under the coverage provided in her father's policy with Erie. During the claim process, she and her father supplied several documents to Erie regarding her medical expenses. On May 1, 1997, she and her father signed an assignment and authorization of benefits under the PIP coverage instructing and directing Erie to pay directly to her treating physician the amount owed him. Thereafter, a check in the amount of $1,756.24 also was issued by Erie to "Lewis A. Schmidt for Minor, Michelle Schmidt" in reference to "Prince George's Hospital Center, Service Date 03-07-1997 to 03-08-1997." The check was negotiated, but neither Schmidt nor her father paid the hospital; rather, they apparently used the funds to purchase a replacement automobile for Michelle. After unsuccessfully demanding payment from Michelle, on November 19, 1999, after she had attained her majority, the hospital sued her for the services rendered. Michelle defended on the grounds that, as a minor, she was legally incapable of entering into an implied contract for emergency medical treatment and that the doctrine of necessaries precluded the hospital from obtaining a money judgment from her when the hospital had failed to name the parent as the primary, legally responsible person.

ISSUE Could a minor, upon reaching the age of majority, be held liable, under the doctrine of necessaries, for medical services rendered during his or her minority if the parent was unable or unwilling to pay for such medical services?

HOLDING Yes. The child could be held liable for such necessaries when the parent was unable or unwilling to pay for the emergency medical treatment.

REASONING Excerpts from the opinion of Judge Harrell:

In the absence of a statute to the contrary, the prevailing modern rule is that a minor's contracts are voidable; nevertheless, it also is well established that a minor may be liable for the value of necessaries furnished to him or her. This doctrine, eponymously referred to as the doctrine of necessaries, is well recognized in Maryland law. . . . They are allowed to contract for their benefit with power in most cases, to recede from their contract when it may prove prejudicial to them, *but in their contract for necessaries, such as board, apparel, medical aid, teaching and instruction, and other necessaries, they are absolutely bound, and may be sued and charged in execution*; but it must appear that the things were absolutely necessary, and suitable to their circumstances, and whoever trusts them does so at his peril, or as it is said, deals with them at arms' length. Their power . . . to contract for necessaries is for their benefit, because the procurement of these things is essential to their existence, and if they were not permitted so to bind themselves they might suffer. [A recent Maryland precedent noted that] "the application of the necessaries doctrine is often limited to when the minor child is living with and supported by his parents" because parents are responsible at common law and by statute for the necessaries of their children. We noted, however, that "where the parent refuses or is unable to furnish necessaries, the infant is liable for necessaries furnished him or her." . . . After considering the various manifestations and applications of this rule in certain other jurisdictions, we resolved that . . . "the doctrine of necessaries is sufficient to hold a minor child liable for medical expenses incurred by him or her if it can be shown that his or her parent is unwilling or truly unable to pay them. This liability will, in turn, give a minor the right to claim medical expenses on his or her own behalf. It would be manifestly unjust to hold a child liable for medical expenses but to deny that child the opportunity to recover those expenses from a wrongdoer. . . . Under such a circumstance, the minor must be allowed to recover medical expenses to the extent that the minor will be liable for such expenses." . . . The rationales underlying [our precedents] recognize that public policy and justice demand that an injured minor have the right to recover incurred medical expenses from a third-party tortfeasor, where the child's parents are unable or unwilling to pay for those expenses, because the medical provider may sue to recover them, either during the child's minority or within the statute of limitations after the child has reached the age of majority. By parity of reasoning, it would seem that such a child, upon attaining adulthood, may be liable in contract to pay for medical necessaries provided to him or her while a minor, if the parents were unable or unwilling to pay for such necessaries.

The father's refusal to apply the insurance proceeds to the debt owed to Respondent—the existence of which he was well aware of as it was the facial premise for which he and Petitioner applied to Erie in the first place—is a clear indication of his unwillingness to pay for Petitioner's medical expenses at a time fairly contemporaneous with the provision of the medical services, i.e., within 60 days. We agree with the Circuit Court, which found that, as an adult, Petitioner is liable for the medical treatment expenses . . . she had incurred while a minor. . . . [She] could be held liable for those medical expenditures provided for her benefit under the doctrine of necessaries, which trumps her defense that she was under the disability of minority when she had entered into the implied promise to pay Respondent for the needed medical treatment. Lastly, we agree that the record supports that Petitioner's father was unwilling to pay for his then minor daughter's medical necessaries, which, in turn, left Petitioner primarily liable for the debt to Respondent. . . . [T]he greater public policy dictates that the former patient pay for the benefits received when given the medically necessary care by the hospital. Whatever unfairness may inhere in this principle is overweighed by the consideration of not placing hospitals and other emergency health care providers in a situation where financially able individuals might avoid paying for necessary medical treatment. . . .

BUSINESS CONSIDERATIONS What policy bases does the court's opinion reflect? Do you agree with the court's rationales?

ETHICAL CONSIDERATIONS Was Michelle behaving in an ethically appropriate fashion when she used the insurance proceeds to buy a car rather than to pay the hospital? Do hospitals have an ethical obligation to treat individuals even in circumstances in which the hospitals know they will never receive payment for the services?

Misrepresentation of Age

What if the minor intentionally misrepresents his or her age? For example, suppose 17-year-old Marcie tells the salesperson at Ace Used Cars that she is 21 and, to "prove it," pulls out a falsified driver's license. If Marcie later tries to avoid the contract with Ace, can Ace argue that this intentional misrepresentation (fraud) prevents rescission? Under the law of most jurisdictions, the minor still can disaffirm the contract. But some states by statute hold that such a misrepresentation completely cuts off the minor's power of disaffirmance. Alternatively, some states allow rescission but force the minor to put the adult back in the position he or she would have been in but for the contract. In other words, in such age-misrepresentation cases, some states will allow Marcie to disaffirm the contract but either will force her to return the car or hold her liable in quasi contract for the reasonable value of the benefit Ace has conferred on her by furnishing her with the car. Also, Marcie probably will have to pay for any damage done to the car while she has had custody of it. Courts may employ some of these alternatives in situations involving minors who have not misrepresented their ages; but when age misrepresentation is present, courts increasingly will hold the minor to a heightened duty of restoration (or even restitution). Given the lack of uniformity among the states, you should check your own jurisdiction's precedents in this regard.

Changing the circumstances of the first example, assume now that Marcie had traded in another car when she had purchased the now-demolished car from Ace. When she avoids the contract, Ace has to return the trade-in to the minor as well in order to fulfill the adult's corresponding duty of restoration. If Ace has already sold this car to a bona fide purchaser—a person who purchases in good faith, for value, and without notice of any defects or defenses affecting the sale or transaction—the minor cannot get the car back (as would be the usual result under the common law) but can recover the price paid to Ace by the third party. This result follows from the fact that the UCC (in § 2-403) covers this transaction. Thus, the UCC, by cutting off the minor's power of disaffirmance in some circumstances, has changed the common law.

When minors like Marcie attempt to disaffirm transactions with adults, the law requires no special words or acts to effect an avoidance. Disaffirmances may be made orally or in writing, formally (by a lawsuit) or informally, directly or indirectly. The public policy considerations permitting a minor to disaffirm his or her contracts are very strong. For example, in *Star Chevrolet Co. v. Green*,[1] the court allowed a minor to disaffirm his contract for the purchase of a car even though the car had been wrecked and the minor had received a settlement from his insurance company. In this case, the minor had previously attempted to disaffirm, but the auto dealer refused to refund his purchase price unless he first repaired the car, which had a blown head gasket. The minor then repaired the car and was driving it when he was involved in an accident that totaled the car. The court allowed the minor to retain the proceeds from his insurance coverage and also to recover the purchase price paid to the dealer less the salvage value of the car. As the court pointed out, when a minor disaffirms a contract, he or she must return any consideration still in his or her possession. But the minor will not be held responsible for any property that was lost, stolen, or destroyed. While this ruling is harsh, it emphasizes the point that adults should avoid contracting with minors.

The minor's power of disaffirmance, whether the contract is executory or executed, ordinarily extends through his or her minority and for a reasonable time after achieving majority. How long is reasonable becomes a question of fact for a judge or jury to decide in light of all the circumstances.

Ratification

Ratification means that the minor in some fashion has indicated (1) approval of the contract made while he or she was an infant and (2) an intention to be bound to the provisions of that contract. Ratification, then, represents the opposite of disaffirmance and cuts off any right to disaffirm. Ratification takes two separate forms: express and implied. Even with express ratifications, or those situations in which the minor explicitly and definitely agrees to accept the obligations of the contract, the policy of protecting minors is so strong that many states require express ratifications to be in writing.

The more common type of ratification occurs indirectly, for example, through conduct that shows approval of the contract, even though the minor has said nothing specifically about agreeing to be bound to it. To illustrate, failure to make a timely disaffirmance constitutes an implied ratification of an executed contract. Thus, a minor who is not diligent in disaffirming within a reasonable time after attaining majority will have impliedly ratified the contract. Such inaction does not ordinarily bring about the rat-

ification of an executory contract, however. Some courts will hold that, by itself, partial payment of a debt usually is not tantamount to ratification, unless payment is accompanied by the minor's express intention to be bound to the contract. In any event, ratification cannot occur until the minor achieves majority status. If ratification were possible beforehand, the law's protection of minors would be meaningless.

Necessaries

Even in the absence of ratification, minors will be liable for transactions whereby an adult has furnished them with "necessaries." *Necessaries* formerly encompassed only food, clothing, and shelter; but the law has broadened the doctrine to cover other things that directly foster the minor's well-being. The basis for the minor's liability is quasi contract, which you learned about in Chapter 9. (Remember that there can be no liability in *contract* law because of a lack of capacity.) If an adult has supplied necessaries to the minor, the law will imply liability for the reasonable value of those necessaries. Often, though, the law will not impose liability on the minor for the cost of necessaries unless the minor's parents are unable to discharge their obligation to support their child and pay for such essentials.

The definition of necessaries depends on the minor's circumstances, or social and economic situation in life. In this sense, the rule is applied somewhat subjectively. Although food, clothing, and shelter are covered, is a fur coat a necessary for which the minor is liable? It may be, depending on the minor's social station. Similarly, loans for medical or dental services or education also may be necessaries in some situations. Numerous cases involve cars; and many courts hold that a car, especially if the minor uses it for coming and going to work, is a necessary for which the minor remains liable. The definition of what constitutes a necessary changes as community values and mores change.

Special Statutes

Legislatures in many states have passed special statutes making minors liable in a variety of circumstances. Under such laws, minors may be responsible for educational loans, medical or dental expenses, insurance policies, bank account contracts, transportation by common carrier (for example, airline tickets), and other expenses. These statutes protect the interests of those persons who deal with minors who, despite their age, exhibit the skills and maturity of adults. The existence of such a statute in the *Schmidt* decision would have made the court's disposition of the case much more straightforward.

Torts and Crimes

The law similarly protects the interests of adults when an adult has suffered losses owing to a minor's torts and crimes. Minors, therefore, generally cannot disaffirm liability for torts and crimes unless the minor is of *tender years*, or too young to understand the consequences of his or her acts. Minors sometimes may escape liability in these areas if the imposition of tort liability will bring about the enforcement of a contract the minor previously has disaffirmed. Note how, in this latter context, the law once again has chosen to protect minors at the expense of adults.

As discussed earlier in Chapter 5, the Federal Trade Commission (FTC) has undertaken a number of initiatives aimed at protecting minors in the on-line environment. Indeed, the 1998 Children's Online Privacy Protection Act (COPPA) grew out of FTC recommendations for congressional action. COPPA in general prohibits on-line service providers from assembling or releasing personally identifiable information collected from a child under the age of 13 without notice to, and the consent of, the child's parents. Such information includes names, addresses, telephone numbers, Social Security numbers, and any other type of information that can facilitate either physical or on-line contact with a child. As the implementing agency for COPPA, the FTC has promulgated rules requiring any Web site operator to provide notice to parents of the site's information practices. Moreover, the operator must employ "reliable" methods to verify that the operator has obtained parental consent prior to the operator's collection, use, or disclosure to third parties or the public (such as through chat rooms) of any personal information about the children. COPPA also requires parental access to any information collected about the children.

Augmenting such protection of minors is the recent congressional concern about the susceptibility of minors to on-line gambling. In addition to proposed federal legislation, such worries have led several banks that offer credit card services to formulate special rules designed to prevent minors from betting online. These public and private initiatives are recent examples of the law's continuing watchfulness regarding minors.

Insane Persons

Like minors, insane persons may lack the capacity to make a binding contract. However, the law in this area is somewhat more complicated.

To be insane, a person must be so mentally infirm or deranged as to be unable to understand what he or she is agreeing to or the consequences attendant upon that agreement. The causes of such disability—lunacy, mental retardation, senility, or alcohol or drug abuse—are irrelevant.

Effects of Transactions by Insane Persons

The contract of a person whom a court has adjudged insane is absolutely void. Only his or her guardian, that is, the person legally responsible for taking care of another who lacks the legal capacity to do so, has the legal capacity to contract on the person's behalf. The contracts of other insane persons are voidable, however. To disaffirm a contract, the person using insanity as a defense must prove that he or she actually was insane at the time of contracting. If the person instead was lucid and understood the nature and consequences of the contract, that person is bound by the contract.

This power of an insane person to avoid contracts also extends to the heirs or personal representative of a deceased insane person. A living insane person's guardian possesses similar powers. Upon regaining sanity, a formerly insane person nonetheless may ratify a contract made during the period of insanity.

Determining whether a transaction by an insane person is void, voidable, or enforceable depends heavily on the facts.

Necessaries

By analogy to the rules covering minors, the law makes insane persons liable for necessaries in quasi contract. The categories of goods and services deemed necessaries for minors generally extend to insane persons. In the context of insanity, fewer controversies should arise regarding whether medical or legal services are necessaries—they probably constitute necessaries for which the insane person remains liable.

Intoxicated Persons

If a person is so thoroughly intoxicated that he or she does not understand the nature or consequences of the agreement being made, the person's mental disability approaches that of an insane person. Hence, under certain circumstances, such a person can disaffirm a given agreement. This power of possible disaffirmance depends, however, on the degree of intoxication involved, which in turn involves a question of fact. Slight degrees of intoxication do not constitute cause for the disaffirmance of a contract.

PURCHASES BY MINORS

Helen's niece, Lindsay, who is 18 years old, recently joined a club that, through a promotion, allowed Lindsay to purchase seven DVDs for $25. Lindsay further committed herself to purchase another five (at an average cost of $14.99 each) over the next two years. Because she would not receive the items for some time, she decided she didn't want to wait and that she wanted to cancel the agreement. So she wrote a letter informing the club that she (Lindsay) was a minor and that she was disaffirming her contract with the club to purchase the seven DVDs now and five additional DVDs in the future. She also demanded, in her disaffirmance of the agreement, that the club return her $25 payment. Afterward, Lindsay was boasting to her Aunt Helen about how clever she had been in this situation. Naturally, Helen was extremely upset when she learned of Lindsay's actions. She asked you to contact Lindsay and talk to her about the legal and ethical implications of her behavior. What will you tell Lindsay?

BUSINESS CONSIDERATIONS Why do firms such as the club involved here continue to woo the teenage market when they know minors can disaffirm such contracts? Does this orientation represent a prudent business strategy?

ETHICAL CONSIDERATIONS Is the law's protection of minors an ethical rule? Do parents have an obligation to act as ethical role models for their children? Does that role diminish in importance once a child reaches a certain age, say 17?

INTERNATIONAL CONSIDERATIONS How do the legal institutions of other countries treat the defense of infancy? If such laws differ from the common law treatment accorded minors, what is the basis for these differences?

Whether the intoxication was involuntary or voluntary may bear on the result, too. If a plaintiff has plied the defendant with liquor, any resulting intoxication may factor into a court's finding of incapacity, fraud, or overreaching that will release the defendant from the agreement. Even voluntary intoxication sometimes can result in a voidable contract if the facts support this conclusion.

Upon regaining sobriety, the formerly intoxicated person may either avoid or ratify the contract. The rules about acting within a reasonable time apply here as well; if the person does not quickly disaffirm the contract, an implied ratification will result. Courts generally are hostile to avoiding contracts on the basis of intoxication except in unusual circumstances.

Aliens

An *alien* is a citizen of a foreign country. Most of the disabilities to which the law formerly subjected an alien have been removed, usually through treaties. Thus, a *legal* alien ordinarily can enter into contracts and pursue gainful employment without legal disabilities, just as any U.S. citizen can. Some states make distinctions based on the alien's right to hold or convey personal property (generally authorized under such statutes) and the right to hold, convey, or inherit real property (some restrictions potentially apply here). *Enemy* aliens, or citizens of countries with whom we officially are at war, cannot enforce contracts during the period of hostility but sometimes can after the war ends. Given the large numbers of illegal aliens in the United States, as well as the governmental actions taken as a consequence of the September 11, 2001, attacks, this area of the law, with its attendant ethical and political questions, promises to be ripe for future developments.

Convicts

In many states, conviction of a felony or treason carries with it certain contractual disabilities. For instance, laws may prohibit convicts from conveying property during their periods of incarceration. Such disabilities, if applicable, exist only during imprisonment. Upon release from prison, these persons possess full contractual rights.

Married Women

Under early common law, married women's contracts were void. The law viewed women as their husbands' property and as otherwise lacking in capacity to make contracts. This common law disability, reflected in Married Women's Property Acts, has been eliminated by statute or by judicial decision in almost all states. Exhibit 12.1 summarizes the contractual capacities of minors, insane persons, intoxicated persons, aliens, convicts, and married women.

EXHIBIT 12.1 Contractual Capacity

Class of Person		Classification of Contract	Exceptions
Minors		Voidable (upon return of consideration to seller)	1. Misrepresentation of age, which eliminates power of rescission in some jurisdictions 2. Failure to rescind within a reasonable time after achieving majority (implied ratification) 3. Express ratification after achieving majority (necessity of a writing in some jurisdictions) 4. Necessaries (liability in quasi contract in some cases if parents are unable to pay) 5. Special statutes making minors liable
Insane persons	Those adjudged insane	Void	1. Capacity by guardians to contract on these insane persons' behalf
	Those insane but not adjudged so by a court	Voidable	1. Ratification possible during periods of lucidity 2. Necessaries (liability in quasi contract in some circumstances)
Intoxicated persons	Slightly intoxicated persons	Valid	
	Seriously intoxicated persons	Voidable	1. Subsequent ratification upon regaining sobriety possible 2. Failure to rescind within a reasonable time after achieving sobriety in involuntary intoxication circumstances (implied ratification)
Aliens	Legal aliens	Valid	1. Some restrictions sometimes regarding ownership of real property or workers' compensation claims
	Enemy aliens during hostilities	Void	
	Enemy aliens after hostilities end	Valid	
	Illegal aliens	Valid	
Convicts	Convicts during incarceration	Void	
	Convicts after release	Valid	
Married women		Valid	1. Some anachronistic restrictions remaining in a few states

The Requirement of Reality (or Genuineness) of Consent

Appearances often are deceptive. The same is true of contract formation; what seems to be a valid agreement may in actuality lack the parties' genuine assent. Put another way, the law has to ascertain whether the consent given by the parties is real or whether the facts actually differ from those to which the parties have outwardly agreed. As a prerequisite for contract formation, the law therefore requires reality (or genuineness) of consent. The existence of fraud, misrepresentation, mistake, duress, undue influence, or unconscionability precludes genuine mutual assent.

Fraud

Fraud is a word everyone uses fairly loosely, mainly because it lends itself to many definitions. At base, it consists of deception or hoodwinking; and it seems to involve a communication of some sort. But as one ancient case notes, "[a] nod or a wink, or a shake of the head or a smile" will do (see *Walters v. Morgan*, 3 Def., F. & J. 718, 724 [1861].) Sometimes even silence will suffice. The essence of fraud is hard to pin down. One common definition states that fraud is a deliberate misrepresentation of a material fact with the intent to induce another person to enter into a contract that will be injurious to that person.[2] If you break this definition down into smaller components, you can see that fraud consists of six elements.

Elements of Fraud

To constitute fraud, the misrepresentation or misstatement first must concern a fact. A *fact* is something reasonably subject to exact knowledge. Thus, statements about the size of a car engine or the dimensions of a real estate parcel involve facts.

To show this first element of fraud, then, the plaintiff will have to prove that the defendant misstated a fact. Predictions, statements of value, and expressions of opinions generally do not equate with misrepresentations of fact. Neither do misstatements of law.

Actually, in any given situation, it may be difficult to distinguish a fact from an opinion. Suppose a car salesperson says to you, "This little dandy will get you down the road at a pretty good clip. It has a great engine. It's a V-6, and those engines have been very serviceable." The first two remarks probably are opinions, also known as "puffs" or "dealer's talk." The statement about the type of engine probably constitutes a fact. You may be unhappy, for instance, if you find a V-8 engine in the car after you purchase it, or if you find out V-6 engines have many problems and the salesperson knows this. You may want to argue that you have been a victim of intentional misrepresentation. On the other hand, courts tend to discount statements of value because of genuine differences in the way people assess things. When Joe says, "That ring is worth a thousand dollars," unless Joe is a jewelry dealer or an expert and the other person is not, most courts will refuse to call Joe's statement a fact. Such nonfactual statements of value ordinarily do not fulfill this first element of a showing of fraud.

The second element of fraud a plaintiff must prove involves the *materiality* of the fact that the defendant allegedly has misstated. A fact is not material unless the plaintiff, when making the decision to enter the contract, considers it a substantial factor. To use the earlier example, if you do not care if the engine is a V-6, the lack of a V-6 in the car you buy makes the fact immaterial. A court will enforce the bargain despite your protestations. The mileage of the car, the number of previous owners, and the extent of any warranties (representations that become part of the contract and that are made by a seller of goods at the time of the sale and that concern the character, quality, or nature of the goods), however, all ordinarily are material. Misstatements about these facts therefore may lead to liability if you prove the other elements of fraud.

The most distasteful element of fraud, as well as the most difficult to prove, is the defendant's knowledge of the falsity of his or her statements. This sometimes is called *scienter*, that is, guilty knowledge (specifically, one party's prior knowledge of the cause of a subsequent injury to another person). In other words, at the time of making the statement, the defendant knew, or should have known, that he or she was misstating an important fact. Outright lies, of course, would meet this third requirement. Interestingly, the defendant also may be liable for reckless use of the truth or for a statement made without verifying its accuracy when verification is possible. To illustrate, assume that a prospective buyer says to the homeowner, "I guess the property line extends to the fence, doesn't it?" The homeowner nods yes, even though the line actually does not extend that far. If the buyer purchases in reliance on this statement, a cause of action in fraud may result.

Closely related to the requirement of knowledge of the falsity of the statement is an *intent to deceive*. As noted earlier, deception is the hallmark of fraud. This element is difficult to disprove if the first three elements have been established, because courts usually can find no satisfactory reason for a defendant's misstatements except as an intent to induce the plaintiff into accepting a "sharp" bargain.

The plaintiff also must prove that he or she *relied* on the deception. Assuming the plaintiff's reliance is reasonable, this showing will not be particularly burdensome. For example, if Tom inspects a lakefront cottage with a front porch that is on the verge of caving into the lake, a court will not allow him to cry "foul" (or "fraud") if the porch crumbles into the water one month after he buys the cottage. The same will be true even if the owner has said the cottage is structurally sound. Clearly, Tom should have been aware of such a *patent* (obvious) defect. Assuming the damage instead derives from a *latent* (hidden, unobservable by the human eye) defect, such as

carpenter ant infestation, Tom may win unless the court thinks Tom's failure to order a pest inspection in itself is unreasonable.

The final element of a plaintiff's proof—*injury*, or *detriment*—normally is not difficult to show. In the last example, Tom can argue that his damages amount to the sum needed to rid the cottage of carpenter ants and to repair the substructure of the dwelling. Alternatively, Tom may ask for rescission of the contract. When a court grants rescission, Tom will turn the cottage over to the original owner; and the owner will make restitution of the price Tom has paid for the property. In the case that follows, the court had to decide whether a *failure* to communicate constituted fraud.

12.2

RHONE-POULENC AGRO, S.A. V. DEKALB GENETICS CORPORATION
272 F.3d 1335 (Fed. Cir. 2001)

FACTS Rhone-Poulenc Agro, S.A. (RPA) and DeKalb Genetics Corporation (DeKalb) entered into a 10-year collaboration aimed at producing herbicide-resistant corn. Pursuant to this collaboration, in 1992, RPA provided DeKalb with new genetic materials containing a mutated corn gene, RD-125. In return, DeKalb was to test the corn and provide RPA with the results of these tests. After successfully growing herbicide-resistant corn plants in its greenhouse in early 1994, DeKalb informed RPA that it would begin field testing the RD-125 in the summer of 1994. The results of these field tests were very encouraging—the corn plants grown in the field were resistant to up to four times the levels ordinarily achieved with Roundup herbicide. However, DeKalb never sent these extremely encouraging results (which were similar to the greenhouse tests) to RPA. Nonetheless, following the field tests, DeKalb began the backcrossing process that would lead to the creation of a marketable line of seeds, thereby ensuring for itself a jump on any potential competition. In 1994, as part of a settlement of its ongoing patent infringement litigation against Monsanto Company (Monsanto), the manufacturer of Roundup, RPA gave to DeKalb what amounted to a complete surrender of RPA's exclusive rights in the RD-125 and related technologies. DeKalb eventually developed a successful glyphosate-tolerant corn line containing RD-125, marketed as Roundup Ready corn, which DeKalb referred to as the "GA21 corn line." In January 1996, DeKalb and Monsanto entered into an agreement to work together on the corn; and DeKalb licensed the GA21 corn line to Monsanto. Sales of Roundup Ready corn seeds began in 1998. RPA thereupon sued DeKalb, claiming that by not

providing RPA with the results of the 1994 Hawaii field tests, DeKalb had fraudulently induced RPA to enter into the 1994 agreement that had granted DeKalb paid-up rights to the RD-125 technology. RPA also sued DeKalb for misappropriation of trade secrets and patent infringement.

ISSUE Did DeKalb fraudulently induce RPA to enter into the 1994 agreement whereby RPA gave DeKalb the rights to the RD-125 technology?

HOLDING Yes. DeKalb defrauded RPA.

REASONING Excerpts from the opinion of Judge Clevenger:

North Carolina requires that, for the remedy of rescission, each element of fraud must be proven by a preponderance of the evidence.... The elements of actual fraud under North Carolina law are [a]

> (1) material misrepresentation of a past or existing fact; (2) the representation must be definite and specific; (3) made with knowledge of its falsity or in culpable ignorance of its truth; (4) that the misrepresentation was made with [the] intention that it should be acted upon; (5) that the recipient of the misrepresentation reasonably relied upon it and acted upon it; and (6) that [resultant] damage to the injured party [occurred].

... The heart of RPA's case for fraud concerns DeKalb's behavior upon learning of the successful Hawaii field test results for corn containing the RD-125 technology.... [RPA's] Dr. DeRose testified that no successful field trials of glyphosate-resistant corn had ever been done . . . , and that due to the number of past failures, he had no specific expectation that the planned field trials would succeed. On September 6, 1994, Dr. Flick of DeKalb learned that the Hawaii field tests had been successful. However, Dr. Flick did not communicate this information to anyone at RPA. Instead, on September 7, 1994, Dr. Flick wrote Dr. Freyssinet of RPA the following letter[:]

> As the results that we have obtained in maize with the glyphosate resistant double mutant maize gene provided by RPA to DEKALB have been very encouraging, we are interested in whether this gene would also function as a selectable marker in soybeans. Is it possible for DEKALB to use this gene in soybeans as a selectable marker?
>
> I will await your answer.

When Dr. Flick was asked in deposition why he did not inform anyone at RPA about the Hawaii field test results, he responded that it would have required him to write a longer letter. . . . Additionally, DeKalb's lawyer Doug Fisher was also aware of the Hawaii field test results. Mr. Fisher and Dr. Flick were involved in preparing the appendix to the 1994 . . . [RPA/DeKalb agreement that had] transferred the RD-125 construct to DeKalb under a paid-up license. Furthermore, RPA put forth evidence tending to show that Mr. Fisher's notes relating to the preparation of the 1994 [a]greement were destroyed by DeKalb in contravention of DeKalb's stated document retention policy. DeKalb argues that no evidence shows that it failed to send the Hawaii test results under a "plan" to cause RPA to enter the 1994 [a]greement. DeKalb further asserts that Dr. Flick's September letter cannot support a finding of deceitful intent. Certainly, it is true that RPA has not introduced a "smoking gun" memo clearly delineating a fraudulent scheme or plan by DeKalb. However, [DeKalb] appear[s] to urge that inferences cannot be drawn from the actions that took place at DeKalb. The evidence produced at trial tended to show that the Hawaii field test results were an important and exciting milestone in the development of glyphosate-tolerant corn. In light of this, it seems odd that Dr. Flick neglected to send these results to anyone at RPA, especially in light of his past actions [of] forwarding . . . the initial field test results and generally keeping RPA informed of research events. Dr. Flick's explanation for his actions was certainly less than convincing. When this evidence is coupled with the testimony regarding the knowledge and actions of DeKalb's lawyer who assisted in procuring a paid-up license to RD-125 for DeKalb, it seems reasonable to infer that DeKalb reasonably calculated and intended to deceive RPA by withholding the Hawaii field test results to gain a strategic advantage in the 1994 [a]greement. DeKalb also argues that there was no substantial evidence that RPA's reliance on DeKalb's alleged fraudulent conduct was reasonable. [DeKalb notes that the] RD-125 construct [was] clearly included in the exhibit attached to the 1994 [a]greement that listed the genetic material subject to the agreement. DeKalb argues that RPA should have inquired about the results of the Hawaii field tests and the potential of the RD-125 construct before signing away exclusive rights to the technology, and that RPA's failure to do so was unreasonable. Certainly, RPA could have done more to police [its] own technology. However, RPA did present testimony that the success of the Hawaii field tests was unexpected, because no one had ever achieved success in the field with glyphosate-tolerant corn before. Furthermore, Dr. DeRose testified that he had a close and friendly relationship with the scientists at DeKalb and "they always sent us this information without asking them when things had worked, so I fully expected to receive information when these experiments were working." The close working relationship between various RPA and DeKalb scientists, as well as their shared past history of prior failure to achieve success in the field, made it reasonable for RPA to assume that silence from DeKalb meant failure. [The court therefore held that] the jury's fraud verdict was supported by substantial evidence. . . .]

BUSINESS CONSIDERATIONS Should RPA have been more aggressive in seeking information about the Hawaii tests? How does a firm draw the line as to how to seek information in such a fashion that protects its own interests but in a way that does not jeopardize the goodwill needed for effective business relationships?

ETHICAL CONSIDERATIONS Many persons—in the United States and abroad—oppose the development and use of genetically modified plants. Construct ethical arguments for and against such scientific advances.

Successful proof of a cause of action in fraud usually justifies *rescission*, or the setting aside of the contract. Hence, such contracts are voidable at the option of the injured party. As mentioned, an alternative to rescission is the recovery of damages sufficient to restore the injured party to the status quo, or the position he or she would have enjoyed had the facts of the transaction mirrored his or her conception of them at the time of acceptance. The facts of each case normally will dictate which remedy a plaintiff will elect to pursue. The injured party, as plaintiff, faces a

NRW

MARKETING AND SALES STRATEGIES

NRW needs to generate revenues very quickly at the outset of its business life if it hopes to survive. As a result, Mai favors a very aggressive approach to the marketing of the firm's products. Carlos, in contrast, prefers a more cautious marketing strategy. Carlos believes that sales representatives who answer questions honestly and completely will build a loyal customer base and that a few lost sales early on are preferable to a number of lost customers in the future. Helen responds that, in the absence of robust sales early on, the company's financial prospects will remain so shaky that NRW will have few worries about customer concerns in the future because such a clientele will be nonexistent. All three have asked for your advice. What will you tell them?

BUSINESS CONSIDERATIONS What sort of policy should a business adopt regarding the information a sales representative can or should communicate to the customer? What factors will influence the firm's decision?

ETHICAL CONSIDERATIONS Suppose a sales representative knows that a customer has an erroneous impression of the product, but no legal obligation for the representative to speak exists. From an ethical perspective, what should the sales representative do? Why?

INTERNATIONAL CONSIDERATIONS Do cultural differences heighten the possibilities that one of the parties will view the sales tactics employed by the other as overly aggressive? If so, what can a firm do to ensure that its sales representatives demonstrate sensitivity to such issues?

---

final pitfall: He or she must act as quickly as possible or, as will be discussed later in this chapter, possibly waive the cause of action.

Silence

No discussion of fraud is complete without a reference to *silence* and its effect on whether a court will grant relief. The common law steadfastly held that "mere silence is not fraud." This conclusion rests on the belief that fraud neces-

sitates some sort of overt communication. Because, by definition, silence denotes the total absence of any statement, the rule arose that one cannot be liable for fraud unless one had said or done something. (Remember the first element that requires a misstatement or misrepresentation of a fact.)

Many jurisdictions, in order to encourage nonconcealment and honesty in business transactions, now reject this rule and hold, for instance, that the seller must inform the buyer of any defects in a house. Similarly, if the buyer asks a question, the seller must answer truthfully and correct any wrong assumptions that the buyer holds. A seller's silence in such instances today may not prevent legal liability. Still, the strict rule is that there generally is no duty to speak (that is, to disclose such facts).

Even the common law, however, deemed some situations so fraught with the possibility of injury or detriment that it placed a duty to speak on the party possessing the information. One of these situations, latent defects, already has been examined.

A duty to speak also arises in situations in which the parties owe each other *fiduciary duties*, or duties that arise from a relationship of trust or confidence that requires one who holds the special position of trust or confidence to act with the utmost good faith and loyalty. For example, an investment advisor should inform all clients of her part ownership in ABC Corporation before she suggests that clients purchase ABC stock. Similarly, in applying for insurance coverage, one cannot be silent if the insurer asks questions about one's medical history. To avoid fraud, one must, for example, disclose the existence of a heart condition. Finally, a statement made in preliminary negotiations that no longer is true at the time of the execution of the contract must be disclosed in order for one to escape a possible lawsuit based on fraud.

Misrepresentation

In general, everything previously discussed about the elements of fraud is true of a cause of action involving misrepresentation, with one notable exception: Misrepresentation lacks the elements of *scienter* and *intent to deceive.* Nevertheless, misrepresentation (often called *innocent misrepresentation* to differentiate it from fraud) can lead to the imposition of legal remedies. The property owner's statement about the property boundaries may amount to innocent misrepresentation if the plaintiff cannot prove scienter. *Misrepresentation,* or the innocent misstatement of a material fact that is relied on with resultant injury, makes the contract voidable at the option of the injured party. Rescission thus remains a possible (and, in many jurisdictions, the exclusive) remedy. Again, the plaintiff must act in a timely manner so as not to waive the cause of action.

Practically speaking, most plaintiffs allege both fraud and misrepresentation in the same lawsuit. Fraud is harder to prove but more desirable from the plaintiff's point of view; successful proof of fraud brings with it the possibility of recovery of damages under the tort of deceit. The elements of deceit are identical to those of fraud. Upon a showing of deceit, a court may award *punitive* damages (damages beyond the actual losses suffered) in addition to the actual (or compensatory) damages normally recoverable for fraud. But even if the plaintiff fails to prove fraud (and its twin, deceit), recovery on grounds of misrepresentation is possible. At the very least, a showing of fraud or misrepresentation will form the basis for rescission.

Exhibit 12.2 describes the elements of misrepresentation and fraud; it shows the analysis a court may follow in determining the presence of either as a defense to a contract.

Mistake

Human nature is such that people often try to unravel transactions because they have made an error about some facet of the deal. Imagine the chaos, however, if courts readily accepted these hindsight arguments. The result would be a decrease in the number of contracts, since people would be wary of dealing with each other. As you probably recognize, such unpredictability would unduly hamper commercial pacts. On the other hand, we have repeatedly stressed the importance of mutual assent in contract law. Thus, the law, on policy grounds, wishes to set the contract aside if the error is so great that it has tainted the parties' consent to the agreement.

The legal doctrine of mistake tries to balance these competing interests. *Mistake* occurs when the parties are wrong about the existence or absence of a past or present fact that is material to their transaction. Note that the parties must be wrong about *material* facts. Thus, legal mistake is not synonymous with ignorance, inability, or inaccurate judgments relating to value or quality. Courts will rescind contracts on the ground of mistake only if the error is so fundamental that it cannot be said that the parties' states of mind were in agreement about the essential facts of the transaction. Mistakes as to law, in contrast, oftentimes will not constitute grounds for rescission of the contract. Two kinds of mistakes exist: unilateral and bilateral (or mutual) mistakes.

EXHIBIT 12.2 The Elements of Fraud and Misrepresentation

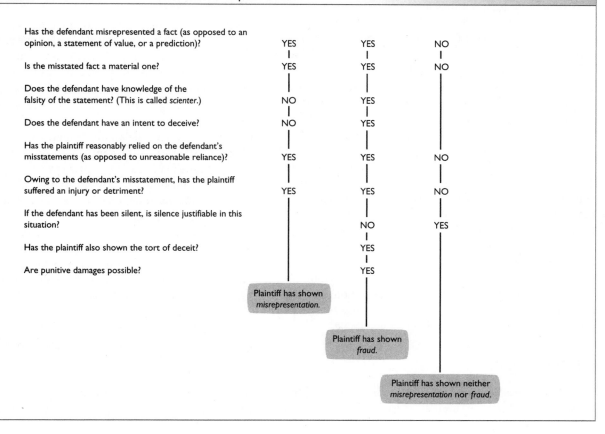

Has the defendant misrepresented a fact (as opposed to an opinion, a statement of value, or a prediction)?	YES	YES	NO
Is the misstated fact a material one?	YES	YES	NO
Does the defendant have knowledge of the falsity of the statement? (This is called *scienter*.)	NO	YES	
Does the defendant have an intent to deceive?	NO	YES	
Has the plaintiff reasonably relied on the defendant's misstatements (as opposed to unreasonable reliance)?	YES	YES	NO
Owing to the defendant's misstatement, has the plaintiff suffered an injury or detriment?	YES	YES	NO
If the defendant has been silent, is silence justifiable in this situation?		NO	YES
Has the plaintiff also shown the tort of deceit?		YES	
Are punitive damages possible?		YES	

Plaintiff has shown *misrepresentation.*

Plaintiff has shown *fraud.*

Plaintiff has shown neither *misrepresentation* nor *fraud.*

Unilateral Mistake

As the term implies, in a unilateral mistake, only one party is mistaken about a material fact. The general rule, with some exceptions, holds that courts will not rescind such contracts.

Unilateral mistakes frequently result from misplaced expectations of value. Let us suppose that Reza goes to an antique store to look for a Duncan Phyfe table. He finds a table he believes to be a Duncan Phyfe and, without mentioning his belief to the store owner, pays a hefty price for it. Later that evening, a friend informs him the table is not a Duncan Phyfe. If Reza tries to avoid the contract, he will not be successful because only he was mistaken about a material fact—that is, that the table was a Duncan Phyfe. He also was mistaken as to value. In such unilateral mistake situations, courts take a hands-off approach and leave the parties with the bargains they have made. Rescission of the contract ordinarily is not granted.

The result here might differ if the store owner knew (or should have known) of Reza's error or in some other fashion acted fraudulently or unconscionably. But the facts in this example do not support such a conclusion; if they did, courts might allow rescission of the contract, despite the unilateral mistake.

Similarly, in situations in which the mistake results from business computations, courts will suspend the general rule of refusing to grant relief for unilateral mistakes. Such situations may arise if a contractor makes an addition error (say $100,000) in computing a bid. The person soliciting the bid generally will choose the lowest bidder. Once the successful contractor/bidder recognizes its mistake, it will wish to rescind the contract. Even though these circumstances involve a unilateral mistake on the bidder's part, it can attempt to show that a court should grant the equitable remedy of rescission (or reformation—a court's correcting a written instrument in order to remove a mistake and to make the agreement conform to the terms to which the parties originally had agreed) because (1) the mistake was of such magnitude that enforcement would be unconscionable, (2) the mistake related to a material aspect of the agreement, (3) the mistake occurred in good faith and in the absence of clear negligence, (4) it would be possible to return the other party to the status quo without causing injury to third parties, and (5) no other circumstances exist that would make the granting of relief inequitable.

Bilateral Mistake

If both parties are in error about the essence of the agreement, bilateral (or mutual) mistake results. Courts will rescind such agreements on the rationale that, owing to a mistake about the existence, identity, or nature of the subject matter of the contract, a valid agreement has not occurred. If a mutual mistake of fact is present, either party may disaffirm this voidable contract unless rescission will cause injuries to innocent third parties. Why? The parties' minds have not met on the salient facts of the transaction. For example, assume an American company contracts with a foreign company (headquartered in New York) for hand-loomed rugs. The firms contract in April; but, unknown to both parties, a warehouse fire had destroyed the rugs in March. The destruction of the subject matter makes the contract voidable on the grounds of bilateral mistake: The parties have made an error regarding a significant fact— that the rugs existed at the time of contract formation.

Ambiguities, or uncertainties regarding the meanings of expressions used in contractual agreements, constitute another cause of mutual mistake. If the American buyer believes that the term rugs means room-sized carpets, but, because of language difficulties, the international seller envisions rugs as smaller, that is, more comparable in size to wall hangings, this ambiguity may constitute mutual mistake. If so, rescission is justifiable.

Reformation

If a court can easily remedy the mistake, a court may *reform* the contract, or rewrite it to reflect the parties' actual intentions. In the ambiguity example, assuming the rugs were obtainable, once the parties recognize the ambiguity, reformation would permit a court to make room-sized rugs the subject matter of the contract. After the parties resort to a court's equitable powers of reformation, the contract will be fully enforceable. Be aware, though, that large backlogs of court cases form a substantial impediment to the availability of reformation as a practical remedy. Therefore, take pains when making a deal to ascertain exactly what your agreement means: You thereby will avoid a great many frustrations (and expenses).

The nature of electronic commerce, especially its reliance on electronic agents and automated programs, has given rise to concerns not only about when assent occurs (a topic covered in Chapter 10) but also about how to handle inadvertent errors. Virtually everyone has either pushed the wrong computer key or at least come close to doing so. To minimize the possibility of someone's unintentionally being bound to a contract, UETA, in § 10, allows one to avoid an automated transaction effected through an inadvertent error. Assuming a B2C transaction, in situations in which B's electronic agent lacks any mechanisms for preventing or correcting an error, the other party (C) may avoid the transaction and the legal consequences caused by the inadvertent error. In other words, if you meant to order two computer games but accidentally ordered 22 because you struck the "2" key twice, you could cancel this transaction if the on-line merchant has not put in place security procedures for detecting changes or errors. Still, to qualify for avoiding the transaction, the consumer, upon learning that the Web site operator believes the consumer has entered into a trans-action, must promptly inform the Web site operator (or Internet merchant) of the error and that he or she had not intended to be bound by the electronic record (the message about the 22 games). Moreover, the consumer cannot have used or received the benefit of the transaction (here, the games). Last, the individual must take all reasonable steps necessary to return any consideration received (again, the games) as a result of the transaction. In so doing, UETA requires the individual's compliance with any reasonable instructions that the firm provides concerning the return or destruction of the items received. Otherwise, rescission of the contract is not allowed. This provision of UETA seeks to encourage on-line firms and those who conduct business through EDIs and other electronic agents to build into their systems security measures aimed at preventing such errors. Accordingly, Internet merchants in B2C transactions com-monly use confirmation screens that reflect the salient details of the transaction and request the consumer to click on a box so as to verify the transaction. Toward the same end, other e-commerce merchants rely on e-mail verifica-tions of the transaction, coupled with a request for the con-sumer to notify the merchant if an error has occurred. Meant by the UETA drafters to supplement any other appli-cable law regarding mistake, this provision notes that when the special provisions do not apply, other law—including the common law rules of mistake—and the parties' contract (if any) will govern the transaction.

UCITA, like UETA, protects consumers who have sent erroneous electronic messages that they did not intend to send by allowing such consumers to use the electronic error as a defense to contract formation. This provision defines an electronic error as one resulting from the on-line firm's use of an automated system that fails to provide a reasonable means for detecting and correcting any such errors. It penal-izes firms that fail to provide such systems. This UCITA pro-vision, § 214, resembles UETA § 10 in that § 214 requires the consumer to act promptly, to notify the other party of the error, and to take any and all actions to put the other party back in the same position it would have enjoyed in the absence of the mistake. To use the previous example, a con-sumer who received 22 games would need to either return all the games or follow the directions of the seller to destroy the 20 unordered copies. Moreover, to qualify for the

defense, the consumer must neither have received any ben-efit or value from the mistake nor have made the informa-tion or benefit available to a third party. Last, § 214 notes that errors in transactions that fall outside UCITA's coverage (for example, credit card transactions) will be determined by the law applicable to credit cards. Section 214, then, does not alter the results reached under other consumer protec-tion laws. Nevertheless, by providing consumers with a spe-cific defense for avoiding contracts that result from electronic errors, UCITA appears to strengthen the protec-tions offered by the common law doctrine of mistake.

Buttressing § 214 is § 206, which allows contract for-mation through the interaction of electronic agents but also empowers courts to grant appropriate relief if the resultant transaction has been induced by mistake or fraud. Section 114's imposition of the duty of good faith, defined in §102 as "honesty in fact and the observance of reason-able commercial standards of fair dealing," helps minimize sharp dealings as well. The same is true of § 209's striking down of any term in a mass license that is unconscionable.

Duress

No genuine assent to the terms of an agreement results if a person assents while under duress. The person who has so assented, then, can ask for rescission of the contract on the ground of duress.

To assert the defense of *duress* means to allege that the other party has forced one into the contract against one's will. To constitute duress, the coercion must be so extreme that the victim has lost all ability to assent freely and volun-tarily to the transaction. Given this definition, courts look for evidence of physical threats or threats that, if carried out, will cause intense mental anguish. Forcing a person to sign a contract at gunpoint, of course, will represent duress. To most courts, so will a spouse's threat to tell the parties' children that the other spouse has committed adultery: If, as a result of this intimidation, the spouse signs over a dis-proportionate share of the marital property, courts can rescind this agreement on the basis of duress. Similarly, courts generally find duress in threats to initiate criminal actions (even if a basis exists) in order to extract a contrac-tual agreement. Courts, however, ordinarily do not see threats of civil suits as constituting duress.

The discussion to this point has focused on personal duress. Recently, the doctrine of economic duress has arisen. Economic duress occurs when one party is forced to agree to a further, wrongful, and coercive demand (usually a price increase) as a consequence of receiving the com-modities or services to which he or she is entitled under the original contract. The party alleging economic duress ordinarily must show (1) wrongful acts or threats by the defendant, (2) financial distress caused by the wrongful acts or threats, and (3) the absence of any reasonable alternative to the terms presented by the wrongdoer (that is, the injured party cannot obtain the goods or services elsewhere). Whether a court will grant a recovery to a plaintiff who alleges economic duress (a theory also known as business compulsion) depends heavily on the particular facts of a given situation.

The earlier example of the hand-loomed rugs illustrates this concept. Assume that the New York–based rug company has the only available hand-loomed rugs, and the American buyer has agreed to pay $2,500 per rug. Economic duress exists if the seller subsequently tells the American buyer (who wants to fill its orders for the rugs) that it can have the rugs only if it is willing to pay $4,000 apiece for them. Basing its decision on the concept of economic duress, a court may force the seller to sell the rugs at the original price of $2,500 or allow the American buyer after the fact to recover any difference in price.

As with most of the reality-of-consent situations discussed in this chapter, contracts made under duress ordinarily are voidable. Hence, rescission may be effected at the option of the injured party *unless* the injured party, by acquiescing in the coercive conduct for an unreasonably long time, ratifies the contract. However, in these cases the conduct exemplifying duress is so extreme that a court sometimes will find the contract void. Threats directed at third parties (such as relatives) may be considered duress of this sort if one party enters into the contract to protect the innocent third party from these threats. The court's use of some of these principles in the next case, *Golden v. McDermott, Will & Emory*, is instructive.

Undue Influence

Closely related to duress is the concept of undue influence. Indeed, many courts view it as a subcategory of duress. Like duress, its existence depends heavily on the facts.

Undue influence is the use of a relationship of trust and confidence to extract contractual advantages. Newspapers are full of examples of such situations. Recall the allegations of undue influence involving nurses who have been named beneficiaries of their patients' sizeable estates or lawyers who have benefited enormously from their clients' testamentary dispositions (that is, those deriving from deceased persons' wills). Since the favored nurse or lawyer by virtue of the relationship enjoyed with the other party has the ability to dominate or overreach the other party, the law often allows the rescission of such contracts. Because of

---

NRW CASE 12.3 | **Manufacturing/Management**

SHOULD THE FIRM AGREE TO THE DEMANDS OF A SUPPLIER?

NRW has entered into a contract with Total Fabricator, Inc. (TFI), a manufacturing company, to assemble 2,000 units of StuffTrakR for $3 per unit. However, because of the likelihood that NRW will succeed, TFI also wants to produce the next 10,000 units at the same price per unit. To do so, TFI refuses to assemble the first 2,000 StuffTrakR units for the agreed-on $3 per unit price unless NRW guarantees that TFI will have the subcontract for the next 10,000 units as well. Both Carlos and Helen know that, for a larger order, they can negotiate a better per unit price; however, they also know that, to ride the present wave of popularity relating to digitized gadgets, they must receive the first 2,000 assembled units immediately and therefore must use TFI. Hence, both firm members seek your advice. What legal risks inhere in TFI's refusal? What legal remedy can NRW seek?

BUSINESS CONSIDERATIONS How does a firm gauge when a "hard-line" approach verges on illegality? Should a firm err on the side of caution and always disavow such an approach?

ETHICAL CONSIDERATIONS Is the intersection of law and ethics represented by the Uniform Commercial Code's section on unconscionability advisable? Does this section represent a statutory abrogation of the principles of freedom of contract that goes too far? Why or why not?

INTERNATIONAL CONSIDERATIONS Is it possible to reach an international consensus on such concepts as unconscionability? Does the CISG address unconscionability, or any similar topics? Do other countries view consumer protection in the way the United States does?

---

the domination by another, the contracting party actually has not exercised his or her free will in entering into the contract, but instead has given effect to the will or wishes of the other party.

The law will presume undue influence in certain circumstances, notably in fiduciary relationships. In the lawyer example just cited, the mere existence of the relationship will require the lawyer to prove that the client made the disposition free from the lawyer's coercion. The

12.3

GOLDEN v. MCDERMOTT, WILL & EMERY
702 N.E.2d 581 (Ill. App. 1st Dist. 1998)

FACTS Bruce Golden worked as a securities lawyer for the law firm of McDermott, Will & Emery (MWE) for 21 years. In 1989, eight years after he had become an income partner, a client he had brought to MWE, Avanti Associates, and its promoter, Timothy Sasak, found themselves subject to a class action suit for securities violations. The suit named MWE as a defendant as well and sought $120 million from the firm. As a result of the suit, MWE's malpractice insurance carrier, Attorney's Liability Assurance Society, Ltd. (ALAS), had to pay the largest claim it had ever covered for a law firm. Golden alleged that owing to the initiation of the Avanti suit, ALAS was hesitant about renewing MWE's policy and wanted Golden removed from the firm. Golden further claimed that MWE at that time postponed his termination because the firm needed his cooperation in the Avanti litigation. Nonetheless, Golden maintained, from the time of the institution of the Avanti suit until his termination about 18 months later, MWE took various steps to limit his participation in partnership business and to reduce his partnership income (for example, he was removed from a client account for which he had done a great deal of work, he was told not to bring in any new business, and so on). In January 1991, the firm reduced Golden's partnership units—and thus his compensation—by one-third.

The day after the settlement of the Avanti litigation, two of MWE's partners (who also were named defendants in the class action) informed Golden the firm was ready to fire him but that he could resign if he wished. The articulated reason for his termination was "lack of production," but Golden asserted that one of the partners later confided that pressure from ALAS was the real reason. Golden ultimately signed a severance agreement that contained a clause releasing the firm from all other claims. In February 1992, Golden accepted the agreed-upon, one-time payment of $225,000 minus a deduction for the draw (an arrangement by which an employee receives a predetermined amount each pay period) the firm had paid to Golden during the period in question. Around the time that Golden signed the severance agreement, he also was having personal problems. He had just lost a lawsuit concerning a major defect in a house he had bought, and his wife was out of work owing to the death of her employer. When Golden sought counseling, the mental health professional reported that the termination had left Golden paranoid, depressed, and dysfunctional. On November 7, 1991, one of the part-

ners who had requested Golden's resignation allegedly told Golden that the management committee, before terminating him, had not taken a vote on his expulsion (as required by the firm's partnership agreement); that Golden would have difficulty finding new legal employment, because ALAS had "blacklisted" him; and that the firm had never asked any other partner to sign such a harsh severance agreement. Filing suit in 1995, Golden claimed that MWE had violated the partnership agreement by not following the termination procedures outlined therein, that the defendant partners had violated their fiduciary duty to him as copartners, and that the firm had committed fraud against him. As part of this lawsuit, Golden moreover argued that the release he had signed was voidable because he had executed it under personal and economic duress.

ISSUE Was the release voidable because Golden had signed it under personal, economic, and/or moral duress?

HOLDING No. The facts failed to show any type of duress. Moreover, Golden's conduct in retaining the consideration for an unreasonable time before the institution of his lawsuit amounted to a ratification of the release.

REASONING Excerpts from the opinion of Judge Cousins:

Golden alleges three closely related types of duress. First, he claims that MWE coerced him by threatening to fire him. Then he says that it practiced economic duress (also known as "business compulsion") by taking unfair advantage of his financial and personal difficulties. Finally he alleges moral duress. Although there are several proposed definitions of duress, the supreme court has defined it as "a condition where one is induced by a wrongful act or threat of another to make a contract under circumstances which deprive him of the exercise of his free will." . . . MWE contends that the pressure it applied to Golden did not constitute duress, because it was not wrongful.

MWE argues that it had a right to expel Golden without cause and that it cannot be duress for it to threaten to do what it has a legal right to do. But while it is true that one must threaten "wrongful" action in order to be guilty of duress, the landmark supreme court case on duress . . . says that the meaning of "wrongful" is "not limited to acts that are criminal, tortious or in violation of a contractual duty, but extends to acts that are wrongful in a moral sense." . . . So even though an employee may be terminable at will, it is not impossible for the threat of discharge to constitute duress. . . . On the other hand, it is not wrongful, and does not constitute duress for an employer to give an employee who is about to be fired the option to resign. . . . So, even if the choice of "resign or be fired" can constitute duress, the choice was not sufficient to constitute duress under the facts as alleged here.

Golden next alleges economic duress or business compulsion. Economic duress occurs where "undue or unjust advantage has been taken of a person's economic necessity or distress to coerce him into making the agreement." . . . These dire circumstances must be such as to overbear the will of the plaintiff. . . . Whether the circumstances did in fact overbear the plaintiff's will is ordinarily a question of fact. . . . However, it is not enough for economic duress that the plaintiff be in great financial or personal difficulty. The defendant must have been in some way responsible for that difficulty. "'[A] duress claim of this nature must be based on the acts or conduct of the other party and not merely on the necessities of the purported victim.'" . . . Assuming, under the facts as alleged, that MWE and the defendant partners were partially responsible for some of Golden's troubles, they still were not responsible for the death of his wife's employer, the loss of her job, or the loss of the lawsuit concerning Golden's house. In our view, the claim of duress lacked this necessary element of responsibility on the part of defendants for the plaintiff's circumstances. . . .

Finally, Golden alleges moral duress. Moral duress is quite similar to economic duress. It "consists in imposition, oppression, undue influence, or the taking of undue advantage of the business or financial stress or extreme necessities or weaknesses of another." . . . "Relief is granted in such cases on the basis that the party benefiting thereby has received money, property, or other advantage which in equity and good conscience he should not be permitted to retain." . . . Golden was a legally sophisticated attorney who negotiated the sever-

ance agreement over the course of several months. Given the dissimilarity of these facts to the above cases, we hold that Golden has not established a claim for moral duress.

Even if the severance agreement were voidable because of duress or a breach of fiduciary duty, we believe that Golden ratified the agreement by his subsequent conduct. "It is well established that the retention of the consideration by one sui juris, with knowledge of the facts will amount to a ratification of a release executed by him in settlement of a claim, where the retention is for an unreasonable time under the circumstances of the case." . . . A victim of fraud who, knowing of the fraud, "accepts the benefits flowing from a contract for any considerable length of time ratifies the contract." . . . Golden accepted a large sum of money as a result of the settlement agreement, despite the fact that he was on notice at that point of facts that he says made the agreement voidable. He retained the money for over five years. This constitutes ratification of the release. . . . Accordingly, given the release's broad terms, it bars Golden's noncontract actions.

BUSINESS CONSIDERATIONS Was the firm justified in firing Golden because of the securities violations lawsuit? Should the firm inform all potential hires that such situations may lead to termination? Or should the firm make such decisions on a case-by-case basis?

ETHICAL CONSIDERATIONS Golden had been a member of the firm for 21 years and was a partner. Do partners as well as professional/personal friends owe each other higher standards of ethical behavior? If so, should the parties here have behaved differently? If the firm had actually capitulated to the pressure brought by its insurer—as Golden alleged—was the firm's conduct appropriate, ethically speaking? As attorneys, all the partners were subject to their profession's canons of ethics. Is society justified in expecting overall higher standards of ethics from professionals (even in areas outside their areas of expertise), owing to their presumably heightened ethical sensitivities?

law will demand that the lawyer, as a fiduciary, act with utmost good faith in dealing with persons who will be predisposed to follow whatever the lawyer advises. Like lawyers, parents may enjoy fiduciary relationships with their children, doctors with their patients, accountants with their clients, and so on. Sometimes it is difficult for courts to determine when the persuasiveness of the fiduciary has become so intense that the other party has lost all vestiges of free will. But when they are convinced that this has occurred, they permit rescission of the challenged contract.

Unconscionability

You may note similarities between the concept of unconscionability, which we addressed in Chapters 9 and 11, and the ideas we discuss in this chapter. Especially in the context of consumer law, some courts have set contracts aside when these courts have found the bargaining power of the parties so unequal as to constitute commercially shocking or unreasonably oppressive conduct. (In Chapter 13, you will learn that some courts call such agreements contracts of adhesion, meaning that one party to the contract, through overreaching, is able to impose its will on the other party.) The Uniform Commercial Code validates this approach in

§ 2-302, but not all states have adopted this section of the UCC. Nevertheless, unconscionability may signal a lack of meaningful assent to a contract and may justify a court's subsequent intervention on behalf of the injured party.

Summary

Certain classes of people may lack capacity, or the legal ability to bind themselves to an agreement and to enforce any promises made to them. For example, the contracts of a minor, usually defined as a person under age 18, often are voidable at the option of the minor, even when the minor has misrepresented his or her age. This power of disaffirmance ordinarily extends through the person's minority and for a reasonable time after attaining majority. After reaching majority, however, a minor may ratify, or approve, the contract. Ratification may be express or implied. Even in the absence of ratification, a minor may be liable for necessaries in quasi contract. The definition of necessaries depends on the minor's station in life and the parents' ability to provide for the minor. Sometimes special statutes broaden a minor's areas of liability. A minor almost always will be liable for any tort or crime unless the minor is very young, or the imposition of tort liability will bring about the enforcement of a contract previously disaffirmed by the minor.

The contracts of insane persons may be void, voidable, or valid. To be insane, a person must demonstrate sufficient mental derangement to be unable to understand that to which he or she is agreeing or the consequences attendant on that agreement. Such agreements are voidable, but contracts entered into during periods of lucidity are enforceable. Upon regaining sanity, a person either may ratify the contract or avoid it. Insane persons are liable for necessaries, just as minors are.

Total intoxication may render a person incapable of entering into a binding contract, but slight intoxication will not. Upon regaining sobriety, the person either may disaffirm or ratify the contract. However, courts generally are hostile to avoiding contracts on the basis of intoxication, except in unusual circumstances.

Aliens (persons who are citizens of foreign countries) may face legal disabilities with regard to contractual capacity. This is especially true of enemy aliens, that is, citizens of countries with whom the United States officially is at war. Convicts and even married women may have limited rights to contract as well. To determine the degree of disability, if any, that exists for these persons, one should consult the relevant state statutes.

To have a valid contract, one also must prove that the assent of the parties is genuine. The existence of fraud, mis-
representation, mistake, duress, undue influence, or unconscionability precludes the reality of consent that serves as the foundation of modern contract law. Fraud is a deliberate misrepresentation of a material fact with the intent to induce another person to enter a contract that will be injurious to that person. Predictions, statements of value, opinions, and misstatements of law do not constitute fraud. Probably the most difficult element to prove is the defendant's knowledge of the falsity of the statement, or scienter. The plaintiff's reliance on the deception must be reasonable, or the plaintiff will be precluded from recovering. Successful proof of fraud makes the contract voidable and justifies rescission. Although the common law held that mere silence is not fraud, exceptions to this doctrine existed even in early common law times. Today, the judicial trend is to force disclosure of material facts if their concealment may injure the other party. Innocent misrepresentation also may result in legal liability. Mistake occurs when the parties are wrong about the existence or absence of a past or present fact that is material to their transactions. Two types of mistakes exist: unilateral (one person is in error) and bilateral/mutual (both parties are in error). Courts generally will not rescind unilateral mistakes unless the other party knows, or should have known, of the mistaken party's error or uses it to take unconscionable advantage of the injured party. In these cases, as in situations involving errors in business computations, courts will allow rescission. If a mutual or bilateral mistake of fact is present, either party can disaffirm the contract. Ambiguity, for example, may lead to rescission. The equitable remedy of reformation allows a court to rewrite a contract to reflect the parties' actual intentions, but courts will not always permit reformation. Duress exists when a person's will has been overridden as a result of another person's threats. Duress may be either personal or economic, the latter occurring when a seller, in order to extract a higher contract price, wrongfully or coercively withholds scarce commodities or services. Undue influence is the use of a relationship of trust and confidence to gain contractual advantages. In certain relationships, the law will presume undue influence. The existence of unconscionability may signal a lack of meaningful assent to a contract and thus constitute grounds for a court's setting the contract aside as well.

Discussion Questions

1. Why do savvy businesspeople say, "Don't deal with minors"? Can minors disaffirm contracts if they have misrepresented their ages at the time of contracting?

2. How long does an infant's power to rescind a contract last?

3. What is *ratification*, and how can it occur?

4. Define *necessaries*.

5. Can an insane or intoxicated person's contracts ever be enforceable? Why or why not?

6. Set out, respectively, the legal requirements of fraud and misrepresentation.

7. How does silence relate to the legal theory of fraud? In what situations does a legal duty to speak arise?

8. Name, define, and explain the remedies for the two types of mistake.

9. Discuss the difference between *duress* and *economic duress*.

10. Define *undue influence*.

Case Problems and Writing Assignments

1. On May 18, 1991, Larry Moeckel, a district manager for the Parke-Davis Division of Warner-Lambert Company (Warner-Lambert), conducted a products seminar for pharmaceutical representatives and physicians at a resort in Phoenix, Arizona. The seminar included several leisure activities, including a cocktail party. After the seminar concluded, Moeckel was driving home in a company-owned car when he collided with a car driven by Cynthia Emmons. Emmons suffered severe injuries and filed this lawsuit, alleging that Moeckel was negligent and that Warner-Lambert was directly and vicariously liable for her injuries. The case proceeded against Moeckel personally and against Warner-Lambert on the vicarious liability theory. On September 20, 1996, the jury, finding that Moeckel had been acting in the scope of his employment at the time of the accident, returned a $2.5 million compensatory damages verdict against Moeckel. As a consequence, Warner-Lambert would be subjected to the punitive damages phase of the trial, scheduled to begin on September 24, 1996. On September 23, 1996, Warner-Lambert, in a settlement offer, stated: "Warner-Lambert is willing to pay the full verdict of $2,500,000 to settle all disputes between the parties. Although . . . there are many appealable issues already in the record, Warner-Lambert would like to resolve the case without further court proceedings. There is every reason to expect that the appellate courts will reverse any award against the defendants or else remand the case for a new trial." Emmons rejected this offer. Later that day, Warner-Lambert faxed to Emmons and her counsel a "final offer of $5,000,000 to settle the case for all parties on all issues." At 4:00 P.M., Emmons accepted the offer and the accompanying confidentiality terms. The judge thereupon dismissed the jury and canceled the punitive damages portion of the trial. Two days later, the trial court held a telephonic conference with all counsel and advised them that the court clerk had inadvertently marked into evidence a letter to the court from the defense counsel concerning the company's indemnification of Moeckel and had sent the exhibit into the jury room. Believing that this exhibit might have led to a larger jury verdict than otherwise might have occurred, Warner-Lambert filed a motion to set aside the settlement agreement. Finding a mutual mistake of fact (the belief of the parties that the jury had based its verdict on the jurors' consideration of only the admitted evidence), the trial judge granted Warner-Lambert's motion to set aside the settlement agreement. Emmons in turn sought enforcement of the agreement. How should the appellate court dispose of this issue? [See *Emmons v. Superior Court*, 968 P.2d 582 (Ariz. App. Div. 1 1998).]

2. Arthur Rawlings and Eleanor Rawlings were married in February 1946. This dispute revolves around a $12,000 life insurance policy Mrs. Rawlings obtained in 1961 through her employer. She originally named Mr. Rawlings as the sole beneficiary of this policy. Mrs. Rawlings's alcoholism forced her to retire from the Nashville Electric Service, and in 1984 she broke her hip while inebriated. Diagnostic X rays of this injury revealed 27 other fractures from previous falls. Mrs. Rawlings did not recover from this latest injury; she was discharged from the hospital to the first of several nursing homes where she spent the rest of her life. After Mrs. Rawlings's mother died in 1985, a dispute arose with Darden Holt, Mrs. Rawlings's brother who lived in Texas. Mr. Holt eventually successfully contested their mother's will. Angered by the will contest, Mrs. Rawlings disinherited Mr. Holt in her 1988 will. Thereafter, Mrs. Rawlings and Mr. Holt reconciled, and Mr. Holt visited his sister two or three times a year between 1988 and 1998. In May 1994, Mrs. Rawlings was admitted to the Bordeaux Hospital. Mr. Rawlings continued to visit her there three to four times per week except when the weather limited his ability to travel. Mrs. Rawlings's mental acuity began to slip as the years went on, and in November 1997 she was diagnosed with senile dementia and depression. She went through periods of confusion, and she was uncommunicative much of the time. By August 1998, Mrs. Rawlings's world consisted only of her room at the Bordeaux Hospital. She was unable to get out of bed, turn over, or bathe and groom herself without assistance. In August 1998, Mr. Rawlings told Mrs. Rawlings that he wanted a divorce. This news upset Mrs. Rawlings. During one of Mr. Holt's visits in October 1998, Mrs. Rawlings told him about Mr. Rawlings's plans to divorce her and asked for his help. Mr. Holt agreed to help and began visiting his sister more frequently. In November 1998, Mrs. Rawlings, with her brother's assistance, took several steps to separate herself from Mr. Rawlings. On

November 11, 1998, Mrs. Rawlings gave Mr. Holt her power of attorney, which he used to change the address where her pension checks were being sent; and Mrs. Rawlings signed a change of beneficiary form naming Mr. Holt as the beneficiary on her life insurance policy. Finally, on November 23, 1998, Mrs. Rawlings executed a new will naming Mr. Holt as her executor and the sole beneficiary of her estate. Thereafter, Mr. Holt returned to his home in Texas, but not before making arrangements to forward all of Mrs. Rawlings's mail to him and using the power of attorney to withdraw $350 from Mrs. Rawlings and Mr. Rawlings's joint account. At the time of the execution of the power of attorney and the change in beneficiary form, Mrs. Rawlings was depressed, and her attending physician had prescribed the smallest dose possible of Prozac for her. A consulting psychiatrist who saw Mrs. Rawlings a few times thought she might have dementia but could not offer an opinion regarding Mrs. Rawlings's competency in mid-November. The attending physician, as well as the hospital's advocacy risk management director (who was present when on November 17, 1998, Mrs. Rawlings signed a durable power of attorney for health care), later testified that she was "of sound mind" and "aware of what she was doing" when she signed this document. According to Mr. Rawlings, however, Mrs. Rawlings began going "in and out" in 1997 and became less communicative. Similarly, Mr. Rawlings's sister testified that Mrs. Rawlings became "a little confused" about 18 months before her death. Mrs. Rawlings died on July 20, 1999. Soon after Mrs. Rawlings's death, Mr. Rawlings contacted the John Hancock Life Insurance Company to obtain the proceeds of Mrs. Rawlings's policy. Only then did he learn that he was no longer the named beneficiary. Mr. Rawlings subsequently sued for the $12,000 life insurance proceeds on the grounds that Mrs. Rawlings had lacked the competency to understand the nature and probable consequences of her actions and that Mr. Holt had procured the power of attorney and the change in the beneficiary form through fraud. The trial court held that Mrs. Rawlings had lacked the capacity to make the changes and that Mr. Holt had procured the changes through undue influence. Should the appellate court affirm this decision? [See *Rawlings v. John Hancock Mutual Life Insurance Company*, 78 S.W.3d 291 (Tenn. Ct. App. 2001).]

3. Verna and Joseph Baum agreed to sell a lot to David Burggraff and his wife, Roberta Rubly-Burggraff, in July 1994. Roberta drafted the contract, and the parties signed it without the advice of counsel. The parties originally became acquainted in April 1993 when the Burggraffs began renting the Baums' house on nearby Patten Point. The couples became close friends, indeed "almost like family." During the summer or fall of 1993, the Burggraffs offered to buy a portion of the Baums' land at Mill Cove. The Burggraffs wanted the lot because it had an ocean view and a potential building site near the water. Negotiations proceeded slowly, however, because the land had been in Verna Baum's family for generations and had sentimental value to her. During this time, the parties discussed in detail their plans for the land, including potential building sites and the importance of limited development so as to preserve the parcel's natural beauty. The Burggraffs planned to build both a primary residence and a cabin on the lot. They wanted the cabin to be located within 75 feet of the water, with the residence in the woods and up the hill from the water. Throughout the negotiations, the parties continued their close relationship and discussed the Burggraffs' building plans frequently. Roberta Rubly-Burggraff, in researching some of the zoning statutes that applied to the land, determined that the general state setback was 100 feet, while the local setback was only 75 feet. Both parties believed, based on her efforts and what they called "common knowledge," that those were the only relevant zoning ordinances applicable to the lot. In April 1995, after the contract was signed, the Burggraffs hired a civil engineer to discuss improving an access road that led to the building site of the primary residence. He then informed the Burggraffs that the land was in the town's Resource Protection District (RPD), which generally extends 250 feet from the water's edge. While the site chosen for the main residence would remain unaffected, the Burggraffs could build neither the access road nor the cabin in the RPD without permits from various local authorities. The Burggraffs thereupon informed the Baums that the lot was in the RPD and asked for a price reduction. After the parties ultimately were unable to come to an agreement, in June 1996 the Burggraffs filed a complaint based on mutual mistake. Would they win this lawsuit? [See *Burggraff v. Baum*, 720 A.2d 1167 (Me. 1998).]

4. Jonathan Ray Adams was born on April 5, 1980, the natural child of Mildred A. Adams and Cecil D. Hylton Jr. Jonathan's parents were never married to each other. On September 8, 1995, after a highly contested lawsuit establishing Hylton's paternity of Jonathan, a paternity order was entered in Dade County, Florida. Jonathan's grandfather, Cecil D. Hylton Sr., died on August 25, 1989. Hylton Sr.'s will established certain trusts for his grandchildren and gave the trustees of the will the authority to determine whether anyone born out of wedlock was an "issue" of Hylton Sr. so as to qualify as a beneficiary of the will. Under the will, Hylton Sr.'s grandchildren and great-grandchildren could potentially receive distributions from the trusts in 2014 and 2021.

On July 11, 1996, Mildred Adams met with attorney Robert J. Zelnick about protecting Jonathan's interest as a beneficiary of the trusts. She had received information leading her to believe that distributions were being made from the trusts to some of Hylton Sr.'s grandchildren. Adams told Zelnick that she had contacted Jonathan's father about these alleged distributions but had not yet received a response from him. Adams explained that she also had contacted the law firm that had prepared Hylton Sr.'s will, but no one would provide her any information about the distributions or whether the estate would recognize Jonathan as a beneficiary. During the meeting, Adams gave Zelnick a copy of the Florida paternity order. Adams explained that she could not afford to pay Zelnick's hourly fee and requested legal services on her son's behalf on a contingency fee basis. At the conclusion of the meeting, Zelnick told Adams that he was unsure whether he would take the case but that he would investigate the matter. Zelnick next spoke with Adams during a telephone conversation on July 18, 1996. He informed her that he had obtained a copy of the will, had reviewed it, and was willing to accept the case "to help her have Jonathan declared a beneficiary of the estate." When Adams went to Zelnick's office the next day, Zelnick explained that the gross amount of the estate was very large. Hence, he "wanted to make sure that she had some understanding of the size of the estate before she entered into this agreement." He further explained that, owing to the continency nature of the agreement, it was impossible to know the ultimate amount of his fee. One July 19, 1996, Adams signed a retainer agreement for Zelnick's firm to represent Jonathan on a one-third contingency fee basis "in his claim against the estate of Cecil D. Hylton." Zelnick's efforts resulted in a January 28, 1998 consent decree that declared Jonathan to be the grandchild and issue of Hylton Sr. and a beneficiary under the trusts Hylton Sr. had created.

In March 1998, Jonathan's father sued Adams and Zelnick, seeking to have the contract with Zelnick declared void. Upon reaching the age of majority, Jonathan joined this litigation. Jonathan disaffirmed the contract and asked the court to declare it void as a matter of law, since the contract with Zelnick did not involve necessaries. Jonathan argued that the 1997 suit was unnecessary because the Florida paternity decree had conclusively established Hylton's paternity and because the trusts could not distribute any funds until the years 2014 and 2021. Hence, Jonathan asserted, the issue was not "ripe for determination." Finally, Jonathan claimed that the contingency fee agreement was unreasonable. The trial court agreed that the contingency fee agreement was void owing to Jonathan's being a minor at the time of the execution of the contract. The court also held that the doctrine of necessaries did not apply, inasmuch as Jonathan, who was within a few years of his majority at the time of the contract, could have adjudicated the issue of his being a beneficiary once he attained majority. Would a contract for legal services fall within the general classes of necessaries that could defeat a defense based on infancy? [See *Zelnick v. Adams*, 561 S.E.2d 711 (Va. 2002).]

5. **BUSINESS APPLICATION CASE** In the 1980s, Michael Mathias (formerly known as Nenad Matjasevic) and Bradley Jacobs worked together in the oil brokerage business in London. In 1989, Jacobs launched a waste management business that eventually became United Waste Services, Inc. Mathias worked amicably for United Waste from 1989 until some time in 1992. Disagreement then arose about whether Jacobs had ever promised Mathias an ownership stake in the company. On June 1, 1992, Mathias and Jacobs seemingly resolved this dispute by entering into two contemporaneous agreements, one terminating Mathias's employment with United Waste (the United Waste agreement) and the other granting him stock options in United Waste (the stock options agreement). The United Waste agreement provided Mathias with a lump sum of $31,200 in back pay, and, for a two-year period, monthly payments of $8,000 and continuing health insurance coverage. In

return, Mathias agreed to several non-compete provisions. The stock options agreement granted Mathias the right to purchase 400,000 shares of United Waste stock, exercisable at $3 per share anytime between June 1, 1994 and May 31, 1999. The options agreement incorporated by reference the non-compete provisions of the United Waste agreement and further provided that the options would be "automatically and unconditionally rescinded and terminated" if Mathias breached the non-compete provisions.

On March 8, 1999, Mathias attempted to exercise the option by tendering a check for $1.2 million, the amount set out in the options agreement; but Jacobs refused to accept it. Mathias consequently filed a lawsuit to recover damages totaling the value of the stock shares on the day Jacobs breached (minus the $1.2 million Mathias was required to pay), plus interest, in addition to specific performance for delivery of the stock shares. Jacobs asserted as an affirmative defense that he had entered the agreements under duress caused by Mathias's threats of economic interference and physical violence. Jacobs described an "atmosphere of threats and intimidation" during the period that he and Mathias had negotiated the agreements. For instance, Jacobs claimed that, while they were discussing Mathias's termination, Mathias brought a cast of unsavory characters to the United Waste offices, including his cousin "Zoran," characterized as a gun-toting Mafia contract killer, and "Little Mike," who "also was described as basically a thug, and frankly made a convincing performance." Perhaps the most menacing Mathias associate was a boxer allegedly employed by Mathias to extort money out of Jacobs. The boxer purportedly arrived unannounced at the United Waste office and poised himself with an intimidating glare in front of Jacobs. The boxer left only after Jacobs called Mathias and threatened to call the police. According to Jacobs, Mathias was perceived to be a threatening person "primarily due to the stories and information that Mike told . . ." about his "violent lifestyle." Finally, Jacobs buttressed his allegation of Mathias's violent personality by associating Mathias with the tumult in the former Yugoslavia, specifically in a book that identified Nenad Matjasevic (Mathias's former name) as an "operative in charge" of carrying out apparent terrorist acts against Croatia. Jacobs also noted that contact information for Arkan and Stojiljkovic, two Serbians purportedly indicted for war crimes in connection with the war in the Balkans, was contained in Mathias's Palm Pilot. In addition to the threat of physical violence, Jacobs asserted that Mathias threatened economic injury to United Waste by issuing ultimatums about hiring "a Mob-connected lawyer . . . to file frivolous lawsuits against the Company and individuals here, to defame, to hurt the Company's business generally, to 'squeeze' the Company. . . ." How should a court rule on this case? [See *Mathias v. Jacobs*, 167 F. Supp. 2d 606 (S.D. N.Y. 2001).]

6. **ETHICAL APPLICATION CASE** On March 19, 1996, Mark, Raelynn, and Milton Ramsden were the high bidders on a dairy farm sold at public auction by Agribank. Farm Credit Services of North Central Wisconsin (FCS), which had financed

the prior owners, Triple L Dairy, also financed the Ramsdens' purchase, which closed on April 17, 1996. Thomas Hass, an Agribank employee and an agent of both Agribank and FCS, was the auctioneer and also handled the details of the Ramsdens' purchase from Agribank.

While Triple L Dairy owned the property, it had complained to Hass, Agribank, and FCS that its cattle were sick and dying. After an investigation and prior to selling the property to the Ramsdens, Agribank, FCS, and Hass learned that an underground gasoline storage tank on the property was leaking and contaminating the soil. On June 15, 1995, Hass had reported to the Department of Natural Resources that the groundwater on the property was contaminated. Thereafter, that agency directed Agribank to remove the underground storage tank and to remedy the contamination to both the soil and the groundwater. Agribank removed the tank, but it did not remedy the contamination. Notwithstanding their knowledge of the contamination and its effect on dairy cows, Agribank and Hass sought to sell the property as a dairy farm.

At the auction, Hass told the Ramsdens, who said they were considering buying the property for a dairy farm, that: (1) Agribank would be responsible for any contamination, cleanup, or problems associated with an underground storage tank that had leaked; (2) the property was suitable for use as a dairy farm; and (3) there was plenty of good, clean water available for the cattle. Hass did not mention the contamination of the groundwater or the deaths of Triple L's cattle. Based on Hass's factual representations and the failure of Hass, Agribank, and FCS to disclose that the groundwater was not fit for consumption and that the prior owner's cattle had died, the Ramsdens bought the property.

On April 18, 1996, the Ramsdens moved their cattle onto the property. By April 20, 1996, the cows began to appear depressed, ceased producing milk, and exhibited sunken eyes, general weakness, bellowing, and a lack of appetite. By April 23, 1996, four of the cows had died. Mark Ramsden also became ill. To determine the cause of these problems, the Ramsdens submitted water samples to the University of Wisconsin at Stevens Point. The samples showed benzene contamination from the underground storage tank that had leaked. The Ramsdens also had a local toxicologist perform a necropsy on one of the dead cows. The toxicologist determined that the cow had died of benzene poisoning as well. As a result of the benzene poisoning, the Ramsdens suffered the loss of 186 head of cattle and the loss of profits from the operation of their dairy. Additionally, Mark Ramsden suffered personal injuries, both physical and emotional, owing to benzene poisoning.

In 1997, the Ramsdens sued Agribank, FCS, and Hass. Hass moved to dismiss the complaint of fraud filed against him. Among other things, he argued that as an agent, he had no duty to disclose his knowledge of the property to the Ramsdens because any disclosures might have been contrary to the interests of his principal, Agribank. Who should win this case?

Should a firm take a "zero-tolerance" stance toward ethical violations by employees, or should a firm base its decisions on the egregiousness of the conduct? What sanctions should a firm impose for ethical violations? [See *Ramsden v. Farm Credit Services*, 590 N.W.2d 1 (Wis. App. 1998).]

7. **CRITICAL THINKING CASE** John Hess was a passenger in a Ford pickup truck on Christmas morning. At an intersection, a car driven by Charles Phillips struck the Ford truck, and the truck rolled over at least one and a half times. Hess suffered severe injuries and is now a paraplegic. Before filing a lawsuit, Hess made a claim against Phillips and his insurance company, Continental Insurance Company. Hess's attorney at the time negotiated with Brad Sommers, the claims adjuster for Continental, and settled Hess's claim against Phillips for $15,000, the policy limit. As part of the settlement, Hess signed a one-page boilerplate release form provided by Continental. This release stated that Hess "releases, acquits and forever discharges Charles Phillips, Continental Insurance and any and all agents and employees, UAC [the underwriters adjusting company] and any and [all] agents and employees and all other persons, firms, corporations, associations or partnerships of and from any and all claims, actions, causes of action, demands, rights, damages, costs, loss of service, expenses and compensation whatsoever" that Hess had or might have as a result of the accident. The release further stated that Hess "declare(s) and represent(s) that . . . this Release contains the entire agreement between the parties hereto. . . ."

Several months after signing the Release, Hess hired a new attorney and filed suit against Ford Motor Company (Ford) and others, alleging negligence, strict liability, and breach of warranty. In a separate lawsuit filed against Phillips and Continental, Hess asked for reformation of the release, specifically that the court strike the language discharging "all other persons, firms, corporations, associations or partnerships of and from any and all claims" on the ground of mutual mistake. At trial, Hess testified that, before he signed the release at his hospital bed, he had asked his first attorney about the contractual language at issue; and his attorney had told him the release was a standard form document. Hess then testified that he had not intended to release Ford from liability. Hess's first attorney testified that he had recommended settling with Phillips for the policy limit of $15,000, because an asset search had revealed that Phillips had no money. He further testified that he had not intended to release Ford and that he had told Hess the release covered only Phillips, his insurance company, and the adjusting company. Finally, the attorney stated that he had bought the Ford pickup truck involved in the accident for use as evidence in litigation against Ford after agreeing to settle with Phillips but before Hess had signed the release. Sommers, the former claims adjuster who had settled the case on behalf of Phillips and Continental, testified that he and Hess's attorney had discussed Hess's intention to sue Ford and others and that Hess's attorney had told him (Sommers) he was settling with Phillips and Continental in order to defray future litigation costs. Sommers also testified that Hess would not have settled and signed the release if it had discharged Ford. Finally, Sommers testified that he (1) had not intended to release Ford; (2) had not prepared the release or chosen the form used; and (3) had intended to protect Phillips and his insurance companies from "future exposure." Who had the stronger argument, Hess or Ford? Why? [See *Hess v. Ford Motor Company*, 117 Cal. Rptr. 2d 220 (2002).]

8. YOU BE THE JUDGE In 1995, 17-year-old David Cooper had been a member of the Aspen Valley Ski Club., Inc., for about nine years and was actively involved in competitive ski racing. At the beginning of the 1995–1996 ski season, David and his mother signed a form entitled "Aspen Valley Ski Club, Inc. Acknowledgment and Assumption of Risk and Release." This form was an exculpatory clause that released the ski club from any liability for any claims that might arise from a member's participation in any ski club events. This release also included a "hold harmless" indemnification clause in which both David and his parents agreed to release the club from liability for future injuries and to assume all known and unknown risks. In short, should a participant such as David incur personal injury (including death) or property damage during his participation in the ski club's programs and activities, he and his parents—not the club or its employees, even if the latter had caused his injuries—would bear the financial responsibility for any such injuries. The release would preclude a participant's suing the club and its employees for torts committed against the minor. On December 30, 1995, David was training for a competitive, high-speed alpine race on a course set by David's coach, John McBride. During a training run, David fell and collided with a tree, sustaining severe injuries, including the loss of vision in both eyes. When David and his parents sued the ski club and McBride for negligence, the lower courts held that the release David's mother had signed was enforceable against David, despite his being a minor both at the time of the signing of the release and at the occurrence of the accident. The state supreme court granted review to determine whether public policy in Colorado permits a parent to release the claims of a minor child for future injuries and whether a parent may enter into an indemnification agreement that shifts the source of compensation for a minor's claim from a tortfeasor (the person or entity that commits a tort) to the parent. Given what you have learned about minors' rights, what particular aspects of parental releases of liability for prospective claims of negligence bring up public policy issues? If *you* were deciding this case, would these public policy aspects cause you to uphold the parents' rights to sign such releases or militate against the parents' having such rights? [See *Cooper v. Aspen Skiing Company*, 48 P.3d 1229 (Colo. 2002).]

Notes

1. 473 So.2d 157, 1985 Miss. LEXIS 2141 (Miss. S. Ct., 1985).
2. A. G. Guest, *Anson's Law of Contracts*, 26th ed. (Oxford: Clarendon Press, 1984), 209–210.

CHAPTER 13

Legality of Subject Matter and Proper Form of Contracts

NRW As NRW increasingly focuses on sales of the StuffTrakR and InvenTrakR, the firm must make certain that its activities, as well as its contracts, involve legal undertakings. Otherwise, statutes and public policy may restrict the firm's ability to contract.

Assuming all their agreements consist of legal subject matter, the firm members plan to put most of these contracts in writing. To do so, they need to know which of their contracts *must* be in writing in order to be enforceable, and which contracts merely *should* be in writing, although they do not have to be. They also will need to understand how detailed their writings need to be and whether any of NRW's written agreements are subject to amendment or alteration by oral testimony.

They are likely to look to you for help as they gain knowledge about these areas of the law. Be prepared! You never know when the firm or one of its members will seek your advice.

AGENDA

The Requirements of Legality of Subject Matter and Proper Form

By this time, you undoubtedly have noted the emphasis U.S. contract law places on bargaining and contract formation through the agreement of the parties. Yet, as with most human activities, the permissible boundaries of such conduct remain limited. Society at large may have a stake in the agreement the parties have forged. An agreement to bribe public officials or to murder someone, for instance, has definite repercussions for society that extend beyond the parties who initiated the bargain. The law, then, imposes a requirement that in order for the bargain to be recognized as a valid contract, the subject matter and purpose of the bargain must be legal. In this sense, the term *illegal contract* constitutes a misnomer; in general, a bargain cannot attain the status of "contract" unless it is legal. Put differently, illegal "contracts" are void. Hence, any bargain, however innocent it seems, that involves a violation of a statute, common law, or public policy is void.

In addition to this last transactional element of contract formation—legality—the Statute of Frauds requires that certain categories of contracts be in proper form—that is, they must be in writing—in order to be enforceable. Such categories include contracts to answer for the debt of another if the debtor defaults, contracts involving interests in land, and several other classifications of contracts. The writing provides evidence that the parties actually entered into the contracts at issue. Once the parties have reduced their contract to writing, application of the parol evidence rule ordinarily means that courts will not admit oral testimony that will alter, add to, or vary the terms of the written agreement. Hence, this chapter will focus on this substantive rule of evidence as well.

Components of Illegality

A widely accepted definition of *illegality*, taken from the Restatement (First) of Contracts § 512, and augmented by the Restatement (Second) of Contracts § 178, states that a bargain is illegal if its performance is criminal, tortious, or otherwise opposed to public policy.[1] Both the subject matter of the bargain and the realization of its objectives must be permissible under state and federal statutes. Sometimes these statutes impose criminal penalties for their violation (for example, an agreement to engage in arson for money). Other statutes, however, may prohibit certain kinds of bargains (for example, a contract with an improperly licensed electrician) without imposing criminal penalties on those who violate these statutes.

The desire to protect the public also underlies the prohibition of bargains involving tortious conduct (for example, an agreement between two parties for the purpose of defrauding a third person).

Similarly, even in the absence of an agreement that violates a statute or requires the commission of a tort (that is, a private or civil wrong), courts may declare as illegal on *public policy* grounds any bargain that will be detrimental to the public at large. Although the concept of public policy may fluctuate as different courts apply different standards, courts increasingly have used this rationale in a variety of contexts in which there appears to be no other basis for protecting the peace, health, or morals of the community. For instance, a bank may offer a rather one-sided night depository agreement in which it refuses to accept liability for a deposit placed in its after-hours slot, even if the loss stems from the negligence of its own employee and the depositor can prove that he or she actually deposited the amount in question with the bank. The concept of public policy—here the protection of depositors' expectations that the bank will take proper care of their deposits and the protection of consumers against one-sided agreements—will permit a court to invalidate such agreements on the grounds of illegality.

A court may characterize such agreements as exculpatory clauses (portions of agreements in which a prospective plaintiff agrees in advance not to seek to hold the prospective defendant liable for certain losses for which the prospective defendant otherwise would be liable) or contracts of adhesion (contracts in which the terms are not open to negotiation; so-called take-it-or-leave-it contracts). A court may construe the agreement as a contract of adhesion if, in these circumstances, depositors may have had no choice but to accept the bank's terms. In general, an illegal bargain is void and hence unenforceable. This ordinarily is true whether the agreement is executory or fully executed. Usually a court merely leaves the parties where it finds them. Neither party, then, can sue the other. Exceptions to the general rule that courts will not give relief to parties who have created an illegal bargain do exist, however.

Mala in Se and *Mala Prohibita* Bargains

Early on, many courts became dissatisfied with the rule that illegal contracts are absolutely void. Some of these courts therefore distinguished between bargains that violate statutes

NRW CASE 13.1 Finance

MALA PROHIBITA CONTRACT SITUATIONS

NRW has obtained a guaranteed offer to provide a $100,000 line of credit, which will be very helpful in facilitating the upcoming expansion or growth of the firm. However, the prospective lender insists on receiving 3 percent simple interest on any balance each month. Carlos, concerned that this interest rate amounts to a usurious loan, asks for your advice. What will you tell him?

BUSINESS CONSIDERATIONS Should lenders gouge their customers who are in desperate need of money by charging these customers the highest possible interest? What factors should a lender (or a borrower) consider when it decides how much interest is appropriate in a credit transaction?

ETHICAL CONSIDERATIONS Is it ethical for a lender to charge the highest interest rate the market will permit? Does such conduct take advantage of the lender's customers? Is it ethical for a borrower to agree to credit terms and then later object because the terms are too high?

INTERNATIONAL CONSIDERATIONS How do lenders in other countries—especially Islamic ones—view interest?

because they are evil *in themselves (mala in se)* and bargains that have been merely *forbidden by statute (mala prohibita)*. The first type (for example, an agreement to murder someone) fell within the general rule and was void. Some courts, however, depending on the nature and effect of the act prohibited by the statute, were prepared to view bargains included within the second type as voidable rather than void.

To illustrate, one case involved the sale of cattle in violation of a law stating that all cattle sold must be tested for brucellosis (a serious disease in cattle) within the 30-day period preceding the sale. The court clearly could have used this statutory violation as a basis for holding the agreement void. Yet the court concluded that this bargain was *mala prohibita*, rather than *mala in se*, because the contract was neither in bad faith nor contrary to public policy, and it therefore enforced the contract.[2]

More recent commentators have criticized the distinction between *mala in se* and *mala prohibita* bargains as invalid because any bargain that violates a statute is absolutely void no matter what underlying rationale the prohibition involves. This conclusion represents the position most widely accepted today. Nevertheless, the continued use of these terms demonstrates the tendency of courts to weigh differences in the degree of evil and accordingly determine the availability of judicial relief.

Courts, however, almost universally recognize two types of agreements as *mala in se* bargains: agreements to commit a crime and agreements to commit a tort. The agreement mentioned earlier involving arson could be called a *mala in se* bargain because the subject matter of the agreement itself, the commission of a crime, is morally unacceptable. The same would be true of an agreement to kill someone, a so-called murder "contract." Neither party can enforce such agreements; they are absolutely void. Likewise, an agreement that involves the commission of a tort is void. Besides fraud, such bargains may involve agreements to damage the good name of a competitor, to inflict mental distress on a third party, or to trespass against another's chattels (articles of personal property) or real property in order to cause injury to the property.

Determining whether a particular activity violates a statute (assuming the activity is not *mala in se*) is more difficult and requires that courts resort first to the words of the underlying statute. Courts then must assess the legislative intent and, finally, examine the social effects of giving or refusing a remedy in the particular situation.

Agreements That Violate Statutes

Courts ordinarily find certain categories of activities in violation of statutes. These undertakings include price-fixing agreements, performances of services without a license, contracts formed on Sunday, wagering, and usurious contracts.

Price-Fixing Agreements

The purpose of price-fixing agreements generally is to restrain competition so as to create a monopoly (the power of a firm to carry on a business or a trade to the exclusion of all competitors) or oligopoly (an economic condition in which a small number of firms dominates a market, but no one firm controls it) in order to control price fluctuations. The Sherman Antitrust Act, the Clayton Act, and the Federal Trade Commission Act are the major federal laws that make such bargains illegal. Price-fixing agreements also may violate state statutes; or, alternatively, courts may invalidate these arrangements on public policy grounds.

Performances of Services without a License

Agreements relating to the performances of services without a license may constitute another type of statutory violation. To protect the public from unqualified persons, state statutes often require (or regulate) the licensing of professions such as law, medicine, and public accountancy and trades such as electrical work, contracting, and plumbing. Before the state grants a license, the would-be practitioner must achieve the required educational qualifications and usually demonstrate minimal competency by successfully passing an examination. In such cases, the absence of a license prevents the professional or tradesperson from enforcing their bargains.

In contrast to such a regulatory licensing scheme, some states require licensing for some activities primarily as a revenue-producing mechanism rather than as a device for protecting the health and welfare of its citizens. If the primary intent of the licensing requirement is to produce revenue, the lack of a license will not affect the contract between the parties.

It pays to remember that courts have fairly wide discretion in these matters and may take into account such factors as the absence of harm resulting from failure to obtain the license, the extent of the knowledge of the persons involved, and the relative "guilt" of the respective parties. If, for example, a court deems the amount forfeited by the unlicensed professional sufficiently large to constitute a penalty, the professional ordinarily will be able to sue for the fee, despite the lack of a license. As mentioned earlier, even in statutes assigning criminal sanctions, courts will look closely at the legislative intent of the statute as they decide whether to give or to withhold remedies.

Sunday Closing Laws

Sunday closing laws (also called "blue laws") are so named because they prohibit the formation or performance of contracts on Sundays. These laws are troublesome because the terms of such statutes vary widely from state to state. The most common type of statute prohibits the conduct of secular business, or one's "ordinary calling" (such as selling merchandise), on Sunday. You may be familiar with Sunday laws that forbid the sale of certain alcoholic beverages. Exceptions usually involve works of charity or necessity, which one can undertake on Sunday without fear of sanctions.

In some jurisdictions, a violation of a Sunday statute voids the contract, unless the party asking for recovery can show, for instance, that he or she had no knowledge that the execution of the contract occurred on Sunday. He or she also can argue that the agreement, though initiated on Sunday, was not accepted until later in the week and thus actually ripened into a contract at that time.

Litigants in some jurisdictions have challenged the constitutionality of such statutes. These laws, by singling out Sunday as a "day of rest" from mercantile activity, may violate the First Amendment's prohibition against a governmentally established religion. State governments' enactments of such laws, therefore, arguably put the interests of one religious group ahead of the interests of others and thus raise constitutional questions.

Wagering Statutes

Wagering contracts and lotteries are illegal in certain states because of statutes prohibiting gambling, betting, and other games of chance. The underlying rationale for these laws focuses on the protection of the public from the crime and familial discord often associated with gambling. To constitute illegal wagering, the activity must involve a person's paying consideration or value in the hope of receiving a prize or other property by chance. Wagering in the legal sense always consists of a scheme involving the artificial creation of risk; hence, insurance contracts or stock transactions in which risk is an inherent feature are not illegal wagers. On the other hand, courts may view raffles as unlawful wagering. For instance, because of the relatively soft demand in the housing market, some enterprising couples in various parts of the country recently have attempted to raffle off their homes. The conduct of these people has violated the wagering statutes of some of these jurisdictions. Additionally, if the participant need not give something of value in order to take part in the activity, it is probably not a lottery and consequently it is probably legal. Note that public lotteries (and gambling casinos) are legal in many states.

On-line gambling represents a fast-growing sector of e-commerce, with an estimated 14.5 million participants annually. This activity has led to a number of recent legal developments. One issue involves whether the transactions of on-line bettors and the provision of such services by on-line casinos—most of which are located in foreign countries—actually break the law. Some experts interpret a 1960s-era federal wire statute that prohibits placing bets on sports by telephone or wire as encompassing Internet transactions and thus banning on-line gambling as well. Several bills aimed at cleaning up such ambiguities have surfaced in Congress in recent years. The gamblers themselves have also offered novel legal theories. Bolstered by the common law rule that gambling or wagering debts are void and thus legally uncollectible, some such compulsive bettors have refused to pay the credit card charges used to finance their betting behavior. In one celebrated case, a gambler defaulted on more than $70,000 in off-shore gambling debts racked up on numerous credit cards. When the card companies sued, she contended that because Internet gambling was illegal in her state, the credit card firms were accessories to a crime. In the subsequent settlement of the case, the credit card companies forgave the debts and paid her attorney's fees. This lawsuit, in conjunction with similar litigation, has led several banks that offer credit card services either to refuse to accept Internet-related gambling charges or to formulate new rules governing this aspect of their business operations. Concerns regarding gambling by minors have played a significant role in the development of such rules, as well as in the proposed legislation. The evolving contours of the law's disposition of such issues consequently bear watching.

Usury Statutes

Usurious contracts occur when a lender loans money at a greater profit (or rate of interest) than state law permits. For usury to exist, there must be a loan of money (or an agreement to extend the maturity of a monetary debt) for which the debtor agrees to repay the principal at a rate that exceeds the legal rate of interest. In addition, the lender must intend to violate the usury laws. If these elements are present, the resultant contract is illegal. In most states, a usurious lender will be unable to collect any interest and also may be subject to criminal or other statutory penalties. In some states, courts deny only the amount of excess interest; the lender can recover the remaining interest and principal. In a few states, the agreement is void; the lender receives no interest or principal.

Because such wide variations exist among state usury laws, it is difficult to generalize one set of rules. Loans to corporations may be exempt from a jurisdiction's usury statutes, for example, as may short-term loans, especially if the lender, in making the loans, will incur large risks.

Acceleration clauses (clauses in contracts that advance the date for payment based on the occurrence of a condition or the breach of a duty) and prepayment clauses (contract clauses that allow the debtor to pay the debt before it is due without penalty) generally are not usurious. The same is true of service fees that reflect the incidental costs of making a loan—filing and recording fees, for example. Sales under revolving charge accounts (open-ended credit accounts) or conditional sales contracts (sales contracts in which the transfer of title is subject to a condition, most commonly the payment of the full purchase price by the buyer) ordinarily are not usurious even if the seller charges a higher-than-lawful rate. Two reasons have been forwarded to justify this position: (1) A bona fide conditional sale on a deferred-payment basis is not a loan of money, and (2) the finance charge is merely a part of an increased purchase price reflective of the seller's risk in giving up possession of personal property (clothes, refrigerators, compact disk players, and the like) that depreciates quickly in value.

Time-price differential sales contracts (contracts with a difference in price based on the date of payment, with one price for an immediate payment and another for a payment at a later date) may or may not be usurious, depending on the applicable state law and/or special consumer protection statutes. Time-price differential sales contracts involve an offer to sell at a designated price for cash (say $6,000 for an entertainment center) or at a higher price on credit (say $7,500). Even though the maximum legal rate of interest in this state may be 18 percent, the 25 percent actual rate represented by the credit price does not involve usury as long as the final price reflects the credit nature of the sale rather than an intent to evade the usury laws.

The trend today is to raise the maximum interest rate and to increase the exceptions to the usury laws. Moreover, federally guaranteed loans allow interest rates that otherwise would violate state law. These factors have seriously eroded the original purpose of usury laws—the protection of debtors from excessive rates of interest. But, as mentioned earlier, little uniformity exists in the various states' usury statutes; it is wise, therefore, to consult these statutes if you have doubts about the legality of a particular transaction.

Agreements That Violate Public Policy

Ample precedents indicate that judges more and more frequently resort to public policy as a basis for invalidating agreements. In holding that a contract is void on public policy grounds, a court is deciding the legality of the agreement in light of the public interests involved. Hence, public policy frequently becomes an alternative ground for finding illegality. To illustrate, a court may strike down a contract to fix prices because the agreement violates statutes (for example, the Sherman Act) or because the agreement will damage the public. However, because *public policy* is such a wide-ranging term, courts, in judging the legality of certain types of bargains, often have to juggle competing interests. Keep this point in mind as you consider the following concepts.

Covenants Not to Compete

Covenants not to compete, also called *restrictive covenants*, are express promises that a seller of a business or an employee who leaves a company will not engage in the same or similar business or occupation for a period of time in a certain geographic area. Such bargains may or may not be legal. If the purpose of these "non-compete clauses" is to protect the recent buyer of a business from the possibility that the seller will set up shop two blocks from the original business establishment or the former employer from the possibility that the ex-employee will sign on with a competitor, the restrictions on the seller or former employee, if *reasonable* in *time* and in *geographic scope*, ordinarily are legal. But, as mentioned earlier, competing policies complicate these situations. It clearly is unfair to unduly shackle the employment opportunities of the seller (or former employee) who must make a living. Similarly, to curtail this person's business or occupational activities in effect insulates the buyer (or former employer) from competition and thereby may result in higher prices. For this reason, when examining these covenants, many courts use public policy considerations.

Usually such covenants are incidental to the sale of a business or to an employment contract and are legal. (Agreements not to compete whose sole purpose is to curtail competition are illegal as restraints on trade—they violate the antitrust laws.) If, however, under the facts and circumstances, a particular covenant not to compete is unreasonably restrictive in time or geographic scope, a court has the power to rewrite the covenant so that it is less restrictive—a process called blue-penciling—and hence reasonable. Bargainers should not expect courts to save them from bad, or illegal, bargains, however. Blue-penciling is relatively rare. In fact, most courts reject this approach and will void the restrictive covenant and construe the agreement without any reference to the covenant not to compete.

The *Standard Register Company v. Cleaver* case, which follows, shows how the legality of a restrictive covenant can become the basis for a lawsuit.

The growth of Internet-based businesses has posed special challenges for courts in the context of non-compete clauses. An interesting intersection of judicial rulings and legislative responses often results. To illustrate, California, the early home of many such start-up companies, views covenants not to compete as void on public policy grounds. California's almost total prohibition on the enforcement of such covenants (the relevant statute recognizes a few narrow exceptions) makes this jurisdiction's business climate especially attractive to Internet firms and thereby encourages the further development of e-commerce in the state. The greater mobility of so-called knowledge workers; the reliance of many e-commerce firms on trade secrecy as their primary basis for protecting their intellectual prop-

---

NRW CASE 13.2   Management

EMPLOYEE AGREEMENTS AND RELEASES

Mai, Helen, and Carlos want any employees (including family members) hired by NRW to sign a covenant not to compete with the firm anywhere in the United States for at least three years after leaving employment with NRW. The firm members have asked you about the advisability of such a policy. What will you tell them?

BUSINESS CONSIDERATIONS What sort of policy regarding covenants not to compete should a business adopt? When would such a covenant be a good idea? When would such a covenant be impracticable? Explain.

ETHICAL CONSIDERATIONS Is it ethical for a firm to routinely require employees to sign covenants not to compete, even if the employee would not have access to any confidential business information? What ethical issues are raised by the use of such covenants?

INTERNATIONAL CONSIDERATIONS Do firms in other countries employ restrictive covenants? On what bases do such firms endorse—or reject—the use of such agreements?

---

erty; the tendency of competitors to buy each other out; and the difficulty of assessing the reasonableness of the time and geographic aspects of these clauses, given the volatility of the on-line environment and the boundaryless dimensions of this market sector, promise to generate significant legal rulings in the future. Watch for these developments. In the meantime, you may find it instructive to check on how your state treats covenants not to compete.

Exculpatory Clauses

Agreements to commit torts are illegal. Indeed, a court has little justification to validate an agreement that stipulates an intentional breach of the duty of reasonable care to others. On the other hand, is there anything illegal about a bargain in which one party tries in advance to limit its liability in a particular set of circumstances? Unfortunately, this question has no clear-cut answer. Courts judge the legality of such *exculpatory clauses*, or bargains in which one person agrees *in advance* to exonerate another person from liability, on a case-by-case basis.

13.1

STANDARD REGISTER COMPANY v. CLEAVER
30 F. Supp. 2d 1084 (N.D. Ind. 1998)

FACTS In 1981, Phil Cleaver became an employee at will for UARCO, Inc., a firm engaged in the sales of printed business items. As such, Cleaver signed a non-compete clause that obligated him to refrain from divulging any of the company's trade secrets or confidential information he might learn while in the company's employ. He further promised—in paragraph 9 of the agreement—that

> [f]or a period of two years following the termination of his employment for any reason whatsoever . . . , [he would] not contact, with a view towards selling any product competitive with any product sold or proposed to be sold by [the] Company at the time of the termination of [his] employment, or sell any product to, any person, firm, association or corporation:
>
> (a) to which [he] sold any product of Company during the year preceding the termination of [his] employment,
>
> (b) which [he] solicited, contacted, or otherwise dealt with on behalf of Company during the year preceding termination of [his] employment.

Cleaver worked for UARCO until 1998, when the company merged with Standard Register Company. Shortly after the merger, Cleaver went to work for Prograde, Inc., a firm engaged in selling printed business materials similar to those sold by UARCO and Standard Register. While at UARCO, Cleaver, as was typical in the industry, had worked for many years to develop customer relationships. For example, it had taken him four years to increase the $350,000 in initial sales to HWI, a major UARCO customer, to $1,000,000 at the time of his departure from Standard Register's employ. In his first four months with Prograde, Cleaver sold over $1,000,000 to HWI and also solicited other UARCO/Standard Register customers whom he previously had serviced. As a consequence, Standard Register sued to enforce the restrictive covenant Cleaver had signed.

ISSUE Were the non-disclosure and non-solicitation provisions in the restrictive covenant valid and enforceable?

HOLDING Yes. The limitations set out by the provisions coincided perfectly with Standard Register's protectable interest in its goodwill (the customers with whom Cleaver had developed a relationship while in UARCO and Standard Register's employ); hence, the provisions were enforceable.

REASONING Excerpts from the opinion of Judge Cosbey:

It is well-settled that Indiana disfavors covenants not to compete as restraints on trade. . . . Such covenants are to be strictly construed against the covenantee and enforced only if reasonable. . . . The issue of reasonableness is a question of law which rests upon facts gleaned from the totality of the circumstances. . . . Whether a covenant contains reasonable restrictions depends upon the legitimate business interests of the employer which might be protected by the covenant, in conjunction with the duration, the geographic area, and the types of activity proscribed. . . .

Standard Register contends that the business interests at stake here include its good will, trade secrets, and confidential information, and that it first seeks to prevent Cleaver from directly or indirectly communicating or divulging trade secrets or confidential information to others, including Prograde. . . . However, when it comes to the specifics as to what it considers "trade secrets," or "confidential information," Standard Register retreated to generalities. . . . On this record, however, Standard Register points to little that would actually classify as a true trade secret. The information as to the identity of Standard Register's customers or potential customers is something that is already readily known in the industry. . . . Thus, Standard Register has failed to show the need for an injunction as to these matters. Nevertheless, Standard Register contends that Cleaver is also trading on its good will, a resource sometimes defined as including the names, addresses and requirements of customers, and the advantage acquired through representative contact with the trade in the area. . . .

However, "good will" is broader, than simply the names, addresses and requirements of customers, or some pricing information, it also includes the advantageous familiarity and personal contact that employees, such as Cleaver, derive from their dealings with the employer's customers. This, of course, is the thrust of the non-solicitation provision . . . of the Salesman's Agreement. In short, the familiarity with customers and their accounts is a protectable interest for the employer, regardless of whether he or she had access to confidential information. . . . Here, though it has not been shown that Cleaver retained truly confidential information upon leaving Standard Register, there has been a showing that there was at least a personal relationship between Cleaver and his customers, particularly HWI. Obviously, Cleaver assiduously courted HWI; indeed, he held out to Prograde the relationship he had developed with HWI (and Centennial Communications as well) as good reasons for hiring him as a salesperson. Moreover, given his long standing relationship with HWI, Cleaver had developed some special skill and knowledge as to the operation of that firm, having promoted UARCO's and Standard Register's "value added" concept of service. . . .

Standard Register had a good will property interest to protect, which means that now we must examine the covenant at paragraphs 9(a) and 9(b) to determine, in light of the interest to be protected, whether it is overly restrictive. . . . The covenant sought to be enforced at paragraph 9 can be no broader than is necessary for the protection of the good will interests of the employer. . . . In imposing these restrictions, the covenant does not seek to define a geographic scope; rather it seeks to recognize that if any good will developed between Cleaver and his customers, it could only have come from Cleaver's personal contacts with them. . . . Thus, while the scope of a covenant can be limited through geographical boundaries, it can also be done by increasing the specificity of the class of persons with whom contact is prohibited because "as the specificity of limitation regarding the class of person with whom contact is prohibited increases, the need for limitation expressed in territorial terms decreases." . . . In other words, the covenant "must be sufficiently specific in scope to coincide with only the legitimate interests of the employer and to allow the employee a clear understanding of what conduct is prohibited." . . . Thus, the specificity of the general class of persons described in paragraph 9(a)

of the covenant is sufficiently precise as to render it enforceable without any further geographic limitations, and it coincides perfectly with what is clearly Standard Register's protectable interest—the buying customers with whom Cleaver has developed a relationship. . . .

Cleaver was in frequent, indeed sometimes weekly, contact with his customers, monitoring their needs and fostering his personal relationship with them. . . . Clearly, Cleaver has been successful in developing such personal relationships with his customers, most particularly HWI, such that upon leaving Standard Register he was able to switch the business to Prograde with virtually no drop-off. This result was achieved by virtue of the trust and confidence that HWI reposed in him (and in reality, in UARCO and Standard Register), an intangible factor that can only be obtained after some considerable period of time. . . . On the other hand, such a limited restraint as is set forth in paragraph 9(a) of the Salesman's Agreement would not be so substantial as to injure Cleaver in that he would only be precluded from soliciting or contracting with former entities to whom he had sold products during the year preceding his termination with Standard Register. Thus, Cleaver would be entirely free to sell to any other potential customers on behalf of Prograde. . . . Based on the foregoing, the Motion for a Preliminary Injunction is hereby granted.

BUSINESS CONSIDERATIONS Why would a business want to include a covenant not to compete in its contracts with its sales force? Why would a business claim that its sales techniques should be protected as trade secrets?

ETHICAL CONSIDERATIONS Is it ethical for a business to prevent former employees from working for any competitors for one or two years after the initial employment ends? Are covenants not to compete ethical?

For example, a dry cleaner may always write on its customers' tickets, "Not responsible for elastic and buttons." The dry cleaner can argue that by signing the tickets, customers agree to hold it harmless for any damages to elastic and buttons. Similarly, restaurants that have signs saying "Not responsible for belongings left in booths" attempt to achieve the same end. In general, these and other agreements in which one party promises not to hold the other liable for tortious or wrongful conduct are legal.

In many jurisdictions, statutes covering workers' compensation, innkeepers, and landlord-tenant relationships make the issue of liability for these particular areas moot. In the absence of statutes or clear precedents, however, courts look closely to see whether the party who agrees to

assume the risk of tortious conduct without any recovery has done so voluntarily. In other words, the courts consider whether the party who has initiated the exculpatory clause has vastly superior bargaining power (or superior knowledge) over the other person. (Recall the bank deposit example earlier in this chapter.) If so, courts may strike down the exculpatory clause as contrary to public policy.

If the court believes an *adhesion contract* exists—that is, a contract drafted by the stronger party in order to force unfavorable terms on the weaker party—the court probably will find the clause contrary to public policy and thus illegal. This finding by no means is an easy task, though. Courts necessarily will weigh a variety of factors, such as the age of the parties, their respective degrees of expertise, their mental condition at the time they signed the clause (was the injured party drunk when he signed the exculpatory clause just before climbing onto the mechanical bull in Joe's Pub?), and whether the language of the clause was in fine print. After analyzing these and other facts and policies, the court assesses the legality of such clauses.

Reed v. University of North Dakota illustrates the disposition of a lawsuit involving an exculpatory clause issue related to participation in a charity event.

13.2

REED v. UNIVERSITY OF NORTH DAKOTA
589 N.W.2d 880 (N.D. 1999)

FACTS In 1989, the University of North Dakota (UND) offered Jace Reed, a Minnesota high school student, a scholarship to play hockey at UND. Reed signed a national letter of intent and played hockey at UND for two years. On September 15, 1991, Reed ran in a 10-kilometer charity road race sponsored by the North Dakota Association for the Disabled (NDAD). Before the race, Reed signed a registration form that, among other things, released the NDAD from all liability for injuries or any claims arising from his participation in the race. According to Reed, UND coaches presented the registration form to him before the race; and he had to sign it to run in the race, which was a mandatory part of the UND hockey team's preseason conditioning program. During the race, Reed became severely dehydrated and suffered extensive damage to his kidneys and liver. As a result, Reed required extensive medical care, including one kidney and two liver transplants, and thereby incurred substantial expenses for medical treatment. He subsequently brought a lawsuit challenging the validity of the release he had signed.

ISSUE Was the release a valid exculpatory clause?

HOLDING Yes. The release was supported by consideration; it was unambiguous; and it contravened no public policy. Hence, the release was fully enforceable against Reed.

REASONING Excerpts from the opinion of Judge Maring:

Reed asserts the release is not enforceable, because it was not supported by consideration. Consideration may be any benefit conferred or detriment suffered. . . . The forbearance of a legal right is a legal detriment which constitutes good consideration. . . . The existence of consideration is a question of law. . . . As part of their preseason conditioning program, the UND hockey players were allowed to run on the same course during NDAD's road race. When the hockey players, including Reed, signed the registration form, they agreed not to hold the participating sponsors responsible for any claims arising from their participation in the event and NDAD agreed to let them run on the course during NDAD's road race. Reed's surrender of a legal right in exchange for NDAD allowing him to run the course during the race constitutes consideration for the release. . . .

Reed contends the release is ambiguous. He asserts he did not contemplate the extreme nature of his injuries, nor the improper medical attention he received after collapsing from dehydration. He claims the phrases "participating sponsors" and "for injuries I may incur as a direct or indirect result of my participation" are vague and ambiguous. He argues there are genuine issues of material fact about the injuries the parties intended to release, thus precluding summary judgment. . . .

Generally, the law does not favor contracts exonerating parties from liability for their conduct . . . contractual exculpatory clauses are strictly construed against the benefitted party, and will not be enforced if they are ambiguous, or release the benefitted party from liability for intentional, willful, or wanton acts. Although exculpatory clauses are strictly construed against the benefitted party, the parties are bound by clear and unambiguous language evidencing an intent to extinguish liability. . . . Although the language of this release is broad, we believe it unambiguously evidences an intent to exonerate NDAD from liability for Reed's injuries. We construe contracts to give effect to the parties' intent, which, if possible, must be ascertained by giving meaning to each provision of the contract. . . . This release was limited to a single event. . . . Reed may not have contemplated he would incur severe complications from dehydration, or allegedly receive improper emergency medical attention after collapsing from dehydration. Reed concedes, however, he was aware of some of the risks inherent to running, and his complaint effectively acknowledged dehydration was a reasonably foreseeable race injury. . . . We believe the consequences of dehydration and the allegation of improper emergency medical care at the race site were within the plain meaning of Reed's assumption of all responsibility for injuries incurred as a direct or indirect result of his participation in the race and his agreement not to hold NDAD responsible for any claims. The plain language of this release would be rendered meaningless if it were construed as not exonerating NDAD from responsibility for the injuries incurred by Reed as a result of his participation in this race. We construe the release to effectuate the intent evidenced in its plain language, and we reject Reed's argument it vaguely and ambiguously described the injuries the parties intended to release. We conclude the release clearly and unambiguously evidences an intent to exonerate NDAD from liability for the injuries incurred by Reed as a result of his participation in this race....

Reed contends the release is against public policy, because he lacked bargaining power to negotiate or alter its terms. In considering whether a release is against public policy, other courts generally have considered: (1) the disparity of bargaining power between the parties in terms of compulsion to sign the agreement and lack of ability to negotiate elimination of the clause, and (2) the types of services provided by the party seeking exoneration, including whether they are public or essential services. . . . Here, any perceived mandatory requirement for Reed to participate in this race involved his relationship with the UND hockey program and not with NDAD. Although NDAD may not have allowed Reed to run in the race if he had not signed the registration form, he was not under any economic or other compulsion from NDAD to sign the release. Under these circumstances, we reject Reed's argument any differences in bargaining power between him and NDAD rendered this release invalid. We conclude the release was not against public policy, and we hold it exonerated NDAD from liability for Reed's negligence claims against NDAD.

BUSINESS CONSIDERATIONS In deciding such a case, should a court take into account the fact that the entities being sued here were a public university and a charitable organization? Or is the nature of the organization irrelevant to the issue of the possible imposition of liability?

ETHICAL CONSIDERATIONS Do athletic programs, in their zeal to ensure a winning record, make too many demands on an athlete's out-of-class time? Is it ethical for the university to condition an athlete's receiving a scholarship on such things as the student's participation in charity events over which the university has no supervisory control? Why or why not?

Exceptions: Upholding Illegal Agreements

The general rule, as mentioned earlier, holds that an illegal bargain is void, and courts will leave the parties to such agreements where they find themselves as a result of the bargain. Despite this general rule, some situations exist in which a party may bring a successful suit based on an illegal agreement. Put differently, one usually cannot sue for enforcement of an illegal executory agreement; but in certain circumstances one may sue if the performance called for in the bargain has been rendered.

Parties Not *in Pari Delicto*

When one of the parties is less blameworthy than the other, the law states that the parties are not *in pari delicto* (they are not equally at fault or equally wrong). This allows the less-blameworthy person to recover if recovery serves the public interest in some way. For instance, the less-blameworthy party may belong to the class of persons a regulatory statute was designed to protect. Such results consequently focus on the conduct of the less-blameworthy party rather than on the illegality of the subject matter of the contract. For example, if Joanne works for a photographer who does not have a license as required by a local ordinance, she still can recover the wages due her if she is unaware of her boss's noncompliance. The law terms the illegality here incidental or collateral to Joanne's bargain.

Repentance

Even if the parties are in *pari delicto*, the law allows recovery by the person who shows repentance by rescinding the illegal bargain before its consummation. For example, assume that a partnership attempts to bribe a state senator to enact favorable legislation. This agreement would be illegal because it harms the public. If one of the partners attempts to rescind the transaction before delivery of the money to the senator, he or she can do so. The law calls this action repentance. Courts justify the partner's recovery of the money he or she earlier directed to the senator because such a result furthers the public interest of deterring illegal schemes.

Partial Illegality

Agreements, as you may recall, may consist of several different promises supported by different considerations. While refusing to enforce those parts of the bargain that are illegal, courts enforce the parts of the bargain that involve legal promises and legal considerations if the courts can sever these legal promises. If, instead, either the illegal promise or the illegal consideration (or both) wholly taints the agreement, courts declare the entire agreement void. The *Standard Register* decision and others like it that involve a restrictive covenant may, in certain circumstances, provide good examples of partial illegality. If a court finds the restrictive covenant unreasonable in scope, the judge may, owing to the clause's illegality, sever it from the rest of the agreement. The court, however, ordinarily enforces the remainder of the contract (the sale of a business, for example), because the balance of the contract is perfectly legal; it is divisible from the illegal portion. In short, after severing the illegal portions, courts will give effect to those provisions that constitute a legal contract. Exhibit 13.1 summarizes the key components of legality as an element of contract formation and enforcement.

The Importance of Form

At this point, you should have a good grasp of the requirements of contract formation: agreement (offer and acceptance), consideration, capacity, reality of consent, and legality. In addition, according to the Statute of Frauds, certain categories of contracts must be in writing to be enforceable. Contracts to answer for the debt of another if the debtor defaults, contracts involving interests in land, contracts not to be performed within one year from the date of their making, promises of executors and administrators to pay a claim against the estate of the deceased out of their own personal funds, contracts made in consideration of marriage, and contracts involving a sale of goods priced at $500 or more, or the lease of goods for $1,000 or more, represent the classifications of contracts that must be in proper form—that is, in writing—in order for the law to give them effect. The writing in these situations provides evidence that the parties did contract about the matters in dispute, and it avoids the perjuries (false statements made under oath during court proceedings) traditionally and historically associated with these categories of contracts. In most other situations, the parties are free to contract orally even though it is unwise to do so.

Moreover, once the parties reduce their agreement to writing, judges necessarily are wary of tampering with the contract. For this reason, the parol evidence rule states that oral testimony ordinarily is not admissible to add to, alter, or vary the terms of a written agreement. In certain situations, parol evidence will be admissible to clear up ambiguities.

EXHIBIT 13.1 The Requirement of Legality as an Element of Contract Formation and Enforcement

Illegality ← → **Legality**

Mala in Se **Bargains** (inherently and completely illegal)
a. "Agreements" to commit crimes
b. "Agreements" to commit torts

Mala Prohibita **Bargains** (illegal because forbidden by statute)
a. Price-fixing agreements
b. Performances of services without a license required under regulatory licensing schemes
c. Sunday closing laws
d. Wagering statutes
e. Usury statutes

Bargains Comprised of Subject Matters That Are Not Tortious, Criminal, or Otherwise Violative of Public Policy

Bargains Involving Public Policy Considerations

a. Covenants not to compete

If *unreasonable* in time and/or geographic scope | If *reasonable* in time and geographic scope

b. Exculpatory clauses

If clauses are in fine print and drafter has vastly superior bargaining power | If clauses are conspicuous and parties have equal bargaining power
c. Agreements in which one party is not *in pari delicto*
d. Agreements in which one party repents before the illegal bargains are consummated
e. Agreements in which the legal portions can be severed from the illegal portions

Reference to the trade usages and customs of a particular industry may dispose of these types of ambiguities. Hence, an understanding of the interplay between the Statute of Frauds and the parol evidence rule will represent a useful adjunct to your understanding of contract law.

Statute of Frauds

The historical ancestor of the present-day Statute of Frauds was called "An Act for the Prevention of Frauds and Perjuries," passed by the English Parliament in 1677. This statute required that specified types of contracts be in writing in order to be enforceable. In other words, because perjury was so widespread in lawsuits involving oral contracts, Parliament decreed that, to be enforceable, certain classes of contracts must be in writing. Thus, the term Statute of Frauds is somewhat misleading, because such statutes deal with the requirement of a writing rather than with reality-of-consent situations like fraud. (In the Statute of Frauds, the term "frauds" refers to the wholesale misrepresentations or perjured statements made to early English courts.) Almost every state has a Statute of Frauds modeled on this original statute.

To reiterate, the Statute of Frauds requires that certain types of contracts be in writing before courts will enforce them. Thus, if the subject matter of the contract involves a type of contract enumerated in the Statute of Frauds, the agreement generally cannot be oral but instead must be in writing before a court will give it effect. The Statute of Frauds never is a legal issue unless a valid contract exists; hence, it becomes an issue only after all the stages of contract formation are present.

The Statute of Frauds also is an affirmative defense (that is, a defense to a cause of action that the defendant must raise) that a person who wants to avoid the enforcement of a contract can assert. A defendant who wishes to utilize this defense must expressly plead it, or it will be waived; if a waiver is found, an oral contract that otherwise would have been unenforceable because of a violation of the Statute of Frauds will be enforced against the defendant. Courts have been somewhat hostile to Statute of Frauds claims because of the injustice such statutes can cause. Consequently, some courts construe these statutes broadly and find various rationales for removing the contract at issue from the coverage of the statute, allowing the court to give effect to oral contracts that otherwise would not be enforceable.

Types of Contracts Covered

The following sections examine six categories of contracts covered by the Statute of Frauds:

1. Contracts to answer for the debt of another if the person so defaults

2. Contracts for interests in land

3. Contracts not to be performed within one year of the date of their making

4. Contracts of executors and administrators of estates

5. Contracts made in consideration of marriage

6. Contracts for the sale of goods priced at $500 or more, and contracts for the lease of goods where the total lease price is $1,000 or more

Contracts to Answer for the Debt of Another If the Person So Defaults

Ordinarily, oral promises between two persons are perfectly valid and enforceable in court. When Linda orally promises to pay George $200 for a used cash register and he orally promises to sell it to her, a contract exists between the two parties. We call such promises original promises because both parties have promised to be *primarily* liable (liable in all events) if something in the transaction should go awry.

Sometimes people agree to be secondarily liable—that is, only in the event someone else (i.e., the debtor) defaults. Such agreements, called *collateral contracts*, are promises to answer for the debt or default of another. Collateral contracts typically involve three persons: the debtor (the original promisor), the creditor (the promisee), and the third party, who generally is called a guarantor (one who promises to answer for the payment of a debt or the performance of an obligation if the person liable in the first instance fails to make payment or to perform). Notice that a collateral contract exhibits definite characteristics:

• There are three parties. However, some three-party transactions—novations, for example—are not collateral contracts. (Novations are substitutions of new contracts in place of preexisting ones by mutual agreement, whether between the same parties or with new parties replacing one or more of the original parties.)

• There are two promises, one original (debtor to creditor) and the other collateral (third party to creditor).

• The second promise is a promise to accept only collateral, or secondary, liability resulting from the default of another.

Since most people would view such collateral promises as somewhat unusual (we generally assume people will be responsible for their own debts but not for another person's), the purpose of this provision of the Statute of

Frauds is to require evidence—through a writing—of this undertaking of possible secondary liability.

The *intent of the parties* determines whether a three-party transaction involves a collateral contract, which must be in writing to be enforceable, or an original contract, which may be enforceable even if oral. For example, if Stein wants his grandson to have a car, he may co-sign the note his grandson has signed with a bank. This is a three-party situation (Stein, his grandson, and the bank), but it is not a collateral contract. Stein and his grandson are joint, original promisors to the bank. The same would be true if Stein had been a surety (a concept discussed in Chapter 11). A surety is a person who promises to pay or to perform in the event the principal debtor fails to do so. As such, Stein is accepting liability in all circumstances. If the grandson defaults on the car payment, the bank can sue either Stein or his grandson. If, however, Stein wishes to be only secondarily liable and the note is phrased accordingly, the contract is a collateral one. In the event of the grandson's default, the bank must sue the grandson *without success before* it can attempt to hold Stein liable. Note that the intent of the parties is crucial in determining the type of contract—original or collateral—that is involved. By requiring any transaction deemed a collateral contract to be in writing, the bank is protecting itself from a defense based on the Statute of Frauds.

Because courts generally are hostile to the Statute of Frauds, they sometimes allow an exception to the rule that a collateral contract must be in writing to be enforceable. This is called the *leading-object* or *main-purpose* exception: When the third party agrees to be liable chiefly for the purpose of obtaining an economic benefit for himself or herself personally, the second promise, even if oral, will be enforceable. Let us change our earlier example to one in which Stein orally tells the bank he will pay if his grandson defaults. When the grandson fails to pay and the bank sues Stein, Stein will use the Statute of Frauds as his defense: No writing exists, and the contract appears to be a collateral one. If the bank nonetheless can prove that before Stein agreed to be liable, Stein knew that the institution was about to force the grandson into bankruptcy, which, in turn, meant that Stein might lose the sizeable loans he had made to his grandson, the bank may be able to show that Stein's "leading object" in making the promise primarily involved preventing economic loss to himself rather than displaying grandfatherly love and generosity. Proving this, the bank can argue that the "main purpose" of Stein's conduct focused on protecting his own economic position vis-à-vis his grandson's impending bankruptcy. Owing to the personal, immediate, pecuniary benefits Stein himself may have realized from the bank's loan, courts will cast aside their usual skepticism concerning such oral promises and impose liability on Stein.

By requiring all promises to be in writing, the wise businessperson or firm avoids such potential legal problems, as illustrated by the *Gallagher* case that follows.

Contracts for Interests in Land Any agreement that involves buying, selling, or transferring interests in land must be in writing to be enforceable. Mortgages (conditional transfers of property as security for a debt), leases (contracts that grant the right to use and occupy realty), easements (limited rights to use and enjoy the land of another), and sales agreements about standing timber and buildings attached to the land also should be in writing to satisfy the Statute of Frauds. Thus, if you orally offer to buy someone's house and the seller accepts your offer, this contract will be unenforceable because it does not comply with the Statute of Frauds.

Courts nevertheless will enforce oral contracts for the sale of land if the purchaser has paid part of the purchase price and, with the seller's consent, takes possession of the land and makes valuable improvements on it. This equitable remedy is called the *doctrine of part performance*. For example, assume Green moves onto Berry's land and, with Berry's oral permission, tears down an old garage, repaints the entire house, and rebuilds a barn, all at Green's expense. Before undertaking these actions, Green also has paid $5,000 to Berry. When Berry later tries to claim an absence of any enforceable contract of sale between the two, a court nonetheless can order specific performance of the contract despite noncompliance with the Statute of Frauds. Courts justify such an exception to the requirement of a writing on the ground that the *conduct* of the parties prior to litigation shows the existence of a contract. Courts in such cases conclude that the parties' actions can be explained only by the actuality of such a contract. To avoid the unjust enrichment of the seller, equity also will give remedies in such situations.

Contracts Not to Be Performed within One Year of the Date of Their Making According to the Statute of Frauds, a promise in a contract that cannot be performed within one year from the date of the making of the agreement must be in writing to be enforceable. To illustrate, an oral promise to haul milk for a dairy producer is invalid under the Statute of Frauds if the milk cannot be hauled in less than one year. This is the case when the parties enter into a contract on December 15, with the term of the contract stated as running from January 1 to December 31 of the next year. Such a contract is one not to be performed within one year of the date of its making (December 15).

13.3

GALLAGHER, LANGLAS & GALLAGHER v. BURCO
587 N.W.2d 615 (Iowa App. 1998)

FACTS Lynn Roose asked that the law firm of Gallagher, Langlas and Gallagher, P.C. (Gallagher) represent her in her dissolution (divorce) action. In August 1994, attorney Thomas Langlas gave Roose a contract in which he requested a $2,000 retainer fee. Roose never signed or returned the contract. She also did not pay the retainer fee in full. Nonetheless, the firm represented Roose in her lawsuit. On April 10, 1995, the Gallagher attorneys met with Roose and her father, Gaylen Burco, and told Burco about the anticipated child custody trial. The firm contended that, during the meeting, Burco agreed to take responsibility for the remainder of Roose's account; Burco later denied the existence of any such agreement. But at the end of the meeting, Burco gave the firm a check for $1,000 to pay the outstanding balance of $814.92 on Roose's account. Before the trial, when another attorney in the firm contacted Burco requesting an additional retainer to secure the fees to be incurred, Burco told her, "My word as a gentleman should be enough. . . . I told Mr. Langlas I would pay and I will pay." When Roose failed to pay her legal fees, in July 1995 the attorneys sent Burco a letter requesting either $5,000 for Roose's legal fees or the signing of a promissory note for that amount. Although neither Roose nor Burco paid the attorneys' fees or signed any notes, the firm represented Roose in the July 1995 trial. After the trial, Burco returned the second letter and promissory note with a notation stating he was not responsible for his daughter's attorneys' fees. When the firm filed an action against Burco and Roose for the unpaid legal fees, Burco denied the allegations and raised the affirmative defense of the Statute of Frauds.

ISSUES Did the parties' dealings show sufficient definiteness to constitute a valid agreement? Was the agreement unenforceable under the Statute of Frauds?

HOLDING Yes to both issues. The agreement constituted a valid contract, but the contract was unenforceable because the collateral promise made by the father was oral.

REASONING Excerpts from the opinion of Judge Streit:

The question is, then, whether the terms of the communications between Burco and the firm were definite enough to form a contract. At the April 10, 1996, meeting, Burco was told the estimated expense of his daughter's custody trial would be approximately $1,000 per day. The firm would not guarantee Burco the trial would only last two or three days. Burco paid $1,000 towards an existing $814.92 bill and said he would pay for future services. Before trial, Burco was pressed for payment or to sign a promissory note. Burco said he would pay and his word was good enough. Burco took an active part in the trial by testifying and participating in conferences with counsel during recesses.

Burco claims his guarantee to pay future legal expenses is too vague and uncertain to form a contract. The dealings described above are definite. Each party's duties are clear. The attorneys were to continue representing Roose in her custody fight. Burco was to pay her legal fees. These terms are as definite as many attorney-fee agreements. These facts are sufficient evidence to prove an oral contract existed. The trial court's finding an oral contract existed between Burco and the firm is supported by substantial evidence. This may not suffice, however. Because the contract was in the nature of a surety or guaranty contract, the evidence or proof of the contract may have to be written. We now consider the statute of frauds. . . .

The statute of frauds requires that certain contracts be evidenced by some kind of writing before they are enforceable. The statute applies to surety contracts—a promise to a creditor to answer for debt, default, or miscarriage of another. . . . In construing [the] Iowa Code section . . . the Iowa Supreme Court has distinguished between collateral and original promises. . . . Original promises are made when the promise to pay the debt of another arises out of new and original consideration between the newly contracting parties. . . . With an original promise the surety has a personal concern in the debtor's obligation and will achieve a personal benefit out of the debtor's obligation. . . . The "leading object of his promise is to secure some benefit or business advantage for himself." . . . Original promises are not within the statute of frauds. . . . Collateral promises are made when a promise is made in addition to an already existing contract and the surety has no personal concern in the debtor's obligation and gains no benefit from the debtor's obligation. The "main purpose" of the promise must not be the benefit of the surety. . . . Collateral promises fall within the statute of frauds. . . .

In addition to ascertaining whether the promisor receives a benefit, we ascertain who the credit was extended to, the promisor or the party who was rendered the services. . . . This intention is ascertained from the promissory words used, the situation of the parties, and all surrounding circumstances when the promise was made. . . .

There is nothing in the record which supports the trial court's conclusion the promise was original rather than collateral except for a vague notion his family was affected by the matter. The evidence shows the benefit to Burco was indirect in that if his daughter won custody of his granddaughter he may get to visit her more. There is no evidence this was Burco's primary motivating factor in promising to pay his daughter's debt. From this record, it cannot be found Burco gained a benefit from his promise. This being so, his promise was collateral rather than original. There is not substantial evidence supporting the court's finding Burco made an original promise which falls outside the statute of frauds. The statute of frauds renders evidence of the contract incompetent and makes it unenforceable. Once a court determines the statute of frauds applies to a contract, it must be determined if there are any exceptions that overcome the statute of frauds. One such exception, if proven, is promissory estoppel. . . . Generally, Iowa cases hold promissory estoppel must be pled in order to rely on it at trial. . . .

The law firm was not required to file a reply to Burco's affirmative defense of the statute of frauds in order to develop the defense of promissory estoppel at trial. . . . At a minimum, however, the law firm was required to urge on appeal promissory estoppel brought Burco's promise outside the statute of frauds. "Failure in the brief to state, argue, or cite authority in support of an issue may be deemed waiver of that issue." . . . The firm has not preserved this issue for appeal.

Because we have found the statute of frauds applies, and the law firm has not raised the doctrine of promissory estoppel on appeal, Burco's oral contract to pay the debt of his daughter may not be enforced. For these reasons, we reverse.

BUSINESS CONSIDERATIONS Should the law firm have taken a "hard-nosed" approach and have refused to represent Roose in the absence of her father's written guarantee of the fees? What are the respective merits and demerits of such an approach?

ETHICAL CONSIDERATIONS Burco's failure to live up to his word exemplifies what some ethicists have identified as the erosion of the worth of a personal oath. Do you agree that formal and informal vows, or promises, do not carry the same depth of commitment they used to reflect? If you do, what are the underlying causes of this phenomenon?

Therefore, under the Statute of Frauds, to be enforceable this agreement must be in writing.

Courts have reacted hostilely to this section of the statute because, when applied, it may harshly affect the parties to the contract. Thus, courts often have limited the coverage of this proviso to situations in which *performance cannot possibly occur within one year's time* (as in our example above). This limitation has led to rather strained results. For example, a bilateral contract in which an employee promises to work for an employer "for the employer's lifetime" in exchange for the employer's promise to pay a monthly salary sounds as if it invariably cannot be performed within one year. Some courts, however, interpret such language to mean that since it is *possible*—though not *probable*—that the employer might die within a year, an oral contract is enforceable despite the Statute of Frauds. Under this approach, if the contract in our earlier example obligated the hauler to transport the milk for "as long as the dairy farmer produces milk," such courts would reason that the dairy farmer possibly could cease operations within one year, thereby making the contract capable of being performed within one year from the date of the making of the contract. Although a remote possibility, the fact that such a

contingency could happen makes the oral contract enforceable and this section of the Statute of Frauds inapplicable. Other courts, nevertheless, will adopt the stricter approach and hold that the contracts at issue in both cases must be in writing to be enforceable.

Some jurisdictions allow recovery for oral contracts that fall under this provision of the Statute of Frauds—that is, because they extend for periods longer than one year—when one party to the contract will be able to complete its performance within one year, even though the other party will be unable to do so. Courts also may apply promissory estoppel, which we discussed in Chapter 10, to allow recovery for otherwise unenforceable contracts.

Contracts of Executors and Administrators of Estates Promises to pay estate claims out of their own personal funds by executors (persons appointed in a will by the testator to administer the estate as established by the will) and administrators (persons empowered by an appropriate court to handle the estate of a deceased person) must be in writing to be enforceable. Since such promises are relatively unusual, the courts require a writing as evidence that the parties actually reached such an agreement.

Contracts Made in Consideration of Marriage

Like the previous category, unilateral promises to pay money or to transfer property in consideration of a promise to marry are so uncommon that the law will enforce such promises only if they are in writing. If the Benson family promises to pay $20,000 and to transfer the ownership of their condominium in Florida to Pat Lloyd—if Pat promises to marry their child—the Statute of Frauds will require the Bensons' promise to be in writing. By analogy, antenuptial (or prenuptial) agreements, into which couples enter before marriage and which typically spell out the disposition of the marital property should the marriage end in divorce, also ordinarily must be in writing to be enforceable.

Contracts for the Sale of Goods Priced at $500 or More, or the Lease of Goods for $1,000 or More

In addition to the five common law categories of contracts that need to be in writing to be enforceable under the Statute of Frauds, the Uniform Commercial Code (UCC) also has several provisions that implicate the Statute of Frauds. The most important of these are UCC §§ 2-201 and 2A-201. Section 2-201 states that contracts for the sale of goods priced at $500 or more are not enforceable unless there is a writing sufficient to indicate that a contract for sale has been made between the parties and the writing is signed by the person against whom enforcement of the contract is sought. Section 2A-201 states that contracts for the leasing of goods calling for total payments of $1,000 or more, excluding payments for options to renew or to buy, are not enforceable unless there is a writing sufficient to indicate that a contract for the lease has been made between the parties and the writing has been signed by the party against whom enforcement is sought. Therefore, according to the Statute of Frauds, a contract for a sale of produce priced at $500 or more (the Code would classify produce as goods, that is, identifiable, movable, personal property) must be in writing. Similarly, a contract for the leasing of a computer with lease payments of $1,000 or more (also classified as goods under the UCC) must be in writing. The Code further states that a writing *is* sufficient even if it omits or incorrectly states a term agreed on, but courts will refuse to enforce the agreement beyond the *quantity* of goods mentioned in such a writing.

Under § 2-201, however, courts will enforce oral contracts if (1) the goods are to be specially manufactured for the buyer and are not suitable for sale to others in the ordinary course of the seller's business; (2) the buyer makes a partial payment or a partial acceptance, although the contract will be enforced only for the portion of goods paid for or accepted; or (3) the party being sued admits in court, or in court documents, that a contract was made for a certain quantity of goods. These same exceptions also apply to lease contracts that otherwise would require a writing.

UCC § 2-201 also contains a novel provision that may trap the unaware merchant, defined by the UCC as a person who deals in goods of this kind, or otherwise, through his or her occupation, holds himself or herself out as having knowledge or skill peculiar to the practice or goods involved in the transaction. Section 2-201 states that a merchant who receives a signed written confirmation from another merchant (for example, "This is to confirm our sale to you of 2,000 bushels of apples, #2 grade, at $1.25/bushel, delivery Tuesday /s/ Seller") and does not object to the confirmation in writing within 10 days is bound to the contract. The policy underlying this result is a familiar one: A valid oral contract on the terms stated must exist if the other party (who, as a merchant, is considered a "pro") does not object to the confirmation. The moral of this section of the UCC is: Merchants, answer your mail, e-mails, and faxes!

Writing

As we have seen in other contexts, the writing required to satisfy the Statute of Frauds may be rather negligible; it may take the form of letters, telegrams, receipts, e-mail, or memoranda. The writing must, at a minimum, identify the parties to the agreement, the subject matter of the agreement, and all material terms and conditions. Several writings may be pieced together as long as they all refer to the same transaction.

Signature

Similarly, anything intended by the parties as a signature will suffice to satisfy the Statute of Frauds. This, of course, would include written signatures; but courts have even held stamped signatures or stationery letterheads to be sufficient. Both parties need not sign the memorandum, as long as the party against whom enforcement is sought, or the party's authorized agent, has signed.

Exhibit 13.2 (pages 316–317) explains the scope of the Statute of Frauds, the elements required to find coverage, and the exceptions to the general rules.

The e-commerce environment has spawned alternative approaches to the common law treatment of the Statute of Frauds. As noted in Chapter 9, the central thrust of UETA is that electronic records, electronic signatures, and the contracts that result from such transactions be treated on a par with their paper-based counterparts. Accordingly, § 7 of UETA provides for the legal recognition of electronic records, electronic signatures, and electronic contracts. UETA in § 2(8) defines an "electronic signature" as an "electronic sound, symbol, or process attached to or logically associated with a record and executed or adopted by a person with the intent to sign the record." An electronic signature, then, ranges from PIN numbers to passwords to clicking on a box labeled "I agree" to encryption devices. Yet, as discussed earlier, UETA does not override otherwise applicable substantive law. Hence, § 8 makes it clear that "while the pen and ink provisions of such other law may be satisfied electronically, nothing in this Act vitiates the other requirement of such laws."[3] Therefore, even though UETA in § 9(a) makes an electronic record or electronic signature attributable to a person as if it were the act of the person, this provision allows the determination of who signed the record to be established by any means (including effective security procedures). Moreover, § 9(b) notes that the evidence used to determine the person to whom the electronic record or signature is attributable can be drawn from the context and surrounding circumstances, including the parties' agreement. Security procedures such as encryption help to verify the identity of the person who sent/signed the electronic record, a problem more prevalent in electronically based transactions (owing to the possibility of hacking) than in paper-based ones. Nevertheless, if the parties dispute the attribution of a signature or record, they may introduce any relevant evidence. An electronic signature that can be attributed to a given person would satisfy the signature requirement of the Statute of Frauds.

Unlike UETA, which does not supplant existing law, UCITA has a Statute of Frauds provision. But like UETA, UCITA's validation of both paper and electronic records encompasses electronic forms of authentication as signatures. Therefore, even though UCITA's Statute of Frauds provision (§ 201) is based on the UCC, UCITA requires an "authenticated record" rather than a signed writing. As noted earlier, a "record" refers to information that is inscribed on a tangible medium (in writing) or that is stored in an electronic, retrievable format. A record becomes authenticated once it is signed or an electronic symbol linked with that record has been executed or adopted. Under UCITA § 201, a contract requiring a contract fee of $5,000 or more is not enforceable unless the party against which enforcement is sought has authenticated a record sufficient to indicate that a contract has been formed and which reasonably identifies the copy or subject matter to which the contract refers. The parties can, however, alter the requirements of this provision to the effect that any future license between them need not be stated in an authenticated record if the party against which enforcement is sought agrees to this alteration in the first authenticated record. The exceptions set out in UCITA § 201 largely mirror the UCC's provisions as to merchants, admissions in court, and

NRW CASE 13.3 Sales/Manufacturing

CHECKING THE MAIL AND E-MAIL

Carlos and Mai want to shut down the plant for two weeks and give all the employees a paid vacation. Carlos and Mai want all three firm members during this same period to attend an international conference that will focus on many subjects of interest to them. Helen is concerned that in these circumstances communications sent to the firm will go unanswered. She suggests that they select an employee to check the daily mail and e-mails during their absence. Carlos and Mai do not like the idea of having an employee read NRW's letters and messages. They assert that because two weeks is not such a long time, all three can catch up with the mail and their e-mails on their return. Helen continues to insist that the firm cannot afford to ignore the communications sent to it for two weeks. They have asked for your advice. What will you tell them? Does the time involved affect your answer?

BUSINESS CONSIDERATIONS Why is it important for businesspeople to read and react to their mail and e-mails in a timely manner? What should a business do to protect itself when it regularly takes telephone orders for the sale of goods and those goods typically cost $500 or more?

ETHICAL CONSIDERATIONS Is it ethical to hold a merchant responsible for communications received but unanswered (or even unread), when the same rules do not apply to a nonmerchant? Why does the distinction between merchants and nonmerchants matter?

INTERNATIONAL CONSIDERATIONS The recent enactment of UETA and E-SIGN recognizes electronic communications as "writings." Are there any similar treaties, statutes, or provisions for the treatment of electronic communications in international trade? Is the recognition of electronic communications as "writings" as important in international trade as it is in the United States?

past performance; but the record must describe the subject matter (for example, the database that is being licensed) or the copies to which the agreement refers rather than goods, as would be the case under the UCC. Notably, the UCITA exceptions also expand on the common law categories as well. To illustrate, UCITA dispenses with the need for a

EXHIBIT 13.2 "The Statute of Frauds"

Types of Contracts Covered (and Which Must be in Writing)	Elements	Exceptions
1. Contracts to answer for the debt of another if the person so defaults	1. There are three parties. 2. There are two promises, one original (debtor to creditor) and the other collateral (third-party guarantor to creditor). 3. The second promise is a promise to accept only secondary liability resulting from the default of another. 4. The intent of the parties determines whether a three-party transaction involves a collateral contract (which must be in writing) or an original contract (which can be oral yet still enforceable).	1. Novations and other three-party transactions are not guaranty contracts but joint, original contracts. 1. The "leading object" or "main purpose" doctrine may apply.
2. Contracts for interest in land	1. The agreement involves buying, selling, or transferring interests in land. 2. Leases, easements, and sale agreements about standing timber and buildings attached to the land also are covered.	1. The doctrine of part performance may take the contract out of the statute.
3. Contracts not to be performed within one year of the date of their making	1. Contracts in which it is impossible to perform the contract completely within one year of the date of the creation of the contract are involved.	1. Courts may circumvent the application of the statute by resorting to the fiction that it is possible (albeit not probable) for the contracts to be performed within one year. 2. Part performance by one party has occurred. 3. Circumstances that justify the application of promissory estoppel exist.

license if the agreement is a license for an agreed duration of one year or less or the license may be terminated at will by the party against which the contract is asserted.

The federal E-SIGN statute, like UETA, validates but does not mandate the use of electronic signatures. In general, E-SIGN permits the use of electronic signatures in circumstances that otherwise would require so-called wet (that is, manual) signatures. Like UETA, E-SIGN does not alter substantive contract law. Nevertheless, some critics argue that E-SIGN's fairly extensive consumer notification procedures may weaken the efficiencies otherwise realized by the statute's blanket endorsement of electronic signatures.

Notably, the Convention on Contracts for the International Sale of Goods (CISG) has no Statute of Frauds provision. Rather, CISG provides that contracts of sale need not be evidenced by a writing and also rejects the necessity of any other requirements as to form.

Parol Evidence Rule

So far we have explored some of the concepts and rules concerning the application of the Statute of Frauds. We now turn to another important facet of contract law, the parol evidence rule. The law predicates this rule on the belief that oral statements should not be admissible to alter, add to, or vary the terms of an integrated, written contract. If the parties appear to have intended the writing as the

EXHIBIT 13.2 *continued*

Types of Contracts Covered (and Which Must be in Writing)	Elements	Exceptions
4. Contracts by executors and administrators of estates	1. The executors or administrators have promised to pay estate claims out of their own personal funds.	
5. Contracts made in consideration of marriage	1. One person has promised another person to pay a given amount or otherwise to perform a contractual duty in order to induce the person to enter a marriage.	
6. Contracts for the sale of goods priced at $500 or more (UCC §2-201) or contracts for the lease of goods for $1,000 or more (UCC § 2A-201)	1. The contract involves the sale or lease of goods. 2. The price of the goods must be at least $500, or the lease is for at least $1,000. 3. The writing is not insufficient if it omits or incorrectly states an agreed-on term, but the contract will be unenforceable beyond the quantity of goods shown in the writing. 4. The writing must be signed by the person (or by his or her authorized agent or broker) against whom enforcement is sought.	1. Between merchants, a written confirmation sent by one party to another must be objected to by the other within 10 days, or the Statute of Frauds will be satisfied. 2. Oral contracts that are enforceable consist of those involving (a) specially manufactured goods not readily resalable in the ordinary course of the seller's business, (b) goods for which payment has been received, (c) goods for which acceptance has been made, or (d) an admission in a court proceeding by the person against whom enforcement is sought that a contract for sale was made.

final expression of their agreement, a court's allowing later oral or written evidence that contradicts that writing will call into question the whole process of reducing one's agreement to writing. The parol evidence rule serves several important purposes. First, it facilitates judicial interpretation by having a single, clear source of proof as to the terms of the agreement between the parties. Second, it emphasizes the importance of the writings between the parties. For instance, assume that Larry and Ahmed sign a contract for the sale of a consulting business. They both agree, in writing, that the price of the business is $16,000. If Larry or Ahmed later tries to argue that the price is higher or lower, and litigation ensues, the parol evidence rule will preclude oral testimony to this effect. Imagine the havoc a contrary rule would cause. By applying the parol evidence rule, courts therefore uphold the sanctity of totally integrated written contracts.

Because the parol evidence rule is designed to further a policy of protecting writings—those instruments representing the final intentions and terms of the parties—it actually is a rule of *substantive law* (the portion of the law that regulates rights, in contrast to law that grants remedies or enforces rights) rather than a rule of evidence.

Exceptions to the Parol Evidence Rule

The preceding notwithstanding, courts will disregard the parol evidence rule and will admit parol evidence in certain circumstances. The following sections describe common circumstances in which the parol evidence rule is not applied.

Partially Integrated Contracts

The policy base that underlies the parol evidence rule is not as compelling in situations in which the contract is partially integrated (that is, the writing is an incomplete statement of the contract). In such cases, although the writing may not be *contradicted* by evidence of earlier terms, it may be *supplemented* by evidence of additional, consistent terms.

Mistake, Fraud, and Other "Reality-of-Consent" Situations

Parol evidence similarly is admissible to show mistake, fraud, duress, and failure of consideration—the kinds of situations covered in Chapter 12. Since the existence of these circumstances casts doubt on the validity of the integrated writing, there is no overwhelmingly persuasive policy reason to justify the exclusion of contradictory oral statements.

Ambiguities and Conditions Precedent

Courts also will allow parol evidence in order to clear up ambiguities and to show that the agreement was not to become binding on the parties before meeting a *condition precedent* (a certain act or event that must occur before the other party has a duty to perform or before a contract exists), such as reduction of the agreement to writing or approval of the contract by a party's attorney. However, courts may allow evidence about a condition precedent only if this evidence does not contradict the written terms of the contract at issue.

Uniform Commercial Code

Sections 2-202 and 2-208 of the UCC concern the parol evidence rule. Basically, the Code recognizes the rule but then weakens its impact by stating that evidence of course of dealing (the parties' previous conduct), usage of trade (a regularly observed practice in a trade), and course of performance (a contract that contemplates repeated occasions of performance) is admissible. Courts also can admit evidence of consistent, additional terms unless they find that the parties intended the writing as a complete and exclusive statement of the terms of the agreement. Moreover, the Code sets up priorities among these types of evidence: The express terms of the agreement control course of performance, course of dealing, and usage of trade. Evidence relating to course of performance, in turn, controls admissions about course of dealing and usage of trade.

Sections 2A-202 and 2A-207 of the UCC provide parallel coverage and treatment of parol evidence in contracts for the leasing of goods.

As was the case with the Statute of Frauds provision, UCITA—in § 301—basically engrafts the common law parol evidence rule onto the parties' "confirmatory records" to protect the integrity of the terms the parties intended as the final expression of their agreement.

To acquire more information about UETA, go to http://www.uetaonline.com. Access http://www.ucitaonline.com for more extensive coverage of UCITA.

Summary

In order for the bargain to be recognized as a valid contract, the law imposes a requirement that the subject matter and purpose of a bargain must be legal. A bargain is illegal if its performance is criminal, tortious, or otherwise opposed to public policy. Some courts distinguish between bargains that violate statutes because they are evil in themselves (*mala in se*) and bargains that are merely forbidden by statute (*mala prohibita*). Many types of bargains (such as price-fixing agreements, bargains in contravention of Sunday laws, wagering agreements, and usurious transactions) violate statutes. Performances of services without a license may make the agreement void if the statute is regulatory. In contrast, if the statute requires licensing as a revenue-enhancing measure, lack of a license will not void the bargain. When deciding cases, judges today look increasingly to public policy factors. Covenants not to compete (promises to refrain from engaging in the same or a similar business for a period of time in a certain geographic area) and exculpatory clauses (agreements in advance to exonerate another from negligence or other torts), if too restrictive or one-sided, may be struck down on public policy grounds. There are some exceptions to the rule that illegal bargains are void. These exceptions include agreements in which the parties are not *in pari delicto*, or of equal blame; agreements in which one party repents before it consummates the illegal bargain; and agreements in which courts can sever the legal portions from the illegal segments.

In accordance with the Statute of Frauds, certain types of contracts must be in writing to be enforceable. These include collateral contracts, contracts for the sale or transfer of interests in land, contracts not to be performed within one year from the date of their making, contracts of executors and administrators of estates, contracts made in consideration of marriage, and contracts for the sale of goods priced at $500 or more, or the lease of goods with payments of $1,000 or more. Nevertheless, very little in the way of a memorandum or signature is necessary to satisfy the Statute of Frauds.

The parol evidence rule states that oral evidence is not admissible to alter, add to, or vary the terms of an integrated, written contract. However, the law will not apply the parol evidence rule in some circumstances: partially integrated contracts; agreements involving mistake, duress, fraud, ambiguity, or conditions precedent; or in some commercial contexts.

Although the Convention on Contracts for the International Sale of Goods (CISG) has no Statute of Frauds provision, UETA, UCITA, and E-SIGN validate electronic forms of signatures.

Discussion Questions

1. What is the difference between a *mala in se* and a *mala prohibita* bargain?

2. What is an exculpatory clause? Is it always legal? Why or why not?

3. What are covenants not to compete? What standards do courts use to judge their legality?

4. Why are wagering and lotteries illegal in various jurisdictions?

5. What is a usurious contract? What kinds of common financing devices would not violate the usury laws?

6. Describe the three most important exceptions to the general rule that an illegal bargain is void.

7. Explain both the historical and the current basis for the Statute of Frauds.

8. What are the most important characteristics of a collateral contract, or a contract to guarantee the debt of another if a person so defaults? Also, explain the exception to the rule that collateral contracts must be in writing.

9. Describe the exceptions to the rule that a contract for a sale of goods priced at $500 or more or the lease of goods with payments of $1,000 or more must be in writing.

10. What is the parol evidence rule? What are the exceptions to the rule?

Case Problems and Writing Assignments

1. Bradley Holcom was a licensed real estate agent who arranged the sale of trust deeds for clients looking to invest in loans for the development of real property. John Roes approached Holcom about investing in trust deeds and, from 1991 to 1993, purchased interests in a number of properties through Holcom. In May 1992, Holcom arranged two $179,000 construction loans to Luz Maria Garcia for the development of two properties in Calexico, California. Each loan was reflected by a promissory note secured by one of the two properties, and each note provided for interest at 15 percent (the senior notes). Holcom also personally made two loans, totaling $50,000, to Garcia for the development of the two properties. A second trust deed on the relevant property secured each of the Holcomb loans (the junior notes). Less than one month later, at a time when Holcom knew of potential problems with the development of the properties, Holcom sold his interests in the junior notes and the second trust deeds to John Roes for $43,000. When Garcia defaulted on the repayment of the loans, the holders of the senior notes threatened foreclosure. To avoid losing his investment in the properties, Roes paid the interest, costs, and penalties due on the senior notes and ultimately paid off the senior notes. He later sued the holders of the senior notes. Specifically, Roes alleged that the senior note holders' violation of California's usury laws entitled him to treble damages for the interest paid under the notes. Would someone other than the debtor—here the holder of a junior encumbrance—have standing to assert a claim under the usury laws? [See *Roes v. Wong*, 81 Cal. Rptr. 2d 596 (Cal. App. 4th Dist. 1999)]

2. Sysco Corporation, a distributor of food and cleaning products, hired Michael Massino, William G. Mitchell, and Scott R. Thomas as marketing associates. After Sysco and the three employees came to terms on the essential aspects of their employment, including salary, benefits, bonuses, and territory, they left their prior employment and reported for work with Sysco. At that point, Sysco asked them to sign a restrictive covenant in which they agreed not to disclose Sysco's confidential and proprietary information. The three also agreed that for a one-year period after the termination of their employment with Sysco, they would not "directly or indirectly, on behalf of [themselves] or for any other entity, business or person other than [Sysco], contact, solicit, or sell to any of the customers of [Sysco] with which [they] solicited or had contact while employed by [Sysco]. . . ." After the three went to work for Maines Paper and Food Service, Inc. and allegedly solicited the business of some of Sysco's customers in Pennsylvania, Sysco sued to enforce the restrictive covenant each had signed. When the defendants argued that no new consideration supported their signing of the restrictive covenant, Sysco submitted that the "extensive and expensive training program" it had provided to the defendants constituted the required consideration. Would a court find this argument compelling? [See *Sysco Corporation v. Maines Paper & Food Service Inc.*, 679 N.Y.S.2d 175 (A.D. 3rd Dept. 1998).]

3. In the early 1990s PMC Corporation, a supplier of thermocouple wire and cable, began to sell its products to Houston Wire & Cable Company, a distributor of wire and cable prod-

ucts. In 1994, PMC and Houston began discussions about entering into a relationship in which PMC would provide training on thermocouple applications and other services to Houston and PMC would become Houston's primary vendor of thermocouple products. In late 1994, PMC's president, John Gehrisch, asked Houston to put in writing its commitment to purchase primarily from PMC. On January 4, 1996, Gehrisch wrote a letter to Tom Adelman, vice president of operations at Houston, in which Gehrisch requested a letter of intent from Houston confirming its recognition of PMC as its primary source for thermocouple products and confirming its intent to purchase thermocouple products amounting to a minimum of $800,000 per year and totaling $2,000,000 in 1995, $3,000,000 in 1996, and $4,000,000 in 1997. This amount represented Houston's total purchases of thermocouple products to cover both its corporate inventory and branch requirements. Although Houston could not guarantee that it would purchase a minimum of $800,000 per year, the parties noted PMC's need for a letter of intent from Houston so PMC could obtain leverage at its bank and would have something to give to the bank when it was negotiating for capital to expand the factory. On January 13, 1995, PMC faxed Houston a draft of a revised agreement. The cover sheet characterized the draft as an intent to purchase that in no way locked Houston into purchases from PMC but merely indicated an intent. On January 17, 1995, Houston signed the revised version, which indicated Houston's acceptance in principle of the January 4 agreement and its addition of the following details:

[Houston] expects to purchase in excess of $2,000,000 of thermocouple products in 1995. . . . While [Houston] cannot commit to exclusive purchase of this total from PMC, [Houston] recognizes PMC as a preferred supplier. As such . . . PMC can expect to receive a major share of the total thermocouple business. It is not unrealistic to project total purchases by [Houston] from PMC to be in the $2,000,000 range in 1995, [$3,000,000 in 1996, and $4,000,000 in 1997]. It is also [Houston's] intent to purchase the major portion of this product from PMC.

After this correspondence, Houston's orders from PMC began to decrease. During a meeting on February 21, 1996, Houston informed PMC that it was planning to purchase the bulk of its thermocouple products from Belden, a competing manufacturer. In 1998, when PMC sued Houston for breach of contract, Houston argued that the writings in question were unenforceable under the Uniform Commercial Code's Statute of Frauds provision because they lacked the required element relating to quantity. Was Houston correct? [See *PMC Corporation v. Houston Wire & Cable Company*, 797 A.2d 125 (N.H. 2002).]

4. Ronald A. Yocca and others brought a class action against The Pittsburgh Steelers Sports, Inc., a National Football League franchise, and others. The Steelers had issued a brochure soliciting the purchase of stadium builder licenses (SBLs) for Heinz Field, a new football stadium then under construction. The brochure indicated that, for a one-time contribution to the cost of building the new stadium, the SBL purchasers would be assigned to a particular seating area (or section) in the stadium

and would have the right to buy season tickets in that section for as many seasons as they wished. The actual seat assignments were to be made after the seats were physically installed in the stadium. The price of the SBLs ranged from $250 to $2,700 depending on where the purchaser wished to sit. The SBL brochure contained colored diagrams of the planned stadium showing the various sections and showing the yard lines of the playing field. The penultimate pages of the SBL brochure was headed "Before you sign" and contained, among other things, the following:

You may apply for any Section you wish as your first preference. To ensure fairness, every application received by the November 30 deadline will be assigned a random computerized priority number and that priority number will be used to assigned both sections and seats. . . . If you are ordering SBLs, you will be mailed a contract by the end of March 1999, notifying you of your Section assignment. The contract must be signed and returned within 15 days. If the completed contract is not returned as required, your season ticket holder discount, seating priority and deposit will be forfeited. . . . Current season ticket holders who apply for [an] SBL Section that corresponds with their current seat location in Three Rivers Stadium will be the first assigned to that Section. If that is your choice, we will try to assign seats as close to your current seat location as the new stadium seating configuration will allow. All other seats in a given SBL Section will be assigned using the random priority number. Assignment of your first preference is not guaranteed.

Interested parties were to fill out the application form and indicate their first, second, and third section choices. Yocca claimed that the defendants mailed two documents to the SBL applicants in October 1999, an "SBL Agreement" and "Additional Terms." The SBL Agreement incorporated by reference the Additional Terms, which, in turn, contained an integration clause stating that "This Agreement contains the entire agreement of the parties with respect to the matters provided for herein and shall supersede any representations or agreements previously made or entered into by the parties hereto." Yocca and the other plaintiffs alleged that they signed the SBL Agreement and paid the remaining installments for their SBLs. The plaintiffs claimed that when they took their seats in Heinz Field for the first time, they realized that the defendants had enlarged some of the SBL sections, causing their individual seats to be outside the SBL sections as depicted in the SBL Brochure, upon which they had relied when they filled out their applications. Yocca therefore submitted that, based on the diagram in the SBL Brochure, he believed that Club I section seats would be somewhat between the 20-yard lines. However, Yocca's seats turned out to be at the 18-yard line. As as a result, he submitted he would be forced to pay the higher Club I price for seats that, according to the SBL Brochure, should have been considered part of the less expensive Club II section and that he would have to do so for as long as he purchased season tickets. In rebuttal, the Steelers and the other defendants claimed that the integration clause in the "Additional Terms" portion of the October 1999 SBL Agreement barred the introduction of the parol evidence the plaintiffs had used to support their breach of contract claim. Evaluate the defendants' allegation that the October 1999 SBL Agreement superseded the parties' prior dealings, as well as the parol evidence rule's possible application to the plaintiffs' allegations. [See *Yocca v. The Pittsburgh Steelers Sports, Inc.*, 806 A.2d 936 (Pa. Comwlth. 2002).]

5. BUSINESS APPLICATION CASE Albert Vajda, a former manager with Arthur Andersen & Company, sued Andersen for damages based on wrongful termination of his employment. Vajda, who had worked at Andersen for over 21 years, claimed that Andersen's employee manual precluded dismissal from employment except for just cause and through procedures that accorded with the company's three-warning policy. Andersen, while contesting the claim that the employee manual had set up enforceable contractual rights, also argued that, in any event, such a contract would be unenforceable under the Statute of Frauds. Discuss the specific provision of the Statute of Frauds on which Andersen had grounded this portion of its contentions and whether a court should agree with Andersen's reasoning. In addition, discuss the steps Andersen could have taken to avoid this litigation. [See *Vajda v. Arthur Andersen & Co.*, 624 N.E.2d 1343 (Ill. App. 1st Dist. 1993).]

6. ETHICAL APPLICATION CASE Video-Trax, Inc. (VTI) opened a checking account at NCNB National Bank of Florida, Nationsbank, N.A.'s predecessor. As part of the deposit agreement, VTI agreed in writing to pay a flat fee when a check presented to the bank for payment exceeded the collected balance in VTI's account. In addition, the agreement stated that the bank charged interest on overdraft sums to the extent those sums exceeded the balances in VTI's account. The rate of interest charged was the bank's prime rate plus 3 percent and was subject to the maximum rate permissible by law. Throughout the history of the parties' banking relationship, several checks were presented for payment against VTI's account when the account contained insufficient funds to cover the checks. Pursuant to the deposit agreement and the bank's policies, the bank exercised its option to either honor or dishonor the checks. If the bank chose not to honor the check, the bank returned the check unpaid. For the duration of the parties' relationship (1992–1997), VTI's account history reflected that, pursuant to this practice, out of a total of 212 checks presented when insufficient funds existed in VTI's account, 92 checks were honored, while 120 checks were returned. The bank calculated the interest charged against the account for overdrafts on the basis of the average daily overdrawn account balance and charged a flat fee of $25 to $27 for each overdraft. VTI ultimately sued the bank on the grounds that the $18,000 assessed as periodic charges for interest, when aggregated with the overdraft fees, constituted "interest" in excess of the lawful maximum amount allowed under state usury laws. According to VTI, the $18,000 so assessed on an average overdraft balance of approximately $6,000 represented a total of over 300 percent in interest. The bank refused to refund any of this alleged "excess interest" on the rationale that the "not sufficient fund

fee" (NSF) and the overdraft fee (OD) were administrative charges commonly utilized in the banking industry to cover processing charges and to deter depositors from overdrawing their accounts. The bank further maintained that NSF and OD fees do not constitute "interest" within the meaning of the usury provisions of the Bank Act and that VTI would be unable to avoid its contractual obligations by claiming protection under the usury laws. Who had the more persuasive argument here—VTI or the bank? [See *Video Trax, Inc. v. NationsBank, N.A.*, 33 F. Supp. 2d 1041 (S.D. Fla. 1999).]

7. CRITICAL THINKING CASE R. E. Haase owned the Whataburger, Inc. franchise rights for Longview, Texas. In 1992, Joseph K. Glazner went to work for Haase as a manager trainee. By the end of 1992, Glazner had been promoted to supervisor for Haase's five Longview Whataburger restaurants. Glazner alleged that in 1994, he and Haase entered into a contract in which Haase agreed to allow Glazner to build an additional Whataburger in south Longview, a part of Haase's franchise area. According to Glazner, Haase promised to help Glazner secure a franchise by guaranteeing the success of Glazner's proposed new restaurant to Whataburger, the corporate franchisor. Glazner further claimed that Haase agreed to sell Glazner his restaurants when Haase decided to retire and that Glazner agreed to sell Haase his proposed restaurant should he (Glazner) ever decide to sell "for some reason." Glazner asserted that the consideration to Haase for this agreement was to be 2 percent of the net sales from Glazner's new restaurant. Although the parties had not entered into an express written agreement, Glazner submitted that the contract's terms either appear in three letters to Whataburger that Haase signed or were incorporated by reference in a letter that Haase had signed, along with a proposed cash flow statement Glazer had prepared that reflected a payment to Haase of 2 percent of the projected net sales.

In May 1995, Glazner quit working for Haase before he (Glazner) had acquired a Whataburger franchise; indeed, Whataburger had refrained from granting any new franchises during the time Glazner had worked for Haase. In November 1996, Haase was granted a Whataburger franchise for a south Longview location and opened a restaurant there in June 1997. At that time, Glazner sued Haase on various theories, including fraud. Haase then asserted the affirmative defense of the Statute of Frauds. On these facts, what would the parties argue, respectively? If the court found that the Statute of Frauds covers the parties' agreement, would this conclusion affect the validity of the fraud claim? [See *Haase v. Glazner*, 62 S.W.3d 795 (Tex. 2001).]

8. YOU BE THE JUDGE Jerie Pacurib was a willing, active participant in an illegal distributor pyramid scheme called Network. Using a promotional, chain-linked "gifting" program, Network led new members to believe that an unlimited pool of possible recruits was readily available to spawn new pyramid boards. In actuality, because Pacurib was a 20th-level investor, just to advance one level would have required an additional 8,388,608 new investors. Thus, because these schemes are doomed to fail, most states—including New York—view them as *malum prohibitum*. New York had specifically addressed the practices in

the Martin Act, which was part of New York's General Business Law. Marlene Terez, one of the "founders" of the "gifting board" of which Pacurib would be a part upon Pacurib's joining Network, orally promised proposed recruits (including Pacurib) that if they joined and thereafter failed to get sufficient new recruits and/or the program did not work, she would return their money. At least one of the trial witnesses who corroborated this promise was a friend of Terez and had no stake in the outcome. Pacurib ultimately paid the $2,000 "gift" required for membership in Network. What would Pacurib argue as her basis for receiving a refund of the $2,000 she paid to Terez? If this case were brought in *your* court, would you find that the illegality of the undertaking precluded any recovery by Pacurib? [See *Pacurib v. Villacruz*, 705 N.Y.S.2d 819 (N.Y. City Civ. Ct. 1999).]

Notes

1. *Restatement (Second) of Contracts* (St. Paul, Minn.: American Law Institute Publishers, 1981), § 178.

2. See *First National Bank of Shreveport v. Williams*, 346 So. 2d 257, 264 (La. App. 1977).

CHAPTER 14

Contract Interpretation and the Rights of Third Persons

AGENDA

NRW Mai, Carlos, and Helen recognize that NRW will enter into a number of contracts in the near future. They plan to put many of their contracts in writing. They would like to know how much technical language, or "trade talk," they can use in their written agreements, and how the courts will interpret this technical language. They also will need to know how detailed their writings should be. Another concern they have is whether any of their written agreements can be amended or altered orally.

Mai, Carlos, and Helen know that third parties have contractual rights in many business situations. For example, they know that a third party's rights are involved each time an intermediary orders parts and supplies that ultimately are to be shipped to NRW. They also know that third-party rights are involved when a shipment is lost or destroyed in the possession of a trucking company. Assume there is a retail distributor who owes NRW $65,000 for inventory that NRW has already delivered. The retailer would like to transfer its current accounts receivable of $40,000 to NRW to discharge its obligation. Should NRW accept this arrangement? What risks would NRW assume? NRW is considering hiring other companies to serve as official repair centers for its StuffTrakR and InvenTrakR. What criteria should be evaluated by NRW before entering into these arrangements with other firms?

These and other questions will arise as you read this chapter. Be prepared! You never know when the firm or one of its members will seek your advice.

Judicial Interpretation

In previous chapters, we stressed the importance of a *meeting of the minds* of the parties to the contract. This phrase highlights one of the essential elements of a contract: The parties must have indicated, by their words or conduct, an intention to agree about some matter. Sometimes the parties do not express their intentions accurately and with complete detail. Because language is not always precise, it may later become apparent that the parties were not binding themselves to identical terms and courses of action. Disputes arise when this variance in expectations is discovered. If the parties cannot resolve these disputes amicably, courts must interpret what the contract "really says."

When the language of the agreement is confusing or ambiguous, *interpretation* is used to determine the meaning of the words and actions of the parties. When this happens, it is likely to be difficult to ascertain the parties' real intent. Problems arise primarily because words are symbols of expression and can take on a multitude of meanings. Words do not exist in a vacuum. Determining how a certain party intended to use words or actions becomes a factual issue. A court must examine each party's understanding and conduct in the situation; it also must be conscious of how other reasonable persons would have understood these words and actions under similar circumstances. In deciding between the competing views, courts often consider the intentions of the parties through a frame of reference known as the "reasonable person." This perspective allows the court to choose the interpretation that would be most consistent with the expectations of a reasonable person in the same circumstances. Unreasonable expectations will not be protected.

Standards

Certain standards of interpretation have evolved over the years. Probably the most common is the standard of *general usage*, or the meaning that a reasonable person who was aware of all operative uses and who was acquainted with the circumstances would attach to the agreement. For example, Leighanne signs an agreement in which she pays $100,000 as a life membership fee for admission to a nursing home. The agreement states that for a trial period of two months, either Leighanne or the nursing home can suspend the agreement. If the agreement is "suspended," the $100,000 (minus $2,000 per month) will be returned. What if Leighanne dies after one month in the home? Can her estate recover the $98,000 by arguing that the agreement was "suspended" during the trial period due to Leighanne's death, or has the life membership fee been paid irrevocably? A court in a similar case applied general usage; it decided

that a reasonable person in Leighanne's position would have understood the provision to mean that until life membership status was obtained, the nursing home should return the money (less the amounts specified) to her estate. The court also asserted that if the nursing home had intended to retain the money in the event of a probationary member's death, it should have expressly stated this fact in the contract. Under different facts, the court might have applied the standard of *limited usage* (the meaning given to language in a particular locale) instead of the standard of general usage.

Rules of Interpretation

To supplement the appropriate standard of interpretation, courts also use *rules of interpretation.* These are also called *rules of construction.* In most states, no one rule is conclusive. Authorities disagree as to the relative importance of these aids to interpretation. You should be aware of the following common rules. Courts should:

- Attempt to give effect to the manifested intentions of the parties.

- Take into account the circumstances surrounding the transaction.

- Examine the contract as a whole in order to ascertain the intentions of the parties.

- Give ordinary words their ordinary meanings and technical words their technical meanings, unless the circumstances indicate otherwise.

- Favor reasonable constructions over unreasonable alternatives.

- Give effect to the main purpose of the agreement and all its parts, if possible.

- Interpret the contract so that specific words or provisions control over general ones.

- Give effect to hand-written words over typed words and typed words over printed ones when there is a conflict. (*Printed words* are the words printed, or *pre*printed, on a form contract.)

- Construe words most strictly against the party who drafted the agreement.

- Interpret contracts affecting the public interest in favor of the public.

These common rules of construction give the court a good "starting point" for interpreting written agreements and help to provide some sense of continuity and consistency in such interpretations.

Conduct and Usage of Trade

The *conduct* of the parties often aids in contract interpretation. If the court is in doubt, it will follow the interpretation placed on the agreement by the parties themselves. For example, when one party for years has accepted as satisfactory a grade of wool that is inferior to that called for by the contract specifications, evidence of this conduct will be admissible in determining how to interpret the other party's performance in relation to the contract specifications. Uniform Commercial Code (UCC) § 2-208 incorporates this rule of interpretation. Section 2-208 also addresses the roles that course of performance, course of dealing, and usage of trade have in contract construction. To characterize a situation involving judicial interpretation, one should answer the following questions:

1. Do the parties claim competing interpretations?
2. Can general usage resolve the conflict?
3. Can limited usage resolve the conflict?
4. Which rules of interpretation should the court employ?
5. How should the court resolve any conflicts among the rules of interpretation?
6. Is there any conduct of the parties or any "trade usage" that should be considered by the court in interpreting the contract?

The Parol Evidence Rule

As was discussed in the previous chapter, the parol evidence rule is an important part of the substantive law. The *parol evidence rule* applies when the parties have a written contract. Once there is a written contract, all previous oral agreements "merge" into the writing, and the written contract cannot be modified or changed by parol evidence.

Under the parol evidence rule, when the parties to a contract reduce their agreement to a writing with the intent that it embody the full and final expression of their bargain, no other expressions—*written or oral*—made prior to or contemporaneous with the writing are admissible in court. However, there are exceptions to the parol evidence rule, and these exceptions provide an important area of judicial interpretation. One of the important exceptions arises when the parties have a writing that is only a *partially integrated* contract. Since the writing does not always provide conclusive proof as to whether the agreement is totally or partially integrated, the court must resolve this issue. Integration will be discussed in the following sections. (In reading the following sections, note that "the parol evidence rule and the problems of interpretation must remain separate if they are to be understood."[1]) Exhibit 14.1 illustrates the parol evidence rule. The Cornell Law School Web site at http://www.law.cornell.edu/ucc/2/2-202.html/ includes § 2-202 of the UCC, Final Written Expression: Parol or Extrinsic Evidence.

Rules of Integration

In general, the more formal and complete the instrument, the more likely a court will conclude that it is a *totally integrated* agreement. Courts use various tests to determine if the contract is totally integrated. One common test is the "face-of-instrument" test, where the court examines the "four corners of the writing" to determine if the parties intended the document to be totally integrated. Other jurisdictions use the "all-relevant-evidence" test, where the court reviews the document and extrinsic evidence to determine if the parties intended a total integration. Some contracts include clauses called *integration* or *merger* clauses. In these clauses, the parties declare that the writing is the full and final expression of all the terms in the agreement. Courts will then interpret the contract as totally integrated unless a party can show that the merger clause was induced by fraud or mistake.

EXHIBIT   14.1   Application of the Parol Evidence Rule

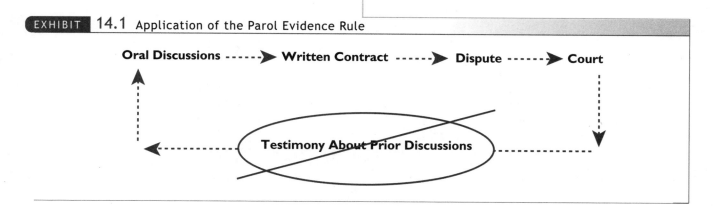

Total Integration

A *totally integrated* contract is one that represents the parties' final and complete statement of their agreement. Such a contract can be neither contradicted nor added to by evidence of prior agreements or expressions. The law assumes that the writing supersedes the terms set out earlier in preliminary negotiations. Exhibit 14.2 illustrates some of the limitations on the use of parol evidence.

Partial Integration

If a writing is intended to be the final statement of the parties' agreement but is incomplete, it is a *partially integrated* contract. Such a writing cannot be contradicted by evidence of earlier agreements or expressions, but it can be supplemented by evidence of additional, consistent terms. Perhaps Leighanne and the nursing home orally agreed that her personal physician (rather than the nursing home's) would provide needed medical care. If the parties leave out this provision, the contract represents a partially integrated writing. Since this provision does not appear to contradict the original agreement, some courts may allow the parties to add it later.

Sometimes the proponent of the parol evidence may acknowledge that there is one agreement but may argue that the parties intended to include only certain terms in the written contract. The proponent argues that it was their intent to leave the remaining terms "in parol." Courts may examine whether the subject matter of the parol evidence was mentioned at all in the contract. If it was, this strongly suggests that the writing was intended to cover that provision. The policy base that underlies the parol evidence rule is not *as* compelling in situations in which the contract is partially integrated (that is, incomplete). In such cases, although the writing may not be contradicted by evidence of earlier terms, it may be supplemented by evidence of additional, consistent terms.

The following example shows how the court may use the rules of integration and the rules of interpretation in resolving a conflict between two parties.

Julian is trying to buy a "fully equipped" car. He enters into a written contract with the dealer for the purchase. The contract specifies that the car will be "fully equipped" upon delivery. When the car is delivered, Julian notices that there is no air conditioning in the car. He complains to the dealer, insisting that a fully equipped car includes air conditioning. The dealer disagrees, stating that fully equipped does not refer to air conditioning. If the parties cannot settle this dispute informally, a court may be asked to settle the case. If the judge believes the writing was a partial integration, he or she will need to scrutinize the entire transaction, including

---

EXHIBIT 14.2 Limitations Imposed on Parol Evidence

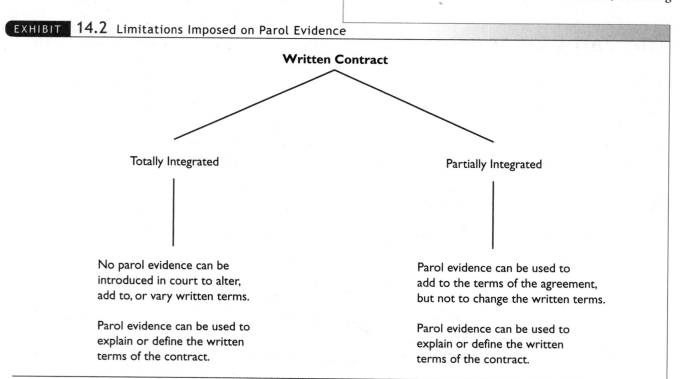

Written Contract

Totally Integrated

No parol evidence can be introduced in court to alter, add to, or vary written terms.

Parol evidence can be used to explain or define the written terms of the contract.

Partially Integrated

Parol evidence can be used to add to the terms of the agreement, but not to change the written terms.

Parol evidence can be used to explain or define the written terms of the contract.

the car salesperson's representations and Julian's expectations. If instead the court decides the writing was a full integration of the agreement, neither the salesperson's representations nor Julian's expectations will be considered. However, if the agreement is fully integrated, a judge may apply the standard of limited usage—the meaning of the term as understood locally and in the trade—to see whether a "fully equipped" car ordinarily includes air conditioning.

Note how the court applied the parol evidence rule and the rules of interpretation to the following case. Should the court have allowed an exception to the parol evidence rule in order to interpret the clause as requested?

Addition of Third Parties to the Contract

A contract affects the legal rights of the parties who directly enter into it. It may also influence the rights of other people. In some situations, these other people are so significant that they have legal rights under the contract and can file a lawsuit to enforce these contractual rights. In some situations, the third person is a significant party to the contract when the contract is initially formed; in others, the third person is added to the contract or affected by the contract at a later time. This next section of the chapter discusses what enforceable legal rights, if any, these third persons have under the contract.

14.1

BIONGHI v. METROPOLITAN WATER DISTRICT OF SOUTHERN CALIFORNIA
83 Cal. Rptr. 2d 388, 199 Cal. App. LEXIS 260 (C.A. 2d Dist. 1999)

FACTS Christina Bionghi, d.b.a. Abacus Technical (Abacus), entered into an integrated, consulting contract with Metropolitan Water District (MWD) in November 1993. Under the contract, Abacus would be paid up to $200,000 a year for providing temporary employees for MWD's Engineering Division. The contract included the provision that "The Agreement may be terminated by [the MWD] 30 days after notice in writing to Consultant of such termination. MWD's only obligation in the event of termination shall be payment for services provided by Consultant up to and including the effective date of termination." The contract was amended effective January 1, 1995, to increase the maximum allowable annual fee to $1,250,000. The amendment did not change the termination clause in the original contract.

Both the original and amended contracts included integration clauses. In the original agreement, the clause read, "It is understood that no alteration or variation of the terms of this Agreement shall be valid unless made in writing and signed by the parties hereto and that no oral understanding or agreements not incorporated herein shall be binding on any of the parties hereto." The amended agreement included a similar clause. Abacus did not dispute that it received 30 days notice.

ISSUE Is the contract reasonably susceptible to an interpretation requiring good cause for termination?

HOLDING No. This interpretation is not consistent with the meaning of the language used.

REASONING Excerpts from the opinion of Judge Armstrong:

[W]e conclude that the language used by the parties is not reasonably susceptible to that interpretation. However, we recognize . . . that the parties may have ascribed such a meaning to the words they used. . . . [T]he extrinsic evidence proffered by Abacus was not admissible here. "The parol evidence rule generally prohibits the introduction of any extrinsic evidence to vary or contradict the terms of an integrated written instrument. It is based upon the premise that the written instrument is the agreement of the parties. Its application involves a two-part analysis: 1) was the writing intended to be an integration, i.e., a complete and final expression of the parties' agreement, precluding any evidence of collateral agreements; and 2) is the agreement susceptible of the meaning contended for by the party offering the evidence? Here, the agreement was integrated. Since there is no dispute about that fact, we turn to the second part of the analysis: is the agreement reasonably susceptible of the meaning contended for by the party offering the evidence? . . . "Although extrinsic evidence is not admissible to add to, detract from, or vary the terms of a written contract, these terms must first be determined before it can be decided whether or not extrinsic evidence is being offered for a prohibited purpose. The fact that the terms of an instrument appear clear to a judge does not preclude the possibility that the parties chose the language of the instrument to express different terms. That possibility is not limited to contracts whose terms have acquired a particular meaning by trade usage, but exists whenever the parties' understanding of the words used may have differed from the judge's understanding. Accordingly, rational interpretation requires at least a preliminary consideration of all credible evidence offered to prove the intention of the parties. Such evidence includes testimony as to the 'circumstances surrounding the making of the agreement . . . including the object, nature and subject matter of the writing . . .' so that the court can 'place itself in the same situation in which the parties found themselves at the time of contracting.' If the court decides, after considering this evidence, that the language of a contract, in the light of all the circumstances, 'is fairly susceptible of either one of the two interpretations contended for . . .' extrinsic evidence relevant to prove either of such meanings is admissible." . . .

[I]t calls for a two-step process. First, the court must determine whether the language of the contract is reasonably susceptible to the meanings urged by the parties. In so doing, the court must give consideration to any evidence offered to show that the parties' understanding of words used differed from the common understanding. If the court determines that the contract is reasonably susceptible of the meanings urged, extrinsic evidence relevant to prove the meaning agreed to by the parties is admissible. . . . [T]he termination clause is not on its face reasonably susceptible to meaning that there can be no termination except on good cause. . . . When Abacus's extrinsic evidence is considered as part of this preliminary step, . . . Abacus did not expose any ambiguity, or establish that the words of the contract were reasonably susceptible to the meaning it urged. The evidence offered by Abacus did not concern the "'circumstances surrounding the making of the agreement'" or allow a court to "'place itself in the same situation in which the parties found themselves at the time of contracting.'" Abacus did not offer evidence concerning either the negotiations, which took place before the contract was executed or the drafting process. . . . There was no evidence of the parties' discussion of the meaning of the termination clause as it is found in the contract . . . There was, in sum, no evidence of the situation the parties were in at the time of contracting. . . .

A good cause limit on the right to terminate is a significant contract term. In our view, a contract which provides that it may be terminated on specified notice cannot reasonably be interpreted to require good cause as well as notice for termination, unless extrinsic evidence establishes that the parties used the words in some special sense. Instead, such a contract allows termination with or without good cause. . . . "Testimony of intention which is contrary to a contract's express terms . . . does not give meaning to the contract: rather it seeks to substitute a different meaning." . . . In sum, the contract here was integrated and in unambiguous terms required only notice for termination. . . . [P]arol evidence was not admissible to prove the terms of the contract. . . . [The California Supreme Court denied the appellant's petition for review, 1999 Cal. LEXIS 4533 (1999).]

BUSINESS CONSIDERATIONS Is it to a business's advantage to require cause to terminate a contract? Who benefits when "cause" is required? Who benefits when "cause" is not required? What should a business do to assure that extrinsic evidence is not introduced into contract disputes? Are "iron-clad" contracts possible?

ETHICAL CONSIDERATIONS When a firm is providing a quality service, is it ethical to terminate a contract with that firm? What ethical duty is owed to consultants? What duty is owed to other suppliers?

Third-Party Beneficiary Contracts

Persons and corporations who immediately receive rights in a contract to which they are not a party are called *beneficiaries*. It is really more appropriate to call this kind of beneficiary a *third person* because the additional person is *not* a party to the contract. However, we shall use the common terminology and refer to this person as a *third party*. In some circumstances the third person is *expected* to receive the benefits under the contract. These third persons are called "intended beneficiaries": they may be able to enforce the contract if the intended benefits are not conferred on them. In other circumstances the third person is not necessarily expected to receive any benefits under the contract.

Any benefits received by these third persons are incidental, or spillover, benefits. Such third persons do not have the right to enforce the contract if they never actually receive the benefits.

The two people who enter into the contract are commonly called the *promisor* and the *promisee*. The *promisor* is the party who promises to perform; the *promisee* is the party to whom that promise is made. A promisor may also be called an *obligor*, and a promisee may be called an *obligee*. Often, in third-party beneficiary contracts, the promise is to deliver goods to or perform a service directly for a third party. For example, Jane is very busy; to save time in shopping for a Father's Day present and mailing it to her father in St. Cloud, Minnesota, she orders a shirt from the Lands' End Web site to be gift wrapped and delivered to her father. This arrangement is a third-party beneficiary contract; her father is the third-party beneficiary. A beneficiary does not need to know about the contract for the contract to be valid.

Many businesses rely primarily on these contracts to achieve financial success. Examples include florist shops, singing telegram companies, mail-order companies that send fruit baskets, and life insurance companies.

Because these third parties are called beneficiaries, it is generally assumed that they receive something beneficial and good, but this is not always the case. In most states, the legal requirement for an *intended beneficiary* is that at least one of the contracting parties, usually the promisee, intended to have goods delivered to or services performed for the third party. The third party may not necessarily desire these goods or services. The beneficiary may, in fact, be displeased on receipt of the goods or services. An example is a singing telegram that embarrasses the recipient or is in poor taste. Some of these issues are addressed in "Third Party Beneficiaries," an article by Larry R. Leiby and David S. Hawkins that can be found at http://www.leibylaw. com/CM/ArticlesandForms/ArticlesandForms46.asp, the Leiby Taylor Stearns Linkhorst & Roberts, P.A. law firm Web site.

An Incidental Beneficiary

The most important factor in determining the rights of a third party is whether the third party is an intended or an incidental beneficiary. When at least one of the original parties to the contract *meant* to affect a noncontracting person by establishing the contract, the noncontracting person is an *intended beneficiary*. Intended beneficiaries have legal rights in the contract. If the benefit or action to the noncontracting party was *accidental*, or *not intended*, this party is an *incidental beneficiary*.

For example, suppose Rosalia, an owner of a vacant city lot, decides to build a high-rise garage on it. Rosalia enters into a contract with a builder to construct the garage. Luke owns the neighboring lot that has a high-rise office building on it; consequently Luke is likely to benefit financially from the construction of the garage. However, if the builder does not complete the construction job and Rosalia does not choose to sue for this breach of contract, Luke will not be able to sue to enforce the contract. In this situation Luke is an incidental beneficiary, because neither the builder nor Rosalia intended to benefit him. Consequently, he has no rights under the contract.

An Intended Beneficiary

An intended beneficiary does not have to be mentioned by name in the contract. It is sufficient for the parties to *clearly intend* to provide the beneficiary with rights under

the agreement. In the absence of a clear expression of such an intent, the contracting parties are presumed to act solely for themselves. Sometimes the intended beneficiary may be one person from a group of people for whose benefit the contract was established. Automobile liability insurance, for example, is a contract between an insurance company and an automobile owner, but insurance is also partially for the benefit of other drivers and pedestrians. These people, who share the road with the insured, would be intended beneficiaries in some states. (*Insureds* are persons or entities covered under an insurance policy.)

Suppose a legal environment professor signs a teaching contract with the university president. Do the students benefit from the employment contract? Of course they do. Are the students intended or incidental beneficiaries? They are one of the primary reasons for soliciting the faculty member's promise to teach, so the students are intended beneficiaries; they do not need to be listed in the contract. In fact, students may not even be specifically mentioned. However, both the faculty member and the university president know that students are one of the primary reasons for the employment contract. Students would be viewed as intended beneficiaries of such faculty contracts in most states. The legal relationships in this example are diagrammed in Exhibit 14.3.

The distinction between intended and incidental beneficiaries is discussed in the following case. See if you agree with the court's determination as to the status of the third-party beneficiaries.

A Donee Beneficiary

The type of relationship between the promisee and the third party may affect the rights of an intended third-party beneficiary. If the promisee means to make a gift to the third party, the third party is a *donee beneficiary*. Life insurance policies are excellent examples of third-party beneficiary contracts. If a husband purchases a $100,000 life insurance policy from Prudential Insurance Company of America and names his wife as the beneficiary, she is a donee beneficiary. The husband has no legal obligation to purchase this insurance. (He might be under a legal obligation to purchase life insurance under some marital contracts or divorce decrees, but this is uncommon.) He is, in reality, planning a gift to his wife that will take effect at his death. She is a donee beneficiary. A donee beneficiary example is shown in Exhibit 14.4 on page 332.

Prudential Insurance Company, the promisor, promises to deliver $100,000 to the promisee's wife if the promisee dies under situations covered by the policy. If Prudential refuses to pay, the wife may sue the company directly as an intended third party. Prudential (the promisor) can use the same legal defenses against the wife (the third party) as it

EXHIBIT 14.3 Intended Beneficiary

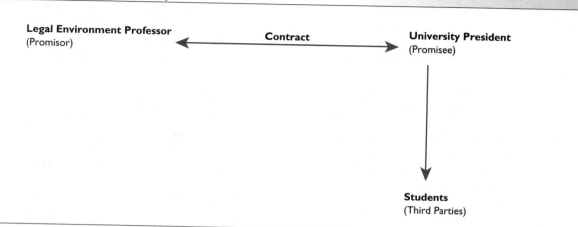

14.2

CHEN v. STREET BEAT SPORTSWEAR, INC.
2002 U.S. Dist. LEXIS 19652 (E.D. N.Y. 2002)

FACTS This suit arose out of violations of the minimum wage and overtime provisions of the Fair Labor Standards Act (FLSA) and New York Labor Law. The manufacturer defendants "hired, retained or contracted with the factory defendants" to produce their sportswear, providing them with garment designs, sewing instructions, textiles, and other materials. Approximately 90 percent of the garments made by the factory defendants were produced for the manufacturer defendants. The employees worked for the defendants from 1996 until 2000 as garment inspectors, hangers, button sewers, iron pressers, or general helpers. The employees worked seven days a week with only one or two days off a year. They often worked from early in the morning until past midnight and into the next morning. The employees were paid either by the piece or by the hour, and were never paid overtime wages. The workers were threatened with the loss of their jobs if they complained or did not comply with the work schedule. The defendants maintained false employment records in an effort to conceal their employment practices.

The manufacturer defendants, including Street Beat, knew or should reasonably have known that the employees were not paid minimum wage and overtime pay. Street Beat had a representative present in the factories about three times a week. Other factory workers had sued Street Beat earlier, and the U.S. Department of Labor (DOL) found that Street Beat had violated the FLSA in the past. On February 26, 1997, the manufacturer defendants signed a Memorandum of Agreement (MOA) with the DOL under which they entered into an ongoing Augmented Compliance Program Agreement (ACPA) to ensure factory compliance with the FLSA. The ACPA imposed several duties on the manufacturer defendants, including but not limited to (1) the precontract evaluation of the economic feasibility, based on the price involved, of a contractor's compliance with the FLSA; (2) the ongoing monitoring of contractor compliance with the FLSA; and (3) in the event that FLSA violations by a contractor were detected by the manufacturer, a suspension of shipment of all goods affected by the violations and payment of all unpaid back wages. The employees claimed that they were third-party beneficiaries to the DOL's contract with Street Beat, and that Street Beat materially beached the terms of that agreement.

ISSUE Are the employees intended beneficiaries of the contract between DOL and Street Beat?

HOLDING Yes. The employees are intended beneficiaries.

REASONING Excerpts from the opinion of Judge I. Leo Glasser:

In New York, a third-party may enforce a contract if that third-party is an intended beneficiary of the contract . . . . The applicable law provides that a non-party to a contract may recover "by establishing (1) the existence of a valid and binding contract between other parties, (2) that the contract was intended for his benefit, and (3) that the benefit to him is sufficiently immediate, rather than incidental, to indicate the assumption by the contracting parties to compensate him if the benefit is lost." . . . A contract is intended for the benefit of a third-party if (1) "no one other than the third party can recover if the promisor breaches the contract or (2) the language of the contract otherwise evidences an intent to permit enforcement by third parties." . . . An intention to benefit a third-party may be gleaned from the contract as a whole and the party need not be named specifically as a beneficiary. . . . [T]he first element with respect to enforcement by third-parties is satisfied because the agreement between the DOL and Street Beat is a valid and binding contract between parties other than the plaintiffs. . . . Based on the language of the agreement . . . , it is strikingly obvious that the entire purpose of the ACPA is to ensure that employees of factories which contract with Street Beat are paid minimum wage and overtime, and that it was they who were directly intended to be benefited. . . . Street Beat entered into the agreement with the DOL to "promote compliance . . . with Section 15(a)(1) of the [FLSA]." Section 15(a) states in pertinent part: "it shall be unlawful for any person . . . to transport, offer for transportation, ship, deliver, or sell in commerce . . . any goods in the production of which any employee was employed in violation . . . of this title." Section 206 of the FLSA provides for minimum wage payments, and Section 207 provides for overtime compensation. . . .

[T]he ACPA explains from the onset, . . . that its purpose is to ensure that factories hired by Street Beat . . . pay their employees minimum wage and overtime. . . . Section 3 [of the ACPA] describes the procedures by which Street Beat agreed to evaluate a potential factory in determining whether to engage in business with that factory. . . . Street Beat must review with the owner of the factory the terms and purposes of the Employer Compliance Program (ECP) and the ACPA; the economic feasibility of the price terms that are involved, in light of compliance with the FLSA; the factory's willingness and ability to fully understand and fully comply with the FLSA; and the obligation of the factory to advise the manufacturer when and if it is unable to meet the requirements of the FLSA. [ECP is a contract between the factory and the manufacturer that obligates the factory to comply with FLSA.] Section 3 further requires that Street Beat document its findings. . . . Street Beat must decline to engage in business with any

factory if Street Beat's evaluation discloses an unreasonable risk that the FLSA will not be complied with. Section 4 states that Street Beat will monitor and enforce full compliance with the FLSA and the ECP . . . and Section 5 describes Street Beat's record keeping obligations of all of its purchases. Section 6 outlines the duties and steps Street Beat must take when it discovers that a factory has failed to comply with the FLSA. . . . Street Beat must notify the DOL, and may be required to provide the DOL with a report, including copies of payroll records for each week the violations occurred, a certification from the factory that the records are accurate, copies of employee paystubs, and copies of payroll checks. . . .

Section 8 outlines the procedures for payment of back wages to the employees of contracting factories. . . . [T]he ACPA specifically provides that Street Beat will pay back wages to employees of contractors who engage in business with Street Beat and who violate the FLSA. Thus, recognizing "a right to performance in the beneficiary," the ACPA evidences an intent to benefit employees . . . Street Beat entered into the MOA as a means of resolving prior complaints . . . Section 9 describes the remedial process for contractor violations, and states . . . that the DOL and Street Beat will attempt to reach an agreement on the total amount to be paid to the affected employees, but, in the absence of a prompt agreement, the DOL will decide the proper amount on its own. . . . [A]n intent to benefit the plaintiffs may otherwise be gleaned from the contract as a whole. . . . Moreover, while Section 10 provides that Street Beat's compliance with the ACPA are [sic] subject to specific performance at the instance of the DOL, this statement does not necessarily preclude enforcement by persons other than the DOL. The manifest purpose of the ACPA is to benefit employees of factories . . . by ensuring that factory workers are paid minimum wage and overtime as required by the FLSA. The plaintiffs in this case are exactly those persons whom the ACPA was intended to benefit. Thus, the plaintiffs may sue on the contract for an alleged breach committed by Street Beat. . . .

BUSINESS CONSIDERATIONS How could Street Beat have prevented this situation? Did the DOL intend to benefit the employees? Did Street Beat?

ETHICAL CONSIDERATIONS Did the defendants treat the employees in an ethical manner? Why?

can against the husband (the promisee). These defenses might include lack of capacity to enter into a contract, lack of mutual assent, illegality in the contract, mistake in contract formation, fraudulent statements about the promisee's health, an improperly formed contract, or can-

cellation of the policy. The promisor would not be obligated to make a payment if the cause of death is excluded by the terms of the contract. In addition, the courts usually disallow recovery by the beneficiary if the promisee failed to perform his or her duty under the contract.[2]

EXHIBIT 14.4 Donee Beneficiary

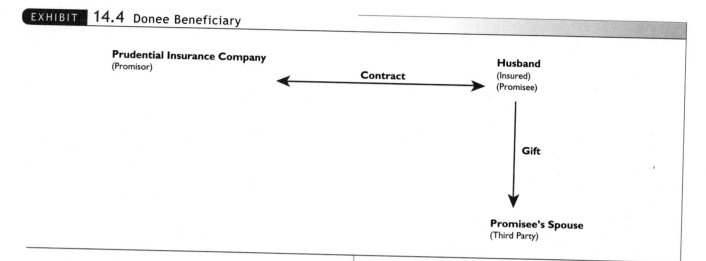

Prudential Insurance Company
(Promisor)

← **Contract** →

Husband
(Insured)
(Promisee)

Gift

↓

Promisee's Spouse
(Third Party)

According to the law in some states, the donee beneficiary's rights cannot be terminated after the contract is made. However, the promisee can still defeat the rights of the donee beneficiary by not performing his or her contractual obligations.[3] In other states, the beneficiary's rights are limited to situations in which the beneficiary knows about the contract and has accepted it verbally or by reliance on its terms. If the beneficiary has accepted the contract, the beneficiary has a vested interest in it. (A *vested interest* is a fixed interest or right to something, even though actual possession may be postponed until later.) In these states, a beneficiary with a vested interest must consent before there can be an effective rescission of the contract. This rule applies to both donee and creditor beneficiaries. (A *creditor beneficiary* is a third party who is entitled to performance because the promisee owes him or her a contractual duty.) Even so, a donee beneficiary cannot prevent the promisee from taking some action that will defeat the rights of the donee beneficiary; for example, breaching the contract by refusing to pay for the goods or services.

A Creditor Beneficiary

The third party is a *creditor beneficiary* if the promisee owes a legal duty to the third party that is being satisfied by the contract. In a contract between a university president and a professor for teaching services, the third-party beneficiaries are students. The students are creditor beneficiaries. This is true even at state-supported universities where tuition payments constitute only a portion of the cost of offering classes.

Another excellent example involves a life insurance policy. A working couple wishes to purchase a house with a $100,000 mortgage. The bank is willing to lend them $100,000 based on the value of the home and both of their salaries. Since the bank feels that the husband cannot afford the monthly payments without his wife's salary, the bank makes the loan contingent on the purchase of mortgage insurance on her life. (*Mortgage insurance* is insurance that will provide funds to pay the mortgage balance on a home if the insured dies.) She agrees to purchase a $100,000 mortgage insurance policy from Metropolitan Life Insurance Company. The bank is a creditor beneficiary. This arrangement is diagrammed in Exhibit 14.5.

If the wife dies during the term of the mortgage, the bank is entitled to sue Metropolitan directly on the insurance contract if Metropolitan refuses to pay. Metropolitan can use any defenses that it had against the wife as defenses against the bank. A third party cannot successfully claim any better rights than those provided in the contract.

If the wife tries to cancel the policy, the bank can successfully sue the wife. Canceling the insurance policy and not replacing it is a breach of the contract. The bank, however, will probably allow the wife to substitute another policy from a different insurance company if the coverage is essentially the same. In practice, if the bank does not trust the wife to make the premium payments, the bank will require her to make the payments through the bank; then, it will be assured that the premium payments are made in a timely manner.

The differences between donee and creditor beneficiaries are not significant. They both have basically the same rights against the promisor. A third party cannot successfully claim any better rights than those provided in the contract. Although many states say that the rights of a creditor beneficiary are directly derived from the promisee, courts usually provide the same type of protection for the donee beneficiary as they do for the creditor beneficiary. The only real differences are their rights against the promisee, and even these

EXHIBIT 14.5 Creditor Beneficiary

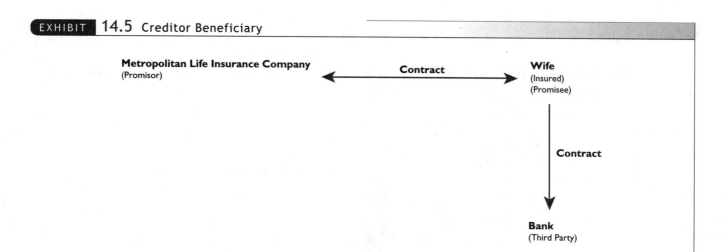

differences are becoming less pronounced. The distinction between creditor and donee beneficiaries is excluded from the Restatement (Second) of Contracts,[4] which relies solely on the distinction between intended and incidental beneficiaries. The American Law Institute publishes Restatements of the Law, some model codes, and other proposals for legal reform. Its Web site includes press releases about its activities and annual reports. It can be accessed at http://www.ali.org. The donee/creditor distinction is also beginning to disappear in some states, such as California.[5]

Analysis of Third-Party Beneficiary Contracts

In analyzing a situation involving a potential third party, the following questions should be addressed:

- Was the additional person involved from the beginning, or was that person added later?

- Did the promisee intend to benefit the third party, or was it an accident?

- Was the promisee making a gift to the third party, or was the promisee fulfilling a contract obligation to the third party?

Defining Assignments and Delegations

If the third person becomes involved after the initial contract formation, that person is *not* a third-party beneficiary. Instead, the relationship may be an assignment or a delega-

tion. To understand the distinction between assignments and delegations, remember the distinction between rights and duties. *Contractual rights* are the parts of the contract a person is entitled to *receive*. Examples include delivery of goods, payment for goods, payment for work completed, and discounts for early payment. Payments owed to car dealers, mortgage companies, finance companies, and collection agencies are rights that are commonly assigned.

Contractual duties are the parts of the contract a person is obligated to *give*. Duties include working an eight-hour day, paying 15 percent interest on credit card charges, and providing repair services. A common example is a general contractor who subcontracts certain duties of a construction job, such as installing the roof. Rights can be assigned, and duties can be delegated. This may be confusing because judges and lawyers are sometimes careless in their use of terminology; however, duties *cannot* be assigned. A common example is a document that states "I assign all my rights and duties in the April 8 note with Gerald Weichmann." The rules of law dealing with delegation will be applied to any attempts to "assign" contractual duties.

Assignments

An *assignment* occurs when a person transfers a contractual right to someone else. The transferor is called the *assignor*, and the recipient is called the *assignee*. The assignor "loses" the contractual right when the right is transferred to another party. The assignor's right has been extinguished, and now it belongs exclusively to the assignee. (*Extinguished* means destroyed or wiped out.) The other party to the original contract, the promisor, now has to deliver the promised goods or services to the assignee. The assignee is

NRW CASE 14.1 Management/Manufacturing

LIABILITY FOR DAMAGES IN SHIPPING

NRW placed an order for 10,000 specialized computer chips from Salma Systems, a manufacturer in Palo Alto, California. NRW was a bit concerned because this was the first time NRW had ordered computer chips from Salma Systems, and the miniaturized computer chips are the most delicate component of the StuffTrakR system. Salma Systems packed the computer chips in two sturdy cardboard boxes, with foam pads between the layers to cushion them. Salma Systems then contracted with Vicente's Trucking to deliver the two boxes to NRW. When the boxes were delivered three weeks later, there was substantial damage to both of the boxes and their contents. NRW believes that the chips were in good condition when Salma Systems sent them, and that the damages occurred during the transportation of the computer chips. They have asked you who is responsible for the damaged goods. What will you tell them?

BUSINESS CONSIDERATIONS What steps could Salma Systems have taken to further reduce the risk of loss? How might Vicente's Trucking and NRW have reduced the risk of loss? How could/should NRW protect its interests in future situations like this one?

ETHICAL CONSIDERATIONS Do Salma Systems and Vicente's Trucking owe NRW ethical obligations in addition to their legal obligations? Why or why not?

INTERNATIONAL CONSIDERATIONS Would the situation change if Salma Systems were headquartered in England, with its manufacturing plant outside London? Is risk of loss treated differently in international shipments of goods than in domestic shipments of goods?

the only party entitled to them. For example, Mira (a tenant) rents a house from Susan (a landlord). Under the terms of the lease, Mira must pay $400 per month for rent. Susan is in default on a small business loan obtained from the bank and assigns the $400 per month rent payment to the bank. Therefore, Susan (the assignor) has relinquished the legal right to the money—that right now belongs exclusively to the assignee, the bank. This situation is diagrammed in Exhibit 14.6. Assignments do not need to take any particular form. Home Business Online, provided

by The Advantage Corporation, has many free legal forms at its Web site at http://www.homebusinessonline.com/a&r/elibrary/legal/index.shtml/. The forms include many types of assignments, for example, assignments of leases and mortgages. The 'Lectric Law Library's business forms also include a variety of assignments for personal and business use. Their Web site is at http://www.lectlaw.com/formb.htm.

Formalities Required for Assignments

Generally, an assignment does not have to follow any particular format. Assignors must use words that indicate an intent to vest a present contract right in the assignee. This means that the assignor intends to transfer the right immediately, not at some time in the future. However, this does not mean that the word *assignment* must be used. A writing is not required unless the state Statute of Frauds applies. This includes the Statute of Frauds' provisions in the UCC as adopted by the individual state. As with other contractual provisions, it is preferable to reduce the assignment to writing. The assignment must contain an adequate description of the rights being assigned.

Consideration, consisting of a bargained-for exchange and a legal detriment (or benefit) for both parties, is *not* required in order to have a valid assignment. (Consideration is discussed in detail in Chapter 11.) Although the assignee need not give up consideration in exchange for the contract right, consideration is generally present. The existence of consideration affects the legal relationship between the assignor and the assignee—that relationship can be either a contract or a gift. However, the relationship is generally a contract, especially in business settings. In our earlier example, Susan (the landlord) assigns the payments to the bank so that the bank will not sue her or take other action to collect. People in business are not in the habit of making gifts to other businesspeople. A gift assignment occurs, for example, when Bradley, a sales representative for a computer company, assigns the 10 percent Christmas bonus he earns to his eldest daughter, Brande, for her college education fund.

Notice of the Assignment

Because an assignment extinguishes the assignor's rights and creates rights only for the assignee, one would assume that the person obligated to perform must be told about the assignment. Surprisingly, this is not a legal requirement; an assignment is perfectly valid even though the person obligated to perform is never informed. An assignee may *want* to give notice to the promisor for a number of reasons, particularly if the assignor is potentially unethical or dishonest.

EXHIBIT 14.6 Assignment

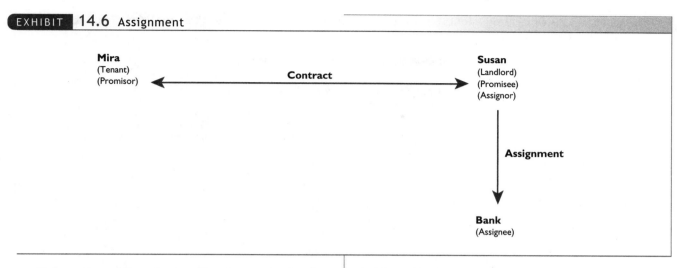

If the person obligated to perform *has* received notice of the assignment and then pays the assignor or delivers performance to the assignor, the person will still be obligated to pay or deliver performance to the assignee. In many instances, the promisor is not told about the assignment, and the assignor receives the performance and then transfers it to the assignee. Suppose the promisor has not been given notice and delivers performance to the assignor, and the assignor does not transfer it to the assignee; then the assignee will be limited to taking action against the assignor. This will be the result even if the assignor has absconded with the funds.

In some cases, assignors have profited by selling the *same* contract right to more than one assignee through mistake, negligence, or fraud. Of course, if the second assignee has notice or knowledge of the prior assignment, that person will receive the assignment *subject* to the rights of the first assignee. In many cases, however, the second assignee lacks notice. If the first assignment is revocable, the fact that a second assignment has occurred still presents a relatively simple problem. Since the first assignment was revocable, the second assignment merely revokes the first.

However, a second assignment presents a much more difficult problem in a few situations. If the second assignee (1) does not know about the first assignment and (2) does not take the assignment subject to the first assignment, and the first assignment is not revocable; then a situation may exist in which two (or more) assignees each believe that he or she will receive the complete performance from the promisor. In these situations a dishonest assignor deceives one or more assignees, usually for the monetary benefit of the assignor.

Of course, dishonest assignors generally disappear with the funds and leave the innocent assignees to resolve their conflicting claims. What are these innocent assignees'

rights under these circumstances? Two broad theories are widely used by the courts to resolve these problems. The first of these theories is based on the belief that the first assignee to receive the assignment receives all the rights; after the first assignment has been made the assignor has nothing left to assign to later assignees. This theory is usually called the *American Rule* or the *first-in-time approach.* The *New York Rule* is a variation of the first-in-time approach and is applied in some states.

For example, if Anita, the promisee, assigns her rights to Joel for value on January 1 and then assigns these same rights to Larry for value on January 15, Joel will receive the rights according to the American rule. The same results are likely to occur under the New York Rule variation. There are two primary exceptions where the first assignee will not "win": (1) if the first assignment is revocable, like an undelivered gift; or (2) if the first assignee fails to obtain documents evidencing the assignment, thus enabling the assignor to "transfer" the rights to a second assignee.

Closely related to the New York Rule is the *Massachusetts Rule,* which is another slightly different first-in-time approach. Under this rule, the first assignee also has priority if the first assignment is not revocable. However, the second assignee will have the priority if the second assignee acquires the assignment in *good faith, for value,* and does any *one* of the following:

1. obtains payment from the promisor,

2. recovers a judgment against the promisor,

3. obtains the promisor's promise to pay the assignee instead of the assignor, or

4. receives delivery of tangible evidence representing the claim.

See Exhibit 14.7, which describes the first-in-time approach.

EXHIBIT 14.7 Multiple Assignments of the Same Rights: The First-in-Time Approach (American Rule)

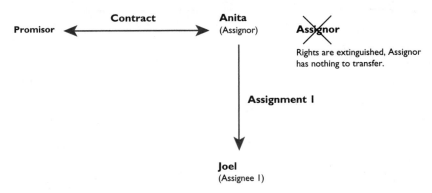

The first assignee takes the rights unless Assignment I is revocable.

Promisor ⟷ **Contract** ⟷ Anita (Assignor)   ~~Assignor~~

Rights are extinguished, Assignor has nothing to transfer.

Assignment I

Joel (Assignee I)

New York Rule
Additional exception: Assignee 1 fails to obtain documents evidencing Assignment 1.

Massachusetts Rule
Assignee 2 will have priority if Assignee 2 obtains the Assignment in good faith, for value, and does one of the following: obtains payment from Promisor, recovers a judgment against Promisor, obtains Promisor's promise to pay, OR receives tangible evidence of the claim.

The American rule and its variations make sense, but neither the basic rule nor either of its variations have been adopted by every state. While many states do follow the American rule, other states apply the rule that the first assignee to actually give notice to the promisor receives the right. This is called the *first-to-give-notice approach* or the *English Rule*, which is followed in California, Florida, and a few other states. In the prior example, if Larry gives notice to the promisor first, he will prevail under the English Rule, provided he takes for value without notice of the prior assignment to Joel. One of the policies underlying this rule is that a prudent assignee, one who is about to pay value for the assignment, will check with the person obligated to perform. The promisor, who has notice of earlier assignments, will tell the prospective purchaser, and this information will prevent additional assignments. The advantage of giving notice should be obvious, especially under the English Rule. Exhibit 14.8 illustrates the first-to-give notice approach.

Under each of these rules of law, the assignor who makes multiple assignments is likely to be held liable for fraud and each of the injured parties can collect his or her damages from the assignor, *if* the assignor can be located, and *if* the assignor still has any assets. (Similar policy problems arise when multiple security interests are created in the same property or there are multiple transfers of the same property.) However, there is nothing inappropriate if a promisee (assignor) divides up the contract rights and assigns *different* contract rights to different assignees. For example, a landlord may assign the January and February rent payments to one assignee and the remaining rent payments to another.

Assignable Rights

Assignments have become an important aspect of our business and financial structure. They are useful techniques for marketing goods and improving cash flow. A common business practice among retail outlets is to sell expensive items on time. The retailer assigns the monthly payments to a credit corporation in exchange for cash, and then uses the cash to buy more merchandise. A simple example of this practice occurs when a buyer purchases an automobile financed through a car dealership. Because of the importance of assignments in commercial transactions, courts are generally predisposed to allow assignments. This favorable perspective is obvious in the courts' treatment of contract assignments. Assignments do not require the approval of the promisor. Even when the promisor objects to the assignment in court, the court will still generally allow it.

To prevent an attempted assignment, the promisor must prove to the court that at least one of the following conditions will exist if the assignment is allowed:

EXHIBIT 14.8 Multiple Assignments of the Same Rights: The First-to-Give Notice Approach (English Rule)

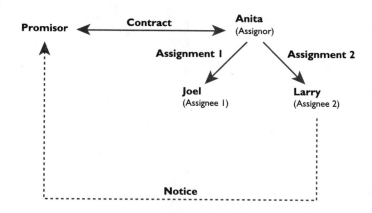

- The assignment will materially change the duty of the promisor.

- The assignment will materially impair the chance of return performance or reduce its value.

- The assignment will materially increase the burden or risk imposed by the contract.

Basically, the promisor must convince the court that he or she will be in a substantially worse position if the assignment is allowed. These requirements are discussed in the Restatement (Second) of Contracts in § 317(2) and are also included in § 2-210(2) of the UCC. These provisions are applicable unless the language of the contract provides otherwise or the assignment is forbidden by statute or is against public policy.

When the promisor is asserting that the assignment materially changes the promisor's duty, the promisor is claiming that he or she will be required to perform a substantially different type or degree of work if the assignment is allowed. Many assignments involve assigning monthly payments. Because this simply requires that the promisor change the address on the payment envelopes, the promisor's duty is not substantially different following the assignment. As an example of a substantially different duty, suppose that Thad (a promisor) agrees to paint the exterior of any one house for $1,200, and he makes this promise to Lynda, who owns a 1,000-square-foot single-level house. Lynda enters into a contract with Thad and then assigns the right to Joanne, who owns a 2,500-square-foot two-story house. Thad might convince the court that this assignment materially affects his duty. However, it is unwise for a promisor to enter into a contract that is ambiguous. Generally, a house painter like Thad will provide a bid that specifies a particular house address to avoid this type of problem.

If the assignment impairs the risk of return performance, it increases the chance that the promisor will not receive consideration from the promisee. For example, Chris wants to have her portrait painted; she locates a talented but struggling artist, Arturo, to paint the portrait for $200. Arturo explains that he needs the money to buy canvas and quality oil paint. Chris agrees to pay him the money on the first of the month, and Arturo is to start the portrait on the 15th. Later, however, Arturo wants to assign that payment to his landlord for unpaid rent. Consequently, Chris may convince the court that allowing this assignment will impair her chance of receiving the portrait since Arturo will still need supplies.

An assignment will not be allowed if it increases the risk or burden of the contract. If Arturo, the artist, tries to assign only $150 of the payment to his landlord, Chris might be able to convince the court that this assignment increases the burden or risk imposed by their contract, because Arturo might purchase inferior materials.

Not all types of assignments are favored. Some types of assignments are considered less desirable and are limited by state law. Common examples are prohibitions or limitations on the assignment of wages. Statutes in Alabama, California, Connecticut, the District of Columbia, Missouri, and Ohio generally prohibit the assignment of future wages. In addition, California, Connecticut, and many other states have special rules that apply to assignments of wages as security for small loans.[6] Recently the legislatures and the courts have also been scrutinizing assignments of post-loss insurance payments. (*Post-loss* means after loss. These are obligations of insurance companies after a covered loss has actually occurred.)

NRW CASE 14.2   Finance

ACCEPTING ACCOUNTS RECEIVABLE AS PAYMENT OF DEBT

All Electronics, Inc. (AEI) is one of NRW's major retail distributors in Chicago. AEI has been suffering financial difficulties for over a year and currently owes NRW $65,000 for StuffTrakR inventory that it has already received. This $65,000 is 90 days past due, which causes Helen some anxiety. AEI has $40,000 in accounts receivable, most of which are current (not past due). AEI has suggested that it transfer its own accounts receivable to NRW. AEI would prefer to do this to discharge its entire obligation, but if this proposal is not acceptable to NRW, then AEI would, at least, like to transfer the accounts as partial payment of the obligation. Mai, Carlos, and Helen have never before accepted another firm's accounts receivable as payment, and they are unsure of the legal implications of doing so. They ask you for advice. What will you tell them?

BUSINESS CONSIDERATIONS In order to decide if this is a sound business decision, what information should NRW obtain? What are the legal and business consequences of such an arrangement? What would be NRW's position if it accepted the transfer?

ETHICAL CONSIDERATIONS Evaluate AEI's ethical perspective as it relates to this series of transactions.

INTERNATIONAL CONSIDERATIONS If AEI were a foreign company, would this change the situation? Do other legal systems allow assignments as readily as the U.S. legal system does?

Contract Clauses Restricting Assignments

Another example of court behavior that favors assignments is the way courts interpret language in the original promisor/promisee contract. Even if the contract states that "no assignment shall be made" or that "there shall be no assignment without the prior consent of the promisor," many courts will still allow the assignment. Courts *may* interpret these clauses as promises or covenants not to assign the rights. The assignor is then held legally responsible for making the assignment and must pay the promisor for any loss caused by the assignment. Often the promisor cannot prove any loss in court, so this is a rather hollow right. These clauses can also be interpreted by courts as preventing the transfer of the contract duties. This latter approach is followed by § 2-210(3) of the UCC. If the contracting parties really want to prevent assignments, they must use clauses such as "all assignments shall be void" or "any attempt at assignment shall be null and void." Most courts will interpret this language as actually removing the power to make assignments.

In the following case, the court addressed the validity of an antiassignment clause. Note that the court focused on the public policy against assignments in this situation, instead of the language used in the contracts.

Warranties Implied by the Assignor

An assignor who makes an assignment for value implies that certain things are true about the assigned rights. These implied warranties exist without any action by the assignor. The assignor's knowledge of the warranties is not required. The warranties include the following: (1) the right is a valid legal right and actually exists; (2) there are no valid defenses or limitations to the assigned right that are not specifically stated or apparent; and (3) the assignor will not do anything to defeat or impair the value of the assignment. These warranties need not be expressly stated but, instead, can be implied. If the assignor breaches the warranties, the assignee can successfully sue. The assignor and assignee may expressly agree to limit or exclude warranties.

Rights Created by the Assignment

An assignee obtains the same legal rights in the contract that the assignor had. If the assignee sues the promisor, the promisor generally may use the same defenses against the assignee as were available against the assignor. Examples of these defenses would include fraud, duress, undue influence, and breach of contract by the assignor. The promisor will not, however, be able to use every conceivable defense against an assignee.

Waiver of Defenses Clause

A waiver of defenses clause in a contract attempts to give the assignee better legal rights than the assignor had. Often such a clause is part of a standard printed contract prepared by the assignee or assignor and signed by the promisor. Generally, the promisor (buyer) is not aware that the contract contains a waiver of defenses clause or does not understand what it means. In the clause, the promisor promises to give up legal defenses in any later lawsuit by the

14.3

SOMERSET ORTHOPEDIC ASSOCIATES, P.A. v. HORIZON BLUE CROSS AND BLUE SHIELD OF NEW JERSEY
345 N.J. Super. 410, 2001 N.J. Super. LEXIS 437 (Superior Ct. App. Div. 2001)

FACTS Paul Vessa, M.D., and his medical practice, Somerset Orthopedic Associates, sought to invalidate an antiassignment provision in health care contracts issued by defendant Horizon Blue Cross and Blue Shield. Horizon is a nonprofit health service corporation authorized and established under the Health Service Corporations Act of New Jersey. Upon payment of a periodic premium, Horizon agrees to pay a certain amount for described health care services contracted for by the subscriber. Horizon provides health benefits through a network of medical providers who have contractually agreed to participate in Horizon's program and render services to subscribers. These providers are called "participating" providers. The contracts between Horizon and the participating providers require the providers to accept set amounts for specified services as payment in full. Horizon is required to pay each participating provider directly.

Nonparticipating providers have not entered into contracts with Horizon to accept agreed-upon payments as payment in full. When a nonparticipating provider performs services, payment may be made by Horizon directly to the subscriber. All Horizon insurance contracts contain an antiassignment provision. In all these contracts, Horizon has preserved its discretionary right to not accept assignment of benefits. A typical clause in such contracts provides: "No assignment or transfer by You of any of Your interest under this Policy is valid unless We consent thereto. However, We may, in Our discretion, pay a Provider directly for services rendered to You."

Plaintiffs were nonparticipating providers who provided health care to a number of patients insured by Horizon. Plaintiffs took assignments of Horizon benefits and submitted them to Horizon for payment. Horizon refused to pay plaintiffs directly, but instead sent payment to the subscriber.

ISSUE Should the court enforce the nonassignment clause or is it contrary to New Jersey law?

HOLDING Yes, the clause should be enforced based on public policy.

REASONING Excerpts from the opinion of Judge Anthony J. Parillo:

It has been long held that any beneficial contract may be assigned, and courts of law will protect the rights of the assignee. . . . [T]he rule is not absolute. Where a contract uses specific and express language sufficiently manifesting an intention to prohibit the power of assignment without the consent of one or more of the contracting parties, courts generally uphold these . . . clauses. . . . [A]lthough the free assignment of . . . [contract rights] may be a valuable goal of public policy, it will not override competing, superior public interests. . . . [T]he validity of anti-assignment clauses in group health care contracts has been upheld almost uniformly in the courts of other states. . . . [T]hese cases conclude that such clauses "are valuable tools in persuading health [care] providers to keep their costs down." . . . [T]hese cases have held that the purported assignment of benefits to a nonparticipating medical provider, in the face of an anti-assignment clause . . . , is void and unenforceable. . . .

New Jersey has adopted the standard advocated by the *Restatement (Second) of Contracts*. Section 317 recognizes the validity of assignments, but specifically identifies important exceptions that limit the assignability of contractual rights:

> (2) A contractual right can be assigned unless
>
> > (a) the substitution of a right of the assignee for the right of the assignor would materially change the duty of the obligor, or materially increase the burden or risk imposed on him by his contract, or materially impair his chance of obtaining return performance, or materially reduce its value to him, or
> >
> > (b) the assignment is forbidden by statute or is otherwise inoperative on grounds of public policy, or
> >
> > (c) [the] assignment is validly precluded by contract.

. . . [A] clear legislative intent allowing such anti-assignment clauses may be . . . gleaned from the overall statutory scheme under which Horizon was established . . . Horizon is a non-profit, tax-exempt corporation operated for the benefit of its subscribers and invested with a public interest. . . . Under the Act, Horizon continues to carry out the essentially public mission . . . of providing available and affordable health insurance to a broad-based community. . . . [T]he Legislature expressly contemplated an in-network of participating medical providers who agree to negotiate pre-arranged costs in exchange for direct payment . . . [F]reedom of choice in selecting physicians was preserved for subscribers who receive . . . reimbursement for payments made by the subscriber to a non-participating medical provider . . . [T]he Legislature recognized . . . the significance of creating a network of participating medical providers and its critical role in the success of this venture. . . . Horizon's ability to control costs and . . . provide affordable health care coverage is directly related to the number of medical providers participating in its program. . . . [I]nherent in its statutory mandate to control costs is a directive to Horizon to encourage broad participation [by] . . . medical providers. . . . [N]on-profit health service corporations . . . rely on anti-assignment clauses as an important inducement to medical providers to join their insurance networks. Obviously, medical providers would have less reason to join if non-participating physicians could garner the same advantages without subjecting themselves to the contractual constraints. . . . This clear expression of legislative intent not only has been recognized by courts of other states interpreting similar legislative schemes, but also within New Jersey's own regulatory structure, as evidenced by the executive department's approval of forms of policies containing the very anti-assignment clauses at issue here. We may infer from such approval that these . . . clauses comport with both the statutory language and the legislative intent . . . We . . . hold that the anti-assignment clause in Horizon's . . . contracts is valid and enforceable. . . .

BUSINESS CONSIDERATIONS Why did Somerset Orthopedic Associates accept the patients' assignments? Why did Horizon refuse to pay Somerset Orthopedic Associates?

ETHICAL CONSIDERATIONS Was it ethical for patients (subscribers) to assign their medical payments to non-participating providers? Why? Was it ethical for nonparticipating providers to accept the assignments and try to collect from Horizon?

assignee. In other words, the promisor agrees not to exert defenses such as fraud in the inducement or breach of warranty against any subsequent assignees. Exhibit 14.9 shows the effect on the promisor/assignee relationship of a valid waiver of defenses clause.

If the waiver of defenses clause is effective, it reduces the promisor's bargaining power. For example, if a purchaser buys a product on time and the product is defective, a common reaction is to stop making payments. A waiver of defenses clause means that the buyer must continue to make the payments.

Consumer groups and government agencies have often opposed waiver of defenses clauses because they reduce a consumer's bargaining power. Such a clause is generally enforceable under § 9-206(1) of the UCC, unless the particular state has a different rule under statutes or court decisions for buyers or lessees of consumer goods. Under the UCC, the assignee is subject to the same defenses as a holder in due course of a negotiable instrument. Some states, including Alaska, Missouri, Ohio, Washington, and the District of Columbia, have statutes that forbid or limit these clauses.[7] The Federal Trade Commission enacted a regulation barring these agreements in contracts by consumers.[8]

Delegations

Assignments and delegations may occur simultaneously. However, it is easier to understand delegations if they are analyzed as independent transfers. In fact, they are completely separate concepts that can and do occur independently. In a *delegation*, the promisor locates a new promisor to perform the duties under the contract. The original promisor is called the delegator, and the new promisor is called the delegatee. For example, suppose Cruz buys a new automobile from a Hyundai dealer. One of the terms of that contract is a promise by the dealer to provide certain warranty work on the car for three years. Later, Carmen, the mechanic employed by the Hyundai dealer, quits, and the dealer contracts with a garage to do the warranty work. This particular delegation is illustrated in Exhibit 14.10. As with assignments, there may be consideration for the delegation, but it is not necessary. If no consideration exists, the delegation is really a gift from the new promisor to the old promisor.

The purchaser of the car (Cruz) can sue the car dealer who made the promise if the warranty work is not performed. The purchaser can also generally sue the garage for failure to perform. In many states, the purchaser can sue both the dealer (delegator) and the garage (delegatee) at the same time, but the courts will allow the purchaser to collect only once.

The relationship between the delegator and the delegatee may be that of a contract or of a gift. If a contract relationship is present, the delegator has the right to sue the delegatee for nonperformance. If a gift relationship is present, the court would hold that the delegatee promised to make a gift in the future but failed to deliver it. Generally, promises to make gifts in the future are not enforceable without promissory estoppel. (*Promissory estoppel* is the

EXHIBIT **14.9** Comparison of the Contract Rights of the Assignor and the Assignee

CONTRACT WITHOUT A WAIVER OF DEFENSES CLAUSE	CONTRACT WITH A VALID WAIVER OF DEFENSES CLAUSE
A. Lawsuit by Assignor	A. Lawsuit by Assignor
Assignor ——✗——▶ Promisor (Defenses)	Assignor ——✗——▶ Promisor (Defenses)
B. Lawsuit by Assignee	B. Lawsuit by Assignee
Assignee ——✗——▶ Promisor (Defenses)	Assignee ——————▶ Promisor (Defenses ✗)

Legend

Plaintiff ——————▶ **Defendant**

——✗——▶ **Lawsuit will not be successful.**

Defe✗ses **Defenses will not be successful.**

(This exhibit assumes that the promisor has valid defenses that can be proven in court.)

doctrine used to enforce a gift promise based on the justifiable reliance of the promisee.)

Delegations do not occur unless the delegatee assumes the contract duties. This assumption can be either expressly stated or implied. The modern trend in court decisions is to imply the assumption of the duties, especially when there is both an assignment and a delegation. Implied assumption of duties is also supported by the Restatement (Second) of Contracts and the UCC. An example of this occurs when the parties state that there is an "assignment of the contract" or an "assignment of all my rights under the contract." Such statements are generally interpreted as indicating (1) an assignment, (2) a delegation of the duties

by the delegator, and (3) an acceptance of the duties by the delegatee unless there is a clear indication of a contrary intention. This position is followed by the UCC § 2-210(4) and the Restatement (Second) of Contracts § 328.

Delegations do not have the favored legal status that assignments do. Courts are more inclined to deny a delegation. If the contract between the promisor and the promisee states that "there shall be no delegations," the courts will prevent delegations. The same is true if the contract requires personal performance. Courts are also more likely to decide that a delegation is unfair to the promisee. Under the UCC § 2-210(1), duties cannot be delegated if the agreement states that there will be no delegation or the promisor has a sub-

EXHIBIT **14.10** Delegation

NRW CASE 14.3   Marketing/Finance

CREATING AUTHORIZED REPAIR CENTERS

StuffTrakR is sold to consumers with a 90-day warranty. Currently, consumers must send the units back to NRW for any necessary warranty work, including repair or replacement. Mai is thinking about identifying certain retailers who are selling StuffTrakR in large cities and designating them as "authorized NRW repair centers." Mai feels this arrangement will improve the marketability of StuffTrakR. However, Mai, Carlos, and Helen are concerned about how this might change their relationships with their distributors. They ask you about the legal and business effects of this decision. What do you tell them and why?

BUSINESS CONSIDERATIONS What are the business advantages of such an arrangement? What are the disadvantages? What types of legal arrangements could NRW have with authorized repair centers? What will be NRW's obligations under these arrangements? If you were assisting NRW in drafting these contracts, what provisions would you include and why?

ETHICAL CONSIDERATIONS Is it ethical to require an authorized repair center to also sell NRW products? Why or why not?

INTERNATIONAL CONSIDERATIONS Should NRW use the same repair system in foreign countries that it uses in the United States? Why or why not?

generally cannot be delegated. Section 2-210(3) of the UCC indicates that a contract clause that prohibits the assignment of "the contract" is to be construed as preventing only a delegation of the contract duties to the assignee.

Analysis of Assignments and Delegations

To characterize an assignment or a delegation situation, one should answer the following questions:

- Was the additional person involved from the beginning or added later?
- Did the additional person undertake to perform a contract duty or become entitled to a contract right? Or both?
- Did the language of the original contract prevent this transfer to an additional person?
- Did the type of rights or duties prevent this transfer to an additional person, because the transfer materially changes the rights or duties of a party?
- Is this transfer forbidden by state statute or public policy?

Uniform Commercial Code Provisions

When the UCC is applicable, businesspeople need to review UCC assignment and delegation provisions. Certain types of assignments are excluded from Article 9 by UCC § 9-104—for example, claims for wages, interests under an insurance policy, claims arising from the commission of a tort, and deposits in banks. Under § 9-201 and § 9-203 of the UCC, provisions of Article 9 may be subordinated to state statutes regulating installment sales to consumers. Section 2-210 of the Code covers assignments and delegations under contracts for the sale of goods. However, some questions concerning assignments are not resolved in either Article 2 or Article 9 of the UCC. (This is only a brief overview of the UCC's provisions.)

stantial interest in having the delegator perform the contract. The Restatement (Second) of Contracts § 318(2) states that delegations should not be allowed if the promisee has a substantial interest in having the delegator control or perform the acts promised. Consequently, personal service contracts

Summary

Interpretation is the process of determining the meaning of words and other manifestations of intent that the parties have used in forging their agreement. Certain standards and rules of interpretation have evolved, based on whether the contract is totally integrated or partially integrated. A totally integrated

contract represents the parties' final and complete statement of their agreement and cannot be contradicted. Similarly, a partially integrated contract is intended to be the parties' final statement, but it is incomplete. It may be supplemented with consistent, additional terms. The conduct of the parties and usage of trade may aid in contract interpretation. The parol evidence rule states that oral evidence is not admissible to alter, add to, or vary the terms of a totally integrated, written contract. If the contract is not totally integrated, the parol evidence rule is not applicable and such evidence is admissible to add to the terms. However, it still cannot be used to alter or to vary the written terms in the contract.

An additional person who is involved in a contract from the beginning may be a third-party beneficiary. If the promisor or promisee meant to affect the third person under the contract, that person will be an intended beneficiary and will have enforceable rights. Intended beneficiaries can file lawsuits to protect their own legal rights. If they sue the promisor, the promisor can use the same defenses that would be valid against the promisee. Creditor beneficiaries can sue a promisee who tries to cancel the contract. Donee beneficiaries generally will not be suc-

cessful in a suit against the promisee because legally the donee beneficiary did not receive the promised gift.

An additional party who becomes involved after the contract is formed may be an assignee or a delegatee. An assignee receives a contract right from the transferor. An assignment extinguishes the contract right of the assignor and sets up this contract right exclusively in the assignee. The assignee is now entitled to performance under the contract. The assignee does not have to notify the promisor of the assignment, but is better protected if he or she *does* give notice. This is especially important if the assignor makes multiple assignments of the same contract right.

In a delegation, a delegatee assumes the transferor's obligation to perform under the contract. The delegator will still be obligated to perform if the delegatee does not. Generally, courts will respect contract clauses that state that there shall be no delegation.

Discussion Questions

1. What is the process of contract interpretation?

2. What is the legal difference between a totally integrated contract and a partially integrated contract?

3. NRW recently reviewed the standard form contracts the firm uses, and it decided to revise some of these contracts. As a part of this revision, Carlos suggested that the firm include a so-called merger clause stating that the written contract represented the parties' agreement, and that the written terms superseded any previous oral communications. Is a "merger clause" a good idea for NRW? Why or why not?

4. How are conduct and usage of trade important in contract interpretation?

5. Legal Hit, Inc. makes contracts to deliver "benefits" to designated third-party beneficiaries. In the contract, Legal Hit agrees to have one of its employees throw a cream pie in the face of any target designated by the promisee. If you hired Legal Hit to deliver a cream pie "greeting" to your boss, what are the legal rights of Legal Hit, you, and your boss?

6. Some states have statutes prohibiting or limiting assignment of wages. What public policies might state legislatures be trying to promote with these statutes?

7. Should waiver of defenses clauses be enforced? What are the advantages and disadvantages of these clauses?

8. Andrew owes Clairise $100. Clairise assigns $25 of this amount to Diane. With knowledge of the assignment, Andrew pays the entire $100 to Clairise. Has Andrew discharged his duty to pay?[9]

9. What are the differences between assignees, delegatees, and third-party beneficiaries? In what ways are they similar?

10. What happens if the assignor assigns the identical contract right to three different assignees? Who should recover from whom? Why?

Case Problems and Writing Assignments

1. Monica Guzman's friend, Barbara Graves, rented a car from AAA Auto Rental (AAA) in Bloomington, Indiana, and listed Guzman as an authorized driver. Guzman telephoned AAA to inform it that she would be driving the rental car to Chicago. At dusk on November 8, 1993, about 25 miles from her destination, the battery light went on in the car. About 10 minutes later, the temperature light came on. Guzman continued to drive the car toward her destination; she passed a couple of exits from the interstate. The car eventually broke down on the interstate. Due to Guzman's failure to stop the car immediately after the warning lights had come on, the car's engine sustained damage from overheating. AAA had the car towed back to Bloomington, where substantial repairs to the car's engine were made, including the resurfacing of the cylinder heads, a valve job, and the replacement of the fan relay switch. The towing and repair bills totaled nearly $1,000. Guzman testified that she had been afraid to pull off the highway. The trial court concluded that Guzman had willfully failed to stop because she was anxious to reach her destination and determined that Guzman had breached the car rental contract when she had

failed to return the car in good and safe mechanical condition. The trial court also found Guzman liable for the damages because she had "committed vandalism by the willful infliction of damage to this car by continuing to drive it after knowing it was not operating properly." The court relied on an Indiana statute governing motor vehicle rental companies and their contracts with customers, which permits rental companies to hold renters responsible for "physical damage to the rented vehicle. . . , resulting from vandalism unrelated to the theft of the rented vehicle." The trial court entered judgment in favor of AAA in the amount of $1,437, which represented the sum of the towing and repair bills and AAA's attorney's fees. Guzman argued that the judgment was incorrect because the car had sustained mechanical, as opposed to physical, damages. She claimed the rental company could recover for mechanical/engine damage only in the event of a collision. Is Guzman's interpretation logical or not? Why? [See *Guzman v. AAA Auto Rental*, 654 N.E.2d 838 (Ind. App. 1995).]

2. Maurice Quinn owned the controlling interest in two banks. William Carroll, a registered securities dealer, advised Quinn to buy American Home Acceptance Corporation (AHAC) "collateralized mortgage obligations," called bonds throughout the case. Carroll informed Quinn that the bonds would receive an "A" rating from Standard and Poor's, an entity of McGraw-Hill Companies. AHAC contracted for a rating from Standard and Poor's, and Standard and Poor's initially rated the bonds "A". On behalf of the banks, Quinn purchased the entire bond issue from AHAC. He could not have purchased the bonds for the banks without the "A" rating. About two and a half years later, Standard and Poor's abruptly reduced the rating to "CCC." Bonds rated "CCC" are considered "junk bonds" and are not investment quality. AHAC defaulted on the bonds, causing the banks a large loss. Was Quinn an intended third-party beneficiary of the contract between AHAC and Standard and Poor's? How could Quinn have better protected the banks' interests? Do most investors rely on rating services such as Standard and Poor's? Is such reliance reasonable? [See *Quinn v. McGraw-Hill Cos.*, 168 F.3d 331, 1999 U.S. App. LEXIS 2294 (7th Cir. 1999).]

3. Barlar Enterprises, a general contractor, was sued for defective construction, and sued, in turn, its subcontractors, including Jeff and Joanne Davis. Pursuant to an American States insurance policy covering the Davises, American States provided counsel and related costs for the Davises' defense. Upon a finding of nonliability on the part of the Davises, the American States attorneys moved for (and were granted) attorneys' fees and costs. This dispute is over the rights to approximately $30,000 in attorneys' fees and costs. On October 31, 1996, the Internal Revenue Service (IRS) sent a Notice of Levy to Barlar, stating that Jeffery Davis owed the government in excess of $150,000 in delinquent taxes and demanding that Barlar release to the government the approximately $30,000 Barlar owed Davis. Barlar, in turn, filed a complaint in state court. Barlar's complaint named the Davises and the IRS as defen-

dants, but neglected to name American States or its attorneys. The government removed the case to federal court. The American States insurance policy stated:

If the insured has rights to recover all or part of any payment we have made under this Coverage Part, those rights are transferred to us. The insured must do nothing after loss to impair them. At our request, the insured will bring "suit" or transfer those rights to us and help us enforce them. . . .

Were the funds assigned to American States at the time the insurance policy was originally issued and, as such, were they never the property of the Davises for attachment by the IRS? [See *Cole v. Barlar Enterprises, Inc.*, 35 F. Supp. 2d 891, 1999 U.S. Dist. LEXIS 6323 (M.D. Fla. Tampa Div. 1999).]

4. On February 8, 1996, Church & Tower entered into a $25.4 million contract with Broward County to design and construct a 1,024-bed inmate facility, known as the North Broward Detention Center. The contract provided that the project was to be substantially completed within 548 days of the "project initiation" date. The anticipated completion date was October 4, 1997. A final certificate of occupancy was not issued until October 28, 1998. Sheriff Ken Jenne of Broward County filed a suit against the construction company alleging that the delay caused him to incur over $13 million in labor and expenses because he had to transport inmates to other counties. Jenne was under a federal court decree to develop a plan for managing the jail population. Was Jenne an intended third-party beneficiary of the construction contract between the county and the construction company so that he could bring a lawsuit? [See *Jenne v. Church & Tower, Inc.*, 814 So. 2d 522, 2002 Fla. App. LEXIS 5226 (Fla. App. 4th Dist. 2002).]

5. **BUSINESS APPLICATION CASE** Kurt L. VanVoorhies was a senior design engineer for General Motors Corporation before he enrolled in graduate school at the University of West Virginia (WVU) to pursue a Ph.D. in engineering. He selected WVU specifically to work with one particular professor, Dr. James E. Smith. Smith and VanVoorhies investigated antennae for wireless power transmission. VanVoorhies's laboratory notebook indicated that he completed the first invention by June 3, 1991. In November 1991, VanVoorhies submitted an invention disclosure form to WVU describing that invention and listing Smith as a co-inventor. The WVU policy on inventions applies to "University personnel," which it defines as "all full-time and part-time members of the faculty and staff, and all other employees of the University including graduate and undergraduate students and fellows of the University." Under the policy, "the University owns worldwide right, title and interest in any invention made at least in part by University personnel, or with substantial use of University resources, and unless otherwise agreed, this Policy applies to any invention conceived or first reduced to practice under terms of contracts, grants or other agreements." The inventor is required to cooperate with WVU in obtaining patents on the inventions. Inventors are compensated with 30 percent of the net royalty income received after subtracting the expenses incurred from

procuring and licensing the patent. The assignment of the first invention to WVU states in part:

The undersigned does (do) hereby sell, assign, transfer and set over unto said assignee, its successors and assigns, the entire right, title and interest in and to said invention or inventions, as described in the aforesaid application, in any form or embodiment thereof, and in and to the aforesaid application; . . . also the entire right, title and interest in and to any and all patents or reissues or extensions thereof to be obtained in this or any foreign country upon said invention or inventions and any divisional, continuation, continuation-in-part or substitute applications which may be filed upon said invention or inventions in this or any foreign country; and the undersigned hereby authorize(s) and request(s) the issuing authority to issue any and all patents on said application or applications to said assignee or its successors and assigns.

VanVoorhies finished his dissertation and received his doctoral degree on December 29, 1993. On February 1, 1994, he began to work at WVU as a postgraduate research assistant professor. VanVoorhies claimed that he invented the second invention in the short interval between receiving his graduate degree and becoming an assistant professor. The second invention was based, at least in part, upon the technology in the first invention. Did VanVoorhies have an obligation to assign the second invention to WVU? Why or why not? [See *University of West Virginia Bd. of Trustees v. VanVoorhies*, 278 F.3d 1288, 2002 U.S. App. LEXIS 1327 (Fed. Cir. 2002).]

6. **ETHICAL APPLICATION CASE** PepsiCo, through its operating division of Pepsi-Cola Company, manufactured and sold soft-drink concentrates for Pepsi-Cola soft-drink products. PepsiCo entered exclusive bottling appointments (contracts) with individual bottlers throughout the United States. A bottling appointment authorized a bottler to manufacture and distribute Pepsi-Cola soft-drink products within a defined, exclusive geographic territory. Bottlers could not directly or indirectly sell Pepsi-Cola soft-drink products in another bottler's territory. Bottlers had a number of other duties including to vigorously promote and distribute the product line. Transshipment of any Pepsi-Cola soft-drink product into the exclusive territory of another bottler undermined that bottler's rights under the bottling contract and posed a threat to the distribution system. PepsiCo enacted a Transshipment Enforcement Program to investigate and fine transshipping bottlers. When a bottler was fined, PepsiCo collected the fine and then paid the money to the offended bottler whose territory was violated. PepsiCo sent periodic memos to bottlers, reassuring them that it would enforce the exclusive territory agreements. Pittsburg Pepsi aggressively marketed Pepsi-Cola soft-drink products in its territory, which included parts of Kansas and Missouri surrounding Pittsburg, Kansas. Bottling Group had the territory that surrounded that of Pittsburg Pepsi. Pittsburg Pepsi complained to PepsiCo that Bottling Group frequently transshipped into its territory. PepsiCo largely ignored these complaints, so Pittsburg Pepsi sued Bottling Group. Could Pittsburg Pepsi be an intended third-party beneficiary of Bottling Group's contract with PepsiCo? Was Bottling Group's behavior ethical or not? Why? [See *Pepsi-Cola Bottling Co. of Pittsburg, Inc. v. PepsiCo, Inc.*, 175 F. Supp. 2d 1288, 2001 U.S. Dist. LEXIS 21429 (D. Kan. 2001).]

7. **CRITICAL THINKING CASE** Ray Larson and his sons, Michael and Robert Larson, contacted Glopak, Inc. They wanted to sell Glopak the intellectual property rights to an invention, a "bag and straw" that allows single-serving beverages in a small pouch that can be used through the enclosed straw. Glopak purchased the rights to the "bag and straw" and agreed to make royalty payments to the Larsons. The Larsons wanted to have their payments accelerated, but Glopak did not consent. Glopak did allow the Larsons to sell their royalty payments to a third party. Dakota Partners purchased the right to receive the royalty payments in exchange for cash advances to the Larsons. Dakota Partners entered into two addenda with Glopak and the Larsons, both containing similar language. Addendum #2 provided, in part:

Glopak was requested by Larson on December 4, 1997, and Glopak has agreed, that payments which become due to Larson under Clauses 7c up to a maximum of Forty Thousand U.S. Dollars ($40,000.00 US) shall be paid to Dakota Partners . . .

Glopak agrees that it shall not offset any amount due under Clauses 7c and that said amount is absolutely due and owing.

Later Glopak discovered that the Larsons were not the rightful owners of the rights to the "bag and straw." Glopak rescinded its agreements with the Larsons and refused to make payments to Dakota Partners. Dakota Partners filed suit against Glopak and the Larsons for breach of contract. The Larsons did not participate in the court suit. The trial court found that the Larsons made fraudulent representations to Glopak and that the contracts between Glopak and the Larsons were properly rescinded. Does the language quoted above contain a waiver of defenses clause? What effect does fraud have on the two addenda between Glopak, the Larsons, and Dakota Partners? [See *Dakota Partners, L.L.P. v. Glopak, Inc.*, 2001 N.D. 168, 634 N.W.2d 520 (N.D. 2001).]

8. **YOU BE THE JUDGE** Arsenal, a London soccer club, has been attacked for "poaching" young players from other clubs. Arsenal has been criticized for offering £1.6 million to the 17-year-old midfielder Fernando Maceda da Silva (Nano). The Spanish football federation has stated that it could not prevent the transfer of Nano, who plays for the Catalan club's youth team for around 60,000 pesetas (£280) a week under a contract with Barcelona. The prevailing view within the Spanish FA is that the Barcelona contract is void because it was signed when Nano was 15; they believe that professional contract terms should not apply before a player's 16th birthday. According to the Spanish FA's general secretary, Gerardo Gonzalez, "We cannot go against fundamental rights, which is the freedom for a footballer to play where he wants. However, it is the desire of the Spanish federation that the best Spanish players play in

our own country." Barcelona still seems determined to hang on to Nano. Nano has stated, "Arsenal want me and I am disposed to go there but Barcelona seem determined to do everything to block me going." If you were the judge deciding this case, how would you interpret the contract between Nano and Barcelona? Can Nano go to Arsenal? Why or why not? How would you rule on signing 15- and 17-year-old players? Com-pare the assignment of players in the United States with player transfers in other countries. How are they similar and how are they different? Do they vary depending on the sport? How? [See Tommy Staniforth, "Football: Arsenal Attacked Over Nano Move," *The Independent* (London), May 21, 1999, Sports, p. 32.]

Notes

1. John Edward Murray Jr., *Grismore on Contracts*, rev., student edition (Indianapolis: Bobbs-Merrill Company, 1965), § 97, p. 152.

2. Walter H. E. Jaeger, ed., *Williston on Contracts*, 3rd ed. (Mount Kisco, N.Y.: Baker Voorhis, 1957), § 395, p. 1066.

3. Ibid., § 396, pp. 1067–1070.

4. *Restatement (Second) of Contracts*, § 302 and Introductory Note to Chapter 14 at pp. 438–439.

5. *Allan v. Bekins Archival Service, Inc.*, 154 Cal. Rptr. 458, 463 n. 8.

6. *Restatement (Second) of Contracts*, Statutory Note to Chapter 15 at 7–9.

7. *Restatement (Second) of Contracts*, Statutory Note to Chapter 15 at 10.

8. 16 C.F.R. § 433.1-.3 (1975, as amended in 1977).

9. *Restatement (Second) of Contracts*, § 326, Comment b, Ill. 1.

Contractual Discharge and Remedies

AGENDA

NRW Mai, Helen, and Carlos realize that NRW may, from time to time, have customers who do not pay their bills as these sums come due. The firm members therefore want to know what rights they will have in such situations. They also will be ordering component parts that must be produced to fairly exact standards. They wonder how they can word their contracts so that they will receive parts of the desired specifications and what they can do if the suppliers do not meet these specifications. They moreover are concerned—both as sellers and as buyers—with the time element in their contracts. How important is the time for performance? All three are unsure about the types of remedies they can seek should their dealings lead to results that differ from what they expected under the contracts.

These and other questions are likely to arise during this chapter. Be prepared! You never know when the firm or one of its members will seek your advice.

Termination of the Contract

When parties contract with one another, each party naturally assumes that the other party will faithfully and satisfactorily perform according to the terms of the agreement. Consequently, whenever the parties do what the contract calls for, the law says that they have discharged their duties under the contract. *Discharge* of a contract involves the legally valid termination of a contractual duty. Upon discharge, the parties have fulfilled their agreement; at this time, the parties' duties and obligations to one another end. The law groups the numerous methods for discharging contracts into four main categories: discharge by performance, discharge by agreement of the parties, discharge by operation of law, and discharge by nonperformance.

Exhibit 15.1 shows various methods for discharging a contract and details both the methods of discharge and the general rules applied to each method.

Despite the parties' original intentions, the possibility exists that one party will fail to live up to the contractual obligations. As you will learn, such nonperformance constitutes a breach of the contract and entitles the injured party to certain remedies, assuming the injured party does not wish to *waive* (or ignore) the breach. A *remedy* is a cause of action resulting from the breach of a contract. After the occurrence of a breach, remedies attempt to satisfy the parties' expectations as of the time of the contract's formation. Remedies fall into two main categories: those resulting from a court's exercise of its powers at law (*legal* remedies) and in equity (equitable remedies, or those arising from the branch of the legal system designed to provide fairness when there was no suitable remedy "at law").

EXHIBIT 15.1 Methods of Discharging Contracts

Type of Discharge

1. Discharge by performance
   a. Complete performance: the parties' exact fulfillment of the terms of the contract.
   b. Substantial performance: less-than-perfect performance that complies with the essential portions of the contract.

2. Discharge by agreement of the parties
   a. Release: the surrender of a legal claim.

   b. Rescission: the voluntary, mutual surrender and discharge of contractual rights and duties whereby the parties are returned to the original status quo.
   c. Accord and satisfaction: an agreement whereby the parties decide to accept performance different from that required by their original bargain and the parties' later compliance with this new agreement.
   d. Novation: a contract that effects an immediate discharge of a previously existing contractual duty, creates a new contractual obligation or duty, and includes as a party to this new agreement one who neither was owed a duty nor obligated to perform in the original contract.

General Rules

1. Completion of the contract on tender of delivery or payment.

1. Applicable only to nonmaterial and nonwillful breaches.
2. The injured party's suit for damages resulting from the minor deviations that have led to substantial (as opposed to complete) performance.

1. Necessitates a writing, consideration, and an immediate relinquishment of rights or claims owed to another.
1. May be either written or oral (subject to the Statute of Frauds), formal or informal, express or implied.

1. Actual agreement and subsequent performance necessary.

1. Assent of creditor and new obligor required.
2. Differs from an accord and satisfaction in that it effects an immediate discharge of an obligation rather than a discharge predicated on a subsequent performance.

EXHIBIT 15.1 *continued*

Type of Discharge	General Rules
3. Discharge by operation of law	
a. Bankruptcy: a court decree/discharge of the debtor's contractual obligations.	1. Revival of the obligation possible if done in compliance with applicable statutory provisions.
b. Statute of limitations: a definite statutory time period during which the plaintiff must commence a lawsuit or be barred forever.	1. Applicable time periods different from state to state.
c. Material alteration of the contract: a serious change in the contract effected by a party to the contract.	1. Must be done intentionally and without the consent of the other party.
4. Discharge by nonperformance	
a. Impossibility: an unforeseen event or condition that precludes the possibility of the party's performing as promised.	1. Discharge stemming from only objective (as opposed to subjective) impossibility. 2. Includes such events as the destruction of the contract's subject matter without the fault of either party, supervening illegality, the death or disability of either party whose performance is essential to the performance of the contract, and conduct by one party that makes performance by the other party impossible.
b. Commercial frustration: the destruction of the essential purpose and value of the contract.	1. Destruction of the value of the contract brought about by a supervening event not reasonably anticipated at the contract's formation. 2. Term *commercially impracticable* used in the UCC.
c. Breach: the nonperformance of the obligations set up by the contract. 1. Complete (or actual) breach.	1. A party's failure to perform a duty material and essential to the agreement; the other party justified in treating the agreement as at an end.
2. Anticipatory breach: an indication in advance by one of the contracting parties that he or she does not intend to abide by the terms of the contract.	1. Covered by both the common law and the UCC.
d. Conditions: limitations or qualifications placed on a promise. 1. Express conditions: those in which the parties explicitly or impliedly in fact set out the limitations to which their promises will be subject.	1. Strict compliance with express conditions necessary to avoid a breach.
2. Constructive conditions: those read into the contract or implied in law in order to serve justice.	1. Substantial compliance with constructive conditions necessary to avoid a breach.
3. Condition precedent: performance contingent on the happening of a future event; resultant discharge of both parties stemming from the failure of the condition precedent.	
4. Condition subsequent: the occurrence of a particular event that cuts off all ongoing contractual duties and discharges the obligations of both parties.	

Although you have probably always used the term "legal remedies" to encompass both types of relief, in this chapter you will learn to identify the sorts of situations in which it is appropriate for a court to order one kind of relief or the other. You also will become aware that these types of remedies usually are mutually exclusive.

Discharge by Performance

Complete Performance

The simplest, most common, and most satisfactory method of discharge consists of *complete performance*. (Yet, as we will see later in this chapter, rendering complete performance may be easier said than done.) If Johnson has agreed to deliver five carloads of grain, and Kreczewski has promised to pay $2,000 per carload, complete performance will occur when Johnson makes the deliveries to Kreczewski and Kreczewski pays Johnson. The parties' exact fulfillment of the terms of the contract satisfies the intent of their agreement and their reason for contracting. Complete performance also extinguishes all the legal duties and rights that the contract originally set up. Note, too, that performance will be complete if one of the parties *tenders* either the grain or the payment (that is, unconditionally offers to perform his or her contractual obligation and can so perform). That person will have completely performed the contract even if the other person does not accept the grain or the payment.

As long as Johnson is fulfilling Kreczewski's reasonable expectations under the contract, discharge by complete performance will ensue once the parties have met their respective obligations under the agreement. If during the course of the deliveries, however, Johnson does not live up to the letter of the agreement as to the quality of the grain sent to Kreczewski, Kreczewski should give Johnson prompt notice of these defects and should state formally that he (Kreczewski) expects complete performance. Kreczewski's failure to take such actions may allow Johnson to argue after the fact that Kreczewski has waived his right to expect complete performance.

Substantial Performance

In some circumstances, one party's performance does not mirror precisely the rights and obligations enumerated in the agreement. In such cases, the other party may question whether this degree of performance adequately fulfills the requisites of the contract. The issue raised by such a question involves the legal sufficiency of less-than-complete performance.

NRW CASE 15.1   Manufacturing/Sales

ENSURING ACCEPTABLE PERFORMANCE

Helen has recently negotiated a preliminary agreement with a plastics manufacturer, PDG Plastiques (PDG), that calls for PDG to produce the plastic housing for the StuffTrakR units. Helen realizes that PDG will need to supply housing of very exact specifications; otherwise, these components will not satisfy NRW's production needs. She has asked for your advice on how to word the final written contract between NRW and PDG to ensure that NRW protects itself and so that the housing will meet NRW's specifications. What advice will you give her?

BUSINESS CONSIDERATIONS Suppose a business is offered a very lucrative contract if it will produce a product to very specific standards. In deciding whether to accept the offer, what factors should the firm consider?

ETHICAL CONSIDERATIONS Is it ethical for a person to enter a contract that requires personal satisfaction with the performance of the other party? What, if anything, would make such a measure unethical?

INTERNATIONAL CONSIDERATIONS Do international standards of quality exist? If so, why are such standards practicable?

The law does not always require exact performance of a contract. Hence, minor deviations from the performance contemplated in the contract may not preclude the discharge of the contract. This type of performance is called substantial performance. Construction of a new house in which the contractor still needs to finish the woodwork or touch up the painting in certain rooms—assuming the contractor has completed everything else—probably constitutes substantial performance. A party who has substantially performed may receive the payment to which the parties have agreed. Because substantial performance represents a type of contract breach, since the performance is not perfect and instead is a notch below the parties' reasonable expectations under the contract, the other party can sue for the damages occasioned by substantial, as opposed to complete, performance.

Two criteria must be met before the doctrine of substantial performance is available to discharge the responsibilities of a performing party. First, the breach must not be material. In other words, the defective performance must not destroy the value or purpose of the contract.[1] Second, the breach must be nonwillful and devoid of bad-faith conduct.

Courts usually are more willing to apply the concept of substantial performance to construction contracts than to sales contracts. Why? A disgruntled buyer has a duty to return or to reject a defective computer, whereas a dissatisfied occupier of land necessarily must keep the defective house or garage. The possibility of the unjust enrichment of the landowner in construction situations makes the doctrine of substantial performance more attractive to courts in these circumstances than in most other commercial contexts.

Discharge by Agreement of the Parties

The parties themselves can specifically agree to discharge the contract. Provisions to that effect may be part of the original contract between the parties or part of a new contract drafted expressly to discharge the initial contract.

Release

Release represents a common method of discharging the legal rights one party has against another. To be valid, a *release* should be in *writing*, should be supported by *consideration*, and should effect an *immediate relinquishment* of rights or claims owed to another. For example, a landowner may sign a release in which he or she agrees, usually in exchange for money, to discharge the builder from the original contractual obligations. Insurance companies commonly execute similar releases that the insured parties must sign before the insurers will pay for the insured parties' injuries or losses.

Rescission

Sometimes the parties may find it advantageous to call off their deal. The law calls this process *rescission*. A contract of rescission is a voluntary, mutual surrender and discharge of contractual rights and duties whereby the law returns the parties to the original status quo. A valid rescission is legally binding. In general, rescission may be either formal or informal, express or implied, and written or oral (subject, you will recall, to the requirements of the Statute of Frauds under § 2-209 of the UCC; moreover, rescissions of realty contracts often must be written).

The simplest method of rescission involves the termination of executory bilateral contracts. If Johnson and Kreczewski in the earlier example *mutually agree to cancel* their transaction, *express rescission* has occurred. On the other hand, they may subsequently agree that Johnson will deliver seven carloads of grain instead of five. Substituting this later agreement for the old one brings about an *implied rescission* of the earlier agreement. However, problems often ensue if the parties attempt rescission of a unilateral contract (or a bilateral contract where one party has fully executed his or her duties). In these situations, some courts, before they will grant rescission, will infer a promise to pay for the performance rendered or require that consideration be paid to the party who has performed. Courts ordinarily resolve these issues by trying to ascertain the intent of the parties; but as we have learned, this task often is difficult.

Accord and Satisfaction

Parties may agree to accept performance different from that required by their original bargain (as discussed in Chapter 11 concerning consideration in unliquidated debt situations). The law calls such an agreement an *accord*. When the parties comply with the accord, *satisfaction* occurs; and discharge of the original claim by *accord and satisfaction* (that is, substituted performance) has resulted. The process of accord and satisfaction requires evidence of assent. Moreover, an accord will not be legally binding unless and until the performance required in the accord (that is, the satisfaction) is rendered.

Novation

Just as the parties may agree to substituted performances, so they may agree to substituted parties. A *novation* is a contract that effects an immediate discharge of a previously existing contractual obligation, creates a new contractual obligation or duty, and includes as a party to this new agreement one who in the original contract was neither owed a duty nor obligated to perform. A novation, then, is a contract in which a new party is substituted for one of the parties in the previous contract. The novation immediately discharges an obligation, whereas in contrast an accord is not executed until performance occurs. As you might expect, both the assent of the person to whom the obligation is owed (usually the creditor) and the assent of the new obligor (third party) are required for a valid novation. The assent of the previous debtor usually is not required, although that party can, if it wishes, disclaim the benefit of the discharge. The novation, in addition, must be supported by valid consideration.

Discharge by Operation of Law

We have seen in other contexts that the law itself can mandate the discharge of certain contracts. As you will learn in Chapter 28, bankruptcy decrees may grant to honest debtors a discharge of contractual obligations by operation of law. Most of the time a creditor will not receive the total owed, and yet the discharge in bankruptcy prevents the creditor from later suing the debtor for nonperformance (usually nonpayment). Most states, however, pursuant to the Bankruptcy Act's provisions, allow the debtor to revive the obligation by a later promise to pay the creditor. This reaffirmation of the debt involves several stringent new requirements under the Bankruptcy Act.

Statutes of limitations in all jurisdictions establish time periods within which, depending on the nature of the claims, litigants must initiate lawsuits. Noncompliance with these statutory time limits may discharge contractual claims by operation of law. For example, one typically must bring claims for breach of common law contracts within six years of the date of the alleged breach. Filing a lawsuit after this time limit makes the claim unenforceable. When the transaction involves a sale of goods, § 2-725 of the UCC states that the injured party ordinarily must file suit within four years of the occurrence of the breach. The underlying claim is discharged by operation of law if the injured party fails to file a lawsuit within this period. These periods of limitations differ from jurisdiction to jurisdiction, so each state's statutes should be checked.

The law also may grant a discharge of any contract that one of the parties to the agreement has materially altered. Before a court will apply this rule, it must be shown that the alteration was done intentionally and without the consent of the other party. Thus, if Johnson, without Kreczewski's permission, changes the carload price of the grain on the written contract from $2,000 to $5,000, Kreczewski can obtain a discharge of the contract through operation of law.

Discharge by Nonperformance

Under certain circumstances, nonperformance may discharge a contract. Still, as mentioned before, do not expect courts to apply these doctrines in order to save you from an unfavorable bargain.

Impossibility

Until the middle of the 19th century, courts rejected outright the doctrine of impossibility as a method of discharging contracts. *Impossibility* as a legal concept refers to an unforeseen event or condition that precludes a party's performing as promised. For instance, events such as these generally discharge contracts: the destruction of the subject matter of the contract without the fault of either party (Johnson's wheat burns before being loaded), supervening illegality (after the contract's formation, the legislature passes a law making it illegal for trains to carry agricultural products into certain states), or conduct by one party that makes performance by the other party impossible (in carrying out other deals, Kreczewski contracts for every possible car so that Johnson cannot procure the necessary cars for their transaction). These examples denote *objective impossibility* (nonperformance of the contract is unavoidable; *no one* could perform the contract in these circumstances).

Another instance of objective impossibility involves the death or disability of either party to a personal services contract (Johnson hires Pollock to paint his portrait, and Pollock has a debilitating heart attack). This contingency forms an exception to the general rule that a contract will be binding and thus not dischargeable except through performance despite the death or disability of either party, unless the parties have agreed otherwise. The contract will not be discharged, however, if another painter is acceptable to Johnson.

On the other hand, courts have held that circumstances involving subjective impossibility (as opposed to objective impossibility) will not discharge contractual obligations. *Subjective impossibility* consists of nonperformance owing to personal, as contrasted to external, impossibility. In such cases, the contract can be performed, but *this particular person* is unable to fulfill the obligations contemplated in the contract. For this reason, nonperformance owing to insolvency, shortages of materials, strikes, riots, droughts, and price increases ordinarily will not discharge contracts. However, some courts temporarily will suspend the duty to perform until the conditions causing the inability to perform have passed. More liberal courts may even discharge the contract if later performance will place an appreciably greater burden on the one obligated to perform. Given this division of opinion, the parties often will try to protect their rights by including express provisions covering the types of contingencies just described. Still, it is up to the courts to evaluate the validity of any such clauses.

Commercial Frustration

Because of the harshness of the general rule that impossibility ordinarily will not discharge the performance called for in a contract, the doctrine of *commercial frustration* (or *frustration of purpose*) has recently emerged as a basis for justifiable nonperformance. Courts will not invoke this doctrine to excuse performance, however, unless the essential purpose and value of the contract have been frustrated. If the parties reasonably could (or should) have foreseen the resultant frustration, courts will hold the nonperforming party to the terms of the bargain. Hence, courts will not utilize this doctrine to release parties from bad bargains. It is important to understand that in these cases performance is possible, but the value of the contract has been frustrated or destroyed by a supervening event that was not reasonably anticipated at the contract's formation. The Uniform Commercial Code uses the term *commercially*

impracticable (§ 2-615) in like fashion to excuse nonperformance in cases of severe shortages of raw materials owing to war, embargo, local crop failure, and other similar reasons. Before courts will allow discharge, these factors must have caused a marked increase in price or must have totally precluded the seller from obtaining the supplies necessary for performance. A recent case that deals with these concepts follows.

Actual Breach

Breach of contract occurs when one or more of the contracting parties fail to perform the obligations set up by the contract. That degrees of breach exist complicates the issue

---

15.1

BUSH v. PROTRAVEL INTERNATIONAL, INC.
746 N.Y.S.2d 790 (N.Y. City Civ. Ct. 2002)

FACTS On May 8, 2001, Alexandra Bush booked an African safari travel package for herself and her fiancé through Micato Safaris, which in turn referred her to ProTravel International, Inc. Bush gave ProTravel $1,516, the required 20 percent deposit. The safari was scheduled to begin on November 14, 2001. Sixty-four days before the safari's start, the events of September 11, 2001, occurred. As a result of the attacks on the World Trade Center, other terrorism alerts, and airline scares, Bush and her fiancé decided almost immediately to cancel the trip. Bush claimed she endeavored to notify ProTravel of her decision; but, as a result of the interruption of telephone service between Staten Island, where she had fled to safety, and Manhattan, where ProTravel maintained an office, she was physically unable to communicate her cancellation order until September 27, 2001. ProTravel conceded that Bush had contacted it that day. Micato acknowledged receiving a fax from ProTravel to that effect on October 4, 2001. ProTravel and Micato's applicable cancellation policy was set out in a brochure referenced in the registration form Bush had completed. Bush maintained she had never received this brochure. The policy imposed a $50 per person penalty for a cancellation occurring more than 60 days prior to departure. For a cancellation occurring between 30 and 60 days prior to departure, the traveler was subject to a penalty equal to 20 percent of the total retail tour rate (here, the deposit Bush had given ProTravel). Assuming a departure date of November 14, 2001, canceling on or before September 14, 2001, would have subjected her to, at worst,

a $50 per person penalty. Any cancellation after that date but on or before October 15, 2001, would have subjected her to the greater 20 percent penalty under the cancellation policy. Bush's cancellation of the trip therefore fell within the time frame that would trigger a 20 percent penalty for cancellation. Consequently, neither ProTravel nor Micato would return the deposit. While ProTravel argued that it was open for business from September 12 onward and furnished phone records to show it could make and receive calls, ProTravel offered no rebuttal to Bush's claim that it was virtually impossible for many days after the terrorist attacks to place a call from Staten Island if such a call were transmitted via the telephone trunk lines in downtown Manhattan. Nevertheless, the defendants submitted that, despite the horrors and communications disruptions visited on New York City in the aftermath of September 11, a contract is a contract, and that since the cancellation call was received, at best, 13 days late, Bush was not entitled to a refund. The defendants characterized the cancellation penalties as mechanisms for covering the costs incurred in planning and preparing for a customer's safari.

ISSUE Did the September 11, 2001, attacks on the World Trade Center and the civil upset spawned by their aftermath constitute the legal defense of impossibility that would entitle Bush to receive a refund of the deposit despite her late cancellation and the contract's cancellation penalties provisions?

HOLDING Possibly. Bush had raised sufficient material issues of fact concerning her inability to cancel the contract by September 15, 2001, which fact would, if established, provide a defense that would warrant a denial of the defendants' summary judgment motion.

REASONING Excerpts from the opinion of Judge Vitaliano:

Though it is true that the black letter of the law establishes the rule that once a party to a contract has made a promise, that party must perform or respond in damages for its failure, even when unforeseen circumstances make performance burdensome, . . . the rule is not an absolute. Where the means of performance have been nullified, making performance objectively impossible, a party's performance under a contract will be excused.

Counsel for the defendants . . . claimed to understand the difficulties encountered by literally every New Yorker in the wake of the disaster at the World Trade Center, but argue that those difficulties do not constitute a valid excuse for the failure . . . to cancel the safari before September 15, 2001. The delay until September 27, 2001, they contend, is inexcusable. Putting aside the sheer insensitivity of their argument, the argument fails to come to grips with . . . Bush's sworn claim that the disaster in lower Manhattan, which was unforeseen, unforeseeable and, certainly, beyond her control, had effectively destroyed her ability and means to communicate a timely cancellation under the contract she had booked . . . with the defendants. To the point, Alexandra Bush claims she could not physically take the steps necessary to cancel on time. . . . Micato and ProTravel, to the contrary, claim she was simply a traveler too skiddish [sic] to travel after September 11th, who wanted to stick the travel professionals she had retained with the bill for her faint heart. Should the defendants establish that to be the case to the satisfaction of the jury or at a bench trial, they will be entitled to judgment. . . . They certainly have not established that as a matter of law now.

Furthermore, the plaintiff's claim of excuse because of the frustration of the means of performance is supported, underscored and punctuated by the official actions taken by civil authorities on September 11, 2001, and in the days that followed. On the day of the attack, a state of emergency had been declared by the Mayor of the City of New York . . . [and by] the Governor of the State of New York. . . . Particularly on the days at the focal point of the argument here, September 12, 13 and 14, 2001, New York City was in the state of virtual lockdown with travel either forbidden altogether or severely restricted. Precedent is plentiful that contract performance is excused when unforeseeable government action makes such performance objectively impossible. . . . Further, in the painful recognition of the obvious and extraordinary dimensions of the disaster that prevented the transaction of even the most time-sensitive business during the days and weeks that followed the September 11th atrocities, the Governor even issued an executive order extending the statute of limitations for all civil actions in every court of our state for a period well-beyond the times Alexandra Bush claims to have communicated her cancellation and Micato acknowledges it received it. . . . In such light, to even hint that Alexandra Bush has failed to raise a triable issue of fact by her argument that the doctrine of impossibility excuses her late cancellation of the safari she booked . . . borders on the frivolous. . . .

It is not hyperbole to suggest that on 11 September 2001, and the days that immediately followed, the City of New York was on a wartime footing, dealing with wartime conditions. The continental United States had seen nothing like it since the Civil War and, inflicted by a foreign foe, not since the War of 1812. Accordingly, it is entirely appropriate for this Court to consider and follow wartime precedents which developed the law of temporary impossibility. Stated succinctly, where a supervening act creates a temporary impossibility, particularly of brief duration, the impossibility may be viewed as merely excusing performance until it subsequently becomes possible to perform rather than excusing performance altogether. . . .

The law of temporary and/or partial impossibility flows from the theory that when a promisor has obligated himself to perform certain acts, which, when taken together are impossible, the promisor should not be excused from being called upon to perform insofar as he is able to do so. . . . So too here, if Alexandra Bush can establish objective impossibility of performance at trial she is entitled to, at minimum, a reasonable suspension of her contractual obligation to timely cancel, if not outright excuse of her untimely cancellation.

BUSINESS CONSIDERATIONS As a consequence of the September 11th attacks, the government set up a fund to compensate businesses that had been destroyed or injured by the events of that day. Do such subsidies represent a practical aspect of the government's exercise of its police power? How can businesses otherwise protect themselves from cataclysmic events like the September 11th attacks?

ETHICAL CONSIDERATIONS Was it unethical for the travel agents to retain Bush's refund? Were her apprehensions about flying to Africa six weeks later too self-serving? Could you provide support for the proposition that, in canceling her trip, she had acted unethically?

somewhat. A *complete or actual* breach of contract involves the nonperformance of a duty that is so material and essential to the agreement that the other party is justified in treating the agreement as at an end. The Uniform Commercial Code in § 2-703 and § 2-711 embraces this common law principle. Actual breach generally discharges the other party's obligation to perform under the terms of the contract. However, rather than cancel the contract upon breach, the injured (or nonbreaching) party may elect instead to hold the nonperforming party to the contract through various types of remedies, which we will discuss later in this chapter.

Anticipatory Breach

Sometimes one of the contracting parties will indicate in advance, through words or conduct, that he or she does not intend to abide by the terms of the contract. To illustrate, if Johnson unequivocally tells Kreczewski before the time performance is due that he will not send the grain as scheduled, Johnson will have wrongfully repudiated the contract. In legal terms, Johnson's action is called *anticipatory breach*, or *anticipatory repudiation*. In this situation, as in actual breaches, the injured party need not limit its potential responses to discharge of the contract.

The Uniform Commercial Code sanctions a kind of anticipatory repudiation in circumstances less definite than those allowable under the common law. Section 2-609 of the Code states that when reasonable grounds for insecurity arise with respect to one party's performance, the other party may demand adequate assurances of due performance and suspend performance until such assurances are forthcoming. If 30 days pass without reply, the party who has demanded the assurances can deem the contract repudiated. Kreczewski's actual or apparent insolvency (the inability to pay one's debts as they become due), for example, may cause Johnson to invoke the provisions of § 2-609. If Kreczewski does not respond within 30 days, Johnson then may treat the contract as repudiated (see § 2-610).

The following case involves a situation in which each of the parties to the contract believes the other is in breach. Reflect on how the court disposed of these contentions.

Conditions

The presence of conditions may result in nonperformance that will justify discharge of a contract as well. A *promise* is a vow or a covenant that places on the promisor a duty to do something or to refrain from doing something. A *condition*, in contrast, is an act or event that limits or qualifies a promise. The condition must occur before the promisor has a duty to perform or to refrain from performing.

NRW CASE 15.2   Management

DEFENSES TO CONTRACT ENFORCEMENT

Helen recalls that one of her professors once mentioned in class that a number of subcontractors who encounter difficulties in meeting their contractual obligations often try to use the defenses of impossibility, commercial impracticability, or commercial frustration to escape liability when they fail to satisfy their contracts. NRW "jobs" out much of its work to subcontractors, and Helen is concerned that these sorts of situations may arise with the firm. She asks you what the firm should do to protect itself. What will you tell her?

BUSINESS CONSIDERATIONS Should a business enter into contracts that it is not sure it can perform and then resort to commercial impracticability as an excuse if it cannot perform as promised? What legal risk is the firm assuming if it uses such an approach to its obligations?

ETHICAL CONSIDERATIONS Is it ethical for a firm to avoid liability by asserting that its promised performance was made impossible or impracticable by some external factor? Is it ethical for a firm to try to collect damages when an external factor made the performance by the other firm impossible or impracticable?

INTERNATIONAL CONSIDERATIONS Does the Convention on Contracts for the International Sale of Goods have provisions relating to impossibility, commercial impracticability, or commercial frustration? How does the CISG treat these areas?

Courts classify conditions in two ways. The first category emphasizes the *timing* of the qualifying occurrence (the condition) in relation to the promised performance. Three subsets of this category include *conditions precedent*, *concurrent conditions*, and *conditions subsequent*. The second category stems from the manner in which the conditions arise. Conditions created by law are deemed *constructive* (or *implied*) *conditions*. In contrast, conditions created by the agreement of the parties themselves are called *express conditions*.

Under the first category (timing), an agreement may explicitly state that a certain act or event must occur before the other party has a duty to perform or before a contract results. If so, a *condition precedent* exists. For example, a

15.2

IN RE CORNELL & COMPANY, INC.
229 B.R. 97 (Bankr. E.D. Pa. 1999)

FACTS Cornell & Company, Inc., a construction company (the debtor), had hired a subcontractor to do part of the painting work for a municipal project for which Cornell was the general contractor. The subcontractor later assigned its fee—$975,000—and the subcontract to Delbert L. Smith Company (the defendant). As was customary in the industry, Cornell retained monies to ensure the defendant's completion of the subcontract. The defendant worked for Cornell for three months before the project started to experience difficulties owing in part to the delays associated with the changes in the federal lead-abatement standards. These difficulties, in turn, led to the debtor's filing for bankruptcy. The defendant continued to work on the project once the debtor became current on all the outstanding sums due. However, when the defendant asked for a reduction in the monies retained by the debtor, the debtor refused, owing to its belief that the defendant had not completed enough work on the project to warrant the requested reduction. The parties' relationship continued to deteriorate; and on November 13, 1996, the defendant permanently departed from the project. Even though it contended only two days' work remained, the defendant submitted it could not finish this work because certain tasks that had to precede its work had been left undone. When the defendant refused thereafter to return, the debtor paid an additional $307,000 to another firm to complete the work. In the subsequent bankruptcy proceeding, the defendant filed a claim of $80,374.83 for the unreleased retainage monies on the project. The debtor maintained that the bankruptcy court should deny the claim because the defendant's failure to complete the work had forced the defendant to retain a new subcontractor to finish the work and to incur significant additional costs. These costs, the debtor argued, reflected the fact that the defendant had completed only about 70 percent of the work.

ISSUE Did the defendant's failure to complete its contractual obligations, in conjunction with its abandonment of the project, constitute a material breach of contract that would justify the bankruptcy court's rejection of the defendant's claim against the debtor?

HOLDING Yes. The defendant's unilateral withdrawal from the job site without completing its contractual duties represented a material breach of the contract that excused the nonbreaching party from fulfilling its obligations under the contract. Hence, the court was justified in rejecting the claim asserted against the debtor by the defendant.

REASONING Excerpts from the opinion of Judge Scholl:

The Defendant failed to complete a substantial portion of the work in question as mandated by the subcontract agreement. . . . Thus, despite the parties' claims of a high of ninety-six (96%) percent completion on the part of the Defendant, and but seventy (70%) percent on the part of the Debtor, our scrutiny of the monies paid to the Defendant from October 1994 through October 1996 reveals that the Defendant completed 86.41% of the subcontract work involved. In light of this conclusion, there is no question that the Defendant's failure to perform any further work on the . . . project pursuant to the terms of the agreement . . . evidenced the Defendant's breach of its agreement with the Debtor. Moreover, the Defendant's abandonment of the project . . . conclusively established the Defendant's material breach of the subcontract agreement.

It is well settled that when a party materially breaches a contractual agreement, the non-breaching party is not required to fulfill its duties under the contract. . . . As a result, a party who has materially breached a contract may not complain if the other party refuses to perform its obligations under the contract. . . . Since it breached the contract, the Defendant is not entitled to request nor recover from the Debtor the release of the retainage monies. Nor has it proven that it performed extra work on the project which the Debtor agreed to compensate over and above the $975,000 contract price. . . . The Defendant maintains that it was justified in not performing the agreement in question as a result of the debtor's failure to make certain that other work necessary to be completed prior to the Defendant's painting was done. . . . We find little merit in these arguments. The prerequisite work was ultimately completed, but even then the Defendant simply refused to return until paid its retainage, which was not yet due to it. Delay in making payment where the amount of the work done is disputed or is being negotiated is not on that basis alone a breach of contract. Rather, a breach occurs on the part of the subcontractor where that party unilaterally, as here, leaves a job site without completing its contractual duties. . . . [A] party who has materially breached a contract may not complain if the other party thereafter refuses to perform. . . . Stated another way, a party at breach has no valid claim against the other party. . . . Since the Defendant failed to introduce any persuasive evidence that would defeat the Debtor's contention that it failed to complete the contract and hence was not entitled to the remainder of the contract price under the requisite "preponderance of the evidence" standard, we must conclude that the claim at issue, based on the Defendant's assertion of an entitlement to the contract balance, must be stricken in its entirety. . . .

BUSINESS CONSIDERATIONS What could the parties have done differently to avoid this litigation? Would informal mediation have avoided a lawsuit?

ETHICAL CONSIDERATIONS Assess the respective ethics of the debtor's refusing to release any of the retainage monies and the defendant's behavior in abandoning the project. Had one party behaved relatively more ethically than the other?

person may promise (for consideration) to buy a car if the seller can deliver the car within 10 days. A duty to buy the car does not arise unless and until the seller fulfills the condition. Thus, the timing of the condition and any later duty to perform go together.

To be a condition precedent rather than a mere promise, the parties must indicate that the condition is an essential, vital aspect of the transaction. If the buyer in our example later wishes to sue for rescission of the contract or for damages on the ground that the seller has not delivered the car on time, the buyer will have to prove that delivery within 10 days is essential to the transaction. A common condition precedent involves a buyer's signing a contract for the purchase of a new house subject to the sale of the buyer's current residence. The buyer views this provision as an important consideration regarding his or her willingness to enter into the contract.

Concurrent conditions, related to conditions precedent in regard to the timing of the condition and the promised performance, obligate the parties *to perform at the same time.* Concurrent conditions (for example, the transfer of goods in exchange for payment) underlie most commercial sales.

A *condition subsequent* is any occurrence that the parties have agreed will cut off an existing legal duty. It also may be a contingency, the happening or performance of which will defeat a contract already in effect. When a sales contract involving grain storage states that the contract will be of no effect if fire destroys the grain, a condition subsequent exists.

Genuine conditions subsequent are rare. What may sound like a condition subsequent—for example, Acme Insurance will not pay for casualty losses if the premises are unoccupied—will be construed by many courts as a condition precedent. Courts that characterize such a provision as a condition subsequent will interpret the clause as stating that the occurrence of the condition (vacant premises) will cut off an existing legal duty (payment of the casualty loss). Other courts will say that it is a condition precedent (the premises must be kept occupied) that merely sounds like a condition subsequent because of the phrasing. This dis-

tinction can be procedurally significant. If it is a condition precedent, the insured has the burden of proof; if it is a condition subsequent, the insurer has the burden of proof. And when the evidence is conflicting, the party who has the burden of proof often loses.

Express conditions (for example, this sale can be consummated only by payment of cash) are those spelled out by the parties explicitly or impliedly in fact. A *constructive condition* is one not expressed by the parties, but rather read into the contract in order to serve justice (that is, the condition is implied in law). Differentiating between an express condition implied in fact and a constructive condition can be difficult. For example, a provision regarding place of delivery normally is a condition precedent in a contract involving grain; but if such a condition is lacking, and in the absence of clear intent, a court may imply that the place for delivery is the seller's place of business (see UCC § 2-308).

Nonperformance of an express condition precedent (such as posting a performance bond) causes a failure of the condition that nullifies the other party's duty to perform and discharges the contract. Similarly, the presence of an express condition subsequent (meaning that the occurrence of a particular event cuts off all ongoing contractual duties) discharges the obligations of both parties. For example, the buyer's returning goods before payment is due under the terms of a contract in which the buyer has reserved this right would constitute discharge of the contract. But to avoid a breach of an express condition, courts ordinarily require strict compliance. In contrast, substantial compliance generally avoids a breach of a constructive condition.

It should be noted that a condition may require one party to perform "to the satisfaction" of the other party. In fact, in certain cases, such as those involving custom tailoring, some courts hold that in order to discharge the contract, the performing party must meet the personal, subjective expectations of the dissatisfied party. Other courts characterize the performance as substantial if the performance rendered will satisfy our old friend, the reasonable person. Courts generally will apply this latter test when the parties base performance not on personal tastes or aesthetic preferences (as may be involved in our custom tailoring example) but rather on satisfaction as to merchantability or mechanical utility (as in the purchase of a car).

Types of Remedies

Upon breach of contract, in order to satisfy his or her expectations as of the time of contract formation, the injured party can choose among various remedies.

The most common legal remedy consists of *damages*. The injured party must *mitigate*, or minimize, these damages; but having fulfilled this legal duty, the injured party at the very least should be able to receive *compensatory damages*, those that will put the party in the same economic position that he or she would have occupied had the other party performed. If the facts permit, the injured party moreover may receive *consequential damages*, those indirect or special damages springing from the effects or aftermath of the breach itself; *punitive damages*, those damages, over and above the actual damages, that a court may award in order to deter the defendant from future malicious conduct; and *liquidated damages*, those agreed on in advance by the parties in the event breach occurs. A court also may award *nominal damages* (a small amount of compensation) for minor, technical contractual breaches that cause no actual losses.

In some situations, money damages will represent inadequate compensation for the loss of the bargain occasioned by the breach. Injured persons in these cases ordinarily resort to *equitable* remedies. These possible modes of relief include *rescission*, the cancellation or termination of the contract through the restoration of the parties to the status quo. Restoration is accomplished by *restitution*— the return of the goods, money, or property involved in the contract or the recovery of the reasonable value of the services rendered. *Specific performance*, the court-ordered enforcement of the contract according to its exact terms, is an alternative type of equitable remedy, as is quasi contract. *Quasi contract*, you may remember, refers to the situation in which a court creates a contract for the parties, despite their wishes and intentions, in order to prevent the unjust enrichment of one party. The remedy available in quasi contract is restitution based, allowing the injured party to recover the reasonable value of the services rendered. *Reformation*, the court's rewriting of a contract in order to remove a mistake and to make the agreement conform to the terms to which the parties originally agreed, and *injunctions*, court-ordered writs directing a person to do or to refrain from doing some specified act, are two other equitable remedies.

It has been said that for every legal wrong the law attempts to provide a legal remedy. This chapter explores some of the contractual remedies that are obtainable. Exhibit 15.2 classifies various common types of contractual remedies. It also notes the fact that an injured party may give up the right to receive the performance called for in the contract.

Damages

When one party breaches a contract, the other party is entitled to payment for lost expectations. The injured party therefore can bring an action for damages. It is not necessary that the injured party have the ability to compute exactly what the damages are, as long as the losses represent the natural and proximate consequences of the breach. In computing damages, courts ask whether the breaching party, as a reasonable person, at the time of contracting should have foreseen that these injuries would result from breach. If the nonperforming party should have foreseen the losses, courts will award damages to the injured party. The amount of damages awarded, of course, will depend heavily on the facts of the case.

Compensatory Damages

The most common type of damages is *compensatory damages*, or those sums of money that will place the injured party in the same economic position that would have been attained had the contract been performed. Such damages also are called *actual* damages. Injured parties may recover only the damages that the parties reasonably can foresee.

The 1854 English case, *Hadley v. Baxendale*,[2] enunciated this doctrine, which courts still widely accept as a limitation on the damages recoverable for breach of contract. Under the *Hadley v. Baxendale* rule, courts ordinarily will confine compensatory damages awards to those losses naturally arising from the breach, or those the parties may have reasonably contemplated or foreseen, at the time of contract formation, as the probable result of a breach of the contract. Compensatory damages include all damages directly attributable to the loss of the bargain previously agreed on by the parties, including lost profits and any incidental expenses incurred as a result of the breach. In a sale of goods, courts, in formulating the actual damages, usually compute the difference between the contract price and the market price. The same ordinarily is true of land contracts. Thus, if Miranda Construction Company, a developer of real estate for its own particular purposes, orders three bulldozers from Welling Machinery Company and, unfortunately, none of the bulldozers functions properly, Miranda should

EXHIBIT 15.2 Types of Contractual Remedies

Type of Remedy	Definition
Legal remedies (money damages)	Those damages resulting from a court's exercise of its power "at law."
Compensatory damages	Damages awarded to a nonbreaching party in order to compensate him or her for the actual, foreseeable harm or loss caused by the breach.
Consequential damages	Indirect or special damages springing from the effects or aftermath (i.e., the consequences) of the breach itself; not recoverable unless the breaching party knew, or should have known, at the time of contract formation, of the potential effect of a breach on the nonbreaching party.
Punitive damages	Unusual damages awarded to punish for willful, wanton, malicious harm caused to a nonbreaching party.
Nominal damages	Inconsequential sums that establish that the plaintiff had a cause of action but suffered no measurable pecuniary loss.
Liquidated damages	A provision in a contract that a stated sum of money or property will be paid, or forfeited if previously deposited, if one of the parties fails to perform in accordance with the contract; enforceable unless unreasonable.
Mitigation of damages	Nonbreaching party's duty to reduce the actual losses, if he or she is able to do so.
Equitable remedies	Remedies arising from a court's use of its powers of equity.
Rescission and restitution	The cancellation or abrogation of a contract and the return of the previously rendered consideration or its value; may be mutually agreed to by the parties to a contract or awarded as a remedy by a court.
Specific performance	An order by a court to render a contractually promised performance.
Quasi contract	A court's requiring that one who has received a benefit pay for the benefit conferred so as to prevent the unjust enrichment of the other party.
Reformation	A court's correction of an agreement to conform to the intentions of the parties.
Injunction	An order requiring a person to act or restraining a person from doing some act.
Waiver of breach	A party's relinquishment, repudiation, or surrender of a right that he or she has to seek a remedy for breach of contract.

be able to recover the general or *direct damages* or losses occasioned by the defective equipment. Miranda's costs of repairing the machines constitute one type of direct loss. Alternatively, if Miranda has to buy new bulldozers at higher prices, Miranda will be able to recover the costs associated with obtaining this substitute performance.

Assuming that Miranda's bad luck continues and Antonelli, a seller with whom Miranda has contracted to buy land for investment purposes, fails to go through with this realty contract, Miranda can sue Antonelli, the reneging seller, for the difference between the price of this piece of land and the one Miranda eventually purchases. Miranda also can sue for such expenses as the additional brokers' fees or commissions involved in obtaining the second parcel of real estate, since these losses flow directly

and foreseeably from Antonelli's breach as well. However, Miranda in both cases must deduct any expenses saved as a result of the breaches.

Consequential Damages

Besides compensatory damages, it also is possible for plaintiffs like Miranda to receive *consequential damages.* Consequential damages are those indirect or special damages springing from the effects or aftermath (that is, the consequences) of the breach itself. Assume that in addition to the contracts mentioned, Miranda loses a grading contract with the city because the bulldozers will not work and, as a result, also loses several rental contracts from retailers who wished to be part of a mall Miranda was planning to develop on the real estate it had tried to purchase. Can Miranda sue Welling and Antonelli for the losses accruing from these special circumstances and not just from the direct breaches? To determine liability or the lack thereof, a court will apply the reasonable person test to see whether such lost contracts were a foreseeable result of Welling's and Antonelli's breaches. A judge will not award purely speculative or conjectural damages; but if a court finds Welling and Antonelli knew, or should have known, at the time of contract formation, of Miranda's circumstances and the potential effect of their breaches on Miranda, it may award incidental or consequential damages. The Uniform Commercial Code in § 2-715 and § 2-710 also recognizes this doctrine.

Duty to Mitigate

In determining whether to award damages and, if so, how to measure them, courts place on the injured party the duty to *mitigate* (minimize) these damages if possible. In other words, the injured party must take affirmative steps to prevent the escalation of the losses brought about by the breaching party.

In our bulldozer example, courts will expect Miranda to attempt to procure substitute bulldozers, assuming this is possible without undue risk or expense. If Miranda does not undertake such reasonable steps, its failure to mitigate damages will preclude its receiving consequential damages. Rather, the court will limit losses to those accruing directly from the breach. But if Miranda can prove it was impossible to obtain substitute bulldozers, most courts will excuse its failure to mitigate. The duty of mitigation does not require the injured party to go to superhuman lengths. If the risks or expenses in mitigation attempts are unreasonably great, no duty to mitigate arises.

Punitive Damages

In contrast to their willingness to make compensatory and consequential damages available to injured parties, courts generally will not allow the recovery of punitive damages in breach of contract situations. *Punitive*, or exemplary, damages are imposed not to compensate the injured party but to punish the wrongdoer so as to deter future conduct of this sort. The old common law rule was that punitive damages never were appropriate for breaches of contract. Though still rare, some statutes now permit the imposition of punitive damages in contractual situations (such as treble damages, a statutory remedy that allows the successful plaintiff to recover three times the damages suffered as a result of the injury) under the antitrust laws. Fur-

thermore, some courts have been willing to grant punitive damages in situations in which one party has acted willfully. An insurance company that unduly delays paying off legitimate contractual claims against it may be subject to punitive damages in order to discourage this type of conduct. If the circumstances so warrant, consumer transactions also may form the basis for an award of punitive damages.

In the past decade, courts have struggled with the issue of whether the due process clause of the Fourteenth Amendment, which requires fundamental fairness, places some outer limits on a jury's otherwise unfettered discretion to award any amount of punitive damages, no matter how gargantuan. The issue has arisen because juries in many cases award huge punitive damages of many times the compensatory damages awarded. The Supreme Court in *Pacific Mutual Life Insurance Company v. Haslip,*[3] held that a punitive damages award of more than $800,000 against an insurer whose agent had defrauded an insured was reasonable and did not violate the insurer's due process rights, even though the award exceeded by more than four times the amount of compensatory damages, was more than 200 times the out-of-pocket expenses incurred by the insured, and greatly exceeded the fine that Alabama law imposed for insurance fraud. The Court based its conclusion on the fact that the procedural and substantive safeguards imposed by state law (including posttrial procedures that required trial courts to scrutinize all such punitive damages awards) ensured the reasonableness of the amount of punitive damages and the rationality of the award in furthering the purposes of deterrence and punishment. In short, the Court held that such safeguards imposed a sufficiently definite and meaningful constraint on the discretion of state juries to award punitive damages to ensure that such awards were not grossly disproportionate to the severity of the offense and were adequate to protect the due process rights of the persons against whom the juries had assessed the punitive damages.

Five years later, relying on *Haslip*, the Court in *BMW of North America, Inc. v. Gore,*[4] for the first time voided a state court's award of punitive damages as unconstitutional under the Fourteenth Amendment's due process clause. The Court held that a $2 million punitive damages award against BMW of North America, Inc. for BMW's fraudulent failure to disclose that it had repainted a new $40,000 car, thereby reducing the vehicle's value by $4,000, was "grossly excessive." The jury apparently had arrived at the $4 million punitive damages figure it had awarded (the state supreme court had remitted—that is, reduced or lowered—the damages to $2 million) by multiplying the $4,000 compensatory damages award by the 1,000 nationwide instances of BMW's similar nondisclosures of minor repairs. The

Court stressed that while Alabama had the right to protect its own citizens through the punishment of firms that engage in deceptive trade practices, such a state would not have the right, by the imposition of a punitive damages award or a legislatively authorized fine, to punish out-of-state activity that was lawful where it had occurred. Hence, the Court viewed this $2 million award as excessive in light of the interest of Alabama consumers and BMW's conduct in Alabama. And while the Court quoted *Haslip* for the proposition that the Court could not "draw a mathematically bright line" with regard to when the ratio between the compensatory and the punitive damages awarded would become unconstitutional, the Court concluded that when, as here, the ratio was "a breathtaking 500:1," any such award must surely "raise a suspicious judicial eyebrow." The Court then held that the grossly excessive award imposed in this case would transcend the constitutional limit. In *Cooper Industries, Inc., v. Leatherman Tool Group, Inc.,*[5] the Court rejected the contention that a jury award of $4.5 million in punitive damages (the jury had awarded $50,000 in compensatory damages) was grossly excessive under *Gore*. The Court further held that courts of appeals should apply a de novo standard (rather than the less demanding abuse-of-discretion standard) when they review district court determinations of the constitutionality of punitive damages awards. The Court continues to fill in the parameters of this important aspect of law, so watch for new developments in this area.

Liquidated Damage

The parties may agree in advance that, upon breach of contract, a certain sum of money will be paid to the injured party. This remedy is called *liquidated damages*. The amount to which the parties have agreed in advance fully satisfies any liability attendant upon the breach that has occurred. Courts will enforce such provisions if (1) the agreed-on amount is reasonable and not out of proportion to the apparent injury resulting from the breach and (2) calculation of the resulting damages in advance and with any accuracy will be difficult, if not impossible. In the context of sales contracts, UCC § 2-718 takes a similar approach.

The contractor mentioned earlier, Miranda, may well find itself subject to such a clause. Construction contracts typically have clauses assessing a per-day charge for delays in completing a building on time. Because it is difficult to ascertain the amount of damages that a breach of such a contract will cause, as long as the per-day charge is reasonable, courts generally uphold these clauses.

Courts will not enforce *penalties*, however. Penalties consist of amounts unrelated to the possible damages that

may occur and usually are excessively large. Such an arbitrary lump sum, even if the parties have agreed to it as satisfaction of a breach, will be void.

Nominal Damages

You have learned that for most breaches of contract, an action for damages may be possible. However, in certain cases, especially those involving a minor, or technical, breach, the injured party sustains no actual losses or damages. A court nevertheless may award a small amount of compensation (say $1) for the breach. This type of remedy is called *nominal damages*. Sometimes a court or jury awards nominal damages because the injured party has not been able to prove the substantial damages that he or she claims to have suffered. Upon proof of a breach, the injured party therefore is entitled only to nominal damages, the token sum that a court will require the defendant to pay as an acknowledgment of the wrongful conduct in which he or she has engaged.

Equitable Remedies

When the "at law" remedy of damages is unavailable, indeterminable, or inadequate, courts in the exercise of their powers of equity may award certain remedies. The plaintiff's eligibility to receive such fairness-oriented relief will depend on the absence of bad faith on the plaintiff's part and similar factors. Simply put, a plaintiff will not necessarily receive equitable remedies just because he or she asks for them. When they are available, the most significant types of equitable relief include rescission and restitution, specific performance, quasi contract, reformation, and injunction.

A court's power to award equitable remedies is discretionary; hence, courts normally will not give equitable remedies if the injured party has "unclean hands" (that is, has shown bad faith or dishonesty); if the injured party has unduly delayed bringing the lawsuit; if a forfeiture (the loss of a right or privilege as a penalty for certain conduct) of property will result from conferring an equitable decree; if the court itself necessarily will have to supervise the implementation of the remedy granted; or if the remedy at law (ordinarily money damages, as you will recall) is available, determinable, and adequate.

Rescission and Restitution

As you saw earlier in this chapter, the parties may voluntarily agree to rescind, or set aside, their contract before rendering performance. This type of rescission discharges the contract. But rescission also may occur as a result of a material breach of the agreement. Rescission in this context refers to the cancellation or termination of the contract through the restoration of the parties to the status quo. Upon such rescission, the injured party may ask for restitution.

Restitution, the return of the goods, money, or property involved in the contract or the recovery of the reasonable value of the services rendered, is the legal term that describes the process by which the parties are returned to their original positions at the time of contract formation. In essence, then, restitution relies on quasi-contractual principles rather than on the original agreement, because once rescission has occurred, the original contract no longer exists.

To avoid the unjust enrichment of the breaching party, the law permits restitution by allowing the plaintiff to sue in quasi contract in order to recover. For this reason, in most jurisdictions, one cannot sue for both damages and restitu-

tion; damages and restitution constitute *mutually exclusive* remedies. The injured party must *elect* (choose) to pursue one remedy or the other. If Miranda has paid Welling for the bulldozers, upon Welling's breach Miranda can treat the contract as at an end (that is, rescind it) and then recover the money (consideration) already paid to Welling in order to avoid the unjust enrichment of Welling. Alternatively, Miranda can sue for damages. The common law *election of remedies* doctrine prevents Miranda from recovering twice.

Note how the judge, in deciding the following case, uses many of these concepts.

Specific Performance

Whenever the remedy represented by damages or restitution is inadequate or unjust, the injured party may ask a court to order *specific performance*. In these cases, a court compels the breaching party to perform according to the exact terms of the agreement.

Courts rely on uniqueness as one factor in deciding whether to grant specific performance. Since land by definition is unique, courts ordinarily grant specific performance for breaches of land contracts. For example, should you try to buy a prairie-style home on the river, money damages for breach of that contract are unfulfilling: Money can buy a house similar to the one in the contract, but not that particular house. The inherent uniqueness of real estate therefore may convince a court to order the breaching party to convey the house to you—that is, give you specific performance—in order that justice may be done.

The same may be said of contracts involving unique goods or *chattels* (articles of movable personal property). If Bogan breaches a contract to sell a Rembrandt painting, in the absence of fraud or illegality, a court can compel Bogan to convey the painting to the buyer. But when the injured party can easily obtain the personal property or chattels, specific performance is an inappropriate remedy: Money damages will be adequate in these cases. Just as damages and restitution generally are mutually exclusive remedies, so too are damages and specific performance.

Money damages ordinarily will not satisfy the parties in situations involving personal services contracts. If these contracts are at issue, courts are reluctant to force the parties into a relationship in which at least one of the parties will be unhappy. For example, when Reggie Jackson wanted to break his contract with the Oakland A's and play for the Yankees, how could the A's be sure Jackson would give his best efforts if he really wanted to play for the Yankees? For this reason, and because courts are reluctant to force a party into what one party may characterize as involuntary servitude, courts ordinarily do not grant specific

15.3

BARKER v. NESS
587 N.W.2d 183 (N.D. 1998)

FACTS Jan M. Ness and Cynthia K. Smith purchased a house that they knew had a water problem in the basement. On July 14, 1993, Ness and Smith sold this home to Karen Barker for $40,000. On March 28, 1996, Barker filed a complaint alleging that Ness and Smith had fraudulently misrepresented the condition of the home as to its structural integrity and the water problems in the basement. In March 1998, after a bench trial, the district court ordered the rescission of the sale of the home. Hence, the district court ordered Barker to restore everything of value received during the ownership of the property to Ness and Smith and to return the property to Ness and Smith. The court also ordered Smith and Ness to pay Barker $33,830.87, a sum arrived at by taking $44,855.87, Barker's total cost of the home, and subtracting the $11,025 in rental income received by Barker from the house, which sum would be returned to Ness and Smith. On appeal, Barker claimed that the district court had erred in denying her a jury trial and in reducing her restitution by the amount she had received as rental income.

ISSUES Was Barker entitled to a jury trial? Should the lower court have deducted the income received on the rental property from the restitution paid to her by the defendants?

HOLDINGS No; in an equitable proceeding, no absolute right to a trial by jury exists. Yes; because rescission necessitates the restoration of the *status quo*, Barker had to remit the rent. But this duty meant that the defendants in turn must remit to Barker the value of the use of the money paid to them for the purchase of the house (that is, the interest earned on the money).

REASONING Excerpts from the opinion of Judge McLees:

An individual who has been induced to enter a contract for the purchase of real estate by fraudulent misrepresentation may elect to affirm the contract, in which case the property is retained and an action is brought for damages. . . . Alternatively, an individual may elect to rescind the contract for fraud and restore everything of value received under the contract. . . . This decision is sometimes referred to as the Election of Remedies Doctrine. . . . Under [this] Doctrine . . . a plaintiff is required to elect between two inconsistent remedies . . . rescission or damage remedies. . . . The plaintiff must elect either to sue for damages (affirm) or to rescind the contract (disaffirm) and seek the return of the consideration given. . . . To effect a rescission at law, the plaintiff must give notice to the defendant of the rescission and . . . must offer to restore to the defendant what was given in the transaction, unless the offer to restore is obviated by an exception to the restoration rule. . . . The restoration of the status quo as a requirement for rescission at law, though part of a legal action, is nevertheless based on the equitable principle that he who seeks equity must do equity. . . . However, the plaintiff does not retain what he received. It is a fundamental principle of equity that parties must be restored to their pre-contractual position. . . . Therefore, once the trial court renders a formal rescission, it must restore each side to its respective pre-contractual position. . . . In this case, Barker, in her complaint, asked the court to cancel the sale of the home and return the ownership of the house to Ness and Smith. There is nothing in the record indicating tender of a notice of rescission and offer to restore sufficient . . . to effect a rescission at law. Therefore, we determine Barker proceeded in equity, seeking a rescission of the sale of the house. Because Barker was pursuing a claim in equity, with other alleged damage claims incidental to and dependent on the claim for rescission, we necessarily hold the district court did not err when it refused to grant Barker a jury trial. . . . Barker argues the district court erred when it reduced her restitution by the value of the rental income she had received while owning the house. The district court . . . found Barker had received rental income while in possession of the home and that those benefits must be restored to Smith and Ness. . . . This symmetrical application requires both parties be returned to their pre-contractual position. In addition to Barker remitting the reasonable use value gained from the transaction, in the absence of some countervailing equitable factor, Ness and Smith must also remit to Barker the value of the use of the money paid them for the purchase of the house. . . .

BUSINESS CONSIDERATIONS How does a person decide whether to sue for damages or for rescission of the contract at issue? On what factors will such a decision hinge?

ETHICAL CONSIDERATIONS Did Ness and Smith have an ethical duty to disclose, prior to Barker's purchase of the house, the water damage? Fully support whatever position you take.

performance in contracts that consist of personal services. The A's instead could sue Reggie and the Yankees for money damages once he became a Yankee.

Quasi Contract/Reformation/Injunction

Two concepts covered on several occasions in the contracts section, quasi contract and reformation, bear mentioning again, this time in the context of equitable remedies. *Quasi contract* involves circumstances in which a court creates a contract for the parties, despite their wishes and intentions, in order to prevent the unjust enrichment of one party. When the parties have not entered into a contract, but one party has knowingly received a benefit to which he or she is not entitled, an unjust enrichment has occurred. Given the absence of a valid contract, the injured party cannot seek contract-related remedies. In the interests of equity and fairness, however, the injured party may receive a restitution-based remedy, the reasonable value of the services rendered. *Reformation*, on the other hand, concerns a court's rewriting of a contract in order to remove a mistake and to make the agreement conform to the terms to which the parties originally agreed. (See the discussion of reformation in Chapter 12.)

An injunction is another type of equitable remedy. An *injunction* is a writ issued by a court of equity ordering a person to do or refrain from doing some specified act. This remedy does not arise often in contractual situations.

Limitations on Remedies

The parties may attempt in advance to limit the remedies available to the injured party. Chapter 13 discussed such efforts in the context of exculpatory clauses. The UCC also permits the parties to limit remedies. However, if an exclusive remedy—as defined in the contract—fails in its essential purpose, UCC § 2-719 permits the injured party to seek any remedies available under the Code. This same section also forbids contractual limitations of consequential damages for *personal* injuries resulting from the use of consumer goods. The UCC dubs limitations on these sorts of damages prima facie unconscionable, or damages that, on their face, are blatantly unfair and one-sided. On the other hand, the UCC does not characterize limitations of damages in purely *commercial* settings in this way.

Waiver of Breach

Even though you have spent a great deal of this chapter studying the various remedies available to an injured party

when the other party breaches the contract, recall that the injured party may be willing to accept less-than-complete performance. The law terms an injured party's giving up the right to receive the performance set out in the contract a *waiver of breach*. Once a waiver of breach occurs, the waiver in effect eliminates the breach; the performance required under the contract continues as if the breach never happened. In essence, waiver of breach precludes the termination or rescission of the contract; it serves as a method of keeping the contract operative between the parties. As usual, the nonbreaching party later can recover damages for anything that constitutes less-than-complete performance. Thus, if only one of the bulldozers delivered to Miranda is slightly defective or if Welling is only slightly late in making what otherwise is a satisfactory delivery, Miranda, in order to receive Welling's performance under the rest of the contract, may choose to waive such breaches.

A waiver of breach ordinarily applies only to the matter waived and not inevitably to the rest of the contract. The same is true of subsequent breaches of the contract: The first waiver normally will not cover additional, later breaches, especially when the later breaches bear no relation to the first one. However, the waiving party may want to stand on his or her rights after the first waiver and indicate unambiguously that he or she will not tolerate future breaches. This action will eliminate the possibility of the breaching party's arguing that the waivers were so numerous and systematic that the breaching party believed less-than-complete performance was acceptable for the duration of the contract. Still, waiver remains a common business response in those circumstances in which the continuation of the contract will further the interests of the injured party.

UCITA's rules regarding contract discharge, breach of contract, and remedies resemble those provided by the UCC. For example, § 601 requires a party's performance to conform to the contract. If the performance fails to do so, in the absence of a waiver, the aggrieved party has a right to a remedy. In turn, the nature and extent of the remedy hinges on whether the failure to perform is minor or material. In this regard, UCITA follows the common law in making distinctions between material and nonmaterial breaches. UCITA § 701 notes that whether a party has breached the contract is determined by the agreement, or in the absence of an agreement, by the act's terms. According to § 701, among other things, a material breach is "a substantial failure to perform a term that is an essential element of the agreement" and the circumstances indicate that "the breach is likely to cause substantial harm to the aggrieved party." Nevertheless, § 701 explicitly states that an aggrieved party is entitled to remedies even for nonmaterial breaches. However, as § 701 makes clear, the aggrieved party can cancel the contract only if the breach is material. UCITA § 702 permits waivers of breach. Furthermore, like the UCC, UCITA § 615 recognizes the doctrine of commercial frustration and anticipatory repudiation (§ 709).

UCITA likewise mirrors the UCC in providing for cumulative remedies, including equitable ones (§ 801), with § 911 covering specific performance, one such equitable remedy.

UCITA also sets out general rules for calculating damages (§ 807); a liquidated damages provision (§ 804); a complicated statute of limitations provision (§ 805); and rules for discontinuing a licensee's access to the software, subscription service, or database that is the subject of the contract (§ 814). Pursuant to § 815, upon the cancellation of the license, the licensor can prevent the continued use of the contractual and informational rights in the licensed information that the licensee possesses. This so-called electronic self-help provision is probably the most controversial aspect of UCITA. Simply put, with the exception of mass-market transactions, UCITA allows a licensor to disable the software or computer program from a remote location if the licensor believes the licensee has breached the contract. Moreover, a licensor that avails itself of this "electronic self-help" method is not liable for any losses caused thereby unless the self-help is wrongful. The procedural safeguards set out in § 816 afford some protections to the licensee; for example, the requirement that the licensee must have separately manifested its assent to a term authorizing the self-help; that the licensor must give 15 days' advance notice; that the licensor must specify the nature of the claimed breach; and that the licensor must provide the licensee with information that will allow the licensee to communicate with the licensor about the claimed breach. Still, the licensor's use of electronic self-help could, for example, shut down a human resources or accounting computerized system and thereby wreak havoc on the licensee's business. Such concerns presumably underlie some states' reluctance to enact UCITA.

Summary

Discharge of a contract refers to the legally valid termination of a contractual duty. Performance may be either complete or substantial, and both degrees of performance ordinarily discharge the contract. The parties themselves may agree to discharge the contract; release, rescission, accord and satisfaction, and novation are examples of this method of discharging contracts. Bankruptcy decrees, the running of statutes of limitations, and material alterations of the contract will justify discharge of a contract by operation of law. In some circumstances, the nonperformance of one of the parties will discharge a contract. Courts that find evidence of destruction of the subject matter, intervening illegality, or conduct by one party that makes performance by the other party objectively impossible will excuse the resultant nonperformance. This is the doctrine of impossibility. In many other situations, however, impossibility will not justify discharge of the contract. The doctrine of commercial frustration consequently has arisen to mitigate the harshness of the common law's rejection of impossibility as a defense to nonperformance. Breach, whether actual or anticipatory, also may bring about discharge of the contract. The nonoccurrence of express conditions precedent and the occurrence of express conditions subsequent, in addition to constructive conditions, may cause discharge of a contract as well.

Upon one party's breach of a contract, the other party is free to pursue several kinds of remedies unless the injured party waives the breach. Remedies fall into two main categories: legal ("at law") and equitable.

Damages are the "at law" remedy. Usually a party sues for compensatory damages, or the amount of money that will place the party in the same economic position that he or she would have enjoyed had the contract been performed. Because the breaching party is liable for the foreseeable consequences of the breach, courts may award these actual losses and may even grant consequential, or special, damages if the facts so warrant. The injured party must mitigate the damages unless doing so will cause unreasonable expense or unreasonable risk. Failure to mitigate will limit the injured party to the recovery of direct losses. Courts impose punitive damages to punish the wrongdoer and to deter future malicious conduct. Some modern courts and statutes reject the old common law rule that punitive damages never can constitute appropriate remedies for breaches of contract. The parties may agree in advance on the sum of money to be paid for breaches of certain types. Such liquidated damages clauses are enforceable unless a court construes them as penalties. If the party sustains no actual damages, a court may award nominal damages.

When the "at law" remedy of damages is unavailable, indeterminable, or inadequate, courts may order equitable remedies. Rescission and restitution constitute one such remedy and involve the termination of the contract through the restoration of the parties to the status quo. Damages and restitution are mutually exclusive remedies, so the injured party must elect (or choose) one remedy or the other. If other damages or restitution will be inadequate, a court may order specific performance. This is an equitable remedy that compels the breaching party to perform according to the terms of the agreement. Courts usually grant specific performance when the subject matter of the contract is unique, but they are reluctant to grant specific performance in suits involving nonunique goods or personal services contracts. Quasi contract, reformation, and injunctions (writs ordering a person to do or refrain from doing some specified act) represent other types of equitable relief.

The injured party may choose to waive the breach in order to keep the contract going between the parties. Waiver of breach, or the injured party's giving up the right to receive the performance set out in the contract, does not preclude the injured party's seeking recovery for damages resulting from the breach, however.

UCITA's provisions on contract discharge, breach of contract, and remedies resemble those provided by the UCC. The "electronic self-help" provision is probably the most controversial aspect of UCITA.

Discussion Questions

1. What are the four main methods of contract discharge?

2. What is *rescission*?

3. Explain fully the doctrine of impossibility and the doctrine of commercial frustration as they relate to contract discharge.

4. What sorts of situations will discharge a contract by operation of law?

5. What is a complete, or material, breach of contract? What are the injured party's options when a complete breach occurs?

6. Name and define the two main types of remedies.

7. Define the *duty of mitigation*.

8. Why does the remedy of restitution differ from an action in damages?

9. Under what circumstances is specific performance an appropriate remedy?

10. What are the legal consequences of waiving a breach of contract?

Case Problems and Writing Assignments

1. The Evanoskis sued All-Around Travel to recover the monies the couple had paid to a travel agency. Mrs. Evanoski's sudden illness on the day of the scheduled departure for the tour precluded the couple's giving the 72-hour advance notice required under the contract with the travel agency. Was this sudden illness an event the couple could not have foreseen or guarded against so as to invoke the doctrine of impossibility of performance? [See *Evanoski v. All-Around Travel*, 682 N.Y. S.2d 342 (Sup. Ct. 1998).]

2. In February 1986, Trans World Airlines, Inc. (TWA) entered into an equipment trust agreement with the Connecticut National Bank (CNB). The agreement, commonly known as a sale/leaseback, provided that CNB would purchase 10 aircraft and approximately 96 jet engines from TWA and then would lease them back to TWA until February 1, 1996. In connection with the lease/purchase, CNB received senior secured trust notes, some of which matured on February 1, 1991 and others of which were scheduled to mature on February 1, 1996. The aggregate original principal of these notes amounted to approximately $312 million, with the principal on the 1991 notes being worth $100 million and the balance being covered by the 1996 notes. The agreement stipulated that TWA would pay all the necessary interest and principal on the notes directly to CNB, as trustee, which, in turn, would pay the note-holders, or the trust beneficiaries. TWA also guaranteed payment to the beneficiaries and agreed to indemnify CNB (reimburse CNB if CNB suffered a loss attributable to TWA's default). Finally, the agreement stated that once the lease had expired and TWA had paid off the loss suffered by that party under the notes, the equipment reverted to TWA.

TWA met its obligations in a satisfactory fashion until January 31, 1991. At that time, TWA failed to make the required payments of approximately $57 million, $9 million of which represented interest on the 1991 and 1996 notes and the other $48 million of which represented the remaining principal on the then-matured 1991 notes. Consequently, CNB failed to pay the beneficiaries, since the agreement specifically obligated CNB to pay the beneficiaries only to the extent that TWA had paid CNB. CNB then demanded the return of its property and the immediate payment of the approximately $81 million presently due as principal on the 1996 notes. Although the agreement specifically afforded CNB these remedies, TWA failed to make any payments and did not return any of CNB's property. Therefore, on March 26, 1991, CNB filed a lawsuit seeking specific performance of the agreement's default remedies, including the return of the equipment located inside and outside the United States, delivery of various records relating to the property, and a permanent injunction preventing TWA from removing any of the property from the United States. TWA argued that a court's requiring specific performance of the agreement's default provisions would be inappropriate because CNB had a remedy at law. In addition, TWA asserted that requiring it to return the property in light of the tremendous ramifications such an order might have on both TWA and the public at large would be inequitable. Should the court grant CNB's motion for summary judgment and order specific performance of the agreement? [See *Connecticut National Bank v. Trans World Airlines, Inc.,* 762 F. Supp. 76 (S.D.N.Y. 1991).]

3. Katherine Lane enrolled her 18-month-old daughter in day care with Kindercare Learning Centers, Inc. On December 9, 1992, Lane dropped off her daughter at Kindercare's facility at lunchtime. Lane's daughter had been prescribed medication, and Lane filled out an authorization form granting Kindercare's employees permission to administer the medication to her daughter that day. Just after 5:00 P.M., one of the employees placed the child, who had fallen asleep, in a crib in the infant room. At approximately 6:00 P.M., the employees, apparently unaware that Lane's daughter was still sleeping in the crib, locked the doors of the facility and went home for the day. Shortly thereafter, Lane returned to the facility to pick up her daughter and found the facility locked and unlit. A police officer who responded to Lane's 911 call looked through a window of the facility and saw the child sleeping in the crib. Another officer then broke a window and retrieved the child from the building. The child was upset after the incident but not physically harmed. When Lane went into the facility to retrieve her daughter's belongings, she apparently found the medication authorization form and observed that it had not been initialed to indicate that an employee had given the medication to the child. As a result of the incident, Lane alleged that she had suffered emotional distress. Michigan law allowed the recovery of emotional damages for breach of contracts of a personal nature but not for breaches involving commercial, or pecuniary, contracts. Should Lane prevail on her claim in this case? [See *Lane v. Kindercare Learning Centers, Inc.,* 588 N.W.2d 715 (Mich. App. 1998).]

4. On January 24, 1995, Mr. and Mrs. Laurence L. Kesterson and Patrick J. Juhl entered into a loan agreement. The terms of the loan agreement were expressed in a letter drafted by Juhl. According to the agreement, Juhl agreed to lend the Kestersons $145,000 in cash. They in turn agreed to pay Juhl $15,000 as a loan fee and to pay Juhl's attorney $15,000 for the preparation of the loan agreement. As security for the loan, the Kestersons provided Juhl with a trust deed to property in Washington and a mortgage on property in Idaho. The value of the two properties substantially exceeded $145,000. The Kestersons further agreed to pay off the loan within six months. Interest on the outstanding balance accrued at an annual rate of 22 percent. In the event they failed to repay the entire loan within six months, they agreed to pay "an additional loan fee" of 20 percent of the gross sales price of each of the two properties pledged as security for the loan. In the loan agreement, Juhl explained the purpose of that fee as follows: "As I have stated to you, a failure on your part to timely repay the loan will cause me significant financial hardship." The agreement did not specify the nature of the "hardship" that Juhl anticipated. Some evidence indicated that Juhl wanted to have the loan

repaid no later than July so that it would be available to him during the building season. As security for the obligation to pay the 20 percent, the Kestersons agreed to execute warranty deeds conveying the 20-percent interest in each of the two properties to Juhl and to deposit the deeds with Juhl's attorney. The attorney could record the deeds in Juhl's name if the Kestersons failed to repay the loan within the required six months. The Kestersons subsequently deposited the full repayment amount—the $145,000 principal and the $22,000 interest—into an escrow account for Juhl. When the money was not immediately released from escrow—apparently because of a construction lien—Juhl declared the Kestersons to be in breach and recorded the two warranty deeds. Meanwhile, the funds in escrow were released on September 15, 1995. In November 1995, the Kestersons sold the Idaho property for $450,000. They continued to own the Washington property, valued at $60,000. When Juhl subsequently claimed a 20 percent interest in each, for a total of $102,000, the Kestersons sued. They alleged that Juhl had breached the loan agreement by recording the warranty deeds in spite of the fact that they had deposited the full repayment into escrow (that is, the deposit into escrow constituted full performance). They also sought a declaration that, in any event, they were not obligated to pay the 20 percent additional loan fee for untimely repayment, because the fee constituted liquidated damages that amounted to an unlawful penalty. Were the Kestersons correct? [See *Kesterson v. Juhl,* 970 P.2d 681 (Or. App. 1998).]

5. **BUSINESS APPLICATION CASE** Franconia Associates (Franconia) and other property owners had participated in a federal program that promoted the development of affordable rental housing in areas conventional lenders traditionally would not serve. Pursuant to this program, the owners, in exchange for low-interest mortgage loans issued by the Farmers Home Administration (FmHA), had agreed to devote the owners' properties to low- and middle-income housing and to abide by related restrictions during the life of the loans. The owners' promissory notes had included provisions concerning prepayment of the loans involved. However, the Emergency Low Income Housing Preservation Act of 1987 (ELIHPA), as amended, placed permanent restrictions on the prepayment of such loans. Franconia and the other owners, filing suit under the Tucker Act, claimed that ELIHPA had abridged the absolute prepayment right set forth in their promissory notes and thereby had effected a repudiation of their contracts. In dismissing these contract claims as untimely under § 2501 of the Tucker Act—which provides that a claim "shall be barred unless the petition thereon is filed within six years after such claim first accrues"—the Court of Federal Claims concluded that the claims first accrued on the ELIHPA regulations' effective date. The Federal Circuit ruled that, if the government's continuing duty to allow the owners to prepay their loans had been breached, the breach had occurred immediately on ELIHPA's enactment date, over nine years before the owners had filed their suit. In holding that the statute of limitations would bar the owners' claims, the court also rejected the owners' argument that ELIHPA's passage qualified as a repudi-

ation, so that their suit would be timely if filed within six years of either the date performance fell due (the date they tendered prepayment) or the date on which they elected to treat the repudiation as a present breach. Should the Supreme Court affirm the Federal Circuit's decision? [See *Franconia Associates v. United States*, 536 U.S. 129 (2002).]

6. ETHICAL APPLICATION CASE Warren Kobatake and other nursery owners whose plants were allegedly damaged by Benlate 50DF, a product manufactured by E.I. Dupont de Nemours and Company, had settled a product liability case with DuPont. Pursuant to the terms of the settlement agreements, the plaintiffs executed general releases in which they released and discharged DuPont from any and all liabilities relating to the fungicide. The parties also covenanted that the release represented the parties' complete agreement. Some time afterward, the plaintiffs discovered information that led them to believe that DuPont had acted improperly and fraudulently during the defense of the previous litigation by, among other things, scheming to destroy harmful evidence and presenting perjured testimony. Accordingly, two years after unearthing these facts, the plaintiffs sought to rescind the settlement agreements on the basis of fraud. What factors would a court consider when it rules on this case? Why would a large, well-known firm like DuPont put its reputation on the line and engage in the ethically questionable behavior alleged here? Would a code of ethics have helped to prevent these improprieties? [See *Kobatake v. E.I. DuPont de Nemours and Company*, 162 F.3d 619 (11th Cir. 1998).]

7. CRITICAL THINKING CASE Howard Mowers, a self-employed chiropractor, purchased a disability insurance policy from Paul Revere Life Insurance Company beginning in July 1989. The policy provided coverage in the event that Mowers became totally disabled with regard to his work. The pertinent contract provision stated: "Total disability means that because of injury or sickness: a. You are unable to perform the important duties of Your Occupation; and b. You are under the regular and personal care of a Physician." The policy also stated that the insured agreed to submit to Independent Medical Exams (IMEs) as often as reasonably required during the pendency of any disability claim. In August 1992, Mowers injured his lower back at work and was forced to reduce his work hours until, eventually, he ceased working entirely. As a consequence, in November 1992, Mowers began receiving disability payments in the amount of $3,760 per month. In the fall of 1993, Paul Revere stopped paying the benefits to Mowers, because it required further confirmation of his injuries. At the request of Paul Revere, Mowers submitted to five IMEs by physicians of the company's choosing between 1993 and 1994. Three of the five examinations explicitly confirmed that he remained totally disabled from his work as a chiropractor. The other two confirmed that Mowers could not lift patients. At that time, Mowers also was under the continuous care of Dr. Gary Witchley. On confirmation of Mowers's continued disability, Paul Revere resumed the payment of the benefits to Mowers. In February 1997, Mowers submitted to a requested

sixth IME, performed by Dr. Warren Rinehart. Dr. Rinehart reported that Mowers might be able to resume part-time work if Mowers limited his practice to conducting IMEs and working only with patients who had cervical vertebrae problems. After Dr. Rinehart's report, Paul Revere made arrangements for two functional capacity evaluations (FCE) for July 28, 1997, and September 3, 1997, to determine the extent of Mowers's disability. Mowers did not attend either evaluation. Effective September 1, 1997, the company stopped paying Mowers benefits. The company based its denial on Dr. Rinehart's opinion that Mowers retained the ability to engage in some aspects of chiropractic. Mowers subsequently filed suit for breach of contract. Paul Revere contended that the court should dismiss the claim because Mowers had failed to perform the condition precedent of submitting to physical examinations as often as reasonably requested by the company. Who had the more persuasive argument here—Paul Revere or Mowers? [See *Mowers v. Paul Revere Life Insurance Company*, 27 F. Supp. 2d 135 (N.D. N.Y. 1998).]

8. YOU BE THE JUDGE Basketball superstar Michael Jordan filed a lawsuit claiming Karla Knafel had attempted to extort additional money from him in exchange for her silence about a relationship they had had a decade ago. Jordan argued that, owing to Knafel's threats to publicly expose that relationship, he had agreed to pay—and had paid her—$250,000. However, he asserted, he had never agreed to pay Knafel any amount—let alone the $5,000,000 she claims he had promised—in addition to the $250,000 already paid to her.

In a countersuit, Ms. Knafel alleged that she and Jordan first met each other at an Indianapolis hotel where she was working as a vocalist. After an NBA referee had introduced her to Jordan, they had numerous long-distance telephone conversations before and after Jordan's marriage on September 2, 1989. When Knafel asked Jordan why he still wanted to see her, he allegedly responded that his marriage to Mrs. Jordan was a "business arrangement," that he considered his wife "hired help," and that he had married Juanita so as to maintain a favorable public image. Knafel and Jordan began a sexual relationship in December 1989. According to Knafel, they always engaged in unprotected sex, apparently out of Jordan's wishes, even though Knafel had voiced her concerns about this matter to Jordan.

When Karla learned she was pregnant in 1991, she believed the child was Jordan's. She refrained from telling Jordan because the Chicago Bulls were en route to winning Jordan's and the team's first NBA championship. When she eventually told Jordan about the pregnancy, he insisted that she have an abortion. Because of her personal beliefs, she refused. According to Knafel, Jordan wanted this relationship to remain out of the public eye because the ensuing damage to his public image would result in reductions in future endorsements. In 1991, Jordan allegedly offered to pay Karla $5,000,000 when he retired from professional basketball in exchange for her agreement not to file a paternity suit against him in a court of law and for her agreement to keep their romantic involvement publicly confidential. Knafel accepted Jordan's offer and, as consideration for his promising payment of $5,000,000 when he retired from professional basketball, she agreed not to file a public paternity action against him and further agreed that she otherwise would keep their romantic relationship publicly confidential. When Karla's child was born in July 1991, Jordan paid certain hospital bills and medical costs regarding the birth and sent roses to her at the hospital. Jordan also paid Karla the sum of $250,000 for the mental pain and anguish that had arisen from her relationship with him.

In point of fact, Jordan was not the baby's father. In October 1993, Jordan announced that he was retiring from the Bulls after three consecutive NBA championships. However, at his retirement press conference, he hinted that he might return to the NBA. In March 1995, Jordan announced his immediate return to the Chicago Bulls. Because Jordan suddenly had "unretired" from professional basketball by returning to the Bulls before the 1995 NBA playoffs, she had not personally contacted Jordan to demand his payment of the $5,000,000 amount that he promised her in 1991. Rather, she allegedly continued to rely on his assurance that he would pay her. However, when, in the summer of 1998, public speculation arose that Jordan soon would retire again, Knafel decided to see Jordan in Las Vegas, Nevada, where he was vacationing. During the course of their conversation, Karla allegedly reminded Jordan of his obligation to pay her the money. He allegedly reaffirmed his 1991 agreement to pay her the $5,000,000 sum and said that he would have his Chicago

lawyer contact her to arrange for payment. He then left the blackjack table, joined two women—neither one of whom was his wife—and disappeared with them. Only a few months after Karla and Jordan met in Las Vegas, he again retired from playing professional basketball.

When Jordan sued Knafel, she counterclaimed that Jordan's failure to pay her constituted a breach of their 1991 contract and his 1998 reaffirmation of it, causing her damages in the amount of $5,000,000 plus interest. Jordan, in contrast, submitted that any alleged agreement for $5,000,000 would be unenforceable because: (i) extortion agreements violate public policy; (ii) there would be no consideration to support any such agreement owing to Knafel's existing obligation to refrain from publicly exposing the relationship; (iii) any such agreement would violate the Statute of Frauds, since there is an absence of any agreement and, hence, a lack of any agreement signed by Jordan; and (iv) any such agreement would be barred by the applicable statute of limitations. If *you* were the judge in this case, how would you rule on these and any other issues germane to this lawsuit? [Pleadings filed on October 14, 2002, and November 14, 2002, by Michael Jordan and Karla Knafel, respectively, in the Circuit Court of Cook County, Illinois; similar information found at http://www.thesmokinggun.com/archive/jordanextort1.html and http://www.thesmokinggun.com/archive/karlaresp1.html (accessed 12/21/2002).]

Notes

1. A material breach, as we will see in later sections of this chapter, occurs when the performance rendered falls appreciably below the level of performance the parties reasonably expected under the terms of the contract. Such a breach discharges the other party from the contract.

2. 156 Eng. Rep. 145 (Ex. 1854).
3. 499 U.S. 1 (1991).
4. 517 U.S. 559 (1996).
5. 532 U.S. 424 (2001).

Sales and Leases

The early common law of contracts was inappropriate—if not inadequate—for a commercial society. The common law was developed in an agrarian society; it reflected the relative importance of land and a corresponding lack of importance for commercial transactions, especially the sale of goods. Over time, however, commercial transactions became increasingly important, and the law became less relevant to the realities of the society. As a result, during the late Middle Ages merchants developed their own set of rules and regulations, the law merchant, as a means for regulating commercial transactions. Eventually, in the 16th century, the law merchant was absorbed into the common law, providing "official" recognition of the growing importance of commercial transactions to the society. The sociological and technological advances of the 20th century made the law merchant as outmoded for this era as the common law had been for the Industrial Revolution. Once again, new rules were developed and codified, first in such statutes as the Uniform Sales Act (USA) and the Uniform Negotiable Instruments Law (NIL), and then later in the Uniform Commercial Code (UCC). The UCC covers multiple areas of commercial law, including the sale of goods (Article 2) and the leasing of goods (Article 2A).

The UCC covers sales and leases within the United States, but not international transactions. Firms involved in international trade also need to be aware of their rights and obligations, but contracts between firms in different nations make such awareness difficult. One potential solution to this problem can be found in the United Nations Convention on Contracts for the International Sale of Goods, the CISG.

The next four chapters discuss how contracts involving the sale or leasing of goods are formed; the rules that govern performance, title, and risk of loss; how warranties and liabilities operate in these transactions; what remedies are available for a breach in a sales contract; and how international laws may affect the sales of goods outside the borders of the United States.

CHAPTER 16

Formation of the Sales Contract: Contracts for Leasing Goods

AGENDA

NRW NRW will be considered a merchant in the sale of its disks and its microchips in the United States. What does it mean to be considered a "merchant" in the sale of goods? Does merchant status carry any special benefits or burdens that nonmerchants do not possess? Why should it matter if NRW is considered a merchant?

The firm expects to sell its products to a significant number of purchasers. Some of these purchasers will also be merchants and some will be consumers. Should the firm negotiate each contract separately, entering into the traditional "give and take" of the marketplace, or would the business be better served by using a standard form contract, basically treating each sale as being virtually the same as every other sale? Does the status of the purchaser have any impact on this decision?

If things go as hoped, NRW will also be making sales to some foreign customers and may have to order some of its chips from foreign suppliers. Will Article 2 of the UCC still govern these transactions, or will some other law control these international contracts?

These and other questions need to be addressed in covering the material in this chapter. Be prepared! You never know when the firm or one of its members will seek your advice.

The common law coverage of contracts provides a good framework for studying agreements between people. As society has progressed and developed in England and in the United States, however, some elements of the common law have become outdated. When this occurs, the law-making bodies often step in to try to resolve the problems presented by a changing society. One early result of this legislative intervention is the Statute of Frauds (the original statute was enacted by the English Parliament in 1677), which requires that certain types of contracts be in writing in order to be enforceable. Another—and more contemporary—example of legislative intervention to help the law keep pace with society is the Uniform Commercial Code (the first UCC was adopted in the United States in 1954). The UCC was developed by the National Conference of Commissioners on Uniform State Laws. It is designed to update and modernize the law of commerce in code form and to reflect modern commercial reality.

Under the early common law, contract law developed primarily to reflect the importance of land in the economy of England. The common law treatment of contracts involving the sale of land was quite extensive, whereas the treatment of contracts for the sale of goods was sparse. As a merchant class began to develop in England, the merchants realized that the common law did not adequately address their contracts or their contractual concerns. As a result, the merchants developed their own law, the law merchant (*lex mercatoria*). Eventually, the law merchant was adopted by Parliament as an official part of English law, giving official status to the merchants and their transactions under the law.

This same legal tradition was followed in the United States after its formation. Because the United States had been a part of England, and because the courts in existence were based on English law, it was natural for the United States to follow English laws initially. By the early 20th century, the law merchant was still in effect, but it was substantially out of date. As a result, the Uniform Sales Act (USA) was enacted to update and modernize the law merchant in the United States. While the USA was significantly more modern than the law merchant, it too was quickly out of date.

The Uniform Commercial Code (UCC) was adopted in 1954 to reflect contemporary commercial practices. The UCC replaced the USA and the NIL (the Uniform Negotiable Instruments Law), among other areas. The Uniform Commercial Code is organized into sections, each covering a different aspect of commercial law. For example, the UCC replaced the USA with Article 2, which governs the sale of goods. Other sections of the Code include Article 2A, which deals with the leasing of goods (many modern transactions involve leasing goods rather than buying them); Article 3, which deals with negotiable instruments (checks, a form of negotiable instrument, are often used to pay for goods); Article 4, which deals with banks and customers; Article

---

NRW CASE 16.1   Management

WHAT TYPE OF LAW WILL MOST AFFECT NRW?

The firm's members have been discussing the various types of law that are likely to affect their business and trying to decide what type of law will be most important in governing their business. Mai is convinced that federal regulatory provisions and statutes will be most important, especially patent law, Federal Communications Commission rules and regulations, and laws affecting computers and computing technology. Helen agrees that federal laws will have a large impact, but she believes that traditional common law principles, especially in the area of contract law, will be most important. Carlos is of the opinion that, because NRW will be selling goods, the most important area of law will be Article 2 of the UCC, at least until the firm begins to make international sales. They have asked you for your opinion. What will you tell them?

BUSINESS CONSIDERATIONS A new business, especially one in a relatively high-tech industry, is likely to be subjected to numerous types of legal and administrative regulations. Is any one type of regulation more important than the others? Should a business try to deduce which areas of law or administrative regulation will most affect it before it begins doing business, or should the firm just seek compliance with *all* areas of the law that affect it?

ETHICAL CONSIDERATIONS Should a business be more concerned with evading regulations, avoiding regulations, or complying with regulations? Explain your reasoning. What ethical issues are raised by efforts to evade regulation? By efforts to avoid regulation?

INTERNATIONAL CONSIDERATIONS Should a business begin planning for possible international transactions from its beginning or wait until it actually has an opportunity to "go international" before it becomes concerned with any possible legal differences in an international contract? Why?

4A, which deals with funds transfers; Article 5, which deals with letters of credit (a standard method of payment, especially when the parties are separated geographically); Article 7, which deals with documents of title (often used in sales of goods between merchants); and Article 9, which deals with secured transactions (goods are often used as collateral when goods are sold on credit).

The UCC has been adopted, in whole or in part, in all 50 states. (Louisiana, with its French heritage and its tradition of following the Napoleonic Code, has not adopted all sections of the Code. In particular, Louisiana has not adopted Article 2 or Article 2A. South Carolina has not adopted Article 2A. All the other states have adopted both articles.) Thus, the coverage and the principles of the Code are applicable virtually nationwide, even though the Code itself is state law. This uniformity allows widespread understanding of the rules and the reasonable expectation that the rules followed in one state are likely to be followed in other states as well.

Although the UCC has basically been adopted throughout the United States, it does not apply internationally unless the parties to an international contract specify that the UCC will control, or unless the contract is entered into in the United States and the parties agree to be governed by U.S. law while also "opting out" of the provisions of the United Nations Convention on Contracts for the International Sale of Goods (CISG). As international trade increases, the need for a uniform set of legal rules and guidelines will increase. The closest thing to a uniform set of international laws governing such trade that we have at present is the CISG, which is similar in many respects to Article 2 of the UCC. Article 2 of the UCC, including the Official Comments, can be accessed at http://www.law.cornell.edu/ucc/2/overview.html, or through the site for the National Conference of Commissioners on Uniform State Laws at http://www.nccusl.org.

The Scope of Article 2

Article 2 of the UCC (Sales) deals with the *sale* of *goods*. This is a somewhat limited topic when compared with all the types of contracts that a party might enter. However, most of us will enter into more contracts for the sale of goods than any other types of contracts.

To understand the scope of Article 2, we need to know what is covered. Thus, we must begin by defining a "sale" and then by defining "goods." According to § 2-106(1) of the UCC, a sale is defined as the passing of title from the seller to the buyer for a price. This is the only definition of a sale in Article 2, but there are several related and similar terms that also need to be examined. For example, the words *contract* and *agreement,* when used in Article 2, refer to either the present or the future sale of goods. *Contract for sale* covers both a present sale and a contract to sell goods in the future. A *present sale* is a sale made at the time the contract is made. *Goods* are defined in § 2-105(1) of the Code. According to that section, goods mean "all things that are movable at the time they are identified to the contract." The Code lists several things that are specifically included as goods, such as specially manufactured items, the unborn young of animals, growing crops, and things attached to land, if they are to be separated from the land for their sale. The Code also specifically excludes some things, declaring them *not* to be goods. Examples are money when used as a payment for sale, investment securities, and things in action, such as rights under a contract yet to be performed. (Things in action are also sometimes referred to as choses in action.)

In the next case the court had to decide whether the contract involved a sale of goods, which would allow the case to be resolved in one manner, or the sale of a service, which would require that the case be resolved in a different manner. Follow the court's reasoning and decide whether you agree with the conclusions the court reached.

Statutory enactments that specifically exempt certain transactions from sales law coverage reflect public policy considerations as determined by the legislatures of the various states. For example, hospitals that provide blood, blood products, and human tissues provide a service that is deemed essential to society. By classifying such procedures as "services" rather than "sales," the legislatures of a significant number of states have opted to protect the hospitals, even if some individuals may suffer grievous loss without the possible recourse options that would be available in a sale of goods.

Transactions under Article 2 must involve two persons. One is the buyer—the person who purchases, or agrees to purchase, the goods. The other person is the seller—the person who provides, or agrees to provide, the goods covered by the contract.

The law of sales is very broad. It covers every sale of goods, whether made by a seller who is a merchant or by one who is a nonmerchant, and whether made to a buyer who is a merchant or to one who is a nonmerchant. Regardless of the status of the parties, Article 2 controls the sale. However, the status of the parties will affect the duties and obligations of the parties involved in the sale; the key factor here is the status of the parties as merchants or nonmerchants.

A merchant is defined as a person who deals in the type of goods involved in the sale, *or* a person who claims to be

16.1

BRANDT v. SARAH BUSH LINCOLN HEALTH CENTER
2002 Ill. App. LEXIS 313 (4th District)

FACTS In December 1998 Brandt was treated at the Sarah Bush Lincoln Health Center for incontinence. The treatment involved having Brandt purchase a ProteGen Sling from the Health Center and then having the sling surgically implanted by the Health Center. Boston Scientific Corporation, the manufacturer of the ProteGen Sling, issued a recall for the slings in January 1999, a month after the treatment here in issue. According to Boston Scientific, the sling did not produce the desired outcome in treating female incontinence. In addition, other problems related to vaginal erosion and dehiscence (a tearing apart or reopening of the surgical wound from the initial implant) were likely to occur in patients who had received implants of the sling. Ms. Brandt reported suffering numerous complications following the implant procedure, including inflammation, pain, bleeding, infections, and erosion of the tissue of her vaginal wall. She eventually had the sling surgically removed in November 1999.

In June 2000, Ms. Brandt filed suit against Boston Scientific and the Health Center, alleging that the defendants had committed torts under negligence and strict liability principles, and also alleging that they should be held liable for breach of the implied warranty of merchantability. (The original complaint was deemed defective under Illinois law because it lacked a required physician's affidavit.) Brandt filed an amended complaint in May 2001. In the amended complaint Brandt alleged the same three counts against Boston Scientific but alleged only breach of the warranty of merchantability against the Health Center. The Health Center filed a motion to dismiss, arguing that Brandt had failed to correct the deficiency in her pleading and also arguing that it was not a "merchant" in the sale of the ProteGen Sling, so that it could not have breached the warranty of merchantability. The trial court granted the motion to dismiss, and Brandt appealed this decision.

ISSUE Was the sale of the ProteGen Sling by the Health Center to Brandt a sale of "goods" under Article 2 of the UCC? [There was also an issue involving whether the allegation of breach of warranty of merchantability involved "healing art malpractice," thus requiring the inclusion of a physician's affidavit under Illinois law.]

HOLDING No. The sale of the sling by the hospital was an incidental aspect of the contract, which was primarily for the provision of services, and thus Article 2 of the UCC did not apply.

REASONING Excerpts from the opinion of Justice Cook:

Plaintiff's amended complaint alleged one count of breach of implied warranty of merchantability under section 2-314 of the UCC against the defendant based upon its sale and distribution of the sling. . . . Section 2-314 of the UCC states:

(1) Unless excluded or modified ***, a warranty that the goods shall be merchantable is implied in a contract for their sale if the seller is a merchant with respect to goods of that kind. ***

(2) Goods to be merchantable must be at least such as

   (a) pass without objection in the trade under the contract description; and ***

   (c) are fit for the ordinary purpose for which such goods are used. . . .

Section 2-104 defines "merchant" to mean: "[A] person who deals in goods of the kind or otherwise by his occupation holds himself out as having knowledge or skill peculiar to the practices or goods involved in the transaction or to whom such knowledge or skill may be attributed by his employment or an agent or broker or other intermediary who by his occupation holds himself out as having such knowledge or skill."

Section 2-102 further provides that the UCC "applies to transactions in goods." . . . Finally, case law established that the warranty provisions do not apply to the rendition of services. . . . The test for applicability of the UCC in Illinois is whether the transaction at issue is predominantly one for the sale of goods with services incidentally involved, or one for the rendition of services with the sale of goods incidentally involved. . . . If the transaction was primarily for services, then the UCC does not apply even if the sale of goods was part of the transaction. . . . Defendant contends that in the instant case, the sale of the sling was a necessary adjunct to the primary function of providing medical services, and therefore the UCC does not apply. We agree. In general, when a person seeks medical care from a hospital, the primary purpose of the transaction is to obtain the hospital's services, not to buy medical supplies or devices. Many courts have declined to allow product liability claims against hospitals based upon the sale of defective medical equipment. . . . A hospital will often use and sell certain tangible items as a necessary part of providing services. However, the thrust of the transaction between patient and hospital is still the provision of services to treat a medical condition. The incidental sale of the product or device that is necessary to render the medical service does not transform the transaction into one primarily for the sale of goods. In this case, plaintiff sought the hospital's services for treatment of a medical condition. The rendition of services was the primary purpose of the transaction. The sale of the sling, though an important part of the services, was incidental to those services. The UCC does not apply. . . .

[On the second issue the court determined that, because Brandt did not allege "healing art malpractice" against the hospital, there was no need for her to attach a physicians' affidavit to her complaint. An allegation of breach of the warranty of merchantability is *not* an allegation of medical malpractice.]

BUSINESS CONSIDERATIONS Should a business that provides goods and services to its customers try to fashion its contracts in a manner that emphasizes the "service" aspect and downplays the "goods" aspect in order to avoid giving warranties? Would such a practice make it more difficult to show the existence of a contract because the transaction would be governed by common law?

ETHICAL CONSIDERATIONS Should a provider of services who also makes "incidental" sales of goods, such as a hospital, inform its customers or patients that the transaction does not carry any warranty protections? Is it ethical if such a provider does not notify the customer or patient, and then relies on precedents such as this case to avoid liability?

(or is recognized as) an expert in the type of goods involved in the sale, *or* a person who employs an expert in the type of goods involved in the sale (§ 2-104). A person who is represented by an agent or a broker or any other intermediary who, by his occupation, holds himself out as an expert is deemed to be a merchant. Any other person is viewed as a nonmerchant.

A merchant is required by the terms of the Code to act in good faith, to cooperate with the other party in the performance of the contract, and to act in a commercially reasonable manner in the performance of the contract. (A commercially reasonable manner means that the conduct must comply with the normal fair dealings and practices of the trade.) A nonmerchant is required to act in good faith and to cooperate with the other party in the performance of the contract. However, a nonmerchant is not required to act in a commercially reasonable manner. Thus, a merchant is held to a higher standard of conduct than is expected of a nonmerchant. Further, merchants are presumed to give an implied warranty of merchantability in their contracts, whereas a nonmerchant does not give such an implied warranty. Obviously, the status of a party as a merchant or as a nonmerchant is an important consideration in determining rights and duties under the sales contract.

Forming the Sales Contract

A contract for the sale of goods under Article 2 is formed in basically the same manner that a contract is formed under the rules of common law. However, a sales contract can be formed with much less formality or rigidity than is

required by common law. While the common law requires an exact agreement, a "mirror image" between the offer and the acceptance, the Code recognizes that a contract exists whenever the parties *act* as if they have an agreement. The common law requires that the acceptance has to comply exactly with all the terms of the offer. Any variation is treated as a counteroffer (an attempt to vary the terms of the original offer) rather than as an acceptance. In an effort to reflect commercial reality, the Code will sometimes recognize a contract that would not be considered binding under the common law.

For example, in § 2-204(2) the Code recognizes that a contract exists even though the time of the agreement is uncertain. Further, in § 2-204(3), the Code permits a contract to stand even though some other terms (such as price or quantity) are omitted from the agreement. Under the common law, the omission of any of these terms would negate the existence of a contract. The courts would rule that the attempt to form a contract failed due to the "indefiniteness of the terms." Under the UCC, if the parties intend to have a contract and if remedies can be found in case there is a breach, the mere lack of some terms is often deemed unimportant. A contract will be found to exist, and the missing terms will be supplied under other provisions of the Code.

As in regular common law, a contract for the sale of goods needs both an offer and an acceptance. These technical requirements are covered by UCC § 2-206, which states that, unless an offer obviously requires otherwise, it can be accepted in any manner reasonable under the circumstances. Suppose the seller received an offer that included the following clause: "Acceptance must be made by sending a white pigeon carrying your note of acceptance tied to its left leg." Under the common law, a seller could accept this offer only by tying a note to the left leg of a white pigeon. If the message was tied to the right leg or if the pigeon was gray, the seller would be deemed to have made a counteroffer. Under the Code, the seller can accept by complying exactly with the terms of the offer (tying a message to the left leg of a white pigeon), by nearly complying (tying a message to either leg of a pigeon, or using a gray pigeon rather than a white one), or by using any other method of accepting that is reasonable under the circumstances. Sometimes, the Code even permits the acceptance of an offer by performing rather than by communicating or by communicating rather than performing, depending upon the terms of the offer and the conduct of the offeree.

For example, an offer to buy goods may call for the offeree to show acceptance of the offer by prompt shipment of the goods. Under the common law, the seller could accept this offer only by making a prompt shipment of the goods. However, under the UCC, the seller can accept this offer, thus creating a contract, in any of the following ways:

- The seller can promptly ship conforming goods to the buyer.

- The seller can promptly ship nonconforming goods to the buyer.

- The seller can notify the buyer that the goods will be shipped promptly.

Thus, the UCC permits acceptance in at least three different ways, while the common law only permitted acceptance in one exact manner. Notice that in the second method of acceptance under the UCC, the seller would not only accept the offer but would also (possibly) breach the contract that was entered into by shipment-as-acceptance. According to § 2-206(1)(b), a seller who receives an order or other offer, with the offer calling for acceptance by prompt shipment, may ship nonconforming goods as an accommodation to the buyer, and the shipment will not be treated as an acceptance of the offer. In order to qualify as an accommodation shipment, however, the seller must seasonably notify the buyer that nonconforming goods have been shipped and that the buyer has the option of accepting these (counteroffered) goods or rejecting them and returning them to the seller at the seller's expense. If the seller fails to give the required seasonable notification, the buyer may treat the goods shipped as an acceptance of the offer—and as a breach of the contract. The prompt shipment constituted an acceptance because it conformed to the terms of the offer, and the contract can be deemed to be breached because the goods do not conform to the terms specified in the offer.

The seller who accepts an offer by means of a prompt or current shipment must be careful for another reason. Assume the seller accepts by promptly shipping the goods but does not notify the buyer that the goods have been shipped. If the buyer neither receives the goods nor hears from the seller within a reasonable time, the buyer may treat the offer as lapsed before acceptance. When this happens, the buyer has no duty to pay for the goods when they finally arrive (if they finally arrive). This could leave the seller with unsold goods at some distant point, no ready buyer for the goods, and no contract remedies available, because, due to lapse, there was no contract and thus no breach by the buyer.

Standard Form Contracts

Very often both parties to the contract are merchants, and they are transacting business over a substantial distance. When this situation occurs, it is common to have the offer made on a standard form prepared by the offeror and the acceptance made on another standard form, this one prepared by the offeree who is trying to accept the offer. (A standard form is a preprinted contract form, often with blanks left in certain key places for later completion as the final contract terms are agreed to by the parties.) Use of a standard form contract frequently would have negated the contract under the common law because the terms included in the two forms are likely to differ, but the Code makes allowance for these differences while recognizing the existence of a contract. Under § 2-207(1), an acceptance that is made within a reasonable time is effective, even if it includes terms that add to or differ from the terms of the original offer. The only exception is when the acceptance is expressly made subject to an agreement with the new or different terms.

If the purported acceptance includes new or different terms, the Code provides a solution. The new terms are treated as proposed additions to the contract. If the contract is between merchants, the new terms become a part of the contract unless one of the following conditions exists:

- The offer explicitly limits acceptance to the terms of the offer.

- The new terms materially alter the contract.

- The offeror objects to the new terms within a reasonable time.

If the contract is not between merchants, the courts will not normally uphold the new terms unless it can be shown that both parties accepted them. If the offeree proposes different terms, § 2-207(3) controls. This section states that when the parties act as if they have a contract, they have a contract. And if they have writings, the writings will be construed consistently, so that an agreement exists. The written contract will consist of the terms on which the parties agree as well as the terms included by one party without any objection by the other party. But it will not include any terms that contradict other terms, or that have been objected to by one of the parties, or that materially alter the basic agreement. Exhibit 16.1 shows how a "conflict of forms" problem would be resolved.

The following case involved one of these "conflict of forms" controversies. Notice how the court resolved this conflict of forms between these merchants, and compare the court's results with Exhibit 16.1.

Firm Offers

Another area that gets special treatment for merchants under the Code is that of firm offers. Under common law, an offer could be freely revoked by the offeror at any time before its acceptance. This right to revoke existed even though the offeror might have "promised" to keep the offer open for some given time period. (If the offeree wanted a guarantee that the offer would remain open, the offeree had to enter into an option contract, giving consideration to the offeror for the benefit of having a guaranteed time period to decide.) Such a situation makes it very difficult for the offeree to make detailed plans based on the offer.

The Code recognizes that the offeree may have to make plans and explore options before accepting an offer, but may still need to be able to rely on the offer being available if and when the decision to accept is reached. The offeree may be harmed if an offer that is supposed to be "open" is revoked. To eliminate this potential problem, the Code guarantees that firm offers cannot be freely revoked before acceptance. Firm offers are given only by merchants. But if a merchant promises in writing to keep an offer open and unmodified for some specified time and signs the writing, a firm offer exists. The offer cannot be revoked by the offeror during the time the offeror agrees to keep the offer open. And if no time is specified, the offer cannot be revoked for a "reasonable time." To place some limit on this, the "reasonable time" cannot exceed three months.

Statute of Frauds

So far, the discussion has focused on the intent to have a contract and the Code's recognition that a contract exists in such a situation. However, some technical rules still exist that will override intent. One of these involves the Statute of Frauds, which requires that a contract for the sale of goods for $500 or more must be in writing in order for it to be enforceable. According to § 2-201 of the Code,

a contract for the sale of goods for the price of $500 or more is not enforceable by way of action or defense unless there is some writing sufficient to indicate that a contract for sale has been made between the parties and signed by the party against whom enforcement is sought or by his authorized agent or broker. A writing is not insufficient because it omits or incorrectly states a term agreed upon but the contract is not enforceable under this paragraph beyond the quantity of goods shown in such writing.

EXHIBIT 16.1 A "Conflict of Forms" Resolution

If the *offer* includes a Term or Clause	If the *acceptance* includes an *Additional* Term or Clause
And the acceptance includes the same term or clause, the term or clause will become part of the contract.	And the offeror does not object to the proposed additional term within a seasonable time, the proposed additional term or clause will become part of the contract, *unless* the proposed additional term materially alters the rights or duties of the parties in performing the contract.
And the acceptance is silent as to the term or clause, the term or clause will become part of the contract.	
And the acceptance includes the opposite of the term or clause, the two conflicting terms cancel one another and the term or clause is not mentioned—positively or negatively—in the contract.	But the offeror *does* seasonably object to the inclusion of the term or clause, the proposed clause will *not* become part of the contract.

16.2

RICHARDSON v. UNION CARBIDE INDUS. GASES, INC.
347 N.J. Super. 524; 790 A.2d 962; 2002 N.J. Super. LEXIS 80 (2002)

FACTS Prior to 1988, Hoeganaes Corporation operated furnace 2S, which was used for annealing iron powder. In 1988 Hoeganaes decided to convert furnace 2S to a distalloy furnace. This conversion required the purchase of a powder transport system to transport iron powder to the input end of the furnace. Hoeganaes purchased this powder transport system from Rage Engineering, Inc. The contract was based on proposal number 3313, submitted by Rage, and on purchase order number 21584, issued by Hoeganaes. The parties subsequently entered into two other contracts, one for the purchase of target boxes and one for the purchase of control logic panels. In each instance, Rage issued a proposal and Hoeganaes then issued a purchase order. On each proposal form prepared by Rage there was a statement that any purchases made were subject to the terms and conditions included by Rage in its proposal and that any contracts made were expressly subject to Rage's terms and conditions. One of these terms was that the purchaser would indemnify Rage and hold Rage harmless against any losses unless those losses were due solely and directly to the negligence or willful misconduct of Rage. Hoeganaes included similar boilerplate language on each of its purchase orders. The Hoeganaes form stated that *its* terms were the sole and exclusive contract of purchase and sale, and further stated that the seller agreed to indemnify and hold the purchaser harmless from any liability arising from the use of the goods being purchased. Neither party objected to any of the terms included in the form of the other party.

Jeffrey Richardson, an employee of Hoeganaes, was injured when furnace 2S exploded on May 13, 1992. Richardson eventually sued numerous parties, including Hoeganaes and Rage, on September 15, 1994, alleging breach of warranty, negligence, and product liability. Rage then cross-complained against Hoeganaes, seeking contractual indemnification based on its proposal forms. This complaint was denied, and the Hoeganaes motion for summary judgment was granted.

ISSUE Did the "knock-out" rule apply in New Jersey when there were conflicting terms in a contract formed under Article 2 of the UCC?

HOLDING Yes. The "knock-out" rule applied, so that the conflicting terms canceled one another, with none of these terms becoming part of the contract.

REASONING Excerpts from the opinion of Judge Braithwaite:

The relevant statutory provision is [UCC] 2-207, which provides as follows:

Additional Terms in Acceptance or Confirmation.

(1) A definite and seasonable expression of acceptance or a written confirmation which is sent within a reasonable time operates as an acceptance even though it states terms additional to or different from those offered or agreed upon, unless acceptance is expressly made conditional on assent to the additional or different terms.

(2) The additional terms are to be construed as proposals for addition to the contract. Between merchants such terms become part of the contract unless:

(a) the offer expressly limits acceptance to the terms of the offer;

(b) they materially alter it; or

(c) notification of objection to them has already been given or is given within a reasonable time after notice of them is received.

(3) Conduct by both parties which recognizes the existence of a contract is sufficient to establish a contract for sale although the writings of the parties do not otherwise establish a contract. In such cases the terms of the particular contract consist of those terms on which the writings of the parties agree, together with any supplementary terms incorporated under any other provisions of this Act.

We address first, Rage's second point, which asserts that the "knock-out" rule should not have been applied to its indemnity clause. This issue has not been addressed previously by our courts in a published opinion. We note that [UCC] 2-207 addresses "additional or different terms," . . . however, where the standard to determine whether additional terms become part of the parties' contract, the word "different" is not employed. [UCC] 2-207 is silent on the question of whether "additional or different terms" means the same thing. . . . There is seemingly no agreement on the matter. . . . It is unclear whether the reference to "different" terms in the acceptance . . . means that the drafters intended "different" to be treated like "additional" terms. . . . Comment . . . six . . . advances the proposition that conflicting terms in exchanged writings must be assumed to be mutually objected to by each party with the result of a mutual "knock-out" of the conflicting terms. Scholars differ on the subject. . . . There are, however, three recognized approaches by the courts to the issue of conflicting terms in contracts under circumstances such as here. . . . The majority view is that the conflicting terms fall out, and, if necessary, are replaced by UCC gap-filler provisions. . . . The minority view is that the offeror's terms control because the offeree's different terms cannot be saved . . . because that section only applies to additional terms. . . . The third view assimilates "different" to "additional" so that the terms of the offer prevail over the different terms in the acceptance only if the latter are materially different. This is the least adopted approach. . . . We conclude that the majority approach, the "knock-out" rule, is preferable and should be adopted in New Jersey. We reach this conclusion because the other approaches are inequitable and unjust and run counter to the policy behind [UCC] 2-207, which addresses a concern that existed at common law. . . .

Now we address Rage's first point . . . [UCC] 2-207(2) sets forth the standard to determine if additional terms of an acceptance become part of the contract . . . the additional terms between merchants become part of the contract unless: (a) the offer expressly limits acceptance to the terms of the offer; (b) they materially alter it; or (c) notification of objection to them has already been given or is given within a reasonable time after notice of them is received. . . . Applying this section here leads inescapably to the conclusion that Rage's indemnification clause did not become part of the contract. . . . Here, the contested provisions addressed indemnity and only became relevant after plaintiff was injured, some three years after the conversion of the furnace was completed. Pursuant to [UCC] 2-207(3), the conduct of the parties recognizes the existence of a contract and the "terms of the particular contract consist of those terms on which the writings of the parties agree, together with any supplementary terms incorporated under other provisions of the Act. Because the parties' writings disagree on indemnity, that term did not become part of the contract.

BUSINESS CONSIDERATIONS Should businesses just blindly rely on the validity of their own forms in forming a sales contract, or should more attention be paid to the terms included by the other party? Should a policy be developed for employees to follow in dealing with such forms?

ETHICAL CONSIDERATIONS Is it ethical to include an indemnity clause in a standard form and expect the other party to agree to provide indemnification for virtually any occurrence under the contract?

The Official Comments state that there are only three definite and invariable requirements for the writing:

1. the writing must evidence a contract for the sale of goods;

2. the writing must be "signed," which includes any authentication; and

3. it must specify a quantity of goods covered by the contract.

An oral agreement that falls within the coverage of the Statute of Frauds is normally unenforceable. However, the Code attempts to recognize modern commercial practices in this area as well. If the parties have any writing (a note, a memorandum, or "other writing") signed by the party being sued, that writing is sufficient to satisfy the statute. (This is the common law rule.) Terms that are omitted or incorrectly stated in the writing will not defeat the proof of the contract's existence. When both parties are merchants, however, a slightly different rule applies. Suppose one merchant sends a written confirmation that would be binding on the sender. Under common law rules, the sender would be bound by the writing, but the other party would not be bound, because he or she did not sign it. Under the UCC, the other merchant will also be bound by this written confirmation unless he or she objects to its contents in writing within 10 days after receiving it. This rule forces merchants to read their forms and to cooperate with other merchants.

The Statute of Frauds requirements have recently evolved in an interesting way. New statutory coverage recognizes the possibility that electronic communications can satisfy the writing requirement, and thus can satisfy the Statute of Frauds. Under the Electronic Signatures in Global and National Commerce Act (E-SIGN)[1] an "authenticated" electronic communication will suffice as a writing if the transaction affects interstate or foreign commerce. Further, the Uniform Electronic Transactions Act (UETA)[2] recognizes "authenticated" electronic communications for intrastate transactions. Thus, electronic communications such as e-mails or faxes will meet the requirement of a "writing" for Statute of Fraud purposes under Article 2 in most intrastate transactions and in all interstate transactions, with the expectation that the UETA will eventually be adopted by virtually all of the states. Numerous sites contain information on the E-SIGN bill, including http://www.mbc.com/ecommerce/ecom_overview.asp; information on the UETA can also be found at numerous sites, including http://www.uetaonline.com.

NRW CASE 16.2   Sales

STANDARD FORM SALES CONTRACTS

NRW will be making most of its sales of StuffTrakR to consumers rather than to merchants. Helen thinks they should use a standard order form for all of the sales to consumers, and that they should word the form in a manner that provides contract protection to NRW. She also suggests that the firm may want to draft a more complex standard form contract for sale of InvenTrakR, which will be sold to merchants. Carlos agrees that a standard order form for consumer purchases is a good idea, but he would prefer to have the firm negotiate orders for InvenTrakR individually, thus encouraging the firm to bargain based on the relative size of the order and the importance of the individual customer. They have asked you for your opinion. What will you tell them?

BUSINESS CONSIDERATIONS Is the standard order form NRW is considering a "standard form contract"? Why might a business want to use a standard form for sales to individuals who are not merchants, but not to merchant buyers? What are the advantages to using a standard form contract?

ETHICAL CONSIDERATIONS If a business uses a standard form contract, should that standard form include "fine print" clauses that are advantageous to the firm, or should it avoid using such language? Why?

INTERNATIONAL CONSIDERATIONS International sales contracts normally do not require *any* writing in order to be valid. What should a business do in order to be certain that it has the contract terms it wants when there is no need for a writing, and its "typical" standard form agreement may not be in effect?

Finally, § 2-201(3) of the Code lists three exceptions to the general provisions of the Statute of Frauds:

1. No writing is needed when the goods are to be specially manufactured for the buyer and are of such a nature that they cannot be resold by the seller in the ordinary course of his or her business, and when the seller has made a substantial start in performing the contract.

2. No writing is needed if the party being sued admits in court or in the legal proceedings that the contract existed.

3. No writing is needed for any portion of the goods already delivered and accepted or already paid for.

When the parties have a written agreement, the parol evidence rule applies; that is, the writing is meant to be the final agreement, and the writing cannot be *contradicted* by any oral agreements made at the same time as, or before, the written document. If the writing is intended as a *total integration* of the agreement, the writing is viewed as the entire contract. No additional terms can be introduced. However, even with a total integration the writing can be *explained* or *supplemented* by additional evidence, including parol (oral) evidence. For example, either party may show that course of dealings, usage of trade, or course of performance gives special meaning to certain terms contained in the writing. If the writing is deemed to be only a partial integration of the contract, evidence can be introduced to show additional terms that are also a part of the contract, even if those terms are not included in the writing. Either party may introduce evidence of additional consistent terms to fill out any apparent gaps in the written agreement.

Course of dealings refers to any prior conduct or contracts between the parties. Prior conduct between the parties sets up a pattern that either party may reasonably expect will be followed in the present setting. *Course of performance* involves repeated performances between the parties in their present contract. If neither party objects to the performance, it is considered appropriate to continue such performance. *Usage of trade* refers to a widely recognized and accepted industry practice. When usage of trade is proven, it is expected to be followed by the parties.

In interpreting a contract, the court will first look to the express language used by the parties. Whenever possible, the court will read the express language of the agreement and then consider the course of performance, any course of dealings, and any usages of trade in a consistent manner. If a consistent interpretation is not possible, however, express terms control any other interpretation. Course of performance controls either course of dealings or usage of trade, and course of dealings controls usage of trade.

Course of dealings and course of performance are normally based on current or prior conduct of the parties with one another. As such, both standards are, or have been, practiced by the parties, and they are readily apparent to both parties and are difficult for either party to deny. Some trade usage patterns are less obvious, especially since the usage of trade may apply to situations in which one (or even both) of the parties are not merchants. For example, in California it is a standard usage of trade to use a formal bill of sale to transfer an automobile, truck, or boat by contract (see Exhibit 16.2 on page 385). It is generally the obligation of the parties to acquaint themselves with the usages of trade that apply and to comply with them if necessary.

Special Rules under Article 2

The basic assumption under Article 2 is that both parties will be acting in good faith, with the seller selling and the buyer buying. And, of course, all is done according to the terms of the contract. If that were all that Article 2 said, the rules of contracts from common law would be more than adequate to cover sales. The true value of the Code's coverage of sales is what it provides if, or when, the contract is defective, incomplete, or unclear in some area.

For example, § 2-302 makes provisions for unconscionable contracts or contract clauses. Unconscionable means so unfair or one-sided as to shock the conscience. Unlike the common law, which presumed that equal bargaining power existed, the Code recognizes that some parties can "force a bargain" on the other party, and such forced bargains may be unconscionable to the party who was forced into the bargain. If the court feels that a contract is unconscionable, it may refuse to enforce the contract. If the court feels that only a clause of the contract is unconscionable, it normally will enforce all of the contract except the challenged clause.

Open Terms

The Code also recognizes that the parties may intend to have a contract even though the contract may omit some elements. In an effort to give the parties the "benefit of their bargain," the Code allows the omitted terms to be filled in by the court. (Remember from Chapter 13 that the court may complete a contract for the parties, but it will not write or make a contract for the parties.)

What happens when, for example, the parties intend to create a contract but fail to set a price? In such a case, § 2-305 controls. Under this section, the price can be set by either of the parties or by some external factor. If nothing is said about price, the price is a reasonable price at the time of delivery of the goods. If the price is to be set by one of the parties, that party must set the price in good faith. A bad-faith price may be treated by the other party as a cancellation of the contract, or the other party may set a reasonable price and perform the contract.

Sometimes the parties set a price and otherwise agree to contract terms, but fail to provide for delivery. Again, the Code provides a method to save the contract and to resolve the problem. Three different delivery sections may be utilized.

First, under § 2-307, the seller can make a complete delivery in one shipment unless the contract allows for several shipments. However, if the seller tenders a partial delivery and the buyer does not object, the seller can continue to make partial shipments until the buyer objects.

NRW CASE 16.3   Management

HOW SHOULD NRW COMMUNICATE WITH ITS CUSTOMERS?

A local retail establishment sent a letter to NRW requesting information on the InvenTrakR. This retailer wanted an idea of how much it would cost to purchase the product for the store's inventory, what would be needed in the way of computer or other technical support, and how long it would take to implement use of the InvenTrakR system in the store. Mai thinks NRW should reply by e-mail, citing its ease and its speed. She believes that if the firm can accustom its clientele to using e-mail, the firm can save a significant amount of money in postage, increase the speed of communications, and be more efficient. Carlos would prefer to reply to the customers in the manner the customers use to initiate contact. He thinks that this will allow the firm to operate in the "comfort zone" of the customer, with long-term benefits because the customers will communicate in the manner to which they are accustomed. Helen agrees with Mai, but she is concerned that e-mail communications, while much quicker, may have negative legal implications. They have asked you to provide some guidance in this area. What will you tell them?

BUSINESS CONSIDERATIONS Communications with customers or potential customers may well have legal implications. Should a business have a policy concerning communications? Should the policy, if one exists, be for all communications, or should it depend on the status of the other party?

ETHICAL CONSIDERATIONS Is it ethical for a business to communicate with a customer in a manner that is

continued

not normal for that customer, thus potentially putting the customer at a disadvantage? Should a business impose its standards on a customer just because the business is more comfortable using those standards, whether in communications or in some other area?

INTERNATIONAL CONSIDERATIONS Getting involved in e-commerce provides a much larger potential customer base and it provides for much quicker communications, both of which can help a business to grow. However, e-commerce also provides the opportunity for customers from other countries to place orders without the business being aware that it is involved in international sales. Should this affect the decision to use electronic communication means in accepting orders or dealing with customers? Should a disclaimer be used to negate orders from international customers until the business is ready to "go global"? Why?

Second, § 2-308 covers the place for delivery. If the contract is silent as to the place of delivery, delivery is at the seller's place of business. (Law students often miss this point. At first glance, it seems illogical. In reality, it is very logical. When a person buys a toaster or a can of beans, that person takes delivery at the store—the seller's place of business.) If the seller has no place of business, delivery is at the seller's residence. If the goods are known by both parties to be at some other place, that place is the proper place for the delivery.

Third, § 2-309 covers the time for delivery. If the contract is silent about when delivery is to occur, delivery is to be within a reasonable time. Reasonable time here means reasonable in both clock time and in calendar time. The seller is to make delivery during normal business hours (clock time), and the seller is not allowed to delay unduly the number of days before delivery (calendar time).

In addition to these rules, the Code resolves several other potential problems. Under § 2-306, the Code specifically allows requirement contracts and output contracts. In a requirement contract, the seller provides all of a certain good that the buyer needs. In an output contract, the buyer purchases all of a certain good that the seller produces. Both types of contracts were often declared unenforceable at common law because they were too indefinite in terms. Exhibit 16.3 on page 386 summarizes the treatment of open terms in a sales contract.

Options

The Code also deals with options. If a contract calls for an unspecified product mix, the assortment of goods is at the buyer's option. If the contract is silent as to how the goods are to be shipped, the shipping arrangements are at the seller's option. However, if a party having an option delays unduly, the other party may act. A party may elect to wait until he or she hears what is being done by the other party or may proceed on his or her own. Thus, if the buyer does not notify the seller of the product mix desired, the seller may delay shipping any goods, and the delay is excused. Or the seller may select his or her own assortment and ship it, provided the act is in good faith. Or the seller may treat the delay as a breach of contract by the buyer and seek remedies for the breach.

Cooperation

As a final and overriding obligation, the parties are required to cooperate with one another in the performance of their duties. Any failure to cooperate or any interference with the performance of the other party can be treated as a breach of contract or as an excuse for a delayed performance.

The Scope of Article 2A

When the National Conference of Commissioners on Uniform State Laws decided to codify the coverage of leases, the drafting committee looked for comparable areas for guidance. Eventually they decided that Article 2 of the UCC was most analogous to leases, and they used this article for guidance in their efforts. The coverage of leases was originally embodied in the Uniform Personal Property Leasing Act, which was approved by the National Conference of Commissioners on Uniform State Laws in 1985. It was decided, however, that this coverage would be better suited for inclusion in the UCC, and the Uniform Personal Property Leasing Act was reworked into its present form as Article 2A. In August 1986, the Conference approved Article 2A for promulgation as an amendment to the UCC. The Council of the American Law Institute approved and recommended the article in December 1986, and the Permanent Editorial Board of the Uniform Commercial Code approved the article in March 1987. As of July 1999, all of the states except Louisiana and South Carolina had adopted Article 2A.

Article 2A applies to "any transaction, regardless of form, that creates a lease."[3] This broad statement provides coverage for a "consumer lease," a "finance lease," or an "installment lease" contract. As used in this article, "lease" means "a transfer of the right to possession and use of goods for a term in return for consideration, but a sale,

EXHIBIT 16.2 Bill of Sale

EXHIBIT 16.2 Bill of Sale

BILL OF SALE

VEHICLE LICENSE NO OR VESSEL CF NO

VEHICLE OR HULL IDENTIFICATION NO	MAKE	BODY TYPE	MODEL	YEAR

FOR MOTOR CYCLE ONLY:

ENGINE NO.

For the sum of _____ Dollars

($ _____) and/or other valuable consideration in the amount of

$ _____ , the receipt of which is hereby acknowledged, I/we did sell,

transfer and deliver to _____

(BUYER)

ADDRESS	CITY	STATE	ZIP CODE

on the _____ day of _____ 19 _____ my/our right, title
and interest in and to the above described vehicle or vessel.

I/WE certify under penalty of perjury that: (1) I/WE are the lawful owner(s)
of the vehicle/vessel and (2) I/WE have the right to sell it, and (3) I/WE guarantee and will defend the title to the vehicle/vessel against the claims and
demands of any and all persons arising prior to this date and (4) the vehicle/
vessel is free of all liens and encumbrances.

Signature
of seller **X** _____ Date _____

ADDRESS	CITY	STATE	ZIP CODE

Courtesy of Bingham Toyota, Clovis, California.

including a sale on approval or a sale or return, or retention or creation of a security interest is not a lease. Unless the context clearly indicates otherwise, the term includes a sublease."[4]

Article 2A is intended to provide the same sort of broad coverage to leases, regardless of form, that Article 2 provides for sales. With the increasing use of leases by both merchants and nonmerchants, such coverage gives a welcome—and necessary—uniformity to this area of the law. Article 2A, including the Official Comments, can be found at http://www.law.cornell.edu/ucc/2A/overview. html or at the NCCUSL Web site, http://www.nccusl.org.

Contracts for Leasing Goods

Much of the coverage from Article 2 was carried into Article 2A, with appropriate changes made to reflect the inherent differences between a sale and a lease. Amendments were also made to Articles 1 and 9 to make these areas consistent with the new coverage of leases as provided in Article 2A. The article is designed to help protect the basic tenets of freedom of contract by permitting the parties to vary certain terms of

EXHIBIT **16.3**   Open Terms in Sales Contracts

Open Term	Treatment	Code Section
Price	The buyer or the seller sets the price in *good faith*, of the contract so provides.	2-305(2)
	The price is a *reasonable price* at the time and place of delivery.	2-305(1)
Delivery	If no place for delivery is mentioned, delivery is at the seller's place of business (or the seller's home if the seller has no place of business).	2-308(a)
	If the goods to the contract are identified, and if both parties know the goods are at a place other than the seller's location, delivery is presumed to occur at the location of the goods.	2-308(b)
	If the time for delivery is not mentioned, delivery is to occur within a reasonable time considering the nature of the goods (calendar time) and the nature of the buyer's business (clock time).	2-309
Payment	Payment is expected at the time and place of delivery unless some other payment terms are specified; payment is to be made in any commercially reasonable manner.	2-310, 2-511(1)
	If the seller insists on payment in cash, but did not specify cash payment in the contract the buyer must be given a reasonable time to procure cash for the payment.	2-511(2)

their lease agreements. At the same time, the parties cannot vary such staples of the UCC as the requirements that the parties act in good faith and in a reasonable manner and that they exercise due diligence and due care.

Article 2A has five parts, as opposed to the seven parts in Article 2. Part 1 contains general provisions. Part 2 covers the formation and construction of lease contracts. Part 3 covers the effect of lease contracts, including enforceability. Part 4 deals with the performance of lease contracts. Part 5 concerns defaults and remedies.

The scope of Article 2A is restricted to leases of goods. It does not include "security leases," which are already provided for in Article 9. Similarly, there is no need for a lessor to file any financing statement or other document in order to protect his or her interest in the leased property. Lessees are entitled to warranty protections similar in scope and coverage to those protections given to buyers of goods under Article 2. Thus, both express and implied warranties are given to lessees.

Parties to a lease, the same as parties to a sale, are classified as merchants or nonmerchants. Protections are provided for a lessee in the ordinary course of business, a person who leases goods in the ordinary course of business and in good faith and without knowledge that the lease is a violation of the rights of a third person.

Article 2A recognizes two basic types of leases, consumer leases and finance leases. It also recognizes an "installment lease" contract, with some special provisions for this type of agreement. A consumer lease is defined as a lease made by a lessor who regularly engages in the business of making leases and made to a lessee (excluding an organization) for personal, family, or household usage. In order to qualify as a consumer lease, the total payments called for, excluding renewals or options to buy, may not exceed $25,000. A finance lease is a lease in which (1) the lessor does not select, manufacture, or supply the leased goods, (2) the lessor acquires the goods in connection with the lease, and (3) either the lessee receives a copy of the contract under which the lessor acquired rights to the goods before the lease is signed or the lessee's approval of the contract under which the lessor acquires rights to the goods is a condition to the effectiveness of the lease contract. An "installment lease" contract is one that authorizes or requires the delivery of goods in separate lots to be separately accepted, even if the contract contains a clause stating that each delivery is to be viewed and treated as a separate lease.

A lease contract may be made in any manner sufficient to show agreement between the parties, including the conduct of the parties. Similarly, a lease contract can be entered even though some of the terms of the contract are omitted, provided that the parties intended to make a lease and there is a reasonably certain basis for giving appropriate remedies in the event of a breach.

Leases may also be subject to the rules providing for firm offers. A merchant who makes a written offer to lease goods to or from another party in a signed writing is deemed to have made an irrevocable offer when that writing gives assurance that the offer will be held open. The offer may not be revoked for the time stated in the writing. If no time period is stated, the offer is irrevocable for a reasonable time. In no event may the period during which the offer is irrevocable exceed three months. Further, any such terms of assurance included on a form prepared by the offeree must be signed by the offeror before the offer is considered "firm," and therefore irrevocable.

The Statute of Frauds for leases requires a writing for any lease that calls for total payments, excluding options for renewals or options to buy, of $1,000 or more. If the total payments are less than $1,000 an oral contract is valid and enforceable. Article 2A also recognizes the same three exceptions to the Statute of Frauds that are recognized under Article 2 if there is no writing and the lease has total payments of $1,000 or more (specially manufactured goods, admission in a legal proceeding by the party against whom enforcement is sought, or to the extent the goods have been received and accepted).

Contracts for the Sale of Goods in an International Setting

Business is rapidly "going global," with international trade increasing each year. A significant portion of international trade involves the sale of goods, with the balance composed of services. Whether goods or services are involved, the trade entails contracts between the parties. Most of these contracts will be performed with few problems—at least legally. However, some of these contracts will not be performed or will not be performed satisfactorily, and legal issues will arise due to the inadequate performance. These legal issues may well present legal problems beyond the "mere" problem of the alleged breach of contract.

There are substantially more than 100 separate nations today, each with its own (somewhat) unique legal system. A business that is involved in international sales of goods may do business with firms in any—or even all—of these separate nations. Familiarity with each of these legal systems would be impractical at best. Yet a person who does business with a person in another nation may be subject to the laws of that other nation in a contract action. Obviously this presents a logistical problem for the international trader.

In addition, many different languages are used in the world. Communication between people who speak different languages can make international trade more difficult than national trade between people who share a common language and a culture. Recall the *Frigaliment Importing Co.* case from Chapter 3. The simple word "chicken" caused serious legal problems in that case. As technological advances are made and as international trade increases, translation problems and misunderstandings are also likely to increase. As the *Frigaliment* case indicates, the potential for confusion or

misunderstanding as to meaning is present with any international sales contract.

Determining which laws are in effect and need to be followed also provides for potential confusion or misunderstanding to a much greater extent in international trade than in domestic trade. This potential for confusion, in turn, has had a negative impact on the growth and development of international trade. Something new was needed to reflect the increasingly international nature of business as the 20th century progressed. This "something new" became the United Nations Convention on Contracts for the International Sale of Goods, the CISG. Information on the CISG and other UN conventions can be found through the home page of the United Nations at http://www.un.org/. From the home page, click on Welcome, then go to international law, then UNCITRAL, then adopted texts. The CISG is listed as an adopted text.

The United Nations Convention on Contracts for the International Sale of Goods

The CISG was drafted at the behest of the United Nations to provide for international sales what Article 2 of the Uniform Commercial Code (UCC) provides in the United States for domestic sales, a uniform set of rules governing sales contracts. There had been earlier attempts to provide regulations for international sales, most notably the efforts arising from the international diplomatic conference in The Hague in 1964.

The United Nations instituted the Conference on International Trade (UNCITRAL) in 1968, charging this conference with the task of unifying the international law governing sales. To help ensure broader acceptance of its actions, the conference was composed of representatives from numerous countries, with broad diversity in the legal traditions and the economic status of the represented states.

Meeting once a year, UNCITRAL took nine years to prepare draft conventions dealing with the international sale of goods and with the formation of international sales contracts. These two drafts were combined into one draft convention in 1978, and that combined convention was submitted to an official diplomatic convention convened in Vienna in 1980 by the United Nations General Assembly.

The final language of the CISG was approved at the Vienna Conference in 1980. Sixty-two nations participated in the Vienna Conference, and these nations helped in the drafting of the Convention. By having such broad participation (one commentator characterized the participants as 22 Western nations, 11 socialist nations, and 29 third-world nations[5]), the Convention provides compromise standards that should eventually prove acceptable to most of the world. There were 20 signatory nations, including the United States. (The U.S. Senate unanimously ratified the CISG in 1986.) The CISG became effective January 1, 1988, for all of the ratifying nations.

As of October 12, 2002, the UN Treaty Section reports that 62 nations have signed or ratified the Convention. These nations are listed in Exhibit 16.4.[6]

Domestically, various nations follow numerous legal traditions, and there are various levels of economic development among the member nations of the United Nations. Both of these differences present problems in deriving a uniform set of laws to govern the international sale of goods. Common law nations, such as England, the United States, and the numerous nations that are—or have been—heavily influenced by England, traditionally follow a less rigid system in forming and performing sales contracts. Civil law nations, including most of Europe except for England, follow a more rigid system in which statutes provide the entire framework of the sales contract. Nations that follow Islamic law, including most of the Middle East, have different expectations regarding contract law. Socialist nations prefer much more controlled terms and allow much less flexibility in forming contracts, establishing prices, and dealing with remedies. Industrialized nations have different expectations than developing—or "third-world"—nations. All of these differences have made the creation and ratification of the CISG very difficult.

Despite these differences, and despite the difficulties, a Convention was agreed on and ratified by 44 (now 62) nations. This Convention holds out the hope for a truly uniform international law governing the sale of goods. In the interim, the CISG may provide the controlling law for international sale-of-goods contracts under two different sets of circumstances:

1. The contract for the sale of goods is made between firms from different countries, if both countries have ratified the Convention.

2. The contract for the sale of goods designates that the law of a particular country will be the applicable law governing the contract, provided that the country whose laws will be applicable has ratified the Convention.

Scope of the CISG

The CISG provides the framework for the international sale of goods in much the same way that Article 2 of the UCC provides the framework for the domestic sale of goods in the United States. However, students should avoid drawing too strict a comparison between the UCC and the CISG. Not all the subjects covered by the UCC are also covered by the CISG, nor does the CISG extend to as many sales as does Article 2. For example, the CISG does not apply to the sale of goods intended for personal or household use unless the seller neither knew nor should have known that the goods were being purchased for personal or household use.[7] By contrast, Article 2 does apply to such purchases by a consumer, even providing warranty protection to the consumer in many such situations.

The CISG applies to contracts for the sale of goods between parties whose places of business are in different states, provided that those different states are signatory states to the CISG, *or* provided that the parties have agreed to follow the laws of one of the two nations and that nation is a signatory state. In addition, the International Chamber of Commerce has recognized the CISG as part of the *lex mercatoria* and regularly applies the terms of the CISG to controversies involving the international sale of goods that are submitted to the International Chamber of Commerce for arbitration.

The following case involved the applicability of the CISG. It also involved a "battle of the forms" issue. After reading the case, determine how you think the case would have been decided under Article 2. If you believe the results would be different, determine why.

One of the interesting aspects of the preceding case is that both parties had included a "choice of laws" clause calling for application of its domestic law, when the domestic law for each was actually the CISG. Obviously, firms need to be more specific in their choice of laws if they do not want the CISG to be controlling.

There are some other significant differences between the UCC and the CISG, and some of these differences may prove troublesome for U.S. businesses (as well as businesses from other common law nations) new to the international marketplace. For example, under common law, in order to have a contract there must be (1) an offer, (2) an acceptance, and (3) consideration. The CISG does not mention "consideration"—a basic element of contract formation in common law countries. Instead, the CISG view is that since consideration is part of the formation of the contract, it relates to the "validity" of the contract. Validity-of-the-contract issues are to be determined by applicable national law, not by the CISG.

Another formation-of-the-contract issue involves acceptance. Unlike consideration, which is a matter to be resolved under applicable national law, the CISG does address the issue of acceptance. Under common law, an acceptance is effective when sent by the offeree (the "mailbox rule"), placing the risk of misdelivery or nondelivery on the

EXHIBIT   16.4 United Nations Convention on Contracts for the International Sale of Goods (Vienna, 1980)

State	Signature	Ratification, Accession (a), Approval (AA), Acceptance (A), Succession (d)	Entry into force
Argentina	.	19 July 1983 (a)	1 January 1988
Australia	.	17 March 1988 (a)	1 April 1989
Austria	11 April 1980	29 December 1987	1 January 1989
Belarus	.	9 October 1989 (a)	1 November 1990
Belgium	.	31 October 1996 (a)	1 November 1997
Bosnia and Herzegovina	.	12 January 1994 (d)	6 March 1992
Bulgaria	.	9 July 1990 (a)	1 August 1991
Burundi	.	4 September 1998 (a)	1 October 1999
Canada	.	23 April 1991 (a)	1 May 1992
Chile	11 April 1980	7 February 1990	1 March 1991
China	30 September 1981	11 December 1986 (AA)	1 January 1988
Colombia		10 July 2001 (a)	1 August 2002
Croatia	.	8 June 1998 (d)	8 October 1991
Cuba	.	2 November 1994 (a)	1 December 1995
Czech Republic	.	30 September 1993 (d)	1 January 1993
Denmark	26 May 1981	14 February 1989	1 March 1990
Ecuador	.	27 January 1992 (a)	1 February 1993
Egypt	.	6 December 1982 (a)	1 January 1988
Estonia	.	20 September 1993 (a)	1 October 1994
Finland	26 May 1981	15 December 1987	1 January 1989
France	27 August 1981	6 August 1982 (AA)	1 January 1988
Georgia	.	16 August 1994 (a)	1 September 1995
Germany	26 May 1981	21 December 1989	1 January 1991
Ghana	11 April 1980	.	.
Greece	.	12 January 1998 (a)	1 February 1999
Guinea	.	23 January 1991 (a)	1 February 1992
Honduras	.	10 October 2002	.
Hungary	11 April 1980	16 June 1983	1 January 1988
Iceland	.	10 May 2001 (a)	1 June 2002
Iraq	.	5 March 1990 (a)	1 April 1991
Israel	.	22 January 2002 (a)	1 February 2003
Italy	30 September 1981	11 December 1986	1 January 1988
Kyrgyzstan	.	11 May 1999 (a)	1 June 2000
Latvia	.	31 July 1997 (a)	1 August 1998
Lesotho	18 June 1981	18 June 1981	1 January 1988
Lithuania	.	18 January 1995 (a)	1 February 1996
Luxembourg	.	30 January 1997 (a)	1 February 1998
Mauritania	.	20 August 1999 (a)	1 September 2000
Mexico	.	29 December 1987 (a)	1 January 1989
Mongolia	.	31 December 1997 (a)	1 January 1999
Netherlands	29 May 1981	13 December 1990 (A)	1 January 1992
New Zealand	.	22 September 1994 (a)	1 October 1995
Norway	26 May 1981	20 July 1988	1 August 1989
Peru	.	25 March 1999 (a)	1 April 2000
Poland	28 September 1981	19 May 1995	1 June 1996
Republic of Moldova	.	13 October 1994 (a)	1 November 1995
Romania	.	22 May 1991 (a)	1 June 1992

EXHIBIT 16.4 Continued

State	Signature	Ratification, Accession (a), Approval (AA), Acceptance (A), Succession (d)	Entry into force
Russian Federation	.	16 August 1990 (a)	1 September 1991
Saint Vincent and the Grenadines	.	12 September 2000 (a)	1 October 2001
Singapore	11 April 1980	16 February 1995	1 March 1996
Slovakia	.	28 May 1993 (d)	1 January 1993
Slovenia	.	7 January 1994 (d)	25 June 1991
Spain	.	24 July 1990 (a)	1 August 1991
Sweden	26 May 1981	15 December 1987	1 January 1989
Switzerland	.	21 February 1990 (a)	1 March 1991
Syrian Arab Republic	.	19 October 1982 (a)	1 January 1988
Uganda	.	12 February 1992 (a)	1 March 1993
Ukraine	.	3 January 1990 (a)	1 February 1991
United States of America	31 August 1981	11 December 1986	1 January 1988
Uruguay	.	25 January 1999 (a)	1 February 2000
Uzbekistan	.	27 November 1996 (a)	1 December 1997
Venezuela	28 September 1981	.	
Yugoslavia		12 March 2001 (d)	effective for Yugoslavia on 27 April 1992, the date of State succession.
Zambia	.	6 June 1986 (a)	1 January 1988
		Parties: 62	

offeror. Under civil law, an acceptance is not effective until it is received by the offeror, placing the risk of misdelivery or nondelivery on the offeree. These two positions are diametrically opposed. This means that in a civil law nation an offer can be revoked by the offeror at any time prior to his or her receipt of an acceptance. In a common law nation, the offer cannot be revoked once an acceptance has been sent by the offeree.

In Article 18(2), the CISG states that an acceptance is effective when it reaches the offeror—the civil law rule. However, it also states, in Article 16(1), that an offer may not be revoked after an acceptance has been sent (even though it may not yet have been received)—a variation on the common law rule. Finally, Article 18(3) says that an acceptance is effective as soon as the offeree shows acceptance by beginning to perform—another concession to common law traditions.

Another difference involves the need for a written agreement for some contracts. Many U.S. firms are used to the applicability of the Statute of Frauds, requiring that a contract for the sale of goods (subject to numerous exceptions) must be in writing if the contract is for $500 or more. These parties may be shocked to learn that the CISG specifically states that oral contracts for the sale of goods are enforceable.[8] Since there is no need for any writing, U.S. firms may believe that they are still in the negotiations (prewriting) stage while their non–U.S. counterparts (especially those from civil law nations) will believe that an oral agreement has been reached and will be expecting performance. If the CISG is the statute governing the sale, a contract may very well exist, and the U.S. firm will have to perform despite the lack of a writing.

Common law nations treat offers as freely revocable at any time prior to acceptance, unless the offeree has an option or unless the parties are governed by the UCC and a merchant has made a firm offer. Civil law countries generally treat an offer that states a time limit as irrevocable. Thus, there is a basic difference between common law and civil law in this area. The CISG generally adopts the common law approach, making the offer freely revocable at any time prior to acceptance. However, there are two important exceptions to this general approach, both based on civil law:

16.3

ASANTE TECHNOLOGIES, INC. v. PMC-SIERRA, INC.
164 F. Supp. 2d 1142; 2001 U.S. Dist. LEXIS 16000

FACTS Asante Technologies, a Delaware corporation with its primary place of business in Santa Clara, California, entered into a contract with PMC-Sierra, Inc., another Delaware corporation, but one with its corporate headquarters in Burnaby, British Columbia, Canada. PMC produces network switchers, electronic components used to connect multiple computers to one another and to the Internet. Asante purchased application-specific integrated circuits (ASICs) from PMC. Asante submitted five different purchase orders to PMC, four through Unique Distributors, the authorized distributor for PMC in California, and the fifth faxed directly to PMC headquarters in British Columbia. For each of these purchase orders, Asante alleged that PMC had promised in writing that the chips would meet certain technical specifications but that the chips delivered by PMC did not meet these specifications. As a result, Asante sued for breach of contract and for breach of express warranties under the provisions of Article 2 of the UCC. PMC removed the case to the federal district court, arguing that the contract was governed by the CISG rather than by the UCC.

ISSUES Should the controlling law in this case be Article 2 of the UCC or the CISG? If the CISG is applicable, does it preempt the coverage of the UCC?

HOLDINGS Since each of the parties to the suit is from a different nation, and each of their home countries have ratified the Convention, the controlling law should be the CISG. Yes; if the CISG is applicable, it will preempt any state law that falls within the scope of the CISG, including Article 2 of the UCC.

REASONING Excerpts from the opinion of Judge Ware:

Defendant asserts that this Court has jurisdiction to hear this case pursuant to 28 U.S.C. 1331, which dictates that the "district courts shall have original jurisdiction of all civil actions arising under the Constitution, laws, or treaties of the United States." Specifically, Defendant contends that the contract claims at issue necessarily implicate the CISG, because the contract is between parties having their places of business in two nations which have the adopted the CISG treaty. The Court concludes that Defendant's place of business for the purposes of the contract at issue and its performance is Burnaby, British Columbia, Canada. Accordingly, the CISG applies. Moreover, the parties did not effectuate an "opt out" of application of the CISG. Finally, because

the Court concludes that the CISG preempts state laws that address the formation of a contract of sale and the rights and obligations of the seller and buyer arising from such a contract, the well-pleaded complaint rule does not preclude removal in this case. . . . Although the general federal question statute . . . gives district courts original jurisdiction over every civil action that "arises under the . . . treaties of the United States," an individual may only enforce a treaty's provisions when the treaty is self-executing, that it, when it expressly or impliedly creates a private right of action. . . . The parties do not dispute that the CISG properly creates a private right of action. . . . The CISG only applies when a contract is "between parties whose places of business are in different States." . . . If this requirement is not satisfied, Defendant cannot claim jurisdiction under the CISG. It is undisputed that Plaintiff's place of business is Santa Clara, California, U.S.A. It is further undisputed that during the relevant time period, Defendant's corporate headquarters, inside sales and marketing office, public relations department, principal warehouse, and most of its design and engineering functions were located in Burnaby, British Columbia, Canada. However, Plaintiff contends that, pursuant to Article 10 of the CISG, Defendant's "place of business" having the closest relationship to the contract at issue is in the United States.

The complaint asserts . . . two claims for breach of contract and a claim for breach of express warranty based on the failure of the delivered ASICs to conform to the agreed upon technical specifications. . . . It appears undisputed that each of these alleged representations regarding the technical specifications of the product was issued from Defendant's headquarters in British Columbia, Canada. . . . Plaintiff next argues that, even if the Parties are from two different nations that have adopted the CISG, the choice of laws provisions in the "Terms and Conditions" set forth by both Parties reflect the parties' intent to "opt out" of application of the treaty. Article 6 of the CISG provides that "the parties may exclude the application of the Convention or, subject to Article 12, derogate from or vary the effects of any of its provisions." . . . Defendant asserts that merely choosing the law of a jurisdiction is insufficient to opt out of the CISG, absent express exclusion of the CISG. The Court finds that the particular choice of law provisions in the "Terms and Conditions" of both parties are inadequate to effectuate an opt out of the CISG. Although selection of a particular choice of law, such as "the California Commercial Code" or the "Uniform Commercial Code" *could* amount to an implied exclusion of the CISG, the choice of law clauses at issue here do not evince a clear intent to opt out of the CISG. For example, Defendant's choice of applicable law adopts the law of British Columbia, and it is undisputed that the CISG *is* the law of British Columbia. . . . Furthermore, even Plaintiff's choice of applicable law generally adopts the "laws of" the State of California, and California is bound by the Supremacy Clause to the treaties of the United States. . . . Thus, under general California law, the CISG is applicable to contracts where the contracting parties are from different countries that have adopted the CISG. In the absence of clear language indicating that both contracting parties intended to opt out of the CISG, and in view of Defendant's Terms and Conditions which would apply the CISG, the Court rejects Plaintiff's contention that the choice of law provisions preclude the applicability of the CISG. . . .

It appears that the issue of whether or not the CISG preempts state law is a matter of first impression. In the case of federal statutes, "the question of whether a certain action is preempted by state law is one of congressional intent. The purpose of Congress is the ultimate touchstone." . . . Transferring this analysis to the question of preemption by a treaty, the Court focuses on the treaty's contracting parties. . . . In the case of the CISG treaty, this intent can be discerned from the introductory text, which states that "the adoption of uniform rules which govern contracts for the international sale of goods and take into account the different social, economic and legal systems would contribute to the removal of legal barriers in inter-

national trade and promote the development of international trade." . . . The CISG further recognizes the importance of "the development of international trade on the basis of equality and mutual benefit." . . . The Court concludes that the expressly stated goal of developing uniform international contract law to promote international trade indicates the intent of the parties to the treaty to have the treaty preempt state law causes of action. The availability of independent state contract law causes of action would frustrate the goals of uniformity and certainty embraced by the CISG. Allowing such avenues for potential liability would subject contracting parties to different states' laws and the very same ambiguities regarding international contracts that the CISG was designed to avoid. As a consequence, parties to international contracts would be unable to predict the applicable law, and the fundamental purpose of the CISG would be undermined. . . .

BUSINESS CONSIDERATIONS Should a business involved in international sales contracts attempt to "opt out" of the coverage of the CISG in order to (hopefully) have any cases decided under more familiar laws? If a business knows that it will be regularly involved in international sales, should that business take steps to familiarize its managers with the provisions of the CISG?

ETHICAL CONSIDERATIONS Is it ethical for businesses from industrialized nations to insist that the other firm "opt out " of the coverage of the CISG and agree to "choose" the laws of the industrialized nation in order to finalize a contract?

1. The offer is irrevocable where the offer states that an acceptance must be made within a stated time.

2. The offer is irrevocable if it was reasonable for the offeror to rely on the offer remaining open, and the offeree did, in fact, rely on the offer remaining open.[9]

Thus, an offer that says the offeree has 20 days to accept is deemed to be irrevocable for the 20-day period even though the offer does not take the form of a firm offer as

provided for in the UCC. In addition, the CISG provides an exception similar to promissory estoppel when the facts of the case make it appear that the offeree relied on the fact that the offer would remain open and will be harmed if the offer is not held open for the time indicated in the offer. (Note that the CISG does not require the offeror to reasonably expect the offeree to rely to his or her detriment, as the common law would.)

Exhibit 16.5 shows some of the significant differences between Article 2 of the UCC and the CISG.

Summary

This chapter introduces the law of sales, Article 2 of the Uniform Commercial Code; the law of leases, Article 2A of the Uniform Commercial Code; and the CISG, the United Nations Convention on Contracts for the International Sale

of Goods. It is important to distinguish sales contracts from other types of contracts. Article 2 attempts to deal with "commercial reality" in the sale of goods, whereas common law developed strict and rigid rules for the treatment of contracts.

EXHIBIT 16.5 A Comparison of UCC Article 2 and the CISG

Article 2	**CISG**
Contract formation requires an offer, an acceptance, and consideration.	Contract formation requires an offer and an acceptance, but there is no requirement of consideration.
Acceptance is generally valid when sent (the "mailbox rule"), even if never received by the offeror.	Acceptance is not valid until received by the offeror.
An offer can generally be revoked at any time prior to acceptance.	An offer can be revoked at any time prior to the time when an acceptance is *sent* even though the acceptance is not valid until received.
A "firm offer" is irrevocable for the time stated, and if no time is stated, for a reasonable time.	An offer that the offeror promises to hold open *or* that the offeree reasonably believes will be held open is irrevocable for the time stated or for a reasonable time.
Contracts for the sale of goods in an amount of $500 or more must be in writing in order to be enforceable.	There is no writing requirement under the CISG, although the parties may, in their agreement, require a writing before a contract exists.

Article 2 also recognizes the difference between a merchant (a person who "specializes" in dealing with a particular type of goods) and a nonmerchant (a "casual dealer" in the goods). The Code provides built-in flexibility in the formation of sales contracts. Intent, rather than form, is the key element in sales. Offers and acceptances are likely to be found if the parties act as if they have an agreement. The Code even provides methods to supply missing terms, if it seems appropriate to do so in order to carry out the wishes and intentions of the parties. The Statute of Frauds remains operative under Article 2, but its provisions are less restrictive than under common law. Three exceptions to the Statute of Frauds are built into the Code, and the past dealings of the parties may also be taken into consideration in deciding what the parties have agreed to do. Some general obligations are imposed on the parties to prevent or minimize abuses of the less rigid rules of Article 2. The parties are required to act in good faith, they may not act unconscionably, and they must cooperate with one another. Performance options are available to either party if the other party fails to cooperate fully or properly.

Article 2A was enacted because of the growing importance of leases in our society. Many people today lease goods rather than purchase them. Historically, leases were governed by common law, whereas sales of goods have been governed by the UCC since 1954. Despite the similarity between a sale of goods and a lease of goods, there was likely to be a different outcome in a lawsuit. For quite some time courts have drawn analogies between leases and sales and then applied Article 2 provisions to leases.

This will no longer be necessary with the enactment of Article 2A.

Work on an international law of sales began in 1930, prior to World War II, when the International Institute for the Unification of Private Law tried to develop uniform coverage in this area. The initial work was submitted to an international conference at The Hague following World War II and resulted in the creation of two conventions, one dealing with the formation of sales contracts and one dealing with the performance of sales contracts. Unfortunately, neither convention was widely adopted. The United Nations created an International Conference on International Trade and charged it with creating an international law governing sales. This led to the United Nations Convention on Contracts for the International Sale of Goods (CISG), which was approved at the Vienna Conference in 1980 and became effective January 1, 1988 for all ratifying nations.

The CISG was created by compromises among the various factions that make up the United Nations. There were disagreements among common law, civil law, and Islamic law nations; between developed and developing nations; and between capitalist and socialist nations. Despite these differences, a convention was created and has been ratified or adopted by 62 nations as of April 2002. The CISG covers formation-of-contracts issues; seller obligations and rights; buyer obligations and rights; and remedies for both sellers and buyers. Ratifying nations have the option of not ratifying all sections of the CISG, but most have opted to follow the entire Convention.

Discussion Questions

1. What does Article 2 of the UCC govern? What does Article 2A of the UCC govern? How is it different from Article 2? What does the CISG govern? How does the coverage in each of these areas differ from the common law of contracts as followed in the United States?

2. The status of "merchant" carries with it certain duties and expectations under the UCC. What are the three separate tests that the UCC uses to determine whether a person in a sales or a leasing contract is a merchant? How are merchants treated differently from nonmerchants under the UCC? Why do you think this difference in treatment exists?

3. What is a *firm offer* under either Article 2 or Article 2A, and how is a firm offer treated differently from a similar offer at common law? Does the CISG have anything analogous to the *firm offer* provisions of the UCC?

4. Generally speaking, how can an offer be accepted under the law of sales? How is this different from the *mirror image* requirement for acceptance at common law? Why does the UCC provide for a different method of acceptance than the common law provides? Are the rules concerning acceptance different under the provisions of the CISG?

5. Assume that a buyer sends the seller a *purchase order,* a form offering to buy a certain quantity of goods. The seller subsequently returns an acknowledgment form accepting the offer. When these two forms are compared, it is discovered that they do not agree on every point. Do the parties have a contract under Article 2? If so, what are its terms? If not, why? Would the same result occur under the provisions of the common law?

6. There are special Statute of Frauds provisions for contracts involving the sale or the leasing of goods under the UCC. According to this provision, when does the Statute of Frauds apply to a sale-of-goods contract? When does the Statute of Frauds apply to a lease-of-goods contract? What are the exceptions to the Statute of Frauds under Article 2 on the law of sales? Are there similar exceptions under Article 2A? When does the CISG require a writing between the parties before there is an enforceable contract for the international sale of goods?

7. Assuming that a contract for the sale of goods is governed by the Statute of Frauds, what constitutes a sufficient writing between merchants to satisfy the Statute of Frauds? What special rules apply to writings between merchants under Article 2? If this contract were for the leasing of goods under the Statute of Frauds provisions of Article 2A, would the same requirements be present?

8. If the sales contract is silent as to the place of delivery, where should delivery occur? If the sales contract is silent as to when delivery is to occur, when should delivery be tendered? Explain fully.

9. In interpreting a written sales contract, the court will permit merchants to use parol evidence to establish course of dealings, course of performance, and usage of trade. What do each of these terms mean, and what is the hierarchy among them if there is a conflict between them? Why should merchants be able to use these concepts to explain or supplement a written contract?

10. Article 2A distinguishes between a *consumer lease* and a *finance lease.* What is the difference between these two types of leases, and why are they distinguished from one another under Article 2A?

Case Problems and Writing Assignments

1. City University of New York (CUNY) solicited "firm" bids for the sale of a used IBM computer system. Finalco submitted the highest bid, and CUNY officially awarded the sale of the computer to Finalco. During the bidding process, the parties discussed the need for signing a formal written document as evidence of the contract; however, no written contract was ever prepared. Finalco decided to withdraw its offer to purchase the computer, stating that its prospective lessee for the system had decided not to proceed with the lease, so Finalco no longer had a reason to purchase the computer system. CUNY made repeated demands for performance by Finalco, to no avail. Finally, CUNY sold the system to a substitute buyer for substantially less money. CUNY then sued Finalco for the difference between the price received from the substitute buyer and the bid Finalco had submitted. Finalco denied liability, claiming that no binding contract was ever entered. Was a written contract necessary in this case before an agreement existed? Had Finalco made a firm offer to CUNY in submitting its bid to purchase the computer system? [See *City University of New York v. Finalco, Inc.,* 514 N.Y.S.2d 244 (A.D.I. Dept. 1987).]

2. Smith-Scharff was a distributor of paper products. One of its customers was P. N. Hirsch, which purchased paper bags imprinted with the P. N. Hirsch logo from Smith-Scharff. The two companies had been doing business almost continuously since 1947. Smith-Scharff kept a supply of Hirsch paper bags in stock so that purchase orders could be filled in a timely manner. Hirsch was aware of this practice and kept Smith-Scharff up to date on its (Hirsch's) business forecasts. When P. N. Hirsch was liquidated and its stores sold to Dollar General, the president of Smith-Scharff promptly called the president of P. N. Hirsch, seeking assurances that the bags Smith-Scharff had in stock would be purchased. He was told that Hirsch would honor all of its commitments. Subsequently, Smith-Scharff sent Hirsch a

bill for $65,000, representing the amount of all Hirsch bags in stock. Over the next six months, Hirsch ordered and paid for $45,000 worth of bags, leaving Smith-Scharff with an inventory of just over $20,000 in Hirsch bags. When no additional orders from Hirsch were forthcoming, Smith-Scharff sued for the $20,000 balance. Was there an enforceable contract between Smith-Scharff and P. N. Hirsch for the sale of these bags? If so, what were the terms of the contract? [See *Smith-Scharff Paper Co. v. P. N. Hirsch & Co. Stores, Inc.*, 754 S.W.2d 928 (Mo. App. 1988).]

3. Jo-Ann, a corporation formed under the laws of Iceland, solicited Alfin, a New Jersey corporation, for permission to sell Glycel products (a line of beauty care products) in Iceland. Jo-Ann also asked for information about other Alfin products. Alfin sent samples of the Glycel products to Jo-Ann, and Jo-Ann then contacted Alfin by telex, stating in part: "We are very excited to be the exclusive distributors for these products in Iceland. We have not received any prices yet. Please send us your net prices on each item as soon as possible." Alfin replied with its own telex, stating prices in terms of a percentage of American retail and asking for opening orders for the products as soon as convenient. At no time did the parties agree as to (1) the duration of the agreement; (2) the quantity of products to be purchased; (3) the timing of payments; (4) inventory levels; or (5) the method for termination. Several months later, a representative of Alfin met with Jo-Ann's representatives. Following this meeting, he recommended that Alfin not deal with Jo-Ann, but rather seek another exclusive distributor in Iceland. Alfin eventually agreed to terms with another Iceland firm, GASA, and Jo-Ann sued for breach of contract. Alfin denied that a contract existed between the parties. Did the parties have an agreement under the UCC, or was the alleged agreement void due to its vagueness and indefiniteness? [See *Jo-Ann, Inc. v. Alfin Fragrances, Inc.*, 731 F. Supp. 149 (D. N.J. 1989).]

4. Kane, a professional photographer, shipped 45 photographic transparencies to Avanti Press via Federal Express. Federal Express lost the transparencies sometime during the shipment. Admitting that it had lost the package, Federal Express paid Kane $100 as per the shipping contract the two parties had entered when Kane shipped the package of transparencies (apparently he decided not to insure the package for its alleged value). Kane then filed suit against Avanti for $67,000, the alleged value of the transparencies. Avanti denied liability. According to Kane, Avanti had requested that he submit the transparencies so that Avanti could consider the pictures for possible inclusion in its greeting card collection, and had even sent Kane a shipping number to use with Federal Express, so that Avanti was paying the shipping fees. Because of these allegations, Kane asserted that Avanti had the risk of loss. Avanti argued that Article 2 did not apply because this was not the sale of goods, but rather of an intangible, the images contained on the transparencies. According to Avanti, since this was not a sale of goods, the risk of loss provisions of Article 2 do not apply, and any claim Kane might have was against Federal Express. Further, under the Federal Express contract, Kane had been paid for his loss. Was this a sale of goods, governed by Article 2 of the UCC, or the sale of an intangible, governed by the common law? Should Article 2 apply by analogy even if this is *not* a sale of goods? [See *Kane v. Federal Express Corp. et al.*, 2001 Conn. Super. LEXIS 2536, 45 U.C.C. Rep. Serv. 2d (Callaghan) 730 (Conn. 2001).]

5. **BUSINESS APPLICATION CASE** During the time relevant to this lawsuit, Industrial Engineering, Inc. machined steel castings into molds for use by Corning Asahi Video Products, a subsidiary of Corning, Inc. In 1989, Industrial began to order steel castings from Waukesha Foundry, Inc. Industrial and Waukesha commenced their relationship and entered into a series of contracts for the sale of metal castings. The typical deal was fairly straightforward. Industrial would telephone Waukesha and place an order for a particular number of castings and then fax a confirming purchase order. The parties disagreed over whether Waukesha would then send an acknowledgement form confirming the order. After manufacturing the castings, Waukesha would ship the order to Industrial. It was undisputed that Waukesha enclosed with each order a packing slip and followed each shipment with an invoice. Printed on each packing slip and invoice was a list of terms and conditions of sale, which included the following:

Buyer agrees he has full knowledge of the conditions printed below, and that the same shall be the sole terms and conditions of the agreement between Buyer and Seller and shall be binding if either (1) the goods referred to herein are delivered to and accepted by Buyer, or (2) if Buyer does not within ten days from date of the Seller's acknowledgement deliver to Seller written objection to said conditions of any part thereof.

Paragraph eight of the conditions of sale, entitled "Warranty," read as follows:

IT IS EXPRESSLY AGREED THAT NO WARRANTY OF MERCHANTABILITY OR FITNESS FOR USE, NOR ANY OTHER WARRANTY, EXPRESS OR IMPLIED, IS MADE BY THE SELLER HEREUNDER. THE FOREGOING STATES THE SELLER'S ENTIRE AND EXCLUSIVE LIABILITY AND BUYER'S EXCLUSIVE AND SOLE REMEDY FOR ANY CLAIM OF DAMAGES IN CONNECTION WITH THE SALE OF THE PRODUCTS HEREUNDER. SELLER WILL IN NO EVENT BE LIABLE FOR ANY SPECIAL OR CONSEQUENTIAL DAMAGES WHATSOEVER.

Industrial placed 60 orders with Waukesha between 1989 and 1993, and Waukesha claims that it sent Industrial a total of 60 acknowledgment forms, 234 packing slips, and 234 invoices during this four-year period. Neither party has offered a precise assessment of how many defective castings Waukesha delivered to Industrial. It appears that Industrial began to track the incidence of faulty castings and to submit documentation to Waukesha identifying faulty castings and seeking credit sometime in 1992. Both parties agree that according to Industrial's records, 31 percent of the castings inspected between April and December 1992 were defective. The last shipment of castings was delivered sometime around early March 1993.

The evidence suggests that the parties operated under an agreement of net payment 30 days after delivery of the castings. However, in August 1992, Waukesha determined that it would no longer extend 30-day credit to Industrial and notified Industrial that payment would henceforth be "COD." Waukesha decided to change the payment terms because of Industrial's delayed payments and outstanding invoices in the summer of 1992 totaling more than $250,000. Industrial did not agree to this change of payment terms and thus ended the relationship. Waukesha filed a lawsuit against Industrial on May 12, 1993, alleging that Industrial owed it $256,304.99 on outstanding invoices. Industrial filed a counterclaim on February 18, 1994, alleging that it had suffered cumulative losses of $1.2 million as a result of Waukesha's failure to deliver conforming castings in a breach of the parties' contract. Did the additional terms included by Waukesha on its acknowledgment forms, packing slips, and invoices become a part of the contract, thus effectively limiting the remedies available to Industrial in the event of any breaches of the contracts? [See *Waukesha Foundry, Inc. v. Industrial Engineering, Inc.*, 91 F.3d 1002 (7th Cir. 1996).]

6. **ETHICAL APPLICATION CASE** Kay McDaniel, widow of William Thomas McDaniel brought suit against Baptist Memorial Hospital, alleging that the hospital was responsible for the wrongful death of her husband. It was charged in the complaint that William McDaniel died on February 5, 1970, from serum hepatitis as a consequence of blood transfusions given to him on November 25, 1969, while a patient in the Baptist Memorial Hospital in Memphis, Tennessee. In the complaint Ms. McDaniel asserted that:

- *the defendant owned, operated, managed, maintained and controlled a certain hospital located in Memphis, Tennessee, wherein it provided, supplied and leased rooms, sold and supplied drugs, blood, medical devices and provided trained, skilled personnel for the needs of patients during their care and treatment in said hospital. It also maintained a blood bank, from which it sold and supplied whole blood to patients in the hospital, including the deceased, William Thomas McDaniel.*

- *The defendant, in the rendition of such medical and hospital services and supplies, did supply, sell and transfuse William Thomas McDaniel on November 25, 1969, with approximately 12 pints of blood from its blood bank.*

- *Such blood as was obtained, supplied, sold and transfused by the defendant to the decedent was defective, impure, and contained deleterious contaminants. And was in an unreasonably dangerous condition at the time of the supplying, sale and transfusing of said decedent; that this blood was expected to and did reach the deceased without substantial change in the condition in which it was sold and supplied; that as a direct and proximate result of its use, the said William Thomas McDaniel was caused to and did contract, serum hepatitis as a result of which, the said William Thomas McDaniel died on February 5, 1970; that therefore, the defendant is strictly liable in tort to plaintiff.*

The hospital denied any liability in this case, insisting that it could not be held liable under these theories because it had not engaged in the sale of goods in this situation. Is strict liability in tort applicable against a hospital in a case of wrongful death alleged to have been caused by serum hepatitis due to transfusion of contaminated blood, even though a Tennessee statute exempts hospitals from liability for breach of implied warranty under the state's Uniform Commercial Code? Is the Tennessee statute constitutional? [See *McDaniel v. Baptist Memorial Hospital*, 469 F.2d 230 (1972).]

7. **CRITICAL THINKING CASE** C-Thru Container Corporation entered into a contract with Midland Manufacturing Company in March 1989. In this contract, Midland agreed to purchase bottle-making equipment from C-Thru and to make commercially acceptable bottles for C-Thru. Midland was to pay for the equipment by giving C-Thru a credit against C-Thru's bottle purchases. The contract stated that C-Thru expected to order between 500,000 and 900,000 bottles in 1989. Finally, the contract also provided that if Midland failed to manufacture the bottles, C-Thru could require Midland to pay the entire purchase price plus interest within 30 days.

Midland picked up the equipment as agreed and later sent a notice to C-Thru that it was ready to begin production. C-Thru never ordered any bottles from Midland but instead purchased its bottles from another supplier at a lower price. In 1992, Midland gave C-Thru notice that it was rescinding the 1989 contract, based on C-Thru's failure to order any bottles. C-Thru did not respond to this notice. Midland later sent C-Thru notice that it was claiming an artisan's lien for the expenses of moving, rebuilding, and repairing the machinery. Midland eventually foreclosed the artisan's lien and sold the machinery.

Approximately one month later, C-Thru notified Midland that Midland had failed to comply with the terms of the contract and that the full purchase price plus interest was due and payable within 30 days. When Midland failed to pay C-Thru the amount requested, C-Thru filed a petition alleging that Midland had breached the contract by being incapable of producing the bottles as agreed to in the contract.

Midland contended that the contract did not require that it demonstrate an ability to manufacture commercially acceptable bottles as a condition precedent to C-Thru's obligation to place an order. C-Thru argued that a material issue of fact existed as to whether Midland was unable to manufacture the bottles, thereby excusing C-Thru's failure to place an order. As proof that Midland could not manufacture the bottles, C-Thru pointed to Midland's failure to provide sample bottles. C-Thru relied on deposition testimony that the practice in the bottle-making industry was for the bottle manufacturer to provide sample bottles to verify that it could make commercially acceptable bottles before the purchaser placed any orders.

In ruling on Midland's motion for summary judgment, the trial court found no sample container requirement in the written contract. The court held that the parol evidence rule precluded consideration of any evidence that the practice in the trade was to provide sample bottles before receiving an order. It concluded that no genuine issue of material fact existed and granted Midland's motion for summary judgment. Should parol evidence of usage of trade be admitted to explain or supplement the written contract between the parties? [See *C-Thru Container Corp. v. Midland Manufacturing Co.*, 533 N.W.2d 542 (Iowa 1995).]

8. YOU BE THE JUDGE This case is a striking example of how a lawsuit involving a relatively straightforward international commercial transaction can raise an array of complex questions. Plaintiff Filanto was an Italian corporation engaged in the manufacture and sale of footwear. Defendant Chilewich was an export-import firm incorporated in the state of New York. On February 28, 1989, Chilewich's agent in the United Kingdom signed a contract with Raznoexport, the Soviet Foreign Economic Association, which obligated it to supply footwear to Raznoexport. Section 10 of this contract—the "Russian Contract"—was an arbitration clause, which read in pertinent part as follows:

All disputes or differences which may arise out of or in connection with the present Contract are to be settled, jurisdiction of ordinary courts being excluded, by the Arbitration at the USSR Chamber of Commerce and Industry, Moscow, in accordance with the Regulations of the said Arbitration.

The first exchange of correspondence between the parties to this lawsuit was a letter dated July 27, 1989, from Chilewich to Filanto, as part of the negotiations to fulfill the Russian Contract. This letter states as follows:

Attached please find our contract to cover our purchases from you. Same is governed by the conditions which are enumerated in the standard contract in effect with the Soviet buyers [the Russian Contract], *copy of which is also enclosed.*

Following an exchange of correspondence, Filanto accepted the contract with Chilewich but attempted to exclude the arbitration provision found in the Russian Contract, which was also included in the original communication to Filanto from Chilewich. The next document in this case, and the focal point of the parties' dispute regarding whether an arbitration agreement existed, was a Memorandum Agreement dated March 13, 1990. This was a standard merchant's memo prepared by Chilewich for signature by both parties confirming that Filanto would deliver 100,000 pairs of boots to Chilewich at the Italian/Yugoslav border on September 15, 1990, with the balance of 150,000 pairs to be delivered on November 1, 1990. This Memorandum included the following provision:

It is understood between Buyer and Seller that [the Russian Contract] *is hereby incorporated in this contract as far as practicable, and specifically that any arbitration shall be in accordance with that Contract.*

Chilewich signed this Memorandum and sent it to Filanto. Filanto at that time did not sign or return the document. Then, on August 7, 1990, Filanto returned the Memorandum Agreement, sued on here, that Chilewich had signed and sent to it in March; although Filanto had signed it, Filanto had also appended a cover letter purporting to exclude the arbitration provisions.

It appears that the parties performed as agreed on September 15, 1990, but that problems arose with the scheduled November 1, 1990 performance. According to the complaint, Chilewich ultimately bought and paid for 60,000 pairs of boots in January 1991, but never purchased the 90,000 pairs of boots that compose the balance of Chilewich's original order. It was Chilewich's failure to do so that formed the basis of this lawsuit, commenced by Filanto on May 14, 1991. Chilewich then filed a motion to stay this action pending an arbitration hearing in Moscow. Filantro moved to enjoin the arbitration, arguing that the matter should be adjudicated in the federal district court. In the alternative, Filantro asserted that if the matter were to be submitted to arbitration, it should be submitted to arbitration in New York. Did the contract require that the parties submit any claims to arbitration, or had Filanto properly excluded arbitration? If arbitration were to be used, where was the arbitration to occur? [See *Filanto, S.p.A. v. Chilewich Int'l Corp.*, 789 F. Supp. 1229 (S.D.N.Y. 1992).]

Notes

1. 15 U.S.C.A. § 7001 et seq.
2. Promulgated by the NCCUSL, the UETA is currently enacted in 39 states, with another 4 states having similar statutes.
3. UCC § 2A-102.
4. UCC § 2A-103(j).
5. Alejandro M. Garro, "Reconciliation of Legal Traditions in the U.N. Convention on Contracts for the International Sale of Goods," *International Lawyer* 23 (summer 1989): 433 at 444.
6. United Nations Treaty Section, April 2002.
7. United Nations, Convention on Contracts for the International Sale of Goods, Article 2.
8. CISG, Article 11.
9. CISG, Article 16(2).

Title and Risk of Loss

A G E N D A

NRW NRW expects to increase sales to retail merchants in the near future, and it will need to decide how it should deliver the goods to its buyers. It will also need to decide what delivery terms it is most comfortable using. There is also a concern about whether the firm will be responsible for any loss or damage to the goods while they are being delivered.

Sales to individual consumers also present a problem. Should the firm give some sort of "satisfaction guarantee" to consumers, or should it just trust that the StuffTrakR will satisfy most, if not all, of its customers? If a "satisfaction guaranteed" selling method is used, who is responsible for any damage to the goods while the customer is deciding whether he or she is satisfied? Be prepared! You never know when the firm or one of its members will seek your advice.

What is *title* and why is it important? What is *risk of loss* and why is it important? Are these two topics related, interrelated, or independent? The answer to these questions is the focus of this chapter.

Title is defined as "the union of all elements (as ownership, possession, and custody) constituting the legal right to control and dispose of property."[1] When a buyer enters into a sales contract he or she expects to *own* the goods once the contract has been performed, that is, he or she expects to acquire *title* to the goods being purchased. The UCC reflects this concern with its definition of a sale. According to § 2-106(1), a *sale* "consists of the passing of title from the seller to the buyer for a price." The section then refers to § 2-401 for an explanation of the "passing of title." We will discuss passing of title in more detail later in this chapter. By contrast, when parties enter into a contract to lease goods, title is not an issue. A lease is defined in § 2A-103(j) as "a transfer of the right to possession and use of the goods for a term in return for consideration." This section goes on to state that a sale, including a sale on approval or a sale or return (both discussed later in this chapter) or the retention or creation of a security interest is *not* a lease. Article 2 of the UCC can be found on-line, including the Official Comments, at http://www.law.cornell.edu/ucc/2/overview.html/ or at the NCCUSL home page, http://www.nccusl.org.

Title to Goods under Article 2 of the UCC

Historical Importance

Under common law and under the Uniform Sales Act, title was of paramount importance. The Uniform Sales Act was concerned with when title passed from the seller to the buyer because it tied many other aspects of the sales contract to the issue of title. For example, the party who had title also had risk of loss. Thus, if the goods were damaged or destroyed after the contract was entered but before the buyer had possession of the goods, the risk of loss for the damaged or destroyed goods was on the party who had title. The Uniform Sales Act determined that title passed when the parties intended for title to pass. If the parties did not specify when they intended title to pass, the Act provided certain guidelines. If the goods had been identified to the contract, title passed at the time of the formation of the contract. If the goods had not yet been identified to the contract when the contract was made, title passed when the goods were subsequently identified to the contract by

the seller and delivered to a carrier for delivery (shipment contract), unless the seller was required to pay for the transportation. In that case, title passed when the goods arrived at the destination (destination contract). Finally, if the goods were sold to the buyer "on approval," title passed to the buyer when the buyer approved the goods. And if the sale specified that the buyer had the right to return the goods (sale or return), title passed to the buyer upon delivery but would revest in the seller upon their return by the buyer.[2]

Although this approach worked, and had worked for literally centuries, it did not really address the practical issue of how to allocate the various risks and responsibilities of modern commercial practice. One source refers to the Uniform Sales Act approach as the "lump concept" approach in which the location of title determined virtually every other aspect or issue in the contract.[3] There was a need for a more "contemporary approach, one that reflected modern commercial concerns and practices, rather than this "lump concept," which blindly located title and then rigidly applied the rules. That more contemporary approach can be found in Article 2 of the UCC.

Risk of loss refers to financial responsibility for goods that are lost, damaged, or destroyed during the performance of a contract. The parties are allowed to expressly agree in the sales contract how risk of loss will be allocated. If they do not so agree, § 2-509 and § 2-510 provide the guidelines for when risk of loss moves from the seller to the buyer. Section 2-509 provides for risk of loss when there is no breach of contract by either party. Section 2-510 discusses the effect of a breach of contract by one of the parties on how risk of loss may be modified or altered due to the breach. These issues are addressed in detail later in the chapter.

The Modern Rule under the UCC

Section 2-401 of the UCC addresses the "passing of title" issue. This section states that title to goods cannot pass under a contract for sale prior to their identification to the contract, and that once the goods are identified the buyer acquires a "special property" in the goods without regard to the location of title. The section provides that, unless the parties otherwise explicitly agree, title passes from the seller to the buyer at the time and place where the seller completes his or her performance with reference to delivery of the goods. If the goods are not to be moved, title passes to the buyer with any documents of title delivered by the seller, and if no documents of title are involved, title passes at the time and place the contract is made. Finally, if the buyer rejects or refuses the goods or revokes his or her acceptance of the goods, title revests in the seller. Since these rules sound strikingly similar to the rules under the Uniform Sales Act, you *might* (should) be asking yourself "What's the big deal?"

The "big deal" is found in the first paragraph of § 2-401, which specifically states that all the rights, duties, and remedies of any party apply without regard to title unless title is specifically referred to in the provisions of the particular section. Thus the UCC has separated the concepts of title and risk of loss in favor of a "narrow approach."[4] The UCC provides for the passage of title from the seller to the buyer for a price (the definition of a sale) and also provides a method of ascertaining the location of title for those instances where it is important, but frees up the concept of risk of loss to allow the parties to address that issue in the context of contract performance and the reasonable expectations of each party. This is a significant improvement from the rigid, title-is-determinative approach of the pre-Code rules.

When *does* the location of title matter in a sales contract? Title might matter for inheritance purposes. For example, if one of the parties to the sales contract dies, the heirs of that party might be able to assert a claim to the goods as part of the estate of the decedent, *if* the decedent had title to the goods. Title might matter for taxation purposes. Suppose that a state imposes a sales tax on any sales of goods within the state. A buyer from that state and a seller from a different state enter into a sales contract. If title passes at the *seller's* location, it can be argued that the sale occurred in the seller's state, so that no sales tax is owed in the buyer's state.[5] And of course, the location of title is still important in the area of creditor rights. A creditor of one of the parties may be able to attach any goods that belong to that party. Thus, creditors are very anxious to know where title lies. This also helps to explain the UCC's treatment of consignments. The Code is very careful in spelling out the rights of each party when creditors are involved. Section 2-402 deals with the rights of creditors of the seller when goods are sold. The rights of an unsecured creditor of the seller are limited by the rights of the buyer to recover the goods once the goods are identified to the contract. In a legal tug-of-war between the buyer and a creditor of the seller, the buyer normally will win if the goods have been identified as the goods covered by the sales contract.

When the seller is a merchant, and he or she sells the goods in the ordinary course of business, the buyer purchases the goods "free and clear" of any claims of the seller's creditors. Should the seller subsequently default on his or her credit obligations, the creditors will *not* have the right to go to the buyer in an effort to repossess the goods. The buyer obtains title from the seller in the contract, and any rights the seller's creditors may possess in the goods are cut off. (More treatment of this topic is found in Chapters 25 and 26 in the coverage of secured transactions, Article 9 of the UCC.) If the seller is a merchant and he or she sells the goods to the buyer *not* in the ordinary course of business, the sale is likely to be treated as a bulk sale, governed by Article 6 of the UCC. In this situation, if the creditors of the seller have a perfected security interest in the goods, those creditors can proceed against the goods in the hands of the buyer. Because the sale is made *not* in the ordinary course of business, the creditors retain their rights. While the buyer acquires title to the goods, he or she acquires that title *subject to* the perfected rights of the seller's creditors.

Exhibit 17.1 shows how title passes under Article 2 of the UCC. These same rules apply whether the seller has valid title or voidable title, a topic discussed in a following section.

What happens when, as sometimes happens, the seller "sells" goods but retains possession? The seller's creditors would normally think that so long as their debtor has possession of the goods, he or she still owns those goods, and the creditors may be able to use the goods to pay the debt if the debtor defaults on his or her credit. But suppose that the debtor defaults on the debt, the creditors show up asserting one or more claims against various goods in the possession of the debtor, and the debtor asserts that he or she sold the goods to another person. Assuming that the purported buyer shows up and presents an apparently valid bill of sale or other receipt, what happens to the creditors of the "seller"? In such a case, the seller's creditors can treat the sale as void if the retention by the seller is fraudulent under state law. Historically, the seller's only defense was to show that he or she was a merchant who retained the goods in good faith in the ordinary course of business, and then only if the goods were retained only for a commercially reasonable time. Thus, a seller who holds identified goods in "layaway" would have a valid defense to a fraudulent retention charge. But a seller who holds the goods without a valid reason could be in trouble.

Different states treat the issue of fraudulent retention differently. Three possible rules exist for a state to follow. In some states, a fraudulent retention by the seller is treated as a conclusive presumption of fraud; if a seller sells goods and then retains possession of those goods for any reason other than a commercial reason, the seller is deemed guilty of fraud. Other states view retention of the goods by the seller after the sale as prima facie proof of fraud; the seller is presumed to be guilty of fraud unless the seller is able to show good cause for the retention. In other states, the retention of the goods by the seller is viewed merely as one bit of evidence, to be viewed together with all the other evidence, in determining whether a fraud has occurred.

EXHIBIT 17.1 The Passing of Title

Method of Delivery by Seller	When Title Passes to Buyer under § 2-401
Delivery by Carrier	
• With a shipment contract	When the seller surrenders the goods to the carrier and makes arrangements for shipment
• With a destination contract	When the carrier tenders delivery to the buyer at the destination
Delivery via Warehouseman	
• With a document of title	When the document is delivered to the buyer (the negotiability of the document is irrelevant)
• Without a document of title	At the time and place of the contract
Personal Delivery by the Seller	
• The seller is a merchant	At the time and place of the contract
• The seller is not a merchant	At the time and place of the contract

Note: If the buyer rejects the goods, whether rightfully or wrongfully, title *revests* in the seller; if the buyer rightfully revokes his or her acceptance, title *revests* in the seller.

The enactment of Article 2A, "Leases," has further complicated this issue. Article 2A specifically recognizes the validity of a sale and leaseback arrangement, provided that the buyer in the sale portion of the deal acts in good faith and gives value for the goods purchased. Sale and leaseback arrangements have become very popular in a number of industries, especially construction, and the increase has presented numerous problems with the former attitude toward sellers who retained possession of the goods following the sale. The specific authorization of this sort of dealing under Article 2A should reduce the problems and help to clarify this area of law.

Sellers with Voidable Title

As a general rule, any person who sells goods can transfer to the buyer only those rights that are equal to or less than the rights the seller possesses in those goods. Thus, the person who has *valid* title (that is, the owner of the goods) can sell the goods and pass valid title to the buyer. A person who has *void* title (that is, a thief) has no true title to the goods and passes void title to the buyer. The true owner of the goods may legally reclaim the goods from the person who bought the goods from the thief, if and when the true owner discovers the location of the goods.

However, a special exception to this general rule exists under Article 2. A person who has *voidable* title may legally transfer rights that are better than he or she possesses in the goods. A person with voidable title may legally pass full and valid title to a buyer if that buyer is a good-faith purchaser for value. For example, a person who acquires goods through fraud or misrepresentation has voidable title to those goods. The person who was defrauded or who was the victim of the misrepresentation may avoid the transaction and recover title to the goods if the avoidance occurs while the defrauding or misrepresenting party still has possession of the goods. However, if the defrauding or misrepresenting party sells the goods to a bona fide purchaser for value before the victim of the wrongdoing makes any attempt to avoid the transaction, the buyer may have full and valid title to the goods.

Voidable title does not exist only in cases such as fraud or misrepresentation. Voidable title also exists in situations involving *entrustment*. An entrustment occurs when there is "any delivery and acquiescence in retention of possession regardless of any conditions expressed between the parties to the delivery or acquiescence and regardless of whether the procurement of the entrusting or the possessor's disposition of the goods has been such as to be larcenous under the criminal law" [UCC § 2-403(3)]. Commonly, an entrustment involves a situation in which possession of the goods is given to a merchant who regularly deals in goods of that kind (often for repairs). The entruster, the person who delivers possession of the goods to the merchant, gives the merchant voidable title, which gives the merchant the legal power to transfer all of the entruster's rights to a buyer who in the ordinary course of business purchases the entrusted goods from the merchant. Thus, an owner who takes his or her goods to a merchant for repairs entrusts those goods to the merchant. If the merchant happens to sell the entrusted goods to a customer in the ordinary course of business, and if the customer acted in good faith, the customer takes valid title to the goods. Of course, the entruster does have rights and remedies against the merchant to whom the goods were entrusted. If the entrustment involves a party who obtains the goods but who is not a merchant in goods of that kind, the entrusted party can transfer good title to any good faith purchaser for value. The following two examples show the difference between an entrustment to a merchant and an entrustment to a nonmerchant.

Betty took her watch to Roger's Jewelry to have it repaired. Roger's sells new and used watches in its normal business dealings. If a customer comes into the store and "purchases" Betty's watch, that customer will own the watch. Betty's only recourse will be to sue Roger's for her loss. By entrusting the watch to Roger's, she gave Roger's the legal power to transfer good title to any buyer in the ordinary course of business who purchases the watch from Roger's.

Roger took his watch to Betty's Radio Shop to have it repaired. Although Betty's does not deal in watches, Betty sometimes repairs watches for her friends, and she agrees to do this for Roger. If a customer comes into Betty's and purchases Roger's watch, Roger may be able to recover the watch from the customer. Since Betty does not deal in watches, the transaction with Roger was not an entrustment to a merchant. However, if the person who bought the watch bought it as a good faith purchaser for value, the buyer would still acquire good title due to the entrustment of the watch to Betty by Roger.

In the following case the court was forced to determine rights in a car between its original owner and a bona fide purchaser for value. Notice how the court resolved this controversy and compare the outcome of the case to the information just covered.

17.1

ALAMO RENT-A-CAR, INC. v. MENDENHALL
937 P.2d 69 (Nev. 1997)

FACTS John Clark, using the alias Thomas Pecora, rented a Lexus automobile from a Nevada Alamo Rent-a-Car location in December 1994. Shortly thereafter, Clark obtained a "quick title" to the car from the State of California, using fraudulent documents with forged signatures of fictitious parties. Clark then sold the car to the Mendenhalls for $34,000 in January 1995. The Mendenhalls made some improvements to the car, had it safety-inspected and smog-tested, and registered the car at their home in Utah. The car was also properly insured and licensed by the Mendenhalls. In March 1995, the Nevada DMV seized the car from the Mendenhalls and returned the auto to Alamo. The Mendenhalls sued in an effort to recover the car, and the trial court ruled that they were bona fide purchasers for value who purchased the automobile without notice that it was stolen, and that they were entitled to ownership and possession of the car. Alamo appealed this ruling, arguing that since Clark was a thief, he never obtained voidable title, and since he never had voidable title, the Mendenhalls could not obtain clear title from him.

ISSUE Did the Mendenhalls acquire good title from Clark in their purchase of the automobile?

HOLDING No. Clark was a thief, he held only void title, and he could not pass good title to any purchasers.

REASONING Excerpts from the opinion of the court (Shearing, Springer, Rose, Young, and Maupin):

[The Nevada UCC § 2-403(1)] provides in pertinent part:

A purchaser of goods acquires all title which his transferor had or had power to transfer... a person with voidable title has power to transfer good title to a good faith purchaser for value. When goods have been delivered under a transaction of purchase the purchaser has such power even though: ...

  c) It was agreed that the transaction was to be a "cash sale"; or

  d) The delivery was procured through fraud punishable as larcenous under the criminal law. ...

The primary questions raised are whether Clark had voidable title to the Lexus when he sold it to the Mendenhalls, and whether the Mendenhalls were, in fact, good faith or bona fide purchasers of the car. If the answer to either of these questions is answered in the negative, the transfer was void. . . . We need not reach the issue of the Mendenhalls' status as bona fide purchasers because we conclude that Clark did not have voidable title. Therefore, even if we assume that the district court properly found the Mendenhalls to be bona fide purchasers, the transfer was void. . . .

Upon concluding that the Mendenhalls were bona fide purchasers, the lower court noted that the California "quick title" furnished by Clark "was accepted by the state of Utah and a new registration and license plates were issued" to the Mendenhalls. Both the Mendenhalls and the lower court seem to equate Clark's fraudulently obtained but facially valid California "quick title" with voidable title capable of transferring ownership. The law does not support this conclusion. Other jurisdictions have considered the effect of a sale by a thief:

The owner of stolen goods is not divested of title therein by the theft, and even though an innocent subsequent purchaser may be treated as having title against everyone but the rightful owner, a sale by the thief . . . does not vest title on the purchaser as against the true owner. . . .

The true owner may recover a stolen motor vehicle . . . from a good-faith purchaser even though the thief had also stolen, or forged, a title certificate, or obtained a title certificate in another state and delivered it to the purchaser. . . .

The fact that the negligence of the owner contributed to or facilitated the theft does not estop the true owner from asserting title. . . .

Because Alamo still had possession of the Lexus' title, Clark could not have had voidable title simply by fraud-ulently obtaining a facially valid California title. Accordingly, the Mendenhalls, even if found to be bona fide purchasers, could not have taken ownership superior to Alamo's. . . . However, because the Mendenhalls were found to be bona fide purchasers, Alamo must be ordered to reimburse the Mendenhalls for any improvements made to the Lexus while in their possession. . . . Accordingly, we reverse the district court's judgment and remand with instructions to award ownership and possession to Alamo and order Alamo to reimburse the Mendenhalls for improvements made to the Lexus while it was in their possession.

BUSINESS CONSIDERATIONS What can a car rental company do to prevent a customer from stealing one of the company's cars, fraudulently titling the car, and then selling it to an innocent third person? What procedures should be in place to minimize the risk of such an occurrence?

ETHICAL CONSIDERATIONS Was it ethical for Alamo to seek recovery of the stolen vehicle from admittedly bona fide purchasers four months after the car was stolen, especially given that the Mendenhalls had purchased the car in good faith before Alamo reported the car as stolen? If Alamo had acted more promptly in reporting the car as stolen, would the Mendenhalls have been protected?

Insurable Interest

"An insurable interest, in its broadest sense, is a relation between the insured and the event insured against such that the occurrence of the event will cause substantial loss or injury of some kind to the insured."[6] As applied to sales or leases, the term insurable interest refers to the right to purchase insurance on goods to protect one's property rights and interests in the goods. Section 2-501 provides the general guidelines for determining whether an insurable interest exists in the sale of goods, and § 2A-218 provides the guidelines for determining whether an insurable interest exists in the leasing of goods. The buyer gains an insurable interest when existing goods are identified to the contract, even if the goods are nonconforming. If the goods are not identified, the buyer gains an insurable interest once identification occurs. Likewise, if the goods are not yet in existence, the buyer gains an insurable interest as soon as the goods come into existence.

The seller has an insurable interest in the goods for as long as the seller retains title to or any security interest in the goods; and either party has an insurable interest if that party also has a risk of loss. Notice that title is not necessary for an insurable interest to exist. Insurance provides an important protection when a party has any risk of loss for the affected goods, so knowing when an insurable interest arises can be extremely important.

In the following case the insurer argued that the insured no longer had an insurable interest at the time the loss occurred, since title to the insured goods had passed to the buyer. Follow the court's reasoning and see if you agree with the decision the court reached.

Risk of Loss under Article 2 of the UCC

The term risk of loss refers to the financial responsibility between the parties if the goods are lost, damaged, or destroyed before the buyer has accepted them. Notice that risk of loss refers to the relationship between the buyer and the seller. It does not refer to the possibility that an independent carrier of the goods or a warehouseman or bailee hired to store the goods may be liable. Nor does it refer to

DESIGN DATA CORP. v. MARYLAND CASUALTY CO.
503 N.W.2d 552 (Neb. 1993)

FACTS Design Data sold a computer plotter and software to HHB Drafting, Inc., for a total of $73,495, and arranged to have the plotter shipped to HHB by Consolidated Freightways. Representatives of HHB alleged that the plotter appeared to be damaged when it arrived at their location. Despite this fact, HHB accepted the plotter. However, after the plotter was set up it did not work, and HHB notified Design Data that it was revoking its acceptance due to the defects in the product that had been delivered.

Design Data then filed a claim with Consolidated Freightways for indemnification for its losses, only to discover that the contract with Consolidated included a "tariff provision" that set the value of the goods at $5 per pound. Accordingly, Consolidated issued a draft to Design Data for $1,700, the amount called for in the "tariff provisions."

Still seeking to recover its loss on the transaction, Design Data then filed a claim with its insurer, Maryland Casualty. Maryland Casualty denied any liability, asserting that Design Data no longer had an insurable interest in the plotter once the buyer accepted the goods. Maryland Casualty also argued that its policy limited its potential liability for goods in transit to a maximum of the transit limit, and if no transit limit was shown, any losses were not covered by the policy.

ISSUES Did Design Data have an insurable interest in the plotter? Did the policy limitation remove any liability from Maryland Casualty?

HOLDINGS Yes, Design Data had an insurable interest in the plotter despite the acceptance by HHB. Yes, the policy language precluded Design Data from seeking any additional recovery from Maryland Casualty.

REASONING Excerpts from the opinion of Chief Justice Hastings:

Maryland Casualty contends that under UCC § 2-509 the risk of loss had passed to the buyer upon the buyer's acceptance of the plotter and that Design Data had no insurable interest at the time the damage was discovered. In pertinent part, § 2-509 provides:

1) Where the contract requires or authorizes the seller to ship the goods by carrier . . .

   b) if it does require him to deliver them at a particular destination and the goods are there duly tendered while in the possession of the carrier, the risk of loss passes to the buyer when the goods are there duly so tendered as to enable the buyer to take delivery.

Maryland Casualty concedes that the risk of loss can be shifted back to the seller if the buyer effectively revokes acceptance, but contends that the key criterion is whether the buyer's acceptance was reasonably induced by the difficulty of discovery of nonconformity before acceptance. . . . Maryland Casualty argues that HHB's rejection was untimely and, thus, an ineffective transfer of the risk of loss, since the buyer's onsite manager had reason to suspect that the plotter had been damaged when the shipment arrived. . . . While HHB had reason to suspect that the plotter was damaged, the nature of the damage was not known until the carton was opened and inspection was made. It was reasonable under the circumstances for [HHB] to allow the Design Data representative who was present to install the plotter to ascertain the extent of the damage. The revocation of acceptance was timely, and thus, the risk of loss remained with the seller, Design Data. Under the terms of the policy, Maryland Casualty was to provide coverage for equipment which Design Data owned, rented, or for which it was legally responsible. Design Data had an insurable interest in the plotter at the time the damage was discovered, and therefore Maryland Casualty's first assignment of error is without merit. . . .

Both parties seem to misconstrue the policy provisions as to losses occurring "in transit." The relevant policy language bears repeating here: "[L]osses that occur while property is in transit are covered up to the transit limit. If no transit limit is shown, these losses won't be covered." . . . The application of "transit limit" must be found within the policy. The plain reading of the policy discloses that the amount of transit limit has been left blank in the policy. No transit limit is shown in the policy, and therefore under the terms of the policy, "these losses won't be covered." . . . The parties in this case simply did not contract for any transit coverage, nor was any premium paid for this coverage. . . . It should now be apparent that Design Data's problem is that it never had "in transit" coverage; it has only vaguely alleged, but failed to establish, that its losses came within the terms of the Maryland Casualty policy. When a breach of an insurance contract is alleged, the plaintiff has the burden of bringing his or her claim within the limitations of the policy. . . .

> BUSINESS CONSIDERATIONS What procedures should a merchant seller of goods establish in order to minimize his or her potential risk of loss in the sales contract he or she enters with customers?

> ETHICAL CONSIDERATIONS Is it ethical for an insurance company to try to avoid liability under a policy that it wrote for one of its customers? Would it be ethical for an insurance company to just pay any claims submitted by its customers without some proof of coverage and loss?

the possible liability of any insurer of the goods or of their delivery. The allocation of risk of loss normally depends on the method of performance called for in the contract, passing from the seller to the buyer once the seller completes his or her delivery obligations under the terms of the contract.

A buyer who has risk of loss must pay the seller for the goods if the goods were properly shipped. This situation arises most commonly in a shipment contract: If the seller shipped conforming goods, but during the journey the goods were damaged, destroyed, or lost, the buyer is liable and must perform the contract as agreed. Of course, the buyer may have recourse against the carrier, the warehouseman, or an insurer for the loss, but such recourse involves a separate contract or relationship and does not affect the buyer's liability to the seller under Article 2.

If the contract involved is a destination contract, the seller bears the risk of loss. In this situation, any lost, damaged, or destroyed goods are the responsibility of the seller. The seller will be required to ship more goods or make up the loss to the buyer in some other manner. And the seller will then have to proceed against the carrier, the warehouseman, or the insurer for any remedies that may be available under the carriage or storage contract or the insurance coverage.

In contracts that do not involve the use of an independent carrier, the risk of loss will frequently depend on the status of the parties, the terms of the contract, and how adequately the parties have performed. Several possibilities are explored next.

Breach of Contract

If the seller breaches the contract by sending nonconforming goods, risk of loss remains with the seller until either the seller cures the defect or the buyer accepts the goods despite the nonconformity. In order for this provision to apply, the goods must be so nonconforming that the buyer may properly reject the tender of delivery. Sometimes the buyer accepts the goods that the seller sends but later finds them to be nonconforming. When this occurs, the buyer often has the right to revoke acceptance. When

accepting the goods, the buyer assumes risk of loss. When the nonconformity is discovered and the acceptance is revoked, what happens? The buyer retains risk of loss, but only to the extent of the buyer's insurance coverage. Any loss in excess of the buyer's insurance rests on the seller because the seller breached the contact. It would not be fair to have the buyer assume risk of loss when the seller is the party at fault in the underlying agreement, nor would it be fair to allow the buyer to recover the complete loss from the seller and also to recover from the insurance company for its payment under the insurance policy.

Sometimes the buyer breaches a contract, usually by repudiation, after the goods are identified but before they are delivered. In such a case, risk of loss has not yet shifted from the seller to the buyer. As a result, the risk still rests on the seller. However, since the buyer is in breach, any loss in excess of the seller's insurance coverage rests on the buyer, for the reasoning just set out. The buyer will face this possible loss only for a commercially reasonable time, at which point the buyer is relieved of the burden of risk of loss. Of course, he or she still faces the burden of being in breach of contract and may well face liability for that breach.

No Breach of Contract

If the contract is not breached, risk of loss is much more technical. It is difficult to determine where risk of loss resides until the entire contract is reviewed. The UCC recognizes four distinct contract possibilities to allocate risk of loss when the contract has not been breached. In addition, the parties can agree by contract to allocate the risk.

The first situation arises in a contract whereby the seller sends the goods by means of a carrier. If the goods are sent by means of a shipment contract, risk of loss passes to the buyer when the goods are delivered to the carrier. This is true even if the seller reserves rights in the goods pending payment. In contrast, the seller may enter into a destination contract with the carrier. Risk of loss then does not pass to the buyer until the goods are properly tendered at the point of destination. Once the goods are made available to the buyer, the buyer has risk of loss.

NRW CASE 17.1 Finance/Management

WHO TAKES THE LOSS?

NRW made a relatively large sale to a new retail customer recently. Initially the firm was delighted. The sale was significant and the new customer, an electronics retail store, had the potential to become a major purchaser of InvenTrakR units. However, the delight turned to concern in short order. As per the contract, NRW shipped the units to the customer via Federal Parcel Service, with terms of FOB the customer's warehouse. Unfortunately, Federal Parcel misplaced the package containing the InvenTrakR units. The day after the scheduled delivery, Helen received a call from the customer, asking where the units were. Helen told the customer that the goods had been shipped and that she would check with Federal Parcel to see where the units were. NRW cannot refill the customer's order at this point in time, and the customer insists that he will sue for breach of contract unless he has the goods he ordered by the end of the week. Helen has asked you what the responsibility of NRW is in this situation, and what rights NRW might be able to assert. What will you tell her?

BUSINESS CONSIDERATIONS What should a company do to ensure that goods are properly tendered at the customer's warehouse? What should a company do to minimize its risk if the goods are lost during shipment?

ETHICAL CONSIDERATIONS Is it ethical for a buyer to threaten to sue the seller for breach of contract when the loss is not the fault of the seller? Does it matter if the buyer was the party that specified the type of delivery or the carrier to be used?

INTERNATIONAL CONSIDERATIONS The parties in this case agreed to use a standard shipping term for carriage of the goods, each assuming that the term referred to the UCC's provisions. Would it have made a difference if one of the parties were in a different nation and they still decided to use the term "FOB"? Why?

risk of loss passes when the buyer receives the document from the seller. If the seller is not to use a negotiable document of title but does use a nonnegotiable document, risk of loss passes only after the buyer has a reasonable opportunity to present the document to the bailee. And sometimes no document at all is used. In such cases, risk of loss passes to the buyer only after the bailee acknowledges the rights of the buyer in the goods.

The third situation arises when the goods are in the possession of the seller and a carrier is not to be used. Under these circumstances, the status of the seller is the key. If the seller is a merchant, risk of loss does not pass to the buyer until the buyer takes possession of the goods. If the seller is not a merchant, risk of loss passes on tender of delivery to the buyer. The following two examples show how risk of loss varies with the status of the seller.

Joan is a used-car dealer. She enters a contract with Bob to sell him a car. She tells Bob that the keys are in the car and to go pick it up at any time. Before Bob gets there, the car is destroyed by a fire. Since Joan is a merchant, she still has risk of loss. She will have to provide Bob with another car or refund his money.

Jack is not a car dealer of any sort. He enters a contract to sell his car to Marie. He tells her the keys are in the car and she can pick it up at any time. This is a tender of delivery. Before Marie gets the car, it is destroyed by a fire. She must bear the loss, since Jack was a nonmerchant.

The fourth set of circumstances applies to a sale on approval. Here risk of loss remains with the seller until the buyer accepts the goods by approval of the sale. Of course, the various ways the buyer can accept should be kept in mind.

Finally, the parties can agree to allocate risk of loss in any way they wish. Risk of loss can be divided in any manner the parties feel is proper. Such an agreement must be very explicit or the Code provisions just discussed will be applied.

Exhibit 17.2 illustrates the allocation of risk of loss under Article 2 of the UCC. It might be helpful to compare how title passes (Exhibit 17.1) with how risk of loss passes. This is a substantial change from the treatment at common law or under the Uniform Sales Act, where title was paramount and risk of loss was simply assigned to the party with title.

In the following case the court had to determine whether the buyer had assumed risk of loss and an insurable interest when the goods that were the subject of the contract were damaged prior to completion of performance by the parties.

The second situation arises when the goods are in the hands of a bailee and they are not to be physically delivered. When the bailee is holding the goods, the contract must be very carefully analyzed. The contract may call for the seller to deliver a negotiable document of title to the buyer. If so,

EXHIBIT 17.2 Allocation of Risk of Loss

Risk of Loss with No Breach of Contract — § 2-509

Method of Delivery by Seller	When Risk of Loss Passes to Buyer
Delivery by Carrier	
• With a shipment contract	When the seller surrenders the goods to the carrier and makes arrangements for shipment
• With a destination contract	When the carrier tenders delivery to the buyer at the destination
Delivery via Warehouseman	
• With a negotiable document of title	When the document is delivered to the buyer
• With a nonnegotiable document of title	After the buyer receives the document *and* has a reasonable time to notify the warehouseman of his or her rights in the goods
• Without a document of title	Upon the warehouseman's acknowledgment of the buyer's rights in the goods once the warehouseman has been notified of the sale
Personal Delivery by the Seller	
• The seller is a merchant	Upon *actual* delivery of the goods to the buyer
• The seller is not a merchant	Upon *tender* of delivery of the goods to the buyer

Risk of Loss with a Breach of Contract — § 2-510

When Breach Is Discovered	Allocation of Risk of Loss
• Tender of delivery fails to conform, buyer rightfully rejects	Risk remains with seller until the seller cures or the buyer accepts the goods despite the nonconformity
• Buyer rightfully revokes an acceptance	Risk is with the buyer to the extent of the buyer's insurance, if any; any loss beyond the buyer's insurance is treated as remaining with the seller from the beginning
• Buyer repudiates or otherwise breaches before risk has passed to the buyer	Risk is with the seller to the extent of the seller's insurance, if any; any loss beyond the seller's insurance lies with the buyer for a commercially reasonable time

Special Problems

The commercial world is crowded with businesses trying to get, or trying to keep, "a foot in the door" or just looking for a new gimmick that will provide an edge. As a result, some special forms of business dealings have arisen. The UCC has attempted to deal with two of these special areas: "sale on approval" and "sale or return." Both forms of business dealings resemble yet another: consignments. The Code deals with these special areas in §§ 2-326 and 2-327.

Sale on Approval

A sale on approval exists if the buyer "purchases" goods primarily for personal use with the understanding that the goods can be returned, even if they conform to the contract. The buyer is given a reasonable time to examine, inspect, and try the goods at the seller's risk. Neither title nor risk of loss passes to the buyer until and unless the buyer accepts the goods. The seller retains both title and risk of loss during the buyer's "approval" period even though the buyer has possession of the goods. The buyer is deemed to have accepted the goods if one of the following occurs:

• The buyer signifies acceptance.

• The buyer does not return the goods.

• The buyer subjects the goods to unreasonable usage.

The following example involves a contract for sale on approval.

Sam "purchases" a new lawn mower with a 30-day "free home trial." He uses the mower six times in three weeks, cutting his lawn and in no way abusing the product. After the third week, Sam returns the mower and refuses to pay the purchase price. Since this was a sale on approval and Sam never approved, he is not responsible for payment.

17.3

VALLEY FORGE INSURANCE CO. v. GREAT AMERICAN INSURANCE
1995 Ohio App. LEXIS 3939 (1995)

FACTS The Kennedys went to John Nolan Ford on Friday, April 7, 1989, to purchase a 1989 Ford Mustang. The parties basically agreed on a deal but were unable to complete the deal since the financing arrangements were not done by the close of the business day. All the other paperwork had been completed, including a New Vehicle Buyer's Order Form, an Agreement to Provide Insurance, and the credit application. John Nolan Ford decided that the financing arrangements would be completed the following Monday and allowed the Kennedys to take the new car home for the weekend. When the Kennedys drove the car home that day, the certificate of title had not passed and the financing arrangements were incomplete.

That evening Mr. Kennedy loaned the car to his brother-in-law, Cella, and allowed Cella to take the car for a drive with one of his friends, Campbell, as a passenger. Cella wrecked the car on the drive, injuring Campbell. The next day Mr. Kennedy informed John Nolan Ford that there had been an accident involving the new Mustang and that the car had been towed to the John Nolan Ford lot. John Nolan Ford was paid for the damages to the Mustang by its insurer, Milwaukee Mutual Insurance Company. On January 26, 1990, Campbell filed suit against Cella and Kennedy for his injuries from the accident. Cella eventually settled for a total of $24,385, the amount being paid by his insurance company, Valley Forge Insurance Company. Valley Forge then sought indemnification from Kennedy's insurer, Great American Insurance Company, and from Milwaukee Mutual, the insurer of John Nolan Ford. Both of the other insurers denied any liability in the case. A declaratory judgment action was heard in the trial court to determine who held the interest in the automobile at the time of the accident. The trial court ruled that John Nolan Ford owned the automobile at the time of the accident and that Milwaukee, as the primary insurer, should indemnify Valley Forge.

ISSUE Did the Kennedys have risk of loss or an insurable interest in the automobile before the contract was finalized?

HOLDING No. Title and risk of loss remained with the seller due to the explicit language of the agreement between the parties, and the Kennedys did not yet have an insurable interest.

REASONING Excerpts from the opinion of the court (Doan, Hildebrandt, and Sundermann):

Both Milwaukee and Great American agree that [the UCC], and not the Certificate of Title Act, applies to the facts of this case. We agree . . . [The UCC] provides, in pertinent part, the following:

unless otherwise explicitly agreed, title passes to the buyer at the time and place at which the seller completes his performance with reference to the physical delivery of the goods, despite any reservation of security interests and even though a document title is to be delivered at a different time or place; and in particular and despite any reservation of security interest by the bill of lading.

Milwaukee argues that the risk of loss and insurable interest had passed because the car had been delivered. Further, Milwaukee states that the Kennedys explicitly agreed to provide insurance. Great American counters that the parties had "otherwise explicitly agreed" in the New Vehicle Buyer's Order that any interest in the car would not pass until "either the full purchase price is paid in cash or a satisfactory deferred payment agreement is executed by the parties[.]" No financing had been arranged at the time of the accident. We agree with Great American's position that the parties had "otherwise explicitly agreed." The parties had clearly agreed to various provisions in the contract. Two terms of the New Vehicle Buyer's Order apply to the situation at bar. Under the "Agreement" provision, the contract states that "it is expressly agreed that the purchaser acquires no right, title or interest in or to the property which he agrees to purchase hereunder until such property is delivered to him and either the full purchase price is paid in cash or a satisfactory deferred payment agreement is executed by the parties hereto[.]" Under the provision designated "Purchasers [*sic*] Acceptance of Motor Vehicle" . . . the contract states that "purchaser hereby agrees as follows * * * to insure said motor vehicle with a licensed and responsible Insurance Company[.]" Milwaukee contends that the language of the "Purchaser's Acceptance" is more specific than the "Agreement." It further argues that the trial court should have construed the contract using the principle that the specific controls the general. While we acknowledge that this principle is useful in construction of some contracts, it is unavailing here. We disagree with Milwaukee that the second term is more specific than the first. The first term specifically addresses the issue of transfer of interest. Because we find the terms equally specific, we will not construe the "Purchaser's Acceptance" to control.

We look instead to another well-established construction principle: "Where there is doubt or ambiguity in the language of a contract it will be construed strictly against the party who prepared it[.]" . . . Applying that principle to this case, we must construe the contract strictly against John Nolan Ford. We hold that the term of the contract under "Agreement" is the term that controls the contract. Therefore, no interest, including insurable interest, had passed at the time of the accident because the full price was not paid nor was a payment plan worked out. Milwaukee also argues that the Kennedys explicitly agreed to provide insurance by signing the "Agreement to Provide Insurance." While the agreement does state that the Kennedys agreed to provide insurance, it is not clear when the Kennedys were to obtain the insurance. In fact, because the agreement refers to an "instalment [*sic*] contract," it is possible that the Kennedys were to provide insurance once a financing agreement was reached. In light of the fact that the agreement is ambiguous, we again construe the contract strictly against the drafter and hold that any agreement to provide insurance was to take effect after financing was obtained. As financing was not obtained, the insurable interest and the risk of loss remained with John Nolan Ford.

This result is bolstered by the comments to Uniform Commercial Code 2-401. . . and by the actions of the parties after the accident. Comment 4 to Uniform Commercial Code 2-401 makes clear that passage of title occurs "when the seller has finally committed himself in regard to specific goods." In this case, to say that John Nolan Ford had finally committed itself to transfer title of a car without financing having been arranged is implausible. That John Nolan Ford had not finally committed itself is demonstrated by John Nolan Ford's actions after the accident. John Nolan Ford accepted the wrecked car and returned the deposit and the trade-in. Clearly, John Nolan Ford believed it still held the interest in the car. We hold that because the parties had otherwise agreed that interest in the car, including insurable interest, would not pass until the financing was complete, John Nolan Ford still had the risk of loss and the insurable interest when the accident occurred.

BUSINESS CONSIDERATIONS Is it a good business practice for a merchant seller to allow buyers to take goods home before the sales contract is complete? How was the possession and use of the car by the Kennedys in this case any different than a "test drive" of a car they were interested in buying?

ETHICAL CONSIDERATIONS Was it ethical for Cella's insurance company to settle the lawsuit by Campbell and then to seek indemnification? Should Valley Forge have insisted that the other insurers be involved in case they ended up bearing the financial responsibility of the accident?

Sale or Return

A sale or return exists if the buyer "purchases" goods primarily for resale with the understanding that the unsold goods may be returned to the seller even if they conform to the contract. In this situation, both title and risk of loss lie with the goods. Goods stolen from the buyer cannot be returned, so they are "sold" to the buyer. The seller must be paid for them. The following example indicates how the purpose of a sale or return differs from the purpose of a sale on approval.

Sam "purchases" some automobile stereo systems from Smooth Sounds, Inc., on a sale-or-return contract. Sam displays one of the stereos in his service station. If a customer wants an auto stereo system, Sam will sell it and install it. Sam can return any unsold units to Smooth Sounds for a refund or for credit on future goods. However, a thief breaks into Sam's station and steals the stereos. Sam must pay Smooth Sounds for the stereos since he cannot return them.

There is a strong presumption that any delivery of goods to a merchant for resale of those goods should *not* be treated as a sale on approval, and that any delivery of goods to a consumer is not a sale or return of those goods.[7] When goods are delivered to a merchant buyer, it is assumed that the transaction is either a normal sale or a sale or return. Similarly, when goods are delivered to a consumer, it is assumed that the transaction is either a normal sale or a sale on approval.

Consignment

In a consignment, the owner of the goods allows a consignee to display and sell the goods for the owner-consignor. The UCC treats such an arrangement as a sale or return unless one of the following occurs:

- The consignor ensures that signs are posted specifying that the goods on display are consigned goods.

- The consignor proves that the creditors of the consignee were generally aware of the consignments.

NRW CASE 17.2   Sales

METHODS OF SELLING

Mai contacted a local computer store to ask if the store might be interested in carrying StuffTrakR units as one of the store's computer-related items. The store seemed interested but did not want to make a commitment to purchase the units. Instead, the store owner asked Mai if NRW might be interested in entering into a "sale or return" arrangement so that if the StuffTrakR units did not sell, the computer store would be able to return them. Mai has asked what you think of the idea, and what risks and benefits might be involved in a sale or return. What will you tell her?

BUSINESS CONSIDERATIONS A firm trying to break into an established industry might have to decide whether it is better to try to gain a market share through price competition or through the use of a nonstandard marketing method such as a sale or return arrangement. What are the benefits of using sale or return rather than reduced price to gain market recognition and share? What are the potential drawbacks to this approach?

ETHICAL CONSIDERATIONS The rights of the creditors of a retail merchant are different in regard to the merchant's inventory if the merchant has goods through a consignment or a sale or return. If the merchant carries inventory under both bases, what are the ethical obligations of that merchant to provide its creditors with adequate information regarding the inventory? What concerns might the seller or the consignor have about the potential claims of the buyer's creditors?

INTERNATIONAL CONSIDERATIONS Does the CISG make provision for either a "sale or return" or a "sale on approval" contract? Assuming that it does not, would the parties be precluded from making such an agreement on their own?

- The consignor complies with the rules for secured transactions under Article 9 of the UCC.

Obviously, the Code has limited, if not eliminated, consignment in the modern business world. Most such arrangements today are treated merely as sale-or-return contracts.

Auctions

Auctions receive special mention in § 2-328. In an auction, the auctioneer, on behalf of the seller, sells the goods to the highest bidder. The auctioneer does not normally give the same warranties to a buyer that other sellers of goods give. A sale at auction is not complete until the auctioneer accepts a bid. Even then, if a bid is made while the auctioneer is in the process of knocking down, the auctioneer may elect to reopen bidding. The goods at an auction are presumed to be put up "with reserve." An auction will be deemed "without reserve" only if, by its terms, it is specifically and expressly stated to be "without reserve." With reserve means that the auctioneer may declare all the bids to be too low and may refuse to accept any bids or to make any sale. In contrast, if the auction is without reserve, the highest bid made must be accepted and a sale made.

What if the seller enters a bid, directly or indirectly, in an effort to drive up the bidding? The winning bidder in such a case may choose to renounce his or her bidding and avoid the sale or may elect to take the goods at the last good-faith bid before the seller entered the bidding.

Leases under Article 2A of the UCC

In much the same manner as under Article 2, Article 2A is not overly concerned with the concept of title. Article 2A specifically separates title and possession. It states that the provisions governing leases apply whether the lessor or a third party has title to the leased goods, and whether the lessor, the lessee, or a third party has possession of the leased goods.

Risk of loss with respect to the leased goods varies depending upon the type of lease involved. In a finance lease, risk of loss passes to the lessee under the provisions of § 2A-219. If the lease is other than a finance lease, risk of loss is retained by the lessor. If the leased goods are in the hands of a bailee and risk of loss is to pass to the lessee, rules similar to those under Article 2 are followed in allocating risk of loss:

- If the goods are in the possession of a bailee and delivery is to occur without movement of the goods, risk of loss passes to the lessee upon the bailee's acknowledgment of the lessee's right to possession of the goods. (Since there is not a sale, there will not be a document of title involved in such a situation.)

- If the goods are to be delivered to the lessee by a carrier, the carriage contract is presumed to be a shipment contract, passing risk of loss to the lessee when the goods are duly delivered to the carrier. If a destination contract is specified, risk of loss passes to the lessee when the goods are duly tendered at the destination.

- If the goods are to be delivered to the lessee by the lessor, passage of risk of loss depends upon the status of the lessor. If the lessor (or the supplier, in the case of a finance lease) is a merchant, risk of loss passes to the lessee when the goods are actually delivered to the lessee. If the lessor is not a merchant, risk of loss passes to the lessee upon tender of delivery.

Article 2A of the UCC can be found online, including the Official Comments, at the NCCUSL home page, http://www.nccusl.org.

Title to Goods under the CISG

Article 1 of the CISG states: "This Convention governs only the formation of the contract of sale and the rights and obligations of the seller and the buyer arising from such a contract. In particular, except as otherwise expressly provided in this Convention, it is not concerned with:

> (a) the validity of the contract or of any of its provisions or of any usage;
>
> (b) the effect which the contract may have on the property in the goods sold."

Thus, the CISG is not concerned with title—or with a number of other issues that seem important to American businesspeople. The CISG "applies to contracts for the sale of goods between parties whose places of business are in different States and either both of those States are contracting States or the rules of private international law lead to the law of a Contracting State."[8] It would seem the Convention treats title as a "validity question," and "validity questions" are resolved by the applicable laws of the forum state rather than under the provisions of the CISG.

Despite the lack of specific treatment of the title issue, however, the CISG does *imply* how title should be treated under the provisions of the Convention. Article 41 obligates the seller to deliver goods that are free from any right or claim of a third party, unless the buyer agreed to take the goods subject to that right or claim, unless the right or claim is based on industrial property or other intellectual property of the third party. (These claims by a third party based on industrial or other intellectual property of the third party are very similar to the UCC's implied warranty against infringements, which is discussed in Chapter 19.)

Thus, while the CISG does not expressly discuss title, there appear to be warranty provisions that assure the buyer will receive title to the goods upon performance by the seller.

Risk of Loss under the CISG

The CISG treats risk of loss in a manner that is very similar to the way in which Article 2 treats risk of loss. Like Article 2, the CISG allocates risk of loss based on how the seller is to deliver the goods to the buyer.

If a common carrier is to be used to transport the goods from the seller to the buyer, the type of carriage contract arranged by the seller determines when risk of loss passes to the buyer. If the sales contract does not designate a destination at which the seller is to deliver the goods, risk of loss passes to the buyer when the goods are handed over to the first carrier.[9] If the seller is obligated to turn the goods over to the carrier at a particular location, risk of loss will pass to the buyer when the goods are handed over to the carrier at that location.[10] The risk of loss will pass to the buyer in either of these circumstances even if the seller is permitted to retain documents that control the disposition of the goods by the carrier.

If the contract for sale is made while the goods are in transit, risk of loss passes to the buyer upon the conclusion of the contract.[11] Thus, if goods are in a ship at sea and the buyer and seller enter into a contract for the sale of those goods, the buyer assumes risk of loss as soon as the contract is entered, and the seller will be able to enforce the contract and collect the contract price even if the goods are lost, damaged, or destroyed while at sea.

If the goods are not to be transported by carrier and are not in transit, the risk of loss passes from the seller to the buyer when the buyer either takes possession of the goods *or* fails to take possession of them within a reasonable time after the goods have been placed at his or her disposal, *if* such failure to take possession is a breach of the contract.[12]

Standard Shipping Terms

If both parties to a sales contract are merchants, it is a fairly common practice for the parties to the contract to agree that the seller will have the goods delivered to the buyer by a third person, a "common carrier." This is such a common occurrence that the parties have developed standardized terms that are used in the contract to describe the carriage by the third party. These standardized terms are a sort of commercial "shorthand" that merchants use. While the terms do describe the carriage, they also carry other important meanings, including an allocation of risk of loss. And once again, the terms used internationally are different—at least in meaning, even if not always in "letters"—from the terms used under the UCC.

Standard Terms under the UCC

Every shipping contract must take one of two positions: It is either a *shipment* contract or it is a *destination* contract. In a shipment contract, once the seller makes a proper contract for the carriage of the goods and surrenders them to the care of the carrier, the goods belong to the buyer. The buyer has title and risk of loss. The seller has performed his or her part of the contract. In contrast, in a destination contract, the seller retains title and all risk of loss until the carrier gets the goods to the buyer or wherever the goods are supposed to go under the contract. The seller has not performed until the goods reach their destination.

Under § 2-303, the parties can agree to allocate or share the risk of loss during transit. This sort of arrangement seems to be the exception rather than the rule, however. Most parties seem to ignore the problem of loss during shipment until a loss occurs. And, at that point, it is too late to begin negotiating about what to do if one occurs. Because of this normal oversight, and because so many shipments use standard terms, the UCC allocates risk of loss when the parties to a contract use any of these standard shipping terms. If the parties do not designate how loss is to be allocated, and if the contract does not specify whether it is a shipment contract or a destination contract, the law presumes that the contract is a shipment contract. Thus, once the seller properly transfers the goods to the carrier and makes arrangements for the transportation of the goods, the title and the risk of loss pass to the buyer.

FOB

FOB means "free on board." A seller frequently quotes a price for the goods to the buyer "FOB." This quoted price represents the total cost to the buyer for the goods (including any transportation or loading expenses incurred) at the place named as the FOB point. The buyer is responsible for any costs incurred beyond the FOB point named in the contract. Free on board may be either a shipment contract term or a destination contract term, depending on the place named. If the contract terms are FOB and the named place is the place of shipment (the seller's location), the contract is a shipment contract. Once the seller has the goods loaded by the carrier, the seller has performed fully. If the contract terms are FOB and the named place is the destination (the buyer's location), the contract is a destination contract. The seller has not performed until the goods arrive at the final point, and thus the seller faces the risk of damages during transit.

FAS

FAS means "free along side" and is a standard shipping term for seagoing transportation. This term is normally followed by the name of a vessel and the name of a port. When a seller quotes the price to the buyer "FAS," the seller is telling the buyer that this is the total cost of the goods, including any expenses incurred, to get the goods to the named location. Again, the buyer is responsible for any costs incurred (loading, transportation, insurance, and so on) beyond the FAS point named in the contract. The seller is required only to get the goods to the named vessel and port. Having done so, the seller has performed. The buyer then has all the risks of loading, transporting, and unloading the goods. The buyer is responsible from the dock of shipment to the buyer's location. There is a recent trend to treat FAS as a seagoing FOB term, with the term being either a shipment contract or a destination contract, depending on the named port. This current usage is gradually replacing the more traditional and more correct treatment of FAS as a shipment contract term, with ex-ship being the more traditional and more correct term for a destination contract.

Ex-Ship

The term ex-ship always involves a destination contract. The seller quotes the buyer an "ex-ship" price, which means the price the buyer is to pay to receive tender of the goods from the named ship at the named dock. Like FAS, ex-ship indicates that the transportation is by sea. However, now the seller is responsible for getting the goods both to the named vessel and port and unloaded from the vessel. Here the seller shoulders the risks of loading, transportation, and unloading the goods. Until the goods reach the destination dock, they are the seller's responsibility.

CIF and C & F

CIF means cost, insurance, freight. C & F means cost and freight. When either of these terms is used, the seller quotes a lump-sum price to the buyer. That single price will include the cost of the goods, the freight to get the goods to the buyer, and possibly the cost of the insurance to cover the goods during the carriage. Both terms are deemed to be shipment contracts, with the buyer assuming all the risks associated with the transportation. Under both terms, the seller pays the carrier for the transportation and then includes these freight charges as part of the price quoted to the buyer. The buyer thus repays the seller for the expenses of the carriage.

No Arrival, No Sale

Under a no arrival, no sale contract, the seller faces the risk of loss if the goods are damaged or destroyed during transit. However, even if the goods are damaged or destroyed, the seller may not be responsible to the buyer to perform the contract. If it can be shown that the seller shipped conforming goods and if it is not shown that the seller caused the loss or damage, the seller is released from the duty to perform. If the goods shipped were not conforming or if the seller caused the loss, however, the seller is still obligated to ship conforming goods.

COD

COD means collect on delivery. COD is a destination contract with a special feature: the buyer is required to pay for the goods on tender by the carrier, but is not permitted to inspect the goods until payment has been made. If the buyer is unable or unwilling to pay on tender, the goods are returned to the seller, and the buyer is likely to be sued and found liable for breach of contract.

Standard Shipping Terms in International Trade (Incoterms)

International sales of goods under the CISG are *expected* to be between merchants, and it is *expected* that the goods will be moved from one nation to another—often after passing by, through, or over several other nations while en route. Very often these goods will be transported by third parties serving as common carriers. And once again, standard terms have been developed to serve as a sort of commercial "shorthand" between the parties to the contract. However, these provisions are not found in the CISG.

In 1936, the International Chamber of Commerce first developed the "International Rules for the Interpretation of Trade Terms," which provide for one uniform meaning for international commercial terms, or incoterms. These incoterms became widely known and followed and are encouraged by trade councils, courts, and international experts. The International Chamber of Commerce has amended the general provisions of these incoterms a number of times, most recently in 1990. These "Incoterms 1990" have no automatic legal standing and are applied only

if the parties agree to accept them and so state in their contract. Because there are terms (e.g., FOB) that are used as incoterms and are also used in the UCC, the parties should also ensure that their contract designates the applicable source of the term. For example, the contract should say FOB

NRW CASE 17.3   **Management/International Business**

SELECTING DELIVERY TERMS FOR INTERNATIONAL SALES

NRW was recently contacted by a European company that is interested in purchasing thousands of Inven-TrakR units, provided that the price is reasonable and that delivery can be made relatively promptly. The firm is very interested in making this contract and has been discussing what method for delivery it should use. Carlos sent an e-mail to the European headquarters of the business and suggested that the units should be sent FOB the seller's warehouse. The buyer replied that it would like to receive the goods much more promptly than that. Carlos was confused by this reply and has asked you if you know what the European company meant by that comment. What will you tell him?

BUSINESS CONSIDERATIONS International sales carry a number of benefits for both parties, but there are also a number of risks, including misunderstandings due to language differences and law differences. How can a business ensure that the terms it uses, especially delivery terms, have the same meaning to both parties?

ETHICAL CONSIDERATIONS Is it ethical for a business to insist that the primary language of its managers be used in all of the international contracts to reduce the chance of misunderstanding the terms of the agreement? What should a business do to protect both parties when a potential contracting party speaks a different language?

INTERNATIONAL CONSIDERATIONS Assume that a seller in one country and a buyer in a second country enter into a sales contract that calls for shipment of the goods via a common carrier. How should the contract address the standard shipping term that the parties agree to in order to ensure that both parties *and* any third parties know exactly which term (UCC or incoterm) the parties intended to use in their contract? Why would this make any difference?

(Incoterms 1990) if the parties want the incoterm interpretation of FOB to control in the contract. It is also important for businesses that do not customarily use incoterms to be very careful in using them. Many American firms use FOB as a matter of course. If these firms are using incoterms, they probably mean to use the term "FCA" in order to provide the same responsibility that "FOB" provides under the UCC.

There are four broad categories of incoterms, with each category placing different burdens and responsibilities on the buyer and the seller. These categories are designated by letters—"E" terms, "F" terms, "C" terms, and "D" terms.

"E" Terms There is only one "E" term, EXW, which stands for "ex-works." Under this term, the seller fulfills its obligation when the goods are made available to the buyer at the seller's premises. The seller is not responsible for loading the goods or for clearing the goods for export. The buyer bears all risks and responsibilities. The "E" term represents the minimum obligation the seller can face.

"F" Terms "F" terms require the seller to hand over the designated goods to a nominated carrier free of any risk or expense to the buyer. There are three basic "F" terms.

The first is FCA, which means free carrier. To satisfy this term, the seller must hand over goods to a named carrier, cleared for export, at the named location. The name of the location will follow the term, as in "FCA London."

The second is FAS, which means free along side. The seller must place goods alongside a named vessel at a named port with all fees and risks covered to that point. The buyer assumes responsibility and risk once the goods reach the docks alongside the named vessel.

The final "F" term is FOB, which means free on board. As an incoterm, FOB transfers risk and responsibility to the buyer as soon as the goods "pass over the ship's rail" at the named destination port. The seller must clear the goods for export under this term, which is used only for sea or inland waterway transportation internationally.

"C" Terms "C" terms imply that the seller must bear certain costs under the contract. There are four "C" terms.

The first "C" term is CFR, which stands for cost and freight, and it is normally followed by a named location such as Lisbon. The seller must clear the goods for export and bears all risks until the goods pass over the ship's rail at the port of shipment. CFR is used only for sea or inland waterway transportation.

The second "C" term is CIF, which is the same as CFR except that the seller must also insure the goods during the carriage. The insurance to be carried need be only a minimum (contract price plus 10 percent) unless the agreement sets a different rate.

The third "C" term is CPT, which means carriage paid to (named location). The seller makes arrangements for shipping the goods to a named location, pays the freight or carriage charges, and delivers the goods to the carrier. At that point, the risk transfers to the buyer.

The final "C" term is CIP, which means cost and insurance paid to (named location). The seller has the same obligations as under CPT, plus the obligation to procure insurance (again at minimum coverage) to protect the buyer's potential risk of loss.

"D" Terms The final type of incoterm is the "D" term, which refers to a named destination; the duty of the seller depends on the particular "D" term used.

The first "D" term is DAF, which means delivered at frontier. The seller must make the goods available and clear the goods for export at a named place, but prior to the clearing of customs at the next country. This term is most common with overland transportation of the goods, normally by rail or by truck.

The second term is DES, which means delivered ex-ship at some named port. The seller must make the goods available to the buyer on board the ship, prior to clearing the goods for import, at the named port. This is a seagoing transportation term.

A similar term, again used with seagoing transportation, is DEQ, which means delivery ex-quay. The seller in a DEQ contract is to place the goods on the quay (dock), cleared for importation, before the risk passes to the buyer.

DDU, which stands for delivered duty unpaid, may be used for any type of transportation. The seller is to get the goods to a named destination with all fees paid except for import fees and costs, which are to be borne by the buyer.

A similar term, again valid with any type of transport, is DDP, which means delivered duty paid. With this term, the seller is to get the goods to the named destination with all costs paid, including import duties and taxes, and cleared for importation.

Exhibit 17.3 compares the standard shipping terms used under Article 2 of the UCC and the incoterms developed by the International Chamber of Commerce. Note that in several cases the *terms* are the same, but the *meaning* of the terms is different. Businesspeople need to exercise care in their international contracts to be certain that the delivery term used carries the meaning the businessperson intended. For more information on incoterms, see http://www.iccwbo.org/home/menu_incoterms.asp/. For more information on the International Chamber of Commerce, see http://www.iccwbo.org.

EXHIBIT 17.3 A Comparison of Standard Shipping: UCC and Incoterms

UCC Terms	Meaning	Incoterms	Meaning
C&F	Cost and Freight—seller quotes buyer a price for the goods plus freight. Buyer has risk of loss.	CFR	Cost and freight—seller clears goods for export and bears all risks until the goods pass over the ship's rails. Used with water transport.
CIF	Cost, Insurance, Freight—same as C&F, plus seller procures insurance in the buyer's name.	CIF	Cost, Insurance, Freight—same as CFR, plus seller insures the goods during transport
		CPT	Carriage Paid To—seller makes arrangements to ship the goods to a named destination, pays the freight, and delivers the goods to the carrier. Buyer takes risk when carrier acquires goods.
		CIP	Cost and Insurance Paid—same as CPT, plus the seller procures insurance to cover the buyer's risk.
		DAF	Delivered at Frontier—seller makes goods available and cleared for export at a named location, but prior to clearance of customs. Normally used for overland transport.
Ex-ship	Ex-ship—seller makes goods available on the dock beside a ship at a named port. Used with water transport. Seller has all risk until the goods reach the dock.	DES	Delivered ex-ship—seller makes goods available on board a ship, prior to clearance for import. Used with water transport.
		DEQ	Delivered ex-quay—seller places goods on the quay (dock) cleared for import before risk shifts to the buyer. Used with water transport.
		DDU	Delivered Duty Unpaid—seller gets goods to a named destination with all fees paid except for import duties. Used with any transport.
		DDP	Delivered Duty Paid—same as DDU, except the seller has also paid import duties, taxes, and fees.
		EXW	Ex-works—seller makes goods available to the buyer at the seller's premises. Buyer is responsible for all risks upon tender of delivery.
		FCA	Free Carrier—seller transfers goods to a named carrier, cleared for export.
FAS	Free Along Side—seller gets the goods to a named vessel at a named port, with all fees paid to that point. Buyer has risk during loading. Used only with water transport.	FAS	Free Along Side—seller gets the goods to a named vessel at a named port, with all fees paid to that point. Buyer has risk during loading. Used only with water transport.
FOB	Free on Board—seller quotes a price for goods, with all fees paid, to the location named. Buyer has risk from that point. Used with all forms of transport.	FOB	Free on Board—seller is responsible for getting the goods "over the rail" of a named vessel at a named port, and cleared for export. Used only with water transport.

EXHIBIT **17.3** *continued*

UCC Terms	Meaning
COD	Collect on Delivery—buyer is to pay for the goods upon tender at the buyer's location. Can be used with any form of transport.
No Arrival, No Sale	Seller has risk during transport, but is excused from additional obligations if the goods are lost or destroyed during carriage.

Summary

In this chapter, we examine the concept and importance of title to goods. Under the UCC, title passes at any time the parties agree. If the parties do not agree, title passes when the seller completes his or her performance. Title can revest in the seller if the buyer refuses to accept the goods, rejects them, or revokes the acceptance. The primary area in which title is important today is that of creditor rights.

The concept of risk of loss is much more important under the Code than it is under common law. Risk of loss refers to the party—buyer or seller—who must bear the burden of lost, damaged, or destroyed goods when the loss occurs during the performance stage of the contract. Risk of loss is allocated in a similar manner both in a sale of goods and in the leasing of goods under a finance lease. In a non–finance lease, risk of loss remains with the lessor throughout the lease.

Some special problems have developed from modern business practices. Before the adoption of the UCC, consignments were frequently used to sell goods. Today, consignments have virtually been replaced by sale-on-approval and sale-or-return contracts. Each of these areas is specifically treated under Article 2. Special treatment is also provided for consignments and for auctions under Article 2.

Article 2A separates title and possession, and allocates risk of loss to the parties based on the type of lease contract involved. In a finance lease, risk of loss passes to the lessee in the same manner as risk of loss passes to the buyer in a sales contract. For example, if a carrier is involved, the passage of risk of loss is determined by whether the delivery is a shipment contract or a destination contract. If the lease is other than a finance lease, risk of loss remains with the lessor and does not pass to the lessee.

The CISG was created by compromises among the various factions that make up the United Nations. There were disagreements among common law, civil law, and Islamic law nations; between developed and developing nations; and between capitalist and socialist nations. Despite these differences, a Convention was created and has been ratified or adopted by 62 nations as of March 1999. The CISG covers formation-of-contracts issues; seller obligations and rights; buyer obligations and rights; and remedies for both sellers and buyers. Ratifying nations have the option of not ratifying all sections of the CISG, but most have opted to follow the entire Convention.

The parties to a sale often use standard shipping terms. The meaning of these "standard terms" will depend on the context in which they are used. If the contract is governed by the UCC, one interpretation applies. However, if the contract involves an international sale of goods, a different interpretation is likely to apply. The UCC classifies any carriage contract as forming either a shipment contract or a destination contract, and imposes the burdens and responsibilities on each party accordingly. In a shipment contract, the buyer bears the risks of loss or damage during transportation. In a destination contract, the seller bears the risks of loss or damage during transportation.

The International Chamber of Commerce developed the "International Rules for the Interpretation of Trade Terms," which provide uniform meanings for these incoterms. Incoterms are broken down into four broad categories, with each category imposing different burdens and responsibilities on the parties to contracts when they use standard shipping terms. The categories are "E" terms, "F" terms, "C" terms, and "D" terms.

Discussion Questions

1. Under Article 2 of the UCC, when does title pass from the seller to the buyer in a sale-of-goods contract? Under the CISG, when does title pass from the seller to the buyer in a sale-of-goods contract?

2. Two parties enter into a sales contract under Article 2 of the UCC. The contract calls for the seller to send the goods to the buyer via a common carrier. The seller would like to use a *shipment* contract, while the buyer would prefer a *destination* contract. What is the legal effect of a *shipment* contract as compared with that of a *destination* contract? How can a party tell if the delivery terms involve a shipment contract or a destination contract?

3. Under Article 2 of the Uniform Commercial Code, when does risk of loss pass from the seller to the buyer? Under Article 2A of the Uniform Commercial Code, when does risk of loss pass from the lessor or supplier to the lessee? When does risk of loss pass from the seller to the buyer under the CISG?

4. Ralph operates a repair shop in the local community. While Ralph repairs all sorts of things, he does not sell anything on a regular basis. Harvey takes his watch to Ralph's Repair Shop and asks Ralph to fix it. After the watch is repaired, but before Harvey returns to pay for the repairs, one of Ralph's employees innocently sells Harvey's watch to another customer. The customer buys the watch in good faith, with no knowledge or notice of Harvey's rights or claims on the watch. Who has title to the watch? What should Harvey do in this situation?

5. Marge, a merchant, sells goods to Dennis, receiving payment in full at the time the contract is made. Dennis is to pick up the goods from Marge's store later in the day. When Dennis arrives to pick up the goods, he discovers that the goods were damaged when they were removed from the showroom floor and taken to the loading dock. Marge insists that, since Dennis has already paid for the goods, he owns them and he is therefore responsible for the loss due to the damage. Is Marge correct or not? Explain your reasoning.

6. George sold some goods to Dana, but George retained possession of the goods. Several of George's creditors discover the location of the goods, and they attempt to attach the goods to cover the debts George owes them. These creditors allege that the sale to Dana is void as to the creditors because George retained possession of the goods after the sale. George and Dana both insist that the transaction is perfectly valid and that the creditors should not be able to assert any rights to the goods. What must George and Dana prove in order to avoid the claims of George's creditors? Has the enactment of Article 2A changed the potential rights of George and Dana?

7. Suppose that goods are to be *consigned* to a merchant for sale. What would the owner-consignor need to show in order to establish that the goods in the hands of the merchant are consigned goods rather than goods that had been sold under a sale-or-return (or other sales) contract? Why might the owner-consignor want or need to establish that a consignment exists?

8. Biltless Mfg. sends goods to Smart Set Co. under a "no arrival, no sale" contract. After the goods are sent but before they arrive, Biltless learns it can double its profit by selling the goods to another buyer in another market. Assume that Biltless is able to recover the goods from the carrier before the goods are tendered to Smart Set. What rights can Smart Set assert against Biltless in this situation? Explain.

9. A lessor entered into a 12-month lease contract with a lessee. The goods leased were to be delivered by a common carrier. The contract between the lessor and the carrier called for a COD delivery. The lessee was to pay the entire lease price plus the delivery fees upon tender of delivery by the carrier. When the carrier tendered delivery, the lessee paid the amount owed, unloaded the goods, and inspected them. Upon inspection it was determined that the goods had been damaged during shipment. Between the lessor and the lessee, who has risk of loss in this situation? What factor(s) are key in deciding this case?

10. A buyer and a seller enter into a contract for the sale of goods, and the parties agree that the goods will be shipped to the buyer "FOB" the buyer's place of business. What does this mean if the contract is governed by the UCC? What does this mean if the contract is an international sale of goods, with the standard terms interpreted as an ICC Incoterm? If the buyer would prefer one interpretation to the other, what can he or she do to ensure that such an interpretation will be used?

Case Problems and Writing Assignments

1. In March 1975, Nahim Amar B., a resident of Mexico, entered into a contract with Karinol, an exporting company operating out of Miami. The terms of the contract, contained in a one-page invoice written in Spanish, called for Amar to purchase 64 electronic watches for $6,006. A notation at the bottom of the contract read: "Please send the merchandise in cardboard boxes duly strapped with metal bands via air parcel post to Chetumal. Documents to Banco de Commercio de Quintano Roo, S.A." There were no provisions in the contract specifically allocating the risk of loss while the goods were in the possession of the carrier, nor were any standard shipping terms used. The evidence established that on April 11, 1975, Karinol properly packaged and shipped the watches to Belize, Central America, to an agent of Amar. The cartons arrived in Belize on

April 15 and were stored in the air freight cargo room. On May 2, Amar's agent opened the boxes and discovered that there were no watches in the boxes. Mr. Pestana, as the representative of Amar (who died in the interim), sued Karinol and its insurer, alleging that the watches were lost or stolen while under the care and control of Karinol and while Karinol had risk of loss. Karinol filed a cross-complaint alleging that Amar had risk of loss and that Karinol was thus not liable. Which party had risk of loss in this case? Why? [See *Pestana v. Karinol Corp.*, 367 So. 2d 1096 (Fla. App. 1979).]

2. In 1989, Michael Heinrich wished to buy a particular model new Ford pickup truck. James Wilson held himself out as a dealer-broker, licensed to buy and sell vehicles. Heinrich retained Wilson to make the purchase, but did not direct Wilson to any particular automobile dealer. Unbeknownst to Heinrich, Wilson had lost his Washington vehicle dealer license the previous year. Wilson negotiated with Titus-Will for the purchase of a Ford pickup truck with Heinrich's desired options. Titus-Will had been involved in hundreds of transactions with Wilson over the years and also was unaware that Wilson was no longer licensed to act as a vehicle dealer.

Wilson gave Heinrich a receipt using a "Used Car Wholesale Purchase Order" that displayed Wilson's alleged vehicle dealer license number. Wilson then ordered the truck from Titus-Will, using his own check to make a $7,000 down payment. The purchase order indicated the truck was being sold to Wilson. "Dealer" was written in the space on the form for tax. Wilson told the Titus-Will salesman handling the sale that he was ordering the truck for resale. On October 13, 1989, Wilson told Heinrich the truck was ready for delivery. Heinrich paid Wilson $15,549.55 as final payment, including tax and license fees. Wilson gave Heinrich copies of the purchase order and an options checklist with corresponding prices. These documents indicated that Wilson was buying the truck from Titus-Will. The Titus-Will salesman had signed off on the options list; Wilson marked it "paid in full" and signed it after Heinrich paid him. On the same day, at Wilson's behest, Heinrich signed a Washington application for motor vehicle title.

Wilson agreed to deliver the truck to Heinrich at Titus-Will on Saturday, October 21, 1989. He arranged with a Titus-Will salesman to deliver a check on the morning of October 21 to a clerk in the Titus-Will office and, in return, to receive the truck keys and paperwork. The clerk accepted Wilson's check for $11,288, postdated to Monday, October 23, 1989, and delivered to Wilson a packet containing the keys to the truck, the owner's manual, an odometer disclosure statement, and a warranty card. Titus-Will did not fill out the warranty card with the name and address of the purchaser because the sale appeared to be dealer to dealer, with the warranty to benefit the ultimate purchaser. Titus-Will retained the manufacturer's certificate of origin. The certificate of origin is apparently a "pre-title" document used to obtain state title documents when a car is sold to a nondealer. Titus-Will, believing this to be a dealer-to-dealer transaction, planned to give the certificate to Wilson when his check cleared. Wilson immediately taped Heinrich's application for title in the rear window of the truck that was parked on the Titus-Will lot. When Heinrich arrived, Wilson gave him the keys and the documents and Heinrich drove off.

Wilson's check did not clear. Titus-Will demanded return of the truck. On November 6, Wilson picked up the truck from Heinrich, telling him he would have Titus-Will make certain repairs under the warranty. Wilson returned the truck to Titus-Will. On November 9, 1989, Wilson admitted to Heinrich that he did not have funds to cover the check to Titus-Will and that Titus-Will would not release the truck without payment. Heinrich sued Titus-Will and Wilson, seeking replevin of the truck and damages of his loss of use. Heinrich obtained a default judgment against Wilson. He also won title to the truck and $3,500 in damages in his trial against Titus-Will, which appealed.

Did Titus-Will entrust the truck to Wilson, giving him voidable title and permitting him to pass valid title to Heinrich, a buyer in the ordinary course of business? From a business perspective, what should Titus-Will have done to protect itself? [See *Heinrich v. Titus-Will Sales, Inc.*, 868 P.2d 169 (Wash. App. 1994).]

3. Malnove manufactures and sells printed folding cartons. Hearthside manufactures, packages, and sells bakery goods. Hearthside purchases millions of printed folding cartons per year to package the cookies it manufactures. The parties entered into a contract for Malnove to manufacture and sell 250,000 Family Favorite boxes to Hearthside. Malnove manufactured and delivered all 250,000 of the Family Favorite boxes, and Hearthside paid for all of the Family Favorite boxes except for the final shipment of 30,000 boxes. Hearthside justifies its refusal to pay for the final shipment by claiming that the purchase price included purchase of the dies and printing plates used in the production of the Family Favorite boxes. Hearthside claims that in the negotiations leading up to the issuance of its purchase order, Malnove stated that the price quotes include "all printing plates and cutting dies necessary to duplicate these cartons."

As of the summer of 1993, pinwheel cookies were Hearthside's best-selling cookie in the Chicago market. Hearthside also began developing a new design and interviewing box manufacturers about this new product. Finally, Malnove and Hearthside finalized negotiations for 500,000 pinwheel cookie boxes. Hearthside selected the volume of boxes and understood that in reliance upon this order, Malnove would proceed to order all of the polyboard it would need to manufacture the boxes. Shortly thereafter, Malnove manufactured all 500,000 pinwheel cookie boxes and delivered the first truckload of 144,000 boxes to Hearthside. Malnove stored the remaining boxes while awaiting further release from Hearthside.

When no further orders were forthcoming, Malnove filed suit seeking payment of the balance due under the Family Favorites contract and also seeking enforcement of the Pinwheel contract. How should the court resolve this case? Which party had title to the 366,000 Pinwheel boxes at the time of the lawsuit? Which party had risk of loss for these boxes? Was there any restriction or limitation on this risk of loss? [See *Malnove Inc. of Nebraska v. Hearthside Baking Co.,* 944 F. Supp. 657 (N.D. Ill. 1996).]

4. Badger was a manufacturer of wood products. In the course of its business operations Badger had borrowed some $3.7 million from Associated Bank, with the three notes Badger had signed being secured by a security agreement properly executed and perfected under the laws of the state of Wisconsin. The security agreements covered numerous Badger assets, including all raw materials and all work in process. In September 1993 Badger defaulted on the three notes and agreed to surrender all of its assets to Associated Bank. These assets included three shipments of wood for making cabinets that had been delivered to Badger by Houghton Wood Products in July and August of 1993. Associated Bank then enforced its security agreement by selling the assets and applying the proceeds from these sales to the debt owed by Badger. Shortly thereafter Houghton filed suit against Badger (and against Associated Bank, by amended complaint), seeking either the amount owed for the purchase of the wood ($25,572.16) or replevin of the wood. According to Houghton, the wood had been delivered to Badger under a sale-on-approval agreement and, by the terms of the contract, Badger had never "approved." Houghton argued that since Badger had never approved, Badger never acquired title, and thus the wood properly still belonged to Houghton. Houghton pointed out that the invoices accompanying the wood shipments stated that the contract was a sale on approval, and that approval could be shown only by payment of the purchase price. Since the purchase price had never been paid, there had never been any approval. Badger and Associated Bank asserted that there was a presumption against viewing any delivery of goods to a merchant as a sale on approval, and that the bank had every right to the wood under this presumption. How should the court resolve this case? What should Houghton have done to maximize its protection in this situation? [See *Houghton Wood Products v. Badger Wood Products,* 538 N.W.2d 621 (Wis. App. 1995).]

5. BUSINESS APPLICATION CASE Arcadia is an independent financier of motor vehicles for retail customers of motor vehicle dealers. Advantage is in the business of renting cars to consumers and occasionally provides vehicles for sale to wholesalers from its fleet of used rental vehicles. Lone Star Used Cars was a licensed motor vehicle dealer that sold used vehicles in Austin, many of which it purchased from Advantage. Advantage and Lone Star had an oral agreement by which Advantage sold vehicles directly to Lone Star for cash. Advantage would deliver the vehicles to Lone Star for inspection, which generally took two weeks. Once Lone Star accepted the vehicles, Advantage would order the titles to the vehicles from its corporate office. Advantage would generally receive the titles two to three weeks after the request was made. Once Advantage received the titles, Advantage would inform Lone Star and Lone Star would provide payment in exchange for the titles to the vehicles. This course of conduct continued over a period of approximately two years, during which time Advantage sold almost 200 vehicles to Lone Star and transferred the titles.

On February 11, 1998, Lone Star entered into a Master Dealer Agreement with Arcadia. Under this agreement, Arcadia agreed to finance retail installment contracts for Lone Star's customers, provided Arcadia approved their creditworthiness, and Lone Star agreed to assign the retail installment contracts to Arcadia. The agreement required Lone Star to submit to Arcadia a certificate of title with any liens thereon released and an application to register ownership in favor of Arcadia. The agreement also required that Lone Star warrant that title to the purchased goods at the time of sale was vested in Lone Star free of all liens and encumbrances.

Between July 4, 1998, and August 24, 1998, Lone Star purported to sell four of the vehicles that it had acquired from Advantage. Lone Star, however, failed to pay Advantage for these vehicles, and Advantage consequently never transferred the certificates of title for the four vehicles to Lone Star. Nevertheless, Lone Star and its customers executed retail installment contracts for the vehicles, and Lone Star assigned the contracts to Arcadia, pursuant to their agreement. Before it approved the transaction, Arcadia was not provided with the certificates of title, because Lone Star did not possess them. Instead, Lone Star provided letters of guarantee of title, representing to Arcadia that the original Texas certificates of title would be submitted within 30 days. Following Arcadia's review and approval of the customers, Lone Star completed the sale of the vehicles to its customers and Arcadia accepted assignment of the retail installment contracts and advanced the amount financed under the contracts to Lone Star, a total of $56,410.86.

Shortly thereafter, Lone Star went out of business. Arcadia then demanded that Lone Star repurchase the retail installment contracts, but Lone Star was unable to do so. Arcadia then demanded that Advantage provide certificates of title to the four vehicles, alleging that it (Arcadia) was a bona fide purchaser of the vehicles in the ordinary course of business, and as such had legal title. When Advantage refused to do so, Arcadia sued Advantage. Which party should win this case? Is Arcadia a bona fide purchaser for value of the vehicles? Were the cars entrusted to Lone Star, so that Arcadia can prevail under the UCC's treatment of entrustment? What policies followed by Arcadia in this case led to the tenuous position it faced at trial? [See *Arcadia Financial, Ltd. v. Southwest-Tex Leasing Co.,* 2002 Tex. App. LEXIS 3648 (2002).]

6. ETHICAL APPLICATION CASE In 1988 Ron Rasmus entered into the business of buying, selling, and raising exotic animals, including ostriches. He conducted these activities at his Hancock County, Iowa, farm. Also in 1988, Gene Baker began purchasing ostriches and other flightless birds (known as ratites) for investment purposes. For some time previously, Baker, a livestock farmer, had been boarding his extra swine at the Rasmus farm. According to their agreement, Baker could place and remove swine at will, and Rasmus was paid out of the profits when the swine were sold. Because this agreement had proven beneficial, Baker chose to enter into an agreement for a similar arrangement to board ostriches. Between the years

1990 and 1993, Baker purchased what eventually became two adult breeding pairs of ostriches. In January 1992 Gene Baker sold one of the breeding pairs to his father, Don Baker, for $25,000. Don Baker also chose to leave the birds in the care of Rasmus under the agreement. On June 18, 1993, Mike Pickard, acting on behalf of Missouri Ratite Center, Inc. (MRC), purchased for MRC the two adult breeding pairs from Rasmus for $75,000. Pickard then proceeded to sell one pair to Gary Prenger for $37,500. Both Prenger and MRC left the ostriches with Rasmus. On September 10, 1993, Gary Baker removed several animals from the Rasmus farm and transported them to his farm, including the breeding pair purchased by the Prengers, the male purchased by MRC (by Pickard), and several juvenile ostriches. The female of the pair claimed by Pickard (MRC) was not found at this time. The female of the Prenger pair later died in January 1994 while at Baker's farm.

On December 22, 1993, Gary and Carol Prenger filed an action in replevin against Gene Baker, alleging he wrongfully retained possession of the birds and requesting return of the birds as well as damages for the value of any birds destroyed or disposed of by Baker. MRC also filed an action in replevin against Baker seeking possession of their pair or the sum of $37,500 in the alternative. Gene Baker alleged that the birds at issue were owned by Donald Baker and himself and they were entitled to possession. Was Rasmus a merchant in ostriches? Were the birds in question entrusted to Rasmus, so that his subsequent sale to the buyers conveyed good title to the buyers? Is it ethical for a merchant to conduct business in such a "loose" manner, especially when he or she is in possession of property belonging to other people? [See *Prenger v. Baker*, 542 N.W.2d 805 (Iowa 1995).]

7. **CRITICAL THINKING CASE** Albu Trading, Inc., purchased a quantity of frozen chicken backs from Allen Family Foods, intending to export the chicken to Romania. Allen delivered the chicken to United States Cold Storage (US Storage) between February 4 and 13, 1998. US Storage notified Albu on May 14 that the chicken was available, and Albu took possession of the chicken on May 18. After taking possession of the

chicken, Albu exported it to Romania. Unfortunately, upon arrival in Romania, the chicken tested positive for salmonella. The chicken was pronounced unfit for import under Romanian law and eventually was destroyed. Albu commenced this litigation to recover the purchase price of the chicken on the theory that the chicken was contaminated when delivered by Allen. If this was true, Allen was in breach of contract and would therefore bear the risk of loss. Allen asserted that the chicken was free of salmonella infection when it was delivered to Albu, so that there was no breach of contract, and that risk of loss passed to Albu when US Storage informed Albu that the chicken was available. What would Albu need to show in order to prevail in this case? What would Allen need to show in order to avoid liability? When did the risk of loss pass to Albu, and what would cause that risk of loss to revert to Allen? [See *Albu Trading, Inc. v. Allen Family Foods, Inc.*, 2001 Del. Super. LEXIS 409 (2001).]

8. **YOU BE THE JUDGE** D'Antonio & Klein, jewelers in Center City, sold a pair of diamond earrings to Robert Nelis for $3,200. The earrings had been placed with the jewelers on consignment by Morton Reiff, who had instructed D'Antonio & Klein not to sell the earrings for less than $13,200. Unfortunately, one of the store's employees mispriced the earrings, omitting the "1" and listing the price at $3,200. When Reiff learned of the sale, he filed a complaint seeking equitable rescission against Nelis, asking the court to negate the sale to prevent Nelis's unjust enrichment due to the large discrepancy between the "true" or "actual" worth of the earrings and the price Nelis paid. Nelis alleged that he purchased the earrings in good faith and without any actual knowledge of the alleged "true" or "actual" worth of the earrings, and moved for summary judgment. Should the court grant Nelis's motion for summary judgment? If this case were argued in *your* court, and you had to decide the case *without a jury*, how would you rule? Be certain that you can explain and justify your reasoning! [See "Bargain Sale" of Earrings OK'd by Superior Court," *Legal Intelligencer*, Regional News, 226, no. 88 (American Lawyer Media, May 7, 2002): 3.]

Notes

1. Bryan A. Garner, ed., *A Handbook of Basic Law Terms* (St. Paul, Minn.: West Group, 1999), 217.
2. Uniform Sales Act, § 19, Rules 1–5.
3. Bradford Stone, *Uniform Commercial Code in a Nutshell*, (St. Paul, Minn.: West Group, 2002), 39–43.
4. Ibid., 43–46.
5. Ibid., 47.
6. Edwin W. Patterson, *Essentials of Insurance Law*, 2nd ed. (New York: McGraw-Hill, 1957), § 22.
7. UCC § 2-306, Official Comments.
8. Explanatory Note by the UNCITRAL Secretariat on the United Nations Convention on Contracts for the International Sale of Goods, Part One, A. 7.
9. CISG, Article 67.
10. Ibid.
11. CISG, Article 68.
12. CISG, Article 69 (1).

Performance and Remedies

AGENDA

NRW NRW purchases parts for its products from several different suppliers and outsources most of its packaging. As a result, the firm has little direct control over the quality of its products. The principals realize that some of the components they buy and some of the units they sell will be defective, and that there is a very real possibility that the firm will be sued or will have to file suit in some of these situations. They are concerned about what they can expect from their suppliers and what duties they owe to their customers. They are also concerned about the types of remedies that may be available to them or that may be asserted against them. They are likely to have a number of questions for you in these areas. Be prepared! You never know when the firm or one of its members will seek your advice.

Performance of a Sales Contract

General Obligations

The performance of a sales contract seems very simple and straightforward. The seller delivers the goods to the buyer, who accepts the goods and pays for them. In practice, this is very often what occurs. However, the exceptions to this simple and straightforward process provide a myriad of possibilities that need to be explored and explained if a businessperson is to be able to protect his or her interests in this area. The performance obligations must be examined, as must the intervening rights of the parties. We have already discussed the topics of *title* (who owns the goods at any particular point in time) and *risk of loss* (who is financially and legally responsible for any loss, damage, or destruction of the goods during performance), as well as "standard shipping terms," and "special problems" in Chapter 17. Those issues may affect the performance obligations of the parties and the availability of remedies, so keep them in mind as you study the materials in this chapter.

To further complicate this seemingly simple and straightforward area, there may well be an issue as to what law governs the transaction, depending upon the domicile of the parties. If both parties are U.S. citizens and the contract is formed within the United States, the applicable law is likely to be Article 2 of the UCC. However, if either—or both—parties are nonresidents of the United States, there is a good chance that some other law will control. If so, the controlling law is increasingly likely to be the CISG, more formally known as the United Nations Convention on Contracts for the International Sale of Goods. While both the UCC and the CISG expect the seller to deliver the goods to the buyer, and then expect the buyer to inspect the goods and pay for them, they differ in a number of ways in deciding how the parties can meet these expectations, and also in treating what happens if one or the other of the parties does not perform as expected. A number of these differences will be addressed in this chapter.

Sales under Article 2 of the UCC

The parties to a sales contract are required by the Uniform Commercial Code to act in good faith. In addition, any merchant who is a party to a sales contract is obligated to act in a commercially reasonable manner. These two standards are broad enough that they could adequately regulate the basic sales contract. The drafters of the Code decided, however, that more specific provisions were needed to supplement these rules and standards.

The most basic and obvious obligation is spelled out in § 2-301. Under that section, the seller is to transfer and deliver conforming goods to the buyer. The buyer is then to accept and pay for the goods so delivered. Both parties are to perform in accordance with the terms of the contract.

Conforming goods are goods that are within the description of the goods as set out in the contract. Payment by the buyer will normally be made at the time and place of delivery and will be made in money. However, the Code permits payment in money, goods, realty, or "other."[1] The manner of payment, whatever the form, will normally be spelled out in the contract.

The Code presumes that both parties will be acting in good faith, with the seller selling and the buyer buying.[2] In addition, if one of the parties to the contract is a *merchant*, the merchant is expected to observe the reasonable commercial standards of fair dealings in the trade.[3] And, of course, everything is being done according to the terms of the contract. If that were all that Article 2 said, the rules of contracts from common law would be more than adequate to cover sales. The true value of the Code's coverage of sales is what it provides if, or when, the contract is defective, incomplete, or unclear in some area. For additional information on Article 2 and its Official Comments, see http://www.law.cornell.edu/ucc/2/overview.html.

Cooperation

As a final and overriding obligation, the parties are required to cooperate with one another in the performance of their respective duties. Any failure to cooperate or any interference with the performance of the other party can be treated as a breach of contract or as an excuse for a delayed performance.

Seller's Duties

The seller in a contract for the sale of goods has a very simple basic duty: the seller is to *tender delivery* of conforming goods according to the terms of the contract. The parties can agree to make delivery in any manner they desire. If they do not agree, or if they simply fail to consider how delivery is to occur, the Uniform Commercial Code covers the topic for them. Section 2-503 explains tender of delivery. The seller has properly tendered delivery by putting and holding conforming goods at the buyer's disposition and then notifying the buyer that the goods are available. Normally, the contract will tell the seller when and where to make the goods "available." When it does not, the seller must make his or her tender at a reasonable time and place, and the buyer must provide facilities suitable for receiving the goods. This all sounds technical and confusing, but in practice delivery is fairly simple. There are five possible ways delivery can occur:

1. The *buyer* personally takes the goods *from* the seller.

2. The *seller* personally takes the goods *to* the buyer.

3. The *seller ships* the goods to the buyer by means of a common carrier.

4. The goods are in the hands of a *third person* (bailee), and *no documents of title* are involved.

5. The goods are in the hands of a *third person* (bailee), and the seller is to deliver some *document of title* to the buyer.

If the seller properly tenders delivery under any of these situations and the goods are conforming, the seller has performed his or her duty under the contract.

Tender entitles the seller to have the buyer accept the goods and entitles the seller to receive payment for the goods. If the buyer and seller make the delivery personally and directly (possibilities 1 and 2), proper tender is obvious. The seller will provide properly packaged goods to the buyer. The buyer will accept the goods and pay for them. Very neat and very simple. If the goods are in the hands of a third person, referred to as a bailee, delivery becomes somewhat more complicated. The seller in these cases must either provide the buyer with a negotiable document of title covering the goods (possibility 5) or get some acknowledgment from the bailee that the goods now belong to the buyer (possibility 4). If the buyer objects to anything less than a negotiable document of title, the seller must provide a negotiable document in order to prove that a proper tender of delivery was made. The UCC treats the topic of documents of title in Article 7. This article, entitled "Warehouse Receipts, Bills of Lading, and Other Documents of Title," specifies the rights and duties of all relevant parties in the handling of documents of title, whether those documents are negotiable or nonnegotiable. In addition to the coverage of a document of title by Parts 1 and 2 (for a warehouse receipt) or Parts 1 and 3 (for a bill of lading), both Parts 4 and 5 of this article deal with warehouse receipts and bills of lading if the document of title is negotiable. In order to reduce the amount of statutory coverage involved, and to avoid the problems of determining whether there has been "due negotiation" of the document making the holder a "holder by due negotiation" (a favored position under the law), most commercial warehousemen and common car-

riers simply issue nonnegotiable documents of title to protect themselves. These two areas limit and control how a seller of stored goods may tender delivery to a buyer.

None of the methods of delivery that have been described is very troublesome. The problems in understanding delivery normally arise when a common carrier enters the picture (possibility 3). Now the seller must give the goods to the carrier, the carrier must transport the goods to the buyer, and the buyer must accept the transported goods and make payment for them. As one might expect, the more parties involved in a transaction, the more likely that problems and confusion will enter the picture.

The seller must provide for reasonable carriage of the goods, taking into account the nature of the goods, the need for speed, and any other factors that will affect delivery. The seller must then obtain and deliver to the buyer any necessary documents concerning the carriage, and the seller must promptly notify the buyer of the shipment. Again, all these steps seem obvious, and none should cause any undue problems or hardships. The problems arise when the parties use technical or legal terms without understanding their meaning. This area generally involves the use of standard shipping terms, a topic discussed in Chapter 17, where we also compared and contrasted the standard shipping terms used in the United States under the UCC with the standard shipping terms used in international sales of goods, incoterms. In the following case the seller did not tender delivery as required by the contract, but argued that it was still entitled to damages. The seller argued that the buyer had failed to provide adequate assurance and had repudiated the contract, thus negating the seller's duty to tender delivery. The court considered each of these issues before rendering its decision.

Intervening Rights

Once the seller's single duty has been performed, the focus of the sales contract shifts. Even though the seller has performed, it is not yet time for the buyer to perform. First, the buyer has an intervening right, the right to inspect the goods. If this inspection results in a discovery of some nonconformity, the seller may have a right to cure the defective performance to avoid a breach. Only after these intervening rights have been exercised or waived does the duty of the buyer to perform arise.

Inspection

The right of the buyer to inspect the goods is covered in § 2-513. This section empowers the buyer to inspect the

ALASKA PACIFIC TRADING CO. v. EAGON FOREST PRODUCTS, INC.
933 P.2d 417 (Wash. App. Div. 1 1997)

FACTS Alaska Pacific (ALPAC) and Eagon entered into a contract for the sale of logs in April 1993. The contract called for ALPAC to ship about 15,000 cubic feet of logs from Argentina to Korea between the end of July and the end of August 1993, and Eagon to pay for the logs following delivery. After April, but before July, the market for logs began to weaken, and ALPAC became concerned that Eagon would attempt to cancel the contract. In fact, the Eagon home office was quite concerned about the weakening market and was discussing its options in the contract, including withholding approval of the shipment and holding ALPAC responsible for any delays. On August 23, ALPAC faxed a letter to Eagon suggesting that the price and volume of the contract be reduced. When ALPAC did not receive a positive reply to this fax, ALPAC believed that the contract was about to be cancelled by Eagon and that Eagon would not accept the logs if they were delivered in Korea as per the contract. As a result, ALPAC canceled the vessel that had been reserved for transporting the logs. After repeated discussion into September (after the logs were already to have been shipped), ALPAC sent a letter to Eagon stating that Eagon had breached the contract by its failure to take delivery of the logs. Eagon responded that ALPAC was the party in breach due to its failure to ship the logs, and that ALPAC's breach excused Eagon's performance. ALPAC filed suit, and Eagon filed a motion for summary judgment. The trial court granted this motion, and ALPAC appealed.

ISSUES Did the conduct of Eagon amount to a repudiation of the contract or a failure to provide adequate assurances? Did ALPAC breach by its failure to ship the logs as per the contract?

HOLDINGS No, Eagon did nothing that amounted to a repudiation, and ALPAC never requested any assurances from Eagon. Yes, ALPAC was in breach for its failure to tender delivery as per the contract.

REASONING Excerpts from the opinion of Judge Agid:

ALPAC's first contention is that it did not breach the contract by failing to timely deliver the logs because time of delivery was not a material term of the contract. ALPAC relies on common law contract cases to support its position that, when the parties have not indicated that time is of the essence, late delivery is not a material breach which excuses the buyer's duty to accept the goods. . . . However, as a contract for the sale of goods, this contract is governed by the Uniform Commercial Code, Article II (UCC II) which replaced the common law doctrine of material breach on which ALPAC relies, with the "perfect tender" rule. Under this rule, "if the goods or the tender of delivery fail in any respect to conform to the contract, the buyer may . . . reject the whole." . . . ALPAC does not dispute that the contract specified a date for shipment, or that the logs were not shipped by that date. Thus, under the applicable "perfect tender" rule, ALPAC breached its duty under the contract and released Eagon from its duty to accept the logs. . . . ALPAC's [next] contention is that summary judgment is inappropriate because a material fact exists about whether it requested assurances from Eagon and Eagon failed to respond. The UCC II provides that:

A contract for sale imposes an obligation on each party that the other's expectation of receiving due performance will not be impaired. When reasonable grounds for insecurity arise with respect to the performance of either party the other may in writing demand adequate assurance of due performance and until he receives such assurance may if commercially reasonable suspend any performance for which he has not already received the agreed return. . . .

ALPAC argues both that written requests are not necessary and that it provided a written request for assurance. . . . Eagon and ALPAC each made assumptions about the other's performance under the contract, but neither clearly expressed a need for assurance. If we were to hold that, in every case where a contract becomes less favorable for one party, general discussions between the parties can be considered requests for assurances, we would defeat the purpose of 2-609. That section demands a clear demand so that all parties are aware that, absent assurances, the demanding party will withhold performance. An ambiguous communication is not sufficient. . . . ALPAC's final contention is that Eagon repudiated the contract prior to the delivery date. It argues that Eagon's concern about the drop in log prices and its difficulty in getting final approval from its head office were sufficient to present a material factual issue about whether Eagon intended to accept the logs. ALPAC correctly argues that the question of anticipatory repudiation is one of fact. . . . This issue, too, may only be decided on summary judgment if, taking all evidence in the light most favorable to the non-moving party, reasonable minds can reach only one conclusion. . . . However communicated, a court will not infer repudiation from "doubtful and indefinite statements that performance may or may not take place."... Rather, the anticipatory breach must be a clear and positive statement or action that expresses an intention not to perform the contract.... Washington courts have refused to hold that a communication between contracting parties that raises doubt as to the ability or willingness of one party to perform, but is not an outward denial, is a repudiation of the contract.... Therefore, as a matter of law, neither Eagon's expressed unhappiness about the drop in timber prices nor its problems completing the contract rises to the level of repudiation. [The grant of summary judgment is] Affirmed.

BUSINESS CONSIDERATIONS Why would ALPAC not just ship the logs to Korea and find out upon tender of delivery whether Eagon was going to perform the contract? Was this a sound *business* decision, even if it turned out to be an unsound *legal* decision?

ETHICAL CONSIDERATIONS Was it ethical for ALPAC to sue Eagon for breach when ALPAC knew that it had not shipped the goods, as called for in the contract? Was it ethical for Eagon to fail to communicate with ALPAC, leaving the impression that Eagon *might* not be willing to accept delivery upon tender? Which company acted more ethically in this case?

goods in any reasonable manner and at any reasonable time and place. This includes inspection after the goods arrive at their destination, if the seller ships the goods. The buyer bears the expense of inspection. This serves two functions: (1) It encourages the buyer to use a more reasonable method of inspection (since the buyer must pay for it), and (2) it eliminates "phantom" inspections, with the expenses billed to the other person. If the inspection reveals that the goods do not conform to the contract, the buyer is entitled to recover the expenses of the inspection from the seller, along with any other damages the buyer may be entitled to recover.

There are two circumstances in which the buyer is required to pay for the goods before being allowed to inspect them. If the contract calls for payment against documents or if it is COD, inspection before payment is not allowed. However, such a preinspection payment is not treated as an acceptance under the Code.

In contrast, if the right to inspect the goods before payment exists, a preinspection payment is treated as an acceptance. If the buyer fails to inspect, or refuses to inspect, or inspects poorly, the buyer may waive some rights. Any defects that should be noticed or discovered by a reasonable inspection may not be raised, argued, or relied on after an unreasonable inspection. The one exception is when the seller promises to correct, or cure, the problem and then fails to do so. In other words, unless the defect is hidden (so that a reasonable inspection would not reveal it), the buyer must "speak now or forever hold his peace."

Cure

Often the buyer will discover, on inspection, that the goods do not conform exactly to the description in the contract. When this happens, the buyer must make a decision. Either (1) the nonconformity is minor, or of little or no consequence, in which case the buyer will normally accept the goods despite the nonconformity; or (2) the goods are too different from those described in the contract to be acceptable. When this happens, the buyer must promptly notify the seller, specifying in detail the problems with the goods that result in nonconformity. If the time for performance has not yet expired, the Code gives the seller a chance to avoid being held in breach. The seller may cure the defect in the goods, putting the goods into conformity with the contract. However, the cure must be completed within the time period in which the original contract was to be performed. No extension of time is permitted without the buyer's permission.

Occasionally, a seller ships nonconforming goods and reasonably expects the buyer to accept them despite the nonconformity. Such an expectation may be realistically based on typical past dealings between the parties, prior performances between the parties, or industry standards. In such a case, if the buyer decides to stand by the literal terms of the contract and refuses to accept the nonconforming goods and so informs the seller, the UCC gives the seller a right to cure even if the time for performance is past. If the seller informs the buyer of an intention to cure the defect, the seller is given a reasonable time to cure by substituting conforming goods so that the seller's performance is in compliance with the contract. The following example addresses this issue.

A merchant seller and a merchant buyer have done business together over several previous contracts, each of which involved the sale of a particular component part the seller uses in its manufacturing process. Each of these previous contracts called for the seller to deliver the component part Brand A. On at least one prior occasion, the seller did not have an adequate supply of Brand A to satisfy the contract, so the seller substituted Brand B (a competing brand with similar characteristics and price), and the buyer accepted the substituted component without objection. In the current contract, the seller once again had an inadequate supply of Brand A and decided to fill the contract by shipping Brand B instead. When the delivery was tendered, the buyer rejected the goods because the component was not Brand A, as called for in the contract. Since the seller reasonably believed that the substitution would be acceptable (based on their prior dealings), the seller will have a reasonable time to ship conforming goods in order to satisfy the contract. If this had been the first time the seller had shipped substitute parts, there would not be a reasonable belief that they would be accepted (unless such a belief was based on industry standards), and there would not be an extension of time to allow the seller to perform.

While a seller who reasonably believes that the substitute goods will be accepted is given an extension of time to satisfy the contract, the seller will not be given unlimited time or opportunity to cure the defect. This has often been a problem in automobile cases.

Buyer's Duties

The buyer's duties with respect to the sales contract arise after the seller's duties have been completed and the intervening rights of the parties have been exercised, if these intervening rights in fact exist in the contract. Since the buyer is not required to inspect the goods, a failure to inspect operates as a waiver, and the buyer's duty to perform arises. If the buyer inspects and discovers a defect, the seller may have a right to cure. If the seller does in fact cure, the duty of the buyer arises. The buyer has a duty to accept the goods and to pay for the goods.

Acceptance

When delivery of the goods is tendered, the buyer has three options:

1. He or she can accept the entire shipment, without regard to the conformity of the goods.

2. He or she can reject the entire shipment, without regard to the conformity of the goods.

3. He or she can accept some of the goods and reject the rest of the shipment.

The buyer's options are illustrated in Exhibit 18.1. If the buyer accepts the entire shipment, the seller may view the contract as properly performed and is entitled to payment for the goods as called for in the contract. If the buyer rejects the entire shipment, either the seller is in breach for tendering delivery of nonconforming goods or the buyer is in breach for rejecting a proper tender of delivery. One of the parties will be entitled to damages due to the breach of the contract by the other party. If the buyer decides to accept some of the goods and to reject the rest, there is a limitation imposed by the Code. The buyer must accept *all* conforming goods and may then *also accept* as many nonconforming goods as he or she desires. This means that the seller breached the contract, at least in part, and that the buyer will be entitled to some remedies.

Obviously, the decision of the buyer to accept—or to reject—the goods is of paramount importance. The UCC states that the buyer accepts the goods, and thus is obligated to pay for them, in a number of ways. After having had a reasonable time to inspect the goods, the buyer is deemed to have accepted them in one of the following ways:

- by signifying that the goods conform to the contract;

- by signifying that the goods do not conform, but that they will be retained and accepted despite the nonconformity;

- by failing to make a proper rejection of the goods if they are nonconforming;

- by doing anything that is not consistent with the seller's ownership of the goods. (Since the buyer is attempting to

EXHIBIT   18.1 Buyer's Options upon Tender of Delivery

Seller Tenders Delivery of Goods:		
Buyer accepts all	Buyer rejects all	Buyer accepts some and rejects the rest
The contract is performed.	The contract is breached and remedies are available to the nonbreaching party.	The buyer must accept all conforming goods and so many of the nonconforming ones as he or she desires.

reject the goods, he or she must treat the goods as if they still belong to the seller. Any conduct by the buyer that is not consistent with this hypothetical ownership of the seller is taken as proof that the buyer owns the goods, and has therefore accepted them!)

As mentioned earlier, acceptance obligates the buyer to pay for the goods at the contract price. It also prevents rejection of the accepted goods unless the defect was hidden or the seller promised to cure the defect and then failed to do so. Also, the acceptance of any part of a commercial unit is treated as an acceptance of the entire commercial unit.

Payment

Once the seller tenders delivery and the buyer accepts (or fails to reject properly), the buyer has a duty to tender payment. Likewise, in the case of a COD contract or a payment against documents, the buyer has a duty to tender payment. The buyer is allowed to tender payment in any manner that is normal in the ordinary course of business, typically by check or draft. A seller who is not satisfied with this can demand cash. But in so doing, the seller must allow the buyer a reasonable extension of time to obtain cash. This would normally be viewed as at least one banking day. Once the buyer tenders payment, the normal contract for the sale of goods is fully performed. Each of the parties received what it wanted, and nothing further is required. However, some contracts present special problems, some of which will be discussed later in the chapter.

In the following case a buyer argued that the seller had not made a "perfect tender" as required by New York law and that he had never accepted the goods tendered by the seller. Note how the court treats conduct of the parties and the performance of each of them in its opinion.

18.2

Y & N FURNITURE, INC. v. NWABUOKU
734 N.Y.S.2d 382 (N.Y.City Civ. Ct. 2001)

FACTS Mr. Nwabuoku entered into a contract to purchase furniture with Y & N Furniture in June 2001. The invoice for the furniture showed a purchase price of $1,500 and indicated that the method of payment was to be by "Beneficial." (This payment method meant that Mr. Nwabuoku wanted to finance his purchase through Beneficial Finance.) Mr. Nwabuoku signed the invoice once in the store and then a second time upon delivery, indicating that the furniture had been received at his home in good condition. He also signed a completed credit application from Beneficial and a Retail Installment Contract specifying how payments were to be made. Shortly after this transaction took place, Mr. Nwabuoku saw a newspaper advertisement in which Y & N offered a credit sale without finance charges. He returned to the store and, at his request, the original Retail Installment Contract was canceled, replaced with a second Retail Installment Contract that called for the same monthly payments, but the second Retail Installment Contract provided that there would be no finance charges if the entire purchase price was paid within 180 days. After signing this second Retail Installment Contract, Mr. Nwabuoku informed Y & N that he no longer wanted the furniture, and he refused to indicate to Beneficial that he accepted the furniture. Without his acknowledgement of acceptance, Beneficial did not purchase the Retail Installment Contract from Y & N. Y & N sued Mr. Nwabuoku for breach of contract. Mr. Nwabuoku denied that he accepted the goods and denied any liability due to his alleged rejection of the furniture.

ISSUES Did Y & N make a "perfect tender" of delivery in this contract? Did Mr. Nwabuoku properly reject the goods?

HOLDINGS Yes, Y & N made a perfect tender. No, Mr. Nwabuoku did not properly reject the goods.

REASONING Excerpts from the opinion of Judge Battaglia:

The buyer's right, generally, to reject the goods for any nonconformity, even one that is trivial, is known as the "perfect tender rule;" it requires "exact performance by the seller of his (sic) obligations as a condition to his (sic) right to require acceptance by the buyer." . . . Although criticized, and modified by case law in some states, the perfect tender rule is still very much the law of New York. . . . However, consistent with the obligation of good faith that is part of every commercial contract . . . the buyer's rejection of the goods must be made in good faith. . . . "Rejection of the goods must be within a reasonable period of time after their delivery or tender. It is ineffective unless the buyer seasonably notifies the seller." . . . If the buyer fails to make an effective rejection, the buyer will be deemed to have accepted the goods. . . . The buyer who accepts the goods must pay the contract price for them . . . even if the goods are nonconforming. . . .

In this case, the evidence at trial was unclear as to how and when Y & N was notified that Mr. Nwabuoku didn't want the furniture. It appears that Y & N may not have been made aware that there was some problem with the transaction until some three weeks after delivery, when Beneficial called Mr. Nwabuoku to determine whether he was satisfied with the furniture. It also appears that Mr. Nwabuoku subsequently executed the second Retail Installment Contract, but there was no evidence of any further discussion with Beneficial. These circumstances might allow a conclusion that Mr. Nwabuoku had accepted the goods, either by failing to make an effective rejection, or by signifying that he would take them. . . . Because the evidence on these circumstances was not as clear as it might have been, the Court will assume instead that the Mr. Nwabuoku's refusal to indicate his acceptance of the furniture to Beneficial constituted a rejection of the goods, and that Y & N was "seasonably notifie[d]." . . .

If Mr. Nwabuoku's rejection had been "rightful," i.e., because the goods did not conform to the contract, he could hold the goods until Y & N came to get them or gave appropriate instructions. In other words, he would have no obligation to return the furniture to Y & N. . . . But it is clear the Mr. Nwabuoku's rejection of the goods was "wrongful" . . . in that there is not even an allegation that the goods failed to conform to the contract. Under these circumstances, and, again assuming a seasonable rejection, must Mr. Nwabuoku pay for the goods, particularly when he has not returned them to Y & N? . . . Mr. Nwabuoku signed his name five times, on three separate occasions, in connection with this transaction: on two separate Retail Installment Contracts, on the credit application, and twice on the invoice—when he agreed to purchase the goods and when he received them. The Court questioned Mr. Nwabuoku about his ability to understand the documents he signed, and found no evidence of overreaching. . . . The Court is aware that this is a consumer contract, but a consumer contract is a contract nonetheless. . . .

The Court concludes, therefore, that a buyer who purports to reject goods under a contract for their sale, when the buyer does not have a good faith belief that the seller's tender is nonconforming in some respect, and when the buyer has not returned the goods to the seller, shall be considered to have accepted the goods and be liable for payment of the contract price. . . . Judgment is awarded to Y & N for $1,500.00, with interest from June 9, 2001, plus disbursements.

BUSINESS CONSIDERATIONS How can a business ensure that its performance is in compliance with the "perfect tender rule"? If a business sells its goods on credit, should it have a policy regarding returns and refunds included on the credit application and/or instrument the customer fills out?

ETHICAL CONSIDERATIONS Is it ethical for a buyer to attempt to avoid contractual obligations by rejecting a tender of delivery that is less than "perfect" even though the goods may fully satisfy the terms of the contract?

Leases under Article 2A of the UCC

Performance of a lease contract under Article 2A is virtually identical to performance of a sales contract under Article 2. The lessor is expected to tender delivery of the leased goods to the lessee as per the contract, and the lessee is expected to accept the goods and to make payments on the lease as per the contract. Prior to acceptance the lessee has the right to inspect the goods and to reject the goods if they are nonconforming. Again, the rejection must be specific. The lessee must notify the lessor of the nonconformity and must give specific details about why or how the goods do not conform. The lessor may then have the opportunity to cure the defect, putting the goods in conformity with the contract.

Article 2A specifies that the lessor is expected to make a *perfect tender*.[4] If the goods or the tender fail in any way to conform to the lease contract, the lessee may reject the goods. Of course, the lessee may also choose to accept the goods despite the nonconformity, and he or she may choose to accept some of the goods while rejecting the rest, provided that all conforming goods are accepted.

Obviously, Article 2A is modeled to a significant extent on Article 2. The manner in which the lessor can tender delivery is virtually the same as the manner in which a seller can tender delivery. The intervening rights of the parties between tender of delivery and acceptance and payment are the same. The need for specificity in rejecting an improper tender is the same. And the options of the lessee are virtually the same as the options of a buyer. For additional information on Article 2A and its Official Comments, see http://www.law.cornell.edu/ucc/2A/overview.html.

Sales under the CISG

The CISG provides the framework for an increasing number of international sale-of-goods contracts. The CISG also expects the seller to tender delivery of the goods to the buyer as per the contract, and it expects the buyer to accept the goods and to pay for them, presuming, of course, that the goods conform to the contract. The CISG also imposes a duty of good faith on the parties.[5] The CISG provides the buyer the opportunity to inspect the goods prior to acceptance, and obligates the buyer to notify the seller of any nonconformity in the goods within a reasonable time. The seller may well have an opportunity to cure any nonconformity in order to avoid a breach. The similarities are obvious, but in practice there are some important differences that a businessperson must keep in mind when dealing in the international environment.

One major difference involves the buyer's right to inspect the goods. U.S. sellers operating under the provisions of the UCC expect their buyers to inspect the goods tendered for delivery and to give specific reasons for any rejection. A failure to properly reject is treated as an acceptance of the goods as tendered, making the buyer liable for the purchase price. Under the CISG, a buyer may not rely on any lack of conformity as a reason to reject the goods unless notice of the nonconformity is given to the seller within a reasonable time. This sounds like the UCC rule, but there is an important difference. The CISG states that there is a time limit of *two years* for the giving of notice, unless the contract includes an agreement setting a different time.[6] To further confuse U.S. firms, even if the buyer fails to give the required notice of nonconformity, Article 44 of the CISG allows the buyer to "reduce the price . . . or claim damages, except for the loss of profit, if he has a reasonable excuse for his failure to give the required notice." The CISG can be viewed at http://www.un.org. You need to click on "Welcome," then on "International Law," then "UNCITRAL," and finally adopted texts to get to the CISG and other conventions of the UN.

Obligations of the Seller

Chapter II of the CISG covers the obligations of the seller of goods under the Convention, and Chapter III covers the obligations of the buyer. These chapters include remedies for breach of the contract among the obligations, which reflects the basic implication of the Convention that a contract for the sale of goods is expected to be performed by both parties to the contract.

The obligations of the seller under the CISG can be found in Articles 30 through 52 of the Convention; these articles are broken down into three sections. The first section is general, calling for the seller to deliver goods, turn over any relevant documents, and surrender any property in the goods as provided in the contract. The second sec-

tion deals with the conformity of the goods and with any claims by third parties. The third section deals with remedies that are available upon breach by the seller (see Remedies under the CISG).

Section I, Articles 31 through 34, describe the obligations of the seller in a contract under the CISG. Under the provisions of Article 31, if the seller is not specifically obligated to deliver the goods at a particular place, then he or she is expected to follow these guidelines:

• If the contract involves carriage of the goods, the seller is to hand the goods over to the first carrier for transmission to the buyer.

• If the goods are not to be carried, the seller is to place the goods at the buyer's disposition either where the goods are known by both parties to be located or at the seller's place of business.

Article 32 deals with contracts involving carriage of the goods by independent carrier. It specifies that the seller must notify the buyer of the consignment of the goods to the carrier, must make the reasonable and necessary contracts for carriage of the goods, and must either procure insurance on the goods or give the buyer sufficient information regarding the goods and the carriage to permit the buyer to procure insurance.

Articles 33 and 34 deal with the proper time for delivery and with the handing over of any necessary documents relating to the goods as a part of the performance duty.

Section II, made up of Articles 35 through 44, deals with conformity of the goods and possible claims by third parties. This section specifies that the goods must be fit for their normal and intended purpose, fit for any particular purpose of which the seller was aware at the time of the contract, and properly packaged in order to be deemed conforming. Conformity is measured at the time when the risk of loss passes to the buyer, although the seller may cure any nonconformity if the goods are delivered prior to the delivery date as set out in the contract. The buyer is expected to examine the goods as promptly as practical and to notify the seller of any nonconformity in a timely manner, or the buyer loses his or her right to object to any nonconformity in the goods delivered. This section was hotly debated at the conference, and a compromise was reached on this topic. The buyer is given special rights here in that the buyer has up to two years to assert that the goods contain a hidden defect. In addition, a buyer who fails to give timely notice of a defect can still deduct the "value" of the defect from the contract price, provided that the buyer has a "reasonable excuse" for a failure to give timely notice.[7]

The seller is also expected to deliver goods to the buyer that are free of any rights or claims of any third parties, and can be held liable to the buyer and to the third party for any violations of this obligation.

Obligations of the Buyer

Chapter III of the CISG covers the obligations of the buyer under the contract, which consist of the duty to accept the goods and to pay for them. This chapter is also broken down into three sections. Section I, composed of Articles 54 through 59, discusses the duty of the buyer with respect to payment of the contract price for the goods. Section II, which consists solely of Article 60, explains taking delivery. Section III, made up of Articles 61 through 65, discusses remedies upon a breach by the buyer (description follows).

Section I specifies the payment obligation of the buyer under a number of different sets of circumstances. If the contract is silent as to payment, the buyer is to pay the price generally charged for such goods at the time and place of the conclusion of the contract. If the price is to be based on weight and the method for determining weight is not specified, it is presumed to be net weight. If no place for payment is specified, the buyer is to pay the seller at the seller's place of business or at the place where any documents are handed over, if payment is to be "against documents." In addition, unless the contract specifies a different time, the buyer is to pay for the goods when the goods or the documents are made available by the seller.

Section II (Article 60) specifies that the buyer is to take delivery by doing all the acts that are necessary and could reasonably be expected in order to allow the seller to deliver the goods, and by actually taking delivery of the goods.

The Reason for Remedies

The overwhelming majority of sales contracts are performed by the parties as expected. The seller tenders conforming goods to the buyer at the time and place of delivery. The buyer then inspects the goods, accepts them, and pays the seller the price agreed to in the contract. Of course, not every tender is letter-perfect; but when the tender of delivery is flawed, the seller normally cures the defect. Again, the parties are left with their bargain as agreed.

In some cases, however, the tender is never made or it is made in so insubstantial a manner that it is treated as a breach of contract. Furthermore, some sellers refuse to cure a defective performance or lack the time to do so, and some buyers refuse to pay the agreed price or are unable to do so. Under these circumstances, the other party must look to remedies to minimize the effect of the breach.

This chapter examines remedies first from the seller's viewpoint and then from the buyer's. In either case, certain remedies will be available at some times and other remedies will be available at other times. The last part of the chapter explores some technical rules that affect how and when remedies may be sought or established.

Seller's Remedies under Article 2

If the buyer wrongfully rejects goods, refuses to pay for the goods, or otherwise breaches the contract, the seller is entitled to remedies. The remedies available to the seller depend on when the buyer breaches. The seller has six possible remedies if the breach occurs before acceptance. If the breach happens after acceptance, the seller has two possible remedies. Exhibit 18.2 summarizes the types of preacceptance and postacceptance remedies available to the seller. Each of these is discussed in turn.

Preacceptance Remedies of the Seller

If the buyer breaches the contract before accepting the goods, the seller may seek up to six different remedies. The seller does not have to choose just one possible remedy: As many of the six can be used as are needed in the particular case.

The first possible remedy is to withhold delivery of the goods. The seller does not have to deliver or continue delivering goods to a buyer who is not willing to perform the contract properly. In addition, if the seller discovers that the buyer is insolvent, the seller may withhold delivery unless the buyer pays all prior charges and the cost of the current shipment.

The second possible seller's remedy is a little more complicated. It is known as stoppage of delivery in transit. To use this remedy, the goods must be in the possession of a third person—a carrier or a bailee. If the seller discovers that the buyer is insolvent, the seller may stop delivery of any goods in the possession of a third person. If the buyer breaches the contract, the seller may also be able to stop the delivery; however, before the seller can stop delivery because of a breach, the delivery must be of a planeload, carload, truckload, or larger shipment. The seller also must make provisions to protect the carrier or the bailee before a stoppage is permitted. The seller must notify the carrier or bailee in enough time to reasonably allow a stoppage and must indemnify that carrier or bailee for any charges or damages suffered because of the stoppage.

EXHIBIT 18.2 Seller's Remedies under Article 2

Preacceptance Remedies

1. Withhold delivery of goods identified to the contract but still in the seller's possession.
2. Stop delivery of goods in transit.
3. Resell the goods, including raw materials purchased to produce the goods, and any goods listed as work in process, resold as scrap, salvage, or other.
4. Sue for the *contract*. This includes the right to identify goods to the contract and the right to complete work in progress.
5. Sue for *damages* suffered due to the breach, whether based on a resale of the goods, lost profits, or some other measure.
6. Cancel any future performance obligations under the contract.

Postacceptance Remedies

1. Sue for the amount still due under the contract.
2. Reclaim/recover the goods (provided that the buyer is insolvent *and* that the seller asserts this right within 10 days of delivery, *or* that the buyer made a written misrepresentation of solvency, which waives the 10-day limit).

The third remedy allows the seller to sue for the contract. This remedy does provide a potential burden to the seller, however. If or when the buyer pays the contract price, the seller must tender delivery of the goods. Thus, a seller who sues for the contract must be prepared to perform the contract upon the buyer's performance.

The fourth seller's remedy gives the seller the right to resell those goods that are still in the seller's possession. A seller who does resell the goods, and who does so in good faith in a commercially reasonable manner, may also be able to collect damages from the buyer. The seller may elect to resell in a public sale or in a private sale and may resell the entire lot of goods as a unit or make the resale by individual units. All the seller has to do is establish that the resale was conducted in a commercially reasonable fashion. This means that the method, time, place, and terms all must be shown to be reasonable. And the seller must give the breaching buyer notice of the sale, if possible. Normally, the issue of reasonableness will be raised in a private sale, but if he or she is given notice, the buyer has little opportunity to defeat the resale. In a public resale, reasonableness is well defined. Except for recognized futures, the resale can be made only on identified goods. It must occur at a normal place for a public sale unless the goods are perishable. The breaching buyer must be given notice of the time and place of the resale. Notice must be given as to where the goods are located so prospective bidders can inspect them. If the seller fails to meet any of these criteria, the resale is not commercially reasonable, and therefore the seller cannot recover any damages. If the seller resells the goods for more than the contract price, an interesting situation arises. If the buyer breached, the seller may keep the excess.

If the buyer rightfully rejected the goods, the seller may still keep the excess, but now the excess is defined as anything above the buyer's security interest.

The fifth option available to the seller is to sue the buyer, either for damages or for lost profits. If the seller has not yet completed the goods or has not yet identified the goods to the contract, the seller normally will be content to sue for damages. In such a situation, damages are determined by taking the difference between the contract price and the market price at the time and place of breach, adding any incidental damages incurred, and then subtracting any expenses avoided. The seller may discover that the damages computed in this manner do not put him or her in as good a position as performance of the contract would have. If so, the seller may instead elect to sue for lost profits. The seller will show the profits that full performance would have netted and sue for this amount plus the recovery of any expenses reasonably incurred due to the breach. The seller may decide to resell the goods and then to sue for any losses or damages not recovered in the resale. If so, the damages are figured by deducting the resale price from the original contract price, adding consequential damages incurred due to the buyer's breach, and then subtracting any expenses saved by not having to deliver the goods to the original buyer.

Remedies 3, 4, and 5 allow the seller to exercise some discretion in the treatment of unidentified goods. If the buyer breaches the contract, the seller may identify goods to the contract that were unidentified before the breach, thus helping to establish damages. Also, the seller may decide either to complete goods that were incomplete or to stop production and resell the goods for scrap. Either of

NRW

SHOULD NRW USE CREDIT SALES TO INCREASE MARKET SHARE?

Helen would like to offer InvenTrakR units to a number of local retailers on credit terms. She is convinced that if the firm can get these local merchants to use the product, the company's name will become well known and the firm will grow more quickly. Carlos is concerned about cash flow, especially during the initial stages of development of the InvenTrakR market. He would prefer to have the firm require payment on delivery, or very shortly thereafter. Helen has argued that extending credit is not such a great risk because the firm can just repossess the product if any buyer defaults. However, Carlos is not sure that the firm will be allowed to "just go in and repossess" any units if the buyer defaults. The firm asks you for advice. What will you tell them?

BUSINESS CONSIDERATIONS A new company in an industry may have trouble getting its product into stores unless it is willing to take some chances, including making credit sales. What should a company do to maximize its protection if it decides to sell goods on credit? Are the Article 2 postacceptance remedies adequate for the firm's protection? Do any other articles, used in conjunction with Article 2, increase the seller's protection?

ETHICAL CONSIDERATIONS Suppose that a credit customer is having a temporary cash flow problem, but will probably be able to meet its debt obligation to your company in the near future. Should your company play "hardball" and demand payment when due, be "caring creditors" who allow the debtor a bit of leeway, or take a position somewhere between these extremes? How can the position you choose be justified ethically?

INTERNATIONAL CONSIDERATIONS Credit sales present certain risks for the seller in *any* circumstances. Are those risks increased if the buyer is in a foreign country? What steps, if any, can a seller take to reduce the risk of extending credit in an international sale?

these options may be used, provided that the seller is exercising reasonable business judgment.

The seller's final preacceptance remedy is the right to cancel. On giving notice to the buyer, the seller can cancel all future performance due to the buyer under the contract.

Cancellation does not discharge the buyer or hinder the seller in collecting or enforcing any other rights or remedies resulting from the breach; it merely terminates the duties of the seller under the contract due to the breach by the buyer.

Postacceptance Remedies of the Seller

Once the goods have been accepted by the buyer and the buyer has breached the contract, the seller may seek either or both of two remedies.

The first of these remedies is by far the more common: the seller may sue the buyer for the price of the goods. Because the buyer has accepted, the buyer's duty to pay is established. Thus, winning the case is almost a certainty. Many buyers who do not pay, however, are unable to pay. They are insolvent. In such a situation, winning the case is a Pyrrhic victory—the winner suffers nearly as much as the loser.

If the buyer has accepted goods and the buyer is insolvent, the seller will possibly seek the second available postacceptance remedy: The seller will attempt to reclaim the goods. To do so, the seller must prove that the following two conditions have been satisfied:

1. The buyer received the goods on credit while insolvent.

2. The seller demanded the return of the goods within 10 days of delivery to the buyer.

This remedy is obviously of limited value, since many businesses operate on credit terms providing for payment after 30 days (or longer) and the seller has only 10 days in which to act. But there is one exception. If the buyer misrepresented his or her solvency in writing to the seller within three months before delivery, the 10-day limit does not apply. In practice, many sellers extend credit in conjunction with a security interest (as provided for in Article 9 of the UCC) to protect themselves from the drawbacks presented by the "reclaim the goods" postacceptance remedy. Otherwise, if the seller discovers that the buyer is unable to pay after the goods have been accepted, the seller may find himself or herself with little hope of ever collecting the full contract price.

It is possible, at least in theory, for a seller to use all eight potential remedies in a single contract upon a breach by the buyer. In order to use all eight possible remedies, the circumstances would have to be unusual (to say the least), and the conduct of the buyer would have to fit within certain guidelines. Although such a confluence of circumstances is highly unlikely, it could happen, as is shown in the following example.

Tara entered into a contract with Jaime that called for Jaime to produce and deliver 1,000 video games to Tara each month for the next 12 months. Tara was to make payments for each shipment within 30 days of receipt. Jaime did not ordinarily allow deferred or delayed payment, but Tara had provided a written financial statement that presented a picture of a very profitable business. (As it turned out, the financial statement was fraudulent; Tara was, in fact, insolvent at the time of the contract.) Jaime purchased sufficient raw materials to produce 8 months' worth of goods and began the manufacturing process. The performance of the contract can be summarized as follows:

1. *The first two monthly shipments were sent to Tara.*
2. *The third monthly shipment was turned over to a common carrier for delivery.*
3. *The fourth monthly shipment was ready for pickup by the common carrier when Jaime learned that Tara was insolvent.*
4. *The goods for monthly shipments 5 through 8 were, at that time, in various stages of "work in process."*
5. *The balance of the raw materials to complete the contract had been ordered by Jaime.*

Jaime decided to seek any and all remedies that might be available under Article 2. Jaime first looked at the preacceptance remedies. He decided to withhold delivery of the fourth shipment to the carrier and to notify the carrier to stop the goods that were already in transit (the third shipment). The goods in shipments 3 and 4 had been identified to the contract, as was the work in process. Jaime decided to stop the work in process and to sell the partially completed goods for scrap. He also decided to resell the completed goods that were stopped in transit and the goods withheld from delivery. Jaime also called Tara and canceled all future performance on the contract due to Tara's insolvency. Jaime sued for damages on shipments 3 through 8 and for lost profits on shipments 9 through 12. Jaime then decided to exercise the postacceptance remedies. He reclaimed all the unsold goods still in Tara's possession from shipments 1 and 2 and sued for the amount due under the contract for all goods that Tara had disposed of before Jaime was able to assert his right to reclaim the goods from Tara.

Buyer's Remedies under Article 2

The buyer also has a range of possible remedies. Like the seller, the buyer's remedy options depend on the timing of the breach. The buyer has six preacceptance and three postacceptance remedies available. These remedies are summarized in Exhibit 18.3. We will discuss each of them in turn.

Preacceptance Remedies of the Buyer

Before the buyer accepts, the seller may breach by nondelivery or by delivery of nonconforming goods. Under either circumstance, the buyer may elect any or all of the following remedies.

The buyer's first remedy is to sue for damages. The buyer is allowed to recover the excess of market price over contract price at the time of breach and at the place of delivery. Any additional damages are added to this amount. The amount is then reduced by any expenses the buyer saved because of the breach.

The second remedy available to the buyer is that of cover. The buyer covers by buying substitute goods from another source within a reasonable time of the breach. If the goods obtained through cover cost more than the contract price, the buyer can collect the excess costs from the breaching seller, plus other expenses incurred in effecting cover.

The third remedy is available if the goods cannot be obtained by cover. The buyer may seek specific performance or replevin. If the goods are unique, the court may order specific performance; the seller will have to deliver the goods in accordance with the contract. If the goods are not unique but are unavailable from other sources at the time, replevin is available. Once the buyer shows an inability to cover, the court will order replevin.

The fourth remedy is probably rare in actual practice. If the seller has identified the goods to the contract, and if the buyer has paid some or all of the contract price, and if the seller becomes insolvent within 10 days of receipt of the payment, the buyer can claim the identified goods. The likelihood of this chain of events occurring is not very high. But if it does occur, the buyer is protected.

The fifth remedy available to the buyer frequently baffles and amazes students: Under appropriate circumstances, the buyer may resell the goods. (Students frequently ask: "How can someone resell goods that were never accepted and thus never sold in the first place?") This remedy becomes available when the seller ships nonconforming goods to the buyer. On receipt of the noncon-

---

EXHIBIT 18.3 Buyer's Remedies under Article 2

Preacceptance Remedies
1. Sue for damages for breach of contract.
2. Cover (buy substitute goods elsewhere), and sue for damages for any losses due to the efforts and expenses of covering.
3. Seek *specific performance* (for unique goods) or *replevin* (for common goods that are temporarily not available through cover).
4. Claim any identified goods still in possession of the seller, *provided that* the goods have already been paid for *and* the seller has become insolvent *and* it is within 10 days of the payment for the goods.
5. Resell any nonconforming goods tendered by the seller.
6. Cancel any further obligations under the contract.

Postacceptance Remedies
1. Revoke the acceptance (requires either a hidden defect that substantially impairs the value of the contract or a failure by the seller to cure after promising to do so in order to get the buyer to accept nonconforming goods).
2. Sue for damages for breach of contract.
3. Use *recoupment* by deducting the alleged damages from the contract price still owed to the seller (the buyer must notify the seller of an intent to recoup before using this remedy).

---

forming goods, the buyer must notify the seller of the nonconformity. Furthermore, if the buyer is a merchant, the buyer must request instructions from the seller as to disposal of the goods. If no instructions are given (or if the seller asks the buyer to resell the goods on the seller's behalf), the buyer must attempt to resell the goods for the seller. The resale must be reasonable under the circumstances. A buyer who does resell the goods will be allowed to deduct an appropriate amount from the sale amount for expenses and commissions, and may then apply the balance of the sale proceeds to the damages resulting from the breach. Any excess must be returned to the seller.

The final preacceptance remedy available to the buyer is the right to cancel. On discovery of a breach by the seller, the buyer may notify the seller that all future obligations of the buyer are canceled. Cancellation will not affect any other rights or remedies of the buyer under contract.

Postacceptance Remedies of the Buyer

Once the buyer has accepted the goods, the focus shifts. A buyer who accepts cannot reject the goods, since accepting and rejecting are mutually exclusive. However, the buyer may be able to revoke the acceptance. Revocation is permitted only if the following criteria are met:

• The defect must have been hidden; or the seller must have promised to cure the defect, but no cure occurred.

• The defect must substantially impair the value of the contract.

While a hidden defect is not necessarily rare, a hidden defect that also substantially impairs the value of the contract may well be rare. If something is so wrong with the goods that the buyer's rights are substantially harmed, that problem would seem to be one that a reasonable inspection should reveal. A substantially impairing defect that is not cured when cure is promised is probably more common.

If the buyer properly revokes acceptance, the buyer is treated as if he or she rejected the initial delivery, and the buyer is then permitted to assert any or all of the available preacceptance remedies that apply to the case.

The buyer may accept the goods and later discover a defect or other breach that is not sufficient to permit a revocation. When this happens, the buyer will select the second possible remedy, suing the seller for damages. Damages are likely to be measured by comparing the value of the goods as delivered with the value that the buyer would have received if the goods that were delivered had conformed to the contract. Damages can also be established as the expense the buyer incurs in having the defects in the goods repaired by a third person.

The third remedy available to the buyer is recoupment, which allows the buyer to deduct damages from the price. Normally, this third remedy will be used together with the second. The buyer must notify the seller that the buyer intends to deduct damages caused by the seller's breach from the contract price still owed to the seller for the contract. If the seller agrees, the matter is concluded. If the seller disagrees, he or she will need to either negotiate with the buyer to reach an agreement or sue the buyer for any alleged underpayment of the balance due on the contract.

ADDRESSING DELIVERY PROBLEMS WITH A SUPPLIER

The firm that supplies the plastic disks for the Stuff-TrakR unit has recently been troubled by labor problems. Its employees were out on strike for several weeks and the company has virtually exhausted its inventory of the disks. When the strike ended last week the president of the company called Mai to let her know that the strike was over and that the company expected to be back in regular production in a matter of days. He also explained that the strike has depleted the company's inventory and that the next scheduled shipment of disks to NRW would be several days late. Mai thinks the firm should be patient with the supplier and let that company get back up to normal production. She points out that NRW can handle the temporary disk shortage with virtually no trouble, and the supplier has been cooperative with NRW in the past. Helen believes that the strike was just a harbinger of problems to come in dealing with the supplier. She would like the firm to cancel its contract due to the delay in delivery, sue for damages, and seek a new supplier. Carlos is concerned that there could be more delays beyond those the supplier anticipates, but he does not want to just drop the contract with the supplier. The members have asked you for your advice on the best alternative for the firm. What will you tell them?

BUSINESS CONSIDERATIONS Does the fact that one or more remedies are available mean that a business should *use* those remedies? Should a business base its decisions on the fact that remedies are available, or should it view remedies as a last resort after all else has failed?

ETHICAL CONSIDERATIONS Is it a better business practice to work problems out in an equitable manner or to hold the other person to the literal terms of the bargain? Should loyalty to a supplier be a factor in deciding whether to sue or to be patient?

INTERNATIONAL CONSIDERATIONS Suppose that NRW decides to purchase the disks from a supplier in Mexico. Would NRW face any additional problems or risks by using a Mexican supplier? Would there be any difference if NRW used a foreign supplier from a non-NAFTA nation?

Modifications

The parties to the contract are allowed to tailor their remedies to fit their particular contract and their particular circumstances. For example, the parties may, by expressly including it in the contract, provide for remedies in addition to the remedies provided by the Uniform Commercial Code. Or they may provide for remedies in lieu of those provided by the Code. Or they may place a limit on the remedies that may be used. If the parties so desire, they can select one remedy that is to be used as the exclusive remedy for their particular contract. (When an exclusive remedy is selected, it must be followed unless circumstances change so that the remedy no longer adequately covers the damages.)

Consequential damages may be excluded or limited by the parties in the contract. Such an agreement will be enforced unless the court finds it to be unconscionable. The parties may also provide for liquidated damages if the provision is reasonable, the difficulty of setting the loss is substantial, and establishing actual loss would be inconvenient, if not impossible. Of course, if the amount designated as liquidated damages is found unreasonable or unconscionable or is deemed to be a penalty, the clause is void.

Sometimes the seller justifiably withholds delivery from the buyer when the buyer has paid part of the contract price. In such a case, the buyer, even though in breach, can recover any payments made in excess of any liquidated damages called for in the contract, or, if there is no liquidated damages amount, the lesser of 20 percent of the total contract value or $500.

Special Problems

In determining when remedies may be obtained and what remedies to seek, several special problems may arise. The court may be asked to determine whether a breach has occurred or whether the contractual performance was excused. If there has been a breach, the courts may need to determine when it occurred. There may be a problem with the expectations of the parties or a question of whether a party is capable of performing as scheduled. And sometimes there is just a special circumstance involved that requires special treatment.

(Anticipatory) Repudiation

Occasionally, one of the parties to a contract will repudiate his or her obligations before performance is due. If such anticipatory repudiation will substantially reduce the value expected to be received by the other party, the other party may choose one of three courses of conduct:

1. He or she may await performance for a commercially reasonable time despite the repudiation.

2. The nonrepudiating party may treat the repudiation as an immediate breach and seek any available remedies.

3. The nonrepudiating party may suspend his or her own performance under the contract until there is a resolution of the problem.

A repudiating party is allowed to retract the repudiation at any time up to and including the date performance is due, if the other party permits a retraction. No retraction is allowed if the nonrepudiating party has canceled the contract or has materially changed his or her position in reliance on the repudiation. A retraction reestablishes the contract rights and duties of each party.

Excused Performance

Sometimes a seller may be forced into a delay in making delivery, may not be able to make delivery, or may have to make only a partial delivery. Normally, this would be treated as a breach. Some of these situations fall into the area of excused performance, however, and hence are not treated as a breach. Performance is excused, in whole or in part, if performance has become impracticable because of the occurrence of some event whose nonoccurrence was a basic assumption of the contract. Also, performance is excused if the seller's delay or lack of performance is based on compliance with a governmental order or regulation.

If the seller has an excuse for less than full performance, the seller must notify the buyer seasonally. If performance will be reduced but not eliminated, the seller is allowed to allocate deliveries among customers in a reasonable manner. On receiving notice of a planned allocation due to some excuse, the buyer must elect whether to terminate the contract or to modify it. Modifying it means accepting the partial delivery as a substitute performance. A failure to modify within 30 days will be treated as a termination.

Adequate Assurances

When the parties enter a contract for the sale of goods, each expects to receive the benefit of the bargain made. If, before performance is due, either party feels insecure in expecting performance, the insecure party may demand

---

NRW CASE 18.3   Finance

NRW

WHAT DAMAGES WOULD BE APPROPRIATE?

NRW entered into a contract with a South American company that ordered $25,000 worth of StuffTrakR units to carry in its stores. When the goods were tendered at the buyer's warehouse, the delivery was refused. The carrier made a second effort to deliver the goods, then notified NRW of the refused tender and asked what it should do with the goods. The contract is governed by the CISG, but the firm's members aren't as familiar with the terms of the CISG as they would like. Mai thinks the firm should have the carrier return the goods to NRW and should then sue the customer for lost profits and expenses incurred. Carlos thinks the firm should insist that the customer pay for the goods rather than have them returned from South America. Helen thinks the firm should seek another buyer in South America, possibly at a reduced rate, and should then decide what to do about the first customer. They have asked you for advice in this situation. What will you tell them?

BUSINESS CONSIDERATIONS The CISG provides the possibility of specific performance as a remedy, regardless of the nature of the goods. It also requires each party to mitigate damages. Does seeking specific performance following a breach help to mitigate damages, or are these two policies contradictory?

ETHICAL CONSIDERATIONS Is it ethical to provide for a remedy that requires a business to do what it promised to do, but then failed to do (specific performance)? Would seeking another remedy be more ethical?

INTERNATIONAL CONSIDERATIONS How do the available remedies differ under the UCC and under the CISG? Should the fact that remedies differ affect the way a business views its contract obligations?

---

assurances of performance. The insecure party must make a written demand for assurance that performance will be tendered when due. Until the assurances are given, the requesting party may suspend performance. If no assurance is given within 30 days of request, it is treated as repudiation of the contract.

Duty to Particularize

When the buyer rightfully rejects goods, the buyer must do so properly. If the goods are rejected owing to a curable defect, the buyer may reject only by stating exactly what the defect is. A failure to do so will preclude the use of that defect to prove breach in court. And if the buyer cannot prove breach, the seller will be deemed to have performed properly. Thus, a failure to particularize can result in the buyer's being required to pay for nonconforming goods or in other liability to the seller.

Statute of Limitations

Any lawsuit for breach of a sales contract must be started within four years of the breach, unless the contract itself sets a shorter time period. (The time period cannot be less than one year.) The fact that a breach is not discovered when it occurs is not material. The time limitation begins at breach, not at discovery. This reemphasizes the need for a buyer to inspect goods carefully and completely in order to protect his or her interests.

Remedies in Leasing Contracts under Article 2A

Article 2A provides for remedies in the event a lease contract is breached. As under Article 2, the remedies available depend to a significant extent on when the breach occurs. A brief synopsis of the remedies is set out below.

Lessor's Remedies

If a lessee wrongfully rejects goods tendered under the lease, wrongfully revokes acceptance, fails to make payments when due, or repudiates the lease, the lessor may:

• cancel the lease contract

• proceed respecting goods not identified to the lease contract

• withhold delivery of the goods and take possession of goods previously delivered

• stop delivery of the goods by any bailee

• dispose of the goods and recover damages, or retain the goods and recover damages, or, in a property case, recover rent

If a lessee is otherwise in default, the lessor may exercise the rights and remedies provided in the lease, as well as those listed in Article 2A.

Lessee's Remedies

If a lessor fails to deliver goods in conformity with the lease contract or repudiates the lease contract, or the lessee rightfully rejects the goods or justifiably revokes acceptance of the goods, then the lessee may:

• cancel the lease contract

• recover as much of the rent and security as has been paid; but in the case of an installment lease contract, the recovery is that which is just under the circumstances

• cover and recover damages as to all goods affected, whether or not they have been identified to the lease contract, or recover damages for nondelivery

If the lessor fails to deliver the goods or repudiates the contract, the lessee may also:

• recover any goods that have been identified to the contract

• obtain specific performance or replevin

If the lessor is otherwise in default under a lease contract, the lessee may exercise the rights and remedies provided in the lease contract and/or those included in Article 2A.

Remedies under the CISG

Remedies for Breach by the Seller

Section III of Chapter II specifies remedies that are available to the buyer upon a breach of the sales contract by the seller. In addition, Articles 74 through 77 provide damages that may be available to either the buyer or the seller upon a breach by the other party. The CISG also specifically states that a party is not deprived of any rights to claim damages if that party seeks other remedies under the Convention as well. If the seller fails to deliver conforming goods or fails to meet any other aspect of the agreement, the buyer may seek any or all of the appropriate remedies from the alternatives shown in Exhibit 18.4.

The case on pages 441–442 involves the assessment of damages when the seller breaches the contract under the CISG. This opinion seems to be the benchmark for buyer remedies under the CISG, and several subsequent cases

---

EXHIBIT 18.4 Buyer's Remedies under the CISG

1. The buyer may require the seller to perform, unless the buyer has chosen another remedy that is inconsistent with performance by the seller.
2. The buyer may require the seller to deliver conforming substitute goods or to cure any nonconformity, if the seller delivered nonconforming goods.
3. The buyer can set an additional time for performance, provided that the seller is notified of this extension. (The buyer may not seek any other remedies during this extended time.)
4. The buyer can declare the contract avoided if the seller does not deliver the goods within the time permitted under the contract (or before the time extension expires).
5. If the seller delivered nonconforming goods, the buyer can reduce the price paid to the seller to reflect the value of the goods delivered.
6. If the seller tenders delivery prior to the agreed delivery date, the buyer can accept or refuse to accept the goods; if the seller tenders delivery of a larger shipment than called for in the contract, the buyer may accept any or all of the excess amount, paying for any accepted goods at the contract rate.

---

have cited it in deciding what damages can be collected upon breach by the seller.

Remedies for Breach by the Buyer

Section III of Chapter III specifies the remedies that are available to the seller upon a breach of the sales contract by the buyer. Again, Articles 74 through 77 provide damages that may be available as well. Recall also that the CISG specifically states that a party is not deprived of any rights to claim damages if that party seeks other remedies under the Convention as well. If the buyer fails to accept delivery of the goods or fails to pay for the goods as agreed, the seller may seek any or all of the appropriate remedies from the alternatives shown in Exhibit 18.5.

Damages

Section II of Chapter IV specifies damages that may be available to either party under the Convention following a breach of the contract by the other party. These damages may be available even if other remedies are also sought by the nonbreaching party.

The basic measure of damages under the CISG is "a sum equal to the loss, including loss of profit, suffered by the other party as a consequence of the breach. Such damages cannot exceed the loss which the party in breach foresaw or ought to have foreseen at the time of the conclusion of the contract."

If the contract is avoided and the buyer then purchases replacement goods, the buyer is entitled to the difference between the price of the replacement goods and the original contract price, plus any other damages computed under the prior damage provisions. If the contract is avoided and the seller then resells the goods, the seller is entitled to the difference between the resale price and the original contract price, plus any other damages computed under the prior damage provisions.

If the contract is avoided and there is a current price for the goods covered by the contract, the nonbreaching party

---

EXHIBIT 18.5 Seller's Remedies under the CISG

1. The seller may require the buyer to pay the contract price, to take delivery of the goods, or to perform any other obligations under the contract, unless the seller has chosen another remedy that is inconsistent with this remedy.
2. The seller can set an additional reasonable time during which the buyer can perform, provided that the buyer is notified of this extension. (The seller may not seek any other remedies during this extended time.)
3. The seller can declare the contract avoided as to any unperformed parts of the contract.
4. If the contract calls for the buyer to specify any form, measurement, or other feature of the goods and he or she fails to do so, the seller may supply such specifications, if he or she does so within a reasonable time.

18.3

DELCHI CARRIER SPA v. ROTOREX CORPORATION
71 F.3d 1024 (2nd Cir. 1995)

FACTS In January 1988, Rotorex agreed to sell 10,800 compressors to Delchi for use in Delchi's "Ariele" line of portable air conditioners. The air conditioners were scheduled to go on sale in the spring and summer of 1988. Prior to executing the contract, Rotorex sent Delchi a sample compressor and accompanying written performance specifications. The compressors were to be delivered in three shipments before May 15, 1988. Rotorex sent the first shipment by sea on March 26. The shipment arrived at the factory in Italy on April 20, and Delchi paid for the shipment by letter of credit. Rotorex sent a second shipment of compressors on or about May 9. Delchi also remitted payment for this shipment by letter of credit.

While the second shipment was en route, Delchi discovered that the first lot of compressors did not conform to the sample model and accompanying specifications. On May 13, after a Rotorex representative visited the Delchi factory in Italy, Delchi informed Rotorex that 93 percent of the compressors were rejected in quality control checks because they had lower cooling capacity and consumed more power than the sample model and specifications. After several unsuccessful attempts to cure the defects in the compressors, Delchi asked Rotorex to supply new compressors conforming to the original sample and specifications. Rotorex refused, claiming that the performance specifications were "inadvertently communicated" to Delchi.

In a faxed letter dated May 23, 1988, Delchi canceled the contract. Although it was able to expedite a previously planned order of suitable compressors from Sanyo, another supplier, Delchi was unable to obtain in a timely fashion substitute compressors from other sources and thus suffered a loss in its sales volume of Arieles during the 1988 selling season. Delchi filed suit against Rotorex alleging breach of contract and failure to deliver conforming goods under the provisions of the United Nations Convention on Contracts for the International Sale of Goods. Rotorex was held liable to Delchi for $1,248,331.87. Rotorex appealed, arguing that it did not breach the agreement, that Delchi is not entitled to lost profits because it maintained inventory levels in excess of the maximum number of possible lost sales, that the calculation of the number of lost sales was improper, and that the district court improperly excluded fixed costs and depreciation from the manufacturing cost in calculating lost profits.

ISSUES Did Rotorex breach the agreement? Is Delchi entitled to lost profits? How should the damages for lost profits be calculated?

HOLDINGS Yes, Rotorex breached the contract. Yes, Delchi is entitled to lost profits. The damages for lost profits are to be calculated under the broad provisions of the CISG.

REASONING Excerpts from the opinion of Circuit Judge Winter:

The district court held, and the parties agree, that the instant matter is governed by the CISG. . . . Because there is virtually no case law under the Convention, we look to its language and to "the general principles" upon which it is based. . . . The Convention directs that its interpretation be informed by its "international character and . . . the need to promote uniformity in its application and the observance of good faith in international trade." . . . Under the CISG, "[t]he seller must deliver goods which are of the quantity, quality and description required by the contract," and "the goods do not conform with the contract unless they . . . [p]ossess the qualities of goods which the seller has held out to the buyer as a sample or model." . . . The CISG further states that "[t]he seller is liable in accordance with the contract and this Convention for any lack of conformity." . . .

The agreement between Delchi and Rotorex was based upon a sample compressor supplied by Rotorex and upon written specifications regarding cooling capacity and power consumption. . . . There was thus no genuine issue of material fact regarding liability, and summary judgment was proper. . . . Under the CISG, if the breach is "fundamental" the buyer may either require delivery of substitute goods, . . . or declare the contract void, . . . and seek damages. . . . In granting summary judgment, the district court held that "[t]here appears to be no question that [Delchi] did not substantially receive that which [it] was entitled to expect" and that "any reasonable person could foresee that shipping non-conforming goods to a buyer would result in the buyer not receiving that which it expected and was entitled to receive." Because the cooling power and energy consumption of an air conditioner compressor are important determinants of the product's value, the district court's conclusion that Rotorex was liable for a fundamental breach of contract under the Convention was proper. We turn now to the district court's award of damages. . . .

A reviewing court must defer to the trial judge's findings of fact unless they are clearly erroneous. . . . The CISG provides:

Damages for breach of contract by one party consist of a sum equal to the loss, including loss of profit, suffered by the other party as a consequence of the breach. Such damages may not exceed the loss which the party in breach foresaw or ought to have foreseen at the time of the conclusion of the contract, in the light of the facts and matters of which he then knew or ought to have known, as a possible consequence of the breach of contract. . . .

The provision is "designed to place the aggrieved party in as good a position as if the other party had properly performed the contract.". . . Rotorex contends . . . that the district court improperly awarded lost profits for unfilled orders from Delchi affiliates in Europe and from sales agents within Italy. We disagree. The CISG requires that damages be limited by the familiar principle of foreseeability. . . . However, it was objectively foreseeable that Delchi would take orders for Ariele sales based on the number of compressors it had ordered and expected to have ready for the season. The district court was entitled to rely upon the documents and testimony regarding these lost sales and was well within its authority in deciding which orders were proven with sufficient certainty.

Rotorex also challenges the district court's exclusion of fixed costs and depreciation from the manufacturing cost used to calculate lost profits. . . . The CISG does not explicitly state whether only variable expenses, or both fixed and variable expenses, should be subtracted from sales revenues in calculating lost profits. However, courts generally do not include fixed costs in the calcu-

lation of lost profits. . . . That is, of course, because the fixed costs would have been encountered whether or not the breach occurred. In the absence of a specific provision in the CISG for calculating lost profits, the district court was correct to use the standard formula employed by most American courts and to deduct only variable costs from sales revenue to arrive at a figure for lost profits. . . .

The Convention provides that a contract plaintiff may collect damages to compensate for the full loss. This includes, but is not limited to, lost profits, subject only to the familiar limitation that the breaching party must have foreseen, or should have foreseen, the loss as a probable consequence. . . . An award for lost profits will not compensate Delchi for the [additional] expenses [incurred]. Delchi's lost profits are determined by calculating the hypothetical revenues to be derived from unmade sales less the hypothetical variable costs that would have been, but were not, incurred. This figure, however, does not compensate for costs actually incurred that led to no sales. Thus, to award damages for costs actually incurred in no way creates a double recovery and instead furthers the purpose of giving the injured party damages "equal to the loss." . . . We affirm the award of damages.

BUSINESS CONSIDERATIONS What obligations are assumed by a seller who provides a sample and/or written specifications concerning the character or quality of goods in a contract under the CISG? How does this compare to the obligations of a seller in a similar situation under Article 2 of the UCC?

ETHICAL CONSIDERATIONS Is it ethical for a firm that has provided written specifications regarding goods it is selling to argue that the writing was "inadvertently" provided to the buyer? What ethical issues are raised by the assertion of such a defense?

can recover the difference between the current price and the contract price, plus any other damages allowed under Article 74, without the need to purchase (by the buyer) or resell (by the seller). In any case, the party seeking damages must take any and all reasonable steps to mitigate damages, or the other party can use the failure to mitigate as grounds for reducing the damages assessed to the level that would have been attained with mitigation.

The international sale and movement of goods should continue to expand over the foreseeable future. This means

the CISG will become increasingly important to the U.S. domestic business environment in the future, although it will not replace the UCC in its importance. Business will need to be aware of the differences between the CISG in international agreements and the UCC domestically, because conduct that is merely a preliminary negotiation under the UCC may well be a binding contract under the Convention.

Summary

Although most sales contracts are fully performed and the performance is normally satisfactory, sometimes a nonperformance occurs. When nonperformance is found, the innocent party usually seeks remedies for breach of contract.

If the buyer fails to perform, the seller's available remedies depend on when the buyer breaches. If the buyer breaches before acceptance of the goods, the seller will seek one or more of six preacceptance remedies. If the buyer accepts the goods and then breaches, the seller will seek one or both of two postacceptance remedies. By the same token, if the seller breaches, the buyer's available remedies will depend on when the seller breaches. If the seller breaches before the buyer accepts the goods, the buyer may seek one or more of six preacceptance remedies. If the seller breaches after the buyer accepts, the buyer has up to three available postacceptance remedies.

Occasionally, a nonperformance turns out not to be a breach. It may involve a special problem that excuses performance or affects the rights of the innocent party. Great care must be exercised by both parties in these special problem areas.

Leases are also normally performed properly by both parties. Again, however, sometimes breaches occur. When they do, the breaching party is held liable for those damages that the nonbreaching party suffers. Article 2A lists specific remedies that are available, and also specifically states that the parties are entitled to those damages called for in the lease contract as well as any of the remedies listed in the article. These Code remedies are very similar in nature and application to the remedies provided by Article 2.

The CISG also provides remedies when the sales contract is breached. The remedies are not very similar to those found in Article 2, nor do they distinguish between pre- and postacceptance remedies. Basically, the nonbreaching party can require the other party to perform the contract unless the nonbreaching party has resorted to other remedies. The nonbreaching party can also extend the time for performance, thus encouraging the other party to perform, or can declare the contract avoided. Of course, numerous other remedies may be available under the other applicable laws of the nation in which the suit is filed.

Discussion Questions

1. What constitutes a proper *tender of delivery* under either Article 2 or Article 2A of the UCC? What constitutes a proper *tender of delivery* under the terms of the CISG? Does the manner of delivery called for in the contract determine what is required in order to have a proper tender of delivery?

2. What is the right of inspection, and how does it affect the performance obligation of the parties in a sale or lease of goods under the UCC?

3. What is meant by "cure," and how does it affect the performance obligation of the parties in a sale or lease of goods under the UCC?

4. How long does a buyer of goods have to inspect the goods and inform the seller of any nonconformities under the UCC? How does this compare with the time for inspection and notification under the CISG? Why is there such a significant difference in the time allowed?

5. Chen, a merchant, sends Roy some goods under a contract. Roy is to receive the goods by December 18. On December 12, Roy receives nonconforming goods from Chen, and Roy promptly calls Chen to inform her of the nonconformity. What are Chen's rights and duties under these circumstances? What can Chen do to avoid being sued for breach of the contract?

6. What is an anticipatory repudiation, and how does it affect contracts formed under the law of sales? Does a repudiation have the same meaning and impact under the law of leases?

7. What is an "adequate assurance," and when does a party to a sales contract have the right to request such an assurance? What is required in order to make a proper request for an adequate assurance?

8. Ace Manufacturing agreed to produce and sell some goods to Sampson. The contract called for 10 shipments of 25 units each. After satisfactorily completing 5 shipments, Ace sent the sixth shipment. Order 7 was then "in process." Sampson wrongfully rejected shipment 6. Ace decided to complete the work on order 7 and to sue Sampson for the contract price on shipments 6 and 7 and for lost profits on the remaining three shipments. Sampson argued that Ace could not complete order 7 at his (Sampson's) expense. Who is correct? Explain.

9. Roberto, the seller, was in possession of goods that Suzanne had wrongfully rejected. Roberto sold the goods to Brenda for one-half the contract price without telling anyone about the sale. Can Roberto collect the unpaid balance of the contract price from Suzanne? Does Suzanne have a claim against Roberto for damages even though Suzanne had initially breached the contract? Explain.

10. Bob and Sam entered into a contract that called for Sam to deliver goods to Bob and for Bob to pay $1,500 for the goods. Bob gave Sam a $500 deposit on the goods. During the contract period, Sam discovered that Bob was insolvent and decided to withhold delivery of the goods to Bob. While Bob admits that he is in breach, he also asserts that he is entitled to restitution for his deposit on the goods. Is Bob entitled to restitution, and, if so, how much can he recover from Sam? Explain.

Case Problems and Writing Assignments

1. In an attempt to feather their nest, as it were, the Doners decided to invest in the burgeoning, albeit risky, ostrich breeding and production industry. Ostriches are promoted as an alternative food source and, coupled with the demand for their feathers and leather, are completely consumable. The potential rewards of the investment are great: Mr. Doner stated that the hen he purchased from the Snapps for $3,000 was worth at least $20,000 three years later, although she had yet to lay a fertile egg. The risks of the business include ostrich infertility and mortality.

   The appellants purchased a "trio" of ostrich chicks by oral agreement from the appellees in 1990 for $9,000. In breeders' parlance, a "trio" means two hens and one male. One male may mate with as many as three hens. The appellants' bid to build a nest egg suffered a bad break in early 1991, when they discovered that their "trio" consisted of two males and one hen. Mr. Doner testified that his first knowledge of the error came when the darker features and feathers of the males appeared. Mr. Snapp testified that it can be difficult to determine an ostrich's sex, and that he had advised Mr. Doner to have the birds' sex confirmed within 90 days of the sale. Mr. Doner denied that he had been so counseled.

   There also was disputed testimony about whether the appellees agreed to exchange a hen for one of the males upon learning of the alleged breach. In any event, no agreement was reached between the parties. Rather than bury their heads in the sand, the appellants traded both of their male ostriches in 1992, one to a Michigan breeder for another male of equal value, and the other to an Indiana supplier for two female chicks. Since ostrich hens do not mature sexually for three years, the younger hens have not been bred. The hen purchased from the appellants has not produced any offspring. The record indicates that the appellants also acquired another hen, now of breeding age, from the Michigan breeder. This particular hen has produced offspring.

   The appellants filed suit against appellees for breach of contract on June 15, 1993. The appellants requested compensatory damages of $15,000 plus lost profits. The appellees filed a motion for summary judgment, asserting that appellants had not raised a genuine issue of material fact on the issue of liability, specifically that the appellants had suffered damage from the alleged breach. The trial judge granted appellees' motion and the appellants appealed. Did the buyers establish that they had suffered any damages in this case? [See *Doner v. Snapp*, 649 N.E.2d 42 (Ohio App. 1994).]

2. Conveying Techniques manufactures and fabricates conveying and material-processing equipment. Lakewood Pipe processes and sells steel pipe for the oil industry and for agricultural irrigation. In 1979, Conveying sold Lakewood a manual hydrostatic testing system. In 1984, Conveying gave Lakewood a written proposal for the construction and installation of an automatic system. The two corporate presidents met soon thereafter and Conveying demonstrated a prototype automatic system. According to Conveying's president (Lee), the president of Lakewood (Tybus) orally agreed to buy the system for $240,000. Tybus denied that he agreed, orally or otherwise. Conveying began construction of the automatic system in late 1984. In December 1984, Lee wrote to Lakewood, summarizing his understanding of the agreement, and reminding Lakewood that all of Lakewood's outstanding accounts receivable must be paid before the system would be installed. (Lee noted that the system had been delayed because Lakewood failed to pay, and Lee was concerned that Lakewood would not pay for the system prior to installation.) In February 1985, Lakewood informed Conveying that it was not in the market for the automatic system. In March, Conveying billed Lakewood for $80,000, determined by taking 30 percent of the contract price as "cancellation charges" on the contract. Did Lakewood breach a contract with Conveying in this case? If so, were the damages properly computed by Conveying? [See *Lakewood Pipe of Texas, Inc. v. Conveying Techniques, Inc.*, 814 S.W.2d 553 (Tex. App. Houston [1st Dist.] 1991).]

3. The Bowens' home had a Carrier heating and cooling system consisting of four exterior and four interior units. They decided to upgrade their system with equipment having a "12 seer rating" or higher to increase the efficiency of the heating and cooling of the house. In furtherance of this goal, they solicited bids from a number of local firms. Foust Plumbing and Heating's bid was accepted. The bid called for Foust to install a new heat pump system, and specified that the seller was to install "four RHEEM 3½ ton heat pump systems with a seer rating of 12." The contract also called for the Bowens to pay $8,159 upon completion of the installation. Shortly after the installation was completed a compressor went out. Foust removed the defective compressor and ordered a replacement. A few months later a second compressor went out. Again, Foust removed the defective compressor and ordered a replacement. In October the Bowens discovered that the new system would not produce any heat. Foust replaced the four interior units, submitting a bill to the Bowens for $1,400 for the work. Despite Foust's best efforts, however, the unit still

produced no heat. At this point Foust told the family that the problem was in their breaker system. An electrician was hired to replace the breaker system in the house at a cost of approximately $200. After the breakers were replaced, there was still no heat from the new system. Finally the Bowens had a second heat and air specialist inspect their system. This second specialist informed the family that the system "did not have a 12 seer rating." The following spring the Bowens hired Ray Buffington, a Carrier dealer, to replace their system. Buffington removed the Rheems units (which are not compatible with Carrier units) and replaced them with larger Carrier equipment, bringing the system up to the 12 seer rating originally sought. The bill for this work was more than $15,000. The Bowens are now suing to revoke their acceptance of the goods provided by Foust and to recover the money paid to Foust under the contract. Foust objects, insisting that too much time has elapsed for the family to revoke its acceptance and denying any liability to them. How should this case be resolved? [See *Bowen v. Foust*, 925 S.W.2d 211 (Mo. App. S.D. 1996).]

4. On September 17, 1987, Ance and Alice Page purchased a new van from the Treadwell Ford automobile dealership, trading in their old car and financing the remainder of the van's $24,500 purchase price through Treadwell. At the time of the purchase, the Pages received warranties from Ford Motor Company, which had manufactured the basic vehicle, and the Zimmer Corporation, which had installed various modifications transforming the vehicle into a conversion van. Treadwell, however, disclaimed all express or implied warranties. Soon after their purchase, the Pages discovered numerous problems with the van, finding a steady stream of leaks around the van's windshield and top and around its side and back doors. There was water damage to the interior. The Pages also discovered that, among other things, the motors controlling the passenger- and driver-side windows malfunctioned, rubber sealing around the back door had come loose, wall panels and a cabinet were broken, the television set and the interior lights would not work at the same time, the stereo speakers often did not work, molding around the television set was loose, the van rattled badly, the paint on the roof had faded, the gas gauge and the cruise control did not work, the front end was misaligned, and the van used three to five quarts of oil per month. On a regular basis the Pages began taking the van for repairs by Treadwell, the authorized agent for warranty work, traveling some 80 miles round trip with another vehicle to drive home each time. Eventually, many of the defects were repaired; but a number were not, with Treadwell indicating that there were certain problems that could not be corrected. The Pages attempted and failed to receive satisfaction through numerous letters and telephone conversations with Treadwell and Ford.

In late 1987, the Pages gave notice to Treadwell of their desire to revoke acceptance of their purchase. Treadwell, however, refused to recognize the Pages' attempt at revocation. On February 21, 1989, the Pages filed suit against Treadwell, Ford, and Zimmer. The jury returned verdicts in favor of Ford and Zimmer, but found that the requisite elements of the revocation claim had been met. The court then permitted the revocation and assessed $7,500 in damages against Treadwell. The Pages and Treadwell appealed. Were the Pages entitled to revoke their acceptance after 10 months without a showing of fraud or breach of warranty by the seller? If they were entitled to revoke, were they also entitled to any damages in this case? What arguments can you present in support of the Pages? In support of Treadwell? Which arguments do you think are more persuasive? [See *Page v. Dobbs Mobile Bay, Inc.*, 599 So. 2d 38 (Ala. Civ. App. 1992).]

5. BUSINESS APPLICATION CASE Firwood and General Tire entered into a contract in which General Tire allegedly agreed to purchase 55 model 1225 post-cure inflators (PCIs), $30,000 machines used by General Tire in its manufacturing process. Following lengthy negotiations between representatives from each company, Firwood transmitted an offer letter stating that the price agreed upon was based on a minimum purchase of 55 PCIs during 1990, and that if General Tire purchased fewer than 55 units the price would be adjusted for each unit. Firwood also asked for a letter of intent showing anticipated purchase dates for the CPI units. Soon thereafter General Tire issued two written purchase orders to Firwood in which it revised prior orders to reflect the new price of $31,216 per PCI—the price level available for purchases of a minimum of 55 units—and encouraged Firwood to have all 55 PCIs available for delivery. Firwood began ordering parts for the PCIs. Six months later General Tire had purchased 22 PCIs from Firwood under the contract. However, when General Tire decided to close its Barrie plant it no longer needed or wanted the remaining PCIs. At that point the 33 remaining PCIs were in the following stages of production: 8 units, 100 percent complete; 5 units, 95 percent complete; and 20 units, 65 percent complete. After learning that General Tire did not intend to complete the purchase of the remaining 35 PCIs at issue in this dispute, Firwood began looking for alternative buyers. General Tire also sought alternative buyers for the PCIs. After three years of searching for alternative buyers, during which it sold a few machines, Firwood was ultimately able to sell the balance of the 33 PCIs intended for General Tire, but at a price below that called for in the contract with General Tire. While looking for buyers, Firwood filled some of its ongoing orders for spare parts with parts that already had been installed in the 33 PCIs intended for General Tire. Although the PCIs themselves were specially made for General Tire, the parts taken from the General Tire PCIs and sold as spare parts were fungible parts regularly sold in Firwood's spare parts business. Eventually Firwood sued General Tire for breach of contract. The district court entered a judgment in favor of Firwood for damages plus interest, and General Tire appealed. Could the seller substitute fungible goods for the goods identified to the contract at the time of the substitution? Did Firwood act in good faith and in a commercially reasonable manner? [See *Firwood Manufacturing Company, Inc. v. General Tire, Inc.*, 96 F.3d 163 (6th Cir. 1996).]

6. **ETHICAL APPLICATION CASE** ConAgra operates grain elevators in various Nebraska locations and a grain merchandising office in Kearney, Nebraska. During 1992, ConAgra bought and sold in excess of 500,000,000 bushels of corn. The Bartlett Partnership conducts a farming operation, and consists of Roger Race, the managing partner and an experienced farmer, and three other farmers. In the summer of 1992, the partnership had approximately 2,800 acres planted in corn near Bartlett, Nebraska. In previous years, this acreage had yielded approximately 130 bushels per acre. Based on this, Race testified that he expected the total yield for 1992 to be approximately 360,000 bushels. The land farmed by the partnership was in the Sandhills and consisted of marginal soil. Because of the soil, more water, fertilizer, and care than normal were required to secure a good crop. In 1992, the partnership undertook an extensive manure-spreading operation to improve the soil. To keep costs down, the partnership started a practice of hauling corn to ConAgra's elevator in Grand Island and then on the way back hauling manure from Hastings to the land the partnership farmed. Race testified that this unusual arrangement prompted the partnership's interest in selling its corn to ConAgra, a fact known to ConAgra.

On or about June 10, 1992, the partnership entered into a series of four contracts for the sale by the partnership and purchase by ConAgra of 300,000 bushels of corn. The first contract called for the delivery of 100,000 bushels of corn sometime in December 1992; the second for the delivery of 70,000 bushels of corn in January 1993; the third for the delivery of 65,000 bushels of corn in February 1993; and the fourth for the delivery of 65,000 bushels of corn in March 1993. Each contract left the price to be determined by the partnership at 20 cents below the daily price of corn on the Chicago Board of Trade. The partnership had the right, up until the time of delivery, to pick the day on which the corn would be priced.

On August 13, 1992, the partnership's crop was severely damaged by a hailstorm. Race called ConAgra on August 17 or 18 to report the hail damage. About a month later, on September 23, 1992, Race called the plant manager and informed him that the salvage value would be close to 70,000 bushels, but to be on the safe side he would like to lock in, or price out, 60,000 bushels. Race testified that at this time he did not understand that there may have been some damages to pay if the partnership could not fulfill its contracts. Later, on November 10, 1992, ConAgra placed a conference call to Race in an attempt to negotiate a settlement of the corn contract. After Race discussed the situation with his partners, the partnership decided that it would try to buy some corn so it could start to fill these contacts. The partnership eventually purchased 60,000 bushels of "wet" corn to dry in its facilities and deliver to ConAgra. Although it had priced out a total of 130,000 bushels of corn, the partnership delivered only 108,503.04 bushels, 100,000 bushels in fulfillment of the first contract and the remainder on the second contract. This left the partnership 61,496.96 bushels short of the corn it had priced out on the second contract and 130,000 bushels short of the corn it had contracted to sell in the third and fourth contracts.

On February 18, 1993, ConAgra bought corn on the market to cover the partnership's unfilled obligations under the contracts at a claimed loss of $11,689.88. ConAgra then sued the partnership to recover its losses due to the breach of contract by the partnership. Was the partnership excused from its performance obligation due to the destruction of its crops in the hailstorm? Is ConAgra entitled to recover its claimed losses based on the cost of cover? Was it ethical for ConAgra to hold the partnership to the literal terms of their contracts after the hailstorm destroyed such a significant portion of the partnership's crop? Would ConAgra be breaching a duty to any other interested parties if it had excused the partnership's duty to perform in this case? [See *ConAgra, Inc. v. Bartlett Partnership*, 540 N.W.2d 333 (Neb. 1995).]

7. **CRITICAL THINKING CASE** Smyers owns and operates Engineered Specialty Products ("ESP"). ESP manufactures and sells resistance welders and quartz crystal X-ray machines called goniometers. Quartz Works is a Massachusetts corporation in the business of purchasing welders, goniometers, and other related equipment and reselling the equipment as a package to businesses that wish to operate quartz crystal manufacturing facilities. In 1992, Quartz Works and ESP began negotiations for Quartz Works to purchase two welders from ESP, and they also explored the possibility of ESP manufacturing two goniometers for Quartz Works. ESP had never manufactured a goniometer, and Quartz Works was aware of this inexperience at the time the negotiations began.

On September 21, 1992, Quartz Works offered to purchase two welders from ESP at a total price of $88,825. At the time of its offer, Quartz Works also sent ESP a check for $66,618.75, representing a 75 percent down payment toward the total. Upon receiving the Quartz Works order, ESP sent back a counteroffer reflecting price adjustments for some of the related parts and a total purchase price of $89,125 for the welders. The invoice that ESP sent back to Quartz Works credited the payment Quartz Works had made and indicated that the total amount due was now $22,506.25. The ESP invoice also included two additional terms. The first read "75% DOWN, 25% BEFORE SHIPMENT." The second provided that, if ESP were not timely paid, a service charge of 1.5 percent per month would be applied to the balance due.

On November 11, 1992, Quartz Works sent another purchase order to ESP. This one was for two single-diffraction goniometers, with accompanying software, and a proposed purchase price of $96,359.80. By its invoice of November 16, 1992, ESP agreed with the proposed price, but again added terms to which Quartz Works apparently did not object. The invoice included the following payment terms: "1/3 DOWN, 90% BEFORE END OF '92, BAL. N/10 [within 10 days after shipment]." It reflected receipt of the one-third payment of $32,199.90 and indicated that the balance due was $64,239.90.

Quartz Works did not pay 90 percent of the total due on the goniometer contract before the end of 1992, and the parties disagreed at trial about the contractual effect of the failure to pay. The record does demonstrate that receipt of the 90 percent payment by the end of the year was a condition of the discount; however, there is no evidence other than testimony that the delivery date was contingent upon that payment by year-end. The parties agree that when the 90 percent payment was not received by the end of 1992, ESP raised the total price of the goniometers to $99,340 and changed the payment terms to one-third down and two-thirds before shipment of the goniometers.

The goniometers were not delivered in February 1993; in fact, they were not shipped until October 1, 1993. During a September 22 meeting, the parties agreed to modify the payment terms of both the welder contract and the goniometer contract. Instead of requiring final payment prior to shipment, as the contracts had originally done, final payment was to be made upon proof of shipment to Quartz Works. The parties agreed that ESP would send a copy of the bills of lading to defendant by facsimile on the day of each shipment, and Quartz Works would send payment by Federal Express that same day for arrival the following day. On September 29, 1993, ESP had the welders crated and placed with Yellow Freight System for shipment and delivery to Quartz Works.

Although Quartz Works received the welders, subsequently sent them to Mongolia, and received payment for them from its customer, Quartz Works has not paid ESP the $22,506.25 which it acknowledges is due under the welder contract. Although Smyers expected payment for the welders on September 30, he did not receive it, and was unable to reach Quartz Works by telephone on September 30 or October 1. He sent a message by facsimile on September 30 informing them that ESP had not received payment for the welders as agreed, and stating that he expected it the following day. Smyers also asked Quartz Works to call if any problems had arisen, but heard nothing in response. At this point, for various reasons, Smyers became anxious about whether he would be paid for the goniometers he was about to ship. Quartz Works had failed to pay for the welders and had also failed to respond to his messages. In addition, Smyers perceived cash flow problems with Quartz Works, and mistrust between ESP and Quartz Works had grown throughout the course of their relationship. Finally, because the welders and goniometers were destined for Mongolia, Smyers feared that his recourse in the event of nonpayment would be severely limited. Smyers nonetheless felt obligated to ship the goniometers on October 1, 1992, as agreed. Instead of shipping the goniometers to Quartz Works, however, he shipped them to ESP as addressee. Again, he immediately sent a copy of the bill of lading to Quartz Works by facsimile. Smyers continued to demand payment for both the welders and the goniometers; Quartz Works continued to ignore his telephone and facsimile messages. The parties had reached an impasse.

Eventually Smyers sued Quartz Works for breach of contract. Quartz Works countersued, alleging that ESP had breached, forcing Quartz Works to "cover" by purchasing goniometers from another source, for a much higher price. Which party was in breach of the contract in this case? Did ESP have a right to request assurances from Quartz Works concerning its ability to pay for the goniometers? Did ESP make a proper written request for assurances? [See *Smyers v. Quartz Works Corp.*, 880 F. Supp. 1425 (D. Kan. 1995).]

8. **YOU BE THE JUDGE** Gottlieb, the founder and president of TVT, invented an improved method for packaging audio and video tape cassettes called the "Biobox." Unlike other packaging methods utilized by the music industry at that time, the Biobox was to be made from cardboard with a flip-open top, in the manner of a cigarette pack. The Biobox was intended to be biodegradable and difficult to duplicate, thus deterring counterfeiting. TVT obtained a patent on this new design. After the record industry expressed interest in the proposed packaging, TVT began to look for a manufacturer to design and construct the machinery required to mass-produce the Biobox. Schubert, a German company, manufactures high-speed packaging systems and holds itself out as the European market leader in innovative packaging solutions. During the period relevant to the Complaint, Schubert marketed its products in the United States through an exclusive agency agreement with Rodico, Inc., a New Jersey–based company.

At a trade show in 1994, Gottlieb met with representatives of Rodico and, following the trade show, commenced discussions with Ekstedt, a Rodico officer who identified himself as being the "Schubert National Sales Manager." Ekstedt informed Gottlieb that Schubert possessed the experience and expertise necessary to develop machinery for the production of the Biobox. Through Rodico, Schubert made a specific bid for the Biobox project. By a written quotation dated October 28, 1994, Rodico proposed to TVT on behalf of Schubert that Schubert manufacture "One (1) Schubert Automatic Erecting, Loading, and Closing System for a Flip Top Cassette Carton" for a price of $800,000.00, based upon an exchange rate of $1.00 to DM 1.4920. The 1994 Quotation also provided that "machine design and electrical components are based on Schubert standards." Ekstedt signed the document as "Schubert National Sales Manager."

The following month, Rodico representatives introduced Gottlieb to Gerhard Schubert, the founder and principal of the company, at an industry trade show in Chicago. At the trade show, Gerhard Schubert represented that he was personally committed to the Biobox project and that his company had the experience and expertise required to design and manufacture an efficient production system. After issuing the 1994 Quotation, Schubert purported to refine its drawings and designs for the Biobox production line. During this period, Gottlieb communicated directly with Schubert officer Cornelis Lindner, who faxed revised designs to TVT's New York office. In February 1995, Gottlieb received from Rodico a revised quotation for "One (1) Schubert Automatic Erecting, Loading, and Closing System for a Flip Top Cassette Carton," again signed by Ekstedt as "Schubert National Sales Mgr." The pricing was "ex-works Crailsheim, Germany" and was based on the existing Deutsche Mark exchange rate. The shipment date was designated as the "end of September 1995." The 1995 Quotation contained an express warranty that the Biobox system would be free of any defect in material workmanship for at least six months from the date of shipment. TVT accepted the 1995 Quotation and paid a 20 percent down payment, in the amount of $172,432.00, to Rodico on behalf of Schubert.

Schubert did not meet the September 1995 shipment deadline and repeatedly pushed back the delivery date. Although the system failed internal Schubert tests, in late August 1997 Schubert sent the Biobox system to TVT for installation. The system performed poorly and did not meet the production rate set forth in the 1995 Quotation. Schubert failed to repair the system, and by the end of 1999 TVT was forced to halt the project. TVT claims that it suffered millions of dollars in damages, including money paid to Schubert for the system and for repairs; money spent on other technicians and equipment to try to fix or replace components; money spent to set up its production facility; money that will have to be spent to replace the facility; money spent on administration of the project; and lost profits. TVT filed suit against Schubert, alleging breach of contract under the provisions of the CISG. Schubert moved to dismiss the complaint on the grounds that TVT's only contract was with Rodico, specifically that TVT has no claim against Schubert due to lack of contractual privity. In addition, Schubert argues that the Court should dismiss the action for lack of personal jurisdiction, or alternatively, on the basis of forum non conveniens, in favor of litigation in Germany. If *you* were hearing the case, how would *you* rule on these motions? If this case were being tried in *your* court, how would *you* rule? [See *TeeVee Toons, Inc. v. Gerhard Schubert, GMBH*, 2002 U.S. Dist. LEXIS 5546 (S.D.N.Y. 2002).]

Notes

1. UCC § 2-304.
2. UCC, § 1-203.
3. Official Comments to UCC § 1-203.
4. UCC § 2A-509(1).
5. CISG, Articles 7(1), 60(a).
6. CISG, Article 39.
7. CISG, Article 44.

Warranties and Product Liability

AGENDA

NRW While most customers will be pleased with the NRW products, some customers will encounter problems. Since the cost of the StuffTrakR is so low, it is unlikely that an individual consumer will complain too much if he or she has a problem with the product, but complaints or lawsuits are still a possibility. The Inven-TrakR is slightly more expensive per unit, but the potential for problems is much greater because this product will be used to track and protect inventory. Thus, any problems with the InvenTrakR could have serious legal and financial implications. As a result, the firm wants to establish a warranty strategy for the firm that will provide appropriate protection for the firm while also providing reasonable protection for the customers. Should the firm attempt to exclude any warranties? Should the firm attempt to impose a liability cap in its contracts? How should warranty information be disseminated to customers? Should different methods be used for consumers than for merchants? These and other questions may arise in this chapter. Be prepared! You never know when the firm or one of its members will seek your advice.

It is increasingly important for businesses to be aware of the scope of warranties and of the potential impact of product liability. A substantial number of very large judgments have been handed down against merchant sellers and manufacturers for breach of warranty or product liability. Many of these judgments have been awarded to consumers of the goods, nonmerchant buyers who have suffered harm when a product did not measure up to the reasonable—or guaranteed—expectations of the consumer purchaser. While it is true that warranty protections also extend to merchant buyers, and that some merchant buyers may have a claim against their sellers based on product liability, this area seems to be more important to nonmerchant buyers who suffer harm from the product in question. This chapter will emphasize the rights of the consumers and the corresponding obligations of the merchant sellers against whom the claims are filed. Remember that a warranty claim involves an alleged breach of contract, and as such this area falls within the broad category of "remedies" (covered in Chapter 18), but it is treated separately because the claims often involve personal injuries suffered by the buyer, not just a loss in value of the goods due to the alleged defect in the goods.

A warranty is defined as "a promise that a proposition of fact is true."[1] Since a warranty involves a promise, it becomes a part of the contract. This is especially important in the sale of goods. Warranty protection is very often the best protection that a buyer can have in a sale. There are two types of warranties in sales: express and implied. (There are also statutory warranty provisions, but these tend to be informational rather than coverage based.) The fact that one type of warranty is present does not mean that the other type is absent. In fact, both types will frequently be present in one contract.

At common law, the courts presume that the parties to a contract have equal bargaining power. The courts also strongly believe in "freedom of contract." Thus, they are reluctant to interfere in the contractual relationship. Historically, the rule of *caveat emptor*—let the buyer beware—was regularly followed. As the commercial world matured, the relative positions of the parties to a sales contract began to change. Businesses grew larger, and the location of the business was more likely to be removed from the location of the individual buyer. It became less likely that the parties would truly have equal bargaining power. It also became less likely that the seller of the goods had also manufactured them. The courts and legislatures began to seek means of protecting consumers. Implied warranties (and statutory warranty provisions) and product liability provided those means. The consumer has thus now become so protected that many people feel the modern rule of commerce is *caveat venditor*—let the seller beware!

NRW CASE 19.1   Marketing and Sales

ADVERTISING THE PRODUCT

Helen wants to advertise the StuffTrakR extensively on television, with ads showing the product in use and suggesting the benefits and time to be saved through its use. Mai and Carlos agree with Helen in principle, but they suggest that the product should be enhanced somewhat in order to "grab" the viewers and, hopefully, really spur sales. They have suggested some exaggerated examples that could be used, including having a StuffTrakR on the family dog. In this scenario, the dog runs off, but the family is able to track it down thanks to the StuffTrakR. The commercial ends with the happy family reunited with its pet, and a voice-over saying something like "Another happy ending, thanks to the StuffTrakR." Helen doesn't like this idea. She thinks the commercials should show only what the product actually does. Further, she is afraid that the commercials might lead to the imposition of liability on the firm if the product doesn't measure up to the commercials. They have asked for your advice. What will you tell them?

BUSINESS CONSIDERATIONS Visual ads can be very effective, especially with the technological devices available today. Computer enhancements can place famous people in contemporary settings, and "morphing" can allow the advertiser to transform products from or to something else. While such ads can be effective, they can also be misleading. How much care should an advertiser take to ensure that an ad does not create express warranties that the advertiser will then have to honor?

ETHICAL CONSIDERATIONS From an ethical perspective, should commercials include some disclaiming language informing the viewers that the commercial was performed under controlled conditions, possibly with special effects and computer enhancement, in order to prevent viewers from getting the wrong idea about the capability of the advertised products?

INTERNATIONAL CONSIDERATIONS In the United States advertising may well lead to the imposition of express warranties on the seller of the advertised goods. Do *you* think the same thing is likely to happen in other countries? Why?

Express Warranties

An express warranty can be given only by the seller; it is not present until such time as the seller gives it. However, once given, such a warranty is said by the UCC to be a part of "the basis of the bargain." Section 2-313 mentions three different ways in which the seller creates an express warranty:

1. Any affirmation of a fact or a promise that relates to the goods creates an express warranty that the goods will match the fact or the promise.

2. Any description of the goods creates an express warranty that the goods will match the description.

3. Any sample or model of the goods creates an express warranty that the goods will conform to the sample or the model.[2]

Any of these three methods creates an express warranty if it is a part of "the basis of the bargain." It is not necessary for the seller to use words such as "warrant" or "guarantee." It is not even necessary for the seller to *intend* to create an express warranty. All that is necessary is that the seller employ one of these methods in a manner that causes the buyer to reasonably believe that a warranty covering the goods has been given.[3]

The Uniform Sales Act, which preceded the UCC, required the buyer to show reliance before an express warranty was found. The UCC seems to have removed the requirement of proving reliance. Instead, reliance appears to be presumed. The rule under the Code is that the seller must disprove the existence of an express warranty. In other words, if the buyer can prove the seller affirmed a fact, described the goods, or used a model or a sample, an express warranty is presumed. To disprove the existence of the warranty, the seller must show proof that the conduct described by the buyer was not the basis of the bargain. If such proof cannot be shown, the express warranty is present and it will be included in the contract.

Express warranties focus on *facts*. Mere opinions of the seller are not taken to be warranties. The seller is also allowed a certain amount of puffing. However, there is often a fine line between opinion and fact, and the seller should be extremely careful. If a statement is quantifiable, it is likely to be treated as a fact. If the statement is relative, it normally will be treated as opinion. Thus, the statement "this car gets 30 miles per gallon" likely would be treated as a warranty. But the statement "this is a good car" likely would not be a warranty. The problem lies with comments that fall between these two extremes.

Exhibit 19.1 illustrates the difficulty faced by the court in deciding whether something is a matter of fact or a matter of opinion. There is a great deal of gray area between things that are obvious facts and those that are obviously opinion, and the court has the task of deciding whether something within this gray area is a fact or an opinion.

If a statement that falls between an obvious fact and an obvious opinion was made by the seller, the court must decide how to interpret this statement in terms of warranty protections. To do so, the court must weigh the relative knowledge of the parties, the reliance (if any) the buyer placed on the seller, the likelihood that the seller was aware of any reliance, and any other pertinent facts that influence the balancing of interests of the two parties. Thus, if the seller conveyed an impression that seemed to be based on facts to the buyer, the court may decide that there was an assertion of facts and therefore may find an express warranty exists, despite the intent of the seller.

The seller also needs to be careful in advertising. Advertisements that claim certain characteristics for a product may also be treated by the courts as affirmations of fact and thus as express warranties. The following example shows

EXHIBIT 19.1 Finding an Express Warranty

Words or Conduct of the Seller
(Can be before, during, or after the contract is made)

Obvious statement of fact—quantifiable and measurable	Possible statement of fact, possible statement of opinion	Obvious statement of opinion—not quantifiable or measurable
Creates an express warranty.	May create an express warranty, depending on other circumstances, including the relative knowledge and expertise of the parties.	Does not create an express warranty; this is mere "puffing" or sales talk.

how an advertisement may be viewed by the court in an express warranty case.

A television advertisement for the Pick Pen Company, manufacturers of disposable ballpoint pens, shows a couple on a picnic. The couple remove a can of fruit juice from the picnic hamper, only to discover that they forgot to bring a can opener. One of them reaches into a pocket, removes a Pick Pen, and uses the uncapped pen to punch a hole in the top of the can. The couple smile, the camera pulls back, and a voice solemnly intones, "Pick Pens! For 79 cents, it's not just a great writing instrument."

A customer who has seen this commercial decides to use his or her Pick Pen to open a can. Unfortunately for the customer—and for the Pick Pen Company—the pen shatters and plastic shards enter the customer's wrist and hand, causing serious injury to the customer during this attempted use. A good argument could be made that the commercial had created a belief in the mind of the customer that this use was expressly warranted by the commercial. If, however, the Pick Pen Company used a disclaimer in the commercial—normally by scrolling script across the bottom of the screen—the courts might be less likely to find that the commercial created an express warranty.

Finally, the Code considers the timing of the statement or conduct from the buyer's perspective. Under § 2-209(1), a modification of a sales contract is valid without consideration. This means that the seller can create an express warranty before the contract is formed (through sales talk, negotiations, or even commercials); while forming the contract (in the language used in the agreement or in oral commitments made while forming the writing); or even after the contract is formed (through continued reassurances to the buyer that he or she has made a "good deal"). As a result, sellers should remember two things:

1. If they know a fact, they should state it honestly.

2. If they do not know a fact, they should not speculate! It is too easy to give an express warranty without realizing it.

Wat Henry Pontiac Co. v. Bradley [4] is one of the landmark cases in express warranty law. In 1944, Mrs. Bradley went to the Wat Henry Pontiac Company to purchase a used car. Mrs. Bradley asked many questions and the seller assured her that the car in question was in good condition. When Mrs. Bradley stated that she had to drive to Camp Shelby, Mississippi, with her seven-month-old child to see her husband, the salesman allegedly said: "This is a car I can recom-

mend" and "It is in A-1 shape." However, Mrs. Bradley was not allowed to take a "test drive" in the car, allegedly because of wartime gas rationing. Eventually, Mrs. Bradley bought the car and drove it home. Several days later, after she set out for Camp Shelby, the car broke down and required extensive repairs. Mrs. Bradley sued for breach of express warranties concerning the car. The sales manager testified that he gave no warranties in the sale and that he had explained to Mrs. Bradley at the time of the sale that there were no warranties covering the car. The court disagreed! The court pointed out that Mrs. Bradley was not generally knowledgeable concerning automobiles, and she was ignorant of all of the facts concerning this car in this case. The defects in the car were hidden, and the buyer was denied the opportunity to take a test drive during which the defects might have been discovered. The seller was an expert in automobiles. He repeatedly reassured her about the quality of the car (albeit in general and nonquantifiable terms) throughout the sale. His statements concerning the condition of the car, when viewed with her inability to personally examine the car prior to the sale, created express warranties and not mere opinion. Many of the principles of express warranty law now included in the Code seem to be based, at least indirectly, on the court's language from this case.

Implied Warranties

As the preceding section pointed out, express warranties are a part of the contract. They are not present until given by the seller. The court will not find an express warranty unless it is created by the seller as a part of the "basis of the bargain." Thus, a careful seller will not give many, if any, express warranties until—and unless—so desired.

In contrast, implied warranties are imposed by operation of law (subject to certain limitations involving the status of the seller). If the circumstances are correct for the imposition of implied warranties, these warranties will automatically be present in the contract unless they are voluntarily "surrendered" by the buyer, generally because the warranties were excluded by the seller. If the language of the contract includes specific language excluding one or more of the implied warranties and the buyer agrees to that language, the buyer has surrendered the protections afforded by the excluded warranties.

The UCC recognizes four types of implied warranties: the warranty of title, the warranty against infringement, the warranty of merchantability, and the warranty of fitness for a particular purpose. Some, all, or none of these warranties may be present in any given sales contract, depending on the circumstances surrounding the transaction and on the status of the seller of the goods.

Warranty of Title

Every contract for the sale of goods carries a warranty of title by the seller unless such a warranty is excluded by specific language warning the buyer that title is not guaranteed or unless the sale is made under circumstances that put the buyer on notice that title is not guaranteed. Absent one of these two conditions, a warranty of title exists to protect the buyer. A warranty of title ensures the buyer of the following:

• The transfer of the goods by the seller is proper.

• The buyer is receiving good title.

• The goods are free of hidden security interests, encumbrances, or liens.

In other words, the buyer is assured that no one may assert a hidden claim to the goods that is superior to the claim of the buyer.

Section 2-312 of the UCC specifies that every seller of goods gives an implied warranty of title unless the contract contains specific language that the warranty is being excluded or the circumstances of the sale are such that the buyer should realize that the seller does not warrant title. Thus, a merchant who is entrusted with goods gives a warranty of title if the merchant sells the entrusted goods to a good-faith purchaser. If the merchant has voidable title to the entrusted goods, the buyer receives good title, and there is no breach of the warranty. However, if the goods entrusted to the merchant have been stolen, the person who purchases the goods from the merchant would receive void title, and the merchant would be liable for breach of the implied warranty of title.

Warranty against Infringement

The implied warranty against infringement is unique in that it can be given by either the buyer or the seller, although it is normally given by the seller. (None of the other implied warranties can be given by the buyer.) The infringement protected against is the rightful claim of any third person concerning the goods.

Patent infringement is probably the most common type of problem dealt with under this warranty, but another area that is becoming increasingly important is copyright infringement. Videotapes, audiotapes, and computer software normally are copyrighted, and all are easy to copy without a great deal of equipment, expertise, or expense. Experts estimate that pirated copies of copyright-protected materials cost each of these industries a tremendous amount of money, possibly even billions of dollars per year. As a result, more attention is being paid to the protection and enforcement of copyrights. As this trend continues, an

---

NRW CASE 19.2 | **Management**

NRW

POTENTIAL PATENT INFRINGEMENT

One of the chip suppliers has recently raised its price for the chips used in the InvenTrakR, and the firm is concerned that if it raises its prices to offset this cost increase it will lose business to some of its competitors. A new chip supplier contacted Mai recently, offering to sell NRW a "knockoff" chip that is virtually identical to the chip provided by the current provider. Mai is concerned that the present chip supplier might have a patent on the chip, and that by purchasing this "knockoff" chip, the firm will be infringing on the patent, thus facing liability. She has asked you for advice on this matter. What will you tell her?

BUSINESS CONSIDERATIONS What sort of policy should a firm have for dealing with items that are likely to be protected by a patent or a copyright? How can a firm be certain that it is not infringing rights when it uses a product?

ETHICAL CONSIDERATIONS Patent litigation can be extremely expensive, and it is not unusual for a court to declare the patent invalid, ruling that the product was not "new, useful, or nonobvious." Is it ethical for a business to infringe a patent, hoping to prevail in court by having the patent declared invalid?

INTERNATIONAL CONSIDERATIONS Suppose that a supplier from another country is offering to provide a "knockoff" chip and that the "model" chip is likely to be protected by a patent. Does the fact that the supplier is from another country affect the issue of potential patent infringement? Are there any international patent protections that may affect your answer? A good starting place for looking into patent law is http://www.patentlawlinks.com/. Also look at http://www.gahtan.com/cyberlaw/.

---

increase in the number of cases involving the warranty against infringement will likely occur.

In order for a seller to give this warranty, the seller must be a merchant who regularly deals in the type of goods involved. A buyer who gives the warranty against infringement need not be a merchant. Any buyer who furnishes specifications to the seller in order to have the seller specially manufacture the goods described warrants against infringement if the seller complies with the specifications.

The following case involved an alleged breach of the warranty of infringement. Notice how the court treats the issue of patent rights in an effort to determine whether there was an infringement.

Warranty of Merchantability

Probably the most commonly breached, and the most commonly asserted, implied warranty is the warranty of merchantability. A warranty of merchantability is given whenever a merchant of goods, including a merchant of food or drink, makes a sale. It is a very broad warranty, designed to assure buyers that the goods they purchase from a merchant will be suitable for the normal and intended use of goods of that kind. Failure to satisfy any of the following six criteria means that the goods are not merchantable and that the warranty has been breached.

1. The goods must be able to pass without objection in the trade, under the description in the contract.

2. If the goods are fungible, they must be of fair average quality within the description.

3. The goods must be suitable for their ordinary purpose and use.

19.1

BONNEAU CO. v. AG INDUSTRIES, INC.
116 F.3d 155 (5th Cir. 1997)

FACTS Bonneau, a manufacturer and distributor of non-prescription eyeglasses, entered into a contract for the manufacturing of display stands for its glasses with AGI. The display stands used the Bonneau "Slide-Hook" system of holding the glasses, which involved a "hang-tag" system and cantilevered arms. Some time after the contract between Bonneau and AGI was made, Magnavision filed suit against Bonneau, alleging that Bonneau's "Slide-Hook" system, specifically the "hang-tag" portion, infringed a patent held by Magnavision. After losing the patent infringement case to Magnavision, Bonneau filed suit against AGI for breach of the warranty against infringement, alleging that the design and manufacturing of the display stands by AGI led to the allegedly inadvertent patent infringement by Bonneau. AGI denied that it had breached the warranty, asserting that Bonneau had provided the specifications for the display stands so that any patent infringement was committed by Bonneau. AGI also filed a counterclaim against Bonneau for breach of contract, alleging that Bonneau had not paid for the display stands under the contract.

ISSUE Did AGI breach the warranty against infringement in its production of the display stands?

HOLDING No, AGI did not breach the warranty against infringement because the design specifications were provided by Bonneau.

REASONING Excerpts from the opinion of the court (Judges Jolly, Jones, and Parker): Bonneau's complaint alleges a cause of action pursuant to [UCC] § 2-312(c). Section 2-312(c) states:

Unless otherwise agreed a seller who is a merchant regularly dealing in goods of the kind warrants that the goods shall be delivered free of the rightful claims of any third person by way of infringement or the like but a buyer who furnishes specifications to the seller must hold the seller harmless against any such claim which arises out of compliance with the specifications. . . .

At the outset, this Court's research discloses very little case law regarding this particular section. As noted by Professors White and Summers, "this section has not been heavily litigated" in the courts. . . . Our main focus concerns the second clause of § 2-312(c), the hold harmless provision, where the buyer furnishes specifications to the seller. However, under the particular facts of this case, we need not delve into a dissection of § 2-312(c) in order to answer the question before us. . . .

We now turn our focus to the district court's grant of AGI's alternative submission in its motion for summary judgment that Bonneau supplied the design specification for the Slide-Hook display system (which was the basis of Magnavision's patent infringement suit) to AGI and, therefore, under § 2-312(c), Bonneau must hold AGI harmless against the patent infringement actions. Bonneau asserts that it merely supplied a "sketch" of the hang-tag to AGI, and that AGI designed and manufactured the Slide-Hook display system according to AGI's own "engineer like" specifications. Thus, Bonneau contends that it did not assume liability for patent infringement either by agreement or under § 2-312(c). AGI counters that Bonneau, and not AGI, designed the display system that was the subject of the patent infringement suits and, therefore, there was no breach of warranty under § 2-312(c). We reject Bonneau's arguments. We recognize that "specification" is not defined in § 2-312(c) or in Article 2 of the [UCC].

However, based on our review of the record, we conclude that the hang-tag design furnished by Bonneau to AGI constitutes a specification under § 2-312(c) which formed the basis for the infringement actions for which Bonneau sought indemnification. The record discloses that the hang-tag design . . . was created by Alice Myer, Bonneau's advertising and display manager, and other Bonneau executives in late January 1991. . . . The hang-tag design specifications which Bonneau furnished to AGI were central to the Slide-Hook display system. Accordingly, we concluded that Myer's design contains sufficient specificity for a competent manufacturer to construct the product, and thus constitutes a "specification" pursuant to §2-312(c). . . . These actions by Bonneau's personnel support the conclusion that Bonneau created the design specifications for the hang-tag Slide-Hook and furnished those specifications to AGI to create a custom hang-tag display stand. Moreover, as Comment 3 to § 2-312(c) recognizes "when the buyer orders goods to be assembled, prepared or manufactured [based] on his own specifications . . . liability will run from the buyer to the seller." . . . Because the statutory language is clear, judicial inquiry into the statute's plain meaning is unnecessary. . . . Thus, because we have concluded that Bonneau furnished the specifications to AGI for the Bonneau Slide-Hook display system, Bonneau's defense costs associated with the patent infringement actions . . . must be borne by Bonneau. . . . Based on the foregoing discussion, we affirm the district court's grant of summary judgment for AGI on Bonneau's breach of warranty claim . . . and on AGI's counterclaim for breach of contract. . . .

BUSINESS CONSIDERATIONS AGI accepted an offer to produce display stands to the specifications of its customer, Bonneau. Should AGI, and similarly situated firms, have a policy in which potential infringements are specifically discussed and included in their contracts? Would such an inclusion have been helpful in this case?

ETHICAL CONSIDERATIONS Bonneau attempted to place the blame for the patent infringement on AGI, seeking to avoid payments due under their contract and also seeking to recover for its fees and losses from the patent infringement case filed by Magnavision. Was this conduct by Bonneau ethical?

4. The goods must be of even kind, quality, and quantity.

5. The goods must be adequately contained, packaged, and labeled as required under the agreement.

6. The goods must conform to the promises and facts contained on the label, if any.

Merchant sellers have been found liable for breaching this warranty because of such things as bobby pins in soft-drink containers, worms in canned peas, a decomposing mouse in a soda bottle, and a hair dye that caused the buyer's hair to fall out.

Because many merchantability cases involve disputes over food and drink, the courts have developed special tests to determine merchantability in these cases. Early cases involving food were decided under the "foreign/natural" test. Under the foreign/natural test, "foreign" objects found in the food do constitute a breach of warranty, whereas "natural" objects found in the food do not constitute a breach. Thus, a chicken bone found in a chicken salad sandwich does not involve a breach because chicken bones are "natural" to chicken. But a cherry pit found in a chicken salad sandwich is "foreign" and thus establishes a breach. While the results under the foreign/natural test were easy to predict, they often seemed unfair. Eventually a somewhat fairer test was developed, the "reasonable expectations" test. The reasonable expectations test has supplanted the earlier foreign/natural test in most, if not all, jurisdictions. Under the reasonable expectations test, the court attempts to establish what a reasonable person expects to find in the food. A reasonable person does not expect to find a "foreign" object in the food, so any foreign object found constitutes a breach. However, a reasonable person may not expect to find a "natural" object in the food either, so that finding such a natural object can also constitute a breach. Thus, a chicken bone in a chicken salad sandwich might show a breach if it is unreasonable to expect to find a bone in such a sandwich. The reasonable expectation in any given case is a question of fact.

One such case, *Webster v. Blue Ship Tea Room,*[5] is considered a classic in the law. The case involved a woman (Webster) who ingested a fish bone while eating a bowl of fish chowder in a Boston restaurant. The bone became lodged in her throat, and she required surgery to remove the bone. The court recognized that Webster was a native New Englander and that she had ordered a seafood dish in a waterfront restaurant in Boston. The court's opinion then treated her presumed knowledge of the preparation of fish chowder, along with a relatively detailed history of fish chowder as a New England dietary staple. The court concluded that a reasonable person eating fish chowder in a New England restaurant would reasonably expect to find fish bones in the chowder, so that the chowder was, in fact, merchantable. This opinion illustrates one approach a court might take in deciding a merchantability-of-food case.

Merchants whose contracts primarily provide services do not give the implied warranty of merchantability for those services. A number of cases involving tainted blood have been decided, with the courts tending to view the provision of blood by a hospital as a "service" rather than a "sale," thus negating any claim that the tainted blood provided to the patient constituted a breach of the warranty of merchantability. Other states have specifically excluded warranty protections in the provision of blood, blood products, and other human tissue.

Warranty of Fitness for a Particular Purpose

Any seller, whether a merchant or a nonmerchant, may give the implied warranty of fitness for a *particular* purpose (remember that the warranty of merchantability refers to fitness for a *normal* purpose). In order for this warranty to come into existence, all of the following conditions must be present:

- The seller must know that the buyer is contemplating a particular use for the goods.

- The seller must know that the buyer is relying on the seller's skill, judgment, or knowledge in selecting the proper goods for the purpose.

- The buyer must not restrict the seller's range of choices to a particular brand or price range or otherwise limit the scope of the seller's expert judgment.

The following case involved quite a few issues. The plaintiff was seeking damages for a wrongful death, arguing that the various defendants should be held liable for product liability and breach of the implied warranty of fitness. Two of the three defendants settled with the plaintiff, but the third denied liability, leading to a trial and then to this appeal.

Warranty Exclusions

The seller can modify or exclude warranties. The simplest way to exclude an express warranty is not to give one. If the seller is careful, no express warranties will exist. Sometimes a seller will create an express warranty orally but will attempt to exclude any express warranties in writing. In this case, the court will turn to UCC § 2-316(1). The court will take the warranty and the exclusion as consistent with one another if possible; otherwise, the warranty will override the exclusion. Excluding or modifying implied warranties is not so easy. To exclude or modify a warranty of merchantability, either orally or in writing, the word

---

NRW CASE 19.3   Sales

WARRANTIES

Carlos recently attended a seminar discussing common problems faced by new businesses, and one of the problems discussed was warranties and the potential liability a firm faces if it breaches its warranties. Carlos became concerned that the firm had not given enough thought to the potential liability that NRW could be facing. He decided to make some recommendations to the others about limiting or excluding their warranties in an effort to avoid liability if something should be wrong. He has asked for your advice. What will you tell him?

BUSINESS CONSIDERATIONS A firm like NRW produces one product that it sells primarily to consumers and another product that it sells exclusively to merchants. Should such a business develop a strategy for its treatment of warranties based on the status of the customer, or should it just follow one warranty strategy for all of its products?

ETHICAL CONSIDERATIONS Is it ethical for a business to advertise in a manner that suggests that the customers are getting a *full* warranty when in fact the customers are getting a *limited* warranty? Is it ethical to attempt to exclude all warranty protections in selling a product to consumers?

INTERNATIONAL CONSIDERATIONS Under the CISG there is no requirement for a writing in order to make a contract. How would a buyer prove that any types of warranties, express or implied, were given in an oral agreement? How would a seller prove that he or she did not give any warranties absent written evidence of a disclaimer or an exclusion?

---

merchantability must be used. If the exclusion is written, the exclusion must be conspicuous. To exclude or modify a warranty of fitness for a particular purpose, the exclusion must be written, and it must be conspicuous; no oral exclusions of fitness are allowed. Under § 2-316(3), it is possible to exclude all implied warranties of quality (which normally do not exclude title or infringement protections) under three sets of circumstances:

1. Language such as "as is" or "with all faults" must be used properly so that the buyer is duly informed that no implied warranties are given.

19.2

BOUVERETTE v. WESTINGHOUSE ELECTRIC CORPORATION
628 N.W.2d 86, 2001 Mich. App. LEXIS 72 (2001)

FACTS David Bouverette was a journeyman electrician with Sebewaing Industries, Inc., an automotive parts stamping company. On June 7, 1995, Bouverette died of an apparent electrocution while working on a control panel manufactured by Medar, Inc. This control panel contained circuit breakers manufactured by Hy Tek Systems. The panel controlled an industrial welding machine designed, built, and sold by Hy Tek. On March 27, 1996, Ms. Bouverette, the widow, filed this action, alleging wrongful death and product liability against Westinghouse and Hy Tek, and alleging, against Westinghouse, negligent design, manufacture, and failure to warn and breach of implied warranty of fitness (defective design and manufacture and inadequate warnings). Hy Tek filed a third-party complaint against Medar, Inc., seller of the electrical control panel to Hy Tek, and Ms. Bouverette filed an amended complaint, alleging negligence and breach of implied warranty against Medar. Before the trial, Bouverette settled with Hy Tek for $75,000 and with Medar for $35,000. The case against Westinghouse then proceeded. The jury returned a verdict for Bouverette on the claims of breach of implied warranty and breach of express warranty. However, the jury found in favor of Westinghouse on the claim of negligence. The jury awarded damages of $111,817 for economic losses and $750,000 for noneconomic losses. The jury found Bouverette 30 percent at fault and defendant 70 percent at fault, resulting in a final judgment of $499,610.90. The court then denied Westinghouse's motions for judgment notwithstanding the verdict (JNOV) or a new trial.

ISSUES Did Bouverette establish a prima facie case of breach of warranty? Can Westinghouse be liable for breach of the implied warranty of fitness if it was not found liable for negligence?

HOLDINGS Yes, Bouverette established a prima facie case of breach of warranty. Yes, Westinghouse can be liable for breach of the warranty of fitness even if it was not liable for negligence.

REASONING Excerpts from the opinion of the court (Judges Holbrook, Hood, and Neff):

Defendant argues that plaintiff failed to establish a prima facie case of breach of implied warranty in the absence of risk-utility evidence, required for claims under either defective design or failure to warn, and, thus, that the trial court erred in denying defendant's motions for a directed verdict and JNOV. We disagree. . . .

Our courts have stated that negligence and breach of implied warranty may, in certain factual contexts, involve the same elements and proofs, both in a failure to warn claim . . . and in a design defect claim. . . . Nonetheless, the theories of negligence and implied warranty remain separate causes of action with different elements. . . . Although in a design defect case the trier of fact must apply "a risk-utility balancing test that considers alternative safer designs and the accompanying risk pared (sic) against the risk and utility of the design chosen," . . . no such specific analysis is required in a failure to warn case. In discussing the importance of risk-utility balancing with regard to the proper scope of warnings, this Court . . . expressly stated that the adequacy of a warning is an issue of reasonableness, and reasonableness is a question of fact. Thus, plaintiff did not fail to establish a prima facie case of breach of implied warranty in failing to satisfy a risk-utility analysis.

When a products liability action is premised on a breach of implied warranty of fitness, the plaintiff must prove that a defect existed at the time the product left the defendant's control, which is normally framed in terms of whether the product was "'reasonably fit for its intended, anticipated or reasonably foreseeable use.'" . . . There was ample evidence to establish a prima facie claim of breach of implied warranty premised on failure to warn. Plaintiff presented evidence that the breaker did not make or break simultaneously as intended when used with an external linkage handle. Further, defendant's instruction and installation manual did not provide a warning in this regard. There was testimony that the manual contained other warnings to electricians and should have warned of the external linkage problem or that the breaker itself should have had a warning label to that effect. Electricians relied on the breaker to shut off power by breaking simultaneously when the handle was in the off position, as did Medar in installing the indicator lights. This evidence presents a question of fact whether defendant's failure to warn of this condition was reasonable given the risk of electrocution. . . . Further, given the evidence, the jury could have found a breach of implied warranty because it was foreseeable that the breaker would be used with the linkage and yet, when one leg of the breaker fused, the breaker handle could be placed in the off position even though electricity was still flowing. The jury could have found that the breaker failed to break simultaneously, as it was intended to do, when the linkage handle was placed in the off position.

Thus, the jury verdict must stand. . . . Defendant argues that the jury's verdict is inconsistent as a matter of law because the jury found no negligence, but did find breach of implied warranty, and an implied warranty cannot be breached absent negligence. We disagree. " 'If there is an interpretation of the evidence that provides a logical explanation for the findings of the jury, the verdict is not inconsistent.' " . . . A court must look beyond the legal principles underlying the plaintiff's causes of action and carefully examine how those principles were argued and applied in the context of the case. . . .

In this case, the court's instructions to the jury provide a plausible explanation for the finding of a breach of implied warranty, but no negligence, on the basis of a failure to warn. The instructions on negligence were expressed in terms of negligent design or manufacture, with no mention of failure to warn. The only mention of failure to warn liability was in the court's instruction on breach of implied warranty.

Given the instructions, it is plausible that the jury found liability on the basis of a failure to warn, and thus found a breach of implied warranty, but did not find that defendant negligently designed or manufactured the breaker, and therefore found no negligence. This is particularly so in this case, given the parties' emphasis on an external linkage as the source of the problem, because defendant was not the manufacturer of the linkage. Moreover, the jury could have found that the breaker itself technically was not defective, but that it was not reasonably fit for the uses intended or foreseeable, i.e., the safety features failed when connected to a linkage handle, which was an intended or foreseeable use. Because the factual situation in this case so closely coincides with the specific language of implied warranty, the jury's findings are logical and consistent. " 'It is fundamental that every attempt must be made to harmonize a jury's verdicts. Only where verdicts are so logically and legally inconsistent that they cannot be reconciled will they be set aside.' " . . . Defendant claims that the jury's verdict was against the manifest weight of the evidence or was improperly influenced by sympathy, passion, or prejudice. A trial court's determination that a verdict was not against the great weight of the evidence will be given substantial deference by this Court. . . . We find no basis for vacating the verdict in this case, where reasonable support for the verdict is found in the evidence and the verdict returned by the jury is unlikely to have resulted from extraneous influences, passion, prejudice, or sympathy. . . .

Defendant presents as its final argument the contention that the trial court erred in failing to reduce (1) the judgment by the amount of Medar's settlement, and (2) the future damages award to present cash value. This issue is not presented in defendant's statement of questions presented and, thus, this Court need not review this issue. Independent issues not raised in the statement of questions presented are not properly presented for appellate review. . . .

BUSINESS CONSIDERATIONS When should a corporate defendant choose to settle a case, and when should a corporate defendant choose to litigate rather than settle out of court? Might Westinghouse have been better served to settle this case prior to trial?

ETHICAL CONSIDERATIONS Is it ethical for a business to settle a case if its management honestly believes that the business did not breach any warranties or commit any negligent acts? Is it ethical for a business to refuse to settle if its management honestly believes that the business did breach one or more warranties or did act in a negligent manner?

2. If the buyer has thoroughly examined the goods or has refused to examine them before the sale, no implied warranty is given for defects that the examination should have revealed.

3. Under course of dealings, course of performance, or usage of trade, implied warranties are not given as a matter of common practice.

Scope of Warranty Protection

If warranties do exist, the next question is, who do they protect? At common law, the answer is simple but unsatisfactory.

Since the warranty is a part of the contract, it extends only to a party in privity of contract. Any party not in privity of contract would not be covered by the warranty, regardless of whether that party was a foreseeable user or consumer of the warranted goods. Thus, the buyer is covered, but no one else is protected. The UCC has changed this. Section 2-318 contains the following three alternative provisions, and each state has selected one of the alternatives:

1. Warranties extend to any member of the buyer's family or household or any guest in the buyer's home if it is reasonable to expect that person to use or consume the goods.

2. Warranties extend to any natural person (human being) who could reasonably be expected to use or consume the goods.

3. Warranties extend to any person (remember, a corporation is a legal person) who could reasonably be expected to use or consume the goods.

The seller may not exclude or modify the extension of the warranties to those third-party beneficiaries.

Statutory Warranty Provisions

Before 1975, consumers faced certain problems in the area of warranty law: many manufacturers disclaimed warranty protection, leaving the consumer with little or no protection, and most manufacturers put the warranty terms inside a sealed package, so the consumer did not even know what warranty provisions were being offered until after the sale was completed. The warranty terms inside the package frequently were in the form of a warranty card. The instructions told the buyer to complete the card and return it to the manufacturer in order to obtain his or her warranties. In fact, these cards often specified that the buyer was agreeing to accept the express warranties the manufacturer was offering as the exclusive warranties in the contract. By completing and returning the card, the buyer was surrendering any implied warranties he or she possessed in exchange for a very restricted (frequently 60- or 90-day) express warranty coverage proposed by the merchant.

As a result of these problems, the Magnuson-Moss Warranty Act was passed and took effect in 1975. This law covers any consumer good manufactured after January 3, 1975. The manufacturer must provide the consumer with presale *warranty information*. The manufacturer also should set up informal settlement procedures to benefit the consumer. The manufacturer does not have to give any express warranties under the statute. However, according to the law, a manufacturer who does give an express warranty must designate it as either full or limited. To qualify as a full warranty, the warranty must meet at least four requirements:

- It must warrant that defects in the goods will be remedied within a reasonable time.

- It must conspicuously display any exclusions or limitations of consequential damages.

- Any implied warranty must not be limited in time.

- It must warrant that if the seller's attempts to remedy defects in the goods fail, the consumer will be allowed to select either a refund or a replacement.

Any warranty that is not full is limited. In a limited warranty, implied warranties may be limited to a reasonable time, frequently the same time as the express warranties

given in the contract by the seller. There may also be limits on when the buyer can select a refund or a replacement.

Note that Magnuson-Moss does not provide warranty protection. All that this law requires is for the manufacturer or seller who deals in consumer goods to inform the consumer of his or her warranty protections. The Magnuson-Moss Warranty Act is a disclosure law, designed to ensure that consumers are made aware of the warranty protections available with different products so that the consumer can make an informed and intelligent choice between products based on all of the available information, including warranty coverage. An interesting Web site for information on warranty protections and the scope of Magnuson-Moss is http://www.mlmlaw.com/library/guides/ftc/warranties/toc.htm. You might also want to visit http://oci.wi.gov/pub_list/pi-069.htm for related information.

Product Liability

While a great deal of energy and emphasis is placed on warranty law and warranty protections, this is not the only area in which buyers and consumers are protected from injuries caused by goods they have purchased or are using. Because they are a part of the contract, warranty protections are obvious to the buyer and the seller. Less obvious to the buyer, and to many sellers, are the other sources of remedies to which the buyer may be entitled. These other remedies may well be broader, they often last longer, and they frequently lead to larger judgments for injured parties. Sellers, in particular, need to be aware of the potential liability they face for injuries caused by the goods they sell beyond the liabilities imposed under warranty law.

Assume that a person is injured while using goods he or she has purchased, and he or she decides to seek remedies for the injury suffered. The first alternative many people consider is a breach of warranty claim. However, in many cases the warranty protections do not extend to the injury suffered, or the warranty protections have expired. When such a situation occurs, the injured party is not necessarily left without remedies. He or she may discover that, although warranty protections are lacking, potential remedies are still available under tort law. The injured party may be able to assert negligence against the manufacturer, or may even be able to establish strict tort liability against the manufacturer or the seller of the goods. See http://www.personalinjuryfyi.com/ or http://www.injuryboard.com/tort10.cfm/ for additional information on this area of law.

Negligence

At common law, negligence can be used in only two circumstances: the buyer can argue breach of duties established by the privity of contract between the parties; or the buyer can argue that the goods are innately dangerous, so that privity of contract is not necessary in order to establish the liability of the seller or the manufacturer.

An injured party trying to establish that the tort of negligence occurred has to show the requisite elements of negligence: duty, breach of duty, harm, and proximate cause. Duty, the first element, is often the most difficult to establish. The injured party has to show that he or she is in privity of contract with the negligent party in order to establish that the seller owes a duty to the buyer. If there is privity, the contractual relationship establishes a duty by the seller to provide reasonably safe goods. The buyer next has to establish that this duty has been breached. This is normally done by showing that the goods provided are not reasonably safe for their intended use. The injured party then has to show that he or she was injured while using the goods and that the injury was *proximately caused* by the seller's breach of duty. This presents a relatively difficult task for the buyer. Even if the buyer can establish that the goods are not reasonably safe, that an injury did occur, and that there is a proximate causative link between the defect and the injury, establishing a duty owed by the manufacturer to the buyer is hard. In most instances, the injured party is in contact only with an innocent intermediate party and not with the negligent manufacturer. The manufacturer would argue that it owes a duty only to its buyer, the intermediate party. The intermediate party would assert that it has not breached any duty owed to the injured party. The lack of privity thus negates the duty element, effectively removing the possibility of suing the manufacturer for negligence.

Historically, an injured user who was able to argue that the goods were innately dangerous had an easier time establishing his or her case, if the innate danger of the goods could be shown. If the goods were found to be imminently or inherently dangerous, privity was not required. However, establishing the imminent or inherent danger of the product is more difficult. A product is deemed to be imminently dangerous if it is reasonably certain to threaten death or severe bodily harm as produced or sold. An item is considered to be inherently dangerous if it is dangerous by its nature. Imminent danger is most commonly found in negligent production; inherent danger is most commonly found in negligent use.

The difficulty of establishing either of these bases for proving that the manufacturer is liable for injuries serves as an effective shield from product liability at common law. However, times change, and so did the law's approach to product liability. In 1916, U.S. courts effectively laid the privity defense to rest in product liability cases. In the landmark case of *MacPherson v. Buick Motor Co.*,[6] the owner of

a Buick automobile was injured when the wooden spoke wheel of his automobile broke while he was driving the car. MacPherson sued Buick for his injuries. Buick denied liability for two reasons. It had not produced the wheel, but rather it had purchased the wheel from a supplier; so if liability attached to the defect in the wheel, the supplier should be the liable party. Buick also claimed lack of privity in that MacPherson had purchased his car from a dealer, not from the Buick Motor Company. The court rejected both arguments made by Buick, allowing the injured plaintiff to recover damages from Buick despite a lack of privity. Other courts quickly adopted the MacPherson rule, and, as a result, privity of contract is seldom asserted as a negligence defense today.

Strict Liability in Tort

The other basis for recovery frequently asserted by an injured party is strict liability in tort (also frequently referred to as strict liability or strict tort liability). Strict liability in tort appears to be a public policy area. It is possible for a manufacturer to disclaim warranty provisions, leaving a purchaser without the protections envisioned by warranty law. Similarly, an injured consumer may not be able to establish the necessary elements for a successful negligence suit. Nonetheless, there seems to be a general feeling that an injured consumer should be able to recover from someone, and the manufacturer is seen as the best available source for recovery. Not only is the manufacturer normally better able to absorb the loss than the injured consumer, but the manufacturer is also in a position to pass the cost on to society in the form of higher prices for the goods.

The basis for this theory of recovery is found in the Restatement (Second) of Torts, § 402A. Section 402A is widely followed by the courts of the United States. The section states:

> *(1) One who sells any product in a defective condition unreasonably dangerous to the user or consumer or to his property is subject to liability for physical harm thereby caused to the ultimate user or consumer, or to his property, if*
>   *(a) the seller is engaged in the business of selling such a product, and*
>   *(b) it is expected to and does reach the user or consumer without substantial change in the condition in which it is sold.*
> *(2) The rule stated in subsection (1) applies although*
>   *(a) the seller has exercised all possible care in the preparation and sale of his product, and*

(b) the user or consumer has not bought the product from or entered into any contractual relation with the seller.

Note that this provision applies only to a merchant, that the goods must be a "defective" product that is "unreasonably" dangerous to the consumer, and that the product must reach the consumer without any substantial change in its condition. If these three criteria are satisfied, and if the consumer is injured using the product, the manufacturer can be held liable even though it used all possible care in the production of the product and even though there is no allegation of negligence.

This basis for liability imposes a substantial potential burden on the manufacturer. The "defective condition unreasonably dangerous to the user or consumer" referred to in part 1 is often measured at the time the injury occurs and not at the time the product was produced. Thus, a manufacturer who produces a product with a long useful life may face liability in the future, due to technological advances in the industry after production of the product but before the product is removed from service. The manufacturer can be found liable under this section for defects in design, defects in construction, or failure to warn the consumer of a known danger commonly faced when using the product. This is one of the reasons for the warning on the blade platform on power lawn mowers ("Keep hands and feet from under mower while in operation"), the warning label on the power cords of electric hair driers ("Keep away from water—Danger"), and other labels or tags on consumer goods. This could also be an argument for planned obsolescence of products. A product whose useful life is supposed to end before too many technological advances can be made is less likely to lead to liability for the manufacturer.

The following case involves an interesting allegation regarding product liability—an allegation that a manufacturer of windows made windows that were too *easy* to open. Observe how the court addresses the issue and then decide if you agree with the conclusion the court reaches.

19.3

SOPRONI v. POLYGON APARTMENT PARTNERS
941 P. 2d 707 (Wash. App. Div. I 1997)

FACTS Shannon Soproni and her 20-month-old son Daniel were visiting Shannon's boyfriend in his apartment. During the visit, Daniel was playing in an upstairs bedroom in the presence of his mother and her boyfriend. He was repeatedly warned by his mother not to play with, open, or close the window near the end of the bed. Nonetheless, when neither of the adults was paying particular attention to him, Daniel climbed onto the window sill, opened the window, and fell from the window to a concrete patio. The fall caused Daniel serious injuries, including long-term neurological harm. Daniel, through his guardian ad litem, filed suit against Polygon Apartment Partners, the developers of the apartment complex, alleging that the partnership was negligent and in violation of safety rules and regulations, including the building code. Polygon denied liability, but argued that, if liability were to be found, the architect of the apartment complex and the manufacturer of the windows should be found comparatively liable as well. Daniel's guardian ad litem then amended the complaint, including the architect and the manufacturer of the windows and argued that the windows were defectively designed, and that the manufacturer failed to provide a warning regarding the ease with which the windows could be opened, thus presenting an unreasonable danger to small children.

ISSUES Were the windows defectively designed? Was the manufacturer's failure to provide a warning that the windows could easily be opened a proximate cause of the accident?

HOLDINGS No, the windows were not defectively designed. No, the failure to provide a warning was not a proximate cause of the accident.

REASONING Excerpts from the opinion of Judge Grosse:

Soproni alleges that the action was brought under the product liability act . . . and that because of the nature of a product liability claim, summary judgment is rarely, if ever, appropriate. Soproni argues that there are always questions of fact as to the reasonableness of the design based upon either of two methods: a risk-utility analysis or a consumer expectation analysis. While we have doubts that Soproni adequately pleaded the case under the product liability act, we will review it on that basis. We hold that even if viewed as a case under the act, it can be decided as a matter of law. The product liability statute . . . provides in pertinent part:

(1) A product manufacturer is subject to liability to a claimant if the claimant's harm was proximately caused by the negligence of the manufacturer in that the product was not reasonably safe

as designed or not reasonably safe because adequate warnings or instructions were not provided. . . .

(2) In determining whether a product was not reasonably safe under this section, the trier of fact shall consider whether the product was unsafe to an extent beyond that which would be contemplated by the ordinary consumer.

To establish a violation of [the statute] Soproni must prove that, at the time of manufacture,

The likelihood that the product would cause plaintiff's harm or similar harms, and the seriousness of those harms, outweighs the manufacturer's burden to design a product that would have prevented those harms or any adverse effect a practical, feasible alternative design would have on the product's usefulness. . . . If the plaintiff fails to establish this, the plaintiff may nevertheless establish liability by showing the product was unsafe to an extent beyond that which would be contemplated by the ordinary consumer. . . .

However, settled law requires that the expectations of the consumer must be the *reasonable* expectations of an ordinary consumer. Thus, under the facts of a particular case, "it may be unreasonable for a consumer to expect product design to depart from legislative or administrative regulatory standards, even if to do so would result in a safer product." . . . The statute itself mandates that the safety of the product must be considered under its ordinary use. Virtually any product manufactured could cause injury if put to certain uses or misuses. Liability

under this state's product liability law is based on the product being unsafe to an extent beyond that which would be contemplated by the ordinary user. . . . A window is for light, air, and egress in case of fire. The window here has not been shown to be "unsafe," only that another window design might or would be safer if used in a similar window application. The window here complied with all codes and standards applicable to its design, manufacture, and use. It performed as it was designed, and performed as a reasonable consumer would expect it to. . . . Here, by admission, Daniel Soproni was repeatedly warned by his mother, who was present, to stay away from the window. The risk of harm was apparent to Shannon Soproni. She warned the child more than once to stay away from the window and directed him not to play with it. She closed the window at least twice. Any failure to warn here was simply not the cause of the harm. The trial court did not err. The decision of the trial court is affirmed.

BUSINESS CONSIDERATIONS **Should a business procure liability insurance as a hedge against potential product liability lawsuits? Is there any protection beyond insurance that a business can rely on to protect it from claims of injured parties?**

ETHICAL CONSIDERATIONS **Is it ethical for an injured consumer to sue the manufacturer or the seller for injuries suffered due to the inattention or carelessness of the injured consumer? To discourage such claims, should there be a public policy providing for recovery of all expenses incurred by a business that prevails in such a suit?**

Leases

Article 2A provides many of the same types of protections to lessees that Article 2 provides to buyers. Thus, when goods are leased, the lessee receives certain warranties, and these warranties are either the same as, or at least analogous to, the warranties given to the buyer in a sale of goods. There are some differences in a few of the warranties, but these differences are due to the difference in the reason the contract is entered. As you can see, these differences are more in style or terminology than in the types of coverage provided. The lessee receives express warranties on the same basis as a buyer of goods does. Express warranties are created when the lessor makes any affirmation of fact or promise that relates to the character, quality, or nature of the goods. These express warranties become part of the basis of the bargain. The lessor also provides express war-

ranties based on descriptions of the goods or by providing any sample or model of the goods being leased. Article 2A of the UCC specifically excludes any statements as to the value of the goods, as well as any statement purporting to be merely the lessor's opinion or commendation of the goods, from attaining the status of an express warranty.

Lessees also receive four implied warranties in their lease contracts. These implied warranties are the warranty against interference, the warranty against infringement, the warranty of merchantability, and the warranty of fitness for a particular purpose. The warranty against interference is similar to the warranty of title under Article 2. It warrants that, during the term of the lease, no person holds a claim to or interest in the goods that will interfere with the lessee's use and enjoyment of the goods. The other three implied warranties are the same for lessees as they are for buyers. Warranties under Article 2A can be excluded in the same manner as under Article 2.

Product liability claims are also available against the lessor or the manufacturer in a lease agreement. The same sorts of claims would be asserted, and the same defenses would be available.

The CISG

The CISG does not expressly provide for warranties as the UCC does. Instead, the warranty protections provided under the CISG are implied from the language of some of the articles of the Convention. Nonetheless, if warranties are found to exist and those warranties are breached, the buyer will be entitled to remedies. Also remember that the CISG is not meant to apply to the sale of goods to consumers under most circumstances, so any breach of warranty claims under the CISG are most likely to involve merchant buyers and merchant sellers. Thus, the remedies sought are quite likely to be "normal" sales remedies rather than remedies given to an injured consumer. As such, the assessment of damages is likely to be much smaller, relating to the value of the contract rather than to personal injury, harm, or loss.

Article 8 of the CISG says that any statements or conduct of either party are to be interpreted according to the intent of the party making the statement or carrying out the conduct. If the intent of the party cannot be determined from the circumstances, statements and conduct are to be interpreted as a reasonable person would interpret them under the circumstances. If the statements or the conduct were intended to create a warranty, *or* if the intent cannot be determined, but a reasonable person would interpret the statements or conduct as creating a warranty, then a warranty has been created. Since this warranty exists because of the intentional conduct of the parties, the warranty would be viewed as an express warranty.

Article 9 provides that the parties are bound by any practices they have established between themselves, and to have impliedly made any common trade usages part of their contract. Thus, if it is normal trade usage to provide warranties in these types of contracts, those warranties will become part of the particular contract unless the agreement specifically excludes such trade usage. These trade usages may well include some implied warranty provisions, especially if one of the parties to the international sale of goods is a U.S. firm which commonly has implied warranties as a part of its trade usage, and the other party knew or should have known of that trade usage.

Article 35 requires the seller to deliver goods that are of the quantity, quality, and description required by the contract and that are contained or packaged in the manner required by the contract. This article goes on to state that, unless otherwise agreed, the goods are nonconforming unless they are fit for their ordinary use and purpose,[7] and are also fit for any particular purpose made known to the seller of the time of the contract.[8] These provisions sound strikingly similar to the UCC's provisions for the implied warranties of merchantability (fit for normal use) and fitness for a particular purpose. The CISG even has a similar limitation on the provisions regarding particular purpose: this finding of nonconformity does not apply in the "particular purpose" area where the circumstances show that the buyer did not rely, or that it was unreasonable for him to rely, on the seller's skill and judgment. Article 35 also states that the goods must be properly contained and packaged, and that the goods must possess the qualities of goods that the seller has held the goods out as possessing, based upon the use of any model or sample. Thus, while the CISG does not use the word "warranty," it contains provisions that require the same sorts of protections as the implied warranty provisions of Articles 2 and 2A of the UCC.

The CISG does not make any provisions for product liability, but then, neither does the UCC. It appears that international sales of goods treat the issue of product liability or negligence under the applicable national laws of the forum court. Of course, the UCC does not provide for product liability or negligence either. These areas are both areas of state law developed through the common law tradition and applied by the forum court when appropriate.

ISO 9000

The CISG is not the only major international agreement involving business and the sale of goods. Numerous free-trade zones have been established in the recent past, greatly affecting trade both within and outside of these zones. (See Chapter 3 for a brief discussion of free-trade zones.) A number of other initiatives that will have an impact on international trade have also been adopted or proposed. It appears that international business will be a focal point for uniform law for the foreseeable future.

Product quality and quality control are topics that have attracted a substantial amount of attention in the global marketplace. The concerns with these topics led to the promulgation and eventual adoption of an international quality control standard, ISO 9000.

The International Organization for Standardization (ISO) is an international agency headquartered in Geneva, Switzerland. The ISO was established to develop uniform international standards in certain specified areas. The ISO is composed of representatives from the national standards organizations of a number of countries; they have joined their efforts in an attempt to create certain uniform international standards. The first major success was in the area of quality control—ISO 9000.

ISO 9000 is not a standard. Rather, it is a mechanism providing a comprehensive review process and guidelines. By following this review process and the guidelines, companies can ensure that their products comply with the quality standards established for their industry. ISO 9000 is a set of five international standards concerning quality management and quality assurance in the production process. Firms that decide to participate in the program register with the national standards body and acquire an ISO number. As the number of registered firms increases, the importance of participation also increases. Many firms that are active in international trade require ISO 9000 participation as a condition of entering a contract. Quality standards may have a significant impact on international sales over the next few years.

It is quite possible that ISO 9000 compliance will become even more important in the future. Not only might ISO certification become mandatory for the importation of goods into some free trade zones, but the presence or absence of ISO 9000 certification might become an aspect of product liability litigation. Firms that possess such certification might, arguably, be deemed to satisfy minimum quality standards for their products unless the injured party can prove some form of negligence or some other basis for recovery. Firms that do not possess the certification might be presumed to lack the necessary minimum quality standards, placing the burden on the firm to establish its lack of liability. Such presumptions are merely speculative now, but as ISO 9000 certification expands, this could change.

Summary

Warranty law and product liability are two major areas of consumer protection—a subject that has been receiving an increasing amount of attention for some years. Warranty protection comes in two broad forms: express warranties, which are given by the seller; and implied warranties, which are imposed by law. There are also statutory warranty provisions, which are primarily concerned with disclosures to consumer-purchasers. Warranties are considered a part of the contract covering the sale of goods. Warranties may be excluded by the seller or surrendered by the buyer. The method of exclusion depends on the type of warranty involved.

Generally speaking, warranties extend to parties other than the buyer of the product, provided that the other parties are foreseeable users or consumers of the product. Each state has adopted one of three alternatives for the extension of warranty protections beyond the buyer of the goods.

The Magnuson-Moss Warranty Act provides statutory coverage in the warranty area. Magnuson-Moss provides for disclosure of the warranty protections extended to purchasers of consumer goods. It does not provide substantive protections for the purchasers, but it does provide a method for making consumer purchasers aware of what sorts of warranty protections are provided in the contract.

Under product liability, the manufacturer or the seller may be held liable because of negligence in making, designing, or packaging the product. The manufacturer may also be held strictly liable, despite any lack of due care. This is true if the product, in its normal use, is imminently or inherently dangerous.

Leases also carry protections for the lessee in the area of warranty law. Lessees can receive express warranties when the lessor creates a belief in the mind of the lessee as to the character, quality, or nature of the goods being leased. Lessees also enjoy the protection of four implied warranties analogous to the implied warranties of Article 2.

The CISG contains language that seems to provide for warranty coverage although the word "warranty" is not used. It provides that statements or conduct of the parties is to be interpreted as the parties intend, and if such intent cannot be ascertained, the statements or conduct is to be interpreted as a reasonable person would interpret them. This can be interpreted as allowing the parties to create express warranties if they so desire, or if a reasonable person would believe they had done so. The CISG also provides that the goods must be fit for their normal use and properly packaged, and must conform to any samples or models provided by the seller in order to be deemed as conforming to the contract. This is similar to the UCC's merchantability provisions. The CISG also states that goods must be suitable for a particular use of which the seller was aware at the time of the contract, unless the buyer can be shown not to have relied on the seller's expertise. This is similar to the UCC's fitness for a particular purpose provisions.

Discussion Questions

1. According to Article 2 of the UCC, what is necessary before a seller is deemed to give a buyer express warranties in a sales contract? What is necessary to give a lessee express warranties in a lease contract under Article 2A? Does the CISG make any provisions for the granting of express warranties in an international sale of goods?

2. What does a seller warrant to the buyer in the implied warranty of title? What does the lessor warrant to the lessee in the implied warranty against interference? Does the CISG have any comparable protections in its coverage?

3. When does a buyer of goods receive an implied warranty of merchantability under Article 2 of the UCC? When does the lessee of goods receive an implied warranty of merchantability under Article 2A of the UCC? What assurances does the buyer or lessee receive with this warranty? Does the CISG provide a warranty of merchantability under its coverage?

4. What is the purpose of the Magnuson-Moss Warranty Act? What is the difference between a full warranty and a limited warranty under the Magnuson-Moss Act?

5. What are the requirements that must be satisfied before a seller will be found liable for strict tort liability under § 402A of the Restatement (Second) of Torts?

6. Laura purchased a tool from Acme Corporation, a merchant. The tool was sold "as is—with no warranties of any kind, either express or implied." Laura was aware of this limitation at the time she purchased the tool. The tool Laura had purchased from Acme had, in fact, been stolen from Owen. Owen was able to trace the tool to Laura, and he was able to reclaim the tool from Laura. Laura is now seeking damages from Acme, alleging that Acme breached the warranty of title in the sale. Acme denies any liability, asserting that the sale "as is" protects it from liability. How should this case be decided?

7. Mildred was planning a dinner party for several of her friends. In preparation for the dinner, she purchased several pounds of seafood from the local grocer. Mildred followed the recipe for her seafood dish and prepared an entrée that looked and smelled wonderful. Unfortunately, the seafood was tainted, and all of Mildred's dinner guests suffered gastrointestinal distress following the meal. Several of the guests and Mildred are considering filing suit against the grocer, alleging that the seafood was not merchantable. The grocer admits that he may be liable to Mildred but denies any warranty liability to any of the guests, pointing out that none of the guests was in privity of contract with the grocer. Is the grocer liable to the guests for breach of the warranty of merchantability? How does the privity of contract assertion affect any potential liability of the grocer?

8. Bob is buying a stereo from Earl. Bob asks Earl about the distortion figures for the stereo. Earl does not know the correct answer, but he does not want Bob to realize his lack of knowledge. What will happen if Earl answers, and his answer is incorrect? How should Earl answer? What will a court look for in trying to determine whether Earl's answer, if he gives one, amounts to a warranty?

9. Warren leased an industrial vacuum sweeper for his business. The vacuum sweeper was advertised as a "wet-dry" vacuum, meaning that it could safely vacuum up either wet or dry objects. However, when Warren was using the vacuum sweeper to vacuum some water that had been spilled on the floor of his business he suffered a serious electrical shock. He filed suit against the vacuum sweeper manufacturer and the business from which he leased the item, alleging breach of express warranties. Both deny liability on two bases: that they did not give any express warranty on the product; and that even if they gave warranties to *purchasers* of the vacuum, they did not give warranties to *lessees* of the product. How should this case be resolved?

10. Rayex sold sunglasses advertised as safe for baseball. A high school athlete was using the baseball sunglasses when he misplayed a fly ball. The ball hit the glasses and they shattered, blinding the athlete in one eye. It was subsequently discovered that the lenses of the sunglasses were unreasonably thin and not impact-resistant. If the injured player decides to sue Rayex, what should be the basis of the lawsuit? If he *must* select just one basis for his lawsuit, should he sue alleging a breach of warranty, negligence on the part of Rayex, or strict product liability? Why did you make the selection you made?

Case Problems and Writing Assignments

1. Koster and each of the other plaintiffs suffered food poisoning from salmonella enteritidis (hereinafter salmonella) after dining at a restaurant operated by Scotch Associates on five separate days in May 1990. Each of the plaintiffs was served different foods and there is no direct evidence that any particular food was the cause of the food poisoning. There is some indication, however, that the raw eggs in the Caesar salad may have been the source of the salmonella. The plaintiffs contend that the restaurant is strictly liable. Scotch Associates responds that principles of strict liability are inapplicable to food served in a restaurant. It also argues that it cannot be liable to the plaintiffs for the harm caused to them because the source of the salmonella was the raw eggs that had been purchased from the third-party defendant and there was no way the restaurant could detect this problem. Is a restaurant selling goods or providing a service? Does the implied warranty of merchantability

attach to meals served in a restaurant? Is a restaurant strictly liable for serving adulterated food? See *Koster v. Scotch Associates*, 640 A.2d 1225 (N.J. Super. L. 1993).]

2. In 1989 TCA decided to update its computer system, which is used to process incoming orders, issue dispatching assignments, and store all distribution records. The information entered into the computer system is stored onto a backup system at 2:00 A.M. every day. TCA entered into an agreement to purchase an IBM computer system from ICC for $541,313.38. TCA subsequently executed a lease agreement that assigned IBM Credit Corporation its right to purchase the IBM equipment from ICC, but TCA retained possession and use of the computer system. The computer system was installed at TCA's offices on December 29, 1989. On December 19, 1990, almost a year later, the computer system went down and one of the disk drives revealed an error code. TCA properly contacted IBM, and IBM dispatched a service person. Although TCA requested a replacement disk drive, the error code indicated that the service procedure was not to replace any components but to analyze the disk drive. TCA had restarted the computer system and did not want to shut it down for the IBM service procedure. IBM informed TCA that replacement was not necessary under the limited warranty of repair or replace, and agreed to return on December 22, 1990, to analyze the disk drive. On December 21, 1990, the same disk drive completely failed, resulting in the computer system being inoperable until December 22, 1990. TCA alleges that the cumulative downtime for the computer system as a result of the disk drive failure was 33.91 hours. This includes the time to replace the disk drive, reload the electronic backup data, and manually reenter data that had been entered between 2:00 A.M. and the time the system failed. TCA alleged that it incurred a business interruption loss in the amount of $473,079.46 due to the disk crash and sued both IBM and ICC based on the failure of the disk drive. The suit alleged strict liability, negligence, breach of implied warranty, and breach of express warranty by both IBM and ICC. Can TCA assert a tort claim under these circumstances? Did the "repair or replace" warranty provisions IBM included in the contract provide the only warranty available to TCA? Was ICC's disclaimer of liability for consequential damages unconscionable? [See *Transport Corporation of America v. International Business Machines Corporation*, 30 F.3d 953 (8th Cir. 1994).]

3. On March 24, 1989, Dorothy Zimmerman was driving her 1987 Volkswagen Golf east on Franklin Road. While in the process of making a left turn, Dorothy's car was struck by a pickup truck that was traveling westbound on Franklin Road. Dorothy was alert and oriented but complained of left knee pain to the emergency medical technician responding to the accident. Dorothy was then transported to St. Alphonsus Hospital where she spoke with Dr. Austin Cushman. Dorothy told Dr. Cushman that she did not recall striking anything within the automobile during the accident and thought that she was relatively uninjured although she did note some pain above her waist on the right side. Shortly after speaking with Dr. Cushman, Dorothy became unresponsive and later died from

what Dr. Cushman concluded was an internal hemorrhage caused by a liver laceration. In Dr. Cushman's opinion, Dorothy's liver was torn from the inside outward when the restraint system in Dorothy's car caused her body to rapidly decelerate immediately after the collision and the entire force of that deceleration was imparted to her abdomen by the seat belt. The Zimmermans' complaint alleged causes of action against Volkswagen for strict product liability, negligence, and breach of warranty and including a claim for hedonic damages. The district court dismissed the Zimmermans' claim for hedonic damages pursuant to Volkswagen's motion, and the breach of warranty claim was dismissed by stipulation. The court subsequently granted Volkswagen's motion for summary judgment, finding that the Zimmermans' claims against Volkswagen were both expressly and impliedly preempted by applicable provisions of the National Traffic and Motor Vehicle Safety Act. The Zimmermans appealed from this ruling. Did the National Traffic and Motor Vehicle Safety Act preempt state law coverage of strict product liability and negligence in this case? Assuming that state law coverage has not been preempted, how should this case be decided? [See *Zimmerman v. Volkswagen of America, Inc.*, 920 P.2d 67 (Idaho 1996).]

4. In 1986, Chrysler Credit Corporation entered into a financing agreement with Preston Highway Chrysler/Plymouth, a car dealership in Louisville, Kentucky. The agreement gave Chrysler a perfected security interest in all of Preston's equipment, furniture, fixtures, machinery, tools, and leasehold improvements. In August 1990, Preston defaulted on the agreement and thereafter voluntarily surrendered all of its assets to Chrysler in September 1990. One of those assets was a Wash Pac unit manufactured by Brite-O-Matic. The Wash Pac unit had been leased by Preston, but there were no records of the lease and Chrysler believed that Preston had purchased the unit from Brite-O-Matic. Subsequently, Chrysler held an auction to dispose of the collateral, and the Wash Pac was purchased by Landmark Motors. Soon after the auction Brite-O-Matic contacted Chrysler claiming that it had title to the Wash Pac and wanted the unit returned. Chrysler then contacted Landmark, explained what had happened, and requested the return of the Wash Pac. Chrysler also offered to refund the purchase price to Landmark. Landmark refused, asserting that it qualified as a bona fide purchaser for value, and that as such it had title to the unit. Who is entitled to the Wash Pac unit? What rights, if any, can Landmark assert against Chrysler? Did Chrysler breach the implied warranty of title in its sale to Landmark? How should the case be resolved? [See *Landmark Motors, Inc. v. Chrysler Credit Corporation*, 662 N.E.2d 971 (Ind. App. 1996).]

5. BUSINESS APPLICATION CASE Craig Cover received a patent from the U.S. Patent Office for a lighting fixture system having a batt of thermal insulation to protect the wiring from heat produced by the bulb. Cover then entered into an exclusive license arrangement with Pacor to commercialize the patent. Thereafter, Pacor began to supply multilayered batts of insulation to Sea Gull, which designated these insulation units as parts number 6254 and 6255. Pacor did *not* mark the insula-

tion units with the patent number as required by law. Pacor sold these units to Sea Gull until 1993. Beginning in 1988, Sea Gull also ordered parts number 6254 and 6255 from Hydramatic. Sea Gull provided Hydramatic with drawings and specifications for the parts and Hydramatic produced and delivered the parts to Sea Gull. When Cover discovered that Sea Gull was purchasing his patented lighting system from someone other than the exclusive license holder (Pacor), he filed suit against both the buyer (Sea Gull) and the producer (Hydramatic) of the allegedly infringing items. Eventually, Cover reached out-of-court settlements with both Sea Gull and Hydramatic. Hydramatic then sued Sea Gull, alleging that Sea Gull had breached the warranty against infringements by providing specifications for specially manufactured goods that infringed a valid patent. Sea Gull denied liability, alleging that it neither knew that the design was for a patented product nor had any notice of the patent in question. Sea Gull also claimed that the federal patent law preempted the enforceability of the UCC, so that Hydramatic should be precluded from seeking recovery. How should this case be resolved? Is the preemption argument asserted by Sea Gull persuasive? What steps should a business that has a patent on a process follow in order to maximize its protection of its rights under the patent? [See *Cover v. Hydramatic Packing Co.,* 83 F.3d 1390 (Fed. Cir. 1996).]

6. **ETHICAL APPLICATION CASE** Dr. Homsy, a former DuPont research engineer, invented Proplast—a semisoft, porous, spongy material—while doing prosthetic research at Methodist Hospital at Houston, Texas, in 1968. Proplast was produced by combining Teflon, carbon, solvents, and other ingredients. Homsy founded Vitek in 1969 to manufacture and distribute his Proplast prosthetic devices while he continued his research at Methodist Hospital. Vitek patented Proplast in 1976. One of the devices Vitek sold was the Proplast Interpositional Implant designed to correct temporomandibular joint disorders (TMJ). When Homsy first attempted to purchase Teflon from DuPont, he was warned by DuPont that Teflon was an "industrial material" that was "not made for medical use." The FDA authorized the sale of Proplast TMJ implants in 1983. Rynders had Proplant implants surgically placed in her jaw by oral surgeons in 1985 to correct her TMJ disorder. The Proplast implants were removed in 1988, at the recommendation of Rynders's oral surgeon, because she continued to suffer from TMJ problems. The oral surgeon observed that the removed implants had fractured and that the bony surfaces of Rynders's TMJ had eroded since the implant procedure. Rynders sued DuPont, alleging product liability, breach of the implied warranties of merchantability and fitness for a particular purpose, strict liability, and negligence. DuPont denied liability. It pointed out the disclaimers and warnings that were sent to Dr. Homsy and to Vitek regarding the inappropriateness of using Teflon in medical procedures. However, Rynders argued that DuPont knew Vitek was using the Teflon for medical purposes and continued to provide Vitek with the Teflon Vitek ordered. She asserted that DuPont had a duty not to sell the product to

Vitek if DuPont knew Vitek was using the product improperly. How should the court resolve this case? Is it ethical for a business to sell its products to a buyer if the business knows—or should know—that the buyer is using the product in a manner that poses a substantial risk to the buyer's customers? Should a business be, in effect, "its brother's keeper" in such a situation? [See *Rynders v. E.I. DuPont, DeNemours & Co.,* 21 F.3d 835 (8th Cir. 1994).]

7. **CRITICAL THINKING CASE** Jackie Tipton, owner and operator of Tipton Motor Company, was attempting to mount a used Michelin tire on what Tipton thought was a 16-inch rim manufactured by Kelsey-Hayes. In reality, the rim was 16.5 inches, causing what is known in the tire industry as a "mismatch" situation. Using a mounting machine, Tipton placed the uninflated tire on the rim and "seated" the tire's bead against the rim's flanges. Once a tire is properly seated it can be safely inflated to its normal operating pressure. However, in a mismatch situation there is a danger of the tire bursting during inflation since it cannot be properly seated due to the mismatch. Tipton removed the tire from the mounting machine and began to inflate it without realizing that the bead was not properly seated. He exceeded the recommended tire pressure while inflating the tire, and the tire exploded. The explosion catapulted the entire tire assembly toward Tipton, striking him and causing severe injuries. Tipton sued Michelin, alleging negligence and strict liability against each of the parties. How should the court resolve this case? Can the court find Michelin liable based on negligence, but not liable based on product liability? [See *Tipton v. Michelin Tire Company,* 101 F.3d 1145 (6th Cir. 1996).]

8. **YOU BE THE JUDGE** Alex Hardy was driving his Chevrolet S-10 Blazer when he was involved in a one-vehicle accident. Hardy was thrown from the vehicle, allegedly because the door latch failed, and he suffered serious and permanent injuries as a result of the accident. Hardy was paralyzed from the waist down. During the trial, Hardy admitted that he had been drinking beer immediately before he began his fateful drive. He also admitted that he was not wearing a seat belt at the time of the accident. Finally, he admitted that he had fallen asleep at the wheel of his vehicle while driving and was asleep at the time of the accident. However, Hardy also asserted that none of these factors was involved in the crash or the subsequent injuries. According to Hardy's theory, the axle of the truck broke, causing the crash. As a result of the crash, the vehicle rolled over, the door latch failed, and Hardy was thrown from the truck. Thus, according to Hardy, the vehicle did not conform to his expectations, the defects were hidden so that a reasonable inspection would not reveal them, and General Motors was in breach of its contract. A jury awarded Hardy $50 million in compensatory damages, and an additional $100 million in punitive damages. General Motors has appealed this case to *your* court. How will *you* rule on this appeal? See "GM Vows to Appeal Verdict," *The National Law Journal,* p. A12 (The New York Law Publishing Company, June 17, 1996).

Notes

1. *Black's Law Dictionary*, rev. 6th ed. (St. Paul, Minn.: West Group, 1990), 1586.
2. UCC § 2-313(1).
3. UCC § 2-313(2).
4. 210 P.2d 348 (Supp. Ct. Okla. 1949).
5. 198 N.E.2d 309 (1964).
6. 217 N.Y. 382, 111 N.E. logo (1916).
7. CISG Article 35(2)(a).
8. CISG Article 35(2)(b).

PART 5

Negotiables

Negotiables can take many forms. Negotiable *instruments* consist of checks, notes, drafts, and certificates of deposit. All of these forms are governed by Revised Article 3 of the Uniform Commercial Code (UCC), "Negotiable Instruments." Checks are also governed to a significant extent by Article 4 of the UCC, "Bank Deposits and Collections." Negotiables can also take the form of negotiable documents of title. Documents of title are governed by Article 7 of the UCC, "Warehouse Receipts, Bills of Lading and Other Documents of Title." Article 8, "Investment Securities," also deals with an area historically included with "negotiables." Our emphasis in this section will be on negotiable instruments, although we will also address negotiable documents to a limited extent.

In general, negotiable instruments are short-term instruments that arise out of commercial transactions. Millions of such instruments are signed each day, not only because they are a safe and convenient means of doing business, but also because they are acceptable in the commercial world as credit instruments and/or as substitutes for money. Documents of title are not as widely used, but they also have an important place in our commercial law.

This part of the text explains how and why negotiables are widely used and accepted in the modern commercial world. In addition, the topics of funds transfers (Article 4A of the UCC), electronic funds transfers and bank-customer relations will be discussed.

CHAPTER 20

Introduction to Negotiables: UCC Article 3 and Article 7

AGENDA

NRW NRW will need an initial source of funds in order to get established. Mai, Carlos, and Helen may need to obtain loans for the business. What will they need to do, and what legal implications may arise if they sign promissory notes on behalf of the firm?

The business will have bills and obligations that it needs to meet periodically. Should NRW try to pay all of its bills in cash, or should the firm have some sort of checking account? If a checking account is opened, what legal rights and duties will be involved for the firm? For the principals?

Many customers of NRW will wish to pay their bills by check. Accepting these checks will create a risk, albeit small, for NRW. Should the firm have a policy against accepting checks in order to avoid this risk? What might such a policy mean for the firm and its chances of success?

NRW will be shipping goods to a number of customers, over a—hopefully—increasing geographic area. The firm will also be receiving shipments from a number of different producers. How should these shipments be handled? Should the firm use negotiable documents of title, or should it insist that all documents of title be nonnegotiable? What legal significance is attached to the negotiability of the documents used by the firm?

These and other questions will arise during our discussion of negotiability law. Be prepared! You never know when the firm or one of its members will seek your advice.

Historical Overview

An industrial or a commercial society needs to have some documents or instruments in order to function efficiently. Documents and instruments provide evidence of the transactions and also provide convenience for their users. When goods are transported or stored, some document is needed to reflect their transportation or their storage. When goods are sold and paid for, unless the sale is a cash transaction, some instrument or documentation is needed to reflect the payment while providing some safety for the parties involved. This is especially true if the transaction is not a "face-to-face" transaction, since sending cash payments by means of the mail or commercial carrier is, at best, somewhat risky.

Negotiable instruments of various types have been present in nearly every society that has developed a substantial commercial system. Instruments very similar to the contemporary promissory note date back to about 2100 B.C. The merchants of Europe were using negotiable documents and instruments on a broad scale by the 13th century. In fact, the use of drafts was so widespread that a substantial portion of the law merchant was devoted to the proper treatment of these instruments.

Negotiable instruments had become so pervasive by the late 19th century that the British Parliament enacted the Bills of Exchange Act in 1882 to govern their use in Great Britain. Following the example of Parliament, the National Conference of Commissioners on Uniform State Laws drafted the Uniform Negotiable Instruments Law (NIL) for the United States in 1896. Each of these statutes merely attempted to codify and formalize the common law rules that had been developed over the years in their respective nations. In the United States, the NIL was designed to unify and codify the rules and laws of each jurisdiction regarding all negotiable commercial documents. However, since negotiable commercial documents included checks, drafts, notes, certificates of deposit, bills of lading, warehouse receipts, and investment securities, the breadth of the topical coverage made the NIL unwieldy and difficult to apply to the commercial world of the 20th century.

One of the objectives of the Uniform Commercial Code (UCC) is to comply more readily with the demands of the modern business world. By the mid-20th century, it was obvious that the coverage of the NIL was too broad. In an effort to reflect "commercial reality," the topical coverage contained in the NIL was updated and divided into different articles, and these articles were then included in the UCC. The original Article 3, "Commercial Paper," dealt only with negotiable *instruments* in their various forms.

Other articles dealt with other aspects of what had been covered for the previous 50-plus years by the NIL.

The Code has been adopted by every state in the union except Louisiana, and Louisiana has adopted some portions, including the original Articles 3 and 4, which deal with commercial paper and with bank-customer relations. However, changes in banking laws and banking practices, and the increased use of instruments that were not covered by the original Article 3 (e.g., "share drafts" issued by credit unions) led the National Conference of Commissioners on Uniform State Laws (NCCUSL) to develop and propose the 1990 revision of Article 3 and the related amendments to Article 4.

Articles 3 and 4 are based on a paper payment system, and that system has changed dramatically. In the early 1950s, about seven billion checks were processed annually.[1] However, the American Banking Association anticipated a major increase in checking activities and developed the MICR[2] line technology, a more efficient method for processing checks. By 1988, the Federal Reserve estimated that approximately 48 billion checks were written annually,[3] and nearly 50 billion checks, worth about $47.4 *trillion* dollars, were written in 2000.[4] See http://www.bankrate.com/msn/news/cc/20020212a.asp/ for more details. There were also some changes in federal banking law, especially in the Expedited Funds Availability Act,[5] and with the Federal Reserve, which enacted Regulation CC.[6]

The revision to Article 3 involved a change of name, to "Negotiable Instruments," and a change in scope, to encompass more types of instruments. The amendments to Article 4, "Bank Deposits and Collections," not only take into account the changes to Article 3 but also more accurately reflect modern banking practices and contemporary usage of instruments. As of May 1999, the Revised Articles 3 and 4 have been adopted in 48 states and the District of Columbia (New York and South Carolina have not yet adopted the revised version). As a result, our coverage here will discuss only Revised Article 3, which will henceforth be referred to simply as Article 3. You can see Article 3 at http://www.law.cornell.edu/ucc/3/overview.html.

In revising Articles 3 and 4, the UCC's treatment of negotiable instruments has been modified to reflect modern commercial reality. The articles now provide statutory treatment that is in line with the advances provided by growth and technology, and with the changes in federal laws and banking practices. You can see Article 4 at http://www.law.cornell.edu/ucc/4/overview.html.

The UCC has also standardized and clarified the rules governing documents of title. Both warehouse receipts and bills of lading are covered in Article 7 of the Code. Article 7 retains many of the traditional rules and views of documents of title, while also codifying the contemporary use of these documents in the U.S. legal system. You can see Article 7 at http://www.law.cornell.edu/ucc/7/overview. html. Each of these articles will be discussed in some detail in the remainder of this chapter.

The Scope of Article 3

Article 3 of the Uniform Commercial Code covers *negotiable instruments*. A negotiable instrument is a written promise or order to pay money to the order of a named person or to bearer. Although Article 3 provides most of the coverage of negotiable instruments, there are also provisions in other articles of the UCC that affect negotiable instruments. For example, a number of definitions from Article 1 apply in Article 3. Article 4, "Bank Deposits and Collections," and Article 9, "Secured Transactions," also affect the coverage of negotiable instruments. In fact, Article 3 specifies that its own provisions are "subject to" the coverage in Articles 4 and 9.[7] The scope of Article 3 is somewhat narrow, restricted solely to negotiable instruments, as defined in § 3-104. Further, § 3-102(a) states that Article 3 does *not* apply to money, to payment orders governed by Article 4A, or to securities governed by Article 8. Thus, one finds that Article 3 covers negotiable instruments but not other types of commercial or negotiable documents, and that two other articles of the Code may supplement, complement, or override the provisions of Article 3. To fall within the coverage of Article 3, an instrument must qualify as a "negotiable instrument." If an instrument does not qualify, it is likely to be governed by common law provisions, primarily in the area of contract law.

The revision to Article 3 provides for substantially different coverage of negotiable instruments and also significantly expands the definition of what constitutes a negotiation instrument. This new treatment is found in § 3-104. This section is important enough, and complex enough, that we have reproduced it virtually in its entirety, with the first portion set out here and the balance set out in Functions and Forms, below.

Section 3-104. Negotiable Instrument.

(a) *Except as provided in subsections (c) and (d), "negotiable instrument" means an unconditional promise or order to pay a fixed amount of money, with or without interest or other charges described in the promise or order, if it:*

1) *is payable to bearer or to order at the time it is issued or first comes into possession of a holder;*

2) *is payable on demand or at a definite time; and*

3) *does not state any other undertaking or instruction by the person promising or ordering payment to do any act in addition to the payment of money, but the promise or order may contain (i) an undertaking or power to give, maintain, or protect collateral to secure payment, (ii) an authorization or power to the holder to confess judgment or realize on or dispose of collateral, or (iii) a waiver of the benefit of any law intended for the advantage or protection of an obligor.*

(b) *"Instrument" means a negotiable instrument.*

(c) *An order that meets all of the requirements of subsection (a) except paragraph (1), and otherwise falls within the definition of "check" in subsection (f) is a negotiable instrument and a check.*

(d) *A promise or order other than a check is not an instrument if, at the time it is issued or first comes into possession of a holder, it contains a conspicuous statement, however expressed, to the effect that the promise or order is not negotiable or is not an instrument governed by this article.*

Thus, the first part of § 3-104 gives us the broad general outline of what constitutes a negotiable instrument. It is an unconditional promise or order to pay a fixed amount of money, and it contains no other "undertaking" or "instruction" by the person who promised or ordered the payment. Notice, also, that a negotiable instrument must be payable "to bearer" or "to order" at the time it is issued or first comes into the possession of a holder *unless* the instrument qualifies as a check. A check will be considered negotiable even if it lacks this wording, the "words of negotiability" that are discussed in Chapter 21. It should also be noted that any writing that looks like an instrument *except a check* will *not* be negotiable (and hence, not an instrument) if it contains a conspicuous statement that it is not negotiable.

This means that a person who issues a *check* must abide by the provisions of Article 3, even if the check does not contain "words of negotiability," but a person who issues any other type of writing that *appears* to be an instrument may opt out of Article 3's coverage by placing a conspicuous term on the face of the instrument excluding it from treatment as a negotiable instrument.

The following case dealt with a criminal law issue, not a common topic to cover when discussing negotiable instruments. Note, however, that the case involved an alleged "uttering" of a money order—an instrument that histori-cally was viewed as *not* being a negotiable instrument. Also notice how the defendants tried to argue for a lesser charge based on their interpretation of a few of the provisions of Article 3.

20.1

STATE OF UTAH, v. BARRICK
2002 Utah App 120; 46 P.3d 770; 445 Utah Adv. Rep. 28; 2002 Utah App. LEXIS 32

FACTS The defendants, Barrick and Johnston, allegedly found or otherwise acquired a money order. At the time of their acquisition, the money order had the signature and address of the purchaser, but the payee line was blank. The purchaser apparently bought the money order to pay a utility bill and did not know either of the defendants. One of the defendants wrote the name "Amber Barrick" on the blank payee line, endorsed the money order, and then cashed it. The defendants were charged with forgery, a third-degree felony under Utah law. The defendants entered a plea of guilty to attempted forgery, conditional upon their right to appeal the denial of their motion to dismiss the forgery charge and their convictions for attempted forgery.

ISSUES Did the filling in of a name on the blank payee line change the legal significance of the instrument? Did the actions of the defendants constitute forgery, or was it merely a theft of lost property, a misdemeanor under Utah law?

HOLDINGS Yes, the filling in of the name changed the legal significance of the instrument. Yes, the conduct of the defendants constituted a forgery under Utah law, and not merely the theft of a lost or mislaid instrument.

REASONING Excerpts from the opinion of Judge Bench:

"In interpreting a statute we give the words their usual and accepted meaning." . . . We first examine the statute's plain language, resorting to other methods of statutory interpretation only if the language is ambiguous. . . . The Forgery Statute provides, in part, that

(1) A person is guilty of forgery if, with purpose to defraud anyone, or with knowledge that he is facilitating a fraud to be perpetrated by any-one, he:

    (a) alters any writing of another without his authority or utters any such altered writing; or

    (b) makes [or] completes . . . or utters any writing so that the writing or the making, [or the] completion . . . or [the] utterance pur-ports to be the act of another, whether the person is existent or nonexistent. . . .

Defendants do not contest that they had "purpose to defraud" or "knowledge" that they were facilitating a fraud. The requirements for forgery . . . are accordingly met. Therefore, we consider Defendants' actions and arguments in the order listed in the Forgery Statute: first looking at the issue of altering a writing without authority as stated in subsection (1)(a), and then con-sidering whether Defendants completed or uttered the writing as specified in subsection (1)(b).

The language of the Forgery Statute is plain and unam-biguous and we "give the words their usual and accepted meaning." . . . "When language is clear and unam-biguous, it must be held to mean what it expresses, and no room is left for construction." . . . Defendants argue that the trial court erred when it concluded that their actions constituted forgery. . . . Defendants contend that their actions did not change the legal significance of the instrument. Subsection (1)(a) of the Forgery Statute states that anyone who "alters any writing of another without his authority" is guilty of forgery. . . . The pur-chaser of the money order did not know either Defen-dant. Therefore, Defendants did not have the authority to alter or add anything to the money order. Inserting Barrick's name into the blank payee line clearly altered the money order. . . . Specifically, the money order was altered by Defendants in at least three respects. First, Defendants' conduct subverted the purchaser's intent as to who was to be paid by the money order. Second, the face of the money order was altered according to the meaning of "alter" by filling in a line that was left blank. Finally, as we discuss below, Defendants' conduct "altered" the writing within the meaning of the Forgery Statute by converting the money order from a bearer instrument to an order instrument, which changes the legal significance of the instrument. . . .

Section [3-109 of the Uniform Commercial Code] delin-eates the difference between a bearer instrument and an order instrument. That section provides, in part, that

(1) A promise or order is payable to bearer if it:

  (a) states that it is payable to bearer or to the order of bearer . . . ;

  (b) does not state a payee; or

  (c) states that it is payable to or to the order of cash or otherwise indicates that it is not payable to an identified person.

(2) A promise or order that is not payable to bearer is payable to order if it is payable to the order of an identified person, or to an identified person or order. A promise or order that is payable to order is payable to the identified person.

A bearer instrument "does not state a payee" while an order instrument is "payable to order if it is payable to the order of an identified person." . . . When Defendants filled in one of their names on the blank payee line, the instrument ceased to be a bearer instrument and became payable to the order of an identified person. The newly created order instrument restricted who could receive payment and changed the obligation of the parties to the money order. . . . Defendants' actions therefore "altered" the writing by changing the instrument from bearer to order, and in the process changed the instrument's legal significance. . . .

Defendants also assert that the term "completes," as used in subsection (1)(b) of the Forgery Statute, refers to the negotiability of the instrument as specified in the UCC. Defendants urge that the money order with a blank payee line was a completed, negotiable instrument. . . . It is well settled by authority that the omission to insert in an instrument the name of a payee is not a feature or a defect which affects negotiability. The effect of the omission to name a payee is to invest any bona fide holder with the authority to fill in the blank left for that purpose by the drawer or maker. Such instruments are payable to the bearer until restricted in their currency as negotiable instruments by the insertion of the name of some particular payee. . . . The court used this language to conclude that the defendant's instrument was a check, although the payee section was left blank. . . . The Forgery Statute states that a person is guilty of forgery if the person completes "any writing so that the writing . . . purports to be the act of another." . . . A money order is clearly a writing . . . and Defendants do not challenge that their writing purported to be the act of another. . . . Based on the ordinary meaning of complete, Defendants "completed" a writing by inserting one of their names into the blank payee line. This action completed an order instrument that prior to the entering of Barrick's name was incomplete as an order instrument, and by so doing purported to be the act of the purchaser in designating Barrick as the intended payee. . . . Accordingly, we conclude that the Defendants also "completed" the writing.

Finally, Defendants contend that they did not "utter" the instrument as the term is used in the Forgery Statute. When the Defendants cashed the forged instrument, they, in effect, uttered the instrument. . . .

We conclude that the trial court did not err in denying Defendants' motion to dismiss, and in finding that Defendants' actions legally constituted the offense of forgery. The decision of the trial court is therefore affirmed.

BUSINESS CONSIDERATIONS Should a business that sells money orders have a policy requiring its employees to warn money order purchasers of the potential danger of financial loss if the money orders are left incomplete? Why would a purchaser *not* have the money order completed by the entity from whom it was purchased?

ETHICAL CONSIDERATIONS Is it ethical to sell money orders to purchasers-remitters with the payee line left blank *and* without warning the customer of the risk? Is an oral warning of the risk sufficient?

Uses of Negotiable Instruments

Negotiable instruments are widely used in our economy: They are used as a substitute for money. They are used for convenience. They are used as credit instruments. They are used to pay bills, to buy things, and to borrow. Some of the most important uses of each type are set out in the following sections.

Checks

The most commonly used type of negotiable instrument is a check. Many people use checks rather than cash for daily purchases. Checks are regularly written to the supermarket for groceries, to the utility companies to pay bills, to the landlord to pay the rent, and to the bank to make loan payments. In addition, many working people receive their salaries or wages in periodic paychecks from their employers. (Of course, many people also now have automatic deposits of their pay made electronically. This is a type of electronic funds transfer, one of the topics discussed in Chapter 24.)

Checks are widely used because they are easily written, easily carried, and widely accepted. Carrying and using checks is safer than carrying and using cash. If a person loses a blank, unsigned check, no harm is likely to occur. All that was lost was a piece of paper. However, if a person loses cash, the money is gone. The bank will not take an unsigned check, but it will take lost money. Great care should be taken with checks, particularly signed ones. A signed check, otherwise blank, is nearly as good as cash. Anyone finding such a check can complete the blanks and possibly receive cash for it as completed, to the detriment of the depositor-"drawer."

The revision to Article 3 recognizes a number of specialized drafts as "checks" within the coverage of § 3-104. Each of these specialized checks has the primary use of serving as a substitute for money. However, they also have some aspect that distinguishes them from traditional or "regular" checks. For example, a cashier's check is a check drawn by a bank against that same bank and then issued to the person who purchased it. Cashier's checks and teller's checks are commonly used by a purchaser who wants to guarantee payment to the payee. Both cashier's checks and teller's checks are treated as "cash equivalents" by the payee, based on the assumption that the bank will honor the check upon presentment.[8] The bank issuing the cashier's or teller's check is referred to as the "obligated bank," and it must honor the check unless the bank itself has a reason for nonpayment. Any alleged defenses by the remitter cannot be used by the bank to avoid liability.[9] Payees are willing to accept either of these checks because the payee knows that there are sufficient funds available, and because the issuing bank is not likely to have any reason not to pay the check upon proper presentment. The case on pages 477–478 dealt with a cashier's check. The court analyzed *when* a cashier's check is transferred, but it also addressed the issue of whether a bank can stop payment on a cashier's check.

A traveler's check is a special type of check used by people who are away from home and want the security of having checks that will be accepted. A traveler's check is signed once by the drawer upon purchase, but it requires a second signing by that same drawer (a countersigning) before it can be negotiated. The payee knows that a bank is holding the funds used to purchase the traveler's check, so there is no danger of insufficient funds; and the payee can compare the countersignature to the "authenticating" original signature, minimizing the risk of a forgery. A credit union check (formerly called a "share draft") is simply a check drawn against a credit union. As banks become more and more specialized, many individuals are turning to credit

unions to handle their personal banking needs simply because the credit union specializes in individual accounts, and the fees imposed are normally substantially less.

Drafts

Businesses often use drafts to pay for merchandise ordered, especially when the buyer and the seller are in

---

NRW CASE 20.1   Finance

COMAKERS FOR COMPANY LOANS

When NRW was first formed, the firm needed to borrow some money. The bank's lending officer seemed very willing to make the loan, but not if the borrower was going to be NRW alone. She insisted that the principals had to be comakers of the note, with each signing the note as both an individual and as a principal of NRW. While they were not comfortable with this arrangement, the three principals agreed to the terms because they needed the funds the loan would provide. Afterward, Mai felt that the bank had treated them unfairly and suggested that they seek a new bank for future activities. Carlos and Helen were not sure they had been treated unfairly. They have asked for your advice. What will you tell them?

BUSINESS CONSIDERATIONS It is common in business classes to discuss the advantages and disadvantages of various forms of business. One advantage that is normally cited for a corporation is limited liability for the investors. However, when a corporation is newly formed, it has no "track record" upon which a bank can rely. Should a bank refuse to lend money to a newly formed corporation until it has established itself? Should it insist that the principals act as copromisors on any loans?

ETHICAL CONSIDERATIONS Is it ethical for the principals in a business to attempt to avoid any potential liability by forming a corporation, an LLP, or an LLC?

INTERNATIONAL CONSIDERATIONS Do other nations provide business organizations that may be more beneficial to the principals than the forms that are available in the United States? Should a businessperson look for a domicile nation based on the potential personal liability he or she might face if the business does not succeed?

20.2

IN RE MORA
218 B.R. 71; 1998 Bankr. LEXIS 218

FACTS On March 1, 1995, the Moras purchased a cashier's check from their California bank in the amount of $24,660.27 made payable to BancBoston Mortgage Corporation. This money was intended to reduce the principal balance owing on the Moras' home mortgage. That same day they placed the cashier's check in the U.S. mail. The next day, March 2, 1995, the Moras filed a voluntary petition under Chapter 7 of the Bankruptcy Code. The cashier's check arrived at BancBoston on March 6, 1995, and on March 7, 1995, was credited toward the principal balance owing on their mortgage.

The Trustee contacted BancBoston and demanded return of the $24,660.27 payment, claiming that it was an illegal postpetition transfer of estate property. In September 1995, BancBoston turned over the money to the Trustee and charged the amount back to the Moras' mortgage account. In July 1996, the Moras filed an amended complaint against the Trustee and Banc-Boston seeking declaratory relief that the returned money was not property of the estate and that the Trustee had converted the money. As an affirmative defense, the Trustee claimed the payment was an avoidable postpetition transfer of estate property. At trial, the court ruled for the Moras and ordered the Trustee to return the payment to BancBoston, finding that the transfer of the cashier's check occurred at the time it was placed in the mail, and that it was placed in the mail prior to the petition.

ISSUE Did the bankruptcy court err in holding that the transfer of an interest in a cashier's check occurs at the time the check is mailed?

HOLDING Yes, the bankruptcy court erred. A transfer of a cashier's check occurs when the check is in the physical possession or control of the intended payee.

REASONING Excerpts from the opinion of Bankruptcy Judge Russell:

Section 549(a) of the [Bankruptcy] Code permits the Trustee to avoid a postpetition transfer of estate property. Section 550(a)(1) permits a trustee to recover the amount of the avoidable transfer from the initial transferee. . . . To avoid a transfer under § 549(a), the Trustee must show that after commencement of the bankruptcy in question, property of the estate was transferred and the transfer was not authorized by the bankruptcy court or the Code. . . . The parties in this case agree, and the

bankruptcy court held, that under California law Debtors had an interest in the cashier's check prior to mailing it to BancBoston. . . . And, Debtors do not contend that mailing the cashier's check to BancBoston was authorized by either the Code or the bankruptcy court. . . . On appeal, the Trustee asserts that Debtor's sending of the cashier's check to BancBoston was an avoidable postpetition transfer of estate property because the check was delivered to and cashed by BancBoston after Debtors filed bankruptcy. Debtors claim they transferred the cashier's check prepetition because it was mailed to BancBoston . . . prior to them declaring bankruptcy.

When a cashier's check is specifically deemed transferred for purposes of § 549(a) appears to be an unanswered question. "Transfer" is broadly defined by the Code as "every mode, direct or indirect, absolute or conditional, voluntary or involuntary, of disposing of or parting with property or with an interest in property, including retention of title as a security interest and foreclosure of the debtor's equity of redemption." . . . Quoting § 101(54)'s legislative history, we have recognized that this definition of transfer includes any transfer of "possession, custody, or control." . . . What constitutes a transfer and when it is complete is a question of federal law. . . . In the absence of any controlling federal law, "property" and "an interest in property" are creatures of state law. . . .

In *In re Lee* . . . the Panel examined whether the transfer of a cashier's check for purposes of § 547(b) occurs at the time it is issued or at the time the check is delivered to its intended recipient. In *Lee* we held that a transfer occurs at the time a cashier's check is delivered. . . . The transfer analysis for § 547(b) and § 549(a) is analogous. . . . However, *Lee* apparently left unclear the crucial question of when delivery is effectuated. Does delivery occur at the time the purchaser of the cashier's check relinquishes physical possession of the check by transmitting it or at the time it is actually received by the intended payee? In this case, the bankruptcy court examined *Lee* and held that delivery was effectuated when the cashier's check was deposited in the mail because Debtors lost physical possession of the check, thereby placing it in the constructive possession of BancBoston. In reaching this conclusion, the bankruptcy court relied upon *Lee*'s determination that under California law the drawer of the cashier's check, Debtors here, have no right to stop payment of the cashier's check once it leaves their physical possession. . . . However, the bankruptcy court's analysis of *Lee* was inaccurate. In *Lee*, we held that "until delivery, the purchaser's property rights in the cashier's check are not transferred to the payee/holder." . . . We stated that the "negotiable instruments provisions [of the California Commercial Code] are predicated on the rights of a holder, and one cannot be a holder without possession." . . . Thus *Lee* equated date of delivery as the date the cashier's check is in the physical possession of the payee. In that case, we explicitly found that the transfer of the cashier's check occurred on the date the intended recipient actually received the check from the debtor. . . .

While not controlling, the Uniform Commercial Code also supports the conclusion we reach. California has largely adopted the U.C.C. . . . Uniform Commercial Code § 3-203(a) . . . defines transfer of a cashier's check as occurring "when it is delivered by a person other than its issuer for the purpose of giving to the person receiving delivery the right to enforce the instrument." "'Delivery' with respect to instruments, documents of title, chattel paper or certificated securities means voluntary transfer of possession." . . . Possession is commonly understood as "the act of having or taking into control." . . .

In this case, it is undisputed that BancBoston was not in physical possession of the cashier's check until March 6, 1995, after Debtors filed their bankruptcy petition on March 2. Nor could BancBoston have taken control of the cashier's check until it physically received it. The bankruptcy court, however, concluded that BancBoston had constructive possession of the cashier's check at the time of mailing because Debtors "could not ask for a return of the cashier's check out of the mail, or divert its delivery, and it is unlikely that the bank which made the cashier's check could honor a request to stop payment." This conclusion is inaccurate. While it is true that Debtors had no right to stop payment of the cashier's check once it left their possession, under the U.C.C. a bank can refuse to pay the cashier's check as an accommodation to its customer.* . . . A rule making transfer of a cashier's check effective merely by mailing it would thus ignore common business practice and common sense. A transfer of a cashier's check for purposes of 11 U.S.C. § 549(a) occurs when the check is in the physical possession or control of the intended payee. The bankruptcy court's conclusion that the cashier's check was in the constructive possession of BancBoston at the time the check was mailed is erroneous. The transfer of the check in this case occurred postpetition and is thus an avoidable transfer of estate property.

We **REVERSE** and direct the bankruptcy court to enter judgment in favor of the Trustee.

*We recognize that it would be unusual for a bank to honor a request not to pay on a cashier's check it issued because the U.C.C. provides banks with every incentive to honor their cashier's checks. Under [§ 3-411(b)] a bank that refuses or stops payment on the cashier's check is potentially liable for expenses, lost interest resulting from nonpayment, and consequential damages if it receives notice of the particular circumstances giving rise to such damages. Section 3-411 is specifically designed to discourage the practice of dishonoring cashier's checks. . . . Nevertheless, the fact that Debtors' bank could choose not to honor the cashier's check is an additional factor in finding that the check was not in the possession of BancBoston merely because it was mailed.

BUSINESS CONSIDERATIONS Why would a business return money paid on one of its customer's accounts to the bankruptcy trustee? Is there a valid business reason for *refusing* to return the money? Does the form of payment (i.e., check, credit card, cash) enter into your decision?

ETHICAL CONSIDERATIONS Is it ethical for a creditor to "return" money paid by one of its customers to a bankruptcy Trustee, and to then adjust the customer's account balance before the customer has had his or her "day in court"?

different states. Drafts may be payable "at sight" (i.e., on demand), or they may be "time drafts" (i.e., they are payable at a future date). Often a seller of goods will send a draft to the buyer for acceptance. If the buyer accepts, he or she has agreed to pay any holder who makes proper presentment. Such a draft is called a trade acceptance.

With the recent liberalization of federal and state banking laws and regulations, a number of changes have occurred in the area of negotiable instruments. One of these changes has been in the area of drafts. Today some financial institutions other than banks offer accounts similar to the checking accounts offered by banks. These drafting accounts offer the same privileges for these depositors as are available to depositors of banks. Technically, however, these are not checking accounts; there are some minor differences.

Promissory Notes

Promissory notes are most often used as instruments of credit. They are also used as evidence to show a preexisting debt. When a person borrows money from a bank, finance company, or other type of commercial lender, the borrower will normally be required to sign a promissory note; this signed note proves the existence of the debt, the amount owed, the manner of repayment, and any other terms important to the loan agreement. Notes are so widely used that special types of notes have developed. Real estate loans normally involve a mortgage note. Automobile loans usually involve an installment note. Many banks also use a device called a commercial loan note or a signature note for short-term unsecured loans (loans made without collateral).

The following case involved two promissory notes, an original note that was dishonored and a second, allegedly nonnegotiable, promissory note that guaranteed payment of the original note. See if you agree with the court's reasoning in this opinion.

Certificates of Deposit

A certificate of deposit (CD) is an instrument issued by a bank evidencing a debt owed to a depositor. These instruments commonly call for the bank to pay to a proper presenter the amount deposited plus interest at a stated future date. Although regularly thought of as a type of special savings account, CDs are really credit instruments. They are

---

20.3

VAUGHN v. DAP FINANCIAL SERVICES, INC.
982 S.W.2d 1; 1997 Tex. App. LEXIS 5659

FACTS DAP Financial Services, Inc. sued Joe Vaughn as the guarantor of a $122,500 promissory note executed by Gierhart/Vaughn Construction Company. On July 25, 1984, Vaughn and Gierhart, vice-president and president, respectively, of Gierhart/Vaughn Construction Company, signed an open continuing guaranty individually agreeing to repay all future loans made by Texas American Bank to their company. The guaranty covered a guaranteed indebtedness of the company up to $500,000. On November 4, 1987, Gierhart, in his capacity as president of Gierhart/Vaughn Construction Company, signed a promissory note with Texas American Bank in the amount of $122,500. No payments were made on the note, which matured on November 3, 1989. Later, Texas American Bank became insolvent, and DAP purchased the note through a loan sale by Team Bank, which was acting as an agent of the FDIC, which in turn was acting as receiver for Texas American Bank. On July 16, 1992, DAP filed suit against the guarantors Vaughn and Gierhart to recover from them individually the unpaid note signed by their company in 1987. Gierhart later filed bankruptcy and was eventually nonsuited. On January 10, 1996, the trial court entered judgment in favor of DAP against Vaughn. Vaughn appealed.

ISSUES Did Vaughn terminate the guaranty? Was DAP a holder of the note? Was the guaranty, a nonnegotiable promissory note, properly assigned to DAP?

HOLDINGS No, Vaughn did not terminate the guaranty. Yes, DAP was a holder of the note. Yes, the guaranty was properly assigned to DAP.

REASONING Excerpts from the opinion of Justice Sam Nuchia:

There is ample evidence in the record to dispose of Vaughn's legal sufficiency challenge. Vaughn testified that he signed the 1984 guaranty. The 1984 guaranty expressly states the guarantor may only terminate the agreement in writing. Vaughn admitted he was bound by the terms of the 1984 guaranty and that he did not terminate it in writing. This evidence is legally sufficient to find that Vaughn did not terminate the 1984 guaranty. . . . Where the parties' intentions are clearly and unambiguously stated in the contract, a court gives effect to the intentions of the parties, as expressed in the contract. . . . The terms of the guaranty contracts are plain and unambiguous, and Vaughn provided no evidence at trial that would contradict the guaranties. Thus, sufficient evidence exists to support the trial court's finding that Vaughn did not terminate the 1984 guaranty. . . . We overrule Vaughn's first point of error.

In his second point of error, Vaughn contends the trial court erred in granting judgment against him because DAP was not a holder of the note or the 1984 guaranty. Vaughn presents several arguments in support of this point of error. Vaughn first argues DAP did not establish the right to recover on the note. To recover on a note through a guaranty, the plaintiff must show: (1) the existence of the note and guaranty; (2) the debtor signed the guaranty; (3) the plaintiff legally owned or held the guaranty; and (4) that a certain balance remains due and owing. . . . The evidence and testimony submitted to the trial court sufficiently establish DAP's right to recover the amount of the promissory note under the 1984 guaranty. The trial court specifically concluded that DAP was a holder in due course of the note pursuant to federal law. The fact that DAP knew of the note's default is of no consequence under the federal holder in due course doctrine. The federal holder in due course doctrine prohibits debtors from asserting personal defenses against the FDIC and subsequent note holders of the FDIC whether or not they satisfy the technical requirements of state law.... In *Hanks v. NCNB Texas Nat'l Bank* ... the court held that where a bank officer stated that copies of a note and guaranty were true and genuine copies, provided principal balances and interest due, and confirmed that the bank was the legal holder and owner of certain notes and guarantees and the sole party to enforce the same, there was legally sufficient evidence to prove legal holder and ownership status. DAP established it was the legal holder and owner of the note and the 1984 guaranty through the testimony of Kenneth R. Smith, executive vice-president of DAP. Smith testified to each of the above components, and Vaughn offered no evidence to the contrary during trial. Therefore, the evidence is legally and factually sufficient to establish the right to recover on the 1984 guaranty.

Vaughn also attacks the sufficiency of the evidence to show a valid transfer of title from Texas American Bank/Galleria to DAP. Although the assignment document only recites that title to the documents passed from Texas American Banks/Dallas to the FDIC, Kenneth Smith, executive vice-president of DAP, testified that DAP purchased this particular loan in a loan sale, after Texas American Bank went defunct. At trial, Vaughn had the opportunity to cross-examine Smith and rebut his testimony; he did neither. Accordingly, the evidence was legally and factually sufficient to demonstrate a valid transfer of title to DAP. Vaughn argues the trial court's finding of fact and conclusion of law that DAP is a holder in due course of the note and the 1984 guaranty are in error. Vaughn contends DAP is not a holder in due course of the note. Vaughn argues DAP had notice the note was in default when DAP purchased it from Team Bank in 1991. . . . However, in its findings of fact and conclusions of law, the trial court specifically concluded that DAP was a holder in due course. . . . Federal common law also prohibits these same defenses against the FDIC and private purchasers from the FDIC. . . .

Vaughn also argues DAP is not a holder in due course of the 1984 guaranty because the 1984 guaranty is not a negotiable instrument. DAP, in its pleadings, conceded that a guaranty is not a negotiable instrument. Chapter 3 of the Texas Uniform Commercial Code (UCC) ... applies only to negotiable instruments. . . . A guaranty agreement is not a negotiable instrument, and is not governed by provisions of the Texas UCC. . . . The federal holder in due course doctrine likewise applies only to negotiable instruments. . . . Because the 1984 guaranty is not a negotiable instrument, DAP cannot be a holder in due course of the 1984 guaranty. . . . The trial court did not dispose of Vaughn's oral termination argument by erroneously holding that DAP was the holder in due course of the 1984 guaranty, and thus, could not submit personal defenses to the 1984 guaranty. Instead, as the reporter's record, findings of fact, and conclusions of law show, the trial court found that Vaughn's attempt to orally terminate the continuing guaranty was ineffective. The fact that the guaranty was a simple contract, and not a negotiable instrument, does not change the trial court's disposition of this case. The continuing guaranty, which was signed by Vaughn and which was in full effect and force, contractually ensured Vaughn's personal liability for any debts of Gierhart/Vaughn Construction Company to Texas American Bank or its assigns. . . . Unless otherwise stipulated, all contracts are freely assignable. . . . A non-negotiable note remains susceptible of assignment, as in the case of any other chose of action. . . . DAP, although not a holder in due course of the guaranty as a negotiable instrument, is the contractual owner of the "guaranteed indebtedness" of Gierhart/Vaughn Construction Company, and the benefit of a contractual continuing guaranty ensuring payment thereof. Pursuant to the plain terms of the continuing guaranty, it is intended for and shall inure to the benefit of Texas American Bank, as well *"as each and every person who shall from time to time be or become the owner or holder of any of the Guaranteed Indebtedness."* As a result, because Vaughn did not terminate the continuing guaranty, Vaughn is contractually liable to DAP for the Guaranteed Indebtedness of Gierhart/Vaughn Construction Company. . . . We overrule Vaughn's second point of error. . . .

The proper remedy is for this Court to reform the judgment. . . . We reform the judgment to read that the award of additional attorney's fees to appellee, in the event of appeal by appellant, is conditioned upon appellee's prevailing on appeal. As reformed, the judgment is affirmed.

BUSINESS CONSIDERATIONS Why would a business buy the debts of a failed bank? Why would the officers of a business agree to guarantee the debts of the business well into the future?

ETHICAL CONSIDERATIONS Is it ethical for a business like DAP to be allowed to purchase debts of a failed bank and to be protected from the assertion of any defenses the debtor might have been able to assert against the bank? Is there a sound ethical reason for providing firms like DAP with holder in due course status in such a situation?

notes of the bank that recognize money "borrowed" by the bank from "depositor," the person who loaned the money to the bank.

Functions and Forms

Negotiable instruments have two major functions: they are designed to serve as a substitute for money, and they are designed to serve as credit instruments. In satisfying either use, they carry certain contract rights, certain property rights, and some special rights due exclusively to their nature as negotiable instruments. Every negotiable instrument is presumed to be a contract, but not every contract is a negotiable instrument. The difference between a contract and a negotiable instrument is one of form. To be negotiable, an instrument must be (1) current in trade and (2) payable in money. These criteria are obviously too broad and too vague to be of much practical significance. Accordingly, Article 3 has more fully defined the requirements an instrument must meet in order to be negotiable. These elements are discussed in detail in Chapter 21.

As mentioned earlier, UCC § 3-104 defines the various types of negotiable instruments. These definitions include the following, as described in the remaining subsections of § 3-104:

(e) *An instrument is a "note" if it is a promise and is a "draft" if it is an order. If an instrument falls within the definition of both "note" and "draft," a person entitled to enforce the instrument may treat it as either.*

(f) *"Check" means (i) a draft, other than a documentary draft, payable on demand and drawn on a bank or (ii) a cashier's check or teller's check. An instrument may be a check even though it is described on its face by another term, such as "money order."*

(g) *"Cashier's check" means a draft with respect to which a drawer and drawee are the same bank or branches of the same bank.*

(h) *"Teller's check" means a draft drawn by a bank (i) on another bank, or (ii) payable at or through a bank.*

(i) *"Traveler's check" means an instrument that (i) is payable on demand, (ii) is drawn on or payable at or through a bank, (iii) is designated by the term "traveler's check" or by a substantially similar term, and (iv) requires, as a condition to payment, a countersignature by a*

person whose specimen signature appears on the instrument.

(j) *"Certificate of deposit" means an instrument containing an acknowledgment by a bank that a sum of money has been received by the bank and a promise by the bank to repay the sum of money. A certificate of deposit is a note of the bank.*

Every instrument must contain either an order or a promise to pay a fixed amount of money. If the instrument contains an order, it is a draft. If the instrument contains a promise, it is a note. The category of drafts includes checks, which are simply specialized forms of drafts. The category of notes includes certificates of deposit, which are simply specialized forms of notes. Drafts, also known as "order paper," are most commonly used as a substitute for money. Notes, also known as "promise paper," are most commonly used as credit instruments, providing proof that credit has been extended and showing evidence of the terms of payment for that credit.

Paper Containing an Order ("Three-Party" Paper)

The distinctive features of paper containing an order (order paper), or three-party paper, are that each instrument contains an order to pay money and that at least three legal roles are involved on each instrument. The order element will be pointed out in the following sections, while the rules governing this class of negotiable instrument will be explained later. The three roles involved on order paper are the drawer, the drawee, and the payee. As noted, this class consists of drafts, including checks in the various forms checks can take.

Drafts

A draft is an instrument in which one party, the drawer, issues an instrument to a second party, the payee. The draft is accepted by the payee as a substitute for money. The payee expects to receive money at some time from the third party, the drawee. The reason the payee expects to receive money from the drawee is contained in the basic form of the instrument. As will be pointed out, the drawer issues an order to the drawee to pay a sum of money. This order, coupled with the three roles involved, distinguishes drafts from promise paper. The components of a draft are shown in Exhibit 20.1 on page 483.

WHERE SHOULD NRW HAVE ITS CHECKING ACCOUNT?

Carlos has his personal checking account with a credit union, and he is very pleased with the service he receives. He is strongly urging the firm to place the NRW account with the credit union to take advantage of the lower fees and what he perceives as more personal service. Mai has dealt with a local bank for several years, and she is also generally pleased with the service and treatment she receives with her bank. Helen has recently opened an account with a large regional bank, and she likes the services available through such a bank. She thinks that this is the sort of bank the firm should utilize for its checking account. While each of the principals can see advantages to having the firm's account with the same bank where at least one of them has a personal account, they have also heard that a commercial bank has certain benefits for a business. They have asked you for your advice. What will you tell them? (Before answering, you might want to contact a local bank and a local credit union for information, suggestions, and guidance.)

BUSINESS CONSIDERATIONS What services would a business want or reasonably expect from a bank? How are these services different from those that an individual would want or reasonably expect on his or her account?

ETHICAL CONSIDERATIONS Many banks today are beginning to charge customers fees and service charges for using an automated teller machine (ATM). Some banks are also imposing fees when a customer enters the bank and uses a human teller when the transaction could have been handled by an ATM. Is the imposition of a fee or a service charge for normal and expected banking services ethical? How does such an arrangement affect a business account, as compared with a personal account?

INTERNATIONAL CONSIDERATIONS Offshore banking in such places as the Cayman Islands receives a lot of publicity, albeit often of a somewhat dubious nature. Should a U.S. firm investigate having its checking accounts or other bank accounts in such banks? Why might a U.S. firm prefer to do its banking in a domestic bank rather than an offshore one?

Checks

The most common type of order paper is a check. A check is a special type of draft. Like a draft, a check necessitates the involvement of three parties, but there are two differences. A check is, by definition, a demand instrument; in contrast, a draft may be a demand instrument or a time instrument. Furthermore, a check must be drawn on a bank or payable at or through a bank; in contrast, anyone may be the drawee on a draft. Article 3 now specifically includes cashier's checks, teller's checks, traveler's checks, and checks drawn against credit unions within the definition of "checks" to better reflect contemporary usage of that term. Exhibit 20.2 shows the various elements of a check.

In the case of both a check and a draft, the drawee is obligated to the drawer. This obligation is normally a debt or contractual obligation owed to the drawer by the drawee. When the drawer orders the drawee to pay, the drawer is directing the drawee as to how the debt or contractual obligation should be discharged or partially discharged. The order to the drawee to pay, coupled with the obligation to pay, assures the payee or a subsequent holder that payment will (normally) be made by the drawee at the appropriate time.

The Order All drafts (including checks) contain an order. The drawer orders the drawee to pay the instrument. The language used is not a request. The drawer does not "ask," or "hope," or even "expect" the drawee to pay. The drawer demands that payment be made. If you look at Exhibit 20.1 or Exhibit 20.2, you will see that the drawer tells the drawee to "Pay to the order of (Payee)." It should also be noted that the *order* is the word "pay"; the phrase "to the order of" is not the order. This phrase is a term of negotiability; its meaning will be explained later, when negotiability is discussed.

The Drawer The person who draws an order instrument, who gives the order to the drawee, and who issues the instrument to the payee is known as the drawer. This person originates the check or the draft. The drawer does not pay the payee directly. The drawee is expected to pay the payee or the holder, upon proper presentment. That is why the drawer gives the drawee the order. The drawer expects the order to be obeyed because of a prior agreement or relationship between the drawer and the drawee. If the order is obeyed, the drawee pays the payee or holder, and both the drawer and the drawee have performed.

The Drawee The party to whom the order on the draft is directed is the drawee. The drawee is told by the drawer to "*Pay* to the order of" the payee. It is the drawee who is expected to make payment to the presenting party. How-

EXHIBIT **20.1** A Bank Draft

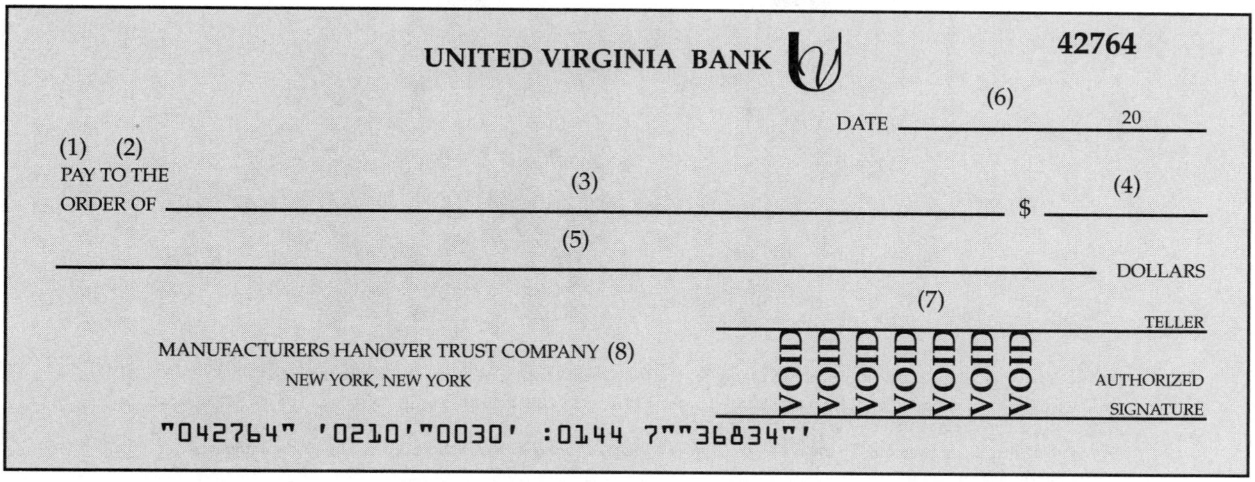

UNITED VIRGINIA BANK   42764

(6)
DATE _____ 20 ____

(1) (2)
PAY TO THE
ORDER OF   (3) $ _____ (4)
_____

(5)
_____ DOLLARS

(7)
TELLER

MANUFACTURERS HANOVER TRUST COMPANY (8)   VOID VOID VOID VOID VOID VOID VOID   AUTHORIZED
NEW YORK, NEW YORK   SIGNATURE

"042764" '0210'"0030' :0144 7""36834"'

Courtesy of Sun Trust Bank (formerly United Virginia Bank), Radford, Virginia. (1) The order. (2) Words of negotiability. (3) The payee.
(4) The amount, in numbers. (5) The amount, in words. (6) The date of issue. (7) The drawer's signature. (8) The drawee.

ever, the drawee has no duty to the payee or to the holder to pay, despite the order. The only duty the drawee has is a duty owed to the drawer. The duty of the drawee is to accept the instrument. Before acceptance, there is only the prospect that the drawee will pay when the time for payment arrives. Once the drawee accepts, the drawee has a contractual obligation to pay the presenter. This relationship is shown in Exhibit 20.3.

The Payee The payee is the person to whom the instrument is originally issued. The payee may be specifically designated, as in "Pay to the order of Jane Doe"; the payee may be an office or title, as in "Pay to the order of Treasurer of Truro County"; or the particular payee may be unspecified, as in "Pay to the order of bearer." The payee may decide to seek payment personally, or the payee may decide to further negotiate the instrument. The words "to the order of"

EXHIBIT **20.2** A Check

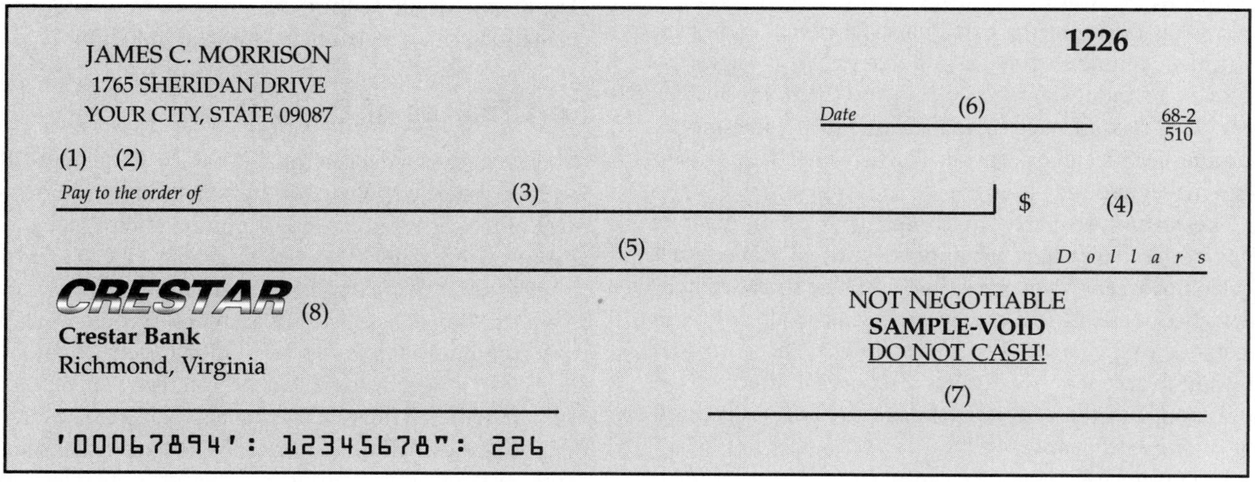

JAMES C. MORRISON   1226
1765 SHERIDAN DRIVE
YOUR CITY, STATE 09087
                                         Date   (6)   68-2
                                                                        510
(1) (2)
Pay to the order of   (3) $ (4)

(5)
_____ Dollars

CRESTAR (8)   NOT NEGOTIABLE
Crestar Bank   SAMPLE-VOID
Richmond, Virginia   DO NOT CASH!

                                                  (7)

'00067894': 12345678": 226

Courtesy of Sun Trust Bank, Radford, Virginia. (1) The order. (2) Words of negotiability. (3) The payee. (4) The amount, in numbers.
(5) The amount, in words. (6) The date of issue. (7) The drawer's signature. (8) The drawee.

EXHIBIT 20.3 The Parties on Order Paper

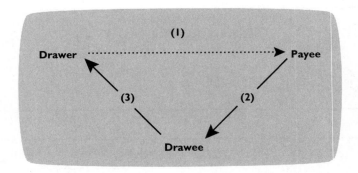

(1) The drawer issues the order instrument to the payee. The instrument contains an order directed to the drawee.

(2) The payee (or an endorsee or holder) presents the order instrument to the drawee in order to collect. The drawee is expected to obey the order directed to it by the drawer.

(3) Assuming that the drawee obeyed the order, the drawer is charged (or his or her account is debited) for the amount of the order instrument.

---

allow the payee to order the drawee to make payment to some other party. (To the order of means to whomever the payee orders, literally allowing the negotiation of the instrument.)

Paper Containing a Promise ("Two-Party" Paper)

The distinctive features of paper containing a promise (promise paper), or two-party paper, are that each such instrument contains a *promise* and that only *two* parties are necessary to fulfill the legal roles involved on the instrument. This class of negotiable instruments involves notes, including certificates of deposit. The two parties are known as the maker and the payee.

The term "two-party" is confusing to many people. Many stores have signs prominently posted stating that they do not accept "two-party checks." These so-called two-party checks are, in reality, checks that have already been negotiated to the payee or to a later holder. The store does not want to accept a check unless it receives it directly from the drawer. But there is no such legal creature as a check that is "two-party paper."

The promise element of promise paper will be pointed out in the following sections, and the rules governing this class of negotiable instrument will be explained later.

Promissory Notes

The promissory note is the oldest known form of negotiable instrument. It is normally used as a credit instrument, executed either at the time credit is extended or as evidence of a pre-existing debt not yet repaid.

In a note, one party (the maker) promises to pay the other party (the payee) a sum of money at some future time. The promise may call for a lump-sum payment, or it may call for installment payments over time. The note may specify the payment of interest in addition to the principal; it may have the interest included in the principal; or it may be interest free. The note may recite details about collateral. Despite any or all of these possibilities, the basic form is constant. Such an instrument is shown in Exhibit 20.4.

Certificates of Deposit

A certificate of deposit (or a CD, as it is frequently called) is a special type of note issued by a bank as an acknowledgment of money received, with a promise to repay the money at some future date. Many people think of a CD as a "time savings account," in contrast to a passbook savings account. In reality, though, a CD is not a savings account at all. It is most commonly a time deposit of money with a bank.

A CD normally pays higher interest than a savings account, with the interest varying according to the amount of time the certificate is to run. Most certificates run for some multiple of six months, and they are available in some multiple of $1,000. However, a number of banks offer CDs for shorter time periods such as 90 days. Some banks are beginning to offer CDs for multiples of $100. One type of CD is shown in Exhibit 20.5 on page 487. Today, many banks offer some variation of a "saver's certificate," which is nonnegotiable, rather than a negotiable certificate of deposit. It appears that the CD is becoming extinct, although some CDs still exist. However, the widespread replacement of CDs with other forms of certificates makes this an area of primarily historic interest.

The Promise Promise paper is so called because it contains a promise. The maker of the instrument *promises* to pay an amount of money to the payee or to a holder. The instrument does not say that the maker "might" pay, or will "probably" pay, or will "agree" to pay. The instrument says that the maker *promises* to pay an amount of money to the payee or to the order of the payee.

The Maker The duties performed by the drawer and the drawee on order paper are effectively combined in promise paper: both duties fall to the maker. The maker makes the promise—"I promise to pay to the order of (the payee)"; the maker issues the instrument to the payee; and the maker pays the instrument upon proper presentment. However, there is one important difference from order paper. While the drawee is not obligated to any holder until acceptance, the maker is liable to a holder from the date of original issue. This obligation is shown in Exhibit 20.6 on page 487.

The Payee As in order paper, the payee is the party to whom the instrument is originally issued. Again, the payee may be specifically designated by name, or designated by title or office, or unspecified. The payee on promise paper is the person to whom the promise is made by the maker. By contrast, the payee on order paper is the person to whom the drawee is directed (ordered) to make payment.

The Scope of Article 7

The UCC treats the topic of documents of title in Article 7. This article, entitled "Warehouse Receipts, Bills of Lading, and Other Documents of Title," specifies the rights and the duties of all relevant parties in the handling of documents of title, whether those documents are negotiable or nonnegotiable. Part 2 of Article 7 deals with warehouse receipts; Part 3 deals with bills of lading; Part 5 deals with the negotiation and transfer of a document of title. Note that these provisions apply to the documents of title

EXHIBIT 20.4 A Promissory Note

FEDERAL BANK

PROMISSORY NOTE

Loan No.

Borrower(s)
Name(s) ———————————————————— and ————————————————————
      first   middle   last   first   middle   last

Address
               (1)   (2)   (3)   (2)
Borrower (jointly and severally if more than one) promises to pay to Federal Savings Bank ("Lender"), or order, in U.S. money, at its office in San Diego, California, or elsewhere Lender designates, principal and interest on unpaid principal from the date advanced until paid, in amount, annual rate and consecutive monthly installments as follows:

Principal $ (4)   Annual Interest Rate   %

Installments $ on the same day of month beginning

Minimum Interest $ 100.00

Interest will be computed on the basis of a 12 month year and 30 day month. The date of payment, whether early or late, will be disregarded for purposes of allocating the payment between principal and interest: each payment will be treated for this purpose as though made on its due date.

EXHIBIT 20.4 *continued*

PREPAYMENT: Full or partial prepayment may be made without penalty except Borrower will pay any minimum interest amount specified. Borrower will tell Lender in writing that Borrower is making a prepayment. Lender will use all prepayments to reduce the principal subject to its right to first apply payments received to any past due interest or other charges. Partial prepayments will not delay the due dates nor change the amount of monthly payments unless Lender agrees in writing to those delays or changes. Full prepayment may be made at any time. Lender may require that partial prepayment be made on the same day as monthly payments are due. Lender may also require that the amount of any partial prepayment be equal to the amount of principal that would have been part of the next one or more monthly payments.

LATE CHARGE: Borrower will pay a late charge of 5% of each installment not paid within 15 days of its due date, or $5.00, whichever is greater.

DEFAULT AND ACCELERATION: If Borrower fails to timely pay any installment when due or to perform any provision contained in any document securing this Note, Lender may, at Lender's option, declare all sums owed hereunder immediately due and payable. Borrower will pay all reasonable expenses and attorney's fees of Lender in any action relating to Borrower's obligations.

SELLER, IF ANY: Borrower intends to use some or all of the loan proceeds to pay _____ , as Seller, amounts due Seller under a contract between Seller and Borrower, dated _____ , Borrower represents that a true and correct copy of the contract has been furnished to Lender and that it contains the entire agreement between Seller and Borrower. The following notice applies only to the named Seller, if any, and to the proceeds hereof paid to said Seller under the described contract.

NOTICE: ANY HOLDER OF THIS CONSUMER CREDIT CONTRACT IS SUBJECT TO ALL CLAIMS AND DEFENSES WHICH THE DEBTOR COULD ASSERT AGAINST THE SELLER OF GOODS OR SERVICES OBTAINED WITH THE PROCEEDS HEREOF. RECOVER HEREUNDER BY THE DEBTOR SHALL NOT EXCEED AMOUNTS PAID BY THE DEBTOR HEREUNDER.

NON-WAIVER: By accepting payment after its due date or after notice of default, Lender will not waive its right to prompt payment when due of other sums, or to declare a default, or to proceed with any remedy it has. Without affecting the liability of anyone else, Lender may release anyone liable, may change payment terms, and add, alter, substitute, or release security.

❏ This Note is secured by a Security Agreement.
❏ This Note is unsecured.

BEFORE SIGNING ORIGINAL, WE RECEIVED AND READ A COMPLETED COPY HEREOF.

(5)

Borrower's Signature	Date	Borrower's Signature	Date
Borrower's Signature	Date	Borrower's Signature	Date

C-1-424 (REV 6/83)   *(Sign Original Only)*

Courtesy of Great American Federal Savings Bank of San Diego and Fresno, California. (1) The promise. (2) Words of negotiability. (3) The payee. (4) The amount borrowed. (5) The signature of the maker.

EXHIBIT 20.5 A Certificate of Deposit

NEGOTIABLE CERTIFICATE OF DEPOSIT

FEDERAL BANK
SAVINGS AND LOAN ASSOCIATION

600 B Street, San Diego, California 92183

NO. **5014**

DATE _____ (1)

THIS CERTIFIES THAT THERE HAS BEEN DEPOSITED IN FEDERAL SAVINGS AND LOAN ASSOCIATION

THE SUM OF _____(2)_____ DOLLARS (3) **VOIDED**
($)

VOIDED

PAYABLE TO THE ORDER OF _____(4)

UPON PRESENTATION AND SURRENDER OF THIS CERTIFICATE PROPERLY ENDORSED AT OFFICE	INTEREST RATE % PER ANNUM	INTEREST AMOUNT	MATURITY DATE	TOTAL AMOUNT PAYABLE
			(5)	(6)

This deposit bears interest from the date hereof to the maturity date at the stated rate computed for the actual number of days elapsed on the basis of a 360-day year payable on the maturity date. This certificate is not payable before maturity and bears no interest after maturity.

(FIXED RATE/ FIXED TERM)

SAN DIEGO FEDERAL SAVINGS AND LOAN ASSOCIATION

(7)

Authorized Signature

Courtesy of Great American Federal Savings Bank (formerly San Diego Federal) of San Diego and Fresno, California.
(1) The date of issue. (2) The amount of the "deposit," in words. (3) The amount of the "deposit," in numbers. (4) The payee. (5) The maturity date. (6) The amount to be paid. (7) The signature of the maker.

---

without regard to their negotiability. While Article 3 deals only with negotiable instruments, Article 7 deals with all relevant documents of title.

Uses and Forms of Documents of Title

The essential use of a document of title is to reflect the rights of the owner when the goods are turned over to the custody and care of a bailee, whether for storage or for carriage. A secondary use of a document of title, especially if the document is negotiable, is to enable the owner to transfer title to the goods without having to reclaim possession of the goods in order to make the sale. The owner can negotiate the document of title, and in so doing the owner also transfers title to the goods to the person receiving the negotiation.

Warehouse Receipts

A warehouse receipt is a document issued by a person who takes goods for storage. There is no particular form

---

EXHIBIT 20.6 The Parties on Promise Paper

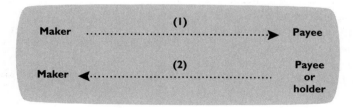

| Maker | ············(1)············▶ | Payee |
| Maker | ◀············(2)············ | Payee or holder |

(1) The maker issues the promise paper to the payee, promising to pay the payee (or a subsequent holder) upon presentment.
(2) The payee (or a subsequent holder) presents the promise paper to the maker, expecting to receive payment as per the promise.

that a warehouse receipt needs to take, but most will contain at least the following provisions:

1. The location of the warehouse

2. The date the receipt for the goods is issued

3. The number of the receipt (receipts are numbered consecutively)

4. A statement as to whether the stored goods will be delivered to the bailor (nonnegotiable) or either to the bearer or to a named person or that person's order (negotiable)

5. The fees and expenses for the storage (unless the goods are stored in a field warehousing arrangement)

6. A description of the goods or the packages stored

7. The signature of the warehouseman or his or her agent

The warehouseman assumes a duty to exercise due care in the handling of the goods and a duty to deliver the goods as agreed in the receipt at the close of the storage period.

The warehouseman assumes liability for any damages to the goods stored with him or her if the damages are caused by a failure to exercise reasonable care. The warehouseman also acquires a warehouseman's lien on the goods for the storage and transportation charges, insurance, and expenses reasonably necessary to preserve the goods.

Bills of Lading

A bill of lading is issued by a carrier who is taking possession and custody of the goods for the purpose of transporting the goods, normally from a seller to a buyer. The person who arranges the transportation is the consignor; the person to whom the goods are to be delivered is the consignee; the carrier is the issuer of the bill of lading. The bill must adequately describe the goods covered by the bill and must designate whether the goods were consigned to a particular consignee (nonnegotiable) or to a named consignee or order or to the consignee or bearer (negotiable). The carrier is liable for any misdescription or irregularity unless the document is properly qualified by words such as "contents of package unknown," "shipper's weight and count," or comparable language. Even then, the alleged qualification may not be sufficient to protect the carrier.

NRW CASE 20.3   Finance/Sales

BILLS OF LADING

A retailer in another state has recently contacted NRW about buying several hundred StuffTrakR units for her store. She believes that the units would be a good addition to the "Notions" rack next to the cash registers and might generate a significant number of impulse purchases among her customers. She liked the price Carlos quoted for the units and stated that she would be willing to make a contract, but only if the goods were shipped to her via negotiable bill of lading, with payment terms of "2/10, net 30." Carlos told her he would let her know the following day. He thinks the firm should agree to give this customer *either* a negotiable bill of lading *or* credit terms, but not both. He has asked for your advice. What will you tell him?

BUSINESS CONSIDERATIONS Should a business have a policy concerning the use of either credit terms or negotiable bills of lading? Does the frequency with which the firm does business with a particular customer affect how you answer this question?

ETHICAL CONSIDERATIONS Should a request from a first-time customer that a negotiable document of title be used raise any concerns or worries? Are there ethical implications to the use of a negotiable document of title that might be avoided if the document were not negotiable?

INTERNATIONAL CONSIDERATIONS. Suppose that a customer from another nation wants to purchase goods from a domestic supplier, and that the customer does not want to pay immediately. What might the supplier suggest that could possibly meet the needs and the concerns of both the foreign purchaser and the domestic supplier? What type of instrument might be used to provide some protection to both parties?

Summary

"Negotiables" are an important part of the modern commercial world. Negotiable *documents* cover goods that are placed in the hands of a bailee, either for storage or for transportation. Negotiable *instruments* are used as a substitute for money or as a credit instrument. Both are governed by the UCC.

Article 3 of the Uniform Commercial Code involves negotiable instruments. These negotiable instruments are "current in trade" and are payable in money. There are two major classes of negotiable instruments, and each major class contains two types of instruments. The first class, paper containing an order ("order paper"), is composed of checks and drafts. Checks and drafts are used primarily as a substitute for money. There are three legal roles involved on "order paper": the drawer, who "draws" (drafts) the instrument and issues the order; the payee, to whom the instrument is issued; and the drawee, the party who is ordered to pay the instrument upon presentment.

The second class of negotiable instruments, paper containing a promise ("promise paper"), is composed of promissory notes and certificates of deposit. Promise paper is used principally as a credit instrument. There are two legal roles involved on promise paper: the maker, who makes the promise to pay and who issues the instrument; and the payee, to whom the instrument is issued.

The recent revision to Article 3 has greatly expanded the concept of "checks," making the article more closely reflect contemporary business practices. The revision also removed some of the older, more technical aspects of negotiable instrument law.

Documents of title, including negotiable documents, are governed by Article 7 of the UCC. The two primary types of documents of title are warehouse receipts, issued by a bailee who accepts goods for storage, and bills of lading, issued by a carrier who accepts possession of goods for transportation. However, Article 7 is much more flexible than Article 3. Any other document which in the regular course of business or financing is treated as a document of title is recognized as falling within the coverage of Article 7.

Discussion Questions

1. Who is expected to make payment on negotiable instruments that are designated as "order paper"? Who is expected to make payment on negotiable instruments that are designated as "promise paper"? Why are different parties expected to pay on these different instruments?

2. What characteristics distinguish a check from other types of drafts? What characteristics distinguish a promissory note from a certificate of deposit?

3. A check or a draft contains a specific type of communication from the drawer to the drawee. What form does this communication take? Why does this communication obligate the drawee to pay the instrument issued by the drawer?

4. Article 3 of the UCC was revised in 1990. Why was Article 3 revised, and what effect did these revisions have on the law governing negotiable instruments?

5. What duty or duties are performed by the "maker" on promise paper? What do we call the party or parties who perform comparable duties on order paper?

6. What are the two major functions of negotiable instruments? Which function is most likely to be involved with the use of a draft or a check? Which function is most likely to be involved with the use of a note or a certificate of deposit?

7. How does Article 3 define a "check"? Why is this definition important in negotiable instrument law? Given the increased use of debit cards and credit cards, why is it necessary for the UCC to pay so much attention to checks and their regulation?

8. What is a document of title under the provisions of Article 7? How is a negotiable document of title different from a non-negotiable document of title?

9. When do the parties to a contract use a warehouse receipt? When do the parties to a contract use a bill of lading? Why do the parties need two different documents of title?

10. What sort of limitation or qualification can a carrier use on a bill of lading to protect itself from liability if the goods delivered are mislabeled or improperly identified? Is it ethical for a carrier to use such language, effectively shielding itself from liability for damages to the goods carried?

Case Problems and Writing Assignments

1. Goss obtained a loan from Trinity Savings, signing a promissory note that called for interest to be adjusted in conjunction with the interest rates on U.S. Treasury Securities. Eventually, a dispute arose between Goss and Trinity, and Goss sued to cancel the note and to recover the excess interest charges that he alleged he had paid under the agreement. Is the instrument here a negotiable instrument, so that the case should be resolved under Article 3 of the UCC, or is the instrument nonnegotiable, so that the case should be resolved under the common law of contracts? Explain. Would your answer be different if the case arose under the former version of Article 3? [See *Goss v. Trinity Savings & Loan Ass'n,* 813 P.2d 492 (Okla. 1991).]

2. The Department of Transportation awarded a contract to Ted's Sheds, Inc., for several metal buildings to be used at various service plazas on the Florida Turnpike. Ted's Sheds provided a Fort Lauderdale address during the bidding process. When the buildings were delivered, the State received an invoice from Ted's Sheds listing its address as Bonita Springs, Florida. The State approved the invoices for payment, and, on February 5, 1987, the comptroller issued a warrant for $16,932 payable to the order of Ted's Sheds and sent it to the Fort Lauderdale address listed on the original bid. On February 12, 1987, Ted's Sheds of Broward, Inc., presented the original warrant to Seminole National Bank. The warrant was endorsed "Ted's Sheds of Broward, Inc.," and was credited to that account by the bank. Sometime thereafter, the agents of Ted's Sheds, Inc., in Bonita Springs stated that they had not received the warrant and requested a duplicate warrant.

   It was then discovered that there were two Ted's Sheds, one in Fort Lauderdale known as "Ted's Sheds of Broward, Inc.," and one in Bonita Springs, known as "Ted's Sheds, Inc." These separate legal entities shared common corporate officers. On February 19, 1987, the comptroller placed a stop payment order on the original warrant, issued a duplicate warrant to Ted's Sheds, and mailed it to Ted's Sheds, Inc., in Bonita Springs. Subsequently, the Federal Reserve Bank of Miami returned the original warrant to the bank, indicating that payment had been stopped by the state treasurer.

   The bank initiated an action some 14 months after the original warrant was returned. In the intervening time, Ted's Sheds of Broward, Inc., was involuntarily dissolved. The bank argued that it had no knowledge of the stop payment order and asserted that it was a "holder in due course" entitled to reimbursement by the State of Florida on the theory that state warrants are negotiable instruments. The State maintained that state warrants are not negotiable instruments under the UCC, and thus the bank was not entitled to repayment of these funds. The trial court entered summary judgment for the bank, and the State appealed. Are state warrants negotiable instruments under Article 3 of the UCC? Is a holder of a state warrant entitled to prejudgment interest on the amount of the warrant? [See *State v. Family Bank of Hallandale,* 623 So. 2d 474 (Fla. 1993).]

3. On October 16, 1989, Harris Trust and Savings Bank sold to Siena Publishers the book inventory and accounts receivable of Bookthrift Marketing following a foreclosure on Bookthrift by the bank. Siena agreed to pay $2,250,000 for the assets on an "as is, where is" basis. The sale was financed by the bank, as evidenced by a demand note signed by the president of Siena dated October 19, 1989. In this demand note, Siena promised to pay to the bank on demand the sum of $2,250,000, representing the purchase price of the Bookthrift assets. Siena also agreed to grant the bank a purchase money security interest in all of Siena's accounts receivable, general intangibles, inventory, and equipment. The bank properly perfected its security interest, filing its UCC-1 with the appropriate offices during November 1989. At some time prior to August 31, 1989, Metro Services, Inc. had provided fulfillment and warehousing services for Bookthrift. (Fulfillment services include the receipt and unloading of books from delivering carriers, storage of the books, picking, counting, packing, loading, and shipping the books, and so forth.) Metro was also indebted to Harris Trust and Savings Bank, and Metro also defaulted on its loans. The bank arranged for NCI to purchase Metro's assets. This sale was consummated on August 31, 1989, with the bank receiving full payment for Metro's debt and NCI purchasing all of Metro's assets except accounts receivable. (This means that NCI did not receive the fulfillment services contract claims against Bookthrift, and thus against Siena.) On August 29, 1990, NCI and Siena entered into a fulfillment services agreement. On March 18, 1992, Siena filed for relief under the Bankruptcy Act. At that time Siena was in default on its fulfillment services agreement with NCI and was unable to pay the note from Harris Bank. Both Harris Bank and NCI claimed priority on the assets of Siena. The bank argued that it had a valid perfected security interest. NCI argued that it had a valid possessory warehouseman's lien, and that this lien had priority over the bank's security interest. Did the fulfillment services agreement give NCI a warehouse receipt on the assets of Siena? Explain. Which party, the bank or NCI, should have priority in this case? Why? Should NCI have adopted a policy to help protect its interests when it entered into a fulfillment services agreement? [See *In Re Siena Publishers Associates,* 149 B.R. 359 (1993).]

4. Lassen is an experienced construction lender. It is his practice before entering into a loan agreement to conduct an independent analysis of the financial condition of the borrower. He conducted such an analysis before making the loans in this case. Lassen had a continuing business relationship with Kopfmann Homes, Inc., a builder in the Minneapolis area. Between 1985 and 1990, Lassen made a number of loans to Kopfmann through an account Lassen had with First Bank. In 1986, on the basis of Lassen's recommendation, Kopfmann opened its own account with First Bank. In early 1990, Lassen entered into two loan agreements with Kopfmann. The contracts called for Kopfmann to construct two homes. Each loan was secured by a mortgage. Later that year, Lassen purchased five cashier's

checks (totaling nearly $170,000) from First Bank and delivered these checks to Kopfmann. Each of the checks was jointly payable to Kopfmann and Chicago Title Insurance Company. Kopfmann presented each of these checks to First Bank without the indorsement of the title company. First Bank accepted each of the checks, depositing the proceeds into Kopfmann's account. Subsequently, Kopfmann defaulted on the two loans from Lassen. Kopfmann also failed to pay the subcontractors on the two construction jobs. Lassen then sued First Bank, alleging breach of contract, conversion, and fraud. Lassen argued that the bank had a duty to ensure that all required indorsements were present on the checks before accepting them. The bank denied liability to Lassen, asserting that he was not a party to the contracts because the checks in question were cashier's checks, with the bank as both drawer and drawee. Did the bank breach its contracts with Lassen, who purchased the cashier's checks, by not obtaining the indorsements of both joint payees on the checks prior to accepting them? Was it ethical for the bank to deny any obligation to Lassen, the purchaser of the cashier's checks, for its failure to require the indorsements of both joint payees? What more could Lassen have done to protect his interests? [See *Lassen v. First Bank Eden Prairie*, 514 N.W.2d 831 (Minn. App. 1994).]

5. **BUSINESS APPLICATION CASE** Universal Premium Acceptance Corporation provides financing to policyholders to pay their insurance premiums. In the fall of 1991, Walter Talbot of the W. Talbot Insurance Agency in Lancaster, Pennsylvania, requested Universal to provide financing for his customers who needed funds to pay premiums on policies issued by the Great American Insurance Company. Universal accepted Talbot's proposal and sent him the necessary documents, including blank drafts. The face of each instrument contained Universal's name and address in the top left corner, and a large UPAC logo in the top center. Below UPAC's address was printed "PAY AND DEPOSIT ONLY TO THE CREDIT OF: _____ INSURANCE CO." with a space for the amount. On the lower right side of the instrument were blanks for the policyholder's name, the insurance agency name, and a line for 'SIGNATURE OF PRODUCER OF RECORD/BROKER/AGENT." In the lower right corner beneath the signature line appeared the name and address of the Landmark Bank. The back of each instrument contained preprinted language: "Acceptance of this draft acknowledges Universal Premium Acceptance Corporation's interest in the unearned or return premium(s) and that we have issued a policy(ies) to the named applicant (insured) in the amount of the premium indicated." Between September 1991 and July 1992, Talbot signed drafts for more than $1 million in favor of Great American but did not deliver them to the insurance company. Instead, he arranged for his confederate to forge the indorsement of Great American and deposit the drafts in an account they opened at defendant York Bank under the name of "Small Businessman's Service Corporation." York deposited the drafts without securing the indorsement of Small Businessman's Service Corporation and transmitted them to Landmark, Universal's bank in St. Louis. As part of the scheme, Talbot and his associate set up a dummy "Great American

Insurance Company" office in Lancaster and furnished its address and telephone number to Universal. To verify that Great American had issued a policy, Universal would contact that office. After assurances from Talbot's cohorts there that the transaction was in order, Universal would then authorize Landmark to pay the draft.

After the fraud was discovered, Talbot was convicted and imprisoned. Universal recovered part of its loss from Talbot and then filed suit in its own behalf and as assignee of Landmark against York. The complaints asserted claims under Articles 3 and 4 of the Uniform Commercial Code as enacted in Pennsylvania, as well as for negligence and conversion. The district court granted summary judgment for York, and Universal appealed, contending that the limiting language as to the payee of the drafts did not permit York to deposit them in the Small Businessman's account, that the fictitious payee provision did not apply, and that the negligence claim should not have been resolved in York's favor. Were the drafts negotiable instruments under Article 3? Did the blank indorsements convert the drafts to negotiable bearer instruments? Is York protected from liability by the fictitious payee rule? What sort of policies or procedures should Universal have established to help prevent this sort of situation from arising? [See *Universal Premium Assurance Corporation v. York Bank and Trust Company*, 69 F.3d 695 (3rd Cir. 1995).]

6. **ETHICAL APPLICATION CASE** On May 1, 1984, Rhyne executed an agreement whereby Rhyne agreed to purchase 50 shares of stock in A & H Millworks, Inc., from Jesse Almond (later deceased). In addition, this agreement gave Rhyne an option to purchase an additional 50 shares of stock. To secure the purchase price of $35,000, Rhyne also executed a document entitled "Promissory Note and Security Agreement."

In either June or September of 1988, after Almond was diagnosed with cancer, Rhyne visited him. During this visit, Rhyne obtained possession of the promissory note and a stock certificate representing the original 50 shares of stock. Only Rhyne and Almond were present during this time.

Margaret Almond filed suit on April 9, 1990, to collect the balance owing on the promissory note. No payment had been made on the promissory note since May 10, 1988. On September 12, 1991, the trial court granted Almond's motion for summary judgment for the balance due on the note plus interest. Did Jesse Almond deliver the "promissory note" to Rhyne with the intent to cancel the note and discharge the debt? What ethical issues are raised by a debtor's claim that a terminally ill creditor canceled the debt just prior to the creditor's death? Did the fact that Rhyne had possession of the note evidencing the debt add probity to his claim of cancellation? [See *Almond v. Rhyne*, 424 S.E.2d 231 (N.C. App. 1993).]

7. **CRITICAL THINKING CASE** Amoco uses platinum to prepare catalysts that are used in reactors at Amoco's six refineries around the country. These catalysts accelerate the refining process in the manufacture of gasoline. During the refining process, some platinum is lost—between 2,000 and 4,000 ounces each year.

Although Amoco owns 280,000 ounces of platinum, it must occasionally lease platinum from other sources. Sloss, who was Amoco's Senior Supply Negotiator until 1992, testified that he leased from metal trading companies that delivered platinum to Amoco's catalyst manufacturers. A particular shipment of platinum, once it is used to prepare catalysts for use in the refining process, can no longer be traced. When leasing, Amoco would issue a holding certificate to the precious metal company from which the platinum had been obtained.

DBL Trading leased metals to companies such as Amoco in order to improve profitability on its precious metals inventory. Metal was also used as collateral by DBL Trading in lending transactions with various banks, including Bank of New York (BNY). The amount of the loans made available by BNY were limited to 95 percent of the daily value of the pledged collateral. BNY would receive a telex from the depository where the collateral was being held, a warehouse receipt, or a holding certificate. The banks' rights in the collateral were reflected in a General Loan and Security Agreement between BNY and DBL Trading, which had been signed in 1982. Three of the four holding certificates at issue in this litigation were accepted by BNY in December 1989. They conformed to previous certificates that BNY had accepted. The fourth certificate was identical in wording to the other three, but was dated January 2, 1990. On February 13, 1990, DBL Trading defaulted on an overnight loan that it had obtained from BNY. BNY immediately began liquidating collateral; after an exchange of communications discussed in detail below, Amoco returned platinum to BNY. It did not do so, however, until April 4, 1990, after this action had been brought. Sloss instructed UOP, Inc., a platinum reclaimer that held platinum in a pool account for Amoco, to transfer 22,230 troy ounces of platinum from Amoco's account to BNY's account. BNY sued Amoco for conversion, alleging that Amoco had refused to turn over the platinum upon the bank's proper demand based on its possession of the holding certificates. Were the holding certificates negotiable documents of title under Article 7, granting the bank the right to immediate transfer upon demand? What should each of the principal businesses in this case have done to better protect their positions? [See *Bank of New York v. Amoco Oil Co.*, 831 F. Supp. 254 (S.D.N.Y. 1993), aff'd 35 F.3d 643 (2nd Cir. 1994).]

8. **YOU BE THE JUDGE** Flatiron Linen, Inc. received a check for $4,100 from one of its customers. The check was drawn against the customer's account at First American State Bank. Flatiron deposited the check at its bank, Colorado National Bank. The check was dishonored by First American the next day due to insufficient funds, and was duly returned to Flatiron. The day after the check was dishonored, the drawer contacted First American State Bank and placed a stop payment order on the check. Several months later, and without knowledge of the stop payment order, Flatiron presented the check to First American. The teller at First American failed to notice the stop payment order and issued a cashier's check payable to the order of Flatiron. Flatiron then deposited the cashier's check into its account with Colorado National Bank and immediately withdrew the full amount in cash. When First American realized what it had done, it contacted Flatiron and informed the company that it intended to dishonor the check. Soon thereafter, Colorado National Bank informed Flatiron that the cashier's check had been dishonored, that the $4,100 had been charged back to Flatiron's account, and that the charge-back resulted in several overdrafts by Flatiron. Flatiron sued First American for the amount of the cashier's check and for all related damages Flatiron incurred due to the overdrafts. This case has been brought in *your* court. How will *you* resolve the case? [See "Good Faith Creditor Acted in Good Faith in Presenting 5-month-old Cashier's Check," *Commercial Lending Litigation News* (LRP Publications, July 20, 2001); *Flatiron Linen, Inc. v. First American State Bank*, No. 99SC 887, Colorado Supreme Court, 2001.]

Notes

1. Prefatory Note to Article 3, *Uniform Commercial Code, 2001 edition* (St. Paul, Minn.: West Group, 2001): 287.
2. Magnetic Ink Character Recognition, the required encoding on all checks issued in the United States.
3. Ibid.
4. "Cards Keep Gaining Ground, but Cash and Checks Are Still King," Bankrate.com, March 6, 2002 (http://www.bankrate.com/msn/news/cc/20020212a.asp).
5. 12 U.S.C.A. §§ 401 et seq.
6. 12 C.F.R. § 229.
7. UCC § 3-102(b).
8. UCC § 3-411, Official Comment.
9. UCC § 3-411.

Negotiability

AGENDA

NRW NRW will be receiving payments from their customers in various ways. While some will pay by cash and some by credit card, most of the customers will pay by issuing a check or a draft. Although they do not anticipate any problems, they will need to know if these checks or drafts are negotiable within the coverage of Article 3, or nonnegotiable and therefore governed by other areas of the law. NRW will also be issuing its own instruments to purchase supplies and materials, to pay bills, and to operate the business. Will the instruments issued by the firm be negotiable? Will it matter if the instruments issued by NRW are *not* negotiable?

The firm will be relying on common carriers a great deal, both for receiving shipments of materials and for shipping finished goods to their commercial customers. These shipments via carrier will use bills of lading. Being relatively new to the operation of a business, Mai, Carlos, and Helen are not very familiar with bills of lading, and they are unsure whether they should use negotiable bills or nonnegotiable bills.

These and other questions will arise during our discussion of negotiability. Be prepared! You never know when the firm or one of its members will seek your advice.

Negotiable instruments have a special place in business law. Every negotiable instrument is a contract and carries with it, at a minimum, the rights that a person would enjoy under contract law. As you remember from contract law, a person possessing rights under a contract can *assign* those rights to another person. The person who assigns his or her rights—the assignor—is expected to give notice to the party who will be conferring the benefits—the obligor—that an assignment has been made, and the assignor will identify the person to whom the rights were transferred—the assignee. You should also remember that the assignee takes the rights assigned under the contract subject to *any* and *every* defense the obligor could assert against the assignor. These two things, taking the benefits subject to any defenses and the need for the assignor to give notice, make assignments a less-than-popular method for transferring benefits under a contract.

While a negotiable instrument is also a contract, it is a contract given special treatment under the law. Because a negotiable instrument is a contract, the benefits called for in the instrument can be assigned, the same as the benefits under other types of contracts can be assigned. But, as we just discussed, assignments are not a very good method for ensuring that the assignee will receive the benefits the assignor is trying to transfer. Unless there is more to it than that, negotiable instruments would just be a specialized type of contract with no particular benefits beyond those of other contracts.

A person in possession of a negotiable instrument by means of a negotiation is called a *holder* (think of the holder as roughly analogous to an assignee for now). The holder of a negotiable instrument has all of the rights of an assignee under contract law, *plus* any rights conferred by Article 3. Although an assignee can assert only rights equiv-alent to those of the assignor, the holder of a negotiable instrument may be able to assert greater rights than those possessed by the person from whom the holder acquired the instrument. In addition, a holder may be able to attain the status of *holder in due course*. The holder in due course of a negotiable instrument will be permitted to collect the money (receive the benefits under the contract), despite virtually any defenses the maker or drawer can assert. (There are some defenses that not even a holder in due course can overcome. The various defenses will be discussed in Chapter 22.) This is the primary reason that negotiable instrument law is so important! A person having the right to enforce a "mere" contract through an assignment would not have this same benefit. The holder of a negotiable instrument has all of the rights of an assignee under contract law, plus any additional rights conferred on him or her by Article 3 of the Uniform Commercial Code (UCC). Not only that, but the instrument, if correctly made or drawn, will move easily through the commercial world as a substitute for money and/or as a credit instrument. Exhibit 21.1 compares the assignment of contract rights with the negotiation of a negotiable instrument.

Different payment options under the UCC are described at http://www.uccpayments.org.

Formal Requirements for Negotiability: Article 3

In order to qualify for the special treatment accorded to negotiable instruments, the document in question must qualify as a *negotiable instrument* under the guidelines as set out in Article 3. Six requirements set out in Article 3 must be

---

EXHIBIT 21.1 Comparison of an Assignment and a Negotiation

Assignment: A is obligated to B under the terms of a contract.

B assigns his rights to C.

C takes the same rights under the contract as B. C will be subject to any and all defenses that A could assert against B, *and* C will not be able to assert any rights against A unless and until A is notified of the assignment.

Negotiation: A is obligated to B and issues a negotiable instrument to cover the obligation.

B negotiates the instrument to C.

C takes the same rights as B, *plus* C has no need to notify A of the negotiation because possession of the instrument is adequate notice. C also takes the rights of a *holder,* and may be able to assert the rights of a *holder in due course.* Thus, C may have greater rights than B and may be able to enforce the instrument against A even if A would be able to avoid honoring the obligation if B were attempting to enforce it.

met before an instrument is deemed negotiable, and the instrument in question must meet each and every one of these requirements in order to fall within the coverage of Article 3. Any missing element removes the instrument from Article 3 and places it under the coverage of the common law. The basic requirements for negotiability are set out in § 3-104(a) of the UCC, which provides the following:

Section 3-104. Negotiable Instrument

(a) Except as provided in subsections (c) and (d), "negotiable instrument" means an unconditional promise or order to pay a fixed amount of money, with or without interest or other charges described in the promise or order, if it:

(1) is payable to bearer or to order at the time it is issued or first comes into possession of a holder;

(2) is payable on demand or at a definite time; and,

(3) does not state any other undertaking or instruction by the person promising or ordering payment to do any act in addition to the payment of money, but the promise or order may contain (i) an undertaking or power to give, maintain, or protect collateral to secure payment; (ii) an authorization or power to the holder to confess judgment or realize on or dispose of collateral; or (iii) a waiver of the benefit of any law intended for the advantage or protection of an obligor.

Two other important definitions must also be reviewed before the discussion of negotiability can commence. Both of these definitions are found in § 3-103, and each defines one of the words used in § 3-104(a). As defined in the article:

Section 3-103. Definitions

(a) In this Article:

(6) "Order" means a written instruction to pay money signed by the person giving the instruction. The instruction may be addressed to any person, including the person giving the instruction, or to one or more persons jointly or in the alternative but not in succession. An authorization to pay is not an order unless the person authorized to pay is also instructed to pay. [Emphasis added]

(9) "Promise" means a written undertaking to pay money signed by the person undertaking to pay. An acknowledgment of an obligation by the obligor is not a promise unless the obligor also undertakes to pay the obligation. [Emphasis added]

These two sections, when read together, give the requirements for a negotiable instrument. Thus, to qualify as a negotiable instrument, the instrument in question must:

- contain a written promise [§ 3-103(a)(9)] or a written order [§ 3-103(a)(6)];

- be signed by the maker (promise paper) [§ 3-103(a)(9)] or by the drawer (order paper) [§ 3-103(a)(6)];

- contain an unconditional promise or order to pay a fixed amount of money, with or without interest or other charges described in the promise or order [§ 3-104(a)];

- be payable *to bearer* or *to order* at the time it is issued or first comes into possession of a holder [§ 3-104(a)(1)];

- be payable *on demand* or *at a definite time* [§ 3-104(a)(2)]; and

- *not* state any other undertaking or instruction by the person promising or ordering payment to do any act in addition to the payment of money [§ 3-104(a)(3)].

These elements are shown in Exhibit 21.2 Remember that every one of the elements must be present with *one* exception—checks do not have to have the "words of negotiability" in order to be negotiable. Other than this one exception, the absence of any element negates negotiability. While the absence of negotiability does not make the paper worthless, the paper is not negotiable under the law; this means that no one in possession of the paper would have the protections afforded by the UCC. The person holding the paper would have only his or her (potential) contract rights under the common law. As you will see in our subsequent discussion, this can be an important consideration for the person in possession of the paper.

It should be emphasized that negotiability has nothing to do with *validity* or *enforceability*. If an instrument is negotiable, this merely means that the instrument is governed by the provisions of Article 3. The enforceability of the instrument or the collection of money called for in the instrument has nothing to do with whether the instrument is negotiable. We will examine each of these elements of negotiability in the following sections. For a more detailed look at Article 3, including the Official Comments, see http://www.law.cornell.edu/topics/negotiable.html/.

Writing Requirement

Commercial paper represents an intangible right, the right to collect money at some time. However, to satisfy the

EXHIBIT   21.2   The Elements of Negotiability

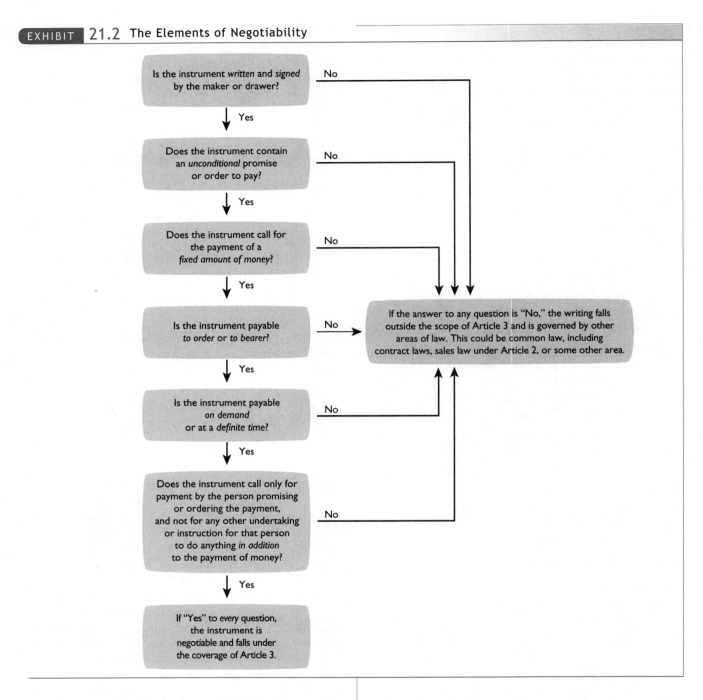

requirements of Article 3, the proof of this right must be tangible. The simplest way to prove that the right exists is to put it in writing. "Writing" is defined in § 1-201(46), which states that "'written' or 'writing' includes printing, type-writing, or any other intentional reduction to tangible form." This is a broader definition than the one originally found in the NIL, and provides a significant amount of flexibility in which the courts can find that a "writing"

exists, thus allowing more types of instruments to be brought within the coverage of Article 3.

For many people, the type of negotiable instrument most frequently encountered is a check. Most checks are in a standard form, preprinted on paper, with magnetic ink to designate the drawee bank and the drawer's account number. Similarly, many drafts are preprinted, in stan-dard form, on paper, with magnetic ink encoding; most certificates of deposit (CDs) are preprinted on paper, with magnetic ink encoding; and many notes are preprinted in a form readily adaptable to the needs of the lender-preparer. These preprinted, standardized forms are familiar, they contain blanks at all the appropriate places to streamline their completion, and they are preencoded with magnetic ink to make computerized processing readily available. However, such convenience is just that—a convenience. It is important to remember that use of a preprinted form is not a necessity in order to have a negotiable instrument.

Commercial paper is equally valid when prepared by handwriting on a scratch pad, or on a blank sheet of paper, or on virtually any other relatively permanent thing. For example, several years ago, on a television series entitled *Love American Style*, a couple was marooned on a desert island. The only thing they had for entertainment was a deck of cards. According to the plot, they spent their time playing gin. When they were rescued, the young woman had won $1 million from her fellow castaway. As evidence, she had a check . . . written on her stomach! Despite the comedic implications, such a check would (theoretically) be valid.

In another (possible apocryphal) example, a disgruntled taxpayer completed his tax return on April 15. When he mailed his return, he included a check for the taxes due and a note. The note said: "You've been trying to get it for years, and you've finally succeeded. Here's the shirt off my back." The note was pinned to his check, which was written on his undershirt. However, the joke was on him. The IRS cashed it!

Signature Requirement

On a check or a draft, an order is given by the drawer. On a note or a CD, a promise is given by the maker. Given the widespread use of preprinted forms as negotiable instruments, some protection from fraud or trickery is needed. The UCC tries to minimize the potential for fakery by requiring a *signature* by the maker or the drawer. A signature is deemed to be an "authentication" of the document or writing to which the signature is attached. As such, it has great legal significance. Most people think of a signature as a manual subscription, an autograph. Although a manual subscription is, obviously, a signature, it is not the only possible type of signature.

A corporation, as an inanimate object, cannot sign its own name. Yet corporations need to "sign" negotiable instruments, particularly checks. The instruments can, of course, be signed by agents of the corporation. But even this is impractical. Some corporations issue thousands of checks each month. An "authorized signer" could spend an

---

NRW CASE 21.1 Finance/Management

SIGNING BUSINESS CHECKS

NRW will be issuing a significant number of checks initially, and the number is likely to increase as the business grows. Carlos, Helen, and Mai have agreed that the firm's checks should be signed by two of them, and all three of their signatures are on file with the bank. However, Helen has pointed out that it will take up a lot of time every month just signing checks, and that there should be a better way for the firm to "sign" its checks, from the perspective of efficiency and time management. She would like to have the firm invest in a software package that will prepare checks, keep a check register, and even sign the checks automatically. They have asked you for advice. What will you tell them?

BUSINESS CONSIDERATIONS Many businesses have lost money because of inadequate internal auditing practices or poor controls, especially in the handling of checking accounts. What sorts of practices and controls should a business have in place to minimize the risk of suffering such losses?

ETHICAL CONSIDERATIONS Is it ethical for a business to try to "play the float" by writing checks before deposits are available, in the hope—or the expectation—that the funds will be available when the checks are presented to the bank?

INTERNATIONAL CONSIDERATIONS Should a business attempt to pay a creditor in another country with a check drawn against a U.S. bank, or should the business use some other method of payment? Why might the foreign party not want a check drawn on a U.S. bank? How might a business pay a foreign creditor other than by check?

---

entire career "autographing" checks for the corporation, laboriously attaching his or her manual subscription to checks, drafts, and notes every working day. While such a position would be boring beyond belief, if "autographs" were the only method of signing, someone would have to occupy such a position in virtually every company.

Fortunately, the UCC solved this problem. The solution is found in § 1-201(39), which states that "'signed' includes any symbol executed or adopted by a party with present intention to authenticate a writing." Thus, the party who is signing an instrument can use *any* symbol he or she desires, so long as the symbol is used with the "present intent" to authenticate the writing. This means that, for example, a corporation can use a stamp or imprinter of some sort to sign checks. Likewise, a negotiable instrument can be signed by affixing an X, or a thumbprint, or any other intentionally affixed symbol. (Note that although a number of banks are now requiring a thumbprint along with the indorsement of the presenter before accepting checks drawn against the bank when the presenter does not have an account with the bank, this is not a "signing" as defined by the Code, merely a protective device for the bank.)

Even though the Code permits the maker or drawer to use any symbol he or she desires to authenticate a writing, care and common sense should be exercised. There are practical problems with adopting any unusual types of signatures. These problems deal more with the acceptability of the instrument than with the negotiability of it. An unusual signature may be so strange that people will be hesitant to accept it or the instrument containing it. The unusual signature also must be proved by the person trying to claim the instrument.

It makes no difference where the instrument is signed. Although it is normal to sign in the lower right-hand corner of the face of the instrument, the signature can be anywhere. For example, in a note beginning "I, Mary Smith, promise to pay," Mary Smith's signature can be placed following the word "I," or Mary Smith can sign in the lower right-hand corner, or the lower left-hand corner, or in any other location on the face of the instrument, and her signature will be sufficient if it appears to a reasonable person that the signature was placed by Mary Smith in an attempt to authenticate the underlying writing.

The following case presented an interesting signature question. The court had to decide if a "telecheck" had been "signed" by the purported "drawer," and in doing so the court had to determine whether a "telecheck" is a negotiable instrument governed by Article 3. Follow the court's reasoning and then decide whether you agree with the conclusion the court reached.

21.1

INTERBANK OF NEW YORK v. FLEET BANK
189 Misc. 2d 20; 730 N.Y.S.2d 208; 2001 N.Y. Misc. LEXIS 270; 45 U.C.C. Rep. Serv. 2d (Callaghan) 167 (2001)

FACTS Interbank commenced this action against Fleet to recover on four drafts in the total sum of $3,361.16, paid out by Interbank from the account of its customer, Dimitrios Tasoulis. Two of the drafts were issued by and made payable to Sprint PCS, and two of the drafts were issued by and made payable to Bell Atlantic Mobile, Inc. These drafts are known commonly in the banking industry as "preauthorized drafts" or "telechecks." These drafts are created when a consumer has agreed to pay for goods or services by allowing the subject vendor to prepare and issue a preauthorized check drawn on the consumer's account at the consumer's designated financial institution. The consumer provides the vendor with the necessary account number and bank at which it is maintained, and the vendor then issues a check drawn on the consumer's account. In this case, Sprint and Bell issued drafts on the account of Tasoulis to pay for telephone services. The drafts contained the typed notation "verbally authorized by your depositor." Bell and Sprint deposited the drafts in their respective accounts at Fleet. The drafts were ultimately paid by Interbank. Thereafter, Tasoulis advised Interbank that he never authorized Bell or Sprint to issue the drafts. Tasoulis executed an affidavit of forgery with respect to each draft, in which he stated that he had never authorized the drafts to be issued. Interbank seeks to recover on the forged drafts. It is Fleet's position that the preauthorized checks herein should be treated like any other check, and that in accordance with the Uniform Commercial Code, a depository bank such as Fleet cannot be liable for accepting a check on which the signature of the drawer is forged, unless it knew that the signature was forged. Interbank's position is that a preauthorized check cannot be treated as an ordinary check and is not a negotiable instrument. Fleet is the depository bank and collecting bank, while Interbank is the drawee and payor bank.

ISSUES Is a "telecheck" a negotiable instrument under the provisions of Article 3? Is the typed notation on the signature a valid signature under the provisions of Article 3?

HOLDINGS Yes to both questions. Under the provisions of Article 3 a telecheck is a negotiable instrument, and the typed notation on the signature line of the telecheck is a valid signature.

REASONING Excerpts from the opinion of Judge Edmead:

Defendant Fleet Bank moves for an order granting it summary judgment dismissing plaintiff Interbank of New York's complaint. This case of first impression considers whether a notation "verbally authorized by your depositor" qualifies as a signature on a check. "First, a drawee who accepts or pays an instrument on which the signature of a drawer is forged is bound on its acceptance and cannot recover back its payment. This rule, first set forth in *Price v. Neal* . . . [decided in *1762*] is followed in section 3-418 of the Uniform Commercial Code and inferentially in section 3-417 . . . and section 4-207 . . . of the Uniform Commercial Code." . . . A forgery is an unauthorized signature . . . and is "wholly inoperative as that of the person whose name is signed." . . . Thus, it is Interbank, the drawee and payor bank, who is liable for the forged signature of its customer, the drawer. . . . "The traditional justification for the result is that the drawee is in a superior position to detect a forgery because he has the maker's signature and is expected to know and compare it; a less fictional rationalization is that it is highly desirable to end the transaction on an instrument when it is paid rather than reopen and upset a series of commercial transactions at a later date when the forgery is discovered."

Section 3-104(1)(a) of the UCC provides that for a writing to be a negotiable instrument it must be signed by the maker or the drawer. Interbank argues that since the subject drafts are not signed by the maker, but merely contain the notation "verbally authorized by your depositor," the subject drafts do not constitute negotiable instruments. UCC 1-201(39) provides that "signed" includes any symbol executed or adopted by a party with a present intention to authenticate a writing. UCC 3-401(2) provides that a signature is made by any word or mark used in lieu of a written signature. In accordance with the above-noted sections of the UCC, if a drawer or maker intended the notation "verbally authorized by your depositor" to authenticate the check and intended that the notation take the place of a written signature, then the check would be a negotiable instrument. Clearly, if Tasoulis had authorized Bell to issue the check with the notation "verbally authorized by your depositor," in place of his written signature, the check would qualify as a negotiable instrument. The only infirmity in the subject drafts is that Tasoulis did not authorize their issuance. Thus, the notation "ver-bally authorized by your depositor," which could constitute a signature under the UCC, is unauthorized. . . . Accordingly, the pre-authorized checks herein should be treated as any other check which contains a forged signature. These pre-authorized checks constitute negotiable instruments. . . . The pre-authorized checks herein should be treated like any other check, to insure that they pass through the system with speed, and to insure that the parties and entities who deal with this type of draft, as it passes through the system, know their rights, responsibilities and liability as to these items, so that they can take steps to avoid loss. In this case, it is Interbank, the drawee and payor bank, who is in the best position to prevent the loss due to forgery. Although the pre-authorized check does not contain the actual handwritten signature of the drawer or maker, Interbank, which has a business relationship with the drawer, is in the best position to determine whether the pre-authorized check was actually authorized by its customer. Fleet, as a collecting and depository bank, which had no relationship with Tasoulis, is not in the best position to determine whether Tasoulis actually authorized the issuance of the check.

Finally, Interbank argues that Fleet has not shown that Bell had the proper authorization from its customer on file to issue the checks as required by the Telemarketing and Consumer Fraud Prevention Act. Any failure on the part of Bell to have the proper authorization on file would only go to the issue of whether Bell is liable to Interbank, but would not affect Fleet's status as a holder in due course. Accordingly, defendant Fleet's motion for summary judgment is granted and the complaint is dismissed against it.

BUSINESS CONSIDERATIONS Telechecks, preauthorized checks, and various other forms of electronic payment options are becoming popular. What sort of policies should a business follow if it decides to accept any of these forms of payment?

ETHICAL CONSIDERATIONS Is it ethical for a business payee to accept a verbal authorization to "sign" a telecheck from one of its purported customers without some form of verification as to the identity of the purported customer? Should the business payee ask to see an actual check from the account to try to ensure that the customer is authorized to use the account number?

A "telecheck" is created when a consumer agrees to pay for goods or services by allowing the subject vendor to prepare and issue a "preauthorized check" drawn on the consumer's account at the consumer's designated financial institution, which contains the notation "verbally authorized by your depositor." Such a writing qualifies as a negotiable instrument (UCC §3-104[1][a]), and should be treated like any other check with respect to risk of loss as it passes through the banking system. The notation "verbally authorized by your depositor" takes the place of a written signature.

Unconditional Promise or Order Requirement

Negotiable instruments are designed to move easily through the commercial world. To serve effectively as a substitute for money, a negotiable instrument must be freely transferable. It also needs to be "current in trade," which means that it must be in a form that people are willing to accept. These needs are met by the requirement that the promise made, or the order given, be unconditional. A person taking possession of a negotiable instrument wants to know that payment can reasonably be expected under *every* circumstance. A prospective holder would not be eager to accept an instrument that says payment *might* be made or will be made *only if* something happens. The holder wants an unconditional promise that the money will be paid.

The Code has gone to great lengths to define "unconditional." Section 3-106 lists the requirements that must be met to make the promise or order conditional. These requirements will be set out here, with a brief explanation inserted between each of the four subsections of the Code section. According to this Code section:

(a) *Except as provided in this section [3-106], for the purposes of [negotiable instruments], a promise or order is unconditional unless it states (i) an express condition to payment, (ii) that the promise or order is subject to or governed by another writing, or (iii) that rights or obligations with respect to the promise or order are stated in another writing. A reference to another writing does not of itself make the promise or order conditional.*

There appears to be a presumption that every promise or order is unconditional unless a condition is obvious from reading the instrument. For example, if an instrument says "payment to be made only if [statement of condition]," that instrument would contain an express condition and would not be negotiable." Similarly, if an instrument contains a clause stating that the payment of the instrument is *governed* by a separate document or writing, the instrument would be conditional and, therefore, nonnegotiable. However, if the instrument merely *refers* to another writing there is no condition attached to payment, and negotiability would not be affected by the reference. Thus, a notation that the instrument is issued as "Payment for Invoice #67542" would not be conditional and such a notation would not affect negotiability.

(b) *A promise or order is not made conditional (i) by a reference to another writing for a statement of rights with respect to collateral, prepayment, or acceleration, or (ii) because payment is limited to resort to a particular source of funds.*

This subsection makes a significant change in the law of negotiable instruments, again emphasizing the effort to remove conditions from written promises or orders unless they are very explicit. Before the revision to Article 3, the "particular fund" doctrine made an instrument conditional, hence negating negotiability, any time the instrument required payment from a particular fund, unless the drawer or maker was a governmental entity. Many students have wondered why a check drawn by a person against his or her personal account was not drawn against a "particular fund." The (technically accurate) explanation was that the check was not drawn against that person's deposited funds, but rather against any or all of the funds in the bank, and the person's account was merely a bookkeeping notation telling the bank where to "post" the check. The answer seemed evasive at best and ignored the premise of the question at worst. This particular rule was confusing, and its demise was long overdue.

(c) *If a promise or order requires, as a condition to payment, a countersignature by a person whose specimen signature appears on the promise or order, the condition does not make the promise or order conditional. If the person whose specimen signature appears on an instrument fails to countersign the instrument, the failure to countersign is a defense to the obligation of the issuer, but the failure does not prevent a transferee of the instrument from becoming a holder of the instrument.*

This subsection appears to be intended specifically to permit the inclusion of traveler's checks within the coverage of Article 3. Notice that the absence of a required countersignature does *not* remove the instrument from the coverage of Article 3, it merely provides a defense for the issuer. The instrument is still negotiable and the person in possession of the instrument is not prevented from being classified as a holder of the instrument.

(d) *If a promise or order at the time it is issued or first comes into possession of a holder contains a statement, required by applicable statutory or administrative law, to the effect that the rights of a holder or transferee are subject to claims or defenses that the issuer could assert against the original payee, the promise or order is not thereby made conditional for the purposes of Section 3-104(a); but if the promise or order is an instrument, there cannot be a holder in due course on the instrument.*

This subsection reflects the Code's recognition of the "Federal Trade Commission Holder in Due Course Rule" as it affects consumer credit transactions (explained in the next chapter), while also recognizing that other statutory or regulatory enactments may also occur in the future. By addressing this issue in general terms, the Code greatly simplifies the task facing courts that would otherwise have to interpret the effect of these enactments on (1) whether they created a condition and (2) whether it would be possible to attain holder in due course (HDC) status under the enactment if it were determined that the provision did not create a condition and that the instrument was therefore negotiable.

In the following case the court addressed whether a promise was unconditional *and* whether the note was payable at a determinable time. The court also had to resolve an allegation that the note in question was not negotiable, and thus that the statute of limitations had expired prior to the commencement of the action. See if you agree with the court's reasoning.

21.2

FIRST WESTERN NATIONAL BANK v. CORONA
2002 Cal. App. Unpub. LEXIS 3563 (Cal. App., 4th App. District, Div. One)

FACTS In November 1990 the Coronas obtained a loan to purchase a single family residence. The loan was secured by a first deed of trust encumbering the property. In October 1991 the Coronas obtained a loan from Directors Mortgage Loan Corporation for home improvements on the property. They signed a promissory note providing for payment of monthly installments of principal and interest and payment in full on or before October 21, 2006. The note included a provision for the lender to notify the debtor of any defaults, and a provision that the entire loan became due and payable upon such notice of default. In October 1993 First Western Bank acquired the note from a prior holder. The Coronas paid all monthly installments through April 1994 but did not pay any further amounts due on the note. Because the Coronas did not pay installments on their home purchase loan note, the holder of that note and first deed of trust (Directors Mortgage Loan Corporation) foreclosed on that deed of trust, eliminating First Western's security interest in the property under its second deed of trust. On September 18, 1998, First Western filed a complaint against the Coronas alleging a cause of action for nonpayment of amounts due under the note. The Coronas demurred to the complaint, asserting that the cause of action was barred by the statute of limitations. First Western disagreed, asserting that its cause of action was filed within the six-year limitations period under California Uniform Commercial Code § 3-118. The Coronas' reply argued that the note was not a negotiable instrument, so that a four-year statute of limitations for actions based on written contracts applied, and not the six-year statute of limitations set out in § 3-118. According to the Coronas, language within the note referring to the fact that the deed of trust secured their obligations made the note conditional and therefore negated negotiability. The trial court disagreed with this contention, overruled the Coronas' demurrer, and ordered them to file their answer to the complaint no later than December 29, 1998. The Coronas filed their answer to the complaint, once again asserting the affirmative defense that the four-year statute of limitations expired before the complaint was filed. At trial, the court entered judgment for First Western and the Coronas appealed.

ISSUE Did the cited language make the note conditional and therefore nonnegotiable?

HOLDING No. The cited language did not constitute a condition. The note was a negotiable instrument and the six-year statute of limitations applied.

REASONING Excerpts from the opinion of Acting Presiding Judge McDonald:

Section 3-118(a) provides: "An action to enforce the obligation of a party to pay a note payable at a definite time shall be commenced within six years after the due date or dates stated in the note or, if a due date is accelerated, within six years after the accelerated due date." . . . The term "note" . . . is a type of negotiable instrument. . . . Section 3-104, subdivision (a) generally defines a "negotiable instrument" as:

"An *unconditional* promise or order to pay a fixed amount of money, with or without interest or other charges described in the promise or order, if it is all of the following:

"(1) Is payable to bearer or to order at the time it is issued or first comes into possession of a holder.

"(2) Is payable on demand or at a definite time.

"(3) *Does not state any other undertaking or instruction by the person promising or ordering payment to do any act in addition to the payment of money*, but the promise or order may contain (i) an undertaking or power to give, maintain, or protect collateral to secure payment, (ii) an authorization or power to the holder to confess judgment or realize on or dispose of collateral, or (iii) a waiver of the benefit of any law intended for the advantage or protection of an obligor." (Italics added.)

Section 3-106 provides, in part:

"(a) Except as provided in this section, for the purposes of subdivision (a) of Section 3-104, *a promise or order is unconditional unless it states* (1) an express condition to payment, (2) *that the promise or order is subject to or governed by another writing*, or (3) that rights or obligations with respect to the promise or order are stated in another writing. *A reference to another writing does not of itself make the promise or order conditional.*

"(b) *A promise or order is not made conditional (1) by a reference to another writing for a statement of rights with respect to collateral, prepayment, or acceleration*, or (2) because payment is limited to resort to a particular fund or source." (Italics added.)

Uniform Commercial Code comment 1 to section 3-106 states in pertinent part:

"For example, a promissory note is not an instrument defined by Section [3-104] if it contains any of the following statements: . . . 2. 'This note is subject to a loan and security agreement dated April 1, 1990[,] between the payee and maker of this note.' It is not relevant whether any condition to payment is or is not stated in the writing to which reference is made. The rationale is that the holder of a negotiable instrument should not be required to examine another document to determine rights with respect to payment. But *[subdivision] (b)(i) permits reference to a separate writing for information with respect to collateral, prepayment, or acceleration*. . . .

We conclude the Note is a negotiable instrument and therefore the six-year statute of limitations period under section 3-118(a) applies in this case. The Note, on its face, satisfies all of the requirements for a negotiable instrument. The Note is payable to the order of the lender. The Note is payable at a definite time (i.e., by monthly installments with the remainder due on October 21, 2006, unless the due date is accelerated by

the holder). The Note is a promise to a pay a fixed amount ($17,500). That promise is unconditional and does *not* state "any other undertaking or instruction by the [Coronas] to do any act in addition to the payment of money." . . . The Note is *not* made conditional by the fact that it includes a provision referring to the deed of trust securing its obligations. . . . "A reference to another writing does *not* of itself make the promise or order conditional." . . . In particular, "a reference to another writing for a statement of rights with respect to collateral, prepayment, or acceleration" does *not* make a note conditional. . . . Therefore, although the Note states that it is secured by a deed of trust that "describes how and under what conditions [the Coronas] may be required to make immediate payment in full of all amounts that [they] owe under this Note," it is *not* conditional. Furthermore, the Note's inclusion of specific language from the deed of trust regarding the deed of trust's acceleration provisions does *not* make the Note conditional. . . . The Note does *not* expressly state that it is subject to or governed by the deed of trust or any other writing. . . . The Note contains an *unconditional* promise to pay by the Coronas. . . . Therefore, the Note is a negotiable instrument and the six-year section 3-118(a) statute of limitations applies to Bank's action to collect amounts due on the Note. . . . Because the six-year section 3-118(a) statute of limitations applies to Bank's action against the Coronas for amounts due on the Note, we conclude the trial court correctly entered judgment for Bank. . . .

The judgment is affirmed.

BUSINESS CONSIDERATIONS First Western Bank waited for a significant amount of time before seeking recourse against the Coronas, and the delay could have precluded the bank's enforcement of its rights. Why would a creditor wait so long before seeking recovery from a defaulting debtor? What sort of policy should a business have for seeking to enforce its rights following a default?

ETHICAL CONSIDERATIONS Did the Coronas act ethically in seeking to avoid paying their debt due to the technicality that the bank waited more than four years to seek its money? Did the bank act ethically by waiting for more than four years before seeking recourse?

Fixed Amount of Money Requirement

In order to serve as a substitute for money, and in order to be current in trade, a negotiable instrument must provide for payment at some point in time, and it must call for

that payment in "money." A holder of a negotiable instrument reasonably expects to know how much money is to be received when the instrument is ultimately paid. The amount is commonly specified exactly, which makes the determination simple, but this is not necessary to satisfy

NRW CASE 21.2   Finance

NRW

PROMISSORY NOTES AND INTEREST RATES

Mai recently contacted the firm's bank, inquiring about current rates on loans. The bank's lending officer informed Mai that the firm had recently been reclassified by the bank and was now eligible for a "prime plus" rate on its loans. When Mai shared this information with the others, Helen was pleased, but Carlos was skeptical. He wanted to know what a prime plus rate meant, exactly, and he also wanted to know if a "note" that called for interest at "prime plus" was negotiable. The principals have asked for your advice. What will you tell them?

BUSINESS CONSIDERATIONS The revisions to Article 3 greatly expanded the permissible terms that can be used in an instrument without affecting negotiability, especially in determining interest on an instrument. Are these changes better or worse for a borrower? To whom is the negotiability of an instrument most important: the maker, the payee, or a holder?

ETHICAL CONSIDERATIONS Is it ethical to use a phrase for describing the interest on an instrument that may be misinterpreted by third persons? Is it ethical to use any unclear or inexact language in an instrument?

INTERNATIONAL CONSIDERATIONS Why might an instrument call for the payment of money in terms other than U.S. dollars? Why might a payee want an instrument to be paid in "foreign" money rather than American dollars?

---

the "fixed amount of money" requirement. Article 3 does not address this requirement specifically. Instead, several sections of the Code need to be read in conjunction to determine what a "fixed amount of money" means. First we will look at how money is defined in the Code; then we will look at how to arrive at a "fixed amount."

Money is defined in § 1-201(24), and the treatment of an instrument that calls for payment in foreign money is explained in § 3-107. According to these sections:

Section 1-201(24). *"Money" means a medium of exchange authorized or adopted by a domestic or foreign government and includes a monetary unit of account established by intergovernmental organization or by agreement between two or more nations.*

Section 3-107. *Instrument Payable in Foreign Money*

Unless the instrument otherwise provides, an instrument that states that it is payable in foreign money may be paid in the foreign money or in an equivalent amount in dollars calculated by using the current bank-offered spot rate at the place of payment for the purchase of dollars on the day on which the instrument is paid.

Thus, money is a medium of exchange that has been authorized or adopted by a government. (The earlier requirement that money was defined as "legal tender" has been rejected in favor of this broader definition.[1]) While an instrument may be worded in terms of "foreign" money, Article 3 permits the payment of that instrument in *either* the foreign currency *or* the equivalent of the foreign currency in U.S. dollars at the time and place of payment of the instrument, *unless* the instrument itself specifies the form of payment. Now that the definition of "money" has been established, we must turn to the meaning of "fixed amount."

Historically, in order to meet the requirement that the instrument called for the payment of a fixed amount of money, the total amount to be paid had to be calculable from the face of the instrument. This requirement raised the "four-corner" rule. All the necessary information for the calculation of the amount to be paid had to be on the face of the instrument, within the "four corners" of the instrument, even if the calculation had not yet been done. This requirement no longer applies under the new standards, at least with regard to interest.

If an instrument calls for the payment of a definite amount, as a check does, the "fixed amount" is obvious. A check for $100 orders the payment of $100 regardless of when the check is presented for payment. Any non–interest bearing instrument provides an easily determined fixed amount of money to be paid. The problem with determining the fixed amount arises when interest is to be paid on the instrument. Given the current practice of variable rate notes, and of tying interest to the "prime rate," the provisions for determining a fixed amount of money needed to be revised, and the old "four-corner" rule needed to be retired. The provisions for interest are set out in § 3-112. An instrument is presumed to be issued without interest unless interest is specifically called for in the instrument.[2] However, if interest is called for in the instrument, the interest will run from the date of the instrument. The significant change in the treatment of interest is found in § 3-112(b), which states:

Interest may be stated in an instrument as a fixed or variable rate or rates. The amount or rate of interest

NRW CASE 21.3   Finance/Management

HOW SHOULD THE FIRM HANDLE A MONEY ORDER?

NRW recently received a writing from one of its customers intended as a payment on the customer's account. The writing had a heading stating that it was a "Money Order," and below this heading it stated "Pay to NRW_____ $100.00." When this payment was received, the principals discussed what it meant and how it should be treated. Helen said that money orders are valid methods of payment and that the firm should just deposit it as it would any other payments. Carlos said that he thought the money order was actually a check, and that the firm should treat it as a check. Mai was of the opinion that both Helen and Carlos were correct, and that it really didn't matter unless the money order was dishonored. They have asked for your advice. What will you tell them?

BUSINESS CONSIDERATIONS Why might a firm be hesitant to accept a "money order" as payment from a customer? Should a firm be more or less confident in collecting on a "money order" than on a check?

ETHICAL CONSIDERATIONS Is it ethical to refuse payments from customers unless the payments are submitted either in cash or by means of a traditional check? Is it ethical for a customer to submit payment in an unusual manner?

INTERNATIONAL CONSIDERATIONS Checks and drafts are well known and widely accepted in the international business environment. Are money orders also well known or widely accepted? Might an attempt to make payment by means of a money order cause a problem in an international transaction?

may be stated or described in the instrument in any manner and may require reference to information not contained in the instrument. If an instrument provides for interest, but the amount cannot be ascertained from the description, interest is payable at the judgment rate in effect at the place of payment of the instrument and at the time interest first accrues.

This means that an instrument can call for the payment of interest at a variable rate, for example "the prime rate," and it still satisfies the fixed amount of money requirement.

Words of Negotiability Requirement: "Pay to the Order of" or "Pay to Bearer"

To be negotiable, even if every other element is present, an instrument generally must contain "words of negotiability." (There is one exception to this rule, which will be discussed next.) The words of negotiability are "Pay to the order of (name of payee)" or some variation of this phrase, or "Pay to bearer" or some variation. The reason these words are so important is that the law reads them as authorizing the free transfer of the instrument. Failing to use one of these terms can be viewed as a denial of the intention to permit free transferability of the instrument, and therefore as a denial of negotiability.

When Article 3 was revised, a special exception was added to this rule as it relates to the treatment of checks. An instrument that meets all of the requirements to be negotiable *except* for being payable "to order" or "to bearer" at the time of its issue, *and* which otherwise falls within the definition of a "check" as set out in § 3-104(f) is a negotiable instrument *and* a check.[3] This is true even if the instrument is described on its face as being some other type of instrument, such as a "money order." Thus, if an instrument is payable on demand and drawn on a bank, and it meets every requirement for negotiability *except* that it does not contain either of the "words of negotiability" phrases, it is still considered a check, and as such it is still negotiable. (At the time of the revision of Article 3, many credit unions were using instruments that stated "Pay to [name of payee], rather than the more widely accepted "Pay to the order of [name of payee]." Since credit union instruments were now to be recognized as checks, and since so many of the instruments using this form were available, the revised Article 3 simply decided to recognize these forms and to carve out a special rule for checks. In addition, this exception prevents a person from simply deleting or striking out the words "the order of" on a preprinted check and thereby removing the paper from the coverage of Article 3.[4])

However, if an instrument other than a check that is otherwise negotiable calls for payment by stating "Pay to Pete Jones" (rather than "Pay to the order of Pete Jones"), it is *not* negotiable. By the terms of the instrument, only Pete Jones is authorized to receive payment; he cannot transfer payment by negotiation (although he may be able to *assign* his right to receive payment under contract law). And since the instrument is not a check, the special exception does not apply. However, an *indorsement* that says "Pay to Pete Jones" would not affect negotiability. Indorsements cannot negate negotiability once it exists, nor can an indorsement "create" negotiability where it did not previously exist. (Negotiability is found from the information contained on the face of the instrument, and an indorsement is normally on the back of the instrument.)

To be payable "to order," the terms of the instrument must state that it is payable to the order or assigns of a specified individual or to a specified individual or to the individual's order. The designated individual may be a person, as in "Pay to Paula Lopez or order"; an office, as in "Pay to the order of the Treasurer of Washington County"; an estate or trust, as in "Pay to the order of the Johnson Estate"; or an unincorporated association, as in "Pay to the XYZ Partnership or order." An instrument payable to order requires an endorsement to be further negotiated.

If no particular individual is designated, the instrument must be payable to bearer to be negotiable. An instrument is payable to bearer when, by its terms, it is payable to bearer or to the order of bearer; or to "cash" or the order of "cash"; or to a named person or bearer, as in "Pay to Joe Jakes or bearer" or "Pay to the order of Joe Jakes or bearer" (§ 3-109). An instrument is also considered payable to bearer if no payee is stated. No indorsement is legally needed to negotiate an instrument payable to bearer, although most holders will request (or demand) an indorsement for added protection. (The meaning and the importance of indorsements is discussed in Chapter 22.)

Determinable Time Requirement: Payable on Demand or at a Fixed Time

A holder wants to know not only how much money will be paid (fixed amount in money), but also *when* payment can be expected. The question of when will depend on the terms of the instrument, but in order to be negotiable the instrument must be payable either on demand or at a definite time. This element of negotiability is discussed in § 3-108 of Article 3, which provides:

(a) A promise or order is "payable on demand" if it (i) states that it is payable on demand or at sight, or otherwise indicates that it is payable at the will of the holder; or (ii) does not state any time for payment.

(b) A promise or order is "payable at a definite time" if it is payable on elapse of a definite period of time after sight or acceptance or at a fixed date or dates or at a time or times readily ascertainable at the time the promise or order is issued, subject to rights of (i) prepayment, (ii) acceleration, (iii) extension at the option of the holder, or (iv) extension to a further

definite time at the option of the maker or acceptor or automatically upon or after a specified act or event.

(c) If an instrument, payable at a fixed date, is also payable upon demand made before the fixed date, the instrument is payable on demand until the fixed date and, if demand for payment is not made before that date, becomes payable at a definite time on the fixed date.

The payee or holder must be able to tell when the instrument is payable by looking at the face of the instrument. Unless the instrument specifies that it is to be paid at some future date (payable at a definite time), it is payable on demand. An instrument is payable on demand when payment is to be made on sight, or at presentment, or when no time for payment is stated. Any form of instrument may be payable on demand, but promise paper (notes and CDs) normally is payable at a definite (future) time and is not payable on demand. A check must be payable on demand, by definition. A draft other than a check may be payable on demand or it may be payable at a definite time.

The following case involved a suit to collect on what was allegedly a promissory note. However, the defendant challenged the negotiability of the "note" by claiming that there was no due date, thus negating negotiability. The defendant also raised a question regarding the legality of the alleged debt due to the fact that some of the "loan" proceeds had not been paid in money. After reading the opinion, decide if you agree with the court's reasoning.

An instrument is payable at a definite time if, by its terms, it is payable at a time that can be determined from its face. This definite time frequently will be some stated future date such as "September 24, 20XX." Or it may be at some time after a stated date, such as "90 days after March 3, 20XX." Either of these dates would be definite even if some provision were made for accelerating the payment date. They also would be definite with a provision for extending the time if the holder has the option of extension, or even if the maker or acceptor has the option of extending the time. However, in this last situation the extension must be a predetermined definite period, not to exceed the original term.

The UCC also stipulates that payment is at a definite time if payment is a stated period after sight (i.e., after presentment). Thus, an instrument calling for payment "60 days after sight" is payable at a definite time even though that definite time cannot be ascertained until after "sight" is established. Although the holder must act (present the instrument to the drawee to establish the date of sight), once the act is done, the date for payment is definite.

CHO v. CHI
2002 Cal. App. Unpub. LEXIS 2664 (Cal. App., 4th App. Dist., Div. One)

FACTS Chang Cho alleged that she loaned $40,000 to Kacy Chi, and that Chi failed to repay the loans. According to Cho, she made an initial loan of $4,000 to Chi in March 1995, and then loaned Chi another $1,000 per month from April 1995 through May 1997, a total of $30,000. Cho also stated that, on occasion, when she did not have enough cash to make the loan, Chi would request that Cho give her (Chi) food stamps instead of cash. Chi agreed to repay the $30,000 in June 1997, and submitted a check for $30,000 in that month as repayment. The check was postdated to September 30, 1997. When Cho deposited the check in October 1997, the bank returned the check unpaid. Cho had also made a separate $10,000 loan to Chi in May 1996. Chi had also attempted to pay that loan by postdated check (that check was dated November 30, 1996), and that check was also returned by the bank upon Cho's attempt to deposit the check. In April 1997 Chi made a $4,000 cash payment to Cho, reducing the total of her debt to $36,000. Cho was concerned that she had no evidence of the debt owed to her by Chi, so she prepared a written document to memorialize the debt and then asked Chi to sign the document. Chi signed the document on August 28, 1997. When the debt remained unpaid, Cho filed suit against Chi in January 1998, alleging breach of contract. Chi demurred to the complaint, alleging that Cho had failed to set forth sufficient facts to support her claim, and also that Cho had not alleged when payment was due under the contract or to whom the money was to be paid. Cho amended the complaint to state that the payment was to be made to Cho and that payment was to be made "upon demand by Cho." According to Cho, only $4,000 of the loan was repaid by Chi. On the other hand, Chi argues that the payments were not a loan, but were in connection with a "kye," described by Chi as a pyramid or lottery played by members of the Korean community. Following presentation of Cho's case, the court granted Chi's motion for nonsuit on the grounds that (1) the alleged "promissory note" did not rise to the level of a negotiable instrument as defined by California Uniform Commercial Code § 3-104 and was therefore unenforceable; (2) the consideration for the agreement was illegal because it involved the transfer of food stamps, rendering the agreement void; and (3) Cho could not establish with sufficient certainty the amount of money consideration she gave Chi other than the food stamps. On appeal, Cho contends that the court erred in granting Chi's motion for nonsuit.

ISSUES Was the "promissory note" signed by Chi a negotiable instrument? Was the underlying agreement illegal, thus nullifying the claim of Cho?

HOLDINGS Yes, the promissory note was a negotiable instrument. No, the underlying agreement was not illegal, although a portion of the agreement was illegal.

REASONING Excerpts from the opinion of Judge Nares:

In opening statement, counsel for Cho argued that the case was a simple one: that Cho had lent Chi $40,000, that Chi had not paid back $36,000 of that amount, and that the agreement was supported by checks Chi had written to Cho, and a "promissory note" evidencing the debt. Counsel for Cho acknowledged that $5,000 of the amount loaned to Chi was in the form of food stamps, but argued that this fact did not affect the enforceability of the debt. Counsel for Cho also noted that it was anticipated that Chi would argue that the money was not for a loan, but Cho's involvement in a "kye," what the defense characterized as a pyramid or lottery game played by members of the Korean community. However, counsel asserted that the evidence would show that there was no such "kye."

Counsel for Chi argued that the "promissory note" did not meet the requirements for negotiable instruments contained in section 3-104 and thus was not enforceable. Counsel for Chi also argued that the evidence would show that the checks and promissory note were only given in recognition that Cho would eventually be paid under the kye, not that Chi was liable for a debt to her. Defense counsel also argued that the claims were not valid because the money was an investment in a "kye," which the defense characterized as an illegal pyramid scheme. Counsel argued that the evidence would show there was no loan, but rather that Cho invested in a kye that fell apart when some members did not pay their share. Defense counsel also argued that there was no contract between Cho and Chi, as Chi was merely the "facilitator" for the kye and not responsible if some participants did not pay their share. Finally, counsel took the position that because some of the consideration for the transaction was in the form of food stamps, the transaction was illegal and could not be enforced by the court. . . .

The court found the promissory note unenforceable because it "did not contain an indication that it was payable on demand or at any other time, or a payment schedule and amount of periodic payments." The court also found that the transaction was illegal because "the alleged loan included an undetermined amount of food stamps." Finally, the court also found that Cho had not proven her damages in an ascertainable amount because "the amount of consideration exclusive of the food stamps was not established." . . .

"A contract must receive such an interpretation as will make it lawful, operative, definite, reasonable, and capable of being carried into effect, if it can be done without violating the intention of the parties." . . . Additionally, if an agreement is silent on any subject, any applicable laws become a part thereof as if "expressly included in the terms of the agreement itself." . . .

Chi argues, and the court found, that the promissory note was unenforceable as it violated the terms of section 3-104 because it failed to state a date for payment or state that it was payable on demand. This argument fails for a couple of reasons. First, section 3-104 merely provides the requisites to a note being considered a "negotiable instrument" under that statute:

"'Negotiable instrument' means an unconditional promise or order to pay a fixed amount of money, with or without interest or other charges described in the promise or order, if it is all of the following: (1) Is payable to bearer or to order at the time it is issued or first comes into possession of a holder. (2) *Is payable on demand or at a definite time.* (3) Does not state any other undertaking or instruction by the person promising or ordering payment to do any act in addition to the payment of money . . ."

Section 3-104 does not by its terms hold that a promissory note is unenforceable if it does not specify a time for payment or that it is payable upon demand. Rather, it states that if a document does not meet the prerequisites set forth in that section it is not subject to the law on negotiable instruments.

Further, even if section 3-104 is applicable to Cho's claim for breach of contract, the promissory note is enforceable. Section 3-108, subdivision (a) provides:

"A promise or order is 'payable on demand' if it (1) states that it is payable on demand or at sight, or otherwise indicates that it is payable at the will of the holder,

or (2) *does not state any time of payment.*" (Italics added.)

Thus, under section 3-108, as with Civil Code section 1657, if a promissory note contains no time for payment, it is interpreted to mean that the money is due upon demand. Accordingly, under either Civil Code section 1657 or sections 3-104 and 3-108, the promissory note is not rendered unenforceable because it specifies no time for repayment. . . . On appeal, Cho does not contend that her transfer of food stamps to Chi as part of the loan transaction was legal or proper. Accordingly, for the purposes of this appeal, we will assume that use of food stamps as a portion of the consideration for the loan to Chi was illegal. The issue presented then is what was the effect of that illegal consideration.

"The consideration of a contract must be lawful. . . ." . . . However, "while the courts generally will not enforce an illegal contract or one against public policy, 'the rule is not an inflexible one to be applied in its fullest rigor under any and all circumstances,' and '[a] wide range of exceptions has been recognized' to enforce contracts 'to avoid unjust enrichment to a defendant and a disproportionately harsh penalty upon the plaintiff.'" . . . In this regard, where the consideration for an agreement is only partly illegal and the legal portion of the consideration is severable, the legal part of the agreement may be enforced. . . . As the court stated . . . "a contract is severable if the court can, consistent with the intent of the parties, reasonably relate the illegal consideration on one side to some specified or determinable portion of the consideration on the other side." . . .

The judgment is reversed. Appellant to recover her costs on appeal.

BUSINESS CONSIDERATIONS In this case Cho made multiple loans to Chi without any evidence of the loans except her word. Is this a good business practice? Should a business have a policy of *always* receiving written evidence of any credit it extends?

ETHICAL CONSIDERATIONS Was it ethical of Chi to argue that Cho was involved in illegal activities, and thus attempt to avoid liability for the debts Chi had incurred? Was the use of an alleged "cultural activity" (the "kye") as a defense ethical?

However, one must be careful in this area. Payment is not at a definite time if it is to occur only upon an act or occurrence that is of uncertain date. For example, an instrument payable "30 days after Uncle Charlie dies" is probably not negotiable, since the holder would have to go outside the instrument to determine the time of occurrence

before the time to pay the instrument could be set. (The language of the revised Article, that a definite time exists if the time or times are "readily ascertainable at the time the promise or order is issued," may change this area. We will have to wait for judicial interpretations to see how broadly or how narrowly this provision will now be construed.)

The "Exclusive Obligation" Requirement

The final requirement for determining negotiability is that the promise or the order contained in the instrument is the only *undertaking* or *instruction* of the person making the promise or giving the order. The person promising or ordering payment must not have any other "undertaking or instruction" to do any other act in addition to payment of the money. The Code uses the terms "undertaking" and "instruction" rather than "promise" or "order" because both promise and order are specifically defined in Article 3 as involving only written promises or orders to pay money.[5] Thus, undertaking and instruction are meant to be broader, and to include oral commitments or other written commitments beyond the coverage of Article 3. The promises and orders governed by this Article are *exclusively* those written promises and orders that call for the payment of money and have no other commitments or obligations tied to the writing.

Construction and Interpretation: Article 3

Article 3 takes a very short-and-simple approach to construction and interpretation. Basically, § 3-114, which covers contradictory terms, provides the coverage in this area. According to this section:

If an instrument contains contradictory terms, type-written terms prevail over printed terms, handwritten terms prevail over both, and words prevail over numbers.

This coverage is very brief and seems to be very specific. However, despite its brevity, this is an area that is likely to require some litigation to provide additional guidelines on how courts plan to interpret ambiguities that do not fall exactly within the language of the section. Judicial decisions will provide the parameters for this area, possibly beyond the simple language of the statutory coverage. For a "black letter law" explanation of negotiability, look at http://lawschool.westlaw.com/blacks/negotiable.asp.

Requirements for Negotiability: Article 7

Article 7 of the UCC covers documents of title. Where Article 3 is very strict in determining whether the Article applies to a particular writing, Article 7 is much more relaxed in determining what it covers. One reason for this difference is that Article 3 applies *only* to negotiable instruments. If a writing is not negotiable it does not fall within the coverage of Article 3 and is governed by other areas of law. However, Article 7 applies to "Warehouse Receipts, Bills of Lading, and Other Documents of Title." In order for Article 7 to apply, all that needs to be shown is that the document in question is a document of title. The negotiability of the document is not relevant to the document's coverage by Article 7. Nonetheless, the negotiability of a document of title may be important, and the Article does have provisions for determining whether a document of title is negotiable. Section 7-104 states that a document of title is negotiable if:

1. by its terms the goods are to be delivered to bearer or to the order of a named person; or

2. where recognized in international trade, if it runs to a named person or assigns.

Every other document of title is deemed to be non-negotiable. In fact, a bill of lading that is consigned to a named person is not made negotiable by a provision specifying that the goods are to be delivered only against an order signed by a named person. Obviously, Article 7 is more concerned with the rights of the parties to the goods than with the rights of the parties in the documents covering the goods.

Whether the document of title is negotiable or non-negotiable, the bailee has a duty of care. If the bailee fails to exercise due care and the goods are damaged or destroyed, the bailee is liable.

Even though Article 7 is more concerned with rights in the goods, there are certain rights to be gained if the document of title is negotiable, especially if the party qualifies as a holder by due negotiation. In addition, a holder by due negotiation can exist only if the document of title is negotiable. (This topic will be covered in more detail in Chapter 23.)

Summary

This chapter examines the technical requirements for negotiability of an instrument under Article 3. The first requirement is that the instrument be written or reduced to tangible form. Next, the instrument must be signed by the maker or the drawer. The promise (for notes or CDs) or the order (for checks or drafts) must be unconditional. The instrument must call for the payment of a fixed amount of money—a medium of exchange authorized or adopted by a domestic or foreign government. In addition, the time of payment must be determinable from the face of the instrument, or it must be payable on demand. Finally, the instrument must contain "words of negotiability." This means it must be payable "to order" or "to bearer," although a special exception for this rule exists if the instrument is in all other respects a check.

Checks do not need to include the "words of negotiability" in order to be treated as negotiable instruments.

In case the instrument contains ambiguities, the Code provides a method of interpretation. Handwriting takes precedence over typing and over printing. Typing takes precedence over printing, and words take precedence over numbers. Article 7 of the UCC governs documents of title, which may be negotiable or nonnegotiable. The requirements for negotiable documents under Article 7 are much less stringent than the requirements under Article 3. Article 7 is more concerned with the goods than with the documents covering the goods, but it does provide some special protections if the document is negotiable and the holder qualifies as a holder by due negotiation.

Discussion Questions

1. How does the UCC define a "signature"? Why is the signature requirement so important in determining whether an instrument is negotiable?

2. In order to qualify as a negotiable instrument, the promise or the order must be "written." How does the UCC define "written," and how is that definition modified for negotiable instruments?

3. What is meant by a "fixed amount of money" under Article 3 of the UCC? How does the Code define "fixed amount"? What is meant by "money"?

4. In order to be a negotiable instrument, the writing must call for payment *either* on demand *or* at a definite time. Why is an instrument that is payable "30 days after sight" considered to be payable at a definite time, while an instrument payable "30 days after my anniversary" is not?

5. Sight drafts are increasingly important as a means of payment in sales contracts. What is meant by "sight" and how is the date of "sight" established?

6. The courts have consistently held that an "IOU is not a negotiable instrument." Below is a typical IOU. Why would such an instrument be deemed nonnegotiable? Be specific.

Betty,   March 17, 20XX

IOU $350

Jane Doe

---

7. A promissory note was issued by Larry to Darryl. The note had the following terms included in the body of the instrument:

   Interest to be paid at 14 percent per annum. [This term was preprinted on the promissory note form.] Interest at 14.5 percent per annum. [This term was typewritten above the preprinted term.] Plus interest. [This term was handwritten in the margin and initialed by both Larry and Darryl.]

   How will interest be computed on this note, and why will that method for computing interest be used?

8. Marvella issued what appeared to be a time draft payable to the order of Herman. The terms of the instrument called for payment "90 days after our marriage." Marvella and Herman were married on January 4 of this year. Subsequently, they got a divorce on March 15. Herman presented the instrument to the drawee 90 days after the wedding date, demanding payment. The drawee refused to pay, and Herman has sued Marvella on the instrument. Will this case be resolved under the provisions of Article 3, or will it be resolved under the provisions of common law? Why?

9. What is required by Article 7 in order for a document of title to be deemed negotiable? Is this more or less rigorous than the requirements for negotiability under Article 3? Why is there a difference in the requirements of negotiability under the two articles?

10. A bill of lading called for the delivery of the goods to Acme, Inc. It went on to specify that delivery was to take place only on receipt of a written order signed by Mr. Aziz. Is this document of title negotiable? Explain.

Case Problems and Writing Assignments

1. The Oaks Apartments Joint Venture and its five partners executed a promissory note payable to the order of Meridian Service Corporation, a wholly owned subsidiary of Meridian Savings Association. The note read, in pertinent part:

   FOR VALUE RECEIVED, THE OAKS APARTMENTS JOINT VENTURE, a Texas Joint Venture . . . promises to pay to the order of MERIDIAN SERVICE CORPORATION, a Texas Corporation . . . the sum of TWO MILLION AND NO/100 DOLLARS ($2,000,000.00) or so much thereof as may be advanced in accordance with the terms of a certain Loan Agreement executed on even date herewith, with interest thereon at the rate provided below.

   The five partners also executed an unconditional personal guaranty of the note, obligating each partner for 20 percent of the total debt. The Oaks Apartments was subsequently sold to Veigel, who assumed the loan obligation in 1985. Veigel then entered into an agreement with Meridian that modified the time and manner of payment. Veigel subsequently defaulted on the note, and Meridian began attempting to collect from Veigel, the partnership, and each of the partners in 1986. In 1987, Meridian foreclosed on the apartment complex and sold it, leaving a deficit of $755,249.06 on the note. Meridian then sued to recover this deficit. (Resolution Trust replaced Meridian as conservator when Meridian failed.) Resolution Trust argued that it was an HDC of the note and the guaranty, not subject to any defenses. The partners objected, alleging that the note was not negotiable, so RTC could not be an HDC.

   Was the note originally signed by Oaks Apartments a negotiable instrument? Is it ethical to try to avoid liability by denying that a note issued by the defendant is negotiable? [See *Resolution Trust Corp. v. Oaks Apartments Joint Venture*, 966 F.2d 995 (5th Cir. 1992).]

2. Butler Manufacturing and a number of other firms stored goods with Americold Corporation. Americold operated an underground warehouse, storing goods in a limestone cave that was originally formed during a mining operation. A fire broke out in the warehouse on December 28, 1991, causing substantial losses and/or damages to the stored goods. Many of the plaintiffs stored business records with Americold. Each firm that stored such business records executed and signed a standard Records Storage Contract. These Records Storage Contracts contained an exculpatory clause excusing Americold from any claims against it for ordinary negligence, and another clause purporting to limit the total amount of damages that could be collected from Americold regardless of the cause of action. Americold argued that the exculpatory clauses should be given full force and effect because the contracts were fairly bargained for, and agreed to, by the parties. They added that there was no unconscionable disparity of bargaining power and that the limitations were an acceptable allocation of risk. Butler and the other plaintiffs argued that the exculpatory clauses violated public policy and also violated the duty of care imposed by § 7-204 of the UCC. They urged the court to negate these clauses and to allow them to recover their damages. How should the court resolve this case? What arguments, if any, can be made for upholding the exculpatory clauses in the contract? What arguments, if any, can be made for ignoring the exculpatory clauses? [See *Butler Manufacturing Co. v. Americold Corporation*, 835 F. Supp. 1274 (D. Kan. 1993).]

3. O'Mara, a West Virginia corporation with its principal place of business in Steubenville, Ohio, operated 15 Bonanza restaurants. O'Mara hired GSD, an accounting firm, to manage its accounting and other financial matters. Included in GSD's services were the computation of O'Mara's weekly federal withholding taxes, preparation of checks for deposit of these taxes, and reconciliation of bank statements. Smith was the sole owner of GSD, and also owned 20 percent of O'Mara. Thompson was the comptroller for both O'Mara and GSD. Smith encountered financial difficulties beginning in 1979, and Smith and Thompson devised a plan whereby Smith would embezzle O'Mara's withholding taxes. This scheme involved indorsing the withholding checks, which were payable to the order of the Heritage Bank, as follows:

   Pay to the order of The First National Bank & Trust Company in Steubenville, Ohio FOR DEPOSIT ONLY GAIL SMITH DEVELOPMENT #009-215, W. Gail Smith.

   Heritage Bank accepted each of these checks with this indorsement and without question. When O'Mara discovered what had happened, it sued Heritage Bank (along with two other banks similarly involved) to recover the funds. The banks denied liability, asserting that the checks as issued were "bearer" instruments, not "order" instruments. Were these checks "bearer paper" so that Heritage Bank acted properly in accepting them? [See *O'Mara Enterprises v. People's Bank of Weirton*, 420 S.E.2d 727 (W.Va. 1992).]

4. On October 13, 1975, Wachovia Bank issued a $20,000 certificate of deposit to "Timmy S. Holloway, Jr., by Rountree Crisp, Sr., Agent." At the time, Timmy was a six-year-old minor. Crisp died on April 5, 1978. On April 11, 1980, Wachovia paid to Marcia Coleman, Timmy's mother, and Louise Crisp, Crisp's widow and Timmy's grandmother, the sum of $26,294.92, purportedly the proceeds then due on the certificate of deposit, upon an indorsement reading "Timothy S. Holloway, Jr., by Estate of George R. Crisp, Sr., Marcia Coleman, Adminx." Coleman twice rolled over the proceeds of the certificate of deposit into new certificates.

   On October 23, 1981, Coleman presented the most recent certificate to Wachovia for payment. Wachovia paid the certificate with a check in the amount of $26,294.92 payable to "Timmy S. Holloway, Jr., by Marcia Coleman." Coleman stated that she did not remember what she did with the $26,294.92 proceeds of that check. No court had appointed Coleman as Timmy's guardian with authority to receive the funds for him. In June 1986, Coleman was appointed Timmy's guardian for purposes of holding real property inherited by Timmy from his grandmother. Shortly before his 18th birthday on September 5, 1987, Timmy's relationship with his mother had deteriorated to the point that he had moved away from her house and to an aunt's house. In the summer of 1988, Timmy was in need of money and his aunt told him about the certificate of deposit left by his grandfather.

Timmy brought an action against Wachovia seeking to recover the original value of the certificate ($20,000) plus interest. Did the bank breach its contract with Crisp when it paid the certificate to Coleman? In this case the bank paid the certificate of deposit upon presentment and demand for payment from the administratrix of the estate of Crisp and the mother of the named payee. What more should the bank have done to ascertain the right of Timmy's mother to act as his "legal guardian" in the handling of this nonnegotiable certificate of deposit? [See *Holloway v. Wachovia Bank & Trust Co.*, 423 S.E.2d 752 (N.C. 1992).]

5. **BUSINESS APPLICATION CASE** Fleetguard, located in Tennessee, was a manufacturer of filter paper. Dixie Box, located in Charleston, packaged merchandise cargo for transportation, mostly for export. Fleetguard entered into an agreement with Dixie Box to package nine rolls of its filter paper in a moisture-proof barrier for international shipment to China. Dixie Box received the paper from Fleetguard in July 1986, and placed it in its warehouse. In August 1986, prior to the packaging and shipment of the paper, a fire occurred at the Dixie Box facility. Fleetguard's paper was damaged by smoke and water and has no salvage value. Fleetguard brought a bailment action to recover the value of the paper. The circuit court held Dixie Box failed to rebut a presumption of negligence in its care of Fleetguard's paper and awarded Fleetguard $21,012.87, the value of the paper. Did Dixie Box use reasonable care in storing Fleetguard's paper? What might Dixie Box have done differently to avoid this problem? [See *Fleetguard, Inc. v. Dixie Box and Crating Company*, 445 S.E.2d 459 (S.C. App. 1994).]

6. **ETHICAL APPLICATION CASE** James H. Creekmore, Jr. and Judith Carolyn Creekmore were the only children of Ruby Lamm Creekmore. During her final illness, Ruby executed a last will and testament that disposed of her assets, including real property, personal effects, and shares of a closely held corporation called Lamm Development Corporation. Until her death, Ruby was an officer and stockholder of the corporation. Under the terms of the will Judith Creekmore was to receive 50 percent of her mother's stock in a life estate, and then Judith and James were to divide the balance of their mother's estate equally. On February 6, 1994, prior to her death, Ruby gave a check for $10,000 to Judith and asked her not to deposit the check until after March 1, 1994, because she did not want the check to appear in her February bank statements, to which James had access. James argued that the check did not constitute a completed gift because it was not cashed prior to the

death of the drawer. James believed that the $10,000 should be a part of the estate, to be divided equally between him and his sister. Was the delivery to Judith Creekmore by her mother of a $10,000 check a completed *inter vivos* gift, and thus properly excluded from the estate? Is it ethical for a relative to challenge the alleged wishes of a decedent in hopes of gaining a larger inheritance? [See *Creekmore v. Creekmore*, 485 S.E.2d 68 (N.C. App. 1997).]

7. **CRITICAL THINKING CASE** Kindy agreed to purchase four diesel engines from Hicks, with Hicks agreeing to deliver the engines to Kindy. The purchase price was $13,000. Kindy agreed to wire transfer $6,500 and to pay the remainder by check. The check was not to be cashed until the engines had been delivered. Kindy wrote and mailed a postdated check to Hicks in June 1989. This check had two different amounts on its face: $6,500 in numbers on the number line, and $5,500 imprinted with a check imprinting machine on the line where words normally appear. Kindy stated that he had intentionally put two amounts on the check, reasoning that the bank would call him to find out which amount was to be paid, allowing him to tell the bank whether to honor the check (if the engines had been delivered) or to dishonor the check (if the engines had not been delivered). Hicks presented the check to the Galatia Bank June 10, 1989, and the bank honored the check for $5,500. A bank employee altered the amount in the normal "number" location, changing the "6" in $6,500 to a "5" so that the amounts in each area were in agreement. The check was subsequently presented to the drawee bank, which refused it. Galatia sued Kindy for the amount of the check. Kindy denied liability, asserting that he had a defense (nondelivery) and that the bank was a mere holder. Was Galatia Bank a holder in due course and thus entitled to recover from Kindy on the check? Do imprinted numbers, located where the words are normally located, take precedence over numbers placed where the numbers are *normally* placed on a check? Does the answer to this question have any implications for businesses that use imprinting machines to "emboss" the amount on checks issued by the company? [See *Galatia Community State Bank v. Kindy*, 821 S.W.2d 765 (Ark. 1991).]

8. **YOU BE THE JUDGE** Thomas J. Stafford was a farmer in Chesterfield County. He had two children, a daughter, June S. Zink, and a son, Thomas L. Stafford. He also developed a residential subdivision on a parcel of land that he owned. He built four houses in the subdivision, each on a separate subdivided lot, and sold each of the four houses. In each instance Stafford took back a purchase money note from the purchaser, with the note secured by a deed of trust. Each of the four notes was payable to the order of Thomas Stafford, and each of the notes was indorsed by Stafford as follows: "Pay to the order of Thomas J. Stafford or June S. Zink, or the survivor." Proceeds from the notes were deposited into a "collection account" with a local bank. The account was maintained in the name of "Thomas J. Stafford and June S. Zink, as joint tenants with right of survivorship." Thomas J. Stafford died, and his son insists that the four purchase money notes and the balance in

the "collection account" properly belonged in the estate, to be distributed according to the will of the deceased. June Zink argues that the notes and the balance of the "collection account" properly belonged to her, as survivor, in accord with the indorsements on the notes and the provision that the account named her as one of the "joint tenants with right of survivorship." The daughter also asserts that the notes were negotiated to her, as evidenced by the indorsements on each, giving her rights. The son argues that the notes were not negotiated—or even transferred—to June Zink, and that the various writings were merely a failed attempt to create a gift. This case has been brought before *your* court. How will *you* decide? What should a person who operates an unincorporated business do to ensure that the assets of the business—or even the business entity—are preserved in the event of his or her death? How could the notes in this case have been written to ensure that the daughter had rights in the notes *ab initio*? [See *Zink v. Stafford*, 509 S.E.2d 833, 1999 Va. LEXIS 19 (1999).]

Notes

1. Official Comments to UCC § 1-201(24), Comment 24.
2. UCC § 3-112(a).
3. UCC § 3-104(c).
4. Official Comments to UCC § 3-104, Comment 2.
5. Official Comments to UCC § 3-104, Comment 1.

CHAPTER 22

Negotiation and Holders in Due Course/Holders by Due Negotiation

AGENDA

NRW NRW will be receiving a number of checks from its customers. How should the checks be handled? How should they be indorsed? Does the method of indorsement make any difference legally?

Occasionally the firm will receive a check that was originally issued to one of the firm's customers as payee, and that customer will then turn the check over to NRW as payment on his or her account. Does it matter if the customer transfers such a check to the firm without indorsing the check? If the firm wants an indorsement, what type of indorsement will the firm be entitled to receive from the transferring customer?

NRW will also be using checks to make payments on the firm's various accounts. If a problem subsequently arises between the payee and NRW, can the firm avoid paying the check because of this problem, or might it be forced to pay the check despite the problem?

If the checks are deposited, when will the funds be available for the firm to use? Suppose that some of the checks they deposit are dishonored by the bank. What rights can the firm assert? Against whom will they be able to assert these rights?

These and other questions may arise during our discussion of the topics in this chapter. Be prepared! You never know when the firm or one of its members will seek your advice.

Transfer

Negotiable instruments are intended to "flow" through the commercial world. In order to "flow," the instrument needs to be freely transferable from person to person. The form these transfers take determines the rights that can be asserted by each person gaining possession of the instrument.

The Uniform Commercial Code (UCC) defines a transfer as a delivery by any person other than the issuer for the purpose of giving the person receiving the instrument the right to enforce the instrument.[1] A transfer, whether by negotiation or not, confers on the transferee the rights possessed by the transferor, including the rights of a holder in due course (HDC) if the transferor has those rights.[2] Thus, as the previous chapter discussed, a transfer of a negotiable instrument is treated like an assignment of a contract right. The transferee receives any and all rights of the transferor. While this is, in effect, the same as an assignment, this is not an ideal position, and if negotiable instruments could only be transferred—treated the same as an assignment—they would not be as readily acceptable as they are in the modern commercial world.

In the following case the court had to address the issue of an heir who acquired possession of a promissory note through a trust established by her father. The makers of the note were attempting to assert the right to recoupment against the note. Notice the importance of holder in due course status in the court's opinion.

22.1

DAVIS v. STARLING
799 So.2d 373, Fla. App. LEXIS 16043 (Fla. App. 2001)

FACTS Dennis and Karla Davis originally leased real property from David Ballou. They conducted a business selling and servicing tractors, as Ballou had previously done. At the time of the lease Ballou allegedly represented that the property was free of any environmental contamination. After a few years, the Davises entered into a contract to purchase the property from Ballou, and in 1994 they executed and delivered to him a purchase money note and mortgage in the amount of $285,000.

Some time later Ballou established a trust, naming himself as trustee, and assigned this mortgage note to the trust. Two years after establishing the trust, Ballou passed away. Upon his death, his surviving spouse and daughter became successor trustees of the trust, and a few weeks later the successor trustees assigned the mortgage to the daughter alone. She was then the owner and holder of the promissory note and mortgage. More than a year after Ballou's death, the Davises discovered that Ballou had installed an underground gasoline storage tank on the property, from which he fueled trucks on site. In 1988, Ballou filled the tank with water and paved over the area, apparently in violation of environmental laws. As a result, the regulatory authorities later found the property contaminated by leaking from the underground tank. The estimated cost of cleaning up the contamination ran from $38,500 to $64,500. Two years after their discovery of the contamination, the Davises brought this declaratory judgment action against the daughter as the holder of the mortgage, seeking to recoup from sums due on the mortgage the costs related to bringing the land into compliance with the environmental laws. The daughter moved for summary judgment, arguing that the Davises had waited too long to assert recoupment. She argued that they should have asserted the recoupment by filing a claim against Ballou's estate and that, having failed to do so, they are barred from asserting recoupment by section 733.710, the nonclaim statute. The trial court agreed and entered judgment in favor of Starling, the transferee of the mortgage. The Davises appealed from this decision.

ISSUES Is recoupment still available for the makers of the note even though the statutory "nonclaim" period has expired? Would the makers be able to use recoupment if Starling were a holder in due course?

HOLDINGS Yes, recoupment is still available in this case. No, recoupment could not be used if the holder qualified for holder in due course status.

REASONING Excerpts from the opinion of Judge Framer:

We have a summary judgment cutting off an attempt by debtors to assert recoupment against the transferee of a mortgage for certain expenses resulting from environmental contamination. The debtors claim that the original mortgagee, who was also their seller, had falsely told them that there was no environmental contamination. Although the time for asserting independent damages claims directly against the estate of the seller has been extinguished by the lapse of the nonclaim statute, we nevertheless conclude that recoupment is not unavailable against the current holder of the mortgage and therefore reverse. . . . The gist of the legal position asserted by debtors is quite straightforward. They contend that as against their seller equity would surely allow them to reduce the amount of the mortgage debt for their economic losses resulting from the seller's misrepresentation as to hidden environmental contamination. As between them and their seller, they argue, they are the wronged party and the seller is the wrongdoer. Thus they ought to be able, they argue, to assert recoupment against the daughter because she succeeded to the ownership of the mortgage, as it were, by being heir to the alleged wrongdoer's estate and not by giving value. That is, the current owner/holder of the note and mortgage securing it did not take the mortgage by purchase for value. In this circumstance, they say, they ought to be able to assert the right of setoff defensively against the holder.

It is true, as debtors argue, that if their seller were alive and still held the mortgage they would be able to state a right of recoupment against him for the misrepresentation. It is also true, however, that any independent claim for damages arising from such a misrepresentation would have been, upon his death, transformed to a claim against his estate. And the holder of the mortgage is equally correct that such an independent claim against the estate expired when the debtors failed to file such a claim with the personal representative before the lapse of section 733.710. At this point, however, to authorize a summary judgment the transferee of the mortgage leaps from the demise of the independent claim to argue that defensive relief by recoupment to reduce the mortgage debt is also barred as well, and for essentially the same reason—the lapse of the non-claim statute. We disagree.

Functionally the debtors seek to reduce the amount of the debt by a "credit" for the costs of curing the environmental contamination. Their action is in the nature of a defense against the original mortgagee/seller for an alleged misrepresentation as to the environmental status of the property later sold, the same property securing the debt. It is well established that a simple holder of a note and mortgage—as opposed to a holder in due course—takes the instruments subject to the personal defenses of the maker against the original payee/mortgagee. . . . The

daughter is merely a holder of the mortgage, rather than a holder in due course, because she gave no value and acquired her interest by virtue of her status as the beneficiary of the trust. . . . Thus the daughter holds the mortgage subject to the same defenses as her father faced when he held it. The question, then, is whether recoupment is one of those defenses the makers of the note and mortgage can now assert.

It has long been the rule in Florida that the defense of recoupment is available even though an underlying claim based on the same facts may be barred as an independent action by the applicable statute of limitations. . . . The theory is that the defense should be viable as long as the claim to which it responds is viable. . . .

Whether recoupment would be equitable depends on the facts proved at trial, but there does not appear to be anything inequitable . . . about the debtors waiting until now to assert recoupment. As long as equity will permit an action on the mortgage by its holder, so too will equity recognize the defense of recoupment. Nor, in allowing a recoupment defense to lessen the amount due on the mortgage by the amount of environmental clean-up costs, does it seem necessary to restore the status quo ante. After all, debtors seek not a rescission of the entire debt but a mere reduction in the amount of the debt by such clean-up expenses as they may prove at a trial. As the trial judge himself said, equity follows the law and cannot be used to eliminate its established rules. In this instance the law and its rules favor recoupment, and so does equity.

Reversed and Remanded for Consistent Proceedings

BUSINESS CONSIDERATIONS Expenses related to environmental clean-ups can be extremely high, posing a serious economic risk to businesses that incur such expenses. Should a business that is purchasing property include a clause addressing responsibility for environmental clean-up expenses, if any should arise? Should a business that is selling property agree to such a clause?

ETHICAL CONSIDERATIONS Is it ethical for a seller to hide potential environmental problems from a purchaser of real estate? Is it ethical for the buyers in a case such as this to proceed against the heirs of the seller?

Negotiation

Obviously, something more is needed to protect the possessor of the negotiable instrument and to facilitate the free flow of negotiable instruments through commercial channels. The UCC provides this "something more" by making

provision for *negotiations* of the instruments and the possibility of special protections for some of the recipients of these negotiations, provided they qualify as *holders in due course.*

The Code defines a negotiation in § 3-201(a) as "a transfer of possession, whether voluntary or involuntary, of an instrument by a person other than the issuer to a person who thereby becomes its holder." The Code then explains what is required to negotiate an instrument in § 3-201(b): "Except for negotiation by a remitter, if an instrument is payable to an identified person, negotiation requires transfer of possession of the instrument and its indorsement by the holder. If an instrument is payable to bearer, it may be negotiated by transfer of possession alone."

For example, a check that says "Pay to the order of Ollie Oliver" must be indorsed by Ollie Oliver along with a transfer of its possession before it can be negotiated. If Ollie simply transfers possession of the check to another person without indorsing it, the transfer would be an assignment. The terms imposed by the drawer—pay to the order of Ollie Oliver—require that Ollie prove he is transferring his rights. His indorsement provides that proof.

In contrast, a check that says "Pay to the order of bearer" does not need to be indorsed to be negotiated. Transfer of possession alone is enough to show negotiation. The terms imposed by the drawer at the time of issue—pay to the order of bearer—tell the drawee that anyone in possession is entitled to payment. However, the recipient of the instrument may well insist on having an indorsement even though none is required, for reasons explained in the next section.

The Code even makes allowance for negotiations that may be subject to rescission by the negotiating party. Section 3-202 addresses this issue, providing that:

(a) *Negotiation is effective even if obtained (i) from an infant, a corporation exceeding its powers, or a person without capacity, (ii) by fraud, duress, or mistake, or (iii) in breach of duty or as part of an illegal transaction.*

(b) *To the extent permitted by other law, negotiation may be rescinded or may be subject to other remedies, but these remedies may not be asserted against a subsequent holder in due course or a person paying the instrument in good faith and without knowledge of facts that are the basis for rescission or other remedy.*

Such protection for the subsequent parties would not be available in a "mere" assignment, but it is available under the provisions of Article 3, providing protection for holders in due course and for parties who pay the instrument in good faith beyond the protections they would enjoy under traditional contract law.

Indorsements

Section 3-204 defines an indorsement. According to this section of the Code:

NRW CASE 22.1   Finance

SHOULD THE FIRM INSIST ON HAVING AN INDORSEMENT?

NRW recently received a complaint from one of its customers. The customer wanted to give the salesperson a check as payment for a StuffTrakR package. The check was originally written by another person and was payable to the order of "bearer." The customer, who was not the drawer, wanted to merely deliver the check to the salesperson as payment for the product, but the salesperson insisted that the customer needed to indorse the check prior to delivering it or it would not be taken as payment. The customer refused to indorse the check, left the store without paying for the product, and called the firm to complain. Carlos believes that the salesperson should have avoided this scene by accepting the check. After all, as he points out, the check was payable to bearer and did not require any indorsements. Mai disagrees, pointing out that the salesperson was protecting the firm by insisting on an indorsement on the check. They have asked for your opinion. What will you tell them?

BUSINESS CONSIDERATIONS Should a business have a policy regarding accepting checks drawn by someone other than the person trying to negotiate the check to the business (so-called two-party checks)? If a business is going to accept checks from a payee or other holder, should the business insist on getting an indorsement? Why?

ETHICAL CONSIDERATIONS Is it ethical for a person who wants to negotiate a check drawn by another person to refuse to indorse the check before transferring it, even if an indorsement is not legally necessary?

INTERNATIONAL CONSIDERATIONS Do indorsements have the same legal meaning in an international setting as they do under the provisions of Article 3 of the UCC? Where would you look in order to find out?

"Indorsement" means a signature, other than that of a signer as maker, drawer, or acceptor, that alone or accompanied by other words is made on an instrument for the purpose of (i) negotiating the instrument, (ii) restricting payment of the instrument, or (iii) incurring indorser's liability on the instrument, but regardless of

the intent of the signer, a signature and its accompanying words is an indorsement unless the accompanying words, terms of the instrument, or other circumstances unambiguously indicate that the signature was made for a purpose other than an indorsement . . .

This means that a signature on a negotiable instrument is *presumed* to be an indorsement unless some other purpose is *unambiguously* shown as the purpose for the signature's placement on the instrument. There are two reasons that this is important. First, any instrument payable "to order" requires an indorsement before it can be further negotiated. Second, and perhaps more important, each and every indorsement is a separate contract added to the contract that the instrument itself represents, and to any other indorsement contracts already present on the instrument. Indorsers are assuming contractual liability to the person to whom they transfer the instrument and to every subsequent holder or transferee of that instrument. For this reason, many people will not accept the negotiation of a bearer instrument unless the holder indorses it. Even though bearer paper may legally be negotiated by delivery alone, the transferee usually demands the added security of an indorsement, thereby adding the indorsement contract and its rights to the rights represented by the instrument itself.

There are two reasons for indorsing an instrument. One reason is to affect negotiation. The other is to affect liability. The indorsements that affect negotiation will tell the holder (1) that another indorsement is needed to negotiate the instrument further (a special indorsement); (2) that no further indorsements are needed in order to negotiate the instrument further (a blank indorsement); or (3) that the instrument has been restricted to some special channel of commerce such as banking (a restrictive indorsement). The indorsements that affect liability either (1) admit and/or agree to honor the contract of indorsement (an unqualified

indorsement) or (2) expressly deny any liability on the indorsement contract (a qualified indorsement). Every indorsement must affect negotiation as well as liability. Thus, each indorsement must fit one of the boxes in the matrix shown in Exhibit 22.1.

Notice that each box in the matrix is numbered. We will use these numbers to refer back to the matrix as we discuss some examples of the various types of indorsements. Throughout the examples, we will be using the check shown in Exhibit 22.2.

Special Indorsements

A special indorsement specifies the party to whom the instrument is to be paid or to whose order it is to be paid. This means that a special indorsement makes (or leaves) the instrument payable "to order." Even if the instrument was issued as bearer paper, a special indorsement will make it payable "to order." The party specified will have to indorse it before it can be negotiated further. Exhibit 22.3 is an example of a special indorsement.

Blank Indorsements

A blank indorsement does not specify the party to whom the instrument is to be paid. The normal form of a blank indorsement is a mere signature by the holder. Such an indorsement makes the instrument bearer paper. As such, it is negotiable by transfer of possession alone, without any need for further indorsements. In Exhibit 22.4 on page 519, a blank indorsement has been added to the previous special indorsement. Note that at this point the check has every indorsement that is necessary for negotiation. Should the check now be lost or stolen, the finder or the thief could effectively negotiate it. To protect against such an occurrence, § 3-205(c) empowers the holder to convert a blank

---

EXHIBIT   22.1   The Indorsement Matrix

	Unqualified	Qualified
Special	(1) Designates the next holder, so an additional indorsement is required; does not deny liability for the indorsement contract.	(2) Designates the next holder so an additional indorsement is required; denies contract liability for the indorsement.
Blank	(3) Does not designate the next holder, making the instruments "bearer paper"; does not deny liability for the indorsement contract.	(4) Does not designate the next holder, making the instrument "bearer paper"; denies contract liability for the indorsement.
Restrictive	(5) Attempts to restrict or limit future negotiation of the instrument, as in "for deposit only"; does not deny liability for the indorsement contract.	(6) Attempts to restrict or limit future negotiation of the instrument, as in "for deposit only"; denies contract liability for the indorsement.

EXHIBIT **22.2** The Check as Issued

> Robert Drawer
> 210 Elm Street
> Anytown, USA
>
> **3728**
> _July 4,_ ___ 20 __XX__
>
> Pay to the order of ____ Sam Shovel ____ $ __1,000.00__
>
> __One Thousand and XX/100 ____ dollars
>
> Last National Bank
> Bigtown, USA
>
> Memo _____
>
> _Robert Drawer_
>
> 11 000000011 01 123456789

indorsement into a special indorsement by writing, above the signature of the indorser, words identifying the person to whom the instrument is now made payable. This is shown in Exhibit 22.5. Here a holder added the words "Pay to Mata Harry, or order" above Charlie Chenn's indorsement. This phrase could have been added by Charlie Chenn when he negotiated the check to Mata Harry. More likely, Mata Harry added the phrase after she received the check from Charlie Chenn. By adding the phrase, he or she has protected Mata Harry against losing her right in the event that she should lose the check or have it stolen.

Restrictive Indorsements

A restrictive indorsement purports to restrict or prohibit any further negotiation of the instrument. Prior to the revision of Article 3 it was not uncommon for a person to use an indorsement that contained a condition restricting

any further negotiation of the instrument, words that indicated the instrument had to be deposited or collected (such as "for deposit," "for collection," or "pay any bank") or some other restriction that specified permissible use or further negotiation of the instrument. Because restrictive indorsements could be used to effectively eliminate the ability to *negotiate* a negotiable instrument, the revision to Article 3 paid special attention to this area. The new rules governing restrictive indorsements are found in § 3-206, which provides:

(a) An indorsement limiting payment to a particular person or otherwise prohibiting further transfer or negotiation of the instrument is not effective to prevent further transfer or negotiation of the instrument.

(b) An indorsement stating a condition to the right of the indorsee to receive payment does not affect the

EXHIBIT **22.3** A Special Indorsement

Pay to Charlie Chenn
Sam Shovel   } (1)

EXHIBIT 22.4 A Blank Indorsement

EXHIBIT 22.4 A Blank Indorsement

right of the indorsee to enforce the instrument. A person paying the instrument or taking it for value or collection may disregard the condition, and the rights and liabilities of that person are not affected by whether the condition has been fulfilled.

(c) *If an instrument bears an indorsement . . . using the words "for deposit," "for collection," or other words indicating a purpose of having the instrument collected by a bank for the indorser or for a particular amount, the following rules apply:*

(1) *A person, other than a bank, who purchases the instrument when so indorsed converts the instrument unless the amount paid for the instrument is received by the indorser or applied consistently with the indorsement.*

(2) *A depository bank that purchases the instrument or takes it for collection when so indorsed converts the instrument unless the amount paid by the bank with respect to the instrument is*

received by the indorser or applied consistently with the indorsement.

(3) *A payor bank that is also the depositary bank or that takes the instrument for immediate payment over the counter from a person other than a collecting bank converts the instrument unless the proceeds of the instrument are received by the indorser or applied consistently with the indorsement.*

Thus, under the new rules, a restrictive indorsement that purports to restrict payment or negotiation may be disregarded by the indorsee, with no affect on the rights or liabilities of the indorsee, unless the restrictive indorsement restricts further negotiation of the instrument to banking channels. When a restrictive indorsement restricts the instrument to banking channels ("for deposit" or "for collection"), it is a valid restriction, and any person who subsequently deals with that instrument without ensuring that the funds are applied consistently with the indorsement is

EXHIBIT 22.5 Conversion of a Blank Indorsement to a Special Indorsement

NRW CASE 22.2   Finance

DEPOSITING COMPANY CHECKS

One of the new employees has been given the responsibility of preparing the deposits made by the company. This employee takes the checks that have been received, stamps the back of each check with a rubber stamp reading "NRW" and the company's address, and then puts the checks in an envelope until they are taken to the bank for deposit. Mai is concerned that the employee is not being careful enough with the checks, and that this treatment poses a potential financial risk to the firm. Carlos thinks that Mai is overreacting. He thinks that since the checks have been indorsed, the firm is safe. However, he wants to be certain, so he has asked for your advice on this matter. What will you tell him?

BUSINESS CONSIDERATIONS How should a business handle checks to reduce its risk of loss through embezzlement, theft of the checks, or other similar problems? Does the method of indorsement used on the checks make any difference?

ETHICAL CONSIDERATIONS Assume that a firm permits its employees to indorse checks in blank, and then suffers a financial loss when some of these checks are stolen and negotiated further. Is it ethical for the firm to blame the employees for mishandling the checks? Should the firm share in the blame for permitting this method of indorsing?

INTERNATIONAL CONSIDERATIONS Should a business use a different type of indorsement for instruments it receives that are to be paid outside the United States? Do types of indorsement used internationally differ from the ones used in the United States? Do similar indorsements have different meanings in an international setting?

deemed guilty of conversion. Thus, the revision to Article 3 establishes that only those restrictive indorsements that restrict the instrument to banking have any meaning or effect, but that the ones that do so restrict the instrument have a very serious and substantial effect.

One possible reason for this change in the treatment of restrictive indorsements is the importance placed on the

negotiability of the instrument governed by Article 3. Remember that negotiability is determined by the information contained on the *face* of the instrument, and that indorsements are normally placed on the *back* of the instrument. Once an instrument as issued satisfies all the tests of negotiability, the instrument is deemed to be negotiable and no indorsement can be allowed to remove its negotiable status.

In Exhibit 22.6, item (5) shows a restrictive indorsement.

It should be noted that each of these sample indorsements refers to the unqualified indorsement column of the matrix set out in Exhibit 22.1. The reason for this is contained in UCC § 3-415, Obligation of Indorser, which provides:

(a) . . . If an instrument is dishonored, an indorser is obliged to pay the amount due on the instrument

(i) according to the terms of the instrument at the time it was indorsed; or (ii) if the indorser indorsed an incomplete instrument, according to its terms when completed [presuming that the completion was authorized]. The obligation of the indorser is owed to a person entitled to enforce the instrument or to a subsequent indorser who paid the instrument under this section.

(b) If an indorsement states that it is made "without recourse" or otherwise disclaims liability of the indorser, the indorser is not liable under subsection (a) to pay the instrument.

Under this section, an indorsement is presumed to be *unqualified*. To be qualified, the indorsement must contain specific words of qualification. An unqualified indorsement carries with it a contractual commitment to pay the amount due on the instrument if there is a dishonor. The indorser is committed to the indorsee (the person to whom the instrument is transferred by indorsement) or to any later holder if the instrument is dishonored and proper notice of the dishonor is given. The normal order of payment among the indorsers is the reverse of the order in which they indorsed the instrument. Thus, on a dishonored check, which had four indorsers, indorser four would collect from indorser three, who in turn would collect from indorser two, who in turn would collect from indorser one. (This is known as the secondary chain of liability and will be discussed in detail in the next chapter.)

A qualified indorsement is one that denies contract liability. The indorser includes words such as "without recourse" in the indorsement. These words have the legal effect of telling later holders that the qualifying indorser will not repay them if the instrument is dishonored. By accepting a qualified indorsement in a negotiation, the later

EXHIBIT 22.6 A Restrictive Indorsement

EXHIBIT 22.6 A Restrictive Indorsement

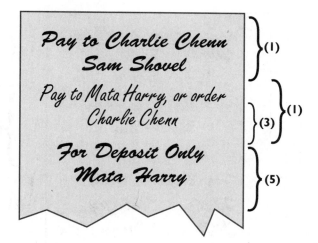

holders also agree to the contract terms of the qualified indorsement. In Exhibit 22.7, each of the earlier indorsements is shown as unqualified; in Exhibit 22.8, the same indorsements are shown as qualified. Note the specific language necessary to change an indorsement from the presumed unqualified indorsement to a qualified indorsement.

Holder

At the beginning of this chapter, we examined the transfer of negotiable instruments. It was pointed out that a *transfer* leaves the transferee in the role of an *assignee*. It also was stated that a *negotiation* leaves the transferee in the role of a *holder*. The role of a holder is important in negotiable instruments. A holder takes an instrument by transfer, giving the holder all of the rights that his or her transferor possessed. However, a holder also acquires personal rights that may well be above and beyond those rights conferred by the transfer. Thus a holder can have better rights than the person from whom the holder received the negotiation. A holder normally acquires contractual rights against several parties involved with the instrument. A holder also normally acquires warranty rights against some parties involved with the instrument. Also, being a holder is an essential element before the party can become a holder in due course, perhaps the most favored position in the law of negotiable instruments.

EXHIBIT 22.7 Unqualified Indorsements

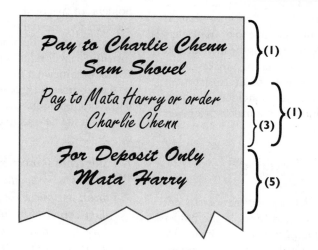

EXHIBIT   22.8 Qualified Indorsements

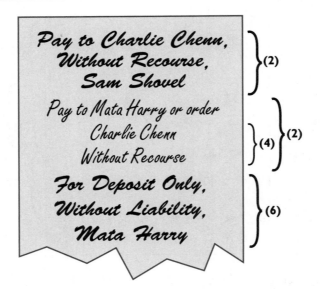

The word "holder" is defined in § 1-201(20). According to the definition:

"Holder," with respect to a negotiable instrument, means the person in possession if the instrument is payable to bearer, or, in the case of an instrument payable to an identified person, if the identified person is in possession.

This definition of "holder" is considerably broader and more inclusive than the definition under the earlier version of Article 3. Prior to the revision, a person had to take possession of an instrument through a voluntary transfer of the instrument in order to qualify as a holder. But now a person can become a holder by gaining possession of the instrument through an involuntary transfer of possession. This means that if an instrument is payable to bearer or has been indorsed in blank, and a person *steals* the instrument, the *thief* becomes a holder![3] A holder has the right to transfer, negotiate, discharge, or enforce the instrument in the holder's own name. However, a holder is subject to any defenses on the instrument that a maker or drawer can assert.

Holder in Due Course

To overcome even one of the defenses on the instrument that may be available to the maker or drawer, the holder needs to acquire *holder in due course* status. Great care needs to be exercised here. The burden of proof for estab-

lishing HDC status lies with the person claiming the status. A holder must prove he or she is a holder in due course; such status is not presumed. A holder or an assignee is subject to any defense the drawer or maker can assert. A holder in due course is subject only to some defenses of the maker or drawer. The holder in due course prevails over most available defenses.

When the NIL was initially enacted, and for quite some time thereafter, instruments commonly remained in circulation for quite a while after they were issued. Under these circumstances, the instruments were regularly treated as substitutes for money, and the protection of the holders of the instrument was a very significant concern. The rules regarding holders in due course were developed to protect holders of negotiable instruments in these situations. Modern commercial practice and changes in banking laws, rules, and regulations has reduced the likelihood that an instrument will remain in circulation for very long today, reducing somewhat the practical importance of the holder in due course rules. Nonetheless, the Code still devotes a considerable amount of attention to HDC status, beginning with the definition of a holder in due course as set out in § 3-302:

(a) Subject to subsection (c) [precluding HDC status for parties who acquire an instrument through extraordinary purchases, acquisitions outside the ordinary course of business, and the like] and Section 3-106(d) [statutory language that removes the availability of HDC status contained on the face of

certain instruments], "holder in due course" means the holder of an instrument if:

(1) the instrument when issued or negotiated to the holder does not bear such apparent evidence of forgery or alteration or is not otherwise so irregular or incomplete as to call into question its authenticity; and

(2) the holder took the instrument (i) for value, (ii) in good faith, (iii) without notice that the instrument is overdue or has been dishonored or that there is an uncured default with respect to payment of another instrument as part of the same series, (iv) without notice that the instrument contains an unauthorized signature or has been altered, (v) without notice of any claim to the instrument described in Section 3-306, and (vi) without notice that any party has a defense or claim in recoupment described in Section 3-305(a).

Thus, in order to qualify as an HDC, the holder must take an instrument that *appears* to be regular, complete, and authentic when he or she acquires the instrument, *and* the instrument must be taken (1) for *value*, (2) in *good faith*, and (3) *without notice* of defects or defenses affecting the instrument.

The appearance of the instrument at the time the holder takes possession of it should not be too difficult to establish. Similarly, the issues of value and good faith are relatively simple to establish. However, the various notice issues can be difficult to prove at times. Each of these three elements of holder in due course status is discussed in the following sections.

For Value

In order to qualify as an HDC, a holder must give *value* for the instrument. Under Article 3, value is more than consideration. Holders in due course merit special protection because they have already *performed* their obligation or they are irrevocably committed to perform. Thus, if they are not protected, they lose more than "opportunity costs." Because they have already performed, they are "out" the value of the performance. If they were not protected on the instrument, they might also wind up being "out" on the instrument, thus causing them to lose twice, the actual loss of their uncompensated performance and the opportunity cost of the unpaid or dishonored instrument.

Section 3-303 sets out five methods of giving value for an instrument. Notice that each method involves actual performance by the holder, not just a commitment to

perform in the future. The first method involves an instrument issued or transferred for a promise of performance, to the extent the promise has been performed. The second method arises when the transferee acquires a security interest or other lien in the instrument, other than a lien obtained in a judicial proceeding. Third, the instrument is issued or transferred as payment of, or as security for, an antecedent claim against any person, whether or not the claim is due. Fourth, the instrument is issued or transferred in exchange for another negotiable instrument. Fifth, the instrument is issued or transferred in exchange for an irrevocable obligation to a third person by the person taking the instrument. Once the holder can prove that value was given, the holder goes on to the next test.

In Good Faith

The next requirement is that the holder must take the instrument in *good faith*. Historically, good faith was defined as "honesty in fact." This provided a relatively simplistic standard, and one that was very hard to measure. It seemed that good faith was assumed, and the person challenging HDC status for a holder had to establish a lack of good faith in order to negate this element of the HDC requirements. This requirement was actually being measured by a negative test. The holder acted with good faith if bad faith was not present. Traditionally, in order to show a lack of good faith, it had to be proved that the holder either had actual knowledge of a defect in the instrument or ignored facts that would have shown the defect. Usually, all the holder needed to do was to allege that he or she had acted in good faith. (This test was referred to by one court as the "white heart, empty head" test because of the presumption that the parties acted with good faith absent some showing of knowledge or gross negligence.) Very few cases involved bad faith.

The revision to Article 3 has changed the requirement of good faith and its measurement significantly. Article 3 now provides in § 3-103(a)(4) that " 'Good faith' means honesty in fact and the observance of reasonable commercial standards of fair dealing." With this new definition of "good faith" the courts require the holder to show that he or she has "observed reasonable commercial standards" in order to establish that he or she has acted with good faith in the transaction. The requirement that a holder must have "observed reasonable commercial standards of fair dealing" provides a relatively broad test that is not specifically defined. Thus, the courts will have to decide whether the holder meets this standard by looking at the context of the transaction. It seems that this section is now more concerned with the fairness of the conduct of the parties than

NRW CASE 22.3   Finance/Management

WHAT CONSTITUTES NOTICE?

NRW received a paper from one of its customers as payment in full of the customer's account. The paper looked like a typical draft except for a statement typed in bold-faced type across the top of the paper. The statement said **"This is NOT a negotiable instrument."** Everything else on the paper had the look and the form of a draft, including the statement "Pay to the order of NRW." When the paper was presented to the person to whom the order was directed, that person refused to honor the writing and returned the paper unpaid. The principals want to know if this is a draft and also what they can or should do. They have asked for your advice. What will you tell them?

BUSINESS CONSIDERATIONS Should a business develop a policy for what types of writing it will accept as payment and what types of writing it will refuse, if offered as payment? Why might such a policy be a good idea?

ETHICAL CONSIDERATIONS Is it ethical for a person to issue what *looks* like a negotiable instrument, but to include a disclaimer of negotiability, thus "opting out" of the coverage of Article 3? What ethical issues are raised by such conduct?

INTERNATIONAL CONSIDERATIONS Might a firm be better off in an international transaction if the "instrument" is not negotiable, thus allowing them to resolve the controversy under some other area of law rather than Article 3? If Article 3 does not apply in *this* case, and if the customer is from another country, what law is likely to be applied to settle the dispute?

with the care with which the parties have acted.[4] This new standard is likely to make "good faith" a much more meaningful test in cases in which HDC status is alleged, and it will be interesting to watch how the courts apply this newer, stricter standard.

Without Notice of Defenses or Defects

The final requirement to establish holder-in-due-course status is that the holder takes the instrument without notice of any defenses or defects on the instrument. Notice is present if a reasonable person would know that there was a defense or a defect, or if a reasonable person would be suspicious and would make further inquiry before accepting the instrument.

The Code provides a broad statement concerning notice in § 3-302(2), but it does not list many specific facts that do or do not constitute notice, leaving this area for judicial interpretation to a much greater extent. According to this section, in order to satisfy the "without notice" requirement, the holder must take the instrument:

(iii) without notice that the instrument is overdue or has been dishonored or that there is an uncured default with respect to payment of another instrument issued as part of the same series, (iv) without notice that the instrument contains an unauthorized signature or has been altered, (v) without notice of any claim to the instrument described in Section 3-306 (claims of a previous holder to recover the instrument or to rescind the negotiation), and (vi) without notice that any party has a defense or claim in recoupment described in Section 3-305.

Thus, to qualify as an HDC, the holder cannot have notice that the instrument is overdue or has been dishonored. He or she also cannot have notice that there is an unauthorized signature or an alteration of the instrument, that another party has asserted a claim to recover the instrument by legal means or to rescind a previous negotiation. And finally, he or she cannot have notice of any *other* defense or claim against the instrument. Of these elements, the fact that an instrument is overdue *will* be apparent on the face of the instrument most of the time. The fact that an instrument has been dishonored *might* be apparent on the face of the instrument (the instrument may have been stamped "NSF" or "Payment Stopped" upon prior presentment to the drawee bank, for example). An alteration also *might* be apparent on the face of the instrument, especially if someone has stricken through something on the instrument and replaced it with something else. But it is quite likely that any defenses or claims against the instrument, and any claims to recover the instrument or to rescind a prior negotiation, will not show on the face of the instrument and will not be apparent to a holder exercising ordinary care in accepting the instrument through a negotiation.

In § 3-304, overdue instruments are defined. According to this section:

(a) an instrument payable on demand becomes overdue at the earliest of the following times:

(1) on the day after the day demand for payment is duly made;

(2) *if the instrument is a check, 90 days after its date; or*

(3) *if the instrument is not a check, when the instrument has been outstanding for a period of time after its date which is unreasonably long under the circumstances of the particular case in light of the nature of the instrument and usage of the trade.*

(b) *With respect to an instrument payable at a definite time the following rules apply:*

(1) *if the principal is payable in installments and a due date has not been accelerated, the instrument becomes overdue upon default under the instrument for nonpayment of an installment, and the instrument remains overdue until the default is cured;*

(2) *if the principal is not payable in installments and the due date has not been accelerated, the instrument becomes overdue on the day after the due date;*

(3) *if a due date with respect to principal has been accelerated, the instrument becomes overdue on the date after the accelerated due date.*

(c) *Unless the due date of principal has been accelerated, an instrument does not become overdue if there is default in payment of interest but no default in payment of principal.*

Other Facts That Are Considered Notice

Some of the things that have traditionally served as notice of a defect or a defense affecting an instrument are set out here. A purchaser of a negotiable instrument has notice of a defect if the instrument is incomplete in some material respect. Thus, a missing signature or a missing amount would be notice. So would a missing date on a time instrument. But a missing date on a demand instrument, such as a check, is not notice since it is not material. It is not material because a demand instrument is payable at issue, and even if it is not dated, it has been issued. The simple fact of its existence proves that it has been issued. Notice of a defect also exists if the instrument is visibly altered or bears visible evidence of a forgery. Notice exists if the instrument is irregular on its face. This means that an erasure or a "striking out" of an obligation of a party or of an amount is notice of a defect. A holder who takes an instrument stamped "NSF" (not sufficient funds), or "Payment Stopped," or "Paid" would have notice of a defense or defect on the instrument. It has been presented, and it has been dishonored or paid. The holder knows this by looking at the face of the instrument.

Facts That Are Not Considered Notice

Traditional interpretations of Article 3 have shown that the following facts, standing alone, are not notice of a defense or defect on the instrument, even if the holder has knowledge of the fact:

- The instrument was antedated or postdated.

- The instrument was issued or negotiated for an executory promise, unless the holder has notice of defenses to the promise.

- Any party has signed as an accommodation party.

- A formerly incomplete instrument was completed.

- Any person negotiating the instrument is or was a fiduciary.

In addition, it is not treated as notice if any party has filed or recorded a document, if the holder would otherwise qualify as an HDC. In addition, before notice is effective, it must be received in a time and a manner that give a reasonable opportunity to act on the information. Notice must be received before the holder receives the instrument. Once the holder has received the instrument, later notice is irrelevant.

In the case on page 526, a number of instruments were drawn against a corporate account and paid by the bank. The corporation against which the instruments were drawn argued that the instruments were irregular on their faces, thus providing notice to the bank and eliminating the possibility that the bank could be an HDC. After reading this opinion, decide whether you agree with the court's decision.

Effect of Holder in Due Course Status

The status of holder in due course is a preferred legal position. The HDC takes an instrument free of personal defenses that the drawer or maker may be able to assert in order to avoid paying the instrument. Although the holder in due course is subject to real defenses, he or she will be able to enforce the instrument against any other defense or defect. This position is far superior to that of a mere holder or an assignee. A holder or an assignee is subject to any and every defense or defect in the instrument, real or personal. In contrast, an HDC takes the instrument subject only to real defenses. The HDC is not subject to personal (sometimes referred to as limited) defenses.

A personal defense is one that affects the agreement for which the instrument was issued. It does not affect or challenge the validity of the instrument. The underlying

PRESTIGE OF BEVERLY HILLS, INC. v. FIRST FEDERAL BANK OF CALIFORNIA
2002 Cal. App. Unpubl LEXIS 1090 (Cal. App., 2nd App. Dist. 2002)

FACTS Amir Shokrian is the president of Prestige, a real estate holding and management company. In 1993 Shokrian opened a checking account for Prestige at First Federal's West Hollywood, California, branch. Shokrian signed an account agreement on behalf of Prestige that authorized First Federal "to act without further inquiry in accordance with any writing bearing the signature(s) of the accountholder(s), as indicated on the face hereof." Shokrian signed the account agreement on both sides as the only signatory on the account. In addition to being president of Prestige, Shokrian was an habitue of Caesars Palace in Las Vegas, which he visited on many occasions between the late 1960s and 1999. As a "high roller," Shokrian often received complimentary hotel rooms, food services, and travel accommodations from Caesars.

In 1992 Shokrian provided a credit application to Caesars to enable him to gamble on credit. Thereafter, when Shokrian wanted to obtain gaming chips from Caesars on credit, he would sign a document known as a "marker." These gambling markers signed by Shokrian are similar to checks: They contain blank lines for "Pay to the Order of," for the dollar amount, and for the payor's signature. They also contain blank lines for the payor's bank name and the date. Above the signature line, the markers also contain a pre-printed statement authorizing Caesars to complete any missing information on the "marker" and to direct the completed instrument to any account from which the payor has the right to withdraw funds. When Shokrian wished to obtain gaming chips on credit, a Caesars employee would present a marker to him at the baccarat table with only the dollar amount filled in. Sometime after Shokrian signed the marker and received chips in exchange, Caesars employees would fill in the missing information including the bank name and account number.

Shokrian traveled to Caesars Palace on July 24 and 25, 1999. On August 2, 1999, three markers dated July 24, 1999, and apparently bearing Shokrian's signature were presented to First Federal for payment to Caesars. First Federal honored the markers and paid Caesars the total sum of $20,000 from Prestige's account. When Shokrian learned that these markers had been paid from the Prestige account, he went to the bank and demanded that the funds be returned to the account. Shokrian denied that he had signed the markers or that he had authorized any charges to the Prestige account. He also executed three copies of an "affidavit of forgery" to support his claim that he had not signed the markers. Despite this, the bank refused to credit the Prestige account for the $20,000. In fact, the bank asked Prestige to close its account and to take its business elsewhere shortly after these events occurred. Prestige filed suit seeking to recover the $20,000.

ISSUES Had Shokrian signed the markers? Were the markers negotiable instruments? Were the markers so irregular on their faces that they provided notice to the bank of a defense or defect? Were the markers void due to the underlying illegality that they were issued to pay gambling debts?

HOLDINGS Yes, the markers were negotiable instruments. Whether Shokrian had signed the markers and whether the markers were so irregular on their faces as to provide notice to the bank of a defect or a defense were both triable issues that need to be resolved on remand. No, the markers were not void due to the underlying illegality.

REASONING Excerpts from the opinion of Judge Perluss:

Prestige filed suit against First Federal for breach of contract, breach of California Uniform Commercial Code section 4-401, negligence and conversion. After answering the complaint, First Federal moved for summary judgment . . . on the ground the markers were properly payable negotiable instruments under the California Uniform Commercial Code and First Federal was therefore obliged to honor them when presented for payment. First Federal also argued that, since it paid the markers, it was a holder in due course.

Prestige opposed the motion, asserting that the markers were not in a form that First Federal was required to honor; that it had not authorized Shokrian to execute gambling markers on its behalf; that the markers were not properly executed by Prestige; that the markers were illegal and unenforceable because they memorialized gambling debts; and that First Federal failed to exercise due care in processing the markers for payment. It also argued that triable issues of fact existed as to whether the markers were properly executed, whether First Federal had breached the account agreement by accepting the markers and whether First Federal exercised reasonable care in accepting the markers for payment. . . .

Taking the parties' evidence at face value, before any evidentiary objections, there is clearly a question of fact as to whether Shokrian executed the markers: Shokrian's declaration states he does not believe he executed them, he did not tell Sizemore he executed them and, in fact, he told Sizemore he had *not* executed them. This is sufficient to raise a triable issue of fact. However, the trial court's order granting summary judgment states that all of plaintiff's objections were overruled and all of defendant's objections were sustained. That ruling left intact all of the evidence proffered by First Federal. Its impact on the evidence proffered by Prestige is less clear. . . . To the contrary, the interrogatory response and the deposition testimony are equivocal in the extreme and fall well short of an admission that Shokrian did indeed sign the markers. The statements that Shokrian "may have" signed the markers or "it could be" his signature on a marker are at best the type of "tacit admissions or fragmentary and equivocal concessions." . . . Indeed, those statements may be reconciled relatively easily with Shokrian's declaration, resulting in the statement, "I may have signed the markers, it could be my signature on the markers, but to this day I do not believe I signed them." These statements simply are not mutually exclusive. Accordingly, the trial court abused its discretion . . . to exclude Shokrian's declaration testimony. When Shokrian's declaration is properly considered, it is clear there is a triable issue as to whether he signed the markers. . . .

First Federal contends that, even if Shokrian did not sign the markers, the judgment should be affirmed on the alternate ground that it was a holder in due course. A holder in due course is one who takes an instrument "(A) for value, (B) in good faith, (C) without notice that the instrument is overdue or has been dishonored or that there is an uncured default with respect to payment of another instrument issued as part of the same series, (D) without notice that the instrument contains an unauthorized signature or has been altered. . . . "[A] party can be a holder in due course only if the instrument 'when issued or negotiated to the holder' did not 'bear such apparent evidence of forgery or alteration or was not otherwise so irregular or incomplete as to call into question its authenticity.' " . . . The trial court ruled no triable issue of fact existed as to whether First Federal was a holder in due course because "there were no irregularities on the face of the markers which were unconditional promises to pay money and defendant bank paid value for them in good faith." This was error.

Although there is no dispute that First Federal took the markers for value and in good faith, there is a triable issue as to whether the markers were so irregular as to give First Federal notice they were forged or otherwise not properly payable on Prestige's account. On their face, the markers indicated they were to be drawn on First Federal Bank, West Hollywood, *Florida*. While First Federal dismisses this as a mere "typographical error,"

we are not prepared to hold this irregularity is insignificant as a matter of law, particularly when combined with the fact that the markers were apparently signed by Shokrian but were not Prestige's preprinted corporate checks and did not identify Prestige as the payor other than by account number. A party has notice of a claim or defense if an instrument is "so irregular as to call into question its validity, terms or ownership or to create an ambiguity as to the party to pay." . . .

Prestige argues that, even if First Federal were a holder in due course, it is still subject to the defense of illegality because of this state's longstanding public policy against gambling on credit. . . . Because this issue may well arise in the trial court on remand, we address it here and hold Prestige may not invoke the defense of illegality against First Federal.

Prestige relies on *Metropolitan Creditors Service v. Sadri* . . . in which the defendant wrote checks for gambling chips in a Nevada casino. The defendant lost the chips playing baccarat and subsequently stopped payment on the checks. . . . In *Metropolitan Creditors* . . . the question was not whether the checks could properly be paid by the defendant's bank, but whether the casino could bring suit against the defendant after he stopped payment on the checks. Nothing in *Metropolitan Creditors*, or in any of the other cases cited by Prestige, holds or even suggests that checks written for gambling debts are void due to illegality in the first instance. Moreover, the parties to the gambling debt—Shokrian and Caesars—are not before the court in this appeal. While we would not hesitate to bar Caesars from collecting against Prestige had it stopped payment on the markers, we decline to apply the public policy against enforcement of gambling debts in an action where neither party has taken part in gambling activities. . . .

The judgment is reversed, and the matter is remanded to the trial court for further proceedings not inconsistent with this opinion. Prestige is entitled to recover its costs on appeal.

BUSINESS CONSIDERATIONS In this case Shokrian had the authority to access the account of Prestige on the basis of his signature alone. What should a business do differently to protect its interests and to prevent misuse of its funds from someone in a position like that occupied by Shokrian?

ETHICAL CONSIDERATIONS Shokrian was recognized by the casino as a "high roller." Is it ethical for a casino to "comp" rooms, meals, and even travel in order to entice such "high rollers" to visit the casino? Should a business permit any of its top management personnel to participate in such gaming activities?

agreement, the reason the instrument was issued, is the point of contention. A real defense, on the other hand, questions the legal validity of the instrument.

Personal Defenses

The most common types of personal defenses are those available on a simple contract, such as failure of consideration, fraud, duress, and breach of warranty. In addition, the holder frequently may be faced with the personal defenses of nondelivery, theft, payment, or any other cancellation.

Most of the simple contract defenses were covered in Part 3, Contracts, and need no further review here. However, fraud does need some added coverage because negotiable instrument law recognizes two types of fraud. One type, fraud in the inducement, is a personal defense. The other type, fraud in the execution, is a real defense.

Fraud in the inducement is a personal defense because the fraud committed is a fraud related to the agreement. The maker or drawer intentionally and knowingly issues a negotiable instrument to the payee. However, this issue is made to support an underlying agreement, and the agreement is based on fraudulent representations. The underlying

contract is voidable because of the fraud, but the instrument is valid, subject only to a personal defense. (Fraud in the execution is discussed in the following section.)

Of the other personal defenses not based on simple contract defenses, only one will be covered here. Nondelivery of the instrument needs special treatment. To issue an instrument, the maker or drawer must deliver the instrument to the payee or to an authorized representative of the payee. If the payee gains possession of the instrument without the knowledge or consent of the maker or drawer, the defense of nondelivery is available against a mere holder. Another type of nondelivery occurs when the maker or drawer gives the payee possession, but with a condition attached before delivery is effective. The condition may be that the payee must perform some act before he or she can treat the instrument as "delivered," and the act is then not performed. Technically, delivery never occurred because the condition was never satisfied, and the defense of nondelivery can be raised as a personal defense.

A holder in due course will not only prevail over any personal defenses of the maker or drawer, he or she can also prevail over a properly perfected security interest under some circumstances. The following case dealt with this issue.

22.3

VAN HATTEM v. DUBLIN NATIONAL BANK
2002 U.S. Dist. LEXIS 2645 (N.D. Tex. 2002)

FACTS On October 31, 1994, Steven A. Van Hattem executed a promissory note in the principal amount of $75,645.60 payable to his brother, James Van Hattem. To secure repayment of the note, Steven granted James a security interest in livestock owned by Steven. On December 6, 1995, James perfected this security interest by filing a financing statement with the Texas Secretary of State. On May 1, 1997, Dublin National Bank made a $390,500 loan to Steven and Pamela, granting a security interest to the bank. On October 22, 1999, Steven's cattle were sold at auction. Dublin National Bank received in excess of $102,000 from the sale but refused to pay James the proceeds from the sale. James then sued Dublin National Bank, alleging conversion and a violation of the Texas Uniform Commercial Code. Dublin National Bank sought summary judgment on the grounds that James did not have an enforceable security interest in the livestock or proceeds and that, even if James did have a security interest, it was unperfected and subordinate to the bank's perfected security interest. Moreover, proceeds received by the bank were in the form of negotiable instruments that the bank took as a holder in due

course, free of any claim of James. There was no conversion of the proceeds, and the default provisions of the UCC are inapplicable because defendant did not take possession of, sell, or otherwise dispose of any collateral.

ISSUES Did the bank take the negotiable instruments as an HDC? Does an HDC of such negotiable instruments prevail over a perfected security interest held by another party?

HOLDINGS Yes to both issues. The bank did take the negotiable instruments as an HDC, and an HDC prevails over a perfected security interest held by another party.

REASONING Excerpts from the opinion of Circuit Judge McBryde:

Steven and his wife, Pamela N. Van Hattem (Pamela), operated a dairy farm near Stephenville, Erath County, Texas. Steven and Pamela first became loan customers of defendant in August 1994, when defendant made a loan to them to finance their purchase of dairy cattle.

Steven is the brother of plaintiff James A. Van Hattem. Starting in 1979, plaintiffs loaned Steven and Pamela money for various purposes, including dairy farm operations. On or about October 31, 1994, Steven executed a promissory note, titled "Note Secured by Second Security Interest in Dairy Cows, payable to plaintiffs in the principal sum of $75,645.60 (the "note"). The note bore a signature line for Pamela, but was not signed by her or by anyone else on her behalf. The note stated: "This note is secured by a second security interest in the dairy cows owned by Steven A. and Pamela N. Van Hattem." . . . Steven also signed a UCC-1 financing statement, which was filed with the Secretary of State of Texas on December 6, 1995. The financing statement likewise listed Steven and Pamela as debtors and had places for each of them to sign. Only Steven's signature appears on the financing statement. . . .

On May 1, 1997, defendant made a $390,500 loan to Steven and Pamela under a United States Department of Agriculture program pursuant to which 90% of the principal amount of the loan was guaranteed by the Farm Service Agency. . . . In connection with that loan, Steven and Pamela each executed a promissory note, a commercial security agreement, a security agreement supplement, a UCC-1 financing statement, a disbursement request and authorization, and a notice of final agreement. Defendant filed its financing statement on May 16, 1997, with the Texas Secretary of State. In their financial statement as of date of loan application, Steven and Pamela did not list any debt owed to plaintiffs. Pursuant to the terms of the 1997 loan and security agreement, Steven and Pamela granted defendant a security interest in all dairy cattle and other livestock owned or thereafter acquired by them.

On October 22, 1999, Steven and Pamela caused their dairy cattle to be sold at auction. Defendant was not aware that the cattle were going to be sold. Prior to the sale, defendant had not made any demand on Steven and Pamela or commenced any sort of default proceedings. After the sale, the auction house called defendant to find out how the proceeds should be paid. Pursuant to defendant's instructions, proceeds of the sale were paid by three checks made payable to defendant and Steven. Steven endorsed the checks and delivered them to defendant. The total amount of the sale checks was $109,774.30. Defendant credited that amount against the debt owed by Steven and Pamela.

At the time defendant received and processed the checks, it did not know that Steven and Pamela, or either one of them, owed any debt to plaintiffs. . . . Defendant contends that plaintiffs' security interest is unenforceable because Pamela did not sign the note or

financing statement. . . . Plaintiffs argue that Steven was authorized to sign the documents on behalf of Pamela. The cases they cite, however, are inapposite, since Steven did not purport to sign the agreements on Pamela's behalf. . . . Here, the documents were clearly drawn for Pamela's signature, but no signature appears above her name on either document. Nevertheless, the court cannot find as a matter of law that the documents were unenforceable as to the interest capable of being conveyed by Steven. Here, the property in which the interest is conveyed is not homestead . . . but what appears to be joint management community property. . . .

As discussed in the preceding subsection of this memorandum opinion and order, plaintiffs cannot show that they had an enforceable security interest in the proceeds from the sale of Steven and Pamela's livestock. Even if they did, defendant contends that it took the sales proceeds, in the form of three negotiable instruments, as a holder in due course, i.e., free from any claim of plaintiffs. A holder in due course is one who takes an instrument for value, in good faith, and without notice that it is overdue or has been dishonored or of any defense against or claim to it on the part of any person. . . . That defendant took the checks for value is undisputed, since the checks were taken in payment of an antecedent debt. . . The "good faith" and "without notice" requirements are likewise met. Objective, rather than subjective, intent controls. . . . Good faith is defined as "honesty in fact in the conduct or transaction concerned." . . . "It is not sufficient that [defendant] had knowledge that would put a reasonable person on inquiry which would lead to discovery. There must be actual knowledge of facts and circumstances which amounted to bad faith." . . . Here, there is no summary judgment evidence of bad faith on the part of defendant. Finally, plaintiffs' filing of their UCC-1 financing statement does not of itself constitute notice sufficient to defeat the rights of a holder in due course. . . . As provided in chapter 9 of the UCC in effect at the time:

> Nothing in this chapter limits the rights of a holder in due course of a negotiable instrument (Section 3.302) . . . and such holders or purchasers take priority over an earlier security interest even though perfected. Filing under this chapter does not constitute notice of the security interest to such holders or purchasers. . . .

For the reasons discussed herein,

The court ORDERS that defendant's motion for summary judgment be, and is hereby, granted; that plaintiffs take nothing on their claims against defendant; and that such claims be, and are hereby, dismissed with prejudice.

BUSINESS CONSIDERATIONS Dublin National Bank did not effectively check for competing security interests on the collateral. Should a business have a policy of checking for competing interests before enforcing its claims against a debtor? Why?

ETHICAL CONSIDERATIONS Although James had perfected his security interest first, Dublin National Bank prevailed in this case due to its status as a holder in due course. Is it ethical for a business that does not have the priority claim on a debtor's assets to take those assets through a "loophole" such as acquiring HDC status? Would Dublin have acted more ethically if it had turned the proceeds over to James and then sought recovery through the federal agency that guaranteed the loan of Steven and Pamela?

Recoupment

On occasion the person who issues a negotiable instrument may be able to assert a claim, not against the instrument, but against payment of the full amount of the instrument. When this happens, the issuer is said to have a claim in recoupment. For example, suppose that a buyer purchases some equipment from a seller, paying for the equipment by issuing a check payable to the order of the seller. The buyer accepts the equipment when it is delivered but discovers a defect in the equipment. The buyer then decides to pay for repairs to the equipment rather than revoke his acceptance of the goods. Although the buyer has accepted the goods, it is quite likely that the seller has breached one or more warranties in the sale. In this case, although the buyer is obligated to pay for the goods (the goods were accepted upon tender of delivery), the buyer also has a claim against the seller for the damages discovered after the acceptance and may well be allowed to reduce the amount owed to the seller for the goods by the amount of the damages ("recouping" his losses). If recoupment is allowed, the issuer pays the amount of the instrument minus the amount of any damages incurred. The instrument is still being paid, but it is not being paid in full!

Under the former version of Article 3, this sort of situation was classified as a general "failure of consideration" and was treated as a personal defense of the issuer. However, this treatment was deemed too vague and was open to too many possible interpretations. As a result, the revision to Article 3 does not mention "failure of consideration," instead preferring to treat specific types of failures more directly. In § 3-305(a)(3), claims in recoupment are specifically covered. According to this section, "the right to enforce the obligation of a party to pay an instrument is subject to the following:

(2) A claim in recoupment of the obligor against the original payee of the instrument if the claim arose from the transaction that gave rise to the instrument; but the claim of the obligor may be asserted against a transferee of the instrument only to reduce the amount owing on the instrument at the time the action is brought."[5]

Section 3-305(b) goes on to state that the right of a holder in due course to enforce the instrument is not subject to any claim of recoupment against a person other than the holder.

This change in emphasis removes a personal defense that existed under the previous coverage of Article 3, failure of consideration. But it allows the issuer of the instrument to "net out" the amount owed on the instrument if the issuer has a claim in recoupment against the original payee, unless the party seeking payment is a holder in due course. This still provides adequate protection for an HDC, it protects other holders who do not possess HDC status to some extent, and it leaves the issuer in the position he or she would occupy under Article 2 while allowing the issuer to use a negotiable instrument to make payment for the goods.

Real Defenses

A real defense, sometimes referred to as a universal defense, challenges the validity of the instrument itself. If a real defense can be established, the negotiable instrument is voided by operation of law, and *no one* can enforce the instrument. Thus, even an HDC will lose to a real defense. It should be kept in mind that if a maker or drawer alleges a real defense, the maker or drawer must establish the defense as real. A failure to do so will normally still leave a valid personal defense, but such a defense will not prevail against a holder in due course. Section 3-305(a)(1) of the UCC lists the four defenses that are valid against an HDC. Two additional potential real defenses, found in § 3-403 and § 3-407, are also discussed here.

Infancy The first real defense is infancy (or minority), but only "to the extent that it is a defense to a simple contract." Infancy refers to the period before a person attains majority status and gains complete contractual capacity. Thus, anyone who is not yet 18 years of age is still, legally, an infant, or a minor. To determine whether infancy is a real defense, state law must be examined. If the statutes or cases in the state where the instrument is issued allow infancy to be asserted as a defense to the underlying contract, the infancy may also be raised as a real defense on the instrument. Even if state law does not give such a broad defense, it is still useful as a personal defense; however, a holder in due course can override that defense.

Duress, Lack of Legal Capacity, or Illegality The second real defense is "duress, lack of legal capacity, or illegality of the transactions which, under other law, nullifies the obligation." Again, the relevant state law will be controlling. If the state statutes or prior cases void the transaction, the instrument is also voided. If not, the defense is merely personal in nature. An example would be the issuance of a check to pay a gambling debt. If gambling agreements are illegal in the state, there is a defense on the instrument, but it is probably only a personal defense. However, if the check contains a notation that it is meant as payment for a gambling debt, the defense becomes real. The instrument itself now reflects the illegality.

Other types of illegality that might affect a negotiable instrument, and hence operate as a real defense on the instrument, include usury, agreements that violate public policy, and attempting to do business in a state when not licensed to do so.

Fraud The third real defense is "fraud that induced the obligor to sign the instrument with neither knowledge nor reasonable opportunity to learn of its character or its essential terms." In this defense, the maker or drawer must prove two things: (1) lack of knowledge of the instrument signed and (2) no reasonable opportunity to discover the nature or terms of the instrument. To establish this defense, the maker or drawer must prove that discovering the nature of the signed instrument was not reasonable at the time of signing. Such proof will be virtually impossible unless the signing person is either illiterate or is involved in a strange set of circumstances. The following hypothetical case illustrates such a setting.

Freddy Hornet, a famous rock musician, was signing autographs outside a theater after a performance. Sonya Smith, among others, shoved a paper in front of Freddy for him to sign. However, the paper she shoved was a promissory note, payable to her order, for $50,000. Freddy signed it without reading it, and Sonya left the theater area. Sonya later sued Freddy to collect the money called for in the note. If Freddy can prove these facts, he may have a real defense and will not have to pay the note.

Check fraud is becoming a significant problem, especially with the growing use of telechecks and preauthorized payments. Several Web sites are devoted to this topic, including http://www.ckfraud.org/. Another site that pro-

vides some guidelines and some suggestions is http://www.cpaonline.com/insite/. While the check frauds referred to at these sites may not qualify as a real defense in every case, it is worth examining these sites for some helpful hints.

Discharge in Insolvency The fourth real defense is a "discharge of the obligor in insolvency proceedings." This area basically refers to a discharge in bankruptcy proceedings. Bankruptcy is a federally guaranteed privilege, and federal law prevails over conflicting state law. The federal bankruptcy law discharges the enforceability of the instrument, creating a statutory real defense on the instrument.

Forgery Section 3-403 of the Code treats a forgery—or any unauthorized signature—as ineffective against anyone except the person who signed. Thus, a forgery of the signature of the drawer of a draft or the maker of a note is ineffective against the person whose signature was forged. However, if the drawer or maker ratifies the signature, the signature becomes authorized, and thus effective against that person. In addition, if the drawer or maker contributed to the forgery, the defense is "reduced" to a personal defense; it is no longer valid against a holder in due course.

Material Alteration Section 3-407 provides that an unauthorized material alteration is a real defense to the extent of the alteration. An HDC can still enforce the instrument as issued, but would have to seek recovery for the altered terms from the person who altered the instrument without authorization. Again, if the drawer or maker contributed to the alteration, the defense becomes merely personal and is not effective against a holder in due course.

Section 3-406 provides the standards for determining whether an unauthorized signature or an unauthorized alteration becomes merely a personal defense. According to this section, "a person whose failure to exercise reasonable care substantially contributes to an alteration of an instrument or to the making of a forged signature on an instrument is precluding from asserting the alteration or the forgery against a person who, in good faith, pays the instrument or takes it for value or for collection."

The Shelter Provision

Remember that we stated earlier in this chapter that a transfer of an instrument is treated like the assignment of rights under contract law. You should also remember that an assignee takes the same rights as were held by his or her assignor. This same rule holds true with the transfer of a negotiable instrument. This provision is spelled out in § 3-203(b), which states:

Transfer of an instrument, whether or not the transfer is a negotiation, vests in the transferee any right of the transferor to enforce the instrument, including any right as a holder in due course, but the transferee cannot acquire rights of a holder in due course by transfer, directly or indirectly, from a holder in due course if the transferee engaged in fraud or illegality affecting the instrument.

This provision, generally known as the "shelter provision," simply states that once an HDC is involved with an instrument, every subsequent holder can assert the rights of an HDC without having to prove his or her status, with one exception. No one who engaged in any act of fraud or other illegality affecting the instrument can then "launder" his or her involvement by having the instrument negotiated to an HDC and then acquiring or reacquiring the instrument and asserting the shelter provision.

Also note that a transferee who takes an instrument by a means other than negotiation may have to establish his or her rights to the instrument and may also have to establish the rights of his or her transferor *as an HDC* in order to make use of the protection of the shelter provision.[6]

Statutory Limitations

The protected status given to holders in due course makes abuses possible. If a payee obtains an instrument by wrongful means and then negotiates it to an HDC, the maker or drawer will nearly always be obliged to pay the instrument. As will be seen in the next chapter, the maker or drawer can sue the payee to recover the money paid. However, the payee must be found to be sued, and the finding may not be easy. If the payee and the HDC are working together, the maker or drawer is easily taken, usually with no chance of recovering.

Because of this potential, the Federal Trade Commission (FTC) passed a regulation in 1976 designed to protect consumers. This regulation modifies the holder in due course rules in some circumstances. If a consumer credit transaction is involved, the instrument used must contain the following notice, printed prominently:

ANY HOLDER OF THIS CONSUMER CREDIT CONTRACT IS SUBJECT TO ALL CLAIMS AND DEFENSES WHICH THE DEBTOR COULD ASSERT AGAINST THE SELLER OF GOODS OR SERVICES OBTAINED HERETO OR WITH THE PROCEEDS HEREOF. RECOVERY HEREUNDER BY THE DEBTOR SHALL NOT EXCEED AMOUNTS PAID BY THE DEBTOR HEREUNDER.

The effect of the rule is to make even an HDC subject to any defenses available against the payee, which is a tremendous protection for the consumer. This rule may have a great impact on the use of consumer credit contracts in the future.

If the notice is present in a consumer credit transaction, any holder of the instrument has agreed by the terms of the instrument to remain subject to any defenses of the maker or drawer. This means that a consumer could avoid payment to any HDC in possession of the instrument if the consumer could avoid payment to the payee. This is true even if the notice is included in a credit contract with a nonconsumer, as is pointed out in *Jefferson Bank & Trust Co. v. Stamatiou.*[7] In that case, Stamatiou purchased a truck from Key Dodge, signing a note that was subsequently assigned to Jefferson Bank & Trust. Although Stamatiou was purchasing the truck for a commercial purpose, the note Stamatiou signed included the FTC's HDC limitation. (Apparently, the sales manager at the dealership used the consumer loan form by mistake.) When the truck broke down, Stamatiou rescinded the contract and ceased making payments on the loan. The bank sued, alleging that it was entitled to recover on the note due to its status as an HDC. Stamatiou raised the FTC restriction on the protections afforded to an HDC and denied liability, and the court agreed with his argument. While the protection was *intended* for consumer credit transactions, it *could* be used in a commercial loan, and would be given full force and effect when it was. Since the clause was in the note, Stamatiou was allowed to assert his personal defense against the bank despite its HDC status and was therefore not obligated to pay the note.

This case is still viewed by many people as the definitive case in this area. The new restriction on HDC status included in the revision to Article 3 is based, at least in part, on this opinion. Section 3-302(g) states that the protections given to a holder in due course are subject to any law limiting the status as a holder in due course in particular classes of transactions. This section is intended to recognize the impact of the FTC's HDC rule, as well as any comparable rules or statutes passed by any state, and to remove any uncertainty as to whether HDC protections exist in such a situation.

Holder by Due Negotiation

When a negotiable document of title is issued calling for delivery of the goods to the order of a named individual, or to bearer, the document of title is negotiable. As such, it can be negotiated by indorsement and delivery (if the goods are to be delivered "to order") or by delivery alone (if the goods are to be delivered "to bearer"). When a document is negotiated to a person who purchases the instrument in good faith and the purchaser takes the document without notice of any defense against or claim to the goods or the document, the instrument has been "duly negotiated." This makes the recipient of the document a *holder by due negotiation* (HDN), a somewhat preferred and protected status in the area of documents of title, although neither as preferred nor as protected as an HDC in the area of negotiable instruments.

A holder by due negotiation is assured of the following rights:

- title to the document.

- title to the goods the document represents.

- all rights accruing under the laws of agency or estoppel, including the right to goods delivered to the bailee after the document was issued.

- the direct obligation of the issuer of the document to hold or to deliver the goods according to the terms of the document and free of any claims or defenses of the issuer except those specified in the document or specified in Article 7.

In contrast, if the document is not negotiable or was not negotiated despite its negotiability, or if the purchaser either did not act in good faith or had notice of a defense or claim against the document, he or she cannot be an HDN. In this situation the recipient acquires only the rights and the title the transferor possesses or has the authority to convey. Further, if the document is nonnegotiable, the rights of the recipient may be defeated by any claims or defenses that arise after the transfer but before the bailee receives notice of the transfer.

Summary

A negotiable instrument can be transferred in a number of ways. The original transfer from the maker or the drawer is an issue. Once issued, the instrument can be further transferred by assignment or by negotiation. An assignment gives the assignee no special rights or protections. In contrast, a negotiation may confer some individual rights on the recipient. When a negotiation occurs, the transferee becomes a holder.

Most negotiations involve the use of an indorsement. Indorsements may affect further negotiation, and they may affect the possible liability of the parties. Special, blank, and restrictive indorsements affect negotiations. Qualified and unqualified indorsements affect liability.

Once a negotiation occurs, the holder has the opportunity to achieve the most favored status in commercial paper: He or she may become a holder in due course. An HDC is a holder who takes an instrument in good faith, for value, and without notice of any defenses or defects on the

instrument. A holder in due course can defeat a personal defense. A real defense will defeat a holder in due course. In addition, a person who takes an instrument *after* a holder in due course is normally allowed to assert the rights of an HDC because of the shelter provision. Thus, once an HDC has possessed the instrument, subsequent parties can assert the rights of an HDC regardless of their status, with a few minor exceptions.

The Federal Trade Commission enacted a special rule in 1976 to protect consumers. The rule denies any protection against any defenses, even for an HDC, on a consumer credit instrument.

Article 7 provides for special protections in handling negotiable documents of title. A person who acquires a negotiable document of title by purchasing the document in good faith without notice of any defenses or defects qualifies as a holder by due negotiation. This status confers benefits beyond the benefits acquired in the document itself.

Discussion Questions

1. Is the distinction between a mere transfer and a negotiation important in determining the rights of a party in possession of a negotiable instrument? Why might this distinction matter to the party in possession of the instrument?

2. How can a holder indorse an instrument to minimize his or her potential secondary liability on the instrument in the event of a dishonor upon presentment? What, if anything, will such an indorsement tell the indorsee?

3. Amita issued Carol a check payable to the order of Carol. Carol sold the check to Lynn, but neglected to indorse it at the time of the sale. At that point, what legal status would Lynn possess? What duty, if any, would Carol owe to Lynn? Would Carol have any different duties or obligations if she had given the check to Lynn as a gift, again without any indorsement?

4. Terry issued a check to Phil. Phil indorsed the check and delivered it to Irene. The name on the payee line of the check

had originally read "Ben," but Terry had crossed out Ben's name and replaced it with Phil's name. To show what he had done, Terry initialed the change on the payee line. Under these circumstances, can Irene qualify as a holder in due course on the check? Explain your reasoning.

5. Ann is in possession of a check that Dan issued to her. She would like to mail the check to her bank to be deposited to her checking account. How should she indorse the check to give herself the maximum possible legal protection, and why does such an indorsement give her this maximum protection?

6. Charles had a note issued by David. Charles discovered that David was about to go through a bankruptcy, so he negotiated the note to Richard. Richard qualified as a holder in due course. David filed for bankruptcy, and Richard sued David to collect on the note. What are Richard's rights against David? Why?

7. Denise issued the following check to Bill:

	October 3, 20XX
Denise	
Freemont Ln.	
Enfield, CT	$ 20.00
Pay to the order of ___ Bill ___	
___ Twenty and no/00 ___ dollars	
	Denise

Bill added the number 2 before the "20.00" and added the words Two Hundred before the "Twenty." He then negotiated the check to Sarah, an HDC, for $220. Sarah presented the check to the bank, but it was dishonored due to nonsufficient funds. Sarah is suing Denise to recover on the check. How much will Denise have to pay Sarah, and why?

8. John's Television Sales and Service offered credit terms to its customers who desired credit. To obtain credit, the customer signed a promissory note for the amount of the credit, and after the customer took the television, John sold the signed note to his bank. The notes John provided did not contain the FTC consumer credit language. If a customer has a personal defense on his or her purchase from John, may the customer raise that defense against the bank as well? Why? Might the customer have a claim against John's Television Sales and Service in this situation?

9. Daryl issued a check payable to the order of Annie. Annie then negotiated the check to Belinda, a holder in due course. Belinda subsequently negotiated the check to Chen, who took the check without giving value. When Chen presented it to the bank, the bank dishonored the check because of a stop payment order placed against the check by Daryl. (Annie did not perform her portion of the contract with Daryl, causing Daryl to issue the stop payment order.) When Chen demanded payment from Daryl for the check, Daryl refused to pay. Daryl is of the opinion that he does not have to pay Chen because he has a defense on the check. Daryl believes that since Chen is not an HDC, Chen cannot enforce the check against Daryl. If Chen sues Daryl on the check, what result will occur? Why?

10. What rights are acquired by a holder by due negotiation, and how are these rights superior to the rights of a person who merely possesses a nonnegotiable document of title?

Case Problems and Writing Assignments

1. Gilliam loaned Westhampton $345,200. As security for this loan, Westhampton assigned three deed of trust notes to Gilliam. These deed of trust notes were apparently issued by White. White refused to pay the notes when they came due, and Gilliam filed suit to collect the notes. Gilliam asserted that he was a holder in due course on the notes and was, therefore, entitled to receive payment even if White had a defense. White asserted that either he never executed the notes or, if he executed them, the execution was the result of fraud and constituted a real defense against enforcement of the notes. According to White, the only document he was aware of signing purported to be a "disclosure statement." White did admit that he had not read the "disclosure statement" very carefully, but that he did not know that the papers he was signing were, in fact, deed of trust notes.

How should the court resolve this case? How much influence would White's experience—or lack of same—in real estate

loans and financing have on your decision? Assume that White had substantial experience in real estate transactions. What should White have done to protect his interests in a situation like this? [See *White v. Gilliam*, 419 S.E.2d 247 (Va. 1992).]

2. Doyle borrowed money from Trinity Savings & Loan, signing a promissory note that included an adjustable interest rate. The interest rate typed on the appropriate blank on the loan form provided for interest in the amount of 11.375 percent per annum. After Doyle signed the note, Trinity "whited out" the interest rate, typed in a new interest rate of 15.875 percent per annum, and appended what were purportedly Doyle's initials to the change. Trinity subsequently sold the note to the Federal National Mortgage Association (FNMA). When the note came due, Doyle refused to pay. He cited the material alteration as a defense to his obligation to Trinity and asserted that the FNMA could not qualify as a holder in due course because the note contained an obvious alteration.

How should this case be decided? What ethical issues are raised when any negotiable instrument has some essential element "whited out," new terms inserted, and initials appended? [See *Doyle v. Resolution Trust Corp.*, 999 F.2d 469 (10th Cir. 1993).]

3. Michigan Insurance Repair Co. (Michigan) entered into a joint venture with Ultimate Construction for the purpose of doing fire damage repair work. One of the jobs they were to perform was on property owned by Booth and the Madias Brothers, and insured by Allstate. Michigan claimed that it advanced funds to Ultimate to pay for the repairs on this property, and that Ultimate promised to have any checks received from Allstate reflect the rights of Michigan to a share of the proceeds. Eventually, Allstate issued a check for $28,964.94 in payment for the work. The check as issued was payable to the order of "Nella and Chutry Booth and Ultimate Construction and Madias Bros., Inc. and Levin & Levin." On the back of the check were the following indorsements (from top to bottom):

For Deposit Only to Acct. #0051255-04

Ultimate Construction Co., Randy Bidlofsky

C.L. Booth, Chutry Booth

Madias Brothers, Inc. (by Nick Madias, President)

Levin & Levin

Pay to the Order of Manufacturers National Bank of Detroit,

For Deposit Only, Ultimate Insurance Repair or Construction

Michigan sued the bank for the amount of the check, claiming that the first indorsement was a restrictive indorsement for deposit to its account, and asserting that the bank violated its duty as imposed by this restrictive indorsement when it deposited the check to the Ultimate account. Was the bank obligated to honor the first restrictive indorsement on this check? Revised Article 3 takes a much harsher attitude toward restrictive indorsements than the prior law. Banks will be much more hesitant to ignore a restrictive indorsement under the revisions. What should a business do to protect itself when it receives a check that has been indorsed restrictively? [See *Michigan Insurance Repair Co., Inc. v. Manufacturers Nat'l Bank of Detroit*, 487 N.W.2d 517 (1992)].

4. An Admaster employee prepared a number of Admaster checks payable to the order of Merrill Lynch, signed the checks without authorization, and deposited the checks in the employee's account with Merrill Lynch. The Admaster employee then used the funds so deposited for his personal transactions with Merrill Lynch. Eventually, Admaster learned that its employee had embezzled these funds, and sued Merrill Lynch to recover the funds taken by the employee. Did Merrill Lynch qualify as a holder in due course on these checks, or did Merrill Lynch have notice of the unauthorized signature, thus negating its HDC status? Should Merrill Lynch have been suspicious of the checks it received from the Admaster employee? Should a business that handles investments and receives large amounts of money be more aware of the likelihood of thefts and embezzlements? Does an investment firm have a higher ethical duty in handling the funds of customers than other types of businesses? [See *Admaster, Inc. v. Merrill Lynch, Pierce, Fenner, & Smith, Inc.*, 583 N.Y.S.2d 408 (N.Y. App Div. 1st Dept. 1992).]

5. **BUSINESS APPLICATION CASE** In the summer of 1987, C. L. Gildroy, a Harvard M.B.A with many years of experience in banking, real estate, and venture capital operations, was a co-owner of the Hyannis Regency Hotel with Robert F. Welch, Stephen C. Jones, and another. Welch and Jones were at the time also owners of the Taunton Regency Hotel, then under construction, in which Gildroy had no interest.

In order to secure funds to complete construction of the Taunton Regency, Welch approached the Taunton Savings Bank (TSB) for a $200,000 loan. Welch represented to TSB that he, Jones, and Gildroy were owners of the Taunton hotel. That representation was false as to Gildroy. Ultimately TSB approved the loan and prepared a promissory note for the signatures of Welch, Jones, and Gildroy. Rather than follow TSB's normal procedure of conducting loan closings with all borrowers present to execute the documents, the responsible TSB officer allowed Welch to take the note out of the bank in order to obtain the signatures of Jones and Gildroy. Welch presented the TSB note to Gildroy in a stack of documents that Welch advised Gildroy were necessary to sign in connection with applications for refinancing the outstanding construction loan for the Hyannis hotel. Without reading the note—which was titled in capital letters, "Taunton Savings Bank Commercial Loan Note and Disclosure $200,000.00" and bore the words, immediately above the signature lines, "If this note is signed by more than one person their liabilities hereunder shall be joint and several"—Gildroy affixed his signature under those of Welch and Jones. In accordance with Welch's instructions, TSB, after receiving the fully executed note from Welch, deposited the $200,000 loan proceeds into Taunton Regency's checking account at TSB. TSB was not aware of Welch's machinations or the circumstances that led to Gildroy's signing the note. Gildroy was not aware of the loan negotiations, the loan, or Welch's deception.

Welch and Jones made required monthly interest payments to TSB on the note for about a year. TSB was then acquired by the plaintiff, New Bedford Institution for Savings (NBIS). Shortly thereafter, payments on the note stopped, and the loan went into default. Gildroy had never been contacted by either TSB or NBIS regarding the loan until the default occurred and NBIS demanded payment. Upon the failure of any of the comakers to remove the default, NBIS commenced this action against them to enforce their joint and several liabilities. While Welch and Jones defaulted, Gildroy defended vigorously, asserting defenses of fraud and want of consideration flowing to him. The judge ruled for Gildroy, holding that neither TSB (because it was the note payee) nor NBIS (because it acquired the note as part of a "bulk transaction") qualified as a holder in due course. Based upon that ruling, the judge deemed Gildroy's lack of consideration to be available against NBIS, as one not a holder in due course under ordinary contract principles. Was TSB and/or NBIS a holder in due course on the note? What policies should the bank have followed to prevent this result? [See *New Bedford Institution for Savings v. C. L. Gildroy*, 634 N.E.2d 920 (Mass. App. Ct. 1994).]

6. **ETHICAL APPLICATION CASE** Harry H. Wagner is the president of Harry H. Wagner & Son, Inc., a residential and commercial construction company located in Lima, Ohio. Wagner has worked for the company, which was founded by his father, for 31 years. In the past 20 years, Wagner & Son has built approximately 156 duplex units, which it owns and leases as residential rental property. The properties had been financed through various local banks at interest rates of 8.0 percent, adjustable in small increments every three to five years. Wagner had no difficulty paying these loans. Wagner eventually sought to refinance these rental properties for estate planning purposes, and approached American Heritage Mortgage Company of Ohio for assistance in arranging and securing this refinancing. Wagner hoped to secure a fixed interest rate of 7 to 8 percent to increase the properties' long-term profitability. Wagner eventually agreed to borrow the money from AMC Bank at a fixed rate of 10.9 percent. Wagner agreed to these terms, at least in part, because he thought that AMC had orally agreed to refinance the loans at a fixed rate between 7 and 8 percent after the loans had "seasoned" for about 12 months. On February 10, 1997, Wagner closed on the loans with AMC by executing approximately 60 notes totaling $11 million at an annual interest rate of 10.9 percent per annum. Thereafter, AMC sold the mortgage notes on the secondary market to various banks.

The properties failed to generate the income necessary to support the note payments at the new, higher rates, and Wagner eventually defaulted on the payments. The various banks that had purchased the notes then declared the debts due and initiated foreclosure proceedings. Wagner objected to the foreclosure proceedings, claiming, among other things, that he had defenses on the notes including fraud, misrepresentation, promissory estoppel, and breach of contract. According to Wagner's assertions, the oral promises from AMC Bank provided him with defenses on the notes and those defenses were good against the various banks that had purchased the notes. Each of the banks claimed to be a holder in due course on any notes held by that bank, and they denied that Wagner's alleged defenses were valid against them. How should this case be resolved? Did the various banks act in good faith in their dealings with AMC? Were the various banks holders in due course of the notes they held? Were the alleged personal defenses raised by Wagner valid against these banks? What ethical issues are raised by the facts in this case? [See *Bankers Trust Company v. Harry H. Wagner & Son, Inc., et al.*, 2001 Ohio App. LEXIS 5947 (Ohio App. 3rd App. Dist. 2001).]

7. **CRITICAL THINKING CASE** In April 1984, Rosenbaum was arrested and charged with the crime of obtaining property by false pretenses. She eventually was convicted of this charge and was transferred to Women's Prison in Raleigh for confinement pending appeal. The trial judge in her case set an appearance bond of $50,000 as a condition for her release during the pen-

dency of the appeal. Unable to raise this sum of money herself, the plaintiff sought assistance from her sister, Louise Knox. Knox initially petitioned the judge for a reduction in the amount of her sister's bond. When this proved unsuccessful, she began approaching members of Ayden's business community in an effort to borrow the money.

Knox's requests generated little interest until she met with Harvey Bowen, a used car dealer. Bowen was not a licensed bondsman, and he barely knew Knox or Rosenbaum. Nevertheless, he agreed to post the bond in exchange for a $7,500 promissory note secured by a deed of trust on Rosenbaum's house. After obtaining Rosenbaum's agreement, Bowen hired an attorney who drafted the necessary loan documents running in favor of Bowen. Bowen's lawyer gave these documents to Knox, who took them to Raleigh where they were signed by her sister. Shortly thereafter, Bowen arranged for a *second* set of documents to be drafted, this time naming W. F. Bulow, the husband of Bowen's niece, as payee of the note and beneficiary of the deed of trust. Other than the substitution of Bulow for Bowen, the two sets of documents were essentially identical. At Bowen's request, Knox took the second set of documents to Raleigh for Rosenbaum's signature, then returned them to Bowen's attorney. The attorney then recorded the deed of trust running in Bulow's favor. Bowen subsequently executed the appearance bond, and Rosenbaum was released from custody. Like Bowen, Bulow had never been licensed as a bondsman by the State of North Carolina. He conceded that he gave no consideration directly to Rosenbaum in exchange for her execution of the note and deed of trust.

Eventually Rosenbaum defaulted on the note and Bulow initiated a foreclosure proceeding on the deed of trust. Rosenbaum objected and sued to prevent the foreclosure proceeding. Rosenbaum asserts that she has a defense to the note, the illegality of the transaction. Bulow argues that he is a holder in due course of the note and should be allowed to enforce the note. Is the note—and the related deed of trust—enforceable? Is Bulow a holder in due course of the note? In deciding this case, what issues are most persuasive to you in reaching your decision? [See *Rosenbaum v. Bulow*, 197 Bankr. LEXIS 555 (E.D. N.C. 1997).]

8. **YOU BE THE JUDGE** Ludmilla recently received a phone call from a telemarketing company. The person who called informed her that she had been selected as a possible winner of a free prize—a bookshelf stereo system. However, in order to claim her prize, Ludmilla was told that she needed to prove her eligibility. She was then asked if she had a checking account. When she answered "yes," she was told that the company needed the numbers from the bottom of the check to verify her eligibility for the prize. Ludmilla read off the numbers to the person, the call ended, and Ludmilla returned to her prior activities without giving the conversation much more thought. The following month Ludmilla discovered that a "telecheck," in the form of a demand draft payable to the order of the telemarketing firm, had been charged against her account. This

telecheck contained all of the correct information but was signed with a typed statement: "signature authorized by customer." Ludmilla demanded that the bank return the funds to her account, but the bank refused. Ludmilla has sued the drawer in an effort to recover her money. The case has been brought in *your* court. What will *you* decide? What factors are most likely to affect your decision? Is it possible for the drawer in this case to be an HDC? See "How to Protect Yourself: Checking Account Numbers—Keep Them Secret," Florida Attorney General's Office, http://myfloridalegal.com/pages.nsf/ 4492d797dc0bd92 f85256cb80055fb97/b101cb6e8c90747085256cc900529bd1! OpenDocument.

Notes

1. UCC § 3-203(a).
2. UCC § 3-203(b).
3. UCC § 3-201, and Official Comment 1.
4. UCC § 3-103(a)(4), and Official Comment 4.
5. UCC § 3-305(a)(3).
6. UCC § 3-203, Official Comment 2.
7. 384 So. 2d 388 (La. 1980).

Negotiables: Liability and Discharge

AGENDA

NRW NRW is likely to receive a few "bad" checks in the course of its business, and the firm will need to know what its rights are in those situations. Since the firm is involved in a technology-intensive industry, Mai, Carlos, and Helen would like to accept "telechecks" as payment for their goods, but they are unsure what their rights and/or liabilities might be with a telecheck. They are especially concerned with what happens if a telecheck is dishonored.

The firm has borrowed money from its bank in order to make some needed improvements. However, the bank recently informed the firm that it had "sold" the firm's note to another financial institution. The principals would like to know what this will do to their potential liability and to the liability of the firm. They would also like to know what impact this will have on their possible future dealings with their bank.

These and other questions will arise during our discussion of negotiable instruments law. Be prepared! You never know when the firm or one of its members will seek your advice.

Basic Concepts

Negotiable instruments are used as a substitute for money. However, at some point, the holder of the instrument is going to want the money for which the instrument has been substituted. Normally, this desire will lead to a presentment to the maker or drawee. In most cases, the maker or drawee then will pay the money as called for by the instrument, the instrument will be canceled, and its commercial life will terminate. Unfortunately, such a series of events does not happen every time. Some makers or drawees refuse to pay the presented instrument—they dishonor it. When this occurs, the issue of secondary liability arises. Some holders inadvertently fail to make a proper presentment. When this occurs, the issue of discharge arises. These possibilities are shown in Exhibit 23.1. You may want to refer back to this exhibit as you move through this chapter, keeping the roles and responsibilities of the various parties in mind.

The Chains of Liability

The term "liability," when used with negotiable instruments, refers to an obligation to pay the negotiable instrument involved. There are several possible types of liability in negotiable instruments. The obligation to pay may be based either on primary liability or on secondary liability. The liability also may be based on contract principles, warranty principles, or the admissions of one of the parties. For more information on liability on instruments, see http://www.law.cornell.edu/topics/negotiable.html/.

Primary Liability

Every negotiable instrument has a primary party, and every negotiable instrument has secondary parties. The primary party is the party who is expected to pay the instrument upon proper presentment. The secondary parties are the parties who face conditional liability if or when the primary party refuses to pay the instrument upon proper presentment.

The maker of a note is the primary party on that note. It is the maker to whom the holder will look for payment, and it is the maker who is normally expected to pay the note on its due date. Similarly, the drawee is the primary party on a check or a draft. It is the drawee to whom the holder will first look for payment of the order instrument, and it is the drawee who is normally expected to pay the order instrument, either on demand or on its due date.

A substantial difference exists between the position of the primary party on a note and that of a primary party on a check or a draft. On a note, the maker is primarily liable as soon as the note is issued. This is because the primary party, the maker, is also the person who gives the promise to pay. The maker is in a contractual relationship with the payee from the time he or she issues the instrument. By contrast, the drawee is normally *not* primarily liable on a check or a draft at the time the check or draft is issued. Primary liability will not arise until a holder presents the instrument and the drawee accepts the instrument as presented. (This is not true if the instrument is a cashier's check, certified check, or teller's check.)

The reason the drawee is not normally liable on an order instrument upon issue is that there are usually two contractual relationships involved in order paper: the first

---

EXHIBIT   23.1 The Movement of a Negotiable Instrument

Issue ····▶ Negotiation(s) ·····▶ Presentment ···▶ Acceptance & Payment (Primary Liability Accepted)
                                                    ↘ Dishonor; Secondary Liability Claims Arise

Issue	The initial negotiation of an instrument. Normal delivery is to the payee, although it also may be delivered to a remitter.
Negotiation(s)	The transfer of an instrument by indorsement and delivery or by delivery alone, in which the transferee becomes a holder.
Presentment	Demand made to the primary party for the acceptance and/or payment of the instrument.
Acceptance	Commitment by the primary party to pay the instrument as presented.
Dishonor	Refusal by the primary party to accept the instrument; activates secondary liability of the prior parties on the instrument.
Payment	

contract is the contract between the drawer and the payee, the reason for the issuance of the instrument; the second contract is between the drawer and the drawee, the reason the drawee is expected to obey the drawer's order upon proper presentment. No contractual relationship exists between the drawee and the payee on the negotiable instrument issued by the drawer unless or until the drawee accepts the instrument, thereby agreeing to honor the order given by the drawer. Thus, a note has a commitment of primary liability from the time of its issue (the maker is legally obligated to the payee or any subsequent holders), but a check or a draft has a mere *expectation* that primary liability will exist at a future time. (The drawee has not yet made a commitment to the payee or any subsequent holders; its commitment is to the drawer.)

On most negotiable instruments the primary party does, in fact, pay the instrument, honoring the primary liability of the instrument. Occasionally, however, the primary party does not honor his or her primary liability. When this happens, the holder of the dishonored instrument may seek recovery from one of the secondary parties on that instrument.

Secondary Liability

The drawer of a check or a draft is obligated to pay that draft or check if the instrument is dishonored.[1] This means that the drawer of the instrument is a secondary party on the instrument. In addition, the payee and any indorsers of any negotiable instrument—a check, a draft, a note, or a certificate of deposit—are each secondary parties on that instrument. Secondary parties face potential secondary liability on the instrument. A secondary party agrees, by acting as either the drawer, the payee, or an indorser, to pay the instrument if certain conditions are met. Remember, though, that secondary liability is conditional liability. The secondary parties can be held liable only if the conditions are satisfied or if the secondary party waives the need for the conditions to be met. To hold a secondary party liable on his or her contract (represented by the indorsement or signing of the instrument), a person holding the instrument must prove all three of the following actions:

1. Presentment of the instrument was properly made or presentment was excused.

2. The primary party dishonored the instrument upon proper presentment.

3. Notice of the dishonor was properly given to the secondary party or notice has been waived or excused.

Recall also that there are two types of potential secondary liability: contractual liability and warranty liability. Any indorsement that is unqualified (indorsements are presumed to be unqualified) gives a contract to the indorsee and to every subsequent holder that, upon proper presentment and dishonor, the indorser will "buy" the instrument back. However, indorsers who use a qualified indorsement deny this contractual liability. Nonetheless, they, too, face potential secondary liability based on the warranties they give upon transfer and/or presentment. (This warranty liability will be discussed later in the chapter.)

Obligation of the Drawer

The drawer of a draft faces potential secondary liability for any drafts issued if the draft is dishonored upon presentment. Section 3-414 spells out the obligations of the drawer:

If an unaccepted draft is dishonored, the drawer is obligated to pay the draft (i) according to its terms at the time it was issued or, if not issued, at the time it first came into possession of a holder, or (ii) if the drawer signed an incomplete instrument, according to its terms when completed. . . . The obligation is owed to a person entitled to enforce the draft or to an indorser who paid the draft under Section 3-415.[2]

If the draft is accepted upon proper presentment, and the acceptance is by a bank, the drawer is discharged.[3] However, if the draft is accepted by a drawee and the drawee is not a bank, the drawer is not automatically discharged. Instead, if the drawee accepts the draft and later dishonors the instrument, the drawer faces the same liability as would be faced by an indorser under the provisions of § 3-415.[4] If the drawer wishes to avoid liability, he or she can issue a draft—but not a *check*—"without recourse." The drawer of a check cannot deny secondary liability in this manner. By using this qualifying language, the drawer is denying his or her potential secondary liability on the draft from the date of issue, thus negating the liability provisions of § 3-414(b). And since the qualifying language is on the face of the instrument, the payee is aware of the denial of secondary liability from the time the draft is issued.

Obligation of the Indorser

In a similar manner, the indorsers of a negotiable instrument have certain obligations. The indorsers of any negotiable instrument face potential secondary liability for any instruments indorsed that are dishonored upon presentment. Section 3-415 spells out the obligations of the indorsers:

(a) Subject to subsections (b), (c), (d), (e), and to Section 3-419(d), if an instrument is dishonored, an indorser is obliged to pay the amount due on the instrument (i) according to the terms of the instrument at the time it was indorsed, or (ii) if the indorser indorsed an incomplete instrument, according to its terms when completed. . . . The obligation of the indorser is owed to a person entitled to enforce the instrument or to a subsequent indorser who paid the instrument under this section.

There are a few exceptions to this basic rule as set out in subsection (a). If the indorser used a qualified indorsement to indorse the instrument, he or she is not liable under subsection (a) to pay the instrument.[5] The indorser is also not liable

1. if notice of any dishonor is required in order to hold the indorser liable, and such notice is not given;[6]

2. if the instrument is accepted by a bank after the indorsement was made;[7] or

3. if the indorsed instrument is a check, and the check is not presented to the drawee bank or deposited within thirty days of the day the indorsement was made.[8]

These chains of liability are shown in Exhibit 23.2.

Establishing Liability

As we showed in Exhibit 23.1, negotiable instruments have a normal movement pattern. The instrument is issued, and it may then be negotiated to one or more holders. At some point in time a holder is expected to make *presentment* of the instrument to the primary party. When presentment is made, one of two things will occur. Either the primary party will *accept* the instrument (and pay it, either at the time of acceptance or at a later time), or the primary party will *dishonor* the instrument, refusing to accept it. If the instrument is accepted, primary liability is accepted and the instrument will be paid and removed from circulation. If the instrument is dishonored, primary liability is refused and secondary liability is activated. These stages are examined in detail in the following sections.

Presentment

Presentment is a demand for acceptance or for payment of a negotiable instrument. The demand is made to the maker of a promise instrument, or to the drawee of an order instrument, or to the acceptor of a previously accepted instrument. The party making presentment is called the presenter. The rules governing presentment have been changed somewhat in the current version of Article 3 to more accurately reflect the treatment of negotiable instruments today. The current rule regarding presentment is found in § 3-501. This section is set out here, with a brief

---

EXHIBIT   23.2 The Chains of Liability on Negotiable Instruments

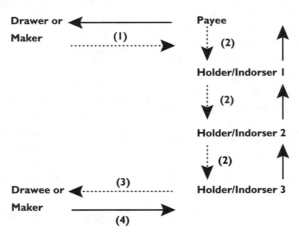

The (potential) primary liability moves in a clockwise manner, following the dashed lines: (1) is the issue, (2) is a negotiation, and (3) is a presentment. If the drawee or maker accepts the instrument, it is paid and discharged. If the drawee or maker dishonors the instrument on presentment (4), secondary liability is activated. Secondary liability moves counterclockwise, following the solid lines. (The number of holder/indorsers may be larger or smaller than the number shown in this exhibit.)

explanation of each subsection immediately following that subsection.

Section 3-501. Presentment

(a) "Presentment" means a demand made by or on behalf of a person entitled to enforce an instrument (i) to pay the instrument made to the drawee or a party obliged to pay the instrument or, in the case of a note or accepted draft payable at a bank, to the bank, or (ii) to accept a draft made to the drawee.

(The holder *demands* payment and/or acceptance from the drawee of order paper or the maker of promise paper. If the instrument is a note payable at a bank or is an accepted draft, the holder demands payment from the bank.)

(b) The following rules are subject to Article 4, agreement of the parties, and clearinghouse rules and the like:
(1) Presentment may be made at the place of payment of the instrument and must be made at the place of payment if the instrument is payable at a bank in the United States; may be made by any commercially reasonable means, including an oral, written, or electronic communication; is effective when received by the person to whom presentment is made; and is effective if made to any two or more makers, acceptors, drawees, or other payees.

(The holder is to make presentment at the proper place. This means at the place of payment of the instrument. If the place of payment is a U.S. bank, presentment *must* be made at that bank. Presentment may be made in any reasonable manner, and is deemed effective when the presentment is received by the primary party.)

(2) Upon demand of the person to whom presentment is made, the person making presentment must (i) exhibit the instrument; (ii) give reasonable identification and, if presentment is made on behalf of another person, reasonable evidence of authority to do so, and . . . sign a receipt on the instrument for any payment made or surrender the instrument if full payment is made.

(The presenting party must satisfy the reasonable demands or requests of the primary party in order to establish the rights of the presenting party. This includes showing the instrument, showing proof of identity, and signing a receipt for any payments made on the instrument.)

(3) Without dishonoring the instrument, the party to whom presentment is made may (i) return the instrument for lack of a necessary indorsement, or (ii) refuse payment or acceptance for failure of the presentment to comply with the terms of the instrument, an agreement of the parties, or other applicable rules of law.

(If the instrument lacks a necessary indorsement at the time of presentment, the primary party can refuse to accept the instrument, and this refusal is *not* treated as a dishonor. It is also deemed *not* to be a dishonor if the primary party refuses to accept or pay the instrument due to an improper presentment for other reasons, including the terms of the instrument itself, an agreement of the parties, or any applicable rules of law regarding presentment.)

(4) The party to whom presentment is made may treat presentment as occurring on the next business day after the day of presentment if the party to whom presentment is made has established a cut-off hour not earlier than 2 P.M. for the receipt and processing of instruments presented for payment or acceptance and presentment is made after the cut-off hour.

(This allows primary parties, especially banks and other financial institutions, to establish an "end of business day" time, and to treat any activities after that time as occurring on the next business day. Thus, a presentment made at 3:00 P.M. on a Tuesday is treated as being made on Wednesday. Since the primary party has a deadline for taking action after a proper presentment, it is important to know the day on which presentment was made.)

The following case dealt with the issue of proper presentment, in particular the right of the drawee to demand "reasonable identification" from the presenter.

The previous version of Article 3 required that presentment be made by mail, or through a clearinghouse, or at a place specified in the instrument. The presentment "at a place specified in the instrument" implied, at least, that the presentment had to be made by the holder by having the holder be physically present *with the instrument* at that place. Thus, presentment required the production of the instrument itself if the presentment was to be proper. This has changed dramatically in the revision to Article 3. Presentment can now be made in the "traditional" manner by using the mail or a clearinghouse, or by physically appearing at the place specified in the instrument. But presentment can also be made *orally* or *electronically*. Obviously, the instrument itself will not be physically present in

23.1

MESSING v. BANK OF AMERICA, N.A.
792 A.2d 312, 2002 Md. App. LEXIS 40 (2002)

FACTS On August 3, 2000, Messing attempted to cash a check for $976 at one of the Baltimore branches of the Bank of America. Messing was the payee on the check, which was drawn against the Bank of America. Messing did not have any accounts with the Bank of America. Messing handed the check to a teller, who confirmed that the drawer had adequate funds on deposit to cover the check and who then "validated" the check by stamping the date, time, account number, and teller number on the back of the check. The check was then returned to Messing for his indorsement. After the check was indorsed, the teller asked Messing for some identification. In response, Messing produced his driver's license and a "major credit card." The teller then copied the information from these two sources to the back of the check. When the teller learned that Messing did not have an account with the bank, the teller returned the check to Messing and requested that he place his "thumbprint signature" on the back of the check. The teller explained that this was bank policy for all non-account holders who presented checks drawn by Bank of America customers to the bank. Messing refused to place his thumbprint on the check, and the teller refused to cash the check. Messing then asked to see the branch manager. Upon entering the manager's office, Messing demanded that the bank cash the check without his "thumbprint signature." The manager explained to Messing that the bank could not do so, that the "thumbprint signature" from non-account holders was a part of the bank's policy and that it was also a part of the contract the bank had with each of its checking account customers. Messing then left the bank with the check in his possession. Messing subsequently filed suit against the bank, seeking a ruling that he had provided adequate identification to the bank, that the bank had wrongfully dishonored the check upon presentment, and that the bank was guilty of conversion.

ISSUES Is it lawful for Bank of America to require a thumbprint signature from non-account holders before it will accept a check drawn against the bank? Did Bank of America dishonor the check upon proper presentment by Messing?

HOLDINGS Yes, it is lawful to require a thumbprint signature from non-account holders. No, the bank did not dishonor the check because the check was never properly presented.

REASONING Excerpts from the opinion of Judge Krauser:

This appeal focuses on one of the most expressive parts of the human body—the thumb: "thumbs up" (approval), "thumbs down" (disapproval), "thumbing one's nose" (defiance), and "thumbing a ride" (requesting transport). Notwithstanding all of the things we ask of this unassuming two-jointed digit, appellee, Bank of America, adds one more task—personal identification. The thumbprint, if Bank of America has its way, will now be one more means by which the identity of a non–account check holder is expressed and confirmed. This idea has of course not met with universal approval, and that is why this matter of first impression is now before us.

Specifically, we are presented with the question of whether Bank of America's practice of requiring non–account check holders to provide a thumbprint signature before it will honor a check is lawful. . . . In addition to the question of the legality of appellee's thumbprint signature program, appellant also raises questions as to whether appellee "accepted," "dishonored," or "converted" appellant's check upon presentment. . . .

For the reasons that follow, we hold that the circuit court did not err in granting summary judgment and dismissing appellant's complaint. Requiring thumbprint signatures for non–account check holders is lawful, and at no time did appellee accept, convert, or dishonor appellant's check. . . .

Appellant contends that the circuit court erred in construing the "reasonable identification" requirement of § 3-501(b)(2) to include a thumbprint signature if demanded by appellee, notwithstanding appellant's proffer of his driver's license and a credit card. § 3-501(b)(2) provides:

Upon demand of the person to whom presentment is made, the person making presentment must (i) exhibit the instrument, (ii) give reasonable identification and, if presentment is made on behalf of another person, reasonable evidence of authority to do so, and (iii) sign a receipt on the instrument for any payment made or surrender the instrument if full payment is made. . . .

Because § 3-501(b)(2) does not define "reasonable identification," appellant maintains that we should look to Title 31, § 103.28 of the Code of Federal Regulations which, according to appellant, does. That regulation was promulgated by the United States Department of the Treasury pursuant to the Bank Secrecy Act. . . . For certain cash transactions exceeding $10,000 per business day, 31 C.F.R. § 103.28 requires that financial institutions handling such transactions verify "the identity . . . of any person or entity on whose behalf such transaction is to be effected." That verification is to "be made by examination of a document, other than a bank signature card, that is normally acceptable within the banking community as a means of identification when cashing checks for nondepositors (*e.g.,* a drivers [sic] license or credit card)." . . . Because 31 C.F.R. § 103.28 recognizes a driver's license or credit card as a reasonable method for establishing "identification when cashing checks for nondepositors," appellant argues that other methods of identification, such as appellee's thumbprint signature program, are unreasonable. We disagree.

While 31 C.F.R. § 103.28 does indicate that a driver's license or a credit card may be an acceptable form of identification for certain transactions in excess of $10,000, it does not, as appellant suggests, preclude appellee from requiring a thumbprint signature of non–account holders who wish appellee to honor their checks. A "drivers license [sic] or credit card," . . . are only examples of the types of identification "normally acceptable within the banking community as a means of identification when cashing checks for nondepositors." Nowhere does 31 C.F.R. § 103.28 suggest that a driver's license and a credit card are the only acceptable forms of identification. Nor does 31 C.F.R. § 103.28 preclude a financial institution from requesting additional or alternative forms of identification. . . .

Appellee's thumbprint requirement is a form of "reasonable identification". . . .

[Section 3-502(b)(2)] provides that if an unaccepted "draft is payable on demand . . . the draft is dishonored if presentment for payment is duly made to the drawee and the draft is not paid on the day of presentment." § 3-502(b)(2). There is no dishonor, however, if presentment fails "to comply with the terms of the instrument, an agreement of the parties, or other applicable law or rule." § 3-501(b)(3). In the words of one authority:

If the presentment is not proper, payment or acceptance may be refused by the presentee and this refusal does not constitute a dishonoring of the instrument. This provision comes into play if the presentment does not comply "with the terms of the instrument, an agreement of the parties, or other applicable law or rule." . . .

It is undisputed that appellee had the authority to refuse payment in accordance with the deposit agreement it had with each account holder, including with the drawer of the check in question. Pursuant to that agreement, appellee was permitted to set "physical and/or documentary requirements" for all those who seek to cash a check with appellee. And because appellee had the authority to refuse payment by agreement with its customer under § 3-501(b)(2)(ii) unless "reasonable identification" was presented, appellant's failure to provide his thumbprint rendered the presentment ineffective and did not result in a dishonor of the check when appellee returned it to him. . . .

As noted, because this appeal involves a request for declaratory judgment, the circuit court must enter "a written declaration of the rights of the parties" or file a "written opinion" which could be treated as such. . . . Because it did not, we shall vacate the judgment and remand the case to the circuit court to enter a written declaration of the rights of the parties consistent with this opinion.

BUSINESS CONSIDERATIONS Why might a bank want a "thumbprint signature" on a check presented by a non-account holder? What is provided by a thumbprint signature that is not provided by more traditional forms of identification, such as a driver's license and a major credit card?

ETHICAL CONSIDERATIONS Is it ethical for a financial institution to ask for a form of identification that might be viewed as an undue invasion of privacy? If a business is not allowed to request a person's Social Security number for identification purposes, why is it ethical to ask for a thumbprint signature?

either an oral or an electronic presentment. Thus, if the parties have agreed to an oral or an electronic presentment, the requirement that the instrument be exhibited by the presenter at the request of the primary party [§ 3-501(b)(2)(i)] does not apply. This would allow an acceptance of the instrument—or a dishonor—by the primary party without that person actually seeing the instrument.

If the presentment is made through the mail, presentment occurs when the mail is received. (This places the

danger of postal delay on the presenting party.) If the presentment is to be made at a specified place and if the person who is to receive it is not there at the proper time, presentment is excused. This makes the drawee or the maker responsible for being at the proper place at the proper time. It also removes a possible worry from the presenting party—that the drawee or the maker will be absent when presentment is due and will then deny that a presentment was ever made to that drawee or maker. If a note is payable at a bank in the United States or a draft is to be accepted at such a bank, the note or draft must be presented at that bank.

The rules of presentment are very important because presentment must be properly made before a dishonor can be shown. Dishonor also must be shown before any secondary party (except the drawer) can be held on his or her liability. The only exception to this rule is if presentment is excused.

The rules that govern presentment are fairly straightforward. The holder must make presentment within a reasonable time, or the presentment is improper. The reasonable time concept has two components: The time must be reasonable in both a clock sense (time of day) and a calendar sense (day of the week). In every case, presentment must be made at a reasonable time of day—that is, during normal working hours. An alleged presentment made at a bank or business address at 3 A.M. would be improper and would not be effective to prove a dishonor. Article 3 as revised has no time requirements for presentment, leaving the determination of whether presentment was made in a timely manner for interpretation based on the terms of the instrument and on other provisions of the Code.

Instruments that are payable at a definite time must be presented on or before the due date in order to establish that proper presentment was made. Demand instruments are treated differently. The holder of a check must present the check to the drawee bank within 90 days of its date or its issue, whichever is later, to hold the drawer liable on that check. A delay beyond this 90-day period will not excuse the drawer from liability on the underlying obligation, but it will excuse the drawer (and any secondary parties) from liability on that particular check. The drawer may be forced to redeem the check by paying cash or by issuing a new negotiable instrument to replace the original check. Indorsers also have an interest in proper presentment. An indorser of a check is released from the contract liability of the indorsement if the check is not presented within 30 days of the date of indorsement. In order to hold the indorsers liable for the indorsement contract on other demand instruments, presentment must be made within a reasonable time from the date of the indorsement. If the instrument is payable at a definite time, the presentment must be made by that time in order to hold the indorser to the indorsement contract.

Once presentment is made, the focus shifts to the maker, drawee, or acceptor. If the presentment is made for acceptance alone (as when a presenter asks a bank to certify a check), the drawee (the bank in this example) has until the close of business the next business day to accept the instrument. (If the holder agrees—in good faith—another business day may be granted to the drawee to decide whether to accept the instrument.) If the presentment is made for acceptance and payment (or for payment alone, if acceptance occurred previously), payment must be made before the close of the business day on which the presentment was made. (Some short delay in paying the instrument is permitted if the drawee, acceptor, or maker needs to investigate whether payment would be proper.) Any delay beyond these time limits is treated as a dishonor of the instrument presented.[9]

Persons receiving a presentment do have some protection. They can require some proof from the presenter of the presenter's right to have the check; requesting this proof is not treated as a dishonor. They can require the presenter to show them the instrument. They can demand reasonable identification of the presenter. They can require a showing of authority to make the presentment. They can demand the surrender of the instrument upon payment in full. If the presenter fails or refuses to comply with any of these requests, the presentment is considered improper. However, the presenter is allowed a reasonable time to comply with any of the requests.

Acceptance

When the drawee decides to accept an instrument, the drawee must sign the instrument. By signing the draft or check, the drawee agrees to honor the instrument as presented. This act of acceptance fixes the primary liability of the drawee. (Remember: An order instrument has no primary liability until it has been accepted by the drawee.)

The acceptance can be made even if the instrument is incomplete, but it must be made for the instrument as presented. Suppose the drawee tries to change the terms of the draft in the acceptance. The presenter can treat this as a dishonor or can agree to the changed terms. However, if this draft-varying acceptance is agreed to by the presenter, the drawer and every prior indorser are discharged from secondary liability on the draft.

If a draft is accepted by a bank, the drawer and any indorsers who indorsed the draft prior to its acceptance are all discharged from secondary liability.

Check fraud has become a major concern. For more information on this topic see Carreker-Antinori, "Provide Your Bank with a Shield of Protection against Check Fraud," Thompson Financial Publishing, at http://www.tfp.com/text/Fraudlink.pdf.

Dishonor

An instrument is dishonored when proper presentment is made and acceptance or payment is refused. A dishonor also occurs when presentment is excused and the instrument is not accepted or paid. Under UCC § 3-501(b)(3)(i), the return of an instrument for lack of a proper indorsement is not a dishonor. The failure of the primary party to accept the instrument within the proper time is also a dishonor. A check returned because of insufficient funds or because of a stop-payment order is dishonored. A refusal by the primary party to accept the instrument is a dishonor, subject to the limitations in § 3-501(b)(3). Dishonor is a denial of primary liability, and it activates the secondary liability of indorsers and of the drawer (refer to Exhibit 23.2, The Chains of Liability on Negotiable Instruments). Remember that before dishonor, the secondary parties faced only potential secondary liability. The act of dishonor may, and usually will, move this liability from potential to actual.

Notice

The holder of a dishonored instrument has an obligation to give notice to prior parties in order to establish their secondary liability. The notice may be given to any or all persons who may be secondarily liable on the instrument, and it may be given by any person who has received notice. Thus, if the presenter-holder gives notice of dishonor to Indorser 2, Indorser 2 may then give notice to Indorser 1, and so on. The notice may be given in any commercially reasonable manner, including oral, written, or electronic communication. It may be given in any terms or in any form, as long as it reasonably identifies the instrument and states that it has been dishonored or has not been paid or accepted.

Article 3 is concerned with protecting the rights of the holder of a dishonored instrument. Allowance is made for an error in the description of the instrument in the notice. A misdescription will not affect the validity of the notice unless it misleads the person being notified. The notice must be given in a timely manner. Again, there has been a significant change in the time limit for notice under the revised Article 3. This new provision is found in § 3-503, which provides that:

(c) Subject to Section 3-504(c), with respect to an instrument taken for collection by a collecting bank, notice of dishonor must be given (i) by the bank before midnight of the next banking day following the banking day on which the bank receives notice of dishonor of the instrument, or (ii) by any other person within 30 days following the day on which the person receives notice of dishonor. With respect to any other instrument, notice of dishonor must be given within 30 days following the date on which dishonor occurs.

NRW CASE 23.1   Finance/Law

DISHONORED CHECKS

One of the checks received from a customer as a payment on an account was returned by the bank for insufficient funds. As is her usual practice, Helen has redeposited the check twice, and both times it was returned dishonored. This is the first time the firm has received a check that the bank did not honor on either the first or the second time it was deposited, and Helen is not sure what the firm needs to do. Carlos remembers hearing something about the need to give notice of a dishonor within three days of the dishonor in order to preserve your rights on a dishonored instrument against prior parties. Mai agrees that notice must be given, but she is not sure that there is a three-day time limit. However, both Carlos and Mai are concerned that by redepositing the check the firm has waived its right to collect from the drawer, and that the amount of the check has been lost. They have asked you for advice. What will you tell them?

BUSINESS CONSIDERATIONS A number of businesses will hold a dishonored check for a short time and then "rerun" the check through the bank in the hope that the drawer has made a deposit and that the check will be honored the second time through banking channels. Is this a good practice or a bad practice? Why? Should the business give the customer who wrote the check notice that the check has been dishonored, but that the firm plans to "rerun" the check soon?

ETHICAL CONSIDERATIONS Most banks impose a service charge on their customers for every check presented against the customer's account and dishonored. Is it ethical to present a check more than once, thus potentially increasing the service charges imposed on the customer by the bank, and to have the business also impose a service charge as the payee for a check that is dishonored? When does submission of a check stop being good business and start being an attempt to punish the drawer for writing a bad check?

INTERNATIONAL CONSIDERATIONS Suppose that a customer has submitted a check drawn against a foreign bank as payment on an account, and that check is dishonored upon presentment. Do the same rules apply for handling the dishonor if the drawee bank is located in a different country? Should a business with international customers have a policy regarding such a situation?

Section 3-504(c) excuses giving notice of the dishonor within these time limits if the delay is caused by circumstances beyond the control of the person giving notice, and if that person acts with reasonable diligence once the reason for the delay is removed. Prior to the revision, the time limit for a bank was the same—its midnight deadline on the next banking day. However, other parties had only three days after they learned of the dishonor to give notice, or they lost their secondary liability contract claim. The new rules are obviously much more favorable for secondary parties.

It is normal for each party to give notice to the party who transferred the instrument to him or her. However, sometimes this transferor cannot be found or, when found, cannot pay. For that reason, a holder should give notice to every prior party who can be located. This increases the chances that the holder eventually will recover on the dishonored instrument.

A failure to give proper or timely notice will operate as a release from the conditional secondary liability for all the secondary parties except the drawer, unless the need to give notice is excused or the need to receive notice is waived. Failure to give notice, or giving improper notice, may release other secondary parties, but it does not release the drawer or maker.

Frequently, the duty to make presentment or to give notice is waived or excused. When these situations arise, § 3-504 of the Code governs the situation. Under subsection (a), a delay in making presentment is excused if any of the following are true:

- The person entitled to make presentment cannot with reasonable diligence make presentment.

- The maker or acceptor has repudiated an obligation to pay the instrument, or has died, or is involved in an insolvency proceeding.

- The terms of the instrument state that presentment is not necessary in order to enforce the obligation of the indorsers or the drawer.

- The drawer or indorser whose obligation is being enforced has waived presentment or otherwise has no reason to expect or right to require that the instrument be paid or accepted.

- The drawer instructed the drawee not to pay or accept the instrument or accept the draft or the drawee was not obligated to the drawer to pay the draft.

Under subsection (b), notice of dishonor is excused if any of the following are true:

- By the terms of the instrument, notice is not necessary to enforce the obligation of a party to pay the instrument.

- The party whose obligation is being enforced waived notice of dishonor.

- Presentment was waived, which also constitutes a waiver of notice.

Types of Liability

A negotiable instrument is a contract with special treatment under the law. One recognition of contract law principles is found in UCC § 3-401. This section states that "a person is not liable on an instrument unless (i) the person signed the instrument, or (ii) the person is represented by an agent or representative who signed the instrument and the signature is binding on the represented person . . ." However, once such a signature is found, the signing—or represented—party faces potential liability. The type of liability depends on the capacity in which it was signed. Again, the Code helps. As was pointed out earlier, § 3-204 states that every signature is presumed to be an indorsement unless the instrument clearly indicates that the signature was made in some other capacity by the signing party.

It is important to remember that there are two types of contracts involved with negotiable instruments. The first type of contract is represented by the instrument itself. The maker of promise paper and the acceptor of order paper give a contract. Each agrees to pay the instrument according to the terms of the instrument at the time of his or her engagement, or as completed if it was incomplete. The drawer of order paper promises to pay any holder or any indorser the amount of the instrument if it is dishonored. The second type of contract is the contract encompassed in the indorsement.

Indorsement Liability

The indorsers of negotiable instruments also give a contract by the act of indorsing, unless the indorsement is qualified. By the act of indorsing, the indorser promises that upon dishonor, and proper notice, he or she will pay the instrument as indorsed to any subsequent holder. The indorsers are presumed to be liable to one another on a dishonored instrument in the order indorsed, moving from bottom to top.

Two other parties may be involved in contractual liability on negotiable instruments: the accommodation party and the guarantor. Each of these parties has special potential contract liability. An accommodation party is a person who

NRW CASE 23.2 Finance

SEEKING RECOVERY FOR A BAD CHECK

One of the checks the firm deposited into its account has been returned by the bank. The check has an "Account Closed" stamp on its face. The check was originally issued by James Smitts, payable to the order of Harriet Rudzinski. Ms. Rudzinski, a customer of the firm, had indorsed the check "Pay to NRW, Harriet Rudzinski" and forwarded it to the firm as payment for some StuffTrakRs she had ordered. Mai has asked you what the firm can do to recover the amount of this check, and from whom the firm should seek recovery. She also wants to know if the firm should refuse to accept indorsed checks payable to the order of someone other than NRW in the future. What advice will you give her?

BUSINESS CONSIDERATIONS Many businesses have a policy of not accepting what they call "two-party checks," checks that were drawn to the order of a payee who now wants to indorse the check over to the business. What reasons might a business have for this policy? Do the protections afforded by Article 3 make such a policy unnecessary?

ETHICAL CONSIDERATIONS Is there an ethical issue raised when a person indorses a check over to a new holder rather than depositing the check into his or her own account and then writing a check to that person? Is it ethical for a business to refuse to accept a check indorsed by the payee when there are legal protections for the business if the check is dishonored?

INTERNATIONAL CONSIDERATIONS When a firm is dealing internationally, the costs and the delays that may be incurred by a dishonor are likely to increase. Should such a firm insist on having customers make payment by some method other than a normal check to reduce this risk? What might the firm reasonably be able to insist on for a preferred method of payment?

signs an instrument to "lend his name," or his credit, to another party. He signs as a favor, usually without getting anything out of the transaction. The accommodation party is liable to subsequent parties in the capacity in which he signed. If required to pay because of his secondary liability, he is entitled to recover from the party for whom he signed

as an accommodator. A person signing an instrument is presumed to be an accommodation party and there is notice to all subsequent holders that the instrument was signed for accommodation if the signature is an anomalous indorsement (any indorsement made by a person who is not a holder of the instrument is considered anomalous), or if the signature is accompanied by words indicating that the indorser is acting as a surety or as a guarantor with respect to the obligations of another party to the instrument.

If the signature of a party to an instrument is accompanied by words indicating unambiguously that he or she is guaranteeing collection rather than guaranteeing the payment of the obligation of another party to the instrument, that party is endorsing as a guarantor. Article 3 has reduced the obligation of a guarantor somewhat. A guarantor is obliged to pay the amount due on the instrument to any person entitled to enforce the instrument, but only if:

- an execution of judgment against the party whose obligation was guaranteed has been returned unsatisfied, or
- the party whose obligation was guaranteed is insolvent or involved in an insolvency proceeding, or
- the party whose obligation was guaranteed cannot be served with process, or
- it is otherwise apparent payment cannot be obtained from the party whose obligation was guaranteed.[10]

The Federal Trade Commission has enacted its Federal Trade Commission Credit Practices Rule, which went into effect in 1985, in an effort to provide some protection to accommodation parties, especially cosigners on notes. This rule requires lenders to provide disclosure to cosigners and other accommodation parties as to the serious nature of signing as an accommodation. This rule is discussed in more detail in Chapter 27.

Warranty Liability

In addition to the basic contract liabilities just discussed, persons who present or transfer negotiable instruments make certain warranties. These warranties also carry with them the possibility of liabilities, and warranty liabilities cannot be disclaimed as easily as contract liabilities. An indorser may deny contract liability by the use of a qualified indorsement, but warranty liability is still present even if the indorsement is qualified, unless the qualified indorsement also specifically excludes warranties. An indorser could qualify the indorsement so that warranties are also excluded, even though indorsing with such a qualification to later holders makes the indorsement highly unusual. The indorser who would use such an indorsement would be well protected, but the instrument would be very difficult to transfer because few subsequent holders would be willing to accept such a negotiation.

The warranties involved in negotiable instruments are set out in § 3-416 and § 3-417 of the UCC. Section 3-416 provides for transfer warranties, while § 3-417 provides for presentment warranties. Any person who transfers an instrument for consideration gives transfer warranties to his or her transferee. In addition, if the transfer is by indorsement the transferee gives the transfer warranties to every subsequent transferee. Notice that the instrument does not need to be negotiated, and the transferee does not have to give value in order to have transfer warranties arise.

The transfer warranties provide protection to the transferee(s) in the following five areas:

1. The warrantor (transferor) is a person entitled to enforce the instrument.

2. All signatures on the instrument are authentic and authorized.

3. The instrument has not been materially altered.

4. The instrument is not subject to a defense or claim in recoupment of any party which can be asserted against the warrantor.

5. The warrantor has no knowledge of any insolvency proceedings commenced with respect to the maker or acceptor or, in the case of an unaccepted draft, the drawer.

Transfer warranties cannot be disclaimed on checks. Notice of any breach of the transfer warranties must be given to the warrantor within 30 days after the claimant has reason to know of the breach of warranty in order to have maximum protection. After 30 days the liability of the warrantor is reduced by any amount the warrantor can show was lost due to the delay.

If an unaccepted draft is presented to the drawee for payment or acceptance and the drawee pays or accepts the draft, the person making presentment and any previous transferees of the draft give presentment warranties to the drawee. The presentment warranties provide the following three protections to the drawee:

1. The warrantor is, or was, at the time the warrantor transferred the draft, a person entitled to enforce the draft or authorized to obtain payment or acceptance of the draft on behalf of a person entitled to enforce the draft.

2. The draft has not been altered.

NRW CASE 23.3　Management/Law

NRW

FORGERIES

NRW received a check from a customer recently as payment for a purchase. Carlos was concerned when the check was received because there seemed to be something unusual about the signature. However, he decided not to do anything about it and the check was included in the firm's deposit. Unfortunately, the check was eventually returned by the bank with a notation that the drawer's signature was a forgery. Carlos is concerned that he may have done something wrong or that the firm may now face liability on the check because he failed to act on his suspicions initially. He asks you if he has done anything wrong and if the firm is now at risk. He also would like to know what the firm's rights are on the check. What will you tell him?

BUSINESS CONSIDERATIONS Should a business have a policy of requiring identification and a specimen signature from any of its customers who want to pay by check? How could such a policy be implemented if the business receives payments by mail?

ETHICAL CONSIDERATIONS Is it ethical for a business to refuse to accept a check if the business doesn't like the way a signature looks? Should businesses select customers on the basis of the legibility of the customer's signature?

INTERNATIONAL CONSIDERATIONS Businesses that deal internationally are quite likely to accept telechecks or some other form of electronic payment. Should a business that does so require some sort of encryption "signature" to authenticate the identity of the person making payment? What issues are raised by electronic payments beyond the issues normally faced with a negotiable instrument?

---

3. The warrantor has no knowledge that the signature of the drawer is unauthorized.

Again, these warranties cannot be disclaimed on a check, and again notice of a claim for breach of the warranty must be given within 30 days of the time the drawee has reason to know of the breach. Any losses suffered by the warrantor as a result of a delay beyond the 30 days reduces the liability of the warrantor.

The new provisions of Article 3 have removed presentment warranty protections from promise paper, have removed the added protections that were formerly available with a qualified indorsement, and have added a time limit within which the person claiming damages based on a breach of warranty must give notice in order to have maximum protection.

Exhibit 23.3 summarizes the order of liability on a negotiable instrument.

Special Problems

As was pointed out earlier, a person's signature, or the signature of a person authorized to represent him or her, must appear on an instrument before that person can be held liable on the instrument. Thus, a forgery or an unauthorized signature is normally of no legal effect. However, an unauthorized signature can be ratified by the named person, and it then becomes fully effective. The rules governing unauthorized signatures can be found in § 3-403. These rules are relatively simple and straightforward:

(a) *Unless otherwise provided in this Article or Article 4, an unauthorized signature is ineffective except as the signature of the unauthorized signer in favor of a person who in good faith pays the instrument or takes it for value. An unauthorized signature may be ratified for all purposes of this Article.*

(b) *If the signature of more than one person is required to constitute the authorized signature of an organi-*

zation, the signature of the organization is unauthorized if one of the required signatures is lacking.

(c) *The civil or criminal liability of a person who makes an unauthorized signature is not affected by any provisions of this Article which make the unauthorized signature effective for the purposes of this Article.*[11]

Any unauthorized signatures are ineffective against the person whose name is signed, unless that person chooses to ratify the signature after the fact. The unauthorized signature is effective against the person who did, in fact, sign, and will expose that person to liability for the signature or it will transfer any rights that the signer might possess in the instrument, provided that the person who takes the instrument takes it for value or pays the instrument in good faith. Unauthorized signings include both forgeries and signatures made without actual, implied, or apparent authority.[12]

Even with such a straightforward set of rules, there are some special circumstances that arise often enough to require special rules and special treatment. In particular, situations involving *imposters* and situations involving *fictitious payees* demand special rules and special treatment beyond the provisions for unauthorized signatures.

The following case involved an alleged fictitious payee. The time period involved overlapped the revisions to Article 3, so the court had to treat some of the checks in the case under the prior law and the balance under the current law. Do you think this made a significant difference to the result?

EXHIBIT 23.3 Liability on a Negotiable Instrument

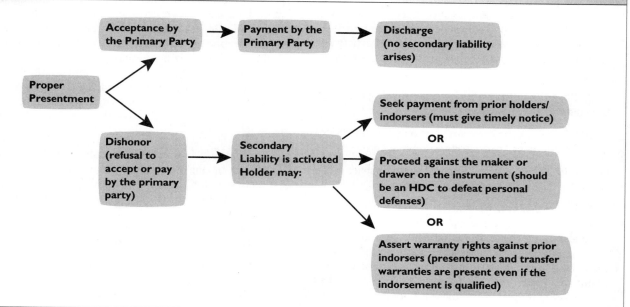

23.2

GUARDIAN LIFE INSURANCE CO. v. MIDLANTIC
30 F. Supp. 2d 720, 1998 U.S. Dist. LEXIS 21471 (1998)

FACTS Mark Weisman was a field representative for The Guardian Life Insurance Company of America (Guardian), a broker for The Guardian Insurance & Annuity Company (GIAC), and an agent/broker for New England Mutual Life Insurance Company (New England). While holding these positions, from January 1990 through June 25, 1995, he engaged in a scheme under which he submitted false claims to the insurance companies in the names of various policyholders and annuity account holders either for loans against the policies or for account withdrawals. The Guardian and GIAC, unaware of the fraudulent scheme, issued checks in the names listed and delivered these checks to Weisman, expecting him to then deliver the checks to the policyholders and annuity account holders. In the same manner, New England also issued checks in the names of its clients and delivered them to Weisman, expecting him to then deliver the checks to the customers. Upon receiving the checks from the companies, Weisman forged the indorsements of the payees and deposited the funds in his personal account with Midlantic Bank. The majority of the indorsements were illegible, although some of the forgeries were legible. Weisman conducted this fraudulent scheme for 5½ years without his conduct being detected or questioned by Midlantic, any of the three employer-drawer insurance companies, or any of the drawee banks. Once the scheme was discovered, Guardian, GIAC, and New England filed suit against Midlantic as the depository bank, and against each of their own drawee banks, alleging conversion, improper payment, negligence, and fraud. The banks, and particularly Midlantic, based their defense on the fictitious payee rule of the UCC.

ISSUE Does the fictitious payee rule provide protection to Midlantic and the drawee banks?

HOLDING Yes, to some extent, but only on the checks on which the banks exercised reasonable care.

REASONING Excerpts from the opinion of District Judge Barry:

Midlantic's position is that § 3-405(1)(c) of New Jersey's Uniform Commercial Code . . . the so-called "faithless employee/fictitious payee" rule—bars plaintiffs' action to recover from Midlantic losses they incurred as a result of Weisman's forged indorsements. Plaintiffs, on the other hand, contend that the "faithless employee/fictitious payee" rule does not apply to Mid-

lantic because Midlantic failed to exercise ordinary care and good faith in accepting for deposit checks containing illegible indorsements. Plaintiffs further argue that, without such a defense, Midlantic is liable for conversion under . . . § 3-419(1)(c).

As part of an effort to establish uniform rules governing the relationships between banks and their customers, the UCC attempts to allocate the losses caused by forged indorsements according to the relative responsibilities of the parties to a given transaction. . . . As a general rule, "forged indorsements are ineffective to pass title." . . . Indeed, an instrument is typically considered "converted . . . when it is paid on a forged indorsement." . . . Thus, a drawee bank generally may not debit a drawer's account when it pays over a forged indorsement. . . . If it does, "the drawer can usually require the drawee bank to recredit the drawer's account" on the basis that the check was not "properly payable" under § 4-401. . . . A drawee bank that has recredited a drawer's account after paying over a forged indorsement can usually shift its loss "upstream," however, to banks that have previously accepted the check (e.g., the depository bank) by way of an action for breach of warranty of good title. . . . As a result, the ultimate loss typically "falls on the party who took the check from the forger [e.g., the depository bank], or on the forger himself." . . .

Section 3-405(1)(c) creates a limited exception to this general rule, however, when an employee, intending the named payee to have no interest in the instrument, causes his or her employer to draw a check made payable to one of its customers. . . . As the comments to 3-405 explain, the "conversion rule of section 3-419 and the warranty rules of sections 3-417 and 3-418" do not apply to the situation where a "faithless employee . . . uses a fictitious-payee scheme to defraud his employer." . . . § 3-405. . . . In such a case, the banks are shielded from liability because of the

> feeling, largely unarticulated, that the loss should be taken by the drawer (employer). [Its] employee, acting within the scope of his authority, caused the loss; [it] is in the best position to prevent it by supervision and by using care in hiring employees; [it] has as good a chance as the bank to distribute the risk to all of society through the use of insurance. . . .

The crux of this court's analysis, therefore, is whether § 3-405(1)(c) applies to Midlantic; if it does, summary judgment must be granted in favor of

Midlantic on the theory that plaintiffs, as Weisman's employers, were in a better position to prevent or ameliorate the consequences of their employee's financial abuses. The 1961 version of . . . § 3-405, which was in effect for all but the last month of Weisman's scheme, provided, in pertinent part, as follows:

(1) An indorsement by any person in the name of a named payee is effective if

(c) an agent or employee of the maker or drawer has supplied him with the name of the payee intending the latter to have no such interest . . .

Given that an employee . . . of the employers/drawers . . . supplied the employers/drawers with the names of payees (the policyholders and annuity contract holders) intending that the payees have no interest in the instruments, Midlantic's argument appears, at first glance, to be viable. The inquiry does not end there, however.

As a threshold requirement, the depository bank (Midlantic) must first show that the forged indorsements on the checks it accepted were "in the name of the named payee." . . . Although the 1961 version of the New Jersey Code does not define or explicate this requirement, courts have consistently required banks to use ordinary care and accept for deposit only instruments where the indorsement is "*substantially identical* to the name of the named payee." . . . As the court . . . held, a "bank may not pay over such an indorsement with impunity" and is not protected by § 3-405 if it does not otherwise satisfy its "obligation of good faith" under § 1-203. . . . Accordingly, the . . . court held that "checks exhibiting *illegible indorsements* . . . raised a question of fact as to whether payment by the bank constituted a lack of 'good faith' on the part of the bank." . . .

The . . . court could, and should, have gone one step further. While the court agrees that a factual question as to the bank's good faith might be raised when it accepts for deposit checks containing illegible indorsements, the acceptance of such checks, more importantly, renders the "faithless employee/fictitious payee" exception inapplicable because, as a matter of law, illegible indorsements do not satisfy the threshold statutory requirement. . . . When this requirement is not satisfied (i.e., when the forged indorsements are not substantially identical to the names of the named payees), the forged indorsements cannot be considered effective as against the drawer and the general rules discussed must apply.

Parenthetically, this analysis is consistent with the following provisions of the current version of the New Jersey Code, which became effective on June 1, 1995:

b. For the purposes of determining the rights and liabilities of a person who, in good faith, pays an instrument or takes it for value or for collection, if an employer entrusted an employee with responsibility with respect to the instrument and the employee . . . makes a fraudulent indorsement of the instrument, the indorsement is effective as the indorsement of the person to whom the instrument is payable *if* it is made in the name of that person. If the person paying the instrument or taking it for value or for collection fails to exercise ordinary care in paying or taking the instrument and that failure substantially contributes to loss resulting from the fraud, the person bearing the loss may recover from the person failing to exercise ordinary care to the extent the failure to exercise ordinary care contributed to the loss. . . .

Once the foregoing analysis is properly understood, applying it to the case at hand is a simple task. The parties have stipulated that the forged indorsements on seventy-six of the ninety-one checks deposited into Weisman's Midlantic account were "illegible." . . . Given this undisputed fact, Midlantic has not satisfied its statutory burden of showing that it accepted for deposit checks containing indorsements that were "substantially identical," . . . or "substantially similar," . . . to the names of the named payees. Summary judgment as to the seventy-six checks containing illegible indorsements must, therefore, be denied. Because there is no genuine dispute regarding the legibility of fourteen of the ninety-one checks, however, and because no genuine issue has been raised regarding any other issue that would preclude summary judgment . . . the court will grant Midlantic's motion as to those fourteen checks pursuant . . . § 3-405(1)(c) . . .

BUSINESS CONSIDERATIONS What steps can a business take to prevent issuing checks to "faithless employees/fictitious payees"? If such a case arises, against whom should the drawer proceed?

ETHICAL CONSIDERATIONS Is it ethical for a business to attempt to have a bank bear the loss for its own careless conduct when the business issues checks payable to a "fictitious payee"? Is it ethical for a bank to attempt to avoid liability after it accepts checks with illegible indorsements?

There are also some special rules in effect for situations involving imposters and for situations involving fictitious payees. These two similar areas each require attention.

An "imposter" is a person who pretends to be the person to whom an instrument is payable. The imposter pretends to be the actual payee in order to induce the issuer of the instrument to deliver the instrument to the imposter, believing that the instrument is being delivered to the intended payee. Situations involving imposters arise when there is a legitimate reason for issuing the instrument and the person named as payee has a legitimate claim to the instrument, but the issuer is tricked into issuing the instrument to a person claiming to be the payee. A "fictitious payee" is a person who obtains an instrument that either (a) is made payable to the order of a legitimate person, but one who has no legitimate claim to the particular instrument, or (b) is made payable to a nonexistent person, a "fictitious" payee.

Section 3-404 covers both imposters and fictitious payees. According to § 3-404:

(a) If an imposter, by use of the mails or otherwise, induces the issuer of an instrument to issue the instrument to the imposter, or to a person acting in concert with the imposter, by impersonating the payee of the instrument or a person authorized to act for the payee, an indorsement of the instrument by any person in the name of the payee is effective as the indorsement of the payee in favor of a person who, in good faith, pays the instrument or takes it for value or for collection.

(b) If (i) a person whose intent determines to whom an instrument is payable . . . does not intend the person identified as payee to have any interest in the instrument, or (ii) the person identified as payee of an instrument is a fictitious person, the following rules apply until the instrument is negotiated by special indorsement:

(1) Any person in possession of the instrument is its holder.

(2) An indorsement by any person in the name of the payee stated in the instrument is effective as the indorsement of the payee in favor of the person who, in good faith, pays the instrument or takes it for value or for collection.

These two subsections seem to place the risk of loss on the issuer of the instrument when an imposter or a fictitious payee is involved. While this is generally true, the provisions of each of these subsections are limited to some extent. If the person who pays the instrument or who takes it for value or for collection does not exercise ordinary care in acquiring the instrument, and if the failure to exercise ordinary care substantially contributes to the loss resulting from paying the instrument, the person suffering that loss can recover the portion of the loss suffered because ordinary care was not exercised.

The following hypothetical cases illustrate these two special problem areas.

Fred stole a radio from Herb. Fred then approached Thelma, told her that he was Herb, and offered to sell the radio to her. Thelma wrote a check payable to the order of Herb to pay for the radio. Under the impostor rule, Fred may effectively indorse the check by writing Herb's name, UCC § 3-403 on unauthorized signatures notwithstanding. Thelma intended to write a check to Herb, Fred pretended to be Herb, so Fred is an imposter and his indorsement of the check in Herb's name is effective against Thelma.

Steve works for Acme. Part of his job is preparing checks to be sent to various suppliers and creditors of the firm and then taking those checks to Mr. Burton to be signed for the company. Steve slipped a check payable to Hall and Associates in among the other checks for Mr. Burton to sign. In fact, no money was owed to Hall and Associates. If Steve later removes the phony check and indorses it "Hall and Associates," the indorsement is valid under the fictitious payee rule, UCC § 3-403 notwithstanding. Steve intended to have a check drawn payable to the order of Hall and Associates, while he also intended for Hall and Associates to have no interest in the check. Thus, the check is payable to a fictitious payee, and Steve's indorsement of the check in the name "Hall and Associates" is effective against Acme.

A related problem area is that of fraudulently indorsed instruments, especially by dishonest employees. Again, the problems in this area are common enough and significant enough to require special attention and treatment under the Code. Section 3-405 addresses the employer's responsibility for fraudulent indorsements by employees. The section uses a broad definition of employees, including independent contractors and employees of independent contractors who are retained by the employer. "Fraudulent indorsement" is defined as:

(i) in the case of an instrument payable to the employer, a forged indorsement purporting to be that of the employer, or

(ii) in the case of an instrument with respect to which the employer is the issuer, a forged indorsement purporting to be that of the person identified as the payee.

Section 3-405 imposes responsibility on the employer for these fraudulent indorsements if a subsequent party took the instrument that contained the fraudulent indorsement in good faith, and either paid the instrument or took it for value or for collection. The fraudulent indorsement is effective against the employer, who will then need to seek recovery from the employee who appended the fraudulent indorsement to the instrument.

One other "special problem" needs to be addressed. On some occasions an instrument is lost, stolen, or destroyed prior to its presentment, and the person who was in possession of the instrument prior to its loss, theft, or destruction would like to collect the amount owed despite the absence of the instrument itself. The situation arises frequently enough that the Code has two sections addressing the problem.

Section 3-309 deals with the enforcement of lost, destroyed, or stolen instruments. Section 3-312 is more specific, dealing with lost, destroyed, or stolen cashier's checks, teller's checks, and certified checks. Under the provisions of § 3-309, a person who is *not* in possession of an instrument will still be allowed to enforce the instrument, if:

(i) the person was in possession of the instrument and entitled to enforce it when the loss of possession occurred,

(ii) the loss of possession was not the result of a transfer by the person or a lawful seizure, and

(iii) the person cannot reasonably obtain possession of the instrument because the instrument was destroyed, its whereabouts cannot be determined, or it is in the wrongful possession of an unknown person or a person that cannot be found and is not amenable to service of process.[13]

Of course, the person seeking to enforce the missing instrument must prove the terms of the instrument and also must prove his or her right to enforce the instrument. And the person seeking to enforce the instrument will not be able to procure a judgment unless the court is assured that the person who will have to pay is adequately protected against loss in the event that another person should surface with a valid claim seeking to enforce the instrument.[14]

Section 3-312 is similar, but more complicated. The drawer or the payee of a certified check, or the remitter or the payee of either a teller's check or a cashier's check, must make a written "declaration of loss" regarding the missing check. This declaration is made under penalty of perjury

and states that the party making the declaration lost possession of the check and that the loss was not the result of a transfer or a lawful seizure, and that possession of the check cannot reasonably be obtained. If the bank pays the claimant the amount of the check and the check itself is subsequently presented to the bank by a person possessing the rights of a holder in due course, the claimant must refund the proceeds to the bank or to the HDC.[15]

The case on pages 556–557 dealt with a claim that certain notes were lost or destroyed, and the party entitled to payment was seeking to collect on the notes. The maker of the notes claimed that the notes had been canceled, thus providing a discharge of his obligations. After reading the case, decide which party had the more persuasive argument.

Discharge

The term "discharge" means to remove liability or potential liability on a negotiable instrument. A discharge can take place in a number of ways. Some methods discharge all the parties, and others discharge only a few. The most important and most common types of discharge are explained in the following sections.

Payment

The most common type of discharge is the payment or other satisfaction of the instrument. In the vast majority of cases, the primary party pays the instrument on presentment and cancels it (or otherwise marks it as paid). If this were not so, negotiable instruments would not be so readily accepted in the commercial world. There are only two exceptions to payment operating as a discharge. A payment will not operate as a discharge when it is made in bad faith to a thief or to a person holding through (receiving the instrument from) or after (receiving the instrument from a party who received it from) a thief. Also, it will not operate as a discharge if the paying party makes a payment that violates a restrictive indorsement. (Note: An intermediary bank or a nondepository bank may be discharged even though it ignores the restrictive indorsement, provided it acts in good faith.) In these examples, the bad faith of the payer does not remove liability. The proper party, the person who should have received payment, is still entitled to payment, and the liability of the wrongfully paying party remains.

Tender of Payment

If a party tenders payment in full to a holder when an instrument is due, or later, and the holder refuses the payment, a discharge occurs. The party tendering payment is

23.3

FALES v. NORINE
644 N.W.2d 513, 2002 Neb. LEXIS 118 (S. Ct. Neb. 2002)

FACTS Virginia Norine died intestate September 7, 1997. She was survived by her son, Irwin Norine, and two granddaughters, Tonia Fales and Mindy Medina. After Virginia died, Irwin was appointed the personal representative of her estate. In March 1999, Irwin prepared an inventory of the estate. In the inventory, among other items, he listed two promissory notes dated January 16, 1996, on which he was the maker and Virginia was the payee. One note was for $67,615.48, plus interest at $8\frac{1}{2}$ percent. The second note was for $115,000, plus interest at $8\frac{1}{2}$ percent. Both notes were due on January 16, 1998. In May 1999, Irwin prepared a proposal for the distribution of the estate, which included both notes as assets of the estate. Both the inventory and the proposal were signed by Irwin and filed with the County Court. Irwin was later removed from the position of personal representative of the estate due to mismanagement, and Fales was appointed to succeed him in June 2000. The notes could not be found at the time Irwin was removed as personal representative of the estate, and have not subsequently been seen. Fales filed suit against Irwin, seeking to recover on the notes under the provisions of § 3-309, dealing with lost, stolen, or destroyed instruments. Irwin denied liability, alleging that Virginia never intended to enforce the notes, and opining that she had probably destroyed or otherwise canceled the notes shortly before her death. At trial Fales presented photocopies of each note. Irwin admitted that the copies were "true and accurate" copies, and that he had signed both of the original notes. The court ruled for Fales, ordering Irwin to pay the notes by 2003, assuming that any possible holders of the notes would come forward by then. Irwin appealed.

ISSUES Did Fales present sufficient evidence to meet the requirements for enforcing a lost, stolen, or destroyed instrument? If so, did the court provide adequate protection for Irwin against any future claims of a holder in due course, should one assert claims with the "lost" notes?

HOLDINGS Yes, Fales presented sufficient evidence. No, the court did not provide sufficient protection for Irwin against potential claims by an HDC.

REASONING Excerpts from the opinion of Justice Connolly:

Norine contends that Fales failed to prove by clear and convincing evidence that (1) Virginia was in possession of the notes and entitled to enforce them when the loss of possession occurred; (2) Virginia did not transfer the notes before her death; and (3) the whereabouts of the notes cannot be reasonably obtained. Fales contends there was sufficient evidence for the jury to find that Virginia was in possession of the notes and had not destroyed them or transferred them before her death. Further, she contends that the evidence showed that she could not determine the whereabouts of the notes. In an action to recover upon lost, destroyed, or stolen instruments, a plaintiff must prove the elements of the claim by clear and convincing evidence. . . . The notes were made payable to Virginia at the time they were executed, and Norine promised to pay them 2 years from the date they were executed. They were therefore due on January 16, 1998. There were no conditions placed on the payments, and the parties have not disputed that the instruments were negotiable. Thus, the enforcement of the notes is governed by § 3-309. Section 3-309(a) provides:

> A person not in possession of an instrument is entitled to enforce the instrument if (i) the person was in possession of the instrument and entitled to enforce it when loss of possession occurred, (ii) the loss of possession was not the result of a transfer by the person or a lawful seizure, and (iii) the person cannot reasonably obtain possession of the instrument because the instrument was destroyed, its whereabouts cannot be determined, or it is in the wrongful possession of an unknown person or a person that cannot be found or is not amenable to service of process. . . .

Section 3-309 was designed to deal with the typical situation of a lost, destroyed, or stolen check or other type of instrument being enforced against the maker by the payee. . . . Although § 3-309 does not deal specifically with lost instruments in the context of probate administration, its application in this context is not entirely without precedent. . . . On the other hand, if a personal representative alleges that the decedent lost possession of an enforceable instrument before the decedent's death, then the personal representative must prove the elements under § 3-309(a), as they relate to the decedent, by clear and convincing evidence.

Fales did not allege that the loss of possession occurred while the notes were in Virginia's possession. There was evidence, however, that Virginia did not destroy or transfer the notes before her death because Norine had possession of them after her death. . . . At trial,

Norine admitted that he had testified in an October 1999 deposition that he had possession of the original notes at that time. . . . [T]he evidence also showed that he had listed the notes as assets on both the inventory of the estate and the proposed distribution. Both documents were signed by Norine and filed with the county court. In the estate inventory, he certified the notes were part of the "true and complete inventory of the property owned by decedent at the time of her death." . . . Under these facts, this court cannot conclude as a matter of law that Fales has failed to prove by clear and convincing evidence that Norine was in possession of the notes after Virginia's death. Norine's own admissions, through earlier deposition testimony and submission of the estate's assets and distribution proposal, strongly indicate that he was in possession of the notes after Virginia's death. . . . He admitted that he had executed and delivered the notes, along with the mortgage and security agreement, verified that the copies were accurate representations of the notes and that the signatures were his. He stated that he was unable to locate the notes after Virginia's death. But given the evidence showing that he was in possession of the notes, the jury could have reasonably concluded that this testimony indicated that he had either lost the notes after her death or intentionally destroyed them. The jury was properly instructed that clear and convincing evidence is that amount of evidence which produces in the trier of fact a firm belief or conviction about the existence of the fact to be proved. . . . Under these facts, this court cannot conclude the jury's verdict was clearly wrong.

Section 3-309(b) provides that a "court may not enter judgment in favor of the person seeking enforcement unless it finds that the person required to pay the instrument is adequately protected against loss that might occur by reason of a claim by another person to enforce the instrument." The comment to § 3-309 provides: "The court is given discretion in determining how adequate protection is to be assured. . . . Under section 3-309 adequate protection is a flexible concept. . . . The type of adequate protection that is reasonable in the circumstances may depend on the degree of certainty about the facts in the case." . . . Under U.C.C. § 3-118 . . . an action to enforce the obligation of a party to pay a negotiable instrument must be commenced within 6 years of the due date or the accelerated due date stated in the note. We conclude that the judgment should be withheld from Fales until January 16, 2004, or 6 years from the date the notes were due. The court's judgment is corrected to that extent. . . .

Affirmed as modified.

BUSINESS CONSIDERATIONS The testimony at trial showed that Virginia kept most of her important papers, including the promissory notes, in a wooden box in a room in her home. From a business perspective, as opposed to a personal one, how should a prudent person store various important papers? Should the treatment of notes and other negotiables be different from "mere" important papers?

ETHICAL CONSIDERATIONS Is it ethical to have someone serve as a personal representative of an estate when that person is also a debtor of the decedent? Should the court or one of the other family members have objected to having the estate handled by a person who owed the estate over $200,000?

discharged to a limited extent. No additional interest can be added to the instrument after the date of the tender, nor can any other costs or attorney's fees be added to the instrument. Any other parties on the instrument (indorsers, drawers, and the like) are totally discharged if, to collect on the instrument, they could theoretically have sued the party who made the tender of payment.

Cancellation and Renunciation

A holder may discharge a party by canceling that party's signature on the instrument or by canceling the instrument itself. Cancellation may be shown either by striking out a portion, such as one signature, or by striking out the entire instrument. It can also be shown by destroying or mutilating a signature or the entire instrument. To be effective, the cancellation must be done intentionally.

Renunciation operates as a discharge whenever the holder delivers a written and signed statement to the discharged party that renounces (gives up) any rights against that person. Such a discharge is good against the renouncing party but not against any later holders, unless they were aware of the renunciation.

Impairment

Under the UCC section on impairment, a holder may elect to release some party from liability on the instrument. Or a holder may decide to release some collateral that is being used to secure payment of the instrument. However, in so doing, the holder also will discharge some or even all of the secondary parties on the instrument. When the holder releases a particular prior party, the holder also releases any other prior party who might have had recourse against the originally released party. In addition, when a holder releases collateral, the holder releases every prior party, since each prior party might have had recourse against the collateral. The following are the only two exceptions to these rules:

1. If a prior party agrees to the release of another party or to a release of the collateral, this prior party is not discharged by the release.

2. If the holder expressly reserves rights against a party, that party is not released or discharged. However, the releases by the holder are also not effective as far as the nondischarged party is concerned. In other words, the party who was expressly not discharged does not have any change in his or her position.

Other Discharges

If a party is a former holder of an instrument and later reacquires it, a partial discharge occurs. Any person who held the note between the two holdings of the reacquiring party is discharged from liability to the reacquiring party. Also, if the reacquiring party strikes out the indorsements of the intervening persons, they are totally discharged on the instrument. For example, if George holds a note, indorses it to Betty, and then buys it back from Betty, Betty is discharged from liability to George.

A fraudulent material alteration also acts as a discharge. If the alteration is fraudulent and material, any party who does not consent to the alteration is totally discharged from liability under most circumstances. A holder in due course may still enforce the instrument as it was originally issued, even though it has been materially altered.

Finally, an undue delay in making presentment operates as a discharge for all prior indorsers. An undue delay in giving notice of a dishonor will also operate as a discharge of all prior indorsers, and may even discharge a drawer or maker.

A good review of negotiable instruments can be found at http://courses.washtenaw.cc.mi.us/~cdgracie/BMG111/SlideShows/18NegotiableInstrum/index.html, a slide show outline of the materials covered under this topic.

Summary

As formal contracts, negotiable instruments carry certain contract responsibilities and liabilities. The maker of promise paper has primary liability on the instrument from its issue date. The drawee of order paper faces potential primary liability. However, once the drawee accepts the instrument, the drawee has primary liability. If the primary liability is denied or refused, every prior holder is secondarily liable. In addition, the drawer of order paper is secondarily liable on a dishonored instrument.

For the holder to enforce the primary liability of the instrument, proper presentment must be made to the maker or drawee. Proper presentment can now be made electronically, as well as through one of the traditional methods. Proper presentment also may include demands made on the presenter for him or her to establish identity. This can include requiring a "thumbprint signature" as part of the identification. At that point, the primary party will either accept the instrument or dishonor it. If dishonor occurs, the holder will give notice to prior parties to establish their secondary liability.

If an instrument is lost, stolen, or destroyed, the party who is entitled to enforce the instrument may still be allowed to seek collection from the primary party. In order to do so, that person will need to establish that loss of possession was not due to a transfer or a lawful seizure, and that he or she cannot reasonably obtain possession of the missing instrument. The person will also need to prove the terms of the instrument *and* his or her right to enforcement. Similar rules apply if the missing instrument is a cashier's check, teller's check, or certified check.

Negotiable instruments carry both contract liability and warranty liability. The warranty liability may be transfer warranty liability or presentment warranty liability. Transfer warranties exist on all negotiable instruments that are transferred for consideration. Presentment warranties apply only to order paper that is presented to the drawee for acceptance or payment.

The final stage for most instruments is discharge. Discharge can be, and normally is, based on payment or satisfaction. Some discharges are partial, discharging either a portion of the liability or a few of the parties. Tender of payment is a partial discharge. Cancellation, renunciation, and impairment are all discharges of some of the secondary parties.

Discussion Questions

1. What is meant by "primary liability" under Article 3, and when does it exist on a negotiable instrument? What is meant by "secondary liability" under Article 3, and when does it exist on a negotiable instrument? Is it possible for a party to be both primarily and secondarily liable on the same instrument at the same time?

2. In order to show proper presentment, what must the presenting party establish? What are the rights of the primary party when a presentment is made? How have these rights changed in light of the increase in check fraud?

3. There are five transfer warranties involved with negotiable instruments. Who gives transfer warranties, and to whom are they given?

4. What is an "impairment" as it relates to discharge of liability on a negotiable instrument? Why is a discharge granted to some of the parties on an instrument when an impairment occurs?

5. What are the presentment warranties associated with negotiable instruments? Who receives the benefit of these warranties? Who gives these warranties? How have presentment warranties changed under the revisions to Article 3?

6. Who or what is an "imposter" under Article 3? Who or what is a "fictitious payee" under Article 3? How is an indorsement by an imposter or by a fictitious payee treated? What reasons exist for this special treatment of the indorsements of imposters and fictitious payees?

7. Presume that a holder makes proper presentment of a negotiable instrument and that the instrument is dishonored upon presentment. The holder now has three options. What are the three options available to the holder of an instrument that has been dishonored after proper presentment? Under what circumstances should the holder pursue each—or all—of the options available? Explain your reasoning.

8. When a person indorses a check, that person gives an additional contract to the indorsee, the contract of indorsement. How long is that indorsement contract valid? What must the indorsee (or a subsequent transferee) do in order to hold the indorser of the check to the indorsement contract?

9. Amy transferred a note to Jim by delivery alone. At the time of the transfer, the maker of the note was involved in an insolvency proceeding. Because of the insolvency proceeding, Jim was unable to collect the note from the maker. What are Jim's rights against Amy? Would it alter his rights if Amy had indorsed and delivered the note to him initially? Why? Suppose that Jim had subsequently indorsed and delivered the instrument to Antoine. What rights could Antoine assert against Jim? Against Amy? Why?

10. José issued an interest-bearing demand note to Loretta, who in turn negotiated the note to Larry. Larry, in turn, negotiated it to Hsin-Min. José offered to pay , Hsin-Min, but Hsin-Min refused the payment. What effect does Hsin-Min's refusal to accept the tender of payment have on the potential secondary liability of each of the other parties who have negotiated the note?

Case Problems and Writing Assignments

1. Myles and Theresa Bryant issued a promissory note payable to the order of Thomas, with monthly installments to begin April 1, 1989. The note recited that payment in full was due if the note were to become two months past due. In November 1989, Thomas sued Myles Bryant for the full amount of the note, alleging that no payments had ever been made. Bryant denied liability, asserting that he and his wife had separated earlier, and that he never received any consideration for the note. He also alleged that Thomas was guilty of fraud in procuring the note and that Thomas had failed to meet several conditions orally agreed to with regard to the note. Would a failure by Thomas to satisfy the conditions to which he agreed when he accepted the note preclude his ability to recover on the note? Would this same failure to satisfy conditions affect a third person taking the note by negotiation from Thomas? Explain your reasoning. [See *Thomas v. Bryant*, 597 So. 2d 1065 (La. App. 2d Cir. 1992).]

2. Erb was a financial consultant at Shearson Lehman in Provo, Utah, rising to the rank of vice-president by 1987. In 1987, Erb was contacted by Matthews, the controller for WordPerfect Corporation and its sister firm, Utah Softcopy, concerning the establishment of several accounts for the firms and for the principals of WordPerfect. Erb established the three accounts and assumed responsibility for managing all three. Shortly thereafter, Matthews delivered a check to Erb for $460,150.23. The check was payable to the order of ABP Investments, and was to be used for the WordPerfect principals. At the time there was no "ABP Investments" account with Shearson, although the WordPerfect principals did business elsewhere under this name. Matthews offered to replace the check with another, payable to the name on the account used at Shearson. However, Erb assured Matthews that there would be no problem with the check as drawn. Erb then opened an account at Shearson in the name ABP Investments and forged the signature of one of the principals. Over the next 11 months, Erb procured and negotiated 37 checks drawn by Shearson Lehman and payable to the order of ABP Investments. The checks, totaling $504,295.30, were all deposited to Erb's personal account at Wasatch Bank, with forged indorsements for ABP Investments. None of the checks contained Erb's indorsement. Eventually, an audit of Erb's handling of the various

WordPerfect accounts revealed the extent of his misappropriations. Shearson settled with WordPerfect for $1,208,903 and then sued Wasatch Bank for negligence, breach of warranty, and conversion. Wasatch denied liability.

Is a depository bank liable to the drawer of a check when the drawer's faithless employee induces the drawer to issue checks, fraudulently indorses them in the name of the specified payee, and absconds with the funds? What ethical considerations are raised by the facts in this case? [See *Shearson Lehman Brothers, Inc. v. Wasatch Bank*, 788 F. Supp. 1184 (D. Utah 1992).]

3. Vincent and Mary Jane Catania were married. They resided on property owned by Vincent's mother and secured by a mortgage. Vincent and Mary Jane were to pay the mortgage and the real estate taxes, but title was to remain in the name of Vincent's mother. In 1977, the mother conveyed title to the property to Joseph Catania, Vincent's brother, without Joseph's knowledge or consent. (He did not learn of his title to the land until some time after 1980, when he received a tax notice from the town of Enfield.) Vincent and Mary Jane divorced in 1980. The divorce decree called for Vincent to pay the mortgage, insurance, and taxes on the property until their youngest child reached the age of 18. The decree also contained certain conditions calling for the sale of the property and the division of the proceeds between Vincent and Mary Jane. In 1982, Vincent arranged for a second mortgage on the property, and Joseph—the owner of record of the property—also signed the loan agreement. Eventually, Vincent defaulted on the mortgage, and Mary Jane paid the bank, receiving an assignment of the mortgage in exchange. Since Vincent had procured relief through bankruptcy, Mary Jane sued Joseph on the note. Joseph asserted that he was merely an accommodation party on the mortgage and was not liable to Mary Jane. Was Joseph an accommodation on the note, or was he a comaker on the note? After deciding this case, ask yourself, "Why would a person indorse a note as an accommodation party"? [See *Catania v. Catania*, 601 A.2d 543 (Conn. App. 1992).]

4. Pauline Pagani was an employee of Maryland Industrial Finishing Company, Inc. (MIFCO) from April 13, 1989, through February 23, 1990. In June 1989, Pagani began embezzling funds by depositing some of MIFCO's checks into her own account at Citizens Bank of Maryland, rather than depositing the checks into MIFCO's account at Citizens. She continued this practice until February 1990, when Brenda Alexander discovered the embezzlement. MIFCO later sued Citizens to recover the funds that were deposited into Pagani's personal account. MIFCO alleged, among other things, that Citizens converted the checks under the UCC, and that Citizens was negligent. At trial, Brenda Alexander testified that MIFCO is a small company with seven employees and that it has had an account with Citizens since 1976. Alexander also testified that she instructed Pagani that when MIFCO received a check from a customer, she should retrieve the invoice from the file, mark it paid, write on it the check information, and then place the invoice in the "paid" file. Pagani was also instructed to indorse the check by stamping the back with two stamps—one with the name and address of MIFCO and the other containing the words "For deposit only." Pagani was then directed to deposit the indorsed checks into MIFCO's account at Citizens Bank and to file a copy of the deposit slip in MIFCO's files. Were the indorsements made by Pagani "unauthorized" because she did not make the indorsements restrictive, as she had been instructed to do? Was the bank liable under conversion, negligence, or breach of warranty theories? What ethical issues are raised by the facts in this case? How might the parties have acted differently if they were more concerned with ethics than with law? [See *Citizens Bank of Maryland v. Maryland Industrial Finishing Co.*, 659 A.2d 313 (Md. 1995).]

5. BUSINESS APPLICATION CASE Texas Stadium Corporation ("TSC") is the lessee of Texas Stadium in Irving, Texas. Candace Pratt worked as an accounts payable clerk for TSC from late 1988 until August 1993. As part of her job, Pratt prepared TSC checks, which were later signed by authorized officers of TSC. While employed at TSC, Pratt embezzled money from TSC. As part of her embezzlement scheme, Pratt established a d/b/a account at Savings of America (SOA) in the name of Candace A. Pratt d/b/a AAA Lawn Maintenance Service and Repair ("AAA"). To effect her embezzlement scheme, Pratt would prepare a check for an actual vendor, and after having the check signed by an authorized officer of TSC, Pratt would alter the check by either changing the payee name to a version of the AAA name or adding the AAA name above the original payee name. Pratt also used other methods to embezzle money from TSC. One such method was to prepare a TSC check in a version of the AAA name and then deposit it into her account once it was signed. Once Pratt obtained the appropriate signatures and deposited the checks in her d/b/a account, SOA then forwarded the checks to TSC's bank, and the checks were paid in due course. In all, Pratt deposited 206 checks in her account, totaling $1,060,052.10. After discovering Pratt's scheme, TSC filed suit against Pratt and SOA to recover the money Pratt embezzled. TSC alleged causes of action against Pratt and SOA for negligence, conversion, money had and received, and breach of warranty. In July 1994, SOA moved for summary judgment on all of TSC's claims. After hearing the evidence and arguments of counsel, the trial judge granted summary judgment in favor of SOA without specifying the basis for his ruling. TSC and Pratt then entered into an agreed judgment. TSC appealed the summary judgment granted in favor of SOA. Was Savings of America liable to TSC on the checks under any of the theories advanced by TSC in its complaint? Should the "fictitious payee" rule protect SOA in this case? What should Texas Stadium Corporation have done differently in order to prevent this sort of loss? [See *Texas Stadium Corporation v. Savings of America*, 933 S.W.2d 616 (Tex. App. Dallas 1996)]

6. ETHICAL APPLICATION CASE On November 1, 1987, four individuals formed a partnership, South Central Investing Associates, for the purpose of "purchasing, developing and/or operating income producing property and related ventures." Approximately 10 months later, the partners incorporated SCI

Professional Associates, Inc. In 1988, Comerica Bank extended South Central a $100,000 line of credit that was secured by the personal guarantees of the partners. In July 1989, Comerica increased the line of credit to $150,000 and subsequently issued a cashier's check for $149,850, listing "South Central Investment Associates" as the payee. In return, South Central executed a promissory note to Comerica. The intended purpose of this unsecured loan was for the purchase of an apartment building. The purchase agreement, however, clearly reflected that SCI was the buyer. The cashier's check was endorsed "SCI Prof. Assoc., Inc." and deposited in SCI's account with Michigan National Bank. Comerica's account with the Federal Reserve Bank was debited for the amount of the check. South Central eventually failed to pay the promissory note when it matured in November 1989; nevertheless, Comerica renewed the note on two subsequent occasions. On March 9, 1990, SCI assumed the loan by executing a promissory note in the amount of $150,000 and securing the note by two parcels of real estate that were owned by SCI. A few months later, two partners were arrested and charged with obtaining money under false pretenses. SCI subsequently failed to pay the note when it matured.

Rather than foreclose on the mortgage, Comerica informed Michigan National on May 17, 1991, that Michigan National had improperly accepted and processed the cashier's check, because the check was improperly endorsed. Michigan National refused to reimburse Comerica the proceeds of the check. Comerica then filed suit on the basis that Michigan National was strictly liable for accepting an improperly endorsed check for deposit under Article 4 of the UCC. Michigan National claimed that it was not responsible because the proceeds of the cashier's check were received by the intended payee, South Central. The trial court granted Comerica's motion for summary disposition, holding that Michigan National was liable because the check had not been endorsed by South Central. Did Michigan National Bank breach the presentment warranties on the cashier's check by accepting an improperly endorsed check? Is it ethical for Comerica to seek recovery from Michigan National when Comerica had continued to deal with the partnership after it had twice ignored defaults on the loan and had renewed the loan on both occasions? [See *Comerica Bank v. Michigan National Bank*, 536 N.W.2d 298 (Mich. App. 1995).]

7. **CRITICAL THINKING CASE** On August 8, 1980, Commercial Mortgage and Finance Company sent a commitment for a construction loan to shareholders of Ledgewood Development Corporation. Hamlett, as president of Ledgewood, and George Zannis, as then-president of Commercial, signed the document, which provided for a $200,000 loan secured by a trust deed on "The Timbers," an undeveloped real estate parcel. The commitment letter stated:

Signature of Corporate President and Secretary (including Corporate seal) will be required. Also the Secretary's Certificate and copy of the resolution of the Board of Directors authorizing such

loan. Personal guarantees will also be required of Mr. & Mrs. McCaslin and Mr. & Mrs. Hamlett.

The minutes of a special meeting of the board of directors of Ledgewood, on September 29, 1980, stated that the board of directors resolved that the president and secretary of Ledgewood were authorized to mortgage the property to Commercial for $200,000 for one year, and the officers were further authorized to execute all necessary notes and other documents to effect the loan. The trust deed was signed by Hamlett and Mansfield as president and secretary, respectively, of Ledgewood. Five trust deed notes were signed by Hamlett and Mansfield in their corporate capacities and by them and Clara Hamlett and Frank McCaslin as individuals. The notes were each due September 30, 1981. A check drawn on Commercial's account, dated September 30, 1980, was made payable to Ledgewood. The following September, Lehman agreed to purchase the property. A contract for the sale of the property to Lehman, dated September 3, 1981, lists the sellers as "Bill Hamlett and Clara Hamlett and Jan Mansfield"; however, the deed conveying the property to Lehman was a corporation warranty deed that listed the grantor as Ledgewood, and it was signed by Hamlett and Mansfield in their corporate capacities.

On September 8, 1981, Commercial sent a letter to Lehman acknowledging his intent to buy "The Timbers" from Ledgewood. The letter provided that Commercial waived the right to enforce the acceleration clause in the trust deed in the event of a sale of the property. The letter further stated, "[t]his waiver does not release the original signers of the Trust Deed Notes in the event of default." The letter also provided for an extension of the loan to September 30, 1982. It was accepted by Lehman. Lehman signed a personal guaranty on September 11, 1981. That guaranty stated that Lehman was guaranteeing the credit given to Ledgewood. On September 30, Ledgewood and the shareholders executed an extension agreement with Commercial and Lehman. This agreement represented that Frank McCaslin and Mansfield had divorced and Frank McCaslin quitclaimed his interest in the property to Mansfield. Commercial released Frank McCaslin from further obligations under the notes and accepted Lehman's guaranty. Commercial agreed to an extension of time for payment of the notes. Final payment for the balance of the debt was due September 30, 1982; all other provisions of the notes remained in effect.

Eight more extension agreements were signed by Lehman and Commercial. Each agreement provided for a one-year extension. The last agreement extended the date of payment to September 30, 1990. Only the agreement executed September 20, 1981, mentioned Ledgewood or the shareholders. In 1984, Lehman submitted to plaintiff his personal financial statement for the purpose of obtaining an extension on the loan. Apparently, Lehman died on April 16, 1990, and, on June 26, 1990, Commercial filed a claim against Lehman's estate for the principal sum and $5,500 interest due on June 30, 1990. Commercial filed the foreclosure complaint on November 5, 1990. The court found that Mansfield was not an accommodation maker but a comaker because the loan was for construction on property owned by her and the other shareholders. Because Mansfield was a comaker, she was not released by any subsequent extensions.

Did Mansfield sign the trust deed notes as a comaker or as an accommodation party? What difference would it make in the outcome of this case? If a person is signing as an accommodation party, should the person note that at the time of signing? [See *Commercial Mortgage and Finance Company v. American National Bank and Trust Company of Chicago*, 624 N.E.2d 933 (Ill. App. 2nd Div. 1993).]

8. YOU BE THE JUDGE Fly by Night Delivery Services owed money to Acme Enterprises for various supplies Fly by Night had recently purchased. Fly by Night purchased a cashier's check from First Federal, the bank regularly used by Fly by Night for its business transactions. The cashier's check was then mailed to Acme, with Fly by Night using priority mail to post the check. A few days later Acme informed Fly by Night that the cashier's check had not arrived and was apparently lost. Acme also promptly notified First Federal of the lost cashier's check and asked First Federal to place a stop payment against the original check and to issue a replacement check payable to the order of Acme Enterprises. First Federal refused to do so, alleging that Acme was not the proper party to make such a request. Acme insists that it has the right to make the request and has filed suit against First Federal. The case has been brought in *your* court. How will *you* decide the case? What factors will be most important in reaching your decision? [See The National Check Fraud Center, *"Other Check Problems: Lost, Stolen, or Destroyed Cashier's Checks, Teller Checks and Certified Checks,"* at http://www.ckfraud.org/problems.html.]

Notes

1. UCC § 3-414(b).
2. Ibid.
3. UCC § 3-414(c).
4. UCC § 3-414(d).
5. UCC § 3-415(b).
6. UCC § 3-415(c).
7. UCC § 3-415(d).
8. UCC § 3-415(e).
9. UCC § 3-502(a).
10. UCC § 3-419(d).
11. UCC § 3-403.
12. UCC § 1-201(43).
13. UCC § 3-309(a).
14. UCC § 3-309(b).
15. UCC § 3-312.

CHAPTER 24

Bank-Customer Relations/ Electronic Funds Transfers

AGENDA

NRW NRW will need to open at least one account, and more than likely it will need several different accounts, with its bank. What sorts of accounts might the firm need? There are several different types of financial institutions in the community, including credit unions, savings and loans, and commercial banks. What sort of financial institution should NRW deal with? Each of the principals in the firm has an ATM card and at least two different types of credit cards. Should the firm also have an ATM card or a credit card?

What are the rights and responsibilities of the firm in its dealings with a bank? Are the rights and responsibilities of a business different than the rights and responsibilities of an individual customer?

How can the firm transfer funds quickly and safely without using checks or other types of negotiable instruments? The firm will receive a number of payments each month by check. How soon after depositing these checks into the firm's account will the funds be available? How can the firm minimize the risk that any checks it accepts may be dishonored by the drawee bank upon presentment?

These or similar questions may arise during our discussion. Be prepared! You never know when the firm or one of its members will seek your advice.

Basic Concepts

In the United States today, nearly every business organization has a checking account. In addition, many, if not most, of the adults in this country have checking accounts. Many workers still receive their pay by check. Checking account information is normally required on credit and loan applications and, increasingly, is asked for on job applications. Millions of checks move through the economic system each day. Yet few people actually understand the basic rules and regulations of the checking system they are using.

A new customer walking into a bank follows the signs that lead to the "New Accounts" desk. Upon sitting down at this desk, the novice depositor is inundated with seemingly trivial information and details. Several different types of accounts—interest plus checking, free checking, ready-reserve checking, and so on—are briefly mentioned in passing; multiple colors and styles of checks are displayed; a "signature card" is handed to the customer with instructions to "sign at the X"; a deposit ticket is prepared; and a deposit is made in the customer's name in a new account. Before really knowing what has happened, the new customer is back on the street, the proud possessor of a personal checking account. More likely than not, the customer has no idea of what all this means legally.

By signing a signature card, the customer has entered a multirole legal relationship with the bank. The signature card represents a contract with the bank that the customer accepts on signing the card, even though he or she probably is unaware of any of its terms or conditions. In addition, the customer is now governed by Article 4 of the Uniform Commercial Code (UCC), which covers Bank Deposits and Collections. Article 4 was revised, together with Article 3, in 1990. As of May 1999, 47 states and the District of Columbia have adopted the revised versions of both Articles (New York, Rhode Island, and South Carolina still follow the earlier versions of both Articles). The customer has entered into an agency relationship and has agreed to a debtor–creditor relationship as well.

The contract that the customer entered into is relatively simple. It covers things like service charges that can be imposed by the bank for various services, minimum balance requirements for the customer's account, and technical terms and conditions. Likewise, the coverage afforded by Article 4 of the Code is fairly simple; basically, it spells out the mandatory rights and duties of each of the parties. These will be dealt with later in this chapter.

The agency portion of the agreement is a complete surprise to most depositors. To put it simply, the bank is the agent and the depositor is the principal. An agent is required to obey any lawful orders of the principal that deal with the agency. This explains, in part, the language used on a check. The depositor (principal) is ordering the bank (agent) to "*Pay* to the order of" someone. The check does not say, "Please pay" or "I would appreciate it if you would pay." It says, "*PAY!*" This language is an order, and the order is usually lawful. Therefore, the bank must obey that order or face possible liability to the depositor for the disobedience, provided that the order issued by the principal is lawful.

The final relationship varies based on the situation. Normally, the customer will have a positive balance in the checking account. As a result, the customer is a creditor of the bank, and the bank is a debtor of the customer. Occasionally, the bank will pay an overdraft on the customer's account. When this happens, the customer has a negative balance in the account, and the roles reverse. Now the bank is a creditor of the customer, and the customer is a debtor to the bank.

The Customer: Rights and Duties

The duties of a bank customer are relatively few and straightforward. The first and main duty of a customer is to act with due care and diligence. Whether writing a check, inspecting a monthly statement, or indorsing a check, and whether making a deposit or cashing a check, the customer is required to act in a careful and reasonable manner. If customers remember that it is their money being handled, and that carelessness could cause them to lose that money, they are more likely to be careful. In addition, the customer is expected to prepare and issue checks in a nonnegligent manner and to exercise reasonable care and promptness in examining statements and items delivered to the customer by the bank.

Customers have several rights they may exercise. They may stop payment on a previously issued check, and they may collect damages from the bank if the bank errs in the handling of the account to the customer's financial detriment. But before they can exercise these rights, customers must show that they have acted properly and/or that the bank has acted improperly. For example, suppose that Louis issues a check to pay for some merchandise. The merchant presents the check to the bank for payment, and the bank dishonors the check. Louis is now likely to have some problems with the merchant. He may have to pay the merchant a "handling fee" or a "service charge" for the returned check. He may face a lawsuit filed by the merchant to collect the amount of the check plus costs and interest. In many states a person may face a criminal charge for passing "hot" (bad) checks. But what if the dishonor was due to an error by the bank, not carelessness or wrongdoing on Louis's part? Louis will still have to settle his own problems with the merchant, but the criminal action will be dropped. And Louis will be able to proceed against the bank for recovery of the damages he might have suffered in this ordeal.

Wrongful Dishonor

According to UCC § 4-402, the bank is liable to its customer for any damages proximately caused by a wrongful dishonor of the customer's check. Note that this section also limits damages *under this Article* to *actual* damages proved by the customer. Those damages may include damages for an arrest or prosecution, or any other consequential damages. While this section restricts damages the customer can recover to actual damages, "other" damages, including punitive damages, might be available under "other rules of law" if the court deems such damages appropriate.[1] (Under the previous version of Article 4, there was some controversy concerning available damages when a check was wrongfully dishonored for a reason other than mistake. The language of § 4-402 was changed to eliminate this controversy by deleting the reference to "dishonor due to mistake" and limiting damages for wrongful dishonor to actual damages.) From the language used in the revision to § 4-402 it sounds as if the customer will end up in a reasonably good position if the bank wrongfully dishonors a check drawn by the customer: The customer will recover the "handling fees," the interest, and any other costs paid to the merchant; the customer will recover any damages related to the arrest; and the bank will end up taking all the losses on this case. In seeking damages from the bank, however, the customer must prove that the bank's conduct was the proximate cause of the losses suffered by the customer. If the bank can show that the customer contributed to the loss, the bank may be able to avoid liability for the dishonor of the customer's check. The following hypothetical case represents the type of problem that might prevent the customer's recovery.

Roberto owed Mustafa $600. Roberto wrote Mustafa a check for the $600 to pay off the debt, but he postdated the check so that he would have time to make a deposit in order to ensure that his account had sufficient funds to cover the check. Unfortunately, Mustafa presented the check to the bank prior to the date on the check (remember, the check was postdated) and before Roberto had an opportunity to make a deposit. The bank dishonored the check and imposed its service charge for returning a check against Roberto's account. Even though the check was presented prior to its date and the bank ignored the date on the check, this would not be a wrongful dishonor. A bank is not obligated to honor a postdating unless the customer has notified the bank in advance[2] and provided an adequate description of the postdated check to allow the bank to act on it. In addition, the bank has no duty to pay an overdraft unless it has a prior agreement with the customer concerning overdrafts on the account. If Roberto has any complaint in this situation it should be made to Mustafa, the party who did not honor the postdating of the check as he (apparently) had agreed to do when he accepted delivery of a postdated check.

In the following case a customer sued the bank for an alleged wrongful dishonor and also argued that the wrongful dishonor was a key factor in a related intentional tort. Follow the court's reasoning and then decide whether you think it reached the right result.

24.1

COLONIAL BANK v. R. D. PATTERSON
788 So. 2d 134; 2000 Ala. LEXIS 492 (Ala. S.Ct. 2000)

FACTS Patterson and Nordness were equal owners and the only members of the board of directors of Resource 100 Management Group, Inc., an employee-leasing agency. Nordness was the president of the corporation, and Patterson was the secretary and treasurer. Resource 100 opened a business account with Colonial Bank. Originally, Nordness was the sole signatory on the account, but later Patterson was added. Some time later, Nordness and Patterson's business relations became strained. Nordness informed Patterson that Resource 100 was in a bad financial condition and could no longer pay either of them a salary. Patterson thereupon began paying his own salary, from the Resource 100 account, using counter checks. Nordness eventually discovered that counter checks were being written on the account. Nordness asked Colonial to find out who the payee was on these counter checks, and Colonial informed him that it was Patterson.

Nordness then asked a Colonial representative how he could have Patterson's name removed from the account, and was advised that he had several options: (1) take the money out of the account and open a new account; (2) take the money out of the account and deposit it in another bank; or (3) present Colonial with a corporate resolution removing Patterson's name from the account. Nordness chose this third alternative. He returned to the bank with two documents: one purporting to dismiss Patterson from the company, and another representing that a resolution by the board of directors had removed Patterson as a signatory on the account. The resolution was signed by Nordness as president and as secretary of Resource 100. Colonial responded by authorizing a stop order on all counter checks. In early 1997, Patterson presented to the bank a counter check payable to himself. Colonial refused to honor the counter check and informed Patterson that his name had been taken off the account, and that Colonial had received documents indicating that Patterson had been removed from Resource 100's board of directors and had been removed as a signatory on the account. Patterson claimed that these documents were erroneous and that he had never been informed of a board of directors meeting and had not consented to the action purportedly taken by the board.

Eventually Patterson sold his interest in Resource 100 to Nordness, but he then filed suit against Colonial Bank, alleging wrongful dishonor of the checks he had presented to the bank and intentional interference with a business relationship. Patterson claims that Colonial was involved in helping Nordness "shove" Patterson out of Resource 100. He argues that Colonial and Nordness engaged in discussions concerning Nordness's possibly "buying" Patterson out of the business. Patterson claims that Blake, the Colonial representative who advised Nordness of ways to remove Patterson's authorization or access to the account, created a plan that would give Nordness control of the company and would aid Colonial in recovering its money on several unpaid loans it had made to Patterson. Colonial denied liability and moved for a judgment as a matter of law (JML) on the allegation of intentional interference with a business relationship. The court denied the motion. The jury awarded Patterson a verdict for compensatory damages of $60,640 and punitive damages of $939,000. The court granted Colonial an offset of $27,274.54, and reduced the punitive damages to $363,840. Colonial appealed from this judgment.

ISSUES Did Colonial wrongfully dishonor the checks presented by Patterson? Did Colonial intentionally interfere with a business relationship, to the detriment of Patterson?

HOLDINGS No, to both issues. The dishonor of the checks was proper under the terms of the account contract. Since the bank had to dishonor the checks, it did not intentionally interfere with a business relationship by so doing.

REASONING Excerpts from the opinion of Justice Lyons:

Colonial argues that the trial court erred in denying its JML motion because, it argues, Patterson did not present substantial evidence as to all of the elements of his claim alleging intentional interference with a business relationship. To defeat a JML motion directed to such a claim, a plaintiff must present substantial evidence of the following elements: (1) the existence of a contract or business relation; (2) the defendant's knowledge of the contract or business relation; (3) intentional interference by the defendant with the contract or business relation; (4) the absence of justification for the defendant's interference; and (5) damage to the plaintiff resulting from the interference. . . .

The tort of intentional interference with business relations was recognized so as to provide a remedy in the situation where a third party intentionally interferes with the relationship of two contracting parties. . . . Moreover, a party to a particular contract cannot, as a matter of law, be liable for tortious interference with that contract. . . .

In the present case, Patterson's claim alleging intentional interference with business relations revolves around the dishonor of a counter check that Patterson presented to Colonial on the Resource 100 account. This dishonor forms the basis of Patterson's argument. Patterson argues that Colonial dishonored the counter check, as a means to accomplish an interference with Patterson and Nordness's stockholder relationship and their negotiations over the sale of stock. He claims that by not releasing any funds from the Resource 100 account to Patterson, Colonial forced Patterson to sell his share of the business because, he says, without funds from that account he had no income, and the sale of his stock allowed Colonial to recover the unpaid balances on its loans to Patterson. Early in the business relationship, and after the Resource 100 account had been established, Patterson and Nordness entered into an agreement with Colonial by which each would be a signatory on the account. Each of them signed documents that related to the account and defined the rules governing the account. The signature-card contract, which both Patterson and Nordness also signed, incorporated Colonial's "Rules and Regulations for Depository Accounts."

These rules and regulations regarding "Business and Organization Account Authorized Representatives" provide:

You agree that each authorized representative shall have full authority, subject to the provisions of the signature card and supporting documents, for all actions relating to your account, including, but not limited to, checks, closing the account, stopping payment, assigning the account or overdrawing the account for both savings and checking accounts.... If there is a dispute between the authorized representative(s) who has signed a signature card, or if one of the authorized representative(s) demands that we not allow other(s) to withdraw money from the account, or if there is a dispute about who is authorized to make withdrawals from an account, we may refuse to allow certain withdrawals by anyone until we are satisfied that the dispute is resolved or the demand is withdrawn. We will not be responsible for any damages you may suffer as a result of our refusal to allow you to withdraw money due to the dispute or demand....

Clearly, Colonial had the prerogative to choose not to honor Patterson's counter check. It is evident in the rules, which both Nordness and Patterson signed, that Colonial reserved the right to withhold funds at the onset of any dispute between authorized representatives, such as Nordness and Patterson. Moreover, Nordness and Patterson agreed, when they signed the signature contract card, that any authorized representative would have full authority for all actions relating to the account. Thus, Nordness, by virtue of the contract between Resource 100 and Colonial, had the authority to inform Colonial to place a stop order on all counter checks; he exercised that authority and Colonial placed the stop order....

Colonial had the legal right to do exactly as it did, given the clear language of the Rules and Regulations for Depository Accounts and the undisputed evidence regarding a dispute between Patterson and Nordness. The conduct of Colonial that Patterson condemns is specifically allowed by the agreement, and Patterson, by characterizing that conduct as conduct taken in bad faith, cannot defeat Colonial's right to take that action....

For Patterson to succeed on his attempt to limit the scope of the rules and regulations so as to prevent them from applying to this transaction, we would have to alter some unambiguous language. The rules regarding restrictions on withdrawals begin with the phrase "In the event of any controversy," and while they contain an illustration concerning a dispute over who makes withdrawals, to confine the operation of the rules to such a circumstance would be to rewrite the agreement. The rules and regulations preclude our imposing on Colonial a liability for refusing to allow withdrawal of money. The dishonor of Patterson's check had precisely that effect—Patterson could no longer draw checks on the business account in order to pay his salary.

Because Patterson's claim alleging intentional interference with business relations is based on Colonial's dishonoring the counter check, and because Colonial, as a party to the business relationship with Patterson and Nordness, had the legal right to take that action, the trial court should have granted Colonial's motion for a JML on Patterson's claim alleging a wrongful interference with a business relationship. The judgment is reversed and a judgment is rendered for Colonial. The cross-appeal is dismissed as moot.

BUSINESS CONSIDERATIONS Nordness submitted a "resolution" from the board of directors of Resource 100 to the bank. This resolution authorized Nordness to remove Patterson as an authorized signer of company checks. Should the bank have accepted this "resolution" without consulting Patterson, especially since the bank knew that Patterson was—or had been—the secretary of the firm?

ETHICAL CONSIDERATIONS Was it ethical for Patterson to pay himself after being told that the firm was in financial difficulty? Was it ethical for Nordness to attempt to remove Patterson as an authorized signer of checks due to their personal disagreements and difficulties?

Stop Payment Orders

A customer has a right to order the bank to pay by issuing a check. The customer also has a right to order the bank *not* to pay by issuing a stop payment order to the bank. If this stop payment order is issued properly, the bank must obey the order to stop payment on the check. The bank may be held liable for any damages proximately caused by its failure to obey a properly issued order to stop payment. Of course, the burden of proving damages is on the customer who issued the stop payment order. The stop payment order must be given to the bank in a time and manner that gives the bank a reasonable opportunity to act on the order. In other words, the bank must receive a complete description of the check (number, payee, amount, date, reason) with enough "lead time" to allow the bank to react to the order. A minimum of a few hours is normally required, but it may take as long as a full

ISSUING A STOP PAYMENT ORDER

NRW recently issued a check to pay for some office supplies, including some letterhead stationery. When the supplies were delivered Mai noticed that the letterhead stationery was not properly centered and that the design seemed to be a bit blurred. While the stationery could be used as is, none of the principals is very happy with the quality of the stationer's work. They would like to issue a stop payment order on the check to the stationer, but they are not sure that this is the right thing to do, fearing that this might cause future problems with the stationer and that the bank may pay the check despite the stop payment order. They have asked you for your opinion. What will you tell them?

BUSINESS CONSIDERATIONS Should a business issue a stop payment order on a check before trying to resolve a controversy over performance with the payee of the check? What drawbacks might there be for trying to resolve the matter first?

ETHICAL CONSIDERATIONS Is it ethical to issue a stop payment order on a check when only a portion of the goods or services for which the check was issued is defective? How might the use of a stop payment order be abused?

INTERNATIONAL CONSIDERATIONS Are stop payment orders available in other nations, or is the stop payment a uniquely American banking service? What problems might arise in using a stop payment order in an international transaction that would not be of the same concern in a domestic transaction?

banking day to get the word out to the bank's various branch offices.

The customer can give either an oral or a written stop payment order. A stop payment order is good for six months, but it lapses after 14 days if the original order was oral and it was not confirmed in writing within that 14-day period. A written order can be renewed for additional six-month periods. Of course, every renewal will entail another service charge.

If the customer properly gives the bank a stop payment order, and the bank pays the check despite the order, the customer may be able to collect damages from the bank. To do

so, the customer will have to prove that he or she suffered damages because the check was paid. To prove this, he or she will have to show that the presenter could not have collected from him or her (the customer) if payment had been stopped by the bank as the customer ordered. If the presenter could enforce the check against the customer (drawer), then the customer will not be able to collect any damages from the bank for paying the check despite the stop payment order. If payment is stopped by the bank, the drawer may be sued by the holder in an effort to recover his or her money.

In the case on pages 569–570 an organization issued a stop payment order on a "bonus" check issued to a former employee upon her retirement. The payee sued, alleging that the stop payment was an illegal retaliation against her for actions taken after her retirement. After reading the case, think about what the organization should have done differently in the events that led to the lawsuit.

The Duty to Inspect Bank Statements

Section 4-406 addresses the customer's duty to inspect his or her bank statements. The bank will periodically send statements to the customer showing the activities on the account for the statement period, typically one month. The statement must *either* include the canceled items (paid checks) *or* provide adequate information for the customer to reasonably be able to identify the items listed on the statement. Section 4-406(a) states that the bank's statement provides sufficient information to the customer "if the item is described by number, amount, and date of payment." If the bank returns the paid items, the customer should retain them for a period of seven years. If the bank does not return the paid items, § 4-406(b) provides that "the person retaining the items [the bank] shall either retain the items or, if the items are destroyed, maintain the capacity to furnish legible copies of the items until the expiration of seven years after receipt of the items." This section adds the requirement that if the customer requests an item from the bank, the bank must provide the requested item or a legible copy of that item within a reasonable time. This is an important provision, because the paid item is proof of payment and may be needed as evidence in a legal proceeding involving the customer.

The customer has certain duties once he or she receives the periodic statement of account. The customer is expected to examine the statement, reconcile his or her account with the statement provided by the bank, and discover and report any unauthorized signatures or alterations on any items included in the statement. Section 4-406(c) provides that the customer must "exercise reasonable promptness" in examining the statement to determine

24.2

ORIGEL v. COMMUNITY ACTION SERVICES
2001 U.S. Dist. LEXIS 1540 (N.D. Ill. Eastern Div. 2001)

FACTS Mary Origel began working for Community Action Services (CASI), a not-for-profit organization, as an administrative assistant on October 3, 1988. When Origel began her employment, she reported to then executive director Michael Perry. As part of her job responsibilities, she prepared employee time sheets, which, in turn, were forwarded to an outside vendor of payroll services for preparation of the actual payroll checks. A check log of every check that was cut documented the amount of the check, the payee, and the reason for the check. Because she was also responsible for the maintenance of all personnel files, Origel had access to all information pertaining to each employee, including administrative personnel. She knew when raises were given as well as when other financial considerations were given to an employee because she prepared the payroll worksheets. Origel worked continuously for CASI on a full-time basis for nearly 11 years until her retirement on July 16, 1999, at age 65. After she retired, on July 31, 1999, Origel signed an affidavit in a Title VII action being brought against CASI by her former supervisor, Michael Perry. The affidavit was filed on August 11, 1999. The Origel affidavit contradicted an affidavit filed by CASI's chairman of the board, Robert Donaldson.

On August 12, 1999, Origel received a check (no. 15505) from CASI dated August 11, 1999, in the amount of $2,500. The check was delivered to Origel's home personally by one of CASI's drivers. The stub for check no. 15505 read "retirement bonus." The check had been signed by Robert Donaldson in his capacity as chairperson and member of the board of directors.

CASI claimed the check was a discretionary "bonus," while Origel contended that it represented the "nondiscretionary" remainder of a raise she had been awarded the previous year. She contended that when she asked Donaldson why she had received a raise that was $2,500 less than another employee, he had told her that, when she retired, she would "get a nice bonus."

On August 18, 1999, a copy of Ms. Origel's affidavit was transmitted to and received by CASI at its office. That same day, a stop payment order was issued on check no. 15505. The board of directors of CASI met on August 24, 1999, and voted to rescind the $2,500 check to Origel. When asked in his deposition whether the board also discussed Origel's affidavit at the meeting,

Chairman Donaldson first said they did and then claimed they did not. Origel deposited the check on August 27, 1999. She did not speak to or correspond with anyone at CASI between August 12 and August 27, 1999. Origel did not learn about the stop payment order until September 3, 1999, when, upon opening her mail, she saw the returned check and her bank's notice that payment on the check had been stopped. She then filed suit against CASI, alleging that the stop payment was made in retaliation for her affidavit, in violation of Title VII of the Civil Rights Act of 1964. CASI moved for summary judgment.

ISSUE Did CASI improperly issue a stop payment order on the check in retaliation for the affidavit filed by Origel?

HOLDING Perhaps. Origel presented sufficient evidence to prevent the granting of a summary judgment. She met her burden of showing that a reasonable jury might find in her favor, and she was entitled to a trial on the issues.

REASONING Excerpts from the opinion of Judge Darrah:

Summary judgment is appropriate when there remains no genuine issue of material fact and the moving party is entitled to judgment as a matter of law. . . . "One of the principal purposes of the summary judgment rule is to isolate and dispose of factually unsupported claims or defenses. . . ." To establish a prima facie case of retaliation under Title VII, Plaintiff must establish that: (1) she engaged in "statutorily protected expression," (in this case, Plaintiff's protected expression consisted of filing an affidavit in a fellow employee's Title VII case); (2) she suffered an adverse, job-related action by her employer; (3) there is a causal link between her opposition to unlawful discrimination and the adverse employment action. . . . Defendant has challenged the second and third elements of Plaintiff's case for retaliation.

Plaintiff contends that Defendant's issuance of a stop payment order on her retirement payment after she retired constituted an adverse employment action or action with a nexus to employment in violation of Title VII. Defendant argues that the cancellation of Plaintiff's retirement payment did not constitute an adverse employment action because: (1) Plaintiff was no longer an employee when the check was canceled; and (2) the cancellation had no nexus to employment. . . .

Former employees have a right to sue their former employers under Title VII's retaliation provision. . . . The Seventh Circuit has noted that "former employees, insofar as they are complaining of retaliation that impinges on their future employment prospects or otherwise has a nexus to employment, do have the right to sue their former employers." . . . Conduct that is related to Plaintiff's former employment is actionable under Title VII. . . .

Defendant has correctly pointed out that Plaintiff has not accepted or sought new employment after retiring from CASI. Therefore, CASI's alleged retaliatory action (canceling the check) cannot be said to affect Plaintiff's future employment prospects. However, the relevant question in this case is whether Defendant's cancellation of the "retirement payment" can be said to have a "nexus" to her employment at CASI. This Court finds that it does, regardless of whether this payment is characterized as a "gift" (the explanation proffered by Defendant) or a "delayed raise" (the explanation proffered by the Plaintiff). Loss of pay or material benefits deriving from employment constitute an adverse employment action. . . . The Court need not resolve the divergent characterizations of this payment on this Motion for Summary Judgment since, in both cases, the payment can be said to be connected (have a nexus) to Plaintiff's performance of services for Defendant. The fact that the check read "retirement bonus" establishes that the employer itself believed that the check bore a nexus to her employment (or more specifically, the cessation of her employment at Defendant).

Plaintiff contends that Defendant's cancellation of her "retirement payment" came as the result of her decision to proffer an affidavit in another case being brought against Defendant. To succeed on her claim of retaliation, Plaintiff must show that there was a causal link between the protected expression and the adverse employment action. If the Defendant offers a "legitimate" reason for the act, the Plaintiff must show that this reason is pre-textual. . . . Defendant has argued that: (1) there was no causal connection because the person who allegedly stopped payment on the check did not know of the affidavit Plaintiff filed; (2) it had a legitimate reason for taking this action because Walker did not have authority to authorize the check, and cancellation of the check was consistent with and came as a result of its policy of not awarding bonuses to administrative personnel.

Plaintiff has made out a prima facie case of retaliation. Although she has proffered no direct evidence, she has offered enough sufficient evidence so that a jury could reasonably conclude that the cancellation was caused by the filing of her affidavit. The fact that Defendant received the affidavit and canceled the check on the same day raises a material issue of fact as to whether there was a causal connection. "Generally, a plaintiff may establish such a link through evidence that the [adverse employment action] took place on the heels of protected activity." . . .

Since the Plaintiff has met her summary judgment burden of showing a causal link, the burden shifts to Defendant to articulate a legitimate reason for stopping payment on the check. . . .

Plaintiff has met her burden of showing that a reasonable jury might conclude that Defendant's proffered explanation is pre-textual. To meet this burden, Plaintiff must "'produce evidence from which a rational trier of fact could infer that the company lied' about its proffered reasons for [her] dismissal . . . if an inference of improper motive can be drawn, there must be a trial." . . .

For the reasons stated herein, Defendant's Motion for Summary Judgment is DENIED.

BUSINESS CONSIDERATIONS Should a not-for-profit organization have different policies and procedures for issuing checks than would be followed by a regular corporation? Should it have different policies and procedures for "bonuses" and other salary-related items?

ETHICAL CONSIDERATIONS Is it ethical for a drawer to issue a stop payment order on a check because the payee has taken some action of which the drawer does not approve? Does it matter if the action is not related to the reason for issuing the check?

whether any of the items paid by the bank were not authorized due to an alteration of the instrument or the presence of a signature of the drawer that was not authorized. If any such items are discovered, the customer must *promptly* give the bank notice of this fact. If the customer fails to exercise "reasonable promptness" in meeting these duties, he or she may be unable to recover from the bank for any unauthorized payments.

According to § 4-406(d), if the bank can prove that a customer failed to exercise reasonable promptness in examining the statement and reporting any problems, the customer will be precluded from asserting against the bank:

(1) the customer's unauthorized signature or any alteration on the item, if the bank also proves that it suffered a loss by reason of the failure; and

NRW CASE 24.2   Finance/Management

UNAUTHORIZED PAYMENTS BY THE BANK

While reconciling NRW's latest bank statement, Helen found a listing for an item that was not reflected in the check register. When she asked, neither Mai nor Carlos could remember issuing a check for the amount of the listed item. Helen wants to call the bank to complain and to demand that the money be recredited to the firm's account, but Carlos thinks that they should wait for the next statement to see if perhaps the bank made a mistake in posting the item to the account and has subsequently discovered and corrected the error. Mai is concerned that if the firm delays, it may be waiving some of its rights. They have asked you for your opinion. What will you tell them?

BUSINESS CONSIDERATIONS Should a business have a policy for reconciliation of its bank statement? If so, what should that policy include? What sort of policy or practice should an individual follow in reconciling his or her bank statement?

ETHICAL CONSIDERATIONS Is it ethical for a bank that has made an unauthorized payment on a customer's account *not* to recredit the account simply because the customer delayed in reporting the transaction? Is it ethical for a customer who delayed reporting an unauthorized payment to still seek recovery from the bank even though the customer's delay may have affected the bank's rights?

INTERNATIONAL CONSIDERATIONS Do banks in other nations provide the same sorts of protections to customers as are provided in Article 4 for such things as unauthorized signatures or material alterations of checks? Would you expect the rights of the customer to be greater or less than in the United States?

---

(2) the customer's unauthorized signature or alteration by the same wrongdoer on any other item paid in good faith by the bank if the payment was made before the bank received notice from the customer of the unauthorized signature or alteration and after the customer had been afforded a reasonable period of time, not exceeding 30 days, in which to examine the item or statement and notify the bank.

These rules make it sound as if the customer *must* (1) examine his or her statement, (2) discover any unauthorized payments made by the bank because the item either contains a signature that was not authorized by the customer or the item was altered without the customer's authorization, and (3) notify the bank of the problem in a reasonably prompt manner not to exceed 30 days, or the customer will lose his or her rights against the bank. However, that is *not* what the rules mean.

The bank can avoid liability to the customer for paying an unauthorized item only if the customer does not give the bank prompt notice *and* the bank can prove that it suffered a loss due to the delay. If the bank cannot prove that it suffered a loss due to the delay, the bank will still be liable to the customer. The real protection for the bank here arises when the *same* wrongdoer has signed more than one item without authority or has altered more than one item without authority, and the bank has paid these subsequent items in good faith. If the customer failed to notify the bank of the problem with reasonable promptness when the first such item was included in a statement, and the bank paid subsequent items in good faith before it was notified, the customer cannot recover for the subsequent items paid by the bank. Since the customer failed to notify the bank with reasonable promptness, the bank can treat these subsequent signatures or alterations by the same wrongdoers as *authorized* by the customer.

The Code seems to limit the customer's right to recover to those situations in which the customer gives reasonably prompt notice, which is not to exceed 30 days. In fact, a customer has one year after the statement or the item is made available to discover and report the unauthorized signature or alteration before he or she is absolutely precluded from asserting the improper payment of any item by the bank.[3]

Finally, even if the customer would otherwise be precluded from recovering from the bank under § 4-406(d), the customer may still have recourse. If the customer can prove that the bank did not exercise ordinary care in paying the item, and that this lack of ordinary care substantially contributed to the customer's loss, the loss will be allocated between the bank and the customer based on the degree of fault that can be allocated to each party.[4] And if the customer can prove that the bank did not pay the item in good faith, the customer can recover for all of his or her loss, and none of the preclusions under § 4-406(d) apply.

The rules regarding examination of the statement require a customer to discover that his or her "signature" was not authorized, or that the item has been altered. These rules do not address the issue of an unauthorized indorsement. Obviously, a drawer should recognize his or her own signature or should be aware that he or she had not authorized a particular item to be signed. Similarly, the customer should be aware of the amount of any items issued and should recognize when such an item has been altered. But the customer cannot be expected to know the indorsement of the payee or of any subsequent holders, so the "reasonable promptness" standard would impose an unreasonable burden on the customer. Accordingly, the Code gives the customer three years from the statement date to discover that an indorsement was not authorized and to notify the bank of this fact.[5]

The Bank: Rights and Duties

The overriding duty of the bank is the duty to exercise ordinary care. Section 4-103(a) allows the parties a certain amount of flexibility, but only within limits. According to this section, the parties can vary the effects of the provisions of Article 4, but the bank cannot disclaim its responsibility for a lack of good faith or for a failure to exercise ordinary care, nor can the bank limit the measure of damages for any lack of good faith or any failure to exercise ordinary care. The "ordinary care" standard is intended to allow banks to change their practices over time as the ordinary standards and practices of the banking industry change, while helping to ensure that any particular bank will be held to the current standards of the industry. To further reflect this intent, § 4-103(b) specifies that "Federal Reserve regulations and operating circulars, clearinghouse rules, and the like have the effect of agreements under subsection (a), whether or not specifically assented to by all parties interested in items handled." Obviously, "all parties interested" would include the bank and the customer, but it may also include indorsers or other parties having an interest in the account.

Banks face other duties beyond those imposed by § 4-103. Since the bank is the agent of the customer, it has the duties of an agent. This means, among other things, that it must obey any lawful orders of the customer. This duty to obey gives the bank a very important right: It can charge to the customer's account any item that is properly payable from the customer's account. The bank can pay the check even if the payment creates an overdraft. The bank can also pay a check that was incomplete when issued and then completed by some later holder. The bank may even know that a holder, and not the drawer, completed the check and still pay it as completed. The only exception is when the bank has notice that the completion was improper or was done in bad faith.

Stale Checks

In accordance with the rules that govern timely presentment, the bank may refuse to honor any "stale" checks.[6] A "stale" check is one that is more than six months old and has not been certified. If the bank dishonors a stale check, it is not liable to the customer for any damages, nor can the dishonor be treated as a wrongful dishonor. Alternatively, the bank may, at its option, honor a stale check. Again, the bank will not be liable for any damages suffered by the customer if it honors the check in good faith. It should be remembered that a written stop payment is good for six months, the period after which a check becomes stale. Suppose a customer issues a written stop payment order. Six months elapse without the check ever being presented, and the customer does not renew the stop payment order. The payee now presents the check to the bank. The check is stale, and a stop payment order had been in effect on that check, but the bank honors the check. If the bank can prove it acted in good faith, it will face no liability for its payment of the stale check the customer once tried to stop.

Death or Incompetence of a Customer

Under traditional agency rules, if the principal dies or becomes incompetent, the agency terminates by operation of law. After this termination, if the agent continues to perform its agency duties, the agent becomes personally liable, and the principal has no liability. (This is the traditional rule for agencies. Many states have modified this rule so that the death of the principal does not automatically terminate the agency if doing so would cause an undue hardship. See Chapter 29 for a detailed discussion of this topic.) This rule would be impractical with negotiable instruments, so the UCC expressly changed it. As applied to the bank-customer relationship, agencies do not automatically end at the instant of the principal's death or incompetence. Under § 4-405(a), the bank is fully authorized to perform its banking functions on the account of a customer who has died or has become incompetent until the bank knows of the occurrence and has had adequate time to react to the news. Even if the bank knows of the customer's death, its power to act is not terminated. Section 4-405(b) permits the bank to continue to honor checks drawn on the account for 10 days after the date of a death unless a stop payment is placed on the account by an interested party.

The Bank's Right of Subrogation

Sometimes banks make mistakes. A bank may honor an instrument covered by a stop payment order, or it may do something else that allows the customer to recover damages from the bank. When this happens, the bank has some protection: It is entitled to subrogation. Subrogation means the bank is given the rights that some other parties could have raised if the bank had not made improper payment. UCC § 4-407 gives the bank three different sets of rights to assert through subrogation:

- the rights of a holder in due course on the item against the maker or drawer;

- the rights of the payee or any other holder of the item against the maker or drawer either on the item or under the transaction out of which the item arose; and

- the rights of the drawer or maker against the payee or any other holders of the item with respect to the transaction out of which the item arose.

Thus, the bank may assert the rights of the drawer, the payee, the holder, or any other interested party in the transaction. From this buffet of rights, the bank can select the set of rights that gives it the greatest likelihood of winning the case.

The Bank's Rights with Legal Notice

A bank may acquire knowledge or receive legal notice affecting a particular item or affecting a customer's account. What must the bank do in this situation? What rights can the bank assert? This area is addressed in § 4-303, which says:

(a) Any knowledge, notice, or stop-payment order received by, legal process served upon, or setoff exercised by a payor bank comes too late to terminate, suspend, or modify the bank's right or duty to pay an item or to charge its customer's account for the item if the knowledge, notice, stop-payment order, or legal process is received or served and a reasonable time for the bank to act thereon expires or the setoff is exercised after the earliest of the following:
(1) the bank accepts or certifies the item;
(2) the bank pays the item in cash;
(3) the bank settles for the item without having a right to revoke the settlement under statute, clearing-house rule, or agreement;
(4) the bank becomes accountable for the amount of the item under Section 4-302 dealing with the payor bank's responsibility for late return of items; or
(5) with respect to checks, a cutoff hour no earlier than one hour after the opening of the next banking day

after the banking day on which the bank received the check and no later than the close of that next banking day or, if no cutoff hour is fixed, the close of the next banking day after the banking day on which the bank received the check.
(b) Subject to subsection (a), items may be accepted, paid, certified, or charged to the indicated account of its customer in any order.

This section specifies the rights of the bank any time a customer of the bank is involved in a bankruptcy proceeding, garnishment, or some other legal process in which one or more parties is seeking to assert a claim against the customer's account. The bank is allowed to pay the item or otherwise settle on the item without liability to the legal claims of third persons, so long as the bank exercises "ordinary care" in handling the item and follows its normal practices and procedures. So long as the bank follows these rules it will not be held liable by a third person asserting a legal claim against the customer for making a "wrongful payment" in contravention of any legal proceedings or other claims asserted by the third person.

The Account Contract

The bank has the right to enforce the terms of its contract with the customer. Among other things, this right allows the bank to impose certain service charges and fees against many of its customers each month. The bank may be able to collect a specific amount every month, it may be able to collect a specific amount in any month the customer's account balance falls below a certain amount, or it may be able to charge a specific amount for every check written by the customer. The bank will impose a service charge for handling a stop payment order. Likewise, it may charge a customer when it pays an overdraft or when it dishonors a check, if honoring it would have created an overdraft. These service charges are specified in the contract formed when the customer signs the signature card.

Special Problems

Two areas deserve further mention: certified checks and unauthorized signatures.

Certified Checks

A certified check is one that has already been accepted by the drawee bank. In other words, the bank has assumed primary liability and agreed to pay the check on a later presentment. Certification can be done at the request of the drawer or of any holder. A refusal by the bank to certify the check is not a dishonor.[7] How does certification occur? Either the drawer or a holder presents the check to the bank and requests certification. If the bank agrees to certify, it follows certain steps. First, it charges the account of the customer and credits its own "Certified Check Account." Thus, the money is held by the bank in the bank's own account, and the customer has already "paid" the amount of the check. Second, the bank punches a hole in the encoded account number of the check to ensure that the check will not be paid a second time on a later presentment. Third, a stamp is made on the face of the check, and the terms of the certification are written into the stamped form.

If the drawer seeks and receives the certification, the drawer remains secondarily liable until final payment. However, if a holder seeks and receives the certification, the drawer and all prior indorsers are discharged from liability.

Unauthorized Signatures

Under UCC § 1-201(43), an unauthorized signature is one made without any authority, express or implied, and it includes a forgery. An unauthorized signature is wholly inoperative against the person whose name was signed unless that person later ratifies the signing. It cannot be used to impose liability on the purported signer. However, in some circumstances, an unauthorized and unratified signature is still binding on the purported signer. According to § 3-406, if a person contributes to the unauthorized signing through negligence, he or she will be held liable to any good-faith holder of the instrument.

Many businesses "sign" checks by means of a stamp. The business may leave the stamp and its checks in a place where they are easily reached by a nonauthorized person (most likely a thief). Such conduct on the part of the business is negligent, and the negligence may lead to the unauthorized "signing." In such circumstances, the business may not later assert the defense that the signing was unauthorized if the holder is a holder in good faith. Notice that the holder does not have to be a holder in due course; the fact that the holder is in good faith is sufficient. The negligence of the wronged party is the key: The wronged party must be negligent, and the negligence must cause the loss. Otherwise, the unauthorized signature cannot be used against the person whose name was signed.

Funds Transfers: Article 4A

Changes in banking laws, the growth of international business, and technology have affected the banking industry to a significant extent since the last quarter of the 20th century. The savings and loan industry crisis of the 1980s led to numerous changes in banking regulations. International trade frequently requires that large amounts of money be transferred from one nation to another quickly. Technology has reduced the need for personnel and made automated banking much simpler. Each of these changes has moved banking ahead, while many of the banking regulations have lagged behind. However, the distance between banking practice and banking regulation is narrowing.

The following case involves an alleged failure to transfer funds under a standing order for the bank to make funds transfers. After reading the case, decide whether you agree with the court's judgment, and then decide whether you believe the bank or the customer was more "right" in this situation.

24.3

TRUSTMARK INSURANCE CO. v. BANK ONE, ARIZONA, N.A.
48 P.3d 485; 2002 Ariz. App. LEXIS 91 (Ariz. App. 2002)

FACTS In February 1995 Trustmark Insurance Company opened a non-interest bearing account with Bank One, Arizona. The account was governed by Bank One's deposit account rules. At the same time Trustmark executed a wire transfer agreement with Bank One. In May 1995 Trustmark sent Bank One a letter regarding a second deposit account. In the instructions for this second account, Trustmark instructed Bank One to retain a minimum balance of $10,000 and to automatically make a wire transfer to Trustmark's interest-bearing account at Harris Bank any time the account balance in account two reached $110,000. This system was followed until August 1996, at which time Bank One automated its wire transfer functions and centralized its wire transfer department. Under the revised system Bank One required a new wire transfer agreement from each of its customers. Letters were sent to each of its customers. The letters informed the customers that uninterrupted wire transfer service could not be guaranteed absent the completion and submission of a new agreement. Trustmark claims that it never received the letter, and Trustmark did not submit a new wire transfer agreement form. In September 1996 the balance in Trustmark's second account reached $110,000 for the first time since July (before the new system went into effect). The balance in account two continued to grow, with no funds transferred until December 1997, by which time the balance was more that $19 million. In early 1998 Trustmark instructed Bank One to transfer all of its funds from account two to Harris Bank, and to then close the account. Following this, Trustmark sued Bank One, alleging a loss of more than $500,000 in lost interest on its funds due to Bank One's failure to make the wire transfers as agreed. According to Trustmark, Bank One had violated the Letter of Agreement and was liable for its failure to make the wire transfers under the provisions of Article 4A of the UCC. Bank One denied any liability, alleging that the Letter of Agreement was not a payment order, so that Article 4A did not apply. At trial the jury awarded Trustmark $573,197.02, plus prejudgment interest and attorneys' fees. Bank One appealed from this judgment.

ISSUE If a banking customer sends a bank a letter of instructions requesting wire transfers of funds upon future occurrences of a specified balance condition in the customer's account, does the letter of instructions constitute a "payment order" under Article 4A of the Uniform Commercial Code?

HOLDING No. As a matter of law, Trustmark does not have a claim under UCC Article 4A, because the Letter of Instructions is not an Article 4A "payment order."

REASONING Excerpts from the opinion of Judge Gemmill:

Bank One argues on appeal that Trustmark's judgment should be reversed as a matter of law because Article 4A of the UCC is not applicable. According to Bank One, the Letter of Instructions was not a "payment order" under Article 4A, and the trial court should not have sent this UCC claim to the jury. . . . Bank One challenges the trial court's submission of the UCC claim to the jury on the basis that the Letter of Instructions is not a "payment order" under Article 4A; therefore the UCC is not applicable, and this claim should have been dismissed as a matter of law. Whether the Letter of Instructions is a "payment order" is initially a question of law that we independently review. . . .

Technological developments in recent decades have enabled banks to transfer funds electronically, without physical delivery of paper instruments. Before Article 4A, no comprehensive body of law had defined the rights and obligations that arise from wire transfers. Article 4A was intended to provide a new and control-ling body of law for those wire transfers within its scope. "The drafters' aim was to achieve national uniformity, speed, efficiency, certainty, and finality in the funds transfer system." . . .

Because there are very few reported decisions—and none from Arizona—interpreting and applying the provisions of Article 4A defining its scope, we have considered primarily the language of the pertinent statutes, the purpose of Article 4A, and the comments of its drafters. In the Prefatory Note to Article 4A, the drafters discussed the funds transfers intended to be covered and several factors considered in the drafting process:

There are a number of characteristics of funds transfers covered by Article 4A that have influenced the drafting of the statute. The typical funds transfer involves a large amount of money. Multimillion dollar transactions are commonplace. The originator of the transfer and the beneficiary are typically sophisticated business or financial organizations. High speed is another predominant characteristic. Most funds transfers are completed on the same day, even in complex transactions in which there are several intermediary banks in the transmission chain. A funds transfer is a highly efficient substitute for payments made by the delivery of paper instruments. Another characteristic is extremely low cost. A transfer that involves many millions of dollars can be made for a price of a few dollars. Price does not normally vary very much or at all with the amount of the transfer. This system of pricing may not be feasible if the bank is exposed to very large liabilities in connection with the transaction. . . .

Article 4A applies only to "funds transfers" as defined in the statute. . . . A "funds transfer" is "the series of transactions, beginning with the originator's *payment order*, made for the purpose of making payment to the beneficiary of the order." . . . Accordingly, to fall within the scope of Article 4A, a transaction must begin with a "payment order."

A "payment order" is defined by the UCC, in pertinent part, as:

An instruction of a sender to a receiving bank, transmitted orally, electronically, or in writing, to pay, or to cause another bank to pay, a *fixed or determinable amount of money* to a beneficiary if:

(a) *The instruction does not state a condition to payment to the beneficiary other than time of payment.* . . .

A recent law review article explains:

By definition, an Article 4A payment order must be unconditional. Therefore, an important scope issue in determining whether Article 4A applies is whether the payment order in question is or is not conditional. . . .

Bank One argues that the Letter of Instructions was not a payment order, because the Letter was not for a "fixed or determinable amount of money" and imposed two conditions other than time of payment: that the account balance always remain $10,000 ("balance condition") and that transfers not occur until subsequent deposits have raised the balance to $110,000 or more ("deposit condition"). Trustmark argues that the conditions at issue were merely conditions regarding the time of payment—that the balance and deposit conditions essentially determined when transfers were to be made. Trustmark asserts that time of payment need not be set by a specific date, but may be set by events such as the bank's receipt of an incoming wire or deposit. However, the amounts to be transferred did not relate to incoming wires for the same amounts or even wires received on the same day of each month. Rather, Trustmark's agent made deposits sporadically and in varying amounts. Therefore, the conditions in the Letter of Instructions required Bank One to continuously monitor Trustmark's account balance to determine whether sufficient deposits had been made to enable the bank to make a transfer that satisfied both the deposit and balance conditions.

Neither party has cited, nor has our own research revealed, any reported decision addressing the precise issue presented: whether a letter of instructions from an account holder to its bank, requesting automatic wire transfers of funds in excess of a minimum balance whenever the total balance equals or exceeds a specified amount, constitutes a "payment order" governed by UCC Article 4A. We conclude that the Letter of Instructions was not a "payment order," because the Letter subjected Bank One to a condition to payment other than the time of payment.

Article 4A applies to discrete, mechanical transfers of funds. Comment 3 to UCC § 4A-104 . . . provides:

The function of banks in a funds transfer under Article 4A is comparable to their role in the collection and payment of checks in that it is essentially mechanical in nature. The low price and high speed that characterize funds transfers reflect this fact. Conditions to payment . . . other than time of payment impose responsibilities on [the] bank that go beyond those in Article 4A funds transfers. . . .

Bank One's obligation to make an ongoing inquiry as to Account Two's balance status removes the Letter of Instructions from the Article 4A definition of a "payment order." . . . Comment 3 to UCC § 4A-104. . . . Conditions other than time of payment "are anathema to Article 4A, which facilitates the low price, high speed, and mechanical nature of funds transfers." . . . Based on the language defining "payment order," the purpose of Article 4A, and the drafters' intent that payment orders be virtually unconditional, we conclude that requiring the bank to continually examine the account balance is a condition to payment other than time of payment. . . . We perceive a qualitative difference between a condition requiring daily monitoring of the account balance and an instruction to wire funds on a specific day. . . .

We reverse the judgment in favor of Trustmark on the UCC claim and vacate the award of attorneys' fees to Trustmark. We affirm the judgment in all other respects.

BUSINESS CONSIDERATIONS In this case Trustmark kept significant funds on deposit with Bank One and with Harris Bank. Should Trustmark have relied on Bank One to automatically transfer funds from an account it controlled to an account with another bank upon the occurrence of certain conditions? What should Trustmark have done differently here?

ETHICAL CONSIDERATIONS Is it ethical for a bank customer to expect the bank to do his or her account management? Is it ethical for a bank to deny liability when it fails to follow an agreement it has made with one of its customers, causing the customer a financial loss?

Bank customers have long had a need for a particular type of funds transfer, the wire transfer. However, this type of funds transfer has not been uniformly regulated until very recently. Now the UCC has developed Article 4A to provide uniform coverage in the area of funds transfers within the United States. As of July 1998, Article 4A had been adopted by all 50 states and the District of Columbia. Funds transfers are commonly used to provide a rapid movement of funds from one account to another without the use of a traditional negotiable instrument. A "funds transfer" is defined in § 4A-104 as follows:

the series of transactions, beginning with the originator's payment order, made for the purpose of making payment to the beneficiary of the order. The term includes any payment order issued by the originator's bank or an intermediary bank intended to carry out the originator's payment order. A funds transfer is com-

FUNDS TRANSFERS

The firm is currently concluding negotiations for a very large sale with a retail store that has locations throughout the southwest. The resulting contract should be for an amount in the high six figures. Carlos is willing to let the retailer pay for the order by check. Helen would prefer that the customer send either a cashier's check or a certified check. Mai has pointed out that, given the "time value" of money, the sooner the firm receives the funds, the better it will be. She thinks that the firm should insist on a wire transfer of the funds as soon as the retailer receives the goods. They all agree that the time value of money is important, and they like Mai's idea, but they want more information before they make a final decision. They have asked you for your opinion. What will you tell them?

BUSINESS CONSIDERATIONS What benefits accrue to a seller who receives payment by wire transfer? What disadvantages does the buyer who pays by wire transfer face? When should a business insist that it be paid by wire transfer rather than by negotiable instrument?

ETHICAL CONSIDERATIONS Is it ethical to ask a buyer to pay for goods by wire transfer upon receipt? Should the buyer be given some sort of discount because the seller will be receiving his or her funds so quickly, as compared with when the funds would be available if the buyer sent a negotiable instrument?

INTERNATIONAL CONSIDERATIONS Should businesses involved in international trade tend to use more funds transfers than negotiable instruments? Domestic funds transfers are governed by Article 4A. What governs international wire transfers?

---

pleted by acceptance by the beneficiary's bank of a payment order for the benefit of the beneficiary of the originator's payment order.

Note that the funds transfer is defined as a *series* of transactions. The person who is transferring the funds—the "originator"—places the funds transfer order with his or her bank. This bank—the "originator bank"—then transfers the funds to the next bank in line—an "intermediary

bank." This intermediary bank, in turn, will transfer the funds to the next bank, until ultimately the funds reach the "beneficiary bank." Once the funds reach the beneficiary bank, they are credited to the account of the beneficiary, completing the funds transfer. Each transaction is deemed to be only between the two parties directly involved. Thus, the transfer between the originating bank and intermediary bank one is a transaction between them, and the originator has no rights against the intermediary bank if something goes awry subsequently with a later transfer.

Section 4A-302 provides guidance for receiving banks in carrying out the funds transfer. If the sender of the funds transfer order specifies how the funds transfer is to be carried out, the receiving bank must follow these specifications. If no specifications are provided, the receiving bank is allowed to use any means that are reasonable under the circumstances, including first-class mail, if such a method is appropriate under the circumstances.

Finally, §4A-108 specifically excludes coverage by Article 4A in any area already governed by the Electronic Funds Transfer Act, as that Act may be amended from time to time. Thus, the UCC will provide state coverage for funds transfers but will defer to federal regulation of Electronic Funds Transfers (EFTs), which are discussed in the next section.

Funds Transfers: Electronic Funds Transfers

Recent technological advances have provided banking with a new method of doing business and with a new type of service. This new method of doing business is the electronic funds transfer (EFT), which allows for computerization of checking accounts and for faster (theoretically), more accurate banking transactions.

Electronic funds transfers are regulated by the Electronic Funds Transfer Act (15 U.S.C. 1693), which became effective in 1980. This statute provides the basic legal framework for EFTs, granting extensive authority to the Board of Governors of the Federal Reserve System. In addition, various agencies are granted enforcement power,[8] with special enforcement power given to the Federal Trade Commission for any areas not specifically reserved to the specialized authority of other named agencies. This method of financial dealing eventually may make the current checking or drafting account obsolete, or nearly so, due to the delays and expenses of handling checks or drafts when compared with electronic banking.

The purpose of the Electronic Funds Transfer Act is "to provide a basic framework establishing rights, liabilities, and responsibilities of participants in electronic fund transfer systems."[9] The primary objective of the statute is the provision of individual consumer rights in electronic funds transfers.

The Act defines an electronic fund transfer as "any transfer of funds, other than a transaction originated by check, draft, or similar paper instrument, which is initiated through an electronic terminal, telephonic instrument, or computer or magnetic tape so as to order, instruct, or authorize a financial institution to debit or credit an account."[10] It also requires any financial institution providing EFTs to its customers to provide those customers with periodic statements for each account that the customer may access through the use of an EFT. These periodic statements must be provided at least monthly for each monthly cycle in which an EFT occurred, or every three months, whichever is more frequent.[11]

Four methods for electronically transferring funds are recognized by the Act: POS transactions; ATM transactions; telephonic transactions; and preauthorized transactions, whether deposits or withdrawals.

Point of Sale (POS) Transactions

The first method is the point-of-sale (POS) transaction, involving the use of a POS terminal and a "debit" card. In a POS transaction, the customer presents the merchant with a debit card, the merchant imprints the card and has the customer sign, and the funds are transferred from the customer's account to the merchant's account. The transaction is similar in format to the use of a credit card, but the merchant should experience no delay in receiving the money from the sale. Unfortunately, the use of a POS transaction is often no faster or safer for the merchant than the use of a check. In most parts of the country, the POS transaction must be processed through a clearinghouse in the same manner as a check, making the transfer of funds to the merchant no faster than it would be with a check. In addition, the cost is slightly higher for a POS transaction than for a check when a clearinghouse is involved.

Debit/ATM Cards

A second, and more familiar, method is the use of automated teller machine (ATM) transfers. The bank customer inserts his or her card in the machine, enters his or her personal identification number (PIN), and selects a transaction. The customer can make a deposit, a withdrawal, a transfer from one account to another, a payment, or a number of other banking transactions.

Telephonic Transactions

If the bank is a participant in a network, the customer may be able to authorize payments to predetermined accounts by phone. Here, the customer calls the bank and, using the buttons on a touch-tone phone, can designate preselected "payees" who will be paid an amount determined by punching in the amount of the "electronic check" so that the funds are automatically transferred.

Preauthorized Transactions

Finally, there are preauthorized automatic payments and preauthorized direct deposits. In both cases, regular amounts are deducted from, or added to, the customer's account balance on designated dates to ensure that payment (or credit) is received without any worries about forgetting to send in the check or driving to the bank to make the deposit.

Rights and Duties with EFTs

In general, a consumer who uses EFTs has the same type of rights and duties as a consumer who has a checking or drafting account with a financial institution. For example, a customer can place a stop payment order on a preauthorized payment by notifying the bank orally or in writing at least three days prior to the date for preauthorized payment. A consumer can recover damages from a financial institution for failure to make EFT payments as instructed, provided the consumer has sufficient funds on deposit.

Numerous protections also exist for the consumer who is using EFTs. For example, consumer liability is limited in case of unauthorized use of an account, provided the consumer gives proper and timely notice to the bank. A consumer is expected to give the bank "proper and timely" notice of the loss or theft of his or her card or other means of access to his or her account in order to minimize liability. If the consumer gives such "proper and timely" notice, the consumer's liability is limited to the lesser of the amount of money or value accessed wrongfully or $50. "Proper and timely" notice is generally defined as notice given within two business days after the consumer learns of the loss or theft. If the consumer gives notice, but the notice is not "proper and timely," his or her liability is still somewhat limited under the statute. In this case liability is the lesser of $500 or the amount of unauthorized electronic funds transfers that occur between the time when the consumer should have given notice (two business days after discovery) and the date on which notice was actually given.

The bank has the burden of proof to establish either that the use was in fact authorized or that the customer did not give proper and/or timely notice.

As the public becomes more familiar and more comfortable with EFTs, the use of this form of money management will grow and develop. As that happens, the use of checks will begin to decline. The decline will be gradual at first, but over the next few decades we may do virtually all our banking electronically.

The Expedited Funds Availability Act

For years bank customers complained about the delays they experienced in gaining access to funds they had deposited. It was fairly common for a bank to impose a "waiting period" of up to 10 days after a check was deposited before the customer was allowed to use the funds. It was also not uncommon for a customer to issue checks that were dishonored by the bank even though the funds were, at least theoretically, available, simply because the check was presented to the bank during the "waiting period" before the customer could use the funds. In an effort to address this problem, Congress passed the Expedited Funds Availability Act[12] (EFAA) in 1988. This act provides federally mandated guidelines for when funds must be made available to the customer.

Under the provisions of the EFAA and Regulation CC,[13] its implementing regulations, there are specified time limits for when a customer can write a check against funds deposited with the bank and for when the customer can withdraw cash from funds deposited with the bank. The Act also takes into account *what* the customer deposited, *where* the deposit was made, and the location of the drawee bank, if the deposit was of a check acquired by the customer. There are also some exceptions written into the law for the treatment of new accounts and for those situations in which a customer has a history of issuing bad checks.

If the customer makes a deposit of cash, a cashier's check, a certified check, a government check, or a check drawn against the customer's bank, or receives a wire transfer, and the deposit is made with a teller, the customer can write checks against the amount deposited the next business day. If the deposit is made at one of the bank's ATMs the customer can write checks against the funds on the second business day after the deposit.

If the customer makes a deposit of a *local* check, but not a check drawn against the customer's bank, the customer can write checks for the first $100 the next business day.

The customer can then write checks for the balance of the check, up to $5,000, on the second business day. If the check is for more than $5,000, the customer cannot write checks on the balance over $5,000 until the *ninth* business day.

If the customer makes a deposit of a *nonlocal* check, once again the customer can write checks for the first $100 the next business day. However, since the check in not local, the customer must wait until the *fifth* business day to write checks for the balance of the check, up to $5,000. And, once again, if the check is for more than $5,000, the customer cannot write checks on the balance over $5,000 until the *ninth* business day.

If the customer would like to withdraw cash, rather than write a check, from the deposited funds, the rules are slightly different. The customer can withdraw up to $100 cash the next business day after the deposit. He or she can then withdraw up to $400 more on the same day that those funds would be available for covering checks, and the balance can be withdrawn in cash the day *after* the funds would be available for covering checks.

Check Truncation

Check truncation, the changing of a check into an electronic or digital image of the check, is about to become a reality. The reason behind this move is to speed up the flow of instruments through the system, although it should also provide significant savings for banks because it will reduce the expenses associated with storage of canceled items.

With check truncation, a drawer presents a check to the merchant payee as in a normal checking transaction. However, the merchant will then swipe the check, creating a machine-readable copy, a "substitute check," which will be processed. The original check is then returned to the drawer. The truncated check (the machine-readable or digital image) will then be transmitted electronically to the bank for processing.

The National Automated Clearing House Association (NACHA), the electronic payment association based in Herndon, Virginia, adopted its final rules on check truncation in October 2001. Among the reasons cited for making this change were that billers would get their money more quickly and more reliably, that automated clearinghouse transactions eliminate "float," and that most banks process automated clearinghouse debits before they process checks, making electronic items more likely to be honored. For more information on NACHA, and to see the Automated Clearing House rules on-line, see http://www.nacha.org/.

The Federal Reserve Board has proposed the Check Truncation Act to Congress. The draft version of this Act would make a substitute (truncated) check the legal equivalent of a paper check and thus make it subject to the provisions of Articles 3 and 4, if it:

1. contains an image that accurately represents all of the information on the front and the back of the original check as of the time the original check was truncated;

2. contains an MICR line that would permit the substitute check to be processed on standard check-sorting equipment;

3. conforms to industry standards for substitute checks; and

4. bears a legend that indicates that it is the legal equivalent of the original check.[14]

The Federal Reserve Board of Governors has a slide presentation addressing the Board's proposed Check Truncation Act online. You can view this slide presentation at http://www.clev.frb.org/market/Conf2001/PaymtSymp/Presentations/final%20Checktruncationact/sld001.htm.

Transferable Records

The Check Truncation Act has a good chance of being enacted by Congress in the near future, moving negotiable instruments into the electronic realm. Telechecks (discussed in Chapter 23), truncated checks, and the recently created "transferable records" point to the likelihood that more and more negotiable instruments will be transformed from their current tangible form to an electronic form or to a digital form.

The term "transferable record" was first used in the Uniform Electronic Transactions Act (UETA) and was then picked up in the Electronic Signatures in Global and National Commerce Act (E-SIGN). Simply stated, a transferable record is the electronic equivalent of a promissory note.[15]

A transferable record cannot be used unless the obligor (the "maker" if it were truly a promissory note) expressly agrees to execute a "negotiable instrument" in electronic form. A further restriction applies in that E-SIGN permits the use of a transferable record only if the obligation is secured by real property. The UETA, by contrast, refers to negotiable instruments and documents without imposing any limitations.

Given the recent growth of electronic transactions, the enactment of such statutes as UETA and E-SIGN, and the proposal of the Check Truncation Act, it is quite possible that transferable records are but the first step in another "revolution" in negotiable instrument law. This is an area of law that is worth watching.

Summary

The most frequently used negotiable instrument is the check. As a result, special attention must be paid to the bank-customer relationship. When a customer opens a checking account, a multirole relationship is created. The bank and the customer have a contract, they are involved in an agency relationship, they have a debtor-creditor relationship, and they are controlled by Article 4 of the UCC and a number of regulations promulgated by the Federal Reserve Board. In addition, a number of statutory enactments also affect the relationship.

Obviously, customers are obligated to obey the terms of the contract with the bank and are expected to exercise reasonable care. They are required to inspect their statements carefully and promptly for any irregularities, alterations, or unauthorized signings, and to notify the bank of any problems encountered with "reasonable promptness." They may also issue stop payment orders to the bank. Since the bank is the agent of its customers, it is obligated to obey such orders.

Banks are required to operate with ordinary care, and to abide by the terms of the contract with the customer. The bank must pay properly drawn checks if the customer has sufficient funds, must obey the lawful orders of the customer to "pay" or to "stop payment," and must act in good faith.

Certified checks and unauthorized signatures can present special problems. A certified check is one that has been accepted by the bank and then circulated through the normal channels of commerce. Unauthorized signings are sometimes caused by the negligence of the customer; in such a case, the bank is not liable for honoring the unauthorized signing.

Funds transfers are the "wave of the future" for banking and for businesses. There are two major areas of funds transfers: electronic funds transfers, governed by the Electronic Funds Transfer Act; and funds (wire) transfers, governed by Article 4A of the UCC. By using the capacity and speed of computers and by eliminating the paper required for traditional checking accounts, funds can be moved more quickly, more accurately, and more efficiently than is possible with checking accounts. This developmental area will continue to grow and spread over the next several years.

The Expedited Funds Availability Act regulates when banks must make funds available to customers. This law has reduced the time that a bank can "hold" funds before the customer can access the monies deposited. The Federal Reserve Board has proposed a new law, the Check Truncation Act, that is expected to greatly increase the speed and ease of handling checks. Check truncation will involve scanning a check and then replacing it with an electronic or digital "duplicate" that will be treated as the equivalent of the check. Transferable records, which are, for lack of a better term, electronic "promissory notes," have also been introduced. The use of transferable records and the potential for truncating checks should, in the near future, bring Articles 3 and 4 and the EFTs into much closer harmony.

Discussion Questions

1. Where do the terms and conditions of the contract between the bank and the customer originate? How many different sources are likely to affect this contract?

2. What is a "stop payment" order? Why must a bank obey a customer's order to "stop payment" on a check? What should a stop payment order include? Can a bank customer issue a "stop payment" order on a preauthorized payment—an EFT—periodically charged to the customer's account?

3. What is the bank's liability to a customer when the bank wrongfully dishonors one of the customer's instruments? What limitations are imposed on this liability?

4. James received his bank statement August 1. He examined the statement and discovered a forgery on August 14. He notified the bank of the forgery on September 3. A second forgery by the same person had been presented to the bank and honored by the bank on September 2. What are James's rights against the bank on the second forged check? Explain fully. Would James have better rights if he had informed the bank of the forgery on August 15? Why?

5. Bob issued a check to Carl. Carl negotiated it to Dave. Dave negotiated it to Edna. Edna went to the bank seeking certification of the check. The bank refused to certify the check for Edna. Has the bank dishonored the check? What are Edna's rights against each of the parties? Why?

6. What is an electronic funds transfer? What current methods can a customer use to transfer funds electronically? What advantages, if any, are provided by EFTs over payment by negotiable instrument?

7. What is required for a customer to place a stop payment order on a preauthorized charge, a type of electronic funds transfer? What liability does the bank face if it fails to honor this stop payment order? How does this compare with the liability of a bank that fails to honor a stop payment order on a check?

8. What is a wire transfer? How are wire transfers regulated under current U.S. law? Why are wire transfers treated differently than electronic funds transfers?

9. What is the Expedited Funds Availability Act and how does it affect the bank-customer relationship? If a customer deposits a $10,000 check drawn on a bank within the same region, when can the customer access the funds deposited? Would this access be different if the check were drawn against a bank from outside the same region as the depository bank?

10. What is "check truncation"? How might the proposed Check Truncation Act affect the bank-customer relationship? What effect, if any, would this act have on a customer's checking account and the related duties of the customer with regard to his or her checking account?

Case Problems and Writing Assignments

1. Brown was the bookkeeper for Reynolds Lumber. Part of Brown's job involved the depositing of checks received by the company into the corporate account. The checks were all indorsed "For Deposit Only." However, the bank permitted the customers to make a "Less Cash" notation on the deposit slip and receive a portion of the check total back in cash. Over the years between 1962 and 1974, Brown expropriated $75,000 by use of the "Less Cash" notation on the deposit slips she took to the bank. When these expropriations were discovered, Reynolds Lumber sued the bank to recover the funds Brown had embezzled. According to Reynolds Lumber, the bank had no authority to permit the bookkeeper to take cash back on checks indorsed "For Deposit Only," so the bank had breached its duty to the customer by allowing this practice. The bank countered that it allowed all its customers this right and that it was a standard banking practice. Which side had the more persuasive argument? Who should have prevailed in this case? [See *J. W. Reynolds Lumber Co. v. Smackover State Bank*, 836 S.W.2d 853 (Ark. 1992).]

2. The checking account Saboya maintained with Banco Santander reflected a zero balance on November 18, 1985, when Saboya simultaneously deposited $100 cash and a counterfeit cashier's check for $26,250. Two days later, Sainz presented a check in the amount of $16,100, payable to Sainz and drawn by Saboya. Sainz was informed that the check was good and could be cashed, but Sainz requested a cashier's check instead. Sainz was then given a cashier's check by Banco Santander in exchange for the check drawn by Saboya. Sainz deposited the cashier's check in the Banco Guipuzcoano, in Spain, receiving

credit for 2,558,870 pesetas. On the same day, Sainz used the proceeds of the cashier's check and some other funds to purchase a 4 million peseta certificate of deposit.

When Banco Santander learned that the cashier's check deposited by Saboya was counterfeit, it stopped payment on the cashier's check it had issued to Sainz. As a result, Banco Guipuzcoano canceled the CD it had issued to Sainz, seized the original amount of the cashier's check (2,558,870 pesetas) from Sainz, and issued a new certificate of deposit for the 1,441,130 peseta difference. Sainz then sued Banco Santander for the losses he suffered due to the alleged wrongful dishonor of the cashier's check he had purchased from the bank. Who should prevail in this case? If Sainz prevails, should he be entitled to compensatory and consequential damages? [See *Sainz Gonzalez v. Banco de Santander-Puerto Rico*, 932 F.2d 999 (1st Cir. 1991).]

3. Duchow's Marine, Inc., financed its inventory of boats with a loan from General Electric Capital Corporation (GECC), which took a security interest in the boats and the proceeds from their sale. The security interest was perfected under Wisconsin law. Duchow's Marine and its owner Roger Duchow (collectively Duchow) promised to deposit proceeds into an account from which they could be disbursed only on GECC's signature. The name on this account at Central Bank was "Duchow Marine, Inc. GE Escrow Account" (the blocked account). Duchow maintained a separate account at Central Bank for revenues from other sources (the regular account). In November 1990, Duchow sold a yacht to Gray Eagle, Inc., and directed the customer to remit $215,370 of the purchase price to the regular account. By issuing this instruction, Duchow set out to defraud GECC.

Gray Eagle instructed its bank to make a wire transfer, giving it the number of Duchow's regular account. Gray Eagle's bank, the "originator's bank," following the convention of Article 4A, asked Banker's Bank of Madison, Wisconsin, to make the transfer on its behalf. The originator's bank performed correctly. As an intermediary bank, Banker's Bank should have relayed the payment order exactly. It didn't. Banker's Bank made the transfer by crediting Central Bank's account at Banker's Bank, but it "bobtailed" the instructions. Banker's Bank told Central Bank (which the UCC calls the "beneficiary's bank") that the credit was for Duchow's benefit. That's all; the payment order omitted account identification. A clerk at Central Bank routed the funds to the first account she found bearing Duchow's name: the blocked account. This credit was made on November 23, 1990. Entirely by chance, Duchow's fraudulent scheme had been foiled. But not for long. Duchow, thinking the funds were in the regular account, promptly wrote a check in an effort to spirit them away. The check appeared on the overdrawn-accounts list of November 29. When contacted, Roger Duchow asserted that the money belonged in the regular account. Central Bank inquired of Banker's Bank, which on November 30 relayed the full payment order, including the number of Duchow's regular account. Without notifying GECC, Central Bank then reversed

the credit to the blocked account, credited Duchow's regular account, and paid the check.

When it discovered what had happened, GECC filed an action seeking to hold Central Bank liable for conversion of its funds. Central Bank impleaded Duchow, but no one believed that he or his firm was good for the money; Duchow did not participate in this case. The parties agreed that Wisconsin supplies the applicable law. Did Central Bank convert funds that properly should have been subject to the control of GECC? What steps should a beneficiary's bank take in a wire transfer when there is a report that the funds were erroneously credited to the wrong account, and that report is more than one week after the funds were originally received by the beneficiary's bank? Is it fair to let the intermediary bank off the hook when its error (failing to relay the entire wire transfer order) was a significant factor in the resulting misallocation of the funds? Should there be some allocation of the loss to the intermediary on ethical grounds? [See *General Electric Capital Corporation v. Central Bank*, 49 F.3d 280 (7th Cir. 1995).]

4. MRF Resources, Ltd. maintained a checking account with Merchant's Bank, as did Galit Diamond, Inc. On May 20, 1993, the bank certified a check drawn by MRF, payable to Galit Diamond in the amount of $58,958. Upon receipt of the check, Galit presented it to Merchant's for payment, and the bank posted the funds to Galit's account on that same day. Shortly thereafter, MRF's president informed Merchant's that the certified check was forged. As a result, the bank placed a hold on Galit's account. Meanwhile, on June 1, Galit presented Merchant's with a funds transfer application accompanied by a check drawn on its Merchant's account in the amount of $30,030. The check was intended to cover a funds transfer for $30,000 and the bank's fee for that service. The application directed a credit to the Israeli bank account of Ilan Gertler, the supplier of approximately 60 percent of Galit's diamond inventory. Without rejecting the application or informing Galit that a hold had been placed on its account, Merchant's held onto the funds transfer application and check. Gertler eventually received the funds, but a week later than expected. Because the late transfer tainted Galit's creditworthiness, Gertler severed its business relationship with Galit, greatly damaging Galit's ability to conduct its business profitably. Galit alleged that Merchant's Bank was liable in damages for wrongfully freezing its account and claimed that Merchant's handling of the certified check violated various provisions of Article 3 of the Uniform Commercial Code, giving rise to liability under Article 4. Merchant's Bank denied any liability. According to Merchant's Bank, the transaction is governed completely by Article 4A, and Article 4A does not make allowance for consequential damages. Galit denied that Article 4A provides exclusive coverage, pointing out that the problem arose from the handling of a cashier's check and thus must be decided under all three articles—3, 4, and 4A. How should this case be decided? What do you think is the key factor in deciding this case? [See "Diamond Dealer Denied Consequential Damages Allegedly Sustained When Bank Delayed Execu-

tion of Funds Transfer," *New York Law Publishing Company, New York Law Journal,* http://www.lexis-nexis.com (October 20, 1997).]

5. BUSINESS APPLICATION CASE In the early 1980s, Robert J. Beshara met Betty J. Mitchell, an assistant cashier with Southern National Bank in Tulsa, Oklahoma. Shortly thereafter, Beshara and Mitchell began a social relationship. In August of 1986, Beshara opened a checking account with Southern National. As a matter of convenience, Beshara had Mitchell conduct virtually all of his banking business by having her make deposits to and withdrawals from his checking account at the bank. However, a few days after he opened his checking account with Southern National, Mitchell, without Beshara's authorization or his knowledge, changed the address on his account to her home address in Sand Springs and added her name as an authorized signer on the account. Subsequently, she began embezzling money from the account. When Beshara's monthly statements were mailed to Mitchell's residence, she altered them so that they would conform with his actual transactions in the account and sent him the false statements. Mitchell periodically embezzled money from Beshara's checking account until late December of 1988, when another employee of Southern National, while conducting a routine internal audit, discovered a large transfer of money from Beshara's account into another account.

On January 9, 1989, with Beshara's checking account showing a balance of $32,425.37, Southern National placed a hold on the account to conduct an internal audit to determine the correct account balance. On March 29, 1989, Beshara's attorney wrote the bank, demanding that Beshara's checking account be released from the hold and that the proper account balance be restored. The bank insisted that it had not completed its audit. In April 1989, Beshara informed the bank that he needed some of his money to pay his income taxes, which were due. The bank offered to loan Beshara the money to pay his taxes but Beshara refused the offer. Five months after Southern National first placed its hold on Beshara's checking account, Beshara wrote two checks against the account. According to Beshara, his attorney advised him to write the checks to determine if the bank continued to hold his checking account and, if so, to provide him with written evidence that the bank was doing so. Southern National refused to honor the checks, marked them "refer to maker," and returned them to their respective payees. On August 10, 1989, Southern National mailed a proof of loss claim to its insurance company requesting reimbursement under a fidelity bond for the losses it suffered as a result of Mitchell's embezzlement. The Hartford Insurance Company issued Southern National three checks for a total of $200,897.64 for reimbursement of its losses as a result of Mitchell's embezzlements . . . nearly two years before it finally restored the funds in Beshara's account.

Beshara sued the bank on August 17, 1989. Seeking actual and punitive damages, Beshara asserted that the bank acted in bad faith, wrongfully refused to honor the checks he wrote, and converted his money. The trial court granted summary judg-

ment in favor of the bank, and Beshara appealed. Was the bank guilty of wrongfully dishonoring the checks Beshara wrote? Was the bank guilty of conversion for the manner in which it handled this account? [See *Beshara v. Southern National Bank,* 928 P.2d 280 (Okla. 1996).]

6. ETHICAL APPLICATION CASE On or before June 7, 1990, Sakoff wrote a check for $98,581.40 on its account at Northern Trust, payable to the order of Zaragoza. Zaragoza deposited the Sakoff check in its account at Bank One on June 7, 1990. Bank One sent the Sakoff check to Northern Trust for payment. On June 13, 1990, it was returned to Bank One, because the funds in Sakoff's account were insufficient to cover the amount of the Sakoff check. Dykstra, a Bank One employee, telephoned Northern Trust upon receiving the returned Sakoff check on June 13 and was told that Sakoff's account did contain sufficient funds to cover the check. On the same day, Dykstra drove to Northern Trust's offices and exchanged the Sakoff check for a Northern Trust cashier's check for $98,581.40. When Bank One sent the cashier's check through the Federal Reserve Bank to Northern Trust for payment, however, Northern Trust refused to honor *this* check.

The reasons for Northern Trust's refusal to pay relate to another check drawn on Zaragoza's account at Bank One, for $103,200, which Zaragoza presumably transferred to Sakoff at about the same time Zaragoza received the Sakoff check for $98,581.40. At some point before June 12, 1990, Sakoff deposited Zaragoza's check into Sakoff's account at Northern Trust. Northern Trust then sent the Zaragoza check to Bank One for collection. Bank One received the check on June 12 but, on June 13, issued notice to Northern Trust, through the Federal Reserve Bank, that it was dishonoring the Zaragoza check, because of insufficient funds in Zaragoza's account. This notice did not reach Northern Trust until after Dykstra had obtained the cashier's check. As a result of Bank One's rejection of the Sakoff check, the funds in Sakoff's account were insufficient to cover the Sakoff check for which Northern Trust had issued its cashier's check.

Could Northern Trust dishonor the cashier's check that it had issued to Bank One? Even if Northern Trust could legally dishonor the cashier's check, would it be ethical for it to do so? What ethical issues are raised by a bank's attempt to dishonor one of the cashier's checks it has issued? [See *Bank One, Merrillville v. Northern Trust Bank/Dupage,* 775 F. Supp. 266 (N.D. Ill. 1991).]

7. CRITICAL THINKING CASE On December 22, 1994, Grain Traders initiated a funds transfer to effectuate the payment of $310,000 to Kraemer. The funds transfer was designed to move money from Grain Traders to Kraemer in one day. Grain Traders issued the payment order to its bank, Banco de Credito Nacional ("BCN"). The funds transfer was to proceed as follows: (1) Grain Traders's account at BCN was to be debited $310,000; (2) the $310,000 was then to be "transferred" to Banque De Credit Et Investissement Ltd. ("BCI") at Citibank by way of a debit to BCN's Citibank account and a corresponding credit in that

amount to BCI's Citibank account; (3) the $310,000 was in turn to be "transferred" from BCI to Banco Extrader, S.A. ("Extrader") by way of an unspecified transaction between BCI and Extrader; and (4) the $310,000 was finally to be transferred to Kraemer by way of a credit to his account at Extrader.

After Grain Traders issued the payment order to BCN, the funds transfer initially proceeded as expected. BCN's account at Citibank was debited $310,000 and BCI's account at Citibank was credited $310,000. At the same time, BCN sent instructions to Citibank, directing Citibank to instruct BCI to instruct Extrader to credit $310,000 to Kraemer. Citibank in turn sent instructions to BCI on the same day, notifying BCI that Citibank had credited its account with $310,000 and instructing BCI to instruct Extrader to credit this amount to Kraemer. Either just before or just after BCI's account at Citibank was credited with the $310,000, however, the BCI account was placed by Citibank on "hold for funds" status. The "hold for funds" status, which was put into place because BCI's account with Citibank was overdrawn by more than $12 million, preventing BCI from making any further withdrawals from the account. Kraemer apparently never received a credit to his Extrader account for the $310,000. Kraemer's affidavit, submitted by Grain Traders, states that on December 28, 1994, just six days after the attempted funds transfer, the government of Argentina ordered Extrader to suspend payments and that Extrader later became insolvent. Likewise, BCI, a Bahamian bank, ceased making payments in January 1995; supervisory authorities in the Bahamas closed it on July 31, 1995. Grain Traders commenced a cause of action against Citibank in November 1995.

Was Citibank liable to Grain Traders for the failure of the funds transfer? What other risks might a business face when it makes a funds transfer under the provisions of Article 4A? Are those other risks greater or less if the transfer is international and is not governed by Article 4A? [See *Grain Traders, Inc. v. Citibank, N.A.*, 960 F. Supp. 784 (S.D.N.Y. 1997).]

8. **YOU BE THE JUDGE** Maria Johnson was a depositor at Republic National Bank. In March 1989, she opened a checking account with the bank by depositing $59,000. From May through July she made a series of cash withdrawals from her account at the bank, eventually depleting the account balance. Unbeknownst to the bank, during this same time period Ms. Johnson's landlord was attempting to have the Department of Health and Rehabilitative Services take action to determine her competency. No action was accomplished during that period, but Ms. Johnson was adjudged incompetent by reason of organic mental syndrome in September 1989. She was 76 years of age at the time of the hearing. The guardian appointed for Ms. Johnson attempted to locate the money she had withdrawn but was unable to ascertain what had happened to it. The guardian then filed suit against the bank to recover the money, alleging that there were "red flags" that should have alerted the bank to the condition of its customer, and that the bank should have taken steps to protect Ms. Johnson. This case has been filed in *your* court. How will *you* rule? In your opinion, does a bank have an obligation—legally or ethically—to "protect" its customers even though those customers have not been declared incompetent at the time of the transactions in question? [See *Republic Nat'l Bank of Miami v. Johnson*, 622 So. 2d 1015 (Fla. App. 1993).]

Notes

1. UCC § 1-106.
2. UCC § 4-401(c).
3. UCC § 4-406(f).
4. UCC § 4-406(e).
5. UCC § 4-111.
6. UCC § 4-404.
7. UCC § 3-409(d).
8. Section 1693o(a).
9. Section 1693(b).
10. Section 1693a(6).
11. Section 1693d(c).
12. 12 U.S.C.A. §§ 4000 et seq.
13. 12 C.F.R. Part 229.
14. Scott A. Anenberg, "FRB Proposes Check Truncation Act," *Electronic Banking Law and Commerce* (Glasser LegalWorks, February 2002): 22.
15. Jane K. Winn, "What Is a 'Transferable Record,' and Who Cares?" *BNA Electronic Commerce & Law Report* (October 25, 2000): 1060.

PART 6

Debtor-Creditor Relations

The use of credit is integral to the U.S. economy. People purchase homes on credit; they purchase automobiles on credit; they purchase major appliances on credit; and they purchase a number of other, less expensive or less valuable items on credit. In addition, businesses often use credit to obtain equipment, raw materials, and inventory. Such widespread use of credit will, on occasion, cause problems for the creditor, as well as presenting a number of concerns to the debtor who may not be able to pay for the credit as originally scheduled or intended.

Secured transactions are used to protect some credit by affording a hedge against losses if or when the debtor defaults on the contract. Secured transactions give the creditor access to the collateral used as security so as to minimize the potential losses that arise when the debtor fails to repay in a timely manner the credit extended to that debtor. The law of secured transactions establishes the requirements for creating the security interest (attachment) and for perfecting the security interest. The law also provides priorities among conflicting creditor claims and sets out a structured method for enforcing the rights of competing creditors in the collateral of the debtor.

Many different types of credit are widely used in the United States, especially by consumers. Collateralized loans of various sorts, whether secured transactions or of another form, signature loans, and credit card transactions are common forms of consumer credit transactions. There are a number of laws designed to provide consumer protections in credit transactions and guidance for the creditors who deal in this area.

Bankruptcy law is intended to give "honest debtors" a fresh start by allowing said honest debtors to eliminate a number of their debts under the appropriate circumstances. The federal bankruptcy laws protect debtors who encounter financial problems beyond their control or their ability to repay, while also seeking to protect the interests of the creditors to a significant extent. There are bankruptcy protections for honest individual debtors and for honest business debtors.

CHAPTER 25

Secured Transactions: Attachment and Perfection

AGENDA

NRW NRW entered the "location device" market at a very opportune time, and it has enjoyed moderate success. However, in order to expand the business and to take advantage of the firm's potential for growth, the business may at times need to borrow money. The principals would like to know how they can borrow money on the most favorable terms available and what sorts of collateral they can use to obtain those terms. They also want to know what granting a security interest in assets they own means to them and to their other creditors.

The firm may also be asked to extend credit to some of its customers. What should NRW expect from its customers to whom it extends credit? How can the firm best protect its interests if it agrees to extend credit? What rights might the firm gain if it retains a security interest in any credit sales?

These and similar questions will arise as you study this chapter. Be prepared! You never know when the firm or one of its members will seek your advice.

The Need for Security

According to an old song, "love makes the world go round." While this may be true, love does not provide much help in the business environment. Indeed, from a business perspective, *credit* may be what makes the *business* world go round. Creditors extend credit with the expectation that they will be repaid, with interest. Generally, the interest rate charged will, to some extent, reflect the risk the creditor believes he or she is assuming. The greater the risk assumed by the creditor, the higher the cost of the credit demanded of the debtor. Debtors realize that they will be expected to pay for the use of credit, but they would prefer to receive as much credit as they need while paying as little for that credit as possible.

Security interests in general, and secured transactions in particular, can be used to help both parties in such credit situations. The creditor is given "security" in the form of a claim against assets of the debtor, thus reducing the risk faced by the creditor. With this lowered risk, the creditor is willing to extend credit to the debtor at a lower cost. The debtor, in turn, is given credit at a lower cost without much, if any, additional risk. Admittedly, the debtor has granted the creditor rights against one or more assets of the debtor in the event that the debtor defaults, but the creditor would have rights against the debtor in the event of a default with or without any security interest.

There are numerous types of security interests that can be used. Many homeowners acquire a mortgage loan to purchase their homes, granting the lender a security interest against the home and the property as security for the loan. Many automobile loans involve a retention by the lender of a lien against the title of the automobile. Some lenders want to take physical possession of the securing asset until such time as the loan is repaid, a method referred to at common law as a *pledge*. In this chapter we will address secured transactions as they are defined—and restricted—by Article 9 of the UCC. This article has recently been amended, and the amendments were significant. The revised Article 9 went into effect January 1, 2001, in most states.

You can see the revised Article 9 and the Official Comments to the article at www.law.cornell.edu/topics/secured_transactions.html.

Credit Financing and Article 9

The UCC, including the original Article 9, was originally put forward in 1951. This original version was basically a compilation of many of the laws and interpretations of secured transactions that were then in existence. Since then Article 9 has been amended several times. The 1962 revision made substantial changes to the law in this area, and the 1972 official text of Article 9 differed substantially from the 1962 official text. While most of the states had adopted the 1972 version of Article 9, some states were still following the 1962 rules. Then in 1999 the NCCUSL completed its far-reaching revision of Article 9 and presented it to the states for consideration and adoption. The reaction was surprising. The states quickly adopted this latest revision, and by January 1, 2001, the newly revised Article 9 was in effect in every state.

The revisions to Article 9 are significant, and while they are meant to simplify the treatment of secured transactions, they require a period of adjustment for businesspeople—and for their attorneys. Among other things, this newest version of Article 9, now simply called "Secured Transactions," expands the scope of property available for secured transactions. For example, the revision permits creditors to create original security interests in deposit accounts and in software that is embedded in goods. Moreover, revised Article 9 has eliminated the need for the multiple filings required by the 1962 and 1972 versions of the Code. Instead, under the revision, creditors will need to file only in the state where the debtor is located. Other than fixture filings, the creditor need only file centrally, not locally. This change replaces the earlier mixed system of centralized and local filings. This new provision also clarifies the place for filing if the debtor is an international entity or individual. Again, the drafters' intent focuses on facilitating such credit arrangements. Revised Article 9 also permits electronic filings, thus making the filing process potentially faster and easier for the creditor. The revision also revamps many of the current rules on priorities when competing creditors assert claims as to certain classes of collateral.

We have already seen that a commercial transaction in one of its simplest forms may involve a sale of goods in which the buyer pays cash and takes possession of the goods. Alternatively, the buyer may use a check or draft to pay for the goods or services. The customer may even use a credit card or a debit card. Each of these methods is used regularly, and each of them has the advantage of simplicity and ease. In this chapter, we examine another method of completing a commercial transaction: The buyer obtains credit from the seller, giving the seller a *security interest* in some assets of the buyer as collateral for the credit extended. Such transactions are frequently governed by UCC Article 9, "Secured Transactions."

The use of secured transactions is very common in business, so an understanding of the material is important to most businesspeople. It is not unusual to have a manufacturer who is a secured creditor in a number of transactions, while simultaneously occupying the role of debtor for one or more credit transactions in which he or she purchased equipment or raw materials. This manufacturer is in the position of having one or more security interests in his or her role as creditor, while also being subject to one or more security interests in his or her role as debtor.

To illustrate how a secured transaction may be used, assume that Bart Brown has opened a new restaurant and he needs to purchase a freezer and a cash register for his new business. He has enough cash on hand to make a substantial down payment toward both of these assets, but he cannot afford to pay the full price for either of them at this time. In this situation, he may be able to enter into a secured transaction with the sellers. For example, he may pay part of the sale price in cash, financing the balance of the price with the sellers. Bart will then receive possession of the items in exchange for giving each of the sellers of the goods a security interest in the equipment being sold. (Such a transaction is called a *purchase-money security interest.*) Using such a security interest "secures" (or ensures) payment by the buyer so that if Bart does not pay one of the sellers, that seller will have a claim against the goods and can repossess those goods in partial satisfaction of the debt owed by Bart. The creditors in this example could also have taken a security interest in assets other than the equipment they were selling to Bart, or they could have taken a security interest in other assets along with a claim against the equipment. Such decisions are left to the creditor and the debtor.

Thus, a secured transaction frequently allows buyers to receive goods sooner than if they had been forced to pay cash, while permitting the creditors (often the sellers, but other creditors may be involved) to protect themselves by retaining the right of repossession of the collateral in the event of a buyer's nonpayment. As we shall see, to ensure that they will have first rights to the equipment (or other collateral) in the event of Bart's default, these creditors must comply with the Article 9 rules relating to attachment, perfection, and priorities. These concepts are developed further in this chapter and in Chapter 26.

The terminology used in Article 9 is fairly specific, and it is important to use these terms correctly in any discussion of secured transactions. Applying this terminology to our example, the two seller-creditors are characterized as the *secured parties* ("a lender, seller, or other person in whose favor there is a security interest, including a person to whom accounts or chattel paper have been sold").[1] Bart, of course, is the *debtor* ("the person who owes payment or other performance of the obligation secured, whether or not he owns or has rights in the collateral, and includes the

seller of accounts or chattel paper").[2] Bart and the seller presumably have entered into a *security agreement* ("the agreement which creates or provides for a security interest").[3] The freezer and cash register constitute *collateral* ("the property subject to a security interest").[4] Article 9's application is very broad: It may cover relatively simple business transactions like the one we have described, or it may extend to more complex forms of business financing, such as accounts receivable financing.

Scope of Article 9

With the revision to Article 9, there was also a change in the scope of the article's coverage. The newly defined scope can be found in § 9-109. This section provides the following definition.

§ 9-109. Scope.

(a) [**General scope of article.**] *Except as otherwise provided in subsections (c) and (d), this article applies to:*

(1) *a transaction, regardless of its form, that creates a security interest in personal property or fixtures by contract;*

(2) *an agricultural lien;*

(3) *a sale of accounts, chattel paper, payment intangibles, or promissory notes;*

(4) *a consignment;*

(5) *a security interest arising under Section 2-401, 2-505, 2-711(3), or 2A-508(5), as provided in Section 9-110; and*

(6) *a security interest arising under Section 4-210 or 5-118.*

The provisions set out in (a)(5) refer to security interests involved in a sale or lease of goods, and allow the creditor to retain a security interest in the goods until such time as the debtor acquires possession of the goods without requiring the creditor to file or otherwise act to perfect his or her interest. The provisions set out in (a)(6) refer to security interests by a bank (§ 4-210) or the issuer of a letter of credit (§ 5-118), to the extent that the bank or the issuer has given value for the instrument or for the letter of credit, without regard to the "normal" rules for creating a security interest otherwise set out in Article 9. These are special rules more fully defining the scope of the article.

Interestingly, the definition of a *security interest,* the key component of the scope of Article 9 is found in UCC § 1-201 (37). According to this definition, a *security interest* means "an interest in personal property or fixtures which secures payment or performance of an obligation. The term also includes any interest of a consignor and a buyer of accounts, chattel paper, a payment intangible, or a promissory note in a transaction that is subject to Article 9." This definition goes on to define several things that are *not* security interests:

• the special property interests of a buyer of goods upon identification of the goods to the contract; or

• the rights of a seller or lessor of goods under Articles 2 or 2A to retain or acquire possession of the goods.

However, in each case a security interest can be acquired, provided the party seeking the interest complies with the terms of Article 9. This section also states that the retention or reservation of title by a seller of goods notwithstanding shipment or delivery to the buyer is limited in effect to the reservation of a security interest in those goods.

The personal property or collateral that will be subject to a security interest takes many forms. Moreover, the Code categorizes collateral according to either (1) the nature of the collateral or (2) its use. Thus, *documents* (warehouse receipts, bills of lading, and other documents of title); *instruments* (drafts, certificates of deposit, stocks, and bonds); *proceeds* (whatever is received upon the sale, exchange, collection, or other disposition of collateral or proceeds); and the three kinds of collateral mentioned earlier—*accounts, chattel paper,* and *general intangibles*—represent the types of collateral the Code classifies primarily on the basis of their nature.

In the following case a patent had been used as collateral, and there was a controversy over the correct place in which to perfect the security interest. Notice how the court balances the interests of the parties, and also how the court addresses the conflict between federal and state law.

25.1

IN RE: CYBERNETIC SERVICES, INC.
252 F.3d 1039, 2001 U.S. App. LEXIS 11750 (9th Cir. 2001

FACTS Matsco, Inc., and Matsco Financial Corporation (Petitioners) have a security interest in a patent developed by Cybernetic Services, Inc. (Debtor). The patent is for a data recorder that is designed to capture data from a video signal regardless of the horizontal line in which the data is located. Petitioners' security interest in the patent was "properly prepared, executed by the Debtor and timely filed with the Secretary of State of the State of California," in accordance with the California Commercial Code. Petitioners did not record their interest with the PTO.

After Petitioners had recorded their security interest with the State of California, certain creditors filed an involuntary Chapter 7 petition against Debtor, and an order of relief was granted. The primary asset of Debtor's estate is the patent. Petitioners then filed a motion for relief from the automatic stay so that they could foreclose on their interest in the patent. The bankruptcy Trustee opposed the motion, arguing that Petitioners had failed to perfect their interest because they did not record it with the PTO.

The bankruptcy court ruled that Petitioners had properly perfected their security interest in the patent by following the provisions of Article 9. Furthermore, the court reasoned, because Petitioners had perfected their security interest before the filing of the bankruptcy petition, Petitioners had priority over the

Trustee's claim in the patent and deserved relief from the stay. Accordingly, the bankruptcy court granted Petitioners' motion. The Bankruptcy Appellate Panel affirmed.

Moldo, the Trustee, then filed this timely appeal.

ISSUE Does the Patent Act or Article 9 of the UCC require the holder of a security interest in a patent to record that interest with the federal Patent and Trademark Office in order to perfect the interest?

HOLDING No. Neither the Patent Act nor Article 9 of the UCC so requires.

REASONING Excerpts from the opinion of Circuit Judge Graber:

As is often true in the field of intellectual property, we must apply an antiquated statute in a modern context. Article 9 of the UCC, as adopted in California, governs the method for perfecting a security interest in personal property. Article 9 applies to "general intangibles," a term that includes intellectual property. . . . § 9-106. The parties do not dispute that Petitioners complied with Article 9's general filing requirements and, in the case of most types of property, would have priority over a subsequent lien creditor. The narrower question in this case is whether Petitioners' actions were sufficient to perfect their interest when the "general intangible" to which the lien attached is a patent. The parties also do not dispute that, if Petitioners were required to file notice of their security interest in the patent with the PTO, then the Trustee, as a hypothetical lien creditor under 11 U.S.C. § 544(a)(1), has a superior right to the patent.

The Trustee makes two arguments. First, the Trustee contends that the Patent Act preempts Article 9's filing requirements. Second, the Trustee argues that Article 9 itself provides that a security interest in a patent can be perfected only by filing it with the PTO. We discuss each argument in turn. . . .

As noted, the Patent Act's recording provision provides that an "assignment, grant or conveyance shall be void as against any subsequent purchaser or mortgagee for a valuable consideration, without notice, unless it is recorded in the [PTO]." . . . In order to determine whether Congress intended for parties to record with the PTO the type of interest that is at issue in this case, we must give the words of the statute the meaning that they had in 1870, the year in which the current version of § 261 was enacted. . . .

The historical meanings of the terms "assignment, grant or conveyance" all involved the transfer of an ownership interest. A patent "assignment" referred to a transaction that transferred specific rights in the patent, all involving the patent's title. . . .

A "grant," historically, also referred to a transfer of an ownership interest in a patent, but only as to a specific geographic area. . . .

Although older cases defining the term "conveyance" in the context of intangible property are sparse, and its historic meaning tended to vary, the common contemporaneous definition was "to transfer the legal title . . . from the present owner to another." . . .

That Congress intended to incorporate the common, contemporaneous meanings of the words "assignment," "grant," and "conveyance" into the Patent Act's recording provision can be seen when § 261 is examined in its entirety. . . . By using the unambiguous words "ownership; assignment," Congress must have intended to introduce the subject that was to follow: the ownership of patents and the assignment thereof. . . .

In summary, the statute's text, context, and structure, when read in the light of Supreme Court precedent, compel the conclusion that a security interest in a patent that does not involve a transfer of the rights of ownership is a "mere license" and is not an "assignment, grant or conveyance" within the meaning of 35 U.S.C. § 261. And because § 261 provides that only an "assignment,

grant or conveyance shall be void" as against subsequent purchasers and mortgagees, only transfers of ownership interests need to be recorded with the PTO. . . .

In the present case, the parties do not dispute that the transaction that gave Petitioners their interest in the patent did not involve a transfer of an ownership interest in the patent. Petitioners held a "mere license," which did not have to be recorded with the PTO. . . .

That the Patent Act refers to securing a patent through a "mortgage" but not through a "pledge" is significant, for both were common methods of using a patent as collateral. . . . It seems then, that by using the term "mortgagee," but not "lien" or "pledge," Congress intended in 1870 for the Patent Act's recording provision to protect only those who obtained title to a patent. . . .

In summary, the historical definitions of the terms" purchaser or mortgagee," taken in context and read in the light of Supreme Court precedent, establish that Congress was concerned only with providing constructive notice to subsequent parties who take an ownership interest in the patent in question. . . .

The Trustee is not a subsequent "mortgagee," as that term is used in 35 U.S.C. § 261, because the holder of a patent mortgage holds title to the patent itself. . . . Instead, the Trustee is a hypothetical lien creditor. The Patent Act does not require parties to record documents in order to provide constructive notice to subsequent lien creditors who do not hold title to the patent.

The Trustee argues that requiring lien creditors to record their interests with the PTO is in line with the general policy behind recording statutes. It may be, as the Trustee argues, that a national system of filing security interests is more efficient and effective than a state-by-state system. However, there is no statutory hook upon which to hang the Trustee's policy arguments. Moreover, we are not concerned with the policy behind recording statutes generally but, rather, with the policy behind 35 U.S.C. § 261 specifically.

Title 35 U.S.C. § 261, as we have demonstrated and as its label suggests, is concerned with patent ownership. In that provision Congress gave patent holders the right to transfer their ownership interests, but only in specific ways. The congressional policy behind that decision was to protect the patent holder and the public for, as the Supreme Court put it, it was obviously not the intention of the legislature to permit several monopolies to be made out of one, and divided among different persons within the same limits. Such a division would inevitably lead to fraudulent impositions upon persons who desired to purchase the use of the improvement, and would subject a party who, under a mistake as to his rights, used the invention without authority, to be harassed by a multiplicity of suits instead of one, and to successive recoveries of damages by different persons holding different portions of the patent right in the same place. . . .

The recording provision, if read to include ownership interests only, is perfectly aligned with that policy. By contrast, a security interest in a patent does not make "several monopolies . . . out of one, . . . divided among different persons within the same limits." . . .

It is worthy of mention that the applicable PTO regulations parallel our interpretation of 35 U.S.C. § 261. Title 37 C.F.R. § 3.11(a) provides that "assignments" must be recorded in the PTO. That regulation also states that "other documents affecting title to applications, patents, or registrations, will be recorded at the discretion of the Commissioner" of Patents and Trademarks. . . . Section 313 of the Manual of Patent Examining Procedure (7th ed. 1998) explains that "other documents" that may be filed include "agreements which convey a security interest. Such documents are recorded in the public interest in order to give third parties notification of equitable interests." . . .

Title 37 C.F.R. § 3.11 is illuminating because it shows that the PTO does not consider security interests to be "assignments, grants or conveyances." Under 35 U.S.C. § 261, certain conveyances—those that transfer an ownership interest—must be recorded to be effective as against a subsequent purchaser or mortgagee. If security interests were "assignments, grants or conveyances," then they would have to be filed to provide constructive notice to a subsequent purchaser or mortgagee, consistent with the Patent Act. As a matter of law and logic, the Commissioner would not have the "discretion" to reject federal filing. . . .

Because the Patent Act does not cover security interests or lien creditors at all, there is no conflict between 35 U.S.C. § 261 and Article 9. Petitioners did not have to file with the PTO to perfect their security interest as to a subsequent lien creditor. . . .

Because 35 U.S.C. § 261 concerns only transactions that effect a transfer of an ownership interest in a patent, the Patent Act does not preempt Article 9, and neither California Commercial Code § 9104(a) nor § 9302(3) applies. Consequently, Petitioners perfected their security interest in Debtor's patent by recording it with the California Secretary of State. They have priority over the Trustee's claim because they recorded their interest before the filing of the bankruptcy petition.

BUSINESS CONSIDERATIONS Why would a business accept a security interest in a general intangible of indeterminant value? What risks might the secured party be taking by accepting a security interest in a patent?

ETHICAL CONSIDERATIONS Did the general creditors act ethically in this case by challenging the validity of a security interest that had been properly perfected under Article 9? Is it ethical to seek a "loophole" in the law to avoid an adverse result?

Goods, the most common type of collateral, are categorized on the basis of their use by the debtor. According to the Code, *goods* include all things that are movable at the time the security interest attaches or that are fixtures.[5] *Consumer goods* consist of those goods used or bought for use primarily for personal, family, or household purposes.[6] Thus, a debtor may give a security interest in his or her furniture or car to a secured party. *Equipment* includes goods used or bought for use primarily in business.[7] Bart's freezer and cash register, as cited in our example, are equipment collateral, as a truck would be for the electric company. Farm products also constitute a type of goods. The Code defines *farm products* as crops, livestock, or supplies used or produced in farming operations.[8] Interestingly, then, a farmer may give a security interest in wheat, corn, cows, or even milk, since the Code covers the products of crops or livestock in their unmanufactured states as well. *Inventory*, defined as goods held by a person for sale or lease or raw materials used or consumed in a business, is another type of goods.[9] Inventory differs from consumer goods and equipment because inventory is held for sale rather than use. Such things as coal or the packaging for goods are inventory, as is a dealer's supply of cars or a merchant's supply of tires, paint, clothing, or toys. The last type of goods that the Code delineates is *fixtures*. Goods are fixtures when they become so related to particular real estate that an interest in them arises under real estate law.[10] Furnaces and central air-conditioning units, once installed in a building, are fixtures.

When goods are used as collateral, the goods must be classified as one—and only one—type of goods. The classifications are mutually exclusive, and the classification is determined by the use made of the goods by the debtor. In borderline cases—for example, a social worker's car or a farmer's pickup—the principal use to which the debtor has put the property determines the type of collateral involved. Because the Code's rules regarding perfection, priorities, and default often turn on the type of collateral involved, as we shall see in Chapter 26, it is important to know which category of collateral is present in a given transaction.

A secured transaction is a *consensual* arrangement between the debtor and the creditor in which the debtor consents to the use of certain of his or her assets as collateral, and the creditor then consents to the granting of credit, subject to the creditor's claim against that collateral. In our earlier example, we can say that Bart Brown and the sellers of both the meat freezer and the cash register have each consented to enter into this commercial transaction. Since personal property is involved (the freezer and register are goods), Bart has agreed to let the sellers retain an interest in the goods until Bart pays for them (a method of ensuring the performance of Bart's obligations); and the sellers, in turn, have agreed to give the goods to Bart now (even though the sellers have not received the total price for them) in exchange for the right to repossess the freezer and register if Bart fails to pay. This transaction therefore fulfills all the requirements of an enforceable security interest.

Given the need for consent between the parties, Article 9 does not apply to a security interest that arises by operation of law rather than through the agreement of the parties. Examples of such situations include a mechanic's lien or a judgment lien asserted against any of the assets of a debtor. For example, assume that Bart, our erstwhile restaurateur, hires a building contractor to renovate the restaurant building. Upon completion of the remodeling Bart is unable to pay for the work. The contractor would be able to assert a mechanic's lien against Bart. The lien represents the money Bart owes for the labor and materials involved in the remodeling of the restaurant. Since Bart and the contractor have not agreed in advance that the contractor will have an interest in Bart's restaurant, this is a nonconsensual arrangement that arises as a consequence of the parties' *status* (the contractor is a creditor who now is using the restaurant as security for the debt Bart owes) rather than as a result of *mutual consent*. It therefore is not an Article 9 security interest.

Similarly, if Bart has previously lost a lawsuit filed by someone Bart injured in a traffic accident, and Bart has not paid the victim the judgment, that victim can assert a judgment lien against property belonging to Bart, giving the victim the right to levy on that property in an effort to satisfy the judgment previously won. Again, there is no agreement between Bart and the judgment creditor that the property will be used as security against the debt, so this is a nonconsensual arrangement and it will not be governed by Article 9.

This result stems in part from the fact that Article 9 does not apply to transactions involving real property or real estate, with the exception of some treatment of fix-

---

NRW CASE 25.1   **Management/Finance**

SOURCES OF FINANCING

The firm needs a quick infusion of capital, and Mai and Helen would like to have the firm borrow some money for the operation of the business. However, they expect that the bank will want some sort of collateral before making any loan to the firm. Neither Mai nor Helen wants to use her personal assets as security for any credit they receive, but they are not sure that NRW has any assets that can be used to secure the loan. They ask you what assets NRW has that might be useful as collateral for any loans they seek. What will you tell them?

BUSINESS CONSIDERATIONS How can businesspeople who are starting a closely held business acquire financing without using their personal assets as collateral? Is it a good idea for the owner-managers of small businesses to have their personal and their professional assets so closely entwined in the business venture?

ETHICAL CONSIDERATIONS Is it ethical for a lender to insist that the owners of a start-up business use their personal assets as security for loans extended to the business? What ethical principles does this situation involve?

INTERNATIONAL CONSIDERATIONS Suppose a business operates a plant in another country, and the business needs to borrow funds to expand the operation. If the firm seeks a loan from a bank in the other country, is the bank likely to want collateral? Will the bank use a security interest similar to one found under Article 9, or is it more likely to use something completely different?

---

tures. Instead, as mentioned, it applies only to consensual security interests in *personal property*. Article 9 has no bearing on land mortgages or on landlords' liens. Article 9 applies to the sale of motor vehicles, although the security interest is shown as a lien on the certificate of title issued by the state. The normal rules of Article 9 apply to vehicles held as inventory by a dealer. In some cases, a transaction, although covered by Article 9, also may be subject to local statutes governing usury, retail installment sales, and the like (for example, the Uniform Consumer Credit Code). In the event of a conflict, the provisions of any such statute, and not Article 9, are controlling.

One test a person can use in deciding whether Article 9 applies is to ask whether the transaction is intended by the parties to have effect as a security interest. If the answer is yes, Article 9 probably covers the transaction.

For an interesting contrast, visit http://www.worldlii.org/catalog/3024.html to see some of the proposals for international security interests.

Attachment: The Creation of a Security Interest

As was previously mentioned, a secured transaction is a consensual relationship between the debtor and the creditor. If the debtor repays the creditor as agreed to by the parties, there is no controversy and no problems will arise. But if the debtor does not repay the creditor, the creditor is quite likely to want to enforce the security interest agreed to by the parties. In order to do so, the creditor needs some proof that such an arrangement exists. This proof is established by *attachment*. Attachment establishes the rights of the creditor versus the debtor, vis-à-vis the collateral covered by the agreement. However, attachment does *not* provide the creditor with any advantage over other, potentially competing, creditors who may seek to enforce their claims against that same collateral.

Attachment creates the security interest in the collateral, and it establishes the rights of the creditor in the collateral.[11] Following attachment the creditor can assert rights superior to those of the debtor in the collateral if or when the debtor defaults on the agreement, usually due to nonpayment of the debt. In addition, attachment is necessary before the creditor can *perfect* his or her interest. (Perfection establishes the rights of the creditor to the collateral against everyone *except* the debtor.)

According to the UCC, there are three requirements that must be met before attachment occurs. These requirements can be met in any order, but until all three are present there can be no attachment. And if there is no attachment, there can be no perfection. Thus, a creditor who fails to attach is an unsecured general creditor, a disfavored position should the debtor default. The three requirements for attachment are:

1. the parties have an agreement that the security interest will attach;

2. the secured party—the creditor—must give value to the debtor; and

3. the debtor must have rights in the collateral.

The requirements for attachment are illustrated in Exhibit 25.1 and are discussed in detail in the sections that follow.

The Security Agreement

The first requirement, the existence of an agreement between the parties, emphasizes the consensual nature of the relationship. This agreement must either be in the form of an *authenticated record* or the secured party must have possession of or control over the collateral. If the secured party has possession or control, the agreement is valid and enforceable even if the agreement is oral. The revision to Article 9 reflects the growing use and acceptance of electronic means of communication. Under prior versions of the article, the security agreement had to be "in writing" and "signed" by the debtor unless the creditor had possession of the collateral.

Section 9-203 (b)(3)(A) states that, unless the secured party is in possession or control of the collateral, the security interest will not be valid unless there is a security agreement "authenticated" by the debtor and containing a description of the collateral. "Authenticated" is defined rather broadly by the Code and includes a signed record or the adoption and execution of a symbol or the encryption of a record, in whole or in part, with the present intent to (1) identify the authenticating party, and (2) adopt or accept the record.[12] "Record" is defined as "information that is inscribed on a tangible medium or which is stored in an electronic or other medium and is retrievable in perceivable form."[13]

If the security agreement is in "record" form, it must contain a description of the collateral, and this description must be sufficient to reasonably identify the collateral. This is a somewhat vague statement, but it is markedly better than the description allowed in the perfection of the interest. In perfection, the parties can use a "supergeneric" description, such as "all the debtor's property." In the security agreement, the collateral must be described with enough detail that it adequately reflects what collateral the parties intend to designate as the security for the agreement. Thus, a statement that the collateral is "all of the debtor's consumer goods" would be too broad, and thus would not be effective. However, a statement that the collateral is "all of the debtor's televisions" would be sufficiently detailed and specific, and would satisfy this requirement.

The security agreement may also contain an *after-acquired property clause*, a clause which specifies that the secured party not only has a claim against the collateral described in the agreement, but also has a claim against any

EXHIBIT 25.1 Attachment of a Security Interest

Agreement between the Debtor and the Secured Party	"Authenticated record" of the agreement with a sufficient description of the collateral
	or
	Oral agreement between the parties and the Secured Party has possession or control of the collateral
Secured Party gives value to the Debtor	Consideration sufficient to support a simple contract
	or
	The Creditor has a preexisting claim against the Debtor
	or
	The Debtor accepts delivery under a preexisting purchase contract
	or
	The Secured Party makes a commitment to give future value
The Debtor has rights or acquires rights in the collateral	Debtor owns or possesses the collateral
	or
	In a sale or lease of goods to the debtor, the goods have been identified to the contract
	or
	The court determines that the debtor otherwise has "rights in the collateral"

property of the type described (for example, equipment) acquired by the debtor after the interest attaches and while the debt is still outstanding, in whole or in part.[14] After-acquired property clauses are relatively common in commercial credit transactions. They are less common in consumer credit transactions. In fact, the Code prohibits the attachment of an after-acquired property clause to consumer goods unless the consumer acquires rights in the goods within 10 days of the time the secured party gave value to the debtor.[15] If the parties intend to include an after-acquired property clause in the agreement, they need to either use the term "after-acquired property" or expressly refer to goods or assets acquired in the future. If they do not, the courts are not likely to recognize any claims on property acquired by the debtor after the agreement has attached.

The Secured Party Gives Value

The purpose of a security interest is to secure payment or performance of an obligation owed to the creditor by the debtor. This payment or performance is in return for something previously done by the creditor—the "giving of value." The UCC defines value in a fairly broad manner in § 1-201 (44). According to this section, a person gives "value" for rights in collateral by acquiring these rights:

a. in return for any consideration sufficient to support a simple contract,

b. as security for a preexisting claim or in partial or total satisfaction thereof,

c. by accepting delivery under a preexisting contract for purchase, or

d. in return for a commitment to give future value. (This commitment must be definite and binding, and not subject to the secured party's subsequent change of mind.)

Once such value is given, the secured party stands to suffer an actual loss if the debtor defaults. This, in turn, justifies allowing the secured party a priority position in the collateral against the debtor, should the debtor default.

The Debtor Acquires Rights in the Collateral

When the parties enter into a security agreement, the creditor agrees to give value to the debtor, and the debtor, in turn, agrees to place his or her *rights* in the collateral as security in the event of nonperformance. Thus, the debtor must have "rights in the collateral" before the security interest can attach. Interestingly, the Code does not define "rights in the collateral," leaving the determination of what this means for the courts to decide. It would appear that the debtor must have either some type of ownership or possessory claim to the collateral in order to show that the debtor has "rights" in the collateral.

Perfection

Thus far, we have focused primarily on the relationship between the creditor and the debtor and how the creditor, by becoming a secured party, may protect his or her interest in the collateral against the debtor if or when the debtor defaults. Yet, in that earlier discussion, we noted that the processes leading to the creation and enforceability of a secured interest give the secured party rights greater than only those of the debtor. They do not confer on the secured party superior rights to the collateral vis-à-vis other creditors and the bankruptcy trustee. Now we turn to a discussion of how secured parties can protect themselves against such third parties who also may be claiming rights in the collateral. *Perfection* is the process by which secured parties establish their position or priority in their claims against the collateral. Perfection is giving notice to "the world" that a particular secured party has a security interest in one or more specific assets of the debtor. Perfection is required in order for a secured party to protect his or her claim against collateral from the clutches of later creditors who also have given value to the debtor, especially when the debtor has used the same assets as collateral for loans from them. Perfection is extremely important in the determination of rights, since it establishes notice and priority. Generally, the Code adopts a "first in time, first in right" approach. The

first secured party to perfect will normally have the highest priority, although there are some exceptions. The topic of priorities among secured parties is addressed in Chapter 26.

There are four possible ways in which perfection can occur. Care needs to be exercised here, since all four methods may not be available in a particular setting or transaction. The possible methods of perfection are:

- Perfection by filing. The secured party files a financing statement, giving notice to the world of his or her interest.

- Perfection by possession of the collateral. The secured party takes possession of the collateral, giving notice to the world of his or her interest.

- Perfection by control of the collateral. The secured party takes control of the collateral, giving notice to the world of his or her interest.

- Automatic perfection. The secured party is automatically perfected *upon attachment* of the security interest, even though there is no notice given to anyone of the existence of the security interest.

Obviously, automatic perfection upon attachment is the easiest method, and the secured party is not required to take any steps beyond attachment. Given the simplicity of this method, every secured party would use this method *every* time if it were always available. Unfortunately for the secured party, this method is not always available. More often than not, especially in commercial credit transactions, automatic perfection is not an option and the secured party must use one of the other three methods in order to properly perfect. The methods of perfection, and when each method is available, are illustrated in Exhibit 25.2. Each of the methods is then described in detail in the following sections.

Perfection by Filing

Location Perhaps the best-known method for perfection is the filing of a financing statement by the secured party. Under the prior law, filing was well known, but it could also be somewhat confusing. The secured party had to determine *where* to file, and the location for filing could vary from state to state. In addition, even if the secured party filed in the correct location, if the debtor moved the collateral it was possible that the secured party would need to refile in a new location in order to retain his or her perfection on the goods. The revision to Article 9 made substantial changes to the filing requirements. Filing is now simpler, the location for filing is much more straightforward, and even the method of filing has changed.

EXHIBIT 25.2 Methods of Perfection

Method of Perfection	Effective with the Following Types of Collateral
Perfection by Filing	Can be used with all types of collateral *except* deposit accounts and letters of credit
Perfection by Possession of the Collateral	Can be used with goods, money, documents, instruments, certificated securities, and tangible chattel paper
Perfection by Control of the Collateral	Can be used with investment properties, deposit accounts, letters of credit, and electronic chattel paper
Automatic Perfection	Can be used with purchase-money security interests (PMSIs) in consumer goods, the sale of payment intangibles and promissory notes, and the assignment of beneficial interests in a decedent's estate

There are also some *temporary* automatic perfections available:

- 20-day "grace period" for a PMSI in equipment, although the secured party must "otherwise perfect" before the expiration of the 20 days in order to have a perfected interest;

- 20 days from attachment if the secured party gives new value and the collateral is a negotiable document, an instrument, or a certificated security;

- 20 days when a secured party makes available to the debtor an instrument, a negotiable document, or goods in possession of a bailee (normally for the debtor to sell the collateral).

According to § 9-301(1), the proper place to file under the new Article 9 is in the jurisdiction where the debtor is located. The location of the collateral no longer matters for most purposes (a few exceptions will be addressed later in the chapter). While this rule seems simple, by itself it still does not tell the secured party where to file. The location depends on the debtor's location, but what does that mean? If the debtor is an individual, the debtor's location is his or her state of residence. And if the debtor has several different residences (for example, a summer home in the Hamptons or a winter home in Florida), the debtor's location is his or her *primary* residence.[16]

If the debtor is a corporation or "registered organization," the debtor is "located" in its state of incorporation.[17] It does not matter where the corporate offices are located, or where any individual store, plant, or operation is located. The "residence" of a corporation is the state in which it was incorporated. This means that a creditor extending credit under a security agreement to a store in California may need to file in Delaware, if the store is part of a chain and the parent corporation was incorporated in Delaware. If the debtor is an organization *other than* a corporation (trusts, partnerships, societies, etc.), the organization is "located" at its place of business. If the organization has more than one place of business, it is located at its chief executive offices.[18] If the federal government is the debtor, the location for filing is the District of Columbia.[19] Finally, if the debtor is foreign there are two possibilities for the proper location to file the security interest. If the debtor is located in a foreign country that has laws governing perfection that are similar to Article 9, especially in allowing the recording of nonpossessory liens, the debtor is located in that foreign country. If the debtor is not located in a country with such laws, the proper place for filing—the "location" of the debtor—is the District of Columbia.[20]

Not only must the secured party know the jurisdiction in which he or she must file in order to properly perfect, the secured party must also perfect in the correct location within that jurisdiction. This requirement caused some confusion prior to the revision of the article because some states required local filing (filing in the county where the collateral was located) while other states required central filing (filing in the state capital of the state in which the collateral was located). In addition, some states required local filing for some types of collateral, but central filing for other types of collateral. Add to this the problems presented if or when the debtor moved the collateral from one state to another, and the potential for confusion and for erroneous filings is obvious. The revised act has virtually eliminated this problem. The secured party is now expected to file *centrally* in the state of the debtor's residence. In addition, the secured party is permitted to file electronically. Thus, in our previous example the California secured creditor will be able to submit a financing statement to the secretary of state in Delaware in order to perfect his or her security interest against the debtor even though the debtor is a store located in California.

There are still a few potential pitfalls under this new system, but they are significantly fewer than existed under the prior law. For example, if the collateral is "related to realty," the secured party must file locally, and not centrally. The filing is in the same office where real estate mortgages would be filed. Such collateral "related to realty" includes minerals, timber to be cut, and fixtures, but it does not include crops.[21] Also, if the debtor is an individual, and he or she moves to another state after the secured party has perfected, the secured party will have a grace period of four months in which to refile in the new state of the debtor's residence in order to retain the security interest. If the secured party does not refile within the four-month window, his or her interest will lapse. While the secured party will still be able to file in the new state of residence, the lapse may well permit other creditors who had been junior to this claim to move up the priority list, dropping the secured creditor whose interest had lapsed to a lower priority position. (Remember, the normal rule is "first in time, first in right.")

Effective Date A filing is considered effective upon the presentation of a financing statement for filing, together with a tender of the filing fees, to the filing officer.[22] The creditor is not responsible for any delays or misfilings of the filing officer. However, the creditor is responsible for making a proper presentation and for proper tender of the filing fees. If the presentation is communicated in a manner or medium that is not authorized by the filing office, it is inappropriate, and thus ineffective. Similarly, if the creditor does not tender an amount equal to or greater than the required filing fee, the attempt to file in invalid.[23]

Once properly filed, the financing statement is effective for a period of five years from the date of filing,[24] and may be continued for additional five-year periods if a continuation statement is properly filed within the last six months before the expiration of the interest.[25]

Sufficiency In order for a filing to be sufficient, it must contain the name of the debtor and the name of the secured party, and indicate the collateral that is covered by the financing statement.[26] In addition, if the financing statement is for collateral "related to realty," the statement must include a description of the real property, and if the debtor does not have an interest of record in the realty, the name of the record owner must be included.[27]

As stated above, the financing statement must contain the name of the debtor. However, this requirement has a more rigorous meaning under the new provisions. If the debtor is a registered organization, the financing statement must contain the official name of the debtor as reflected in the public record of the jurisdiction of organization. In a similar vein, if the debtor is a decedent's estate, the financing statement must provide the name of the decedent and indicate that the debtor is an estate. If the debtor is a trust, that fact must be reflected. Thus, the secured party must exercise care that the statement contains the *official* name, and not some variation of that name or a different name under which the debtor is doing business. If the financing statement contains only the debtor's trade name, the filing is not sufficient to put other creditors on notice.[28]

At the same time, the drafters did not want to erect too many barriers to the sufficiency of filings. Article 9 has a stated policy that if the financing statement substantially complies with the requirements of § 9-502, that filing is sufficient even if it contains minor errors, so long as those errors are not seriously misleading. In addition, even if there is an error in the name of the debtor in the filing, the filing is sufficient if a search of the records using the debtor's correct name and using the filing office's "standard search logic" (a computer term relating to how a computer program searches for files) would disclose the financing statement; the statement is sufficient despite the technical error in the statement.[29]

In the following case, decided under the prior version of Article 9, there were questions as to the sufficiency of the description of the collateral and of the identification of the debtor. After reviewing the court's opinion, decide whether the same result would occur under the new statute.

Finally, the financing statement can use "supergeneric" terms to describe the collateral, even though such terms are not permitted in the security agreement. Thus, a description of the collateral as "all the debtor's assets" is permissible and serves as adequate notice to any subsequent creditors.

Perfection by Possession

The secured party can perfect his or her interest by taking physical possession of the collateral. In this situation, commonly referred to as a pledge, the perfection is effective as soon as the secured party takes possession and lasts for so long as the secured party retains possession.

25.2

WEST IMPLEMENT COMPANY, INC. v. FIRST SOUTH PRODUCTION CREDIT ASSOCIATION
815 So. 2d 1164, 2002 Miss. LEXIS 148 (Miss. 2002)

FACTS On February 2, 1998, FSPCA made a loan in the amount of $750,000 to Mouton Farms Partnership. The partnership is composed of Napanee Planting Company, Inc., Benoit Planting Company, Inc., and the Virginia Amy Mouton Marital Trust. The security agreement for the loan granted FSPCA a security interest in Mouton Farms' equipment, among other things. The equipment list attached to the security agreement specifically lists a model 9600 John Deere Combine. FSPCA filed a financing statement with the Bolivar County Chancery Clerk's office on January 10, 1997, and with the Mississippi Secretary of State on January 14, 1997.

In February 1998, West took the John Deere combine from Mouton Farms as a trade-in on a new combine. West relied on the oral statements of the Mouton Farms representative that there were no existing liens on the combine. West conducted no further research to verify this assertion, despite the fact that the Mouton Farms representative provided West with an address and tax identification number for Mouton Farms.

In its order granting summary judgment, the trial court found that there were no material disputed facts, but that the parties did disagree as to the legal sufficiency of the description of the collateral and the legal sufficiency of the identification of the debtor in FSPCA's financing statement. The trial court found this to be an issue of law, not of fact. The trial court then made an analysis of the law pertaining to that issue and granted summary judgment in favor of FSPCA.

ISSUE Did the trial court err in finding that FSPCA's financing statement sufficiently identified the John Deere combine as collateral and sufficiently identified the debtor as Mouton Farms?

HOLDING No. The statement sufficiently identified both the collateral and the debtor.

REASONING Excepts from the opinion of Justice Diaz:

West argues that the trial court "misapprehended its function as a trier of fact" in granting the motion for summary judgment and did not view the case in the light most favorable to the nonmoving party as required by Miss. R. Civ. P. 56(c). In support of its argument that the legal sufficiency of the identification of the collateral or the debtor in a financing statement is a question of fact, West cites *In re Strickland* . . . (holding that "the determination of whether an error in a financing statement is seriously misleading must turn on the facts of

the particular case"). Unlike West, we interpret *Strickland* as holding that whether there is an error in a financing statement is a question of law, and whether that error is seriously misleading is a question of fact. As such, the trial court was within its authority to determine, as a matter of law, whether there was an error in the financing statement. We must now determine whether the trial court was correct in its finding that there was no error in the financing statement and, consequently, no question of fact.

Miss. Code Ann. § 75-9-402(1) (1972) provides in pertinent part:

> A financing statement is sufficient if it gives the names of the debtor and the secured party, is signed by the debtor, gives an address of the secured party from which information concerning the security interest may be obtained, gives a mailing address of the debtor, and contains a statement indicating the types, or describing the items, of collateral. . . .

The purpose of the filing system under Article 9 of the Uniform Commercial Code is to provide notice to potential creditors of preexisting liens. . . . Under the Article 9 system, "what is required to be filed is not, as under chattel mortgage and conditional sales act, the security agreement itself, but only a simple notice which may be filed before the security interest attaches or thereafter." . . .

Many courts have been faced with this question of whether the description of the collateral in a financing statement is sufficient. In one such case, a bankruptcy trustee sought priority over a secured creditor for certain collateral described as "machinery and equipment" in the financing statement because the financing statement indicated that a security agreement was attached when it was not. The court held that the description, "equipment and machinery" was sufficient, even without the security agreement. . . .

One court has found the description, "consumer goods" located at a particular address, a sufficient description to put a subsequent searcher on notice of a possible preexisting security interest. . . .

Here, there was no error in the financing statement concerning the description of the collateral. The terms "equipment and machinery" should put a searcher on notice that a 9600 model John Deere combine may be included in the secured interest property. As such, there is no question of fact as to whether an error was misleading, as there was no error. Therefore, we affirm the trial court's grant of summary judgment against West.

West next argues that, if it had made a search, it would not have found FSPCA's security interest in the combine because FSPCA filed its lien under the wrong name of the debtor. West claims that FSPCA should have identified the debtor under "Mouton Farms d/b/a Mouton Farms Partnership" instead of "Mouton Farms Partnership."

Again, Miss. Code Ann. § 75-9-402 provides in part:

(1) A financing statement is sufficient if it gives the names of the debtor and the secured party, is signed by the debtor, gives an address of the secured party from which information concerning the security interest may be obtained, gives a mailing address of the debtor, and contains a statement indicating the types, or describing the items, of collateral. . . .

(7) A financing statement sufficiently shows the name of the debtor if it gives the individual, partnership or corporate name of the debtor, whether or not it adds other trade names or the names of partners. . . .

(8) A financing statement substantially complying with the requirements of this section is effective even though it contains minor errors which are not seriously misleading.

Here, FSPCA did supply the partnership name of the debtor as required by statute. Thus, there is no error in the financing statement regarding the identification of the debtor.

Even more support for the trial court's grant of summary judgment is found in *Strickland*. There, the court was presented with the opposite issue of whether the use of the debtor's trade name in the financing statement, Strickland Builders Mfg. Company and Strickland Builders and Supply Company, rather than the debtor's correct legal name, James Terence Strickland, rendered the financing statements seriously misleading. In deciding that the error was not seriously misleading, the court found that "if the debtors' trade name is sufficiently similar to its real or corporate name and therefore not seriously misleading, then perfection of the creditor's security interest should remain intact. . . ."

Clearly, the statute required FSPCA to use the debtor's partnership name. Furthermore, even when filers do not use the individual, partnership or corporate name of the debtor, but instead err and use the trade name of the debtor, that error is not fatal to perfection of the security interest if the names are sufficiently similar. Although inconsequential in light of the fact that FSPCA correctly identified the debtor, it is interesting to note that the alleged trade name of the debtor, "Mouton Farms," could not be any more similar to the partnership name of the debtor, "Mouton Farms Partnership." . . .

BUSINESS CONSIDERATIONS What did West do wrong in this situation? What should West have done to prevent the problems it encountered?

ETHICAL CONSIDERATIONS Did West act ethically in attempting to have the financing statement declared invalid when West's own failure to adequately search the records led to West's failure to become aware of a prior perfected interest?

There is no need to file any statements or worry about any continuations or renewals. However, the secured party must properly store, maintain, and care for the collateral while it is in his or her possession.

Perfection by possession can be used if the collateral is in the form of negotiable documents, goods, instruments, money, or tangible chattel paper. The secured party can also perfect by possession if the collateral is in the form of certificated securities and the secured party takes delivery of the securities under the provisions and guidelines of § 8-301.[30]

If the collateral is in the possession of a third person, the secured party is deemed to be "in possession," and therefore to be perfected, if the person in possession of the collateral authenticates a record acknowledging that it is holding the collateral for the benefit of the secured party.

Perfection by Control

If a security interest is held in investment property, deposit accounts, letter-of-credit rights, or electronic chattel paper, the secured party is allowed to perfect by taking control of the collateral. The requirements for control of investment property are spelled out in § 8-106, the Investment Securities article. The secured party has perfection by control of a deposit account if the secured party is the bank with which the account is maintained, or the debtor, the bank, and the secured party have agreed in an authenticated record that the bank will follow the instructions of the secured party with respect to the deposit account.[31] The secured party has control of a letter-of-credit right to the extent that the secured party has any right to payment or performance by the issuer of the letter-of-credit, if the issuer has consented to an assignment of the proceeds of the letter-of-credit to the secured party.[32] Finally, the secured party has control of an electronic chattel paper if there is only one authoritative copy of the record, that copy identifies the secured party as the assignee of the record, and the authoritative copy is communicated to and maintained by the secured party or his or her designated custodian.[33]

Automatic Perfection

Automatic perfection upon attachment has limited availability under the revised act. The reasons for allowing automatic perfection relate to commercial convenience, especially in credit transactions involving consumers, or because there are other protections available to the creditor under other areas of the law.

PMSI in Consumer Goods A purchase-money security interest (PMSI) in consumer goods is automatically perfected for five years upon attachment. There is no need for the secured party to take any additional steps or to incur any additional expenses in order to be perfected, provided that the secured party and the consumer-debtor have entered into a security agreement.[34] A purchase money security interest arises when the secured creditor provides either the money or the credit to allow the consumer to purchase the collateral. In return, the consumer agrees to use the asset just purchased with the credit as the collateral to secure the agreement. Remember that this applies only to a PMSI for consumer goods, goods that are purchased primarily for personal or household use. Also, if the consumer goods purchased are to become fixtures, the secured party cannot rely on automatic perfection. He or she must file a financing statement in order to perfect this interest despite the PMSI nature of the transaction.

Other Automatic Perfections The Code makes provision for several other types of transactions that have automatic perfection and that do not require any additional steps by the secured party. These transactions are listed here without explanation.

- The assignment of a beneficial interest in a decedent's estate

- The assignment of accounts or payment intangibles, so long as the assignment does not constitute a significant portion of the assignor's outstanding accounts or payment intangibles

- The sale of promissory notes or payment intangibles

NRW CASE 25.2   Finance

PERFECTING A SECURITY INTEREST

NRW recently made a large sale to one of its customers in the Midwest. The sale was made on credit, and the firm retained a security interest in the goods. A proper security agreement was prepared and signed by the customer, and the firm prepared a financing statement so that it could file and perfect its interest. However, a disagreement has arisen as to where and how to perfect. Carlos thinks that the firm should file the financing statement in the state where the customer is located, since that is where the units were shipped. Mai insists that the statement must be filed where the customer is incorporated, regardless of where any of the stores or the inventory happen to be located. They have asked for your advice. What will you tell them?

BUSINESS CONSIDERATIONS What policies should a business that regularly enters into secured transactions as a creditor develop to ensure that it will properly perfect its security interests? Would these policies be different under the prior version of Article 9?

ETHICAL CONSIDERATIONS Is it ethical for a creditor to use "supergeneric" descriptions of collateral in its financing statements when the security agreement requires a more specific description?

INTERNATIONAL CONSIDERATIONS Suppose the customer-debtor in a secured transaction is domiciled in another country. Where should the secured party file its financing statement? What factors will affect your answer to this question?

Temporary Automatic Perfections There are also several areas in which the law grants the secured party an automatic perfection, but the perfection period is temporary. These are also listed here without explanation.

- A secured party who has a security interest in negotiable documents, certificated securities, or instruments, and who gives new value to the debtor is automatically perfected for 20 days from the time of attachment even if the debtor retains possession of the collateral.

- If the secured party delivers goods or negotiable documents covering the goods, for the purpose of allowing the debtor to sell or exchange the goods, or for the purpose of loading, shipping, or storing the goods, the secured party is temporarily perfected for 20 days on the goods or the documents.

- Similarly, if the secured party delivers instruments or certificated securities to the debtor for the purpose of sale, exchange, collection, renewal, or registration, the secured party is temporarily perfected on the instruments or the certificated securities.

Lease Intended as Security

As we have noted, Article 9 broadly defines the term *security interest* as an interest in personal property or fixtures that secures payment or performance of an obligation. One of the assets of the Code derives from the flexibility of such a sweeping definition. In fact, courts have had few problems in recognizing the existence of a security interest in most circumstances. However, one area *has* presented some difficulty to the courts, the area of leases. If the parties enter into a lease, the lessor retains title to the goods, and there is no need for the lessor to comply with the provisions of Article 9 in order to protect his or her interest in the leased goods. However, some "leases" appear to be disguised sales rather than true leases. In such a transaction the lessor is attempting to circumvent the requirements of Article 9 by *calling* the transaction a lease when it is, in fact, a credit sale with a security interest. These "leases" are recognized by Article 9 as secured transactions and are subject to all the requirements of any similar Article 9 transactions.

The adoption of Article 2A of the UCC, "Leases," did not resolve this problem, nor was it adequately resolved under the provisions of the previous version of Article 9. The revision of Article 9 attempts to address the issue more directly. In § 1-201 (37) the Code states:

Whether a transaction creates a lease or a security interest is determined by the facts of each case; however, a transaction creates a security interest if the consideration the lessee is to pay the lessor for the right to possession and use of the goods is an obligation for the term of the lease, not subject to termination by the lessee, and

(a) the original term of the lease is equal to or greater than the remaining economic life of the goods,

(b) the lessee is bound to renew the lease for the remaining economic life of the goods or is bound to become the owner of the goods,

(c) the lessee has an option to renew the lease for the remaining economic life of the goods for no additional consideration or nominal additional consideration upon compliance with the lease agreement, or

(d) the lessee has an option to become the owner of the goods for no additional consideration or nominal additional consideration upon compliance with the lease agreement.

NRW CASE 25.3   Finance

NRW

MOVING COLLATERAL

NRW has been selling a significant number of Stuff-TrakRs in New York, and has, on occasion, had difficulty in providing an adequate supply of the units to meet the requests of its customers. Helen has suggested that the firm should establish a warehouse facility in New York to provide better and quicker service to its customers in the northeast. She believes that having a ready supply of StuffTrakR units in the region will actually help to increase sales. Carlos is concerned that the firm's creditors may be opposed to this relocation of inventory, especially the firm's bank, which has a security interest in the inventory to secure a line of credit. He thinks the firm should at least notify the bank of this plan. While Helen does not think that the bank will object, she would like to know what you think they should do. They have asked you for your opinion. What will you tell them?

BUSINESS CONSIDERATIONS Should a debtor in a secured transaction adhere to a policy of informing the creditor any time removal of the collateral from the jurisdiction occurs? Why or why not? What can the creditor in this situation do to maximize its protection in the event the collateral is removed from the jurisdiction without notice?

ETHICAL CONSIDERATIONS Is it ethical for a debtor to remove collateral from the jurisdiction without notifying the creditor? Is it ethical for the creditor to demand notice from the debtor in advance before the debtor can move the collateral?

INTERNATIONAL CONSIDERATIONS Would your answer be different if NRW were planning to establish a warehouse facility in another country rather than another state? Why?

While this section expressly provides that the facts of each case will determine whether a given transaction creates a lease or a security interest, it does provide some guidelines to help the courts in making this determination. If the lessee has the right to terminate the lease and to return the goods at any time, the transaction is a "true" lease. If the lessee does not have this right, *and* if the lessee has the option to purchase the goods at the end of the lease for either no or nominal consideration, this is a disguised secured transaction. In addition, if the goods will have no remaining economic value at the conclusion of the lease, this is a secured transaction.

The next case involved the question of whether a lease was a "true" lease or a lease intended as security. Notice how the court resolved the issue, and then decide whether the same result would occur under the new version of Article 9.

25.3

IN RE ARCHITECTURAL MILLWORK OF VIRGINIA, INC.
226 B.R. 551 (Bankr. W.D. Va. 1998)

FACTS The debtor, Architectural Millwork of Virginia, Inc., filed a Chapter 11 bankruptcy petition on March 25, 1998. Prior to the filing date, Associates Leasing, Inc. and the debtor on May 16, 1996, entered into a truck lease agreement, providing for the lease of a 1995 Freightliner vehicle. Then, on August 2, 1996, River Ridge Supply (RRS) and the debtor entered into a conditional sales contract regarding a Komatsu forklift. Contemporaneous with the execution of the Komatsu agreement, RRS assigned to Associates all RRS's rights under the agreement. The Komatsu agreement gave the debtor the option to purchase the forklift for one dollar after the debtor had made all the scheduled payments. The Freightliner agreement, in contrast, permitted the debtor to purchase the truck at the end of the "lease" period at the price that represented the residual value of the truck. When the debtor filed its Chapter 11 petition, the question before the court centered on whether the equipment leases were "true" leases or disguised "security agreements."

ISSUE Were the leases in question "true" leases and thus subject to the bankruptcy laws, or were the leases intended as security and hence covered under Virginia's Commercial Code?

HOLDING The Komatsu agreement was a lease intended as security that fell under the coverage of Virginia's Commercial Code, not the federal bankruptcy laws. However, the Freightliner agreement involved a true lease that, according to the bankruptcy laws, the debtor either must assume or reject.

REASONING Excerpts from the opinion of Bankruptcy Judge William E. Anderson:

The Court's ruling on Associates's motion turns on whether the agreements in question are true leases or, in fact, security agreements, for purposes of Bankruptcy Code § 365. Such a determination is made by reference to state law. . . . Accordingly, a careful analysis of the relevant state code provisions is in order. Virginia has adopted the Uniform Commercial Code. Of particular importance to this case, the first paragraph of Virginia Code § 8.1-201(37) reads as follows.

> (37) 1. "Security interest" means an interest in personal property or fixtures which secures payment or performance of an obligation. . . . Whether a lease is intended as security is to be determined by the facts of each case; however, (a) the inclusion of an option to purchase does not of itself make the lease one intended for security, and (b) *an agreement that upon compliance with the terms of the lease the lessee shall become or has the option to become the owner of the property for no additional consideration or for a nominal consideration does make the lease one intended for security.*

Although this first paragraph of the statute requires the Court to examine the facts of each case in characterizing a transaction, "the plain language of the statute creates a security interest in property as a matter of law if the parties' contract allows the lessee to become the owner of the leased property for nominal or no additional consideration upon compliance with the terms of the lease." . . .

Applying this rule to the two agreements involved in this case produces mixed results. The Komatsu agreement clearly provides for the option to purchase the forklift for one dollar after all scheduled payments are completed. Consequently, the Court finds that this transaction was, in fact, a security agreement for purposes of Bankruptcy Code § 365 and dispenses with that portion of Associates's motion. Although this conclusion is well supported by the law, the Court also notes that neither the evidence submitted by Associates nor the arguments of its memoranda refute or even seriously address the characterization of the Komatsu agreement. Associates has focused on the more difficult issue of the Freightliner agreement.

Although the Freightliner agreement does not provide an option to purchase the equipment for one dollar, the debtor nonetheless argues that the purchase option is for nominal consideration. Associates, in turn, asserts that no option to purchase even exists in the Freightliner agreement. Instead, Associates argues that the agreement includes a final adjustment clause in paragraph 8 that requires the sale of the property at the end of the lease. If the proceeds are more than the residual value set forth in the agreement, then a credit is given to the debtor. If, however, the sale proceeds are less than the residual value, the debtor is charged the difference. . . .

Contrary to Associates suggestion, however, the Court treats the final adjustment clause in this case as simply an option for the debtor to purchase the equipment at the end of the lease at the price set by the residual value, $9,625.00. . . . The result, of course, is that an option to purchase is created.

The characterization of the final adjustment clause as an option to purchase, however, is only a step in the process of determining whether the Freightliner agreement is a disguised security agreement and not a true lease. The Court returns to the remaining provisions of Virginia Code § 8.1-201(37) to resolve this question.

2. Whether a transaction creates a lease or security interest is determined by the facts of each case; however, a transaction creates a security interest if the consideration the lessee is to pay the lessor for the right to possession and use of the goods is an obligation for the term of the lease not subject to termination by the lessee, and:

(a) The original term of the lease is equal to or greater than the remaining economic life of the goods;

(b) The lessee is bound to renew the lease for the remaining economic life of the goods or is bound to become the owner of the goods;

(c) The lessee has an option to renew the lease for the remaining economic life of the goods for no additional consideration or nominal additional consideration upon compliance with the lease agreement; or

(d) The lessee has an option to become the owner of the goods for no additional consideration or nominal additional consideration upon compliance with the lease agreement.

. . . As conceded by the debtor, the relevant portions of this statute are found in the main body of paragraph two and in subsection (d). Under this analysis, if (i) the debtor cannot avoid paying Associates the value of the payments due under the lease, and (ii) the debtor can become the owner of the Freightliner for nominal or no consideration upon compliance with the lease terms, then the transaction creates a security interest.

The first of these two conditions exists in this case. While the debtor could terminate the lease early, it cannot avoid or terminate the obligation to pay Associates the value of the consideration due under the agreement, whether payable at the natural end of the lease or upon earlier termination. The Court agrees with the analysis of the debtor on this point as outlined in its initial memorandum. . . . The Court finds that the Freightliner agreement requires payment to Associates of the present value, upon early termination, of exactly what it would be paid upon the natural termination of the lease. . . .

Having satisfied the first condition of paragraph 2, the Court looks to the second condition. If any of the four criteria detailed in the subsections (a) through (d) are also met, then the Freightliner agreement is not a true lease. The debtor, of course, asserts that subsection (d) is satisfied. Associates, in contrast, strongly contends that the residual value purchase price of $9,625.00 may not be characterized as nominal consideration under subsection (d).

The Court sides with Associates and finds that this option to purchase for the residual value is not, in fact, for no consideration or for nominal consideration. Although the Court declines to speculate on where the line would be drawn for what constitutes nominal consideration, clearly $9,625.00 does not qualify as such, particularly in light of the agreement's capitalized cost of only $38,500.00. Furthermore, the testimony of both parties indicates that the $9,625.00 residual value was a fair estimate, when made at the time the agreement was executed, of the vehicle's value at the conclusion of the lease payments. Consequently, it is not clear from the evidence before the Court that the parties expected for the debtor to recognize much, if any, equity in the vehicle. Nor is it clear that the only economically sensible course for the debtor would be to exercise the option to purchase the vehicle. . . . As a result, the Court finds that the option price in this case is not nominal. . . .

As noted previously, the parties' testimony indicated that the $9,625.00 residual value was a fair estimate, when made at the time the agreement was executed, of the vehicle's anticipated value at the conclusion of the lease payments. Again, the Court does not find the resulting option price of $9,625.00 to be nominal consideration under these circumstances. Furthermore, the Court finds that little, if any, equity was anticipated by the parties.

After analyzing the Freightliner agreement and weighing all of the facts and arguments presented by the parties, the Court finds that the Freightliner agreement is a true lease. The Freightliner agreement transferred the right to possession and use of a vehicle to the debtor for a term. The lease included an option to purchase the vehicle; however, that option was for more than just nominal consideration. The equity, if any, created in the lessee in this case is minimal and is therefore of limited significance to the debtor's argument that this lease should be considered as a security agreement. . . .

BUSINESS CONSIDERATIONS Why would a seller prefer to characterize a lease as a true lease rather than as a lease intended as security? Why would competing creditors prefer to characterize a lease as a lease intended as security rather than as a true lease?

ETHICAL CONSIDERATIONS Has a seller who recognizes the legal distinctions between a true lease and a lease intended as security acted unethically toward the lessee-debtor if the seller couches the arrangement as a true lease but asks for monthly payments that in effect mean the lessee will pay twice the fair market value of the item leased?

Proceeds

The final point we should make about security interests and perfection is that the Code allows a secured party's interest to reach the *proceeds* of the debtor's disposition of the collateral. If the debtor disposes of the collateral, whatever the debtor receives in exchange for that collateral is deemed proceeds. Assuming that the secured party had properly perfected his or her security interest in the original collateral, his or her interest will automatically be perfected in the proceeds under the original perfection. And so long as the proceeds are identifiable, the secured party will retain his or her perfection over those proceeds. However, if the proceeds received by the debtor are in the form of cash,

the secured party is perfected in the proceeds only for a period of 20 days.

Suppose the debtor disposes of the collateral for cash, and then uses the cash to purchase some new asset. This newly purchased asset is referred to as "second-generation proceeds," and the secured party will need to file a new financing statement that adequately describes these second-generation proceeds in order to retain his or her perfection.

The Legal Information Institute has information on Article 9 at http://www.law.cornell.edu/topics/secured_transactions.html. It provides an interesting contrast to compare some of this information with that available at http:/www.ebrd.com/pubs/sectrans/main.htm, which addresses international issues in the area of secured transactions.

Summary

A secured transaction provides added protection to the creditor in the event the debtor defaults on his or her obligation. If the debtor does not pay the creditor as agreed, the creditor's security interest will allow the creditor to repossess the collateral used as security. A secured transaction typically involves a secured party, a debtor, a security agreement, and collateral. The Code categorizes collateral according to its nature or its use. One type of collateral is goods; the different classes of goods are mutually exclusive. Collateral also may consist of documents, instruments, letters of credit, proceeds, accounts, chattel paper, and general intangibles. Article 9 applies to consensual security interests in personal property or fixtures but not to those arising by operation of law. It covers leases meant as security but not "true" leases.

Attachment is the process by which the secured party creates an enforceable security interest in the collateral. A signed security agreement, in conjunction with the occurrence of other events, provides evidence that attachment has occurred. Perfection refers to the method by which a secured party gives notice to the world of his or her security interest. Perfection protects the secured party against claims asserted against the collateral by later creditors of the debtor. Perfection can take place in one of four ways: (1) by the creditor's filing of a valid financing statement, (2) by the creditor's possession of the collateral, (3) by the creditor's control of the collateral, and (4) by automatic perfection. The method of perfection that the secured party should use often depends on the type of collateral involved. If filing is the applicable method, the creditor must use a legally effective financing statement. The revision to Article 9 provides for a simplified filing system. Generally, filing of the financing statement occurs centrally, normally with the office of the secretary of state of the debtor's home state. If the debtor is a corporation, this means the state of incorporation. If the debtor is foreign, the filing may have to be in his or her home nation, or it may be effective if filed in the District of Columbia. Filings may also be made electronically, and the description of the collateral may use "supergeneric" terms such as "all the assets of the debtor."

Discussion Questions

1. What is a secured transaction? Why would a creditor want to enter into a secured transaction rather than a normal credit transaction?

2. Define a security interest. How is a security interest created under the provisions of Article 9?

3. Revised Article 9 recognizes four different methods for perfection of a security interest. What are these methods, and when can each of them be used?

4. If Will does not pay Carla, the mechanic who fixes his car, and she obtains a judgment against him, does Carla have an Article 9 security interest in Will's car? Why or why not?

5. What is the difference between a true lease and a lease intended as security? How does the UCC distinguish between these two types of "leases"?

6. What is attachment under Article 9, and what are the requirements that must be met before an attachment is valid?

7. What must be included in a security agreement? How may the collateral be described? When must a security agreement be in writing?

8. How accurate must the description of collateral be in a financing statement? How does this compare with the accuracy required of the description in the security agreement?

9. What kinds of defects cause a financing statement to be ineffective?

10. What problems might arise for the bank if Debbie Dunn has given the bank a security interest in bulldozers and she subsequently moves the bulldozers from Indiana to Michigan? Would it matter if Debbie Dunn moved from Indiana to Michigan, but the bulldozers remained in Indiana?

Case Problems and Writing Assignments

1. On about August 20, 1986, John J. and Clara Lockovich purchased a 22-foot 1986 Chapparel Villian III boat from the Greene County Yacht Club for $32,500. The Lockoviches (the debtors) paid $6,000 to the club and executed a security agreement/lien contract that set forth the purchase and finance terms. In the contract, the Lockoviches granted a security interest in the boat to the holder of the contract. When Gallatin National Bank paid the club $26,757.14 on the Lockoviches' behalf, the club assigned the contract to Gallatin. Gallatin then filed financing statements in the appropriate Greene County office and with the secretary of the Commonwealth of Pennsylvania. Greene County was the county in which Gallatin was located, but the Lockoviches resided in Allegheny County. The filing of the financing statements therefore was ineffective to perfect the security interest in the boat. The Lockoviches, by failing to remit payments as required, subsequently defaulted under the terms of the security agreement they had signed with Gallatin. Before Gallatin could take action, the Lockoviches filed for relief under Chapter 11 of the Bankruptcy Code. Gallatin then sought, pursuant to the security agreement, to enforce its rights. On October 2, 1989, the Bankruptcy Court, in denying Gallatin's motion, held that because Gallatin had failed to perfect its security interest in the boat by filing, it was an unsecured creditor. Pursuant to the bankruptcy laws, as a holder of an unperfected security interest, Gallatin's right to the boat remained inferior to that of the debtor-in-possession, a hypothetical lienholder. To perfect its purchase money security interest in the boat, would Gallatin need to file a financing statement? [See *In re Lockovich*, 124 B.R. 660 (Bankr. W.D. Pa. 1991).]

2. On or about October 11, 1997, Grieb Printing Company, the debtor, executed a lease of equipment with Bayer Financial Services. The lease was for 48 months, had a monthly payment of $4,108.71, and gave the debtor the option to purchase the equipment at the end of the lease for one dollar. The lease, which was executed by the debtor's CEO, granted Bayer a security interest in the equipment and authorized Bayer or its agents to sign and execute on the lessee's behalf any and all necessary documents to effect any filings, including the filing of any such financing or continuation statements without further authorization. On October 6, 1997, Bayer filed a financing statement on the equipment. Pursuant to the lease agreement, Bayer signed the financing statement on behalf of the debtor as the debtor's "attorney-in-fact." Before doing so, Bayer did not request that the debtor sign the lease. Bayer then properly filed the financing statement. Approximately five months after obtaining the equipment, the debtor filed a Chapter 7 bankruptcy petition. When the bankruptcy trustee moved to sell the equipment in which Bayer claimed an interest, the trustee

argued that Bayer's interest in the collateral was unperfected. The trustee based its contention on the Kentucky statutory provision that makes invalid any filing of a financing statement not signed by an individual authorized to sign on behalf of the corporate debtor. Was the signature that Bayer, the creditor, had placed on the financing statement for the debtor valid under Kentucky law and thus sufficient to protect the creditor's security interest? [See *In re Grieb Printing Company*, 230 B.R. 539 (Bankr. W.D. Ky. 1999).]

3. In 1993, Kenneth W. Gibson, an employee of United Airlines, obtained a Visa card from the airline's credit union. Gibson did not give the credit union any collateral to secure this extension of credit at the time of the issuance of the Visa card. The interest rate for charges always had been 12.96 percent per annum. In 1996, the Gibsons (Kenneth and his wife, Ramona) borrowed approximately $23,000 from the credit union. In connection with the 1996 loan, the Gibsons executed a loan and security agreement that provided that the balance due to the credit union would accrue interest at the rate of 8.9 percent per annum. Pursuant to the terms of the 1996 agreement, the Gibsons gave the credit union a security interest in collateral consisting of two cars and Mr. Gibson's shares in the credit union. The back of the 1996 loan and security agreement set out a series of preprinted terms and conditions. One of these preprinted terms and conditions—the so-called dragnet clause—purported to make the collateral security for any debt owed by either of the Gibsons to the credit union as well as for the 1996 loan obligation. The Gibsons later contended that no one representing the credit union pointed this language out to them in 1996. The 1996 loan and security agreement also contained a preprinted provision (a "choice of law" clause) stating that the agreement "shall be governed by and construed in accordance with the laws of the State of Illinois."

When the Gibsons, who resided in California, ultimately filed a petition for an adjustment of debts under Chapter 13 of the Bankruptcy Code, Mr. Gibson owed the credit union $4,846.06 on the Visa card and the Gibsons owed the credit union $14,759.97 on the 1996 loan obligation. The value of the collateral was sufficient to cover both obligations. The credit union filed two proofs of claim in the Chapter 13 case, one for the Visa card debt and one for the 1996 loan obligation. Originally, only the 1996 loan claim had been described as secured; the Visa claim had been described as unsecured. However, shortly thereafter, the credit union, in an amended claim, asserted secured status for the Visa claim as well. The Gibsons characterized the dragnet clause as unenforceable and the Visa claim as unsecured. How should a court dispose of this case? [See *In re Gibson*, 234 B.R. 776 (Bankr. N.D. Cal. 1999).]

4. On June 18, 1993 and July 24, 1994, Cheqnet Systems, Inc. (the debtor) signed promissory notes with Citizens First Bank of Fordyce. Prior to filing a petition under Chapter 7 of the Bankruptcy Code, the debtor engaged in the business of check collection. Specifically, the debtor would contract with merchants and promise to pursue the recovery of returned and uncollected checks. The debtor then would remit a portion of any such checks recovered to the merchants. The notes the debtor had signed with the bank granted the bank "a . . . security interest in the property described in the documents executed in connection with the note as well as other property designated as security for the loan now or in the future. Assignment of Contract with Walmart Stores, Inc., and Second Mortgage on Commercial Building More Particularly Described on Mortgaged Date 6-18-93." Other documents, including the mortgage but not including the financing statement the bank later referenced in its motion for summary judgment, were executed with the notes. It was not until nearly three years after the signing of the first note that the debtor and the bank, in April 1996, executed and filed with the appropriate state and local offices a UCC-1 financing statement that listed other collateral. During the Chapter 7 proceedings, the trustee alleged that the bank would not enjoy a perfected security interest in the property of the estate because the security documents failed to properly reference the collateral. The bank, in turn, moved for a summary judgment on the grounds that, as a matter of law, it had perfected its security interest in the debtor's accounts and contract rights as of the date of the filing of the bankruptcy petition. Should the judge grant the bank's summary judgment motion and thus endorse the bank's argument that the bank's security interest had attached? [See *In re Cheqnet Systems, Inc.*, 227 B.R. 166 (Bankr. E.D. Ark. 1998).]

5. BUSINESS APPLICATION CASE Gregory Westfall, a resident of Missouri, purchased a Kenworth tractor-trailer truck from Rush Truck Centers of Texas, Inc. In order to finance the purchase of the Kenworth, Westfall signed a security agreement in favor of Rush; in the same security agreement Rush assigned its interest to Associates Commercial Corporation. The security agreement contained the Associates logo in the upper-left hand corner of the first page, and the legend "ORIGINAL FOR ASSOCIATES" appeared at the bottom of each of the five pages in the security agreement. The security agreement stated that Westfall would keep the Kenworth at P.O. Box 367, Mountain Grove, Missouri, or Oklahoma. Westfall testified at the bankruptcy hearing that the Rush salesperson offered Westfall the option of titling the Kenworth in Texas or Missouri. Westfall stated that he was already aware that he would have to pay Missouri sales taxes if he titled the Kenworth in Missouri. After Westfall indicated he wanted to title the Kenworth in Oklahoma, the salesperson referred him to Pro-Cert, Inc., a titling company in Oklahoma. Pro-Cert subsequently prepared an Oklahoma lien entry form that identified the collateral as the Kenworth, gave the name and address of the secured party, set out the name and address of the debtor (with a fictitious address in Oklahoma), and showed the assignee as Associates Commercial Corp. in Irving, Texas. Westfall immediately removed the Kenworth to his home state, Missouri, and never

operated the Kenworth in Oklahoma. Neither Associates nor Rush ever perfected their respective liens in Missouri.

Missouri law recognizes vehicle liens that are perfected in another state. Hence, a Missouri resident can purchase a vehicle in another state; and the lender or seller can perfect its lien under the laws of its state before the vehicle is moved to Missouri. Thus, if the buyer brings the vehicle to Missouri and never registers it, the creditor still has a valid lien. Missouri statutes recognize a lien that was valid in the state in which the vehicle was located at the time of perfection. Westfall ultimately defaulted on the loan and returned the Kenworth to Rush sometime before filing a Chapter 7 bankruptcy petition on April 16, 1998. During the bankruptcy proceedings, Associates pointed to the statute stating that as to goods issued under a certificate of title, perfection is governed by the law of the jurisdiction "issuing the certificate until four months after the goods are removed from that jurisdiction and thereafter until the goods are registered in another jurisdiction." Associates also claimed that no other creditor would suffer any harm if Missouri recognized the lien, since the only title available for the Kenworth clearly noted Associates's lien. Was Associates a secured creditor that thus had priority over the bankruptcy trustee's lien, or was Associates a general unsecured creditor whose rights were subordinate to those of the trustee? [See *In re Westfall*, 227 B.R. 734 (Bankr. W.D. Mo. 1998).]

6. **ETHICAL APPLICATION CASE** SouthTrust Bank, N. A. extended a line of credit to Environmental Aspects, Inc. (EAI), Environmental Aspects of North Carolina's parent corporation, in June 1994. EAI executed a note and a security agreement evidencing that loan, and SouthTrust perfected its security interest by filing in the appropriate statewide and local office financing statements listing EAI as the debtor. Throughout 1995 and 1996, the bank, based on invoices submitted by those companies, advanced funds to EAI and its subsidiary corporations. Typically, SouthTrust would credit funds received from EAI of NC against the outstanding balance of SouthTrust's loans to EAI. Some of the advances of funds on the loans made to EAI in 1995 and 1996, then, were approved based on SouthTrust's review of EAI of NC's invoices identifying that company's accounts receivable and SouthTrust's belief that the subsidiaries and the parent corporation were operating as a single business represented by EAI. Although SouthTrust apparently knew of the existence of EAI of NC, SouthTrust at that time neither required EAI of NC to execute a security agreement nor filed financing statements to perfect its interest in property owned by EAI of NC or any other subsidiary. When EAI defaulted on its SouthTrust loans, EAI and its subsidiary corporations executed an October 31, 1997, agreement in which the subsidiaries agreed to be responsible for the obligations of the 1996 loan. Therefore, in November 1997, SouthTrust filed financing statements listing EAI and EAI of NC, among others, as debtors.

Meanwhile, back in September 1996, approximately 11 months before SouthTrust filed these financing statements

naming EAI of NC as a debtor, EAI of NC had executed a security agreement in favor of Advanced Analytics Laboratories, Inc. On December 27 and 31, 1996, AAL filed financing statements with the appropriate statewide and local offices. When asked to identify the debtor on the financing statements, AAL named EAI—the same legal entity listed as the debtor on SouthTrust's 1994 financing statements. Both the description boxes on the financing statements, located immediately below the debtor's name, and the debtor's signature lines on the statements contained the words "See Exhibit A attached for description and debtor's signature" and "See Exhibit A attached." The security agreements that were attached to the financing statements as Exhibit A and filed with the appropriate offices, both in the introductory paragraphs and on the signature pages, noted that the debtor was EAI of NC. The agreements also were signed by Dennis L. Mast as president of EAI of NC.

In April 1998, EAI and EAI of NC filed for bankruptcy under Chapter 11, and AAL subsequently filed a motion to determine the priority of the security interests held by SouthTrust. In granting summary judgment for AAL, the bankruptcy court concluded that AAL had perfected its security interest in the assets of EAI of NC in December 1996, 11 months before SouthTrust had perfected an interest in those assets in November 1997. The court concluded that AAL had properly perfected its interest because its financing statements, while containing minor errors, were not seriously misleading. Was the financing statement in which AAL had erroneously listed the debtor as EAI, but attached to which were security agreements that correctly noted the debtor as EAI of NC, sufficient to protect AAL's security interest? Is it ethical for a secured creditor to attempt to enforce its interest at the expense of other creditors when it made an error in filing that may have misled the other creditors? [See *In re Environmental Aspects, Inc.* 235 B.R. 378 (Bankr. E.D. N.C. 1999).]

7. **CRITICAL THINKING CASE** In August 1991, Expeditors International of Washington, Inc. began providing transportation-related services for CFLC, Inc., formerly known as Everex Systems, Inc. These services included freight forwarding, ocean shipping, and customs brokerage. For 17 months prior to Everex's filing its bankruptcy petition, Expeditors handled Everex's export and import shipments and thus was in continuous possession, either directly or through its agents, of Everex's goods. Expeditors billed Everex on Expeditors's regular invoices, which were issued contemporaneously with receipt of the shipments. From August 1991 until January 1993, Expeditors sent approximately 330 invoices that contained fine print on the reverse side entitled "Terms and Conditions of Service." The language of paragraph 15 stated:

15. General Lien on Any Property. The Company shall have a general lien on any and all property (and documents relating thereto) of the Customer, in its possession, custody or control or en route, for all claims for charges, expenses or advances incurred by the company in connection with any shipments of the Customer and if such claim remains unsatisfied for thirty (30) days after demand for its payment is made, the Company may sell at public auction or private sale . . . the goods, wares and/or merchandise, or so much thereof as may be necessary to satisfy such lien. . . .

Everex never signed these invoices or any agreement with Expeditors regarding the printed invoice terms. Moreover, the parties neither discussed nor expressly bargained over Section 15 of the invoice or any other provision on the reverse side of the invoice. Furthermore, Everex failed to object to the invoice terms prior to its bankruptcy; and Expeditors did not attempt to enforce Section 15 until October 29, 1992. At that time, Expeditors notified an Everex employee that Expeditors would be asserting its lien on the Everex goods in its possession until Everex made payments on the outstanding invoices.

Prior to the filing of the bankruptcy petition, the parties continued their normal business operations. At the time of Everex's bankruptcy filing, Expeditors thus was in possession of Everex property valued at $81,402. Expeditors claimed that Everex owed a balance of almost $43,000 for the past-due invoices and that Expeditors held a security interest in the Everex property because the invoices amounted to a security agreement. Expeditors subsequently filed a complaint in which it asked the bankruptcy court to determine the validity, priority, and extent of the claimed lien. Did Expeditors's preprinted invoice terms create an Article 9 security interest in Everex's property, either explicitly or through a course of dealing analysis? [See *In re CFLC, Inc.*, 166 F.3d 1012 (9th Cir. 1999).]

8. YOU BE THE JUDGE Bank of the West (BOW) and ITT Commercial Finance Corporation are commercial lenders. Over the course of several years, both BOW and ITT had lent money to the same debtor, a fledgling microcomputer dealership that had operated initially as a sole proprietorship run by Carlos Chacon and doing business under the trade name "Compucentro USA." Coronado Bank (CB) and Texas National Bank (TNB) had made loans to the sole proprietorship in August 1988 and February 1990, respectively. They had filed financing statements in the office of the secretary of state of the state of Texas to perfect their security interests in a broad class of current and after-acquired property under the names "Carlos Chacon d/b/a/ Compucentro USA" and "Carlos R. Chacon and Lorena Chacon d/b/a Compucentro USA." BOW subsequently had purchased these loans and thus held the security interests originally filed by CB and TNB.

On November 26, 1990, Carlos Chacon incorporated the sole proprietorship under the name "Compu-Centro, USA, Inc." On December 12, 1990, using the letterhead of the sole proprietorship bearing the name "Compucentro USA," Chacon informed BOW of the incorporation. The letter stated: "Enclosed please find copies of our newly incorporated license. As you finalize the paperwork on our loan, you [m]ay want to reflect that we are incorporated." On January 28, 1991, BOW filed with the secretary of state a notice of assignment of

the interest underlying CB's 1988 filing; and, on March 11, 1991, BOW similarly filed a notice of assignment of the interest underlying TBN's 1990 filing. These assignment notices did not reflect the debtor's recent incorporation. Rather, they listed the debtor's name as "Chacon, Carlos d/b/a/ Compucentro, USA" and "Carlo R. Chacon and Lorena Chacon d/b/a Compucentro USA," respectively. BOW also independently extended financing to the new corporation and on January 18, 1991, filed a new financing statement covering a broad class of current and after-acquired property and specifying the name of the debtor as "Compucentro, USA, Inc." This filing left out the hyphen in the corporation's legal name.

On October 1, 1991, ITT agreed to extend a line of credit for inventory purchases to Compu-Centro, USA, Inc. On October 14, 1991, ITT filed a financing statement covering a broad class of current and after-acquired property and specifying the name of the debtor as "Compu-Centro, USA, Inc." In the course of conducting a credit review of the corporation, ITT learned, through a loan application and credit report, that Compu-Centro, USA, Inc. had existed before its November 1990 incorporation with a different name and business structure. ITT also possessed financial documents of the Chacons that listed a $68,000 liability to BOW for a loan. ITT did not investigate further; and, on October 18, 1991, ITT obtained an official search of the secretary of state's records concerning the name "Compu-Centro, USA, Inc." ITT's filing was the sole filing reflected on the search report.

In the course of its business, Compu-Centro, USA, Inc. entered into a contract with the federal government to supply a medical center with computers. Neither ITT nor BOW provided Compu-Centro, USA, Inc. with the funding used to obtain these computers. Compu-Centro, USA, Inc. thereafter established an account at BOW in which the firm deposited only the proceeds. In 1993, by a check drawn on the BOW account, Compu-Centro, USA, Inc. paid BOW $300,000 out of the $1.3 million received as proceeds of the government contract. The purpose of the payment was to satisfy, in part, the outstanding balance on the debt owed to BOW. BOW did not instruct Compu-Centro, USA, Inc. to make payment out of these proceeds and never offset or froze the account.

At the time of the payment, Compu-Centro, USA, Inc. was in default on its obligation to ITT in the amount of $117,795.14. Consequently, on March 7, 1994, ITT filed an action seeking a declaratory judgment regarding the priority of its security interest in the collateral of Compu-Centro, USA, Inc., and alleging that BOW had converted the proceeds of the government contract. This case has been brought in *your* court. How will *you* resolve this controversy? Would your decision be different if you were to decide this case under the revised Article 9 than if it were decided under the prior version of the article? [See *U.C.C. Bulletin* (Eagan, Minn.: West Group, May 1999), 6–7; also see *ITT Commercial Finance v. Bank of the West*, 166 F. 3d 295 (5th Cir. 1999).]

Notes

1. UCC § 9-102 (a)(72).
2. UCC § 9-102 (a)(28).
3. UCC § 9-102 (a)(73).
4. UCC § 9-102 (a)(12).
5. UCC § 9-102 (a)(44).
6. UCC § 9-102 (a)(23).
7. UCC § 9-102 (a)(33).
8. UCC § 9-102 (a)(34).
9. UCC § 9-102 (a)(48).
10. UCC § 9-102 (a)(41).
11. UCC § 9-203 (a).
12. UCC § 9-102 (a)(7).
13. UCC § 9-102 (a)(69).
14. UCC § 9-204 (a).
15. UCC § 9-204 (b)(1). See also the federal "Credit Practice Rules," 16 C.F.R. § 444; 12 C.F.R. § 227. Under these rules, both the Federal Trade Commission and the Federal Reserve Board prohibit the creation of non–purchase money, nonpossessory liens in household goods.
16. UCC § 9-307 (b)(1).
17. UCC § 9-307 (e).
18. UCC § 9-307 (b)(2)–(3).
19. UCC § 9-307 (h).
20. UCC § 9-307 (c).
21. UCC § 9-501.
22. UCC § 9-516 (a).
23. UCC § 9-516 (b).
24. UCC § 9-515 (a).
25. UCC § 9-515 (d).
26. UCC § 9-502 (a).
27. UCC § 9-502 (b).
28. UCC § 9-503 (c).
29. UCC § 9-506 (c).
30. UCC § 9-313.
31. UCC § 9-104.
32. UCC § 9-107.
33. UCC § 9-105.
34. UCC § 9-309 (1).

CHAPTER 26

Secured Transactions: Priorities and Enforcement

AGENDA

NRW If NRW is going to grow and prosper, it will need funding. While the principals expect to generate profits from their operation, they realize that profits alone are not likely to provide the funding the firm will need. And since they do not want to sell any ownership interests, they know they will need to borrow money occasionally. They also realize that the firm will need collateral for these loans, but the firm does not have many different types of assets that can be used. As a result, they wonder if it is possible to use the *same* assets as collateral for more than one loan, and what effect this might have on any prospective creditors.

The firm will also be making a number of substantial sales of their inventory to retail purchasers, and many of these sales will be made on credit. The principals understand the need to make credit sales, but they would like to protect themselves and the firm as much as possible by retaining a claim on the merchandise they sell on credit. What type of security interest or other claim on the goods can the firm use in these situations? What will provide the greatest protection to the firm if any of its customers default?

If the firm should default on its obligations, what rights can its creditors assert against the firm and against any collateral used to secure the credit? If a customer defaults, what rights can the firm assert against that customer?

These and other questions are likely to arise during your study of this chapter. Be prepared! You never know when the firm or one of its members will seek your advice.

In a perfect world, debtors always repay their debts when they are due and creditors do not have to worry about when—or if—they will be repaid. However, the world in which we live is not perfect. Sometimes debtors don't pay their debts when they are due. In fact, sometimes the debtors never repay their obligations. As a result, creditors do worry about when and if they will be repaid. This is one of the main reasons that creditors seek security interests and then take the time and trouble to perfect those interests.

In Chapter 25 we discussed the process of creating a security interest by attachment, and the process of perfecting that security interest, thus giving notice to the world of the secured party's claim against some of the assets of the debtor. If each debtor dealt with only one creditor, we would not need such rules. In that situation, if the debtor defaulted on his or her obligations, everything the debtor owned would be available for the creditor's use in satisfying the creditor's claims. But in reality, debtors are likely to have multiple creditors, and each of those creditors may need to assert claims against assets of the debtor if the debtor defaults on his or her obligations. This is another reason for secured transactions—to allow secured creditors to assert claims against particular assets of the debtor that have been accepted as collateral on the obligation. Even this is not foolproof, though, since some debtors will use the same collateral as security for several loans or credit transactions. As a result, we need to have rules for establishing priorities among conflicting creditors, both secured and unsecured. We also need rules governing what the creditors can do if the debtor defaults and the creditors have to resort to the collateral in order to satisfy their claims, or at least a portion of their claims. That is the thrust of this chapter.

While many of these rules are found in revised Article 9, there is also an interplay between the provisions of Article 9 and various other state and federal laws in determining priorities. Not all creditor claims are based on a security interest. There may also be claims based on judgments or judgment liens, statutory liens, possessory liens, or the claims asserted by a trustee in bankruptcy. The rules for determining which creditor has priority, and where each of the competing creditors stands in relation to the other creditors and to the collateral is the primary focus of this chapter.

You can view revised Article 9, along with the Official Comments, at http://www.law.cornell.edu/topics/secured_transactions.html.

Priorities

A secured party's priority over other creditors can have enormous practical importance. If a debtor defaults on his

or her obligation, the parties with the highest priority are the creditors most likely to be able to recover most, if not all, of the money owed to them without having to resort to a trial. Creditors with lower priority, "junior" creditors, may well be prevented from accessing the collateral and may be forced to seek other methods of collecting from the debtor, including filing suit.

In addition, the debtor may not simply default. He or she may seek relief and protection in bankruptcy. The one catastrophe every creditor probably fears the most in any credit situation is the bankruptcy of the debtor. The reason is simple: In the event of bankruptcy an automatic stay is entered, which prevents the creditors from proceeding against the debtor. If the creditor participates in the bankruptcy proceeding, he or she runs the risk of receiving only a few cents on every dollar loaned to the debtor.

Yet, as we have seen, a creditor who attains the status of a perfected secured party can maximize the chances of recovering the money owed, even in a bankruptcy proceeding. This status gives the creditor first claim on the collateral and thus the best chance (generally by selling the collateral) of realizing most, if not all, of the debt. A perfected secured party, then, will have priority over general (or unsecured) creditors and lien creditors, including the trustee in bankruptcy. After the secured party has disposed of the collateral, any money in excess of that owed to the secured party may be applied to the claims of these other creditors. In many instances, however, no money remains to satisfy these latter claims. Thus, we cannot overemphasize the importance of becoming a secured party.

In the material to follow, we will first examine priorities among competing security interests. We will then look at the priorities between secured creditors and lien holders. We will finish our coverage of priorities by discussing the conflict between secured creditors and the trustee in bankruptcy.

Conflicting Security Interests

A creditor holding a properly perfected security interest has numerous advantages. As a result, most creditors strive to achieve this status. However, most debtors have either a limited number of assets to use as collateral, or a limited number of *types* of assets (equipment, inventory, etc.) to use as collateral. This fact, in turn, leads to the possibility that several secured parties will claim a security interest in the same collateral. When this happens, how can we determine who among this class of favored parties has priority? Or, in other words, who has "first dibs" on the collateral?

Article 9 spells out the rules for priority among conflicting security interests in § 9-322, which provides that:

(a) [***General Priority Rules***] *Except as otherwise provided in this section, priority among conflicting security interests and agricultural liens in the same collateral is determined according to the following rules:*

(1) *Conflicting perfected security interests and agricultural liens rank according to priority in time of filing or perfection. Priority dates from the earlier of the time a filing covering the collateral is first made or the security interest or agricultural lien is first perfected, if there is no period thereafter when there is neither filing nor perfection.*

(2) *A perfected security interest or agricultural lien has priority over a conflicting unperfected security interest or agricultural lien.*

(3) *The first security interest or agricultural lien to attach or become effective has priority if conflicting security interests or agricultural liens are unperfected.*

This is not as complicated as it sounds. The Code follows a "first-in-time, first-in-right" approach in deciding priority. According to this section, the first security interest to *file or perfect* has priority over any conflicting security interests in the same collateral. Thus, if two creditors, each claiming the same collateral as security, both file financing statements seeking to perfect their interests, the first to file would have priority since this creditor won the "race" to record the interest. The second creditor would be subordinate to the first creditor's claim even if the second creditor was the first to attach his or her interest, or the first to give value to the debtor.

Notice that the priority is determined by the first to file *or* perfect. It is quite possible that one creditor may file his or her interest *before* that interest attaches, thus establishing his or her priority position at the time of filing. In this example, since there has not yet been an attachment, this interest, while *filed,* is not perfected. A second, competing creditor might then take possession of the collateral, thus perfecting his or her security interest in the collateral by possession. If the first creditor then has his or her interest attach, probably by giving value to the debtor, the first creditor would have priority on the collateral. Since this creditor filed first, this creditor was first in time and will also be first in right. Note, however, that this creditor must have a perfected interest in order to have priority. If the creditor

files first, but his or her interest never attaches, the interest is never perfected. And if it is never perfected, it cannot have priority over a perfected interest.

If for some reason none of the competing parties has perfected its security interest, the first interest to attach enjoys priority. Relying on attachment alone as a vehicle for attaining priority, however, generally makes little sense because an unperfected secured creditor will not enjoy a preferred status in bankruptcy proceedings. In addition, any of the competing creditors can move ahead of the first party to attach simply by perfecting. While the creditor whose interest attached first is celebrating his or her priority position, one or more of the "losing" creditors can file or otherwise perfect, and by so doing gain a priority over the earlier attachment. Remember, to gain priority over other secured parties, other creditors or claimants, and over the trustee in bankruptcy, it is imperative to perfect the security interest as soon as possible. Normally this will entail filing a financing statement, if filing is an acceptable mode for perfecting this particular security interest. If filing is not appropriate, the secured creditor needs to perfect his or her interest as soon as possible in the appropriate manner.

Exceptions

While the Code generally follows the first-in-time, first-in-right approach to determining priority among conflicting security interests, there is an exception. A properly perfected security interest will not prevail over a purchase-money security interest, a PMSI, that is properly perfected even if the PMSI arises later in time. There are also two situations in which a perfected security interest is cut off by the sale of the collateral despite the prior perfection of the security interest covering the collateral prior to the sale. One such situation involves a buyer in the ordinary course of business and the other involves a bona fide purchaser of consumer goods. Each of these is discussed subsequently.

Purchase-Money Security Interests

According to § 9-324, a perfected purchase-money security interest in goods, other than inventory or livestock, has priority over a conflicting security interest in the same goods.[1] Further, a perfected purchase-money security interest in inventory has priority over conflicting security interests in the same inventory, as well as over any proceeds from the sale of that inventory, provided that the secured creditor has met two criteria: (1) the creditor has perfected the purchase-money security interest by filing before the debtor receives possession of the inventory, and (2) the creditor sends an authenticated notification to any holder of a conflicting security interest stating that the creditor expects to acquire a purchase-money security interest in the inventory, and that notice is received by the conflicting creditor before the debtor acquires the inventory.[2] If the PMSI is in livestock, the creditor also must perfect by filing before the debtor acquires the livestock, and must notify any conflicting creditors by authenticated notification before the debtor acquires the livestock.[3]

You should recall from Chapter 25 that a purchase-money security interest arises when the secured creditor provides the credit with which the debtor purchases the assets that will be used as collateral to secure the credit. Thus, a debtor who purchases a new computer from a computer company on credit, using the computer as security for the debt, has entered into a PMSI transaction. Similarly, if the debtor goes to the bank to borrow money in order to purchase the computer, and agrees to give the bank a security interest in the computer as collateral, a PMSI transaction is involved.

Generally speaking, a PMSI has priority over any other type of security interest, regardless of when the other interest attached or was perfected. This may seem unfair at first glance, but it actually makes sense from a business perspective. The debtor who enters into a PMSI transaction has not affected his or her net worth, so prior creditors are no worse off than before the transaction, and they may be better off, depending on the value of the new asset. The debtor's assets will increase by the value of the collateral purchased, and his or her liabilities will increase by the amount of the new debt secured by the new asset. If the debtor finances 100 percent of the transaction, both debits and credits increase by the same amount. If the debtor pays 20 percent down and finances the balance, the debtor's assets increase by the value of the new collateral, but decrease by the 20 percent down payment, a net increase of 80 percent of the asset's value. The liabilities also increase by 80 percent of the asset's value.

You should also recall from Chapter 25 that goods are classified according to their primary use in the hands of the purchaser-debtor. If a debtor acquires goods for personal or household use, those goods are viewed as consumer goods. If the debtor acquires the goods for the purpose of using them in the operation of a business, the goods are viewed as equipment. If the goods are acquired for use in a farming operation, they are deemed to be farm goods. And if the goods are acquired by the debtor with the intention to resell them as part of his or her business, the goods are inventory. The reason for this attention to the classification of the goods is that a purchase-money security interest can be perfected in different ways depending on the classification of the goods.

A PMSI in consumer goods is automatically perfected upon attachment, and the perfection is valid for five years. The creditor needs to do nothing beyond attachment in order to enjoy the special priority status of the PMSI. This normally means that the creditor needs only to enter into a security agreement with the debtor. There are numerous reasons for this special treatment, including the fact that consumer goods are not likely to be resold, and that this treatment helps to reduce the cost to consumers who are involved in consumer credit transactions.

A PMSI in equipment must be filed or otherwise perfected in order to protect the creditor. Since the collateral is equipment, and since the debtor is likely to need the equipment in order to operate his or her business, this normally means that the creditor will file in order to perfect. The creditor will enjoy the special priority accorded a PMSI if the interest is perfected at the time the interest attaches or within 20 days after the debtor receives the equipment. The same rules apply for farm goods other than livestock. Again, the creditor is required to file before, or within the 20 days after, the debtor receives the farm goods.

If the PMSI is in inventory or livestock, the creditor must file before the debtor acquires the property, and must also provide authenticated notification to any conflicting creditors before the debtor acquires the collateral in order for the creditor to properly perfect the PMSI.

If a creditor has an interest in equipment, farm goods, inventory, or livestock that otherwise qualifies as a PMSI, but fails to perfect this interest properly, the creditor will lose his or her "PM" status, but still retains an "SI." This means that an equipment creditor who failed to file within the 20-day grace period, but did file thereafter, would be a secured creditor with a perfected interest, but the interest would *not* be a PMSI and the creditor would not enjoy the special priority rules. Rather, he or she would now be subject to the first in time, first in right provisions of a regular security interest.

We know that a properly perfected PMSI has special priority over other security interests, but which creditor has priority if there are multiple PMSIs in the same collateral? While this situation is likely to be rare, it does occur on occasion. Previous versions of Article 9 did not address this issue, leaving it for the courts to decide on a case-by-case basis. The revision to Article 9 provides a statutory solution to the problem. If a seller and a lender each claim a PMSI in the same collateral, the *seller* of the goods has priority over a lender.[4]

You can find some additional information on PMSIs, and other aspects of secured transactions, at http://www.wsba.org/media/publications/barnews/default.htm

To those who see this "super priority" for purchase-money secured parties as unfair to prior secured creditors, the drafters of the Code offer the following policy justifications. The notification procedures required by the Code when the PMSI involves inventory or farm products will tip off the earlier creditor that the debtor is "double financing." At this point, the earlier creditor who believes that he or she is vulnerable may curtail any future advances to the debtor. And, assuming that the security agreement so provides and that this earlier creditor gives notice to the debtor, it may be argued that such double financing constitutes a condition of default, allowing the creditor to demand payment from the debtor. The earlier creditor has means of protecting his or her interest, while the debtor is allowed access to new sources of credit. Remember, the earlier creditors still have priority for the collateral on which they perfected, and they may have a secondary claim on the newly acquired assets covered by the PMSI.

If the security interest covers noninventory collateral (such as equipment, farm products other than livestock, or consumer goods), a purchase-money secured party has pri-

ority over prior secured parties without the need to give notice to those prior secured parties. Why is less required (a 20-day grace period for filing and no need to give notice to holders of previously filed security interests if the covered collateral is equipment or farm products; automatic perfection for consumer goods) if one wishes to attain priority in noninventory collateral? Apparently, the drafters of the Code believed that arrangements for periodic advances against incoming property are unusual outside the inventory field; thus, they did not think there was a need to notify noninventory secured parties. The case that follows illustrates how a court can dispose of lawsuits involving assertions of purchase-money security interests.

Buyers in the Ordinary Course of Business

Businesses that sell goods from inventory need to make sales in order to be profitable. The creditors who finance the inventory do so knowing that the goods are likely to be sold. If the debtor is successful, the collateral used to secure the

---

26.1

GENERAL ELECTRIC CAPITAL COMMERCIAL AUTOMOTIVE FINANCE, INC. v. SPARTAN MOTORS, LTD.
675 N.Y.S.2d 626 (N.Y. App. Div. 2 Div.. 1998)

FACTS On September 28, 1983, a predecessor of General Electric Capital Commercial Automotive Finance, Inc. (GECC) entered into an inventory security agreement with Spartan Motors, Ltd. in connection with Spartan's "floor plan" financing of the dealership's inventory. Pursuant to that agreement, GECC acquired a blanket lien, otherwise known as a "dragnet" lien, on Spartan's inventory so as to secure a debt in excess of $1,000,000. The agreement defined inventory as "All inventory, of whatever kind or nature, wherever located, now owned or hereafter acquired, and all returns, repossessions, exchanges, substitutions, replacements, attachments, parts, accessories and accessions thereto and thereof, and all other goods used or intended to be used in conjunction therewith, and all proceeds thereof (whether in the form of cash, instruments, chattel paper, general intangibles, accounts or otherwise)." This security agreement was duly filed in the appropriate state and local offices.

On July 19, 1991, Spartan signed a new wholesale security agreement with General Motors Acceptance Corporation (GMAC), in which GMAC agreed to finance—or "floor plan"—Spartan's inventory.

GMAC's security agreement was duly filed. In addition, the following certified letter dated July 17, 1991, officially notified GECC of GMAC's competing security interest in Spartan's inventory:

> This is to notify you that General Motors Acceptance Corporation holds or expects to acquire purchase money security interests in inventory collateral which will from time to time hereafter be delivered to Spartan Motors Ltd. of Poughkeepsie, New York, and in the proceeds thereof. Such inventory collateral consists, or will consist, of the types of collateral described in a financing statement, a true copy of which is annexed hereto and made a part hereof.

On May 7, 1992, Spartan paid $121,500 of its own money to acquire a 1992 600 SEL Mercedes-Benz. Six days later, on May 13, 1992, GMAC reimbursed Spartan; and the vehicle was placed on GMAC's floor plan. On July 7, 1992, Spartan paid $120,000 of its own money to acquire a second 1992 600 SEL Mercedes. Two days later, on July 9, 1992, GMAC reimbursed Spartan for that amount and placed the second vehicle on its floor plan. A few months later, on or about

October 2, 1992, GECC, seeking $1,180,999.98 in money then due to GECC under its agreement with Spartan, as well as a determination of who had priority in the two unsold Mercedes-Benzes, commenced this action against Spartan. Soon thereafter, Spartan filed a bankruptcy petition and ceased doing business. Among the assets appropriated and sold by GMAC were the two Mercedes-Benz automobiles, which were auctioned for $194,500. GECC subsequently claimed that, by so doing, GMAC had converted the two vehicles in violation of GECC's antecedent security interest.

ISSUE Did GMAC's agreement with Spartan create a purchase-money security interest that would give GMAC priority over GECC's blanket lien, even though GMAC had not advanced funds to Spartan until after the dealership had purchased vehicles on its own?

HOLDING Yes. Because GMAC was "obligated" to give value to enable Spartan to acquire rights in the two Mercedes-Benzes and the purchase and loan transactions were only days apart, Spartan's purchases and GMAC's reimbursements were sufficiently "closely allied" to have given GMAC a purchase-money security interest in the vehicles in question.

REASONING Excerpts from the opinion of Judge Friedmann:

A perfected purchase-money security interest provides an exception to the general first-in-time, first-in-right rule of conflicting security interests. Thus, a perfected purchase-money security interest in inventory has priority over a conflicting prior security interest in the same inventory.... However, as the Supreme Court, Dutchess County, observed, the purported purchase-money security interest must fit within the Uniform Commercial Code definition to qualify for the exception.

Uniform Commercial Code § 9-107 defines a "purchase-money security interest" as a security interest:

(a) taken or retained by the seller of the collateral to secure all or part of its price; or

(b) taken by a person who by making advances or incurring an obligation gives value to enable the debtor to acquire rights in or the use of collateral if such value is in fact so used.

The issue here is therefore whether GMAC's payment as reimbursement to Spartan *after* it had acquired the two Mercedes-Benz vehicles on two different occasions qualifies as an "advance" or "obligation" that enabled Spartan to purchase the cars, such that GMAC acquired a purchase-money security interest in the vehicles. The arguments *against* finding a purchase-money security interest under these circumstances are basically twofold:

Firstly, of the few courts to construe Uniform Commercial Code § 9-107 (b), many have been reluctant to decide that a purchase-money security interest has been created where, as here, title to and possession of the merchandise have passed to the debtor *before* the loan is advanced. Secondly, the literal wording of the agreement between GMAC and Spartan appears to accord GMAC purchase-money secured status only when the finance company paid Spartan's "manufacturer, distributor or other seller" *directly*. As the Supreme Court noted, nothing in GMAC's contract with Spartan appears to contemplate any obligation on the part of the financier to "reimburse" the auto dealership for funds that the latter had already expended to purchase merchandise....

If under UCC 9-107 (b) neither the chronology of the financing nor the configuration of the cash flow is, without more, dispositive ... how can we tell if a loan transaction is sufficiently "closely allied" to a purchase transaction to qualify for purchase-money status?

One factor that courts have considered is simple temporal proximity—that is, whether the value is given by the creditor "more or less contemporaneously with the debtor's acquisition of the property" ... However, it should be noted that early drafts of UCC 9-107 contained an additional subdivision (c), which envisioned a purchase-money interest to the extent of value advanced for the purpose of financing new acquisitions within 10 days of the debtor's receiving possession of the new goods, *even though the value was not in fact used to pay the price*. The subdivision was deleted, according to the sponsors, because it extended the purchase-money interest too far.... It appears, then, that mere closeness in time is but another mechanical circumstance to be considered—a significant clue, but not one dispositive of the relationship between the transactions.

The authorities are agreed that the critical inquiry, as in all contract matters, is into the intention of the parties.... "In determining whether a security interest exists, the intent of the parties controls, and that intent may best be determined by examining the language used and considering the conditions and circumstances confronting the parties when the contract was made." ... In assessing the relationship of the transactions, the test should be whether the availability of the loan was a factor in negotiating the sale, and/or whether the lender was committed at the time of the sale to advance the amount required to pay for the items purchased....

Applying these principles to the matter before us: (1) The record establishes that GMAC's reimbursements to Spartan following its two Mercedes-Benz purchases were only six and two days apart, respectively. (2) GECC does not dispute GMAC's contention that a postpurchase reimbursement arrangement was common in the trade, as well as routine in Spartan's course of dealing with GMAC and its other financiers, depending upon the circumstances of the purchase. . . . In the language of Uniform Commercial Code § 9-107 (b): GMAC was committed to give value to enable the car dealership to acquire rights in the collateral. The value so extended was intended to and in fact did enable Spartan to acquire the two Mercedes-Benzes, as GECC does not seriously suggest that without GMAC's backing Spartan could have afforded to purchase the expensive vehicles. Accordingly, the literal requirements of Uniform Commercial Code § 9-107 (b) are satisfied, notwithstanding the inverted purchase-loan chronology. . . . Because GMAC's loans were "closely allied" with Spartan's inventory acquisitions, GMAC enjoys a purchase-money security interest in the contested merchandise. . . .

Under the UCC, the identification of a secured party's collateral is adequate if it is "reasonably" specific. Normally, the designation of the generic "type" of collateral covered by a security agreement will be found to be sufficient. . . . Moreover, the purpose of judicial inquiry is solely to establish, first, whether the written description may reasonably be construed to include the disputed property, and secondly, whether the parties intended that the description include that property. . . . Here, GMAC's security agreement and its timely notice to GECC adequately specified the precise nature of the vehicular inventory to which its lien attached, such that GECC should have been alerted to GMAC's claim to the two Mercedes-Benzes; and, as discussed above, it is clear that GMAC and Spartan intended these vehicles to be covered by their financing agreement. . . .

Accordingly, the Supreme Court erred when it found that, having financed the two vehicles at issue here by way of reimbursements—"the very opposite of an advance"—GMAC did not acquire a purchase-money security interest pursuant to Uniform Commercial Code 9-107 (b). Rather, since GMAC has established—and GECC does not deny—that GMAC was "obligated" to give value to enable Spartan to acquire rights in the two Mercedes-Benzes, and the purchase and loan transactions were only days apart, it is clear that Spartan's purchase and GMAC's subsequent reimbursement were sufficiently "closely allied" to give GMAC a purchase-money security interest in the subject vehicles. . . .

BUSINESS CONSIDERATIONS Assume you work for GMAC and that your boss has asked you to redraft the instruments connected with this case so as to ensure that the firm in the future unquestionably will enjoy the status of a purchase-money secured party. Although the staff counsel will write the final draft, what language will you incorporate in this first draft?

ETHICAL CONSIDERATIONS Was Spartan behaving in an unethical fashion when it engaged two "floor plan" financiers? Would your answer differ if you discovered that Spartan had begun dealing with GMAC because it (Spartan) was behind in its payments to GECC?

credit will leave the possession of the debtor at the time of the sale. But what if the debtor sells the goods and then fails to make payments to the secured creditor? Will the creditor be permitted to proceed against the buyer of the goods, enforcing his or her security interest against the purchaser?

According to § 9-320(a), a buyer in the ordinary course of business takes the goods free from any security interests valid against the seller even if the security interest is perfected and the buyer knows of its existence. (There is an exception to this rule if the buyer is buying farm goods from a person engaged in farming operations.)

The key point to this rule, which effectively "cuts off" the perfected security interest of the creditor, is that the sale is in the *ordinary* course of business. The debtor is simply doing what the debtor was expected to do. He or she is selling inventory to customers. The creditor loses his or her claim against the inventory that has been sold, but the creditor is automatically perfected on the proceeds from that sale, so the creditor is in no worse position than before. In addition, most security interests covering inventory are floating liens that will automatically attach to the replacement inventory the debtor acquires in restocking. And absent this rule, it would be very difficult for the debtor to make sales to customers. If a customer had to worry about whether the debtor would pay his or her creditors, with the customer being subject to the repossession of the goods if the debtor did not pay, the customer would hesitate to make a purchase.

Is should also be noted that this rule does not apply if the sale is made *not* in the ordinary course of business. For example, a bulk sale in which the buyer purchases a significant portion of the debtor's inventory and/or equipment does not cut off the rights of the secured creditor in the items sold. In this situation the security interest remains valid and enforceable against the buyer, and if the debtor defaults, the creditor can enforce the interest against the buyer. The buyer, in turn, would then have to sue the seller for any losses suffered due to the seller's default.

Although many people use the terms *bona fide purchaser* and *buyer in the ordinary course of business* interchangeably, they are distinct concepts. We more appropriately term a consumer who has bought goods from another consumer in an occasional sale a bona fide purchaser. Buyers in the ordinary course of business, in contrast, are purchasers who are buying from a seller who routinely sells from inventory or otherwise regularly engages in such transactions.

Bona Fide Purchasers of Consumer Goods

Another class of persons who may have "priority" of a sort over a previously perfected security interest is the *bona fide purchaser* of consumer goods. However, before this exception applies, several conditions must be met. According to § 9-320(b), a buyer of goods who purchases the goods from a consumer takes the goods free of any security interests that may exist in those goods, if:

• the buyer buys the goods without knowledge of the security interest,

• the buyer purchases the goods "for value,"

• the buyer purchases the goods for his or her own personal or household use, and

• the buyer purchases the goods before a financing statement covering the goods is filed by the creditor.

This means that a consumer who buys goods from a consumer and gives value for the goods will take the goods free of any security interest that the seller granted, provided that the buyer did not know of the security interest, and that the secured party had not filed to perfect. Since many, if not most, consumer credit transactions of the type likely to be involved in this type of sale involve a PMSI in the covered goods, and since a PMSI in consumer goods is automatically perfected without filing, it is quite likely that the consumer buyer will take the goods "free and clear" of any interests of the secured party.

Other Exceptions

Two other exceptions need to be mentioned before we complete our discussion of conflicting security interests. The revision to Article 9 permits a secured party holding a security interest in a negotiable instrument or in chattel paper to perfect this interest by filing. (Under the prior law the creditor had to take possession in order to perfect such an interest in negotiable instruments, with the exception of a 21-day "grace period" if the instrument represented pro-

---

NRW CASE 26.1   Finance

NRW

SECURITY INTEREST

The firm recently sold 100 StuffTrakRs on credit to a local retail store. NRW retained a security interest in these units and properly perfected its interest by filing in the appropriate office in a timely manner. Unfortunately, the principals have learned that this retail store is having serious financial problems and may be forced to go out of business. They ask you if they can assert their security interest against the units still in the store's possession if the retailer ultimately should default on the contract. They also want to know what rights, if any, they can assert against any customers who purchased a StuffTrakR from the store if the store eventually defaults on its obligations to the firm. What will you tell them?

BUSINESS CONSIDERATIONS What should a business creditor that holds a perfected security interest do if or when it hears that one of its debtors is having financial difficulties? How can the business creditor protect its interests without jeopardizing the future of the debtor?

ETHICAL CONSIDERATIONS Assuming that it would be legal to do so, would it be ethical for a secured creditor to seek enforcement of its security interest against buyers in the ordinary course of business who purchased collateral from a retail seller that also was a debtor of the secured creditor?

INTERNATIONAL CONSIDERATIONS Assume that a business creditor extends credit to a chain of stores that is organized in another country but doing business in this country. If the creditor properly perfects under Article 9, can the creditor assert the same rights against the foreign company that it could assert against a U.S.-based company? How would the creditor perfect a security interest against a foreign-based company?

---

ceeds from the sale of other, covered collateral.) While filing in now a permissible method of perfection, it may not be as effective as the creditor would like. Most people who are purchasing a negotiable instrument or a chattel paper are not going to run a record search prior to acquiring the instrument or the paper to determine whether it is subject to a security interest. Such conduct would be unreasonable for the purchaser and would significantly slow down commercial transactions. As a result, the new version of Article 9 addresses these issues in § 9-330.

Under this section, a purchaser of chattel paper has priority over a security interest in the chattel paper, if the chattel paper represents proceeds from the sale of inventory by the debtor, the purchaser gave new value for the paper and took the paper in the ordinary course of his or her business, and the paper itself did not indicate that it had already been assigned to a third party.[5] If the purchaser purchases a negotiable instrument, and qualifies as a holder in due course following this purchase, the purchaser-HDC takes priority over any security interests filed against the negotiable instrument.[6]

Conflicts between Security Interests and Liens

As you should already have surmised, secured creditors may face a number of conflicting claims against the collateral in which a security interest has been granted by the debtor. Among the types of claims that may conflict with the secured creditors are the various types of liens that another creditor of the debtor may assert. These liens may take the form of *judicial* liens, *statutory* liens, and *consensual* liens. We will look at the effect each of these types of liens may have on the priority of a perfected security interest in the next section.

Judicial Liens

A judicial lien is a lien acquired by the creditor in a judicial proceeding. The most common method for creating a judicial lien is for the winning party in a lawsuit to have the sheriff, or some other court official, levy on the assets of the debtor. Section 9-102 (a)(52) defines a lien creditor as:

(a) a creditor that has acquired a lien on the property involved by attachment, levy, or the like;
(b) an assignee for the benefit of creditors from the time of assignment;
(c) a trustee in bankruptcy from the date of the filing of the petition; or
(d) a receiver in equity from the time of appointment.

In a conflict between a secured creditor and a judicial lien holder, the interests are generally viewed as being equal, and the courts apply the "first-in-time, first-in-right" rule to determine the priority among the creditors. Thus, if the security interest is perfected before the judicial lien attaches, the secured party will have priority.[7] Also, if the creditor makes any "future advances" to the debtor, these future advances will also have priority over an intervening judicial lien, if the future advances are made within 45 days after the judicial lien attaches. And if the creditor has no knowledge of the judicial lien or the future advance is made because of a commitment made without knowledge of the judicial lien, the 45-day limit does not apply.[8]

Notice in the definition set out above that each of the judicial liens *except* the one created by attachment or levy also provides for when the lien attaches. For a judicial lien created by attachment or levy, state law controls as to when the interest attaches. Most states hold that the interest attaches at the time of the levy, which means when the sheriff takes physical control of the asset. However, a few states treat the lien as attaching when the court clerk issues a writ of attachment.

Statutory Liens

Statutory liens arise as a result either of a statutory provision establishing the lien, or under common law traditions and customs. Statutory liens are often obtained by landlords against their tenants, artisans or mechanics against the party for whom they have performed work, and attorneys who have not been paid for legal services rendered on behalf of the debtor. Tax liens also are statutory liens. A statutory lien may be possessory or nonpossessory. A possessory statutory lien attaches to the debtor's property when the lienholder takes possession of the collateral. For example, if a person takes his or her car to a mechanic for a tune-up, the mechanic has a possessory statutory lien on the car until he or she is paid for the services. If the owner does not pay, the mechanic is allowed to retain possession until such time as payment is made. However, if the mechanic releases the car to the customer, the mechanic has surrendered the lien and is, at that point, merely an unsecured general creditor. A possessory lien has priority over a properly perfected security interest, regardless of when either arose, unless the statute that creates the lien expressly makes the lien subordinate to a security interest.[9]

Some interesting special rules apply to a tax lien. If a debtor fails to pay his or her federal taxes, a tax lien is created by statute. This lien arises at the moment of "assessment" by the IRS, even though no one except IRS knows of the existence of the assessment or the related lien at that time. This lien is valid against all property owned by the debtor, or anything subsequently acquired by the debtor. However, the Federal Tax Lien Act specifies that a properly perfected security interest that was perfected prior to the attachment of the tax lien will prevail over the tax lien.[10] In addition, the IRS has ruled that a PMSI will also prevail over a tax lien, even if the PMSI arises after the tax lien attaches, provided that the PMSI is properly perfected.[11]

Consensual Liens

Consensual liens arise by agreement of the parties. While a secured transaction is a type of consensual lien, that is not the type we are discussing here. The consensual liens that are likely to conflict with a secured transaction are likely to involve mortgages on real estate, often in conflict with a secured interest in a fixture.

A fixture is a good that has become so related to a parcel of real property that any interest in the fixture arises under real property law.[12] Unlike other security interests, an interest in fixtures must be filed locally in the office where a mortgage would be filed. It must also include a legal description of the real property, and it must contain the name of the owner of the property, if the owner is not also the debtor.[13]

If the creditor is financing the construction of a building and has properly perfected a construction mortgage, his or her security interest has priority over any conflicting security interests. This would include a PMSI in fixtures that is perfected before the fixture is attached to the realty or within the 20 days after it is so attached.[14] In any other situation involving a fixture, if the interest in the fixture is a PMSI, and if the secured party perfects by filing before the fixture is attached to the realty or within 20 days after it is attached, the PMSI in the fixture will have priority.[15] If the security interest in the fixture in not a PMSI, or if it is a PMSI that is not timely filed, the interest in the fixture is subordinate to any interests in the realty that were recorded prior to the filing of the interest in the fixture.[16]

Conflicts between Security Interests and the Trustee in Bankruptcy

When a debtor petitions for relief under the provisions of the Bankruptcy Act, or is involuntarily petitioned into bankruptcy, several things happen. (Bankruptcy is discussed in detail in Chapter 28, and several of these points will be treated more expansively there.) The bankruptcy court enters an order for relief and issues an automatic stay. This automatic stay halts any legal proceedings involving the debtor, including any rights of the secured party to proceed

---

NRW CASE 26.2   Finance

PURCHASE-MONEY SECURITY INTEREST

NRW sold several StuffTrakRs to a customer on credit and retained a purchase-money security interest in the units. (Since the units were sold to a consumer there was no need for the firm to file, so taking a security interest seemed like a good idea.) The customer is in default on the debt, and the firm would like to enforce its interest in the units. Carlos learned that two of the units are in the possession of a repairperson whom the customer had hired to work on them. Carlos wants to know what rights the firm has in this situation and also whether the firm can insist that the repairperson turn over the StuffTrakRs to NRW due to its perfected security interest. He also would like to know whether the lack of a filing might reduce the firm's rights in this situation. What will you tell him?

BUSINESS CONSIDERATIONS Why might a secured creditor, in order to obtain possession of the collateral itself, want to pay a person who has a possessory lien stemming from repairing the collateral? What can the creditor do if it decides not to redeem the collateral from the possessory lien holder?

ETHICAL CONSIDERATIONS Is there an ethical reason for allowing a possessory lien holder to gain priority over a properly perfected security interest? What ethical considerations justify such a rule?

INTERNATIONAL CONSIDERATIONS If NRW were operating in Mexico, would it have similar rights to the rights in can assert under Article 9 in the United States? Would your answer be different if NRW were operating in Canada?

---

against the debtor for any default on the underlying debt. In addition, in a Chapter 7 proceeding—the most common type—a trustee is appointed to "manage" the debtor's estate for the benefit of the debtor's unsecured creditors.

The trustee in bankruptcy is treated as a judicial lien holder. As was discussed earlier, a judicial lien is subordinate to a prior perfected security interest. As a result, it would seem as if the secured party is in good position. While there are some obstacles, such as the automatic stay provisions, the secured party retains his or her priority. Given this priority position and the general protections afforded a perfected security interest, what could possibly go wrong? As it turns out, several things could go wrong, depending on the circumstances of the case and the timing of the creation of the security interest.

The trustee is expected to marshal the debtor's assets, prepare an inventory of those assets, and investigate any claims against those assets. This would include the claims of any secured parties and any lien holders. The trustee will determine, under the provisions of the Bankruptcy Code, whether any of these claims were valid against the debtor's estate at the time the bankruptcy petition was filed. If they were, the collateral subject to any such claims is normally released to the secured creditor or the lien holder. (The secured party can also attempt to get a release from the automatic stay in order to be allowed to repossess the collateral.)

Also, the trustee may decide to challenge the validity of the security interest. In this situation, the trustee will attempt to show either that the security interest is fraudulent against any of the unsecured creditors or that the interest is a voidable preference. If either can be shown, the interest is set aside and the secured party becomes an unsecured general creditor for purposes of the bankruptcy proceeding. If the debtor transfers property, or an interest in property, while he or she is insolvent, and the transfer is for less than "fair consideration," the transfer is presumed to be fraudulent and will be declared invalid. If the security interest involves a transfer of property, or an interest in property, and it is made for a preexisting debt, and the debtor is insolvent at the time of the transfer and the transfer is made within 90 days of the petition, the transfer can be challenged as a voidable preference. Thus, while the perfected secured creditor retains his or her priority over the trustee as a hypothetical judicial lien holder, that priority can be lost if the trustee can successfully challenge the creation of the security interest under either of these criteria.

Enforcement of the Security Interest

Default

Thus far, we have considered the methods by which a secured party can protect his or her interest in the collateral. Neither the debtor nor the secured party, however, wants to consider the possibility that the debtor will *default*, or fail to meet the obligations set out in the security agreement. Still, this contingency sometimes occurs, and is, in fact, the reason for seeking a security interest in the first place.

The default of the debtor represents a bittersweet moment for the secured party. On the one hand, default distresses the secured party because it reveals that the debtor may be unable or unwilling to pay the debt to the secured party. But, on the other hand, the secured party has worked hard to preserve his or her status. The secured party has a position that is superior to any unsecured lenders, he or she has established a priority position against other secured parties and lien holders, and upon the debtor's default, has certain rights to the collateral. Part 6 of revised Article 9 addresses default and the enforcement of the security interest. It also addresses the rights of the debtor following a default. We will examine these rules in the balance of the chapter.

Interestingly, the Code does not define the term default. Basically, the parties decide what events constitute default, and the security agreement may well embody these conclusions. Basically default means whatever the security agreement says it means. Nonpayment by the debtor perhaps constitutes the easiest definition of default. But default clauses often are broad and lengthy. Security agreements also typically include *acceleration clauses* by which the secured party demands that all obligations be paid immediately. In the absence of bad faith and unconscionability, courts routinely uphold these clauses whenever the secured party can show that the debtor has defaulted.

Upon default, the secured party may resort to various alternative remedies. Using non-Code remedies, the secured party may become a judgment creditor, may garnish the debtor's wages, or may replevy the goods. Of course, the secured party may also choose to use the remedies provided in Article 9. Code remedies include strict foreclosure (retention of the collateral in satisfaction of the debt) and resale of the collateral. The secured creditor's rights after default are spelled out in § 9-601:

(a) After default, a secured party has the rights provided in this part and, except as otherwise provided in Section 9-602, those provided by agreement of the parties. A secured party:

(1) may reduce a claim to judgment, foreclose, or otherwise enforce the claim, security, interest, or agricultural lien by any available judicial procedure; and

(2) if the collateral is documents, may proceed either as to the documents or as to the goods they cover.

(b) A secured party in possession of collateral or control of collateral . . . has the rights and duties provided in Section 9-207.

(c) The rights under subsections (a) and (b) are cumulative and may be exercised simultaneously.

Obviously, the secured creditor has substantial protections when the debtor defaults. The creditor needs to be aware, however, that there may be problems if he or she attempts to use all available remedies simultaneously. It is possible

NRW CASE 26.3   Finance

DEFAULT

Third Bank holds a perfected security interest in some of NRW's inventory, and the perfection is by possession (through a field warehousing arrangement). Third Bank is asserting that NRW has defaulted on its obligations and that it (Third Bank) intends to seek recovery under the provisions of Article 9. Helen and Carlos ask you what obligations or liabilities Third Bank may owe to NRW under these circumstances, and what obligations or liabilities NRW may owe to Third Bank. What will you tell them?

BUSINESS CONSIDERATIONS What factors should a secured creditor consider before it decides whether to seek a recovery under Article 9 or under common law? Why might a business decide to forgo its Article 9 protections and seek a non-Code remedy?

ETHICAL CONSIDERATIONS Is it ethical for a secured creditor to elect *not* to enforce its security interest upon default by the debtor? What impact might such a decision have on the other creditors of the defaulting debtor?

INTERNATIONAL CONSIDERATIONS Suppose that a debtor maintains a sizeable bank account in another country. Could a secured creditor obtain a writ of garnishment from a U.S. court in order to garnish that bank account? What problems might the creditor encounter in attempting to do so?

---

that the simultaneous exercise of remedies in a particular case may constitute abusive behavior or harassment, thus giving rise to liability despite the apparently permissive language of § 9-601(c).[17]

Assuming that the debtor has defaulted, what can the secured creditor do? Let us examine these rights, first by looking at the non-Code remedies and then by looking at the remedies available under the Code.

Non-Code Remedies

The Code says that, upon default, secured parties may seek a court judgment, may foreclose, or may otherwise enforce the security agreement by any available judicial procedure. Accordingly, secured parties can use their Code remedies of repossession and resale with the possibility of a deficiency judgment for which the debtor is liable, or they can follow the non-Code remedy of becoming judgment creditors whereby they file suit, obtain a judgment, and have the sheriff use a writ of execution to levy on the goods and then sell the goods at a public sale. The proceeds of this sale are paid to the secured party. Another non-Code alternative to levying on the goods involves garnishment. Garnishment can be used on any assets of the debtor that are in the possession of a third party, including bank accounts and wages or salary. If the creditor seeks a garnishment of the debtor's wages, he or she will be limited to receiving only a set percentage of the debtor's wages, as determined by state statute. There may be certain advantages to the creditor from seeking non-Code remedies. This is especially true if the collateral has substantially declined in value. However, most creditors elect the tidier and speedier remedies provided by the Code, most likely the remedies of repossession and disposition by resale or lease.

Code Remedies

Right of Repossession

Article 9 gives the creditor the right to take possession of the collateral if the debtor defaults, unless the parties have agreed to the contrary. This action, generally called a "repossession" even if the creditor never previously possessed the collateral, is the essential first step if the creditor is seeking his or her Code remedies. The act of repossession may be a simple affair with no controversies and no problems, or it may be substantially different.

The secured party may decide to use the "self-help" method of repossessing. This involves a repossession by the secured party without the use of any judicial procedures or any court officers. However, while the Code specifically permits "self-help," it also states that the creditor may not *breach the peace* in effecting the repossession.[18] Technically, this means that the creditor is allowed to personally take possession of the collateral from the debtor, but must stop any such efforts if continuation would involve a breach of the peace. Thus, if the debtor or some other person who is present objects to the act of repossession, the creditor must stop. Of course, he or she can try again later. Similarly, the creditor is not allowed to enter the debtor's property in order to make a repossession if doing so involves breaking and entering. However, most courts have upheld a repossession even though the creditor entered onto the debtor's property without permission, thereby committing a trespass. The courts have reasoned that a "mere" trespass, without more, is not enough to constitute a breach of the peace. Courts have also upheld repossessions made through trickery, but not if the trickery involves impersonating a police officer or other court official. The courts have prohibited the use of force or the threat of force in making a repossession, including the fact that the collection agent is armed. If the collection agent is armed, he or she has used an "implied threat" in order to complete the repossession, and this constitutes a breach of the peace.

In the next case the court addressed the issue of whether a breach of the peace occurred during a repossession. After reading the opinion, decide whether you think the court adequately treated the issues raised.

26.2

GILES v. FIRST VIRGINIA CREDIT SERVICES, INC.
149 N.C. App. 89; 560 S.E.2d 557; 2002 N.C. App. LEXIS 127 (N.C. App. 2002)

FACTS Joann Giles entered into an installment sale contract on or about January 18, 1997, for the purchase of an automobile. The contract was assigned to First Virginia, which obtained a senior perfected purchase-money security interest in the automobile. The terms of the contract required Joann Giles to make 60 regular monthly payments to First Virginia. The contract stated that Joann Giles's failure to make any payment due under the contract within 10 days after its due date would be a default. The contract contained an additional provision agreed to by Joann Giles that stated:

> If I am in default, you may consider all my remaining payments to be due and payable, without giving me notice. I agree that your rights of possession will be greater than mine. I will deliver the property to you at your request, or you may use lawful means to take it yourself without notice or other legal action. . . .

During the early morning hours of June 27, 1999, Professional Auto Recovery, at the request of First Virginia, repossessed the locked automobile from plaintiffs' front driveway. According to First Virginia, the account of Joann Giles was in arrears for payments due on May 2, 1999, and June 2, 1999, and pursuant to the terms of the contract, repossession was permitted.

In an affidavit filed by plaintiffs in opposition to First Virginia's motion for summary judgment, plaintiffs' neighbor, Glenn A. Mosteller, stated that he was awakened around 4:00 A.M. by the running of a loud diesel truck engine on the road outside his house. He added that he got up to see what was going on when the truck did not leave, and that he saw a man run up the Giles's driveway, where their car was parked. Shortly thereafter the car came "flying out back down the driveway making a loud noise and starting screeching off. . . . I got to the phone, called the Giles and told them someone was stealing their car. . . . About 5 minutes later a police car came up and pulled into the Giles' yard. Then another police car came then a Sheriff's Deputy car came. Then another police car came. . . .

There was a great commotion going on out in the street and in our yard all to the disturbance of the quietness and tranquility of our neighborhood. . . . It scared me and it scared the Giles."

Joann Giles stated in a deposition that she was awakened by Mr. Mosteller's telephone call in which he told her that someone was stealing her car. She stated she ran to see if the automobile was parked outside and confirmed that it was gone. Plaintiffs testified in their depositions that neither of them saw the car being repossessed but were only awakened by their neighbor after the automobile was gone. During the actual repossession, no contact was made between Professional Auto Recovery and plaintiffs, nor between Professional Auto Recovery and Mr. Mosteller.

The Giles filed a complaint against First Virginia and Professional Auto Recovery for wrongful repossession of the automobile. They further alleged that the removal of the automobile constituted a breach of the peace in violation of state law.

First Virginia filed an answer stating the automobile was repossessed due to the default of Joann Giles in making the payments to First Virginia on a loan secured by the automobile. First Virginia stated that N.C. Gen. Stat. § 25-9-503 permitted a secured lender to peaceably repossess its collateral upon default by a debtor and that such repossession could not, as a matter of law, constitute conversion of the collateral or an unfair or deceptive trade practice. First Virginia moved to dismiss plaintiffs' complaint for failure to state a claim.

ISSUE Did the repossession of the automobile involve a breach of the peace in violation of state law?

HOLDING No. The repossession was properly done under state law and there was no breach of the peace.

REASONING Excerpts from the opinion of Judge McGee:

Our Courts have long recognized the right of secured parties to repossess collateral from a defaulting debtor without resort to judicial process, so long as the repossession is effected peaceably. . . .

The General Assembly did not define breach of the peace but instead left this task to our Courts, and although a number of our appellate decisions have considered this self-help right of secured parties, none have clarified what actions constitute a breach of the peace.

[UCC] § 9-503, at issue in this appeal, has been replaced by [UCC] § 9-609 . . . which states that a secured party, after default, may take possession of the collateral without judicial process, if the secured party proceeds without breach of the peace. In Number 3. of the Official Comment to the new statutory provision, our General Assembly continued to state that, "like former Section 9-503, this section does not define or explain the conduct that will constitute a breach of the peace, leaving that matter for continuing development by the courts." . . . The General Assembly clearly may further define and/or limit the time, place and conditions under which a repossession is permitted, but it has not yet done so. . . .

In a case addressing the issue of whether prior notice of repossession is required under . . . § 9-503, our Court stated that repossession can be accomplished under the statute without prior notice so long as the repossession is peaceable. . . . Without specifically defining breach of the peace, our Court explained that "of course, if there is confrontation at the time of the attempted repossession, the secured party must cease the attempted repossession and proceed by court action in order to avoid a 'breach of the peace.'" . . . This indicates, as argued by First Virginia, that confrontation is at least an element of a breach of the peace analysis.

In that breach of the peace has not heretofore been clarified by our appellate courts, but instead only vaguely referred to, we must construe this term as the drafters intended. "In construing statutes the court should always give effect to the legislative intent." . . . "The intent of the Legislature may be ascertained from the phraseology of the statute as well as the nature and purpose of the act and the consequences which would follow from a construction one way or another." . . . In determining what conduct constitutes a breach of the peace we consider each of these contributing elements. . . .

The courts in many states have examined whether a breach of the peace in the context of the UCC has occurred. Courts have found a breach of the peace when actions by a creditor incite violence or are likely to incite violence. . . .

Other courts have expanded the phrase breach of the peace beyond the criminal law context to include occurrences where a debtor or his family protest the repossession. . . .

If a creditor removes collateral by an unauthorized breaking and entering of a debtor's dwelling, courts generally hold this conduct to be a breach of the peace. . . . Removal of collateral from a private driveway, without more however, has been found not to constitute a breach of the peace. . . . Additionally, noise alone has been determined to not rise to the level of a breach of the peace. . . .

Many courts have used a balancing test to determine if a repossession was undertaken at a reasonable time and in a reasonable manner, and to balance the interests of debtors and creditors. . . . Five relevant factors considered in this balancing test are: "(1) where the repossession took place, (2) the debtor's express or constructive consent, (3) the reactions of third parties, (4) the type of premises entered, and (5) the creditor's use of deception." . . .

Relying on the language of our Supreme Court . . . plaintiffs argue that the "guiding star" in determining whether a breach of the peace occurred should be whether or not the public peace was preserved during the repossession. . . . Plaintiffs contend "the elements as to what constitutes a breach of the peace should be liberally construed" and urge our Court to adopt a subjective standard considering the totality of the circumstances as to whether a breach of the peace occurred. . . .

Based upon our review of our appellate courts' treatment of breach of the peace in pre-UCC and UCC cases, as well as in other areas of the law, the purposes and policies of the UCC, and the treatment other jurisdictions have given the phrase, we find that a breach of the peace, when used in the context of . . . § 9-503, is broader than the criminal law definition. A confrontation is not always required, but we do not agree with plaintiffs that every repossession should be analyzed subjectively, thus bringing every repossession into the purview of the jury so as to eviscerate the self-help rights duly given to creditors by the General Assembly. Rather, a breach of the peace analysis should be based upon the reasonableness of the time and manner of the repossession. We therefore adopt a balancing test using the five factors discussed above to determine whether a breach of the peace occurs when there is no confrontation.

In applying these factors to the undisputed evidence in the case before us, we affirm the trial court's determination that there was no breach of the peace, as a matter of law. Professional Auto Recovery went onto plaintiffs' driveway in the early morning hours, when presumably no one would be outside, thus decreasing the possibility of confrontation. Professional Auto Recovery did not enter into plaintiffs' home or any enclosed area. Consent to repossession was expressly given in the contract with First Virginia signed by Joann Giles. Although a third party . . . was awakened by the noise of Professional Auto Recovery's truck . . . neither of the plaintiffs were awakened by the noise of the truck, and there was no confrontation between either of them with any representative of Professional Auto Recovery. . . .

There is no factual dispute as to what happened during the repossession in this case, and the trial court did not err in granting summary judgment to First Virginia on this issue. . . .

BUSINESS CONSIDERATIONS Should a business give notice to defaulting debtors before attempting to repossess the collateral, or is it better to rely on the element of surprise in order to effect repossessions?

ETHICAL CONSIDERATIONS Is it ethical for a creditor to use "self-help" methods of repossession? What ethical issues are raised by the creditor removing something from the debtor's property under cover of darkness?

Needless to say, this aspect of the Code has spawned numerous lawsuits. In general, courts assess such factors as whether the secured party entered the debtor's home or driveway without permission and whether the debtor agreed to the repossession. Although it is difficult to make generalizations in this area, if the creditor repossesses an automobile from a public street and the debtor fails to object to this procedure, most courts will hold no breach of the peace has occurred. Nevertheless, in recent years, some questions have arisen as to the constitutionality of this "self-help" provision of the Code. Specifically, some have argued that repossession without notice to the debtor may deprive the debtor of due process rights.[19]

Self-help is not the only alternative available to the creditor in seeking repossession of the collateral. The agreement may require the debtor to assemble the collateral at some specified place upon default by the debtor.[20] If the debtor refuses to assemble the collateral according to the agreement after being asked to do so by the creditor, the courts are likely to compel the debtor to do so.

If the collateral is equipment, the creditor also has the right to disable the collateral, thus making it unusable, on the debtor's premises. The creditor is also allowed to dispose of the collateral by sale or otherwise without removing it from the debtor's premises.[21]

If the creditor does repossess the collateral, he or she is expected to take reasonable care of the collateral while it is in his or her possession. This includes properly storing the collateral, maintaining it, and so forth.[22]

"Realizing" on the Collateral

Once the secured party is in possession of the collateral, he or she must decide how to proceed. The Code authorizes the creditor to "sell, lease, license, or otherwise dispose" of the collateral.[23] Thus, the creditor must decide whether to keep the collateral in satisfaction, either total or partial, of the debt, or to dispose of the collateral. However, there are some restrictions that may affect what the creditor does or how the creditor does it.

Strict Foreclosure After default and repossession, the secured party may decide to retain the collateral in complete satisfaction of the debt.[24] This remedy is generally referred to as *strict foreclosure,* although that term is not used in the Code. Strict foreclosure is not always available as an alternative for the creditor, but if it is available it may be an attractive choice. If the collateral is likely to appreciate in value or if the potential costs of any additional action are likely to be prohibitive, strict foreclosure will provide a simple and expedient method for ending the proceedings.

Strict foreclosure cannot be used if the collateral is classified as consumer goods, *and* if the debtor has repaid at least 60 percent of the of the cash price of the goods or the amount of the loan. Instead, the creditor must dispose of the collateral within 90 days of the date of repossession. If the creditor fails to do so, he or she can be held liable for the tort of conversion, or the consumer debtor can sue for actual damages plus punitive damages, set by the Code as either (1) the finance charges plus 10 percent of the loan amount, or (2) the time-price differential plus 10 percent of the cash price.[25]

If the collateral is not classified as consumer goods, or if it is consumer goods but the debtor has not repaid at least 60 percent of the cash price or the amount of the loan, the creditor may be allowed to use strict foreclosure. However, before strict foreclosure can be used, the creditor must send an authenticated notice to the debtor and to any conflicting creditors, stating his or her intention to retain the collateral in total or partial satisfaction of the debt.[26] If any of these parties object to the creditor's proposed retention within 20 days of the date the notice was sent, the creditor may not use strict foreclosure. Instead, he or she will be required to dispose of the collateral.[27]

In the next case the court addressed an unusual situation, the use of strict foreclosure by a creditor when a promissory note was the collateral.

26.3

HARRIS v. KEY BANK, N.A.
193 F. Supp. 2d 707; 2002 U.S. Dist. LEXIS 1187 (W.D. N.Y. 2002)

FACTS In June 1984, plaintiffs sold an apartment building on St. Paul Street in Rochester to the partners. As part of the $775,000 purchase price, the partners executed a promissory note for the benefit of plaintiffs in the amount of $195,000. As security for this note, the partners gave plaintiffs a second mortgage on the property.

In May 1985, in a completely separate transaction, plaintiffs borrowed $150,000 from Key Bank. Plaintiffs executed a demand note for the benefit of the bank in the amount of $150,000. As security for that note, plaintiffs assigned to Key Bank the $195,000 St. Paul Street Note and the second mortgage interest that secured it.

In time, both the partners and plaintiffs began having difficulty making their monthly payments on their respective notes. For several years, with the blessing of plaintiffs, the partners sent their payments on the St. Paul Street Note directly to Key Bank and not to plaintiffs, in order to fulfill the partners' obligation to plaintiffs and plaintiffs' obligation to the bank simultaneously. Various other proposals concerning the parties' obligations were made and considered over the years, but in early 1994, Key Bank sold plaintiffs' Key Bank Note to the partners, doing business as "Lass" or "Last" Associates, for $75,000, which was the remaining balance on the note at that time, along with the $195,000 St. Paul Street Note and the second mortgage interest that secured it.

In April 1994, Lass Associates demanded that plaintiffs pay the $75,000 balance on the Key Bank Note within 15 days. When plaintiffs failed to do so, Lass Associates served on plaintiffs written notice, pursuant to U.C.C. §9-505(2), that Lass Associates proposed to retain the assigned collateral, that is, the St. Paul Street Note and second mortgage, in full satisfaction of the Key Bank Note. Plaintiffs neither objected to nor responded to this notice, although it is not entirely clear from plaintiffs' deposition testimony and that of their then attorney, David Berlowitz, why that was so.

Thereafter, plaintiffs sued the partners to enforce the St. Paul Street Note. The court ruled that since the bank had repledged the Key Bank Note to Lass Associates and Lass Associates had foreclosed on that note, Lass Associates was now the owner of the St. Paul Street Note, and plaintiffs did not have standing to enforce it. Plaintiffs then brought this action against Key Bank, alleging that the bank impaired the value of plaintiffs' collateral when it transferred the collateral and the Key Bank Note to Lass Associates.

ISSUES Did Key Bank impair the value of the collateral by transferring the note to Lass Associates? Did Lass Associates properly use strict foreclosure in this situation?

HOLDINGS No, Key Bank did not impair the value of the collateral. Yes, Lass Associates properly used strict foreclosure in this situation.

REASONING Excerpts from the opinion of Chief Judge David G. Larimer:

After reviewing the record, I find that Key Bank is entitled to summary judgment. The undisputed facts show that the alleged injury to plaintiffs was caused not by any wrongful action of the bank, but by plaintiffs' own failure to object or otherwise respond to Lass Associates' proposal to keep the collateral, *i.e.*, the St. Paul Street Note and second mortgage, in full satisfaction of plaintiffs' debt on the Key Bank Note.

At his deposition, plaintiff Ben Harris testified that after plaintiffs received Lass Associates' notice under Uniform Commercial Code . . . § 9-505(2), plaintiffs "told [their] attorney to reject it." . . . He stated that he understood the implication of the warning contained in the notice that Lass Associates would retain the St. Paul Street Note and mortgage if plaintiffs did not respond within twenty-one days. . . .

Shirley Harris testified in similar fashion. . . . She testified that after plaintiffs received the notice from Lass Associates, she called Berlowitz and told him to reject the proposal. She said that Berlowitz "made light of it," and told her "there's nothing to this. . . ." He also allegedly told her that plaintiffs should have no direct contact with Lass Associates. . . .

In fact, Ben Harris did prepare a letter rejecting Lass Associates' proposal, which he gave to Berlowitz for his approval. . . . The letter stated that Lass Associates' proposal was "entirely out of the question. The mortgage is obviously worth considerably more than the demand note." . . . Mr. Harris testified, however, that Berlowitz never responded to him about the letter, and that Harris did not send the letter to Lass Associates because Berlowitz had instructed him not to contact Lass Associates directly. . . .

Berlowitz himself testified at his deposition in the instant action that he "was having daily conferences" with plaintiffs around the time when they received the § 9-505(2) notice, "so [he] would assume that [he] did have conferences with [plaintiffs] concerning [Ben Harris's] letter."... He testified that he explained plaintiffs' options to them, and that if plaintiffs rejected Lass Associates' proposal, Lass Associates could commence an action on the note against plaintiffs. He stated that plaintiffs were concerned that if Lass Associates obtained a judgment against them, Lass Associates would have a lien on other real property owned by plaintiffs. . . . Berlowitz testified that he explained to plaintiffs that if they accepted Lass Associates' proposal, Lass Associates would not be able to commence an action against them. . . . According to Berlowitz, it was plaintiffs' decision not to respond to Lass Associates' notice, after plaintiffs had been made aware of all their options. . . .

Whichever version of these events is true, the undisputed fact is that plaintiffs received Lass Associates' § 9-505(2) notice, and understood its meaning and the implications of not responding or objecting to it. For whatever reason, whether due to their attorney's inaction or their own decision, plaintiffs did not respond to the notice.

The important point is that, when the bank transferred the Key Bank Note to Lass Associates, it was not a foregone conclusion that Lass Associates would end up retaining the collateral, or that plaintiffs would lose their rights in the collateral. Nor was that conclusion inevitable when Lass Associates sent the notice to plaintiffs. When plaintiffs received the notice, they had options other than doing nothing. Under § 9-505(2), had plaintiffs objected within twenty-one days after the notice was sent, Lass Associates would have been required to dispose of the collateral under § 9-504. That section provides that a "secured party after default may sell, lease or otherwise dispose of any or all of the collateral in its then condition or following any commercially reasonable preparation or processing." It goes on to state the order in which the proceeds of disposition must be applied (*e.g.* to the secured party's expenses, the satisfaction of the secured indebtedness, etc.), and that "if the security interest secures an indebtedness, the secured party must account to the debtor for any surplus, and, unless otherwise agreed, the debtor is liable for any deficiency." . . .

Plaintiffs, then, had the option of timely objecting to Lass Associates' proposal to effect a strict foreclosure, and by doing so, they could have prevented Lass Associates from simply retaining the collateral in satisfaction of plaintiffs' debt. Had an objection been lodged, there

could have been a substantial surplus, had the Lass Associates sold the St. Paul note in a commercially reasonable manner. But, whether a surplus or a deficiency could have resulted has no bearing on the ultimate issue here, *i.e.*, whether the bank somehow impaired the collateral by transferring it to Lass Associates.

The fundamental problem with plaintiffs' claim is that when Lass Associates sent plaintiffs the § 9-505(2) notice, plaintiffs stood in no different position than if the bank had kept the note, and had sent plaintiffs a § 9-505(2) notice itself. Certainly, there could be no claim that the bank would have somehow violated its duties under the U.C.C. by acting in that fashion, when the U.C.C. itself expressly permits the secured party in possession to take such action.

Similarly, Key Bank could have sold the Key Bank Note to *any* third party, not just to Lass Associates, and that third party could then have proposed to retain the collateral in the same manner that Lass Associates did. Plaintiffs do not appear to contend, nor is there any authority, that *any* sale of the Key Bank Note to anyone would have constituted a violation of the bank's duties, either under the U.C.C. or the common law. Under New York law, a party's rights under a contract are generally considered to be freely assignable, unless the contract provides otherwise. . . . Here, the document by which plaintiffs assigned the St. Paul Street Note and mortgage to Key Bank implicitly provided that the bank could assign the note and mortgage to a third party, since it stated that plaintiffs assigned the note and mortgage "unto the assignee [*i.e.*, Key Bank], and to the successors, legal representatives and assigns of the assignee forever." . . .

Just as the bank itself, had it not sold the Key Bank Note, could have proposed to retain the collateral on default, so could any buyer or assignee of the Key Bank Note have done so. That the assignee happened to be Lass Associates and not some other party did not affect plaintiffs' rights and obligations in the event that the assignee gave plaintiffs notice under § 9-505(2).

Regardless of who held the note, then, the holder had the right to give notice of its proposal to retain the collateral in satisfaction of the debt under § 9-505(2). At that point, plaintiffs had two options: object within twenty-one days, or remain silent, which is what they did. If they chose the former route, then the secured party, regardless of whether it was Lass Associates, Key Bank, or someone else, would have been obligated to dispose of the collateral in a commercially reasonable manner under § 9-504 with the surplus, if any, going to plaintiffs. If plaintiffs remained silent, and failed to timely redeem the collateral . . . then the secured party could have simply retained the collateral, and plaintiffs' rights as well as their obligations relating to the debt or collateral would have been extinguished. . . .

The bank's relationship with plaintiffs was a creditor-debtor one, and not principally a fiduciary relationship. . . . [It] would be absurd to think that Key Bank could never take its own interests into account, or that plaintiffs' interests had to be absolutely paramount at all times and in all situations. Obviously it would have been in *plaintiffs'* best interests for Key Bank simply to have forgiven their debt altogether, but the law imposes no duty on a creditor to do so. Rather, "at common law, and implicitly under the Uniform Commercial Code, a creditor may assign its rights and transfer possession of collateral without the knowledge or consent of the debtor, as long as the debtor's right to redeem upon payment of the debt is not impaired." . . . That is precisely what the bank did here. Plaintiffs retained the same right to redeem after the bank's transfer to Lass Associates that they would have had, had the bank itself, or any other transferee, exercised its rights under § 9-505.

Plaintiffs' failure to object to Lass Associates' notice, whether the result of their own informed decision or their attorney's negligence or questionable advice, is what caused plaintiffs to lose the value of the collateral, and that failure to act is not Key Bank's fault.

For these reasons, then, I find that all of plaintiffs' remaining claims must be dismissed. As stated, Key Bank's duties under the U.C.C. and under common law are essentially one and the same: not to impair or destroy the collateral or plaintiffs' right to redeem. Key Bank did not violate that duty. . . .

BUSINESS CONSIDERATIONS **When should a secured creditor attempt to use strict foreclosure rather than disposal of the collateral? Should a business that regularly enters into secured transactions develop a policy regarding the use of strict foreclosure?**

ETHICAL CONSIDERATIONS **Is it ethical for a creditor to propose strict foreclosure when the creditor knows that the collateral has a value substantially in excess of the balance of the debt?**

An interesting change to Article 9 is the provision allowing strict foreclosure as *partial* settlement of the debt. The law now permits the creditor to notify the debtor and any conflicting creditors that he or she plans to retain the collateral in partial satisfaction of the debt, with the balance still due and owing. In order to use strict foreclosure for partial satisfaction, the creditor must once again give the authenticated notice to the debtor and to the conflicting creditors, and once again, if any of these parties objects within 20 days the creditor may not retain the collateral in partial satisfaction of the debt. But there is an additional requirement here, and a limitation. Before the creditor can retain the collateral as partial satisfaction, the debtor must *consent* in an authenticated record. And if the goods are consumer goods, the creditor may not use strict foreclosure as a partial satisfaction.[28]

Disposition by Sale As was pointed out above, the secured party is allowed to "sell, lease, license, or otherwise dispose of the collateral." In fact, secured parties use this remedy of *foreclosure by sale* much more frequently than strict foreclosure. The liberality of the Code's provision for resale allows the secured party to realize the highest resale price possible and, at the same time, to reduce the possibility of a *deficiency judgment* (the debtor's liability for the difference between the amount realized at resale and the amount owed to the secured party). In this way, both the secured party and the debtor benefit.

The sale may be either public or private, subject always to the requirement that the method, manner, time, place, and terms of such sale be commercially reasonable.[29] A public sale, or auction, is the more ordinary occurrence; but the Code encourages private sales when, as often is the case, a private sale through commercial channels will increase the chances for a higher resale price. If the debtor or a competing creditor should subsequently challenge the reasonableness of the sale, the burden of proof is on the creditor, who must establish that the sale was made in a commercially reasonable manner.[30]

In order to establish that the sale was made in a commercially reasonable manner, the creditor must first show that he or she gave proper notice of the sale. This notice must be given to the debtor, to any sureties or guarantors of the debtor, and to other creditors that are claiming an interest in the collateral. These "other" creditors include any creditors of record and any creditors who have notified the repossessing creditor of an interest in the collateral. The only exceptions to the notice requirement are if (1) the goods are perishable and are likely to decline in value, or (2) the goods are sold by the creditor in a recognized market.[31]

The Code also specifies how the proceeds from the disposition of the collateral are to be applied. According to § 9-615, the proceeds are first applied to the expenses incurred in the sale. This includes the cost of repossession and storage, the cost of the sale itself, and any legal expenses and attorney's fees. If there are still funds available, these funds are applied to the debt owed to the creditor who repossessed and then disposed of the collateral. Again, if there are still funds available, these funds are distributed to junior secured creditors who have sent an authenticated demand for payment. These creditors are paid in order of priority. If any funds remain, the surplus is paid to the debtor. If the funds are inadequate to cover any of the first three categories, the debtor is liable for the deficiency.

Debtors' Rights

Because the debtor has the right to redeem the collateral at any time before the secured party has disposed of it, it is possible that no sale will ever occur. *Redemption* consists of the debtor's tendering payment of all obligations due, including the expenses incurred by the secured party in retaking and preparing the collateral for disposition (usually by sale), thereby extinguishing the secured party's security interest in the collateral. Such expenses also may encompass attorney's fees and legal expenses. A debtor who can accomplish redemption before sale or strict foreclosure can retain the collateral. The debtor can waive the right to redeem *after* default, but cannot waive this right before default.[32]

Secured Parties' Duties

Besides having to observe the previously mentioned duties regarding disposition of the collateral, secured parties also have the duty of taking reasonable care of the collateral while it is in their possession, either before or after default. They are liable for any losses caused by their failure to meet this obligation, but they do not lose their security interests if such a loss occurs. Unless the parties otherwise have agreed, the secured party can charge to the debtor the payment of reasonable expenses, such as insurance and taxes, incurred in the custody, preservation, or use of the collat-

eral. Moreover, the Code places the risk of accidental loss or damage on the debtor to the extent of any deficiency in insurance coverage. The secured party also may hold as additional security any increase in the value of or any profits (except money) received from the collateral, but the secured party either should turn over any money so received to the debtor or apply it to reduce the secured obligation. There is a duty to keep the collateral identifiable except for fungible collateral that may be commingled. The secured party either may repledge the collateral on terms that do not violate the debtor's right to redeem it or use the collateral (for example, in an ongoing business, the continued operation of equipment that has been given as security) if this will help to preserve it or its value.

Once the secured party defrays the expenses of holding the collateral, as mentioned earlier, the secured party must turn over any remaining proceeds to the debtor. On the other hand, the debtor remains liable for any deficiency— the difference between the available proceeds and the amount of outstanding indebtedness and expenses— unless the parties otherwise have agreed or state law eliminates this obligation.

Debtors sometimes try to argue that the amount received from the sale of the collateral (the usual basis for computing deficiencies or surpluses), if lower than the collateral's market value, makes the sale commercially unreasonable. But courts ordinarily respond unfavorably to such arguments as long as fraud is not present and the secured party has attempted in good faith to attract buyers. Similarly, these arguments generally will not affect the rights of the purchaser at the sale; the purchaser takes the collateral free and clear of such claims if the purchase is made in good faith.

You can find information on secured transactions at http://www.law.cornell.edu/topics/secured_transactions. html. You may also want to visit http://www.law. georgetown.edu/olin/papers/wallac1a.html for an interesting paper on international initiatives in this area.

Summary

The rules on priorities represent the Code's attempt to decide who, among validly perfected secured parties, has superior rights to the collateral. In general, the Code validates a first-in-time, first-in-right approach. Thus, if competing security interests have been perfected by filing, the first to be filed has priority, whether the security interest attached before or after filing. If neither party has filed, the first party to perfect has priority. And if no one has per-

fected, the first interest to attach has superior rights to the collateral.

Some exceptions to these priority rules exist. For instance, a properly perfected purchase-money security interest has priority over other security interests, even if the other interest were perfected first. Similarly, in some situations, bona fide purchasers of consumer goods and buyers in the ordinary course of business may defeat prior perfected interests. A secured party may also face competing claims against his or her collateral asserted by lien holders. The lien may be classified as a judicial lien, a statutory lien, or a consensual lien. Generally, a conflict between a lien and a security interest is decided by the "first-in-time, first-in-right" rule, unless the lien is possessory, in which case the lien is likely to prevail so long as the creditor retains possession. Likewise, certain liens that arise by operation of law have priority over perfected security interests in the collateral.

When a debtor defaults, the secured party may pursue either non-Code or Code remedies. Under the Code, the secured party may take possession of the collateral and either retain it in complete or partial satisfaction of the debt (strict foreclosure) or dispose of it, most often by public or private sale (foreclosure by sale). In either case, if the secured party is to escape Code liability, notification of the debtor and perhaps other parties must take place. The secured party's right of strict foreclosure may be limited in certain situations. If a sale is undertaken, the secured party must conduct it in a commercially reasonable manner. Assuming a sale has occurred, the Code also enumerates the order in which the proceeds of a sale should be applied. The debtor's redeeming the collateral prior to foreclosure may cut off the secured party's right to foreclosure by sale or strict foreclosure. When the secured party is in possession of the collateral either before or after default, he or she must take reasonable care of the collateral. Failure to live up to this and other duties subjects the secured party to potential liability for any losses caused thereby, to possible damages under a statutory formula, and to the possible denial of the right to a deficiency judgment. Debtors ordinarily are liable for any deficiency that remains after the sale or other disposition of the collateral.

Discussion Questions

1. Why is the issue of priority important to a secured creditor or to a lien holder?

2. Explain what is meant by a purchase-money security interest. Also explain why purchase-money secured parties are given priority over other secured parties.

3. List the rules for becoming a properly perfected purchase-money secured party in inventory collateral and in noninventory collateral. Why are there different rules for proper perfection of a PMSI depending on the type of collateral involved?

4. What is a bona fide purchaser? Does such a purchaser always take goods free of any security interest covering the goods? How does this person differ from a buyer in the ordinary course of business?

5. When does a secured party have priority over the holder of a common law lien? When does a security interest become subordinate to a later lien?

6. What is default, and how does default affect the rights of the parties to a security agreement?

7. What kinds of non-Code remedies can the secured party pursue if the debtor defaults on his or her obligations? When can the secured party decide to pursue these non-Code remedies?

8. What is a "repossession"? When can the secured party repossess collateral? What restrictions are imposed on the repossessing party?

9. Explain the requirements necessary for effecting strict foreclosure. What limitations restrict the creditor's right to use strict foreclosure?

10. Assume that a secured creditor has repossessed collateral from a defaulting debtor. The creditor has decided not to use strict foreclosure. What must the creditor do in order to ensure that he or she preserves all of his or her rights and also that the rights of the debtor are not infringed?

Case Problems and Writing Assignments

1. On April 27, 1992, Darro and Tracy Long purchased a 1980 Ford Escort for $2,795 from Auto Credit, Inc. They made a cash down payment of $300 and financed the balance of the purchase price. The terms of the financing required the Longs to pay $38.84 per week for 84 weeks. The Longs made six timely payments on the vehicle. On June 17, 1992, however, the Longs notified Auto Credit that they intended to make no further payments; and they returned the vehicle to Auto Credit. The car was in virtually the same condition as when the Longs had purchased it, with the exception that they had driven it 3,500 miles. The balance due for the vehicle at the time was $2,594.02. On June 17, 1992, Auto Credit notified the Longs that if they failed to pay the remainder of the balance within 10 days, the car would be sold at a private sale by the end of June. Auto Credit actually sold the car on August 12 at the Billings Auto Auction for $150. After Auto Credit deducted $229.47, a sum representing its expenses from the sale and finance charges, an additional $79.47 was charged to the Longs' account. Auto Credit subsequently filed a court action to recover a deficiency of $2,934.15. The Longs counterclaimed for damages on the grounds that the sale was commercially unreasonable under UCC §9-504. In whose favor should the judge rule? [See *Auto Credit, Inc. v. Long,* 971 P.2d 1237 (Mont. 1998).]

2. Ford Motor Credit Company hired Badgerland Auto Recovery, Inc. to repossess a Ford Bronco II from Florence Hollibush, who was behind in her payments and who had had a poor record of making the required payments under her installment contract with FMCC. Badgerland's employee testified that at about midnight on January 18, 1990, he arrived at Hollibush's tavern. Her vehicle was parked in front of the tavern, and the employee hooked the Bronco up to his tow truck. He saw a man looking out of the tavern window at him and entered the tavern to tell the man who he was. He spoke with Hollibush and with William Finn, Hollibush's fiancé. Finn called an attorney and then stated that he would call the sheriff's office. Hollibush observed Finn's conversation and occasionally would say something. Finn told Badgerland's employee: "You are not going to take the Bronco"; but shortly after that, the employee left with Hollibush's automobile. Although Hollibush and Finn's description of the repossession differed considerably from the description given by Badgerland's employee, both testified that Finn had told the employee not to take the automobile. Did the Badgerland employee's subsequent repossession in disregard of the statement not to repossess the car constitute a breach of the peace under § 9-503? Why or why not? [See *Hollibush v. Ford Motor Credit Company*, 508 N.W.2d 449 (Wis. App. 1993).]

3. On December 13, 1997, the debtor, Karen H. Johnson, purchased a new 1998 Honda from College Park Honda and received delivery of the car. At that time, several documents, including a retail installment contract and a buyer's order, were executed. Johnson subsequently failed to obtain third-party financing for the purchase of the car. On December 24, 1997, Johnson filed a voluntary Chapter 7 petition in bankruptcy; and on January 1998, Johnson notified College Park of that fact. Also on January 2, College Park and Johnson executed a security agreement and another buyer's order. On January 28, 1998, the debtor again informed College Park that she had filed a bankruptcy petition. On February 6, 1998, College Park repossessed the 1998 Honda. College Park knew that, at the time of the transaction, Johnson lived in the District of Columbia. To perfect a security interest in an automobile under the law of the District of Columbia, the secured party must note its lien on the certificate of title. The bankruptcy trustee ultimately sued the dealership to force College Park to turn over the repossessed car. In these circumstances, what was the status of College Park? Who held superior rights to the car, College Park or the bankruptcy trustee? [See *In re Johnson*, 230 B.R. 466 (Bankr. D. D.C. 1999).]

4. SMS Financial, L.L.C. sued ABCO Homes, Inc. and H. Eugene and Richard E. Abbott, the makers of a promissory note SMS had purchased from the Federal Deposit Insurance Corporation. The background facts indicated the following: On July 17, 1991, the FDIC had sent to each maker a notice of intent to foreclose on the collateral securing the note. On December 17, 1991, the FDIC had sent a second notice of intent to foreclose on the collateral to H. Eugene Abbott and ABCO. The July 17, 1991, letter demanded that the makers pay such indebtedness in full on or before August, 16, 1991. The notice also provided that if the makers failed to pay this sum to the FDIC by such date, the FDIC would exercise its legal rights and remedies to collect such indebtedness, including, but not limited to, foreclosure of the deed of trust and the sale of the property covered thereby in accordance with the terms of the deed of trust. The FDIC subsequently leased the collateral (bowling alley equipment) to Amwest Savings on January 21, 1992, and ultimately sold it to Amwest on September 3, 1992. The Abbotts later argued that the FDIC's failure to provide them with adequate notice of the lease of the collateral made the FDIC's disposition of the collateral commercially unreasonable. The Abbotts also submitted that the sale violated UCC §9-504(c) because, in effect, the FDIC had sold the collateral to itself in a private sale, since Amwest, the purchaser of the collateral, was the FDIC's agent at the time of the sale of the equipment. Should the appellate court affirm the lower court's entry of a summary judgment in favor of the Abbotts? [See *SMS Financial, Limited Liability Company v. ABCO Homes, Inc.*, 167 F.3d 235 (5th Cir. 1999).]

5. **BUSINESS APPLICATION CASE** Biglari Import Export, Inc., the debtor, operates the Ritz Oriental Rug Gallery. In 1986, Biglari borrowed operating capital from the International Bank of Commerce (IBOC) and granted IBOC a lien on its inventory of rugs. Later in the lending relationship, IBOC became concerned about Biglari's business and loan performance and asked that some of the rugs be pledged to the bank. Biglari complied and ultimately delivered 40 rugs into IBOC's possession. IBOC stored the rugs in a storage room in its bank building. The room, though not designed as a collateral storage vault, is the same room in which the bank stores its own records. It has a concrete floor, no windows, and no public access. The room is located toward the rear of the building, on an upper level, and is the only room on that level. A winding stairway leads to a vestibule area, which has one door opening out to a fenced courtyard and one door into the employee-only area of the bank. The bank keeps this back door locked, and only bank officers have a key to this door.

According to the witnesses, the rugs were removed from this room on two occasions only, once in July 1988 and again in March 1990. On both occasions, Biglari took out the rugs and brought them back. In March 1990, Biglari removed all 40 rugs so they could be aired out in the sun and mothballed (the standard procedure for maintaining the quality of the rugs). On that particular occasion, while the bank officer in charge of this loan was on his lunch hour, two Biglari employees picked up the rugs. The employees told bank personnel that the loan officer had approved their coming by to pick up the rugs, and someone from the bank let them into the storage room. No one had the employees sign any paperwork relative to checking out the rugs. Three days later, after the mothballing process, two Biglari employees brought the rugs back to the bank. At that time, no one from the bank checked the bundles to be sure all 40 rugs were there. The rugs were returned to the storage room, where they remained undisturbed. During an inventory of the rugs taken at the bank in December 1990, the bank came up 10 rugs short. Later, during its bankruptcy proceedings, Biglari argued that the judge should reduce IBOC's secured claim by the value of the 10 rugs because of IBOC's alleged failure to take reasonable care of the collateral in its possession. Had IBOC used reasonable care in the custody and preservation of Biglari's rugs? (See *In re Biglari Import, Inc.*, 130 B.R. 43 (Bankr. W.D. Tex. 1991).]

6. **ETHICAL APPLICATION CASE** On April 25, 1997, Michael T. Eustler, a motor vehicle repossessor, arrived at the home of Jon Douglas Alexander in Rockbridge County, Virginia, to repossess Alexander's car. Alexander asked if he could remove his "personal property" from inside the car, and Eustler agreed. At the subsequent trial, Alexander testified that a muscular disorder had left him partially disabled for many years. He stated further that the vehicle contained legal documents that pertained to his longstanding (but pending) disability claim, as well as some "tools of his profession." Alexander testified that he related these facts to Eustler and that Eustler agreed to allow the removal of these items. However, according to Alexander, Eustler "jacked up" the vehicle while Alexander was partially seated in the car and demanded that Alexander provide him with the keys. Alexander testified that he went into his house and returned with the keys, which he put on top of the car. Alexander also brought with him an unloaded rifle, which he placed in a flowerbed near the vehicle. Alexander stated that because Eustler then approached Alexander in a "belligerent manner," Alexander, out of a fear for his personal safety and his property, retrieved the rifle. At first, Alexander testified, he held the rifle at his side. But when Eustler continued to advance toward Alexander, Alexander raised the rifle to his shoulder and pointed the rifle at Eustler. Eustler's version of the facts differed from Alexander's. Eustler testified that Alexander went into the house and returned with a rifle. Eustler stated that Alexander then opened the left rear door and began to remove items from the back seat. Eustler stated that when he approached the vehicle, Alexander raised the rifle and said, "I could drop you right there." Eustler testified that he immediately returned to his truck, left the premises, and called the police. The police later recovered an unloaded rifle from Alexander's home.

Alexander subsequently was convicted of brandishing a weapon. On appeal, he argued the judge had committed reversible error when the judge had refused to instruct the jury that Virginia precedents recognize brandishing a firearm as lawful resistance to the repossession of personal property. Should a debtor be able to threaten to use deadly force to stave off a "self-help" repossession? Did the repossessor act ethically in this situation? If not, what could or should he have done differently? Does the leeway given to secured creditors under the "self-help" provision implicitly condone unethical behavior on their part? [See *Alexander v. Commonwealth of Virginia*, 508 S.E.2d 912 (Va. App. 1999).]

7. **CRITICAL THINKING CASE** In March 1989, Mark J. Zimmermann, an attorney, joined a law firm called GGM, P.C. Pursuant to a shareholders' agreement, Zimmermann financed the capital contribution expected of him by executing, in favor of Texas Commerce Bank, N.A. (TCB), a promissory note for $50,000 and by pledging the GGM shares so purchased as collateral for the note. Two years later, Zimmermann signed a second shareholders' agreement, which, among other things, provided for the firm's repurchasing the shares of a defaulting shareholder and for the firm's terminating the agreement should a dissolution of the firm occur. In June 1992, owing to spiraling financial difficulties, GGM began the process of dissolving and winding down its business affairs. As a consequence, Zimmermann's employment was terminated. In September 1992, GGM's creditors instituted involuntary bankruptcy proceedings against GGM, but in 1993, the case was converted to a Chapter 7 proceeding. The bankruptcy court subsequently approved GGM and TCB's right to purchase the shareholders' notes, including Zimmermann's, which had been in default for several months. When Zimmermann refused the bankruptcy trustee's demand for payment of the note, the trustee sued Zimmermann. At trial, Zimmermann argued that a secured creditor must either retain the collateral or sell it and that because TCB had retained the collateral (here the pledged stock), it had elected to do so in complete satisfaction of the debt. Hence, Zimmermann argued, he was under no obligation to pay the note. Does Article 9 require a creditor to sell or otherwise dispose of the stock pledged as collateral prior to bringing a cause of action against the debtor to collect on the unpaid balance of the debt? [See *In re GGM, P.C.*, 165 F.3d 1026 (5th Cir. 1999).]

8. **YOU BE THE JUDGE** In late 1988, the corporate owners of several radio stations entered into a loan agreement with the predecessor in interest of MLQ Investors, L.P. The loan documents purported to create a security interest in the station owners' intangible personal property, including all Federal Communications Commission (FCC) broadcast licenses, to the extent permitted by law. In the event of default, the lender was authorized to obtain a court judgment enabling it to sell the collateral and to apply the proceeds to the outstanding debt. Between 1988 and 1994, the station owners defaulted on the loans and failed to pay taxes to the Internal Revenue Service. MLQ's predecessor in interest had perfected its security interest under the loan documents in December 1988 and January 1989, and subsequently had filed continuation statements. The IRS's first tax lien on the station owners' property arose in 1991. The station owners' debt to MLQ ultimately exceeded the combined value of the owners' assets; hence, in 1994, MLQ filed suit against the station owners and two guarantors for breach of contract, foreclosure of the security interest, and breach of guarantees. MLQ also sought the appointment of a receiver and injunctive relief. In May 1994, after the district court had appointed a receiver, the parties stipulated that the proceeds were to be distributed in accordance with the bankruptcy laws. In late November 1994, the district court entered orders authorizing the receiver (assuming the receiver could secure FCC approval for the

transfer of the broadcast licenses) to sell all the assets of the radio stations at a private sale and to disburse the sales proceeds to MLQ. One of the guarantors, Walter A. Heusser, appealed this decision on the grounds that a creditor could not obtain a valid security interest in an FCC broadcasting license and consequently would be unable to perfect this interest under the UCC. This case has been brought in *your* court. How will *you* resolve these issues: Can a creditor perfect a security interest in an FCC broadcasting license? If so, would the creditor's security interest have priority over IRS tax liens filed on the debtor's property? [See *MLQ Investors, L.P. v. Pacific Quadracasting, Inc.*, 146 F.3d 746 (9th Cir. 1998).]

Notes

1. UCC § 9-324 (a).
2. UCC § 9-324 (b), (c).
3. UCC § 9-324 (d), (e).
4. UCC § 9-324(g) and Comment 13.
5. UCC § 9-330 (a).
6. UCC § 9-330 (d).
7. UCC § 9-317 (a)(2).
8. UCC § 9-323 (b).
9. UCC § 9-333 (b).
10. 26 U.S.C. § 6323 (a), (h)(1).
11. Rev. Rul. 68-57, 26 C.F.R. §301.6321-1 (1968).
12. UCC § 9-102 (41).
13. UCC § 9-502 (b).
14. UCC § 9-334 (h).
15. UCC § 9-502 (b).
16. UCC § 9-334 (c).
17. UCC § 9-601, Official Comment 5.
18. UCC § 9-609 (b).
19. See, for example, *Fuentes v. Shevin*, 407 U.S. 67 (1972); *Mitchell v. W.T. Grant Co.*, 416 U.S. 600 (1974).
20. UCC § 9-609 (c).
21. UCC § 9-609 (a)(2).
22. UCC § 9-207.
23. UCC § 9-610.
24. UCC § 9-620.
25. UCC § 9-620 (e).
26. UCC § 9-621.
27. UCC § 9-620.
28. UCC § 9-620 (g).
29. UCC § 9-610 (b).
30. UCC § 9-626 (a)(2).
31. UCC § 9-611 (d).
32. UCC § 9-623.

Other Credit Transactions

A G E N D A

NRW NRW recently received an offer from a firm in Canada that seems promising for the firm. The offer included a statement that payment was to be made by a *letter of credit* if the firm decided to accept the offer. The principals are not sure exactly what is involved with the use of a letter of credit, but they want to find out because they are interested in the offer. Mai has heard of a "standby letter of credit," and she would like to know if this is the same thing or a different form of an "ordinary" letter of credit.

While Mai, Carlos, and Helen are primarily concerned with the operation and the success of NRW, each also has other concerns. Each has his or her share of the normal wants and needs of other young professionals. Mai would like to buy a new car, Carlos wants to purchase a house, and Helen would like to travel. They realize that they need to wait for these things if they are to pay cash, but they also realize that they can use credit to get them. But they question whether the cost of the credit is worth the reduced waiting period to enjoy these things sooner.

Each of them has several credit cards, and they each regularly receive offers of new credit cards in the mail. Some of these offers carry very attractive interest rates, and they would like to know whether they should just keep their current cards or opt to take some of the cards they are offered.

One of the firm's employees recently came to Helen asking for an advance on his pay. When asked why he needed the money, he explained that he was past due on a "payday loan" and was worried about getting too far behind and losing everything. Helen had never heard of a "payday loan," and she would like to know what it is and how it compares with a regular loan.

These or similar questions may arise during our discussion. Be prepared! You never know when the firm or one of its members will seek your advice.

The use—and occasional misuse—of credit is an integral part of contemporary American life. Businesses very often will be both a creditor and a debtor during their normal business cycle. A business may need to obtain credit in order to provide its goods and services to its customers, and then may need to grant credit to its customers in order for the customers to purchase the goods or services. Many of these credit transactions take the form of secured transactions, a topic covered in considerable detail in the previous two chapters. However, a significant number fall outside the coverage of Article 9. The types of credit used by businesses vary widely. Any given business may use letters of credit, covered by Article 5 of the UCC, or promissory notes, covered by Article 3. Similar items are likely to be used by the business when it extends credit to its customers.

Consumers also use credit. Many consumers use credit to purchase major items, such as homes, automobiles, and major appliances. While the major appliance purchases may well be governed by Article 9, other purchases may fall outside its coverage. Both the home loan and the automobile loan, while secured by collateral, are outside the provisions of secured transactions coverage. Many consumers also use credit for smaller purchases, such as clothing, gasoline, and groceries, among other items. For example, a significant number of college students purchase their books and supplies on credit, and students often pay their tuition by means of credit. These transactions also fall beyond the scope of Article 9. In fact, most of these latter transactions do not involve collateral in any sense. These are unsecured credit transactions. Some unsecured credit is procured through the use of promissory notes or credit cards. A relatively recent—and controversial—form of unsecured credit that is used by consumers is the "payday loan." These loans often have an API (annual percentage rate) in *triple digits,* with interest in some cases exceeding 900 percent per annum.

Letters of Credit

Letters of credit are perhaps the most unique area regulated by the Uniform Commercial Code. The original Article 5 was one of the few areas covered in the UCC that was not based on some form of prior codification.[1] The laws governing letters of credit prior to the enactment of the UCC were derived primarily from court opinions rather than statutory enactments, and there were not that many cases addressing the issue. As a result, the original article was intended to establish "an independent theoretical frame for the further development of letters of credit."[2] The statutory goal of Article 5 was originally stated to be "(1) to set a substantive theoretical frame that describes the function and legal nature of letters of credit; and (2) to preserve procedural flexibility in order to accommodate further developments of the efficient use of letters of credit."[3]

The current version of Article 5, which was revised in 1995, reflects the increasing importance of this method of payment. It is estimated that nearly $500 billion in standby letters of credit are now issued annually, with some $250 billion of those originating in the United States.[4] As the use of letters of credit has grown, so has the statutory and code coverage of the area. International letters of credit are regulated by the Uniform Customs and Practices (UCP), which have been revised four times since the 1950s. The current version (UCP 500) became effective in 1994. Article 5 of the UCC regulates domestic letters of credit, although many letters of credit also include language stating that the letter is subject to the Uniform Customs and Practices. In addition the United Nations has proposed a Convention dealing with Independent Guarantees and Standby Letters of Credit through UNCITRAL.

By now you are probably thinking that, while all of this background is fascinating, you still do not know what is meant by a "letter of credit." Stated as simply as possible, a letter of credit is a device designed to reassure both the buyer and the seller in a transaction, especially a long-distance transaction, that each party will receive the benefit of his or her bargain. For example, suppose that a buyer and a seller enter into a sales contract. The seller may be unwilling to deliver any goods until such time as he or she is paid for the goods. But the buyer is equally unwilling to pay for any goods until he or she has received the goods and can verify their conformity to the contract. This position might well result in a failure to complete the contract, to the detriment of both parties and possibly to their respective economies. One alternative, discussed under Negotiable Instruments (Chapters 20–24), is to use a *sight draft.* While the use of such an instrument increases the level of comfort of both the buyer and the seller, it still leaves a bit to be desired. The drawee must accept the sight draft before there is any obligation to honor the instrument, leaving the seller at the mercy of the drawee to a significant degree.

A letter of credit helps to eliminate this concern, giving the seller a greater degree of control and thus a greater sense of confidence that he or she will be paid. With a letter of credit the *applicant* (the buyer) obtains a commitment from the *issuer* (the buyer's bank) that the issuer will honor the letter of credit upon the issuing bank's receipt of certain specified documents from the *beneficiary* (the seller). The specified documents that must be presented to the issuing bank will normally include (1) a draft drawn by the seller in the seller's favor against the buyer, (2) a bill of lading covering the goods, (3) an invoice, (4) an inspection certificate, (5) an insurance certificate, and (6) any other documents that might be necessary to show performance by the seller.

When a letter of credit is used, the risk to the parties is minimized. The seller knows that he or she will be paid by the issuing bank once the seller ships the goods and provides the required documents to the issuing bank. The buyer knows that he or she will receive a bill of lading that will enable the buyer to obtain the goods from the carrier. The buyer also knows that the goods have been inspected, so that it is reasonable to think the goods are conforming; that the goods are insured, so that the risk of loss during transit is minimized; and that any other necessary documentation has been satisfied.

Revised Article 5 expressly states that the letter of credit is independent of the underlying transaction for which it was issued.[5] In a reflection of modern commercial practices, the revision to Article 5 authorizes the use of electronic technology in the creation, transmission, and presentment of a letter of credit.[6] The letter of credit in deemed to be irrevocable unless the letter itself expressly provides for revocation,[7] which is of great benefit to the beneficiary (the seller). The code also requires the issuer to dishonor any letter that does not strictly conform, under standard customs and practices, to the terms and conditions contained in the letter of credit.[8] This requirement of "strict compliance" provides protection to the applicant (the buyer), while the limitation as to how "strict" the compliance must be (under standard customs and practices) provides the issuer with some flexibility based on the industry standards of the issuer.

The issuer *is* permitted to dishonor a letter of credit if a required document is forged or materially fraudulent. Under the provisions of § 5-109, if a presentation is made to the issuer that appears on its face to strictly comply with the terms of the letter of credit, but a required document is forged or materially fraudulent, or if honoring the letter would facilitate a material fraud on the applicant or the issuer, the issuer may dishonor the letter. The right to dishonor is limited to some extent. The letter must be honored if the presentation is demanded by a person who has given value in good faith without notice of the forgery or fraud. In addition, an applicant can prevent the honoring of the letter of credit. According to § 5-109(b):

If an applicant claims that a required document is forged or materially fraudulent or that honor of the presentation would facilitate a material fraud by the beneficiary on the issuer or the applicant, a court of competent jurisdiction may temporarily or permanently enjoin the issuer from honoring a presentation or grant similar relief against the issuer or other persons only if the court finds that:

(1) the relief is not prohibited under the law applicable to an accepted draft or deferred obligation incurred by the issuer;

(2) a beneficiary, issuer, or nominated person who may be adversely affected is adequately protected against loss that it may suffer because the relief is granted;

(3) all of the conditions to entitle a person to the relief under the law of this State have been met; and

(4) on the basis of the information submitted to the court, the applicant is more likely than not to succeed under its claim of forgery or material fraud and the person demanding honor does not qualify for protection under subsection (a)(1).

The case on pages 638–640 deals with an attempt to enjoin payment of a letter of credit. The case also involves an alleged conflict between Article 5 and the UPC. Observe the court's treatment of the issues and how letters of credit are handled differently from other documents we have discussed in other parts of the text.

There are numerous Web sites that deal with letters of credit. One such site, which also provides an overview of numerous other banking services, is http://www.iboc.com/.

Unsecured Credit

In an *unsecured credit* arrangement, the creditor agrees to grant credit to the debtor without the use of any collateral. In such an arrangement, the creditor is relying on the debtor to repay the loan or to honor the debt without the benefit of some form of security in the event the debtor defaults on the obligation. Thus, the creditor will *either* restrict the debtors to whom such credit is extended to those debtors who are deemed better credit risks, *or* the creditor will charge a significantly higher interest rate for the credit because of the added risk.

Unsecured credit may take the form of a *signature loan*, in which the lender agrees to make the loan on the basis of the borrower's signature alone. Unsecured credit is also found with most public utility accounts (telephone, electricity, water, etc), bank credit cards (e.g., Visa and Master-Card), and travel and entertainment cards (e.g., American

27.1

MID-AMERICA TIRE, INC. v. PTZ TRADING LTD.
768 N.E.2d 619, 2002 Ohio LEXIS 1291 (Ohio S. Ct. 2002)

FACTS Gary Corby, an independent tire broker operating as Corby International, approached John Evans, the owner of Transcontinental Tyre Company of Wolverhampton, England, about purchasing and then reselling tires to buyers in the United States. Evans was an agent for PTZ Trading, Ltd. Evans, in turn, contacted Aloysius Siever, a German tire broker who was also an agent for PTZ. Siever had an arrangement with a sole distributor of Michelin surplus tires from France that would allow the parties to acquire the required tires. In the meantime, Corby contacted Paul Chappell, an independent tire broker in California who worked as an independent contractor for Tire Network, Inc., to see if Chappell would be interested in importing "gray market" Michelin tires into the United States. ("Gray market" tires are tires that are imported and marketed in a region at a greatly reduced rate without the knowledge or approval of the manufacturer.) Corby told Chappell that he could offer 50,000 to 70,000 Michelin tires per quarter at 40 to 60 percent below the U.S. market price on an exclusive and ongoing basis. The quantity of tires being offered was too great for Chappell and/or Tire Network to handle, so Chappell contacted Mid-America Tire and Jenco Marketing, Inc., to see if they would be interested in participating in the deal. When they agreed, the deal was struck with Corby.

Initially Corby provided a list of mud and snow tires that were immediately available. Chappell asked Corby if he could include some "highway" tires as well, since the snow tire season was virtually over. Despite the request for "highway" tires, Corby continued to submit lists of mud and snow tires. He also included on his list tires that were not normally sold in the United States. In addition, Corby was trying to sell tires that had their serial numbers sanded off, which could not be legally imported into the United States. Despite these problems, the buyers continued to try to work with Corby to acquire the tires. Corby informed Chappell that nothing further could be done to satisfy their agreement until such time as a letter of credit was provided to protect the European parties in the transaction. As a result, First National Bank issued an irrevocable letter of credit in favor of PTZ. The letter was drawn against the Mid-America account and was for an initial amount of $517,260.33. The letter of credit specified that shipping terms were to be "exworks any European location," and that "the credit is subject to the Uniform Customs and Practices for Documentary Credit (1993 Revision), International Chamber of Commerce—Publication 500."

When the buyers eventually learned that the prices they were to pay *exceeded* the price the tires were sold for at retail in the United States, and that Corby did not have the exclusive rights to surplus Michelin, they informed Corby that they were withdrawing their offer to purchase any tires and were canceling the letter of credit. At that point Siever informed the buyers that he had the letter of credit, that he was shipping the tires he had on hand immediately, and that he intended to present the letter for payment. The following day Mid-America sought an injunction against First National's honoring the letter of credit. The court granted a preliminary injunction, and then, at trial, granted a permanent injunction based on the apparent fraud that led to the issuance of the letter. The court of appeals reversed. According to the court of appeals, the documents submitted were in strict compliance with the letter. The court also noted that the letter stated that the UCP was to govern, and the UCP has no provision for enjoining payment based on fraud. Given the lack of sanctions under the UCP, the court of appeals ruled that the letter should be honored. Mid-America and Jenco appealed from this decision.

ISSUES Is a fraud in the inducement of the issuance of a letter of credit grounds for a court to grant injunctive relief against the payment of that letter of credit to the beneficiary who perpetrated the fraud? Does the UCP preclude the issuance of an injunction against payment of a letter of credit?

HOLDINGS Yes, fraud in the inducement by the beneficiary provides sufficient grounds for the court to issue an injunction against payment of the letter of credit. No, the UCP does not preclude the issuance of an injunction when there is a fraud involved in the issuance of the letter of credit.

REASONING Excerpts from the opinion of Judge Alice Robie Resnick:

PTZ argues, and the court of appeals held, that appellants should be denied injunctive relief under R.C. 1305.08(B) because they have an adequate remedy at law. Appellants claim that the common-law requirement of irreparable injury is not one of the prerequisites for injunctive relief . . . and that, in any event, Mid-America does not have an adequate legal remedy.

It is well settled that an injunction will not issue where there is an adequate remedy at law. . . . However, there is one exception to this rule. "It is established law in Ohio that, when a statute grants a specific injunctive remedy to an individual or to the state, the party requesting the injunction 'need not aver and show, as under ordinary rules in equity, that great or irreparable injury is about to be done for which he has no adequate remedy at law.' " . . . We hold, therefore, that in order for a court of competent jurisdiction to enjoin the issuer of a letter of credit from honoring a presentation . . . the court must find that the applicant has no adequate remedy at law.

In actions to enjoin honor on the basis of fraud, courts usually find that the applicant has an adequate remedy at law where the alleged injury is capable of being measured in pecuniary terms. While there is some authority to the contrary, most courts find that the availability of a monetary damage award for fraud in the underlying contract constitutes an adequate legal remedy, even if the applicant must travel overseas and submit to the uncertainties of foreign litigation in order to obtain it. On the other hand, the availability of a damage award is usually held to be inadequate where resort to foreign courts would be futile or meaningless, where the beneficiary is insolvent or may abscond with the money drawn, where honoring a draft would likely force the applicant into bankruptcy, or where the determination of damages would be difficult or speculative. . . .

Although R.C. Chapter 1305 is the primary source of law governing LCs in Ohio, it "is far from comprehensive." UCC 5-103, Official Comment 2 (1995). It is designed to cover only "certain rights and obligations arising out of transactions involving letters of credit." . . . It is intended to be supplemented by various principles of law and equity that will often apply to help determine those rights and obligations. . . . And subject to certain exceptions, it allows the parties to vary the effect of its provisions "by agreement or by a provision stated or incorporated by reference in an undertaking." . . . The parties in this case have specifically adopted the UCP as applicable to the present undertaking. In fact, "many letters of credit, domestic and international, state that they shall be governed by the UCP." . . . "When rules of custom and practice are incorporated by reference, they are considered to be explicit terms of the agreement or undertaking." . . . The question that naturally arises from such an incorporation is whether and to what extent R.C. Chapter 1305 will continue to apply to the undertaking. In other words, when a particular LC states that it is subject to the UCP, what is the resulting relationship between the UCP and R.C. Chapter 1305 with regard to

that transaction? . . . This is not a situation where one complete set of rules is substituted for another. The scope of the UCP is basically different from that of Article 5. "Because of their different scope, Article 5 [of the UCC] covers some important areas not covered by the UCP, and the UCP covers some important areas not covered by Article 5." . . . Each of these bodies of rules will apply to govern the undertaking in their respective areas of coverage, and both will apply concurrently in the event of any overlapping consistent provisions. . . . It is only when the UCP and R.C. Chapter 1305 contain overlapping inconsistent provisions on the same issue or subject that the UCP's terms will displace those of R.C. Chapter 1305. Thus, when a particular LC states that it is subject to the UCP, the UCP's terms will replace those of R.C. Chapter 1305 only to the extent that "there is a direct conflict between a provision of the UCP and an analogous provision of R.C. Chapter 1305." . . . In other words, "the UCP terms are permissible contractual modifications . . . when a rule explicitly stated in the UCP . . . is different from a rule explicitly stated in Article 5." . . .

Thus, the fact that the credit in this case was expressly made subject to the UCP is not dispositive. Instead, the determinative issue is whether a direct conflict exists between the UCP and R.C. Chapter 1305 as to the availability of injunctive relief against honor where fraud is claimed . . . [Article 5] . . . provides:

"If an applicant claims that a required document is forged or materially fraudulent or that honor of the presentation would facilitate a material fraud by the beneficiary on the issuer or applicant, a court of competent jurisdiction may temporarily or permanently enjoin the issuer from honoring a presentation." . . . Because "the UCP 'is by definition a recording of practice rather than a statement of legal rules,' [it] does not purport to offer rules which govern the issuance of an injunction against honor of a draft." . . . Thus, the UCP's silence on the issue of fraud "should not be construed as *preventing* relief under the 'fraud in the transaction' doctrine, where applicable law permits it." . . . In fact, the overwhelming weight of authority is to the effect that Article 5's fraud exception continues to apply in credit transactions made subject to the UCP. These courts hold, in one form or another, that the UCP's failure to include a rule governing injunctive relief for fraud does not prevent the applicant from obtaining such relief under Article 5. Stated variously, these courts recognize that there is no inherent conflict between the UCP's statement of the independence principle and Article 5's remedy against honor where fraud is charged. Instead, this is merely a situation where Article 5 covers a subject not covered by the UCP. . . .

Based on all of the foregoing, the judgment of the court of appeals is hereby reversed, and the permanent injunction as granted by the trial court is reinstated.

Judgment reversed.

BUSINESS CONSIDERATIONS Should a business be willing to arrange for a letter of credit before it has been convinced that the beneficiary of that letter is able to satisfy its obligations under the contract? What sorts of protections exist for the applicant in this type of situation without resorting to injunctive relief?

ETHICAL CONSIDERATIONS Is it ethical for a seller to insist on the establishment of a letter of credit naming the seller as beneficiary before the seller has arranged to satisfy the terms of the contract? Did Corby and his associates act in an ethical manner in this case?

NRW CASE 27.1   Finance

NRW

CHOOSING LOAN TERMS

Carlos recently began looking for a short-term loan to cover the cost of some renovation work he is doing on an old car. After getting terms and conditions from a number of different prospective lenders, he decided that one of the local banks provided him with the best options. The loan officer at the bank gave Carlos two options: a signature loan with a single payment due in six months, and an APR of 10.5 percent; or an installment loan with 12 equal monthly payments and an APR of 9.75 percent. The signature loan would be made without any collateral, while the installment loan would require that Carlos provide some collateral to secure the loan. Carlos has asked you which of these two loans would be better for him. What will you tell him?

BUSINESS CONSIDERATIONS Although the installment loan has a lower interest rate, Carlos will end up paying more money and more interest to the bank if he chooses the installment loan. Why might a businessperson prefer a lower rate, longer term loan when such a loan actually increases the amount to be repaid?

ETHICAL CONSIDERATIONS Is it ethical for a bank to require collateral for a loan in order to grant a lower rate, when the bank was willing to make essentially the same loan to a customer without collateral?

INTERNATIONAL CONSIDERATIONS Suppose that a business wanted to borrow money from its bank in order to invest in a business venture in another country. What concerns might such a loan application raise with the bank that would not necessarily be present for a similar loan to invest in a domestic business venture?

Express, Diners Club, Carte Blanche). Public utility accounts are regulated by the various state public utility regulatory commissions and by contract law. Credit cards and travel and entertainment cards are discussed in a later section of this chapter. Other types of unsecured credit transactions will be discussed next.

Regulation of unsecured credit transactions is primarily a matter of state law. Federal regulation of these transactions is primarily concerned with ensuring that information is provided to the debtor prior to the creation of the debt, and with acceptable methods of collection in the event the debtor defaults on the agreement. Under Title I of the federal Consumer Credit Protection Act, better known at the "Truth in Lending Act" (TILA), creditors must provide credit applicants with certain information as to the cost of the credit. This information must be provided in a standard format and in a standard terminology. The most important information that must be given to the applicant is the "APR," the annualized percentage rate to be charged in the transaction. This information must be provided in writing, and the writing must be clear and conspicuous. Failure to provide the necessary information in the appropriate format may subject the creditor to various penalties and liabilities. (For more detailed coverage of TILA, see Chapter 38.)

The case on pages 641–642 involved a claim by the debtor that the creditor had failed to properly explain the cost of the credit, in violation of the disclosure requirements of TILA. After reading the case, decide whether you agree with the assertions of the debtor.

If a debtor defaults on the credit arrangement, the creditor is allowed to use various methods to enforce his or her claim. For example, the "self-help" provisions discussed in the coverage of secured transactions may be available in certain cases. However, with an unsecured credit transaction, the creditor does not have access to any "self-help" provisions because there is no collateral. The creditor may seek a writ of attachment or a writ of garnishment, or the creditor may elect to file suit for breach of contract. While these methods are often successful, they are time consuming and relatively expensive. As a result, many creditors

27.2

COELHO v. PARK RIDGE OLDSMOBILE, INC.
2001 U.S. Dist. LEXIS 14652 (N.D. Ill. 2001)

FACTS Coelho bought a 1999 Mitsubishi Montero Sport SUV from Park Ridge Oldsmobile on June 26, 1999. He was given the choice of either a $1,500 rebate or financing at a below-market rate. Coelho chose the below-market financing option and entered into a retail installment contract with Park Ridge (PRO), which immediately assigned the contract to Mitsubishi Motors Credit of America (MMCA). Two months later, on August 26, 1999, Coelho brought suit against Park Ridge and MMCA, claiming that the contract violates both the Truth in Lending Act (TILA) and the Illinois Consumer Fraud Act (ICFA) by failing to adequately disclose the total cost of the credit on the contract. Specifically, Coelho alleged that because Park Ridge withheld the $1,500 rebate money when he chose to purchase the SUV on credit, this constituted a finance charge, which the contract fails to disclose. After the court dismissed the complaint against MMCA, Coelho filed an amended complaint in which he maintained his TILA claim against Park Ridge and alleged that MMCA and Mitsubishi Motors violated the ICFA and the Illinois common law rules against fraudulent misrepresentation. According to the amended complaint, the defendants had a policy of selling cars to "cash customers" for $1,500 less than the price charged to "credit customers." Coelho claimed that this $1,500 difference was a finance charge imposed on the credit customers, and that it was not disclosed in the contract.

ISSUE Is the "cost difference" between cash customers and credit customers a "finance charge" that must be disclosed in the retail installment contract?

HOLDING Yes. The "cost difference" was an expense related to a credit purchase, and as such it must be disclosed as a finance charge.

REASONING Excerpts from the opinion of District Judge Joan B. Gottschall:

TILA was enacted "to assure a meaningful disclosure of credit terms so that the consumer will be able to compare more readily the various credit terms available to him and avoid the uninformed use of credit, and to protect the consumer against inaccurate and unfair billing and credit card practices." . . . "TILA requires creditors to disclose clearly and accurately to consumers any finance charge that the consumer will bear under the credit transaction. These stringent disclosure requirements are designed to prevent creditors from circumventing TILA's objectives by burying the cost of credit in the price of the goods sold." . . . In addition, the Federal Reserve Board issued regulations implementing TILA, commonly referred to as Regulation Z. . . . A "finance charge" is defined by TILA as the "sum of all charges, payable directly or indirectly by the person to whom the credit is extended, and imposed directly or indirectly by the creditor as an incident to the extension of credit." . . . Regulation Z provides that a finance charge "includes any charge payable directly or indirectly by the consumer and imposed directly or indirectly by the creditor as an incident to or a condition of the extension of credit." . . . Regulation Z specifically provides that finance charges include "discounts for the purpose of inducing payment by a means other than credit." . . . Coelho claims that if he had purchased the car for cash, "he would have paid a cash price for the car $1,500 less than the cash price of his financed transaction." . . . This constitutes "a charge that is avoidable by paying cash." . . . Because Coelho was not offered the rebate, the $1,500 is a condition to the extension of credit. This constitutes a finance charge as defined by TILA and must be disclosed as such. . . . It is undisputed that PRO did not disclose the rebate as a finance charge.

Defendants argue first that the $1,500 rebate was actually available to some customers who purchased Mitsubishi vehicles on credit. Thus, defendants argue that the rebate was not a condition to the extension of credit, and not a finance charge. This raises a question of fact, the resolution of which is inappropriate on a motion to dismiss. However, even if the rebate were available to *some* customers on credit, it appears that the question is whether it was a condition to the extension of credit to Coelho and customers like him. . . . Coelho sufficiently alleges that the rebate was such a condition. The second amended complaint states that "no purchaser who takes advantage of the [special financing], with the exception of purchasers of 1999 Galants and Diamantes, is eligible to receive a dealer cash rebate." . . . The court accepts this as true. Therefore, defendants' first argument fails.

Second, defendants point to the Official Staff Commentary to Regulation Z. Specifically, the commentary . . . states that in a credit sale transaction, a seller's or manufacturer's rebate offered to prospective purchasers may be "either reflected in the Truth in Lending disclosures or *disregarded in the disclosures*" of the amount of credit extended, or "amount financed" (emphasis added). Defendants argue that this part of the Official Staff Commentary should apply to the present case because it involves a rebate. This argument fails. First, the commentary discusses rebates offered in a *credit sale transaction*. In the present case *no* rebate was offered in Coelho's credit transaction; rather, a rebate was withheld. In addition, this Official Staff Commentary discusses what the creditor may disclose as the "amount financed"; however, the $1,500 in the present case is a "finance charge." The commentary is inapplicable.

Finally, defendants argue that the rebate constitutes "seller's points," which are explicitly excluded under Regulation Z. . . . The Official Staff Commentary to that section of Regulation Z states that seller's points "include any charges imposed by the creditor *upon the noncreditor seller* of property for providing credit to the buyer or for providing credit on certain terms" (emphasis added). As an example, the commentary points to real estate transactions guaranteed or insured by governmental agencies. "A 'commitment fee' paid by a noncreditor seller (such as a real estate developer) to the creditor should be treated as seller's points." . . . This exception is inapplicable to the present case. First, PRO is not a noncreditor seller; it is both the seller and creditor. Second, there has been no allegation that any charges were imposed on PRO for providing credit to Coelho or any other customers.

Defendants offer a creative argument as to why the court should recognize the rebate as seller's points, asserting that Mitsubishi plays the role of the noncreditor seller, which "pays to secure low interest financing from the dealership . . . " assuming that Mitsubishi and MMCA are separate entities. . . . The court disagrees with this interpretation of the Official Staff Commentary. First, the plain language of the commentary states that it applies to charges imposed on a "noncreditor seller." Mitsubishi is not the seller in this case, and PRO is not a noncreditor. No matter who the defendants insert as the operative party, the commentary cannot apply. Second, if the court were to agree with defendants' argument, it would render the definition of "finance charge" meaningless as applied to auto financing cases such as this one. . . . The court does not think that the Federal Reserve Board intended such a result. PRO's motion to dismiss is denied as to the TILA claim. . . . PRO's only argument—that there was no fraud because it did not violate TILA—fails. Defendant Park Ridge Oldsmobile's motion to dismiss is denied. Defendants Mitsubishi Motor Sales of America's and Mitsubishi Motors Credit of America's joint motion to dismiss is granted.

BUSINESS CONSIDERATIONS Why would a business that extends credit to its customers want to exclude the "lost" rebate in its TILA calculations? What harm is done to the customer in this situation?

ETHICAL CONSIDERATIONS Is it ethical for a business that extends credit to its customers to attempt to hide the cost of that credit? Is it ethical for a customer to elect a below-market interest rate rather than a rebate, and then to complain that he or she was treated unfairly?

---

choose to hire a collection agent in an attempt to collect the unpaid balance owed. Historically, such debt collection agencies developed a bad reputation. They were known to engage in various types of harassing behavior in their effort to "encourage" the debtor to pay the debt. As a result, the Fair Debt Collection Practices Act was passed. This Act applies only to persons who are attempting to collect debts owed to another person, and not to the actual creditor who is acting on his or her own behalf in seeking recovery. However, most creditors also follow the guidelines of the Act in the interests of following sound and fair business practices.[9] (The Fair Debt Collection Practices Act is also covered in detail in Chapter 38.)

The federal regulation in this area is effective in providing debtors with information regarding the cost of the credit and protecting defaulting debtors from some unfair or improper collection practices, but it is not very effective as to the terms of the credit agreement. Regulation of the terms and conditions of unsecured credit transactions is left to the states. State regulation in this area includes limits on the interest rates and other finance charges that may be imposed, possible "cooling-off" periods for the debtor in some transactions, and other terms and details of the transaction. Each state establishes its own maximum permissible interest rates for various types of loans or credit transactions. If the creditor charges a rate in excess of the state's maximum, the interest is *usurious*. Since usury is defined as charging an illegal rate of interest,[10] the contract is tainted with illegality. In some states, the charging of a usurious rate of interest voids the entire contract. In other states, the interest portion is voided due to the illegality, although the debtor still must repay the principal. Some states void the usurious interest, substituting the state interest maximum into the agreement on the theory that the parties meant to charge only the highest legal rate.

In some states there is a single usury provision for all types of credit. However, most states have different usury rates for different types of credit. A closed-end unsecured loan will have one rate; an installment loan with collateral will have another rate; revolving credit arrangements (credit cards) will have still another rate. It is important for a business that extends credit—and an individual who uses credit to make purchases—to be aware of the state rules in this area.

State regulation also extends to other terms and conditions of the credit arrangement. Among the areas of coverage that may be encountered here are the following:

- The Uniform Consumer Credit Code (adopted by 11 states)[11]

- State consumer loan acts

- State home solicitation sales acts

- Negotiable Instruments Law (Articles 3 and 4 of the UCC)

- Contract law

Again, familiarity with the applicable state statutes will help to ensure that the businessperson who extends credit is acting in a proper manner, and that the individual who is using credit is acting in the most appropriate manner.

Installment Loans

Installment loans are loans for a fixed time period and with fixed periodic payments. Installment loans usually require a monthly payment. While installment loans may be secured or unsecured, many consumer installment loans are secured by some form of collateral. Some of these loans will fall within the coverage of Article 9. For example, if a person purchases a refrigerator on credit and uses the refrigerator as collateral for the loan, the credit arrangement is a purchase money security interest, and Article 9 governs the transaction. However, if a person purchases a car on credit, using the car as collateral for the loan, the transaction falls outside the coverage of Article 9. This transaction will be governed by the state certificate of title rules rather than by Article 9.

Installment loans are subject to many of the same regulatory provisions as unsecured loans. At the federal level the lender is still governed by TILA, and the Fair Debt Collection Practices Act still applies to attempts to collect past due accounts by collection agencies. At the state level, the transaction is still covered by Article 3 of the UCC if a promissory note is involved, as is likely. In addition, the Uniform Consumer Credit Code may apply to the transaction, *if* the transaction takes place in one of the 11 states that have adopted the UCCC, and *if* the debtor is a consumer. Since

the parties are involved in a contract, the state laws governing contracts also apply. And if the state has a retail installment sales act, or similar legislation, the provisions of that act will also apply to the transaction.

Mortgage loans involve loans in which real estate is used as collateral by the debtor to secure the credit. Mortgage loans are commonly installment loans, but the repayment term tends to be much longer. For example, many mortgage loans have a repayment period of 30 years. By contrast, most of the other types of installment loans have a repayment term of 5 years or less. Since real estate is used as collateral in a mortgage loan, the interest of the state in regulating the transaction is obvious, and state regulations in this area are substantial. However, there are also some important federal regulations that must be met by the parties, particularly the creditor.

The most important federal regulation is, once again, TILA. Debtors must be made aware of the cost of the credit prior to entering the transaction. Given the length of time involved, and the relative size of the credit involved—mortgages are frequently the largest debt a consumer will assume—the need for full and accurate disclosure is obvious. A second area of coverage at the federal level is the Real Estate Settlement Procedures Act (RESPA), which became effective in 1974. RESPA is also a disclosure act. Home mortgage lenders are required to provide loan applicants with a good-faith estimate of all settlement and closing costs associated with the loan. The lender must also inform the applicant if any of the settlement business is being referred to a company affiliated with the lender. The applicant must be informed as to the possibility that the loan will be transferred at some point in time. If the loan is transferred, both the lender and the new holder of the note must also notify the debtor at that time. Finally, the lender must provide the borrower with a list of the actual settlement and closing costs at the time the loan is formally closed.

Most states have a number of statutes that apply to mortgage loans. Included among these statutes are

- mortgage lending acts

- mortgage banker and broker acts

- secondary mortgage acts

- home improvement contract acts

State law will also have provisions regarding the warranties that the seller provides to the buyer, statutes governing recording of the deed, and various other aspects. These provisions will be covered in detail in Chapter 41.

Credit Cards

Credit cards have become ubiquitous in the United States. A significant percentage of adults have at least one credit card, and most people are likely to have several different credit cards at any point in time. There are three basic types of credit cards: bank cards such as MasterCard, Visa, and Discover; travel and entertainment cards such as American Express, Carte Blanche, and Diners Club; and store or merchant cards such as Sears, J.C. Penney, Exxon, Texaco, and so on. Bank cards and travel and entertainment cards are widely accepted at a variety of locations. By contrast, store or merchant cards are normally accepted only by the stores or merchants who issue the cards. Credit cards involve open-ended credit, and they are often viewed differently from loans for purposes of usury provisions and other state credit coverage. The holder of the card is regarded by the courts as being involved in a "revolving credit" arrangement rather than a loan, and the methods for computing charges and fees are different than the methods used in a "standard" loan. Nonetheless, the number of people who hold credit cards, and the widespread usage of credit cards, has necessitated a great deal of coverage at both the federal and the state levels.

Federal regulation in this area is based, once again, on the Truth in Lending Act (TILA). The provisions for credit card protection are found in the Truth in Lending Act Regulations (Regulation Z), Subpart B, which deals with "open-ended credit."[12] The credit card issuer must provide a full disclosure of the costs associated with the card, as would be expected under TILA. However, the regulations go much farther.

Section 226.12 (a) prohibits the issuing of unsolicited credit cards. This section states that no credit card may be issued unless it is issued in response to an application from the recipient (the application can be made orally or in writing) or it is a renewal of, or substitution for, a card that has previously been issued and accepted. At this time there is no prohibition against *solicitation* of applications by the card issuer, but the solicitation may not include the card itself. It is not a defense for the card issuer to send a card that requires a telephone call to an "activation center" before the card can be used. The courts have viewed this as an *issuance*, not as a *solicitation* subject to an oral application (the phone call to the activation center). Regulation Z has recently been updated. A summary of the update can be found at http://www.federalreserve.gov/boarddocs/press/boardacts/2001/200112142/. Bankers Online also has some interesting information on Regulation Z at http://www.bankersonline.com/articles/v01n06/v01n06a4.html.

NRW CASE 27.2   Finance

CHOOSING A CREDIT CARD

Recently each of the principals of NRW has been receiving credit card solicitations in the mail and by telephone. Most of these solicitations inform the recipient that she or he has been "preapproved" for the credit card in question. These solicitations also state that the card has a very attractive interest rate, such as 2.9 percent, and that there will be no fee for any transfers of the balances from any other credit cards to this new one. Mai states that she has heard about "teaser" rates, and also that some of her friends have had problems with changes in the interest rates on cards they accepted. She asks you for your advice regarding these solicitations. What will you tell her?

BUSINESS CONSIDERATIONS Most college students have minimal income, at best, and yet they regularly receive credit card solicitations from a multitude of credit card issuers. Why would a credit card issuer solicit an application from a person who is probably either unemployed or underemployed, and likely to remain so at least until graduation?

ETHICAL CONSIDERATIONS Is it ethical for a credit card issuer to use a "teaser" rate to procure applications and then to change the rate on the cards at some time in the near future, such as after six months? Is it ethical for a credit card company to change the interest rate the first time a customer is late with his or her payments?

INTERNATIONAL CONSIDERATIONS Should credit card companies solicit applications from international students who are attending college in the United States but are likely to return to their home nations upon graduation? What sorts of problems might issuing a card to such a student present for the company? For the student?

TILA also limits the liability of card holders in the event that their cards are used without authorization. If a credit card is lost or stolen, the card holder faces a maximum liability of $50 for unauthorized use of the card, and the liability is only for use of the card *before* the issuer is notified of the loss or theft. Once the card issuer is notified, the liability of the card holder ends. However, a different limit applies if the card holder consents to the use of his or her card by another, only to find out that the other person did not use the card as the card holder expected. In this situation, the card holder can be held liable for any charges incurred by the person who is using the card until such time as the card holder notifies the credit card issuer and cancels the "permissive" use of the card by the other person.

Regulation Z also prohibits "offsets" by the card issuer. The card issuer cannot take any action to offset credit card indebtedness by unilaterally asserting a claim on the card holder's funds on deposit with the issuer of the card. However, if the offset is part of a consensual security agreement between the card issuer and the card holder, an offset is permissible. Similarly, the card issuer can proceed against funds on deposit on the basis of a judgment obtained against the card holder, an attachment by the card issuer, or a written plan from the card holder permitting periodic offsets against a credit card balance.

Other federal regulations also apply to credit card use. The Equal Credit Opportunity Act requires businesses that regularly extend credit as a part of their business to make credit available without discrimination. The Fair Credit Billing Act provides a method for card holders to challenge any alleged billing errors without liability until the alleged error is investigated. And the Unsolicited Credit Card Act protects the customer from potential liability for misuse of credit cards issued without that person's application.

State regulation of credit cards tends to be more enabling than restrictive. However, the state usury provisions regarding credit cards still apply. State contract laws are applicable to the credit card relationship between the issuer and the customer. Further, when store or merchant cards are used, there is the possibility that the store or the merchant will retain a security interest in the purchased item, thus making the transaction subject to the provisions of Article 9 of the UCC.

FTC Consumer Credit Rules

The Federal Trade Commission has enacted two special *credit practice* rules designed to provide consumer debtors with protections they might not otherwise enjoy under the various other areas of law. The first of these rules is the Federal Trade Commission Holder in Due Course Rule, in effect since 1976. The second is the Federal Trade Commission Credit Practices Rule, in effect since 1985.

The Federal Trade Commission Holder in Due Course rule requires the inclusion in consumer credit contracts of

---

NRW CASE 27.3 Finance/Management

NRW

THE RISKS OF COSIGNING

One of Helen's friends has encountered some financial difficulties since she graduated from college, but it appears that she has managed to turn her life around. In fact, she has recently discovered a business opportunity that has tremendous potential and she believes that the risk factor for the opportunity is acceptable. Unfortunately, she lacks the resources to take advantage of the opportunity on her own, and none of the local bankers is willing to lend her the money unless she has more collateral or a cosigner. Since she lacks the collateral to secure the loan on her own, she approached Helen about acting as a cosigner. She also promised Helen a share of the profits from the business, if it is as successful as she thinks it will be. Helen would like to help her friend, but she is concerned about the potential liability if she agrees to act as a cosigner. Helen is worried not only for herself but also for the possibility that she might be putting Carlos, Mai, and NRW at risk. She has asked you for advice. What will you tell her?

BUSINESS CONSIDERATIONS Many businesses have a policy that prohibits the business from cosigning on loans except under extraordinary circumstances. Why might a business have such a policy?

ETHICAL CONSIDERATIONS From an ethical perspective, how should a business view requests to serve as a cosigner on a loan? Which constituent groups are jeopardized by cosignings if the borrower defaults? Which constituent groups might benefit from cosigning a loan?

INTERNATIONAL CONSIDERATIONS Suppose that a business was asked to serve as a cosigner on an international venture that had tremendous potential for profit but also carried a significant element of risk. As an inducement, the person seeking a cosigner offers the business a share of the profits from the venture. Assuming that the business would like to get involved, what might it consider doing in this situation to protect its interests?

---

a statement that the debtor retains all rights, claims, and defenses that the consumer could have asserted against the seller, even against holders in due course of the consumer credit instrument. This rule does not apply to real estate transactions or to credit card transactions.

The second rule makes it an unfair trade practice for a seller or creditor in a consumer credit transaction to make a contract containing a confession of judgment clause or a waiver of exemptions clause. Nor can the seller or creditor make a contract containing a wage assignment provision or a nonpossessory security interest in household goods or furnishing, except in the form of a purchase money security interest.

This second rule also has a special disclosure requirement when a cosigner is involved in a credit arrangement. The required disclosure statement reads as follows:

You are asked to guarantee this debt. Think carefully before you do. If the borrower doesn't pay the debt you will have to. Be sure you can afford to pay if you have to, and that you want to accept this responsibility.

You may have to pay up to the full amount of the debt if the borrower does not pay. You may also have to pay late fees or collection costs, which increase this amount. The creditor can collect this debt from you without first trying to collect from the borrower. The creditor can use the same collection methods against you that can be used against the borrower such as suing you, garnishing your wages, etc. If this debt is ever in default that fact becomes a part of your credit record.

This notice is not the contract that makes you liable for the debt.

Failure to include this notice is an unfair trade practice under the provisions of the Federal Trade Commission Act.

Payday Loans

One of the fastest-growing areas in consumer lending is the "payday loan." These loans are also perhaps the most controversial topic in consumer lending. In a payday loan a borrower goes to a lender to borrow funds "until payday." These loans are usually for a short period of time, ranging from a few days to a few weeks. In exchange for the loan, the borrower writes a check payable to the order of the lender and dated for the borrower's next payday. The check written by the borrower is for the amount of the loan plus any fees and interest to be paid. (A variation of this involves the borrower writing a check for the amount of the loan and then receiving the amount of the loan minus the fees.) When the borrower's check comes due, the borrower can either let the lender present the check to his or her bank or roll the loan over by "buying back" the check (issuing a new check for the amount of the "repurchased" check plus any new fees). Such rollovers may or may not be limited by applicable state laws or by the agreement between the borrower and the lender. The Community Financial Services Association has a code for its members that limits any customer to three rollovers on any one loan.[13]

Most payday loans are for relatively small amounts of money, normally from $100 to $500. The most common fee for a $100 loan is $15,[14] which works out to an APR of as much as 390 percent.

Nineteen states prohibit payday loans. However, a loophole in federal banking regulations permits payday lenders to operate even in those states. If a payday lender enters into an arrangement with a national bank, the bank is allowed to "export" its loan rates to any state in which it operates. Thus, a national bank may enter into an arrangement with a payday lender in which the bank "makes" the loan and then sells it to the payday lender, or it may carry the loan and pay the payday lender a "finder's fee" for finding the customer.[15]

By one estimate, payday loans will number between 55 million and 69 million loans this year, with gross revenues of $10 billion to $14 billion, and fees of $1.6 billion to $2.2 billion.[16]

The Federal Trade Commission has an Internet site that raises some questions about payday loans. This site is at http://www.ftc.gov/bcp/conline/pubs/alerts/pdayalrt.htm. For a view of payday loans from the lender's perspective, visit http://www.payday-loan-usa.com/.

A bill has been introduced in Congress that would prohibit any FDIC-insured bank from participating, either directly or indirectly, in payday lending. In addition, a number of recent state laws have addressed the issue, and more states are expected to follow soon. In the interim, it appears that payday loans will be a significant factor in the area of consumer credit.

The following case addresses a number of issues that are of concern when payday loans are involved. Among the issues are whether TILA applies to such loans, and whether these loans violate state consumer protection statutes or the state usury laws. After reading the case, evaluate the court's opinion and decide whether you agree with the court's results.

27.3

ARRINGTON v. COLLEEN, INC.; LEACH V. MR. CASH, INC.
2000 U.S. Dist. LEXIS 20651 (Md. 2000)

FACTS These two cases involved claims filed against the corporate defendants and several named individuals for alleged violations of the Truth in Lending Act (TILA), Regulation Z, and the civil provisions of the Racketeer Influenced and Corrupt Organizations Act (RICO). The case also involved allegations of violations of the Maryland Consumer Loan Law (MCLL) and the Maryland Consumer Protection Act (MCPA). All of these alleged violations are based on the practice of making "pay day loans" or "deferred deposit check-cashing services" by the corporate defendants. In a payday loan, the customer borrows a sum of money for a short term, "until payday," from the lender. In exchange for the cash received, the customer writes the lender a check for the amount of the loan plus the fees and the interest connected to the loan. On "pay day" the lender then deposits the check into its account. Prior to the presentment of his or her check, the customer can normally get an extension to the next pay day by writing a new check for the amount of the old check, plus the fees and the interest for the new time period, and recovering the older check in exchange for the newer check.

ISSUES Do TILA and Regulation Z govern "pay day" loans? Do the Maryland Consumer Loan Law and/or the Maryland Consumer Protection Act also govern "pay day" loans?

HOLDINGS Yes, these loans are subject to the provisions of TILA and of Regulation Z. Yes, these loans are also subject to the provisions of the Maryland Consumer Loan Law and the Maryland Consumer Protection Act.

REASONING Excerpts from the opinion of Judge Andre M. Davis:

In both cases, plaintiffs have asserted several federal claims. In Count I, plaintiffs assert claims under the federal Truth In Lending Act ("TILA") . . . and its accompanying Regulation Z, which requires consumer lenders to disclose interest rates and certain other information deemed critical by Congress to facilitate the informed use of consumer credit. . . . Plaintiffs also invoke this court's supplemental jurisdiction . . . by asserting in Counts II, III and IV state law claims brought under the Maryland Consumer Loan Law ("MCLL"), which requires consumer lenders to make disclosures generally consistent with those required by TILA . . . prohibits lending at usurious rates . . . and requires persons engaged in consumer lending to be licensed by the Maryland Department of Labor, Licensing and Regulation. . . . In addition, plaintiffs assert in Count VI claims under the Maryland Consumer

Protection Act ("MCPA"), which prohibits false or misleading statements or other factual representations which have the tendency to deceive the customer. . . . It is defendants' position that the MCLL does not regulate the transactions here at issue and further, that if in fact these transactions are regulated, the MCLL does not give sufficient notice to persons engaging in these transactions of that fact; and, finally, that if these transactions are regulated by the MCLL, the defendants were justified in relying on an informal letter opinion issued in 1996 by the former Commissioner of Financial Regulation, H. Robert Hergenroeder, that "deferred deposit check cashing" services did not constitute consumer lending under the MCLL (the "Hergenroeder letter"). For these reasons, defendants argue, the determination of whether these transactions are consumer loans and thus regulated by the MCLL presents "novel" and "complex" issues of state law which are best resolved by the courts of Maryland. . . . I disagree.

The question of the proper characterization for the transactions at issue in the cases at bar has not been specifically addressed by the Maryland Court of Appeals. This does not mean, however, that the question raised by these cases invariably presents a "novel and complex" issue of law. Quite the contrary, there are instances, of which I am convinced this is one, where the Court of Appeals has not had occasion to rule on the particulars of an issue but where its prior cases in the same or a related context . . . provide, in conjunction with the relevant portions of the Maryland Code . . . more than sufficient information upon which a federal court may reliably predict how the Maryland Court of Appeals will resolve open questions of state law. . . . The lack of case law does not make the [claims] unintelligible to this Court. . . . Defendants' proffer of the Hergenroeder letter does not change my analysis. I rely on the considerations discussed by the Court of Appeals in *Baltimore Gas & Elec. Co v. Public Service Comm'n of Maryland* . . . and applied in *Haigley v. Department of Health and Mental Hygiene* . . . which convince me that the Hergenroeder letter is entitled to very little, if any, weight.

In light of the foregoing, the issues raised by the complaints in these cases are not so novel or complex as to warrant my declining the exercise of supplemental jurisdiction over the state law claims. . . .

Defendants contend that plaintiffs have failed to state a claim under the TILA. In arguing against the application of the TILA to their businesses, defendants are swimming against a strong current as every court that has examined the issue has concluded that the TILA applies to transaction [sic] of the sort at issue in these cases.

All defendants argue that it is not clear that TILA and Regulation Z apply to the transactions at issue here. They direct my attention to a proposed change to the Federal Reserve Board of Governors' (the "Board") official interpretation of Regulation Z, which implements TILA. . . . The change—or "addition," since so far as I can tell it did not change or contradict prior policy—which became final on March 24, 2000, clarified the Board's position that payday lending or deferred deposit check cashing services were covered by Regulation Z. In accordance with normal Board procedures, compliance of payday lenders with Regulation Z is "optional" until October 1, 2000, and mandatory thereafter.

Prior to the Board's clarification of its official interpretation, neither the Board nor any other authoritative body had interpreted TILA or Regulation Z to exempt these transactions. In fact, federal courts have, since 1997, interpreted TILA and Regulation Z to apply to these transactions. . . . By virtue of the unambiguous federal authority on the application of TILA and Regulation Z to these transactions, and given the absence of any authority or interpretation to the contrary . . . I am persuaded that plaintiffs have stated claims under TILA and Regulation Z against the defendants.

The individual defendants argue that plaintiffs have failed to allege sufficient facts establishing that they are "creditors" under TILA. The purpose of TILA is to require consumer lenders to disclose their interest rates clearly and conspicuously so that consumers can make informed decisions when shopping for credit. . . .

TILA applies to "creditors" engaging in open- and closed-end credit transactions. . . . Plaintiffs have sufficiently alleged that the corporate defendants, Colleen and Mr. Cash together with their operating entities, are in the business [of] extending credit and were the parties to whom the customers' checks were made payable. . . . Plaintiffs have also sufficiently alleged that the defendant offered consumer credit for which defendants charged a fee . . . These allegations place Colleen and Mr. Cash in the category of creditors targeted by TILA. . . .

Since defendants have not in their motions demonstrated to my satisfaction that plaintiffs can prove "no set of facts in support of [plaintiffs'] claim[s] that would entitle [them] to relief." . . . the TILA claims will not be dismissed as to the individual defendants.

TILA claims must be brought within one year from the date of the occurrence of the violation. . . . Transactions in which there was a failure to disclose occurring prior to January 20, 1999, for the Arrington plaintiffs are barred. . . . Transactions in which there was a failure to disclose occurring prior to February 11, 1999, for the Leach plaintiffs are barred. . . . While the allegations with respect to the Leaches do not definitively establish that they were subject to failures to disclose within the limitations period on the initiation of their transactions in "approximately February [and March] of 1999," they have also alleged a series of "rollover" transactions over a period of approximately eight weeks . . . which would represent separate "occurrences" of the failure to disclose within the TILA limitations period. . . . Since all claims filed by the plaintiffs were filed within the one-year TILA limitations period, they also were filed within the general three-year limitations period for MCLL claims. . . . The usury provisions of the Maryland Code provide a six-month statute of limitations for usury running from the time the loan is "satisfied." . . . Claims based on loans which were satisfied before August 11, 1999, are barred for the Leach plaintiffs. . . . For the reasons set forth above and on the record on July 13, 2000, defendants' motions to dismiss, except as to Count II . . . are denied. The motions for summary judgment are denied.

BUSINESS CONSIDERATIONS Why would a national bank want to be affiliated with a payday loan company? Why would a payday loan company want to be affiliated with a national bank?

ETHICAL CONSIDERATIONS Do firms that make payday loans act in an ethical manner, or do they prey on the people least able to afford the cost of the credit they offer?

Summary

While secured transactions form an important part of debtor-creditor relations, they are not the only type of credit transactions involved in this area. This is especially true of consumer credit transactions, where the use of secured transactions under Article 9 tends to be limited to purchase money security interests for furniture and major appliances. There are a number of credit devices that can be used besides secured transactions. Some of these devices are more likely to be used by businesses, while others are more likely to be used by consumers.

Letters of credit are used by businesses as a means of protecting both the seller, who is assured of being paid if he or she complies with the conditions set out in the letter, and the buyer, who is assured that no funds will be released until the conditions established by the buyer have been satisfied by the seller. The buyer, known as the "applicant," establishes the letter of credit with his or her bank, the "issuer." The seller, known as the "beneficiary," provides certain specified documents to the bank to show that the goods called for have been shipped, or are ready for shipment. If the seller provides all of the required documentation, the funds are released by the bank.

Unsecured credit is fairly commonly used by both businesses and consumers. Many banks grant *signature loans* to their better customers, and most businesses and consumers rely on unsecured credit for the use of public utilities. The regulation of unsecured credit transactions is primarily a matter of state law. Included in the state regulation is the topic of usury. Every state has a maximum interest rate that can be charged; excessive interest is deemed usury, and is illegal. The federal regulation of unsecured credit is primarily concerned with ensuring that information is provided to the debtor prior to the creation of the debt, and with acceptable methods of collection in the event the debtor defaults on the agreement. Title I of the federal Consumer Credit Protection Act (TILA) requires creditors to provide credit applicants with certain information as to the cost of the credit. This information must be provided in a standard format and in a standard terminology. The most important information that must be given to the applicant is the "APR," the annualized percentage rate to be charged in the transaction.

Installment loans are closed-end loans, calling for a fixed periodic payment for a predetermined number of periods, normally a monthly payment. Installment loans may be secured or unsecured, although most consumer installment loans are secured by some form of collateral. Some of these loans will fall within the coverage of Article 9. However, if a person purchases a car on credit, using the car as collateral for the loan, the transaction falls outside the coverage of Article 9, and this transaction will be governed by the state certificate of title rules rather than by Article 9. Installment loans are subject to many of the same regulatory provisions as are unsecured loans. Federal regulation is primarily under TILA and the Fair Debt Collection Practices Act. State coverage includes Article 3 of the UCC, if a promissory note is involved. The Uniform Consumer Credit Code may apply to the transaction. State laws governing contracts will also apply, as will any state statutes governing retail installment sales or similar legislation.

Mortgage loans involve loans in which real estate is used as collateral by the debtor to secure the credit. Mortgage loans are commonly installment loans, but the repayment term tends to be much longer than other types of installment loans. Mortgage loans often have a repayment period of 15, 20, or 30 years. Both federal and state regulations apply to these transactions.

The most important federal regulation in real estate lending is, once again, TILA. A second important area of federal coverage is the Real Estate Settlement Procedures Act (RESPA), which is also a disclosure act. Home mortgage lenders are required to provide loan applicants with a good-faith estimate of all settlement and closing costs associated with the loan. Other information that must be disclosed includes referrals to any company affiliated with the lender, and information about possible transfers of the loan to subsequent parties. State coverage in this area includes mortgage lending acts, mortgage banker and broker acts, secondary mortgage acts, and home improvement loan acts.

Credit card coverage is primarily at the federal level, although some state regulation exists. The main source of federal coverage is Regulation Z, the regulations enacted in support of TILA. Among the prohibitions found under Regulation Z are these: credit card issuers are prohibited from issuing unsolicited credit cards; credit card holders are liable only up to $50 for unauthorized usage of the card; and the issuer is prohibited from using offsets to recover credit card payment deficiencies from deposit accounts of the credit card holder. State law in this area is primarily enabling, although state usury law can have an impact on credit card holders and issuers.

The Federal Trade Commission has issued two credit practice rules designed to provide some protection and some information to consumer debtors. The first, the FTC Holder in Due Course Rule, requires the inclusion of language allowing a consumer debtor to retain and use any defenses against subsequent HDCs on a consumer credit note. The second is a disclosure statement warning cosigners of the potential liability faced by cosigning on a loan or credit application.

Payday loans have experienced tremendous growth over the past decade. These loans, normally made for short time periods and for relatively small amounts of money, are readily available virtually anywhere in the nation. Many payday loan companies have reached agreements with national banks, allowing the payday loan company to operate in states that would otherwise prohibit them from operating. Federal regulation of this area has been proposed but not yet enacted.

Discussion Questions

1. What is a *letter of credit,* and why are letters of credit important in commercial transactions? How does a letter of credit differ from a *sight draft?*

2. What is an unsecured credit transaction? Why would a creditor extend unsecured credit to a debtor? What are some common types of unsecured credit that most consumers are likely to use?

3. What distinguishes a mortgage loan from other types of installment loans? Why is there a different type of coverage for a mortgage loan than for an installment loan taken to purchase an automobile?

4. What are the different types of credit cards? How does a "bank card" differ from a "travel and entertainment card"?

5. What information does TILA require a creditor to provide to a debtor prior to the extension of credit? What is the format in which this information must be presented?

6. What is the rule regarding unsolicited credit cards? When can a credit card issuer legally issue a credit card under Regulation Z?

7. What liability does a credit card holder face if his or her card is lost or stolen, and the finder or thief charges several hundred dollars of goods and services to the card?

8. What liability does a credit card holder face if he or she allows a friend to use the card, and that friend charges several hundred dollars of goods and services to the card beyond what the holder authorized the friend to charge?

9. How does the FTC rule regarding cosigners provide protection to potential co-signers of credit instruments or agreements?

10. What is a *payday loan?* Why are payday loans so controversial?

Case Problems and Writing Assignments

1. In 1994, Bank of America sent an unsolicited credit card application to Cauffiel at his place of business, Galaxie Corporation. Although Cauffiel is the sole shareholder of Galaxie, the application was addressed to Cauffiel individually. Unbeknownst to Galaxie, Cauffiel, or Bank of America, Diadette Mejia, an employee of Galaxie, intercepted and completed the application, putting Cauffiel as the primary card holder and herself as the secondary card holder. She also changed the billing address to her private residence. In response to the application, Bank of America issued credit cards in the primary name of Cauffiel with Mejia as the secondary card holder. From October 1994 to February 1996, Mejia made unauthorized purchases and cash advances amounting to more than $116,000 using the credit card. She paid the monthly credit card statements by forging Cauffiel's signature on stolen checks drawn on the bank account of Galaxie. In February 1996, Cauffiel informed Bank of America of Mejia's criminal conduct and arrest, at which time the bank conducted a fraud investigation and closed the account. Cauffiel and Galaxie Corporation sued Bank of America for damages, alleging that Bank of America was negligent in issuing the credit card to Mejia. The district court granted summary judgment to Bank of America, citing the fact that Galaxie was the only injured party in this case and determining that Bank of America owed no duty to Galaxie under these facts. Cauffiel and Galaxie Corporation appealed this ruling. Should the court of appeals uphold the district court's determination? [See *Galaxie Corporation v. Bank of America, N.A.,* 165 F.3d 27, 1998 U.S. App. LEXIS 22696 (6th Cir. 1998).]

2. Towers World Airways, Inc. leased a corporate jet and hired Schley as the pilot for the jet. The jet was used by Towers for flights that Towers booked, and it was also used for other charter flights that were not booked by Towers. In February 1988, Towers applied for and received a credit card from PHH Aviation Systems. Towers gave the credit card to Schley, instructing him that it was to be used only for the purchase of fuel and other airline-related expenses when the jet was being used in connection with Towers flights. Despite these instructions, Schley charged more than $89,000 on the card for charter flights that were not booked by Towers. Towers canceled the card in August 1988 and filed suit seeking a declaratory judgment that it was liable only for $50 on the credit card. According to Towers, the charges by Schley were unauthorized, so that Towers faced only a maximum liability of $50 under the provisions of Regulation Z. PHH disagreed, asserting that Schley was an authorized user of the card and that Towers was liable for all aircraft-related charges made by Schley while the card was in effect. How should this case be resolved? [See *Towers World Airways, Inc. v. PHH Aviation Systems, Inc.,* 933 F.2d 174 (2nd Cir. 1991).]

3. American Loan was a financial institution licensed by the Illinois Department of Financial Institutions. It was in the business of making so called payday loans, that is, small, short-term loans, to individuals whom American Loan characterized as posing a high risk of default. These payday loans were offered to the public at annual interest rates of 261 percent to 521 percent. Because of the extraordinarily high interest rates, these loans were primarily made to individuals to whom more traditional forms of credit were unavailable. On October 2, 1998, Jackson obtained a payday loan from American Loan to be repaid on October 15, 1998. On October 12, 1998, Jackson "renewed" her loan in order to gain more time in which to repay the debt.

Upon renewal, Jackson was issued a receipt stating that an "extension fee" had been assessed to her in the amount of $35.00. Subsequently Jackson secured at least two additional payday loans from American Loan and on at least two more occasions "renewed" these loans and received receipts listing extension fees. Jackson sued American Loan for allegedly violating the terms of TILA. According to Jackson, American Loan did not provide adequate disclosure of the finance terms when Jackson renewed the payday loans, and did not properly list the "extension fees" as finance charges, as required by TILA. Is American Loan guilty of violating TILA for either of these alleged offenses? Explain. Was it ethical to make payday loans or grant extensions at the interest rates charged? [See *Jackson v. American Loan Company, Inc.,* 1999 U.S. Dist. LEXIS 9143 (N.D. Ill. 1999).]

4. On several occasions between 1988 and 1992, Draiman used his American Express Platinum Card to purchase airline tickets through the Travel Dimensions travel agency. Draiman provided Travel Dimensions with his Platinum Card number, and when he needed tickets he would call and place an order. Travel Dimensions would send the tickets to Draiman and the bill to American Express. American Express would then secure payment from Draiman by including the cost of the tickets plus applicable financing charges in its periodic billing statement. On January 21, 1992, Draiman canceled his Platinum Card. Sometime thereafter Draiman deposited an undisclosed sum of money with Travel Dimensions. On July 20, 1992, Draiman purchased four El Al tickets to Israel at $2,077 each, for a total cost of $8,308. Draiman instructed Travel Dimensions to pay for the El Al tickets by drawing upon his deposited funds. Travel Dimensions did not honor that request—instead it charged the amount against the number that it had for Draiman's Platinum Card. American Express knew nothing of Draiman's deposit with, or his instructions to, Travel Dimensions. When American Express received the $8,308 charge from Travel Dimensions, that triggered its reinstatement policy, as set out in these terms in the cardholder agreement:

If you ask us to cancel your account, but you continue to use the Card, we will consider such use as your request for reinstatement of your account. If we agree to reinstate your account, this Agreement or any amended or new Agreement we send you will govern your reinstated account.

American Express does not communicate with cardholders to confirm that it is in fact their desire to revive their accounts. In accordance with its written policy, American Express reinstated Draiman's Platinum Card on August 26, 1992, and billed him $8,308. Draiman later actually used the El Al tickets (each of which had his Platinum Card number printed on its face) to travel to Israel. On October 15, 1993, Draiman paid American Express $3,399.98 of the $8,308 total and threatened suit if it tried to collect the $4,908.02 balance, citing purported violations of the Fair Credit Billing Act, TILA, and other applicable laws. When American Express attempted to collect the debt, the threatened legal action ensued on Janu-

ary 11, 1995, with one twist: Draiman filed not only on his own behalf but also on behalf of a purported class of similarly aggrieved persons.

Did American Express violate the unsolicited credit card provisions of TILA? Was this an unauthorized use of the card, limiting the liability of the cardholder to $50? [See *Draiman v. American Express,* 892 F. Supp. 1096, 1995 U.S. Dist. LEXIS 10195 (N.D. Ill. 1995).]

5. **BUSINESS APPLICATION CASE** On March 18, 1992, the Foxes entered into a contract to purchase the photography business of Color Mate Photo, Inc., a corporation owned by Jack Bedford. The contract called for the Foxes to pay $350,000 for the photography business. As part of the purchase price, the Foxes executed two promissory notes on March 18, 1992. The first note, for $245,000, was payable to the order of Color Mate, Inc. The second note, for $30,000, was payable to the order of Jack Bedford. The notes executed on March 18 carried interest in excess of the legal limit for Arkansas at that time, and the Foxes alleged Bedford knew that the notes carried this illegal interest rate. The Foxes testified that they learned from their banker that the rate on the notes exceeded the legal limit in 1992, but they continued to make payments on the note despite this information. Under Arkansas law, if a borrower pays interest at a usurious rate, the borrower can recover as damages twice the interest paid. Mr. Fox testified that in 1995 he calculated how much interest had been paid to date, and then subtracted double that amount from the principal balance and realized that, if he objected, he would owe $45,000 to pay off the loan. He did the calculations again in 1996, discovering that he could now pay off the loan and receive slightly more than $13,000 back. The Foxes continued to pay on the notes until 1997, at which point they sued, raising the usury issue and seeking the recovery of double the interest paid, which amounted to $231,009.96 on the first note and $28,286.96 on the second note. Bedford objected to the claim. First, Bedford argued that the parties had actually reached their agreement regarding the sale on November 6, 1991, at which time the interest rate was still legal, and that the rate was "locked in" on that date, making the interest on the notes later executed legal. Second, Bedford argued that the Foxes should be estopped from raising the issue of usury now when they had known of the alleged usury from the beginning and had knowingly made the payments with the intent to subsequently sue in an effort to recover double the interest.

The interest rate called for in the note would have been legal in November 1991, but was illegal in March 1992. Was the contract usurious, or was the rate "locked in" before the notes were executed, making the interest rate within the legal limit? If the contract was usurious, were the Foxes estopped from raising the usury claim? [See *Bedford v. Fox,* 333 Ark. 509, 970 S.W.2d 251, 1998 LEXIS 381 (1998).]

6. **ETHICAL APPLICATION CASE** Shelley Swift filed a class action complaint against First USA Bank, First Credit Card Services, USA, and Premiere Communications, Inc., alleging violations of the Truth in Lending Act. Swift was seeking actual, statutory,

and punitive damages, as well as injunctive relief. The complaint alleged the following: First USA Bank issues credit cards to consumers throughout the United States; First Credit Card Services USA provides marketing services and credit card servicing to credit card issuers such as First USA; and Premiere Communications is a telecommunications company that provides telephone services to consumers nationwide. In January 1998, Swift received a credit card solicitation from Defendants in the mail. The cover letter discussed the benefits of the Platinum Connect card ("Connect Card"), which was enclosed with the letter. The letter stated:

Introducing the First USA Platinum Connect card. Whether you decide to use it as a calling card, a Pre-Approved credit card, or both, you'll receive one free hour of long distance calling. Use your new Platinum Connect card to make all your calls AND purchases. Having one card for both your calling and credit card needs is a great convenience. Because not only is it one card to carry, it is also just one bill to pay every month.

You're Pre-Approved!

Just call 1 (800) 335-2453 to activate your card today. Activating your card is simple, since you're already Pre-Approved. Just call 1 (800) 335-2453 by January 30, 1998, to get your free hour of domestic long distance calling, and if you choose, to take advantage of the credit card and/or calling card features.

The card member agreement further disclosed that Premiere would provide telecommunications services in conjunction with the credit card. Included with the solicitation was a VISA credit card that could be activated by calling an 800 number. Swift had not applied or otherwise requested a credit card from Defendants prior to receiving Defendants' solicitation in the mail, and Swift had never been a customer of Defendants. Swift alleged that this constituted the issuance of an unsolicited credit card in violation of federal law and that all three defendants were involved in the issuance of such cards. Was the inclusion of the VISA card with the application solicitation the issuance of an unsolicited credit card? Which, if any, of the defendants could be held liable *if* this constituted the issuance of an unsolicited credit card? Is it ethical for a credit card issuer to send unsolicited cards to prospective customers in the hope that the customer will accept the cards? [See *Swift v. First USA Bank,* 1999 U.S. Dist. LEXIS 8208 (N.D. Ill. 1999).]

7. **CRITICAL THINKING CASE** In 1977 Newport applied to First Wisconsin for a corporate MasterCard account. The town obtained the credit card to enable its clerk to charge fuel for the town hall, but the application did not state that fact. The application stated that Newport

shall be liable for all credit extended to any person presenting [the] charge card until company delivers written notice that such card

has been lost or stolen or returns such card advising in writing that the authority of the agent or employee named thereon has been revoked.

The bank opened the account and issued the credit card in the name of "Town of Newport." The town clerk used the card not only for official purposes but also to charge hotel and restaurant expenses and clothing and gift shop purchases for her personal use. The personal purchases were made at unspecified dates from 1980 through April 1983. The town did not notify the bank of any improper or unauthorized use.

15 U.S.C. § 1643 provides in relevant part:

(a)(1) A cardholder shall be liable for the unauthorized use of a credit card only if—. . . (B) the liability is not in excess of $ 50; . . .

15 U.S.C. § 1602(o) provides:

The term "unauthorized use," as used in [15 U.S.C. § 1643], means a use of a credit card by a person other than the cardholder who does not have actual, implied, or apparent authority for such use and from which the cardholder receives no benefit.

The trial court held that although the town clerk was authorized to possess the card and to use it for business-related purposes, she had no authority to use it for personal purchases. Since the town received no benefit from the personal purchases, the court concluded that the town's liability was limited to $50. First Wisconsin National Bank appealed this judgment for $50 against the Town of Newport. Were the purchases in question an "unauthorized use" of the credit card, consequently limiting the town's liability to $50? Did the failure of the town to properly supervise the use of the card amount to an "authorization" of the use made by the town clerk? Should the town be estopped from raising the alleged unauthorized use due to its failure to raise the issue in a timely manner? [See *MasterCard v. Town of Newport,* 396 N.W.2d 345; 1986 Wisc. App. LEXIS 3810 (Wisc. 1986).]

8. **YOU BE THE JUDGE** Guaranteed Credit, Inc. advertised that it would provide its customers with a major credit card, regardless of the applicant's credit history, upon receipt of a one-time up-front payment from the applicant. When the applicant made this payment, Guaranteed Credit, Inc. would deposit the funds and then supply the applicant with a list of companies and banks in the customer's geographic area that offered major credit cards. One of the applicants complained about this practice to the Federal Trade Commission. The FTC investigated, decided that this constituted an unfair and deceptive trade practice, and issued a cease and desist order. Guaranteed Credit, Inc. denied that it was doing anything improper and filed suit against the FTC. This case has been brought in *your* court. How will *you* decide? [See Bob Garver, "FTC Turns Up Heat on Scam Artists," *American Banker,* Washington Section (September 6, 2002): 3.]

Notes

1. "Prefatory Note to Article 5," *Uniform Commercial Code, 2001 ed.* (St. Paul: West Group, 2001), 541–543.

2. *Uniform Commercial Code in a Nutshell, 5th ed.* Bradford Stone (St. Paul, Minn.: West Group, 2002), 521.

3. Ibid., 522.

4. "Prefatory Note" at 541.

5. UCC § 5-103(d) and § 5-108(f).

6. UCC § 5-102(a)(14) and § 5-104.

7. UCC § 5-106(a).

8. UCC § 5-108.

9. "Summary of Consumer Credit Laws," U.S. Department of Commerce, 1999.

10. *Black's Law Dictionary*, 6th ed. (St. Paul: West Group, 1990), 1545.

11. Colorado, Idaho, Indiana, Iowa, Kansas, Maine, Oklahoma, South Carolina, Utah, Wisconsin, Wyoming.

12. 15 U.S.C.S. 12, C.F.R. § 226.12.

13. Ibid.

14. Marcy Gordon, "Payday Loans Targeted in Report," *Financial News* (AP Online, November 13, 2001).

15. John Hackett, "Ethically Tainted," *Consumer Lending*, 3, no. 11 (American Banker-Bond Buyer, November 2001): 48.

16. Ibid.

Bankruptcy

AGENDA

NRW Mai, Carlos, and Helen have invested virtually everything they own in NRW. They are aware that any business venture can be risky, but they are making every effort to operate their business as safely and as profitably as possible. Still, they realize that NRW could encounter some difficulties that would force them to terminate the business. They wonder whether they should consider bankruptcy if that should happen.

They also realize that, no matter how carefully they operate NRW, they cannot control the business practices of their customers or their suppliers. It is possible that some of these parties may face financial problems and could even resort to bankruptcy. They are concerned about what NRW will be able to do if this situation should arise.

Since Mai, Carlos, and Helen have invested so much time and energy into NRW, they would like to know if it would be possible to "salvage" the business if they encounter financial problems. They wonder if liquidating the business is the only option available if they have serious problems. In addition, Carlos has heard that bankruptcy can be a business strategy in some situations. He doesn't understand how going bankrupt could ever be part of the strategy of a successful business. He would like to learn more about this so that he and the other principals can plan for any contingency that the firm might face.

Each of the principals also has personal debts and obligations. Since NRW is the primary source of income for each of them, they would like to know what their alternatives as individuals would be if the firm should fail. Would they be forced into a liquidation, or is there another avenue they could take under the provisions of the bankruptcy law? What is meant by a "fresh start," and who is entitled to have a "fresh start"?

These or similar questions may arise during our discussion. Be prepared! You never know when the firm or one of its members will seek your advice.

Historical Background

Sometimes people have trouble paying their debts. When this problem arises, what should the creditor and/or the debtor do? How should a society address the problem of defaulting debtors? Perhaps the society will decide that the debtor should be punished. "In medieval Italy, when a businessman did not pay his debts, it was the practice to destroy his trading bench. From the Italian for broken bench, 'banca rotta,' comes the term bankruptcy."[1] This *banca rotta* showed the community that the businessman did not pay his debts, which undoubtedly caused him to be subjected to ridicule and to distrust. In addition, the broken trading bench made it difficult, if not impossible, to continue to ply his trade. How, then, was he to earn enough money to repay his creditors?

The first official law regarding bankruptcy in England was passed in 1542, during the reign of King Henry VIII. Under this law, a bankrupt individual was viewed as a criminal and could be punished for his crime, if convicted. The punishment for a conviction ranged from incarceration in debtors' prison to execution![2] Over time the seriousness of the "crime" of bankruptcy was reduced, and by the 18th century those people in England who were unable or unwilling to pay their debts were very commonly thrown into debtors' prison. A debtor might remain in prison for years waiting for friends or family to raise the funds necessary to repay the debt, or for the creditors to agree to the debtor's release. Less commonly, the debtor might agree to some form of indentured servitude, agreeing to work for a preset number of years at little or no salary to repay the debt.

To prevent such treatment of debtors in this country, the founding fathers made provisions in the Constitution to allow "honest debtors" to make a "fresh start" by providing for relief in the form of bankruptcy. Article I, Section 8, of the U.S. Constitution says: "The Congress shall have the Power . . . to establish . . . uniform Laws on the subject of Bankruptcies throughout the United States."

It should be noted that the Constitution only *allows* Congress to establish uniform laws on bankruptcy. There is no constitutional *requirement* that Congress provide bankruptcy laws or relief. In fact, while four separate bankruptcy acts were passed in the 19th century, three of them were very short lived, and they did not have wide application or protection for the debtors. The first U.S. Bankruptcy Act was passed in 1800 and repealed in 1803. This act applied only to individuals and it provided minimal discharge of debts. The second bankruptcy act, passed in 1841 and repealed in 1842, also applied only to individuals, and also provided for only minimal discharge of debts. The Civil War led to the enactment of the Bankruptcy Act of 1867. This act, which was repealed in 1878, was the first to apply to corporations as well as to individuals, and it also provided for a greater degree of relief from the debts of the bankrupt. The final bankruptcy law of the 19th century, and the longest lived of these laws, was the Bankruptcy Act of 1898. This act made provision for the use of "equity receiverships" as a means of protecting and preserving businesses, and it also provided broader protection for individuals.[3]

The Great Depression led to a number of amendments to the Bankruptcy Act of 1898. These amendments were especially important to business debtors because they formalized the reorganization provisions used in Chapter XI bankruptcy proceedings. These amendments were found in the Bankruptcy Act of 1933, the Bankruptcy Act of 1934, and the Chandler Act of 1938.[4]

In 1978, Congress passed a new law, the Bankruptcy Reform Act, which took effect October 1, 1979. The Bankruptcy Reform Act had two major purposes. It was designed to provide for fair and equitable treatment of the creditors in the distribution of the debtor's property, and, more importantly, it was designed to give an honest debtor a fresh start. The Reform Act attempted to modernize the bankruptcy coverage, providing treatment for both the debtor and the creditors that was consistent with the credit-intensive, consumer-oriented society of the late 20th century. The Bankruptcy Reform Act contained the first major changes in the bankruptcy laws in 40 years. This new law provided stronger reorganization provisions under the new Chapter 11 and also provided stronger protection for individual debtors in the repayment plan provisions of Chapter 13. The reform act contained many changes, but it also contained a number of defects. Perhaps the most significant defect was its treatment of bankruptcy judges. The Supreme Court declared the Bankruptcy Reform Act unconstitutional in *Northern Pipeline Construction Co. v. Marathon Pipe Line Co.*[5] Although the Supreme Court had declared the Bankruptcy Reform Act unconstitutional, the bankruptcy courts were allowed to operate under an "emergency rule" suggested by the Judicial Conference of the United States and accepted by the U.S. Court of Appeals.

Congress eventually responded to the problems identified by the Supreme Court when it enacted the Bankruptcy Amendments and Federal Judgeship Act of 1984. This act was intended to clarify the jurisdictional authority of the bankruptcy courts and to resolve the constitutional problems discovered in the Bankruptcy Reform Act. At the same time, Congress made the amended bankruptcy coverage more sensitive to the needs of the creditors and made some effort to reduce or eliminate the problem of debtor abuses that had occurred under the former bankruptcy laws.

Additional changes were made to the act with the Bankruptcy Reform Act of 1994, again with the aim of balancing protections while ensuring that the basic purpose of bankruptcy was maintained. While far from perfect, the Bankruptcy Reform Act and the accompanying Bankruptcy Amendments and Federal Judgeship Act and the Bankruptcy Reform Act of 1994 are a vast improvement over the 1898 act they replaced.

A number of people do not believe that the current bankruptcy laws are appropriate. The argument has been made that bankruptcy is too easy to obtain and that the current provisions do not adequately protect the creditors. This debate has been taken up in Congress, which has been debating a *new* Bankruptcy Reform Act that would significantly reduce the availability of liquidation proceedings. This proposed revision is discussed at the end of the chapter. If enacted, it will constitute a tremendous change in bankruptcy as it is currently viewed in the United States.

Although the Constitution seemingly calls for exclusive federal control of this area, the bankruptcy laws coexist with state law in some areas. In fact, state law often is used to define problems or to provide solutions to bankruptcy problems. For example, each state has its own exemption provisions, a listing of the assets that an honest debtor can retain following a bankruptcy. While there are federal exemptions that might be available to the debtor, state law determines whether the debtor can choose between the state and the federal exemptions or whether the debtor must choose the state's exemption provisions.

The Bankruptcy Reform Act has (from a business law perspective) three major operative sections, called chapters. These chapters are Chapter 7, Liquidation; Chapter 11, Reorganization; and Chapter 13, Adjustments of Debts of an Individual with Regular Income. A fourth important operative section, Chapter 12, Adjustment of Debts of a Family Farmer with Regular Annual Income, was added under the Bankruptcy Amendments in 1984.

In a Chapter 7 proceeding, the debtor's nonexempt assets are sold, the proceeds are distributed to the creditors, and a discharge is (normally) granted. Under Chapters 11, 12, and 13, the debtor restructures and rearranges finances and (possibly) organization so that the creditors will be paid, hopefully in full, but at least more than in a liquidation proceeding.

The Bankruptcy Reform Act (1978)

The Bankruptcy Reform Act called for a whole new adjudicative system of bankruptcies. Under the act, each U.S.

district court was to contain a separate, adjunct bankruptcy court. These bankruptcy courts were to be staffed by bankruptcy judges, each of whom was to serve a 14-year term, with their salaries to be determined annually by Congress. The bankruptcy judges were to be appointed by the president, subject to approval by the Senate. It was hoped that this new system, which replaced "referees" acting through the district courts, would simplify and speed up bankruptcy proceedings. Unfortunately, this process was declared unconstitutional, jeopardizing the entire reform effort.

Bankruptcy Amendments and Federal Judgeship Act of 1984

The Bankruptcy Amendments and Federal Judgeship Act of 1984 went into effect on July 10, 1984. This act addresses the problems presented by the *Northern Pipeline* opinion by restructuring and redefining the bankruptcy court system and its jurisdiction. In addition, it makes a number of substantive changes to the Bankruptcy Reform Act and its coverage.

Under the new law, bankruptcy judges are still appointed for a term of 14 years, and their salaries are still established by Congress. However, since the tenure and the salary both are established by statute and are subject to changes by the legislature, the bankruptcy judges are still not Article III judges, the original problem addressed by the court in *Northern Pipeline*. (Article III federal judges are appointed "during good behavior," that is, for life, if the judge so desires. In addition, the compensation of Article III judges "shall not be diminished during their continuance in office."[6]) The appointments are made by the U.S. court of appeals in which the district court is located from a slate of nominees recommended by the judicial councils of each circuit. Only persons who apply to the judicial council for a judgeship may be considered for recommendation by the court of appeals. The judicial council is to submit a list of three nominees for each judgeship. The court of appeals will then either select one of the nominees or reject all of them and request a new submission.

Since these bankruptcy judges are not Article III judges, the bankruptcy courts have only limited jurisdiction under the law. The 1984 Bankruptcy Amendments grant exclusive and original jurisdiction in all bankruptcy matters to the U.S. district court. The district court may then refer any or all such cases to the bankruptcy court for adjudication. After referral to the bankruptcy court, however, the case may be withdrawn by the district court, either on its own motion or on the motion of any party to the proceedings, "for cause shown."

The Bankruptcy Reform Act of 1994

The Bankruptcy Reform Act of 1994 makes several substantial changes in the bankruptcy law. It also created a National Bankruptcy Review Commission charged with studying issues and problems related to bankruptcy.

The National Bankruptcy Review Commission was composed of nine members and it was designed to be as nonpartisan as possible. Three of the members, including the chair of the commission, were appointed by the president. The speaker of the house, the president pro tempore of the Senate, the minority leader of the House, and the minority leader of the Senate each named one member. The chief justice of the United States named the remaining two members. Its initial term was two years and seven months, with the initial appointments to be made within 60 days after enactment of the bill. The initial commission's term expired in July 1997. In the commission's report to Congress, one of its strongest recommendations called for some unification of the exemption provisions available to debtors, either by eliminating state "opt-out" provisions, eliminating state exemptions, or putting a limit on exemptions. The commission ceased to exist on November 19, 1997 (Public Law 103-394), but its recommendations are likely to influence the next revisions or amendments to the bankruptcy code.

Numerous substantive changes to the Bankruptcy Code were included in the Bankruptcy Reform Act of 1994. Among the more important of these changes are the following:

- Compensation for trustees is now set at "25 percent of the first $5,000 or less, 10 percent of any amount in excess of $5,000 but not in excess of $50,000, 5 percent of any amount in excess of $50,000 but not in excess of $1,000,000, and reasonable compensation not to exceed 3 percent of such moneys in excess of $1,000,000."[7]

- The debt limit for Chapter 13 debtors is increased from $450,000 to $1,000,000, and the dollar amounts for involuntary petitions, priorities, and exemptions are doubled.[8]

- Future adjustments for these dollar amounts are included in the act on a three-year cycle, beginning April 1, 1998. These adjustments will be based on the Consumer Price Index for All Urban Consumers published by the Department of Labor, rounded to the nearest $25 amount.

- Purchase-money security interests are given a 20-day grace period for perfection to reflect the majority of state law provisions now in effect, an increase from the 10-day grace period previously allowed.

- Independent sales representatives are classified as employees and are entitled to the same priority status as employees for purposes of claims against the debtor.

- Limited liability partnerships are treated in bankruptcy as they would be treated in a nonbankruptcy proceeding (limited liability partnerships are discussed in Business Organizations in Chapters 32 to 34), reflecting the growing recognition of this relatively new form of business.

- Debtors who are represented by an attorney may reaffirm debts without the need for a separate reaffirmation hearing as required under the provisions of the original Bankruptcy Reform Act.

- The nondischargeability of "loading up" debts is triggered at $1,000 rather than $500.

- Bankruptcy fraud is now recognized as a crime. This crime involves filing a petition or a document or making a false representation with the intent to devise a scheme to defraud under Chapter 11.

- A streamlined treatment is provided for small businesses (businesses involved in commercial or business activities other than solely real estate and with liquidated debts of $2,000,000 or less) seeking relief under Chapter 11.

- Small business investment companies are not eligible for relief in bankruptcy.

Initially, the Bankruptcy Reform Act of 1994 seemed to balance the interests of the debtors and the creditors, providing a more workable structure than the previous coverage. However, in practice creditors do not seem to be receiving the benefits envisioned in drafting the Act. This is one of the leading factors behind the push for a *new* reform act.

Chapter 7: Liquidation, a "Straight" Bankruptcy

To many people, the term bankruptcy means just one thing—a liquidation of the debtor's assets in order for the debtor to obtain a discharge from his or her debts. This form of bankruptcy carries negative connotations to many people. A number of people view a straight bankruptcy, or a Chapter 7 proceeding, as an admission of failure. Rather than a fresh start for an honest debtor, they feel that it is a "cop-out" by a "deadbeat." Times are changing, however. More and more people are beginning to realize that a liquidation is a financial and legal option designed to help a person who has been flooded by debt. The stigma of failure is being removed, and the number of Chapter 7 proceedings increases annually. For example, in 1990, there were 725,484 bankruptcy petitions filed, of which 515,337 were for relief under Chapter 7, and 199,186 were for relief under Chapter 13. By 1996, the number of petitions filed had increased to 1,042,110, of which 712,129 were for relief under Chapter 7, and 316,024 were for relief under Chapter 13.[9] Nonbusiness bankruptcies composed 91 percent of the petitions in 1990 and 95 percent of the petitions in 1996.[10]

There are two types of Chapter 7 bankruptcies: voluntary and involuntary. Voluntary bankruptcies are initiated by the debtor. Involuntary bankruptcies are initiated by some combination of creditors of a debtor. The overwhelming majority of bankruptcy petitions are filed voluntarily by the debtor.[11] Any person, firm, or corporation may file a voluntary bankruptcy petition under Chapter 7, with *five* exceptions:

1. Railroads
2. Government units
3. Banks
4. Savings and loan associations
5. Insurance companies

In addition, any person, firm, or corporation may be subjected to an involuntary petition under Chapter 7, with *seven* exceptions:

1. Railroads
2. Government units
3. Banks
4. Savings and loan associations
5. Insurance companies
6. Farmers (a farmer is defined as an individual who received more than 80 percent of gross income in the prior year from the operation of a farm that he or she owns and operates)
7. Charitable corporations

The filing fees connected to the various bankruptcy chapters are established by law. For example, effective December 29, 1999, a Chapter 7 proceeding has a filing fee of $200 plus a $45 administration fee. For Chapter 11 proceedings, the filing fee is $800. Chapter 13 requires a $185 filing fee plus a $30 administrative fee.[12]

Voluntary Bankruptcy Petition

The debtor who files a voluntary petition does not need to be insolvent. If a debtor desires to eliminate his or her debts, the debtor can file the petition, consent to the court's jurisdiction, go through the proceedings, and hopefully receive a discharge. In theory, a debtor with $1 million in cash and total debts of $250 can file for bankruptcy. In practice, such an event is extremely unlikely.

The 1984 Bankruptcy Amendments made a major substantive change in this area. Prior to the 1984 act, bankruptcy was viewed as a right of the debtor, and the needs of the debtor or the creditors were not considered by the court. As a result, some creditors alleged that some debtors were abusing the bankruptcy system, using Chapter 7 proceedings to eliminate unsecured debts they could have repaid in full. The law now permits the bankruptcy judge to hold a hearing designed to determine the need of the debtor for the relief being sought. If the judge feels that granting the relief will be a substantial abuse of Chapter 7, the petition can be dismissed.

In addition, the law requires that all debtors be made aware of the alternative provisions of Chapter 13 repayment plans before they are allowed to file a Chapter 7 petition. By so doing, it is hoped that more debtors will elect a repayment plan rather than a liquidation procedure. This will work to the benefit of the creditors and may also help a number of debtors by allowing them to retain more of their assets than they would under a Chapter 7 liquidation.

Involuntary Bankruptcy Petition

Often a debtor will get deeply in debt and try to avoid bankruptcy. When this happens, the creditors may decide to petition the debtor into bankruptcy against his or her will. They do so by initiating an involuntary bankruptcy proceeding.

A debtor who does not fall within one of the exempted groups is potentially subject to an involuntary petition. The vast majority of debtors in this country do not fit into one of these exceptions. That does not make most debtors automatically subject to an involuntary petition, however. The creditors who file the petition must show that three criteria—one related to the *conduct* of the debtor, one to the *number* of creditors of the debtor, and one to the *unsecured debt* of the debtor—are satisfied before they may file an involuntary petition against the debtor.

Debtor Conduct The petitioning creditors must establish that the debtor is "guilty" of one of two acts: either the debtor is not paying debts as they become due, or the debtor appointed a receiver or made a general assignment for the benefit of the creditors within the 120 days that preceded the filing of the petition. (Under the latter test, the receiver or assignee must have taken possession of the debtor's property.)

Number of Petitioning Creditors The petition filed with the court must be signed by the "proper number" of creditors. The proper number of creditors for a particular debtor is determined by the total number of creditors the debtor has. If the debtor has a total of 12 creditors or more, at least *3* creditors must sign the petition. If the debtor has fewer than 12 creditors, only *1* creditor must sign the petition, although more may choose to do so.

Debt Requirement The creditors who file the petition must have an aggregate claim against the debtor of at least $10,000 that is neither secured nor contingent. This means that a debtor with less than $10,000 in general unsecured debts may not be involuntarily petitioned into bankruptcy. It also explains why more than the minimum number of creditors (from the "number of petitioning creditors" requirement) will often need to sign the petition.

The following example shows one problem that petitioning creditors may face.

Bob has 7 creditors. He has made no payments to any of them for four months. He owes Ralph, one of the creditors, $6,000, of which $2,000 is secured by collateral. Ralph wants to file an involuntary petition against Bob. Since Bob is not paying his debts as they come due, the "conduct" requirement is satisfied. Since Ralph has less than 12 creditors, only one of his creditors must sign the petition to satisfy the "number" requirement. However, unless one or more of Bob's other creditors—with a (combined) claim of at least $6,000 in unsecured debt— will join Ralph on a petition, Ralph cannot institute an involuntary petition. His unsecured claim of $4,000 does not satisfy the "debt" requirement.

In this example, Ralph also needs to exercise care prior to filing the petition. If a debtor is involuntarily petitioned into bankruptcy, the debtor may deny that he is bankrupt and request a trial on this issue. A debtor who wins such a trial can collect damages from the creditors who signed the petition.

The Bankruptcy Proceeding

Once a petition is filed, the judge will issue an order for relief (unless the debtor files an answer denying bankruptcy and demands a trial). At this point, the proceeding is in motion, and it will continue until the final orders are entered. Upon entering the order for relief, the judge promptly appoints a trustee from a panel of private trustees. This trustee takes possession of—and legal title to—the debtor's property and begins the administration of the debtor's estate. (At the first creditors' meeting, a new trustee may be selected. If creditors having collective claims of at least 20 percent of the unsecured claims against the debtor request an election, the creditors can select a "permanent" trustee. If no such request is made, the court-appointed trustee serves throughout the proceedings.)

The Trustee

The trustee is the key figure in the bankruptcy proceeding, representing the debtor's estate and attempting to preserve this estate to protect the interests of the unsecured creditors. The estate that the trustee preserves is made up of all the property the debtor has when the case is begun and any property the debtor acquires within the 180 days following the petition-filing date, reduced by any collateral removed from the estate and by the exempt assets of the debtor. The trustee must gather all of these assets, liquidate them, and generally handle the creditors' claims. The trustee also raises objections to the granting of a discharge if the debtor gives cause to do so. The trustee may be helped by a creditors' committee, a group of at least 3 and at most 11 unsecured creditors who consult with the trustee as needed.

The trustee is responsible for representing the interests of the general unsecured creditors in the bankruptcy petition. While the trustee takes legal title to the debtor's estate, the creditors have equitable title—this means that the trustee possesses the estate for the benefit of the creditors. The trustee's job is difficult and demanding. Under the Bankruptcy Act, both individuals and corporations may serve as trustees, although corporations need to be authorized to perform this function in their corporate charter. In order for an individual to serve as trustee, he or she must be "competent to perform the duties of a trustee." The trustee must also satisfy a residency requirement by residing or having an office in the district where the case is pending or in an adjacent district. Under current bankruptcy law, the U.S. Attorney General prescribes qualifications for appointment to a panel of trustees. The U.S. Trustee sets up such a panel for the bankruptcy court; the bankruptcy judge appoints the trustee in each bankruptcy case from this panel. The appointment of a trustee is basically a mechanical chore, with the trustees appointed on a rotational basis. This method of appointment has virtually eliminated a common complaint under the prior law—that the trustees were appointed by friendly judges, were too close to the judges in too many instances, and were not always qualified for the role.

Interestingly, the 1994 bankruptcy bill restored the former method for appointing trustees in Chapter 11 proceedings. Under Chapter 11, to an extent, any interested party may call for a meeting of the creditors in order to elect a trustee, provided the meeting is called within 30 days of the court's appointment of an operating trustee. There is some expectation that similar provisions will be enacted regarding Chapter 7 trustees in the near future.

Automatic Stay Provision

The filing of a petition in bankruptcy operates as an *automatic stay*, placing any legal actions involving the debtor "on hold." The automatic stay operates to stop lawsuits instituted by the debtor, allowing the trustee the opportunity to settle these cases, bringing any judgment into the bankruptcy estate. The automatic stay also works against creditors who are involved in any legal actions against the debtor. The creditors must suspend any legal actions already commenced and must delay filing any new actions, pending the outcome of the bankruptcy proceedings. Similarly, the creditors may not initiate any repossession actions against the assets of the debtor. This automatic stay provision is designed to ensure that all the creditors are afforded equitable treatment under the bankruptcy proceedings by preventing any one creditor from gaining an advantage through his or her actions at the expense of the other creditors.

The Creditors' Meeting

The court will call for a meeting of the creditors within a reasonable time of the order for relief. The debtor, the trustee, and the creditors—but not the judge—will all attend this meeting. The debtor is expected to provide schedules of anticipated income, assets and their locations, and debts and liabilities at that time and to submit to an examination by the creditors concerning the debtor's assets, liabilities, and anything else the creditors feel is important. Although the debtor may not like it, it is best to cooperate fully: A refusal to cooperate may result in a denial of discharge. At this first creditors' meeting, the trustee is required to orally advise the debtor as to the possible repercussion from filing for bankruptcy relief and to explain to the debtor about other bankruptcy chapters that the debtor might want to utilize in lieu of a Chapter 7 liquidation proceeding.

The Debtor

The debtor also has certain duties to perform. The debtor must file a relatively detailed series of schedules that are intended to reveal his or her financial position so that (1) the bankruptcy court can properly evaluate the need for relief and (2) the interests of the various creditors can be protected. The debtor must provide a list of creditors, both secured and unsecured, the address of each creditor, and the amount of debt owed to each. The debtor also must provide a schedule of his or her financial affairs and a listing of all property owned, even if that property will be claimed as an exempt asset. Finally, the debtor must provide a list of current income and expenses. This list may show that the debtor should be in a Chapter 13 repayment plan rather than a Chapter 7 liquidation proceeding. If it does, the court may, on its own motion, dismiss the Chapter 7 proceeding following a hearing and encourage the debtor to refile under Chapter 13. However, the law also carries with it a presumption that the debtor is entitled to receive the order of relief for whatever chapter he or she has chosen. The schedules are prepared by the debtor under oath and signed. Knowingly submitting false information in these schedules is a crime under the bankruptcy law.

The debtor also must cooperate fully with the trustee and surrender all property to the trustee. Finally, the debtor must attend any and all hearings and comply with all orders of the court. If this is done, a discharge will normally result.

Exemptions

The debtor can exempt some assets from the trustee's liquidation. The exempted assets are intended to provide the foundation for the "fresh start" bankruptcy grants to those honest debtors who successfully complete the bankruptcy proceeding and receive a discharge. This exemption is, surprisingly, governed to a significant extent by state statutes, which determine what the debtor is allowed to exempt. If state law permits, the debtor may elect to take *either* the state exemptions *or* the federal exemptions. If no such choice is allowed by state law, the debtor must take the state exemptions. Under no circumstances may the debtor take both sets of exemptions. For any particular state's exemption provisions, visit the appropriate state Web site. An excellent starting point is http://www.law.cornell.edu/topics/bankruptcy.html/. The Web site for the Virginia state exemptions can be found at http://virginia-bankruptcy.com/.

Thirty-six states have elected the override provision, requiring the debtor to take the state exemptions and prohibiting the debtor from using the federal exemptions. In addition, even if the debtor is in one of the 14 states that allow the choice of either the federal or the state exemptions, another limitation has been imposed by the 1984 Bankruptcy Amendments. In a joint filing, both the husband and the wife must select the same exemptions, either state or federal. They no longer will be allowed to select the exemptions individually, allowing one spouse to take the federal exemptions and the other to select the state exemptions.

Certain types of property are exempt under most state statutes. Typically, a debtor who elects (or is required) to take the state exemptions will be able to retain the following types of assets for his or her fresh start:

- Some cash (the amount varies from state to state)

- Residence or homestead

- Clothing

- Tools of the trade

- Insurance

- A cemetery plot

- An automobile (the value varies from state to state, as do the criteria)

- Funds invested in a retirement plan

- Jewelry (the value varies from state to state, although wedding and engagement rings are frequently exempt without regard to value)

- Heirlooms

- Furniture and household items

In addition, the debtor is allowed to exempt some benefits for public policy reasons:

- Veterans' benefits

- Social Security benefits

- Unemployment compensation benefits

- Disability benefits

- Alimony

The federal exemptions, as provided for under the Bankruptcy Reform Act, allow the debtor to exempt the following property from the proceeding if state law allows the debtor to select the federal exemptions:

- The debtor's aggregate interest in real property or personal property that the debtor or a dependent of the debtor uses as a residence, up to $15,000.

- If the "aggregate interest" in the debtor's residence is less than $15,000, the unused portion of the $15,000 in a joint petition or $7,500 in an individual petition may be used as a "wild card," exempting anything the debtor desires.

- The debtor's interest in one automobile, up to $2,400.

- The debtor's interest in household furnishings, household goods, wearing apparel, appliances, books, animals, crops, or musical instruments primarily held for personal use of the debtor, up to $400 in value per item and up to $8,000 aggregate.

- The debtor's aggregate interest in items of jewelry, up to $1,000.

- The debtor's aggregate interest in any tools of the debtor's trade, including books, up to $1,500.

- The debtor's aggregate interest in any other property, up to $800.

- Any unmatured life insurance policies owned by the debtor.

- Professionally prescribed health aids.

- The debtor's right to receive certain benefits, such as Social Security, veterans' benefits, disability or unemployment benefits, alimony, child support, and some pension or annuity payments.

- The debtor's right to receive—or property traceable to—any awards under victims' reparation laws, some wrongful death benefits, some life insurance payments, recoveries from bodily injury claims, and payments of the loss of future earnings. (Several of these are limited to the amount that is reasonably necessary to support the debtor and/or any dependents of the debtor. The bodily injury payments are limited to $15,000, excluding pain and suffering.)

The Bankruptcy Reform Act also permits a debtor to convert goods from nonexempt classes to exempt classes before filing the bankruptcy petition. In addition, if there is a lien on, or security interest attached to, otherwise exempt property, the debtor can redeem it—which automatically exempts it—by paying off the lien-holding creditor.

Secured Creditors

Once the debtor has selected those assets to be exempted for a "fresh start," the trustee must communicate with the secured creditors concerning their status. Each secured creditor must make a selection. Secured creditors may (1) elect to take their collateral in full satisfaction of their claims; (2) dispose of the collateral, applying the proceeds to the debt and surrendering any surplus to the trustee to be included in the bankruptcy estate; (3) dispose of the collateral and participate as unsecured creditors to the extent they are not satisfied by the collateral; or (4) have the trustee dispose of the collateral, pay the secured creditors the proceeds realized (up to the debt amount), and allow the creditors to participate as unsecured creditors for any balance owed.

Allowable Claims

Once the permanent trustee has assumed control of the estate and the exempt property has been removed from the estate, the serious business of bankruptcy begins. Those claims of creditors that are "allowable" must be filed. Only allowable debts may participate in the distribution of the estate. Allowable claims may be filed by the debtor, a creditor, or even the trustee, but they must be filed within six months of the first creditors' meeting.

Virtually every debt of the debtor that existed prior to the entry of the order for relief will be treated as an "allowable" claim. The court will *not* allow any claims that would be unenforceable against the debtor outside of the bankruptcy proceeding, such as claims based on fraud or duress by the person asserting the claim. In addition, the court will *not* allow any claims for interest accruing after the petition date. The automatic stay provision of a bankruptcy proceeding stops the accrual of interest on any claims of the creditor.

There are also two classes of claims that are allowable, but with a limit on the amount of the claims allowed. If the debtor has violated a lease agreement, the landlord's claim under the broken lease agreement is allowable, but for a limited amount. The landlord is entitled to recover any rent already due and payable, and is also allowed to recover for future rent under the lease. However, the claim for future rent is limited to the *greater* of one year's rent or 15 percent of the balance of the lease (with a three-year maximum), plus any unpaid rent already due and payable. Similarly, if the debtor has breached any employment contracts, the employees may assert their claims for damages due to the breach. The employees will be entitled to any wages already due and payable, and they will also be entitled to claim lost future wages, but only for a maximum of one year of unpaid future compensation. The following example illustrates these restrictions.

Milady Formal Wear, Inc. leased office space from River City Realty, signing a 30-year lease in June 2000. Milady also hired a sales manager, signing her to a five-year employment contract in June 2000. In August 2000 Milady hired a designer, signing a three-year employment contract, with an option for another three years. After an auspicious start, Milady encountered financial difficulties, culminating in the filing of a bankruptcy petition in January 2003. At the time of the petition, Milady was four months behind on its rent to River City Realty, and it had been unable to pay its sales manager or its designer for three months.

River City Realty will have an allowable claim for the 4 months of rent already due and payable, plus a claim for the breached lease, which still had 27 years and 6 months remaining. However, the claim for the balance of the lease is restricted to the greater of 1 year or 15 percent of the balance, with an absolute maximum of 3 years. Thus, River City Realty will be entitled to an allowable claim for 40 months of rent; 4 months already owed plus 3 years for the future rent.

Each of the employees will also have an allowable claim against Milady. The sales manager will have an allowable claim for three months' wages already due and payable, plus an additional allowable claim for future wages of up to one year. Since the sales manager signed a five-year contract, and the contract still has two years and four months remaining, she has an allowable claim for one year's future compensation. The designer will have a claim for the three months that Milady is in arrears, and will have a claim for future compensation for the remaining six months on the original employment contract. The three-year option will not be considered, nor will any part of it be allowed.

Recovery of Property

While administering a debtor's estate, a trustee may discover that the debtor committed certain improper actions. A trustee who discovers such conduct is obligated to recover the transferred property for the benefit of the unsecured creditors. These improper acts fall into two major categories: voidable preferences and fraudulent conveyances.

Voidable Preferences A voidable preference is a payment made by a debtor to one or a few creditors at the expense of the other creditors in that particular creditor class. This is not as complicated as it may seem at first glance. A transfer is deemed a preference and therefore voidable if all the following five conditions are met:

1. The transfer benefits a creditor.

2. The transfer covers a preexisting debt.

3. The debtor is insolvent at the time of the transfer. (A debtor is presumed to be insolvent during the 90 days preceding the date of the petition; this presumption is rebuttable by the debtor.)

4. The transfer is made during the 90 days preceding the petition date.

5. The transfer gives the creditor who receives it a greater percentage of the creditor's claim than fellow creditors will receive as a result of the transfer.

A transfer is not deemed a preference if it fits any one of the following tests:

- The transfer is for a new obligation, as opposed to a pre-existing debt.

- The transfer is made in the ordinary course of business.

- The transfer involves a purchase-money security interest.

- The transfer is a payment on a fully secured claim.

- The transfer is for normal payments made to creditors within 90 days prior to the petition, if the payments total less than $600 per creditor.

Fraudulent Conveyances A fraudulent conveyance is a transfer by a debtor that involves actual or constructive fraud. Actual fraud is involved if the debtor intended to hinder or delay a creditor in recovering a debt. Such a transfer will occur if the debtor transfers assets to a friend or a relative, or hides assets, to prevent any creditors from foreclosing on the assets. Constructive fraud is involved when the debtor sells an asset for inadequate consideration and as a result of the sale becomes insolvent, or if the debtor is already insolvent at the time of the unreasonable sale. It is also deemed constructive fraud to engage in a business that is undercapitalized.

Any fraudulent conveyance made during the year preceding the petition may be set aside by the trustee under federal law. In addition, some state statutes permit the avoidance of such conveyances during the preceding two to five years. The trustee uses the time period that most strongly favors the creditors.

The case on pages 665–667 addresses the issue of fraudulent conveyances. Follow the court's reasoning and then decide whether you believe that the transfer in question was, in fact, fraudulent.

Distribution of Assets

Once the trustee has gathered and liquidated all available assets and admitted all allowable claims, the estate is distributed to the creditors. The Bankruptcy Reform Act contains a mandatory priority list of debts. Each class of creditors takes its turn, and no class may receive any payments until all higher-priority classes are paid in full. All creditors within a given class will be paid on a pro rata basis until either the claims are paid in full or the estate is exhausted.

The highest priority of claims is the expense of handling the estate. All the costs incurred by the trustee in preserving and administering the bankruptcy must be paid first.

NRW CASE 28.1   Finance

WAS THIS A FRAUDULENT CONVEYANCE?

NRW has purchased a significant amount of its chips from the same firm for quite some time. This firm has a reputation for high-quality products and competitive prices. Ninety days ago the president of this firm contacted Helen offering to sell NRW some new chips. The quantity the firm was offering was larger than any order NRW had placed before, but the price was especially attractive. After a short deliberation, Helen accepted the offer. Now NRW has learned that this supplier has been involuntarily petitioned into bankruptcy, and that the trustee appointed to handle the bankruptcy is investigating all sales made by the company in the past six months. The trustee believes that several of the company's sales were fraudulent conveyances, with the selling price for the goods so far below fair market value that the buyers should have been suspicious. Helen does not believe that she did anything wrong in accepting the offer to buy the equipment, but she is not sure what evidence the trustee would need in order to establish that a fraudulent conveyance occurred. She has asked you for advice. What will you tell her?

BUSINESS CONSIDERATIONS Should a business accept an offer that looks "too good to be true" without investigating the reason for the offer, or should the business just be grateful for the opportunity and try to take advantage of it? Why?

ETHICAL CONSIDERATIONS What ethical issues are raised when a buyer is offered a price that seems unreasonably low? Is it ethical to accept such an offer without investigating the circumstances behind the offer? Is it ethical to refuse such an offer to the detriment of your firm?

INTERNATIONAL CONSIDERATIONS What actions might a trustee or the bankruptcy court take if a debtor involuntarily petitioned into bankruptcy transferred a significant portion of its assets or inventory to one of its operations located in another country?

The next class of claims involves debts that arise in the ordinary course of business between the date the petition is filed and the date the trustee is appointed.

The third and fourth priorities are interrelated. Priority 3 is wages earned by employees of the debtor during the 90

28.1

IN RE MICHAEL v. FRIERDICH
294 F.3d 864, 2002 U.S. App. LEXIS, Bankr. L. Rep (7th Cir. 2002)

FACTS In early 1998 Michael Frierdich was a director and the treasurer of Columbia Centre, Inc., a closely held company, and owned 360 of its outstanding 1,000 shares. Paul Frierdich (his brother) and Joe Koppeis held the remaining shares. (Paul and Michael Frierdich both submitted affidavits saying that Columbia Centre never issued stock certificates to its shareholders. A certificate—"Certificate # 6"—evidencing Frierdich's shares turned up but had never been signed.) The stock record book was also lost. At this time Frierdich and Oswald were contemplating marriage. In anticipation of this marriage they decided to enter into a prenuptial agreement under which Frierdich would transfer his stock in Columbia Centre, Inc. to Oswald, and Oswald would waive any interest in Frierdich's estate.

The couple became engaged on January 7, 1998, and on January 8, 1998, Frierdich executed a "Stock Transfer/Stock Power" document assigning his interest in the Columbia Centre stock to Oswald and granting power of attorney to the officers of the Columbia Centre to transfer the stock on the company books. This document was mailed to Paul Frierdich on January 16, 1998. Paul Frierdich responded on February 10, 1998, informing the couple that the transfer was taken care of. Unfortunately, Oswald never received a stock certificate and no notation on the (missing) stock record book was ever made.

In August or September of 1998, Koppeis and Paul Frierdich approached Michael Frierdich, seeking to purchase his Columbia Centre stock from him. Michael pointed out that the stock had been transferred to Oswald, but he continued to negotiate with the prospective buyers, finally agreeing to sell for a total of $400,000. Despite Michael's assertion that the proper seller should be Oswald, the final agreement listed Michael as the seller and warranted that he had title to the stock. The sale was completed, Michael received a check payable to his order for $400,000, and he promptly indorsed and deposited the check in Oswald's account. In a letter to the bank, however, Frierdich informed the bank that he had deposited the check as a gift to his wife.

In February 1999 Frierdich was involuntarily petitioned into bankruptcy. The schedules he submitted to the court showed that he had debts of $8,530,395, and assets of $1,200. At the time of the petition there were 12 lawsuits pending against Frierdich. Five of these suits had been pending prior to September 10, 1998.

The claims on file showed debts in excess of $400,000 prior to January 1, 1998. The trustee filed suit against Oswald, seeking to avoid the transfer of the $400,000 as a fraudulent conveyance. Oswald argued that the conveyance was not fraudulent since it was in support of a prenuptial agreement. She also argued that the transfer took place in January 1998 and was thus exempt from challenge because it occurred more than one year before the petition was filed. The bankruptcy judge entered summary judgment in favor of the trustee. Oswald appealed, and the District Court affirmed. Oswald then appealed to the Circuit Court.

ISSUES Was the transfer of the $400,000 a fraudulent conveyance? Did the transfer occur within one year of the date of the bankruptcy petition?

HOLDINGS Yes, the transfer was a fraudulent conveyance. Yes, the transfer took place within one year of the petition date.

REASONING Excerpts from the opinion of Judge Evans:

Michael Frierdich is a Chapter 7 debtor, which means, in simplest terms, that he does not have enough assets to pay off a staggering amount of debt. This case, between the bankruptcy trustee (Mottaz) and Frierdich's wife (Oswald), turns on when Frierdich transferred shares of stock (or their proceeds, worth $400,000) to Oswald. The answer to that question affects whether Mottaz can upset the transfer and obtain its proceeds for distribution to Frierdich's creditors. Oswald, who would just as soon keep the $400,000, has already had two swings at this issue. She lost before the bankruptcy judge and the district judge. We will ring her up on strikes. . . .

This case implicates two avoidance provisions of the federal bankruptcy code. Title 11 U.S.C. § 548(a)(1)(A) provides that a trustee may avoid a transfer by a debtor made "within one year before the date of the filing" of the bankruptcy petition if the debtor "made such transfer . . . with actual intent to hinder, delay, or defraud any entity to which the debtor was or became . . . indebted." Title 11 U.S.C. § 544(b)(1) allows the trustee to commandeer the rights of an unsecured creditor who could have avoided the transfer under applicable law, in this case the Illinois Fraudulent Transfer Act. . . . For our purposes the key difference between these two avoidance routes is that the Illinois Fraudulent Transfer Act does not contain a one-year "look back" provision. Thus if the transfer in the present case occurred in January of 1998, it occurred more than one year before the

February 17, 1999, bankruptcy filing and would fall outside of § 548's one-year "look back" provision. Mottaz would then be relegated to avoiding the transfer under § 544. If, on the other hand, the transfer did not occur in January, but rather occurred when the proceeds of the stock sale were deposited in September 1998, the transfer would fall within one year of the February 1999 bankruptcy filing and could be avoided, if there was actual intent to defraud, under § 548(a)(1)(A). The burden of proving a fraudulent transfer under § 548 is on the trustee. . . . So to the key issue we turn: whether Frierdich transferred his Columbia Centre stock to Oswald in January of 1998. Under the bankruptcy code,

> a transfer is made when such transfer is so perfected that a bona fide purchaser from the debtor against whom applicable law permits such transfer to be perfected cannot acquire an interest in the property transferred that is superior to the interest in such property of the transferee . . .

This provision presumes a "transfer," which the bankruptcy code defines as "every mode, direct or indirect, absolute or conditional, voluntary or involuntary, of disposing of or parting with property or with an interest in property." . . . Although this definition of transfer is obviously federal, its references to "property" and "interest in property" require an analysis of whether a property interest was created under state law. . . . Columbia Centre is an Illinois corporation and the parties and courts below have applied Illinois law, so we apply it as well. . . .

Oswald argues that she acquired the stock pursuant to a prenuptial agreement under which she waived her interest in Frierdich's estate in exchange for the stock transfer. This qualifies her, she argues, for "protected purchaser" status under section 303 of Article 8 of the Illinois Commercial Code. . . . Section 8-303(a) defines a "protected purchaser" as "a purchaser of a certificated or uncertificated security" who gives value, does not have notice of an adverse claim to the security and obtains "control" of the security. . . . Oswald charges ahead to argue that she can show value, no notice and control, and thus concludes that she acquired an interest as a "protected purchaser." She has put the cart before the horse. To be a "protected purchaser" she must first show that she is a "purchaser" of the security, which, unfortunately for her, is the key issue in this case. A "purchaser" (to no one's surprise) is "a person who takes by purchase." . . . The Code adds that a purchase "includes taking by sale, discount, negotiation, mortgage, pledge, lien, issue or reissue, gift or any other voluntary transaction creating an interest in property." . . . Oswald claims to have taken by prenuptial agreement.

That argument confronts two problems. First, even assuming the parties had a valid agreement pursuant to which Frierdich would transfer the stock, delivery is required to effectuate the transfer. . . . And, on that point, Oswald hits a snag. . . . Even assuming Oswald's premise that the shares were uncertificated, she cannot show delivery. Delivery of an uncertificated security occurs when "the issuer registers the purchaser as the registered owner," . . . or "another person . . . either becomes the registered owner of the uncertificated security on behalf of the purchaser or, having previously become the registered owner, acknowledges that it holds for the purchaser." . . . Oswald cannot prevail under section 8-301(b)(1) because Columbia Centre never registered her as the owner of the stock. (Its stock book was missing.) . . .

The second problem with Oswald's "prenuptial" theory is that, even apart from a failure of delivery, she never obtained an enforceable interest in the stock. Illinois law requires that a premarital agreement be in writing. . . . The writing that purports to be the prenuptial agreement in this case consists of two matching "waivers," one signed by Oswald, the other signed by Frierdich. Nowhere does Oswald's waiver recite the stock transfer, which occurred 3 months prior to this time, as connected to the waiver. Oswald's waiver merely states that her interest was limited to stock (purportedly) in her possession already. The fact that Frierdich voluntarily transferred the stock to "calibrate" the estates 3 months earlier did not give Oswald an interest, enforceable in law or equity, in the stock. Accordingly, Oswald did not take an interest in the stock until Frierdich deposited the proceeds from its sale into her account in September of 1998. That transfer was 5 months before the February 1999 bankruptcy filing and, therefore, well within the one-year provision of 11 U.S.C. § 548. The transfer is therefore voidable if it was done with actual intent to defraud under 11 U.S.C. § 548(a)(1)(A).

We find nothing wrong with the bankruptcy judge's conclusion that there was no dispute that Frierdich transferred the proceeds with actual intent to defraud. Direct proof of actual intent to defraud is not required—indeed, it would be hard to come by—and a trustee can prove actual intent by circumstantial evidence. . . . Courts often look to "badges of fraud" as circumstantial evidence. . . . These "badges" include: whether the debtor retained possession or control of the property after the transfer, whether the transferee shared a familial or other close relationship with the debtor, whether the debtor received consideration for the transfer, whether the transfer was disclosed or concealed, whether the debtor made the transfer before or after being threatened with suit by creditors, whether the transfer involved substantially all of the debtor's assets, whether the debtor absconded, and whether the debtor was or became insolvent at the time of the transfer. . . . The trustee presented evidence that Frierdich transferred a substantial sum of money, $400,000, to a close relative, his wife, and received nothing in return. In Frierdich's own words to Union Planters Bank, the transfer was a "gift." He made this gift in the midst of his own financial demise. The bankruptcy judge did not err by taking judicial notice of the schedules filed in the underlying bankruptcy proceeding. . . . Those schedules indicate that as of February 17, 1999, Frierdich's balance sheet was a sorry $8,529,195 in the red. They also reveal that five lawsuits against Frierdich were pending prior to September 10, 1998. Although a debtor's schedules, often filed months after the time of transfer, may not be probative of the earlier time, it simply blinks reality to think that Frierdich incurred $8,530,395 worth of debt and

(innocently) dwindled his assets to $1,200 in the 5 months between September 1998 and February 1999. . . . In sum, no reasonable fact finder could conclude that Frierdich did not have an actual intent to defraud his creditors in September 1998 . . . AFFIRMED.

BUSINESS CONSIDERATIONS The debtor in this case had incurred substantial debts. What policies or procedures might his creditors have followed so that the creditors did not end up in such an unfavorable position? Should the creditors object to a discharge, hoping to recover more of the money they are owed than they will receive if a discharge is granted?

ETHICAL CONSIDERATIONS Is it ethical for a corporation, even a closely held corporation, to "lose" its stock book and then take no steps to recover, reproduce, or replace it? What ethical issues are raised by such conduct?

days preceding the petition, up to a maximum of $4,000 per employee. Priority 4 is unpaid contributions by an employer to employee benefit plans, if they arise during the 180 days before the petition, up to $4,000 per employee. However, these claims are reduced by any claims paid in Priority 3. Thus, the maximum priority for each employee is a total of $4,000. Any claims in excess of this amount go to the bottom of the list.

The fifth priority is given to grain farmers who have a claim against the owner or operator of a grain storage facility and to U.S. fishermen who have a claim against individuals who operate a fish storage or fish-processing facility. In either case, the priority is limited to $4,000 per individual creditor.

The sixth priority is claims by consumers for goods or services paid for but not received. The maximum here is $1,800 per person as a priority, with any surplus claim going to the bottom of the list.

As of 1994, alimony, maintenance agreements or obligations, and child support were granted the next priority, being inserted into the list above obligations owed to the government. This placement reflects the increasing public policy position of "family values" and a desire to help protect spouses or ex-spouses, especially those with children. To further emphasize this change, the payment of alimony, maintenance, or child support is specifically not a voidable preference, nor are such payments subject to the automatic stay provisions of other debts and obligations of the debtor.

The final priority claim is in favor of debts owed to government units. This class consists basically of taxes due during the three years preceding the petition.

After all priority claims are paid, the balance of the estate is used to pay general unsecured creditors. When all unsecured creditors have been paid in full, any monies left are paid to the debtor. Normally, the funds will not cover the general creditor claims, and a pro rata distribution is necessary. This leaves the creditors with less money than they were owed. The debtor must hope for a discharge to make the balance of the claims uncollectible. Exhibit 28.1 summarizes the distribution of proceeds in a Chapter 7 bankruptcy proceeding.

The Discharge Decision

A discharge can be granted only to an individual and only if he or she is an honest debtor. A discharge will be denied if the debtor made a fraudulent conveyance or does not have adequate books and records. In addition, a debtor will be denied a discharge if he or she refuses to cooperate with the court during the proceedings. Furthermore, a discharge will not be granted if a discharge was received during the previous six years. A denial of discharge means that the unpaid portions of any debts continue and are fully enforceable after the proceedings end.

Even if a discharge is granted, some claims are not affected. Under the Bankruptcy Reform Act, certain debts continue to be fully enforceable against the debtor even though the debtor received a discharge. The following 11 major classes of debts are not affected by a discharge:

1. Taxes due to any government unit

2. Loans where the proceeds were used to pay federal taxes

EXHIBIT 28.1 Distribution of Proceeds in a Chapter 7 Bankruptcy Proceeding

Priority 1:   Expenses of the bankruptcy.

If any funds remain,

Priority 2:   Debts arising in the ordinary course of business between the petition date and the date a trustee is appointed (pro rata if necessary).

If any funds remain,

Priority 3:   Wages earned during the 90 days preceding the petition by employees of the debtor but not yet paid, to a maximum of $4,000 per employee (pro rata if necessary).

If any funds remain,

Priority 4:   Fringe benefits earned during the 180 days preceding the petition by employees of the debtor but not yet paid, to a maximum of $4,000 per employee (pro rata if necessary). Priorities 3 and 4 combined cannot exceed $4,000 per employee.

If any funds remain,

Priority 5:   Claims of grain farmers against grain storage facilities, and/or of U.S. fishermen against fish storage or fish-processing facilities, limited to $4,000 per creditor (pro rata if necessary)

If any funds remain,

Priority 6:   Claims by consumers for goods or services paid for but not received, up to $1,800 per consumer (pro rata if necessary).

If any funds remain,

Priority 7:   Claims against the debtor for alimony payments, separate maintenance payments, or child support.

If any funds remain,

Priority 8:   Debts owed to the government, especially for taxes owed for the previous three years.

If any funds remain,

General unsecured creditors: pro rata, together with any excess over the priority claims set out above.

When no funds remain, or when all eight levels have been treated, the court makes a *discharge* decision.

---

3. Debts that arose because of fraud by the debtor concerning his or her financial condition

4. Claims not listed by the creditors or by the debtor in time for treatment in the proceedings

5. Debts incurred through embezzlement or theft

6. Alimony

7. Child support

8. Liabilities due to malicious torts of the debtor

9. Fines imposed by a government unit

10. Claims that were raised in a previous case in which the debtor did not receive a discharge

11. Student loans, unless the loan is at least five years in arrears

In addition to these 11 classes of debts, the 1984 Bankruptcy Amendments addressed the problem of debtors who "load up" with debts just prior to filing a petition, expecting to use the bankruptcy proceeding to discharge these recently incurred debts. Under the law, any debtor purchases from one creditor of $1,000 or more in luxury goods or services that are incurred within 40 days of the petition are presumed to be nondischargeable. Similarly, any cash advances of $1,000 or more that are received from one creditor within the 20 days prior to the petition are presumed to be nondischargeable. The debtor will have the burden of proof and will have to convince the court that these debts were not fraudulently incurred with the intent to have these debts discharged. Notice that a discharge is possible but that the debtor has the burden of proof!

Finally, even if a discharge is granted, it may be revoked. If the trustee or a creditor requests a revocation of the discharge, the request may be granted. The request must be made within one year of the discharge, and the debtor must have committed some wrongful act, such as fraud during the proceedings. The possibility of revocation encourages the debtor to remain honest.

On some occasions, a debtor who has been granted a discharge in bankruptcy may decide that he or she wants to repay the creditor despite the discharge. A debtor who truly wants to repay the debt may voluntarily reaffirm the debt and then repay it. However, the requirements for a reaffirmation were substantially increased by the 1984 Bankruptcy Amendments. Prior to the 1984 amendments, debtors could reaffirm any debts at virtually any time. Too often this led to debtors reaffirming debts out of a sense of guilt following the discharge and putting themselves in the same sort of financial position that originally led to the petition. As a result, the 1984 amendments require that any reaffirmations be made in writing and filed with the court. In addition, the written agreement must be filed before the debtor is granted a discharge. If the debtor has an attorney, the attorney must file a declaration that the debtor was fully informed of his or her rights and voluntarily agreed to the reaffirmation, and that the agreement will not impose an undue hardship on the debtor or his or her dependents. If the debtor does not have an attorney, the court must approve the reaffirmation, and the court will not grant approval unless the repayment is in the best interests of the debtor. For an illustration of a Chapter 7 proceeding and a comparison with the other bankruptcy chapters, see Exhibit 28.2 at the end of this chapter.

Chapter 11: Reorganization Plans

Many people have the mistaken idea that Chapter 7 proceedings are all the Bankruptcy Reform Act covers. While a Chapter 7 proceeding is the most common type of bankruptcy, several other types of proceedings are also available under the Bankruptcy Reform Act including: a reorganization under Chapter 11, which is normally used by businesses; and a wage earner's repayment plan under Chapter 13, which is available only for individual debtors. None of these plans calls for a liquidation of the debtor's assets in order to cover the debts; and under these plans, the credi-

tors can reasonably expect to be paid more than they would receive under a liquidation proceeding. In fact, many times the creditors will be paid in full by the debtor. While a Chapter 7 bankruptcy relies on the debtor's assets as of the petition date, plus those assets acquired during the proceedings, each of these other chapters involve plans that rely on the debtor's future earnings.

Chapter 11 bankruptcy proceedings, known as reorganizations, are designed to allow the debtor to adjust his or her financial situation, restructuring the business financially in order to save the enterprise. Chapter 11 is used by debtors to avoid liquidations. Although reorganizations are

---

NRW CASE 28.2 Finance

CHAPTER 11 BANKRUPTCY

Mail-Mart, a mail-order retail business, is one of NRW's largest customers. Over the past several months it has ordered nearly $12,000 worth of Stuff-TrakRs, which has been one of Mail-Mart's largest selling "novelty" items. However, business has been in decline for Mail-Mart for some time, and it recently filed a petition seeking relief under Chapter 11 of the Bankruptcy Act. At the time of the filing Mail-Mart owed NRW nearly $10,000 and had been steadily falling behind on its payments. Mail-Mart has filed a reorganization plan that would have it making payments to its creditors for a longer time period, and would also reduce or eliminate the interest it would normally pay on any of its debts. Helen thinks that Mail-Mart's plan will put NRW in a poor cash flow position, and she would like the firm to vote against the plan as proposed by Mail-Mart. Mai is also concerned about the cash flow consequences, but thinks that the firm can handle the situation, provided that Mail-Mart pays the entire balance due. She is concerned that if the creditors oppose the plan, Mail-Mart will be forced to liquidate and NRW will receive only a fraction of the money owed. They have asked you what the firm should do in this situation, and they also want to know what rights, if any, NRW can assert. What will you tell them?

BUSINESS CONSIDERATIONS Any time a business extends credit to a customer, that business assumes the risk of default or bankruptcy by the customer. What can a business like NRW do to protect itself, short of

continued

refusing to make credit sales? Why would a business *not* decide to deal strictly on a cash-and-carry basis?

ETHICAL CONSIDERATIONS Suppose that a customer is encountering financial difficulties and facing the possibility of failure. That customer asks for an extension of the time for making its payments. What considerations would cause a creditor to agree to the extension? When should the creditor take a hard-line stance and refuse to vary the payment terms?

INTERNATIONAL CONSIDERATIONS Suppose that a firm is incorporated in another country, but doing business in the United States, and that this firm encounters financial difficulties that threaten its survival. Can the firm seek protection under the bankruptcy laws of the United States even though it is incorporated in another country? What concerns would such a filing raise among the creditors?

designed primarily for use by corporate debtors, individuals are also allowed to use the reorganization format. The major advantage of a reorganization is that it allows a business to continue despite its debts. In fact, if the court approves a reorganization plan, it will force the creditors who object to go along with the plan despite their objections. Normally the creditors will receive more of the money owed to them in a reorganization than they would receive in a liquidation under Chapter 7.

Any debtor who can use Chapter 7, except stockbrokers and commodity brokers, can also use Chapter 11. Moreover, railroads, which are prohibited from using Chapter 7, can take advantage of the provisions of Chapter 11. Like a liquidation proceeding, a reorganization may be either voluntary or involuntary. The limitations for an involuntary petition under Chapter 11 are the same as those for a liquidation petition.

The Proceedings

Once the petition has been filed, the court will do three things:

1. It will enter an order for relief.

2. It will appoint a trustee, if requested to do so by any interested party.

3. It will appoint creditor committees to represent the creditors. (Equity security holders will be represented by a separate committee.)

Remember that the *automatic stay* provisions also apply in this chapter. When a petition is filed, any legal actions involving the debtor are subject to an automatic stay, freezing those legal proceedings until the bankruptcy proceedings have been concluded.

The court may appoint a trustee, although that is not necessary in Chapter 11. In fact, if no interested party *asks* for the appointment of a trustee, no trustee will be appointed. Instead, the debtor is permitted to retain possession and control of the assets and/or the business (such a debtor is referred to as a debtor-in-possession). This *debtor-in-possession* is deemed to have the same basic duties as a trustee, including the fiduciary duty owed to the creditors. The committees appointed by the court will meet with the trustee, if one is appointed, or with the debtor-in-possession, if no trustee is appointed, to discuss the treatment of the proceedings. The committees also will investigate the debtor's finances and financial potential, and they will help prepare a plan for reorganizing the enterprise that will benefit all the interested parties.

In the event that no one asks for the appointment of a trustee, the court may decide to appoint an *examiner*. The examiner or the trustee will investigate the debtor, the debtor's business activities, and the debtor's business potential. On the basis of this investigation, a recommendation will be made to the court. The recommendation may be a reorganization plan, or it may be a suggestion that the proceedings be transferred from Chapter 11 to Chapter 7 (liquidation) or to Chapter 13 (wage earner plan, if the debtor is an individual). The court normally will follow such a recommendation unless a good reason not to follow it is presented.

The Plan

The purpose of a reorganization is to develop a plan under which the debtor can avoid liquidation while somehow managing to satisfy the claims of the creditors. Obviously, the right to propose a plan can be very important. If the debtor remains in possession (i.e., no trustee is appointed), only the debtor can propose a plan during the first 120 days after the order for relief is entered. Any interested party (debtor, creditor, stockholder, or trustee) can propose a plan under any of three conditions:

1. If a trustee is appointed, any interested party can propose a plan at any time until a plan is approved by the court.

2. If the debtor fails to propose a plan within the 120-day period, any interested party can propose a plan.

3. If the debtor proposes a plan within 120 days, but it is not accepted by all affected classes of creditors within 180 days of the order for relief, any interested party can propose a plan to the court.

The 1994 Bankruptcy Reform Act includes provisions for a "fast track" reorganization for small-business debtors. This "fast-track" reorganization is covered in § 1121(c). To be eligible for this provision, the business must be a "small business" *and* it must elect to be considered a "small business." Small business is defined in § 101(51C) as a business with less than $2 million in noncontingent liquidated liabilities. If the debtor business has as its primary activity the owning or managing of real estate it is not allowed to use the fast track option. The debtor in a fast track reorganization must file a plan within 100 days, rather than the 120 days granted under a "regular" Chapter 11. All plans must be filed within 160 days, as opposed to the 180 days granted under a "regular" Chapter 11.

For a plan to be confirmed, it must designate all claims by class as well as specify which classes will be impaired and which will not be impaired. It must also show how the plan can be implemented successfully. Among the factors that the court will examine in reviewing a plan are the following:

• plans to sell any assets

• plans to merge, consolidate, or divest

• plans to satisfy, or modify, any liens or claims

• plans to issue new stock to generate funds

If new stock is to be issued, it must have voting rights. No new nonvoting stock may be issued under a reorganization plan. Each class of creditors that is impaired is allowed to vote on the plan.

According to § 1129(a), the court can confirm a plan *only if* a number of requirements are met. Included in this list of requirements are the following:

1. the plan was proposed in good faith and not by any means forbidden by law;

2. any payments made or to be made under the plan for services, costs, and expenses in connection with the plan have been approved by, or are subject to approval by, the court;

3. with respect to each impaired class of claims or creditors, each holder of a claim or interest within the class

   a. has accepted the plan, or

   b. will receive or retain property of a value that is not less than the amount that class or claim would receive or retain if the debtor were liquidated under Chapter 7;

4. if a class of claims is impaired, at least one class of claims that is impaired has accepted the plan; and

5. confirmation of the plan is not likely to be followed by a liquidation.

A class is deemed to have accepted the plan if creditors having at least two-thirds of the dollar amount involved and more than one-half of the total number of creditors vote in favor of the plan. If a creditor class is not impaired by the plan, it does not need to approve the plan. Creditor classes whose claims will be impaired under the plan *must* vote on the plan, and at least one of these impaired classes must approve the plan [§ 1129(a)(10).] This requirement sounds very straightforward, but even this has an exception, the so-called cramdown provisions found in § 1129(b), which is discussed below.

Despite the vote, no plan can be accepted or rejected by the creditors. The final word is left to the court. The court will hold a hearing on the plan, and the court can confirm or reject it. The court *can* confirm a plan if it is accepted by at least one class of creditors. If all the creditor classes approve the plan, the court normally will confirm it. Similarly, if all the creditor classes reject the plan, the court will reject it. The vote of the creditor classes provides the court with guidance, but the final decision lies with the court, subject to the limitations imposed by the statute.

The court will look at the plan's fairness to each interested group, especially those creditors impaired by the plan. The court also will look at the viability of the plan. If the court feels the plan will not work or is not fair, it can order the proceedings converted to a Chapter 7 liquidation. This last-ditch power encourages everyone involved to act in good faith, since Chapter 11 usually is better than Chapter 7 for all concerned.

Once the court approves a plan, it becomes binding on all of the interested parties affected by the plan. Suppose that a creditor class objects to the plan and votes against it. Despite this objection, if the court approves the plan, it will be binding on the disgruntled creditor class. In this situation the court is using the cramdown provision; the plan is being "crammed down" the throats of the dissenting creditors.

Section 1129(b) allows the court to bypass the restrictions imposed by § 1129(a) and to confirm a plan, at the request of the proponent of that plan, if the plan does not discriminate unfairly and is fair and equitable, with respect to each class of claims that is impaired by the plan and has not accepted the plan.

The following case involved the potential use of the cramdown provision and also the possibility that the proceedings would be removed to Chapter 7. Did the court make the proper decision? What would *you* have done?

28.2

FORT KNOX MINI WAREHOUSE, INC.
2002 Bankr. LEXIS 909 (N.D. Iowa, 2002)

FACTS Fort Knox Mini Warehouse, Inc., the Debtor corporation in this Chapter 11 proceeding, operated a self-storage business at 5300 J Street S.W., Cedar Rapids, Iowa. Donald Nemec was the sole shareholder of the business. He and his wife, JoAnn Nemec, were both actively involved in the operation of the business. Fort Knox provided both short- and long-term storage space to individuals and businesses in units of varying sizes and costs. Fort Knox also operated a temperature-controlled self-storage facility at 301 F Avenue N.W. and a residential property at 622 3rd Street N.W. The F Avenue and 3rd street properties were not owned by Fort Knox, but were operated by it under an operating agreement with the owners, Donald Nemec and JoAnn Nemec. This agreement provided that Fort Knox collect the rental income and pay the associated expenses attributable to those properties.

This Chapter 11 petition was precipitated by foreclosure of mortgages held by Guaranty Bank. These mortgages encumbered the real estate owned by Fort Knox and certain real estate owned by Donald and JoAnn Nemec. Mr. and Mrs. Nemec personally guaranteed much of the secured debt of Fort Knox to Guaranty Bank. A judgment was entered in favor of Guaranty Bank on August 21, 2001, in the Iowa District Court for Linn County for $1,097,104.05 plus interests and costs. Of that amount, $916,455.55 was specifically a judgment against Fort Knox. Fort Knox filed for Chapter 11 protection on October 12, 2001. The U.S. Trustee filed a Motion to Dismiss or Convert on May 24, 2002. It is asserted that the profit and loss statements filed in this case reflected that Fort Knox had shown a loss in most months since the filing of the petition and was delinquent on property taxes for the prior three biannual tax periods. Additionally, current property taxes were accruing at a rate of approximately $2,100 per month. Donald Nemec testified that the gross revenue for the company was trending upward. In addition, he was willing to contribute the proceeds from a promissory note owed to Donald Nemec, personally, by Walnut Creek Storage Partners, Ltd., a limited partnership, in the amount of $150,000. Mr. Nemec's son was the principal participant in Walnut Creek, the developer of a real estate project in Mansfield, Texas. Although, the note was scheduled to mature on March 9, 2003, Donald Nemec testified that Walnut Creek should be able to satisfy that obligation by October 2002.

The U.S. Trustee noted that the case had been on file in excess of nine months. The business continued to experience losses and accumulated taxes since the filing of the petition that it would be unable to pay. Guaranty Bank joined in the U.S. Trustee's motion for the same reasons and further stated that collection of the $150,000 would be speculative, and even if the note were collected, the $150,000 would not be enough to reduce the secured debt to a point where the monthly interest payments would amortize secured debt. Finally, Guaranty Bank asserted that Fort Knox's income statement showed a net loss through April 2002. For these reasons, the U.S. Trustee and Guaranty Bank sought dismissal or conversion of the case.

ISSUES Should the reorganization plan be approved by the court despite the objection of Guaranty Bank and the trustee? If not, should the court dismiss or convert the case?

HOLDINGS No, the plan should not be approved over the objections of the bank and the trustee. Yes, the case should be dismissed or converted to a Chapter 7 proceeding.

REASONING Excerpts from the opinion of Chief Bankruptcy Judge Paul J. Kilberg:

A bankruptcy court has broad discretion under 11 U.S.C. § 1112(b) to either dismiss a case or convert a case from a Chapter 11 reorganization to a Chapter 7 liquidation.... Dismissal or conversion is appropriate if "cause" exists and it is in the "best interests of creditors and the estate." ... It is therefore incumbent upon the court to determine, as a threshold matter, whether "cause" exists.

Section 1112(b) sets forth specifically enumerated examples of "cause" including the "continuing loss to or diminution of the estate and absence of a reasonable likelihood of rehabilitation." ... The burden of proof in a motion for conversion or dismissal rests squarely upon the moving party....

The first aspect of § 1112(b)(1) requires a showing of a "continuing loss to or diminution of the estate." ... This element can be satisfied by demonstrating that the debtor incurred continuing losses or maintained a negative cash flow position after the entry of the order for relief. . . . Movants have established a continued diminution of the estate. The main asset in the

Debtor's estate is the property consisting of land and buildings located at 5300 J. Street S.W., Cedar Rapids, Iowa. As indicated on Debtor's monthly reports, this property had a value of approximately $1,300,000 on October 12, 2001, the date the Chapter 11 petition was filed. As of May 2002, this property has depreciated in value to roughly $900,000. Guaranty Bank is the holder of a foreclosure judgment in the original amount of $1,097,104 with interest accruing at $258.77 per day from August 1, 2001. This obligation continues to accumulate despite Debtor's adequate protection payments to the Bank in the amount of $7,000 per month. In addition, there are unpaid and delinquent property taxes. Not only is Debtor behind $ 42,000 for the three previous bi-annual tax periods, but the current property taxes, which are accruing at a rate of approximately $2,100 per month, also have not been addressed. Debtor's monthly profit and loss statements indicate that Debtor has realized a profit in only three of the last nine months. . . . These figures, even though not positive, do not represent Debtor's true level of financial distress. The financial statements are incomplete. The Profit and Loss Statement does not make provision for depreciation expenses for the year 2002 or any property taxes. The record indicates that a post-petition profit would have been non-existent had Debtor included these expenses in the monthly reports. It is apparent that Debtor's estate continues to incur losses. This Court concludes that the first element of § 1112(b)(1) has been satisfied.

The second aspect of § 1112(b)(1) requires a showing of an "absence of a reasonable likelihood of rehabilitation." This test is satisfied if the state of the debtor's financial affairs is such that it is unable to re-establish itself on a firm or sound base. . . . The concept of rehabilitation necessarily hinges upon establishing a cash flow from which current obligations can be satisfied. . . . The Court must evaluate whether Debtor can emerge as an economically viable enterprise capable of servicing its obligations under a plan. . . . This finding in turn requires an assessment of the feasibility of the debtor's proposal for rehabilitation, as contained in the Debtor's plan of reorganization together with the disclosure statement, under a cramdown scenario. . . . This Court will give Debtor the benefit of the doubt and apply the foregoing analysis to the most recent Plan submitted by the Debtor. Feasibility contemplates the probability of actual performance of plan provisions or whether the things to be done under a plan of reorganization can be done as a practical matter under the facts. . . . To be feasible, a Chapter 11 plan must offer a reasonable prospect of success and be workable. . . . "Sincerity, honesty and willingness are not sufficient to make the plan feasible

and neither are visionary promises." . . . Debtor's monthly reports do not contain information sufficient to enable a hypothetical, reasonable investor, as defined in 11 U.S.C. § 1125(a)(2), to make an informed judgment about the Plan of Reorganization as required by 11 U.S.C. § 1125(a)(1). The monthly reports combine the income from Debtor's operations with that from the F Avenue and 3rd Street properties. The F Avenue and 3rd Street properties are not owned by Debtor, but have been operated by it under agreement with the owners Donald Nemec and JoAnn Nemec. Under this operating agreement, Debtor is obligated to collect the rental income and pay the associated expenses. The Disclosure Statement further states that this arrangement is beneficial to Debtor because the rental income exceeds the expenses. It must be noted that Donald Nemec's testimony is the only evidence as to the existence of this agreement.

Based upon the evidence presented, it is impossible to discern whether the income from these properties can be classified as property of the estate. As they stand, the monthly reports may seriously misrepresent Debtor's financial condition by inflating its gross revenue. It is the opinion of this Court, however, that even if the cash flow projections are based on the inflated monthly reports, Debtor does not have sufficient cash flows to produce a feasible Plan. Cash flow projections must be based upon objective facts. . . . The Court will give Debtor the benefit of the doubt when evaluating projections. The projections, however, must be based on more than wishful thinking. Historical data is one source of objective evidence upon which projections may be premised. . . . Debtor projects an average positive monthly cash flow of approximately $1,575. The cash flow projection assumes that gross revenue will reach $13,000 per month. Debtor testified that gross revenue has trended upward over the past nine months and such a trend would justify a projection of $13,000 per month. It is the conclusion of this Court, however, that an upward trend in operating income is not supported by the record. Moreover, the historical data shows that Debtor has only recognized gross revenue in excess of $13,000 in two of the last nine months. . . . Debtor has not offered additional facts which would convince this Court that its projections are not the result of wishful thinking. . . .

This Court must conclude that Debtor has failed to show that the plan is feasible on this basis, for purposes of a § 1112(b) analysis. . . . The record proves that Debtor has done poorly since the filing of the Chapter 11 petition. It continues to lose money and has new accruing obligations which cannot be paid. The success of Debtor's Plan depends largely on its ability to cut expenses, obtain outside funding, and collect on a $150,000 note that matures in March of 2003. Not only are Debtor's income and expense projections fanciful, but it is speculative to assume that Debtor will obtain outside financing or collect on the note. As such, this Court must conclude that the U.S. Trustee has established grounds to dismiss or convert this case. It is the opinion of this Court that converting this case would cause unnecessary administrative expenses to be incurred. Accordingly, for the reasons stated, the Chapter 11 case should be dismissed.

BUSINESS CONSIDERATIONS When should a business facing financial distress attempt to reorganize, and when should it decide to just go out of business? What factors should the business look at in making such a decision?

ETHICAL CONSIDERATIONS Was it unethical for Mr. Nemec to report income from assets not owned by Fort Knox in an effort to show that the business could be made profitable? How should he have reported the income potential of the business?

Chapter 11 as a Corporate Strategy

Reorganizations have recently taken on an interesting twist. A number of corporations, some of which are very large and successful, have availed themselves of Chapter 11 to escape or avoid potentially onerous debts or obligations. Johns-Manville was, at one time, a giant in the asbestos industry. When the effect of asbestos on health became known, Johns-Manville was faced with potential liability to its customers and employees that could have literally reached billions of dollars. Despite the size and success of the firm, such liability would have destroyed Johns-Manville. Rather than await the imposition of such a liability, Johns-Manville went to court seeking a reorganization under Chapter 11. The firm proposed the establishment of a trust fund to be used for victims entitled to compensation due to asbestos-related health problems.[13] The court approved the reorganization plan, and the firm endowed the trust with millions of dollars and continued to operate the business. The firm recently paid its first dividends in several years and has once again assumed its position on the *Fortune* 500 list.

Similar strategies have been used to escape other potentially disastrous liabilities. Several firms have recently used Chapter 11 to avoid burdensome labor contracts. In fact, the use of Chapter 11 to reject a collective bargaining agreement is prevalent enough to have a section of the Bankruptcy Code that addresses this issue. Section 1113, "Rejection of Collective Bargaining Agreements," specifies the conditions under which a collective bargaining agreement can be rejected as a part of the debtor's reorganization plan. The court can approve such a proposal only if:

- the debtor has made a proposal to the authorized representatives of the employees which provides for any modifications that are necessary to permit the reorganization, and that assures that all affected parties are treated fairly and equitably;

- the authorized representative of the employees has rejected the proposal without good cause; and

- the balance of the equities, in the eyes of the court, clearly favors rejection of the collective bargaining agreement despite the action of the authorized representative of the employees.

For an illustration of a Chapter 11 proceeding and a comparison with the other bankruptcy chapters, see Exhibit 28.2 at the end of this chapter.

Chapter 13: Repayment Plans

Chapter 13 of the Bankruptcy Reform Act is designed to allow a debtor with a regular source of income to adjust his or her debts in a manner that (hopefully) will repay all creditors. Chapter 13 plans are available only to individual debtors; they cannot be used by corporations. As a further restriction, they are available only to debtors who have less than $1 million of debt, with a maximum of $750,000 in secured debts and a maximum of $250,000 in unsecured debts. (Prior to the 1994 Bankruptcy Act, the debt ceilings for a Chapter 13 repayment plan limited the debtor to no more than $100,000 in unsecured debts and no more than $350,000 in secured debts.) There is also a cost-of-living adjustment (COLA) provision in the 1994 Bankruptcy Act. The debt ceiling for Chapter 13 proceedings will be adjusted for inflation every three years, thus (hopefully) allowing this relief to keep up with inflation and negating the need for periodic amendments. The debt ceilings in effect prior to October 6, 1994, made Chapter 13 unavailable to many farmers, which led to the creation of Chapter 12. The increase in consumer debt, coupled with inflation from 1978 through 1994, made the debt ceiling an impediment to the public policy objectives of Chapter 13 proceedings and led to the upward revision on allowable debt and to the inflation adjustment mechanism now in effect. Debtors who exceed the debt ceiling will have to use Chapter 7, Chapter 11, or some nonbankruptcy alternative.

Chapter 13 is available only by means of a voluntary petition. The debtor can seek relief under this option, but the creditors cannot force a debtor to enter a repayment plan. (However, the threat of forcing a debtor into Chapter 7 may persuade the debtor that Chapter 13 is in his or her best interests.)

The Proceedings

In many respects, a repayment plan is the simplest bankruptcy proceeding for an individual debtor. The debtor files a voluntary petition seeking relief. The court will issue an order for relief, an automatic stay takes effect, and a trustee will be appointed. The trustee will perform the investigation normally followed under a reorganization, but only if the debtor operates a business. In addition, the trustee will carry out the plan proposed by the debtor, if the plan is approved by the court.

The Plan

The debtor must file a proposed repayment plan with the court. The plan must provide equal treatment to each creditor claim within any given class of creditors. This does not mean that each class must be treated equally—only that within each class, every creditor must be treated equally. The plan also must make some provisions for clearing up any defaulted debts or defaulted payments on debts. The plan must not call for payments beyond a three-year period, unless the court feels that a longer period is necessary. Even then, the plan must be carried out within five years.

The court will approve the plan if the following conditions are met:

• The plan complies with the provisions of Chapter 13. (This includes the minimum payment provisions discussed later.)

• The plan appears to be fair to all parties.

• The plan is in the best interests of the creditors.

• It appears that the debtor can conform to the plan.

• The plan proposes to pay at least as much as would have been paid under Chapter 7.

Once approved, the plan is binding on all parties, with or without their consent. At that point, the debtor must turn over to the trustee enough of the debtor's income to make the payments called for under the plan.

If the debtor performs the plan as approved, the court will grant a discharge. The discharge terminates all debts provided for in the plan—if they are dischargeable in a liquidation—that received their full share under the plan. In addition, the court can intercede and grant a discharge during the plan, even though the plan has not been completely carried out. The court will do so only if the following three factors are present:

1. The debtor cannot complete the plan owing to circumstances beyond the debtor's control.

2. The general (lowest-priority) creditors have received at least as much as they would have received in a liquidation.

3. The court does not feel it is practical to alter the plan.

NRW CASE 28.3 | **Finance/Management**

CHAPTER 13 BANKRUPTCY

When NRW first began operations, it hired Stephanie as an executive secretary. Stephanie has been a wonderful secretary, and the principals have become very fond of her. Stephanie recently encountered some financial difficulties and asked for an advance on her pay. While the firm has no formal policy regarding advances, the principals generally agree that advances on pay should not be given. However, since Stephanie has been with the firm from the beginning, and since the firm values her contributions, it was agreed that the firm would advance her $2,000. Several weeks after receiving this advance, Stephanie filed for relief under Chapter 13 of the Bankruptcy Act. Among the creditors she listed was NRW, listing it for the amount of the advance. She listed total debts of $22,500, all unsecured except for a car loan from her bank. Her only assets are her car, her computer, her clothing, and her job. She currently takes home $275 per week. In her repayment plan she proposes that she would make weekly payments of $37.50 for the next three years. (NRW would receive $5 per week, or a total of $780, under this plan.) Stephanie is single; she shares an apartment with a friend and her share of the monthly rent is $190. Her car payments to the bank are $211. Carlos is quite upset at this turn of events, and he has asked you if this repayment plan is likely to be approved by the Bankruptcy Court. What would you tell him? Why?

BUSINESS CONSIDERATIONS Should a business have a formal policy regarding employee salary advances?

continued

What can a business do to protect itself from situations such as this if the business does, in fact, allow employees to receive advances on their pay?

ETHICAL CONSIDERATIONS Suppose that an employee "takes advantage" of the employer by getting an advance on his or her pay, and then lists that advance as a creditor's claim in bankruptcy. Should the firm retaliate against the employee through a firing or a reassignment? How should the employee be treated following his or her seeming mistreatment of the employer?

INTERNATIONAL CONSIDERATIONS Suppose that a debtor files a petition for relief under Chapter 13 of the Bankruptcy Act and submits a plan for repayment that is approved by the court. What effect will the court's approval of this plan have on a creditor from another nation? Will another nation recognize the "fresh start" and the discharge of this debt owed to one of its citizens or corporations, even if the debt arose in the United States?

The likelihood of such a court intervention during the plan is not very high, but the option is there. And, once again, the desire to provide a fresh start for an honest debtor is obvious.

In 1993, the Supreme Court handed down its opinion in *Rake v. Wade*.[14] Wade held a long-term promissory note from Rake, with the note secured by a home mortgage. Wade was classified as an "oversecured" mortgagee because the value of the home was significantly higher than the balance owed on the note. The Court allowed Wade to collect interest, both pre- and post-petition, from Rake even though the note was silent on this matter and state law would not have allowed Wade to recover such interest.

Congress did not like the Court's opinion in *Rake v. Wade*. The Bankruptcy Reform Act of 1994 contains a section intended to overrule the court's opinion. The discussion of the 1994 act included this observation:

Interest on Interest. This provision is applicable in Chapter 11, 12 and 13 cases, and provides that if a plan cures a default, the liability for interest is to be determined in accordance with the agreement and nonbankruptcy law. The purpose is to overrule Rake v. Wade . . . , *which required the payment of interest on mortgage arrearages when the chapter 13 debtor attempted to cure the default and reinstate the mortgage even if not contained in the agreement and not required by State law.*[15]

1984 Bankruptcy Amendments

The Bankruptcy Amendments of 1984 have tightened the requirements for a Chapter 13 repayment plan. The new standards also reduce the burden on the courts, since the good faith of the debtor is not an issue. Rather, a more tangible standard than the apparent good faith of the debtor has been substituted.

The Bankruptcy Reform Act of 1984 allows any unsecured creditor to block the debtor's proposed repayment plan, but only if the plan does not meet one of two criteria:

1. The plan calls for the payment of 100 percent of the creditor's claim.

2. The plan calls for the debtor to pay 100 percent of all income not necessary to support the debtor's immediate family for at least three years.

Unless the debtor shows that the plan satisfies one of these two criteria, the Chapter 13 repayment plan will be rejected by the court. The debtor will then have to file a new plan, change over to a Chapter 7 proceeding, or withdraw the petition. Note that these are the *only* criteria available for a creditor to challenge a proposed repayment plan. The creditors do not have a right to "approve" the plan, or even to vote on the plan.

Under the 1978 Bankruptcy Reform Act, debtor payments under a repayment plan did not begin until the plan was confirmed by the court. This gave many debtors a four- to six-month "grace period" in which the debtor retained all of his or her assets but made no payments, to the detriment of the creditors. The 1984 Bankruptcy Amendments call for payments to begin within 30 days of the filing of the plan, subject to confirmation of the plan by the court. The debtor makes these payments to the trustee, who holds the monies paid until confirmation of the plan by the court and then distributes them to the various creditors. If the debtor fails to make payments to the trustee in a timely manner, the plan can be dismissed by the court.

Finally, the 1984 Bankruptcy Amendments provide for the possible modification of the plan after it is confirmed. The trustee, the debtor, or any creditor can petition the court to increase or decrease the debtor's payments whenever the debtor's circumstances or income warrant such a modification. Prior to the 1984 Amendments, decreases were possible, but increases were not permitted.

In the following case, a debtor was asking the court to reopen a Chapter 13 plan in order to modify the plan.

The three bankruptcy alternatives discussed in this chapter are each designed to give an honest debtor a fresh start. An individual may use any of them, and most businesses can use two. Exhibit 28.2 compares these three bankruptcy alternatives.

28.3

IN THE MATTER OF ZURN
290 F.3d 861, 2002 U.S. App. LEXIS 9163 (7th Cir. 2002)

FACTS Mary Zurn sued Aldo Botti, an attorney who represented her in a divorce proceeding, alleging numerous counts of wrongdoing. Botti countersued Zurn for damages, including an allegation that Zurn had still not paid her legal fees from the divorce proceeding. The net result of these suits was a judgment in Botti's favor from the Illinois court. The court awarded Botti nearly $180,000. Zurn decided to file a petition in bankruptcy rather than pay Botti the amount of the judgment. However, the bankruptcy court decided that it would abstain from any decisions regarding the Zurn-Botti controversy until the parties had exhausted their appeals in Illinois. Ultimately Zurn filed a plan promising payment in full to all of her creditors, including Botti. Zurn paid the amount claimed by Botti, the court approved her plan, and the federal proceedings were dismissed in 1996.

Meanwhile the litigation continued in Illinois. In March 1998 the state's appellate court reversed the judgments to the extent that they had required Zurn to pay Botti. Three of Zurn's claims against Botti were decided in Botti's favor, but the court ruled that Zurn's claim for battery had been dismissed improperly. At this point Botti should have returned the money Zurn had paid to satisfy the judgments, but he did not. The appellate decision left each side with unresolved legal claims against the other, but neither took timely steps to resume the litigation in the trial court. Illinois requires a litigant that wants to continue the proceedings after an appeal to act within a reasonable period after the appellate mandate (which issued in November 1998). Botti never attempted to reinstate his suit seeking legal fees, and Zurn did not attempt to proceed with her battery claim against Botti. After allowed 13 months to pass, Zurn moved to reopen the bankruptcy proceeding. She asked the bankruptcy judge to order Botti to return the money that had been paid under the plan. A few weeks later (in January 2000) she tried to reinstate the litigation in the state's trial court. Both the bankruptcy judge and the state judge said no. The state judge concluded that Zurn's request was untimely, and after initially granting some of the relief Zurn had requested, the bankruptcy judge changed his mind, deciding that Zurn had not provided adequate reasons for the bankruptcy court to reopen the proceedings. Zurn appealed.

ISSUE Should the bankruptcy court reopen *this* case after the plan has been carried out to completion?

HOLDING No. The issues raised by the appellant should more properly be heard in a state court, and not in the bankruptcy court.

REASONING Excerpts from the opinion of Circuit Judge Easterbrook:

Bankruptcy Judge Wedoff concluded that Zurn had not supplied adequate cause to reopen the proceedings under 11 U.S.C. § 350(b), that it was not possible to "enforce the plan" (as Zurn had requested in a separate motion) because the plan had been carried out to the letter, and that state rather than federal tribunals offer the right forums for final resolution of the disputes between Zurn and Botti.

Zurn did not appeal within the state system, but she did ask a district judge to review the bankruptcy judge's decision. The district judge agreed with the bankruptcy judge's bottom line but gave different reasons. He concluded, first, that reopening is barred by the Rooker-Feldman doctrine . . . and, second, that Zurn has no remaining state remedies and thus is not entitled to restitution. Bankruptcy courts implement entitlements under state law . . . and if as a matter of Illinois law Zurn has lost her right to restitution then there is no claim to vindicate in bankruptcy. Dismayed by this turn of events—the bankruptcy judge sent her claim to state court, while the district judge wiped it out—Zurn has appealed to us.

The district court characterized its decision as one affirming the bankruptcy judge's decision to abstain rather than interfere with state litigation. If that is the right understanding, then 28 U.S.C. § 1334 (d) blocks appellate review. But the district judge's use of language was imprecise. The bankruptcy judge discussed abstention (particularly the consequences of the 1995 decision to abstain), but his *judgment* in these proceedings was not one of abstention. Instead the bankruptcy judge denied Zurn's motion to enforce the plan, a decision that is not abstention of any flavor. Indeed, it would have been possible to abstain in 2000 only after first reopening the bankruptcy. Judge Wedoff rescinded his initial act of reopening; the district court affirmed. That is incompatible with abstention. Moreover, by the time this dispute returned to the district judge, all proceedings in state court were over. There was nothing to abstain in favor of—nor was there any pending bankruptcy case that would proceed while the state courts handled the matters from which the federal court had abstained. The questions on the table in 2000 concerned the consequences of decisions the state courts already had rendered. Because the federal court was not asked in 2000 to interfere with or take over a pending state suit in order to value a claim in bankruptcy, it also could not "abstain" within the meaning of § 1334(c). What the court actually did was decline to reopen a bankruptcy proceeding under § 350(b) and hold that the plan did not need "enforcement" because no one had departed from its provisions. Because that decision ended the litigation in the district court, we have jurisdiction under 28 U.S.C. § 158(d).

Neither of the district judge's substantive reasons is correct. The *Rooker-Feldman* doctrine instantiates the principle that only the Supreme Court of the United States may modify a judgment entered by a state court in civil litigation. Zurn did not ask the federal court to review or alter the state courts' decisions; she argued, instead, that the appellate decision has a particular legal consequence (that Botti must make restitution). That may be right or wrong, but deciding whether it is right does not transgress *Rooker-Feldman*. Federal law does not undercut efforts to enforce state judgments. Nor was it right to say that Zurn's delay in attempting to reinstate her suit obliterated her opportunity to obtain restitution. Illinois entertains independent actions for restitution, when a judgment that has been satisfied later is reversed. . . . Whether such an independent suit would be appropriate in light of other circumstances that are not in the record (such as whether Zurn has made a timely demand of Botti for restitution) is something on which we offer no comment. It is enough to say that Zurn retains at least a potential for restitution under state law.

Although neither of the district judge's reasons is convincing, its judgment nonetheless is correct, for the reason given by the bankruptcy judge. Zurn's bankruptcy ended in 1996. The plan of reorganization has been fully implemented; there is nothing to "enforce" and no reason to reopen and alter the plan. Zurn's belief that anyone who has been a debtor in bankruptcy has eternal access to federal court for all disputes related in some way to the debts handled in the bankruptcy proceeding is incompatible not only with *Pettibone* but with many other cases, none of which Zurn discusses. . . . Suppose that a Chapter 13 plan called for a debtor to pay in full for a car, and thus retain title, and that after the confirmation of the plan a warranty dispute occurred. Would the bankruptcy judge be called on to determine whether the car's transmission had been repaired to the debtor's satisfaction? Certainly not; the federal role ended with the decision that the car would be paid for and retained rather than abandoned. Other disputes concerning the car belong to state tribunals. . . . Zurn conceded at oral argument that disputes of this kind could not be brought back to federal court but argues that her dispute differs because the state litigation was ongoing at the time of the federal bankruptcy. But that was equally true in *Pettibone*, where the bankruptcy court abstained and left resolution of the parties' dispute to state tribunals. After the bankruptcy ended, the parties could not agree on the effect in the state cases of the automatic stay in bankruptcy; even though this dispute (unlike the Zurn-Botti imbroglio) was related to federal law, we held in *Pettibone* that jurisdiction once relinquished stays relinquished. When a bankruptcy court abstains and permits state courts to handle pending litigation, the parties must thereafter look to the state courts to handle their *complete* dispute and may not drag selected issues back to the bankruptcy forum years later.

Section 350(b) allows a district judge to reopen a bankruptcy proceeding, but use of that power is reserved for matters such as the correction of errors . . . amendments necessitated by unanticipated events that frustrate a plan's implementation, and the need to enforce the plan and discharge. . . . Reversal of a civil judgment that created a claim against the estate does not warrant reopening; reversal affects the amount of a given claim, not the plan's provisions for satisfying claims. Zurn's plan promised payment in full; and if events mean that "in full" is less than the debtor anticipated, still this does not call the plan itself into question. It just provides an occasion for the use of whatever remedies Zurn has under state law.

It is unfortunate that Botti's obduracy has prolonged this dispute. Lawyers should comply with their legal duties—including the duty to make restitution . . . — rather than compel former clients to resort to still more litigation to vindicate their rights. Behavior such as Botti's brings the legal profession into disrepute. . . . If litigation must continue, however, the right forum is state court, just as the bankruptcy judge concluded.

Affirmed

BUSINESS CONSIDERATIONS What should Zurn have done when the Illinois appellate court overturned the damage award to Botti?

ETHICAL CONSIDERATIONS Is it ethical for a person who loses a lawsuit to file a petition in bankruptcy to avoid paying the judgment? Is it ethical for a person who has a judgment overturned on appeal to fail to return the money paid to satisfy the judgment? Which party was more ethical in this case?

EXHIBIT **28.2** A Comparison of the Bankruptcy Alternatives

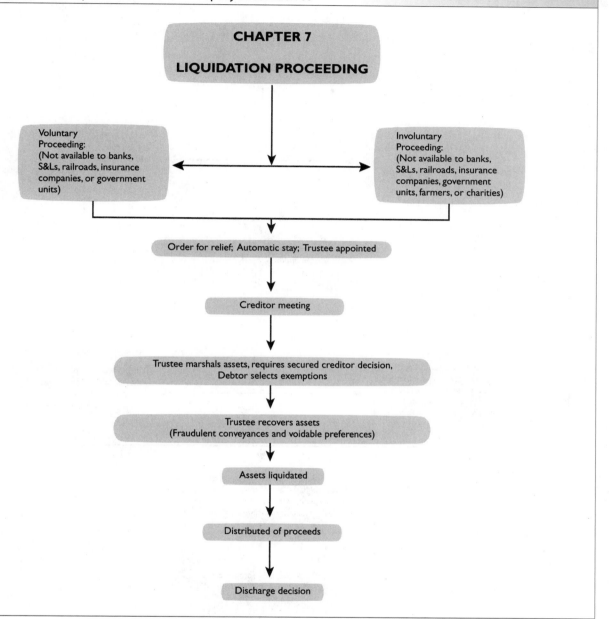

CHAPTER 7

LIQUIDATION PROCEEDING

Voluntary Proceeding:
(Not available to banks, S&Ls, railroads, insurance companies, or government units)

Involuntary Proceeding:
(Not available to banks, S&Ls, railroads, insurance companies, government units, farmers, or charities)

Order for relief; Automatic stay; Trustee appointed

Creditor meeting

Trustee marshals assets, requires secured creditor decision, Debtor selects exemptions

Trustee recovers assets
(Fraudulent conveyances and voidable preferences)

Assets liquidated

Distributed of proceeds

Discharge decision

EXHIBIT 28.2 *continued*

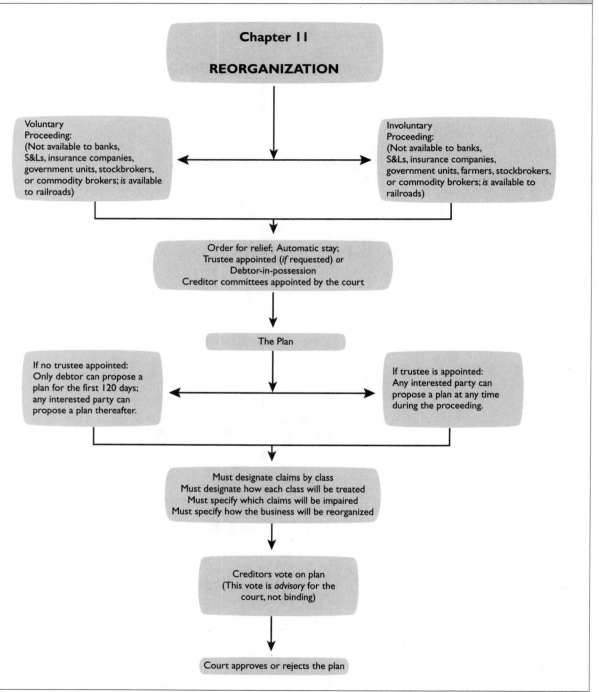

EXHIBIT 28.2 *continued*

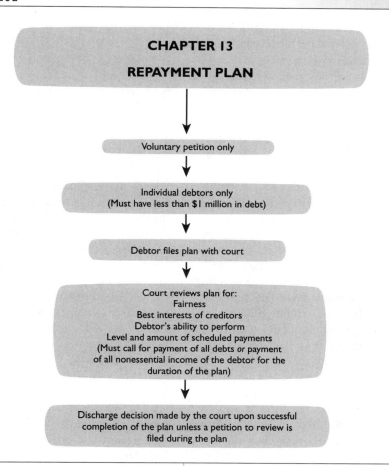

The [Proposed] Bankruptcy Reform Act

Despite the improvements that have been made in the bankruptcy laws since the Bankruptcy Reform Act of 1978 was passed, a number of people continue to complain about the bankruptcy provisions. To many creditors, bankruptcy is considered too easy to use, too readily available, and too often abused by the debtors taking advantage of its provisions. The U.S. Chamber of Commerce—a staunch advocate of bankruptcy reform—provides some interesting data in support of this position. According to the U.S. Chamber of Commerce,[16] in 1997, 1.33 million consumer bankruptcy petitions were filed. These bankruptcies erased $40 billion in consumer debt. They further cite the fact that, according to *Investor's Business Daily,* in 95 percent of all Chapter 7 proceedings *no* assets are liquidated—meaning that there is virtually *no* money available for the creditors at the conclusion of the proceeding. It is estimated that consumer bankruptcies costs each family in the United States $550 a year in higher costs for credit, goods, and services.[17] As a result, a new Bankruptcy Reform Act has been introduced, and it has an excellent chance of being passed by Congress.

The current version of the proposed Bankruptcy Reform Act includes means testing for any debtor seeking relief under Chapter 7, a defined "median income" level that will be applied to Chapter 13 proceedings, and new time restrictions for when a debtor may seek relief in bankruptcy under various possible scenarios, among other changes.[18]

The new means test proposed for Chapter 7 is somewhat complicated. The debtor will have to prepare a schedule of "current monthly income" based on the monthly average of all household income received for the six months preceding the petition. Deductions are then taken from this average monthly income, based on the criteria set out in the statute (these criteria are intended to provide the debtor with enough income to live a relatively normal, though hardly extravagant, life). If the debtor has average monthly income remaining after the deductions are taken, and that remaining balance is $166.67 per month or more, the debtor is presumed to be abusing the bankruptcy system, and he or she will be removed from the Chapter 7 proceeding. If the debtor has less than $166.67 per month, but at least $100 per month, abuse is presumed if the balance would pay at least 25 percent of the debtor's unsecured debts over five years. If the debtor has less than $100 per month remaining after the deductions, abuse of the system is never presumed.

Chapter 13 repayment plans would have to provide for the repayment of secured claims in equal installments. In addition, the debtor will be expected to pay all claims in full with interest or the debtor will be required to pay all of his or her defined "median income" for five years. And there are additional debts that will not be discharged upon successful completion of the plan. Among these are claims based on fraud of the debtor, including credit card misuse, claims based on "unfiled, late-filed, and fraudulent tax returns," and claims of creditors who were not notified in time to allow them to assert their claims in the proceeding.

The proposed reform act is supposed to be "needs based," and to provide protection for the creditors as well as the debtor. In an effort to help avoid the perceived "system abuses" that are of such concern today, there is also an expectation that debtors will be required to take some form of credit counseling or credit management class before a discharge will be granted.

Bankruptcy in the International Environment

Bankruptcy is not just an American—or even an Anglo-American—phenomenon anymore. There are numerous international statutes and treatments for bankruptcy, and as business becomes more global it is likely that other statutes and treatments will be enacted. For example, UNCITRAL, the United Nations international trade law body, is developing its "Model Law on Cross-Border Insolvency" with the intention of urging cooperation between the states that are affected, providing greater legal certainty for trade and investment, and ensuring fair and efficient administration in order to protect the interests of all interested parties. The draft of this model law can be found at http://www.uncitral.org/english/texts/insolven/ml+guide.htm. The European Union has developed its own regulations for insolvency proceedings within the Union. These regulations can be found at http://www.abiworld.org/international/euinso.html/. Insolvency laws for 28 different nations besides the United States are cited at the American Bankruptcy Institute Web site, http://www.abiworld.org/international/foreign.html.

The development and recognition of various insolvency statutes and treaties should be an important and an exciting aspect of international business over the next several years.

Summary

Federal law governs the topic of bankruptcy, which is designed to give an honest debtor a fresh start. The Bankruptcy Reform Act, which took effect in October 1979, provided for the establishment of bankruptcy courts as a separate branch of the U.S. district court system. These courts were to be presided over by bankruptcy judges who specialized in handling bankruptcy petitions. Following a constitutional challenge to the bankruptcy courts established by the Bankruptcy Reform Act, the Bankruptcy Amendments and Federal Judgeship Act of 1984 modified these bankruptcy courts and severely restricted the authority of the courts and judges. The Bankruptcy Reform Act of 1994 added a number of additional provisions designed to close loopholes and to further balance the rights of the parties in a bankruptcy proceeding. This act also includes a built-in adapter in an effort to keep the dollar amounts involved in bankruptcy current without the need to amend the Code every few years.

Under Chapter 7 (Liquidation), bankruptcy can be initiated by the debtor's voluntary petition or the creditors' involuntary petition against the debtor. Five types of "public interest" corporations are prohibited from filing a voluntary petition; any other debtor may file such a petition, even if solvent. Creditors may file an involuntary petition against most debtors, although there are seven classes of debtors who are exempt from an involuntary petition. Even for those debtors who are legally subject to an involuntary petition, there are safeguards. An involuntary petition can be filed only if the debtor is "guilty" of specified conduct, the proper number of creditors join the petition, and the proper amount of unsecured debts is involved.

Once the petition is filed, a judge appoints a trustee to administer the bankrupt's estate. The trustee is to preserve the estate for the protection of the unsecured creditors. The debtor is allowed some exemptions so that a fresh start is possible, but the rest of the estate is available for settling debts. Secured creditors must choose between removing themselves and their collateral from the bankruptcy or surrendering their security interest and participating in the proceedings. Once the exempt property and the collateral securing certain loans is removed, the balance of the estate is liquidated and the proceeds are applied to the allowable claims of the creditors.

The proceeds are applied first to priority classes set up by the Bankruptcy Reform Act. After all priority classes are paid in full, the remaining proceeds are applied to the claims of the unsecured creditors. The debtor will then seek a discharge. If the debtor has been honest and has cooperated, a discharge will probably be granted. If not, the debts will continue.

An embattled debtor need not always go through liquidation in order to make a fresh start; other bankruptcy and nonbankruptcy remedies may work equally well.

Under bankruptcy, the debtor may seek a reorganization under Chapter 11 or a repayment plan under Chapter 13. Each of these requires court approval of a plan, and each requires the debtor to propose the plan in good faith.

In a reorganization, the debtor adjusts his or her financial position to allow a business to continue. In a repayment plan, the debtor proposes a method of repaying debts over a three- to five-year period. Good faith and fairness are essential in any plans before they will be approved by the courts. Recently, Chapter 11 has been used as a corporate strategy, allowing corporations to escape liabilities or obligations that the firm feels are blatantly unfair or may lead to the demise of the organization.

There is a proposed Bankruptcy Reform Act that, if enacted, would substantially change this area of law. Debtors would be restricted from using Chapter 7 under many circumstances and would be forced to resort either to Chapter 13 and a repayment plan, or to nonbankruptcy alternatives, to resolve their financial woes.

There is an increasing international development of insolvency laws and regulations. Many of these laws seem to be more concerned with assuring that creditors are paid than with providing a fresh start for an honest debtor. Since more and more businesses are involved in international and multinational activities, the availability of some sort of international remedies is likely to continue to grow.

Discussion Questions

1. What are the two major purposes of the 1978 Bankruptcy Reform Act? What public policy considerations support these two purposes? What public policy considerations oppose these two purposes?

2. What are the five classes of debtors who cannot file a voluntary petition for a Chapter 7 bankruptcy? What are the seven classes of debtors who cannot be involuntarily petitioned into Chapter 7 bankruptcy? What are the public policy considerations for excluding these debtors from a Chapter 7 bankruptcy proceeding?

3. Before a debtor can be involuntarily petitioned into bankruptcy, the petitioning creditors must satisfy three tests. What are they? Why must these tests be satisfied prior to the imposition of an involuntary bankruptcy proceeding?

4. On August 1 of last year, Martha filed a voluntary bankruptcy petition, seeking relief under Chapter 7 of the Bankruptcy Code. Included among the debts she listed on her schedule of assets and liabilities were a $30,000 loan with 18 percent interest per annum from Last Bank and Trust dated June 1 of last year; an employment contract with her housekeeper for the next three years; and a lease on her apartment that runs for five more years. She has not paid her housekeeper for the past two months, nor has she paid her rent for the past three months. What portion of each of these debts will be allowable in the bankruptcy proceeding?

5. What does it mean when a debtor "loads up" with debts prior to filing a bankruptcy petition? How does bankruptcy law deal with this problem? Is this treatment an appropriate solution to the problem of debtors who load up with debts in anticipation of bankruptcy?

6. Why are alimony and child support obligations not discharged in a bankruptcy proceeding? Is such a rule good or bad, from a public policy perspective? Do the same justifications apply to not permitting the discharge of taxes or student loans?

7. What role does the examiner play in a reorganization under Chapter 11? How is this different from the role that a trustee plays in a Chapter 11 reorganization? How is the role of the trustee different in Chapter 11 from his or her role in Chapter 7?

8. The 1984 Bankruptcy Amendments provide some rather specific guidelines for a repayment plan under Chapter 13. What does the court look at in deciding whether to approve a repayment plan under these guidelines? How does this differ from the requirements for a repayment plan under the original Bankruptcy Reform Act? What can a creditor do to challenge a plan under Chapter 13?

9. What can the court do under a repayment plan if, owing to a change in circumstances, the debtor cannot complete the plan as approved by the court? Who may ask the court to intercede and to change the repayment plan?

10. What public policy considerations might lead a court to prefer a Chapter 11 reorganization over a Chapter 7 liquidation for a corporation seeking relief in bankruptcy? What considerations will lead the court to order a removal from Chapter 11 to Chapter 7 when a corporation files its petition for reorganization under Chapter 11?

Case Problems and Writing Assignments

1. Certain transfers made before the filing of a petition in bankruptcy may be avoided as impermissibly preferential. However, a trustee may not so displace a security interest for a loan used to acquire the encumbered property if, among other things, the security interest is "perfected on or before 20 days after the debtor receives possession of such property." On August 17, 1994, Diane Beasley purchased a 1994 Ford and gave petitioner, Fidelity Financial Services, a promissory note for the purchase price, secured by the new car. Twenty-one days later, on September 7, 1994, Fidelity mailed the application necessary to perfect its security interest to the Missouri Department of Revenue. Two months after that, Beasley sought relief under Chapter 7 of the Bankruptcy Code. After the proceeding had been converted to one under Chapter 13, Richard V. Fink, the trustee of Beasley's bankruptcy estate, moved to set aside Fidelity's security interest. He argued that the lien was a voidable preference, and the enabling loan exception did not apply because Fidelity had failed to perfect its interest within 20 days after Beasley received the car. Fidelity responded that Missouri law treats a lien on a motor vehicle as having been "perfected" on the date of its creation (in this case, within the 20-day period), if the creditor files the necessary documents within 30 days after the debtor takes possession. The Bankruptcy Court set aside the lien as a voidable preference, holding that Missouri's relation-back provision could not extend the 20-day perfection period imposed by § 547(c)(3)(B). Fidelity appealed to the U.S. District Court for the Western District of Missouri, which affirmed on substantially the same grounds, as did the Court of Appeals for the Eighth Circuit, holding a transfer to be perfected "when the transferee takes the last step required by state law to perfect its security interest." May a creditor invoke this "enabling loan" exception if it performs the acts necessary to perfect its security interest more than 20 days after the debtor receives the property, but within a relation-back or grace period provided by the otherwise applicable state law? [See *Financial Services, Inc. v. Fink*, 522 U.S. 211. 118 S. Ct. 651. 1998 U.S. LEXIS 456 (1998).]

2. On March 29, 1993, Kenneth W. Bass proposed that he give his 152-acre farm in Dane County, Wisconsin, to his daughter Marcia Fillion, and her husband, with the conditions that Fillion assume the $18,000 mortgage on the farm and forgive another $5,000 debt her father owed her, and also that Bass retain a life estate in the buildings on the property. Fillion agreed, and a deed specifying these terms was drawn up and signed. Bass claimed that at the same meeting, as part of the same transaction, Fillion agreed to support her father for the rest of his life. Fillion disputed this version, claiming that the only conditions to the gift of the farm were included in the deed. In June 1994, Marcia and Robin Fillion (and their three children) moved onto the farm. Then in September, they moved from a trailer on the farm to the house also occupied by Bass. At this point, the Fillions began paying for the mortgage, taxes, gas, and food.

Unfortunately for all concerned, the relationship between Bass and the Fillions became acrimonious almost immediately. After about two years of domestic disturbances, Bass filed a civil action in state court seeking to eject the Fillions from the farm and to rescind the deed giving the farm to Marcia Fillion. During this state court litigation, Bass and the Fillions agreed to sell 40 acres of the farm to the Wisconsin Department of Natural Resources (leaving 112 acres). The proceeds were used to satisfy a sales tax lien incurred by Bass, and the balance was paid to the mortgagee. Just days before Bass's motion for partial summary judgment was to be heard by the state court, the Fillions filed a Chapter 13 bankruptcy petition. On the date of the hearing before the state court, the Fillions did not appear, but Bass and the state court were notified of the bankruptcy filing. In violation of the automatic stay imposed by a voluntary bankruptcy filing, Bass requested a default judgment against the Fillions for ejectment. This constituted a continuation of a judicial proceeding against the debtors, and was prohibited by § 362(a)(1) of the Bankruptcy Code. The Fillions filed their Chapter 13 plan in September 1997. This plan proposed to sell part of the farm and to use the proceeds to satisfy the claims of creditors, including Bass. Bass objected to this plan, claiming that the plan was not feasible. Bass also initiated an adversary proceeding in the bankruptcy court on his rescission claim. The bankruptcy court denied the objection to the Chapter 13 plan and granted summary judgment to the Fillions on the rescission claim. Bass appealed both adverse decisions to the district court, which affirmed. He then appealed these decisions. Should the court approve a repayment plan over the objection of a creditor of the debtors? [See *In re Fillion*, 1999 U.S. App. LEXIS 14220 (7th Cir. 1999).]

3. Bustop Shelters entered into several contracts with Classic. These contracts called for Classic to install 400 shelters at designated bus stops from kits provided by Bustop, to perform periodic maintenance on the installed shelters, and to clean each of the shelters weekly. Bustop and Classic subsequently filed suits against one another, each alleging breach of the contract by the other. Classic prevailed, receiving a damage award in the amount of $440,000. As a result, Bustop filed for relief under Chapter 11, availing itself of the automatic stay provision before Classic could enforce its judgment. Bustop proceeded to submit a reorganization plan under Chapter 11 during its 120-day exclusive period. In this plan, Bustop listed three classes of creditors: Class 1, Citizens Bank, based on a fully secured loan; Class 2, unsecured creditors owed between $201 and $20,000; and Class 3, unsecured creditors owed more than $20,000. (The only creditor in Class 3 was Classic.) The creditors in Classes 1 and 2 approved the plan, while the Class 3 creditor (Classic) rejected it. Bustop then asked the court to approve the plan, despite this rejection by Class 3, under the "cramdown" provisions of the Bankruptcy Code. Classic objected to this request. According to Classic, there should have been only two classes of creditors: Class 1, secured credi-

tors, and Class 2, unsecured creditors. According to Classic, the secured creditors were not impaired by the plan, while the unsecured creditors were impaired. If the unsecured creditors were treated as a single class, this class would have rejected the plan, negating the availability of the "cramdown" provisions. How should the court resolve these issues? [See *Bustop Shelters of Louisville v. Classic Homes*, 914 F.2d 810 (6th Cir. 1990).]

4. Holt purchased a 1988 Ford Aerostar, signing a promissory note and security agreement with Dana Federal Credit Union to finance the purchase. This loan was executed in connection with an open line of credit extended by Dana to Holt on March 22, 1988. On May 22, 1995, Holt filed a voluntary petition for relief under Chapter 7 of the Bankruptcy Code. In his schedule of debts, Holt listed Dana as an unsecured creditor with a claim of $6,012.87. (There were only four other unsecured creditors listed, each with a claim of less than $300.) Dana asserted it was owed $7,926.88. The Aerostar was not listed among Holt's assets, and the court presumed that either the van had already been repossessed or it had no value as of the petition date. Holt proposed to discharge in full his debt to Dana through the Chapter 7 proceeding; Dana objected to the discharge by asserting that Holt had knowingly and fraudulently made numerous false oaths and that he failed to explain the loss of assets that occurred immediately preceding the petition. According to Holt's schedule of assets, he had $7 in cash, $400 in his checking account, and $25 in his savings account on the petition date. However, three days prior to the petition date Holt had a checking account balance of more than $2,350, and a savings account balance of more than $4,500. Holt also denied depositing any of his severance pay of $9,162 in either his checking or savings accounts, although bank records indicated that he had deposited $4,500 in each of the accounts on the day that he received the severance pay check. Should the court deny a discharge to a debtor who cannot satisfactorily explain the dissipation of his assets immediately preceding his petition for relief under the Bankruptcy Code? [See *Matter of Holt*, 190 B.R. (Bankr. N.D. Ala. 1996).]

5. BUSINESS APPLICATION CASE Bank of America was the major creditor of 203 North LaSalle Street Partnership. The Bank loaned North LaSalle some $93 million, secured by a non-recourse first mortgage on North LaSalle's principal asset, 15 floors of an office building in downtown Chicago. In January 1995, North LaSalle defaulted, and the Bank began foreclosure in a state court. In March, North LaSalle responded with a voluntary petition for relief under Chapter 11 of the Bankruptcy Code, which automatically stayed the foreclosure proceedings. The North LaSalle's principal objective was to ensure that its partners retained title to the property so as to avoid roughly $20 million in personal tax liabilities, which would fall due if the Bank foreclosed. North LaSalle proceeded to propose a reorganization plan during the 120-day period when it alone had the right to do so. The Bankruptcy Court rejected the Bank's motion to terminate the period of exclusivity to make way for a plan of its own to liquidate the property and instead extended the exclusivity period. The value of the mortgaged property was less than the balance due the Bank, which elected to divide its undersecured claim into secured and unsecured deficiency claims.

Under the plan, North LaSalle separately classified the Bank's secured claim, its unsecured deficiency claim, and unsecured trade debt owed to other creditors. The Bankruptcy Court found that North LaSalle's available assets were prepetition rents in a cash account of $3.1 million and the 15 floors of rental property worth $54.5 million. The secured claim was valued at the latter figure, leaving the Bank with an unsecured deficiency of $38.5 million. North LaSalle's plan also provided the following: (1) The Bank's $54.5 million secured claim would be paid in full between 7 and 10 years after the original 1995 repayment date. (2) The Bank's $38.5 million unsecured deficiency claim would be discharged for an estimated 16 percent of its present value. (3) The remaining unsecured claims of $90,000, held by the outside trade creditors, would be paid in full, without interest, on the effective date of the plan. (4) Certain former partners of North LaSalle would contribute $6.125 million in new capital over the course of 5 years (the contribution being worth some $4.1 million in present value), in exchange for the Partnership's entire ownership of the reorganized debtor. The last condition was an exclusive eligibility provision: the old equity holders were the only ones who could contribute new capital. The Bank objected and, as the sole member of an impaired class of creditors, thereby blocked confirmation of the plan on a consensual basis. North LaSalle, however, took the alternate route to confirmation of a reorganization plan, forthrightly known as the judicial "cramdown" process for imposing a plan on a dissenting class.

Can a debtor's prebankruptcy equity holder contribute new capital and receive ownership interests in the reorganized entity, despite any objections by a senior class of impaired creditors? Should the court use the cramdown process in this case to approve the plan over the objections of the Bank? [See *Bank of America National Trust and Savings Association v. 203 North LaSalle Street Partnership*, 119 S. Ct. 1411; 1999 U.S. LEXIS 3003 (1999).]

6. ETHICAL APPLICATION CASE Poor applied to Chase Visa for a credit card in May 1997. The application incorporated a "Chase Visa Balance Transfer Form" inviting Poor to "complete this form today to pay off your outstanding balances at a low fixed APR of just 7.9%. You can transfer one, two, or three balances to your new Chase Visa." Poor accepted the invitation when she applied for a Chase Gold Visa account, requesting the transfer of $3,400.00 of debt from her MBNA MasterCard and $2,600.00 from a Choice Visa account. In a letter dated June 9, 1997, Chase notified Poor that it had approved her application and had opened her new Gold Visa account with a $7,300.00 credit limit. The missive went on to state: "As you requested, we are transferring the following balances to your new account: Payee MBNA America, Amount $3,400.00 Check 5000 Status Balance Transferred." Poor claims to have received her Chase gold card on June 17, 1997. Chase effected the $3,400.00 payment to MBNA by a check and that check "cleared" on June 20, 1997. On that date Chase charged $3,400.00 to Poor's Visa account. On June 26, 1997, Poor withdrew $350.00 cash on credit through

the Chase account. Poor had been involved in a disabling automobile accident on June 8, 1997, and the injuries she suffered led to unemployment. Poor and her husband filed a joint Chapter 7 petition on August 19, 1997. Chase argued that the obligations created by two transactions—a $3,400.00 balance transfer and a $350.00 credit cash withdrawal—were excepted from Poor's Chapter 7 discharge. It argued that the debts came within § 523(a)(2)(C)'s nondischargeability presumption on "loading up" debts. Did the balance transfer qualify as a "cash advance," and thus as a "loading up" debt under the provisions of the Bankruptcy Code? [See *In re Poor*, 219 B.R. 332 (1998).]

7. CRITICAL THINKING CASE Petitioner owned several residential properties in and around Hoboken, New Jersey, one of which was subject to a local rent control ordinance. In 1989, the Hoboken Rent Control Administrator determined that petitioner had been charging rents above the levels permitted by the ordinance and ordered him to refund to the affected tenants $31,382.50 in excess rents charged. Petitioner did not comply with the order. Petitioner subsequently filed for relief under Chapter 7 of the Bankruptcy Code, seeking to discharge his debts. The tenants filed an adversary proceeding against petitioner in the Bankruptcy Court, arguing that the debt owed to them arose from rent payments obtained by "actual fraud" and that the debt was therefore nondischargeable under 11 U.S.C. § 523(a)(2)(A). They also sought treble damages and attorney's fees and costs pursuant to the New Jersey Consumer Fraud Act. Following a bench trial, the Bankruptcy Court ruled in the tenants' favor. The court found that petitioner had committed "actual fraud" and that his conduct amounted to an "unconscionable commercial practice" under the New Jersey Consumer Fraud Act. As a result, the court awarded the tenants treble damages totaling $94,147.50, plus reasonable attorney's fees and costs. Noting that courts had reached conflicting conclusions on whether § 523(a)(2)(A) excepts from discharge punitive damages (such as the treble damages at issue here), the Bankruptcy Court sided with those decisions holding that § 523(a)(2)(A) encompasses all obligations arising out of fraudulent conduct, including both punitive and compensatory damages. The court observed that the term "debt," defined in the Code as a "right to payment," plainly encompasses all liability for fraud, whether in the form of punitive or compensatory damages. And the phrase "to the extent obtained by," the court reasoned, modifies "money, property, services, or credit," and therefore distinguishes not between compensatory and punitive damages awarded for fraud but instead between money or property obtained through fraudulent means and money or property obtained through nonfraudulent means. Here the entire award of $94,147.50 (plus attorney's fees and costs) resulted from money obtained through fraud and is therefore nondischargeable.

Does the Bankruptcy Code bar the discharge of treble damages awarded on account of the debtor's fraudulent acquisition of "money, property, services, or credit," or does the exception encompass only the value of the "money, property, services, or credit" the debtor obtains through fraud? [See *Cohen v. DeLaCruz*, 118 S. Ct. 1212, 1998 U.S. LEXIS 2119 (1998).]

8. YOU BE THE JUDGE Jefley, Inc. owned and operated four retail supermarkets. In 1997 Jefley filed a voluntary Chapter 11 bankruptcy petition, at least in part due to large claims against the debtor and its owner (Jefley) by the Internal Revenue Service. The IRS was seeking to recoup untaxed profits from a fraudulent scheme involving improper remittances of manufacturers' discount coupons. The debtor then submitted a reorganization plan that included closing its least profitable store and eliminating some of its administrative staff positions. It also negotiated a "pot" plan of reorganization calling for the debtor to remit, for the benefit of unsecured creditors, $100,000 on the effective date of the plan and then $175,000 annually for the next six years. These payments would result in a recovery of between 10 percent and 38 percent percent for unsecured creditors, depending on the outcome of objections to certain of the claims. A hearing on the plan was scheduled, and this hearing led to a finding of the following facts: The debtor is a party to two collective bargaining agreements with the United Food and Commercial Workers Union. The first, with Local 56, includes 25 to 28 butchers, wrappers, and sellers of meat and seafood. The other, with Local 1360, includes 110 to 119 retail clerks. The debtor wanted to modify both labor contracts in order to reduce labor costs by about $720,000, with approximately $125,000 coming from the modification with Local 56 and the remaining $595,000 from modification with Local 1360, to comply with the terms of the plan. This proposal also contemplated a reduction in the combined salaries of Jefley and his wife, Joni, who works on a regular but less than full-time basis as an administrator, from $670,000 to $350,000 annually. The proposed modifications to the union contracts included reductions in vacation times, holidays, and personal days; a freeze on employees' pensions and health and welfare contributions; an increase from 16 hours to 20 hours in the minimum weekly work time necessary to qualify for health and welfare benefits; reductions of premiums for working on Sundays; and the placement of a cap of $10.00 on cashiers' hourly rates. The proposal also included a "snapback," whereby one-third of the profits generated in excess of projections were to be disbursed to union members. Local 56 agreed to the proposal, but Local 1360 voted against the proposed modifications. Local 1360 also questioned the salaries and benefits paid to Jefley and his wife. In reply, Jefley testified that he needed $90,000 net annually to pay his personal share of restitution due as a result of the coupon fraud and $30,000 to send his two children, described as having an attention deficit disorder and reading problems, respectively, to remedial schools. Jefley and his family also receive the full use of a 1997 Landcruiser rented by the debtor for $950 monthly and full health and welfare benefits. Jefley is now asking the court to allow him to reject the collective bargaining agreement with Local 1360 and to then approve his plan as submitted. This proceeding has been brought before *your* court. Will *you* allow the debtor to reject the collective bargaining agreement in order to effectuate his reorganization plan? Explain. [See *In re Jefley, Inc.*, 219 B.R. 88; 1998 Bankr. LEXIS 211 (Bankr. E.D. Penn. 1998).]

Notes

1. "A Brief History of Bankruptcy in the U.S.," *2001 Bankruptcy Yearbook and Almanac*, found at http://www.bankruptcydata.com/Ch11History.htm/.

2. Ibid.

3. Ibid.

4. Ibid.

5. 458 U.S. 50 (1982).

6. U.S. Constitution, Article III, Section 1.

7. Bankruptcy Reform Act of 1994, 11 U.S.C. § 326.

8. Ibid., § 109(e).

9. Administrative Office of the U.S. Courts, Statistical Tables for the Federal Judiciary, http:www.census.gov/statab/.

10. Ibid.

11. Ibid. In 1990, there were 723,886 voluntary petitions out of 725,484. In 1996, some 1,040,915 of 1,042,110 petitions were voluntary.

12. "Bankruptcy Filing Fee Increase," *Nolo Law for All*, http://www.nolo.com/lawstore (accessed 9/2/2002).

13. See, for example, "Reshaping Corporate America," *Management Accountant* 71, no. 9 (March 1990): 21; "Court Reverses Own Ruling: Negotiations Over Revised Manville Payout Plan to Continue," *Business Insurance* 27, no. 21 (May 1993): 2; Kevin J. Delaney, *Strategic Bankruptcy* (Berkeley: University of California Press, 1992).

14. 113 S. Ct. 2187 (1993).

15. H.R. 5116 § 306.

16. "Bankruptcy Reform," *U.S. Chamber of Commerce*, http://www.uschamber.com/policy/bankruptcy (accessed 3/19/99).

17. "Gekas Introduces Bankruptcy Reform Act for 106th Congress," George W. Gekas, U.S. Congressman, 17th District of Pennsylvania (February 24, 1999).

18. "Major Effects of the Consumer Bankruptcy Provisions of the 2002 Bankruptcy Legislation (H.R. 333 Conference Report)," prepared by Eugene R. Wedoff, Chief Judge, U.S. Bankruptcy Court, Northern District of Illinois.

Agency

People *dream* of being in two places at once. For example, they could be at work and a still take in that movie they want to see. Or they could attend that fundraiser *and* play a round of golf. Obviously, this must remain a dream because it is a physical impossibility. However, the law has found a way to do legally what cannot be done physically, and it is a good thing the law has managed to do so. Without this legal flexibility, business as we know it could not be conducted. But through the "magic" provided by the law, a person can *legally* be in more than one place at the same time. A person can literally be in one location, and simultaneously, through his or her agent, that same person can effectively be in a second place, or a third, or even an unlimited number of places. By using an agent, a person can legally be in more than one place at a time.

An agent is a person empowered to "be you" within the scope of the agency. Whatever the agent hears in the agency, the law treats as if you "heard it." Whatever the agent says in the agency, the law treats as if you "said" it. Whatever an agent does in the agency, the law holds you responsible for, as if you "did" the act. In other words, you are legally responsible for your agent's conduct, but only when the conduct is within the scope of the agency.

A businessperson derives obvious benefits from "being" in many places at the same time; however, if the agent does not act properly, many problems may arise. Part 6 explores these areas, discussing the various benefits and problems that may occur in the course and scope of an agency.

Agency: Creation and Termination

AGENDA

NRW NRW started out as a small firm, and its principals did most of the work themselves. But as the business grows they will need to hire more workers, and these workers will have varied duties and responsibilities within the firm. As a result, Mai, Carlos, and Helen will need to understand the duties and responsibilities associated with the different jobs being performed. They will also need to understand their responsibilities and obligations owed to employees and to members of the public with whom the employees may interact. What types of relationships might be involved? Is it possible that the firm may be responsible for the actions of its employees?

NRW does not plan to make its own deliveries to its customers. In dealing with consumers, NRW will mail the StuffTrakRs that are ordered. In dealing with retailers, NRW plans to hire a common carrier to deliver the InvenTrakR units and, eventually, the StuffTrakR units ordered directly by its customers. If a common carrier is used, what is the legal relationship between NRW and the carrier? Is it possible that NRW can be held liable for any wrongful conduct by the carrier or by its drivers?

Mai is also concerned that some of the employees may decide to copy the concepts and the products that NRW has developed in order to start their own competing business. She is especially concerned that the salespeople, who already have a relationship with the firm's customers, would be in a position to compete effectively almost immediately. Is this a valid concern? What does NRW need to do to protect itself from such competition by former—or current—employees?

These and other questions will arise during our discussion of agency law. Be prepared! You never know when the firm or one of its members will seek your advice.

Agency Law and Agency Relationships

Agency law concerns the relationships between workers and the people who hire workers. It involves their duties and responsibilities both to each other and to the public at large. No one can really avoid agency law; almost everyone at some time works as an employee or hires an employee. Moreover, agency relationships arise not only in business situations but also in nonbusiness situations. Suppose that Marty has some books that are due back to the university library, but Marty has a review session that he cannot afford to miss. Marty asks Karen, a friend who is already going to the library, if she would take the books back for him. If Karen agrees to do so, she will be acting an as *agent* for Marty.

Most agency relationships do not require litigation because they function smoothly. To resolve the legal problems that do arise, one must look to agency law, contract law, and tort law. In most of these areas, the court will place significant reliance on state law. Much of the law of agency has been studied by the American Law Institute and is discussed in its publication, Restatement (Second) of Agency. (You can visit the American Law Institute (ALI) Web site at http://www.ali.org/.) The Restatements are treatises that summarize detailed recommendations of what the law should be on a particular subject. Although Restatements are not legislature- or court-made law, they become part of the legal precedents when courts rely on them and incorporate them into court decisions. (Legal *precedents* are prior court cases that control future decisions. See Chapter 1 for a more detailed discussion of precedents.) The three agency chapters in this book rely on the provisions found in the Restatement (Second) of Agency for the formulation of majority rules and for general guidance in the discussion of agency law.

You should note that the position of your state may vary from that in the Restatement. You should check for variations followed in your state when issues arise. The Restatement (Second) of Agency explains some key terms:

- Agency is the fiduciary relation which results from the manifestation of consent by one person to another that the other shall act on his [sic] behalf and subject to his control, and consent by the other so to act.

- The one for whom action is to be taken is the principal.

- The one who is to act is the agent.[1]

An *agency relationship* is consensual in nature. It is based on the concept that the parties mutually agree that (1) the agent will act on behalf of the principal; and (2) the agent will be subject to the principal's direction and control. The agreement can be expressed or implied. In addition, the parties must be competent to act as principal and agent. A distinguishing characteristic is that an agent represents the principal and derives his or her authority from the principal. (You can visit the Cornell Law School Web site at http://www.law.cornell.edu/topical.html for an overview of agency law. Using the topical outline, look under Enterprise Law—Agency.)

Analysis of Agency Relationships

While most agency relationships do not involve litigation, sometimes litigation will occur. When problems arise, you will need to determine which aspect of the agency relationship is involved in order to properly determine what the result should be. To analyze a situation involving an agency relationship, ask these questions:

- Was the dispute between the principal and the agent?

- Was the agency formed voluntarily by the principal and the agent, or is there some other relationship between the parties?

- Did the parties have the capacity to perform their roles as the principal and the agent?

- What authority did the principal vest in the agent?

- Did the agent enter into a contract with a third person or commit a tort or crime harming a third person?

Restrictions on Creating an Agency Relationship

Agency law affects a broad range of situations, from a small partnership with two partners and no employees up to and including a corporation with thousands of employees, and from a highly skilled developer of computer peripherals to a 16-year-old babysitter. In fact, everything a corporation does, it does through agents. Agency is integral to business as it is conducted in the world today, and business as we know it could not exist without the use of agency law or something very closely akin to it.

There are few restrictions on who can form agency relationships and what can be done through agency relationships. In order to form a *lawful* agency relationship, the agreement must specify legal acts for the agent to perform. An agreement to distribute illegal drugs such as "crank," for example, could not be the basis for the creation of a lawful agency relationship. Since the basic agreement specifies an illegal act, no agency is created. An overview of agency law is available at 'Lectric Law Library, http://www.lectlaw.com/d-a.htm, under the letter A for Agent.

Capacity to Be a Principal

With the exception of minors and mental incompetents, any person can appoint an agent. It is generally true that any person having capacity to *contract* has capacity to employ a servant agent or a nonservant agent. (The distinction between these two agents is that a principal has more control over the actions of the former than over those of the latter. The distinction will be discussed in more detail later in this chapter.) Since agency is a consensual relationship, the principal must have capacity to confer a legally operative consent.[2]

Some states have determined that a minor lacks capacity to be a principal. In other states, a minor has the capacity to be a principal, but the agency relationship is voidable. The Restatement (Second) of Agency, § 20, takes the second position. In this second group of states, the agreements entered into by the minor's agent will also be voidable to the same extent as the minor's own contracts. The key to understanding this concept is to remember that the contract is really entered into by the principal. The agent is not a party to the contract, he or she is merely a "facilitator" in the formation of the agreement.

Capacity to Be an Agent

Generally, anyone can be an agent. Strange as it seems, even persons who do not have the capacity to act for themselves—for example, minors or insane persons—can act as agents for someone else. It is the capacity of the *principal*, not that of the agent, that controls. Obviously, however, principals should exercise care to appoint agents who are able to make sound decisions.

Duties an Agent Can Perform

A principal "appoints" an agent to deal with the public. Generally, an agent can be assigned to do almost any legal task. There are, however, some nondelegable duties such as the following:

• an employer's duty to provide safe working conditions.[3]

• a person's duty under some contract terms.

• a landlord's duty to tenants.

• a common carrier's duty to passengers. (A *common carrier* is a company in the business of transporting people or goods for a fee and serving the general public.)

• a person's duty under a license issued to that person.

• the duty of a person engaged in inherently dangerous work to take adequate precautions to avoid harm.

Other nondelegable duties are defined by various state statutes. Each state statute is distinct. If the duty is nondelegable and the principal attempts to delegate the duty to someone else, the principal will be personally liable if the task is not properly completed. When a duty is nondelegable, the tasks can be delegated but the responsibility for their proper completion cannot.

Types of Agency Relationships

General and Special Agents

The distinction between general and special agents is a matter of degree. A *special agent* is employed to complete one transaction or a simple series of transactions. The relationship covers a relatively limited period and is not continuous. A *general agent* is hired to conduct a series of transactions over time. The amount of discretion the agent has is immaterial in making the distinction between general and special agents. (*Discretion* is the right to use one's own judgment in selecting between alternatives.) The expertise of the agent is also immaterial.

In deciding whether an agent is a general agent or a special agent, courts should examine all of the following factors:

• the number of acts that will need to be completed to achieve the authorized result.

• the number of people who will need to be dealt with before achieving the desired result.

• the length of time that will be necessary to achieve the desired result.[4]

The manager of an electronics store is likely to be viewed as a general agent. He or she can reasonably be expected to have an ongoing, relatively permanent position with broad, general authority. In contrast, a person who collects a payment from a customer of the store on a one-time basis is a special agent. Categorizing an agent who is between these two extremes can be difficult. As Exhibit 29.1 shows, a continuum of relationships exists between the roles of special agents and those of general agents.

Gratuitous Agents

Payment is not necessary in a principal-agent relationship. If a person volunteers services without an agreement or an expectation of payment, that person may still be an agent. The requirements for a *gratuitous agency* are that one person volunteers to help another and the second person accepts this "free" assistance. For example, Susie offers to help Joel with his paper route. While she is driving to a customer's home to deliver a newspaper, she fails to stop at a stop sign and collides with Ray's vehicle. The courts *can* find that Susie works for Joel and therefore that Joel is liable for the damage Susie causes. Another example is if Beth is not feeling well the morning her legal environment homework is due. Angelica, a sorority sister, is in the same class. Beth asks Angelica to deliver the paper for her. Angelica arrives at class late and the instructor deducts late points from both Beth's paper and Angelica's paper. Beth will be held responsible for Angelica's acts. Note that, with few exceptions, the rights and duties of a gratuitous agent are the same as those of an agent who is being compensated. The primary differences are that the gratuitous agent can freely terminate his or her duty by giving notice to the principal that he or she will not continue. Since the gratuitous agent is not being compensated, there is no contract with

the principal, and thus no breach by the agent when he or she resigns, with or without advance notice.

Servants and Independent Contractors

Most workers are *either* servants or independent contractors. The distinction between the terms *servant* and *independent contractor* is confusing, partly because authors and judges apply differing definitions to these terms and partly because common usage differs from legal usage. This text uses the definitions of the Restatement (Second) of Agency. Under legal definitions, servants and employees are generally synonymous.[5] We generally use the term *servant* to describe someone who is subject to the control of his or her *master*. Either servants or independent contractors can also be agents. Agents have the authority to perform "legal acts." In other words, agents can represent their principals in contractual or other dealings with third parties.

Servants

A master is a special type of principal who has the right to tell his or her worker both what to do and how to do it. The worker then is included in a special class of workers called *servants* or *employees*. (The more modern term is *employee*.) A *servant* is one who works physically for the hiring party. A *master* (employer) has a right to control how the task is accomplished by the servant (employee). The actual exercise of this control is not necessary; it is

---

EXHIBIT 29.1 Distinction between Special Agents and General Agents

Relevant factors:	Special Agent	General Agent
Frequency of acts	Few acts or simple series of acts	Many acts or long series of acts
Number of people who will be contacted	Few people	Many people
Length of service	Short period of time	Longer period of time
Irrelevant factors:		
Discretion granted to agent		
Expertise of agent		

The exact number of people contacted and length of time are subject to interpretation by the court. This line constitutes a continuum and not discrete categories.

sufficient that the master has the *right* to control. Thus, interns in hospitals, airline pilots, sales clerks, and officers of corporations are commonly servants.

The distinction between servants and independent contractors is important, because a principal is rarely liable for the unauthorized *physical* acts of an independent contractor. Principals sometimes label a worker as an independent contractor in an attempt to escape liability, but the courts will look behind the designation and make a judgment about the true nature of the relationship. The distinction between servants and independent contractors is also important in determining rights and benefits under unemployment insurance laws, workers' compensation laws, income taxation, the Employee Retirement Income Security Act of 1974 (ERISA), employment discrimination, bankruptcy exemptions, and similar statutes and court precedents.

The distinction between an independent contractor and a servant is represented in Exhibit 29.2. Remember that this distinction is material only when there is a question about whether the hiring party is responsible for the physical acts of the worker. When the worker has entered into a contract for his or her employer, it is irrelevant whether the worker is a servant or an independent contractor.

Independent Contractors

An *independent contractor* is hired to complete a task for someone else. The physical acts of the independent contractor are not controlled or subject to the control of the hiring party. Instead, the independent contractor relies on his or her own expertise to determine the best way to complete the job. Anyone who contracts to do physical work for another does so as either a servant or an independent contractor. It is, however, possible for two people to have multiple working relationships between them and one person can be a servant as to some duties and an independent contractor as to others.

Courts look at many factors in distinguishing between servants and independent contractors. In addition to considering the *right* to control, courts commonly consider the following factors:

- whether the worker hires assistants
- whether payment is by the number of hours worked or by the job completed
- what is the length of time for which the services are to be performed
- who supplies the tools and equipment to be used
- where is the work being performed
- whether the worker is engaged in a distinct occupation or independent business
- whether the work is a part of the regular business of the principal

The court examined the working relationships of a truck driver in the case on pages 696–697. See if you agree with the court's determination of the status of the parties.

Independent contractors may be agents, but that is not a necessary condition for being an independent contractor. This is shown in Exhibit 29.3. If the independent contractor does not represent the hiring party or act for the hiring party in legal or contractual matters with third parties, the independent contractor is not the hiring party's agent. For example, a nonagent independent contractor who is building a house on an owner's lot cannot bind the owner to a contract. In these situations, the independent contractor does not owe the hiring party any fiduciary duties. A *fiduciary duty* is the legal duty to exercise the highest degree of loyalty and good faith in handling the affairs of another; a *fiduciary* is a person who owes a special duty of good faith and loyalty due to his or her status. Fiduciary relationships include attorney-client, priest-confessor, husband-wife, and

EXHIBIT 29.2 Distinction between Servants and Independent Contractors

Does the hiring party have the right to:	Servant	Independent Contractor
Control results (outcome)	Can control results	Can control results as specified in the agreement
Control physical acts (methods)	Can control specific details	Lack of control over details

The amount of control is subject to interpretation by the court. This line constitutes a continuum and not discrete categories.

29.1

HATHCOCK v. ACME TRUCK LINES, INC.
262 F.3d 522, 2001 U.S. App. LEXIS 19693 (5th Cir. 2001)

FACTS Acme transports equipment, materials, and supplies throughout the country. Bobby Hathcock, pursuant to a written agreement, leased his truck to Acme. The third paragraph of the lease agreement provides:

> As consideration for the use of the Leased Equipment . . . Lessee [Acme] agrees to pay Lessor [Hathcock] (70%) percent of the "Earned Revenue derived by the Lessee from the Leased Equipment [Hathcock's truck]," . . . less driver's wages; payroll taxes (including FICA and other deductions); cost of medical or hospitalization insurance, if applicable; . . . and such other costs or payments made by Lessee by reason of driver employment and less any "Operating costs and expenses," . . . which are incurred by Lessee in connection with the use and/or operation of the Leased Equipment. . . .

Acme gave Hathcock the option of choosing and designating the driver of his truck or allowing Acme to supply the driver for his truck. Hathcock chose to drive the truck himself. Pursuant to the lease agreement, Hathcock allocated 10 percent of his Lessor's revenue to driver's wages. Acme informed Hathcock that he would be paid by two separate checks, one for the lease of his truck and the other to him as the designated driver of that truck. This was consistent with company policy. In another writing, Acme told Hathcock of the fixed percentage of the driver's wages that it would deduct from the rental check to cover those driver-related costs specified in the lease as chargeable to Hathcock.

ISSUE Was Hathcock an employee and/or an independent contractor of Acme?

HOLDINGS Both. Hathcock was an employee when he was operating the truck on Acme's business: he was an independent contractor when he was leasing the truck to Acme.

REASONING Excerpts from the opinion of Circuit Judge Wiener:

Hathcock bases his claims on the proposition that Acme and only Acme is responsible for FICA, FUTA, and SUTA taxes. [FICA refers to Social Security or Federal Insurance Contribution Act taxes. FUTA refers to Federal Unemployment Tax Act taxes. SUTA refers to the state analogues of the FUTA taxes.]. . . . The legality of the payment system employed by Acme depends in large part on its statutory and contractual ability to treat Hathcock as an owner-lessor for some purposes while treating him as an employee for others. . . . Because most of Acme's lessor-owners do not choose to drive their own trucks, Acme's two-check system is the norm, and is commercially logical as well. . . . Hathcock's capacity vis-à-vis Acme when he drove the truck is material. If he were Acme's employee, then he created a portion of Acme's FICA, FUTA, and SUTA tax liability, making Acme's withholdings from Hathcock's driver paycheck not merely proper but mandated by state and federal tax law. Conversely, if Hathcock were an independent contractor when wearing his driver's hat, withholding monies from his rental check to cover Acme's employee expenses would have been improper. In fact, if Hathcock were an independent contractor when he drove, Acme would not have been responsible for withholding and remitting income, FICA, FUTA, and SUTA taxes because Acme is required to do that for its employees only.

Courts have developed various tests to differentiate employees from independent contractors. Case law from both Texas and Louisiana recognizes "the right to control an employee's conduct" as the most important component of the determination. The state appellate court in . . . [precedents] explained that Texas courts analyze five factors in determining the employer's degree of control: (1) the independent nature of the workman's business; (2) the workman's obligation to furnish necessary tools, supplies, and materials; (3) the workman's right to control the progress of the work except as to the final results; (4) the time for which the workman is employed; and (5) whether the workman is paid by time or by job. Similarly, we have evaluated employment relationships in the context of Title VII [*Title VII* is part of the Civil Rights Act that prohibits employment discrimination and harassment based on race, sex, religion, and national origin] and the ADEA [Age Discrimination in Employment Act] by using a hybrid economic realities/common law control test that focuses on whether the alleged employer had the right to hire and fire, the right to supervise, the right to set the work schedule, paid [sic] the employee's salary, withheld taxes, provided benefits, and set the terms and conditions of employment. And, in examining employee status under an FLSA [Fair Labor Standards Act] claim, we considered five factors: (1) degree of control exercised by the alleged employer; (2) the extent of the relative investments of the worker and alleged employer; (3) the degree to which the worker's opportunity for profit or loss is determined by the employer;

(4) the skill and initiative required in performing the job; and (5) the permanency of the relationship.

Under each of the foregoing tests, the instant facts mandate a conclusion that an employer-employee relationship existed when Hathcock drove the truck for Acme, regardless of his contemporaneous ownership of the vehicle and his independent contractor role as its lessor. Acme treated Hathcock as an employee for tax purposes and withheld mandated federal and state income and social security taxes from his driver's paycheck, and paid Hathcock, the driver, a regular salary as an employee. When he drove, the terms and conditions of Hathcock's employment were set by Acme: He had to submit to Acme's medical and driving requirements; he was subject to discipline for violation of Acme's personnel policies, including anti-harassment, drug testing, and 401(k) Plan; he was subject to discharge by Acme for violations of its Driver Manual; he was bound to work exclusively for Acme; and while doing so he had to drive a truck sporting the Acme logo at all times. In addition, Acme covered the costs of advertising, employing administrative staff, and soliciting business, including all business for Hathcock. He had no outside or personal customer base; he was "on-call" for Acme at all times; he did not participate in setting prices or rates for his deliveries; and Acme owned all permits and transportation rights required for Acme drivers, including Hathcock. The relationship between Acme and its drivers, including Hathcock, has always been of an indefinite duration. Finally, Acme showed that the IRS conducted an employment tax compliance check in 1996, and found no fault with Acme's accounting, deductions, or treatment of drivers as employees. . . . Hathcock's ability to pick his delivery route and work details does not evince sufficient initiative to allow him to be classified as an independent contractor as a matter of law. . . . [Here, we assume that when driving the truck Hathcock was discharging his driver obligations, including pick-up and delivery of items pursuant to Acme's business. When Hathcock drove his own truck for the limited purpose of discharging his contractual obligation of truck maintenance and service, then he was acting in the capacity of lessor.]

BUSINESS CONSIDERATIONS Hathcock's CPA characterized him as an independent contractor. Should that have any effect on the decision? Does it appear that Hathcock was misled or defrauded? Why? What else could Acme do in the future to assure that its lessors and drivers understand the terms of the agreements?

ETHICAL CONSIDERATIONS If the contracts and memorandums were clear when Hathcock signed them, is it ethical to sue Acme? Why?

agent-principal. Ordinary business transactions, such as contracts, do *not* create fiduciary relationships. Agents do owe fiduciary duties to their principals. Agents represent the principal in legal matters and must act with the utmost fairness and good faith.

Independent contractors who are also agents (1) have fiduciary duties, and (2) can bind their principals to contracts. For example, attorneys owe their clients fiduciary duties when they negotiate settlements and then agree to them on the clients' behalf. On the other hand, attorneys are not the clients' servants. Legal clients have no control over when their attorneys come to work in the morning or when they leave work at the end of the day. These relationships are represented in Exhibit 29.4.

EXHIBIT 29.3 Independent Contractors May Also Be Agents

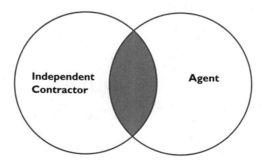

The shaded area indicates independent contractors who are also agents.

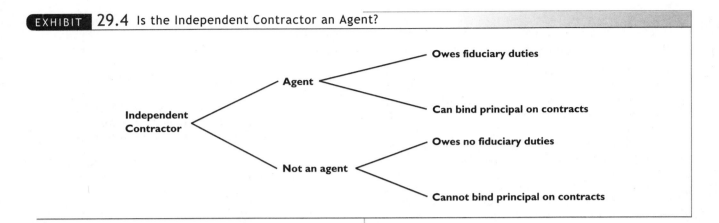

EXHIBIT 29.4 Is the Independent Contractor an Agent?

When legal questions concern fiduciary duties or contracts, the worker will simply be identified as an agent, rather than applying the cumbersome term "independent contractor agent."

Responsibility for Independent Contractors

Contract Liability Principals who engage independent contractors as agents will be liable on the contract *if* the contract was authorized. Authorization is discussed in detail in Chapter 30. This liability complies with the general rule for agents.

Tort Liability A person who hires an independent contractor is generally not responsible to third parties for the independent contractor's physical wrongdoings. However, there are a number of common exceptions to this general rule, depending on the laws of the forum state. Some of these rules are stated in the Restatement (Second) of Torts.[6] These exceptions include:

- The independent contractor is hired to engage in ultra-hazardous activities.[7]

- The independent contractor is hired to commit a crime.

- The hiring party reserves the right to supervise or control the work.[8]

- The hiring party actually directs the independent contractor to do something careless or wrong.[9]

- The hiring party sees the independent contractor do something wrong and does not stop it.

- The hiring party fails to adequately supervise the independent contractor.

- The hiring party is negligent in selecting the independent contractor.[10]

In many states, the trend has been to increase the number of situations in which the hiring party can be held liable. For example, some courts have reduced the standard for holding the employer liable from hiring an independent contractor to perform *ultrahazardous* activities to hiring an independent contractor to perform merely *hazardous* activities. In other words, in some states a person can be held liable when he or she hires an independent contractor to engage in hazardous activities. This results in a substantial increase in the potential liability of the employer. Remember, the independent contractor is also liable for his or her own wrongdoings, regardless of whether the hiring party is liable.

The independent contractor generally cannot recover from the hiring party if he or she is injured while working. In other words, he or she is not covered by workers' compensation. Employees of the independent contractor, however, have been permitted to recover from the independent contractor. This is because the employees are servants and the independent contractor is *their* master. Servants of independent contractors have sued the hiring party on the seven theories listed above. State law and the hiring party's behavior will determine whether the servant is successful.[11] In the case on pages 699–700, the court of appeals wrestled with a number of issues, including whether Rountree's activity was inherently dangerous.

Duties of the Agent to the Principal

The agent must protect the interests of the principal, as the duties discussed in the following sections show. Some of the duties overlap. In fact, when an agent breaches one duty, most likely he or she will breach others as well.

AMTRAK v. ROUNTREE TRANSPORT AND RIGGING, INC.
286 F.3d 1233, 2002 U.S. App. LEXIS 4956 (11th Cir. 2002)

FACTS An Amtrak passenger train was traveling on a railroad track of CSX when it collided with a hauler rig owned by Rountree. The Rountree rig was transporting a combustion turbine to a power plant being built by the Kissimmee Utility Authority (KUA). KUA had entered into an agreement with CSX to construct and use a private road to cross over CSX's tracks. KUA contracted with General Electric (GE) for the purchase and delivery of some customized power generation equipment including the turbine. GE contracted with S&S, who agreed to purchase and customize the equipment. S&S contracted with a transportation broker, WOKO, to deliver certain pieces of the equipment. WOKO contracted with Rountree to have the turbine transported to the plant.

Rountree decided to transport the turbine using a road tractor that pulled a hauler rig. The massive vehicle had 13 axles and 8 pivot points, and it weighed over 290,000 pounds. The crew first attempted to turn the transport vehicle left onto the crossing, but a utility pole prevented this maneuver. The crew then turned the vehicle around and approached the railroad crossing from the opposite direction in order to make a right-hand turn. The project supervisor and the rear driver of the transport vehicle inspected the elevation of the crossing. They concluded that the vehicle would clear the crest of the crossing if the vehicle were elevated to its maximum height using the hydraulic system. After raising the height, the crew attempted to maneuver the vehicle over the railroad crossing. The crew realized that the cargo beds still would not clear the crest. It would have to be raised further through a shimming procedure, where pieces of metal are inserted into certain crevices in the vehicle. The project supervisor believed that the vehicle could be removed from the tracks more quickly if the crew shimmed the load on the tracks. He feared that if the crew tried to back the vehicle completely off the crossing, it would jackknife and be stuck there. The crew proceeded to shim the load with the vehicle on the tracks. Members of the Rountree crew had heard that an Amtrak train was due to pass the railroad crossing by 1:00 p.m. The Amtrak train collided with the vehicle after it was shimmed, but before the vehicle had time to proceed forward over the crossing. The collision destroyed the rig and the turbine and hurt some of the crew and passengers on the train.

The parties sued each other and the various insurance companies. Applying Florida's comparative negligence

law, the jury determined that Rountree was 59 percent at fault, CSX was 33 percent at fault, and Amtrak was 8 percent at fault. The trial court ruled that transporting a combustion turbine was inherently dangerous as a matter of law, and that consequently WOKO, S&S, and GE were liable for Rountree's negligence. That ruling was appealed to this court.

ISSUE Is transporting a turbine inherently dangerous work under Florida law?

HOLDING Yes, it is an inherently dangerous activity.

REASONING Excerpts from the opinion of Circuit Judge Birch:

Under Florida law, an owner, contractor, or employer is not liable for injury caused by an independent contractor's negligence, unless the owner, contractor, or employer's own active negligence caused or contributed to the injury. An exception to this rule is the inherently dangerous work doctrine, which applies when the work to be performed by the independent contractor "is inherently or intrinsically dangerous." An activity is inherently dangerous if the "danger *inheres in the performance of the work*," and "it is sufficient if there is a recognizable and substantial danger inherent in the work, even though a major hazard is not involved." The activity . . . must be such that "in the ordinary course of events its performance would probably, and not merely possibly, cause injury if proper precautions were not taken." If the activity is found to be inherently dangerous, then the "one engaged in or responsible for the performance of [the] work . . . is said to be under a nondelegable duty to perform, or have others perform, the work in a reasonably safe and careful manner." Generally, it is a fact question for the jury whether a particular activity is inherently dangerous. The trial court nonetheless may rule that an activity is inherently dangerous as a matter of law if there is "some statute or case law designating the activity as inherently dangerous," or if there is a "sufficient record of undisputed facts" upon which the decision can be based. . . . Florida courts often have held that particular activities are inherently dangerous as a matter of law.

. . . [W]e conclude that the district court had a sufficient basis for concluding that transport of the combustion turbine was inherently dangerous as a matter of law. . . . The district court noted that the combustion turbine itself was tremendous in size, constituting an 82-ton, 14-foot high, 14-foot wide, and 57-foot long piece of machinery. . . . [T]he district court pointed to the quantum of regulations dealing with the transport of oversized items like the turbine as indicative of the inherent dangerousness involved. . . . Florida strictly regulates the transportation of oversized items . . . , and . . . state law specifically addresses the moving of heavy equipment across railroad crossings. . . . [T]he Florida Department of Transportation, the City of Tampa, and Polk County all required special permits before the turbine could be transported.

GE and S&S used a special "transportation broker" to arrange for the transport of the turbine on a specially-equipped vehicle. Unique measures then had to be taken by Rountree before it could transport the turbine. . . . All of these factors, when taken together, provide ample justification for the district court's conclusion on the inherent dangerousness issue. . . . Finally, we point out that the use of special hydraulics on the hauler rig to raise or lower its height makes this case similar to the operation of a crane, which Florida courts, on numerous occasions, have held is an inherently dangerous activity. . . . Rountree's failure to move the transport vehicle from the railroad crossing was a function of the unique dangers that arose in transporting an over-sized piece of machinery like the combustion turbine. . . . The issue here is whether a principal (S&S) can be liable for the conduct of its contractor's (WOKO's) subcontractor (Rountree). We . . . conclude that . . . S&S can be held vicariously liable for Rountree's negligence. . . . By contracting with GE, S&S assumed the duty of providing for the safe transport of the turbine. As part of its contractual duties, S&S arranged for the inherently dangerous activity of having the turbine transported in a specially-equipped vehicle. Because transport of the turbine constituted inherently dangerous work, the duty of S&S to provide for the safe transport of the turbine was nondelegable. . . . When a duty is nondelegable, "responsibility, i.e., ultimate liability, for the proper performance of that undertaking may not be delegated." . . . S&S remained ultimately liable for the transport of the turbine. . . .

BUSINESS CONSIDERATIONS What can a business like GE or S&S do to avoid liability for an independent contractor's negligence? How can a business reduce the probability of injury?

ETHICAL CONSIDERATIONS What is the moral duty of Rountree's crew to the people on the Amtrak train? Why?

Duty of Good Faith

The duty of *good faith* is also called the *fiduciary* duty, and the rule is that every agent owes the principal the obligation of faithful service. The most common violations of this duty include concealing essential facts that are relevant to the agency, obtaining secret profits, and self-dealing. Suppose the principal is searching for a parcel of agricultural land, and the agent locates a suitable parcel. The agent arranges for its sale to the principal without first informing the principal that the agent owns a one-third interest in the parcel. In this case, the agent has violated his or her fiduciary duty to the principal.

Duty of Loyalty

An agent has a duty to be loyal to the principal and to protect the principal's best interests. Accordingly, an agent must not compete with the principal, work for someone who is competing with the principal, or act to further the agent's own interests. An agent may not use his or her agency position for personal benefit at the expense of the principal. Such self-dealings involve a breach of the duty of loyalty. The following example shows a variation on a common problem many businesses must confront—employee conversion of firm assets.

André works in the marketing division of a large company. One of his responsibilities is to purchase supplies for the division. He tells Katie, the division chief, that the division has Zip® disks no one is using, and that there is not enough room in the supply storage area for new supplies that have been ordered. André indicates that he will solve this problem by taking the "surplus" Zip disks home.

If André takes the disks home, he will breach his fiduciary duties to the company, and he will have engaged in a poor business practice. He will be setting a bad example for the other employees and he will fail to search for alternatives that would be more beneficial to the division and the company. There are a number of better options available to the division: trade the disks for supplies with the other divisions; return the disks to the vendor (seller) for a credit; or keep the disks for future use. Perhaps the employees who use Zip disks already have a supply at their workstations and they will come to the supply room when their supply runs out.

If André is permitted to take unused supplies home, this might encourage him to order supplies that he wants at home with the hope that he will be able to use them himself. Katie should resolve this conflict of interest as soon as possible.

Duty to Obey All Lawful Instructions

Agents must follow all *lawful* instructions as long as doing so does not subject them to an unreasonable risk of injury *and* the instructions are in the course and scope of the agency. This is true even if agents think the instructions are capricious or unwise. Agents must repay their principals for damages suffered by their principals because they failed to follow lawful instructions that were in the course and scope of their employment.

Duty to Act with Reasonable Care

An agent has a duty to act as a reasonably careful agent would under the same circumstances. Again, if the agent fails to live up to this obligation and it causes the principal a loss, the agent will be obliged to reimburse the principal. For example, Sita hired Lydia to manage her investments. Lydia was considering various options, when Stan suggested that she make a private loan secured by a parcel he owned. Stan and a business associate both told Lydia that the parcel was worth $50,000. Based on their statements, Lydia made a loan of $45,000 secured by the property. She did not visit the parcel prior to making the loan. When Stan failed to make the mortgage payments, Lydia began foreclosure proceedings. Then she discovered that the property was worth about $4,000 due to its irregular size and location. Lydia will be liable to Sita for the loss. A reasonable person would look at the property, get an independent appraisal of its value, and consider comparable sales in the area *prior* to making this type of loan.

Duty to Segregate Funds

The agent has a duty to keep personal funds separate from the principal's funds. If the agent wrongfully uses the principal's funds to purchase something, the court can impose a trust. (A *trust* is an arrangement in which the legal title is separated from the equitable or beneficial ownership of the asset). The court treats the situation as though the purchase were made for the benefit of the principal from the beginning. A trust imposed by a court to prevent unjust enrichment is called a *constructive trust*. Constructive trusts are discussed in Chapter 44.

Duty to Account for Funds

An agent has a duty to account for money received. This is really a combined function of recordkeeping and delivery of the funds. The funds usually must be delivered to the principal (or an authorized third party). If the money was received while the agent was *not* in the course and scope of the employment, the agent has a duty to return the proceeds to the third party. Compare the agent's duty in each of the following two examples for an illustration of how this duty is applied.

Kamal is a sales representative for Fida, Inc. Kamal is authorized to receive payments from the customers with whom he deals. He takes a potential client to dinner to discuss possible orders the client might place with Fida. The client, impressed with the presentation Kamal makes during the meal, places an order for $10,000 worth of goods, writing a check as payment in full for the goods ordered. Although Kamal is technically "off the clock," this sale would be considered to have occurred in the course and scope of Kamal's employment, and he would be expected to account to Fida for the proceeds from the sale.

Bhudi is also a sales representative for Fida, Inc., but he is not *authorized to accept payments for goods he sells for the principal. He takes his wife to dinner to celebrate their anniversary. While they are eating, a client of Fida recognizes Bhudi as an employee of the firm. The client approaches Bhudi's table and hands Bhudi a check for $10,000 as payment for goods ordered from Fida the previous week. Bhudi is technically "off the clock," and he is not authorized to receive payments for his principal. In this situation, Bhudi would be expected to return the check to the client and to explain to the client that the check should be sent directly to Fida, the principal.*

Duty to Give Notice

The *duty to give notice* requires an agent to inform the principal about material facts that are discovered within the scope of the agent's employment. For example, if a tenant gives an apartment manager notice that the tenant will move out at the end of the month, it is assumed that the manager will inform the owner. In fact, the principal may be bound by this notice even though the agent failed to inform the principal. It is said that the notice is "imputed" to the principal.

Duty to Perform the Contract

If the relationship between the agent and principal *is* a contract, the agent must perform the duties specified in the contract. Normally the agent's promise to act is interpreted

THE RISKS OF HIRING SALESPEOPLE

NRW has decided that it needs to expand its geographic market if it is to be successful in the industry. In order to expand sales geographically, the firm will need sales representatives to work in the new regions. While Carlos does not mind doing some traveling for the business, he does not want to spend too much time "on the road." Neither Mai nor Helen enjoys business travel, and both would prefer to stay in the office doing their primary jobs. Carlos, Mai, and Helen recognize that they will need to hire sales representatives for NRW, but they are hesitant to do so. Mai is concerned that any sales agents would be able to cultivate a customer base, copy the NRW products, and then start a competing business using what NRW has taught the agent. Carlos is concerned that the firm will not have adequate control over the agents. Helen does not feel that either of these is a valid concern. She believes there are protections available to the firm but is not sure exactly what those protections are. She has asked for your input about the potential problem. What will you tell her?

BUSINESS CONSIDERATIONS What policies should a firm establish to maximize its protection in the event an agent violates his or her duty? What are the legal rights of a principal whose agent attempts to utilize technological information obtained in the course of employment for the personal benefit of that agent?

ETHICAL CONSIDERATIONS What are the ethical implications of acting as a sales agent for a firm that produces a highly technical product? What ethical principles would preclude an agent from attempting to establish a business in competition with his or her former principal based on either the knowledge or the customers he or she developed as an agent?

INTERNATIONAL CONSIDERATIONS Are there international protections available for a firm that is producing a product that is based on intellectual properties? Does the firm have to take any special steps to acquire international protection of its intellectual property rights?

as being only a promise to make reasonable efforts to achieve the desired result. Consequently, the agent will not be liable for a breach of contract if he or she fails to satisfy the promised act. The agent normally will not be held liable unless he or she fails to make reasonable efforts. The agent is expected to try to notify the principal if he or she is unable to perform. For example, an agent who accepts a listing to sell a lot is not guaranteeing that the lot will be sold at the listed price. The agent is committing to make reasonable effort to try to sell the lot at that price.

Duties of the Principal to the Agent

Many of the duties of the principal may be specified in the contract between the principal and the agent. In general, the principal has the following obligations to the agent:

- to pay the agent per the agreement
- to maintain proper accounts so that compensation and reimbursement will be correct
- to provide the agent with the means to do the job
- to continue the employment for the time period specified in the agreement

With the exception of gratuitous agents, agents are entitled to be paid under the terms of their agreements with their principals. Some types of agents are entitled to compensation under special arrangements such as commission sales. These unique situations are usually mentioned in the written contract. For example, in some states real estate agents are entitled to their commissions if they find a buyer who is ready, willing, and able to buy the parcel. This is true even if the transfer does not occur because of destruction of the building, the buyer's inability to obtain a loan, or some other circumstance. Some states follow a different rule, whereby a sale must close before a real estate commission is earned.

In addition, if the worker is a servant, his or her master has an obligation to provide the servant with a reasonably safe place to work and safe equipment to use. This obligation is based on common law *and* state and federal safety statutes, such as the federal Occupational Safety and Health Act (OSHA). Under OSHA, the secretary of labor *may* pass regulations permitting workers to refuse to work under hazardous conditions.[12] A master also owes a servant an obligation to compensate him or her for injuries under state workers' compensation laws. Workers' compensation laws are discussed in Chapters 31 and 40.

Principals also owe nonservant agents a duty to provide the means to do the job, but the principals' obligations are more limited than when workers are servants. For example, the principal may have the duty to provide the architect's sketches to the builder.

Termination of the Agency Relationship

Agreement of the Parties

An agency relationship is governed in the first instance by the agreement between the principal and the agent. Commonly the contract will be established for a set period. For example, assume a real estate agent has a listing to sell a house according to certain terms. One of the terms may specify the period for which the contract is going to run, say 90 days; that agreement, therefore, will terminate at the end of 90 days.

The parties can consent to amend the agency agreement to terminate the agency relationship early or to extend it. For example, if the house in the prior example is not sold within 90 days, the owner and agent may specifically extend the agency agreement for an additional 60 days.

If the parties consent to the continuation of the agency relationship beyond the period originally stated, this consent may be implied as a renewal of the original contract for the same period and under the same conditions. This is true only if they have not specifically altered the terms and conditions of the original agreement.

Agency at Will

If the agency agreement does not specify a set date, a set period, or a set occurrence that will terminate it, the relationship is an *agency at will*. This is also called an employment at will. Either party can terminate the relationship by giving notice to the other. The principal or agent does not need cause or justification to terminate the relationship. This is consistent with the theory that agency is a voluntary relationship between the parties. Either party can decide to terminate it. Traditionally, it was perceived that the two parties were relatively equal in their bargaining position and that, consequently, this rule was fair.

The traditional concept of an agency at will is being eroded rapidly. In addition, courts are recognizing various theories for recovery by the discharged agent. Adoption of these theories of recovery vary depending on the situation and state law. Three common examples follow:

1. The courts are recognizing a breach of employment contract, that is, an express or implied agreement that the employment will not be terminated *or* will not be terminated without following a specific set of procedures. For example, union-management contracts called collective bargaining agreements gener-

NRW CASE 29.2 Management

PROTECTING AGAINST WORKPLACE VIOLENCE

Carlos has become very concerned about workplace violence. This topic was discussed in a seminar he recently attended and was cited as one of the fastest-growing problem areas in the 2000s. One example cited in the seminar involved a manager who fired an employee for using drugs at work. The dismissed employee became verbally abusive, and he had to be physically removed from the workplace. At that point he went home to get his hunting rifle, returned to the plant with the rifle, and proceeded to shoot the manager and four of his former co-workers.

Although Carlos is unsure exactly how to best protect the managers and employees, he believes the firm should at least keep a gun in the office suite for protection if such a situation should arise at NRW. However, he is concerned about potential liability for the firm if something were to happen. He asks for your advice and for any suggestions you have. What will you tell him?

BUSINESS CONSIDERATIONS Workplace violence is not just a legal problem. It also presents serious business implications. What policies should a business establish to protect its employees and its business operation from workplace violence? Should a business establish policies for some sort of intervention or counseling prior to the dismissal of an employee?

ETHICAL CONSIDERATIONS What should a firm do, from an ethical perspective, before it fires an employee? Is having a gun in the office area an ethical solution to the potential threat of violence in the workplace?

INTERNATIONAL CONSIDERATIONS Obtaining and possessing a firearm is much more difficult in some nations than it is in the United States. What problems might be caused in a foreign office if a business has an established policy requiring the presence of an armed guard or a handgun in the manager's office area? How should such a policy be tailored to ensure compliance with local laws and customs?

ally contain express agreements that prevent the dismissal of union employees without a showing of cause *and* the following of specific procedures. Implied contracts often are based on procedures, policies in personnel manuals, interviews, and advertisements for workers.

2. Courts are also recognizing a tort of bad-faith discharge, where the employee has a right of continued employment and has developed a relationship of trust, reliance, and dependency on the employer. It is based on an implicit understanding between the agent and principal that they will deal honestly and fairly with each other. Bad faith is usually evidenced by fraud, malice, or oppression. This is sometimes considered a breach of a covenant of good faith and fair dealing.

3. Some states are holding an employer liable for a tortious discharge if the termination violates public policy. This is based on the theory that employees should not have to forfeit their positions because they act in a manner that supports some *important* public policy. For example, this basis is commonly used to protect whistle-blowers, e.g., employees who report safety violations to OSHA or violations of environment protection laws to EPA. Many federal and state statutes now have antiretaliation provisions that principals cannot retaliate against agents who complain to agencies, file reports, or testify against them. For example, public policy provisions are used to protect employees who testify in court about the employers' criminal activity.

Most states recognize implied agreements and public policy exceptions. A few recognize the tort of bad-faith discharge. States may not recognize any of these theories or they may recognize some combination of them. Most of the court cases involve servants instead of independent contractors.

There are other public policy prohibitions on firing agents at will. If the agent was fired on the basis of gender, race, religion, or national origin, or some other violation of civil rights, the courts may decide that the principal cannot terminate the relationship. In 1991, the National Conference of Commissioners on Uniform State Laws approved the Model Employment Termination Act 2 (META), which provides some protection for agents at will. It has not been adopted by any states.[13]

Companies should maintain careful records documenting the reasons a worker is discharged, even if an agency at will is involved. Companies are particularly likely to have difficulty when they terminate a worker after a number of years of successful employment, including frequent promotions and commendations for the worker. The courts generally use the terms "employer" and "employee" when discussing both agency at will and wrongful discharge.

Notice that wrongful discharge has been used to prevent employers from firing employees, but employees in employment-at-will relationships are still free to quit at any time and for any reason. In the case on pages 705–706, the court addressed the firing of four agents at will.

The use of an employee handbook or employment manual can be beneficial to an employer in establishing a formal guide for what each party to the employment can expect of the other. However, the handbook can also be somewhat burdensome because it is likely to impose standards for management that must be followed in order to protect the rights of the employees. This is especially true if the handbook or manual becomes part of the employment contract, either expressly or by implication. A number of companies and universities have put their employee handbooks online. The College of William and Mary Employee Policy Manual is available at http://www.dhrm.state.va.us/hrpolicy.htm. (Is the employee manual for your university online? Locate it.)

Fulfillment of the Agency Purpose

Logically, an agency relationship terminates when the purpose for which it was created has been fulfilled. It does not make sense to continue the relationship beyond that time.

Revocation

Principals can revoke or terminate the authority of their agents to act on their behalf. They should directly notify their agents of the termination. The notice that the agency relationship is being terminated, moreover, should be clear and unequivocal. Indirect notice will *sometimes* be sufficient—for example, hiring a second agent to complete all the duties of the first agent. Due to the agent's obligation to obey, the principal can terminate the agency at any time. This is true even though there was an agreement that the agency relationship would continue longer. Even a statement in the agreement that the agency cannot be terminated does not affect the principal's ability to terminate it. Although the principal may have the *ability* to terminate the agency, he or she may not have the legal *right* to do so; in such a case, the agency can be terminated, but the principal may be liable for damages if this termination is a breach of contract.

Renunciation

Renunciation occurs when the agent notifies the principal that he or she will no longer serve as an agent. In other words, the agent resigns. Since an agency relationship is

29.3

BARON v. PORT AUTHORITY OF NEW YORK AND NEW JERSEY
271 F.3d 81, 2001 U.S. App. LEXIS 24353 (2nd Cir. 2001)

FACTS Patricia Gayle Baron, Lisa Diaz, Laura L. Toole, and Amos Ilan were four managerial employees of the Port Authority of New York and New Jersey (the Port Authority). Each contended that "job security" was of "great importance" and a "substantial factor" in his or her decision to accept and continue employment with the Port Authority. Throughout their employment, the Port Authority issued "employment manuals" explaining that in the event of a reduction in force (RIF), any decision as to whom to fire would be based on past performance and seniority. One such manual, the Port Authority Instructions (PAIs), provided that in the event of an RIF, the termination of employees would proceed from lowest performance category to highest, with seniority governing terminations in any particular performance category. The PAIs were not distributed to the employees, but instead were provided only to division and department heads, supervisors, and the Port Authority library. The employees contended that they were encouraged to refer to the library's copies of the PAIs. The PAIs expressly contemplated amendment and alteration. The introductory section of the PAIs provided: "[The PAIs] are subject to modification, in general or for any particular instance and retroactively or otherwise, in the discretion of the Executive Director." The PAI regarding consideration of merit and seniority during an RIF was modified three times since its promulgation in 1975. A second writing containing the policy, the Guide for Port Authority Personnel (the Guide), was issued to Baron when she was hired. It was no longer distributed when the other employees commenced employment with the Port Authority. The Guide stated that although the Port Authority might need to eliminate positions "for reasons of economy and efficiency," "in the event of any reduction in the work force, merit and ability as well as length of service and salary step will be considered in deciding how the reduction will be accomplished." The employees also claimed that over the course of their employment, they were orally assured by Port Authority supervisors that merit and seniority would be considered in the event of an RIF. They contended that these writings and accompanying oral assurances, taken together, gave rise to an implicit contractual obligation on the part of the Port Authority to take merit and seniority into consideration in the event of an RIF.

On September 7, 1995, the commissioners of the Port Authority authorized an RIF. On that day, the commissioners also eliminated the merit and seniority provision of the PAIs and replaced it with the following:

Each affected department director, consistent with sound business and policy discretion and in order to improve [the] effectiveness and efficiency of the Port Authority, [should] identify the particular employees who are subject to involuntary removal[.]

The Port Authority identified and notified approximately 316 persons, including these employees, that their positions would be eliminated in 30 days.

ISSUE Were the employees terminated in violation of an implied contract?

HOLDING No, their termination was not in violation of an implied contract.

REASONING Excerpts from the opinion of Chief Judge John M. Walker Jr.:

In New York, it has long been "settled" that "an employment relationship is presumed to be a hiring at will, terminable at any time by either party." . . . This presumption can be rebutted, however, by establishing an "express limitation in the individual contract of employment" curtailing an employer's right to terminate at will. Policies in a personnel manual specifying the employer's practices with respect to the employment relationship, including the procedures or grounds for termination, may become a part of the employment contract. . . . To establish that such policies are a part of the employment contract, an employee . . . must prove that (1) an express written policy limiting the employer's right of discharge exists, (2) the employer (or one of its authorized representatives) made the employee aware of this policy, and (3) the employee detrimentally relied on the policy in accepting or continuing employment. The New York Court of Appeals has admonished . . . that "routinely issued employee manuals, handbooks and policy statements should not lightly be converted into binding employment agreements." . . .

Here, the plaintiffs' implied contract claims fail because none of the writings identified by the parties . . . constitutes a written express limitation on the Port Authority's right to hire, fire, promote, demote, transfer or take any other employment action it deems otherwise appropriate. To the contrary, the disclaimers at the front of both the Port Authority Guidebook and the PAIs expressly and specifically disavow any intent on the Port Authority's part to accept contractual limitations on its rights as an at-will employer. For example, the Guidebook's disclaimer stated that the Guidebook is a "guide to help" employees and not a "rule book." The PAIs' disclaimer was even more explicit: the PAIs are "not intended to create any rights or presumptions," do not "impose any standards or obligations," and are "solely for internal Port Authority guidance." These disclaimers plainly convey the Port Authority's intention that the provisions in the Guidebook and PAIs are non-binding. No understanding by the plaintiffs to the contrary would have been objectively reasonable. . . . [T]he disclaimers in the Port Authority Guide and the PAIs are sufficiently clear to defeat as a matter of law the plaintiffs' implied contract claims. . . . The New York Court of Appeals' recent decision in [precedents] . . . makes clear that "conspicuous disclaiming language" in an employee handbook "preserves [the employer's] . . . at will employment relationship with" its employees as far as the provisions in an employee handbook are concerned. . . . [W]here a sufficiently unambiguous disclaimer, conspicuously placed in the employee handbook such that the employee reasonably could be expected to read it is at issue, . . . the implied contract claim may be dismissed as a matter of law. . . . [I]n light of the general clarity with which the disclaimers in the Port Authority Guide and the PAIs disavow any contractual intent, the Port Authority "clearly preserved" its rights as an at-will employer of the plaintiffs. Accordingly, the Port Authority was not contractually obligated to consider plaintiffs' seniority or merit in terminating them. . . .

BUSINESS CONSIDERATIONS What would you recommend to a business that wants to maintain an at-will relationship with its employees? Why?

ETHICAL CONSIDERATIONS Should an employer consider seniority when implementing an RIF? What ethical theories would support the use of seniority? Why?

voluntary, an agent can renounce. However, the agent may be liable to the principal if the renunciation is a breach of their contract.

Operation of Law

In the legal system, operation of law means that rights or liabilities are created without the parties' acting in a particular manner or even intending the rights to occur. Sometimes operation of law will automatically terminate an agency relationship without any additional action. These situations include:

- when the agent dies

- when either party becomes insane

- when the principal becomes bankrupt

- when the agent becomes bankrupt, if the bankruptcy affects the agency

- when the agency cannot possibly be performed (e.g., when the subject matter of the agency is destroyed)

- when an unusual and unanticipated change in circumstances occurs that destroys the purpose of the agency relationship

- when a change in law makes completion of the agency relationship illegal

The traditional rule is that the death of the principal also terminates the agency relationship immediately. Because this rule can cause hardship, many states modified their laws to implement a more liberal approach. Under this more liberal rule, the death of the principal does not immediately terminate the agency relationship *if* immediate termination will cause a hardship.

When the relationship is terminated by the operation of law, usually it is unnecessary to give notice to the other party or to the public at large. This rule is discretionary, and a court may decide to require notice if lack of notice causes a great hardship.

Importance of Notice

When an agent or a principal terminates the agency relationship early, the agent or principal has a duty to notify the other party so that the other party does not waste effort on a relationship that no longer exists. If the principal revokes the agency relationship and does not notify the agent, the principal is obligated to indemnify the agent for liabilities that the agent incurs in the proper performance of his or her duties.[14]

It may be crucial to notify third parties even if it is not legally required, such as in termination by operation of law. The agent may find it advantageous to provide notice, but the principal will find notice even more important. If the principal fails to notify a third party, the third party may

NRW CASE 29.3   Management

SHOULD AN EMPLOYER HAVE AN EMPLOYEE HANDBOOK?

NRW has grown since its early days, and expects to continue to grow in the future. The firm now has 25 regular, full-time employees. The employees have been loyal to NRW, and the firm is appreciative of their contributions. However, the economy has slowed somewhat and a few of the employees are concerned about their job security with the firm. Mai, Carlos, and Helen would like to reassure the employees, without making any guarantees they may not be able to honor if the downturn continues. Mai suggests that NRW should write an employee handbook/ employment manual to reassure the employees and to establish an employment policy framework for the firm. She thinks the handbook should address a number of issues, including length of employment and procedures for discharge. She has asked for your advice. What will you tell her?

BUSINESS CONSIDERATIONS Should NRW adopt an employee handbook? What are the advantages and disadvantages of a handbook? What should it say about the length of the employment or grounds for discharge?

ETHICAL CONSIDERATIONS Is it ethical for a business to "assure" employees about their status when the business is not willing to make guarantees? What would an act utilitarian do in this situation? What would an *immoral* manager do? What would an *amoral* manager do?

INTERNATIONAL CONSIDERATIONS Suppose that an American business opens a facility in another country. Do U.S. labor laws and employee protection statutes apply to workers in the foreign facility? Does it make a difference if the employees are American citizens assigned to the foreign locale, or if they are foreign nationals?

transfer money such as a rent payment to the agent with the expectation that the agent will forward the funds to the principal. Remember that the agent ordinarily has a duty to do so. If the agent is unhappy with the termination, there is a risk that the agent may unlawfully abscond with the money.

The notice can take various forms. The preferred method is to personally notify the third person by mail, e-mail, electronically transmitted facsimile copy, telephone, or telegram. Personal notice is generally required for all third parties who have had dealings with the agent. The names, addresses, and telephone numbers of these customers are usually in the company data banks or the agent's files. The advantage of using e-mail or an electronically transmitted facsimile copy is that it is fast, and there is written proof of the notification. Without written proof, the third party may deny receiving the notice. Notice should be distributed promptly, since one of its purposes is to prevent losses caused by a disgruntled agent who feels that the termination is unjust.

In addition, the law accepts notice by publication (also called constructive notice). Usually, such notice is published in the legal notices in the newspaper. This is the only type of notice that is practical for members of the public who are aware of the agency, but who have not had previous dealings with the agent.

The principal will be protected if the third party actually knows that the agency relationship has been terminated, even if the third party did not receive notice from the principal (i.e., the third party may have heard about the termination from the agent or from someone else).

Breach of Agency Agreement

Generally the principal has the power to terminate the agency, even if the principal does not have the right. If the principal wrongfully revokes the agent's authority, the agent can sue for breach of express or implied contract. Many principal-agent contracts contain provisions for arbitrating disputes between them. Arbitration is discussed in Chapter 6. If there is an anticipatory breach and the principal notifies the agent in advance of the breach, the agent can sue the principal immediately for the anticipated damages. The agent, at his or her election, may decide to wait until after the contract period and then sue for actual damages. In either case, the agent has an obligation to *mitigate damages* or to keep them as low as possible by searching for another similar position with another principal in the same locality. Mitigating damages is discussed more fully in Chapter 15.

Summary

Agency relationships center on the agreement between a principal and an agent that the agent will act for the benefit of the principal. The principal must have the capacity to consent to the relationship. The agent need not have contractual capacity. Most agents are compensated. An agent who does not receive compensation is called a gratuitous agent.

In analyzing the legal rights of the parties, one must determine whether the worker is a servant or an independent contractor. An independent contractor is hired to complete a job. The hiring party does not direct how the independent contractor does the task. In contrast, a master can exert a great deal of control over a servant and how the servant performs the assigned duties. Because the master can control the servant, the master is more likely to be held financially responsible for the servant's physical acts.

An agent has a duty to act in good faith, to act loyally, to obey all lawful instructions, to act with reasonable care, to segregate funds, to account for all funds, and to give notice.

An agency relationship may terminate at a specified time agreed on by the parties, at the will of the parties, or after the purpose of the agency has been fulfilled. It can be revoked or renounced by one of the parties or terminated by operation of law. Even in an agent-at-will situation, the employer can be successfully sued for breach of an expressed or implied employment contract, bad-faith discharge, or tortious discharge in violation of public policy.

A principal generally has the power to terminate an agency relationship even if the termination is wrongful.

Discussion Questions

1. NRW hired Raúl as a distributor of its goods. However, NRW also required that Raúl help with unloading all the shipments as they arrive at the loading dock. Was Raúl a servant, independent contractor, or both?

2. Juan hired Jack to deliver one cord of pine wood for the fireplace in the house Juan rented. Jack usually just dumps the wood in the driveway—a practice known as a driveway delivery. However, this time he decided to help Juan stack the wood in the garage. Juan was standing in the garage as Jack backed the truck into position. However, Jack backed the truck too far, damaging both the truck and the garage wall. Was Jack a servant or an independent contractor? Who was liable to the injured third party (the landlord), and why? Who would have been liable if the truck had injured Juan? Why?

3. Antonio was a real estate broker. He knew that Jacinta wanted to make a bid on a parcel of land, and he offered to deliver the bid for her. She wrote out the bid and gave it to Antonio. Antonio attended the auction and failed to submit Jacinta's bid. However, he did submit the bids of other parties. Jacinta did not discover this until it was too late to submit a bid, so she lost the opportunity to purchase the parcel. Jacinta's bid would have been successful. What rights did Jacinta have?

4. Ron worked for Acme Grocery Store. One day while Ron was unloading produce from a truck, Jimmy stopped by to talk to him. Jimmy got into the truck and, while handing the boxes to Ron, carelessly dropped a box on a person walking down the alley. Who was responsible for the injury, and why? Is it relevant that Jimmy was not being paid? If so, why?

5. Peter hired Andy to purchase some goods for him on the open market. While Andy was obtaining prices from vendors, Ted offered Andy a $100 rebate if Andy purchased the goods from Ted; Andy did so and kept the $100 for himself. What were the rights of the parties? Why?

6. Elaine worked as a travel agent for World Travel, Inc. As an incentive, a cruise ship line offered travel agents one free passage on a cruise for every 25 paying passengers they booked on the line. The cruise ship line felt that this practice was good public relations. Elaine earned two free passages. Who was entitled to these passages, and why? Should Elaine's customers be concerned about this practice? Why or why not?

7. Rick was hired to serve as a deck hand on Marsha's fishing boat. One day Marsha ordered him to scrape and repaint a portion of the hull just above the water line. (The boat was not in dry dock.) Rick was directed to perform the task sitting on the rope ladder suspended above the water. Rick complained that he was tired, the job was dirty and dangerous, and the duty was not discussed when he accepted the job as deck hand. What rights did Rick have? What rights did Marsha have?

8. Steve managed a 200-unit apartment complex, which the owners wanted to convert to condominiums. The city council scheduled a hearing on the issue. Instead of sending the notice to the owners, the council sent the notice to Steve. What were the rights and obligations of the parties? Why?

9. Andrea acted as an agent for principals wishing to purchase small businesses. She was trying to assist Rudy in the purchase of a doctor's office for a reasonable price. Rudy called her on her cell phone while she was out of town on other

business. She returned the call while she was in the hotel lobby during the evening reception hour. During the discussion with Rudy she revealed most of the details of the business, including an analysis of the business's income statements, projected business, and a reasonable purchase price. Did Andrea violate any duties owed to Rudy? Why?

10. Sarah signed a written contract stating that her agency relationship would last for four years and that she would have the irrevocable right to take orders from customers for children's educational software on behalf of her principal. In an attempt to downsize and economize, however, her principal fired her. What rights did Sarah have?

Case Problems and Writing Assignments

1. José Torres was a self-employed gardener doing business as José Torres Gardening Service from 1980 to 1988. He performed weekly gardening services at a number of homes in Torrance, California, including the home of Michael and Ona Reardon. In 1988, the Reardons began discussing the possibility of having Torres trim a 65- to 70-foot tree in their front yard. An agreement was reached in mid-June that Torres would trim the tree for $350. David Boice, the Reardons' neighbor, was present during the final discussion. Boice indicated that he was concerned about a large branch of the tree that overhung his house. He feared that the branch would fall onto his roof. Torres and one helper arrived at 11:00 A.M. on June 20 to do the job. The Reardons were not at home. Boice was at home working in his garage workshop and he reminded Torres about the branch. Periodically, Boice came out to watch the progress. He mentioned that Torres was not using safety lines and Torres responded that he did not need them. Torres used a chain saw to cut the larger branches. When Torres was ready to cut the branch that overhung Boice's house, Boice came out to hold a rope tied to the branch. He was going to pull on it so the branch would not fall on his roof. Torres was wearing a safety belt, but it was not attached to the tree. He did not have enough line to reach a branch that could support his weight. Torres claimed that Boice pulled on "Boice's rope" when Torres did not expect it, causing Torres to lose control of the chain saw and fall. Torres became a paraplegic due to the fall and sued the Reardons. Was Torres a servant of the Reardons and, therefore, entitled to workers' compensation? [See *Torres v. Reardon*, 5 Cal. Rptr. 2d 52 (Cal. App. 2nd Dist. 1992).]

2. Industry specialists contend that employees playing games on company computers create significant costs for businesses. A 1993 survey of 1,000 corporations by a software company found that workers spend an average of 5.1 hours a week doing non-job-related tasks on their company computers. This includes playing games. It is estimated that this costs the nation $10 billion annually in lost productivity. Governor George Allen of Virginia has ordered that games be *deleted* from *all* state-owned computers, including those of university faculty members. To quote an administrative memo, "[T]ime spent by employees playing such games should be considered an improper use of taxpayer funds." The ban, which eliminates playing games during breaks and lunchtime, is raising questions among Virginia employees. Assume you are a high-level corporate manager. What approach would you take and why? What are the advantages of this approach? Is Virginia taking an ethical approach to this problem? Why or why not? [See Rajiv Chandrasekaran, "No More Games for Virginia Employees," *The Fresno Bee* (January 10, 1995), D10.]

3. Robert T. Darden was an insurance "agent" who worked for Nationwide Mutual Insurance Co. Under their written contract Darden was enrolled in a Nationwide "insurance agents retirement plan," which provided that Darden would forfeit his retirement benefits if he sold insurance for a competitor within one year of retirement and within 25 miles of his prior business location. Darden began selling for a competitor and Nationwide implemented the forfeiture provision. Darden sued under the federal Employee Retirement Income Security Act of 1974 (ERISA). Only employees have rights under ERISA. Was Darden an employee or an independent contractor when he worked for Nationwide? Was the Nationwide "insurance agents retirement plan" subject to ERISA? [See *Nationwide Mutual Insurance Co. v. Darden*, 503 U.S. 318 (1992).]

4. Robert Jones worked for Western States operating heavy equipment. When the equipment broke down, he was assigned a position in the cyanide leach pit. Previously Jones had attended one of his employer's safety courses, where he had learned about the dangers of absorption of cyanide and the need to avoid contact with open wounds. Since Jones had an open wound from surgery, he asked to be assigned an alternate position. He was then fired for insubordination. Was Robert Jones wrongfully discharged? Why or why not? Analyze the ethical perspective of Western States. [See *Western States Minerals Corp. v. Jones*, 819 P.2d 206 (Nev. 1991).]

5. **BUSINESS APPLICATION CASE** James Matthew Hutchings, a pipe fitter/rigger, was assigned to work on board the vessel *M/V Candy Lady* in order to assist with off-loading groceries and equipment from the boat to the Chevron platform. A relief crew of three men was being lowered in a personnel basket from the platform to the vessel by a crane located on Chevron's platform. The personnel basket fell and struck Hutchings, pinning him to the deck. He was unable to grab the personnel basket because there was only one tag line attached to it. At the time of the accident, Hutchings was an employee of Danos & Curole Marine Contractors, Inc. (Danos), an independent contractor of Chevron. Danos and Chevron had signed a contract whereby Danos would provide various services for Chevron at the site. The contract contained no provision that Chevron could retain control of the operations; however, it also did not state that Chevron could not retain operational control over

the work. While Danos assumed contractual responsibility for safety, the contract was ambiguous about whether Chevron relinquished control over the day-to-day operations of the work to Danos. An accident report was completed by Quent B. Gilbert, who listed himself on the report as "Chevron Representative Preparing Report." In addition, Hutchings stated that "Danny" Ragus, Chevron's company man, was the person from whom he generally received instructions, and that a Chevron representative was supervising the Danos employees on the day of the accident. The crane operator responsible for lowering the personnel basket stated that he reported to the Chevron supervisor. Could Chevron legally be held liable for Hutchings's injuries? [See *Hutchings v. Chevron U.S.A. Inc.*, 1999 U.S. Dist. LEXIS 2079 (E.D. La. 1999).]

6. ETHICAL APPLICATION CASE Michael A. Haddle was an at-will employee. A federal grand jury indictment in March 1995 charged Haddle's employer, Healthmaster, Inc., and Garrison and Kelly, officers of Healthmaster, with Medicare fraud. Haddle cooperated with the federal agents in the investigation prior to the indictment. He also appeared to testify before the grand jury pursuant to a subpoena, but did not testify due to the lack of time. Haddle was also expected to appear as a witness in the criminal trial resulting from the indictment. Garrison and Kelly were barred by the Bankruptcy Court from participating in the affairs of Healthmaster. Haddle claimed they conspired with G. Peter Molloy, Jr., one of the remaining officers of Healthmaster, to have him fired, both to intimidate Haddle and to retaliate against him for his attendance at the federal court proceedings. Section 1985(2) of the Civil Rights Act of 1871 prohibits conspiracies to "deter, by force, intimidation, or threat, any party or witness in any court of the United States from attending such court, or from testifying to any matter pending therein, freely, fully, and truthfully, or to injure such party or witness in his person or property on account of his having so attended or testified." Could Haddle state a claim for damages by alleging that a conspiracy proscribed by § 1985(2) induced his employer to terminate his at-will employment? How could this business avoid the problems caused by the firing of Haddle? Analyze the ethics of Healthmaster *if* it did engage in Medicare fraud. Was Haddle a whistle-blower? Analyze Haddle's ethics. [See *Haddle v. Garrison*, 119 S. Ct. 489 (1998).]

7. CRITICAL THINKING CASE Five-year-old Valerie Lakey was playing in a wading pool in North Carolina when she was trapped by suction from water being pumped through the drain in the bottom of the pool. The drain cover, manufactured by Sta-Rite Industries, Inc. was not properly screwed into place. Her parents sued a number of entities on her behalf. The claim against Sta-Rite was based on theories of defective design and failure to warn. Sta-Rite selected an attorney to represent it in pretrial matters and at trial. Sta-Rite had two insurance policies including a $500,000 self-insured retention and an excess insurance policy issued by Zurich Re (U.K.) Ltd. with a limit of $20 million. Zurich hired its own attorney, Mark Kreger, who participated in pretrial discussions with Sta-Rite regarding settlement strategy. The jury rendered a compensatory damage verdict in favor of plaintiffs in the amount of $25 million. The parties then settled prior to the punitive damage portion of the trial. Sta-Rite then filed suit against Zurich, claiming that Zurich owed it a fiduciary duty of good faith which Zurich breached by refusing to pay its policy limits of $20 million in response to a settlement offer. Was Zurich an agent of Sta-Rite that owed Sta-Rite a duty of good faith? [See *Sta-Rite Industries, Inc. v. Zurich Re (U.K.) Ltd.*, 178 F.3d 883 (7th Cir. 1999).]

8. YOU BE THE JUDGE Joseph Szaller was employed by the Red Cross for three and a half years as a medical team manager. In this capacity, he supervised several other staff members and was responsible for collecting blood from volunteer donors on bloodmobiles in Howard County, Maryland. On February 22, 2001, Szaller placed a telephone call to an anonymous Red Cross hotline. During this call, he reported various blood handling and staff training deficiencies, which he believed violated Food and Drug Administration (FDA) regulations and provisions of a 1993 consent decree between the FDA and the Red Cross regarding training and quality assurance. (A *consent decree* is a court decree agreed to by the parties. In this case, the FDA and the Red Cross agreed to the decree.) Szaller was suspended from work the day after he called the hotline, and his employment with the Red Cross was terminated on March 7, 2001. Joseph Szaller claims that the American National Red Cross and the American Red Cross Greater Chesapeake and Potomac Blood Services Region wrongfully discharged him in violation of Maryland law. He contends that he was unlawfully terminated for reporting alleged violations of FDA regulations and a consent decree to a Red Cross hotline. Did Szaller's discharge violate a clear mandate of Maryland public policy and was it therefore a wrongful discharge under Maryland law? What about the public policy in most states? [See *Szaller v. American National Red Cross*, 2002 U.S. App. LEXIS 10727 (4th Cir. 2002).]

Notes

1. *Restatement (Second) of Agency* (Philadelphia: American Law Institute, 1958), § 1.
2. Ibid., § 20, Comment b.
3. Ibid., § 492, Comment a.
4. Ibid., § 3, Comment a.
5. Exceptions occur in areas of unemployment compensation and workers' compensation statutes. These statutes often require that the worker is being paid.

6. *Restatement (Second) of Torts* (Student Edition) (St. Paul, Minn.: American Law Institute, 1965), Chapter 15.
7. Ibid. Section 423 discusses highly dangerous activities; § 427A discusses abnormally dangerous activities; § 413 and § 416 address work that creates a peculiar risk.
8. Ibid., § 414.
9. Ibid., § 410.
10. Ibid., § 411.

11. For example, the California Supreme Court recently decided that an employee of an independent contractor is barred from suing the hiring party for negligently hiring that independent contractor. See *Camargo v. Tjaarda Dairy,* 2001 Cal. LEXIS 3799, 108 Cal. Rptr. 2d 617 (2001), where Camargo was an employee of Golden Cal Trucking when he was killed on the property of Tjaarda Dairy. His widow sued the dairy for negligently hiring Golden Cal Trucking. The court denied her claim. It felt that this would, in effect, provide a way around the state workers' compensation provisions. Two companion cases also deal with servants of independent contractors—*McKown v. Wal-Mart Stores, Inc.,* 2002 Cal. LEXIS 465, 115 Cal. Rptr. 2d 868 (2002) and *Hooker v. Department of Transportation,* 2002 Cal. LEXIS 464, 115 Cal. Rptr. 2d 853 (2002).

12. *Whirlpool Corp. v. Marshall,* 445 U.S. 1 (1980).

13. On August 8, 1991, the National Conference of Commissioners on Uniform State Laws approved the Model Employment Termination Act 2 (Proposed Official Draft, 1991), commonly called META, which addresses these issues. To date, no states have adopted this model act. (Information on the current status of adoptions of Uniform State Laws provided in an e-mail from Katie Robinson, Communications Officer, NCCUSL, November 7, 2002.)

14. Harold Gill Reuschlein and William A. Gregory, *Hornbook on the Law of Agency and Partnership,* 2nd ed. (St. Paul, Minn.: West, 1990), § 89(b), 151–152.

Agency: Liability for Contracts

AGENDA

NRW NRW will use agents in the conduct of its business. Consequently, the firm needs to decide whether NRW should be a disclosed, an undisclosed, or a partially disclosed principal. The firm also needs to decide what authority NRW should expressly grant to its agents, what additional authority these agents will have, and whether there is some means of limiting the authority of the agents.

Helen is concerned that salespeople will negotiate contracts with buyers and distributors that NRW has not authorized and that NRW will find these contracts unacceptable. What can Helen do to alleviate her concern? In general, what steps should NRW take with its sales force to reduce the risk of this type of problem?

What steps should NRW agents take to minimize their personal liability on contracts they negotiate for NRW?

NRW will deal with the agents of suppliers and retailers. In these relationships, NRW will be the third party. What rights will NRW have against these agents and their principals?

These and other questions will arise during our discussion of agency law. Be prepared! You never know when the firm or one of its members will seek your advice.

A Framework for Contractual Liability

An agent may have many and varied duties. These duties often include negotiating contracts on behalf of the principal. This chapter addresses the obligations of the parties in these contracts, and the potential liability of the agent, the principal, and/or the third party when problems arise during the performance of these contracts.

While the same broad concepts generally apply, agency law varies from state to state. In addition to applying any given state's rules of agency law, the court will often be influenced by the reasonable expectations of the third party; that is, how the third party reasonably perceives the situation. This perception, coupled with the specific laws of a given jurisdiction, may well influence the results in a particular case.

The distinction between servants and nonservants is *not* significant when the agent has entered into a contract on behalf of the principal. As a result, the courts will treat both types of agents the same in contract cases. Remember, though, that the distinction *is* significant if the agent commits a tort in the course and scope of employment. Because the distinction is irrelevant in contract cases, it is logical to only use the term *agent* in this chapter.

In looking at the potential liability that might arise in a contract case, the prime issue for consideration is whether the principal authorized the agent to enter into the contract. This may affect any possible claims the principal, the agent, or the third party might assert against one another. Another important factor is whether the principal's identity is to be revealed to the third party. The principal may be classified as a disclosed, an undisclosed, or a partially disclosed principal. Each classification has implications for the potential liability of the agent, the third person, and the principal. The status of the principal in this regard is determined when the agent and the third party enter the contract; the legal relationships are fixed at that time. These issues, among others, will be discussed in detail in the rest of this chapter.

Imposing Liability on the Principal

Regardless of the principal's classification, the principal will not be liable for every act committed by his or her agent or for every contract signed by the agent. To determine whether the principal should be held liable, the court will examine whether the agent was authorized to enter into this type of contract. Authority can be established in a number of different ways, normally referred to as *types of authority*. Types of authority can overlap in a given situation, adding confusion for the business student. The types of authority are listed in Exhibit 30.1.

For the third party to enforce the contract agreed to by the agent or to recover a judgment against the principal for breach of contract, all that needs to be shown is that *one* type of authority exists. In fact, if the third person can establish that *apparent* authority exists in the agent, the principal can be held liable to the third person even though the agent's conduct was *not* actually authorized by the principal. Even if the principal had expressly forbidden the conduct, the principal will be held liable if the agent possessed the apparent authority to perform the act. Remember, though, that the authority to act as an agent usually includes authority to act only for the benefit, *not* the detriment, of the principal. This establishes some limitations on the agent's apparent authority. See The Principles of European Contract Law, Chapter 3—Completed and Revised Version 1998, at the Universtiteit Antwerpen Web site at http://www.ufsia.ac.be/~estorme/PECL2en3.html for a discussion of an agent's ability to enter into a contract for the principal in Europe.

Actual Authority

Actual authority is the authority that the principal actually grants to the agent and that will establish the limits of what the agent should do in the performance of his or her duties. If the agent acts within the limits of actual authority, the agent will not be liable to the principal for any conduct he or she undertakes on the job, even if the results are negative for the principal. Actual authority may be expressed by the principal, it may be incidental to the performance of the agent's job, or it may be implied from the context of the overall agency agreement. The principal may ratify conduct of the agent, thus making the conduct "authorized" from the outset. And in some cases the authority may arise due to the existence of an emergency that must be dealt with by the agent without the opportunity to seek guidance from the principal.

Express Authority

Express authority occurs when the principal informs the agent that the agent has authority to engage in a specific act or to perform a particular task. Generally, express authority need not be in writing; and, in most cases, it is not. For example, a principal may say to her secretary, "Please order more stationery." Courts often strictly construe the words the principal uses when giving the authority. If the principal says to the agent, "Locate premises for another card

EXHIBIT 30.1 Rights of a Third Party to Sue a Principal

Principal —— (Appointment) ——> Agent   [Agent is the *representative* of the principal. Legally the agent's actions are treated as *if* done by the principal.]

Agent —— (Interacts) ——> Third Person   [Third person can treat the agent's conduct as equivalent to the principal performing the action, *provided* the agent possesses authority.]

Third Person —— (Sues) ——> Principal   [The third party can sue the principal for conduct of the agent, provided that the conduct was authorized *or* within the course and scope of employment.]

Types of Authority an Agent may possess:

- Express
- Ratification
- Incidental
- Implied
- Emergency
- Apparent
- Estoppel

shop," usually the court will interpret this to mean that the agent is authorized only to *find* the premises and not authorized to actually purchase the store. Therefore, an agent should interpret the instructions narrowly or ask for clarification of the scope of authority.

Ratification Authority

Ratification authority occurs when the agent does something that was unauthorized at the time, and the principal approves it later. Ratification requires approval by the principal after the agent forms the contract and after the principal has knowledge of the material facts. When a principal ratifies a contract, the principal must ratify the whole agreement. The principal cannot elect to ratify parts of the contract and disregard the less advantageous parts.

Furthermore, the principal does not need to communicate the ratification verbally to anyone.[1] Generally, ratification may occur by an express statement or may be implied by the principal's conduct indicating an intent to affirm the agent's actions. An example of implied ratification occurs when the principal retains and uses goods delivered under a contract that was originally unauthorized *after* learning of the contract and its terms. Another example of implied ratification occurs when a principal initiates a lawsuit to enforce the terms of such an agreement. The ratification needs to follow the same format required of the original authorization. This means that in a limited number of situ-

ations the ratification will have to be in writing. If the agent/third-party contract must be in writing under the Statute of Frauds, then the ratification must be written, too. (The *Statute of Frauds* is a statute that requires some contracts to be in writing to be enforceable.)

Courts have imposed additional limitations on the doctrine of ratification. Both the principal and the agent must have been capable of forming a contract when the original contract occurred *and* when it was ratified. The *relation back doctrine*, as used in this context, states that *if* the contract is properly ratified, it is as if the contract were valid the whole time. Modern courts will not apply the relation back doctrine if it will injure an innocent party who obtains rights in the contract between the time of the original contract formation and the ratification.

Ratification cannot occur if important contract terms are concealed from the principal. Ratification will be effective only if the principal knows all the relevant facts. Also, the agent must have *purported* to act for the principal (indicated that he or she was acting for the principal) when the agent entered into the contract. If the agent did not reveal his or her agency capacity or if the agent was working for an undisclosed principal, there can be no ratification.

Incidental Authority

In most cases, the principal does not discuss the grant of power in detail, if at all. Generally, the agent is given a brief explanation of his or her authority or he or she is given an objective to accomplish on behalf of the principal. This brief grant of express authority includes the power to do all acts that are incidental to the specific authority that is discussed. *Incidental authority* reasonably and necessarily arises in order to enable the agent to complete his or her assigned duties. Suppose an agent is provided with merchandise that is to be sold door to door. The agent will reasonably and necessarily have incidental authority to deliver the merchandise and to collect the purchase price. Incidental authority is also referred to as *incidental powers.*

Implied Authority

Implied authority is based on the agent's position *or* on past dealings between the agent and the third party. One type of implied authority arises when an agent is given a title and a position. It is implied that the agent can enter into the same types of contracts that people with this title normally can. A vice-president of sales and marketing, for example, will have implied authority to purchase advertising in newspapers and on radio and to contract with an advertising agency for a new ad campaign. The agent will

have this authority because *most* vice-presidents of sales and marketing have such authority. In other words, it is customary. When the principal confers the title on the agent, the agent acquires the implied power that accompanies it.

In the alternative, implied authority may exist because of a series of similar dealings in the past between the agent and the third party. If the principal did not object to the past transactions, it is assumed that the principal authorized the earlier contracts and that this type of transaction is within the agent's power. For example, if a secretary customarily orders office supplies for a business on a monthly basis, the secretary has implied authority to continue ordering office supplies in this manner.

Implied authority may exceed express authority. The third party can recover a judgment in court on the basis of this implied authority if (1) the third party reasonably believed that the agent had some particular authority, and (2) the third party was unaware that the authority was lacking. Both elements are required.

There is often more than one type of authority present. The court in the following case considered express, implied, and apparent authority. (*Apparent authority* exists when the principal creates the appearance that the agent acts with authority.)

30.1

OPP v. WHEATON VAN LINES, INC.
231 F.3d 1060, 2000 U.S. App. LEXIS 27460 (7th Cir. 2000)

FACTS Shelley Opp lived in California with her husband, Richard Opp, until they sought a divorce in August 1996. In June 1997, Ms. Opp contacted Soraghan Moving and Storage, an agent of Wheaton Van Lines, to move her personal property from California to Illinois. She provided Soraghan with a list of her items. Linda Kloempken, a Soraghan employee, phoned Ms. Opp to give her an estimate of the moving charges. Ms. Opp then notified Kloempken that she wanted to insure her property for its full value of $10,000.00. Soraghan movers conducted a "walk-through" of the California residence. Kloempken then faxed to Ms. Opp an "Estimate/Order for Service" form. Ms. Opp signed the form. According to Kloempken, she explained to Ms. Opp that the phrase "shipper to advise" meant that Ms. Opp or her representative must advise the mover at the time the shipment was picked up whether Ms. Opp would like full replacement coverage of $10,000.00. According to Ms. Opp, she was never informed that the person releasing her property in California would have to sign anything, declare any value for her property, or do anything other than give the movers access to her belongings. The estimate form

also provided a location where Ms. Opp could designate someone as her "true and lawful representative," but she made no such designation.

On the day of the move, the movers called Ms. Opp in Illinois to notify her that their arrival at the California home would be delayed by a half-hour due to a flat tire. Ms. Opp then phoned Mr. Opp at his office and asked him to go to the house, open the door, and "let the movers in." Ms. Opp also told Kloempken that "someone" would be at the California home to give the movers access to her property. While the movers were loading the property, Mr. Opp signed the bill of lading on a line that indicated that he was Ms. Opp's authorized agent. While the parties agree that Mr. Opp signed the bill of lading, they dispute whether he made the notation that limited the carriers' liability to $.60 per pound. Mr. Opp also signed an inventory of the property that indicated that he was its "owner or authorized agent." After the movers left, Mr. Opp called Ms. Opp to tell her that the movers "picked up your stuff." On July 8, 1997, the truck carrying Ms.

Opp's belongings was struck by a train, damaging most of her property. The carriers claimed that their liability was limited to $.60 per pound.

ISSUE Did Mr. Opp have express, implied, or apparent authority to limit the carriers' liability?

HOLDING Maybe. Mr. Opp *may* have had implied or apparent authority. Summary judgment on this issue was incorrect; it should be submitted to a trial court.

REASONING Excerpts from the opinion of Circuit Judge Manion:

According to Ms. Opp, . . . she never authorized Mr. Opp to sign the bill of lading and limit the carriers' liability. . . . Ms. Opp's . . . claim requires us . . . to determine whether Mr. Opp had the authority to act as Ms. Opp's agent and limit the carriers' liability when he signed the bill of lading. . . . We also note that the Illinois law of agency, as well as the federal common law of agency, accord with the *Restatement.* [The court considered federal law because of a federal statute that was involved.] . . . "An agent's authority may be either actual or apparent . . . " . . . "[O]nly the words or conduct of the alleged principal, not the alleged agent, establish the [actual or apparent] authority of an agent."

We . . . note that the record clearly demonstrates that Mr. Opp never received the express authority to represent Ms. Opp and to limit the carriers' liability. "An agent has express authority when the principal explicitly grants the agent the authority to perform a particular act." There is no evidence . . . that Ms. Opp explicitly granted authority to Mr. Opp to bind her to an agreement that limited the carriers' liability. . . . Ms. Opp stated in her affidavit that she never requested or intended Mr. Opp to do anything other than to open the door and allow the movers to remove her property. And the record contains no testimony from Mr. Opp. Because the record provides no counter affidavits that establish an explicit agency relationship between Ms. and Mr. Opp, we must accept Ms. Opp's affidavit as true. . . .

We next determine whether Mr. Opp had the implied authority to limit the carriers' liability. "Implied authority is actual authority that is implied by facts and circumstances and it may be proved by circumstantial evidence." "An agent has implied authority for the performance or transaction of anything reasonably necessary to effective execution of his express authority." . . . Thus we must determine whether it was reasonably necessary for Mr. Opp to sign the bill of lading in order to execute his express authority to open the door to give the movers access to Ms. Opp's property. The carriers argue that because Ms. Opp allegedly knew that the bill of lading had to be signed when her property was picked

up, . . . Ms. Opp's request for Mr. Opp to tender the goods to the movers also included the necessary authority for him to sign the bill of lading. But . . . , Ms. Opp only told Mr. Opp to open the door. She made no request for him to sign anything, or to make any agreement as to the carriers' liability. Ms. Opp also testified that she was never informed that the person releasing her property in California would have to sign a bill of lading and declare a value for her property. . . . [T]he record contains no testimony from Mr. Opp at all . . . thus it is unclear whether he ever implied from Ms. Opp's request that he was also authorized to limit the carriers' liability, or whether he merely thought that he was signing forms to confirm that Ms. Opp's goods were taken from the home. The record also lacks testimony from any of the movers who picked up Ms. Opp's personal property . . . , and we have no indication from them what Mr. Opp understood about the significance of his signature. . . . Thus we conclude that there is insufficient evidence to support a grant of summary judgment for the carriers on this issue.

We . . . then consider whether Mr. Opp had the apparent authority to sign the bill of lading and limit the carriers' liability. Under the doctrine of apparent authority, "a principal will be bound not only by the authority that it actually gives to another, but also by the authority that it appears to give." "Apparent authority arises when a principal creates, by its words or conduct, the reasonable impression in a third party that the agent has the authority to perform a certain act on its behalf." Thus we must determine whether the evidence demonstrates that Ms. Opp's words or conduct created a reasonable impression in the carriers that Mr. Opp had the authority to sign the bill of lading and limit their liability. The carriers argue that they reasonably believed that Mr. Opp had the authority to sign the bill of lading because Ms. Opp allegedly knew that a bill of lading had to be signed when her goods were picked up, she had arranged for the carriers to contact Mr. Opp to preside at the prior walk-through, and she had also arranged for Mr. Opp to be the only person present at the California home to tender the goods. But material facts in the record also justify a reasonable inference that Mr. Opp did not have . . . apparent authority. . . . It is undisputed that Ms. Opp told Kloempken at Soraghan that she wanted the full replacement value of $10,000.00 on her goods, which is reflected on Wheaton's . . . form. Ms. Opp never designated a "lawful representative" on the space provided on the estimate form, and thus Wheaton's own form lacked any indication that Mr. Opp was her agent. . . . Ms. Opp testified that the carriers never informed her that the person releasing her property in California would have to sign anything, declare any value for her property, or do anything other than to give the movers access to her belongings. . . . And there is no evidence in the record that . . . Ms. Opp ever discussed the valuation of her property with Mr. Opp. . . .

BUSINESS CONSIDERATIONS How could the parties have better handled the receipt of Ms. Opp's belongings and the signing of the bill of lading? How could the parties have done a better job preparing for trial?

ETHICAL CONSIDERATIONS Is it ethical for the movers to claim that their liability is limited? Does the fact that the movers "knew" Ms. Opp wanted replacement value on her goods affect your answer? Why?

Emergency Authority

Emergency authority is inherent in all agency relationships. It need not be expressed. It provides the agent with authority to respond to emergencies, even though the principal and agent never discussed the type of emergency or how to respond to it. Suppose Galen, the owner of a jewelry store, leaves Andrea, his manager, in charge and goes out for supper. While Galen is absent, a fire starts in the stockroom. In an effort to contain the fire, Andrea rushes to the hardware store next door and "buys" four fire extinguishers on credit. Galen must pay for the fire extinguishers because Andrea had emergency authority to purchase them.

Emergency authority will be found when all the following circumstances exist:

• An emergency or unexpected situation occurs that requires prompt action.

• The principal cannot be reached in sufficient time for a response or advice.

• The action taken by the agent is reasonable in the situation and it is expected to benefit the principal.

Apparent Authority

Apparent authority occurs when the principal creates the appearance that an agency exists or that the agent has certain powers. Here, the representation of authority is made to the third party rather than to the agent.[2] Apparent authority is based on the conduct of the *principal,* not the conduct of the agent; the conduct of the principal must cause a reasonable third party to believe that a particular person has authority to act as the principal's agent. An agent with apparent authority may or may not also have actual authority to perform the same acts on behalf of the principal.

Apparent authority may be created by intentional or careless acts of the principal and reasonable reliance by the third party. Obviously, if the third party knows the agent does not have this authority, the reliance cannot be reasonable, and there can be no apparent authority.

In some cases, apparent authority exists even though there is no real agent. The person acting in the agent's role may be considered a *purported agent* (that is, one who claims to be an agent). Sometimes this purported agent is an agent who has been terminated, and sometimes the person never was an agent. For example, suppose a company fires Nathan, a sales representative, but neglects to collect its samples, displays, and order forms from him. Nathan then takes a number of customer orders and disappears with the cash deposits. The company will have to return the deposits or credit the deposits to the customers' orders, because Nathan still has apparent authority to take orders. To help prevent this situation, the company should require Nathan to return the company's sales materials at the time his employment is terminated.

When an agency relationship is terminated, a principal should take certain steps to terminate apparent authority. The principal should inform the agent that the relationship is terminated, call or send notices to people who have dealt with that agent, and sometimes advertise in newspapers and trade journals that the relationship is terminated. The principal should collect all identification tags, samples, displays, order forms, and any other materials that can be used as evidence of the agency relationship. These items are *indicia* of the agency relationship.

Sometimes the principal never employed the purported agent, and yet the principal's conduct may cause the principal to be liable for the "agent's" actions. For example, a department store may not require its clerks to wear identifying jackets, vests, or even name tags. Suppose Rosa, a customer, selects some merchandise and walks toward a cash register. In place of a clerk, JoLynne, another customer, steps behind the cash register, "rings up" Rosa's sale, puts the merchandise in the bag, and pockets the payment. In this case, the store cannot charge Rosa again for the merchandise; it is bound by the acts of JoLynne, the purported agent.

Before applying apparent authority, some courts require that the principal's actions give rise to a reasonable belief in the agent's authority and that there be detrimental reliance on the part of the third party.[3] A number of factors need to be considered; the existence of apparent authority is a factual issue to be determined in each case.

A third party must act reasonably or the court will not apply the concept of apparent authority. The third party must take into consideration the facts and circumstances surrounding the transaction and the type of action involved. Sometimes, based on the information available, the third party must investigate further before reasonably relying on apparent authority.

Apparent authority may be used to hold a principal liable on contracts entered into by the agent. It *ordinarily* will not be used to make a principal accountable for physical harm caused by the agent through negligence, assault, trespass, and similar torts.

The federal court of appeals grappled with whether the attorney had apparent authority in the following case. The majority of the court decided to certify the question to the District of Columbia Circuit Court of Appeals for a ruling on this issue of the law.

30.2

MAKINS v. DISTRICT OF COLUMBIA
277 F.3d 544, 2002 U.S. App. LEXIS 780 (D.C. Cir. 2002)

FACTS Brenda Makins had been employed in the District of Columbia's Department of Corrections. John Harrison began representing Makins as her attorney after she received a notice of termination from the Department. Harrison and Makins did not have a written retainer agreement. The district judge referred Makins's case to a magistrate judge, who ordered the "lead attorney(s) for the parties" to appear before him for a settlement conference. The order required that the "parties shall either attend the settlement conference or be available by telephone for the duration of the settlement conference." Makins did not attend the settlement conference, but she spoke to Harrison several times on the phone. Harrison and the attorneys for the District reached an agreement to settle the case, but Makins refused to sign it. According to Makins, she never agreed to settle her case because "getting [her] job back had to be part of any agreement." Harrison contended that Makins told him to do "what you think is right, I trust you," and that she agreed to the actual settlement.

ISSUE Could Harrison bind Makins to a settlement agreement even though he did not have actual authority?

HOLDING Yes, Harrison could have apparent authority. This question was certified to the District of Columbia courts for an answer since there was no precedent.

REASONING Excerpts from the opinion of Circuit Judge Randolph:

Aside from cases in which a settlement agreement is sought to be enforced against the United States or in which there is a statute conferring lawmaking power on federal courts, we adopt local law in determining whether a settlement agreement should be enforced. The local law on this subject is, unfortunately, not much developed. The District of Columbia Court of Appeals treats settlement agreements as contracts. In run-of-the-mill contract cases, the D.C. Court of Appeals relies on § 27 of the *Restatement (Second) of Agency* to determine whether an agent has the authority to enter into a binding agreement on behalf of the principal. The local court distinguishes . . . between an agent's "actual authority" and his "apparent authority." Actual "authority," according to the *Restatement's* definition, means that the agent has the power "to affect the legal relations of the principal by acts done in accordance with the principal's manifestations of consent to him."[4] For settlement purposes, attorney Harrison possessed actual authority in certain respects. Makins manifested her consent [to] Harrison's attending the settlement conference on September 12, to negotiating on her behalf and, if her testimony is believed, to settling the case, but only on the condition that she got her job back.

We must assume . . . that Makins never gave Harrison actual authority to settle the case without the condition she specified. . . . As agents for their clients, attorneys without actual authority may have "apparent authority" to bind their clients to agreements. The local court has not, however, addressed the precise question presented here: may an attorney negotiating in the client's absence bind the client to a settlement agreement if the attorney has led opposing counsel to believe he had actual authority from the client to settle the case? . . . [A]n opinion of the local court . . . holds that "regardless of the good faith of the attorney, absent specific authority, an attorney cannot accept a settlement offer on behalf of a client." On the face of it, the statement leaves no room for apparent authority. . . . [However,] the case is at odds with the same court's later pronouncement. . . . There was . . . no occasion for the court to consider whether an opposing party could enforce a settlement agreement when the other party's attorney possessed only apparent authority. . . .

Makins herself concedes that if Harrison had apparent authority . . . the agreement he negotiated could be enforced. . . . Apparent authority, according to the widely-accepted rule in the *Restatement,* can arise from "written or spoken words or any other conduct of the principal which, reasonably interpreted, causes the third person to believe that the principal consents to have the act done on [her] behalf by the person purporting to act for [her]." While actual authority depends on communications between the client and the attorney—the principal and the agent—apparent authority under the *Restatement* turns on the client's communication to the third party. . . . As the D.C. Court of Appeals put it, "apparent authority is derived from the principal's representations to the third-party rather than to the agent."

Given the local court's adoption of the *Restatement,* and its willingness to look at treatises to establish the general rules of law pertaining to agency issues, . . . the local court faced with this issue might turn to the recently-issued *Restatement (Third) of the Law Governing Lawyers* to aid analysis. *The Restatement of the Law Governing Lawyers* parallels the *Restatement of Agency's* approach to authority: "A lawyer's act is considered to be that of the client in proceedings before a tribunal or in dealings with a third person if the tribunal or third person reasonably assumes that the lawyer is authorized to do the act on the basis of the client's (and not the lawyer's) manifestations of authorization."[5] . . . [T]he *Restatement* adds: "Apparent authority exists when and to the extent a client causes a third person to form a reasonable belief that a lawyer is authorized to act for the client"; and "Generally a client is not bound by a settlement that the client has not authorized the lawyer to make by express, implied, or apparent authority. . . ."

. . . [C]ertain decisions in litigation are the client's, and the client's alone to make. Like the decision to enter a plea of guilty or to pursue an appeal in a civil or criminal case, the decision whether to settle a case and on what terms is reserved to the client. . . . As to settlements, the client therefore must manifest to the third party that his lawyer has the authority to compromise the case. If the matter is in doubt, third parties can protect themselves by "obtaining clarification of the lawyer's authority." Settlements are thereby facilitated while the client's prerogatives are preserved. The key here is that the client, not the lawyer, must indicate to the third party that the lawyer is authorized to act. . . . [A]lthough "simply retaining a lawyer confers broad apparent authority on the lawyer" regarding some matters, it "does not extend to matters, such as approving a settlement, reserved for client decision. . . ." . . . Neither the District nor the magistrate ever heard from Makins, in person or by telephone [during the settlement conference]. . . . The client's manifestations to the third party must be with respect to settlement, not the general conduct of the litigation. If it were otherwise, an attorney would nearly always have apparent authority to end the case despite the wishes of his client. . . . "The apparent authority of an agent arises when the principal places the agent in such a position as to mislead third persons into believing that the agent is clothed with authority which in fact he does not possess." . . . [A]pparent authority can arise from something other than statements of the principal. . . . The "something other" usually consists of "the ordinary habits of persons in the locality, trade or profession"[6]—in other words, custom and usage. . . . [I]t may be that it is customary for lawyers in the District to enter into binding, oral settlement agreements without the opposing side receiving some manifestation of assent—orally or in writing . . . from the client. . . . It may also be that the D.C. Court of Appeals would decide that a client's authorizing his attorney to attend a settlement conference and negotiate on the client's behalf is, in itself, enough to confer apparent authority. . . . [The issue is referred to the D.C. Court of Appeals for clarification.]

BUSINESS CONSIDERATIONS How can parties protect themselves from attorneys entering into settlement agreements without authority? How can parties protect themselves from apparent authority arising from the custom and usage in the locality? What techniques can generally be used to prevent unauthorized acts of agents?

ETHICAL CONSIDERATIONS Was it ethical for Harrison to accept on behalf of Makins? Why?

Authority by Estoppel

Authority by estoppel prevents a principal who has misled a third party from denying the agent's authority. This is also called *ostensible authority.* It occurs when the principal *allows* the purported agent to pass himself or herself off as an agent and does not take steps to prevent the purported agent's representation.

Estoppel authority may occur by itself or in conjunction with other types of authority. When there is only estoppel authority and no other authority, estoppel authority will be used solely for the protection of the third party. It will not constitute the basis of a successful lawsuit by the principal against the third party. It creates rights for the third party and liabilities for the principal; it protects the third party and provides reimbursement for the third party's injuries. As with other doctrines of agency law, the courts are weighing the respective rights of two relatively innocent people—the third party and the principal. The purported agent can be sued for fraud, but generally that person cannot be located or has insufficient funds to cover the resulting losses. (*Fraud* is the intentional misrepresentation of a material fact.)

Authority by estoppel is illustrated in Exhibit 30.2 and in the example that follows.

Roy was walking to class one Wednesday when he passed Grace and David, who were standing next to Roy's car. He overheard Grace pointing out all the car's features to David. It was evident that Grace was trying to sell the car to David on Roy's behalf. Roy thought this amusing and did not stop to explain the truth. He went to class instead. He later learned that David made a $200 down payment on the car and that Grace disappeared with the money.

In a lawsuit between David and Roy, David will prevail. The court can apply agency by estoppel and decide that Roy is estopped (prevented) from denying that Grace was his agent. Roy knew that Grace was pretending to be Roy's agent, and Roy easily could have denied this. Roy's failure to speak helped to cause David's loss. The court will protect David by allowing him to recover.

Note that Grace would also be liable to David if she could be located. She would be liable under fraud and breach of warranty of authority. (*Warranties of authority* are implied warranties that the agent is an agent for the principal and is permitted to act in this manner.)

Imputing the Agent's Knowledge to the Principal

In addition to being liable for contracts entered into by an agent, a principal may be legally responsible for information known to the agent but not actually known by the principal. This concept is called *imputing knowledge*. Because an agent has a duty to inform the principal about important facts that relate to the agency, it will be assumed that the agent has performed this duty. This duty, commonly called the duty to give notice, was discussed in Chapter 29. If the agent fails to perform this duty and the failure causes a loss, the principal—not the third party—should suffer the loss. Courts justify this result because the principal selected the agent, placed the agent in a position of authority, and had (legal) control over the agent.

The agent's knowledge is not always imputed to the principal. Before a principal will be bound by knowledge received by the agent, generally the agent must have actual or apparent authority to receive this type of knowledge. In addition, the information received by the agent must relate to the subject matter of the agency. For example, if Valora, the principal, owns a real estate firm, a movie theater, and a hardware store, and Dimas, the agent, works in the hardware store, knowledge that Dimas obtains about the real estate firm will *not* be imputed to Valora. The knowledge must be within the scope of the agency.

Disclosed Principal

When an agent clearly discloses that he or she is representing a principal and identifies the principal, the principal is *disclosed*. In these situations, the principal may be

EXHIBIT 30.2 Authority by Estoppel

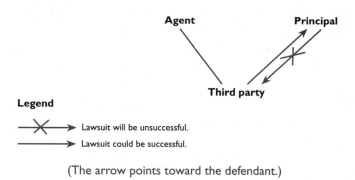

Legend

→ Lawsuit will be unsuccessful.

→ Lawsuit could be successful.

(The arrow points toward the defendant.)

bound to the contract by any of the types of authority that have been discussed. Exhibit 30.3 illustrates a disclosed principal.

Liability of the Agent

Normally, when an agent indicates that he or she is entering into a contract on behalf of the disclosed principal, the agent will not be liable for the contract. It is clearly understood that the third party should look to the principal alone for performance. As with most legal rules, there are exceptions. For example, if the agent fails to represent his or her capacity as such, the agent will be personally bound. In addition, the agent will be bound if he or she intends to be bound. For example, the agent may say, "You can rely on me," or "You have my word on it."

Why would an agent want to be liable on the principal's contract? Why would an agent want to undertake additional liability? An agent might do this if it is necessary to make a sale. The prospective buyer may be unsure about the principal and his or her reputation or financial backing. Perhaps the prospect has a long working relationship with the agent, so the agent's guarantee of performance persuades the prospect. The agent does not have valid grounds to complain if he or she is accepted at his or her word. The third party generally will prefer to sue the principal on the contract instead of the agent, since the principal often has more assets.

The third party, then, has legal rights against both the agent and the disclosed principal in these circumstances. (See the Center for Computer-Assisted Legal Instruction [CALI][7] Web site at http://www.cali.org/fellows/grids/businessorgs.html for a discussion of the liability of agents and principals.) This does not mean that the third party can collect twice. The third party is limited to one reimbursement. The traditional approach also required the third party to make an *election* to sue either the agent *or* the principal. Obviously, an important factor in this decision is who has the funds to pay a judgment. If the third party sues the principal and loses, he or she will be barred from then suing the agent. The reverse is also true. The more modern approach permits the third party to sue both the principal and the agent *together*. However, either defendant can require the third party to make an election prior to judgment.

Warranty of Authority

Whenever an agent of a disclosed principal enters into a contract, the agent makes all of the following implied warranties. The agent does not state these warranties; they are implied by the situation.

NRW CASE 30.1 Sales/Management

NRW

HONORING SALES AGENT'S CONTRACTS

NRW appointed several sales agents. Each agent was assigned a territory, and each was provided with an "order book" containing standard order forms. These order forms contain the list price for NRW products. One of the sales agents called on a large retail outlet in another state. The retailer expressed an interest in buying a large quantity of StuffTrakR units, but only if NRW would give the retailer a 10 percent discount on the order. The sales agent agreed to these terms and completed the order form, including an indication of the 10 percent discount. Once the form was completed and signed by the sales agent and the store's representative, a copy was faxed to NRW. When Carlos received the copy of the order, he was livid. He knows that the discount will remove virtually all the profit from the sale, but he fears that the firm is bound by the signed order. He asks you whether NRW must honor this contract. What will you tell him?

BUSINESS CONSIDERATIONS What can a firm do to protect itself from overly zealous sales agents? Should a firm have a policy in place for handling situations such as this, or should each case be handled on an individual basis? How should the business communicate with the buyer in this sort of situation in order to (a) avoid the contract, and (b) retain the buyer as a future customer?

ETHICAL CONSIDERATIONS Is it ethical for a firm to refuse to honor a commitment made by one of its agents, even if the agent exceeded his or her authority? Is it ethical for a buyer to utilize its size to force special concessions from a sales agent beyond those normally granted by the firm?

INTERNATIONAL CONSIDERATIONS Suppose that the buyer was in another country, and that the buyer *claims* that the agent made an oral commitment for a discount. Would such an oral promise, if proven, be valid? Why?

- The disclosed principal exists and is competent.

- The agent is an agent for the principal.

- The agent is authorized to enter into this type of contract for the principal.

EXHIBIT 30.3 Disclosed Principal

> # NRW
>
> Mai Nguyen
> Sales Agent for NRW
> 9876 Appian Way
> Maineville, OH 44444
> 513-555-8375 phone
> 513-555-8376 fax
> mai@nrw.com

The third party can sue the agent to recover for losses that are caused by the breach of warranty of authority. Perhaps the third party has losses because he or she did not receive the goods covered by the contract. Further, suppose the principal is not responsible for the losses because the agent is not authorized to enter into this type of contract. The third party can sue the agent for the breach of warranties.

If the agent fears that he or she does not have the authority to enter into this type of contract, the agent may be concerned about the warranties of authority. He or she would be wise, then, to negate the warranties. This can be accomplished by stating that there is no warranty or by specifically stating to the third party the limitations on the agent's actual authority. The latter situation is illustrated in the following example.

Rhoda hires Beth as an agent and tells her to locate a parcel of agricultural real estate. Beth locates a parcel that meets Rhoda's specifications. Edele, the owner of the parcel, wants Beth to sign the purchase contract, but Beth is not sure whether she has authority to sign. If she fully and truthfully discloses the situation surrounding her authority to Edele, Beth will negate the implied warranty of authority. If Edele still wishes to sign the contract with Beth, he will assume the responsibility, and the loss, if the contract is not authorized. Edele would be relying on his own judgment.

The agent may be liable for fraud if the agent intentionally misrepresents his or her authority. Exhibit 30.4 illustrates the agent's liability.

Liability of the Third Party

Lawsuit by the Principal When a principal has been disclosed from the beginning, the third party realizes, or should realize, that the principal has an interest in the contract. The principal can successfully sue the third party on

Exceptions:

- agent fails to represent capacity
- agent intends to be bound
- agent breaches warranties of authority
- agent commits fraud

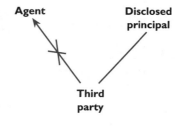

Legend

✕——▶ Lawsuit will be unsuccessful.

(The arrow points toward the defendant.)

the contract, if the agent was authorized to enter into this type of contract for the principal. In other words, the third party will be liable if there is express, implied, incidental, emergency, apparent, or ratification authority. The third party will not be liable if the only type of authority is estoppel authority.

Lawsuit by the Agent Normally, the agent has no right to sue the third party on a contract. An agent *may* successfully sue the third party if the agent can show that he or she has an interest in the contract. The most common type of interest is one in which the agent is entitled to a commission on a sale. For example, M.J., a real estate broker (the agent) enters into a contract with a buyer on behalf of Yolanda, a homeowner (the principal). M.J. is entitled to a 6 percent commission payable from the proceeds of the sale. If the buyer (the third party) breaches the contract, M.J. can sue to recover the lost commission. (In this type of case, Yolanda may decide that it is not worth suing, but M.J. may feel that it is.)

An agent may successfully sue the third party when the agent intends to be bound to the original contract. This rule is based on equitable principles. If the agent is potentially liable to the third party, the third party should be potentially liable to the agent, too. In some cases, a principal may transfer to the agent the right to file the lawsuit. In these cases, also, the agent can sue on the contract. These relationships are illustrated in Exhibit 30.5.

Undisclosed Principal

An *undisclosed* principal is one whose existence and identity are unknown to the third party. There are many valid reasons why a principal might want to be undisclosed—to be able to negotiate a deal, to negotiate a better deal, or to conceal either an investment in a project or a donation to a charity. Exhibit 30.6 illustrates an undisclosed principal.

There may be situations where the third party would have refused to contract with the principal and the principal and his or her agent decide to mislead the third person in order to obtain the contract. If the agent and principal agree that the principal should remain undisclosed for the purpose of defrauding the third party, the third party can have the contract set aside by proving this fraud in the court. However, the third party cannot have the contract set aside in court on the basis of fraud merely because the identity of the principal was not disclosed. The third party must show that the identify of the principal is a material fact. The fact that the principal prefers to remain undisclosed to the third person is not sufficient in itself to establish fraud or any other type of wrongdoing.

Liability of the Agent

When the principal is completely undisclosed, the third party believes that he or she is contracting with the agent and that the agent is dealing for himself or herself. Based on the third party's knowledge, that assumption is rational. If there is a default on the contract, the third party can sue the agent. As far as the third party is concerned at the time of contracting, there are only two parties to the contract: the third party and the agent. Thus, the agent is liable to the third person for any breach of the contract.

Liability of the Principal

If the third party later discovers the identity of the principal, the third party can sue the principal. The principal will be held liable if the agent was authorized to enter into this type of contract for the principal. As mentioned before, traditionally with an undisclosed principal the third party must make an election to sue either the agent *or* the principal. There is one important exception, however, if the

---

EXHIBIT 30.5 **Rights of an Agent of a Disclosed Principal to Sue a Third Party**

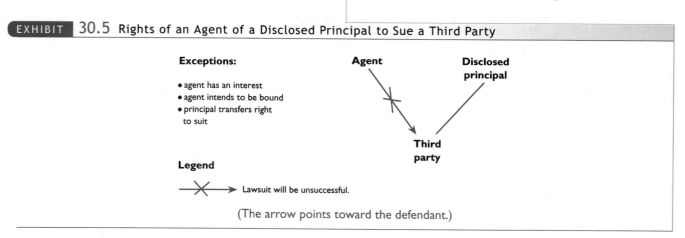

NRW CASE 30.2   Sales/Management

THE WARRANTY OF AUTHORITY

When one of the firm's sales agents was discussing InvenTrakR with a potential customer, the customer expressed interest in the product but was also concerned about an "overreliance" on technology for inventory control. The customer was concerned that the product might malfunction, causing the store significant losses. The agent told the customer that, while it was not normal company policy, she was certain that NRW would be willing to guarantee that the InvenTrakR system would not malfunction, and that the firm would probably be willing to give a three-year guarantee against any losses due to system failures. The customer agreed to purchase the system, but only if the agent included this three-year guarantee on the order form and gave the customer a copy of the form. The agent did so, and the form was signed by the agent and the customer. When the agent sent the order form to NRW, Helen was furious. She would like to cancel the agreement but isn't sure she or the firm has the authority to do so. Helen has asked you about the legal implications of this situation. What will you tell her?

BUSINESS CONSIDERATIONS How can a firm protect itself from an agent who knowingly exceeds his or her authority in order to make a sale? Is an agent legally liable to the customer if the agent knowingly exceeds the authority granted by the principal?

ETHICAL CONSIDERATIONS Does an agent have an ethical obligation to disclose to the third person any conduct that might exceed the authority given to the agent? Does the agent have an ethical obligation to inform the principal if or when the agent exceeds his or her authority?

INTERNATIONAL CONSIDERATIONS If the customer in this case was from another country, would the provisions of either the CISG or NAFTA protect NRW from any conduct by the agent that exceeded his or her authority?

---

third party sues the agent and loses *before* discovering the principal. In that case, the third party is not considered to have made an election and will be permitted to sue the principal later.

Liability of the Third Party

The third party may not be the one who suffers damages because of a breach of contract but may, in fact, be the one who commits the breach. Since the third party thought he or she was liable to the agent, it is logical to allow the agent to sue the third party. The law allows this action.

Under some circumstances, the undisclosed principal may, in his or her own name, also be able to sue the third party. There are some limitations, however. Generally, the principal can file a lawsuit by himself or herself only if the contract is assignable. (*Assignable* means that the right is legally capable of being transferred from one person to another. See Chapter 14 for a discussion of assignments and of assignable contracts.) If the contract is assignable, the position of the third party will not be jeopardized by either an assignment or the suit by the principal. Since the agent can assign the contract to anyone, the principal should be able to enforce the contract rights as if those rights had been assigned to the principal. Either way, the third party will be in the same position. Remember that the third party will not have to pay both the agent and the principal: the third party will have to pay damages only once. This relationship is shown in Exhibit 30.7.

Remember that the principal may not be able to sue in his or her own name because the contract is not assignable, or the principal may still wish to keep his or her identity secret. If either of these situations occur, the principal can still arrange for the agent to file the lawsuit in the agent's name.

Partially Disclosed Principal

A *partially disclosed* principal is one whose existence is known to the third party but whose identity is not. In other words, the agency is disclosed, but the principal's identity is not yet disclosed. For example, suppose that Hector Dias works as an agent for Smith Manufacturing. Hector approaches Beheshti Tool and Die to have some work done for Smith Manufacturing. However, he does not mention Smith Manufacturing by name. Hector then negotiates a contract with Beheshti Tool and Die and signs the contract. Instead of signing with a full disclosure of his position, Hector signs the contract as "Hector Dias, agent." Obviously, in this situation Beheshti Tool and Die would know that the contract was with the principal, but it would not (yet) know the identity of the principal. If the contract is breached and the work is not paid for as scheduled, who can Beheshti Tool and Die sue to recover its damages?

EXHIBIT 30.6 Undisclosed Principal

> ## PROPERTY LOCATION SYSTEMS
>
> Mai Nguyen
> 9876 Appian Way
> Maineville, OH 44444
> 513-555-8375 phone
> 513-555-8376 fax
> mai@yahoo.com

The rules that are applied to partially disclosed principals are similar to those applied to undisclosed principals. The principal may be sued if the contract is breached, and the suit will be successful if the principal authorized the actions of the agent. Once again, the third party can be required to make an election to sue the principal *or* the agent. If the principal suffers damages, he or she can sue the third party. The contract need not be assignable, because the third party knew that another party in interest, the partially disclosed principal, was involved. Exhibit 30.8 illustrates a partially disclosed principal.

The general rule is that when an agent is working for a partially disclosed principal, the agent will be personally liable for the contract. The third party is probably relying on the agent's reputation and credit because the third party knows the identity of the agent but does not know the identity of the principal. It is unlikely that the third party is relying on the reputation and credit of the unrevealed principal, a principal who could be anyone. The third party is probably relying on the reputation and credit of the agent, a party who is known to the third party and with whom the third party decided to conduct business. An exception arises if the contracting parties agree that the agent will not be held liable. This agreement may occur if the agent indicates that he or she will not be bound and the third party does not object to this limitation.

Analysis of Agent's Contracts with Third Parties

To characterize a contract situation involving any type of principal, one should answer the following questions:

- Was the person acting as an agent for the hiring party?

- Did the agent enter a contract on behalf of the hiring party or make contractual promises?

- Was the agent acting within the scope of his or her contractual authority? What type or types of authority were present?

EXHIBIT 30.7 Rights of an Undisclosed Principal

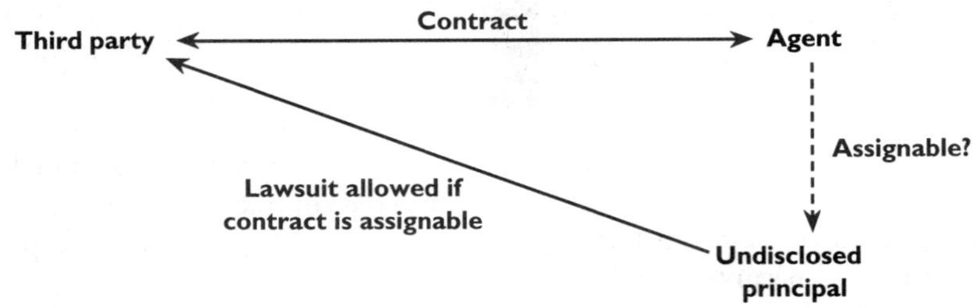

EXHIBIT 30.8 Partially Disclosed Principal

> Mai Nguyen
> Sales Agent
> 9876 Appian Way
> Maineville, OH 44444
> 513-555-8375 phone
> 513-555-8376 fax
> mai@yahoo.com

• Was the hiring party a disclosed, undisclosed, or partially disclosed principal?

• Did the third party make an election to sue the agent or principal?

• Is the agent liable for the contractual promises?

Contract between the Principal and the Agent

The Need for a Writing

The agency relationship is consensual in nature. It actually will be a contract if the principal and agent both give up consideration, which is generally the case. As with other contracts, the Statute of Frauds may apply and require written evidence of the contract in order for the contract to be enforceable. The provisions of the Statute of Frauds that are most likely to apply are those relating to contracts that cannot possibly be performed within one year and contracts involving the sale of real estate. Even if the Statute of Frauds does not apply, it is wise to write out the contractual provisions.

The *equal dignities rule* also requires that some agency agreements be in writing. This rule states that the agent/principal contract deserves (requires) the same dignity as the agent/third-party contract, as shown in Exhibit 30.9. If contract A *must* be written, then contract B *must* be written. For example, if the agent is hired to locate and purchase goods costing more than $500, the UCC Statute of Frauds requires that the agent/third-party contract be in writing, consequently the principal/agent contract must also be in writing.

Covenants Not to Compete

Covenants in Employment Contracts Some employment contracts contain *covenants* (promises) that the agent will not work for a competing firm. The contract may provide that (1) the agent will not moonlight with the competition, or (2) the agent will not compete with the principal after this employment relationship is terminated. The

EXHIBIT 30.9 Equal Dignities Rule

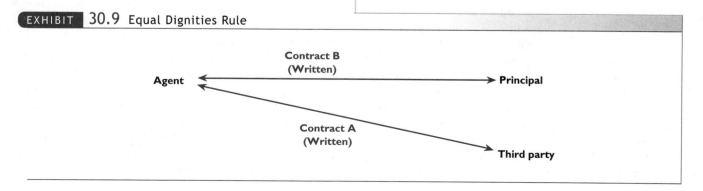

second provision is usually applicable if the agent either quits or is fired. Some contracts contain both prohibitions.

Competing legal considerations arise in disputes about these covenants. On the one hand, the agent agrees not to compete. Perhaps the agent desperately wants the position and feels that he or she will not be hired unless he or she signs the covenant. The agent may not have equal bargaining power with the principal. Generally, parties *are* bound by their contract provisions. On the other hand, it may be a hardship on the agent to unduly restrict his or her ability to locate another position. In addition, it will be detrimental to society if people are not allowed to seek the occupations for which they are most highly qualified. For these reasons, courts scrutinize covenants not to compete to determine whether the covenant is legal. As a rule, courts do not favor covenants not to compete. The covenant will be illegal if the court concludes that it is against public policy.

To determine whether the covenant is against public policy, the court will examine its reasonableness. The court will look at the situation surrounding the employment to see whether the principal has a legitimate interest in preventing the competition.

Covenants in Sales Contracts Covenants not to compete are also prevalent in contracts in which the owner of a business sells the business to a buyer and the buyer obtains a promise that the previous owner will not compete with him or her. In such cases, the buyer has an interest in not having competition from the seller. Generally, the buyer pays a larger purchase price so that the seller will sell the goodwill of the business and sign a covenant not to compete with the buyer. (*Goodwill* means the good name and reputation of a business and its resulting ability to attract clients.) Courts are more inclined to enforce covenants not to compete in the sale of a business.

Enforceable Restrictions Additional requirements exist for a valid covenant not to compete. The time and area specifications of the covenant must be reasonable. What is reasonable, moreover, depends on the type of employment. Covenants containing time periods of two to five years are generally acceptable to the courts. The limitation is controlled by the time period during which the agent is able to draw contacts away from the principal or the time period in which these contacts still have value.

The covenant also must be reasonable in the area or distance specified. Another way to consider this is to ask the following question: How far will customers or clients travel to do business with the agent? The answer depends on the field of the agent's expertise. For example, a patient might travel halfway across the country to see a world-famous

---

NRW CASE 30.3   Manufacturing/Management

NRW

CREATING EMPLOYMENT CONTRACTS TO PROTECT TECHNOLOGY

NRW has been more successful than anticipated, and it is producing StuffTrakR at nearly full capacity. In order to keep up with demand, the firm will need to expand its production capacity, including the hiring of new employees. There have also been several suggestions for improvements in the product from a number of customers, and NRW would like to hire some engineers to help implement these suggested changes. However, the firm is concerned that some of the new employees might reveal (or "borrow") the technology the firm has developed, to the detriment of NRW. They ask you what protections they have or could build into their employment contracts to help protect them. What advice will you give them?

BUSINESS CONSIDERATIONS How can a firm prevent employees from revealing or taking confidential business information or technology? What practical protections are available to a firm that is trying to protect a trade secret?

ETHICAL CONSIDERATIONS Is it ethical for an employee to utilize information gained in a previous position to benefit a competitor of the former employer? Is it ethical to restrict a former employee from using knowledge or information gained in a job when that knowledge or information makes the former employee a more productive or valuable individual? How can these competing interests be balanced?

INTERNATIONAL CONSIDERATIONS Are there any restrictions on what technology should be shared with foreign countries? Why? Are there products that should not be distributed in foreign countries? If so, what are they?

---

heart transplant specialist, but many patients will not even go across town to see a general practitioner.

If the principal has a legitimate business interest and the covenant is reasonable, the principal can sue the breaching agent or former agent for an injunction and/or contract damages. However, a principal may structure a covenant not to compete that is too broad. The courts apply one of two approaches in such cases. In one approach, the court declares the covenant void and ignores it. The agent then can do whatever he or she wishes with impunity. A less common approach is for the court to reform (modify) the contract to make its restrictions reasonable.

Courts may examine the following criteria in determining whether to enforce a covenant not to compete in an *employment* contract:

- Is the restraint reasonable in the amount of protection it affords the principal, or is it excessive?

- Is the restraint unreasonable because it is unduly harsh on the agent?

- If the agent works for a competitor, will that threaten irreparable injury to the principal?

- Does the principal have a legitimate interest in preventing competition by the agent? Is the agency relationship of a unique and unusual type?

Some state statutes hold that a principal cannot prevent an ordinary employee from engaging in competition once the employment is over.[8]

A covenant not to compete usually is not required in order to prevent an agent from divulging trade secrets or customer lists after the employment is terminated. Under common law, this behavior is a violation of the agent's duties of loyalty. (The duty of loyalty is discussed in Chapter 29.) See the Patent Examiner Newsletter sponsored by the law firm of Arent, Fox, Kintner, Plotkin, and Kahn for a basic discussion of patent protection. It is located at http://www.arentfox.com/quickguide/businesslines/intlprop/patentexaminer/newsalerts/corpusurviv/corpsurviv.html. The following case addressed the requirements for a valid covenant not to compete in North Carolina.

30.3

THE MANUAL WOODWORKERS & WEAVERS, INC. v. THE RUG BARN, INC.
2001 U.S. Dist. LEXIS 21502 (W.D.N.C. Asheville Div. 2001)

FACTS Manual Woodworkers & Weavers (plaintiff) was a North Carolina-based business that produced textiles for sale. Rug Barn was a competitor of the plaintiff, manufacturing similar products. Marvin Allen and Kenneth Kane were former salaried employees of plaintiff who were hired by Rug Barn after they left plaintiff's employ. Both men signed contracts with plaintiff, which provided in Paragraph 7:

(a) Following termination of Employee's employment with Employer, whether voluntary or otherwise, Employee shall not engage in any business, either alone, with another, or on behalf of another, that competes with any product being designed, manufactured, distributed, retailed, planned or proposed by Employer at the time Employee's employment terminates; and Employee shall not provide any services or advice to any person or entity that competes with any product being designed, manufactured, distributed, retailed, planned or proposed by Employer at the time Employee's employment terminates. . . .

(c) The covenants set forth in this Paragraph Seven (7) shall have force and effect only for a period of three (3) years following Employee's termination of employment with Employer . . .

(d) Except as expressly stated in Paragraph 7(b), the covenants set forth in this Paragraph Seven

(7) shall have force and effect only in the following areas: . . .

(1) In the following countries: the United States of America; Virgin Islands; Grand Cayman Islands; Canada; Japan; Singapore; Italy; Finland; Sweden; Norway; Germany; Belgium; France; Great Britain; Puerto Rico; Australia; New Zealand; Austria; South Korea; Spain; India; or Saudi Arabia; . . .

(2) In the following areas of the United States: Florida; Georgia; South Carolina; North Carolina; Virginia; West Virginia; District of Columbia; Maryland; Delaware; New Jersey; New York; Connecticut; New Hampshire; Rhode Island; Massachusetts; Maine; Vermont; Pennsylvania; Ohio; Kentucky; Tennessee; Alabama; Mississippi; Louisiana; Arkansas; Missouri; Illinois; Indiana; Michigan; Wisconsin; Iowa; Minnesota; North Dakota; South Dakota; Nebraska; Kansas; Oklahoma; Texas; New Mexico; Colorado; Wyoming; Montana; Idaho; Utah; Arizona; Nevada; California; Oregon; Washington; Alaska; or Hawaii; or . . .

(3) In the following areas of Canada: Yukon; Northwestern Territory; British Columbia; Alberta; Saskatchewan; Manitoba; Ontario; Quebec; Newfoundland; New

Brunswick; Nova Scotia; or Prince Edward Island. . . .

ISSUE Was the agreement not to compete unenforceable as a matter of law?

HOLDING Yes, it was overly broad and unenforceable as a matter of law.

REASONING Excerpts from the opinion of United States Magistrate Judge Max O. Cogburn Sr.:

[T]he moving party [for summary judgment] has the burden . . . to show that there are no genuine issues for trial. . . . [T]here is no dispute that North Carolina law governs. . . . The North Carolina appellate courts have consistently held . . . [quoting from various North Carolina opinions]:

Covenants not to compete between an employer and employee are "not viewed favorably in modern law." To be enforceable, a covenant must meet five requirements—it must be (1) in writing; (2) made a part of the employment contract; (3) based on valuable consideration; (4) reasonable as to time and territory; and (5) designed to protect a legitimate business interest of the employer. The reasonableness of a non-compete agreement is a matter of law for the court to decide. . . . The employer must show that the territory . . . is no greater than necessary to secure the protection of its business. . . . If the territory is too broad, "the entire covenant fails since equity will neither enforce nor reform an overreaching and unreasonable covenant." . . . In evaluating reasonableness as to time and territory restrictions, we must consider each element in tandem. . . . Although either . . . standing alone may be reasonable, the combined effect of the two may be unreasonable. . . . A five-year time restriction is the outer boundary which our courts have considered reasonable. . . . To prove that a geographic restriction . . . is reasonable, an employer must first show where its customers are located and that the geographic scope of the covenant is necessary to maintain those customer relationships. The employer must show that the territory embraced by the covenant is no more than necessary to secure the protection of its business. . . . In . . . [precedents], we set forth a six-part test to determine whether the geographic scope of a covenant not to compete is reasonable. The six factors are: (1) the area or scope of the restriction; (2) the area assigned to the employee; (3) the area where the employee actually worked; (4) the area in which the employer operated; (5) the nature of the business involved; and (6) the nature of the employee's duty and his knowledge of the employer's business operation. . . .

. . . [This] agreement would prevent defendants from working for direct competitors . . . ; however, it would also prevent them from working for any number of other textile concerns which manufacture, but do not directly market, items for ultimate sale in the gift market. As to geographic scope, the agreement seeks to prevent defendants from going to work for any "competitor." . . . [A] single sale to a single customer in a given foreign country was enough to include that country in the non-compete agreement. . . . Both individual defendants appear to have been involved in the manufacturing end of plaintiff's business, not sales or marketing. . . . [Therefore, the area assigned to the employee test, designated number 2] would have little relevance. . . . One [individual] defendant may have had knowledge of the manufacturing process and the customers who placed orders, while the other knew the supply chain. . . . North Carolina law allows plaintiff to negotiate a non-compete agreement designed to secure the protection of its business. The problem in this case is that plaintiff attempts to impose a geographic limitation, which is based on marketing, to employees who were engaged in manufacturing. . . . [T]he terms of the agreement are not connected to any legitimate business concern, such as the lawful protection of trade secrets, and can only be construed as an unlawful attempt to keep employees from seeking better jobs at better pay. North Carolina law is unequivocal that, standing alone, a covenant that an employee will not compete with his former employer is not viewed favorably. . . . With respect to geographic limitations, plaintiff must show that the territory embraced by the negative covenant is no greater than necessary to secure the protection of its business or goodwill. The geographic limitation asserted would cover all states in the Union, its territories and possessions, and 21 foreign countries. . . . When . . . time and geographic limitations are viewed together, the court can only conclude that such agreement is unenforceable as overly broad as a matter of law. . . .

BUSINESS CONSIDERATIONS What should a business do to protect its customers and trade secrets from employees who decide to leave? What techniques offer the most protection? When should a covenant not to compete extend beyond the country in which it is signed? Why?

ETHICAL CONSIDERATIONS Was it ethical for the plaintiff to enter into these covenants not to compete with its employees? Why? What ethical theory are you applying in your decision?

Summary

The type of principal affects the rights and obligations of the agent, the principal, and the third party. A disclosed principal is one whose identity and existence are known to the third party. When the principal is disclosed, the principal can sue and be sued on the contract if there is express, implied, incidental, emergency, apparent, or ratification authority. These types of authority often overlap. If only authority by estoppel exists, it will be applied to protect a third party but not to protect the principal. Information received by the agent within the course and scope of the job generally will be imputed to the principal. Usually, the agent of a disclosed principal will not be bound on the contract itself, but the agent may be responsible for breach of warranty of authority. The third party will be liable to the principal on the contract and to the agent if the agent has an interest or intends to be bound.

A partially disclosed principal is one whose existence is known but whose identity is not. In situations with partially disclosed principals, the agent will be held liable on the contract because the third party is relying on the agent's reputation. When the principal is undisclosed, the third party thinks he or she is dealing only with the agent. In this situation, the agent will be bound on the contract because the third party believes that the agent is a party to the contract.

The agency agreement must be in writing, *if* this is required by either the Statute of Frauds or the equal dignities rule. Covenants not to compete may be valid if the principal has a legitimate interest in preventing the competition, provided that the limitation is reasonable in the length of time and the area specified.

Discussion Questions

1. Sasha, a secretary, often orders office supplies, such as photocopy paper, tablets, and pens, for her employer. One day, Sasha orders a personal computer and has it delivered to her home. Sasha has the bill sent to her employer. Based on the information provided, does Sasha have authority to do this? Why or why not? What additional information would be helpful? Why?

2. Mai, Carlos, and Helen have recently been issued NRW cell phones. Even though Helen's husband Elliot is not part of the business enterprise, he commonly answers "her" cell phone when she is busy. Assume Elliot makes representations about NRW products. Could NRW be held liable for his statements? What if Helen's 14-year-old nephew answers the cell phone and promises delivery within two weeks?

3. What are the business implications of people representing themselves as working for or on behalf of NRW? When is the firm legally obligated for the actions of these people? What are the public relations implications of successfully denying that an alleged agent was working on behalf of the firm?

4. Besides collecting samples, displays, and order forms, what else should a principal do to terminate the apparent authority of an agent who is being fired?

5. Bonnie buys a house through Angie, who is a real estate agent. Before the sale is completed, Angie recommends that they have an appliance inspector examine the house. Angie makes the arrangements. Joe, the inspector, says that all the major appliances are in proper working order. Bonnie completes the sale and is now living in the house. Joe, however, has not been paid yet. Who is obligated to pay Joe? Why?

6. What is a partially disclosed principal? How might partial disclosure occur? How do the rights and liabilities of an agent for a partially disclosed principal differ from those of an agent for an undisclosed principal?

7. Carmo farms 200 acres planted with grape vines. His neighbor has an additional 100 acres planted with grapes, which are for sale. Since Carmo and his neighbor have been feuding for 12 years, the neighbor will not sell the land to Carmo. Therefore, Carmo hires Rose to act as his agent without revealing his identity. Rose buys the land and starts to transfer it to Carmo. Upon discovering this, the neighbor tries to stop the transfer. What are the legal rights of the parties in this situation?

8. Why are warranties of authority applicable only when there is a disclosed principal?

9. Lisa has charges on her telephone bill that she does not understand. The bill states that billing inquiries should be made by calling (800) 555-2941. She calls the number and speaks with Venus. Venus says that she will remove the charges; the charges, however, are not removed. Is Lisa entitled to have them removed? Do you think Venus had authority for her statement? Why or why not?

10. Is it reasonable for a fast-food chain to require all new employees to sign an agreement that they will not work for another fast-food restaurant for six months after leaving the chain? Is it legal? Can an ex-employee legally reveal the recipe for a chain's special blend of 11 herbs and spices? Why or why not?

Case Problems and Writing Assignments

1. Jason Weimer leased and operated a farm owned by Brugger Corporation. When a new lease was negotiated in 1987, Grant McQueen, a manager for Brugger, agreed Brugger would pay for some necessary repairs to the irrigation system. Weimer negotiated with Tri-Circle to make the repairs. Weimer indicated that he had authority from Brugger to arrange for this work. Tri-Circle was directed to set up a separate billing for Brugger for this work, and to send the bill to Weimer. When Weimer received the first bill for $9,769, he verified the amount and forwarded the bill to Brugger. Brugger sent Tri-Circle a check for this amount. A second billing for $11,540 was sent to Weimer, approved by him, and forwarded to Brugger. This second bill was not paid and Tri-Circle sued. Who is liable for this second bill and why? [See *Tri-Circle, Inc. v. Brugger Corp.*, 829 P.2d 540 (Idaho App. 1992).]

2. Margaret Farris was injured in a fall at the J.C. Penney store in downtown Philadelphia. She hired attorney Timothy Booker to represent her in connection with the incident. At about noon on the second day of trial, settlement discussions began. Later that day, in a meeting with both Booker and Renee Berger, the counsel for J.C. Penney, the judge asked Berger if her client would authorize her to settle the case for $20,000. Berger secured the necessary authority and communicated that fact to Booker. Berger then saw Booker enter a witness room with Farris, where the two remained for about five minutes. Booker then informed Berger that the $20,000 settlement offer had been accepted. To the contrary, Farris actually told Booker that she did not want the case to be settled until her medical treatment was complete. Nonetheless, Booker and Berger told the judge that the $20,000 settlement figure was acceptable. The entire in-court proceeding with respect to the settlement lasted approximately three minutes. The District Court later found that Farris either did not hear or did not understand what was happening until after the jury had been dismissed. After leaving the courtroom briefly, Farris reentered the courtroom. Farris told Berger that she had never authorized Booker to settle the case. Did Booker have apparent authority to settle the case? [See *Farris v. J.C. Penney Company, Inc.*, 176 F.3d 706, 1999 U.S. App. LEXIS 9357 (3rd Cir. 1999).]

3. Ticor employed Kenneth Cohen as a title insurance salesman. (*Title insurance* insures the buyer of real property, or a lender secured by real property, against defects in the legal title to the property.) Cohen began working at Ticor in 1981, shortly after graduating from college. Within six years he was a senior vice president in charge of several major accounts. His clients have consisted almost exclusively of real estate attorneys in large New York law firms. Ticor and Cohen, both represented by attorneys, entered into an Employment Contract on October 1, 1995. There were extensive negotiations over its terms, including the 180-day covenant not to compete. Cohen was made one of the highest paid Ticor sales representatives, being guaranteed annual compensation of $600,000, consisting of a base salary of $200,000 plus commissions. In addition to compensation, Cohen received expense account reimbursements that by 1997 exceeded $150,000 per year. On April 20, 1998, TitleServ, a direct competitor of Ticor, offered to employ Cohen. TitleServ agreed to indemnify Cohen by paying him a salary during the six-month period (i.e., the 180-day hiatus from employment) in the event that the covenant not to compete was enforced. Cohen admitted to speaking with 20 Ticor customers about TitleServ before submitting his letter of resignation, and telling each of them that he was considering leaving Ticor and joining a competitor firm. Cohen maintained that this was an effort on his part to learn more information about TitleServ, including its ability to service the New York market and the opportunity he was being offered. Cohen insisted he never discussed transferring any business from Ticor to TitleServ, nor did he discuss any specific deals. However, this assertion is undermined by Cohen's deposition testimony concerning conversations with Martin Polevoy of the Bachner Tally law firm, in which he admitted he directly solicited Polevoy's business for TitleServ and eventually secured a promise that Polevoy would follow him by taking his firm's business to TitleServ. Is the covenant not to compete valid? Should the court enforce the covenant with an injunction? Are other damages appropriate? What should a business do to protect its customers and trade secrets from employees who decide to leave? What techniques offer the most protection? [See *Ticor Title Insurance Co. v. Cohen*, 173 F.3d 63, 1999 U.S. App. LEXIS 9998 (2nd Cir. 1999).]

4. BDO was a national accounting firm with 40 offices throughout the United States. Jeffrey Hirshberg began employment in BDO's Buffalo office in 1984 and in 1989 was promoted to the position of manager. As a condition of receiving the promotion, Hirshberg was required to sign a "Manager's Agreement." In it Hirshberg expressly acknowledged that a fiduciary relationship existed between him and the firm by reason of his having received various disclosures, which would give him an advantage in attracting BDO clients. Hirshberg agreed that if, within 18 months following the termination of his employment, he served any former client of BDO's Buffalo office, he would compensate BDO "for the loss and damages suffered" in an amount equal to one and one half times the fees BDO had charged that client over the last fiscal year of the client's patronage. Hirshberg resigned from BDO in October 1993. BDO submitted a list of 100 former clients of its Buffalo office, allegedly lost to Hirshberg, who were billed a total of $138,000 in the year he left the firm's practice. Hirshberg denied serving some of the clients, claimed that a substantial number of them were personal clients he had brought to the firm through his own outside contacts, and that with respect to some clients, he had not been the primary BDO representative servicing the account. Is the "reimbursement clause" requiring Hirshberg to compensate BDO for serving

any client of the firm's Buffalo office a valid and enforceable restrictive covenant? How could BDO improve its protection from accountants who leave its employment? What documentation would assist BDO in proving its case and the appropriate amount of damages? [See *BDO Seidman v. Hirshberg*, 712 N.E.2d 1220, 1999 N.Y. LEXIS 860 (C.A.N.Y. 1999).]

5. **BUSINESS APPLICATION CASE** Late in 1991, Jo Daviess hired Arlyn Hemmen to serve as its controller. Jo Daviess was a farm service cooperative located in the northwestern Illinois community of Elizabeth, a town of approximately 700 people. Prior to this, Hemmen had worked for a number of banks. As Jo Daviess's controller, Hemmen maintained the company's books and accounts, reviewed and reconciled its bank statements, prepared monthly operating statements and other financial reports, and supervised his coworkers in the absence of the office manager.

Jo Daviess maintained two accounts with Elizabeth State Bank (ESB): (1) an operating account, into which the company deposited all of its revenue and out of which it paid for its day-to-day expenses; and (2) an account reserved for the company's payroll. *ESB* maintained an account, referred to as the treasury tax and loan (TT&L) account, into which the bank's commercial customers deposited the federal income tax that they withheld from their employees' paychecks. Jo Daviess periodically transferred funds out of its operating account into either its payroll account or the bank's TT&L account. Pursuant to the terms of the operating account, only authorized signers could withdraw or transfer funds from that account. Hemmen was never a signer on the operating account. He did have the authority to sign checks drawn on the payroll account. Hemmen regularly prepared checks drawn on the operating account, both to pay Jo Daviess's suppliers and to transfer funds into one of the other accounts. These checks would be presented to the company's general manager for signature. For purposes of transferring funds into the TT&L account, Hemmen would prepare a check payable to the order of ESB. Jo Daviess did not owe any money to the bank; the only legitimate reason for making a check payable to the bank would be to accomplish a transfer of funds from the operating account to the TT&L account.

Beginning in January 1992, Hemmen began to embezzle money from Jo Daviess. Periodically, he would prepare a check on the company's operating account payable to the order of ESB, as if he were making a deposit into the TT&L account. He would then present the check to the general manager, who signed the check assuming that the proceeds were destined for the TT&L account. Hemmen would divert the proceeds of the checks to his own use in one of several ways. Hemmen presented the check to an ESB teller and requested that a portion of the check be deposited into the TT&L account, with the balance to be disbursed to him either in cash or one or more cashier's checks payable to Hemmen's creditors, or he would present the check and have the entirety of the proceeds issued to him. Bank personnel did not realize that Hemmen was diverting the proceeds to his own use; Hemmen would explain that the cash and cashier's checks were necessary in order to pay for supplies, parts, or some other legitimate company expense. Hemmen would make a false entry in Jo Daviess's internal records indicating that the cash or cashier's check issued to him was used to pay for something.

ESB was aware that Hemmen was not an authorized signer on Jo Daviess's operating account and Jo Daviess never indicated to the bank that Hemmen had authority to withdraw funds from that account. The bank acceded to Hemmen's requests for cash and cashier's checks without first consulting with Jo Daviess to confirm his authority to receive the proceeds of these checks. The bank did not even ask him to endorse the checks. It was the bank's custom to honor such requests. There was nothing that Jo Daviess did or said that induced the bank to comply with Hemmen's requests. Jo Daviess officials had never discussed with ESB whether Hemmen could legitimately receive the proceeds of any checks payable to the bank. Mutual Service Casualty Company (Mutual), which insured Jo Daviess, compensated the company for its loss. Mutual then filed suit against ESB.

Did Hemmen have either actual or implied authority to receive funds from Jo Daviess's operating account? Is Jo Daviess's system of bank accounts common business practice? What could Jo Daviess do to improve its banking and bookkeeping practices? What should ESB do to improve its procedures? [See *Mutual Service Casualty Insurance Company v. Elizabeth State Bank*, 265 F.3d 601, 2001 U.S. App. LEXIS 20667 (7th Cir. 2001).]

6. **ETHICAL APPLICATION CASE** Kent Garver owned and operated Paramark Financial Services, a division of Paramark Insurance Corporation. Garver marketed insurance policies and annuities for 40 to 50 companies, including Legacy. Legacy marketed insurance products underwritten by American National Insurance Company (ANICO), as well as other insurance companies. The contract between Legacy and Garver specified that Garver was an independent contractor. Garver was paid on a commission basis, and Legacy retained no rights of control over Garver's actions except that he was forbidden to place client funds for Legacy products into his own company account.

Jimmie Alverson's accountant, William Jordan, referred Alverson to Garver in January 1995. Alverson had retired from his employment and had withdrawn his retirement funds of $275,000. He sought to invest them elsewhere. Alverson was shown a sales illustration for ANICO annuities and researched the company before meeting with Garver. Garver suggested that Alverson purchase ANICO annuities. The annuities were to be purchased in $50,000 increments. Alverson agreed and delivered the proceeds of his retirement accounts to Garver. On April 19, 1995, Alverson signed an ANICO application for a single $50,000 annuity. Garver sent Legacy the application, along with a $50,000 check payable to ANICO. Garver invested only $50,000 in ANICO annuities and transferred the balance of Alverson's money into the "Hallmark High Yield Fund." The

Hallmark fund was actually controlled by Garver's own company, Paramark Financial Services. The ANICO annuity turned out to be a legitimate investment, but the money invested in the Hallmark fund was lost when Garver's company went under. Seeking recovery of his lost funds, Alverson filed this action against ANICO, Legacy, and Garver. Was Garver an agent of Legacy and/or ANICO? Did he have apparent or ostensible authority to act on their behalf? Analyze Garver's ethical perspective. Does Alverson bear some ethical responsibility for his loss? [See *Alverson v. American National Insurance Company*, 2002 U.S. App. LEXIS 3132 (6th Cir. 2002) (Not recommended for full-text publication.).]

7. **CRITICAL THINKING CASE** The Musicians and Employers' Pension Fund was maintained for the purpose of providing retirement and related benefits. Steven Scott was a company that employed musicians to perform for its clients at functions such as weddings or bar mitzvahs. Steven Scott signed various collective bargaining agreements with Local 802, the musicians' union, and was required to make contributions to the Pension Fund at specified rates.

Steven Scott entered into 15 settlement agreements with William Moriarity, Local 802 president and Pension Fund trustee. Each agreement included the following terms: (1) Steven Scott agrees to pay a certain sum of money to the Pension Fund for certain listed employees; (2) the agreement is in full settlement of all monetary claims against Steven Scott through a specified date; (3) the agreement binds Local 802, the Pension Fund, and Steven Scott; and (4) each party, including Moriarity, "acknowledges, represents, and warrants that they are authorized to enter into, execute, deliver, perform, and implement the agreement." Each agreement was signed by two parties: Joseph Mileti, an officer and duly authorized agent for Steven Scott, and Moriarity. Steven Scott sent the union 15 settlement checks, accompanied by a three-page settlement agreement and a list of employee names and contribution amounts. It is common practice for employers to send their checks and employee lists to Local 802. Local 802 forwarded the agreements and checks to the Pension Fund. Pension Fund clerical workers, who were in charge of processing all contributions, processed the checks. Each check was accompanied by a settlement agreement, which unequivocally stated that the check was in full settlement of all obligations owed by Steven Scott.

As a Pension Fund trustee and Local 802 president, Moriarity was authorized to collect Pension Fund contributions from employers. However, Moriarity was not authorized to unilaterally enter into settlement agreements that were in full satisfaction of any debts owed to the Pension Fund. Only the Board of Trustees of the Pension Fund had the authority to enter into such agreements or delegate such authority to two or more trustees. Steven Scott was not aware of this limitation on Moriarity's authority, and a copy of the union document containing this limitation was not mailed to Steven Scott until June 1995. Did these agreements bind the Pension Fund? What can a business, union, or pension fund do to reduce the risk that agents will exceed their authority? What business practices would reduce the application of apparent and ratification authority? [See *Trustees of the American Federation of Musicians and Employers' Pension Fund v. Steven Scott Enterprises, Inc.*, 40 F. Supp. 2d 503, 1999 U.S. Dist. LEXIS 3410 (S.D.N.Y. 1999).]

8. **YOU BE THE JUDGE** William Powell authorized Debbie Powell, his wife, to obtain a rate quote and an application from Nationwide Mutual Insurance Company for coverage of his two vehicles. Debbie contacted the Nationwide agent from whom she had obtained her own policy, which included Underinsured Motorist (UIM) coverage. (*Underinsured Motorist coverage* pays the insured if another motorist who has insufficient insurance injures her.) South Carolina requires companies to tell applicants about UIM coverage and whether or not it is included in their policy. Debbie informed the agent that her husband desired liability coverage of $100,000 on his two vehicles and that he wanted "full coverage" as he had with his then current insurer. Debbie met with the agent's assistant, Sherry Volz, and at Volz's direction signed William's name beside several "X" marks on various forms. One of the signatures was in a space indicating that the insurance applicant (William) did not wish to purchase UIM coverage. Another signature was in a space confirming that the applicant had read the explanation of UIM coverage contained in the form. Debbie did not know what UIM coverage was, nor did Volz explain it to her. Additionally, Volz never asked Debbie whether William had authorized her to apply for insurance or reject UIM coverage on his behalf, and Debbie never told Volz that she was so authorized. William was displeased when he learned that Debbie had applied for a policy, but when Debbie assured him that the resulting policy would contain the "full coverage" that he desired, he chose not to rescind the application. Accordingly, when Volz contacted William, he told her that he wanted the policy. Volz did not ask William whether Debbie had been authorized to act on his behalf, nor did she specifically inquire as to whether William desired UIM coverage. Nationwide subsequently issued the policy with William listed as the named insured and Debbie listed as a driver. Although the policy, which Nationwide sent William, indicated that it did not provide UIM coverage, William never read the policy and continued to believe that UIM coverage was included. William never rescinded, modified, or canceled the policy, and he paid the premium. Shortly after he had renewed the policy for an additional six months, Debbie was driving one of William's vehicles when she was involved in an accident caused by another driver. She sustained injuries in excess of the other driver's limits. When she subsequently made a claim under William's policy, Nationwide made payments for property damage, towing, and automobile rental but denied that the policy provided UIM coverage. Did Debbie have authority to "reject" the UIM coverage for William? If so, what type of authority existed? If this case were filed in *your* court, how would *you* rule? [See *Nationwide Mutual Insurance Company v. Powell*, 2002 U.S. App. LEXIS 10562 (4th Cir. 2002).]

Notes

1. *Restatement (Second) of Agency* (Philadelphia: American Law Institute, 1958), § 97.

2. Warren A. Seavey, *Handbook of the Law of Agency* (St. Paul, Minn.: West, 1964), § 8D, p. 19.

3. *General Overseas Films, Ltd. v. Robin International, Inc.,* 542 F. Supp. 684 (S.D. N.Y. 1982), at 688, n. 2.

4. *Restatement (Second) of Agency* (Philadelphia: American Law Institute, 1958), § 7.

5. *Restatement (Third) of the Law Governing Lawyers* (Philadelphia: American Law Institute, 1998), § 27.

6. *Restatement (Second) of Agency* (Philadelphia: American Law Institute, 1958), § 49 comment c.

7. CALI is a nonprofit consortium of over 180 law schools and affiliates. It develops computer-based tutorials.

8. See, for example, California Business and Professions Code, § 16600.

Agency: Liability for Torts and Crimes

AGENDA

NRW As the business grows, NRW will be hiring a number of new employees. Some of these new employees will be making deliveries of the products, while others will be working at one of the firm's facilities. What happens if one of the employees making deliveries for the firm commits a tort, causing injury to a third person? Will NRW be liable for the damages, will the employee be liable, or will the liability be joint and several? If NRW is held liable, will the firm have any recourse against the employee for the damages incurred? What should NRW consider in hiring delivery people? What financial risk is involved with hiring delivery people, and how can NRW best minimize this risk?

Suppose that some of the employees in the firm's warehouse are involved in some form of "horseplay" during the day, and that one of the employees is injured as a result. What liability might NRW face in this situation? What protections are available for the firm to either prevent or minimize the potential financial risk the firm might face? What duties does NRW owe its employees?

Mai, Carlos, and Helen designed work shirts with the NRW logo for the employees in the warehouse and for the delivery personnel. They liked the idea of using the shirts to promote the firm and decided they would also make up T-shirts that could be given away at various functions. They also gave some of these T-shirts to family members and friends to help publicize the firm. Suppose that one of their relatives or friends commits a tort, injuring a third person, while wearing a T-shirt with the firm's logo. Is it possible for the third person to hold NRW liable on the theory that the relative or friend was advertising for the firm and was therefore engaged in a business-related activity for which the firm should be held liable?

These and other questions will arise during our discussion of agency law. Be prepared! You never know when the firm or one of its members will seek your advice.

Servant's Liability

Servants engage in physical activities or labor on behalf of the master. These activities frequently bring the servant into close contact with members of the general public. When the servant is careless or overly aggressive, there is a good chance that one or more of these members of the public will be injured. This chapter discusses the servant's and the master's responsibility to the public for these types of injuries. As we will see, these relationships can occur in business and nonbusiness settings.

Vicarious liability is legal responsibility for the wrong committed by another person, in this case the servant. Vicarious liability for torts involves different policy considerations from those surrounding an agent's ability to bind the principal in business dealings with third persons. In contract matters, there is generally a conscious desire to interact with the public and a conscious decision to enter into business arrangements with the public by means of the agent. In most tort situations, however, neither the master nor the servant desires that the tort occur. But once the tort has occurred, someone has to suffer the financial burden, even if that someone is the innocent victim. Who should pay? The master? The servant? Or the third person?

The general rule of tort law is that everyone is liable for his or her own torts. This general rule is followed in agency law. Since the servant committed the tort, the servant can normally be held liable for the harm that occurs. The fact that the servant is working for the master at the time of the tort does not alter the general rule. However, this general rule is supplemented under the rules of agency to be discussed in this chapter. Refer to Chapter 7 for a more complete discussion of specific torts. You can also find some information on tort law and tort liability at http://www.law.cornell.edu/topics/torts.html/.

Master's Liability: *Respondeat Superior*

When the servant commits a tort that harms a third person, the servant should be responsible for the harm. However, in agency law, some circumstances exist in which the master can *also* be held liable for the torts committed by the servant. (For a good, brief description of master liability and the underlying policy see the CCH Business Owner's Toolkit online at http://www.toolkit.cch.com/text/P04_7335.asp.) Notice that in these situations the master is being held liable for the conduct of the servant. Since the

servant is also liable for his or her tortious conduct, the liability is said to be *joint and several*. This means that *either* party may be held liable individually (several liability) or that *both* parties may be held liable (joint liability).

Respondeat superior is the theory under which masters are held liable for the torts of their servants even though the masters are not personally at fault. Literally, it means "let the master answer." It is also referred to as a "deep-pockets" theory, based on the belief that the master's pockets are likely to be "deeper" (i.e., they hold more money) than those of the servant. The *respondeat superior* doctrine is one of the many legal theories that attempts to balance competing interests. In this situation, the competing interests are the rights of the injured party to receive compensation for injuries suffered versus the right of the master to avoid liability for acts not actually committed by him or her. Is it better to compensate the victim by holding the master liable, or is it better to "protect" the master, even though the victim may not be able to recover for his or her injuries?

For example, if Myesha has suffered $175,000 in injuries from an automobile accident caused by the negligence of Sondra, a servant, and Sondra has a total net worth of only $50,000, Sondra cannot fully compensate Myesha. However, if the master is a multimillion-dollar corporation, the master *can* fully compensate Myesha. In these circumstances, the court must evaluate all the facts and determine whether *respondeat superior* should be applied in this particular case. If *respondeat superior* applies, the victim will be allowed to recover from the master; if not, the victim may seek recovery only from the servant. (This chapter generally uses the traditional terms *master* and *servant* because *respondeat superior* is limited to master-servant relationships.)

Respondeat superior has been justified on numerous grounds in court opinions and in legal treatises. The justifications for holding the master liable for wrongful acts of the servant include the following:

- The master will be more careful in choosing servants in order to avoid liability.

- The master will be more careful in supervising servants in order to avoid liability.

- The liability for servants is a cost of conducting business.

- The master is the person benefiting from the servant's actions.

- The master can purchase liability insurance.

- The person with the power to control the conduct should be the person to bear financial responsibility.

• The master can better afford the costs, especially when compared with an innocent third person who is injured by the servant's conduct.

Respondeat superior is not based on the idea that the master did anything wrong. Rather, it involves a special application of the doctrine of strict liability. *Strict liability* is liability for an action simply because it occurred and caused damage, not because it is the fault of the person who must pay. The master hired the servant and the servant then did something wrong while carrying out his or her obligation to the master, so the master should pay for the wrongdoing. Courts tend to apply a "but for" test in deciding whether to assign liability to the master. "But for" the existence of the master-servant relationship, no harm would have resulted. In other words, someone should pay, and the master is best able to pay and afford the loss; therefore, the master must pay. However, *respondeat superior* does require a wrongful act by a servant for which the master can be held liable, and a legally defensible reason for holding the master liable for the wrongful act of the servant. It is not sufficient that the servant committed a wrongful act and that a third person was injured by that act. The wrongful act must be one over which the master can be held legally responsible. It must be an act the master should legally have controlled. This idea is illustrated in *Girard v. Trade Professionals, Inc.* (Case 31.1).

The principal's *right to control* is really what distinguishes servants from nonservants. A principal who has the right to control may be called a *master,* and the worker may be called a *servant.* Remember that *respondeat superior* applies only to servants. It does not apply to nonservants because the principal lacks control over the conduct of the nonservants and, thus, is not a "master" in these situations.

Respondeat superior also does not make the master an insurer for every act of the servant. The master is liable for only those actions that are within the *course* and *scope* of the employment. Therefore, the issue in most cases based on *respondeat superior* involves a decision as to whether the servant was acting within the course and scope of his or her employment when the tort was committed. To resolve this question, it is important to know the servant's duties, working hours, state of mind, assigned location, and the master's right to control the worker. It is also important to know whether the servant has deviated from his or her route and/or routine, whether the servant has any history of similar sorts of conduct, and any other factors that might show whether the conduct was an extreme deviation from what the master should reasonably have expected. It is immaterial if the master fails to exert actual control over how the worker completes the tasks as long as the master

has the right to use this control. *Respondeat superior* has been criticized by "masters" on the grounds that it is unconstitutional, but the Supreme Court recently affirmed that *respondeat superior* is not fundamentally unfair or unconstitutional.[1] In most jurisdictions there seems to be a trend toward increasing the master's liability, even for intentional torts or serious wrongs committed by the servant, such as rape.

Factors Listed in the Restatement of Agency

The Restatement (Second) of Agency indicates the factors that should affect the determination of whether a servant is within the scope of his or her employment. The factors include the following:

General Statement

(1) *Conduct of a servant is within the scope of employment if, but only if:*
   (a) *it is of the kind he is employed to perform;*
   (b) *it occurs substantially within the authorized time and space limits;*
   (c) *it is actuated, at least in part, by a purpose to serve the master; and*
   (d) *if force is intentionally used by the servant against another, the use of force is not unexpectable by the master....*[2]

(2) *In determining whether or not the conduct, although not authorized, is nevertheless so similar to or incidental to the conduct authorized as to be within the scope of employment, the following matters of fact are to be considered:*
   (a) *whether or not the act is one commonly done by such servants;*
   (b) *the time, place, and purpose of the act;*
   (c) *the previous relations between the master and the servant;*
   (d) *the extent to which the business of the master is apportioned between different servants;*
   (e) *whether or not the act is outside the enterprise of the master or, if within the enterprise, has not been entrusted to any servant;*
   (f) *whether or not the master has reason to expect that such an act will be done;*
   (g) *the similarity in quality of the act done to the act authorized;*

(h) *whether or not the instrumentality by which the harm is done has been furnished by the master to the servant;*

(i) *the extent of departure from the normal method of accomplishing an authorized result; and*

(j) *whether or not the act is seriously criminal.*[3]

In many cases, certain factors may indicate that the servant is within the scope of employment and other factors may indicate the contrary. For example, suppose that Eric, a servant, is involved in a traffic accident while driving a truck owned by Micheala, the master, and used in Micheala's business. At the time of the accident Eric is legally under the influence and will be held liable for the accident. While Micheala in this example furnishes the truck (the instru-mentality), she probably has no reason to suspect that Eric will drive under the influence of alcohol (engage in this conduct). Should the court impose liability on Micheala in this situation under the theory of *respondeat superior*? There is no absolute answer to this question. Each case is different, and no one factor controls this decision; the judge or jury weighs all the factors involved to reach a decision. Since the triers of fact exercise a lot of discretion in these cases, fact situations that seem very similar may result in markedly different decisions by different courts. In the following case, the court addressed the Kansas rules of *respondeat superior* and negligent hiring. Negligent hiring is discussed in more detail later in this chapter. Note how the court used *servant*, *employee*, and *agent* interchangeably. The court did this both in its own language and in the quoted material.

31.1

GIRARD v. TRADE PROFESSIONALS, INC.
2001 U.S. App. LEXIS 15772 (10th Cir. 2001) (Unpublished opinion)

FACTS On May 22, 1997, Roger Anders was driving home from work when his vehicle and a vehicle driven by Jerome Girard collided. Girard sustained severe injuries. At the time of the accident, Trade Professionals, Inc. employed Anders. In 1997, Anders, a journeyman electrician, contacted Trade Professionals about employment. Trade Professionals sent him an application. During his interview and on the application, Trade Professionals asked if Anders had his own transportation and could get to job sites, but Trade Professionals did not ask Anders about his driving record, which contained multiple violations. Trade Professionals did not require employees to own cars. DeVries Electric Company contacted Trade Professionals to locate an electrician to work on a project in Kansas. Trade Professionals in turn contacted Anders to fill the position. Anders went to Kansas and rented lodging. Because he was working out of town, Trade Professionals provided him with what they called a "per diem," which amounted to three dollars per hour above his standard wage. The contractor decided what the per diem would be. The payment of a per diem is common in this industry; the money is understood to be compensation for the costs of meals, lodging, and so forth, which are incurred by employees who are working out of town. (This use of the term "per diem" is not technically correct because this was really an increase in Anders's hourly wage. For consistency, the court decided to continue to use the term.) Trade Professionals did not directly pay for any of Anders's travel-related expenses. Representatives of DeVries and Trade Professionals testified that Anders's job duties were those of an electrician, and DeVries said that Anders's duties did not include driving. While he was in Kansas, Anders generally drove his own truck to work or got a ride with a coworker. On the day of the accident, Anders left work after his shift was over, stopped for gasoline, and proceeded to drive toward his temporary lodging. En route, Anders collided with Girard's vehicle.

ISSUE Was Girard entitled to a trial on *repondeat superior* and/or negligent hiring? Was the district court correct in granting summary judgment to Trade Professionals on these issues?

HOLDINGS No, Girard was not entitled to a full trial on these issues. Yes, the district court was correct in granting summary judgment.

REASONING Excerpts from the opinion of Circuit Judge Nathaniel R. Jones:

[T]he district court's order should only be affirmed if . . . there is no genuine issue as to any material fact and . . . the moving party is entitled to a judgment as a matter of law. . . .

. . . The Kansas Supreme Court has held that:

An employer is liable for the tortious acts of his employee only under special circumstances. Special circumstances exist when the employee is (1) on the employer's premises, (2) performing work for the employer, or (3) using the employer's chattel, (4) when the employer voluntarily assumes a duty to control the employee, or (5) when the employer negligently retains a known incompetent or unfit employee.

... Girard seeks to impose liability on Trade Professionals under the second and fifth of these circumstances. A principal is only liable for the torts of his agent if at the time the tort was committed the agent was acting within the scope of his authority or employment....

> Under Kansas law the liability of an employer for the negligent acts of his employee is controlled by a determination as to whether, at the time of the act complained of, the employee was engaged in the furtherance of the employer's business to such a degree that the employer had the right to direct and control the employee's activities. Liability does not attach to the employer if there is only incidental furtherance of the employer's business.

... Thus, the primary factor to be considered is whether the principal had control over the agent. "If the principal had no right to direct and control the agent at the time in question, the principal is not vicariously liable to third parties for the agent's negligence." Accordingly, ... the Supreme Court of Kansas held that "an employer is not liable for injuries caused by an employee whose 'actual work for the company had ceased for the day.'" ... Here, Anders' shift was over. He was under no instruction to go to his home and he had no duty to perform on the way. He was free to go wherever he pleased, by whatever form of transportation he desired, and to do whatever he wanted. Thus, he was no longer under the control of his employer, and he was not furthering Trade Professionals' business. Therefore, Trade Professionals cannot be liable for the accident [under *respondeat superior*]. ... [... [N]umerous courts have held that employers are not generally liable for the acts of their employees on the employees' way to and from work, and the rule has come to be known in various jurisdictions as the "going [to] and coming rule." ... ("Because an employee usually does not begin work until he reaches his employer's premises, his going to and coming from work is generally considered outside the course of his employment unless he has a duty to perform en route.")]

Under Kansas Law, "[a] master may be liable for injuries to a third person which are the direct result of the incompetence or unfitness of his servant where the master was negligent in employing the servant or in retaining him in employment when the master knew or should have known of such incompetence or unfitness of the servant." [An employer's direct liability for negligent hiring is independent from the vicarious liability of an employer under the doctrine of *respondeat superior.*] ... [T]he Kansas Supreme Court recently explained this cause of action as follows.

> In order to find an employer liable for negligently hiring or retaining an employee, there must be some causal relationship between the dangerous propensity or quality of the employee, of which the employer has or should have knowledge, and the injuries suffered by the third person; the employer must, by virtue of knowledge of the employee's particular quality or propensity, have reason to believe that an undue risk of harm exists to others as a result of continued employment of that employee; and the harm which results must be within the risk created by the known propensity.

... [T]he court said that none of the [precedent] cases,

> should be unduly extended to find that a duty comes into existence whereby an employer must ascertain the detailed history of every employee, whether criminal or not, and terminate the employment of an individual who is performing acceptable services and is clearly not unfit or incompetent, but who does pose some degree of risk due to previous actions.

... Anders was on his own time. He was merely using his own truck to transport himself home. The actions at issue took place away from the place of business, and he was not carrying out his employer's business. Thus, there was no "nexus to the employer's operations." Based on the Kansas Supreme Court's refusal to impose liability for negligent hire where the employee is acting without a nexus to the employer's business, we affirm the district court's grant of summary judgment on ... [the negligent hire] issue. ...

BUSINESS CONSIDERATIONS How could Trade Professionals improve its hiring practices? Can you think of variations in the facts that would result in liability for Trade Professionals? What would they be?

ETHICAL CONSIDERATIONS Is it ethical to sue a master for injuries caused by a servant during the servant's commute from work?

Time and Place of Occurrence

Two of the factors that courts analyze in determining the course and scope of employment are the time and place of the act[4]—whether the tort occurred on the work premises and whether it occurred during work hours. One of the factors affecting the court's decision in the *Trade Professionals* case (Case 31.1) was that Anders was not on the work premises at the time of the tort.

Failure to Follow Instructions

A master can be held liable for a servant's acts even though the master instructed the servant not to perform a specific act or commit torts. The disobedience of the servant does not necessarily exempt the master from liability. If this were not true, a master could avoid all liability by simply instructing all of his or her servants not to commit any torts during the course of employment.

Failure to Act

A master can also be held liable under *respondeat superior* when the servant fails to act as directed, as shown in the following example.

Sammy, a railroad switch operator, is supposed to throw a switch on the track at the same time every day. One day, he carelessly fails to do so, causing a train to derail, and passengers on the train to be injured. The master (the railroad) is liable for Sammy's negligence in this situation. Sammy was negligent by failing to act as instructed.

Respondeat superior does not decrease the servant's liability for wrongdoing, but it makes an additional party, the master, also liable. In many legal situations, such as the one just described, multiple parties may be held liable for a single occurrence.

Identifying the Master

Another problem that may arise is deciding *who* the master is. Who controls the manner in which the servant will do the work? The master, or employer, is the one who not only can order the work done, but also can order how it will be done. Identifying the master is especially complex in cases involving borrowed servants. In these cases, who *is* the master? Is it the lending master, the borrowing master, or both? Again, the important factors are the course and scope of the employment and the master's ability to control the servant. Consider the following example:

Jamal works for Computer, Inc., which is having its office remodeled by Interiors Redone, LLP. (LLP signifies that the business is operating as a Limited Liability Partnership. LLPs are discussed in greater detail in Chapters 32–34.) Since the contractors doing the work are understaffed, Jamal's supervisor tells Jamal to help them. In this situation, Computer, Inc., is referred to as the general master and Interiors Redone, LLP is referred to as Jamal's special master. (The meanings of general

---

NRW CASE 31.1   Management

LIABILITY FOR DRIVERS MAKING DELIVERIES

As NRW's business has expanded, the firm has begun to hire drivers to make deliveries of the product to customers, especially retail outlets. Carlos recently read an article in the local newspaper about a case in which the driver of a delivery van caused an accident. The county trial court entered a judgment against the employer of the driver for $1.5 million. Carlos is concerned that a similar case would destroy NRW if the firm employed a driver who caused an accident. Carlos has asked you if there is any way for the firm to avoid liability while still hiring drivers to make deliveries for the firm. What will you tell him?

BUSINESS CONSIDERATIONS How can a business minimize its potential financial risk when one of its servants is guilty of negligence? What policies should a business initiate to provide the best possible protection when hiring servants who will be driving company-owned vehicles?

ETHICAL CONSIDERATIONS Would it be ethical for a firm to state that its delivery personnel are independent contractors, and then to require all of its drivers to drive their personal vehicles, and to provide proof of adequate insurance coverage?

INTERNATIONAL CONSIDERATIONS Suppose that one of NRW's drivers is making a delivery to a customer in Canada and is involved in an accident there. Would the same rules apply in this situation? What if the delivery and the accident occurred in Mexico? Would NAFTA influence the case, or would it be tried under other legal principles?

---

master and special master here are similar to those used to define general and special agents in Chapter 29.) Jamal is classified as a borrowed servant.

Assume that the supervisor for Interiors Redone, LLP instructs Jamal to paint the walls in the main lobby of the building. After painting the walls in the main lobby, Jamal fails to put up Wet Paint signs. We will assume that Jamal was negligent. A customer brushes against the wall and wet paint ruins her clothes. Who is Jamal's master at the time of his negligent act? Who will be held liable under respondeat superior? *Recall that Jamal will also liable for his negligence.*

Some courts will decide that both Computer, Inc. and Interiors Redone, LLP are liable. Jamal was subject to the control of both, and his actions benefited both. Other courts will conclude that Interiors Redone, LLP is liable because Jamal was working primarily for Interiors Redone,

LLP at the time of the negligence. Still other courts will hold Computer, Inc. liable because ultimately Jamal was subject to its control and it supplied his paycheck. To avoid the uncertainties caused by borrowed servants, prudent masters enter into agreements about which master will be liable when a servant is "loaned" to another master and/or obtain liability insurance for the servants' acts. In the following case, the two employers argued about who was liable for a borrowed servant's acts.

31.2

NVR, INC. v. JUST TEMPS, INC.
2002 U.S. App. LEXIS 3746 (4th Cir. 2002) (Unpublished opinion)

FACTS Just Temps was in the business of supplying temporary laborers for construction and warehouse work. NVR, a developer and builder of single and multi-family homes used temporary labor providers, including Just Temps. NVR required all such companies to enter into a standard contract to govern the parties' relationship. The contract contained an indemnification provision whereby Just Temps "agreed to indemnify NVR . . . for . . . any and all liabilities, losses, and costs . . . regardless of cause, arising from or connected with . . . any alleged personal injury, death, or property damage arising from or connected with the Work" that Just Temps laborers were performing for NVR.

When placing an order for Just Temps labor, NVR usually advised Just Temps of the particular tasks involved and the amount of weight the temporary laborers would be required to lift. One of the tasks typically assigned to such laborers was the moving of empty or partially filled 100-pound propane cylinders. NVR had several such cylinders at the Durham Manor Project to fuel open-flame heaters called "salamanders," which were used to dry newly taped and spackled drywall. At the time of the explosion and fire, two salamanders were in operation, one on the ground floor and the other on the third floor. The salamanders were connected by long rubber hoses to two 100-pound propane cylinders positioned considerable distances away from the operating heaters.

Willie Everett had not worked before at the Durham Manor Project. When he arrived there, he reported to Kenneth Dudley, NVR's on-site project supervisor, who initially assigned Everett and a coworker from Just Temps the task of moving bricks. When that task was completed, Dudley asked the workers to move four partially filled propane cylinders from behind the building to the parking area on the opposite side of the building, where the cylinders would be refilled by

NVR's propane gas supplier. Everett and his coworker began moving the cylinders by rolling them upright through the building. Josef Kokes, a masonry subcontractor, heard a loud hissing noise coming from within the building and asked Everett's coworker about the noise. The coworker replied that Everett was in the building "releasing gas because [the cylinder] got too heavy for him to carry." An explosion occurred and a fire spread rapidly throughout the building. Michael Newberry, a certified fire investigator, concluded that the explosion and fire were the result of Everett's release of the propane gas.

ISSUE Which company was liable for Everett's acts?

HOLDING This was a question for the trial court. The district court's grant of summary judgment was incorrect.

REASONING Excerpts from the court's opinion (Circuit Judges Niemeyer, Traxler, and Senior Circuit Judge Hall):

. . . The borrowed servant doctrine arose as a means of determining which of two employers, the general employer or the borrowing employer, should be held liable for the tortious acts of an employee whose conduct injured a third party and who, although in the general employ of the former, was performing a task for the latter. ("When . . . an attempt is made to impose upon the master the liability for [the servant's tortious acts], it sometimes becomes necessary to inquire who was the master at the very time of the negligent act or omission.") The [U.S.] Supreme Court summed up the doctrine as follows: "One may be in the general service of another, and, nevertheless, with respect to particular work, may be transferred . . . to the service of a third person, so that he becomes the servant of that person, with all the legal consequences of the new relation."[5]

. . . [W]e agree with NVR that application of the borrowed servant doctrine does not resolve the ultimate issue presented. Under Maryland law, in cases like this one between a general employer and a borrowing employer, "whatever the status of an employee under the 'borrowed servant' doctrine, the parties may allocate between themselves the risk of any loss resulting from the employee's negligent acts." . . . Thus, if the parties contractually agreed that one or the other of them should bear the risk of a particular employee's negligent acts, that employee's status under the borrowed servant doctrine is immaterial.

Here, the contract clearly allocated the risk of Everett's negligence to Just Temps. Specifically, Just Temps expressly agreed to indemnify NVR for "all liabilities, losses, and costs . . . arising from or connected with . . . any alleged personal injury, death, or property damage arising from or connected with the Work" that Everett was performing for NVR. The indemnification provision made clear, however, that Just Temps was not required to indemnify NVR for "any liability attributable solely to the negligence of NVR or its affiliates," a term that NVR presumably placed in its standard form contract to ensure that the . . . indemnification provision comported with Maryland law. See [precedents] . . . (holding that clauses in construction contracts providing for indemnity against the results of one's sole negligence are void as against public policy). Essentially then, by virtue of the indemnification clause, Just Temps contractually agreed to bear the financial burden of any damage caused in whole or in part by any Just Temps laborer, including Everett.

. . . All of the cases cited by Just Temps involve disputes between an employee and one of the employers. None of the cases involve a dispute between a general employer and a borrowing employer in which the employers contractually allocated the risk of the loss that materialized. . . .

BUSINESS CONSIDERATIONS What could a construction company do to reduce the likelihood that an employee will cause an accident? Did Everett have the knowledge and wisdom to do the job? Who is responsible for assuring that employees have the knowledge and wisdom to do the assigned work?

ETHICAL CONSIDERATIONS Did Everett owe NVR a moral duty? Did he breach any moral duty? Why? How would NVR feel about Everett's release of the propane even if there were no explosion?

The fact pattern in Case 31.2 is relatively simple. In more complex cases, it is helpful to draw a diagram of the relationships of the parties.

A closely related problem occurs when one servant appoints another servant (a subservant) to complete his or her tasks. Under *respondeat superior,* who is responsible for the torts of the subservant? If the servant had authority to appoint the subservant, the master will be held liable for the subservant. However, if the servant lacked authority, generally the servant will be liable as the "master" under *respondeat superior.* The primary justification for this rule is that the servant is the one with the right to control the subservant.

Crimes and Intentional Torts

Courts are more reluctant to hold a master liable under *respondeat superior* for intentional wrongs such as *assault* (a threat to touch someone in an undesired manner) and *battery* (unauthorized touching without legal justification or consent) than they are for negligence on the part of the servant. In fact, some courts still follow the traditional rule that a master is not responsible for the intentional acts of his or her servant. The modern view, however, is that a master is liable if the servant advanced the master's interests or the servant believed that his or her conduct was advancing the master's interests. Consequently, masters can be held liable under *respondeat superior* for intentional torts such as slander, libel, invasion of privacy, and assault and battery. Many criminal acts are also torts, and the master may be held civilly liable under *respondeat superior* for the financial losses suffered by the victim of the servant's criminal act even if the master is not held liable for the criminal conduct of the servant. *Respondeat superior* is not used to impose criminal liability on the master.

Courts will hold a master liable for some of a servant's serious wrongdoings, but not for others. The question is often one of degree. How serious was the tort or crime? Should the master have expected it? Is there much variance between the assigned tasks and the wrongdoing? There seems to be a trend toward increasing the masters' liability. In these cases the courts frequently examine the underlying policies for *respondeat superior.*

Direct Liability of the Principal

The agent must be a servant before *respondeat superior* will be applied. However, principals may be held *directly* responsible for some of the wrongs committed by their agents, even if the agents are not servants. For example, the

WHEN IS MAI "OFF THE CLOCK"?

Mai, Carlos, and Helen designed T-shirts with the NRW logo. They gave shirts to family members and friends to help publicize the firm. Mai liked to wear her T-shirt to the gym. One day, while wearing her shirt, Mai had a disagreement with Eslanda, another member of the gym, about who was next to use the weight bench. Eslanda claimed that Mai hit her. Mai denied the claim. Eslanda threatened to sue Mai for battery and intentional infliction of emotional distress, and to sue NRW for *respondeat superior* for Mai's torts. Assuming that Eslanda can prove that Mai hit her, can she successfully sue NRW for damages? Is Mai advertising for NRW, thereby making her conduct "job related?"

BUSINESS CONSIDERATIONS Should a business expect to be held liable whenever any person acts negligently or in a tortious manner while wearing a shirt (or other item of apparel) that advertises the firm? Should it matter if the person wearing the logo is, or is related to, a manager of the "advertised" firm?

ETHICAL CONSIDERATIONS Is it ethical for the plaintiff in a tort case to sue the wealthiest potential defendant, regardless of the degree of fault that may attach to that defendant? Is it ethical for a business to derive the benefits of "free advertising" when people wear its logo on their apparel and yet to deny liability when those same people act in a tortious manner?

INTERNATIONAL CONSIDERATIONS Would the result be any different if Mai were on an overseas business trip and using the exercise room of the hotel when the incident arose? What if Mai were on vacation in another country rather than on a business trip?

principal is liable if the principal *instructed* the agent to commit the wrong, did not properly supervise the agent, ratified or approved the agent's tort, or was negligent in the selection of the agent. (Negligent hiring is discussed in greater detail in the following section.)

Criminal law may also apply to a principal when an agent commits a crime. For example, a principal can be criminally liable based on his or her own fault. If a principal directs or encourages an agent to engage in criminal activity, the principal will probably be held personally liable

for such acts as conspiracy, solicitation, or being an accessory to the crime. (In a *conspiracy,* the participants plan the criminal behavior together. However, in a *solicitation,* one person convinces another to engage in the criminal activity. As an *accessory to the crime,* one person assists the primary actor in the commission of the crime.) In addition, some criminal statutes create liability for the principal even though the principal does not intend to violate the statute or does not know of the illegal act or condition. For example, state liquor laws often specify that tavern or restaurant owners are liable if minors are served alcohol in their bars. In most states, this is true whether or not the owner approves of such action or even knows that it has occurred. Other examples include statutes that prohibit the sale of impure food or beverages, no matter who is at fault. The purpose of these statutes is to assure that the principals take every possible precaution to ensure that such activities do not occur in their establishments; this is accomplished by imposing liability on them if these statutes are violated.

Negligent Hiring

Careful selection of employees is important to an employer. An employer wants to know if the applicant will do a good job and work well with other members of the staff. In addition, an employer does not want to hire an applicant who will not follow instructions or work within the guidelines established by the employer. Such an employee may be likely to commit torts or harm members of the public while in the course and scope of employment, creating potential liability for the employer.

An employer can be held liable for negligent hiring if he or she is careless in the hiring process. In many states, negligent hiring also applies to the hiring of agents and independent contractors. However, since most of the cases involve employees, we will use the employee/employer terminology. The number of suits based on negligent hiring is on the rise. (Negligent hiring or selection of independent contractors was also discussed briefly in Chapter 29.) *Negligent hiring* assumes that if the company had investigated the applicant's past, it would have learned of the prior antisocial conduct of the applicant, and then the employer would not have hired the person. However, the employer hired the employee and placed the employee in a position where he or she could harm someone. (For a good description of how to avoid negligent hiring, see the Quicken.com Web site at http://www.quicken.com/cms/viewers/article/small_business/40071/ and the CCH Business Owner's Tool Kit at http://www.toolkit.cch.com/text/P05_1515.asp.) Under the theory of negligent hiring, an employer owes a duty to customers and to the public at large. Depending on state law, the employer may also be liable to his or her other employees and agents. In many states, the employee's acts are not required to be in the course and scope of the employment in order to impose liability for negligent hiring. A relatively recent Florida case, *Tallahassee Furniture Co. v. Harrison*, illustrates these principles:

John Allen Turner, an employee of Tallahassee Furniture Company, delivered a couch to Elizabeth Harrison. (The couch was purchased by her father, a stockholder in the furniture company.) Three months later Turner returned and asked Harrison for a receipt for the broken television she had given him on the delivery date because, he said, they thought he had stolen it. Then he asked to use her bathroom. After gaining access to her home, he brutally beat and stabbed her. Following these events, Harrison filed criminal charges against Turner. In addition to these criminal charges, she sued Tallahassee Furniture Company for her damages, alleging negligent hiring and negligent retention. The employee had a criminal record including several charges of battery. He had been voluntarily committed to a psychiatric hospital two times, where he was diagnosed as a paranoid schizophrenic: he claimed to hear voices telling him to kill himself and telling him to kill other people. He had a known history of drug abuse and he had been fired from his last job. Harrison prevailed in court because the court found that the employer failed to use adequate measures to determine Turner's qualifications for the job or to discover problems with his past conduct. When Turner was hired for the job, the company did not ask him to complete a job application. Company management testified that if they had known of Turner's history, they would not have hired him as a delivery person. The court decided that the company should have known of his history, and held the company liable for its failure to act reasonably in hiring Turner.[6]

In negligent hiring cases, the question before the court normally will be whether the employer exercised the level of care that, under all the circumstances, the reasonably prudent employer would exercise in choosing or retaining an employee for the particular duties to be performed. The courts then consider the reasonableness of the employer's efforts to inquire into the applicant's background. In the Tallahassee Furniture Company case, the court held that the employer was guilty of negligent hiring. The employer's duty depends on the type of position for which it is hiring. This duty is particularly high when the employer is hiring maintenance workers and delivery people who will go into homes and apartments of customers.

The liability for negligent hiring poses some difficult practical problems for employers. How does an employer obtain all the necessary information about an applicant, *without* illegally violating his or her right to privacy? What is the employer's responsibility to learn about the applicants' character and background? An employer must consider both federal and state laws. In addition, there are difficult moral questions involving an applicant's privacy and employer's desire (or need) to know. Exhibit 31.1 contains some practical advice on hiring. Exhibit 31.2 compares the direct and the vicarious liability of the principal.

It is common to sue the employer for negligent hiring and under *respondeat superior*. In the case on pages 748–749 the court considered both theories.

Indemnification

When a master pays a third person under *respondeat superior* for injuries caused by the servant's unauthorized acts, the master is entitled to *indemnification* (the right to be repaid) from the servant. Unlike most other theories, *respondeat superior* is not based on the fault of the master; it only creates legal liability for the master. The master should be entitled to recover from the person who caused the loss—the servant—so the law permits reimbursement. As a practical matter, the master generally will have insurance to cover the liability he or she incurred. Remember that the servant normally will not have sufficient funds to cover the liability either to the victim or to the master. If the servant is still employed by the master, the master may be able to withhold part of the reimbursement from each paycheck until the master is completely repaid. Continuing to employ the servant, however, may increase the likelihood that the master will be liable for any similar wrongs by the servant in the future under *respondeat superior* or negligent retention.

Sometimes an *agent* may be held liable to the third person due to the commission of a tort, but the agent may then be entitled to indemnification from the principal. (We are using *agent/principal* terminology in this paragraph rather than *master/servant* terminology because these are the terms used in the Restatement [Second] of Agency.) The agent's right to reimbursement will depend on the particular facts of the case. Such cases are based either on contract law or on the law of restitution.[7] Courts are influenced by what they believe to be just, considering the business and the nature of the particular relationship between the principal and the agent.[8] Under the Restatement, an agent is entitled to indemnification *if* the agent, at the direction of

---

EXHIBIT 31.1 Steps to Reduce Liability for Negligent Hiring

Remember to check the limits of local, state, and federal employment law.

1. Obtain a completed job application.

2. Obtain a release so that the employer can check criminal records, mental health records, and credit histories.

   Most commonly, if the applicant will not sign a release he or she will not be hired.

   This is especially important if past history or mental condition creates a potential threat to customers.

3. Conduct a detailed job interview. Ask about "breaks" in employment.

4. Ask about convictions, not arrests. Arrest records are protected in many states.

5. Be diligent about checking with prior employers.

   Did the employee leave on good terms?

   Would the prior employer hire him or her again?

   Don't limit the inquiry to prior positions at this employer in cases of potential promotions, demotions, or lateral transfers.

6. Check on alcohol and drug use, particularly if this occurs on the job and/or interferes with job performance.

   An employer generally cannot prohibit alcohol use by adults during their own time, unless it interferes with work.

7. Ask about driver's license, tickets, and driving accidents if the applicant will be driving on business.

8. Check on potential mental or emotional problems.

9. Consider hiring a professional investigator. The cost may be justified.

10. Keep a written record of the investigation to show the steps taken, questions asked, etc.

11. Remember to consider the nature of the employment.

    Is the employee going to enter customers' homes?

    Is the employee going to have access to a passkey?

---

the principal, commits an act that constitutes a tort but the agent believes that the act is not tortious.[9] In other words, the agent must act in good faith. Obviously, if an agent completes a task that he or she knows to be illegal or tortious, the agent is not entitled to indemnification.[10]

Exhibit 31.3 illustrates the relationships among the primary parties when the servant commits a tort. The ser-

vant's right to indemnification is questionable because the courts require that the servant was following the master's instructions in good faith before being entitled to indemnification. The master's *right* to indemnification is established by law. The master's ability to collect, however, is questionable because, realistically, many servants cannot afford to reimburse the master.

EXHIBIT 31.2 Liability of Master

Courtesy of Deborah Kemp

MIDDLEBROOKS v. HILLCREST FOODS, INC.
256 F.3d 1241, 2001 U.S. App. LEXIS 15528 (11th Cir. 2001)

FACTS On November 22, 1996, the members of the marching band of North Atlanta High School were on the way home from an out-of-town football game. Around midnight, they stopped in Commerce, Georgia, to eat. The buses parked at McDonald's, and most of the band members remained there. A group numbering at least 20 or 25, including an adult chaperone, went to the Waffle House owned by Hillcrest Foods. Some of the students ordered and received food and drinks; some ordered, but received only their drinks or nothing; and others were not waited on. The cook, Hal Hanley, who is white, was taking some food off the grill when he turned and said that the motherfuckers who weren't buying anything were going to have to get out and that he was not going to serve any niggers. (At trial, Hanley admitted using profanity, but denied using a racial epithet.) Two of the plaintiffs heard both the profanity and the racial epithet, one heard the profanity, and the other five heard nothing.

Hanley then called 911. He stated that a "bus load of black people" was in the Waffle House and that some were throwing things, which had hit him in the head. He also said, "Y'all need to send somebody down here to clear 'em all out before I get a damn knife to the son of a bitches." Hanley told a Waffle House server that people were throwing things at him, and she responded, "Oh, I didn't know that." Hanley asked the responding officer, Sergeant Russ Myers, to clear the group from the restaurant. Myers asked them to leave, and they complied. Hanley then locked the door and turned the lights off. The band members congregated in the Waffle House parking lot and then walked back to McDonald's. Most were upset, and some were crying. When the band members returned to their buses and left, the lights were back on at the Waffle House and there were customers inside the restaurant.

Hanley testified that the band group was loud and boisterous and that at least two students threw coffee creamers at him. Hanley, who has only a partial left arm, testified that at least three students called him a cripple. None of the other witnesses testified that anyone threw things at Hanley or ridiculed him. Myers testified that when he arrived at the Waffle House, the band members were not unruly or loud and they appeared to be behaving very well.

The chaperone and seven of the band members, all of whom are African American, brought claims against Hanley and Hillcrest for racial discrimination and for intentional infliction of emotional distress. The plaintiffs characterized their feelings after the incident as humiliation, embarrassment, disbelief, shock, shame, and disgust. The plaintiffs who did not hear the language firsthand learned of it shortly thereafter. The jury found for Hillcrest on the discrimination claim, but found in favor of Middlebrooks and the seven band members on the intentional infliction of emotional distress claim.

ISSUE Can Hillcrest be held liable based on *respondeat superior* or the negligent hiring of Hanley?

HOLDING Yes. Hillcrest can be held liable for the intentional infliction of emotional distress by Hanley.

REASONING Excerpts from the opinion of Circuit Judge John R. Gibson:

Respondeat superior and negligent hiring or retention were alternate theories under which the jury could find Hillcrest liable for Hanley's actions. A master is liable for the torts of its servant if they are committed in the prosecution and within the scope of the master's business. Under Georgia law, "as a general rule, the determination of whether an employee was acting within the scope of his employment is a question for the jury; however, in plain and indisputable cases, the court may decide the issue as a matter of law." This is not a case that falls within the "plain and indisputable" exception. Hanley was cooking when he turned and used offensive language. He identified himself as a Waffle House employee when he called the police, and he told the responding officer that he was in charge. Hanley testified that he believed he was doing his job when he called the police. He also testified that he had to handle the situation because no manager was present at Waffle House that night. Based on this evidence, a reasonable jury could conclude that Hanley acted within the scope of his employment.

Under Georgia law, liability for negligent hiring or retention requires evidence that the employer knew or should have known of the employee's propensity to engage in the type of conduct that caused the plaintiff's injury. Hanley testified that Hillcrest's district manager knew that he had been involved in an earlier altercation with a customer where a server called the police. During this altercation, the customer came over the counter, and Hanley defended himself with a knife in an attempt to cut the customer's throat. Another Hillcrest manager testified that it would not surprise him to learn that Hanley would use profanity or make racist remarks, although he would be surprised that Hanley used this language in front of customers. A reasonable jury could conclude that Hillcrest knew or should have known of Hanley's propensity to engage in the sort of conduct that occurred in this case. . . . [A] reasonable jury could find that Hanley acted within the scope of his employment and that Hillcrest negligently retained him . . .

Hillcrest's argument rests on its mistaken belief that the company itself must have taken some action that justifies an award of punitive damages. Under Georgia law, an employer is liable for punitive damages for the acts of its agent if the agent's conduct is sufficient to support an award of punitive damages. Hanley's actions—including the use of profanity and a racial epithet, calling the police, and having the students removed from Waffle House—are the sort of willful misconduct that suffices to present a jury question on whether

the Middlebrooks group was entitled to punitive damages. . . .

Hillcrest also argues that evidence of Hanley's previous altercation with a customer should not have been admitted because it was irrelevant and its prejudicial effect outweighed any potential probative value. The district court held that the evidence was relevant to the issues of negligent hiring or retention and punitive damages. Because the probative value of this evidence was not outweighed by any prejudice, the district court did not abuse its discretion by ruling it admissible. . . .

BUSINESS CONSIDERATIONS What should an employer do to prevent swearing and racial epithets by employees? What should an employer do when it starts having problems with an employee?

ETHICAL CONSIDERATIONS What duty did the Waffle House owe to its customers? What duty did Hanley owe to his employer?

Analysis of a Servant's Torts

To characterize a tort situation, one should answer the following questions:

• Was the person acting as a servant for the hiring party?

• Did the servant commit a tort?

• Was the servant acting within the course and scope of the job?

• Is the servant entitled to indemnification from the master? Is the master entitled to indemnification from the servant?

Remember that the servant is ultimately the one who is liable for the tort, unless he or she is entitled to indemnification from the master. The master may also be liable in his or her own right.

Injury on the Job

Courts generally use the terms *employer* and *employee* when discussing injuries on the job. Consequently, the same terminology is used here. An employer has a duty to provide

EXHIBIT 31.3 Liability for Tortious Injury to a Third Person

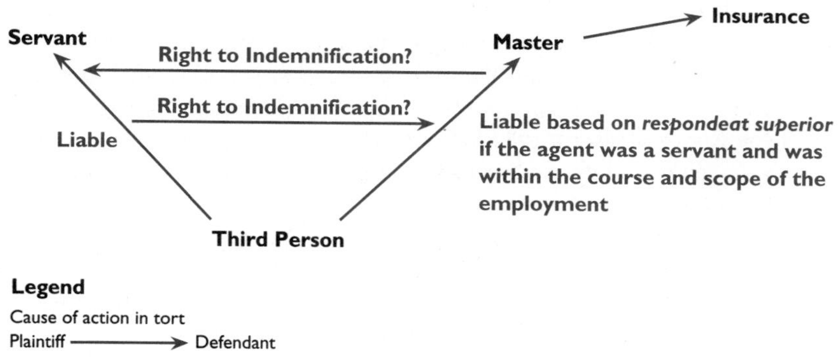

Legend
Cause of action in tort
Plaintiff ———→ Defendant

NRW

CD BURNERS AND COMPANY COMPUTERS

NRW is considering the purchase of a CD burner to produce promotional materials for the company. Mai recently read an article about CD burners being used to copy music or videos from the Internet. In 2001, more blank CDs were sold than prerecorded CDs. Entertainer Sheryl Crow calls CD burning "shoplifting."[11] Mai is concerned that NRW might be held civilly or criminally liable if employees use its CD burner to make unauthorized copies. What will you tell her?

BUSINESS CONSIDERATIONS What can a business do to minimize its risk that employees will use CD burners and other computer equipment in inappropriate ways? What policies and practices should the business establish? List some of the inappropriate ways that employees could use computer equipment.

ETHICAL CONSIDERATIONS What should NRW do if it discovers that its employees are burning music and/or video CDs on its equipment? What is its moral duty? What is the ethical perspective of people who burn CDs of music from the Internet? Why?

INTERNATIONAL CONSIDERATIONS It is possible to copy music or videos from Web sites throughout the world. How does this affect NRW's legal and moral duty? Since countries have different copyright laws, what law should apply to copying? Should it be the law where the copying actually takes place, the location of the Web site, or where the work is copyrighted?

employees with a reasonably safe place to work and reasonably safe equipment to use at work. Both the place and equipment should be appropriate to the nature of the employment. For example, some places—such as college classrooms—are relatively safe. Other places, like submarines, drilling platforms, and coal mines[12] are likely to be dangerous under the best of circumstances. If the workplace is not safe, the employer should warn employees about unsafe conditions that the employees may not discover even if they are reasonably careful.[13] For a good overview of workers' compensation statutes including special statutes for federal workers and maritime workers, see the Legal Information Institute at Cornell Law School, http://www.law.cornell.edu/topics/workers_compensation.html/.

Although courts sometimes apply similar rules to employees and independent contractors, there are distinct differences in their legal relationships. Nevertheless, courts have, on occasion, allowed independent contractors to recover for injuries sustained on the job.[14]

Under the common law, if an employee is hurt at work, the employer can utilize a number of defenses to avoid an obligation to the employee. Negligence by the employee and the employee's assumption of the known risk are two such defenses. For example, the employee might have been driving a truck too fast for icy road conditions, or the employee might not have been wearing safety goggles provided by the employer. Assumption of the risk, contributory negligence, and its modern counterpart—comparative negligence—are discussed in detail in Chapter 7.

Sometimes the work itself may be inherently dangerous.[15] Absent a statute to the contrary, an employer is *not* legally liable to an employee who is injured by a risk that is inherent in the work.[16] For example, some states have a "firefighter's rule" that prevents firefighters, peace officers, and/or other emergency professionals from recovering for on-the-job injuries.[17] The employer may also have a duty to warn if the danger is not commonly known, but the employer knows or should know of the risk inherent in the job.[18]

At common law, the *fellow employee doctrine* also acts to bar recovery by the employee. Traditionally, this concept was called the *fellow servant doctrine*. More recent court cases and treatises call it the fellow employee doctrine. For a brief definition, see the Rupp's Insurance & Risk Management Glossary on the Web at http://www.nils.com/rupps/fellow-servant-rule.htm. Under this theory, an employee cannot recover damages for work-related injuries if the damages are caused by another employee of the same employer. Like assumption of the risk, this doctrine acts as a complete bar to recovery. This rule is applicable to many worksite accidents. Most of the time, when an employee is injured on the job, the injury is caused not by the employer but by another employee at the jobsite. One justification suggested for this doctrine is that the employer is often remote from the worksite. The employee, on the other hand, is likely to know of hazards at work and to know of careless fellow employees. Another justification used to support the doctrine is that an employee "assumes the risk" of being injured by coworkers. The existence of the fellow employee doctrine encouraged the development of state workers' compensation statutes.

Workers' Compensation

Under workers' compensation statutes, payments are made to injured workers for injuries suffered on the job. Generally, these statutes do not apply the common law defenses. In some states, particular types of workers are not covered under the workers' compensation statutes.[19] For example, in New Mexico agricultural workers are not covered under the state statute.[20] For a Web site with links to the state agencies administering workers' compensation, see http://www.comp.state.nc.us/ncic/pages/all50.htm sponsored by Robert W. McDowell, Webmaster, North Carolina Industrial Commission.

Workers' compensation statutes may seem to be the opposite extreme from the fellow employee doctrine. They are not based on the fault of the employer, and the employer's negligence need not be shown in court. The worker needs to show only that his or her injury was caused in the course and scope of the job. In many states, the policies underlying these statutes are to "provide prompt and limited compensation benefits for job-related injuries and to facilitate the employee's speedy return to employment without regard to fault."[21] In other words, these statutes are intended to be "economic insurance" for workers. These statutes exist in most states and provide for a fixed schedule of compensation for listed injuries. Moreover, workers can easily determine how much they are entitled to receive. Therefore, this procedure allows for the quick settlement of claims and discourages many lawsuits. When workers' compensation statutes are applied, the statute generally provides the exclusive remedy for the worker. In other words, legal action against the employer based on other theories is prohibited. This is often called the *exclusivity requirement*.

State statutes vary in format. Some states have organized a fund to which the employers contribute, and injured employees collect from the fund. Some states allow employers to purchase insurance or to establish their own funds. In most states, the employee is allowed to recover even if he or she was negligent in causing the injury, assumed the risk, or was injured by a fellow employee. The injured employee generally receives compensation according to a schedule of payments, depending on the type of disability and how long the employee is unable to work. The AFL-CIO, a federation of America's labor unions, has prepared a comparison chart with state workers' compensation data and placed it on the Internet at http://www.aflcio.org/yourjobeconomy/safety/wc/upload/comptable.pdf. Workers' compensation statutes vary in the following respects:

- Some cover only major industrial occupations.
- Some exclude small shops with few employees.
- Some exclude injuries caused intentionally by the employer or other workers.

Because of the variations, it is important to examine the particular statute at issue.

If the workers' compensation statute does not apply, generally the employee will be permitted to sue based on common law theories. (Workers' compensation is also discussed in Chapter 40.)

Summary

A servant is liable for his or her own tortious and criminal acts. The fact that the servant was working at the time is immaterial. The fact that the master may also be liable to the third person is irrelevant as well.

A master may be liable for the acts of his or her servants. Much of this liability is based on the doctrine of *respondeat superior*. A master is liable for the torts committed by a servant if the servant was acting within the course and scope of the employment. The courts have discussed many policy reasons for enforcing *respondeat superior*. These include: masters are encouraged to be careful in selecting servants; masters are encouraged to be careful in supervising servants; liability is a necessary expense of conducting business; the master is benefiting from the servant's acts; the master can purchase liability insurance; the master has control; and the master can better afford these costs.

Numerous factors are used in analyzing what activity is "within the course and scope of the employment." There is no formula, however. Courts look at the factors and determine if *respondeat superior* should be applied. Even though a court holds a master liable to the third person under *respondeat superior*, this does not mean that the master necessarily will bear the ultimate loss. The master generally will be entitled to indemnification from the servant, although such indemnification may not be practical. The master may also have purchased insurance for this risk.

In rare cases, the principal may owe the agent the duty to reimburse the agent for money he or she paid to third persons. A principal may also be held directly liable if he or she commits a tort or a crime; this liability is not based on *respondeat superior*. It includes situations in which a principal directs an agent to commit a crime or tort or is negligent in selecting or retaining an agent.

The employer has a duty to provide a reasonably safe place to work. At a minimum this includes furnishing appropriate tools and equipment, adherence to safety regulations, and proper supervision. Injuries to employees on the job are normally covered by workers' compensation statutes. State statutes vary as to who is covered, the amount of compensation, and how the payment is funded.

Discussion Questions

1. David hires Annabelle as a housekeeper. Her main duties are to remain in the house and clean, prepare meals, and do the laundry. One afternoon, Annabelle receives a call from One-Day Drycleaners. David's suit is ready to be picked up. Annabelle decides to go and get the suit in her car. On the way back to David's home, she runs a red light and hits Julie's car. The police officer at the scene says that Annabelle's intoxication is the main cause of the accident. Annabelle had a few drinks with her lunch. David knew that Annabelle had a drinking problem when he hired her and that she is trying to stop drinking. Who is responsible for the damage to Julie's car, and why?

2. Samantha has just started working as an accountant for Big Five Accounting Firm. On her first audit, Samantha's supervisor sends her to get the coffee and doughnuts every morning. One morning, on the way to get the doughnuts, Samantha does not notice that the traffic has stopped in front of her, and she collides with Claudia's car. Who is responsible for the damage to Claudia's car, and why?

3. Consuelo prepares a joint tax return for Sammy and Lenora Johnson during her first year at Big Five Accounting Firm. However, she does not prepare the return correctly, and the IRS assesses an additional $4,000 in taxes and penalties. What rights do the Johnsons have? Why?

4. After class in the afternoon, Jim has a job delivering floral arrangements for Flowers by Flo. Flo often instructs Jim not to give his friends rides in the truck when he makes deliveries. One day, Jim sees Nanci, a classmate, waiting for the bus. He is going toward her home, so he gives her a ride. On the way, Jim carelessly drives off the side of the road, and Nanci is injured. Who is liable to Nanci for her injuries, and why?

5. Helen had the NRW company name, logo, and phone numbers painted on her husband's truck, even though Elliot does not work for NRW. One day while driving to his job, Elliot is involved in a traffic accident. Can Erin, the driver of the other vehicle, successfully sue NRW, claiming that Elliot is advertising for the firm?

6. Saul works for Central Cable Co. installing the cable for cable television in residential areas. The company needs water to repave the street after the cable is installed. Without permission, Saul uses water from Rosemary's tap. When Rosemary arrives home from work and sees this, she is furious. Her water bill is based on usage, and Saul has been using her water all day. Who is liable to Rosemary, and why?

7. Luis makes deliveries for Superior Meat Packing Company. On Wednesday, he complains to the company mechanic that his truck is not braking correctly. The mechanic says he will check it out immediately. On Thursday afternoon, the brakes fail, and Luis is unable to stop the truck. He collides with a telephone pole and suffers neck and back injuries. Who is liable? Why?

8. Beatrice owns three car dealerships—Toyota, Chevrolet, and Honda—which are located at the major intersection of College Avenue and Main Street. The Chevrolet dealership in located north of College Avenue and faces College Avenue. The Honda and Toyota dealerships are located south of College Avenue and face Main Street. Her sales force is authorized to sell vehicles at any of the dealerships. Sales people and clients often jaywalk across College Avenue. Repair people also jaywalk across the street. If potential clients are hit by a car travelling on College Avenue, who would be liable and why? If her servants are injured while jaywalking, who would be liable? Why?

9. Joe's Pizza Parlor advertises that their pizza will arrive at the customer's home hot and tasty within 30 minutes. Their television and radio commercials promise customers that if the pizza does not arrive within 30 minutes of ordering, the pizza will be free. The drivers have the primary responsibility for timely delivery. If a driver delivers more than one late pizza a week, he or she must pay for the additional pizzas from his or her paycheck. The delivery area is limited to a 20-mile radius from Joe's. Drivers are responsible for late delivery, even when the kitchen is busy. During busy periods, like Monday night football games, the pizzas are sometimes boxed 20 minutes after the placement of the order. Drivers compensate by driving fast to abide by the guarantee. Under the work contract, drivers supply their own vehicle and their own automobile insurance. Who is responsible if one of Joe's drivers has an accident? Why? What changes in policy could be implemented to reduce the likelihood of an accident?

10. Some employers ask applicants questions that may violate federal or state law. For example, an employer may mention his or her own children and ask the applicant if he or she has any children. An employer may ask what educational degrees the applicant has and where and when they were earned in order to calculate approximate age. What are the advantages and disadvantages of these inquiries to the employer? What about to the society at large? Assume that the employer is using this information to discriminate against parents or older people. What is the moral perspective of the employer?

Case Problems and Writing Assignments

1. The University of California Board of Regents has decided to sue doctors who ran a fertility clinic at the University of California (UC) Irvine campus. The University has agreed to pay more than $16.7 million to infertile couples who tried to obtain help at the Center for Reproductive Health. The work was primarily done at fertility clinics in Orange and San Diego counties from 1986 to 1995. Drs. Ricardo Asch and Jose Balmaceda allegedly took women's eggs without consent and used them to create children for other infertile patients. Dr. Asch said the University settled 106 patient claims to make him look bad. The University is still trying to settle the last seven claims. The doctors, who deny wrongdoing, fled the country in 1995 when they were indicted by a federal grand jury on charges of mail fraud and conspiracy to defraud patients of their genetic material.

   Cornell University also filed a legal action against the Regents, UC Irvine, and the doctors for Cornell's share of any damages awarded to two former patients whose embryos were used at Cornell without the patients' consent. Should the Regents and UC Irvine be entitled to reimbursement from the doctors involved? Why or why not? Should Cornell University be entitled to reimbursement from the Regents, UC Irvine, and/or the doctors? Why or why not? [See "UC Board Sues Doctors, Fertility Specialists Cost the University System Over $16.7m," *The Fresno Bee*, July 18, 1999, p. A13.]

2. Fred Remillard operates 12 McDonald's franchises in western New York State. Two of his employees, Michael Huffcut and Rose Hasset, who worked at separate restaurants 60 miles apart, had an affair. When they were not able to meet, they left "lovey-dovey" messages for each other on their voice mail boxes at work. It is alleged that Remillard listened to the messages, tape-recorded them, and even played them back to Michael's wife, Lisa Huffcut. The affair is over and the Huffcuts have reconciled. Michael and Lisa are suing McDonald's Corporation and Remillard for $1 million each. They claim their rights to privacy were violated and that they suffered from intentionally inflicted emotional distress, embarrassment, loss of reputation, and loss of income. What right to privacy should employees have in this context, and would non-employees have a greater right to privacy? Should voice mail recordings be protected by privacy considerations? What arguments can employers make that they should be able to monitor and record messages on company voice mail systems and electronic mail systems? Was Remillard's behavior reasonable in this situation? [See Ben Dubbin, "Voice Mail Love Affair Turns Privacy Issue Public," *The Fresno Bee*, January 23, 1995, p. A6.]

3. Charlotte H. Enger went to the Giant of Maryland store to purchase some groceries. While she was in the store, Kenneth M. Brown, the store's manager, saw a piece of celery that had fallen on the floor in the produce area, and he directed Geo Asfaw, a produce clerk, to pick up the celery. Asfaw refused to do so, walked toward Brown, stood within an inch of Brown's face, and stated: "You don't know who I am. I'm the devil. I'm going to burn you." Brown stepped back, and he "motioned" to Julio Rivera, a store employee, "to come over . . . to witness what [Asfaw] had said. . . ." Rivera approached Asfaw from behind, touched him on the shoulder, and said, "Hey, man." Asfaw pushed Rivera and assaulted him with karate kicks and punches. As Asfaw was attacking Rivera, Asfaw's foot almost hit Enger in her face. After Asfaw finished attacking Rivera, Asfaw decided to leave the store, and he began to walk toward the door. While leaving, he began to remove a nametag that was affixed to a red jacket that store employees were required to wear. The plaintiff testified: "And I thought, well, he's going to try to leave. And I said [to Asfaw], where are you going? What is your name? Why are you taking—and he just looked at me. And I said, why are you taking off your name tag? And then he slugged me, just pow! Just reached around and I went flying across the floor." Asfaw attacked Enger by delivering a "karate type of blow" to her chest. As a result of the impact from the blow, she sustained injuries to her foot and ankle. The trial court used the following jury instruction over the defendant's objection: "An act is within the scope of employment if it is incidental to the employer's business and is done to further the employer's interest. If an employee departs so far from his duties that his acts are no longer for his employer's benefit, then his acts are not within the scope of his employment. However, if the tortious act of the employee arose out of an activity which was within the employee's scope of employment or within the ordinary course of business, then that act may be considered to be within the scope of employment." Did the court err in instructing the jury on the doctrine of *respondeat superior*? Should a business establish procedures for handling aggressive employees or employees who have lost control? What policies might a business establish? Should Enger have intervened in the dispute? Why or why not? Was it ethical for Enger to intervene in the fight and then complain when she was injured? [See *Giant of Maryland, Inc. v. Enger*, 257 Va. 513, 1999 Va. LEXIS 71 (Va. 1999).]

4. Paul Brierly was a co-op student attending Shelby County Vocational School and he was working with Alusuisse under the supervision of David Ellison. Alusuisse manufactured materials for packaging and labeling foods and medicines. The printing press components gradually developed a buildup, which the workers eliminated by disassembling the components and running them through a "large-parts washing machine." The washing machine was similar to a dishwasher, but the solvent cleaning solutions used had low flash points and were highly flammable. Three days before the accident, the seal on the main pump of the parts washing machine broke and flammable solvent leaked. The employee shut the washer down. Employees took a number of precautions to minimize the possibility of a fire hazard. Before welding, Alusuisse took additional safety measures including: "(1) water was placed in the pit below the machine so as to prevent sparks from igniting any dried solvent residue left behind from the leaking pump; and (2) welding blankets were placed on and around the filter

basket housing and parts washing machine." The lead maintenance man, Reinhold Ritzi decided that he would do the
welding because he had more experience. Wordlow, Ellison,
and Ritzi apparently believed that the parts washing room had
been monitored with the "LEL" meter, a device used to
measure the "lowest explosive limit" of solvent vapor in an
area before a flammable source, like a welder, is introduced.
The meter had not been used. Each of the men involved stated
that they had assumed that one of the others had obtained the
readings. A "fire watch" crew was assembled. Wordlow and
other maintenance crew members, including Brierly, stood by
with fire extinguishers watching for stray sparks that could
ignite a fire. Brierly, the least experienced member of the crew,
was almost 12 feet away from the welding site, further away
than any of the other crew members. A spark ignited solvent
fumes inside the parts washing machine, causing an explosion.
The explosion blew off the steel door of the parts washing
machine, and the door struck Brierly, resulting in his death.
Wordlow, Ritzi, and one other worker also suffered injuries.
Can Brierly's administrator proceed with a tort action against
Alusuisse and Ellison? [See *Brierly v. Alusuisse Flexible Packaging, Inc.*, 1999 U.S. App. LEXIS 11927 (6th Cir. 1999).]

5. **BUSINESS APPLICATION CASE** Dusty Lewis, 18, was arrested
after a resident of the Dakota Woods apartments called police
and claimed that Lewis had raped her. Lewis had been assigned
the 8 P.M. to 3 A.M. shift, patrolling the apartment complex.
Lewis was arrested early Monday during his first shift at work.
Lewis was hired as a security guard that Saturday by Guard
Express in Fresno and given a temporary card until appropriate
background checks cleared and the state could issue a license.
Lewis has a misdemeanor conviction as a juvenile for driving
without a license. Department spokesman Jay Van Rein said, "If
you have a misdemeanor or felony conviction, you can't use a
temporary card at all. If he had a misdemeanor conviction,
then it was illegal for him to have that card." The victim and her
boyfriend and child lived in the apartment. Lewis contended
that he is a friend of the boyfriend and that he visited the
woman during his lunch break and used her phone. He contended that he did not assault her. Eddie Rodriguez, general
manager of Guard Express, stood by Lewis. He said that Lewis
knew the victim for several years. Rodriguez also said that he
had been in the guard business for six years, he knew about the
misdemeanor conviction, he believed that issuing the temporary card was correct, and that he used sound judgment in
hiring Lewis. Assume that Lewis did assault the victim. Who
should be civilly liable for the assault—Lewis, Rodriguez,
Guard Express, and/or Dakota Woods apartments? Why? What
can an employer do to improve its hiring of security guards?
[See Matthew Kreamer, "Guard's Permit at Issue," *The Fresno
Bee*, August 18,1999, pp. A1 and A10.]

6. **ETHICAL APPLICATION CASE** Owen Hart was a 33-year-old
wrestler with the World Wrestling Federation (WWF), wrestling
under the name "Blue Blazer." He was fatally injured at a pay-for-
view event called "Over the Edge," sponsored by WWF. As he was
being lowered from the ceiling into the ring by a guy wire, he fell

about 50 feet, hitting his head. The exact cause of the accident
was under investigation. Some theories include that he was never
properly connected to the harness; the harness malfunctioned;
the harness may have caught on the feathers of Hart's costume;
or Hart may have released it too soon. Hart was not trained as a
stunt man. Thousands of fans in the arena watched the event,
and many of them initially thought that it was a gag. Robert
McCome, a 15-year-old spectator, said, "We thought it was a doll
at first. We thought they were just playing with us. We were really
shocked when we found out that it was no joke."

Vince McMahon, WWF owner, vowed that this particular
stunt will not be repeated by any WWF performer, but he has
not ruled out other dangerous stunts. "In its quest for higher
ratings and its competition with WCW, the WWF has 'raised
the bar' with more dangerous stunts."[22] A memorial to Owen
Hart was taped by WWF.

This case poses a multitude of questions and issues, including
the following: Was Owen Hart a servant or an independent
contractor in this case? Does an accidental death such as this
encourage or discourage attendance at future events? Is it ethical to ask servants to perform dangerous stunts for the purpose of notoriety, ratings, and selling tickets? Are these
performers being respected as individuals or are they being
used merely as a means to greater profit? [See Kia Shant'e
Breaux, "Wrestler Hart Dies in Plunge at Arena," *The Fresno
Bee*, May 24, 1999, p. A8; Nova Pierson, "Wrestler Falls to
Death: WWF Star Owen Hart Killed in Ring Accident,"
Toronto Sun, May 24, 1999, Sports, p. 5; M. L. Curly, "Pro
Wrestling: McMahon: Stunts Like Hart's Won't Be Repeated,"
Detroit News, May 28, 1999, Sports, p. F2.]

7. **CRITICAL THINKING CASE** Christina Furey, an operating room
technician, assisted Dr. William Bradford Adkins with a
cesarean delivery. After closing the incision, Adkins allegedly
pressed the surgical staple gun to Furey's shoulder and shot a
staple into her arm. The gun was unsterile. The staple pene-
trated her skin and tissue and had to be removed with a Kelly
clamp. The incident occurred at Medical Center Hospital, which
is now called University Hospital. The Bexar County Hospital
District employed Furey. At the time, Adkins was a second-year
resident in obstetrics and gynecology at the University of Texas
Health Science Center (UTHSC). Adkins admitted that the District served as his paymaster but that UTHSC had control over
him. A Graduate Medical Training Agreement governed the
medical training and employment in question. It was signed by
Dr. Adkins, by John A. Guest as president and chief executive
officer of the District, and by a Dr. Forland on behalf of the
Dean of the Medical School for UTHSC. The agreement provided that the District did not have a legal right to control the
medical resident's tasks performed at the District's hospital.
However, the agreement also provided that the District would
pay the resident an annual stipend and provide such employee
benefits as leave time, insurance, workers' compensation, and
parking privileges. The agreement also required the resident to
become familiar with and abide by the House Staff Manual, the
bylaws of the medical-dental staff, and the policies, rules, and

regulations of the District. Jack Park, an attorney employed by UTHSC, stated in his affidavit that according to the agreement and as a matter of implementation and practice, the UTHSC controlled the details of the work performed by the house staff physicians like Adkins. The UTHSC recruited, sponsored, trained, and made the decisions as to whether the house staff physicians remained in the program. Schedules, rotations, and the details of the practice of medicine were made under the direction of faculty. All physicians, including medical residents, were under some control of the Hospital District. Dr. John Guest, president of the district, understood that the resident doctor "is working for both organizations." They are "being funded by the Bexar County Hospital District. They are under the supervision of the Health Science Center. . . . And the control of the Health Science Center." He also stated that liability coverage was provided by UTHSC and the District provided funding. They worked under the faculty of the medical school.

Was Dr. Adkins an employee of UTHSC, which is a state entity (entitled to sovereign immunity),[23] or was he an employee of the Bexar County Hospital District (the District)? Were Dr. Adkins's acts committed in the course of employment? Was Adkins's behavior ethical? Is "horseplay" in an employment setting inherently unethical, or does the ethical nature of the conduct depend on the results that may arise due to the horseplay? [See *Adkins v. Furey*, 1999 Tex. App. LEXIS 3887 (Tex. App. 4 Dist. San Antonio 1999).]

8. **YOU BE THE JUDGE** Donna Ivy was a bus driver in the City of Visalia. On September 25, 2000, around noon, Jerry William Knight hijacked the bus she was driving and raped her at knifepoint. Knight was sentenced to 89 years in prison for this crime. Ivy filed suit against the City because the silent alarm on the city-owned bus malfunctioned. The alarm was supposed to activate "Call Police" signs on the front and rear of the bus, sound a loud ringer in the dispatcher's office, and flash the bus number on a small screen in the dispatcher's office. The "Call Police" signs went on, but the ringer in the dispatcher's office did not. Ivy contended that if the alarm system had worked properly she would have been rescued. (A cell phone user did eventually call police after seeing the "Call Police" sign from the rear of the bus.) Ivy sued the City because it owns the bus system. The City contended that it is not liable because bus drivers are not city employees and the alarm system is the responsibility of Laidlaw Transportation, Inc., the independent contractor that managed and maintained the bus system. The City alleges that Ivy chose to sue the City because Ivy is receiving temporary disability checks from the workers' compensation system and that Ivy cannot sue Laidlaw, her employer. If this case were brought in *your* court, how would *you* rule? Who is responsible for providing Ivy with a safe workplace? Is this a nondelegable duty? [See Lewis Griswold, "Raped City Bus Driver Sues Visalia Over Alarm," *The Fresno Bee*, July 13, 2002, p. B4.]

Notes

1. *Pacific Mutual Life Insurance Co. v. Haslip*, 111 S. Ct. 1032 (1991).
2. *Restatement (Second) of Agency* (Philadelphia: American Law Institute, 1958), § 228(1).
3. Ibid., § 229(2).
4. Ibid., § 229(2)(b).
5. See *Standard Oil Co. v. Anderson*, 212 U.S. 215, 220 (1909).
6. See *Tallahassee Furniture Co. v. Harrison*, 583 So. 2d 744, 1991 Fla. App. LEXIS 7598 (Fla. App. 1st Dist. 1991). The Florida Supreme Court denied the petition for review in *Tallahassee Furniture Co. v. Harrison*, 595 So. 2d 558, 1992 Fla. LEXIS 152 (1992).
7. Warren A. Seavey, *Handbook of the Law of Agency* (St. Paul, Minn.: West, 1964), § 168, p. 265.
8. *Restatement (Second) of Agency* (Philadelphia: American Law Institute, 1958), § 438(2)(b).
9. Ibid., § 439(c) and Comment on Clause (c).
10. Harold Gill Reuschlein and William A. Gregory, *Hornbook on the Law of Agency and Partnership*, 2nd ed. (St. Paul, Minn.: West, 1990), § 89(B), pp. 151–152.
11. In 2001, 1.1 billion blank CDs were sold compared to 968 million prerecorded CDs. See Steve Morse, "CD Burning Protests Still Fall on Deaf Ears," *The Fresno Bee*, May 5, 2002), pp. H1 and H2.
12. On July 24, 2002, nine coal miners were trapped in a mine near Somerset, Pennsylvania, when they accidentally broke through the wall of a nearby mine. Fortunately, this time the miners were all rescued. (See Judy Lin, "Rescuers Bring Coal Miners to Safety," *Las Vegas Review-Journal*, July 28, 2002, Newsline Second Front Page, pp. 3A and 7A.
13. *Restatement (Second) of Agency*, § 492.
14. *Rodney* v. *U.S.*, No. 77-4028 (9th Cir. 1980); *Cioll v. Bechtel Corp.*, No. 733794 (San Francisco City Super. Ct., April 23, 1981).
15. Many of the professional and volunteer rescue workers from the 9/11 disaster at the World Trade Center Twin Towers are suffering from some form of respiratory problems. Workers at the site and residents of the area have been exposed to pollutants that are harmful if inhaled, such as asbestos, lead, mercury, and pulverized glass. See Richard Perez-Pena, "Cleaning Set for Exteriors Near 9/11 Site," *New York Times*, April 6, 2002, p. B1, and Margaret Ramirez, "WTC Clinic Opens; Clinton Urges $90 M More for Initiative," *Newsday*, August 6, 2002.
16. *Restatement (Second) of Agency*, § 499.
17. The South Carolina Supreme Court recently refused to adopt such a rule. See "S. Carolina High Court Rejects Firefighter's Rule," *National Law Journal*, Case, 24, no. 38 (June 3, 2002): B4.
18. *Restatement (Second) of Agency* § 499, Comment (c).
19. For example, see Cal. Labor Code § 3352 (2001) for a listing of people not considered employees under California workers' compensation law.
20. See 52-1-6, Application of Provisions of Act, Part A, of the New Mexico Statutes Annotated 1978/Chapter 51 Worker's Compensation.
21. *Sussman v. Florida East Coast Properties*, 557 So. 2d 74 (Fla. App. 3rd Dist. 1990) at 75.
22. M. L. Curly, "Pro Wrestling: McMahon: Stunts Like Hart's Won't Be Repeated," *Detroit News*, May 28, 1999, Sports, p. F2.
23. The Texas Tort Claims Act does not apply to claims "arising out of assault . . . or any other intentional tort." Tex. Civ. Prac. & Rem. Code § 101.057(2).

Business Organizations

Should the entrepreneur "go it alone" in a sole proprietorship? If so, the entrepreneur will have both absolute authority and total responsibility. Should a partnership be formed? For many businesses, the simplicity of a partnership makes it an ideal form, but the entrepreneur should be aware that a partnership entails the sharing of management powers and duties. Should a corporation be formed? The corporate form offers a number of advantages, including limited personal liability and the ability to franchise, but corporations are subject to heavy federal regulation and taxation.

Part 8 compares and contrasts these three main forms of business—proprietorship, partnership, and corporation—by showing the legal steps taken in their formation, operation, and termination. In addition, this part discusses several variations of these forms, such as limited liability partnerships and limited liability companies. Finally, franchising and securities regulation are addressed.

Formation of a Business

AGENDA

NRW Mai, Carlos, and Helen realize they have a product—StuffTrakR—that will have broad public appeal. Hence, they need to consider what form of business organization is best for them as owners. They will also want to consider which type of organization will be best for producing, marketing, and distributing this product. Since they are already involved together, should they just form a partnership? What legal implications might arise in such an organization? Should the firm incorporate? If it does, should it "go public," selling stock to investors to help acquire badly needed capital? Could Mai, Carlos, and Helen lose control of the business to an outsider if the firm went public? Is there a business form that will allow for outside investment without the fear that the investors might take control of management? What benefits are offered by one of the newer forms of organization, an LLP or an LLC? For purposes of Part 8, we will assume that the entrepreneurs are wrestling with these issues.

These and other questions will arise as you read this chapter. Be prepared! You never know when the firm or one of its members will seek your advice.

Selecting a Business Form

As we will see, no one form of business organization is perfect. Each has some advantages that the others lack; and each has some drawbacks the others avoid. Deciding on the proper form can be one of the most important decisions a businessperson will make. Fortunately, a great deal of information is available to help with this decision. The U.S. Small Business Administration provides information about forming and expanding businesses at its Web site at http://www.sba.gov/. Delaware Intercorp publishes an article entitled "What Other Steps Might You Need to Take?" at http://www.delawareintercorp.com/else.htm. This site discusses some of the necessary steps in forming a business. The site also provides incorporation services and encourages businesses to incorporate in Delaware. The Center for Computer-Assisted Legal Instruction (CALI)[1] Web site at http://www.cali.org/fellows/grids/businessorgs.html includes an outline of the various forms of business organizations. The decision to choose a type of business organization should never be made lightly or automatically. All "pros" and "cons" for each available alternative should be weighed carefully before a decision is made.

Businesses that purchase franchises can operate in any form allowed by state law unless the contract with the franchisor contains restrictions. (Franchise has multiple meanings in the law. In this context, a *franchise* is the right to engage in business using a particular trademark at a particular location or in a particular territory. Franchises are discussed in detail in Chapter 35.). Information about particular franchises and forming a business is available at Be The Boss, The Virtual Franchise Expo at http://www.betheboss.com/. It includes information on franchising your business, listing your franchise for sale, and buying a franchise in Canada or Mexico. For a helpful discussion about what form of business you should use to operate your franchise, see Entrepreneur.com's Web site at http://www.entrepreneur.com/Your_Business/YB_Node/0,4507,143,00.html/. Some states also provide information about choosing a business form. For example, see the Secretary of State of Iowa Web site at http://www.sos.state.ia.us/business/handbookintro.html/. California lists the key steps necessary to forming a business at http://www.ss.ca.gov/business/resources.htm.

Historical Overview of Partnerships

The partnership form of business organization is very old. It can be traced back to ancient Babylon and perhaps came into existence even earlier. It was widely used by the Romans during the height of the Roman Empire. In fact, Roman merchants introduced the partnership throughout Europe as they conducted trade with the peoples conquered by the Roman legions. England was one of the nations that "discovered" the Roman partnership. Later, English common law modified this form of organization slightly and utilized it in the development of the British Empire, including the colonies in North America that later became the United States.

The United States followed the English common law of partnerships for quite some time. Partnership law in the United States, however, has now been codified. Much of the codification has occurred under the leadership of the National Conference of Commissioners on Uniform State Laws (NCCUSL), which prepares uniform acts that it encourages state legislatures to adopt. The NCCUSL Web site includes information about the uniform acts and current projects. It is located at http://www.nccusl.org. The University of Pennsylvania Law School maintains the NCCUSL archives at http://www.law.upenn.edu/bll/ulc/ulc_frame.htm. The archives contain the full text of the uniform laws. Depending on the state, the controlling law today is found in the Uniform Partnership Act (UPA)[2] or the Revised Uniform Partnership Act (RUPA)[3] for general partnerships. In 1997 the NCCUSL amended RUPA to include limited liability for partners in registered limited liability partnerships.

As partnership law continues to evolve, there are a number of significant changes. RUPA has moved away from viewing the partnership as an aggregate of the partners to viewing it as a separate entity. This is called an *entity approach* and is expressly stated in § 201. Consequently, the partnership can sue and be sued in the partnership name.[4] Under RUPA, partnership property is owned in the partnership name. A partner has his or her partnership interest but is not a co-owner of specific partnership property.[5] RUPA has also changed some of the dissolution rules. A dissolution no longer occurs every time a partner leaves. Generally, a partnership can buy the interest of the partner who leaves.[6] "Partnerships based upon aggregate theory are simply more fragile than partnerships based upon entity theory."[7] RUPA also permits, but does not require, the filing of statements when the partnership is formed, dissolved, or merged with another partnership, or if there are limitations on partnership authority.[8] Other sections of RUPA explicitly state rules that were implicit in the UPA, or build on provisions in the Revised Uniform Limited Partnership Act (RULPA), which is discussed in the following paragraph.[9]

Rules for limited partnerships are codified in either the Uniform Limited Partnership Act (ULPA 1916) or the

Revised Uniform Limited Partnership Act (RULPA or ULPA [1976]). (A *limited partnership* is a partnership where some partners' liability is limited to their contribution.) In 1976, the NCCUSL approved RULPA[10] and in 1985 amended it.[11] Some form of RULPA has been adopted by every state except Louisiana and Vermont. (Officially, NCCUSL refers to them as ULPA [1916], ULPA [1976], and ULPA [1976] with 1985 amendments. Unofficially, NCCUSL and most writers refer to the 1976 revision as RULPA. We will call it RULPA.) There is now a new version called the Uniform Limited Partnership Act Revision that was finalized by the NCCUSL in 2001. The 2001 draft of the Uniform Limited Partnership Act (ULPA 2001) is available at http://www.law.upenn.edu/bll/ulc/ulc_frame.htm. ULPA (1916) has little effect today since it is followed only in Vermont. Louisiana does not follow either act.[12]

Partnerships are formed for a variety of reasons. Many professionals, for example, enter partnerships because they are not allowed to incorporate under the applicable state law. (In the sense used here, a *professional* is a member of a "learned profession," such as a doctor, a lawyer, or an accountant.) Some people enter partnerships to avoid the technical steps and expense required to form a corporation. (A *corporation* is an artificial person or legal entity created by or under the authority of a state or nation. It is owned by a group of persons known as stockholders or shareholders.) Other people form partnerships because it seems appropriate, sometimes without giving the matter serious consideration.

A partnership has many of the best features of the other major types of business organizations—proprietorships, limited partnerships, and corporations—but also some of the worst features. (A *proprietorship* is a solely owned business with legal rights or exclusive title vested in one individual. It is relatively easy to form.) A partnership is relatively easy to form, and the formation is normally informal. Like a corporation, a partnership may have a wider financial base than a proprietorship, and like a corporation, the partnership has more expertise from which to draw. A partnership can be a simple, oral agreement by two people. On the other extreme, it can be very complex with multiple levels of partners with various rights and obligations for the parties at each level.

One disadvantage to a partnership is that it is not "perpetual" as a corporation may be. A partnership will dissolve eventually. Also, the partners face unlimited liability for business-related conduct, as does a sole proprietor. Shareholders in a corporation, in contrast, have limited liability.

Exhibit 32.1 compares the different types of business organizations, while Exhibit 32.2 on page 764 addresses the complexity of forming any particular type of organization.

Partnerships Defined

Uniform Partnership Act

Section 6(1) of the Uniform Partnership Act defines a partnership. According to this section, a partnership has five characteristics. It is:

1. An association
2. Of two or more persons
3. To carry on a business
4. As co-owners
5. For profit.

The 16 words in the definition are deceptively simple. In fact, a tremendous amount of interpretation often is involved in fitting an organization into the definition of a partnership. To illustrate the potential problem, we will discuss the terms in the order listed.

An Association The courts have consistently held that a partnership must be entered voluntarily; that is, no one can be forced to be a partner against his or her will. Thus, *an association* has been interpreted as being "a voluntarily entered association." Being realistic, the courts also realize that people occasionally disagree. The test for voluntariness is the willingness to associate at the time of *creation* of the relationship. Later disagreements will not automatically destroy the partnership. Thus, an *association* means a mutual and unanimous assent to be partners jointly and severally at the time of the agreement.

Of Two or More Persons *Persons* here is interpreted broadly. It means persons in the biological sense, or persons in the legal sense, or persons in any other sense—in other words, two or more identifiable entities that elect to associate. Each partner may be a human being, a corporation, a partnership, or even a joint venture. (A *joint venture* is a commercial or maritime enterprise undertaken by several persons jointly; an association of two or more persons to carry out a single business enterprise for profit.) For good suggestions on how to select your partner(s), see Entrepreneur.com's Web site at http://www.entrepreneur.com/Your_Business/YB_Node/0,4507,146,00.html/.

To Carry on a Business The third element of the definition has two separate segments. First, it must be determined whether there is a business. A *business* is defined as any trade, occupation, or profession; so most associations meet this test. Next, it must be determined whether the business is being carried on. *Carrying on* implies some *continuity*. A business must be fairly permanent and lasting in

EXHIBIT 32.1 A Comparison of Different Types of Business Organizations

	Proprietorship	Partnership	Limited Partnership[a]
Creation	Proprietor opens the business, subject to state and local licensing laws and regulations.	Partners enter into an agreement, either orally or in writing; no formalities are required.	Partners enter into a partnership agreement and file a written form designating the limited partners and the general partners.
Termination	Proprietor closes the business; death, insanity, or bankruptcy of the owner also terminates the business.	Partners agree to dissolve the partnership; death, bankruptcy, or withdrawal of any partner also dissolves the partnership.[b] The terms of the agreement or a court order may dissolve the partnership. Liquidation of the assets after a dissolution winds up the business.	Partners follow same procedure as for a partnership, but with a difference in the order of distributing assets in case of a dissolution and liquidation of the business.
Taxation[c]	All business profits are taxed as regular income of the owner; there are no federal income taxes on the business, per se.	The business must file a federal tax return, but it is for information only. The income of the business is taxed as regular income to the partners.	The same tax procedure is followed as for a regular, general partnership.
Liability	Proprietor has unlimited personal liability. First, business assets will be used, and then the personal assets of the owner.	Partners have unlimited personal liability. First, business assets will be used, and then the personal assets of the partners. The partners are jointly and severally liable for the debts.	General partners have unlimited personal liability. First, business assets will be used, and then the personal assets of the general partners. The general partners are jointly and severally liable for the debts. Limited partners are only liable to the extent of their contribution.
Advantages	Simplicity of creation; complete ownership and control of the firm.	Informality of creation; greater potential for expertise and capital in management (because there is more than one manager).	Somewhat greater flexibility than a general partnership; increased opportunities to raise capital.
Disadvantages	Limited capital; limited expertise; limited existence (when the owner dies, the business terminates).	Limited existence; lack of flexibility; potential liability.	Some rigidity in ownership and decision making; personal liability of general partners; limited existence.

a. This applies to limited partnerships under the Revised Uniform Limited Partnership Act after the 1985 amendments.
b. This applies to partnerships under the Uniform Partnership Act.
c. Any change in the business form may result in substantial tax consequences for the business and for its owners.
d. This may also be an advantage.

EXHIBIT 32.1 *continued*

Limited Liability Partnership	Corporation	Limited Liability Company
Partners enter into a partnership agreement and the partnership files a copy or some other notice with the state.	Parties prepare and file *formal* legal documents known as articles of incorporation with the state of incorporation; they must comply with any relevant state or federal security statutes or regulations.	LLCs may be formed by two or more members, who enter into an agreement. Generally, LLCs must file articles of organization with the state government.
Partners follow same procedure as for a general partnership.	Parties close the business, liquidate all business assets, surrender the corporate charter, and distribute the assets as per state law; termination may also be due to state action revoking the charter.	Statute and/or agreement will probably limit the term of the LLC: State laws vary on whether the association can be renewed for an additional period.
The same tax procedure is followed as for a regular, general partnership.	A normal corporation is treated as a separate taxable entity and pays taxes on its profits. Any dividends are also taxed to the stockholders. This is called "double taxation." A Subchapter S corporation, regulated by the IRS, is taxed as if it were a general partnership despite its corporate status. A Subchapter S corporation is treated differently only for federal tax purposes. States may also tax them as partnerships.	Most LLCs can make an election to be taxed as either a corporation or a partnership. The LLC may have different taxation for state and federal purposes.
Partner is liable without limit for his/her own wrongs and wrongs of people the partner directly supervises; the partner's liability is limited to the partner's contribution for the wrongs of others.	Stockholders are *not* personally liable for debts of the corporation, so there is limited liability. Stockholders may lose their investment in the corporation if it fails.	All members are liable for association debts only to the extent of their capital contribution(s).
Limited liability except for a partner's own wrongs and the wrongs of people the partner directly supervises.	Longevity, including the potential for perpetual existence; potentially unlimited access to capital and to expertise; freely transferable ownership; limited personal liability of the owners.	Limited liability for all the members.
Unlimited liability for partner's own wrongs; only permitted in some states.	"Double taxation" (except for Subchapter S corporation); much more federal regulation; considerably more state regulation; formality and rigidity of the organization.	LLC statutes vary greatly from state to state. Professionals may not be permitted to form an LLC, depending on the state. There may be limitations on the transferability of shares.[d] Selling interests in an LLC may be subject to state and federal securities regulations. LLCs may have a limited term of existence.[d]

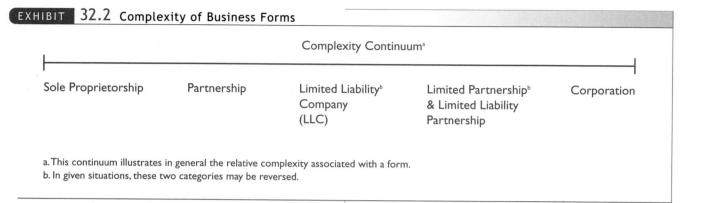

EXHIBIT 32.2 Complexity of Business Forms

Complexity Continuum[a]

| Sole Proprietorship | Partnership | Limited Liability[b] Company (LLC) | Limited Partnership[b] & Limited Liability Partnership | Corporation |

a. This continuum illustrates in general the relative complexity associated with a form.
b. In given situations, these two categories may be reversed.

order to be carried on. If a business appears to be short term, it is quite possible that the court will rule that no partnership exists. If the other elements of a partnership are present, however, the short-term business may qualify as a joint venture instead.

As Co-owners The fourth element is probably the most important and the most confusing. Co-ownership does not refer to a sharing of title on the assets used in the business. Instead, it refers to a sharing of ownership of the *business itself*. The business is an intangible asset. A business often uses assets of a tangible nature, but it need not own any tangible assets. For example, several accountants may enter a partnership. The partnership owns a business that provides services, and services are intangible. The accountants may lease an office; they may rent furniture; they may not own a single tangible asset, and yet they co-own a business. How, then, is one to know if people involved in a business are co-owners? The simplest way is to look at the agreement the people made when the business began. If the agreement states that they are partners, or co-owners, of the business, they *are* co-owners. But all too often the agreement is ambiguous, unclear, or oral. In such a situation, the agreement is of no help in resolving the co-ownership question. Then the courts must look beyond the agreement.

The courts normally will look at how the parties treat profits. If the parties share profits, or net returns, there is *prima facie* evidence that a partnership exists—that is, the partnership is presumed to exist unless disproved by evidence to the contrary. The sharing of profits creates a rebuttable presumption that a partnership was formed. (A *rebuttable presumption* is a legal assumption that will be followed until a stronger proof or presumption is presented.) The burden then shifts to the parties to *disprove,* or to rebut, the presumption. Note that under the provisions of RUPA, the sharing of profits is recharacterized as an evidentiary presumption, rather than *prima facie* evidence.[13]

The UPA recognizes five rebuttals.[14] If one of the parties can prove that profits were shared for one of the following reasons, no partnership exists. If such proof is not made, the sharing of profits establishes that a partnership did exist. The rebuttal is valid if profits are shared for one of the following purposes:

- As payment of a debt, by installments or otherwise (a promissory note or a judgment note should be produced as evidence)

- As payment of wages to an employee or of rent to a landlord

- As payment of an annuity to the representatives of a deceased partner

- As payment of interest on a loan (again, some document probably will be necessary)

- As payment of consideration in the sale of goodwill or other property, whether by installment payments or otherwise

For Profit The fifth and final element of the definition of a partnership is probably the easiest to show. A partnership must operate *for profit*. To be specific, all that is needed is a *profit motive*. If the business was created to generate profits and to return these profits to the owners of the business, this test for the existence of a partnership is satisfied. Thus, nonprofit associations cannot, by definition, be partnerships. However, an unprofitable business can be a partnership, provided that profits are the goal of the business. In short, the court is looking at the motive of the organization, not the financial bottom line.

In the following case the court analyzed whether the parties had formed a partnership. The court used the California statute based on the UPA (1914). In California, RUPA became effective January 1, 1999, and applies only to partnerships formed on or after that date.[15]

IN RE NIELSEN
2002 Cal. App. Unpub. LEXIS 5621 (Cal. Ct. App., 2d Dist., Div. 3 2002)
(Not to be published in the official reports.)

FACTS In 1973, Sharon, age 14, and Timothy, age 22, married. On September 12, 1989, they separated. On April 23, 1991, Timothy filed an action for dissolution of marriage. Sharon filed a civil complaint and the two cases were consolidated. The trial court awarded Sharon Nielsen the sum of $477,918 as her interest in the family partnership. There was no formal written partnership agreement. When Sharon married Timothy, he told her he was a partner in the family business with his parents, Rodney and Elaine, and his brother, Terry. The family business was developing and leasing residential real properties using the name "Four Winds Development." The family held annual partnership meetings, which Sharon sometimes attended. Both Timothy and Sharon used gas credit cards bearing the name "Four Winds Development." Everyone in the family wore T-shirts with the business name. Timothy worked with his father and mother in the family business. Timothy collected rents, which he gave to Elaine. He obtained new tenants for the rental properties. Timothy also assisted the family business in construction projects. He was involved with at least 11 different construction or remodeling projects. Timothy also investigated locations for the construction of a trailer park. Timothy had authority to write checks on some of the business bank accounts.

Sharon also worked for the family business by performing monthly typing services and miscellaneous services, such as cleaning. Sharon frequently answered the family business phone. Timothy and Rodney provided Sharon with telephone training. She made appointments for potential renters to view properties. Timothy and Elaine discouraged Sharon from seeking employment outside the family business. At one point, Sharon needed extra money for additional medical expenses. Elaine asked Sharon not to baby-sit for the extra money. Elaine increased Sharon and Timothy's "draw" to cover the additional medical expenses. Sharon was not paid wages for her work. Instead of receiving wages, Timothy and Sharon received a weekly "allowance" or "draw." Elaine disbursed Timothy and Sharon's allowance of $50 per week, gradually increasing it to $250. The words "draw" or "Tim's draw" were on their "allowance" checks, which were always written on business checks. Whenever Timothy and Sharon needed additional funds for items like a television or refrigerator, Timothy could always obtain the money from Rodney and Elaine. Sharon and Timothy never had to pay rent while living in the properties owned by the family. Timothy performed some work outside of the family business. Timothy also transferred these wages to Elaine.

In 1986, Rodney, Elaine, Timothy, Sharon, Terry and Cheryl (Terry's spouse at that time) undertook the purchase of two units located on Green Lane. Rodney and Elaine advanced the purchase price. Timothy and Terry performed the construction work. When the project was sold, Rodney and Elaine received their initial investment. The proceeds were divided on a one-third basis to each couple, Rodney and Elaine, Timothy and Sharon, and Terry and Cheryl. The 1986 and 1987 federal income tax returns for Timothy and Sharon showed they had either a 25 percent or 33⅓ percent interest in the rental income and expenses for nine real properties. Rodney and Elaine's returns also showed their corresponding shares.

ISSUE Is there substantial evidence to support the finding of a partnership?

HOLDING Yes, there is substantial evidence to support the lower court's decision.

REASONING Excerpts from the opinion of Judge Kitching:

The intent of the parties, as determined from the totality of the circumstances, is the primary factor for determining the existence of a partnership. . . . [T]he record contains substantial evidence . . . to support the finding of a partnership. In 1949, the Legislature adopted the Uniform Partnership Act (UPA) [and included it as part of the corporation statute]. . . . Corporations Code section 15006 . . . defined a partnership as "an association of two or more persons to carry on as co[-]owners a business for profit." [California Corporations Code] Section 15007 . . . identified some of the factors for determining the existence of a partnership . . . : "In determining whether a partnership exists, these rules shall apply: . . . (3) The sharing of gross returns does not of itself establish a partnership . . . (4) The receipt by a person of a share of the profits of a business is *prima facie* evidence that he is a partner in the business, but no such inference shall be drawn if such profits were received in payment: (a) As a debt by installments or otherwise. (b) As wages of an employee or rent to a landlord. . . . (d) As interest on a loan, though the amount of payment vary [sic] with the profits of the business."

. . . [T]he intention of the parties is the primary factor in determining the existence of a partnership. " . . . The rules to establish the existence of a partnership . . . should be viewed in the light of . . . the intent of the parties [as] revealed in the terms of their agreement, conduct, and the surrounding circumstances when determining whether a partnership exists." Additionally, "some degree of participation by partners in [the] management and control of the business is one of the primary elements of partnership." However, "the apportionment of duties will not affect the character of the relationship; one partner may be given the sole right of management." The fact that one partner "contributed labor and skill rather than capital does not preclude the existence of a partnership."

. . . Substantial evidence supports the conclusion that Timothy and Sharon contributed capital to the partnership. Timothy turned over his wages to Elaine. . . . The fact that Timothy and Sharon did not contribute an equal amount of capital to the partnership does not negate the existence of the partnership. . . . Timothy and Sharon provided skill and labor to the family business, receiving a weekly "draw" in consideration. Timothy provided construction and leasing services, and Sharon provided clerical and cleaning services. . . . Substantial evidence supports the conclusion that Timothy also participated in the management of the family business. . . .

Receipt of profits from a business is *prima facie* evidence of a partnership unless an exception applies. . . . "[T]he fact that the profits and losses were not equally shared does not necessarily compel a conclusion that no partnership existed. Although a partnership generally contemplates an equal sharing of the profits and losses, . . . the division may be left to the agreement of the parties." Even if the parties did not share profits during the 1986 to 1989 time frame, what is important about the tax returns is that the parties expressed a clear and unmistakable intent to allocate partnership shares according to a detailed schedule. This is clear evidence of the Nielsen family's intent to operate its business as a partnership and allocate shares accordingly. . . . [I]t would be reasonable to conclude that Timothy and Sharon received such a mediocre weekly "draw" in anticipation of the future disbursement of partnership proceeds. . . .

BUSINESS CONSIDERATIONS What practices could a family business use to avoid the problems the Nielsen family experienced?

ETHICAL CONSIDERATIONS Is it ethical to exclude Sharon from the partnership when she is no longer part of the family? Why? What ethical perspective is illustrated by Rodney and Elaine?

Limited Partnership

A limited partnership can be created by two or more persons, as long as at least one person is designated a limited partner. (A *limited partner* is a partner who furnishes certain funds to the limited partnership and whose liability is restricted to the funds provided.) There must be at least one general partner also. With the exception of classifying the partners, a limited partnership has the same characteristics as a general partnership set up under RUPA. A limited partnership is more formal than a general partnership, however. In order to set up a limited partnership, the partners must sign and swear to a written certificate that details all the important elements of the partnership agreement. This certificate must be filed with the public official specified in the state statutes where the limited partnership is created.

A limited partner is so called because a limited partner has *limited liability*. In other words, a limited partner is not personally liable for any obligations of the partnership. However, there is a price to pay for this protection: A limited partner is precluded from management of the business. A limited partner who takes part in management loses the limited status[16] and may be treated as a general partner, subject to unlimited personal liability. This loss of protection occurs only in suits by third persons who actually know of the limited partner's participation in the management of the business. Limited partners who act as agents or employees of a general partner or of the firm or who advise the general partners about business are not considered to be "involved in management." The partnership agreement *may* grant voting rights to limited partners under RULPA, which specifically addresses the types of acts that by themselves will not be considered control.[17]

A limited partnership must be set up in accordance with the controlling state laws governing limited partnerships—either ULPA, which is followed in Vermont, or RULPA, which is followed in all the other states, except Louisiana. Louisiana follows its own statutes. Although most of the topical coverage is essentially the same, there are some technical differences between ULPA and RULPA. Under RULPA, for example, the certificate of agreement forming the limited partnership must be filed with the secretary of state for the state in which the limited partnership is formed. The revised act also calls for profits and losses to be shared on the basis of capital contributions unless the agreement specifies some other distribution. The distribution and the liquidation of assets upon termination of the entity are treated differently under the revised act than under ULPA. One of the interesting aspects of RULPA is § 1105, which specifies that any cases not provided for in the revised act are to be governed by the provisions of ULPA. Our discussion will center on RULPA, since it has been adopted by 48 states. Any parties who plan to establish a limited partnership, however, need to check the applicable statute for the state of origin.

Throughout this chapter and Chapters 33 and 34, we will discuss the majority rule contained in RULPA.

Partnership Property

Although no partnership is *required* to own property, most partnerships do, in fact, own some property. Even if the partnership chooses not to own property, it must have access to possession and use of some physical assets. And this access and use may lead to ownership, at least under the UPA and in the eyes of the court.

Section 8 of UPA defines partnership property for general partnerships. Under this section, the following kinds of property are deemed to be *partnership property* (property owned by the partnership rather than the partners as individuals):

- All property originally contributed to the partnership as a partner's capital contribution(s)

- All property acquired on account of the partnership

- All property acquired with partnership funds, unless a contrary intention is shown

- Any interest in real property that is acquired in the partnership name

- Any conveyance to a partnership in the partnership name, unless a contrary intention is shown

If an individual partner wants to retain personal ownership but allow the partnership to use property, he or she should be extremely cautious. Unless the intention is made obvious, the property the partner thinks he or she still owns may legally belong to the partnership. (The reason this is so important is discussed in detail in Chapter 34, which covers dissolution.)

The Partnership Agreement

A partnership is created by agreement of the partners. The agreement is a contract, and it may be oral, unless it falls within the Statute of Frauds. In other words, no formality is required in setting up a general partnership. (Note, how-

---

NRW CASE 32.1 | Finance/Management

OBTAINING NECESSARY CAPITAL

Mai and Carlos believe that the firm needs a large infusion of capital in order to succeed. They have suggested that the firm incorporate and "go public" by offering stock for sale. Mai and Carlos believe that the firm can incorporate, sell 45 percent of the stock, and acquire enough funds to establish the business financially. Helen is opposed to the idea of selling any stock. She feels that such a sale opens up the possibility that an "outsider" could—by purchasing stock in the future—take control of the business. As an alternative, Helen mentions that she has heard about some kind of partnership that might be used to raise money without surrendering any control. Mai and Carlos ask you if you know what type of partnership Helen is talking about. What do you tell them? What alternatives might exist for the entrepreneurs that will allow them to raise capital and at the same time retain control of the firm? What will you advise them to do?

BUSINESS CONSIDERATIONS What factors should a firm consider in evaluating methods to obtain capital? How important is maintaining control of the enterprise?

ETHICAL CONSIDERATIONS Is it ethical to sell interests in NRW solely to obtain funds and not provide the purchasers with any control over the firm? Is this using investors solely as a means to NRW's ends?

INTERNATIONAL CONSIDERATIONS If NRW seeks foreign investors, are there some forms of business organization that it should avoid? Are there some forms that may *not* be used if foreign investors are involved?

---

ever, the formal requirements for creating a limited partnership, which we have already discussed.) Under RUPA, the partnership agreement is primary, and can include written, oral, or implied agreements. For the most part, the agreement takes priority over RUPA: The statute covers matters not addressed in the partnership agreement.[18]

A reasonably prudent, cautious person is expected to take great care in negotiating the basic partnership agreement and then reducing the agreement to written form. Yet all too often a partnership is begun with little or no detailed negotiation. Case 32.1, *In re Nielsen*, is an example of this. Even if the parties are very careful, situations may arise that were never considered and, therefore, are not covered by the agreement. To minimize the harm such situations can create, the UPA imposes certain rules, which apply unless the agreement provides otherwise. It also specifies certain areas that the agreement must cover.

Imposed Rules

Unless the agreement between the parties states otherwise, the following rules are imposed on general partnerships by operation of law:

- Each partner is entitled to an equal voice in the management of the business.

- Each partner is entitled to an equal share of profits, without regard to capital contributions. (RULPA takes the totally opposite approach for limited partnerships.)

- Each partner is expected to share any losses suffered by the business in the same proportion as profits are to be shared.

- The books of the partnership are to be kept at the central office of the business. (RUPA considers access to the partnership books so important that the partnership agreement cannot waive a partner's right of access.)[19]

In addition, some rules are imposed and must be followed by the general partners, no matter what the agreement says. Any attempt to modify these rules in the agreement is contrary to public policy, so any modification will be deemed void. Some of these rules are:

- Each general partner is deemed to be an agent for the partnership and for each partner, as long as the partner is acting in a business-related matter.

- Each general partner is personally liable, without limit, for torts or contracts for which the partnership has insufficient assets to cover the debt or liability.

- Each general partner is expected to devote service to the partnership only and not to any competing business ventures.

Express Terms

In addition to those terms imposed by law, the partnership agreement should cover some other areas. For instance, the agreement should designate the name of the business. This name cannot be deceptively similar to the name of any other company or business, and it cannot mislead the public as to the nature of the business. (If a limited partnership is involved, the name should reflect this fact.)

The agreement should cover the duration of the business—how long the partnership will last. Such an understanding in the beginning can avoid serious disagreements later. It also should cover the purpose of the business. Understanding the business's functions not only makes it easier to operate the business but also helps to avoid any controversies later.

Finally, the agreement should discuss in detail how, or if, a partner can withdraw from the business. In this area, the rights of a withdrawing partner should be very carefully spelled out so that no one, including a court, will misconstrue the agreement's terms.

Of course, any other items the partners feel should be included can be discussed, agreed on, and included. In fact, the more detailed the original agreement, the better. A carefully drawn, well-thought-out agreement will always benefit honest partners. Where RUPA has been adopted, it will provide terms for the partners only if they failed to specify the terms themselves.

Limited Liability Partnerships

Limited liability partnerships (LLPs) are a relatively new form of business organization. The first statute was enacted in Texas in 1991 partially as a response to suits against partnerships arising out of the saving and loan failures.[20] LLPs are currently permitted in most states. Sometimes the enabling legislation is passed as amendments to the state's partnership act or as part of the state's limited liability company act. The 1997 amendments to RUPA, enacted by a majority of the states, expressly provide for limited liability partnerships.[21] Information on LLPs is available in a number of locations. General information can be found at the West Legal Directory's Web site at http://www.wld.com and http://www.coollawyer.com/webfront/bizfilings/LLP.php. In addition, the Iowa Secretary of State Web site provides a discussion of how to form an LLP at http://www.sos.state.ia.us/business/limliabpart.html, and California has the forms and fee schedule for forming an LLP at http://www.ss.ca.gov/business/llp/llp_formsfees.htm.

The advantage of an LLP over a general partnership is, as the name implies, the limit on the liability of the partners. In an LLP, a partner's personal assets are protected from liability claims against the partnership. There is variation in state laws on the protection afforded partners in an LLP. Generally, under RUPA, the protection is from all liability for partnership obligations.[22] The exception to this is liability created by the partner himself or herself. In other words, a partner has unlimited liability for his or her own wrongdoings and limited liability for the wrongdoings of others. Generally, the statutes broadly interpret the partner's own wrongs to include the wrongs of persons under that partner's direct supervision and control. Under RUPA, the liable partner is still entitled to indemnification from the partnership: however, other partners are not required to make contributions to the partnership when partnership assets are not sufficient.[23]

Many enterprises that were general partnerships have become LLPs. However, as RUPA points out, the decision to become an LLP should not be taken lightly. Like other decisions about business forms, it involves some serious consideration. RUPA suggests that each partner should consider a "personal liability calculus." Each partner gives up the right to receive contributions from other partners in exchange for being relieved of the obligation to contribute toward the personal liability of the other partners. The following factors are relevant in the decision: the size of the business; the type of business; the number of partners; the amount of insurance; and the relative risk of each partner's business practice.[24]

RUPA provides that a decision to change from a regular partnership to an LLP is a major partnership event. The change requires the same percentage vote that is required to amend the partnership agreement.[25] When a partnership votes to become an LLP, the liability "shield" applies, notwithstanding any inconsistent provisions in the partnership agreement.

RUPA requires an election to become a limited liability partnership. The partnership must register with the state. In addition, it must identify itself as an LLP to those with whom it does business. The registration and identification requirements provide clear notice of the limited liability status. Creditors will evaluate creditworthiness accordingly.[26] Generally under RUPA, the LLP status remains effective until it is revoked by a vote of the partners or is canceled by the secretary of state for failure to file an annual report or pay the required annual fees.[27]

Under RUPA, LLPs are treated as partnerships in all respects.[28] This permits reliance on partnership law to answer many of the questions that might arise. Some states have not adopted the 1997 RUPA amendments and may treat an LLP differently in some respects. Even though most states have adopted RUPA, some of them have adopted different LLP statutes. Some states will not permit professionals to use LLPs. Other states permit professionals to form LLPs but may require the professional LLPs to purchase liability insurance. For example, South Carolina requires professional LLPs to carry a minimum of $100,000 of insurance.

Taxation of Partnerships

For taxation purposes, the partnership form of business can be either an advantage or a disadvantage. Basically, the partnership is not taxed, but the individual partners are taxed on the receipts of the firm. Federal income tax rules and regulations do not recognize the partnership as a taxable entity. The firm must file an annual federal tax return, but the return is for information purposes only. Each partner is taxed on his or her share of the firm's profits for the year, whether these profits are distributed to the partners or not. Each partner is also taxed on the capital gains and takes the deductions for capital losses that the firm experiences during the tax year. Limited partnerships and LLPs are taxed as partnerships, too. The Internal Revenue Service provides tax advice and information at its Web site at http://www.irs.ustreas.gov/. The page on starting a business is at http://www.irs.ustreas.gov/businesses/small/article/0,,id=99336,00.html.

Many states also treat the partnership as a mere conduit for the transfer of income to the partners. In these states, the partnership is not taxed, but the partners are taxed on the firm's income whether it is distributed or retained by the firm for reinvestment or expansion.

Historical Overview of Corporations

It is not known when the first corporation was created, but some evidence suggests that people began to recognize the concept of corporate personality as early as the time of Hammurabi (about 1750 B.C.). Certainly by Roman times, vestiges of corporateness had appeared through royal fiat. (A *fiat* is an order issued by legal authority.) From its very origins, the concept of corporateness depended on government authority. The *fiction theory*—that a corporation is an artificial legal person separate from its shareholders—probably developed from the papacy's desire to accommodate priests who had taken vows of poverty forbidding them to hold property. Since controlling the activities and finances of these clergymen was very lucrative, the church devised a way (the corporation) to allow church officers to own property. This separation of the artificial person from the natural person spawned the modern view that the corporation, not the shareholders, owns the corporate property and that shareholders ordinarily are not liable for debts incurred by the corporation. The development of the law merchant, the forerunner of modern commercial law, mirrored these and similar views of corporateness.

By the 17th century, English monarchs had tightened control over corporations, which were deemed to exist by virtue of concessionary grants of power from the state. Not surprisingly, the concession theory was part of the common law heritage that remained with American colonists after they gained independence from Britain. At first, Americans viewed corporations with suspicion because several well-known, unsavory schemes had been perpetrated through use of the corporate form. However, suspicions reduced over time as the advantages of corporations became apparent. As the corporate form developed, however, each state jealously guarded its power over these artificial creatures. This careful regulation of corporations, augmented now by federal securities statutes, remains an essential characteristic of the law of corporations in the United States.

Corporate Nature

We define a *corporation* as an artificial person created under the statutes of a state or nation, organized for the purpose set out in the application for corporate existence. A corporation is an invisible, intangible, artificial person. Therefore, because it is considered a person, the corporation ordinarily enjoys most of the rights that natural (flesh-and-blood) persons possess. For example, it is a citizen and a resident of the state in which it has been incorporated. Thus, under the Fourth Amendment, it cannot be the object of unreasonable searches or seizures. Similarly, under the Fourteenth Amendment, it must be afforded its rights of due process and equal protection. In addition, a corporation assumes the nationality of either the nationality and/or the residence of the persons controlling it (called the *aggregate test),* or the nation in which it was incorporated or where it has its principal place of business (dubbed the *entity test).*

Advantages of the Corporate Form

The popularity of the corporation as a business form results from its comparative advantages over other types of business organizations. These advantages include:

- *Insulation from liability.* Corporate debts are the responsibility of the corporation. The shareholders' liability ordinarily is limited to the amount of their investment; creditors of the corporation normally cannot reach the shareholders' personal assets to pay for corporate debts.

- *Centralization of management functions.* Centralizing the management functions in a small group of persons pos-

sessing management expertise avoids some of the friction that may plague partnerships.

- *Continuity of existence.* The corporation continues to exist in the eyes of the law even after the deaths of the officers, directors, or shareholders, or the withdrawal of their shares. This potential for perpetual existence provides stability. A corporation exists in perpetuity unless a specific length of time is stated in its articles of incorporation.

- *Free transferability of shares.* This creates opportunities for access to outside capital (as well as allowing investors to sell their interests without the need for unanimous approval or the dissolution of the firm).

These attributes unquestionably convince many large and small businesses to employ the corporate form. In a given situation, however, another form may better suit the business's needs. This is a decision that requires careful thought and the advice of knowledgeable experts, such as a lawyer, accountant, or investment adviser. There are also distinct disadvantages that may result from choosing the corporate form.

Formation of a Corporation

The process of forming a corporation involves complicated issues that demand the attention of well-versed professionals. One of these considerations consists of choosing the most desirable type of corporation for the particular circumstances. There are a number of Internet companies that provide general information about incorporating and provide the necessary paperwork. For example, some basic information on incorporating and Subchapter S corporations is included in the Business Filings Incorporated Web site at http://www.bizfilings.com/learning/incfaq.htm. Another important decision is where to incorporate. Although there are some federal statutes, most corporate activity is controlled by state law.

Types of Corporations

The *public-issue private corporation* is the best-known type of private corporation. We are all familiar with American Telephone & Telegraph (AT&T), General Motors (GM), International Business Machines (IBM), General Electric (GE), and other large public-issue corporations. The central advantage of public-issue corporations is their access to capital in the form of new shares. The shareholder, however, has very little say in the management of such giant concerns. Corporations may also attempt to raise capital by franchising their products or services. The corporation raises funds by selling a "franchise" to investors, who purchase the right to market the products or services to others under the franchise name. These investors, known as franchisees, agree to operate the franchise under the guidance and control of the franchisor in exchange for the use of the name and reputation of the franchise.

There is another type of private corporation, the *close corporation*. This form limits the ownership and management of the firm to a select few shareholders and restricts the transferability of shares in order to consolidate control. Close corporations allow a firm to enjoy many of the advantages of the corporate form without giving up the day-to-day control more commonly associated with sole proprietorships or general partnerships. An inherent disadvantage of close corporations, on the other hand, stems from a lack of free transferability of shares; these shares are often not as liquid or saleable as those of public-issue corporations.

Private corporations may also include *professional corporations,* organized for conducting a particular occupation or profession. Doctors, lawyers, dentists, and accountants may find it advantageous financially (because of tax and pension benefits, for example) to form such corporations. Most states have special statutes regulating professional corporations. Typically, these statutes limit share ownership in such corporations to duly licensed professional persons. Despite the limited liability offered by the corporate form, under these statutes the professional is ordinarily personally liable for his or her own malpractice or similar torts as well as for any such acts performed by others who are under the professional's supervision.

A city is an example of a *public* or *municipal corporation.* We often call some public utilities *quasi-public corporations* because they are private corporations that, nevertheless, furnish public services such as electricity, gas, or water.

Corporations are generally for-profit. But *nonprofit corporations,* or those organized for charitable purposes, also exist. Special statutes in some jurisdictions regulate educational institutions, charities, private hospitals, fraternal orders, religious organizations, and other types of nonprofit corporations.

Promoters

Despite the negative connotation of the word, promoters may be vital to the formation of the corporation. Although the law does not require the services of promoters as a precondition to incorporating, *promoters* begin the process of forming a corporation by procuring sub-scribers for the stock or by taking other affirmative steps toward incorporating. Thus, promoters facilitate the creation of the corporation by bringing interested parties together and by encouraging the venture until the corporation is formed. Promoters are also labeled *preincorporators.*

Promoters' activities bring up a host of legal issues. Since the promoter is working on behalf of an entity not yet created, questions arise as to who is liable on contracts made on the corporation's behalf before its inception: the promoter or the corporation? The general rule is that the promoter will be liable for goods and services rendered to him or her before the corporation's formation. However, after formation, the corporation may become liable for the promoter's contracts (and possibly torts) by novation, or by adoption or ratification of the promoter's contracts. (In this context, *novation* means a new contract that replaces the old contract and substitutes the corporation for the promoter. It releases the promoter from his or her liability. *Ratification* is accepting an act that was unauthorized when committed and becoming bound to that act upon its acceptance.) In most cases, this liability is joint and does not eliminate the promoter's personal liability. The promoter's liability *will* be eliminated if there is a novation or an express release of liability.

The *possibility* of double-dealing is inherent in the process of promotion. For this reason, the law treats promoters as owing fiduciary duties to the corporation. Therefore, the promoter must act in good faith, deal fairly, and make full disclosure to the corporation. The liability of promoters as fiduciaries is not as pervasive a problem today as in the past because of the disclosures mandated by the Securities Act of 1933. In a few cases, however, the promoter has had to give back to the corporation secret profits, embezzled funds, and other damages. Therefore, anyone desiring to act as a promoter should seek professional advice in advance.

Articles of Incorporation

The document that signals the official existence of the corporation is the *articles of incorporation.* State statutes prescribe the contents of the articles. Typically the articles include:

- The name of the corporation
- Its purpose
- Its duration
- The location of its principal office or registered agent (A *registered agent,* also called a resident agent, is a person designated by a corporation to receive service of process within the state.)

- Its powers and its capital structure (that is, the number of shares and minimum *stated capital*, the latter is the amount of consideration received by the corporation for all its shares)

- Its directors and their names (these people are usually the incorporators)

- The signatures of the incorporators (in most jurisdictions they do not have to be shareholders)

Once the incorporators file the articles with the appropriate state official (ordinarily, the secretary of state) and pay all the required filing fees, the state issues a formal *certificate of incorporation*, or license.

Corporate Charter/Certificate of Incorporation

In most states, corporate existence begins with the issuance of the certificate of incorporation by the secretary of state. After the state issues such a certificate, the state normally will not interfere with this grant of power. Unless the corporation by its conduct poses a definite and serious danger to the welfare of the state's citizens (for example, by engaging in wholesale fraud), the state will honor the certificate and allow the corporation to conduct its usual business without obstruction. Exhibit 32.3 represents a typical certificate of incorporation.

Organizational Meeting

In some jurisdictions, official corporate existence does not begin when the certificate of incorporation is issued; it begins after the first organizational meeting of the corporation. The organizational meeting is important because it is during the meeting that (1) bylaws are adopted, (2) the preincorporation agreements are approved, and (3) officers are elected.

Bylaws

Bylaws are the rules and regulations adopted by a corporation for the purpose of self-regulation, especially of day-to-day matters not covered by other documents. These ordinarily are not filed in a public place as the articles of incorporation are. Bylaws constitute the corporation's internal rules for the governance of its own affairs. They must, however, be consistent with the jurisdiction's corporate statute and the corporation's articles. Bylaws typically list the location(s) of the corporation's offices and records; describe the meetings of the shareholders and the directors;

set out the powers and duties of the board of directors, officers, and executive committee; establish the capitalization of the corporation; and establish the methods for conducting the corporation's business, such as execution of contracts, signatures on deeds, and notices of meetings.

De Jure versus *De Facto* Corporations

As we have seen, it is relatively easy to obtain corporate status if one *carefully* follows the required statutory procedures. Even so, errors occur, so it is necessary to examine the consequences of failure to comply with the statutory requirements. *Defective incorporation*, as this concept is called, may be a matter of degree. If the defect in formation (or noncompliance with the incorporation statute) is slight, the law characterizes the corporation as *de jure* (valid by law). The general rule is that where there has been substantial compliance with all steps necessary for incorporation, the resultant entity is a de jure corporation. If an address is wrong in a provision mandating an address or a relatively insignificant provision has been overlooked, courts will not invalidate corporate status. Such minor flaws ordinarily will not cause the loss of de jure status.

Sometimes, however, the defect involved is so serious that the law cannot consider the corporation as de jure. Corporateness and all its attributes may still be retained, however, if certain conditions are met: (1) a law exists under which the business could have been incorporated; (2) there was a good-faith effort to comply with the statute; and (3) there was some use or exercise of corporate powers. Such entities are called *de facto* corporations (corporations in fact, if not in law). Only the state can attack the existence of a de facto corporation. Hence, if the state does not bring an action to dissolve its certificate (or its charter), the firm will enjoy all the powers and privileges that exist in the corporate form.

This result is probably fair. Even if the defects in compliance are serious, if both the entity and third parties dealt with each other in the belief that corporateness existed, fulfilling the expectations of the parties seems justifiable. Yet the law should scrutinize the parties' nonfulfillment of statutory requirements in order to avoid frustrating legislative intent. In recent years, statutory provisions have increasingly reflected the view that the issuance of a certificate of incorporation will create a presumption that the corporation has been validly formed (that is, it has attained de jure status) except in actions brought by the state. If the state has not issued a certificate, the presumption is that corporate status is not yet realized. In this case, third parties can hold individual shareholders personally liable. These developments have greatly eroded the importance of the de facto doctrine, but some courts have continued to make distinctions between de jure and de facto corporations. It is, therefore, important to understand both the historical backdrop and the modern trends in this area of the law.

EXHIBIT 32.3 Certificate of Incorporation

STATE OF INDIANA
OFFICE OF THE SECRETARY OF STATE

CERTIFICATE OF INCORPORATION

OF

. . . ., INC. . . . .

. . . .

I, EDWIN J. SIMCOX, Secretary of State of Indiana, hereby certify that Articles of Incorporation of the above Corporation, in the form prescribed by my office, prepared and signed in duplicate by the incorporator(s), and acknowledged and verified by the same, have been presented to me at my office accompanied by the fees prescribed by law; that I have found such Articles conform to law; that I have endorsed my approval upon the duplicate copies of such Articles; that all fees have been paid as required by law; that one copy of such Articles has been filed in my office; and that the remaining copy of such Articles bearing the endorsement of my approval and filing has been returned by me to the incorporator(s) or his (their) representatives; all as prescribed by the provisions of the

INDIANA GENERAL CORPORATION ACT
. . . .

. . . ., *as amended.*
NOW, THEREFORE, *I hereby issue to such Corporation this Certificate of Incorporation, and further certify that its corporate existence has begun.*

In Witness Whereof, I have hereunto set

my hand and affixed the seal of the State

of Indiana, at the City of Indianapolis,

this. . . . .*day of*

. . . ., *20*. . . . .

. . . .
EDWIN J. SIMCOX, *Secretary of State*

By. . . . .
Deputy

Courtesy of Douglas D. Germann, Sr., Attorney-at-Law, Mishawaka, Indiana.

NRW CASE 32.2   Management

DE JURE VERSUS DE FACTO CORPORATIONS

Mai and Carlos have just about decided that the benefits of incorporating NRW outweigh the disadvantages of the corporate form. They are unsure, however, about the legal steps involved in incorporation and ask your advice as to what they must do to incorporate. What will you advise them to do?

BUSINESS CONSIDERATIONS What advice and guidelines can you suggest to NRW to ensure that it forms a de jure corporation rather than a de facto corporation?

ETHICAL CONSIDERATIONS Is it ethical to grant the benefits of limited liability and perpetual existence to a business with only partial compliance with the state statute? Would it be more ethical, due to some minor flaw in formation of the enterprise, to treat the stockholders as partners? If the creditor or supplier believed it was a de jure corporation when it dealt with the business, is it ethical for the creditor or supplier to complain about the status after the fact?

INTERNATIONAL CONSIDERATIONS If NRW incorporates, how will its status as a corporation affect its business transactions in foreign countries? Will it matter if the firm is a de facto, but not a de jure, corporation?

Corporate Powers

The articles of incorporation may set forth the powers of the corporation. Such provisions actually may be redundant because state statutes normally specify what corporations can permissibly do. These express powers include the ability (1) to conduct business, (2) to exist perpetually (unless the articles define a shorter period or the state dissolves the corporation), (3) to sue and be sued, (4) to use the corporate name or seal, and (5) to make bylaws. In addition, a corporation possesses implied powers to do everything reasonably necessary to conduct its business. Typical implied powers consist of holding or transferring property, acquiring stock from other corporations, borrowing money, executing commercial paper, issuing bonds, effecting loans, reacquiring the corporation's own shares, and contributing to charity. Statutes may enumerate these and other implied powers.

Ultra Vires Acts

As noted earlier, corporations have more power today than they did years ago. The strict application of the concession theory held that corporate status was a privilege (in contrast to a right), so that corporate acts outside the legal boundaries were considered to be ultra vires and therefore void. *Ultra vires* means beyond the scope or legal power of a corporation as established by the corporation's charter or by state statute. When sued, corporations could use ultra vires as a defense to enforcement of a contract. A corporation's use of this doctrine to avoid contractual duties has become largely outmoded since (1) the advent of implied powers, (2) a relaxation of the concession theory, and (3) an increase in permissible corporate purposes. Thus, the modern trend is to curtail application of the ultra vires doctrine as a defense unless the action is a public wrong or forbidden by statute. State statutes have either abolished the *defense* of ultra vires or greatly limited its application. The statutes usually continue to permit suits only in three situations:

1. Shareholder injunctive actions against the corporation (*Injunctive actions* are suits asking a court of equity to order a person to do or to refrain from doing some specified act.)

2. Shareholder suits on behalf of the corporation to recover damages caused by an impermissible act

3. Proceedings by the state to dissolve the corporation because of repeated violations of applicable law

For practical purposes, these situations constitute the only areas where the ultra vires doctrine will still be applied.

Taxation of Corporations

The tax treatment of corporations stems from the law's recognition of corporations as separate entities for federal income tax purposes. Often this is a disadvantage of the corporate form. The corporation pays taxes on its income as earned. When this income is distributed to shareholders in the form of dividends, it produces taxable income for them. This structure brings about so-called double taxation. Moreover, because corporate losses are not passed on to the shareholders, shareholders do not receive the tax advantages that otherwise accompany such losses.

The creation of what the Internal Revenue Code terms an *S corporation* (regular corporations are dubbed *C corporations*) may offset these tax drawbacks and provide tax relief. Subchapter S of the Internal Revenue Code permits certain corporations to avoid corporate income taxes and, at the same time, to pass operating losses on to their shareholders. In this sense, federal tax laws covering S corporations are similar to the laws covering partnerships, although there are a few differences. Attaining S corporation status involves an elective procedure and the necessity for strict compliance with statutory requirements.

In order to elect Subchapter S status, the business must:

- Be a domestic small-business corporation (To be a domestic corporation, it must be incorporated and organized in the United States. Foreign corporations, certain banks, and insurance companies may not become S corporations.)

- Have only one class of stock issued and outstanding

- Have 75 or fewer shareholders (Congress has raised the number of shareholders permitted in recent years.)

- Have no nonresident alien shareholders (If a resident alien moves outside the United States, the election will be terminated.)

- Have only qualifying shareholders (Individuals, estates, and certain trusts qualify as shareholders, but partnerships, corporations, limited liability companies, LLPs, and nonqualifying trusts are not eligible.)

- Have the consent of all the shareholders

- Not exceed the maximum allowable passive investment income

In order to make a proper election, the consent must be made in writing on IRS Form 2553 in a timely and proper manner. Once the election occurs, renewals are unnecessary; S status remains in effect as long as none of the events that can trigger loss of the election occurs. An S corporation may be subject to state and local incomes taxes.

Disregarding the Corporate Entity

We have seen that the law sometimes will recognize corporateness when the incorporation has been defective. Now we will examine situations that call for disregarding the corporate entity even when there has been compliance with the incorporation statute.

The usual rule is that the shareholders in a corporation enjoy limited liability. Because the corporation is an entity separate from the shareholders, the law normally will not be interested in who owns or runs the corporation. Sometimes, though, it will be necessary to *pierce the corporate veil*

in order to serve justice. In other words, the law will ignore the shield that keeps the corporation and its shareholders' identities separate. For example, the corporate veil will be "pierced" when the corporate form is being used to defraud others or to achieve similar illegitimate purposes. Courts may pierce the corporate veil to place liability on the shareholder who is using the corporate form without permission. Courts examine the facts closely to see if a particular situation justifies disregarding corporateness. Put another way, if the corporation is a mere "shell" or "instrumentality," or in reality is the "alter ego" of the shareholder, courts can use their powers of equity to impose liability on the controlling shareholders.

The law may impose personal liability on a shareholder, despite the fact that these are corporate liabilities. Examples include (1) when the shareholder is the sole shareholder in an association that is so thinly capitalized initially that it cannot reasonably meet its obligations, or (2) when the shareholder is draining off the corporation's assets for his or her own personal use. In this case, there will be no personal liability. This is not to say that "one-person" corporations are always candidates for disregarding the corporate entity—quite the contrary. The usual rule is that the law will not disregard corporateness if there has been no domination by the shareholder for an improper purpose (such as fraud or evasion of obligations) with resultant injury to the corporation, third parties, or the public at large. Courts will uphold corporateness as long as the controlling shareholder (1) keeps corporate affairs and transactions separate from personal transactions, (2) adequately capitalizes the business initially and forgoes the draining off of corporate assets, (3) incorporates for legitimate reasons (tax savings, limitation of liability, and so on); and (4) directs the policies of the corporation toward its own interests, not personal ones. These same principles, in general, apply to situations involving parent/subsidiary (that is, affiliated) companies, which also pose problems of whether corporateness should be retained or disregarded. In the parent/subsidiary situation, there are two general theories for holding the parent liable for the acts of the subsidiary: alter ego (piercing the corporate veil) and agency principles (the amount of control the parent exercises over the subsidiary). Case 32.3 involves piercing the entity of a limited liability company (LLC). Most states are using the corporation rules regarding "piercing the veil" for LLCs as well as for corporations. Exhibit 32.4 illustrates these points.

Note in the case on pages 777–778 how the U.S. Supreme Court compared the concepts of piercing the corporate veil with direct liability under the Comprehensive Environmental Response, Compensation, and Liability Act of 1980 (CERCLA).

EXHIBIT	32.4 Piercing the Corporate Veil

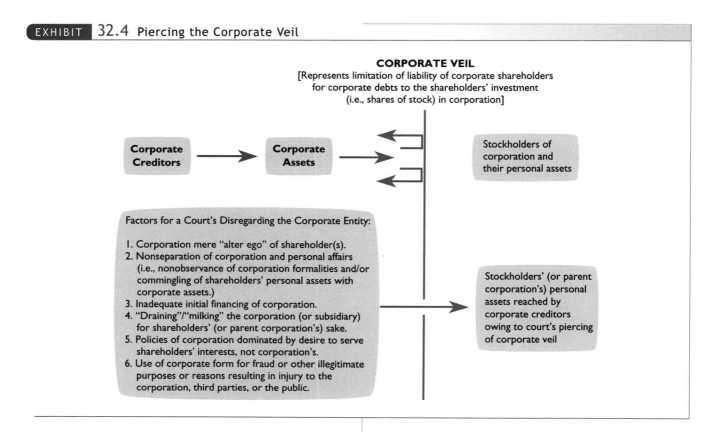

CORPORATE VEIL
[Represents limitation of liability of corporate shareholders
for corporate debts to the shareholders' investment
(i.e., shares of stock) in corporation]

Corporate Creditors → Corporate Assets → Stockholders of corporation and their personal assets

Factors for a Court's Disregarding the Corporate Entity:

1. Corporation mere "alter ego" of shareholder(s).
2. Nonseparation of corporation and personal affairs (i.e., nonobservance of corporation formalities and/or commingling of shareholders' personal assets with corporate assets.)
3. Inadequate initial financing of corporation.
4. "Draining"/"milking" the corporation (or subsidiary) for shareholders' (or parent corporation's) sake.
5. Policies of corporation dominated by desire to serve shareholders' interests, not corporation's.
6. Use of corporate form for fraud or other illegitimate purposes or reasons resulting in injury to the corporation, third parties, or the public.

Stockholders' (or parent corporation's) personal assets reached by corporate creditors owing to court's piercing of corporate veil

Limited Liability Companies

Limited liability companies (LLCs) are a hybrid form of business organization. The state enabling statute that allows LLPs may be the same state statute that authorizes LLCs. In general, businesspeople need to remember that state statutes vary, and what is true of New York LLCs may not be true of Florida LLCs. Some states allow for much flexibility while others are more restrictive.

Historical Overview of Limited Liability Companies

The first LLC statute was enacted in Wyoming in 1977. After enactment, however, a number of questions arose about the federal income tax treatment of an LLC and how sister states would treat Wyoming LLCs. Florida adopted the next LLC statute in 1982, primarily to attract foreign capital to the state.[29] All 50 states and the District of Columbia now recognize LLCs. Many states also recognize out-of-state LLCs and/or permit registration of foreign LLCs. For an overview of how LLCs are treated, visit the Limited Liability

Company Web site sponsored by Steven E. Davidson, which has a State Comparison Chart with the date the LLC statute was enacted, filing fees, and state taxation of LLCs. It is at http://www.llcweb.com/State%20Comparison.htm.

The purpose of LLCs is to provide limited liability for all investors, who are called members. (*Limited liability* means that investors may lose their investments in the enterprise, but not their personal assets.) LLCs have an advantage over limited partnerships because a general partner is not required. A limited partnership must have at least one general partner who is personally liable for the partnership's debts. With an LLC, each member's liability is limited to his or her capital investment. Many state statutes require LLCs to file articles of organization with the state similar to the articles of incorporation filed by corporations. Generally, state law permits corporations, nonresident aliens, partnerships, and trusts to be members of an LLC. LLCs are based on state statutes, so the provisions vary from state to state. Generally, the statutes dictate the following characteristics:

- The LLC must be formed by two or more members.[30]

- The LLC must have a stated term of duration not to exceed 30 years.

32.2

UNITED STATES v. BESTFOODS
524 U.S. 51, 1998 U.S. LEXIS 3733 (1998)

FACTS The United States brought this action for the costs of cleaning up industrial waste generated by a chemical plant under CERCLA. Ott Chemical Co. (Ott I) began manufacturing chemicals at a plant near Muskegon, Michigan. Its intentional and unintentional dumping of hazardous substances significantly polluted the soil and ground water. CPC International Inc. [now Bestfoods] incorporated a wholly owned subsidiary to buy Ott I's assets in exchange for CPC stock. The new company, also dubbed Ott Chemical Co. (Ott II), continued chemical manufacturing and continued to pollute its surroundings. CPC retained the managers of Ott I as officers of Ott II. Several Ott II officers and directors were also given positions at CPC, and they performed duties for both corporations.

By 1981, the federal Environmental Protection Agency had undertaken to see the site cleaned up, and its plan called for expenditures well into the tens of millions of dollars. The United States filed this action, but by that time, Ott I and Ott II were defunct. The parties stipulated that the Muskegon plant was a "facility" within the meaning of CERCLA, that hazardous substances had been released at the facility, and that the United States had incurred reimbursable costs to clean up the site. The Supreme Court granted certiorari to resolve a conflict among the Circuits over the extent to which parent corporations may be held liable under CERCLA for operating facilities ostensibly under the control of their subsidiaries.

ISSUE Is a parent corporation liable for a polluting facility owned or operated by a subsidiary?

HOLDING Not usually; however a parent corporation may be liable if the corporate veil is pierced or the parent corporation actively participated in, and exercised control over, the operations of the facility itself. In the latter case, it is an operator of the facility under CERCLA.

REASONING Excerpts from the opinion of Justice Souter:

It is a general principle of corporate law . . . that a parent corporation (so-called because of control through ownership of another corporation's stock) is not liable for the acts of its subsidiaries. . . . Thus . . . "the exercise of the 'control' which stock ownership gives to the stockholders . . . will not create liability beyond the assets of the subsidiary. That 'control' includes the election of directors, the making of bylaws . . . and the doing of all other acts incident to the legal status of stockholders. Nor will a

duplication of some or all of the directors or executive officers be fatal." . . . [T]here is an equally fundamental principle of corporate law, . . . that the corporate veil may be pierced and the shareholder held liable for the corporation's conduct when, . . . the corporate form would otherwise be misused to accomplish certain wrongful purposes . . . on the shareholder's behalf. . . . Nothing in CERCLA purports to rewrite this well-settled rule . . . .

CERCLA liability may turn on operation as well as ownership, and nothing in the statute's terms bars a parent corporation from direct liability for its own actions in operating a facility owned by its subsidiary. . . . In such instances, the parent is directly liable for its own actions. . . . CERCLA's "operator" provision is concerned primarily with direct liability for one's own actions. . . . It is this direct liability that is properly . . . at issue here. Under the . . . language of the statute, any person who operates a polluting facility is directly liable for the costs of cleaning up the pollution. This is so regardless of whether that person is the facility's owner, the owner's parent corporation or business partner. . . . [T]he difficulty comes in defining actions sufficient to constitute direct parental "operation." . . . To sharpen the definition for purposes of CERCLA . . . , an operator must manage, direct, or conduct operations specifically related to pollution, that is, operations having to do with the leakage or disposal of hazardous waste, or decisions about compliance with environmental regulations. . . . "The question is not whether the parent operates the *subsidiary*, but rather whether it operates the *facility*, and that operation is evidenced by participation in the activities of the facility. . . . Control of the subsidiary, if extensive enough, gives rise to indirect liability under piercing doctrine, not direct liability under the statutory language." . . . The analysis should . . . have rested on the relationship between CPC and the Muskegon facility itself. . . . "[I]t is entirely appropriate for directors of a parent corporation to serve as directors of its subsidiary, and that fact alone may not serve to expose the parent corporation to liability for its subsidiary's acts." . . . [D]irectors and officers holding positions with a parent and its subsidiary can and do 'change hats' to represent the two corporations separately, despite their common ownership. . . . The Government would have to show that, despite the . . . presumption to the contrary, the officers and directors were acting in their capacities as CPC officers and directors, and not as Ott II officers and directors, when they committed those acts. . . . [T]he statute . . . must be read to contemplate "operation" as including the exercise of direction over the facility's activities. . . . Yet another possibility . . . is that an agent of the parent with no hat to wear but the parent's hat might manage or direct activities at the facility.

. . . [T]he acts of direct operation that give rise to parental liability must necessarily be distinguished from the interference that stems from the normal relationship between parent and subsidiary. Again norms of corporate behavior . . . are crucial reference points. . . . "Activities that involve the facility but which are consistent with the parent's investor status, such as monitoring of the subsidiary's performance, supervision of the subsidiary's finance and capital budget decisions, and articulation of general policies and procedures, should not give rise to direct liability." The critical question is whether, in degree and detail, actions directed to the facility by an agent of the parent alone are eccentric under accepted norms of parental oversight of a subsidiary's facility. There is . . . some evidence that CPC engaged in just this type and degree of activity at the Muskegon plant. . . . G.R.D. Williams worked only for CPC . . . and thus, his actions were of necessity taken only on behalf of CPC. . . . He "actively participated in and exerted control over a variety of Ott II environmental matters," and he "issued directives. . . ." We think that these findings are enough to raise an issue of CPC's operation of the facility through Williams's actions. . . .

BUSINESS CONSIDERATIONS What should a business do to avoid responsibility for a wholly owned subsidiary? Why?

ETHICAL CONSIDERATIONS Should CPC be responsible for the expenses, since it benefited from Ott's activities?

- All members of the LLC must have limited liability to the extent of their invested capital plus any additional capital contribution contractually promised by the members.

- The LLC members' shares are not freely transferable. (Due to this requirement, LLCs are not appropriate where a large number of investors is anticipated.)

- The central management must be elected by the members.

The statutes also require that the entity indicate in its name that it is an LLC. Most states require the use of "limited liability company," "limited company," "L.L.C." or "L.C." in the title.

Most states require the following information in the LLC's articles of organization:

- Name

- Duration

- Purpose

- Address of the initial registered office and the name of the initial registered agent at that address

- Statement that the LLC is to be managed by a manager or group of managers or a statement that it will be managed by the members

- Name and address of each initial manager or managers, if applicable, or each initial member

- Name and address of each organizer (Organizers serve the role of promoters in LLCs.)

The articles of organization must be filed with the state. Often the filing fee is less for articles of organization than it is for articles of incorporation. For a state-by-state comparison of filing fees for corporations and LLCs, see http://www.incorporateabusiness.com/state.htm. Many states limit what type of business can form an LLC. For example, professional practices and insurance businesses may not be authorized to form LLCs.

Taxation of Limited Liability Companies

The IRS enacted new regulations that greatly simplify the federal taxations of LLCs. Unless the entity is actually a corporation or deemed to be a corporation under the regulations, it can elect pass-through tax treatment. Consequently, single-member LLCs, where they are permitted, can be taxed as sole proprietorships. Multiple-member LLCs can be taxed as partnerships if they are properly structured. (More exactly, they are taxed as limited partnerships with no general partners.) The LLC should follow the rules for filing an Entity Classification Election on IRS Form 8832, commonly called a "check-the-box" election. You can see Form 8832 at the IRS Web site at http://www.irs.gov/pub/irs-pdf/f8832.pdf/. The default for failing to file the form is that most LLCs will be taxed as pass-through entities. There are still uncertainties in the taxation of LLCs because of a lack of IRS rules and court cases, but, the new regulations have greatly simplified questions of tax status for LLCs. The rules pertaining to LLCs in existence prior to January 1, 1997, are a little more complex. In addition, state income tax systems may not honor the federal tax election.

Flexibility and Variance

One of the primary disadvantages of LLCs is that they are a new form of business enterprise. There is not an established body of law interpreting state statutes. Consequently, it is difficult to predict how the law will be applied in specific situations. This problem increases when an LLC operates in multiple states due to the variance in statutes. Which state's laws will be applied? Many statutes authorizing the creation of LLCs include statements that other states *should* honor and enforce the law under which the LLC is formed. However, these provisions have limited effect. One characteristic on which LLC statutes vary is whether people offering professional services can form an LLC.[31] Many states will not permit an LLC to continue in perpetuity as a corporation can. Most LLC statutes or the LLC articles greatly restrict the transferability of shares. Some states, including Arkansas, Colorado, Idaho, Missouri, North Carolina, and Texas,[32] allow one person to form an LLC. Another unresolved issue is whether the selling of LLC interests falls under the applicable state and/or federal securities laws. The SEC's position appears to be that LLCs consisting of a large number of members are required to file under the 1933 and 1934 securities statutes. One factor in the determination is whether the members actually manage the enterprise or whether the entity uses centralized managers. It has also been suggested that members in an LLC can distribute profits and losses in different proportions than the membership interests. For example, four members with a 25 percent interest each could agree to give one member 50 percent of the profits and losses.[33]

The NCCUSL drafted a Uniform Limited Liability Company Act in 1995 and amended it in 1996.[34] In addition, there is a Prototype Limited Liability Company Act issued by a committee of the American Bar Association Section on Business Law. States have already enacted their own particular version of an LLC enabling statute.[35] However, uniform legislation may be slowly adopted by the states.

The court in the following case considered whether the corporate law doctrine of piercing the veil could be applied to a Wyoming LLC.

32.3

KAYCEE LAND AND LIVESTOCK v. FLAHIVE
2002 Wyo. 73, 2002 Wyo. LEXIS 78 (2002)

FACTS This question of law was certified to the Wyoming Supreme Court. Under the state statute, the court relied on the factual determinations made by the trial court, which include:

1. Flahive Oil & Gas is a Wyoming Limited Liability Company with no assets at this time.

2. [Kaycee Land and Livestock] entered into a contract with Flahive Oil & Gas LLC allowing Flahive Oil & Gas to use the surface of its real property.

3. Roger Flahive is and was the managing member of Flahive Oil & Gas at all relevant times.

4. [Kaycee Land and Livestock] alleges that Flahive Oil & Gas caused environmental contamination to its real property. . . .

5. [Kaycee Land and Livestock] seeks to pierce the LLC veil and disregard the LLC entity of Flahive Oil & Gas Limited Liability Company and hold Roger Flahive individually liable for the contamination.

6. There is no allegation of fraud.

ISSUE In the absence of fraud, can the veil of an LLC be pierced in the same manner as that of a corporation?

HOLDING Yes, it can be pierced.

REASONING Excerpts from the opinion of Justice Kite:

As a general rule, a corporation is a separate entity distinct from the individuals comprising it. . . . The concept of piercing the corporate veil is a judicially created remedy for situations where corporations have not been operated as separate entities as contemplated by statute and, therefore, are not entitled to be treated as such. . . .

We note that Wyoming was the first state to enact LLC statutes. . . . Wyoming's statute is very short and establishes only minimal requirements for creating and operating LLCs. It seems highly unlikely that the Wyoming legislature gave any consideration to whether the common-law doctrine of piercing the veil should apply to the liability limitation granted by that fledgling statute. It is true that some other states have adopted specific legislation extending the doctrine to LLCs while Wyoming has not. However, that situation seems more attributable to the fact that Wyoming was a pioneer in the LLC arena and states which adopted LLC statutes much later had the benefit of years of practical experience during which this issue was likely raised. . . . Lack of explicit statutory language should not be considered an indication of the legislature's desire to make LLC members impermeable. . . .

[W]e are left to determine whether applying the well established common law to LLCs somehow runs counter to what the legislature would have intended had it considered the issue. In that regard, it is instructive that: "Every state that has enacted LLC piercing legislation has chosen to follow corporate law standards and not develop a separate LLC standard." Statutes which create corporations and LLCs have the same basic purpose—to limit the liability of individual investors with a corresponding benefit to economic development. Statutes created the legal fiction of the corporation being a completely separate entity which could act independently from individual persons. If the corporation were created and operated in conformance with the statutory requirements, the law would treat it as a separate entity and shelter the individual shareholders from any liability caused by corporate action, thereby encouraging investment. However, courts throughout the country have consistently recognized certain unjust circumstances can arise if immunity from liability shelters those who have failed to operate a corporation as a separate entity. Consequently, when corporations fail to follow the statutorily mandated formalities, co-mingle funds, or ignore the restrictions in their articles of incorporation regarding separate treatment of corporate property, the courts deem it appropriate to disregard the separate identity and do not permit shareholders to be sheltered from liability to third parties for damages caused by the corporations' acts.

We can discern no reason, in either law or policy, to treat LLCs differently than we treat corporations. If the members and officers of an LLC fail to treat it as a separate entity as contemplated by statute, they should not enjoy immunity from individual liability for the LLC's acts that cause damage. . . . Most, if not all, of the expert LLC commentators have concluded the doctrine of piercing the veil should apply to LLCs. . . . It also appears that most courts faced with a similar situation—LLC statutes which are silent and facts which suggest the LLC veil should be pierced—have had little trouble concluding the common law should be applied and the factors weighed accordingly.

Certainly, the various factors which would justify piercing an LLC veil would not be identical to the corporate situation for the obvious reason that many of the organizational formalities applicable to corporations do not apply to LLCs. The LLC's operation is intended to be much more flexible than a corporation's. . . . It would be inadvisable in this case, which lacks a complete factual context, to attempt to articulate all the possible factors to be applied to LLCs in Wyoming in the future. For guidance, we direct attention to commentators who have opined on the appropriate factors to be applied in the LLC context. . . .

We clearly stated: "Fraud is, of course, a matter of concern in suits to disregard corporate fictions, but it is not a prerequisite to such a result." . . . Thus, even absent fraud, courts have the power to impose liability on corporate shareholders. This same logic should naturally be extended to the LLC context. We have made clear that: "Each case involving the disregard of the separate entity doctrine must be governed by the special facts of that case." Determinations of fact are within the trier of fact's province. The district court must complete a fact intensive inquiry and exercise its equitable powers to determine whether piercing the veil is appropriate under the circumstances presented in this case. . . .

BUSINESS CONSIDERATIONS What should a business owner do to avoid personal liability for the acts of an LLC?

ETHICAL CONSIDERATIONS Is it ethical for Kaycee Land and Livestock to try to pierce the entity veil when it dealt with the Flahive LLC? Should Roger Flahive be held responsible for the LLC's activities because he benefited from them?

Other Types of Business Organizations

There are three other types of business organizations that are very similar to partnerships, yet qualify as their own business forms: partnerships by estoppel, mining partnerships, and joint ventures. These forms are introduced below.

Partnerships by Estoppel

Technically, no partnership can exist without an agreement. A third person, who is dealing with someone who *claims* to be a partner but is not, may be able to proceed against the partnership and/or the alleged partner. Such a situation may lead to a partnership by estoppel. (*Estoppel* is a legal bar or impediment that prevents a person from claiming or denying certain facts as a result of the person's past conduct.) To use estoppel, three facts must be shown:

1. Someone who is not a partner was held out to be a partner by the firm.

2. The third person justifiably or reasonably relied on the holding out.

3. The person will be harmed if no liability is imposed.

NRW

NRW CASE 32.3 Finance

LIMITED LIABILITY WITHOUT DOUBLE TAXATION

Mai and Carlos have decided to incorporate NRW in order to take advantage of the corporate form, including the protection of limited liability. Helen, however, is concerned that the firm will face "double taxation" if it incorporates. She knows that other methods of organization exist whereby NRW can gain limited liability but not be subject to double taxation. She is unsure what those methods are, however, or how NRW could organize under one of them. Helen asks you what methods are available for organizing the business with limited liability for members of the firm but without double taxation. What will you tell her?

BUSINESS CONSIDERATIONS What factors should be considered by a group of people *before* they decide on the appropriate form of organization? Is there a single best form for businesses?

ETHICAL CONSIDERATIONS What is the ethical duty of a business in regard to the tax code? Is it ethical to select a particular form of organization to avoid or reduce taxation?

INTERNATIONAL CONSIDERATIONS Would a firm encounter problems doing business internationally if it adopts one of the "new" business organization forms? Might an LLC have problems internationally that a corporation would not face?

This theory is also called ostensible partnership. RUPA continues most of the prior law of partnerships by estoppel under the new name of "purported partner."[36] Partnership by estoppel is a particular problem for young business enterprises that share space—for example, newly licensed accountants. If you will be sharing office space, avoid these problems by making sure to observe the following advice:

• Maintain your own identity. This includes using your own letterhead, business cards, and plaques on office doors.

• Arrange for separate entries on the building directory.

• Maintain your own telephone lines. If you share a receptionist, try to assure that incoming calls are answered with individual names.

• Do not use a group name. If one is used, it should include a disclaimer of joint responsibility *everywhere* it appears, for example, on business cards and telephone listings.

• Be careful to be accurate when talking about the business relationship to business associates and friends. Do not say you are "with" the other individuals or refer to the other individuals as "partners."

• Remind the other individuals to use care, also.

• Be careful if you share work or clients with the others in the office. Clearly identify the working relationship to the client.[37]

Mining Partnerships

A *mining partnership* is a uniquely American creation. It is a partnership, but it has special characteristics not found in a nonmining partnership. It is an association of several owners of a mine for cooperation in working the mine. In a regular partnership, a partner cannot sell his or her interest or leave the interest to his or her heirs in a will without dissolving the partnership. In a mining partnership, however, the selling of an interest or the bequeathing of an interest by will is permitted.

One theory about how this special treatment evolved is that during the California gold rush, after partners discovered gold, one partner would suddenly and "mysteriously" have a fatal accident that left the mine to the surviving partner. In an effort to extend the life span of successful miners, mining partnership laws were developed. The death of a partner merely brought another partner, the deceased partner's heir, into the business. Thus, no advantage was gained by the death of a partner.

Joint Ventures

A *joint venture* has all the characteristics of a partnership except one. It is not set up to "carry on a business." A joint venture, by definition, is established to carry out a limited number of transactions, very commonly a single deal. As soon as that deal or those transactions are completed, the joint venture terminates. Why is this form important? The agency power in a joint venture is limited; thus, a member of the venture is not as likely to be held responsible for the conduct of the other members of the venture. Also, the death of a joint venturer does not automatically dissolve the joint venture. In all other respects, partnership law is applicable.

Summary

Every business enterprise must have an organizational form, choosing among a proprietorship, a partnership, a limited partnership, a limited liability partnership (LLP), a limited liability company (LLC), and a corporation. A partnership has the advantages of being easily formed and of having multiple contributors, whose different opinions and expertise are always available. A partnership also has the disadvantages of somewhat limited existence and unlimited personal liability for each general partner. A partnership is defined in the UPA as an association of two or more persons carrying on a business as co-owners for profit. This definition requires that the partners voluntarily agree to enter the business and that the business be somewhat permanent in nature. Co-ownership is the key element of the definition. This element is so important that a sharing of profits by the people involved creates a presumption of co-ownership, which, in turn, creates a presumption that a partnership exists.

A limited partnership is similar to a regular, or general, partnership with a few exceptions: There must be at least one general partner and at least one limited partner who may not participate in the management of the business. Somewhat formal documents must be prepared and correctly filed in order to establish the limited partnership.

An LLP is a relatively new development. In an LLP, a partner is personally liable for his or her own wrongs and for the wrongs of people he or she supervises. A partner will not be personally liable for the wrongs of other partners.

A corporation is an artificial entity created by the state and endowed with certain powers by the state. The filing of the articles of incorporation signals the corporation's official beginning, but some jurisdictions require the issuance of a certificate of incorporation or an organizational meeting before the corporation can attain corporate status. In general, corporate status will not be lost if substantial compliance with incorporation statutes occurs; courts will view the entity as a *de jure* (legal) corporation. Courts will even grant corporate status to *de facto* (in fact, but not in law) corporations on the fulfillment of certain requirements. The modern trend is to presume de jure status, except in actions brought by the state.

Corporations enjoy certain express and implied powers. Years ago courts held that corporations were not responsible for *ultra vires* acts (those beyond the power of the corporation), but the law now limits the application of this doctrine to a few specialized situations.

At times, courts will disregard corporate status even when complete compliance with the state statute has taken place. "Piercing the corporate veil" in order to impose personal liability on a shareholder will occur when the corporation becomes the means for furthering illegitimate ends.

LLCs have a number of advantages over the older forms of business. The LLC can be a hybrid of the generally favorable features of partnerships and corporations. Generally the formation of the LLC is an attempt to provide for pass-through tax treatment, including both income and active losses, and to insulate personal assets from the LLC's debts. Many state statutes restrict the transferability of LLC shares and limit the life of the organization. Care must be used in establishing an LLC. Members must conform to the applicable state statute. In order to be entitled to partnership tax treatment on the federal level, the LLC should comply with the new IRS rules on election.

There are three additional forms of business operation. The first is *partnership by estoppel,* where there is no partnership agreement, but the parties act as if there were an agreement, to the detriment of some third party. This is also called a purported partner situation. The other two types of organizations are mining partnerships and joint ventures. Both have special rules that separate them from ordinary general partnerships.

Discussion Questions

1. Bob, Carol, and Ted set up a partnership. Later, Bob and Ted want to bring in Alice as a fourth partner. Carol, however, objects to allowing Alice to enter. A vote is taken, and Alice receives two votes of approval and one of disapproval. Will Alice be admitted as a fourth partner? Explain your answer.

2. Raylon, Tim, and Dennis have a business concept they are sure will succeed if they can establish it properly. Unfortunately, they are short of capital and cannot afford to begin the business without financial support. Marge is willing to put up the necessary capital, but she is unwilling to face the liability of a general partner. Therefore, Marge agrees to be a limited partner in the business. What must the parties do to establish a limited partnership under RULPA?

3. Larry and Vincente form a partnership. Vincente contributes $10,000. Larry, on the other hand, lets the partnership use an office building he owns, rent free. Three years later, the business dissolves. Vincente claims the building is partnership property. Larry claims he still owns the building personally. Who is correct, and why?

4. Hans and Ruth enter a partnership, but Hans does not want Ruth to be his agent or to participate in managing the business. What should he do to see that his wishes are carried out?

5. Name five advantages of corporations as business associations.

6. How does a *de jure* corporation differ from a *de facto* corporation? What requirements are necessary for a corporation to acquire de facto status?

7. Assume that a partnership has decided to incorporate its business to protect the personal assets of the partners. What must they do to avoid having the corporate veil pierced? What advice and guidelines can you provide them?

8. Discuss the express and implied powers of corporations. What is the *ultra vires doctrine*, and what are the circumstances in which it may be applied?

9. Jesse, José, and Esmeralda want to form an LLC that will be taxed as a partnership. What type of taxation do they desire? What should they do to help assure taxation as a partnership?

10. Mohammed and Eliza are partners. In order to get a loan, they tell the bank that Denise is also a partner. Relying on Denise's credit, the bank makes the loan. Mohammed and Eliza default, and the bank sues Denise. What must the bank prove in order to hold Denise liable for the loan?

Case Problems and Writing Assignments

1. Rhode Island Builders Association's (RIBA's) executive director, Ross Dagata, decided to enter into an agreement with Sherman Exposition Management, Inc. (SEM), a Massachusetts-based professional show owner and producer, for future productions of the RIBA home shows at the Providence Civic Center. This is called the 1974 Agreement. The preamble to the 1974 Agreement announced that "RIBA wishes to participate in such shows as sponsors and partners." The term of the Agreement was five years, renewable by mutual agreement. "RIBA further agreed (i) to sponsor and endorse only shows produced by SEM, (ii) to persuade RIBA members to exhibit at those shows, and (iii) to permit SEM to use RIBA's name for promotional purposes." In turn, SEM undertook "to (i) obtain all necessary leases, licenses, permits and insurance, (ii) indemnify RIBA for show-related losses "of whatever sort," (iii) accord RIBA the right to accept or reject any exhibitor, (iv) audit show income, and (v) advance all the capital required to finance the shows. Net show profits were to be shared: 55% to SEM; 45% to RIBA." In contemporaneous conversations relating to the meaning of the term "partners," Manual Sherman, SEM's president, informed RIBA's Dagata that he "wanted no ownership of the show," because he was uncertain about the financial prospects for home shows in the Rhode Island market. Although SEM owned other home shows, which it produced outside Rhode Island, Sherman consistently described himself simply as the "producer" of the RIBA shows. In 1994, after a series of assignments and contract renewals agreed to by RIBA, Southex acquired SEM'S interest under the 1974 Agreement. After a period of discord, RIBA entered into a contract with another producer and began work on the 2000 home show. Was there a partnership between RIBA and SEM, Southex's predecessor? Was there a partnership by estoppel? [See *Southex Exhibitions, Inc. v. Rhode Island Builders Association, Inc.*, 279 F.3d 94, 2002 U.S. App. LEXIS 1997 (1st Cir. 2002).]

2. William Gosselin sued his former attorney, James O'Dea, for mishandling an employment claim. He also sued attorneys Marshall Field, William Hurley, Raymond Webb, and Arthur Sullivan. These lawyers practiced law in Lowell, Massachusetts, using the name of Field, Hurley, Webb & Sullivan. (Field, Hurley, Webb, and Sullivan were not partners, but they shared office space and some expenses.) O'Dea had an office with them. In the lobby of the building, the directory listed "Field, Hurley, Webb, Sullivan, Attorneys at Law" followed by the names of Field, Hurley, Sullivan, and O'Dea. O'Dea told Gosselin that he was "with" Field, Hurley, Webb & Sullivan. Prior to hiring O'Dea, Gosselin checked on the reputation of Field, Hurley, Webb & Sullivan, because Gosselin wanted to hire an attorney with an established firm behind him. Gosselin had meetings with O'Dea at the Field, Hurley, Webb & Sullivan office. He met with Sullivan when O'Dea was not available. Gosselin's wife also met with Sullivan. Was there a partnership by estoppel? [See *Gosselin v. Webb*, 242 F.3d 412, 2001 U.S. App. LEXIS 3979 (1st Cir. 2001).]

3. Abrahim & Sons Enterprises and 42 other independent dealers operated Shell or Texaco gasoline stations in southern California. All dealers leased their stations from, and had dealer agreements with, Shell or Texaco. In 1998, Shell and Texaco addressed growing concerns about declining oil prices, declining profits, and increased competition by combining their refining and retail marketing activities into an LLC, called Equilon Enterprises. They contributed all of their western refining and marketing assets to Equilon and assigned the gas station leases and dealer agreements to Equilon. Shell transferred title of its real property to Equilon by deed. Shell and Texaco, as the sole members of Equilon, received 100 percent of the ownership interests in the LLC. Texaco's SEC form stated that Texaco and Shell jointly controlled Equilon. The individual gas stations continued to sell Shell and Texaco products under their same leases and agreements. The California Business & Professions Code § 20999.25(a) reads in relevant part:

In the case of leased marketing premises as to which the franchisor owns a fee interest, the franchisor shall not sell, transfer, or assign to another person the franchisor's interest in the premises unless the franchisor has first . . . made a bona fide offer to sell, transfer, or assign to the franchisee the franchisor's interest in the premises. . . .

Did the contribution of assets by Shell and Texaco to Equilon require Shell and Texaco to first offer to sell the stations to the independent dealers? [See *Abrahim & Sons Enterprises v. Equilon Enterprises, LLC*, 2002 U.S. App. LEXIS 15847 (9th Cir. 2002).]

4. George Randall Patin, Laura Wier Patin, Catherine Irene Boley, and Darin Lane Watkins were involved in a boating accident while operating a boat manufactured by Thoroughbred Power Boats, Inc. and purchased by the Patins from Thunder Marine, Inc. Three separate lawsuits were consolidated. The Patins, Boley, Watkins, and the Patins' insurance company (plaintiffs) subsequently became aware that Thoroughbred had ceased doing business. The plaintiffs filed amended complaints naming Steven Stepp and Velocity Power Boats as additional defendants. Consequently, Thoroughbred, Stepp, and Velocity are all defendants. The trial court found the following relevant facts:

Until August 1996, Stepp manufactured [pleasure] boats through Thoroughbred Power Boats, Inc. In August 1996, Thoroughbred ceased manufacturing and selling pleasure boats. In August 1996, Velocity Power Boats, Inc. began manufacturing and selling pleasure boats. Beginning in August 1996, Stepp manufactured his boats through Velocity. . . . The boats manufactured by Velocity after July 1996 were essentially the same boats that had been manufactured by Thoroughbred. Thoroughbred and Velocity were wholly owned by Steven Stepp and his wife. Steven Stepp and his wife were the only officers and board members of Thoroughbred and Velocity. Thoroughbred and Velocity shared the same address and telephone numbers. After August 1996 Steven Stepp leased the same property to Velocity that he had leased to Thoroughbred prior to August 1996. [Before] August 1996, Thoroughbred "leased" its employees; and after July 1996, many of the same "leased" employees became the "leased" employees of Velocity. . . . By check dated August 13, 1996, Velocity transferred $80,000 to Thoroughbred. On or about September 5, 1996, $60,000 was transferred from Velocity to Thoroughbred. . . . Steven Stepp's testimony was less than credible. . . . Steven Stepp did not provide a satisfactory or believable rational [sic] for the transformation of Thoroughbred and Velocity in 1996. That Thoroughbred might have an obligation as a result of a judgment in this lawsuit was a factor in Steven Stepp's decision to discontinue the manufacture of boats through Thoroughbred and begin production through Velocity. . . . Velocity is the successor corporation of Thoroughbred. . . . Velocity is merely a continuation of its predecessor, Thoroughbred. Velocity is and Thoroughbred was the alter ego of Steven Stepp. . . .

Should the corporate veil of Thoroughbred and Velocity be pierced to reach Stepp? [See *Patin v. Thoroughbred Power Boats Inc.*, 294 F.3d 640, 2002 U.S. App. LEXIS 11382 (5th Cir. 2002).]

5. BUSINESS APPLICATION CASE Omnibus Financial Group, LLC, was formed by four investor-members in 1996. It was down to two, John Valinote and Stephen Ballis, by mid-1997. In 1999 Valinote stopped participating in the firm's management. Early in 2000 Valinote decided to withdraw from the foundering concern and asked Ballis for an "exit strategy." Ballis then initiated the buy-sell clause of Omnibus's operating agreement. The procedure specified, common in closely held businesses, allows one investor to set a price on the shares (for an LLC, the membership interests); next the other investor decides whether to buy the first investor's interest, or sell his own, at that price. The possibility that the person naming the price can be forced either to buy or to sell keeps the first person honest. Nothing in the operating agreement prescribes how investments are to be valued for this purpose. (A mechanical valuation for use in the event of a member's death or resignation does not apply to voluntary transactions among members.) Ballis named a price of –$1,581.29 for each 1 percent interest in Omnibus, implying a total of –$79,064.25 for the 50 percent stake that each of the two held. Valinote then decided to sell his interest to Ballis at that price—effectively paying Ballis $79,064.25 to take his 50 percent off his hands. At the time, Omnibus owed Valinote exactly that sum to repay a loan that Valinote had made to the firm. So in March 2000 Valinote surrendered his interest to Ballis, who became the sole owner of Omnibus Financial Group. No money changed hands. Valinote could have acquired Ballis's interest on the same terms but must have thought that the real value was even lower than the negative price that Ballis had specified. In December 2000, Omnibus defaulted on a $200,000 debt to a bank. The bank then collected on the guarantees of this debt that Valinote and Ballis had made. Omnibus was effectively broke, but Ballis was not. Valinote demanded that Ballis indemnify him for his $100,000 share of the loan guarantee and for any future payments that Valinote might be required to make on other guarantees. Ballis refused. Was Ballis liable to Valinote on the loan guarantees? [See *Valinote v. Ballis*, 295 F.3d 666, 2002 U.S. App. LEXIS 12672 (7th Cir. 2002).]

6. ETHICAL APPLICATION CASE Patricia Holmes and Sandra Kruger Lerner became friends. Sandra Lerner is a successful entrepreneur and an experienced businessperson. She and her husband were the original founders of Cisco Systems. She received a substantial amount of money when she sold her interest in Cisco, which she invested in a venture capital limited partnership called "& Capital Partners." At Lerner's mansion outside of London, Holmes developed her own nail color. On July 31, 1995, the two women returned from England and stayed at Lerner's West Hollywood condominium. Lerner and Holmes worked with the colors in a nail kit to try to recreate the purple color Holmes had made in England. Holmes said that she wanted to call the purple color she had made "Plague." The two women decided that "Urban Decay" was a good name for their concept. Lerner said to Holmes: "This seems like a good [thing], it's something that we both like, and isn't out there. Do you think we should start a company?" Holmes responded: "Yes, I think it's a great idea." Lerner told Holmes that they would have to do market research, determine how to have the polishes produced, and that there would be many things they would have to do. They did not separate out which tasks each of them would do, but planned to do it all together. Lerner went to the telephone and called David Soward, the general partner of & Capital, and her business consultant. Holmes heard her say, "Please check Urban, for the name, Urban Decay, to see if it's available and if it is, get it for us." Holmes knew that Lerner did not joke about business and was certain that Lerner was serious about the new business. The telephone call to secure the trademark for Urban Decay confirmed in Holmes's mind that they were forming a business based on the concepts they had origi-

nated in England and at the kitchen table that day. Holmes knew that she would be taking the risk of sharing in losses as well as potential success, but the two friends did not discuss the details at that time. Although neither of the two women had any experience in the cosmetics business, they began work on their idea immediately. Holmes and Lerner discussed their plans for the company and agreed that they would attempt to build it up and then sell it.

The participants in the business attended meetings that they called board meetings. They discussed financing, and Soward reluctantly agreed to commit $500,000 toward the project. Urban Decay was financed entirely by & Capital, the venture capital partnership composed of Soward as general partner, and Lerner and her husband as the only limited partners. Holmes was spending four to five days a week at the warehouse. Holmes was reimbursed for mileage, but received no pay for her work. Holmes inquired about her role in Urban Decay a number of times. When it became obvious that they were excluding her, she initiated this lawsuit. Did Holmes and Lerner form a partnership? Was Lerner's behavior ethical? Why or why not? [See *Holmes v. Lerner*, 1999 Cal. App. LEXIS 774, 88 Cal. Rptr. 2d 130 (Cal. Ct. App. 1st Dist. Div. 1, 1999).]

7. CRITICAL THINKING CASE Exchange Point LLC asked the court to quash or modify a subpoena issued by the Securities and Exchange Commission (SEC) on First Union National Bank with respect to Exchange Point's bank account. Exchange Point is a single-member LLC organized under Delaware law. Alon Moussaief is the sole owner and president of Exchange Point. Exchange Point operates as a conduit in check cashing for Israeli clients. For example, a person in Israel will cash a check at one of Exchange Point's Israeli affiliate's offices, and the Israeli affiliate will forward the check to Exchange Point's U.S. office. The check will then be cleared through Exchange Point's bank account at

First Union. Exchange Point also has engaged in wire transfers for customers. The SEC's investigation involved allegations that certain entities may have manipulated the prices of certain securities in a scheme to defraud investors. The SEC had information that certain funds may have been wired through Exchange Point's account at First Union. The SEC issued a subpoena duces tecum on First Union. A "customer" of a financial institution may object to a government subpoena of bank records to that institution under the Right to Financial Privacy Act of 1978 (RFPA). A "customer" is defined under RFPA as "any person or authorized representative of that person who utilized or is utilizing any service of a financial institution." A "person" is defined in RFPA as "an individual or a partnership of five or fewer individuals." An LLC under Delaware law is similar to a limited partnership. Was Exchange Point a "person" under RFPA with standing to object to the subpoena? [See *Exchange Point LLC v. United States Securities and Exchange Commission*, 1999 U.S. Dist. LEXIS 8766 (S. D. N.Y. 1999).]

8. YOU BE THE JUDGE PricewaterhouseCoopers and Ernst & Young changed the form of their enterprises to that of an LLP. Other accounting firms are considering making the same change. These changes are occurring because New York amended its law during the summer of 1994 to permit accounting firms to form LLPs. Assume that the change in the form of these firms has been challenged in your court due to its potential impact on parties who may sue these firms at a later date. How will you address these issues, and how will you resolve the case? Why is this new form of business so popular with the major accounting firms? Will it be this popular with smaller firms? What should a business consider before deciding to adopt this form of organization? [See "Three Accounting Firms Now Limited Partnerships," *Wall Street Journal*, August 2, 1994, p. A8.]

Notes

1. CALI is a nonprofit consortium of over 180 law schools and affiliates. It develops computer-based tutorials.
2. Officially, this is the UPA (1914). The following states have adopted UPA (1914): Georgia, Indiana, Kentucky, Maine, Massachusetts, Michigan, Mississippi, Missouri, Nevada, New Hampshire, New York, North Carolina, Ohio, Pennsylvania, Rhode Island, South Carolina, Utah, and Wisconsin. E-mail from Katie Robinson, Communications Officer, National Conference of Commissioners on Uniform State Laws (NCCUSL), September 16, 2002.
3. The NCCUSL made the Revised Uniform Partnership Act available in 1992. Officially, it is the Uniform Partnership Act or UPA (1992). Unofficially, it is called RUPA. The commissioners further amended it in 1993 and 1994; in 1994, they released UPA (1994), which is basically the 1992 version with the 1993 and 1994 amendments. The following states have adopted the 1994 version of RUPA (without the 1997 amendments): Connecticut, West Virginia, and Wyoming. The 1997 amendments provided for limited liability partnerships. The following states have adopted the RUPA with the 1997 amendments: Alabama, Alaska, Arizona, Arkansas, California, Colorado, Delaware, District of Columbia, Florida, Hawaii, Idaho, Illinois, Iowa, Kansas, Maryland, Minnesota, Montana, Nebraska, New Jersey, New Mexico,

North Dakota, Oklahoma, Oregon, Puerto Rico, South Dakota, Tennessee, Texas, U.S. Virgin Islands, Vermont, Virginia, and Washington. In 2002 it was introduced in the Rhode Island legislature. Four of these states—Arizona, California, Puerto Rico, and Virginia—have enacted a Limited Liability Partnership Equivalent. "A Few Facts about the Uniform Partnership Act (1994)(1997)," NCCUSL Web site, http://www.nccusl.org/nccusl/uniformact_factsheets/uniformacts-fs-upa9497.asp (accessed 9/4/02).
4. "Revised Uniform Partnership Act Reflects Modern Business Practices, 28 Jurisdictions Have Now Updated Venerable 80-year-old Partnership Law," NCCUSL Web site, http://www.nccusl.org.
5. See "Uniform Partnership Act (1994)," NCCUSL Web site, http://www.nccusl.org/nccusl/uniformact_summaries/uniformacts-s-upa1994.asp (accessed 9/4/02).
6. See note 4.
7. See note 5.
8. Ibid.
9. Revised Uniform Partnership Act § 602 Comment 1 and § 601 Comments 1 and 5.
10. The following states have adopted ULPA (1976) (RULPA): California, Connecticut, Maryland, Michigan, Montana, Missouri,

Nebraska, New Jersey, South Carolina, Washington, and Wyoming. E-mail from Katie Robinson, Communications Officer, National Conference of Commissioners on Uniform State Laws, November 4, 2002.

11. The following states have adopted ULPA (1976) or RULPA with the 1985 amendments: Alabama, Alaska, Arizona, Arkansas, Colorado, Delaware, District of Columbia, Florida, Georgia, Hawaii, Idaho, Illinois, Indiana, Iowa, Kansas, Kentucky, Maine, Massachusetts, Minnesota, Mississippi, Nevada, New Hampshire, New Mexico, New York, North Carolina, North Dakota, Ohio, Oklahoma, Oregon, Pennsylvania, Rhode Island, South Dakota, Tennessee, Texas, U.S. Virgin Islands, Utah, Vermont, Virginia, West Virginia, and Wisconsin. See note 10, e-mail. The NCCUSL has enacted the 2001 Revision of the Uniform Limited Partnership Act (ULPA 2001). It has been approved by the American Bar Association, but it has not yet been adopted by any state. See "A Few Facts about the Uniform Limited Partnership Act," NCCUSL Web site, http://www.nccusl.org/nccusl/uniformact_factsheets/uniformacts-fs-ulpa.asp (accessed 12/27/02).

12. See note 10, e-mail.

13. Revised Uniform Partnership Act § 16202(c)(3).

14. Uniform Partnership Act § 7(4).

15. Cal. Corp. Code § 16111. California has adopted RUPA with the 1997 amendments, although it uses its own Limited Liability Partnership Act.

16. Uniform Partnership Act § 303.

17. "Revised Uniform Limited Partnership Act, a Summary," NCCUSL Web site, http://www.nccusl.org/summary/ulpa.html/ (accessed 10/11/99).

18. See note 4.

19. See note 5.

20. Excerpt entitled Limited Liability Partnership from *West's Encyclopedia of American Law* published at http://www.wld.com/conbus/weal/wlimlpar.htm/ (accessed 12/27/02).

21. Note 3 lists the states that have adopted RUPA with the 1997 amendments.

22. Revised Uniform Partnership Act, Addendum.

23. Ibid.

24. Revised Uniform Partnership Act, Addendum.

25. Revised Uniform Partnership Act § 1001(b).

26. "A Few Facts about the Uniform Partnership Act (1994)(1997)" (revised 10/1/99), NCCUSL Web site, http://www.nccusl.org/factsheet/upa-fs.html/ (accessed 10/11/99).

27. Revised Uniform Partnership Act, Addendum.

28. See note 26.

29. Carol J. Miller and Radie Bunn, "Limited Liability Companies—A Taxing Alternative." Paper presented at the annual meeting of the Academy of Legal Studies in Business, August 11, 1994.

30. Some states permit one person to form an LLC, as does the Uniform Limited Liability Company Act. "Uniform Limited Liability Company Act: Limited Liability Companies, A Kind of Business Organization," NCCUSL Web site, http://www.nccusl.org/nccusl/uniformact_summaries/uniformacts-s-ullca.asp (accessed 9/4/02).

31. California specifically forbids LLCs from providing professional services, Cal. Corp. Code § 17000 (1996). An earlier draft, however, allowed professional limited liability companies in Chapter 9. The Uniform Limited Liability Company Act, drafted by the NCCUSL, expressly permits professional LLCs (in § 101(3)).

32. Miller and Bunn, note 29.

33. Fred S. Steingold, *The Legal Guide for Starting & Running a Small Business* (Berkeley, Calif.: Nolo Press, 1992), 1/20.

34. The states that have adopted the Uniform Limited Liability Company Act are Alabama, Hawaii, Illinois, Montana, South Carolina, South Dakota, U.S. Virgin Islands, Vermont, and West Virginia. "A Few Facts About the Uniform Limited Liability Company Act, NCCUSL Web site, http://www.nccusl.org/nccusl/uniformact_factsheets/uniformacts-fs-ullca.asp (accessed 9/4/02).

35. For an analysis of the three general forms for LLCs, see Miller and Bunn, note 29.

36. Revised Uniform Partnership Act § 308.

37. John W. Marshall, "Partnership by Estoppel—Liability by Surprise" in the *Boston Bar Journal*, May/June 2002, at http://www.bostonbar.org/members/bbj/bbj0506_02/casefocus_estoppel.htm (accessed 12/27/02).

Operation of a Business Organization

AGENDA

NRW When NRW was being established, Mai, Carlos, and Helen were unsure as to what form of business they should select for NRW. If they chose to form a partnership, how would they delegate authority and responsibility for the decisions that need to be made? How would they share profits and responsibility? If they were to decide to incorporate, how should the corporation be structured? Obviously, it will be a for-profit enterprise, but should it be publicly owned or closely held? If they did decide to incorporate the business, what legal steps must they follow in managing and operating the firm? How would these steps compare to those followed in a partnership, a limited partnership, or a limited liability company? Can they be compelled to distribute profits, or can they retain the firm's earnings to help it grow?

These and other questions will arise during our discussion of business organizations. Be prepared! You never know when the firm or one of its members will seek your advice.

NOTE: Throughout this section the organization form selected by NRW may vary from one NRW problem to the next. This is done to allow you to evaluate the problems presented on the basis of different organizational options. If the facts of a particular case state that NRW has adopted a particular form, answer the question based on the implications for that particular form. If no particular form is specified, assume that NRW is operating as a partnership, but the principals are considering the benefits—and the burdens—of changing the structure to another of the available forms.

Operation of a Partnership

A partner has certain rights by virtue of his or her status as a partner. These rights *may* be limited or defined by the partnership agreement, the type of partnership formed, and any statutory restrictions. If there is no agreement to limit the rights, each partner is a manager for the enterprise, an agent for every other partner, and a principal of every other partner. As a result, all the regular rules of agency apply. This means, among other things, that each partner is a fiduciary of the other partners, and that when a partner deals with some third party, the firm is bound by the conduct of that partner if the conduct was apparently or actually authorized. Remember that if the partnership is a limited partnership or a limited liability partnership, some of these rules will be modified. This discussion focuses on general partnerships.

Rights of the Partners

A person who enters a partnership acquires certain rights. Some of these rights are gained through the agreement, and some are gained through the terms of the Uniform Partnership Act (UPA)[1] or the Revised Uniform Partnership Act (RUPA).[2] This book cannot cover all the rights that might be included in the agreement, but it can examine some of those rights imposed by the uniform acts.

Management

By virtue of his or her status as a partner, each partner is entitled to an equal voice in management. In conducting the ordinary business of the partnership, a majority vote controls. In order to conduct any extraordinary business, a unanimous vote is required.[3] A matter is considered extraordinary if it changes the basic nature or the basic risk of the business.

While the UPA requires that each partner be given an equal voice in managing the business, the partners are allowed to agree on the definition of "equal." Such an agreement can be beneficial to a dynamic business. If the partnership is forced to conduct its business by majority vote, opportunities may be lost because a vote cannot occur quickly enough to take advantage of them as they arise.

To avoid this problem, many partnership agreements *define* the management voice of each partner. Remember that the agreement must include such a definition to be valid. For instance, a partnership composed of Ali, Ben, Chris, and Dee might provide the following management divisions:

- Ali is in charge of purchasing inventory.
- Ben is in charge of marketing.
- Chris is in charge of accounting and personnel.
- Dee is in charge of computer software and office organization.
- Any other areas are governed by a vote.

Under such an agreement, Ben can make marketing decisions immediately, without needing to meet with the partners to vote on the issue. Likewise, Ali can decide matters concerning purchasing; Chris can make personnel decisions; and Dee can upgrade the virus-scanning software without first consulting the other partners. Absent such an agreement, each partner has a truly equal voice in management, with decisions made by majority vote.

RUPA permits but does not require the filing of a statement of partnership authority with the appropriate state office.[4] The statement can be used to limit the capacity of a partner to act as an agent of the partnership and to limit a partner's capacity to transfer property on behalf of the partnership. A partnership is not required to file such a statement. The partnership's existence is not dependent upon the filing of *any* statement. If the statement is filed, it has an impact upon a third party dealing with the partnership. It can grant extraordinary authority to partner(s) and/or limit the ordinary authority of partner(s). If the third party deals with a partner with authority provided in the statement, the third party is assured that the partnership will be bound. Any limitation upon a partner's authority, however, generally does not affect any third party who does not know about the statement.[5] The statement concerns the authority of the partners to bind the partnership to third persons. The relationship among the partners is governed by the partnership agreement or RUPA, and not by the statement of partnership authority.

Reimbursement

Each partner is entitled to repayment by the partnership for any money spent to further the interests of the partnership. In addition, each partner is entitled to interest on the advances or payments made, unless the agreement says otherwise. Each partner is also entitled to a return of his or her capital contribution at the close of the partnership, provided enough money is present after all the other liabilities have been satisfied.[6] (*Capital contribution* is money or assets invested by the business owners to commence or promote an enterprise.)

NRW

LIABILITY IN A GENERAL PARTNERSHIP

Assume that NRW is continuing to operate as a general partnership. Helen, a partner, signed a contract with a marketing consulting firm to develop a new marketing plan at a cost of $20,000. She entered this contract without consulting with the other partners in the firm, believing that the new consultants would improve NRW's opportunity to establish its niche in the industry. Unfortunately, when the plan was implemented, it was a disaster. Mai thinks that Helen should have consulted with the partners before signing the contract and asks you whether NRW and/or the other partners are liable for this contractual agreement. What will you tell her? In this situation what is Helen's personal liability to the consulting firm and/or NRW?

BUSINESS CONSIDERATIONS Assume that a partnership does not want an individual partner to unilaterally enter into specialized service contracts for the firm. What should the partnership do to prevent such conduct? How could a statement of authority under RUPA affect the result?

ETHICAL CONSIDERATIONS Suppose that an individual partner *does* enter into a contract without consulting with his or her partners. Is it ethical for the firm to refuse to honor the contract because the partners did not discuss it? Why or why not?

INTERNATIONAL CONSIDERATIONS Do similar rules regarding the agency authority of each partner exist in other countries? How should a partnership authorize a contract with a firm from another country?

Profits and Losses

Unless the agreement states otherwise, each partner is entitled to an equal share of the profits of the business. The profits are not automatically divided in the same percentage as capital was contributed, nor are they automatically divided in any other unequal manner. Profits are the only remuneration to which any partner is always entitled.[7] No partner is automatically permitted to draw a salary from the enterprise even if that partner devotes extra time to running the business. However, the agreement can be worded in such a manner that a partner receives a salary

from the business, with the remaining profits then divided in some predetermined manner. Any salary provision for partners must be expressly set out in the agreement. Losses are divided among the partners in the same ratio as profits are shared, unless the agreement expressly provides for a different allocation of losses.

Books and Records

Each partner is entitled to free access to the books and records of the business. This includes the right to inspect the records and to copy them as the partner sees fit. Similarly, each partner is expected to give, and entitled to receive, detailed information on any matter that affects the partnership.[8]

Partnership Property

Under the UPA, each partner is a co-owner of partnership property with the other partners. This ownership is called a tenancy in partnership.[9] A *tenancy in partnership* is a special form of property ownership found only in partnerships, in which each partner has an equal right to possess and to use partnership assets for partnership purposes. This tenancy entitles the partner to possess the property for partnership purposes, but not to possess it for nonpartnership purposes. However, if all the partners agree to a nonpartnership usage, such a usage is allowed. This tenancy also carries with it a right of survivorship; if a partner dies, the other *partners* own the property. The heirs of the deceased partner do not inherit it if any other partners are still surviving. Thus, the last surviving partner will own the partnership property individually. The heirs of the last partner may not possess the property except for partnership purposes.

Recall that a majority of the states have now adopted RUPA. RUPA has moved away from viewing the partnership as an aggregate of the partners to viewing it as a separate entity.[10] RUPA states simply that since a partnership is a separate entity, its property belongs to it and not to the partners.[11] A partner has his or her partnership interest but is not a co-owner of specific partnership property.[12] This is a significant departure from the UPA.

Right to an Account

Any general partner is entitled to a formal *account*—that is, a statement or record of business transactions or dealings—if he or she feels mistreated in the partnership.[13] Specifically, any partner who is excluded from the business or from use of business properties is entitled to an account. And the UPA provides for an account in any other circumstances that render it just and reasonable. In effect, any time an internal argument or disagreement arises about the business operation, the courts will say an account is just and reasonable.

Each partner is a fiduciary for every other partner and is expected to account to the other partners and to the partnership for any benefits received or any profits derived without the knowledge and consent of the other partners.[14]

Duties of the Partners

Agency Duties

Each general partner is an *agent* of the partnership and of every other partner. Thus, any conduct by a partner that is *apparently* authorized is binding on the partnership. Because each partner is *personally* liable for partnership debts, such an act makes each partner at least *potentially* personally liable.

This obviously creates a possible financial hazard to the partners. To reduce the danger that a reckless partner can present, the UPA restricts some agency power. Under UPA § 9(3), there is no apparent authority to do any of five specific acts unless unanimously approved. These five acts are as follows:

1. Making an assignment for the benefit of creditors by transferring partnership property to a trust for the creditors of the business (*Assignment for the benefit of creditors* is an assignment in trust made by debtors for the payment of their debts.)

2. Selling or otherwise disposing of the goodwill of the business (*Goodwill* is the favorable reputation of an established and well-conducted business.)

3. Performing any act that makes it impossible to carry on the business

4. Confessing a judgment against the partnership (In this context, *confessing a judgment* is an acknowledgment in court that the partnership is legally to blame. Standard-form contracts may provide that the party contracting with the partnership has authority to confess judgment against it.)

5. Submitting a partnership claim or liability to an arbitrator (An *arbitrator* is an independent person chosen by the parties or appointed by statute. The issues are submitted to the arbitrator for settlement outside of court.)

Notice the scope of these acts. The first three frustrate business, and the last two remove the partners' rights to their "day in court." Except for these five situations, any other act of a partner within the scope of apparent authority is binding.

Since each partner is an agent, *notice* given to any partner on a partnership matter is as valid as notice given to each of the partners.[15] This is simply the application of basic agency law to a partnership/agency situation. Similarly, knowledge gained, or *remembered,* while one is a partner is imputed to each partner.

If a partner acts, or fails to act, within the course and scope of the business, and the act or omission causes harm to a third person, the partnership is liable to the third person, as is the partner who committed the tort.[16] The other partners face joint and several liability for torts. Under RUPA, the liability of the partnership and the partners is joint and several for *all* debts of the partnership. However, RUPA defines joint and several liability in a different sense than is commonly used in law. Generally, RUPA requires the creditor to exhaust the partnership's assets before going against the individual partners.[17]

Likewise, if a partner *misapplies* money or property of a third person that is in the possession of the partnership, the partnership is liable. All the partners, or each of them, may need to answer for the breach of trust by one partner.[18] Again, the liability is joint and several.

Obviously, being a partner *may* be hazardous to your financial health. Even if you are a careful, cautious person, you face potential financial liability, maybe even disaster, from the conduct of your partners. What rights do you have that protect you? What rights are available for the protection of any partner from the excesses of another partner?

One such right protects the other partners and the partnership from a creditor of a partner. For example, assume that Ali, Bill, and Cindi are partners. The business is very profitable, and Bill and Cindi are solvent. However, Ali is in deep financial trouble. Several of Ali's creditors sue Ali to collect their claims. They win the suit, only to discover that Ali cannot pay the judgment from his personal assets. Can these creditors foreclose on Ali's share of the partnership assets? No. All the creditors can do is to get a charging order from a court.[19] A *charging order* is a court order permitting a creditor to receive a portion of the profits from the operation of a business; it is especially common in partnership situations. Under a charging order, the debtor/partner's *profits* are paid to the creditors until the claims are completely paid. Thus, the partnership can continue, and Bill and Cindi are protected. Only Ali, the debtor, suffers.

On the other hand, suppose that the partnership is in financial difficulty but that some of the partners are solvent. Can the partnership's creditors proceed directly against the individual partners, bypassing or ignoring the assets of the firm? No. Generally, the creditors of the firm must first proceed against the assets of the firm.[20]

Fiduciary Duties

Another protection given to the partners is the legal status assigned to each partner. Each member of a partnership is a *fiduciary* of the other partners and of the business itself.[21] The fiduciary position carries with it certain responsibilities and certain duties. Each partner is required to account for, and to surrender to the firm, any profits derived from the business or from the use of business assets. No partner is allowed to have a conflict of interest with the partnership. And each partner is entitled to indemnification from a partner who causes a loss or liability from misconduct in the course and scope of employment. The RUPA explicitly addresses the fiduciary duties of partners to each other, including the obligations of loyalty, due care, and good faith.[22]

Rights of Third Persons Who Deal with Partnerships

When partners are dealing internally, each is aware of the rights and duties of the other partner(s). Each general partner should know the terms of the basic agreement and the limits of his or her authority. A third person who deals with the partnership, however, has no such advantage. Any nonpartner who deals with the firm must rely on *appearances*. As a result, a third person who deals with the partnership may be given certain rights by the court that are contrary to the basic partnership agreement.

Contracts

As noted earlier, each partner is an agent of the partnership. Thus, if a partner negotiates a contract on behalf of the partnership, that partner is negotiating as an agent. From agency law, we know that if the agent has the *apparent authority* to perform an act, the principal is bound by the act. The same rule applies here. If the partner has the apparent authority to enter the contract, the partnership is bound to honor the contract. Under the prior law, partners were jointly liable on partnership contracts. Under RUPA, the liability of the partnership and the partners is joint and several for all obligations of the partnership. (Remember that RUPA defines joint and several liability in a different sense.[23])

In many instances, the partner has the actual authority to enter the contract. If so, the partnership is obviously bound, and the partner who negotiated the contract is no more liable than the other partners.

In some cases, the partner has the apparent authority to enter the contract but lacks the actual authority. (Recall, for example, the division of duties discussion earlier in this chapter.) Under these circumstances, the partnership must still honor the contract with the third person. But the partner who negotiated the contract will be liable to the partnership for any losses that arise because the partner exceeded his or her authority.

In still other cases, the partner does not have even apparent authority. If the partner exceeds his or her authority and negotiates a contract, the negotiating partner is personally obligated to perform, but the firm is *not* liable on the agreement.

When the court examines these agreements, the apparent authority of the partner is of overriding importance. When deciding the scope of authority, courts often look at the type of business the firm is conducting. If the partnership buys and sells as its primary business purpose, the court views the partnership (unofficially) as a *trading* partnership. If the primary business purpose is to provide services, the court views it (unofficially) as a *nontrading* partnership. In a trading partnership, the partners are presumed to have broad powers. In a nontrading partnership, partners are deemed to have much narrower powers. A partner in a trading partnership is presumably authorized to perform *any* management-related duties. In contrast, a partner in a nontrading business is apparently authorized to do only those things reasonably necessary to further the main business purpose of the partnership.

A third person who is dealing with a partnership for the first time needs to exercise care. The partner with whom the third person is dealing may exceed his or her authority, and the resulting contract will not be binding on the partnership.

Borrowing in the Partnership Name

Perhaps the most important area in which the court applies the trading-versus-nontrading distinction is in the borrowing of money. In a trading partnership, the firm deals from inventory. Inventory must be purchased, and purchases require money. Thus, a partner in a trading partnership has the apparent authority to borrow money in the firm's name.

In a nontrading partnership, the need for money is less obvious. As a result, the courts are less apt to impose liability on the firm for a loan that was made to a single partner even though that partner borrowed the money in the partnership name.

Torts and Crimes

Again, remember that each partner is an agent for every other partner. Under agency law, when an agent commits a *tort*, the agent is liable as the tortfeasor. (A *tortfeasor* is a wrongdoer, the one who commits a tort.) The principal may also be liable, jointly and severally with the agent, under the theory of *respondeat superior*. If the injured person can establish that the partner was performing in "the course and scope of employment," that individual partner and the partnership are liable for the tort. Their liability is joint and several in the traditional sense. Under prior law, the partnership and all the partners are jointly and severally liable in the traditional sense. Under RUPA, the liability of the partnership and the other partners is joint and several for all debts of the partnership. No distinction is made for liability for contracts or torts. Recall that RUPA defines joint and several liability in a different sense.[24] For an example, assume Mary, Ned, and Oscar are partners. Ned is driving to a business meeting to represent the firm in some negotiations. On the way to the meeting, Ned runs a stop sign and hits Sam. Since Ned was on a job-related errand, Ned and the partnership are liable to Sam. The other individual partners will be liable only when the partnership assets are exhausted.

If the tort is willful and malicious, however, the firm is normally not liable. Assume Oscar, another of the partners, is driving to a business meeting to represent the firm and sees Tom crossing the street. He is still angry with Tom for an insult from long ago. Oscar accelerates the car and intentionally runs over Tom. Since the tort was willful and malicious, neither Mary nor Ned nor the firm is liable to Tom. However, if the willful and malicious tort is one that furthers any business interests of the firm, the partnership *may* be held liable despite the intentional nature of the tort.

And even if the intentional tort is not related to the business purpose, the partnership can still be held liable, provided that it assents to or ratifies the tortious conduct.

If a partner commits a crime, what liability do the non-criminal partners face? For most crimes, the other partners are not liable. Most crimes require a specific criminal intent. To be convicted of such a crime, a person must commit it or aid and abet in its commission. (To *aid and abet* means to help, assist, or facilitate the commission of a crime.) Unless evidence of involvement is shown, only the partner who committed the crime will be liable. However, some crimes can be committed without a specific criminal intent. Such crimes are normally *regulatory* in nature; in other words, these crimes involve violations in administrative areas rather than violations in traditional criminal areas. If one of these crimes is committed, all the partners are criminally liable.

Operation of a Limited Partnership

Although a limited partnership is an actual partnership, the limited partners are more like investors than regular partners. They have contributed cash, property, or services, and in exchange they receive an interest or "share." Courts often treat the limited partners like investors in limited liability companies or corporations. In the following case, the court examined the *limited* partners' right to inspect records. As you would expect, the inspection rights of a limited partner are more restricted than those of general partners. Note that the investors in the limited partnership are also referred to as shareholders and unit holders in this opinion. This probably reflects their true nature. (The case was heard in a *Court of Chancery*, a court of equity.)

33.1

MADISON AVENUE INVESTMENT PARTNERS, LLC v. AMERICA FIRST REAL ESTATE INVESTMENT PARTNERS, L.P.
2002 Del. Ch. LEXIS 97 (Del. Ch. New Castle 2002)

FACTS The plaintiffs are Madison Avenue Investment Partners, LLC and Madison Partnership Liquidity Investors 104, LLC (MLI 104). They are both Delaware limited liability companies, together called Madison. Madison became limited partners by investing in the defendants, which are various limited partnerships called collectively the Partnerships, Defendants, or America First. Madison has attempted to sell its units in the Partnerships to the general partner on multiple occasions. On January 30, 2001, Madison contacted the general partner to demand that the Partnership be liquidated. On March 22, 2001, Madison demanded access to the Partnerships' books and records, with the stated purpose of determining "whether to increase its holdings and whether liquidation would be in the best interests of the respective limited partners and shareholders. . . ." Each request stated Madison's purpose in seeking access to the specified books and records as "to properly value its investment." America First agreed to provide some of the documents. However, Madison decided that the information provided was inadequate to allow for a proper valuation.

ISSUE Is Madison entitled to inspect the Partnership books?

HOLDING Yes. Madison is entitled to inspect most of the records, but Madison must first sign a satisfactory confidentiality agreement.

REASONING Excerpts from the opinion of Vice Chancellor Stephen P. Lamb:

[Note: All section references are to the Delaware Revised Uniform Limited Partnership Act.] . . . Section 17-305 of Delaware's Revised Uniform Limited Partnership Act [DRULPA] . . . provides limited partners with the right to inspect . . . "information regarding the status of the business and financial condition of the limited partnership" and "other information regarding the affairs of the limited partnership as is just and reasonable." This statutory right is limited by three conditions. . . . First, the limited partner must establish that it has complied with the provisions respecting the form and manner of making demand for obtaining such information. It is conceded that Plaintiffs have complied with these provisions. Second, the demand must be reasonable and for a purpose reasonably related to the limited partner's interest as a limited partner. This condition is the basis for the proper purpose analysis. . . . Third, the right is subject to such reasonable standards "as may be set forth in the partnership agreement or otherwise established by the general partners." This condition is the basis for the analysis . . . of what items constitute "books and records" of the Partnerships. . . . Section 17-305(b) . . . allows general partners to refuse disclosure to limited partners of any information that the partnership is required by law or contract to keep confidential or which might damage the partnership if disclosed. This condition is the basis for the scope of inspection analysis. . . .

Under Section 17-305(a) . . . , the right to obtain books and records . . . is expressly made subject to "such reasonable standards . . . as may be set forth in the partnership agreement or otherwise established by the general partner[]." . . . [S]uch standards may "govern[] what information and documents are to be furnished. . . ." There is no evidence in this case that the . . . general partners ever "established" standards governing access to information. . . . The Partnership Agreements are contracts to be construed like any other contract. . . . Here, the context [of the Partnership Agreements] suggests that the phrase "shall include" was not used to confine the statutory right of inspection to the items listed in the Partnership Agreements. . . . These facts suggest that the Partnership Agreements need to be interpreted in

tandem with the statute. . . . [I]t would have been a simple matter for the drafters of these [contract] provisions to include language clearly stating an intention to supplant or restrict the statutory right of inspection. . . . The items Plaintiffs seek easily fall within the ambit of their statutory right . . . [T]he court concludes that the items sought by Plaintiffs are "books and records" of the Partnerships.

. . . [T]he next inquiry is . . . whether Plaintiffs have stated a proper purpose for their request. . . . "[The] limited partner's right to inspect books and records and to otherwise access information regarding the partnership is limited to 'purpose[s] reasonably related to the limited partner's interest as a limited partner.'" . . . "It is settled law in Delaware that valuation of one's shares is a proper purpose for the inspection of corporate books and records." . . . [O]nce an acceptable primary purpose is established, any secondary purpose or even ulterior motive is irrelevant. . . . ". . . [However, it] must not be for a purpose adverse to the best interests of the [entity]." . . . To some extent, Defendants' concern reflects a fear that Madison will attempt to gain an unfair informational advantage over the others, including existing limited partners, with the information it has requested. This is a legitimate concern and one that Defendants are empowered by the DRULPA to address. To allay these concerns and give effect to the statutory rights of the general partners, the final order will condition the right of access . . . on the execution of a satisfactory confidentiality agreement governing the treatment of the documents and information made available to Plaintiffs. . . .

It is fair to conclude that Madison seeks to obtain a better valuation of its investment than is possible using only the market price for units and the information that is publicly available in SEC filings. . . . [T]he fact that a plaintiff has previously valued its interest in an entity should not . . . preclude its ability to seek additional information in its efforts to do so anew. . . .

The court . . . concludes that the production of all limited partnership agreements between Real Estate Investment Partners and its subsidiaries is reasonably necessary to valuing Madison's investment in that partnership. . . . [T]he production of all mortgage, loan, note and debt agreements for the Partnerships (and the Real Estate Investment Partners subsidiaries) is not reasonably necessary to value Madison's investment. . . . While it is no doubt possible for Madison to forecast the likelihood that such a liquidation . . . will occur, . . . such information falls short of what is reasonably necessary for Madison to currently value its units. . . . [T]he production of all non-public financial statements specifically relating to the real estate held or owned by the Partnerships is not necessary to value Madison's investment. Nevertheless, the court concludes that non-public financial statements specifically relating to the subsidiary partnerships through which Real Estate Investment Partners invests are reasonably necessary to value Madison's investment in that partnership. . . . [T]he aggregated financial statements of the partnership as a whole mask the performance and value of the individual properties and can make it difficult to value the partnership as a whole. . . . [T]o the extent the books and records of Real Estate Investment Partners contain such information, they will be made available to Plaintiffs.

BUSINESS CONSIDERATIONS How could Madison have better protected its investment? What procedures and practices could the Partnerships or related entities have established if they did not want to reveal this information? Do you think the court-ordered confidentiality agreement will be effective? Why? Are investors becoming more concerned about the underlying value of their investments? Why?

ETHICAL CONSIDERATIONS Would it be ethical for Madison to obtain the books and records to gain an advantage over the other limited partners? Why?

Operation of a Limited Liability Company

Nine states have adopted the Uniform Limited Liability Company Act.[25] All the other states and the District of Columbia have enacted their own versions of Limited Liability Companies (LLCs) statutes, which have diverse provisions. As the number of LLCs increases, legislatures and courts create laws concerning their operation. Generally, it is easier to operate an LLC than a corporation, but many rules of corporation law are also being applied to LLCs. (Attorney Steven E. Davidson maintains The Limited Liability Company Web site. It includes basic information about LLCs and a state-by-state comparison chart. He also markets kits for forming LLCs from the site, which is located at http://www.llcweb.com/index.html. Business Filings Incorporated has a chart comparing the state filing fees for corporations, limited liability companies, and nonprofits at http://www.bizfilings.com/pricing/index.html.)

Many of the practical aspects of other business forms are also being applied to LLCs. Some LLCs have a complicated structure for members. There may be the managing members, voting members, and "regular members" who have control over all matters that are not reserved to the managing members and voting members. LLCs may have buyback procedures that require members who terminate their employment with the LLC to sell their shares back to it at a set price. There may be restrictions on a member's ability to transfer ownership interests. For example, an LLC operating agreement may include: "No member shall sell, assign, transfer, pledge or encumber any interest in the Company without the prior written consent of the Manager and the other Members. Any person acquiring rights with respect to any interest in the Company in a trans-

action which is an Adverse Act shall not be deemed a substituted Member and shall be restricted to the right to receive any distributions made with respect to such interest."[26]

Statutes may specify the manager's legal liability. For example, under the Arkansas statute a manager of an LLC is not liable to the company or other members unless he or she engages in "gross negligence or willful misconduct."[27] In Maryland, a majority interest holder owes a fiduciary duty to the minority interest holders.[28] In the following case, the Illinois Court of Appeals examined the fiduciary duties of a member in a member-managed LLC. Note how Illinois refers to corporate law to resolve some LLC issues.

Operation of a Corporation

The officers and the board of directors bear the responsibilities for both the day-to-day operations and the overall policies of a corporation. They also act as agents for the corporation. The management of the entity is centralized. Directors, officers, and controlling shareholders are often called "managers" for the sake of simplicity. The managers are ultimately answerable to the shareholders (the owners). Shareholders exert only indirect control, generally through the election of directors. Exhibit 33.1 shows the legal relationship between the three primary groups. Some writers contend that the legal model is inaccurate and that often the board of directors actually controls the stockholders instead. When individual shareholders are displeased with the management or performance of a firm, the shareholders are likely to do the "Wall Street walk" by selling their shares and walking away. (FindLaw for Business has an article entitled "Board of Directors" at http://sv.biz.findlaw.com/management/board.html/. Its focus is establishing the board of directors and selecting board members.)

33.2

ANEST v. AUDINO
773 N.E.2d 202, 2002 Ill. App. LEXIS 581 (Ill. App. 2nd Dist. 2002)

FACTS Bill Anest obtained a default judgment against David Audino and then levied against his interest in Precision Pour, LLC. Anest later purchased that interest at a sheriff's sale. Precision Pour sold a product called the BLM 2000, a beer line cleaning device. Precision Pour was the exclusive distributor of the device in the United States in 1997 and 1998. Prior to Anest's purchase, the members of Precision Pour were Audino, Leon Teichner, and William Schilling. Subsequently, when Precision Pour was insolvent and needed additional capital, Anest bought membership units and lent it money. The company changed from a manager-managed limited liability company to a member-managed limited liability company. The court vacated the sheriff's sale and ordered Audino's interest returned.

On October 29, 1999, Ronald Panter's office faxed a notice of an "emergency meeting" of Precision Pour to be held on November 1. Panter was Precision Pour's attorney. The notice stated that the purpose was "to discuss changing the business relationship of the company from a nonexclusive distributor to an importer and the ramifications thereof." Section 7.3 of the operating agreement states that at least five days' notice must be provided to members before a membership meeting. On November 1, Anest, Teichner, Schilling, Iseberg (another member), and the LLC's attorneys attended the emergency meeting. The parties discussed an offer from BLM International, Limited, for a five-year exclusive distributorship agreement of the BLM 2000. Teichner claimed that the offer had to be acted upon by November 1. BLM International was concerned about Precision Pour's financial ability and requested a letter of credit. Precision Pour was, in fact, insolvent. A vote was taken as to whether the members would contribute additional funds to the company. The members voted no. After the emergency meeting, another meeting took place among Anest, Teichner, and Schilling, at which they agreed to exercise the exclusive distributorship offer. On December 9, Anest, Iseberg, Schilling, and Teichner formed BLM Technologies, LLC. Anest was the company's manager and put up the funds to secure the letter of credit.

ISSUES Did Anest owe Audino fiduciary duties? Was the BLM 2000 a corporate opportunity of Precision Pour?

HOLDINGS Yes, Anest did owe Audino fiduciary duties. Yes, under state law it was a corporate opportunity.

REASONING Excerpts from the opinion of Justice Callum:

[T]he Limited Liability Company Act . . . states that members in a member-managed limited liability company owe to each other the fiduciary duties of loyalty and care. . . . [S]ection 15-3 applies to all limited liability companies as of January 1, 2000. . . . [A]n entity in existence on January 1, 1998, was required to elect to be governed by the . . . amendments to the Act. . . . [D]uring the relevant period here, there was no direct statutory basis to assert the existence of fiduciary duties between members of limited liability companies. . . . Audino has presented no evidence that Precision Pour elected to be governed by the amended Act. . . . Prior to amendment, section 10-10 of the Act . . . stated as follows:

(a) A member of a limited liability company shall be personally liable for any act, debt, obligation, or liability of the limited liability company or another member or manager to the extent that a shareholder of an Illinois business corporation is liable in analogous circumstances under Illinois law.

(b) A manager of a limited liability company shall be personally liable for any act, debt, obligation, or liability of the limited liability company or another manager or member to the extent that a director of an Illinois business corporation is liable in analogous circumstances under Illinois law.

This provision instructs us to review the law of corporations. . . . Individuals who control corporations owe a fiduciary duty to their corporations and their shareholders. Directors and officers of a corporation have a duty " 'to deal openly and honestly' with each other, and to 'exercise the utmost good faith and honesty in all dealings and transactions.' . . . " Shareholders in a close corporation owe to each other fiduciary duties similar to those of partners in a partnership. . . . They owe a duty of loyalty to the corporation and to other shareholders. Minority shareholders may owe a duty of loyalty to a close corporation under certain circumstances. . . . Anest held a 12½% membership interest in the company and was a creditor. . . . Precision Pour was a member-managed entity effective as of July 13, 1999. . . . Anest was more than a minority shareholder; he had management responsibilities in the company. His role in the entity was . . . akin to that of an officer or director in a corporation. . . .

Having found a prima facie case that Anest owed a fiduciary duty to Audino, we must next determine whether he breached that duty. . . . [C]ommentators generally assume that members and managers of limited liability companies may not divert company opportunities. . . . The corporate opportunity doctrine provides that a fiduciary cannot usurp a business opportunity that was developed through the use of corporate assets. . . . A corporate opportunity is defined as a "proposed activity [that] is reasonably incident to the corporation's present or prospective business and . . . in which the corporation has the capacity to engage." When a corporate fiduciary wants to take advantage of a business opportunity that is within the company's line of business, the fiduciary must first disclose and tender the opportunity to the corporation before he or she takes advantage of it, notwithstanding the fiduciary's belief that the corporation is legally or financially incapable of taking advantage of the opportunity. The evidence establishes that the distributorship offer was developed with Precision Pour's assets. Precision Pour was involved in many capacities in promoting the BLM 2000. . . . [They were working on regulatory approval.] In 1997 and 1998, Precision Pour was the exclusive distributor of

the BLM 2000 in the United States. . . . Audino testified that Schilling worked with Coors while Coors tested the device. . . . [W]hen corporate assets are used to develop an opportunity, "the fiduciary is estopped from denying that the resulting opportunity belongs to the corporation whose assets were misappropriated, even if it was not feasible for the corporation to pursue the opportunity or it had no expectancy in the project." . . .

[W]e observe . . . that the opportunity was not properly disclosed and tendered. . . . [T]he so-called emergency meeting was called with a notice that admittedly violated the . . . operating agreement. . . . [W]e believe that a five-day notice could have been given . . . because the offer was still available on December 9, when BLM Technologies accepted it. . . .

BUSINESS CONSIDERATIONS Could BLM Technologies properly accept the opportunity? If so, how?

ETHICAL CONSIDERATIONS What is the ethical perspective of Anest? Why? Would you want to do business with him? Why?

Increasingly, shareholders are walking away when they do not trust the accuracy of the corporate financial records. The National Conference of Commissions on Uniform State Laws (NCCUSL) approved a new Uniform Securities Act (USA) on August 1, 2002.[29] Like other uniform acts, the USA is a *state* act. If adopted, it would replace or supplement existing state securities laws. It prohibits fraud in the sale of securities and imposes registration requirements for brokers and investment advisors.[30] The federal government also has enacted a number of securities laws. (Securities laws are discussed in more detail in Chapter 36.)

The United States is not the only nation concerned with the conduct of its corporations. Here are a few examples of how corporations are established in other nations. The Corporation Act (1985) of the Parliament of South Australia is located at http://www.sca.org.au/lochac/del/aia.html. The Irish Companies Act (1963) is located at http://193.120.124.98/ZZA33Y1963.html.

Rights of the Shareholders

Stock Certificates

Shareholders exert indirect control over the corporation by virtue of their ownership of shares; the more they

own, the more power they wield. Ownership is generally evidenced by stock certificates, which became prevalent in the United States by the late 1800s. They were often elaborately designed and played a role as financial document, advertising pitch, and public relations ploy. The stock certificate is becoming obsolete, especially in large publicly traded companies. Ownership is increasingly evidenced by an "electronic book entry."[31]

Types of Stock Owned

A shareholder may own *common stock,* which allows the shareholder to receive dividends, to vote on corporate issues, and to receive property upon the corporation's liquidation. Or, the shareholder may own *preferred stock,* which, as its name suggests, confers priority with regard to dividends, voting, or liquidation rights. Furthermore, within the preferred stock, several classes, or series, may exist that set out different gradations of priority for each class. Under most state statutes, the articles of incorporation must spell out the preferences; such preferences generally will not be implied.

The most common preference involves priority with regard to *dividends* (cash, property, or other shares that the board of directors declares as payment to shareholders). For example, preferred stockholders may receive dividends paid at a specified rate (for example, 7 percent) before any other classes of stock receive any dividends. If any funds for dividends remain after payment to the various classes of

EXHIBIT 33.1 Legal Model of Corporate Governance

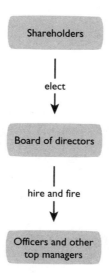

preferred stockholders, preferred shareholders may have *participation* rights; that is, they take part in this additional distribution of dividends with the common shareholders.

In addition to dividend and participation rights, preferred shareholders may receive corporate assets before any other stockholder if the corporation is liquidated. After the debts of the corporation are paid, preferred shareholders with liquidation preference are the first to receive the par value of their stocks plus any outstanding dividends. (*Par value* is the face value assigned to a stock and printed on the stock certificate.) Common stockholders receive corporate assets only if sufficient assets remain to pay their stocks' par values. If there are any additional assets after payment to the common stockholders, the preferred and common shareholders normally share this balance in proportion to their shares. Preferred shareholders also may enjoy *conversion* rights (the shareholder's option to change preferred stock into common stock or corporate bonds) and/or *redemption* rights (the corporation's right to buy the shares in certain authorized circumstances). These features are summarized in Exhibit 33.2. For more information about types of stocks and investing, see the Web site of Investopedia.com. Consult their glossary at http://www.investopedia.com/dictionary/ and tutorials at http://www.investopedia.com/university/.

Shareholders' Meetings

Notice In general, the corporation must send written notice of the meeting to all shareholders of record. Statu-tory and bylaw provisions often spell out the procedures for giving notice. Such notice ordinarily contains the time, date, and place of the meeting, as well as a statement of the purpose of the meeting. Most statutes require at least 10 days' notice before a meeting can legitimately be conducted. States are beginning to provide for the use of electronic media in shareholder meetings, including notice of meetings.[32] Shareholders can expressly waive the notice requirement in writing before or after the meeting, or they can impliedly waive it by not protesting the lack of notice. (Home Business Online, provided by The Advantage Corporation, has many legal forms at its Web site at http://www.homebusinessonline.com/a&r/elibrary/legal/index.shtml. It includes waivers of notice for shareholders' meetings and board of director meetings.)

Quorum Shareholder meetings cannot take place in the absence of a quorum. State statutes and corporate bylaws or articles usually state the percentage of *outstanding shares*, or shares entitled to vote, that constitutes a quorum. A majority of such votes is usually necessary; yet some states authorize articles of incorporation that set the quorum requirement at one-third of all outstanding shares. Delaware permits a corporation to conduct shareholder meetings by "remote communication" under some conditions. The board of directors can choose whether to use "remote communication" and how the meeting will be conducted.[33] As technology advances, the shareholders at remote sites may be able to be counted as part of the quorum and to vote. Ballots submitted by "electronic

EXHIBIT 33.2 Stock Characteristics

Type of Stock	Characteristics
Common	Basic shares issued by a corporation; they generally have a lower priority for dividends and distribution of assets upon dissolution.
Preferred	Shares that include special rights to dividends and/or distribution of assets upon dissolution
Cumulative Preferred	Shares that include the right to a specified dividend; any unpaid dividends owed to these shareholders must be paid before dividends can be paid on the common stock
Convertible Preferred	Shares that include the shareholder's right to convert them into another type of stock; generally they are convertible into common stock or corporate bonds
Redeemable Preferred	Shares that the corporation can repurchase according to the terms of the redemption agreement

transmission" will satisfy the written ballot requirement of the Delaware statute.[34]

Dissident shareholders (those who disagree with the actions of management) may prevent a quorum by not attending meetings; but the law remains unsettled as to whether a subsequent walkout of dissident shareholders, once a quorum is present, invalidates the meeting.

Election and Removal of Directors

One of the foremost powers held by shareholders is their capacity to elect and remove directors. Although the articles of incorporation usually designate the people who are to serve as the initial directors, these directors may serve only until the first annual meeting. At that time, the shareholders may elect some (or all) of them to the board of directors. If vacancies occur on the board because of deaths or resignations, the shareholders normally vote to fill these vacancies. The articles of incorporation or bylaws, however, may permit the directors to fill these posts. Directors usually serve staggered terms. This means that only a certain proportion of directors (for example, one-third) will be up for reelection at any given meeting. Such staggered terms ensure continuity of leadership on the board. In recent years, there has been a trend toward adding outsiders to the board of directors. *Outsiders* are directors who are not shareholders or corporate officers.

Shareholders have *inherent* power (that is, power regardless of the articles or bylaws) to remove a director for cause. Previous cases have upheld the exercise of such rights when directors have engaged in embezzlement or other misconduct; have failed to live up to their duties to the corporation; or have undertaken unauthorized acts. The director, of course, may appeal his or her removal to a court of law. Statutes, articles of incorporation, and bylaws may also allow removal without cause.

Amendment of the Bylaws

Bylaws are provisions intended to regulate the corporation and its management. To be valid, bylaws must comply with state incorporation statutes and the articles of incorporation. Shareholders retain inherent power to amend (or repeal) bylaws. State law generally mandates the proportion of outstanding shares needed to approve an amendment. (For an example of bylaws, visit the Web site for Educause, Inc., a not-for-profit corporation, which maintains not only its bylaws but also its articles of incorporation and information about its trustees at http://www.educause.edu/coninfo/cearticles.html.

Voting

The voting rights exercised by shareholders at meetings allow them *indirect control* of the corporation and the board of directors. All shareholders of record as of the date of the shareholders' meeting ordinarily appear on the voting list and can vote. Shareholders can either be present at the meeting and vote in person, or they can assign their voting rights to others, who then vote their shares for them by proxy. (A *proxy* is a person appointed and designated to act for another, especially at a public meeting. The term *proxy* can be used to designate either the person or the document used to appoint the person.) If a shareholder in a public-issue corporation does not want to participate personally in the meeting, he or she can sign a proxy, giving the proxy holder authority to act as his or her agent.[35] Exhibit 33.3 shows a proxy. Delaware permits stockholders to appoint proxies by transmitting telegrams, cablegrams, or other electronic transmissions.[36]

Whoever controls large blocs of proxies in a public-issue corporation may, in effect, dictate the outcome of the election. For this reason, management (and sometimes dissident stockholders) in such corporations may solicit proxies in order to consolidate voting power. Not surprisingly, then, vicious proxy fights have occurred at various

EXHIBIT **33.3** Proxy

_____, a California Corporation.

The undersigned, as record holder of the shares of stock of _____ , described above, revokes any previous proxies and appoints _____ as the undersigned's proxy to attend the special shareholders' meeting on _____ , and any adjournment of that meeting.

The proxy holder is entitled to cast a total number of votes equal to, but not exceeding _____ which the undersigned would be entitled to cast if the undersigned were personally present.

The undersigned authorizes the undersigned's proxy holder to vote and otherwise represent the undersigned with regards to any business that may come before this meeting in the same manner and with the same effect as if the undersigned were personally present.

THIS PROXY MAY BE REVOKED AT ANY TIME IN WRITING.

Dated: _____ , 20 _____

Courtesy of Robyn Esraelian, Richardson, Jones and Esraelian, Attorneys-at-Law, Fresno, California.

---

times in U.S. corporations. Because of the high stakes and the possibilities for abuse, federal law now ensures that proxy solicitations are carried out fairly. Within the corporation, impartial parties called inspectors, judges, or tellers oversee the election to ensure fairness (see Chapter 36).

In most corporate matters, a shareholder can cast one vote for each share held. This is called *straight voting*. Unless the voting involves an extraordinary corporate matter (such as dissolution, merger, amendment of the articles of incorporation, or sale of substantially all the assets), the decision made by a majority generally controls. Thus, votes of more than 50 percent for any ordinary corporate matter usually bind the corporation. In extraordinary matters, statutes may require a higher proportion (for example, two-thirds) of votes for the action taken to be legally binding.

To offset shareholders who own large blocs of votes and who may therefore be able to wield significant control, most state statutes today either permit or require *cumulative voting*. Cumulative voting applies only to the election of directors and is a method for ensuring some minority representation on the board.

The following example illustrates the difference between straight and cumulative voting. Assume that at the annual shareholders' meeting, three directors will be elected from a field of six candidates—Umberto, Victoria, Wally, Xavier, Yvette, and Zack. Under straight voting, shareholder Amir, who owns 100 shares, can cast 100 votes for each of three directors, say Umberto, Victoria, and Wally. If, instead, cumulative voting is used, Amir can cast 300 votes (the number of votes equals the number of shares times the number of directors being elected). Amir can cast 300 votes for Umberto or can divide 300 votes among the candidates

in any proportion he wishes (e.g., 150 for Umberto, 100 for Victoria, and 50 for Yvette). In this fashion, Amir's votes accumulate—hence, the term cumulative voting. The ability of a minority shareholder to have an impact on the election of directors thus becomes more formidable under cumulative voting than under straight voting.

To dilute any advantage that the minority might gain through cumulative voting, management may stagger the terms of directors, reduce or enlarge the size of the board, or remove directors elected by the minority. To counter such steps, lawmakers in many jurisdictions have passed statutory provisions that protect cumulative voting rights by making such steps illegal or by mandating statutory formulas that safeguard the beneficial effects of cumulative voting.

Voting trusts, like proxies and cumulative voting, represent devices used to consolidate votes for control. A shareholder can create a voting trust by transferring to trustees the shares he or she owns. (In this context, *trustees* are persons in whom a power to vote is vested under an express or implied agreement.) Once the shareholder has entered into such a trust, the shareholder has no right to vote the shares until the trust terminates. The trustees issue a *voting trust certificate* to the shareholder to indicate that the shareholder retains all rights incidental to share ownership except voting. In contrast to proxies, which are generally revocable, voting trusts are normally irrevocable. State statutes, however, usually limit the duration of voting trusts to a specified time period, such as 10 years (with possible extensions).

Pooling agreements are similar to voting trusts. In such agreements, each shareholder agrees to vote the shares he or she owns in a specified way. Both voting trusts and pooling agreements remain valid and enforceable as long as they do not, in effect, preempt the directors' managerial functions. This could happen if the shareholders who enter into these arrangements are also directors. For example, it is legal for the shareholders to agree through voting trusts or pooling agreements to vote for director Ali at the annual election of directors (even if director Ali is also one of the shareholders who enters into the arrangement). However, voting trusts or pooling arrangements to bring about the dismissal of the chief executive officer (CEO) normally will be unenforceable. Why? Selection of officers is ordinarily a function of the directors.

Shareholders of close corporations probably utilize voting trusts and pooling arrangements more than their counterparts in publicly held corporations. Modern statutes recognize that close corporations are more similar to partnerships than most other business entities. Consequently, some states will enforce agreements that treat shareholders as if they were directors, when all the shareholders are parties to the agreement. Such statutory developments illustrate the law's ability to change whenever modifications become necessary.

Dividends

Most shareholders buy shares of for-profit, public-issue corporations primarily to receive dividends. Such shareholders normally care more about dividends than about control. We have spoken of a *right* to receive dividends, but that constitutes a very loose use of the term "right." Actually, there is no absolute right to receive dividends. The power to declare dividends resides with the board of directors. Shareholders cannot compel the directors to declare dividends without proving bad faith. The directors alone decide, first, *if* dividends will be distributed. If so, they also determine the timing, type, and amount of the dividend.

Of course, shareholders hope to receive the financial profits represented by dividends. *Cash dividends* are the most common type. However, the dividend may also take the form of *property* or *stocks*. If cash dividends are involved, the directors must make certain that the dividends will be paid from a *lawful source*. In general, statutes limit the sources of dividends to *current net profits* (those earned in the preceding accounting period) or *earned surplus* (the sum of the net profits retained by the corporation during all previous years of existence). Any declaration of dividends that will impair the corporation's *original capital structure* (the number of shares originally issued times their stated value) is illegal and may subject the directors and shareholders to personal liability. Similarly, payment of dividends during the corporation's insolvency or any payment that will bring about insolvency or financial difficulties is illegal. Exhibit 33.4 illustrates the decision-making process in declaring dividends.

As noted earlier, preferred stockholders enjoy priority with regard to the distribution of dividends. Preferred shareholders are also protected from improper dividend declarations. Directors normally cannot declare dividends if the declaration will jeopardize the liquidation preferences of the preferred shareholders. (*Liquidation preferences* are priorities given to creditors and shareholders when the enterprise is terminated and the assets are distributed.) Once a dividend is lawfully declared, preferred stockholders receive their dividends first. Common stockholders receive dividends only if adequate funds remain after the preferred stockholders have been paid. Sometimes preferred stockholders have *participating* preferred stock. This means they not only receive their original dividend but also share (or participate) with the common stockholders in any dividends that are paid after the preferred stockholders have received their initial dividends. In other words, participating preferred stockholders may be able to dip into the dividend fund twice. Usually, however, preferred stock is nonparticipating.

There is another complexity in declaring preferred dividends. Preferred dividends may be *cumulative,* which means that the sum (or accumulation) of all unpaid prior preferred dividends must be paid before common shareholders receive any dividends. In contrast, in *noncumulative* preferred dividends, the preferred stockholder receives only the dividend preferences for the *current accounting period,* and the common stockholders then receive their dividends should any funds remain. Under this type of preference, the preferred shareholders lose all dividends for any years in which the directors have chosen not to declare a dividend.

Preemptive Stock Rights

Sometimes it is necessary for a corporation to increase its capital by issuing new shares. This is an extraordinary matter involving amendment of the articles of incorporation because the original number of shares and their par value will be changed. Shareholders must vote on the issuance of these new shares. A shareholder's interest in this matter extends beyond voting rights. For example, assume Bonnie owns 10 shares of Samp Corporation. Samp's original capitalization involved 100 shares sold at $100 each ($10,000 stated capital). At that time, Bonnie owned 10 percent of Samp Corporation (10 shares/100 total shares). If Samp issues another 100 shares as a result of the amending of the articles, Bonnie then will own 5 percent of the corporation (10 shares/200 total shares). As a result of this new capitalization, her voting power will decrease proportionately. Her right to receive dividends and corporate assets on liquidation will also decrease.

EXHIBIT 33.4 The Decision to Issue Dividends: A Flowchart

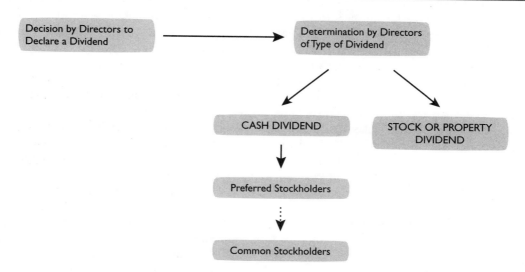

The following diagrams illustrate cash dividends involving special types of preferred stock:

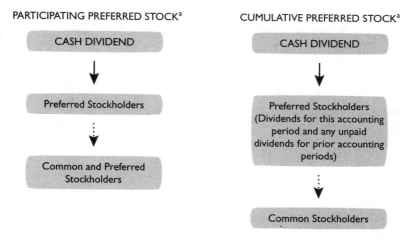

- - - - - Stockholders receive dividends only if sufficient funds remain.

a. Preferred stock can be both participating and cumulative.

Realizing the unfairness of this sequence of events, courts began to protect the Bonnies of the corporate world by a doctrine called *preemptive rights.* These courts promoted the notion that the right of first refusal inheres in stock ownership. These rights are particularly important in closely held corporations. Before the corporation can sell to anyone else, it must offer to sell to Bonnie the number of shares that will restore her proportionate share of ownership. Bonnie, in effect, can preempt the rights of other would-be purchasers of the stock because she can purchase before they have the chance to do so. Once the corporation notifies Bonnie of her preemptive rights, she has a limited time to exercise them. If she does not take advantage of the offer, she waives her rights of preemption.

Preemptive rights normally apply only to new shares issued for cash and will not apply to shares issued in exchange for property (such as a commercial building) or services (such as shares issued to lure a CEO to Samp), or to shares issued as share dividends, or to treasury stock (stock originally issued but subsequently reacquired by the corporation). In this last situation, there is no new issue and, hence, no reduction in Bonnie's proportionate interest in Samp Corporation. In the two prior situations, preemptive rights may cripple the corporation's financing efforts and obstruct the corporation's legitimate, profit-maximizing activities, such as acquiring property and recruiting top-flight executives. Because of the possible frustration of these worthwhile aims, courts and statutes alike deny Bonnie's preemptive rights, even though her ownership interest will still be diluted. In addition, judicial and statutory treatment of Bonnie's preemptive rights might be different in a publicly held (as opposed to a close) corporation.

Inspection of Corporate Books and Records

The rights of shareholders to inspect corporate records arise from both common law doctrines and express statutory provisions. In light of the recent situations such as Enron and MCI Worldcom, shareholders may increase the amount and frequency of their inspection of corporate records. In general, shareholders have access to such corporate materials as stockholder lists; minutes of shareholders' meetings; minutes of board or officers' meetings; financial records, such as books of account or other periodic summaries; and business documents, including tax returns, contracts, and office correspondence or memoranda.

At common law, inspection rights were qualified (rather than absolute) because shareholders needed to demonstrate that the reason for inspection involved a "proper purpose." Shareholders had to show that the motivation for the inspection related to their status as a shareholder. Requests for shareholder lists to communicate with shareholders about corporate matters, or corporate financial records to determine the value of shares, the propriety of dividends, or possible mismanagement would ordinarily qualify as proper purposes. On the other hand, shareholder requests that ask for information to learn trade secrets for the benefit of the corporation's competitors or to bring *strike suits* (those without any real merit) in order to impede management normally will constitute improper purposes. Assuming the inspection is for a proper purpose, the shareholder generally can employ attorneys, accountants, and other personnel to aid in examining records, making copies or summaries, and the like. Note the similarity between a limited partner's inspection rights (Case 33.1, *Madison Avenue Investment Partners, LLC v. America First Real Estate Investment Partners, L.P.*) and those of a shareholder.

Most statutes require a showing of proper purpose; but once the shareholder has made an initial showing of a proper purpose, the burden of proof shifts to the corporation to rebut the presumption by showing an improper purpose on the part of the shareholder. Sometimes statutes change the burden of proof or the party who has the burden, depending on the type of record being requested. Statutes may also restrict inspection rights to only certain shareholders (for example, those who have held their shares for at least six months or who own at least 5 percent of the outstanding shares). These statutory restrictions, however, do not eliminate the shareholder's common law inspection rights. But, as mentioned, the shareholder, not the corporation, has the burden of proving proper purpose under these common law doctrines.

Federal securities law and state statutes that mandate annual disclosure of profits and losses, officer compensation, and so on have made inspection rights somewhat less important. The information made available to the shareholder under these statutes encompasses the type of information that previously shareholders could obtain only by exercising their rights of inspection.

Transfer of Shares

As discussed earlier, ownership of share (stock) certificates signifies ownership of a portion of the corporation. Thus, these shares are the shareholder's property. Shareholders, like other owners of property, generally can transfer their shares to someone else (by gift or sale). A transfer of shares generally occurs through endorsement and delivery of the stock certificate in conjunction with a surrender of the certificate for subsequent reissue to the new owner by the corporation's secretary or, in a large corporation, by its transfer agent. Stock exchange rules regulate the conduct of transfer agents, who are professionals who help the corporate secretary with the myriad details attendant on large-scale transfers of stocks. Transfers of stock in these situations, including the actual physical transfers of stock certificates, cause numerous administrative headaches. Recent developments, such as when a brokerage firm holds title to stock through bookkeeping entries rather than possession of actual certificates, will likely lead to the abolition of stock certificates and their replacement by computer printouts.

Generally, the right to transfer stock remains unfettered. Restrictions placed on the stock itself, however, may limit this right of transferability. It is easy to understand why these restrictions may be advisable. Such restrictions commonly occur in close corporations. We have already discussed the fact that close corporations are like partnerships in that the controlling shareholders actively take part in the day-to-day management of the corporation. Consequently, shareholders in close corporations often attempt to preserve their control over the corporation through voting trusts and pooling arrangements. Such attempts at consolidation of power will be meaningless without restrictions on the stock's transferability.

Courts try to balance the legitimate interests of the shareholders in limiting ownership to a few congenial shareholders with the competing right of a shareholder to transfer his or her property. In our legal system, this right of alienation is considered to be inherent in the ownership of property. (*Right of alienation* is the right to transfer ownership to another.) A *right of first refusal*, where the shareholder who wishes to sell must first offer his or her shares to the corporation or to the other shareholders, is enforceable as a valid restriction on transfer. It is considered to be a reasonable restraint on alienation. A common valid restriction is "No shareholder may encumber or dispose of his or her shares except (1) by sale only if such shareholder first offers his or her shares to the corporation, or to the other shareholders, on the same terms as such shareholder can sell to a bona fide prospective purchaser and (2) by gift, bequest, or intestate descent to, or in trust for, certain described members of such shareholder's family." In contrast, a restriction that states that "these shares are nontransferable" will probably be unreasonable and, therefore, unenforceable.

The restriction must be conspicuously placed on the stock certificate to be valid. A conspicuous notice is meant to protect any subsequent purchaser of the shares by informing him or her of the restriction. If this notice is missing, the purchaser will not be bound by the restriction unless he or she otherwise has notice of it. If the restriction is reasonable and appears on the face of the stock certificate, however, the corporation can refuse to transfer the shares to the purchaser. The purchaser's remedy involves forcing the seller to return the money paid for the shares.

If the transfer satisfies all legal requirements, including the applicable provisions of Article 8 of the Uniform Commercial Code (UCC) and state securities laws, the purchaser (transferee) pays the price asked and the shareholder (transferor) then endorses and delivers the stock to the purchaser. The corporation, when notified, must register the transfer and change corporate records to denote the new ownership. This is necessary to guarantee the new owner the rights incidental to stock ownership in the corporation.

Liabilities of the Shareholders

As we learned in Chapter 32, one of the most significant advantages of the corporate form is the limited liability afforded to shareholders. In other words, the shareholders risk only their investment. Except for situations in which courts can disregard the corporate entity, shareholders normally do not become personally liable for corporate debts. In this section, we will look at some other circumstances that may cause a shareholder to be personally liable for obligations of the corporation. (For a discussion of stock and capitalization, see the definitions listed by 1-800-attorney.com at http://www.1-800-attorney.com/li/legal_topics.cfm?i_Display=2&LN_ID=67.)

Watered Stock

At the time of the formation of the corporation, the articles of incorporation spell out its *capital structure*. The money to operate the corporation initially results from the issuance of securities to investors. The authorization for such securities ordinarily occurs early in the formation process, probably by board action at the organizational meeting.

The consideration the corporation receives for these shares constitutes the stated capital of the corporation. The board of directors establishes a fixed value for each share of such capital stock (for example, $10 per share). This is called *par value stock*. The corporation may also issue no-par value stock, which has no fixed value but may be sold at whatever price the directors deem reasonable (called *stated value*). No-par value shares permit a corporation to issue stock in return for corporate assets that currently are worth little but have the possibility of high, though speculative, returns (such as technological developments).

If no statutory provisions exist to the contrary, the corporation may issue shares in exchange for any lawful consideration, including cash received, property received, or services actually rendered. Just as the board of directors generally sets the price of the shares, it also normally fixes the value of the property received or services rendered. As long as the board makes these decisions in good faith and in the absence of fraud, courts will not impose legal liability on the directors for these decisions.

However, the shareholder who receives shares of a corporation that are issued as fully paid, when in fact the full par or stated value has not been paid by the purchaser, owns *watered stock*. The shareholder is personally liable for the deficiency, that is, "the water." For example, if a shareholder pays $8 per share and the par value or stated value is $10 per share, the shareholder is liable to the corporation for the $2 per share deficiency.

Watered-stock problems normally arise in situations in which services have been rendered in exchange for stock. For example, suppose a firm incorporates and issues $4,000 worth of its shares to Eduardo in exchange for his efforts in developing a talking medicine container. If Eduardo's efforts are later found to be worth only $2,000, Eduardo will be liable for $2,000 worth of watered stock. Usually Eduardo's liability is to the corporation, but some states will allow corporate creditors to impose liability on Eduardo if the firm becomes insolvent and unable to meet its obligations as they come due. A later purchaser from Eduardo normally will not be liable for watered stock, however, because the rule regarding watered stock applies only to initial corporate issuances and purchases of stock.

The use of no-par value stock and the impact of federal and state securities regulation have greatly reduced the incidence of suits alleging liability for watered stock. Still, shareholders should be aware of this legal doctrine.

Stock Subscriptions

Stock subscriptions are agreements by investors ("subscribers") to purchase shares in a corporation. The law views a subscription as an offer. However, most state statutes make subscriptions irrevocable for a certain period unless the subscription itself provides otherwise. A subscriber may enter into such agreements either before or after the corporation's formation. If the stock subscription occurs before the corporation's formation (usually as a result of promoters' activities), some states treat the subscription as an offer that is automatically accepted by the corporation upon its formation, creating a valid contract. Other states, however, require formal acceptance of the subscription (offer) before a valid contract between the subscriber and the corporation arises.

Because an accepted stock subscription constitutes a contract, various types of liabilities arise if it is breached. Thus, the corporation can sue the subscriber for the subscription price if the subscriber refuses to pay as agreed. In some cases, creditors of a corporation that has become insolvent may force the subscriber to pay the amount owed on the subscription. By the same token, the subscriber can sue the corporation if the corporation refuses to issue the shares that are the object of the subscription. As in the case of watered stock, securities laws have reduced the incidence of shareholder liability for stock subscriptions.

Illegal Dividends

We noted earlier that cash dividends must be paid from a lawful source. Any declaration of dividends that will impair the original capital structure of the corporation is illegal and may subject both the directors and the shareholders to personal liability. Shareholders who receive an illegal dividend are liable for its return if the corporation is insolvent at the time the dividend is paid. In such cases, the corporation's creditors can sue the shareholders directly for the amount of

the illegal dividend. If the corporation is solvent when an illegal distribution takes place and remains solvent even after it, however, only shareholders who knew the dividend was illegal (e.g., from an improper source) must repay the dividend to the corporation. Innocent shareholders can retain the dividends. Directors who have been held financially liable for distributing illegal dividends can force shareholders who knew of the illegal dividends to pay the amounts received back to the directors. The shareholders and directors thus share liability in such circumstances.

Dissolution

Dissolution signals the legal termination of the corporation's existence. It may occur *voluntarily* (by actions of the incorporators or shareholders), or *involuntarily* (by court actions initiated by the state or a shareholder). It is important to note that majority (or controlling) shareholders may incur liability if the purpose of the dissolution is to freeze out minority stockholders and to strip them of rights or profits they would otherwise enjoy. The basis of this liability is that controlling shareholders owe fiduciary duties to minority shareholders. Generally speaking, controlling shareholders must exert control for the benefit of all shareholders, not just for themselves. Majority shareholders may be personally liable for dissolutions that prejudice the interests of minority shareholders while substantially enhancing the interests of majority shareholders.

Rights and Duties of the Managers

Board of Directors

The right to manage the affairs of the corporation falls squarely on the board of directors. Although shareholders, the ultimate owners of the corporation, retain the power to elect and remove directors, this prerogative does not give shareholders a direct voice in management. Nor can shareholders compel the board to take any action. The directors are not agents of the shareholders; they owe loyalty primarily to the corporation. As we discussed, however, different rules may apply if the corporation is a close corporation. (*Directors & Boards* is a quarterly journal of articles on serving as director or CEO. It maintains a Web site with select articles at http://www.directorsandboards.com/.)

Number and Qualifications The articles of incorporation usually name the initial directors. Older statutes required at least three directors, but the modern trend—

due, in part to the increased numbers of close corporations—is to permit as few as one or two directors. To avoid deadlocks, the articles or bylaws usually authorize an uneven number of directors.

Unless otherwise provided in the relevant statutes, articles, or bylaws, directors need not be either shareholders in the corporation or residents of the state where the corporation has its principal place of business. Where there are qualifications for directors, the election of unqualified persons is voidable, not void. In other words, until the corporation employs proper proceedings to displace the unqualified directors, the law considers them *de facto directors* (that is, directors in fact if not in law). Consequently, most of their acts as directors are effective, and de facto directors must live up to the same corporate duties and standards as qualified directors do. Directors generally have the right to appoint interim replacements on the board when vacancies arise owing to the death, resignation, or incapacity of a director.

Term of Office Directors serve for the time specified in state statutes, unless the articles or bylaws limit the term to a shorter period. Directors usually serve for one year unless the corporation has set up a *classified board* (a board divided into classes of directors with staggered election dates). Directors continue to hold office until the shareholders elect their successors and the latter take office. Thus, sitting directors do not automatically drop off the board at the end of their terms.

Sometimes shareholders remove directors before their terms on the board end. Shareholders may remove directors for cause. For cause was the only basis for removal at common law. Modern statutes relax this standard by permitting a majority of shareholders to remove directors at any time during their terms without cause. In those jurisdictions that require cumulative voting, however, directors cannot be removed if the number of votes cast for retention would have been sufficient to elect those directors to the board. In most jurisdictions, directors who have been removed can seek court review of such dismissals to determine if the proper procedures were followed.

Meetings Traditionally, the board could validly exercise its powers only when acting collectively, not individually. The law emphasized the value of decision making arrived at through collective debate, deliberation, and judgment. For this reason, statutes set out rules permitting the board to act only when it was formally convened. Moreover, directors traditionally had to be present to vote (they could not vote by proxy or send substitutes to deliberate for them). Directors could vote only at a properly announced and formal meeting.

Today, most modern statutes dispense with the formalities previously required of directors' meetings. Thus, even though the bylaws usually fix the times for regular or special board meetings, statutes today allow meetings to occur even without prior notice. To make a meeting valid, however, either before or after the meeting each absent director must—in writing—waive the right to prior notice, consent to the meeting, or approve the minutes of the meeting.

Similarly, some states even allow the board to act without a meeting, assuming the articles or bylaws permit informal action, as long as all directors consent and file their consents in the corporate minute book. In fact, telephone conference calls suffice in several states. In Delaware the directors can use all forms of teleconferencing, videoconferencing, and other communication means as long as the participants can "hear" each other.[37] In California, the directors can also meet by "chat room" meetings or committee meetings over the Internet.[38] Given this trend toward informality, the board can hold its meetings anywhere unless the articles or bylaws declare otherwise. Meetings outside the corporation's state of incorporation or principal place of business are, in general, perfectly legal.

Unless the articles or bylaws set a higher or lower percentage, a simple majority of the directors ordinarily constitutes a quorum. Actions taken by a quorum of directors are binding on the corporation. Two important questions still arise in any discussion about quorums. First, can directors who intentionally miss a meeting to prevent a quorum later question the validity of the action taken at the meeting? Since different cases have produced different results, you should check the law on this matter in your particular jurisdiction. Second, can directors count toward the quorum (or vote) if the board will be voting on matters in which they are personally interested? Modern statutes generally allow directors to participate as long as there has been compliance with statutory provisions meant to ensure fairness to the corporation (such as disclosure of the interest). When there is no statutory provision, the case results vary from jurisdiction to jurisdiction. Some cases have allowed interested directors to be counted; other cases have not.

Directors usually cannot agree in advance about how they will vote on corporate matters. Such a formal agreement is not binding because it is against public policy; directors owe fiduciary duties to the corporation and must be free to exercise their judgment in a totally unrestricted fashion. Such agreements may be valid, however, among directors in a close corporation if all the shareholders-directors agree to the plan.

Delegation of Duties Most statutes authorize the board of directors to delegate managerial authority to officers and executive (or other) committees. A common example of a specialized committee is the compensation committee. Such delegations of duties ensure the smooth running of the day-to-day affairs of the corporation and promote efficiency by utilizing the expertise of the various committee members.

If no statutory provisions specifically allow the delegation of duties, courts will interpret any attempts at delegation very strictly. Moreover, if the delegations become too broad and pervasive, such actions will probably be void because it is too great a relinquishment of the board's management functions. Similarly, attempts to place control of the corporation in fewer persons than the entire board of directors will be illegal (even in close corporations), because the corporation deserves the best efforts of all its directors, who, in turn, owe fiduciary duties to the corporation. Delegation of authority to arbitrators, management consultants, or others outside the ranks of directors and officers becomes extremely difficult to justify legally.

Compensation In the past, the corporation had no duty to compensate directors for their services. Older cases ruled that directors were not to be paid for their services unless the articles or bylaws authorized the compensation before the directors had rendered the services. Even under these circumstances, however, directors could receive payment for extraordinary services taken at the board's request (such as recruitment of executive officers), despite the lack of a prearranged, specific agreement. The payment is based on quasi-contractual grounds. Today, although many corporations still pay their directors little or no compensation, an increasing number of corporations do pay rather hefty sums. Since directors are subject to ever-expanding duties and potential liability, compensation seems more justifiable. Directors often are not substantial shareholders, and consequently they do not profit as owners of the firm.

The directors normally determine the salaries of the officers of the corporation. Possible conflict of interest concerns may arise when directors also serve as officers because, in effect, the directors will be participating in setting their own salaries. As noted earlier in the discussion of quorum requirements, statutes may empower interested directors to vote on these issues as long as disclosure of the interest has been made and the transaction is otherwise fair to the corporation. The board can hire officers to serve for periods longer than the board's tenure as long as the period involved is reasonable in length. The amount of compensation paid to officers also must be reasonable. The compensation package commonly consists of salary, bonuses, share options, profit sharing, annuities, and deferred-compensation plans. Large compensation packages may be attacked as a "waste" of corporate assets by the directors.

Corporate salaries in the millions of dollars are not uncommon today. Moreover, it has become a relatively common strategy for the board to give "golden parachute" packages to their chief executive officers when the corporation is the target of a hostile takeover attempt. (*Golden parachutes* pay the officers a hefty salary after their severance from the corporation in return for doing no additional work.) Since the acquirer will be obligated to pay these inflated salaries after the acquisition, golden parachutes become a strategy for fending off a takeover attempt. Golden parachutes raise controversial questions about possible conflicts of interest and waste of corporate assets.

Liabilities State corporation statutes, common law doctrines, and federal securities and antitrust laws may impose liability on a director for noncompliance with the duties or requirements set out in those doctrines and statutes. Directors, by the very nature of their positions, make numerous decisions, collectively and individually. Increasingly, the performance of these duties subjects directors to potential personal liability, either individually or with the other members of the board who have approved or engaged in the forbidden conduct. Directors must use great caution in order to avoid liability in the form of civil damages or criminal fines. Scrutiny of directors' decisions is likely to increase in the light of recent problems, such as those at Enron and Adelphia.

Although not always the case, today it is legal—indeed, common—for corporations to *indemnify* (pay back or reimburse) their directors for liabilities accruing from their corporate positions. Through indemnification, directors are reimbursed by the corporation for the losses and expenses incurred from litigation brought against them personally for actions undertaken in their corporate capacities. Statutes may limit the right of indemnification in certain circumstances. For instance, indemnification for criminal fines may be prohibited when directors have knowingly engaged in illegal activities. Statutes often empower corporations to purchase liability insurance for their directors, officers, and other employees to cover nonindemnifiable liabilities. These policies are commonly called *D and O liability insurance*—for directors and officers' liability and reimbursement policies. Exhibit 33.5 summarizes the management responsibilities in a corporation.

Other Rights Because directors alone have the right to declare dividends, they may be personally liable for improper dividends. (We have already discussed the shareholders' potential liability for improper dividends.)

Directors may enter into agreements about how they will vote as directors. But if such agreements unduly hamper

EXHIBIT 33.5 Management of the Corporation

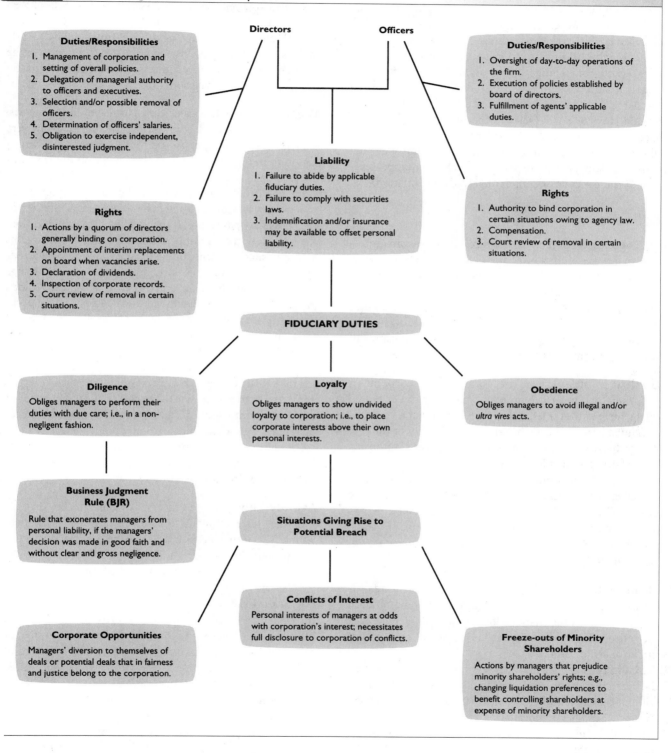

Directors   **Officers**

Duties/Responsibilities
1. Management of corporation and setting of overall policies.
2. Delegation of managerial authority to officers and executives.
3. Selection and/or possible removal of officers.
4. Determination of officers' salaries.
5. Obligation to exercise independent, disinterested judgment.

Duties/Responsibilities
1. Oversight of day-to-day operations of the firm.
2. Execution of policies established by board of directors.
3. Fulfillment of agents' applicable duties.

Liability
1. Failure to abide by applicable fiduciary duties.
2. Failure to comply with securities laws.
3. Indemnification and/or insurance may be available to offset personal liability.

Rights
1. Actions by a quorum of directors generally binding on corporation.
2. Appointment of interim replacements on board when vacancies arise.
3. Declaration of dividends.
4. Inspection of corporate records.
5. Court review of removal in certain situations.

Rights
1. Authority to bind corporation in certain situations owing to agency law.
2. Compensation.
3. Court review of removal in certain situations.

FIDUCIARY DUTIES

Diligence
Obliges managers to perform their duties with due care; i.e., in a non-negligent fashion.

Loyalty
Obliges managers to show undivided loyalty to corporation; i.e., to place corporate interests above their own personal interests.

Obedience
Obliges managers to avoid illegal and/or *ultra vires* acts.

Business Judgment Rule (BJR)
Rule that exonerates managers from personal liability, if the managers' decision was made in good faith and without clear and gross negligence.

Situations Giving Rise to Potential Breach

Conflicts of Interest
Personal interests of managers at odds with corporation's interest; necessitates full disclosure to corporation of conflicts.

Corporate Opportunities
Managers' diversion to themselves of deals or potential deals that in fairness and justice belong to the corporation.

Freeze-outs of Minority Shareholders
Actions by managers that prejudice minority shareholders' rights; e.g., changing liquidation preferences to benefit controlling shareholders at expense of minority shareholders.

the board's managerial functions, the agreements will be void on public policy grounds. These agreements ordinarily will be valid, however, in close corporations in which *all* the shareholder-directors have assented to the terms.

The rights of directors to inspect corporate records are even more compelling than shareholders' rights. Why? Access to corporate records is essential if directors are to discharge their fiduciary duties and decision-making functions. Many states characterize the directors' right of inspection as absolute. Yet this right will probably be lost if directors abuse the right by using it for an improper purpose that damages the corporation, such as misappropriation of trade secrets or confidential trade information.

Officers

The selection or removal of officers represents an important managerial function of the board of directors. While directors are responsible for the overall policies of the corporation, officers conduct the day-to-day operations of the firm and execute the policies established by the board. These lines of authority are well established in American law. The directors should manage, and the officers should carry out the management goals delegated to them by the directors.

Qualifications Officers are agents of the corporation and, therefore, must live up to the fiduciary duties placed on agents. Statutes often name the officers that a corporation must have, and usually either these statutes or the corporate bylaws specify each respective officer's authority. Typical officers include president, vice-president, secretary, and treasurer (or comptroller). The top executive may also be called the chairman of the board, the chief executive officer (CEO), or the general manager. The same person ordinarily can serve in more than one position, but some statutes prohibit the same person from serving as both president and secretary.

Term of Office The board ordinarily appoints the officers, who serve at the will of the directors. Some modern statutes, on the other hand, allow the shareholders to elect the officers. Either the board or the president can appoint junior or senior officers.

Officers usually serve at the pleasure of the board because the board in most jurisdictions can remove an officer with or without cause, even when the officer has a valid employment contract. But after removal *without cause,* the corporation may be liable in damages to the former officer for breach of the employment contract. As we shall see later in this chapter, the directors normally escape personal liability if they have removed the officer in accordance with the *business judgment rule;* that is, they have exercised due care while making corpo-

rate decisions. (For an interesting article about the business judgment rule published at the Washburn Law School Web site see "The Business Judgment Rule in Kansas: From Black and White to Gray," at http://washburnlaw.edu/wlj/41-1/articles/staa.pdf.) In rare instances, the state, the courts, or the shareholders can remove officers. These instances nearly always involve a removal with cause.

Compensation In earlier times, officers, like directors, traditionally served without pay because they usually were shareholders who expected their investment in the corporation to multiply by virtue of their work on the corporation's behalf. Thus, there was no need to supplement these corporate profits with a salary. Today, since neither directors nor officers are required to be shareholders, the corporation usually pays a prearranged, fixed salary. In addition, the corporation commonly adds to this salary such benefits as profit-sharing plans, bonuses, share options, deferred-compensation plans, pensions, annuities, and other fringe benefits like health care and expense accounts. Golden parachutes may also be included. Such compensation packages often turn out to be substantial indeed.

Compensation, to be lawful, should be reasonable and not represent waste of corporate assets. If waste is present, both directors and officers may be liable to the corporation for this waste. Courts have even ordered officers to return amounts deemed excessive to the corporation. The amount of officers' compensation has been an issue recently, particularly in corporations that are doing poorly. Some of these corporations filed for protection under the bankruptcy laws while they provided substantial compensation packages to the officers of the business.

Agency Law Because officers are agents of the corporation, they have authority to bind the corporation. To help with this section, you should review the material on agency in Chapters 29 through 31. Briefly, an officer's authority may be actual (either express or implied) or apparent.

Express authority derives from state statutes, the articles, or the bylaws. Any of these three sources may spell out the duties, responsibilities, and authority of the respective officers. The bylaws are the most common source of express authority. Under express authority, the corporation has determined the boundaries within which the officer shall act on behalf of the corporation.

Implied authority, on the other hand, is derived by virtue of the office or title of the person. Corporate presidents have implied authority to direct meetings and to act on behalf of the corporation with regard to transactions occurring in the ordinary and regular course of business. For example, a president normally has authority to hire real estate brokers for the purpose of selling corporate property.

Yet the president cannot validly sell or mortgage corporate assets without the approval of the board (and sometimes that of the shareholders). The president can have authority, however, to bind the corporation to sale or service contracts arising in the usual course of business; for instance, the president of a grain elevator can authorize purchases of wheat from local farmers. Courts sometimes uphold expansions of authority for presidents who are CEOs or general managers.

Vice-presidents normally possess no authority by virtue of their office. Similarly, the treasurer and the secretary cannot normally bind the corporation. The law ordinarily limits them to fairly ministerial intracorporate functions. Some jurisdictions, however, do give the treasurer authority to write, accept, endorse, and negotiate corporate checks and promissory notes.

Corporate officers may have *apparent authority* to bind the corporation. Apparent authority arises when the corporation, by its actions, indicates to a third party that an officer or agent is empowered to engage in certain transactions on behalf of the corporation. The corporation's actions can be intentional or careless. In addition, to constitute apparent authority the third party's reliance must be reasonable. When apparent authority exists, the contract will be binding on the corporation and the third party.

Subsequent *ratification* or approval of previously unauthorized acts will also bind the corporation. Even if the president had no prior authority to buy real estate, a later board resolution that approves the purchase constitutes a ratification and binds the corporation to the completion of the transaction.

Liabilities Officers who attempt to contract on behalf of the corporation without authority may be personally liable to the other contracting party. Nondisclosure of the fact that the officer is acting on behalf of the corporation, even when the officer's actions are authorized, will also lead to the personal liability of the officer. This is really an application of general agency law. Officers who commit torts may be personally liable to the injured party, but the corporation may also be liable for torts committed by the officer during the scope of his or her employment under the doctrine of *respondeat superior*. *Respondeat superior* will be applied by the court only if the tort is in "the course and scope" of the employment.

Fiduciary Duties Owed to the Corporation

Directors, officers, and controlling shareholders owe fiduciary duties to the corporation and sometimes to shareholders and creditors. The source of these duties is the fact that directors, officers, and controlling shareholders occupy a position of trust and faith with regard to the corporation and other constituencies. Generally speaking, these obligations fall into three broad categories: the duty of obedience, the duty of diligence (or due care), and the duty of loyalty. These duties may arise from statute but, more often, they issue from case law.

Obedience Directors, officers, controlling shareholders, and other corporate managers must restrict their actions and those of the corporation to lawful pursuits. Any action taken beyond the scope of the corporation's power is an illegal, *ultra vires* act. By definition, violation of a positive rule of law or statute constitutes an illegal act. Any such actions by managers violate the duty of obedience and may subject them to personal liability. (For an example of the statutory coverage on this area, see the Maine statute on *ultra vires* acts, which is located at http://janus.state.me.us/legis/statutes/13-A/title13-Asec203.html.)

NRW CASE 33.2   Management/Finance

AVOIDING LIABILITY

Helen, as you recall, contracted for a unique marketing plan that she fully expected would be successful. Unfortunately, the plan was a disaster, and the firm lost a significant amount of money on the plan. While the firm will weather this financial storm, the setback made Helen consider what might have happened if the firm were publicly owned. She is afraid that if this situation occurred in a publicly held firm, she might have been dismissed and/or held personally liable for the losses. Helen has asked you what liabilities she would have faced if NRW had been publicly owned at the time she made the decision to enter the marketing plan. What will you tell her?

BUSINESS CONSIDERATIONS What must a manager be able to show in order to avoid liability for a decision gone bad? Is this a difficult defense to establish? Why or why not?

ETHICAL CONSIDERATIONS What ethical duties do managers owe to the firm and/or the shareholders? To whom do managers owe the greatest duty?

INTERNATIONAL CONSIDERATIONS Would Helen's liability be any different if the firm were a multinational corporation (MNC)? Would the nation of incorporation influence the potential liability that Helen, or any other officer or director, might face?

Diligence Because corporate managers act on behalf of the corporation, they are obligated to perform their duties with the amount of diligence or due care that a reasonably prudent person would exercise in the conduct of his or her own personal affairs in the same or similar circumstances. You probably notice the familiar ring of this language. We discussed this kind of standard when we addressed negligence (see Chapter 7). Basically, the duty of due care obliges a corporate manager to perform his or her duties in a nonnegligent fashion. Note that the law does not expect a director, officer, or controlling shareholder to be perfect or all-knowing. Honest errors of judgment will not lead to liability for breach of the duty of diligence. If liability were imposed in such situations, who would ever consent to be a director or officer?

Instead, the law excuses the conduct if the manager has made the error in good faith and without clear and gross negligence. This is the *business judgment rule*. A jury must decide whether the manager's decision satisfies the business judgment rule or is grossly negligent and, hence, unacceptable. A manager who is ill-prepared because he or she fails to attend corporate meetings or pays no attention to corporate affairs may incur liability for breach of the duty of diligence. Similarly, failure to fire an obviously unworthy employee, failure to obtain casualty insurance, failure to heed warning signs suggesting illegal conduct (such as embezzlement), or reliance on unreasonable statements by attorneys or accountants may lead to liability.

Nonetheless, the manager will incur liability only for such losses caused by his or her own negligent conduct. Consequently, if a director formally dissents about a matter that is later held to be negligent, that director will avoid liability. If the director does not dissent, it is usually no defense that the director was only a figurehead or served without pay. However, a manager's reasonable reliance on expert reports, such as those by accountants or attorneys, usually exonerates the manager from liability unless violations of securities acts are involved.

The Delaware Supreme Court in the following case considered the interrelationship between the business judgment rule and a charter provision. The charter provision under the Delaware statute allows corporations to provide additional protection for directors.

33.3

EMERALD PARTNERS v. BERLIN
787 A.2d 85, 2001 Del. LEXIS 525 (Del. 2001)

Notice: This opinion has not been released for publication in the permanent law reports. Until released, it is subject to revision or withdrawal.

FACTS Emerald Partners, a New Jersey limited partnership and a shareholder in May Petroleum, Inc., filed this action to stop a merger between May, a Delaware corporation, and 13 Subchapter S corporations owned by Craig Hall, the chairman and chief executive officer of May. Hall originally proposed the merger. At that time he was the holder of 52.4 percent of May's common stock. The board of directors of May consisted of Hall and Berlin, the inside directors, and Florence, Sebastian, and Strauss, the outside directors. (These directors were named as defendants.) The outside directors hired Bear Stearns & Company to act as investment advisor and render a fairness opinion to the board and the stockholders. On the basis of company valuations and the Bear Stearns fairness letter, the transaction contemplated that Hall would receive 27 million May common shares in exchange for the merger of the Hall corporations with May. This would increase Hall's shareholding to 73.5 percent of May's outstanding common stock. May and the Hall corporations entered into a proposed merger agreement on November 30, 1987. On February 16, 1988, May issued a proxy statement to shareholders that described May, the Hall corporations, and the proposed merger terms. The May shareholders approved the merger on March 11, 1988, and the merger was completed on August 15, 1988. Following the consummation of the merger, Emerald Partners continued its class and derivative actions against the merger, resulting in numerous rulings by the Court of Chancery and the Supreme Court.

ISSUE Did the Court of Chancery in its most recent opinion fail to follow the Supreme Court's instruction by not conducting an entire fairness analysis?

HOLDING Yes, the Court of Chancery must decide the issue of entire fairness.

REASONING Excerpts from the opinion of Justice Holland:

When shareholders challenge actions by a board of directors, generally one of three standards of judicial review is applied: the traditional business judgment rule, an intermediate standard of enhanced judicial scrutiny, or the entire fairness analysis. The applicable standard of judicial review often controls the outcome of the litigation on the merits.... The directors of Delaware corporations have a triad of primary fiduciary duties: due care, loyalty, and good faith.... [T]he shareholders of a Delaware corporation are entitled to rely upon their board of directors to discharge each of their three primary fiduciary duties at all time[s]. . . . The purpose of Section 102(b)(7) was to permit shareholders . . . to adopt a provision in the certificate of incorporation to exculpate directors from any personal liability for the payment of monetary damages for breaches of their duty of care, but not for duty of loyalty violations, good faith violations and certain other conduct. Following the enactment of Section 102(b)(7), the shareholders of many Delaware corporations approved charter amendments containing these exculpatory provisions with full knowledge of their import.

The business judgment rule is a presumption that "in making a business decision the directors of a corporation acted on an informed basis, in good faith and in the honest belief that the action taken was in the best interests of the company [and its shareholders]." The business judgment rule operates as a procedural guide for litigants and as a substantive rule of law. "As a procedural guide, the business judgment presumption is a rule of evidence that places the initial burden of proof on the plaintiff." To rebut the . . . [presumption], a shareholder . . . has the burden of proving that the board of directors . . . violated any one of its triad of fiduciary duties: due care, loyalty, or good faith. If a shareholder plaintiff fails to meet this evidentiary burden, the business judgment rule operates to provide substantive protection for the directors and for the decisions that they have made. If the presumption of the business judgment rule is rebutted, however, the burden shifts to the director defendants to prove to the trier of fact that the challenged transaction was "entirely fair" to the shareholder plaintiff.

... [T]his Court held that evidence of how the board of directors discharged all three of its primary fiduciary duties has "probative substantive significance throughout an entire fairness analysis and . . . must permeate that analysis, for two reasons." First, a substantive finding of entire fairness is only possible after examining and balancing the nature of the duty or duties that the board breached in a contextual comparison to how the board otherwise properly discharged its fiduciary responsibilities. Second, the determination that a board has failed to satisfy the entire fairness standard will constitute the basis for a finding of substantive liability.

... [T]he circumstances . . . implicate the entire fairness standard. Hall, as Chairman and Chief Executive Officer of both May and the Hall corporations and sole owner of the Hall corporations, "clearly stood on both sides of the transaction." . . . "[A]t the time the parties entered the proposed merger agreement . . . , Hall owned 52.4% of May common stock" [making him a controlling stockholder] . . . [W]e held that "Emerald Partners has made a sufficient showing through factual allegations that entire fairness should be the standard by which the directors' actions are reviewed.... When the entire fairness standard of review is applicable, . . . judicial analysis must begin with an examination of the process by which the directors discharged their fiduciary responsibilities, notwithstanding the existence of a Section 102(b)(7) charter provision. . . .

> The concept of fairness has two basic aspects: fair dealing and fair price. The former embraces questions of when the transaction was timed, how it was initiated, structured, negotiated, disclosed to the directors, and how the approvals of the directors and the stockholders were obtained. The latter aspect of fairness relates to the economic and financial considerations of the proposed merger, including all relevant factors: assets, market value, earnings, future prospects, and any other elements that affect the intrinsic or inherent value of a company's stock. However, the test for fairness is not a bifurcated one as between fair dealing and price. All aspects of the issue must be examined as a whole since the question is one of entire fairness.

... Upon remand, the Court of Chancery must analyze the factual circumstances, apply a disciplined balancing test to its findings on the issue of fair dealing and fair price, and articulate the basis upon which it decides the ultimate question of entire fairness. If the Court of Chancery determines that the transaction was entirely fair, the director defendants have no liability for monetary damages. The Court of Chancery should address the Section 102(b)(7) charter provision only if it makes a determination that the challenged transaction was not entirely fair. The director defendants' Section 102(b)(7) request for exculpation must then be examined in the context of the completed judicial analysis that resulted in a finding of unfairness. The director defendants can avoid personal liability for paying monetary damages only if they have established that their failure to withstand an entire fairness analysis is exclusively attributable to a violation of the duty of care. . . .

BUSINESS CONSIDERATIONS In this case what could the Board of Directors do to reduce the chance of litigation on its decision?

ETHICAL CONSIDERATIONS Was it ethical for Hall to propose a merger of his Subchapter S corporations with May Petroleum? What is Hall's ethical perspective? Why?

Loyalty Because directors, officers, and controlling shareholders enjoy positions of trust with the corporation, they must act in good faith and with loyalty toward the corporation and its shareholders. The undivided loyalty expected of fiduciaries means that managers must place the interests of the corporation above their own personal interests. Sometimes these corporate interests and personal interests collide, and it becomes necessary to resort to applicable statutes and case law. Notice that there is such a collision between Hall and May Petroleum in the prior case. Usually such collisions involve (1) corporate opportunities or (2) conflicts of interest.

The *corporate opportunity doctrine* forbids directors, officers, and controlling shareholders from diverting to themselves business deals or potential deals that in fairness or in justice belong to the corporation. Personal gains at the expense of the corporation represent a breach of the managers' fiduciary duties. A corporate opportunity is commonly found (1) if the manager discovers the opportunity in his or her capacity as director, and (2) it is reasonably foreseeable that the corporation will be interested in the opportunity because it relates closely to the corporation's line of business. Notice how the court addressed business opportunities in Case 33.2, *Anest v. Audino*. Then consider this example:

Juanita is a director in a real estate development corporation (Coast-to-Coast Properties, Inc.) and Joel offers to sell property to Juanita because he knows she is a director of Coast-to-Coast Properties, Inc., Juanita should not buy the property for herself. To do so will violate her duty of loyalty. If the corporation might reasonably be interested in the land for its corporate development program, Juanita must disclose this opportunity to the corporation. Once she has given the corporation this right of first refusal, Juanita ordinarily can purchase the property in her own right, but only after the corporation refuses the opportunity or is financially unable to implement the purchase.

If Juanita breaches the duty of loyalty and purchases the land for herself, corporate remedies will include damages (the profits Juanita makes as a result of the sale) or the imposition of a constructive trust. (A *constructive trust* is a trust imposed by law to prevent the unjust enrichment of the person in possession of the property, the purported owner). A court will treat Juanita as a trustee who is holding the property for the benefit of the corporation. A court then can force Juanita to convey the property to Coast-to-Coast Properties, Inc. and to pay Coast-to-Coast any profits she realized on the transaction.

The most common example of a possible conflict of interest occurs when a director, officer, or controlling shareholder personally contracts with the corporation. *Emerald Partners v. Berlin*, Case 33.3, discusses a conflict of interest. To continue with the previous example:

Juanita, a director of Coast-to-Coast Properties, Inc., is willing to sell a piece of her own property to the corporation. Because of her personal interests, Juanita will undoubtedly hope to make as much money as possible on the transaction. Yet her position as a director of Coast-to-Coast Properties, Inc. obligates her to accept as low a price as possible in order to benefit the company. Juanita obviously faces a difficult dilemma. Most states will allow the transaction (1) if Juanita makes a full disclosure of her interest to the board of directors of Coast-

---

NRW CASE 33.3 **Finance**

SUBCHAPTER S CORPORATIONS

Mai, Carlos, and Helen have decided either to incorporate NRW as a Subchapter S corporation or to remain a general partnership. They are concerned, however, about the need to satisfy several of the more burdensome and/or time-consuming aspects of corporate existence. They need to know what requirements they will face as a Subchapter S corporation in such matters as annual meetings, distribution of authority, tax returns, and rights of shareholders. They also need to know how these requirements might vary if they were just to remain a partnership. What advice will you give them?

BUSINESS CONSIDERATIONS What business criteria are important in making the decision to adopt any particular business form? What personal factors should a businessperson consider?

ETHICAL CONSIDERATIONS Will the businesspeople have different ethical duties if they operate the business as a partnership as compared to a corporation? Why or why not?

INTERNATIONAL CONSIDERATIONS Is a Subchapter S corporation permitted to invest in foreign countries? Are foreign nationals permitted to own stock in a Subchapter S corporation?

to-Coast before the board begins its deliberations on the proposed contract, and (2) if the resultant contract is fair and reasonable to the corporation. If Juanita does not fully disclose her interest or if the terms of the contract are unfair or unreasonable, however, the contract will be voidable by the corporation.

An additional concern in these situations stems from whether Juanita (who is called an interested director) should be allowed to vote on the contract. At common law, Juanita could not vote—or even be counted toward the quorum—at the meeting where the matter was to be discussed. Although modern statutes (and articles or bylaws) vary, in general, Juanita can vote and be counted toward the quorum if, as noted earlier, she discloses her interest and the resultant contract is fair to the corporation.

A recent development in the conflict of interest area occurs when directors and officers trade in corporate stock. Although generally they are selling the stock on the open market, they may be tempted to postpone announcements or to "camouflage" transactions on the balance sheets in order to dispose of their shares first. These issues will be discussed in greater detail in Chapter 36.

As previously discussed, the duty of loyalty also prohibits directors, officers, or controlling shareholders from prejudicing minority shareholders' rights. This includes freezing out minority shareholders through such actions as forcing dissolution of the corporation or modifying the distribution of assets on liquidation.

In the context of corporate takeovers, allegations of breach of fiduciary duties commonly arise. As the sophistication of both the "raider" and the target corporation has increased, directors of the target have responded creatively to initiate a host of defensive moves meant to blunt the would-be acquiring firm's desire for the target corporation. This has led to the development of thrusts and countermeasures such as greenmail and poison pills. (*Greenmail* is the process by which a firm threatens a corporate takeover by buying a significant portion of a corporation's stock and then selling it back to the corporation at a premium when the corporation's directors and executives, fearing for their positions, agree to buy the firm out. A *poison pill* is any strategy adopted by the directors of a target firm in order to decrease their firm's attractiveness to an acquiring firm during an attempted hostile takeover.) The critical issue remains whether the law will approve of these deterrent efforts.

Summary

Each partner has certain rights in the business by virtue of his or her status as a general partner. These rights may be limited or defined by the agreement. If no agreement exists, each partner has an equal voice in management, a right to an equal share of profits or losses, equal access to books and records of the enterprise, and an equal right to use partnership property for partnership purposes.

Each general partner is an agent for every other partner and is a principal of every other partner. As a result, all the rules of agency apply. Each partner is a fiduciary of the other partners. When a partner deals with some third party, the firm is bound by the conduct if it was apparently or actually authorized. Partners are jointly and severally liable for the contracts of the partnership under RUPA. However, RUPA generally requires the firm's creditor to exhaust the partnership assets before going after the partners' individual assets. Agency principles also apply to the torts of a partner. If the tort is in the course and scope of employment, the partners are jointly and severally liable. RUPA again uses the same definition of joint and several liability.

Limited partners are more like investors. They are not automatically entitled to access all the books and records. They do not have the right to manage the firm.

Limited liability companies (LLCs) are now authorized in all states. Courts and legislatures are wrestling with the various issues that arise with LLCs. Many concepts in corporate law are also being applied to LLCs.

Ownership of corporate shares carries with it certain rights. The rights shareholders enjoy may vary depending on the type of stock involved. Ownership of common stock permits the shareholder to receive dividends (without priority) and to vote on corporate issues. In contrast, ownership of preferred stock confers priority as to dividends, voting, and/or liquidation rights. In addition, preferred stock may have participation rights, conversion rights, and/or redemption rights.

Shareholders' meetings provide the vehicle by which both common and preferred stockholders exercise their most significant control over the corporation. Corporate bylaws usually require an annual meeting (primarily for election of directors) and may authorize special meetings. Such meetings ordinarily cannot occur without prior notice and a quorum. One of the shareholders' foremost powers involves the election and removal of directors. Shareholders have inherent power to remove a director for cause and also may have power to remove a director without cause. They may also amend or repeal the bylaws.

Shareholders can cast their votes either in person or by proxy. For most corporate matters, straight voting is used. However, for the election of directors, many state statutes either permit or require cumulative voting. Cumulative voting protects the interests of minority shareholders but may be countered by such strategies as staggered terms for directors. Other devices used to consolidate voting power include voting trusts and pooling arrangements. These devices are especially useful in close corporations.

Shareholders' rights to inspect corporate records arise from both common law doctrines and express statutory provisions. Ordinarily, if a shareholder can demonstrate a proper purpose for requesting access to the records, the shareholder will be able to examine certain corporate documents.

Shareholders may be liable to the corporation or creditors for watered stock, and a subscriber may be liable to the corporation or to creditors if the subscriber breaches a stock subscription. Declaration and distribution of illegal dividends may subject both directors and shareholders to personal liability. Controlling shareholders also may incur liability if the purpose of the corporation's dissolution is to freeze out minority stockholders and to strip these stockholders of rights or profits they would otherwise enjoy.

The right to manage the corporation falls squarely on the board of directors. Shareholders cannot compel directors to take any action, because the directors are not the agents of the shareholders but, rather, owe loyalty *primarily* to the corporation. The modern trend is to lower the number of directors and to lessen the traditionally stringent rules concerning directors' qualifications.

Most statutes authorize the board of directors to delegate managerial authority to officers and executive committees. Broad delegations of authority to persons outside the directorial ranks are usually invalid.

Directors may or may not receive compensation from the corporation. The directors normally determine officers' compensation. Such compensation packages are usually legal if reasonable in amount. Otherwise, a shareholder can attack the compensation as a waste of corporate assets.

Performance of directorial duties may lead to personal liability for directors. Occasionally, the corporation will indemnify the directors for liabilities accruing from their corporate positions. Directors have the right to declare dividends, enter into agreements, and inspect corporate records.

The board of directors ordinarily appoints the officers, who serve at the will of the directors. Officers are agents of the corporation and, thus, must live up to the fiduciary duties placed on agents.

Directors, officers, and controlling shareholders owe fiduciary duties to the corporation. Broadly speaking, these duties fall into three categories: the duty of obedience, the duty of diligence (or due care), and the duty of loyalty. The duty of obedience forbids *ultra vires* acts. The business judgment rule constitutes a defense to liability for violation of the duty of diligence. Under this rule, the manager will not be liable if he or she makes an erroneous decision in good faith and without clear and gross negligence. The duty of loyalty, among other things, precludes directors, officers, and controlling shareholders from usurping corporate opportunities or prejudicing the corporation because of undisclosed conflicts of interest.

Discussion Questions

1. Tim and Ed are partners. Tim, however, is tired of the business and sells it to Eugenia. Ed objects to the sale and sues to have it declared void. Eugenia claims Tim has the apparent authority to sell. How should the court rule, and why?

2. Manpal and Barbara are partners. Barbara calls a customer and says the firm will not be able to deliver certain goods on time. The customer immediately sues for anticipatory breach. Manpal objects to the suit, saying the customer has no grounds to expect a breach. Do you agree? Explain.

3. April, Jim, and Dan are partners in a retail business. Dan borrows $10,000 from the bank to "buy more goods." The loan is made in the partnership name. Dan, however, takes the money to Las Vegas and loses it all at the roulette table. If the bank sues April and Jim on the loan, what should be the result? Explain. Would the results be the same under the UPA and the RUPA? Why?

4. Define the following in the context of shareholders' meetings: (a) proxies, (b) straight voting, (c) cumulative voting, (d) voting trusts, and (e) pooling agreements.

5. Explain how a shareholder secures the right to inspect corporate documents.

6. How can liability arise for watered stock, stock subscriptions, illegal dividends, and dissolution?

7. What are the limitations on directors' delegations of authority to officers and corporate committees?

8. Briefly enumerate the rights and liabilities of directors. How do officers' rights and liabilities differ from those of directors?

9. In what ways can corporate managers prevent charges of conflicts of interest from being levied against them?

10. Assume NRW has decided to incorporate. What should they consider in choosing members for the board of directors? Why are these factors important?

Case Problems and Writing Assignments

1. The Red Hawk partnership, consisting of 20 (1 deceased) limited partners and one corporate general partner, G&A, was formed in 1986. Pursuant to their partnership agreement, the Partners contributed capital which ultimately they allocated to two distinct partnership projects, Timber Knolls and Chestnut Woods. In 1987, Red Hawk and Cedar Ridge entered into a joint venture agreement forming the Chestnut Woods Partnership, with both Red Hawk and Cedar Ridge as general partners. Under the joint venture agreement, Red Hawk would provide the capital funds for the project and Cedar Ridge would provide the general management. Cedar Ridge agreed to act as both the managing partner and the general contractor of the project. Cedar Ridge had the right to incur liabilities on behalf of the partnership, borrow money in the name of the partnership, and incur reasonable and legitimate expenses related to Chestnut Woods. Red Hawk and Cedar Ridge entered into a second and distinct joint venture agreement to form the Timber Knolls partnership. Red Hawk contributed $2.3 million and Cedar Ridge again agreed to act as both the managing partner and the general contractor. The Timber Knolls project never commenced operations. The Red Hawk Partners entered into an agreement with Cedar Ridge requiring the latter to return Red Hawk's capital contribution. This money was returned to the limited partners.

   Cedar Ridge, as general contractor for Chestnut Woods, entered into a written subcontract with Henkels & McCoy, Inc. (Henkels), to have Henkels furnish the labor, materials, and equipment for the installation of the storm and sanitary sewer systems for the project. Cedar Ridge agreed to pay Henkels a fixed price of $300,270 under the contract. Henkels completed the installation of the storm and sewer systems but Chestnut Woods defaulted in making the payments due under the contract. Henkels filed a lawsuit against Cedar Ridge and Red Hawk, followed by a lawsuit against G&A. In both suits, Henkels obtained a judgment that was not paid. Henkels brought suit against the limited partners of Red Hawk. Are the limited partners obligated to return capital contributions distributed to them in violation of their partnership agreement? [See *Henkels & McCoy, Inc. v. Adochio*, 138 F.3d 491, 1998 U.S. App. LEXIS 4101 (3rd Cir. 1998).]

2. Southwest Breeders, Inc., an Oklahoma corporation, had offered to sell shares of its stock to Jack Agosta. At the time, Southwest Breeders' articles of incorporation allowed the corporation, through its officers and directors, to issue no more than 50,000 shares of its stock at $1 per share. On March 31, 1986, Agosta purchased 15,000 shares of the stock. Agosta later discovered that the officers and directors had, on December 27, 1985, issued to themselves 1,370,000 shares at below-par value, clearly in excess of the amount allowed by the articles of incorporation. Southwest Breeders subsequently filed an amendment of its articles of incorporation with the secretary of state that authorized it to increase the number of shares of its stock from 50,000 to 50,000,000. Agosta filed suit to rescind his contract, seeking $6,000 in damages for his purchase of the overissued stock. Agosta then filed a motion for summary judgment, which the trial court granted on the ground that the sale of the overissued stock to Agosta constituted a sale of nonexistent stock for which the officers and directors remained personally liable. On appeal, Southwest Breeders alleged that the trial court had erred in characterizing the sale of stock to Agosta as unauthorized and, therefore, void. How should the appellate court rule? [See *Agosta v. Southwest Breeders, Inc.*, 810 P.2d 377 (Okla. App. 1991).]

3. Charles Zwick served as Southeast Banking Corporation's chairman and chief executive officer. He was ousted from his $500,000-a-year job in January 1991 and he signed a severance agreement for $1.25 million, consisting of monthly payments of $41,667 spread over two and a half years. Although once the leading corporate lender in Florida, Southeast's banks were failing. Due to pressure from regulatory entities, such as the Comptroller of the Currency, and from shareholders, Southeast stopped paying Zwick the agreed-upon sum after only a few months. Zwick then sued Southeast for breach of contract. The Comptroller of the Currency argued that regulators acted within their lawful powers by cracking down on golden parachutes extended to departing executives at failing institutions. Zwick's attorney, however, maintained that regulators, in these circumstances, unlawfully interfered with valid and legal contracts when they brought pressure to bear on Southeast to cease payments under the severance arrangement. Why might a business decide to provide golden parachutes to its key executives? How does such a decision affect the duty of the board of directors to its other constituents? [See Joann S. Lublin, "Firms Rethink Lucrative Severance Pacts for Top Executives as Criticism Swells," *Wall Street Journal*, November 11, 1991, p. B1.]

4. Thomas Scanlon had been employed by Steel Suppliers, Inc., a company engaged in warehousing and distributing structural steel, for 30 years. He had served as president and a director. On November 21, 1984, Steelvest, Inc., a corporation owned by William Lucas, purchased the assets of Steel Suppliers for approximately $5 million. After this purchase, Steelvest continued Steel Suppliers as a separate, unincorporated division under the same name. At Lucas's request, Scanlon agreed to stay on as president and general manager of Steel Suppliers. He also subsequently became a director of Steelvest and a member of its executive committee. Scanlon's employment with Steel Suppliers continued for 11 months after the purchase by Steelvest. During these 11 months, Scanlon began to formulate a plan to start and incorporate his own steel business, which would compete directly with Steelvest. Toward this end, he sought the advice of counsel, contacted potential investors, and sought financing. He disclosed none of these activities to any representative of Steelvest. Furthermore, he recruited two CEOs of major Steelvest clients to invest in his new company. Scanlon resigned

from his employment with Steel Suppliers and Steelvest on October 15, 1985. One day prior to this, on October 14, Scanlon had completed most of the necessary arrangements for setting up his new business, including the signing of documents for the purchase of property to be used as the site for the business. Immediately after Scanlon's resignation from Steelvest, he, along with the other investors, incorporated Scansteel Service Center, Inc., which began actual operations soon thereafter. Nine office and supervisory employees of Steelvest resigned to take employment with Scansteel. On June 2, 1986, Steelvest instituted an action against Scansteel and Scanlon, alleging a breach of fiduciary duties by Scanlon and a conspiracy on the part of the investors and the bank that had provided the financing for the formation of Scansteel. Did Scanlon breach his fiduciary duties to Steelvest by planning and organizing a directly competitive business? [See *Steelvest, Inc. v. Scansteel Service Center, Inc.*, 807 S.W.2d 476 (Ky. 1991).]

5. BUSINESS APPLICATION CASE On June 7, 1996, General Motors Corporation (GM), a Delaware corporation, effected a split-off of its wholly owned subsidiary, Electronic Data Systems Holding Corporation (EDS). The terms of the transaction provided for (1) an exchange of GM Class E shares for EDS shares on a one-to-one basis; (2) new information technology service agreements between GM and EDS; and (3) a $500 million lump sum cash transfer payment from EDS to GM. Before the split-off, GM had three classes of common stock: GM 1-2/3 common stock, GM Class E common stock, and GM Class H common stock. The latter two classes of stock, so-called tracking stocks, derived their value from the GM operations to which they were tied. While dividends payable to holders of GM 1-2/3 common stock were based on GM's total income, dividends payable to holders of Class E common stock were tied to EDS's income, and dividends payable to holders of Class H common stock were based upon the income of GM's wholly owned subsidiary, GM Hughes Electronics Corp. The certificate of incorporation and bylaws provided a formula to ensure a proper accounting of earnings attributable to each stock.

On August 7, 1995, GM announced that it planned to pursue a split-off of EDS to holders of GM Class E common stock. GM determined that it would only consummate a transaction that was tax-free and that would not trigger Class E shareholders' right to redeem their shares. Under GM bylaws, a subcommittee of GM directors, the Capital Stock Committee (or the Committee) was charged with charting a course for the split-off. The purported aim of the Committee was to structure a process that would protect the interests of all of GM's various classes of shareholders. The Committee put together two management teams, one consisting of GM officers and the other consisting of EDS officers. The teams were charged with negotiating the terms and conditions of the split-off. The GM team was authorized to use the assistance of GM's treasurer's office staff and legal staff, and also engaged outside counsel and a financial advisor. The EDS team was responsible for negotiating the terms of the transaction from the perspective of the

holders of GM Class E common stock. The EDS team was authorized to use its own financial and legal staffs, and also engaged outside counsel and financial advisors. In connection with the split-off, the financial advisors were to receive a fee in the total amount of $7.5 million, $6.5 million of which was contingent upon consummation of the split-off. Negotiations began on various issues. The Capital Stock Committee suggested that the GM board promulgate a series of directives.

On March 22, 1996, the GM and EDS teams recommended to the Capital Stock Committee the terms of the split-off. On March 31, 1996, the GM board approved the split-off, subject to the approval of a majority of the holders of each of (1) the GM 1-2/3 common stock, voting separately as a class; (2) the GM Class E common stock, voting separately as a class; and (3) all classes of GM common stock, voting together. The GM board agreed to recommend to the GM shareholders the terms of the split-off. The shareholders approved the split-off. Did the board violate the business judgment rule? Was the shareholder vote coerced or based on false statements? [See *Solomon v. Armstrong*, 1999 Del. Ch. LEXIS 62 (Del. Ch. New Castle 1999).]

6. ETHICAL APPLICATION CASE William Granewich was a shareholder and director in a closely held corporation called Founders Funding Group, Inc. (FFG). Granewich, Ben Harding, and Jeannie Alexander-Hergert each owned one-third of the stock. They were all directors, officers, and employees of FFG. They agreed to accept inadequate compensation from the corporation, with the expectation that they would be well compensated in the future. They were each going to receive the same amount of compensation. They also agreed that they would be "employed continually and perpetually by the corporation." The business became quite successful. On May 5, 1993, Harding and Alexander-Hergert met with Granewich and told him that he was removed as a director, officer, and employee effective immediately. Harding and Alexander-Hergert, acting on behalf of the corporation, hired attorney Michael Farrell to provide legal services to the corporation. Granewich claimed that Farrell assisted the other shareholders in amending the corporate bylaws, removing Granewich as director, and taking action to dilute the value of Granewich's interest in the corporation. Granewich sued Farrell. Was Farrell liable to Granewich? What ethical issues are raised? [See *Granewich v. Harding*, 985 P.2d 788, 1999 Ore. LEXIS 383 (Sup. Ct. Ore. 1999).]

7. CRITICAL THINKING CASE Archer Daniels Midland (ADM) is an agribusiness giant and global producer of goods such as corn syrup, vegetable oil, and ethanol. Its slogan is "supermarket to the world." ADM was besieged by a group of irate institutional shareholders at its annual stockholders' meeting in October 1996. *Institutional shareholders* purchase shares for an institution, such as a pension fund, trust fund, mutual fund, insurance company, or bank. Just prior to the meeting, ADM had pled guilty to federal charges that it had fixed prices of lysine and citric acid. It had agreed to pay a $100 million criminal fine. In addition, it owed $90 million in related civil settle-

ments. Many of the institutional shareholders blamed the company's troubles on the unusually close relationship between ADM's management and its board of directors. Of the 17-person board of directors, 10 were current or former executives of ADM or relatives of Dwayne Andreas, the CEO. A number of the other directors were loyal to Andreas. The shareholders felt that the board failed to adequately oversee the company's operations due to its lack of independence. The institutional shareholders proposed a number of changes including that a majority of the directors should be outsiders; Andreas should resign; and there should be secret shareholder voting. The proposals failed. What changes should ADM make to its organizational structure? Why? [See Kurt Eichenwald, "The Tale of the Secret Tapes," *New York Times*, November 16, 1997, pp. B1 and B10; Nancy Millman, "ADM's New CEO: Allen Andreas," *Chicago Tribune*, April 18, 1997, p. 1; Richard A. Melcher, Greg Burns, and Douglas Harbrecht, "It Isn't Dwayne's World Anymore," *Business Week*, November 18, 1996, p. 82; Sharon Walsh, "Andreas Creates Executive 'Team'," *Washington Post*, November 1, 1996, p. F3; and Kurt Eichenwald, "Archer Daniels Midland Agrees to Big Fine for Price Fixing," *New York Times*, October 15, 1996, pp. A1, C3.][39]

8. YOU BE THE JUDGE Adelphia Communications Corporation was the cable television company founded by John Rigas. Five former executives—John Rigas (chief executive officer), his sons, Timothy Rigas (chief financial officer) and Michael Rigas (vice-president for operations), Michael Mulchey (former director of internal reporting), and James Brown (vice-president for finance)—were indicted on September 23, 2002.

U.S. authorities accused the Rigases of hiding debt and looting the company. The criminal indictment charged 24 counts of conspiracy and fraud, including that the Rigases: (1) used company money to cover $250 million in personal stock purchases and build a golf course, and (2) failed to disclose $2.3 billion in loans to the family. Authorities alleged that the Rigases made phony bookkeeping entries to make it appear that the company's debt was declining and its operating performance was improving. Shareholders, Adelphia, and the U.S. Securities and Exchange Commission (SEC) have filed more than 40 lawsuits against the Rigases. Federal prosecutors wanted the Rigases to forfeit $2.5 billion. The independent directors removed Rigas from control of Adelphia in May 2002; the company filed for Chapter 11 bankruptcy in June. In July 2002, the SEC filed a civil fraud suit accusing the Rigases of "rampant self-dealing."

Originally Brown entered a plea of innocent. However as part of a plea bargain, on November 14, 2002, Brown pleaded guilty to conspiracy to commit fraud, securities fraud, and bank fraud. He faced a maximum of 45 years in prison under the plea. Brown admitted to the court that he conspired with John, Timothy, and Michael Rigas and Michael Mulchey to cheat investors. He said he overstated earnings, lied to Moody's Investor Service and several banks, and issued misleading statistics about the number of subscribers the cable company had. Presumably, Brown will aid the investigators by telling them how the financial statements were manipulated. Brown's testimony could be particularly damaging to Timothy Rigas, who was the chief financial officer and Brown's supervisor.

There is also a legal battle over the family's money. In August 2002, John Rigas was about to sell two properties, when the bankruptcy court blocked the sales of the parcels. The court can implement a freeze on the family assets. A freeze of assets is common in cases like this. Partial freezes are also common. The court will have to decide "How to balance the family's right to pay for their defense with creditors' desire to safeguard money that they contend was stolen."

The family would like to have the case moved to district court. The stated reason is that the bankruptcy court lacks the necessary expertise to handle the legal issues under the Racketeer Influenced and Corrupt Organizations Act (RICO) and the federal securities laws. However, bankruptcy courts also may be more protective of unpaid creditors than the district court. There is also a question of whether the bankruptcy filing under Chapter 11 will prevent the five defendants from receiving payments under the director and officer liability policies. The bankruptcy judge hearing the case said that the former Adelphia executives can request $300,000 each from Adelphia D and O liability insurance policies to cover legal bills and defend fraud suits by investors. According to the ruling by Judge Robert E. Gerber, the men could ask the 3 insurers to advance legal fees and other costs of their defense. The judge also stated that if the insurance companies deny coverage, the men may not sue to demand payments until after the criminal cases are over. Assume that the judge's ruling has been appealed to *your* court. How will *you* decide? [See "Adelphia's Rigases Plead Not Guilty," digitalMass at Boston.com, October 3, 2002, http://digitalmass.boston.com/news/2002/10/03/adelphia.html; and "Former Adelphia VP Pleads Guilty to Fraud Charges," CNN, November 14, 2002, http://www.cnn.com/2002/LAW/11/14/adelphia.plea/index.html.]

Notes

1. Uniform Partnership Act (UPA) refers to the 1914 act drafted by the National Conference of Commissioners on Uniform State Laws (NCCUSL). The following 18 states have adopted UPA (1914): Georgia, Indiana, Kentucky, Maine, Massachusetts, Michigan, Mississippi, Missouri, Nevada, New Hampshire, New York, North Carolina, Ohio, Pennsylvania, Rhode Island, South Carolina, Utah, and Wisconsin. E-mail from Katie Robinson, Communications Officer, NCCUSL, September 16, 2002.

2. The following states have adopted the 1994 version of RUPA, without the 1997 amendments: Connecticut, West Virginia, and Wyoming. The 1997 amendments provide for limited liability partnerships. The following jurisdictions have adopted RUPA with the

1997 amendments: Alabama, Alaska, Arizona, Arkansas, California, Colorado, Delaware, District of Columbia, Florida, Hawaii, Idaho, Illinois, Iowa, Kansas, Maryland, Minnesota, Montana, Nebraska, New Jersey, New Mexico, North Dakota, Oklahoma, Oregon, Puerto Rico, South Dakota, Tennessee, Texas, U.S. Virgin Islands, Vermont, Virginia, and Washington. In 2002 it was introduced in the Rhode Island legislature. Four of these—Arizona, California, Puerto Rico, and Virginia—have enacted a Limited Liability Partnership Equivalent. "A Few Facts about the Uniform Partnership Act (1994)(1997)," NCCUSL Web site, (accessed 9/4/02), http://www.nccusl.org/nccusl/uniformact_factsheets/uniformacts-fs-upa9497.asp.

3. Uniform Partnership Act § 18(h).

4. Revised Uniform Partnership Act § 303.

5. "Uniform Partnership Act (1994)," NCCUSL Web site (accessed 9/4/2002), http://www.nccusl.org/nccusl/uniformact_summaries/uniformacts-s-upa1994.asp (accessed 9/4/2002).

6. Uniform Partnership Act § 18(a), (b), and (c).

7. Ibid., § 18(f).

8. Ibid., §§ 19 and 20.

9. Ibid., § 25.

10. Revised Uniform Partnership Act § 201.

11. Revised Uniform Partnership Act § 203.

12. See note 5.

13. Uniform Partnership Act § 22.

14. Ibid., § 21.

15. Ibid., § 12.

16. Ibid., § 13.

17. Revised Uniform Partnership Act §§ 306 and 307.

18. Uniform Partnership Act § 14.

19. Ibid., § 28.

20. Revised Uniform Partnership Act § 307(d).

21. Uniform Partnership Act § 21.

22. See note 2, "A Few Facts."

23. Revised Uniform Partnership Act §§ 306 and 307.

24. Ibid.

25. The jurisdictions that have adopted the Uniform Limited Liability Company Act are Alabama, Hawaii, Illinois, Montana, South Carolina, South Dakota, U.S. Virgin Islands, Vermont, and West Virginia. See note 2, "A Few Facts."

26. *Ault v. Brady*, 2002 U.S. App. LEXIS 11684 (8th Cir. 2002), Unpublished Opinion, footnote 6.

27. Ark. Code Ann. § 4-32-402(1) (Repl. 2001).

28. *Robinson v. Geo Licensing Company, L.L.C.*, 173 F. Supp. 2d 419, at 427, 2001 U.S. Dist. LEXIS 18867 (Md. 2001).

29. E-mail from Katie Robinson, Communications Officer, NCCUSL, September 9, 2002.

30. "New Uniform Securities Act Approved, Law Governing Regulation of Securities by States Modernized," NCCUSL Web site, Press Release, Section: Newsroom, August 5, 2002 http://www.nccusl.org/nccusl/pressreleases/pr080502_SEC.asp (accessed 9/4/02).

31. "The Art of the Market" (book excerpt), *Fortune*, September 27, 1999, pp. 230–239. Book excerpt from Bob Tamarkin and Les Krantz, with commentary by George LeBarre, *The Art of the Market* (New York: Stewart Tabori & Chang, 1999).

32. Del. Code Ann. § 232 (2000) provides that stockholders *may* consent to notice by "electronic transmission." New York Bus. Corp. Law § 605 (1988) and Conn. Gen. Stat. Ann. § 33-603 (c) (2) (2000) authorize electronic notice of shareholders' meetings. Delaware enacted a revision to its corporate code effective 1 July 2000. It permits Delaware corporations to use electronic transmissions in additional aspects of corporate affairs. It includes a definition of "electronic transmission." The purpose of the amendments are to (1) enable corporations to use them but not require their use; (2) operate fairly and maintain the balance of powers and responsibilities among corporate constituents, (3) anticipate technological advances; (4) be flexible; and (5) permit economic efficiency and cost savings. Prior to passage of the statute, only electronic proxies by shareholders were permitted. Delaware permits stockholders to consent to notice by "electronic transmission" under Section 232 of the corporate code. The Securities and Exchange Commission (SEC) has also issued two releases providing for the use of electronic media in a limited number of situations. James L. Holzman and Thomas A. Mullen, "A New Technology Frontier for Delaware Corporations," 4 Del. L. Rev. 55 (2001).

33. Del. Code Ann. § 211. Holzman and Mullen, note 32.

34. Ibid.

35. A common reason for not participating is because the meeting is far from the shareholder's home.

36. Del. Code Ann. § 212 (c)(2). Electronic proxies were permitted prior to the 2000 revisions. Holzman and Mullen, note 32.

37. Del. Code Ann. § 141 (i). Holzman and Mullen, note 32.

38. Cal. Corp. Code § 307. This provision in the California Code was enacted on a trial basis until January 2003. Holzman and Mullen, note 32.

39. ADM did eventually change its governance process. Andreas would share power as part of a four-person executive committee. Four managers stepped down from the board, several others were replaced, and two executives implicated in the price-fixing scandal left the company, including Andreas's son and heir apparent. In April 1997, Andreas, age 79, finally retired as CEO; he retained the title of chairman of the board. He was succeeded by his nephew, G. Allen Andreas, as CEO.

For more information about the price-fixing scandal, see Ronald Henkoff, "Behind the ADM Scandal: Betrayal," *Fortune*, February 3, 1997, pp. 82–87, and Mark Whitacre's interview with Ronald Henkoff, "I Thought I Was Going to Be a Hero," *Fortune*, February 3, 1997, pp. 87–91.

CHAPTER 34

Business Terminations and Other Extraordinary Events

AGENDA

NRW NRW may be a big success in developing and marketing StuffTrakR and InvenTrakR. On the other hand, the enterprise may fail miserably. If the firm is a success, it is likely that a large corporation may wish to acquire NRW. Mai, Carlos, and Helen do not wish to give up ownership of the company at this time, and they would resist any takeover efforts. If the other firm persists in its efforts to acquire NRW, how can our entrepreneurs prevent a takeover? What legal or ethical restrictions may limit NRW's actions? If the enterprise is a failure, Mai, Carlos, and Helen are afraid that they will lose everything they have acquired over the years. How can they protect their assets while providing adequate support to the firm to give it an opportunity to succeed?

These and other questions will arise as you read this chapter. Be prepared! You never know when the firm or one of its members will seek your advice.

Termination of a Franchise

When a franchisee terminates his or her business, the termination must follow the rules discussed in this chapter based on the form of the business. (A *franchisee* has purchased the right to sell goods or services using the name, goodwill, techniques, and/or recipes of the franchisor.) In addition, the termination will be controlled by the franchise contract. The franchise agreement, discussed in detail in Chapter 35, may contain a number of restrictions. It may prohibit the sale or transfer of the franchise to another entity without the permission of the franchisor. Any restrictions on transfer may greatly reduce the value on termination of the franchise and any specialty assets. The assets such as goodwill and brand name may have no value to the franchisee due to these restrictions.

Termination of a Sole Proprietorship

The termination of a sole proprietorship is a relatively simple matter. The owner simply pays the business debts and then the remaining assets belong to him or her. As an alternative, the owner might sell the business to someone else. Care must be used to assure that business liabilities are handled correctly, however. Often, but not always, this is an obligation undertaken by the buyer. The parties should discuss existing liabilities and who will pay them. The U.S. Chamber of Commerce provides news and information to assist small-business owners at http://www.uschamber.org/default.htm.

Termination of a Partnership under UPA

The ending of a partnership is different from what most people expect. The *partnership* may end while the business *enterprise* continues; if so, a dissolution occurs. Or the partnership and the business enterprise may both end. If so, a dissolution and a winding up occur. (A *winding up* consists of paying the accounts and liquidating the assets of a business for the purpose of making distributions and dissolving the concern.) The 'Lectric Law Library's business forms include a variety of partnership and corporation documents. Its Web site is at http://www.lectlaw.com/formb.htm. A dissolution is diagrammed in Exhibit 34.1. Note that a dissolution does not necessarily result in a termination of the business.

Dissolution of a Partnership

Technically, a *dissolution* is "the change in the relation of the partners caused by any partner ceasing to be associated in the carrying on as distinguished from the winding up of the business."[1] This means that any time a partner leaves the business, the partnership is dissolved. The change in the relations of the partners changes the basic structure and nature of the partnership, "dissolving" the former partnership.

The fact that a partner leaves the business does not mean that the *business* must cease to exist. The remaining partners may be able to continue the business, or they may need to terminate the business. Their options depend on the method and manner of dissolution.

The Uniform Partnership Act (UPA) lists several different causes of dissolution.[2] Any of these events will cause a dissolution of the partnership, but they may not require a winding up of the business. We shall examine these causes of dissolution next. Note that references in this chapter to the Uniform Partnership Act (UPA) are to the UPA (1914), which 18 states still follow.[3]

Without Violation of the Agreement

A dissolution may be caused by the terms of the partnership agreement. For example, the time period established in the agreement may expire, or the original purpose of the partnership may be fulfilled. If a partnership was established to operate for two years, and two years have elapsed, the partnership is dissolved. If a partnership was established to sell 100 parcels of land, and all the land has been sold, the partnership is dissolved. Of course, a new agreement may be made to extend the time or to modify the purpose, if the partners so desire.

If the agreement does not specify a particular time period or a particular, limited purpose, a partner may simply decide to quit. Unless the agreement denies this right to withdraw, such a decision operates as a dissolution without violation of the agreement.

All the partners may decide to terminate the partnership. If so, the partnership is dissolved without violating the agreement. This is true even if a definite time period was specified and that time has not yet expired. And it is true *even if* a particular purpose was declared and the purpose has not yet been achieved.

Finally, a partnership is dissolved if any partner is expelled from the partnership by the others; this dissolution does not violate the agreement *provided* that the agree-

---

EXHIBIT 34.1 **Partnership Dissolution under the Uniform Partnership Act (UPA)**

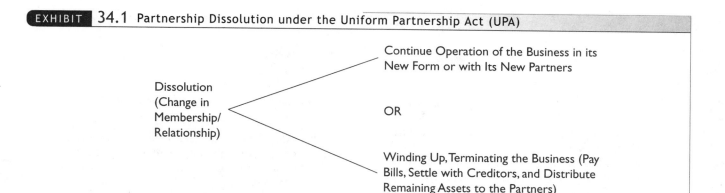

Dissolution (Change in Membership/Relationship)

Continue Operation of the Business in its New Form or with Its New Partners

OR

Winding Up, Terminating the Business (Pay Bills, Settle with Creditors, and Distribute Remaining Assets to the Partners)

---

ment permits the expulsion. Thus, if Xavier, Yvette, and Zara vote to remove Patricio from the firm, and the agreement permits such a vote, the partnership is dissolved without violation of the agreement.

Normally, a dissolution in accord with the agreement will lead to a winding up *unless* the agreement itself provides for a continuation of the business. If the agreement does not specify that a continuation is permitted, the partner who causes the dissolution may demand that a winding up take place. Such a demand must be obeyed, even though it normally will harm the remaining partners who may wish to continue the business. Thus, every partnership agreement should contain some provisions for continuing the business. (Of course, an *expelled* partner cannot demand a winding up of the business if the expulsion was done in good faith by the other partners.)

In Violation of the Agreement

No one can be forced to be a partner against his or her will. Thus, any partner has the *power* to withdraw from any partnership at any time—but a partner does not necessarily have the *right* to withdraw at any time. A withdrawing partner may violate the terms of the partnership agreement by withdrawing. If so, the remaining partners may continue the business if they desire, even though the partnership has been (technically) dissolved. The partner who withdrew in violation of the agreement has no right to demand or require a winding up.

Similarly, the partner who withdraws in violation of the agreement does not have the right to demand that the business be continued. Once a partner withdraws in violation of the agreement, the remaining innocent partners may decide to do whatever they believe is most appropriate; when a partner withdraws in violation of the agreement all of the options concerning the business belong to the remaining partners.

In the case on pages 822–823, the Texas Supreme Court addressed a dissolution issue when it considered whether a law partnership could expel a partner.

By Operation of Law

A partnership may also be dissolved by operation of law, if any one of the following three events occurs:

1. Something happens that makes it unlawful for the business to continue or for the partners to continue the business. (Thus, a law that prohibits anyone from selling elephant tusks will terminate a partnership in the tusk-selling business. And a partnership that loses its import license will be dissolved even though importing itself is still legal.)

2. A partner dies.

3. A partner or the partnership becomes bankrupt.

By Court Order

The final method for dissolving a partnership is by court order. As explained in § 32 of the UPA, a court will order a dissolution only if *asked* to do so. The person who wants to dissolve the partnership must petition the court; the court will not go searching for partnerships that should be dissolved.

Most commonly, the petitioning person is one of the partners or a representative of one of the partners. Even if a petition is filed, dissolution is not automatic. The court must have *grounds* to grant the request. The following grounds will justify a dissolution by court decree:

• Insanity of any partner

• Incapacity, other than insanity, of a partner that prevents that partner from performing the contractual duties called for in the agreement

34.1

BOHATCH v. BUTLER & BINION
977 S.W.2d 543, 1998 Tex. LEXIS 13 (Sup. Ct. 1998)

FACTS Colette Bohatch became an associate in the Washington, D.C., office of Butler & Binion in 1986. John McDonald, the managing partner of the office, and Richard Powers, a partner, were the only other attorneys in the Washington office. The office worked almost exclusively for Pennzoil. Bohatch was made partner in February 1990. She then began receiving internal firm reports showing the number of hours each attorney worked, billed, and collected. From reviewing these reports, Bohatch became concerned that McDonald was overbilling Pennzoil. She discussed the matter with Powers. Together they reviewed and copied portions of McDonald's time diary. Bohatch's review of McDonald's time entries increased her concern. On July 15, 1990, Bohatch met with Louis Paine, the firm's managing partner, to report her concern. Paine said he would investigate. The following day, McDonald met with Bohatch and informed her that Pennzoil was not satisfied with her work and wanted her work to be supervised. Bohatch testified that this was the first time she had ever heard criticism of her work for Pennzoil. The next day, Bohatch repeated her concerns to other members of the firm's management committee. Paine and Burns reviewed the Pennzoil bills and supporting computer printouts and discussed the allegations with Pennzoil in-house counsel John Chapman, the firm's primary contact with Pennzoil. Chapman, who had a long-standing relationship with McDonald, responded that Pennzoil was satisfied that the bills were reasonable.

In August, Paine met with Bohatch and told her that the firm's investigation revealed no basis for her contentions. He added that she should begin looking for other employment, but that the firm would continue to provide her a monthly draw, insurance coverage, office space, and a secretary. After this meeting, Bohatch received no further work assignments from the firm. In January 1991, the firm denied Bohatch a year-end partnership distribution for 1990 and reduced her tentative distribution share for 1991 to zero. In June, the firm paid Bohatch her monthly draw and told her that this draw would be her last. Finally, in August, the firm gave Bohatch until November to vacate her office. By September, Bohatch had found new employment. She filed this suit on October 18, 1991, and the firm voted formally to expel her from the partnership three days later.

ISSUE Can the partnership expel Bohatch for reporting suspected overbilling by another partner? Did the partnership err in the manner that they terminated Bohatch?

HOLDING Yes, a partnership has the right to expel a partner for reporting her suspicions about overbilling. Yes, the partnership violated its agreement in Bohatch's termination.

REASONING Excerpts from the opinion of Justice Craig T. Enoch:

We have long recognized as a matter of common law that "the relationship between . . . partners . . . is fiduciary in character, and imposes upon all the participants the obligation of loyalty to the joint concern and of the utmost good faith, fairness, and honesty in their dealings with each other with respect to matters pertaining to the enterprise." . . . Yet, partners have no obligation to remain partners; "at the heart of the partnership concept is the principle that partners may choose with whom they wish to be associated." The issue presented, one of first impression, is whether the fiduciary relationship between and among partners creates an exception to the at-will nature of partnerships; that is, in this case, whether it gives rise to a duty not to expel a partner who reports suspected overbilling. . . . [N]either statutory nor contract law principles answer the question of whether the firm owed Bohatch a duty not to expel her. The Texas Uniform Partnership Act addresses expulsion of a partner only in the context of dissolution of the partnership. . . . [A]s provided by the partnership agreement, Bohatch's expulsion did not dissolve the partnership. . . . [T]he new Texas Revised Partnership Act does not have retroactive effect and thus does not apply. . . .

[T]he partnership agreement contemplates expulsion of a partner and prescribes procedures to be followed, but it does not specify or limit the grounds for expulsion. . . . Courts in other states have held that a partnership may expel a partner for purely business reasons. . . . [C]ourts recognize that a law firm can expel a partner to protect relationships both within the firm and with clients. . . . [M]any courts have held that a partnership can expel a partner without breaching any duty in order to resolve a "fundamental schism." . . . The fiduciary duty that partners owe one another does not encompass a duty to remain partners . . . Bohatch . . . [asks] this Court to recognize that public policy requires a limited duty to remain partners—i.e., a partnership must retain a whistleblower partner. . . . [She argues] that such an extension of a partner's fiduciary duty is necessary because permitting a law firm to retaliate against a partner who in good faith reports suspected overbilling would discourage compliance with rules of professional conduct and thereby hurt clients. . . . A partnership exists solely because the partners choose to place personal confidence and trust in one another. . . . [When a partner accuses another partner, this] may have a profound effect on the personal confidence and trust essential to the partner relationship. Once such charges are made, partners may find it impossible to continue to work together to their mutual benefit and the benefit of their clients.

We are sensitive to the concern . . . that "retaliation against a partner who tries in good faith to correct or report perceived misconduct virtually assures that others will not take these appropriate steps in the future." . . . [On the other hand,] [t]he threat of tort liability for expulsion would tend to force partners to remain in [an] untenable circumstance—suspicious of and angry with each other—to their own detriment and that of their clients whose matters are neglected by lawyers distracted with intra-firm frictions. . . . We emphasize that our refusal to create an exception to the at-will nature of partnerships in no way obviates the ethical duties of lawyers. Such duties sometimes necessitate difficult decisions, as when a lawyer suspects overbilling by a colleague. The fact that the ethical duty to

report may create an irreparable schism between partners neither excuses failure to report nor transforms expulsion . . . into a tort. We hold that the firm did not owe Bohatch a duty not to expel her for reporting suspected overbilling by another partner.

The court of appeals concluded that the firm breached the partnership agreement by reducing Bohatch's tentative distribution for 1991 to zero without the requisite notice. The firm contests this finding on the ground that the management committee had the right to set tentative and year-end bonuses. However, the partnership agreement guarantees a monthly draw of $7,500 per month regardless of the tentative distribution. . . . [T]he firm's right to reduce the bonus was contingent upon providing proper notice to Bohatch. The firm does not dispute that it did not give Bohatch notice that the firm was reducing her tentative distribution. . . . [The firm breached the partnership agreement.]

BUSINESS CONSIDERATIONS Would a partnership want to encourage the reporting of unethical or illegal practices? Why? What can a partnership do to encourage reporting?

ETHICAL CONSIDERATIONS From the information provided, was Bohatch acting ethically? Why? What is her ethical perspective? Was the firm behaving ethically? Why?

- Misconduct by any partner that makes continued operation of the business difficult

- Intentional or repeated breach of the agreement by a partner, or any behavior that makes the continuation of the business impossible or impractical

- Evidence that the business can be continued only at a loss with no prospect of a profit turnaround in the near future

- Any other circumstances that, in the court's opinion, justify dissolution as the equitable response

Note that insanity does *not* automatically dissolve the partnership; a petition must be filed seeking dissolution. If the remaining partners wish to continue the business with an insane partner, they have the right to do so.

It is also possible that some person may purchase the interest of a partner and then decide to seek a court-ordered dissolution.[4] Such a court order may be granted only if one of two sets of circumstances can be shown:

- The agreement had a specific term or a particular purpose that has been fulfilled or satisfied.

- The partnership was a partnership at will at the time of the purchase. (At will means it has no specific date or circumstance to bring about a dissolution.)

In the following case, the court analyzed when the dissolution occurred under the Pennsylvania UPA. Notice how the court wrestled with the interaction between the state partnership law and federal bankruptcy law.

Termination under RUPA

The Revised Uniform Partnership Act (RUPA) has modified the partnership termination rules due to its adoption of the entity theory.[5] Partnerships under the entity theory are more durable than partnerships based on the aggregate theory.[6] The entity theory provides a conceptual basis for continuing the firm despite a partner's withdrawal or expulsion. An example of this shift in perspective is the addition of sections in RUPA on partnership "mergers" and "conversions." For example, two or more partnerships may merge and form a new partnership. A general partnership can convert to a limited partnership and vice versa.

WOSKOB v. WOSKOB (IN RE WOSKOB)
2002 U.S. App. LEXIS 19751 (3rd Cir. 2002)

FACTS Leah and Victor Woskob formed the Legends Partnership to construct, own, and operate the Legends, an apartment building in State College, Pennsylvania. Leah and Victor were married to each other. Each held a 50 percent interest under the Partnership Agreement. In January 1997, Leah and Victor separated. During the divorce proceedings (which apparently never became final), Victor prevented Leah from receiving any distributions from the partnership. On April 15, 1997, the court awarded Leah the exclusive right to manage and derive income from the Legends. Victor filed a bankruptcy petition under Chapter 11, which he later withdrew. The petition included his 50 percent of the partnership. The partnership tax returns for 1997 and 1998, both signed and filed by Leah, continued to list both Victor and Leah as general partners of the partnership. On January 12, 1999, Victor died in an automobile accident. In his will, he named his four children as beneficiaries of his estate and his parents, Alex and Helen Woskob (the Woskobs), as executors to administer the estate. Within 15 days of Victor's death, Leah notified the Woskobs that she intended to dissolve the partnership and purchase Victor's interest. Under the agreement, Leah had 30 days from the date of an act of dissolution or 90 days from the death of a partner to exercise this option. Based on the written opinion of the partnership's accountant, Leah advised the Woskobs that Victor's interest was worth negative $33,944 and that the estate was not entitled to any payments for his interest. The Woskobs opposed this sale to Leah.

ISSUE Did Leah exercise her option to purchase her late husband's interest in the partnership in a timely manner?

HOLDING Yes, her exercise was timely. The case was remanded to the District Court to determine whether Leah validly exercised her option following Victor's death.

REASONING Excerpts from the opinion of Judge José L. Fuentes:

Because Leah and Victor formed and managed the Legends Partnership in Pennsylvania, we apply the law of Pennsylvania in determining the . . . date of dissolution. The Uniform Partnership Act (UPA), as adopted by Pennsylvania, defines the "dissolution" of a partnership as "the change in the relation of the partners caused by any partner ceasing to be associated in the carrying on, as distinguished from the winding up, of the business."

The timeliness of Leah's attempt to exercise her option . . . depends upon the partnership's date of dissolution. Dissolution can be caused by decree of court or automatically through operation of law. . . . When dissolution occurs through operation of law and without the need for a judicial decree, the date of dissolution is the date of the first effective act of dissolution. . . . When a partnership is dissolved by decree of court, the date of dissolution is ordinarily the date upon which the court decrees the dissolution. . . . [N]o court ever decreed the dissolution of the Legends Partnership. . . . If the partnership was not dissolved before Victor's death, it was certainly dissolved upon his death. . . . The question before us is whether any other events . . . [dissolved] the partnership . . . prior to Victor's death. . . .

[The Pennsylvania UPA] provides that dissolution is caused, "by the expulsion of any partner from the business . . . in accordance with such a[n] [expulsion] power conferred by the agreement. . . ." . . . The full text makes clear that not all partner expulsions are sufficient to cause automatic dissolution through operation of law. Only those expulsions that are in accordance with an expulsion power conferred by the . . . agreement will cause an immediate dissolution. . . . § 8354(a) . . . provides the following general rule:

On application by or for a partner, the court shall decree a dissolution whenever:

(1) A partner has been declared a lunatic in any judicial proceeding or is shown to be of unsound mind.

(2) A partner becomes in any other way incapable of performing his part of the partnership contract.

(3) A partner has been guilty of such conduct as tends to affect prejudicially the carrying on of the business.

(4) A partner willfully or persistently commits a breach of the partnership agreement or otherwise so conducts himself in matters relating to the partnership business that it is not reasonably practicable to carry on the business in partnership with him.

(5) The business of the partnership can only be carried on at a loss.

(6) Other circumstances render a dissolution equitable.

It is not difficult to see how the acts of one or more partners to exclude another partner . . . could serve as grounds for dissolution under the broad language of §§ 8354(a)(4) or (a)(6). Such acts of exclusion by a partner would . . . tend to make it "not reasonably practicable to carry on the business in partnership with him" . . . [and] would constitute a circumstance that "renders a dissolution equitable." The key point . . . is that when such acts of exclusion are not committed "in accordance with [an expulsion] power conferred by the agreement . . . ," they do not result in the instantaneous dissolution of the partnership. They merely serve as grounds by which a court can decree a dissolution. . . . [B]ecause the alleged acts of exclusion . . . by Leah and Victor were not in accordance with an expulsion power explicitly conferred by the Partnership Agreement, they did not cause the dissolution of the partnership. At the very most, such . . . acts could have served as grounds for dissolution if either Leah or Victor had applied for a dissolution by decree of court. . . . Since neither of them did so, the claimed exclusions are irrelevant to the . . . date of dissolution. . . .

This . . . raises the question of whether the bankruptcy of a general partner results in the dissolution of the partnership. . . . Under § 8353 [of the Pennsylvania UPA], the bankruptcy of a partner . . . does . . . cause the automatic dissolution of the partnership. . . . We must also consider, however, the role of federal bankruptcy law and the impact of its interplay with state partnership law. . . . [Section] 365(c)(1) and § 365(e)(2)(A) [of the Bankruptcy Code] are applicable to executory contracts only when the non-debtor party "does not consent to [the] assumption or assignment" at issue. . . . When a partner files for bankruptcy, a co-partner may not want to continue in the partnership with the debtor because, "upon securing bankruptcy-court protection, a general partner who becomes a debtor-in-possession of her personal estate necessarily assumes responsibilities to her creditors that conflict with her responsibilities to her co-partners." Subsections 365(c) and 365(e)(2) will prevent a debtor in bankruptcy from continuing to serve as a partner, however, only when a non-debtor partner does not consent to continue in the partnership with the debtor. . . . [T]here is no evidence . . . that Leah objected to having Victor remain as her general partner after he had filed his bankruptcy petition. In fact, the record demonstrates that Leah, with full knowledge that Victor had filed for bankruptcy, continued to regard Victor as her general partner. . . .

BUSINESS CONSIDERATIONS What provisions should Leah and Victor have included in their partnership agreement? Why?

ETHICAL CONSIDERATIONS Was it ethical for Victor to exclude Leah from the partnership? Why?

RUPA adopted the term "dissociation," and § 601 discusses the events that cause a partner's dissociation.[7] These events will sound familiar. As summarized and paraphrased below, a partner is dissociated if:

1. The partnership has notice that the partner wants to withdraw now or at a later date specified by the partner.[8] (The section calls this "notice of the partner's express will.")

2. An event occurs that is specified in the agreement as causing the partner's dissociation.

3. A partner is expelled pursuant to the partnership agreement.

4. There is a unanimous vote of the other partners to expel a partner under certain circumstances listed in RUPA.

5. Any partner or the partnership can apply to the court to have a partner expelled if:

   a. The partner engaged in wrongful conduct that adversely and materially affected the partnership business.

   b. The partner willfully or persistently committed a material breach of the agreement or of a duty owed to the partnership or other partners under § 404 of RUPA.

   c. The partner engaged in conduct that makes it not reasonably practical to carry on the business in partnership with him or her.

6. The partner becomes a debtor in bankruptcy;[9] executes an assignment for the benefit of creditors; seeks, consents, or agrees to the appointment of a trustee, receiver, or liquidator of that partner or substantially all that partner's property; or fails to have the appointment of a trustee, receiver or liquidator canceled or postponed within 90 days after appointment.

7. If the partner is an individual, the partner's death;[10] the appointment of a guardian or general conservator for the partner; or a judicial determination that the partner has become unable to perform his or her partnership duties under the agreement.[11]

Under RUPA, a partner has the power to withdraw at any time even though he or she may not have the right to do so.[12] A partner who wrongfully withdraws is liable to the partnership and to the other partners for any damages caused by the withdrawal.[13] A partner who dissociates wrongfully is not entitled to participate in the winding up of the firm.[14] A dissociated partner remains a partner for some limited purposes and retains some residual rights and duties. He or she is a partner for some purposes but a former partner for other purposes. Section 701 provides that in most situations there is a buyout of the dissociating partner's interest, rather than a winding up of the business. Section 801 specifies the situations in which the dissociation of a partner causes a winding up of the business.

A dissociation is diagrammed in Exhibit 34.2. Note that a dissociation does not necessarily result in a termination of the business.

Continuation of the Partnership Business

Once a dissociation (RUPA) or a dissolution (UPA) occurs, an important decision must be made. Will the business terminate through a winding up, or will the business continue? In most cases, an ongoing business is more valuable than the assets that make up the business; in other words, the whole is greater than the sum of its parts. Thus, the remaining partners normally want to continue operating the business if they can possibly do so. This may not be satisfactory to a withdrawing partner, however. For this reason, the partners should consider the problem of a continuation when they draw up the original agreement, and they should make provisions for the problem at that time.

The remaining partners have the *right* to elect to continue the business under any one of the following circumstances:

- The withdrawing partner withdraws in violation of the agreement.

- The withdrawing partner consents to the continuation when he or she could have demanded a termination and winding up.

- The agreement permits a continuation following a dissociation or dissolution.

Unless one of these circumstances occurs, a dissociation or dissolution will be followed by a winding up.

Withdrawing Partners

Anytime the business is continued following a withdrawal, the continuing partners have a duty to the withdrawing partner. The withdrawing partner must be both indemnified (secured against anticipated losses) and bought out. The purpose of the indemnification is to protect the withdrawing partner from any claims of creditors of the partnership. The withdrawing partner is still liable for any debts owed that arose during his or her membership in the partnership. Without an indemnification agreement, a withdrawing partner might be tempted to force a winding up in order to minimize his or her potential liability. But the indemnification agreement is assurance that the continuing partners will repay any losses the withdrawing partner may suffer on account of partnership obligations.

Withdrawing partners are also entitled to payment for their interest in the business at the time of withdrawal, including any undistributed profits. However, if a withdrawal is in violation of the partnership agreement, the continuing partners may first deduct *damages*, based on breach of contract theories. The amount of these

---

EXHIBIT 34.2 Partnership Dissociation under the Revised Uniform Partnership Act (RUPA)

Dissociation of Partner[a]

→ Continue Operation of the Business
Buyout of Dissociated Partner

OR

Dissolution and Winding Up (Pay Bills, Settle with Creditors, and Distribute Assets to the Partners)

[a] Although dissociation is a new term in RUPA, it is really a withdrawal or removal of a partner.

damages should adequately cover the harm caused by the breach.

The continuing partners may pay former partners in a lump sum and settle the matter. If they do not, or cannot, make a lump-sum payment, the withdrawing partners are allowed to elect how payment will be made. They can either (1) receive interest on the unpaid portion until they receive payment in full or (2) elect to receive a portion of profits that corresponds to the unpaid portion of their share until they are paid in full. This election must be made at the time of withdrawal, however, and once made, it cannot be modified unless the continuing partners agree to the change.

Entering Partners

Occasionally, a new partner is brought into the business. When this happens, a continuation obviously occurs. No one wants to enter a business in order to see it go through a winding up. The continuation is treated slightly differently, however, when a new partner enters the firm. As a partner, the new entrant is liable for the debts of the partnership. But existing creditors did not rely on the new partner's credit rating when they decided to extend credit to the (previous) partnership. As a result, it seems unfair to impose unlimited liability on the new partner. UPA § 41(7) resolves this problem by specifying that the new partner is liable to preexisting creditors only up to the amount of his or her capital contribution. In other words, an entering partner has limited liability to preexisting creditors but faces unlimited personal liability with respect to future creditors. This rule is continued under RUPA.[15]

Winding Up the Partnership

Winding up is the termination of the business enterprise. In winding up, one must marshal and liquidate the assets of the business and then distribute the proceeds of this process to the proper parties. (To *marshal* means to collect assets or claims against others so that the firm's debts can be paid. To *liquidate* means to settle with creditors and debtors and apportion any remaining assets to the partners.)[16]

General Partnerships

The priority for distributing the proceeds is set out in UPA § 40. The first priority is the claims owed to creditors who are not partners. If the proceeds are sufficient to pay this class entirely, they will be so paid. Any surplus carries over to the next priority class. Any deficit will cause two things to happen: (1) a pro rata distribution of the proceeds within the class; and (2) a collection of the balance from the personal assets of the partners, jointly and severally.

The second priority in receiving the proceeds is claims owed to the partners as *creditors* of the business. Again, any surplus will be applied to the next priority class, and any deficit will be made up from the personal assets of the partners. Note that a partner who wishes to be treated as a creditor of the firm will need to present clear and convincing evidence of the debt. It is normally presumed that any monies advanced to the firm were advanced as a capital contribution, not as a loan. The court probably will demand some written proof, such as a promissory note, that the funds were meant as a loan. Without such proof, the court will probably determine that it was a capital contribution.

The third priority is the return of the capital contributions of the partners. Any surplus will be carried over to the fourth and final priority. Any deficit will be allocated among the partners pro rata.

The fourth and final priority category is profits. Any monies left over after all the other classes have been satisfied will be distributed as profits, according to the terms of the partnership agreement. There can be no deficit here.

Creditors of the partnership have first claim on any partnership assets. If the partnership is actually in bankruptcy, the Bankruptcy Reform Act of 1978 §723 provides that partnership creditors can recover from the individual partners at the same time as the individual creditors of the partners.

If an individual partner cannot pay his or her creditors, the creditors of the individual partner can claim against that partner's partnership interest. However, these creditor claims are limited by UPA § 28. Usually, if the partnership is solvent, the creditors of the individual partner will be given a charging order by the court. (A *charging order* is a court order permitting a creditor to receive profits from the operation of a business; it is especially common in partnership situations.) This charging order allows the business to continue to operate and minimizes the amount of disruption to the partnership, while providing some recovery for the creditor.

The three examples that follow illustrate how the various interested parties may be treated in a dissolution of a partnership and a winding up of the business. In each example, there are three partners—Jerrod, Carmen, and Eric—whose net worths are shown. In addition, each partner has made the capital contributions specified, and Jerrod has made a loan to the firm. Notice the effect the different asset positions of the partners have on the partners individually.

Partners	Personal Assets	Personal Liabilities	Net Worth
Carmen	$ 80,000	$ 40,000	$ 40,000
Eric	40,000	100,000	(60,000)
Jerrod	100,000	20,000	80,000

Each partner has already contributed $50,000 to the partnership; moreover, profits and losses are to be shared equally. Jerrod has already loaned the firm $30,000 (there is a signed promissory note for this loan).

Example 1 Further assume that the partnership has $200,000 in proceeds and $290,000 in liabilities to regular creditors, plus the $30,000 owed to Jerrod.

Step 1. Partnership proceeds are distributed to regular creditors (priority 1), leaving a deficit of $90,000.

Step 2. Each partner owes an additional $30,000 to priority 1 creditors. However, Eric has no money, and so Jerrod and Carmen must pay the full $90,000 between them (Jerrod will pay $50,000 and Carmen will pay $40,000) and hold claims against Eric (Jerrod for $20,000, and Carmen for $10,000). Both Carmen and Eric are now insolvent.

Step 3. Under priority 3, Jerrod, Carmen, and Eric each owe Jerrod $10,000. Jerrod "pays" himself, and Carmen and Eric each owe Jerrod $10,000.

Consequently, Jerrod had a net worth of $80,000, which has decreased to $30,000 plus $40,000 in debts owed by Carmen and Eric. Carmen had a net worth of $40,000, which has decreased to ($10,000), including the amount that Carmen owes Jerrod. Carmen also has a claim of $10,000 against Eric. Eric had a net worth of ($60,000), which has technically decreased to ($100,000).

Example 2 Assume instead that the partnership has $309,000 in proceeds and $300,000 in liabilities to regular creditors, plus the $30,000 owed to Jerrod.

Step 1. The priority 1 debts are paid in full, and the $9,000 surplus is carried over.

Step 2. Priority 2 debts are paid until the money runs out. Thus, Jerrod receives the $9,000 carried over from priority 1 and is still owed $21,000. Jerrod "pays" himself $7,000; Carmen pays Jerrod $7,000; Eric owes $7,000. Eric is insolvent, and Jerrod probably will not collect from Eric.

Consequently, Jerrod, who had a net worth of $80,000, now has increased it to $96,000 plus a $7,000 debt owed by Eric. Carmen had a net worth of $40,000, which has decreased to $33,000. Eric had a net worth of ($60,000), which has technically decreased to ($67,000).

Example 3 Assume instead that the partnership has $500,000 in proceeds, $200,000 in liabilities to regular creditors, and the $30,000 owed to Jerrod.

Step 1. Priority 1 debts are paid in full, leaving a surplus of $300,000.

Step 2. Priority 2 debts are paid in full (Jerrod gets his $30,000), leaving a $270,000 surplus.

Step 3. Priority 3 is taken care of next. Each partner receives a full return of his or her capital contribution, leaving a surplus of $120,000.

Step 4. The final priority is satisfied; the $120,000 is distributed as profits, with $40,000 going to each of the partners.

In addition, the partners will also be paid in full in this case. Jerrod receives:

$30,000 loan payment
$50,000 return of capital
$40,000 profits
$80,000 prior net worth
$200,000 new net worth

Carmen and Eric each receive:

$50,000 return of capital
$40,000 profits
$90,000 distribution

Consequently, Carmen had a net worth of $40,000, which has increased to $130,000. Eric had a net worth of ($60,000), which has increased to $30,000.

Limited Partnerships

A change in the limited partners does not dissolve the partnership. Under most statutes and agreements, new general or limited partners can be added only with the written consent of all the limited partners. (The law firm of Donlevy-Rosen & Rosen, P.A. has published an article entitled "Limited Partnerships: A Closer Look" at http://www.assetprotectionnews.com/apn4-1-fr.html.)

The distribution of assets in a limited partnership is substantially different from that in a normal, general partnership. Also, the Uniform Limited Partnership Act (ULPA) and the Revised Uniform Limited Partnership Act (RULPA) differ in their treatment of distributions. We will discuss the latter because the vast majority of states follow RULPA. The Revised Act calls for distribution in the following order:

• Claims of nonpartner creditors and claims of partners as creditors

• Any amounts owed to former partners prior to their withdrawal from the firm

- Return of capital contributions of all partners

- The remainder distributed as profits to all of the partners

The two examples that follow illustrate how various interested parties may be treated in a dissolution of a limited partnership and a winding up of the business under RULPA. In each example, there are two general partners—Alice and Bob—and two limited partners—Chuck and Diane. The financial positions and contributions of each of the four are set out as follows.

Partners	Personal Assets	Personal Liabilities	Net Worth
Alice	$150,000	$ 75,000	$ 75,000
Bob	375,000	135,000	240,000
Chuck	100,000	150,000	(50,000)
Diane	200,000	185,000	15,000

Each partner has already contributed $75,000 to the firm. The general partners are to receive 30 percent of the profits each, and the limited partners are to receive 20 percent of the profits each. Chuck has already loaned the firm an additional $50,000 and has a signed promissory note.

Example 1 Further assume the partnership has $400,000 in proceeds and $500,000 in liabilities to nonpartner creditors. Under RULPA, the distribution is as follows:

Step 1. Claims of creditors, both partner and non-partner, are first priority. Here, the $400,000 in proceeds are allocated to the $550,000 in debt owed to nonpartners and to Chuck. These debtors are paid at the rate of approximately 73 percent each, which is calculated by dividing $400,000 by $550,000. The balance of $150,000 in debt is owed by the general partners individually. Since Alice and Bob have the funds, they share this liability equally.

Step 2. Amounts owed to former partners are paid next; however, there are no former partners in this example.

Step 3. Capital contributions of all partners are returned. Since the firm has no money left, the general partners are personally liable for this $300,000 ($75,000 times 4) claim. Bob "pays" himself, and he pays Chuck and Diane $75,000 each. Since Alice already owes Bob, she does not collect $75,000 from him. Alice "pays" herself and owes Bob $75,000 for her share of the payments to Chuck and Diane.

Step 4. Remaining funds are distributed as profits; however, no funds remain in this example.

Example 2 Assume instead that the partnership has $500,000 in proceeds and $100,000 in liabilities to nonpartner creditors. Under RULPA, the distribution is as follows:

Step 1. Claims of creditors, both partner and non-partner, are satisfied first. The entire $150,000 owed is paid, leaving $350,000.

Step 2. Any amounts owed to former partners are paid; however, there are none in this example.

Step 3. Capital contributions of all partners are returned. The entire $300,000 is paid, leaving a balance of $50,000.

Step 4. The balance is distributed as profits. Each general partner gets $15,000 (30 percent each), and each limited partner gets $10,000 (20 percent each).

Changes in Corporate Structure

In Chapter 33, we briefly touched on the subject of dissolution when we discussed shareholders' rights in the event of corporate liquidation. So far, though, we have paid scant attention to fundamental changes in the corporate structure that may endanger the rights of shareholders and creditors. We will now focus on actions bringing about some of these fundamental changes—dissolution, merger and consolidation, sale of substantially all the corporate assets, and stock acquisition. (CNN and *Money* magazine have joined to provide financial information at http://money.cnn.com/.)

Exhibit 34.3 illustrates these four major changes in corporate structure.

Liquidation of the Corporation

The process of *liquidation* consists of winding up the affairs of a business in order to go out of business, that is, marshaling assets and subsequently converting those assets to cash in order to pay the claims of creditors. During this winding up, the corporation pays all debts and creditors from the corporate assets and then distributes any remaining assets to the shareholders. The process of *dissolution*, which denotes the end of the corporation's legal existence, may immediately precede or follow liquidation. Although the terms "dissolution" and "liquidation" are often used together, they are not synonymous.

Throughout the liquidation period, the corporation has all the rights and powers reasonably necessary to effect

EXHIBIT   34.3 Fundamental Changes in Corporate Structure

MERGER OR CONSOLIDATION

Rationales:
- Economies of scale
- Knowledge (i.e., acquisition of "know-how")
- Diversification
- Securing of competitive advantages
- Tax savings
- Utilization of assets
- Preservation of management prerogatives

Formalities:
- Both boards' adoption of merger plan
- Both corporations' shareholder approval (usually 2/3 of outstanding shares or more needed) unless short-form merger involved
- Filing of plan with state
- Issuance of certificate of merger
- Provision of appraisal rights to dissenting shareholders and compliance with statutory procedures covering such rights, including:
  (a) Dissenting shareholders' written notice of objection to merger
  (b) Dissenting shareholders' written demand on corporation for fair market value/fair market of shares
  (c) On failure to agree, either corporation or dissenting shareholders petition court for an appraisal proceeding

Effect:
- Assets, rights, and liabilities of acquired firm assumed by surviving firm by operation of law
- Dissolution of acquired firm

SALE OF SUBSTANTIALLY ALL THE ASSETS

Formalities:
- Simpler than merger procedures
- Approval only by seller's shareholders (i.e., approval of buyer's shareholders unnecessary)
- Provision of appraisal rights to seller's dissenting shareholders and compliance with applicable statutory procedures
- Compliance with statutory provisions protecting creditors' rights
- These formalities not applicable to sale, in the regular course of business, of substantially all the assets created by the corporation

Effect:
- Liabilities of seller ordinarily not assumed by purchaser by operation of law

STOCK ACQUISITION

Formalities:
- Simpler than procedures for merger or sale of substantially all the assets
- Compliance with all applicable state statutes and federal securities laws
- Neither board action nor shareholder approval by either corporation needed: necessary only for shareholders of target firm to decide to sell to would-be acquirer or refrain from selling
- Transactions may be deemed de facto mergers and set aside by courts

DISSOLUTION

Voluntary (Initiated by shareholders)	**Involuntary** (Initiated by shareholders or other entities)
Formalities:	Types:
- Board recommendation	- At request of state, owing to
- Shareholder approval (usually 2/3 of outstanding shares or more needed)	(a) Securities fraud; or (b) Noncompliance with state statutory procedures (e.g., failure to pay taxes or file annual reports)
- Filing of notice to creditors	- At request of shareholders, owing to
- Filing of certificate of dissolution	(a) Mismanagement; or (b) Deadlock among directors or controlling shareholders so serious as to warrant dissolution
- Liquidation of corporation either before or after dissolution	- At request of creditors, owing to the need to preserve creditor's rights

liquidation. Moreover, during this period the corporation can sue and be sued. Under most statutes, the board of directors continues the management of the corporation unless there is a court ordered dissolution and liquidation. In the latter case, the court may appoint a receiver to oversee the liquidation. (A *receiver* is an unbiased person appointed by a court to receive, preserve, and manage the funds and property of a party.) If the directors unlawfully continue the business after dissolution and beyond the time reasonably necessary to wind up the corporation's affairs, they may become personally liable for the corporation's debts. Therefore, the directors (and controlling shareholders) must be cautious during the liquidation process. The law firm of Faegre and Benson, LLP, maintains an article entitled "Fulfill Your Duties at the Helm of a Sinking Ship," which provides guidance for directors of failing companies at http://www.faegre.com/articles/article_671.asp. Note that not all companies undergoing liquidation are failing.

State statutes normally protect creditors during liquidation because the creditors have rights superior to those of the stockholders. The statutes require the corporation to notify creditors of dissolution and liquidation so that these creditors can file their claims against the corporation in a timely manner. A creditor who receives notice but does not file a claim may lose the right to sue later on this claim. Retention of this right, on the other hand, allows the creditor to recoup from shareholders any distributions of corporate assets that have occurred before payment of creditors' claims. To protect creditors, the law characterizes the illegal distributions as held "in trust" for the benefit of the creditors. The directors also may incur liability for distributions illegally declared up to the amount of the unpaid claims.

After the corporation has satisfied its debts to its creditors, the shareholders ordinarily receive their proportionate share of the remaining net assets. As discussed earlier, however, the articles of incorporation may set out one or more classes of shares as meriting liquidation preferences over another class or classes of shares. For instance, preferred stockholders usually receive their shares of the net assets before holders of common stock do. (Note, however, that preferred shareholders *never* receive payment before creditors do.) But if the preferred shareholders do not enjoy liquidation preferences, they will participate with the common shareholders on a share-for-share basis. Sometimes the articles give the preferred shareholders both liquidation preferences and participation rights with the common shareholders. Because cash is the usual method for satisfying liquidation preferences, the corporation may need to sell its assets to raise the amount required to pay these preferences. Under most statutes, the corporation can distribute property instead of cash in satisfying liquidation preferences; but it will be illegal to favor some shareholders through grants of property (as when a corporation gives controlling shareholders valuable patents or trademarks) while doling out cash to minority shareholders.

Dissolution of the Corporation

Dissolution involves termination of the corporation as a *legal entity*, or juristic person. The term *dissolution* is not synonymous with *liquidation*, which refers to the winding up or termination of the corporation's business or affairs. Corporate existence remains impervious to most events, including such unusual occurrences as bankruptcy or the cessation of business activities. Dissolution represents an extraordinary circumstance, or an organic change in corporate structure, that must occur formally in order to have legal effect. Dissolutions are of two types: voluntary and involuntary.

Voluntary Dissolution

As we learned in Chapter 32, corporations theoretically can exist perpetually. On the other hand, a corporation's articles may limit the period of corporate life to, say, 10 years. Alternatively, the incorporators may decide at some point to end the corporation's existence, even though the articles specify the perpetual duration of the corporation. In both cases, such voluntary dissolutions must be carried out through formal procedures.

Statutes ordinarily set out the requirements for these nonjudicial, voluntary dissolutions. Typically, these statutes mandate (1) board action recommending dissolution, (2) shareholder voting to approve the dissolution (usually by the holders of two-thirds of the outstanding shares), and/or (3) filing of a notice to creditors prior to dissolution.

On compliance with these and any other necessary procedures, a certificate of dissolution is filed with the secretary of state or other designated state officer. At this time, the dissolution is legally effective. Remember, though, that liquidation may follow or precede dissolution; so it is possible that some limited corporate activity may occur after dissolution. In voluntary liquidation, the shareholders share proportionately—subject, of course, to any liquidation preferences—in the net assets of the corporation that remain after satisfaction of creditors' claims. As discussed in earlier chapters, some courts prohibit dissolutions that freeze out minority shareholders, especially if a controlling shareholder initiates the dissolution. Also, be aware that the rules regarding dissolutions may vary when a close corporation, instead of a publicly held corporation, is involved.

Involuntary Dissolution

Occasionally, the state, the shareholders, or the corporation's creditors may request the dissolution of the corporation because of wrongdoing or prejudice to shareholders or creditors. Such judicial proceedings are involuntary because the corporation itself is not asking for dissolution. Involuntary dissolutions by their very nature occur less frequently than voluntary ones.

Dissolution at the Request of the State Because the corporation is a creation of the state, the state retains the power to rescind the corporation's certificate when the corporation's actions present a clear danger to the public. For instance, the state may ask for involuntary dissolution of a corporation that has engaged in systematic securities fraud. More often, however, grounds for involuntary dissolution involve noncompliance with state requirements, such as failure to pay taxes or to file annual reports.

Rather than seek dissolution, the state may seek suspension of the corporation. *Suspension* works as a deprivation of the corporation's right to conduct its business and certain other powers, but is not as drastic or as permanent a remedy as dissolution. When the firm is once again in compliance with the corporate statutes, the corporation can be reinstated.

Dissolution at the Request of Shareholders Shareholders can petition the courts for dissolution of the corporation. Statutes generally authorize shareholder actions based on freeze-outs (or oppression) of minority shareholders' interests, allegations of corporate waste of assets, and other examples of corporate mismanagement. Courts sometimes order dissolutions in similar circumstances even in the absence of express statutory provisions. Deadlock among directors or shareholders constitutes an additional ground for involuntary dissolution. For example, courts intervene when a shareholder shows that the deadlock among directors or controlling shareholders has so paralyzed the corporation that it can no longer conduct its business advantageously.

As a less severe alternative, some state statutes permit the appointment of a provisional (or temporary) director who breaks the deadlock and thus allows the corporation to continue functioning. Statutes also may allow holders of a majority of the corporation's outstanding shares to purchase the shares owned by the shareholders who are requesting dissolution. Statutes may contain provisions setting out a minimum number of shareholders (for example, one-third of the corporate shareholders) who must join in the petition for involuntary dissolution before it can be presented to a court.

In contrast to these potential actions, shareholders in close corporations frequently agree in advance that upon the occurrence of a certain event, such as deadlock, each shareholder will be able to request dissolution. Courts ordinarily enforce such agreements.

Dissolution at the Request of Creditors The theory of corporate personality normally prevents creditors from compelling the involuntary dissolution of the corporation. But in order to protect creditors' rights during dissolution and liquidation, statutes require prior notice to creditors. Statutes also allow the appointment of a receiver who takes over the corporation's business and conducts it for the benefit of the creditors. In some circumstances, creditors can petition for the involuntary bankruptcy of the corporation to preserve their rights. Neither the appointment of a receiver nor the institution of involuntary bankruptcy proceedings results in the dissolution of the corporation, however. As we have seen, formal statutory procedures spell out the necessary steps for implementing this fundamental change in corporate structure. Courts are reluctant to force dissolution and generally do so only if they have no other alternative.

Corporate Merger and Consolidation

Like dissolutions, mergers and consolidations bring about fundamental, or organic, changes in the corporation's structure. Dissolution is also related to these two concepts because dissolution of a corporation (or corporations) occurs automatically when either a merger or a consolidation occurs. The procedures for carrying out a merger or consolidation are similar to dissolution procedures. The National Conference of Commissioners on Uniform State Laws (NCCUSL) currently is working on a drafting project entitled *Conversion or Merger of Different Types of Business Organizations Act.*[17] (A drafting project begins when the NCCUSL convenes a committee to study an area of law. Following this study, the committee then drafts a proposal for a uniform act. When the draft is complete, it is submitted to the NCCUSL for its approval.)

Technically, a merger differs from a consolidation. In a *merger,* one corporation (called the *acquirer* or *acquiring firm*) purchases another firm (called the *acquired* or *disap-*

pearing firm) and absorbs it into itself. This new entity is called the *survivor corporation;* the acquired firm no longer exists.

A *consolidation* is similar, except that in a consolidation two or more existing corporations combine to form a wholly new corporate entity. Since most statutes treat the procedures for mergers and consolidations as if the two were identical transactions, this part of our discussion focuses only on mergers. But, as noted, they are analytically different ways of bringing about major changes in corporate structure.

Rationales for Merger

For various reasons, the last four decades have witnessed a phenomenal upsurge in the number of mergers.[18] We will review some more common motivations.

Economies of Scale *Economies of scale* refer to reductions in per-unit costs resulting from larger plant size. A merger may permit a firm to achieve economies of scale and thus to compete much more efficiently: The larger the firm, the easier it is for the firm to receive discounts on sales and advertising and thereby to achieve lower costs. Accumulation of resources resulting from merged firms also facilitates access to financing. Two beer producers that merge generally present a more attractive credit risk for lending institutions than a wine business operating from someone's basement. Large firms may engage in more research and development. A merged firm, for example, ordinarily is able to allocate more funds to these activities. The capital in the struggling wine business, in contrast, typically goes for electricity, rent, and other overhead costs. The vintner may want to invest in research on capping methods or grape hybrids, but economies of scale make such research and development much more feasible in large firms. Mergers can cut costs by allowing the new firm to reduce the number of workers. Mergers between manufacturers and customers (called *vertical mergers*) may lessen transaction costs, also bringing about economies of scale.

As you will learn in Chapter 37, a firm can use economies of scale to drive out smaller, less efficient firms through its dominance due to size and wealth ("deep pockets"). Antitrust laws generally protect the competitive environment from any retaliatory, abusive conduct by large firms. In the absence of antitrust concerns, mergers to effect economies of scale are legal and customary.

Knowledge Often a larger company will merge with a smaller company because the latter possesses valuable technological information or know-how. An established computer firm, for example, may find a merger with a software firm valuable if the software firm has made important technological breakthroughs. Thinking back to economies of scale, it may well be cheaper for the computer firm to purchase the software firm and its patents, trademarks, and trade secrets than to expend research and development funds necessary to create similar software. Furthermore, the merged firm may be able to retain the staff of the smaller firm and thereby realize future gains from these persons' collective expertise and inventive capacities.

Diversification The 1970s marked a large increase in the number of mergers undertaken for the purpose of diversification. Many firms jumped into areas previously unrelated to their principal lines of business through conglomerate mergers. (*Conglomerate mergers* are mergers between noncompeting firms in different industries.) Diversification minimizes the risks that are inherent in being restricted to one industry and the risks caused by economic cycles. It permits a company to gain access to new technologies, markets, skills, and workers. For instance, a traditional retailer may acquire an e-commerce firm. Critics of diversification have argued that diversification dilutes capital markets by making it easier for a diversified company to hide its actual profits and losses. These authorities maintain that lending institutions' abilities to assess creditworthiness are impaired by corporate diversification resulting from mergers. Investors will have the same problems in evaluating company stock. These concerns, coupled with some experts' fears about the implications of the excessive concentrations of economic power represented by diversified companies, argue for limiting conglomerate mergers. At this time, governmental regulators are not enforcing a strict policy against conglomerate mergers. (Antitrust enforcement policies often change with the political and economic climate of the country.) Even without regulatory concerns, a company should limit its mergers to firms that are similar in culture and related to its core competencies. Recently there have been concerns about the acquisitions by Amazon[19] and Medtronic.[20]

Competition Inherent in much of what we have discussed so far is an underlying desire to control, if not curtail, competition. One firm clearly does not want to be at the mercy of another firm in times of scarcity. Therefore, a merger between a supplier of aluminum and a fabricator of aluminum, for instance, seems a viable strategy for cutting down on some of the supply-side uncertainties. Naturally, though, antitrust concerns may also lurk in mergers designed to control the competitive process, so caution is warranted. A merger with a competitor may permit the new firm to raise its prices.

One example of such a problem involved the planned merger between Microsoft and Intuit in 1996. When the proposed merger was announced, the Justice Department objected on the grounds that competition in the software market would be harmed. Eventually, Microsoft withdrew its offer rather than enter a prolonged and expensive legal battle over the competitive effect of the proposed merger.[21]

Other Rationales Other rationales for mergers include tax savings, utilization of cash-rich assets to infuse businesses that need such assets for expansion and growth, and preservation of rights of management. Critics of the last rationale have argued that many mergers occur because of the egos of important management officials who want to become the executive officers of even bigger companies. Such "power trips," these critics assert, lead to the possible sacrifice of shareholders' interests, personnel displacement, and the uprooting of smaller corporations from the local community of which they were an integral part. The latter was a concern in the recent proposal to sell Hershey Foods Corporation.[22] The controversies over hostile takeovers, "golden parachutes," "poison pills," and defensive mergers (for example, mergers in which Abaristo Corporation merges with Chimalis Corporation to avoid Abaristo's being taken over by Belloma Corporation) often surface in such criticisms as well.

Procedure

Board of Directors Whatever the rationale for the merger, once the firms have decided to merge, state statutes set out the steps that must be followed in bringing about the merger. Such statutes generally require that each corporation's board of directors adopt a merger plan that includes (1) the names of each corporation and the surviving corporation, (2) the appropriate terms and conditions of the merger, (3) the method for converting the acquired firm's securities into the securities of the acquiring firm (stock for cash, stock for stock, and the like), and (4) any amendments to the articles of the acquiring corporation that have resulted from the merger. Thorny problems can arise from these procedures.

Shareholders After each of the boards of directors has adopted a merger plan, the shareholders of both corporations ordinarily must approve the merger. As with dissolutions, normally the holders of two-thirds of the outstanding shares must approve this fundamental change, although in a few states approval by a simple majority of the holders of the outstanding stock suffices.

In some states, statutes dispense with the necessity for shareholder approval in *short-form mergers* (those involving

---

NRW CASE 34.1 Finance/Management

NRW

SHOULD NRW DIVERSIFY?

Carlos read about the opportunities in operating franchises in an entrepreneurship magazine. Carlos has suggested that NRW might want to purchase an ice cream franchise to provide a steady source of cash until NRW establishes its reputation and builds a regular market. He feels that an ice cream shop will do a steady business and that the funds generated from this shop should carry the firm for the first year or two. Mai and Helen, however, are unsure about this suggestion and ask for your opinion. What legal complications might arise if NRW tries to expand into the operation of an ice cream shop?

BUSINESS CONSIDERATIONS What are the advantages and disadvantages of diversification by a newly formed business? What information should a firm obtain in order to make an informed decision in this instance?

ETHICAL CONSIDERATIONS Does a business have any duties to expand or not expand when an opportunity presents itself? Do these duties vary depending on the business form of the enterprise—corporation, limited liability company, limited partnership, partnership, or sole proprietorship?

INTERNATIONAL CONSIDERATIONS What additional information should a firm obtain if the business selling the franchises is formed in a foreign country? What additional risks might be faced if the franchisor is foreign?

---

a merger between a subsidiary and a parent company that owns 90 to 100 percent of the subsidiary's stock). Because the parent's ownership interest is so high, a vote of approval is a mere formality; therefore requiring such a vote makes little practical sense.

Once all the required steps have been followed, the directors file the plan with the appropriate state office. After the state approves this plan, the surviving corporation receives a certificate of merger and can begin conducting business.

Effect of Merger

Once the state issues the certificate of merger, the acquired corporation ceases to exist; only one corporation survives. The survivor takes on all the assets, rights, and liabilities of the disappearing (acquired) corporation by operation of law. This means, among other things, that creditors of the acquired corporation are now the creditors of the survivor corporation. Lawsuits, like product liability cases, pending against the acquired corporation, if successful, will be paid by the survivor corporation.

Appraisal Rights

Thus far, we have focused on the positive qualities of a merger from the point of view of those who want it. In any given merger, however, persons will object to, or dissent from, the merger. Many people believe it is unfair to require someone to become a shareholder in a new corporation that may be totally different from the one in which he or she originally invested. Therefore, statutes in most states give dissenting shareholders appraisal rights. *Appraisal rights* allow dissenters to sell their shares back to the corporation for cash for the market value or fair market value of the shares. (*Market value* is the current price the stock will sell for on a stock exchange. *Fair market value* is the current price for selling an asset between an informed willing buyer and an informed willing seller.) In this way, a dissenting shareholder can avoid becoming a shareholder in the survivor corporation and still protect his or her original investment.

To be eligible for appraisal rights, a shareholder ordinarily must follow a set statutory procedure. Although the state statutes vary, in general, such statutes require the following steps:

- The dissenter must send a written notice of his or her objection to the merger before the meeting at which the merger will be considered.

- The shareholder must make a written demand on the corporation for the fair value of the shares after the merger has been approved.

- The corporation must then make a written offer to purchase at a price it believes represents the fair value (or the fair market value) of the shares.

- If the corporation and the dissenting shareholder disagree about the fair value of the shares, either party may petition a court to determine the fair value in an appraisal proceeding.

Valuation of shares is quite complicated and requires a sophisticated understanding of valuation issues. This task becomes somewhat easier if the stock is traded on the New York, American, Tokyo, or other stock exchanges; in such cases, a court will place great importance on the market price of the stock when assigning a fair value to it. Other-

NRW CASE 34.2 Finance/Management

HOW TO DISCOURAGE A TAKEOVER

NRW has had success in developing and marketing the StuffTrakR. This product has been featured in articles in business journals and in the news. As a result of this success and the publicity, Tempo Electronics, Inc. wishes to acquire NRW. Tempo Electronics specializes in personal, portable electronics. Mai, Carlos, and Helen have a meeting (which you attend) and decide they are not ready to sell the firm. They ask for your advice about resisting this takeover attempt. Assume that NRW is a regular (Subchapter C) corporation. What can Mai, Carlos, and Helen legally do to discourage or prevent a takeover? What legal limitations may restrict their options? Why is this problem less likely with a Subchapter S corporation?

BUSINESS CONSIDERATIONS From a practical perspective, what can a business do to discourage or prevent a takeover? Which techniques are most effective? Why?

ETHICAL CONSIDERATIONS From an ethical perspective, what can a business do to discourage or prevent a takeover? What ethical limitations may restrict its options?

INTERNATIONAL CONSIDERATIONS Would NRW have different options if Tempo Electronics were incorporated in another country?

wise, a court usually will arrive at its valuation determination by weighing a number of factors, including market price, investment value, net asset value, and dividends.

Some jurisdictions deny appraisal rights for certain types of mergers (for example, shareholders of the parent company in a short-form merger may have no appraisal rights) and certain types of corporations (those with stock listed on a national securities exchange or those with more than 2,000 shareholders). Since appraisal rights generally represent the exclusive remedy for a dissenting shareholder who opposes a merger, the shareholder must use vigilance in complying with the strict statutory provisions and short time periods involved.

The Delaware Supreme Court, in *Weinberger v. UOP, Inc.,*[23] revamped their state appraisal remedy, by expanding the scope of the appraisal process, thereby making it more appropriate in minority freeze-out cases. The court approved the use of cash-out mergers to eliminate minority interests in a firm. The court held that appraisal should be a minority shareholder's exclusive remedy in most cases. Still, the court provided for judicial review of majority action where "fraud, misrepresentation, self-dealing, deliberate waste of corporate assets, or gross and palpable overreaching are involved."[24] Since then, Delaware courts have permitted minority shareholders to challenge the "entire fairness" even when the alleged harm could have been remedied in an appraisal. Where directors are on both sides of a transaction, they have the burden of demonstrating the "entire fairness" of the transaction, which has two aspects: fair dealing (or procedural fairness) and fair price. The fair dealing prong "embraces questions of when the transaction was timed, how it was initiated, structured, negotiated, disclosed to the directors, and how the approvals of the direc-tors and stockholders were obtained."[25] Fair price "relates to the economic and financial considerations of the proposed merger, including all relevant factors: assets, market value, earnings, future prospects, and any other elements that affect the intrinsic or inherent value of a company's stock."[26] In many states other than Delaware, the trend is still to view appraisal as the sole check on conflicts of interest by majority shareholders. It will be interesting to see which states decide to follow the Delaware approach.

In the following case, the court examined the rights of a minority shareholder under Michigan law. The court referred to Delaware law, not because it was precedent, but because Delaware is often considered the leading state in corporate matters. There were no direct Michigan precedents. The opinion in this case includes an interesting discussion of appraisal rights.

34.3

KRIEGER v. GAST
179 F. Supp. 2d 762, 2001 U.S. Dist. LEXIS 18678 (W.D. Mich. S.D. 2001)

FACTS Gast, a Michigan corporation, was engaged in the business of manufacturing and selling compressors, pumps, and related items. Defendant Warren E. Gast, his family, and three Gast directors, Allan Westmaas, William E. Johnson, and Jay Van Den Berg, held the majority of the stock in Gast. Westmaas, Johnson, Van Den Berg, Warren E. Gast and Kevin C. Gast, Warren's son, are the Director Defendants. All the shares of Gast were privately held; there was no established market for the stock. Gast had a policy of repurchasing shares of stock for 75 percent of book value. Because some repurchases involved substantial amounts, Gast decided to increase liquidity for its shareholders.

Gast retained McDonald & Company to assist it in exploring financing arrangements. McDonald & Company presented several alternatives, including selling a substantial minority interest to an outside investor as part of a "Private IPO." In the Private IPO, Gast would sell a substantial minority interest to an outside investor and incur substantial bank debt that would be used to redeem some of the existing stock and reduce the number of outstanding shares. A Private IPO would provide the desired liquidity, allow share redemption proceeds to be taxed at capital gains rather than at ordinary tax rates, and permit the existing shareholders to maintain control of the company. Gast negotiated a sale with RDV Corporation (RDV). Gast and RDV agreed that the shares of all shareholders other than directors and members of Warren Gast's family would be cashed out. Thus, the minority shareholders would not be included in the Private IPO. A special meeting of Gast shareholders was held for the purpose of voting on the merger. Prior to the meeting, a notice was sent to Gast shareholders informing them of the details of the merger. A new corporation called Gast Investment Corporation (GIC) was being created by the majority shareholders to hold their shares. The notice included a copy of the agreement and plan of merger between Gast and GIC. It informed the shareholders that GIC would vote its shares in favor of the merger and that the minority shareholders would receive $140 for each share. The notice also contained a copy of the dissenters' rights statute under the Michigan Business Corporation Act (MIBCA) and described the details of the recapitalization. The merger was approved at the August 21 meeting following a shareholder vote. Krieger attended the meeting and voted against the merger. However, Krieger did not exercise his right to an appraisal.

Later, IDEX, another company, purchased Gast for approximately $118 million. Those shareholders who continued to own an interest in Gast after the 1996 recapitalization realized an additional $43 million.

ISSUES Would Michigan permit an "entire fairness" challenge as a remedy in addition to appraisal rights? Did the defendants fail to disclose material information about the merger? Were the Director Defendants shielded from liability?

HOLDINGS No, Michigan would not adopt an "entire fairness" test. No, the material information was disclosed. **Yes, the Director Defendants were shielded from liability.**

REASONING Excerpts from the opinion of District Judge Gordon J. Quist:

[Krieger alleged that the defendants had a plan to underpay the shareholders and then later sell the company at a substantial profit. The court concluded that he failed to prove the existence of any such plan.]

[T]he Court must also address this issue: whether Michigan courts would permit the same type of "entire fairness" challenge to a freeze-out merger outside of an appraisal proceeding as permitted under Delaware law. . . . Weinberger [*Weinberger v. UOP, Inc.*, 457 A.2d 701 (Del. 1983)] is the most significant opinion issued by the Delaware Supreme Court in recent years dealing with the treatment of minority shareholders in freeze-out mergers. . . . Without the benefit of any guidance from Michigan courts . . . , this Court predicts that Michigan courts would not adopt the entire fairness test used by Delaware courts . . . [T]his Court believes that Michigan courts . . . would hold that appraisal is the sole remedy available to a minority shareholder, . . . so long as the shareholder's complaint is that he was paid less than the fair value of his shares. The "entire fairness" test is at odds with [the appraisal] . . . approach. . . . [T]his conclusion does not undermine the Court's . . . determination that Krieger may maintain a breach of fiduciary duty claim if he can show that Defendants failed to disclose information that a reasonable shareholder would have considered material to . . . whether to seek an appraisal. . . .

Section 703a specifies the information that must be included in a notice to shareholders of a meeting for approval of a merger or share exchange. . . . In addition, § 764 provides that if dissenters' rights are available to shareholders, the notice must include a copy of the MIBCA sections governing dissenters' rights. [These requirements were met.] . . . While . . . in some situations a director's compliance with statutory requirements may be insufficient to relieve the director from liability for breach of fiduciary duties, in this case there is a specific statute governing the timing and procedure for disclosure of the information. . . . [T]his Court cannot ignore the Michigan legislature's decision on this issue. While . . . a shareholder must decide whether or not to dissent without the benefit of financial information, a shareholder who seeks to dissent need only vote against the transaction and deliver notice to the corporation before the date of the vote. The shareholder is not required to make the decision to seek appraisal until after he receives all of the information specified in § 769. . . . [T]here was no material omission in the Notice. . . .

The [1988] amendment [to Gast's articles] states that a director is not personally liable to the shareholder for a breach of the director's fiduciary duty, with relevant exceptions for: (i) breaches of the duty of loyalty; (ii) acts or omissions not in good faith or involving intentional misconduct or a knowing violation of the law; (iii) or a transaction from [which] the director derived an improper personal benefit. The limitation of liability provision was authorized by . . . the MIBCA. . . . A director's disclosure violation may implicate either the duty of loyalty or the duty of care. . . . [W]here a plaintiff's evidence fails to show that a disclosure violation amounted to a breach of the duty of loyalty or satisfied one of the other exceptions to liability, the directors will be shielded from liability. . . . Krieger has failed to establish that . . . a material misstatement or omission occurred . . . as the result of bad faith or was knowingly or intentionally made. . . . [T]he Director Defendants are shielded from personal liability under Gast's articles of incorporation.

BUSINESS CONSIDERATIONS Gast wanted to increase liquidity because Warren Gast was nearing retirement age and his children were not interested in the company. What other options are available to a closely held company in these circumstances? Why?

ETHICAL CONSIDERATIONS Did the Defendant Directors behave ethically? Why? Is it good public policy to reduce director liability? Why?

Sale of Substantially All the Assets

Rather than acquire another firm through a merger, a corporation can instead buy all, or substantially all, of another firm's assets. For example, a shipping company may buy the ships of a rival company as an alternative to merging with it. This method of acquisition enjoys favor over a merger because it has less procedural complexity. Approval by the shareholders of the acquired firm ordinarily is necessary, but approval by the acquiring firm's shareholders is not. Even then, a sale of substantially all the assets made in the regular course of the corporation's business (as when a corporation is formed to build a tanker, and the tanker is then sold to an oil company) would not normally require shareholder approval. Shareholder approval thus becomes

NRW CASE 34.3   Finance/Management

MERGERS AND ACQUISITIONS

A business that provides a key component for the production of StuffTrakR is experiencing financial difficulties. If this firm fails, NRW will need to find another source for this component, probably at a substantially higher cost per unit. The owner of the business has proposed either selling his firm to NRW or merging with NRW. If NRW buys the firm, it will consume a substantial amount of cash. If NRW agrees to merge, the manufacturer of the component part wants 20 percent of the common stock in NRW. Mai, Carlos, and Helen have asked your advice as to their best course of conduct. What do you recommend?

BUSINESS CONSIDERATIONS Should a business have a policy regarding potential mergers, or should it analyze and decide on each opportunity separately as it arises?

ETHICAL CONSIDERATIONS What duties does a business owe to its supplier in a situation like the one confronting NRW? What duties does it owe its owners and other constituents?

INTERNATIONAL CONSIDERATIONS If we assume that NRW is a Subchapter S corporation, would the proposed merger affect the firm's status if the new stockholder were a foreign entity? How might a foreign owner affect the permissible forms of business organization for NRW?

necessary only in the event of a fundamental change in the corporate structure (that is, the disposal of operating assets in order to terminate the corporation's business activities). Most states provide appraisal rights for dissenting shareholders in these circumstances as well. In addition, various methods of protecting creditors are included in the statutes governing sales of substantially all the assets. In a merger, the acquiring firm takes on all the liabilities of the acquired firm by operation of law, but this is not ordinarily the case when all or substantially all the assets are sold. Corporate statutory provisions, the provisions on bulk transfers in UCC Article 6, and decisional law have been developed to give creditors remedies if such sales prejudice their rights.

Stock Acquisition

An alternative method for acquiring the business of another corporation involves stock acquisitions. Instead of buying substantially all the assets of a corporation, the acquiring corporation's directors may decide to buy the stock of the "acquired" corporation. Because the acquisition implicates only the acquired corporation's individual shareholders, who can decide for themselves whether to sell at the price offered for the stock, the directors of the acquired corporation have no right to approve or disapprove the stock acquisition. Similarly, no requirements usually exist for shareholder approval or appraisal rights. However, federal securities laws may apply to such corporate takeovers, as we will see in Chapter 36.

Because sales of substantially all the assets and stock acquisitions may have the ultimate effect of mergers, some companies have characterized their acquisitions in one of these fashions in order to avoid the strict statutory procedures required of mergers. Transactions that take the *form* of sales of assets or stocks but nevertheless have the *effect* of mergers are called *de facto mergers*. Because shareholders and creditors can be injured through de facto mergers, courts where the doctrine is recognized can set aside the transactions and require compliance with the relevant merger statutes (shareholder approval, appraisal rights, and so on).

Termination of a Limited Liability Company

As we mentioned in the prior chapter, the law of Limited Liability Companies (LLCs) is based on laws of other business organizations. (For example, the CCH Business Owner's Toolkit provides an article about using charging orders with LLCs at http://www.toolkit.cch.com/text/P12_4476.asp.)

Summary

Under the UPA, when a partnership undergoes a change in the relationship among the partners, a dissolution occurs. Thus, a withdrawal by any partner is a dissolution, whether the agreement allows such conduct or not. Likewise, a dissolution will occur when the purpose of the agreement has been carried out or when its time has expired. A dissolution will happen by operation of law (1) if a partner dies; (2) if any partner goes bankrupt; or (3) if the purpose becomes illegal, or the partners cannot legally continue in the business. A dissolution can also happen by court order. When a dissolution occurs because a partner withdraws, the remaining partners may be allowed to continue the business. If they do, then the withdrawing partner must be bought out and indemnified. The RUPA discusses dissociation instead of dissolution.

Often the partnership must be wound up if a dissolution occurs. In a winding up, the assets of the firm are marshaled and liquidated, and the proceeds are distributed according to law. In a general partnership under the UPA, the proceeds must be used first to pay debts that the partnership owes to nonpartner creditors. Next, the creditors who are also partners must be paid. After that, the partners recover their capital contributions. Anything left is distributed as profits.

The process of liquidation (or winding up) of a corporation occurs when it pays all debts and creditors from the corporate assets and then distributes any remaining assets to the shareholders. Directors may incur personal liability if they continue the business of the corporation beyond the time reasonably necessary to wind up the corporation's affairs. Creditors who have preserved their claims against the corporation can recoup from shareholders any distributions of assets that happened prior to payment of creditors. Directors may also incur liability for the remaining unpaid claims. After creditors' claims have been satisfied, the shareholders normally receive the proportion of the remaining net assets represented by their proportionate ownership, subject to any liquidation preferences that the corporation has authorized.

Dissolution of a corporation involves the termination of the corporation as a legal person. It is not synonymous with the term "liquidation," which refers to the winding up of the corporation's business. Dissolutions may be either voluntary or involuntary. Statutes set out the formal requirements for a voluntary dissolution. Typically, voluntary dissolution involves board action, shareholder approval, and notice to creditors. Upon voluntary dissolution, the shareholders share proportionately in the net assets that remain after satisfaction of creditors' claims. Involuntary dissolutions— those effected by judicial proceedings—occur less frequently than voluntary dissolutions.

The state can rescind or suspend the corporation's certificate when the corporation's actions present a clear danger to the public. When the corporation complies again with the statutes, the state often orders the corporation's reinstatement. Shareholders also can petition the courts for dissolution of the corporation. Statutes sometimes limit the conditions under which shareholders can petition for involuntary dissolution. Creditors normally cannot compel involuntary dissolution of the corporation.

Mergers and consolidations can bring about fundamental changes in the corporation's structure. Technically, mergers and consolidations differ, because in a merger one firm absorbs another, whereas in a consolidation both firms combine to produce a wholly new entity. The increase in mergers stems from a desire to effect economies of scale, to gain technical knowledge, to diversify, to control competition, and to avoid taxes. The negative aspects of mergers include the possible sacrifice of shareholders' interests, personnel displacement, and the uprooting of firms from the local community. State statutes set out the procedures necessary for bringing about a merger. The directors ordinarily adopt a merger plan, which the shareholders of both firms must approve. Shareholder approval is not necessary in short-form mergers. After the state approves the filed merger plan, the surviving corporation receives a certificate of merger and can begin conducting business. At this time, the acquired corporation ceases to exist. The surviving corporation takes on all the assets, rights, and liabilities of the acquired corporation by operation of law.

Most state statutes permit appraisal rights for stockholders who object to the merger. Appraisal rights allow dissenters to sell their shares back to the corporation for cash equal to the shares' fair market value. To be eligible for appraisal rights, shareholders usually must follow a set statutory procedure.

Rather than merge, a corporation instead can buy all or substantially all the assets of another firm. This method of acquisition entails far fewer procedures than a merger. Care must be taken to avoid de facto mergers, which are transactions that take the form of either a sale of substantially all the assets or a stock acquisition but have the effect of a merger.

Discussion Questions

1. Julio is an equal partner is an accountancy partnership with Justin and Alex. However, Julio is engaged to Christy. Julio and Christy wish to establish their own accountancy partnership after their marriage. Julio is unsure of his obligations to his current partners and their obligations to him. He also wants to continue to provide accounting advice and tax return preparation for some of his present clients even after he has established an office with Christy. What legal rights and obligations does Julio have? What decision do you recommend Julio make and why?

2. Abner, Bert, and Lois are partners in a bakery. Abner, however, suffers a nervous breakdown and is placed in a mental institution. Abner's wife demands Abner's share of the business, alleging that his insanity has dissolved the partnership. Discuss her allegation.

3. Demetrio is in a partnership, but is also heavily in debt. One of his creditors has gone to court and obtained a charging order against Demetrio's share of the business. Under what circumstances can this creditor seek a court-ordered dissolution of the business?

4. Maria entered an existing partnership as a new partner in 2000. She contributed $20,000 at that time. By 2002, her share had grown to $50,000. How much can creditors who had claims predating Maria's entry into the firm collect from Maria's share of the business? From her personal assets?

5. Given the following figures, work out the final financial position of each of the partners (net worth, cash, amounts owed, amounts receivable) following a winding up of their general partnership business:

	Bill	Charles	Larry	BCL Partnership
Assets	$70,000	$50,000	$50,000	$200,000
Liabilities	20,000	45,000	85,000	190,000
Capital contribution	50,000	25,000	25,000	
Profits	50%	25%	25%	

6. Given the following figures, work out the final financial position of each of the partners (net worth, cash, amounts owed, amounts receivable) following a winding up of their business under the RULPA.

	Beth	Cheryl	Linda (Limited Partner)	B & C (The Firm)
	(General Partners)			
Assets	$67,500	$123,250	$87,900	$350,000
Liabilities	24,000	101,000	86,400	200,000
Capital contribution	50,000	50,000	100,000	
Loans to firm	0	5,000	7,000	
Share of profit	35%	35%	30%	

7. Who can bring about an involuntary corporate dissolution? What procedures must be followed?

8. In 1999, Mattel Inc. acquired the Learning Company for $3.8 billion. Five months after the merger Mattel announced that due to problems at the Learning Company, it would have a $50 million to $100 million third-quarter after-tax loss. "A Mattel spokesman said that the company had done due diligence on the Learning Company and that its problems came as a big surprise." However, analysts say that the problems at the Learning Company were well known for years prior to the merger. What constitutes due diligence for the managers at the acquiring company? What can an investor do to protect him- or herself?[27]

9. Explain the meaning and importance of *appraisal rights*.

10. Why in a given case will a sale of substantially all the corporate assets be preferable to a merger?

Case Problems and Writing Assignments

1. A limited partnership was created in 1982 to provide cellular telephone service in the Los Angeles area. The limited partnership, known as the Los Angeles SMSA Limited Partnership (Los Angeles Partnership) had three partners: U.S. Cellular, AirTouch Cellular, and GTE Wireless Incorporated (GTE). The Los Angeles Partnership Agreement includes Section 13.1 which provides that the general partner may "transfer or assign" its general partner's interest only with the consent of all the other partners. AirTouch Cellular owns a 40 percent general partner interest. Vodafone AirTouch (Vodafone) is the ultimate parent of AirTouch Cellular. AirTouch Communications, Inc. owned all of the stock of AirTouch Cellular when AirTouch Cellular first acquired its partnership interest. AirTouch Communications is a wholly owned subsidiary of Vodafone. Cellco is a joint venture (or alliance) created in 1999 between Bell Atlantic Corporation and Vodafone. Under the Alliance Agreement, Vodafone would transfer all its U.S. wireless interests to Cellco. In April 2000, AirTouch Communications transferred all of its AirTouch Cellular stock to Cellco. Thus, AirTouch Cellular remains the 40 percent general partner of the Los Angeles Partnership and it also retains its limited partnership interest, but Cellco now owns all of Air-Touch Cellular's stock. AirTouch Cellular remains a bona fide operating company, with thousands of employees, substantial assets, interests in wireless systems throughout California, and general partnership interests in other communities in addition to Los Angeles. When AirTouch Communications transferred the AirTouch Cellular stock to Cellco, did it withdraw as the general partner under the agreement and give up control to Cellco? [See *United States Cellular Investment Company of Los Angeles, Inc. v. GTE Mobilnet, Inc.*, 281 F.3d 929, 2002 U.S. App. LEXIS 2618 (9th Cir. 2002).]

2. Horizon/CMS Healthcare appealed the final judgment in favor of Southern Oaks Health Care, Inc. Horizon was a large, publicly traded provider of both nursing home facilities and management for nursing home facilities. It wanted to expand into Osceola County, where Southern Oaks was already operating. Horizon and Southern Oaks decided to form a partnership to own the proposed facility. They agreed that Horizon would manage both the Southern Oaks facility and the new Royal Oaks facility. Southern Oaks and Horizon entered into several partnership and management contracts in 1993. In 1996, Southern Oaks filed suit alleging numerous defaults and breaches of the 20-year agreements. The court ordered that the

partnerships be dissolved, finding that "the parties to the various agreements . . . are now incapable of continuing to operate in business together" and that because it was dissolving the partnerships, "there is no entitlement to future damages. . . ."

The pertinent contracts provided in Section 7.3, "Causes of Dissolution":

. . . [T]he Partnership shall be dissolved in the event that: (a) the Partners mutually agree to terminate the Partnership; (b) the Partnership ceases to maintain any interest (which term shall include, but not be limited to, a security interest) in the Facility; (c) the Partnership, by its terms as set forth in this Agreement, is terminated; (d) upon thirty (30) days prior written notice to the other Partner, either Partner elects to dissolve the Partnership on account of an Irreconcilable Difference which arises and cannot, after good faith efforts, be resolved; . . . (g) pursuant to a court decree; or (h) on the date specified in Section 2.4.

The term "irreconcilable difference" used in the above quote is defined in the contracts as:

[A] reasonable and good faith difference of opinion between the Partners where either (i) the existence of the difference of opinion has a material and adverse impact on the conduct of the Partnerships' Business, or (ii) such difference is as ́to (x) the quality of services which is or should be provided at the long-term care facilities owned by the Partnership, (y) the adoption of a budget for a future fiscal year, or (z) any matter requiring unanimous approval of the Partners under the terms of this Agreement. . . .

Did Horizon wrongfully cause the dissolution of the partnership? [See *Horizon/CMS Healthcare Corporation v. Southern Oaks Health Care, Inc.*, 732 So. 2d 1156, 1999 Fla. App. LEXIS 4902 (Fla. App. 5th Dist. 1999).]

3. Don Tyson, chairman of Tyson Foods, met with Jim Keeler, the president of WLR Foods. They discussed Tyson's acquiring WLR. Keeler presented Tyson's offer to WLR's board of directors, which rejected the offer. Tyson made a tender offer to acquire WLR stock for $30 per share—the market price was only $19.25. The WLR board met on January 28, 1994, to obtain legal and investment advice. The board met again on February 4, 1994, and rejected Tyson's tender offer. At that time the board approved lucrative severance packages for some of the officers and employees. They adopted a *poison pill* that would issue shares to existing shareholders if the tender offer was successful. The purpose of the poison pill was to make the tender offer less attractive to Tyson and to dilute Tyson's interest in WLR if the tender offer was successful. Did the WLR board behave properly? WLR is a Virginia corporation and Virginia has an antitakeover statute. Is the Virginia statute or federal law controlling in this situation? Why? [See *WLR Foods, Inc. v. Tyson Foods, Inc.*, 869 F. Supp. 419 (W.D. Va. 1994); 65 F.3d 1172 (4th Cir. 1995).]

4. Frank Sorenson replaced worn-out brake assemblies and clutch disks containing asbestos for Fowler Oliver Sales, Inc. from 1964 to 1971 and 1977 to 1993. The parts were used in Oliver brand and White Farm brand tractors and combines. The Oliver brand name was discontinued sometime after Oliver was purchased by White Farm. Fowler was a White Farm dealership of new equipment but continued to provide service and maintenance on the discontinued Oliver product line as well as the White Farm product line. In 1985, White Farm was placed in involuntary bankruptcy by its creditors. On October 9, 1985, Allied entered into an Asset Purchase Agreement with White Farm in which Allied would purchase White Farm assets related to the manufacturing of tractors, planters, and tillage equipment. Allied agreed to issue and deliver to White Farm 340,000 shares of a new series of preferred stock. The Agreement specifically provided that:

Allied shall not assume or in any way become liable for, any claims, liabilities or obligations or [sic] any kind or nature, whether accrued, absolute, contingent or otherwise, or whether due or to become due or otherwise arising out of the events or transactions of facts which shall have occurred prior to the final closing date except as expressly assumed by Allied . . .

The bankruptcy court ruled that White Farm was authorized to immediately consummate the acquisition agreement with Allied and that the reorganization assets should immediately be transferred to Allied free and clear of all liens, claims, and encumbrances. On November 11, 1987, the bankruptcy court confirmed a plan of reorganization. In 1986, Allied entered into new dealer contracts with a number of White Farm dealers, including Fowler. Allied also began selling replacement brakes and clutches to dealers of old Oliver and White Farm brand tractors and combines.

Sorenson became sick in late 1993 and died on April 24, 1994, of mesothelioma from asbestos exposure. The doctor who diagnosed Sorenson with mesothelioma stated that the latency period for the effects of asbestos exposure is 30 to 50 years. He concluded that Sorenson must have been exposed to asbestos prior to 1986, when Allied bought White Farm's assets. Sandra Sorenson, his wife, brought a claim against Allied alleging that Allied supplied the brakes and clutches that Sorenson inspected, serviced, and repaired. Is Allied liable as a successor of White Farm? [See *Sorenson v. Allied Products Corporation*, 706 N.E.2d 1097, 1999 Ind. App. LEXIS 361 (Ind. Ct. App. 3d Dist. 1999).]

5. BUSINESS APPLICATION CASE Jeffrey D. Gilbert instituted a statutory appraisal action as the sole dissenting stockholder of M.P.M. Enterprises, Inc. following MPM's merger into a subsidiary of Cookson Group, PLC. Prior to the merger, MPM was a Delaware corporation, headquartered in Franklin, Massachusetts. It was engaged in the design, manufacture, and distribution of screen printers. Business was very good in the 1980s and early 1990s. In March 1995, MPM and Cookson signed an Agreement of Merger, which the parties consummated on May 2, 1995. Gilbert owned 600 shares of MPM's common stock and 200 shares of MPM's preferred stock or 7.273 percent of MPM. Under the terms of the merger, Gilbert would have received $4.56 million.

Gilbert chose to exercise his statutory appraisal right and filed suit. MPM presented expert testimony concerning MPM's going concern value at the date of the merger from William A. Lundquist and Gilbert presented expert testimony from

Kenneth W. McGraw. As is often the case, these experts came up with widely divergent appraisal values. Lundquist placed MPM's going concern value at $81.7 million. McGraw placed MPM's going concern value at $357.1 million. Lundquist arrived at his appraisal value through two separate discounted cash flow (DCF) analyses. He constructed both a "sell-side" DCF (representing the transaction from MPM's point of view) and a "buy-side" DCF (representing the transaction from a buyer's point of view). Lundquist compared the values derived from the buy-side analysis to the terms of the merger, as well as two earlier offers for equity interests in MPM from Dover Technologies and TA Associates, Inc. McGraw performed two analyses: a DCF analysis and a comparative public companies analysis. McGraw took the values from each of these approaches, weighted them equally, and arrived at a fair market value for MPM's equity at the date of the merger of $357.1 million.

In evaluating the various approaches, the Court of Chancery settled on a DCF analysis as the best method for discerning MPM's going concern value at the date of the merger. Did the Court of Chancery commit legal error or abuse its discretion by applying an appraisal analysis that accorded no weight to the terms of the merger giving rise to the appraisal action or to the terms of two prior offers for equity stakes in the subject corporation? [See *M.P.M. Enterprises, Inc. v. Gilbert*, 731 A.2d 790, 1999 Del. LEXIS 205 (Sup. Ct. 1999).]

6. ETHICAL APPLICATION CASE Minority shareholders, including Phil Neal, challenged an appraisal, pursuant to Delaware statutes, of approximately 120,000 shares of the stock of Alabama By-Products Corporation (ABC). Following a short-form merger between ABC and Drummond Holding Corporation, effective August 13, 1985, Drummond absorbed ABC. The ABC minority shareholders were cashed out, pursuant to the merger, and received $75.60 per share. That consideration reflected the $75.00 per share paid to ABC shareholders pursuant to a tender offer less than six months earlier, plus a $0.60 quarterly dividend omitted in 1985. After a six-day trial, the Court of Chancery concluded that the fair value of ABC stock on August 13, 1985, was $180.67 per share and that Neal and the other minority shareholders were entitled to that amount plus interest. ABC, however, contended that the Court of Chancery committed an error of law when determining value in a statutory appraisal proceeding. Was it proper for the Court of Chancery to consider the majority shareholders' wrongdoing when determining the value of the dissenting shareholders' stock in a statutory appraisal hearing? [See *Alabama By-Products Corporation v. Neal*, 588 A.2d 255 (Del. 1991).]

7. CRITICAL THINKING CASE Cadbury Schweppes PLC, a London group, and Dr Pepper–Seven-Up Cos., Inc., are competitors in the soft-drink market. Cadbury is offering to purchase all the shares of Dr Pepper that it does not currently own, which is about 75 percent of the company. After an 18-month negotiation period, Cadbury increased its initial offer to a cash price of $33 per share. A few days prior to the offer, the closing price of Dr Pepper on the New York Stock Exchange was $30.50. Dr Pepper shareholders were urged to accept the offer.

After Cadbury had acquired about one-quarter of Dr Pepper, Dr Pepper began taking steps to make a takeover more difficult. During the negotiation, John Albers, Dr Pepper chairman, kept forcing the price up until the price seemed about right. Observers noted that Dr Pepper got about all it could from Cadbury. Cadbury will finance the deal by a variety of techniques, including asking shareholders to accept extra stock in lieu of cash dividends, borrowing funds, and offering preferred stock for purchase. Cadbury will also assume Dr Pepper's $828.4 million debt.

According to the deal, Cadbury will be entitled to sell Dr Pepper worldwide; however, it will receive only the U.S. rights to sell Seven-Up brands. (Pepsi owns the international rights to Seven-Up brands.) As Cadbury's group finance director, David Kappler, stated, "What we are really buying is brands." Cadbury expects to assume third place in the U.S. soft drink market with this acquisition.

Should Dr Pepper shareholders accept the offer? Is it beneficial to them? Is it beneficial to Cadbury and/or Cadbury's shareholders? What ethical considerations are raised by takeover bids? Are there different ethical considerations for hostile takeovers compared with relatively friendly takeovers? [See Dirk Beveridge, "Cadbury Hits on Right Bid for Dr Pepper," *The Fresno Bee*, January 27, 1995, p. C1.]

8. YOU BE THE JUDGE On October 5, 1999, it was announced that MCI/WorldCom agreed to buy Sprint for $115 billion. These firms were No. 2 and 3 in the U.S. long-distance industry. According to some sources, the combined MCI Worldcom/Sprint would have 30 percent of the market. The Federal Communications Commission had not yet approved this deal.

Tele-Trend tracks consumer telecommunications spending and behavior. (Tele-Trend collects data from actual household bills.) According to Tele-Trend, the merger of SBC and Ameritech, Inc. would create the second largest U.S. residential communications company based on dollar market share. MCI/WorldCom's acquisition of Sprint would create the fourth largest firm. AT&T, which recently acquired TCI, would continue as No. 1. Third place would be the new combination of Bell Atlantic and GTE, called Verizon. Together these four new firms would have more than 70 percent of the market.

The global market is also consolidating rapidly. Deutsche Telekom has tried to expand—its bid to acquire Telecom Italia failed in May 1999. It also tried to buy Sprint; this effort failed on October 5, 1999, when it was announced that Sprint would be acquired by MCI/WorldCom, Inc. Deutsche Telekom is having difficulty competing even in Europe. The German government owns a 66 percent stake in Deutsche Telekom. This protects it from a hostile takeover. However, government officials are hinting that the government will begin to sell off its interest. It has already acquired a British mobile phone company, One-2-One, for top dollar. Some analysts contend that Deutsche Telekom paid too much. The German government's interests may have caused difficulty in its bids to acquire other companies such as Telecom Italia. It has a 10 percent interest in

Sprint. Deutsche Telekom acquired Voicestream, the U.S. mobile phone operator.

Assume that a group of shareholders object to the MCI/WorldCom–Sprint purchase, and they have filed suit in your court to prevent it. How will *you* decide this case? What factors will *you* consider? [See Gail Edmondson, with Jack Ewing, Stephen Baker, and Bill Echikson, "Time Is Running Out," *Business Week International Editions* (October 25, 1999), International Business, Germany, p. 26; "1999's Mergers Create New 'Top Four' Telecommunications Companies, Says Tele-Trend Report," *PR Newswire,* October 21, 1999, Financial News; "MCI WorldCom/Sprint Deal Would Link the No. 2 and No. 3 Players. Is This Anti-Competitive?" *Investor's Business Daily* October 14, 1999, p. A8; Peter Thal Larsen, "The Year the Giants Chose to Merge: M&A," *Financial Times* (London), May 11, 2001, Survey–FT 500, p. 10.][28]

Notes

1. Uniform Partnership Act § 29.

2. Uniform Partnership Act § 31.

3. The following states have adopted UPA (1914): Georgia, Indiana, Kentucky, Maine, Massachusetts, Michigan, Mississippi, Missouri, Nevada, New Hampshire, New York, North Carolina, Ohio, Pennsylvania, Rhode Island, South Carolina, Utah, and Wisconsin. E-mail from Katie Robinson, Communications Officer, National Conference of Commissioners on Uniform State Laws, September 16, 2002.

4. Uniform Partnership Act §§ 27 and 28.

5. The following states have adopted the 1994 version of RUPA, without the 1997 amendments: Connecticut, West Virginia, and Wyoming. The 1997 amendments provided for limited liability partnerships. The following states have adopted RUPA with the 1997 amendments: Alabama, Alaska, Arizona, Arkansas, California, Colorado, Delaware, District of Columbia, Florida, Hawaii, Idaho, Illinois, Iowa, Kansas, Maryland, Minnesota, Montana, Nebraska, New Jersey, New Mexico, North Dakota, Oklahoma, Oregon, Puerto Rico, South Dakota, Tennessee, Texas, U.S. Virgin Islands, Vermont, Virginia, and Washington. In 2002 it was introduced in the Rhode Island legislature. Four of these states—Arizona, California, Puerto Rico, and Virginia—have enacted a Limited Liability Partnership Equivalent. "A Few Facts about the Uniform Partnership Act (1994)(1997)," NCCUSL Web site, (accessed 9/4/02). http://www.nccusl.org/nccusl/uniformact_factsheets/uniformacts-fs-upa9497.asp.

6. "Uniform Partnership Act (1994)," NCCUSL Web site, http://www.nccusl.org/nccusl/uniformact_summaries/uniformacts-s-upa1994.asp (accessed 9/4/02).

7. The special rules for dissociating partners that are partnerships, corporations, trusts, estates, or other types of business entities have been omitted from this discussion.

8. If the partner specifies a future date, other partners can still dissociate before the date specified.

9. Under RUPA, this includes a person who files a voluntary petition or against whom an involuntary petition is ordered under any chapter of the Bankruptcy Code.

10. Usually, the deceased partner's transferable interest in the partnership will pass to his or her estate, and then the partnership will buy it out under Article 7 of RUPA.

11. The drafters intended for this to include physical incapacity. Revised Uniform Partnership Act § 601, Comment 8.

12. Revised Uniform Partnership Act § 602 addresses a partner's power to dissociate and wrongful dissociation.

13. Section 603 of the Revised Uniform Partnership Act addresses the effect of a partner's dissociation.

14. Revised Uniform Partnership Act § 804.

15. Revised Uniform Partnership Act § 306 (a) and (b).

16. Liquidation is described in the Uniform Partnership Act § 40 and the Revised Uniform Partnership Act § 807.

17. NCCUSL Web site, http://www.nccusl.org/nccusl/draftingprojects.asp (accessed 8/18/02).

18. In 2000, there were substantial changes in the Fortune 500 companies due to mergers. The rate and size of mergers may have slowed somewhat since then due to the economy, falling share prices, and government scrutiny of proposed mergers. See Peter Thal Larsen, "The Year the Giants Chose to Merge: M&A," *Financial Times* (London), May 11, 2001, Survey–FT 500, p. 10.

19. Katrina Brooker, "Amazon vs. Everybody," *Fortune* (November 8, 1999): 120–129.

20. Bethany McLean, "How Smart Is Medtronic Really?" *Fortune* (October 25, 1999): 173–180.

21. Microsoft's dominance of the software market is under consideration by Commissioner Mario Monti, Europe's (EU's) Competition Commissioner. Clayton Hirst, "The Lowdown: Bush Hates Him, Brown Hates Him and EMI Hates Him, So What's Mr. Monti Doing Right?" *Independent on Sunday* (London), June 24, 2001, Business, p. 5.

22. Andrew Ross Sorkin, "Hershey Trust Halts Auction Despite Offer of $12 Billion," *New York Times,* September 18, 2002, and Sherri Day and Andrew Ross Sorkin, "Candy Giants Both Show New Faces in Failed Deal," *New York Times,* September 19, 2002.

23. 457 A.2d 701 (Del. 1983).

24. Ibid., 714, quoted in *Krieger v. Gast,* 179 F. Supp. 2d 762, 2001 U.S. Dist. LEXIS 18678 (W.D. Mich., S.D. 2001) at 775.

25. Ibid., 711, quoted in *Krieger v. Gast,* note 24.

26. Ibid., 714, quoted in *Krieger v. Gast,* note 24.

27. Gretchen Morgenson, "Market Watch: On the Acquisitions Road, Stay Alert to the Hazards," *New York Times* Late Edition-Final, October 10, 1999, Sec. 3, p. 1.

28. Postscript: The merger between MCI/WorldCom and Sprint was blocked by Commissioner Mario Monti, Europe's (EU's) Competition Commissioner. Clayton Hirst, "The Lowdown: Bush Hates Him, Brown Hates Him and EMI Hates Him, So What's Mr. Monti Doing Right?" *Independent on Sunday* (London), June 24, 2001, Business, p. 5. It was also blocked by U.S. regulators. "Worldcom Scandal: Timeline," *Atlanta Journal and Constitution,* June 27, 2002, Home Edition, Business, p. 3D, which includes a time line of WorldCom's financial difficulties.

Franchising

NRW A friend has informed the members of the firm that they should consider franchising NRW. Such a distributional system could give the firm access to new financing and allow it to expand its market. Therefore, NRW would like to know what establishing a franchising system for the production and sale of StuffTrakR and InvenTrakR would involve. NRW also would find it helpful to have information concerning the potential risks and/or benefits franchising might provide. These and other questions are likely to arise in the course of this chapter.

Be prepared! You never know when the firm or one of its members will seek your advice.

The Significance of Franchising as a Business Method

Although franchising began in the United States over a century ago when breweries licensed beer gardens as a means of distributing their products, franchising did not become recognized as a distinct method of doing business until after World War II.[1] Since then, and especially in the last 20 years, franchising has significantly helped the United States achieve its position as the world's largest market.

Presently more than 1,500 U.S. companies encompassing more than 75 different industries use the franchise method for distributing their goods or services both domestically and internationally.[2] The types of businesses that use franchise systems include the following: automobile dealerships; gasoline stations; restaurants; convenience stores; soft drink bottlers; nonfood merchandising businesses (such as drug, electronics, cosmetics, and home furnishings companies); travel agencies; hotels, motels, and campgrounds; automobile and truck rental services; printing and copying services; tax preparation firms; real estate businesses; accounting firms; cleaning services; lawn and garden services; laundry services; equipment rental businesses; early childhood education and daycare centers; beauty salons; bioenvironmental services; check cashing/financial services; dating services; and Internet services. The breadth of these activities led analysts to estimate that franchising accounted for $1 trillion in annual U.S. sales in 2000.[3]

Overall, franchising has developed into an important and popular method of marketing and distribution. This chapter examines why this phenomenon has occurred.

Definition

No universally accepted definition of the word *franchise* exists. The following definition, taken from the Washington Franchise Investment Protection Act, § 19.100.010(4), is typical:

(a) An agreement, express or implied, oral or written, by which: (i) A person is granted the right to engage in the business of offering, selling, or distributing goods or services under a marketing plan prescribed or suggested in substantial part by the grantor or its affiliate; (ii) The operation of the business is substantially associated with a trademark, service mark, trade name, advertising, or other commercial symbol designating, owned by, or licensed by the grantor or its affiliate; and (iii) The person pays, agrees to pay, or is required to pay, directly or indirectly, a franchise fee.

Service marks (distinctive symbols designating the services offered by a particular business or individual), trademarks (distinctive marks or symbols used to identify a particular company as the source of its products), and logotypes (identifying symbols) indicate the origin of goods and services. The person or firm that grants a franchise to another is called the *franchisor*. The person receiving the franchise is known as the *franchisee*. Franchises, or retail businesses involving sales of products or services to consumers, fall into three general categories:

1. *Trade name franchising*, in which the franchisee purchases the right to be identified with the franchisor's trade name (for example, True Value Hardware) but does not distribute particular products exclusively under the franchisor's name.

2. *Product distributorships*, in which a manufacturer/franchisor licenses a franchisee to sell its product either exclusively or with other products via a limited distribution network. The franchisee often has the exclusive right to sell the product in a designated area or territory. Examples of such franchises include automobiles (Chevrolet), gasoline products (Shell or Marathon), and soft drinks (Pepsi-Cola).

3. *Pure franchises* (also called business format franchises), in which a franchisee operates a business under the franchisor's trade name and is identified as a member of a select group of persons who deal in this particular business format. In exchange for the franchise, the franchisee ordinarily must follow a standardized or prescribed format as to the franchisor's methods of operation and may be subject to the franchisor's control with regard to the materials used in making the product, site selection, the design of the facility, the hours of the business, the qualifications of personnel, and the like. Fast-food restaurants, hotels, and car rental agencies often conduct business in this type of franchise.[4]

As a result of the closings of gasoline stations and automobile and truck dealerships, the overall number of product distributorships has decreased since 1972.[5] In contrast to this decrease in distributorships, pure franchises have increased in number. Large franchisors (those with 500 or more units each) should continue to dominate this category of franchising; most of these large franchisors engage either in restaurant businesses or in the retailing of automotive products and services. Analysts expect service-related fields, such as carpet cleaning and home-repair activities; business support services; and educational products and services to provide the most significant areas of future growth.[6] For some ideas of the types of opportunities available in a franchise, visit the FranchiseHandbook at http://www.franchise1.com.

Benefits of Franchising

Whatever form the particular franchise takes, the advantages of a franchise system as a method of doing business make it attractive to both potential franchisees and franchisors. The benefits to franchisees include the following:

- The opportunity to start a business despite limited capital and experience

- The goodwill that results from marketing a nationally known, high-quality trademark or service mark, which not only benefits the individual franchisees but also raises customer acceptance throughout the system

- The availability of the franchisor's business expertise in such areas as inventory control, warehousing, advertising, market research, and product innovation

- An assured supply of materials, the use of bulk-buying techniques, and access to training and supervision

The benefits to franchisors include:

- The franchisee's investment of capital

- The goodwill and other advantages flowing from the franchisee's entrepreneurial abilities, including the enhanced value of the trademark or service mark

- The availability of an assured distribution network, which brings about economies of scale in labor costs, produces a more certain demand curve, and reduces wide fluctuations in sales

- A larger asset base, which makes the franchisor better able to secure credit, enhance profits, avoid financial risks, attract the best talent, lobby for favorable legislation, and defray litigation costs.[7]

Simply put, the franchisor and the franchisee are able to accomplish more together than they can through individual effort. In an era of increasing vertical integration, some observers view franchising as the last bastion for the independent businessperson. Franchising provides independent businesspeople with the means of opening and operating their own businesses, and it allows small businesses to compete with mammoth corporations. In addition, franchising fosters the expansion of an established product or service. It also may bring about the rescue of an otherwise failing business.

By lowering barriers to entry, franchising as a type of business system furthers many of the antitrust policies you will learn about in Chapter 37. It thus provides social and economic benefits to the public at large as well as to individual consumers. On the other hand, the franchisor's often extensive control over the franchisee's conduct of the business, together with other aspects of the franchisor/franchisee relationship, has spawned complicated legal questions. The remainder of this chapter considers some of these issues. Exhibit 35.1 catalogues more fully both the advantages and disadvantages of franchising from the franchisees' and the franchisors' respective points of view.

Franchising Compared with Other Business Relationships

A franchise generally involves a form of marketing or distribution in which one party grants to another the right or privilege to do business in a specified manner in a particular place over a certain period of time. It sometimes has been difficult to distinguish franchising from other types of business relationships. The distinction nonetheless may be legally important, since in recent years virtually every state has passed laws dealing specifically with franchising, and the Federal Trade Commission (FTC) has established regulations covering franchising. Until trouble develops, the two parties may view the holder of the right to do business in a prescribed manner as an independent contractor. But when the grantor terminates its business relationship with the holder, the holder, in order to fall under the protection of such statutes, may try to characterize the relationship as a franchise. Even before the relationship between the two parties sours, governmental agencies tend to see the relationship as one of employment, not of independent contracting. If the holder of the privilege is an employee or agent rather than an independent contractor, the law requires the grantor to pay withholding and Social Security taxes, federal minimum wages, and workers' compensation. In addition, in such circumstances, the grantor may be subject to the provisions of other labor laws and private antitrust suits.

EXHIBIT   35.1   Franchising Advantages and Disadvantages

For Franchisees

Advantages

- Quicker start-up time

- Initial and ongoing management training and support

- The goodwill that results from marketing a nationally known, high-quality trademark or service mark, which raises customer acceptance

- Standardized quality of goods and services

- Access to national advertising programs

- Possible, but often limited, financial support from the franchisor

- Proven products and business formats

- Benefits resulting from the franchisor's experience

- Centralized buying power—potentially leading to lower costs

- Advice as to site selection

- Territorial protection

- Increased likelihood of success compared to other business formats

Disadvantages

- Costliness (e.g., required franchise fees and royalties, the latter of which may be payable even if the firm fails to make a profit)

- Limited scope for creativity and independence owing to the franchisor's strict control over operating standards and procedures (i.e., "assistance" becoming control)

- Requirements to buy supplies, equipment, etc. from the franchisor, or from suppliers approved by the franchisor

- Limitations on product lines

- Market saturation, with the franchisor allowing many franchises in the same area

- Training programs that promise more than they deliver

- Restrictions on growth stemming from a defined sales territory

- Burdensome paperwork/accountability

For Franchisors

Advantages

- A relatively quick way to grow with limited capital

- Ability to grow without the cost and inconvenience of identifying and developing key managers internally

- Potential for gaining a share of a regional or national market relatively quickly

- Franchisees' investment of capital

- Increased income from franchisees through fees and ongoing royalty payments

- Goodwill and other advantages flowing from the franchisees' entrepreneurial abilities, including the enhanced value of the trademark or service mark

- The availability of an assured distribution network, which brings about economies of scale in labor costs, produces a more certain demand curve, and reduces wide fluctuations in sales

- A larger asset base, which makes the franchisor better able to secure credit, enhance profits, reduce financial risks, attract the best talent, lobby for favorable legislation, and defray litigation costs

Disadvantages

- Actions of one franchisee can reflect badly on the entire franchise

- Monitoring and policing of franchisees

- Conflicts with franchisees who want to do things differently

- Laws protecting franchisees from terminations

Sources: Norman Scarborough and Thomas Zimmerer, *Effective Small Business Management,* 6th ed. (Upper Saddle River, N.J.: Prentice Hall, 2000), 104–114; Harold Brown, *Franchising—Realities and Remedies,* 2nd ed. (New York: Law Journal Press, 1978), 6–12.

It is especially difficult to classify the relationship if the holder of the privilege is a distributor. As we have already noted, a distributor may be a franchisee. Yet, depending on the details surrounding the distributor's relationship with its supplier, it also is possible that a distributor instead is an employee, a consignee (a person to whom goods are shipped for sale and who generally can return all unsold goods to the consignor), or an independent contractor. As you might expect, courts, in making such determinations, delve deeply into the particular facts at issue (most notably evidence of the grantor's degree of control over the distributor).

The Internet has hundreds of franchising sites. One that has relatively balanced information is Bison.com, which can be accessed at http://www.bison.com.

Still, the law is fairly well settled with regard to certain issues: *Cooperatives, concessionaires,* joint ventures, general partnerships, and sales agencies ordinarily are not deemed franchises. Note, however, that a partnership can enter into a franchising agreement, acting as either a franchisor or a franchisee. In addition, as you will learn in Chapter 36, a franchise agreement usually does not amount to a security under federal or state law because the distributors/franchisees invest their own efforts in the franchise and do not expect to obtain benefits solely from the efforts of others. In other words, the typical franchising arrangement lacks the "passive investment" component generally associated with certain types of securities.

In the following case, the court had to decide whether the business relationship at issue involved a franchise arrangement.

Setting Up the Franchising Relationship

To recruit franchisees, franchisors usually advertise in such periodicals as *Inc., Entrepreneur,* and so on. The franchisor typically sends "franchise kits" to those who answer the advertisements. Ordinarily, this franchise kit points out in glowing terms the potential for success in this particular business. To the uninitiated layperson or the businessperson with little previous experience and limited capital—those who may be most inclined to enter a franchising arrangement—the franchisor's promotional documents, market studies, and statistics seem highly persuasive. Even at the outset, then, the franchisee relies heavily on the franchisor for guidance. But, as we will see, the pervasiveness of the franchisor's control often leads to subsequent legal difficulties.

Although many variables are involved, the details of a franchising arrangement usually follow a set pattern. Once

---

NRW CASE 35.1   Management

FRANCHISING NRW

During a recent firm meeting, Helen suggested that the firm should consider franchising NRW. Helen stated that, by franchising, NRW could rapidly expand into a number of states that the firm would be unable to reach for quite some time under its current operating system. If Mai and Carlos subsequently ask you for your advice concerning the benefits and the risks of franchising, what would you tell them?

BUSINESS CONSIDERATIONS Why might a relatively small but dynamic business want to consider franchising? Why might this same firm prefer to avoid franchising or otherwise permitting outsiders to have access to its products or ideas?

ETHICAL CONSIDERATIONS Is it ethical for a franchisor to be able to control the conduct of its franchisees as completely as many franchisors do? Explain your reasoning.

INTERNATIONAL ISSUES A number of American corporations have enjoyed considerable success with franchises in other nations. What special risks may be involved with franchising internationally? What special benefits may accrue to such franchisors?

---

the parties have established initial contact and have decided to enter into a franchising relationship, the parties first typically sign a detailed agreement. In this agreement, the franchisor grants to the franchisee the right to use the mark or standardized product or service in exchange for a franchise fee. The franchisor then uses its real estate expertise to designate a specific franchise location, designs and arranges for the standardized construction of the facility, and installs fixtures and equipment therein. In exchange for an advertising fee (usually a percentage of gross sales) paid by the franchisee, the franchisor intensively advertises the product. In addition, the franchisor creates training programs, prepares training manuals, and sets out stringent guidelines—even for the hiring of personnel, the personnel's dress and grooming standards, and the like—for the day-to-day operation of the business.

Once the franchise becomes operative, the franchisee must follow the procedures delineated in the franchisor's confidential operating manual or risk termination of the franchise. This manual usually mandates strict accounting

35.1

EAST WIND EXPRESS, INC. v. AIRBORNE FREIGHT CORPORATION
974 P.2d 369 (Wash. App. Div. 2 1999)

FACTS Airborne Freight Corporation conducts a nationwide delivery service for packages from the pick-up point to the packages' ultimate destination. Airborne receives packages at one of several stations located around the country; and from there the packages go to Wilmington, Ohio, for sorting and routing to the ultimate destination station. Once at the destination station, either an Airborne employee or an independent contractor under a cartage contract (a contract involving the carrying of goods by trucks) delivers the packages. By sending a letter, including a sample contract, to potential cartage contractors within a given geographic area, Airborne invites bids for pick-up and delivery service.

Beginning in 1990, East Wind Express, Inc. held a cartage contract with Airborne. Pursuant to a new contract signed in 1993, East Wind was to provide pick-up, transport, and delivery of shipments between Airborne's customers and Airborne's facilities in northern Oregon. The customer contacted Airborne, at which time Airborne generated the pick-up information and relayed it to an East Wind driver. While delivering packages that recently had arrived from Airborne's sorting facility, East Wind picked up the package from the customer and delivered it to the Airborne facility. Airborne billed the customer and was responsible for the package from pick-up to the ultimate destination. East Wind could not receive any portion of any charges made by Airborne to its shippers. Rather, Airborne paid East Wind based on the average number of packages East Wind carried per day. The 1993 contract further provided that "usage of the Airborne trademarks or [trade name] on vehicle(s) and driver uniforms shall constitute an advertising service, the compensation for which is included in the agreed to rates reflected in SCHEDULE A of this Agreement." East Wind chose to put the Airborne logo on its trucks; its drivers wore Airborne uniforms; and East Wind was required to maintain the trucks, uniforms, and logos according to standards established by Airborne. When the relationship between East Wind and Airborne subsequently deteriorated, Airborne terminated the contract. East Wind thereupon sued Airborne for alleged violations of Washington's franchise act. In its summary judgment motion, Airborne asserted that, as a matter of law, the contract between East Wind and Airborne did not constitute a franchise and that Airborne therefore could properly terminate its relationship with East Wind at will.

ISSUE Was East Wind a franchisee entitled to the protections of Washington's Franchise Act?

HOLDING No. East Wind was an independent contractor hired by Airborne to pick up and deliver Airborne's customers' packages. Since East Wind refrained from marketing, selling, or distributing Airborne's services to Airborne's customers, East Wind was not a franchisee.

REASONING Excerpts from the opinion of Judge J. Robin Hunt:

[The Washington state] legislature enacted the Washington Franchise Investment Protection Act (FIPA) to curb franchisor sales abuses and unfair competitive practices. . . . [The] FIPA defines franchising, regulates the sales of franchises through registration and disclosure requirements, and provides a "franchisee bill of rights." . . . Registration and disclosure prevent fraud in franchise sales, and the "bill of rights" ameliorates the non-negotiable nature of the franchisor-franchisee relationship. . . . [According to the applicable statute,] a franchise is

> (a) An agreement, express or implied, oral or written, by which: (i) A person is granted the right to engage in the business of offering, selling, or distributing goods or services under a marketing plan prescribed or suggested in substantial part by the grantor or its affiliate; (ii) The operation of the business is substantially associated with a trademark, service mark, trade name, advertising, or other commercial symbol designating, owned by, or licensed by the grantor or its affiliate; and (iii) The person pays, agrees to pay, or is required to pay, directly or indirectly, a franchise fee.

To establish that it is a franchisee, East Wind must demonstrate that: (1) Airborne granted it the right to offer, sell, or distribute goods or services under a marketing plan substantially provided by Airborne; (2) operation of its business was substantially associated with Airborne's trademark; and (3) it paid Airborne a franchise fee. . . . East Wind cannot meet this test. Airborne's service is package delivery, which it markets and sells directly to customers. East Wind delivered and picked up some of Airborne's packages, but it did not market or sell this service to individual customers. Rather, the customer called Airborne, which then noted the shipment in its computer system. The East Wind dispatcher, working from an Airborne-provided computer terminal, radioed an East Wind driver and coordinated East Wind's pickup and delivery of Airborne's shipments for Airborne's customers. Airborne sold the service to its customers, and East Wind provided delivery of the packages. Airborne did not grant to East Wind the right to offer, to sell, or to distribute any goods or services under a marketing scheme substantially provided by Airborne. Therefore, East Wind was not Airborne's franchisee. . . . East Wind merely provided transportation services for Airborne. East Wind did not offer, sell, or distribute to the customers who ship goods with Airborne. We hold that East Wind did not have a franchise relationship with Airborne. East Wind is therefore not entitled to the benefits of FIPA, and Airborne was entitled to terminate East Wind's cartage contract at will. . . . We affirm the trial court's grant of summary judgment to Airborne.

BUSINESS CONSIDERATIONS Assume the CEOs of East Wind and Airborne have asked you to prepare a memo in which you explain how the respective companies could have avoided the litigation in which they found themselves embroiled. What ideas would you stress most heavily?

ETHICAL CONSIDERATIONS The contract between these parties apparently did not characterize the parties' relationship. Given the absence of such language, was East Wind's assertion that it fell under the protection of the state's franchise laws ethical? Did either party, ethically speaking, have the right to stake out the moral high ground?

procedures and authorizes the franchisor to inspect the books and records at any time. The franchisee customarily pays to the franchisor a set royalty fee (a payment made in exchange for the granting of a right or a license). The franchisee pays the royalty fee (usually based on a certain percentage of the gross sales), on a monthly or semi-monthly basis. The franchise agreement normally obligates the franchisee to secure liability insurance to protect the franchisee and franchisor against casualty losses and tort suits. Usually, the franchisee has the responsibility of meeting state requirements regarding workers' compensation as well.

The last two areas customarily covered in the franchise agreement—quality control and termination—pose most of the potential legal problems. It is easy to understand the franchisor's desire for quality control: Only by maintaining uniform standards of quality and appearance can the franchisor preserve its reputation and foster the public's acceptance of its product. For this reason, franchisors typically obligate the franchisee to buy products and supplies from them at set prices or from suppliers who can meet the franchisors' exacting specifications and standards.

Critics of such franchisor-mandated provisions have argued that, practically speaking, the franchisee will have a difficult time finding suppliers who will meet the franchisor's specifications, with the result that, under the guise of quality control, franchisees often must pay inflated prices for supplies. The anticompetitive effects of such contractual provisions therefore can give rise to federal and state antitrust issues. The same is true of other commonly employed franchisor practices: vertical pricing policies (for example, forcing franchisees to charge specified retail prices, a practice known as resale price maintenance), vertical non-price restraints (for instance, restricting franchisees to specific territories), and tying arrangements (forcing franchisees to buy a less desirable product—the

tied product—to obtain the more desirable tying product). The legality of such practices defies easy classification. Any such determination turns on a wide variety of factors, including analyses of market structure that enable courts to gauge the pro- or anticompetitive impact, as well as the reasonableness, of such restraints. Given the complexities inherent in such fact-specific inquiries and the intricate interrelationships of the applicable legal precedents, franchisors should seek the advice of counsel as to the advisability of carrying out such strategies. Franchisees similarly should contact their lawyers if their business relationship with the franchisors reflects such practices.

The termination provisions of a franchising agreement also constitute legal pitfalls for the unwary. The franchise agreement ordinarily sets out the duration of the franchise (say 10 years) and usually contains provisions for renewals after this time period has passed. As part of the covenants, or promises, made about the term of the agreement, the franchisee usually agrees to a covenant not to compete for a set time period after the termination of the franchise. The conditions of default that lead to termination, such as a franchisee's insolvency or failure to pay monthly or semi-monthly fees when due, are reproduced in the franchise agreement. In these and other "for cause" situations, the agreement normally calls for the franchisor to give the franchisee time (for example, 10 days) to cure these instances of default. Most agreements provide for notice of termination, and the existing state laws on franchising generally set out a required notice period (say 90 days) before the franchisor can effect a termination.

When prospective franchisees lack business acumen, they are likely to accept without question the 30- to 50-page agreement that the franchisor typically offers. This disparity in bargaining power has led to the passage of state and federal laws and the promulgation of administrative regulations designed to protect franchisees when they enter

NRW CASE 35.2   Management

POTENTIAL PROBLEMS WITH FRANCHISING

Helen seems to be convinced that franchising NRW is an excellent idea and that the firm should move with all due speed to establish franchises in the neighboring states. Mai and Carlos are both hesitant to proceed without further investigation. They ask you what potential problems NRW might encounter in establishing franchises, especially from an agency and a liability perspective. What will you tell them?

BUSINESS CONSIDERATIONS If it establishes franchises, what steps should a business take to ensure that the law will not view the franchisees as the employees or agents of the franchisor? Why should a firm take such steps?

ETHICAL CONSIDERATIONS Is it ethical to use franchising to expand a business venture while simultaneously trying to avoid the traditional liability areas businesses face as they expand? How does franchising affect the ethical duties a business owes to its constituents?

INTERNATIONAL CONSIDERATIONS Suppose that NRW decides to grant a franchise to a firm in Mexico. Will NAFTA be a help or a hindrance to such an arrangement? Suppose instead that the franchisee is located in England; what effect will the EU's rules and regulations have on that arrangement?

their agreements (through mandated disclosures) and upon termination (through notice provisions). By closely scrutinizing franchise agreements, courts, too, increasingly have tried to protect franchisees.

Most litigation involving franchises has centered on the termination provisions in the franchising agreement. Because termination can leave the franchisee with little to show after years of effort and expense, courts, whenever possible, try to find a basis of relief so the franchisee is not without a remedy. However, courts will not force franchisors to stick with obviously inept franchisees.

For information about franchise-related Web sites, check out http://www.franchise.org, a site that lists other publications dealing with franchising issues. Governmental agencies, such as the Federal Trade Commission (http://www.ftc.gov, the Small Business Administration (http://

www.sbaonline.sba.gov/workshops/franchises), and the International Trade Administration (http://www.ita.doc.gov) provide useful on-line information about franchising as well.

Decisional Law and Statutes Affecting Franchising

Courts have been sensitive to the issue of damages in the franchising context. This is particularly true in circumstances involving terminations, because upon termination the franchisee may be left with nothing. Termination provisions, especially when coupled with transferability terms that allow the franchisor to reject potential buyers, may clothe the franchisor with an inordinate amount of power vis-à-vis the franchisee.

In shaping relief, as we have seen, courts can turn to common law, their own powers of equity, and/or applicable statutes. Some of the statutes mentioned earlier were designed by their drafters to correct perceived abuses and overreaching by franchisors; indeed, few regulations pertain to the conduct of franchisees. Clearly, such statutes have improved the bargaining position of franchisees, but some critics have argued that they also make franchise systems more rigid and encourage litigation. Many state legislatures have passed special laws to protect automobile dealers from excessive competition. These statutes typically require that a franchisor who wishes to establish a new dealership or to relocate an existing one must give notice to established automobile dealers and to the state motor vehicle regulatory agency. This notice provision allows established dealers to object to the granting of any additional dealership licenses and thereby to protect their economic stakes in a particular territory. In *New Motor Vehicle Board of California v. Orrin W. Fox Co.*,[8] the Supreme Court upheld a California statute of this type even though Fox had argued that the statute violated antitrust laws and was unconstitutional on grounds of due process.

On the federal level, the Automobile Dealers' Franchise Act, also known as the Automobile Dealers' Day in Court Act (15 U.S.C. § 1221), in a similar fashion allows a terminated dealer to bring a federal court action seeking retention of the franchise if the dealer can prove that the franchisor has conducted the termination in bad faith and coercively. The federal Petroleum Marketing Practices Act (15 U.S.C. § 2801) protects motor fuel distributors and dealers from arbitrary terminations as well. However, even with these statutes, courts have allowed franchisors to terminate franchisees for such reasons as misconduct, or alternatively, failure to meet sales quotas, to observe quality standards, to maintain appropriate investment levels, and the like. Nevertheless, the presence of these laws helps to ensure that the bargaining power between franchisors and franchisees will be more commensurate and balanced. The following case illustrates these points.

35.2

COFFEE v. GENERAL MOTORS ACCEPTANCE CORPORATION
5 F. Supp.2d 1365 (S.D. Ga. 1998)

FACTS LMC Motors, Inc., which operated a General Motors dealership in Eastman, Georgia, and General Motors Acceptance Corporation (GMAC) were involved in an inventory financing arrangement. L. Mitchell Coffee Jr. was the president and sole shareholder of LMC. Under the "floor plan" financing arrangement at issue here, the lender (GMAC) provided a line of credit to the dealership (LMC), which the dealership would use to finance the purchase of vehicles from the manufacturer (GM). GMAC extended a $1.5 million line of credit to LMC so that LMC could finance up to 80 vehicles. GMAC, however, frequently adjusted the number of vehicles it would finance—and hence the amount it would advance on LMC's behalf—based on a 60-day supply of vehicles, the number the dealership was likely to sell in a two-month period. According to GMAC, this "60-day-supply" rule was standard company policy and also constituted an accepted guideline within the automobile industry. GMAC also periodically adjusted LMC's credit limit based on LMC's sales rates and other financial criteria, such as liquidity and capitalization. GMAC admitted that, under these policies, it had "suspended" LMC's line of credit on two different occasions: once from February to September 1990, and again from March to July 1993. According to GMAC, the company initiated the 1990 suspension at Coffee's request after GMAC's discovery that LMC had $650,000 in previously undisclosed, off-balance-sheet debts. According to Coffee, however, GMAC refused to "reinstate" the line of credit until Coffee had made an additional $100,000 capital contribution to LMC. The 1993 suspension, on the other hand, was initiated by GMAC because a check from LMC to GMAC had been returned for insufficient funds. GMAC therefore conditioned reinstatement of the credit line on satisfaction of several financial criteria, including an additional capital contribution by Coffee.

On April 5, 1994, GMAC advised LMC that it intended to terminate the inventory financing arrangement and would make a formal demand for payment in 90 days. On July 5, 1994, GMAC demanded payment of the principal amount outstanding on the line of credit, plus the accrued interest on that amount. To shore up LMC's finances, at about the same time, Coffee entered into negotiations with two individuals—Frank Andrews and Woody Butts—regarding their potential investment in LMC. Andrews, Butts, and Coffee subsequently formed ABC Motors in July 1994; ABC Motors in turn executed an asset purchase agreement with LMC. GMAC thereafter provided floor plan financing to ABC Motors. Although LMC timely paid all amounts owed to GMAC under the terms of the agreement, LMC incurred substantial operating losses during its existence. Coffee alleged that GMAC's repeated and unjustified reductions in LMC's credit limit and GMAC's consequent refusal to finance the purchase of new vehicles at certain critical times had precipitated these losses. GMAC, on the other hand, attributed LMC's losses to poor management and further claimed that it was justified—and in fact authorized under the agreement—in adjusting LMC's credit limit and in terminating the financing relationship. In 1996, Coffee sued GMAC for having allegedly breached its contract with LMC and for having violated the Automobile Dealers' Day in Court Act. GMAC thereupon moved for summary judgment.

ISSUES Had GMAC, by adjusting LMC's credit limit, breached GMAC's contract with LMC? Had GMAC acted with "good faith" as required under the Automobile Dealers' Day in Court Act?

HOLDINGS As to both issues, maybe yes, maybe no. The existence of genuine issues of fact as to both claims made summary judgment inappropriate at this time.

REASONING Excerpts from the opinion of District Judge Dudley H. Bowen Jr.:

[The court noted that the loan agreement between LMC and GM had provided that GMAC would extend to LMC a $1,500,000 line of credit, subject to certain terms and conditions. Moreover, in paragraph 3 of this document, the parties had agreed that GMAC could,]

at its option, terminate the line of credit and refuse to advance funds hereunder upon the occurrence of any of the following: [1] a default by

LMC in the payment or performance of any obligation hereunder or under any other agreement entered into with GMAC; [2] the institution of a proceeding in bankruptcy, receivership or insolvency by or against LMC or its property; [3] an assignment by LMC for the benefit of creditors; [4] cancellation of LMC's General Motors franchise; [5] the filing of a notice of any tax lien against any of LMC's property; [6] a misrepresentation by LMC for the purpose of obtaining credit or an extension of credit; [7] a refusal by LMC, upon request by GMAC, to furnish financial information to GMAC at reasonable intervals or to permit GMAC to examine LMC's books and records. . . .

Plaintiffs [LMC and Coffee] contend that GMAC was obligated under this contract to finance up to $1.5 million worth of vehicles, and that GMAC could refuse to advance funds or terminate the line of credit only upon the occurrence of one of the events enumerated in paragraph 3 of the Loan Agreement. Therefore, Plaintiffs claim, GMAC breached the contract in four distinct ways: (1) by refusing to advance funds to the full extent of LMC's line of credit; (2) by adjusting LMC's line of credit based upon criteria not contained in the contract; (3) by imposing additional terms and conditions upon LMC and Coffee which were not contained in or authorized by their agreement; and (4) by terminating the line of credit in the absence of any event of default.

GMAC, on the other hand, contends that it was not unconditionally obligated to advance $1.5 million on behalf of LMC. Indeed, GMAC argues that it is entitled to summary judgment on Plaintiffs' breach of contract claim because nothing in the relevant documents required it to advance the full amount of LMC's line of credit. Contrary to GMAC's argument, however, the Loan Agreement expressly states that GMAC "will advance funds in payment of property so acquired or held in an amount not to exceed the aggregate amount of the line of credit." . . . It is true, as GMAC argues, that it was only required to advance funds in payment of vehicles that LMC purchased from GM. However, nothing in the contract documents gave GMAC authority to adjust the number of vehicles that LMC could purchase, nor was the decision to advance funds placed in GMAC's discretion. Under the plain language of the agreement, GMAC was required to advance up to, though not more than, $1.5 million on LMC's behalf. . . . If GMAC had wished to retain discretion over the lending decision it easily could have inserted language to that effect in the form contract. GMAC was unconditionally obligated to advance up to $1.5 million on LMC's behalf for the purchase of vehicles, and thus it would appear that GMAC's failure to advance funds, or its conditioning funds upon the satisfaction of extra-contractual requirements, constituted a breach of this agreement.

Nevertheless, it would be premature to grant summary judgment in favor of Plaintiffs on this issue, as there may have been a modification of the agreement. . . . GMAC's modification argument . . . is . . . as follows: GMAC had the authority to terminate the agreement at any time; thus, when GMAC reduced LMC's credit limit and imposed conditions upon the extension of further credit, it implicitly agreed to forego its right to terminate the line of credit in exchange for Plaintiffs' acceptance of the new terms. Therefore, GMAC argues, the parties modified their original agreement and GMAC is not liable for breach. . . .

GMAC was obligated under the terms of the written agreement to advance up to $1.5 million on LMC's behalf for its inventory purchases. GMAC had no authority under this agreement to adjust LMC's line of credit or otherwise restrict the availability of funds, and GMAC could not terminate the line of credit in the absence of one of the contingencies identified in paragraph 3 of the Loan Agreement. Nevertheless, a genuine issue of fact remains as to whether one of these contingencies occurred, and therefore there is a genuine issue of fact as to whether the parties modified their agreement. Accordingly, summary judgment is not appropriate for either Plaintiffs or GMAC on the breach of contract claim. . . .

The Automobile Dealers' Day in Court Act (ADDCA) . . . "is a remedial statute enacted to redress the economic imbalance and unequal bargaining power between large automobile manufacturers and local dealerships, protecting dealers from unfair termination and other retaliatory and coercive practices." . . . The statute permits an "automobile dealer" to bring suit against an "automobile manufacturer" for "the failure of said automobile manufacturer . . . to act in good faith in performing or complying with any of the terms of the franchise, or in terminating, canceling, or not renewing the franchise with said dealer." . . .

GMAC first argues that Coffee lacks standing to sue in his individual capacity under the ADDCA because he is not an "automobile dealer" within the meaning of the Act. . . . Indeed, it is readily apparent from the various agreements between LMC and GM that Coffee was considered essential to the dealership's operations. . . . Moreover, Coffee had personally guaranteed LMC's indebtedness to GMAC, and thus his personal wealth was substantially intertwined with the dealership's financial affairs. Therefore, I conclude that Coffee has standing to assert a claim under the ADDCA.

Second, GMAC argues that it is entitled to summary judgment on Plaintiffs' ADDCA claim because Plaintiffs cannot show that GMAC failed to act in good faith. . . . GMAC contends that because it has put forward evidence tending to show that it acted out of concern over LMC's financial difficulties, it has shown that it had objectively valid reasons for its conduct. Thus, GMAC argues, Plaintiffs were required to present evidence of an ulterior motive to avoid summary judgment. Because Plaintiffs have not come forward with any such evidence, GMAC contends that it is entitled to summary judgment on the Plaintiffs' ADDCA claim. . . . Here, there is evidence in the Record that GMAC had legitimate concerns about LMC's performance and that GMAC treated LMC like other financially troubled dealerships. There is some evidence, however, that GMAC acted in a coercive and intimidating manner in its dealings with the Plaintiffs. Also, it is notably undis-

puted that Plaintiffs timely met all financial obligations under their agreements with GMAC. At this stage in the litigation, it remains a jury question whether GMAC acted with the requisite bad faith. Accordingly, GMAC's Motion for Summary Judgment is denied on Plaintiffs' ADDCA claim. . . .

BUSINESS CONSIDERATIONS Given the existence of state franchise laws, do franchisors need the protections offered by such federal laws as the Automobile Dealers' Day in Court Act? Do such acts tip the balance too far in favor of franchisees? Do these enactments represent an unwarranted intrusion by federal law into areas traditionally regulated by the states?

ETHICAL CONSIDERATIONS Evaluate both GMAC's and LMC's actions from the perspective of the Golden Rule. Did one party behave better, ethically speaking, than the other?

The FTC has promulgated a trade regulation rule on franchise disclosure meant to satisfy the same aims that underline the Automobile Dealer's Day in Court Act and the Petroleum Marketing Practices Act. This 1979 rule, and state laws that mandate similar disclosure provisions, have helped to do away with the abuses associated with the sale of franchises. Continuing investigations of the franchise industry under the power to prohibit deceptive and unfair trade practices granted to the FTC by the Federal Trade Commission Act should effectively reinforce these other regulatory measures.

You can access the FTC Franchise Rule at http://www. ftc.gov/bcp/franchise/netrule.htm. You also may find it interesting to check to see if your state is one of the 15 that have state franchise law administrators that can provide additional information concerning state-specific disclosure requirements.

Furthermore, antitrust laws, such as the Sherman Antitrust Act and the Clayton Act, may apply to various aspects of the franchising relationship. We learned earlier that, as a condition of using their trademark or service mark, franchisors often attempt to impose on franchisees territorial restrictions and restrictions on supplies or prices that may run afoul of the antitrust laws. Consumer protection statutes also may affect the franchising relationship: Franchises that extend credit on installments or through charge accounts may be subject to various truth-in-lending statutes. In addition to its requirement of good faith, the UCC's warranty provisions and its section on unconscionability may be applicable to franchising operations. Since the law on franchising at this time appears to be unset-

tled yet proliferating, a thoughtful examination of such laws by franchisors and franchisees alike seems warranted.

Challenges to Franchising Regulatory Statutes

Some franchisors have bridled at the passage of such franchising statutes because they view these laws as serious limitations on their freedom to contract and to manage their businesses. Consequently, franchisors have raised constitutional arguments against these laws. The parts of the Constitution relied on in these challenges include the following:

- *Impairment of the obligation of contracts.* The Constitution prohibits a state from passing a law that makes substantive changes in contractual rights.

- *Due process.* The Fourteenth Amendment bans vague, standardless laws.

- *Federal supremacy.* Article VI of the Constitution makes federal law the supreme law of the land. Thus, a state franchising law that conflicts with a federal law (say the Lanham Act's regulation of trademarks or the Federal Arbitration Act) will be unconstitutional.

- *Interstate commerce.* Article I, § 8 of the Constitution prohibits the states from placing undue burdens on interstate commerce.

Note how the court disposed of the constitutional issue raised by the plaintiffs in the following case.

35.3

EQUIPMENT MANUFACTURERS INSTITUTE v. JANKLOW
300 F.3d 842 (8th Cir. 2002)

FACTS Equipment Manufacturers Institute (EMI) is a trade association consisting of 141 manufacturers of agricultural, construction, forestry, materials handling, and utility equipment. AGCO Corporation, Case Corporation, John Deere & Company, and New Holland are manufacturers of agricultural equipment and members of EMI. The relationships between the manufacturers and the dealers that market and service the manufacturers' machinery are governed by dealership agreements that establish the respective rights and duties of each party, as well as the essential structure of the parties' business relationships. Sections 37-5-1, 37-5-2, and 37-5-3 of the South Dakota Codified Laws, in force since 1951, make it a class 1 misdemeanor for a manufacturer "to coerce or attempt to coerce" a dealer to take certain actions, or to cancel a dealership agreement "unfairly, without due regard to the equities of the dealer and without just provocation." These protections were augmented by the passage of a 1999 law that provided certain restrictions for dealership contracts for machinery (the act). Section 2 of this 1999 act sets forth five circumstances that do not constitute cause for termination of a dealership contract, including

> (2) Refusal by the dealer to purchase or accept delivery of any machinery, parts, accessories, or any other commodity or service not ordered by the dealer unless such machinery, parts, accessories, or other commodity or service is necessary for the operation of machinery commonly sold in the dealer's area of responsibility, . . .

Each of the manufacturers asserted that a substantial number of their relationships with South Dakota dealers are governed by dealership agreements in existence before July 1, 1999, the effective date of the act. Hence, the manufacturers claimed that Section 2 of the act violated the Contract Clauses of the U.S. and South Dakota constitutions because the act's provisions impair preexisting dealership contracts.

ISSUE Did Section 2 of the 1999 act violate the Contract Clause?

HOLDING Yes. Because Section 2 represents a substantial impairment of preexisting contractual relationships and because the act has no legitimate and significant public purpose, Section 2 unconstitutionally burdens the preexisting dealership agreements at issue.

REASONING Excerpts from the opinion of Judge Goldberg:

The first part of the Contract Clause test is whether Section 2 of the Act substantially impairs pre-existing dealership agreements. In *General Motors Corp.* v. *Romein*, 503 U.S. 181 (1992), the Supreme Court set forth a three-part test to determine whether a substantial impairment of a contractual relationship exists. This "inquiry has three components: [1] whether there is a contractual relationship, [2] whether a change in law impairs that contractual relationship, and [3] whether the impairment is substantial." . . . In the current case, the first component is clearly satisfied, as neither party disputes that contracts between the manufacturers and dealers exist. . . . It remains, then, to determine whether Section 2 impairs the pre-existing dealership contracts, and whether that impairment is substantial.

The Manufacturers contend . . . that several contractual terms within the pre-existing dealership agreements have been impaired, including: (a) terms governing a change in dealership executive management or ownership; (b) terms about dealers' stocking machinery parts and accessories; (c) terms covering the manufacturer's attempts to further penetrate the market; (d) terms regarding a dealer's sale of another line-make of machinery; and (e) terms about required dealer participation in advertising and promotional activities. . . .

Under Section 2(2) of the Act, a manufacturer does not have cause to terminate a dealership contract if the dealer refuses to "purchase or accept delivery of any machinery, parts, accessories, or any other commodity or service not ordered by the dealer unless such machinery, parts, accessories, or other commodity or service is necessary for the operation of machinery commonly sold in the dealer's area of responsibility."

[Hence,] Section 2 of the Act impairs specific contractual rights contained in the preexisting dealership agreements. Therefore, the second component for determining whether the dealership agreements are substantially impaired by Section 2 of the Act is satisfied. . . .

The third component of the inquiry for determining whether the dealership agreements are substantially impaired is to ascertain whether Section 2 of the Act "has, in fact, operated as a substantial impairment of a contractual relationship." . . . This Court will consider "the extent to which the [parties'] reasonable contract expectations have been disrupted . . ."

Under all the dealership contracts before this Court, the dealer has the burden of proving to the manufacturer the fitness of a prospective owner or manager of a dealership. . . . Any change in ownership or executive management without the manufacturer's approval is cause for termination of the dealership agreement. . . . [However,] Section 2(1), [in] [s]hifting this burden to the manufacturer, substantially impairs the terms of the pre-existing dealership agreement, especially given the special nature of the relationship between dealers and manufacturers. Among the distinctive features typical of that relationship are the credit that manufacturers extend to dealers; the intangible factors manufacturers use in choosing dealers; and the extensive degree to which dealers represent the manufacturers to the public. . . .

To evaluate prospective dealers, manufacturers typically consider factors such as experience in agricultural and other equipment sales; financial status; development of a business, personnel and marketing plan; management talent; willingness to be involved in the day-to-day operations of the dealership; dedication, character, trustworthiness, personality, energy, enthusiasm, intelligence, customer relations skills, and similar qualities; competency of staff; business acumen; and commitment to the manufacturer's products. . . . Manufacturers conduct this extensive review of potential dealers because if the dealership becomes insolvent, the manufacturer's reputation in the community may suffer and its customers may be left without a local dealership for repairs and parts. . . .

Therefore, assuming that Section 2(1) of the Act was not reasonably foreseeable, . . . manufacturers' contract expectations about their control of the representatives of their products are substantially disrupted... Section 2(1) of the Act is therefore a substantial burden on the contractual rights of manufacturers under the pre-existing dealership agreements. . . .

The second step in analyzing the nature of Section 2 of the Act's impairment on pre-existing dealership agreements is to ascertain whether previous regulation affects the nature of the impairment, i.e., whether the impairment was foreseeable. Although Section 2 of the Act substantially impairs the contractual rights bargained for in the pre-existing dealership agreements . . . if previous regulation of the relationship between manufacturers and dealers made the terms of Section 2 of the Act foreseeable, then Section 2 of the Act does not substantially impair the pre-existing dealership agreements in violation of the Contract Clause. . . . Parties' expectations of future regulation are important in determining whether contractual rights are substantially impaired because parties bargained for terms in the contract based on those expectations; if those expectations were fulfilled, the Court will not now relieve parties of their obligations. . . .

In the current case, agricultural machinery manufacturer-dealer relationships were previously regulated. . . . These regulations, in force since 1951, made it a Class 1 misdemeanor for manufacturers "to coerce or attempt to coerce" a dealer to take certain actions, or for a manufacturer to cancel a dealership agreement "unfairly, without due regard to the equities of the dealer and without just provocation." However, the 1951 statutes, unlike Section 2 of the [present] Act, do not regulate [the] terms of a contract.

In contrast, Section 2 of the Act purports to place extensive limitations on freely-negotiated arrangements, and thus exceeds what the manufacturers could have reasonably anticipated in light of the previous South Dakota regulation. . . .

[T]he sparse legislative history reinforces that the suspect purpose of the Act is to directly change the obligations of the manufacturers and dealers, as illustrated by its title, "An Act to provide certain restrictions for dealership contracts for machinery." . . . [A]ny claim that its purpose is to benefit farmers and rural communities is belied by the fact that only implement dealers and manufacturers attended [the] committee hearings on the Act, and the record contains no evidence of farmers' participation. . . .

It is clear that the only real beneficiaries under the Act are the narrow class of dealers of agricultural machinery. . . . As the case law makes clear, such special interest legislation runs afoul of the Contract Clause when it impairs pre-existing contracts. . . . Without evidence of a significant and legitimate public purpose underlying Section 2 of the Act, Section 2 is void as applied to dealership agreements in existence before July 1, 1999. . . .

For all the foregoing reasons, this Court finds and concludes that Section 2 of the Act . . . is not based on a significant and legitimate public purpose, sufficient to justify the substantial impairment that its provisions have on dealership agreements in effect prior to the Act's effective date. The grant of partial summary judgment of the district court on the Contract Clause claim is reversed, and the Manufacturers' motion for summary judgment is granted. . . .

BUSINESS CONSIDERATIONS Is it a good business practice to challenge a statutory change when the effect of that change is detrimental to the business? Should the affected businesses seek a legislative solution rather than a judicial one in such circumstances?

ETHICAL CONSIDERATIONS Is it ethical to challenge a statute that adversely affects one's business purely because of the negative business impact? Is such a challenge consistent with the Social Contract Theory?

QUALITY CONTROL OVER FRANCHISES

The firm members have decided to franchise NRW, and they plan to offer franchises to investors in each of the neighboring states. They are concerned, however, with quality control and the preservation of the image and the name the firm has established. They ask for your advice as to how they can make provisions for these issues in the franchise agreement. What advice will you give them?

BUSINESS CONSIDERATIONS Why might a franchisor want to control the materials used by the franchisees in operating their franchises? How much freedom should the franchisor grant to the franchisees, and how much control should the franchisor exercise for the sake of company image and consistency?

ETHICAL CONSIDERATIONS Is it ethical for a franchisor to require the franchisee to purchase materials and supplies from the franchisor? Would it be more ethical for the franchisor to allow the franchisee to act as he or she desires, but to make termination of the franchise easier if the franchisee fails to meet certain quality standards?

INTERNATIONAL CONSIDERATIONS Franchisors often include guidelines dealing with such standards as employee uniforms. Franchisees are expected to adhere to these provisions. Might the cultural values of the franchisee possibly conflict with such provisions? If so, how should this conflict be handled to the mutual satisfaction of both parties?

The Franchising Environment

Industry Statistics

Industry promotional literature and trade groups such as the International Franchise Association (IFA) for decades have touted franchising as a particularly robust and viable method of conducting business. While no one disputes the high level of general interest in franchising—governmental reports note that franchises account for approximately 40 percent of all retail sales in the United States—these reports and other academic studies of the franchising environment dispute the accuracy of the data that, for instance, indicate low failure rates for franchises.[9] The methodologies of industry advocates for franchising have probably resulted in flawed data, so the would-be franchisee should be cautious. Since independent empirical research has questioned what these glowing numbers really mean, the wise potential entrepreneur who is drawn to franchising will view these statistics with some skepticism.[10]

International Markets

These imperfect data have not stanched the expansion of U.S. franchises abroad. Indeed, governmental studies suggest that U.S. franchisors will continue to pierce international markets, despite the numerous problems inherent in complying with the local laws of other nations. According to industry analysts, approximately one in seven franchisors establishes franchises outside its home country. Canada remains the most important market for U.S. franchisors. As recent statistics show, Canada represented about one-third of all U.S. international outlets; Japan constituted the second-largest foreign outlet; and Australia ranked third. Interestingly, in a similar fashion, Canada, Mexico, Japan, the United Kingdom, and the continental European countries are setting up an increasing number of franchises in the United States. The international ramifications of franchising thus should become even more significant as the growth of communication and transportation systems makes consumer preferences more similar around the world and as the advantages of franchising become more apparent to the counterparts of the United States.

Yet another factor that will spur the increasing internationalization of franchising is the industry's heightened reliance on the Internet for the dissemination of franchisee-specific information, internal supply-chain management, promotional efforts to reach prospective franchisees, advertising, and sales leads. In addition, some franchises themselves (for example, Web site design firms) base their services on technology. Hence, industry sources not surprisingly tout the prospects of such expanded uses of the Internet as a distinct advantage of the franchising form of doing business, both internationally and domestically.

Still, the borderless nature of the e-commerce environment raises special challenges and concerns, particularly for franchisees, wherever they are located. In conventional brick-and-mortar franchising relationships, the franchisee, as we have seen in other contexts, often can object to the granting of a new franchise within its territory. Moreover, the duty of good faith and the doctrine of unconscionability protect the individual franchisee from franchisor behavior that arguably invades—or encroaches upon—the actual or perceived rights of an existing franchisee. However, the capacity of an e-franchisor to displace the sales of a land-based franchisee with sales from the franchisor's own Web site looms as a serious threat to the customary, decentralized nature of conventional franchising arrangements. If the consumer can obtain the desired product online, he or she presumably will have few incentives to patronize the local franchisee's place of business. Hence, a franchisor that wishes to integrate an e-commerce presence into an existing franchise network must take into account the "commercial marriage" aspects of the franchisor-franchisee relationship, the interdependence of both parties, and the common vision both participants share with regard to the franchising system.[11] A franchisor's strategy of allocating to franchisees the revenues generated from the franchisor-created Web site or letting franchisees fulfill Internet-originated orders and retain the revenues realized thereby goes a long way toward preserving the vital dimensions of franchising relationships. Put differently, the transition to an e-tailing presence requires the franchisor and franchisees to thoughtfully and candidly discuss the contours of such an emergent e-business strategy, as well as of the commercial realities that the newly configured business will face. The development of an e-commerce model that accommodates only the interests of the franchisor invites franchisee dissatisfaction and enhances the probability of litigation, thus threatening the overall viability of the franchise system itself.

Summary

Franchising has become a significant method of doing business both in the United States and abroad. A franchise is an agreement in which one person pays a fee in exchange for a license to use a trademark, service mark, or logotype while one engages in the distribution of goods or services. The person or firm granting the franchise is called the franchisor; the person receiving the franchise is known as the franchisee. Franchises fall into three general categories: trade name franchising, product distributorships, and pure (or business format) franchises. For both franchisees and franchisors, the advantages of franchising make it an attractive method of doing business. Courts have had some problems in distinguishing franchise relationships from other types of business relationships, such as independent contracting. Yet such a distinction may be important under state and federal franchising laws, tax laws, labor laws, and antitrust laws. Some areas of the law are settled: Cooperatives, concessionaires, joint ventures, general partnerships, and sales agencies generally are not deemed the legal equivalent of a franchise. Neither is a franchise considered a security.

To ensure product uniformity and to protect the goodwill associated with its trademark or service mark, the franchisor strictly controls the franchise relationship. Two areas ordinarily covered in the franchise agreement—quality control and termination—pose the most numerous legal problems. State and federal laws may cover these two aspects of the agreement, and a wise franchisor should take care not to run afoul of these laws by pressing for unreasonable provisions or terms. Special industry laws at both the federal and state levels also may protect franchisees. The Federal Trade Commission's franchise disclosure regulations, antitrust laws, consumer protection statutes, and the Uniform Commercial Code constitute further bases for controlling abusive behavior by franchisors. Franchisors have challenged such statutes on constitutional grounds, sometimes successfully.

In the last few years, academicians and other experts have questioned the accuracy of industry-generated franchising data. Hence, the would-be franchisee should treat these data with caution. No one doubts that franchising will continue to play an important role in domestic retail sales, however. Similarly, the international aspects of franchising should continue to gain in significance in the coming decades as more sophisticated communication and transportation systems allow for global dissemination of goods and services.

Discussion Questions

1. Name eight different types of businesses that use franchising as their distributional method. Then list and describe the three main classifications of franchises.

2. Define *franchise*.

3. Describe four benefits of franchising for the franchisee and franchisor, respectively.

4. For what purposes does the law make distinctions between franchising and other types of business relationships such as independent contracting?

5. Briefly explain the steps involved in setting up a franchising arrangement and describe what areas the franchising agreement normally covers.

6. Discuss why quality control and termination clauses are important to franchisors and how these same provisions nevertheless pose legal pitfalls for franchisors.

7. Enumerate the types of statutes that franchisees can use to curb the power of franchisors.

8. What four constitutional bases have franchisors used to challenge franchising statutes?

9. Why should a would-be franchisee approach industry-generated data concerning franchising with caution?

10. Name the three most important international markets for U.S. franchisors.

Case Problems and Writing Assignments

1. Domino's Pizza, Inc. is a fast-food service company that sells pizza through a national network of over 4,200 stores. Domino's is the second largest pizza company in the United States, with revenues in excess of $1.8 billion per year. A franchisee joins the Domino's system by executing a standard franchise agreement with Domino's. Pursuant to the franchise agreement, the franchisee receives the right to sell pizza under the "Domino's" name and format. In return, Domino's Pizza receives franchise fees and royalties. The essence of a successful nationwide fast-food chain is product uniformity and consistency. Uniformity benefits franchisees because customers can purchase pizza from any Domino's store and be certain the pizza will taste exactly like the Domino's pizza with which they are familiar. Hence, individual franchisees need not build up their own goodwill. Uniformity also benefits the franchisor. It ensures the brand name will continue to attract and hold customers, thereby increasing franchise fees and royalties.

For these reasons, Section 12.2 of Domino's standard franchise agreement requires that all pizza ingredients, beverages, and packaging materials used by a Domino's franchisee conform to the standards set by Domino's. Section 12.2 also provides that Domino's may, in its "sole discretion require that ingredients, supplies and materials used in the preparation, packaging, and delivery of pizza be purchased exclusively from [it] or from approved suppliers or distributors." Domino's further reserves the right "to impose reasonable limitations on the number of approved suppliers or distributors of any product." To enforce these rights, Domino's retains the power to inspect franchisee stores and to test materials and ingredients. Section 12.2 is subject to a reasonableness clause providing that Domino's must "exercise reasonable judgment with respect to all determinations to be made by [it] under the terms of this [a]greement." Under the standard franchise agreement, Domino's sells approximately 90 percent of the $500 million in ingredients and supplies used by Domino's franchisees. These sales, worth some $450 million per year, form a significant part of Domino's profits. Franchisees purchase only 10 percent of their ingredients and supplies from outside sources. With the exception of fresh dough, Domino's does not manufacture the products it sells to franchisees. Instead, it purchases these products from approved suppliers and then resells them to the franchisees at a markup.

The plaintiffs in this case consisted of 11 Domino's franchisees and the International Franchise Advisory Council, Inc. (IFAC), a Michigan corporation made up of approximately 40 percent of the Domino's franchisees in the United States and aimed at promoting the franchisees' common interests. The plaintiffs contended that Domino's has a monopoly in "the $500 million aftermarket [of] sales of supplies to Domino's franchisees" and has used its monopoly power to unreasonably restrain trade, limit competition, and extract supra-competitive profits. To support their claims, the plaintiffs alleged that (1) they attempted to lower costs by making fresh pizza dough on site, but Domino's increased the processing fees and altered the quality standards and inspection practices for store-produced dough, thereby eliminating all the potential savings and financial incentives for the plaintiffs to make their own dough; (2) Domino's prohibited stores that produced dough from selling this dough to other franchisees, even though the dough-producing stores were willing to sell dough at a price 25 percent to 40 percent below Domino's price; (3) Domino's blocked IFAC's attempts to buy less expensive ingredients and supplies from other sources in that Domino's intentionally issued ingredient and supply specifications so vague that potential suppliers could not provide would-be purchasers with meaningful price quotations; and (4) Domino's refused to sell fresh dough to franchisees unless the franchisees purchased other ingredients and supplies from Domino's. As a result of these and other alleged practices, the plaintiffs maintained that each franchisee store now pays between $3,000 and $10,000 more per year for ingredients and supplies than it would in a competitive market—costs that in turn are passed on to consumers.

When the lower court dismissed all the antitrust claims, owing to the plaintiffs' failure to allege a relevant market, the plaintiffs appealed. Did the ingredients, supplies, and materials used by and in the operation of pizza franchise stores qualify as a relevant market for purposes of the franchisees' monopolization and attempted monopolization claims against the franchisor? Did the franchisor-approved dough that the franchise agreement required franchisees to use qualify as a separate market for the franchisees' claim that the franchisor had unlawfully tied the sale of such dough to the franchisees' purchase of other ingredients and supplies? [See *Queen City Pizza,*

Inc. v. Domino's Pizza, Inc., 124 F.3d 430 (3rd Cir. 1997), cert. denied sub nom. *Baughans, Inc. v. Domino's Pizza, Inc.*, 523 U.S. 1059 (1998).]

2. Babak Mebtahi became a Chevron, U.S.A., Inc. franchisee in 1997. In 1999, Chevron audited Mebtahi's station because Chevron had expected it to be generating a larger volume of sales. The audit concluded that Mebtahi had underreported and underpaid his sales tax for 1998 by several thousand dollars and that the federal income tax and state sales taxes for 1998 were missing. Chevron thereafter sent Mebtahi a notice of termination because of his failure to comply with the applicable tax laws. Mebtahi attributed the admitted underreporting and underpayment of the 1998 sales taxes to his following the suggestion of his accountant. Advising Mebtahi that he was paying too much in sales taxes, the accountant recommended that Mebtahi either seek a refund from the state or understate his current sales so as to recoup the overpayments. Because seeking a refund would result in an audit and the attendant inconvenience, Mebtahi chose the latter method (which his accountant later conceded was not the most fitting choice). When Mebtahi subsequently challenged his termination under the Petroleum Marketing Practices Act (PMPA), Chevron argued that the statute allows terminations for the franchisee's failure "to comply with any provision of the franchise relationship, which provision is both reasonable and of material significance to the franchise relationship." The statute also permits terminations on the "occurrence of an event which is relevant to the franchise relationship and as a result of which termination of the franchise or nonrenewal of the franchise relationship is reasonable. . . ." The statute provided that such events include the "knowing failure of the franchisee to comply with [f]ederal, [s]tate, or local laws . . . relevant to the operation of the marketing premises. . . ." Was Chevron's termination of Mebtahi in these circumstances permissible? [*Chevron, U.S.A., Inc. v. Mebtahi*, 148 F. Supp. 2d 1019 (C. D. Cal. 2000).]

3. Northeast Express Regional Airlines Inc. (NERA) and Precision Valley Aviation, Inc. (PVA) were two regional commuter airlines with principal operations in the state of Maine. In 1989, Northwest Airlines, Inc. was seeking to strengthen its presence in New England by expanding its jet capacity in Boston, Massachusetts. To further that goal, on May 2, 1989, Northwest entered into an Airline Service Agreement (ASA) with PVA and on January 5, 1990, it entered into a similar agreement with NERA. Both ASAs were amended by various letter agreements that provided PVA and NERA with additional compensation. Both ASAs expired by their own terms on December 1, 1994. Pursuant to the terms of these ASAs, both PVA and NERA identified their respective commuter airlines as a "Northwest Airlink" and flew under Northwest's designation code, colors, and logo. These ASAs provided that Northwest would pay NERA and PVA for each passenger flown and ticketed on a Northwest flight, based on a "straight-rate prorate" formula. Both NERA and PVA gave Northwest letters of credit as security for a $2 million advance made by Northwest at the inception of the parties' relationship. Both

agreements contained an integration clause stating that the ASAs constituted the full agreement between the parties and could be modified only by a duly executed subsequent writing. Additionally, the ASAs stated that the agreements were to be governed by the laws of the state of Minnesota. NERA and PVA, while operating under the ASAs, requested continual financial accommodations from Northwest, concessions that Northwest often granted and evidenced by a written amendment to the ASAs. On May 25, 1994, Northwest sent written notice of default to PVA and NERA and provided each with notice that the ASAs would terminate in six months. On May 28, 1994, NERA and PVA filed voluntary petitions for relief under Chapter 11 of the Bankruptcy Code. In the ensuing bankruptcy litigation, NERA and PVA claimed they were franchisees under the Minnesota Franchise Act. Using the facts of this case and the principles discussed in this chapter, evaluate NERA and PVA's claims. [See *In re Northeast Express Regional Airlines, Inc.*, 228 B.R. 53 (Bankr. D. Me. 1998).]

4. Lithuanian Commerce Corporation (LCC) had served as the exclusive Lithuanian distributor of L'eggs pantyhose for Sara Lee Hosiery, the manufacturer of L'eggs pantyhose. LCC alleged that while it was Sara Lee's exclusive Lithuanian distributor, Sara Lee donated a large number of pantyhose to areas neighboring Lithuania. LCC claimed that this action created a black market for pantyhose in Lithuania and hampered LCC's sales of L'eggs pantyhose. After LCC complained about Sara Lee's so-called dumping of pantyhose in the Baltic, the two parties reached a settlement in which Sara Lee provided LCC with a large number of Mexican-made pantyhose at no cost. LCC alleged that the Mexican pantyhose Sara Lee provided pursuant to this latter agreement were defective or, at the very least, significantly different from the American versions of the L'eggs styles of pantyhose LCC had previously received from Sara Lee. LCC claimed that, as a result of the poor quality of these Mexican-made pantyhose, LCC's business suffered both in the lost profits it should have realized had the pantyhose been of standard quality and in the loss of customer goodwill that LCC experienced.

In response, Sara Lee submitted that LCC had examined samples of the pantyhose and, therefore, that LCC had had full knowledge of the nature and quality of the Mexican-made pantyhose. Further, Sara Lee asserted counterclaims which alleged that LCC and its principals, Algis Vasys and Laima Zajanckauskiene, had made false claims in their advertisements for L'eggs pantyhose by claiming that L'eggs pantyhose have medicinal and therapeutic value, and that LCC had failed to pay invoices due to Sara Lee.

LCC received mail at its New Jersey office, and Mr. Vasys conducted one business meeting there, meeting with the CEO of another international company to investigate the possibility of establishing a distributorship arrangement between LCC and that international firm. LCC is not authorized to sell pantyhose in New Jersey or anywhere in the United States. Rather, all LCC's sales take place in Lithuania, Latvia, Estonia, and Kaliningrad.

LCC subsequently sued Sara Lee for damages based on breach of warranty and for violations of the New Jersey Franchise Practices Act (NJFPA). Sara Lee argued that LCC had failed to present sufficient evidence on which a jury could reasonably assess damages. Sara Lee further argued that LCC was not a franchisee because the NJFPA applies only to an arrangement, the performance of which contemplates or requires the franchisee to establish or maintain a place of business within the state of New Jersey. Thus, according to Sara Lee, a franchise would exist under the NJFPA if: (1) a "community of interest" between the franchisor and the franchisee existed; (2) the franchisor granted a "license" to the franchisee; and (3) the parties contemplated that the franchisee would maintain a "place of business" in New Jersey. For which company should the judge rule, LCC or Sara Lee? [See *Lithuanian Commerce Corporation, Ltd. v. Sara Lee Hosiery*, 23 F. Supp. 2d 509 (D. N.J. 1998).]

5. BUSINESS APPLICATION CASE The plaintiffs were gasoline service station dealers operating Shell-branded gasoline stations in California, Texas, and New York under franchise agreements. The plaintiffs sued on behalf of themselves and others similarly situated who had received, or would receive in the future, renewal franchise agreements consisting of "retail facility leases," "retail sales agreements," and other related documents. The plaintiffs alleged that the retail facility leases and retail sales agreements contain unlawful waivers, forfeitures, penalties, limitations of liability, unconscionable penalties in the form of liquidated damages, and unreasonable restraints on the alienation (that is, the sale or transfer) of the franchisee's interest in the franchise in the form of a unilateral consent clause giving the franchisors the unilateral right to approve or disapprove of a proposed sale or conveyance of the franchisee's interest in the franchise. The plaintiffs claimed that all these provisions were not offered in good faith or in the normal course of business, but instead were designed to eliminate lessee-dealers in favor of company-operated stations. The plaintiffs submitted that the Petroleum Marketing Practices Act (PMPA) applied to the documents because the cover letter accompanying the renewal franchise agreements constituted a "constructive termination" of their franchise relationship. The cover letter stated:

If you do not sign and return the Lease and other enclosed documents in a timely manner, be advised that Equilon will issue without further warning a non-rescindable notice of non-renewal pursuant to the terms of the Petroleum Marketing Practices Act.

The plaintiffs characterized the cover letter as showing the defendants' clear and unequivocal intent to terminate the plaintiffs as dealers if the agreements were not signed "as is." The plaintiffs did not allege, however, that the defendants had actually issued a formal notice of nonrenewal under the PMPA to any plaintiff or that any plaintiff's franchise relationship actually had been terminated. In short, the plaintiffs were asserting a "constructive termination" theory. The defendants moved to dismiss this case because the plaintiffs had failed to establish the termination or nonrenewal of their franchise relationships as required by the PMPA's threshold requirements for franchisees' bringing suit. Who had the stronger arguments here, the plaintiffs or defendants? [*Abrams Shell v. Shell Oil Company*, 216 F.Supp. 2d 634 (S.D.TX. 2002).]

6. ETHICAL APPLICATION CASE In 1998, the Roy Rioux dealership in Westborough, Massachusetts, ceased operations. Shortly thereafter, Mazda Motor of America, Inc. (Mazda) investigated possible new locations for a combined Lincoln-Mercury Mazda dealership. By 1999, Mazda identified the intersection of Route 9 and Walnut Street as the site of a potential replacement dealership. At that time, Mazda notified Nicholas Gallo, an owner of Gallo Mazda, that he would soon receive a letter informing him that Mazda intended to establish a new dealership. Mazda did not inform Mr. Gallo that the site of the new dealership was in Shrewsbury and Mr. Gallo did not make any inquiries with respect to its precise location. During that same period, Gallo, at Mazda's request, was in the process of moving its dealership facility from its Shrewsbury Street location to its present site at 70 Gold Star Boulevard in Worcester. On August 16, 1999, Mazda notified Gallo by certified mail of its intention to establish a new Mazda dealership "at the Southwest corner of Route 9 and Walnut Street in Westboro [sic], Massachusetts." Mazda further advised Gallo that it anticipated that the new dealership would begin operation in January 2000 or shortly thereafter.

Although that notice provided Gallo with the correct street address of the proposed Route 9 dealership, it inaccurately identified the site as being in Westborough rather than in Shrewsbury. At the time he received Mazda's notice letter, Nicholas Gallo understood that, pursuant to the protest procedures of Chapter 93B of the Massachusetts franchise law, his dealership was required to notify Mazda of its intent to sue within 30 days of receipt of the letter. Based upon the notice letter, Gallo assumed that the new dealership would effectively replace the Rioux franchise in Westborough. The day after receiving the notice letter, Nicholas Gallo allegedly conferred with his business associate, Alfred Gallo, and they agreed that they would not protest the establishment of the new dealership because Westborough was sufficiently distant to give Gallo "enough space to compete equally."

Gallo Mazda contended that it did not become aware of the Shrewsbury location of the new Mazda dealership until March 2001 when one of its employees noticed a sign for the new dealership at the construction site even though Mazda had long since begun construction at that site. On March 28, 2001, Nicholas Gallo informed Mazda's regional general manager that he was both surprised and displeased that the new dealership was in Shrewsbury rather than in Westborough. Almost three months later, on June 21, 2001, Gallo sent a letter to Mazda challenging Mazda's establishment of the Shrewsbury dealership and Mazda's failure to provide Gallo with adequate notice. If Mazda's notice was adequate, Gallo could not sue under 93B because Gallo's notice of intent to sue would have been untimely. Mazda claimed that the reference to the Walnut Street intersection gave Gallo adequate notice that was, in any event, sufficient to promote a "prelitigation" dialogue between the parties. Who should win this lawsuit? [*Gallo Motor Center*

Corporation v. Mazda Motor of America, Inc., 190 F. Supp. 2d 188 (D. Mass. 2002).]

7. CRITICAL THINKING CASE The Mitsubishi keiretsu (the traditional Japanese form of conglomerate) is a well-known manufacturer of heavy equipment, including forklift trucks. In June 1985, To-Am Equipment Co., Inc. entered into a dealership agreement for these forklifts with a company affiliated with Mitsubishi, Machinery Distribution, Inc. (MDI). In 1992 MDI became part of a new entity, MCFA, which assumed MDI's role in the contract. Since 1973, To-Am had been servicing, renting, and repairing forklifts in South Chicago. Over the years it also had sold a number of different brands of forklifts, including those made by Clark, Yale, and Hyster, although prior to its contract with MCFA it had sold only used forklifts. Before allowing To-Am to become a Mitsubishi dealer, MCFA required To-Am to relocate to a larger showroom. To-Am complied and moved to Frankfort, Illinois.

During the years it served as a Mitsubishi dealer, To-Am continued to handle used forklifts manufactured by Mitsubishi's competitors—in other words, the dealership did not require exclusivity on To-Am's part. On the other hand, the agreement conferred on To-Am an exclusive Area of Primary Responsibility (APR), consisting of four Illinois counties and one county in Indiana, in which MCFA did not have, and had agreed to refrain from creating, a competing dealership. Under the 1985 contract, To-Am was required to participate in Mitsubishi's warranty program. This meant, among other things, that To-Am had to maintain trained personnel and provide prompt warranty and nonwarranty service on all Mitsubishi products within its APR. To comply with these requirements, To-Am participated in all of MCFA's training programs, apparently for the most part at To-Am's own expense.

Article III, paragraph 14 of the agreement expressly required To-Am to "maintain an adequate supply of current [MCFA] sales and service publications." To-Am did so by keeping a master set of manuals in its parts department, a second set in its service department, and additional manuals in its mobile service vehicles (a necessity in this business). MCFA had provided one set of these manuals in 1985 when To-Am became a distributor; but thereafter To-Am had to order additional manuals for the other locations where it kept manuals, for updating, and for replacing obsolescent manuals. MCFA invoiced To-Am for these additional manuals, and over the years To-Am paid more than $1,600 for them. At trial, MCFA argued that it had updated To-Am's manuals with all new releases free of charge and that it viewed one full set (which it claimed to have supplied to To-Am) as an "adequate supply." Other evidence, however, indicated that MCFA dealers, including To-Am, did not receive free updates and that one set was inadequate for a dealer of To-Am's size.

In February 1994, MCFA notified To-Am that, in accordance with Article XI, paragraph 1 of the agreement, which permitted either party to terminate upon 60 days' written notice "or as required by law," MCFA was terminating the dealership agreement effective April 2, 1994. This step was a blow to To-Am's business, even though after MCFA's action To-Am continued to service, repair, lease, and rent Mitsubishi forklift trucks, and continued to service and repair other brands of forklift trucks. The reason was simple: Mitsubishi forklifts were the only new vehicles that To-Am had been selling. Even though new truck sales are themselves relatively low profit generators for dealers, such sales can create substantial downstream business, ranging from trade-ins that could be resold as used equipment or carried as rental equipment, to service and parts sales. While dealer profit margins on new equipment sales might be as low as 3 percent, the margins on these downstream business opportunities ranged from 30 to 50 percent. Thus, the loss of To-Am's line of new trucks had ripple effects on its business extending far beyond the immediate lost sales.

In 1995, To-Am sued MCFA for violations of the Illinois Franchise Disclosure Act (owing to the allegedly wrongful termination of To-Am's franchise without good cause) and for breach of contract by MCFA (for MCFA's failure to repurchase To-Am's inventory following this termination). In rebuttal, MCFA contended that To-Am had failed to pay a sufficient franchise free as defined by the Franchise Disclosure Act (which requires a payment in excess of $500) and thus could not be considered a franchisee. If you were the judge, how would you decide this case? [See *To-Am Equipment Co., Inc. v. Mitsubishi Caterpillar Forklift America, Inc.*, 152 F.3d 658 (7th Cir. 1998).]

8. YOU BE THE JUDGE The Massachusetts legislature enacted General Laws Chapter 93B to prevent unfair methods of competition and unfair or deceptive acts among motor vehicle manufacturers, distributors, and dealers. Specifically, Chapter 93B prohibits the improper granting of a franchise to an additional franchisee who would conduct its dealership operations from a place of business situated within the relevant market area of an existing franchisee representing the same line make. The legislature further defines the "relevant market area" as the more narrowly defined and circumscribed geographical area immediately surrounding the dealer location within which it obtained at least two-thirds of (1) its retail sales of new motor vehicles of said line make or (2) its retail service sales. In setting out this definition, the legislature hoped to provide a bright-line test for determining a motor vehicle dealer's relevant market area. An existing dealer has standing to contest the establishment of a new dealership if the add point is within the existing dealer's relevant market area. (The automotive industry defines the "add point" as the location at which an automobile manufacturer proposes to establish a new automobile dealership.)

When American Honda Motor Company, Inc. (Honda) sought to establish a new Honda dealership in Westborough, Massachusetts, approximately 11 miles east of Lundgren Honda (Lundgren), Lundgren notified Honda of its (Lundgren's) intent, pursuant to Chapter 93B, to protest the award of the new dealership. In the earlier litigation between the parties, the Massachusetts supreme court had determined that the relevant geographic market consists of "a geographical area circular in shape, though not a perfect circle, and contiguous to the existing dealer's location." Given the court's clarification of the shape of the relevant market, the parties made the definition of "service sales" the focus of this second lawsuit.

Using a method called geocoding, Lundgren maintained that the add point fell within its relevant market. Geocoding entails an expert's taking the information from each service sale, consisting of the customer's address, repair order number, and dollars spent, and putting these data into a software program that sorts the data geographically by producing a latitude and longitude for each repair order so that each can be plotted on a map. In this case, the software was able to geocode 89.4 percent of the service sales data (that is, that percentage of the addresses were positively and exactly located). The remaining faulty data were plotted at the geographic center of their respective zip codes. On the other hand, the zip code distribution method, the analysis favored by Honda, summarizes and sorts the dealership's service sales according to zip codes. The expert then distributes the sales within each zip code as random dots on a map. The dots that comprise the closest two-thirds of the service sales immediately surrounding the dealership in question constitute the relevant market area.

Not surprisingly, the methodology utilized by each side supported the position it had taken—Honda's expert concluded that the add point fell just outside Lundgren's relevant market

area, while Lundgren's expert found that it fell on the line forming the outer boundary of Lundgren's relevant market area. Lundgren contended that the total number of service customers, the total number of repair orders, and the total dollar value of repairs were all valid indicia of service sales. It further asserted that if either the total number of customers or the total number of service dollars was used to determine service sales, the add point fell within Lundgren's relevant market area. Honda, on the other hand, argued that the number of service customers and the dollar volume of sales were not reasonable definitions of "service sales" and that geocoding was an unreliable method for computing and plotting the data. It was undisputed that if service sales was defined by the number of repair orders (as opposed to the dollar volume or number of customers), the add point would fall outside Lundgren's relevant market area.

Suppose this case is brought in *your* court. Which party do *you* think has the stronger argument here? Why? In making your decision, should you take into account the fact that Lundgren's present position (that one could analyze service sales using the number of service customers and repair order dollars rather than relying solely on the number of repair orders) was inconsistent with the position it had taken in the earlier litigation? Explain fully. [*American Honda Motor Company, Inc. v. Bernardi's, Inc.*, 188 F. Supp. 2d 27 (D. Mass. 2002).]

Notes

1. Harold Brown, *Franchising—Realities and Remedies*, 2nd ed. (New York: Law Journal Press, 1978), 1; Norman Scarborough and Thomas Zimmerer, *Effective Small Business Management*, 6th ed. (Upper Saddle River, N.J.: Prentice Hall, 2000), 104–114.
2. International Franchise Association Educational Foundation, Inc. and FRANDATA Corporation, The Profile of Franchising, Vol. III: A Statistical Abstract of 1998 UFOC Data, available at http://www. franchise.org.
3. Ibid.
4. Scarborough and Zimmerer, note 1, 103.
5. International Franchise Association, note 2, 94.
6. Ibid.
7. Brown, note 1, 6–12; Scarborough and Zimmerer, note 1, 104–114.
8. 439 U.S. 96 (1978).
9. Timothy Bates, Survival Patterns among Newcomers to Franchising, 13 *J. Bus. Venturing* 113, at 116 (1998). See also J. Howard Beales III and Timothy J. Muris, The Foundations of Franchise Regulation: Issues and Evidence, 2 *J. Corp. Fin.* 157–197 (1995).
10. Bates, ibid., 116–118.
11. Andrew Terry, The E-Business Challenge to Franchising, 30 *Australian Bus. L. Rev.*, 227, 240 (2002).

Securities Regulation

AGENDA

NRW The firm members have incorporated NRW, and they are now considering taking the firm public in order to raise money for needed expansion and growth. They therefore will consider issuing stocks, bonds, and debentures to the public. They also will need to know how these offerings may affect their liability and moreover what they must do in order to comply with the federal securities laws. Furthermore, they must acquire an understanding of how they can comply with the applicable state securities regulations. In addition, the firm is considering an expansion into the international marketplace. If this expansion occurs, Mai, Helen, and Carlos are likely to have questions about the Foreign Corrupt Practices Act and its impact on their dealings. These and other questions may arise as you study this chapter.

Be prepared! You never know when the firm or one of its members will seek your advice.

Federal Laws

In Chapters 31 and 32, we briefly examined some provisions of the 1933 and 1934 Securities Acts. It is not possible in one chapter to discuss fully the complex interplay of federal and state securities laws, but we will attempt to understand the broad outlines of this complicated area of the regulation of business.

Securities regulation has come to be known as "federal corporate law." This label in large measure stems from the extensive federal laws and the rules set forth by the Securities and Exchange Commission (SEC), the federal agency charged with primary responsibility for the enforcement and administration of the federal laws covering securities, public utility holding companies, trust indentures, investment companies, and investment advisers. The SEC consists of five members appointed by the president for five-year terms. To ensure impartiality, securities law requires that no more than three of the commissioners be members of the same political party. The SEC and its staff generally have enjoyed a high-quality reputation among securities professionals. The SEC Web site can be explored at http://www.sec.gov/.

The Securities Act of 1933

The Securities Act of 1933 (the '33 Act) defines a *security* as "any note, stock, treasury stock, bond, debenture, evidence of indebtedness, . . . or participation in any profit-sharing agreement, . . . investment contract, . . . fractional undivided interest in oil, gas, or other mineral rights, or, in general, any interest or instrument commonly known as a 'security.'" The Supreme Court in *Gould v. Ruefenacht*, 471 U.S. 701 (1985), held that where an instrument bears the label "stock" and possesses all the characteristics typically associated with stock, the instrument is a "security"; in such cases, a court need not look beyond the character of the instrument to the economic substance of the transaction.

But in other situations in which the instrument bears no such label, courts oftentimes must construe what the statutory term *investment contract* means. Relying on *SEC v. J.W. Howey Co.*, 328 U.S. 293 (1946), subsequent case decisions interpreting this phrase have made it clear that, in this sense, a security involves (1) an investment of money (2) in a common enterprise (3) whereby the investor has no managerial functions but instead expects to profit solely from the entrepreneurial or managerial efforts of others. For this reason, court determinations of what constitutes a security based on this so-called economic reality test have been broad and far-reaching. Courts have construed investments in condominiums, citrus groves, and cattle, when others have been employed to manage such assets, as securities subject to the federal securities laws.

The '33 Act basically is a disclosure statute meant to protect the unsophisticated investing public. By requiring the registration of most securities when they initially are offered and by enforcing various antifraud provisions, the '33 Act ensures such protection.

In the following case, the court based its disposition of whether the opportunity to buy shares on a virtual Web site constituted an investment contract—and hence a security—under the federal securities laws' registration and antifraud provisions on the *Howey* decision. Note also the detailed analysis the court undertook in reaching its conclusion.

Procedures Section 5 is the heart of the '33 Act. It provides that any security that is not exempt must be registered with the SEC before a firm can sell it through the mails or through any facility of interstate commerce, such as securities exchanges (organized security markets in which investors buy and sell securities at central locations). All U.S. issuers now are required to utilize EDGAR, the SEC's electronic data gathering, analysis, and retrieval system, when the firms engage in any initial public offering (IPO). The corporation issuing the security must file a *registration statement* with the SEC and provide investors and would-be investors with a *prospectus*—a document presented by a corporation or its agents that announces the issuance of corporate securities, states the nature of the securities and the financial status of the issuing firm, and asks the general public to purchase the securities covered. The registration statement contains detailed information about the plan for offering and distributing the security, the names and salaries of managers and others who control the corporation, a description of the security, and information about the issuer and its business, including detailed financial reports. The prospectus must contain similar information in summary form.

The underlying purpose of both the registration statement and the prospectus is the protection of the unsophisticated investor. These documents purport to inform a prospective investor of everything he or she should know before a purchase of a security occurs. Some critics argue, however, that the SEC requires so much information that an unsophisticated investor can make little sense of the myriad details that appear in the registration statement and the prospectus. These commentators believe the SEC's "overregulation" actually has undercut the worthy purposes of the '33 Act. Still, the SEC's recent emphasis on the use of plain English in such documents should help to mitigate such concerns. For information about the SEC's efforts in this regard, check out http://www.sec.gov/news/extra/handbook.htm.

SECURITIES AND EXCHANGE COMMISSION v. SG LTD.
265 F.3d 42 (1st Cir. 2001)

FACTS SG Ltd. operated a "StockGeneration" Web site in which purchasers could buy shares in the 11 "virtual companies" listed on the site's "virtual stock exchange." SG arbitrarily set the purchase and sale prices of each of these imaginary companies in biweekly "rounds" and guaranteed that investors could buy or sell any quantity of shares at posted prices. SG focused on one particular virtual enterprise, the so-called privileged company. SG advised potential purchasers to pay "particular attention" to shares in the privileged company and boasted that investing in those shares was a "game without any risk." To this end, its Web site announced that the privileged company's shares would unfailingly appreciate "on average at a rate of 10 percent monthly (this is approximately 215 percent annually)." To add plausibility to this representation and to allay anxiety about future pricing, SG published prices of the privileged company's shares one month in advance.

While SG conceded that a decline in the share price was theoretically possible, it assured prospective participants that, owing to several distinct revenue streams, the share price for the privileged company could not fall by more than 5 percent in a round. According to SG's representations, capital inflow from new participants provided liquidity for existing participants who might choose to sell their virtual shareholdings. As a backstop, SG pledged to allocate an indeterminate portion of the profits derived from its Web site operations to a special reserve fund designed to maintain the price of the privileged company's shares. As a further hedge against adversity, SG alluded to the availability of auxiliary stabilization funds that could be tapped to ensure the continued operation of its virtual stock exchange. SG's Web site contained lists of purported "big winners," an Internet bulletin board featuring testimonials from supposedly satisfied participants, and descriptions of incentive programs that held out the prospect of rewards for such activities as the referral of new participants and the establishment of affiliate Web sites.

At least 800 persons, paying real cash, purchased virtual shares in the virtual companies listed on SG's virtual stock exchange. By the spring of 2000, SG had deposited $7.4 million in Latvian and Estonian bank accounts. In late 1999, however, participants began to experience difficulties in redeeming their virtual shares. At about the same time, SG stopped responding to participant requests for the return of funds, yet continued to solicit new participants through its Web site. The SEC subsequently filed a civil action alleging that SG's operations constituted a fraudulent scheme that violated the registration and antifraud provisions of the federal securities laws. Accordingly, the SEC sought injunctive relief, disgorgement, and civil penalties. The district court dismissed the complaint on the grounds that the virtual shares were not securities but instead a clearly marked and defined game that lacked a business context. The SEC appealed this decision.

ISSUE Did the transaction in the privileged company's shares constitute transactions in securities?

HOLDING Probably. The SEC had alleged a set of facts that, if proven, supported its contention that the opportunity to invest in the privileged company constituted an invitation to enter into an investment contract within the jurisdictional reach of the federal securities laws.

REASONING Excerpts from the opinion of Judge Selya:

The applicable regulatory regime rests on two complementary pillars: the Securities Act of 1933 . . . and the Securities Exchange Act of 1934. . . . These statutes employ nearly identical definitions of the term 'security.' Congress intended these sweeping definitions to encompass a wide array of financial instruments, ranging from well-established investment vehicles (e.g., stocks and bonds) to much more arcane arrangements. . . . Included in this array is the elusive . . . concept of an investment contract.

Judicial efforts to delineate what is—and what is not—an investment contract are grounded in the seminal case of *SEC v. W. J. Howey* Co., 328 U.S. 293 (1946). The *Howey* Court established a tripartite test to determine whether a particular financial instrument constitutes an investment contract (and, hence, a security). . . . Under it, an investment contract comprises (1) the investment of money (2) in a common enterprise (3) with an expectation of profits to be derived solely from the efforts of the promoter or a third party. . . . This formulation must be applied in light of the economic realities of the transaction. . . . In other words, substance governs form. . . .

The Supreme Court has long espoused a broad construction of what constitutes an investment contract, aspiring "to afford the investing public a full measure of protection." . . . The investment contract taxonomy thus "embodies a flexible rather than a static principle, one that is capable of adaptation to meet the countless and variable schemes devised by those who seek the use of the money of others on the promise of profits." . . .

Over time, courts have classified as investment contracts a kaleidoscopic assortment of pecuniary arrangements that defy categorization in conventional financial terms, yet nonetheless satisfy the *Howey* Court's three criteria. . . .

[T]he district court drew a distinction between what it termed "commercial dealings" and what it termed "games." . . . Characterizing purchases of the privileged company's shares as a "clearly marked and defined game," the court concluded that since that activity was not part of the commercial world, it fell beyond the jurisdictional reach of the federal securities laws. . . . In so ruling, the court differentiated SG's operations from a classic Ponzi or pyramid scheme on the ground that those types of chicanery involved commercial dealings within a business context. . . .

Contrary to the district court's view, however, this locution does not translate into a dichotomy between business dealings, on the one hand, and games, on the other hand, as a failsafe way for determining whether a particular financial arrangement should (or should not) be characterized as an investment contract. *Howey* remains the touchstone for ascertaining whether an investment contract exists—and the test that it prescribes must be administered without regard to nomenclature. . . . As long as the three-pronged *Howey* test is satisfied, the instrument must be classified as an investment contract. . . . Once that has occurred, "it is immaterial whether the enterprise is speculative or non-speculative or whether there is a sale of property with or without intrinsic value." . . . It is equally immaterial whether the promoter depicts the enterprise as a serious commercial venture or dubs it a game. . . .

To sum up, *Howey* supplies the appropriate template for identifying investment contracts within the overarching ambit of the federal securities laws. Contrary to the district court's conclusion, this template admits of no exception for games or gaming. Thus, the language on SG's website emphasizing the game-like nature of buying and selling virtual shares of the privileged company does not place such transactions beyond the long reach of the federal securities laws. . . .

The first component of the *Howey* test focuses on the investment of money. The determining factor is whether an investor "chose to give up a specific consideration in return for a separable financial interest with the characteristics of a security." . . . We conclude that the SEC's complaint sufficiently alleges the existence of this factor.

To be sure, SG disputes the point. It argues that the individuals who purchased shares in the privileged company were not so much investing money in return for rights in the virtual shares as paying for an entertainment commodity (the opportunity to play the Stock-Generation game). This argument suggests that an interesting factual issue may await resolution—whether participants were motivated primarily by a perceived investment opportunity or by the visceral excitement of playing a game. Nevertheless . . . the SEC's complaint memorializes . . . SG's representation that participants could "firmly expect a 10% profit monthly" on purchases of the privileged company's shares. That representation plainly supports the SEC's legal claim that participants who invested substantial amounts of money in exchange for virtual shares in the privileged company likely did so in anticipation of investment gains. Given the procedural posture of the case, no more is exigible to fulfill the first part of the *Howey* test. . . .

The second component of the *Howey* test involves the existence of a common enterprise. . . . Courts are in some disarray as to the legal rules associated with the ascertainment of a common enterprise. . . . Many courts require a showing of horizontal commonality—a type of commonality that involves the pooling of assets from multiple investors so that all share in the profits and risks of the enterprise. . . . Other courts have modeled the concept of common enterprise around fact patterns in which an investor's fortunes are tied to the promoter's success rather than to the fortunes of his or her fellow investors. This doctrine, known as vertical commonality, has two variants. Broad vertical commonality requires that the well-being of all investors be dependent upon the promoter's expertise. . . . In contrast, narrow vertical commonality requires that the investors' fortunes be "interwoven with and dependent upon the efforts and success of those seeking the investment or of third parties." . . .

Thus far, neither the Supreme Court nor this court has authoritatively determined what type of commonality must be present to satisfy the common enterprise element. . . . The case at bar requires us to take a position on the common enterprise component of the *Howey* test. We hold that a showing of horizontal commonality—the pooling of assets from multiple investors in such a manner that all share in the profits and risks of the enterprise—satisfies the test. . . .

Here, the pooling element of horizontal commonality jumps off the screen. The defendants' website stated that: "The players' money is accumulated on the SG current account and is not invested anywhere." . . . Thus, as the SEC's complaint suggests, SG unambiguously represented to its clientele that participants' funds were pooled in a single account used to settle participants' on-line transactions. Therefore, pooling is established. Of course, horizontal commonality requires more than pooling alone; it also requires that investors share in the profits and risks of the enterprise. . . .

We conclude, without serious question, that the arrangement described in the SEC's complaint fairly can be characterized as either a Ponzi or pyramid scheme, and that it provides the requisite profit-and-risk sharing to support a finding of horizontal commonality. Taking as true the SEC's allegation that SG's ability to fulfill its pecuniary guarantees was fully predicated upon the net inflow of new money, the fortunes of the participants were inextricably intertwined. As long as the privileged company continued to receive net capital infusions, existing shareholders could dip into the well of funds to draw out their profits or collect their commissions. But all of them shared the risk that new participants would not emerge, cash flow would dry up, and the underlying pool would empty. . . . For present purposes, it is enough that the SEC's allegations, taken as true, satisfy the common enterprise component of the *Howey* test. . . .

The final component of the *Howey* test—the expectation of profits solely from the efforts of others—is itself divisible. . . . The Supreme Court has recognized an expectation of profits in two situations, namely (1) capital appreciation from the original investment, and (2) participation in earnings resulting from the use of investors' funds. . . . These situations are to be contrasted with transactions in which an individual purchases a commodity for personal use or consumption. . . .

The SEC posits that SG's guarantees created a reasonable expectancy of profit from investments in the privileged companies, whereas SG maintains that participants paid money not to make money, but, rather to acquire an entertainment commodity for personal consumption. . . . [T]he district court accepted SG's thesis. . . . We do not agree. . . .

SG flatly guaranteed the investments in the shares of the privileged company would be profitable, yielding monthly returns of 10% and annual returns of 215%. In our view, these profit-related guarantees constitute a not-very-subtle form of economic inducement, closely analogous to [the language used in cases holding that a security existed.] This is not to say that SG's gaming language and repeated disclaimers are irrelevant. SG has a plausible argument . . . that no participant in his or her right mind should have expected guaranteed profits from purchases of privileged company shares. But this argument, though plausible, is not inevitable. In the

end, it merely gives rise to an issue of fact . . . regarding whether SG's representations satisfy *Howey's* expectation-of-profit requirements. . . .

We turn now to the question of whether the expected profits can be said to result solely from the efforts of others. The courts of appeals have been unanimous in declining to give literal meaning to the word "solely" in this context, instead holding the requirement satisfied as long as "the efforts made by those other than the investor are the undeniably significant ones, those essential managerial efforts which affect the failure or success of the enterprise." . . .

SG's alleged scheme meets the literal definition of "solely." According to the SEC's allegations, SG represented to its customers the lack of investor effort required to make guaranteed profits on purchases of the privileged company's shares, noting, for example, that "playing with [the] privileged shares practically requires no time at all." SG was responsible for all the important efforts that undergirded the 10% guaranteed monthly return. As the sole proprietor of the StockGeneration website, SG enjoyed direct operational control over all aspects of the virtual stock exchange. . . . SG's payment of referral bonuses to participants who introduced new users to the website does not require a different result. Even if a participant chose not to refer others to the StockGeneration website, he or she still could expect, based on SG's profit-related guarantees, to reap monthly profits from mere ownership of the privileged company's shares. Accordingly, the SEC's complaint makes out a triable issue on whether participants expected to receive profits derived solely from the efforts of others. . . .

Giving due weight to the economic realities of the situation, we hold that the SEC has alleged a set of facts which, if proven, satisfy the three-part *Howey* test and support its assertion that the opportunity to invest in the shares of the privileged company, described on SG's website, constituted an invitation to enter into an investment contract within the jurisdictional reach of the federal securities laws. . . .

BUSINESS CONSIDERATIONS Would serious investors view an Internet "stock game" as an investment rather than a diversion, albeit an amusement that carried with it the potential for substantial returns?

ETHICAL CONSIDERATIONS Was SG acting ethically when it placed this "game" on the Internet and encouraged people to "invest" in these "companies"? What, if anything, could SG have done to act in a more ethical manner in this situation?

Although the '33 Act prohibits all offers to buy or sell prior to the filing of a registration statement, some activities can take place before this filing. For example, the issuer (the corporation selling the stock) typically enlists the services of third parties, such as underwriters, who agree to help the issuer finance the stock offering. Underwriters are persons or institutions that, by agreeing to sell securities to the public and to buy those not sold, ensure the sale of corporate securities. During this prefiling period, then, the issuer can enter into preliminary negotiations with such underwriters. Next, during the registration process's so-called waiting period, the SEC has 20 days in which to examine the registration statement. If the registration statement is complete and accurate, it becomes effective at the end of this 20-day waiting period.

During this period, the issuer or underwriter can accept oral purchase orders. However, the SEC limits written advertisements to "tombstone ads," so designated because they are boxed in the shape of a tombstone, and limits written information to preliminary "red herring" prospectuses, so dubbed because of the red lettering on them, to the effect that a registration statement has been filed but is not yet effective.

After the registration statement becomes effective but before any sale can occur—this is the so-called posteffective period—the issuer or underwriter must provide virtually every would-be investor with a prospectus (the so-called statutory prospectus) that sets out the information required by the statute. The issuer must make sure the information contained in the prospectus remains accurate during the posteffective period as well; otherwise, the sale of the securities will not be legal. These rules reinforce the '33 Act's "truth-in-securities" policies.

Exemptions The '33 Act exempts certain *classes of securities* from the registration and prospectus requirements discussed above. Note, however, that there are no exemptions from the antifraud provisions, which we will examine in the next section of this chapter. The exempted classes include securities issued by federal and state governments and banks; short-term notes; issues by nonprofit organizations; issues by savings and loan associations subject to state or federal regulation; any security futures product that is cleared by a registered clearing agency and traded on a national exchange; issues by common carriers subject to the jurisdiction of the Surface Transportation Board; certain qualifying employee pension plans; insurance policies and certain annuities subject to regulation by state authorities; and intrastate issues of securities.

In addition, the '33 Act exempts certain *transactions*: private offerings (those that do not involve public offerings of securities, as is the usual case); transactions by persons other than issuers, underwriters, or dealers; certain brokers'

and dealers' transactions; and small public issues (defined generally as transactions up to $5 million that involve sales only to "accredited investors"). As the latter exemption shows, SEC rules oftentimes may limit the issuers who qualify, the aggregate offering price, the number and qualifications of investors, the manner in which the issuer conducts the offering, the resale of the shares, and the like. In short, the SEC has established prerequisites and complex rules that firms must follow if they hope to secure an exemption from the registration process for this and certain other transactions.

For instance, in one famous case, Ralston Purina Co. had sold nearly $2 million of unregistered stock to its "key employees." The key employees who had purchased the stock included shop and dock foremen, stenographers, copywriters, clerical assistants, and veterinarians. Because it had made offers to only a few of its employees, Ralston Purina construed its actions as falling under the "private offering" exemption. Asserting that the aim of the '33 Act is to protect investors by promoting full disclosure of the information thought necessary for informed investment decisions, the Supreme Court concluded that Ralston Purina had not shown that the employees involved here had enjoyed access to the kind of information that registration would disclose. Thus, the Court held that this attempted private offering (or "private placement") was not a bona fide exempt transaction and that registration under the 1933 Act should have occurred.[1]

Antifraud Provisions In addition to registration requirements, the '33 Act contains several antifraud provisions. Section 12 prohibits oral or written misstatements of material facts or omissions of material facts necessary to keep the statements from being misleading in the circumstances in which they were made. Section 17 is a general antifraud provision that makes it unlawful for any person to use the mails or interstate commerce to employ any device or scheme that will defraud another person or to engage in any transaction, practice, or course of business that defrauds or deceives the purchaser. Basically, § 17 makes illegal any form of fraud, untrue statement of a material fact, or omission of a material fact involving the sale of any securities in interstate commerce or through the mail.

Section 27A of the 1995 Private Securities Litigation Reform Act (PSLRA) redefines when liability exists for certain misleading "forward-looking" statements. The PSLRA represents one of the most sweeping and comprehensive reforms of the nation's securities laws in the last two decades. Designed to reassert legislative control over securities fraud litigation, the PSLRA sets out specific procedural and substantive rules with regard to these and other sections of the

'33 Act. To encourage corporate executives to offer investors more meaningful information, § 27A, the so-called safe harbor provision, exempts from liability filed registration documents containing certain types of forward-looking statements (including projections of revenues, income, earnings per share, and company plans or objectives relating to certain products or services) by certain issuers and underwriters. (Significantly, this "safe harbor" is not applicable to IPOs.) To fall within the available safe harbor, a forward-looking statement (either oral or written) should be accompanied by meaningful cautionary statements identifying important factors that would cause actual results to differ materially from those projected in the forward-looking statements. Registration statements consisting of traditional "boilerplate" language in which the issuer's purported cautionary statements mention "lack of demand," "an increase in competition," and so on presumably would not suffice. But information relating to the issuer's business that discusses the possible loss of a major customer or a serious glitch in the development of technology for a product in the prototype stage would fulfill the statutory requirements for a "meaningful cautionary statement."

Besides providing encouragement for executives to offer investors more meaningful information, other central aims of the PSLRA include the discouragement of class action suits brought for frivolous—or purely entrepreneurial—reasons (so-called strike suits) and the preservation of such suits in situations in which shareholders in fact have been the victims of securities fraud. The act accomplishes these goals by codifying stringent pleading requirements for certain private actions under the '34 Act (but not the '33 Act) and by awarding sanctions (for example, costs and attorney's fees) for a party's failing to fulfill these pleading requirements. Given the PSLRA's complexities as well as those that generally inhere in the issuance of securities, anyone who contemplates issuing securities should seek the counsel of professionals who specialize in the securities field.

Liabilities and Remedies The potential liabilities spawned by the '33 Act also constitute a significant reason for seeking competent advice. Section 11 imposes civil liability for any registration statement that contains untrue statements of a material fact or omissions of material facts that would make the registration statement misleading in the circumstances in which a purchaser buys the securities. Such a purchaser can receive as damages an amount not exceeding the price paid for the securities.

Section 11 places liability on every person who signed the registration statement; on every person who was a director or was named in the registration statement as about to become a director; on every accountant, engineer, appraiser, or any

---

NRW CASE 36.1 Finance/Management

NRW

ISSUING STOCK IN NRW

Mai, Helen, and Carlos want to issue stock in NRW to generate funds for the expansion of the firm. They believe that, if successful, this IPO will result in a huge inflow of cash for the firm. However, they also know that the firm's IPO is likely to be subject to regulation under the Securities Act of 1933. They ask you what they will need to do to qualify for an exemption from registration under the '33 Act, or, in the alternative, what they will need to do to comply with the registration requirements. What advice will you give them?

BUSINESS CONSIDERATIONS Why might a business prefer a potentially smaller inflow of funds if this meant that the firm qualified for an exemption from registering under the '33 Act? What factors should a firm consider in deciding whether the registration requirements justify a larger public offering?

ETHICAL CONSIDERATIONS Is it ethical for a firm to tailor its securities offerings to avoid registration of the securities under the '33 Act? Are the directors of a business acting ethically toward their constituents if they fail to consider a security-issuing plan that legally avoids registration?

INTERNATIONAL CONSIDERATIONS Could the firm possibly avoid SEC regulations by only offering the stock to potential investors through a foreign market, such as the markets in London or Tokyo? What potential drawbacks might exist for such a decision?

---

other professional expert whose statement or report appears in the registration statement; and on every underwriter. By showing that they acted with "due diligence," all such persons, except the issuer, may escape liability.

This statutory defense of "due diligence" varies as to the type of defendant involved and whether the misrepresentations or omissions are found in the "expertised" or "nonexpertised" portions of the registration statement. The defense generally is available to anyone who, after reasonable investigation, had reasonable grounds to believe, and did believe, that the registration statement was accurate and did not omit material facts that were either required or necessary to make the statement not misleading.

A landmark, pre-PSLRA case, *Escott v. BarChris Construction Corp.*[2] illustrates many of these concepts. Suing under § 11 of the '33 Act, the purchasers of certain securities of BarChris Construction Corporation alleged that the registration statement filed with the SEC concerning this stock had contained materially false statements and material omissions. The defendants included the persons who had signed the registration statement (primarily directors and officers), the underwriters (investment bankers), and Peat, Marwick, Mitchell & Co. (BarChris's auditors). The court framed the issues as whether the registration statement had included materially false statements and material omissions and, if so, whether the defendants had successfully shown the statutory defense—that is, that they had acted with due diligence. The court concluded that the registration statement had included materially false statements and material omissions. Moreover, the court determined that only the outside directors had been able to sustain even a part of their "due diligence" defense (and they could show due diligence only with respect to the "expertised" portion of the registration statement).

The court emphasized that a material fact is a fact that, had it been correctly stated or disclosed, would have deterred the average prudent investor from purchasing the securities in question. Therefore, BarChris's overstatement of its sales and gross profits and its understatement of its liabilities in 1961 constituted material facts. But the prospectus statements about BarChris's status in December 1960 consisted of rather minor and hence nonmaterial errors. On the other hand, the prospectus's 1961 balance sheet had contained material errors. Nonetheless, although the due diligence statutory defense had been available to all the defendants except the issuer, BarChris, none of the inside directors and officers had sustained the due diligence defense with respect to either the "expertised" (financial reports prepared by accountants) or the "unexpertised" portions of the registration statement. The outside directors similarly had not sustained their due diligence defense as to the unexpertised part of the registration statement, primarily because they had neither familiarized themselves with its contents nor questioned its major points. On the other hand, the outside directors, because of their confidence in the auditors, Peat, Marwick, Mitchell & Co., had shown due diligence regarding the expertised portion of the statement. Like the inside directors and officers, the underwriters and the auditors had failed to establish the due diligence defense with respect to either portion of the registration statement.

In this context, note that the PSLRA changes § 11's longstanding joint and several liability rules, in which each defendant potentially was liable for all the damages awarded to the plaintiff, to a standard that embraces proportionate liability. The PSLRA grounds this change on the rationale that the imposition of joint and several liability in the past had led to a plaintiff's joining "deep pocket" defendants (lawyers, accountants, underwriters, and directors) in the lawsuit, even though these persons bore little responsibility for the plaintiff's injuries.

These defendants often felt overwhelming pressures to settle—even if the suits were meritless—so as to avoid the enormous damage awards recoverable by plaintiffs in huge class action suits. Hence, the PSLRA adopts a "fair share" rule approach to liability in general and applies this rule in specific to outside directors who have refrained from "knowingly" violating the securities laws. These outside directors ordinarily will be liable only for the portion of damages attributable to their percentage of responsibility. In enacting this legislation, Congress hoped to give qualified persons an incentive to sit on the boards of start-up and high-technology companies without becoming apprehensive about their possible exposure to grossly disproportionate liability. It is important to note that the PSLRA applies solely to the allocation of damages; the PSLRA otherwise preserves the plaintiff's § 11 claims against all other defendants as well as the rights of contribution and settlement set out in the '33 Act. Nor does the PSLRA change the state-of-mind requirements of § 12 and § 17 as reflected in the '33 Act and Court holding.

Additionally, § 12 exacts civil liability from any person who sells securities through the mails or in interstate commerce by means of a prospectus or oral communication that includes misrepresentations or omissions of necessary material facts. Such persons can avoid liability if they can show that they did not know, and in the exercise of reasonable care could not have known, about the untruths or omissions. The injured party can sue only the person who actually sold the security but can rescind the sale and recover the price paid for the security. The PSLRA amends § 12 to allow a defendant to escape liability if he or she can prove that the depreciation in the value of the security resulted from factors unrelated to the alleged misstatement or omission (for example, from a general market decline). Thus, purchasers suing under the '33 Act's civil liability provision must prove that the alleged misstatements or omissions actually *caused* their losses. In *Gustafson v. Alloyd, Inc.,*[3] the Supreme Court held that § 12 claims can arise only from initial stock offerings and not from a private sale agreement. The Court reasoned that such a contract is not held out to the public as a prospectus (that is, the document that solicits the public to acquire securities). Hence, the Court held, under the plain meaning of the statute—as reinforced in § 10—a "prospectus" must set out the information contained in the registration statement required in public offerings. Because a private contract indisputably does not have to specify the information enumerated in a registration statement, the Court rejected the argument that the contract in question was tantamount to a prospectus. In addition to § 12's civil liabilities, § 17's antifraud provisions may be used as a basis for criminal liability. Moreover, § 24 sets up criminal sanctions for willful

violations of the '33 Act. The '33 Act, and several other laws affecting securities, is discussed at http://www.sec.gov/about/laws.shtml.

Note how the court in the following decision used many of these concepts in disposing of the case.

36.2

IN RE NATIONSMART CORPORATION SECURITIES LITIGATION
130 F.3d 309 (8th Cir. 1997), cert. denied, 524 U.S. 927 (1998)

FACTS NationsMart Corporation was formed in 1992 with the goal of applying the low-price, one-stop shopping concept, made successful by Wal-Mart and Kmart "supercenters," to the dry cleaning, laundry, and shoe repair markets. After filing a registration statement and a prospectus with the Securities and Exchange Commission (SEC), on December 22, 1993, NationsMart commenced an initial public offering (IPO) of two million units at $7.00 per unit. The prospectus stated that NationsMart expected to raise $11.7 million in its public offering and that it intended to use the net proceeds to fund the 51 existing NationsMart stores and to open 108 new stores by November 1994 and 600 new stores by 1998. The prospectus contained detailed financial data about NationsMart, a discussion and analysis of the company's financial situation as well as the results of its operation, and its strategy for future growth.

The prospectus acknowledged that NationsMart had previously experienced financial losses but stated that NationsMart's management believed that, based on a "financial model," projected income from existing stores, in conjunction with the proceeds of the public offering, would "significantly improve the capital resources of the Company and thereby address certain of the going concern conditions." Another section of the prospectus included some of the risks investors faced in buying the offered units, such as NationsMart's limited operating history and the absence of a prior market for its shares; its dependence on leases from Wal-Mart, Kmart, and other "host retailers"; and its need for additional financing in the future. The prospectus also cautioned that NationsMart's financial model reflected "only the best judgment of management" and was subject to conditions beyond the company's control.

On July 14, 1994, NationsMart announced that it was experiencing slower-than-expected growth and that it would open 35 to 45 fewer stores than the prospectus had anticipated. NationsMart also disclosed that it had settled a "whistle-blower" lawsuit with a former executive who had sued NationsMart after her discharge in March 1994. Following these announcements, Nations-

Mart's common stock fell to $1.875 and continued to decline until mid-1995, when the stock was delisted.

A 1994 class action filed against NationsMart and its underwriters alleged, among other things, violations of §§ 11 and 12 of the '33 Act. The plaintiffs alleged that the defendants had made false statements in, and had omitted material information from, the prospectus, specifically that the defendants had known that the company would not be able to implement the business plan outlined in the prospectus with the proceeds of the offering. The plaintiffs also submitted that, in the months before the effective date of the public offering, the defendants had failed to disclose the fact that the favorable trends described in the prospectus were not likely to materialize; that the costs to operate existing NationsMart stores and to open new stores were rising; and that corporate overhead was increasing. The district court dismissed the § 11 claim owing to the plaintiffs' failure under Federal Rule of Civil Procedure 9(b) to meet the requirement that one plead "the circumstances constituting fraud or mistake" with particularity. The plaintiffs subsequently appealed this part of the court's ruling.

ISSUE Did Rule 9(b)'s particularity requirement apply to claims under § 11 of the '33 Act?

HOLDING No. The particularity requirement of Rule 9(b) was inapplicable to such claims because proof of fraud or mistake is not a prerequisite to establishing liability under § 11 of the '33 Act.

REASONING Excerpts from the opinion of Chief Judge Richard S. Arnold:

Section 11 imposes civil liability on persons preparing and signing materially misleading registration statements. . . . A registration statement is materially misleading if it contains an untrue statement of material fact or if it omits a material fact necessary to prevent the statement from being misleading. . . . Any person who purchases a registered security is entitled to sue under this section. . . . Section 11 imposes "a stringent standard of liability on the parties who play a direct role in a registered offering." . . . To establish a prima facie § 11 claim, a plaintiff need show only that he bought the security and that there was a material misstatement or omission. Scienter is not required for establishing liability under this section. . . . The liability of the issuer of a materially misleading registration statement is "virtually absolute, even for innocent misstatements." . . . Persons beside the issuer who face liability under § 11—which includes anyone who signed the registration statement, such as officers, directors, and underwriters—must prove that, after reasonable investigation, they had reasonable grounds to believe that the statement was not materially misleading. . . . In their complaint, the plaintiffs made clear that they did not allege in the context of their § 11 claim that the defendants were liable for fraudulent or intentional conduct. . . . Therefore, their claim should not have been dismissed for failing to comply with Rule 9(b). . . . The allegations of innocent or negligent misrepresentation, which are at the heart of a § 11 claim, would survive. The plaintiffs' case should not have been dismissed because they alleged more than was necessary to recover under § 11 of the Securities Act. We recognize that other courts have sometimes applied Rule 9(b) to claims brought under §§ 11 and 12(2) of the Securities Act of 1933. Such claims are said to be subject to Rule 9(b) when they are "grounded in fraud." . . . Defendants ask that we follow these authorities and affirm the dismissal of the §§ 11 and 12 (2) counts of this complaint for failure to comply with Rule 9(b). We decline to do so for two reasons. First, the complaint in this case expressly disavows any claim of fraud in connection with the § 11 and § 12(2) counts. . . . In addition, a pleading standard which requires a party to plead particular facts to support a cause of action that does not include fraud or mistake as an element comports neither with Supreme Court precedent nor with the liberal system of "notice pleading" embodied in the Federal Rules of Civil Procedure. . . . Rule 9(b) imposes a heightened pleading requirement for allegations of fraud and mistake; but . . . § 11 does not require proof of fraud for recovery. The Supreme Court has held that federal courts may not apply the heightened pleading standard of Rule 9(b) outside the two specific instances—fraud and mistake—explicitly found in the Rule. . . . Given the broad scope of liability under § 11 and the liberal pleading requirements of Federal Rule 8(a), these allegations are sufficient to state a claim. Therefore, the District Court should not have dismissed the complaint under Rule 12(b)(6).

The District Court also based its dismissal of part of the plaintiffs' § 11 claim on the "safe harbor" provision of SEC Rule 175, which protects "forward-looking statements" made in documents filed with the SEC. Under this regulation, a "forward-looking statement" can include statements containing projections of revenue, income, earnings per share, capital expenditures, dividends, or capital structure; statements of management's future plans and objectives; and statements of future economic performance contained in the management's discussion and analysis of financial conditions. . . . A forward-looking statement is protected from liability under the Securities Act of 1933 and "shall be deemed not to be a fraudulent statement . . . unless it is shown that such a statement was made or reaffirmed without a reasonable basis or was disclosed other than in good faith." . . . "Fraudulent" for purposes of Rule 175 does not mean fraud in the traditional sense, but instead simply denotes any of the bases of liability under the Securities Act, including liability under § 11. . . . Therefore, material misstatements in a registration statement may be protected from § 11 liability if they are forward-looking. Many of the statements in the Prospectus challenged by the plaintiffs were indeed forward-looking. The plaintiffs challenged NationsMart's projections that it would open 108 new stores by 1994 and 600 new stores by 1998; that the proceeds from the public offering would be sufficient to cover the plans for expansion; and that NationsMart's history of operating losses would give way to future growth. . . . The plaintiffs did not argue in their complaint or before the District Court that these statements were not forward-looking; rather, they alleged that the defendants' statements "were false and had no reasonable basis because [the defendants] knew that there were no valid assumptions underlying the projections." . . . Forward-looking statements are not protected by Rule 175 if they are not generally believed, if they lack a reasonable basis, or if the speaker knows of undisclosed facts which seriously undermine the accuracy of the statement. . . . However, the District Court held that the plaintiffs could not avoid the "safe harbor" of SEC Rule 175 by claiming that the defendants had no reasonable basis for their projections because, under Rule 9(b), the plaintiffs did not plead specific facts which showed that the statements either had no reasonable basis or were not believed by the defendants. . . . However, the claims in these cases were brought only under § 10(b) of the Securities Exchange Act of 1934, which requires proof of fraud as one of its elements. Application of the specificity requirement of Rule 9(b) would be appropriate if the "safe harbor" protected the defendant from a cause of action involving true fraud. But § 11 claims do not involve fraud, and the plaintiffs did not have to plead specific facts to avoid the safe-harbor rule. . . .

The District Court also dismissed the plaintiffs' § 11 claim because, according to the Court, the Prospectus contained numerous statements which "bespoke caution" and warned investors of the financial risks they were taking when they bought stock in Nations-Mart. This Court has recognized that specific cautionary statements in offering materials which disclose potential investment risks may defeat a plaintiff's claim that the offering materials were materially misleading under federal securities law. . . . Cautionary statements, however, cannot be general risk warnings or mere boilerplate; they must be detailed and specific. . . . The Prospectus contained a section labeled "Risk Factors" which warned of potential problems NationsMart faced as a growing company. . . . Many of the warnings of short-term risks to investors, however, were generic and nonspecific. The complaint alleges that the defendants did not adequately warn investors of the potential risks faced by NationsMart between the time of the offering and October 1994, when the Prospectus admitted that the company would have to find new sources of revenue. Many statements in the Risk Factors section—such as the warning that "there can be no assurance that any of the Company's Centers or that the Company as a whole will generate income from operations or provide cash from operating activities in the future"—do not provide the sort of detail that would "bespeak caution" to a potential investor. Though the Prospectus did state that "the Company expects to continue to incur net losses and negative cash flow from operations during 1994 and 1995," . . . There is no warning anywhere in the Prospectus detailing the specific risk that NationsMart would continue to face severely declining profits and ballooning corporate overhead in the short term,

between the date of the offering, December 1993, and October 1994, which threatened the company's ability to operate.

In addition, the bespeaks-caution doctrine cannot immunize the defendants from liability under § 11 if they omitted material information from the offering materials. . . . In their complaint, the plaintiffs alleged that NationsMart's management failed to disclose specific facts indicating that its judgment was flawed. . . . If taken as true, these allegations would call into question whether management was in fact exercising its "best judgment" in formulating the company's financial model, as it claimed in the Prospectus. . . . Because of inadequate and nonspecific warnings of short-term risks, and because of the plaintiffs' allegations that the defendants omitted material information from the Prospectus, the bespeaks-caution doctrine cannot, simply as a matter of pleading, defeat the plaintiffs' § 11 claim. . . .

BUSINESS CONSIDERATIONS Should a firm put in place specific policies aimed at ensuring that the statements made in the prospectus and the registration statement fall within the "safe harbor" rule, or should the firm evaluate all such statements on a case-by-case basis? Explain your reasoning.

ETHICAL CONSIDERATIONS If you were to consider the "safe harbor" rule and the "bespeaks caution" doctrine from an ethical (as opposed to a legal) perspective, would you support these concepts? Why?

The Securities Exchange Act of 1934

Whereas the 1933 Act deals with the initial issuance of securities, the Securities Exchange Act of 1934 (the '34 Act) regulates the secondary distribution of securities. As such, the '34 Act's jurisdiction extends to the registration and distribution of securities through national stock exchanges, national securities associations, brokers, and dealers. The '34 Act also covers proxy solicitations of registered securities, regulates tender offers, limits insider trading, forbids short-swing profits, and in general tries to eliminate fraud and manipulative conduct with respect to the sale or purchase of securities. Thus, in many ways the '33 and '34 Acts are similar and supplement each other. But the reach of the '34 Act, with its supervision of national exchanges and over-the-counter sales of securities, is even broader than that of the '33 Act.

Registration and Reporting The '34 Act requires any issuer who trades securities on a national stock exchange to register with the SEC. In addition, any firm engaged in

interstate commerce with total assets of over $5 million and at least 500 shareholders must comply with the registration provisions of § 12. For violations of § 12, the SEC can revoke or suspend the registration of the security involved.

Like the '33 Act, the '34 Act tries to ensure that the investing public will have sufficient information about publicly traded securities when these investors make their decisions about whether to buy stocks. Hence, the '34 Act mandates certain disclosures by firms covered by the act when the securities are listed with national exchanges or traded over the counter. Basically, these obligatory disclosures include detailed registration statements similar to the information required under the '33 Act as well as annual and quarterly reports. SEC Forms 8-A, 8-K, 10-K, and 10-Q, which companies use for compiling this information, are complex and contain substantial numbers of facts and figures relating to the companies' businesses. Other SEC provisions impose liability on the company for damages resulting from an investor's reliance on misleading statements contained in any such documents.

Proxy Solicitations A *proxy* is an assignment by the shareholder of the right to vote the shares held by the shareholder. Since proxies become a device for consolidating corporate power and control, one cannot underestimate their importance both to management and to those "dissident" shareholders who wish to oust the present management. Because of the high stakes involved for both competing factions, it is vitally important that the information provided to shareholders be accurate. If shareholders receive misleading information, they will make their decision regarding who should be given their proxies—management or dissidents—in ignorance of the facts. To prevent such abuses, § 14 of the '34 Act makes it illegal for a company registered under § 12 to solicit proxies in a manner that violates the SEC rules and regulations that protect the investing public. Section 14 also sets out rules mandating disclosure of pertinent information to shareholders at corporate meetings even when no solicitation of proxies will occur.

The disclosure required of proxy solicitations includes a proxy statement, which contains detailed information, and a proxy form, on which the shareholder can note his or her approval or disapproval of each proposal that will be decided at the corporation's meeting. Before either the corporation or the dissidents send proxies to shareholders, the SEC must approve the statement and the form. These preliminary proxies must be filed with the SEC at least 10 days before they are sent to shareholders. If the meeting involves the election of directors, any proxy statement also must include an annual report detailing, among other things, the financial aspects of the company (including a graph that analyzes the company's performance) and the company's executive compensation plans and arrangements (including "golden parachutes"). Similarly, as mentioned earlier, any proxy contest requires full disclosure of all pertinent facts regarding the matters under consideration, such as the identity of all participants in the proxy contest and the reasons for the proxy solicitation.

Section 14 furthermore authorizes the inclusion of shareholder proposals of no more than 500 words in any management-backed proxy solicitation. This SEC rule allows any eligible shareholder to express an opinion regarding the recommendations management has made without incurring the significant costs involved in an independent proxy solicitation. This aspect of § 14 thus attempts to preserve the balance of power between management and the insurgents so as to safeguard the democratic aspects of the corporation.

As you probably have surmised, management usually opposes the inclusion of such proposals. SEC rules authorize the exclusion of proposals, under state law, that are not "proper subjects" for action by shareholders, proposals that center on personal claims or grievances, proposals that are not significantly related to the corporation's business, and proposals that are substantially similar to a proposal submitted but not approved within the past five years. In disputes over whether the corporation can exclude the proposal, the SEC normally decides who is correct. Management bears the burden of proof regarding why it properly excluded the proposal. Shareholder proposals have dealt with management compensation, company policies allegedly leading to discrimination or pollution, and even opposition to the Vietnam War. Shareholder proposals, however, usually are unsuccessful.

The corporation ordinarily pays for the expenses incurred in proxy contests if either management or the insurgents win. The law is unsettled as to whether the corporation should pay the costs of a contest if management loses, but the trend is to make the corporation (not the managers themselves) pay even in those circumstances.

Liability for misleading proxy statements or those that omit a material fact necessary to make the statement true and not misleading is absolute. Any person who sells or buys securities in reliance on such statements can recover from the corporation.

Tender Offers In addition to regulating proxies, since 1968 the Williams Act, codified in § 13 and § 14, also has regulated tender offers or takeover bids, whether hostile or friendly, wherein one publicly held corporation (the "tender offeror") attempts to acquire control of another publicly held company (the "target"). Section 14, in conjunction with § 13, sets forth filing and registration requirements for any person who becomes the owner of more than 5 percent of any class of securities registered under § 12. In general, these provisions force the offeror to provide the target company's shareholders with the names of the offerors and their interests, the purpose of the takeover, the method of disposing of the target firm's stocks and assets, and so forth. Additionally, any statements the management of the target firm makes in opposition to the merger also must be filed with the SEC. Provisions for liability under this aspect of the '34 Act are similar to those instituted for violations of the proxy rules.

Insider Trading Directors, officers, and controlling shareholders may violate the federal securities laws if they engage in "insider trading." We noted that the '34 Act makes such activities illegal and sets out possibilities of far-ranging liability. Section 10(b) of the '34 Act makes unlawful any manipulative or deceptive device used through the mails or in interstate commerce in connection with the purchase or sale of any security. By providing for liability for any fraudulent or deceitful activity that involves misleading material facts or omissions of material facts that would make a statement misleading in the circumstances in which it was made, SEC Rule 10(b)-5 augments § 10(b).

When material inside information is involved, the insider *either* must publicly disclose the information so as to ensure that the investing public that does not have access to the information will remain free from prejudice *or* abstain from trading in the securities.

Nevertheless, it is difficult to judge when information is important enough to be considered "material." *Basic Incorporated v. Levinson,*[4] a Supreme Court case involving the company's public statements concerning the possibility of a merger, provides guidelines in this important area. In the *Basic* decision, the Court reiterated that the standard of materiality set forth in *TSC Industries, Inc. v. Northway* will govern future § 10(b) and Rule 10(b)-5 cases. In short, materiality depends on the significance the reasonable investor would place on the withheld or misrepresented information. If, as noted in the *TSC Industries* case, there is a substantial likelihood that the disclosure of the omitted fact would have been viewed as significant by a reasonable investor, the information is material. Hence, the Court identified no valid justification for artificially excluding from the definition of materiality information concerning merger discussions, which otherwise would be considered significant to the trading decision of a reasonable investor, merely because the parties (or their representatives) had failed to reach an agreement-in-principle as to price and structure. The Court noted that the lower courts in this case had accepted a presumption, created by the fraud-on-the-market theory and subject to rebuttal by Basic, that persons who had traded Basic shares had done so in reliance on the integrity of the price set by the market; but that because of Basic's material misrepresentations, that price had been fraudulently depressed. Requiring plaintiffs to show a speculative state of facts—that is, how they would have acted if omitted material information had been disclosed or if the misrepresentations had not been made—would place an unnecessarily unrealistic evidentiary burden on the Rule 10(b)-5 plaintiff who had traded on an impersonal market. Because most publicly available information is reflected in the market price, the Court stressed, an investor's reliance on any public material misrepresentations, therefore, may be presumed for purposes of a Rule 10(b)-5 action. Nevertheless, any showing that severs the link between the alleged misrepresentation and either the price received (or paid) by the plaintiffs, or their decision to trade at a fair market price, will be sufficient to rebut the presumption of reliance. According to the Court, materiality in the merger context depends on the probability that

the transaction will be consummated and its significance to the issuer of the securities. Simply put, materiality depends on the facts and must be determined on a case-by-case basis. Courts may apply a presumption of reliance supported by the fraud-on-the-market theory; that presumption, however, is rebuttable.

Although § 10(b) does not expressly provide for civil liability, it, as a broad antifraud provision, applies to any manipulative or deceptive device used in connection with any purchase or sale of any security by any person; there are no exemptions from coverage. Similarly, Rule 10(b)-5 has been applied to the activities of corporate insiders—directors, officers, controlling shareholders, employees, lawyers, accountants, bankers, consultants, and anyone else who has access to material inside information that may affect the price of the stock. Prior to 1980, persons considered insiders included even those who purchased or sold stock based on tips provided directly or indirectly by directors, officers, and the like. Hence, the SEC considered, for example, a barber who overheard a director's discussion of an upcoming business trip and bought stock based on this market information an insider as well. But the *Chiarella v. United States*[5] case has cast some doubt on whether such remote "tippees" should be liable.

Chiarella was a printer who worked for a firm that printed takeover bids. Although the identities of the firms had been left blank, Chiarella—using the information contained in the documents he was preparing for printing—was able to deduce the names of the target companies. Without disclosing his knowledge, Chiarella purchased stock in the target companies and sold the stock when the takeover attempts became public knowledge. Chiarella thereby gained $30,000 in 14 months. The SEC indicted him on 17 counts of violating § 10(b) and Rule 10(b)-5 of the '34 Act.

However, the Supreme Court held that neither Section 10(b) nor Rule 10(b)-5 would apply to Chiarella. In the Court's view, he was not a corporate insider, a fiduciary, or a tippee. Rather, he was a complete stranger who had dealt with the sellers only through impersonal market transactions. The Court therefore believed that affirming Chiarella's conviction would recognize a general duty between all participants in market transactions to forgo actions based on material, nonpublic information. Therefore, the Court concluded that the imposition of such a broad duty, departing as it would from the established doctrine that duty arises from a specific relationship between two parties, would be ill-advised.

According to the *Chiarella* case, then, the mere possession of inside information does not create a legal duty owed to faceless market participants. The Supreme Court's decision in *Dirks v. Securities and Exchange Commission,*[6] by emphasizing the basic principle that only some persons, under some circumstances, will be barred from trading while they are in possession of material, nonpublic information, appears to reinforce *Chiarella*'s holding.

In 1973, Raymond Dirks was an officer of a New York broker/dealer firm that specialized in providing investment analyses of insurance company securities to institutional investors. On March 6, Ronald Secrist, a former officer of Equity Funding of America, told Dirks that the assets of Equity Funding, a diversified corporation primarily engaged in selling life insurance and mutual funds, had been vastly overstated as the result of fraudulent corporate practices. Stressing that various regulatory agencies had failed to act on similar charges made by Equity Funding employees, Secrist urged Dirks to verify the fraud and to disclose it publicly. Although neither Dirks nor his firm owned or traded any Equity Funding stock, some of Equity Funding's clients and investors ultimately sold their holdings in Equity Funding as a result of information that Dirks had shared with them during his investigation. The SEC also subsequently investigated Dirks's involvement and found that his repeating of confidential corporate information had violated securities rules. However, since he had played an important role in bringing Equity Funding's massive fraud to light, the SEC merely censured (that is, formally reprimanded) him.

The Supreme Court found that Dirks, as a tippee of material nonpublic information received from the insiders of a corporation with which Dirks was unaffiliated, in these circumstances had no duty to abstain from the use of such inside information. The Court based its holding on the following grounds: The tippers had been motivated by a desire to expose fraud rather than from a desire either to receive personal benefits or to bestow valuable information on him so that he could derive monetary benefits from what they had told him.

Hence, in the absence of personal gain to the insider, there was no breach of duty to the stockholders. Similarly, in the absence of such a breach by the insider, there could be no derivative breach by someone like Dirks. In short, tippees in Dirks's position would inherit no duty to disclose or abstain until a breach of the insider's fiduciary duty had occurred. Dirks's conduct, therefore, had not violated the antifraud provisions of the '33 or '34 Acts.

The *Chiarella* and *Dirks* cases thus appear to limit significantly the concept of who an "insider" is for § 10(b) purposes. According to *Chiarella*, "outsiders"—those who are not in positions of trust or confidence within the companies involved in the litigation—can escape the duty to abstain from trading on nonpublic material information, unless they are actual tippees of insiders. Reinforcing *Chiarella*, *Dirks* holds that tippees of insiders who have divulged material inside information out of motives other than personal gain may avoid liability as well. Because the tippees' potential liability derives from the insiders' fiduciary duties to the corporation, the absence of any breach of those duties by the insiders leads to a finding of no breach on the tippees' part, either.

For years after these decisions, the SEC continued to prosecute the outsiders and their tippees on the theory that outsiders' misappropriation of nonpublic material information works a fraud on the securities market or constitutes fraud as to the outsiders' employers, owing to the outsiders' breach of a fiduciary duty or similar relationship of trust and confidence. As such, the SEC reasoned, this fraudulent conduct violates the securities laws' insider-trading prohibitions. In 1997, in *United States v. O'Hagan*,[7] the Supreme Court finally resolved the split among the federal circuit courts of appeals that had developed as to the legal validity of this so-called misappropriation (or "fraud-on-the-market") theory. There the Court held that one who traded in securities using confidential information misappropriated through a breach of a fiduciary duty owed to the source of the confidential information would violate both § 10(b) and Rule 14c-3(a)'s "disclose or abstain" rule because such a misappropriation involves "deceptive" conduct "in connection with" a securities transaction.

As a further clarification of the misappropriation theory, in 2000 the SEC issued Rule 10b-5-1, which prohibits insiders from trading "on the basis of" material nonpublic information. According to the rule, a purchase or sale of a security of an issuer is "on the basis" of material nonpublic information about that security or issuer if the person making the purchase or sale was aware of the information when the person engaged in the purchase or sale. One accused of violating the rule can assert a number of affirmative defenses; including the fact that he or she had entered into a binding contract of purchase or sale before becoming aware of the information; he or she had instructed another to purchase or sell the security for the account of the person giving the instructions; or the person had adopted a written plan for trading securities according to a written formula or a computer program and the purchase or sale that occurred was pursuant to the contract, instruction, or plan and effected without the person's subsequently influencing how, when, or whether to effect purchases or sales. Any other person who, pursuant to the contract, instruction, or plan, did exercise influence must have been unaware of the material nonpublic information when doing so.

Also issued was Rule 10b-5-2, which provides a nonexclusive definition of the circumstances in which a person has a duty of trust or confidence for purposes of the "misappropriation" theory of insider trading under Section 10(b) and Rule 10b-5. The rule is specifically limited to violations "based on the purchase or sale of securities on the basis of, or the communication of, material nonpublic information misappropriated in breach of a duty of trust or confidence." The rule, directed at family relationships (husband and wife, parent and child, and siblings), creates a rebuttable rule that a person who receives material nonpublic information from such a family member had a duty of trust and confidence with regard to such information. The relative who has allegedly violated the rule can assert as an affirmative defense the fact that "he or she neither knew nor reasonably should have known that the person who was the source of the information expected that the person would keep the information confidential, because of the parties' history, pattern, or practice of sharing and maintaining confidences, and because there was no agreement or understanding to maintain the confidentiality of the information." The other two situations that may give rise to liability stem from circumstances in which a person agrees to maintain information in confidence or those in which the person who shares the material nonpublic information has, with regard to the alleged violator, "a history, pattern, or practice of sharing confidences, such that the recipient of the information knows or reasonably should know that the person communicating the material nonpublic information expects that the recipient will maintain its confidentiality."

In a related vein, the SEC in 2000 promulgated Regulation FD—fair disclosure—which bars public companies from disclosing material nonpublic information to securities analysts and institutional investors without also disclosing such information publicly. Any such selective disclosures arguably create a conflict of interest for analysts, since they may be more likely to review the firm positively, thereby appreciating the stock's value. The rule has generated controversy because many companies see the potential for liability as leading to the disclosure of less—rather than more—information. The SEC brought its first enforcement actions under the regulation in 2002. You might find it interesting to access the SEC's Web site to determine how many such enforcement actions the SEC has undertaken. You can do so by visiting http://www.sec.gov.

The *Zandford* case that follows represents a recent gloss on the type of conduct that will constitute fraud "in connection with the purchase or sale of a security."

36.3

SECURITIES AND EXCHANGE COMMISSION v. ZANDFORD
535 U.S. 813 (2002)

FACTS Charles Zandford, a securities broker, persuaded William Wood, an elderly man, to open a joint investment account for himself and his mentally retarded daughter. The Woods gave Zandford discretion to manage the $419,225 account and a general power of attorney to engage in securities transactions without prior approval. When Mr. Wood died a few years later, all the money he had entrusted to Zandford was gone. Zandford was subsequently indicted on federal wire fraud charges for selling securities in the Woods' account and for making personal use of the proceeds. The SEC then filed a civil complaint alleging that Zandford had violated § 10 of the Securities Exchange Act of 1934 and Rule 10b-5 by engaging in a scheme to defraud his client and by misappropriating approximately $343,000 worth of securities without the client's knowledge or consent. After the broker's conviction for wire fraud, the SEC moved for partial summary judgment on the theory that the criminal judgment estopped (precluded) the broker from contesting facts that established a violation of § 10(b) and Rule 10b-5. The district court granted the SEC's motion. However, the Court of Appeals for the Fourth Circuit reversed and remanded with directions to dismiss the complaint on the grounds that the wire fraud conviction had failed to establish that the alleged fraud was connected with the sale of a security within the meaning of § 10(b) and Rule 10b-5 because the alleged sales of the client's securities were merely incidental to the broker's alleged fraud in absconding with the proceeds.

ISSUE Would a broker's alleged conduct of selling his customer's securities with the intent to misappropriate the proceeds constitute fraud "in connection with the purchase or sale of a security" as required for the SEC to establish a civil securities fraud claim against the broker under § 10(b) and Rule 10b-5 of the '34 Act?

HOLDING The broker's alleged conduct in selling his customer's securities and using the proceeds for his own benefit would constitute fraud in connection with the purchase or sale of a security within the meaning of § 10(b) and Rule 10b-5, where, among other factors: (1) The SEC had consistently interpreted the statute and rule broadly to cover brokers who sold customers' securities with the intent to misappropriate the proceeds; (2) this interpretation was reasonable and thus entitled to deference; and (3) the sales of the securities and the broker's conversion of the proceeds were not independent events, because each sale was made without the customer's knowledge or consent and for the purpose of furthering the broker's fraudulent scheme.

REASONING Excerpts from the opinion of Justice Stevens:

Between 1987 and 1991, respondent [Zandford] was employed as a securities broker in the Maryland branch of a New York brokerage firm. In 1987, he persuaded William Wood, an elderly man in poor health, to open a joint investment account for himself and his mentally retarded daughter. According to the SEC's complaint, the "stated investment objectives for the account were 'safety of principal and income.' " The Woods granted Zandford discretion to manage their account and a general power of attorney to engage in securities transactions for their benefit without prior approval. . . .

Section 10(b) of the Securities Exchange Act makes it "unlawful for any person . . . to use or employ, in connection with the purchase or sale of any security . . . , any manipulative or deceptive device or contrivance in contravention of such rules and regulations as the [SEC] may prescribe." Rule 10b-5, which implements this provision, forbids the use, "in connection with the purchase or sale of any security," of "any device, scheme, or artifice to defraud" or any other "act, practice, or course of business" that "operates . . . as a fraud or deceit." . . . Among Congress' objectives in passing the Act was "to insure honest securities markets and thereby promote investor confidence" after the market crash of 1929. . . . More generally, Congress sought " 'to substitute a philosophy of full disclosure for the philosophy of *caveat emptor* and thus to achieve a high standard of business ethics in the securities industry'." . . . Consequently, . . . the statute should be "construed 'not technically and restrictively, but flexibly to effectuate its remedial purposes.' " . . . In its role in enforcing the Act, the SEC has consistently adopted a broad reading of the phrase "in connection with the purchase or sale of any security." It has maintained that a broker who accepts payment for securities that he never intends to deliver, or who sells customer securities with the intent to misappropriate the proceeds, violates § 10(b) and Rule 10b-5. . . . This interpretation of the ambiguous text of § 10(b), in the context of formal adjudication, is entitled to deference if it is reasonable. . . . For the reasons set forth below, we think it is. While the statute must not be construed so broadly as to convert every common-law fraud that happens to involve securities into a violation of § 10(b), neither the SEC nor this Court has ever held that there must be a misrepresenta-

tion about the value of a particular security in order to run afoul of the Act. . . .

The SEC claims respondent engaged in a fraudulent scheme in which he made sales of his customer's securities for his own benefit. Respondent submits that the sales themselves were perfectly lawful and that the subsequent misappropriation of the proceeds, though fraudulent, is not properly viewed as having the requisite connection with the sales; in his view, the alleged scheme is not materially different from a simple theft of cash or securities in an investment account. We disagree. According to the complaint, respondent "engaged in a scheme to defraud" the Woods beginning in 1988, shortly after they opened their account, and that scheme continued throughout the 2-year period during which respondent made a series of transactions that enabled him to convert the proceeds of the sales of the Woods' securities to his own use. . . . The securities sales and respondent's fraudulent practices were not independent events. This is not a case in which, after a lawful transaction had been consummated, a broker decided to steal the proceeds and did so. Nor is it a case in which a thief simply invested the proceeds of a routine conversion in the stock market. Rather, respondent's fraud coincided with the sales themselves . . . [E]ach sale was made to further respondent's fraudulent scheme; each was deceptive because it was neither authorized by, nor disclosed to, the Woods. With regard to the sales of shares in the Woods' mutual fund, respondent initiated these transactions by writing a check to himself from that account, knowing that redeeming the check would require the sale of securities. Indeed, each time respondent "exercised his power of disposition for his own benefit," that conduct, "without more," was a fraud. . . . In the aggregate, the sales are properly viewed as a "course of business" that operated as a fraud or deceit on a stockbroker's customer. [As was the case in numerous Supreme Court precedents,] the SEC complaint describes a fraudulent scheme in which the securities transactions and breaches of fiduciary duty coincide. Those breaches were therefore "in connection with" securities sales within the meaning of § 10(b). Accordingly, the judgment of the Court of Appeals is reversed, and the case is remanded for further proceedings consistent with this opinion.

BUSINESS CONSIDERATIONS Assume your CEO has asked you to summarize the present state of the law regarding insider trading and to put on a training session for the benefit of your colleagues. What concepts will you stress? Why?

ETHICAL CONSIDERATIONS What ethical considerations did Zandford's conduct raise? To forestall this kind of conduct, should a firm promulgate an ethics code? If so, what points should this code emphasize?

Short-Swing Profits Section 16(b) also is aimed at gains by corporate insiders. This provision of the '34 Act requires everyone who is directly or indirectly the owner of more than 10 percent of any security registered under § 12 or who is a director or officer in a § 12 corporation to make periodic filings with the SEC. In these SEC filings, each must disclose the number of shares owned and any changes in the number of shares held.

This section, designed to prevent unfair use of information obtained by virtue of an inside position in the corporation, forces insiders to disgorge (that is, give up ill-gotten gains and return to the corporation) any profits they realize from the purchase or sale of any security that takes place in any time period of less than six months—that is, *short-swing profits*. Section 16(b) is inapplicable to any transaction in which the beneficial owner was not an owner at both the time of purchasing and the time of selling; on the other hand, directors and officers face liability if they held their positions at the time of either sale or purchase. Interestingly, though, § 16(b) covers transactions that fit the enumerated criteria even when the transactions were not actually based on inside information. In essence, then, it is a preventative section. Thus, if director Wallis sells stock in Continuing Corp. for $5,000 and five months later buys an equal number of shares for $3,000, Wallis will have to pay back to the corporation the $2,000 in profits so realized.

Note that in a merger case involving § 16(b), *Gollust v. Mendell,*[8] the Supreme Court held that a plaintiff who had properly instituted a § 16(b) action as the owner of a security of the issuer had standing to continue to prosecute the action even after a merger involving the issuer had resulted in exchanging the stockholder's interest in the issuer for stock in the issuer's new corporate parent.

Liabilities and Remedies The '34 Act creates a private right of action for those who have dealt in securities on the basis of misleading registration statements (liability pursuant to §§ 12 and 18), tender offers (§ 13), and proxy solicitations (§ 14). Under § 16(b), the corporation or a shareholder suing in a derivative action for the benefit of the corporation may recover short-swing profits realized by officers, directors, and shareholders controlling at least 10 percent of the securities involved. Private actions under § 10(b) and Rule 10(b)-5, the catchall antifraud provision, may be brought by any purchasers or sellers of any securities against any person who has engaged in fraudulent conduct, including a corporation that has bought or sold its own shares. Recall in this context that the PSLRA of 1995 preserves the state-of-mind requirements set out in the '34 Act and interpreted in subsequent Supreme Court and other court holdings.

The early § 10(b) cases had expansively imposed liability under § 10(b) and Rule 10(b)-5. However, in *Ernst & Ernst v. Hochfelder*, 425 U.S. 185 (1976), *reh'g. denied*, 425 U.S. 986 (1976), the Supreme Court limited the reach of § 10(b) in that the Court required a private person to prove that the securities law violator intended to deceive, manipulate, or defraud the injured party. After *Hochfelder*, proof of negligent conduct alone will not constitute a violation of § 10(b). Similarly, *Santa Fe Industries, Inc. v. Green*, 430 U.S. 462 (1977), which held that the term *fraud* in § 10(b) and Rule 10(b)-5 would not cover management's breach of fiduciary duties in connection with a securities transaction, signals somewhat of a retreat from the Court's prior, expansive view of possible liability under § 10(b).

Yet the SEC's ability (under the Insider Trading Sanctions Act of 1984) to penalize insider traders up to three times the amount of the profit gained or the loss avoided as a result of the unlawful purchase or sale suggests the availability of potent remedies aimed at discouraging securities laws' violations. Such penalties are payable to the U.S. Treasury; private parties cannot seek relief based on this act. The act also increases the criminal penalties that can be levied against individual violators from $10,000 to $100,000.

In addition, the Insider Trading and Securities Fraud Enforcement Act of 1988 creates an express private right of action in favor of market participants who traded contemporaneously with those who violated the '34 Act or SEC rules by trading while in possession of material, nonpublic information. This 1988 act supplements all other existing express and implied remedies and does not limit either the SEC's or the attorney general's authority to assess penalties for illegal use of material, nonpublic information. However, the 1988 legislation limits the damages one can receive in such private actions to the profits gained or losses avoided by the illegal trading (less any disgorgement ordered in an SEC action brought under the 1984 Act). The 1988 Act also allows private individuals who provide information that leads to the imposition of penalties to receive a bounty of up to 10 percent of any penalty.

Although the 1988 legislation considerably bolsters the remedies provided under the 1984 Act, Congress in 1988—as it had done in 1984 as well—declined to expand the definition of illegal insider trading under the misappropriation theory to include trading by anyone who merely is in possession of material, nonpublic information. Some legislators rejected the "possession" test as unduly broad, and others thought the law should prohibit only the improper use of such information. In short, Congress in the 1988 amendments ultimately declined to add any express definition of insider trading to the '34 Act.

Nonetheless, the legislative history of the 1988 Act reflects a clear endorsement of the misappropriation theory as articulated by lower federal courts and as approved subsequently by the Supreme Court in *O'Hagan.* Indeed, both the 1984 and the 1988 acts seem to represent a congressional backlash directed at the perceived leniency of the Supreme Court's holdings in the *Chiarella* and *Dirks* cases.

The Securities Enforcement Remedies and Penny Stock Reform Act of 1990 further augmented the SEC's enforcement powers and its ability to set penalties and seek disgorgement for insider trading. The act authorizes the SEC to issue cease and desist orders and require the alleged violator to comply with any terms and conditions the SEC may specify. In addition, the act gives courts the power to prohibit violators from serving as officers or directors of public companies if the violators' conduct demonstrates "substantial unfitness to serve" as officers or directors. As its name suggests, the statute overhauled the penny stock industry as well.

Those who advocate more potent remedies for violations of the securities laws and who disagree with the *Chiarella* and *Dirks* holdings were dealt a harsh blow by the Supreme Court in *Central Bank of Denver v. First Interstate Bank of Denver, NA.*[9] By further limiting the scope of the implied remedies available to litigants under the '34 Act, this case built on these earlier precedents. Prior to 1994, plaintiffs often sued not only the person who violated a specific provision of the securities acts but also those who "aided and abetted" the wrongdoer. By bringing "aiding" and "abetting" cases under § 10(b) and Rule 10(b)-5, a plaintiff could expand the number of persons from whom he or she could seek damages (several courts had held that "aiders" and "abettors," along with the primary violator, were jointly and severally liable). Simply put, the plaintiff was assured of a "deep pocket" because the plaintiff could recover from the most solvent defendant. Alternatively, the court, by requiring each defendant to contribute to the overall monetary award granted to the successful plaintiff, could distribute the damages among all the defendants. Because the '34 Act was silent as to a defendant's potential liability for aiding and abetting and as to the right of contribution, it was only a matter of time before the issue reached the Supreme Court.

In *Central Bank,* the Court concluded that Congress never intended to impose secondary liability under § 10(b) and that the '34 Act consequently does not reach those who aid and abet but instead prohibits only the making of a material misstatement (or omission) or the commission of a manipulative act. However, the Court refrained from holding that secondary actors (like accountants) are always free from liability under the act. Rather, such secondary actors may be held liable as primary actors if the plaintiff can prove all the requirements for primary liability,

---

NRW CASE 36.2   Finance/Management

NRW

INSIDER TRADING RULES UNDER THE '34 ACT

NRW stock is being sold on a national exchange, subjecting the firm to regulation under the '34 Act. The initial public reaction to the firm and its prospects has been good, and the stock has had steady increases in its market price. NRW is currently negotiating with a small firm that has "know-how" that will speed up the response time for both NRW products. This new technology accordingly holds great promise for increased sales. No one outside the immediate family is aware of these negotiations. Mai, Helen, and Carlos want to purchase a significant number of NRW shares before the news "leaks out" about the negotiations. However, they are concerned that if they do so, they will be guilty of insider trading. They ask you what they should do to avoid liability under the '34 Act in this situation. What will you tell them?

BUSINESS CONSIDERATIONS What should the officers, directors, and controlling shareholders of a firm whose stock is publicly traded be concerned about when they trade in their firm's securities? What can the firm do to minimize its potential liability when an insider trading scandal erupts?

ETHICAL CONSIDERATIONS Is it ethical for an insider to trade in securities when he or she has information that is not yet available to the general public? Is it ethical to prevent people from using the knowledge or information they have acquired through their jobs to make a profit based on that knowledge or information? Can these two areas be reconciled, ethically speaking?

INTERNATIONAL CONSIDERATIONS If NRW is offering its securities on a foreign exchange, must it provide information to prospective purchasers in the language of that foreign country, or may it submit its information in English? What impact, if any, will requiring the submission of the information only in the language of that foreign nation have on NRW?

---

including a material misstatement (or omission) on which a purchaser or seller of securities has relied. The federal courts presently are split over the threshold required for a secondary actor's conduct to constitute primary liability. Some, under the "bright line" test, will find primary liability only if the defendant makes a material misstatement or omission. Other courts, though, predicate liability on the "substantial participation" of the defendant. At some point, the Supreme Court presumably will provide a definitive answer to such questions.

Interestingly, in enacting the PSLRA, Congress refused to give an express private right of action for aiding and abetting; hence, the *Central Bank* ruling survives the PSLRA. This 1995 act, however, does give the SEC enforcement authority to bring actions against aiders and abettors.

Recall that the PSLRA sets out a "fair share" rule of proportionate liability for those who have engaged in "non-knowing" violations. Joint liability will befall only those who knowingly violate the securities law. As in the '33 Act, the plaintiffs who sue for damages will have to prove that the alleged misstatements actually caused their losses. The PSLRA further requires the calculation of damages based on the mean trading price of the stock (the average daily trading price of the stock determined as of the close of the market each day during the 90-day period after the dissemination of any information that corrects the misleading statement or omission).

Experts have posited that the PSLRA will have a dramatic impact on private actions brought under Rule 10(b)-5. Since the representations that form the basis of such actions often involve forward-looking statements, the "safe harbor" rule probably will lessen the incidence of such actions. Presumably, the PSLRA's pleading rules that require that scienter be pleaded with particularity in lawsuits involving the '34 Act (as opposed to the '33 Act) similarly will dampen the ardor of class action lawyers and plaintiffs who used to rush to the courthouse to file class action suits whenever a major company announced a sharp decline in the company's stock.

In 1997, Congress passed the Securities Litigation Uniform Standards Act (SLUSA) to require that certain securities fraud class actions, involving specified types of securities, be brought in the federal courts. Congress enacted this legislation to close an apparent loophole in the PSLRA—that plaintiffs were avoiding the federal heightened pleading requirements simply by filing their lawsuits in state courts. Critics have pointed out that, in failing to establish a uniform pleading standard—another deficiency in the PSLRA—and in encouraging (at the federal level) the very "forum-stopping" it was trying to eliminate, the 1997 act has created more issues than it has solved.

Besides the remedies allowable under the '33 and '34 Acts, the Supreme Court's opinion in *Sedima S.P.R.L. v. Imrex Co., Inc.*[10] which apparently allowed securities cases to be brought under the Racketeer Influenced and Corrupt Organizations Act (RICO) for a time represented a signifi-

cant remedial vehicle as well. However, the PSLRA brings to an end this chapter in the history of securities litigation. By removing fraud as a predicate act for the purposes of a private civil action based on RICO except in certain rare instances, the PSLRA has turned this past remedy for securities violations into little more than a legal artifact.

Yet since the late 1980s, the Supreme Court has validated, under the provisions of the Federal Arbitration Act, arbitration of both RICO and securities act claims. In a related vein, then, in *First Options of Chicago, Inc. v. Kaplan*,[11] the Supreme Court held that whenever it is clear that the opposing sides have agreed to submit the question to arbitration, a court should defer to the arbitrator's decision. In all other circumstances, federal courts have wide latitude to review the arbitrator's determination and to come to an independent conclusion regarding this issue. In giving courts authority to "second-guess" arbitrators on this procedural issue, the Supreme Court disappointed securities industry organizations that had urged the Court to restrict such judicial authority so as to make the arbitration process more streamlined and speedier. Nonetheless, particularly with regard to disputes between investors and their brokers, arbitration represents an increasingly significant possible remedy for investors. Some securities experts, though, in the past have raised questions concerning the legal validity of mandatory arbitration of disputes between securities firms and their employees, especially those involving charges of employment discrimination or harassment. The Supreme Court recently answered this question in *Circuit City Stores, Inc. v. Adams*.[12] There the Court upheld the arbitration of employment contracts under the Federal Arbitration Act. Watch for developments in this area. For more information on the '34 Act, visit http://www.sec.gov/about/laws.shtml.

Securities and Exchange Commission Actions

The '34 Act empowers the SEC to conduct investigations of possible violations of the securities laws. Many times such investigations lead to censure or, alternatively, culminate in a consent decree signed by the alleged wrongdoer in exchange for less stringent sanctions. But the SEC also can order an administrative hearing conducted by an administrative law judge to determine if penalties are in order with respect to any security, person, or firm registered with the SEC. As mentioned earlier, revocation of registration or suspension of the distribution of the security (or the activities of the person or firm) are two of the enforcement powers that the SEC possesses. The SEC itself may review the hearing officer's decision and, if necessary, modify the sanctions originally levied.

A party adversely affected by a final SEC order can seek review of such an order in a federal circuit court of appeals.

Besides administrative proceedings, the SEC can, on a "proper showing" of a reasonable likelihood of further violations, bring court actions to enjoin violations of the securities laws. The SEC also can refer cases to the Justice Department, which then mounts criminal actions against willful violators of securities laws and rules.

Sarbanes-Oxley Act of 2002

The SEC has engaged in a great deal of rulemaking owing to the accounting scandals involving such firms as Enron, Global Crossing, and WorldCom, as well as the auditing role of Arthur Andersen, LLP in such misconduct. These improprieties led to the enactment of the Sarbanes-Oxley Act of 2002.[13] Aimed at restoring investor confidence that had plummeted because of these far-reaching financial wrongdoings, the sweeping reforms set out in the legislation target various dimensions of corporate governance, financial disclosure, and the auditing function. Most provisions of the act apply to U.S. public companies and to non-U.S. public companies listed in the United States. Put differently, the new legislation covers all issuers that are required under the '34 Act to file periodic reports with the SEC. The most important aspects of the 2002 Act and the relevant sections include:[14]

CEO/CFO certification CEOs and CFOs of U.S. and non-U.S. public companies must personally certify to the SEC that their companies' annual and quarterly reports reflect financial statements that are appropriate and fair (§ 302). CEOs and CFOs who knowingly certify reports that do not comport with the requirements of the act are subject to a $1 million fine and a term of imprisonment of up to 10 years (or both). For making improper certifications "willfully," CEOs and CFOs face a maximum fine of $5 million and imprisonment of a maximum of 20 years (or both) (§ 1350). These sanctions are in addition to other penalties that can be assessed under federal securities laws. CEOs and CFOs must certify that they have reviewed the report and, based on their knowledge, the report does not contain an untrue statement of a material fact or omit to state a material fact necessary in order to make the statements made, in light of the circumstances under which such statements were made, not misleading (§ 302). Moreover, this provision of the act makes it clear that all CEOs and CFOs bear the responsibility for establishing, maintaining, and designing external controls in such a fashion that the discovery of material information is assured. All such officers furthermore must evaluate the efficacy of these internal controls within the 90-day period prior to the report and specify in their report their conclusions in this regard. Each CEO or CFO who signs a report also must reveal to the company's auditors and the auditing committee all the deficiencies in the auditing system that the CEOs and CFOs deem significant and any fraud on the part of management or other employees who play a significant role in the internal controls process. Lastly, the officers who sign the reports must indicate any significant changes in the internal controls or any other factors that could significantly affect the controls since the officers' last evaluation of the internal controls process (§ 302).

Establishment of audit committees/corporate governance All public companies must set up an audit committee comprised solely of independent directors; the committee must hire and oversee the outside auditors and establish procedures for processing complaints about accounting matters, internal controls, or auditing matters (§ 301). The committee must include at least one member who is a "financial expert," although the committee additionally must have the authority to engage independent counsel and other advisers from funding provided by the issuer (§ 407).

Prohibitions on loans to directors and executive officers With some exceptions, U.S. companies and non-U.S. companies listed in the U.S. are prohibited from making personal loans (directly or through a subsidiary) or otherwise extending credit to such corporate personnel (§ 402).

Restrictions on executive compensation and service as directors or officers CEOs and CFOs must disgorge incentive-based compensation and any profits derived from trading whenever an accounting restatement occurs (§ 304); the SEC also can prohibit individuals from serving as directors or officers of public companies (§ 1105).

Bans on trading during benefit plan blackouts Directors and executive officers of U.S. and non-U.S. public companies may not engage in trading in the company's equity securities during any blackout period in which the company's employees are prohibited from trading in company stock held in pension funds (§ 306).

Adoption of a code of ethics Public companies must disclose whether they have adopted a corporate ethics code for their senior financial officers and must immediately disclose publicly any changes in, or waivers of, any such code (§ 406).

Accelerated reporting of insider transactions Changing the earlier rule that mandated reporting within

10 days of the execution of such transactions, the act obligates insiders (executive officers, directors, and greater-than-10 percent beneficial owners of equity securities in U.S. public companies) to report to the SEC any transactions in their company's equity securities within two days after trading in the securities (§ 403).

Disclosure of and material changes in financial conditions of off-balance-sheet transactions

The act requires the SEC to issue rules, based on a study of enforcement actions taken in the preceding five years, requiring the disclosure of such transactions, as well as other areas of reporting most susceptible to fraud (§ 704). Furthermore, public companies must make any and all "rapid and current" (i.e., real-time) disclosures of material changes in their financial conditions or operations as the SEC may require through future rule-making (§ 409).

Increased frequency of SEC reviews

The SEC must review all public companies' filings at least every three years (§ 408).

Creation of additional criminal penalties

The act sets out several new criminal offenses, including those involving conspiracies, fraud, and violations of securities law (§ 902 and § 802). Individuals who willfully violate the securities law face penalties of $5 million (a sum increased from the $1 million imposed previously) and a term of imprisonment of up to 20 years (thus doubling the previous maximum term of 10 years). For willful violations, corporations are subject to $25 million in fines (up from $2.5 million) (§ 906). Pursuant to the act, the U.S. Sentencing Commission must review the sentencing guidelines for certain "white collar"—and other—crimes (§ 1104, § 805, and § 905).

Whistleblower protection

Public company employees who lawfully provide information to their supervisors, the U.S. government, or Congress concerning conduct that the employees reasonably believe violate U.S. securities or anti-fraud laws are protected from retaliatory discharge or other adverse employment actions taken against the employees owing to the whistleblowing (§ 806). Employees whose rights have been violated can seek such remedies as reinstatement; back pay; and special damages remedies, including attorney's fees and the costs of litigation. This whistleblowing protection is available to contractors, subcontractors, and agents of U.S. companies as well.

Audit independence/rotation

The act lists eight categories of non-audit services functions—bookkeeping; the design and implementation of financial information systems; appraisal or valuation services, fairness opinions, or contribution-in-kind reports; actuarial services; internal audit outsourcing services; management functions or human resources; broker or dealer, investment adviser, or investment banking services; legal services and expert services unrelated to the audit; and any other service that the auditor oversight board may specify—that auditors cannot provide contemporaneously with audits (§ 201). The audit committee must give advance authorization for all other non-audit services (e.g., tax work) (§ 202). Because the act expressly includes the term "audit services" as encompassing the provision of comfort letters and securities underwritings, pre-approval of such matters is unnecessary. The act in addition requires the rotation of audit partners every five years and directs the Comptroller General to conduct a study of audit firm rotation (§ 203). Lastly, the act bars former audit firm employees from serving in senior executive positions (for example, as CEOs, CFOs, controllers, chief accounting officers, or the equivalent) at an audit client's firm for one year (§ 206).

Creation of an auditor oversight board

One of the cornerstones of the act is its creation of a self-regulatory board that will promulgate auditing standards and regulate accounting firms that function as auditors for public companies (§ 101). The board will consist of five members, no more than two of whom may be certified public accountants. An accounting firm's registration with this board is a pre-condition of the firm's providing auditing services for a public company (§ 102). The board must conduct annual inspections of firms that audit more than 100 public companies and must inspect all other auditing firms at least once every three years (§ 104). The purpose of the inspections is to gauge the auditing firms' compliance with the professional accounting standards and the rules adopted by both the board and the SEC, and with other laws and regulations that relate to the preparation of auditors' reports and accountants' liability. As part of its regulatory authority, the board can investigate and discipline firms and individual accountants for potential violations of the securities laws (§ 105).

The board must notify the SEC of the investigation and coordinate all investigatory activities with the SEC, since the SEC has oversight and enforcement authority over the board. The board can impose monetary sanctions on a registered firm or its supervisory personnel for violations unearthed by a board investigation. Sanctions can result from the activities of control persons as well if the firm or any of its supervisory personnel fails to adequately supervise such persons. Neither the firm nor its supervisory personnel will be liable if the firm has in place procedures that it reasonably expects will prevent and detect violations and the firm and its supervisory personnel have reasonably complied with such procedures. For each knowing or intentional violation by an individual, the board can assess fines of up to $750,000. For violations by a firm, a maximum penalty of $15 million is possible. Nonmonetary sanctions include suspension of a firm's registration with the board, thus precluding the firm from engaging in the auditing of any public company (§ 105). The funding for the board's activities will derive from annual fee assessments placed on public companies in accordance with the firms' relative market capitalizations (§ 109).

The act additionally requires public companies to fund the activities of the Financial Accounting Standards Board (FASB). The act directs the SEC to adopt a principles-based accounting system and allows the SEC to recognize a private organization such as FASB as a generally accepted accounting practices (GAAP) standard-setting body so long as this body meets certain requirements (§ 108).

Prohibitions on securities analysts' conflicts of interests The act requires the adoption of rules that would prevent conflicts of interests on the part of securities analysts (§ 501). In this context, the SEC-approved rules on this subject adopted by the National Association of Securities Dealers (NASD) and the New York Stock Exchange (NYSE) earlier in 2002 presumably would suffice.

Attorney professional responsibility The act requires the SEC to establish professional conduct standards for lawyers who represent public companies. Among other things, such standards would obligate corporate attorneys to report evidence of material violations of securities laws, breaches of fiduciary duty, or similar violations to the company CEO or general counsel. If the CEO or general counsel fails to respond appropriately, the attorneys must provide such information to the audit committee or the entire board of directors (§ 307).

Bankruptcy/Litigation Reform The act makes debts arising under the securities laws non-dischargeable in bankruptcy (§ 803) and extends the statute of limitations in private securities fraud actions to the earlier of five years after the alleged violation or two years after its discovery (§ 804) (the law previously mandated the filing of a private securities lawsuit within three years of the alleged violation and within one year of the discovery of the violation).

Studies of investment banks, violators, and enforcement actions The act also directs the Comptroller General to conduct a study meant to discern whether investment banks and financial advisers assisted public companies such as Enron and Global Crossing in manipulating their earnings and obscuring their true financial conditions (§ 705). The SEC also is to consider and report on the number of securities professionals who have been found to have aided and abetted violations of the securities laws; the range of sanctions imposed; and the amount of disgorgement, restitution, or other fines and payments assessed against and collected from such violators (§ 703). A similar mandate applies to enforcement actions taken by the SEC with regard to violations of reporting requirements and restatements of financial statements in the preceding five years (§ 704).

State Regulation

Because the assorted federal statutes preserve the states' power to regulate securities activities, any transactions involving securities may be subject to state law as well as federal law. Such varied state laws, often called "blue sky" laws, prior to 1996 normally included three types of provisions: (1) antifraud stipulations, (2) registration requirements for brokers and dealers, and (3) registration prerequisites for the sale and purchase of securities. Congress's enactment of the National Securities Markets Act of 1996, however, has preempted most such state regulation of securities. In many ways, this 1996 federal act merely codifies the securities regimes previously followed by most states. For instance, state laws frequently exempted from registration the same classes of securities exempted under the '33 Act and additionally often exempted stocks listed on the major stock exchanges. Exempted transactions customarily included private placements and isolated nonissuer transactions. The 1996 law's restructuring of the states' authority to regulate securities specifically mandates such exemptions, as well as one for investment securities issued by companies. The states still retain specific regulatory authority over penny stocks and small intrastate offerings exempted under the '33 Act. Moreover, the states can require the payment of fees for notice filings (notifications of the sale of securities within the state) and can bring enforcement actions related to broker fraud or other illegal conduct.

It is also useful to remember that, in this context, the Securities Litigation Uniform Standards Act of 1998 (SLUSA), discussed earlier in the chapter, preempts lawsuits involving class actions (and consolidated actions of more than 50 plaintiffs) based on state law allegations of fraud with respect to "covered securities" (i.e., the classes of securities exempted from "blue sky" regulation under the 1996 act).The passage of SLUSA in effect overruled

Matsushita *Electric Industrial Co., Ltd. v. Epstein,*[15] a case in which the Supreme Court interpreted the full faith and credit clause of the U.S. Constitution as meaning that any federal courts must give a class action settlement judgment in a state court the same preclusive effect the settlement would have had in the state court, notwithstanding the fact that the settlement at issue had released claims under the'33 Act (over which the state court had no jurisdiction) and claims under the '34 Act were then pending on appeal in a separate action in the federal courts.

Last, you should note that in 1956, the National Conference of Commissioners on Uniform State Laws drafted a Uniform Securities Act meant for adoption by the states. This attempt at uniformity for resolving securities questions among the various states has not been wholly successful, however.

For future reference, pay heed to the ramifications of such uniform laws, federal legislation, Supreme Court holdings, and SEC rule-making and enforcement actions. This rich interplay has substantial effects on the conduct of everyday business operations in the United States.

To access the extensive information compiled on the SEC's Web site, go to http://www.sec.gov. By clicking on the EDGAR database, you can examine firsthand information filed electronically by numerous companies.

Anyone who wishes to lodge an investor complaint should access http://www.sec.gov/complaint/cf942sec7040.htm. E-mailing cyberfraud@nasaa.org will put one in contact with the North American Securities Administrators Association, Inc., an organization composed of securities commissioners from all 50 states.

The Foreign Corrupt Practices Act

One additional topic merits attention. On December 19, 1977, President Jimmy Carter signed into law the Foreign Corrupt Practices Act (FCPA). The FCPA resulted from post-Watergate congressional hearings about questionable payments made to foreign officials by hundreds of U.S. firms, including Exxon, Northrop Corporation, Lockheed Aircraft Company, Gulf Oil, and GTE Corp. Testimony revealed that, in order to land sizeable contracts for themselves, companies had given foreign officials large payments, or bribes. In their own defense, these U.S. firms argued that foreign officials often demanded such payments as a condition of doing business and that without such "grease" payments, or sums paid to facilitate transactions by minor governmental functionaries, bureaucratic

---

NRW CASE 36.3 Marketing/International

NRW

HOW SHOULD NRW "BEHAVE" IN FOREIGN MARKETS?

NRW is investigating the possibility of selling the firm's products internationally. Carlos thinks he recalls learning in one of his management classes that bribery of governmental officials as a way of procuring business is a common occurrence in many countries. Carlos therefore advocates following that old adage, "When in Rome, do as the Romans do." He consequently supports giving NRW's sales personnel a "slush fund" the staff can use for bribing the appropriate officials in whichever country they target for obtaining sales. Mai and Helen suggest that Carlos immediately undertake a close reading of the FCPA. What will the FCPA teach Carlos about the advisability of embracing bribery as a corporate strategy?

BUSINESS CONSIDERATIONS The International Chamber of Commerce in recent years has added antibribery provisions to its organizational rules. The Organization for Economic Cooperation and Development similarly has advocated that its member states criminalize the bribery of foreign officials. What policies should a business institute to ensure compliance with the provisions of the FCPA and these other organizations' rules? Do you believe that the FCPA hampers the ability of U.S. firms to compete in a global market? Why or why not?

ETHICAL CONSIDERATIONS Does the FCPA improve the ethical conduct of U.S. firms? Does the FCPA represent a type of "cultural imperialism" in which the United States expects the rest of the world to accede to its view of what is—or is not—ethical?

INTERNATIONAL CONSIDERATIONS If NRW establishes franchises in other nations, should it include, as a condition of retaining the franchise, a restriction requiring each franchisee to comply with the terms of the FCPA?

---

red tape would have brought business dealings to a complete halt.

Congressional investigators found that such questionable payments often took the form of secret slush funds, dubious transfers of funds or assets between subsidiaries and parent companies, improper invoicing methods (for example, false payments for goods or services that never were received), and bookkeeping practices designed to camouflage improper payments or procedures. Indeed, these corrupt practices by U.S. corporations even included payments to engineer the overthrow of foreign governments hostile to U.S. business interests and bribes to foreign officials to keep competitors out of certain countries. To compound the improprieties, these same firms often deducted such so-called business expenses from their tax returns.

Since accounting irregularities, including secret funds and falsified or inadequate books, were most often used to make these questionable payments and bribes, Congress attempted to put an end to these practices by enacting the FCPA. Containing both antibribery provisions and accounting standards, the FCPA itself amends §§ 13(a) and 13(b)-2 of the Securities Exchange Act of 1934. The FCPA's antibribery sections provide criminal penalties for actions taken by issuers (firms subject to the '34 Act) or any domestic concern (even those not subject to the '34 Act) when an officer, director, employee, agent, or stockholder acting on behalf of such businesses corruptly uses the mail or any instrumentality of interstate commerce either to offer or actually to pay money (or anything of value) to foreign officials for the purpose of influencing foreign officials to assist the firm "in obtaining or retaining business for or with, or directing business to, any person."[16] In addition, it is unlawful under the FCPA to offer or to give payments or gifts for similar purposes to any foreign political party (or officials or candidates thereof) or to any person who the U.S. concern knows will transmit the payment or thing of value to any of the classes of persons specifically prohibited from receiving such bribes.[17]

Gifts or payments that are lawful under the written laws and regulations of the foreign country involved or that constitute bona fide reasonable expenditures (such as travel or lodging) incurred by such persons during the performance of a contract with the foreign government do not fall within the FCPA's proscriptions. Moreover, these antibribery provisions do not extend to payments made to these classes of persons when the payments' purpose is to expedite or facilitate the performance of "routine governmental action." Hence, "grease" payments to obtain permits or licenses to do business in the foreign country, visas, work orders, phone service, police protection, or inspections are legal as long as the employee receiving them is not a person known as someone who is acting as a conduit for governmental officials to whom the FCPA forbids corrupt payments or gifts.

However, decisions by foreign officials to award or continue business with a particular party are not included in the definition of routine governmental action.[18] Purely commercial bribery of corporate officials who lack governmental

connections and who do not act as conduits for governmental officials thus appears to be legal, but business records, in order to comply with the FCPA's accounting standards described below, should reflect such payments. Recent amendments to the FCPA empower the attorney general, after consultation with the SEC and others, to issue guidelines describing specific types of conduct that satisfy the strictures of the act and, when requested by firms, to issue opinions as to whether certain specified prospective conduct by these firms conforms with the act. Once promulgated, these regulations and advisory opinions should greatly facilitate U.S. firms' attempts to comply with the FCPA.

Although all individuals and domestic concerns (which can include corporations, partnerships, sole proprietorships, or any other sort of association) are subject to the FCPA antibribery provisions, only issuers subject to the SEC's jurisdiction must comply with the FCPA's accounting standards. These recordkeeping standards require issuers to do the following:

(A) *make and keep books, records, and accounts, which, in reasonable detail, accurately and fairly reflect the transactions and dispositions of the assets of the issuer; and*

(B) *devise and maintain a system of internal accounting controls sufficient to provide reasonable assurances that—*

  (i) *transactions are executed in accordance with management's general or specific authorization;*

  (ii) *transactions are recorded as necessary (i) to permit preparation of financial statements in conformity with generally accepted accounting principles or any other criteria applicable to such statements, and (ii) to maintain accountability for assets;*

  (iii) *access to assets is permitted only in accordance with management's general or specific authorization; and*

  (iv) *the recorded accountability for assets is compared with the existing assets at reasonable intervals and appropriate action is taken with respect to any differences.*[19]

Because they largely eliminate the possibility of secret slush funds for bribing foreign officials, these provisions are beneficial. Yet the statute gives no specific guidelines for setting up a particular internal control system. Rather, it leaves the choice of the particular system to the individual firm. The statute's vagueness therefore confused some businesspeople as to what type of recordkeeping system will suffice. Given the FCPA's criminal penalties for knowingly failing to comply, this is not an idle worry.

Further compounding such apprehensions is the SEC's promulgation of far-ranging regulations designed to promote the reliability of the information requested in the FCPA's recordkeeping provisions. These regulations prohibit both the falsification of accounting records and misleading statements made by an issuer's directors or officers to auditors or accountants during the preparation of required documents and reports.

The FCPA imposes criminal penalties—corporate fines of a maximum of $2 million for violations and a maximum of five years' imprisonment and/or $100,000 in fines for willful violations by corporate individuals—and individual civil penalties not to exceed $10,000. These should adequately deter U.S. corporations and corporate personnel engaged in international business from such illegal activities. Adding further strength to these criminal penalties, the FCPA prohibits a corporation from indemnifying its employees against liability under this act.[20] Other remedies available under the '34 Act, such as injunctions, also may be used in the enforcement of the FCPA by the Justice Department and the SEC, which share the enforcement responsibilities relating to the act.

Critics of the FCPA argue that its provisions and resultant regulations have greatly increased both U.S. businesses' costs of doing business and the enforcement agencies' costs, all of which negatively affect the public. On the other hand, such laws and supplementary regulations carry the attendant advantages of heightened investor information and fewer scandals involving U.S. bribery of foreign officials.

Since the FCPA is of relatively recent vintage, case law interpreting it is sparse. Because of the legal, social, and ethical issues it involves the FCPA promises to remain a controversial law. The Department of Justice has a Web site detailing the FCPA at http://www.usdoj.gov/criminal/fraud/fcpa.html.

Since the mid-1990's, Internet-based securities transactions have increased dramatically. The development of extensive computerized trading signals a major shift in the traditional makeup of the financial services industry. Would-be investors no longer are limited to placing orders through brick-and-mortar stock exchanges but instead can utilize electronic market systems such as that of the National Association of Securities Dealers Automated Quotations (NASDAQ) system. Such would-be market participants have at their fingertips (or their computer screens) a wide variety of market mechanisms ranging from on-line brokerage firms to bulletin boards that provide price information. Owing to these advances in technology, myriad companies have gravitated to the Internet as a means of reaching potential investors. In short, the Internet offers considerable opportunities for not only educating investors and increasing their sophistication, but also enhancing the speed and efficiency of market transactions.

As underscored by the establishment of EDGAR in the mid-1980s, the securities industry and the SEC were in the vanguard of those who viewed e-commerce as a desirable setting for doing business. Nonetheless, the problems discussed in other chapters infuse the on-line securities environment: heightened opportunities for fraud and market manipulation, the jurisdictional questions that accrue from the borderless nature of electronic transactions, and compliance concerns, to name but a few. Still, electronic securities transactions do not necessarily bring up brand new concerns—indeed, cyber-investing implicates legal issues very similar to those deriving from conventional securities transactions. Hence, in the last few years, the SEC has issued releases, rules, no action letters, and other guidelines aimed at reducing investor and industry uncertainty.

With the exchange markets in a state of transition—alternative trading systems (ATSs) now compete with traditional brokerage houses—guaranteeing compliance with the securities laws' requirements of adequate disclosure, as well as ensuring the accuracy and integrity of market information, has become more complicated. For example, because information posted on a Web site could constitute an offer, the SEC has regulated on-line registration processes, including prospectus requirements. As early as the mid-1990s, the SEC issued a no action letter concerning "road shows," an industry method of marketing offerings. Road shows involve the transmission of management-initiated meetings with brokers, analysts, portfolio managers, institutional traders, and individual investors during the waiting period before a registration statement takes effect. Electronically promulgated road shows permit the communication of information to a wider audience of potential investors and reduce the costs of the offering. The SEC likewise has allowed private placement offers to be disseminated by e-mail. Through interpretive releases, the SEC similarly has authorized the electronic delivery of a wide array of documents, including prospectuses; annual reports; and proxy and tender offer materials. SEC rules also permit brokers, dealers, investment advisers, and transfer agents to deliver confirmations electronically. The SEC's "safe harbor" rules currently authorize issuers and underwriters to engage in a variety of communications—including electronic ones during the pre-filing period, depending on the type of issue and the offering involved.

In sum, the evolution of liberalized rules concerning electronic transactions has continued to take into account the policies that underlie conventional investment transactions:

the need for notice and adequate disclosure to investors, as well as parity of information, whether the communications are based on paper or electronic formats. Yet because of the special challenges posed by electronic transactions, recent SEC releases have mandated firms' obtaining investors' consent as a precondition to the use of such a medium. Issuers also must ensure the investors' ability to download and retain a copy of the electronic communication and honor the investors' right to insist on the delivery of a paper copy. Electronic delivery of information and documents moreover obligates trading firms to ensure the security and integrity of investor communications and to provide mechanisms for receiving paper copies in cases in which electronic delivery fails or is otherwise flawed.

Besides rulemaking directed primarily at individual investors, the SEC has regulated alternative trading systems (ATSs), particularly electronic communications networks (ECNs), as well. ECNs bring buyers and sellers together for electronically executed trades; however, ECNs ordinarily do not trade as broker-dealers. Rather, ECNs match up subscribers' buy and sell orders and charge both parties a fee for acting as an agent. ECNs also charge nonsubscriber fees for quotations. While ECNs have driven down execution costs, they put other market makers, such as NASDAQ, at a competitive advantage because NASDAQ cannot charge fees. After deciding to integrate ATSs into the national market system, the SEC in 1998 issued final rules under which ATSs can decide to register as either broker-dealers or exchanges. The SEC's handling of the technological advances represented by ATSs reflects a regulatory approach designed to promote marketwide fairness and integrity. Try to keep abreast of such developments.

While it has been appropriate for the SEC to serve as the driving force in the development of Internet-based securities transactions, the states have not been idle—about 30 have adopted rules related to electronic intrastate placements. This represents an important, recently emerging dimension of blue-sky regulation.

Summary

The Securities Act of 1933 and the Securities Exchange Act of 1934 extensively regulate securities. In essence, a "security" involves instruments that are labeled as stock and possess all the characteristics typically associated with stock, as well as an investment in an enterprise whereby the investor has no managerial functions but instead expects to profit solely from the efforts of others. The '33 Act basically is a disclosure statute meant to protect the unsophisticated investing public. To further this purpose, the '33 Act requires the issuer of an initial distribution of stock to file a detailed registration statement with the SEC and to furnish a prospectus to virtually all potential investors. Until the registration statement becomes effective, selling and promotional activities remain limited. The '33 Act exempts certain classes of securities from its registration and prospectus requirements.

The '33 Act also exempts certain transactions such as private offerings. It contains several antifraud provisions and may impose civil liability for violations. One section places liability on everyone who signed the registration statement, was named as a director, contributed an expert opinion to the statement, or underwrote the issue. All such persons, except the issuer, may escape liability if they can show they acted with "due diligence." Other sections of the '33 Act establish civil and criminal liability.

The '34 Act regulates the secondary distribution of securities. Its reach therefore is even broader than that of the '33 Act. The '34 Act covers proxy solicitations and tender offers, limits insider trading, forbids short-swing profits, and in general tries to eliminate fraud and manipulative conduct with respect to the sale or purchase of securities. According to the '34 Act, any issuer who trades securities on a national stock exchange must register with the SEC. Like the '33 Act, it mandates certain disclosures by the firms that it covers when the securities are listed with national stock exchanges or traded over the counter. Regulation of proxy solicitations is an important facet of the '34 Act. In order to further the democratic aspects of corporations, it authorizes the inclusion in management proxy solicitations of shareholder proposals that involve "proper subjects." Liability for misleading proxy statements is absolute, as is liability for misleading statements made during tender offers or takeover bids. The '34 Act also prohibits insider trading because of the injury to the investing public that otherwise may ensue. When material inside information is involved, the insider must either publicly disclose the information or refrain from trading in the securities. Under the '34 Act's section on short-swing profits, directors, officers, and beneficial shareholders in certain corporations must refrain from buying or selling securities within a six-month period. The Private Securities Litigation Reform Act of 1995 limits class action suits to situations in which shareholders in fact have been the victims of securities fraud and discourages suits brought for frivolous—or entrepreneurial—purposes. This statute's adoption of a proportionate approach to liability for damages represents Congress's attempt to attract high-quality professionals to the boards of directors of start-up companies. The Securities Litigation Uniform Standards Act of 1998 requires that certain securities fraud class actions, involving specified types of securities, be brought in the federal courts.

The Securities and Exchange Commission can conduct administrative hearings with respect to securities violations and can seek injunctions to stop continuing violations. State securities laws usually set up antifraud provisions and registration requirements for brokers and dealers and for the sale of securities. The Sarbanes-Oxley Act of 2002 targets various dimensions of corporate governance, financial disclosure, and the auditing function as the linchpins of its reforms of the accounting and securities industries. Since 1977, the Foreign Corrupt Practices Act has forbidden U.S. businesses from making payments to foreign officials for the purpose of obtaining foreign business. Noncompliance with the FCPA's anti-bribery provisions and recordkeeping standards may subject individuals or corporations to civil or criminal penalties.

Discussion Questions

1. What, essentially, is a *security*?

2. Explain the primary purposes of the Securities Act of 1933 and the Securities Exchange Act of 1934.

3. List the types of information the '33 Act requires a registration statement to include.

4. What are "tombstone ads" and "red herring" prospectuses?

5. List the '33 Act's exempt classes of securities and transactions.

6. Explain what a *proxy* is, and describe the SEC rules surrounding proxy solicitations.

7. What are the '34 Act's provisions regarding insider trading?

8. Discuss the laws regarding short-swing profits and why the '34 Act prohibits these profits.

9. Enumerate the liabilities and remedies possible under both the '33 and '34 Acts (including the PSLRA of 1995 and the Sarbanes-Oxley Act of 2002 amendments as well).

10. Explain the enforcement powers held by the SEC and how state regulation of securities differs from federal regulation.

Case Problems and Writing Assignments

1. After California had deregulated its utility industry in 1997, Scott J. Levine and his wife, Sabrina Levine, formed Friendly Power Company LLC (FPC-LLC). A few months later, they formed Friendly Power Company, Inc. (FPL-Inc.), as well as Friendly Power Franchise Company (FPC-Franchise). FPC-LLC became a utility company licensed to operate in California, while FPC-Franchise was incorporated in Colorado. All three companies are located in Miami Lakes, Florida. Under a so-called franchise agreement, FPC-Franchise entered into a contract with FPC-Inc. giving FPC-Franchise the authority to enter into exclusive licenses with franchise operators who in turn would convert residential customers to Friendly Power. Under this agreement, FPC-Franchise would give FPC-Inc. 90 percent of the monies generated from the sales of these franchises. The franchise agreement that FPC-Franchise in turn signed with its "franchisees" contained the following provisions: FPC-Franchise would pay two dollars for every household that a franchise converted to Friendly Power. Each franchise was assigned a protected geographical territory, and each was required to achieve and maintain a 5 percent market share of the electric power customers in its protected territory within five years from the date of its franchise agreement.

Ultimately, FPC-Franchise sold 17 franchises priced between $200,000 and $600,000 each. Several of these franchisees consisted of telemarketing operations aimed at attracting investors who would buy partnership units in various franchises. According to the franchise agreements, 40 percent of the investors' funds would go to Friendly Power as payment for the purchase price of the franchises. An additional 40 percent of the investors' funds would go to the telemarketing operations as payment for their services. The remaining 20 percent of the investors' monies would be held for future working capital once the franchise's escrowed funds had been exceeded. At that point, the investors would be entitled to 50 percent of Friendly Power's net profits on sales to residential customers in the franchise territory. However, FPC-Franchise early on notified the investors that they likely would not see a profit for quite some time after their initial investment. In the meantime, the franchise agreement permitted Friendly Power to use the investors' funds as capital for its business of providing electrical power to commercial customers in the state of California. Each Friendly Power franchise consisted of between 50 and 94 partners. Each investor in addition signed a participation agreement, which mandated that each investor be involved in the day-to-day operations of the franchise and actively participate in one or more of the management committees responsible for overseeing and conducting the franchise.

Friendly Power began providing electricity to its customers on May 1, 1998. By July 17, 1998, FPC-Franchise had released only the San Francisco franchise's escrow fund. In contrast, by this time, Friendly Power had received $2.4 million from 308 investors. On July 17, 1998, when the SEC froze all of Friendly Power's assets, Friendly Power no longer could buy power. With its funds frozen and its credit terminated, Friendly Power on August 8, 1998 notified the California Energy Commission that it would no longer be able to provide power to its customers; all the customers reverted to their respective previous utility providers. The SEC subsequently alleged that the Levines and Friendly Power had offered unregistered securities for sale in violation of the '33 Act. Were the "franchises" at issue here securities? [*SEC v. Friendly Power Company LLC,* 49 F. Supp 2d 1363 (S.D. Fla. 1999).]

2. Prior to March 15, 1999, Ronald Bleakney was vice-president of Natural Microsystems Corporation (NMC) and responsible for directing sales activities for NMC in North America, South America, and Europe. On that date, he tendered his resignation. He continued to bear the title of "senior vice-president for sales" at NMC, but the resignation was effectively accepted on March 22, 1999, after which time he had few, if any, substantive duties commensurate with the title. In October 1998, Bleakney had purchased 400 shares of NMC and had sold these same shares in November 1998. Bleakney also purchased additional shares in April 1999. Bleakney claimed he paid $111,988 to NMC for the shares sold on November 9, 1998, for approximately $92,004, resulting in a net personal loss of $19,984. Bleakney held the purchases made on April 20, 1999, and April 22, 1999, for more than a year. NMC provided some guidance to employees concerning all executive/insider stock trading, including but not limited to § 16(b). In Bleakney's dealings, including the transactions of April 20, 1999, and April 22, 1999, the issue of sale and purchase as these relate to § 16(b) was never raised. Bleakney relied on the company's advice and believed his transactions to be in accordance with § 16(b)'s rules and regulations, as further evidenced by the production of Form 4 by NMC agents and the appropriate approval on such forms by NMC's legal counsel. On November 1, 2000, NMC made a demand on Bleakney for the payment to it of the short-swing profits that this suit sought to recover. Had Bleakney violated § 16(b)'s prohibitions against short-swing profits? Could Bleakney use as his defense that he was not *in pari delicto* owing to the fact that NMC had failed to caution him about his potential liability under § 16(b)? Would the fact that Bleakney's transactions had resulted in an aggregate net loss insulate him from § 16(b) liability? Explain fully. [See *Donoghue v. Natural Microsystems Corporation,* 198 F. Supp. 2d 487 (S.D.N.Y. 2002)

3. Alan Carr, a Canadian, owned Europe and Overseas Commodity Traders, S.A. (EOC), a venture capital company incorporated in Panama. EOC had an account with the London branch of Banque Paribas, a French bank. In October 1993, Carr was visiting England. On October 7, John Arida, an account manager at Paribas's London office, informed Carr that a substantial amount of cash had accumulated in EOC's account. Arida thereupon offered to recommend an attractive investment opportunity for the money. Carr said he expressed interest in the proposal, but explained that he was preparing to leave for Florida on the 9th and thus would be happy to hear more after his arrival in Florida. In a series of telephone conversations that began on October 14, Carr and Arida resumed their discussion of EOC's investment in the Paribas Global Bond Futures Fund (the Fund). Carr subsequently alleged that Arida had misled him by conveying the following inaccurate information: (a) that the Fund was overseen by Paribas's proprietary trading desk; (b) that the investors' capital in the Fund was traded along with Paribas's own capital; and (c) that the Fund traded securities based primarily on technical as opposed to fundamental considerations. In reliance on these statements, Carr claimed that he, while in Florida, ordered $1,800,000 in purchases for EOC. Arida claimed that Carr was in England when Carr ordered the first purchase of Fund shares. However, the documents Arida offered in support of this allegation were inconclusive. Carr thereafter sued Paribas for, among other things, violating the '33 Act owing to the sale of unregistered securities. Under SEC regulations and securities law precedents, U.S. courts would have jurisdiction over the transactions involved here if the conduct at issue would have the effect of creating a market for such unregistered securities in the United States. Did the securities sold to EOC fall under the registration requirements of the '33 Act and thus give the court subject matter jurisdiction over the sales to EOC? Explain. [See *Europe and Overseas Commodity Traders, S.A. v. Banque Paribas London,* 147 F.3d 118 (2d Cir. 1998).]

4. Valence Technology, Inc. was founded in 1989 to develop new battery technology. In May, 1992, after announcing that it was developing a new solid electrolyte rechargeable battery, Valence raised $33 million in an IPO. Valence advertised its batteries as having an extended life cycle compared to conventional rechargeable batteries. Valence announced that it was focusing in particular on applying this technology to the commercial manufacture of batteries for use in cellular telephones and laptop computers. After Valence had raised $82.8 million in a second IPO, in December 1992 Valence announced the conclusion of a $100 million contract with Motorola, which was to begin using Valence's batteries in its cellular telephones in 1994.

On February 15, 1993, the March issue of *Forbes* magazine published an article about Valence entitled "Story Stock." The article claimed that while "the folks at Valence can put on a good show" in demonstrating prototypes of their battery, the investment community remained largely ignorant of "what is really energizing this stock . . . insiders unloading shares for a price hundreds of times what they paid, an underwriting firm . . . [that helps] them do that, and journalists who . . . take at face value the boastful pronouncements of the company's publicity department." According to the article, although

Valence's battery "works beautifully in the lab," "the world doesn't know" whether it will "last" or if it can be "made cheaply." The article took particular aim at Carl Berg, Valence's largest shareholder. It noted his participation in two other Silicon Valley enterprises through which he had made large profits even though the companies themselves had suffered financially. According to the article, "outside investors may do poorly, but Berg usually gets his money out."

Valence and its officers made several public pronouncements in response to the *Forbes* article. Lev Dawson, then the CEO of Valence, sent to *Forbes* a letter (that Valence later distributed to shareholders) describing the article as "inaccurate." The press follow-up to the *Forbes* article was modest. The *San Francisco Chronicle* published a story on February 27, 1993, reiterating the *Forbes* article's claim that "there was no reliable evidence that the batteries will work as advertised." *Bloomberg Business News,* in contrast, in a February 17, 1993, wire story entitled "Valence Chairman Calls Forbes Article 'Inaccurate,'" reported Dawson's response to the *Forbes* article. Later press coverage resumed its largely positive tone: September 1993, stories in the *Dow Jones Wire Service* and the *Wall Street Journal* reported Valence's announcement that it would deliver the batteries for the Motorola contract in the coming year. Neither story mentioned the *Forbes* article.

The week after the publication of the *Forbes* article, Valence's stock dropped from about $15.00 per share to $12.50 per share. Two days later, on February 25, it rose back to $15.00 and by September 28, had reached $20.00. In December 1993, Valence completed its third public offering, raising $51.5 million. On May 3, 1994, Valence announced that it was unable to meet Motorola's specifications and that it would not be delivering batteries under that contract as planned. On that day, Valence's stock dropped from $9.50 to $5.25. On August 9, 1994, when Valence announced that it was abandoning its new battery technology, Valence's stock dropped to $3.375.

When James L. Berg and other investors sued Valence for securities fraud under § 10(b) and Rule 10b-5, the defendants claimed that the statute of limitations would bar the plaintiffs' claims. Specifically, the defendants maintained that the *Forbes* article had placed the plaintiffs on "inquiry notice" of the possibility of fraud more than one year before they had sued. Did the *Forbes* article raise sufficient suspicion of fraud to cause a reasonable investor to investigate the matter further and thus trigger the running of the one-year limitations' period? Explain fully. [See *Berry v. Valence Technology, Inc.*, 175 F.3d 699 (9th Cir. 1999).]

5. BUSINESS APPLICATION CASE Computer Associates International, Inc. (CA) is in the business of designing and marketing computer software products. In July 1991, CA's chairman, Charles Wang, approached the chairman and chief executive officer of On-line Software International, Jack Berdy, to discuss the possibility of CA's acquiring On-Line. Berdy owned 1.5 million shares of On-Line stock, representing approximately 25 percent of the company's outstanding shares. Berdy

and Wang, as well as Sanjay Kumar, the chief operating officer of CA, negotiated extensively over the price that CA would pay for On-Line's stock. Negotiations over the terms of a non-compete agreement proceeded concurrently with negotiations over the purchase price. CA insisted that Berdy and other On-Line executives, who would be leaving the company following the acquisition, agree not to compete with CA for a specified period of time. Berdy initially resisted entering into a non-compete agreement. At one point in the negotiations, CA offered to purchase On-Line's stock (which was then trading at approximately $10 per share on the New York Stock Exchange) for $14 per share and to pay Berdy $9 million for a seven-year non-compete agreement. However, On-Line's board of directors viewed CA's offer of $14 per share as too low and believed that the $9 million offered to Berdy for his agreement not to compete was too high. CA and On-Line ultimately agreed that CA would offer to purchase On-Line's stock for $15.75 per share and that CA would pay Berdy $5 million for a five-year non-compete agreement.

On August 15 and 16, 1991, an unusually large amount of trading in On-Line stock occurred, prompting the NYSE to ask On-Line about the unusual trading activity. Around noon on August 16, On-Line and CA reached their agreement at $15.75 per share. Later that day, each company issued a press release announcing that it had reached an agreement in principle with the other, although On-Line's press release also noted that "no assurance can be given that a transaction between On-Line and Computer Associates of any sort will occur." After issuing their respective August 16 press releases, CA and On-Line agreed that the transaction would take the form of a tender offer and a follow-up merger. Accordingly, on August 20, CA's board of directors approved a merger agreement, a stock purchase and non-competition agreement (the Berdy agreement), and several related agreements. On August 21, On-Line's board unanimously approved the merger agreement, recommended the transaction to On-Line shareholders, and authorized the necessary filings with the SEC.

Pursuant to the Berdy agreement, LWB Merge Inc., CA's wholly owned subsidiary, purchased Berdy's On-Line stock for $15.75 per share, the same price that CA had offered to all other On-Line shareholders. In addition to the non-compete clause, the Berdy agreement also provided that Berdy could not tender his shares in the tender offer and that if another bidder made a better offer, LWB retained an option to purchase Berdy's shares for $15.75 per share. The non-compete clause did not restrict Berdy, who had been a medical student since 1989, from "engaging in the design, development, marketing, licensing or sale of computer software designed for use in the medical industry, in the biological sciences or as a teaching aid for educational purposes."

On August 21, 1991, CA and On-Line executed the merger agreement, obligating CA to commence the tender offer "as promptly as practicable"; and CA, LWB, and Berdy executed the Berdy agreement. On August 22, CA and On-Line issued a joint press release announcing that the two companies had entered into an agreement and that CA "will make a tender offer today" and conduct a follow-up merger. The same day, August 22, CA filed with the SEC and disseminated to On-Line shareholders the offer to purchase all shares of On-Line stock not owned by Berdy for $15.75 per share. After a majority of On-Line shareholders had tendered shares to CA, CA and LWB completed the acquisition of On-Line with the follow-up merger.

Joel Gerber, an On-Line shareholder, subsequently brought this action individually and on behalf of a class of On-Line shareholders who had tendered On-Line stock to CA in the tender offer. The complaint alleged that several defendants (including CA, Wang, Kumar, and Berdy) had violated SEC Rule 14d-10, as well as various other provisions of the federal securities laws, by offering and paying more consideration to Berdy for his On-Line shares than it had offered or paid to other On-Line shareholders. Gerber claimed that, because Berdy was disengaging from the business to pursue his medical studies, CA was not genuinely concerned about the possibility of his competing and that the $5 million payment to him, while nominally consideration for Berdy's non-compete agreement, actually represented additional compensation to ensure that CA would acquire Berdy's large block of On-Line shares. CA, on the other hand, insisted that it genuinely feared potential competition from Berdy and that the entire $5 million was consideration for Berdy's agreement not to compete. The defendants in moving to dismiss the Williams Act claims argued that the tender offer did not begin until August 22, 1991, and that the Berdy agreement, which was executed on August 21, had preceded the tender offer. The district court denied the motion, concluding as a matter of law that the tender offer had commenced on August 16, 1991, when CA had issued its first press release. Had a violation of the Williams Act occurred here? [*See Gerber v. Computer Associates International, Inc.*, 303 F.3d 126 (2d Cir. 2002).]

6. ETHICAL APPLICATION CASE Life Partners, Inc. (LPI) arranges transactions relating to viatical settlements and performs certain post-transactional administrative services. A viatical settlement is an investment contract pursuant to which an investor acquires an interest in the life insurance policy of a terminally ill person—typically an AIDS victim—at a discount of 20 to 40 percent, depending on the insured's life expectancy. When the insured dies, the investor receives the insurance benefits. The investor's profit is the difference between the discounted purchase price paid to the insured and the death benefits collected from the insurer, less transaction costs, premiums paid, and other administrative expenses. LPI sells fractional interests in insurance policies to retail investors, who may pay as little as $650 and buy as little as 3 percent of the benefits of a policy. In order to reach its customers, LPI uses some 500 commissioned "licensees," mostly independent financial planners. For its efforts, LPI's net compensation is roughly 10 percent of the purchase price after the payment of referral and other fees. Brian Pardo, LPI's chairman, claimed

that LPI was by far the largest of about 60 firms serving the rapidly growing market for viatical settlements; in 1994 the company accounted for more than half of the industry's estimated annual revenues of $300 million. In 1995, the SEC sued LPI. Specifically, the SEC contended that the fractional interests marketed by LPI are securities and that LPI had violated the '33 and '34 Acts by selling the viatical settlements without first complying with the registration and other requirements of those acts. In rebuttal, LPI argued that (1) viatical settlements are exempt from the securities laws because they are insurance contracts within the meaning of the McCarran-Ferguson Act; and (2) the fractional interests sold by LPI are not in any event securities within the meaning of the '33 and '34 Acts. Who had the stronger argument, LPI or the SEC? Would you characterize LPI's activities—investing in the life insurance policies of terminally ill persons—as an example of admirable ethics? Why? [See *SEC v. Life Partners, Inc.*, 87 F.3d 536 (D.C. Cir. 1996).]

7. CRITICAL THINKING CASE James Herman O'Hagan was a partner in the law firm of Dorsey & Whitney in Minneapolis, Minnesota. In July 1988, Grand Metropolitan PLC (Grand Met), a company based in London, England, retained Dorsey & Whitney as local counsel to represent Grand Met regarding a potential tender offer for the common stock of the Pillsbury Company, headquartered in Minneapolis. Both Grand Met and Dorsey & Whitney took precautions to protect the confidentiality of Grand Met's tender offer plans. O'Hagan in fact did no work on the Grand Met representation. Dorsey & Whitney withdrew from representing Grand Met on September 9, 1988. Less than a month later, on October 4, 1988, Grand Met publicly announced its tender offer for Pillsbury stock. While Dorsey & Whitney was still representing Grand Met, O'Hagan began purchasing call options for Pillsbury stock. When Grand Met announced its tender offer, O'Hagan sold his Pillsbury call options and common stock at a profit of more than $4.3 million. After investigating O'Hagan's transactions, the Securities and Exchange Commission (SEC) alleged that O'Hagan had defrauded his law firm and its client, Grand Met, by using for his own trading purposes material, nonpublic information regarding Grand Met's planned tender offer. A conversation between O'Hagan and the Dorsey & Whitney partner heading the firm's Grand Met representation constituted the nonpublic information O'Hagan allegedly had misappropriated from the firm. O'Hagan was charged with 20 counts of mail fraud; 17 counts of securities fraud, in violation of § 10(b) of the '34 Act and SEC Rule 10b-5; 17 counts of fraudulent trading in connection with a tender offer, in violation of § 14(e) of the '34 Act and SEC Rule 14e-3(a); and three counts of violating federal money laundering statutes. After his conviction and his being sentenced to a 41-month term of imprisonment, the Court of Appeals for the Eighth Circuit reversed all of O'Hagan's convictions. Liability under § 10(b) and Rule 10b-5, the Eighth Circuit held, may not be grounded on the "misappropriation theory" of securities fraud on which the prosecution had relied. This court also held that Rule 14e-

3(a)—which prohibits trading while in possession of material, nonpublic information relating to a tender offer—exceeds the SEC's § 14(e) rulemaking authority because the rule contains no breach of fiduciary duty requirement. The Eighth Circuit further concluded that O'Hagan's mail fraud and money laundering convictions, resting as they did on violations of the securities laws, could not stand once the reversal of the securities fraud convictions had occurred. Was O'Hagan, a person who had traded in securities for personal profit, and had used confidential information misappropriated in breach of a fiduciary duty to the source of the information, guilty of violating § 10(b) and Rule 10b-5? Had the Commission exceeded its rulemaking authority by adopting Rule 14e-3(a), which proscribes trading on undisclosed information in the tender offer setting, even in the absence of a duty to disclose? [See *U.S. v. O'Hagan*, 521 U.S. 642 (1997).]

8. YOU BE THE JUDGE Steven G. Cooperman and five other purchasers of the common stock of Individual, Inc. sued Individual, its board of directors, and the underwriters who had participated in Individual's March 1996 IPO. The plaintiffs claimed that the defendants had made materially false and misleading statements and had omitted material facts in connection with the registration statement and prospectus for the IPO. Specifically, the plaintiffs alleged that the defendants had failed to disclose that, at the time the IPO became effective, a conflict exited between Yosi Amram—

the director, founder, chief executive officer, and president of Individual—and a majority of the board of directors about the strategic direction the company should take. In 1989, Yosi Amram had founded the company, a provider of electronic customized information services, and was largely responsible for the firm's rapid growth. According to the plaintiffs, Amram believed that the company should grow and expand through rapid, often costly, acquisitions of new businesses. The majority of the board, however, believed that Individual should grow through building its core business by, among other things, expanding the subscriber base, extending its information base and providers, and enhancing its knowledge processing systems. The prospectus did not disclose the existence of any disagreement between Amram and the majority of the board. Instead, the prospectus stated that the company's future objective was to maintain growth through the development of Individual's existing core business. The plaintiffs further maintained that, owing to this conflict, Amram ultimately had left Individual and thereby had caused a sharp decline in the company's stock. Hence, the plaintiffs alleged that the defendants' failure to disclose the conflict between Amram and the majority of the board at the time of the IPO constituted an omission of a material fact in violation of § 11 of the '33 Act. If this case were brought in *your* court, would *you* rule in favor of Cooperman and the other plaintiffs? [See *Cooperman v. Individual, Inc.*, 171 F.3d 43 (1st Cir. 1999).]

Notes

1. *Securities and Exchange Commission v. Ralston Purina Co.*, 346 U.S. 119 (1953).
2. 283 F. Supp. 643 (S.D. N.Y. 1968).
3. 513 U.S. 561 (1995).
4. 485 U.S. 224 (1988).
5. 445 U.S. 222 (1980).
6. 463 U.S. 646 (1983).
7. 521 U.S. 642 (1997).
8. 501 U.S. 115 (1991).
9. 511 U.S. 164 (1994).
10. 473 U.S. 479 (1985).
11. 514 U.S. 938 (1995).
12. 532 U.S. IDS (2001).
13. Pub. L. No. 107-204, 116 Stat. 747 (2002).

14. John T. Bostelman, Robert E. Buckholz Jr., David B. Harms, Robert W. Reeder III, Andrew D. Soussloff, Donald C. Walkovik, Richard C. Morrissey, and George H. White III, "Enactment of Broad Accounting, Corporate Governance Reform Act Brings New Prohibitions Requirements for Executives and Auditors," 71 U.S.L.W. 2114-2128 (August 20, 2002), published almost contemporaneously with the enactment of the statute, provides both the framework for the textual discussion and an excellent and detailed analysis of the act.
15. 516 U.S. 367 (1996).
16. 15 U.S.C. § 78(dd-1), (dd-2).
17. Ibid.
18. Ibid.
19. Ibid., § 78(m).
20. Ibid., § 78(ff).

Government Regulation of Business

Government regulation of business is a controversial area. There are people who believe that such regulation is an inappropriate exercise of governmental power and that the nation would be better served by significantly less government regulation or intervention into the business environment. These people would prefer a return to a laissez-faire economy. Other people believe that the government does not go far enough in regulating business and that the nation would be better served by a government that was more actively involved in the regulation and operation of business.

However, for better or for worse, government regulation of business is a fact of business life, and, given the corporate scandals of 2002, it is likely to increase before there is any thought given to a decrease in the amount or the scope of regulation. At this time the federal government regulates competition through the Sherman, Clayton, Robinson-Patman, and

Federal Trade Commission Acts. It also provides consumer protection through a myriad of consumer credit and product safety acts. The federal government provides environmental protection through the National Environmental Policy Act (NEPA) and the EPA, and a multitude of statutes dealing with a variety of environmental issues, including clean air and clean water. Finally, the government regulates labor and employment, addressing concerns of organized labor and of individual employees through various statutes.

Governmental regulation is closely related to the social contract theory discussed in Chapter 2. It is also an area that invites controversy concerning whether business should be proactive or reactive as it attempts to meet its social and legal obligations and expectations while simultaneously attempting to make a profit and satisfy its constituents. Throughout the rest of this section of the text, consider the social contract theory and the benefits and burdens the social contract places on business. Also consider the benefits to businesses that become proactive as opposed to those that remain reactive.

Antitrust Law

AGENDA

NRW NRW has entered the market for its product on the "ground floor," providing a good that virtually no one else is providing. This has placed the firm in a position to take control of a significant part of the market. This potential market position has benefits, but it also carries risks. The firm may be able to generate large profits and gain "name" recognition, allowing it to remain profitable for quite some time. However, it may also lead to charges that NRW is improperly maintaining its position or otherwise violating the antitrust laws. The firm needs to be aware of the scope of the various antitrust laws, and it needs to take steps to ensure that it does not violate any of these laws. It will also need to be aware of what constitutes an "unfair trade practice." This is all new territory for the firm and its principals, and may lead to a significant number of questions.

Be prepared! You never know when the firm or one of its members will seek your advice.

The Basis of Regulatory Reform

For the first 114 years of U.S. history, business had a fairly free field in which to work. There was little federal regulation and little effective state regulation. The courts and the federal government took a "hands-off" attitude toward business. In such an environment, Cornelius Vanderbilt, buccaneering railroad tycoon of the 1800s, was able to crow, "What do I care about the law? Hain't I got the power?"

The tide began to turn in the late 1800s as the public tired of the irresponsible behavior of some of the so-called *robber barons*. The press began to call for reforms and for protection from "big business." Finally, in 1890, a beachhead was established with the passage of the Sherman Antitrust Act. While the Sherman Antitrust Act began the era of government regulation, it proved to be inadequate in curbing business excesses. One of the problems with the Sherman Act is that the act is *remedial*, applying to situations only *after* the conduct has occurred and the harm has been inflicted. In an effort to provide *preventative* protections, Congress subsequently bolstered the antitrust area with the passage of the Clayton Act and the Federal Trade Commission Act, both in 1914, and once again with the Robinson-Patman Act, an amendment to § 2 of the Clayton Act, which was passed in 1936. As international trade has increased, and with the potential for international trade to affect the domestic market, the Sherman Act was amended in 1982 with the passage of the Foreign Trade Antitrust Improvement Act. We will examine the effectiveness of this comprehensive statutory package over the balance of this chapter.

The Sherman Antitrust Act

Congress passed the Sherman Antitrust Act in 1890. The purpose of the act was to preserve the economic ideal of a pure-competition economy. To reach this ideal, the Sherman Act prohibits combinations that restrain trade, and it prohibits attempts to monopolize any area of commerce. Violations of the act can result in fines, imprisonment, injunctive relief, and civil damages.

Section 1: Contracts, Combinations, or Conspiracies in Restraint of Trade

The Sherman Act is a fairly short statute, but its few words cover a great number of actions. Section 1 states:

Every contract, combination in the form of trust or otherwise, or conspiracy, in restraint of trade or commerce among the several States, or with foreign nations, is hereby declared to be illegal. Every person who shall make any contract or engage in any combination or conspiracy hereby declared to be illegal shall be deemed guilty of a felony, and, on conviction thereof, shall be punished by fine not exceeding $10,000,000 if a corporation, or, if any other person, $350,000, or by imprisonment not exceeding three years, or by both said punishments, in the discretion of the court.[1]

(The original statute provided that the crime was a misdemeanor and called for a maximum fine of $5000, with a maximum imprisonment of one year for anyone convicted of violating the act.) Violations of § 1 require a contract, a combination, or a conspiracy. Each of these three require two or more persons acting in concert in some manner that restrains trade or commerce among the states or with a foreign nation before a violation can be found. One person cannot be guilty of a § 1 violation, since one person is acting alone, by definition.

As originally enacted, § 1 presented problems to the courts. Because nearly every contract can, at least in theory, be viewed as a restraint of trade, the prohibition against contracts "in restraint of trade" seemed too broad. In fact, if this section were to be interpreted literally, virtually all business dealings that affect interstate commerce (including foreign trade) could, theoretically, be prohibited by § 1 of the Sherman Act. As a result, the courts initially interpreted the Sherman Act very narrowly. The courts were willing to rule against combinations or conspiracies "in restraint of trade," but had a more difficult time ruling that any contracts were "in restraint of trade." However, the courts *did* rule that some union activities were combinations or conspiracies in restraint of trade, and thus constituted violations of § 1 of the Sherman Act. Unfortunately, these rulings tended to promote—rather than hinder—the "big business" of the era. Interpretations of this sort worked in such a way that the objective of the act was virtually negated.

The Rule of Reason Eventually, the Supreme Court found a method for evaluating conduct, particularly contracts, that allegedly restrains trade among the several states in violation of § 1 of the Sherman Act. In *Standard Oil Co. of New Jersey v. United States*[2] the "rule of reason" concept was introduced to the Supreme Court. According to this "rule," the Sherman Act does *not* prohibit *every* contract, combination, or conspiracy in restraint of trade among the several states. Rather, the Act prohibits only those contracts, combinations, or conspiracies that *unreasonably* restrain trade among the several states. If the contract, combination, or conspiracy is *reasonable* under the circumstances, the conduct is not in violation of the law. By applying this "rule" the Court can determine whether a defendant accused of violating the Act conducted his or her business in a reasonable manner and adhered to the law, or acted in an unreasonable manner in violation of the law. Although the Court determined in this particular case that the conduct by Standard Oil of New Jersey was unreasonable, the Court did accept, in theory, this defense. Thus was born the "rule of reason" defense to charges of violations of §1 of the Sherman Act.

Once it was established, the "rule of reason" defense provided business with an opportunity that it lost no time in using to its best advantage. Given a sufficient amount of time to prepare a defense, almost any business can develop a strong argument that its conduct was "reasonable" under the circumstances. Because of the results that the rule of reason produced, the courts had to reevaluate their approach. The amended approach retained the rule of reason but added a new category: The courts declared some conduct to be so lacking in social value as to be an automatic violation of § 1. These actions, called *per se* violations, tend to contradict directly the economic model of pure competition.

Per se Violations As noted in the preceding section, the courts restricted the availability of the rule of reason defense for alleged Sherman Act violations by the imposition of per se violations. The acts that are deemed to be per se violations are acts that are inherently contradictory to the economic theory of pure competition. If a firm is found guilty of a per se violation, it is not permitted to defend its conduct; it will be found guilty of the alleged violation of the Sherman Act by definition.

Historically the per se violations under the Sherman Act, § 1, were:

- Horizontal price-fixing (agreements on price among competitors)

- Vertical price-fixing (agreements on price among suppliers and customers)

- Horizontal market divisions (agreements among competitors as to who can sell in which region)

- Group boycotts (agreements among competitors not to sell to a particular buyer or not to buy from a particular seller)

Clearly, few businesses would be careless (or stupid) enough actually to overtly agree to such conduct. As a result, the courts have had to infer such agreements from the conduct of the parties. For example, in the area of price-fixing, if the courts find that the parties have acted in a manner that amounts to conscious parallelism, a violation is likely to be found. Conscious parallelism, by itself, is not conclusive proof of a violation of § 1. However, it is to be weighed—and weighed heavily—by the courts in determining whether a § 1 violation is present. Generally, conscious parallelism coupled with some other fact, however slight, is sufficient to support a jury verdict of price-fixing in violation of § 1. But if the conduct of the firms amounts only to price leadership, no violation is present. How can anyone distinguish conscious parallelism from price leadership? There is no answer to this problem; it poses a Gordian knot for the court every time it is raised.

Both the rule of reason and the economic theory of competition seemed to be invoked by the court in a recent case.[3] Sears, Roebuck and Company applied for membership with Visa, USA, the association of credit card issuers who offer the Visa card in the United States. The association denied the application by Sears, and Sears filed suit against Visa, USA, alleging that the credit card association was combining or conspiring illegally in an effort to prevent Sears from issuing Visa cards. The court found that the harm to competition would be greater if the association admitted Sears than if Sears were prevented from joining the association. According to the court, the credit card industry was better served by having Visa, MasterCard, American Express, Diners/Carte Blanche, and Discover (issued by and through Sears). Competition was keen, and the market was highly competitive. Admitting Sears to the association would reduce the number of competitors in the credit card industry and would seriously harm banks that would issue Visa in head-to-head competition with Sears for the potential Visa customers in the market. According to the court, the association acted in a reasonable manner under the circumstances. Under the rule of reason, the conduct of Visa, USA, was reasonable and therefore appropriate. It did not violate § 1 of the Sherman Act.

"Quick Look" Analysis The courts have recently added a third method for evaluating allegations that certain conduct violates § 1 of the Sherman Act. This method, the *"quick look"* analysis, provides a "middle ground" between the rule of reason and the per se violations. Under the quick look analysis a defendant firm that is charged with what has historically been treated as a per se violation is given an opportunity to rebut the presumption that the conduct is automatically anticompetitive, and thus to avoid conviction under the per se standards. If the court agrees with the rebuttal evidence of the defendant firm, the court removes the conduct from the per se category and applies a "rule of reason" analysis to the case.

Under the traditional approach, the per se rule absolutely prohibits certain conduct, denying the firms accused of violating the act the opportunity to show that there is a business justification for the conduct. By contrast, the rule of reason allows the accused firms an opportunity to present a business justification, and thus to avoid being held in violation of the statute. When a quick look analysis is applied, the courts allow the firms charged with traditional per se violations to present a business justification. The quick look, gives these firms the opportunity to show that there *is* a business justification for their conduct, and that they should not be found in violation of the law.

In 1967, the U.S. Supreme Court ruled that nonprice vertical restrictions imposed by a supplier on its customers was a per se illegal market division.[4] The following year, the Court ruled that a maximum resale price-fixing arrangement was also illegal per se.[5] However, by 1979 the Court had begun to restrict the application of the per se doctrine, beginning to apply the quick look analysis to certain types of cases. In *Broadcast Music, Inc. v. CBS, Inc.*[6] the Court upheld the right of an association of music copyright holders to establish a common price for the "blanket license" of their compositions. In rejecting the challenge by CBS, the Court stated that, in determining whether to apply the rule of reason or the per se rules, the court should decide "whether the practice facially appears to be one that would always or almost always tend to restrict competition and decrease output," or is "one designed to increase economic efficiency and render markets more, rather than less, competitive." This formulation provides the framework for the quick look analysis.

To date the quick look has been limited in its application to some vertical restraints and some cooperative pricing agreements. Thus, while horizontal price-fixing, horizontal market divisions, and group boycotts still are viewed as per se violations, some vertical market division cases and some maximum price arrangement cases have been evaluated under the quick look provisions. In addition, some tying arrangements are now being evaluated under a quick look analysis. The businesses charged with violations of § 1 of the Sherman Act are allowed the opportunity to rebut the presumption of anticompetitive effect in these cases. If they are successful, the case is decided under the rule of reason. If they are not, the conduct is found to be a violation of § 1 of the Sherman Act per se.

Another change to the Sherman Act occurred in 1982 when Congress passed the Foreign Trade Antitrust Improvement Act,[7] an amendment to the Sherman Act that addressed antitrust issues involving foreign trade. The FTAIA was intended to facilitate the *exporting* of domestic goods by providing an exemption from the provisions of the Sherman Act for export transactions that did not injure the U.S economy, thus relieving exporters from competitive disadvantage in foreign trade.[8] The Act precludes subject matter jurisdiction over claims by foreign plaintiffs against defendants when the situs of the injury is overseas and the injury arises from effects in the nondomestic market.[9] In order to meet this objection, the Act provides that its provisions do "not apply to conduct involving trade or commerce (other than import trade or import commerce) with foreign nations unless:

(1) such conduct has a direct, substantial, and reasonably foreseeable effect . . .

    (a) on trade or commerce which is not trade or commerce with foreign nations, or on import trade or commerce with foreign nations; or

    (b) on export trade or export commerce with foreign nations, or a person engaged in such trade or commerce in the United States; and

(2) such effect gives rise to a claim under the provisions of sections 1 to 7 of this title [the Sherman Act], other than this section."[10]

The following case involves an alleged violation of the Sherman Act, and the argument by the defendants that their conduct was protected due to the provisions of the FTAIA. Notice how the court, in this case of first impression, addressed these issues, and then decide whether you agree with the conclusions the court reached.

Section 2: Monopolizing and Attempts to Monopolize

Section 2 of the Sherman Act is nearly as brief as § 1 and is equally as broad. Section 2 makes the following provision:

Every person who shall monopolize, or attempt to monopolize, or combine or conspire with any other person or persons, to monopolize any part of the trade or commerce among the several States, or with foreign nations, shall be deemed guilty of a felony, and, on conviction thereof, shall be punished by a fine not exceeding $10,000,000 if a corporation, or, if any other person, $350,000, or by imprisonment not exceeding three years, or by both said punishments, in the discretion of the court.

(The original statute provided that the crime was a misdemeanor, and called for a maximum fine of $5,000, with a maximum imprisonment of one year for anyone convicted of violating the act.)

37.1

KRUMAN v. CHRISTIE'S INTERNATIONAL PLC
284 F.3d 384 (2nd Cir. 2002)

FACTS Christie's, a United Kingdom corporation, and Sotheby's, a Michigan corporation, are respectively the world's first and second largest auctioneers of fine art, antiques, collectibles, and other items, together controlling 97 percent of the market. Christie's and Sotheby's conduct auctions at various locations around the world, including London and New York City. At these auctions, in return for the auctioneer's services, the purchaser of an auctioned item pays the auctioneer a "buyer's premium," while the seller of the auctioned item pays the auctioneer a "seller's commission." These fees are calculated as a percentage of the purchase price of the auctioned item. From late 1992 until at least February 7, 2000, the defendants agreed to set the buyer's premiums charged by Christie's and Sotheby's at identical levels. On November 2, 1992, Sotheby's announced it would increase its buyer's premiums from 10 percent to 15 percent for the first $50,000.00 of the purchase price. On December 22, 1992, Christie's declared an identical increase in its buyer's premiums. The defendants allegedly agreed not to reduce these premiums.

The defendants also agreed to set their seller's commissions at identical levels. Prior to March 1995, the defendants would permit clients to negotiate smaller seller's commissions. On or about March 10, 1995, Christie's announced it would implement a fixed schedule of nonnegotiable seller's commissions ranging between 2 percent and 10 percent depending on the value of the item to be sold. On April 13, 1995, Sotheby's stated it would implement a fixed schedule of nonnegotiable seller's commissions substantially identical to the schedule set by Christie's. Moreover, the defendants allegedly conspired to coordinate their policies and procedures in other areas. They agreed to restrict the ability of sellers to negotiate the terms of loans they received before the sale of their works, exchanged preferred client lists, and otherwise monitored each other's businesses to prevent cheating. After the Justice Department initiated an antitrust investigation in 1997, on January 28, 2000, Christie's admitted it had uncovered information relevant to the investigation and disclosed that it had been granted conditional amnesty by the Justice Department in exchange for its cooperation with federal authorities. Soon after the announcement by Christie's, a number of litigants filed class action lawsuits alleging that Christie's and Sotheby's had violated the antitrust laws through price-fixing. These lawsuits were consolidated into one action in the Southern District of New York and on April 20, 2000, the district court certified a class (the "domestic class") consisting of "all persons who purchased from or sold through defendants items offered at or sold through defendants' non-Internet auctions held in the United States between January 1, 1993, and February 7, 2000. The district court ruled that the FTAIA was applicable to the case, but granted the defendants' motion to dismiss due to the court's decision that the conduct did not have the requisite effect on domestic conduct to be regulated by the Sherman Act. The plaintiffs appealed.

ISSUE Does a transnational price-fixing conspiracy that affects commerce both in the United States and in other countries inevitably give persons injured abroad in transactions otherwise unconnected with the United States a remedy under our antitrust laws?

HOLDING Yes, so long as the conduct has a "direct, substantial and reasonably foreseeable effect in the United States," and the conduct is properly subject to adjudication under the Sherman Act.

REASONING Excerpts from the opinion of Circuit Judge Katzmann:

The plaintiffs allege that the defendants entered into an agreement to fix the prices they charged for their services as auctioneers. Part of the agreement was directed at fixing the prices in foreign auctions. Section 1 of the Sherman Act proscribes "every contract, combination . . . or conspiracy, in restraint of trade or commerce among the several States, or with foreign nations. . . ." A price-fixing agreement is unlawful *per se* under the Sherman Act, meaning that it is illegal regardless of whether it affects prices or reduces competition in a market. . . . Before turning to the FTAIA, we find it helpful to begin with a discussion of the application of the antitrust laws to conduct directed at foreign markets. The antitrust laws strive to foster competition in our domestic markets. . . . While the antitrust laws do not extend to conduct that exclusively affects foreign markets . . . anticompetitive conduct directed at foreign markets can also directly affect the competitiveness of our domestic markets. There is a distinction between anticompetitive conduct directed at foreign markets that only affects the competitiveness of foreign markets and anticompetitive conduct directed at foreign markets that directly affects the competitiveness of domestic markets. The antitrust laws apply to the latter sort of conduct and not the former. Our markets benefit when antitrust suits stop or deter any conduct that reduces competition in our markets regardless of where it occurs and whether it is also directed at foreign markets. On the other hand, our markets do not benefit when antitrust suits stop or deter anticompetitive conduct directed at foreign markets without an effect on our markets. Ever since Judge Learned Hand's seminal opinion in *United States v. Aluminum Co. of America* . . . it has been clear that the focus in determining whether the antitrust laws govern conduct is the conduct's effect on the domestic market rather than the situs of the conduct itself. Under what was called the "effects test," foreign conduct was actionable under our antitrust laws if it was intended to affect domestic commerce and actually did so. . . . In contrast, "we should not impute to Congress an intent to punish all whom its courts can catch, for conduct which has no consequences within the United States." . . . The Supreme Court recently reaffirmed these fundamental principles when it stated that "it is well established by now that the Sherman Act applies to foreign conduct that was meant to produce and did in fact produce some substantial effect in the United States." . . .

In this Circuit, though, we have recognized that an unmodified "effects test" is too broad in its regulation of conduct. If conduct affecting foreign markets has a substantial but beneficial effect on our markets, such conduct does not implicate the concerns of the antitrust laws, which are meant to protect our markets from negative effects. Thus, just prior to the passage of the FTAIA, we modified the "effects test" by giving the term "effect" a specific and narrower meaning than its common usage. In *National Bank of Canada*, we held that we only have jurisdiction to hear an antitrust claim arising out of conduct directed at foreign markets if the conduct had the "effect" of "injuries to United States commerce which reflect the anticompetitive effect either of the violation or of anticompetitive acts made possible by the violation. . . ." In other words, under *National Bank of Canada*, the antitrust laws apply to anticompetitive conduct directed at foreign markets only if such conduct injures domestic commerce by

either (1) reducing the competitiveness of a domestic market; or (2) making possible anticompetitive conduct directed at domestic commerce. The first prong of the *National Bank of Canada* test would clearly encompass a situation where anticompetitive conduct is directed at both foreign and domestic markets and actually reduces the competitiveness of the domestic market. The mere fact that such conduct targets a foreign market in addition to a domestic market does not mean that it should be exempt from our antitrust laws. If such a course of conduct is successful and reduces the competitiveness of our markets, it would certainly fall within our antitrust laws. The second prong of the *National Bank of Canada* test encompasses a situation where anticompetitive conduct is directed only at a foreign market, but has the effect of allowing a separate course of conduct that directly affects the competitiveness of our domestic markets. Again, because such conduct affects the competitiveness of our domestic markets, the antitrust laws apply. . . . Ultimately, however, the only issue we resolve on this appeal is whether the Sherman Act applies to the conduct that is the basis for the plaintiffs' action, and we find that it does. While the defendants ask this Court to affirm the district court's dismissal based on their lack of standing and improper venue arguments, because the district court did not address these issues in its opinion granting the motion to dismiss, we remand the case so that the district court may examine these issues in the first instance. For the reasons stated above, we affirm in part, vacate in part, and remand the case for further proceedings consistent with this opinion.

BUSINESS CONSIDERATIONS Why might a business agree to enter into a price-fixing arrangement with its primary competitor? Should a business conduct its international operations in a manner that violates its domestic laws if such conduct is legal in a foreign setting?

ETHICAL CONSIDERATIONS Is it ethical to have a law that seems to allow conduct by domestic firms in foreign markets when that same conduct would be illegal in the domestic market? What justification might exist for such statutory treatment?

Note that § 2 can be violated *either* by one person acting alone *or* by multiple parties acting in concert. In contrast, § 1 can be violated only by multiple parties acting together. (To avoid confusion, remember that it takes two people to violate § 1, while it takes only one person to violate § 2.)

Many people have the mistaken idea that monopolies are prohibited by § 2. In fact, no law prohibits having monopoly power. The prohibition in § 2 of the Sherman

Act is against *monopolizing*, that is, seeking a monopoly or attempting to keep a monopoly once one is attained. Either act is monopolizing and is illegal under § 2. Having a monopoly, however, is not illegal.

Obviously, very few "pure" monopolies exist in the U.S. market, and those often exist for a valid reason, such as the so-called natural monopolies. Some areas, for example, may be served by only one railroad or have only one source of electric

NRW CASE 37.1 Sales/Management

DOES NRW HAVE A MONOPOLY IN THE RELEVANT MARKET?

While NRW has enjoyed success in its initial entry into the market, the firm has hardly become dominant in its industry. Nevertheless, the firm's major competitor in the Indiana-Illinois region recently filed for protection under the bankruptcy law and closed its operations in this two-state region. As a result, NRW now controls more than 70 percent of the market in the Indiana-Illinois market. Carlos jokingly stated that, with the withdrawal of this competitor, NRW now is in a position to monopolize the Indiana-Illinois market. Mai replied that the firm does not have a large enough share of the national market to be accused of monopolizing. However, Helen remembers something about relevant product markets, and she is concerned that the firm *could* be accused of violating § 2 of the Sherman Act if it acts improperly in the region. She has asked for your opinion. What will you tell her?

BUSINESS CONSIDERATIONS Is there any problem with a business gaining a dominant position in its market? Should a business aim for a lesser degree of control to avoid potential problems under the Sherman Act, or should it maximize its potential, dealing with the Sherman Act problems if or when they arise?

ETHICAL CONSIDERATIONS Section 2 of the Sherman Act prohibits monopolizing, and a "virtual-monopoly" position is defined by the courts as controlling 70 percent or more of the relevant product market. Economic theory states that a monopoly exists when an industry contains only one firm. Is it ethical for the courts to define a virtual-monopoly position differently than economic theory defines monopoly position, when the purpose of the Sherman Act is to provide for industrial conduct that is more in line with economic theories and economic competition?

INTERNATIONAL CONSIDERATIONS Suppose that NRW decides to export its product, and it enters into price-fixing agreements that are likely to result in its virtual control of the market in some foreign markets. Can NRW be prosecuted under the Sherman Act if it enters into such an arrangement?

power. However, the provisions of § 2 do not require that a "pure" monopoly exist. Monopoly *power* may be present even if an area of commerce has several businesses in existence and seemingly competing with one another. If a firm is found to dominate an industry, it may also be found to possess monopoly power. As a rule of thumb, control of 70 percent or more of the *relevant market* is deemed to be sufficient to establish that the firm has monopoly power. However, defining the relevant market may be difficult. In determining the relevant market, the courts must determine the relevant *geographic* market—where the product is sold—and the relevant *product* market—what is being sold or provided by the seller. In so doing, the courts examine the *product* produced by the challenged firm, *substitute* goods produced by other firms, and the elasticity of demand between the challenged product and the substitutes. If the courts find that the firm controls 70 percent or more of this relevant market with its product, the firm will be found to possess monopoly power under the courts' interpretation of § 2 of the Sherman Act. If the firm possesses less than 70 percent of the relevant market, it lacks monopoly power under § 2 of the Sherman Act.

United States v. E. I. DuPont de Nemours and Co.[11] is a landmark in U.S. antitrust law involving relevant product market. Dupont acquired the exclusive U.S. right to produce cellophane from the French patent holder of the process. By 1947, Dupont had acquired 75 percent of the cellophane market in the United States, which led the Justice Department to file charges against Dupont for violating § 2 of the Sherman Act. At trial, Dupont admitted that it controlled the market for *cellophane*, but denied that it controlled the relevant product market. According to Dupont, the relevant product market was for *flexible wrapping materials*, including aluminum foil, wax paper, saran wrap, and various other materials. In this broader market, Dupont had only a 20 percent market share. The Court agreed with Dupont's argument, establishing a precedent for the determination of relevant product market.

When a dominant position in the relevant product market is present, there is a presumption that § 2 was, or is, violated. However, a number of defenses exist to rebut this presumption. The dominant firm may argue that it is not attempting to retain its power, or that it acquired its position legally, or that its position was "thrust upon" it. Any of these defenses is sufficient to prevent a § 2 prosecution.

The next hypothetical case shows how the defense can be applied:

Ralph developed a new product, Kleenzall, which does what other soaps or cleansers do, except that it does it better and is cheaper. Kleenzall is good for washing dishes, clothes, floors, walls, and even hair. Kleenzall is so good a product that Ralph has 95 percent of every cleanser and soap market. The major soap producers sue Ralph for monopolizing the industry in violation of the Sherman Act, § 2. The court, however, finds that Ralph is not guilty. He did nothing wrong in acquiring his market share. Rather, this monopoly was "thrust upon" him by sheer efficiency. However, if Ralph subsequently takes steps to prevent other firms from entering the cleanser market or acts in any manner that seems to be precluding or preventing competition, he may be found guilty of monopolizing. Possessing his monopoly power is legal, but attempting to retain it is illegal!

The government in a number of monopolization cases over the years has used the Sherman Act quite successfully, beginning with *Standard Oil Co. v. United States*,[12] decided in 1911. The Standard Oil Company was found guilty of monopolizing, using regional price-cutting to drive competition out of the market and then asserting domination over that market segment. The court ordered Standard Oil broken up into a number of smaller companies, effectively ending its ability to dominate the domestic oil market. The Justice Department was also successful in attacking American Tobacco, Alcoa, and AT&T. However, the last major Sherman Act success came with the breaking up of the telephone monopoly in 1982, until the government managed to obtain a conviction against Microsoft in 2000.

In the Microsoft case, the judge found that Microsoft was guilty of monopolizing and was also guilty of illegal tying arrangements. He ordered that the company be broken into two separate companies, one handling the Windows operating system and the other handling Internet Explorer, Microsoft Office, and all other Microsoft holdings. These two companies were to remain separate and independent for at least 10 years.

The judge also prohibited Microsoft from taking any actions against computer makers who support competing technologies, required that the Windows system had to be sold at the same price to all computer makers, and ordered that Microsoft disclose certain parts of the Windows source code to software developers in order to ensure that newly developed software would be compatible with the Windows system.

Microsoft has subsequently reached a settlement with the Justice Department and nine of the states that participated in the initial case. This settlement would avoid the breakup of the firm, although numerous other remedies would be imposed. While some of the states that initially joined in the complaint are not participating in the settlement, it appears that Microsoft will survive this action without being broken into two or more companies. But the success of the government in gaining a conviction shows that the potential for using the Sherman Act continues.

Remedies

When a Sherman Act violation is shown, both criminal and civil remedies are available. As originally enacted, the Sherman Act did not provide for individual remedies. Instead, the law provided only for governmental prosecution of the prohibited conduct. However, § 4 of the Clayton Act[13] authorizes civil remedies for violations of *any* antitrust statutes, including the Sherman Act. Under this section "any person who shall be injured in his business or property by reason of anything forbidden in the antitrust laws may sue therefore . . . and shall recover threefold the damages by him sustained, and the cost of suit, including a reasonable attorney's fee."[14] In addition, as was previously mentioned, an individual who is convicted of a violation of the Sherman Act can be fined up to $350,000 and can receive up to three years in prison; a corporation that is convicted can be fined up to $10 million. Also, § 4 of the Sherman Act provides that an injunction can be issued against the prohibited conduct. For more information on the Sherman Antitrust Act, visit http://www.bartleby.com/65/sh/ShermanA.htm or http://www.usdoj.gov/atr/foia/divisionmanual/ch2.htm to view the text of the act.

The Clayton Act

By 1914, Congress realized that the Sherman Act alone was not sufficient to solve the major business problems of the country. The Sherman Act was remedial in nature: If a problem existed, the Sherman Act could be used to help correct the problem. Unfortunately, it is possible (if not probable) that by the time the "remedy" is sought the injured party has suffered irreparable harm or has ceased to exist as a business entity. Nothing, however, was available to prevent a problem from developing. In an effort to correct this regulatory deficiency, Congress decided to enact some preventative legislation. The result was the Clayton Act, which was designed to nip problems "in their incipiency." The Clayton Act has four major provisions addressing antitrust conduct, each directed toward a different potential problem. And, as previously discussed, the Clayton Act has a number of other provisions dealing with implementation of the antitrust laws, including the provision for treble damages for violations of any of the antitrust laws.

Section 2: Price Discrimination

The first regulating section of the Clayton Act, § 2, prohibits price discrimination. The original § 2 made it illegal for a *seller* to discriminate in price between different purchasers unless the price difference could be justified by a difference in costs. This provision soon placed a number of sellers in a terrible bind. Major purchasers often demanded special prices from sellers. If the sellers refused, they lost the business; if they agreed, they violated the law. This placed some sellers in an untenable position, while shielding the buyers—who often initiated the price discrimination—from liability, since the law applied only to the seller. As a result, § 2 was amended in 1936 when the Robinson-Patman Act became law. Under the Robinson-Patman Act, *buyers* were prohibited from knowingly accepting a discriminatory price. In addition, the act prohibited buyers from knowingly accepting indirect benefits such as dummy brokerage fees and promotional kickbacks. And, of course, sellers were still prohibited from granting discriminatory prices to their customers absent a cost differential justifying the price.

In interpreting and applying the provisions of the Robinson-Patman Act, the courts have developed a "checklist" of elements that are required in order to find that a firm is guilty of violation the law. It appears that all of these elements must be present before a violation will be found. The elements are:

- There must be discrimination in price, a different price must be charged to two or more different buyers.

- There must be at least two consummated sales. Mere offers will not suffice; there must be at least two contracts involved.

- There must be a difference in price quoted by the "same seller."

- At least one of the sales must cross state lines. Since this is a federal statute, interstate commerce must be involved before the statute applies.

- The sales must either be contemporaneous or they must occur within a relevant time period.

- The sale must relate to "commodities."

- The goods sold must be of "like grade and quality."

- The law applies only to goods that will be used, consumed, or resold within the United States.

- There must be a showing of an adverse affect on competition.[15]

The mere fact that a different price is granted to different buyers is not enough to assure a conviction for price discrimination. In fact, a number of potential defenses exist.

- The person accused of price discrimination can defend against the charge by showing that he or she is meeting, but not beating, the price being offered by a competitor.

- The accused can also defend by showing that the lower price is being offered because of obsolescence, seasonal variations, or damage to the goods being sold.

- The accused can also show that the price differential is based on legitimate cost savings based on quantity discounts, and that such discounts are generally available to any other customers who place orders of sufficient size.

- The accused can avoid being found liable for charging two different prices—a normal price and a reduced price—if it can show that the reduced price is realistically available to any individual customer, but that the particular customer chose not to take advantage of this reduced price for whatever reason.[16]

Standard Oil Co. (of Indiana) v. FTC, a landmark opinion, involved an allegation of price discrimination and a defense of meeting—but not beating—the competition. Standard Oil was selling gasoline to four large "jobbers" in the Detroit area at a lower price than to numerous smaller competitors in the same market. Standard showed that its lower price for the "jobbers" was only to meet—and not to beat—the price of a competitor, thus allowing Standard to retain its customers. The court accepted this defense, finding that Standard Oil was not guilty of price discrimination.

The Robinson-Patman Act also changed the standards needed to show a violation. Under the original § 2, it was necessary to show that general competition had been harmed, but under the Robinson-Patman Act, it is sufficient to prosecute on a showing that a competitor was injured. There are two types of injuries that the courts look for when hearing a Robinson-Patman case: a *primary-line injury* and a *secondary-line injury*. A primary-line injury involves competition at the seller's level. The seller is providing discriminatory prices in order to gain a competitive advantage over one of the seller's competitors. A secondary-line injury involves competition at the buyer's level. One or more of the buyers who receive the discriminatory price are given an advantage over one or more of the buyer's competitors who did not receive the same price.

The following case involves an allegation of price discrimination in violation of the Robinson-Patman Act. It also involves an agreement between two parties that seemingly violates the antitrust laws.

37.2

FRANK SEXTON ENTERPRISES, INC. v. SODIAAL NORTH AMERICA CORPORATION
2002 U.S. Dist. LEXIS 373 (E.D. Pa. 2002)

FACTS Frank Sexton Enterprises, Inc. (FSE) is a closely held corporation. Since its formation in 1990, FSE has engaged in the business of wholesaling butter, eggs and cheese purchased from others and then resold to food service companies and retail grocery markets. The company uses the trade name Sommer Maid. SODIAAL North American Corporation (SNAC) did business from 1990 through 1999 through four operating divisions. The two divisions that supplied Sommer Maid during part of the 1990s were the Keller's Division and the Mayfair Division. During the relevant period, Keller's packaged butter that was obtained from Mayfair creamery and other butter manufacturers in the Midwest and West. Sommer Maid purchased packaged butter from several manufacturers and packagers, including Keller's, which it stored and delivered to food service companies and retail grocery markets. The relationship between the parties derived from a long-standing personal relationship between two industry veterans. Frank Sexton entered the industry in 1970. In 1975, he became president of AMPI's Sommer Maid Division, and in 1990 he purchased the assets of Sommer Maid from AMPI and formed FSE. Thompson was the general manager of Keller's before and after its acquisition by SNAC, and had considerable autonomy in his operation of the division.

In late 1989, Sexton and Thompson began discussing potential business opportunities should Sexton purchase the assets of the Sommer Maid division of AMPI. When this actually occurred in September 1990, Sexton and Thompson formalized their prior discussions by agreeing to cooperate in an effort to control their markets. The terms of the agreement provided, among other things, that the companies would continue to sell to their present customers without competition from the other, and, as to customers supplied by both, the companies would do what was necessary to maintain the same percentage allocation of business. The agreement was to be effectuated in part by the refusal of each party to "quote" a competitive price to a customer of the other or to offer to sell to a shared customer at a price lower than that of the other. When sales to shared customers declined or increased, suggesting a price differential, the parties would respectively raise or lower prices to maintain the agreed upon allocation of business. In Sexton's words, "we would carry this into the next millennium and pretty much own the market" as "we would be unencumbered by competitive pricing of our accounts." The agreement was never memorialized in any writing.

Arthur Thompson retired as general manager in December 1992, and the troubles soon began. FSE asserts that beginning in late 1993, Keller's refused to fill butter orders for Sommer Maid, raised the overage to Sommer Maid higher than that charged to retail purchasers, solicited Sommer Maid's customers and provided "market protection" to customers. FSE alleged that SNAC breached an oral agreement between the parties when it refused to fill plaintiff's orders for packaged butter, raised prices for butter it did sell to plaintiff, and solicited plaintiff's customers. FSE also alleged that SNAC engaged in discriminatory pricing in violation of the Robinson-Patman Act, to FSE's disadvantage. FSE sought $60 million in damages. SNAC contended that, even assuming there was an oral agreement as described by FSE, it involved the allocation of customers, price-fixing, and exchange of pricing information and thus would be illegal and unenforceable. As to FSE's Robinson-Patman Act claim, SNAC contended that FSE had failed to offer any proof of price discrimination or antitrust damages.

ISSUE Did SNAC breach its contract with FSE? Was SNAC guilty of price discrimination in violation of the Robinson-Patman Act in its dealings with FSE beginning in 1993?

HOLDINGS No, the contract, if it existed, was a contract at will from which either party could withdraw at any time. No, there was no evidence of any price discrimination by SNAC in its dealings with FSE.

REASONING Excerpts from the opinion of Judge Waldman

An oral contract that does not specify a definite term of duration or set prescribed conditions which determine the duration is terminable at will by either party. . . . Also, it is uncontested that the agreement involved the sale of goods and is thus governed by the Uniform Commercial Code. Under the Code, a contract that provides for successive performance but is indefinite in duration may, unless otherwise agreed, be terminated by either party at any time. . . . The Pennsylvania Supreme Court has recognized that the Code did not change prior law governing contracts of indefinite duration. . . . The contract at issue was clearly one of indefinite duration and thus terminable at will. By the fall of 1993, defendants effectively terminated any agreement concerning non-solicitation of customers and in 1994, any agreement regarding unilateral price increases. . . . Upon recognition that the contract had been terminated, plaintiff was free to continue ordering from Keller's or place its orders elsewhere. To the extent that the parties continued to conduct business following the termination, this amounted to a series of individual transactions at a price set by defendants in the familiar role of vendor and vendee. . . . Plaintiff alleges that defendants violated § 2(a) of the Robinson-Patman Act, 15 U.S.C. § 13(a), by charging higher prices to Sommer Maid than Keller's direct-purchasing retailers. To sustain a § 13(a) claim, a plaintiff must show that the commodities in question are sold in commerce, the commodities sold are of like grade and quality, there is discrimination in price between different purchasers and such discrimination caused injury to competition. In Robinson-Patman Act cases, it is useful to distinguish the vertical relationship between the discriminatory seller, the favored and unfavored buyer, and the impact of the alleged price discrimination. . . . Where a seller engages in price discrimination, the injury may fall on several different parties. A primary-line injury harms the competitors of the discriminating seller. A secondary-line injury harms the disfavored buyers vis-à-vis the favored buyers of the discriminating seller. A third-line injury falls upon the customers of the purchasers. Plaintiff contends that it was a customer and competitor of Keller's and may thus assert a claim for primary-line or secondary-line injury. Plaintiff has cited no case in which a plaintiff was permitted to assert both types of injury. In any event, there is absolutely no evidence of record that Sommer Maid competed with any favored purchaser of Keller's butter, a prerequisite to establishing secondary-line injury in a price discrimination case. . . . The essence of plaintiff's claim is that defendants diverted business from Sommer Maid, much of it from shared customers, through discriminatory pricing. This is a primary-line injury.

Price discrimination means "selling the same kind of goods cheaper to one purchaser than to another." . . . To show discrimination, a plaintiff must show that the sales were made contemporaneously. . . . Defendants correctly note that plaintiff has failed to present any records or other evidence showing contemporaneous sales by defendant of butter to plaintiff at a price higher than that at which it sold butter to retail customers. After extensive discovery including thirty depositions and the production of thousands of documents including sales records and invoices for all accounts on which plaintiff bases its claim of injury, plaintiff has presented no competent evidence that in any given week defendants sold butter to any customer at a lower price than that charged to plaintiff. . . . Defendants correctly note that it is also not enough even for a plaintiff which has shown price discrimination to prove injury to its own business. A plaintiff must also demonstrate a reasonable possibility that competition in the pertinent market has been harmed as a result of the price differential. . . . Plaintiff has failed to make any such showing. To the contrary, it clearly appears from the record that the private label butter market was highly competitive during the pertinent period. Indeed, what plaintiff essentially complains about in this case is the diversion of business by defendants through competitive pricing and plaintiff's loss of profits from reducing prices to meet the competition or loss of business because of it. Plaintiff has shown no more than defendants' decision after Mr. Thompson stepped down as General Manager of Keller's to terminate an unwritten agreement to allocate business and stifle competition. Although the agreement contemplated the sale of substantial quantities of products, it is not evidenced by any writing and, in the absence of any term of duration, was terminable at will by either party. Moreover, insofar as the agreement blatantly provided for an allocation of customers and suppression of competition, its enforcement would violate public policy. Plaintiff has not shown contemporaneous sales at disparate prices as required to sustain any Robinson-Patman Act claim, let alone any such action by defendants which injured competition. Plaintiff cannot sustain its claims on the competent evidence of record. Defendants are entitled to summary judgment.

BUSINESS CONSIDERATIONS One of the issues in this case was the term of the alleged contract. Why would a business enter into a contract at will rather than a contract for a fixed term? Assuming the agreement is legal, what benefits accrue in an "at will" agreement that would make this a preferable term, rather than establishing a set time for the agreement to run?

ETHICAL CONSIDERATIONS Is it ethical to enter into an apparently illegal agreement and then to sue the other party when that party terminates—or even breaches— such an agreement?

In a case from Puerto Rico,[17] an interesting Robinson-Patman issue was raised. Caribe BMW purchased new automobiles directly from the manufacturer. Caribe's competitors in the market purchased their new BMWs from a wholly owned subsidiary of the manufacturer and were able to purchase at a lower price than that offered to Caribe. The court ruled that a manufacturer and its wholly owned subsidiary are a single entity for purposes of applying the Robinson-Patman Act so that there was a discriminatory pricing practice in effect, entitling Caribe to remedies for violation of the act. (This ruling involves the "single seller" test, the third item in the list on page 907.)

The "Executive Legal Summary" discussing the Robinson-Patman Act can be found at http://www. businesslaws.com/els18.htm.

Section 3: Exclusive Dealings and Tying Arrangements

The second major prohibition under the Clayton Act is found in § 3. This section bans exclusive-dealing contracts and tying arrangements when their "effect may be to substantially lessen competition or tend to create a monopoly." Notice again the preventive intent of the act: Actual harm need not be shown, merely the *likelihood* that harm will eventually occur.

In an exclusive-dealing contract, one party requires the other party to deal with him, and him alone. For example, the seller tells the buyer that unless the buyer buys only from the seller, and not from the seller's competitors, the seller will not deal with the buyer. For such a demand to be effective, the seller must be in a very powerful market position.

In a tying arrangement, one party—usually the seller—refuses to sell one product unless the buyer also takes a second product or service from the seller. For example, a manufacturer of cosmetics might refuse to sell a facial moisturizer unless the buyer agrees to purchase the manufacturer's soap. Usually for this sort of arrangement to work, the seller needs a highly valued, unique product to which he or she can "tie" a commonly available product. As a defense to a charge that such an arrangement lessens competition or creates a monopoly, the seller may attempt to show that the tied product is tied for quality control reasons. To do so, the seller must prove that no competitors produce a competing product that works adequately with the controlled product.

The Supreme Court has ruled that a "not insubstantial" amount of commerce must be affected in order to have an illegal tying arrangement.[18] The Ninth Circuit went even further, ruling that there is no requirement for multiple purchasers in order to have an illegal tying arrangement,[19] so long as the effect on commerce is not insubstantial. The amount involved was approximately $100,000 per year for an indeterminate number of years, and the court ruled that such an amount was sufficiently substantial to allow the trial to proceed even though only one firm was precluded from the market due to the tying arrangement. This could, potentially, open up a number of claims for damages due to tying arrangements by firms that believed there had to be multiple purchasers affected before § 3 of the Clayton Act was applicable.

NRW CASE 37.2   Management/Manufacturing

TYING ARRANGEMENTS

A regional manufacturer of scanners has approached NRW with what it considers a "can't miss" deal. The manufacturer wants to produce a scanner that can be used only with the NRW InvenTrakR units. According to the president of this company, the two firms can each use the success of the other firm to gain a larger market share in their respective industries. Although the idea is intriguing, the firm is afraid there may be some legal implication they have overlooked. They ask you what you think of the idea. What advice will you give them?

BUSINESS CONSIDERATIONS What potential problems could arise under the various antitrust laws from tying your product to the products of another firm? Could this be considered an attempt by each firm to monopolize its respective industry? Is this more or less of a problem than would be faced if a firm tied one of its products to another of its products?

ETHICAL CONSIDERATIONS What ethical issues are raised when one firm ties its products to the products of another firm? Is it ethical to put the stakeholders of one firm in a position where those stakeholders are relying on the performance of another firm for success?

INTERNATIONAL CONSIDERATIONS In the United States, basically, a firm must act and then await results if the firm is considering conduct that may or may not violate antitrust provisions. In the European Union, firms can ask for a "negative clearance," seeking advance permission to do something that, eventually, may be determined to violate the Union's rules of competition. What are the benefits of a system that provides guidance in advance of conduct through the use of something like a "negative clearance"?

Section 7: Antimerger Provisions

The third major section of the Clayton Act, § 7, concerns mergers. As originally written, the only prohibited type of merger was one in which the stock of another firm was acquired with the effect "substantially to lessen competition, or [to] tend to create a monopoly." This prohibition was so narrow that it was rather easily evaded by merging firms.

To broaden the scope of the law, Congress amended § 7 in 1950 by passing the Celler–Kefauver Act. The amended § 7 prohibits the acquisition of stock or assets of another firm that may tend to have a negative effect on any line of commerce. As a result, firms are now subject to § 7 in almost any type of merger—horizontal, vertical, or conglomerate. A horizontal merger is one between competing firms; a vertical merger is one between a firm and one of its major suppliers or customers; a conglomerate merger is one between firms in two noncompeting industries.

Not all mergers are prohibited by § 7. The government must establish that if the merger is allowed, the result "may be to substantially lessen competition" in an industry. For example, as a challenge to a merger, the government might argue that a "concentration trend" has been established, or that one of the firms was a "potential entrant" into one of the industries affected by the merger. The government would thus argue that the industry after the proposed merger was less competitive than the industry prior to the proposed merger. The burden then shifts to the defendants to justify the proposed merger by showing that the effect is not a likely substantial lessening of competition. For example the merging firms might raise the "failing-company" doctrine, showing that without the merger one of the firms would have gone out of business. If one of the firms would have gone out of business anyway, the same number of firms remain in the industry following the merger as would have existed without the merger, and jobs were saved with the firm that would otherwise have ceased to exist. The following example illustrates the failing-company doctrine.

Fred's Stereo is in severe financial difficulty. Irv's Interstate Sound Store, the largest stereo dealer in the region, buys Fred's. Under the failing-company doctrine, if Fred's would have gone bankrupt, the merger with Irv's is probably permissible. (Of course such a merger would be less likely to be challenged if the firm taking over Fred's had not been the largest competitor in the region. In such a case, the merged firms would be better able to compete with Irv's, the largest firm, and might be able to show that competition would be enhanced with the merger even if Fred's was not about to go out of business.)

Section 8: Interlocking Directorates

The final substantive section of the Clayton Act is § 8. This section prohibits interlocking directorates. In other words, no one may sit on the boards of directors of two or more competing corporations if either of the firms has capital and surplus in excess of $1 million and if a merger between them violates any antitrust law.

The Clayton Antitrust Act can be found at http://www.stolaf.edu/people/becker/antitrust/statutes/clayton.html, and additional information can be found at http://www.bartleby.com/65/cl/ClaytonAA.html.

The Federal Trade Commission Act

The year 1914 was a very busy year for antitrust regulation. Congress passed not only the Clayton Act but also the Federal Trade Commission Act, which did two important things:

1. It created the Federal Trade Commission (FTC) to enforce antitrust laws, especially the Clayton Act.

2. In § 5, it provided a broad area of prohibitions to close loopholes left by other statutes.

Section 5 of the act prohibits "unfair methods of competition" and "unfair and deceptive trade practices." This broad language permits the FTC to regulate conduct that technically might be beyond the reach of the other, more specific antitrust statutes. The area of unfair and deceptive trade practices was intentionally made broad and somewhat vague to grant the FTC the leeway to proceed against any commercial practices that seem to be unfair or deceptive under the circumstances. If the statute is specific, businesspeople will find methods to circumvent it, methods that may be unfair or deceptive but within the technical limits of the law. The strength of the law has been its breadth, as well as the willingness of the FTC to attack practices that had been followed for many years.

The case on pages 912–914 involves an FTC allegation of unfair trade practices by one of the leaders in the toy industry. The facts also seem to indicate that there were primary-line and secondary-line price discrimination issues, and possible Sherman Act implications.

To further strengthen the FTC position, a violation can be found without proof of any actual deception. A mere showing that there is a "fair possibility" that the public will be deceived is sufficient to establish that the conduct is unfair and deceptive. In addition, if a representation made by a company is ambiguous, with one honest meaning and one deceptive meaning, the FTC will treat it as deceptive and as a material aspect of the transaction so that remedies are available.

If the FTC opposes a business practice as unfair or deceptive, it issues a cease-and-desist order. The business must stop the challenged conduct or face a fine for disobeying the order. The fine is $5,000 per violation. This may sound small, but realize that each day the order is ignored constitutes a separate violation. Thus, ignoring the

TOYS "R" US, INC. v. FEDERAL TRADE COMMISSION
221 F.3d 928, 2000 U.S. App. LEXIS 18304 (7th Cir. 2000)

FACTS TRU is a giant in the toy retailing industry. It sells approximately 20 percent of all the toys sold in the United States, and in some metropolitan areas its share of toy sales ranges between 35 percent and 49 percent. The variety of toys it sells is staggering: over the course of a year, it offers about 11,000 individual toy items, far more than any of its competitors. As one might suspect from these figures alone, TRU is a critical outlet for toy manufacturers. It buys about 30 percent of the large, traditional toy companies' total output and it is usually their most important customer. According to evidence before the Commission's administrative law judge (ALJ), even a company as large as Hasbro felt that it could not find other retailers to replace TRU—and Hasbro, along with Mattel, is one of the two largest toy manufacturers in the country, accounting for approximately 12 percent of the market for traditional toys and 10 percent of a market that includes video games.

Toys are sold in a number of different kinds of stores. At the high end are traditional toy stores and department stores, both of which typically sell toys for 40 to 50 percent above their cost. Next are the specialized discount stores—a category virtually monopolized by TRU today—that sell at an average 30 percent markup. General discounters like Wal-Mart, K-Mart, and Target are next, with a 22 percent markup, and last are the stores that are the focus of this case, the warehouse clubs like Costco and Pace. The clubs sell toys at a slender markup of 9 percent or so. The toys customers seek in all these stores are highly differentiated products. The little girl who wants Malibu Barbie is not likely to be satisfied with My First Barbie, and she certainly does not want Ken or Skipper. The boy who has his heart set on a figure of Anakin Skywalker will be disappointed if he receives Jar Jar Binks, or a truck, or a baseball bat instead. Toy retailers naturally want to have available for their customers the season's hottest items, because toys are also a very faddish product, as those old enough to recall the mania over Cabbage Patch kids or Tickle Me Elmo dolls will attest. What happened in this case, according to the Commission, was fairly simple. For a long time, TRU had enjoyed a strong position at the low-price end for toy sales, because its only competition came from traditional toy stores that could not or did not wish to meet its prices, or from general discounters like Wal-Mart or K-Mart, which could not offer anything like the variety of items TRU had and whose prices were not too far off TRU's mark.

The advent of the warehouse clubs changed all that. They were a retail innovation of the late 1970s: the first one opened in 1976, and by 1992 there were some 600 individual club stores around the country. Rather than earn all of their money from their markup on products, the clubs sell only to their members, and they charge a modest annual membership fee, often about $30. As the word "warehouse" in the name suggests, the clubs emphasize price competition over service amenities. In an effort to protect its market share, TRU persuaded—or coerced—the major toy manufacturers to agree to a proposal developed by TRU that would effectively preclude serious competition by the warehouse outlets. These agreements, according to the FTC, constituted both vertical and horizontal price-fixing. The Commission concluded, upon an extensive administrative record, that TRU had acted as the coordinator of a horizontal agreement among a number of toy manufacturers. The agreements took the form of a network of vertical agreements between TRU and the individual manufacturers, in each of which the manufacturer promised to restrict the distribution of its products to low-priced warehouse club stores, on the condition that other manufacturers would do the same. This practice, the Commission found, violated § 5 of the Federal Trade Commission Act, 15 U.S.C. § 45. It also found that TRU had entered into a series of vertical agreements that flunked scrutiny under antitrust's rule of reason. TRU appealed that decision, attacking both the sufficiency of the evidence supporting the Commission's conclusions and the scope of the Commission's remedial order.

ISSUE Did the evidence support the decision reached by the FTC? Did the FTC abuse its discretion in formulating its remedy in the case?

HOLDINGS Yes, under the substantial evidence rule there was adequate evidence to support the decision. No, the Commission did not abuse its discretion in formulating its remedy in this case.

REASONING Excerpts from the opinion of Circuit Judge Diane P. Wood.

The antitrust laws, which aim to preserve and protect competition in economically sensible markets, have long drawn a sharp distinction between contractual restrictions that occur up and down a distribution chain—so-called vertical restraints—and restrictions that come about as a result of agreements among competitors, or horizontal restraints. Sometimes, however, it can be hard as a matter of fact to be sure what kind of agreement is at issue. This was the problem facing the Federal Trade Commission ("the Commission") when it brought under its antitrust microscope the large toy retailer Toys "R" Us (TRU).... The Commission first noted that internal documents from the manufacturers revealed that they were trying to expand, not to restrict, the number of their major retail outlets and to reduce their dependence on TRU. They were specifically interested in cultivating a relationship with the warehouse clubs and increasing sales there. Thus, the sudden adoption of measures under which they decreased sales to the clubs ran against their independent economic self-interest. Second, the Commission cited evidence that the manufacturers were unwilling to limit sales to the clubs without assurances that their competitors would do likewise.... Once the special warehouse club policy (or, in the Commission's more pejorative language, boycott) was underway, TRU served as the central clearinghouse for complaints about breaches in the agreement. The Commission gave numerous examples of this conduct in its opinion.... Last, the Commission found that TRU's policies had bite. In the year before the boycott began, the clubs' share of all toy sales in the United States grew from 1.5% in 1991 to 1.9% in 1992. After the boycott took hold, that percentage slipped back by 1995 to 1.4%. Local numbers were more impressive.... In 1989, over 90% of the Mattel toys Costco and other clubs purchased were regular (i.e. easily comparable) items, but by 1993 that percentage was zero. Once again, the Commission's opinion is chock full of similar statistics.... Based on this record, the Commission drew three central conclusions of law: (1) the TRU-led manufacturer boycott of the warehouse clubs was illegal *per se* under the rule enunciated in *Northwest Wholesale Stationers, Inc. v. Pacific Stationery & Printing Co.*... (2) the boycott was illegal under a full rule of reason analysis because its anticompetitive effects "clearly outweighed any possible business justification"; and (3) the vertical agreements between TRU and the individual toy manufacturers, "entered into *seriatim* with clear anticompetitive effect, violate section 1 of the Sherman Act."... These antitrust violations in turn were enough to prove a violation of FTC Act § 5, which for present purposes tracks the prohibitions of the Sherman and Clayton Acts.... In TRU's opinion, this record shows nothing more than a series of separate, similar vertical agreements between itself and various toy manufacturers. It believes that each manufacturer in its independent self-interest had an incentive to limit sales to the clubs, because TRU's policy provided strong unilateral incentives for the manufacturer to reduce its sales to the clubs. Why gain a few sales at the clubs, it asks, when it would have much more to gain

by maintaining a good relationship with the 100-pound gorilla of the industry, TRU, and make far more sales?

We do not disagree that there was some evidence in the record that would bear TRU's interpretation. But that is not the standard we apply when we review decisions of the Federal Trade Commission. Instead, we apply the substantial evidence test, which we described as follows in another case in which the Commission's decision to stop a hospital merger was at issue:

> Our only function is to determine whether the Commission's analysis of the probable effects of these acquisitions on hospital competition in Chattanooga is so implausible, so feebly supported by the record, that it flunks even the deferential test of substantial evidence....

That is a horizontal agreement ... it has nothing to do with enhancing efficiencies of distribution from the manufacturer's point of view. The typical story of a legitimate vertical transaction would have the manufacturer going to TRU and asking it to be the exclusive carrier of the manufacturer's goods; in exchange for that exclusivity, the manufacturer would hope to receive more effective promotion of its goods, and TRU would have a large enough profit margin to do the job well. But not all manufacturers think that exclusive dealing arrangements will maximize their profits. Some think, and are entitled to think, that using the greatest number of retailers possible is a better strategy. These manufacturers were in effect being asked by TRU to reduce their output (especially of the popular toys), and as is classically true in such cartels, they were willing to do so only if TRU could protect them against cheaters. *Northwest Stationers* also demonstrates why the facts the Commission found support its conclusion that the essence of the agreement network TRU supervised was horizontal. There the Court described the cases that had condemned boycotts as *"per se"* illegal as those involving "joint efforts by a firm or firms to disadvantage competitors by either directly denying or persuading or coercing suppliers or customers to deny relationships the competitors need in the competitive struggle."... The boycotters had to have some market power, though the Court did not suggest that the level had to be as high as it would require in a case under Sherman Act § 2. Here, TRU was trying to disadvantage the warehouse clubs, its competitors, by coercing suppliers to deny the clubs the products they needed. It accomplished this goal by inducing the suppliers to collude, rather than to compete independently for shelf space in the different toy retail stores.... TRU's efforts to deflate the Commission's finding of market power are pertinent only if we had agreed with its argument that the Commission's finding of a horizontal agreement was without support. Horizontal agreements among competitors, including group boycotts, remain illegal per se in the sense the Court used the term in *Northwest Stationers*. We have found that this case satisfies the criteria the Court used in *Northwest Stationers* for condemnation without an extensive inquiry into market power and economic pros and cons: (1) the boycotting firm has cut off access to a supply, facility or market necessary for the boycotted firm (i.e. the clubs) to compete; (2) the boycotting firm possesses a "dominant" position in the market (where "dominant" is an undefined term, but plainly chosen to stand for something different from antitrust's term of art "monopoly"); and (3) the boycott, as we explain further below, cannot be justified by plausible arguments that it was designed to enhance overall efficiency. . . . We address the market power point here, therefore, only in the alternative. TRU seems to think that anticompetitive effects in a market cannot be shown unless the plaintiff, or here the Commission, first proves that it has a large market share. This, however, has things backwards. As we have explained elsewhere, the share a firm has in a properly defined relevant market is only a way of estimating market power, which is the ultimate consideration. . . . The Supreme Court has made it clear that there are two ways of proving market power. One is through direct evidence of anticompetitive effects. . . . The other, more conventional way, is by proving relevant product and geographic markets and by showing that the defendant's share exceeds whatever threshold is important for the practice in the case. . . . The Commission found here that, however TRU's market power as a toy retailer was measured, it was clear that its boycott was having an effect in the market. It was remarkably successful in causing the 10 major toy manufacturers to reduce output of toys to the warehouse clubs, and that reduction in output protected TRU from having to lower its prices to meet the clubs' price levels. Price competition from conventional discounters like Wal-Mart and K-Mart, in contrast, imposed no such constraint on it, or so the Commission found. In addition, the Commission showed that the affected manufacturers accounted for some 40% of the traditional toy market, and that TRU had 20% of the national wholesale market and up to 49% of some local wholesale markets. Taking steps to prevent a price collapse through coordination of action among competitors has been illegal at least since *United States v. Socony-Vacuum Oil Co.* . . . Proof that this is what TRU was doing is sufficient proof of actual anticompetitive effects that no more elaborate market analysis was necessary. . . . We conclude that the Commission's decision is supported by substantial evidence on the record, and that its remedial decree falls within the broad discretion it has been granted under the FTC Act. The decision is hereby Affirmed.

BUSINESS CONSIDERATIONS Why would a major producer of toys, such as Mattel or Hasbro, agree to the type of arrangement proposed in this case by Toys "R" Us? Why would a manufacturer be so concerned about keeping one customer, albeit the major customer, happy at the expense of all of its other customers?

ETHICAL CONSIDERATIONS Is it ethical to use a position of power to garner benefits in a contract? Assuming that it is ethical, at least in some circumstances, when does such conduct "cross the line" and become unethical?

order for one week costs $35,000 in fines; for a month, $150,000 in fines; and so on.

In recent years, the FTC has become particularly concerned about two business practices: deceptive advertising and "bait-and-switch" advertising. In an effort to force truth in advertising, the FTC has been carefully studying the commercials run by corporations and, in many cases in which the advertising was deemed especially misleading, ordering corrective advertising.

Bait-and-switch advertising involves advertising a product at an especially enticing price to get the customer into the store (the "bait") and then talking the customer into buying a more expensive model (the "switch") because the advertised model is sold out or has some alleged defect. An advertiser who refuses to show the advertised item to the customer or who has insufficient quantities on hand to satisfy reasonable customer demand is engaging in an unfair trade practice in violation of § 5 of the FTC Act.

Unfair Trade Practices

Some common law unfair trade practices, such as palming off goods and violating trade secrets, also deserve mention. Palming off involves advertising, designing, or selling goods as if they were the goods of another. The person who is palming off goods is fraudulently taking advantage of the goodwill and brand loyalty of the imitated producer. This practice also frequently involves patent, copyright, or trademark infringements.

Trade secrets are special processes, formulas, and the like that are guarded and treated confidentially by the holder of the trade secret. Employees of a firm that has trade secrets must not betray their loyalty to the firm by revealing the trade secrets to others. To do so is a tort, and the employee can be held liable for any damages suffered by the employer. In addition, the firm or person who receives the information is guilty of appropriating the trade secret, and use of the secret can be stopped by injunction; the recipient of the information will also be liable for damages suffered by the trade secret holder. As we just mentioned, palming off frequently involves the infringement of a patent, a copyright, or a trademark. These three areas, along with a few others, such as service marks and trade names, are protected by federal statutes.

A patent is a federally created and protected monopoly power given to inventors. If a person invents something that is new, useful, and not obvious to a person of ordinary skill in the industry, the inventor is entitled to a patent. In exchange for making the method of production public, the patent grants the inventor an exclusive right to use, make, or sell the product for 20 years. If anyone violates this exclusive right, the patent holder can file an infringement suit. If the court upholds the patent, the infringer will be enjoined from further production and will be liable for damages to the holder of the patent.

A copyright, protected by the Copyright Office of the Library of Congress, is the protection given to writers, artists, and composers. The creator of a book, song, work of art, or similar item has the exclusive right to the profits from the creation for the life of the creator plus 50 years. Any infringement can result in an infringement action in federal court, with injunctive relief and damages being awarded to the holder of the copyright.

A trademark is a mark or symbol used to identify a particular brand name or product. Copying the trademark of a competitor or using a symbol deceptively similar to that of a competitor is a violation of the Lanham Act of 1946, and the violator is subject to an injunction and the imposition of damages.

Exemptions

Some conduct appears to violate various antitrust laws, and yet the actor is never challenged for the conduct. Many people are confused by this lack of action, questioning why that party is allowed to do something when others are not allowed to do the same thing. The reason is probably that the particular party belongs to a group specifically exempted from antitrust coverage.

Labor unions are exempt from the provisions of the Sherman Act by the Norris-LaGuardia Act, passed in 1932. They are also exempt from the Clayton Act by § 6 of the Clayton Act. The exemption applies only to "labor disputes" and normal union activities.

Farm cooperatives are also exempt from antitrust coverage so long as they are engaged in the sale of farm produce. (A number of other exemptions exist, but they have little impact on business law.)

NRW CASE 37.3   Management/Marketing

WHAT IS AN "UNFAIR TRADE PRACTICE?"

World-Mart, one of NRW's largest customers, recently placed an order for a large number of StuffTrakRs. The order was so much larger than normal that Helen called the purchasing manager to verify the number of units being ordered. The purchasing manager told Helen that World-Mart plans to launch a "you can't lose" advertising campaign. The idea is that customers will be told that *if* they buy the product from World-Mart, and *if* they also buy a StuffTrakR, they "can't lose" the product. The company's marketing department thinks this is a wonderful ad campaign that will benefit both World-Mart and NRW. However, Helen is afraid that this might be viewed as an unfair trade practice, possibly even a variation of "bait and switch" advertising. Before she agrees to fill the order, she would like your opinion as to whether there is anything wrong with the campaign, and whether any problems might reflect badly on NRW. What advice will you give her?

BUSINESS CONSIDERATIONS Is a manufacturer responsible for the conduct of its customers when that conduct involves potential violations of antitrust law? What responsibility should a manufacturer have for the conduct of its customers after the sale is completed?

ETHICAL CONSIDERATIONS Is it ethical for a manufacturer to deal with a customer if the manufacturer believes that customer is violating the law or public policy, and using the products of the manufacturer in this illegal conduct? Does the manufacturer have an ethical duty to report the suspected improper conduct to a government agency?

INTERNATIONAL CONSIDERATIONS Suppose a U.S. firm has a customer in another country, and the firm knows that this customer is using the firm's products in a manner that violates the competition laws of the foreign country. Does the U.S. firm have any legal liability in the other country for the misuse of its product? Does it have an obligation not to sell the product to the other firm, knowing that the product will be used in an illegal manner in the other country?

Summary

Since 1890, the federal government has regulated business in an attempt to ensure competition in the marketplace. This legislative effort is referred to as antitrust law. The cornerstone of antitrust law is the Sherman Act, which prohibits joint conduct that unreasonably restricts competition, and attempts to monopolize any area of trade or commerce. Some conduct is considered so lacking in social value that it constitutes a per se violation. Other questionable conduct is measured under the "rule of reason." Recently a third test, the "quick look" analysis has been developed. This allows a defendant firm to rebut the presumption of harm to competition with some of the traditional per se violations. If the rebuttal is found persuasive by the court, the case is decided under the rule of reason. In any case, if a violation is found, the injured parties are entitled to recover treble damages from the violators. The Sherman Act has also been amended by the Foreign Trade Antitrust Improvement Act, which attempts to restrict Sherman Act enforcement to conduct that affects domestic trade. The FTAIA exempts export trade from coverage of the Sherman Act unless the conduct has a direct and substantial impact on the domestic markets involved.

While the Sherman Act was effective in attacking conduct that reduced or eliminated competition in a number of industries, it did not suffice in *preventing* violations. The Sherman Act is remedial in nature, applying only to a situation *after* harm—often irreparable—has occurred. As a result, Congress enacted some preventative legislation, laws designed to *prevent* economic or competitive harm before it causes irreparable injury. One of these statutes is the Clayton Act, which prohibits price discrimination, exclusive-dealing contracts and tying arrangements, some types of mergers, and interlocking directorates. The price discrimination provisions were expanded and strengthened by the enactment of the Robinson-Patman Act, and the antimerger provisions were expanded and strengthened by the enactment of the Celler-Kefauver Act. The purpose of the Clayton Act is to stop anticompetitive conduct "in its incipiency." In order to do this, the government can attack conduct within the regulated areas if the effect of such conduct may be to substantially lessen competition in any line of trade or commerce. Notice that the government does not have to prove that competition will be harmed; it merely must show that competition is likely to be harmed. This provides a powerful tool to the government in its antitrust campaigns.

As a means of protecting competition, Congress passed the Federal Trade Commission Act. This act has two major aspects: It created the Federal Trade Commission to act as a watchdog in the antitrust area, and it prohibits unfair and deceptive trade practices. There are numerous other unfair trade practice areas as well, but most of these are regulated under state law.

Discussion Questions

1. Section 1 of the Sherman Act is intended to protect competition by prohibiting restraints on trade. In order to apply this section, the court frequently uses the so-called rule of reason. What is the rule of reason, and how does it affect § 1 of the Sherman Act?

2. The courts have decided that a number of actions are likely to be so anticompetitive that the conduct cannot be defended under the rule of reason analysis. These actions have been deemed per se violations of § 1 of the Sherman Act. What are the traditional per se violations? What public policy or economic theory considerations justify treating these actions as violations per se?

3. Recently the Supreme Court has recognized an exception to the per se violation standards. This exception involves a "quick look" analysis in which the defendant firm or firms can rebut the presumption that the challenged conduct is a violation of § 1 per se. Does this quick look analysis reflect a better public policy approach to enforcing the Sherman Act than the strict per se interpretation it is supplanting, at least in some areas of antitrust analysis?

4. What is "conscious parallelism," and how does it relate to § 1 of the Sherman Act? What is "price leadership," and how does it relate to § 1 of the Sherman Act? How can a person distinguish conscious parallelism from price leadership?

5. Can a firm totally dominate an industry and not be guilty of monopolizing in violation of § 2 of the Sherman Act? Can a firm be found guilty of monopolizing an industry if it controls only three-quarters of the relevant market?

6. Section 2 of the Clayton Act prohibits price discrimination; however, it has been found to be less effective than originally expected. As a result, the Robinson-Patman Act was passed to supplement the provisions of § 2 of the Clayton Act. What are the major prohibitions that the Robinson-Patman Act added to § 2 of the Clayton Act?

7. What is the major difference in philosophy between the coverage of the Sherman Act and the coverage of the Clayton Act and the Federal Trade Commission Act? Which philosophy is more effective in protecting competition?

8. What is "bait-and-switch" advertising or selling, and why is such conduct treated as an unfair trade practice under the

provisions of the Federal Trade Commission Act? What must a firm show to avoid prosecution if it is accused of bait-and-switch advertising?

9. Samantha is a major shirt manufacturer. She sells shirts at one price but gives a quantity discount on orders of 5,000 shirts or more. Only two of Samantha's customers, out of 600 total customers, can take advantage of this quantity discount.

Is Samantha in violation of any antitrust laws? Explain your reasoning.

10. Archaic Airlines advertises that it "gets you there ON TIME more often than any other airline." In fact, Archaic has a very bad record as to arriving on time, with over half of its flights arriving more than 30 minutes late. What might the FTC do to Archaic in regard to this advertising campaign?

Case Problems and Writing Assignments

1. The Detroit Auto Dealers Association (DADA) is a trade association in Detroit to which most of the automobile dealers in the Detroit area belong. In 1960 DADA voted to close dealer showrooms on several weekday evenings. In 1973, DADA voted to close dealer showrooms on Saturdays. As a result of these two votes, automobile dealer showrooms in Detroit were virtually all closed at the same times, effectively precluding shopping for new cars during those hours. The Federal Trade Commission viewed this conduct as a restraint of trade, and initiated an administrative action against DADA and its members, alleging a violation of the Sherman Act. According to the FTC, the members of DADA had conspired or combined to set uniform hours for having the showrooms open in restraint of trade. How should this case be resolved? [See *Detroit Auto Dealers Association, Inc. v. FTC*, 95 F.2d 457 (6th Cir. 1992).]

2. Discon, Inc. sold "removal services"—the removal of obsolete telephone equipment—through Materiel Enterprises Company, a subsidiary of NYNEX Corporation, for the use of New York Telephone Company, another subsidiary of NYNEX. Materiel Enterprises began to purchase "removal services" from AT&T Technologies rather than Discon, and Discon filed suit, alleging that the arrangement between AT&T, Materiel Enterprises, and NYNEX violated the Sherman Act. According to Discon, Materiel Enterprises paid AT&T more than Discon had charged for the same services. Materiel Enterprises then passed these higher costs on to New York Telephone, which, in turn, passed the higher costs on to consumers. (This was permitted by the New York regulatory agency, which characterized the costs as approved service charges.) Discon also alleged that Materiel Enterprises received a year-end "rebate" from AT&T Technologies and then shared this "rebate" with NYNEX. According to its complaint, Discon alleged that this conduct amounted to a prohibited group boycott which had, in effect, driven Discon out of business. Does this conduct amount to a prohibited group boycott? Would the argument put forward by Discon be stronger if the firms were not interrelated? [See *NYNEX Corp. et al. v. Discon, Inc.*, 119 S. Ct. 493, 1998 U.S. LEXIS 8080 (1998).]

3. Warner-Lambert is the producer of Listerine mouthwash. Listerine has been produced, without a change in the formula, since 1879. From its inception in 1879 to 1972, Listerine was represented in advertising as a beneficial treatment for colds, cold symptoms, and sore throats. In 1972, the Federal Trade Commission issued a cease-and-desist order prohibiting such

advertising claims in the future. In addition, the FTC ordered Warner-Lambert to run corrective advertising to remove any lasting impressions implanted with the public that Listerine was an effective cold and sore throat medicine. Warner-Lambert agreed to stop running the challenged ads but objected to running the corrective ads. Can the FTC require a company to run corrective advertising to remedy the alleged harm done by prior misleading or deceptive advertising? Is it ethical for a business to make claims in its advertising without knowing that it can substantiate any claims the ads make? [See *Warner-Lambert Co. v. FTC*, 562 F.2d 749 (D.C. Cir. 1977).]

4. The National Collegiate Athletic Associate, an association of major colleges, voted to restrict the number of television appearances permitted by the football teams of member schools. The NCAA also reached an agreement with the broadcast networks that guaranteed each member school a minimum price for broadcast rights to the games of each school televised by the networks. The Board of Regents of the University of Oklahoma challenged this restriction on the number of games any school was permitted to have televised, alleging that this was an illegal restriction in violation of the Sherman Act. The NCAA defended its action, alleging that such a horizontal restriction was necessary in order to guarantee that the product—televised college football games—was to remain available. How should the court resolve this case? Should these allegations be deemed per se violations, if proven, or should they be subjected to a quick look analysis? [See *National Collegiate Athletic Association v. Board of Regents of the University of Oklahoma*, 468 U.S. 85 (1984).]

5. BUSINESS APPLICATION CASE Barkat U. Khan and his corporation entered into an agreement with State Oil Company to lease and operate a gas station and convenience store owned by State Oil. The agreement provided that Khan would obtain the station's gasoline supply from State Oil at a price equal to a suggested retail price set by State Oil, less a margin of 3.25 cents per gallon. Under the agreement, Khan could charge any amount for gasoline sold to the station's customers, but if the price charged was higher than State Oil's suggested retail price, the excess was to be rebated to State Oil. Khan could sell gasoline for less than State Oil's suggested retail price, but any such decrease would reduce their 3.25 cents-per-gallon margin. About a year after Khan began operating the gas station, they fell behind in lease payments. State Oil then gave notice of its intent to terminate the agreement and commenced a state

court proceeding to evict Khan. At State Oil's request, the state court appointed a receiver to operate the gas station. The receiver operated the station for several months without being subject to the price restraints in Khan's agreement with State Oil. According to Khan, the receiver obtained an overall profit margin in excess of 3.25 cents per gallon by lowering the price of regular-grade gasoline and raising the price of premium grades. Khan sued State Oil alleging in part that State Oil had engaged in price-fixing in violation of § 1 of the Sherman Act by preventing Khan from raising or lowering retail gas prices. According to the complaint, but for the agreement with State Oil, Khan could have charged different prices based on the grades of gasoline, in the same way that the receiver had, thereby achieving increased sales and profits. State Oil responded that the agreement did not actually prevent Khan from setting gasoline prices, and that, in substance, Khan did not allege a violation of antitrust laws by their claim that State Oil's suggested retail price was not optimal. The district court found that the allegations in the complaint did not state a per se violation of the Sherman Act because they did not establish the sort of "manifestly anticompetitive implications or pernicious effect on competition" that would justify per se prohibition of State Oil's conduct, and that Khan had failed to demonstrate antitrust injury or harm to competition. The district court held that Khan had not shown that a difference in gasoline pricing would have increased the station's sales; nor had they shown that State Oil had market power or that its pricing provisions affected competition in a relevant market. Khan appealed this decision. Did State Oil's pricing scheme, which established a maximum price, constitute a per se violation of the Sherman Act? [See *State Oil Company v. Khan*, 522 U.S. 3, 118 S. Ct. 275, 1977 U.S. LEXIS 6705 (1997).]

6. **ETHICAL APPLICATION CASE** The California Dental Association (CDA) is a voluntary nonprofit association of local dental societies to which some 19,000 dentists belong, including about three-quarters of those practicing in the state. The CDA lobbies and litigates in its members' interests, and conducts marketing and public relations campaigns for their benefit. The dentists who belong to the CDA through these associations agree to abide by a Code of Ethics including the following § 10:

Although any dentist may advertise, no dentist shall advertise or solicit patients in any form of communication in a manner that is false or misleading in any material respect. In order to properly serve the public, dentists should represent themselves in a manner that contributes to the esteem of the public. Dentists should not misrepresent their training and competence in any way that would be false or misleading in any material respect. . . .

The CDA has issued a number of advisory opinions interpreting this section, and through separate advertising guidelines intended to help members comply with the Code and with state law the CDA has advised its dentists of disclosures they must make under state law when engaging in discount advertising. Responsibility for enforcing the Code rests in the first instance with the local dental societies, to which appli-

cants for CDA membership must submit copies of their own advertisements and those of their employers or referral services to assure compliance with the Code. The local societies also actively seek information about potential Code violations by applicants or CDA members. Applicants who refuse to withdraw or revise objectionable advertisements may be denied membership; and members who, after a hearing, remain similarly recalcitrant are subject to censure, suspension, or expulsion from the CDA.

The Federal Trade Commission brought a complaint against the CDA, alleging that it applied its guidelines so as to restrict truthful, nondeceptive advertising, and so violated § 5 of the FTC Act. The complaint alleged that the CDA had unreasonably restricted two types of advertising: price advertising, particularly discounted fees, and advertising relating to the quality of dental services. An administrative law judge (ALJ) held the Commission to have jurisdiction over the CDA. The ALJ also found that the CDA had unreasonably prevented members and potential members from using truthful, nondeceptive advertising, to the detriment of both dentists and consumers of dental services, in violation of § 5 of the FTC Act. The FTC treated the CDA's restrictions on discount advertising as illegal per se, but also stated that the price advertising (as well as the nonprice) restrictions were violations of the Sherman and FTC Acts under an abbreviated rule-of-reason analysis.

Does the jurisdiction of the FTC extend to the California Dental Association (CDA), a nonprofit professional association? Is it ethical for the FTC to decide that the conduct in question is a per se violation, or should a more detailed examination be undertaken? Does a "quick look" analysis suffice to justify finding that certain advertising restrictions adopted by the CDA violated the antitrust laws? [See *California Dental Association v. Federal Trade Commission*, 119 S. Ct. 1604; 1999 U.S. LEXIS 3606; 143 L. Ed. 2d 935 (1999).]

7. **CRITICAL THINKING CASE** An aircraft landing system is composed of three component parts: the landing gear, the wheels and brakes (sold together as a package), and the brake control system. A few large firms currently dominate the industry. AlliedSignal manufactures wheels and brakes. B.F. Goodrich manufactures landing gear and wheels and brakes. Coltec manufactures landing gear through its subsidiary Menasco Aerospace, Ltd. The only other major player in this industry is a French company that manufactures landing gear under the name Messier-Dowty, and wheels and brakes under the name Messier-Bugatti. AlliedSignal and Coltec currently operate under a Strategic Alliance Agreement ("SAA") that provides for cooperation between AlliedSignal and Coltec in the preparation of joint bids on landing systems. Their principal competitor in these bids is B.F. Goodrich, which generally pairs its wheels and brakes with its own landing gear.

The proposed merger between B.F. Goodrich and Coltec would bring Coltec's aircraft landing gear division under the control of B.F. Goodrich and result in a single large domestic manufacturer of aircraft landing gear. If the merger were to proceed, B.F. Goodrich–Coltec would control approximately

64 percent of the worldwide market for landing gear for wide-body jets, 44 percent of the worldwide market for landing gear for narrow-body jets, and 59 percent of the worldwide market for landing gear for U.S. military jets. AlliedSignal alleges several harms resulting from the proposed merger. First, in preparing joint bids and the integrated landing systems that result, AlliedSignal and Coltec have shared confidential proprietary information. AlliedSignal is concerned that B.F. Goodrich would have access to this information once Coltec is under B.F. Goodrich's control. In its capacity as a landing gear purchaser, AlliedSignal alleges that B.F. Goodrich could use its market power to charge it uncompetitive prices for landing gear. Last, AlliedSignal fears that B.F. Goodrich could leverage its dominant postmerger position in domestic landing gear production to favor B.F. Goodrich's own wheels and brakes over those of AlliedSignal in the formation of integrated landing systems. Neither the Federal Trade Commission nor the Department of Defense (which reviewed the merger because of the parties' status as defense contractors) has objected to the merger. AlliedSignal claims antitrust injury in part from an increase in the price of landing gear it purchases as a landing systems integrator. The SAA, though it does provide for shared information and cooperation, does not regulate the price Coltec may charge for its landing gear. Therefore, B.F. Goodrich–Coltec could fully comply with the SAA and still cause AlliedSignal antitrust injury by charging uncompetitive prices. AlliedSignal's antitrust claims do not arise under the SAA and hence are not subject to arbitration.

To show some likelihood of success on the merits of its § 7 claim, AlliedSignal had to demonstrate (1) that the effect of the merger had some likelihood of substantially lessening competition or tending to create a monopoly and (2) that AlliedSignal had some likelihood of being within the class of plaintiffs with standing to assert the likely antitrust injuries. The district court found that AlliedSignal had made the requisite showing of likely anticompetitive effects and found two possible bases for AlliedSignal's antitrust standing.

Did the proposed merger between B.F. Goodrich, Coltec Industries, and Menasco Aerospace, Ltd. violate § 7 of the Clayton Act? Did the district court abuse its discretion in rendering its opinion? [See *AlliedSignal, Inc. v. B.F. Goodrich Co.*, 1999 U.S. App. LEXIS 13993 (7th Cir. 1999).]

8. **YOU BE THE JUDGE** Sun Microsystems, Inc. has filed suit against Microsoft Corp., alleging numerous claims for illegal tying, monopolization, and exclusive dealing. Sun's suit alleges that Microsoft's actions undermined the ability of Sun's Java technology to offer an alternative to the Windows operating system. Sun bases its suit, at least in part, on the finding by the U.S. Court of Appeals for the District of Columbia Circuit that Microsoft engaged in a series of illegal acts to choke off the distribution channels for the Navigator browser and Java platform.

The complaint alleges that Microsoft violated the Sherman Act, §§ 1 and 2, by:

- illegally maintaining a monopoly in the Intel-compatible PC operating system market;

- illegally monopolizing the Web browser market;

- unlawfully tying the Internet Explorer browser to the Windows operating system;

- attempting to monopolize the workgroup server operating system market (workgroup servers connect to and interoperate with PCs to perform a variety of functions, including file management, printing, and communications);

- illegally tying the Windows workgroup server operating system to the PC operating system;

- unlawfully tying its IIS Web server to the workgroup operating system (a Web server sends Web pages to client computers over the Internet or other computer network);

- unlawfully tying its .NET "middleware" platform to its PC and workgroup server operating systems;

- engaging in exclusive dealing and other exclusionary agreements with Internet service providers, computer manufacturers and other companies; and

- illegally monopolizing the market for office productivity suites.

The complaint seeks injunctive relief, compensatory damages, treble damages under the Sherman Act, costs, and attorney's fees.

This case has been brought in *your* court. What must Sun show in order to establish that Microsoft is guilty of monopolizing in violation of § 2 of the Sherman Act? How will *you* decide this case? [See "Sun Microsystems Files Antitrust Suit Against Microsoft," *E-Business Law Bulletin*, Antitrust, 3, no. 8 (May 2002, Andrews Publications, Inc.): 12.

Notes

1. 15 U.S.C. § 1.
2. 221 U.S. 1 (1911).
3. *SCFC ILC, Inc. v. Visa, USA, Inc.*, 36 F.3d 958 (10th Cir. 1994).
4. *United States v. Arnold, Schwinn & Co.*, 388 U.S. 365 (1967).
5. *Albrecht v. Herald Co.*, 390 U.S. 145 (1968).
6. 441 U.S. 1 (1979).
7. 15 U.S.C. § 6a.
8. *Carpet Group Int'l v. Oriental Rug Importers Ass'n*, 227 F.3d 62 (2000).
9. *Den Norske Stats Oljeselskap As v. Heereman VOF*, 241 F.3d 420 (2001).
10. 15 U.S.C. § 6a.
11. 351 U.S. 377 (1956).
12. 221 U.S. 1 (1911).

13. 15 U.S.C. § 15.

14. 15 U.S.C. § 15(a).

15. List compiled from "Executive Legal Summary," a publication of *Business Laws, Inc.* (1997).

16. Ibid.

17. *Caribe BMW, Inc. v. Bayerische Werke Aktiengesellschaft,* 19 F.3d 745 (1st Cir. 1994).

18. *Jefferson Parish Hospital District #2 v. Hyde,* 466 U.S. 2, 104 S. Ct. 1551 (1984).

19. *Datagate, Inc. v. Hewlett-Packard Co.,* 60 F.3d (9th Cir. 1995).

Consumer Protection

AGENDA

NRW NRW plans to sell its products to customers both directly and indirectly. For direct sales, the firm is considering extending credit to some customers. The firm members would like to identify the consumer protection statutes NRW needs to follow if it does extend credit to these customers. Mai, Helen, and Carlos also want to know what information they can expect to receive if they seek a credit report on prospective employees. Because a significant number of NRW's customers will be consumers, all three are concerned about consumer product safety. Should NRW be apprehensive, or should the firm not worry about the federal Consumer Product Safety Commission's possible jurisdiction over NRW's StuffTrakRs?

These and other questions are likely to arise as you study this chapter. Be prepared! You never know when the firm or one of its members will seek your advice.

Consumer Credit: The Need for Regulation

For many years, state laws regulated consumer credit activities. But the lack of uniformity among such laws, coupled with the increasing need to protect consumers from fraudulent practices, erroneous information found in credit reports, discrimination in the extension of credit, and harassing debt-collection practices has led to the enactment of numerous federal laws. Product safety also remains a significant issue for the vast majority of the American public. In this chapter, we consider the most noteworthy of these consumer protection laws.[1]

Consumer credit has become a gargantuan business in the United States and increasingly draws the attention of federal lawmakers and regulators. On a given day, we in the United States purchase 500,000 appliances, 40,000 motor vehicles, and 15,000 homes on credit.[2] The ubiquity of such credit transactions in turn has led to a giant industry involving the sale of credit reports by credit bureaus. To generate the two million such reports that are sold every working day, credit bureaus retain information on 90 percent of the adults in our country—some 170 million people.[3]

The Consumer Credit Protection Act

Title I of the Consumer Credit Protection Act of 1968, more commonly known as the Truth in Lending Act (TILA), represents the landmark modern consumer protection law. After its enactment, other federal legislation followed.

TILA, in essence, is a disclosure statute designed to force creditors to inform consumers, via a standardized form and terminology, of the actual costs of credit. This information enables consumers to make more informed decisions about credit. Indeed, to comply with TILA, creditors, prior to the consummation of a credit transaction, must provide every consumer with a separate disclosure statement that satisfies the dictates of both TILA and the Federal Reserve Board (FRB), which enforces TILA. Failure to comply with TILA's disclosure provisions subjects the creditor to various civil, criminal, and statutory liabilities.

Although primarily a disclosure statute, TILA also regulates transactions in which a consumer uses his or her home as collateral for a loan (that is, for home equity or home improvement loans), with the exception of transactions involving the purchase or initial construction of a home. For situations covered by the statute, TILA allows a three-day cooling-off period, during which the consumer may decide to rescind (cancel) the loan. Congress apparently wanted to allow the consumer the opportunity to reconsider any transaction that may encumber the consumer's title to his or her home. The power of rescission potentially lasts for three years from the consummation of the transaction or the sale of the property, whichever occurs first.[4]

Upon its initial enactment, TILA resulted in a great deal of litigation that benefited consumers, much to the chagrin of the lending industry. Largely in response to lobbying efforts by lenders, Congress in 1980 enacted the Truth in Lending Simplification and Reform Act, which the FRB subsequently labeled the "new" truth in lending act. Designed avowedly to simplify the disclosures mandated by the 1968 act (which, according to the FRB, resulted in consumer confusion owing to the detail required), the 1980 act makes creditor compliance easier. But experts debate whether providing consumers with less information actually furthers the law's overriding purpose of enhancing the consumer's ability to shop meaningfully for credit. Litigation under the new act nonetheless has decreased dramatically. In response to litigation stemming from the part of TILA that deals with home equity loans, Congress in 1995 amended that portion of TILA to give lenders some relief from the numerous class action suits that in the mid-1990s had sought the remedy of rescission for the entire class. Hence, these amendments, among other things, provide retroactive and prospective relief from liability for certain types of creditor finance charges.

Regulation Z promulgated by the FRB summarizes the scope of TILA. Therefore, one always should read the statute in conjunction with this regulation. In general, Regulation Z covers persons who regularly offer or extend credit to consumers who seek to use the credit for personal, family, or household purposes and the transaction is subject to a finance charge or, by written agreement, is payable in four or more installments. In the initial disclosure statement, the creditor in a clear and conspicuous manner must provide the consumer with detailed information in a meaningful sequence concerning finance charges (including interest, time differential charges, service charges, points, loan fees, appraisal fees, and certain insurance premiums), any other charges, the creditor's retention of a security interest, and a statement of billing rights that respectively outlines the consumer's rights and the creditor's responsibilities.

In addition, creditors must furnish the consumer with periodic statements that disclose various items: the previous balance, credits, the amount of the finance charge, the annual percentage rate charged, the closing date of the billing cycle, the new balance, the address to be used for notice of billing errors, and so on. The creditor also must promptly credit consumer payments and refund credit balances. A consumer must notify a creditor in writing of an alleged billing error within 60 days of the creditor's transmitting the bill to the consumer. TILA and Regulation Z tell the consumer exactly how to satisfy these notification procedures. Within 30 days after receiving notification from the consumer, the creditor must acknowledge in writing the disputed bill or item. And no later than 90 days after receipt of the consumer's notice, the creditor either must correct the disputed bill or, alternatively, explain in writing why the creditor believes the account is correct and supply copies of documented evidence of the consumer's indebtedness.

A creditor who complies with these provisions has no further obligations to the consumer, even if the consumer continues to make substantially the same allegations regarding the alleged error. Until the dispute is settled, however, the creditor may not do the following: try to collect the cost of the disputed item; close or restrict the consumer's account during the controversy, although the creditor can apply the disputed amount to the consumer's credit limit; or make or threaten to make an adverse report that the consumer is in arrears or that his or her bill is delinquent because of nonpayment of the disputed amount. Any creditor who fails to comply with these provisions forfeits the amount in dispute, plus any finance charges, provided the amount does not exceed $50.

These requirements cover "open-end" credit transactions, such as those accomplished pursuant to credit cards (Visa, MasterCard, American Express, and so forth) or department store revolving charge accounts. If you check a credit card bill, you will notice that it sets out the information required under Regulation Z.

Regulation Z (as well as TILA) also applies to "closed-end" credit transactions, such as consumer loans from finance companies; credit purchases of cars, major appliances, and furniture; and real estate purchases. Different disclosure rules exist for closed-end transactions.

Other provisions of TILA prohibit the issuance of a credit card except in response to an oral or written request or application and limit the liability of the cardholder to $50 in cases of unauthorized use of the card if the cardholder notifies the creditor of an unauthorized use because of the loss or theft of the card. In some circumstances, a person who knowingly and fraudulently uses or traffics in counterfeit access devices (that is, credit cards, plates, codes, account numbers, or any means of account access) and during a one-year period obtains $1,000 in value as a result of this conduct, is subject to a maximum fine of not more than the greater of $100,000 or twice the value obtained by the offense, or imprisonment of not more than 10 years (or both).

Remedies sought by individuals for creditors' violations of TILA include actual damages and statutory damages of twice the finance charges (but not less than $100 or more than $1,000). Class actions for actual damages as well as statutory damages of the lesser of $500,000 or 1 percent of the creditors' net worth also are possible. Awards of attorney's fees to successful litigants are available under the statute, too. Criminal penalties for each willful and knowing failure to make the proper disclosures required by the act include fines of not more than $5,000 and one year's imprisonment. Several agencies—the FRB and the Federal Trade Commission (FTC), for example—have responsibility for the administrative enforcement of TILA. Defenses to liability include the expiration of the one-year statute of limitations (for disclosure violations), creditor bona fide clerical errors, and the creditor's timely correction of an error. Information about TILA can be found in a number of places. The FDIC has information at http://www.fdic.gov/regulations/laws/rules/6500-200.html. Information about Regulation Z is also available at numerous sites, including http://www.mortgage-mart.com/regz.html. *Pfennig v. Household Credit Services, Inc.* illustrates many of these concepts.

You should be aware that in 2001, the Federal Reserve Board (FRB) issued an interim rule covering electronic disclosures under TILA. However, the FRB suspended the mandatory compliance date for when the rule would go into effect because it wanted to consider adjustments to the rule so as to provide additional flexibility. It is generally assumed that the Board's delay of the mandatory effective date stemmed in part from the rule's possible inconsistencies with the federal Electronic Signatures in Global and National Commerce Act (E-SIGN), which became law in 2000. As discussed in the contracts section and other chapters, E-SIGN recognizes electronic documents and signatures to be equally as valid as paper documents and handwritten signatures. This federal act also permits creditors to make consumer disclosures in electronic form as long as the creditors otherwise meet the requirements of the federal statute. Critical to the fulfillment of E-SIGN is the consumer's affirmative consent to receiving the disclosures electronically. Prior to obtaining consent, creditors must meet certain other conditions, including giving the consumer a clear and conspicuous statement of the right or option to obtain the disclosure in nonelectronic form and the means by which the consumer, after consenting to the electronic disclosures, can obtain a paper copy of them and whether a fee will be imposed for the copy. Moreover, E-SIGN denies the validity or enforceability of any record that is in a form incapable of being retained and accurately reproduced. This part of the federal act also sets out rules regarding the consumer's access to such records.

38.1

PFENNIG v. HOUSEHOLD CREDIT SERVICES, INC.
295 F. 3d 522 (6th Cir. 2002)

FACTS Sharon R. Pfennig held a credit card originally issued by an affiliate of Household Credit Services, Inc. in 1993, but in which MBNA America Bank, N.A. acquired an interest in 1998, when MBNA bought Household's credit card portfolio. The companies originally established Pfennig's credit limit at $2,000 but subsequently allowed her to increase that limit when she attempted to make a purchase that pushed her credit limit over the originally agreed upon credit limit. After extending Pfennig's credit limit, the companies assessed her an over-limit charge of $29.00 a month for every month her balance remained over the original limit. Pfennig subsequently alleged that the company had omitted this charge from the finance charge calculation on her monthly statement and instead had posted it to her account as a new purchase or debit on which the company had calculated additional finance charges. In a class action brought against Household and MBNA, Pfennig (the named plaintiff) claimed that the resultant penalty—which often amounted to an annual percentage rate (APR) of nearly 60 percent on credit extended over the limit—violated TILA. Specifically, Pfennig argued that the defendants should have disclosed that fee as a finance charge.

ISSUE Was the $29.00 over-limit fee that the defendants had charged Pfennig a finance charge that the defendants were required to disclose to Pfennig under TILA?

HOLDING Yes. TILA states that the amount of the finance charge equals the sum of all charges payable by one to whom credit is extended as an incident to the extension of credit. Because the defendants had charged the plaintiff a $29.00 over-limit fee after they had agreed to extend her additional credit, TILA would apply. Hence, they must disclose that fee as a finance charge. Further, to the extent TILA and Regulation Z conflict in this regard, the unambiguous language of TILA would control.

REASONING Excerpts from the opinion of Judge Clay:

Plaintiff [Ms. Pfennig] argues that the plain language of TILA mandates that Defendants include as a finance charge the monthly fee imposed on [Pfennig's] monthly statement for exceeding her credit limit. She admits that Regulation Z, promulgated by the FRB, has excluded from the definition of the term "finance charge" fees imposed for exceeding a credit limit. However, she argues that the regulation conflicts with the plain language of the statute, and in such cases, the Supreme

Court has held that courts must ignore the regulation so as to give effect to the statute. She further contends that TILA is a consumer protection statute and must be constructed liberally so as to prevent the type of action in which the Defendants are now engaged.

Defendants contend that the district court properly dismissed Plaintiff's complaint because Regulation Z excludes over-limit fees from the definition of finance charge. They argue that Regulation Z's exclusion of over-limit fees from the definition of the finance charge is rationally based and not contrary to TILA, and that the Supreme Court and this Court have stressed that courts should defer to the FRB's interpretation of TILA. Finally, Defendants claim that they acted in good faith compliance with Regulation Z when they failed to disclose the over-limit fee as a finance charge, and that pursuant to [TILA], they are therefore immune from civil liability....

The purpose of TILA is "to assure a meaningful disclosure of credit terms so that the consumer will be able to compare . . . the various credit terms available to him and avoid the uninformed use of credit and to protect the consumer against inaccurate and unfair credit billing and credit card practices." . . . Because of TILA's purpose of protecting consumers in credit transactions, . . . the statute must be construed liberally in the consumer's favor....

TILA, however, is not exhaustive. Congress delegated to the FRB the authority "to elaborate and expand the legal framework governing the commerce in credit." . . . The Supreme Court has recognized that TILA is a highly technical act and that deference should be given to the FRB's interpretation of the Act as long as such interpretations are not irrational. Section 1605(a) defines "finance charge" as follows:

> Except as otherwise provided in this section, the amount of the finance charge in connection with any consumer credit transaction shall be determined as the sum of all charges, payable directly or indirectly by the person to whom the credit is extended, and imposed directly or indirectly by the creditor as an incident to the extension of credit....

Similar to TILA, Regulation Z defines "finance charge" as "the cost of consumer credit," including "any charge payable directly or indirectly by the consumer" and imposed by the creditor as a result of the extension of credit. . . . Regulation Z excludes from this definition of finance charge "charges for actual unanticipated late payment, for exceeding a credit limit, or for delinquency, default, or a similar occurrence." . . .

[T]he district court found that it was bound to give deference to the FRB's interpretation of the term finance charge, and dismissed Plaintiff's complaint because of Regulation Z's exclusion of over-limit fees from the definition of finance charge. . . . We disagree with Defendants and the district court for several reasons. First, . . . we have held that TILA, as a remedial statute, must be given a liberal interpretation in favor of consumers in order to protect them in credit transactions. . . . Thus, TILA must be interpreted liberally in Plaintiff's favor in the instant case. Further, despite the language in . . . Regulation Z, we believe the fee imposed in this case falls squarely within the statutory definition of a finance charge. . . . TILA defines finance charge as the sum of "*all charges*" paid by the person to whom credit is extended and assessed by the creditor "as an incident to the extension of credit." . . . Plaintiff alleges that Defendants imposed the $29.00 over-limit fee after she requested and was granted additional credit. Had Defendants not granted Plaintiff's request for additional credit, which resulted in her exceeding her credit limit, they would not have imposed the over-limit fee. Thus, under a plain reading of § 1605(a) and the general rules of statutory interpretation, the $29.00 fee was imposed incident to the extension of credit to Plaintiff, and pursuant to TILA, Defendants were obligated to disclose the fee as a finance charge on her monthly statement. . . .

Defendants could have declined her request. Instead, they granted it, and then charged her a $29.00 fee for doing so. Plaintiff would have breached the terms of her original credit agreement but for Defendants' willingness to renegotiate the agreement. Because Defendants knowingly allowed Plaintiff to exceed her credit limit and charged her a fee incident to this extension of credit, that fee is by definition a finance charge. . . . On its face, Regulation Z expressly states that charges imposed for exceeding credit limits are excluded from the "finance charge." . . . Consequently, even if the statute required Defendants to disclose this fee as a finance charge, unequivocally Regulation Z did not. . . . Thus, pursuant to TILA, Defendants may not be held liable for damages for such omission; however, [on remand,] Plaintiff may proceed with her claim against Defendants for equitable relief. . . .

BUSINESS CONSIDERATIONS Why would a business want to *exclude* a charge such as this from the category of "finance charges"? What benefit would accrue to the business if this were excluded as a finance charge?

ETHICAL CONSIDERATIONS Is it ethical for a credit-granting business to agree to extend additional credit to a customer and then to charge that customer a service charge for so doing, without disclosing the charge prior to the extension of such additional credit? Is it ethical for a customer to request additional credit and then to complain when there is a fee attached to the extension asked for by the customer?

The congressional history of E-SIGN specifically refers to TILA disclosures as consumer protection laws unaffected by E-SIGN's provisions, and E-SIGN grants authority to governmental agencies like the FRB to promulgate regulations that implement E-SIGN. Commentators therefore have assumed that the FRB's suspension of the mandatory compliance date derived in part from its recognition that it may have exceeded its authority. For example, the interim rule requires creditors to send the applicable disclosures to the consumer's e-mail address or to post them to a Web site. Any disclosures posted to a Web site must remain available at that site for not less than 90 days. These burdensome requirements raise significant questions as to their validity under E-SIGN, especially since the required use of e-mail imposes a technology-specific requirement that E-SIGN would prohibit. Furthermore, the FRB has exempted from the coverage of the interim rule certain advertisements, credit and charge card applications, and solicitations. In apparently removing these activities from the disclosure provisions set out by E-SIGN, the

FRB seemingly is refusing to recognize the preemptive authority of federal law. Should other state and federal regulators impose similar restrictions, the end result might be to thwart electronic commerce. Such an outcome clearly would be at odds with E-SIGN's purposes.

Given these policy considerations, the uncertainties that attend the interim rule, and the costs for creditors to reconfigure their computer software to implement electronic credit transactions, many experts anticipate that most creditors will refrain from electronic credit transactions until a final version of the rule is issued. Watch for developments in this area.

The Fair Credit Reporting Act

Banks and other lenders, would-be secured creditors (about whom we learned in Chapters 25 and 26), landlords, insurance companies, department stores, and employers often seek information about consumers. Moreover, as we have noted, credit transactions pervade domestic (and international) life. Virtually everyone in our country has a credit card, and each credit card use becomes part of the credit history of the user. Credit-reporting agencies (or bureaus) in turn summarize this information into credit (or consumer) reports and sell these reports to lenders, landlords, insurers, retailers, and employers. Credit-reporting agencies may be either local or national in scope.

Given the statistics cited earlier, one readily understands the importance of credit bureaus to the U.S. economy. Credit bureaus continually update the information they hold regarding consumers—by some estimates, a total of two billion pieces of information concerning private consumer transactions and two million pieces of public record information (that is, bankruptcies, tax liens, foreclosures, court judgments, and so forth) are reported each month.[5] Although credit-reporting services both facilitate a given consumer's access to various avenues of credit and speed up credit transactions, the centralization of these vast stores of information covering virtually the entire adult population has spawned concerns about the accuracy of the information and the adequacy of the safeguards employed by these agencies to protect the privacy of individual consumers. Indeed, studies have shown that one-half of all credit reports contain erroneous information;[6] and a litany of consumer complaints chronicles the denials of credit based on false information and the difficulties inherent in correcting such records.

Given these abuses, Congress in 1970 passed the Fair Credit Reporting Act (FCRA) as a part of the Consumer Credit Protection Act. Congress enacted the FCRA to require consumer-reporting agencies to adopt reasonable procedures for meeting the needs of commerce for consumer credit, personnel, insurance, and other information in a manner that is fair and equitable to the consumer and ensures the confidentiality, accuracy, relevancy, and proper use of such information. It applies, then, to all persons or entities that collect information concerning a consumer's creditworthiness, credit standing, credit capacity, character, general reputation, personal characteristics, or mode of living when third parties use this information either to deny or to increase the amount charged for credit or insurance used primarily for personal, family, or household purposes.

In addition, the FCRA applies whenever such information is used for the purposes of employment, governmental benefits or licenses, insurance underwriting, or other legitimate business transactions. Credit reports and licenses issued for any other reasons require a court order or the permission of the consumer.

Interestingly, the FCRA does not apply to all such credit reports but only to those compiled by any entity that *regularly* engages in the practice of disseminating or evaluating consumer credit or other information concerning consumers for the purpose of furnishing consumer reports to third parties. Thus, the act covers credit reports generated by credit bureaus, whose reports ordinarily set out only financial information about the consumer in question— bank accounts, charge accounts and other indebtedness, creditworthiness, marital status, occupation, income, and perhaps some nonfinancial information. The act also covers credit-reporting bureaus whose reports focus not so much on credit information of the type compiled by credit bureaus but rather involve more personal information typically gathered through interviews with neighbors, colleagues, and the like. In short, whether the report centers respectively on financial matters or on investigatory matters pursuant to a prospective employment or landlord/tenant relationship, both types of credit reports raise significant privacy issues.

In placing obligations on third-party users of credit information and those credit agencies or bureaus that report information about consumers, the FCRA attempts to protect such consumers from invasion of privacy and breach of confidentiality. It expressly obligates every consumer-reporting agency to maintain reasonable procedures designed to avoid violations of the act. Among other things, this obligation means that such agencies must report only accurate and up-to-date information and report these data only to those persons or entities eligible to receive the information.

Congress in enacting this legislation unfortunately set out no test for ensuring the relevancy of the information. Thus, while agencies must report information that is accurate and up to date, consumers have little recourse against credit bureaus and credit-reporting bureaus that report irrelevant information (for example, political beliefs or lifestyle issues) that arguably encroaches on a given subject's privacy.

Besides setting out limitations on consumer-reporting agencies, the FCRA places on both reporting agencies and users certain obligations regarding the proper disclosure of the information compiled. The limitations on the uses of such information discussed earlier (employment, governmental benefits or licenses, insurance underwriting, or any other legitimate business purpose) fulfill this goal, and the act requires that every consumer-reporting agency undertake reasonable procedures to verify that the users of the information furnished use the report for only these purposes. Reasonable procedures include prospective users' identifying themselves and certifying the purpose for which they are seeking the information. Prospective users

---

NRW CASE 38.1 Management

CREDIT-REPORTING AGENCIES

NRW recently fired one of its employees. Following this firing, a credit-reporting agency has contacted the firm and has asked questions about the former employee. Fearing possible liability for the firm under the Fair Credit Reporting Act if the information reported by the firm turns out to be inaccurate or if the agency misuses the information, Mai believes that NRW should not answer the questions. Helen does not see these reservations as legitimate concerns. Rather, Helen thinks that NRW should provide the information, especially since NRW uses this credit-reporting agency when NRW seeks information concerning prospective employees. Helen and Mai ask your opinion on this matter. What will you advise them?

BUSINESS CONSIDERATIONS Should a business establish a policy for providing information concerning employees—or former employees—to credit-reporting agencies? What factors would affect the formation of such a policy?

ETHICAL CONSIDERATIONS Is it ethical for a former employer to provide information about a former employee to a credit-reporting agency? How can the employer, from an ethical perspective, relate the employment performance of a person to the latter's creditworthiness?

INTERNATIONAL CONSIDERATIONS Many people in the United States have raised concerns about the amount and the nature of personal information that is so readily available through credit-reporting agencies. Is similar information about individual consumers available in other countries? Does the gathering of such information have the same legal implications in other countries?

---

also must certify that they will use the information only for this—and no other—purpose.

Users of consumer reports similarly must satisfy certain statutory obligations. Unless the report is an investigative one concerning employment for which the consumer has not yet specifically applied, users of investigative consumer reports must notify the consumer, in advance of the preparation of the report, that he or she may be the subject of an investigation concerning his or her character, general repu-

tation, personal characteristics, and mode of living. Moreover, whenever a user of a consumer report denies credit, insurance, or employment or charges a higher rate for credit or insurance and bases the denial or increase wholly or in part on the information contained in a credit report, the user must advise the consumer of the adverse action and supply the name and address of the reporting agency that compiled the report. Adverse actions involving only denial of credit or an increased charge for the extension of credit pursuant to information obtained from persons other than a consumer-reporting agency obligate the user, upon request, to disclose to the consumer the nature (but not the source) of the information. In this latter situation, the user also must inform the consumer of his or her statutory right to learn of the information that caused the adverse decision.

Consumers' rights, then, in addition to the FCRA's prohibition on the use of inaccurate and outdated information, include notification of an agency's reliance on adverse information contained in consumer reports. Moreover, by statute the consumer enjoys limited access to any files concerning him or her and the right in certain circumstances to correct erroneous information. The information that the consumer can receive from a consumer credit-reporting agency includes the nature and substance of all information (except medical information) in its files concerning the consumer, the sources of information (except for the sources of information compiled pursuant to investigative reports), and the recipients of any consumer reports that the agency has furnished concerning the consumer for employment purposes within the last two years or for any purpose within the one-year period preceding the request.

Note that under the FCRA the consumer cannot actually see his or her file. Moreover, the information shown to the consumer may differ from what the creditor sees; the consumer's credit score often is omitted. When the consumer directly conveys such questions to the reporting agency, the agency within 30 days of notification by the consumer must verify or delete the disputed information. The reporting agency must, within five days, notify the furnishee of the information that the consumer disputes the information. At that point, the furnisher of the information has a similar duty to verify or correct the information furnished to the reporting agency—and must do so within the reporting agency's 30-day window. Alternatively, the firm can "certify" the information and "reinstate" it in the file if the 30 days have passed and the information has been deleted. If the agency's reinvestigation fails to resolve the dispute to the consumer's satisfaction, the consumer can file a statement that sets forth the nature of the dispute. The agency must clearly note in any subsequent consumer report containing the disputed information that the consumer disputes the information and provide either the consumer's statement or a clear and accurate codification or summary thereof. At the request of the consumer, the agency must send a similar notice to any users that the consumer can identify as having received within the last two years a report concerning employment or having received within the last six months a report for any other purpose. The statute expressly mandates that the agency clearly and conspicuously disclose to the consumer his or her right to make such a request.

The FCRA sets out civil remedies for violations of the act. For willful failure to comply with the act, suits for compensatory or punitive damages are possible; for violations stemming from negligent noncompliance, an injured consumer can recover only compensatory damages. In addition, for either type of violation, the injured party who successfully sues can recover court costs and attorney's fees. The affirmative defense available to the reporting agency is that it reported accurate information and that the information was issued for a permissible purpose. Otherwise, the plaintiff's recovery will hinge on whether the reporting agency followed "reasonable procedures" that were aimed at complying with the act.

Given these standards for determining liability, identity theft cases pose special problems. Identity theft occurs when the thief co-opts the victim's identity and establishes a credit history in the victim's name. Typically, the thief then either depletes the victim's bank accounts or establishes new credit-based accounts in the victim's name. The thief typically continues with this course of conduct until caught or until the newly established accounts are canceled owing to nonpayment. At this point, the victim is in the dubious position of having to prove he or she should not face liability to the bilked creditors. However, establishing that one was not the debtor on the accounts or loans in question can be complex—creditors usually continue their collection efforts despite the victim's protestations. In some cases, the victim never recovers financially from the adverse credit reports. This is certainly not an idle worry: Recent statistics indicate that identity theft amounts to $400 million annually in credit card losses.

To avoid such situations, some firms are employing biometric identifiers—those based on the personal characteristics (e.g., handprints or retinal scans) of the consumer rather than numeric identifiers such as Social Security numbers, PINs, credit card numbers, or passwords. Because the Internet—the primary medium of contracting in such situations—has attracted grifters, there is a heightened need for either regulatory or private solutions (or both). How the law handles such matters will have a significant effect on the willingness of consumers to engage in e-commerce transactions.

The Federal Trade Commission (FTC), about which you learned in Chapter 37, functions as the principal enforcement agency for violations of the FCRA, because the law views violations of the act as unfair or deceptive trade practices. As such, the FTC can order various administrative remedies (such as cease-and-desist orders) against consumer-reporting agencies, users, or other persons not regulated by other federal agencies (such as the Federal Reserve Board) with enforcement authority over credit-reporting agencies' and users' activities. The Fair Credit Reporting Act, including amendments, can be viewed at the FTC's Web site, http://www.ftc.gov/os/statutes/fcra.htm.

In *TRW, Inc. v. Andrews*, 534 U.S. 19 (2001), the Supreme Court ruled that the FCRA's two-year statute of limitations ordinarily begins to run on the date on which the defendant made a wrongful credit request, not when the plaintiff discovered that the credit request had been made. In short, the Court rejected the notion that a general discovery rule, other than the one specified in the statute, applies to a court's determination of the date on which the statute had begun to run. In so deciding, the Court laid to rest a split that recently had divided the various circuit courts of appeals.

Congress's passage of the Gramm-Leach-Bliley Act (GLB), the Financial Modernization Act of 1999, carries serious implications for consumers' rights under the FCRA. Intended to facilitate affiliations among banks, securities firms, and insurance companies so as to consolidate these financial services, the act allows merging firms to combine the nonpublic financial information of their respective customers into new databases that contain personally identifiable information (PII) about the customers. However, GLB provides consumers with new protections against the transfer and use of their nonpublic personal information by such financial institutions. Specifically, GLB requires the major federal regulators of financial services—for example, the Federal Trade Commission (FTC), the Federal Reserve Board, and the Comptroller of the Currency—to establish standards that protect the security and confidentiality of customer records and information and prohibit unauthorized access to or the use of such records or information when such unauthorized access could result in substantial harm or inconvenience to any customer. GLB's privacy regulations are designed to restrict the transfer of nonpublic personal information beyond the affiliated firms. Accordingly, a financial institution in general may not disclose such information unless the institution provides the consumer with notice that the information may be disclosed and gives the consumer the opportunity to direct that such information not be disclosed, along with an explanation of how the customer can exercise the nondisclosure option. The required disclosure can be in writing, in electronic format, or in any other form permitted by the regulations. Customers have the right to "opt out"—that is, to say no—to the sharing or selling of personal information with nonaffiliated third parties. Exceptions to the prohibition on the disclosure of nonpublic information include disclosures made to a consumer reporting agency in accordance with the FCRA or from a consumer report reported by a consumer reporting agency. Financial institutions, at the time of establishing a relationship with a customer and at least annually during the term of the relationship, must provide the customer with a clear and conspicuous disclosure of these policies and practices with regard to (1) disclosures of nonpublic personal information to affiliates and nonaffiliated third parties, including the categories of information that may be disclosed; (2) disclosures of former customers' nonpublic information; and (3) protection of consumers' nonpublic personal information. Enforcement of GLB will be the responsibility of the FTC, state insurance authorities, and the federal agencies responsible for financial institutions. GLB states that nothing in its privacy provisions should be construed to modify, limit, or supersede the operation of the FCRA.

The "opt-out" consent provisions of GLB have been criticized as leaving a financial institution free to market to any third party any information it has about the consumer or the consumer's account except for the actual account numbers and access codes (unless the consumer does opt out).

An interesting intersection with the Equal Credit Opportunity Act, which will be discussed later, has come to light. Specifically, the relevant regulatory bodies have determined that because information related to age bears upon a consumer's credit capacity and is used in decisions concerning credit eligibility, a report of information that implicates age is a consumer report under the FRCA. Under this interpretation, the remaining information is then subject to the GLB, since it fulfills part of the definition of "nonpublic personal information" that includes "personally identifiable personal information."

Yet another thought-provoking interpretation has arisen from the TILA Staff Commentary, specifically the determination that payday loans are extensions of credit subject to TILA. Payday loans are single-payment, short-term small loans advanced in return for personal checks. Also called "deferred deposits," "cash advances," or "check loans," such arrangements typically involve a debtor who writes a personal check for the amount of the loan plus a fee (generally a percentage of the loan). The lender agrees not to deposit the check until the consumer's next payday, or up to 14 days. When the loan is due, the consumer can either redeem the check for cash; allow the check to clear through a bank; or, by paying another fee, extend the loan for another two weeks. If a consumer extends the loan several times, triple-digit interest rates result. The degree of state regulation (if any) over such practices varies greatly.

One troubling aspect of these arrangements is that numerous payday lenders have partnered with banks to evade the application of state usury laws that restrict the effective rates of interest that can be lawfully charged. Because such lenders usually realize high rates of return (25 to 60 percent is standard), both they and state officials (who will receive tax revenues from these operations, estimated as generating $2.4 billion in fees and interest) may resist any and all attempts to crack down on the industry.

Advocates argue that the lenders serve a useful purpose—tiding over people who have short-term cash problems—while critics view the practices as predatory and injurious to consumer welfare. You might want to investigate how your state handles payday loans.

The Equal Credit Opportunity Act

When Congress first passed the Equal Credit Opportunity Act (ECOA) in 1974, it prohibited only discrimination based on sex or marital status whenever creditors extend credit. Congress at that time was responding to evidence showing that creditors more often denied credit to single women than to single men and that married, divorced, and widowed women could not get credit in their own names. Instead, these women had to obtain credit in their husbands' names.

To broaden the protections available to low-income consumers and give them access to credit commensurate with that enjoyed by more affluent consumers, Congress in 1976 amended the statute to also prohibit discrimination based on race, religion, national origin, age (provided the applicant has the capacity to contract), receipt of public assistance benefits, and the good-faith exercise of rights under the Consumer Credit Protection Act (that is, TILA). Although part of TILA, ECOA covers more than consumer credit transactions. In short, ECOA covers any creditor who deals with any applicant in any aspect of a credit transaction.

Federal Reserve Board (FRB) Regulation B (extensively revised in 1985), the implementing regulation for ECOA, broadly defines a credit transaction as involving every aspect of an applicant's dealings with a creditor regarding an application for credit or an existing extension of credit including but not limited to information requirements; investigation procedures; standards of creditworthiness; terms of credit; the furnishing of credit information, revocation, alteration, or termination of credit; and collection procedures. Assignees who regularly participate in the decision of whether or not to extend credit are included as well. ECOA and Regulation B exempt certain transactions, such as those made pursuant to special-purpose credit programs designed to benefit an economically disadvantaged class of persons. A person whose only participation in a credit transaction is the honoring of a credit card is not a creditor, either. Partial exemptions also exist for public utility services credit transactions (that is, public utilities can ask questions about an applicant's marital status) and incidental consumer credit transactions, such as those involving physicians, hospitals, and so on.

Since creditors as a precondition of extending credit generally evaluate applicants' creditworthiness, Regulation B sets out rules that creditors must follow in making such evaluations and forms that creditors can use to ensure that they do not discriminate on any of the prohibited bases while they undertake these evaluations. In addition, ECOA

requires creditors to give notice to applicants of any actions taken by the creditors concerning the applicants' requests for credit. Information about the Equal Credit Opportunity Act as provided by the FTC is available at http://www.ftc.gov/bcp/conline/pubs/credit/ecoa.htm. In *Riethman v. Berry*, the judge addressed many of these principles.

Creditor actions typically take three forms: approval of the application; extension of credit under different terms than those requested; or an adverse action (for example, denial of the application). Regulation B then prescribes a notification regime specifically tailored to the type of action taken. Exhibit 38.1 represents a communication that generally will satisfy these notification requirements. Creditors typically must send such a notification within 30 days of receiving a completed application.

Remedies under ECOA include actual damages and/or punitive damages, to a maximum of $10,000 for individual actions or a maximum of $500,000 (or 1 percent of the creditor's net worth—whichever is greater) for class actions. Equitable relief, attorney's fees, and costs also may be granted. A two-year statute of limitations generally applies. The usual administrative remedies are available as

---

38.2

RIETHMAN v. BERRY
287 F. 3d 274 (3d Cir. 2002)

FACTS Harold C. Riethman had retained Berry & Culp, a law firm, to represent him in his divorce proceedings. He then retained the firm in connection with an ensuing child custody battle with his former wife. The initial fee agreement between Riethman and counsel dated February 20, 1995 (the 1995 agreement) provided for billing on a monthly basis. In 1998, at Riethman's request, the parties modified their 1995 agreement to permit Riethman to make smaller progress payments instead of paying the full amount due each month. Although Vicki Hagel, Riethman's new wife, had not been a party to the 1995 agreement, she signed the 1998 agreement. During the custody trial, a fee dispute between Berry & Culp and Riethman and Hagel culminated in Berry & Culp's withdrawing as counsel. Riethman and Hagin subsequently sued Berry & Culp on the grounds that the firm's fee agreement failed to comply with various requirements of the Equal Credit Opportunity Act (ECOA) and the Truth in Lending Act (TILA).

ISSUE Was the law firm a "creditor" under ECOA and TILA?

HOLDING No. Because the law firm's fee agreements did not allow its clients to defer payment for a mone-

tary debt, property, or services, ECOA and TILA were inapplicable to the parties' business relationship.

REASONING Excerpts from the opinion of Judge Sloviter:

In enacting the ECOA, Congress found that "there is a need to insure that the various financial institutions and other firms engaged in . . . extensions of credit exercise their responsibility to make credit available with fairness, impartiality, and without discrimination on the basis of sex or marital status." . . . The congressional statement of purpose continues: "Economic stabilization would be enhanced and competition among the various financial institutions and other firms engaged in the extension of credit would be strengthened by an absence of discrimination on the basis of sex or marital status, as well as by the informed use of credit which Congress has heretofore sought to promote" . . . The Act makes it unlawful for any creditor to discriminate against any applicant with respect to any aspect of a credit transaction on the basis of race, color, religion, national origin, sex or marital status or age; because all or part of the applicant's income derives from any public assistance program; or because the applicant has in good faith exercised any right under the Consumer Credit Protection Act . . . ECOA defines a "creditor" as "any person who regularly extends, renews, or continues credit" . . . (Regulation B). "Credit," in turn, is defined as "the right granted by a creditor to a debtor to defer payment of debt or to incur debts and defer its payment or to purchase property or services and defer payment therefore" . . . Riethman and Hagel contend that Berry & Culp were creditors because they regularly extended credit by providing legal services without requiring immediate payment . . . [A] random cross-section of Berry & Culp's billing agreements and invoices . . . provided for outstanding charges to be paid in full within thirty days, with an interest charge to be imposed on unpaid balances. Riethman and Hagel concede that "these fee agreements, . . . were almost identical to the [1995 agreement]." Of the ten clients whose bills the District Court considered, Berry & Culp continued to perform legal services for at least half despite the failure of some clients to pay bills as they became due. The District Court rejected the contention that Berry & Culp were creditors because, other than Riethman and Hagel under the 1998 agreement, none of Berry & Culp's defaulting clients had a "right" to defer payment. . . . We agree with the District Court. The hallmark of "credit" under . . . ECOA is the right of one party to make deferred payment. The courts have consistently so held. . . . "Absent a right to defer payment for a monetary debt, property or services, . . . ECOA is inapplicable." Riethman and Hagel appear to contend that Berry & Culp's failure to enforce their right to prompt payment gave their clients a unilateral right to defer payments. This position is inconsistent with ordinary principles of contract interpretation. . . . Even if Berry & Culp failed to strictly enforce their rights against tardy clients, the express terms of their fee agreements plainly manifest their right to prompt and full payments. Contrary to Riethman and Hagel's suggestion, the fact that counsel permitted . . . clients to pay by check or credit card, or provided legal services prior to receiving a retainer, does not alone bring them within . . . ECOA. Riethman and Hagel have not identified any language in the legislative history of . . . ECOA that suggests that Congress was thinking about payment of legal fees when it enacted . . . ECOA. . . . We do not suggest that lawyers are ipso facto exempt from the statute. [However, imposing] a requirement of simultaneous performance would transform into credit transactions "countless transactions in which compensation for services is not instantaneous. . . . Such indiscriminate application of . . . ECOA is not appropriate." . . . Similarly, in addition to attorneys' fees, Riethman and Hagel's interpretation of the ECOA would embrace doctors' fees, dentists' fees, accountants' fees, psychologists' fees and virtually all other professional fees. In view of the statutory purpose underlying the ECOA, it seems implausible that Congress intended to cover not only banks and other such financial institutions but also all professions. The Federal Reserve Board's Regulation B defines "extending credit" and "extension of credit" as . . . "the continuance of existing credit without any special effort to collect at or after maturity" . . . Riethman and Hagel suggest that this regulation demonstrates that Berry & Culp's leniency toward enforcing their contractual rights subjects them to . . . ECOA. But this provision of Regulation B presupposes an already existing credit relationship between the parties. Unless the fee agreements themselves are credit transactions, the failure of Berry & Culp to collect after "maturity" cannot be an extension of credit. Because the fee agreements do not themselves extend credit, failure to enforce them was not the continuance of existing credit. Even assuming [the] 1998 agreement did extend credit, it is clear that [the] 1995 agreement did not. Nor did the agreements of the other clients reviewed by the District Court. Therefore, the defendant law firm cannot be equated with one "who regularly extends, renews, or continues credit." . . . The other statute on which Riethman and Hagel base their claim, the Truth in Lending Act (TILA), is designed to strengthen the national economy by enhancing the informed use of credit. It requires creditors to accurately and meaningfully disclose all credit terms. . . . Under the TILA, a "creditor" is, in relevant part, a person or entity which regularly extends consumer credit. . . . Similarly to the ECOA, the TILA defines "credit" as "the right granted by a creditor to a debtor to defer payment of debt or to incur debt and defer its payment." . . . In addition, the Federal Reserve's TILA regulation . . . specifically defines the TILA statutory term "regularly" as extending credit within the last twelve months "more than 25 times." Riethman and Hagel concede that the "ECOA applies to a broader category of cases than [the TILA]." . . . Berry & Culp did not grant clients the right to defer payment. It follows that the TILA is inapplicable.

BUSINESS CONSIDERATIONS Could Barry & Culp have drafted its agreements in such a fashion as to foreclose the kinds of arguments Riethman and Hagel made here? Explain fully.

ETHICAL CONSIDERATIONS At Riethman's request, the 1998 agreement permitted him to make smaller progress payments instead of paying the full amount due each month, an outcome that presumably benefited him financially. Given these facts, did he and his new wife behave unethically in instituting this litigation against Berry & Culp? Why or why not?

EXTENDING CREDIT

NRW has been discussing credit sales to consumers. While Carlos and Mai realize that direct sales to consumers—often on credit terms established by the firm—probably will increase sales substantially, they also agree that some of these customers inevitably will default. To minimize the risk of default, Helen proposes that the firm should extend credit only to consumers who have a minimum family income and a minimum credit bureau rating. All other applicants would be rejected. While the firm's members agree that this policy sounds like a good idea, they wonder whether this proposed strategy will violate the law. If they ask for your advice, what will you tell them?

BUSINESS CONSIDERATIONS The extension of consumer credit is likely to increase the sales of a business, but it also will increase losses because of bad debts and defaults. When NRW decides whether to provide credit to its consumer customers, what factors should the firm consider? Should a firm that decides to extend credit to consumer debtors revisit the decision periodically and reevaluate it?

ETHICAL CONSIDERATIONS Is it ethical for a firm to decide not to extend credit to its consumer debtors, thereby possibly precluding lower-income customers from acquiring the product? Is it more ethical to provide such consumer credit, even though the firm may forgo some of its profits because of defaults?

INTERNATIONAL CONSIDERATIONS Suppose that NRW has the opportunity to sell a significant number of units in other countries, but only if it is willing to make the sales on credit. What problems might the firm encounter by extending credit in an international transaction? Is it more likely that the debtors will be merchants rather than consumers in this situation? What effect, if any, will that possibility have on your answer?

well. The enforcement agencies in addition can ask the U.S. attorney general to institute civil actions against any creditor who has engaged in a pattern or practice of denying or discouraging credit applicants in violation of the act.

In 1999, the FRB published a proposed rule permitting creditors to use electronic disclosures in some circumstances to fulfill the requirements of ECOA. The FRB later put the rule on hold owing to the enactment of E-SIGN. In 2002, the FRB published an interim final rule that amended Regulation B to provide for electronic disclosures. Under this interim final rule, a creditor can make ECOA disclosures electronically as long as the creditor complies with the consumer consent provisions of E-SIGN. In addition, the interim final rule imposes a clear and conspicuous standard on electronic disclosures (but not on conventional paper notifications). A creditor can communicate electronic disclosures either through e-mail or by posting the disclosures on its Web site. A creditor who chooses to post the disclosures must in addition send an "alert notice" that informs consumers of the availability of the information and can do so either by e-mail or postal mail. If a creditor receives actual notice of a nondelivery, it must attempt a redelivery based on the consumer's address as noted in its file. There is no requirement of verification that the consumer actually received the disclosures. The Staff Commentary notes that it considers an electronic document delivered once the creditor either sends an e-mail or sends the alert notice and posts the information on the Web site. In the case of a redelivery, the time of delivery is the time the creditor initially tried to send the documents.

Critics of the interim final rule submit that the Web site posting alternative, especially if the creditor chooses to inform the consumer by postal mail, seems to erode the requirement that a creditor provide reasons for any adverse actions taken. Using criticisms similar to those leveled at TILA's interim rule, which requires retention of Web site notices for 90 days, detractors of the ECOA final interim rule point out that it may contradict E-SIGN's record retention rules. The final interim rule has other provisions that detractors view as violative of E-SIGN's consumer consent requirements, too.

The Fair Debt Collection Practices Act

Congress in 1977 passed the Fair Debt Collection Practices Act (FDCPA) as Title V of the Consumer Credit Protection Act (TILA). This part of TILA regulates the activities of those who collect bills owed to others (including attorneys who regularly engage in consumer debt-collection activity, even when the activity consists of litigation).[7] The act specifically exempts from its coverage the activities of secured parties, process servers, and federal or state

EXHIBIT 38.1 Form C-2 Sample Notice of Action Taken

Dear Applicant:

Thank you for your recent application. Your request for [a loan/a credit card/an increase in your credit limit] was carefully considered, and we regret that we are unable to approve your application at this time, for the following reason(s):

YOUR INCOME:

_____ is below our minimum requirement.

_____ is insufficient to sustain payments on the amount of credit requested.

_____ could not be verified.

YOUR EMPLOYMENT:

_____ is not of sufficient length to qualify.

_____ could not be verified.

YOUR CREDIT HISTORY:

_____ of making payments on time was not satisfactory.

_____ could not be verified.

YOUR APPLICATION:

_____ lacks a sufficient number of credit references.

_____ lacks acceptable types of credit references.

_____ reveals that current obligations are excessive in relation to income.

OTHER: _____

The consumer reporting agency contacted that provided information that influenced our decision in whole or in part was [name, address, and [toll-free] telephone number of the reporting agency]. The reporting agency is unable to supply specific reasons why we have denied credit to you. You do, however, have a right under the Fair Credit Reporting Act to know the information contained in your credit file. You also have a right to a free copy of your report from the reporting agency, if you request it no later than 60 days after you receive this notice. In addition, if you find that any information contained in the report you receive is inaccurate or incomplete, you have the right to dispute the matter with the reporting agency. Any questions regarding such information should be directed to [consumer reporting agency].

If you have any questions regarding this letter, you should contact us at [creditor's name, address, and telephone number].

NOTICE: The federal Equal Credit Opportunity Act prohibits creditors from discriminating against credit applicants on the basis of race, color, religion, national origin, sex, marital status, age (provided the applicant has the capacity to enter into a binding contract); because all or part of the applicant's income derives from any public assistance program; or because the applicant has in good faith exercised any right under the Consumer Credit Protection Act. The federal agency that administers compliance with this law concerning this creditor is [the name and address as specified by the appropriate agency listed in Appendix A].

SOURCE: 12 Code of Federal Regulations § 202 (App.C) (2002).

employees who are attempting to collect debts pursuant to the performance of their official duties.

Congress intended the law to eliminate abusive, deceptive, and unfair debt-collection practices and thereby to protect consumers. The act thus limits the manner in which a debt collector can communicate with the debtor. For example, the statute expressly prohibits any communications made without the consumer's consent at an unusual or inconvenient time, that is, before 8:00 A.M. and after 9:00 P.M. local time at the debtor's location. The debt collector, moreover, cannot communicate with the debtor at the debtor's place of employment if the debt collector knows or has reason to know that the debtor's employer prohibits the consumer from receiving such communications. In addition, in most circumstances, if the debt collector knows an attorney represents the consumer with respect to the debt, the debt collector can contact only the attorney, not the debtor. A debt collector typically cannot communicate with third parties (for example, the debtor's neighbors, coworkers, or friends) concerning the collection of the debt, either.

Prior to 1996, debt collectors had to disclose in all communications that the purpose of the communication (whether oral or written) involved the collection of a debt and that the debt collector would use any information so received for that purpose. Since 1996, the debt collector need disclose the previously required information only in its initial communication (whether oral or written) with the debtor. Pursuant to this recent amendment, the debt collector, as to all subsequent communications, must disclose only that the communication is from a debt collector.

The statute also permits the cessation of further communication with the debtor if he or she in writing notifies the debt collector that he or she refuses to pay the debt and wishes all communications to stop. At that point, the debt collector can advise the consumer only of the termination of further efforts to collect the debt or of the debt collector's intention to invoke any available remedies.

Similarly, debt collectors must refrain from unfair or unconscionable means of debt collection. For example, the debt collector is prohibited from accepting postdated checks, making collect phone calls to debtors, or adding amounts—interest, fees, or expenses—not expressly allowed by the underlying debt agreement or by state law.

So that the debtor can dispute the debt if he or she has grounds to do so, the act requires the bill collector to send the debtor a written verification of the debt. The debtor then has 30 days in which he or she must dispute the debt in writing; otherwise, the debt collector can assume the validity of the debt.

The FTC has primary enforcement responsibilities under the FDCPA. Civil remedies of actual damages plus additional damages, not to exceed $1,000, that the court can set are possible in individual suits. In class actions, $1,000 per person may be awarded; but the total damages so awarded cannot exceed the lesser of $500,000 or 1 percent of the debt collector's net worth.

Under a separate statute, a criminal penalty of $1,000 or a sentence of one year's imprisonment, or both, may be imposed on anyone who, during the course of debt-collection efforts, uses the words "federal," "national," or "the United States" to convey the false impression that the communication originates from, or in any way represents, the United States or any of its agencies or instrumentalities. Successful litigants may recover costs and attorney's fees as well. The FTC lists the Fair Debt Collection Practices Act and related links at http://www.ftc.gov/os/statutes/

NRW CASE 38.3   Finance/Management

NRW

DEBT COLLECTION

Several of NRW's credit customers have fallen behind in making their credit payments; a few have even defaulted. All efforts by the firm to collect these amounts have failed, and Mai and Helen think that the firm should hire a collection agency to recover the firm's money. Carlos, preferring a low-key approach to collection, wants the firm to write to these customers and remind them of their obligation to repay the debts. The firm members all agree that they would like to recover the funds, but they remain unsure of the legal implications of various collection efforts. They ask you what they should do. What will you advise them?

BUSINESS CONSIDERATIONS Why would a business be willing to hire a debt-collection agency to recover past due accounts? What factors should a business consider before it takes such a step?

ETHICAL CONSIDERATIONS Is it ethical for a business to turn its debt collections over to an independent third party who was not involved in the extension of credit? Is it ethical for a firm to accept collections that the debt-collection agency may have acquired in an unethical manner?

INTERNATIONAL CONSIDERATIONS How would a business attempt to collect a debt owed by a foreign debtor without resorting to a judicial proceeding? Do the perceived difficulties of collecting from a foreign customer make a firm less likely to extend credit in an international sale of goods?

---

fdcpajump.htm. Consider these principles as you analyze *Veillard v. Mednick.*

The Uniform Consumer Credit Code

Designed to replace state laws governing consumer credit, the Uniform Consumer Credit Code (UCCC) resulted from the drafting efforts of the National Conference of Commissioners on Uniform State Laws and was meant to make consistent the widely varying state laws concerning installment sales and loans, revolving charge accounts, home solicita-

38.3

VEILLARD v. MEDNICK
24 F. Supp. 2d 863 (N.D. Ill. 1998)

FACTS Doctors Service Bureau, Inc. (DSBI) has been a licensed collection agent in Illinois since 1989. Richard Mednick, an attorney licensed in Illinois, is listed in the telephone book, *Sullivan's Law Directory, Index to Law Firms, Martindale-Hubbell Law Directory*, and directory assistance as an attorney. Mednick employs non-attorneys to collect debts. Patrick Veillard is a resident of New York who became indebted to Nations Credit Commercial Corporation through the use of a credit card. Nations sent Veillard's debt to DSBI, which in turn retained Mednick to collect the money. Mednick's office then sent Veillard an unsigned collection letter, dated October 6, 1997, seeking to obtain the money owed to Nations. The letterhead used in the letter was from "RICHARD M. MEDNICK AND ASSOCIATES," but the letter itself did not explicitly mention that Mednick and Associates is a law firm or that Mednick is an attorney. The body of the letter stated:

DEAR PATRICK VEILLARD:

Your seriously past-due account has been placed with us for collection.

Unless you notify this office within 30 days after receiving this notice that you dispute the validity of the debt or any portion thereof, this office will assume this debt is valid. If you notify this office in writing within 30 days from receiving this notice, this office will obtain verification of the debt or obtain a copy of a judgment and mail you a copy of such judgment or verification. If you request this office in writing within 30 days after receiving this notice, this office will provide you with the name and address of the original creditor, if different from the current creditor.

Your best interest will be served by resolving this matter as soon as possible as our client shows this obligation to be due immediately.

Yours truly,

J. Dancer

for Richard M. Mednick

Debt Collector

THIS IS AN ATTEMPT TO COLLECT A DEBT. ANY INFORMATION OBTAINED WILL BE USED FOR THAT PURPOSE.

Veillard claimed that Mednick and DSBI had violated the FDCPA because the letter created the false impression that the communication had originated with Mednick, a lawyer who was not actually involved in the collection of the debt. Although the letter did not expressly state that Mednick is an attorney, Veillard argued that the letter conveyed this impression because it was on letterhead, a convention generally associated with the legal profession. According to Veillard, by using letterhead that suggested the letter was from a law firm, Mednick and DSBI were being deceptive in violation of the act. Veillard also submitted that the letter overshadowed and contradicted the validation notice requirement. Specifically, Veillard contended, the statement "Your best interest will be served by resolving this matter as soon as possible as our client shows this obligation to be due immediately" is likely to induce the debtor to pay within the validation period so as to avoid legal action.

ISSUE Did the dunning letter at issue here violate the FDCPA?

HOLDING Yes. A dunning letter written on a law firm's letterhead could have led an unsophisticated consumer to be deceived or misled into thinking an attorney was involved in the matter. Moreover, the statement urging the debtor to pay the debt as soon as possible overshadowed the notification that the debtor had 30 days in which to challenge the validity of the debt and thus was another violation of the FDCPA.

REASONING Excerpts from the opinion of District Judge Ruben Castillo:

Congress enacted the FDCPA in 1977 "to eliminate abusive debt collection practices by debt collectors." . . . To this end, the Act sets certain standards for debt collectors' communications with debtors. Among them is a requirement that debt collectors advise debtors of their rights to dispute the debt and demand verification . . . a ban on false and misleading statements in collection letters . . . and a prohibition against collecting a debt through "unfair or unconscionable fees beyond the amount in arrears," . . . Additionally, it is unlawful to "design, compile, and furnish any form knowing that such form would be used to create the false belief in a consumer that a person other than the creditor of such consumer is participating in the collection of or in an attempt to collect a debt such consumer allegedly owes such creditor, when in fact such person is not so participating." . . .

The Seventh Circuit evaluates communications from debt collectors "through the eyes of the unsophisticated consumer." . . . The unsophisticated consumer is a hypothetical consumer whose reasonable perceptions will be used to determine if collection messages are deceptive or misleading. . . . This standard presumes a level of sophistication that "is low, close to the bottom of the sophistication meter," . . . and "protects the consumer who is 'uninformed, naive, or trusting,'" . . . Still, the standard "admits an objective element of reasonableness," which "protects debt collectors from liability for unrealistic or peculiar interpretations of collection letters." . . .

Veillard claims that Mednick and Bureau violated §§ 1692e, 1692e(3), 1692e(5), 1692e(10), and 1692f of the FDCPA, and Bureau violated § 1692j, when they sent a letter out purporting to be from an attorney who was not actually involved in handling the file. Section 1692e states that a debt collector "may not use any false, deceptive, or misleading representation . . . with the collection of any debt." Section 1692e(3) prohibits any "false representation or implication that any individual is an attorney or that any communication is from an attorney." Section 1692e(5) bars debt collectors from threatening "any action that cannot legally be taken or that is not intended to be taken." Collectors violate § 1692e(10) when they use "any false representation or deceptive means to collect . . . any debt." Under § 1692f, a debt collector may not use unfair or unconscionable means to collect or attempt to collect any debt. Finally, § 1692j states that "it is unlawful to design, compile, and furnish any form knowing that such form would be used to create the false belief in a consumer that a person other than the creditor . . . is participating in the collection of . . . the debt." . . .

An attorney sending dunning letters must be directly and personally involved in the debt collection to comply with the strictures of FDCPA . . . the use of an attorney's letterhead and his signature on collection letters could give consumers the false impression that the letters are communications from an attorney . . . and that

> an unsophisticated consumer, getting a letter from an 'attorney,' knows the price of poker has just gone up. And that clearly is the reason why the dunning campaign escalates from the collection agency, which might not strike fear in the heart of the consumer, to the attorney, who is better positioned to get the debtor's knees knocking. . . .

The . . . court held that using the term "attorney" without an attorney actually working on the file was confusing as a matter of law. . . . Although the letter is unsigned, it comes from "J. Dancer for Richard M. Mednick." Dancer is referred to as a debt collector; however, by stating that Dancer wrote the letter on behalf of Mednick, the unsophisticated debtor could logically conclude that Mednick supervised the file. Thus the question is whether an unsophisticated debtor would be misled into believing that Mednick is a lawyer. Mednick and Bureau argue that, because the word "attorney" is not in the letter, the unsophisticated consumer would not be misled or deceived into believing anything other than that the letter came from a collection agency. They contend that only a very sophisticated and extremely suspicious consumer would investigate whether Mednick has a law license. In addition, they argue that because other professionals such as architects, engineers, real estate, and life insurance people use "and associates," an unsophisticated consumer could not reasonably believe the letter came from a law firm.

The defendants' arguments are unpersuasive. In today's world, a person does not need to have a Sullivan's Directory or other legal publication to determine that Richard Mednick and Associates is a law firm. The unsophisticated consumer need only request a telephone number from directory assistance to determine that Mednick and Associates is a law firm. In addition, it would be unusual for a non-lawyer, using the connotation "and Associates," to be involved in the business of collecting debts. The circumstances surrounding the disputed letter could lead an unsophisticated consumer to believe that Richard Mednick and Associates is a law firm prepared to take legal action on the debt. . . .

Accordingly, we hold as a matter of law that Mednick and Bureau violated §§ 1692e, 1692e(3), and 1692(10). We grant Veillard's motion for summary judgment on these issues. In addition, we conclude that Bureau violated § 1692j and grant Veillard's motion for summary judgment on that issue. . . .

As to Veillard's § 1692e(5) claim, we find that, as a matter of law, the letter does not contain any specific or implied threat that legal action will be taken against him. There is nothing in the letter that refers to legal action and the mere inference that legal action could be taken because the letter is on law firm letterhead is [insufficient] for § 1692e(5) purposes. . . . Therefore, we grant defendants' motion for summary judgment on that issue. . . .

To ensure that consumers have a fair chance to dispute and demand verification of their debts, § 1692g requires debt collectors to send debtors a "validation notice". A validation notice must explain that the debtor has 30 days to dispute the validity of all or a portion of the debt. . . . If the debtor disputes the debt, the collector must cease collection efforts until it sends information verifying the debt. . . . If the debtor does not dispute the debt, the collector may assume it is valid. . . . A validation notice that explains the debtor's right to contest a debt nevertheless violates § 1692g if the notice is somehow overshadowed or otherwise contradicted by accompanying or subsequent messages. . . . The court found the letter did just that because it left the debtor without "a clue as to what he was supposed to do before real trouble begins." . . .

Veillard contends that the letter's 30-day notification information conflicts with the sentence "your best interest will be served by resolving this matter as soon as possible as our client shows this obligation to be due immediately," and creates confusion in violation of § 1692g. We see no distinction between "make payment immediately" and "this obligation to be due immediately." Both phrases convey the same message: a payment is due immediately on the debt. The confusion here is that Mednick does not explain what will happen if Veillard disputes the validity of the debt. One sentence could have cleared up the confusion: "If you should dispute this debt, we will discontinue collection efforts immediately until we verify that the debt is accurate." . . . Accordingly, we find the letter in violation of § 1692g. . . .

BUSINESS CONSIDERATIONS Why would rational, profit-maximizing firms conduct themselves as Mednick and DSBI did here? How should firms in this type of situation transact business?

ETHICAL CONSIDERATIONS Was the conduct of the defendants ethical? From an ethical perspective, how should debt-collection firms act?

tion sales, home improvement loans, and truth in lending. Its drafters wished to do for consumer law what the Uniform Commercial Code had done for commercial law.

First promulgated in 1968 and later revised in 1974, the UCCC has failed to gain wide acceptance. To date, only 11 states have enacted it; and many of them have chosen to replace the UCCC's provisions with their own. Still, it represents an additional statutory attempt to benefit consumers.

The Consumer Product Safety Act

The Consumer Product Safety Act of 1972 established the Consumer Product Safety Commission (CPSC). An independent federal regulatory agency, the CPSC consists of five members appointed by the president with the advice and consent of the Senate. The CPSC has authority over a great number of consumer products; but products expressly excluded from the Commission's jurisdiction include tobacco and tobacco products, motor vehicles, pesticides covered under FIFRA (a statute discussed in Chapter 39), firearms and ammunition, food, and cosmetics.

To help protect the public from injuries from consumer products, the Commission can do the following: set and enforce safety standards; ban hazardous products; collect information on consumer-related injuries; administratively order firms to publicly report defects that could create substantial hazards; force firms to take corrective action (repair, replacement, or refund) with regard to substantially hazardous consumer products in commerce; seek court orders for recalls of imminently hazardous products; conduct research on consumer products; and engage in educational outreach programs for consumers, industry, and local government.

Products banned by the CPSC include certain all-terrain vehicles, unstable refuse bins, lawn darts, tris (a chemical flame-retardant once found in children's apparel), products containing asbestos, and paint containing lead. Products subject to CPSC standards include matchbooks, automatic garage door openers, bicycles, cribs, rattles, disposable lighters, toys with small parts, and the like.

Summary

Various federal and state statutes protect consumers' rights. The Consumer Credit Protection Act of 1968, better known as the Truth in Lending Act (TILA), mandates the disclosure (via a standardized form and terminology) of the actual costs of credit so as to enable consumers to make more informed decisions about credit. Failure to comply with the act's disclosure provisions (or with its implementing regulation, Regulation Z) subjects the creditor to various civil, criminal, and statutory liabilities. The Fair Credit Reporting Act of 1970 requires consumer-reporting agencies to adopt reasonable procedures for guaranteeing the accuracy of information disseminated in credit reports. The act also limits the uses that one can make of such information. Consumers enjoy a variety of rights under the statute, including notification of an agency's reliance on adverse information and mechanisms for disputing the accuracy of information contained in files. Civil, criminal, and administrative remedies are available under the act. The Equal Credit Opportunity Act of 1974 (ECOA) prohibits discrimination based on sex, marital status, race, religion, national origin, age (provided the applicant has the capacity to contract), receipt of public assistance benefits, and the good-faith exercise of rights under TILA. Regulation B extensively implements ECOA by, among other things, setting out the rules that creditors must follow when they evaluate the creditworthiness of any applicant and when they provide notification to the consumer of the action taken. The remedies available for

violations of ECOA resemble those granted under TILA. The Fair Debt Collection Practices Act of 1974 (FDCPA) regulates the activities of debt collectors. Congress intended the law to eliminate abusive, deceptive, and unfair debt-collection practices and thereby to protect consumers. The act limits the manner in which the debt collector can communicate with the debtor and limits the third parties whom the debt collector can contact about the debt. Remedial awards are similar to those granted under other statutes, but the Federal Trade Commission has primary enforcement responsibilities under the FDCPA. The Uniform Consumer Credit Code represents yet another statute—this time at the state level—that protects consumers. The Consumer Product Safety Act established the Consumer Product Safety Commission (CPSC). The CSPC regulates hazardous products and can even ban those that pose imminent hazards to the public.

Discussion Questions

1. Explain the disclosures a creditor typically must make to the consumer under the Truth in Lending Act (TILA).

2. Describe the remedies available for a creditor's violation of the Truth in Lending Act (TILA).

3. Explain in detail the coverage of the Fair Credit Reporting Act (FCRA).

4. Delineate the civil remedies that are permitted—and prohibited—by the Fair Credit Reporting Act (FRCA).

5. Explain what Regulation B of the Equal Credit Opportunity Act (ECOA) requires of creditors for compliance.

6. Outline the general requirements of the Fair Debt Collection Practices Act (FDCPA).

7. Set out the civil and criminal penalties that can result from violations of the Fair Debt Collection Practices Act (FDCPA).

8. Explain the underlying purposes of the Uniform Consumer Credit Code (UCCC).

9. Describe in detail the powers enjoyed by the Consumer Product Safety Commission (CPSC).

10. Mention some of the products subject to the standards set by the Consumer Product Safety Commission and some of the products it has banned.

Case Problems and Writing Assignments

1. In 1994, Gregory Hawthorne opened a checking account at a Washington, D.C., branch of Citicorp Data Systems, Inc. (Citibank). Three years later, Hawthorne withdrew all the funds from his Citibank account before moving from Washington, D.C., to New York City. In December 1997, Citibank sent him an invoice alleging an overdraft balance of $2,600 on his Washington, D.C., account. After comparing his records with the Citibank charges, Hawthorne discovered that he owed less than claimed by Citibank. He wrote to Citibank on May 8, 1998, detailed the discrepancies, and enclosed a check for the amount that his records indicated was owed. Citibank did not respond to Hawthorne's claim of a discrepancy. Instead, Citibank sent him numerous computer-generated letters demanding payment and, at various times, threatened either "collection action," legal action, or referral of the matter to a credit-reporting bureau. Hawthorne tried numerous times, by phone and by letter, to explain to Citibank the nature of his

dispute. Citibank neither cleared up the matter over the phone nor indicated in any letter to Hawthorne that it acknowledged that a discrepancy might exist.

On January 17, 2001, Hawthorne purchased his credit report from Experian, a leading credit-reporting bureau. That report included an entry from Citibank indicating that Hawthorne was more than 60 days in arrears. On February 14, 2001, Hawthorne wrote to three of the largest credit-reporting agencies (Experian, Trans Union, and Equifax) and disputed Citibank's report against his account. On February 26, 2001, Hawthorne received from a director of executive communications at Citibank a letter (the first non-form one) indicating that Citibank could not find any discrepancies in his account, that he currently owed a balance of $2,167.97, and that Citibank might be unable to resolve disputes involving statements that are three or four years old. In April 2001, when

Hawthorne sought a home mortgage loan, only one lender offered Hawthorne a loan; and four days before the closing, that lender demanded an additional .875 percent on the interest rate. Hawthorne alleged that the lack of lending options and the lender's last-minute interest rate hike had resulted from Citibank's report to the credit-reporting agencies that Hawthorne was a "bad debt." Further, Hawthorne claimed that the difficulty he had experienced in obtaining a mortgage served as evidence that the Citibank discrepancy continued to have a negative, ongoing effect on his credit.

Section 1681i(a)(2) of the FCRA provides in relevant part that when "a consumer reporting agency receives notice of a dispute from any consumer . . . the agency shall provide notification of the dispute to any person who provided any item of information in dispute. . . ." Section 1681i(a)(2) further states that "the consumer reporting agency shall promptly provide to the person who provided the information in dispute all relevant information regarding the dispute that is received by the agency from the consumer. . . ." Among other things, the FCRA creates a private right of action by which consumers may bring suit for damages against "any person" who violates or fails to comply with "any requirement imposed" under Section 1681. As defined in §1681a, the term "person" means "any individual, partnership, corporation, . . . association, government or governmental subdivision or agency, or other entity." Would the FCRA allow a consumer like Hawthorne to sue a furnisher of information such as Citibank for damages? [*See Hawthorne v. Citicorp Data Systems, Inc.*, 216 F. Supp. 2d 45 (E.D. N.Y. 2002).]

2. The plaintiffs, Glenn A. Fuller, Vera J. Fuller, Charles J. Curry, and Norma Curry, were members of a property owners' association. The defendants, members of a law firm, had sent the plaintiffs the following letter:

The Association is attempting to resolve [past due maintenance assessments] and move forward through the following offer:

(1) For those who have not paid since 1997 or prior, you must pay the amount of $ 75.00 for the last quarter of 1997, $ 360.00 total for the four (4) quarters of 1998, $ 90.00 for the first quarter of 1999, plus $ 50.00 for attorney fees for this collection letter. If these amounts, in total are received within thirty (30) days, the Association will take no further action to collect the prior delinquent amounts or to assess or collect for attorney's fees and costs.

(2) Alternatively, the Association will accept a Quit Claim Deed in return for your payment of the above owed sums, depending on your particular circumstance.

(3) In the event that you do not choose one of the two above options and communicate that acceptance to the undersigned on or before thirty (30) days from the date this letter is sent, we shall proceed to enforce through the filing of a lawsuit against all of the delinquent owners.

Unless, within thirty days after the receipt of this correspondence you dispute the validity of the amounts due, the amount due will be assumed to be valid. If you dispute the amount due, we would appreciate you submitting any docu-

mentation or evidence that you have in support of your contention that the amounts due are not correct.

This is an attempt to collect a debt and any information obtained will be used for that purpose.

Under the Fair Debt Collection Practices Act, the plaintiffs alleged that the defendants (1) by failing to state the "amount of debt," had violated § 1693 (a)(1); (2) by contradicting and overshadowing the validation notice had violated §§ 1692g(a) and 1692e(10); (3) by falsely representing a remedy available to the creditor had violated § 1692e(4); and (4) by using false representations and deceptive means in attempting to collect debts had violated § 1692e. The defendants argued that: (1) the maintenance assessments were not debts for the purposes of the FDCPA, and (2) they accordingly were not debt collectors under the statute. Given the facts of this case, how should the court rule? [See *Fuller v. Becker & Poliakoff, P.A.*, 192 F. Supp. 2d 1361 (M.D. Fla. 2002).]

3. On October 19, 1987, John Venesio Graciano Jr. completed a credit application by which he sought to borrow $6,300 from East Cambridge Savings Bank to purchase an automobile. Graciano listed another person's Social Security number as his and indicated that he worked for New England Tea & Coffee in Malden, Massachusetts. On October 27, 1987, the bank verified Graciano's employment at New England Tea and Coffee and approved his application. Unbeknownst to the bank, Graciano was using someone else's Social Security number, and that someone else had a very similar name—John Victor Graziano Jr., the plaintiff in this case. The plaintiff and Graciano had different addresses, different places of employment, and different dates of birth. And, of course, the plaintiff and Graciano had different, albeit similar, names. The bank nonetheless failed to ascertain the true identity and Social Security number of its loan applicant, Graciano. On October 30, 1987, Graciano signed a promissory note for $4,500 and was given a bank draft in that amount, payable to him and the dealer from whom he was purchasing the automobile.

After Graciano failed to make any payments on the note, on June 30, 1988, the matter was referred to the bank's attorney for collection. The attorney sought and, on February 14, 1989, recovered for the bank a judgment against Graciano in the amount of $6,315.64. Prior to and after this judgment, the bank requested consumer reports on Graciano on at least three occasions: July 18, 1988, February 11, 1992, and November 25, 1992. The bank made each request so that it could obtain information as to the whereabouts of Graciano and thereby facilitate the bank's efforts to collect its judgment. By entering into the computer system the Social Security number Graciano had falsely provided to the bank (that is, the plaintiff's Social Security number), the bank thereafter requested the first report on Graciano. The bank received two reports, one for Graciano and one for the plaintiff. The bank requested the second and third reports after it already knew or should have known that two individuals with similar names were using the same Social Security number. The plaintiff claimed that he never had requested any credit or taken a loan from the bank. Nor, he asserted, had he ever been a customer of the bank.

On December 10, 1992, the plaintiff received a letter from an attorney for the bank, informing the plaintiff that, as he currently owed the bank $8,589.27, the plaintiff should contact the attorney for the purpose of working out an agreeable payment plan. The letter was addressed to the plaintiff's correct address, but the name on the letter was "John V. Graciano." Before being contacted by the bank's attorney, the plaintiff had been aware that someone had been misusing his Social Security number for employment purposes. Indeed, on March 12, 1991, the plaintiff had advised the Social Security Administration that his number was being misused. Bringing suit against the bank, the plaintiff subsequently claimed that the bank's actions of requesting credit reports—pursuant to its collection efforts—represented a violation of the FCRA because the bank had willfully obtained the plaintiff's consumer reports under false pretenses. Should the court accept the plaintiff's contentions? [See *Graziano v. TRW, Inc.*, 877 F. Supp. 53 (D. Mass. 1995).]

4. Brenda Johnson paid for merchandise at a 7-Eleven with a check for $2.64. The check bounced and was referred to the defendant lawyer, Jesse Riddle, whose firm specializes in collecting dishonored checks. In fact, Riddle and Associates's clients include such large corporations as K-Mart, Circle K, and 7-Eleven (Southland Corporation). Consequently, Riddle and his firm receive between 700,000 and 1.2 million dishonored checks per year. Utah law permits a service charge on dishonored checks as long as the charge does not exceed $15. The state's shoplifting statute, on the other hand, imposes civil liability on an "adult who wrongfully takes merchandise by any means" in the amount of the retail price of the item plus "an additional penalty" of up to $500, with costs and attorney's fees. The defendant demanded payment for the value of the check plus a statutory penalty of $250. The plaintiff paid the defendant $17.64 (the value of the check plus the $15 service charge), which he accepted. The plaintiff later brought a class action under the FDCPA on the grounds that the statute prohibits a debt collector from using "unfair or unconscionable means to collect or attempt to collect any debt," which is defined in § 1692f(1) as the collection of any amount "unless such amount is expressly authorized by the agreement creating the debt or permitted by law." Had Riddle violated the FDCPA? [See *Johnson v. Riddle*, 305 F.3d 1107 (10th Cir. 2002).]

5. **BUSINESS APPLICATION CASE** Turner was a 47-year-old woman with an eighth-grade education. E-Z Check Cashing (EZ) is co-owned and managed by Ricky Edwards. Edwards operates four check-cashing businesses, three of which also perform pawn broking services. The "check-cashing" transactions conducted by EZ differ from the usual "check-cashing" transactions at a bank. EZ's business consists of "deferred presentment" transactions in which a customer writes a check to EZ in an amount that includes (1) a principal amount the customer receives immediately in cash, plus (2) an additional

"service fee" to be collected at least 30 days later. At the end of the 30-day period, the customer may (1) repay the principal amount and service fee and retrieve the uncashed check, (2) pay only the service fee and write a new check for the principal amount and service fee, or (3) allow the business to deposit the original check. A "Good Faith Estimate of Settlement Charges" is appended to the agreement. In this document, EZ describes the transaction as a loan. Before agreeing to "cash a check" for a customer, EZ investigates the customer's check-writing history through two national databases and requires the customer to provide references. If a customer has no outstanding bad checks and otherwise is deemed acceptable, EZ will "cash" the check. This means that EZ will advance the customer cash in the amount of the principal portion of the check and hold the check for 30 days. It costs EZ 45 cents per check to investigate a customer's check-writing history.

Turner's series of transactions with EZ began on July 2, 1996, when she borrowed $300.00. Pursuant to this "check-cashing" agreement, Turner wrote a check to EZ for $405.00, which included the $300.00 cash advancement to Turner, plus $105.00 in service fees. At the end of 30 days, Turner could either pay EZ $105.00 in cash and provide another check in the amount of $405.00 (to be held for the next 30 days) or do nothing, at which time EZ would deposit the original $405.00 check, in settlement of the principal amount of the cash advanced originally and the associated charges. On July 31, the due date, Turner chose to pay a service charge of $105.00 and to defer payment on the principal ($300.00) for an additional 30 days. She did so again and again for each of the following seven months, thus deferring the deposit of her $405.00. Through these transactions, Turner paid EZ $840.00 over an eight-month period.

Finally, on April 4, 1997, Turner failed to pay the $105.00 service fee, and EZ deposited her $405.00 check. When that check was dishonored because of the closure of her bank account, Edwards, in a letter dated April 11, 1997, threatened Turner with criminal prosecution unless she reimbursed EZ for the amount of the returned check ($405.00), plus a check recovery fee of 10 [sic] percent of the check amount ($81.00). In May 1997, Turner filed a Chapter 7 bankruptcy petition; and on June 19, 1997, she filed a lawsuit alleging violations of TILA and Regulation Z by EZ. Turner claimed that EZ had failed (1) to provide the disclosures required by TILA and Regulation Z; (2) to make the required disclosures conspicuously in writing; (3) to properly disclose the finance charges; and (4) to state accurately the annual percentage rate (APR), all of which omissions allegedly violated TILA and Regulation Z. Did TILA cover a deferred presentment check-cashing transaction? Did the creditor's disclosures violate TILA? [See *Turner v. E-Z Check Cashing of Cookeville, TN, Inc.*, 35 F. Supp. 2d 1042 (M.D. Tenn. 1999).]

6. **ETHICAL APPLICATION CASE** Mirama Enterprises, Inc., d/b/a Aroma Housewares Company, is a California corporation that distributes to retailers in the United States and abroad a variety

of electric kitchen appliances. From February or March 1996 until February or March 1998, Aroma distributed a juice extractor, model ACJ-250, in the United States. The juicer was manufactured in China by Semco, which is headquartered in Taiwan. The juicer contains several parts: the base, the upper housing, containers for juice and pulp, the grater/filter, the cover/chute, and the plunger. The separate plastic plunger pushes fruit and vegetables down through the chute onto the rotating grater/filter, which is a flat metal plate with sharp metal teeth. The produce is pulverized, sending juice into one container and pulp into the other. The packet of instructions included with the juicer instructed consumers to "Remove all pits (peaches, plums, etc.), large seeds (melons, etc.), and stems before placing food in Chute. Items such as these may damage the unit." Consumers were also told: "Do not clean any part of the Juice Extractor with an abrasive cleaner. Do not put any part of the Juice Extractor in dishwasher or boiling water."

In early January 1998, Aroma received at least one complaint from a consumer whose juicer had broken. In response, on January 12, 1998, Mr. Fred Ying, an Aroma employee, tested six juicers for more than four hours. When applying extra force on the plunger, the plunger was scratched by the grater/filter; but the grater/filter did not break and the lid remained intact. For two juicers, an abnormally high pressure load of 145 pounds was placed on the plunger. The plungers were scratched and the juicers' blades broke, but the lids of the juicers remained intact; and the broken blade was contained inside the juicer. Another employee, in conducting a single test of a single juicer, stood on the plunger. The juicer's blade came in contact with the base and the juicer stopped running but did not shatter. Aroma was unable to reach any conclusions regarding the failure incidents at the time, other than to speculate that, perhaps, consumers were disregarding clear directions not to wash their juicers in hot water or in a dishwasher and thereby were compromising the integrity of the product.

On or about February 2, 1998, consumer Richard Norton called Aroma to report that his juicer had shattered. Failing to receive any communications from Aroma, Mr. Norton followed up with a letter in capitalized letters that stated that the juicer, "Suddenly exploded, throwing with great violence pieces of the clear plastic cover and shreds of the razor-sharp separator screen as far as eight feet in my kitchen. Needless to say, but I will, the suddenness and violence of the explosion shattered the peace of my home and frightened me greatly." In the next few months, at least six additional consumers informed Aroma of other shatterings, all of which had caused cuts and other serious injuries. At least one consumer reported that the juicer had "exploded" like a bomb and that she viewed the product as unsafe. In total, prior to November 16, 1998, Aroma knew of 23 such incidents, 19 of which had resulted in injuries to at least 22 persons. Seven of these incidents resulted in medical treatment for the affected consumers. Aroma continued to view these incidents as stemming from consumer misuse of the product.

On November 16, 1998, Aroma filed a preliminary report with the Consumer Product Safety Commission (CPSC). The CPSC received the company's final report in February 1999 and recalled the juicer on June 30, 1999. The evidence at trial showed that of the 23 consumers who had notified Aroma of their juicers shattering, seven also had contacted the CPSC—one in March, one in May, one in June, and four in September and October. On June 8, 1998, Aroma first learned that these consumers had contacted the CPSC. Aroma also provided extensive evidence that the CPSC had been aware of problems with juicers made by other companies, including a 1993 recall of one type of juicer and the issuing of a preliminary determination that another juicer presented a substantial hazard. All told, from 1995 to 1997, the CPSC recalled juicers from four different manufacturers.

Under the Consumer Product Safety Act, a manufacturer, distributor, or retailer of a consumer product must immediately inform the CPSC if any of them obtains information that reasonably supports the conclusion that the product has a defect that creates a substantial risk to the public or creates an unreasonable risk of serious injury or death. In short, if a covered firm believes its product, through a defect or otherwise, poses a significant threat to consumers, the act requires the firm to report such information within 24 hours. Had Aroma received sufficient notice of the problems with the juicers so as to trigger Aroma's obligation to report the product's defects? Did the CPSC's awareness of the problems eliminate Aroma's duty to report? Assess Aroma's ethics in this situation as well. What, for example, are the costs and benefits of evading such disclosure provisions? [See *U.S. v. Mirama Enterprises, Inc.*, 185 F. Supp. 2d 1148 (D.C. Cir. 2002).]

7. CRITICAL THINKING CASE A Marin County, California, woman who lost $70,000 while gambling online with 12 credit cards sued MasterCard, Visa, and the banks that had issued the credit cards. She argued that because gambling is illegal in California, the credit card companies never should have authorized her charges. She claimed that the credit card companies in effect are aiding and abetting illegal Internet gambling and making a lot of money from these activities. In a related vein, a Minneapolis attorney recently filed a class action lawsuit alleging that credit card firms' fomenting such illegal on-line gambling amounts to racketeering and precludes the companies from collecting on the debts (state laws oftentimes make the collection of gambling debts unenforceable). The operators of on-line gambling Web sites argued that Internet gambling is legal in the absence of laws specifically outlawing it—only a few states explicitly ban Internet gambling, although many prosecutors construe a federal law banning interstate sports betting over the telephone and state laws banning gambling in general as providing a basis for prohibiting on-line gambling. For the 300 Web sites that offer such gambling, business is booming, with revenues expected to exceed $20.8 billion by 2005. Should a business that provides products or services that involve addictive and harmful behavior

take steps to protect its customers from the adverse consequences if the customers' conduct becomes addictive? What responsibility does the business have to the customer or to society for the harm resulting from addictive behavior "aided and abetted" by the goods or services provided by the company to the addict? Is it ethical for a consumer credit-granting business, especially credit card companies, to provide a means for its customers to participate in addictive behavior on credit, even if such activities are legal? [See Tom Lowery, "Debtors Take Credit Cards to Task for Allowing Bets," *USA Today*, August 17, 1999, p. B1; *Datamonitor*, "Bright Future for Online Gambling," July 14, 2001, http://nua.com.]

8. YOU BE THE JUDGE In 1999, Congress enacted the Gramm-Leach-Bliley Act (GLBA) to enhance competition in the financial services industry by eliminating many federal and state law barriers to affiliations among banks and securities firms, insurance companies, and other financial providers. Title V of the GLBA contains a number of provisions designed to protect the privacy of "nonpublic personal information" (NPI) that consumers provide to financial institutions, thereby reflecting the congressional policy that each financial institution has an affirmative and continuing obligation to respect the privacy of its customers and to protect the security and confidentiality of those customers' nonpublic personal information. Accordingly, by requiring that the financial institution provide the consumer with notice of the institution's disclosure policies and the opportunity for the consumer to "opt out" of disclosure, the GLBA restricts the ability of a "financial institution" to disclose NPI to a nonaffiliated third party. The GLBA further mandates that an unaffiliated third party recipient of NPI "shall not, directly or through an affiliate of such receiving third party, disclose such information to any other person that is a nonaffiliated third party of both the financial institution and such receiving third party, unless such disclosure would be lawful if made directly to such other person by the financial institution." To implement its disclosure restrictions, the GLBA gives the FTC and other agencies broad rulemaking authority to promulgate such regulations as may be necessary to carry out the purposes of the act with respect to the financial institutions subject to their jurisdiction. Trans Union, LLC, a credit-reporting agency (CRA) under the Fair Credit Reporting Act, challenged the regulations promulgated by the FTC and other federal agencies to implement the privacy provisions of the GLBA. Trans Union contended that the regulations unlawfully restrict a CRA's ability to disclose and reuse certain consumer information because (1) a CRA is not a "financial institution" subject to the FTC's rulemaking authority under the GLBA; (2) the regulations' definition of the statutory term "personally identifiable financial information" is overbroad; (3) the regulations' restrictions on the reuse of information are inconsistent with the GLBA; and (4) the challenged regulations infringe Trans Union's right of free speech under the First Amendment. If this case were in *your* court, how would *you* rule? [See *Trans Union, LLC v. FTC*, 295 F.3d 42 (D.C. Cir. 2002).]

Notes

1. See, for example, Jonathan Sheldon, ed., *Fair Credit Reporting Act*, 3rd ed. (Boston: National Consumer Law Center, 1994). This and other National Consumer Law Center publications, such as Ernest L. Sarason, ed., *Truth in Lending* (1986); Gerry Azzata, ed., *Equal Credit Opportunity Act* (1988); and the annual cumulative supplements to these works provide more detailed information on consumer law, as does Gene A. Marsh, *Consumer Protection Law in a Nutshell* (St. Paul, Minn.: West Group, 1999) and Howard J. Alperin and Ronald F. Chase, *Consumer Law: Sales Practices and Credit Regulation* (Minneapolis: West, 1986).

2. Jonathan Sheldon, ed., *Fair Credit Reporting Act*, 3rd ed. (Boston: National Consumer Law Center, 1994), 31.

3. Ibid.

4. *Beach v. Ocwen Federal Bank*, 523 U.S. 410, 419 (1998).

5. Sheldon, *Fair Credit Reporting Act*, 32.

6. Ibid.

7. *Heintz v. Jenkins*, 514 U.S. 291, 299 (1995).

Environmental Protection

A
G
E
N
D
A

NRW NRW will manufacture its StuffTrakR units at several factories in the United States. The firm wants to make its factories as similar as possible but has concerns about the differing state environmental protection standards that will force the company to adapt location-specific responses to such laws. The firm members want each community to view NRW as a "good neighbor." Accordingly, they want to know what they must do to meet this objective. In particular, they seek a corporate strategy that will ensure that the firm refrains from polluting these respective communities in any fashion. As NRW opens new facilities, Mai, Helen, and Carlos in addition desire that the firm meets or exceeds the requirements of federal law. What sorts of environmentally friendly technologies should they install in their facilities? These and other questions are likely to arise as you study this chapter.

Be prepared! You never know when the firm or one of its members will seek your advice.

The Environmental Protection Agency

Environmental law constitutes an extremely complex, pervasive, and controversial area of the law. Acronym-laden and composed of highly technical statutes and regulations, environmental law poses genuine challenges to students and legal practitioners alike. Hence, in this chapter we will highlight only some of the most important principles.[1]

During the heyday of environmental protection efforts in the 1970s, the United States, by taking the first steps aimed at halting the destruction of our planet's biodiversity, distinguished itself. The United States did so largely through statutory engraftments onto common law nuisance principles. A nuisance involves the unlawful use of one's own property so as to injure the rights of another. Enforcement of nuisance laws prohibits interference with the rights of others; however, though providing the framework for modern-day statutory environmental law, such laws proved inadequate to solve the sheer magnitude of the problems these laws must address.

Congress instead chose to opt for a statutory approach that leaves enforcement largely to an administrative agency called the Environmental Protection Agency (EPA), itself established by executive order in 1970. In general, the EPA has the power to enforce environmental laws, adopt regulations, conduct research on pollution, and assist other governmental entities concerned with the environment. To enforce federal environmental laws, the EPA can subject suspected violators to administrative orders and civil penalties and can refer criminal matters to the Department of Justice as well.

The laws Congress passes and the EPA enforces consider the economic aspects of environmental law; take a technological approach to environmental concerns; mandate risk assessment in the implementation of these laws; and use the imposition of liability, sometimes even strict liability, as a hammer to ensure compliance. Early legislation required compliance primarily by business and industry, especially the chemical industry. In the last 15 years, however, small businesses and state and local governments increasingly have borne the burden of the compliance costs associated with environmental issues.

Hence, the virtual absence of any legislative enactments in the 1990s may indicate the increasing politicization of this area of the law. In general, what seems a simple (and valid) argument—take all steps necessary to save our environment—is complicated by the staggering costs involved. To illustrate, the EPA's 2004 budgetary request totals $7.6 billion, the sum it deems necessary to support its numerous programs and initiatives.[2] Moreover, EPA figures (which many critics argue may be underestimated by as much as a multiple of 30) place the costs to local taxpayers for environmental compliance in the year 2000 at over $32 billion (in 1986 dollars), an estimate that does not take into account the costs imposed on businesses and consumers.[3] Another article estimates that compliance with all governmental regulations in 1995, including environmental laws, cost U.S. businesses $600 billion (calculated in 1991 dollars).[4] Critics of such environmental regulations question whether the benefits derived from compliance outweigh these gargantuan costs; they suggest the money spent on complying with environmental mandates might be better spent on education, medical research, and the like.[5] Pro-environmentalists, however, argue that we have no choice but to protect our environment. Simply put, it is the only one we have—if we ruin it, we cannot replenish or replace it. The EPA maintains a Web site at http://www.epa.gov.

The National Environmental Policy Act

The National Environmental Policy Act of 1969 (NEPA) became effective when President Nixon signed it into law in 1970. Congress enacted NEPA as a means of furthering a national policy to encourage a productive and harmonious relationship between people and the environment. Congress also viewed NEPA as a vehicle for promoting efforts to eliminate environmental damage and thereby enhance the health and welfare of the citizenry.

Section 101 of NEPA declares that it is the federal government's continuing responsibility, in cooperation with state and local governments and other concerned private and public organizations, to use all practicable means, consistent with other essential national policy considerations, to attain the broadest range of beneficial uses of the environment (including the preservation of healthy and aesthetically and culturally pleasing surroundings) while at the same time avoiding the degradation of the environment, risks to health and safety, and other undesirable or unintended consequences. In fulfilling this purpose, NEPA directs that, to the fullest extent possible, all agencies of the federal government live up to these environmental responsibilities.

Environmental Impact Statement

NEPA effectuates this goal primarily by requiring virtually all federal agencies to prepare a detailed environmental impact statement (EIS) whenever the agency proposes legislation, recommends any actions, or undertakes any activities that may affect the environment. Among other things, an EIS must:

- Describe the anticipated impact that the proposed action will have on the environment

- Describe any unavoidable adverse consequences of the action or activity

- Examine the possible alternative methods of achieving the desired goals

- Distinguish between long-term and short-term environmental effects

- Describe the irreversible and irretrievable commitments of resources that will occur if the proposed action is implemented

The statute requires wide dissemination of the EIS in draft form to other federal, state, and local agencies; the president; and the Council on Environmental Quality (the CEQ, whose importance is discussed in the next section).

Given the substantial data gathering necessary for successful compliance with the prerequisites of an EIS, many agencies have tried to exempt themselves from having to prepare this statement. However, the numerous court decisions since 1970 indicate that the following criteria show a need for an EIS: (1) a proposed federal action (2) that is "major" and (3) that has a significant impact on the environment. Courts have made the definitional thresholds for points 1 and 2 law; hence, if a federal agency has control over the proposed action (no matter how small the undertaking, or even if it is regional in scope), coupled with a substantial commitment of resources, the EIS requirement applies. Similarly, court decisions under point 3 have not limited interpretations of the term "environment" solely to the natural environment (lakes, rivers, wetlands, wilderness areas, beaches, and so forth). The broad goals of the act (for example, the preservation of aesthetically and culturally pleasing surroundings, including the historical aspects of our national heritage) support the view that projects covered by NEPA involve more than just proposals that have an impact on various natural habitats. On the other hand, Congress clearly did not intend to require an EIS for every conceivable federal project, even though all such proposed activities in some fashion affect the quality of life of the citizenry.

Hence, considerable litigation has centered around the content of the EIS. CEQ regulations set out detailed requirements that cover the preparation of an EIS. The agency first makes an "environmental assessment" (an EA) of the need for an EIS. An interdisciplinary, interagency evaluation of the need for the proposed action; the likely environmental effects of the proposed action; the alternatives to the proposed action; and the agency, interest group, and public comments received concerning the proposal all factor into the EA as well.

Unless the agency makes a "finding of no significant impact" (that is, a FONSI), the agency, by determining the scope—or subject matter—of the EIS, begins the preparation of the EIS. Court and agency decisions have held that agencies cannot avoid the application of NEPA by breaking up long-term projects—for example, highway, flood control, and hydroelectric projects that cover wide areas—into segments that in and of themselves separately seem to show no environmental risks even though the overall project does. The EIS must adequately discuss the consequences of each alternative, including the alternative that the agency take "no action" on a given problem.

In deciding whether to include a given alternative, courts use a "rule-of-reason" test that gauges whether a reasonable person would view the alternative as sufficiently significant to merit an extended discussion. The EIS need not mention implausible or purely speculative alternatives. Besides the scope of the EIS, the timing of the EIS also has spawned litigation. Agencies contemplating any action that has environmental repercussions must make sure that the preparation of the EIS occurs sufficiently in advance of the commencement of the project so that the EIS makes an important, practical contribution to the decision-making process rather than serving merely as a rationalization or justification for decisions already made by the agency.

Robertson v. Methow Valley Citizens Council,[6] a landmark case construing NEPA, held that NEPA does not require federal agencies to include in each EIS either a fully developed plan detailing the steps the agency would take to mitigate adverse environmental impacts or a worst-case analysis. Rather, according to the Supreme Court, the statutory requirement that a federal agency contemplating a major action prepare such an EIS ensures that the agency, in reaching its decision, will have available, and will carefully consider, detailed information concerning significant environmental impacts. Simply by focusing the agency's attention on the environmental consequences of a proposed project, NEPA ensures that important effects will not be overlooked or underestimated only to be discovered after resources have been committed. According to the Court, publication of an EIS, both in draft and final form, also gives the public the assurance that the agency in its decision-making process indeed has considered environmental concerns and, perhaps more significantly, provides a springboard for public comment. The EIS moreover offers those governmental bodies that regulate development of the environment adequate notice of the expected consequences and the opportunity to plan and implement corrective measures in a timely manner. In the Court's view, the sweeping policy goals announced in NEPA thus are realized through a set of "action-forcing" procedures that require that agencies take a "hard look" at the environmental consequences and that provide for broad dissemination of relevant environmental information. This "hard look," however, need not include the formulation and adoption of a complete mitigation plan, the Court emphasized. It would be inconsistent with NEPA's reliance on procedural mechanisms—as opposed to substantive, result-based standards—to demand a fully developed plan to mitigate environmental harm before an agency can act. Simply put, the Court explained, it now is well settled that NEPA by itself does not mandate particular results but simply prescribes the necessary process. If the adverse environmental effects of the proposed action are adequately identified and evaluated, the agency is not constrained by NEPA from deciding that other values outweigh the environmental costs.

Council on Environmental Quality

The responsibility for ensuring the success of the EIS process falls to the Council on Environmental Quality (CEQ). Established by NEPA as an advisory council to the president, the CEQ develops regulations covering EISs and otherwise plays a leading role in developing and recommending to the president national policies that will foster and promote the improvement of the environmental quality of the nation. The CEQ assists and advises the president in the preparation of the Environmental Quality Report, which the president by law submits annually to Congress. By statute, the three-member CEQ can maintain a staff to help keep it abreast of developing environmental issues. Although the EPA represents the primary enforcement agency for federal environmental laws, courts give the CEQ's guidelines and regulations great deference.

Amendments to NEPA in the late 1970s set up a nine-member Science Advisory Board to provide scientific information to the EPA administrator (the head of the agency) and various other congressional bodies that address scientific and technical issues affecting the environment. These amendments also give to the EPA administrator the task of coordinating environmental research, development, demonstration, and educational programs to minimize unnecessary duplication of programs, projects, and research facilities. Centralizing these responsibilities within the EPA and its staff facilitates the achievement of both NEPA's mandates and the broader environmental objectives and challenges facing the nation.

Air Pollution

The impurities, dirt, and contaminants that a variety of sources emit into the air fall generally into five different classes. The first class is *carbon monoxide*—a colorless, odorless, poisonous gas produced by burning fossil fuels. Discharges from car engines represent the largest source of carbon monoxide. The second class is *particulates*—liquid or solid substances produced by facilities using stationary fuel combustion and other industrial processes. Sources ranging from factories to home furnaces emit such particles. The third class is *sulfur oxides*—corrosive, poisonous gases caused by use of sulfurous fuels. Electrical utility power plants and industrial plants emit most sulfur oxides. The fourth class is *nitrogen oxides*—gases produced by the very hot burning of fuel. These derive from stationary combustion plants, such as steel mills, and transportation vehicles such as trains, trucks, and buses. Once emitted into the atmosphere, sulfur oxides combine with nitrogen oxides to form "acid rain." Finally, the fifth class—*hydrocarbons*—consists of particulates derived from unburned and wasted fuel. Unlike carbon monoxide, hydrocarbons in and of themselves are nontoxic. However, when hydrocarbons combine in the atmosphere with nitrogen oxides, complex secondary pollution—known as smog—often results. Smog, then, causes respiratory difficulties, eye and lung irritation, damage to trees and other vegetation, offensive odors, and haze.

However, it is nearly impossible to gauge with precision the so-called threshold or safe levels and/or dangerous levels of air pollution. Regulators therefore are relegated to setting exposure levels that kick in only when demonstrable adverse effects already have occurred. As a result, risk management continues to be a problematic issue in this area of environmental law.

As we shall see, the Clean Air Act and its amendments reflect this and other complexities: the ever-expanding recognition of the health risks associated with pollution, rapidly changing technologies, a veritable explosion of scientific data relating to air pollution, and industry resistance to policymakers' attempts to redress this problem.

The Clean Air Act

The Clean Air Act is an oft-amended, lengthy (the statute itself is approximately 300 pages long), technical, complex, and comprehensive approach to combating air pollution. Efforts to regulate air pollution actually began in the 1950s when Congress supplied technical and financial assistance to the states to help control interstate pollution in some circumstances.

The first federal Clean Air Act, enacted in 1963, concentrated on controlling emissions from stationary industrial sources (the "tall-stack" types of facilities). Only four years later, Congress, in the Air Quality Act of 1967, saw the need to pass amendments that address the problem of mobile air emissions from sources such as cars and trucks. The 1967 amendments established atmospheric areas as well as air quality control regions and called for the development of state plans to implement these ambient air standards. Under these early enactments, each state retained primary responsibility for ensuring the air quality within its own borders.

The 1970 Amendments

To achieve national air quality standards as well, the 1970 amendments, by establishing timetables for meeting state goals, appreciably strengthened the federal role in combating air pollution. Under these provisions, the administrator of the EPA is responsible for establishing national ambient air quality standards (NAAQS) for air pollutants that reasonably would be anticipated to endanger the public health or welfare.

The 1970 amendments directed the administrator to establish two kinds of standards: (1) primary standards that, in the judgment of the administrator and allowing for an adequate margin of safety, are necessary in order to protect the public health; and (2) secondary standards that, in the judgment of the administrator, are necessary to protect the public welfare—crops, livestock, buildings, and the like—from any known or anticipated adverse effects associated with such air pollutants in the ambient air.

These amendments also require each state, after reasonable notice and public hearings and within nine months of the promulgation of any NAAQS, to submit to the EPA a state implementation plan (SIP) setting out how the state proposes to implement and maintain that standard within its air quality control regions (AQCRs). Before the EPA administrator can approve it, the SIP must provide for the establishment and operation of procedures necessary to monitor and control ambient air quality as well as for a program to enforce emissions regulations. Any SIP must allow for the attainment of primary standards "as expeditiously as practicable" but in no case later than three years from the date the administrator approves the plan. The state must attain secondary standards within a "reasonable time." Once approved, an SIP has the force of both federal and state law.

The EPA administrator originally promulgated NAAQS for particulates, sulfur dioxide, carbon monoxide, nitrogen oxide, ozone, and hydrocarbons. In 1978, the EPA adminis-

trator also added lead, which can cause retardation and brain damage in children, to this list and in 1983 revoked the hydrocarbon standard.

The 1977 Amendments

Congress realized that the achievement of its national air quality objectives would necessitate strict timetables aimed at forcing cleanup actions by industry and government. Hence, the 1970 amendments contemplated prompt action. But by 1977 it had become clear that the original timetables were too optimistic. The 1977 Clean Air Act amendments therefore allowed delays in compliance in certain situations. By 1977, Congress also recognized that achievement of the nation's air quality objectives must encompass not only existing stationary sources and motor vehicles but also new stationary sources, new motor vehicles, and hazardous pollutants (such as asbestos, mercury, and vinyl chloride) produced by either existing or new sources. In addition, in 1977 Congress characterized this new undertaking as a federal responsibility; thus, Congress directed the EPA to establish such nationally uniform emission standards.

The 1990 Amendments

The 1990 amendments retain the basic strategies of the 1970 and 1977 amendments but also set new compliance dates for many of the deadlines established under the 1977 amendments that had come and gone.

Title I of these amendments, by mandating overall reductions of emissions within six years, attacks urban air pollution—particularly ozone concentrations.

Title II, by strengthening tailpipe emission standards for all cars and trucks and forcing manufacturers to design a certain number of clean-fuel cars each year, tackles mobile sources of emissions.

Title III requires the EPA to set permissible emission standards for some 190 toxic pollutants. In setting these standards, the administrator must consider the costs associated with achieving that standard, as well as the substances' health and environmental impacts.

Title IV for the first time sets up timetables aimed at specifically limiting emissions of nitrogen oxide and sulfur dioxide, the chief components of acid rain, by the year 2000. Focusing on the major emitting facilities, phase one of this title forces these facilities to achieve sulfur emissions of 2.5 pounds per million BTUs by 1995. Phase two, which must be achieved by the year 2000, cuts the allowable emissions to 1.2 pounds per million BTUs. Interestingly, this title contains economic incentives that allow complying facilities to "bank" or transfer emissions credits so as to use reductions of a given magnitude at one site to justify an increase in emissions levels at another site. Although some litigation has arisen over the mechanics of this trading, it does represent an economic-incentives approach to pollution control (similar to the Clean Water Act's permit process that we shall discuss later) that many environmental economists over the years have championed.

Title V sets up a permit system aimed at controlling emissions by major point sources—buildings, structures, facilities, or installations that emit air pollution. This portion of the amendment gives the EPA and state agencies that control air pollution the authority to regulate atmospheric discharges that may damage the general welfare or health and safety of the citizenry. Industry groups have criticized the permit system as an unnecessary regulatory impediment to private enterprise. However, this system highlights the fact that Congress views atmospheric emissions as intrusions on publicly held and environmentally essential ecological systems, rather than as absolute rights, and thus allows appropriate agencies to regulate them.

Title VI for the first time regulates (and provides for the eventual phaseout of) various chlorofluorocarbons, hydrochlorofluorocarbons, and carbon tetrachlorides that bring about the depletion of the ozone layer. In this fashion, Title VI mirrors Title IV's provisions concerning acid rain.

Title VII strengthens the act's civil and criminal investigation, recordkeeping, and enforcement provisions. These new provisions allow the EPA to impose penalties in a more expeditious fashion and permit citizens' suits that address allegedly unreasonable EPA delays in enforcement and repeated violations by emitters.

The remaining titles set out various miscellaneous provisions, including the institution of a program to monitor and improve air quality standards along the United States/Mexico border; the establishment of an interagency task force to conduct research on air quality; and the retraining of workers laid off or terminated as a consequence of a firm's compliance with the Clean Air Act.

Enforcement mechanisms under the Clean Air Act include administrative penalties (not to exceed $25,000 per day per violation), orders issued by the administrator of the EPA, and criminal actions brought by the U.S. attorney general, including fines of $1,000,000 for each violation and/or imprisonment of up to 15 years in cases where one knowingly releases hazardous air pollutants into the ambient air. In setting civil penalties, the administrator or the courts may take into account the size of the business, the economic impact of the penalty on the business, the violator's full compliance history and good-faith efforts to

comply, the duration and seriousness of the violation, and so forth. Those mounting successful citizens' suits may receive attorney's fees and recoup their court costs as well.

According to a 1996 EPA report, the concentrations of five major air pollutants—carbon monoxide, lead, nitrogen dioxide, particulate matter, and sulfur dioxide—declined by an average of about 7 percent in 1995, with the latter pollutant decreasing by 17 percent.[7] The levels of ozone, however, increased by 4 percent, although the overall trend for the last 10 years indicates a reduction in this pollutant.[8] The report also notes that air quality data over the last 25 years show an emissions decline among these six pollutants of about 29 percent while gross domestic product increased by about 99 percent during the same period.[9] The EPA interprets these data as indicative of the fact that the United States can reduce air pollution without sacrificing economic growth. On the other hand, a report authored by certain environmental groups in August 1999 noted that more states had exceeded the ozone levels in 1999 than in 1998 and that many of the nation's most popular summer vacation spots had ozone levels that rivaled (and sometimes exceeded) those from nearby urban areas. Although the heat wave of 1999 undoubtedly affected these air pollution levels, they are a source of concern.[10] To ameliorate such problems, the EPA in 1999 budgeted $507 million to reduce air pollution, including $65 million to develop the states' monitoring of fine particulates, for which the agency announced specific standards in 1997. *Whitman v. American Trucking Associations, Inc.* a recent case, challenged the legality of these very standards. The 2004 EPA budgetary request for reducing air pollution amounts to $617 million. The EPA has a very informative Web site, "The Plain English Guide to the Clean Air Act," at http://www.epa.gov/oar/oaqps/peg_caa/pegcaain.html.

Water Pollution

The Clean Water Act

The Clean Water Act, like the Clean Air Act, exemplifies the complexities involved in regulating a resource that affects virtually every sphere of human activity. Both also exemplify the so-called technology-forcing approach to environmental law.

Passed in 1972 as the Federal Water Pollution Control Amendments (FWPCA), the act was renamed the Clean Water Act when Congress amended it in 1977. Both FWPCA and the Clean Water Act owe doctrinal debts to several earlier federal forays into water pollution control, including the Rivers and Harbors Act of 1899, the Water Pollution Control Act of 1948 (and its 1956 amendments),

39.1

WHITMAN v. AMERICAN TRUCKING ASSOCIATIONS, INC.
531 U.S. 457 (2001)

FACTS Section 109(a) of the Clean Air Act requires the EPA administrator to promulgate national ambient air quality standards (NAAQS) for each air pollutant for which "air quality criteria" have been issued under § 108. Pursuant to § 109(d)(1), the administrator in 1997 revised the ozone and particulate matter NAAQS. Various private parties and several states (the respondents) challenged the revised NAAQS on several grounds. The District of Columbia Circuit Court of Appeals found that, under the Administrator's interpretation, § 109(b)(1)—which instructs the EPA to set standards "the attainment and maintenance of which . . . are requisite to protect the public health" with "an adequate margin of safety"—delegated legislative power to the administrator in contravention of the U.S. Constitution. Hence, the court remanded the NAAQS to the EPA. The court of appeals also declined to depart from its rule that the EPA, in setting the NAAQS, may not consider implementation costs. Moreover, it held that, although certain implementation provisions for the ozone NAAQS contained in Part D, Subpart 2, of Title I of the Clean Air Act did not prevent the EPA from revising the ozone standard and designating certain areas as "nonattainment areas," those provisions, rather than the more general provisions contained in Subpart 1, constrained the implementation of the new ozone NAAQS. Accordingly, the court rejected the EPA's argument that it lacked jurisdiction to reach the implementation question because no "final" implementation action had occurred.

ISSUE Would the Clean Air Act preclude the EPA from considering the costs when the agency promulgates NAAQS?

HOLDING Yes. When it sets primary and secondary NAAQS under the Clean Air Act, the EPA cannot consider implementation costs. Moreover, although the EPA has the authority to construe the statute, its interpretation of the provisions relating to the implementation of the revised ozone standards was unreasonable.

REASONING Excerpts from the opinion of Justice Scalia:

Section 109(b)(1) instructs the EPA to set primary ambient air quality standards "the attainment and maintenance of which . . . are requisite to protect the public health" with "an adequate margin of safety." . . . Were it not for the hundreds of pages of briefing respondents have submitted on the issue, one would have thought it fairly clear that this text does not permit the EPA to consider costs in setting the standards. The language, as one

scholar has noted, "is absolute." . . . The EPA, "based on" the information about health effects contained in the technical "criteria" documents compiled under § 108(a)(2), is to identify the maximum airborne concentration of a pollutant that the public health can tolerate, decrease the concentration to provide an "adequate" margin of safety, and set the standard at that level. Nowhere are the costs of achieving such a standard made part of that initial calculation. . . . Even so, respondents argue, many more factors than air pollution affect public health. In particular, the economic cost of implementing a very stringent standard might produce health losses sufficient to offset the health gains achieved in cleaning the air—for example, by closing down whole industries and thereby impoverishing the workers and consumers dependent upon those industries. That is unquestionably true, and Congress was unquestionably aware of it. Thus, Congress had commissioned in the Air Quality Act of 1967 (1967 Act) "a detailed estimate of the cost of carrying out the provisions of this Act; a comprehensive study of the cost of program implementation by affected units of government; and a comprehensive study of the economic impact of air quality standards on the Nation's industries, communities, and other contributing sources of pollution." . . . The 1970 Congress, armed with the results of this study . . . not only anticipated that compliance costs could injure the public health, but provided for that precise exigency. Section 110(f)(1) of the CAA [Clean Air Act] permitted the Administrator to waive the compliance deadline for stationary sources if . . . sufficient control measures were simply unavailable and "the continued operation of such sources is *essential . . . to the public health* or welfare." . . . Other provisions explicitly permitted or required economic costs to be taken into account in implementing the air quality standards. . . .

Accordingly, to prevail in their present challenge, the respondents must show a textual commitment of authority to the EPA to consider costs in setting NAAQS under §109(b)(1). And because §109(b)(1) and the NAAQS for which it provides are the engine that drives nearly all of Title I of the CAA . . . that textual commitment must be a clear one. Congress, we have held, does not alter the fundamental details of a regulatory scheme in vague terms or ancillary provisions—it does not, one might say, hide elephants in mouseholes. . . .

Their first claim is that §109(b)(1)'s terms "adequate margin" and "requisite" leave room to pad health effects with costs concerns. . . . [W]e find it implausible that Congress would give to the EPA through these modest words the power to determine whether implementation costs should moderate national air quality standards. . . . That factor is *both* so indirectly related to public health *and* so full of potential for canceling the conclusions drawn from direct health effects that it would surely have been expressly mentioned in §§108 and 109 had Congress meant it to be considered. Yet while those provisions describe in detail how the health effects of pollutants in the ambient air are to be calculated and given effect, . . . they say not a word about costs. . . . The text of §109(b), interpreted in its statutory and historical context and with appreciation for its importance to the CAA as a whole, unambiguously bars cost considerations from the NAAQS-setting process. . . . We therefore affirm the judgment of the Court of Appeals on this point. . . .

Section 109(b)(1) of the CAA, which to repeat, we interpret as requiring the EPA to set air quality standards at the level that is 'requisite'—that is, not lower or higher than is necessary—to protect the public health with an adequate margin of safety, fits comfortably within the scope of discretion permitted by our precedent. We therefore reverse the judgment of the Court of Appeals remanding for reinterpretation that would avoid a supposed delegation of legislative power. . . . The final two issues . . . concern the EPA's authority to implement the revised ozone NAAQS in areas whose ozone levels currently exceed the maximum level permitted by that standard. The CAA designates such areas as "nonattainment," . . . and it exposes them to additional restrictions over and above the implementation requirements imposed generally by §110 of the CAA. These additional restrictions are found in the five substantive subparts of Part D of Title I. Subpart 1 . . . contains general nonattainment regulations that pertain to every pollutant for which a NAAQS exists. Subparts 2 through 5 . . . contain rules tailored to specific individual pollutants. Subpart 2, added by the Clean Air Act Amendments of 1990, . . . addresses ozone. . . . The dispute before us here, in a nutshell, is whether Subpart 1 alone (as the agency determined), or rather Subpart 2 or some combination of Subparts 1 and 2, controls the implementation of the revised ozone NAAQS in nonattainment areas. . . . Respondents argued below that the EPA could not revise the ozone standard, because to do so would trigger the use of Subpart 1, which had been supplanted (for ozone) by the specific rules of Subpart 2. The EPA responded that Subpart 2 did not supplant but simply supplemented Subpart 1, so that the latter section still "applies to all nonattainment areas for all NAAQS, . . .

including nonattainment areas for any revised ozone standard." In other words, the EPA was arguing that the revised standard could be issued, despite its apparent incompatibility with portions of Subpart 2, *because it would be implemented under Subpart 1 rather than Subpart 2.* It is unreasonable to contend, as the EPA now does, that the Court of Appeals was obligated to reach the agency's preferred result, but forbidden to assess the reasons the EPA had given for reaching that result. The implementation issue was fairly included within the respondents' challenge to the ozone rule, which all parties agree is final agency action ripe for review. Our approach to the merits of the parties' dispute is the familiar one of *Chevron U.S.A. Inc. v. Natural Resources Defense Council, Inc.* . . . If the statute resolves the question whether Subpart 1 or Subpart 2 (or some combination of the two) shall apply to revised ozone NAAQS, then "that is the end of the matter." . . . But if the statute is "silent or ambiguous" with respect to the issue, then we must defer to a "reasonable interpretation made by the administrator of an agency." . . . We cannot agree with the Court of Appeals that Subpart 2 clearly controls the implementation of revised ozone NAAQS . . . because the statute [is] to some extent ambiguous. . . . [For the agency to] use a few apparent gaps in Subpart 2 to render its textually explicit applicability to nonattainment areas under the new standard utterly inoperative is to go over the edge of reasonable interpretation. The EPA may not construe the statute in a way that completely nullifies textually applicable provisions meant to limit its discretion. . . . We therefore find the EPA's implementation policy to be unlawful, though not in the precise respect determined by the Court of Appeals. After our remand, and the Court of Appeals' final disposition of this case, it is left to the EPA to develop a reasonable interpretation of the nonattainment implementation provisions insofar as they apply to revised ozone NAAQS. . . . .

BUSINESS CONSIDERATIONS Justice Thomas, in a concurring opinion, wondered whether on a future day (the parties had not raised this issue), the Court might wish to ask itself if the legislature had delegated too much power to administrative agencies. Do administrative agencies have too much authority over U.S. firms?

ETHICAL CONSIDERATIONS Does a purely ethical approach to air pollution mandate adherence to a "zero-tolerance" policy? Is it ethical for society to be expected to pay for the "spillover" costs of pollution not borne by the polluter?

the Water Quality Act of 1965, and the 1970 Water Quality Improvements Act.

Congress in the Clean Water Act set as the primary aim of this legislation the restoration and maintenance of the chemical, physical, and biological integrity of the nation's waters as well as national goals for the achievement of this objective. These goals include, within certain timetables, the elimination of discharges of pollutants into navigable rivers; the elimination of the discharge of toxic pollutants in toxic amounts; water quality sufficient to protect fish, shellfish, and wildlife and to provide recreation in and on the water; federal assistance for the construction of publicly owned waste treatment works; the development and implementation of (1) areawide waste treatment management planning procedures designed to control pollutants at their sources in each state and (2) programs to control point and nonpoint sources of pollution; and research efforts aimed at developing the technology necessary to eliminate the discharge of pollutants into the nation's navigable waters, the waters of the continental shelf, and the oceans.

Under the Clean Water Act, the federal role regarding water policy takes precedence over the states' role, since the administrator of the EPA, in cooperation with the appropriate federal and state agencies, has the responsibility for developing comprehensive programs for preventing, reducing, and eliminating water pollution. For example, the Clean Water Act prohibits discharges into navigable waters unless one has a permit to do so. Subsequent EPA regulations and court decisions under the commerce clause make it clear that the term *water* encompasses all waters used in foreign or interstate commerce: rivers, territorial seas, wetlands, interstate lakes, streams, and ponds. The states, by enforcing the federally mandated standards in a manner much like that previously discussed under the Clean Air Act, augment this extensive federal regime. Each state must submit a plan describing how it intends to implement water quality standards applicable to interstate waters and meet the effluent limitation guidelines promulgated by the EPA administrator (the term "effluent" pertains to the outflow of materials).

The Clean Water Act targets two areas for pollution control and regulation: point sources, such as pipes, ditches, channels, wells, animal feeding operations, or floating vessels that emit water pollutants; and nonpoint sources, such as farms and other agricultural activities, forest lands, mining, and forestry. Congress and the EPA view effluent limitations and ambient water control standards, in conjunction with a permit program, as a technology-based means of eliminating most pollution from point sources. The onus is on the polluter to choose abatement procedures—even costly ones—designed to eliminate water pollution at the source of its discharge. However, Congress and the EPA see technology as having fewer beneficial effects on pollution from nonpoint sources.

Although this view is debatable, the fact that Congress makes distinctions in this fashion has significant legal implications: Point sources must comply with the applicable effluent limitations and must obtain—and satisfy—any and all relevant permits. Nonpoint sources remain exempt from both requirements, although they do have to comply with applicable state management programs.

The Clean Water Act attempts, on a case-by-case basis, to resolve questions about whether the point source designation applies to a given polluter. But the act itself sets out three mechanisms for regulating discharges from point sources: effluent limitations (EL), water quality standards (WQS), and pollution discharge permits issued pursuant to the national pollutant discharge elimination system (NPDES) permit program.

Effluent Limitations The first of these, EL, involve industry-specific restrictions on the number of pounds of a given pollutant that a given point source can discharge per day or per week into navigable waters. The Clean Water Act mandates the use of technology to reduce the quantities, rates, and concentrations of the chemical and biological effluent released from point sources and has as its ultimate goal the complete eradication of such industrial pollutants. The allowable EL depend on the industrial processes utilized in a given industry, the available technology, and cost factors.

Water Quality Standards In contrast to EL, WQS derive from the designated uses of the navigable waters involved (for example, fish and wildlife propagation, recreation, agriculture, or industry), as well as their use and value for navigation. The Clean Water Act gives the EPA authority to oversee the states' development of minimum ambient standards for particular lakes, rivers, and streams. Then, once a state achieves its desired water standards, the state must comply with EPA-mandated antidegradation standards that ensure the state's continued maintenance of these desired WQS.

Prior to 1972, pursuant to the FWPCA, federal water pollution control efforts centered on these state WQS plans and had as their goal the elimination of pollutant discharges into all navigable bodies of water by 1985. Enforcement remained problematic, however, because authorities could not act on a given discharge until the pollution had lowered the quality of the affected water below the water's specified ambient level. Enforcement also faltered when multiple polluters had discharged effluent into the same body of water, since it was hard to prove the contribution each had made to lowering the specified ambient levels of the entire body of water.

The 1972 amendments illustrate Congress's intent to use EL as the main supplement to the ambient water standards and, therefore, the primary weapon for controlling point source–generated pollution. These amendments reserve the application of WQS to those situations wherein compliance with the applicable EL nevertheless may interfere with the maintenance of water quality in certain areas.

National Pollutant Discharge Elimination System

The NPDES program, however, by forcing each point-source polluter to obtain a permit, forms the linchpin of these federal antipollution efforts. To obtain a permit, a given point source (other than publicly owned wastewater works) must comply with the EL by using within a certain time frame (but no later than 1977) the "best practicable control technology available" (BPT) as defined by the EPA administrator. Point sources that discharge nonconventional pollutants, such as ammonia, chlorine, or iron, are subject to a phased-in timetable and the standards of "best available control technology economically achievable" (BAT) by 1983. The EL for conventional pollutants, such as suspended solids like oil or grease and fecal coliform, must achieve the standard known as "best conventional control technology" (BCT). For discharges of heat from point sources, the 1972 amendments allow a unique variance system designed to ensure the elimination of pollution and the propagation of a balanced, indigenous population of shellfish, fish, and wildlife. These amendments also establish "pretreatment standards" that industrial facilities discharging into municipal wastewater treatment systems must meet to preclude them from evading the NPDES permit program and discharging effluent directly into city sewers. Publicly owned treatment works (POTWs), that is, municipal wastewater treatment facilities, by 1977 must meet the secondary treatment standards or the even more stringent EL needed to ensure WQS. Both BPT and BAT allow those setting the EL to take into account cost considerations when they compute the degree of effluent reduction attainable under either standard, although BAT standards take cost into account to a lesser degree.

The 1972 amendments leave enforcement primarily to the states but allow a variety of federal enforcement mechanisms as well. In permitting citizens to bring lawsuits to enforce the EL set out in state or federal permits or to enforce EPA orders, the 1972 amendments appreciably strengthened the FWPCA.

Just as Congress had amended the Clean Air Act in 1977, so, too, Congress amended the FWPCA that same year. As mentioned earlier, besides renaming the act, the 1977 amendments authorize the EPA to grant some extensions of the 1977 BPT deadlines on a case-by-case basis. The 1977 amendments also apply the BCT standard to conventional pollutants and therefore replace the BAT standard for all pollutants except toxic and nonconventional ones.

The 1977 amendments reflect an especially stringent approach to toxic pollutants—those that, if ingested, inhaled, or assimilated, can cause death, disease, cancer, physical deformity, behavioral abnormality, or genetic mutation. The Clean Water Act requires the administrator of the EPA to publish a list of toxic pollutants, including asbestos, arsenic, copper, cyanide, lead, mercury, polychlorinated biphenyls (PCBs), and vinyl chloride, and, by July 1, 1984, to establish industry-specific EL that reflect the BAT. Under applicable law, the administrator even can establish a zero tolerance for certain EL if the EPA deems such actions necessary to provide an ample margin of safety or to attain the applicable WQS. Moreover, the cost-benefit analysis that the EPA can consider in establishing EL for conventional pollutants is not available to the agency when it sets EL reflecting the BAT for toxic and nonconventional pollutants.

In the Water Quality Act of 1987, Congress amended the Clean Water Act so as to extend the compliance deadlines for toxic pollutants to 1989 and for some secondary treatment plants to 1988. These amendments also tried to maintain WQS by requiring the states to identify the navigable bodies of waters within the state that, without additional action to control nonpoint sources of pollution (for example, runoffs from agricultural or urban uses), cannot reasonably be expected to attain or maintain applicable WQS. The states then must set up a management program and schedules for implementing the best management practices to control pollution emanating from nonpoint sources to the navigable waters within the state and to improve the quality of such waters.

The NPDES, then, is the vehicle by which the EPA—or the state—can issue permits to any discharger of any pollutant on the condition that the individual discharger agrees to abide by all EL and other pollution standards within a certain time period. Those denied an NPDES permit by the EPA can seek court review in a U.S. circuit court of appeals, as can those whose application permits issued under a state program have been vetoed by the EPA. Variances under the NPDES permit program are possible for those facilities that show that they fundamentally differed with respect to the factors considered by the administrator when he or she established the EL applicable to those facilities and that the alternative requirement (variance) will not result in a non-water quality environmental impact markedly more adverse than the impact considered by the EPA administrator in establishing the national EL at issue.

In response to the oil spill caused by the wreck of the *Exxon Valdez* in 1989, Congress passed the Oil Pollution Act of 1990. Although it amends the Clean Water Act, the act is modeled after CERCLA, a statute we will discuss later, in that it sets up a comprehensive system for removing oil spills caused by vessels or offshore facilities and a trust fund approach for paying the costs and damages from all such spills.

Negligent violations of the Clean Water Act can subject violators to a maximum fine of $25,000 per day of violation and/or one year's imprisonment. Knowing violations increase the possible fines to a maximum of $50,000 per day of violation and/or three years' imprisonment. With some exemptions, an individual who knowingly violates the act and thereby endangers another shall, upon conviction, face fines of not more than $250,000 and/or 15 years' imprisonment. Organizations convicted of such violations may face fines of $1,000,000. The administrator of the EPA can set civil fines of $25,000 per day of violation but in setting these fines can take into consideration the factors mentioned in the Clean Air Act's civil enforcement provisions. Administrative penalties vary, depending on the type of violation: a maximum of $10,000 per violation and a maximum aggregate amount ranging from $25,000 to $125,000. The citizens' suit provisions and awards are similar to those set out in the Clean Air Act.

In 1999, the Clinton administration dedicated $645 million to its "Clean Water Action Plan," whereby the EPA will spearhead a far-reaching new initiative to clean up U.S. rivers, lakes, and coastal waters. Among other things, this program increases the grants given to states for the implementation of water quality improvement projects and places a high priority on efforts aimed at restoring and protecting the national wetlands. The EPA Web site for the Clean Water Act is at http://www.epa.gov/region5/water/cwa.htm.

In *Friends of the Earth, Inc. v. Laidlaw Environmental Services (TOC), Inc.*, the Supreme Court clarified the issues of standing and mootness in environmental cases.

39.2

FRIENDS OF THE EARTH, INC. v. LAIDLAW ENVIRONMENTAL SERVICES (TOC), INC.
528 U.S. 167 (2000)

FACTS Laidlaw Environmental Services (TOC), Inc., bought a facility in Roebuck, South Carolina, that included a wastewater treatment plant. Shortly thereafter, the South Carolina Department of Health and Environmental Control (DHEC), acting under the Clean Water Act, granted Laidlaw a National Pollutant Discharge Elimination System (NPDES) permit. The permit authorized Laidlaw to discharge treated water into the North Tyger River but limited, among other things, the discharge of pollutants into the waterway. Laidlaw began to discharge various pollutants, including mercury, an extremely toxic pollutant, into the waterway repeatedly (on 489 occasions between 1987 and 1995), thereby exceeding the limits set by the permit.

On April 10, 1992, Friends of the Earth (FOE) and other environmental groups notified Laidlaw of their intention to file a citizen suit against it under the act, after the expiration of the requisite 60-day notice period. On the last day before FOE's 60-day notice period expired, DHEC and Laidlaw reached a settlement requiring Laidlaw to pay $100,000 in civil penalties and to make "every effort" to comply with its permit obligations. After FOE initiated this suit, but before the district court rendered judgment on January 22, 1997, Laidlaw violated the mercury discharge limitation in its permit 13 times and committed 13 monitoring and 10 reporting violations. In issuing its judgment, the district court found that Laidlaw had gained a total economic benefit of $1,092,581 as a result of its extended period of noncompliance with the permit's mercury discharge limit; nevertheless, the court concluded that a civil penalty of $405,800 was appropriate. In particular, the district court found that the judgment's "total deterrent effect" would be adequate to forestall future violations, given that Laidlaw would have to reimburse the plaintiffs for significant legal fees and that Laidlaw had itself incurred significant legal expenses. The court declined to order injunctive relief because Laidlaw, after the commencement of the lawsuit, had achieved substantial compliance with the terms of its permit. FOE appealed the amount of the district court's civil penalty judgment but did not appeal the denial of declaratory or injunctive relief. The Fourth Circuit, assuming, for the sake of argument, that FOE had initially had standing, held that the case had become moot once Laidlaw complied with the terms of its permit and the plaintiffs failed to appeal the denial of equitable relief. The court reasoned that the only remedy currently available to FOE, civil penalties payable to the government, would not redress any injury FOE had suffered. The court added that FOE's failure to obtain relief on the merits precluded the recovery of attorney's fees or costs because such an award is available only to a "prevailing or substantially prevailing party" under § 1365(d).

ISSUE Had the defendant's compliance with the environmental laws, effected after the commencement of the lawsuit, rendered FOE's citizen suit moot?

HOLDING No. FOE had standing to bring the lawsuit. FOE's claim for civil penalties did not automatically become moot once the company had come into substantial compliance with its permit.

REASONING Excerpts from the opinion of Justice Ginsburg:

Under § 505(a) of the Act [CWA], a suit to enforce any limitation in an NPDES permit may be brought by any "citizen," defined as "a person or persons having an interest which is or may be adversely affected." Sixty days before initiating a citizen suit, however, the would-be plaintiff must give notice of the alleged violation to the EPA, the State in which the alleged violation occurred, and the alleged violator.... "The purpose of notice to the alleged violator is to give it an opportunity to bring itself into complete compliance with the Act and thus . . . render unnecessary a citizen suit." ... Accordingly, ... citizens lack statutory standing under § 505(a) to sue for violations that have ceased by the time the complaint is filed.... The Act [CWA] also bars a citizen from suing if the EPA or the State has already commenced, and is "diligently prosecuting," an enforcement action....

The Act authorizes district courts in citizen-suit proceedings to enter injunctions and to assess civil penalties, which are payable to the United States Treasury. In determining the amount of any civil penalty, the district court must take into account "the seriousness of the violation or violations, the economic benefit (if any) resulting from the violation, any history of such violations, any good-faith efforts to comply with the applicable requirements, the economic impact of the penalty on the violator, and such other matters as justice may require." In addition, the court "may award the costs of litigation (including reasonable attorney and expert witness fees) to any prevailing or substantially prevailing party, whenever the court determines such award is appropriate." ... The Constitution's case-or-controversy limitation on federal judicial authority, Art. III, § 2, underpins both our standing and our mootness jurisprudence, but the two inquiries differ in respects

critical to the proper resolution of this case. Because the Court of Appeals was persuaded that the case had become moot and so held, it simply assumed without deciding that FOE had initial standing. But because we hold that the Court of Appeals erred in declaring the case moot, we have an obligation to assure ourselves that FOE had Article III standing at the outset of the litigation.... *Lujan* v. *Defenders of Wildlife*, ... held that, to satisfy Article III's standing requirements, a plaintiff must show (1) it has suffered an "injury in fact" that is (a) concrete and particularized and (b) actual or imminent, not conjectural or hypothetical; (2) the injury is fairly traceable to the challenged action of the defendant; and (3) it is likely, as opposed to merely speculative, that the injury will be redressed by a favorable decision. An association has standing to bring suit on behalf of its members when its members would otherwise have standing to sue in their own right, the interests at stake are germane to the organization's purpose, and neither the claim asserted nor the relief requested requires the participation of individual members in the lawsuit. . . . Laidlaw contends first that FOE lacked standing from the outset even to seek injunctive relief, because the plaintiff organizations failed to show that any of their members had sustained or faced the threat of any "injury in fact" from Laidlaw's activities. In support of this contention Laidlaw points to the District Court's finding, made in the course of setting the penalty amount, that there had been "no demonstrated proof of harm to the environment" from Laidlaw's mercury discharge violations.... The relevant showing for purposes of Article III standing, however, is not injury to the environment but injury to the plaintiff. . . . Focusing properly on injury to the plaintiff, the District Court found that FOE had demonstrated sufficient injury to establish standing.... [T]he affidavits and testimony presented by FOE in this case assert that Laidlaw's discharges, and the . . . members' reasonable concerns about the effects of those discharges, directly affected those affiants' recreational, aesthetic, and economic interests. These submissions present dispositively more than the mere "general averments" and "conclusory allegations" found inadequate in *National Wildlife Federation*. Laidlaw argues next that even if FOE had standing to seek injunctive relief, it lacked standing to seek civil penalties. . . . Civil penalties offer no redress to private plaintiffs, Laidlaw argues, because they are paid to the government, and therefore a citizen plaintiff can never have standing to seek them.... It can scarcely be doubted that, for a plaintiff who is injured or faces the threat of future injury due to illegal conduct ongoing at the time of suit, a sanction that effectively abates that conduct and prevents its recurrence provides a form of redress. Civil penalties can fit that description. To the extent that they encourage defendants to discontinue current violations and deter them from committing future ones, . . . [they] afford redress to citizen plaintiffs who are injured or threatened with injury as a consequence of ongoing unlawful conduct. . . . Here, the civil penalties sought by FOE carried with them a deterrent effect that made it likely, as opposed to merely speculative, that the penalties would redress FOE's injuries by abating current violations and preventing future ones—as the district court reasonably found when it assessed a penalty of $ 405,800. . . .

Satisfied that FOE had standing under Article III to bring this action, we turn to the question of mootness. The only conceivable basis for a finding of mootness in this case is Laidlaw's voluntary conduct—either its achievement by August 1992 of substantial compliance with its NPDES permit or its more recent shutdown of the Roebuck facility. It is well settled that "a defendant's voluntary cessation of a challenged practice does not deprive a federal court of its power to determine the legality of the practice." . . . In accordance with this principle, the standard we have announced for determining whether a case has been mooted by the defendant's voluntary conduct is stringent. . . . Standing doctrine functions to ensure, among other things, that the scarce resources of the federal courts are devoted to those disputes in which the parties have a concrete stake. In contrast, by the time mootness is an issue, the case has been brought and litigated, often (as here) for years. To abandon the case at an advanced stage may prove more wasteful than frugal. This argument from sunk costs does not license courts to retain jurisdiction over cases in which one or both of the parties plainly lacks a continuing interest. . . . But the argument surely highlights an important difference between the two doctrines. . . . In its brief, Laidlaw appears to argue that, regardless of the effect of Laidlaw's compliance, FOE doomed its own civil penalty claim to mootness by failing to appeal the district court's denial of injunctive relief . . . this argument misconceives the statutory scheme. . . . Denial of injunctive relief does not necessarily mean that the district court has concluded there is no prospect of future violations for civil penalties to deter. Indeed, it meant no such thing in this case. The district court denied injunctive relief, but expressly based its award of civil penalties on the need for deterrence. . . . In accordance with this aim, a district court in a Clean Water Act citizen suit properly may conclude that an injunction would be an excessively intrusive remedy, because it could entail continuing superintendence of the permit holder's activities by a federal court—a process burdensome to court and permit holder alike. Laidlaw also asserts, in a supplemental suggestion of mootness, that the closure of its Roebuck facility, which took place after the court of appeals issued its decision, mooted the case. . . . [Yet] FOE points out, for example—and Laidlaw does not appear to contest—that Laidlaw retains its NPDES permit. These issues have not been aired in the lower courts; they remain open for consideration on remand. . . . For the reasons stated, the judgment of the United States Court of Appeals for the Fourth Circuit is reversed, and the case is remanded for further proceedings consistent with this opinion.

BUSINESS CONSIDERATIONS Laidlaw continued to dump pollutants in the river on almost 500 occasions in an eight-year period. Presumably, it was not an environmentally oriented (or a so-called green) company. Had it desired to do so, how could Laidlaw have inculcated a corporate culture that valued environmental concerns? Is "being green" good for a business's "bottom line"? Explain.

ETHICAL CONSIDERATIONS Assume the Court had decided this case on ethical—as opposed to legal—grounds. Would the Court have arrived at the same decision?

Safe Drinking Water Act

As an adjunct to the Clean Water Act, the Safe Drinking Water Act (SDWA), enacted in 1974 and amended in 1986, regulates water supplied by public water systems to home taps. The passage of this legislation stems from congressional awareness of the contaminants that have seeped into groundwater supplies and *aquifers* and that have caused cancer and other serious diseases and organ damage. The more than 200 reported instances of illnesses caused by waterborne microorganisms and parasites—including an earlier outbreak involving the water supply in Milwaukee, Wisconsin, and more recent ones in Washington County, New York, and Clark County, Washington—underscore the seriousness of this problem. As a consequence, the EPA has reiterated publicly the two SDWA rules that address microbial contamination such as the *e. coli* illnesses linked to some of these outbreaks.[11]

Under SDWA, the EPA must promulgate national primary drinking water regulations (NPDWRs) that in turn set maximum contaminant levels (MCLs) or, alternatively, require specific treatment techniques designed to reduce contaminants to acceptable levels. By using the most economically and technologically feasible treatment techniques available, public water supply operators must try to meet these MCL standards or goals (where no adverse

NRW CASE 39.1   Manufacturing/Management

NRW

MINIMIZING LIABILITY FOR TOXIC SMOKE

One of the NRW manufacturing facilities has been spewing a great deal of smoke recently, thus causing some concern among the firm's principals that the location may be in violation of the Clean Air Act. An industrial engineer has analyzed the location and reported that the smoke consists of asbestos, vinyl chloride, and various other particulates that represent by-products of the production process for the NRW units. The firm wants to take steps to reduce the pollution emanating from the plant and thereby avoid any potential liability for violating environmental statutes. The principals ask you what they should do in this situation. What advice will you give them?

BUSINESS CONSIDERATIONS Should a business spend more money at the time of plant construction in order to be "ahead of the game" in pollution control and reduction, or should the firm be satisfied with meeting current environmental standards, even though it knows that these standards may change in the future? What factors would influence such a decision?

ETHICAL CONSIDERATIONS Is it ethical for a business to do less than it could do in the area of environmental protection if the business is meeting the existing legal requirements and industry standards? Is it ethical for a business, in order to be more environmentally protective, to exceed legal requirements and industry standards—at a cost to the shareholders?

INTERNATIONAL CONSIDERATIONS Many nations have less stringent environmental protection statutes than those in effect in the United States. Might a firm that knows it cannot operate without producing significant air pollution want to relocate to one of these other nations? What risks might arise from such a decision?

effects on health occur). Variances from these NPDWRs are possible under certain circumstances. The 1986 amendments require the EPA to take more aggressive action to establish standards for 83 specific contaminants, to promulgate a national priority list of known contaminants, and to establish MCL goals and NPDWRs for at least 25 of the contaminants on this list. The 1996 amendments, among other things, for the first time develop a risk-based method to identify drinking water contaminants that could pose a threat to human health.

The 1996 amendments, in addition, require the EPA to publish, by February 6, 1998, a list of contaminants that are known or anticipated to occur in public water systems and may require regulation. An additional list of such contaminants must be published every five years thereafter. Moreover, the amended law requires the EPA to determine every five years whether to regulate at least five of the listed contaminants. Under these amendments, the EPA, when identifying these contaminants, must take into account their danger to sensitive populations such as infants, children, pregnant women, the elderly, and people with illnesses. In its identification method, the EPA will consider factors such as the potential adverse health effects, information on concentrations in drinking water supplies, human exposure via drinking water and other sources, and data uncertainty. This approach will be used to identify and classify contaminants that are not currently regulated and to reevaluate already regulated contaminants. Because microbial contaminants pose unique challenges, the EPA will use a similar but separate approach for their identification. As of 1999, SDWA regulated about 83 contaminants.[12] Beginning January 1, 2000, the EPA will require large systems—those that serve over 10,000 people—to monitor their systems for 12 contaminants that the EPA anticipates will occur, as well as for the targeted 36 unregulated contaminants for which the EPA has established approved test methods.[13] The EPA estimates the cost of such monitoring programs at nearly $40 million over the five-year period, 2000–2004.[14]

States may have primary enforcement responsibilities under SDWA if they have adopted drinking water regulations no less stringent than the national standards and if they have implemented adequate monitoring, inspection, recordkeeping, and enforcement procedures. If the EPA has primary responsibility, the enforcement provisions of the act resemble those under the Resource Conservation and Recovery Act (RCRA) discussed later in this chapter.

Noise Pollution

Noise Control Act of 1972

Probably owing to the fact that noise seems less noxious to us than filthy water or sulfurous-smelling air, Congress did not address the issue of noise until 1972 when it passed the federal Noise Control Act. Prior to that time, litigants seeking remedies to limit the increasingly higher decibel levels caused by post–World War II urbanization and mechanization relied on common law nuisance theories.

MINIMIZING LIABILITY FOR WATER POLLUTION

The firm has just learned that one of its facilities is discharging effluents into the local drainage system and that this system drains into the community's primary water reservoir. The effluents from this particular facility contain contaminant concentrations that frequently exceed the standards for the community. The firm members desire to avoid any legal problems or liabilities, and they also want to ensure that they refrain from harming the community. They ask you what they should do. What will you tell them?

BUSINESS CONSIDERATIONS Should a business attempt to work with local government officials to reduce pollution, or should the business "go it alone" in an effort to act in the most efficient manner possible? Why might working with the local government be advisable? Why might such an approach be unhelpful?

ETHICAL CONSIDERATIONS Is it more ethical for a firm to reveal that it has been polluting, but is taking steps to stop its polluting activities, or for a firm to attempt to hide past pollution, while at the same time it is working to reduce or eliminate pollution in the future? Explain your response.

INTERNATIONAL CONSIDERATIONS What provisions for preventing water pollution exist in the member nations of NAFTA? Do these provisions adequately protect the three nations' shared waterways?

Compared to many of the other statutes discussed in this chapter, this act is simple and straightforward. Recognizing the noise generated by transportation vehicles and equipment, machinery, and appliances as a growing danger to the health and welfare of U.S. citizens—particularly those residing in urban areas—Congress placed the primary responsibility for controlling such noise on state and local governments. However, Congress expressly noted that federal oversight and action are necessary for noise sources in commerce when control of such sources will require uniform national treatment. Hence, the statute preempts the states' regulation of emissions standards for major noise sources such as construction equipment, transportation equipment, motors or engines, and electrical equipment. For these sources, the EPA must promulgate regulations that are necessary to protect the public health and welfare with an adequate margin of safety. The EPA also has the power to fashion regulations for any nonmajor product for which noise emissions standards are feasible and requisite to protect the public health and welfare. To coordinate federal noise control policies, this legislation empowers the EPA to file status reports concerning all federal agencies' noise research and noise control programs, to enforce the labeling of products (including imported ones) as to the level of noise emitted by the products, and to prohibit the removal of noise control devices.

The 1978 amendments, called the Quiet Communities Act, reinforce the significant role that state and local governments play in noise control. The amendments provide federal financial and technical assistance aimed at facilitating state and local research related to noise control and developing noise abatement plans. Similar to the remedies we have seen in other statutes, civil and criminal penalties are possible for violations of the Noise Control Act, as are citizens' suits.

Land Conservation and Pollution

The protection and preservation of land constitute the most obvious areas of federal environmental regulation. As early as the presidency of Theodore Roosevelt, concern for protecting the environment and preserving America's natural resources surfaced in the United States. Land that is open to public use, called the public domain, consists in particular of land owned and/or controlled by the federal government, today comprises nearly 677 million acres. Hence, federally controlled land, national parks, and wildlife refuges occupy about as much land as the subcontinent of India does. In addition to the federal regulation and control of federal lands, a number of federal statutes regulate private land. The following sections discuss some of the most significant of these regulations.

The Toxic Substances Control Act

The Toxic Substances Control Act (TSCA) passed by Congress in 1976 represents the first statutory enactment that comprehensively addresses toxic chemicals and their impact on health and the environment. Congress passed this law for three reasons: (1) to develop data detailing the effect of chemical substances and mixtures on health and the environment by those who manufacture and process such chemicals (that is, industry); (2) to provide adequate governmental authority to regulate chemicals that present an unreasonable risk of injury to health or the environment and to take steps with regard to those chemicals that are imminent hazards; and (3) to ensure the exercise of this governmental authority so as to avoid impediments or unnecessary economic barriers to technological innovation while at the same time to fulfilling the primary purpose of TSCA—avoiding unreasonable risk of injury to health or the environment.

Like NEPA, then, it focuses on risk assessment. But note that TSCA, by giving authority to the EPA to regulate chemicals even before they come onto the market, screens pollutants before humans and the environment are exposed. The TSCA also permits the government to consider the sum total of the health and environmental hazards caused by a given chemical or mixture.

Despite these lofty purposes, the legislative history of TSCA shows that Congress chose not to seek a risk-free environment. Granted, Congress requires the administrator of the EPA, after he or she receives notice of the proposed manufacture of any new substances, to subject these chemical substances and mixtures to testing and thereby ensure the development of test data by manufacturers. TSCA similarly mandates premanufacture notifications for such substances and the regulation of the postmanufacturing distribution of the chemicals.

Yet Congress, by requiring the EPA to test and regulate only those chemicals that pose an "unreasonable risk" of injury to health or the environment, has given the EPA a great deal of discretion. This includes consideration of the relative costs of the various test protocols and methodologies that firms, in order to perform the required testing, may need to utilize. In actual practice, the EPA has taken a lax view toward what it will require of companies that provide test data. Similarly, although the EPA can choose among several options, including prohibiting the manufacturing, processing, or distributing of any substance that poses an unreasonable risk, the statute directs the EPA, in arriving at its decision, to use the least burdensome requirements. As a consequence, the EPA has stopped the manufacture and/or distribution of only a minuscule number of chemical substances.

Nevertheless, the statute authorizes the EPA to regulate *imminent hazards*—those that present imminent and unreasonable risks of widespread injury to health or the environment—through emergency judicial relief leading to an injunction and/or seizure of the chemicals or substances. A special section of TSCA sets out a timetable for phasing out the manufacture of PCBs. Other provisions allow for civil and criminal penalties and carry over the citizens' lawsuit provisions set out in other acts.

For information about TSCA's programmatic review of new chemicals, access http://www.epa.gov/opptintr/newchems/accomplishments.htm.

The Federal Insecticide, Fungicide, and Rodenticide Act

Given the importance of agriculture in our country's history, it is no surprise that Congress passed a federal Insecticide Act in 1910. Surprisingly, this act was aimed at protecting farmers from becoming victims of unsavory and fraudulent marketing practices rather than at protecting the environment.

In 1947, owing to the proliferation of pesticides and insecticides, Congress responded to those newly emerging, but as yet embryonic, environmental concerns when it passed the Federal Insecticide, Fungicide, and Rodenticide Act (FIFRA). This early version of FIFRA mandated the registration of "economic poisons [pesticides] involved in interstate commerce and the inclusion of labels, warnings, and instructions on such pesticides." The 1962 publication of Rachel Carson's *Silent Spring*, which cataloged the environmental risks and dangers created by pesticides, insecticides, and herbicides, in conjunction with litigation based on the use and sale of DDT, prodded Congress into action.

In 1970, the newly established EPA became responsible for the enforcement of FIFRA, and, in 1972, Congress passed the Federal Environmental Pesticide Control Act (FEPCA). FEPCA, in amending FIFRA, changes FIFRA's focus from labeling to concerns for the environment. Under FIFRA as amended, all persons who distribute or sell pesticides must register them with the EPA. The EPA will register a pesticide if the administrator determines that the pesticide, when used in accordance with widespread and common practice, will not generally cause unreasonable adverse effects on the environment. The EPA can register any approved pesticide for general use, restricted use (for example, by exterminators), or both. The EPA subsequently can cancel the registration of any pesticide that fails to live up to this standard and can suspend a registration whenever such action is necessary to prevent an imminent hazard.

Although, like NEPA and TSCA, FIFRA is at heart a risk-assessment statute, the 1975 and 1978 amendments make it clear that in determining "unreasonable adverse effects on the environment" the EPA must take into account the benefits, as well as the costs, associated with the use of the pesticide. It is possible, then, for the EPA to register an economically beneficial pesticide even though it might pose harm to health or the environment.

FIFRA sets out several types of unlawful acts, all of which, in general, involve the sale of unregistered or mislabeled pesticides. It also authorizes "stop sale" and/or seizure orders by the EPA. Furthermore, civil and criminal penalties are available under the act.

Despite the fact that applicants must provide data in support of any application, the EPA has been able to assure the safety of only a handful of the 50,000 pesticides currently on the market. Similarly, the EPA has canceled or suspended the registration of only a few pesticides—for example, DDT, kepone, and chlordane. In part to appease the critics who had advocated amendments to FIFRA that would address these issues, Congress enacted the Food Quality Protection Act of 1996 (FQPA). FQPA mandates more stringent health standards for the EPA's pesticide reviews so as to ensure the wholesomeness of the American food supply and in particular to protect children from the health threats posed by pesticide residues. Reducing young children's exposure to lead constitutes another dimension of the EPA's initiatives in this regard. Pursuant to its oversight, the EPA will remove harmful pesticides from the market or restrict the uses of each pesticide and thereby minimize dietary exposure to such potentially toxic substances. The 2004 EPA budget request accordingly provides $150 million to be used in support of FQPA. Part of these efforts will center as well on strengthening the homeland security activities related to the identification of antimicrobials that could counter the effects of the potential bio-agents that terrorists could unleash against the United States.

The Resource Conservation and Recovery Act

Another act passed in 1976, the Resource Conservation and Recovery Act (RCRA), is a broader statute than TSCA and FIFRA. RCRA encompasses all types of waste, including hazardous and toxic waste and waste generated by households across the country. The predecessors of RCRA include the Solid Waste Disposal Act of 1965 and the Resource Recovery Act of 1970. RCRA, a more comprehensive statute, stemmed from congressional awareness of the environmental problems posed by the generation and disposal of wastes of all types.

Although oftentimes referred to as solid waste, waste actually takes the form of liquids, gases, sludges, and semisolids as well. All of us undoubtedly recognize the complexities associated with the disposal of the billions of tons of household waste generated annually. At some point, virtually everything we buy ends up in a landfill or at some other type of disposal site. The pollution control efforts that we already have studied—emissions and wastewater sludge, for example—ironically also create waste. Moreover, the characteristics of such waste have changed over the years. The toxic substances considered earlier add yet another dimen-

sion to the waste disposal calculus. In short, we presently are paying the price for decades of dumping solid waste on land. We also are running out of room for land-based disposal sites; few communities, owing to fears of groundwater contamination, want to accept other states' waste.

RCRA indicates Congress's understanding that it may no longer view waste disposal as a purely state or local problem. Rather, Congress sees waste disposal as national in scope and concern and, therefore, worthy of federal assistance in the development and application of new and improved methods of waste reduction and disposal practices as well as potential new energy sources. As yet another technology-forcing statute, RCRA therefore clothes the EPA with the power to regulate nonhazardous solid waste and to oversee the management and disposal of hazardous waste.

With regard to nonhazardous solid waste, RCRA provides federal technical and financial assistance to states that voluntarily develop environmentally sound methods of solid waste disposal, including recycling. These state management plans, which resemble the SIPs discussed under the Clean Air Act, must follow EPA guidelines and, among other things, protect ground and surface water from contamination brought on by leachings (oozing of water that contains soil, sediment, chemicals; and other impurities) and runoffs. Any approved state plan must distinguish between sanitary landfills and open dumps; the latter must be closed or upgraded to eliminate health hazards and minimize potential health hazards.

By making lawful only dumping into a solid waste facility that complies with the EPA's criteria for a sanitary landfill, Congress apparently intends to abolish open dumping, even in states that do not develop a state solid waste management program. RCRA also obligates the EPA to publish the names of all the open dump sites in the United States. This public list presumably will spur states to take action to eliminate the environmental and health hazards associated with these sites and encourage citizens' suits.

The EPA's powers to regulate hazardous waste under RCRA far exceed its powers over nonhazardous solid waste. Adopting what one court has called "cradle-to-grave" regulation, the EPA sets out stringent standards covering those who own or operate treatment, storage, or disposal facilities (TSDFs). Such persons or entities must obtain permits issued by the EPA or the states authorized to issue such permits. RCRA mandates that the EPA identify and list hazardous waste (that is, solid waste that, among other things, can cause or significantly contribute to an increase in serious irreversible illness or pose a substantial present or potential threat to the environment) on the basis of several criteria: toxicity, persistence, degradability in its nature, potential for accumulation in tissue, and other related factors such as flammability or corrosiveness. (Interestingly, RCRA excludes nuclear waste from its coverage.) EPA regulations thus list certain chemicals, each identified by so-called EPA hazardous waste numbers.

The EPA, aided by the permit, recordkeeping, labeling, container usage, and report provisions of RCRA, relies on a manifest system to track hazardous waste from the cradle to the grave and to ensure that everyone from the generator of the waste, through the transporter, and to the operator of the disposal facility meets and maintains the applicable federal regulatory standards. Since the 1984 amendments to RCRA, even small generators of hazardous waste must supply this extensive documentation. By setting minimum technological requirements (for example, the provision of two or more liners and a leachate collection system) and groundwater monitoring for both new and existing sanitary landfills, these amendments also phase out land disposal of hazardous wastes. In addition, the 1984 amendments broadly regulate leaking underground storage tanks and, like CERCLA (discussed next), set up a federal trust to remediate leaks under certain circumstances. In 1989, Congress initiated in certain northeastern and midwestern states a demonstration program for tracking the disposal of medical waste products.

Like the Clean Air Act and the Clean Water Act, the permit system established under RCRA provides the EPA with broad enforcement powers. Civil and criminal penalties are available for violations of RCRA, as are citizens' suits. Furthermore, under RCRA, the EPA can seek injunctive relief if the handling, transport, storage, or disposal of solid or hazardous waste presents an imminent and substantial endangerment to health or the environment. The 1984 RCRA amendments extend the coverage of this provision even to past or present generators, transporters, or operators who have contributed or are contributing to an activity that presents such an imminent danger. Subsequent court decisions have construed this as a strict liability provision akin to its counterpart in CERCLA.

The Comprehensive Environmental Response, Compensation, and Liability Act

The Comprehensive Environmental Response, Compensation, and Liability Act (CERCLA), perhaps better known as the "Superfund," was passed in 1980. In this enactment, Congress meant to fill in the gaps left by TSCA and RCRA, neither of which had regulated hazardous waste disposal sites, as the infamous Love Canal disaster unfortunately all too aptly demonstrated.

CERCLA authorizes the administrator of the EPA to regulate "hazardous substances," including those deemed toxic or hazardous under the Clean Water Act, TSCA, or RCRA, which, when released into the environment, may present substantial danger to the public health or welfare, or the environment. The act specifically excludes petroleum and natural gas from the definition of hazardous substances.

Any owner or operator of a vessel or offshore or onshore facility engaged in the storage, treatment, or disposal of hazardous waste must notify the EPA of any release of hazardous materials. This notification aids the EPA's implementation of a national contingency plan (NCP), which, under CERCLA, establishes the procedures and standards for responding to releases of hazardous substances, pollutants, and contaminants and for setting priorities to deal with such substances. The act gives the president authority to undertake any response (including short-term emergency removal and long-term remedial actions) consistent with the NCP that he or she deems necessary to protect the public health or welfare or the environment. CERCLA also gives the government the injunctive or administrative authority to compel private parties to take steps to abate all imminent and substantial endangerment to the public health or welfare, or the environment, caused by the actual or threatened release of hazardous substances from a facility.

CERCLA imposes liability for all costs of removal or remedial action incurred by federal or state governments that are not inconsistent with the NCP; for all other necessary costs of any response incurred by any other person when such costs are consistent with the NCP; and damages to, or loss of, natural resources resulting from the release of hazardous substances.

Recent court decisions have construed this part of CERCLA as a strict liability standard that can result in joint and several liability among responsible generators, owners, operators, transporters, and so on, up to $50,000,000 in toto. For releases or threats of releases caused by willful misconduct or willful negligence, this limitation on liability does not apply. The statute itself sets out defenses to liability for releases or threats of releases caused by acts of God, acts of war, or by an act or omission of a third party who was not an agent or employee (for example, a third party's leachate runoffs). Innocent landowners also escape liability, but the burden of proof necessary to sustain this defense makes it virtually unusable.

In the following case, the Supreme Court provided some definitive guidance on the issue of who could face liability for hazardous waste in situations involving parent-subsidiary corporations. (This case also appears in Chapter 32, but the emphasis in that chapter is on the liability of a parent for conduct by a subsidiary.)

UNITED STATES v. BESTFOODS
524 U.S. 51 (1998)

FACTS In 1957, Ott Chemical Co. (Ott I) began manufacturing chemicals at a plant near Muskegon, Michigan. The firm's intentional and unintentional dumping of hazardous substances significantly polluted the soil and ground water at the site. In 1965, CPC International Inc. (CPC) incorporated a wholly owned subsidiary to buy Ott I's assets in exchange for CPC stock. The new company, also dubbed Ott Chemical Co. (Ott II), continued its chemical manufacturing operations and further polluted the surroundings. CPC retained the managers of Ott I, including its founder, president, and principal shareholder, Arnold Ott, as officers of Ott II. Arnold Ott and several other Ott II officers and directors also were given positions at CPC, and they performed duties for both corporations. In 1972, CPC sold Ott II to Story Chemical Company, which operated the Muskegon plant until its bankruptcy in 1977.

Shortly thereafter, the Michigan Department of Natural Resources (MDNR) examined the site for environmental damage and found the land littered with thousands of leaking and even exploding drums of waste, and the soil and water saturated with noxious chemicals. The MDNR subsequently sought a buyer who would be willing to contribute toward the property's cleanup; and after extensive negotiations, Aerojet-General Corp. in 1977 arranged for the transfer of the site from the Story bankruptcy trustee. To purchase the property, Aerojet created a wholly owned California subsidiary, Cordova Chemical Company (Cordova/California), and Cordova/California in turn created a wholly owned Michigan subsidiary, Cordova Chemical Company of Michigan (Cordova/Michigan), which manufactured chemicals at the site until 1986. By 1981, the federal EPA had undertaken to the cleanup of the site through a long-term remedial plan that called for expenditures well into the tens of millions of dollars. To recover some of that money, in 1989 the United States filed this action under § 107 of CERCLA and named five defendants as responsible parties: CPC (which later changed its name to Bestfoods), Aerojet, Cordova/California, Cordova/Michigan, and Arnold Ott. (By that time, Ott I and Ott II were defunct.) At the trial in the district court, the primary issue centered on whether CPC and Aerojet, as the parent companies of Ott II and the Cordova companies, had owned or operated the facility within the meaning of § 107(a)(2).

ISSUE Could parent corporations face liability under CERCLA for operating facilities ostensibly controlled by their subsidiaries?

HOLDING Yes. When (but only when) the corporate veil may be pierced, a parent corporation may be charged with derivative CERCLA liability for its subsidiary's actions in operating a polluting facility. Under the plain language of § 107(a)(2), any person who operates a polluting facility is directly liable for the costs of cleaning up the pollution, and this is so even if that person is the parent corporation of the facility's owner.

REASONING Excerpts from the opinion of Justice Souter:

It is a general principle of corporate law that a parent corporation (so-called because of control through ownership of another corporation's stock) is not liable for the acts of its subsidiaries. CERCLA does not purport to reject this bedrock principle, and the Government has indeed made no claim that a corporate parent is liable as an owner or an operator under § 107(a)(2) simply because its subsidiary owns or operates a polluting facility. But there is an equally fundamental principle of corporate law, applicable to the parent-subsidiary relationship as well as generally, that the corporate veil may be pierced and the shareholder held liable for the corporation's conduct when . . . the corporate form would otherwise be misused to accomplish certain wrongful purposes, most notably fraud, on the shareholder's behalf. CERCLA does not purport to rewrite this well-settled rule, either, and against this venerable common-law backdrop, the congressional silence is audible . . . . CERCLA's failure to speak to a matter as fundamental as the liability implications of corporate ownership demands application of the rule that, to abrogate a common-law principle, a statute must speak directly to the question addressed by the common law. . . .

The Court of Appeals was accordingly correct in holding that when (but only when) the corporate veil may be pierced, may a parent corporation be charged with derivative CERCLA liability for its subsidiary's actions. . . .

Under the plain language of the statute, any person who operates a polluting facility is directly liable for the costs of cleaning up the pollution. . . . This is so regardless of whether that person is the facility's owner, the owner's parent corporation or business partner, or even a saboteur who sneaks into the facility at night to discharge its poisons out of malice. If any such act of operating a corporate subsidiary's facility is done on behalf of a parent corporation, the existence of the parent-subsidiary relationship under state corporate law is simply irrelevant to the issue of direct liability. . . .

This much is easy to say; the difficulty comes in defining actions sufficient to constitute direct parental "operation." Here of course we may again rue the uselessness of CERCLA's definition of a facility's "operator" as "any person . . . operating" the facility . . . which leaves us to do the best we can to give the term its "ordinary or natural meaning." . . . In a mechanical sense, to "operate" ordinarily means "to control the functioning of; run. . . . So, under CERCLA, an operator is simply someone who directs the workings of, manages, or conducts the affairs of a facility. To sharpen the definition for purposes of CERCLA's concern with environmental contamination, an operator must manage, direct, or conduct operations specifically related to pollution, that is, operations having to do with the leakage or disposal of hazardous waste, or decisions about compliance with environmental regulations. With this understanding, we are satisfied that the Court of Appeals correctly rejected the District Court's analysis of direct liability. But we also think that the appeals court erred in limiting direct liability under the statute to a parent's sole or joint venture operation, so as to eliminate any possible finding that CPC is liable as an operator on the facts of this case. . . .

In addition to (and perhaps as a reflection of) the erroneous focus on the relationship between CPC and Ott II, even those findings of the District Court that might be taken to speak to the extent of CPC's activity at the facility itself are flawed, for the District Court wrongly assumed that the actions of the joint officers and directors are necessarily attributable to CPC. The District Court emphasized the facts that CPC placed its own high-level officials on Ott II's board of directors and in key management positions at Ott II, and that those individuals made major policy decisions and conducted day-to-day operations at the facility: "Although Ott II corporate officers set the day-to-day operating policies for the company without any need to obtain formal approval from CPC, CPC actively participated in this decision-making because high-ranking CPC officers served in Ott II management positions." . . .

In imposing direct liability on these grounds, the District Court failed to recognize that "it is entirely appropriate for directors of a parent corporation to serve as directors of its subsidiary, and that fact alone may not serve to expose the parent corporation to liability for its subsidiary's acts." . . . This recognition that the corporate personalities remain distinct has its corollary in the "well established principle [of corporate law] that directors and officers holding positions with a parent and its subsidiary can and do 'change hats' to represent the two corporations separately, despite their common ownership." . . . Since courts generally presume "that the directors are wearing their 'subsidiary hats' and not their 'parent hats' when acting for the subsidiary," . . . it cannot be enough to establish liability here that dual officers and directors made policy decisions and supervised activities at the facility. The Government would have to show that, despite the general presumption to the contrary, the officers and directors were acting in their capacities as CPC officers and directors, and not as Ott II officers and directors, when they committed those acts. The District Court made no such enquiry here, however, disregarding entirely this time-honored common law rule. . . .

We accordingly agree with the Court of Appeals that a participation-and-control test looking to the parent's supervision over the subsidiary, especially one that assumes that dual officers always act on behalf of the parent, cannot be used to identify operation of a facility resulting in direct parental liability. Nonetheless, a return to the ordinary meaning of the word "operate" in the organizational sense will indicate why we think that the Sixth Circuit stopped short when it confined its examples of direct parental operation to exclusive or joint ventures, and declined to find at least the possibility of direct operation by CPC in this case.

In our enquiry into the meaning Congress presumably had in mind when it used the verb "to operate," we recognized that the statute obviously meant something more than mere mechanical activation of pumps and valves, and must be read to contemplate "operation" as including the exercise of direction over the facility's activities. . . . The Court of Appeals recognized this by indicating that a parent can be held directly liable when the parent operates the facility in the stead of its subsidiary or alongside the subsidiary in some sort of a joint venture. . . . We anticipated a further possibility above, however, when we observed that a dual officer or director might depart so far from the norms of parental influence exercised through dual officeholding as to serve the parent, even when ostensibly acting on behalf of the subsidiary in operating the facility. . . . Yet another possibility, suggested by the facts of this case, is that an agent of the parent with no hat to wear but the parent's hat might manage or direct activities at the facility.

Identifying such an occurrence calls for line drawing yet again, since the acts of direct operation that give rise to parental liability must necessarily be distinguished from the interference that stems from the normal relationship between parent and subsidiary. Again norms of corporate behavior (undisturbed by any CERCLA provision) are crucial reference points. Just as we may look to such norms in identifying the limits of the presumption that a dual officeholder acts in his ostensible capacity, so here we may refer to them in distinguishing a parental officer's oversight of a subsidiary from such an officer's control over the operation of the subsidiary's facility....

The critical question is whether, in degree and detail, actions directed to the facility by an agent of the parent alone are eccentric under accepted norms of parental oversight of a subsidiary's facility.... There is, in fact, some evidence that CPC engaged in just this type and degree of activity at the Muskegon plant. The District Court's opinion speaks of an agent of CPC alone who played a conspicuous part in dealing with the toxic risks emanating from the operation of the plant. G.R.D. Williams worked only for CPC; he was not an employee, officer, or director of Ott II ... and thus, his actions were of necessity taken only on behalf of CPC. The District Court found that "CPC became directly involved in environmental and regulatory matters through the work of ... Williams, CPC's governmental and environmental affairs director. Williams ... became heavily involved in environmental issues at Ott II." ... He "actively partici-

pated in and exerted control over a variety of Ott II environmental matters," . . . and he "issued directives regarding Ott II's responses to regulatory inquiries," ... We think that these findings are enough to raise an issue of CPC's operation of the facility through Williams's actions, though we would draw no ultimate conclusion from these findings at this point. . . . Prudence thus counsels us to remand, on the theory of direct operation set out here, for reevaluation of Williams's role, and of the role of any other CPC agent who might be said to have had a part in operating the Muskegon facility....

BUSINESS CONSIDERATIONS Assume the CEO has asked you to study the *Bestfoods* case and to supply her with a draft policy that, when enacted, will govern the firm's relationship with its subsidiaries as to environmental matters. In preparing this draft, you will need to identify both the opportunities the Court's holding provides to the parent corporation for avoiding liability as well as the threats of vicarious or direct liability that might be imposed on the parent. What points will you include in this document?

ETHICAL CONSIDERATIONS Would the Supreme Court have arrived at a different decision if it had grounded its conclusions on ethics rather than the law? What ethical factors might have influenced the Court's decision?

To finance governmental cleanups and remedial actions in those situations in which the government cannot identify or find the parties responsible for the damage, CERCLA establishes a Hazardous Substance Superfund. The Superfund Amendments and Reauthorization Act of 1986 (SARA), an incredibly complex statute, among other things increased the fund from the $1.6 billion originally enacted to $8.5 billion through 1991. The authorization for general fund payments to the Superfund expired in 1995. Various excise taxes on petroleum and chemical feedstocks, appropriations from general revenues, and the costs recovered from responsible parties currently furnish the monies for the Superfund. The 2004 EPA budget authorized $1.1 billion for the Superfund.

To implement a cleanup plan, the EPA, using a scientific model, must place the site on the national priorities list of waste sites that present the greatest danger to the public health or welfare. When the EPA decides remedial action is appropriate for a given site, it notifies all "potentially responsible parties" (PRPs)—present and past owners or operators, including, since the passage of SARA, state and local governments; generators; and transporters.

If no defenses are available to the PRPs, the EPA, through feasibility studies, begins to negotiate with these parties in order to arrive at a settlement of the total costs. Since liability

is joint and several, the PRPs usually find it advisable to allocate financial responsibility among themselves and to present their settlement agreement to the EPA for its approval. Special statutory provisions cover settlements, which generally take the form of a consent decree or an administrative order setting forth the terms of the settlement.

Exhibit 39.1 summarizes the environmental acts and statutes—enacted from 1895 through 1996—that are discussed in this chapter.

Wildlife Conservation

The Endangered Species Act

The Endangered Species Act of 1973 (ESA) in § 7 states that each federal agency, in consultation with the secretary of the interior, must ensure that no agency action is likely to jeopardize the continued existence of an endangered or threatened species or result in the destruction or adverse modification of any critical habitat of such species. It is the world's first attempt to protect wildlife in a comprehensive manner so as to prevent the extinction of various animals and plants. Indeed, according to scientific estimates, the world loses approximately 100 species per day.[15]

EXHIBIT 39.1 Representative Environmental Statutes (1895–1996)

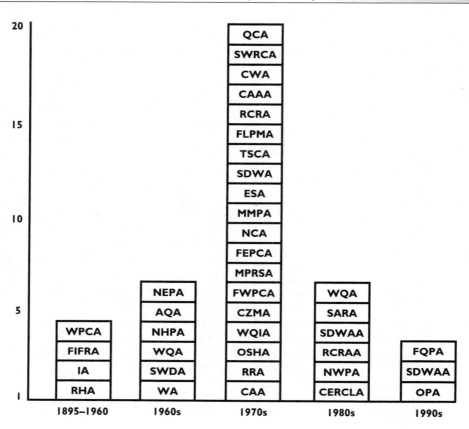

RHA	Rivers and Harbors Act (1899)
IA	Insecticide Act (1910)
FIFRA	Federal Insecticide, Fungicide, and Rodenticide Act (1947)
WPCA	Water Pollution Control Act (1948)
WA	Wilderness Act (1964)
SWDA	Solid Waste Disposal Act (1965)
WQA	Water Quality Act (1965)
NHPA	National Historic Preservation Act (1966)
AQA	Air Quality Act (1967)
NEPA	National Environmental Policy Act (1969)
CAA	Clean Air Act (1970)
RRA	Resource Recovery Act (1970)
OSHA	Occupational Safety and Health Act (1970)
WQIA	Water Quality Improvements Act (1970)
CZMA	Coastal Zone Management Act (1970)
FWPCA	Federal Water Pollution Control Act (1972)
MPRSA	Marine Protection, Research and Sanctuaries Act (1972)
FEPCA	Federal Environmental Pesticide Control Act (1972)
NCA	Noise Control Act (1972)
MMPA	Marine Mammal Protection Act (1972)
ESA	Endangered Species Act (1973)
SDWA	Safe Drinking Water Act (1974)
TSCA	Toxic Substances Control Act (1976)
FLPMA	Federal Land Policy and Management Act (1976)
RCRA	Resource Conservation and Recovery Act (1976)
CAAA	Clean Air Act Amendments (1977)
CWA	Clean Water Act (1977)
SWRCA	Soil and Water Resources Conservation Act (1977)
QCA	Quiet Communities Act (1978)
CERCLA	Comprehensive Environmental Response, Compensation, and Liability Act (1980)
NWPA	Nuclear Waste Policy Act (1982)
RCRAA	Resource Conservation and Recovery Act Amendments (1984)
SDWAA	Safe Drinking Water Act Amendments (1986)
SARA	Superfund Amendments and Reorganization Act (1986)
WQA	Water Quality Act (1987)
OPA	Oil Pollution Act (1990)
SDWAA	Safe Drinking Water Act Amendments (1996)
FQPA	Food Quality Protection Act (1996)

NRW CASE 39.3 Management/Ethics

PURCHASING A POSSIBLE WASTE SITE

Given the robustness of the sales of the firm's products, NRW is contemplating an expansion of its manufacturing facilities. Carlos has learned of a site that seems advantageous, in that it is close to the firm's present facility and the major interstate highway that runs nearby. When Carlos mentions this parcel of land, Helen reminds him that years ago a plastics plant was located there. She wonders whether the owners of that plant properly disposed of the vinyl chloride, phosgene gas, and other toxic chemicals used in the manufacture of plastics. Hence, she expresses some apprehensions about buying the property without checking out these issues. Brushing aside Helen's reservations, Carlos wants to move forward quickly. Just as he is about to make an offer on the real estate, he has second thoughts and calls you. How will you respond to Carlos's summary of Helen's concerns?

BUSINESS CONSIDERATIONS When a firm decides to purchase property, why should it concern itself with the possibility of earlier pollution on the site? Explain why such environmental issues should rank high or low on the firm's priorities as it contemplates the acquisition of a given property.

ETHICAL CONSIDERATIONS Is it ethical for a firm to ignore the possibility that a parcel of land is polluted and thus take a "wait-and-see" attitude regarding this possibility? Or will a firm that tries to emulate admirable ethics be more proactive in such circumstances?

INTERNATIONAL CONSIDERATIONS How do other nations handle the issue of solid waste disposal? Do nations with lax—or nonexistent—statutory coverage offset the gains made by countries that are attempting to provide safe environmental solutions in this area?

Since 1973, the Endangered Species Act has helped bring about stabilization or improvement of the conditions of 270 threatened or endangered species, including the national symbol of the United States, the bald eagle.[16] But its impact reaches beyond the borders of the United States because its prohibitions concerning the international trading of wildlife and its protection of the American habitats of migrating birds implicate transnational interests as well.

The national commitment to protecting species and their habitats invokes more than mere sentimentality or altruism—fully 40 percent of all ingredients in prescription medicines (including digitalis and penicillin) derive from plants, animals, and microorganisms.[17] The loss of a species therefore may involve the loss of the medicinal capacity to save thousands of lives.

The provisions of the Endangered Species Act that preserve genetic diversity help ensure blight- and disease-resistant plants.[18] The harm to wildlife represented by pesticides mirrors the preservation of healthy ecosystems mandated by the Clean Air Act and other statutes discussed in this chapter—clearly a vital national (and international) interest. In 1995, for example, recreational activities in the United States related to wildlife (hunting, fishing, hiking, and so on) totaled $50 billion.[19] Similarly, commercial and recreational fishing resulted in over 100,000 jobs.[20] However, a report issued by the EPA in 2002 noted that state assessments of water quality indicated that nearly 40 percent of rivers, 45 percent of lakes, and more than half of the estuaries were too polluted to support their designated uses, such as fishing and swimming.[21] The declining fish stocks in our nation's navigable waters, lakes, oceans, and contiguous waters and the attendant loss of gainful employment illustrate the economic dimensions of wildlife protection.

Celebrated cases under the Endangered Species Act wherein dam or road construction projects were halted to protect the habitat of fish or butterflies, for example, have led to public controversies of great magnitude. *Babbitt v. Sweet Home Chapter of Communities for a Great Oregon*, 515 U.S. 687 (1995) represents a recent landmark decision in this regard. The Secretary of the Interior defined "harm," as used in the Endangered Species Act, to include modifications to the habitat of wildlife when such modifications are likely to actually kill or injure wildlife. He then denied or refused several requests for permits based on this definition. Sweet Home, an organization made up of landowners, loggers, and their customers, challenged this definition, arguing that the secretary's definition was too broad, and that its implementation caused economic harm to the members of Sweet Home. The Supreme Court upheld the secretary's interpretation, noting that Congress had granted broad discretion to the secretary in this area. Note, too, how the Supreme Court, in disposing of this case, relied on *Chevron U.S.A. Inc. v. National Resources Defense Council, Inc.* as a leading precedent.

Some noted jurists have submitted that courts deciding environmental cases should accord standing to the trees, animals, and so forth involved in the litigation. Yet, as some recent cases show,[22] the constitutional requirement of having a case or controversy before the litigant will have standing to bring a lawsuit represents a formidable procedural obstacle to environmental interest groups seeking to block further development of land (for example, logging on U.S. Forest Service land). The doctrine of ripeness, which holds that the facts of a case must have developed sufficiently to permit the trier of fact to make an intelligent and useful decision, similarly is another procedural stumbling block that thwarts such pro-environmental efforts to challenge agency land and resource management plans.[23] Whether the Supreme Court continues to be receptive to disposing of such cases on these procedural grounds warrants your continued attention.

Enforcement and Remedies

In the last few years, the EPA has aggressively enforced environmental laws. During fiscal year 1998, the EPA brought a total of 2,782 enforcement actions, the second highest combined total in the agency's history.[24] These referrals included 677 criminal and civil cases that netted over $180 million in penalties and fines.[25] In contrast, a recent report indicates that in 2002, the first full year of the Bush administration, the EPA recovered only $51 million in civil fines, about half of what was collected on average in the last three years of the Clinton administration.[26] Cost recovery actions at Superfund sites and commitments made by responsible parties pursuant to Superfund cleanups annually return substantial amounts of money to governmental coffers as well. Enforcement of the environmental laws is "big business."

International Aspects

Environmental regulation is on the rise not only in the United States but around the world as well. While some European countries—Germany and the Netherlands, for example—have traditionally undertaken regulatory efforts that rival those of the United States, in many other countries environmental laws are nonexistent or at best embryonic. The environmental contamination and degradation found in post-Communist Eastern European countries, besides providing telling examples of what results from lax environmental standards, have discouraged much-needed privatization and foreign investments.

Realizing the need for environmental oversight and modeling its efforts on U.S. legislation, the European Union has adopted the Eco-audit Management and Audit Scheme (EMAS) Regulation that mandates environmental registers at each plant to catalog pollution emissions, land contamination, and the like; public disclosure of such environmental statements; and external verification of the company's environmental management system. Recently enacted environmental laws covering products now regulate product features (such as shape and recyclability), labeling, packaging, hazardous chemicals, and waste (its generation, transboundary shipment, etc.).[27] These laws also ban certain products such as asbestos, heavy metals, and vinyl chloride.

Such efforts are a harbinger of the future, since South American and Asian nations of necessity will soon recognize the need to enact environmental laws as well. Closer to home, the passage of the North American Free Trade Agreement (NAFTA), about which you learned in Chapter 3, also shows sensitivity to environmental concerns. A subsequent environmental side agreement between the United States and Mexico attempts to address the degradation of the environment along their border. In 1999, the EPA budgeted $396 million for reducing transboundary threats to human health and shared ecosystems (especially along the United States/Mexico border). The EPA's 2004 budgetary request for reducing global and cross-border environmental risks is more modest: $264 million. Part of the 1999 funds were used to implement the Montreal Protocol on Substances that Deplete the Ozone Layer, a treaty to which the United States is a signatory nation. Pursuant to this treaty, the EPA will establish and enforce rules aimed at controlling the production and emission of ozone-depleting compounds and identifying safer alternatives that curtail ozone depletion. Moreover, the trade talks occurring during the Uruguay Round of the General Agreement on Tariffs and Trade (GATT), also discussed in Chapter 3, involve environmental issues, as does the Kyoto Protocol. This latter initiative requires industrialized countries to reduce, by 2008–2012, their combined greenhouse gas emissions by at least 5.2 percent compared to 1990 levels. As of February 2003, the Convention had received 188 instruments of ratification.[28] However, by the terms of the Convention, the Kyoto Protocol will not go into effect until the emissions of the signing parties total 55 percent of the global emissions of Annex I countries. (Annex I countries are the so-called developed nations. These countries account for 39 percent of global carbon dioxide emissions.) The United States, an Annex I nation, withdrew from the Convention in 2001. Despite the number of nations that have submitted instruments of ratification, the signatories do not yet reach the threshold requirement to put the Kyoto Protocol into effect. You can get more information on the Kyoto Protocol at http://www.iea.org/ieakyoto/index.htm.

Summary

Environmental law involves complicated issues and highly technical statutes. The National Environmental Policy Act of 1969 mandates that virtually all federal agencies prepare detailed EISs whenever any agency undertakes any activities that may affect the environment.

The Clean Air Act, enacted in 1963 and amended subsequently, takes a technology-forcing approach to air pollution. It directs the EPA to establish national ambient air quality standards and state implementation plans that set out how the state proposes to implement and maintain those standards within its air quality regions. The 1990 amendments attack urban air pollution brought on by motor vehicle emissions, toxic pollutants, and acid rain. Among other things, beyond controlling emissions from mobile sources, these amendments set up a permit process aimed at minimizing emissions from major point sources. Civil, criminal, and administrative actions (including citizens' suits) are possible for violations of the act.

The Clean Water Act, so named in 1977 after having been enacted under a different name in 1972, sets out an extensive, joint federal and state comprehensive program for preventing, reducing, and eliminating water pollution. It does so by regulating both point and nonpoint sources. The three mechanisms used to regulate discharges from point sources include effluent limitations, water quality standards, and the national pollutant discharge elimination system's permit program. States also must comply with EPA-mandated antidegradation standards designed to ensure the maintenance of desirable water quality standards. The Clean Water Act sets out a timetable and the technological standards to be used for permit holders' compliance with the act. It takes an especially stringent approach to toxic pollutants such as asbestos, mercury, lead, PCBs, and so forth. The penalties imposed for violations of the Clean Water Act resemble those set out in the Clean Air Act.

The Safe Drinking Water Act of 1974 regulates the water supplied by public water systems to home taps. This act uses EPA-issued national primary drinking water regulations that have as their goal the reduction of contaminant levels in drinking water. States may have primary enforcement responsibilities under SDWA if they have adopted drinking water regulations no less stringent than the national standards and if they have implemented adequate monitoring, inspection, recordkeeping, and enforcement procedures.

The Noise Control Act of 1972 leaves to the federal government control over noise sources that require national uniformity of treatment or protection of the public health and welfare with an adequate margin of safety. Otherwise, the primary responsibility for controlling noise lies with state and local governments. The remedies granted for violations of this act resemble those permitted under the previous acts.

The Toxic Substances Control Act of 1976, by giving authority to the EPA to regulate chemicals before they come onto the market, screens pollutants before humans and the environment are exposed to these substances' effects. Yet its worthy goals have been undercut by the EPA's laxness in requiring companies to provide test data, coupled with the congressional mandate requiring the testing and regulation only of chemicals that pose an "unreasonable risk" of injury to health or the environment. Besides the civil and criminal penalties set out in other acts, TSCA authorizes the EPA to regulate "imminent hazards" through emergency judicial relief leading to an injunction or seizure of the chemicals at issue.

The Federal Insecticide, Fungicide, and Rodenticide Act of 1947 mandates the registration of all insecticides and pesticides with the EPA. The EPA will register only those products that, when used in accordance with widespread and common practice, will not generally cause adverse effects on the environment. The EPA subsequently can cancel the registration of any pesticide that fails to live up to this standard and can suspend a registration whenever necessary to prevent an imminent hazard. Recent amendments to FIFRA—specifically the Food Quality Protection Act of 1996—set out stringent standards aimed at ensuring the wholesomeness of the U.S. food supply and protecting children from the health threats posed by pesticide residues. Civil and criminal penalties, as well as EPA "stop sale" or seizure orders, are available under FIFRA.

The Resource Conservation and Recovery Act of 1976 requires the EPA to regulate nonhazardous solid waste, typically through approved state management plans. The EPA's "cradle-to-grave" regulation of hazardous waste involves a permit/manifest system that covers those who own or operate treatment, storage, or disposal facilities. Under RCRA, the EPA enjoys broad enforcement powers. Anyone involved in the handling, transport, storage, or disposal of solid or hazardous waste that presents an immediate and substantial endangerment to health or the environment faces the imposition of strict liability.

The Comprehensive Environmental Response, Compensation, and Liability Act (or "Superfund"), by regulating hazardous waste disposal sites, fills in the gaps left by RCRA and TSCA. Pursuant to the National Contingency

Plan, CERCLA authorizes cleanups of hazardous waste sites and makes generators, owners, operators, and transporters of hazardous wastes strictly liable for such response costs. CERCLA also establishes a "Superfund" to finance cleanups whenever the government cannot identify the parties responsible for the damage. The Superfund Amendments and Reauthorization Act of 1986 has increased the money allocated to the Superfund.

The Endangered Species Act of 1973, by protecting the critical habitats of wildlife, attempts to conserve endangered or threatened species of plants and animals. Celebrated cases under the act wherein dam or road construction projects were halted to protect the habitat of fish or butterflies, for example, have led to public controversies of great magnitude. International efforts to improve the environment in this and other nations are on the rise and therefore bear watching.

Discussion Questions

1. Describe fully when an agency needs to prepare an environmental impact statement (EIS) and the general prerequisites of an EIS.

2. Explain in detail the manner in which the Clean Air Act addresses the problem of air pollution.

3. Explain the following three Clean Water Act mechanisms and their importance to the fulfillment of the act's dictates: effluent limitations, water quality standards, and the national pollutant discharge elimination system's permit program.

4. How does the Safe Drinking Water Act differ from the Clean Water Act?

5. How has Congress allocated the responsibility for noise control among the federal government and state and local governments?

6. Explain Congress's threefold purpose in enacting the Toxic Substances Control Act.

7. How does the Federal Insecticide, Fungicide, and Rodenticide Act differ from TSCA?

8. How do the Resource Conservation and Recovery Act and the Comprehensive Environmental Response, Compensation, and Liability Act, respectively, regulate waste?

9. Explain some of the more significant economic aspects of the Endangered Species Act.

10. Describe three of the international aspects of environmental law.

Case Problems and Writing Assignments

1. The reality of an ever-increasing backlog of spent nuclear fuel (SNF) in temporary storage has created a national problem. Temporary on-site storage of SNF holds approximately 38,500 metric tons of SNF. But licensed nuclear reactors are expected to generate an additional 70,000 metric tons of SNF, at the least, over their commercial lifetimes. In 1982, Congress passed the Nuclear Waste Policy Act (NWPA). NWPA requires the Department of Energy to construct a permanent repository for the disposal of SNF. Pursuant to the terms of NWPA, the Department of Energy entered into a contractual agreement with all utilities that control one or more nuclear reactors to accept the SNF generated by these reactors no later than January 31, 1998. However, the Department of Energy estimates that, at the earliest, it will not have a permanent repository to receive SNF until 2010.

Hence, a consortium of utility companies formed Private Fuel Storage, L.L.C. (PFS) as a temporary solution to the storage problem. PFS thereafter proposed to build an off-site, private SNF storage facility on a portion of the reservation of the plaintiffs, the Skull Valley Band of Goshute Indians in Utah. On May 20, 1997, PFS entered into a lease of tribal reservation lands with the Skull Valley Band to allow the construction of

an SNF storage facility. After the Bureau of Indian Affairs (BIA) conditionally approved the lease, PFS submitted a license application to the Nuclear Regulatory Commission (NRC) in which PFS sought to construct and operate the proposed SNF storage facility. The NRC has yet to rule on PFS's application.

The state of Utah objected strenuously to PFS's plan. Indeed, Governor Leavitt proposed, and the Utah Legislature passed, five pieces of legislation directed at blocking the proposed facility. The plaintiffs, the Skull Valley Band and PFS, sued for declaratory and injunctive relief from the application of these Utah laws. The defendants—several high-ranking officials in the Utah state government—then filed a counterclaim alleging that (1) the NRC has no authority to license a private, for-profit, off-site storage facility; (2) an NRC license will necessarily violate the National Environmental Policy Act and therefore be invalid; (3) the Skull Valley Band has not lawfully approved the lease; (4) the conditional approval of the lease by the BIA occurred in violation of governing laws and rules; and (5) any BIA approval of the lease will be invalid as a breach of the government's trust obligations. The plaintiffs asserted (1) that the passage of state licensing schemes for the storage and transportation of SNF duplicates the NRC's licensing procedures and therefore is preempted by federal law under the supremacy clause and (2) that the Utah statutes violate the commerce clause.

In moving for judgment on the pleadings, the defendants first argued that the plaintiffs lacked standing. In short, the defendants claimed that, because federal law prohibited the plaintiffs from operating an off-site, private SNF facility, the plaintiffs had not alleged a violation of a legally cognizable interest. Consequently, the defendants submitted, the plaintiffs had not shown the standing required for a court to exercise jurisdiction over the matter. The defendants next argued that the plaintiffs' claims are not ripe because the NRC has yet to grant PFS a license for the facility. The plaintiffs countered that Utah's enactment of various laws aimed at thwarting the construction and operation of an SNF facility, by creating uncertainty about whether it is futile for the plaintiffs to attempt to obtain a license from the NRC and whether the costs imposed by the laws make the construction of the facility prohibitively expensive, render the issue ripe for adjudication. In whose favor should the court rule? [See *Skull Valley Band of Goshute Indians v. Leavitt*, 215 F. Supp. 2d 1232 (D. Utah 2002).]

2. Solid Waste Agency of Northern Cook County (SWANCC) is a consortium of 23 suburban Chicago cities and villages that joined an effort to locate and develop a disposal site for baled nonhazardous solid waste. SWANCC ultimately chose as its solid waste disposal site an abandoned sand and gravel pit with excavation trenches that had evolved into permanent and seasonal ponds Because the operation called for filling in some of the ponds, SWANCC contacted the Army Corps of Engineers (Corps) to determine if a landfill permit was required under § 404(a) of the Clean Water Act. This section authorizes the Corps to issue permits allowing the discharge of dredged or fill material into "navigable waters." The act defines "navigable waters" as "the waters of the United States," and the Corps' regulations define such waters to include intrastate waters, "the use, degradation or destruction of which could affect interstate or foreign commerce." In 1986, the Corps had attempted to clarify its jurisdiction, stating, in what has been dubbed the "Migratory Bird Rule," that § 404(a) extends to intrastate waters that provide habitat for migratory birds. Asserting jurisdiction over the site pursuant to that rule, the Corps refused to issue a § 404(a) permit. The Corps based its determination on the fact that approximately 121 bird species had been observed at the site, including several known to depend on aquatic environments for a significant portion of their life requirements. Thus, on November 16, 1987, the Corps formally "determined that the seasonally ponded, abandoned gravel mining depressions located on the project site, while not wetlands, did qualify as 'waters of the United States' . . . based upon the following criteria: (1) the proposed site had been abandoned as a gravel mining operation; (2) the water areas and spoil piles had developed a natural character; and (3) the water areas are used as habitat by migratory [birds that] cross state lines." SWANCC thereafter filed suit, claiming that the

Corps had exceed its statutory authority in interpreting the Clean Water Act to cover nonnavigable, isolated, intrastate waters based upon the presence of migratory birds and, in the alternative, that Congress lacked the power under the commerce clause to grant such regulatory jurisdiction. Who should prevail in this litigation— SWANCC or the Corps? [See *Solid Waste Agency of Northern Cook County v. United States Army Corps of Engineers*, 531 U.S. 159 (2001).]

3. In September 1994, the City of Middletown, New York, sought proposals for a solid waste management facility to meet its waste disposal needs, as well as to avoid the rising costs of disposal at private landfills. The City eventually accepted the proposal of Pencor-Masada Oxynol, L.L.C. (Masada) to construct a first-of-its-kind facility that would convert the cellulose component of sewage sludge and municipal garbage into ethanol. Masada projected that the facility could process 230,000 tons per year (tpy) of solid waste and 49,000 tpy of sewage sludge, producing approximately 7.1 million gallons of ethanol from these and other waste inputs.

The Clean Air Act mandates that the EPA promulgate NAAQS for certain pollutants. State governments, in turn, have the opportunity to establish and administer permit programs, subject to EPA oversight, that will ensure that the NAAQS are achieved and maintained. In 1977, Congress amended the Clean Air Act and its implementing regulations to establish the Program for the Prevention of Significant Deterioration of Air Quality (the PSD program), which seeks to prevent the significant deterioration of air quality in areas of the country that have achieved the NAAQS. In such areas, the PSD program imposes stringent controls on the construction or modification of "major" stationary sources of pollution. Before a permit for construction or modification of a new "major" stationary source can be issued, the applicant must conduct detailed analyses of the potential impact of the source on air quality and the surrounding environment. In order to categorize such complex sources of air pollution, the EPA looks to the "primary activity" of the facility in question. If the primary activity is one that falls under one of the 28 kinds of "major source" specifically identified by the Clean Air Act, the lower 100 tpy threshold will apply; otherwise the "default" 250 tpy threshold obtains. Even where the primary activity of a multipurpose facility places it within the default 250 tpy applicability threshold, the EPA may determine that the facility contains an "embedded" source of air pollution that must be classified separately under the PSD program. It is the policy of the EPA that if the embedded source involves the kind of activity that is subject to the 100 tpy applicability threshold, and if that source emits more than 100 tpy of a regulated air pollutant, the embedded source will be subject to PSD requirements, even if the facility as a whole is not.

Each Title V operating permit that a state proposes to issue must be submitted to the EPA for review, following the close of public commentary on the draft permit. The EPA may object to the issuance of a permit within 45 days of submission if the administrator determines that the permit is "not in compliance with the applicable requirements of [the act]. The administrator must issue a timely objection if "the petitioner demonstrates to the Administrator that the permit is not in compliance with the requirements of [the act], including the requirements of the applicable implementation plan."

It was undisputed that the Masada facility would require a Title V operating permit. However, during the course of its evaluation of Masada's application, questions arose as to whether the facility would be subject to the PSD program. The EPA had initially determined that the "embedded chemical plant process" aspects of the Masada facility meant that the PSD program would apply.

In early December 1999, the EPA changed its initial assessment to a determination that the primary purpose of the facility was waste collection processing. As for the emissions from the gasifier and package boiler, an EPA regional official concluded that most of the steam produced by the gasifier and package boiler supported the hydrolysis/cooking step, which is important for breaking down the municipal solid waste into reusable components. Although the hydrolysis/cooking step could be considered part of the ethanol production process, she asserted that the regional office had determined that the step more appropriately belonged with the waste processing aspect. She further explained that counting the hydrolysis/cooking step as part of the facility's waste processing activities meant that more than 80 percent of the steam produced by the gasifier and package boiler would have to be considered as supporting waste processing. Accordingly, under the support facility approach, the gasifier and package boiler were not a primary part of the embedded chemical process plant.

After NYSDEC's issuance of the final permit to Masada, the EPA did not object to the permit within the 45-day period specified by the Clean Air Act. However, the EPA subsequently received 35 petitions from 29 different persons, including Robert LaFleur, requesting the EPA to object to the issuance of the permit. LaFleur, who was the president of an environmental consulting firm retained by the Houses, two individuals representing a nearby shopping center, argued that (a) both the NYSDEC's decision and the EPA's change of opinion were motivated by political, rather than scientific, considerations; (b) the primary activity of the plant was chemical processing, not waste disposal, because the plant used waste only as an ingredient in the production of ethanol, thus "converting" waste rather than "disposing" of it; (c) most of the personnel and payroll at the facility would be dedicated to chemical processes; and (d) the gasifier's emissions should be counted as part of the chemical processing activity of the facility, thereby triggering the requirements of the PSD program, because the gasifier supported the production of ethanol by eliminating the residue (lignin) that resulted from that process. In response, the administrator concluded that LaFleur and the other petitioners had failed to carry their burden of showing that the PSD program's requirements

applied to the facility. After the issuance of this order, LaFleur filed a lawsuit claiming that the administrator's decision constituted abuse of discretion. The EPA, in turn, argued that LaFleur lacked standing. Who should prevail in this litigation? [See *LaFleur v. Whitman*, 300 F.3d 256 (2d Cir. 2002).]

4. Dow Chemical Company, while under the control of and at the direction of the federal government, operated a plant that produced synthetic rubber during World War II. The need for rubber during the war effort was critical. Hence, the government, even though it did not manufacture the product, owned the site and all the equipment and materials, knew what the manufacturer was doing, had unfettered control over all the manufacturing activities and approved of them, had an agency relationship that would ordinarily require it to indemnify the manufacturer for its actions, and had made an express written promise to hold the manufacturer harmless for what it had done during the war effort. When Cadillac Fairview/California, a land developer, sued Dow and the government for damages to cover the expenses of investigating the soil pollution that had resulted from the wartime production of rubber, Dow counterclaimed for indemnity and contribution under CERCLA. In deciding the case, the district court found for the plaintiff and allocated 100 percent of the remediation expenses to the government. Did the district court abuse its discretion in placing all the response costs on the government? [See *Cadillac Fairview/California v. Dow Chemical Company*, 299 F.3d 1019 (9th Cir. 2002).]

5. BUSINESS APPLICATION CASE Cropscience U.S.A. Holding, Inc. (Aventis) genetically engineered a corn seed to produce a protein known as Cry9C that is toxic to certain insects. The seeds are marketed under the brand name StarLink. Garst Seed Company is a licensee that produced and distributed StarLink seeds. Aventis attempted to register StarLink with the EPA, which is responsible for regulating insecticides under FIFRA. The EPA noted that Cry9C had several attributes similar to known human allergens and therefore issued only a limited registration that permitted StarLink's use for such purposes as animal feed, ethanol production, and seed increase, but prohibited its use for human consumption. Consequently, segregating this genetically engineered seed from non-StarLink corn, which was fit for human consumption, became of utmost importance.

To prevent StarLink corn from entering the food supply and because corn replicates by the transfer of pollen from one corn plant to another (including cross-pollination from one breed to another), the EPA required special procedures with respect to StarLink. These included mandatory segregation methods to prevent StarLink from commingling with other corn in cultivation, harvesting, handling, storage, and transport, and a 660-foot "buffer zone" around StarLink corn crops to prevent cross-pollination with non-StarLink ones. The limited registration also made Aventis responsible for ensuring these restrictions were implemented, and obligating it (a) to inform farmers of the EPA's requirements for the planting, cultivation, and use of StarLink; (b) to instruct farmers growing StarLink as to how to store and dispose of the StarLink seeds, seed bags, and plant detritus; and (c) to ensure that all farmers purchasing StarLink seeds signed a contract binding them to these terms before permitting them to grow StarLink corn.

StarLink was distributed throughout the United States from approximately May 1998 through October 2000. The limited registration initially limited StarLink cultivation to 120,000 acres. In January 1999, Aventis petitioned the EPA to raise this limit to 2.5 million acres. The EPA agreed, subject to an amended registration that required, among other things, that Aventis (a) inform purchasers ("growers"), at the time of StarLink seed corn sales, of the need to direct StarLink harvest to domestic feed and industrial nonfood uses only; (b) require all growers to sign a "grower agreement" outlining field management requirements and stating the limits on StarLink corn use; and (c) deliver a grower guide (that set out the provisions stated in the grower agreement) with all seed. Over this 29-month period, StarLink cultivation expanded from 10,000 acres to 350,000 acres.

In October 2000, after numerous reports that human food products had tested positive for Cry9C, a wave of manufacturers issued recalls for their corn products. On October 12, 2000, Aventis, at the EPA's urging, applied for a cancellation of the limited registration, effective February 20, 2001. Fear of StarLink contamination nonetheless continued to affect corn markets. As a consequence, many U.S. food producers stopped using U.S. corn, replacing it with imported corn or corn substitutes. South Korea, Japan, and other foreign countries terminated or substantially limited imports of U.S. corn. Grain elevators and transport providers began to mandate expensive testing on all corn shipments.

The plaintiffs alleged that the widespread StarLink contamination of the U.S. corn supply resulted from the defendants' failure to comply with the EPA's requirements. The plaintiffs alleged that Aventis failed to include the EPA-mandated label on some StarLink packages; to notify, instruct, and remind StarLink farmers of the restrictions on StarLink use; to set up proper segregation methods and buffer zone requirements; and to require StarLink farmers to sign the obligatory contracts. Prior to the 2000 growing season, Aventis allegedly instructed its seed representatives that it was unnecessary for them to advise StarLink farmers to segregate their StarLink crops or to create buffer zones because Aventis believed the EPA would amend the registration to permit StarLink for human consumption. In July 2001, however, an EPA Scientific Advisory Panel reaffirmed its previous position on StarLink's allergenic qualities. Further, the FDA has declared StarLink to be an adulterant under the Food, Drug and Cosmetic Act. The plaintiffs, a nationwide class of corn farmers, alleged, among other theories, common law claims for negligence, strict liability, nuisance, and conversion. The defendants argued that FIFRA preempted all such claims and that the lawsuit accordingly should be dismissed. Would you agree with the plaintiffs or the defendants? [See *In re StarLink Corn Products Liability Litigation*, 212 F. Supp. 828 (N.D. Ill. 2002).]

6. ETHICAL APPLICATION CASE The Endangered Species Act of 1973 (ESA) makes it unlawful for any person to "take" endangered or threatened species and defines take to mean "harass, harm, pursue," "wound," or "kill." In the regulations relating to the act, the secretary of the interior further defines harm to include "significant habitat modification or degradation where it actually kills or injures wildlife." Sweet Home Chapter of Communities for a Great Oregon includes small landowners, logging companies, and families dependent on the forest products industries in the Pacific Northwest and the Southeast, as well as organizations that represent these groups' interests. Sweet Home, challenging the statutory validity of the regulation defining "harm," sued Bruce Babbitt, the secretary of the interior. Sweet Home's complaint for a declaratory judgment challenged the regulation on its face, specifically that the application of the regulation to the red-cockaded woodpecker, an endangered species, and the northern spotted owl, a threatened species, had economically injured its constituent groups. The district court upheld the secretary's definition, but the court of appeals reversed. In defining "harm" to include habitat modification, had the secretary reasonably construed Congress's intent? [See *Babbitt v. Sweet Home Chapter of Communities for a Great Oregon*, 515 U.S. 687 (1995).]

7. CRITICAL THINKING CASE Power Engineering Company (PEC) has operated a metal refinishing and chrome electroplating business in Denver, Colorado, since 1968. Each month PEC produces over 1,000 kilograms of waste, including arsenic, lead, mercury, and chromium. This waste is covered by RCRA and is defined as "hazardous." After the Colorado Department of Public Health and Environment (CDPHE) learned of a discharge of hexavalent chromium into the Platte River, it conducted inspections of PEC and discovered that chromium emanating from PEC was the source of this groundwater contamination. The agency also found that PEC had treated, stored, and disposed of hazardous wastes without a permit. The CDPHE issued a notice of violation in June 1993 and in July 1994. The CDPHE issued a final administrative compliance order on June 13, 1996, requiring PEC to comply with hazardous waste laws, to implement a cleanup plan for the chromium-contaminated soil, to conduct frequent inspections, and to submit periodic reports. When PEC failed to comply with this order, CDPHE, on December 23, 1996, assessed civil penalties of $1.13 million. When PEC thereafter refused to pay these penalties, CDPHE brought suit in state court to force PEC's compliance with both orders. On March 23, 1999, the Colorado state court found that the final administrative compliance order and the administrative penalty order were enforceable as a matter of law. Before the issuance of the CDPHE final administrative compliance order, the EPA had filed a lawsuit seeking financial reassurances from PEC owing to the ongoing RCRA violations. Once the state order was promulgated, PEC argued that *res judicata* (a rule of civil law that states that a person cannot be sued more than once by the same party for the same civil wrong) would bar the enforcement of the EPA's suit. How should the court decide

this case? [See *U.S. v. Power Engineering Company*, 303 F.3d 1232 (10th Cir. 2002).]

8. YOU BE THE JUDGE The advertising and sale of pesticides over the Internet pose potential enforcement problems for the EPA. Hence, this emerging e-market is a cause for concern. Assume that the EPA, after developing a compliance strategy under FIFRA and other environmental laws, has targeted certain e-commerce practices, ranging from the sale of nonregistered pesticides to advertising claims that are at odds with the pesticides' registrations. Assume further that a group of e-tailers affected by the EPA's policies has challenged the policies in your court. What arguments would *you* expect both parties to make, and how would *you* rule on these issues? [See 70 *U. S. L. W.* 2732 (May 21, 2002).]

Notes

1. John Henry Davidson and Orlando E. Delogu, *Federal Environmental Regulation*, 2 vols. (Salem, N.H.: Butterworth Legal Publishers, 1994); Roger W. Findley and Daniel A. Farber, *Environmental Law in a Nutshell*, 4th ed. (Minneapolis: West, 1996); and William H. Rodgers Jr., *Handbook on Environmental Law*, 2nd ed. (Minneapolis: West, 1994) provide more detailed and comprehensive information concerning environmental law.

2. This, and all other information and figures relating to 2004, can be found at http://www.epa.gov.

3. Thomas DiLorenzo, "Federal Regulations: Environmentalism's Achilles Heel," *USA Today Magazine*, September 1994, p. 48.

4. Linda Grant, "Shutting Down the Regulatory Machine," *U.S. News & World Report*, February 13, 1995: 70.

5. Ibid.

6. 490 U.S. 332 (1989).

7. "Concentrations of Five Major Air Pollutants Drop by Average 7 Percent but Ozone Up 4 Percent," 27 *Environment Reporter* 1803 (Bureau of National Affairs, Inc.: Washington, D.C.), 1996.

8. Ibid.

9. Ibid.

10. "Ozone Levels Worse in 1999 than in 1998, with Vacation Spots Hit Hard, Report Says," 30 *Environment Reporter* 742–743 (Bureau of National Affairs, Inc.: Washington, D.C.), 1999.

11. "Federal Rules in Place to Protect against E.Coli Outbreaks," 30 *Environment Reporter* 983 (Bureau of National Affairs: Washington, D.C.), 1999.

12. "Up to 30 Unregulated Contaminants to Be Monitored under Final EPA Rule," 30 *Environment Reporter* 983 (Bureau of National Affairs: Washington, D.C.), 1999.

13. Ibid.

14. Ibid.

15. Tim Eichenberg and Robert Irvin, "Congress Takes Aim at Endangered Species Act," *The National Law Journal*, February 13, 1995, p. A21.

16. Ibid.

17. Ibid., pp. A21 and A22.

18. Ibid., p. A22.

19. Ibid.

20. Ibid.

21. "Report Shows Nearly 40 Per Cent of Rivers, Lakes, Half of Estuaries Do Not Support Uses, 33 *Environment Reporter* 2163 (Bureau of National Affairs, Inc.: Washington, D.C.), 2002.

22. See, e.g., *Ohio Forestry Association v. Sierra Club*, 523 U.S. 726 (1998) and *Steel Co. v. Citizens for a Better Environment*, 523 U.S. 83 (1998).

23. Ibid.

24. "Agency Reports Progress in 1998 Actions, Says Conclusions Unaffected by Data Errors," 30 *Environment Reporter* 525 (Bureau of National Affairs: Washington, D.C.), 1999.

25. Ibid.

26. Meredith Preston, "EPA Collects Less in Civil Fines in 2002 than in Final Clinton Years, Report Says," 33 *Environment Reporter* 2466 (Bureau of National Affairs: Washington, D.C.), 2002.

27. Turner Y. Smith Jr., "Environmental Regulation on the Rise Worldwide," *National Law Journal*, September 19, 1994, pp. C15 and C16.

28. The Convention and Kyoto Protocol, http://unfccc.int/resource/convkp.html.

Labor and Fair Employment Practices

AGENDA

NRW As NRW grows and prospers, it will hire more employees. The firm therefore will need to ensure that it complies with all applicable federal and state laws regulating labor and employment. NRW also may have to deal with one or more unions. The firm must make certain that it uses fair employment practices and thus avoids any prohibited discrimination in its hiring and promotion practices. In this regard, the firm must take steps to protect against sexual harassment; and it must provide a reasonably safe work environment as well. The firm in addition will have concerns about Social Security, workers' compensation, and unemployment insurance. Each of these areas requires careful attention to detail and strict compliance with the applicable laws and regulations.

These and other issues are likely to arise during your study of this chapter. Be prepared! You never know when the firm or one of its members will seek your advice.

Labor law and fair employment law provide the framework under which workers—particularly unions—operate and under which employees are regulated and protected. Labor law deals with the relationship between management and the workers. It defines unfair labor practices and unfair management practices, among other things. Fair employment practices law deals with employer rights and responsibilities that help to guarantee the equitable treatment of all the employees within the organization. Most of these protections consist of federal regulations, although important state laws also exist. Exhibit 40.1 provides an overview of the most significant statutes relating to labor and fair employment laws. We will discuss these statutes as we progress through the material in this chapter.

Labor

Federal Statutes

Unions are a fact of life in the United States today. But this was not always so. Violence and bloody battles between employers and pro-union workers marked the rise of unionism in this country. The courts, moreover, were as hostile as most employers to unions. In fact, in the 1800s and early 1900s, both state and federal courts saw common law criminal conspiracies, tortious interference with contract, or antitrust violations in workers' concerted activities such as strikes or picketing (union activity in which persons stand near a place of work affected by an organizational drive or a strike in order to influence workers regarding union causes). Although Congress had passed the Clayton Act in 1914 in part to shield unions from liability under the antitrust laws, subsequent Supreme Court decisions had narrowed this newly won statutory protection.

Norris-LaGuardia Act (1932) Responding to these developments, Congress passed the Norris-LaGuardia Act in 1932. This act immunized certain activities—peaceful refusals to work, boycotts (concerted refusals to deal with firms so as to disrupt their business), and picketing, for example—from federal court action. The act barred the issuance of federal injunctions in the context of labor disputes as well as the institution of *yellow dog* contracts (that is, promises to refrain from union membership as a condition of employment). It thus allowed employees to organize and to engage in collective bargaining free from court or employer intervention, as long as the concerted activity did not involve wildcat strikes (unauthorized withholdings of services or labor during the term of a contract), violence, sabotage, trespass, and the like.

The Norris-LaGuardia Act signaled a policy aimed at keeping the courts out of the labor field. Free from regula-

tion, then, employees and employers, by using the economic weapons appropriate to each side, fought for their respective goals. The unions resorted to strikes, picketing, and boycotts; the employers used discharges of employees.

The Wagner Act (1935) In 1935, Congress passed the Wagner Act, also called the National Labor Relations Act. This legislation heralded the beginning of an *affirmative*—as opposed to a neutral—approach to labor organizations. In § 7 of the Wagner Act, Congress approved the right of employees to organize themselves and "to form, join, or assist labor organizations, to bargain collectively through representatives of their own choosing, and to engage in concerted activities for the purpose of collective bargaining or other mutual aid or protection." The right to refrain from engaging in concerted activities is protected as well. Buttressing § 7 is § 8, which enumerates employer *unfair labor practices* (activities that are prohibited by law as injurious to labor policies), such as coercion of or retaliation against employees who exercise their § 7 rights, domination of unions by employers, discrimination in employment (hiring and firing, for instance) designed to discourage union activities, and refusals by employers to bargain collectively and in good faith with employee representatives (that is, with unions). Section 9 sets out the process by which the employees in the appropriate bargaining unit can conduct secret elections for choosing their representative in the collective bargaining process. The Wagner Act also established a new administrative agency, the National Labor Relations Board (NLRB), to oversee such elections and also to investigate and remedy unfair labor practices. Section 10 permits the appropriate federal circuit court of appeals to review any NLRB order. A 1937 case, *NLRB v. Jones & Laughlin Steel Corp.*, upheld the constitutionality of the Wagner Act.[1]

The Taft-Hartley Act (1947) After the passage of the Wagner Act, unions grew appreciably in size and influence. As a result, the power balance between employees and employers became so pro-union that in 1947 Congress passed legislation meant to counter the perceived excesses of the NLRB and pervasive court deference to its orders.

The Taft-Hartley Act, also called the Labor Management Relations Act (LMRA), attempted to curb union excesses. It amended § 8 of the Wagner Act to prohibit certain unfair labor practices by unions, including engaging in *secondary boycotts* (union activities meant to pressure parties not involved in the labor dispute and to influence the affected employer), forcing an employer to discriminate against employees on the basis of their union affiliation or lack of union affiliation, refusing to bargain in good faith,

EXHIBIT 40.1 Representative Statutes Affecting Labor and Employment

Wagner Act (National Labor Relations Act) [1935]	Allows employees to organize and to engage in collective bargaining; enumerates employer unfair labor practices; establishes the National Labor Relations Board [NLRB].
Taft-Hartley Act (Labor Management Relations Act) [1947]	Prohibits unfair labor practices by unions; separates the NLRB's functions; empowers courts to grant various civil and criminal remedies; creates the Federal Mediation and Conciliation Service.
Landrum-Griffin Act (Labor Management Reporting and Disclosure Act) [1959]	Requires extensive reporting of unions' financial affairs; allows civil and criminal sanctions for union officers' financial wrongdoings; mandates democratic procedures in the conduct of union elections and meetings.
Title VII of the Civil Rights Act [1964]	Prohibits discrimination in the terms, conditions, and privileges of employment on the basis of race, color, religion, sex, or national origin.
Equal Pay Act [1963]	Prohibits discrimination in wages on the basis of sex.
Age Discrimination in Employment Act [1967]	Protects certain workers (in general those aged 40 or older) from discrimination in employment based on age.
Rehabilitation Act [1973]	Directs federal contractors to take affirmative action with regard to "otherwise qualified" handicapped individuals.
Pregnancy Discrimination Act [1978]	Protects workers from pregnancy-related discrimination.
Immigration Reform and Control Act [1986]	Prohibits immigration-related discrimination based on national origin or citizenship status.
Americans with Disabilities Act [1990]	Protects disabled workers from employment discrimination.
Civil Rights Act [1991]	Amends earlier statutes to broaden the scope of protections afforded under antidiscrimination law; prohibits "race norming" of employment tests; in some circumstances, allows compensatory and punitive damage awards and jury trials.
Family and Medical Leave Act [1993]	Mandates that eligible employees receive up to 12 weeks of leave during any 12-month period for certain family or medically related events.
Occupational Safety and Health Act [1970]	Mandates safe and healthful workplace conditions.
Social Security Act [1935]	Provides federal benefits to the aged, the disabled, and other "fully insured" workers.
Federal Unemployment Tax Act [1954]	Provides (through a coordinated federal and state effort) economic security for temporarily unemployed workers.
State Workers' Compensation Statutes	Provide financial benefits to reimburse workers for workplace-related injury or death.

requiring an employer to pay for services not actually performed by an employee (*featherbedding*), and *recognitional picketing* (prohibited picketing in which a union attempts to force recognition of a union different from the currently certified bargaining representative). Congress also amended § 7 to allow employees to refrain from joining a union and participating in its collective activities.

In addition, the Taft-Hartley Act, by separating the NLRB's functions, cut back the authority of the board. The Office of General Counsel took on the prosecution of the board's unfair labor practices cases, leaving to the five-person board the decision-making (or *adjudicatory*) function. This reconfiguration significantly changed the nature of the NLRB, which had served simultaneously as both prosecutor and decision maker under the Wagner Act.

The Taft-Hartley Act also empowered courts of appeals to set aside NLRB findings concerning unfair labor practices cases, authorized district courts to issue labor injunctions requested by the NLRB for the purpose of stopping unfair labor practices, set out the possibility of fines and imprisonment for anyone resisting NLRB orders, and provided for civil remedies for private parties damaged by secondary boycotts or various union activities.

Other sections (1) protect the employer's right of free speech (by refusing to characterize as unfair labor practices an employer's expressions of its opinions about unionism when they contain no threats of reprisal), (2) preserve the employees' rights to engage in peaceful informational picketing (picketing for the purpose of truthfully advising the public that an employer does not employ members of, or have a contract with, a labor organization), and (3) prohibit *closed shop* agreements (contracts that obligate the employer to hire and retain only union members). *Union*

shop clauses (requiring an employee, after being hired, to join a union in order to retain his or her job) are legal. The Taft-Hartley Act also created a Federal Mediation and Conciliation Service for settling disputes between labor and management. To foster conciliation efforts further, the act established a cooling-off period that the parties must observe in certain circumstances before strikes can occur. It also preserved the power of states, under their right-to-work laws, to invalidate other union devices designed to consolidate the unions' hold on workers.

The following recent case construed the NLRB's authority under the NLRA to fashion remedies for unfair labor practices involving undocumented, illegal aliens.

40.1

HOFFMAN PLASTIC COMPOUNDS, INC. v. NATIONAL LABOR RELATIONS BOARD
535 U.S. 137 (2002)

FACTS Hoffman Plastics Compounds, Inc. hired Jose Castro on the basis of documents appearing to verify his authorization to work in the United States, but laid him and others off after they supported a union-organizing campaign at Hoffman's plant. The National Labor Relations Board found that the layoffs violated the National Labor Relations Act (NLRA) and ordered backpay and other relief. At a compliance hearing before an administrative law judge (ALJ) to determine the amount of backpay, Castro testified that he had been born in Mexico; that he had never been legally admitted to, or authorized to work in, this country; and that he had gained employment with Hoffman only after tendering a birth certificate belonging to a friend born in Texas. Based on this testimony, the ALJ found that the Immigration Reform and Control Act of 1986 (IRCA), which makes it unlawful for employers to knowingly hire undocumented workers or for employees to use fraudulent documents to establish employment eligibility, precluded the board from awarding Castro relief. Citing its precedent that held that the most effective way to further the immigration policies embodied in the IRCA is to provide the NLRA's protections and remedies to undocumented workers in the same manner as to other employees, the board reversed with respect to the backpay award. The court of appeals denied review and enforced the board's order.

ISSUE Did the board have the authority to award backpay to an employee who, although illegally laid off pursuant to an employer unfair labor practice, was an undocumented alien?

HOLDING No. The board's backpay award ran counter to the underlying policies of the IRCA, policies the board had no authority to enforce or administer.

REASONING Excerpts from the opinion of Chief Justice Rehnquist:

This case exemplifies the principle that the Board's discretion to select and fashion remedies for violations of the NLRA, though generally broad . . . is not unlimited. . . . Since the Board's inception, we have consistently set aside awards of reinstatement or backpay to employees found guilty of serious illegal conduct in connection with their employment. . . . We have accordingly never deferred to the Board's remedial preferences where such preferences potentially trench upon federal statutes and policies unrelated to the NLRA. . . .

[The *Sure-Tan, Inc. v. NLRB* decision] followed this line of cases and set aside an award closely analogous to the award challenged here. There we confronted for the first time a potential conflict between the NLRA and federal immigration policy, as then expressed in the Immigration and Nationality Act (INA). . . . Two companies had unlawfully reported alien-employees to the INS in retaliation for union activity. Rather than face INS sanction, the employees voluntarily departed to Mexico. The Board investigated and found the companies acted in violation of . . . the NLRA. The Board's ensuing order directed the companies to reinstate the affected workers and pay them six months' backpay.

We affirmed the Board's determination that the NLRA applied to undocumented workers, reasoning that the immigration laws "as presently written" expressed only a "'peripheral concern'" with the employment of illegal aliens. . . . "For whatever reason," Congress had not "made it a separate criminal offense" for employers to hire an illegal alien, or for an illegal alien "to accept employment after entering this country illegally." . . .

[quoting *Sure-Tan*]. Therefore, we found "no reason to conclude that application of the NLRA to employment practices affecting such aliens would necessarily conflict with the terms of the INA." . . .

With respect to the Board's selection of remedies, however, we found its authority limited by federal immigration policy. . . . Thus, to avoid "a potential conflict with the INA," the Board's reinstatement order had to be conditioned upon proof of "the employees' legal reentry." . . . Similarly, "with respect to backpay . . . [t]he employees must be deemed 'unavailable' for work (and the accrual of backpay therefore tolled) during any period when they were not lawfully entitled to be present and employed in the United States." . . . "In light of the practical workings of the immigration laws," such remedial limitations were appropriate even if they led to "the probable unavailability of the NLRA's more effective remedies." . . .

It is against this decisional background that we turn to the question presented here. . . . [W]here the Board's chosen remedy trenches upon a federal statute or policy outside the Board's competence to administer, the Board's remedy may be required to yield. Whether or not this was the situation at the time of *Sure-Tan*, it is precisely the situation today. In 1986, two years after *Sure-Tan*, Congress enacted IRCA, a comprehensive scheme prohibiting the employment of illegal aliens in the United States. . . . IRCA "forcefully" made combating the employment of illegal aliens central to "the policy of immigration law." . . . It did so by establishing an extensive "employment verification system" . . . designed to deny employment to aliens who (a) are not lawfully present in the United States, or (b) are not lawfully authorized to work in the United States. . . . This verification system is critical to the IRCA regime. To enforce it, IRCA mandates that employers verify the identity and eligibility of all new hires by examining specified documents before they begin work. . . . If an alien applicant is unable to present the required documentation, the unauthorized alien cannot be hired. . . .

Similarly, if an employer unknowingly hires an unauthorized alien, or if the alien becomes unauthorized while employed, the employer is compelled to discharge the worker upon discovery of the worker's undocumented status. . . . Employers who violate IRCA are punished by civil fines . . . and may be subject to criminal prosecution. . . . IRCA also makes it a crime for an unauthorized alien to subvert the employer verification system by tendering fraudulent documents. . . . It thus prohibits aliens from using or attempting to use "any forged, counterfeit, altered, or falsely made document" or "any document lawfully issued to or with respect to a person other than the possessor" for purposes of

obtaining employment in the United States. . . . Aliens who use or attempt to use such documents are subject to fines and criminal prosecution. . . . There is no dispute that Castro's use of false documents to obtain employment with Hoffman violated these provisions.

Under the IRCA regime, it is impossible for an undocumented alien to obtain employment in the United States without some party directly contravening explicit congressional policies. Either the undocumented alien tenders fraudulent identification, which subverts the cornerstone of IRCA's enforcement mechanism, or the employer knowingly hires the undocumented alien in direct contradiction of its IRCA obligations. The Board asks that we overlook this fact and allow it to award backpay to an illegal alien for years of work not performed, for wages that could not lawfully have been earned, and for a job obtained in the first instance by . . . criminal fraud. . . . [H]owever . . . awarding backpay to illegal aliens runs counter to policies underlying IRCA, policies the Board has no authority to enforce or administer. Therefore, as [the Court has] consistently held in like circumstances, the award lies beyond the bounds of the Board's remedial discretion.

The Board contends that awarding limited backpay to Castro "reasonably accommodates" IRCA, because . . . such an award is not "inconsistent" with IRCA. . . . What matters here, and what sinks . . . the Board's claims, is that Congress has expressly made it criminally punishable for an alien to obtain employment with false documents. There is no reason to think that Congress nonetheless intended to permit backpay where but for an employer's unfair labor practices, an alien-employee would have remained in the United States illegally, and continued to work illegally, all the while successfully evading apprehension by immigration authorities. . . . Far from "accommodating" IRCA, the Board's position, recognizing employer misconduct but discounting the misconduct of illegal alien employees, subverts it. . . .

The Board admits that had the INS detained Castro, or had Castro obeyed the law and departed to Mexico, Castro would have lost his right to backpay. . . . We therefore conclude that allowing the Board to award backpay to illegal aliens would unduly trench upon explicit statutory prohibitions critical to federal immigration policy, as expressed in IRCA. It would encourage the successful evasion of apprehension by immigration authorities, condone prior violations of the immigration laws, and encourage future violations. However broad the Board's discretion to fashion remedies when dealing only with the NLRA, it is not so unbounded as to authorize this sort of an award.

Lack of authority to award backpay does not mean that the employer gets off scot-free. The Board here has already imposed other significant sanctions against Hoffman—sanctions Hoffman does not challenge. . . . These include orders that Hoffman cease and desist its violations of the NLRA, and that it conspicuously post a notice to employees setting forth their rights under the NLRA and detailing its prior unfair practices. . . . Hoffman will be subject to contempt proceedings should it fail to comply with these orders. . . . As we concluded in *Sure-Tan*, "in light of the practical workings of the immigration laws," any "perceived deficiency in the NLRA's existing remedial arsenal," must be "addressed by congressional action," not the courts. . . . In light of IRCA, this statement is even truer today. . . . The judgment of the Court of Appeals is reversed. . . .

BUSINESS CONSIDERATIONS Employer verification of the alien's lawful authority to work in the United States is a cornerstone of the IRCA. Hoffman attempted to verify Castro's status. What policies should Hoffman adopt so as to ensure that its verification system is more foolproof than the system it followed at the time of Castro's hiring? How can it, in addition, ensure the even-handed application of its hiring policies to both alien and domestic applicants? Be specific.

ETHICAL CONSIDERATIONS Many documented and undocumented workers live in the United States but send a large percentage of their salaries to their families in their home countries. Formulate an argument that it is unethical to do so. Then formulate an argument that the workers' decisions in this regard are ethical.

In settling a similarly contentious issue that had plagued the NLRB's oversight of the health care industry in recent years—whether certain nurses in health care facilities could be considered supervisors and thus be excluded from bargaining units involving nurses—the Supreme Court in 2001 made a twofold determination. The Court first held that the party asserting that an employee is a supervisor has the burden of proving such supervisory status. Second, the Court invalidated the NLRB's current test for determining supervisory status under the NLRA.[2]

The Landrum-Griffin Act (1959) By the 1950s, Congress had unearthed substantial corruption among union leadership. Union members had been prejudiced by officers' plundering of union treasuries and by these officers' often tyrannical treatment of the rank-and-file members.

In 1959, Congress responded with the Landrum-Griffin Act, also called the Labor Management Reporting and Disclosure Act (LMRDA). As this latter title suggests, the act requires extensive reporting of financial affairs; allows civil and criminal sanctions for financial wrongdoings by union officers; and, by providing a "bill of rights" for union members regarding elections and meetings, mandates democratic procedures in the conduct of union affairs. In addition, the Landrum-Griffin Act amended portions of the Taft-Hartley Act to outlaw *hot cargo* clauses (provisions in contracts requiring the employer to cease doing business with nonunion companies).

Taken together, these acts apply to almost all employers and employees, excluding federal, state, and local government employers and employees; employers covered under the Railway Labor Act; agricultural workers; domestic

workers; independent contractors; and most supervisors. Even though government workers are not covered, they can organize themselves under the authority of Executive Order 11491, entitled Labor-Management Relations in the Federal Service, promulgated in 1969. In addition, about two-thirds of the states have enacted laws permitting collective bargaining in the public sector for state and municipal employees. Such executive orders and statutes ordinarily forbid strikes by public employees (such as police officers and firefighters), but such strikes nevertheless have occurred in recent years. The arrival of collective bargaining in the public sector is relatively new, but it promises to have significant implications for the future as our economy becomes more service oriented and the number of government employees proliferates.

Further Issues Although we cannot describe fully the pervasive regulation of labor embodied in the Wagner, Taft-Hartley, and Landrum-Griffin acts, we will highlight a few of the more important issues.

Questions invariably arise when employees select their bargaining representative. The Wagner Act sets forth the procedures that must be followed during this process. Briefly, these procedures include, upon a required showing of employee interest, the union's petitioning for an election that will lead to its recognition as the exclusive bargaining representative of the employees. The NLRB decides whether the election has been conducted validly and, if so, certifies the union as the exclusive bargaining agent.

The employer, who ordinarily resists the election/ representation process, may attempt to "decertify" the union. The employer typically argues that the employees do not constitute an appropriate bargaining unit (that is, the employees have different duties, skills, or responsibilities) or that the union has engaged in unfair labor practices. The NLRB initially adjudicates such complaints, but the circuit courts of appeals can review final NLRB orders. In many cases, the employer prevails.

Not to be outdone, unions usually have alleged unfair labor practices by employers during the certification process. Consequently, these affairs often become real donnybrooks of contradictory allegations because each side is fighting for the economic power signified by union representation or the lack of such representation.

The certification process may raise property issues as well, because organizers ordinarily wish to distribute union literature to employees in firms where they hope ultimately to hold a certification election. The right to engage in protected activity mandated by the Wagner Act thus clashes with the employer's property rights and the efficient conduct of its business. Board decisions generally invalidate the soliciting of employees and the distributing of literature during working hours and in working areas as long as such restrictions do not unduly interfere with the free exercise of employee rights guaranteed by the Wagner Act. As mentioned earlier, during this process, it is likewise permissible for the employer to state its views about unionism unless these statements convey a threat against pro-union employees or promise a benefit to anti-union employees.

Once the bargaining representative has been empowered, the Wagner Act requires *good-faith bargaining* by both the employer and the union. This, of course, is a nebulous term; in essence, it mandates both sides' meeting and discussing certain issues with as much objectivity as possible. The duty to bargain in good faith does not absolutely presume agreement between the parties. Under this duty, an employer cannot bypass the union to deal directly with the employees.

The Wagner Act requires good-faith bargaining over "wages, hours, and other terms and conditions of employment." Basically, then, the duty to bargain covers only those topics that have a direct impact on the employees' job security. Decisions that are not essentially related to conditions of employment but rather are managerial decisions "which lie at the core of entrepreneurial control"[3] fail to suffice as mandatory bargaining subjects. Pay differentials for different shifts, piecework and incentive plans, transfers, fringe benefits, and severance pay are mandatory subjects. Courts have had more trouble classifying bonuses and meals provided by the employer. Managerial decisions to terminate the company's business or to shut down a plant are ordinarily *permissive*, or nonmandatory, subjects. An employer, however, might be forced to bargain about the *effects* of such decisions, such as severance pay (wages paid upon the termination of one's job), that impinge on the conditions of employment.

Although the labor laws view collective bargaining as the parties' meeting, asserting their positions, stating their objections to the other party's position, and disclosing the information necessary for each side to arrive at an informed decision, both sides permissibly can use economic weapons outside the bargaining room. Hence, employee strikes or work stoppages and employer lockouts do not in themselves violate the duty to bargain in good faith. An employer's unilateral granting of a wage increase without notice to the union during the process of negotiations does constitute bad-faith bargaining, however. On the other hand, such unilateral changes made after bargaining has reached an impasse are legal.

The NLRB can require either side that has refused, directly or indirectly, to bargain in good faith to begin bargaining and to cease and desist from any unfair labor practice that has accompanied the bad-faith bargaining. The board also can use such powers for ending violations of any of the employer or union unfair labor practices that have occurred outside the bargaining context.

NLRB orders are not self-enforcing, however; they become law only when imposed by a federal circuit court of appeals. Because litigation is time consuming, these limitations on the NLRB's enforcement powers sometimes make policing the actions of maverick employers or unions difficult. Board hearings and resultant orders, if resisted, bring on court scrutiny. If the court affirms the NLRB order, the court issues an injunction. In the meantime, however, the allegedly unfair labor practices may have continued and may have successfully stifled the employer or employee interests at issue.

BE&K Construction Company v. NLRB, 536 U.S. 516 (2002), illustrates the complexities inherent in these issues. There, the Supreme Court held that the NLRB had exceeded its statutory authority when it found an employer had filed a reasonably based but ultimately unsuccessful lawsuit against a labor union guilty of an unfair labor practice. The employer viewed the unions' lobbying, handbilling, litigation, and institution of grievance proceedings as attempts to delay its steel modernization project that employed nonunion workers. Hence, the employer's suit against the union's alleged secondary boycotts prohibited by the NLRA and violations of the Sherman Act. In the meantime, two unions filed unfair labor practices complaints against the employer. At the conclusion of the employer's federal suit, the NLRB determined that the unions' conduct constituted protected activity under § 8(a)(1), that the employer's suit was motivated by that conduct, and that remedies therefore were appropriate. To avoid what it deemed the "difficult" First Amendment issues, the Supreme Court decided the case by opting for a narrow interpretation of § 8(a)(1), which, as noted earlier in the chapter, prohibits employers from interfering with employees' exercise of rights related to self-organization, collective bargaining, and other concerted activities. The Court held that employers' reasonably based, unsuccessful suits against unions, even when these suits were motivated by the unions' NLRA-protected activity, would fall outside the coverage of the statute. In so holding, the Court cut back on the NLRB's remedial powers.

The application of federal labor laws to an increasingly digitized workplace, specifically the intersection of employer-instituted rules concerning technology and the employees' rights to engage in concerted activities under Section 7 of the Wagner Act, has put many of the issues just discussed in a new light. Accordingly, the National Labor Relations Board recently has faced such questions as the degree of statutory protection the federal labor laws grant to employees' use of e-mail, the appropriate bargaining unit when employers have no fixed work location but rather conduct all their business electronically, and union access to employees in a virtual workplace. Similarly, the precedents for deciding the access issues discussed earlier in the chapter derive from theories of real property (which is characterized by discrete physical boundaries), rules concerning what constitutes work areas (also characterized by discrete physical boundaries), and distinct separations between working hours and nonworking hours. E-mail and related technologies blur these distinctions, thereby raising questions as to the advisability of attempting to engraft these stringent, place-bound rules onto the virtual workplace. Simply, put, the realities of a digitized environment may force the employer's "business only" computer usage policies to give way to unions' right of access. The customary methods of organizing traditional workplaces—face-to-face communications, handbilling, and home visits—provide unions with several options for encouraging workers to join the bargaining unit at issue. While the union may view such personalized contacts as the preferred choice during solicitation drives, they are not the union's only alternative.

In contrast, such face-to-face interactions are absent in the digitized workplace. The time-honored conversations around the water cooler have been largely replaced by discussions via e-mail. In such situations, the employer's denial of access to e-mail may, practically speaking, foreclose all communications to the members of the community. Hence, employers should exercise caution when they tie no-solicitation rules to their e-mail policies. Broad prohibitions on the use of an e-mail system may constitute an unfair labor practice, since denial of access to e-mail systems will arguably result in a greater interference with employees' rights to engage in concerted activities than

---

NRW CASE 40.1 Management

UNIONS

NRW has been wildly successful, and the firm has increased its workforce significantly. One of the newly hired workers, a strong union advocate, has started discussing the possibility of forming a union at NRW. Several of the employees, reasoning that a strong bargaining representative will help them, seem to favor forming a union. Others, including a number of the original employees, oppose the formation of a union. They believe that Mai, Helen, and Carlos have treated the workers fairly and that a union will set up an "us versus them" mentality that will not be in the best long-term interests of the firm or the employees. Carlos is concerned that such discussions will divide the loyalty of the workers and thereby harm the firm. He asks you what the firm can legally do to prevent the formation of a union and what it must legally do if the employees decide to proceed. What will you tell him?

BUSINESS CONSIDERATIONS What should a business do if it learns that its employees are considering petitioning the NLRB for a union certification election? Should the business take steps to discourage the formation of a union, or should the business wait and then choose a course of conduct after the vote?

ETHICAL CONSIDERATIONS Is it ethical for a business to take affirmative steps to thwart union-organizing activities if the management of the firm honestly believes that the introduction of a union will have harmful long-term effects on the business?

INTERNATIONAL CONSIDERATIONS How are labor negotiations handled in other nations? Are unions more common in other nations than they are in the United States? In other nations, is labor more likely to be protected by statutory provisions?

---

would be the case in traditional, physical, workplace settings. Another offshoot of organizational efforts—the potential use of electronic ballots in representation elections—may change the future contours of labor law as well. Given the numerous issues and the present unsettled nature of the law, you will do well to pay heed to such developments and the effect they will have on labor-management relationships in the future.

State Law

The supremacy clause of the Constitution empowers Congress to pass laws, such as the federal labor laws, that will preempt the states' regulation of labor. Supreme Court decisions construing the labor laws (which are silent on the issue of preemption) have held that federal preemption powers are broad. Because of the NLRB's expertise and a desire for uniformity of case results, federal laws ordinarily will oust the states' jurisdiction in activities that arguably are protected or prohibited by federal labor statutes.

Matters that only peripherally affect the federal statutory scheme or matters that are of deep local concern may constitute legitimate state interests that state law (and courts) therefore may regulate. The law in this area is unsettled and the cases controversial; generally, however, state courts can adjudicate lawsuits involving damages from violence or other criminal or tortious activity, retaliatory discharges, and those causes of action covering all employers and employees exempted under federal statutes.

Employment

Fair Employment Practices Laws

Besides this extensive federal and state regulation of labor, several federal and state statutes designed to ensure equal employment opportunity for persons historically foreclosed from the workplace have come into existence since 1964.

Civil Rights Act of 1964 Foremost among these laws is the Civil Rights Act of 1964. Title VII of that statute prohibits discrimination in employment on the basis of race, color, religion, sex, or national origin. Under Title VII, an employer cannot lawfully make decisions to hire; discharge; compensate; or establish the terms, conditions, or privileges of employment for any employee based on the categories just enumerated.

In addition, an employer cannot segregate, limit, or classify employees or applicants for employment in discriminatory ways. Moreover, a union cannot discriminate against or refuse to refer for employment or apprenticeship programs any individual because of race, color, religion, sex, or national origin. And employment agencies cannot discriminate with respect to referrals for jobs or use advertisements indicating a discriminatory preference or limitation.

Furthermore, none of the three groups (employers, unions, or employment agencies) can discriminate against any individual because the individual has opposed unlawful employment practices. An employer that relegates blacks to manual labor jobs or an employment agency or labor organization that refers only white males for executive jobs or only women for nursing or secretarial jobs is in violation of Title VII.

Title VII's coverage, in general, extends to employers in interstate commerce that have on their weekly payrolls at least 15 full- or part-time employees[4] for at least 20 weeks per year, to any national or international labor organizations that consist of at least 15 members or that operate a hiring hall, and to employment agencies that regularly procure employees for employers or work opportunities for potential employees. Because of amendments added in 1972, Title VII currently covers most federal, state, and local governmental and educational employees as well.

Title VII authorized the creation of the Equal Employment Opportunity Commission (EEOC), a bipartisan, five-member group appointed by the president. The EEOC presently serves as the enforcement agency for Title VII, the Pregnancy Discrimination Act of 1978, the Equal Pay Act of 1963, the Age Discrimination in Employment Act of 1967, the Rehabilitation Act of 1973, the Americans with Disabilities Act of 1990, the Civil Rights Act of 1991, and other statutes. The EEOC also can bring lawsuits relating to broad patterns and practices of discrimination. Complaints by individual grievants or charges filed by the EEOC or state fair employment or human rights commissions may trigger the EEOC's jurisdiction.

The jurisdictional requirements for successful suits under Title VII are complex. In brief, a charge must be filed within 180 days or 300 days after the alleged discrimination has occurred, the latter time period being applicable in *deferral* states (those that have their own fair employment practices commissions). In deferral states, the local commission has exclusive jurisdiction for 60 days, at which point the EEOC has concurrent jurisdiction over the charge.

If the EEOC has retained jurisdiction for at least 180 days and has decided no reasonable cause exists to file an action on behalf of the grievant, the EEOC may issue a right-to-sue letter to the grievant. Within 90 days of receiving the right-to-sue letter, the grievant must file suit in the appropriate district court or, generally speaking, lose the right to sue. Under its National Enforcement Plan, the EEOC can certify that it will be unable to investigate the claim in 180 days and immediately issue a right-to-sue letter. Besides the EEOC's resultant cost savings, this plan has resulted in dramatic increases in the number of lawsuits filed in the federal courts.

Moreover, because the process is grievant oriented and because judges do not expect laypersons to write complaints that resemble legal briefs, courts give grievants considerable leeway in describing and recognizing when discrimination arguably has happened. Two recent Supreme Court cases reinforce this proposition. The first held that a plaintiff suing under federal employment discrimination law need not plead a prima facie case in order to survive a motion to dismiss. Put differently, such a plaintiff does not have to allege circumstances supporting an inference of discrimination. Rather, all the complainant need do is set out a short and plain statement that gives fair notice of what the claim is and the grounds upon which the plaintiff's case rests.[5] The second case upheld an EEOC regulation that allows a complainant to "verify" at a later date an unsworn discrimination charge that the plaintiff had filed in a timely manner. In making this determination, the Supreme Court resolved a split in the various circuit courts of appeals as to whether a late verification of a charge could "relate back" to an otherwise timely filing.[6] In addition to these relaxations of formalities that might make the complaint process otherwise overly legalistic and technical, the conciliation orientation of the process makes it possible to clear up the grievance before litigation even becomes necessary. Still, one should remember that procedural pitfalls dot this entire area of the law.

Substantive pitfalls also may snare the unaware employer, since many employment practices that seem neutral actually may lead to discrimination. For instance, in the early 1970s, several cases involved testing procedures and mandatory high school diplomas. These cases show that selection criteria that seem outwardly neutral may foreclose blacks and other protected persons from jobs merely because statistically fewer blacks than whites graduate from high school. Selection criteria that require a certain score on an aptitude test or a high school diploma may, as a landmark case notes, "operate as 'built-in' headwinds for minority groups and [may be] unrelated to measuring job capability. . . . [Title VII] proscribes not only overt discrimination but also practices that are fair in form, but discriminatory in operation. The touchstone is business necessity. If an employment practice which operates to exclude [minorities] cannot be shown to be related to job performance, the practice is prohibited."[7]

Any job requirement that prevents a disproportionate number of blacks or other minorities from securing employment or promotion has a *disparate impact* (that is, an unequal effect) on minorities and may be illegal. The employer then has the burden of proving that the requirement is job related. The EEOC has issued guidelines for selecting employees, but these guidelines do not have the force of law. Nonetheless, if courts so wish, they may give these EEOC guidelines considerable deference.

Besides facing liability stemming from disparate impact, employers also may be liable for the *disparate treatment* of

their employees. Such cases ordinarily arise when an employer allows whites or males to break rules without punishment but institutes penalties if blacks or women break the same rules. A 1976 case, *McDonald v. Santa Fe Trail Transportation Co.*, also held that whites can sue for racial discrimination when they receive disparate treatment.[8] In this case, the employer had accused two whites and one black of misappropriating a shipment of antifreeze. The company fired both white employees but retained the black worker. The Supreme Court concluded that Title VII prohibits all forms of racial discrimination, including *reverse discrimination* of this type. The term reverse discrimination refers to claims by whites that they have been subjected to adverse employment decisions because of their race and the application of employment discrimination statutes designed to protect minorities.

The allegations of reverse discrimination that spring from another source—affirmative action plans—pose some of the most controversial issues in the area of fair employment practices involving race. Title VII places on the employer the duty to maintain a racially balanced workforce. Yet if the employer takes affirmative steps—slotting certain apprenticeship openings for blacks, for example—to bring about such racial balance, these actions may adversely affect the white incumbents who wish to take part in these training programs. Two diametrically opposed policies clash here: the interests of the minority candidate who in the past has been disadvantaged because of race and of the white incumbent worker who has taken no part in this discrimination but who now, because the employer is seeking to bring about equality of opportunity for black workers, must lose employment opportunities.

In these situations, whites occasionally have brought suits alleging reverse discrimination. Though not a Title VII case, the 1978 landmark decision *Regents of the University of California v. Bakke*[9] (discussed in Chapter 5), represented the Supreme Court's first holding in this thorny area. *Bakke* involved a white student who alleged that the University of California at Davis, by rejecting his application for medical school and admitting 16 minority students with credentials inferior to his, had discriminated against him on the basis of his race, in violation of the Fourteenth Amendment. The Court, in a very complex opinion, held that university quota systems that absolutely prefer minority candidates are illegal (the university had reserved 16 spots out of 100 for minorities) but that a university in its admissions process may take race into account. This issue has recently resurfaced in the context of law school and medical school admissions in several states' public universities. Watch for the legal developments spawned by this still-controversial issue.

Reverse discrimination becomes an even more nettlesome issue in the private sector, where employers may face charges by the EEOC if they do not aggressively engage in affirmative action and may face suits by white workers alleging reverse discrimination if they do. In *United Steelworkers of America v. Weber*,[10] the Supreme Court addressed this particular dilemma. In this case, the United Steelworkers of America and Kaiser Aluminum & Chemical Corporation (Kaiser) had entered into a master collective-bargaining agreement covering 15 Kaiser plants. The agreement included an affirmative action plan aimed at eliminating racial imbalances in Kaiser's workforce. This plan reserved for black employees 50 percent of the openings in Kaiser training programs until Kaiser's percentage of skilled black craftworkers equaled the percentage of blacks in the local labor force. Brian Weber, a white worker who had accrued more seniority than some of the black workers selected for the training program, was rejected as a trainee. Weber sued, alleging that Kaiser's affirmative action plan constituted reverse discrimination against white workers and, because of Kaiser's use of race in the selection of apprentices for training programs, violated Title VII's ban on discrimination. The Supreme Court held that a private, voluntary, race-conscious affirmative action plan, such as that at issue here, did not violate Title VII's prohibition against racial discrimination. In the Court's view, one of the purposes of Title VII involves opening up job opportunities traditionally closed to blacks; thus, Kaiser's self-evaluation efforts to eliminate its racially imbalanced workforce were appropriate. Moreover, because the Kaiser plan opened up opportunities for blacks without unnecessarily trammeling the interests of white workers, its affirmative action plan was legal. But the Supreme Court's holding in *Adarand Constructors, Inc. v. Peña*, a public sector case decided on constitutional grounds (and discussed in Chapter 5), may generate court challenges to such race-conscious affirmative action plans.[11] Future legal developments therefore warrant your attention.

Besides racial discrimination, Title VII also prohibits religious discrimination. Sincere religious beliefs (or the lack thereof) are protected under Title VII. Cases typically arise when a job shift necessitates work on the day the employee considers his or her Sabbath. If a person's religion forbids work on Fridays after sundown, for instance, Title VII mandates that the employer make a "reasonable accommodation" to the employee's beliefs unless to do so would pose an "undue hardship" on the conduct of the business.

The 1977 case *Trans World Airlines, Inc. v. Hardison*,[12] however, by holding that an employer does not have to undertake an accommodation that requires more than a minimal expense or that violates a collective bargaining agreement, has severely undercut the guarantees represented by Title VII. Furthermore, under other provisions of Title VII, educational institutions may make religion a bona fide occupational qualification (BFOQ). A BFOQ constitutes a defense to charges of discrimination based on religion, sex, or national origin (but not to charges of racial discrimination) and consists of a situation in which one of these categories is essential to the performance of the job. Pursuant to this statutorily enumerated BFOQ, the University of Notre Dame, for example, may hire only Roman Catholic professors if it so wishes.

Bona fide occupational qualifications also may constitute a limited defense to charges of sex discrimination. For example, it is not a violation of Title VII for a movie director to cast only women in women's roles. Issues implicating the ban on sex discrimination include stereotypes about the ability to perform a job (such as an employer who thinks only men can be heavy equipment operators and only women can be child care providers), height/weight requirements that are not job related (women usually are smaller than men), and so-called sex-plus cases. In the last, the employer adds a selection criterion for women that is not added for men (such as when women with preschool-aged children are not hired but men who have such children are).

By imposing on employers liability for sexual advances or requests for sexual favors made by the employer's agents and supervisory employees (so-called quid pro quo sexual harassment) and for sexual misconduct that creates an intimidating, hostile, or offensive working environment for women (so-called *hostile environment* harassment), recent Title VII cases have protected women from sexual harassment in the workplace. In doing so, the latter line of cases has relied on *Meritor v. Vinson*,[13] the landmark Supreme Court case that held that an employer could face liability for harassment that created a hostile or offensive working environment, even though the plaintiff had suffered no "tangible" losses of an "economic character." Yet, based on its belief that the lower courts had not sufficiently fleshed out the facts, the *Meritor* Court declined to issue a definitive ruling on employer liability. While the Court called for the application of agency principles to the issue of an employer's liability for a supervisor's conduct, the Court elaborated very little beyond this statement.

Since *Meritor*, the various courts of appeals and employers have struggled with the issue of how to apply agency principles in determining whether an employer would be liable for the conduct of its supervisors in situations involving sexual harassment. *Burlington Industries, Inc. v. Ellerth*, the case that follows, answers this important question.

BURLINGTON INDUSTRIES, INC. v. ELLERTH
524 U.S. 742 (1998)

FACTS Kimberly Ellerth quit her job after 15 months as a salesperson in one of Burlington Industries's many divisions, allegedly because she had been subjected to constant sexual harassment by one of her supervisors, Ted Slowik. Burlington did not view Slowik, a mid-level manager who had authority to hire and promote employees, subject to higher approval, as a policymaker. Against a background of repeated boorish and offensive remarks and gestures allegedly made by Slowik, Ellerth emphasized three incidents in which one could construe Slowik's comments as threats to deny her tangible job benefits. For instance, on one occasion, while on a business trip, Slowik allegedly made remarks about Ellerth's breasts. When she gave him no encouragement, Slowik allegedly told her to "loosen up" and warned her that he could make her "life very hard or very easy at Burlington." Ellerth refused all of Slowik's advances, yet suffered no tangible retaliation and was, in fact, promoted once. Despite her knowledge that Burlington had a policy against sexual harassment, Ellerth never informed anyone in authority about Slowik's conduct. In filing this lawsuit, Ellerth alleged Burlington had engaged in sexual harassment and had forced her constructive discharge in violation of Title VII of the Civil Rights Act of 1964. (A constructive discharge is a termination of employment that results from an employer's making the employee's working conditions so intolerable that the employee feels compelled to leave.) The district court granted Burlington summary judgment. Reversing the district court, the Seventh Circuit produced a decision consisting of eight separate opinions and no consensus as to a controlling rationale.

ISSUE Under Title VII of the Civil Rights Act of 1964, could an employee who refuses the unwelcome and threatening sexual advances of a supervisor, yet suffers no adverse, tangible job consequences, recover against the employer without showing the employer is negligent or otherwise at fault for the supervisor's actions?

HOLDING Yes. An employer may be held liable for a supervisor's harassing acts even if the employer was not aware of them. But the employer may assert an affirmative defense under which an employer may escape liability when no adverse job action has been taken against the employee. To prove this defense, the employer must show that it (the employer) took reasonable care to prevent and quickly redress any harassment and that the plaintiff unreasonably failed to make use of employer remedies or otherwise to avoid harm.

REASONING Excerpts from the opinion of Justice Kennedy:

At the outset, we assume an important proposition yet to be established before a trier of fact. It is a premise assumed as well, in explicit or implicit terms, in the various opinions by the judges of the Court of Appeals. The premise is: a trier of fact could find in Slowik's remarks numerous threats to retaliate against Ellerth if she denied some sexual liberties. The threats, however, were not carried out or fulfilled. Cases based on threats which are carried out are referred to often as *quid pro quo* cases, as distinct from bothersome attentions or sexual remarks that are sufficiently severe or pervasive to create a hostile work environment. The terms *quid pro quo* and hostile work environment are helpful, perhaps, in making a rough demarcation between cases in which threats are carried out and those where they are not or are absent altogether, but beyond this are of limited utility.... When a plaintiff proves that a tangible employment action resulted from a refusal to submit to a supervisor's sexual demands, he or she establishes that the employment decision itself constitutes a change in the terms and conditions of employment and thus becomes actionable under Title VII.... Because Ellerth's claim involves only unfulfilled threats, it should be categorized as a hostile work environment claim which requires a showing of severe or pervasive conduct.... For purposes of this case, we accept the District Court's finding that the alleged conduct was severe or pervasive. . . . The case before us involves numerous alleged threats, and we express no opinion as to whether a single unfulfilled threat is sufficient to constitute discrimination in the terms or conditions of employment. . . . We must decide, then, whether an employer has vicarious liability when a supervisor creates a hostile work environment by making explicit threats to alter a subordinate's terms or conditions of employment, based on sex, but does not fulfill the threat.

We turn to principles of agency law, for the term "employer" is defined under Title VII to include "agents." . . . In express terms, Congress has directed federal courts to interpret Title VII based on agency principles. . . . As *Meritor* [*v. Vinson*] acknowledged, the *Restatement (Second) of Agency* (1957) (hereinafter *Restatement*) is a useful beginning point for a discussion of general agency principles. . . . Section 219(1) of the *Restatement* sets out a central principle of agency law: . . . An employer may be liable for both negligent and intentional torts committed by an employee within the scope of his or her employment. Sexual harassment under Title VII presupposes intentional conduct. While early decisions absolved employers of liability for the intentional torts of their employees, the law now imposes liability where the employee's "purpose, however misguided, is wholly or in part to further the master's business." The Restatement defines conduct, including an intentional tort, to be within the scope of employment when "actuated, at least in part, by a purpose to serve the [employer]," even if it is forbidden by the employer. . . . Thus, although a supervisor's sexual harassment is outside the scope of employment because the conduct was for personal motives, an employer can be liable, nonetheless, where its own negligence is a cause of the harassment. An employer is negligent with respect to sexual harassment if it knew or should have known about the conduct and failed to stop it. Negligence sets a minimum standard for employer liability under Title VII; but Ellerth seeks to invoke the more stringent standard of vicarious liability.

Restatement 219(2)(d) concerns vicarious liability for intentional torts committed by an employee when the employee "was aided in accomplishing the tort by the existence of the agency relation" (the aided in the agency relation standard). . . . In a sense, most workplace tortfeasors are aided in accomplishing their tortious objective by the existence of the agency relation: Proximity and regular contact may afford a captive pool of potential victims. Were this to satisfy the aided in the agency relation standard, an employer would be subject to vicarious liability not only for all supervisor harassment, but also for all co-worker harassment, a result endorsed by neither the EEOC nor any court of appeals that has considered the issue. . . . The aided in the agency relation standard, therefore, requires the existence of something more than the employment relation itself. . . . Every [court of appeals that has] considered the question has found vicarious liability when a discriminatory act results in a tangible employment action. . . . In *Meritor* we acknowledged this consensus. . . . When a supervisor makes a tangible employment decision, there is assurance the injury could not have been inflicted absent the agency relationship. A tangible employment action in most cases inflicts direct economic harm. As a general proposition, only a supervisor, or other person acting with the authority of the company, can cause this sort of injury. . . . Tangible employment actions are the means by which the supervisor brings the official power of the enterprise to bear on subordinates. . . . The decision in most cases is documented in official company records; and [the decision] may be subject to review by higher level supervisors. . . . For these reasons, a tangible employment action taken by the supervisor becomes for Title VII purposes the act of the employer. Whatever the exact contours of the aided in the agency relation standard, its requirements will always be met when a supervisor takes a tangible employment action against a subordinate. In that instance, it would be implausible to interpret agency principles to allow an employer to escape liability. . . . Whether the agency relation aids in commission of supervisor harassment which does not culminate in a tangible employment action is less obvious. . . . On the one hand, a supervisor's power and authority invest his or her harassing conduct with a particular threatening character, and in this sense, a supervisor always is aided by the agency relation. . . . On the other hand, there are acts of harassment a supervisor might commit which might be the same acts a co-employee would commit, and there may be some circumstances where the supervisor's status makes little difference... and [neither the EEOC nor any court has endorsed vicarious liability in such circumstances.

Hence, an accommodation of] agency principles of vicarious liability for harm caused by the misuse of supervisory authority, as well as Title VII's equally basic policies of encouraging forethought by employers and [eliminating the need for objecting employees to take action leads us to] adopt the following holding: An employer is subject to vicarious liability to a victimized employee for an actionable hostile environment created by a supervisor with immediate (or successively higher) authority over the employee. When no tangible employment action is taken, a defending employer may raise an affirmative defense to liability or damages, subject to proof by a preponderance of the evidence. . . . The defense [is comprised] of two necessary elements: (a) that the employer exercised reasonable care to prevent and correct promptly any sexually harassing behavior and (b) that the plaintiff employee unreasonably failed to take advantage of any preventive or corrective opportunities provided by the employer or to avoid harm otherwise. While proof that an employer had promulgated an anti-harassment policy with complaint procedures is not necessary in every instance as a matter of law, the need for a stated policy suitable to the employment circumstances may appropriately be addressed in any case when [the parties litigate] the first element of the defense. And while proof that an employee failed to fulfill the corresponding obligation of reasonable care to avoid harm is not limited to showing any unreasonable failure to use any complaint procedure provided by the employer, a demonstration of such failure will normally suffice to satisfy the employer's burden under the second element of the defense. No affirmative defense is available, however, when the supervisor's harassment culminates in a tangible employment action, such as discharge, demotion, or undesirable reassignment. . . .

BUSINESS CONSIDERATIONS Assume your employer has asked you to draft a policy that takes into account the *Ellerth* holding. What will you identify as the main provisions of this policy? Why?

ETHICAL CONSIDERATIONS Argue for or against the following proposition: A company's tolerating a work environment rife with sexual innuendos and insults is just as unethical as a company's tolerating a work environment rife with racial or ethnic slurs.

Faragher v. City of Boca Raton,[14] a companion case decided the same day as *Ellerth,* involved allegations of hostile environment sexual discrimination. Faragher, a female lifeguard, and a coworker alleged that during five years of employment, one supervisor touched them inappropriately on a number of occasions and another made offensive comments and gestures. According to the district court's undisputed findings, the harassment was pervasive and severe enough to be actionable, and the supervisors in question had unlimited authority over the lifeguards. The district court also found that the city had failed to disseminate among the beach employees its policy against sexual harassment, had failed to keep track of supervisors, and had provided no assurance that employees could bypass the harassing supervisors when employees made complaints. Under these circumstances, the Supreme Court concluded, the city would not be able to mount a successful affirmative defense of the type enunciated in *Ellerth.* Hence, the Court found the city vicariously liable for its supervisory employees' sexual harassment of the two women, since the Court could not find that the city had exercised reasonable care to prevent the supervisors' harassing conduct.

Although most cases have involved harassment of women by men, men who face harassment from women supervisors have standing to sue under Title VII as well. Moreover, in yet another recent case, the Supreme Court in *Oncale v. Sundowner Offshore Services, Inc.*[15] held that workplace sexual harassment is actionable under Title VII when the offender and the victim are the same sex. Joseph Oncale, a male, worked as a roustabout on an oil platform in the Gulf of Mexico. He alleged that his male coworkers forcibly subjected him to sexually humiliating actions, physically assaulted him in a sexual manner, and threatened to rape him. Although the lower courts had held that same-sex sexual harassment is never actionable under Title VII, the Court declared that "nothing in Title VII necessarily bars a claim of discrimination because of . . . sex" merely because the plaintiff and the defendant (or the person charged with acting on behalf of the defendant) are of the same sex.[16] Moreover, to support an inference of discrimination based on sex, the Court explained, the harassing conduct need not be motivated by sexual desire. The Court also rejected the employer's contention that the Court's

recognizing same-sex harassment claims would make Title VII "a general civility code" for the workplace.[17] Rather, the Court stressed that the application of common sense, coupled with an appropriate sensitivity to the social context in which the conduct occurred (for example, a football coach's swatting a player on the buttocks as the player runs onto the field would not be the equivalent of similar conduct directed at the coach's secretary, either male or female); this approach would "enable courts and juries to distinguish between simple teasing or roughhousing among members of the same sex, and conduct which a reasonable person in the plaintiff's position would find severely hostile or abusive."[18]

Employers thus face potentially large recoveries if they fail to take corrective actions to end sexual harassment once they know, or should have known, that it had occurred. Wise employers should establish and then vigorously enforce policies against sexual harassment. To illustrate, in 1994 a female secretary in one of the largest law firms in the country won a $3.5 million judgment against the firm and the partner who allegedly had harassed numerous women over a 14-year period. More recently, in 1999, Ford Motor Company agreed to pay $7.5 million in damages and millions more in training costs as part of its settlement of an EEOC-initiated sexual harassment complaint brought on behalf of female workers in two Chicago area plants. This settlement followed the 1998 one involving Mitsubishi Motor Manufacturing Company's record-breaking $34 million agreement to settle a similar case at its Normal, Illinois, plant.

The Pregnancy Discrimination Act of 1978, passed by Congress as an amendment to Title VII, dictates that an employer treat pregnancy in the same fashion as any other disability. To do otherwise constitutes actionable sex discrimination. *International Union UAW v. Johnson Controls, Inc.*[19] illustrates an interesting gloss on the Pregnancy Discrimination Act. Johnson Controls, Inc.'s battery-manufacturing process used lead, occupational exposure to which entails health risks, including the risk of harm to a fetus carried by a female employee. After eight of its employees had become pregnant while maintaining blood lead levels exceeding that noted by the Occupational Safety and Health Administration (OSHA) as critical for a worker planning to have a family, Johnson Controls announced a policy barring all women, except those whose infertility could be medically documented, from jobs involving actual or potential lead exposure exceeding the OSHA standard. The International Union UAW, a group including employees affected by the company's fetal-protection policy, filed a class action in the district court and claimed that the policy constituted sex discrimination violative of Title VII of the Civil Rights Act of 1964. The district court granted summary judgment for Johnson Controls, and the court of appeals affirmed.

The question before the Supreme Court focused on whether Johnson Controls's sex-specific fetal-protection policy, in which the company had excluded fertile female employees from certain jobs because of its concern for the health of the fetuses the women might conceive, violated Title VII's ban on sex discrimination. According to the Court, by excluding women with childbearing capacity from lead-exposed jobs, Johnson Controls's policy created a facial classification based on gender and explicitly discriminated against women on the basis of their sex under Title VII. Moreover, in using the words "capable of bearing children" as the criterion for exclusion, the policy explicitly classified on the basis of potential for pregnancy, which classification, under the Pregnancy Discrimination Act, constitutes explicit sex discrimination. According to the Court, the bias in Johnson Controls's policy was obvious: The company gives fertile men, but not fertile women, a choice as to whether they wish to risk their reproductive health for a particular job. Johnson Controls's fetal-protection policy therefore explicitly discriminated against women on the basis of their sex. In the Court's view, the Pregnancy Discrimination Act of 1978, in which Congress explicitly provided that, for purposes of Title VII, discrimination "on the basis of sex" includes discrimination "because of or on the basis of pregnancy, childbirth, or related medical conditions" also bolstered this conclusion. In other words, for all Title VII purposes, discrimination based on a woman's pregnancy is, on its face, discrimination because of her sex. Johnson Controls's use of the words "capable of bearing children" illustrated that it explicitly had classified on the basis of potential for pregnancy.

Moreover, the Court stressed, the beneficence of an employer's purpose does not undermine the conclusion that an explicit, gender-based policy is sex discrimination. Nevertheless, under § 703(e)(1) of Title VII, an employer may discriminate on the basis of "religion, sex, or national origin in those certain instances where religion, sex, or national origin is a bona fide occupational qualification [BFOQ] reasonably necessary to the normal operation of that particular business or enterprise." And while Johnson Controls argued that its fetal-protection policy falls within the so-called third-party safety exception to the BFOQ,

Supreme Court cases have stressed that discrimination on the basis of sex because of safety concerns is allowed only in narrow circumstances. In the present case, the unconceived fetuses of Johnson Controls's female employees, however, were neither customers nor third parties whose safety is essential to the business of battery manufacturing. No one can disregard the possibility of injury to future children. Yet the BFOQ is not so broad that it transforms this deep social concern into an essential aspect of battery making. Consequently, the employer must direct its concerns about a woman's ability to perform her job safely and efficiently to these aspects of the woman's job-related activities that fall within the "essence" of the particular business. Johnson Controls's professed moral and ethical concerns about the welfare of the next generation would not suffice to establish a BFOQ of female sterility. Decisions about the welfare of future children, the Court concluded, must be left to the parents who conceive, bear, support, and raise them rather than to the employers who hire those parents.

In addition to prohibiting various types of sex discrimination, Title VII's ban on national origin discrimination similarly prevents harassment in the form of ethnic slurs based on the country in which one was born or the country from which one's ancestors came. Repeated ethnic jokes and other derogatory statements directed at one's ethnic origins in a given case may constitute national origin discrimination.

National origin discrimination often takes the form of "covert discrimination." To illustrate, height/weight requirements may foreclose Spanish-surnamed Americans from employment opportunities, as may language difficulties or accents. If an employer fails to hire a worker on the basis of such criteria, the employer must prove that the criteria are job related.

Narrow BFOQs may exist in national origin cases. It is legal to hire a French person to be a French chef, for example. It also is legal to refuse to hire non–American citizens (because the prohibition against national origin discrimination in Title VII does not include citizenship)[20] unless the discrimination in favor of citizens has the purpose or effect of discrimination on the basis of national origin. The protected categories under Title VII do not include alienage in and of itself. Likewise, it is not a violation of Title VII for an employer to refuse to hire persons who are unable to obtain security clearances because they have relatives in countries that are on unfriendly terms with the United States.

Immigration Reform and Control Act of 1986 On the other hand, the Immigration Reform and Control Act of 1986 (IRCA), although principally aimed at stemming the flow of illegal aliens into the United States, out of fairness

NRW CASE 40.2   Management

HIRING REQUIREMENTS

From its inception, NRW has had a policy of refusing to hire any full-time, nonfamily applicants who are not at least high school graduates. The firm's members have included this requirement in the firm's hiring manual because they believe that any high-tech firm—and NRW is high-tech—needs a well-educated workforce if it is to succeed. Mai recently has noticed this provision in the personnel manual, and she is concerned that this requirement makes NRW vulnerable to lawsuits claiming that the firm is guilty of racial discrimination in its hiring practices. She asks you what she should do in this situation. What advice will you give her? Why?

BUSINESS CONSIDERATIONS Should a business have a policy for any situation in which it decides to change the requirements an applicant must meet to be considered for a position? What factors should any such policy include? Could a firm's changing its job descriptions or hiring qualifications lead to possible legal vulnerabilities?

ETHICAL CONSIDERATIONS Would it be ethical for a business to establish higher job requirements for a given position than are absolutely necessary to perform the described job? What ethical concerns would such a job description raise? What should a company do to act ethically, as well as legally, in this situation?

INTERNATIONAL CONSIDERATIONS One reason often cited for the exodus of firms to other countries is the lower wages paid in those other countries, a factor often coupled with those nations' laxness regarding environmental regulation. Should a firm consider such aspects in deciding where to locate—or relocate—one of its plants? Should the firm be more concerned with pay or with the likely level of education and/or training the prospective employees will possess?

---

also bans immigration-related discrimination based on national origin or citizenship status. This act therefore prohibits an employer's turning away job applicants because they appear to be aliens or noncitizens. Besides being narrower in scope than Title VII (the IRCA covers only hiring, recruitment of workers for a fee, and discharges), Title VII also preempts this act whenever Title VII covers the conduct in question. The IRCA's legislative history makes it clear that Congress did not intend this act to expand the rights granted under Title VII. The *Hoffman* decision (Case 40.1) is a recent Supreme Court interpretation of the relationship between the IRCA and federal labor law, specifically the National Labor Relations Act (the NLRA).

Equal Pay Act of 1963 In addition to Title VII, several other federal statutes protect various classes of persons. The Equal Pay Act of 1963 prohibits discrimination in wages on the basis of sex. Therefore, men and women performing work in the same establishment under similar working conditions must receive the same rate of pay if the work requires equal skill, equal effort, and equal responsibility. Different wages may be paid if the employer bases the differential on seniority, merit, piecework, or any factor other than sex (for example, participation in training programs).

The Age Discrimination in Employment Act of 1967 The Age Discrimination in Employment Act of 1967 (ADEA), in general, protects workers aged 40 or older from adverse employment decisions based on age. BFOQs based on safety or human and economic risks—age 55 retirement for police officers, for instance—may be upheld, as may differentiation in age based on a bona fide seniority system and discharges or disciplinary actions undertaken for good cause. The Supreme Court recently held that a plaintiff who alleges discrimination under the ADEA does not have to show, as part of his or her prima facie case, that the employer replaced the plaintiff with a worker under age 40 (*O'Connor v. Consolidated Coin Caterers Corporation*).[21] According to the Court, the fact that one person in the protected class has lost out to another person in the protected class is irrelevant, so long as the plaintiff can show that he or she has lost out because of his or her *age*.

Another recent case, *Oubre v. Entergy Operations, Inc.*,[22] held that a release of all claims against her employer that the employee had signed as a part of a termination agreement would not bar the employee's subsequent lawsuit based on the ADEA. The Supreme Court based its holding on the employer's noncompliance with the Older Workers Benefit Protection Act (OWBPA) passed by Congress in 1996 as an amendment to the ADEA. Specifically, the Court held that, under the OWBPA, Oubre's waiver had not been knowing and voluntary because the waiver had failed to comply with the requirements of the statute. Specifically, this attempted waiver was flawed in that it had not given Oubre sufficient time to consider her options; it had failed to provide her with a seven days' period in which to change her mind; and the waiver had omitted any specific references to ADEA claims. Hence, the Court concluded, the waiver was ineffective and thus would not bar

HARASSMENT POLICY

NRW employs several drivers who operate company trucks delivering the firm's products to customers. Each driver is assigned a particular truck. Sam, one of the drivers, took a personal leave day. Another driver, Toni, was assigned the truck that Sam normally drives. At the end of the day, Toni informed Carlos that Sam had taped several "girlie" pictures to the dashboard of the delivery truck and that she found the pictures sexist and insulting. Carlos apologized to Toni and promised to look into the situation. Carlos later sought your advice as to what liability could arise from these circumstances. What would you tell him?

BUSINESS CONSIDERATIONS Should a business establish a strong policy addressing discrimination and harassment before any complaints arise, or should the business wait until there is a problem and then address that particular problem? If the business decides to become proactive, what sorts of conduct should its policy cover?

ETHICAL CONSIDERATIONS Is it ethical for a business to prohibit the free speech of some of its employees if other employees find such speech offensive? How can an employer protect the freedoms and rights of each employee and simultaneously protect all employees from discrimination and harassment?

INTERNATIONAL CONSIDERATIONS Do the cultural values and mores of a nation affect the employment laws of that nation? How might differing values affect a business that opens operations in another nation? How might such differences affect the business's employment policies?

her bringing a subsequent ADEA action, despite her failure to return the monies she had received for signing the release. Owing to this holding, a prudent employer will take steps to ensure the firm's strict compliance with OWBPA whenever the firm provides terminated employees with an agreement that includes a waiver of age-related claims.

The Rehabilitation Act of 1973

The Rehabilitation Act of 1973 directs federal contractors to take affirmative action with respect to "otherwise qualified" handicapped individuals. A handicapped individual includes any person who "has a physical or mental impairment which substantially limits one or more of such person's major life functions, has a record of such impairment, or is regarded as having such an impairment." Federal contractors must make "reasonable accommodation" to such a person's impairments unless to do so would pose an "undue hardship" on the operation of their programs.

The Americans with Disabilities Act of 1990

The Americans with Disabilities Act of 1990 (ADA) seeks to redress discrimination against individuals with disabilities and to guarantee such individuals equal access to public services (including public accommodations and transportation), public services operated by private entities, and telecommunications relay services, to name a few.

Title I, which prohibits employment discrimination, adopts the Rehabilitation Act of 1973 definition of handicap but uses the more up-to-date term disability. The ADA, in requiring an employer to provide "reasonable accommodation to the known physical or mental limitations" of a person with a disability unless such accommodation "would impose an undue hardship on the operation of the business" of the covered entity, obviously continues to borrow heavily from the 1973 act. Reasonable accommodation under the ADA includes such actions as making existing facilities accessible to and usable by persons with disabilities, restructuring jobs, and providing part-time or modified work schedules.

However, the act does not require the employer to implement any job accommodation if the employer can demonstrate that the accommodation would impose an "undue hardship" on the operation of the business. The ADA defines *undue hardship* as an action requiring "significant difficulty or expense" with reference to the following factors: (1) the nature and cost of the accommodation; (2) the size, type, and financial resources of the specific facility where the accommodation would have to be made; (3) the size, type, and financial resources of the covered employer; and (4) the covered employer's type of operation, including the composition, structure, and functions of its workforce and the geographic separateness and administrative or fiscal relationship between the specific facility and the covered employer.

The legislative history indicates that the "significant difficulty or expense" standard encompasses any "action that is unduly costly, extensive, substantial, disruptive, or that will fundamentally alter the nature of the program." Significant, too, is the fact that in defining "undue hardship," Congress rejected all attempts to put a cap on the level of difficulty or expense that would constitute an "undue hardship," including an amendment to create a presumption that the cost of any accommodation exceeding 10 percent of the annual salary of the position in question constitutes an "undue hardship."

The employment discrimination provisions under Title I cover employers that have on their weekly payrolls 15 or more full- or part-time employees for each working day in each of 20 or more calendar weeks in the current or preceding calendar year. Hence, the ADA's provisions apply to an estimated 3.9 million business establishments and 666,000 employers. Like the Civil Rights Act of 1964, the ADA covers employers, employment agencies, labor organizations, and joint labor/management committees, but exempts religious entities. Thus, the ADA's coverage goes beyond that of the Rehabilitation Act of 1973, which applies only to employers doing business with the federal government. The ADA in addition expressly protects employees or applicants who have completed (or who are participating in) a drug rehabilitation program and no longer are engaging in the use of illegal drugs. Without fear of violating the ADA, employers can, however, impose sanctions against employees who currently are using illegal drugs and may hold such employees (and/or employees who are alcoholics) to the same performance and conduct standards to which it holds other employees, even if the unsatisfactory performance or behavior is related to the employees' drug use or alcoholism. The ADA also protects from discrimination persons who have AIDS or who are HIV-positive. Indeed, in *Bragdon v. Abbott*,[23] the Supreme Court's first pronouncement on the ADA, the Court held that an individual infected with the human immunodeficiency virus (HIV) can invoke the protections of the ADA, even if the virus that causes AIDS is in its asymptomatic phase. The Court, however, stopped short of characterizing HIV infection as a *per se* disability under the ADA.[24] The Court instead remanded the case for an assessment of whether the plaintiff-patient's HIV infection posed a significant threat to the health and safety of others so as to justify the defendant-dentist's refusal to treat the plaintiff in his office.[25]

At the congressional hearings for the ADA, experts testified that it potentially would cover about 43 million Americans and that its enactment therefore might cause a flood of litigation. Indeed, the EEOC itself predicted that complainants would file between 12,000 and 15,000 charges during the first year the statute took effect—a prediction borne out by the number of actual filings.[26] From 1992 to the fall of 2001, the agency resolved almost 169,000 ADA-related charges.[27] As with any comparatively new legislation, the overall impact of the ADA remains unclear. In addition to the costs associated with the hiring process and those resulting from the predicted increases in litigation

under the act, the expenses of converting existing facilities to make them accessible to individuals with disabilities obviously concern many employers, particularly small firms. Yet data from a pre-ADA survey of federal contractors showed that the compliance costs and workplace changes incurred under the Rehabilitation Act of 1973 for half of the companies amounted to zero dollars and for 30 percent of the companies less than $500. In only 8 percent of the cases did the changes cost more than $2,000.

Various circuit courts of appeals had struggled with the ADA issue that is the focus of the following case. Note how the Supreme Court disposed of the conflicting holdings that had developed in these appellate courts.

Besides the *Toyota* holding, the Court in 2002 announced three other significant decisions with regard to the ADA. The first involved Mario Echazabal, who had sought employment with Chevron U.S.A., Inc. but was unsuccessful owing to an abnormal liver, a condition that, according to Chevron's doctors, would be aggravated by continued exposure to toxins at Chevron's refinery where Echazabal had been working for a Chevron subcontractor. After Echazabal underwent a second physical exam, Chevron asked the contractor employing Echazabal either to reassign him to a job without exposure to harmful chemicals or to remove him from the refinery altogether. The contractor laid Echazabal off in early 1996. Echazabal subsequently filed suit, claiming that Chevron had violated the ADA by refusing to hire him or even to let him continue working in the plant, because of a disability, his liver condition. In rebuttal, Chevron cited an EEOC regulation permitting the defense that a worker's disability on the job would pose a "direct threat" to his or her health. This EEOC regulation represented an extension of an affirmative defense set out in the ADA, namely, that employers can screen out workers who pose a direct threat to the health or safety of "other individuals" (that is, coworkers) in the workplace. The Court held that the EEOC regulation in question was a reasonable interpretation of the ADA and thus entitled to deference by courts. Hence, Chevron could refuse to hire Echazabal.[28]

US Airways, Inc. v. Barnett,[29] the second case, involved an employee who had injured his back while working in a cargo-handling position at US Airways. He invoked his seniority rights and transferred to a less physically demanding mailroom position. Under US Airways's seniority system, that position, like others, periodically became open to seniority-based employee bidding. In 1992, Barnett learned that at least two employees senior to him intended to bid for the mailroom job. He thereupon asked US Airways to accommodate his disability-imposed limitations by making an exception that would allow him to remain in the

40.3

TOYOTA MOTOR MANUFACTURING, KENTUCKY, INC. v. WILLIAMS
534 U.S. 184 (2002)

FACTS Ella Williams worked on the Toyota Motor Manufacturing, Kentucky, Inc. assembly line from 1990 to 1996. In her first year of employment, her duties included work with pneumatic tools that caused pain in her hands, wrists, and arms. Toyota's in-house medical service diagnosed her as having various impairments, including carpal tunnel syndrome. For the next two years, Toyota assigned Williams to various modified-duty jobs. Dissatisfied with these accommodations, Williams filed suit under the ADA. As a part of the 1993 settlement of this suit, she agreed to a reassignment involving a four-phase, quality control, inspection regime. Williams satisfactorily performed the tasks required by the first two phases. But in 1996, Toyota announced that all quality control workers must be able to rotate through all four phases of the quality control processes. When the third phase, which required workers to hold their hands and arms at shoulder height for several hours at a time, was added to Williams's rotations, she began to experience pain in her neck and shoulders. After being diagnosed with various medical conditions, Williams requested an accommodation that would allow her to return to doing only her original two quality control jobs, which she claimed she still could perform without difficulties.

The parties disputed what happened next. Williams said Toyota refused her request and forced her to continue work on the third phase, thereby worsening her physical injuries. According to Toyota, Williams simply began missing work on a regular basis. On December 6, 1996, the last day Williams worked at the plant, Williams's treating physicians placed her on a no-work-of-any-kind restriction. On January 27, 1997, Toyota, citing her poor attendance record, fired Williams. Williams subsequently sued Toyota under the ADA on the rationale that Toyota's failure to reasonably accommodate her disability made her termination illegal. The district court determined that Williams was not disabled under the ADA because her self-avowed capacity to perform some assembly and inspection tasks meant that she was not substantially limited in performing manual tasks. Reversing the district court, the court of appeals held that, in order for Williams to demonstrate she had a disability for ADA purposes, as a result of a substantial limitation on her ability to perform the major life activity of performing manual tasks, she had to show that her manual disability involved a class of manual activities affecting the ability to perform tasks at work. The court of appeals found that Williams had satisfied this test, since her ailments prevented her from doing the tasks associated with certain jobs involving repetitive work with hands and arms extended at or above shoulder levels for extended periods of time.

ISSUE At the time she had sought an accommodation, was Williams substantially limited in performing manual tasks and therefore disabled under the ADA?

HOLDING No. The court of appeals, in finding that Williams was disabled, had failed to apply the proper standard for making this determination. The court had erred in analyzing only a limited class of manual tasks and in failing to ask whether Williams's impairments prevented or restricted her from performing tasks that are of central importance to most people's daily lives.

REASONING Excerpts from the opinion of Justice O'Connor:

The question presented by this case is whether the Sixth Circuit properly determined that [Williams] was disabled under subsection (A) of the ADA's disability definition at the time that she sought an accommodation from [Toyota]. . . . The parties do not dispute that [Williams's] medical conditions, which include carpal tunnel syndrome, myotendinitis, and thoracic outlet compression, amount to physical impairments. The relevant question, therefore, is whether the Sixth Circuit correctly analyzed whether these impairments substantially limited [Williams] in the major life activity of performing manual tasks. Answering this requires us to address an issue about which the EEOC regulations are silent: what a plaintiff must demonstrate to establish a substantial limitation in the specific major life activity of performing manual tasks. [The] consideration of this issue is guided first and foremost by the words of the disability definition itself. "Substantially" in the phrase "substantially limits" suggests "considerable" or "to a large degree." . . . The word "substantial" thus clearly precludes impairments that interfere in only a minor way with the performance of manual tasks from qualifying as disabilities. . . . "Major" in the phrase "major life activities" means important. . . . "Major life activities" thus refers to those activities that are of central importance to daily life. In order for performing manual tasks to fit into this category—a category that includes such basic abilities as walking, seeing, and hearing—the manual tasks in question must be central to daily life. If each of the tasks included in the major life activity of performing manual tasks does not independently qualify as a major life activity, then together they must do so. That these terms need to be interpreted strictly to create a demanding standard for qualifying as disabled is confirmed by the first section of the ADA, which lays out the legislative findings and purposes that motivate the Act. . . . When it enacted the ADA in 1990, Congress found that "some 43,000,000 Americans have one or more physical or mental disabilities." . . . If Congress intended everyone with a physical impairment that precluded the performance of some isolated, unimportant, or particularly difficult manual task to qualify as disabled, the number of disabled Americans would surely have been much higher. . . .

We therefore hold that to be substantially limited in performing manual tasks, an individual must have an impairment that prevents or severely restricts the individual from doing activities that are of central importance to most people's daily lives. The impairment's impact must also be permanent or long-term. . . . It is insufficient for individuals attempting to prove disability status under this test to merely submit evidence of a medical diagnosis of an impairment. Instead, the ADA requires those "claiming the Act's protection . . . to prove a disability by offering evidence that the extent of the limitation [caused by their impairment] in terms of their own experience . . . is substantial." . . . That the Act defines "disability" "with respect to an individual," . . . makes clear that Congress intended the existence of a disability to be determined in such a case-by-case manner. . . . An individualized assessment of the effect of an impairment is particularly necessary when the impairment is one whose symptoms vary widely from person to person. Carpal tunnel syndrome, one of [Williams's] impairments, is just such a condition. While cases of severe carpal tunnel syndrome are characterized by muscle atrophy and extreme sensory deficits, mild cases generally do not have either of these effects and create only intermittent symptoms of numbness and tingling. . . . Studies have further shown that, even without surgical treatment, one quarter of carpal tunnel cases resolve in one month, but that in 22 percent of cases, symptoms last for eight years or longer. . . . Given these large potential differences in the severity and duration of the effects of carpal tunnel syndrome, an individual's carpal tunnel syndrome diagnosis, on its own, does not indicate whether the individual has a disability within the meaning of the ADA.

The Court of Appeals' analysis of [Williams's] claimed disability suggested that in order to prove a substantial limitation in the major life activity of performing manual tasks, a "plaintiff must show that her manual disability involves a 'class' of manual activities," and that those activities "affect the ability to perform tasks at work." . . . Both of these ideas lack support. The Court of Appeals relied on our opinion in *Sutton v. United Air Lines, Inc.*, for the idea that a "class" of manual activities must be implicated for an impairment to substantially limit the major life activity of performing manual tasks. . . . But *Sutton* said only that "when the major life activity under consideration is that of working, the statutory phrase 'substantially limits' requires . . . that plaintiffs allege that they are unable to work in a broad class of jobs." . . . Because of the conceptual difficulties inherent in the argument that working could be a major life activity, we have been hesitant to hold as much, and . . . need not decide this difficult question today. In *Sutton*, we noted that even assuming that working is a major life activity, a claimant would be required to show an inability to work in a "broad range of jobs," rather than a specific job. . . . But *Sutton* did not suggest that a class-based analysis should be applied to any major life activity other than working. Nor do the EEOC regulations. In defining "substantially limits," the EEOC regulations only mention the "class" concept in the context of the major life activity of working. . . . ("With respect to the major life activity of working[,] the term substantially limits means significantly restricted in the ability to perform either a class of jobs or a broad range of jobs in various classes as compared to the average person having comparable training, skills and abilities"). Nothing in the text of the Act, our previous opinions, or the regulations suggests that a class-based framework should apply outside the context of the major life activity of working. While the Court of Appeals in this case addressed the different major life activity of performing manual tasks, its analysis circumvented *Sutton* by focusing on [Williams's] inability to perform manual tasks associated only with her job. This was error. When addressing the major life activity of performing manual tasks, the central inquiry must be whether the claimant is unable to perform the variety of tasks central to most people's daily lives, not whether the claimant is unable to perform the tasks associated with her specific job. Otherwise, *Sutton*'s restriction on claims of disability based on a substantial limitation in working will be rendered meaningless because an inability to perform a specific job always can be recast as an inability to perform a "class" of tasks associated with that specific job.

There is also no support in the Act, our previous opinions, or the regulations for the Court of Appeals' idea that the question of whether an impairment constitutes a disability is to be answered only by analyzing the effect of the impairment in the workplace. Indeed, the fact that the Act's definition of "disability" applies not only to Title I of the Act, . . . which deals with employment, but also to the other portions of the Act, which deal with subjects such as public transportation . . . and privately provided public accommodations, . . . demonstrates that the definition is intended to cover individuals with disabling impairments regardless of whether the individuals have any connection to a workplace. Even more critically, the manual tasks unique to any particular job are not necessarily important parts of most people's lives. As a result, occupation-specific tasks may have only limited relevance to the manual task inquiry. In this case, "repetitive work with hands and arms extended at or above shoulder levels for extended periods of time," . . . the manual task on which the Court of Appeals relied is not an important part of most people's daily lives. The court, therefore, should not have considered [Williams's] inability to do such manual work in her specialized assembly line job as sufficient proof that she was substantially limited in performing manual tasks.

At the same time, the Court of Appeals appears to have disregarded the very type of evidence that it should have focused upon. It treated as irrelevant "the fact that [Williams] can . . . tend to her personal hygiene [and] carry out personal or household chores.". . . Yet household chores, bathing, and brushing one's teeth are among the types of manual tasks of central importance to people's daily lives, and should have been part of the assessment of whether [Williams] was substantially limited in performing manual tasks. The District Court noted that at the time [Williams] sought an accommodation from [Toyota], she admitted that she was able to do the manual tasks required by her original two jobs in [quality control]. . . . In addition, according to [Williams's] deposition testimony, even after her condi-

tion worsened, she could still brush her teeth, wash her face, bathe, tend her flower garden, fix breakfast, do laundry, and pick up around the house. . . . The record also indicates that her medical conditions caused her to avoid sweeping, to quit dancing, to occasionally seek help dressing, and to reduce how often she plays with her children, gardens, and drives long distances. . . . But these changes in her life did not amount to such severe restrictions in the activities that are of central importance to most people's daily lives that they establish a manual-task disability as a matter of law. On this record, it was therefore inappropriate for the Court of Appeals to grant partial summary judgment to [Williams] on the issue of whether she was substantially limited in performing manual tasks, and its decision to do so must be reversed. . . .

BUSINESS CONSIDERATIONS The Court declined to decide the question of whether working is a major life activity under the ADA. What arguments could one offer in support of the proposition that working is—or is not—such an activity? Why was the Court reluctant to tackle this question?

ETHICAL CONSIDERATIONS Some phases of Toyota's quality control inspection regime entailed tasks most employees would view as unpleasant. Suppose the phase that had caused Williams to ask for an accommodation involved such an undertaking. Would it be ethical for a firm such as Toyota to grant what some nondisabled workers might view as preferential treatment (that is, assigning a less demanding job) of the person who asks for an accommodation? Conversely, would it be ethical for a firm to refuse to assign such a task to the person requesting the accommodation?

mailroom. After permitting Barnett to continue his mailroom work for five months while it considered the matter, US Airways eventually decided not to make an exception. When Barnett lost his job, he brought an ADA lawsuit. US Airways claimed that the presence of a seniority system virtually always trumps a conflicting request for accommodation because any significant alteration of the seniority policy would result in an undue hardship for both the company and any nondisabled employees. In short, US Airways argued that since an accommodation would provide a "preference"—in the sense that it would permit the worker with a disability to violate a rule that others must obey—that fact, in and of itself, would automatically show that the accommodation is not "reasonable." The Supreme Court agreed, holding that such an accommodation, in the form of an assignment to a particular position, ordinarily would conflict with the rules of an employer's established sen-

iority system and thus would be sufficient to show that the accommodation is not reasonable under the ADA. Moreover, such a showing usually entitles the employer to summary judgment on this issue. Nevertheless, the employee with a disability remains free to present evidence of special circumstances that would make an exception to the seniority rules reasonable in the particular case.

In the third decision, the Supreme Court ruled that plaintiffs who bring private actions under the Rehabilitation Act and the ADA cannot receive punitive damages. Rather, such plaintiffs' remedies are limited to compensatory damages, the type of damages ordinarily granted under traditional contract law.[30]

Civil Rights Act of 1991 Congress enacted the Civil Rights Act of 1991 after a two-year struggle. Interestingly, Congress in part passed this act to overturn a series of 1989 and 1991 Supreme Court cases that had significantly eroded the rights of complainants alleging employment discrimination. Thus, the act reflected Congress's displeasure with the present Court's judicial attitude toward civil rights cases. The act, in its amendments of Title VII, therefore reaffirms the holdings of such cases as *Griggs v. Duke Power Co.*[31] The 1991 act's amendments to § 1981 of the Civil Rights Act of 1866 also specify that this statute covers all forms of racial discrimination in employment (including racial harassment).

Besides these pro-complainant provisions, the act mandates the impartial use of tests and thus prohibits "race norming" of employment tests. In other words, employers must record and report actual scores and will be unable to modify scores, use different cutoff scores, or otherwise adjust the results of employment-related tests on the basis of race, color, religion, sex, or national origin even if employers have taken these actions to assure minority inclusion in the applicant pool. In a similar vein, the act effects no changes regarding what constitutes lawful affirmative action and/or illegal reverse discrimination. It also restricts challenges to court-ordered consent decrees by individuals who had a reasonable opportunity to object to such decrees or whose interests were adequately represented by another party.

The act does broaden the scope of federal antidiscrimination law. It makes clear that Americans employed abroad by U.S.-owned or U.S.-controlled firms can avail themselves of the protection of Title VII, the ADA, and the ADEA, unless compliance with these laws will constitute a violation of the host country's laws. The act moreover extends coverage of the antidiscrimination laws to congressional employees and executive branch political appointees and sets up discrete internal mechanisms for addressing such claims. Nevertheless, in 2001 the Supreme Court held that state employees cannot sue their employers for damages under the ADA because Congress had exceeded its power under the Fourteenth Amendment to enforce the equal protection clause when it applied the ADA to state workers.[32] In holding such suits barred by the Eleventh Amendment, the Court added the ADA to the growing list of federal statutes that cannot be enforced against states that refuse to consent to such suits (a year earlier, the Court had reached the same conclusion with regard to the ADEA).[33] Hence, under both the ADA and the ADEA, such states are entitled to immunity from private damage suits.

The act furthermore broadens the categories of victims who can seek compensatory and punitive damages based on intentional discrimination, although it provides for caps of $50,000 to $300,000 (depending on the size of the employer's workforce) for discrimination based on the complainant's disability, sex, or religion. The Supreme

Court recently held in *Pollard v. E.I. DuPont de Nemours & Company*[34] that front pay—money awarded for lost compensation during the period between the court judgment and reinstatement or in lieu of reinstatement—is not an element of compensatory damages under the Civil Rights Act of 1991. Hence, an award for hostile environment sexual harassment under Title VII was not subject to the act's damages cap of $300,000. The Court concluded that, because front pay (the more modern term for "backpay," the language used at the time of Title VII's enactment) is a remedy authorized under § 706(g), Congress had not limited the availability of such awards in the 1991 act. Instead, in this more recent statute, Congress had sought to expand the available remedies by permitting the recovery of compensatory and punitive damages in addition to previously available remedies such as front pay. Any complainant eligible for compensatory or punitive damages may request a jury trial as well. The act also allows successful complainants to recover expert witness fees in addition to attorney's fees.

Other amendments deal with the availability of interest payments for delayed awards, extensions of filing deadlines for lawsuits brought against the government, notification by the EEOC to the complainant when the EEOC dismisses charges under the ADEA, and a longer statute of limitations period for a claimant who brings an action under the ADEA. The act obligates the EEOC to establish a Technical Assistance Training Institute for entities covered by the laws the EEOC enforces. In addition, the act mandates an EEOC outreach/education program for individuals who historically have been the object of employment discrimination. Title II of the act, the Glass Ceiling Act of 1991, sets up a commission to study why impediments to the advancement of women and minorities exist and to make recommendations for eliminating such barriers. Businesses that show substantial efforts to advance such groups to management and decision-making positions are eligible to receive national awards recognizing their efforts.[35]

Given the comparative recency of this novel landmark legislation, subsequent court decisions will answer the various questions spawned by the act. In 1994, the Supreme Court in *Landgraf v. USI Film Products*[36] answered one such question—whether the 1991 act applies retroactively to Title VII cases pending on appeal at the time of its enactment—by holding that it does not. Even more significantly, a 1999 Supreme Court case—*Kolstad v. American Dental Association*[37]—held that courts may award punitive damages in Title VII cases without a showing of "egregious" misconduct in addition to proof of the employer's state of mind. Although punitive damages had been available under Title VII since the passage of the Civil Rights Act of 1991, the lower courts had imposed a variety of standards for imposing such damages against employers that violate the statute. In resolving the split in the circuit courts of appeals as to the standard of conduct needed for an employer to face liability for punitive damages, the Court stressed that the 1991 act limits compensatory and punitive damages awards to cases of intentional discrimination (as opposed to cases relying on the "disparate impact" theory of discrimination) and further conditions the availability of punitive damages on a showing that the defendant engaged in a discriminatory practice "with malice or with reckless indifference to the federally protected rights of an aggrieved individual."[38] Hence, according to the Court, an award of punitive damages is predicated on the defendant's state of mind and does not require—as the court of appeals erroneously had held—a showing of egregious or outrageous discrimination independent of the employer's state of mind. Citing the *Ellerth* case, the Court further held that in the punitive damages context, an employer may not be held vicariously liable for the discriminatory employment decisions of managerial agents where these decisions are contrary to the employer's good faith efforts to comply with Title VII.[39]

You should visit http://www.eeoc.gov/stats, a site that sets out numerous statistics relating to the various types of charges under Title VII, the Equal Pay Act, the ADEA, and the ADA. The EEOC litigation statistics, in particular, show some interesting trends. Note the gargantuan monetary benefits achieved through the agency's enforcement efforts.

Family and Medical Leave Act of 1993 The first major piece of legislation passed under the Clinton administration was the Family and Medical Leave Act of 1993 (FMLA). Regulations promulgated by the Department of Labor obligate certain employers of 50 or more persons to do the following: formulate a family leave policy, revise employee handbooks and policy manuals so that they are consistent with such a policy, alter any inconsistent policies, and prepare for the paperwork required under the act.

Divided into six titles and 26 sections, the FMLA covers public employers of any size and private employers that have on their weekly payrolls 50 or more employees during each of 20 or more calendar workweeks in the current or preceding calendar year. Employees eligible to take leave under the act must have worked for the employer for at least 12 months and for at least 1,250 hours in the 12 months immediately preceding the commencement of any leave taken under the act. Employees who work at job facilities that employ fewer than 50 persons remain ineligible for FMLA leave unless the employer has 50 or more employees working within a 75-mile radius of any worksite. Part-time employees count, but laid-off employees do not.

Section 102 of the FMLA provides generally that "an eligible employee shall be entitled to a total of 12 work weeks of leave during any 12 month period" for the following family-related events: (1) the birth of a child; (2) the placement of a child with the employee for adoption or foster care; (3) the care of a seriously ill spouse, child, or parent; and (4) a serious health condition of the employee that makes him or her unable to perform any of the essential functions of his or her job.

The FMLA does not require the employer to pay for any leave taken under the act. However, eligible employees can use any accrued vacation or personal leave for FMLA purposes. Similarly, an eligible employee may elect to use any paid leave—sick, family, or disability leave—in accordance with the terms of the employer's leave policies. In fact, the employer can require employees to exhaust all "banked" personal, sick, and vacation leave as part of the 12 weeks' leave. In such cases, though, the FMLA prohibits employers from imposing more stringent conditions on leave taken under the act than the employers would require under their own leave plans. The act moreover obligates employers to reinstate an employee who has used FMLA leave to the employee's former position or to one that involves "substantially equivalent skill, effort, responsibility, and authority."

Interestingly, the FMLA exempts the highest-paid 10 percent of salaried employees within the aforementioned 75-mile radius from the right to reinstatement after they have taken a leave. In short, the FMLA allows an employer to refuse restoration of employment to these "key employees" if an employer can show that "substantial and grievous" economic injury would occur if the key employees were restored to their respective original positions. The regulations never set forth a precise test for calculating the level of hardship that an employer must sustain before it can deny reinstatement (or restoration) to key employees, however.

Once the employer has determined that a given worker is a key employee, the employer, upon the key employee's request for leave, must notify the employee in writing of this determination. The employer's failure to comply with the specific notification requirements delineated in the regulations will cause the forfeiture of its rights to deny reinstatement (or restoration). Furthermore, the employer cannot require an employee to "requalify" for such benefits as life or disability insurance or profit-sharing plans once the worker completes his or her FMLA leave.

Although the act itself does not specifically define the term *family*, the regulations do and they apparently contemplate coverage of a wide spectrum of persons beyond the traditional family unit. The regulations define spouse as a husband or wife recognized as such for purposes of marriage under state law (including common law marriages in jurisdictions that recognize these relationships). Partners in same-sex unions presumably do not qualify for benefits and protection under the FMLA. The parental relationship described in the act can be either biological or one that is *in loco parentis*; but parents "in law" are not included. *Son or daughter* means a biological, adopted, or foster child, a stepchild, a legal ward, or a child of a person standing *in loco parentis* and who either is under 18 or at least 18 and incapable of self-care owing to mental or physical disability. The regulations define a person who is *in loco parentis* as including anyone with day-to-day responsibilities to care for and financially support a child. A biological or legal relationship specifically is not required under the regulations.

The act defines a *serious health condition* as "an illness, injury, impairment, or physical or mental condition that involves inpatient care in a hospital, hospice, or residential facility or continuing treatment by a health care provider." According to the regulations, a *serious health condition* is one that requires either an overnight stay in a hospital; a period of incapacity requiring an absence from work of more than three days and involving continuing treatment by a health care provider; or continuing treatment for a chronic or long-term health condition that, if left untreated, likely will result in a period of incapacity for more than three days. Prenatal care and care administered for a long-term or chronic condition that is incurable (such as Alzheimer's disease) and for which condition the person is not receiving active treatment by a health care provider are included as well.

Given this broad threshold for eligibility, many businesspeople fear that the FMLA will be susceptible to abuse by employees who show tendencies toward chronic, unjustified absenteeism. The medical certification requirements set out under the act, however, do offer a hedge against employee abuse of the FMLA's provisions. According to the act, the employer may require the employee to produce medical documentation of the need for medical leave in many circumstances. The health care professionals who provide such certifications ordinarily furnish specific information about the medical facts underlying the condition that has triggered the need for a leave, the commencement date, and the probable duration of the leave. In strictly circumscribing the information an employer can obtain from a certifying health care professional, the act, among other things, prohibits the employer from requesting additional information from such a provider. Rather, if an employer doubts the validity of the certificate produced by the employee, the employer can, at its own expense, require a second opinion by a health care provider of its choice, so long as the doctor is not "employed on a regular basis by the employer."

The act also allows employees to take *intermittent leave*, that is, "leave taken in separate blocks of time due to a single illness or injury, rather than for one continuous period of time, and may consist of leave of periods from an hour or more to several weeks." Intermittent leave can consist of leave taken for medical appointments, chemotherapy, and the like. (The regulations require the employee to give notice to the employer of the need for intermittent leave, but the regulations are more lenient regarding notification for unforeseeable leave.) Employees instead may opt for a *reduced leave* schedule, which the regulations define as a reduction in an employee's usual number of working hours per week or in the hours per workday.

Intermittent or reduced leave taken for the purpose of caring for a family member or for a serious health condition of the employee requires only the fulfillment of the applicable certification standards; it is not necessary for the employee to obtain the employer's permission in advance. The employer and employee must agree to any intermittent or reduced leave that the employee takes for the birth or adoption of a child, however.

The act allows an employer to require an employee who has requested intermittent or reduced leave to transfer to another position. The transfer must be temporary, and the new position must reflect equivalent pay and benefits (if not equivalent duties). Employers also have the right, consistent with the leave being taken, to transfer an employee to a part-time position. These transfer provisions give the employer some leeway to place the affected employee in a position that more easily accommodates recurrent and unpredictable absences.

The act requires the employer to post notices regarding the FMLA at the worksite. An employer's failure to post these notice requirements at the worksite subjects the employer to fines of up to $100 per offense. Furthermore, if the employer has reduced its policies to writing, the employer must include information concerning the FMLA and its entitlements in all employee handbooks. In the absence of such written policies, the employer must provide written guidance as to an employee's rights and obligations under the FMLA whenever an employee requests leave under the act.

Like other federal fair employment practices laws, the FMLA contains antidiscrimination/antiretaliation provisions. Violations of these provisions may result in civil lawsuits, liquidated damages, or administrative remedies. The Department of Labor's Web site—http://www.dol.gov/—provides detailed information about the FMLA.

Other Protections The Vietnam Era Veterans' Readjustment Assistance Act of 1974, various executive orders, and the Civil Rights Acts of 1866 and 1871 form alternative bases for guaranteeing equal access to the workplace. State law often augments this extensive federal scheme as well.

Occupational Safety and Health Act

Congress passed the Occupational Safety and Health Act, better known as OSHA, in 1970. This act attempts to assure safe and healthful workplace conditions for working men and women. The act does so by authorizing enforcement of the standards developed under the act (through the Occupational Safety and Health Administration); by assisting and encouraging the states' efforts to assure safe and healthful working conditions; and by providing for research, information, education, and training in the field of occupational safety and health, through the National Institute for Occupational Safety and Health (NIOSH).

The act covers most employers and employees, including agricultural employees, nonprofit organizations, and professionals (such as doctors, lawyers, accountants, and brokers). In fact, the act reaches almost any employer that employs at least one employee and whose business in any way affects interstate commerce. Atomic energy workers, however, are exempted.

Because personal illnesses and injuries arising from the workplace produce significant burdens in terms of lost production, lost wages, medical expenses, and disability payments, Congress designed an act meant to highlight the existence of such factors and to provide standards for preventing future illnesses, injuries, and losses. To this end, OSHA sets out methods by which employers can reduce workplace hazards and foster attention to safety. The act further authorizes the secretary of labor to set mandatory occupational safety and health standards for businesses covered under the act and to create an Occupational Safety and Health Review Commission for hearing appeals from OSHA citations and penalties. In *Martin v. Occupational Safety and Health Review Commission*,[40] the Supreme Court held that when this "split enforcement" structure (that is, the secretary's powers of enforcement and rulemaking versus the commission's adjudicatory powers) leads to reasonable but conflicting interpretations of an ambiguous OSHA regulation promulgated by the secretary of labor, courts should defer to the secretary's interpretations.

To help ensure that no employee suffers diminished health, functional capacity, or life expectancy as a result of work experiences, OSHA requires each employer to furnish to its employees a safe and healthful workplace, one that is free from "recognized hazards" that may cause or are likely to cause death or serious physical harm to employees. An example of a recognized hazard might include excessive toxic substances in the air.

OSHA allows inspectors to enter the workplace to inspect for compliance with regulations. Upon an employer's refusal to admit the inspector, OSHA regulations now require a warrant. The refusal in and of itself does not constitute probable cause for the issuance of the warrant. But the standards for demonstrating the need for the warrant are relatively easy to meet and ordinarily do not impede OSHA's functions very much. Employers normally do not know in advance of an inspector's arrival. By writing to the secretary of labor, employees may request an inspection if they believe a violation that threatens physical harm exists.

Inspections typically involve a tour through the business and an examination of each work area for compliance with OSHA standards. After the inspector has informed the employer of the reason for the inspection, the inspector will give the employer a copy of the complaint (if one is involved) or the reason for the inspection if it results from an agency general administrative plan. When an employee has initiated the complaint, OSHA by request will withhold the employee's name. An employer representative and an employee-selected representative generally accompany the inspector on this walk-around tour. The inspector may order the immediate correction of some violations, such as blocked aisles, locked fire exits, or unsanitary conditions. The inspector additionally reviews the records OSHA requires the employer to maintain, including records of deaths, injuries, illnesses, and employee exposure to toxic substances. After the inspection, the inspector and employer engage in a closing conference, during which they discuss probable violations and methods for eliminating these violations. The inspector then files his or her report with the commission.

Citations and proposed penalties may be issued to the employer, and a copy of these will be sent to the complaining party, if there is one. Normally, no citation is issued if a violation of a standard or rule lacks an immediate or direct relationship to safety or health, although a notice of a minimal violation (without a proposed penalty) may be sent to the employer even in these situations. OSHA requires the prominent posting of citations in the workplace.

Penalties, when imposed, are severe: fines of up to $70,000 for each violation may be levied for willful or repeated violations. An employer also will be fined up to $7,000 for each serious violation—one in which there is a "substantial probability" that the consequences of an accident resulting from the violation will be death or serious harm. Employers can defend by showing they did not, and could not with the exercise of "reasonable diligence," know about the condition or hazard. For even nonserious violations (such as a failure to paint steps and banisters or to post citations), fines of up to $7,000 are possible. Prison terms are possible in the event of willful violations that cause an employee's death. The OSHA Commission assesses these penalties in light of the size of the employer's business, the seriousness of the violation, the presence or absence of employer good faith, and the past history of violations.

An employer that wishes to contest any penalties can resort to the procedures established by the commission. In general, these require an investigation and a decision by an administrative law judge. The commission, in turn, can review this decision. An employer that still disagrees with the decision can appeal to the appropriate federal circuit court of appeals for review, as can the secretary of labor if he or she disagrees with the commission's decision.

Upon proof of inability to comply because of the unavailability of materials, equipment, or personnel to effect the changes within the required time, employers may request temporary exemptions from OSHA standards. Permanent exemptions may be granted when the employer's method of protecting employees is as effective as that required by the standard. Needless to say, such exemptions are not granted retroactively.

Other provisions of OSHA protect employees from discrimination or discharge based on filing a complaint, testifying about violations, or exercising any rights guaranteed by the act. The act prohibits employees from stopping work or walking off the job because of "potential unsafe conditions at the workplace" unless the employee, through performance of the assigned work, would subject "himself [or herself] to serious injury or death from a hazardous condition at the workplace."

In *Whirlpool Corp. v. Marshall*,[41] the Supreme Court held that the secretary of labor has the authority to promulgate a regulation allowing workers to refuse to perform in hazardous situations. According to the Court, the promulgation of the regulation was a valid exercise of the authority granted the secretary of labor under the Occupational Safety and Health Act, especially given the act's fundamental purpose of preventing occupational deaths and serious injuries.

Social Security

The Social Security Act, first enacted in 1935 as part of President Franklin D. Roosevelt's New Deal policies, has spawned numerous controversies. Current debate about Social Security centers on fears that the system will become bankrupt and on proposed plans to allay this possibility.

By *Social Security*, most people mean the federal old-age, survivors', and disability insurance benefits plan. Broad in scope, Social Security benefits today are payable to workers, their dependents, and their survivors. Through the Supplemental Security Income (SSI) program administered by the Department of Health and Human Services, the federal Social Security system also makes payments to the blind, the disabled, and the aged who are in need of these benefits. The states also can supplement this pervasive federal scheme if they so choose.

In general, federal Social Security benefits are computed on the worker's earning records. A *fully insured* worker is one who has worked at least 40 quarters (10 years). To use 2003 as an example, such workers will earn one quarter of coverage for each $890 in earnings, whether wages, farm wages, or income from self-employment, up to a maximum of four quarters. Fully insured workers who receive retirement benefits include retired workers, 62 years and older; their spouses, or divorced spouses, 62 and older; spouses of any age who care for a child entitled to benefits; and children or grandchildren under 18 (or 19 if a student) or of any age if disabled before age 22. Additionally, survivors' benefits go to certain classes of fully insured workers, as do disability benefits for qualified workers.

Be aware, however, that computing Social Security benefits involves complicated arithmetical formulas noting the worker's age; date of retirement, disability, or death; and yearly earnings history. Cost-of-living escalators tied to the consumer price index (that is, the measurement of how the price of a group of consumer goods changes between two time periods) in certain circumstances may raise benefits as well.

Disability benefits—those granted to a worker who has been disabled at least five months—are computed in a similar manner, subject to some limitations for younger disabled workers. Additionally, for eligibility, the worker must prove that he or she no longer can engage in substantial gainful employment. The disability must be expected to last at least 12 months or to result in death.[42] Finally, the worker, if near retirement age, must have sufficient quarters of coverage to be considered fully insured and must have worked at least 20 quarters of the last 40 quarters before the disability began. Blind persons and some younger workers who become disabled face less stringent eligibility requirements. Receipt of benefits paid under workers' compensation or other federal, state, or local disability plans may lessen the amount of benefits received from Social Security.

Monthly payments made to a retired or disabled worker's family or to the survivors of an insured worker are equal to a certain percentage (usually 50 or 75 percent) of the worker's benefits. For example, if a worker were entitled to $379 per month in benefits, the worker's spouse or ex-spouse who was married to the worker for at least 10 years and is not now married will receive $189.50 or $284.25 in monthly benefits. The act limits the amount one family can receive in total benefits. Similarly, benefits for a nondisabled child who no longer is attending high school normally end at age 18. Lump-sum death benefits to eligible persons cannot exceed $255. In 2003, a worker at full retirement age (currently 65 and two months or older) could earn unlimited amounts without loss of benefits. All other workers would face reductions in benefits according to set formulas depending on age and maximum earnings of $11,520 to $30,720. Social Security coverage extends to most types of employment and self-employment. Among those excluded, however, are employees of the federal government and railroad workers.

A 1999 Supreme Court decision concerning benefits, *Cleveland v. Policy Management Systems Corporation*,[43] involved an interesting intersection of Social Security law and the ADA. After suffering a stroke and losing her job, Carolyn Cleveland had obtained Social Security Disability Insurance (SSDI) benefits owing to her claim that she was unable to work because of her disability. The week before her SSDI award, she filed suit under the Americans with Disabilities Act of 1990 (ADA), contending that her former employer, Policy Management Systems Corporation, had discriminated against her because of her disability. The lower court concluded that Cleveland's claim that she was totally disabled for SSDI purposes estopped her (that is, prevented her from asserting the claim) from proving an essential element of her ADA cause of action, namely, that she could "perform the essential functions" of her job, at least with "reasonable . . . accommodation." The Fifth Circuit affirmed, holding that the application for or receipt of SSDI benefits creates a rebuttable presumption that a recipient is estopped from pursuing an ADA claim and that Cleveland had failed to rebut the presumption. The Supreme Court ruled that pursuit and receipt of SSDI benefits would not automatically estop a recipient from pursuing an ADA claim or erect a strong presumption against the recipient's success under the ADA. However, the Court stressed that, to survive a summary judgment motion, an ADA plaintiff cannot ignore her SSDI contention that she is too disabled to work, but must explain why that contention is consistent with her ADA claim that she can perform the essential functions of her job, at least with reasonable accommodation.[44]

Those who have been denied benefits may utilize certain administrative steps to appeal an SSA decision. Usually, such persons file a request for reconsideration within 60 days of the date of the initial determination. The agency then conducts a thorough and independent review of the evidence. After this reconsideration, a person who remains adversely affected can file for a hearing or review by an administrative law judge (ALJ). After the hearing, the ALJ issues a written decision that in understandable language sets out his or her findings of fact. All parties receive copies of this decision. The decision is binding unless appealed to the Appeals Council of the SSA or to a federal district court.

The Federal Insurance Contribution Act (FICA) taxes paid by employees and employers on wages earned by workers not only fund Social Security retirement benefits but also help provide qualified persons with hospital insurance. Called Medicare, this protection normally is available to persons 65 years and older and to some disabled persons under 65. Medicare (Part A) covers doctors' services, hospital care, some nursing home care, certain home health services, and hospice care. In 2003, the FICA tax rate paid was 7.65 percent on a maximum of $87,000 in employee wages. The Medicare portion of that amount was 1.45 percent. In 1993, Congress removed the maximum base amount (formerly $135,000); hence, since 1994, the employer must match the employee's portion. Aside from such costs, the record-keeping burdens involved with compliance under the Social Security Act also irk many employers.

In addition to receiving Medicare Part A, qualified persons can pay for a government-subsidized plan called Medicare Part B that will cover medical services beyond hospitalization, such as doctors' services and related medical expenses involving outpatient and rehabilitation costs, ambulance services, lab tests, and the like. In order to fill in the gaps in health care protection left by the Medicare program, some persons also purchase Medicare supplemental insurance ("Medigap" insurance) from insurance companies. Another program, Medicaid, provides broad medical assistance to "categorically needy" individuals.

Unemployment Insurance

In addition to retirement, disability, and Medicare benefits, Social Security covers unemployment insurance through the Federal Unemployment Tax Act (FUTA). Unemployment insurance represents a coordinated federal and state effort to provide economic security for temporarily unemployed workers. The funds used in the unemployment insurance system come from taxes, or "contributions," paid predominantly by employers. In a few states, employees also pay these taxes. Those contributing pay federal taxes, which the government uses to administer the federal/state program, as well as state taxes, which the state uses to finance the payment of weekly benefits to unemployed workers.

Various credits allowed under federal law significantly reduce the amount of taxes paid in federal contributions. Essentially, computation of the taxes paid by the employer/employees is based on a specified percentage of wages. "Wages" include anything paid as compensation for employment and thus may consist of salaries, fees, bonuses, and commissions. Since 1983, the amount of wages subject to federal taxes for unemployment compensation is at most $7,000 for each employee per calendar year. In 1999, the

FUTA applied at a rate of 6.2 percent on the first $7,000 of covered wages. The federal government allows a credit for FUTA sums paid to the state, however. State contribution rates may vary, but most have set a standard rate (such as 5.4 percent). Hence, the amount to be paid to the Internal Revenue Service (IRS) could be as low as 0.8 percent.

State rates, almost without exception, utilize "experience rating" or "merit rating" systems whereby the rate employers pay reflects each individual employer's experience with unemployment. Under such systems, employers whose workers suffer the most involuntary unemployment pay higher rates than employers whose workers suffer less unemployment. Since the aim of unemployment compensation involves the achievement of regular employment and the prevention of unemployment, such systems provide incentives to employers to keep their workforces intact and thereby to perpetuate the goals of these laws.

State provisions regarding the criteria for eligibility and the amount of benefits vary greatly. For instance, in different jurisdictions, unemployment compensation may not be available to employees discharged for cause, to those who quit their jobs without cause, or to those who refuse to seek or accept a job for which they are qualified.

Workers' Compensation

Workers' compensation statutes are not the same as unemployment statutes, although both concern the welfare of workers. Workers' compensation laws in the various states attempt to reimburse workers for injuries or death arising in the employment context. "Compensation" in this area therefore does not refer to wages or salaries but rather to the money paid by the employer to indemnify the worker for employment-related injury or death. The employer usually self-insures; buys insurance; or, as discussed earlier, pays money into a state insurance fund at a "merit" or "experience" rate reflective of the employer's actual incidence of employee injuries. By utilizing administrative proceedings in front of a workers' compensation board, injured workers then receive compensation for their injuries in the form of medical care and disability benefits, the latter often based on a specific statutory scale (such as 60 percent of average weekly wages up to $100 in average weekly wages for 26 weeks).

Workers' compensation acts thus impose *strict liability* on the employer for injuries to employees during the scope of their employment. These laws first arose out of lawmakers' concern for employees injured as a result of increased industrial mechanization, but these acts serve other functions as well. For instance, through such statutes, employees can receive compensation without engaging in costly litigation; and the employer, by passing these costs on to consumers, can recoup the costs of workers' compensation. Both sides benefit, because the employee receives reimbursement for the injuries suffered and the employer's liability to the employee usually ends there; that is, the statutes ordinarily prohibit the employee from suing the employer in a court of law. Such acts, then, are grounded in public policy concerns.

The classes of employees covered by such acts depend on the particular statute involved. Agricultural, domestic, or casual laborers often are not covered because the right to compensation ordinarily depends on the nature of the work performed, the regularity of such work, and/or the status of the worker (that is, whether, at the time of the injury, the worker was working as an independent contractor for someone else).

To be covered, an employee ordinarily must be a worker—that is, a person who performs manual labor or similar duties. For this reason, workers' compensation statutes presumably do not cover directors, officers, or stockholders. Yet under the dual capacity doctrine, such persons can receive compensation if, when they suffer injury, they are performing the ordinary duties of the business. For example, a general manager of a tree-pruning service who is injured while pruning trees will be able to recover. If the general manager instead were working as an independent contractor (not for the corporation), he or she normally would be ineligible to receive workers' compensation.

Typically, however, just about any employment-related injury or disease makes the covered employee eligible for workers' compensation. For this reason, even a negligent employee usually can recover for injuries suffered while he or she was in the employment relationship. Contrast this statutory result with what would occur at common law: The employer could use the employee's contributory negligence as a complete bar to recovery.

Recent decisions allow recoveries for occupational diseases such as asbestosis, for work-related stress, and even for injuries suffered before or after working hours. Although workers' compensation takes the place of an employee's suing the employer for the injuries suffered, employees still can maintain product liability suits against manufacturers or suppliers and also can sue any fellow employees who cause their injuries.

The digital age has had a profound impact on the workplace. Computers have replaced typewriters as the foremost medium for producing documents. They have also supplanted telephones as the primary mode of communication. In addition, the Internet has made conducting research and finding information much easier—one can access data while at one's computer terminal instead of having to go to a library. E-mail technologies alone have improved (or at least substantially accelerated) both inter- and intra-firm exchanges. Consequently, employees' usage of computers has enlarged employees' control over their working hours (through telecommuting, job-sharing, and flex-time), increased productivity, lowered costs, and raised employee morale. Despite these salutary aspects, the proliferation of technology has multiplied the challenges that inhere in the employment context, particularly for employers.

The alternative working arrangements made possible in an Internet-based world, though novel variations, still implicate many traditional workplace issues—for instance, whether the workers in question are employees or independent contractors. As discussed in Chapters 31 and 35, such distinctions become legally important not only for the possible application of the federal antidiscrimination laws, workers' compensation, unemployment compensation, and Social Security (as well as other taxation matters), but also for the calculation of wages and the provision of benefits. To illustrate, the employer generally need not pay overtime to independent contractors. However, distinguishing between employees and independent contractors in the Internet environment can be especially problematic, given the fact that start-up companies often demand long hours from their workers. A misclassification can subject the employer to costly penalties, including the payment of retroactive overtime and overdue employee withholding taxes. The trend toward staffing jobs with temporary workers ("temps") merely exacerbates the problem.

The on-line recruiting revolution, which experts say has grown since 1999 at a rate of 150 percent annually, has brought about similar transformations in the employment arena. In particular, employers who wish to attract younger staff recognize that they must have in place a recruiting strategy that takes into account these workers' tendency to use the Internet as their job-search tool of choice. The resultant proliferation of company Web sites that not only list job openings but many times solicit résumés has led to the issue of when a person becomes an "applicant" under federal law. Federal guidance as of 2002 defined an applicant as "a person who has indicated an interest in being considered for hiring, promotion, or other employment opportunities." The question of when one becomes an applicant is not an idle inquiry because the federal enforcement agencies, notably the Equal Employment Opportunity Commission (EEOC) and the Office of Federal Contract Compliance Programs (OFCCP), mandate that employers collect EEO data on all applicants. The compilation of these data, which focus on race, gender, and ethnicity, enable federal contractors to discharge their duty to undertake affirmative action with regard to certain pro-

tected groups. In past years, "applicants" consisted of the people who walked into a personnel or recruiting office, filled out an application, and provided the requested EEO data. It was relatively simple for employers to manage the documentation/data collection responsibilities as to such persons. Nowadays, anyone seeking employment can, with a keyboard stroke, send off generic resumes to the Web sites of innumerable firms. Employers thus fear that the current guidance could lead to the conclusion that anyone who submits a résumé to the company's Web site is an applicant, thus triggering the collection of EEO data from that individual. This would be true regardless of whether a given employer has any openings, is recruiting, or is even accepting applications. Employers believe this interpretation would impose costly, time-consuming, and unjustified burdens on them without providing the countervailing benefits desired by the enforcement agencies (for example, guaranteeing an applicant pool that is as large as possible and ensuring recruiting practices that are fair, inclusive, and nondiscriminatory). They also harbor misgivings about the fact that such a gloss on the language could lead to frivolous lawsuits by unqualified persons. Owing to the gravity of this issue, the pertinent agencies in 2002 assembled a taskforce to come up with a reasonable clarification of the range of possible definitions.

Besides having to sort out such uncertainties, employers furthermore must recognize that frivolous litigation represents only one aspect of their possible legal exposure. Indeed, the very nature of the technology heightens the potentiality for legal liability in a variety of contexts. For instance, e-mail can be the basis for hostile-working-environment sex discrimination under Title VII of the Civil Rights Act of 1964. Typical cases involve employees' uploading, downloading, or displaying inappropriate content (for example, pornographic materials on a firm's electronic bulletin board) or employees' using e-mail to make unwelcome sexual overtures to another person. Companies therefore will want to monitor any shared systems (such as bulletin boards) to identify and remove any inappropriate content. Employers bent on minimizing litigation, then, will adopt an antiharassment policy that makes it clear that this policy also covers usage of the firm's e-mail system.

Besides technology-related claims of discrimination, liability can arise from defamatory statements, copyright violations, and the disclosure of trade secrets or other proprietary information. Hence, preventing such claims represents a powerful rationale for monitoring employees' usage of the Internet or e-mail. One common misconception is that deleting files destroys e-mail; however, a cottage industry of retrieval specialists who can unearth potentially damaging messages for use as evidence in subsequent litigation by plaintiffs has recently emerged. This development serves as yet another employer justification for employee monitoring aimed at preventing abusive and improper uses of the company's computer system.

Still, before implementing any monitoring regime, employers should inform employees (ideally through a written policy or employee handbook that employees sign at the time of employment) that employee Internet and e-mail usage are intended only for company business and may be monitored. A well-crafted policy will inform employees of the types of conduct that constitute illegal or improper use and the bases for discipline and discharge under the policy. Nonetheless, employers should confine monitoring activities to work-related e-mail and target specific problems (e.g., the lessened productivity stemming from employees' "surfing" the Internet during working hours) rather than totally banning all personal e-mail and Internet usage. (In this regard, some employers dedicate a computer terminal that employees can use for a limited duration for personal e-mails—during their breaks, for example—as long as the usage is lawful and nondisruptive of ordinary business operations.)

The policy moreover should state that because the firm owns the computers and maintains the underlying network and server, employees have no expectations of privacy regarding e-mail and Internet usage and consent both to monitoring and to the employer's disclosure of the results of any monitoring. Employees who wish to challenge such work rules have limited options because the federal Constitution does not protect private sector employees—owing to the absence of state action—in the same way it protects public sector (governmental) employees. Even as to public sector employees, prior notice of the surveillance generally will defeat even these employees' expectations of privacy. Similarly, the rights of freedom of speech and the prohibition on unreasonable searches and seizures as spelled out in the federal Constitution and federal statutory law typically do not curtail the employer's right to monitor either. (A few states have enacted laws pertaining specifically to the monitoring of e-mail, so one should check the reach of these statutes.) Because most people view working as a major life activity, you should make a conscious effort to keep abreast of the evolution of the legal rules that will affect the technological dimensions of employment in the future.

Summary

The Wagner, Taft-Hartley, and Landrum-Griffin acts set out a pervasive federal scheme for the regulation of labor. This blueprint of federal labor law broadly regulates employees' rights to organize and to engage in concerted activities in furtherance of their objectives. Both employees and employers are protected from unfair labor practices. The National Labor Relations Board retains jurisdiction over labor disputes, oversees elections, arbitrates disputes about the duty to bargain, and almost wholly preempts the states' jurisdiction over labor matters, except for criminal violations or torts, retaliatory discharges, and the like.

A host of federal statutes extensively regulates fair employment practices. Title VII of the Civil Rights Act of 1964 prohibits employers, labor organizations, or employment agencies from engaging in employment discrimination based on race, color, religion, sex, or national origin. The Equal Employment Opportunity Commission enforces many of these federal laws and sets out the complex procedures with which a grievant must comply. Employment criteria that have a disparate impact on minorities are illegal unless the employer can show that the criteria are job related. Employers also may be liable for the disparate treatment of their employees. The issue of reverse discrimination remains controversial in the Title VII context. Limited defenses based on bona fide occupational qualifications (BFOQs) are available for the protected categories of religion, sex, and national origin; a BFOQ never can be based on race, however. The Immigration Reform and Control Act of 1986, the Equal Pay Act of 1963, the Age Discrimination in Employment Act of 1967, the Rehabilitation Act of 1973, the Americans with Disabilities Act of 1990, the Civil Rights Act of 1991, the Family and Medical Leave Act of 1993, and other federal statutes protect qualified individuals against employment discrimination. State law often supplements this comprehensive federal scheme.

The Occupational Safety and Health Act attempts to ensure safe and healthful working conditions for American workers. Inspections of the workplace provide a mechanism for realizing this statutory goal. Warrantless inspections conducted after the owner refuses entry to the inspector are illegal. Workers, in contrast, legally can walk off the job if performance of the work assignment can lead to serious injury or death.

Federal and state Social Security benefits aid workers, the disabled, the blind, and the aged. Computations of benefits are complex. Those who have been denied benefits may utilize certain administrative steps to appeal such agency decisions.

Unemployment insurance is designed to provide economic security for temporarily unemployed workers. The contributions paid into the insurance fund stem from a specified percentage of wages paid by the employer or employee. State taxable wage bases may differ from the federal figure, and state provisions regarding the criteria for eligibility and the amount of benefits vary greatly.

State workers' compensation statutes attempt to reimburse workers for injuries or death resulting from the employment relationship. In return, such statutes generally prohibit the employee from suing the employer in a court of law. The classes of employees covered in such acts depend on the particular statute involved; but eligible employees may recover for occupational diseases, injuries resulting from the employee's own negligence, and injuries sustained before or after working hours. Workers' compensation statutes ordinarily do not preclude an employee's maintaining either a product liability suit against a manufacturer or a suit against a fellow employee who caused the injuries at issue.

Discussion Questions

1. List a few of the rights guaranteed and the practices prohibited by the Wagner, Taft-Hartley, and Landrum-Griffin acts.

2. Describe a few of the issues and enforcement problems involved in the collective-bargaining process.

3. Explain the boundaries of state regulation of labor.

4. What are the protected classes of employees under Title VII?

5. Define and describe the two methods by which an employee can show liability for discrimination on the basis of the protected categories set out in Title VII.

6. Why is the issue of reverse discrimination such a difficult problem?

7. Define *bona fide occupational qualification*.

8. Name other statutes that guarantee fair employment, and explain how these more recent statutes build on earlier fair employment statutes.

9. Describe a typical OSHA inspection.

10. Name the classes of persons eligible for Social Security, unemployment insurance, and workers' compensation.

Case Problems and Writing Assignments

1. Under Pennsylvania's Workers' Compensation Act, once an employer becomes liable for an employee's work-related injury—because liability either is uncontested or is no longer at issue—the employer or its insurer must pay for all "reasonable" and "necessary" medical treatment. To assure that only medical expenses meeting these criteria are paid, and in an attempt to control costs, Pennsylvania amended its workers' compensation system. These amendments provided that a self-insured employer or private insurer may withhold payment for disputed treatment pending an independent "utilization review," as to which, among other things, the insurer files a one-page request for review with the State Workers' Compensation Bureau. The Bureau in turn forwards the request to a "utilization review organization" (URO) of private health care providers, and the URO determines whether the treatment is reasonable or necessary.

The plaintiffs—employees and employee representatives—subsequently filed this suit under 42 U.S.C. § 1983 against various Pennsylvania officials, a self-insured public school district, and a number of private workers' compensation insurers. The plaintiffs alleged that, in withholding benefits without predeprivation notice and an opportunity to be heard, the state and the private defendants, acting "under color of state law," had deprived the plaintiffs of property in violation of due process. The district court dismissed the private insurers from the suit on the ground that they are not "state actors." This court also later dismissed the state officials and school district on the ground that the act does not violate due process. Disagreeing as to both issues, the Third Circuit held that a private insurer's decision to suspend payment under the act constitutes state action. This court, emphasizing the parties' assumption that employees have a protected property interest in workers' compensation medical benefits, held that due process requires that payments of medical bills not be withheld until the employees have had an opportunity to submit their view in writing to the URO as to the reasonableness and necessity of the disputed treatment. Did this comprehensive state regulation of workers' compensation convert private insurance companies' actions into state action sufficient to trigger the due process clause of the Fourteenth Amendment? Did the injured workers have a constitutionally protected property interest in receiving payments for medical bills prior to the completion of a "utilization review" evaluation of the treatment plan? [See *American Manufacturers Mutual Insurance Co. v. Sullivan*, 526 U.S. 40 (1999).]

2. On February 27, 1995, Abner J. Morgan Jr., a black male, filed a charge of discrimination and retaliation against the National Railroad Passenger Corporation (Amtrak) with the EEOC and cross-filed with the California Department of Fair Employment and Housing. Morgan alleged that during his employment with Amtrak, he was "consistently harassed and disciplined more harshly than other employees on account of

his race." The EEOC issued a notice of right to sue on July 3, 1996, and Morgan filed this lawsuit on October 2, 1996. While some of the allegedly discriminatory acts about which Morgan complained occurred within 300 days of the time in which he had filed his charge with the EEOC, many took place prior to that time period. Amtrak filed a motion, arguing, among other things, that it was entitled to summary judgment on all incidents that had occurred more than 300 days before the filing of Morgan's EEOC charge. The district court, holding that the company could not be liable for conduct occurring before May 3, 1994, because that conduct fell outside the 300-day filing period, granted partial summary judgment to Amtrak. Morgan appealed. The United States Court of Appeals for the Ninth Circuit reversed, relying on its previous articulation of the continuing violation doctrine, which allows courts to consider conduct that would ordinarily be time barred as long as the untimely incidents represent an ongoing unlawful employment practice. When determining liability in hostile work environment suits under Title VII, may courts consider acts that have occurred outside the applicable statute of limitations time period? [See *National Railroad Passenger Corporation v. Morgan*, 536 U.S. 101 (2002).]

3. Karen Sutton and Kimberly Hinton, severely myopic twin sisters, had uncorrected visual acuity of 20/200 or worse. However, with corrective measures, both functioned identically to individuals without similar impairments. They applied to United Airlines, Inc., a major commercial airline carrier, for employment as commercial airline pilots but were rejected because they did not meet United's minimum requirement of uncorrected visual acuity of 20/100 or better. Consequently, they filed suit under the ADA. The district court dismissed the plaintiffs' complaint for failure to state a claim upon which relief could be granted. The court held that the plaintiffs were not actually disabled under subsection (A) of the disability definition because they could fully correct their visual impairments. The court also determined that the plaintiffs were not "regarded" by United as disabled under subsection (C) of this definition, either. Instead, the court concluded, the plaintiffs had alleged only that United regarded them as unable to satisfy the requirements of a particular job—global airline pilot. In the district court's view, these allegations were insufficient to state a claim that the plaintiffs were regarded as substantially limited in the major life activity of working. Employing similar logic, the Tenth Circuit Court of Appeals affirmed the district court's decision. Should the assessment of whether one is disabled within the meaning of the ADA be determined with reference to measures that mitigate the individual's impairment, including, in this instance, eyeglasses and contact lenses? [See *Sutton v. United Air Lines, Inc.*, 527 U.S. 471 (1999).]

4. Teresa Harris worked as a manager at Forklift Systems, Inc., an equipment rental company, from April 1985 until October 1987. Charles Hardy was Forklift's president. Throughout Harris's time at Forklift, Hardy frequently insulted her because of her gender and often made her the target of unwanted sexual innuendos. Hardy told Harris on several occasions, in the presence of other employees, "You're a woman, what do you know" and "We need a man as the rental manager"; at least once, he told her she was "a dumb a__ woman." Again, in front of others, he suggested that the two of them "go to the Holiday Inn to negotiate [Harris's] raise." Hardy occasionally asked Harris and other female employees to retrieve coins from his front pants pocket. He also threw objects on the ground in front of Harris and other women and asked them to pick up the objects. In addition, he made sexual innuendos about Harris and other women's clothing. In mid-August 1987, Harris complained to Hardy about his conduct. Hardy, saying he was surprised that Harris was offended, claimed he was only joking and apologized. He also promised he would stop; and based on this assurance, Harris stayed on the job. But in early September, Hardy began anew. While Harris was arranging a deal with one of Forklift's customers, he asked her, again in front of other employees, "What did you do, promise the guy . . . some [sex] Saturday night"? On October 1, Harris collected her paycheck and quit. Claiming that Hardy's conduct had created an abusive work environment for her because of her gender, Harris subsequently sued Forklift. The U.S. District Court for the Middle District of Tennessee found this to be "a close case" but held that Hardy's conduct had not created an abusive environment. The court found that some of Hardy's comments offended Harris, and would offend the reasonable woman, but that the remarks were not so severe as to be expected to seriously affect Harris's psychological well-being. Nor, the court concluded, had Hardy created a working environment so poisoned as to be intimidating or injurious to Harris. In focusing on the employee's psychological well-being, the district court was following Sixth Circuit precedents. In a brief, unpublished decision, the U.S. Court of Appeals for the Sixth Circuit affirmed. To be actionable as "abusive work environment" sexual harassment, must the defendant's conduct seriously affect the plaintiff's psychological well-being or lead the plaintiff to suffer injury? [See *Harris v. Forklift Systems, Inc.*, 510 U.S. 17 (1993).]

5. BUSINESS APPLICATION CASE In his application for employment with Waffle House, Inc., Eric Baker agreed that "any dispute or claim" concerning his employment would be "settled by binding arbitration." All prospective Waffle House employees were required, as a condition of employment, to sign an application form containing a similar mandatory arbitration agreement. Baker began working as a grill operator at a Waffle House restaurant on August 10, 1994. Sixteen days later, he suffered a seizure at work and soon thereafter was discharged. Baker did not initiate arbitration proceedings in 1994; but, in 2001, he filed charges with the EEOC. Specifically, Roberts claimed that his discharge violated the ADA. The EEOC charged Waffle House with disability discrimination and requested injunctive relief, as well as backpay, reinstatement, and damages—both compensatory and punitive—in order to make Baker whole. Waffle House filed a petition under the Federal Arbitration Act (FAA) to compel arbitration or, alternatively, to dismiss the EEOC's action. The district court denied this motion. The cir-

cuit court of appeals concluded that, because the EEOC was not a party to the otherwise valid and enforceable arbitration agreement between Waffle House and Roberts and because the EEOC has independent statutory authority to bring suit in any district court where venue is proper, the arbitration agreement would not foreclose such an enforcement action. Nevertheless, the court of appeals limited the EEOC's remedies to injunctive relief and precluded the agency from seeking victim-specific relief. The court based this determination on its conclusion that the FAA policy favoring the enforcement of private arbitration agreements outweighs the EEOC's right to proceed in federal court when it seeks primarily to vindicate private, rather than public, interests. Several circuit courts of appeals had split on the issue of whether private arbitration agreements would prevent the EEOC from pursuing victim-specific relief in suits brought on behalf of employees who had agreed to arbitrate employment-related disputes. How should the Supreme Court resolve this question? [See *EEOC v. Waffle House, Inc.*, 534 U.S. 279 (2002).]

6. **ETHICAL APPLICATION CASE** Tracy Ragsdale began working at a Wolverine World Wide, Inc. factory in 1995. In 1996, she was diagnosed with Hodgkin's disease. Her prescribed treatment involved surgery and months of radiation therapy. Though unable to work during this time, she was eligible for seven months of unpaid sick leave under Wolverine's leave plan. Ragsdale requested and received a one-month leave of absence on February 21, 1996, and then asked for a 30-day extension at the end of each of the seven months that followed. Wolverine granted the first six requests, and Ragsdale missed 30 consecutive weeks of work. Throughout the first six months of her absence, Wolverine held open her position, maintained her health benefits, and paid her premiums. However, Wolverine did not notify her, as required under FMLA regulations, that 12 weeks of the absence would count as her FMLA leave. In September, when Ragsdale sought a seventh 30-day extension, Wolverine advised her that she had exhausted her seven months under the company plan. Her condition persisted, so she requested more leave or permission to work on a part-time basis. Wolverine refused and terminated her when she did not return to work.

Ragsdale thereafter filed suit against Wolverine. Relying on the FMLA regulation that provides that if an employee takes medical leave "and the employer does not designate the leave as FMLA leave, the leave taken does not count against an employee's FMLA entitlement," Ragsdale pointed out that Wolverine had failed to make the required designation. Ragsdale therefore argued that her 30 weeks of leave would not count against her FMLA entitlement. Consequently, she asserted, when she was denied additional leave and terminated after 30 weeks, Wolverine had illegally discharged her, owing to the statutory guarantee of 12 more weeks. She accordingly sought reinstatement, backpay, and other relief. Should the Supreme Court uphold this regulation, or should the Court invalidate it because the regulation, in effect, would require a company to provide more than 12 weeks of leave, a result that would conflict with the statute? Who was entitled to stake out the moral high ground here, Ragsdale or Wolverine? Why? [See *Ragsdale v. Wolverine World Wide, Inc.*, 535 U.S. 81 (2002).]

7. **CRITICAL THINKING CASE** Eastern Associated Coal Corporation and the United Mine Workers of America (UMA) were parties to a collective-bargaining agreement. The agreement specified that, in arbitration, in order to discharge an employee, Eastern must prove it had "just cause." Otherwise, the arbitrator would order the employee reinstated. The arbitrator's decision was final. James Smith worked for Eastern as a member of a road crew, a job that required him to drive heavy, trucklike vehicles on public highways. As a truck driver, Smith was subject to Department of Transportation (DOT) regulations requiring random drug testing of workers engaged in "safety-sensitive" tasks. In March 1996, Smith tested positive for marijuana. Eastern thereupon sought to discharge Smith. When the union took Smith's case to arbitration, the arbitrator concluded that Smith's positive drug test did not amount to "just cause" for discharge. Instead, the arbitrator ordered Smith's reinstatement, provided that Smith (1) accept a suspension of 30 days without pay, (2) participate in a substance abuse program, and (3) undergo drug tests at the discretion of Eastern (or an approved substance abuse professional) for the next five years.

Between April 1996 and January 1997, Smith passed four random drug tests. But in July 1997, he again tested positive for marijuana; and Eastern once more sought to discharge Smith. The union again went to arbitration, and the arbitrator again concluded that Smith's use of marijuana did not amount to "just cause" for discharge, owing to two mitigating circumstances: First, Smith had been a good employee for 17 years. And, second, Smith had sworn that a personal/family problem had caused this one-time lapse in drug usage. The arbitrator therefore ordered Smith's reinstatement subject to five more rigorous conditions. Eastern, seeking to have the arbitrator's award set aside, argued that the award contravened a public policy aimed at prohibiting the operation of dangerous machinery by workers who test positive for drugs. The district court, while recognizing a strong regulation-based public policy against drug use by workers who perform safety-sensitive functions, held that Smith's conditional reinstatement did not violate that policy and ordered enforcement of the award. The Court of Appeals for the Fourth Circuit affirmed the reasoning of the district court. The various circuit courts of appeals had reached different results on this question. How should the Supreme Court dispose of this issue? [See *Eastern Associated Coal Corporation v. United Mine Workers of America*, 531 U.S. 57 (2000).]

8. **YOU BE THE JUDGE** Sanderson Plumbing Products, Inc. manufactures toilet seats and covers. Roger Reeves (age 57), Russell Caldwell (age 45), and Joe Oswalt (age 35) all worked in the Hinge Room. Caldwell supervised the other two employees; Oswalt managed the "special line"; and Reeves, who had worked for Sanderson for 40 years, kept the time sheets and attendance records of the Hinge Room employees. In the summer of 1995, Caldwell informed Powe Chesnut, the director of manufacturing and the husband of company pres-

ident Sandra Sanderson, that "production was down" in the Hinge Room because employees were often absent and were "coming in late and leaving early." Because the monthly attendance reports did not indicate a problem, Chesnut ordered an audit of the Hinge Room's time sheets for July, August, and September of that year. According to Chesnut's testimony, that investigation revealed "numerous timekeeping errors and misrepresentations on the part of Caldwell, Reeves, and Oswalt." Following the audit, Chesnut and two other executives recommended to Sanderson that Reeves and Caldwell be fired. In October 1995, Sanderson discharged both Reeves and Caldwell. In June 1996, Reeves filed a lawsuit claiming that he had been fired because of his age in violation of the Age Discrimination in Employment Act of 1967 (ADEA).

At trial, Sanderson contended that it had discharged Reeves owing to his failure to maintain accurate attendance records, while Reeves attempted to demonstrate that Sanderson's explanation was a pretext for age discrimination. Reeves introduced evidence that he had accurately recorded the attendance and hours of the employees under his supervision and that Chesnut, whom Oswalt described as wielding "absolute power" within the company, had shown age-based animus in his dealings with Reeves. The district court denied Sanderson's motion for judgment as a matter of law. Subsequently, the jury returned a verdict in favor of Reeves. In reversing this decision, the Fifth Circuit conceded that Reeves may well have offered sufficient evidence for the jury to have found that Sanderson's explanation

was pretextual. However, the court asserted that Reeves nevertheless may have failed to present sufficient evidence to show that he had been fired because of his age. In finding the evidence insufficient, the court weighed the additional evidence of discrimination introduced by Reeves against other circumstances surrounding his discharge, including the facts that Chesnut's age-based comments were not made in the direct context of Reeves' termination; there was an absence of any allegations that the other individuals who had recommended his firing had been motivated by age; two of those officials were over 50; all three Hinge Room supervisors were accused of inaccurate recordkeeping; and several of Sanderson's managers were over 50 at the time of Reeves's discharge.

The Supreme Court granted certiorari on the issue posed by this case—an issue that had divided the various circuit courts of appeals—namely, whether an employer could prevail on summary judgment when it has offered a legitimate, nondiscriminatory reason for an adverse job action and the plaintiff has characterized the proffered reason as constituting a mere pretext for discrimination. Put differently, would a plaintiff's showing of a prima facie case of discrimination (as defined in *McDonnell Douglas Corp. v. Green*), combined with sufficient evidence for a reasonable factfinder to reject the employer's nondiscriminatory explanation for its decision, be adequate to sustain a finding of liability for intentional discrimination? If *you* were a Supreme Court justice, how would *you* rule? [See *Reeves v. Sanderson Plumbing Products, Inc.*, 530 U.S. 133 (2000).]

Notes

1. 301 U.S. 1 (1937).
2. *National Labor Relations Board v. Kentucky River Community Care, Inc.*, 532 U.S. 706 (2001).
3. *Fibreboard Paper Products Corp. v. NLRB*, 379 U.S. 203, 223 (1964).
4. *Walters v. Metropolitan Educational Enterprises, Inc.*, 519 U.S. 202 (1997).
5. *Swierkjewicz v. Sorema NA*, 534 U.S. 506 (2002).
6. *Edelman v. Lynchburg College*, 535 U.S. 106 (2002).
7. *Griggs v. Duke Power Co.*, 401 U.S. 424, 431–432 (1971).
8. 427 U.S. 273 (1976).
9. 438 U.S. 265 (1978).
10. 443 U.S. 193 (1979), *reh'g denied*, 444 U.S. 889 (1979).
11. 515 U.S. 200 (1995).
12. 432 U.S. 63 (1977).
13. 477 U.S. 57 (1986).
14. 524 U.S. 775 (1998).
15. 523 U.S. 75 (1998).
16. Ibid., 79.
17. Ibid., 80.
18. Ibid., 81–82.
19. 499 U.S. 187 (1991).
20. *Espinoza v. Farah Mfg. Co., Inc.*, 414 U.S. 86 (1973).
21. 519 U.S.1040 (1996).
22. 522 U.S. 422 (1999).
23. 524 U.S. 624 (1998).
24. Ibid, 641–642.
25. Ibid., 655. The Court has continued to struggle with the definition

of what constitutes a disability. See *Sutton v. United Air Lines, Inc.*, 527 U.S. 471 (1999). See also *Murphy v. United Parcel Service, Inc.*, 527 U.S. 516 (1999) (the question of whether hypertension is a disability must be addressed without consideration of mitigating measures).
26. See http://www.eeoc.gov.stats (accessed 1/3/02).
27. Ibid.
28. *Chevron U.S.A., Inc. v. Echazabal*, 536 U.S. 73 (2002).
29. 535 U.S. 391(2002).
30. *Barnes v. Gorman*, 536 U.S. 181 (2002).
31. 401 U.S. 424 (1971).
32. *Board of Trustees of the University of Alabama v. Garrett*, 531 U.S. 356 (2001).
33. *Kimel v. Florida Board of Regents*, 528 U.S. 62 (2000).
34. 532 U.S. 843 (2001).
35. See *BNA Employee Relations Weekly* (Special Supplement: Civil Rights Act of 1991) (November 11, 1991), pp. S1–S6.
36. 511 U.S. 244 (1994).
37. 527 U.S. 526 (1999).
38. Ibid., 534.
39. Ibid., 542.
40. 499 U.S. 144 (1991).
41. 445 U.S. 1 (1980).
42. In *Barnhart v. Walton*, 535 U.S. 212 (2002), the Supreme Court upheld the Social Security Administration's interpretation of this statutory provision.
43. 526 U.S. 795 (1999).
44. Ibid., 798.

Property Protection

In the United States, the right to own property is one of our most fundamental rights. A primary concern of our founders was preserving the right to pursue and maintain property. This is evident in the Constitution, especially in the search and seizure limits of the Fourth Amendment and the due process clause of the Fifth Amendment. The Constitution balances the right to own property with the need for government to maintain order and promote the good of society. Hence, Congress has the right of eminent domain, or the right to take private lands if they are necessary for public use. Balancing the rights of businesses and individuals with the needs of government is a pressing issue in today's society.

Part 10 examines how local, state, and federal laws treat property and property rights, as well as the manner in which property is transferred. This part addresses real property and personal property. Moreover, this part examines an increasingly significant type of property—intellectual property—and how the law attempts to address the new challenges technology poses for business.

Real Property and Joint Ownership

A G E N D A

NRW A number of property issues will arise as NRW conducts business. For example, Mai, Carlos, and Helen will need to purchase or rent real property for manufacturing plants and warehouse space. What must they know when they engage in these undertakings? If NRW makes a purchase, what type of deed would it prefer? Why? Mai has a barn on her property. NRW would like to renovate the barn into a warehouse. If the land is not zoned for commercial use, can NRW lawfully do this? What problems may arise from such a renovation?

Carlos read an article about a firm purchasing an office building for its own office and renting out the remaining space to other companies. He believes that this may provide NRW with a method of paying for an office building from the rents generated by leasing the excess space, and he has suggested that the firm consider this as a relatively inexpensive means for acquiring its own office building. What should NRW consider before implementing such a plan?

Helen and Elliot plan to purchase some land on which to build a vacation home. They want to be sure that, if something happens to one of them, the property will automatically pass to the surviving spouse. What is the best way to arrange this? What legal implications may arise from such an arrangement? Why?

Assume an NRW debtor is a joint owner in an apartment complex. If this debtor defaults on his or her obligations to the firm, can NRW attach the debtor's interest in the apartment complex and force a sale of the property to satisfy its claim? What issues would affect NRW's rights? These and other questions will arise during our discussion of real property. Be prepared! You never know when the firm or one of its members will seek your advice.

Property Rights

There are two distinctly different meanings for *property*. First, the term means an object that is subject to ownership, a valuable asset. Second, property means a group of rights and interests that are protected by the law, commonly called "a bundle of rights." A multitude of rights are associated with property ownership. Ownership entitles a person to use the property personally, to give someone else the use of the property, to rent the use of the property to someone else, or to use the property to secure a loan. The owner may sell the property, make improvements to the property, or abandon the property. Courts commonly note that this "bundle of rights" includes the rights to enjoy and use the property; to economically exploit the land based on present and potential uses; and to exclude others from occupancy or use of the property.

Ownership of real property normally entitles the owner to continued use and enjoyment of the property in its present condition. For example, suppose you own a house with a beautiful view of the mountains. If someone purchases an adjacent lot and starts constructing a three-story house that will block your view, you can sue for an injunction to prohibit that person from interfering with the view. Such a lawsuit will succeed in some states.[1] Many states also recognize that property owners have the right of support from adjoining lands; the right to use bodies of water adjacent to the property; limited rights to the airspace above it; the right to things growing on it; the right to things attached to it; and the right to things, like minerals, below its surface. However, owners or prior owners may have transferred some of these rights. Many communities now recognize and protect the right to have sun fall on existing solar collectors.

Classification of Property

Property is divided on two dimensions. Real property is land and things that are growing on the land, attached to the land, or erected on the land. Everything else is considered personal property. Property is also divided into tangible and intangible property. Tangible property is property that has a physical, material existence—it can be seen and touched. Tangible real property includes soil, crops, and buildings. Laptop computers and desks are examples of tangible personal property. On the other hand, intangible property has a conceptual existence, but no physical existence—it cannot be touched. Copyrights and patents, discussed in detail in Chapter 43, are examples of intangible personal property. Intangible real property consists of nonpossessory interests in lands. Some examples are an *easement* (the right to use the land of another, for example, the right to drive across a private road), a *license* (a revocable, personal privilege to enter the land of another. Traditionally, tickets for concerts and admission to golf courses are licenses), and a *profit* (the right to enter the real estate of another and take some part of the land or some product of the land, such as oil, sand, or trees). Exhibit 41.1 illustrates the classification of property, showing both the common law and civil law terms. We will use the common law terms used by most states.

Real Property Defined

Definition of Real Property

This chapter deals with *real property* or, as it is commonly called, *real estate*. Significant differences exist

---

EXHIBIT 41.1 Classification of Property

Property can be "classified" on two dimensions.

Real/Immovable	Tangible/Corporeal—Land, trees, buildings, etc.
	Intangible/Incorporeal—Easements, licenses, profits, etc.
Personal/Movable	Tangible/Corporeal—Goods, personal computers, cars, etc.
	Intangible/Incorporeal—Negotiable instruments, patents, copyrights, etc.

Common law title/Civil law title

The rules may vary depending on the jurisdictions.

Courtesy of Deborah Kemp

between real and personal property. Real property is land and things that are permanently attached to the land, including buildings, roadways, and storage structures. Property that is permanently attached to buildings is also considered real property and is called a *fixture*. Personal property consists of everything else capable of being owned.

Definition of a Fixture

A *fixture* is property that at one time was movable and independent of real estate, but became attached to it. Examples are water heaters, central air-conditioning units, furnaces, built-in ovens, installed dishwashers, bathroom sinks, and copper pipes for plumbing. A builder who is constructing a house will buy a water heater, take it to the construction site, and permanently attach it to the plumbing lines and the gas or electric lines. After the personal property has been attached, it becomes a fixture.

In determining whether an item is a fixture as opposed to personal property, courts will look at the reasonable expectations and understandings of most people. For instance, most people would be shocked if they bought a house and, when they moved in, discovered that the sellers had removed the handles on the kitchen cabinets and the plates over the light switches. The same buyers, however, expect the sellers to remove the tables, chairs, and other furniture. Ceiling lights are fixtures, while table lamps are household goods. Plants in a flower bed are real property; plants in pots are personal property. Wall-to-wall carpeting is real property; area rugs are personal property. Refrigerators, mirrors, and paintings are generally personal property but may be treated as real property if they are an integral part of the building.

In making this determination, courts also consider how much damage would occur to the overall property if the item in question were removed.

The Nature of Plants

Another issue concerns plants: Are they real property (real estate) or personal property? Real estate includes plants that are growing on the land, such as fruit and shade trees, tomatoes, strawberries, artichokes, and trees that are being grown for timber. If a farmer sells land with crops still growing on it, the farmer is clearly selling real estate.

Sometimes a farmer or another landowner may sell the plants but keep the land. In this case, did the landowner sell real or personal property? The common law rule is that if the plants were still growing when the title passed to the buyer, the sale was of real estate. (*Common law* in this context is the body of law that has developed from prior case decisions, customs, and usage. *Title* is the legal ownership

of property or the evidence of that ownership.) If the title passed after the plants were severed from the land, the sale was of personal property. This rule is difficult to apply because in many instances the buyer and seller never discuss when title should pass.

Since the common law rule was difficult to apply, the Uniform Commercial Code (UCC) now uses a different test for the situation where the owner is selling the plants but retaining the land. The UCC test is generally much easier to apply. Under it, the determining factor is *who* is going to remove the plants or trees. If the *buyer* is going to remove them, the buyer has purchased real property. If the seller is going to remove them, the sale is of personal property. After defining the difference between real and personal property, the UCC generally is not concerned with real estate, although some sections of the UCC discuss crops and fixtures. A few states still follow the common law rule, and some states use their own rules.

State Governance

Property laws vary from state to state. The laws of a state where the real property is located govern the land, regardless of the residence of the owner. For example, if you live in Wyoming but own land in Florida, Florida law governs your transactions with respect to the Florida real property.

Federal Regulation

While private ownership of property endows the owner with a substantial number of rights, there are limitations imposed on the owner. For example, use of the land is likely to be regulated by local zoning ordinances. In addition, there are a number of federal regulations that impose restrictions and limitations on the rights of the owner. These regulations often reflect public policy considerations in which the rights of the society at large are placed above the rights of the individual property owner.

Title III of the Americans with Disabilities Act (ADA) regulates property that is open to the public. These properties are commonly called *public accommodations* and include motels, hotels, restaurants, movie theaters, and retail stores. Under the act, newly constructed public accommodations must be designed to accommodate handicapped individuals. Architects and builders must comply with regulations established by the Department of Justice (DOJ). Generally, new structures must be designed and built to be readily accessible to and usable by individuals with disabilities unless it is structurally impossible to do so. When existing structures are being renovated, the areas being renovated must be made accessible too. The act itself does not specify the types of accommodation necessary. Court decisions and the DOJ regulations will provide some guidance in interpreting the statute. Critics of the statute claim that the act is ambiguous as to what handicaps must be accommodated and what accommodations are required. Under the statute, disabled Americans can initiate private litigation or the Justice Department can bring litigation. In addition to damages, violators may be subject to civil penalties of up to $50,000 for the first violation and penalties of up to $100,000 for subsequent violations. Note that the ADA also includes employment provisions that are administered by the EEOC.[2] The ADA is discussed in greater detail in Chapter 40.

The Civil Rights Act prohibits discrimination in the sale of homes. In the following case, the U.S. Supreme Court examined whether a broker–owner of a realty firm could be held vicariously liable for racial discrimination.

41.1

MEYER v. HOLLEY
2003 U.S. LEXIS 902 (2003)

FACTS* Emma Mary Ellen Holley and David Holley, an interracial couple, met with Triad Realty's agent Grove Crank. They asked about new houses between $100,000 and $150,000; Crank showed them only more expensive houses. The Holleys located a home listed by Triad on their own. Triad agent Terry Stump told them that the asking price was $145,000. The Holleys offered to pay the asking price and to put $5,000 in escrow to hold the house until they closed escrow on their existing home. Stump told the Holleys that their offer seemed fair. Brooks Bauer, the builder-seller, also thought the offer seemed fair, but indicated that the offer would have to go through Triad. Later, Stump told Mrs. Holley that more experienced agents in the office (including Crank) felt that $5,000 was insufficient to hold the house. The Holleys did not increase their offer. Triad never presented the original offer to Bauer. When Bauer inquired about the status of the offer, Crank allegedly used racial invectives, telling Bauer that he did not want to deal with those "n—" and calling them a "salt and pepper team." Bauer later sold his house for less than the Holleys' offer.

ISSUE Does the Fair Housing Act impose personal liability without fault upon David Meyer, the officer-owner of Triad, for the unlawful activity of Triad's employee or agent?

HOLDING No. The Act imposes liability without fault upon the employer, but not upon its officers or owners.

REASONING Excerpts from the opinion of Justice Breyer:

The Fair Housing Act . . . forbids "any person or other entity whose business includes engaging in residential real estate . . . transactions to discriminate." . . . It adds that "person" includes, for example, individuals, corporations, partnerships, associations, labor unions, and other organizations.

. . . [I]t is well established that the Act provides for vicarious liability. This Court has noted that an action brought for compensation by a victim of housing discrimination is, in effect, a tort action. And the Court has assumed that, when Congress creates a tort action, it legislates against a legal background of ordinary tort-related vicarious liability rules and . . . intends its legislation to incorporate those rules. . . . It is well established that traditional vicarious liability rules ordinarily make principals or employers vicariously liable for acts of their agents or employees in the scope of their authority or employment. . . . And in the absence of special circumstances it is the corporation, not its owner or officer, who is the principal or employer, and thus subject to vicarious liability. . . . The Restatement [of Agency] § 1 specifies that the . . . principal/agency relationship demands not only control (or the right to direct or control) but also "the manifestation of consent by one person to another that the other shall act on his behalf . . . and consent by the other so to act." . . . A corporate employee typically acts on behalf of the corporation, not its owner or officer.

. . . The Court of Appeals held that the Act made corporate owners and officers liable for the unlawful acts of a corporate employee. . . . We do not agree. . . . Congress said nothing in the statute or in the legislative history about extending vicarious liability in this manner. And Congress' silence, while permitting an inference that Congress intended to apply ordinary background tort principles, cannot show that it intended to apply an unusual modification of those rules. Where Congress . . . has not expressed a contrary intent, the Court has drawn the inference that it intended ordinary rules to apply. . . . This Court has applied unusually strict rules only where Congress has specified that such was its intent. . . .

[T]he Department of Housing and Urban Development (HUD), the federal agency primarily charged with the implementation and administration of the statute, has specified that ordinary vicarious liability rules apply. . . . And we ordinarily defer to an administering agency's reasonable interpretation of a statute. . . .

[According to HUD, the language] was designed to make clear that "a complaint may be filed against a directing or controlling person with respect to the discriminatory acts of another only if the other person was acting within the scope of his or her authority as employee or agent of the directing or controlling person." HUD also specified that, by adding the words "acting within the scope of his or her authority as employee or agent of the directing or controlling person," it disclaimed any "intent to impose absolute liability" on the basis of the mere right "to direct or control."

. . . [W]e have found no convincing argument in support of the Ninth Circuit's decision to apply nontraditional vicarious liability principles. . . . The Ninth Circuit underscored the phrase "or has the right to direct or control the conduct of another person." Its opinion did not explain . . . why the Ninth Circuit did not read these words as modified by the subsequent words that limited vicarious liability to actions taken as "employee or agent of the directing or controlling person." Taken as a whole, the regulation . . . says that ordinary . . . rules of vicarious liability should apply. . . .

The Ninth Circuit . . . referred to an owner's or officer's "non delegable duty" not to discriminate in light of the Act's "overriding societal priority." And it added that "when one of two innocent people must suffer, the one whose acts permitted the wrong to occur is the one to bear the burden." "[A] nondelegable duty is an affirmative obligation to ensure the protection of the person to whom the duty runs." . . . Such a duty imposed upon a principal would "go further" than the vicarious liability principles we have discussed . . . to create liability "although [the principal] has himself done everything that could reasonably be required of him," and irrespective

of whether the agent was acting with or without authority. The Ninth Circuit identifies nothing in the language or legislative history of the Act to support the existence of this special kind of liability. . . . In the absence of legal support, we cannot conclude that Congress intended, through silence, to impose this kind of special duty of protection upon individual officers or owners of corporations—who are not principals . . . in respect to the corporation's unlawfully acting employee.

Neither does it help to characterize the statute's objective as an "overriding societal priority." We agree with the characterization. But we do not agree that the characterization carries with it a legal rule that would hold every corporate supervisor personally liable without fault for the unlawful act of every corporate employee whom he or she has the right to supervise. . . . [W]hich "of two innocent people must suffer," and just when, is a complex matter. We believe that courts ordinarily should determine that matter in accordance with traditional principles of vicarious liability—unless, of course, Congress, better able than courts to weigh the relevant policy considerations, has instructed the courts differently. . . . We have found no different instruction here.

. . . The Ninth Circuit did not decide whether other aspects of the California broker relationship, when added to the "right to control," would . . . establish the necessary relationship. But in the absence of consideration of that matter by the Court of Appeals, we shall not consider it. . . . [The decision of the Ninth Circuit is vacated and remanded.]

BUSINESS CONSIDERATIONS What should a real estate office do to encourage agents to comply with federal and state laws?

ETHICAL CONSIDERATIONS If Crank discriminated against the Holleys, was his behavior ethical? Why or why not? What is David Meyer's moral responsibility to the Holleys?

* The detailed facts are from the Ninth Circuit decision in *Holley v. Crank*, 258 F.3d 1127 (9th Cir. 2001).

Acquisition of Real Property

Ownership of land and things growing on the land is a society-based concept. The idea that individuals can own land, trees, and plants is prevalent in European countries and the United States; however, it is not universal. A notable exception is found in Native American cultures.

Original Occupancy

Original occupancy (original entry) occurs when the government allows the private ownership of land that was previously owned by the government. In the United States, title may have been acquired by grant from either the U.S. government or other countries that colonized here. Original occupancy may be accomplished under an outright grant to specific people or families, or it may have occurred under homestead entry laws. *Homestead entry laws* are laws that allowed settlers to claim public lands by entering the land, filing an application with the government, and paying any required fees. Homesteading was a popular way to settle large amounts of land during pioneer days in the United States, but it is not generally available today.

Voluntary Transfer by the Owner

The owner of real property may sell, trade, or give title to another by executing (signing) a deed. The recipient can be a private individual, business entity, or government body. In any of these cases, the transfer of title occurs by the execution and delivery of a written deed of conveyance. A *deed* is the type of title evidence that is used for real estate, and it indicates who owns the land. The Statute of Frauds requires a written document for contracts conveying an interest in land in order for that contract to be enforceable in court. This document must adequately describe the property and the interest that is being transferred. A deed is used to convey title to the real estate from the grantor to the grantee. The deed must adequately describe the land being transferred, and it will generally include the following items:

- The names of the grantor(s) (transferor) and the grantee(s) (transferee)

- The amount of consideration, if any, that was paid by the grantee

- A statement that the grantor intended to make the transfer (commonly called *words of conveyance*)

- An adequate description of the property (the street address by itself will not be sufficient; usually this description contains information provided by a private or government survey)

- A list and description of any ownership rights that are not included in the conveyance, such as mineral rights, oil rights, or easements (*Easements* are the rights to the access and use of someone else's real estate.)

- The quantity of the estate conveyed

- Any covenants or warranties from the grantor or grantee (Some covenants or warranties may be implied under state law; others may be expressed in the deed, such as that the grantee can never permit alcohol to be sold on the premises. Usually the deed specifies that these covenants are binding on the grantee and his or her heirs and legal transferees.)

- The signature of the grantor or grantors

Types of Deeds There are three major types of deeds. While each type conveys rights to the grantee, the rights conveyed and the warranties that are included vary significantly among the three deeds.

A *warranty deed* contains a number of implied covenants (or promises) made by the grantor to the effect that a good and marketable title is being conveyed. All the following covenants are included:

- Covenant of title (The grantor owns the estate or interest that he or she is purporting to convey.)

- Covenant of right to convey (The grantor has the power, authority, and right to transfer this interest in the property.)

- Covenant against encumbrances (There are no encumbrances on the property except for those listed on the deed; encumbrances include easements, mortgages, and similar restrictions on ownership.)

- Covenant of quiet enjoyment (The grantor promises that the grantee's possession or enjoyment of the property will not be disturbed by another person with a lawful claim of title.)

- Covenant to defend (The grantor promises to defend the grantee against any lawful or reasonable claims of a third party against the title of the grantee. This usually includes providing a legal defense in court, if it is necessary.)

A *grant deed* contains fewer promises than a warranty deed. Basically, it includes only a covenant that the grantor has not conveyed this property interest to anyone else. The grantor also promises that all the encumbrances are listed on the deed.

With a *quitclaim deed*, the grantor makes no promises about his or her interest in the property. The grantor simply releases to the grantee any interest in the property that he or she *may* possess.

Delivery of the Deed To complete a transfer of real property, the grantor *must* deliver the deed to the grantee or have it delivered to the grantee by a third person. The delivery establishes the grantor's intention to transfer the property.

Instead of handing the deed directly to the grantee, the grantor may use a third person to make the transfer. Sometimes, as in a real estate sales transaction, it is important to use an impartial third party to assist in the transfer and to protect both the buyer and seller. This third party has the obligation of supervising the transfer, including such activities as (1) collecting the deed, (2) collecting the funds, (3) checking that past utility bills, liens, and tax bills have been paid, (4) prorating real estate taxes, (5) prorating interest payments if a mortgage is being assumed, and (6) assuring that the parties have fulfilled any conditions, such as repairs and inspections of the premises. This procedure is called an escrow and is a common method of transferring property in some states. The person who supervises this type of delivery may be an attorney, an *escrow officer* (an employee of a bank or escrow company who oversees the escrow transaction), or another agent.

Recording of the Deed Recording is accomplished by filing the deed with the proper authority, usually the county clerk or county recorder. The recorder files the deed or a copy of it in a deed book. Deed books usually are arranged in chronological order. The recorder also enters information about the transfer in an index, which is organized by the names of the grantors and grantees or by the location of the property. The index simplifies the task of locating information about a particular parcel. The recording gives the whole world "notice" of the transfer to this grantee. Recording is not a legal prerequisite to the transfer, but it does establish the grantee's interest in the property, and in many states recorded deeds have precedence over unrecorded deeds.

Transfer by Will or Intestate Succession

A person can arrange to transfer real property by provisions in a valid will. If a person does not have a valid will, the property will pass by the intestate succession statute of the state where the property is located. An *intestate succession statute* is a statute that determines who will receive assets if a *decedent* does not have a valid will disposing of them. This statute will determine who inherits the property if a valid will does not exist. (Wills and intestate succession are discussed in detail in Chapter 44.)

Protection of Real Property

Real property is subject to loss by operation of law; it can also be lost due to actions of the government, of another person, or of nature. This loss is generally involuntary on the part of the owner. To prevent it, the owner should be alert to these potential causes of loss.

Involuntary Transfers by Operation of Law

An owner who defaults on a mortgage or trust deed may lose the property due to the default. The lender may

NRW CASE 41.1 Management

PROTECTION AGAINST CLAIMS ASSERTED BY MATERIAL PROVIDERS

Assume that Mai decides to have the furnace inspected at the NRW plant before the cold weather begins. Immediately following the inspection, the service person informs Mai that the furnace has a cracked heat exchanger and that the unit must be shut off until it is repaired. Since the system will be idled anyway, NRW decides to replace the furnace with a new energy-efficient unit installed by Cool Air, Inc. Cool Air, Inc., is a licensed heating-and-cooling contractor that sells, installs, and services furnaces and air-conditioning units. Carlos expresses some concern about having the work done by Cool Air, because he believes that this will give Cool Air a claim against the firm and its assets if there are any problems in making payments. However, he recognizes the need for heat in the plant during the winter months. Carlos asks you how NRW can be protected against claims asserted by suppliers. What will you tell him?

BUSINESS CONSIDERATIONS Should an installer in this situation insist on having firm members serve as cosigners on the contract as protection against any possible default by the firm? Should the firm members be concerned if they are asked to serve as cosigners on the contract?

ETHICAL CONSIDERATIONS Suppose that the service person knows that the current furnace could be repaired, but that it would not last very long even with repairs. Should he or she try to talk the customers into purchasing a new furnace in order to protect their long-term interests, or should he or she make the repairs (a short-term solution) knowing that a new furnace will be needed soon? How should this sort of issue be handled from an ethical perspective?

INTERNATIONAL CONSIDERATIONS The furnace will be considered a fixture, and as such it will be treated as real property in the United States. Do other countries treat fixtures as real property? Is such a classification important for creditors? Why?

institute foreclosure proceedings and take possession of the real estate by following the appropriate state laws. Usually, the property will be sold at a foreclosure sale.

In most states, if the owner has not paid a court judgment, the judgment creditor may ask the court for a writ of execution. Following the applicable state procedures, the sheriff will attach the property and sell it at a judgment sale. (Under state law, some property, both real and personal, may be exempt from attachment under a judgment sale.)

If the owner has not paid people who supplied labor or materials for the premises, these suppliers may also be able to force a sale under state law. These workers may have mechanics' liens for the value of the supplies or services rendered to improve the property. Even if they do not force a sale of the real property, generally they can prevent a voluntary sale by the owner unless they are paid from the proceeds.

Involuntary Transfers by Government Action

Government bodies have the right to take private lands if they are necessary for public use. This is called the right of *eminent domain*. Under this doctrine, the government must have a legitimate public use for the land and must pay the owner a reasonable amount for it.

A different type of taking occurs when the government enacts land use laws. Zoning and planning laws restrict how property may be used. They may prevent certain types of structures from being built on the property; for example, some areas may be limited to single-family residences. Or certain industries may not be permitted to operate plants in particular areas because of the air pollution these plants would produce. Sometimes these ordinances restrict the number and placement of establishments that sell alcohol. Commonly, bars are not allowed within one-quarter mile of public schools. In order to be valid, zoning and planning laws must be based on a compelling government interest, and the restrictions must be reasonable. Two of the federal statutes that restrict land use are the National Historic Preservation Act (1966)[3] and the National Environmental Policy Act (1969).[4] Cornell Law School's LII provides an overview of land use law and links to statutes, court decisions, and other materials at http://www.law.cornell.edu/topics/land_use.html.

The constitutionality of zoning laws was addressed in the landmark U.S. Supreme Court case *Lucas v. South Carolina Coastal Council*,[5] and the cases that have followed it. (See Case Problems and Writing Assignments 1 in this chapter.) In the following case, the U.S. Supreme Court addressed whether a landowner who was denied permission to fill marshland was entitled to sue under the takings clause of the Constitution. (The case is being heard on a Writ of Certiorari to the state supreme court.) The Court discussed "ripeness." A case must be *ripe* before a court will decide it, which means that the facts are sufficiently developed to permit the court to make an intelligent and useful decision.

41.2

PALAZZOLO v. RHODE ISLAND
533 U.S. 606, 2001 U.S. LEXIS 4910 (2001)

FACTS In 1959, Anthony Palazzolo decided to invest in three undeveloped, adjoining parcels in the town of Westerly. Palazzolo and associates formed Shore Gardens, Inc. (SGI) to purchase and hold the property. Palazzolo later bought out his associates and became the sole shareholder. SGI submitted applications to state agencies to fill substantial portions of the parcel. Most of the property was salt marsh subject to tidal flooding and would require considerable fill before structures could be built. SGI's 1962 application to fill the entire property was denied for lack of essential information. A similar proposal was filed a year later. A third application proposed more limited filling of the land for use as a private beach club. The Rhode Island Department of Natural Resources agreed to the third proposal but then withdrew its consent.

In 1971, Rhode Island enacted legislation creating the Council, an agency charged with the duty of protecting the state's coastal properties. Regulations promulgated by the Council designated salt marshes as protected "coastal wetlands," on which development is greatly limited. In 1978 SGI's corporate charter was revoked and title to the property passed to Palazzolo as the sole shareholder.

In 1983 Palazzolo applied to the Council requesting permission to construct a wooden bulkhead and to fill the entire marshland area. The Council rejected the application. Palazzolo submitted a more specific and limited proposal to build a private beach club, which was denied by the Council.

Palazzolo then filed suit, alleging that the property had been "taken" from him by the continued refusal of the state to allow him to develop and to use the land.

ISSUES Is Palazzolo's takings claim ripe for decision? Did Palazzolo's acquisition of title after the effective date of the regulations bar his claim? Was Palazzolo deprived of all value in the property?

HOLDINGS Yes, Palazzolo's claim was ripe. No, his suit was not barred because he acquired title after the effective date. No, he was not deprived of all value.

REASONING Excerpts from the opinion of Justice Kennedy:

The Takings Clause of the Fifth Amendment, applicable to the States through the Fourteenth Amendment, prohibits the government from taking private property for public use without just compensation. The clearest sort of taking occurs when the government encroaches upon or occupies private land for its own proposed use. Our cases establish that even a minimal "permanent physical occupation of real property" requires compensation. . . . In [precedents], the Court recognized that there will be instances when government actions do not encroach upon or occupy the property yet still affect and limit its use to such an extent that a taking occurs. . . . [A] regulation which "denies all economically beneficial or productive use of land" will require compensation under the Takings Clause. . . . Where a regulation places limitations on land that fall short of eliminating all economically beneficial use, a taking nonetheless may have occurred, depending on a complex of factors including the regulation's economic effect on the landowner, the extent to which the regulation interferes with reasonable investment-backed expectations, and the character of the government action. These inquiries are informed by the purpose of the Takings Clause, which is to prevent the government from "forcing some people alone to bear public burdens which, in all fairness and justice, should be borne by the public as a whole." . . .

The Court [in precedents] held that a takings claim challenging the application of land-use regulations is not ripe unless "the government entity charged with implementing the regulations has reached a final decision regarding the application of the regulations to the property at issue." . . . The central question in resolving the ripeness issue . . . is whether petitioner obtained a final decision from the Council determining the . . . use for the land. . . . A landowner . . . is prohibited from filling or building residential structures on wetlands adjacent to Type 2 waters [as is the case here], . . . but may seek a special exception from the Council to engage in a prohibited use. The Council is permitted to allow the exception, however, only where a "compelling public purpose" is served. The proposal to fill the entire property was not accepted under Council regulations and did not qualify for the special exception. . . . There is no indication the Council would have accepted the application had petitioner's proposed beach club

occupied a smaller surface area. To the contrary, it ruled that the proposed activity was not a "compelling public purpose." . . .

[A] landowner may not establish a taking before a land-use authority has the opportunity, using its own reasonable procedures, to decide and explain the reach of a challenged regulation. . . . [A] takings claim based on a law or regulation . . . depends upon the landowner's first having followed reasonable and necessary steps to allow regulatory agencies to exercise their full discretion in considering development plans for the property, including the opportunity to grant any variances or waivers allowed by law. . . . Government authorities . . . may not burden property by imposition of repetitive or unfair land-use procedures in order to avoid a final decision. . . . [T]he Council's decisions make plain that the agency interpreted its regulations to bar petitioner from engaging in any filling or development activity on the wetlands. . . . The rulings of the Council . . . leave no doubt on this point. . . .

[N]ot all of petitioner's parcel constitutes protected wetlands. . . . [There is an upland site.] [T]he strict "compelling public purpose" test does not govern proposed land uses on property in this classification. Council officials testified . . . that they would have allowed petitioner to build a residence on the upland parcel. . . . Ripeness doctrine does not require a landowner to submit applications for their own sake. Petitioner is required to explore development opportunities on his upland parcel only if there is uncertainty as to the land's permitted use. . . . It was stated in the petition for certiorari that the uplands on petitioner's property had an estimated worth of $200,000. . . . [This figure was cited as fact in the State's brief and was accepted by the trial court.] . . . [R]ipeness cannot be contested by saying that the value of the non-wetland parcels is unknown. . . .

[T]he limitations the wetland regulations imposed were clear from the Council's denial of his applications, and there is no indication that any use involving any substantial structures or improvements would have been allowed. Where the state agency . . . entertains an application from an owner and its denial of the application makes clear the extent of development permitted, . . . federal ripeness rules do not require the submission of further and futile applications. . . .

When the Council promulgated its wetlands regulations, the disputed parcel was owned not by petitioner but by the corporation of which he was sole shareholder. When title was transferred to petitioner by operation of law, the wetlands regulations were in force. The state court held the postregulation acquisition of title was fatal to the claim for deprivation of all economic use. . . .

The right to improve property . . . is subject to the reasonable exercise of state authority, including the enforcement of valid zoning and land-use restrictions. . . . The Takings Clause . . . in certain circumstances allows a landowner to assert that a particular exercise of the State's regulatory power is so unreasonable or onerous as to compel compensation. . . . [A] new zoning ordinance can limit the value of land without effecting a taking because it can be understood as reasonable by all concerned[;] other enactments are unreasonable and do not become less so through passage of time or title. Were we to accept the State's rule, the postenactment transfer of title would absolve the State of its obligation to defend any action restricting land use, no matter how extreme or unreasonable. . . . This ought not to be the rule. . . . A blanket rule that purchasers with notice have no compensation right when a claim becomes ripe is too blunt an instrument to accord with the duty to compensate for what is taken. . . .

[The Rhode Island Supreme Court] held that all economically beneficial use was not deprived because the uplands portion of the property can still be improved. . . . Petitioner accepts the Council's contention and the state trial court's finding that his parcel retains $200,000 in development value. . . . A regulation permitting a landowner to build a substantial residence on an 18-acre parcel does not leave the property "economically idle." . . .

BUSINESS CONSIDERATIONS What can a business do to avoid some of the problems faced by Palazzolo?

ETHICAL CONSIDERATIONS Can the Council's decision to deny the application be justified on an act utilitarian basis that it provided the greatest good for the greatest number? Why or why not? Should Rhode Island have taken the property by eminent domain instead of denying Palazzolo the opportunity to develop the land? Why?

Private Restrictions on Land Use

Generally, an owner can use property as he or she wishes. Sometimes the government uses land use regulation to limit the uses. (*Land use regulations* are laws that regulate the possession, ownership, and use of real property.) *Restrictive covenants* also limit how land may be used. These are private agreements between landowners on the use of the property and may take the form of building restrictions or *covenants, conditions, and restrictions* (CC&Rs). These are the techniques used by condominiums and planned developments to control the building on and use of the lots. Restrictive covenants may be enforced by private lawsuits *if* they are lawful. Formerly, restrictive covenants were used to enforce racial segregation, with the covenant stating that no owner could sell his or her property to a nonwhite person. The U.S. Supreme Court declared that restrictive covenants based on race are illegal in the landmark decision of *Shelley v. Kraemer*.[6]

Adverse Possession

Adverse possession occurs when an individual tries to take title and possession of real estate from the owner. A person who has physical possession of real property has better legal rights to that property than anyone else, except for the true owner and people who claim possession through the true owner. If the possession is of an adverse nature and it continues for a sufficient length of time, the adverse possessor may actually take ownership from the true owner.

For possession to be adverse, it must be actual, open, and notorious. *Actual* possession means that the adverse possessor is actually on the land and is using the real estate in a reasonable manner for that type of land—as a residence, a farm, a ranch, or a business office. It is not sufficient that the adverse possessor state that he or she is using the land; actual use is required.

For possession to be *open*, it must be obvious that the adverse possessor is on the property. It will not be sufficient if the person stays out of sight during the day and walks around the property only at night. Openness is required to reasonably put the owner and the rest of the world on notice that the adverse possessor is using the property.

Finally, for possession to be *notorious*, it must be adverse or hostile to the true owner. Generally, people who occupy or use the property with the owner's permission, such as co-owners and renters, cannot be adverse possessors.

The required holding period varies from state to state and is specified by state statute, ranging from 5 to 30 years. Entry under color of title may affect the holding period. Entering under *color of title* means that the holder thought that he or she had a legal right to take possession of the real property and had title to it. For example, a person with a defective deed would enter under color of title. Some states specify a shorter holding period if the holder entered under color of title and/or if the holder paid real estate taxes. In some states, the payment of real estate taxes is a necessary requirement for adverse possession; in some others, color of title is required. The possession must be continuous for

NRW CASE 41.2 Management

ZONING RESTRICTIONS

Mai has a large barn on her rural, residential property. This barn has been vacant for quite some time; and Mai thinks that, with minor renovations, it will make an excellent warehouse from which to ship StuffTrakR and InvenTrakR. Helen points out that the property is zoned for residential and agricultural use, not for commercial activities, and such a use might be criminal without the proper zoning. Carlos thinks that, since NRW is a closely held business, such restrictions do not apply. Mai, Carlos, and Helen seek your advice. What will you tell them?

BUSINESS CONSIDERATIONS What are the advantages and disadvantages of renovating the barn into an NRW warehouse? What factors should the closely held business consider in making this sort of decision? Would different factors enter into the decision for a publicly owned corporation? A partnership?

ETHICAL CONSIDERATIONS Among the factors that might affect any decisions on this issue are: Will there be an increase in traffic and/or noise in the neighborhood? How will such a use affect the neighbors? What ethical obligations exist for NRW under these circumstances?

INTERNATIONAL CONSIDERATIONS How, if at all, do other countries regulate land use? Do other countries use zoning as a method for restricting land use within a given community?

the specified time period. However, the adverse possessor may leave the property for short periods to go to work, to classes, or on a brief vacation. He or she may not leave the property for an extended period of time.

The policy behind the doctrine of adverse possession is to encourage the use of land, a very valuable resource. The doctrine tends to encourage the use of land by someone else, if the owner is not using it. As the old adage says, possession may be nine-tenths of the law. This doctrine applies only to privately owned real property, however; government land may not be taken by adverse possession.

If the owner is not able to use or rent the property, he or she should periodically check to make sure that no one is using it. If it is being used without permission, the owner should take prompt legal steps to remove the occupant,

or the owner may learn a very expensive lesson about the effect of adverse possession on his or her title to the land.

Easements

In some situations, a person may be entitled to use the land of another in a particular manner. This right is called an *easement*. An easement is not a right to *own* the property. Rather, it is the right to *use* the property in a particular manner. An easement may belong to a particular person, called an easement in gross, or it may run with the land. The latter means that the easement belongs to the owner of a particular parcel of land, called the *dominant parcel*. The parcel that is subject to the easement is the *servient parcel*.

An easement may be an *express* easement; that is, it was stated by the person who created the easement. Or it can be created by *prescription*, which is much like adverse possession: A person starts to use the servient parcel openly and, after the state's statutory period, he or she will be entitled to continue the use. Easements also are created by *contract*, when an owner of property sells someone a right to use it. For example, an owner may sell an easement to an oil company to come onto the property to drill exploratory oil wells. An easement can also be created by *necessity*. The most common example of necessity occurs when an owner divides a parcel and deeds a landlocked portion to someone else; the only method of access is across the servient estate. (*Landlocked* means that the land is surrounded by land owned by others.) A requirement for an easement by necessity is that both parcels were originally one large parcel.

Easements can also be created by *implication*. This can occur when a parcel is divided, and the owner of the dominant parcel needs to use the servient parcel. However, the proof of need is not required to be as great as it is for an easement by necessity. For example, suppose an owner of a parcel of land decides to sell the northeast corner of the parcel. The owner had previously run a sewer system from this northeast corner to the main sewer line through the rest of the parcel. The buyer can reasonably expect to use the same sewer line when he or she owns the northeast corner. It would be *possible* to run a new sewer line to the northeast corner, but it was implied that the new owner could use the existing one.

The manner and type of use are restricted by the easement. A person who exceeds the amount of use that is permitted under the easement will lose the easement, and his or her rights will be extinguished.

In the following case, the court interpreted the scope of the easement acquired by the federal government under eminent domain.

CANOVA v. SHELL PIPELINE COMPANY
290 F.3d 753, 2002 U.S. App. LEXIS 8746 (5th Cir. 2002)

FACTS The U.S. Department of Energy exercised the power of eminent domain to acquire easements and property in Louisiana to facilitate the development of the Strategic Petroleum Reserve (SPR), as authorized by the Energy Policy and Conservation Act (EPCA). Among the interests acquired was an easement across property belonging to Carlo Canova, necessary to the construction and operation of a 37-mile pipeline connecting two government facilities. The Strategic Petroleum Reserve Management Office decided to lease this pipeline to reduce operating costs and increase government revenue. Equilon successfully bid on the lease of the pipeline. Under the lease, Equilon had the right to use the pipeline to transport oil commercially in exchange for rental payments and assumption of responsibility for maintenance of the pipeline.

ISSUE Does Equilon's use of the pipeline fall outside the scope of the easement taken by the Government?

HOLDING No, Equilon's use is permissible.

REASONING Excerpts from the opinion of Circuit Judge Reavley:

The issue before us is the nature of the estate or interest in land taken and paid for by the United States, and whether the government's lease of the pipeline to Equilon for commercial use exceeds the scope of that interest. . . . [W]e are first confronted with a choice of law problem: do we look to federal common law, or state property law? . . . In the present case, . . . the interest in the Declaration [of Taking] defines the taking in common law terms (an "easement"), and Louisiana civil law uses an entirely different terminology (predial and personal servitudes) for classifying limited interests in land. Because Louisiana law does not speak in terms of "easements" at all, we apply general common law principles in determining the government's interest.

Using common law property principles, the interest described in the instant Declaration of Taking resembles an easement in gross, which runs in favor of a person (natural or legal), rather than a dominant estate. At common law, easements in gross were historically presumed to be non-transferable, but the almost universally accepted rule is now that easements in gross taken for commercial purposes, particularly public utility purposes such as railroads, telephone lines, and pipelines, are freely transferable property interests.

But having established the general type of interest in land at issue, . . . we must still determine the effect of lan-guage in the Declaration of Taking pertaining to the purposes for which the taking was made. Easements may be limited not only as to physical scope, but also as to purpose. The Declaration of Taking . . . provides that the easement is acquired "for the location, construction, operation, maintenance, alteration, repair and patrol of the multipipelines in the establishment, management, and maintenance of the Strategic Petroleum Reserve." . . . In construing a declaration of taking, "the intention of the United States as author of the declaration, to be gathered from the language of the entire declaration and the circumstances surrounding it, must be considered." Our job is not to strictly construe the declaration in favor of the landowner . . . but to determine what interest in land the government has already taken and paid for. . . .

[W]e accept the argument that the reference to SPR purposes does not impose an additional limitation on the scope of the interest in land taken by the government. . . . Canova's interpretation that any end use of the pipeline must be for SPR purposes is at odds with the easement's character as assignable. Assignable means, "that can be assigned; transferable from one person to another, so that the transferee has the same rights as the transferor had." Because no entity but the government can use the pipeline for SPR purposes, a restriction on use to that end would render virtually meaningless the clause authorizing assignment. . . . Second, there is another possible explanation for inclusion of the language referring to the SPR. . . . The federal Declaration of Takings Act requires "[a] statement of the authority under which and the public use for which said lands are taken." The reference to the . . . [SPR], followed immediately by a citation to the EPCA, is consistent with the statutorily mandated recitation of purpose. The government's separate recitation of public uses for the condemned land also provides that "the said land has been selected for acquisition by the United States for the Strategic Petroleum Reserve and for such other uses as may be authorized by Congress or by Executive Order," which is strong if not conclusive evidence that the estate in land taken is not itself limited in scope to SPR purposes. Third, reading the Declaration informed by common law property principles, the government's interpretation of the easement is more consistent with the typical focus on the burden placed on the servient estate rather than the intended purpose behind the use of the easement. Courts might find an additional burden on the fee where the commercial enterprise or public utility use is no longer the same, for example where a railroad easement is used or leased for the construction of telephone lines, or where an agricultural easement holder uses the easement for recreation. [A *fee interest* is the broadest form of real estate ownership, an absolute interest in which the owner is entitled to the entire property and can transfer it during life and at death. It is also called a fee or a fee simple.] In contrast, where the change to an easement's use is "merely one of quality and not substance," there is no added burden to the underlying fee simple estate.... [I]n this light, it makes little sense to think that the government would have reserved an interest in land that hinged on the intended purpose behind the same physical use, especially when the easement is "perpetual and assignable." We need not determine whether the scope of the easement is effectively limited to use for "pipeline purposes." i.e. "for the location, construction, operation, maintenance, alteration, repair and patrol of the multipipelines," because there is no argument or evidence to suggest that Equilon's use under its lease with the United States in any way falls outside of this possible limitation on scope. We find that the Declaration of Taking's statement that the pipeline easement is taken for use "in the establishment, management, and maintenance of the Strategic Petroleum Reserve" is not a restriction on the scope of the easement as an interest in land. Equilon's use is thus not unlawful as outside the scope of the interest taken. . . .

The EPCA authorizes the Energy Secretary to "acquire by purchase, condemnation, or otherwise, land or interests in land for the location of storage and related facilities" to the extent "necessary or appropriate" to implement the Strategic Petroleum Reserve plan. . . . The EPCA is lacking in language mandating eternal use of SPR facilities for SPR purposes, recognizing that needs can change and that the Secretary should retain flexibility to dispose of such property that is no longer needed or being fully utilized. . . . [W]e find nothing in the EPCA that prohibits Equilon's lease of the pipeline for commercial use, given the statute's express provision that facilities acquired under the EPCA may be leased, sold, or otherwise disposed of as necessary or appropriate to implement the government's SPR plan. . . .

BUSINESS CONSIDERATIONS Could Canova have better protected his interests? How?

ETHICAL CONSIDERATIONS Is it ethical for the government to acquire an easement and then to transfer it to a private company? Why or why not?

---

* Shell Oil Company and Texaco, Inc. formed Equilon Enterprises, LLC, in January 1998. Both companies contributed assets they owned in the West and Midwest United States. Shell owned 56 percent of Equilon and Texaco owned 44 percent. In 2001, Shell acquired Texaco's interest in Equilon; in 2002, Equilon became Shell Oil Products U.S. The agreement to establish Equilon is discussed in Case Problem and Writing Assignment 3 in Chapter 32 of this book.

Sources: *Abrahim & Sons Enterprises v. Equilon Enterprises, LLC,* 2002 U.S. App. LEXIS 15847 (9th Cir. 2002), "Agreement on U.S. Acquisition Strengthens Shell's Global Downstream Position" on the Shell Web site at http://www.shellus.com/news/relations/features/feature45.html (accessed 1/1/03), and Equilon Enterprises Web site at http://www.equilon.com/index.html (accessed 1/1/03).

Rental of Real Property

Types of Tenancies

The owner of real property may decide to allow another person or persons to use the property. If the owner is willing to exchange temporary possession of the property for money or other consideration, there is a rental agreement. Most students are tenants because they live in a university dormitory, an apartment near campus, or a house rented with others. The National Conference of Commissioners on Uniform State Laws (NCCUSL) has enacted the Uniform Residential Landlord and Tenant Act. It has not yet been adopted by any state.[7] (The NCCUSL makes uniform acts available in association with the University of Pennsylvania Law School. The Uniform Residential Landlord and Tenant Act is available at http://www.law.

upenn.edu/bll/. The NCCUSL site can then be accessed.) There are a number of other interesting sites addressing landlord-tenant issues that may be of interest to the typical student-tenant. For example, the Legal Information Institute (LII) at Cornell Law School publishes an article entitled "Landlord-Tenant Law: An Overview" at their Web site at http://www.law.cornell.edu/topics/landlord_tenant.html and Nolo Publishing Co. includes articles on a number of landlord-tenant issues, including roommates, at its Web site at http://www.nolo.com/lawcenter/index.cfm?catID/42F1A487-5FDD-45C5-84A2E323ABF31CC5/.

Tenancies are governed by the rules of both contract law and real estate law. Several basic types of tenancies exist, which are based on the length of the rental period. These include tenancies for a fixed term, periodic tenancies, tenancies at will, and tenancies at sufferance.

A *tenancy for a fixed term* is a tenancy for a set period of time; the beginning and ending dates are established.

Generally, the Statute of Frauds requires a written lease if the tenancy is for one year or longer. Such tenancies automatically end at the set time. (Some states have set a maximum allowable term for a tenancy for a fixed term.) If the tenant has not vacated the premises by the end of the lease period, the landlord can explicitly execute a new lease with the tenant or can elect to treat the tenant's actions as an implicit renewal of the lease for another term of the same length. However, an implicit renewal cannot exceed one year due to the Statute of Frauds.

A *periodic tenancy* starts at a specific time and continues for successive periods until terminated. It may be established to run from year to year, month to month, week to week, or for some similar period. Either party may terminate it after proper notice. The lease normally specifies how much notice is necessary and to whom the notice should be addressed. In a periodic tenancy the beginning date of the tenancy is specified, but the ending date is not.

A *tenancy at will* can be terminated any time at the desire of *either* the landlord or the tenant.

A *tenancy at sufferance* is one in which the tenant enters into possession properly and with the landlord's permission but wrongfully remains in possession after the period of the tenancy.

Rights and Duties of Tenants

The tenant rents the right to exclusive possession and control of the premises, which means that the tenant is the only one entitled to be in possession. Generally, the lease specifies that the property can be used only for a particular, stated purpose. Some leases specify that the property can be used only for lawful purposes.

At common law, the landlord is not entitled to enter the premises. The landlord often obtains permission from the tenant to enter the premises either on an ad hoc basis or because such a right is reserved in the lease. Even at common law, the landlord has the right to enter the premises in case of an emergency.

If the tenant is a business, it may need to install trade fixtures, such as neon signs, commercial refrigeration units, and industrial ovens. If a tenant attaches trade fixtures to the property, the tenant is allowed to remove them before the end of the lease. But if the removal causes any damage, the tenant must repair the damage. Even though the common law provides for trade fixtures, it is advisable for the parties to address them in the written lease. For clarity, the specific trade fixtures can even be listed in the lease. The parties' memories may not be accurate after a long-term lease, for example, 20 or 30 years. The Center for Commer-

cial Real Estate provides helpful information on commercial leases at http://www.centerforcommercialrealestate.com/.

Under a normal lease, the landlord is required to make sure the property is in good condition for the purposes specified in the lease and must maintain the property in good condition. Tenants do not have an obligation to make major improvements or repairs. However, a tenant may contractually agree to make certain modifications or improvements. For example, in exchange for an exceptionally low rent, a tenant might agree to remodel a property at his or her own expense. In such a case, it is wise to specify who will pay for these improvements and who will get the benefit of them at the end of the lease.

Warranty of Habitability Some states have held that an implied warranty of habitability exists in residential housing leases. That is, the landlord impliedly promises that the premises will be fit for living—for example, that the heating system will work, that there will be running water, and that there will be indoor plumbing. When the courts recognize this warranty, the tenant can use a breach of warranty as a basis for terminating a lease, as a means of reducing the rent, or as a defense for nonpayment of the rent.

Constructive Eviction Most states recognize an implied covenant that the owner will protect the tenant's right to quiet enjoyment (use) of the premises. Constructive eviction occurs when the owner does not protect this interest of the tenant and allows a material interference with the tenant's enjoyment of the premises. Suppose, for example, that you rent an apartment and that living in the unit next door is a person whose habit of playing drums in the middle of the night is interfering with your sleep. Although your neighbor's behavior is in violation of the lease, the landlord will not enforce the lease provisions. The landlord's behavior may constitute constructive eviction, which will allow you to escape the lease and to move out without any further liability to pay rent. However, if you do not take some action promptly, the court may decide that you waived your right to complain about the noise. And even if you plan to act promptly, you would be well advised to consult with an attorney before declaring that you have been constructively evicted. Otherwise, you may have improperly broken your lease agreement and may be liable for the balance of the lease.

Assignments and Subleases The transfer of the tenant's entire interest in the lease is an *assignment*. If the tenant transfers only part of his or her interest and retains the balance, the transfer is a *sublease*. (Note that this terminology is slightly different from that in Chapter 14.)

Ordinarily, assignments and subleases are allowed unless the lease specifically provides that they are not. Most leases do prohibit assignments and subleases without the prior written approval of the landlord.

Rights and Duties of Landlords

Landlords have the right to retake possession of their property at the end of the lease. In most rental situations, the landlord expressly reserves the right to terminate the lease if the tenant breaches any promises contained in it, including the promise to adequately care for the property.

Rent Rent is the compensation that the landlord receives in exchange for granting the tenant the right to use the landlord's property. Most leases require the tenant to pay the rent in advance. Many landlords require that tenants pay the first and last month's rent in advance, which provides added protection for the landlord. If the tenant is behind in paying the rent, it usually takes a number of weeks to force the tenant to leave the premises. If the tenant has not paid the rent, the landlord has a number of available options. The landlord can sue for the rent that has not been paid or can start procedures to have the tenant *evicted* (removed) from the premises. In some states, the landlord has a lien on the tenant's personal belongings that are on the premises. This allows a form of self-help called a *lockout*: the landlord locks the tenant out of the premises while all the tenant's personal property is inside. For example, North Carolina law allows a landlord to gain possession of the property by peaceable means, including lockouts.[8]

States generally select one of the following approaches to determine the amount of self-help allowed to a landlord who is entitled to possession of the premises:

1. A landlord can use necessary and reasonable self-help.

2. A landlord must rely only on the remedies provided by the courts.

Or

3. A landlord can gain possession by *peaceable* means.

Damage by the Tenant When a tenant moves into an apartment or home, the tenant and the landlord or the landlord's agent should walk through the home and check for any damage. The attorney general's office for Washington State maintains a checklist for tenants moving into a home or apartment at http://www.wa.gov/ago/consumer/lt/LTChecklist.pdf that may be useful for tenants in any

state. The tenant and landlord should also walk through the property when the tenant moves out. The landlord has the right to reimbursement from the tenant for any damage caused by the tenant. For example, if Rudy, a tenant, negligently fills his waterbed, and it leaks and causes substantial damage to the premises, Rudy is liable for the damage. Tenants are also responsible for any damage caused to the premises by their guests. This right to collect for damages exists at common law and is usually stated in the lease. The tenant is responsible for damage caused negligently or intentionally but not for *ordinary wear and tear*—the deterioration that occurs through ordinary usage.

Security Deposits For protection, the landlord will usually collect a security deposit. This money is to be used after the tenant has vacated the premises to repair any damage negligently or intentionally caused by the tenant. It is not to be used to clean the premises or to repair normal wear and tear. As such, a security deposit generally cannot be used to repaint walls that have become dirty through normal use. It can be used to replace doors in which holes have been punched, however. Any money that remains should be returned to the tenant within a reasonable period after the tenancy terminates. Some states have statutes that establish when the landlord must return the security deposit. Rentlaw.com has published information about security deposits and a brief summary of some state laws on security deposits at http://www.rentlaw.com/securitydeposit.htm.

Duty to Protect a Tenant and His or Her Guests Landlords generally have the same responsibility to their tenants' guests as they do to the tenants themselves. The landlord does not warrant that the premises are safe, but the landlord does have the duty to warn the tenant of *latent defects*—defects that are not immediately obvious and of which the tenant may not be aware. This duty of the landlord extends only to latent defects that the landlord knew or should have known existed.

Rights after Abandonment by a Tenant If the tenant wrongfully abandons the premises during the term of the lease, the landlord has various options. The landlord can make a good-faith effort to find a suitable tenant, but if one cannot be found, the landlord can leave the premises vacant and collect the rent from the tenant who abandoned the premises. The tenant is legally obligated to pay the rent, and the landlord can obtain a court judgment for the payment. Practically, the landlord will be able to collect *if* the tenant can be located and is solvent. If the landlord is able to rerent the premises, he or she is technically renting the

LONG- OR SHORT-TERM LEASE?

NRW wants to rent a new plant in order to expand its production and shipping capacities. The firm has located a parcel that is ideal for its needs: it has good access, adequate space, and a reasonable rent. NRW prefers a relatively long-term lease, due in part to the renovations NRW will need to make to the leased property. The landlord, however, is willing to sign only a five-year lease. He is willing to insert a clause stating that the lease will be renewable for additional periods of five years each, subject to certain conditions. Because the landlord is not willing to meet the terms proposed by NRW, Mai, Carlos, and Helen ask you whether the firm should sign the lease. What advice will you give them? What additional information would be helpful?

BUSINESS CONSIDERATIONS What terms should be included in the lease in order to protect NRW's rights? What concerns should Mai, Carlos, and Helen have with regard to the renovations? How should they protect themselves and their interests?

ETHICAL CONSIDERATIONS Suppose a prospective tenant explains planned renovations for a rental property during the negotiations. The landlord recognizes that the building will be worth a great deal more in rent with the renovations and decides to negotiate a shorter lease term than was originally anticipated. Does such conduct raise any ethical concerns? Why? How should such a situation be treated from an ethical perspective?

INTERNATIONAL CONSIDERATIONS Assume that the plant is outside the United States. How would its location affect your decision to rent the plant? Would the fact that it is in another country encourage you to seek a longer term at a guaranteed rent? Why?

premises on the tenant's behalf. If a lower rent is obtained, the original tenant is liable for the difference.

As an alternative, the landlord can repossess the premises and rerent them on his or her own behalf. The original tenant who abandoned the premises is relieved of any liability for additional rent. If the landlord is able to rerent the premises for more money, the landlord will benefit. There may be a factual issue of whether the rerenting is for the landlord's or the tenant's behalf.

Legislative Trends

Landlord and tenant laws are undergoing change. Two federal statutes address discrimination in housing—the Civil Rights Act of 1866 and the Civil Rights Act of 1968. The 1968 Fair Housing Act, which is contained in the later Civil Rights Act, is the basis for most of the recent litigation and is the more comprehensive of the two acts. (It is discussed in Case 41.1.) As originally passed, it prohibits discrimination based on race, color, religion, or national origin. Discrimination based on sex was added in 1974, and discrimination based on familial status was included in 1988. Familial status includes having children under 18 years of age. The U.S. Department of Housing and Urban Development (HUD) provides information on real property issues for both consumers and businesses, including landlords, tenants, and victims of discrimination at http://www.hud.gov/. Examples of illegal discrimination based on race, religion, national origin, sex, age, familial status, or disability include:

- Advertising or making any statement that indicates a preference for people of a particular group

- Falsely stating that no rental unit is available

- Setting more restrictive standards for certain tenants, such as higher income levels

- Refusing to rent to members of certain groups

- Terminating a tenancy for a discriminatory reason

- Setting different terms for some tenants than others, for example, having an inconsistent policy for late rent payments

- Refusing to make reasonable accommodations for disabled tenants, such as refusing to allow a guide dog or other service dog

The 1988 amendment increased the amount of protection by providing three methods for enforcement: (1) the Department of Housing and Urban Development can initiate a lawsuit in federal court or before an administrative law judge, *if* all the parties agree; (2) the person subjected to the discrimination can file a suit in either state or federal court, and the court may award actual damages, punitive damages, or equitable relief; or (3) the U.S. attorney general can file a suit if a pattern or practice of discrimination exists. As with most statutes, there are exceptions. For example, single-family units owned by a private investor with fewer than four houses *may* be exempt from the act as a whole, and housing solely for the elderly (over

62 years of age) is exempt from the age discrimination provisions.

Some states are very protective of tenants' rights. Other states are more protective of the landlord than of the tenant. Recent examples of pro-tenant legislation include laws that require the payment of interest on security deposits or prevent retaliatory eviction. *Retaliatory eviction* occurs when a landlord evicts a tenant who has filed complaints about violations of law, including building or health code violations. To recover for retaliatory eviction, generally, the tenant must prove *all* of the following elements:

- The tenant's complaint was *bona fide,* reasonable, and serious in nature.

- The tenant did not create the problem himself or herself.

- The complaint was filed before the landlord began the eviction proceedings.

- The primary reason the landlord began the eviction proceedings was to retaliate against the tenant for filing the complaint.

In some states, retaliatory eviction has been prohibited by court decisions and not legislative statutes.

Some states and/or cities have rent control statutes that prohibit landlords from raising the rent.[9] Although rent control is intended to protect tenants, many economists argue that it is ineffective. They argue that instead it creates a shortage of rental housing, because investors choose other investments that provide a higher rate of return. Also, landlords may not provide necessary repairs. After unsatisfactory results, rent controls are being abolished in some areas. Massachusetts's voters abolished rent controls in 1994. The California legislature enacted a statute, effective in 1999, allowing landlords to raise the rents on vacant apartments even where there are local rent controls.[10]

Joint Ownership of Property

Joint ownership exists when two or more people have concurrent title to property; that is, they own the property at the same time. There are five forms of joint ownership: tenancy in common, joint tenancy with rights of survivorship, tenancy by the entireties, community property, and partnership property. (Chapter 32 discusses partnership property; it is not covered in this chapter.) Generally, these forms of joint ownership can apply to personal property as well as real property. Most of these forms can be created

voluntarily by the tenants, or they can be created by someone else for the tenants.

A legal characteristic of most forms of joint ownership is that each of the co-owners (the tenants) has an undivided right to use the whole property. Thus, the parcel described on the deed is not divided equally among the tenants; instead, each of them has the right to use all the property. If a dispute arises about the use of the property that the tenants are unable to resolve among themselves, they can file their complaint with the court. The primary remedies available to resolve such a dispute are (1) to sell the property and divide the proceeds or (2) to divide the property equitably and give each tenant a separate parcel. Both of these are considered actions for partition. Note that because the usable value of adjoining parcels may differ, the separate segments may differ in size and shape. Exhibit 41.2 summarizes joint ownership of property. Since state law governs property rights, there may be some variation from state to state.

Tenancy in Common

A *tenancy in common* occurs when two or more people own the same property. Each tenant has an undivided right to use the whole property. Usually, a tenancy in common is indicated by words like "Peluso and Paulovich, as tenants in common" on the deed or other evidence of title. If the deed simply says "Peluso and Paulovich," most courts will presume that they are tenants in common.

There is no legal limit on the number of tenants in a tenancy in common. Practically speaking, however, if there are too many tenants, conflicts will probably arise among them regarding the use of the property. Each tenant may sell, assign, or give away his or her interest. A tenant may also will away his or her interest in a valid will. If the tenant has no valid will, then the interest in the tenancy will pass to his or her heirs under the state intestate succession statute. (Chapter 44 discusses wills and intestate succession in greater detail.) A creditor of an individual tenant can attach his or her interest in the tenancy in common.

Tenants in common do not have to have equal interests in the property. For example, if there are four tenants in common, one may have a one-half interest, one may have a one-quarter interest, and the other two may have a one-eighth interest each.

Joint Tenancy with Rights of Survivorship

A *joint tenancy with rights of survivorship* occurs when two or more people own property together. Again, there is

EXHIBIT 41.2 Comparison of Forms of Joint Ownership

Remember that because property rights are governed by state law, a wide variation may exist from state to state.

	Tenancy in Common	Joint Tenancy with Rights of Survivorship	Tenancy by the Entireties	Community Property
Requirements for Creation				
Requires equal ownership interests		•	★	★
Restricted to married couples			★	★
Limited to two people			★	★
Restricted to human beings		✓	★	★
Applicable to both real and personal property	★	✓	✓	★
Rights of One Tenant Acting Alone to Transfer or Encumber His or Her Share Without the Consent of the Others				
May use the whole property (undivided right to the whole)	★	★	★	★
May be transferred by will	★			★
May not be transferred by will		★	★	
Will pass to surviving tenants at death, if there is no valid will[b]		★	★	✓[a]
Will pass to intestate heirs at death, if there is no valid will	★			✓[a]
May be sold during life	★[c]	✓		✓ •
May be mortgaged or assigned during life	★[c]	✓		✓
May be transferred by gift during life	★[c]	✓		
May be attached by a creditor of a tenant[d]	★	★		■

a. Most community property states have different intestate succession provisions for the passage of separate property and community property. The community property commonly passes to the surviving spouse if there is no valid will provision covering this property.

b. In some type of tenancies, courts would say the interest "remains" with the surviving cotenants instead of "passing" to them.

c. Generally, a tenant in common will have this power. However, in many states, if the tenancy in common is between spouses and consists of real estate, the signature of the second spouse will be required.

d. Creditors of the husband and wife may attach Tenancies by the Entireties and Community Property.

★The trait applies to the specific form of joint ownership.

✓This is true in most states.

• This is true in many situations.

■ This depends on state law and the situation, including when and how the debt was incurred.

no legal maximum number of tenants. However, the practical question remains: How many cotenants can get along with one another? As in a tenancy in common, each tenant has an undivided right to use the whole property. Generally, each tenant has an equal interest in the property. Joint tenancies differ from tenancies in common in that when one tenant dies, his or her interest passes to the remaining cotenants. The survivors continue to hold an undivided interest in the whole property. Generally, a will does not have any effect on a joint tenancy with rights of survivorship. (There is a movement in the U.S. legal community that advocates changing state laws regarding the ability to will joint tenancies and insurance policies. A few courts are devising theories to this effect.) The interest in the cotenancy property will pass from one tenant to another immediately on death by operation of law. Eventually, the tenant who outlives the others will own the complete interest. In most states, corporations are not allowed to be joint tenants because corporations do not die. The law firm of Donlevy-Rosen & Rosen, P.A. has published an article entitled "Traps & Pitfalls of Do-It-Yourself Asset Protection: *Don't Do It Yourself!*" which discusses the problems with joint tenancy. It is at http://www.assetprotectionnews.com/apn3-3-fr.html.

Because of the survivorship feature, joint tenancies often are used as substitutes for wills. Given the potential for disputes during life, however, this practice may be unwise. In addition, in most states if a joint tenant wrongfully causes the death of another joint tenant, he or she will not be allowed to benefit and will be prevented from taking the decedent's interest.

Joint tenancies may be divided during a court action for partition. In most states, a joint tenant can sell, make a gift of, or assign his or her interest during his or her life. A creditor of the joint tenant can attach the interest. A transferee of the joint tenant will take the interest as a tenant in common. A transferee includes a purchaser, a donee, an assignee, or a creditor who obtains rights through the attachment procedure. The transferee does not receive the survivorship rights of a joint tenant because the other joint tenants never agreed to share the risk of survivorship with the transferee.

Tenancy by the Entireties

In a *tenancy by the entireties*, two tenants, who must be husband and wife, share the property. Each tenant is a joint owner in the whole property. This type of ownership has a survivorship feature: If one spouse dies, the survivor receives the whole property. Unlike joint tenants with rights of survivorship, many states allow a tenant who wrongfully caused the death of his or her spouse (cotenant) to benefit and to take title to the whole. Generally, only creditors of the family unit can attach entireties property. One spouse normally cannot unilaterally dispose of his or her interest, unless the parties obtain a legal separation or a divorce. The tenants can, however, agree to sever the tenancy. A valid will does not affect distribution of entireties property. Tenancies by the entireties are not recognized in all states; for example, community property states do not have tenancy by the entireties.

Community Property

Community property is recognized in eight states—Arizona, California, Idaho, Louisiana, Nevada, New Mexico, Texas, and Washington—as well as the Commonwealth of Puerto Rico. This discussion emphasizes the general features of community property laws, which vary from state to state. Louisiana community property law is most dissimilar, because it is based on Louisiana's French heritage. The community property laws in the other states are based predominantly on Spanish civil law.[11] Remember, too, that community property laws are also evolving.

Community property is a form of co-ownership that can occur only between husband and wife. It is based on the concept that financially the marriage is a partnership. One-half of most of the property that is acquired or accumulated during marriage belongs to each spouse. Technically, this assumes that one-half of each asset belongs to the husband and one-half belongs to the wife. Thus, most states require that both the husband and the wife sign any deeds to transfer real property. In most states, this requirement does not extend to personal property. In fact, the names of both spouses do not have to appear on the community property or on any title evidence to the property. For example, although a paycheck may bear the name of only one spouse, it is nonetheless community property and, as such, belongs to both spouses. The primary source of community property for most couples is wages and earnings.

A couple begins to form community property once they are married. In most situations, they stop forming community property once they establish separate residences. In a divorce proceeding, the community property usually is divided.

This is not meant to imply that a married couple will have only community property. Each may own property separately, just as in separate property states. (*Separate property states* are states in which married couples cannot create community property.) Separate property normally includes the following:

- Property owned by either spouse before their marriage

- Property given to *one* spouse alone by gift, by will, or by intestate succession

- Property that is acquired with separate property funds

In addition, in some states—California, for example—income, rents, or profits earned from separate property are also separate property; in other states—Idaho, Texas, and Louisiana—this income is community property if received during the marriage. In Louisiana, a husband or wife can file a declaration that this income should be separate property instead of community property. All property other than that previously mentioned is usually community property.

For most purposes, a husband and wife can contractually agree to split their community property into two shares of separate property. However, if they are careless and mix their respective separate properties and/or community properties, it may all become community property. If the property becomes so mixed that it cannot be separated into community and separate property, the courts say that it is hopelessly commingled and treat all of it as community property.

Community property does not have a survivorship feature. A spouse can will his or her share of the community property to someone else. If the decedent does not have a valid will, most intestate succession statutes provide that the property will pass to the surviving spouse.

The NCCUSL adopted the Uniform Marital Property Act.[12] When it is enacted by a state legislature, it modifies the property rights of married couples and makes the state more like a community property state. Wisconsin adopted the Act in 1983.[13] Initially, a number of other states introduced the bill; however, none have adopted it.[14]

Distinguishing among the Forms of Joint Ownership

The words used on the deed or other title evidence are controlling as to whether the tenants are tenants in common, joint tenants with rights of survivorship, or tenants by the entireties. If the language on the deed is not clear, under state law there will be a presumption as to the form of joint ownership. If the tenants are husband and wife, most states will presume that the property is community property or entireties property. If the state recognizes neither form of ownership, it will presume a joint tenancy with the right of survivorship. If the tenants are not related to each other by marriage, most states will presume that they are tenants in common.

Transfer on Death Ownership

Transfer on death or pay on death ownership should be distinguished from forms of joint ownership. When an owner opens a bank account, purchases securities, or acquires other assets, he or she may designate the form of ownership as transfer or pay on death. Transfer on death (TOD) is used for investment securities. Pay on death (POD) is generally used for bank accounts. The NCCUSL has drafted a Uniform Transfer on Death Security Registration Act that has been adopted in 46 states and the District of Columbia.[15] (The Uniform TOD Security Registration Act is available at the NCCUSL archives by going to http://www.law.upenn.edu/bll/ulc/ulc_frame.htm and selecting the act.) With this type of ownership, the recipient does not have an interest in the asset during the owner's life and cannot withdraw the assets or mortgage them. The recipient is entitled to the assets only at the owner's death, if the owner has not changed the title evidence to indicate a new recipient. These forms of ownership are relatively new, but they are becoming popular as substitutes for wills. Transfer on death ownership is also discussed in Chapter 44.

Summary

Property ownership includes title to the property and the right to control possession of the property. Real property consists of land and objects that are built on the land, growing on the land, and/or permanently attached to the land. A fixture is property that was personal in nature before it was permanently attached to the land or a building.

Real property can be acquired by a grant from the government or by transfer from the owner. An owner may trade, sell, give, or will the property or leave it to another person by

intestate succession. Lifetime transfers will be described in a deed; the deed will be delivered to the grantee; and, in most cases, the deed will be recorded. Although not legally required, recording protects the grantee and the public.

An owner may lose title to or use of the property because of unpaid debts, government restrictions on the use of the land, or eminent domain. An owner may also lose his or her interest by the adverse possession of another person. Easements can restrict the owner's use of the property.

An owner can enter into a rental agreement called a lease. Under a lease, a tenant is entitled to the exclusive possession of the owner's real estate. The lease is the contract that will govern many terms of the landlord-tenant relationship. Under modern law, the landlord must repair the premises. A tenant who negligently or intentionally damages the property is liable for the cost of those repairs. The landlord can require a security deposit in order to assure that there are funds for making such repairs. The tenant is justified in leaving the premises when there is constructive eviction. A landlord can evict a tenant if the tenant fails to pay the rent. Commercial leases may contain different provisions than the leases of houses or apartments.

Two or more people, called cotenants, can own an interest in the same piece of property at the same time. They may be tenants in common, in which case each tenant owns an undivided right in the whole parcel and there are no survivorship rights. Or they may be joint tenants with rights of survivorship. Such tenants can dispose of their interests during life; at death, their interest will pass to the remaining cotenants by operation of law. Tenants in a tenancy by the entireties must be husband and wife. In community property states, a husband and wife can create community property; most of the assets that they acquire during their marriage will probably be community property. The form of ownership is relevant to a business entity that may desire to purchase the asset from one or more tenants, or the business entity may be a creditor that wishes to attach the tenancy property. Joint ownership provides rights immediately; transfer on death or pay on death ownership provides rights to the recipient only after the owner has died.

Discussion Questions

1. After Al's mother and father died, Al, who is responsible for their estate, decides to sell their home. After locating buyers for the property and entering into a sales contract with them, Al removes the petunias, his father's prize-winning roses, and a load of topsoil that is on the flower beds. The buyers are unhappy about this. Who has the right to these items? Why?

2. Describe the typical provisions included in a warranty deed. How is a warranty deed different from a quitclaim deed?

3. Kim moves onto a piece of real estate in California. He begins to use the property in an open, actual, and notorious manner and continues to do so for five years. He also pays the real estate taxes on this parcel. The applicable holding period is five years. Who owns this parcel? Why? Is it material that Jasmine, the original owner, also paid real estate taxes? What are the legal rights of the parties? Why?

4. Domingo and Rosie are neighbors. In 1970, Rosie built a fence around her property. However, she did not have the boundary surveyed, and the fence was built four feet into Domingo's property. Who owns this four-foot strip of land now? Why?

5. Why is it difficult for a lessee (tenant) to be successful as an adverse possessor?

6. Carmen is a tenant who has complained to the health inspector about a rodent infestation in her apartment complex. Should the court protect Carmen from eviction? Why or why not?

7. Suppose that a business wishes to rent premises to use as a sports bar in a shopping mall. What provisions might the business want to include in the lease? Why?

8. NRW is considering purchasing an office building and renting the excess office space to others. Carlos thinks that this would be a good idea. It would provide some diversification. In the future, when NRW expands, it can refuse to renew leases and expand into the tenant-occupied areas. What are the advantages and disadvantages of this idea? Why?

9. Why might a person want to establish a joint tenancy with rights of survivorship with another person who is not a relative?

10. How is community property made or acquired in a community property state?

Case Problems and Writing Assignments

1. In the late 1970s, David H. Lucas and others were involved in extensive residential development on the Isle of Palms, a barrier island east of Charleston, South Carolina. In 1986, Lucas paid $975,000 for two residential lots for his personal investment, intending to build single-family homes on the lots. At the time, the lots were zoned for single-family residential use and there were no other restrictions on them. In 1988, the state legislature passed the Beachfront Management Act, based on an official report that the beaches named in the act were seriously eroding. The act directed the South Carolina Coastal Council to establish a baseline and permanently prohibited the building of *any* inhabitable structures between the baseline and the ocean. The legislature concluded that the area was not stabilized and setback lines were required to protect people and property from storms, high tides, and beach erosion. No exceptions were allowed under the act. When the baseline was established, Lucas's lots were between the baseline and the ocean, thereby preventing Lucas from building any inhabitable

structures on either of his parcels. Did the state take Lucas's property in violation of the Fifth Amendment of the Constitution, which prohibits the taking of property without due process of law? Must the state pay Lucas for the lots because the act deprived him of all economically viable use of the property? [See *Lucas v. South Carolina Coastal Council*, 112 S.Ct. 2886 (1992).]

2. In March 1994, Neil Fisher purchased a novel home in Coconut Grove, Florida, for $310,000. Built in 1967, the house is surrounded by dense trees and has a mature oak tree that grows through a roofed area in the backyard called the "outdoor living room." Fisher wants to remove the tree that he claims has grown too large for its location. He contends that the tree is ruining the brick floor around it and is causing cracks in the house foundation. However, a county law provides that homeowners can be fined as much as $25,000 for removing a specimen tree more than 18 inches in diameter without a permit. The law applies even if the tree is on the homeowner's lot. This tree exceeds 18 inches in diameter. Government officials have denied Fisher's request for a permit. These statements summarize the attitude of the local residents: "This is like the Rio Grande or the Amazon. . . . You have to put your foot down somewhere to maintain your neighborhood," said Michael Goldstein of the Coconut Grove Council. Ted Stahl, cochair of the council stated, "There has been too much slaughtering of trees that have been here for years and years. . . . This tree is a part of the land." Should Fisher be permitted to remove the tree on his lot? Why or why not? Is this county law ethical? Why or why not? [See Charles Struse, "Man Can't Remove Oak in Own Home, *The Fresno Bee*, May 29, 1994, p. D7.]

3. This dispute is between neighbors who live in adjoining subdivisions. The parcel in dispute is where the backyards of Robert and Rusty Silacci and Richard and Janet Abramson converge. Toro Creek runs through the Silacci property. It is the section across Toro Creek and next to Abramson's property that is the portion in dispute. The parcel is about 1,600 square feet in size. David Scott, who previously owned the Abramsons' parcel, placed a three-foot-high picket fence completely around the parcel in question. At the time the land actually belonged to Carlton. Carlton had given permission to Scott and his other neighbors to take flood-control measures beside Toro Creek. Carlton sold his property and eventually it was developed into Toro Hills Estates. Monterey County required the developer to grant a scenic easement along Toro Creek where there are trails used by hikers and those on horseback. The developer promised that it would not build any structures or gardens that would affect this easement. The developer sold a lot to Bob Franscioni in 1989. "A month after the sale, Chamberlain [the developer] wrote Abramson to say that his rear fence was encroaching on Franscioni's lot. Chamberlain offered to relocate the fence to the correct boundary line. Abramson replied that he believed he was entitled to keep the property located inside of his fence. Later in 1989 Abramson wrote Franscioni suggesting that Franscioni grant him an easement. Franscioni,

who had no use for the disputed parcel, talked to Abramson about it and gave him oral permission to use the land. Abramson testified at trial, however, that he did not believe he needed Franscioni's permission, and that he would have continued to use the land without it." Nothing further happened until 1991, when Dinna Silacci purchased the lot from Franscioni. She offered to rent the property to Abramson for $50 per year. She also recorded a consent to use the property "to stop adverse use by Abramson." Abramson did not respond to the offer to lease the property, so she informed him that her son would remove the fence. Dinna Silacci then transferred the property to her son, Robert Silacci, who initiated this lawsuit. Do the Abramsons have the right to continue to use this enclosed yard based on a prescriptive easement? [See *Silacci v. Abramson*, 53 Cal. Rptr. 2d 37 (Cal. App. 1996).]

4. In 1974 the original grantor, Albert Christiana, filed in the Columbia County Clerk's Office a map of a four-lot subdivision. In 1975 he deeded one of the parcels to plaintiffs: a 0.76-acre lot set forth on the filed map as Parcel "K" which included an easement over a proposed 50-foot-wide private roadway leading to the public highway. The deed specifically refers to the filed map on which the four lots, the private roadway, and a cul-de-sac (located at the interior end of the roadway) are depicted. Thereafter, Christiana, without the aid of a surveyor, had a cul-de-sac created in a location somewhat different from, but in proximity to, that depicted on the filed map. To this day, a narrow driveway connects the disputed area with the public highway. In 1977 plaintiffs, also without the aid of a surveyor and relying on the misplaced cul-de-sac, erected a house on what they believed was their property; the house was actually built within a portion of the mapped cul-de-sac, entirely outside their property. Christiana and his successors conveyed the remaining three lots in the subdivision. The deeds to these three lots conveyed a fee interest in the private roadway as tenants in common where, by contrast, plaintiffs' deed had conveyed only an easement over that roadway.

From 1977 to 1993, none of the other lot owners attempted to use any portion of the mapped cul-de-sac, nor did they object to the location of plaintiffs' house. In 1993 plaintiffs had their property surveyed, revealing their encroachment. Shortly thereafter, with full knowledge of plaintiffs' encroachment, defendant RMF Partners purchased Parcel "O" from Christiana's successor, as an undeveloped 1.70-acre lot that borders the mapped cul-de-sac within which plaintiffs' house has stood since 1977. In 1994 plaintiffs commenced this suit to quiet title with respect to the area of their encroachment based on adverse possession. RMF answered and asserted a counterclaim. (*Quiet title* is a legal proceeding to establish that the petitioner is the owner of property.) After the commencement of this action, the other two lot owners deeded their interest in the disputed area to plaintiffs. The Supreme Court determined that plaintiffs had, by adverse possession, acquired "the land upon which their residence and immediate improvements are located" (New York calls its general jurisdiction trial court the Supreme Court.) Did the plaintiffs acquire title by adverse possession to the property on which they built their house in 1977? [See *Guardino v. Colangelo*, 691 N.Y.S.2d 664, 1999 N.Y. App. Div. LEXIS 6539 (Sup. Ct. N.Y., App. Div., 3d Dept., 1999).]

5. **BUSINESS APPLICATION CASE** Golden West Baseball Co. (club) owns the California Angels baseball team. In 1964, the club was anxious to relocate the Angels from Dodger Stadium, which had been their home stadium. The club wanted their own stadium and also felt that the terraced parking at Dodger Stadium was not suitable. In negotiations with Anaheim's mayor, the club said that it would need about 150 acres, a stadium with approximately 45,000 seats, parking for 12,000 automobiles, and adequate ingress and egress from the property. The club entered into an agreement with the city of Anaheim (city) to have a stadium built and then to use the stadium and parking facilities on game days. The agreement was for a 35-year term with a 30-year renewal option. Numerous draft agreements were exchanged before the final draft. The agreement provided that Anaheim would provide all facilities and equipment, including the parking areas on game days. The city also wished to lease the facilities for other purposes to assist in defraying the costs of construction. The agreement provided that the areas not needed would remain under the city's exclusive control. The contract stated that the city may use the area "except to the extent occupied by the stadium, and to the extent necessary to provide the minimum parking for stadium use." Negotiations began in 1977 to move the Los Angeles Rams (football team) to the Anaheim Stadium. The city entered into an agreement to build an office complex at the site of the stadium, as part of that negotiation and as an inducement to the Rams to move. The club wanted to prevent the construction. One of its main concerns was whether there would be adequate parking on game days. Is the club's agreement to use the stadium property a lease? Should the club have foreseen this problem? How could the club have protected its interests? [See *Golden West Baseball Co. v. City of Anaheim*, 31 Cal. Rptr. 2d 378 (Cal. App. 1994).]

6. **ETHICAL APPLICATION CASE** Marvin Wright filed this action against Bogs Management, Inc., Robert Bogs and Phyllis Bogs (the Bogs defendants), and the Village of Lansing and the Lansing Police Department (Village). In 1997, Marvin Wright was living at an apartment in Lansing, Illinois, that had been leased to his brother-in-law, Reginald Washington. Due to nonpayment of rent, Bogs served Wright with a 5-Day Notice on June 14, 1997. On July 23, 1997, Bogs served Wright and Washington with a Summons and Complaint in Forcible Entry and Detainer seeking possession of the property and rent money. (A *forcible entry and detainer proceeding* is a summary proceeding to recover possession of premises unlawfully or forcibly detained.) On July 24, 1997, a judgment was entered in favor of Wright and Washington due to a defective 5-Day Notice given by Bogs. Immediately following the judgment, Bogs served another 5-Day Notice. Wright alleges that, later that same day, Phyllis Bogs cursed him, using vulgar language and several racial slurs directed toward him. When Wright threatened to sue Phyllis Bogs for her remarks, she

tried to have him arrested for assault. Upon arriving at the apartment complex, the police informed Phyllis Bogs that Wright's threat to sue did not constitute an assault. On July 31, 1997, the Bogses filed another Complaint in Forcible Entry and Detainer seeking possession and money damages. On August 15, 1997, Phyllis Bogs posted notices barring Wright from the apartment complex. The Bogses then called the Lansing Police Department and informed the officers that Wright was a "trespasser." Wright alleges that he informed the officers that there was a Forcible Entry and Detainer action pending. Wright also claims that one police officer told him that Ms. Bogs carries a lot of political weight in the Village and "damn near owns just about everything in Lansing." The following day Wright went to the Lansing Police Department where he explained to the lieutenant that the forcible entry and detainer case was scheduled for August 22, 1997. The lieutenant told Wright: "Those laws don't mean anything to me. You would have to let the court decide that matter." Wright went back to the Lansing Police Department, where he spoke with the captain. The captain told Wright that he was aware of the circumstances, but that there was nothing he could do and that Ms. Bogs "carries a lot of weight in the Village of Lansing, and that the Lansing Police Department is not going to go against Phyllis Bogs." Wright complains that the Lansing Police Department and the Bogses conspired to have him arrested and charged with "criminal trespass to real property." Wright was detained for approximately three hours. He was acquitted of "criminal trespass to real property." Should Wright's claims of illegal lockout and intentional infliction of emotional distress be dismissed? How should the Bogses have handled the situation? What is Ms. Bogs's ethical perspective? Why? [See *Wright v. Bogs Management, Inc.*, 1999 U.S. Dist. LEXIS 7747 (N. D. Ill., E. Div. 1999).]

7. **CRITICAL THINKING CASE** Del Monte Dunes submitted an application to develop a parcel of land within the city of Monterey. Although the zoning requirements permitted the development of more than 1,000 units for the entire parcel, the landowners' proposal was limited to 344 units. The city's planning commission denied the application but stated that a proposal for 264 units would receive favorable consideration. The landowners submitted a revised proposal for 264 units. The planning commission again denied the application saying a plan for 224 units would be received with favor. The landowners prepared a proposal for 224 units, which the planning commission denied. The landowners appealed to the city council, which referred the project back to the commission, with instructions to consider a proposal for 190 units. The landowners reduced the scope of their proposal. The planning commission rejected the landowners' proposal. The council again overruled the commission, finding the proposal conceptually satisfactory and in conformance with previous decisions. The landowners' final plan was designed, in accordance with the city's demands, to provide the public with a beach, a buffer zone between the development and the adjoining state park, and view corridors so the buildings would not be visible

to motorists on the nearby highway; the proposal also called for restoring and preserving as much of the sand dune structure and natural buckwheat habitat as possible.

The planning commission denied the development plan. The city council also denied the final plan, declining to specify measures the landowners could take to satisfy the concerns raised by the council. The council did not base its decision on the landowners' failure to meet any of the specific conditions earlier prescribed by the city. After five years, five formal decisions, and 19 different site plans, Del Monte Dunes decided the city would not permit development of the property under any circumstances. Del Monte Dunes commenced a lawsuit against the city. Eventually, the district court submitted some of the claims to a jury. The jury delivered a general verdict for Del Monte Dunes on the takings claim and awarded $1.45 million in damages. Was this matter properly submitted to the jury? [See *City of Monterey v. Del Monte Dunes at Monterey, Ltd.*, 119 S. Ct. 1624, 1999 U.S. LEXIS 3631 (1999).]

8. YOU BE THE JUDGE Santa Monica, California, may have the toughest rent control law in the United States. Santa Monica is currently governed by members of a political party called Santa Monicans for Renters' Rights (SMRR). (SMRR is pronounced "smur.") Rents there average about $552 a month. By one estimate, this is 30 percent below market value. When Santa Monica created its rent control program, it was aware that rent control might encourage landlords to "economize" on maintenance or convert properties to other uses such as condos. To maintain its rent control program, the local rent control board has 250 pages of regulations, a staff of 50, and an annual budget of $4.2 million.

John Rodriguez, a barber and owner of three small apartment buildings, says "They're using our money to give to other people without any proof whatsoever that those people are in need." Until 1986, landlords could not even go out of business. A California law has been enacted that permits landlords, even in Santa Monica, to go out of business.

In 1990, Santa Monica landlord Phyllis Anderson paid each of her tenants $3,500 to vacate their apartments. She still is unable to convert her six-unit apartment building to another use. If she sold her building to someone else, the purchaser would be restricted by the same rules.

Suppose a group of landlords challenges this law in *your* court. How will *you* rule in this case? Would you consider investing in rental property in a community where there is rent control? Why or why not? What would you do if *you* were the owner when rent control was initiated? [See "Slow Death for Rent Control," *Fortune*, August 5, 1996, pp. 24, 26.]

Notes

1. This is not always the case. In the classic case of *Fontainebleau Hotel Corp. v. Forty-Five Twenty-Five, Inc.*, 114 So. 2d 367 (Fla. 1959), the court held that there were no rights to sunlight or view.
2. Laura M. Litvan, "The Disabilities Law: Avoid the Pitfalls," *Nation's Business* (January 1994): 25–27.
3. 16 U.S.C. §§ 461 et seq.
4. 42 U.S.C. §§ 4321 et seq.
5. 112 S. Ct. 2886 (1992).
6. 334 U.S. 1 (1948).
7. "Residential Landlord and Tenant Act Summary," NCCUSL Web site (accessed 1/1/03), http://www.nccusl.org/nccusl/.
8. See *Spinks v. Taylor*, 278 S.E.2d 501 (N.C. 1981).
9. Currently, communities in only five states have rent control. Those states are California, District of Columbia, Maryland, New Jersey, and New York. Shae Irving, Kathleen Michon, and Beth McKenna, *Nolo's Encyclopedia of Everyday Law*, 4th ed. (Berkeley, Calif: Nolo, 2002).
10. "Slow Death for Rent Control," *Fortune* (August 5, 1996): 24, 26.
11. For an excellent discussion of the historical basis for community property law in each state, see W. S. McClanahan, *Community Property Law in the United States* (Lawyers Cooperative and Bancroft-Whitney, 1982), ch. 1–3. For an interesting discussion of the origins of community property in Europe and its adoption in other countries, see William Q. DeFuniak and Michael J. Vaughn, *Principles of Community Property*, 2nd ed. (Tucson: University of Arizona Press, 1971), ch. II.

12. For a copy of the act as adopted by the NCCUSL, see 9A Uniform Laws Annotated (U.L.A.) 97 (1987) and pocket parts. The NCCUSL has changed the Uniform Marital Property Act to the Model Marital Property Act. E-mail from Katie Robinson, Public Affairs Coordinator, NCCUSL, November 26, 2002.
13. See Wisconsin 1983, Act 186, Effective 1-1-86, Wis. Stat. Ann §§ 766.001 to 766.97.
14. "A Few Facts about the Uniform Marital Property Act," NCCUSL Web site (accessed 11/24/02), http://www.nccusl.org/nccusl/uniformact_factsheets/uniformacts-fs-umpa.asp.
15. The Uniform TOD Security Registration Act has been adopted by Alabama, Alaska, Arizona, Arkansas, California, Colorado, Connecticut, Delaware, District of Columbia, Florida, Georgia, Hawaii, Idaho, Illinois, Indiana, Iowa, Kansas, Kentucky, Maine, Maryland, Massachusetts, Michigan, Minnesota, Mississippi, Missouri, Montana, Nebraska, Nevada, New Hampshire, New Jersey, New Mexico, North Dakota, Ohio, Oklahoma, Oregon, Pennsylvania, Rhode Island, South Carolina, South Dakota, Tennessee, Utah, Vermont, Virginia, Washington, West Virginia, Wisconsin, and Wyoming. New York and North Carolina have introduced bills to adopt the act. "A Few Facts about the TOD Security Registration Act," NCCUSL Web site (accessed 1/1/03), http://www.nccusl.org/nccusl/uniformact_factsheets/uniformacts-fs-tsra.asp.

Personal Property and Bailments

AGENDA

NRW In addition to owning real property, as discussed in Chapter 41, NRW owns personal property. For example, NRW owns the rights to produce and sell StuffTrakR and InvenTrakR. How can Mai, Carlos, and Helen protect this asset? What type of property is it? What are the rights and obligations that accompany ownership? How can NRW best protect its property?

NRW was interviewing a number of applicants for positions in its factory. After all of the applicants left, Carlos noticed two umbrellas in the waiting room. What should Carlos do with them? Does NRW have any sort of claim on the umbrellas? If so, what is the basis for its claim?

NRW leases equipment from an electronics firm. Helen is concerned that NRW may be liable for any damages to the equipment and, consequently, feels this equipment should be insured by NRW during the lease period. Carlos disagrees, arguing that, in leases of industrial equipment, the party leasing the equipment assumes the risk relating to damages. Who is correct? Why? When NRW rents extra delivery trucks, what are the legal rights of the lessor and NRW?

These and other questions will arise during our discussion of personal property. Be prepared! You never know when the firm or one of its members will seek your advice.

Ownership of Property

Classifications of Property

The concepts of property rights and joint ownership discussed in Chapter 41 apply to personal property as well. As noted in that chapter, real estate is land and everything constructed on or otherwise permanently attached to the land or to any of the buildings. All property that is not classified as real property is personal property.

Like real property, personal property is divided into two categories: tangible and intangible. *Tangible* personal property is property that is movable and can be felt, tasted, or seen. It has texture, color, size, a temperature, and similar characteristics. Examples of tangible personal property include textbooks, pens, briefcases, calculators, computers, cell phones, and pagers.

Intangible personal property cannot be reduced to physical possession; it cannot be held in a person's hand. It may, however, be reduced to legal possession and is often very valuable. Intangible personal possessions include things such as shares of stock, bank accounts, traveler's checks, insurance proceeds, patent rights, copyrights, accounts receivable, and corporate goodwill. A physical thing may just *represent rights*. A good example of this is money—without a government willing and able to stand behind its money, money is just metal or colored paper. Another example of a tangible representation is a patent. The right to use an invention or process is intangible; however, a patent holder applies to the U.S. government and if the application is approved, he or she receives a document from the patent office and a patent number. The valuable right is the right to use and sell the invention. The government paperwork evidences that right. The distinction between tangible and intangible personal property is not significant in most contexts and does not control the parties' legal relationships.

The traditional label for a piece of personal property is a *chattel*. Chattels are divided into chattels real, chattels personal, and chattels personal in action. A *chattel real* involves an interest in land, but the chattel *itself* is personal—for example, a leasehold. The owner of the chattel real does not own the land but does have valuable legal rights involving or associated with the land. *Chattels personal* are tangible, movable personal property such as desks, chairs, markers, and overhead projectors. A *chattel personal in action*, also called a *chose in action*, is the right to file a lawsuit or to bring legal action.

Components of Ownership

The three components of ownership that are important with respect to real property are also important with respect to personal property. These components are ownership, possession, and title. *Ownership* includes all the rights related to the ownership of property. *Possession* includes the right to control the property by having it in one's custody or by directing who shall have custody of it. The concept of *title* includes both the current legal ownership of the property and the method of its acquisition. Title also refers to the written evidence of ownership that appears on a certificate of title for property, such as a stock certificate or a certificate of title for an automobile.

Acquisition of Personal Property

Original Possession

Original possession occurs when the owner is the first person to possess the property. In other words, the owner created the ownership rather than receiving it by transfer from another person. One way to obtain ownership by original possession is to create the property through physical or mental labor; Sanjay, an artist, for example, acquires ownership through original possession by creating a painting or a sculpture.

Another way to obtain ownership by original possession is to take something that has never been owned before and reduce it to possession, as when someone pans for gold in a wilderness area and takes possession of any nuggets found. When a person creates property, there is usually no dispute about who actually owns it. Disputes do arise, however, when people are hunting or trapping wild animals. For example, suppose that a group of hunters is about to trap a fox when Spiro, a farmer, spots the fox near some chicken coops and shoots it. A dispute may then ensue about who owns the fox. A court would probably decide that Spiro owned the fox and its pelt because the hunters had not yet taken actual possession of the fox: They had not reduced the fox to their possession. Spiro took control over it first.[1] Today, state statutes may declare that the state is the owner of wild animals, unless the animal was hunted or trapped in accordance with state hunting statutes.

Voluntary Transfers of Possession

Individuals can also acquire real and personal property by having it transferred to them voluntarily by the previous owner. The transfer can occur by purchase, gift, gift *causa mortis*, inheritance, or intestate succession. Exhibit 42.1 illustrates the methods of transfer.

Purchases The most common way to acquire property owned by another is to *purchase* it. When property is sold

EXHIBIT **42.1** **Transfer of Ownership from the Owner to "Recipient"**

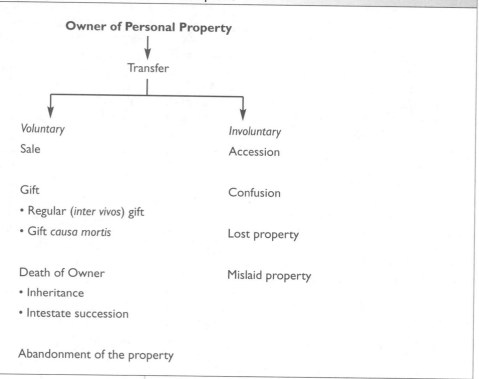

Owner of Personal Property

Transfer

Voluntary	*Involuntary*
Sale	Accession
Gift	Confusion
• Regular (*inter vivos*) gift	
• Gift *causa mortis*	Lost property
Death of Owner	Mislaid property
• Inheritance	
• Intestate succession	
Abandonment of the property	

by the previous owner, there is an exchange of consideration: The buyer gives up one form of property, often money, and the seller gives up another form of property. Sometimes the parties *barter*, or exchange goods or services for the property. Bartering is becoming increasingly popular for goods; organizations even exist to assist businesses in locating other businesses with which to barter.

Gifts A person can also obtain ownership of property through a *gift*. The person who transfers the property is called the *donor*, and the person who receives the property is called the *donee*. Three requirements must be satisfied for a valid transfer by gift.

First, the donor must *intend* to make a present gift—that is, to transfer the property without receiving full and fair consideration. This includes the intent to pass title to the donee now, and not in the future. For example, if the donor says, "I want you to have this" the donor is showing a *present intent* to make the transfer. By contrast, if the owner says "I want you to have this next Sunday," the donor is showing a *future intent* to make a transfer. Since there is no present intent, it is not a present transfer and it is not a valid gift. In most gift situations, the donor is freely giving up the property without receiving any consideration at all. Sometimes it is difficult to determine whether the intent of

the donor was to make a gift or, alternatively, to sell or to lend the property. This is particularly true if the donor has died or if the donor and the donee have had a disagreement. However, if the transfer is to be treated as a valid gift, it must be shown that the donor's intent was to make a gift.

The second requirement for a valid gift is that the donor *deliver* the gift property to the donee. When the donor hands the gift to the recipient, *actual delivery* occurs. Sometimes actual delivery is not practical because of the situation of the parties or the type of property being transferred. Consequently, courts permit *constructive delivery*. Assume Roberto, a hospitalized man, has some antique coins hidden in a secret location in his house and he wants to give them to his son, Fernando. Roberto can give Fernando the keys to the house and the location of the coins, thereby effecting constructive delivery of the gift property.

The third requirement for a valid gift is *acceptance* by the donee. The donee must be willing to take the property from the donor. In most cases, this is not an issue. However, a donee may refuse to accept a gift if the donee feels it will "obligate" him or her to the donor, as when a sales agent making a bid for a contract offers the purchasing agent a two-week vacation in Hawaii. Sometimes a donee may refuse a gift because the gift property has little use or value to the donee or creates legal liabilities for the donee. For instance, Firhana, a donee, might refuse a gift of real estate if it is substandard tenement housing that has many building code violations.

A transfer by gift may be subject to a *transfer tax* (tax on the ability to transfer assets) such as a gift tax. If so, usually the donor must pay the tax. See the Internal Revenue Service Web site for a good, brief description of the federal gift tax at http://www.irs.gov/formspubs/page/0,,id%3d12906,00.html and a fill-in gift tax return (Form 709) at http://www.irs.gov/pub/irs-fill/f709.pdf. The Legal Information Institute of the Cornell Law School maintains an overview of estate and gift tax law, including relevant sections of the Internal Revenue Code, IRS Regulations, court cases, and other links at http://wwwsecure.law.cornell.edu/topics/estate_gift_tax.html. It has the Internal Revenue Code in a hypertext and searchable format at http://www4.law.cornell.edu/uscode/26/.

Most state and federal gift taxes also apply when the transfer is for less than full and adequate consideration. An example would be when the donor receives something back in exchange for the "gift," such as nominal consideration. *Nominal consideration* means that the consideration is very small in proportion to the value of the property. For example, if Markus, a donor, transfers a diamond ring worth $700,000 to Andrea, a donee, for $5, the value of the gift will be treated as the fair market value of the ring ($700,000) less the $5 that was paid for it. Any gift tax is figured on this amount ($699,995) and Markus is obligated to pay the tax. The gift is *not* subject to income tax when Andrea receives it.

If the donor intends to make a gift, delivers the property, and the donee accepts it, the transfer is a valid gift. Once transfer of a gift has been completed, it generally cannot be revoked. A completed gift is also called an *executed gift*. The power of the donor to revoke the gift and reacquire the property is considered inconsistent with surrendering control of the property. The donor cannot legally take the property back from the donee, no matter how much the donor wants or needs to have it returned. In most cases a completed gift is final. However, the gift can be set aside or revoked if the donee engaged in fraud, duress, or undue influence that resulted in the making of the gift. *Fraud* is the use of a false statement of material fact in order to obtain a gift. *Duress* is the wrongful use of force and *undue influence* is the wrongful use of a position or relationship of trust and confidence to obtain a gift. Note that fraud, duress, and undue influence can also be grounds to set aside a contract.

There are a few other cases where a gift may be revocable. Conditions that make a gift revocable *may* be stated by words or inferred from the circumstances. Justice may require the creation of a condition even though the donor had no condition in mind. A majority of the states consider engagement rings to be conditional gifts; courts reason that an engagement ring is given as a pledge or symbol of the promise to marry. States are divided over whether this is an implied condition or an express condition. Many states recognize that an engagement ring is given subject to the implied condition that if the marriage does not take place either because of death, a disability recognized by the law, breach of the promise by the donee, or mutual consent to call off the engagement, the gift must be returned. The ring becomes the absolute property of the donee only if the marriage takes place. A smaller number of states require that the donor prove an express condition in order to have the ring returned. It becomes the absolute property of the donee only if the marriage takes place. When the marriage fails to occur due to the fault of the donor, courts take one of two primary approaches to engagement rings, the fault rule or the no-fault rule. The majority of states are using the fault rule, but an increasing number of jurisdictions are adopting the no-fault rule. Under the no-fault rule devised by many states, absent an agreement to the contrary, the ring must be returned to the donor regardless of the circumstances surrounding the termination of the engagement.

In the following case, the Pennsylvania Supreme Court addressed the gift of an engagement ring. Three justices dissented from the majority opinion. The Pennsylvania Supreme Court later denied a Petition for Reargument, 1999 Pa. LEXIS 3747 (1999).

A promise to make a gift at some time in the future is not binding on the promisor. The promisor can change his or her mind with impunity. However, an executory promise to make a gift may be enforceable in the case of *promissory estoppel*. This equitable doctrine is applied by the courts to avoid injustice. It is based on the concept that the promisor makes a definite promise that he or she expects, or should reasonably expect, will induce the donee to act or refrain from acting based on the promise. The donor will be held to his or her promise to prevent injustice.

Certain types of property require special formalities before the owner can make gifts of them. To transfer a *chose in action* (a right to bring legal action), the transferor must make an assignment of the right. An *assignment* is a formal transfer of a contract right. (Assignments are discussed in detail in Chapter 14.) To transfer negotiable instruments, the transferor must make either an assignment or a negotiation. (*Negotiable instruments* are formal written documents used as credit instruments or as substitutes for money. Examples include checks, drafts, promissory notes, and certificates of deposit.)

Gifts fall into three categories: *inter vivos* gifts, testamentary gifts, and gifts *causa mortis. Inter vivos gifts* are

42.1

LINDH v. SURMAN
560 Pa. 1, 1999 Pa. LEXIS 3498 (1999)

FACTS Rodger Lindh proposed marriage to Janis Surman. He presented her with a diamond engagement ring that he purchased for $17,400. Rodger testified that the price was less than the ring's market value because he was a "good customer" of the jeweler's, having previously purchased a $4,000 ring for his ex-wife and other expensive jewelry for his children. Janis, who had never been married, accepted Roger's marriage proposal and the ring. Discord developed in the relationship, and Rodger broke the engagement and asked for the return of the ring. At that time, Janis obliged and gave Rodger the ring. Rodger and Janis reconciled; Rodger again proposed marriage and offered the ring to Janis. For a second time, Janis accepted. However, later Rodger called off the engagement and asked for the return of the ring. Janis refused.

ISSUE Must a donee of an engagement ring return the ring or its equivalent value when the donor breaks the engagement?

HOLDING Yes. Janis must return the ring to Roger.

REASONING Excerpts from the opinion of Madame Justice Newman:

Pennsylvania law treats the giving of an engagement ring as a conditional gift. . . . Where the parties disagree . . . is: (1) what is the condition of the gift (i.e., acceptance of the engagement or the marriage itself), and (2) whether fault is relevant to determining return of the ring. . . . "[T]he promise to return an antenuptial gift made in contemplation of marriage if the marriage does not take place is a fictitious promise implied in law." . . . Our caselaw clearly recognizes the giving of an engagement gift as having an implied condition that the marriage must occur in order to vest title in the donee; mere acceptance of the marriage proposal is not the implied condition for the gift.

Janis' argument that Pennsylvania law does not permit the donor to recover the ring where the donor terminates the engagement has some basis in the few Pennsylvania authorities that have addressed the matter. The following language from [a prior case] implies that Janis' position is correct:

> We think that it [the engagement ring] is always given subject to the implied condition that if the marriage does not take place either because of the death, or a disability recognized by the law on the part of either party, or by breach of the contract by the donee, or its dissolution by mutual consent, the gift shall be returned.

Noticeably absent from the recital by the court of the situations where the ring must be returned is when the donor breaks the engagement. Other Pennsylvania authorities also suggest that the donor cannot recover the ring when the donor breaks the engagement. . . . This Court, however, has not decided the question of whether the donor is entitled to return of the ring where the donor admittedly ended the engagement. In the context of our conditional gift approach to engagement rings, the issue we must resolve is whether we will follow the fault-based theory. . . .

Under a fault-based analysis, return of the ring depends on an assessment of who broke the engagement, which necessarily entails a determination of why that person broke the engagement. A no-fault approach, however, involves no investigation into the motives or reasons for the cessation of the engagement and requires the return of the engagement ring simply upon the nonoccurrence of the marriage.

The rule concerning the return of a ring founded on fault principles has superficial appeal because, in the most outrageous instances of unfair behavior, it appeals to our sense of equity. Where one fiancée has truly "wronged" the other, depending on whether that person was the donor of the ring or the donee, justice appears to dictate that the wronged individual should be allowed to keep, or have the ring returned. However, the process of determining who is "wrong" and who is "right," when most modern relationships are complex circumstances, makes the fault-based approach less desirable. A thorough fault-based inquiry would not only end with the question of who terminated the engagement, but would also examine that person's reasons. In some instances the person who terminated the engagement may have been entirely justified in his or her actions. This kind of inquiry would invite the parties to stage the most bitter and unpleasant accusations against those whom they nearly made their spouse, and a court would have no clear guidance with regard to how to ascertain who was "at fault."

A ring-return rule based on fault principles will inevitably invite acrimony and encourage parties to portray their ex-fiancées in the worst possible light, hoping to drag out the most favorable arguments to justify, or to attack, the termination of an engagement. Furthermore, it is unlikely that trial courts would be presented with situations where fault was clear and easily ascertained. . . .

The approach that has been described as the modern trend is to apply a no-fault rule to engagement ring cases. Courts that have applied no-fault principles to engagement ring cases have borrowed from the policies of their respective legislatures that have moved away from the notion of fault in their divorce statutes. . . . [T]his trend represents a move "towards a policy that removes fault-finding from the personal-relationship dynamics of marriage and divorce." . . . [B]y 1986, . . . all fifty states had adopted some form of no-fault divorce. . . . We agree with those jurisdictions that have looked towards the development of no-fault divorce law for a principle to decide engagement ring cases, and the inherent weaknesses in any fault-based system lead us to adopt a no-fault approach to resolution of engagement ring disputes.

. . . [W]e still must address the original argument that the donor should not get return of the ring when the donor terminates the engagement. . . . In other words, we are asked to adopt a no-fault approach that would always deny the donor return of the ring where the donor breaks the engagement. We decline to adopt this modified no-fault position, and hold that the donor is entitled to return of the ring even if the donor broke the engagement. We believe that the benefits from the certainty of our rule outweigh its negatives, and that a strict no-fault approach is less flawed than a fault-based theory or modified no-fault position.

BUSINESS CONSIDERATIONS Are there any circumstances in which a business or its key people would want to make a conditional gift? Why might this be something the business or its key people would want to do?

ETHICAL CONSIDERATIONS Is it ethical for Rodger to seek the return of the ring in court? Why? Is it ethical for Janis to keep the ring? Why?

---

made while the transferor is still alive; they are lifetime gifts. *Testamentary gifts* are completed when the owner dies; they are the types of gifts that a person puts in a will and are commonly called *testamentary transfers*. These transfers do not actually take place until death. Gifts *causa mortis* must meet special requirements about the donor's intention.

Gifts *Causa Mortis* Gifts *causa mortis* occur while the property owner is still alive. The donor is making the gift because he or she expects to die soon; generally, the donor is contemplating death from a specific cause. The requirements for a gift *causa mortis* are that (1) the donor must intend to make the gift, (2) the gift must be made in contemplation of death, (3) the gift property must be actually or constructively delivered, and (4) the donor must die from the contemplated cause. If the donor does not die from the contemplated cause, the gift will be revoked. In this case, the donor or the donor's estate can reclaim the gift property. Since the donor was motivated, at least in part, by the expectation of death, it is logical that if the donor does not die, he or she should be able to have the property returned. There is a trend in some states that makes the cause of death immaterial if the donor actually dies.

A gift *causa mortis* is a legal concept and is distinct from various tax concepts that require some lifetime gifts to be included in the estate for tax purposes.

Inheritances A person can receive property from the estate of someone who dies. If the person who died has a valid will covering the property, the recipient specified in the

will receives the property by inheritance. Like gifts, inheritances may be subject to state and/or federal transfer taxes.

Property Received by Intestate Succession The property of a person who dies without a valid will is transferred to the recipients by intestate succession. If some property is omitted from the decedent's will, it will also pass by intestate succession. The people who receive this property in this situation are specified in the state intestate succession statute. As with other death-time transfers, this transfer may be subject to estate or inheritance taxes. Transfers by wills and intestate succession statutes are discussed in greater detail in Chapter 44.

Involuntary Transfers of Possession

Custody of or title to property may be involuntarily transferred by the true owner. Such a situation occurs when there is accession or confusion or when property is lost or mislaid.

Accession *Accession* occurs when a person takes property that he or she does not own and adds to it. Accession can be interpreted as addition or augmentation. For example, Alcides takes some lumber that belongs to Garvin and makes it into a dining room table. The question that arises is: Who owns the dining room table? Should it be Garvin, the person who owned the lumber, or Alcides, who worked on the lumber and changed its nature? The court examines a number of factors in making its decision on this question;

the most important is whether the worker, Alcides in our example, knew that he or she had no right to the lumber. As with many legal problems, the court weighs the conflicting equities.

Title *normally* remains with the rightful owner of the property, the lumber in our example, and is not transferred to the laborer. Depending on the circumstances, the courts may determine that the laborer is an *innocent trespasser* who believes that his or her use of the property is lawful. An innocent trespasser does not acquire title *simply* by adding labor and additional materials. The innocent trespasser *will* acquire title, however, under any one of the following conditions:

• Because of the work effort, the original property has lost its identity. (The innocent trespasser took iron ore and made it into steel.)

• A great difference exists in the relative values of the original property and the new property. (The innocent trespasser took a rough diamond and cut and polished it into a beautiful pear shape.)

• A completely new type of property has been created, and the innocent trespasser has added the major portion of it. (The innocent trespasser placed her notebook on a table in the library. After selecting a couple of references, the trespasser sat down and started to write her research paper. Much later the trespasser discovered that she had sat at the wrong table and used someone else's notebook.)

If the innocent trespasser does acquire title by accession, the trespasser is obligated to pay the rightful owner for the value of the property taken. This value will be based on the worth of the property at the time the trespasser took it. These cases are really exceptions to the general rule that the trespasser usually does not acquire title.

If title to the property stays with the original owner, the innocent trespasser can recover for the value of the services rendered in improving the property. If the owner were allowed to keep these improvements without payment, the owner would have an unjust enrichment and the innocent trespasser would suffer an unjust loss. The owner is obligated to pay for the reasonable value of the improvements. This is comparable to the theory underlying quasi contracts; however, there are minor differences.

A *willful trespasser*—one who knows he or she has no right to the property—cannot acquire title to the new property. The transfer of title under such conditions would permit willful trespassers to benefit from their wrongdoings and might even encourage them to try such an action again. A willful trespasser is liable for any damages that he or she caused and will not be entitled to any compensation for improvements made to the property through his or her efforts.

Suppose, for example, Marti takes some bricks she finds in her neighbor Asa's yard. Marti knows she is not entitled to the bricks, but since she thinks Asa does not want them, she decides to go ahead and use them to build a barbecue. Although heavy, the barbecue is movable, and Asa is entitled to have it. Marti is not entitled to any money for her labor in building the barbecue. If Asa incurs any financial damages because he was planning to use the bricks in another manner, he can recover the damages from Marti.

In rare instances, title may pass to the willful trespasser solely because the owner permits it. In other words, the owner does not want the improved property. However, the original owner may collect the value of the improved property from the willful trespasser. In our example, if Asa decides that he does not want the barbecue, he may allow the title to pass to Marti by default, and he can collect from Marti the value of the brick barbecue instead of the value of the bricks alone. Such action occurs only at the option of the original owner.

Some legal disputes involve cases in which a third party has purchased the property created by the trespasser. Generally, the dispute is between the original owner and the third-party purchaser. To be protected, the third party must be a bona fide purchaser for value. A *bona fide purchaser for value* is a person who buys property in good faith, for a reasonable value, and without actual or constructive knowledge that there are any problems with the transfer. The bona fide purchaser will have the same rights and liabilities as the trespasser. If the original owner could have recovered the property from the trespasser, he or she can obtain it from the bona fide purchaser. Good-faith purchasers do have the right to remove any additions or improvements that they have personally made if this can be done without harming the property. For example, if Ruben, a bona fide purchaser, added a modem to a computer, the modem could be removed without harming the computer.

Confusion *Confusion* occurs when the personal, fungible property of two or more people is mixed together and cannot be separated. *Fungible property* includes things such as sand, gravel, wheat, corn, rye, oil, and gasoline, and generally consists of very small particles or grains. When wheat of the same type and quality belonging to two different farmers is mixed together, confusion occurs: The particles of wheat cannot be separated and returned to their respective owners.

Confusion may be caused by the wrongdoing of one of the owners or may occur without any misconduct. Generally, confusion is voluntary and lawful. For example, farmers often store their fungible crops, such as corn, in the same storage bin or silo. If confusion occurs *without misconduct,* the farmers receive an undivided interest in the new confused mass. If the corn in the bin is sold, the farmers divide the proceeds in proportion to the amount they put into the bin. If there are any losses, the farmers divide them proportionately.

If the confusion is caused by *intentional wrongdoing,* different rules apply. If the new mixture is not divisible, title to the whole mass will pass to the innocent party. Therefore, it is to the wrongdoer's benefit to show that the new mass is divisible. If the wrongdoer can prove that the new mass is divisible and that the mixture has at least the same *unit value* (value per ton, pound, gallon, etc.) as the property belonging to the innocent party, the wrongdoer will be entitled to a share of the new mass. The wrongdoer must prove what amount or share belongs to him or her. The court will probably be suspicious of the wrongdoer. The wrongdoer's proof must be clear and convincing.

Lost or Mislaid Property *Lost property* is property that has been unintentionally lost by the true owner. The owner does not know where the property was lost or where it may be retrieved. For example, Sandrine's scarf falls out of her car when a friend gets into the vehicle. No one notices this. The scarf, lying beside the road, would be lost property. A person who finds lost property has good title to the property, except for the claims or rights of the true owner. The true owner can recover the property from the finder. The finder of lost property generally is entitled to keep possession of it pending the assertion of rights by the true owner, unless a statute or ordinance provides that possession should be given to the police. Normally the rights of the true owner will lapse after some statutory time period, giving the finder absolute rights to the found property.

Mislaid property is property that was intentionally set somewhere by the owner. The manner of placement and the location of the property indicate whether the owner merely forgot to pick up the property or lost it. For example, if Meta, a student, left her calculator on a classroom desk, the calculator would be mislaid, not lost. The owner of mislaid property usually will be able to remember where the property was left and reclaim it. Again, the finder of mislaid property has good title against everyone except the true owner.

A critical distinction exists between *title to* the property and *possession of* the property. Although the finder of the mislaid property has good title, he or she is not entitled to possession. The owner of the premises where the property is found or the person in charge of the premises is entitled to hold the mislaid property. This is because when the true owner remembers where the mislaid property was left, he or she will return to that location to retrieve it. It is logical to leave the personal property on the premises to make it easier for the true owner to reclaim it.

Note that the owner of the premises is entitled to *hold* mislaid property, but not lost property. However, if the finder of the lost or mislaid property was a trespasser on the real estate, the owner of the premises has title to the personal property that was found.

To increase the likelihood that the true owner will be able to reclaim the property, some state statutes and local ordinances require the finder of lost and/or mislaid property to complete certain steps before becoming the final owner. These statutes generally have two requirements:

1. That a specified type of notice be placed in the newspaper

2. That the property be given to the police to be claimed by the true owner

If the property is not claimed within a stated period, the police will allow the finder to claim it.

Abandoned Property

Sometimes an owner is no longer interested in owning a piece of personal property and may *abandon* it, often by throwing it away without intending to reclaim it or by relinquishing it to someone else without intending to retake possession. If the property is relinquished to someone else, that person will become the new owner of the property. Generally, this type of transfer will be considered a gift. If the property is thrown away, any person who finds the property and reduces it to possession will acquire title. The property will once again be subject to original possession. For example, Dina leaves her old desk on the street in front of her house. Javier is passing the house, sees the desk set out by the curb, and claims the desk by removing it from the street and taking it home. If the desk had been abandoned by Dina, Javier has acquired title by original possession of the abandoned property.

The person who locates the property must ascertain if the property has truly been abandoned, rather than lost or mislaid. The owner's intent is not always obvious from the situation. Courts generally consider these three factors in deciding if the owner intended to give up possession: (1) the location of the property, (2) the value of the property, and (3) the utility of the property. Property with low value and usefulness found in someone's trash can has probably been abandoned.

Property Lost at Sea and Salvage Rights

On occasion property is "lost" at sea, either by being jettisoned from a ship, often to lighten the load during a storm, or by the sinking of the ship. Such property is subject to salvage, and special rules have been developed to address the issue of such salvage. In maritime law, salvage refers to "a compensation allowed to persons by whose assistance a ship or its cargo has been saved, in whole or in part, from impending danger, or recovered from actual loss, in cases of shipwreck, derelict, or recapture."[2]

The purpose of salvage law is to regulate the salvaging of a distressed vessel or its cargo. Federal admiralty courts have the authority to grant exclusive salvage rights and salvage awards to salvors who have the intention and the ability to save the property. Once a salvor is granted salvage rights, it must demonstrate that its efforts are (1) undertaken with due diligence, (2) ongoing, and (3) clothed with some prospect for success in order for it to maintain its rights. There is no set formula with which to measure the due diligence of a salvor. Salvors may be temporarily absent from the wreck site without giving up their dominion over the wreck. A salvor has not abandoned its salvage operations by a temporary absence from the wreck site in conjunction with an intention to return.

In the following case, the court addressed the right of R.M.S. Titanic, Inc. to claim the assets of the *Titanic*.[3] The district court obtained in rem jurisdiction over the ship. *In rem jurisdiction* means the court has authority over the property, in this case the ship. Writ of certiorari was denied by the U.S. Supreme Court at *R.M.S. Titanic, Inc. v. Wrecked & Abandoned Vessel*, 2002 U.S. LEXIS 6520 (2002).

42.2

R.M.S. TITANIC, INC. v. THE WRECKED AND ABANDONED VESSEL
286 F.3d 194, 2002 U.S. App. LEXIS 6799 (4th Cir. 2002)

FACTS In 1993, R.M.S. Titanic, Inc. (RMST) commenced this action against the *Titanic*. The district court declared RMST salvor-in-possession. In its order dated June 7, 1994, the court stated:

> The Court FINDS AND ORDERS that R.M.S. Titanic, Inc. is the salvor-in-possession of the wreck . . . and that R.M.S. Titanic, Inc. is the true, sole and exclusive owner of any items salvaged from the wreck of the defendant vessel in the past and, so long as R.M.S. Titanic, Inc. remains salvor-in-possession, items salvaged in the future, and is entitled to all salvage rights. . . .

The district court confirmed its understanding that it was RMST's intention to display *Titanic* artifacts and to try to recover its money out of admissions to the display rather than selling them. RMST has continued to conduct salvage operations and to display the artifacts. In 1999, the court was concerned because of a change in corporate management. The district court issued additional orders restating that RMST cannot sell artifacts from the *Titanic*.

ISSUE What are RMST's rights in the *Titanic*?

HOLDING RMST has the right to salvage the ship and it has a salvor's lien against the assets.

REASONING Excerpts from the opinion of Circuit Judge Niemeyer:

A salvor in admiralty is one who voluntarily saves life or property at sea. Because of the dangers of the sea . . . the law of admiralty for almost 3,000 years has . . . held that those who voluntarily come to the assistance of fellow seamen in distress and perform salvage are entitled to be rewarded. . . . By saving property at sea, salvors do not become the property's owner; rather, they save it for the owners and become entitled to a reward from the owner or from his property. . . . The reward provides an incentive for rendering salvage service at sea, and courts of admiralty have long enforced claims to this award against owners. . . .

The principal method of enforcing a salvor's award is through the recognition of a salvor's lien in the property saved. . . . This maritime lien arises from the moment salvage service is performed, and . . . secures the payment of the as-yet-to-be-determined salvage award. Such liens are a temporary encumbrance of the property saved, lasting only until payment of a salvage award can be made. . . . [T]he maritime lien enforcement process . . . parrots the lien foreclosure process in civil law. The process begins when the salvor commences an in rem proceeding in admiralty against the property. . . . The salvor must provide notice of the in rem proceeding to the owner, other lienholders, and potential claimants to the property. . . . If the owner appears and pays the salvage reward determined by the court, the lien is discharged and the owner takes the property clear of the salvage lien. . . . [I]f the owner does not appear, then the case continues as an in rem action, and the court determines the award, sells the property, and, from the proceeds, pays the salvor. Any remainder from the sale is remitted to the owner. If the owner is no longer living, the court presumably pays the excess to the owner's heirs, and, if there are no heirs, to the state according to its escheat law.

If the sale of the salvaged property yields too little to satisfy the salvor's lien . . . then all of the proceeds from the sale of the salvaged property are paid to the salvor. Courts have held that an award cannot exceed the value of the property itself. Even if it does, though, in an in rem proceeding, there certainly cannot be a deficiency judgment against the owner because the action is against the property and any judgment therefore is limited to the value of the property. . . . If it becomes apparent . . . that the proceeds of any sale would clearly be inadequate to pay the salvor its full reward, then the court might, as a matter of discretion, award the salvor title to the property in lieu of the proceeds of sale, thus saving the costs of sale. The salvor does not have a direct right, however, to title in the property. . . . It is critical to note that . . . the salvor receives a lien in the property, not title to the property, and as long as the case remains a salvage case, the lienholder cannot assert a right to title even though he may end up with title following execution or foreclosure of the lien. . . .

This . . . does not mean that a salvage case could not be converted into a finds case. . . . Under finds law, "title to abandoned property vests in the person who reduces that property to his or her possession." Before such a conversion is made . . . the prerequisites for divesting title under the law of finds must be satisfied. . . . [RMST does not argue that the *Titanic* had been abandoned and that RMST is entitled to full title to the entire ship and the artifacts. Clear and convincing evidence of abandonment is a requirement under the law of finds.]

[T]he court gave RMST the exclusive right to salvage artifacts from the *Titanic* and to obtain a reward through enforcement of its salvor's lien in the artifacts. If and when RMST abandons its role as salvor or the court dispossesses RMST of that role, the unsalvaged wreck will remain as any other unsalvaged wreck at the bottom of the sea, subject to salvage service by others.

Many . . . basic principles of salvage and lien law have been overlooked by RMST. . . . [I]t has . . . argued that the district court should have taken into account RMST's financial viability. But this issue has no relevance to whether RMST is entitled to enforce its salvage lien against the artifacts. . . . RMST is not entitled to a guarantee that it remain in business as a viable company to conduct salvage services. Surely if RMST abandoned its efforts, others would take over. In this case, other potential salvors have unsuccessfully petitioned the district court to do exactly that. . . . And if no others were to do so, then the wreck of the *Titanic* would lie unsalvaged as it did for the first 75 years after it sank. . . .

RMST must first complete the salvage service that it intends to perform and have its reward determined, unless it intends to seek periodic awards. Only after its reward is determined can it seek to enforce the lien against the artifacts themselves. Yet none of these necessary steps had taken place. . . . No determination of a reward had been made; no one had submitted an appraisal of the artifacts or testified that sale of the artifacts would produce an inadequate sum to satisfy the lien. The determination of the reward itself is an involved process that encompasses evaluation of the salvage services. . . . Thus, . . . the court could only have given RMST exclusive possession of the artifacts pending further necessary proceedings. . . .

BUSINESS CONSIDERATIONS Is an attempt to salvage the *Titanic* a wise business decision? Why or why not?

ETHICAL CONSIDERATIONS What is RMST's ethical duty to the heirs of the original owners of the property? Who are the current "owners" of the property?

Protection of Personal Property

If an owner of personal property fails to protect the property adequately, it may be taken by someone else. Sometimes this taking is legal, but often it is not. In either case, the owner will suffer a temporary or permanent loss. To protect against such a loss, the owner should be aware of the means—legal or illegal—by which property may be

taken, including conversion, escheat, an unclaimed property statute, judicial sale, and mortgage foreclosure or repossession of property. The owner should also note that insurance could be purchased to reduce the risk of some of these losses.

Conversion

Conversion occurs when one person takes the personal property of another, usually the owner, and treats it as his or her own property. It is unauthorized and unjustified

DESTRUCTION OF PERSONAL PROPERTY

NRW encountered a fairly serious problem at its office last week. Mai was going to lunch with Ray Goodall, an old friend of hers. Ray met Mai at the NRW office. Ray is a computer consultant who designs software systems for various clients. While waiting for Mai, Ray noticed that NRW was using an old version of a virus scan and protection system he had designed. When Gussie, the NRW secretary, left the room, Ray installed the latest version of his virus scan and protection software on the system. He did this without the knowledge or permission of Mai or Gussie. Although Ray meant no harm, and in fact had only the best of intentions, there was a problem with his new software. During his installation, he erased a substantial portion of NRW's records, which were on the hard drive. Even though a hard copy of all these records exists, a large portion of them had not yet been saved to Zip disks. As a result, NRW will have to pay Gussie overtime in order to recreate the files on the computer. Mai would prefer not to sue a friend, but she doesn't know what she can or should do. Mai asks for your advice. What will you tell her?

BUSINESS CONSIDERATIONS How should a business handle a delicate situation such as the one between NRW and Ray? What should a business do to protect itself from being put into this sort of predicament?

ETHICAL CONSIDERATIONS What ethical obligation does Ray owe to NRW? Is it ethical to require employees to use a password in order to prevent nonemployees or unauthorized personnel from gaining access to company computers? Do the new laws such as Uniform Electronic Transactions Act (UETA) affect your answer?

INTERNATIONAL CONSIDERATIONS There is significant concern today about terrorist attacks and also about computer security. Hackers may access a computer from virtually anywhere in the world, if that computer is connected to the Internet. Should a business store company records on computers that do not have Internet access in order to eliminate the potential threat to the system by hackers, both foreign and domestic?

interference, whether permanent or temporary, with the owner's use and control of property. A transitory interference constitutes trespass to personal property rather than conversion. A more lengthy interference constitutes conversion. However, the interference does not have to be a permanent taking. Under the theory of conversion, the owner can sue the taker for the return of the property, called *replevin,* or for money to replace the property. Conversion is the tort equivalent of a number of crimes, including theft, armed robbery, embezzlement, and obtaining property by false pretenses. In a criminal proceeding, the state will protect its interest in having citizens abide by the law. In a civil proceeding, the individual will protect his or her property rights.

Conversion *can* occur when the owner of personal property voluntarily releases the property to another person, who then uses the property in a manner different from that originally authorized. For example, if Moisis, the owner of an automobile, leaves his vehicle with a car dealer for repairs and the dealer uses it as a demonstrator, the dealer is liable if the automobile is damaged while a prospective customer is taking it for a test drive. In a suit for conversion, Moisis generally prefers to have the personal property returned and repaired, if necessary. Another option available to the owner under the laws of most states is to force the wrongdoer to keep the personal property and to pay for it. The price will be its value at the time the property was taken. This remedy is granted only at the election of the owner. It is not available at the request of the wrongdoer.

Escheat

When the rightful owner of property cannot be located, the property can *escheat,* or revert, to the state government. The effect of escheat is that the property is given to the government. Usually the escheating property is in a third person's custody, and then possession is transferred to the state. The policy behind this doctrine is that the state is more deserving of the property than anyone else if the true owner cannot be found. Escheat tends to occur when a person dies and the heirs or relatives cannot be located. (*Heirs* are the people who actually inherit property from the decedent.) In effect, the state becomes the person's heir. It also can occur when a person does not keep careful financial records and so forgets about small bank accounts, stocks and bonds, or other assets. Often there is an assumption that the owner has died if the owner does not contact the property holder after a period of time.

Escheat is governed by the appropriate state statute, and the rules vary from state to state. Often, escheated property becomes part of the state's general fund. For a specified period after the escheat, the rightful owner can reclaim the property from the state. To successfully reclaim the property, however, the rightful owner will need adequate proof of identity and of a right to the property. Many states have replaced all or part of their escheat laws with unclaimed property statutes, which are discussed in the next section. Ryan and Company maintains a Web site on Unclaimed Property and Escheat Law, including information and links to unclaimed property directories and state laws, at http://www.ryanco.com/gateway/unclaim.html.

Unclaimed Property Statutes

Many states have enacted unclaimed property statutes, which differ from escheat statutes. In escheat laws, title passes to the government; in unclaimed property acts title does not transfer to the government. Unclaimed property acts provide definitions for when the property is "unclaimed." For purposes of these statutes, the term *unclaimed property* replaces the term *abandoned property*. The acts generally prescribe the following steps:

- the holder is required to report to the state that it has unclaimed property;

- the holder attempts to formally notify the owner;

- the property is transferred to the state;

- and the state once again tries to notify the owner.

The state then holds the property for the owner in perpetuity.[4] The advantage of giving custody to the state is to conserve and maintain the property for the owner. Otherwise, the holder with custody of the property may assess fees and deplete the asset.[5] These fees are called *dormancy charges*. Unclaimed property acts generally place restrictions on dormancy charges.[6] The National Conference of Commissioners on Uniform State Laws (NCCUSL) proposed the Uniform Disposition of Unclaimed Property Act (1954), which was enacted by 32 states.[7] The act was followed by the Uniform Unclaimed Property Act in 1981, which was enacted in 27 states.[8] The most recent act is the Uniform Unclaimed Property Act (1995),[9] which replaces both of the previous statutes.[10]

The Uniform Unclaimed Property Act changes the common law of abandoned property and the law of escheat for intangible personal property. Although it is generally limited to intangible personal property, it does provide rules for tangible personal property that is in safe deposit boxes. The Uniform Unclaimed Property Act (1995) is available online through the NCCUSL Archives at the University of Pennsylvania Law School at http://www.law.upenn.edu/bll/ulc/

fnact99/1990s/uupa95.htm. It has been adopted by Arizona, Arkansas, Indiana, Kansas, Louisiana, Maine, Michigan, Montana, New Mexico, North Carolina, and West Virginia.[11] It states: "Property is unclaimed if, for the applicable period of time . . . the apparent owner has not communicated in writing or by other means reflected in a contemporaneous record prepared by or on behalf of the holder, with the holder concerning the property or the account in which the property is held, and has not otherwise indicated an interest in the property."[12] The act is an attempt to streamline the process of dealing with unclaimed property. The NCCUSL encourages passage of the 1995 act because:

- The state will be the custodian for unclaimed property and the property becomes available to the state as a source of revenue.[13]

- The unclaimed property is preserved for the owners. The state is the perpetual custodian until the real owner claims the property.

- When multiple states claim the same property, the act provides a system of priorities to resolve the conflict.

- The periods of abandonment have been shortened. Most property will be unclaimed after five years; however, special rules apply to certain types of property.[14]

- Collection rules and reporting procedures have been improved. Penalties for noncompliance have been increased.

- The act provides the powers and procedures to assist and encourage interstate cooperation.

- Uniformity among the states would benefit both the states and the owners.[15]

The federal government has also enacted an unclaimed deposits act, which was amended in 1993.

Judicial Sale

When a person loses a civil lawsuit, the court may order that person to make payment to the other party. This order by the court is called a *judgment,* and the person entitled to payment is a *judgment creditor.* If the person does not make the required payment, additional action may be necessary. This action commonly consists of an execution of judgment. The person who is entitled to payment procures a writ of execution from the clerk of court's office. With this writ, the sheriff can seize the debtor's property and sell it. This is called a *judicial sale* or a *sheriff's sale.*

After reimbursing the costs of the sheriff's office in seizing this asset, selling it, and executing on it, the remaining money is then given to the judgment creditor to satisfy the judgment. If the amount received exceeds the expenses and the judgment, the excess is generally transferred to the property owner. However, the treatment of this excess is governed by state law and by the type of judgment. Notices of judicial sales are often included with other legal notices in the newspaper. A purchaser at a judicial sale buys the rights that the seller (the sheriff) had to sell. The sheriff's office generally does not *warrant* (promise) that it is entitled to sell the property. In addition, the true owner *may* have a limited period within which he or she may redeem the property, even if it is in the hands of a third-party purchaser. State law governs the amount of money that would be owed to the third party.

Repossession of Property

A lender who wants to protect an interest in a loan may create a security interest in some collateral. If the lender follows the requirements for creating and perfecting a security interest, the lender will have a security interest in the property. Security interests are discussed in detail in Chapters 25 and 26. If the borrower does not repay the loan under the terms of the contract, the lender can *repossess* (retake) the property. Usually the lender prefers to have cash and, thus, will sell the collateral. If the collateral is real estate, the loan is called a *mortgage,* and taking possession of the property is called a *mortgage foreclosure.* A person who buys repossessed property or foreclosed property buys only the seller's legal interest. The purchaser may lose the property if the foreclosure or repossession was wrongful.

Bailments of Personal Property

A *bailment* arises when a person delivers custody of personal property to someone else. The *bailor* is the owner of the property, and the *bailee* is the one who has possession of (but not title to) the property. Whenever an owner allows another person to have custody of the owner's personal property, a bailment exists. It is understood that the bailee is to use the property in a specific way. For example, if the attendants of a parking garage drive a customer's car for any purpose other than parking or safeguarding it, they breach their duty as bailees. It is further understood that the bailee is to return the property at the end of the bailment.

If the bailee is giving up consideration, a contract also exists. If Emma rents a car from Silva's Car Rental Company, a bailment relationship exists. Emma is the bailee and

Silva's Car Rental Company is the bailor. Their relationship will be governed by *both* the rules of bailments and the rules of contracts. However, a contract is not a requirement for a bailment. A bailment can occur gratuitously. All the following elements are necessary for a bailment:

- The bailor must retain the right to reclaim/recover the goods.

- The possession of the property must be delivered to the bailee.

- The bailee must accept possession.

- The bailee must have possession of the property for a specific purpose and must have temporary control of the property.

- The parties must intend that the property will be returned to the bailor unless the bailor directs that the property be delivered to another person.

A bailment is not a sale of personal property. A sale involves a transfer of title and requires an exchange of consideration. A permanent change of possession occurs with the sale. It is not always easy to recognize whether a situation is a bailment. A particularly controversial question is whether parking in a garage constitutes a bailment or the rental of a space to park a car. Generally, the question is resolved by examining whether the driver has relinquished control over the car. If the driver retains control of the vehicle by driving into a self-service parking lot, parking the car, locking it, and removing the keys, courts will decide that there was a license of space. At the other extreme, if a person drives to a hotel where an attendant parks the car, keeps the keys, and gives the driver a claim check, there is a bailment. Transfer of possession of the car is essential. However, courts have held that the *keys* do not necessarily have to be surrendered. Media Values has a Web site on bailments that provides more information. This site can be accessed at http://www.mediavalue.com/bailment_defined1.htm.

Bailee's Duty of Care

Disputes often arise when the property is damaged while in the hands of the bailee. In a lawsuit, the issue concerns whether or not the bailee took proper care of the property. The answer will depend on provisions in local statutes, the language of any bailment contract, and the type of bailment. In the following case, the court discussed the bailor's claim that the bailee was responsible for damage to its property.

42.3

HARTFORD FIRE INSURANCE COMPANY v. B. BARKS & SONS, INC.
1999 U.S. Dist. LEXIS 7733 (E.D.Pa. 1999)

FACTS Barks is a corporation that is in the business of freezing and maintaining perishable food items in its refrigerated warehouse for its customers. In the fall of 1996, Ocean Spray stored cranberries in Barks's warehouse. During the 1996 cranberry season, the temperatures inside Barks's warehouse allegedly increased. Ocean Spray subsequently notified Barks of claims for spoilage losses suffered as a result of the alleged elevated temperature inside Barks's warehouse. As part of this lawsuit, Barks sought indemnity from Hartford for the claims of Ocean Spray for food spoilage pursuant to its commercial general liability policy and its commercial inland marine policy. Hartford employed an investigator, Otis Wright, to examine the Barks's warehouse. Wright concluded that the temperature inside Barks's warehouse increased because the heat emitted from the large quantity of cranberries being stored inside the warehouse exceeded the capacity of the refrigeration system.

On July 28, 1998, Ocean Spray filed a cross-claim against Barks, alleging that its cranberries were damaged while being stored at Barks's warehouse during the fall of 1996 because of high temperatures, which were the result of the breakdown or failure of Barks' refrigeration equipment.

ISSUE Is Ocean Spray entitled to summary judgment on its bailment and/or negligence claims?

HOLDING No. Ocean Spray is not entitled to a judgment as a matter of law since there are a number of material facts to be resolved.

REASONING Excerpts from the opinion of Judge Herbert J. Hutton:

Summary judgment is appropriate "if the pleadings, depositions, answers to interrogatories, and admissions on file, together with the affidavits . . . show that there is no genuine issue as to any material fact and that the moving party is entitled to a judgment as a matter of law." . . . Personal property . . . generally means "all property other than real estate." . . . (Pennsylvania Landlord-Tenant Act defines agricultural crops, whether harvested or growing, as personal property). . . .

Ocean Spray is seeking compensation for spoilage to its cranberries, which were being stored at defendant Barks' warehouse in September of 1996 through June of 1997. Ocean Spray filed a . . . claim against Barks . . . setting forth counts for breach for [sic] bailment agreement and negligence.

Ocean Spray contends that Barks breached its bailment agreement with Ocean Spray as a matter of law and, therefore, judgment should be entered against Barks and in favor of Ocean Spray. Bailment involves "delivery of personalty for the accomplishment of some purpose. . . . [A]fter the purpose has been fulfilled, it shall be redelivered to the person who delivered it, otherwise dealt with according to his directions or kept until he re-claims it." A cause of action for breach of a bailment agreement involves a shifting burden of proof. First, Ocean Spray, as bailor, must put forth evidence of a prima facie case: that it delivered personalty to Barks, the bailee; that it made a demand for return of the property; and the bailee failed to return the property, or returned it in damaged condition. Once the prima facie case is met, Barks, the bailee, must come forward with evidence "accounting for the loss." If the bailee fails to do so, it is liable for the loss because it is assumed the bailee failed to exercise reasonable care required by the agreement. If the bailee successfully puts forth "evidence showing that the personalty was lost and the manner in which it was lost, and the evidence does not disclose a lack of due care on his part, then the burden of proof again shifts to the bailor who must prove negligence on the part of the bailee."

Although not clearly spelled out, case law indicates the bailee's burden of "accounting for the loss" encompasses a showing the bailee was not negligent and/or his actions were not the cause of the loss. . . . Accordingly, on Ocean Spray's bailment claim, Barks bears an initial burden of putting forth evidence it was not negligent and/or that it did not cause the damage to Ocean Spray's cranberries. Ocean Spray satisfies the prima facie case. No dispute exists regarding whether Ocean Spray's cranberries were in Barks' care, that Ocean Spray made a demand for their return, and the cranberries were damaged. Also no dispute exists that the cranberries were damaged by elevated temperatures. . . . Barks . . . produced evidence of Ocean Spray's own negligence in causing the spoilage of the cranberries. Evidence shows that Ocean Spray delivered cranberries to Barks straight from the bog. The cranberries were moist and warm when they arrived on the dock at Barks, two conditions that made it more difficult to bring down the temperature of the cranberries in the freezer. Ocean Spray did not take precautions by shipping its cranberries in refrigerated tractor-trailers.

Ocean Spray has put forth evidence that the refrigeration unit at Barks' warehouse experienced failures during the relevant time. . . . Ocean Spray contends that Barks' negligence caused the elevated temperatures, which resulted in the spoiled cranberries. This issue of comparative negligence . . . shifts the burden back to Ocean Spray to demonstrate that it was Barks' negligence, and not Ocean Spray's own negligence, that caused the spoilage of the cranberries. . . . No issue exists as to whether the cranberries were stored at Barks' facility and then spoiled. Many factual disputes exists [sic] as to why the cranberries spoiled. Under these circumstances, issues of material fact exist as to whether a bailment was breached. Accordingly, Ocean Spray's motion for partial summary judgment on its breach of bailment . . . claim is denied.

In order to sustain a cause of action in negligence, a plaintiff must show that: (1) defendant owed them a duty of care; (2) defendant breached that duty; (3) a causal link existed between the breach of duty and plaintiff's injury and harm; and (4) damages. Pennsylvania courts hold that the existence of a duty "is predicated on the relationship existing between the parties at the relevant time." . . . [T]he Court cannot find as a matter of law that Barks breached its duty of care to Ocean Spray. Accordingly, Ocean Spray's motion for partial summary judgment on its negligence claim is denied. . . .

BUSINESS CONSIDERATIONS What could the bailor or bailee have done to reduce the likelihood of loss in the case? What could a storage facility do to reduce the number of claims of loss?

ETHICAL CONSIDERATIONS Would it be ethical for Ocean Spray to deliver wet, warm cranberries to the facility? Why or why not? What is Ocean Spray's ethical perspective?

Classifications of Bailments

Bailments are divided into types based on who benefits from the bailment relationship. The classification affects the bailee's obligation and his or her liability if any damage occurs to the property. This responsibility is summarized in Exhibit 42.2.

Bailor Benefit Bailments When the bailment is established solely to benefit the bailor, the bailee will be responsible only for gross negligence in caring for the property. An example of a *bailor benefit bailment* is when Sergio, the owner, leaves his laptop computer with Melvin, his friend, until Sergio returns from his lunch. When Sergio returns from lunch he discovers that his laptop computer was knocked off a table and damaged. He alleges that Melvin should be liable for the damages since they occurred while Melvin was a bailee in possession of the laptop. Melvin

denies liability, asserting that the bailment was for Sergio's benefit so that Melvin can be held liable only for gross negligence, and that there is no evidence that Melvin was grossly negligent in this situation. The degree of negligence that can be attributed to Melvin is a question of fact that will need to be determined by the court if this case goes to trial. What is considered to be gross negligence in court will depend on the circumstances and the evidence presented.

Mutual Benefit Bailments When a bailment is established for the benefit of both the bailor and the bailee, a *mutual benefit bailment* exists. Both parties expect to gain from the bailment relationship. In such bailments, the bailee is responsible for ordinary negligence. A mutual benefit bailment occurs, for example, when Constance, the owner of a suit, takes her suit to a dry-cleaning establishment. Constance will benefit by having the suit cleaned and

EXHIBIT 42.2 The Responsibility of the Bailee

Type of Bailment	Who Will Benefit	The Bailee Will Be Liable for . . .
Bailor benefit	Bailor (owner)	Gross negligence
Mutual benefit	Bailor and bailee	Ordinary negligence
Bailee benefit	Bailee (possessor)	Slight negligence

pressed. The dry cleaner will benefit because it is going to be paid. The dry cleaner will be responsible if it carelessly cleans the suit in cleaning fluid that is too hot and causes the suit to shrink. *Hartford Fire Insurance Company v. B. Barks & Sons, Inc.* (Case 42.3) involved a mutual benefit bailment.

Bailee Benefit Bailments When a bailment is established solely for the benefit of the bailee, a *bailee benefit bailment* exists. The bailee will be responsible for slight negligence in caring for the property. When Lance loans his car to Rob, a fraternity brother, to drive to a job interview, a bailee benefit bailment occurs. Since the bailor (Lance, in our example) is receiving no benefit from this arrangement, the bailee (Rob, in our example) will be held responsible for any damages occurring to the bailed item if the bailee was negligent in even a slight manner. Again, the question of negligence is a question of fact to be determined by the court, if the case is taken to trial.

Constructive Bailments

Many states also recognize constructive bailments. *Constructive bailments* occur even though there is no formal agreement between the owner of the property and the possessor of the property, who lawfully comes into possession. The court may determine that the possessor should be treated as a constructive bailee in order to serve justice. A constructive bailee may also be called a *bailee by operation of law*. An example would be if a warehouse were sold to Filzah. The transfer documents did not mention the grain inside the warehouse at the time of the transfer. The prior owner of the warehouse was a bailee of the grain, and Filzah would become the constructive bailee of the grain.[16]

Limitations on a Bailee's Liability

Some states and localities have statutes or ordinances that provide maximum limits on the liability of the bailee in certain types of bailments.

If the bailment is based on a contract, the terms of the contract may increase or decrease the liability of the bailee. A *quasi-public bailee* offers services to the public. For example, he or she may operate a common carrier, a garage, a hotel, or a public parking lot. A quasi-public bailee generally will not be permitted to limit his or her liability contractually unless specifically permitted to do so by statute. Even when a statute permits a bailee to restrict liability, any limitation on liability must be reasonable.

A private bailee can restrict his or her liability under the terms of the agreement *if* this restriction does not conflict

---

NRW CASE 42.2   Manufacturing/Management

NRW

SHOULD NRW PURCHASE INSURANCE ON LEASED PRODUCTION EQUIPMENT?

NRW leases some of its production equipment from a large electronics firm. This equipment is extremely expensive and relatively fragile. Helen is concerned that NRW will be responsible for any damage to the equipment. She feels that NRW should procure insurance to protect the firm from liability in the event the equipment is damaged. Carlos, however, insists that the electronics firm is responsible for maintenance and bears the risk of loss for any damage done to the equipment. He asserts that, since the equipment was leased for industrial use, the electronics firm alone is responsible. They ask you which of their positions is correct. What will you tell them?

BUSINESS CONSIDERATIONS The leasing of equipment creates a bailment, but it also entails a contract for the lease of goods, governed by Article 2A of the UCC. Does Article 2A change the common law treatment of bailments in this sort of situation? Does the lessor or the lessee bear the risk of loss if leased equipment is damaged during the lease, presuming that the equipment is being used by the parties in the manner expected?

ETHICAL CONSIDERATIONS From an ethical perspective, and without regard to who is legally responsible for risk of loss, how should NRW behave in this situation? Is it ethical to underinsure a piece of equipment if the insuring party knows that the other party legally bears the risk of loss? Is it ethical to overinsure a piece of equipment in the hope that the insurer will not notice the overinsurance in the event of a loss?

INTERNATIONAL CONSIDERATIONS If the lessor was a foreign company, how would that affect the situation? Would Article 2A still cover the contract, or would a different law be controlling? What effect would it have if the insurance company were incorporated in another country?

---

with the real purpose of the contract between the bailee and the bailor. The bailee must inform the bailor of any limitation on the bailee's liability. Most courts hold that a

DISCLAIMERS TO AVOID LIABILITY

Carlos was in Chicago recently to meet with a potential client. He drove his rental car to a downtown parking garage in which the parking attendants park the cars and retain the keys. Carlos decided he would not need his overcoat, so he left it on the passenger seat of the car. He handed the attendant the keys to the car, took his claim check, and left for his appointment. When Carlos returned later that day to reclaim the car, he discovered his overcoat was missing. When Carlos complained to the attendants, they denied any knowledge of the loss, and they also pointed to the back of the claim check. The back of the ticket contained the following clause: "The management is not responsible for any personal property or electronic devices left in parked cars. The customer assumes any and all risk of loss for items left in the vehicle."

Carlos does not believe that the garage should be able to avoid liability in this manner. He asks you for advice. What will you tell him?

BUSINESS CONSIDERATIONS Is it a good business practice for a firm to use exculpatory clauses, especially those placed on the back of "claim checks," in an effort to avoid liability? What could/should the parking garage do to reduce the likelihood that its customers will suffer a loss? What could/should the customers do to reduce the likelihood that they will have a loss?

ETHICAL CONSIDERATIONS Is it ethical for a business to include exculpatory clauses on the back of "claim checks"? Is it ethical for a business to attempt to deny liability for the losses suffered by its customers? Is it ethical for a customer to blame the business for losses caused by the carelessness of the customer?

INTERNATIONAL CONSIDERATIONS If Carlos had been conducting his meeting in another country, would the same sort of rules regarding bailments apply? What rule would the courts apply in deciding who was responsible for Carlos's lost overcoat?

printed ticket stub or a posted notice on the premises does not adequately inform the bailor of the limitations *unless* the bailor's attention is directed to the sign or the ticket stub.

Termination of a Bailment

A bailment terminates at the end of the period that the parties specify or when a specified condition occurs. If the bailment was for an indefinite time, it may be terminated at the will of either the bailor or the bailee. A bailment terminates when the purpose or performance of the bailment has been completed. If either party causes a material breach of the bailment relationship, the victim can terminate the bailment and the wrongdoer will be liable for any damages he or she caused. The bailment terminates if the bailed property is destroyed or becomes unfit or unsuitable for the purpose of the bailment. Generally, a bailment also terminates by operation of law if death, insanity, or bankruptcy of either party makes performance by the bailee impossible.

Bailee's Duty to Return the Property

A bailee has a general duty to return the bailor's property to the bailor; however, there are exceptions to this rule. The bailee is not liable to the bailor if the property is lost, destroyed, or stolen through no fault of the bailee. The bailee is not liable if the property is taken away by legal process such as an attachment for a sheriff's sale. The bailee is not liable if the property is claimed by someone who has a better legal right to possession than the bailor has.

Sometimes a bailee has a duty to return the property to someone other than the bailor. For example, there may be a duty to "return" the property to a transferee who has bought the property from the bailor. A common business practice involves transferring property to a warehouse or common carrier that has an obligation to hold this property and then transfer it to a purchaser who presents a receipt or bill of lading.

The bailee does not have to return the property if the bailee has a lien on it. Many states have statutes that allow the bailee to keep the property in his or her possession until the bailor pays for the bailment; this is called a *possessory lien*. If the bailor fails to make payment, most statutes permit the bailee to sell the property. A common type of bailee's lien is a mechanic's lien, which arises when services have been performed on personal property. For example, if a garage repairs an automobile and Lupe, the owner, does not have the money to pay for the repairs, the garage can keep the automobile until Lupe pays. In most cases, the bailee loses the lien if the bailee willingly releases the goods to the bailor, for example, if the bailor comes to reclaim the property and the bailee releases it without receiving payment. Generally, there is no bailee's lien if the bailor and bailee agree at the beginning that the bailor is going to pay on credit.

Summary

Personal property is classified as tangible or intangible property based on its physical characteristics. Discussions of legal interests in property revolve around ownership rights, title, and possession. Often, one business has title to property, but another business has possession. Title to personal property can be acquired by original possession, by voluntary transfer from the owner to the transferee, or by involuntary transfer from the owner. A transferee of personal property generally will not acquire any better title than the transferor had. This is true even though the transferee thought that the transferor had good title. This limitation on title is especially important in judicial sales, sales of repossessed property, conversion, confusion, and accession.

When property is lost, the owner does not know where the property is. The finder is entitled to lost property; the only one with a superior claim is the true owner. Mislaid property was set down, but the owner failed to pick it up before he or she left. The finder of mislaid property must leave the personalty with the owner or manager of the premises because the true owner may remember where the property is and

return to retrieve it. The owner of the premises is entitled to hold the mislaid property. The finder has good title to the mislaid property; only the true owner has a superior claim.

Ownership of property may escheat to the state when a custodian of property cannot locate the owner. A more modern approach is unclaimed property statutes; when a custodian cannot locate the owner, possession of the property may pass to the state. Under these statutes title does not pass to the state. The true owner can claim the property at any time by following the state claim procedures.

A bailment occurs when the owner-bailor transfers the possession of personal property to someone else, the bailee. The owner keeps title. After the purpose of the bailment has been completed, generally possession is returned to the owner. Many businesses, such as dry cleaners and repair shops, basically deal in bailment relationships. The bailee's obligation is influenced by any contract between the bailee and the bailor. The bailee's duty of care is affected by whether it is a bailor benefit bailment, a mutual benefit bailment, or a bailee benefit bailment relationship.

Discussion Questions

1. What are the differences between title and possession?

2. What happens if the donor of a gift *causa mortis* dies but not from the expected cause? Who is likely to complain in such a situation?

3. Takashi takes a piece of rough turquoise stone, polishes it, and sets it in a silver setting in a necklace. Takashi reasonably believes that he found the stone on public land. In reality, he had found it on private land, where Arlene, the owner, had mined it and placed it in a pile for polishing. Who owns the jewelry and why? What are the legal rights of the parties?

4. Is an umbrella on a desk likely to be lost or mislaid property? Why? If the umbrella is on the floor, is it likely to be lost or mislaid property? Why?

5. Ric visits José's Mexican Restaurant for lunch and hangs his coat on the coatrack provided for that purpose. When he leaves, Ric walks out and leaves his coat. Kelly finds it. Who is entitled to title of the coat? Why? Who is entitled to possession of the coat? Why?

6. Twice a year the city of Cedarville has a large trash pickup. At this time, the trash collectors will take nonhazardous waste items they would normally refuse. Marcela hauls an old washing machine to the curb and adds it to her pile of other debris. Wayne drives by and picks up her washing machine, puts it in his truck, and drives away. Who legally owns the washing machine and why?

7. Define *escheat*. What is its purpose? How do escheat statutes differ from unclaimed property statutes?

8. What are the requirements for a bailment relationship?

9. What legal rights does a bailor have when a bailee has damaged the property or allowed someone else to damage it?

10. NRW is considering purchasing a fleet of cars for key employees. NRW would purchase four vehicles and assign them to employees who could operate them for both business and personal use. What are the advantages and disadvantages of such a plan? Why?

Case Problems and Writing Assignments

1. There is a 30,000-square-foot facility in Scottsboro, Alabama, nicknamed "The Lost Luggage Capital of the World." "The Unclaimed Baggage Center offers anything from designer clothing to sporting goods, and adds about 7,000 new items a day—2 million a year."[17] All but one of the U.S. airlines send lost luggage here. Airlines give up tracking the owners after 90 days. The store also obtains merchandise from trains, trucks, and ships. Store spokesman Brock Warner says, "Of all lost

bags, only .005 comes here, so statistically, it's pretty incredible."[18] The firm sells both the luggage and its contents. The store tries to sell items for 50 to 60 percent less than the retail price, according to Warner. Some of the more expensive items are appraised and then sold for about half the appraised value, for example, a 6-carat diamond ring that was appraised at $50,000 to $60,000. Other valuable items are sold at auction, such as Egyptian artifacts dating to 1567 B.C. and numbered Salvador Dali prints. The store has a concierge to help customers find lodgings or a place to dine. E-commerce has also reached the Unclaimed Baggage Center, and you can now order online at http://www.unclaimedbaggage.com/. If a visitor to the center discovers her suitcase, is she entitled to have it returned? Why or why not? Sometimes the owner's name and telephone numbers are clearly marked on the luggage (inside or outside). Would that affect your decision? [See "Sightings," *New Orleans Times-Picayune*, April 22, 1999, p. E2; "North Alabama Store for Who-Knows-What Drawing National Attention," *Associated Press State & Local Wire* (March 8, 1999), PM Cycle; and "Their Loss Could Be Your Find," *Raleigh (N.C.) News and Observer*, June 13, 1999, p. H2.]

2. RMS *Titanic*, Inc. (RMST) filed a complaint asking the court to declare it to be the sole and exclusive owner of any items salvaged from the RMS *Titanic*. Notice was given to other potential salvors and interested parties via publication. The court entered an order on June 7, 1994, conferring salvor-in-possession status on RMST. On February 20, 1996, John A. Joslyn filed a motion asking the court to rescind its order. RMST had a number of outstanding liens and encumbrances against certain *Titanic* artifacts. RMST had a number of outstanding debts. Despite its debt load, RMST remained a financially viable entity. It had a number of exhibition contracts signed or pending. RMST's marketing partner had organized two cruises to the wreck site to generate income to finance the 1996 salvage operations. This type of salvage operation is highly speculative and the expedition costs are high. Because RMST does not sell the artifacts it recovers, it was even more difficult to raise money. Since the 1994 expedition, RMST had not visited the site of the wreck, but RMST had been involved in a number of onshore activities since that time including exhibits. The company had begun selling the coal retrieved from the vessel to the public (the coal lumps were not considered artifacts). RMST has been committed to its role as "caretaker" of the retrieved artifacts and has kept its promise to maintain and preserve the *Titanic* artifacts. RMST planned an expedition for August 1996 and was finalizing an agreement to permit the production of a two-hour documentary detailing this event. Should RMST's status as salvor-in-possession be rescinded? [See *RMS Titanic, Inc. v. Wrecked and Abandoned Vessel*, 924 F. Supp. 714, 1996 U.S. Dist. LEXIS 6600 (E.D. Va. 1996).]

3. Joyce Ferrucci was a guest at the Showboat Hotel & Casino in Atlantic City, New Jersey. While a guest at the hotel, she stayed in room 1104. She did not have exclusive possession and control of room 1104, because Showboat Hotel & Casino had the ability to enter the room. The defendant's agents, servants, and employees would enter rooms for cleaning, maintenance, noise complaints, and security matters. Ferrucci had the right to occupy room 1104 for a limited time subject to the rules and procedures of the hotel. When walking past the bed in the room, Joyce Ferrucci took approximately four steps before her body twisted and she fell over the corner of the bed. Ferrucci claimed the bed was defective and caused her to fall. Ferrucci claimed her foot became stuck on something protruding from the bed. It is unclear if the protrusion was metal or wood. Ferrucci claimed the hotel owner engaged in the bailment of products, including furniture and beds in hotel rooms, to guests of their hotel. She contended that the hotel retained title and delivered furniture, including the bed, to Ferrucci for a particular purpose, creating a bailment. Did the hotel create a bailment? Why or why not? [See *Ferrucci v. Atlantic City Showboat, Inc.*, 51 F. Supp. 2d 129, 1999 U.S. Dist. LEXIS 8698 (Dist. of Conn. 1999).]

4. William Seebold, president of Eagle Boats, was contacted by *Trailer Boats*, a boating magazine, about doing a feature article on a motorboat manufactured by Eagle and including pictures taken on Grand Lake in Oklahoma. At the time of the inquiry, a boat owned by Hoppies Village Marina (Hoppies) was in the Eagle Boats repair facility undergoing minor paint repairs. This boat was a 1991 Seebold Eagle 265 Limited Edition motorboat with a 1990 Buccaneer Deluxe Tri-Axle trailer. This boat is considered "to be the 'cadillac' of motorboats in its class." Seebold contacted Paul Hopkins, the owner of Hoppies, and Michael Atkinson, the sales manager there. Hopkins agreed to loan this boat and trailer to Eagle Boats, Ltd., and William Seebold, president of Eagle Boats. It was also agreed that the magazine article would include information about the boat, Eagle Boats, Ltd., and Hoppies Village Marina. Seebold would transport the boat to Oklahoma and then return it to Hoppies using Hoppies's trailer.

The night before the magazine demonstration, Seebold parked the boat, trailer, and Eagle's truck in the parking lot of the motel. They were parked near the roadway parallel to the fence across the parking lot from the one dusk-to-dawn light. The trailer did not have a locking device that would lock it onto the truck. The truck itself was locked. No one was left to guard the boat and it was not locked in any manner. Although other boats and trailers were in the parking lot, this was the most expensive boat there. It was also the closest to the road. Both the boat and trailer were stolen between 11:00 P.M. and about 5:00 A.M. Seebold offered evidence that failure to use locks is common in the industry. He testified that at his facility, he simply chains the boats together and locks the chain. He also produced sworn statements by Hopkins and Atkinson that it is common not to use locking devices. Seebold admitted that he could have put a chain around the boat and trailer and locked it to the truck; he did not have a chain with him. Suit was filed by a group of insurance underwriters that had issued a policy on this boat, had paid Hoppies for its losses and was subrogee of its claim against the defendants. Did the bailee fail to exercise proper care over the bailed property? [See *Institute of London v. Eagle Boats, Ltd.*, 918 F. Supp. 297 (E.D. Mo. 1996).]

5. BUSINESS APPLICATION CASE In or about late May or early June 1997, Manchester Equipment Co., Inc.'s president, Barry Steinberg, was telephoned by a "David Lancaster," who identified himself as a vice-president of Time-Warner, Inc. Time-Warner had been one of Manchester's established customers, and Lancaster indicated that he wished to purchase a large quantity of computers for a special promotional event. Having never dealt with Lancaster before, Manchester's sales manager, William Breen, made a few telephone calls to various contacts in the Time-Warner corporate family, as well as to a colleague at Toshiba, to confirm Lancaster's identity. All of these contacts confirmed Lancaster's existence, and one Time-Warner employee advised Breen that Lancaster worked out of an office at 75 Rockefeller Plaza in New York City. Shortly thereafter, Manchester received a purchase order, dated June 4, 1997, from Lancaster requesting that Manchester ship the computers to the "Time/Warner Distribution Center" at 700 A Street in Wilmington, Delaware. Not being familiar with this address, Breen again contacted a friend at Time-Warner, who confirmed that the address was legitimate. Satisfied that it was dealing with a bona fide order, Manchester shipped $496,250 worth of computers to 700 A Street in Wilmington. There was no "Time/Warner Distribution Center" located at the address. In the interim, Lancaster contacted American Way Moving & Storage Company, a warehouse located at 700 A Street in Wilmington. Lancaster explained that he was a Time-Warner executive in need of some warehouse space on a month-to-month basis for some of his office equipment, and that his drivers would pick up the equipment shortly after its delivery. American Way agreed to rent a portion of its warehouse and was informed to expect a shipment soon thereafter. Three shipments of computers from Manchester to "Time Warner Dist. Ctr." arrived at American Way in mid-June, and the warehouse personnel stored the shipments in Lancaster's rented space. Lancaster's drivers promptly appeared and took possession of the computers. It is undisputed that American Way had no knowledge that Lancaster had not paid Manchester for the computers at the time they were released to the pickup drivers; indeed, Manchester and American Way had never communicated with each other. Lancaster's scam was revealed when Manchester's invoices, mailed to Lancaster's alleged office at 75 Rockefeller Plaza, were returned as "undeliverable." As it turned out, "David Lancaster" was an imposter and Manchester was not paid for its half a million dollars worth of computers. Time-Warner agreed to pay Manchester $185,000, presumably because its agents incorrectly confirmed that Lancaster and the Time-Warner Distribution Center were legitimate. Manchester also sued American Way to recover the remaining funds. Manchester contended that American Way breached its "bailment duty" by neglecting to take "reasonable and appropriate measures of identification and verification" before turning over the computers to Lancaster's drivers. Did American Way breach its "bailment duty" in this manner? Was there a constructive bail-

ment? [See *Manchester Equipment Co., Inc. v. American Way Moving & Storage Co., Inc.*, 47 Fed. Appx. 189, 2002 U.S. App. LEXIS 20702 (3rd Cir. 2002) (Unpublished Opinion).]

6. ETHICAL APPLICATION CASE John Moore was treated by Dr. David Golde at the UCLA Medical Center. John had hairy-cell leukemia. Dr. Golde discovered that John's blood contained substances that were valuable in medical research. In October 1967, John's spleen was removed at the recommendation of Dr. Golde. Prior to the surgery, Dr. Golde made arrangements to take portions of John's spleen to a separate research unit. Dr. Golde also arranged to draw John's blood when John visited the UCLA Medical Center. Dr. Golde did not inform John of his plan to conduct research or obtain John's permission. Dr. Golde established a cell line from John's blood and the Regents of the University of California acquired a patent on the cell line. Dr. Golde arranged for the commercial development of the cell line. As part of the arrangement Dr. Golde received 75,000 shares of Genetics Institute stock. Genetics Institute also agreed to pay Dr. Golde and the Regents at least $330,000 over three years. Did Dr. Golde and/or the Regents convert John's property? Why? Did Dr. Golde fail to obtain informed consent or violate his fiduciary duty? Why? What should Dr. Golde, the Regents, and Genetics Institute have done? What ethical issues are raised in this case? [See *Moore v. The Regents of the University of California*, 793 P.2d 479 (Cal. 1990).]

7. CRITICAL THINKING CASE Commonwealth Edison Company (Com Ed) and its defined-benefit pension plan brought suit under ERISA against the administrator of the Illinois Uniform Disposition of Unclaimed Property Act, seeking a declaration that ERISA preempts the Illinois statute to the extent that the statute regulates such plans. (ERISA is a federal statute regulating employee retirement programs. *Preempt* means that the federal government takes over a subject to the exclusion of the state government.) Illinois seeks to apply the Uniform Act to benefits payable under Com Ed's pension plan that are not claimed by a plan beneficiary within five years. When benefits are due to a participant in the plan, the plan writes a check to the participant. Until the participant deposits or cashes the check and the check is paid by the plan through the system for clearing bank transactions, the money due the participants remains in the plan's coffers. It is placed in a separate account as soon as the check is written, but if the check isn't cashed within a year the money is retransferred to the general account and is available to pay other participants. Com Ed does not and could not (without adverse tax consequences) impose a deadline on when the beneficiary may cash his or her check. It could be five, or ten, or even more than ten years after the check was written. All this time the plan will have the use of the money due the beneficiary. Were the plan to be terminated, the administrator would have a legal duty to search and make provision for missing beneficiaries. But until then, the plan's only duty of search is whatever is implicit in the fiduciary obligation that ERISA imposes on plans. The Com Ed plan owes about $125,000 to beneficiaries who have not yet cashed or deposited their checks even though more than five years have

passed since the checks were written. The state wants this money. The plan wants to retain it. Com Ed wants the plan to retain it too, because the more money in the plan, the less money Com Ed will be required to contribute to the plan to make sure that it has sufficient funds to meet its obligations. The parties are arguing over who gets to keep the interest on this money—the plan, and perhaps ultimately Com Ed, or the state. Is the state of Illinois entitled to hold the funds from the uncashed checks? [See *Commonwealth Edison Company v. Vega*, 174 F.3d 870, 1999 U.S. App. LEXIS 7215 (7th Cir. 1999). The U.S. Supreme Court denied certiorari at 1999 U.S. LEXIS 5826 (1999).]

8. YOU BE THE JUDGE Alex Popov claims that he caught Barry Bonds's 73rd home-run baseball on October 7, 2001, at Pacific Bell Park. It was the last day of the 2001 season. Popov, who at least touched the ball with his glove, says that the ball was wrestled away from him. In the end, Patrick Hayashi ended up with the ball. Popov claims he was mugged by Hayashi. The parties were not able to resolve their dispute in three mediation sessions. Experts say the ball could be sold for more than $1 million. It is locked in a safety deposit box under the judge's order. Assume that Popov files suit in *your* court to reclaim the baseball. How will *you* decide this case? Why? What additional information would be helpful in making your decision? [See "Claims on Bonds' 73rd Go to Trial," *Newsday*, Nassau and Suffolk Edition, October 16, 2002, Sports, p. A60, and Dean E. Murphy, "A Ball in the Hand Is Worth a Lot—to the Lawyers," *New York Times*, October 16, 2002, Sec. A, p. 16, column 3.]

Notes

1. The classic case on this subject is *Pierson v. Post*, 3 Cal. R. 175 (N.Y. 1805).
2. *Black's Law Dictionary*, 6th ed. (St. Paul, Minn.: West, 1990), 1340.
3. There have been numerous lawsuits since the wreck of the *Titanic* was discovered. *R.M.S. Titanic, Inc. v. Wrecked and Abandoned Vessel*, 924 F. Supp. 714, 1996 U.S. Dist. LEXIS 6600 (E.D. Va. 1996) is commonly referred to as Titanic I. The court addressed RMST's right to continue its salvage operations as the sole salvor-in-possession. In Titanic II , more properly referred to as *R.M.S. Titanic, Inc. v. The Wrecked & Abandoned Vessel*, 9 F. Supp. 2d 624, 1998 U.S. Dist. LEXIS 9347 (E.D. Va. 1998), the court dealt with jurisdictional issues that arise because the wreck lies in international waters. That decision was affirmed in part, reversed in part, and remanded in *R.M.S. Titanic, Inc. v. Haver*, 171 F.3d 943, 1999 U.S. App. LEXIS 5154 (4th Cir. 1999). The appellate court expressed concerns about the court decision that only the salvor-in-possession could view or photograph the wreck.
4. National Conference of Commissioners on Uniform State Laws (NCCUSL) Web site, "Summary Uniform Unclaimed Property Act (1995)," http://www.nccusl.org/nccusl/uniformact_summaries/uniformacts-s-uupa1995.asp (accessed 11/26/02).
5. NCCUSL Web site, "Why States Should Adopt the Uniform Unclaimed Property Act (1995)," http://www.nccusl.org/nccusl/uniformact_why/uniformacts-why-uupa.asp (accessed 1/6/03).
6. See note 4, "Summary Uniform Unclaimed Property Act (1995)."

7. See note 5, "Why States Should Adopt the Uniform Unclaimed Property Act (1995)."
8. Ibid.
9. NCCUSL Web site, "A Few Facts About the Uniform Unclaimed Property Act (1995)," http://www.nccusl.org/nccusl/uniformact_fact-sheets/uniformacts-fs-uupa.asp (accessed 11/26/02).
10. Ibid.
11. In 2002, it was introduced in Mississippi. See "A Few Facts," ibid.
12. See note 4, "Summary Uniform Unclaimed Property Act (1995)."
13. For example, in 1994 California collected $277 million in unclaimed property; $81 million was subsequently reclaimed. See note 5, "Why States Should Adopt the Uniform Unclaimed Property Act (1995)."
14. See note 4, "Summary Uniform Unclaimed Property Act (1995)."
15. See note 5, "Why States Should Adopt the Uniform Unclaimed Property Act (1995)."
16. *German National Bank v. Meadowcroft*, 95 Ill. 124, 1880 WL 10015 (Ill.) and *Christensen v. Hoover*, 643 P.2d 525 (Colo. 1982).
17. "North Alabama Store for Who-Knows-What Drawing National Attention," *Associated Press State & Local Wire* (March 8, 1999), PM Cycle.
18. Ibid.

Intellectual Property, Computers, and the Law

AGENDA

NRW NRW is a high-tech operation with much of its product development based on patent law. As a result, the firm is very concerned about the protections afforded under U.S. patent law and about the effectiveness of a patent in the international arena. The firm members also have registered the StuffTrakR and InvenTrakR names as trademarks, and they would like to protect these marks to the greatest extent possible. One apprehension Mai, Helen, and Carlos have is that, as the first innovations in the field, both products, respectively, may become synonymous with the class of products of which each is a part. The firm members therefore question what they can do to prevent this contingency from depriving them of their trademarked names. They are also worried that someone will steal their ideas and duplicate their products at a lower per unit price. They want to know what steps they can take to prevent this sort of misappropriation. These and other questions are likely to arise as you study this chapter. Be prepared! You never know when the firm or one of its members will seek your advice.

Intellectual Property

In this chapter, we will examine the law's treatment of intellectual property, or the property that comes from the human capacity to create. The body of law that addresses intellectual property derives from a variety of common law, state, and federal statutory and nonstatutory sources. Intellectual property law encompasses several substantive legal areas: copyrights, patents, trademarks, trade secrets, and unfair competition. We will use computers as a special illustration of the importance of intellectual property to U.S. businesses and international competitors.

In the intellectual property arena, several public policies coalesce to serve two goals; these policies both ensure incentives to create so as to guarantee a wider array of products and services in the marketplace and promote competition so as to provide public access to intellectual creations. By granting property rights (sometimes even monopolies) to creators, the law serves the first goal; and by limiting the duration of such exclusive rights and/or circumscribing the rights thereby granted in order to maximize the amount of information found in the public domain, the law facilitates the second goal. This area of the law also seeks to protect creators and businesspeople from injurious trade practices.

Through your study of the material in this chapter, then, you will learn how this hodgepodge of disparate legal doctrines affects business. Also, you will see how the law attempts to reconcile the tension between those who, in order to protect investments or ownership rights in intellectual property, want to restrict others from the free use of this type of property, and those who, in furtherance of free markets, argue for largely unrestricted access to such information and inventions.

Exhibit 43.1 sets out the broad categories of intellectual property.

Copyrights

The U.S. Constitution in Article I, Section 8 authorizes Congress "to promote the progress of science and the useful arts." In conferring statutory protection on artistic works created by writers, artists, and composers, Congress as early as 1790 exercised this constitutional power. The most important of the early copyright laws, the Copyright Act of 1909, remained virtually unchanged until January 1978, when the present copyright statute, the Copyright Act of 1976, became effective. In reality, vestiges of the 1909 act remain with us, however, since it still covers works created

prior to January 1, 1978. The Berne Convention Implementation Act of 1988, which became effective in March 1989, further amended the 1976 act. Under these 1988 amendments, works published after March 1, 1989, do not need a copyright notice. Hence, one first must ascertain which law governs a given copyrighted work and proceed accordingly.

Section 102 of the Copyright Act of 1976 protects any original works of authorship fixed in any tangible medium of expression now known or later developed, from which they can be perceived, reproduced, or otherwise communicated, either directly or with the aid of a machine or a device. Works of authorship include, but are not limited to, (1) literary works; (2) musical works, including any accompanying music; (3) pantomimes and choreographic works; (4) pictorial, graphic, and sculptural works; (5) motion pictures and other audiovisual works; (6) sound recordings; and (7) architectural works. Hence, copyright laws traditionally have protected *only expressions of ideas*, not the ideas themselves. Procedures, plans, methods, systems, concepts, and principles are not copyrightable either.

The Copyright Office of the Library of Congress administers copyrights in the United States. Among other things, the Copyright Office registers copyrights; issues certificates of registration; keeps records of copyright registrations, licenses, and assignments; and oversees deposits of copyrighted materials. Unlike the Patent and Trademark Office's stringent and detailed oversight of patents and trademarks (subjects we shall discuss later), the Copyright Office merely determines whether applications involve copyrightable subject matter and have fulfilled all the registration requirements. In 2000, the Copyright Office registered 515,100 (both U.S. and foreign) works.[1]

To be copyrightable, the works of authorship listed in § 102 must show originality. Courts have construed this term to involve at the very least minimal creative intellectual activity. Works of authorship moreover must be fixed in tangible form. The notes dancing in a creator's head do not become copyrightable until the songwriter puts the notes and words on paper or records the resultant melody (that is, the creator fixes the song in a tangible medium of expression). Section 101 of the 1976 act defines a work as "fixed" in a tangible medium of expression when its embodiment in a copy or phono record, by or under the authority of the author, is sufficiently permanent to permit it to be perceived, reproduced, or otherwise communicated for a period of more than transitory duration. This provision also states that fixation can occur simultaneously with transmission; therefore, radio or television broadcasts of live sporting events fall under this copyright protection if recordings or tapes of the events are occurring concurrently with the broadcasts.

EXHIBIT 43.1 An Overview of Intellectual Property Law

Copyrights

- Cover original works of authorship
- Encompass works fixed in a tangible medium of expression
- Include literary works; musical works; pantomimes and choreographic works; pictorial, graphic, and sculptural works; motion pictures and other audiovisual works; sound recordings; and architectural works
- Form the basis for protecting certain semiconductor chips from piracy

Patents

- Inventions that are novel
- Inventions that are useful
- Inventions that consist of nonobvious subject matter
- Inventions that fall within the statutory categories of patentable subject matter (i.e., any process, machine, manufacture, composition of matter, and any new and useful improvement thereof) or that are genetically engineered living matter

Intellectual Property [A "Bundle of Rights"]

Trademarks

- Consist of any word, name, symbol, device, or any combination thereof
- Used to distinguish the services of one person from another and to indicate the source of the goods
- Must be distinctive, arbitrary, and fanciful or have acquired a "secondary meaning"
- May include the distinctive features of a product (i.e., "trade dress"), such as the product's shape, packaging, logo, or artwork

Trade Secrets

- Consist of any formula, pattern, device, or compilation of information used in a business and which gives the owner a differential competitive advantage
- Can include "know-how," manufacturing processes, customer lists, and any other proprietary information used continuously in the business
- Must be maintained as a secret
- Cannot consist merely of common knowledge
- Cannot be duplicated easily through "reverse engineering"

Courts typically grant more limited copyright protection to useful articles (that is, pictorial, graphic, or sculptural works). Only if the creator can show aesthetic or conceptual elements separable from the utilitarian aspects of the article will the article become copyrightable. Bicycle racks or wrought iron benches, for example, that began as pieces of sculpture are primarily utilitarian rather than aesthetic objects. Hence, the creators of these items typically cannot register them for copyright protection. This policy furthers the goal of increasing competition between useful goods and thus benefits the public more than a creator's being granted a statutory monopoly over utilitarian goods. In short, in these instances, copying benefits the public more than would insulating the item from competition.

The Copyright Office similarly will not accept applications involving typeface designs or fonts. Copyright law, however, does protect compilations of materials—for example, collective works (such as anthologies or encyclopedias) or directories, catalogs, and automated databases. But the research that involves only labor (a mere reordering or alphabetizing of materials) and very little creativity, is afforded minimal protection under the copyright laws. A leading Supreme Court interpretation of this area of the law, *Feist Publications, Inc. v. Rural Telephone Service Co., Inc.,* 499 U.S. 340 (1991), held that the white pages of a telephone directory were not entitled to copyright protection because the raw data involved only facts. According to the Court, facts—like ideas—are uncopyrightable. And since the selection of listings (subscribers' names, towns, and telephone numbers) lacked the modicum of creativity necessary to turn mere selection into copyrightable expression, the competitor's use of the listings in the white pages was lawful.

Derivative works—for example, a motion picture screenplay based on a novel—are copyrightable as well, as long as one has the right to use the original work and the derivative work varies substantially from the original, or the transformation involves substantial artistic skill, judgment, or labor.

The *New York Times Inc. v. Tasini* case that follows provides an interesting—and still controversial—illustration of the extension of copyright law to electronic technologies.

Protection and Infringement

A copyright, in essence, consists of a bundle of exclusive rights that enables the copyright owner—usually the author or one to whom the author has transferred rights—to exploit a work for commercial purposes. These exclusive rights include

- reproducing the copyrighted work;
- preparing derivative works (or adaptations) based on the copyrighted work;

- distributing copies or phono records of the copyrighted work;
- performing publicly literary, musical, dramatic, and choreographic works, pantomimes, and motion pictures or audiovisual works; and
- displaying publicly the works themselves or individual images of the works mentioned as well as pictorial, graphic, or sculptural works.

Therefore, to prove an infringement of a copyrighted work, the owner typically must show by circumstantial evidence (since the existence of direct evidence would be rare) that the defendant had access to the copyrighted work and that the owner's work shows either striking or substantial similarities to the defendant's. Once the trier of fact determines copying has occurred, a finding of unlawful appropriation will result from the plaintiff's showing substantial similarities between the defendant's work and the plaintiff's.

43.1

NEW YORK TIMES COMPANY, INC. v. TASINI
533 U.S. 483 (2001)

FACTS Between 1990 and 1993, Jonathan Tasini and five other freelance authors wrote newspaper and magazine articles for the New York Times Company, Newsday, Inc., and Time, Inc. The authors had registered copyrights in the various articles. The three print publishers had engaged the authors as independent contractors under agreements that made no references to the authors' consenting to the subsequent placement of the articles in electronic databases. The print publishers nevertheless licensed the right to copy and sell the articles to several electronic publishers, including Lexis/Nexis, which placed the articles in their respective databases. Containing millions of files with individual articles from thousands of collective works, these databases for the most part enabled users to retrieve the articles in isolation from the other stories originally published in the same periodical edition. When the freelance authors sued for copyright infringement, the print and electronic publishers argued that § 201(c) of the Copyright Act permitted them to reproduce and distribute articles "as part of that particular collective work" to which the authors had contributed "as part . . . of any revision" thereof, or "as part of any later collective work in the same series." The district court granted the publishers' summary judgment motion on the rationale that on-line publication constituted a "revision" of the collective work that

§ 201(c) would permit. The Second Circuit reversed, holding that the "revision" privilege for collective works applies only to later editions of a particular issue, not to the publication of articles in a database.

ISSUE Did § 201(c) of the Copyright Act, which authorizes the copyright owners of collective works to reproduce and distribute each separate contribution as part of that particular collective work or any revision of that collective work, permit the print publishers to license the articles for publication in electronic databases?

HOLDING No. Section 201(c) would not authorize the copying at issue here. The print and electronic publishers were not sheltered by § 201(c), because the databases reproduce and distribute articles standing alone and out of context. As such, the articles had not been reproduced and distributed "as part of that particular collective work" to which the author contributed, "as part of . . . any revision" thereof, or "as part of . . . any later collective work in the same series." Hence, because the privilege accorded in § 201(c) did not override the authors' copyrights, both the print publishers and the electronic publishers had infringed the freelance authors' copyrights.

REASONING Excerpts from the opinion of Justice Ginsburg:

Under the Copyright Act, as amended in 1976, "copyright protection subsists . . . in original works of authorship fixed in any tangible medium of expression . . . from which they can be perceived, reproduced, or otherwise communicated." . . . When, as in this case, a freelance author has contributed an article to a "collective work" such as a newspaper or magazine, . . . the statute recognizes two distinct copyrighted works: "Copyright *in each separate contribution to a collective work* is distinct from copyright in the *collective work as a whole*. . . ." § 201(c) (emphasis added). Copyright in the separate contribution "vests initially in the author of the contribution" (here, the freelancer). . . . Copyright in the collective work vests in the collective author (here, the newspaper or magazine publisher) and extends only to the creative material contributed by that author, not to "the preexisting material employed in the work," § 103(b). . . . See also *Feist Publications, Inc. v. Rural Telephone Service Co.* . . . (copyright in [a] "compilation"—a term that includes "collective works" . . . —is limited to the compiler's original "selection, coordination, and arrangement"). . . .

Prior to the 1976 revision . . . authors risked losing their rights when they placed an article in a collective work. Pre-1976 copyright law recognized a freelance author's copyright in a published article only when the article was printed with a copyright notice in the author's name. . . . When publishers, exercising their superior bargaining power over authors, declined to print notices in each contributor's name, the author's copyright was put in jeopardy. . . . The author did not have the option to assign only the right of publication in the periodical; such a partial assignment was blocked by the doctrine of copyright "indivisibility." . . . Thus, when a copyright notice appeared only in the publisher's name, the author's work would fall into the public domain, unless the author's copyright, in its entirety, had passed to the publisher. . . .

In the 1976 revision, Congress . . . rejected the doctrine of indivisibility, recasting the copyright as a bundle of discrete "exclusive rights," . . . each of which "may be transferred . . . and owned separately," § 201(d)(2). . . . Congress also provided, in § 404(a), that "a single notice applicable to the collective work as a whole is sufficient" to protect the rights of freelance contributors. And in § 201(c), Congress codified the discrete domains of "copyright in each separate contribution to a collective work" and "copyright in the collective work as a whole." Together, § 404(a) and § 201(c) "preserve the author's copyright in a contribution even if the contribution does not bear a separate notice in the author's name, and without requiring any unqualified transfer of rights to the owner of the collective work." . . .

Section 201(c) both describes and circumscribes the "privilege" a publisher acquires regarding an author's contribution to a collective work: "In the absence of an express transfer of the copyright or of any rights under it, the owner of copyright in the collective work is presumed to have acquired *only* the privilege of reproducing and distributing the contribution as part of that particular collective work, any revision of that collective work, and any later collective work in the same series." (Emphasis added.)

A newspaper or magazine publisher is thus privileged to reproduce or distribute an article contributed by a freelance author, absent a contract otherwise providing, only "as part of" any (or all) of three categories of collective works: (a) "that collective work" to which the author contributed her [or his] work, (b) "any revision of that collective work," or (c) "any later collective work in the same series." In accord with Congress' prescription, a "publishing company could reprint a contribution from one issue in a later issue of its magazine, and could reprint an article from a 1980 edition of an encyclopedia in a 1990 revision of it; the publisher could not revise the contribution itself or include it in a new anthology or an entirely different magazine or other collective work." . . .

Essentially, § 201(c) adjusts a publisher's copyright in its collective work to accommodate a freelancer's copyright in her [or his] contribution. If there is demand for a freelance article standing alone or in a new collection, the Copyright Act allows the freelancer to benefit from that demand; after authorizing initial publication, the freelancer may also sell the article to others. . . . It would scarcely "preserve the author's copyright in a contribution" as contemplated by Congress, . . . if a newspaper or magazine publisher were permitted to reproduce or distribute copies of the author's contribution in isolation or within new collective works. . . .

In the instant case, the Authors wrote several Articles and gave the Print Publishers permission to publish the Articles in certain newspapers and magazines. It is undisputed that the Authors hold copyrights and, therefore, exclusive rights in the Articles. . . . It is clear, moreover, that the Print and Electronic Publishers have exercised at least some rights that § 106 initially assigns exclusively to the Authors: LEXIS/NEXIS' central discs and Uri's CD-ROMs "reproduce . . . copies" of the Articles, § 106(1); UMI, by selling those CD-ROMs, and LEXIS/NEXIS, by selling copies of the Articles through the NEXIS Database, "distribute copies" of the Articles "to the public by sale," § 106(3); and the Print Publishers, through contracts licensing the production of copies in the Databases, "authorize" reproduction and distribution of the Articles, § 106. . . .

Against the Authors' charge of infringement, the Publishers do not here contend the Authors entered into an agreement authorizing reproduction of the Articles in the Databases.... Nor do they assert that the copies in the Databases represent "fair use" of the Authors' Articles.... Instead, the Publishers rest entirely on the privilege described in § 201(c). Each discrete edition of the periodicals in which the Articles appeared is a "collective work," the Publishers agree. They contend, however, that reproduction and distribution of each Article by the Databases lie within the "privilege of reproducing and distributing the [articles] as part of . . . [a] revision of that collective work," § 201(c). The Publishers' encompassing construction of the § 201(c) privilege is unacceptable . . . for it would diminish the Authors' exclusive rights in the Articles.

In determining whether the Articles have been reproduced and distributed "as part of" a "revision" of the collective works in issue, we focus on the Articles as presented to, and perceptible by, the user of the Databases. . . . In this case, the three Databases present articles to users clear of the context provided either by the original periodical editions or by any revision of those editions. The Databases first prompt users to search the universe of their contents: thousands or millions of files containing individual articles from thousands of collective works (i.e., editions), either in one series . . . or in scores of series. . . . When the user conducts a search, each article appears as a separate item within the search result. In NEXIS and NYTO, an article appears to a user without the graphics, formatting, or other articles with which the article was initially published. In GPO, the article appears with the other materials published on the same page or pages, but without any material published on other pages of the original periodical. In either circumstance, we cannot see how the Database perceptibly reproduces and distributes the article "as part of" either the original edition or a "revision" of that edition.

One might view the articles as parts of a new compendium—namely, the entirety of works in the Database. In that compendium, each edition of each periodical represents only a miniscule fraction of the ever-expanding Database. The Database no more constitutes a "revision" of each constituent edition than a 400-page novel quoting a sonnet in passing would represent a "revision" of that poem. "Revision" denotes a new "version," and a version is, in this setting, a "distinct form of something regarded by its creators or others as one work." . . . The massive whole of the Database is not recognizable as a new version of its every small part.

Alternatively, one could view the Articles in the Databases "as part of" no larger work at all, but simply as individual articles presented individually. That each article bears

marks of its origin in a particular periodical (less vivid marks in NEXIS and NYTO, more vivid marks in GPO) suggests the article was previously part of that periodical. But the markings do not mean the article is currently reproduced or distributed as part of the periodical. The Databases' reproduction and distribution of individual Articles—simply as individual Articles—would invade the core of the Authors' exclusive rights under § 106....

Invoking the concept of "media neutrality," the Publishers urge that the "transfer of a work between media" does not "alter the character of" that work for copyright purposes.... That is indeed true.... But unlike the conversion of newsprint to microfilm, the transfer of articles to the Databases does not represent a mere conversion of intact periodicals (or revisions of periodicals) from one medium to another. The Databases offer users individual articles, not intact periodicals. In this case, media neutrality should protect the Authors' rights in the individual Articles to the extent those Articles are now presented individually, outside the collective work context, within the Databases' new media....

Under § 201(c), the question is not whether a user can generate a revision of a collective work from a database, but whether the database itself perceptibly presents the author's contribution as part of a revision of the collective work. That result is not accomplished by these Databases....

The Publishers warn that a ruling for the Authors will have "devastating" consequences.... The Databases, the Publishers note, provide easy access to complete newspaper texts going back decades. A ruling for the Authors, the Publishers suggest, will punch gaping holes in the electronic record of history [, a concern] echoed by several historians, ... but discounted by several other historians....

Notwithstanding the dire predictions from some quarters, ... it hardly follows from today's decision that an injunction against the inclusion of these Articles in the Databases (much less all freelance articles in any databases) must issue. . . . The parties (Authors and Publishers) may enter into an agreement allowing continued electronic reproduction of the Authors' works; they, and if necessary the courts and Congress, may draw on numerous models for distributing copyrighted works and remunerating authors for their distribution. . . . In any event, speculation about future harms is no basis for this Court to shrink [the] authorial rights Congress established in § 201(c)....

We conclude that the Electronic Publishers infringed the Authors' copyrights by reproducing and distributing the Articles in a manner not authorized by the Authors and not privileged by § 201(c). We further conclude that the Print Publishers infringed the Authors' copyrights by authorizing the Electronic Publishers to place the Articles in the Databases and by aiding the Electronic Publishers in that endeavor. We therefore affirm the judgment of the Court of Appeals.

BUSINESS CONSIDERATIONS If your firm were in the print or electronic publishing business, what policies would you institute in the aftermath of this case? What implications would *Tasini* hold for authors' conduct of their business affairs?

ETHICAL CONSIDERATIONS Justice Stevens's dissenting opinion noted that "[t]he majority is correct that we cannot know in advance the effect of today's decision on the comprehensiveness of electronic databases. We can be fairly certain, however, that it will provide little, if any benefit to either authors or readers" (at 523). In short, he apparently viewed the freelance authors as sacrificing the greater good (the promotion of the broad availability of literature, music, and the other arts) for their own self-serving, financial interests. Had the Court decided this case on ethical grounds, would it have held for the electronic publishers? Why or why not?

Under the right of reproduction, the Copyright Act itself allows for certain exceptions; for example, reproductions of nondramatic musical works, such as operas or motion picture sound tracks, subject to compulsory licensing under the act, do not constitute infringements if the user complies with certain conditions, including the payment of royalties to the owner. By the same token, the act exempts from the exclusive rights enjoyed by the copyright holder imitations of sound recordings (when the reproductions go beyond a mere "lifting" of the original expression) and reproductions transmitted by public educational or religious broadcasters under certain conditions. Without violating the copyright laws, one also can reproduce pictures of copyrighted useful art (like the bike rack) or architectural works. In addition, in certain circumstances, libraries can make reproductions of works needed to preserve or secure their collections or archives and of works, subject to some limitations, requested by library users.

The copyright holder's exclusive right to distribute the work differs from the exclusive right to reproduce the work. Under this right of distribution, the copyright owner can control the initial sale or distribution of the work to the public but, except in some situations involving the rentals of records, cannot control any subsequent transfers of the work. Sales of pirated works do not constitute "initial sales," so sellers of pirated works may find themselves subject to an infringement action even if the sellers are unaware that the compact disks, tapes, or records were pirated.

The exclusive right of public performance is subject to various exemptions as well. For example, a bar or restaurant that displays a standard-sized television so that its patrons can watch it free of charge does not infringe the copyright of a program broadcast on the television set. Similarly, pupils can perform copyrighted works in the course of face-to-face teaching activities in the classroom, as opposed to performing the work in a school play open to the public. Record shops, without violating the copyright laws, also can play songs and show public performances as a means of promoting sales.

Compulsory licensing sections in the act apply to cable television systems' secondary transmissions of primary broadcasts, satellite retransmissions, operators of electronic video game arcades, and operation of jukeboxes (even though, under the Berne Convention, jukeboxes were covered under voluntary—as opposed to compulsory—licenses through 1999).

The American Society of Composers, Authors, and Publishers (ASCAP) and Broadcast Music, Inc. (BMI) act as agents for owners of copyrights and issue licenses on behalf of such authors. After securing a license from ASCAP or BMI, a radio or television station can perform any of the works of any authors these societies represent. Each society, in turn, pays the royalties so received to the authors and monitors the stations' compliance with the licenses granted. This system results in greater efficiencies than one that requires each station to negotiate separately with each artist and for each artist individually to police copyright law compliance. The exceptions for the exclusive right to display the work correlate with those just discussed under the right of public performance.

Anyone who violates any of the copyright owner's exclusive rights provided in the statute or who imports copies or phono records into the United States in violation of the statute is an infringer of the copyright or the right of the author, as the case may be. The courts have imposed liability for infringements that are either direct or contributory—that is, those that induce or materially contribute to another person's direct infringement.

A defendant's most common defense against charges of infringement is the "fair use" doctrine. The statute itself states that the fair use of a copyrighted work for purposes of criticism, comment, news reporting, teaching (including multiple copies for classroom use), scholarship, or research is not an infringement of the copyright. The statute then sets out a nonexhaustive list of factors courts shall consider when they determine whether the use made of a work in any particular case is a fair use. These factors include

• the purpose and character of the use, including whether such use is of a commercial nature or is for nonprofit educational purposes;

• the nature of the copyrighted work;

• the amount and substantiality of the portion used in relation to the copyrighted work as a whole; and

• the effect of the use on the potential market for or value of the copyrighted work.

The statute further states that the fact that a work is unpublished shall not itself bar a finding of fair use if a court, after considering all the above factors, makes such a distinction.

Various professional groups have set out guidelines to ensure that copying done, for example, by libraries and/or by teachers for classroom use, falls under either express statutory exemptions or the fair use doctrine. These efforts underscore the importance of complying with the Copyright Act.

The fair use doctrine sometimes implicates parody, or a work in which one person imitates another's work so as to ridicule the latter. The importance of parody in our country's history has led many courts to protect parodic uses of a copyrighted work, despite the owner's unwillingness to grant a license to the parodist. In *Campbell v. Acuff-Rose Music, Inc.*[2] the Supreme Court wrangled with these very issues.

In 1964, Roy Orbison and William Dees had written a rock ballad called "Oh, Pretty Woman" and had assigned their rights in it to Acuff-Rose Music, Inc. Acuff-Rose registered the song for copyright protection. A quarter century later, Luther Campbell, a member of the rap music group 2 Live Crew, wrote a song entitled "Pretty Woman." On July 5, 1989, 2 Live Crew's manager informed Acuff-Rose that 2 Live Crew had written a parody of "Oh, Pretty Woman"; that the group would afford all credit for ownership and authorship of the original song to Acuff-Rose, Dees, and Orbison; and that the group would pay a fee for the use it wished to make of the song. Acuff-Rose refused this requested permission. Despite Acuff-Rose's refusal, 2 Live Crew released records, cassette tapes, and compact discs of "Pretty Woman" in a collection of songs entitled "As Clean as They Wanna Be." The albums and compact discs identify the authors of "Pretty Woman" as Orbison and Dees and the publisher as Acuff-Rose. Almost a year later, after the sale of nearly a quarter of a million copies of "As Clean as They Wanna Be," Acuff-Rose sued 2 Live Crew for copyright infringement.

Reasoning that the commercial purpose of 2 Live Crew's song was no bar to "fair use," that 2 Live Crew's version was a parody, that 2 Live Crew had taken only that which was necessary to "conjure up" the original in order to parody it, and that it was extremely unlikely that 2 Live Crew's song

would lessen the demand for the original, the district court granted summary judgment for 2 Live Crew. The court of appeals, arguing that the "blatantly commercial purpose" of the 2 Live Crew song prevented this parody from constituting a fair use of a copyrighted work, reversed the lower court's decision. The Supreme Court held that 2 Live Crew's commercial parody constituted a fair use of the copyrighted work. In the Court's view, because the group merely parodied the original song, 2 Live Crew had not infringed on Acuff-Rose's copyright of "Oh, Pretty Woman." Despite its commercial intent, 2 Live Crew, in an effort to satirize the original song, could borrow from "Oh, Pretty Woman" and in so doing not contravene the Copyright Act.

You can access this case at http://supct.law.cornell.edu/supct/index/php. You will find the Court's analysis of the four factors relating to fair use very instructive.

The identity of the owner of a copyright ordinarily poses few problems because the original author usually is the owner. But co-ownership over "joint works" does exist. "Works for hire," or works prepared by an employee within the scope of his or her employment (for example, architectural drawings), or work specifically commissioned for use as an instructional text (for example, this textbook) and considered as works for hire belong, respectively, to the employer or to the person who commissions the works. Works prepared by an employee of the U.S. government as a part of that person's official duties enjoy no copyright protection; rather, these works fall within the public domain and generally can be copied at will. By putting the transfer (or assignment) in writing and by recording such actions with the Copyright Office, one can transfer ownership of copyrights.

Since the Berne Convention Implementation Act, which took effect on March 1, 1989, it is not necessary, to ensure copyright protection, that an author put the copyright notice, the copyright symbol, the author's name, and the date of the first publication on the work. However, such notice still is necessary for works copyrighted under the 1976 act and published (that is, released to the public) before March 1, 1989. The 1976 act allows the omission of the required notice in certain limited circumstances, but failure to include the required notice generally results in loss of copyright protection.

Hence, as mentioned earlier, one first must determine which law governs the copyrighted work in question. Registering the work with the Copyright Office remains advisable, however, because registration makes proof of infringement easier in some cases and makes the owner eligible for certain types of damages, court costs, and attorney's fees.

Under the 1976 act, federal copyright commences with the fixation of the work in a copy or phono record for the first time. The duration of a copyright covered by the 1976 act (that is, works created on or after January 1, 1978) generally is the life of the author plus 70 years. After that time, the law presumes the work has passed into the public domain and therefore is not copyrightable.

Remedies

Civil remedies for infringements include injunctions, impoundment and destruction of infringing items, and damages. Plaintiffs can choose between actual damages, including the infringer's profits attributable to the infringement if the court, in computing the damages, did not take these into account, or statutory damages ranging from a minimum of $500 to $20,000 for all infringements involved in the action with respect to one work. A court may increase the damages to $100,000 for willful infringements. Similarly, the court may lower the damages to $100 if the infringer can prove it was unaware that its actions constituted an infringement. The court in its discretion can award court costs to either party and may award attorney's fees to either prevailing plaintiffs or prevailing defendants.[3]

Criminal penalties range from a minimum of $10,000 and one year's imprisonment (or both) to a maximum of $25,000 and one year's imprisonment (or both) for the first offense involving willful infringement and a maximum of $50,000 and two years' imprisonment (or both) for subsequent offenses.

International Dimensions

As noted earlier, U.S. copyright laws have undergone some changes since the United States became a member of the Berne Convention (the International Union for the Protection of Literary and Artistic Works) in March 1989. The Berne Convention makes national treatment of copyrights the linchpin of the treaty. In other words, each member nation must automatically extend the protection of its laws to the other signatory nations' nationals and to works originally published in a member nation's jurisdiction. The Berne Convention is not self-executing; each member nation therefore must enact implementing legislation.

The United States has taken a minimalist approach to compliance with the Berne Convention; in other words, it has not accepted in toto every provision of the treaty. But since the United States has enacted into law many of the treaty's provisions, it is important to U.S. intellectual property law. Apropos of this, the World Intellectual Property Organization's December 1996 treaties have updated the Berne Convention to reflect the changes in information technology and to set intellectual property standards for the digital age. These new treaties, among other things,

---

NRW CASE 43.1　Management

COPYRIGHT INFRINGEMENT

Mai has come up with what she believes is a creative idea for a commercial for StuffTrakR. She has described it to Helen and Carlos, and they also think it could be a very successful ad. In the ad Mai envisions an extraterrestrial, finding itself marooned on earth, tries to "call home" to get one of its fellow extraterrestrials to rescue it. At first, the extraterrestrial cannot find its phone; but then it remembers its StuffTrakR unit can help in locating the phone. StuffTrakR comes through, and as the extraterrestrial dials, the voice of the announcer then describes the benefits of the StuffTrakR, concluding with the admonition, "Don't leave home without it." The firm members ask you if this ad involves any copyright infringement problems. What will you tell them?

BUSINESS CONSIDERATIONS Why do businesses use the voices, names, and likenesses of famous people to sell their products? Are these types of ads less effective if the advertiser uses unknown people to show the use of the product?

ETHICAL CONSIDERATIONS Is it ethical for a business to use computer imaging to place famous people who have died into commercials with contemporary stars or contemporary settings? What ethical concerns does using the likenesses of deceased celebrities raise?

INTERNATIONAL CONSIDERATIONS Do international agreements and/or treaties like the Berne Convention actually improve the protections available to a copyright owner, or do they merely provide a method for the copyright holder to maximize his or her protection? Is coverage of a copyright automatically increased due to these agreements and treaties, or does the holder have to take affirmative steps in order to ensure that he or she enjoys the added protection?

---

have closed some loopholes that had left the U.S. recording industry without copyright protection in the international arena.

The Universal Copyright Convention (UCC), administered by the United Nations, represents another international treaty that covers copyrights. Although it imposes fewer substantive requirements on copyrights than does the Berne Convention, some Berne Convention members also have joined the UCC as a means of establishing relationships concerning copyrights with UCC members who have not signed the Berne Convention.

Recent amendments to GATT (the General Agreement on Tariffs and Trade) expand the protections afforded to copyrighted works, including computer programs. The European Union's "Directive on the Legal Protection of Computer Software," slated to cover EU members as of January 1, 1993, represents another promising initiative in the international arena.

Computers

Copyright law also covers computers. Although it was unclear whether computer programs were copyrightable under the 1909 act, the Copyright Office began accepting computer programs for registration as books as early as 1964, despite the misgivings of register officials. At the time of the passage of the 1976 act, the "jury," in the form of the National Commission on New Technological Uses (CONTU), was still out regarding the copyrightability of computer software. However, by adding the phrase "computer program" and certain other provisions exempting the copying of computer programs from the 1976 act's infringement provisions, the Computer Software Copyright Act of 1980 amended the 1976 act. As a result of these amendments, today, few doubts remain as to the copyrightability of computer programs despite the omission of this phrase from the listed categories of proper subject matters for copyright protection.

Under the 1980 amendments, "[a] 'computer program' is a set of statements or instructions to be used directly or indirectly in a computer in order to bring about a certain result." According to the 1980 amendments, computer databases also are copyrightable as "compilations" or "derivative works." Infringements of copyrights—for example, unauthorized copying, distribution, or derivation—do not occur if the owner (that is, a copyright holder) of a copy of a computer program only makes or authorizes the making of a new copy or adaptation when the copy is an essential step in the utilization of the program in conjunction with a machine (that is, for use with the owner's computer) or for archival purposes (that is, for making backup copies in case the original copy is accidentally destroyed). The fair use doctrine, whereby your professor uses computer software for an in-class performance or display, and libraries reproduce and distribute copyrighted works, including computer software in some circumstances, apparently does not constitute infringement either. The act presently does not differentiate, for infringement purposes, between human-readable or machine-readable copies; copies in either form

may constitute infringements unless the copying falls into one of these exemptions.

Yet controversies still abound owing to the fact that the 1976 act continues the longstanding expression/idea dichotomy of copyright law. This duality, that the program as written is protectible but the unique ideas contained in the program are not, of course looms as a significant impediment to software developers who wish to copyright their manuals: It is easy to produce competing products once the ideas underlying the original package become known. Thus, when the developers meet the required statutory criteria, the manuals will be copyrightable, but the formats may not be.

Similarly, the audiovisual display aspects of a video game may be copyrightable whereas the idea behind the game—a crazy character that "munches" everything, for instance—or the game per se ordinarily will be ineligible for copyright protection. The same may be true in general of flowcharts, components of machines, and printed circuit boards that do not have computer programs embedded in them; these normally are not copyrightable. The unsettled state of the law in this area merely complicates developers' problems.

Apple Computer, Inc. v. Franklin Computer Corporation[4] was an early but significant decision regarding the application of the copyright laws to computer software, particularly computer operating systems. Apple Computer, Inc. had filed suit against Franklin Computer Corporation for copyright infringement owing to Franklin's copying of 14 of Apple's operating system computer programs (collections of systems software programs designed to help someone else program or use a computer and that allow the computer to execute programs and manage programming tasks) for use with Franklin's ACE 100 personal computer.[5] Franklin admitted it had copied Apple's programs and ROM chips (read-only memory chips on which the data and information used to run computer operating systems are affixed; chips that can be "read" by a computer program but generally cannot be changed or altered). Franklin argued it had done so because it had not been feasible to write its own operating system programs.[6] Franklin also asserted that the Apple programs were uncopyrightable subject matter because the object code on which the programs relied as not a "writing." (Object code translates source code into lower-level language, consisting of numbers and symbols that the computer converts into electronic impulses or machine language). Moreover, according to Franklin, the programs were "processes," "systems," or "methods of operation" unprotected by law.[7] This opinion addressed the important issue of whether the object code, which is not readable by people, is a "writing" within the Copyright Act's coverage and hence copyrightable; or instead, given its normal use, whether the object code is a method of operation or a system, which is not copyrightable.[8] In holding that Apple's computer programs, whether in source code (human-readable version of the program that gives instructions to the computer) or in object code embedded in ROM chips, constitute "literary works" protected under the Copyright Act of 1976 from unauthorized copying from either their object code or source code version, the court answered a question that had vexed early software developers.[9]

The new avenues for providing, disseminating, and reproducing information occasioned by the Internet and other electronic publishing media have raised questions about the application of copyright law to works promulgated in electronic formats. The *Tasini* case provides an apt illustration of this point in the context of collective works and electronic databases. Similarly, Apple Computer, Inc., Microsoft Corporation, and Hewlett-Packard Company recently have litigated the copyrightability of the visual display aspects of computer user interfaces. The *Napster* litigation concerning music file-swapping services continues to have far-reaching implications for the billion-dollar recording industries' major players. The emerging contours of the law therefore dictate caution so as to avoid infringements. Simply put, the existence of extensive computer networks and the ease with which people can make perfect digital copies available almost instantaneously have pushed traditional copyright principles nearly to their snapping point. Vigilance is needed because of the breadth of the author's rights—those of reproduction, distribution, display, and performance—that are protected under the copyright laws and the facility with which users can manipulate visual, musical, and audiovisual materials.

The nature of digitized communications would appear to make Internet Service Providers (ISPs) especially vulnerable to claims of contributory infringement stemming from their subscribers' usage of copyrighted materials. Indeed, the difficulties of policing third-party users' postings when copyright holders allege infringement have created genuine challenges for ISPs. The congressional response to this problem was the passage of the Digital Millennium Copyright Act of 1998 (DMCA). The DMCA not only amends the Copyright Act but also implements the World Intellectual Property Organization (WIPO) Copyright Treaty and the WIPO Performances and Phonograms Treaty.

The DMCA protects "service providers" (in general, Internet service providers, Internet access providers, and on-line service providers, hereinafter referred to as ISPs) from liability for on-line copyright infringements when they do not exercise control over the copyrighted materials that others distribute on such systems. To warrant this exemption from liability, ISPs must satisfy certain condi-

tions, such as the establishment and enforcement of reasonable procedures aimed at protecting intellectual property from such distributions. These procedures must include the adoption of a policy that accommodates and does not interfere with standard technical measures that identify and protect copyrighted works. The statute defines such measures as those developed pursuant to a broad consensus of copyright owners and service providers, those available to all persons on reasonable and nondiscriminatory terms, and those that do not impose substantial costs on ISPs or substantial burdens on their systems. These procedures also must include a policy that provides for the termination of subscribers who are repeat infringers.

The statute specifically exempts ISPs from monetary or equitable relief (including injunctions) for (1) the intermediate and transient storage of materials that occurs in the course of the service provider's transmitting, routing, or providing connections for material through a system or network controlled or operated by the service provider (i.e., transitory network communications); (2) system caching (the process by which computers speed up the execution of instructions and retrieve data, such as the capacity to hold a given Web page in the computer's memory for a long period of time); (3) storage of material at the direction of a user of the service provider's system; and (4) linking (through information location tools, such as a search engine, a directory, an index, or a hypertext link) users to an on-line location that contains infringing material or that involves infringing activities. The act sets out certain conditions that ISPs must fulfill to merit each of the exemptions. The act further exempts from liability nonprofit educational institutions, as well as any service provider that, in good faith, disables access to, or removes, materials or activities that have been subject to a claim of infringement or that involve circumstances in which an infringement is apparent. This latter exemption applies regardless of whether the material or activities are ultimately determined to constitute infringement.

To enjoy immunity from legal liability, each ISP must inform the Copyright Office of the agent it has designated to receive notice of alleged copyright infringements. Besides notice, the ISP also must specify the process it will use for investigating any such claims and removing the materials in question. Experts often refer to this process as "a notice and take down" procedure. In the absence of notice, the ISP cannot be liable. Once the ISP receives proper notification, it can avoid liability by promptly removing or disabling access to the infringing material. The statute further sets out the rules for the ISP's restoring service in circumstances in which restoration is justified.

The WIPO amendments center on the protection of technological measures that control access to copyrighted works. To prevent the piracy of copyrighted works and unauthorized access and copying, owners oftentimes use encryption techniques. This part of the DMCA prohibits the circumvention of such protective technological systems. The statute, however, treats actual acts of circumvention differently from the manufacturing and marketing of a device or service that has as its purpose the circumvention of such technological measures. In making this distinction, the act ensures the public's ability to make fair use of copyrighted works. The right of fair use, which the DMCA specifically states is not affected by the act, would in effect be nullified if the owner could install technological measures that prevented all copying of the copyrighted work. This part of the act also sets out exemptions for law enforcement, intelligence, and other governmental activities; nonprofit libraries, archives, and educational institutions; reverse engineering designed to achieve interoperability with another program; encryption research aimed at detecting the flaws and vulnerabilities of such encryption technologies; circumventions undertaken in order to test the security of a computer system or network if accomplished with the authorization of the owner; circumventions designed to protect a measure or work that collects personally identifying information about the on-line activities of an individual; and a court's consideration of a component or part in a device that has as its sole purpose the prevention of minors' access to Internet materials.

These anticircumvention provisions have figured recently in litigation involving programs that can decrypt digital video disk (DVD) content and the security measures designed to protect on-line music (yet another ramification of the *Napster* litigation). Given the huge economic stakes and the ever-changing technology involved in such cases, companies presumably will continue this zealous protection of their rights through resort to the courts. These developments bear watching.

Patents

The same provision of the Constitution that provides the basis for copyright protection furnishes the grounds for patents. Congress's power to promote the progress of science and the useful arts secures for inventors, rather than authors, the exclusive right to their respective discoveries. Today, most experts lump the terms "useful arts," "inventors," and "discoveries" with patent rights and leave the promotion of science through writings to copyright law.

Since the first patent statute in 1790, the statutory categories of patentable subject matter have consisted of

- any process (the earlier term was "art," but the term "process" now includes a process, art, or method);

- machine;

- manufacture;

- composition of matter, including certain nonnaturally occurring plants, such as hybrids;[10] and

- any new and useful improvement thereof.

The Supreme Court has held that such utility patents may cover genetically engineered living matter as well. As in copyright law, ideas per se are not patentable. Neither are laws of nature (for example, "for every action there is an equal and opposite reaction"), mathematical formulas, scientific truths or principles, methods of doing business, and mental processes.

Utility patents last for 20 years from the filing date, after which time the monopoly granted to the patentee (that is, the holder of the patent) ends. *Design patents* (that is, patents involving original, ornamental designs for articles of manufacture) last for only 14 years from the date of the grant of the patent. Once either type of patent protection ends, others can make, use, or sell the invention with impunity.

To be patentable, an invention must demonstrate novelty. In other words, prior art must show an absence of anything substantially identical to the claimed invention; the claimed invention therefore must be unanticipated. Public knowledge or use of the invention by others in this country before the application for the patent indicates a lack of novelty. The public use or sale of the invention more than one year prior to the application for the patent thus will result in the denial of a patent.

Just as it is hard to imagine an invention that lacks novelty, so too, it is difficult to imagine as worthy of patent protection an invention that lacks utility. Both the Constitution and the Patent Act of 1952 describe protected discoveries and inventions as "useful" ones. Hence, to deserve protection under the patent laws, the inventor's discovery must provide significant current benefits to society.

Last, an invention must consist of nonobvious subject matter. In other words, if the differences between the subject matter one seeks to patent and prior art are such that the subject matter as a whole will be obvious, at the time the invention is made, to a person having ordinary skill in the art to which the subject matter pertains, the invention does not warrant protection.

These three requirements clearly overlap. The ingenuity that underlies inventions goes beyond the mere carrying forward of an old idea. Yet Thomas Alva Edison, one of our greatest inventors, surely captured another aspect of invention when he noted that it involves 1 percent inspiration and 99 percent perspiration!

By making an application to the U.S. Patent and Trademark Office (PTO), inventors who believe they have met these requirements begin the process of receiving a patent. This application includes a declaration that the applicant first discovered the invention for which he or she solicits the patent; any drawings necessary to explain the patent; detailed descriptions, specifications, and disclosures (including all prior art) of the subject matter the applicant claims as his or her invention; and the required filing fees. The substantive information provided in the specifications should (1) enable any person skilled in the art to make or use the invention after the expiration of the term of the patent and (2) inform the public of the limits of the monopoly asserted by the inventor for the life of the patent.

The Commissioner of Patents and Trademarks will issue a patent if the PTO examiner to whom the commissioner has given the application approves the application. Applicants who receive rejection notices, usually owing to the examiner's finding prior art or the existence of "double-patenting" (the act prohibits the granting of two patents for the same invention), can appeal to the PTO Board of Patent Appeals and Interferences and then either to the U.S. Court of Appeals for the Federal Circuit or the U.S. District Court for the District of Columbia. Stringent time periods apply to the entire process.

In 1999, the Supreme Court in *Dickinson v. Zurko*,[11] settled a split in the circuit courts of appeals when the Court held that the appropriate standard of review for the Federal Circuit to apply to issues of fact in appeals from the PTO is not the more stringent "clearly erroneous" standard but instead the standard set out in the Administrative Procedure Act (APA). Hence, the Federal Circuit must follow the APA and set aside only those agency factual determinations that the court finds to be arbitrary, capricious, an abuse of discretion, or unsupported by substantial evidence.

The PTO reports that in 2000, it granted a record 176,000 patents, an increase of about 9 percent over 1999's figures.[12] Patents issued to international residents (with Japan leading the way) accounted for about 45 percent of such patents.[13] In 1999, residents of California received the most domestically issued patents, about 20 percent of the total issued to U.S. residents.[14]

Protection and Infringement

Given the economic value of patents, this area of the law tends to invite litigation between parties with adverse interests. Holders of patents (that is, patentees) typically bring patent infringement actions when they believe someone has encroached on or invaded the area covered by the claims the patentee has made concerning the patent. The Patent Act covers direct infringements, indirect infringements, and contributory infringements.

A *direct infringement* involves a party who, without the patent holder's permission, makes, uses, or sells the patented invention in the United States during the term of the patent. For example, Video, Inc. manufactures and sells tracking devices that are almost identical to NRW's products. In this case, NRW has grounds to bring an action for direct infringement.

The act also covers *indirect infringements*. These may take the form of inducements to infringe, in which another party has directly infringed on the patentee's patent and has actively and knowingly aided and abetted an infringement by a third party. For example, Video, Inc. sells a joggers' watch with a locator device that, when mixed with other components, infringes on NRW's patent for the Stuff-TrakR. Video, Inc. then sells its watches and components to See and Speak, which, following Video, Inc.'s instructions, also manufactures the watches. Since Video, Inc. knows that a direct infringement will result from its actions, Video, Inc. has induced See and Speak to infringe NRW's patent.

Finally, the act covers *contributory infringements*, in which another party sells a material component of a patented invention and knows that the component has been specially made or adapted for use in a patented invention and that infringement will occur. For example, Video, Inc. sells to See and Speak a process consisting of a rainproof, computerized timing mechanism specially made for NRW (the mechanism has no substantial, noninfringing use), and Video, Inc. knows See and Speak will use the process to infringe the patentee's invention. Video, Inc. is liable as a contributory infringer while See and Speak becomes liable as a direct infringer once it uses the process.

One can engage in a direct infringement even though one is totally ignorant of the existence of a patent, since the issuance of a patent serves as constructive notice to the world of the patent's existence. On the other hand, indirect infringements involving inducements or contributory infringements require knowledge on the defendant's part before courts can impose liability.

Persons sued for patent infringement will try to overcome the presumption of validity and prove that the patent is invalid owing to some omitted condition of patentability (for example, novelty); infringement cannot exist in the absence of a valid patent. Abuse of patent provides another defense to infringement actions. For instance, if a patentee uses the patent as a means of engaging in anticompetitive activities and for the purpose of extending its monopoly beyond that granted by Congress, any infringement action brought by the patentee will be unsuccessful. Activities that violate the antitrust laws, such as illegal tie-ins and other activities discussed in Chapter 37, when used in conjunction with a patent, will lead to a finding of noninfringement. Refusing any and all requests to license the patent does not constitute patent misuse, however.

The Supreme Court in 1996 held that when an infringement action involves the interpretation of a patent claim (that is, the portion of the patent document that defines the scope of the patentee's rights), such an interpretation is a question of law exclusively within the province of the court; juries are not empowered to engage in such interpretive activities. However, juries can decide questions of fact, such as whether infringement has occurred.[15]

The judicially created "doctrine of equivalents," used to help judges answer such questions of law, has occupied numerous courts' attention over the years. During the extensive disclosure that attends the application process, the applicant describes what is claimed as the parameters of the patent, explains how the claimed invention differs from prior art, and the like. This is a complex process that usually involves complicated scientific principles. Moreover, the PTO examiner's investigation may ultimately result in a claimed invention that is much narrower in scope than that originally sought. The entire process leading up to the grant of the patent is called the patent's prosecution history. In other words, the patentee, during the prosecution of the patent, creates a record that should fairly notify the public that the patentee has relinquished the right to claim a particular subject matter as falling within the reach of the patent. When a subsequent invention that appears to infringe the patent granted at the conclusion of this demanding process surfaces, the holder of the patent (the patentee) typically alleges infringement based on the doctrine of equivalents (that is, the newer invention falls within the claims disclosed when the patentee received its patent). However, what has been called "prosecution history estoppel" limits the application of the doctrine of equivalents. In short, once the patent has been granted, a rebuttable presumption that a claim amendment was made for a substantial reason relating to patentability (thereby invoking prosecution history estoppel) comes into play. The patentee can overcome this presumption by showing that the underlying reason it provided for the amendment did not relate to the requisites for attaining patentability. Put differently, many courts construed the doctrine of equivalents as precluding a patentee from obtaining under this doctrine coverage of subject matter that it had relinquished during the prosecution of its patent application.

It was against this backdrop that the following case, in which the Supreme Court attempts to spell out the scope of the doctrine of equivalents and its relationship to prosecution history estoppel, arose. The *Festo Corporation* decision, which illustrates the complexities inherent in the process of achieving patent protection, thus serves as a cautionary tale to the would-be business practitioner-inventor.

Remedies

Remedies for actionable patent infringement include damages and equitable relief in the form of injunctions. The statute directs courts to award damages in an amount adequate to compensate the patentee (the holder of the patent) for the infringement (such amounts will include lost profits attributable to the infringement) but in no event less than a reasonable royalty representative of the infringer's use of the invention.

The act also allows courts to impose costs and to award reasonable attorney's fees to the prevailing party in exceptional cases, such as circumstances involving clear fraud and wrongdoing or in circumstances in which the court believes the award of attorney's fees will prevent gross injustice. But given the huge size of the attorney's fees in typical patent cases, courts rarely award such fees.

In either jury or nonjury trials, courts have authority to treble the damages assessed. A court's award of damages denies the infringer its ill-gotten gains and also restores to the patentee the benefits he or she would have derived from the monopoly had the infringing sales not occurred. The Patent Act expressly allows courts to use expert testimony for determining the damages or royalties that would be reasonable under the circumstances.

The 1999 Supreme Court case of *Florida Prepaid Post-secondary Education Expense Board v. College Savings Bank*[16] restricted the power of Congress to provide a judicial forum for violations of intellectual property rights. Striking down a 1992 amendment to the patent laws in which Congress had expressly abrogated the states' sovereign immunity from claims of patent infringement, the Supreme Court characterized the 1992 changes as an invalid exercise of power under the Fourteenth Amendment's due process clause. In so holding, the Court noted that the lack of evidence of widespread patent infringement by the states, as well as Congress's failure to consider the adequacy of state remedies for patent infringement, precluded Congress from invoking its powers under the Fourteenth Amendment to eliminate state immunity from patent infringement suits.[17]

International Dimensions

Given the value of patent rights, patent law (like copyright law) now has international dimensions. Prior to international treaties, an inventor had to patent the invention in

43.2

FESTO CORPORATION v. SHOKETSU KINZOKU KOGYO KABUSHIKI COMPANY, LIMITED
535 U.S. 722 (2001)

FACTS Festo Corporation owns two patents for an improved magnetic rodless cylinder, a piston-driven device that relies on magnets to move objects in a conveying system. When the patent examiner rejected the initial application for the first patent because of defects in description, Festo amended the application to add new limitations stating that the device would contain a pair of one-way sealing rings and that its outer sleeve would be made of a magnetizable material. The second patent, also amended during a reexamination proceeding, added the sealing rings limitation. After Festo began selling its device, the respondents (SMC) entered the market with a similar device that uses one two-way sealing ring and a nonmagnetizable sleeve. Festo filed suit, claiming that SMC's device was so similar that it infringed Festo's patents under the doctrine of equivalents. SMC argued that the prosecution history of Festo's patents would estop (prevent) Festo from making this claim. SMC emphasized that Festo had disclosed the sealing rings and the magnetized alloy for the first time in the amended applications. According to SMC, these amendments narrowed the earlier applications, surrendering alternatives that are the very points of difference in the competing devices—the sealing rings and the type of alloy used to make the sleeve. Because Festo had narrowed its claims in these ways in order to obtain the patents, SMC claimed, Festo was now estopped from saying that these features are immaterial and that SMC's device is an equivalent of its own.

The district court disagreed, ruling that Festo's amendments were not made to avoid prior art. Therefore, the district court held that the amendments were not the kinds that give rise to estoppel. The Court of Appeals for the Federal Circuit affirmed this decision. After the Supreme Court vacated this holding as a result of the Court's intervening decision, *Warner-Jenkinson v. Hilton Davis Chemical Co.*, the Federal Circuit ultimately concluded that prosecution history estoppel barred Festo from asserting that the accused device infringed its patents under the doctrine of equivalents. The court held that estoppel arises from any amendment that narrows a claim to comply with the Patent Act, not only from amendments made to avoid prior art. The court further held that when estoppel applies, it stands as a complete bar against any claim of equivalence for the element that was amended. In the court's view, a complete-bar rule, under which estoppel bars all claims of equivalence to the narrowed element, would promote certainty in the determination of infringement cases.

ISSUE Would prosecution history estoppel bar Festo from asserting that SMC's device had infringed its patents under the doctrine of equivalents?

HOLDING Prosecution history estoppel could apply to any claim amendment made to satisfy the Patent Act's requirements, not just to amendments made to avoid the prior art. However, estoppel need not bar a suit against every equivalent to the amended claim element.

REASONING Excerpts from the opinion of Justice Kennedy:

The patent laws "promote the Progress of Science and useful Arts" by rewarding innovation with a temporary monopoly. U.S. Const., Art. I, § 8, cl. 8. The monopoly is a property right; and like any property right, its boundaries should be clear. This clarity is essential to promote progress, because it enables efficient investment in innovation. A patent holder should know what he owns, and the public should know what he does not. For this reason, the patent laws require inventors to describe their work in "full, clear, concise, and exact terms," 35 U.S.C. § 112, as part of the delicate balance the law attempts to maintain between inventors, who rely on the promise of the law to bring the invention forth, and the public, which should be encouraged to pursue innovations, creations, and new ideas beyond the inventor's exclusive rights. . . . Unfortunately, the nature of language makes it impossible to capture the essence of a thing in a patent application. The inventor who chooses to patent an invention and disclose it to the public, rather than exploit it in secret, bears the risk that others will devote their efforts toward exploiting the limits of the patent's language. . . . However, the language in the patent claims may not capture every nuance of the invention or describe with complete precision the range of its novelty. If patents were always interpreted by their literal terms, their value would be greatly diminished. Unimportant and insubstantial substitutes for certain elements could defeat the patent, and its value to inventors could be destroyed by simple acts of copying. For this reason, the clearest rule of patent interpretation, literalism, may conserve judicial resources but is not necessarily the most efficient rule. The scope of a patent is not limited to its literal terms but instead embraces all equivalents to the claims described. . . . It is true that the doctrine of equivalents renders the scope of patents less certain. It may be difficult to determine what is, or is not, an equivalent to a particular element of an invention. If competitors cannot be certain about a patent's extent, they may be deterred from engaging in legitimate manufactures outside its limits, or they may invest by mistake in competing products that the patent secures. In addition the uncertainty may lead to wasteful litigation between competitors, suits that a rule of literalism might avoid. These concerns with the doctrine of equivalents, however, are not new. Each time the Court has considered the doctrine, it has acknowledged this uncertainty as the price of ensuring the appropriate incentives for innovation, and it has affirmed the doctrine over dissents that urged a more certain rule. . . . Prosecution history estoppel requires that the claims of a patent be interpreted in light of the proceedings in the PTO during the application process. Estoppel is a "rule of patent construction" that ensures that claims are interpreted by reference to those "that have been cancelled or rejected." . . . The doctrine of equivalents allows the patentee to claim those insubstantial alterations that were not captured in drafting the original patent claim but which could be created through trivial changes. When, however, the patentee originally claimed the subject matter alleged to infringe but then narrowed the claim in response to a rejection, he [or she] may not argue that the surrendered territory comprised unforeseen subject matter that should be deemed equivalent to the literal claims of the issued patent. . . . A rejection indicates that the patent examiner does not believe the original claim could be patented. While the patentee has the right to appeal, his [or her] decision to forgo an appeal and submit an amended claim is taken as a concession that the invention as patented does not reach as far as the original claim. . . . Were it otherwise, the inventor might avoid the PTO's gatekeeping role and seek to recapture in an infringement action the very subject matter surrendered as a condition of receiving the patent. Prosecution history estoppel ensures that the doctrine of equivalents remains tied to its underlying purpose. Where the original application once embraced the purported equivalent but the patentee narrowed his claims to obtain the patent or to protect its validity, the patentee cannot assert that he lacked the words to describe the subject matter in question. The doctrine of equivalents is premised on language's inability to capture the essence of innovation, but a prior application describing the precise element at issue undercuts that premise. In that instance the prosecution history has established that the inventor turned his attention to the subject matter in question, knew the words for both the broader and narrower claim, and affirmatively chose the latter.

The first question in this case concerns the kinds of amendments that may give rise to estoppel. [Festo] argues that estoppel should arise when amendments are intended to narrow the subject matter of the patented invention, for instance, amendments to avoid prior art, but not when the amendments are made to comply with requirements concerning the form of the patent application. . . . [Yet] a narrowing amendment made to satisfy any requirement of the Patent Act may give rise to an estoppel. . . . As that court explained, a number of statutory requirements must be satisfied before a patent can issue. The claimed subject matter must be useful, novel, and not obvious. 35 U.S.C. §§ 101–103 . . . In addition, the patent application must describe, enable, and set forth the best mode of carrying out the invention. § 112. . . . [Festo] contends that amendments made to comply with § 112 concern the form of the application and not the subject matter of the invention. The PTO might require the applicant to clarify an ambiguous term [or] to improve the translation of a foreign word. . . . In these cases, [Festo] argues, the applicant has no intention of surrendering subject matter and should not be estopped from challenging equivalent devices. . . . If a § 112 amendment is truly cosmetic, then it would not narrow the patent's scope or raise an estoppel. On the other hand, if a § 112 amendment is necessary [to secure the patent] and narrows the patent's scope—even if only for the purpose of better description—estoppel may apply. A patentee who narrows a claim as a condition for obtaining a patent disavows his claim to the broader subject matter, whether the amendment was made to avoid the prior art or to comply with § 112. [One] must regard the patentee as having conceded an inability to claim the broader subject matter or at least as having abandoned his right to appeal a rejection. In either case estoppel may apply. [Festo] concedes that the limitations at issue—the sealing rings and the composition of the sleeve—were made for reasons related to § 112, if not also to avoid the prior art.

Our conclusion that prosecution history estoppel arises when a claim is narrowed to comply with § 112 gives rise to the second question presented: Does the estoppel bar the inventor from asserting infringement against any equivalent to the narrowed element or might some equivalents still infringe? The Court of Appeals held that prosecution history estoppel is a complete bar, and so the narrowed element must be limited to its strict literal terms. . . . By amending the application, the inventor is deemed to concede that the patent does not extend as far as the original claim. It does not follow, however, that the amended claim becomes so perfect in its description that no one could devise an equivalent. After amendment, as before, language remains an imperfect fit for invention. The narrowing amendment may demonstrate what the claim is not; but it may still fail to capture precisely what the claim is. There is no reason why a narrowing amendment should be deemed to relinquish equivalents unforeseeable at the time of the amendment and beyond a fair interpretation of what was surrendered. Nor is there any call to foreclose claims of equivalence for aspects of the invention that have only a peripheral relation to the reason the amendment was submitted. . . . This view of prosecution history estoppel is consistent with [Supreme Court] precedents and respectful of the real practice before the PTO. While this Court has not weighed the merits of the complete bar against the flexible bar in its prior cases, [it has] consistently applied the doctrine in a flexible way, not a rigid one. . . . The Court of Appeals ignored the guidance of *Warner-Jenkinson*, which . . . made it clear that the doctrine of equivalents and the rule of prosecution history estoppel are settled law. The responsibility for changing them rests with Congress. . . . Fundamental alterations in these rules risk destroying the legitimate expectations of inventors in their property. [A] . . . bright-line rule . . . would have provided more certainty in determining when estoppel applies but at the cost of disrupting the expectations of countless existing patent holders. We rejected that approach. . . .

Just as *Warner-Jenkinson* held that the patentee bears the burden of proving that an amendment was not made for a reason that would give rise to estoppel, we hold here that the patentee should bear the burden of showing that the amendment does not surrender the particular equivalent in question. . . . The patentee, as the author of the claim language, may be expected to draft claims encompassing readily known equivalents. A patentee's decision to narrow his claims through amendment may be presumed to be a general disclaimer of the territory between the original claim and the amended claim. . . . There are some cases, however, where the amendment cannot reasonably be viewed as surrendering a particular equivalent. The equivalent may have been unforeseeable at the time of the application; the rationale underlying the amendment may bear no more than a tangential relation to the equivalent in question; or there may be some other reason suggesting that the patentee could not reasonably be expected to have described the insubstantial substitute in question. In those cases the patentee can overcome the presumption that prosecution history estoppel bars a finding of equivalence. This presumption is not, then, just the complete bar by another name. Rather, it reflects the fact that the interpretation of the patent must begin with its literal claims, and the prosecution history is relevant to construing those claims. When the patentee has chosen to narrow a claim, courts may presume the amended text was composed with awareness of this rule and that the territory surrendered is not an equivalent of the territory claimed. In those instances, however, the patentee still might rebut the presumption that estoppel bars a claim of equivalence. The patentee must show that at the time of the amendment, one skilled in the art could not reasonably be expected to have drafted a claim that would have literally encompassed the alleged equivalent. On the record before us, we cannot say [that Festo] has rebutted the presumptions that estoppel applies and that the equivalents at issue have been surrendered.

BUSINESS CONSIDERATIONS The Court opts for a flexible rule for deciding cases of this sort. For a businessperson, what are the advantages of such a rule? What are the drawbacks?

ETHICAL CONSIDERATIONS Had the Court decided this case on ethical grounds, who would have won?

each foreign jurisdiction and in accordance with the law of that particular nation.

To overcome these inefficiencies and complexities, the Paris Convention for the Protection of Industrial Property, administered by the World Intellectual Property Organization, came into existence in 1883. About 140 nations, including the United States, are members of the Paris Convention. Like the Berne Convention, the Paris Convention, by emphasizing the concept of national treatment in which each member can determine the nature and extent of the substantive protections afforded to patents, may not fully protect patented inventions in a given situation. Moreover, the Paris Convention has done little to alleviate the need for separate filings in each signatory nation's jurisdiction, and it has no enforcement mechanisms for policing violations of the convention.

Owing to these shortcomings, the Patent Cooperation Treaty (PCT) became effective in 1978. The PCT's procedures—especially the filing system—allow inventors in the 96 or so nations, including the United States, that have signed the treaty to use one filing for securing patent rights in the jurisdictions represented by the signatory nations. The present GATT round and NAFTA, international efforts discussed in Chapter 3, also provide transnational patent protection to inventors. In particular, the recent GATT changes appear to involve reasonable steps that will result in further harmonization of the international treatment of patents.

Computers

Neither the old law nor the significant amendments to the patent laws contemplated the inclusion of computer or program-related inventions within these classifications. As a result, by the 1960s, the PTO and the Court of Customs and Patent Appeals (CCPA) had drawn strict battle lines regarding the patentability of computer programs and other software. The CCPA was for it; the PTO against it.

Although it was clear that computer programs met the first requirement of patentability, that is, that they potentially arose under one of the four categories of patentable subject matter (process or machine, presumably), doubts existed as to whether software fulfilled the remaining conditions of patentability. Those arguing for patentability viewed computer systems consisting of both hardware and software either as a process (a method for operating a machine) or as a physical component of the hardware itself and thus protected by the machine requirement, with the program being one element in the overall apparatus. Other authorities, by characterizing software as ideas standing alone, laws of nature, scientific truths or principles, algorithms (mathematical formulas), mental steps, printed matter, functions of a machine, and/or methods of doing business, however, relegated computer software to areas lying outside patent protection. Indeed, for many years that was the fate that befell program-related invention cases, since questions arose as to whether an invention containing as one of its elements a computer program implementing such an algorithm was patentable.

Many precedents relied on the so-called preemption test in which the PTO was obliged to examine whether the patent claim on the software would wholly preempt (that is, seize upon to the exclusion of others) the other uses of the algorithm (that is, calculations, formulas, or equations). If so, the invention fell into one of the categories of nonstatutory subject matter and was unpatentable because the claim merely recited a mathematical algorithm. If, instead, the algorithm was but one of several steps or procedures leading to the transformation of the data into a wholly different state or thing, the invention complied with the statutory subject matter and was patentable.

After several cases in the 1970s holding computer-related inventions unpatentable, the Supreme Court in *Diamond v. Diehr*[18] applied the preemption test and held that a process for curing synthetic rubber, which includes in several of its steps the use of a mathematical formula and a programmed digital computer, was patentable subject matter. *Diamond v. Diehr* involved the question of the patentability of a computer program used as an integral part of a machine. A subsequent CCPA decision, *In re Pardo*,[19] ruled that a compiler program, one designed to convert a high-level programming language into binary or machine code so as to translate source code to object code, may alone constitute patentable subject matter.

Emerging technology-related issues include the patenting of on-line expert systems (Priceline.com has applied for approximately 200 patents in the general field of digital systems and processes, especially those concerning on-line auction systems) and of technologies involving linking, interactive TV, voice compression, and handwriting recognition, to name but a few. Stay alert as to these emerging developments.

Trademarks

From their inception, trademarks have served as a means by which tradespeople and craftspeople identify goods as their own. Indeed, archaeologists have found centuries-old artifacts bearing such trade symbols. In further recognition of the social and economic dimensions of such marks, the medieval guilds used trademarks as a means of controlling quality and fostering customer goodwill. Statutes as early as the 13th century codified these ideas. These early statutory developments sought to prohibit "palming off," or one producer's passing off its goods as the goods of a competitor and, through this "free-riding" on the established customer base and goodwill of a competitor, thus taking away sales from the other.

Present-day trademark law, by protecting against consumer confusion as to the origin of goods, advances this goal. In contrast to patents, no analogous constitutional foundation for the protection of trademarks exists. Rather, as we have seen in earlier chapters, the commerce clause provides the basis for the federal regulation of trademarks. However, both federal and state laws protect trademarks.

Over the years, an extensive body of state trademark law had developed in the common law, principally through the state common law relating to unfair competition. The 1946 Lanham Act, the most important federal protection of trademarks, provides a structure by which the enforcement of these common law principles can occur through federal oversight and thereby builds on these common law roots. Just as the Lanham Act allows the registration of various marks, so too, some states have statutory registration provisions. The PTO oversees the federal registration of trademarks. The number of trademarks issued jumped from 24,700 in 1980 to 191,900 in 2000.[20]

Protection and Infringement

The Lanham Act defines a trademark as any word, name, symbol, device, or any combination thereof used to identify and distinguish the services of one person from the services of others and to indicate the source of the goods even if the source is unknown. This definition underscores the fact that a trademark always exists pursuant to commercial activity or use and may cover an extensive array of things, including the distinctive features of the product (that is, "trade dress") such as the product's shape, the product's packaging, the logo or artwork on the product, and so on. All these aspects may be worthy of trademark protection.

Well-known trademarks include Coca-Cola, Pepsi, Tide, Chanel, Mercedes-Benz (and its logo), Ralph Lauren, Nike (and its "swoosh" logo), Kodak, and so forth. Trademark law also protects service marks—those that identify and distinguish services rather than products (for example, McDonald's, United Airlines, or Prudential Insurance); certification marks—those that identify the goods and services of others as having certain characteristics (for example, the Good Housekeeping seal of approval or the Underwriters' Laboratories seal); and collective marks—those that signify membership in a group and the goods or services produced by the group (for example, the Wool Council or the Beef Council).

To deserve protection, the trademark—whatever its form—must be distinctive. Arbitrary, fanciful, and suggestive terms by definition are distinctive. Calling a brand of gasoline "Marathon" on the one hand seems arbitrary, but this designation also suggests mobility and successfully reaching a chosen destination, presumably two of our goals when we put gasoline in our tanks. "Snuggles" as a name for laundry softeners, "Pampers" as a name for disposable diapers, and "Coppertone" as a name for suntan oils clearly meet these tests.

Note that all these marks embody some degree of imaginativeness. Without distinctiveness, identifying the source of the goods and avoiding consumer confusion become decidedly more difficult. Such marks in themselves also serve narrow marketing functions. Purely descriptive marks—adjectives such as "sweet" or "chicken"; geographic designations like "California" or "New York" in reference to wines; and people's surnames like L.L. Bean and Marriott Hotels used as marks—do not qualify as distinctive until they have acquired "secondary meaning." In other words, when the consumer public no longer views the marks as purely descriptive terms but rather as indicative of the source of the goods or products, the marks have become distinctive. In a similar vein, common geometric shapes, flowers, or slogans, for instance, generally lack the required characteristic of distinctiveness and will not merit trademark status unless the owner can demonstrate secondary meaning.

The Lanham Act specifically provides that the PTO commissioner may accept as prima facie evidence of distinctiveness proof that the mark has been in substantially exclusive and continuous use in interstate commerce for five years. Even though one cannot place nondistinctive marks on the Principal Register of trademarks, owners, as a means of protecting against international infringements of the mark, often place such marks on the Lanham Act's Supplemental Register.

In *Wal-Mart Stores v. Samara Brothers, Inc.*, 529 U.S. 205 (2000), the Supreme Court held that "trade dress" (the packaging or design of a product) would be protectible under the Lanham Act only if the product's design had become distinctive owing to the acquisition of secondary meaning. In reaching this conclusion, the Court relied on *Qualitex Company v. Jacobson Products Company, Inc.*[21] where the Court had determined that nothing in the basic objectives of trademark law presents any obvious theoretical objection to the use of color alone as a trademark where that color has attained a secondary meaning and therefore identifies and distinguishes a particular brand (and thus indicates its "source"). The case that follows builds on these two earlier precedents.

Generic terms can never qualify for trademark protection. This result derives from the fact that a generic term, that is, one that merely refers to the group of products or services of which this item is a part, cannot identify the specific source or tradesperson from which the goods originate. Trademark law shows numerous examples of words that have passed into generic usage and thereby have lost their trademark status. Aspirin, calico, cellophane, escalator, linoleum, shredded wheat, thermos, yo-yo, and zipper are a few such formerly trademarked terms.

A deceptive mark, for example, a personal security service that superimposes its logo over the seal of the United States and thereby falsely gives the impression of a connection with the U.S. presidency, cannot obtain trademark status. Neither can an immoral, scandalous, or offensive mark.

Similarly, the Lanham Act specifically precludes trademark status for marks that disparage any person (living or dead), institution, belief, or national symbol; use without consent the name, portrait, or signature of a living person; use the name, portrait, or signature of a deceased U.S. president during the lifetime of his or her spouse without the spouse's consent; and/or so resemble an already registered mark as to be likely to cause confusion, mistake, or deception.

The law recognizes as the owner of the mark the person or entity that first uses—and then continues to use—the mark in trade and affixes it to goods or services. Under federal law, before one can register the mark on the Lanham Act's Principal Register, one must demonstrate prior use or a bona fide good faith intent to use the mark in the future

43.3

TRAFFIX DEVICES, INC. v. MARKETING DISPLAYS, INC.
532 U.S. 23 (2001)

FACTS Marketing Displays, Inc. (MDI) had patented a "dual-spring design" mechanism that keeps temporary road signs, as well as other outdoor signs, upright in adverse wind conditions. According to MDI, buyers and users recognized its sign stands (marketed under the name "WindMaster") because the patented design was visible near the base of the sign. After MDI's patents had expired, TrafFix Devices, Inc. began marketing sign stands (called WindBusters) that incorporated a dual-spring mechanism copied from MDI's design. MDI subsequently sued TrafFix for trademark infringement (based on the similar names), trade dress infringement (owing to the copying of the dual-spring design), and unfair competition. TrafFix counterclaimed using antitrust theories. The district court ruled in favor of MDI on the trademark claim and rejected TrafFix's antitrust claims, results affirmed by the Sixth Circuit. The two courts disagreed, however, with regard to the trade dress claim, leaving this as the only issue before the Supreme Court in this case.

ISSUE Was MDI's trade dress protectible under federal law?

HOLDING No. MDI's dual-spring design was a functional feature for which no trade dress protection would exist. Trade dress could be protected under federal law, but the person arguing for such protection in an infringement action must prove that the matter it seeks to protect is not functional.

REASONING Excerpts from the opinion of Justice Kennedy:

It is well established that trade dress can be protected under federal law. The design or packaging of a product may acquire a distinctiveness [that] serves to identify the product with its manufacturer or source; and a design or package [that] acquires this secondary meaning, assuming other requisites are met, is a trade dress [that] may not be used in a manner likely to cause confusion as to the origin, sponsorship, or approval of the goods. In these respects protection for trade dress exists to promote competition. As [the Court] explained [in 2000, in] *Wal-Mart Stores, Inc. v. Samara Brothers, Inc.*, . . . various Courts of Appeals have allowed claims of trade dress infringement [based] on the general provision of the Lanham Act [that] provides a cause of action to one who is injured when a person uses "any word, term name, symbol, or device, or any combination thereof . . . which is likely to cause confusion . . . as to the origin,

sponsorship, or approval of his or her goods." . . . Congress confirmed this statutory protection for trade dress by amending the Lanham Act to recognize the concept. Title 15 U.S.C. § 1125 (a)(3) . . . provides: "In a civil action for trade dress infringement under this chapter for trade dress not registered on the principal register, the person who asserts trade dress protection has the burden of proving that the matter sought to be protected is not functional." This burden of proof gives force to the well-established rule that trade dress protection may not be claimed for product features that are functional [quoting *Qualitex v. Jacobson*]. . . . And in *Wal-Mart* . . . [the Court was] careful to caution against misuse or over-extension of trade dress [because] . . . "product design almost invariably serves purposes other than source identification." . . . Trade dress protection must subsist with the recognition that in many instances there is no prohibition against copying goods and products. In general, unless an intellectual property right such as a patent or copyright protects an item, it will be subject to copying. As the Court has explained, copying is not always discouraged or disfavored by the laws [that] preserve our competitive economy. . . . Allowing competitors to copy will have salutary effects in many instances. "Reverse engineering of chemical and mechanical articles in the public domain often leads to significant advances in technology." . . .

The principal question in this case is the effect of an expired patent on a claim of trade dress infringement. A prior patent . . . has vital significance in resolving the trade dress claim. A utility patent is strong evidence that the features therein claimed are functional. If trade dress protection is sought for those features[,] the strong evidence of functionality based on the previous patent adds great weight to the statutory presumption that features are deemed functional until proved otherwise by the party seeking trade dress protection. Where the expired patent claimed the features in question, one who seeks to establish trade dress protection must carry the heavy burden of showing that the feature is not functional, for instance by showing that it is merely an ornamental, incidental, or arbitrary aspect of the device. [This] rule . . . bars the trade dress claim, for MDI did not, and cannot, carry the burden of overcoming the strong evidentiary inference of functionality based on the disclosure of the dual-spring design in the claims of the expired patents. [The] statements made in the patent applications and in the course of procuring the patents demonstrate the functionality of the design. MDI does not assert that any of these representations [is] mistaken or inaccurate, and this is further strong evidence of the functionality of the dual-spring design. In finding for MDI on the trade dress issue the Court of Appeals gave insufficient recognition to the importance of the expired utility patents, and their evidentiary significance, in establishing the functionality of the device. The error likely was caused by its misinterpretation of trade dress principles in other respects. As [the Court has] noted, even if there has been no previous utility patent[,] the party asserting trade dress has the burden [of] establish[ing] the non-functionality of [the] alleged trade dress features. MDI could not meet this burden. Discussing trademarks, [the Court has] said "in general terms, a product feature is functional," and cannot serve as a trademark, "if it is essential to the use or purpose of the article or if it affects the cost or quality of the article." [quoting *Qualitex*] . . . Expanding upon the meaning of this phrase, [the Court has] observed that a functional feature is one the "exclusive use of [which] would put competitors at a significant non-reputation-related disadvantage." . . . The Court of Appeals in the instant case seemed to interpret this language to mean that a necessary test for functionality is "whether the particular product configuration is a competitive necessity." . . . This was incorrect as a comprehensive definition. As explained in *Qualitex*, . . . a feature is also functional when it is essential to the use or purpose of the device or when it affects the cost or quality of the device. The *Qualitex* decision did not purport to displace this traditional rule. . . .

The Court has allowed trade dress protection to certain product features that are inherently distinctive [and] not functional. . . . The trade dress in those cases did not bar competitors from copying [the] functional product design features. In the instant case, beyond serving the purpose of informing consumers that the sign stands are made by MDI (assuming it does so), the dual-spring design provides a unique and useful mechanism to resist the force of the wind. Functionality having been established, whether MDI's dual-spring design has acquired secondary meaning need not be considered. . . . In a case where a manufacturer seeks to protect [the] arbitrary, incidental, or ornamental aspects of features of a product found in the patent claims, such as arbitrary curves in the legs or an ornamental pattern painted on the springs, a different result might obtain. There the manufacturer could perhaps prove that those aspects do not serve a purpose within the terms of the utility patent. The inquiry into whether such features, asserted to be trade dress, are functional by reason of their inclusion in the claims of an expired utility patent could be aided by going beyond the claims and exam-

ining the patent and its prosecution history to see if the feature in question is shown as a useful part of the invention. No such claim is made here, however. MDI in essence seeks protection for the dual-spring design alone. The asserted trade dress consists simply of the dual-spring design, four legs, a base, an upright, and a sign. MDI has pointed to nothing arbitrary about the components of its device or the way they are assembled.

The Lanham Act does not exist to reward manufacturers for their innovation in creating a particular device; that is the purpose of the patent law and its period of exclusivity. The Lanham Act, furthermore, does not protect trade dress in a functional design simply because an investment has been made to encourage the public to associate a particular functional feature with a single manufacturer or seller. The Court of Appeals erred in viewing MDI as possessing the right to exclude competitors from using a design identical to MDI's and to require those competitors to adopt a different design simply to avoid copying it. MDI cannot gain the exclusive right to produce sign stands using the dual-spring design by asserting that consumers associate it with the look of the invention itself. Whether a utility patent has expired or there has been no utility patent at all, a product design [that] has a particular appearance may be functional because it is "essential to the use or purpose of the article" or "affects the cost or quality of the article." . . . TrafFix . . . argue[s] that the Patent Clause of the Constitution, Art. I, § 8, cl. 8, of its own force, prohibits the holder of an expired utility patent from claiming trade dress protection. . . . [However, the Court] need not resolve this question. If, despite the rule that functional features may not be the subject of trade dress protection, a case arises in which trade dress becomes the practical equivalent of an expired utility patent, that will be time enough to consider the matter.

BUSINESS CONSIDERATIONS Has the Court in this case involved itself in "slippery slope" reasoning? In other words, has the Court failed to take into account the practical business problems spawned by this ruling? What are some difficulties businesses might face as they try to abide by this decision?

ETHICAL CONSIDERATIONS When TrafFix commenced its business, it sent an MDI product abroad to have it reverse engineered (that is, copied). The Court indicated in this case that the law does not always discourage copying because allowing copying will bring about salutary results in many instances. Is copying a competitor's product unethical? Explain.

in commerce, the affixation requirement, and use of the mark in interstate commerce.

When the PTO receives the application for registration, it undertakes an examination of the mark similar to that conducted with regard to applications for patents. An examiner checks the application for compliance with the statutory prerequisites and makes sure the proposed mark is not confusingly similar to previously registered marks. Once the examiner completes this investigation, assuming he or she approves the mark, the PTO publishes the mark in its *Official Gazette.*

Anyone who believes the registration may damage himself or herself can, within 30 days, file an opposition with the PTO. Once registration has occurred, one, in some cases, can sue for cancellation of the mark. After exhausting all administrative remedies (including appeals to the Trademark Trial and Appeal Board), aggrieved unsuccessful applicants, or those who unsuccessfully allege opposition or cancellation, can sue in either the Court of Appeals for the Federal Circuit or a U.S. district court. Once granted, registration ordinarily lasts for 10 years and is renewable for 10-year periods so long as the mark remains in commercial use. Registration on the Supplemental Register offers fewer protections but, as discussed earlier, may prove advantageous for those who wish to register marks in countries other than the United States.

The law protects the trademark owner from infringement when the infringer's use will likely cause an appreciable number of consumers to be confused about the source of the goods or services. The factors courts have used to determine the "likelihood of confusion" include, but are not limited to, the following:

- similarities in the two marks' appearance, sound, connotation, meaning, and impression;

- similarities in the customer base, sales outlets (that is, "trade channels"), or the character of the sale ("impulse" versus "nonimpulse" sales);

- the strength of the mark;

- evidence of actual confusion; and

- the number and nature of similar marks on similar or related products and services.

As in patent law, one can be guilty of contributory infringement as well.

Defenses to infringement include "fair use." As we have noted earlier, one can use one's surname—even if it is the same as another famous, trademarked name like McDonald's, Campbell's, or Hilton—as long as one's use does not create the likelihood of consumer confusion. Abandonment of the mark, whether actual (that is, discontinuation of the use of the mark with the intent not to resume usage) or constructive (acts or omissions by the owner that bring about loss of distinctiveness), constitutes a defense to infringement as well. The Lanham Act expressly provides that nonuse of the mark for two consecutive years constitutes prima facie evidence of an intent to abandon the mark.

The plaintiff's registration of the mark on the Principal Register gives him or her certain advantages in an infringement action, since registration serves as prima facie evidence of the mark's validity and the registrant's exclusive right to use the mark in connection with the goods or services described in the registration. Ordinarily, then, at least until the mark becomes incontestable, defendants challenging the validity of the mark must prove the registrant's noncompliance with the prerequisites of the Lanham Act (or the common law). Incontestability status derives from the registrant's continuous use of the mark in interstate commerce for five consecutive years, the absence of any decision adverse to the registrant's claim of ownership or any pending proceeding, and the registrant's filing an affidavit to this effect with the commissioner of the PTO.

Attainment of incontestability status gives the registrant of the mark a decided edge. For example, loss of an incontestable mark can occur only through cancellation of the mark, in certain limited statutorily enumerated circumstances, or through the challenger's showing one of the statutorily enumerated defenses to incontestability. Such defenses, among others, include proof that the mark is generic; registration or incontestability has been obtained fraudulently; the registrant has abandoned the mark; the mark falls within the aforementioned categories prohibited as deceptive marks; or the use of the mark constitutes a violation of the antitrust laws. Moreover, in the context of descriptive products or services, incontestability, in effect, substitutes for proof of secondary meaning. Hence, even though the registrant of a generic mark can never use incontestability to protect the mark, owing to this presumption of secondary meaning, the registrant of a merely descriptive mark can avail himself or herself of the protection represented by the incontestability doctrine. On the other hand, one can assert fair use and certain equitable defenses against even an incontestable mark.

Remedies

The Lanham Act sets out certain statutory remedies for trademark infringement, including the equitable remedies of an injunction or an accounting to recover the profits the defendant unfairly has garnered from the infringing use. In addition, the plaintiff may recover actual damages, and the

NRW CASE 43.2 Management

TRADEMARK INFRINGEMENT

A new competitor in the tracking devices market has recently unveiled its new logo, which is very similar to the trademark NRW has been using since its inception. Mai wants NRW to file a trademark infringement suit against this firm. Helen and Carlos, expressing concern, point out that NRW does not have a particularly distinctive name or symbol and that the firm's name is used as an adjective for virtually all products that locate either personal items or inventory. They fear that, if they institute litigation, NRW may lose its right to protect its trademark. The firm members ask for your advice. What will you tell them?

BUSINESS CONSIDERATIONS How can a business protect its trademark so that the trademark does not become a generic term for the product it is intended to promote? Should a business consider changing its logo periodically so as to make the logo appear "fresh" and "new" to the public?

ETHICAL CONSIDERATIONS What ethical concerns derive from a firm's apparent copying of the logo of a more successful rival? If a firm attempts to prevent any competitors from using a trademarked logo even remotely similar to its own, is it behaving in an ethically admirable fashion?

INTERNATIONAL CONSIDERATIONS Suppose that a foreign producer is alleged to be guilty of trademark infringements related to products being imported into the United States. Are there any provisions that will allow the government to prohibit such importing unless the producer ceases the alleged infringements? What rights can the trademark holder assert in this situation?

court in its discretion can treble these damages if the circumstances (for example, willfulness or bad faith on the infringer's part) so dictate. The court similarly can adjust the amount recovered for lost profits to a figure the court considers "just." The court can award court costs and in exceptional cases may award reasonable attorney's fees to the prevailing party. Special rules apply to counterfeit marks. Treble damages, attorney's fees, and prejudgment interest awards usually result from the use of such marks.

In a companion case to the patent law holding mentioned earlier, the Supreme Court in *College Savings Bank v. Prepaid Postsecondary Education Expense Board*,[22] held that Congress had overstepped its constitutional powers when it amended the Lanham Act in 1992 to abrogate states' immunity from false advertising suits filed in federal court. According to the Court, the protection against false advertising set out in § 43(a) of the Lanham Act does not implicate property rights protected by the due process clause. Consequently, Congress could not rely on its remedial powers under the Fourteenth Amendment to abrogate state sovereign immunity.

International Dimensions

The Paris Convention mentioned earlier in our discussion of patent law applies to trademarks. The "national treatment" rationale of the Paris Convention affords to trademark holders from member nations the same protection a nation grants to its own nationals—no more and no less. Under this rationale, one can register a trademark in another member nation either by complying specifically with that nation's requirements or by registering the mark in one's home country. Member nations then cannot refuse to register any such marks unless the mark is confusingly similar to a preexisting mark, or the mark is nondistinctive, immoral, deceptive, or uses the insignia of a member nation without that nation's consent.

The requirements of U.S. trademark law (for example, use in trade and commerce as a prerequisite to registration and the cancellation provisions of U.S. law) decidedly limit the usefulness of the Paris Convention to many international applicants. The same shortcomings discussed earlier—the lack of substantive guarantees, enforcement mechanisms, and a centralized filing system—have led to the creation of the Madrid Protocol and the Trademark Registration Treaty, although neither of these initiatives has attracted very many members. The United States, for example, has refused to sign either treaty. The recent changes under GATT, however, seem promising, since they provide heightened protections against international infringement and piracy of trademarked products.

The proliferation of e-commerce has highlighted a number of trademark issues. One of the most interesting of these involves the relationship between trademark rights and domain names. Domain names are the Internet addresses used by firms, organizations, and individuals. A typical domain name might be ABCCorp.com. The familiar part of a domain name that refers to *.org*, *.com*, *.net*, or *.edu* is the top-level domain name (TLD). These designations are limited to a small number of categories. The remainder of the domain name (ABC Corp.) is assigned and monitored by a nonprofit organization, Network Solutions, Inc. (NSI). NSI's domain name protocol extends to e-mail, as well as to World Wide Web, addresses, the latter of which are known as universal resource locators (URLs). NSI assigns domain names on a first-come, first-serve basis for a fee. As long as no other party has registered the name, NSI will grant the request. That the name may be confusingly similar to another name will not preclude the registration of the name either. In this sense, the NSI processes are at odds with fundamental trademark law principles.

This ease of registration has led to the phenomenon called "cybersquatting," whereby enterprising opportunists have registered famous brands and trademarks. The owner of the famous brand or trademark (or name) subsequently may have to pay a hefty fee to obtain the rights to the domain name. A great deal of litigation has ensued over such issues (for example, Toys R Us sought an injunction against adultsrus.com, a site that sold sexual devices and clothing).

As a consequence, in 1999, Congress passed the Anticybersquatting Consumer Protection Act, which imposes liability on a person who has a bad-faith intent to profit from a registered mark and who registers, traffics in, or uses a domain name that is identical or confusingly similar to a distinctive or famous mark protected under trademark law. The act sets out various factors for determining the existence of bad faith, including whether the person has offered to sell the domain name to the mark's owner for financial gain without having any intent to use the domain name in the bona fide offering of any goods and services, or the person's prior conduct that indicates a pattern of such conduct. An intent to divert consumers from the mark owner's on-line locations to a site accessible under the domain name that could harm the goodwill represented by the mark, either for commercial gain or with the intent to tarnish or disparage the mark, by creating a likelihood of confusion as to the source of the mark constitutes bad faith as well. This, and the other factors, attempt to eliminate the high-handed, extortion-like activities previously engaged in by "cyber-pirates" or "cyber-squatters" such as adultsrus.com. Yet a person can defend against a finding of bad faith, specifically by showing that he or she believed and had reasonable grounds to believe that the use of the domain name was a fair use or otherwise lawful. Remedies under the act are limited to a court order for the forfeiture or cancellation of the domain name or the transfer of the domain name to the owner of the mark. However, these remedies are in addition to any other civil actions or remedies possible under the Lanham Act. For example, trademark owners in such circumstances might bring actions for palming off, unfair competition, trademark dilution, or infringement as well.

Besides litigation under the Anticybersquatting Consumer Protection Act, trademark owners can use the dispute resolution procedures of the Internet Corporation for Assigned Names and Numbers (ICANN). In general, a complainant who alleges trademark rights in a name that is identical or confusingly similar to a domain name may initiate a complaint with a dispute resolution provider. The complainant also must show that the domain name was registered and is being used in bad faith and that the registrant has no rights or legitimate interests in the domain name. Bad faith registration may be evidenced by several factors, including a person's registration of a domain name primarily for the purpose of selling the domain name registration to the complainant/owner of the mark for valuable consideration in excess of the documented out-of-pocket costs directly related to the domain name.

The relief that the administrative panel can grant is limited to the cancellation or transfer of the domain name in question, but the complainant's use of the ICANN arbitration procedures does not preclude court actions. Furthermore, a court decision under the Anticybersquatting Consumer Protection Act takes precedence over an ICANN arbitration panel's decision. The ICANN dispute resolution procedures are advantageous in that they generally provide quicker and cheaper relief. Still, because the institution of litigation may bring about a suspension of the arbitration proceedings, it may be more cost efficient in the long run to proceed under the federal anticybersquatting act.

You can obtain a copy of ICANN's policy by accessing http://www.icann.org/dndr/udrp/uniform-rules.htm. For a telling list of ICANN proceedings, go to http://www.icann.org/udrp.

Given the complexities associated with domain names, e-businesses need to engage in planning regarding which names they will register, which potential infringers they will pursue, and which remedies they will seek. A strategic plan that fails to take account of such matters is impracticable.

Trade Secrets

Protection

Trade secrecy law provides an alternative method for protecting intellectual property, and a firm therefore can use it to protect "know-how" or other information that gives the firm a differential competitive advantage over its competitors who either are unaware of or do not use the information. We already have seen some of the limitations on the protection of software under copyright law, in that only the written expression of the software and not the ideas embodied in it are protectible, and under patent law, in that strict compliance with statutory requirements is necessary for patentability.

However, various state and common law doctrines, such as trade secrets, unfair competition, and misappropriation, may apply to certain aspects of software—including know-how, information, and ideas—and thus encompass concepts too nebulous for copyright or patent protection. These doctrines may cover computer hardware as well. According to the Restatement (First) of Torts, § 757(b), a trade secret may include:

[a]ny formula, pattern, device or compilation of information which is used in one's business, and which gives [one] an opportunity to obtain an advantage over competitors who do not know or use it. The subject matter of a trade secret must be secret . . . so that, except by the use of improper means, there would be difficulty in acquiring the information.

In determining whether given information is a trade secret, courts generally consider:

- The extent to which the information is known outside the owner's business

- The extent to which it is known by employees and others involved in the business

- The extent of measures taken by the owner to guard the secrecy of the information

- The value of the information to the owner and to its competitors

- The amount of effort or money expended by the owner in developing the information

- The ease or difficulty with which others could properly acquire or duplicate the information

To qualify as a trade secret, the know-how, manufacturing processes, customer lists, or other proprietary information must be used continuously in the business. In addition, the business, by ensuring the physical security of the information, limiting disclosure only to those who actually need the information in order to complete their jobs, and putting those who have access to the information on notice that the firm expects them to retain it in confidence, must guard the secrecy of the information. For example, NRW may require employees to sign confidentiality agreements and restrictive covenants, review papers that employees will present publicly, conduct exit interviews with departing employees, and so on. One need only take reasonable precautions—as opposed to those deriving from Herculean efforts or gargantuan costs—to guard and/or prevent access to the proprietary information.

Common knowledge is not protectible under trade secrecy law because such knowledge presumably is of little value to the owner of the information. Similarly, if through reverse engineering one can easily acquire or duplicate the information, it may not qualify as a trade secret.

Liability

Courts ground liability for misappropriation of a trade secret on two principal theories: (1) breach of contractual or confidential relations (note the way in which courts often blur the distinction between contract and tort law) and (2) acquisition of the information through improper means. Under the first line of reasoning, courts will prohibit persons in an agency (including employment) and/or a fiduciary relationship from disclosing or using information acquired in the course of employment. As we saw in Chapter 12, sometimes an employee expressly promises not to compete with the employer for a given period of time in a given geographical area if the employee leaves this particular job. In the absence of such an express contract, courts generally will not imply such a restrictive covenant. But in some circumstances—for example, where a third party learns of confidential information from the employee—the law *will* imply a confidential relationship between the third party and the owner of the trade secret. In such circumstances, the third party's disclosure or use of the information will represent actionable misappropriation.

The law also imposes liability for impropriety in the methods used to acquire the trade secret. The law will not countenance conduct that falls below generally accepted standards of commercial morality. If a competitor of NRW induces the firm's key engineer to disclose proprietary information, the competitor will have acquired the information through improper means. Liability similarly will result from the acquisition of information through bribery, commercial espionage, or other illegal conduct such as fraud, theft, and trespass. However, as we discussed earlier, information obtained through simple reverse engineering, independent discovery, or the owner's failure to take reasonable and inexpensive precautions probably does not involve improper means and thus represents a lawful acquisition of information.

Remedies

Remedies for misappropriation of a trade secret include injunctions and actions for damages. Such damages may include the plaintiff's lost profits, the profits made by the defendant, or the royalty amount a reasonable person would have agreed to pay. State criminal laws may apply to misappropriations of trade secrets as well.

On the federal level, the Economic Espionage Act of 1996 (EEA) seeks to punish a broad spectrum of activity that interferes with an owner's proprietary rights in commercial trade secrets. In establishing a comprehensive and systemic approach to trade secret theft and economic espionage, the EEA facilitates investigations and prosecutions by federal authorities. In enacting the EEA, Congress apparently was responding to the losses—estimated at $1.5 billion in 1995[23] alone—resulting from competitors' activities (the "raiding" of employees, for example) and misappropriations by foreign enterprises. Hence, the substantive provisions of the EEA address "economic espionage," including activities on behalf of foreign instrumentalities, and "theft of trade secrets" resulting from certain domestic commercial endeavors. Prohibited activities include misappropriating, concealing, procuring by fraud or deception, possessing, altering or destroying, copying, downloading-uploading, or conveying trade secrets without permission.

The EEA thus seeks to proscribe "traditional" acts of misappropriation, that is, when conversion removes protectible information from the owner's control, as well as "nontraditional" methods—when "the original property never leaves the control of the rightful owner, but the unauthorized duplication or misappropriation effectively destroys the value of what is left with the rightful owners."[24] The sanctions that can be levied against those who engage in such prohibited activities include fines, imprisonment, and criminal forfeiture. Organizations acting in concert with or on behalf of foreign instrumentalities may be fined no more than $10 million. Other organizations may be fined no more than $5 million. Individuals acting in concert with or on behalf of foreign instrumentalities may be fined no more than $500,000 or imprisoned no more than 15 years, or both.[25] Other individuals also may be fined or imprisoned up to 10 years (or both). The criminal forfeiture provision permits the seizure and forfeiture of the property used to facilitate the misappropriation or impermissible possession of a trade secret. The EEA thus mirrors the broad seizure powers enjoyed by the government under antidrug enforcement criminal statutes.[26] Try to keep abreast of the developments that stem from this relatively new statute.

Computers

The owner of software may find it advantageous to use trade secret protection. This mechanism avoids the public registration required to devise and enforce rights under the

---

NRW CASE 43.3   Management

PATENT OR TRADE SECRET?

The firm has invested a great deal of time, energy, and money in the development of its two products, and NRW wants to derive as much protection for these inventions as the law allows. Helen believes the firm will receive the greatest protection by applying for patents on the products and then for additional patents on each development as NRW improves the products. Carlos prefers to treat NRW's processes as trade secrets and not make the information publicly available. All three ask for your advice. What will you tell them?

BUSINESS CONSIDERATIONS What factors should an inventor consider in deciding to seek a patent? What drawbacks inhere in one's seeking a patent?

ETHICAL CONSIDERATIONS Is it ethical for a firm to copy a patented item and then hope that it can prevail in any litigation that results from the patent holder's suit against the firm? Is it ethical for a firm to attempt to enforce questionable patents and to use the expense of litigation as a means of preventing competitors from making the product?

INTERNATIONAL CONSIDERATIONS Patent protections have been significantly expanded by treaty. Do similar international agreements and/or treaties protect trade secrets? Should a firm that is active internationally patent a new process or treat it as a trade secret? Why?

---

patent and copyright laws. However, because maintaining the secrecy of the proprietary information in question may be difficult and because lack of secrecy constitutes one of the primary defenses to a charge of trade secret misappropriation, the owner of the trade secret should implement various mechanisms to ensure secrecy.

Actions that employers can take to protect trade secrets about software (or hardware) include the creation of nondisclosure, noncompetition, and confidentiality agreements with employees. Employers also should limit physical access to areas where the development of privately and exclusively owned (proprietary) software is taking place as well as to storage areas. All software and documents containing trade secrets should bear proprietary labels; and, to ensure the security of the information, the software should use encrypted code (code typed in one set of symbols and interpreted by the machine as another) so that only those who have the key for unscrambling it can make the program intelligible. Last, employers should provide constant reminders to employees about secrecy obligations and conduct exit interviews with departing employees regarding the information the company considers proprietary.

The licensing of software, in order to preserve secrecy, mandates special steps by the owner of the software. Besides restricting disclosures by the licensee, the licensor-owner should limit the rights the licensee retains in the software by virtue of the license, prohibit copying except for use or archival purposes, formulate special coding techniques to identify misappropriated software, distribute the software in object code as opposed to source code, and stipulate that the breach of any confidentiality provision will result in the immediate termination of the licensing agreement.

As we have seen, it is easier for a court to discern a relationship between the owner of the trade secret and the person or entity using or disclosing the trade secret than it is for a court to ascribe property concepts to the trade secret. Why? It is difficult to determine where general information, which is unprotectible, leaves off and proprietary information in the form of the trade secret, which is protectible, begins. Courts often derive these relationships impliedly from the parties' status as employer/employee, vendor/buyer, and the like. However, the parties cannot enjoy a confidential relationship unless a protectible trade secret first exists. Once it does, though, the trade secret may last perpetually unless the owner loses the differential advantage it affords.

As we learned earlier, the loss of a protectible trade secret may occur through another party's independent discovery of the secret or any other legitimate means, such as reverse engineering or the public dissemination of the knowledge underlying the trade secret through either a failure to keep the information secret or flaws in the methods the owner has employed to ensure secrecy. Mass distribution of software copies to those with whom the software owner has a confidential relationship generally does not eliminate trade secret protection as long as the owner otherwise has taken precautions to preserve secrecy.

Exhibit 43.2 summarizes some of the most significant aspects of the various categories of intellectual property discussed in this chapter.

Also, check out the wide array of interesting information about copyrights, patents, and trademarks you can find at http://www.census.gov.

Unfair Competition

Our system of law allows, in the name of "competition," rather free-wheeling activities. However, courts will give remedies to those injured by activities such as solicitation of a former employer's customers or employees, competition between an employee and his or her employer while the employee still works for the employer, wrongful terminations by the employer, and "palming off" of one's goods as those of another.

Protection and Remedies

The common law and statutory restrictions on "unfair competition" often form the legal bases on which aggrieved persons in these circumstances sue. Misappropriation, another basis for relief, derives from the common law principles of unfair competition and often becomes a "catch-all" theory used in situations in which patent, copyright, and trade secret law do not cover the aspect of the business in dispute. One note of caution is in order, however. The Supreme Court in several decisions has held that federal law will preempt such state causes of action if they interfere with federal policies.[27]

Palming off occurs when a competitor tries to divert another firm's patronage or business to itself by deceptively "palming off" (or "passing off") his or her goods or services as originating from the other firm. It represents the oldest theory of unfair competition. The common law recognized the unfairness of one firm's "free-riding" on the effort, investment, and goodwill of another and thus granted injunctions and/or damages to those injured by such palming off.

Such activities often involved the wrongdoer's misrepresenting or copying the plaintiff's trademark or trade dress. The Lanham Act, in outlawing trademark infringement, basically "federalizes" these common law theories, although it changes them in certain significant ways. Indeed, § 43(a) of the Lanham Act also provides protection to commercial people even in the absence of federal trademark registration; hence, it has carved out broad civil remedies for commercial activities that affect interstate commerce.

Section 43(a) creates three different types of "unfair competition" claims:

1. "palming off" (or "passing off") claims under which the act prohibits any person's falsely designating the origin of particular goods or services if these false designations are likely to cause confusion, mistake, or deception with regard to this person's affiliation or connection to another person's goods, services, or commercial activities;

2. false advertising claims; and

3. product disparagement claims (that is, derogatory, false, injurious statements about a competitor's product, service, or title).

EXHIBIT 43.2 Intellectual Property

Type	Copyright	Patent	Trademark	Trade Secret
What Protected	Original works of authorship—literary, musical, dramatic, dance, art, audiovisual works, and sound recordings—expressed in a tangible medium	Process, machine, manufacture, composition of matter, improvements, plants, and genetically engineered matter	Word, name, symbol, device, trade dress, or mark that indicates the source of goods or services	Formula, pattern, device, or compilation of information that gives the owner an advantage over competitors
Not Protected	Ideas, procedures, methods, systems, facts	Ideas, laws of nature, mathematical formulas, scientific truths, methods, processes	Purely descriptive terms, generic terms, some geographic marks, and deceptive marks	Nonsecrets
Standards	Original Fixed in tangible medium	Novel Useful Nonobvious	Distinctive or fanciful Has acquired secondary meaning	Used in business Secret Not susceptible to simple reverse engineering
Rights	Make copies Distribute copies Reproduce the work Prepare derivative works Perform or display publicly	Exclusive right to make and market the invention	Exclusive right to use the mark	Right to use and exclude others
Limitations	Fair use First sale Archival copying Some performance-related restrictions	Abuse of patent PTO grant mere presumption	Fair use Abandonment	Termination of protection upon discovery of secret through lawful means
Length	Life plus 70 years	20 years (utility) 14 years (design)	Extensions every 10 years through perpetuity	Perpetuity (potentially)
How	Automatic No need to file	Apply to PTO, describe and disclose the art, and pay fees	Apply to PTO	Common law doctrine
Remedies	Civil, including damages and injunctions, and criminal	Civil, including damages (possible treble damages) and injunctions	Civil, including damages (possible treble damages) and injunctions	Civil, including damages and injunctions, and criminal
International	Berne Convention since 1989 WIPO	Paris Convention/WIPO Patent Cooperation Treaty	Paris Convention Trademark Law Treaty of 1994	None

Courtesy of Deborah Kemp

To recover under § 43(a), the plaintiff must show that the defendant's activities affected interstate commerce; the defendant made material, false, misleading, or deceptive statements or designations that led to a likelihood of confusion among consumers; and actual or the likelihood of injury to the plaintiff.

While consumers ordinarily have no standing to sue (only injured competitors do), § 43(a), by allowing injunctive relief upon the plaintiff's showing a likelihood of damage, indirectly protects consumers' interests; the plaintiff need not show the defendant's actual diversion of patronage or trade. A showing of such a loss of business will be necessary if the plaintiff seeks money damages, however. Otherwise, the remedies ordinarily available for infringement of trademarks apply to § 43(a) claims.

The Federal Trade Commission (FTC), discussed in Chapters 5 and 37, has jurisdiction over "unfair or deceptive acts or practices in or affecting commerce." The FTC's enforcement mechanisms, particularly the wide latitude the FTC has in fashioning cease and desist orders, represents yet another avenue for protecting the owners of intellectual property from unfair trade practices. In the international arena, the Paris Convention protects its signatories against unfair trade practices.

Antidilution Statutes

In recent years, the legal system has begun to recognize that competitive injury can result even if the parties are not competitors and even if there is an absence of confusion as to the source of the goods. In other words, the law in some circumstances will protect one who owns strong, distinctive, well-known marks from another's use of an identical or similar mark if such use is likely to tarnish, degrade, or dilute the distinctive power of the mark. The states that have enacted these so-called antidilution statutes recognize that even nonconfusing uses of identical or similar marks over time may gradually erode the distinctive value of the mark, as well as advertising and other public promotional efforts the mark owner has undertaken to promote product goodwill and to capture as well as retain market share.

In granting relief, state courts, as well as federal courts under their diversity jurisdiction, have utilized the dilution doctrine. As we learned in Chapter 5, the law protects truthful, nondeceptive commercial speech. Hence, like the 2 Live Crew case we considered under copyright law, some cases brought under the dilution theory implicate aspects of the First Amendment, particularly if the defendant's use involves parody.

Celebrated dilution cases have included Pillsbury's seeking to enjoin a company that portrayed and marketed Pillsbury's trade figures, "Poppie Fresh" and "Poppin' Fresh," in obscene sexual positions; General Electric's seeking to enjoin an underwear company that used an electric light bulb on its underwear named "Genital Electric"; and Coca-Cola's seeking to enjoin a poster captioned "Enjoy Cocaine" in script similar to that used in the Coca-Cola trademark. These cases illustrate the tension between the owner's desire to protect its mark from tarnishment and the value our society from its inception has placed on parody. Note, too, that only owners of distinctive marks can sue under such statutes, since only they have marks capable of suffering dilution or erosion.

The recently enacted Federal Trademark Dilution Act of 1995 adds to rather than replaces state antidilution statutes. This act codifies as federal law the principle that no one can undertake a diluting use of a famous mark even in circumstances in which there is an absence of the likelihood of customer confusion as to the source of the goods. This statute apparently has ushered in a new era of federal trademark protection, an era that potentially will greatly expand the protection afforded to famous, strong, distinctive marks. Be alert for the legal developments that will result from this congressional act.

The Semiconductor Chip Protection Act of 1984

Congress's enactment of the Semiconductor Chip Protection Act of 1984 as an amendment to the copyright laws affords developers of integrated circuits a 10-year monopoly over their resultant semiconductor chips. Although it contains ideas common to copyright, patent, and trade secret law, this act creates a new class of intellectual property law.

Congress directed the legislation at both domestic and international chip pirates who in the past had merely taken chips apart, reconstructed the circuit design on the chip (known as the mask), and then made copies of the original chip. As long as copyright law did not protect semiconductor chips (they were deemed utilitarian/useful articles and hence uncopyrightable even though the circuit diagrams might be), there was clearly an incentive for pirates to reap profits by copying while at the same time avoiding the mammoth costs associated with developing the chips. By prohibiting reverse engineering that has as its end purpose the copying of the chip, the act eliminates this result but, by allowing reverse engineering leading to the creation of a new chip, preserves current law.

Protection and Remedies

The act itself protects only mask works, or the layouts of the integrated circuits that appear on the chips. It does not protect the semiconductor chips themselves; any other product that performs the function of chips, such as circuit boards; or works embodied in mask works, such as computer programs. Indeed, not all mask works are protected either. For instance, if the mask work is not "fixed" in a semiconductor chip, as is the case of information merely stored on diskettes, or if the mask work embodies designs that are commonplace and unoriginal, the act is inapplicable. The duration of the protection is 10 years from the time of registration or the first commercial exploitation of the mask work, whichever occurs first. The process of registration contains special procedures for protecting proprietary information.

The same remedies generally available under the copyright laws relating to infringement—injunctions, damages, attorney's fees, and import exclusion and seizure—apply in this context, except that criminal sanctions are unavailable. Some provisions of the act protect the mask works of non-pirating foreign companies under certain circumstances as well.

Although interpretive questions undoubtedly will arise as the first cases begin to appear under this act, note that this statute, at the time of its enactment, represented the first new area to be covered by federal intellectual property law in approximately 100 years.

Summary

Intellectual property encompasses several substantive areas of the law: copyrights, patents, trademarks, trade secrets, and unfair competition. Computers constitute an especially apt illustration of the significance of intellectual property both in the United States and in the international arena. Intellectual property law strives to serve two oftentimes competing goals: ensuring incentives to create a wider array of products and services in the marketplace while at the same time providing public access to intellectual creations and promoting competition. The law serves the first goal when it grants property rights (sometimes even monopolies) to creators and the second when it limits the duration of such exclusive rights and/or circumscribes the rights thus granted so as to maximize the amount of information found in the public domain. This area of the law also seeks to protect creators and businesspeople from injurious trade practices.

The copyright laws protect any original works of authorship. To be copyrightable, works of authorship must show originality and must be fixed in a tangible medium of expression. Ideas are not copyrightable. A copyright in essence consists of a bundle of exclusive rights that enables the copyright owner—usually the author or one to whom the author has transferred rights—to exploit a work for commercial purposes. To ensure copyright protection, one must ascertain the governing law: the 1909 Copyright Act, the 1976 Copyright Act, or the Berne Convention. Violations of any of the copyright owner's exclusive rights constitute infringement. The courts have imposed liability for both direct and contributory infringement. The most common defense against charges of infringement is the "fair use" doctrine. Civil remedies for infringement include injunctions, impoundment and destruction of infringing items, and damages. Criminal penalties also are available. The Digital Millennium Copyright Act of 1988 protects Internet service providers from liability for online copy infringements when they do not exercise control over the copyrighted materials that others distribute on such systems, assuming the service providers fulfill certain conditions.

The Patent Act of 1952 grants to inventors the exclusive right to their respective discoveries that consist of patentable subject matter. The Supreme Court has held that such utility patents may cover genetically engineered living matter as well. As in copyright law, ideas per se are not patentable. Utility patents last for 20 years from the filing date, while design patents last for only 14 years from the date of the grant of the patent, after which time the monopoly granted to the patentee ends. At that point, others can make, use, or sell the invention with impunity. To be patentable, an invention must demonstrate novelty, utility, and nonobviousness. Obtaining a patent involves detailed disclosures to the Patent and Trademark Office. Infringements may be either direct or contributory and may consist of inducements to infringe. Persons sued for patent infringement may claim lack of patentability or patent misuse as a defense. Remedies for infringement include injunctive relief as well as damages.

Over the years, an extensive body of state trademark law has developed in the common law, principally through the state common law relating to unfair competition. By providing a structure by which the enforcement of these common principles can occur through federal oversight, the 1946 Lanham Act—the most important federal protection of trademarks—builds on these common law roots. The Lanham Act defines a trademark as any word, name, symbol, device, or any combination thereof used to identify and distinguish the services of one person from the services of others and to indicate the source of the goods, even if the source is unknown. This definition underscores the fact that a trademark always exists pursuant to commercial activity or use and may cover an extensive array of things, including the distinctive features of the product (that is, "trade dress") such as the product's shape, the product's packaging, the logo or artwork on the product, and so on. To deserve protection, the trademark—whatever its form—must be distinctive; generic terms never can qualify for trademark protection. Purely descriptive marks do not qualify as distinctive until they have acquired "secondary meaning."

Trade secret law protects proprietary information that gives the owner a differential advantage over his or her competitors. To merit protection, the information must be secret and used continuously in the business. The law does not protect as trade secrets either common knowledge or information easily acquired from reverse engineering. Misappropriation can occur through breach of contractual or confidential relations or the use of improper means to acquire the secret. Remedies include injunctions and damages actions. State and federal criminal laws may apply to such misappropriations as well.

In "federalizing" common and state law unfair competition claims, the Lanham Act allows recovery on three bases: (1) "palming off," (2) false advertising, and (3) product disparagement. State and federal "antidilution" laws also protect one who owns a strong, distinctive, well-known mark from another's use of an identical or similar mark if such use is likely to tarnish, degrade, or dilute the distinctive power of the mark. As we have seen in other contexts, parody may constitute a defense to actions brought under this theory. The Anticybersquatting Consumer Protection Act imposes liability for bad-faith registrations and uses of domain names.

The Federal Trade Commission also has authority to protect the owners of intellectual property from unfair trade practices. Several international treaties regulate intellectual property as well.

Discussion Questions

1. What does the law require before it will grant copyright protection?

2. What factors constitute "fair use" under the Copyright Act?

3. What does the law mandate before it will grant patent protection?

4. What is a trademark, and what does the law require before it will grant trademark protection?

5. What factors will a court use to determine a "likelihood of confusion" under trademark law?

6. What advantages derive from the registration of a trademark on the Lanham Act's Principal Register?

7. What must one do to protect information as a trade secret? In determining whether information constitutes a trade secret, what factors might a court consider?

8. Name and define the theories on which courts ground liability for misappropriation of a trade secret.

9. Explain in detail how the Lanham Act protects against unfair competition.

10. Explain fully the international protections accorded to various types of intellectual property.

Case Problems and Writing Assignments

1. On April 19, 1982, Wayne Pfaff filed an application for a patent on a computer chip socket. Section 102(b) of the Patent Act of 1952 provides that no person is entitled to patent an "invention" that has been "on sale" more than one year before filing a patent application. Therefore, April 19, 1981, would constitute the critical date for purposes of the "on-sale" bar of § 102(b); if the one-year period had begun to run before that date, Pfaff would lose his right to patent his invention. Pfaff commenced work on the socket in November 1980, when representatives of Texas Instruments asked him to develop a new device for mounting and removing semiconductor chip carriers. In response to this request, he prepared detailed engineering drawings that described the design, the dimensions, and the materials to be used in making the socket. Pfaff sent those drawings to a manufacturer in February or March 1981. Prior to March 17, Pfaff showed a sketch of his concept to representatives of Texas Instruments. On April 8, 1981, they provided Pfaff with a written confirmation of a previously placed oral purchase order for 30,100 of his new sockets for a total price of $91,155. In accordance with his normal practice, Pfaff did not make and test a prototype of the new device before he offered to sell the invention in commercial quantities. The manufacturer took several months to develop the customized tooling necessary to produce the device, so Pfaff did not fill the order until July 1981.

The evidence therefore indicated that Pfaff first reduced his invention to practice (that is, he fully assembled the invention and used it) in the summer of 1981. The socket achieved substantial commercial success before Patent No. 4,491,377 (the '377 patent) was issued to Pfaff on January 1, 1985. After the issuance of the patent, Pfaff brought an infringement action against Wells Electronics, Inc., the manufacturer of a competing socket. Wells prevailed when a court found no infringement had occurred. After Wells began to market a modified device, Pfaff brought this suit, alleging that the modifications infringed six of the claims in the '377 patent. The district court held that two of those claims were invalid because they had been anticipated in the prior art. Nevertheless, the court concluded that four other claims were valid and that various models of Wells's sockets had infringed upon three of these claims. The district court rejected Wells's § 102(b) defense because Pfaff had filed the application for the '377 patent less than a year after he had reduced the invention to practice.

The court of appeals reversed, finding all six claims invalid. Four of the claims described the socket that Pfaff had sold to Texas Instruments prior to April 8, 1981. Because that device had been offered for sale on a commercial basis more than one year before the patent application was filed on April 19, 1982, the appeals court concluded that those claims were invalid under § 102(b). That conclusion rested on the court's view that as long as the invention was "substantially complete at the time of sale," the one-year period would begin to run, even though the invention had not yet been reduced to practice. Did the commercial marketing of a newly invented product mark the beginning of the one-year period even though the invention had not yet been reduced to practice? [See *Pfaff v. Wells Electronics, Inc.*, 525 U.S. 55 (1998).]

2. Vornado Air Circulation Systems, Inc., manufactures patented fans and heaters. Vornado sued Duracraft Corp., a competitor, for trade dress infringement of the spiral grill design used in its fans. In 1995, the Tenth Circuit held that Vornado had no protectible trade dress rights in the grill design (*Vornado I*). Nevertheless, four years later on November 26, 1999, Vornado lodged a complaint with the U.S. International Trade Commission against The Holmes Group, Inc., claiming that Holmes's sale of fans and heaters with a spiral grill design infringed Vornado's patent and the same trade dress held unprotectible in *Vornado I*. Several weeks later, Holmes filed this action against Vornado in the district court. Holmes sought a declaratory judgment that its products did not infringe Vornado's trade dress and an injunction restraining Vornado from accusing it of trade dress infringement in promotional materials. Vornado's answer asserted a compulsory counterclaim alleging patent infringement.

The district court granted Holmes the declaratory judgment and injunction it had sought. The court explained that the collateral estoppel effect of *Vornado I* (that is, the conclusiveness of this prior judgment) precluded Vornado from relitigating its claim of trade dress rights in the spiral grill design. The court therefore rejected Vornado's contention that an inter-

vening Federal Circuit case that had disagreed with the Tenth Circuit's reasoning in *Vornado I* constituted a change in the law of trade dress that warranted the relitigation of Vornado's trade dress claim. The court also stayed all proceedings related to Vornado's counterclaim, adding that the counterclaim would be dismissed if the declaratory judgment and injunction entered in favor of Holmes were affirmed on appeal.

Vornado thereupon appealed to the Court of Appeals for the Federal Circuit. Notwithstanding Holmes's challenge to its jurisdiction, the Federal Circuit vacated the district court's judgment and remanded the case for consideration of whether the "change in the law" exception to collateral estoppel applied in light of *TrafFix Devices, Inc. v. Marketing Displays, Inc.*, a case decided after the district court's judgment and which resolved a circuit split involving *Vornado I* and the aforementioned precedent. The U.S. Court of Appeals for the Federal Circuit is vested with exclusive jurisdiction over final decisions of U.S. district courts whose jurisdiction was based in whole or in part on 28 USC § 1338. Section 1338(a), in granting federal district courts original jurisdiction over any civil action "arising under" federal patent law, uses the same operative language as 28 USC § 1331, which grants district courts original jurisdiction over all civil actions arising under federal law. The Supreme Court precedent of *Christianson v. Colt Industries Operating Corp.* requires courts to apply the same test to determine whether a case arises under § 1338(a) as under § 1331. Moreover, the so-called well-pleaded-complaint rule has long governed whether a case "arises under" federal law for purposes of § 1331. With regard to § 1338(a), the well-pleaded-complaint rule provides that whether a case "arises under" patent law must be determined from what necessarily appears in the plaintiff's statement of his or her own claim in the bill or declaration. The plaintiff's well-pleaded complaint must "establish either that federal patent law creates the cause of action or that the plaintiff's right to relief necessarily depends on resolution of a substantial question of federal patent law." Would the Federal Circuit have jurisdiction over a case in which the complaint did not allege a claim under patent law but the answer contained a counterclaim that did? [See *The Holmes Group, Inc. v. Vornado Air Circulation Systems, Inc.*, 535 U.S. 826 (2002).]

3. Mavety Media Group, Ltd. published *Black Tail*, an adult entertainment magazine featuring photographs of both naked and scantily clad African-American women. On June 7, 1990, Mavety filed a PTO application seeking federal registration of its trademark "Black Tail," based on Mavety's bona fide intention to use the mark in connection with goods identified as "magazines." In accordance with the regulation governing the filing of an amendment to allege the first use of the mark, Mavety provided published issues of *Black Tail*. The examiner ultimately refused registration because the mark consists of or comprises immoral or scandalous matter. The examiner expressly relied on a dictionary reference defining "tail" as "sexual intercourse—usu. considered vulgar." On August 15, 1991, Mavety, responding to the examiner's decision, contended that a substantial composite of the population would

not interpret the mark to be a reference to sexual intercourse but rather as a reference to "the rear end," a meaning not usually considered vulgar. Mavety supported its contention with the magazine specimens of record that depicted the use of the mark—for example, on the magazine cover above a photograph of a woman displaying her derriere. Mavety also provided newspaper articles showing that many consumers would interpret "Black Tail" as connoting the full evening dress worn by men at formal occasions and thus the quality, class, and experience of an expensive lifestyle, consistent with the familiar genre of adult entertainment magazines such as *Playboy* and *Penthouse*. In addition, Mavety argued that the federal trademark register contains numerous marks consisting of words with nonsexual primary meanings that nonetheless have sexual connotations. When the Trademark Trial and Appeal Board (TTAB) of the PTO affirmed the examiner's refusal to register Mavety's mark, Mavety instituted a lawsuit in the Court of Appeals for the Federal Circuit. How should that court rule in this case? Explain fully. [See *In re Mavety Media Group, Ltd.*, 33 F.3d 1367 (Fed. Cir. 1994).]

4. In 1989, the Northern Metropolitan Foundation for Health Care, Inc. (NMF) and Morris Klein, its executive director, undertook to develop an assisted living facility in the town of Ramapo, New York. To develop the design of the facility, NMF hired two architectural firms: Albert Schunkewitz and Partners and Jerome Meckler Associates. Schunkewitz and Meckler retained Albert Sparaco Jr. to prepare a site plan of the development project for submission to the Ramapo planning board. (A site plan is a development plan for a plot of land. It specifies the existing land conditions, including topography, boundaries, and physical structures, and can also specify the proposed improvements to the site.) Schunkewitz and Meckler had prepared "conceptual sketch architectural drawings" of the building's "footprint"—the shape or outline of the building on the land surface—and surrounding parking areas. They provided these drawings to Sparaco for integration into the site plan. Sparaco in turn hired Robert Torgerson, a landscape architect and independent contractor, to assist in developing the site plan. Sparaco's personal contribution to the creation of the site plan was minimal. He supervised Torgerson in the refinement of Schunkewitz and Meckler's drawings and made several adjustments in response to suggestions from Ramapo officials. Financial constraints led NMF to dismiss Meckler, leaving Schunkewitz as the sole architect on the project.

In August 1993, Sparaco formalized his involvement in the project and executed an agreement with Schunkewitz and NMF. The contract provided that the surveyor's drawings and plans would not be used by the client "for the completion of this project by others, except by a separate agreement in writing, and with appropriate compensation to the surveyor." The contract also provided that NMF was not to "copy, reproduce, or adapt the drawings" without Sparaco's written consent. In December 1993, Sparaco completed the site plan, which the Ramapo authorities approved. The final version of the plan was a 14-page document that incorporated a rendering of (1) the existing physical characteristics of the site and (2) the proposed physical improvements to the site. In December 1996, Sparaco obtained a certificate of copyright for the site plan. He registered the site plan under the category of a "map" and "technical drawing." In his application for registration, Sparaco listed only himself as the "author" of the site plan.

Dissatisfied with the building design, NMF removed Schunkewitz from the project and hired Graham & Alexander (G&A), a construction management firm, to oversee the continuation of the project's development. NMF also retained Dahn & Krieger Architects Planners PC (D&K) to provide architectural services. D&K's responsibilities related only to the design of the building. NMF's agreement with D&K stated that "the building footprint and shell shall be in general conformance" with Sparaco's site plan. When D&K proposed changes to the design and footprint of the building, Sparaco offered to prepare an amended site plan if he received an additional payment. NMF rejected the offer and assigned the responsibility of creating an amended plan to Lawler, Matusky, Skelly Engineers LLP (LMS). Thomas B. Vanderbeek, an LMS employee, served as the primary engineer on the project. In order to accommodate D&K's new building design and footprint, LMS and Vanderbeek made several digital modifications to Sparaco's plan, including adjustments to the "utility connections" and "proposed gradings." When NMF submitted this amended site plan to the authorities, the amended site plan included the legend, "This site plan [is] based on [an] approved plan set entitled 'Heritage House' by A.R. Sparaco, Jr. . . . ." According to a Ramapo senior official, the revised plan was basically a copy of the approved A.R. Sparaco plan with several minor changes involving the sedimentation and erosion control plan and the landscaping plan. The amended plan also copied Sparaco's boundary survey, topographical contour lines, parking lot and shape, location of driveway, and curbs, and the original building front. With the use of the amended site plan, the project was completed by November 1998.

Sparaco subsequently filed a lawsuit alleging that the defendants had copied his site plan to create a derivative work in violation of the Copyright Act and had falsely designated the origin of the amended plan in violation of the Lanham Act and New York state laws that prohibit unfair competition. Sparaco's complaint also alleged that NMF and Klein had breached their 1993 agreement with Sparaco by using his site plan without his written authorization. With regard to the copyright claim, Sparaco contended that his depiction of the existing characteristics of the site falls within the Copyright Act's protection either of maps or original compilations. The defendants submitted that the site plan, in setting forth the physical characteristics of the site, implicated only facts, which, under the *Feist* case, are not copyrightable. The district court had granted the defendants' summary judgment motion. Would you agree with this ruling? [See *Sparaco v. Lawler, Matusky, Skelly, Engineers, LLP*, 303 F.3d 460 (2d Cir. 2002).]

5. BUSINESS APPLICATION CASE Adobe Systems, Inc., one of the leading software development and publishing companies in the

United States, sells copyrighted software products, including Adobe Illustrator, Adobe Pagemaker, and Adobe Acrobat. Adobe contends that it distributes its software products under license to a network of distributors and original equipment manufacturers. These distributors sign license agreements that permit them to engage in limited redistribution to entities or individuals authorized by Adobe. Adobe claims all Adobe software products are subject to shrink-wrap end user license agreements (EULAs) that prohibit copying or commercial redistribution. Adobe also makes "Educational" versions of its software packages available for license to students and educators at a discount. Adobe Educational distributors are licensed to transfer Educational software only to resellers who have signed off- or on-campus educational reseller agreements (OCRAs) with Adobe. In turn, any OCRA requires that the redistribution of educational software be limited to students and educators. Adobe asserts that the Educational versions are prominently marked "Education Version—Academic ID Required" and include the legend, "Notice to users: Use of the enclosed software is subject to the license agreement contained in the package."

Stargate Software, Inc. is a discount software distributor wholly owned by Leonid Kelman. Neither Stargate nor Mr. Kelman is an authorized distributor of Adobe products. In 1997, Stargate began acquiring software from two businesses, Dallas Computers and D.C. Micro, Inc. with the majority of the software being Adobe Educational software. Adobe contended that Stargate's suppliers acquired Adobe Educational software from Adobe Educational distributor Douglas Stewart Co. pursuant to valid OCRAs. However, Stargate alleged that all the Adobe software products that Stargate sold had been purchased through either D.C. Micro, Inc. or Dallas Computers. Between March 1998 and April 1999, Stargate purchased between 1,795 and 2,189 packages of Educational software produced by Adobe. Stargate distributed this Educational software at below-market prices to retail customers and unauthorized resellers through magazine advertisements, trade shows, auction Web sites, and its own Web site. Adobe learned of this practice, made a trap purchase of the Educational software in April 1999, and filed suit against Stargate and Mr. Kelman soon thereafter.

Adobe alleged that Stargate had infringed Adobe's copyrights by obtaining and selling the Educational versions of Adobe software without authorization from Adobe. Stargate claimed that it was the rightful owner of the Adobe software products and that, pursuant to the "first sale" doctrine, codified at § 109 of the Copyright Act, Adobe had no right to stop the sales of this software. Section 106 of the Copyright Act outlines the exclusive rights enjoyed by owners of a copyright including the exclusive right "to distribute copies . . . of the copyrighted work to the public by sale or other transfer of ownership, or by rental, lease, or lending." Under this provision, the copyright owner would have the "right to control the first public distribution of an authorized copy . . . of his work, whether by sale, gift, loan, or some rental or lease arrangement." But § 109(a) of the act makes clear that "the copyright owner's rights under § 106(3) cease with respect to a particular copy . . . once he has parted with ownership of it." One significant effect of § 109(a) is to limit the exclusive right to distribute copies to their first voluntary disposition, and thus negate copyright owner control over the further (or "downstream") transfer to a third party. Thus, under the first sale doctrine, a sale of a lawfully made copy terminates a copyright holder's authority to interfere with subsequent sales or distributions of that particular copy.

Although Stargate conceded that Adobe retains title to the objective coded software of the intellectual property contained on the CD-ROM, Stargate nevertheless claimed that whenever there is a sale, Adobe has parted with title to that particular copy of its copyrighted intellectual property, thereby divesting itself of the exclusive right to vend that particular copy. In essence, Stargate submitted that each time Adobe is paid by a distributor or reseller for a package of software, it has "received its rewards" for that package and has parted with title to that particular copy. Stargate maintained that an examination of the "economic realities" of the initial transaction between Adobe and its distributors indicates that Adobe's distribution of its educational software constitutes a sale, rather than a license of each particular copy. Had Adobe, through its OCRAs and EULAs, transferred ownership of each particular copy of its software to its distributors, D.C. Micro, Inc. and Dallas Computers, Inc., thereby fulfilling the first sale doctrine? Should the court deny Adobe's motion for summary judgment owing to copyright infringement? [See *Adobe Systems, Inc. v. Stargate Software, Inc.,* 216 F. Supp. 1051 (N.D. Cal. 2002).]

6. **ETHICAL APPLICATION CASE** Wanda and Christopher Cavalier created copyrighted works involving several characters featured in children's stories. Their main character, Nicky Moonbeam, an anthropomorphic moon, teaches children to overcome their fears (including fear of the dark) and encourages children to follow their dreams. The Cavaliers copyrighted these works from 1992 to 1995. From 1995 through 1998, the Cavaliers submitted more than 280 pages, including their copyrighted works, to Random House, Inc. and the Children's Television Workshop, Inc. (CTW). The first submission consisted of two stories—"Nicky Moonbeam: The Man in the Moon" and "Nicky Moonbeam Saves Christmas"—and the design for a "moon night light" to be built directly into the back cover of a "board book" (that is, a book with sturdy, thick pages, designed for use by young children). Later submissions in 1996 and 1998 consisted of "pitch materials" that included detailed illustrations, ideas for general story lines and television programs, specific traits of the Nicky Moonbeam characters, and the goals of the Nicky Moonbeam stories. After face-to-face meetings with the Cavaliers regarding their submissions, Random House and CTW rejected their works. Soon thereafter, in February 1999, Random House and CTW jointly published the books *Good Night, Ernie* and *Good Night, Elmo,* and, in September 1999, CTW aired the animated television series *Dragon Tales.*

"Nicky Moonbeam: The Man in the Moon" is an approximately 3500-word story. Its main characters are Nicky Moonbeam and Daisy, a five-year-old child. Nicky is a childlike figure drawn with a full moon head. He has egg-shaped eyes, a humanlike nose, and a mouth, with moon rocks or craters on his face. Nicky has star friends who have faces drawn in the upper point of the stars, with small, lidded eyes and no nose. In the latest version of the story, Nicky is sad and lonely because he cannot stop dreaming about meeting a child. Nicky sails the Dream Weaver, a sailboat propelled by moonbeams, to Earth where he meets Daisy. Nicky takes Daisy for a ride in the night sky on his boat. Daisy floats on a cloud that looks like a dragon while Nicky balances on an airplane-shaped cloud. Nicky and Daisy return to Earth where they play at the beach. Nicky does not want to leave, but Daisy convinces him to return to the sky and continue his "man in the moon" job, comforting and encouraging children.

The Cavaliers' second story, "Nicky Moonbeam Saves Christmas," is told in 1,700–2,500 words (depending on the version). In this story, Rudolph the reindeer is sick and cannot guide Santa on his rounds. Santa's chief elf summons Nicky to the North Pole where he learns about Santa's dilemma. Daisy, who has traveled with Nicky to the North Pole on the Dream Weaver boat, suggests that Nicky lead Santa's sleigh using his moonbeams to light the way. Nicky completes Santa's rounds just as Nicky's moonbeams are exhausted.

The Cavaliers' "night light in the sky" idea was that the back cover of a board book featuring Nicky Moonbeam would extend some distance beyond the front cover and the pages, so that a portion of the inside of the back cover would be visible on the right-hand side, both when the book was closed and when it was being read. On the extended (visible) portion of the inside back cover would be a night light in the shape of a pearly white moon with black eyes and pink cheeks. Stars would surround the moon night light. The "on" button for the moon night light would be a small circle with a star on it, positioned below and to the right of the night light. Once a child pushed the button in the circle, the light would shine and stay on for a full minute.

The Cavaliers also suggested a "Just Imagine" book series featuring Nicky Moonbeam; proposed the use of "Nicky Badges" and "Glow Stars"; described and illustrated the concept of a "star tree," from which characters could pluck a star; illustrated a small girl floating on a dragon-shaped cloud; introduced Nicky's "school in the sky"; and created a "fear of the dark" checklist to be packaged with its first story or television episode on that theme.

Good Night, Ernie and *Good Night, Elmo* are both five-page board books featuring these Sesame Street Muppet characters. In *Good Night, Ernie*, told in 74 words, Ernie wonders about the stars and takes an imaginary journey in the night sky. He wonders how many stars there are, and counts them as he sits on a crescent moon. He wonders where the stars go during the day, how the stars stay bright, and how he can help them shine. All of this "wondering" makes Ernie tired. Ernie returns to his bed, which is floating in the sky surrounded by stars. He and the stars, which have ping-pong ball-shaped eyes touching a round bulbous nose, wish each other good night.

In *Good Night, Elmo*, told in 119 words, Elmo notices the moon shining on his pillow. The moon invites him to "hop on" its moonbeam and "take a ride" through the night sky, where Elmo races a shooting star, sees the cow jumping over the moon, and begins jumping like the cow. All of that jumping tires Elmo, and he rides a moonbeam back to his bed, where he begins to fall asleep as the moon shines through his window. The moon on the cover has ping-pong-ball-shaped eyes touching a round bulbous nose.

A star night light, surrounded by stars, is built into the extended inside back cover to the right of the free pages of *Good Night, Ernie*. A comparable moon night light is built into the extended inside back cover of *Good Night, Elmo*. The instructions for the night light are identical for both books: "To turn on Ernie's [Elmo's] night light, press the star button. It turns off by itself."

The *Dragon Tales* series features friendly talking dragons that take children on adventures to teach them how to "face their fears, and to find ways of coping with everyday problems, like making friends and learning new skills." When Emmy, a six-year-old, and Max, her four-year-old brother, move into a new home, they discover Dragon Land, a brightly colored fantasy world in which the children see talking trees, a rainbow river, gnomes, giants, and other fanciful creatures and geography. One of the dragon characters is a wise old teacher who teaches at the "School in the Sky." In the "Forest of Darkness" episode, a character who is afraid of the dark is sent on a mission to find the "Star Tree" and return with one of its "Star Seeds." In conjunction with that episode, CTW marketed a "fear of the dark" checklist.

The Cavaliers subsequently filed in district court, claiming copyright infringement, trademark infringement, and false designation of origin under the Lanham Act. The Cavaliers alleged that Random House and CTW had copied and appropriated their works, including the Nicky Moonbeam characters, illustrations, text, and night light. The trial court granted Random House and CTW's motion for summary judgment on the following grounds: (1) The Cavaliers' general story lines in which anthropomorphic moon and stars ease children's fears of sleeping in the dark, and the depiction of related scenes and stock characters ("scenes-a-faire") were not protectible by copyright; (2) *Good Night, Ernie, Good Night, Elmo*, and *Dragon Tales* were not substantially similar to the copyright-protectible material in the Cavaliers' works; and (3) given the lack of substantial similarity, the Cavaliers' Lanham Act claims also failed. How should the appellate court rule in this case? Would it rule differently if it had decided this case on ethical—as opposed to legal—grounds? [See *Cavalier v. Random House, Inc.*, 297 F.3d 815 (9th Cir. 2002).]

7. **CRITICAL THINKING CASE** The litigation between the parties brought out the following information: Barbie was born in Germany in the 1950s as an adult collector's item. Over the years, Mattel, Inc. transformed her from a doll that resembled a "German street walker," as she originally had appeared, into a glamorous, long-legged blonde. Barbie has been labeled both

the ideal American woman and a bimbo. She has survived attacks both psychic (from feminists critical of her fictitious figure) and physical (more than 500 professional makeovers). She remains a symbol of American girlhood, a public figure who graces the aisles of toy stores throughout the country and beyond. With Barbie, Mattel created not just a toy but a cultural icon. In 1997, Aqua, a Danish band, produced the song "Barbie Girl," on the album *Aquarium*. The female singer (a band member who sings in a high-pitched, doll-like voice), who calls herself Barbie, is "a Barbie girl, in [her] Barbie world." She tells her male counterpart (named Ken), "Life is plastic, it's fantastic. You can brush my hair, undress me everywhere/Imagination, life is your creation." And off they go to "party." The female singer further explains, "I'm a blond bimbo girl, in a fantasy world/Dress me up, make it tight, I'm your dolly." "Barbie Girl" singles sold well; and, to Mattel's dismay, the song made it onto the Top 40 music charts. Mattel sued the music companies that had produced, marketed, and sold "Barbie Girl": MCA Records, Inc., Universal Music International Ltd., Universal Music A/S, Universal Music & Video Distribution, Inc., and MCA Music Scandinavia AB (collectively, MCA). Mattel's theories included trademark infringement, dilution of its mark under the Federal Trademark Dilution Act (FTDA), and unfair competition. MCA in turn challenged the district court's jurisdiction under the Lanham Act and its personal jurisdiction over the foreign defendants, Universal Music International Ltd., Universal Music A/S, and MCA Music Scandinavia AB. MCA also argued that its conduct fell within the FTDA's exemption that permits uses that, though potentially dilutive, involve noncommercial or fully constitutionally protected speech. Evaluate the strength of the arguments each party will make in its own behalf and then decide who should win. [See *Mattel, Inc. v. MCA Records, Inc.*, 296 F.3d 894 (9th Cir. 2002).]

8. YOU BE THE JUDGE DirecTV, Inc. sued NDS Group, a Rupert Murdoch–controlled company that manufactures "smart" cards that prevent the piracy of digital television signals. Although it at one point had a contract with NDS with regard to such "smart" card technology, DirecTV ultimately moved its encryption technology in-house. In September 2002, DirecTV sued NDS on several theories, including misappropriation of trade secrets. DirecTV retained the Los Angeles office of Jones, Day, Reavis and Pogue as its outside legal counsel for this lawsuit. Documents filed in court indicated that DirecTV delivered to the law firm about 27 boxes of confidential materials related to the case. To facilitate the management of these documents, the law firm in turn hired Uniscribe Professional Services, a Norwalk, Connecticut, document-copying service that does imaging work for not only law firms but accounting firms, investment banks, universities, and museums. Owing to the sensitivity of the documents, Uniscribe set up an imaging center at the law firm's offices and greatly restricted the number of persons who had access to these materials. Michael Peker, a Uniscribe employee who did have access to the materials, enlisted the assistance of his nephew, a 19-year-old University of Chicago student named Igor Serebryany, after the firm indicated its desire that the copying work proceed more quickly. The law firm had not approved the hiring of Serebryany.

During the course of his work, Serebryany allegedly came across information concerning the design and architecture of DirecTV's latest "P4 access card" technology, a device that prevents free access to digital television signals by the company's 11 million subscribers. Serebryany allegedly distributed this information—which cost DirecTV about $25 million to develop—to several Internet sites that cater to hackers. Court documents indicated that Serebryany removed copies of the documents from the law firm's offices, took them to his own home, and used his father's computer to send electronic copies of the information to at least three Web site operators. Serebryany apparently was motivated by a desire to facilitate the hacking community's activities rather than by personal monetary gain. Given your knowledge of intellectual property law, on what civil and criminal bases for suing Serebryany would you expect this litigation to focus? If *you* were the judge, how would *you* dispose of each of these theories? [See Debora Vrana, "U. of C. Student Arrested for Document Piracy," *Chicago Tribune*, January 3, 2003, sec. 1, p. 15, col. 1.]

Notes

1. Department of Commerce, Bureau of the Census, *Statistical Abstract of the United States*, 121st ed. (Washington, D.C.: 2001), 495.
2. 510 U.S. 569 (1994).
3. *Fogerty v. Fantasy, Inc.*, 510 U.S. 517 (1994).
4. 714 F.2d 1240 (3d Cir. 1983), *cert. dismissed*, 464 U.S. 1033 (1984).
5. Ibid., 1244.
6. Ibid., 1245.
7. Ibid., 1250.
8. Ibid., 1240–1241.
9. Ibid., 1249. For a more recent disposition of a similar case, see *Lotus Development Corporation v. Borland International, Inc.* 49 F.3d 807 (1st Cir. 1995), *aff'd*, 516 U.S. 233 (1996).
10. *J.E.M. Ag Supply v. Pioneer High-Bred International, Inc.*, 534 U.S. 124 (2001).

11. 527 U.S. 150 (1999).
12. Department of Commerce, Bureau of the Census, *Statistical Abstract of the United States*, 121st ed. (Washington, D.C.: 2001), 494.
13. Ibid.
14. Ibid.
15. *Markman v. Westview Instruments, Inc.*, 517 U.S. 370 (1996).
16. 527 U.S. 627 (1999).
17. Ibid.
18. 450 U.S. 175 (1981).
19. 684 F.2d 912 (CCPA 1982).
20. Department of Commerce, Bureau of the Census, *Statistical Abstract of the United States*, 121st ed. (Washington, D.C.: 2001), 494.
21. 514 U.S. 159 (1995).
22. 527 U.S. 666 (1999).

23. Greenlee, "Spies Like Them: How to Protect Your Company from Industrial Spies," 31 *Management Accounting* 78 (December 1996).

24. Chaim A. Levin, "Trade-Secret Thieves Face Fines, Prosecution," *National Law Journal,* January 27, 1997, p. C13.

25. Ibid.

26. Ibid., p. C12.

27. *Sears, Roebuck & Co. v. Stiffel Co.,* 376 U.S. 225 (1964); *Compco Corporation v. Day-Brite Lighting, Inc.,* 376 U.S. 234 (1964); *Bonito Boats, Inc. v. Thunder Craft Boats, Inc.,* 489 U.S. 141 (1989).

CHAPTER 44

Wills, Estates, and Trusts

A G E N D A

NRW Like many small business owners, Mai, Carlos, and Helen are concerned about protecting their estates. Mai's parents are independent and live in their own home now, but she is concerned that at some time in the future they may become dependent on her financially, and she would like to develop a plan for dealing with this contingency if it arises. Helen is married, and she would like to have a plan that provides some protection for her husband if anything should happen to her. How should Helen write her will to protect Elliot, her husband? After hearing Helen's concerns about her will, Carlos decided that he also wanted to prepare a will. He recently read the book *How to Avoid Probate!* by Norman F. Dacey. As a result, he would like to avoid probate in the administration of his estate. What are the advantages and disadvantages of avoiding probate in Carlos's estate?

With a small business, continuity is important. Mai, Carlos, and Helen don't want NRW to stop operating for a significant period of time if anything should happen to one of them. They are also concerned with the potential financial impact on them and their families if NRW were to fail. How can Mai, Carlos, and Helen control medical and financial decisions if they become extremely ill and/or incompetent? What should they do with their respective interests in NRW in order to protect the enterprise? Can they transfer their interests in NRW to family members? What restrictions would be appropriate? Would a trust be proper? Who could serve as the trustee?

These and other questions will arise during our discussion of wills, estates, and trusts. Be prepared! You never know when the firm or one of its members will seek your advice.

The Transfer of an Estate

Almost everyone has an estate, no matter how modest it might be. It may consist only of compact disks, a television, and a 10-speed bike; conversely, it may consist of some office buildings, rental houses, sizeable money market accounts, and shares in a business, whether a closely-held enterprise like NRW or a publicly traded corporation. This chapter deals with critical planning decisions—what happens to an estate when someone dies—and addresses techniques for transferring an estate, usually to family members and friends. The discussion is general because the rules vary significantly from state to state.

Under the U.S. Constitution, state law governs property transfers, including wills. The probate codes in the states vary greatly. *Probate* is the procedure for verifying that a will is authentic and its provisions should be implemented. *Probate codes* are state statutes that deal with the estates of incompetents and people who have died with or without a valid will. One example is the South Carolina Probate Code, which is listed on the state Web site at http://www.scstatehouse.net/. (From the home page, click on Research, then go to Code of Laws, Title/Chapter List. Chapter 62 is the Probate Code.) For links to other state probate codes, go to the Cornell Law School Web site at http://www.law.cornell.edu/topics/state_statutes3.html#probate/ and look under the heading "Probate."

The *Uniform Probate Code* is a statute drafted by the National Conference of Commissioners on Uniform State Laws (NCCUSL) for adoption by the states as their probate code. Its purposes are to unify state laws and respond to complaints that probate procedures are too complicated, costly, and time consuming. It was completed by the NCCUSL in 1969 and has undergone revision since then.[1] The Web site of the NCCUSL contains information about the uniform acts including information about which states have adopted the act and why the act should be adopted, at http://www.nccusl.org/nccusl/default.aspx/. The Archives of the NCCUSL includes the complete text of the uniform acts. The Archives are maintained by the University of Pennsylvania Law School at http://www.law.upenn.edu/bll/ulc/ulc_frame.htm. This chapter discusses many widely adopted sections. The American Law Institute (ALI) has published the Restatement (Third) of the Law of Property, which is a treatise on wills and other donative transfers. The Restatement itself is not a statute; however, when a court relies on a section it becomes part of the precedents of the state.

Wills

In a will, a person indicates who should inherit his or her property at death.[2] The law that controls the validity of a person's will is the law of his or her domicile. (*Domicile* is a person's permanent home and principal residence. It is the place to which a person will return after traveling.) A will provides an opportunity to name a guardian for any minor children the person may have. In fact, a will is the only way parents can specify who will raise a minor child if they both die. If parents do not use this technique for naming a guardian, the court will appoint one; and the court may not choose the best person. For example, grandparents may no longer be physically or emotionally capable of raising a young child. Since the court is not aware of their limitations, the court may appoint the grandparents as guardians. The parents (and the courts) have the option of dividing the guardian's duties and appointing someone to care for the child's physical needs while appointing someone else to care for his or her financial needs and manage the inheritance. This option is valuable if one person is not competent in caring for *both* the child and the finances, but would be very competent in caring for one of them.

A will is also the place to name a personal representative for the estate. (*Personal representative* is a person who manages the financial affairs of another or an estate.) The personal representative nominated in the will is generally the one appointed by the court, if he or she is able to serve. The judge will appoint an alternate if the nominee is dead, disabled, or incompetent. The will should also contain a residuary clause for all the property that is not specifically mentioned elsewhere in the will. (A *residuary clause* is a clause that disposes of the remainder or the residual of an estate.) It is not advisable to include burial instructions in a will because often the will is not located and read until after the funeral. Such instructions are better contained in a separate document, with copies distributed to the personal representative, close family members, and the attorney.

Some changes in family relationships affect the validity of a will. Children who are born after a will is executed (signed) receive a share of the estate as *after-born children.* After-born children generally are entitled to their *intestate share,* the portion of the estate that a person is entitled to receive under state law if there is no valid will. If a marriage occurs after a will has been executed, the new spouse also will take a share of the estate. A divorce will change an existing will, too. In most states, a divorce with a property settlement will revoke gifts willed to the ex-spouse; however, a few states, including California, still require a revocation by the *testator* (a man who makes a will) or *testatrix* (a woman who makes a will). In this chapter, we will use the term *testator* to refer to a man or a woman.

To make changes in a will, it is not necessary to write a completely new document. The testator can simply make the desired changes in a *codicil*, a separate written document that modifies an existing will. The codicil also acts to confirm the unchanged will provisions. Care should be taken to assure that the will and the codicil read together will make sense. To be valid, a codicil must satisfy the same requirements as a will.

The testator may destroy the effect of a will by making a new will and stating in the new will that the old will is revoked. This is commonly called a *revocation clause*. If the new will does not specifically revoke the old will, the courts in some states will try to interpret the two wills together. In such a case, the new will revokes the older will only to the extent that they contain contradictory or inconsistent provisions. A testator can also cancel an old will by physically destroying the signed original, with the intention of revoking it.

Wills can be categorized by the manner in which they are formed. Generally, wills can be *formal, holographic,* or *nuncupative.* Wills also can be categorized by the types of dispositions they contain.

Formal Wills

The most common type of will is called a *formal,* or attested, will. It is generally drafted by an attorney and printed by the attorney's staff. A will prepared by a competent attorney is more likely to achieve the desired results than one prepared by a layperson. Familiarity with the terminology of wills is important because the words used in the will often have a special significance that differs from their ordinary meaning. In addition, each state has its own technical requirements.

A will *can* be a very lengthy document, and it must be executed in strict compliance with the procedures specified in the state statute. Generally, the testator must sign the will at the end of the document in the presence of at least two witnesses. Some states require more than two witnesses. At least one state requires four. The testator *must* ask these two individuals to act as witnesses to the will. The witnesses must be disinterested persons; that is, they must have no interest in any of the property passing under the will or by intestate succession. The primary purposes of witnesses are to swear that the signatures are valid and to swear that the testator was lucid and seemed competent. In most states, the will also must be dated.

California, Maine, and Wisconsin have a special type of formal will called a *statutory will.* This will is so named because it has been approved by the state legislature, and the language used in the will is specified in the state probate statute. Printing companies in the state can print form wills using the approved language. A form will is sold to an individual testator who fills in the appropriate names and executes the will. Despite its title, a statutory will is a formal will, and consequently it must be witnessed by two disinterested witnesses. The American Bar Association's Section of Real Property, Probate and Trust Law maintains a Web site with answers to common questions about estate planning and related topics at http://www.abanet.org/rppt/public/home.html.

Holographic Wills

Holographic wills (called *olographic wills* in some states) are required to be written, signed, and usually dated in the testator's own handwriting. Although not universally accepted, they are allowed in a number of states, including Alaska, Arizona, Arkansas, California, Colorado, Idaho, Kentucky, Louisiana, Mississippi, Montana, Nebraska, Nevada, New Jersey, North Carolina, North Dakota, Oklahoma, Pennsylvania, South Dakota, Tennessee, Texas, Utah, Virginia, West Virginia, and Wyoming. Holographic wills also are allowed under the Uniform Probate Code, § 2-503.

A testator who writes a holographic will runs the risk of not expressing his or her intentions properly and not complying with the technical requirements that may affect a will under state law. The testator may be unaware of and hence unable to take advantage of techniques to reduce costs and taxes. An attorney or an accountant with tax expertise may be able to make recommendations that will greatly reduce the taxes.

Most of the states that allow holographic wills require that they be dated. They do not, however, have to be witnessed. Traditionally, holographic wills have to be written completely in the testator's handwriting with *no* printed or typed matter included on the document. Recently, some courts and legislatures have become more lenient about accepting printed matter on a holographic will. For example, the California legislature enacted a statutory change requiring only that the signature and the material provisions be in the testator's handwriting.[3] Also, a court may accept the will if the printed matter is not an integral part of the will. Many of the states that allow holographic wills require that the will be kept with the important papers of the *decedent.* The purpose of this requirement is to assist in establishing the testator's intent to make a will and ascertaining that the document was important to him or her.

Nuncupative Wills

Nuncupative, or oral, wills are permitted in a number of states under limited circumstances. Usually, nuncupative wills can be used only to dispose of personal property; this is true in Kansas, Nebraska, Virginia, and Washington. Georgia, however, allows real property to pass in this manner. Some states place a limit on the value of the property transferred by a nuncupative will. The Uniform Probate Code makes no provision for nuncupative wills, and many states do not permit them.

Nuncupative wills also are restricted to certain situations. Generally, an oral will is valid (1) if it is made by a civilian who anticipates death from an injury received the same day or (2) if it is made by a soldier in the field or a sailor on a ship who is in peril or in fear of death. Because of the dangers inherent in military service and duty at sea, some states recognize a separate category of wills called *soldiers' and sailors' wills* (also sometimes called *soldiers' and seamen's wills*). These states may exempt soldiers and sailors from the usual requirements for oral or written wills.[4]

Two or three disinterested witnesses must hear a nuncupative will, at least one of whom must have been asked by the decedent to act as a witness. This requirement is helpful in distinguishing between nuncupative wills and oral instructions to change a written will or a plan to change a will. Many statutes require that the nuncupative will be written down within 30 days and/or *probated* (that is, established in probate court as genuine and valid) within six months from the time it was spoken.

Matching Wills

Wills also can be categorized by the types of dispositions they contain. For example, married couples or business partners (like Mai, Carlos, and Helen) may have matching provisions in their wills. *Matching wills* are appropriate when the testators have identical testamentary objectives. For this reason, they are also called *reciprocal wills*. These wills may be mutual, joint, or contractual.

Mutual wills are separate wills in which the testators, usually a husband and wife, have matching provisions in their respective wills. For example, the separate will of each spouse might provide for "the transfer of my assets to my spouse. If my spouse does not survive me, then my assets shall be divided equally among my children."

In *joint wills,* two people sign the same document as their last will and testament. Usually, the dispositive provisions are the same. Joint wills are not recommended. Many state courts have difficulty analyzing the legal relationship between the two signers. The difficulty normally arises after the first person dies and the second person wants to change the will. The issue is whether the second person can modify the will or is he or she contractually obligated to leave it unchanged. This conflict may cause court trials and appeals. As is the case with any lengthy trial and appeal, a large amount of the estate may be expended in trying to resolve the legal rights of the parties.

In *contractual wills,* people enter into a valid contract in which one or more of them promise to make certain dispositions in their wills. This agreement must meet the usual requirements for a valid contract, including consideration and the absence of fraud and undue influence. (*Undue influence* is the wrongful use of influence to get a person to write certain provisions in a will.) This arrangement lacks flexibility, but it may be desirable in some situations. If it is desirable, it is preferable to make a separate agreement to avoid the interpretive problems of joint wills.

Requirements for a Valid Will

The requirements for a valid will vary from state to state and apply to formal, holographic, and nuncupative wills. A person must be an adult at the time the will is executed in order for it to be valid. The modern rule is that anyone 18 or older can execute a valid will. Eighteen is the age used in the Uniform Probate Code and the Model Execution of Wills Act. The Model Act, written by the NCCUSL, is intended as an example for states to follow in drafting their own laws. All states have now adopted the age of 18, with the following exceptions: Alabama (age 19), Louisiana (age 16), and Wyoming (age 19).[5]

A testator must also have *testamentary capacity,* sufficient mental capability or sanity to execute a valid will. Often wills contain the declaration, "I, Jane Doe, being of sound mind and body. . . ." This statement is *not* necessary. In addition, a person need not be physically healthy to write or sign a valid will. However, *actual* testamentary capacity is required at the time the will is signed. The courts narrowly define actual testamentary capacity. The common requirements are that the person understands the nature and extent of his or her assets, knows who his or her close relatives are, and understands the purpose of a will.[6] In many states, even a prior adjudication of incompetency will not automatically invalidate a will on the grounds of insanity. If any relatives suspect that a decedent was incompetent when he or she executed the will, some of them will probably contest it. One of the purposes of having disinterested witnesses is so that they will be able to testify about the testator's apparent competency at the time the will was executed.

A recent technique developed to assist with proof of competence and volition is a *self-proved (self-proving) will*. This special type of formal will is accepted under the Uniform Probate Code. The purpose of a self-proved will is to reduce the amount of proof necessary when the testator dies and the will is offered for probate.[7] This is achieved by preparing and attaching sworn *affidavits* (written statements made under oath) to the will when it is signed. The sworn affidavit states that the will is signed in compliance with the law. (In some states, the testator and the witnesses must sign the will before a notary public or other officer authorized to administer oaths.) The affidavits may include an optional statement that the witnesses believe that the testator is of sound mind and is acting of his or her own volition and without undue influence. Generally, then, the witnesses are not needed when the will is actually submitted for probate unless someone contests the will.

As noted earlier, the testator must sign formal or holographic wills. Many states require that a proper signature appear at the end of the document.

In the following case, the court addressed the validity of a self-proving will under the Texas statute.

44.1

ESTATE OF GRAHAM
69 S.W.3d 598, 2001 Tex. App. LEXIS 8481 (Tex. Ct. App., 13th Dist., 2001)

FACTS Francis John Graham died in 1998 at the age of 83 years. His wife predeceased him, and he had no children. Mr. Graham executed a will leaving his entire estate to the two daughters of his full sister (the will proponents). His seven remaining nieces and nephews, children of Mr. Graham's half-sister (will contestants), challenge the will.

ISSUES Was the will executed with the formalities required by the Texas Probate Code? Did Mr. Graham lack testamentary capacity or was he subjected to undue influence?

HOLDINGS Yes, the will was properly executed. No, Mr. Graham had testamentary capacity and he was not subjected to undue influence.

REASONING Excerpts from the opinion of Justice Bonner Dorsey:

Section 59 of the Texas Probate Code . . . states that, except where otherwise provided by law, a will must be (1) in writing, (2) signed by the testator and (3) be attested by two or more credible witnesses above the age of fourteen years who shall subscribe their names thereto in their own handwriting in the presence of the testator. . . . The will itself shows that it was in writing and signed by the testator. . . . While a self-proved will can still be challenged, the self-proving affidavit constitutes prima facie evidence of the will's execution. . . . An affidavit . . . that is in substantial compliance with the affidavit form set forth in Texas Probate Code § 59(a) will make the will self-proved. . . . [This affidavit is in substantial compliance.]

. . . In order to execute a valid will,

> The testator must have been of sound mind at its execution; and by this is meant that he must have been capable of understanding the nature of the business he was engaged in, the nature and extent of his property, the persons to whom he meant to devise and bequeath it, the persons dependent upon his bounty, and the mode of distribution among them; that he must have had memory sufficient to collect in his mind the elements of the business to be transacted, and to hold them long enough to perceive, at least, their obvious relations to each other, and be able to form a reasonable judgment as to them; and that he was not under the influence of an insane delusion, either in regard to his property or the natural and proper objects of his bounty, which affected the disposition he was about to make.

. . . The Texas Supreme Court has said that the proper inquiry in a will contest on grounds of testamentary incapacity is the condition of the testator's mind on the day the will was executed. If there is no direct testimony of acts, demeanor or condition indicating that the testator lacked testamentary capacity on the date of execution, the testator's mental condition on that date may be determined from lay opinion testimony based upon the witnesses' observations of testator's conduct either prior or subsequent to the execution. . . . [T]o successfully challenge a testator's mental capacity with circumstantial evidence from time periods other than the [day of signing] . . . the will contestants must establish (1) that the evidence offered indicates a lack of testamentary capacity; (2) that the evidence is probative of the testator's capacity (or lack thereof) on the day the will was executed; and (3) that the evidence provided is of a satisfactory and convincing character. . . . Mr. Graham . . . was fully aware that he was making a will bequeathing his entire estate to his two nieces. . . .

A document is not a will unless it is executed with testamentary intent. "To give the instrument the legal effect either of a will or other revocation of former wills it must be written and signed with the present intention to make it a will or revocation." "It is essential . . . that the maker shall have intended to express his testamentary wishes in the particular instrument." . . . We find abundant evidence that Mr. Graham intended the document signed on March 8, 1996, to be his will. Not only does the language on the document itself clearly indicate that it is Mr. Graham's Last Will and Testament, but it clearly bequeaths his estate to his two nieces. . . . The notary and a witness both stated that he knew he was signing his will and he asked them to witness and acknowledge it for him. Further, Cynthia Baumgardner stated in her affidavit that Mr. Graham approached her and asked her to re-type the handwritten will that he had made out. [Ms. Baumgardner worked for Margaret Hoelscher, his income tax preparer.] The fact that he wrote it out by hand before having it typed up indicates that Mr. Graham intended the document to be his will and understood the contents of the document. [Testamentary intent is proven.] . . .

Before a will can be set aside because of undue influence, the contestant must prove: (1) the existence and exertion of an influence; (2) the effective operation of that influence so as to subvert or overpower the testator's mind at the time of the execution of the testament; and (3) the execution of a testament which the maker would not have executed but for such influence. Not every influence exerted on a person is undue. It is not undue unless the free agency of the testator was destroyed and the will produced expresses the wishes of the one exerting the influence. . . . Courts have long recognized that the exertion of influence that was or became undue is usually a subtle thing and by its very nature usually involves an extended course of dealings and circumstances. . . . In the absence of direct evidence all of the circumstances shown or established by the evidence should be considered. . . . Factors to be considered when determining whether undue influence exists in a particular case are:

(1) the nature and type of relationship existing between the testator, the contestants and the party accused of exerting such influence;

(2) the opportunities existing for the exertion of the type of influence or deception possessed or employed;

(3) the circumstances surrounding the drafting and execution of the testament;

(4) the existence of a fraudulent motive;

(5) whether there has been an habitual subjection of the testator to the control of another;

(6) the state of the testator's mind at the time of the execution of the testament;

(7) the testator's mental or physical incapacity to resist or the susceptibility of the testator's mind to the type and extent of the influence exerted;

(8) words and acts of the testator;

(9) weakness of mind and body of the testator, whether produced by infirmities of age or by disease or otherwise;

(10) whether the testament executed is unnatural in its terms of disposition of property.

. . . We find the record devoid of any evidence of undue influence. . . .

BUSINESS CONSIDERATIONS Should the bookkeeper have allowed Cynthia Baumgardner, her employee, to type Mr. Graham's will? Why or why not?

ETHICAL CONSIDERATIONS The will contestants alleged a number of legal grounds to set aside the will, but they did not have much evidence. Did the will contestants act in an ethical manner? Is it ethical for any potential heirs to challenge the wishes of the decedent as to the disposition of his or her estate?

Testamentary Dispositions and Restrictions

A person has quite a bit of freedom in the dispositions that he or she may make in a will. These provisions are very important to the testator, and the court generally will give effect to them. But a person's ability to make testamentary dispositions has limits. While these restrictions vary from state to state, there are some common restrictions that are found in a significant number of states. We will discuss some of them in this section.

One of the most common restrictions addresses the concerns that arise when a person wills too large a portion of his or her estate to charity, to the detriment of the family. The prohibitions against doing so are found in *mortmain,* or fear of death, statutes, and they operate to restrict the types and amounts of charitable gifts that will be upheld in a will.

Another widely prohibited disposition is a trust that is established for too long a period of time. (A *trust* is an arrangement in which one person or business holds property and invests it for another.) The allowable length of time is specified in the rule against perpetuities, which is discussed briefly in the section of this chapter on private trusts.

In addition, most states do not allow the testator to will money to pets. Animals are not legal beneficiaries under wills or trusts. However, some states do allow the testator to establish an honorary trust for the benefit of the animal. (An *honorary trust* is an arrangement that does not meet the requirements for a trust and thus is not enforceable, but it may be carried out voluntarily.) Where permitted, the testator is restricted in the amount that may be placed in an honorary trust. The trust is limited to an amount of assets that is not excessive with respect to the animal's reasonable needs.

Will provisions can be set aside if they are against public policy. Examples include provisions that encourage beneficiaries to get divorced or that separate children from their parents. Obviously, a person cannot will away someone else's property (for example, the spouse's half of the community property) or property that passes by operation of law, as in a joint tenancy with rights of survivorship. (*Community property* is a special form of joint ownership between husband and wife permitted in certain states, known as community property states.)

If a testator suspects that someone will want to contest the will, a *no-contest clause* may be inserted in it. Basically, such a clause indicates that if a person contests the validity of the will in court, that person will not inherit any assets from the estate. The no-contest clause is used as a threat by the testator, and in that sense it may be effective; however, many states do not enforce no-contest clauses or they make exceptions to them. Regardless of a state's approach to no-contest clauses, if the person is successful in having the will declared invalid, that person can inherit. In other words, the no-contest clause will be invalid along with the rest of the will. Depending on the circumstances, the contestant may inherit under a prior will or under the state intestate succession statute.

Contrary to popular belief, a person is not required to leave assets to family members and other relatives. In common law states, there is an exception to this rule for a spouse: A widow or widower who is not willed at least a statutory minimum amount often can *elect against the will* (that is, choose to take a preset minimum percentage of the estate rather than the amount provided by the will). (*Common law states* are states in which married couples cannot create community property.) Other family members may be excluded, but a testator should mention them and the fact that they are being excluded. This is often accom-

plished by leaving them a nominal amount, such as $5 or $10. If the testator fails to do this, the omitted family members can claim that they were *preterminated* (forgotten) heirs. (*Heirs* are persons who actually inherit property from the decedent.) Courts generally will award intestate shares to preterminated heirs on the grounds that the omission was a mistake. In addition, the omission of a close family member can indicate that the testator was mentally incompetent.

Actual heirs may receive their shares under different theories or philosophies. In writing a will, a testator may select between per capita (per head) or per stirpes (per line) distribution of assets. In *per capita* distribution, each beneficiary in the described group receives an equal share, no matter how many generations he or she is below the decedent. For example, in a gift to the decedent's children and grandchildren, each one would receive an equal share. This is true whether or not the grandchild's parent is alive. In contrast, in a *per stirpes* distribution to the decedent's children and grandchildren, each child of the decedent receives an equal share. If any child has already died, his or her children would equally divide that child's share. If a child is still alive, his or her offspring would not directly receive any assets. This is also called taking by right of representation. (The *right of representation* is the right of children to inherit in their parent's place, if the parent is deceased.) Exhibit 44.1 illustrates the distinction between a per stirpes and a per capita gift made to children and grandchildren.

The Uniform Probate Code introduced a new type of distribution called *per capita at each generation*: it is also called *per capita with representation*. For this method of distribution, the shares are determined at the first generation at which there are *any* living issue. (*Issue* are lineal descendants, such as children, grandchildren, and great-grandchildren.) This generation might be children, grandchildren, or even great-grandchildren. Once the shares are established for each line, then the issue of any deceased line member divides that line member's share. As you might assume, per capita at each generation distribution is really a hybrid between regular per stirpes and per capita distributions. Strict per stirpes distribution, by contrast, always divides the shares at the first generational level below the decedent, even though no one at that level is still alive. Exhibit 44.2 illustrates the difference between per capita at each generation and strict per stirpes distributions. Most states use the per capita at each generation rule in their intestate statutes. If a will or trust does not provide a clear indication about which approach should be used, the courts look to the intestacy statutes of that state. Consequently, most states will use a per capita at each generation approach if the will or trust is ambiguous. A person writing a will or trust can select which of these three methods he or

EXHIBIT 44.1 Testamentary Distributions to Surviving Children and Grandchildren

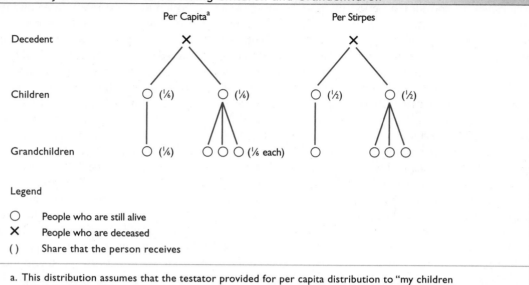

a. This distribution assumes that the testator provided for per capita distribution to "my children and grandchildren."

she prefers and can include a clear statement to that affect. Individuals will have different ideas about which method is most fair.

Wills can be set aside (ignored) by the court if they were signed because of fraud in the inducement, fraud in the execution, duress, or undue influence, which was discussed in *Estate of Graham* (Case 44.1). These concepts are used in wills cases in much the same manner as they are used in contract situations. The Legal Information Institute, main-

tained by the Cornell Law School, provides an overview of estates and trusts, including information about state adoptions of the Uniform Probate Code, and recent court cases at http://www.law.cornell.edu/topics/estates_trusts.html/. A person might also wish to make a gift of his or her organs at death. The person must comply with the state laws concerning organ donations. Most states have adopted the Revised Uniform Anatomical Gift Act (1987) to make it easier to obtain organs.[8]

EXHIBIT 44.2 Testamentary Distributions to Surviving Children and Grandchildren

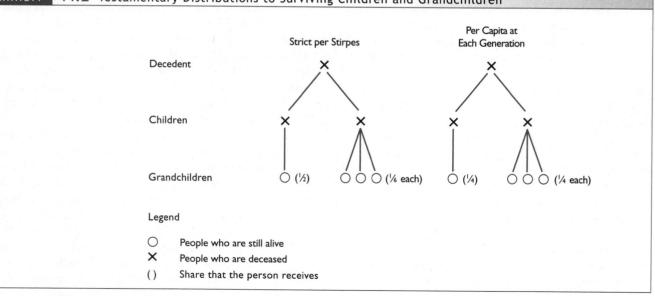

Intestate Succession

For various reasons, people often fail to sign or to execute a valid will. States provide for the transfer of the assets of these people by enacting a state intestate succession statute. People who die without a valid will are said to have died *intestate*. Sometimes, especially with holographic wills, people fail to provide for the disposition of *all* their assets. In a properly drafted will, such disposition is assured by the use of a residuary clause that states: "I leave all the rest and residue of my estate to. . . ." Any assets *not* covered by the will provisions pass by intestate succession.

The intestacy statutes vary from state to state. The intestate law of the decedent's domicile governs passage of personal property; intestate law where the property is located governs real property. Some states have different provisions for the passage of personal property and the passage of real property within the state's control.

Community property states provide for different chains of distribution for community property and separate property. As mentioned in Chapter 41, community property is a form of joint ownership between husband and wife. In states that allow this form of joint ownership, most property that is acquired during marriage is owned one-half by the husband and one-half by the wife.

Generally, legislators enact a statute to dispose of property in the manner they think most people would desire. For example, under the Uniform Probate Code, if the decedent leaves a surviving spouse but no surviving issue or parent(s), the surviving spouse takes all the intestate property.[9] If there are surviving issue who are issue of both the decedent and the surviving spouse, the spouse takes the first $50,000 plus one-half the balance of the estate. The issue would share the rest by per capita at each generation.[10]

These intestate provisions are applicable to separate property states and to separate property in community property states under the Uniform Probate Code. Exhibit 44.3 summarizes the Uniform Probate Code intestate succession provisions for separate property.

EXHIBIT 44.3 Intestate Succession under the Uniform Probate Code[a]

Survivors	Spouse's Share	Remainder of Estate to Others
Spouse (if there is no issue or parent of decedent)	100%	Not applicable
Spouse and issue, all of whom are also issue of the surviving spouse	First $50,000, plus ½ the balance	To the issue, if they are of the same degree of kinship, equally[b]
Spouse and issue, one or more of whom are not issue of the surviving spouse	½ to the spouse	To the issue, if they are of the same degree of kinship, equally[b]
Spouse and parent(s) (if there is no surviving issue)	First $50,000, plus ½ the balance	To parent or parents equally
Issue of decedent (if there is no surviving spouse)	Not applicable	To the issue, if they are of the same degree of kinship, equally[b]
Parent(s) (if there is no surviving spouse or issue)	Not applicable	To parent or parents equally
Issue of parents (if there is no surviving spouse, issue, or parents)	Not applicable	To the issue of the parents or either parent by representation[b]
Grandparents and issue of grandparents (if there is no surviving spouse, issue, parents, or issue of a parent)	Not applicable	½ to paternal grandparent(s) or to their issue[b] if they are both deceased; ½ to maternal grandparent(s) or to their issue[b] if they are both deceased; if there is no grandparent or issue on one side, that share goes to the other side

a. This is a representation of the Uniform Probate Code §§ 2-101-103. It does not reflect the alternative provisions for community property states.

b. These transfers are made per capita at each generation.

NRW CASE 44.1   Management/Personal Law

PROVIDING FOR NRW AND THE FAMILIES

Helen and Elliot are both in excellent health. Helen is pleased with the success and growth of NRW and with its future prospects. Elliot is also doing well in his career. Retirement for either of them is a long way into the future. However, Helen would like to plan now for the future and for any unexpected eventualities. She would also like to make certain that Mai and Carlos could continue to own and operate the firm if anything happens to her, while at the same time providing for her loved ones. She has asked you for advice as to what she can or should do to ensure her wishes are carried out. What advice will you give her?

BUSINESS CONSIDERATIONS What might Mai, Carlos, and Helen do to assure that they continue to operate NRW without any outside interference? Would they be better served by establishing a trust or by making specific provisions in each of their wills?

ETHICAL CONSIDERATIONS Suppose a person decides to write a will and must decide whether to select distribution of the estate per capita, per stirpes, or per capita at each generation. What ethical issues should be considered in making such a decision? Is it ethical to use either a will or a trust in an effort to delay or avoid taxes?

INTERNATIONAL CONSIDERATIONS Are wills and the passing of one's estate to whomever one prefers a common practice in most nations, or is it more common in Anglo-American legal systems? If one of our entrepreneurs were a foreign national from a civil law nation, how might that affect estate planning issues?

Transfer of Business Interests

Participants in closely held businesses, like NRW, have unique estate planning needs regardless of the business form being utilized. In other words, these problems arise with partnerships, corporations, limited liability companies, and so on. When the members desire to maintain the firm and keep the key people in control of it, they may choose some type of buy-sell arrangement. The members enter into an agreement that when a member retires or dies, the member (or his or her estate) will sell the ownership interest to the business itself or to the remaining members. The contract should state what events will "activate" the buy-sell agreement, who will buy the interest, at what price, and whether the sale is mandatory.

One of the difficult issues is the price. The members should strive to set a price that is fair to the other members *and* their families. Generally, members will want to be fair because they do not know whether they will be the buyer or the seller. A specific price could be set, but that might not be a just one, especially if the firm has grown over time. The members could set a price by formula, use an appraiser, or use some form of arbitration. The agreement can be structured so that the business owners retain their proportionate ownership. An awkward financial issue is how the buyers will pay for the interest. The business may have grown quite valuable and the buyer(s) may lack liquidity. One solution is for the purchase price to be paid over time, for example, the business could make payments out of its profits. Another solution is for the purchaser(s) to buy life insurance on the owners to fund the buy-sell agreement.

Yet another variation of this is the right of first refusal, where the business or other owners do not necessarily have to buy the interest. It is simply offered to them first.

Probate and Estate Administration

Probate hearings are a series of hearings in probate court in which the judge makes sure that the estate is being properly administered. The judge will conduct a hearing if any *interested party,* such as a beneficiary, heir, or creditor, contests the validity of the will. For example, an interested party may complain that the testator lacked capacity to make a will; the testator was subject to undue influence, duress or fraud; or the will was not executed in compliance with state law. The judge confirms whether the will is valid and was properly executed under state law. Even after the judge has accepted the validity of the will, this judicial order can be revoked if it is shown that the will was fraudulently offered for probate. The judge supervises the personal representative in the completion of his or her duties.

If the decedent had a valid will that named a representative, that person will be called an *executor.* A court-appointed representative will be called an *administrator.* (Some localities still use the more traditional terminology of calling male representatives executors or administrators, and female representatives executrixes or administratrixes.) The administrator will be appointed according to any guidelines provided in the state probate code. Some states require that an executor or an administrator reside in the same state as the decedent. There usually is a minimum age of 18.

The concept of administering an estate is relatively simple. The personal representative of the estate must advertise in newspapers of general circulation in order to locate the creditors of the deceased. Some states may require personal notice to creditors if the personal representative knows their identity. If a creditor does not file a claim against the estate in a timely manner, the claim will be barred. The representative will also collect the assets of the decedent, collect money owed to the decedent, pay the lawful debts owed by the decedent, pay the necessary expenses of estate administration, and pay any state and/or federal taxes. It is often necessary to sell assets to make these disbursements. The remaining assets are then distributed to the proper beneficiaries. A court generally will oversee this procedure through probate hearings.

The personal representative is responsible for the proper administration and probate of the estate and has fiduciary duties to the lawful beneficiaries of the estate. Personal representatives must make sure that the duties mentioned in this section are properly completed. They have a significant responsibility, for which they receive a fee. They can be *surcharged* (assessed a fee by the court for failure to follow fiduciary duties) from their personal funds if they violate their duties by failing to perform as required or by performing incorrectly. Some common examples of wrongdoing include failure to pay taxes, failure to probate the will, failure to sell assets that are declining in value, failure to minimize taxes, failure to sell assets at a fair price, self-dealing such as selling estate or trust assets to oneself or to a friend, and fraud.

In many jurisdictions, the judge can reduce the commissions paid to the personal representative and the fees paid to the attorney and accountant if they are excessive. Executors, administrators, and, in many states, attorneys usually are paid based on a percentage of the value of the assets in the estate. In some states, maximum fees are established in the probate code.

Avoiding Probate

Often, people believe that it is wise to avoid probate. Examples of property that is not subject to probate include entireties property, joint tenancy with rights of survivorship, and life insurance paid to a named beneficiary. (Refer to Exhibit 41.2 in Chapter 41 for more detail on the forms of joint ownership.) New forms of ownership are being originated that also avoid probate, for example, pay-on-death ownership. When the owner dies, the survivor becomes the next owner. The survivor does not have an interest during the owner's life; consequently that person cannot access the funds and the owner does not require the other person's signature before making transactions involving the property. It is currently available for bank accounts and some government securities, and some states permit pay-on-death registration for securities. The Uniform Transfer on Death Security Registration Act permits investment securities to be held in pay-on-death form, which the Act calls Transfer on Death or TOD. Most states have enacted the Uniform Act.[11]

If, during life, a person places assets into a trust with named beneficiaries, these assets will not be probated. Another option for the property owner is to enter into a valid contract that provides, in part, for the passage of property at the owner's death. All these arrangements may serve as substitutes for a valid will and, depending on state law, may escape the technical requirements of the state statute of wills. However, even assets that are not subject to probate may still be subject to an *estate tax* assessed on the total net (taxable) value of the estate and/or an *inheritance tax* (assessed on transfers of estate assets at the owner's death (with the inheritance tax the rates vary depending on the decedent's relationship to the recipient). A valid will may be advisable even when an owner is trying to avoid probate. The owner may later acquire property that will not avoid probate, such as paychecks and inheritances from other decedents.

Avoiding probate of an estate may reduce the amount of time necessary for the administration of that estate. In the case of joint tenancies with rights of survivorship, one owner will have immediate access to these assets at the other owner's death, although some states restrict this immediate access for bank accounts and safe deposit boxes. An important consideration for some people is the additional privacy afforded by avoiding probate. Probate, like most court proceedings, is part of the public record; anyone who is so inclined can read the will and the inventory of assets. Costs usually are assessed in the probate of an estate; some, such as fees for filing court documents, are nominal. The amount of some fees may be based on the amount and value of probate assets; avoiding probate or reducing the amount of probate assets eliminates or reduces these costs. Probate costs increase markedly when lawsuits arise concerning the validity of the will, its interpretation, or asset distribution. These *will contests* reduce the amount of assets to be distributed to the beneficiaries. Sometimes these contests are caused by poorly drafted wills or holographic wills.

Probate costs and taxes may increase significantly if a person dies intestate or without prudent estate planning. Nolo (Law for All) has a Web site for Wills & Estate Planning at http://www.nolo.com/lawcenter/auntie/index.cfm/catID/FD1795A9-8049-422C-9087838F86A2BC2B/.

Avoiding probate has some disadvantages. The extent to which these concerns are disadvantageous will depend on the people involved and the method used to avoid probate. Some of the techniques—for example, establishing and operating out of a trust—require additional paperwork and attention to detail. Avoiding probate may also create a higher inheritance or estate tax liability on the decedent's estate or on the estates of other family members. In probate, the creditors of the decedent are located and paid, and the estate is discharged of all further obligation to them. Without probate, there is no discharge from potential creditors' claims. In addition, the purpose of probate is to protect lawful beneficiaries and creditors. This may be particularly important when beneficiaries are not knowledgeable or are confused. The court can intervene to protect them from unscrupulous people. Unfortunately, this purpose is not always served effectively under some state probate codes and procedures.

Thus, it is not always advantageous to avoid probate. As with any estate-planning decision, consideration must be given to the individuals and the assets involved. One factor that is often overlooked is that nonprobate assets are generally subject to estate or inheritance taxation.

Legislative sympathy exists for reducing some of the procedures involved in probate. Texas and Washington began permitting executors to perform at least some functions without court supervision. This is called *independent administration,* as distinguished from the more traditional *supervised administration.* In Texas, the testator may indicate that the executor is an *independent executor.* When this occurs, the executor conducts all duties outside the court, except for probating the will and filing an inventory, appraisal of assets, and list of claims against the estate. The Washington provision is similar and is implemented if the testator executes a *nonintervention will.*

The Uniform Probate Code has followed and expanded these examples. Under the Uniform Probate Code, all administrations are unsupervised unless the personal representative or any interested party requests a court ruling to the contrary.[12] Supervised administration, however, is still the majority rule.

The Uniform Probate Code also includes provisions for informal probate with simplified procedures in many situations. A number of states have declined to adopt simplified procedures on the grounds that they do not provide adequate protection from abuses by dishonest and/or incompetent personal representatives.

Transfer Taxes

Federal Transfer Taxes

The federal government taxes the owner when he or she exercises the right to transfer property. This may take the form of gift taxes if the owner transfers the asset during lifetime. You can view a federal gift tax return, Form 709, at the IRS Web site at http://www.irs.gov/pub/irs-pdf/f709.pdf and the instructions at http://www.irs.gov/pub/irs-pdf/i709.pdf. If the transfer is effective on death, a federal estate tax may be due. Estate taxes treat the entire estate as one unit, subject to certain exclusions, deductions, and credits. You can view a federal estate tax return, Form 706, at the IRS Web site at http://www.irs.gov/pub/irs-pdf/f706.pdf and the instructions at http://www.irs.gov/pub/irs-pdf/ i706.pdf. See Exhibits 44.4 through 44.6 on pages 1105–1107 for a simplified explanation of federal transfer taxes. These exhibits are intended to illustrate federal estate taxes and do not use the technical terms. They are correct as of the time of printing; however, tax laws can change very quickly. Recent tax acts increased the credit amount over the next couple of years; consequently, more estate assets can transfer without taxes. The increases are illustrated in Exhibit 44.6. Federal transfer tax rates are progressive, as are federal income tax rates. The federal transfer tax system consists of an estate tax, a gift tax, and a generation-skipping transfer tax. The generation-skipping transfer tax is discussed in the Disadvantages of Trusts section of this chapter. The system attempts to detect and tax all transfers.

Foreign countries have different tax structures. For example, currently there are no estate or inheritance taxes in Canada.[13]

State Transfer Taxes

A few states have gift taxes.[14] States may also have either estate taxes[15] or inheritance taxes.[16] In inheritance taxes, each recipient's share or inheritance is taxed separately. Inheritance taxes are generally based on the recipient's relationship to the decedent and the value of the assets received. The trend seems to be to abolish state inheritance and estate taxes. Most states will impose a "pickup tax" equal to the amount of the credit for state death taxes on the federal estate tax return.[17]

Retirement Plans

People are living longer today, and with this increased longevity comes increased concerns about income during

EXHIBIT **44.4** Overview of the Federal Estate Tax

Gross Estate

        Deduct: Claims, debts, and allowable taxes

                        Administration and funeral expenses

Adjusted Gross Estate

        Deduct: Marital deduction

                        Charitable deduction

Taxable Estate

        Add: Adjusted taxable gifts[a]

Base Amount for Estate Tax

        Calculate tentative estate tax on the base amount using the Estate Tax Rate Schedule in Exhibit 44.5.

        Deduct: Gift tax payable on adjusted taxable gifts[a]

                        Estate Tax Credit from Exhibit 44.6

                        Credit for state death taxes paid (Maximum permitted per IRS table)[b]

Net Federal Estate Tax

a. The federal system is a partially unified system where prior taxable gifts influence the estate tax rates. Consequently, the adjusted taxable gifts are added into the tax base. The gift tax payable is deducted later in the calculation.

b. In states with independent death taxes, the state estate or inheritance taxes may be much greater than the credit for state death taxes. States that do not assess estate or inheritance taxes generally impose a tax equal to the amount of the credit on those estates that are subject to federal estate taxes. The estate will have to pay this amount to either the state or federal government. This is generally called a state "pickup tax."

retirement. Retirement plans are very complex and have both income tax and transfer tax consequences for the family. There are also significant financial and tax effects for the employer. For many people, their pension or retirement plans may be one of their largest assets.

Some plans are employer plans. One type is a *defined-benefit plan*, where the employer promises to pay the retiree a set benefit based upon a percentage of the employee's average earnings and the number of years worked under the plan. The funds for the employees are pooled together; however, the employer keeps separate records on the amount each employee earns. Payments may be made monthly beginning with retirement, or there may be a lump-sum payment at retirement. The retiree may have a choice, or the plan may require one type of payment. The type of payment will have tax consequences. These plans are common for people employed by the military, many unions, and many large companies.

A *defined-contribution plan* is an employer plan where the employer promises to contribute a certain amount to the plan each year, generally a percentage of the worker's earnings. Each employee has a separate account, and the money is invested. When an employee retires, the amount the employee receives is based on the amount contributed plus the earnings. At retirement, payments to the retiree may be periodic or by a lump sum. Again, the type of payment will affect taxation.

Durable Powers of Attorney and Living Wills

Durable powers of attorney can be used to make future financial or medical decisions. A person may create a durable power of attorney because the maker is concerned that he or she may become unavailable, incapacitated, or incompetent. The maker executes a formal document appointing another person to make decisions for the maker. If the appointment is solely for decisions about medical treatment it is called a *durable power of attorney for health care*. A legal durable power of attorney is "durable" because it does not terminate when the maker becomes incompetent.

EXHIBIT 44.5 Estate Tax Rate Schedule

Gross estate taxes are calculated on the estate tax base. Find the appropriate line in the table below. Subtract the amount in column A from the base amount. Multiply the difference by the amount in column D. This is the tax on the excess. Add the tax on the excess to the tax amount from column C. These are the figures for 2002.

A Taxable Amount Over	B Taxable Amount Not Over	C Tax on Amount in Column A	D Rate of Tax on Excess Over Amount in Column A (Percent)
0	10,000	0	18
10,000	20,000	1,800	20
20,000	40,000	3,800	22
40,000	60,000	8,200	24
60,000	80,000	13,000	26
80,000	100,000	18,200	28
100,000	150,000	23,800	30
150,000	250,000	38,800	32
250,000	500,000	70,800	34
500,000	750,000	155,800	37
750,000	1,000,000	248,300	39
1,000,000	1,250,000	345,800	41
1,250,000	1,500,000	448,300	43
1,500,000	2,000,000	555,800	45
2,000,000	2,500,000	780,800	49
2,500,000	—	1,025,800	50

People often include a *living will* as part of their estate plan. This document does not dispose of assets at the owner's death. It explains how the individual feels about certain medical treatments, especially life-prolonging treatment, when the patient is very ill and recovery is doubtful, and it does not appoint someone to make decisions for the maker. The document often states that the living will requests should be honored "if there is no reasonable expectation of recovery." This is often subject to medical interpretation and the medical experts may not agree on this issue. Living wills are popular because of recent developments in medical research that allow a patient to live even though there is little hope of recovery. Problems arise when a patient is physically incapable of making and/or communicating his or her desires about potential medical treatments. Living wills are legal in most states; but compliance with the state statute, of course, is critical.

Trusts Defined

A *trust* is a fiduciary relationship where specific property is transferred to the care of a trustee, or manager. Trusts may be voluntary arrangements created by the property owner, or they may be legal arrangements imposed by the courts or implied by the law in order to reach a fair result. In a trust, legal title and equitable ownership rights are split between two or more people. One person has the legal right to the asset; another person has the beneficial right to the use and enjoyment of the asset. ALI has published the

Decedents Dying in	Unified Credit	Gross Estate Plus Adjusted Taxable Gifts Exceeds[a]
2002 & 2003	$ 345,800	$1,000,000
2004 & 2005	$ 555,800	$1,500,000
2006, 2007 & 2008	$ 780,800	$2,000,000
2009	$1,455,800	$3,500,000

a. This column indicates the amount of gross estate and lifetime taxable gifts together that can be transferred before the estate will be subject to federal estate taxes.

Restatement (Second) of the Law of Trusts, which is a treatise of trust law and includes recommendations on many aspects of trusts. ALI is drafting the third edition of the Restatement of the Law of Trusts. The rules for investors already have been revised and published and ALI is revising the other sections.[18]

Express Trusts

Trusts that are created voluntarily by the owner of the property are called *express trusts.* (Trusts that are created by operation of law are discussed in the section of this chapter on implied trusts.) The owner transfers real or personal property to a trustee for the benefit of a named person. During the period of the trust, the trustee manages the property and pays the income to the people specified in the *trust deed* (a legal document that specifies the recipients of a trust, their interests, and how the trust should be managed; it is also called a *deed of trust*). If the trust is to take effect during the owner's life, it is called an *inter vivos* (lifetime or living) trust. If it is to take effect at death, it is called a *testamentary trust.* Testamentary trusts are usually included as part of the will and do not have a separate trust deed. They must comply with the state's statute of wills.

Generally, at least three people are needed for an express trust: a creator, a trustee, and one or more beneficiaries. A creator also may be called a *settlor* or a *trustor*. The *creator* is the one who establishes the trust and is usually the person who puts assets into the trust. The *trustee*, who may be a person or a business entity, is in charge of managing the assets. *Corpus, res,* or *principal* are the names used for the assets. The *beneficiaries* are the recipients. Depending on the trust instrument, the beneficiaries may receive the income from the assets, the assets themselves, or both. The

Uniform Principal and Income Act of 1997 provides procedures on how to separate principal and income in estates and trusts.[19] Once assets are placed in the trust (or estate), the distinction may be quite complex and includes issues of whether principal or income should be used to pay expenses and taxes. The Act updates two prior Uniform Acts to conform with modern trust investment practices. Consideration is not required to establish a trust.

To be valid, a trust must meet a few requirements. The intention or purpose of the creator must be expressed—for example, by stating that "this trust is established for my children's college educations." In many cases, though, the courts have concluded that the intention of the creator may be inferred from his or her actions if this intention is not stated. Creators commonly establish trusts for one of these purposes: to provide for more than one beneficiary; to protect beneficiaries from themselves and from overreaching by others; and to legally reduce taxes.

Under the Statute of Frauds, most trust deeds must be in writing because they cannot possibly be performed within one year. Even if the Statute of Frauds did not require a writing, it would be foolish to have oral trust provisions. Many potential legal problems do not arise until after the creator has died. Trusts generally contain lengthy and complex provisions about what the trustee can and cannot do; these certainly should be reduced to writing.

A trust may terminate when its purpose is completed or when its term is over. Under some circumstances, the trust may terminate by mutual agreement of all the beneficiaries, or when it becomes uneconomical. Depending on the trust deed, the power to terminate the trust may rest with the trustee, the creator, or someone else. When the trust is terminated, the trust assets are transferred to the specified *remainder beneficiaries* (persons with an interest in what remains in the trust corpus after use by the income

PROTECTING AGAINST FINANCIAL HARDSHIPS

Helen's mother suffered from Alzheimer's disease for three years prior to her death. One of Carlos's brothers was seriously injured in an industrial accident in Spain and spent several years on life support before dying. As a result, Mai, Carlos, and Helen have observed the suffering and the financial hardships that people endure in such a situation. They are determined to do everything in their power to protect their families from this sort of ordeal. They have each asked you for advice on methods for dealing with these sorts of situations. What advice will you give them?

BUSINESS CONSIDERATIONS What can a closely held firm do to protect itself and its constituents in the event a primary policy maker of the firm suffers from a debilitating disease or injury? Should a business have a policy or procedure in place in the event such a situation arises? What if the person is unaware that he or she has become incompetent, such as may occur with Alzheimer's disease or some types of senility? Could a firm purchase insurance to ease the strain? What type(s) of insurance might be appropriate?

ETHICAL CONSIDERATIONS Suppose a person establishes a durable power of attorney for health care issues. What criteria should the "attorney" use in making decisions? Should the "attorney" be concerned only with the wishes of the "maker," or should the desires of the other family members also be considered?

INTERNATIONAL CONSIDERATIONS Assume that Carlos has relatives in Spain who depend on him to supplement their income. Does the nationality of the beneficiaries affect estate planning? How?

beneficiaries.) The *income beneficiaries* are persons with an income interest in the trust.

A *revocable trust* is one that can be revoked or canceled by the creator. In rare instances, the creator may give this power to another individual. This trust usually becomes permanent and irrevocable at the death of the creator. On the other hand, an *irrevocable trust* is one that may not be terminated during the specified term of the trust. Once the assets are placed in trust, they usually must remain there for the term of the trust under the conditions specified in the trust deed.

Whether a trust is revocable or irrevocable depends on the trust document. It is always wise to specify this aspect of the trust; otherwise, state law will govern the trust. In most states, the trust will be irrevocable unless the creator has stated a contrary intention in the trust deed. In a minority of states, including California, it will be presumed to be revocable unless a contrary intention is expressed.

There are various categories of express trusts, based on the clauses contained in the trust deed. A specific trust may contain provisions in more than one of these categories. This sampling of trust provisions indicates the variety that is possible with trusts.

Private Trusts and the Rule against Perpetuities

A *private trust* is one that is not created for the general public good. The beneficiaries of this type of trust are individual citizens and not society as a whole. A private trust is limited by the time period specified in the *rule against perpetuities*. The rule against perpetuities is really a common law rule that prohibits the remote vesting of trust or property interests. It requires that an interest vest within the time limit set by the rule or the interest is invalid. The rule does not apply to interests that are already vested, that is, nonforfeitable, even if the beneficiary will not receive the vested interest until far into the future. The distinction between interests that are vested and those that are not is subtle. This illustration should help. If a trustee had tickets to a concert in three months, beneficiaries with vested interests would be assured that they are entitled to a ticket, even though the concert is in the future. Beneficiaries without vested interests do not know yet whether they will receive a ticket.

Section 1 of the Uniform Statutory Rule Against Perpetuities, drafted by the NCCUSL, states the general rule as follows: "A nonvested property interest is invalid unless: (1) when the interest is created, it is certain to vest or terminate no later than 21 years after the death of an individual then alive; or (2) the interest either vests or terminates within ninety years after its creation." The Uniform Statutory Rule Against Perpetuities with 1990 Amendments has been adopted in about half the states.[20]

Charitable Trusts

A *charitable trust* is a trust where a charity is the beneficiary, and it receives the money for a public purpose. A qualified charity for tax purposes is a corporation organized for religious, charitable, scientific, literary, or educational purposes, including the encouragement of art and the prevention of cruelty to children or animals. Charities also include the United States or any state or political subdivision or any veterans' organization or its departments or posts.[21] Transfers to charities, either outright or in trust, may pass tax free. However, the strict requirements of the Internal Revenue Service must be met. In addition, the charitable organization must qualify under state and federal rules. An organization that qualifies for federal tax purposes may not qualify for state tax purposes. The opposite is also true. California, for example, requires that the organization be a California charity or a national charity that is going to use the assets in California. To qualify for favorable tax treatment under federal law, a trust with char-

itable and noncharitable beneficiaries must meet the stringent requirements imposed by the 1969 Tax Reform Act. In most states, charitable trusts are excluded from the rule against perpetuities.

If the original charitable purpose cannot be fulfilled, a court of equity may apply the *cy pres* doctrine, which permits the court to modify the trust in order to follow the creator's charitable intention as closely as possible. This is usually accomplished by substituting another charitable beneficiary with a similar purpose for the charity initially specified. Before a substitution can occur, it must be shown that the original charity no longer exists or that the original terms no longer apply.

In the following case the trustees petitioned the court to apply the *cy pres* doctrine. Notice the rules used by the court.

44.2

IN RE MARY HOLBROOK RUSSELL MEMORIAL SCHOLARSHIP FUND
730 N.Y.S.2d 702, 2001 N.Y. Misc. LEXIS 322 (Surrogate's Ct., Nassau County 2001)

FACTS The settlors/trustees of an inter vivos charitable trust seek a court order permitting them to terminate the trust. By instrument dated April 2, 1969, the settlors created a trust, the Mary Holbrook Russell Memorial Scholarship Fund, to provide scholarships to students at the Cathedral School of St. Mary, a school in the Episcopal Diocese of Long Island. The trust was named in honor of a former dean and teacher at the Cathedral School of St. Mary. The settlors/trustees established the trust with a minimum amount and public funds were donated to it.

Article FIRST provides in part:

> The trust is organized, and shall be operated, exclusively for educational purposes; in particular, to provide total or partial scholarships for worthy students at The Cathedral School of St. Mary, Garden City, New York (the School), an organization exempt from Federal income tax under section 501(c)(3) of the Internal Revenue Code of 1954, as amended. Such scholarships may include payment of or contributions toward room and board, as well as tuition. The students for whom scholarships shall be provided shall be selected by the Trustees from among lists submitted to the Trustees by the School designating students at, or applicants for admission as students to, the School who require financial assistance, total or partial, in order to attend the School.

An amendment dated September 15, 1969 provides:

> In the event of dissolution of the Trust for any reason, the Trustees shall distribute the entire trust estate to an organization or organizations exempt from taxation under, or in accordance with the purposes recited in, the provisions of Section 501 (c) (3) of the Internal Revenue Code of 1954 or corresponding provisions of future revenue laws.

In 1989, the school merged with the Cathedral School of St. Paul. The trust continued to pay scholarships to female students attending the merged school. By 1991, the school incurred substantial debt and later closed.

In 1995, the trustees of the Mary Holbrook Russell trust petitioned the Surrogate's Court for an order permitting the distribution of the trust corpus (currently in the amount of $65,084) to Mount Holyoke College, the alma mater of Mary Holbrook Russell. The trustees, being of advanced age, sought to terminate the trust rather than continue it with a corpus comprised of a modest sum. In a decision dated September 27, 1995, the court determined that the petition was premature in that it had not been determined that the school would permanently close. The trustees filed this second petition for an order permitting the trust funds to be paid to Mount Holyoke College. The trustees contended that they were authorized to make the distribution under the trust amendment.

ISSUE Should the trustees be permitted to terminate the trust by paying the funds to Mount Holyoke College?

HOLDING No, the trustees should decide on an appropriate beneficiary for the trust funds.

REASONING Excerpts from the opinion of Judge John B. Riordan:

This is a charitable trust. A trust for the advancement of education is for a charitable purpose.[22] The settlors could initially have provided that a charitable beneficiary was to be selected in the discretion of the trustees. The discretionary power was, however, conferred by amendment. Article FOURTH of the trust provided that Article FIRST could not be "amended unless such amendment shall be necessary to exempt the Trust from taxation under the provisions of section 501 (a) of the Internal Revenue Code." The amendment not only required the trustees to apply the funds to a charitable purpose it broadened the power of the trustees to apply the funds to any charitable purpose. The amendment violated the terms of the original trust. Where public contributions are made to a charitable fund the contributions must be applied to the originally stated purpose. The persons who contributed to the trust prior to the amendment are entitled to have their contributions applied to the original purpose.

Under these circumstances it is appropriate to apply the doctrine of *cy pres*. The requirements for *cy pres* are (1) the trust must be charitable in nature; (2) the language of the instrument when read in light of all attendant circumstances must indicate a general rather than specific charitable intent; and (3) the particular purpose for which the trust was created has failed or become impossible or impracticable to achieve. The second condition is satisfied by the language of the instrument and the fact that the fund is substantially comprised of public gifts. Liberally construed the trust instrument expresses a general intention to provide an education to students at an institution supervised by the Episcopal Church. Further, where a charitable trust is funded with public gifts, the donors are presumed to have a general charitable intent. The third condition is met because the school has apparently closed.

The trustees seek to pay the corpus of the trust to Mount Holyoke College. They contend that the college is an appropriate beneficiary because Mary Holbrook Russell was committed to advancing the education of women. Mary Holbrook Russell was not the settlor of this trust nor was she a donor. Under the doctrine of *cy pres* the court must ensure that trust corpus is applied for a charitable purpose falling within the settlors' purpose. It must enforce the intent of the public donors as well. To determine the intention of the settlors the court looks to the trust instrument. . . . The charitable gifts under this trust had several components: (1) to promote the education (2) of female students (3) at an institution affiliated with the Episcopal Church. In applying *cy pres* the court should attempt to satisfy all components. The proposed gift to Mount Holyoke College does not achieve that result.

The trustees are directed to submit an alternative proposal for selection of a beneficiary. . . . The petition is denied to the extent that it seeks an order directing distribution of the corpus . . . to Mount Holyoke College. . . .

BUSINESS CONSIDERATIONS What should a corporate trustee like a bank trust department do in a situation like this? Why?

ETHICAL CONSIDERATIONS Is it ethical to change the purpose of a trust after a number of people have donated money based on the original stated purpose? Under what circumstances, if any, is it ethical to go to court and have a trust modified after the death of the settlor?

Additional Types of Express Trusts

A trust that will accumulate income is called an *accumulation trust*. The trustee will not disburse the income to or for the use of the income beneficiaries or remainder beneficiaries. The earnings will be reinvested in the trust for the period of time specified. Most states restrict the length of time that a private trust can accumulate income to the identical time period prescribed by the *rule against perpetuities*.

A *sprinkling trust* is one that gives the trustee the power to determine which income beneficiaries should receive income each year and how much they should receive. A prudent creator should provide the trustee with some standards to use in making this decision. Income that is not distributed in any particular year is added to the corpus, as in an accumulation trust.

As the name implies, a *spendthrift trust* is established when one or more of the beneficiaries are spendthrifts and need to be protected from their own imprudent spending habits. They are permitted in most, but not all, states. This type of trust also may be used if the beneficiary is unduly subject to manipulation and/or control by family members and friends. Generally, the beneficiary (1) cannot anticipate the receipt of income or corpus from a spendthrift trust, (2) cannot assign it to creditors or borrow against it, and (3) will not necessarily receive all the income earned in any one year. Income will be paid to the beneficiary only when actually necessary. The trustee often will pay it directly to the creditor for services ordered by the trustee. Under some circumstances, creditors *may* be able to attach the trust assets.

A *discretionary trust* allows the trustee to pay or not to pay the income or principal at his or her discretion. It is commonly used in states that either do not allow or greatly restrict spendthrift trusts. In these situations, the creator may name an affectionate family member as an alternate beneficiary and, when the primary beneficiary has difficulties with creditors, the trustee makes the distributions to the alternate. It is hoped that the alternate will feel a moral obligation to care for the primary beneficiary.

Advantages of Trusts

One of the advantages of trusts over other methods of transferring assets is the flexibility that trusts permit. With an outright gift, the gift property belongs to the beneficiary. If that transfer turns out to be inappropriate, generally the transferor cannot change it. With gifts in trust, the trustee maintains control over the assets for a specified period of time under the instructions in the trust deed. For example, a trust can be established for one's children so that each will receive a third of his or her share of the corpus when he or she reaches 25, 30, and 35.

Another aspect of this flexibility is that funding a trust can occur over a period of time. A trust deed can be written to permit the creator to add assets to the trust later. In fact, the trust deed can be written so that other people can add assets to the creator's trust. Moreover, trust income can be paid out to the income beneficiaries based on equal shares, percentages, or need. Beneficiaries can receive the income in a lump sum at the end of the trust or annually, quarterly, monthly, or as needed.

Disadvantages of Trusts

The flexibility of trusts can be an advantage; by the same token, lack of flexibility can be a disadvantage. If a trust is irrevocable and an emergency arises or circumstances change, the trustee generally will be constrained by the trust deed. If the creator did not anticipate this occurrence in the document, the trustee may not be able to modify his or her actions to fit the situation. Another disadvantage of trusts is fees. Rarely is a trustee willing to undertake the responsibility of being a trustee without receiving a fee.

Trusts may also increase the amount of taxes that must be paid, depending on the nature and terms of the trust. Under the tax codes, trusts are taxed in complex ways. Before establishing a trust, one should determine (1) who will pay income tax on its income, (2) who will have the advantage of any income tax deductions, (3) whether the trust will be subject to gift taxes, (4) whether the trust will be subject to estate and/or inheritance taxes when the creator or a beneficiary dies, and (5) whether the trust will be subject to any generation-skipping transfer taxes. A *generation-skipping transfer tax* is a tax imposed on some trust and nontrust transfers to a recipient who is two or more generations younger than the donor. For example, a man who makes a gift to his granddaughter rather than to his daughter makes a generation-skipping transfer. All the tax considerations listed here are complex, with varying tax rates, deductions, exclusions, exemptions, and credits.

Selection of Trustees and Executors

Because trustees and executors have broad powers and broad discretion, it is important to select them wisely. Successor trustees and executors may also be named in a trust or a will in case the first person named is unable or unwilling to serve as the personal representative. If a decedent does not have a valid will naming a suitable executor, the probate court will appoint an administrator for the estate. In such a case, the owner of the assets will have no say in the selection. Trustees may be appointed to invest and protect the estates of the people who are mentally incompetent. Administrators, executors, and trustees may be referred to as *fiduciaries,* since each one has a fiduciary duty to protect the rights of the creator and the beneficiaries.

The legal requirements for who may be a fiduciary are very simple. In most states, the fiduciary must be 18 years of age or older. Some states also require that the fiduciary be a resident of the state. It generally simplifies transactions if the fiduciary does reside in the state.

A common consideration in selecting a fiduciary is whether to select a *corporate fiduciary,* such as the trust department of a bank, or an *individual fiduciary,* such as a family member or a friend. A corporate fiduciary usually does not die or dissolve, often has the expertise needed to do a competent job, and does not need to be bonded for the faithful performance of its duties. Although corporate trustees may last forever, individual trust officers do not. Often, a creator or testator will select a bank because of past dealings with a particular trust officer. Remember, however, that the trust officer may leave or die. Moreover, some corporate trust departments do not earn a very good rate of return on the assets that they invest. The same may be true, though, for any individual trustee. Corporate trustees will require a fee, but they may be willing to negotiate and handle the trust for a smaller fee. Many states have statutes that prescribe the maximum fees.

Individual trustees may be willing to serve without fees. They also may have more knowledge about the business and family members than corporate trustees have. In addition, they may be personally concerned for the well-being of the beneficiaries; they may, however, be biased toward certain beneficiaries. In fact, they may be so closely involved with the family that they will be subject to overreaching by family members.

A decision to choose a corporate trustee may be affected by the selection of individuals available to serve in that capacity. A trustee should be honest, mature, competent, impartial, and knowledgeable and should have the ability and time to make sound business decisions. Obviously, the final selection of any personal representative should depend on the facts and circumstances of each case.

Duties of Trustees and Executors

The trustee has two primary duties in relation to the property in his or her care. First, the trustee is supposed to preserve and protect the trust corpus. This includes identifying the assets, protecting them, and safeguarding them. The other primary function of the trustee is to make the assets productive. In other words, the trustee is supposed to invest and manage the assets to produce income for the beneficiaries. This task must be accomplished without violating the trustee's other duties.

The trustee has some other, more specific duties. They include an obligation to follow the terms of the trust and a duty of care that must be exercised in administering someone else's property. The rule, as stated by a majority of courts, is that a trustee must exercise the degree of *care, skill, and prudence* that a reasonably prudent businessperson would exercise in dealing with his or her own property. This standard is applied whether the person actually possesses the necessary skill and knowledge. A majority of the states have enacted the Uniform Prudent Investor Act (1994) to provide guidance to trustees.[23] The Act takes a portfolio approach to the trust assets, where the court reviews the portfolio as a whole. Under the prior law, still followed in some states, a trustee who lost money on any one investment could successfully be sued, even if the trust assets as a whole had a substantial increase in value. The Uniform Act position is consistent with the concept of a well-rounded portfolio of investments, common in financial planning today. The Act also makes fundamental

---

NRW CASE 44.3   Management/Personal Law

CREATING A TRUST

Carlos would like to create a trust to provide for the education and support of his two nephews in Spain, until each nephew reaches the age of 25. He has asked you what he should include in the proposed trust instrument and also what pitfalls or problems he should seek to avoid in creating the trust. What will you tell him?

BUSINESS CONSIDERATIONS Would it be wise to appoint a business associate as the trustee of a trust? How much latitude should a trustee be given in administering such a trust?

ETHICAL CONSIDERATIONS Is it prudent or ethical to appoint a family member, close family friend, or business associate as trustee? What ethical issues would such an appointment raise? What advantages might such a person have as the trustee?

INTERNATIONAL CONSIDERATIONS What additional issues arise because the nephews are Spanish nationals? What additional information is needed?

---

changes in the way trustees invest, gives trustees broader choices in making investments, and yet still holds them to a strict standard of care.

The trustee also has a duty of loyalty. There are, in reality, two primary aspects of this duty. One is an obligation not to take advantage of situations involving conflicts of interest. In many instances, the trustee has an obligation to avoid even potential conflicts of interest. Obviously, then, a trustee should not personally enter into a transaction with the trust. Such a transaction usually is a breach of fiduciary duty and consequently is voidable and can be set aside. The other aspect of the duty of loyalty is to be as impartial as possible among the beneficiaries. Impartiality is not always possible because there is a natural conflict between the income beneficiaries and the remainder beneficiaries. (Remainder beneficiaries are also called *principal* beneficiaries or *corpus* beneficiaries.) The Uniform Principal and Income Act of 1997 provides guidance on what is income and what is corpus.

As stated by Justice Putnam of the Massachusetts Supreme Judicial Court in the classic decision *Harvard College v. Amory,* "All that can be required of a trustee . . . is that he shall conduct himself faithfully and exercise sound discretion. He is to observe how men of prudence, discretion, and intelligence manage their own affairs, not in regard to speculation, but in regard to the permanent disposition of their funds, considering the probable income, as well as the probable safety of the capital to be invested."[24]

It is commonly stated that a trustee has a duty not to delegate, but this is really just a cautionary note. Not every act of trust administration must be completed by the trustee personally. A trustee may delegate to others the performance of any act or the exercise of any power when it is consistent with the trustee's general duty of care owed to the beneficiaries. In other words, the trustee may employ agents when a reasonably prudent owner of the same type of property with similar objectives would employ agents. In addition, the trustee must exercise due care in selecting and supervising agents. The Uniform Prudent Investor Act (1994) authorizes trustees to utilize portfolio managers and investment advisors.

The trustee must be careful in selecting trust investments. This generally includes a duty to diversify the types of investments. The statutes in many states list or define what investments a trustee may make. These are often called *legal investments*. A creator, however, may grant a trustee the specific power to invest in nonlegal investments. Such a provision gives the trustee broader investment power, *but* it does not remove the general obligation to invest wisely. Obviously, this duty does not imply that the trustee guarantees that all investments will increase in value or that no money will be lost. Generally, trustees limit themselves to conservative investments. The standard test of whether a trustee has fulfilled this obligation is whether other prudent investors, *at that time,* would have chosen other, better investments; the judgment should not be made in hindsight. The trustee may be surcharged for unwise investment decisions and must pay personally for any losses caused by negligent decisions. Under the common law, the trustee may not offset profits on other investments against these losses. The Uniform Prudent Investor Act changes this rule in a majority of states.

The trustee has a duty to maintain clear and accurate records regarding the administration of the trust. This obligation, called the *duty to account,* includes recording the location and type of assets and the receipt and expenditure of income. In some jurisdictions, the trustee must file periodic accountings with the court. In others, it is sufficient for the trustee to account to the trust beneficiaries.

The trustee must not mix his or her personal funds with trust funds, a situation known as *commingling of assets.* The trustee may not borrow money or mortgage trust property unless that power was expressly provided in the trust document. The trustee *will* have the incidental authority to carry out ordinary duties.

The executor's duties parallel those of a trustee. They both have fiduciary duties to the beneficiaries. The executor is responsible for filing estate and inheritance tax returns, paying the applicable taxes, and filing accounts with the probate court. The executor should generally try to complete the estate work and distribute the remaining assets quickly and prudently. This will help prevent a loss in the value of assets.

Implied Trusts

The owner of the assets voluntarily and intentionally creates express trusts. Implied trusts, on the other hand, are created by operation of law—they are either implied by the law or imposed by the courts. Implied trusts may arise in the context of an express trust, but that is not a legal requirement.

Resulting Trusts

A *resulting trust* is based on the owner's presumed intention and occurs when the owner of property disposes of the property but the disposition is not complete. The owner fails to make a complete, effective disposition of all his or her equitable interests. (A disposition will be considered complete if the state rules of trust interpretation determine who receives the interests.) A portion of the owner's interest reverts to the owner or the owner's heirs. A resulting trust will occur only if the owner is acting in good faith. This type of trust most commonly occurs under any one of the following circumstances:

- The owner does not state who should acquire a beneficial interest, such as a remainder interest; for example, the owner transfers a vacation home to a cousin for 10 years.

- The owner does not state what should happen under certain unanticipated situations; for example, a child dies before his or her parents.

- The express trust is not enforceable because it is not in the proper form; for example, the owner fails to name the beneficiaries.

- The express trust fails completely or in part, because it is illegal, impractical, *or* impossible or because a beneficiary refuses an interest in the trust; for example, a charitable purpose becomes impractical and the court finds *cy pres* inapplicable.

A resulting trust also may occur when a person purchases real property with his or her own money and puts the title in the name of another person. The law presumes that the purchaser intends that the recipient hold the property as "trustee" for the purchaser. This is often called a *purchase money resulting trust.* The presumption may be rebutted by evidence that the purchaser has a different intention. In many states, the courts will presume that the purchaser intends a gift, *if* the purchaser and transferee are closely related.

Constructive Trusts

A *constructive trust* is actually an equitable remedy where the court imposes a trust to redress a wrong or to prevent unjust enrichment. A court of equity imposes this trust when a person gains legal title to property but has an equitable duty to transfer the property to someone else. The following are some examples of how this trust can occur:

- A person takes title as a trustee, but the trust is not enforceable; for example, a trustee receives assets under an oral trust that is unenforceable under the Statute of Frauds. To allow the trustee to keep the property would create unjust enrichment.

- A person obtains property by breaching a fiduciary duty; for example, an employee embezzles company funds.

- A person is either guilty of a wrong or would receive unjust enrichment. Depending on state law, the person may be guilty of fraud, conversion, theft, duress, or murder of the transferor. Some situations may involve mistake. For example, the transferor may own two lots and sell one lot to the transferee, but the deed mistakenly mentions both lots. The court will impose a constructive trust on the second lot for the benefit of the transferor.

Constructive trusts are not limited to these situations. As with other equitable remedies, constructive trusts are created to correct unfair results.

In the following case, the court addressed the interrelationship between the remedy of constructive trust in Ohio and federal bankruptcy law. When the court uses the term prepetition, it means before the bankruptcy petition was filed.

44.3

POSS v. MORRIS (IN RE MORRIS)
260 F.3d 654, 2001 U.S. App. LEXIS 18266 (6th Cir. 2001)

FACTS Marilyn E. Morris wished to relocate her business from Newbury, Ohio, to Rock Creek, Ohio. She was unable to secure conventional financing. John Poss, a longtime friend, loaned her $17,500 to purchase a 17.5-acre parcel. Morris took title to the property. Poss did not execute a mortgage. The only evidence of the loan was a note that provided for repayment over 15 years. Morris made some payments to Poss, but they did not comply with the terms of the note. Morris convinced Poss to finance the construction of a building on the property. Poss advanced an additional $149,750 without taking any security interest. To maximize his tax position, Poss leased from Morris the two-and-one-half acres on which the business was to be located. He constructed the building to Morris's specifications and then leased the structure to her for 15 years with a monthly payment intended to amortize his own payments. Neither one made any lease payments.

Morris obtained a $40,000 mortgage on the property without Poss's knowledge. When Poss learned about the mortgage, he filed suit on the note and obtained a judgment. Morris failed to pay the judgment, so Poss brought a foreclosure action. Poss also brought a second action to recover the lease payments due for the building. The court consolidated the suits and entered judgment for Poss. The parties tried to negotiate their differences and when that was not successful, Poss filed a forcible entry and detainer action to remove Morris from the property. Then the parties executed a settlement agreement requiring Morris to vacate the building by January 1, 1994 and convey a specific 7.735-acre parcel to Poss within 60 days. The judges in two actions entered judgments adopting the agreement. Morris requested relief from the judgment. Her request was denied and she was ordered to comply with the judgment. Poss obtained an order from the court requiring the county recorder to convey the 7.735-acre parcel to him. The court issued a writ to the sheriff to seize the property. On September 8, 1995, Morris filed a voluntary petition for bankruptcy under Chapter 13, listing the 17.5-acre property and the debts associated with it.

ISSUE Is Poss entitled to a constructive trust on the property?

HOLDING Yes, Ohio law impressed a constructive trust on the property in favor of Poss prior to the day on which Morris filed her bankruptcy petition.

REASONING Excerpts from the opinion of Circuit Judge Alice M. Batchelder:

[The bankruptcy code] does not authorize bankruptcy courts to recognize a constructive trust based on a creditor's claim of entitlement to one. . . . [O]ur task is to determine whether Ohio law impressed the property in dispute with a constructive trust prior to the time Morris filed her petition. The Ohio Supreme Court has defined a constructive trust as:

> A trust by operation of law which arises contrary to intention . . . against one who, by fraud, actual or constructive, by duress or abuse of confidence, by commission of wrong, or by any form of unconscionable conduct, artifice, concealment, or questionable means, or who in any way against equity and good conscience, either has obtained or holds the legal right to property which he ought not, in equity and good conscience, hold and enjoy. It is raised by equity to satisfy the demands of justice.

Under this definition, constructive trust is a remedy used by courts for the prevention of fraud, unjust enrichment, or other inequitable conduct. Further, the Ohio Supreme Court has counseled the imposition of a constructive trust "where it is against the principles of equity that the property be retained by a certain person even though the property was acquired without fraud." As a prerequisite to the imposition of a constructive trust, a case must give rise to jurisdiction by a court of equity. . . . Ohio follows the traditional rule of the common law that regards contracts for the conveyance of real property as falling within the jurisdiction of courts of equity because of the inherent inadequacy of any legal remedy. . . . Equitable jurisdiction in Ohio extends broadly so that a court may fashion any relief just and appropriate for the circumstances. . . . [U]nder Ohio law a contract for the conveyance of real property falls squarely within the equitable jurisdiction to fashion an appropriate remedy. Essentially, Ohio courts will use the remedy of constructive trust "where there is some ground . . . upon which equity will grant relief." In these situations, Ohio law creates an equitable duty to convey property. . . . [I]t is clear that a constructive trust . . . attached to the property prepetition. . . . [Ohio] Judge Yost found that following the settlement Poss had an enforceable contract for conveyance of the property. Under Ohio law, this contract is enforceable in equity, and . . . Morris had a duty to convey the property. Where such a duty exists, a constructive trust arises by operation of law. . . . [The] language of Judge Yost's opinion emphasizing that Morris retained legal ownership of the property reinforces our conclusion that Morris held equitable title in constructive trust for Poss. . . . [A]nother fact convinces us that this case does not involve an ordinary equitable interest . . . : the "contract" between the parties here is the order of a court. The interest of the Ohio judiciary in ensuring the efficacy of its judgments gives the settlement a heightened basis for equitable relief and calls for imposition of a constructive trust. . . .

Under Ohio law, "where a person holding title to property is subject to an equitable duty to convey it to another" a constructive trust arises by operation of law and attaches to that property. . . . Judge Yost determined that the parties' interests in the disputed property changed when Poss and Morris entered into the settlement agreement. At that point Judge Yost determined that Morris no longer retained equitable title to the property. We have already concluded that by imposing a duty on Morris to convey the property this agreement impressed the property with a constructive trust by operation of law. Although our research has failed to locate authority directly on point, we think that Ohio law creates a constructive trust at the moment the law imposed an equitable duty on Morris to convey the property. Whether . . . that duty arose when the parties entered into the settlement agreement or the . . . court adopted the settlement . . . , it is clear that Ohio law impressed the property with a constructive trust long before Morris filed her petition for bankruptcy. . . . Under section 541(d), "property of the estate" includes all property to which the debtor holds legal title, except "to the extent of any equitable interest in such property that the debtor does not hold. Because the debtor does not own an equitable interest in property he holds in trust for another, that interest is not 'property of the estate.' " . . . Because the property had been impressed by operation of state law with a constructive trust more than ninety days prior to the filing of Morris's petition for bankruptcy, equitable title in the property never became property of the estate, and Morris holds no interest in the property. . . .

BUSINESS CONSIDERATIONS How should Morris and Poss have handled their business dealings? What behaviors caused the most problems?

ETHICAL CONSIDERATIONS Did Morris treat Poss in an ethical manner? Why or why not?

Summary

A will states how a person would like to have property pass at his or her death. This property includes business assets, such as patents, copyrights, and ownership interests in business enterprises. For a will to be valid, a person must intend it to be his or her will, the person must have testamentary capacity, and the will must conform to the state's statutory requirements. Some legal documents, such as trusts and deeds for property, can act as substitutes for will provisions. In the absence of a valid will, the property passes by intestate succession, which is controlled by state law. A formal will is drafted by an attorney, the state legislature (with statutory wills), or the testator. This is the most common type of will. It must be signed by the testator and witnessed by two disinterested witnesses. Self-proved wills can permit the probate of the will without locating the witnesses. Some states also permit nuncupative (oral) wills and holographic (handwritten) wills.

Most estates are subject to probate proceedings. During the hearings, the probate court oversees the proper administration of the estate by the personal representative. The representative must pay debts, collect assets, pay taxes, and distribute assets to the beneficiaries.

Living wills explain the individual's desires concerning medical treatment, if the maker is unable to speak for him-self or herself. Durable powers of attorney allow the maker to designate a person to make financial or medical decisions for him or her. These documents are especially important to health care providers.

An express trust is an arrangement whereby the owner of assets voluntarily places the legal ownership in a trustee and the equitable ownership in one or more beneficiaries. Creators are motivated to establish trusts for many purposes, including the following: (1) to protect beneficiaries from themselves and creditors, (2) to free beneficiaries from the responsibilities of asset management, (3) to split an asset or estate among multiple beneficiaries, (4) to test a pattern of transfers before finalizing it, (5) to save taxes, and (6) to increase flexibility. The trustee is obligated to manage the trust assets prudently. Trustees are often business entities. Trusts can be flexible and are established to accommodate numerous situations, but they may be expensive because of trustee's fees and added tax burdens. Care must be utilized in selecting an appropriate trustee, because a trustee has broad discretion in managing the trust. The trustee must exercise due care in selecting investments for the trust. He or she may be surcharged for making careless decisions or violating his or her fiduciary duties.

Discussion Questions

1. What problems may occur if a person chooses to write a holographic will? What advantages might there be to writing a holographic will?

2. Rufino has inherited a million dollars from his parents' estate. Rufino, who has an extremely low IQ, wants to have his attorney write a will leaving his estate to his gardener and excluding his nieces and nephews. Can such a will be valid? If so, under what circumstances?

3. Karina is writing a new will. She is quite displeased with her sister. She intends to include the following statement in her will: "To my sister, Rosa, I leave nothing. She has lied and cheated and will never amount to anything." Karina asks for your advice. What would you recommend and why?

4. Rachael bequeaths the remainder of her estate "to Bank of America in trust to pay all the income to Bill for life, and on Bill's death to transfer the remainder to Bill's issue who are still alive." Bill dies without having any issue.

The will has no provision controlling this situation. What will happen? Why?

5. What will be the intestate distribution under the Uniform Probate Code when a husband dies survived by his wife and his mother?

6. Distinguish strict per stirpes distributions from per capita at each generation distributions. When will the shares be the same? When will they be different?

7. What are the differences between estate taxes and inheritance taxes?

8. How do defined-benefit plans and defined-contribution plans differ?

9. What are the advantages and disadvantages of living wills?

10. Executors and trustees may be asked to serve without fees. Why might they be reluctant to do so? Under what circumstances might they be willing to do so?

Case Problems and Writing Assignments

1. Margarita Savain executed a will on October 7, 1983 (will #1). Savain was admitted to the hospital early in May 1992, and she was apparently dying. One of the medicines administered to her was Demerol, a narcotic painkiller. As a consequence, there was conflicting information about her state of mind while she was on the medication. While in the hospital, she signed another will (will #2). In this will, she left all her property to her "good friend" and tenant, John Shack. John Shack contacted an attorney on May 8, 1992. The attorney prepared will #2 according to Shack's instructions and delivered it to the hospital the same day. Shack paid for the preparation of the will. The attorney did not know Savain prior to the signing of the will. The signing of will #2 was witnessed by Shack's employer and a hospital nurse, Ms. Melisano, who was instructed to act as a witness by her supervisor. Melisano said that when she arrived in the hospital room, Shack, his employer (who had recommended the attorney to Shack), and the attorney were already there. She asked if they had read the will to Savain and they indicated that they had. It was not read again in her presence. Savain signed the document and Melisano signed at the request of the attorney. Savain did not make any statements about the document, although the attesting clause said it was her will. The discussion at the time centered around Savain's return to her home and getting food for her.

   On May 12, 1992, Savain executed a third instrument (will #3), naming Ecedro Rabsatt as the sole beneficiary of her estate. Rabsatt had been a close friend of Savain's for a long time. Will #3 was drafted by Rita James, a nonlawyer who used to work as a legal secretary. Savain met with James several weeks prior to entering the hospital to outline the will provisions. James was not paid for preparing will #3. The attesting witnesses were Rabsatt's cousin, Randolph Thomas, and James's common law husband, Alvin Canton. (A *common law husband* is a husband who did not participate in the usual wedding ceremony with a legal marriage license. The states that recognize common law marriages generally require that the couple consistently live together and tell people that they are husband and wife.) Both had a long-time relationship with Rabsatt. Thomas testified that, at the signing, Savain never discussed the fact that the document was her will. He also indicated that Rabsatt, not Savain, asked him to sign the document. Savain died on May 24, 1992. Were wills #2 and/or #3 executed properly? Did John Shack and his employer behave ethically? Did Ecedro Rabsatt and his friends and relatives behave ethically? Did Melisano have a duty to speak out if Savain seemed incompetent or confused? To whom should she communicate her concerns? [See *Rabsatt v. Estate of Savain*, 878 F. Supp. 762 (D.V.I. 1995).]

2. The elderly Ms. Annie Bell Smith was diagnosed with terminal lung cancer in December 1994. On January 31, 1995, she executed a will leaving the bulk of her estate to her brother-in-law, Caesar Smith and his wife Lois Smith, who were assisting Ms. Smith and providing her with care. The will also named Caesar Smith as sole executor. Ms. Smith executed another will on March 10, 1995, while she was hospitalized. Ms. Smith's cousin, Dorothy Davis-Murchison, had been coming to town to visit Ms. Smith since learning of her terminal illness. Murchison was at the hospital at the time of the execution of the March will. This will made some specific bequests to friends and family members, including an invalid brother, but left the bulk of the estate to Murchison. It provided a specific bequest to Murchison as well as naming her the residuary beneficiary. In the event that Murchison failed to survive the testatrix, the property was to go to Murchison's daughter. Murchison's name was also handwritten into a space provided for the recipient of any remaining balances on all bank accounts; the name "Lois Smith" had been written in the space but was lined through and initialed "A.B.S." There was also a handwritten provision, again apparently initialed by the testatrix, appointing Murchison as executor. The will bore Murchison's own initials on a change in a bequest to Ms. Smith's brother. The will made no mention of Caesar Smith or any provision for him or for his wife Lois; Ms. Smith later commented to Lois that Murchison had "rewritten her will" and that Lois was not mentioned. On March 20, 1995, Murchison accompanied Ms. Smith to the probate court, where Ms. Smith's January will was on file. Ms. Smith was on oxygen and appeared to be clad in a nightgown or robe. Murchison did most of the talking. Ms. Smith's January will was withdrawn and a will dated March 10, 1995, was filed. The probate judge, who in his capacity as private attorney had drafted the January will, told Ms. Smith that he wanted to make a copy of the January will before she withdrew it. Murchison cautioned Ms. Smith to write "cancelled" or "revoked" on the January will. Ms. Smith wrote "revoked" across the January will, or the judge or Murchison wrote it at Smith's direction, and the judge made a copy of it. Murchison took photographs of Ms. Smith's actions in the probate court. Toward the end of her illness, Ms. Smith was suffering a lot of pain and was often medicated. She died April 16, 1995. The original January will was not found after her death; Murchison maintained that Ms. Smith had torn it up. Caesar Smith petitioned to probate the copy of the January will. Murchison petitioned to probate the March will. After a two-day trial, a jury determined that the January will was not revoked. Was Ms. Smith's January will validly revoked? [See *Murchison v. Smith*, 508 S.E.2d 641, 1998 Ga. LEXIS 1010 (Ga. 1998).]

3. Patrick M. Martin challenged the sale of estate property by Alice M. Karlebach, executor of the estate of Rose Gennett Martin. Rose was Karlebach's mother and Martin's grandmother. At the time of her death, Rose owned 35 of the 80 outstanding shares in Refrigeration Supplies Distributors, Inc. (RSD), a family business. Karlebach, who is Martin's aunt, is an officer, director, and shareholder in RSD. Rose's will made Martin a beneficiary of one-sixth of her residuary estate. The

will also named Karlebach executor. To pay estate taxes, Karlebach decided to sell a portion of the estate's RSD shares to RSD. RSD and Karlebach hired Cronkite & Roda, an independent professional appraiser, to place a value on the shares. In September 1995, Cronkite & Roda told Karlebach and RSD that the 35 RSD shares were worth $9.7 million, or approximately $277,142.86 per share, on the date of Rose's death. Following a vote of RSD's board of directors, RSD redeemed 22.5 shares for $6.235 million in November 1995. Martin alleged that Karlebach had secured the probate court's approval of the estate accounting without informing the court that she had a conflict of interest with respect to the sale of the shares. The IRS began an audit of the estate tax return. It told Karlebach that it disputed the redemption value of the shares. On December 10, 1997, Martin filed a petition to vacate the sale of the shares. The petition contended that the sale was voidable at his request because Karlebach, as executor, had breached her duty under the Probate Code not to purchase estate property indirectly without his consent. Should the court grant Martin's request to set aside the sale of the shares? [See *Martin v. Karlebach*, 1999 Cal. App. LEXIS 599, 86 Cal. Rptr. 2d 37 (Cal. Ct. App. 2nd Dist. 1999), Petition for Review Denied by the California Supreme Court, 1999 Cal. LEXIS 6924 (Cal. 1999).]

4. Mr. LaVern and Mrs. Amelia Wiemer entered into a trust agreement, with Havana Bank as trustee, to enable them to purchase and work a farm. As part of the financial arrangement, Northwestern Mutual executed a $70,000 first mortgage on the farm; Havana held the second mortgage. After Mr. Wiemer died, Havana took $8,000 from the trust account and paid itself part of its own second mortgage. Consequently, the trust was unable to make the next payment to Northwestern, and Northwestern foreclosed on the first mortgage. Did the trustee breach its trust duties? [See *Northwestern Mutual Life Insurance Co. v. Wiemer,* 421 N.E.2d 1002 (Ill. App. 1981).]

5. BUSINESS APPLICATION CASE Milton Hershey founded the Hershey chocolate company. He also established Hershey, Pennsylvania, to support the plant and his employees. He was successful and his business grew. He provided numerous services to the community and engaged in philanthropic acts including the establishment of the Milton Hershey School, which has been called the "ritziest orphanage in history." Hershey played an active role in the boys' orphanage during his life. The school now admits girls and students no longer have to be orphans. In 1918, he established a trust with all his Hershey stock and made the school the beneficiary. (Milton Hershey's will is available online through the Milton Hershey School Alumni Association Web site, along with his trust agreement and related court documents, at http://www.mhsaa.org/Lib/. Click on Legal for a directory of the documents.) Consequently, the trust became the majority shareholder of the company. Hershey and his three top advisers were on the board of Hershey trust. During Hershey's life, the leaders of the trust, the chocolate company, and the town's key institutions were the same people. In the 1970s, the trustees began to be uncomfortable with the fact that Hershey Foods

stock made up 80 percent of the trust corpus. A couple techniques were used to create a little diversification. In December 2001, a representative from the state attorney general's office suggested to the trustees that they should further diversify the trust assets, so, in 2002, they told Hershey Foods to look for a buyer. They received two viable offers: one for $12.5 billion from Wrigley and one for $11.2 billion from a combination of Nestlé and Cadbury Schweppes. Despite the fact that these companies had agreed to maintain the employees and facilities in Hershey, Pennsylvania, the townspeople began a protest. Said Bruce McKinney, "We weren't going to stand by and let someone tear apart the quilt. The community came together in a firestorm of protest to fulfill the prophecy of Mr. Hershey."[25] What should the trust do when it is mostly invested in one company? Does it matter if the founder of the company and the settlor of the trust are the same person? To whom do the trustees owe fiduciary duties? [See Kristine Larsen, "Sweet Surrender," *Fortune* (October 14, 2002): 224–234).]

6. ETHICAL APPLICATION CASE Ted Williams was a baseball legend and he was the last major league hitter to bat better than .400 in a season. He died recently at the age of 83. According to his daughter Barbara Joyce Williams Ferrell, he wanted to have his body cremated and the ashes spread over the Florida Keys, which is confirmed by his will. Her half-brother, John Henry Williams, however, had the body moved to the Alcor Life Extension Foundation in Scottsdale, Arizona, to be frozen. Albert Cassidy, executor of Williams's estate, says that he changed his mind after writing the will. Barbara wants to go ahead and have Williams cremated. She claims that her half-brother wants to sell Williams's DNA. What should be done with Williams's body? Why? Assume that John Henry Williams does want to sell the DNA. Should there be any restrictions on the selling of DNA? What should they be? [See "Lawyer Says Williams Wanted to Be Cremated," *USA Today,* July 9, 2002; Laura Parker, "Williams' Will, Wishes May Be in Conflict," *USA Today,* July 16, 2002.]

7. CRITICAL THINKING CASE In December 1998, Dr. Warren Sisson retained Attorney Shari Jankowski to prepare his will and other estate planning documents. Dr. Sisson informed her that he was suffering from bladder and prostate cancer, did not want to die intestate, and wished to prepare a will that would pass his entire estate to his brother, Thomas Sisson. Dr. Sisson is alleged to have said that he was particularly interested in ensuring that none of his estate pass to his other brother, John Sisson, from whom he was estranged. Jankowski prepared a will and other estate planning documents in accordance with Dr. Sisson's instructions. Thomas Sisson says he contacted Jankowski to tell her that Dr. Sisson wanted to finalize his estate planning documents quickly because of his deteriorating condition. On February 1, 1999, Jankowski and two employees of her law firm visited Dr. Sisson in the nursing home for the purpose of witnessing his execution of those documents. Dr. Sisson executed all of the estate planning documents except his will. After Jankowski raised an issue regarding whether the will should include provisions for a

contingent beneficiary, Dr. Sisson expressed his desire to insert such a clause, thereby providing that his estate would pass to a charity in the event Thomas predeceased him. Dr. Sisson's testamentary intent was clear: the unexecuted will accurately expressed his intent to pass his entire estate to Thomas, but simply omitted provision for a contingent beneficiary. Jankowski left a "seriously ill" client (Dr. Sisson) without obtaining his signature on the will when there were other alternatives. These alternatives included: (a) modifying the will immediately by inserting a brief, handwritten amendment providing for a contingent beneficiary, or (b) modifying the will at her office and returning later that day to secure Dr. Sisson's signature under the requisite formalities, or (c) advising Dr. Sisson to execute the will as drafted to avoid the risk of dying intestate (which he plainly wished to avoid) and simply arranging to have him execute a codicil later providing for the contingent beneficiary. Three days later Jankowski returned with the revised will. It was not executed, however, because she did not believe Dr. Sisson was then competent to execute it and left without securing his signature. After February 4, 1999, Jankowski made no attempt to determine whether Dr. Sisson had regained sufficient testamentary capacity to execute his will. On February 16, 1999, Dr. Sisson died intestate and his $2 million estate did not pass entirely to Thomas, as Dr. Sisson had intended. Under New Hampshire law can Thomas sue Jankowski and her law firm for malpractice? Should he be able to do so? [See *Sisson v. Jankowski*, 2002 U.S. Dist. LEXIS 1946 (D.N.H. 2002) (Not for publication.).]

8. YOU BE THE JUDGE Dana Ewell's father, mother, and sister were murdered in their home on April 19, 1992, Easter weekend. Dana is accused of hiring Joel P. Radovich, his former college roommate, to murder his family in order to split their $8 million estate. The prosecutor has asked for the death penalty against both men. Both defendants have pleaded not guilty. After the murders, Dana was made the trustee of the affairs of Glee Mitchell, his 90-year-old maternal grandmother. Investigators contend he spent about $93,000 of estate funds for the care of Glee Mitchell, who resides in a Turlock convalescent home. Initially, he withdrew funds from Mitchell's accounts at the rate of about $1,000 a month for his own use. The rate of withdrawal increased, and, prior to his arrest, he withdrew funds at the rate of about $10,000 a month. Meanwhile, he wrote many checks from the trust account, including checks for more than $15,000 to a Fresno law firm, checks for $5,500 in flying lessons for Radovich, checks for almost $40,000 for his girlfriend, Monica Zent, and checks for $2,500 to Neiman Marcus. Checks were also written to the Fresno County Library and the RD Fund for the Blind and for car detailing, doctors, pest control, utility bills, cleaning, and magazine subscriptions. Reports indicate that Dana spent over $160,000 on himself and his friends. He even incurred fees for excessive activity on some of Mitchell's accounts. Spokespersons for Dana indicate that Mitchell was always generous with family members and that Mitchell encouraged Dana to spend even more money on himself. Does a business or charity have an obligation to scrutinize the source of checks received to determine if the check is drawn on a trust account? Is this an overwhelming burden to place on businesses or charities? Why or why not? [See Jerry Bier, "Third Ewell Judge Ousted," *The Fresno Bee*, January 26, 1996, pp. B1, B3; Tom Kertscher, "Ewell Allegedly Misused $160,000," *The Fresno Bee*, June 19, 1995, pp. A1, A10; Tom Kertscher, "Ewell Uncles Win Round: Aunt Can't Move Money," *The Fresno Bee*, April 7, 1995, pp. A1, A14.]

Notes

1. The following states have adopted all or almost all of the Uniform Probate Code: Alaska, Arizona, Colorado, Hawaii, Idaho, Maine, Michigan, Minnesota, Montana, Nebraska, New Jersey, New Mexico, North Dakota, Pennsylvania, South Carolina, South Dakota, Utah, and Wisconsin. The District of Columbia, the Virgin Islands, and all the other states, except Louisiana, have adopted some sections of the code. Some of these states have adopted whole sections or articles of the code. "A Few Facts about the Uniform Probate Code," NCCUSL Web site, http://www.nccusl.org/nccusl/uniformact_factsheets/uniformacts-fs-upc.asp (accessed 12/03/02) and a telephone conversation with Katie Robinson, Public Affairs Coordinator, NCCUSL, on March 24, 2000.

2. Milton Hershey was the founder of Hershey chocolate. His will, trust, and related documents are available online through the Milton Hershey School Alumni Association Web site at http://www.mhsaa.org/Lib/.

3. California Probate Code, § 6111(a).

4. 79 *American Jurisprudence 2d, Wills,* §§ 733, 740 (Rochester, N.Y.: Lawyers' Cooperative, 1962); kept current with periodic updates.

5. *The Book of the States,* 1990–91 ed., Vol. 28 (Lexington: Council of State Governments, 1990), p. 417.

6. 79 *American Jurisprudence 2d, Wills,* §§ 733, 740 (Rochester, N.Y.: Lawyers' Cooperative, 1962); kept current with periodic updates.

7. See California Probate Code, § 329, for an example of a probate code section permitting self-proving wills.

8. The Revised Uniform Anatomical Gift Act (1987) has been adopted in Arizona, Arkansas, California, Connecticut, Hawaii, Idaho, Indiana, Iowa, Minnesota, Montana, Nevada, New Hampshire, New Mexico, North Dakota, Oregon, Pennsylvania, Rhode Island, U.S. Virgin Islands, Utah, Vermont, Virginia, Washington, and Wisconsin. "A Few Facts about the Uniform Anatomical Gift Act (1987)," NCCUSL Web site, http://www.nccusl.org/nccusl/uniformact_factsheets/uniformacts-fs-aga87.asp (accessed 12/03/02).

9. Uniform Probate Code, § 2-102(1).

10. Ibid, §§ 2-102(3), 2-103, and 2-106 as amended in 1990.

11. The Uniform TOD Security Registration Act has been adopted by Alabama, Alaska, Arizona, Arkansas, California, Colorado, Connecticut, Delaware, District of Columbia, Florida, Georgia, Hawaii, Idaho, Illinois, Indiana, Iowa, Kansas, Kentucky, Maine, Maryland, Massachusetts, Michigan, Minnesota, Mississippi, Missouri, Montana, Nebraska, Nevada, New Hampshire, New Jersey, New Mexico, North Dakota, Ohio, Oklahoma, Oregon, Pennsylvania,

Rhode Island, South Carolina, South Dakota, Tennessee, Utah, Vermont, Virginia, Washington, West Virginia, Wisconsin, and Wyoming. New York and North Carolina have introduced bills to adopt the act. "A Few Facts about the TOD Security Registration Act," NCCUSL Web site, http://www.nccusl.org/nccusl/uniformact_why/uniformacts-why-utsra.asp (accessed 1/7/03), and "Why States Should Adopt the Uniform TOD Security Registration Act," NCCUSL Web site, http://www.nccusl.org/nccusl/uniformact_why/uniformacts-why-utsra.asp (accessed 1/7/03).

12. Uniform Probate Code, § 3-502.

13. Gary Dick, Insurance & Estate Preservation, Web site at http://www.mnsi.net/~gdick/estateplan.html (accessed 12/5/02).

14. The only states that still have a gift tax are Connecticut, Delaware, Louisiana, North Carolina, and Tennessee. Joshua S. Rubenstein and Eileen Caulfield Schwab, "Historic New York Estate and Gift Tax Reform," *New York Law Journal*, August 20, 1997, p. 1.

15. The states that have an independent estate tax are Ohio and Oklahoma. Ibid.

16. The states that have an independent inheritance tax are Delaware, Indiana, Iowa, Kansas, Kentucky, Louisiana, Maryland, Michigan, Nebraska, North Carolina, Pennsylvania, South Dakota, and Tennessee. In Mississippi, Montana, and New Jersey, the death tax is limited to the death tax credit for property passing to spouses and descendants. These states have an inheritance tax for property passing to other people. Ibid.

17. The states that limit their death tax to the federal state death tax credit are Alabama, Alaska, Arizona, Arkansas, California, Colorado, Connecticut, District of Columbia, Florida, Georgia, Hawaii, Idaho, Illinois, Maine, Massachusetts, Minnesota, Mississippi, Missouri, Montana, Nevada, New Hampshire, New Jersey, New Mexico, New York, North Dakota, Oregon, Rhode Island, South Carolina, Texas, Utah, Vermont, Virginia, Washington, West Virginia, Wisconsin, and Wyoming. Ibid.

18. American Law Institute Catalog Web site, http://www.ali.org/ali/Trusts.htm (accessed 12/4/02).

19. The Uniform Principal and Income Act has been adopted by Alabama, Arizona, Arkansas, California, Colorado, Connecticut, District of Columbia, Florida, Hawaii, Idaho, Indiana, Iowa, Kansas, Maine, Maryland, Missouri, Nebraska, New Jersey, New Mexico, New York, North Dakota, Oklahoma, Pennsylvania, South Carolina, Tennessee, Virginia, Washington, West Virginia, and Wyoming. "A Few Facts about the Uniform Principal and Income Act," NCCUSL Web site, http://www.nccusl.org/nccusl/uniformact_factsheets/uniformacts-fs-upia.asp (accessed 12/03/02).

20. The Uniform Statutory Rule Against Perpetuities Act with 1990 amendments has been adopted in Alaska, Arizona, California, Colorado, Connecticut, District of Columbia, Florida, Georgia, Hawaii, Indiana, Kansas, Massachusetts, Michigan, Minnesota, Montana, Nebraska, Nevada, New Jersey, New Mexico, North Carolina, North Dakota, Oregon, South Carolina, South Dakota, Tennessee, Utah, Virginia, Washington, and West Virginia. "A Few Facts about the Uniform Statutory Rule Against Perpetuities Act," NCCUSL Web site, http://www.nccusl.org/nccusl/uniformact_factsheets/uniformacts-fs-usrap.asp (accessed 12/03/02).

21. Internal Revenue Code, § 2055.

22. *Restatement (Second) of Trusts*, § 370.

23. The Uniform Prudent Investor Act has been adopted by Alaska, Arizona, Arkansas, California, Colorado, Connecticut, District of Columbia, Hawaii, Idaho, Illinois, Indiana, Iowa, Kansas, Maine, Massachusetts, Michigan, Minnesota, Missouri, Nebraska, New Hampshire, New Jersey, New Mexico, North Carolina, North Dakota, Ohio, Oklahoma, Oregon, Pennsylvania, Rhode Island, South Carolina, Tennessee, Utah, Vermont, Virginia, Washington, West Virginia, and Wyoming. Maryland has adopted an act that is substantially similar to the uniform act. "A Few Facts about the Uniform Prudent Investor Act," NCCUSL Web site, http://www.nccusl.org/uniformact_factsheets/uniformacts-fs-upria.asp (accessed 12/03/02).

24. 9 Pick. 446, 461 (1930).

25. Kristine Larsen, "Sweet Surrender," *Fortune* (October 14, 2002): pp. 224–234, at 226.

The Constitution of the United States

PREAMBLE

We the People of the United States, in Order to form a more perfect Union, establish Justice, insure domestic Tranquility, provide for the common defense, promote the general Welfare, and secure the Blessings of Liberty to ourselves and our Posterity, do ordain and establish this Constitution for the United States of America.

ARTICLE I

Section 1. All legislative Powers herein granted shall be vested in a Congress of the United States, which shall consist of a Senate and House of Representatives.

Section 2. The House of Representatives shall be composed of Members chosen every second Year by the People of the several States, and the Electors in each State shall have the Qualifications requisite for Electors of the most numerous Branch of the State Legislature.

No Person shall be a Representative who shall not have attained to the Age of twenty five Years, and been seven Years a Citizen of the United States, and who shall not, when elected, be an Inhabitant of that State in which he shall be chosen.

Representatives and direct Taxes shall be apportioned among the several States which may be included within this Union, according to their respective Numbers, which shall be determined by adding to the whole Number of free Persons, including those bound to Service for a Term of Years, and excluding Indians not taxed, three fifths of all other Persons. The actual Enumeration shall be made within three Years after the first Meeting of the Congress of the United States, and within every subsequent Term of ten Years, in such Manner as they shall by Law direct. The number of Representatives shall not exceed one for every thirty Thousand, but each State shall have at Least one Representative; and until such enumeration shall be made, the State of New Hampshire shall be entitled to chuse three, Massachusetts eight, Rhode Island and Providence Plantations one, Connecticut five, New York six, New Jersey four, Pennsylvania eight, Delaware one, Maryland six, Virginia ten, North Carolina five, South Carolina five, and Georgia three.

When vacancies happen in the Representation from any State, the Executive Authority thereof shall issue Writs of Election to fill such vacancies.

The House of Representatives shall chuse their Speaker and other Officers; and shall have the sole Power of Impeachment.

Section 3. The Senate of the United States shall be composed of two Senators from each State, chosen by the Legislature thereof, for six Years; and each Senator shall have one Vote.

Immediately after they shall be assembled in Consequence of the first Election, they shall be divided as equally as may be into three Classes. The Seats of the Senators of the first Class shall be vacated at the Expiration of the second Year, of the second Class at the Expiration of the fourth Year, and of the third Class at the Expiration of the sixth Year, so that one third may be chosen every second Year; and if Vacancies happen by Resignation or otherwise, during the Recess of the Legislature of any State, the Executive thereof may make temporary Appointments until the next Meeting of the Legislature, which shall then fill such Vacancies.

No Person shall be a Senator who shall not have attained to the Age of thirty Years, and been nine Years a Citizen of the United States, and who shall not, when elected, be an Inhabitant of that State for which he shall be chosen.

The Vice President of the United States shall be President of the Senate, but shall have no Vote, unless they be equally divided.

The Senate shall chuse their other Officers, and also a President pro tempore, in the Absence of the Vice President, or when he shall exercise the Office of President of the United States.

The Senate shall have the sole power to try all Impeachments. When sitting for that Purpose, they shall be on Oath or Affirmation. When the President of the United States is tried, the Chief Justice shall preside: And no Person shall be convicted without the Concurrence of two thirds of the Members present.

Judgment in Cases of Impeachment shall not extend further than to removal from Office, and disqualification to hold and enjoy any Office of honor, Trust or Profit under the United States: but the Party convicted shall nevertheless be liable and subject to Indictment, Trial, Judgment and Punishment, according to Law.

Section 4. The Times, Places and Manner of holding Elections for Senators and Representatives, shall be prescribed in each State by the Legislature thereof: but the Congress may at any time by Law make or alter such Regulations, except as to the Places of chusing Senators.

The Congress shall assemble at least once in every Year, and such Meeting shall be on the first Monday in December, unless they shall by Law appoint a different Day.

Section 5. Each House shall be the Judge of the Elections, Returns and Qualifications of its own Members, and a Majority of each shall constitute a Quorum to do Business; but a smaller Number may adjourn from day to day, and may be authorized to compel the Attendance of absent Members, in such Manner, and under such Penalties as each House may provide.

Each House may determine the Rules of its Proceedings, punish its Members for disorderly Behaviour, and, with the Concurrence of two thirds, expel a Member.

Each House shall keep a Journal of its Proceedings, and from time to time publish the same, excepting such Parts as may in their Judgment require Secrecy; and the Yeas and Nays of the Members of either House on any question shall, at the Desire of one fifth of those Present, be entered on the Journal.

Neither House, during the Session of Congress, shall, without the Consent of the other, adjourn for more than three days, nor to any other Place than that in which the two Houses shall be sitting.

Section 6. The Senators and Representatives shall receive a Compensation for their Services, to be ascertained by Law, and paid out of the Treasury of the United States. They shall in all Cases, except Treason, Felony and Breach of the Peace, be privileged from Arrest during their Attendance at the Session of their respective Houses, and in going to and returning from the same; and for any Speech or Debate in either House, they shall not be questioned in any other Place.

No Senator or Representative shall, during the Time for which he was elected, be appointed to any civil Office under the Authority of the United States, which shall have been created, or the Emoluments whereof shall have been encreased during such time; and no Person holding any Office under the United States, shall be a Member of either House during his Continuance in Office.

Section 7. All Bills for raising Revenue shall originate in the House of Representatives; but the Senate may propose or concur with Amendments as on other Bills.

Every Bill which shall have passed the House of Representatives and the Senate, shall, before it become a Law, be presented to the President of the United States; If he approve he shall sign it, but if not he shall return it, with his Objections to that House in which it shall have originated, who shall enter the Objections at large on their Journal, and proceed to reconsider it. If after such Reconsideration two thirds of that House shall agree to pass the Bill, it shall be sent, together with the Objections, to the other House, by which it shall likewise be reconsidered, and if approved by two thirds of that House, it shall become a Law. But in all such Cases the Votes of both Houses shall be determined by Yeas and Nays, and the Names of the Persons voting for and against the Bill shall be entered on the Journal of each House respectively. If any Bill shall not be returned by the President within ten Days (Sundays excepted) after it shall have been presented to him, the Same shall be a Law, in like Manner as if he had signed it, unless the Congress by their Adjournment prevent its Return, in which Case it shall not be a Law.

Every Order, Resolution, or Vote to which the Concurrence of the Senate and House of Representatives may be necessary (except on a question of Adjournment) shall be presented to the President of the United States; and before the Same shall take Effect, shall be approved by him, or being disapproved by him, shall be repassed by two thirds of the Senate and House of Representatives, according to the Rules and Limitations prescribed in the Case of a Bill.

Section 8. The Congress shall have Power to lay and collect Taxes, Duties, Imposts and Excises, to pay the Debts and provide for the common Defence and general Welfare of the United States; but all Duties, Imposts and Excises shall be uniform throughout the United States;

To borrow Money on the credit of the United States;

To regulate Commerce with foreign Nations, and among the several States, and with the Indian Tribes;

To establish an uniform Rule of Naturalization, and uniform Laws on the subject of Bankruptcies throughout the United States;

To coin Money, regulate the Value thereof, and of foreign Coin, and fix the Standard of Weights and Measures;

To provide for the Punishment of counterfeiting the Securities and current Coin of the United States;

To establish Post Offices and post Roads;

To promote the Progress of Science and useful Arts, by securing for limited Times to Authors and Inventors the exclusive Right to their respective Writings and Discoveries;

To constitute Tribunals inferior to the supreme Court;

To define and punish Piracies and Felonies committed on the high Seas, and Offenses against the Law of Nations;

To declare War, grant Letters of Marque and Reprisal, and make Rules concerning Captures on Land and Water;

To raise and support Armies, but no Appropriation of Money to that Use shall be for a longer Term than two Years;

To provide and maintain a Navy;

To make Rules for the Government and Regulation of the land and naval Forces;

To provide for calling forth the Militia to execute the Laws of the Union, suppress Insurrections and repel Invasions;

To provide for organizing, arming, and disciplining, the Militia, and for governing such Part of them as may be employed in the Service of the United States, reserving to the States respectively, the Appointment of the Officers, and the Authority of training the Militia according to the discipline described by Congress;

To exercise exclusive Legislation in all Cases whatsoever, over such District (not exceeding ten Miles square) as may, by Cession of particular States, and the Acceptance of Congress, become the Seat of the Government of the United States, and to exercise like Authority over all Places purchased by the Consent of the Legislature of the State in which the Same shall be, for the Erection of Forts, Magazines, Arsenals, dock-Yards, and other needful Buildings;—And

To make all Laws which shall be necessary and proper for carrying into Execution the foregoing Powers, and all other Powers vested by this Constitution in the Government of the United States, or in any Department or Officer thereof.

Section 9. The Migration or Importation of such Persons as any of the States now existing shall think proper to admit, shall not be prohibited by the Congress prior to the Year one thousand eight hundred and eight, but a Tax or Duty may be imposed on such Importation, not exceeding ten dollars for each Person.

The Privilege of the Writ of Habeas Corpus shall not be suspended, unless when in Cases of Rebellion or Invasion the public Safety may require it.

No Bill of Attainder or ex post facto Law shall be passed.

No Capitation, or other direct, Tax shall be laid, unless in Proportion to the Census or Enumeration herein before directed to be taken.

No Tax or Duty shall be laid on Articles exported from any State.

No Preference shall be given by any Regulation of Commerce or Revenue to the Ports of one State over those of another; nor shall Vessels bound to, or from, one State, be obliged to enter, clear, or pay Duties in another.

No Money shall be drawn from the Treasury, but in Consequence of Appropriations made by Laws; and a regular Statement and Account of the Receipts and Expenditures of all public Money shall be published from time to time.

No Title of Nobility shall be granted by the United States: And no Person holding any Office of Profit or Trust under them, shall, without the Consent of the Congress, accept of any present, Emolument, Office, or Title, of any kind whatever, from any King, Prince, or foreign State.

Section 10. No State shall enter into any Treaty, Alliance, or Confederation; grant Letters of Marque and Reprisal; coin Money; emit Bills of Credit; make any Thing but gold and silver Coin a Tender in Payment of Debts; pass any Bill of Attainder, ex post facto Law, or Law impairing the Obligation of Contracts, or grant any Title of Nobility.

No State shall, without the Consent of the Congress, lay any Imposts or Duties on Imports or Exports, except what may be absolutely necessary for executing its inspection Laws: and the net Produce of all Duties and Imposts, laid by any State on Imports or Exports, shall be for the Use of the Treasury of the United States; and all such Laws shall be subject to the Revision and Controul of the Congress.

No State shall, without the Consent of Congress, lay any Duty of Tonnage, keep Troops, or Ships of War in time of Peace, enter into any Agreement or Compact with another State, or with a foreign Power, or engage in War, unless actually invaded, or in such imminent Danger as will not admit of delay.

ARTICLE II

Section 1. The executive Power shall be vested in a President of the United States of America. He shall hold his Office during the Term of four Years, and, together with the Vice President, chosen for the same Term, be elected, as follows:

Each State shall appoint, in such Manner as the Legislature thereof may direct, a Number of Electors, equal to the whole Number of Senators and Representatives to which the State may be entitled in the Congress: but no Senator or Representative, or Person holding an Office of Trust or Profit under the United States, shall be appointed an Elector.

The Electors shall meet in their respective States, and vote by Ballot for two Persons, of whom one at least shall not be an Inhabitant of the same State with themselves. And they shall make a list of all the Persons voted for, and of the Number of Votes for each; which List they shall sign and certify, and transmit sealed to the Seat of the Government of the United States, directed to the President of the Senate. The President of the Senate shall, in the presence of the Senate and House of Representatives, open all the Certificates, and the Votes shall be counted. The Person having the greatest Number of Votes shall be the President, if such Number be a Majority of the whole Number of Electors appointed; and if there be more than one who have such Majority, and have an equal Number of Votes, then the House of Representatives shall immediately chuse by Ballot one of them for President; and if no Person have a Majority, then from the five highest on the List the said House shall in like Manner chuse the President. But in chusing the President, the Votes shall be taken by States, the Representation from each State having one Vote; A quorum for this Purpose shall consist of a Member or Members from two thirds of the States, and a Majority of all the States shall be necessary to a Choice. In every Case, after the Choice of the President, the Person having the greatest Number of Votes of the Electors shall be the Vice President. But if there should remain two or more who have equal Votes, the Senate shall chuse from them by Ballot the Vice President.

The Congress may determine the Time of Chusing the Electors, and the Day on which they shall give their Votes; which Day shall be the same throughout the United States.

No Person except a natural born Citizen, or a Citizen of the United States, at the time of the Adoption of this Constitution, shall be eligible to the Office of President; neither shall any Person be eligible to that Office who shall not have attained to the Age of thirty five Years, and been fourteen Years a Resident within the United States.

In Case of the Removal of the President from Office, or of his Death, Resignation, or Inability to discharge the Powers and Duties of the said Office, the Same shall devolve on the Vice President, and the Congress may by Law provide for the Case of Removal, Death, Resignation or Inability, both of the President and Vice President, declaring what Officer shall then act as President, and such Officer shall act accordingly, until the Disability be removed, or a President shall be elected.

The President shall, at stated Times, receive for his Services, a Compensation, which shall neither be encreased nor diminished during the Period for which he shall have been elected, and he shall not receive within that Period any other Emolument from the United States, or any of them.

Before he enter on the Execution of his Office, he shall take the following Oath or Affirmation:—"I do solemnly swear (or affirm) that I will faithfully execute the Office of President of the United States, and will to the best of my Ability, preserve, protect and defend the Constitution of the United States."

Section 2. The President shall be Commander in Chief of the Army and Navy of the United States, and of the Militia of the several States, when called into the actual Service of the United States; he may require the Opinion, in writing, of the principal Officer in each of the executive Departments, upon any Subject relating to the Duties of their respective Offices, and he shall have Power to grant Reprieves and Pardons for Offenses against the United States, except in Cases of Impeachment.

He shall have Power, by and with the Advice and Consent of the Senate, to make Treaties, providing two thirds of the Senators present concur; and he shall nominate, and by and with the Advice and Consent of the Senate, shall appoint Ambassadors, other public Ministers and Con-

suls, Judges of the supreme Court, and all other Officers of the United States, whose Appointments are not herein otherwise provided for, and which shall be established by Law: but the Congress may by Law vest the Appointment of such inferior Officers, as they think proper, in the President alone, in the Courts of Law, or in the Heads of Departments.

The President shall have Power to fill up all Vacancies that may happen during the Recess of the Senate, by granting Commissions which shall expire at the End of their next Session.

Section 3. He shall from time to time give to the Congress Information of the State of the Union, and recommend to their Consideration such Measures as he shall judge necessary and expedient; he may, on extraordinary Occasions, convene both Houses, or either of them, and in Case of Disagreement between them, with Respect to the Time of Adjournment, he may adjourn them to such Time as he shall think proper, he shall receive Ambassadors and other public Ministers; he shall take Care that the Laws be faithfully executed, and shall Commission all the Offices of the United States.

Section 4. The President, Vice President and all civil Officers of the United States, shall be removed from Office on Impeachment for, and Conviction of, Treason, Bribery, or other high Crimes and Misdemeanors.

ARTICLE III

Section 1. The judicial Power of the United States, shall be vested in one supreme Court, and in such inferior Courts as the Congress may from time to time ordain and establish. The Judges, both of the supreme and inferior Courts, shall hold their Offices during good Behaviour, and shall, at Times, receive for their Services, a Compensation, which shall not be diminished during their Continuance in Office.

Section 2. The judicial Power shall extend to all Cases, in Law and Equity, arising under this Constitution, the Laws of the United States, and Treaties made, or which shall be made, under their Authority;—to all Cases affecting Ambassadors, other public Ministers and Consuls;—to all Cases of admiralty and maritime Jurisdiction;—to Controversies to which the United States shall be a Party;—to controversies between two or more States;—between a State and Citizens of another State;—between Citizens of different States;—between Citizens of the same State claiming Lands under Grants of different States; and between a State, or the Citizens thereof, and foreign States, Citizens or Subjects.

In all Cases affecting Ambassadors, other public Ministers and Consuls, and those in which a State shall be a Party, the supreme Court shall have original Jurisdiction. In all the other Cases before mentioned, the supreme Court shall have appellate Jurisdiction, both as to Law and Fact, with such Exceptions, and under such Regulations as the Congress shall make.

The Trial of all Crimes, except in Cases of Impeachment, shall be by Jury; and such Trial shall be held in the State where the said Crimes shall have been committed; but when not committed within any State, the Trial shall be at such Place or Places as the Congress may by Law have directed.

Section 3. Treason against the United States, shall consist only in levying War against them, or in adhering to their Enemies, giving them Aid and Comfort. No Person shall be convicted of Treason unless on the Testimony of two Witnesses to the same overt Act, or on Confession in open Court.

The Congress shall have Power to declare the Punishment of Treason, but no Attainder of Treason shall work Corruption of Blood, or Forfeiture except during the Life of the Person attainted.

ARTICLE IV

Section 1. Full Faith and Credit shall be given in each State to the public Acts, Records, and judicial Proceedings of every other State. And the Congress may by general Laws prescribe the Manner in which such Acts, Records and Proceedings shall be proved, and the Effect thereof.

Section 2. The Citizens of each State shall be entitled to all Privileges and Immunities of Citizens in the several States.

A Person charged in any State with Treason, Felony, or other Crime, who shall flee from Justice, and be found in another State, shall on Demand of the executive Authority of the State from which he fled, be delivered up, to be removed to the State having Jurisdiction of the Crime.

No Person held to Service or Labour in one State, under the Laws thereof, escaping into another, shall, in Consequence of any Law or Regulation therein, be discharged from such Service or Labour, but shall be delivered up on Claim of the Party to whom such Service or Labour may be due.

Section 3. New States may be admitted by the Congress into this Union; but no new State shall be formed or erected within the Jurisdiction of any other State; nor any State be formed by the Junction of two or more States, or Parts of States, without the Consent of the Legislatures of the States concerned as well as the Congress.

The Congress shall have Power to dispose of and make all needful Rules and Regulations respecting the Territory or other Property belonging to the United States; and nothing in this Constitution shall be so construed as to Prejudice any Claims of the United States, or of any particular State.

Section 4. The United States shall guarantee to every State in this Union a Republican Form of Government, and shall protect each of them against Invasion; and on Application of the Legislature, or of the Executive (when the Legislature cannot be convened) against domestic Violence.

ARTICLE V

The Congress, whenever two thirds of both Houses shall deem it necessary, shall propose Amendments to this Constitution, or, on the Application of the Legislatures of two thirds of the several States, shall call a Convention for proposing Amendments, which, in either Case, shall be valid to all Intents and Purposes, as Part of this Constitution, when ratified by the Legislatures of three fourths of the several States, or by Conventions in three fourths thereof, as the one or the other Mode of Ratification may be proposed by the Congress; Provided that no Amendment which may be made prior to the Year One thousand eight hundred and eight shall in any Manner affect the first and fourth Clauses in the Ninth Section of the first Article; and that no State, without its Consent, shall be deprived of its equal Suffrage in the Senate.

ARTICLE VI

All Debts contracted and Engagements entered into, before the Adoption of this Constitution, shall be as valid against the United States under this Constitution, as under the Confederation.

This Constitution, and the Laws of the United States which shall be made in Pursuance thereof; and all Treaties made, or which shall be made, under the Authority of the United States, shall be the supreme Law of the Land; and the Judges in every State shall be bound thereby, any Thing in the Constitution or Laws of any State to the Contrary notwithstanding.

The Senators and Representatives before mentioned, and the Members of the several State Legislatures, and all executive and judicial Officers, both of the United States and of the Several States, shall be bound by Oath or Affirmation, to support this Constitution; but no religious Test shall ever be required as a Qualification to any Office or public Trust under the United States.

ARTICLE VII

The Ratification of the Conventions of nine States, shall be sufficient for the Establishment of this Constitution between the States so ratifying the Same.

AMENDMENT I [1791].

Congress shall make no law respecting an establishment of religion, or prohibiting the free exercise thereof; or abridging the freedom of speech, or the press; or the right of the people peaceably to assemble, and to petition the Government for a redress of grievances.

AMENDMENT II [1791].

A well regulated Militia, being necessary to the security for a free State, the right of the people to keep and bear Arms, shall not be infringed.

AMENDMENT III [1791].

No Soldier shall, in time of peace be quartered in any house, without the consent of the Owner, nor in time of war, but in a manner to be prescribed by law.

AMENDMENT IV [1791].

The right of the people to be secure in their persons, houses, papers, and effects, against unreasonable searches and seizures, shall not be violated, and no Warrants shall issue, but upon probable cause, supported by Oath or Affirmation, and particularly describing the place to be searched, and the persons or things to be seized.

AMENDMENT V [1791].

No person shall be held to answer for a capital, or otherwise infamous crime, unless on a presentment or indictment of a Grand Jury, except in cases arising in the land or naval forces, or in the Militia, when in actual service in time of War or public danger; nor shall any person be subject for the same offense to be twice put in jeopardy of life or limb; nor shall be compelled in any criminal case to be a witness against himself, nor be deprived of life, liberty, or property, without due process of law; nor shall private property be taken for public use, without just compensation.

AMENDMENT VI [1791].

In all criminal prosecutions, the accused shall enjoy the right to a speedy and public trial, by an impartial jury of the State and district wherein the crime shall have been committed, which district shall have been previously ascertained by law, and to be informed of the nature and cause of the accusation; to be confronted with the Witnesses against him; to have compulsory process for obtaining witnesses in his favor, and to have the Assistance of counsel for his defence.

AMENDMENT VII [1791].

In suits at common law, where the value in controversy shall exceed twenty dollars, the right of trial by jury shall be preserved, and no fact tried by a jury, shall be otherwise re-examined in any Court of the United States, than according to the rules of the common law.

AMENDMENT VIII [1791].

Excessive bail shall not be required, no excessive fines imposed, nor cruel and unusual punishments inflicted.

AMENDMENT IX [1791].

The enumeration in the Constitution, of certain rights, shall not be construed to deny or disparage others retained by the people.

AMENDMENT X [1791].

The powers not delegated to the United States by the Constitution, nor prohibited by it to the States, are reserved to the States respectively, or to the people.

AMENDMENT XI [1798].

The judicial power of the United States shall not be construed to extend to any suit in law or equity, commenced or prosecuted against one of the United States by Citizens of another State, or by Citizens or Subjects of any Foreign State.

AMENDMENT XII [1804].

The Electors shall meet in their respective states and vote by ballot for President and Vice-President, one of whom, at least, shall not be an inhabitant of the same state with themselves; they shall name in their ballots the person voted for as President, and in distinct ballots the person voted for as Vice-President, and they shall make distinct lists of all persons voted for as President, and of all persons voted for as Vice-President, and of the number of votes for each, which lists they shall sign and certify, and transmit sealed to the seat of the government of the United States, directed to the President of the Senate;—The President of the Senate shall, in the presence of the Senate and House of Representatives, open all the certificates and the votes shall then be counted;—The person having the greatest number of votes for President, shall be the President, if such number be a majority of the whole number of Electors appointed; and if no person have such majority, then from the persons having the highest numbers not exceeding three on the list of those voted for as President, the House of Representatives shall choose immediately, by ballot, the President. But in choosing the President, the votes shall be taken by states, the representation from each state having one vote; a quorum for this purpose shall consist of a member or members from two-thirds of the states, and a majority of all the states shall be necessary to a choice. And if the House of Representatives shall not choose a President whenever the right of choice shall devolve upon them, before the fourth day of March next following, then the Vice-President shall act as President, as in the case of the death or other constitutional disability of the President. The person having the greatest number of votes as Vice-President, shall be the Vice-President, if such number be a majority of the whole number of Electors appointed, and if no person have a majority, then from the two highest numbers on the list, the Senate shall choose the Vice-President; a quorum for the purpose shall consist of two-thirds of the whole number of Senators, and a majority of the whole number shall be necessary to a choice. But no person constitu-

tionally ineligible to the office of President shall be eligible to that of the Vice-President of the United States.

AMENDMENT XIII [1865].

Section 1. Neither slavery nor involuntary servitude, except as a punishment for crime whereof the party shall have been duly convicted, shall exist within the United States, or any place subject to their jurisdiction.
Section 2. Congress shall have power to enforce this article by appropriate legislation.

AMENDMENT XIV [1868].

Section 1. All persons born or naturalized in the United States, and subject to the jurisdiction thereof, are citizens of the United States and of the State wherein they reside. No State shall make or enforce any law which shall abridge the privileges or immunities of citizens of the United States; nor shall any State deprive any person of life, liberty, or property, without due process of law; nor deny to any person within its jurisdiction the equal protection of the laws.
Section 2. Representatives shall be appointed among the several States according to their respective numbers, counting the whole number of persons in each State, excluding Indians not taxed. But when the right to vote at any election for the choice of electors for President and Vice President of the United States, Representatives in Congress, the Executive and Judicial officers of a State, or the members of the Legislature thereof, is denied to any of the male inhabitants of such State, being twenty-one years of age, and citizens of the United States, or in any way abridged, except for participation in rebellion, or other crime, the basis of representation therein shall be reduced in the proportion which the number of such male citizens shall bear the whole number of male citizens twenty-one years of age in such State.
Section 3. No person shall be a Senator or Representative in Congress, or elector of President and Vice President, or hold any office, civil or military, under the United States, or under any State, who, having previously taken an oath, as a member of Congress, or as an officer of the United States, or as a member of any State legislature, or as an executive or judicial officer of any State, to support the Constitution of the United States, shall have engaged in insurrection or rebellion against the same, or given aid or comfort to the enemies thereof. But Congress may by a vote of two-thirds of each House, remove such disability.
Section 4. The validity of the public debt of the United States, authorized by law, including debts incurred for payment of pensions and bounties for services in suppressing insurrection or rebellion, shall not be questioned. But neither the United States nor any State shall assume or pay any debt or obligation incurred in aid of insurrection of rebellion against the United States, or any claim for the loss or emancipation of any slave; but all such debts, obligations and claims shall be held illegal and void.
Section 5. The Congress shall have power to enforce, by appropriate legislation, the provisions of this article.

AMENDMENT XV [1870].

Section 1. The right of citizens of the United States to vote shall not be denied or abridged by the United States or by any State on account of race, color, or previous condition of servitude.
Section 2. The Congress shall have power to enforce this article by appropriate legislation.

AMENDMENT XVI [1913].

The Congress shall have power to lay and collect taxes on incomes, from whatever source derived, without apportionment among the several States, and without regard to any census or enumeration.

AMENDMENT XVII [1913].

The Senate of the United States shall be composed of two Senators from each State, elected by the people thereof, for six years; and each Senator shall have one vote. The electors in each State shall have the qualifications requisite for electors of the most numerous branch of the State legislatures.

When vacancies happen in the representation of any State in the Senate, the executive authority of each State shall issue writs of election to fill such vacancies; *Provided,* That the legislature of any State may empower the executive thereof to make temporary appointments until the people fill the vacancies by election as the legislature may direct.

This amendment shall not be construed as to affect the election or term of any Senator chosen before it becomes valid as part of the Constitution.

AMENDMENT XVIII [1919].

Section 1. After one year from the ratification of this article the manufacture, sale, or transportation of intoxicating liquors within, the importation thereof into, or the exportation thereof from the United States and all territory subject to the jurisdiction thereof for beverage purposes is hereby prohibited.

Section 2. The Congress and the several States shall have concurrent power to enforce this article by appropriate legislation.

Section 3. This article shall be inoperative unless it shall have been ratified as an amendment to the Constitution by the legislatures of the several States, as provided in the Constitution, within seven years from the date of the submission hereof to the States by the Congress.

AMENDMENT XIX [1920].

The right of citizens of the United States to vote shall not be denied or abridged by the United States or by any State on account of sex.

Congress shall have power to enforce this article by appropriate legislation.

AMENDMENT XX [1933].

Section 1. The terms of the President and Vice President shall end at noon on the 20th day of January, and the terms of Senators and Representatives at noon on the 3d day of January, of the years in which such terms would have ended if this article had not been ratified; and the terms of their successors shall then begin.

Section 2. The Congress shall assemble at least once in every year, and such meeting shall begin at noon on the 3d day of January, unless they shall by law appoint a different day.

Section 3. If, at the time fixed for the beginning of the term of the President, the President elect shall have died, the Vice President elect shall become President. If a President shall not have been chosen before the time fixed for the beginning of his term, or if the President elect shall have failed to qualify, then the Vice President elect shall act as President until a President shall have qualified; and the Congress may by law provide for the case

wherein neither a President elect nor a Vice President elect shall have qualified, declaring who shall then act as President, or the manner in which one who is to act shall be selected, and such person shall act accordingly until a President or Vice President shall have qualified.

Section 4. The Congress may by law provide for the case of the death of any of the persons from whom the House of Representatives may choose a President whenever the right of choice shall have devolved upon them, and for the case of the death of any of the persons from whom the Senate may choose a Vice President whenever the right of choice shall have devolved upon them.

Section 5. Sections 1 and 2 shall take effect on the 15th day of October following the ratification of this article.

Section 6. This article shall be inoperative unless it shall have been ratified as an amendment to the Constitution by the legislatures of three-fourths of the several States within seven years from the date of its submission.

AMENDMENT XXI [1933].

Section 1. The eighteenth article of amendment to the Constitution of the United States is hereby repealed.

Section 2. The transportation or importation into any State, Territory, or possession of the United States for delivery or use therein of intoxicating liquors, in violation of the laws thereof, is hereby prohibited.

Section 3. This article shall be inoperative unless it shall have been ratified as an amendment to the Constitution by conventions in the several States, as provided in the Constitution, within seven years from the date of the submission hereof to the States by the Congress.

AMENDMENT XXII [1951].

Section 1. No person shall be elected to the office of the President more than twice, and no person who has held the office of President, or acted as President, for more than two years of a term to which some other person was elected President shall be elected to the office of the President more than once. But this Article shall not apply to any person holding the office of President when this Article was proposed by the Congress, and shall not prevent any person who may be holding the office of President, or acting as President, during the term within which this Article becomes operative from holding the office of President, or acting as President during the remainder of such term.

Section 2. This article shall be inoperative unless it shall have been ratified as an amendment to the Constitution by the legislatures of three-fourths of the several States within seven years from the date of its submission to the States by the Congress.

AMENDMENT XXIII [1961].

Section 1. The District constituting the seat of Government of the United States shall appoint in such manner as the Congress may direct:

A number of electors of President and Vice President equal to the whole number of Senators and Representatives in Congress to which the District would be entitled if it were a State, but in no event more than the least populous State; they shall be in addition to those appointed by the States, but they shall be considered, for the purposes of the election of President and Vice President, to be electors appointed by a State; and they shall meet in the District and perform such duties as provided by the twelfth article of amendment.

Section 2. The Congress shall have power to enforce this article by appropriate legislation.

AMENDMENT XXIV [1964].

Section 1. The right of citizens of the United States to vote in any primary or other election for President or Vice President, for electors for President or Vice President, or for Senator or Representative in Congress, shall not be denied or abridged by the United States or any State by reason of failure to pay any poll tax or other tax.

Section 2. The Congress shall have power to enforce this article by appropriate legislation.

AMENDMENT XXV [1967].

Section 1. In case of the removal of the President from office or of his death or resignation, the Vice President shall become President.

Section 2. Whenever there is a vacancy in the office of the Vice President, the President shall nominate a Vice President who shall take office upon confirmation by a majority vote of both Houses of Congress.

Section 3. Whenever the President transmits to the President pro tempore of the Senate and the Speaker of the House of Representatives his written declaration that he is unable to discharge the powers and duties of his office, and until he transmits to them a written declaration to the contrary, such powers and duties shall be discharged by the Vice President as Acting President.

Section 4. Whenever the Vice President and a majority of either the principal officers of the executive departments or of such other body as Congress may by law provide, transmit to the President pro tempore of the Senate and the Speaker of the House of Representatives their written declaration that the President is unable to discharge the powers and duties of his office, the Vice President shall immediately assume the powers and duties of the office as Acting President.

Thereafter, when the President transmits to the President pro tempore of the Senate and the Speaker of the House of Representatives his written declaration that no inability exists, he shall resume the powers and duties of his office unless the Vice President and a majority of either the principal officers of the executive department or of such other body as Congress may by law provide, transmit within four days to the President pro tempore of the Senate and the Speaker of the House of Representatives their written declaration that the President is unable to discharge the powers and duties of his office. Thereupon Congress shall decide the issue, assembling within forty-eight hours for that purpose if not in session. If the Congress, within twenty-one days after receipt of the latter written declaration, or, if Congress is not in session, within twenty-one days after Congress is required to assemble, determines by two-thirds vote of both Houses that the President is unable to discharge the powers and duties of his office, the Vice President shall continue to discharge the same as Acting President; otherwise, the President shall resume the powers and duties of his office.

AMENDMENT XXVI [1971].

Section 1. The right of citizens of the United States, who are eighteen years of age or older, to vote shall not be denied or abridged by the United States or by any State on account of age.

Section 2. The Congress shall have power to enforce this article by appropriate legislation.

AMENDMENT XXVII [1992].

No law, varying the compensation for the services of the Senators and Representatives, shall take effect, until an election of Representatives shall have intervened.

The Uniform Commercial Code

(Adopted in fifty-two jurisdictions; all fifty States, although Louisiana has adopted only Articles 1, 3, 4, 7, 8, and 9; the District of Columbia; and the Virgin Islands.)

The Code consists of the following articles:

Art.
1. General Provisions
2. Sales
2A. Leases
3. Negotiable Instruments
4. Bank Deposits and Collections
4A. Funds Transfers
5. Letters of Credit
6. Repealer of Article 6—Bulk Transfers and [Revised] Article 6—Bulk Sales
7. Warehouse Receipts, Bills of Lading and Other Documents of Title
8. Investment Securities
9. Secured Transactions
10. Effective Date and Repealer
11. Effective Date and Transition Provisions

ARTICLE 1: General Provisions

PART 1: Short Title, Construction, Application and Subject Matter of the Act

§ 1-101. Short Title.

This Act shall be known and may be cited as Uniform Commercial Code.

§ 1-102. Purposes; Rules of Construction; Variation by Agreement.

(1) This Act shall be liberally construed and applied to promote its underlying purposes and policies.

(2) Underlying purposes and policies of this Act are
   (a) to simplify, clarify and modernize the law governing commercial transactions;
   (b) to permit the continued expansion of commercial practices through custom, usage and agreement of the parties;
   (c) to make uniform the law among the various jurisdictions.

(3) The effect of provisions of this Act may be varied by agreement, except as otherwise provided in this Act and except that the obligations of good faith, diligence, reasonableness and care prescribed by this Act may not be disclaimed by agreement but the parties may by agreement determine the standards by which the performance of such obligations is to be measured if such standards are not manifestly unreasonable.

(4) The presence in certain provisions of this Act of the words "unless otherwise agreed" or words of similar import does not imply that the effect of other provisions may not be varied by agreement under subsection (3).

(5) In this Act unless the context otherwise requires
   (a) words in the singular number include the plural, and in the plural include the singular;
   (b) words of the masculine gender include the feminine and the neuter, and when the sense so indicates words of the neuter gender may refer to any gender.

§ 1-103. Supplementary General Principles of Law Applicable.

Unless displaced by the particular provisions of this Act, the principles of law and equity, including the law merchant and the law relative to capacity to contract, principal and agent, estoppel, fraud, misrepresentation, duress, coercion, mistake, bankruptcy, or other validating or invalidating cause shall supplement its provisions.

§ 1-104. Construction Against Implicit Repeal.

This Act being a general act intended as a unified coverage of its subject matter, no part of it shall be deemed to be impliedly repealed by subsequent legislation if such construction can reasonably be avoided.

§ 1-105. Territorial Application of the Act; Parties' Power to Choose Applicable Law.

(1) Except as provided hereafter in this section, when a transaction bears a reasonable relation to this state and also to another state or nation the parties may agree that the law either of this state or of such other state or nation shall govern their rights and duties. Failing such agreement this Act applies to transactions bearing an appropriate relation to this state.

(2) Where one of the following provisions of this Act specifies the applicable law, that provision governs and a contrary agreement is effective only to the extent permitted by the law (including the conflict of laws rules) so specified:
   Rights of creditors against sold goods. Section 2–402.
   Applicability of the Article on Leases. Sections 2A–105 and 2A–106.
   Applicability of the Article on Bank Deposits and Collections. Section 4–102.
   Governing law in the Article on Funds Transfers. Section 4A–507.
   Letters of Credit, Section 5–116.
   Bulk sales subject to the Article on Bulk Sales. Section 6–103.
   Applicability of the Article on Investment Securities. Section 8–106.
   Law governing perfection, the effect of perfection or nonperfection, and the priority of security interests and agricultural liens. Sections 9–301 through 9–307.
   As amended in 1972, 1987, 1988, 1989, 1994, 1995, and 1999.

§ 1-106. Remedies to Be Liberally Administered.

(1) The remedies provided by this Act shall be liberally administered to the end that the aggrieved party may be put in as good a position as if the other party had fully performed but neither consequential or special nor penal damages may be had except as specifically provided in this Act or by other rule of law.

(2) Any right or obligation declared by this Act is enforceable by action unless the provision declaring it specifies a different and limited effect.

§ 1-107. Waiver or Renunciation of Claim or Right After Breach.

Any claim or right arising out of an alleged breach can be discharged in whole or in part without consideration by a written waiver or renunciation signed and delivered by the aggrieved party.

§ 1-108. Severability.

If any provision or clause of this Act or application thereof to any person or circumstances is held invalid, such invalidity shall not affect other provisions or applications of the Act which can be given effect without the invalid provision or application, and to this end the provisions of this Act are declared to be severable.

§ 1-109. Section Captions.

Section captions are parts of this Act.

PART 2: General Definitions and Principles of Interpretation

§ 1-201. General Definitions.

Subject to additional definitions contained in the subsequent Articles of this Act which are applicable to specific Articles or Parts thereof, and unless the context otherwise requires, in this Act:

(1) "Action" in the sense of a judicial proceeding includes recoupment, counterclaim, set-off, suit in equity and any other proceedings in which rights are determined.

(2) "Aggrieved party" means a party entitled to resort to a remedy.

(3) "Agreement" means the bargain of the parties in fact as found in their language or by implication from other circumstances including course of dealing or usage of trade or course of performance as provided in this Act (Sections 1–205 and 2–208). Whether an agreement has legal consequences is determined by the provisions of this Act, if applicable; otherwise by the law of contracts (Section 1–103). (Compare "Contract".)

(4) "Bank" means any person engaged in the business of banking.

(5) "Bearer" means the person in possession of an instrument, document of title, or certificated security payable to bearer or indorsed in blank.

(6) "Bill of lading" means a document evidencing the receipt of goods for shipment issued by a person engaged in the business of transporting or forwarding goods, and includes an airbill. "Airbill" means a document serving for air transportation as a bill of lading does for marine or rail transportation, and includes an air consignment note or air waybill.

(7) "Branch" includes a separately incorporated foreign branch of a bank.

(8) "Burden of establishing" a fact means the burden of persuading the triers of fact that the existence of the fact is more probable than its non-existence.

(9) "Buyer in ordinary course of business" means a person that buys goods in good faith, without knowledge that the sale violates the rights of another person in the goods, and in the ordinary course from a person, other than a pawnbroker, in the business of selling goods of that kind. A person buys goods in the ordinary course if the sale to the person comports with the usual or customary practices in the kind of business in which the seller is engaged or with the seller's own usual or customary practices. A person that sells oil, gas, or other minerals at the wellhead or minehead is a person in the business of selling goods of that kind. A buyer in ordinary course of business may buy for cash, by exchange of other property, or on secured or unsecured credit, and may acquire goods or documents of title under a pre-existing contract for sale. Only a buyer that takes possession of the goods or has a right to recover the goods from the seller under Article 2 may be a buyer in ordinary course of business. A person that acquires goods in a transfer in bulk or as security for or in total or partial satisfaction of a money debt is not a buyer in ordinary course of business.

(10) "Conspicuous": A term or clause is conspicuous when it is so written that a reasonable person against whom it is to operate ought to have noticed it. A printed heading in capitals (as: NON-NEGOTIABLE BILL OF LADING) is conspicuous. Language in the body of a form is "conspicuous" if it is in larger or other contrasting type or color. But in a telegram any stated term is "conspicuous". Whether a term or clause is "conspicuous" or not is for decision by the court.

(11) "Contract" means the total legal obligation which results from the parties' agreement as affected by this Act and any other applicable rules of law. (Compare "Agreement".)

(12) "Creditor" includes a general creditor, a secured creditor, a lien creditor and any representative of creditors, including an assignee for the benefit of creditors, a trustee in bankruptcy, a receiver in equity and an executor or administrator of an insolvent debtor's or assignor's estate.

(13) "Defendant" includes a person in the position of defendant in a cross-action or counterclaim.

(14) "Delivery" with respect to instruments, documents of title, chattel paper, or certificated securities means voluntary transfer of possession.

(15) "Document of title" includes bill of lading, dock warrant, dock receipt, warehouse receipt or order for the delivery of goods, and also any other document which in the regular course of business or financing is treated as adequately evidencing that the person in possession of it is entitled to receive, hold and dispose of the document and the goods it covers. To be a document of title a document must purport to be issued by or addressed to a bailee and purport to cover goods in the bailee's possession which are either identified or are fungible portions of an identified mass.

(16) "Fault" means wrongful act, omission or breach.

(17) "Fungible" with respect to goods or securities means goods or securities of which any unit is, by nature or usage of trade, the equivalent of any other like unit. Goods which are not fungible shall be deemed fungible for the purposes of this Act to the extent that under a particular agreement or document unlike units are treated as equivalents.

(18) "Genuine" means free of forgery or counterfeiting.

(19) "Good faith" means honesty in fact in the conduct or transaction concerned.

(20) "Holder" with respect to a negotiable instrument, means the person in possession if the instrument is payable to bearer or, in the cases of an instrument payable to an identified person, if the identified person is in possession. "Holder" with respect to a document of title means the person in possession if the goods are deliverable to bearer or to the order of the person in possession.

(21) To "honor" is to pay or to accept and pay, or where a credit so engages to purchase or discount a draft complying with the terms of the credit.

(22) "Insolvency proceedings" includes any assignment for the benefit of creditors or other proceedings intended to liquidate or rehabilitate the estate of the person involved.

(23) A person is "insolvent" who either has ceased to pay his debts in the ordinary course of business or cannot pay his debts as they become due or is insolvent within the meaning of the federal bankruptcy law.

(24) "Money" means a medium of exchange authorized or adopted by a domestic or foreign government and includes a monetary unit of account established by an intergovernmental organization or by agreement between two or more nations.

(25) A person has "notice" of a fact when

    (a) he has actual knowledge of it; or

    (b) he has received a notice or notification of it; or

    (c) from all the facts and circumstances known to him at the time in question he has reason to know that it exists.

A person "knows" or has "knowledge" of a fact when he has actual knowledge of it. "Discover" or "learn" or a word or phrase of similar import refers to knowledge rather than to reason to know. The time and circumstances under which a notice or notification may cease to be effective are not determined by this Act.

(26) A person "notifies" or "gives" a notice or notification to another by taking such steps as may be reasonably required to inform the other in ordinary course whether or not such other actually comes to know of it. A person "receives" a notice or notification when

    (a) it comes to his attention; or

    (b) it is duly delivered at the place of business through which the contract was made or at any other place held out by him as the place for receipt of such communications.

(27) Notice, knowledge or a notice or notification received by an organization is effective for a particular transaction from the time when it is brought to the attention of the individual conducting that transaction, and in any event from the time when it would have been brought to his attention if the organization had exercised due diligence. An organization exercises due diligence if it maintains reasonable routines for communicating significant information to the person conducting the transaction and there is reasonable compliance with the routines. Due diligence does not require an individual acting for the organization to communicate information unless such communication is part of his regular duties or unless he has reason to know of the transaction and that the transaction would be materially affected by the information.

(28) "Organization" includes a corporation, government or governmental subdivision or agency, business trust, estate, trust, partnership or association, two or more persons having a joint or common interest, or any other legal or commercial entity.

(29) "Party", as distinct from "third party", means a person who has engaged in a transaction or made an agreement within this Act.

(30) "Person" includes an individual or an organization (See Section 1–102).

(31) "Presumption" or "presumed" means that the trier of fact must find the existence of the fact presumed unless and until evidence is introduced which would support a finding of its non-existence.

(32) "Purchase" includes taking by sale, discount, negotiation, mortgage, pledge, lien, issue or re-issue, gift or any other voluntary transaction creating an interest in property.

(33) "Purchaser" means a person who takes by purchase.

(34) "Remedy" means any remedial right to which an aggrieved party is entitled with or without resort to a tribunal.

(35) "Representative" includes an agent, an officer of a corporation or association, and a trustee, executor or administrator of an estate, or any other person empowered to act for another.

(36) "Rights" includes remedies.

(37) "Security interest" means an interest in personal property or fixtures which secures payment or performance of an obligation. The term also includes any interest of a consignor and a buyer of accounts, chattel paper, a payment intangible, or a promissory note in a transaction that is subject to Article 9. The special property interest of a buyer of goods on identification of those goods to a contract for sale under Section 2–401 is not a "security interest", but a buyer may also acquire a "security interest" by complying with Article 9. Except as otherwise provided in Section 2–505, the right of a seller or lessor of goods under Article 2 or 2A to retain or acquire possession of the goods is not a "security interest", but a seller or lessor may also acquire a "security interest" by complying with Article 9. The retention or reservation of title by a seller of goods notwithstanding shipment or delivery to the buyer (Section 2–401) is limited in effect to a reservation of a "security interest". Whether a transaction creates a lease or security interest is determined by the facts of each case; however, a transaction creates a security interest if the consideration the lessee is to pay the lessor for the right to possession and use of the goods is an obligation for the term of the lease not subject to termination by the lessee, and

    (a) the original term of the lease is equal to or greater than the remaining economic life of the goods,

    (b) the lessee is bound to renew the lease for the remaining economic life of the goods or is bound to become the owner of the goods,

    (c) the lessee has an option to renew the lease for the remaining economic life of the goods for no additional consideration or nominal additional consideration upon compliance with the lease agreement, or

    (d) the lessee has an option to become the owner of the goods for no additional consideration or nominal additional consideration upon compliance with the lease agreement.

A transaction does not create a security interest merely because it provides that

    (a) the present value of the consideration the lessee is obligated to pay the lessor for the right to possession and use of the goods is substantially equal to or is greater than the fair market value of the goods at the time the lease is entered into,

    (b) the lessee assumes risk of loss of the goods, or agrees to pay taxes, insurance, filing, recording, or registration fees, or service or maintenance costs with respect to the goods,

    (c) the lessee has an option to renew the lease or to become the owner of the goods,

    (d) the lessee has an option to renew the lease for a fixed rent that is equal to or greater than the reasonably predictable fair market rent for the use of the goods for the term of the renewal at the time the option is to be performed, or

    (e) the lessee has an option to become the owner of the goods for a fixed price that is equal to or greater than the reasonably predictable fair market value of the goods at the time the option is to be performed.

For purposes of this subsection (37):

    (x) Additional consideration is not nominal if (i) when the option to renew the lease is granted to the lessee the rent is stated to be the fair market rent for the use of the goods for the term of the renewal determined at the time the option is to be performed, or (ii) when the option to become the owner of the goods is granted to the lessee the price is stated to be the fair market value of the goods determined at the time the option is to be performed. Additional consideration is nominal if it is less than the lessee's reasonably predictable cost of performing under the lease agreement if the option is not exercised;

    (y) "Reasonably predictable" and "remaining economic life of the goods" are to be determined with reference to the facts and circumstances at the time the transaction is entered into; and

    (z) "Present value" means the amount as of a date certain of one or more sums payable in the future, discounted to the date certain. The discount is determined by the interest rate specified by the parties if the rate is not manifestly unreasonable at the time the transaction is entered into; otherwise, the discount is determined by a commercially reasonable rate that takes into account the facts and circumstances of each case at the time the transaction was entered into.

(38) "Send" in connection with any writing or notice means to deposit in the mail or deliver for transmission by any other usual means of communication with postage or cost of transmission provided for and properly addressed and in the case of an instrument to an address specified thereon or otherwise agreed, or if there be none to any address reasonable under the circumstances. The receipt of any writing or notice within the time at which it would have arrived if properly sent has the effect of a proper sending.

(39) "Signed" includes any symbol executed or adopted by a party with present intention to authenticate a writing.

(40) "Surety" includes guarantor.

(41) "Telegram" includes a message transmitted by radio, teletype, cable, any mechanical method of transmission, or the like.

(42) "Term" means that portion of an agreement which relates to a particular matter.

(43) "Unauthorized" signature means one made without actual, implied or apparent authority and includes a forgery.

(44) "Value". Except as otherwise provided with respect to negotiable instruments and bank collections (Sections 3–303, 4–210 and 4–211) a person gives "value" for rights if he acquires them

(a) in return for a binding commitment to extend credit or for the extension of immediately available credit whether or not drawn upon and whether or not a chargeback is provided for in the event of difficulties in collection; or

(b) as security for or in total or partial satisfaction of a pre-existing claim; or

(c) by accepting delivery pursuant to a preexisting contract for purchase; or

(d) generally, in return for any consideration sufficient to support a simple contract.

(45) "Warehouse receipt" means a receipt issued by a person engaged in the business of storing goods for hire.

(46) "Written" or "writing" includes printing, typewriting or any other intentional reduction to tangible form.

§1-202. Prima Facie Evidence by Third Party Documents.

A document in due form purporting to be a bill of lading, policy or certificate of insurance, official weigher's or inspector's certificate, consular invoice, or any other document authorized or required by the contract to be issued by a third party shall be prima facie evidence of its own authenticity and genuineness and of the facts stated in the document by the third party.

§ 1-203. Obligation of Good Faith.

Every contract or duty within this Act imposes an obligation of good faith in its performance or enforcement.

§ 1-204. Time; Reasonable Time; "Seasonably".

(1) Whenever this Act requires any action to be taken within a reasonable time, any time which is not manifestly unreasonable may be fixed by agreement.

(2) What is a reasonable time for taking any action depends on the nature, purpose and circumstances of such action.

(3) An action is taken "seasonably" when it is taken at or within the time agreed or if no time is agreed at or within a reasonable time.

§ 1-205. Course of Dealing and Usage of Trade.

(1) A course of dealing is a sequence of previous conduct between the parties to a particular transaction which is fairly to be regarded as establishing a common basis of understanding for interpreting their expressions and other conduct.

(2) A usage of trade is any practice or method of dealing having such regularity of observance in a place, vocation or trade as to justify an expectation that it will be observed with respect to the transaction in question. The existence and scope of such a usage are to be proved as facts. If it is established that such a usage is embodied in a written trade code or similar writing the interpretation of the writing is for the court.

(3) A course of dealing between parties and any usage of trade in the vocation or trade in which they are engaged or of which they are or should be aware give particular meaning to and supplement or qualify terms of an agreement.

(4) The express terms of an agreement and an applicable course of dealing or usage of trade shall be construed wherever reasonable as consistent with each other; but when such construction is unreasonable express terms control both course of dealing and usage of trade and course of dealing controls usage trade.

(5) An applicable usage of trade in the place where any part of performance is to occur shall be used in interpreting the agreement as to that part of the performance.

(6) Evidence of a relevant usage of trade offered by one party is not admissible unless and until he has given the other party such notice as the court finds sufficient to prevent unfair surprise to the latter.

§ 1-206. Statute of Frauds for Kinds of Personal Property Not Otherwise Covered.

(1) Except in the cases described in subsection (2) of this section a contract for the sale of personal property is not enforceable by way of action or defense beyond five thousand dollars in amount or value of remedy unless there is some writing which indicates that a contract for sale has been made between the parties at a defined or stated price, reasonably identifies the subject matter, and is signed by the party against whom enforcement is sought or by his authorized agent.

(2) Subsection (1) of this section does not apply to contracts for the sale of goods (Section 2–201) nor of securities (Section 8–113) nor to security agreements (Section 9–203).

As amended in 1994.

§ 1-207. Performance or Acceptance Under Reservation of Rights.

(1) A party who with explicit reservation of rights performs or promises performance or assents to performance in a manner demanded or offered by the other party does not thereby prejudice the rights reserved. Such words as "without prejudice", "under protest" or the like are sufficient.

(2) Subsection (1) does not apply to an accord and satisfaction.

As amended in 1990.

§ 1-208. Option to Accelerate at Will.

A term providing that one party or his successor in interest may accelerate payment or performance or require collateral or additional collateral "at will" or "when he deems himself insecure" or in words of similar import shall be construed to mean that he shall have power to do so only if he in good faith believes that the prospect of payment or performance is impaired. The burden of establishing lack of good faith is on the party against whom the power has been exercised.

§ 1-209. Subordinated Obligations.

An obligation may be issued as subordinated to payment of another obligation of the person obligated, or a creditor may subordinate his right to payment of an obligation by agreement with either the person obligated or another creditor of the person obligated. Such a subordination does not create a security interest as against either the common debtor or a subordinated creditor. This section shall be construed as declaring the law as it existed prior to the enactment of this section and not as modifying it. Added 1966.

Note: *This new section is proposed as an optional provision to make it clear that a subordination agreement does not create a security interest unless so intended.*

ARTICLE 2: Sales

PART 1: Short Title, General Construction and Subject Matter

§ 2-101. Short Title.

This Article shall be known and may be cited as Uniform Commercial Code—Sales.

§ 2-102. Scope; Certain Security and Other Transactions Excluded From This Article.

Unless the context otherwise requires, this Article applies to transactions in goods; it does not apply to any transaction which although in the form of an unconditional contract to sell or present sale is intended to operate only as a security transaction nor does this Article impair or repeal any statute regulating sales to consumers, farmers or other specified classes of buyers.

§ 2-103. Definitions and Index of Definitions.

(1) In this Article unless the context otherwise requires
    (a) "Buyer" means a person who buys or contracts to buy goods.
    (b) "Good faith" in the case of a merchant means honesty in fact and the observance of reasonable commercial standards of fair dealing in the trade.
    (c) "Receipt" of goods means taking physical possession of them.
    (d) "Seller" means a person who sells or contracts to sell goods.

(2) Other definitions applying to this Article or to specified Parts thereof, and the sections in which they appear are:
"Acceptance". Section 2–606.
"Banker's credit". Section 2–325.
"Between merchants". Section 2–104.
"Cancellation". Section 2–106(4).
"Commercial unit". Section 2–105.
"Confirmed credit". Section 2–325.
"Conforming to contract". Section 2–106.
"Contract for sale". Section 2–106.
"Cover". Section 2–712.
"Entrusting". Section 2–403.
"Financing agency". Section 2–104.
"Future goods". Section 2–105.
"Goods". Section 2–105.
"Identification". Section 2–501.
"Installment contract". Section 2–612.
"Letter of Credit". Section 2–325.
"Lot". Section 2–105.
"Merchant". Section 2–104.
"Overseas". Section 2–323.
"Person in position of seller". Section 2–707.
"Present sale". Section 2–106.
"Sale". Section 2–106.
"Sale on approval". Section 2–326.
"Sale or return". Section 2–326.
"Termination". Section 2–106.

(3) The following definitions in other Articles apply to this Article:
"Check". Section 3–104.
"Consignee". Section 7–102.
"Consignor". Section 7–102.
"Consumer goods". Section 9–109.
"Dishonor". Section 3–507.
"Draft". Section 3–104.

(4) In addition Article 1 contains general definitions and principles of construction and interpretation applicable throughout this Article.
As amended in 1994 and 1999.

§ 2-104. Definitions: "Merchant"; "Between Merchants"; "Financing Agency".

(1) "Merchant" means a person who deals in goods of the kind or otherwise by his occupation holds himself out as having knowledge or skill peculiar to the practices or goods involved in the transaction or to whom such knowledge or skill may be attributed by his employment of an agent or broker or other intermediary who by his occupation holds himself out as having such knowledge or skill.

(2) "Financing agency" means a bank, finance company or other person who in the ordinary course of business makes advances against goods or documents of title or who by arrangement with either the seller or the buyer intervenes in ordinary course to make or collect payment due or claimed under the contract for sale, as by purchasing or paying the seller's draft or making advances against it or by merely taking it for collection whether or not documents of title accompany the draft. "Financing agency" includes also a bank or other person who similarly intervenes between persons who are in the position of seller and buyer in respect to the goods (Section 2–707).

(3) "Between merchants" means in any transaction with respect to which both parties are chargeable with the knowledge or skill of merchants.

§ 2-105. Definitions: Transferability; "Goods"; "Future" Goods; "Lot"; "Commercial Unit".

(1) "Goods" means all things (including specially manufactured goods) which are movable at the time of identification to the contract for sale other than the money in which the price is to be paid, investment securities (Article 8) and things in action. "Goods" also includes the unborn young of animals and growing crops and other identified things attached to realty as described in the section on goods to be severed from realty (Section 2–107).

(2) Goods must be both existing and identified before any interest in them can pass. Goods which are not both existing and identified are "future" goods. A purported present sale of future goods or of any interest therein operates as a contract to sell.

(3) There may be a sale of a part interest in existing identified goods.

(4) An undivided share in an identified bulk of fungible goods is sufficiently identified to be sold although the quantity of the bulk is not determined. Any agreed proportion of such a bulk or any quantity thereof agreed upon by number, weight or other measure may to the extent of the seller's interest in the bulk be sold to the buyer who then becomes an owner in common.

(5) "Lot" means a parcel or a single article which is the subject matter of a separate sale or delivery, whether or not it is sufficient to perform the contract.

(6) "Commercial unit" means such a unit of goods as by commercial usage is a single whole for purposes of sale and division of which materially impairs its character or value on the market or in use. A commercial unit may be a single article (as a machine) or a set of articles (as a suite of furniture or an assortment of sizes) or a quantity (as a bale, gross, or carload) or any other unit treated in use or in the relevant market as a single whole.

§ 2-106. Definitions: "Contract"; "Agreement"; "Contract for Sale"; "Sale"; "Present Sale"; "Conforming" to Contract; "Termination"; "Cancellation".

(1) In this Article unless the context otherwise requires "contract" and "agreement" are limited to those relating to the present or future sale of goods. "Contract for sale" includes both a present sale of goods and a contract to sell goods at a future time. A "sale" consists in the passing of title from the seller to the buyer for a price (Section 2–401). A "present sale" means a sale which is accomplished by the making of the contract.

(2) Goods or conduct including any part of a performance are "conforming" or conform to the contract when they are in accordance with the obligations under the contract.

(3) "Termination" occurs when either party pursuant to a power created by agreement or law puts an end to the contract otherwise than for its

breach. On "termination" all obligations which are still executory on both sides are discharged but any right based on prior breach or performance survives.

(4) "Cancellation" occurs when either party puts an end to the contract for breach by the other and its effect is the same as that of "termination" except that the cancelling party also retains any remedy for breach of the whole contract or any unperformed balance.

§ 2-107. Goods to Be Severed From Realty: Recording.

(1) A contract for the sale of minerals or the like (including oil and gas) or a structure or its materials to be removed from realty is a contract for the sale of goods within this Article if they are to be severed by the seller but until severance a purported present sale thereof which is not effective as a transfer of an interest in land is effective only as a contract to sell.

(2) A contract for the sale apart from the land of growing crops or other things attached to realty and capable of severance without material harm thereto but not described in subsection (1) or of timber to be cut is a contract for the sale of goods within this Article whether the subject matter is to be severed by the buyer or by the seller even though it forms part of the realty at the time of contracting, and the parties can by identification effect a present sale before severance.

(3) The provisions of this section are subject to any third party rights provided by the law relating to realty records, and the contract for sale may be executed and recorded as a document transferring an interest in land and shall then constitute notice to third parties of the buyer's rights under the contract for sale.

As amended in 1972.

PART 2: Form, Formation and Readjustment of Contract

§ 2-201. Formal Requirements; Statute of Frauds.

(1) Except as otherwise provided in this section a contract for the sale of goods for the price of $500 or more is not enforceable by way of action or defense unless there is some writing sufficient to indicate that a contract for sale has been made between the parties and signed by the party against whom enforcement is sought or by his authorized agent or broker. A writing is not insufficient because it omits or incorrectly states a term agreed upon but the contract is not enforceable under this paragraph beyond the quantity of goods shown in such writing.

(2) Between merchants if within a reasonable time a writing in confirmation of the contract and sufficient against the sender is received and the party receiving it has reason to know its contents, its satisfies the requirements of subsection (1) against such party unless written notice of objection to its contents is given within ten days after it is received.

(3) A contract which does not satisfy the requirements of subsection (1) but which is valid in other respects is enforceable

(a) if the goods are to be specially manufactured for the buyer and are not suitable for sale to others in the ordinary course of the seller's business and the seller, before notice of repudiation is received and under circumstances which reasonably indicate that the goods are for the buyer, has made either a substantial beginning of their manufacture or commitments for their procurement; or

(b) if the party against whom enforcement is sought admits in his pleading, testimony or otherwise in court that a contract for sale was made, but the contract is not enforceable under this provision beyond the quantity of goods admitted; or

(c) with respect to goods for which payment has been made and accepted or which have been received and accepted (Sec. 2–606).

§ 2-202. Final Written Expression: Parol or Extrinsic Evidence.

Terms with respect to which the confirmatory memoranda of the parties agree or which are otherwise set forth in a writing intended by the parties as a final expression of their agreement with respect to such terms as are included therein may not be contradicted by evidence of any prior agreement or of a contemporaneous oral agreement but may be explained or supplemented

(a) by course of dealing or usage of trade (Section 1–205) or by course of performance (Section 2–208); and

(b) by evidence of consistent additional terms unless the court finds the writing to have been intended also as a complete and exclusive statement of the terms of the agreement.

§ 2-203. Seals Inoperative.

The affixing of a seal to a writing evidencing a contract for sale or an offer to buy or sell goods does not constitute the writing a sealed instrument and the law with respect to sealed instruments does not apply to such a contract or offer.

§ 2-204. Formation in General.

(1) A contract for sale of goods may be made in any manner sufficient to show agreement, including conduct by both parties which recognizes the existence of such a contract.

(2) An agreement sufficient to constitute a contract for sale may be found even though the moment of its making is undetermined.

(3) Even though one or more terms are left open a contract for sale does not fail for indefiniteness if the parties have intended to make a contract and there is a reasonably certain basis for giving an appropriate remedy.

§ 2-205. Firm Offers.

An offer by a merchant to buy or sell goods in a signed writing which by its terms gives assurance that it will be held open is not revocable, for lack of consideration, during the time stated or if no time is stated for a reasonable time, but in no event may such period of irrevocability exceed three months; but any such term of assurance on a form supplied by the offeree must be separately signed by the offeror.

§ 2-206. Offer and Acceptance in Formation of Contract.

(1) Unless other unambiguously indicated by the language or circumstances

(a) an offer to make a contract shall be construed as inviting acceptance in any manner and by any medium reasonable in the circumstances;

(b) an order or other offer to buy goods for prompt or current shipment shall be construed as inviting acceptance either by a prompt promise to ship or by the prompt or current shipment of conforming or nonconforming goods, but such a shipment of non-conforming goods does not constitute an acceptance if the seller seasonably notifies the buyer that the shipment is offered only as an accommodation to the buyer.

(2) Where the beginning of a requested performance is a reasonable mode of acceptance an offeror who is not notified of acceptance within a reasonable time may treat the offer as having lapsed before acceptance.

§ 2-207. Additional Terms in Acceptance or Confirmation.

(1) A definite and seasonable expression of acceptance or a written confirmation which is sent within a reasonable time operates as an acceptance

even though it states terms additional to or different from those offered or agreed upon, unless acceptance is expressly made conditional on assent to the additional or different terms.

(2) The additional terms are to be construed as proposals for addition to the contract. Between merchants such terms become part of the contract unless:

    (a) the offer expressly limits acceptance to the terms of the offer;

    (b) they materially alter it; or

    (c) notification of objection to them has already been given or is given within a reasonable time after notice of them is received.

(3) Conduct by both parties which recognizes the existence of a contract is sufficient to establish a contract for sale although the writings of the parties do not otherwise establish a contract. In such case the terms of the particular contract consist of those terms on which the writings of the parties agree, together with any supplementary terms incorporated under any other provisions of this Act.

§ 2-208. Course of Performance or Practical Construction.

(1) Where the contract for sale involves repeated occasions for performance by either party with knowledge of the nature of the performance and opportunity for objection to it by the other, any course of performance accepted or acquiesced in without objection shall be relevant to determine the meaning of the agreement.

(2) The express terms of the agreement and any such course of performance, as well as any course of dealing and usage of trade, shall be construed whenever reasonable as consistent with each other; but when such construction is unreasonable, express terms shall control course of performance and course of performance shall control both course of dealing and usage of trade (Section 1–205).

(3) Subject to the provisions of the next section on modification and waiver, such course of performance shall be relevant to show a waiver or modification of any term inconsistent with such course of performance.

§ 2-209. Modification, Rescission and Waiver.

(1) An agreement modifying a contract within this Article needs no consideration to be binding.

(2) A signed agreement which excludes modification or rescission except by a signed writing cannot be otherwise modified or rescinded, but except as between merchants such a requirement on a form supplied by the merchant must be separately signed by the other party.

(3) The requirements of the statute of frauds section of this Article (Section 2–201) must be satisfied if the contract as modified is within its provisions.

(4) Although an attempt at modification or rescission does not satisfy the requirements of subsection (2) or (3) it can operate as a waiver.

(5) A party who has made a waiver affecting an executory portion of the contract may retract the waiver by reasonable notification received by the other party that strict performance will be required of any term waived, unless the retraction would be unjust in view of a material change of position in reliance on the waiver.

§ 2-210. Delegation of Performance; Assignment of Rights.

(1) A party may perform his duty through a delegate unless otherwise agreed or unless the other party has a substantial interest in having his original promisor perform or control the acts required by the contract. No delegation of performance relieves the party delegating of any duty to perform or any liability for breach.

(2) Except as otherwise provided in Section 9–406, unless otherwise agreed, all rights of either seller or buyer can be assigned except where the assignment would materially change the duty of the other party, or increase materially the burden or risk imposed on him by his contract, or impair materially his chance of obtaining return performance. A right to damages for breach of the whole contract or a right arising out of the assignor's due performance of his entire obligation can be assigned despite agreement otherwise.

(3) The creation, attachment, perfection, or enforcement of a security interest in the seller's interest under a contract is not a transfer that materially changes the duty of or increases materially the burden or risk imposed on the buyer or impairs materially the buyer's chance of obtaining return performance within the purview of subsection (2) unless, and then only to the extent that, enforcement actually results in a delegation of material performance of the seller. Even in that event, the creation, attachment, perfection, and enforcement of the security interest remain effective, but (i) the seller is liable to the buyer for damages caused by the delegation to the extent that the damages could not reasonably by prevented by the buyer, and (ii) a court having jurisdiction may grant other appropriate relief, including cancellation of the contract for sale or an injunction against enforcement of the security interest or consummation of the enforcement.

(4) Unless the circumstances indicate the contrary a prohibition of assignment of "the contract" is to be construed as barring only the delegation to the assign4ss of the assignor's performance.

(5) An assignment of "the contract" or of "all my rights under the contract" or an assignment in similar general terms is an assignment of rights and unless the language or the circumstances (as in an assignment for security) indicate the contrary, it is a delegation of performance of the duties of the assignor and its acceptance by the assignee constitutes a promise by him to perform those duties. This promise is enforceable by either the assignor or the other party to the original contract.

(6) The other party may treat any assignment which delegates performance as creating reasonable grounds for insecurity and may without prejudice to his rights against the assignor demand assurances from the assignee (Section 2–609).

As amended in 1999.

PART 3: General Obligation and Construction of Contract

§ 2-301. General Obligations of Parties.

The obligation of the seller is to transfer and deliver and that of the buyer is to accept and pay in accordance with the contract.

§ 2-302. Unconscionable Contract or Clause.

(1) If the court as a matter of law finds the contract or any clause of the contract to have been unconscionable at the time it was made the court may refuse to enforce the contract, or it may enforce the remainder of the contract without the unconscionable clause, or it may so limit the application of any unconscionable clause as to avoid any unconscionable result.

(2) When it is claimed or appears to the court that the contract or any clause thereof may be unconscionable the parties shall be afforded a reasonable opportunity to present evidence as to its commercial setting, purpose and effect to aid the court in making the determination.

§ 2-303. Allocations or Division of Risks.

Where this Article allocates a risk or a burden as between the parties "unless otherwise agreed", the agreement may not only shift the allocation but may also divide the risk or burden.

§ 2-304. Price Payable in Money, Goods, Realty, or Otherwise.

(1) The price can be made payable in money or otherwise. If it is payable in whole or in part in goods each party is a seller of the goods which he is to transfer.

(2) Even though all or part of the price is payable in an interest in realty the transfer of the goods and the seller's obligations with reference to them are subject to this Article, but not the transfer of the interest in realty or the transferor's obligations in connection therewith.

§ 2-305. Open Price Term.

(1) The parties if they so intend can conclude a contract for sale even though the price is not settled. In such a case the price is a reasonable price at the time for delivery if

(a) nothing is said as to price; or

(b) the price is left to be agreed by the parties and they fail to agree; or

(c) the price is to be fixed in terms of some agreed market or other standard as set or recorded by a third person or agency and it is not so set or recorded.

(2) A price to be fixed by the seller or by the buyer means a price for him to fix in good faith.

(3) When a price left to be fixed otherwise than by agreement of the parties fails to be fixed through fault of one party the other may at his option treat the contract as cancelled or himself fix a reasonable price.

(4) Where, however, the parties intend not to be bound unless the price be fixed or agreed and it is not fixed or agreed there is no contract. In such a case the buyer must return any goods already received or if unable so to do must pay their reasonable value at the time of delivery and the seller must return any portion of the price paid on account.

§ 2-306. Output, Requirements and Exclusive Dealings.

(1) A term which measures the quantity by the output of the seller or the requirements of the buyer means such actual output or requirements as may occur in good faith, except that no quantity unreasonably disproportionate to any stated estimate or in the absence of a stated estimate to any normal or otherwise comparable prior output or requirements may be tendered or demanded.

(2) A lawful agreement by either the seller or the buyer for exclusive dealing in the kind of goods concerned imposes unless otherwise agreed an obligation by the seller to use best efforts to supply the goods and by the buyer to use best efforts to promote their sale.

§ 2-307. Delivery in Single Lot or Several Lots.

Unless otherwise agreed all goods called for by a contract for sale must be tendered in a single delivery and payment is due only on such tender but where the circumstances give either party the right to make or demand delivery in lots the price if it can be apportioned may be demanded for each lot.

§ 2-308. Absence of Specified Place for Delivery.

Unless otherwise agreed

(a) the place for delivery of goods is the seller's place of business or if he has none his residence; but

(b) in a contract for sale of identified goods which to the knowledge of the parties at the time of contracting are in some other place, that place is the place for their delivery; and

(c) documents of title may be delivered through customary banking channels.

§ 2-309. Absence of Specific Time Provisions; Notice of Termination.

(1) The time for shipment or delivery or any other action under a contract if not provided in this Article or agreed upon shall be a reasonable time.

(2) Where the contract provides for successive performances but is indefinite in duration it is valid for a reasonable time but unless otherwise agreed may be terminated at any time by either party.

(3) Termination of a contract by one party except on the happening of an agreed event requires that reasonable notification be received by the other party and an agreement dispensing with notification is invalid if its operation would be unconscionable.

§ 2-310. Open Time for Payment or Running of Credit; Authority to Ship Under Reservation.

Unless otherwise agreed

(a) payment is due at the time and place at which the buyer is to receive the goods even though the place of shipment is the place of delivery; and

(b) if the seller is authorized to send the goods he may ship them under reservation, and may tender the documents of title, but the buyer may inspect the goods after their arrival before payment is due unless such inspection is inconsistent with the terms of the contract (Section 2–513); and

(c) if delivery is authorized and made by way of documents of title otherwise than by subsection (b) then payment is due at the time and place at which the buyer is to receive the documents regardless of where the goods are to be received; and

(d) where the seller is required or authorized to ship the goods on credit the credit period runs from the time of shipment but postdating the invoice or delaying its dispatch will correspondingly delay the starting of the credit period.

§ 2-311. Options and Cooperation Respecting Performance.

(1) An agreement for sale which is otherwise sufficiently definite (subsection (3) of Section 2–204) to be a contract is not made invalid by the fact that it leaves particulars of performance to be specified by one of the parties. Any such specification must be made in good faith and within limits set by commercial reasonableness.

(2) Unless otherwise agreed specifications relating to assortment of the goods are at the buyer's option and except as otherwise provided in subsections (1)(c) and (3) of Section 2–319 specifications or arrangements relating to shipment are at the seller's option.

(3) Where such specification would materially affect the other party's performance but is not seasonably made or where one party's cooperation is necessary to the agreed performance of the other but is not seasonably forthcoming, the other party in addition to all other remedies

(a) is excused for any resulting delay in his own performance; and

(b) may also either proceed to perform in any reasonable manner or after the time for a material part of his own performance treat the failure to specify or to cooperate as a breach by failure to deliver or accept the goods.

§ 2-312. Warranty of Title and Against Infringement; Buyer's Obligation Against Infringement.

(1) Subject to subsection (2) there is in a contract for sale a warranty by the seller that

(a) the title conveyed shall be good, and its transfer rightful; and

(b) the goods shall be delivered free from any security interest or other lien or encumbrance of which the buyer at the time of contracting has no knowledge.

(2) A warranty under subsection (1) will be excluded or modified only by specific language or by circumstances which give the buyer reason to know that the person selling does not claim title in himself or that he is purporting to sell only such right or title as he or a third person may have.

(3) Unless otherwise agreed a seller who is a merchant regularly dealing in goods of the kind warrants that the goods shall be delivered free of the rightful claim of any third person by way of infringement or the like but a

buyer who furnishes specifications to the seller must hold the seller harmless against any such claim which arises out of compliance with the specifications.

§ 2-313. Express Warranties by Affirmation, Promise, Description, Sample.

(1) Express warranties by the seller are created as follows:

(a) Any affirmation of fact or promise made by the seller to the buyer which relates to the goods and becomes part of the basis of the bargain creates an express warranty that the goods shall conform to the affirmation or promise.

(b) Any description of the goods which is made part of the basis of the bargain creates an express warranty that the goods shall conform to the description.

(c) Any sample or model which is made part of the basis of the bargain creates an express warranty that the whole of the goods shall conform to the sample or model.

(2) It is not necessary to the creation of an express warranty that the seller use formal words such as "warrant" or "guarantee" or that he have a specific intention to make a warranty, but an affirmation merely of the value of the goods or a statement purporting to be merely the seller's opinion or commendation of the goods does not create a warranty.

§ 2-314. Implied Warranty: Merchantability; Usage of Trade.

(1) Unless excluded or modified (Section 2–316), a warranty that the goods shall be merchantable is implied in a contract for their sale if the seller is a merchant with respect to goods of that kind. Under this section the serving for value of food or drink to be consumed either on the premises or elsewhere is a sale.

(2) Goods to be merchantable must be at least such as

(a) pass without objection in the trade under the contract description; and

(b) in the case of fungible goods, are of fair average quality within the description; and

(c) are fit for the ordinary purposes for which such goods are used; and

(d) run, within the variations permitted by the agreement, of even kind, quality and quantity within each unit and among all units involved; and

(e) are adequately contained, packaged, and labeled as the agreement may require; and

(f) conform to the promises or affirmations of fact made on the container or label if any.

(3) Unless excluded or modified (Section 2–316) other implied warranties may arise from course of dealing or usage of trade.

§ 2-315. Implied Warranty: Fitness for Particular Purpose.

Where the seller at the time of contracting has reason to know any particular purpose for which the goods are required and that the buyer is relying on the seller's skill or judgment to select or furnish suitable goods, there is unless excluded or modified under the next section an implied warranty that the goods shall be fit for such purpose.

§ 2-316. Exclusion or Modification of Warranties.

(1) Words or conduct relevant to the creation of an express warranty and words or conduct tending to negate or limit warranty shall be construed wherever reasonable as consistent with each other; but subject to the provisions of this Article on parol or extrinsic evidence (Section 2–202) negation or limitation is inoperative to the extent that such construction is unreasonable.

(2) Subject to subsection (3), to exclude or modify the implied warranty of merchantability or any part of it the language must mention merchantability and in case of a writing must be conspicuous, and to exclude or modify any implied warranty of fitness the exclusion must be by a writing and conspicuous. Language to exclude all implied warranties of fitness is sufficient if it states, for example, that "There are no warranties which extend beyond the description on the face hereof."

(3) Notwithstanding subsection (2)

(a) unless the circumstances indicate otherwise, all implied warranties are excluded by expressions like "as is", "with all faults" or other language which in common understanding calls the buyer's attention to the exclusion of warranties and makes plain that there is no implied warranty; and

(b) when the buyer before entering into the contract has examined the goods or the sample or model as fully as he desired or has refused to examine the goods there is no implied warranty with regard to defects which an examination ought in the circumstances to have revealed to him; and

(c) an implied warranty can also be excluded or modified by course of dealing or course of performance or usage of trade.

(4) Remedies for breach of warranty can be limited in accordance with the provisions of this Article on liquidation or limitation of damages and on contractual modification of remedy (Sections 2–718 and 2–719).

§ 2-317. Cumulation and Conflict of Warranties Express or Implied.

Warranties whether express or implied shall be construed as consistent with each other and as cumulative, but if such construction is unreasonable the intention of the parties shall determine which warranty is dominant. In ascertaining that intention the following rules apply:

(a) Exact or technical specifications displace an inconsistent sample or model or general language of description.

(b) A sample from an existing bulk displaces inconsistent general language of description.

(c) Express warranties displace inconsistent implied warranties other than an implied warranty of fitness for a particular purpose.

§ 2-318. Third Party Beneficiaries of Warranties Express or Implied.

Note: If this Act is introduced in the Congress of the United States this section should be omitted. (States to select one alternative.)

Alternative A

A seller's warranty whether express or implied extends to any natural person who is in the family or household of his buyer or who is a guest in his home if it is reasonable to expect that such person may use, consume or be affected by the goods and who is injured in person by breach of the warranty. A seller may not exclude or limit the operation of this section.

Alternative B

A seller's warranty whether express or implied extends to any natural person who may reasonably be expected to use, consume or be affected by the goods and who is injured in person by breach of the warranty. A seller may not exclude or limit the operation of this section.

Alternative C

A seller's warranty whether express or implied extends to any person who may reasonably be expected to use, consume or be affected by the goods and who is injured by breach of the warranty. A seller may not exclude or limit the operation of this section with respect to injury to the person of an individual to whom the warranty extends.

As amended 1966.

§ 2-319. F.O.B. and F.A.S. Terms.

(1) Unless otherwise agreed the term F.O.B. (which means "free on board") at a named place, even though used only in connection with the stated price, is a delivery term under which

    (a) when the term is F.O.B. the place of shipment, the seller must at that place ship the goods in the manner provided in this Article (Section 2–504) and bear the expense and risk of putting them into the possession of the carrier; or

    (b) when the term is F.O.B. the place of destination, the seller must at his own expense and risk transport the goods to that place and there tender delivery of them in the manner provided in this Article (Section 2–503);

    (c) when under either (a) or (b) the term is also F.O.B. vessel, car or other vehicle, the seller must in addition at his own expense and risk load the goods on board. If the term is F.O.B. vessel the buyer must name the vessel and in an appropriate case the seller must comply with the provisions of this Article on the form of bill of lading (Section 2–323).

(2) Unless otherwise agreed the term F.A.S. vessel (which means "free alongside") at a named port, even though used only in connection with the stated price, is a delivery term under which the seller must

    (a) at his own expense and risk deliver the goods alongside the vessel in the manner usual in that port or on a dock designated and provided by the buyer; and

    (b) obtain and tender a receipt for the goods in exchange for which the carrier is under a duty to issue a bill of lading.

(3) Unless otherwise agreed in any case falling within subsection (1)(a) or (c) or subsection (2) the buyer must seasonably give any needed instructions for making delivery, including when the term is F.A.S. or F.O.B. the loading berth of the vessel and in an appropriate case its name and sailing date. The seller may treat the failure of needed instructions as a failure of cooperation under this Article (Section 2–311). He may also at his option move the goods in any reasonable manner preparatory to delivery or shipment.

(4) Under the term F.O.B. vessel or F.A.S. unless otherwise agreed the buyer must make payment against tender of the required documents and the seller may not tender nor the buyer demand delivery of the goods in substitution for the documents.

§ 2-320. C.I.F. and C. & F. Terms.

(1) The term C.I.F. means that the price includes in a lump sum the cost of the goods and the insurance and freight to the named destination. The term C. & F. or C.F. means that the price so includes cost and freight to the named destination.

(2) Unless otherwise agreed and even though used only in connection with the stated price and destination, the term C.I.F. destination or its equivalent requires the seller at his own expense and risk to

    (a) put the goods into the possession of a carrier at the port for shipment and obtain a negotiable bill or bills of lading covering the entire transportation to the named destination; and

    (b) load the goods and obtain a receipt from the carrier (which may be contained in the bill of lading) showing that the freight has been paid or provided for; and

    (c) obtain a policy or certificate of insurance, including any war risk insurance, of a kind and on terms then current at the port of shipment in the usual amount, in the currency of the contract, shown to cover the same goods covered by the bill of lading and providing for payment of loss to the order of the buyer or for the account of whom it may concern; but the seller may add to the price the amount of the premium for any such war risk insurance; and

    (d) prepare an invoice of the goods and procure any other documents required to effect shipment or to comply with the contract; and

    (e) forward and tender with commercial promptness all the documents in due form and with any indorsement necessary to perfect the buyer's rights.

(3) Unless otherwise agreed the term C. & F. or its equivalent has the same effect and imposes upon the seller the same obligations and risks as a C.I.F. term except the obligation as to insurance.

(4) Under the term C.I.F. or C. & F. unless otherwise agreed the buyer must make payment against tender of the required documents and the seller may not tender nor the buyer demand delivery of the goods in substitution for the documents.

§ 2-321. C.I.F. or C. & F.: "Net Landed Weights"; "Payment on Arrival"; Warranty of Condition on Arrival.

Under a contract containing a term C.I.F. or C. & F.

(1) Where the price is based on or is to be adjusted according to "net landed weights", "delivered weights", "out turn" quantity or quality or the like, unless otherwise agreed the seller must reasonably estimate the price. The payment due on tender of the documents called for by the contract is the amount so estimated, but after final adjustment of the price a settlement must be made with commercial promptness.

(2) An agreement described in subsection (1) or any warranty of quality or condition of the goods on arrival places upon the seller the risk of ordinary deterioration, shrinkage and the like in transportation but has no effect on the place or time of identification to the contract for sale or delivery or on the passing of the risk of loss.

(3) Unless otherwise agreed where the contract provides for payment on or after arrival of the goods the seller must before payment allow such preliminary inspection as is feasible; but if the goods are lost delivery of the documents and payment are due when the goods should have arrived.

§ 2-322. Delivery "Ex-Ship".

(1) Unless otherwise agreed a term for delivery of goods "ex-ship" (which means from the carrying vessel) or in equivalent language is not restricted to a particular ship and requires delivery from a ship which has reached a place at the named port of destination where goods of the kind are usually discharged.

(2) Under such a term unless otherwise agreed

    (a) the seller must discharge all liens arising out of the carriage and furnish the buyer with a direction which puts the carrier under a duty to deliver the goods; and

    (b) the risk of loss does not pass to the buyer until the goods leave the ship's tackle or are otherwise properly unloaded.

§ 2-323. Form of Bill of Lading Required in Overseas Shipment; "Overseas".

(1) Where the contract contemplates overseas shipment and contains a term C.I.F. or C. & F. or F.O.B. vessel, the seller unless otherwise agreed must obtain a negotiable bill of lading stating that the goods have been loaded on board or, in the case of a term C.I.F. or C. & F., received for shipment.

(2) Where in a case within subsection (1) a bill of lading has been issued in a set of parts, unless otherwise agreed if the documents are not to be sent from abroad the buyer may demand tender of the full set; otherwise only one part of the bill of lading need be tendered. Even if the agreement expressly requires a full set

    (a) due tender of a single part is acceptable within the provisions of this Article on cure of improper delivery (subsection (1) of Section 2–508); and

    (b) even though the full set is demanded, if the documents are sent from abroad the person tendering an incomplete set may nevertheless require payment upon furnishing an indemnity which the buyer in good faith deems adequate.

(3) A shipment by water or by air or a contract contemplating such shipment is "overseas" insofar as by usage of trade or agreement it is subject to the commercial, financing or shipping practices characteristic of international deep water commerce.

§ 2-324. "No Arrival, No Sale" Term.

Under a term "no arrival, no sale" or terms of like meaning, unless otherwise agreed,

(a) the seller must properly ship conforming goods and if they arrive by any means he must tender them on arrival but he assumes no obligation that the goods will arrive unless he has caused the non-arrival; and

(b) where without fault of the seller the goods are in part lost or have so deteriorated as no longer to conform to the contract or arrive after the contract time, the buyer may proceed as if there had been casualty to identified goods (Section 2–613).

§ 2-325. "Letter of Credit" Term; "Confirmed Credit".

(1) Failure of the buyer seasonably to furnish an agreed letter of credit is a breach of the contract for sale.

(2) The delivery to seller of a proper letter of credit suspends the buyer's obligation to pay. If the letter of credit is dishonored, the seller may on seasonable notification to the buyer require payment directly from him.

(3) Unless otherwise agreed the term "letter of credit" or "banker's credit" in a contract for sale means an irrevocable credit issued by a financing agency of good repute and, where the shipment is overseas, of good international repute. The term "confirmed credit" means that the credit must also carry the direct obligation of such an agency which does business in the seller's financial market.

§ 2-326. Sale on Approval and Sale or Return; Rights of Creditors.

(1) Unless otherwise agreed, if delivered goods may be returned by the buyer even though they conform to the contract, the transaction is

(a) a "sale on approval" if the goods are delivered primarily for use, and

(b) a "sale or return" if the goods are delivered primarily for resale.

(2) Goods held on approval are not subject to the claims of the buyer's creditors until acceptance; goods held on sale or return are subject to such claims while in the buyer's possession.

(3) Any "or return" term of a contract for sale is to be treated as a separate contract for sale within the statute of frauds section of this Article (Section 2–201) and as contradicting the sale aspect of the contract within the provisions of this Article or on parol or extrinsic evidence (Section 2–202). As amended in 1999.

§ 2-327. Special Incidents of Sale on Approval and Sale or Return.

(1) Under a sale on approval unless otherwise agreed

(a) although the goods are identified to the contract the risk of loss and the title do not pass to the buyer until acceptance; and

(b) use of the goods consistent with the purpose of trial is not acceptance but failure seasonably to notify the seller of election to return the goods is acceptance, and if the goods conform to the contract acceptance of any part is acceptance of the whole; and

(c) after due notification of election to return, the return is at the seller's risk and expense but a merchant buyer must follow any reasonable instructions.

(2) Under a sale or return unless otherwise agreed

(a) the option to return extends to the whole or any commercial unit of the goods while in substantially their original condition, but must be exercised seasonally; and

(b) the return is at the buyer's risk and expense.

§ 2-328. Sale by Auction.

(1) In a sale by auction if goods are put up in lots each lot is the subject of a separate sale.

(2) A sale by auction is complete when the auctioneer so announces by the fall of the hammer or in other customary manner. Where a bid is made while the hammer is falling in acceptance of a prior bid the auctioneer may in his discretion reopen the bidding or declare the goods sold under the bid on which the hammer was falling.

(3) Such a sale is with reserve unless the goods are in explicit terms put up without reserve. In an auction with reserve the auctioneer may withdraw the goods at any time until he announces completion of the sale. In an auction without reserve, after the auctioneer calls for bids on an article or lot, that article or lot cannot be withdrawn unless no bid is made within a reasonable time. In either case a bidder may retract his bid until the auctioneer's announcement of completion of the sale, but a bidder's retraction does not revive any previous bid.

(4) If the auctioneer knowingly receives a bid on the seller's behalf or the seller makes or procures such as bid, and notice has not been given that liberty for such bidding is reserved, the buyer may at his option avoid the sale or take the goods at the price of the last good faith bid prior to the completion of the sale. This subsection shall not apply to any bid at a forced sale.

PART 4: Title, Creditors and Good Faith Purchasers

§ 2-401. Passing of Title; Reservation for Security; Limited Application of This Section.

Each provision of this Article with regard to the rights, obligations and remedies of the seller, the buyer, purchasers or other third parties applies irrespective of title to the goods except where the provision refers to such title. Insofar as situations are not covered by the other provisions of this Article and matters concerning title became material the following rules apply:

(1) Title to goods cannot pass under a contract for sale prior to their identification to the contract (Section 2–501), and unless otherwise explicitly agreed the buyer acquires by their identification a special property as limited by this Act. Any retention or reservation by the seller of the title (property) in goods shipped or delivered to the buyer is limited in effect to a reservation of a security interest. Subject to these provisions and to the provisions of the Article on Secured Transactions (Article 9), title to goods passes from the seller to the buyer in any manner and on any conditions explicitly agreed on by the parties.

(2) Unless otherwise explicitly agreed title passes to the buyer at the time and place at which the seller completes his performance with reference to the physical delivery of the goods, despite any reservation of a security interest and even though a document of title is to be delivered at a different time or place; and in particular and despite any reservation of a security interest by the bill of lading

(a) if the contract requires or authorizes the seller to send the goods to the buyer but does not require him to deliver them at destination, title passes to the buyer at the time and place of shipment; but

(b) if the contract requires delivery at destination, title passes on tender there.

(3) Unless otherwise explicitly agreed where delivery is to be made without moving the goods,

    (a) if the seller is to deliver a document of title, title passes at the time when and the place where he delivers such documents; or

    (b) if the goods are at the time of contracting already identified and no documents are to be delivered, title passes at the time and place of contracting.

(4) A rejection or other refusal by the buyer to receive or retain the goods, whether or not justified, or a justified revocation of acceptance revests title to the goods in the seller. Such revesting occurs by operation of law and is not a "sale".

§ 2-402. Rights of Seller's Creditors Against Sold Goods.

(1) Except as provided in subsections (2) and (3), rights of unsecured creditors of the seller with respect to goods which have been identified to a contract for sale are subject to the buyer's rights to recover the goods under this Article (Sections 2–502 and 2–716).

(2) A creditor of the seller may treat a sale or an identification of goods to a contract for sale as void if as against him a retention of possession by the seller is fraudulent under any rule of law of the state where the goods are situated, except that retention of possession in good faith and current course of trade by a merchant-seller for a commercially reasonable time after a sale or identification is not fraudulent.

(3) Nothing in this Article shall be deemed to impair the rights of creditors of the seller

    (a) under the provisions of the Article on Secured Transactions (Article 9); or

    (b) where identification to the contract or delivery is made not in current course of trade but in satisfaction of or as security for a pre-existing claim for money, security or the like and is made under circumstances which under any rule of law of the state where the goods are situated would apart from this Article constitute the transaction a fraudulent transfer or voidable preference.

§ 2-403. Power to Transfer; Good Faith Purchase of Goods; "Entrusting".

(1) A purchaser of goods acquires all title which his transferor had or had power to transfer except that a purchaser of a limited interest acquires rights only to the extent of the interest purchased. A person with voidable title has power to transfer a good title to a good faith purchaser for value. When goods have been delivered under a transaction of purchase the purchaser has such power even though

    (a) the transferor was deceived as to the identity of the purchaser, or

    (b) the delivery was in exchange for a check which is later dishonored, or

    (c) it was agreed that the transaction was to be a "cash sale", or

    (d) the delivery was procured through fraud punishable as larcenous under the criminal law.

(2) Any entrusting of possession of goods to a merchant who deals in goods of that kind gives him power to transfer all rights of the entruster to a buyer in ordinary course of business.

(3) "Entrusting" includes any delivery and any acquiescence in retention of possession regardless of any condition expressed between the parties to the delivery or acquiescence and regardless of whether the procurement of the entrusting or the possessor's disposition of the goods have been such as to be larcenous under the criminal law.

(4) The rights of other purchasers of goods and of lien creditors are governed by the Articles on Secured Transactions (Article 9), Bulk Transfers (Article 6) and Documents of Title (Article 7).

As amended in 1988.

PART 5: Performance

§ 2-501. Insurable Interest in Goods; Manner of Identification of Goods.

(1) The buyer obtains a special property and an insurable interest in goods by identification of existing goods as goods to which the contract refers even though the goods so identified are non-conforming and he has an option to return or reject them. Such identification can be made at any time and in any manner explicitly agreed to by the parties. In the absence of explicit agreement identification occurs

    (a) when the contract is made if it is for the sale of goods already existing and identified;

    (b) if the contract is for the sale of future goods other than those described in paragraph (c), when goods are shipped, marked or otherwise designated by the seller as goods to which the contract refers;

    (c) when the crops are planted or otherwise become growing crops or the young are conceived if the contract is for the sale of unborn young to be born within twelve months after contracting or for the sale of crops to be harvested within twelve months or the next normal harvest season after contracting whichever is longer.

(2) The seller retains an insurable interest in goods so long as title to or any security interest in the goods remains in him and where the identification is by the seller alone he may until default or insolvency or notification to the buyer that the identification is final substitute other goods for those identified.

(3) Nothing in this section impairs any insurable interest recognized under any other statute or rule of law.

§ 2-502. Buyer's Right to Goods on Seller's Insolvency.

(1) Subject to subsections (2) and (3) and even though the goods have not been shipped a buyer who has paid a part or all of the price of goods in which he has a special property under the provisions of the immediately preceding section may on making and keeping good a tender of any unpaid portion of their price recover them from the seller if:

    (a) in the case of goods bought for personal, family, or household purposes, the seller repudiates or fails to deliver as required by the contract; or

    (b) in all cases, the seller becomes insolvent within ten days after receipt of the first installment on their price.

(2) The buyer's right to recover the goods under subsection (1)(a) vests upon acquisition of a special property, even if the seller had not then repudiated or failed to deliver.

(3) If the identification creating his special property has been made by the buyer he acquires the right to recover the goods only if they conform to the contract for sale.

As amended in 1999.

§ 2-503. Manner of Seller's Tender of Delivery.

(1) Tender of delivery requires that the seller put and hold conforming goods at the buyer's disposition and give the buyer any notification reasonably necessary to enable him to take delivery. The manner, time and place for tender are determined by the agreement and this Article, and in particular

    (a) tender must be at a reasonable hour, and if it is of goods they must be kept available for the period reasonably necessary to enable the buyer to take possession; but

    (b) unless otherwise agreed the buyer must furnish facilities reasonably suited to the receipt of the goods.

(2) Where the case is within the next section respecting shipment tender requires that the seller comply with its provisions.

(3) Where the seller is required to deliver at a particular destination tender requires that he comply with subsection (1) and also in any appro-

priate case tender documents as described in subsections (4) and (5) of this section.

(4) Where goods are in the possession of a bailee and are to be delivered without being moved

(a) tender requires that the seller either tender a negotiable document of title covering such goods or procure acknowledgment by the bailee of the buyer's right to possession of the goods; but

(b) tender to the buyer of a non-negotiable document of title or of a written direction to the bailee to deliver is sufficient tender unless the buyer seasonably objects, and receipt by the bailee of notification of the buyer's rights fixes those rights as against the bailee and all third persons; but risk of loss of the goods and of any failure by the bailee to honor the non-negotiable document of title or to obey the direction remains on the seller until the buyer has had a reasonable time to present the document or direction, and a refusal by the bailee to honor the document or to obey the direction defeats the tender.

(5) Where the contract requires the seller to deliver documents

(a) he must tender all such documents in correct form, except as provided in this Article with respect to bills of lading in a set (subsection (2) of Section 2–323); and

(b) tender through customary banking channels is sufficient and dishonor of a draft accompanying the documents constitutes non-acceptance or rejection.

§ 2-504. Shipment by Seller.

Where the seller is required or authorized to send the goods to the buyer and the contract does not require him to deliver them at a particular destination, then unless otherwise agreed he must

(a) put the goods in the possession of such a carrier and make such a contract for their transportation as may be reasonable having regard to the nature of the goods and other circumstances of the case; and

(b) obtain and promptly deliver or tender in due form any document necessary to enable the buyer to obtain possession of the goods or otherwise required by the agreement or by usage of trade; and

(c) promptly notify the buyer of the shipment.

Failure to notify the buyer under paragraph (c) or to make a proper contract under paragraph (a) is a ground for rejection only if material delay or loss ensues.

§ 2-505. Seller's Shipment under Reservation.

(1) Where the seller has identified goods to the contract by or before shipment:

(a) his procurement of a negotiable bill of lading to his own order or otherwise reserves in him a security interest in the goods. His procurement of the bill to the order of a financing agency or of the buyer indicates in addition only the seller's expectation of transferring that interest to the person named.

(b) a non-negotiable bill of lading to himself or his nominee reserves possession of the goods as security but except in a case of conditional delivery (subsection (2) of Section 2–507) a non-negotiable bill of lading naming the buyer as consignee reserves no security interest even though the seller retains possession of the bill of lading.

(2) When shipment by the seller with reservation of a security interest is in violation of the contract for sale it constitutes an improper contract for transportation within the preceding section but impairs neither the rights given to the buyer by shipment and identification of the goods to the contract nor the seller's powers as a holder of a negotiable document.

§ 2-506. Rights of Financing Agency.

(1) A financing agency by paying or purchasing for value a draft which relates to a shipment of goods acquires to the extent of the payment or purchase and in addition to its own rights under the draft and any document of title securing it any rights of the shipper in the goods including the right to stop delivery and the shipper's right to have the draft honored by the buyer.

(2) The right to reimbursement of a financing agency which has in good faith honored or purchased the draft under commitment to or authority from the buyer is not impaired by subsequent discovery of defects with reference to any relevant document which was apparently regular on its face.

§ 2-507. Effect of Seller's Tender; Delivery on Condition.

(1) Tender of delivery is a condition to the buyer's duty to accept the goods and, unless otherwise agreed, to his duty to pay for them. Tender entitles the seller to acceptance of the goods and to payment according to the contract.

(2) Where payment is due and demanded on the delivery to the buyer of goods or documents of title, his right as against the seller to retain or dispose of them is conditional upon his making the payment due.

§ 2-508. Cure by Seller of Improper Tender or Delivery; Replacement.

(1) Where any tender or delivery by the seller is rejected because non-conforming and the time for performance has not yet expired, the seller may seasonably notify the buyer of his intention to cure and may then within the contract time make a conforming delivery.

(2) Where the buyer rejects a non-conforming tender which the seller had reasonable grounds to believe would be acceptable with or without money allowance the seller may if he seasonably notifies the buyer have a further reasonable time to substitute a conforming tender.

§ 2-509. Risk of Loss in the Absence of Breach.

(1) Where the contract requires or authorizes the seller to ship the goods by carrier

(a) if it does not require him to deliver them at a particular destination, the risk of loss passes to the buyer when the goods are duly delivered to the carrier even though the shipment is under reservation (Section 2–505); but

(b) if it does require him to deliver them at a particular destination and the goods are there duly tendered while in the possession of the carrier, the risk of loss passes to the buyer when the goods are there duly so tendered as to enable the buyer to take delivery.

(2) Where the goods are held by a bailee to be delivered without being moved, the risk of loss passes to the buyer

(a) on his receipt of a negotiable document of title covering the goods; or

(b) on acknowledgment by the bailee of the buyer's right to possession of the goods; or

(c) after his receipt of a non-negotiable document of title or other written direction to deliver, as provided in subsection (4)(b) of Section 2–503.

(3) In any case not within subsection (1) or (2), the risk of loss passes to the buyer on his receipt of the goods if the seller is a merchant; otherwise the risk passes to the buyer on tender of delivery.

(4) The provisions of this section are subject to contrary agreement of the parties and to the provisions of this Article on sale on approval (Section 2–327) and on effect of breach on risk of loss (Section 2–510).

§ 2-510. Effect of Breach on Risk of Loss.

(1) Where a tender or delivery of goods so fails to conform to the contract as to give a right of rejection the risk of their loss remains on the seller until cure or acceptance.

(2) Where the buyer rightfully revokes acceptance he may to the extent of any deficiency in his effective insurance coverage treat the risk of loss as having rested on the seller from the beginning.

(3) Where the buyer as to conforming goods already identified to the contract for sale repudiates or is otherwise in breach before risk of their loss has passed to him, the seller may to the extent of any deficiency in his effective insurance coverage treat the risk of loss as resting on the buyer for a commercially reasonable time.

§ 2-511. Tender of Payment by Buyer; Payment by Check.

(1) Unless otherwise agreed tender of payment is a condition to the seller's duty to tender and complete any delivery.

(2) Tender of payment is sufficient when made by any means or in any manner current in the ordinary course of business unless the seller demands payment in legal tender and gives any extension of time reasonably necessary to procure it.

(3) Subject to the provisions of this Act on the effect of an instrument on an obligation (Section 3–310), payment by check is conditional and is defeated as between the parties by dishonor of the check on due presentment.
As amended in 1994.

§ 2-512. Payment by Buyer Before Inspection.

(1) Where the contract requires payment before inspection non-conformity of the goods does not excuse the buyer from so making payment unless

    (a) the non-conformity appears without inspection; or

    (b) despite tender of the required documents the circumstances would justify injunction against honor under this Act (Section 5–109(b)).

(2) Payment pursuant to subsection (1) does not constitute an acceptance of goods or impair the buyer's right to inspect or any of his remedies.
As amended in 1995.

§ 2-513. Buyer's Right to Inspection of Goods.

(1) Unless otherwise agreed and subject to subsection (3), where goods are tendered or delivered or identified to the contract for sale, the buyer has a right before payment or acceptance to inspect them at any reasonable place and time and in any reasonable manner. When the seller is required or authorized to send the goods to the buyer, the inspection may be after their arrival.

(2) Expenses of inspection must be borne by the buyer but may be recovered from the seller if the goods do not conform and are rejected.

(3) Unless otherwise agreed and subject to the provisions of this Article on C.I.F. contracts (subsection (3) of Section 2–321), the buyer is not entitled to inspect the goods before payment of the price when the contract provides

    (a) for delivery "C.O.D." or on other like terms; or

    (b) for payment against documents of title, except where such payment is due only after the goods are to become available for inspection.

(4) A place or method of inspection fixed by the parties is presumed to be exclusive but unless otherwise expressly agreed it does not postpone identification or shift the place for delivery or for passing the risk of loss. If compliance becomes impossible, inspection shall be as provided in this section unless the place or method fixed was clearly intended as an indispensable condition failure of which avoids the contract.

§ 2-514. When Documents Deliverable on Acceptance; When on Payment.

Unless otherwise agreed documents against which a draft is drawn are to be delivered to the drawee on acceptance of the draft if it is payable more than three days after presentment; otherwise, only on payment.

§ 2-515. Preserving Evidence of Goods in Dispute.

In furtherance of the adjustment of any claim or dispute

    (a) either party on reasonable notification to the other and for the purpose of ascertaining the facts and preserving evidence has the right to inspect, test and sample the goods including such of them as may be in the possession or control of the other; and

    (b) the parties may agree to a third party inspection or survey to determine the conformity or condition of the goods and may agree that the findings shall be binding upon them in any subsequent litigation or adjustment.

PART 6: Breach, Repudiation and Excuse

§ 2-601. Buyer's Rights on Improper Delivery.

Subject to the provisions of this Article on breach in installment contracts (Section 2–612) and unless otherwise agreed under the sections on contractual limitations of remedy (Sections 2–718 and 2–719), if the goods or the tender of delivery fail in any respect to conform to the contract, the buyer may

    (a) reject the whole; or

    (b) accept the whole; or

    (c) accept any commercial unit or units and reject the rest.

§ 2-602. Manner and Effect of Rightful Rejection.

(1) Rejection of goods must be within a reasonable time after their delivery or tender. It is ineffective unless the buyer seasonably notifies the seller.

(2) Subject to the provisions of the two following sections on rejected goods (Sections 2–603 and 2–604),

    (a) after rejection any exercise of ownership by the buyer with respect to any commercial unit is wrongful as against the seller; and

    (b) if the buyer has before rejection taken physical possession of goods in which he does not have a security interest under the provisions of this Article (subsection (3) of Section 2–711), he is under a duty after rejection to hold them with reasonable care at the seller's disposition for a time sufficient to permit the seller to remove them; but

    (c) the buyer has no further obligations with regard to goods rightfully rejected.

(3) The seller's rights with respect to goods wrongfully rejected are governed by the provisions of this Article on Seller's remedies in general (Section 2–703).

§ 2-603. Merchant Buyer's Duties as to Rightfully Rejected Goods.

(1) Subject to any security interest in the buyer (subsection (3) of Section 2–711), when the seller has no agent or place of business at the market of rejection a merchant buyer is under a duty after rejection of goods in his possession or control to follow any reasonable instructions received from the seller with respect to the goods and in the absence of such instructions to make reasonable efforts to sell them for the seller's account if they are perishable or threaten to decline in value speedily. Instructions are not reasonable if on demand indemnity for expenses is not forthcoming.

(2) When the buyer sells goods under subsection (1), he is entitled to reimbursement from the seller or out of the proceeds for reasonable expenses of caring for and selling them, and if the expenses include no selling commission then to such commission as is usual in the trade or if there is none to a reasonable sum not exceeding ten per cent on the gross proceeds.

(3) In complying with this section the buyer is held only to good faith and good faith conduct hereunder is neither acceptance nor conversion nor the basis of an action for damages.

§ 2-604. Buyer's Options as to Salvage of Rightfully Rejected Goods.

Subject to the provisions of the immediately preceding section on perishables if the seller gives no instructions within a reasonable time after notification of rejection the buyer may store the rejected goods for the seller's account or reship them to him or resell them for the seller's account with reimbursement as provided in the preceding section. Such action is not acceptance or conversion.

§ 2-605. Waiver of Buyer's Objections by Failure to Particularize.

(1) The buyer's failure to state in connection with rejection a particular defect which is ascertainable by reasonable inspection precludes him from relying on the unstated defect to justify rejection or to establish breach

    (a) where the seller could have cured it if stated seasonably; or

    (b) between merchants when the seller has after rejection made a request in writing for a full and final written statement of all defects on which the buyer proposes to rely.

(2) Payment against documents made without reservation of rights precludes recovery of the payment for defects apparent on the face of the documents.

§ 2-606. What Constitutes Acceptance of Goods.

(1) Acceptance of goods occurs when the buyer

    (a) after a reasonable opportunity to inspect the goods signifies to the seller that the goods are conforming or that he will take or retain them in spite of their nonconformity; or

    (b) fails to make an effective rejection (subsection (1) of Section 2–602), but such acceptance does not occur until the buyer has had a reasonable opportunity to inspect them; or

    (c) does any act inconsistent with the seller's ownership; but if such act is wrongful as against the seller it is an acceptance only if ratified by him.

(2) Acceptance of a part of any commercial unit is acceptance of that entire unit.

§ 2-607. Effect of Acceptance; Notice of Breach; Burden of Establishing Breach After Acceptance; Notice of Claim or Litigation to Person Answerable Over.

(1) The buyer must pay at the contract rate for any goods accepted.

(2) Acceptance of goods by the buyer precludes rejection of the goods accepted and if made with knowledge of a non-conformity cannot be revoked because of it unless the acceptance was on the reasonable assumption that the non-conformity would be seasonably cured but acceptance does not of itself impair any other remedy provided by this Article for non-conformity.

(3) Where a tender has been accepted

    (a) the buyer must within a reasonable time after he discovers or should have discovered any breach notify the seller of breach or be barred from any remedy; and

    (b) if the claim is one for infringement or the like (subsection (3) of Section 2–312) and the buyer is sued as a result of such a breach he must so notify the seller within a reasonable time after he receives notice of the litigation or be barred from any remedy over for liability established by the litigation.

(4) The burden is on the buyer to establish any breach with respect to the goods accepted.

(5) Where the buyer is sued for breach of a warranty or other obligation for which his seller is answerable over

    (a) he may give his seller written notice of the litigation. If the notice states that the seller may come in and defend and that if the seller does not do so he will be bound in any action against him by his buyer by any determination of fact common to the two litigations, then unless the seller after seasonable receipt of the notice does come in and defend he is so bound.

    (b) if the claim is one for infringement or the like (subsection (3) of Section 2–312) the original seller may demand in writing that his buyer turn over to him control of the litigation including settlement or else be barred from any remedy over and if he also agrees to bear all expense and to satisfy any adverse judgment, then unless the buyer after seasonable receipt of the demand does turn over control the buyer is so barred.

(6) The provisions of subsections (3), (4) and (5) apply to any obligation of a buyer to hold the seller harmless against infringement or the like (subsection (3) of Section 2–312).

§ 2-608. Revocation of Acceptance in Whole or in Part.

(1) The buyer may revoke his acceptance of a lot or commercial unit whose non-conformity substantially impairs its value to him if he has accepted it

    (a) on the reasonable assumption that its nonconformity would be cured and it has not been seasonably cured; or

    (b) without discovery of such non-conformity if his acceptance was reasonably induced either by the difficulty of discovery before acceptance or by the seller's assurances.

(2) Revocation of acceptance must occur within a reasonable time after the buyer discovers or should have discovered the ground for it and before any substantial change in condition of the goods which is not caused by their own defects. It is not effective until the buyer notifies the seller of it.

(3) A buyer who so revokes has the same rights and duties with regard to the goods involved as if he had rejected them.

§ 2-609. Right to Adequate Assurance of Performance.

(1) A contract for sale imposes an obligation on each party that the other's expectation of receiving due performance will not be impaired. When reasonable grounds for insecurity arise with respect to the performance of either party the other may in writing demand adequate assurance of due performance and until he receives such assurance may if commercially reasonable suspend any performance for which he has not already received the agreed return.

(2) Between merchants the reasonableness of grounds for insecurity and the adequacy of any assurance offered shall be determined according to commercial standards.

(3) Acceptance of any improper delivery or payment does not prejudice the party's right to demand adequate assurance of future performance.

(4) After receipt of a justified demand failure to provide within a reasonable time not exceeding thirty days such assurance of due performance as is adequate under the circumstances of the particular case is a repudiation of the contract.

§ 2-610. Anticipatory Repudiation.

When either party repudiates the contract with respect to a performance not yet due the loss of which will substantially impair the value of the contract to the other, the aggrieved party may

(a) for a commercially reasonable time await performance by the repudiating party; or

(b) resort to any remedy for breach (Section 2–703 or Section 2–711), even though he has notified the repudiating party that he would await the latter's performance and has urged retraction; and

(c) in either case suspend his own performance or proceed in accordance with the provisions of this Article on the seller's right to identify goods to the contract notwithstanding breach or to salvage unfinished goods (Section 2–704).

§ 2-611. Retraction of Anticipatory Repudiation.

(1) Until the repudiating party's next performance is due he can retract his repudiation unless the aggrieved party has since the repudiation cancelled or materially changed his position or otherwise indicated that he considers the repudiation final.

(2) Retraction may be by any method which clearly indicates to the aggrieved party that the repudiating party intends to perform, but must include any assurance justifiably demanded under the provisions of this Article (Section 2–609).

(3) Retraction reinstates the repudiating party's rights under the contract with due excuse and allowance to the aggrieved party for any delay occasioned by the repudiation.

§ 2-612. "Installment Contract"; Breach.

(1) An "installment contract" is one which requires or authorizes the delivery of goods in separate lots to be separately accepted, even though the contract contains a clause "each delivery is a separate contract" or its equivalent.

(2) The buyer may reject any installment which is non-conforming if the non-conformity substantially impairs the value of that installment and cannot be cured or if the non-conformity is a defect in the required documents; but if the non-conformity does not fall within subsection (3) and the seller gives adequate assurance of its cure the buyer must accept that installment.

(3) Whenever non-conformity or default with respect to one or more installments substantially impairs the value of the whole contract there is a breach of the whole. But the aggrieved party reinstates the contract if he accepts a non-conforming installment without seasonably notifying of cancellation or if he brings an action with respect only to past installments or demands performance as to future installments.

§ 2-613. Casualty to Identified Goods.

Where the contract requires for its performance goods identified when the contract is made, and the goods suffer casualty without fault of either party before the risk of loss passes to the buyer, or in a proper case under a "no arrival, no sale" term (Section 2–324) then

(a) if the loss is total the contract is avoided; and

(b) if the loss is partial or the goods have so deteriorated as no longer to conform to the contract the buyer may nevertheless demand inspection and at his option either treat the contract as voided or accept the goods with due allowance from the contract price for the deterioration or the deficiency in quantity but without further right against the seller.

§ 2-614. Substituted Performance.

(1) Where without fault of either party the agreed berthing, loading, or unloading facilities fail or an agreed type of carrier becomes unavailable or the agreed manner of delivery otherwise becomes commercially impracticable but a commercially reasonable substitute is available, such substitute performance must be tendered and accepted.

(2) If the agreed means or manner of payment fails because of domestic or foreign governmental regulation, the seller may withhold or stop delivery unless the buyer provides a means or manner of payment which is commercially a substantial equivalent. If delivery has already been taken, payment by the means or in the manner provided by the regulation discharges the buyer's obligation unless the regulation is discriminatory, oppressive or predatory.

§ 2-615. Excuse by Failure of Presupposed Conditions.

Except so far as a seller may have assumed a greater obligation and subject to the preceding section on substituted performance:

(a) Delay in delivery or non-delivery in whole or in part by a seller who complies with paragraphs (b) and (c) is not a breach of his duty under a contract for sale if performance as agreed has been made impracticable by the occurrence of a contingency the nonoccurrence of which was a basic assumption on which the contract was made or by compliance in good faith with any applicable foreign or domestic governmental regulation or order whether or not it later proves to be invalid.

(b) Where the causes mentioned in paragraph (a) affect only a part of the seller's capacity to perform, he must allocate production and deliveries among his customers but may at his option include regular customers not then under contract as well as his own requirements for further manufacture. He may so allocate in any manner which is fair and reasonable.

(c) The seller must notify the buyer seasonably that there will be delay or non-delivery and, when allocation is required under paragraph (b), of the estimated quota thus made available for the buyer.

§ 2-616. Procedure on Notice Claiming Excuse.

(1) Where the buyer receives notification of a material or indefinite delay or an allocation justified under the preceding section he may by written notification to the seller as to any delivery concerned, and where the prospective deficiency substantially impairs the value of the whole contract under the provisions of this Article relating to breach of installment contracts (Section 2–612), then also as to the whole,

    (a) terminate and thereby discharge any unexecuted portion of the contract; or

    (b) modify the contract by agreeing to take his available quota in substitution.

(2) If after receipt of such notification from the seller the buyer fails so to modify the contract within a reasonable time not exceeding thirty days the contract lapses with respect to any deliveries affected.

(3) The provisions of this section may not be negated by agreement except in so far as the seller has assumed a greater obligation under the preceding section.

PART 7: Remedies

§ 2-701. Remedies for Breach of Collateral Contracts Not Impaired.

Remedies for breach of any obligation or promise collateral or ancillary to a contract for sale are not impaired by the provisions of this Article.

§ 2-702. Seller's Remedies on Discovery of Buyer's Insolvency.

(1) Where the seller discovers the buyer to be insolvent he may refuse delivery except for cash including payment for all goods theretofore delivered under the contract, and stop delivery under this Article (Section 2–705).

(2) Where the seller discovers that the buyer has received goods on credit while insolvent he may reclaim the goods upon demand made within ten days after the receipt, but if misrepresentation of solvency has been made to the particular seller in writing within three months before delivery the ten day limitation does not apply. Except as provided in this subsection the seller may not base a right to reclaim goods on the buyer's fraudulent or innocent misrepresentation of solvency or of intent to pay.

(3) The seller's right to reclaim under subsection (2) is subject to the rights of a buyer in ordinary course or other good faith purchaser under this Article (Section 2–403). Successful reclamation of goods excludes all other remedies with respect to them.

§ 2-703. Seller's Remedies in General.

Where the buyer wrongfully rejects or revokes acceptance of goods or fails to make a payment due on or before delivery or repudiates with respect to a part or the whole, then with respect to any goods directly affected and, if the breach is of the whole contract (Section 2–612), then also with respect to the whole undelivered balance, the aggrieved seller may

(a) withhold delivery of such goods;

(b) stop delivery by any bailee as hereafter provided (Section 2–705);

(c) proceed under the next section respecting goods still unidentified to the contract;

(d) resell and recover damages as hereafter provided (Section 2–706);

(e) recover damages for non-acceptance (Section 2–708) or in a proper case the price (Section 2–709);

(f) cancel.

§ 2-704. Seller's Right to Identify Goods to the Contract Notwithstanding Breach or to Salvage Unfinished Goods.

(1) An aggrieved seller under the preceding section may

(a) identify to the contract conforming goods not already identified if at the time he learned of the breach they are in his possession or control;

(b) treat as the subject of resale goods which have demonstrably been intended for the particular contract even though those goods are unfinished.

(2) Where the goods are unfinished an aggrieved seller may in the exercise of reasonable commercial judgment for the purposes of avoiding loss and of effective realization either complete the manufacture and wholly identify the goods to the contract or cease manufacture and resell for scrap or salvage value or proceed in any other reasonable manner.

§ 2-705. Seller's Stoppage of Delivery in Transit or Otherwise.

(1) The seller may stop delivery of goods in the possession of a carrier or other bailee when he discovers the buyer to be insolvent (Section 2–702) and may stop delivery of carload, truckload, planeload or larger shipments of express or freight when the buyer repudiates or fails to make a payment due before delivery or if for any other reason the seller has a right to withhold or reclaim the goods.

(2) As against such buyer the seller may stop delivery until

(a) receipt of the goods by the buyer; or

(b) acknowledgment to the buyer by any bailee of the goods except a carrier that the bailee holds the goods for the buyer; or

(c) such acknowledgment to the buyer by a carrier by reshipment or as warehouseman; or

(d) negotiation to the buyer of any negotiable document of title covering the goods.

(3) (a) To stop delivery the seller must so notify as to enable the bailee by reasonable diligence to prevent delivery of the goods.

(b) After such notification the bailee must hold and deliver the goods according to the directions of the seller but the seller is liable to the bailee for any ensuing charges or damages.

(c) If a negotiable document of title has been issued for goods the bailee is not obliged to obey a notification to stop until surrender of the document.

(d) A carrier who has issued a non-negotiable bill of lading is not obliged to obey a notification to stop received from a person other than the consignor.

§ 2-706. Seller's Resale Including Contract for Resale.

(1) Under the conditions stated in Section 2–703 on seller's remedies, the seller may resell the goods concerned or the undelivered balance thereof.

Where the resale is made in good faith and in a commercially reasonable manner the seller may recover the difference between the resale price and the contract price together with any incidental damages allowed under the provisions of this Article (Section 2–710), but less expenses saved in consequence of the buyer's breach.

(2) Except as otherwise provided in subsection (3) or unless otherwise agreed resale may be at public or private sale including sale by way of one or more contracts to sell or of identification to an existing contract of the seller. Sale may be as a unit or in parcels and at any time and place and on any terms but every aspect of the sale including the method, manner, time, place and terms must be commercially reasonable. The resale must be reasonably identified as referring to the broken contract, but it is not necessary that the goods be in existence or that any or all of them have been identified to the contract before the breach.

(3) Where the resale is at private sale the seller must give the buyer reasonable notification of his intention to resell.

(4) Where the resale is at public sale

(a) only identified goods can be sold except where there is a recognized market for a public sale of futures in goods of the kind; and

(b) it must be made at a usual place or market for public sale if one is reasonably available and except in the case of goods which are perishable or threaten to decline in value speedily the seller must give the buyer reasonable notice of the time and place of the resale; and

(c) if the goods are not to be within the view of those attending the sale the notification of sale must state the place where the goods are located and provide for their reasonable inspection by prospective bidders; and

(d) the seller may buy.

(5) A purchaser who buys in good faith at a resale takes the goods free of any rights of the original buyer even though the seller fails to comply with one or more of the requirements of this section.

(6) The seller is not accountable to the buyer for any profit made on any resale. A person in the position of a seller (Section 2–707) or a buyer who has rightfully rejected or justifiably revoked acceptance must account for any excess over the amount of his security interest, as hereinafter defined (subsection (3) of Section 2–711).

§ 2-707. "Person in the Position of a Seller".

(1) A "person in the position of a seller" includes as against a principal an agent who has paid or become responsible for the price of goods on behalf of his principal or anyone who otherwise holds a security interest or other right in goods similar to that of a seller.

(2) A person in the position of a seller may as provided in this Article withhold or stop delivery (Section 2–705) and resell (Section 2–706) and recover incidental damages (Section 2–710).

§ 2-708. Seller's Damages for Non-Acceptance or Repudiation.

(1) Subject to subsection (2) and to the provisions of this Article with respect to proof of market price (Section 2–723), the measure of damages for non-acceptance or repudiation by the buyer is the difference between the market price at the time and place for tender and the unpaid contract price together with any incidental damages provided in this Article (Section 2–710), but less expenses saved in consequence of the buyer's breach.

(2) If the measure of damages provided in subsection (1) is inadequate to put the seller in as good a position as performance would have done then the measure of damages is the profit (including reasonable overhead) which the seller would have made from full performance by the buyer, together with any incidental damages provided in this Article (Section 2–710), due allowance for costs reasonably incurred and due credit for payments or proceeds of resale.

§ 2-709. Action for the Price.

(1) When the buyer fails to pay the price as it becomes due the seller may recover, together with any incidental damages under the next section, the price

    (a) of goods accepted or of conforming goods lost or damaged within a commercially reasonable time after risk of their loss has passed to the buyer; and

    (b) of goods identified to the contract if the seller is unable after reasonable effort to resell them at a reasonable price or the circumstances reasonably indicate that such effort will be unavailing.

(2) Where the seller sues for the price he must hold for the buyer any goods which have been identified to the contract and are still in his control except that if resale becomes possible he may resell them at any time prior to the collection of the judgment. The net proceeds of any such resale must be credited to the buyer and payment of the judgment entitles him to any goods not resold.

(3) After the buyer has wrongfully rejected or revoked acceptance of the goods or has failed to make a payment due or has repudiated (Section 2–610), a seller who is held not entitled to the price under this section shall nevertheless be awarded damages for non-acceptance under the preceding section.

§ 2-710. Seller's Incidental Damages.

Incidental damages to an aggrieved seller include any commercially reasonable charges, expenses or commissions incurred in stopping delivery, in the transportation, care and custody of goods after the buyer's breach, in connection with return or resale of the goods or otherwise resulting from the breach.

§ 2-711. Buyer's Remedies in General; Buyer's Security Interest in Rejected Goods.

(1) Where the seller fails to make delivery or repudiates or the buyer rightfully rejects or justifiably revokes acceptance then with respect to any goods involved, and with respect to the whole if the breach goes to the whole contract (Section 2–612), the buyer may cancel and whether or not he has done so may in addition to recovering so much of the price as has been paid

    (a) "cover" and have damages under the next section as to all the goods affected whether or not they have been identified to the contract; or

    (b) recover damages for non-delivery as provided in this Article (Section 2–713).

(2) Where the seller fails to deliver or repudiates the buyer may also

    (a) if the goods have been identified recover them as provided in this Article (Section 2–502); or

    (b) in a proper case obtain specific performance or replevy the goods as provided in this Article (Section 2–716).

(3) On rightful rejection or justifiable revocation of acceptance a buyer has a security interest in goods in his possession or control for any payments made on their price and any expenses reasonably incurred in their inspection, receipt, transportation, care and custody and may hold such goods and resell them in like manner as an aggrieved seller (Section 2–706).

§ 2-712. "Cover"; Buyer's Procurement of Substitute Goods.

(1) After a breach within the preceding section the buyer may "cover" by making in good faith and without unreasonable delay any reasonable purchase of or contract to purchase goods in substitution for those due from the seller.

(2) The buyer may recover from the seller as damages the difference between the cost of cover and the contract price together with any incidental or consequential damages as hereinafter defined (Section 2–715), but less expenses saved in consequence of the seller's breach.

(3) Failure of the buyer to effect cover within this section does not bar him from any other remedy.

§ 2-713. Buyer's Damages for Non-Delivery or Repudiation.

(1) Subject to the provisions of this Article with respect to proof of market price (Section 2–723), the measure of damages for non-delivery or repudiation by the seller is the difference between the market price at the time when the buyer learned of the breach and the contract price together with any incidental and consequential damages provided in this Article (Section 2–715), but less expenses saved in consequence of the seller's breach.

(2) Market price is to be determined as of the place for tender or, in cases of rejection after arrival or revocation of acceptance, as of the place of arrival.

§ 2-714. Buyer's Damages for Breach in Regard to Accepted Goods.

(1) Where the buyer has accepted goods and given notification (subsection (3) of Section 2–607) he may recover as damages for any non-conformity of tender the loss resulting in the ordinary course of events from the seller's breach as determined in any manner which is reasonable.

(2) The measure of damages for breach of warranty is the difference at the time and place of acceptance between the value of the goods accepted and the value they would have had if they had been as warranted, unless special circumstances show proximate damages of a different amount.

(3) In a proper case any incidental and consequential damages under the next section may also be recovered.

§ 2-715. Buyer's Incidental and Consequential Damages.

(1) Incidental damages resulting from the seller's breach include expenses reasonably incurred in inspection, receipt, transportation and care and custody of goods rightfully rejected, any commercially reasonable charges, expenses or commissions in connection with effecting cover and any other reasonable expense incident to the delay or other breach.

(2) Consequential damages resulting from the seller's breach include

    (a) any loss resulting from general or particular requirements and needs of which the seller at the time of contracting had reason to know and which could not reasonably be prevented by cover or otherwise; and

    (b) injury to person or property proximately resulting from any breach of warranty.

§ 2-716. Buyer's Right to Specific Performance or Replevin.

(1) Specific performance may be decreed where the goods are unique or in other proper circumstances.

(2) The decree for specific performance may include such terms and conditions as to payment of the price, damages, or other relief as the court may deem just.

(3) The buyer has a right of replevin for goods identified to the contract if after reasonable effort he is unable to effect cover for such goods or the circumstances reasonably indicate that such effort will be unavailing or if the goods have been shipped under reservation and satisfaction of the security interest in them has been made or tendered. In the case of goods bought for personal, family, or household purposes, the buyer's right of replevin vests upon acquisition of a special property, even if the seller had not then repudiated or failed to deliver.

As amended in 1999.

§ 2-717. Deduction of Damages From the Price.

The buyer on notifying the seller of his intention to do so may deduct all or any part of the damages resulting from any breach of the contract from any part of the price still due under the same contract.

§ 2-718. Liquidation or Limitation of Damages; Deposits.

(1) Damages for breach by either party may be liquidated in the agreement but only at an amount which is reasonable in the light of the anticipated or actual harm caused by the breach, the difficulties of proof of loss, and the inconvenience or nonfeasibility of otherwise obtaining an adequate remedy. A term fixing unreasonably large liquidated damages is void as a penalty.

(2) Where the seller justifiably withholds delivery of goods because of the buyer's breach, the buyer is entitled to restitution of any amount by which the sum of his payments exceeds

    (a) the amount to which the seller is entitled by virtue of terms liquidating the seller's damages in accordance with subsection (1), or

    (b) in the absence of such terms, twenty per cent of the value of the total performance for which the buyer is obligated under the contract or $500, whichever is smaller.

(3) The buyer's right to restitution under subsection (2) is subject to offset to the extent that the seller establishes

    (a) a right to recover damages under the provisions of this Article other than subsection (1), and

    (b) the amount or value of any benefits received by the buyer directly or indirectly by reason of the contract.

(4) Where a seller has received payment in goods their reasonable value or the proceeds of their resale shall be treated as payments for the purposes of subsection (2); but if the seller has notice of the buyer's breach before reselling goods received in part performance, his resale is subject to the conditions laid down in this Article on resale by an aggrieved seller (Section 2–706).

§ 2-719. Contractual Modification or Limitation of Remedy.

(1) Subject to the provisions of subsections (2) and (3) of this section and of the preceding section on liquidation and limitation of damages,

    (a) the agreement may provide for remedies in addition to or in substitution for those provided in this Article and may limit or alter the measure of damages recoverable under this Article, as by limiting the buyer's remedies to return of the goods and repayment of the price or to repair and replacement of nonconforming goods or parts; and

    (b) resort to a remedy as provided is optional unless the remedy is expressly agreed to be exclusive, in which case it is the sole remedy.

(2) Where circumstances cause an exclusive or limited remedy to fail of its essential purpose, remedy may be had as provided in this Act.

(3) Consequential damages may be limited or excluded unless the limitation or exclusion is unconscionable. Limitation of consequential damages for injury to the person in the case of consumer goods is prima facie unconscionable but limitation of damages where the loss is commercial is not.

§ 2-720. Effect of "Cancellation" or "Rescission" on Claims for Antecedent Breach.

Unless the contrary intention clearly appears, expressions of "cancellation" or "rescission" of the contract or the like shall not be construed as a renunciation or discharge of any claim in damages for an antecedent breach.

§ 2-721. Remedies for Fraud.

Remedies for material misrepresentation or fraud include all remedies available under this Article for non-fraudulent breach. Neither rescission or a claim for rescission of the contract for sale nor rejection or return of the goods shall bar or be deemed inconsistent with a claim for damages or other remedy.

§ 2-722. Who Can Sue Third Parties for Injury to Goods.

Where a third party so deals with goods which have been identified to a contract for sale as to cause actionable injury to a party to that contract

    (a) a right of action against the third party is in either party to the contract for sale who has title to or a security interest or a special property or an insurable interest in the goods; and if the goods have been destroyed or converted a right of action is also in the party who either bore the risk of loss under the contract for sale or has since the injury assumed that risk as against the other;

    (b) if at the time of the injury the party plaintiff did not bear the risk of loss as against the other party to the contract for sale and there is no arrangement between them for disposition of the recovery, his suit or settlement is, subject to his own interest, as a fiduciary for the other party to the contract;

    (c) either party may with the consent of the other sue for the benefit of whom it may concern.

§ 2-723. Proof of Market Price: Time and Place.

(1) If an action based on anticipatory repudiation comes to trial before the time for performance with respect to some or all of the goods, any damages based on market price (Section 2–708 or Section 2–713) shall be determined according to the price of such goods prevailing at the time when the aggrieved party learned of the repudiation.

(2) If evidence of a price prevailing at the times or places described in this Article is not readily available the price prevailing within any reasonable time before or after the time described or at any other place which in commercial judgment or under usage of trade would serve as a reasonable substitute for the one described may be used, making any proper allowance for the cost of transporting the goods to or from such other place.

(3) Evidence of a relevant price prevailing at a time or place other than the one described in this Article offered by one party is not admissible unless and until he has given the other party such notice as the court finds sufficient to prevent unfair surprise.

§ 2-724. Admissibility of Market Quotations.

Whenever the prevailing price or value of any goods regularly bought and sold in any established commodity market is in issue, reports in official publications or trade journals or in newspapers or periodicals of general circulation published as the reports of such market shall be admissible in evidence. The circumstances of the preparation of such a report may be shown to affect its weight but not its admissibility.

§ 2-725. Statute of Limitations in Contracts for Sale.

(1) An action for breach of any contract for sale must be commenced within four years after the cause of action has accrued. By the original agreement the parties may reduce the period of limitation to not less than one year but may not extend it.

(2) A cause of action accrues when the breach occurs, regardless of the aggrieved party's lack of knowledge of the breach. A breach of warranty occurs when tender of delivery is made, except that where a warranty explicitly extends to future performance of the goods and discovery of the breach must await the time of such performance the cause of action accrues when the breach is or should have been discovered.

(3) Where an action commenced within the time limited by subsection (1) is so terminated as to leave available a remedy by another action for the same breach such other action may be commenced after the expiration of

the time limited and within six months after the termination of the first action unless the termination resulted from voluntary discontinuance or from dismissal for failure or neglect to prosecute.

(4) This section does not alter the law on tolling of the statute of limitations nor does it apply to causes of action which have accrued before this Act becomes effective.

ARTICLE 2: Amendments (Excerpts)[1]

PART 1: Short Title, General Construction and Subject Matter

* * * *

§ 2-103. Definitions and Index of Definitions.

(1) In this article unless the context otherwise requires

* * * *

(b) "Conspicuous", with reference to a term, means so written, displayed, or presented that a reasonable person against which it is to operate ought to have noticed it. A term in an electronic record intended to evoke a response by an electronic agent is conspicuous if it is presented in a form that would enable a reasonably configured electronic agent to take it into account or react to it without review of the record by an individual. Whether a term is "conspicuous" or not is a decision for the court. Conspicuous terms include the following:

(i) for a person:

(A) a heading in capitals equal to or greater in size than the surrounding text, or in contrasting type, font, or color to the surrounding text of the same or lesser size;

(B) language in the body of a record or display in larger type than the surrounding text, or in contrasting type, font, or color to the surrounding text of the same size, or set off from surrounding text of the same size by symbols or other marks that call attention to the language; and

(ii) for a person or an electronic agent, a term that is so placed in a record or display that the person or electronic agent cannot proceed without taking action with respect to the particular term.

(c) "Consumer" means an individual who buys or contracts to buy goods that, at the time of contracting, are intended by the individual to be used primarily for personal, family, or household purposes.

(d) "Consumer contract" means a contract between a merchant seller and a consumer.

* * * *

(j) "Good faith" means honesty in fact and the observance of reasonable commercial standards of fair dealing.

(k) "Goods" means all things that are movable at the time of identification to a contract for sale. The term includes future goods, specially manufactured goods, the unborn young of animals, growing crops, and other identified things attached to realty as described in Section 2–107. The term does not include information, the money in which the price is to be paid, investment securities under Article 8, the subject matter of foreign exchange transactions, and choses in action.

* * * *

(m) "Record" means information that is inscribed on a tangible medium or that is stored in an electronic or other medium and is retrievable in perceivable form.

(n) "Remedial promise" means a promise by the seller to repair or replace the goods or to refund all or part of the price upon the happening of a specified event.

* * * *

(p) "Sign" means, with present intent to authenticate or adopt a record,

(i) to execute or adopt a tangible symbol; or

(ii) to attach to or logically associate with the record an electronic sound, symbol, or process.

* * * *

PART 2: Form, Formation, Terms and Readjustment of Contract; Electronic Contracting

§ 2-201. Formal Requirements; Statute of Frauds.

(1) A contract for the sale of goods for the price of $5,000 or more is not enforceable by way of action or defense unless there is some record sufficient to indicate that a contract for sale has been made between the parties and signed by the party against whom which enforcement is sought or by the party's authorized agent or broker. A record is not insufficient because it omits or incorrectly states a term agreed upon but the contract is not enforceable under this subsection beyond the quantity of goods shown in the record.

(2) Between merchants if within a reasonable time a record in confirmation of the contract and sufficient against the sender is received and the party receiving it has reason to know its contents, it satisfies the requirements of subsection (1) against such party the recipient unless notice of objection to its contents is given in a record within 10 days after it is received.

(3) A contract which does not satisfy the requirements of subsection (1) but which is valid in other respects is enforceable

(a) if the goods are to be specially manufactured for the buyer and are not suitable for sale to others in the ordinary course of the seller's business and the seller, before notice of repudiation is received and under circumstances which reasonably indicate that the goods are for the buyer, has made either a substantial beginning of their manufacture or commitments for their procurement; or

(b) if the party against whom which enforcement is sought admits in the party's pleading, or in the party's testimony or otherwise under oath that a contract for sale was made, but the contract is not enforceable under this paragraph beyond the quantity of goods admitted; or

(c) with respect to goods for which payment has been made and accepted or which have been received and accepted (Sec. 2–606).

(4) A contract that is enforceable under this section is not rendered unenforceable merely because it is not capable of being performed within one year or any other applicable period after its making.

* * * *

§ 2-207. Terms of Contract; Effect of Confirmation.

If (i) conduct by both parties recognizes the existence of a contract although their records do not otherwise establish a contract, (ii) a contract is formed by an offer and acceptance, or (iii) a contract formed in any manner is confirmed by a record that contains terms additional to or different from those in the contract being confirmed, the terms of the contract, subject to Section 2–202, are:

(a) terms that appear in the records of both parties;

(b) terms, whether in a record or not, to which both parties agree; and

(c) terms supplied or incorporated under any provision of this Act.

* * * *

PART 3: General Obligation and Construction of Contract

* * * *

§ 2-312. Warranty of Title and Against Infringement; Buyer's Obligation Against Infringement.

(1) Subject to subsection (2) there is in a contract for sale a warranty by the seller that

(a) the title conveyed shall be good, good and its transfer rightful <u>and shall not, because of any colorable claim to or interest in the goods, unreasonably expose the buyer to litigation;</u> and

(b) the goods shall be delivered free from any security interest or other lien or encumbrance of which the buyer at the time of contracting has no knowledge.

<u>(2) Unless otherwise agreed a seller that is a merchant regularly dealing in goods of the kind warrants that the goods shall be delivered free of the rightful claim of any third person by way of infringement or the like but a buyer that furnishes specifications to the seller must hold the seller harmless against any such claim that arises out of compliance with the specifications.</u>

(3) A warranty under this section may be disclaimed or modified only by specific language or by circumstances that give the buyer reason to know that the seller does not claim title, that the seller is purporting to sell only the right or title as the seller or a third person may have, or that the seller is selling subject to any claims of infringement or the like.

§ 2-313. Express Warranties by Affirmation, Promise, Description, Sample; **Remedial Promise.**

<u>(1) In this section, "immediate buyer" means a buyer that enters into a contract with the seller.</u>

*   *   *   *

<u>(4) Any remedial promise made by the seller to the immediate buyer creates an obligation that the promise will be performed upon the happening of the specified event.</u>

§ 2-313A. Obligation to Remote Purchaser Created by Record Packaged with or Accompanying Goods.

<u>(1) This section applies only to new goods and goods sold or leased as new goods in a transaction of purchase in the normal chain of distribution. In this section:</u>

<u>(a) "Immediate buyer" means a buyer that enters into a contract with the seller.</u>

<u>(b) "Remote purchaser" means a person that buys or leases goods from an immediate buyer or other person in the normal chain of distribution.</u>

<u>(2) If a seller in a record packaged with or accompanying the goods makes an affirmation of fact or promise that relates to the goods, provides a description that relates to the goods, or makes a remedial promise, and the seller reasonably expects the record to be, and the record is, furnished to the remote purchaser, the seller has an obligation to the remote purchaser that:</u>

<u>(a) the goods will conform to the affirmation of fact, promise or description unless a reasonable person in the position of the remote purchaser would not believe that the affirmation of fact, promise or description created an obligation; and</u>

<u>(b) the seller will perform the remedial promise.</u>

<u>(3) It is not necessary to the creation of an obligation under this section that the seller use formal words such as "warrant" or "guarantee" or that the seller have a specific intention to undertake an obligation, but an affirmation merely of the value of the goods or a statement purporting to be merely the seller's opinion or commendation of the goods does not create an obligation.</u>

<u>(4) The following rules apply to the remedies for breach of an obligation created under this section:</u>

<u>(a) The seller may modify or limit the remedies available to the remote purchaser if the modification or limitation is furnished to the remote purchaser no later than the time of purchase or if the modification or limitation is contained in the record that contains the affirmation of fact, promise or description.</u>

<u>(b) Subject to a modification or limitation of remedy, a seller in breach is liable for incidental or consequential damages under Section 2–715, but the seller is not liable for lost profits.</u>

<u>(c) The remote purchaser may recover as damages for breach of a seller's obligation arising under subsection (2) the loss resulting in the ordinary course of events as determined in any manner that is reasonable.</u>

(5) An obligation that is not a remedial promise is breached if the goods did not conform to the affirmation of fact, promise or description creating the obligation when the goods left the seller's control.

§ 2-313B. Obligation to Remote Purchaser Created by Communication to the Public.

<u>(1) This section applies only to new goods and goods sold or leased as new goods in a transaction of purchase in the normal chain of distribution. In this section:</u>

<u>(a) "Immediate buyer" means a buyer that enters into a contract with the seller.</u>

<u>(b) "Remote purchaser" means a person that buys or leases goods from an immediate buyer or other person in the normal chain of distribution.</u>

<u>(2) If a seller in advertising or a similar communication to the public makes an affirmation of fact or promise that relates to the goods, provides a description that relates to the goods, or makes a remedial promise, and the remote purchaser enters into a transaction of purchase with knowledge of and with the expectation that the goods will conform to the affirmation of fact, promise, or description, or that the seller will perform the remedial promise, the seller has an obligation to the remote purchaser that:</u>

<u>(a) the goods will conform to the affirmation of fact, promise or description unless a reasonable person in the position of the remote purchaser would not believe that the affirmation of fact, promise or description created an obligation; and</u>

<u>(b) the seller will perform the remedial promise.</u>

<u>(3) It is not necessary to the creation of an obligation under this section that the seller use formal words such as "warrant" or "guarantee" or that the seller have a specific intention to undertake an obligation, but an affirmation merely of the value of the goods or a statement purporting to be merely the seller's opinion or commendation of the goods does not create an obligation.</u>

<u>(4) The following rules apply to the remedies for breach of an obligation created under this section:</u>

<u>(a) The seller may modify or limit the remedies available to the remote purchaser if the modification or limitation is furnished to the remote purchaser no later than the time of purchase. The modification or limitation may be furnished as part of the communication that contains the affirmation of fact, promise or description.</u>

<u>(b) Subject to a modification or limitation of remedy, a seller in breach is liable for incidental or consequential damages under Section 2–715, but the seller is not liable for lost profits.</u>

<u>(c) The remote purchaser may recover as damages for breach of a seller's obligation arising under subsection (2) the loss resulting in the ordinary course of events as determined in any manner that is reasonable.</u>

(5) An obligation that is not a remedial promise is breached if the goods did not conform to the affirmation of fact, promise or description creating the obligation when the goods left the seller's control.

*   *   *   *

§ 2-316. Exclusion or Modification of Warranties.

* * * *

(2) Subject to subsection (3), to exclude or modify the implied warranty of merchantability or any part of it in a consumer contract the language must be in a record, be conspicuous and state "The seller undertakes no responsibility for the quality of the goods except as otherwise provided in this contract," and in any other contract the language must mention merchantability and in case of a record must be conspicuous. Subject to subsection (3), to exclude or modify the implied warranty of fitness the exclusion must be in a record and be conspicuous. Language to exclude all implied warranties of fitness in a consumer contract must state "The seller assumes no responsibility that the goods will be fit for any particular purpose for which you may be buying these goods, except as otherwise provided in the contract," and in any other contract the language is sufficient if it states, for example, that "There are no warranties which extend beyond the description on the face hereof." Language that satisfies the requirements of this subsection for the exclusion and modification of a warranty in a consumer contract also satisfies the requirements for any other contract.

(3) Notwithstanding subsection (2):

(a) unless the circumstances indicate otherwise, all implied warranties are excluded by expressions like "as is", "with all faults" or other language which in common understanding calls the buyer's attention to the exclusion of warranties, makes plain that there is no implied warranty, and in a consumer contract evidenced by a record is set forth conspicuously in the record; and

(b) when the buyer before entering into the contract has examined the goods or the sample or model as fully as desired or has refused to examine the goods after a demand by the seller there is no implied warranty with regard to defects which an examination ought in the circumstances to have revealed to the buyer; and

(c) an implied warranty can also be excluded or modified by course of dealing or course of performance or usage of trade.

* * * *

§ 2-318. Third Party Beneficiaries of Warranties Express or Implied.

(1) In this section:

(a) "Immediate buyer" means a buyer that enters into a contract with the seller.

(b) "Remote purchaser" means a person that buys or leases goods from an immediate buyer or other person in the normal chain of distribution.

Alternative A to subsection (2)

(2) A seller's warranty whether express or implied to an immediate buyer, a seller's remedial promise to an immediate buyer, or a seller's obligation to a remote purchaser under Section 2–313A or 2–313B extends to any natural person who is in the family or household of the immediate buyer or the remote purchaser or who is a guest in the home of either if it is reasonable to expect that the person may use, consume or be affected by the goods and who is injured in person by breach of the warranty, remedial promise or obligation. A seller may not exclude or limit the operation of this section.

Alternative B to subsection (2)

(2) A seller's warranty whether express or implied to an immediate buyer, a seller's remedial promise to an immediate buyer, or a seller's obligation to a remote purchaser under Section 2–313A or 2–313B extends to any natural person who may reasonably be expected to use, consume or be affected by the goods and who is injured in person by breach of the warranty, remedial promise or obligation. A seller may not exclude or limit the operation of this section.

Alternative C to subsection (2)

(2) A seller's warranty whether express or implied to an immediate buyer, a seller's remedial promise to an immediate buyer, or a seller's obligation to a remote purchaser under Section 2–313A or 2–313B extends to any person that may reasonably be expected to use, consume or be affected by the goods and that is injured by breach of the warranty, remedial promise or obligation. A seller may not exclude or limit the operation of this section with respect to injury to the person of an individual to whom the warranty, remedial promise or obligation extends.

* * * *

PART 5: Performance

* * * *

§ 2-502. Buyer's Right to Goods on Seller's Insolvency.

(1) Subject to subsections (2) and (3) and even though the goods have not been shipped a buyer who that has paid a part or all of the price of goods in which the buyer has a special property under the provisions of the immediately preceding section may on making and keeping good a tender of any unpaid portion of their price recover them from the seller if:

(a) in the case of goods bought by a consumer, the seller repudiates or fails to deliver as required by the contract; or

(b) in all cases, the seller becomes insolvent within ten days after receipt of the first installment on their price.

(2) The buyer's right to recover the goods under subsection (1) vests upon acquisition of a special property, even if the seller had not then repudiated or failed to deliver.

(3) If the identification creating the special property has been made by the buyer, the buyer acquires the right to recover the goods only if they conform to the contract for sale.

* * * *

§ 2-508. Cure by Seller of Improper Tender or Delivery; Replacement.

(1) Where the buyer rejects goods or a tender of delivery under Section 2–601 or 2–612 or except in a consumer contract justifiably revokes acceptance under Section 2–608(1)(b) and the agreed time for performance has not expired, a seller that has performed in good faith, upon seasonable notice to the buyer and at the seller's own expense, may cure the breach of contract by making a conforming tender of delivery within the agreed time. The seller shall compensate the buyer for all of the buyer's reasonable expenses caused by the seller's breach of contract and subsequent cure.

(2) Where the buyer rejects goods or a tender of delivery under Section 2–601 or 2–612 or except in a consumer contract justifiably revokes acceptance under Section 2–608(1)(b) and the agreed time for performance has expired, a seller that has performed in good faith, upon seasonable notice to the buyer and at the seller's own expense, may cure the breach of contract, if the cure is appropriate and timely under the circumstances, by making a tender of conforming goods. The seller shall compensate the buyer for all of the buyer's reasonable expenses caused by the seller's breach of contract and subsequent cure.

§ 2-509. Risk of Loss in the Absence of Breach.

(1) Where the contract requires or authorizes the seller to ship the goods by carrier

(a) if it does not require the seller to deliver them at a particular destination, the risk of loss passes to the buyer when the goods are delivered to the carrier even though the shipment is under reservation (Section 2–505); but

(b) if it does require the seller to deliver them at a particular destination and the goods are there tendered while in the possession of the carrier, the risk of loss passes to the buyer when the goods are there so tendered as to enable the buyer to take delivery.

(2) Where the goods are held by a bailee to be delivered without being moved, the risk of loss passes to the buyer

    (a) on the buyer's receipt of a negotiable document of title covering the goods; or

    (b) on acknowledgment by the bailee to the buyer of the buyer's right to possession of the goods; or

    (c) after the buyer's receipt of a non-negotiable document of title or other direction to deliver in a record, as provided in subsection (4)(b) of Section 2–503.

(3) In any case not within subsection (1) or (2), the risk of loss passes to the buyer on the buyer's receipt of the goods.

*   *   *   *

§ 2-513. Buyer's Right to Inspection of Goods.

*   *   *   *

(3) Unless otherwise agreed, the buyer is not entitled to inspect the goods before payment of the price when the contract provides

    (a) for delivery on terms that under applicable course of performance, course of dealing, or usage of trade are interpreted to preclude inspection before payment; or

    (b) for payment against documents of title, except where such payment is due only after the goods are to become available for inspection.

*   *   *   *

PART 6: Breach, Repudiation and Excuse

*   *   *   *

§ 2-605. Waiver of Buyer's Objections by Failure to Particularize.

(1) The buyer's failure to state in connection with rejection a particular defect or in connection with revocation of acceptance a defect that justifies revocation precludes the buyer from relying on the unstated defect to justify rejection or revocation of acceptance if the defect is ascertainable by reasonable inspection

    (a) where the seller had a right to cure the defect and could have cured it if stated seasonally; or

    (b) between merchants when the seller has after rejection made a request in a record for a full and final statement in record form of all defects on which the buyer proposes to rely.

(2) A buyer's payment against documents tendered to the buyer MADE WITHOUT RESERVATION OF RIGHTS PRECLUDES RECOVERY OF THE PAYMENT FOR DEFECTS APPARENT ON THE FACE OF THE DOCUMENTS.

*   *   *   *

§ 2-607. Effect of Acceptance; Notice of Breach; Burden of Establishing Breach After Acceptance; Notice of Claim or Litigation to Person Answerable Over.

*   *   *   *

(3) Where a tender has been accepted

    (a) the buyer must within a reasonable time after the buyer discovers or should have discovered any breach notify the seller; however, failure to give timely notice bars the buyer from a remedy only to the extent that the seller is prejudiced by the failure and

    (b) if the claim is one for infringement or the like (subsection (3) of

Section 2–312) and the buyer is sued as a result of such a breach the buyer must so notify the seller within a reasonable time after the buyer receives notice of the litigation or be barred from any remedy over for liability established by the litigation.

*   *   *   *

§ 2-608. Revocation of Acceptance in Whole or in Part.

*   *   *   *

(4) If a buyer uses the goods after a rightful rejection or justifiable revocation of acceptance, the following rules apply:

    (a) Any use by the buyer that is unreasonable under the circumstances is wrongful as against the seller and is an acceptance only if ratified by the seller.

    (b) Any use of the goods that is reasonable under the circumstances is not wrongful as against the seller and is not an acceptance, but in an appropriate case the buyer shall be obligated to the seller for the value of the use to the buyer.

*   *   *   *

§ 2-612. "Installment Contract"; Breach.

*   *   *   *

(2) The buyer may reject any installment which is non-conforming if the non-conformity substantially impairs the value of that installment to the buyer or if the non-conformity is a defect in the required documents; but if the non-conformity does not fall within subsection (3) and the seller gives adequate assurance of its cure the buyer must accept that installment.

(3) Whenever non-conformity or default with respect to one or more installments substantially impairs the value of the whole contract there is a breach of the whole. But the aggrieved party reinstates the contract if the party accepts a non-conforming installment without seasonably notifying of cancellation or if the party brings an action with respect only to past installments or demands performance as to future installments.

*   *   *   *

PART 7: Remedies

§ 2-702. Seller's Remedies on Discovery of Buyer's Insolvency.

*   *   *   *

(2) Where the seller discovers that the buyer has received goods on credit while insolvent the seller may reclaim the goods upon demand made within a reasonable time after the buyer's receipt of the goods. Except as provided in this subsection the seller may not base a right to reclaim goods on the buyer's fraudulent or innocent misrepresentation of solvency or of intent to pay.

*   *   *   *

§ 2-705. Seller's Stoppage of Delivery in Transit or Otherwise.

(1) The seller may stop delivery of goods in the possession of a carrier or other bailee when the seller discovers the buyer to be insolvent (Section 2–702) or when the buyer repudiates or fails to make a payment due before delivery or if for any other reason the seller has a right to withhold or reclaim the goods.

*   *   *   *

§ 2-706. Seller's Resale Including Contract for Resale.

(1) In an appropriate case involving breach by the buyer, the seller may resell the goods concerned or the undelivered balance thereof. Where the resale is made in good faith and in a commercially reasonable manner the

seller may recover the difference between the <u>contract price and the</u> resale price together with any incidental <u>or consequential</u> damages allowed under the provisions of this Article (Section 2–710), but less expenses saved in consequence of the buyer's breach.

* * * *

§ 2-708. Seller's Damages for Non-Acceptance or Repudiation.

(1) Subject to subsection (2) and to the provisions of this Article with respect to proof of market price (Section 2–723)

    <u>(a)</u> the measure of damages for non-acceptance by the buyer is the difference between the <u>contract price and the</u> market price at the time and place for tender together with any incidental <u>or consequential</u> damages provided in this Article (Section 2–710), but less expenses saved in consequence of the buyer's breach; <u>and</u>

    <u>(b) the measure of damages for repudiation by the buyer is the difference between the contract price and the market price at the place for tender at the expiration of a commercially reasonable time after the seller learned of the repudiation, but no later than the time stated in paragraph (a), together with any incidental or consequential damages provided in this Article (Section 2–710), but less expenses saved in consequence of the buyer's breach.</u>

(2) If the measure of damages provided in subsection (1) <u>or in Section 2–706</u> is inadequate to put the seller in as good a position as performance would have done then the measure of damages is the profit (including reasonable overhead) which the seller would have made from full performance by the buyer, together with any incidental <u>or consequential</u> damages provided in this Article (Section 2–710).

§ 2-709. Action for the Price.

(1) When the buyer fails to pay the price as it becomes due the seller may recover, together with any incidental <u>or consequential</u> damages under the next section, the price

    (a) of goods accepted or of conforming goods lost or damaged within a commercially reasonable time after risk of their loss has passed to the buyer; and

    (b) of goods identified to the contract if the seller is unable after reasonable effort to resell them at a reasonable price or the circumstances reasonably indicate that such effort will be unavailing.

* * * *

§ 2-710. Seller's Incidental <u>and Consequential</u> Damages.

<u>(1)</u> Incidental damages to an aggrieved seller include any commercially reasonable charges, expenses or commissions incurred in stopping delivery, in the transportation, care and custody of goods after the buyer's breach, in connection with return or resale of the goods or otherwise resulting from the breach.

<u>(2) Consequential damages resulting from the buyer's breach include any loss resulting from general or particular requirements and needs of which the buyer at the time of contracting had reason to know and which could not reasonably be prevented by resale or otherwise.</u>

<u>(3) In a consumer contract, a seller may not recover consequential damages from a consumer.</u>

* * * *

§ 2-713. Buyer's Damages for Non-Delivery or Repudiation.

(1) Subject to the provisions of this Article with respect to proof of market price (Section 2–723), <u>if the seller wrongfully fails to deliver or repudiates or the buyer rightfully rejects or justifiably revokes acceptance</u>

<u>(a)</u> the measure of damages <u>in the case of wrongful failure to deliver</u> by the seller <u>or rightful rejection or justifiable revocation of acceptance by the buyer</u> is the difference between the market price at the time <u>for tender under the contract</u> and the contract price together with any incidental or consequential damages provided in this Article (Section 2–715), but less expenses saved in consequence of the seller's breach; and

<u>(b) the measure of damages for repudiation by the seller is the difference between the market price at the expiration of a commercially reasonable time after the buyer learned of the repudiation, but no later than the time stated in paragraph (a), and the contract price together with any incidental or consequential damages provided in this Article (Section 2–715), but less expenses saved in consequence of the seller's breach.</u>

* * * *

§ 2-725. Statute of Limitations in Contracts for Sale.

(1) <u>Except as otherwise provided in this section, an action for breach of any contract for sale must be commenced within the later of four years after the right of action has accrued under subsection (2) or (3) or one year after the breach was or should have been discovered, but no longer than five years after the right of action accrued. By the original agreement the parties may reduce the period of limitation to not less than one year but may not extend it; however, in a consumer contract, the period of limitation may not be reduced.</u>

(2) <u>Except as otherwise provided in subsection (3), the following rules apply:</u>

    <u>(a) Except as otherwise provided in this subsection, a right of action for breach of a contract accrues when the breach occurs, even if the aggrieved party did not have knowledge of the breach.</u>

    <u>(b) For breach of a contract by repudiation, a right of action accrues at the earlier of when the aggrieved party elects to treat the repudiation as a breach or when a commercially reasonable time for awaiting performance has expired.</u>

    <u>(c) For breach of a remedial promise, a right of action accrues when the remedial promise is not performed when due.</u>

    <u>(d) In an action by a buyer against a person that is answerable over to the buyer for a claim asserted against the buyer, the buyer's right of action against the person answerable over accrues at the time the claim was originally asserted against the buyer.</u>

(3) <u>If a breach of a warranty arising under Section 2–312, 2–313(2), 2–314, or 2–315, or a breach of an obligation other than a remedial promise arising under Section 2–313A or 2–313B, is claimed the following rules apply:</u>

    <u>(a) Except as otherwise provided in paragraph (c), a right of action for breach of a warranty arising under Section 2–313(2), 2–314 or 2–315 accrues when the seller has tendered delivery to the immediate buyer, as defined in Section 2–313, and has completed performance of any agreed installation or assembly of the goods.</u>

    <u>(b) Except as otherwise provided in paragraph (c), a right of action for breach of an obligation other than a remedial promise arising under Section 2–313A or 2–313B accrues when the remote purchaser, as defined in sections 2–313A and 2–313B, receives the goods.</u>

    <u>(c) Where a warranty arising under Section 2–313(2) or an obligation other than a remedial promise arising under 2–313A or 2–313B explicitly extends to future performance of the goods and discovery of the breach must await the time for performance the right of action accrues when the immediate buyer as defined in Section 2–313 or the remote purchaser as defined in Sections 2–313A and 2–313B discovers or should have discovered the breach.</u>

    <u>(d) A right of action for breach of warranty arising under Section 2–312 accrues when the aggrieved party discovers or should have dis-</u>

covered the breach. However, an action for breach of the warranty of non-infringement may not be commenced more than six years after tender of delivery of the goods to the aggrieved party.

*   *   *   *

ARTICLE 2A: Leases

PART 1: General Provisions

§ 2A-101. Short Title.

This Article shall be known and may be cited as the Uniform Commercial Code—Leases.

§ 2A-102. Scope.

This Article applies to any transaction, regardless of form, that creates a lease.

§ 2A-103. Definitions and Index of Definitions.

(1) In this Article unless the context otherwise requires:

(a) "Buyer in ordinary course of business" means a person who in good faith and without knowledge that the sale to him [or her] is in violation of the ownership rights or security interest or leasehold interest of a third party in the goods buys in ordinary course from a person in the business of selling goods of that kind but does not include a pawnbroker. "Buying" may be for cash or by exchange of other property or on secured or unsecured credit and includes receiving goods or documents of title under a pre-existing contract for sale but does not include a transfer in bulk or as security for or in total or partial satisfaction of a money debt.

(b) "Cancellation" occurs when either party puts an end to the lease contract for default by the other party.

(c) "Commercial unit" means such a unit of goods as by commercial usage is a single whole for purposes of lease and division of which materially impairs its character or value on the market or in use. A commercial unit may be a single article, as a machine, or a set of articles, as a suite of furniture or a line of machinery, or a quantity, as a gross or carload, or any other unit treated in use or in the relevant market as a single whole.

(d) "Conforming" goods or performance under a lease contract means goods or performance that are in accordance with the obligations under the lease contract.

(e) "Consumer lease" means a lease that a lessor regularly engaged in the business of leasing or selling makes to a lessee who is an individual and who takes under the lease primarily for a personal, family, or household purpose [, if the total payments to be made under the lease contract, excluding payments for options to renew or buy, do not exceed $_____].

(f) "Fault" means wrongful act, omission, breach, or default.

(g) "Finance lease" means a lease with respect to which:

    (i) the lessor does not select, manufacture or supply the goods;

    (ii) the lessor acquires the goods or the right to possession and use of the goods in connection with the lease; and

    (iii) one of the following occurs:

        (A) the lessee receives a copy of the contract by which the lessor acquired the goods or the right to possession and use of the goods before signing the lease contract;

        (B) the lessee's approval of the contract by which the lessor acquired the goods or the right to possession and use of the goods is a condition to effectiveness of the lease contract;

        (C) the lessee, before signing the lease contract, receives an accurate and complete statement designating the promises and warranties, and any disclaimers of warranties, limitations or modifications of remedies, or liquidated damages, including those of a third party, such as the manufacturer of the goods, provided to the lessor by the person supplying the goods in connection with or as part of the contract by which the lessor acquired the goods or the right to possession and use of the goods; or

        (D) if the lease is not a consumer lease, the lessor, before the lessee signs the lease contract, informs the lessee in writing (a) of the identity of the person supplying the goods to the lessor, unless the lessee has selected that person and directed the lessor to acquire the goods or the right to possession and use of the goods from that person, (b) that the lessee is entitled under this Article to any promises and warranties, including those of any third party, provided to the lessor by the person supplying the goods in connection with or as part of the contract by which the lessor acquired the goods or the right to possession and use of the goods, and (c) that the lessee may communicate with the person supplying the goods to the lessor and receive an accurate and complete statement of those promises and warranties, including any disclaimers and limitations of them or of remedies.

(h) "Goods" means all things that are movable at the time of identification to the lease contract, or are fixtures (Section 2A–309), but the term does not include money, documents, instruments, accounts, chattel paper, general intangibles, or minerals or the like, including oil and gas, before extraction. The term also includes the unborn young of animals.

(i) "Installment lease contract" means a lease contract that authorizes or requires the delivery of goods in separate lots to be separately accepted, even though the lease contract contains a clause "each delivery is a separate lease" or its equivalent.

(j) "Lease" means a transfer of the right to possession and use of goods for a term in return for consideration, but a sale, including a sale on approval or a sale or return, or retention or creation of a security interest is not a lease. Unless the context clearly indicates otherwise, the term includes a sublease.

(k) "Lease agreement" means the bargain, with respect to the lease, of the lessor and the lessee in fact as found in their language or by implication from other circumstances including course of dealing or usage of trade or course of performance as provided in this Article. Unless the context clearly indicates otherwise, the term includes a sublease agreement.

(l) "Lease contract" means the total legal obligation that results from the lease agreement as affected by this Article and any other applicable rules of law. Unless the context clearly indicates otherwise, the term includes a sublease contract.

(m) "Leasehold interest" means the interest of the lessor or the lessee under a lease contract.

(n) "Lessee" means a person who acquires the right to possession and use of goods under a lease. Unless the context clearly indicates otherwise, the term includes a sublessee.

(o) "Lessee in ordinary course of business" means a person who in good faith and without knowledge that the lease to him [or her] is in violation of the ownership rights or security interest or leasehold interest of a third party in the goods, leases in ordinary course from a person in the business of selling or leasing goods of that kind but does not include a pawnbroker. "Leasing" may be for cash or by exchange of other property or on secured or unsecured credit and includes receiving goods or documents of title under a pre-existing lease contract but does not include a transfer in bulk or as security for or in total or partial satisfaction of a money debt.

(p) "Lessor" means a person who transfers the right to possession and use of goods under a lease. Unless the context clearly indicates otherwise, the term includes a sublessor.

(q) "Lessor's residual interest" means the lessor's interest in the goods after expiration, termination, or cancellation of the lease contract.

(r) "Lien" means a charge against or interest in goods to secure payment of a debt or performance of an obligation, but the term does not include a security interest.

(s) "Lot" means a parcel or a single article that is the subject matter of a separate lease or delivery, whether or not it is sufficient to perform the lease contract.

(t) "Merchant lessee" means a lessee that is a merchant with respect to goods of the kind subject to the lease.

(u) "Present value" means the amount as of a date certain of one or more sums payable in the future, discounted to the date certain. The discount is determined by the interest rate specified by the parties if the rate was not manifestly unreasonable at the time the transaction was entered into; otherwise, the discount is determined by a commercially reasonable rate that takes into account the facts and circumstances of each case at the time the transaction was entered into.

(v) "Purchase" includes taking by sale, lease, mortgage, security interest, pledge, gift, or any other voluntary transaction creating an interest in goods.

(w) "Sublease" means a lease of goods the right to possession and use of which was acquired by the lessor as a lessee under an existing lease.

(x) "Supplier" means a person from whom a lessor buys or leases goods to be leased under a finance lease.

(y) "Supply contract" means a contract under which a lessor buys or leases goods to be leased.

(z) "Termination" occurs when either party pursuant to a power created by agreement or law puts an end to the lease contract otherwise than for default.

(2) Other definitions applying to this Article and the sections in which they appear are:

"Accessions". Section 2A–310(1).
"Construction mortgage". Section 2A–309(1)(d).
"Encumbrance". Section 2A–309(1)(e).
"Fixtures". Section 2A–309(1)(a).
"Fixture filing". Section 2A–309(1)(b).
"Purchase money lease". Section 2A–309(1)(c).

(3) The following definitions in other Articles apply to this Article:

"Accounts". Section 9–106.
"Between merchants". Section 2–104(3).
"Buyer". Section 2–103(1)(a).
"Chattel paper". Section 9–105(1)(b).
"Consumer goods". Section 9–109(1).
"Document". Section 9–105(1)(f).
"Entrusting". Section 2–403(3).
"General intangibles". Section 9–106.
"Good faith". Section 2–103(1)(b).
"Instrument". Section 9–105(1)(i).
"Merchant". Section 2–104(1).
"Mortgage". Section 9–105(1)(j).
"Pursuant to commitment". Section 9–105(1)(k).
"Receipt". Section 2–103(1)(c).
"Sale". Section 2–106(1).
"Sale on approval". Section 2–326.
"Sale or return". Section 2–326.
"Seller". Section 2–103(1)(d).

(4) In addition Article 1 contains general definitions and principles of construction and interpretation applicable throughout this Article.

As amended in 1990 and 1999.

§ 2A-104. Leases Subject to Other Law.

(1) A lease, although subject to this Article, is also subject to any applicable:
(a) certificate of title statute of this State: (list any certificate of title statutes covering automobiles, trailers, mobile homes, boats, farm tractors, and the like);
(b) certificate of title statute of another jurisdiction (Section 2A–105); or
(c) consumer protection statute of this State, or final consumer protection decision of a court of this State existing on the effective date of this Article.

(2) In case of conflict between this Article, other than Sections 2A–105, 2A–304(3), and 2A–305(3), and a statute or decision referred to in subsection (1), the statute or decision controls.

(3) Failure to comply with an applicable law has only the effect specified therein.

As amended in 1990.

§ 2A-105. Territorial Application of Article to Goods Covered by Certificate of Title.

Subject to the provisions of Sections 2A–304(3) and 2A–305(3), with respect to goods covered by a certificate of title issued under a statute of this State or of another jurisdiction, compliance and the effect of compliance or noncompliance with a certificate of title statute are governed by the law (including the conflict of laws rules) of the jurisdiction issuing the certificate until the earlier of (a) surrender of the certificate, or (b) four months after the goods are removed from that jurisdiction and thereafter until a new certificate of title is issued by another jurisdiction.

§ 2A-106. Limitation on Power of Parties to Consumer Lease to Choose Applicable Law and Judicial Forum.

(1) If the law chosen by the parties to a consumer lease is that of a jurisdiction other than a jurisdiction in which the lessee resides at the time the lease agreement becomes enforceable or within 30 days thereafter or in which the goods are to be used, the choice is not enforceable.

(2) If the judicial forum chosen by the parties to a consumer lease is a forum that would not otherwise have jurisdiction over the lessee, the choice is not enforceable.

§ 2A-107. Waiver or Renunciation of Claim or Right After Default.

Any claim or right arising out of an alleged default or breach of warranty may be discharged in whole or in part without consideration by a written waiver or renunciation signed and delivered by the aggrieved party.

§ 2A-108. Unconscionability.

(1) If the court as a matter of law finds a lease contract or any clause of a lease contract to have been unconscionable at the time it was made the court may refuse to enforce the lease contract, or it may enforce the remainder of the lease contract without the unconscionable clause, or it may so limit the application of any unconscionable clause as to avoid any unconscionable result.

(2) With respect to a consumer lease, if the court as a matter of law finds that a lease contract or any clause of a lease contract has been induced by unconscionable conduct or that unconscionable conduct has occurred in the collection of a claim arising from a lease contract, the court may grant appropriate relief.

(3) Before making a finding of unconscionability under subsection (1) or (2), the court, on its own motion or that of a party, shall afford the parties

a reasonable opportunity to present evidence as to the setting, purpose, and effect of the lease contract or clause thereof, or of the conduct.

(4) In an action in which the lessee claims unconscionability with respect to a consumer lease:

(a) If the court finds unconscionability under subsection (1) or (2), the court shall award reasonable attorney's fees to the lessee.

(b) If the court does not find unconscionability and the lessee claiming unconscionability has brought or maintained an action he [or she] knew to be groundless, the court shall award reasonable attorney's fees to the party against whom the claim is made.

(c) In determining attorney's fees, the amount of the recovery on behalf of the claimant under subsections (1) and (2) is not controlling.

§ 2A-109. Option to Accelerate at Will.

(1) A term providing that one party or his [or her] successor in interest may accelerate payment or performance or require collateral or additional collateral "at will" or "when he [or she] deems himself [or herself] insecure" or in words of similar import must be construed to mean that he [or she] has power to do so only if he [or she] in good faith believes that the prospect of payment or performance is impaired.

(2) With respect to a consumer lease, the burden of establishing good faith under subsection (1) is on the party who exercised the power; otherwise the burden of establishing lack of good faith is on the party against whom the power has been exercised.

PART 2: Formation and Construction of Lease Contract

§ 2A-201. Statute of Frauds.

(1) A lease contract is not enforceable by way of action or defense unless:

(a) the total payments to be made under the lease contract, excluding payments for options to renew or buy, are less than $1,000; or

(b) there is a writing, signed by the party against whom enforcement is sought or by that party's authorized agent, sufficient to indicate that a lease contract has been made between the parties and to describe the goods leased and the lease term.

(2) Any description of leased goods or of the lease term is sufficient and satisfies subsection (1)(b), whether or not it is specific, if it reasonably identifies what is described.

(3) A writing is not insufficient because it omits or incorrectly states a term agreed upon, but the lease contract is not enforceable under subsection (1)(b) beyond the lease term and the quantity of goods shown in the writing.

(4) A lease contract that does not satisfy the requirements of subsection (1), but which is valid in other respects, is enforceable:

(a) if the goods are to be specially manufactured or obtained for the lessee and are not suitable for lease or sale to others in the ordinary course of the lessor's business, and the lessor, before notice of repudiation is received and under circumstances that reasonably indicate that the goods are for the lessee, has made either a substantial beginning of their manufacture or commitments for their procurement;

(b) if the party against whom enforcement is sought admits in that party's pleading, testimony or otherwise in court that a lease contract was made, but the lease contract is not enforceable under this provision beyond the quantity of goods admitted; or

(c) with respect to goods that have been received and accepted by the lessee.

(5) The lease term under a lease contract referred to in subsection (4) is:

(a) if there is a writing signed by the party against whom enforcement is sought or by that party's authorized agent specifying the lease term, the term so specified;

(b) if the party against whom enforcement is sought admits in that party's pleading, testimony, or otherwise in court a lease term, the term so admitted; or

(c) a reasonable lease term.

§ 2A-202. Final Written Expression: Parol or Extrinsic Evidence.

Terms with respect to which the confirmatory memoranda of the parties agree or which are otherwise set forth in a writing intended by the parties as a final expression of their agreement with respect to such terms as are included therein may not be contradicted by evidence of any prior agreement or of a contemporaneous oral agreement but may be explained or supplemented:

(a) by course of dealing or usage of trade or by course of performance; and

(b) by evidence of consistent additional terms unless the court finds the writing to have been intended also as a complete and exclusive statement of the terms of the agreement.

§ 2A-203. Seals Inoperative.

The affixing of a seal to a writing evidencing a lease contract or an offer to enter into a lease contract does not render the writing a sealed instrument and the law with respect to sealed instruments does not apply to the lease contract or offer.

§ 2A-204. Formation in General.

(1) A lease contract may be made in any manner sufficient to show agreement, including conduct by both parties which recognizes the existence of a lease contract.

(2) An agreement sufficient to constitute a lease contract may be found although the moment of its making is undetermined.

(3) Although one or more terms are left open, a lease contract does not fail for indefiniteness if the parties have intended to make a lease contract and there is a reasonably certain basis for giving an appropriate remedy.

§ 2A-205. Firm Offers.

An offer by a merchant to lease goods to or from another person in a signed writing that by its terms gives assurance it will be held open is not revocable, for lack of consideration, during the time stated or, if no time is stated, for a reasonable time, but in no event may the period of irrevocability exceed 3 months. Any such term of assurance on a form supplied by the offeree must be separately signed by the offeror.

§ 2A-206. Offer and Acceptance in Formation of Lease Contract.

(1) Unless otherwise unambiguously indicated by the language or circumstances, an offer to make a lease contract must be construed as inviting acceptance in any manner and by any medium reasonable in the circumstances.

(2) If the beginning of a requested performance is a reasonable mode of acceptance, an offeror who is not notified of acceptance within a reasonable time may treat the offer as having lapsed before acceptance.

§ 2A-207. Course of Performance or Practical Construction.

(1) If a lease contract involves repeated occasions for performance by either party with knowledge of the nature of the performance and opportunity for objection to it by the other, any course of performance accepted or acquiesced in without objection is relevant to determine the meaning of the lease agreement.

(2) The express terms of a lease agreement and any course of performance, as well as any course of dealing and usage of trade, must be construed whenever reasonable as consistent with each other; but if that

construction is unreasonable, express terms control course of performance, course of performance controls both course of dealing and usage of trade, and course of dealing controls usage of trade.

(3) Subject to the provisions of Section 2A–208 on modification and waiver, course of performance is relevant to show a waiver or modification of any term inconsistent with the course of performance.

§ 2A-208. Modification, Rescission and Waiver.

(1) An agreement modifying a lease contract needs no consideration to be binding.

(2) A signed lease agreement that excludes modification or rescission except by a signed writing may not be otherwise modified or rescinded, but, except as between merchants, such a requirement on a form supplied by a merchant must be separately signed by the other party.

(3) Although an attempt at modification or rescission does not satisfy the requirements of subsection (2), it may operate as a waiver.

(4) A party who has made a waiver affecting an executory portion of a lease contract may retract the waiver by reasonable notification received by the other party that strict performance will be required of any term waived, unless the retraction would be unjust in view of a material change of position in reliance on the waiver.

§ 2A-209. Lessee under Finance Lease as Beneficiary of Supply Contract.

(1) The benefit of the supplier's promises to the lessor under the supply contract and of all warranties, whether express or implied, including those of any third party provided in connection with or as part of the supply contract, extends to the lessee to the extent of the lessee's leasehold interest under a finance lease related to the supply contract, but is subject to the terms warranty and of the supply contract and all defenses or claims arising therefrom.

(2) The extension of the benefit of supplier's promises and of warranties to the lessee (Section 2A–209(1)) does not: (i) modify the rights and obligations of the parties to the supply contract, whether arising therefrom or otherwise, or (ii) impose any duty or liability under the supply contract on the lessee.

(3) Any modification or rescission of the supply contract by the supplier and the lessor is effective between the supplier and the lessee unless, before the modification or rescission, the supplier has received notice that the lessee has entered into a finance lease related to the supply contract. If the modification or rescission is effective between the supplier and the lessee, the lessor is deemed to have assumed, in addition to the obligations of the lessor to the lessee under the lease contract, promises of the supplier to the lessor and warranties that were so modified or rescinded as they existed and were available to the lessee before modification or rescission.

(4) In addition to the extension of the benefit of the supplier's promises and of warranties to the lessee under subsection (1), the lessee retains all rights that the lessee may have against the supplier which arise from an agreement between the lessee and the supplier or under other law.
As amended in 1990.

§ 2A-210. Express Warranties.

(1) Express warranties by the lessor are created as follows:
(a) Any affirmation of fact or promise made by the lessor to the lessee which relates to the goods and becomes part of the basis of the bargain creates an express warranty that the goods will conform to the affirmation or promise.
(b) Any description of the goods which is made part of the basis of the bargain creates an express warranty that the goods will conform to the description.
(c) Any sample or model that is made part of the basis of the bargain creates an express warranty that the whole of the goods will conform to the sample or model.

(2) It is not necessary to the creation of an express warranty that the lessor use formal words, such as "warrant" or "guarantee," or that the lessor have a specific intention to make a warranty, but an affirmation merely of the value of the goods or a statement purporting to be merely the lessor's opinion or commendation of the goods does not create a warranty.

§ 2A-211. Warranties Against Interference and Against Infringement; Lessee's Obligation Against Infringement.

(1) There is in a lease contract a warranty that for the lease term no person holds a claim to or interest in the goods that arose from an act or omission of the lessor, other than a claim by way of infringement or the like, which will interfere with the lessee's enjoyment of its leasehold interest.

(2) Except in a finance lease there is in a lease contract by a lessor who is a merchant regularly dealing in goods of the kind a warranty that the goods are delivered free of the rightful claim of any person by way of infringement or the like.

(3) A lessee who furnishes specifications to a lessor or a supplier shall hold the lessor and the supplier harmless against any claim by way of infringement or the like that arises out of compliance with the specifications.

§ 2A-212. Implied Warranty of Merchantability.

(1) Except in a finance lease, a warranty that the goods will be merchantable is implied in a lease contract if the lessor is a merchant with respect to goods of that kind.

(2) Goods to be merchantable must be at least such as
(a) pass without objection in the trade under the description in the lease agreement;
(b) in the case of fungible goods, are of fair average quality within the description;
(c) are fit for the ordinary purposes for which goods of that type are used;
(d) run, within the variation permitted by the lease agreement, of even kind, quality, and quantity within each unit and among all units involved;
(e) are adequately contained, packaged, and labeled as the lease agreement may require; and
(f) conform to any promises or affirmations of fact made on the container or label.

(3) Other implied warranties may arise from course of dealing or usage of trade.

§ 2A-213. Implied Warranty of Fitness for Particular Purpose.

Except in a finance of lease, if the lessor at the time the lease contract is made has reason to know of any particular purpose for which the goods are required and that the lessee is relying on the lessor's skill or judgment to select or furnish suitable goods, there is in the lease contract an implied warranty that the goods will be fit for that purpose.

§ 2A-214. Exclusion or Modification of Warranties.

(1) Words or conduct relevant to the creation of an express warranty and words or conduct tending to negate or limit a warranty must be construed wherever reasonable as consistent with each other; but, subject to the provisions of Section 2A–202 on parol or extrinsic evidence, negation or limitation is inoperative to the extent that the construction is unreasonable.

(2) Subject to subsection (3), to exclude or modify the implied warranty of merchantability or any part of it the language must mention "merchantability", be by a writing, and be conspicuous. Subject to subsection (3), to exclude or modify any implied warranty of fitness the exclusion must be by a writing and be conspicuous. Language to exclude all implied

warranties of fitness is sufficient if it is in writing, is conspicuous and states, for example, "There is no warranty that the goods will be fit for a particular purpose".

(3) Notwithstanding subsection (2), but subject to subsection (4),

(a) unless the circumstances indicate otherwise, all implied warranties are excluded by expressions like "as is" or "with all faults" or by other language that in common understanding calls the lessee's attention to the exclusion of warranties and makes plain that there is no implied warranty, if in writing and conspicuous;

(b) if the lessee before entering into the lease contract has examined the goods or the sample or model as fully as desired or has refused to examine the goods, there is no implied warranty with regard to defects that an examination ought in the circumstances to have revealed; and

(c) an implied warranty may also be excluded or modified by course of dealing, course of performance, or usage of trade.

(4) To exclude or modify a warranty against interference or against infringement (Section 2A–211) or any part of it, the language must be specific, be by a writing, and be conspicuous, unless the circumstances, including course of performance, course of dealing, or usage of trade, give the lessee reason to know that the goods are being leased subject to a claim or interest of any person.

§ 2A-215. Cumulation and Conflict of Warranties Express or Implied.

Warranties, whether express or implied, must be construed as consistent with each other and as cumulative, but if that construction is unreasonable, the intention of the parties determines which warranty is dominant. In ascertaining that intention the following rules apply:

(a) Exact or technical specifications displace an inconsistent sample or model or general language of description.

(b) A sample from an existing bulk displaces inconsistent general language of description.

(c) Express warranties displace inconsistent implied warranties other than an implied warranty of fitness for a particular purpose.

§ 2A-216. Third-Party Beneficiaries of Express and Implied Warranties.
Alternative A

A warranty to or for the benefit of a lessee under this Article, whether express or implied, extends to any natural person who is in the family or household of the lessee or who is a guest in the lessee's home if it is reasonable to expect that such person may use, consume, or be affected by the goods and who is injured in person by breach of the warranty. This section does not displace principles of law and equity that extend a warranty to or for the benefit of a lessee to other persons. The operation of this section may not be excluded, modified, or limited, but an exclusion, modification, or limitation of the warranty, including any with respect to rights and remedies, effective against the lessee is also effective against any beneficiary designated under this section.

Alternative B

A warranty to or for the benefit of a lessee under this Article, whether express or implied, extends to any natural person who may reasonably be expected to use, consume, or be affected by the goods and who is injured in person by breach of the warranty. This section does not displace principles of law and equity that extend a warranty to or for the benefit of a lessee to other persons. The operation of this section may not be excluded, modified, or limited, but an exclusion, modification, or limitation of the warranty, including any with respect to rights and remedies, effective against the lessee is also effective against the beneficiary designated under this section.

Alternative C

A warranty to or for the benefit of a lessee under this Article, whether express or implied, extends to any person who may reasonably be expected to use, consume, or be affected by the goods and who is injured by breach of the warranty. The operation of this section may not be excluded, modified, or limited with respect to injury to the person of an individual to whom the warranty extends, but an exclusion, modification, or limitation of the warranty, including any with respect to rights and remedies, effective against the lessee is also effective against the beneficiary designated under this section.

§ 2A-217. Identification.

Identification of goods as goods to which a lease contract refers may be made at any time and in any manner explicitly agreed to by the parties. In the absence of explicit agreement, identification occurs:

(a) when the lease contract is made if the lease contract is for a lease of goods that are existing and identified;

(b) when the goods are shipped, marked, or otherwise designated by the lessor as goods to which the lease contract refers, if the lease contract is for a lease of goods that are not existing and identified; or

(c) when the young are conceived, if the lease contract is for a lease of unborn young of animals.

§ 2A-218. Insurance and Proceeds.

(1) A lessee obtains an insurable interest when existing goods are identified to the lease contract even though the goods identified are nonconforming and the lessee has an option to reject them.

(2) If a lessee has an insurable interest only by reason of the lessor's identification of the goods, the lessor, until default or insolvency or notification to the lessee that identification is final, may substitute other goods for those identified.

(3) Notwithstanding a lessee's insurable interest under subsections (1) and (2), the lessor retains an insurable interest until an option to buy has been exercised by the lessee and risk of loss has passed to the lessee.

(4) Nothing in this section impairs any insurable interest recognized under any other statute or rule of law.

(5) The parties by agreement may determine that one or more parties have an obligation to obtain and pay for insurance covering the goods and by agreement may determine the beneficiary of the proceeds of the insurance.

§ 2A-219. Risk of Loss.

(1) Except in the case of a finance lease, risk of loss is retained by the lessor and does not pass to the lessee. In the case of a finance lease, risk of loss passes to the lessee.

(2) Subject to the provisions of this Article on the effect of default on risk of loss (Section 2A–220), if risk of loss is to pass to the lessee and the time of passage is not stated, the following rules apply:

(a) If the lease contract requires or authorizes the goods to be shipped by carrier

(i) and it does not require delivery at a particular destination, the risk of loss passes to the lessee when the goods are duly delivered to the carrier; but

(ii) if it does require delivery at a particular destination and the goods are there duly tendered while in the possession of the carrier, the risk of loss passes to the lessee when the goods are there duly so tendered as to enable the lessee to take delivery.

(b) If the goods are held by a bailee to be delivered without being moved, the risk of loss passes to the lessee on acknowledgment by the bailee of the lessee's right to possession of the goods.

(c) In any case not within subsection (a) or (b), the risk of loss passes to the lessee on the lessee's receipt of the goods if the lessor, or, in the case of a finance lease, the supplier, is a merchant; otherwise the risk passes to the lessee on tender of delivery.

§ 2A-220. Effect of Default on Risk of Loss.

(1) Where risk of loss is to pass to the lessee and the time of passage is not stated:

(a) If a tender or delivery of goods so fails to conform to the lease contract as to give a right of rejection, the risk of their loss remains with the lessor, or, in the case of a finance lease, the supplier, until cure or acceptance.

(b) If the lessee rightfully revokes acceptance, he [or she], to the extent of any deficiency in his [or her] effective insurance coverage, may treat the risk of loss as having remained with the lessor from the beginning.

(2) Whether or not risk of loss is to pass to the lessee, if the lessee as to conforming goods already identified to a lease contract repudiates or is otherwise in default under the lease contract, the lessor, or, in the case of a finance lease, the supplier, to the extent of any deficiency in his [or her] effective insurance coverage may treat the risk of loss as resting on the lessee for a commercially reasonable time.

§ 2A-221. Casualty to Identified Goods.

If a lease contract requires goods identified when the lease contract is made, and the goods suffer casualty without fault of the lessee, the lessor or the supplier before delivery, or the goods suffer casualty before risk of loss passes to the lessee pursuant to the lease agreement or Section 2A–219, then:

(a) if the loss is total, the lease contract is avoided; and

(b) if the loss is partial or the goods have so deteriorated as to no longer conform to the lease contract, the lessee may nevertheless demand inspection and at his [or her] option either treat the lease contract as avoided or, except in a finance lease that is not a consumer lease, accept the goods with due allowance from the rent payable for the balance of the lease term for the deterioration or the deficiency in quantity but without further right against the lessor.

PART 3: Effect of Lease Contract

§ 2A-301. Enforceability of Lease Contract.

Except as otherwise provided in this Article, a lease contract is effective and enforceable according to its terms between the parties, against purchasers of the goods and against creditors of the parties.

§ 2A-302. Title to and Possession of Goods.

Except as otherwise provided in this Article, each provision of this Article applies whether the lessor or a third party has title to the goods, and whether the lessor, the lessee, or a third party has possession of the goods, notwithstanding any statute or rule of law that possession or the absence of possession is fraudulent.

§ 2A-303. Alienability of Party's Interest Under Lease Contract or of Lessor's Residual Interest in Goods; Delegation of Performance; Transfer of Rights.

(1) As used in this section, "creation of a security interest" includes the sale of a lease contract that is subject to Article 9, Secured Transactions, by reason of Section 9–109(a)(3).

(2) Except as provided in subsections (3) and Section 9–407, a provision in a lease agreement which (i) prohibits the voluntary or involuntary transfer, including a transfer by sale, sublease, creation or enforcement of a security interest, or attachment, levy, or other judicial process, of an interest of a party under the lease contract or of the lessor's residual interest in the goods,

or (ii) makes such a transfer an event of default, gives rise to the rights and remedies provided in subsection (4), but a transfer that is prohibited or is an event of default under the lease agreement is otherwise effective.

(3) A provision in a lease agreement which (i) prohibits a transfer of a right to damages for default with respect to the whole lease contract or of a right to payment arising out of the transferor's due performance of the transferor's entire obligation, or (ii) makes such a transfer an event of default, is not enforceable, and such a transfer is not a transfer that materially impairs the prospect of obtaining return performance by, materially changes the duty of, or materially increases the burden or risk imposed on, the other party to the lease contract within the purview of subsection (4).

(4) Subject to subsection (3) and Section 9–407:

(a) if a transfer is made which is made an event of default under a lease agreement, the party to the lease contract not making the transfer, unless that party waives the default or otherwise agrees, has the rights and remedies described in Section 2A–501(2);

(b) if paragraph (a) is not applicable and if a transfer is made that (i) is prohibited under a lease agreement or (ii) materially impairs the prospect of obtaining return performance by, materially changes the duty of, or materially increases the burden or risk imposed on, the other party to the lease contract, unless the party not making the transfer agrees at any time to the transfer in the lease contract or otherwise, then, except as limited by contract, (i) the transferor is liable to the party not making the transfer for damages caused by the transfer to the extent that the damages could not reasonably be prevented by the party not making the transfer and (ii) a court having jurisdiction may grant other appropriate relief, including cancellation of the lease contract or an injunction against the transfer.

(5) A transfer of "the lease" or of "all my rights under the lease", or a transfer in similar general terms, is a transfer of rights and, unless the language or the circumstances, as in a transfer for security, indicate the contrary, the transfer is a delegation of duties by the transferor to the transferee. Acceptance by the transferee constitutes a promise by the transferee to perform those duties. The promise is enforceable by either the transferor or the other party to the lease contract.

(6) Unless otherwise agreed by the lessor and the lessee, a delegation of performance does not relieve the transferor as against the other party of any duty to perform or of any liability for default.

(7) In a consumer lease, to prohibit the transfer of an interest of a party under the lease contract or to make a transfer an event of default, the language must be specific, by a writing, and conspicuous.

As amended in 1990 and 1999.

§ 2A-304. Subsequent Lease of Goods by Lessor.

(1) Subject to Section 2A–303, a subsequent lessee from a lessor of goods under an existing lease contract obtains, to the extent of the leasehold interest transferred, the leasehold interest in the goods that the lessor had or had power to transfer, and except as provided in subsection (2) and Section 2A–527(4), takes subject to the existing lease contract. A lessor with voidable title has power to transfer a good leasehold interest to a good faith subsequent lessee for value, but only to the extent set forth in the preceding sentence. If goods have been delivered under a transaction of purchase the lessor has that power even though:

(a) the lessor's transferor was deceived as to the identity of the lessor;

(b) the delivery was in exchange for a check which is later dishonored;

(c) it was agreed that the transaction was to be a "cash sale"; or

(d) the delivery was procured through fraud punishable as larcenous under the criminal law.

(2) A subsequent lessee in the ordinary course of business from a lessor who is a merchant dealing in goods of that kind to whom the goods were entrusted by the existing lessee of that lessor before the interest of the subsequent lessee became enforceable against that lessor obtains, to the extent

of the leasehold interest transferred, all of that lessor's and the existing lessee's rights to the goods, and takes free of the existing lease contract.

(3) A subsequent lessee from the lessor of goods that are subject to an existing lease contract and are covered by a certificate of title issued under a statute of this State or of another jurisdiction takes no greater rights than those provided both by this section and by the certificate of title statute. As amended in 1990.

§ 2A-305. Sale or Sublease of Goods by Lessee.

(1) Subject to the provisions of Section 2A–303, a buyer or sublessee from the lessee of goods under an existing lease contract obtains, to the extent of the interest transferred, the leasehold interest in the goods that the lessee had or had power to transfer, and except as provided in subsection (2) and Section 2A–511(4), takes subject to the existing lease contract. A lessee with a voidable leasehold interest has power to transfer a good leasehold interest to a good faith buyer for value or a good faith sublessee for value, but only to the extent set forth in the preceding sentence. When goods have been delivered under a transaction of lease the lessee has that power even though:

    (a) the lessor was deceived as to the identity of the lessee;

    (b) the delivery was in exchange for a check which is later dishonored; or

    (c) the delivery was procured through fraud punishable as larcenous under the criminal law.

(2) A buyer in the ordinary course of business or a sublessee in the ordinary course of business from a lessee who is a merchant dealing in goods of that kind to whom the goods were entrusted by the lessor obtains, to the extent of the interest transferred, all of the lessor's and lessee's rights to the goods, and takes free of the existing lease contract.

(3) A buyer or sublessee from the lessee of goods that are subject to an existing lease contract and are covered by a certificate of title issued under a statute of this State or of another jurisdiction takes no greater rights than those provided both by this section and by the certificate of title statute.

§ 2A-306. Priority of Certain Liens Arising by Operation of Law.

If a person in the ordinary course of his [or her] business furnishes services or materials with respect to goods subject to a lease contract, a lien upon those goods in the possession of that person given by statute or rule of law for those materials or services takes priority over any interest of the lessor or lessee under the lease contract or this Article unless the lien is created by statute and the statute provides otherwise or unless the lien is created by rule of law and the rule of law provides otherwise.

§ 2A-307. Priority of Liens Arising by Attachment or Levy on, Security Interests in, and Other Claims to Goods.

(1) Except as otherwise provided in Section 2A–306, a creditor of a lessee takes subject to the lease contract.

(2) Except as otherwise provided in subsection (3) and in Sections 2A–306 and 2A–308, a creditor of a lessor takes subject to the lease contract unless the creditor holds a lien that attached to the goods before the lease contract became enforceable.

(3) Except as otherwise provided in Sections 9–317, 9–321, and 9–323, a lessee takes a leasehold interest subject to a security interest held by a creditor of the lessor.
As amended in 1990 and 1999.

§ 2A-308. Special Rights of Creditors.

(1) A creditor of a lessor in possession of goods subject to a lease contract may treat the lease contract as void if as against the creditor retention of possession by the lessor is fraudulent under any statute or rule of law, but retention of possession in good faith and current course of trade by the lessor for a commercially reasonable time after the lease contract becomes enforceable is not fraudulent.

(2) Nothing in this Article impairs the rights of creditors of a lessor if the lease contract (a) becomes enforceable, not in current course of trade but in satisfaction of or as security for a pre-existing claim for money, security, or the like, and (b) is made under circumstances which under any statute or rule of law apart from this Article would constitute the transaction a fraudulent transfer or voidable preference.

(3) A creditor of a seller may treat a sale or an identification of goods to a contract for sale as void if as against the creditor retention of possession by the seller is fraudulent under any statute or rule of law, but retention of possession of the goods pursuant to a lease contract entered into by the seller as lessee and the buyer as lessor in connection with the sale or identification of the goods is not fraudulent if the buyer bought for value and in good faith.

§ 2A-309. Lessor's and Lessee's Rights When Goods Become Fixtures.

(1) In this section:

    (a) goods are "fixtures" when they become so related to particular real estate that an interest in them arises under real estate law;

    (b) a "fixture filing" is the filing, in the office where a mortgage on the real estate would be filed or recorded, of a financing statement covering goods that are or are to become fixtures and conforming to the requirements of Section 9–502(a) and (b);

    (c) a lease is a "purchase money lease" unless the lessee has possession or use of the goods or the right to possession or use of the goods before the lease agreement is enforceable;

    (d) a mortgage is a "construction mortgage" to the extent it secures an obligation incurred for the construction of an improvement on land including the acquisition cost of the land, if the recorded writing so indicates; and

    (e) "encumbrance" includes real estate mortgages and other liens on real estate and all other rights in real estate that are not ownership interests.

(2) Under this Article a lease may be of goods that are fixtures or may continue in goods that become fixtures, but no lease exists under this Article of ordinary building materials incorporated into an improvement on land.

(3) This Article does not prevent creation of a lease of fixtures pursuant to real estate law.

(4) The perfected interest of a lessor of fixtures has priority over a conflicting interest of an encumbrancer or owner of the real estate if:

    (a) the lease is a purchase money lease, the conflicting interest of the encumbrancer or owner arises before the goods become fixtures, the interest of the lessor is perfected by a fixture filing before the goods become fixtures or within ten days thereafter, and the lessee has an interest of record in the real estate or is in possession of the real estate; or

    (b) the interest of the lessor is perfected by a fixture filing before the interest of the encumbrancer or owner is of record, the lessor's interest has priority over any conflicting interest of a predecessor in title of the encumbrancer or owner, and the lessee has an interest of record in the real estate or is in possession of the real estate.

(5) The interest of a lessor of fixtures, whether or not perfected, has priority over the conflicting interest of an encumbrancer or owner of the real estate if:

    (a) the fixtures are readily removable factory or office machines, readily removable equipment that is not primarily used or leased for use in the operation of the real estate, or readily removable replacements of domestic appliances that are goods subject to a consumer lease, and before the goods become fixtures the lease contract is enforceable; or

(b) the conflicting interest is a lien on the real estate obtained by legal or equitable proceedings after the lease contract is enforceable; or

(c) the encumbrancer or owner has consented in writing to the lease or has disclaimed an interest in the goods as fixtures; or

(d) the lessee has a right to remove the goods as against the encumbrancer or owner. If the lessee's right to remove terminates, the priority of the interest of the lessor continues for a reasonable time.

(6) Notwithstanding paragraph (4)(a) but otherwise subject to subsections (4) and (5), the interest of a lessor of fixtures, including the lessor's residual interest, is subordinate to the conflicting interest of an encumbrancer of the real estate under a construction mortgage recorded before the goods become fixtures if the goods become fixtures before the completion of the construction. To the extent given to refinance a construction mortgage, the conflicting interest of an encumbrancer of the real estate under a mortgage has this priority to the same extent as the encumbrancer of the real estate under the construction mortgage.

(7) In cases not within the preceding subsections, priority between the interest of a lessor of fixtures, including the lessor's residual interest, and the conflicting interest of an encumbrancer or owner of the real estate who is not the lessee is determined by the priority rules governing conflicting interests in real estate.

(8) If the interest of a lessor of fixtures, including the lessor's residual interest, has priority over all conflicting interests of all owners and encumbrancers of the real estate, the lessor or the lessee may (i) on default, expiration, termination, or cancellation of the lease agreement but subject to the agreement and this Article, or (ii) if necessary to enforce other rights and remedies of the lessor or lessee under this Article, remove the goods from the real estate, free and clear of all conflicting interests of all owners and encumbrancers of the real estate, but the lessor or lessee must reimburse any encumbrancer or owner of the real estate who is not the lessee and who has not otherwise agreed for the cost of repair of any physical injury, but not for any diminution in value of the real estate caused by the absence of the goods removed or by any necessity of replacing them. A person entitled to reimbursement may refuse permission to remove until the party seeking removal gives adequate security for the performance of this obligation.

(9) Even though the lease agreement does not create a security interest, the interest of a lessor of fixtures, including the lessor's residual interest, is perfected by filing a financing statement as a fixture filing for leased goods that are or are to become fixtures in accordance with the relevant provisions of the Article on Secured Transactions (Article 9).
As amended in 1990 and 1999.

§ 2A-310. Lessor's and Lessee's Rights When Goods Become Accessions.

(1) Goods are "accessions" when they are installed in or affixed to other goods.

(2) The interest of a lessor or a lessee under a lease contract entered into before the goods became accessions is superior to all interests in the whole except as stated in subsection (4).

(3) The interest of a lessor or a lessee under a lease contract entered into at the time or after the goods became accessions is superior to all subsequently acquired interests in the whole except as stated in subsection (4) but is subordinate to interests in the whole existing at the time the lease contract was made unless the holders of such interests in the whole have in writing consented to the lease or disclaimed an interest in the goods as part of the whole.

(4) The interest of a lessor or a lessee under a lease contract described in subsection (2) or (3) is subordinate to the interest of

(a) a buyer in the ordinary course of business or a lessee in the ordinary course of business of any interest in the whole acquired after the goods became accessions; or

(b) a creditor with a security interest in the whole perfected before the lease contract was made to the extent that the creditor makes subsequent advances without knowledge of the lease contract.

(5) When under subsections (2) or (3) and (4) a lessor or a lessee of accessions holds an interest that is superior to all interests in the whole, the lessor or the lessee may (a) on default, expiration, termination, or cancellation of the lease contract by the other party but subject to the provisions of the lease contract and this Article, or (b) if necessary to enforce his [or her] other rights and remedies under this Article, remove the goods from the whole, free and clear of all interests in the whole, but he [or she] must reimburse any holder of an interest in the whole who is not the lessee and who has not otherwise agreed for the cost of repair of any physical injury but not for any diminution in value of the whole caused by the absence of the goods removed or by any necessity for replacing them. A person entitled to reimbursement may refuse permission to remove until the party seeking removal gives adequate security for the performance of this obligation.

§ 2A-311. Priority Subject to Subordination.

Nothing in this Article prevents subordination by agreement by any person entitled to priority.
As added in 1990.

PART 4: Performance of Lease Contract: Repudiated, Substituted and Excused

§ 2A-401. Insecurity: Adequate Assurance of Performance.

(1) A lease contract imposes an obligation on each party that the other's expectation of receiving due performance will not be impaired.

(2) If reasonable grounds for insecurity arise with respect to the performance of either party, the insecure party may demand in writing adequate assurance of due performance. Until the insecure party receives that assurance, if commercially reasonable the insecure party may suspend any performance for which he [or she] has not already received the agreed return.

(3) A repudiation of the lease contract occurs if assurance of due performance adequate under the circumstances of the particular case is not provided to the insecure party within a reasonable time, not to exceed 30 days after receipt of a demand by the other party.

(4) Between merchants, the reasonableness of grounds for insecurity and the adequacy of any assurance offered must be determined according to commercial standards.

(5) Acceptance of any nonconforming delivery or payment does not prejudice the aggrieved party's right to demand adequate assurance of future performance.

§ 2A-402. Anticipatory Repudiation.

If either party repudiates a lease contract with respect to a performance not yet due under the lease contract, the loss of which performance will substantially impair the value of the lease contract to the other, the aggrieved party may:

(a) for a commercially reasonable time, await retraction of repudiation and performance by the repudiating party;

(b) make demand pursuant to Section 2A–401 and await assurance of future performance adequate under the circumstances of the particular case; or

(c) resort to any right or remedy upon default under the lease contract or this Article, even though the aggrieved party has notified the repudiating party that the aggrieved party would await the repudiating party's performance and assurance and has urged retraction. In addition, whether or not the aggrieved party is pursuing one of the foregoing remedies, the aggrieved party may suspend performance or, if the aggrieved party is the lessor, proceed in accordance with the provisions of this Article on the lessor's right to identify goods to the lease contract notwithstanding default or to salvage unfinished goods (Section 2A–524).

§ 2A-403. Retraction of Anticipatory Repudiation.

(1) Until the repudiating party's next performance is due, the repudiating party can retract the repudiation unless, since the repudiation, the aggrieved party has cancelled the lease contract or materially changed the aggrieved party's position or otherwise indicated that the aggrieved party considers the repudiation final.

(2) Retraction may be by any method that clearly indicates to the aggrieved party that the repudiating party intends to perform under the lease contract and includes any assurance demanded under Section 2A–401.

(3) Retraction reinstates a repudiating party's rights under a lease contract with due excuse and allowance to the aggrieved party for any delay occasioned by the repudiation.

§ 2A-404. Substituted Performance.

(1) If without fault of the lessee, the lessor and the supplier, the agreed berthing, loading, or unloading, facilities fail or the agreed type of carrier becomes unavailable or the agreed manner of delivery otherwise becomes commercially impracticable, but a commercially reasonable substitute is available, the substitute performance must be tendered and accepted.

(2) If the agreed means or manner of payment fails because of domestic or foreign governmental regulation:

(a) the lessor may withhold or stop delivery or cause the supplier to withhold or stop delivery unless the lessee provides a means or manner of payment that is commercially a substantial equivalent; and

(b) if delivery has already been taken, payment by the means or in the manner provided by the regulation discharges the lessee's obligation unless the regulation is discriminatory, oppressive, or predatory.

§ 2A-405. Excused Performance.

Subject to Section 2A–404 on substituted performance, the following rules apply:

(a) Delay in delivery or nondelivery in whole or in part by a lessor or a supplier who complies with paragraphs (b) and (c) is not a default under the lease contract if performance as agreed has been made impracticable by the occurrence of a contingency the nonoccurrence of which was a basic assumption on which the lease contract was made or by compliance in good faith with any applicable foreign or domestic governmental regulation or order, whether or not the regulation or order later proves to be invalid.

(b) If the causes mentioned in paragraph (a) affect only part of the lessor's or the supplier's capacity to perform, he [or she] shall allocate production and deliveries among his [or her] customers but at his [or her] option may include regular customers not then under contract for sale or lease as well as his [or her] own requirements for further manufacture. He [or she] may so allocate in any manner that is fair and reasonable.

(c) The lessor seasonably shall notify the lessee and in the case of a finance lease the supplier seasonably shall notify the lessor and the lessee, if known, that there will be delay or nondelivery and, if allocation is required under paragraph (b), of the estimated quota thus made available for the lessee.

§ 2A-406. Procedure on Excused Performance.

(1) If the lessee receives notification of a material or indefinite delay or an allocation justified under Section 2A–405, the lessee may by written notification to the lessor as to any goods involved, and with respect to all of the goods if under an installment lease contract the value of the whole lease contract is substantially impaired (Section 2A–510):

(a) terminate the lease contract (Section 2A–505(2)); or

(b) except in a finance lease that is not a consumer lease, modify the lease contract by accepting the available quota in substitution, with due allowance from the rent payable for the balance of the lease term for the deficiency but without further right against the lessor.

(2) If, after receipt of a notification from the lessor under Section 2A–405, the lessee fails so to modify the lease agreement within a reasonable time not exceeding 30 days, the lease contract lapses with respect to any deliveries affected.

§ 2A-407. Irrevocable Promises: Finance Leases.

(1) In the case of a finance lease that is not a consumer lease the lessee's promises under the lease contract become irrevocable and independent upon the lessee's acceptance of the goods.

(2) A promise that has become irrevocable and independent under subsection (1):

(a) is effective and enforceable between the parties, and by or against third parties including assignees of the parties, and

(b) is not subject to cancellation, termination, modification, repudiation, excuse, or substitution without the consent of the party to whom the promise runs.

(3) This section does not affect the validity under any other law of a covenant in any lease contract making the lessee's promises irrevocable and independent upon the lessee's acceptance of the goods.

As amended in 1990.

PART 5: Default

A. In General

§ 2A-501. Default: Procedure.

(1) Whether the lessor or the lessee is in default under a lease contract is determined by the lease agreement and this Article.

(2) If the lessor or the lessee is in default under the lease contract, the party seeking enforcement has rights and remedies as provided in this Article and, except as limited by this Article, as provided in the lease agreement.

(3) If the lessor or the lessee is in default under the lease contract, the party seeking enforcement may reduce the party's claim to judgment, or otherwise enforce the lease contract by self-help or any available judicial procedure or nonjudicial procedure, including administrative proceeding, arbitration, or the like, in accordance with this Article.

(4) Except as otherwise provided in Section 1–106(1) or this Article or the lease agreement, the rights and remedies referred to in subsections (2) and (3) are cumulative.

(5) If the lease agreement covers both real property and goods, the party seeking enforcement may proceed under this Part as to the goods, or under other applicable law as to both the real property and the goods in accordance with that party's rights and remedies in respect of the real property, in which case this Part does not apply.

As amended in 1990.

§ 2A-502. Notice After Default.

Except as otherwise provided in this Article or the lease agreement, the lessor or lessee in default under the lease contract is not entitled to notice of default or notice of enforcement from the other party to the lease agreement.

§ 2A-503. Modification or Impairment of Rights and Remedies.

(1) Except as otherwise provided in this Article, the lease agreement may include rights and remedies for default in addition to or in substitution for

those provided in this Article and may limit or alter the measure of damages recoverable under this Article.

(2) Resort to a remedy provided under this Article or in the lease agreement is optional unless the remedy is expressly agreed to be exclusive. If circumstances cause an exclusive or limited remedy to fail of its essential purpose, or provision for an exclusive remedy is unconscionable, remedy may be had as provided in this Article.

(3) Consequential damages may be liquidated under Section 2A–504, or may otherwise be limited, altered, or excluded unless the limitation, alteration, or exclusion is unconscionable. Limitation, alteration, or exclusion of consequential damages for injury to the person in the case of consumer goods is prima facie unconscionable but limitation, alteration, or exclusion of damages where the loss is commercial is not prima facie unconscionable.

(4) Rights and remedies on default by the lessor or the lessee with respect to any obligation or promise collateral or ancillary to the lease contract are not impaired by this Article.

As amended in 1990.

§ 2A-504. Liquidation of Damages.

(1) Damages payable by either party for default, or any other act or omission, including indemnity for loss or diminution of anticipated tax benefits or loss or damage to lessor's residual interest, may be liquidated in the lease agreement but only at an amount or by a formula that is reasonable in light of the then anticipated harm caused by the default or other act or omission.

(2) If the lease agreement provides for liquidation of damages, and such provision does not comply with subsection (1), or such provision is an exclusive or limited remedy that circumstances cause to fail of its essential purpose, remedy may be had as provided in this Article.

(3) If the lessor justifiably withholds or stops delivery of goods because of the lessee's default or insolvency (Section 2A–525 or 2A–526), the lessee is entitled to restitution of any amount by which the sum of his [or her] payments exceeds:

    (a) the amount to which the lessor is entitled by virtue of terms liquidating the lessor's damages in accordance with subsection (1); or

    (b) in the absence of those terms, 20 percent of the then present value of the total rent the lessee was obligated to pay for the balance of the lease term, or, in the case of a consumer lease, the lesser of such amount or $500.

(4) A lessee's right to restitution under subsection (3) is subject to offset to the extent the lessor establishes:

    (a) a right to recover damages under the provisions of this Article other than subsection (1); and

    (b) the amount or value of any benefits received by the lessee directly or indirectly by reason of the lease contract.

§ 2A-505. Cancellation and Termination and Effect of Cancellation, Termination, Rescission, or Fraud on Rights and Remedies.

(1) On cancellation of the lease contract, all obligations that are still executory on both sides are discharged, but any right based on prior default or performance survives, and the cancelling party also retains any remedy for default of the whole lease contract or any unperformed balance.

(2) On termination of the lease contract, all obligations that are still executory on both sides are discharged but any right based on prior default or performance survives.

(3) Unless the contrary intention clearly appears, expressions of "cancellation," "rescission," or the like of the lease contract may not be construed as a renunciation or discharge of any claim in damages for an antecedent default.

(4) Rights and remedies for material misrepresentation or fraud include all rights and remedies available under this Article for default.

(5) Neither rescission nor a claim for rescission of the lease contract nor rejection or return of the goods may bar or be deemed inconsistent with a claim for damages or other right or remedy.

§ 2A-506. Statute of Limitations.

(1) An action for default under a lease contract, including breach of warranty or indemnity, must be commenced within 4 years after the cause of action accrued. By the original lease contract the parties may reduce the period of limitation to not less than one year.

(2) A cause of action for default accrues when the act or omission on which the default or breach of warranty is based is or should have been discovered by the aggrieved party, or when the default occurs, whichever is later. A cause of action for indemnity accrues when the act or omission on which the claim for indemnity is based is or should have been discovered by the indemnified party, whichever is later.

(3) If an action commenced within the time limited by subsection (1) is so terminated as to leave available a remedy by another action for the same default or breach of warranty or indemnity, the other action may be commenced after the expiration of the time limited and within 6 months after the termination of the first action unless the termination resulted from voluntary discontinuance or from dismissal for failure or neglect to prosecute.

(4) This section does not alter the law on tolling of the statute of limitations nor does it apply to causes of action that have accrued before this Article becomes effective.

§ 2A-507. Proof of Market Rent: Time and Place.

(1) Damages based on market rent (Section 2A–519 or 2A–528) are determined according to the rent for the use of the goods concerned for a lease term identical to the remaining lease term of the original lease agreement and prevailing at the times specified in Sections 2A–519 and 2A–528.

(2) If evidence of rent for the use of the goods concerned for a lease term identical to the remaining lease term of the original lease agreement and prevailing at the times or places described in this Article is not readily available, the rent prevailing within any reasonable time before or after the time described or at any other place or for a different lease term which in commercial judgment or under usage of trade would serve as a reasonable substitute for the one described may be used, making any proper allowance for the difference, including the cost of transporting the goods to or from the other place.

(3) Evidence of a relevant rent prevailing at a time or place or for a lease term other than the one described in this Article offered by one party is not admissible unless and until he [or she] has given the other party notice the court finds sufficient to prevent unfair surprise.

(4) If the prevailing rent or value of any goods regularly leased in any established market is in issue, reports in official publications or trade journals or in newspapers or periodicals of general circulation published as the reports of that market are admissible in evidence. The circumstances of the preparation of the report may be shown to affect its weight but not its admissibility.

As amended in 1990.

B. Default by Lessor

§ 2A-508. Lessee's Remedies.

(1) If a lessor fails to deliver the goods in conformity to the lease contract (Section 2A–509) or repudiates the lease contract (Section 2A–402), or a lessee rightfully rejects the goods (Section 2A–509) or justifiably revokes acceptance of the goods (Section 2A–517), then with respect to any goods involved, and with respect to all of the goods if under an installment lease contract the value of the whole lease contract is substantially impaired

(Section 2A–510), the lessor is in default under the lease contract and the lessee may:

(a) cancel the lease contract (Section 2A–505(1));

(b) recover so much of the rent and security as has been paid and is just under the circumstances;

(c) cover and recover damages as to all goods affected whether or not they have been identified to the lease contract (Sections 2A–518 and 2A–520), or recover damages for nondelivery (Sections 2A–519 and 2A–520);

(d) exercise any other rights or pursue any other remedies provided in the lease contract.

(2) If a lessor fails to deliver the goods in conformity to the lease contract or repudiates the lease contract, the lessee may also:

(a) if the goods have been identified, recover them (Section 2A–522); or

(b) in a proper case, obtain specific performance or replevy the goods (Section 2A–521).

(3) If a lessor is otherwise in default under a lease contract, the lessee may exercise the rights and pursue the remedies provided in the lease contract, which may include a right to cancel the lease, and in Section 2A–519(3).

(4) If a lessor has breached a warranty, whether express or implied, the lessee may recover damages (Section 2A–519(4)).

(5) On rightful rejection or justifiable revocation of acceptance, a lessee has a security interest in goods in the lessee's possession or control for any rent and security that has been paid and any expenses reasonably incurred in their inspection, receipt, transportation, and care and custody and may hold those goods and dispose of them in good faith and in a commercially reasonable manner, subject to Section 2A–527(5).

(6) Subject to the provisions of Section 2A–407, a lessee, on notifying the lessor of the lessee's intention to do so, may deduct all or any part of the damages resulting from any default under the lease contract from any part of the rent still due under the same lease contract.

As amended in 1990.

§ 2A-509. Lessee's Rights on Improper Delivery; Rightful Rejection.

(1) Subject to the provisions of Section 2A–510 on default in installment lease contracts, if the goods or the tender or delivery fail in any respect to conform to the lease contract, the lessee may reject or accept the goods or accept any commercial unit or units and reject the rest of the goods.

(2) Rejection of goods is ineffective unless it is within a reasonable time after tender or delivery of the goods and the lessee seasonably notifies the lessor.

§ 2A-510. Installment Lease Contracts: Rejection and Default.

(1) Under an installment lease contract a lessee may reject any delivery that is nonconforming if the nonconformity substantially impairs the value of that delivery and cannot be cured or the nonconformity is a defect in the required documents; but if the nonconformity does not fall within subsection (2) and the lessor or the supplier gives adequate assurance of its cure, the lessee must accept that delivery.

(2) Whenever nonconformity or default with respect to one or more deliveries substantially impairs the value of the installment lease contract as a whole there is a default with respect to the whole. But, the aggrieved party reinstates the installment lease contract as a whole if the aggrieved party accepts a nonconforming delivery without seasonably notifying of cancellation or brings an action with respect only to past deliveries or demands performance as to future deliveries.

§ 2A-511. Merchant Lessee's Duties as to Rightfully Rejected Goods.

(1) Subject to any security interest of a lessee (Section 2A–508(5)), if a lessor or a supplier has no agent or place of business at the market of rejection, a merchant lessee, after rejection of goods in his [or her] possession or control, shall follow any reasonable instructions received from the lessor or the supplier with respect to the goods. In the absence of those instructions, a merchant lessee shall make reasonable efforts to sell, lease, or otherwise dispose of the goods for the lessor's account if they threaten to decline in value speedily. Instructions are not reasonable if on demand indemnity for expenses is not forthcoming.

(2) If a merchant lessee (subsection (1)) or any other lessee (Section 2A–512) disposes of goods, he [or she] is entitled to reimbursement either from the lessor or the supplier or out of the proceeds for reasonable expenses of caring for and disposing of the goods and, if the expenses include no disposition commission, to such commission as is usual in the trade, or if there is none, to a reasonable sum not exceeding 10 percent of the gross proceeds.

(3) In complying with this section or Section 2A–512, the lessee is held only to good faith. Good faith conduct hereunder is neither acceptance or conversion nor the basis of an action for damages.

(4) A purchaser who purchases in good faith from a lessee pursuant to this section or Section 2A–512 takes the goods free of any rights of the lessor and the supplier even though the lessee fails to comply with one or more of the requirements of this Article.

§ 2A-512. Lessee's Duties as to Rightfully Rejected Goods.

(1) Except as otherwise provided with respect to goods that threaten to decline in value speedily (Section 2A–511) and subject to any security interest of a lessee (Section 2A–508(5)):

(a) the lessee, after rejection of goods in the lessee's possession, shall hold them with reasonable care at the lessor's or the supplier's disposition for a reasonable time after the lessee's seasonable notification of rejection;

(b) if the lessor or the supplier gives no instructions within a reasonable time after notification of rejection, the lessee may store the rejected goods for the lessor's or the supplier's account or ship them to the lessor or the supplier or dispose of them for the lessor's or the supplier's account with reimbursement in the manner provided in Section 2A–511; but

(c) the lessee has no further obligations with regard to goods rightfully rejected.

(2) Action by the lessee pursuant to subsection (1) is not acceptance or conversion.

§ 2A-513. Cure by Lessor of Improper Tender or Delivery; Replacement.

(1) If any tender or delivery by the lessor or the supplier is rejected because nonconforming and the time for performance has not yet expired, the lessor or the supplier may seasonably notify the lessee of the lessor's or the supplier's intention to cure and may then make a conforming delivery within the time provided in the lease contract.

(2) If the lessee rejects a nonconforming tender that the lessor or the supplier had reasonable grounds to believe would be acceptable with or without money allowance, the lessor or the supplier may have a further reasonable time to substitute a conforming tender if he [or she] seasonably notifies the lessee.

§ 2A-514. Waiver of Lessee's Objections.

(1) In rejecting goods, a lessee's failure to state a particular defect that is ascertainable by reasonable inspection precludes the lessee from relying on the defect to justify rejection or to establish default:

(a) if, stated seasonably, the lessor or the supplier could have cured it (Section 2A–513); or

(b) between merchants if the lessor or the supplier after rejection has made a request in writing for a full and final written statement of all defects on which the lessee proposes to rely.

(2) A lessee's failure to reserve rights when paying rent or other consideration against documents precludes recovery of the payment for defects apparent on the face of the documents.

§ 2A-515. Acceptance of Goods.

(1) Acceptance of goods occurs after the lessee has had a reasonable opportunity to inspect the goods and

(a) the lessee signifies or acts with respect to the goods in a manner that signifies to the lessor or the supplier that the goods are conforming or that the lessee will take or retain them in spite of their nonconformity; or

(b) the lessee fails to make an effective rejection of the goods (Section 2A–509(2)).

(2) Acceptance of a part of any commercial unit is acceptance of that entire unit.

§ 2A-516. Effect of Acceptance of Goods; Notice of Default; Burden of Establishing Default after Acceptance; Notice of Claim or Litigation to Person Answerable Over.

(1) A lessee must pay rent for any goods accepted in accordance with the lease contract, with due allowance for goods rightfully rejected or not delivered.

(2) A lessee's acceptance of goods precludes rejection of the goods accepted. In the case of a finance lease, if made with knowledge of a nonconformity, acceptance cannot be revoked because of it. In any other case, if made with knowledge of a nonconformity, acceptance cannot be revoked because of it unless the acceptance was on the reasonable assumption that the nonconformity would be seasonably cured. Acceptance does not of itself impair any other remedy provided by this Article or the lease agreement for nonconformity.

(3) If a tender has been accepted:

(a) within a reasonable time after the lessee discovers or should have discovered any default, the lessee shall notify the lessor and the supplier, if any, or be barred from any remedy against the party notified;

(b) except in the case of a consumer lease, within a reasonable time after the lessee receives notice of litigation for infringement or the like (Section 2A–211) the lessee shall notify the lessor or be barred from any remedy over for liability established by the litigation; and

(c) the burden is on the lessee to establish any default.

(4) If a lessee is sued for breach of a warranty or other obligation for which a lessor or a supplier is answerable over the following apply:

(a) The lessee may give the lessor or the supplier, or both, written notice of the litigation. If the notice states that the person notified may come in and defend and that if the person notified does not do so that person will be bound in any action against that person by the lessee by any determination of fact common to the two litigations, then unless the person notified after seasonable receipt of the notice does come in and defend that person is so bound.

(b) The lessor or the supplier may demand in writing that the lessee turn over control of the litigation including settlement if the claim is one for infringement or the like (Section 2A–211) or else be barred from any remedy over. If the demand states that the lessor or the supplier agrees to bear all expense and to satisfy any adverse judgment, then unless the lessee after seasonable receipt of the demand does turn over control the lessee is so barred.

(5) Subsections (3) and (4) apply to any obligation of a lessee to hold the lessor or the supplier harmless against infringement or the like (Section 2A–211).

As amended in 1990.

§ 2A-517. Revocation of Acceptance of Goods.

(1) A lessee may revoke acceptance of a lot or commercial unit whose nonconformity substantially impairs its value to the lessee if the lessee has accepted it:

(a) except in the case of a finance lease, on the reasonable assumption that its nonconformity would be cured and it has not been seasonably cured; or

(b) without discovery of the nonconformity if the lessee's acceptance was reasonably induced either by the lessor's assurances or, except in the case of a finance lease, by the difficulty of discovery before acceptance.

(2) Except in the case of a finance lease that is not a consumer lease, a lessee may revoke acceptance of a lot or commercial unit if the lessor defaults under the lease contract and the default substantially impairs the value of that lot or commercial unit to the lessee.

(3) If the lease agreement so provides, the lessee may revoke acceptance of a lot or commercial unit because of other defaults by the lessor.

(4) Revocation of acceptance must occur within a reasonable time after the lessee discovers or should have discovered the ground for it and before any substantial change in condition of the goods which is not caused by the nonconformity. Revocation is not effective until the lessee notifies the lessor.

(5) A lessee who so revokes has the same rights and duties with regard to the goods involved as if the lessee had rejected them.

As amended in 1990.

§ 2A-518. Cover; Substitute Goods.

(1) After a default by a lessor under the lease contract of the type described in Section 2A–508(1), or, if agreed, after other default by the lessor, the lessee may cover by making any purchase or lease of or contract to purchase or lease goods in substitution for those due from the lessor.

(2) Except as otherwise provided with respect to damages liquidated in the lease agreement (Section 2A–504) or otherwise determined pursuant to agreement of the parties (Sections 1–102(3) and 2A–503), if a lessee's cover is by lease agreement substantially similar to the original lease agreement and the new lease agreement is made in good faith and in a commercially reasonable manner, the lessee may recover from the lessor as damages (i) the present value, as of the date of the commencement of the term of the new lease agreement, of the rent under the new lease agreement applicable to that period of the new lease term which is comparable to the then remaining term of the original lease agreement minus the present value as of the same date of the total rent for the then remaining lease term of the original lease agreement, and (ii) any incidental or consequential damages, less expenses saved in consequence of the lessor's default.

(3) If a lessee's cover is by lease agreement that for any reason does not qualify for treatment under subsection (2), or is by purchase or otherwise, the lessee may recover from the lessor as if the lessee had elected not to cover and Section 2A–519 governs.

As amended in 1990.

§ 2A-519. Lessee's Damages for Non-Delivery, Repudiation, Default, and Breach of Warranty in Regard to Accepted Goods.

(1) Except as otherwise provided with respect to damages liquidated in the lease agreement (Section 2A–504) or otherwise determined pursuant to agreement of the parties (Sections 1–102(3) and 2A–503), if a lessee elects not to cover or a lessee elects to cover and the cover is by lease agreement that for any reason does not qualify for treatment under Section

2A–518(2), or is by purchase or otherwise, the measure of damages for non-delivery or repudiation by the lessor or for rejection or revocation of acceptance by the lessee is the present value, as of the date of the default, of the then market rent minus the present value as of the same date of the original rent, computed for the remaining lease term of the original lease agreement, together with incidental and consequential damages, less expenses saved in consequence of the lessor's default.

(2) Market rent is to be determined as of the place for tender or, in cases of rejection after arrival or revocation of acceptance, as of the place of arrival.

(3) Except as otherwise agreed, if the lessee has accepted goods and given notification (Section 2A–516(3)), the measure of damages for non-conforming tender or delivery or other default by a lessor is the loss resulting in the ordinary course of events from the lessor's default as determined in any manner that is reasonable together with incidental and consequential damages, less expenses saved in consequence of the lessor's default.

(4) Except as otherwise agreed, the measure of damages for breach of warranty is the present value at the time and place of acceptance of the difference between the value of the use of the goods accepted and the value if they had been as warranted for the lease term, unless special circumstances show proximate damages of a different amount, together with incidental and consequential damages, less expenses saved in consequence of the lessor's default or breach of warranty.

As amended in 1990.

§ 2A-520. Lessee's Incidental and Consequential Damages.

(1) Incidental damages resulting from a lessor's default include expenses reasonably incurred in inspection, receipt, transportation, and care and custody of goods rightfully rejected or goods the acceptance of which is justifiably revoked, any commercially reasonable charges, expenses or commissions in connection with effecting cover, and any other reasonable expense incident to the default.

(2) Consequential damages resulting from a lessor's default include:
    (a) any loss resulting from general or particular requirements and needs of which the lessor at the time of contracting had reason to know and which could not reasonably be prevented by cover or otherwise; and
    (b) injury to person or property proximately resulting from any breach of warranty.

§ 2A-521. Lessee's Right to Specific Performance or Replevin.

(1) Specific performance may be decreed if the goods are unique or in other proper circumstances.

(2) A decree for specific performance may include any terms and conditions as to payment of the rent, damages, or other relief that the court deems just.

(3) A lessee has a right of replevin, detinue, sequestration, claim and delivery, or the like for goods identified to the lease contract if after reasonable effort the lessee is unable to effect cover for those goods or the circumstances reasonably indicate that the effort will be unavailing.

§ 2A-522. Lessee's Right to Goods on Lessor's Insolvency.

(1) Subject to subsection (2) and even though the goods have not been shipped, a lessee who has paid a part or all of the rent and security for goods identified to a lease contract (Section 2A–217) on making and keeping good a tender of any unpaid portion of the rent and security due under the lease contract may recover the goods identified from the lessor if the lessor becomes insolvent within 10 days after receipt of the first installment of rent and security.

(2) A lessee acquires the right to recover goods identified to a lease contract only if they conform to the lease contract.

C. Default by Lessee

§ 2A-523. Lessor's Remedies.

(1) If a lessee wrongfully rejects or revokes acceptance of goods or fails to make a payment when due or repudiates with respect to a part or the whole, then, with respect to any goods involved, and with respect to all of the goods if under an installment lease contract the value of the whole lease contract is substantially impaired (Section 2A–510), the lessee is in default under the lease contract and the lessor may:
    (a) cancel the lease contract (Section 2A–505(1));
    (b) proceed respecting goods not identified to the lease contract (Section 2A–524);
    (c) withhold delivery of the goods and take possession of goods previously delivered (Section 2A–525);
    (d) stop delivery of the goods by any bailee (Section 2A–526);
    (e) dispose of the goods and recover damages (Section 2A–527), or retain the goods and recover damages (Section 2A–528), or in a proper case recover rent (Section 2A–529)
    (f) exercise any other rights or pursue any other remedies provided in the lease contract.

(2) If a lessor does not fully exercise a right or obtain a remedy to which the lessor is entitled under subsection (1), the lessor may recover the loss resulting in the ordinary course of events from the lessee's default as determined in any reasonable manner, together with incidental damages, less expenses saved in consequence of the lessee's default.

(3) If a lessee is otherwise in default under a lease contract, the lessor may exercise the rights and pursue the remedies provided in the lease contract, which may include a right to cancel the lease. In addition, unless otherwise provided in the lease contract:
    (a) if the default substantially impairs the value of the lease contract to the lessor, the lessor may exercise the rights and pursue the remedies provided in subsections (1) or (2); or
    (b) if the default does not substantially impair the value of the lease contract to the lessor, the lessor may recover as provided in subsection (2).

As amended in 1990.

§ 2A-524. Lessor's Right to Identify Goods to Lease Contract.

(1) After default by the lessee under the lease contract of the type described in Section 2A–523(1) or 2A–523(3)(a) or, if agreed, after other default by the lessee, the lessor may:
    (a) identify to the lease contract conforming goods not already identified if at the time the lessor learned of the default they were in the lessor's or the supplier's possession or control; and
    (b) dispose of goods (Section 2A–527(1)) that demonstrably have been intended for the particular lease contract even though those goods are unfinished.

(2) If the goods are unfinished, in the exercise of reasonable commercial judgment for the purposes of avoiding loss and of effective realization, an aggrieved lessor or the supplier may either complete manufacture and wholly identify the goods to the lease contract or cease manufacture and lease, sell, or otherwise dispose of the goods for scrap or salvage value or proceed in any other reasonable manner.

As amended in 1990.

§ 2A-525. Lessor's Right to Possession of Goods.

(1) If a lessor discovers the lessee to be insolvent, the lessor may refuse to deliver the goods.

(2) After a default by the lessee under the lease contract of the type described in Section 2A–523(1) or 2A–523(3)(a) or, if agreed, after other default by the lessee, the lessor has the right to take possession of the goods. If the lease contract so provides, the lessor may require the lessee to assemble the goods and make them available to the lessor at a place to be designated by the lessor which is reasonably convenient to both parties. Without removal, the lessor may render unusable any goods employed in trade or business, and may dispose of goods on the lessee's premises (Section 2A–527).

(3) The lessor may proceed under subsection (2) without judicial process if that can be done without breach of the peace or the lessor may proceed by action.

As amended in 1990.

§ 2A-526. Lessor's Stoppage of Delivery in Transit or Otherwise.

(1) A lessor may stop delivery of goods in the possession of a carrier or other bailee if the lessor discovers the lessee to be insolvent and may stop delivery of carload, truckload, planeload, or larger shipments of express or freight if the lessee repudiates or fails to make a payment due before delivery, whether for rent, security or otherwise under the lease contract, or for any other reason the lessor has a right to withhold or take possession of the goods.

(2) In pursuing its remedies under subsection (1), the lessor may stop delivery until

(a) receipt of the goods by the lessee;

(b) acknowledgment to the lessee by any bailee of the goods, except a carrier, that the bailee holds the goods for the lessee; or

(c) such an acknowledgment to the lessee by a carrier via reshipment or as warehouseman.

(3) (a) To stop delivery, a lessor shall so notify as to enable the bailee by reasonable diligence to prevent delivery of the goods.

(b) After notification, the bailee shall hold and deliver the goods according to the directions of the lessor, but the lessor is liable to the bailee for any ensuing charges or damages.

(c) A carrier who has issued a nonnegotiable bill of lading is not obliged to obey a notification to stop received from a person other than the consignor.

§ 2A-527. Lessor's Rights to Dispose of Goods.

(1) After a default by a lessee under the lease contract of the type described in Section 2A–523(1) or 2A–523(3)(a) or after the lessor refuses to deliver or takes possession of goods (Section 2A–525 or 2A–526), or, if agreed, after other default by a lessee, the lessor may dispose of the goods concerned or the undelivered balance thereof by lease, sale, or otherwise.

(2) Except as otherwise provided with respect to damages liquidated in the lease agreement (Section 2A–504) or otherwise determined pursuant to agreement of the parties (Sections 1–102(3) and 2A–503), if the disposition is by lease agreement substantially similar to the original lease agreement and the new lease agreement is made in good faith and in a commercially reasonable manner, the lessor may recover from the lessee as damages (i) accrued and unpaid rent as of the date of the commencement of the term of the new lease agreement, (ii) the present value, as of the same date, of the total rent for the then remaining lease term of the original lease agreement minus the present value, as of the same date, of the rent under the new lease agreement applicable to that period of the new lease term which is comparable to the then remaining term of the original lease agreement, and (iii) any incidental damages allowed under Section 2A–530, less expenses saved in consequence of the lessee's default.

(3) If the lessor's disposition is by lease agreement that for any reason does not qualify for treatment under subsection (2), or is by sale or otherwise, the lessor may recover from the lessee as if the lessor had elected not to dispose of the goods and Section 2A–528 governs.

(4) A subsequent buyer or lessee who buys or leases from the lessor in good faith for value as a result of a disposition under this section takes the goods free of the original lease contract and any rights of the original lessee even though the lessor fails to comply with one or more of the requirements of this Article.

(5) The lessor is not accountable to the lessee for any profit made on any disposition. A lessee who has rightfully rejected or justifiably revoked acceptance shall account to the lessor for any excess over the amount of the lessee's security interest (Section 2A–508(5)).

As amended in 1990.

§ 2A-528. Lessor's Damages for Non-acceptance, Failure to Pay, Repudiation, or Other Default.

(1) Except as otherwise provided with respect to damages liquidated in the lease agreement (Section 2A–504) or otherwise determined pursuant to agreement of the parties (Section 1–102(3) and 2A–503), if a lessor elects to retain the goods or a lessor elects to dispose of the goods and the disposition is by lease agreement that for any reason does not qualify for treatment under Section 2A–527(2), or is by sale or otherwise, the lessor may recover from the lessee as damages for a default of the type described in Section 2A–523(1) or 2A–523(3)(a), or if agreed, for other default of the lessee, (i) accrued and unpaid rent as of the date of the default if the lessee has never taken possession of the goods, or, if the lessee has taken possession of the goods, as of the date the lessor repossesses the goods or an earlier date on which the lessee makes a tender of the goods to the lessor, (ii) the present value as of the date determined under clause (i) of the total rent for the then remaining lease term of the original lease agreement minus the present value as of the same date of the market rent as the place where the goods are located computed for the same lease term, and (iii) any incidental damages allowed under Section 2A–530, less expenses saved in consequence of the lessee's default.

(2) If the measure of damages provided in subsection (1) is inadequate to put a lessor in as good a position as performance would have, the measure of damages is the present value of the profit, including reasonable overhead, the lessor would have made from full performance by the lessee, together with any incidental damages allowed under Section 2A–530, due allowance for costs reasonably incurred and due credit for payments or proceeds of disposition.

As amended in 1990.

§ 2A-529. Lessor's Action for the Rent.

(1) After default by the lessee under the lease contract of the type described in Section 2A–523(1) or 2A–523(3)(a) or, if agreed, after other default by the lessee, if the lessor complies with subsection (2), the lessor may recover from the lessee as damages:

(a) for goods accepted by the lessee and not repossessed by or tendered to the lessor, and for conforming goods lost or damaged within a commercially reasonable time after risk of loss passes to the lessee (Section 2A–219), (i) accrued and unpaid rent as of the date of entry of judgment in favor of the lessor (ii) the present value as of the same date of the rent for the then remaining lease term of the lease agreement, and (iii) any incidental damages allowed under Section 2A–530, less expenses saved in consequence of the lessee's default; and

(b) for goods identified to the lease contract if the lessor is unable after reasonable effort to dispose of them at a reasonable price or the circumstances reasonably indicate that effort will be unavailing, (i) accrued and unpaid rent as of the date of entry of judgment in favor of the lessor, (ii) the present value as of the same date of the rent for the then remaining lease term of the lease agreement, and (iii) any incidental damages allowed under Section 2A–530, less expenses saved in consequence of the lessee's default.

(2) Except as provided in subsection (3), the lessor shall hold for the lessee for the remaining lease term of the lease agreement any goods that have been identified to the lease contract and are in the lessor's control.

(3) The lessor may dispose of the goods at any time before collection of the judgment for damages obtained pursuant to subsection (1). If the disposition is before the end of the remaining lease term of the lease agreement, the lessor's recovery against the lessee for damages is governed by Section 2A–527 or Section 2A–528, and the lessor will cause an appropriate credit to be provided against a judgment for damages to the extent that the amount of the judgment exceeds the recovery available pursuant to Section 2A–527 or 2A–528.

(4) Payment of the judgment for damages obtained pursuant to subsection (1) entitles the lessee to the use and possession of the goods not then disposed of for the remaining lease term of and in accordance with the lease agreement.

(5) After default by the lessee under the lease contract of the type described in Section 2A–523(1) or Section 2A–523(3)(a) or, if agreed, after other default by the lessee, a lessor who is held not entitled to rent under this section must nevertheless be awarded damages for non-acceptance under Sections 2A–527 and 2A–528.

As amended in 1990.

§ 2A-530. Lessor's Incidental Damages.

Incidental damages to an aggrieved lessor include any commercially reasonable charges, expenses, or commissions incurred in stopping delivery, in the transportation, care and custody of goods after the lessee's default, in connection with return or disposition of the goods, or otherwise resulting from the default.

§ 2A-531. Standing to Sue Third Parties for Injury to Goods.

(1) If a third party so deals with goods that have been identified to a lease contract as to cause actionable injury to a party to the lease contract (a) the lessor has a right of action against the third party, and (b) the lessee also has a right of action against the third party if the lessee:

(i) has a security interest in the goods;

(ii) has an insurable interest in the goods; or

(iii) bears the risk of loss under the lease contract or has since the injury assumed that risk as against the lessor and the goods have been converted or destroyed.

(2) If at the time of the injury the party plaintiff did not bear the risk of loss as against the other party to the lease contract and there is no arrangement between them for disposition of the recovery, his [or her] suit or settlement, subject to his [or her] own interest, is as a fiduciary for the other party to the lease contract.

(3) Either party with the consent of the other may sue for the benefit of whom it may concern.

§ 2A-532. Lessor's Rights to Residual Interest.

In addition to any other recovery permitted by this Article or other law, the lessor may recover from the lessee an amount that will fully compensate the lessor for any loss of or damage to the lessor's residual interest in the goods caused by the default of the lessee.

As added in 1990.

REVISED ARTICLE 3: Negotiable Instruments

PART 1: General Provisions and Definitions

§ 3-101. Short Title.

This Article may be cited as Uniform Commercial Code–Negotiable Instruments.

§ 3-102. Subject Matter.

(a) This Article applies to negotiable instruments. It does not apply to money, to payment orders governed by Article 4A, or to securities governed by Article 8.

(b) If there is conflict between this Article and Article 4 or 9, Articles 4 and 9 govern.

(c) Regulations of the Board of Governors of the Federal Reserve System and operating circulars of the Federal Reserve Banks supersede any inconsistent provision of this Article to the extent of the inconsistency.

§ 3-103. Definitions.

(a) In this Article:

(1) "Acceptor" means a drawee who has accepted a draft.

(2) "Drawee" means a person ordered in a draft to make payment.

(3) "Drawer" means a person who signs or is identified in a draft as a person ordering payment.

(4) "Good faith" means honesty in fact and the observance of reasonable commercial standards of fair dealing.

(5) "Maker" means a person who signs or is identified in a note as a person undertaking to pay.

(6) "Order" means a written instruction to pay money signed by the person giving the instruction. The instruction may be addressed to any person, including the person giving the instruction, or to one or more persons jointly or in the alternative but not in succession. An authorization to pay is not an order unless the person authorized to pay is also instructed to pay.

(7) "Ordinary care" in the case of a person engaged in business means observance of reasonable commercial standards, prevailing in the area in which the person is located, with respect to the business in which the person is engaged. In the case of a bank that takes an instrument for processing for collection or payment by automated means, reasonable commercial standards do not require the bank to examine the instrument if the failure to examine does not violate the bank's prescribed procedures and the bank's procedures do not vary unreasonably from general banking usage not disapproved by this Article or Article 4.

(8) "Party" means a party to an instrument.

(9) "Promise" means a written undertaking to pay money signed by the person undertaking to pay. An acknowledgment of an obligation by the obligor is not a promise unless the obligor also undertakes to pay the obligation.

(10) "Prove" with respect to a fact means to meet the burden of establishing the fact (Section 1–201(8)).

(11) "Remitter" means a person who purchases an instrument from its issuer if the instrument is payable to an identified person other than the purchaser.

(b) [Other definitions' section references deleted.]

(c) [Other definitions' section references deleted.]

(d) In addition, Article 1 contains general definitions and principles of construction and interpretation applicable throughout this Article.

§ 3-104. Negotiable Instrument.

(a) Except as provided in subsections (c) and (d), "negotiable instrument" means an unconditional promise or order to pay a fixed amount of money, with or without interest or other charges described in the promise or order, if it:

(1) is payable to bearer or to order at the time it is issued or first comes into possession of a holder;

(2) is payable on demand or at a definite time; and

(3) does not state any other undertaking or instruction by the person promising or ordering payment to do any act in addition to the payment of money, but the promise or order may contain (i) an under-

taking or power to give, maintain, or protect collateral to secure payment, (ii) an authorization or power to the holder to confess judgment or realize on or dispose of collateral, or (iii) a waiver of the benefit of any law intended for the advantage or protection of an obligor.

(b) "Instrument" means a negotiable instrument.

(c) An order that meets all of the requirements of subsection (a), except paragraph (1), and otherwise falls within the definition of "check" in subsection (f) is a negotiable instrument and a check.

(d) A promise or order other than a check is not an instrument if, at the time it is issued or first comes into possession of a holder, it contains a conspicuous statement, however expressed, to the effect that the promise or order is not negotiable or is not an instrument governed by this Article.

(e) An instrument is a "note" if it is a promise and is a "draft" if it is an order. If an instrument falls within the definition of both "note" and "draft," a person entitled to enforce the instrument may treat it as either.

(f) "Check" means (i) a draft, other than a documentary draft, payable on demand and drawn on a bank or (ii) a cashier's check or teller's check. An instrument may be a check even though it is described on its face by another term, such as "money order."

(g) "Cashier's check" means a draft with respect to which the drawer and drawee are the same bank or branches of the same bank.

(h) "Teller's check" means a draft drawn by a bank (i) on another bank, or (ii) payable at or through a bank.

(i) "Traveler's check" means an instrument that (i) is payable on demand, (ii) is drawn on or payable at or through a bank, (iii) is designated by the term "traveler's check" or by a substantially similar term, and (iv) requires, as a condition to payment, a countersignature by a person whose specimen signature appears on the instrument.

(j) "Certificate of deposit" means an instrument containing an acknowledgment by a bank that a sum of money has been received by the bank and a promise by the bank to repay the sum of money. A certificate of deposit is a note of the bank.

§ 3-105. Issue of Instrument.

(a) "Issue" means the first delivery of an instrument by the maker or drawer, whether to a holder or nonholder, for the purpose of giving rights on the instrument to any person.

(b) An unissued instrument, or an unissued incomplete instrument that is completed, is binding on the maker or drawer, but nonissuance is a defense. An instrument that is conditionally issued or is issued for a special purpose is binding on the maker or drawer, but failure of the condition or special purpose to be fulfilled is a defense.

(c) "Issuer" applies to issued and unissued instruments and means a maker or drawer of an instrument.

§ 3-106. Unconditional Promise or Order.

(a) Except as provided in this section, for the purposes of Section 3–104(a), a promise or order is unconditional unless it states (i) an express condition to payment, (ii) that the promise or order is subject to or governed by another writing, or (iii) that rights or obligations with respect to the promise or order are stated in another writing. A reference to another writing does not of itself make the promise or order conditional.

(b) A promise or order is not made conditional (i) by a reference to another writing for a statement of rights with respect to collateral, prepayment, or acceleration, or (ii) because payment is limited to resort to a particular fund or source.

(c) If a promise or order requires, as a condition to payment, a countersignature by a person whose specimen signature appears on the promise or order, the condition does not make the promise or order conditional for the purposes of Section 3–104(a). If the person whose specimen signature appears on an instrument fails to countersign the

instrument, the failure to countersign is a defense to the obligation of the issuer, but the failure does not prevent a transferee of the instrument from becoming a holder of the instrument.

(d) If a promise or order at the time it is issued or first comes into possession of a holder contains a statement, required by applicable statutory or administrative law, to the effect that the rights of a holder or transferee are subject to claims or defenses that the issuer could assert against the original payee, the promise or order is not thereby made conditional for the purposes of Section 3–104(a); but if the promise or order is an instrument, there cannot be a holder in due course of the instrument.

§ 3-107. Instrument Payable in Foreign Money.

Unless the instrument otherwise provides, an instrument that states the amount payable in foreign money may be paid in the foreign money or in an equivalent amount in dollars calculated by using the current bank-offered spot rate at the place of payment for the purchase of dollars on the day on which the instrument is paid.

§ 3-108. Payable on Demand or at Definite Time.

(a) A promise or order is "payable on demand" if it (i) states that it is payable on demand or at sight, or otherwise indicates that it is payable at the will of the holder, or (ii) does not state any time of payment.

(b) A promise or order is "payable at a definite time" if it is payable on elapse of a definite period of time after sight or acceptance or at a fixed date or dates or at a time or times readily ascertainable at the time the promise or order is issued, subject to rights of (i) prepayment, (ii) acceleration, (iii) extension at the option of the holder, or (iv) extension to a further definite time at the option of the maker or acceptor or automatically upon or after a specified act or event.

(c) If an instrument, payable at a fixed date, is also payable upon demand made before the fixed date, the instrument is payable on demand until the fixed date and, if demand for payment is not made before that date, becomes payable at a definite time on the fixed date.

§ 3-109. Payable to Bearer or to Order.

(a) A promise or order is payable to bearer if it:

    (1) states that it is payable to bearer or to the order of bearer or otherwise indicates that the person in possession of the promise or order is entitled to payment;

    (2) does not state a payee; or

    (3) states that it is payable to or to the order of cash or otherwise indicates that it is not payable to an identified person.

(b) A promise or order that is not payable to bearer is payable to order if it is payable (i) to the order of an identified person or (ii) to an identified person or order. A promise or order that is payable to order is payable to the identified person.

(c) An instrument payable to bearer may become payable to an identified person if it is specially indorsed pursuant to Section 3–205(a). An instrument payable to an identified person may become payable to bearer if it is indorsed in blank pursuant to Section 3–205(b).

§ 3-110. Identification of Person to Whom Instrument Is Payable.

(a) The person to whom an instrument is initially payable is determined by the intent of the person, whether or not authorized, signing as, or in the name or behalf of, the issuer of the instrument. The instrument is payable to the person intended by the signer even if that person is identified in the instrument by a name or other identification that is not that of the intended person. If more than one person signs in the name or behalf of the issuer of an instrument and all the signers do not intend the same person as payee, the instrument is payable to any person intended by one or more of the signers.

(b) If the signature of the issuer of an instrument is made by automated means, such as a check-writing machine, the payee of the instrument is determined by the intent of the person who supplied the name or identification of the payee, whether or not authorized to do so.

(c) A person to whom an instrument is payable may be identified in any way, including by name, identifying number, office, or account number. For the purpose of determining the holder of an instrument, the following rules apply:

(1) If an instrument is payable to an account and the account is identified only by number, the instrument is payable to the person to whom the account is payable. If an instrument is payable to an account identified by number and by the name of a person, the instrument is payable to the named person, whether or not that person is the owner of the account identified by number.

(2) If an instrument is payable to:

(i) a trust, an estate, or a person described as trustee or representative of a trust or estate, the instrument is payable to the trustee, the representative, or a successor of either, whether or not the beneficiary or estate is also named;

(ii) a person described as agent or similar representative of a named or identified person, the instrument is payable to the represented person, the representative, or a successor of the representative;

(iii) a fund or organization that is not a legal entity, the instrument is payable to a representative of the members of the fund or organization; or

(iv) an office or to a person described as holding an office, the instrument is payable to the named person, the incumbent of the office, or a successor to the incumbent.

(d) If an instrument is payable to two or more persons alternatively, it is payable to any of them and may be negotiated, discharged, or enforced by any or all of them in possession of the instrument. If an instrument is payable to two or more persons not alternatively, it is payable to all of them and may be negotiated, discharged, or enforced only by all of them. If an instrument payable to two or more persons is ambiguous as to whether it is payable to the persons alternatively, the instrument is payable to the persons alternatively.

§ 3-111. Place of Payment.

Except as otherwise provided for items in Article 4, an instrument is payable at the place of payment stated in the instrument. If no place of payment is stated, an instrument is payable at the address of the drawee or maker stated in the instrument. If no address is stated, the place of payment is the place of business of the drawee or maker. If a drawee or maker has more than one place of business, the place of payment is any place of business of the drawee or maker chosen by the person entitled to enforce the instrument. If the drawee or maker has no place of business, the place of payment is the residence of the drawee or maker.

§ 3-112. Interest.

(a) Unless otherwise provided in the instrument, (i) an instrument is not payable with interest, and (ii) interest on an interest-bearing instrument is payable from the date of the instrument.

(b) Interest may be stated in an instrument as a fixed or variable amount of money or it may be expressed as a fixed or variable rate or rates. The amount or rate of interest may be stated or described in the instrument in any manner and may require reference to information not contained in the instrument. If an instrument provides for interest, but the amount of interest payable cannot be ascertained from the description, interest is payable at the judgment rate in effect at the place of payment of the instrument and at the time interest first accrues.

§ 3-113. Date of Instrument.

(a) An instrument may be antedated or postdated. The date stated determines the time of payment if the instrument is payable at a fixed period after date. Except as provided in Section 4–401(c), an instrument payable on demand is not payable before the date of the instrument.

(b) If an instrument is undated, its date is the date of its issue or, in the case of an unissued instrument, the date it first comes into possession of a holder.

§ 3-114. Contradictory Terms of Instrument.

If an instrument contains contradictory terms, typewritten terms prevail over printed terms, handwritten terms prevail over both, and words prevail over numbers.

§ 3-115. Incomplete Instrument.

(a) "Incomplete instrument" means a signed writing, whether or not issued by the signer, the contents of which show at the time of signing that it is incomplete but that the signer intended it to be completed by the addition of words or numbers.

(b) Subject to subsection (c), if an incomplete instrument is an instrument under Section 3–104, it may be enforced according to its terms if it is not completed, or according to its terms as augmented by completion. If an incomplete instrument is not an instrument under Section 3–104, but, after completion, the requirements of Section 3–104 are met, the instrument may be enforced according to its terms as augmented by completion.

(c) If words or numbers are added to an incomplete instrument without authority of the signer, there is an alteration of the incomplete instrument under Section 3–407.

(d) The burden of establishing that words or numbers were added to an incomplete instrument without authority of the signer is on the person asserting the lack of authority.

§ 3-116. Joint and Several Liability; Contribution.

(a) Except as otherwise provided in the instrument, two or more persons who have the same liability on an instrument as makers, drawers, acceptors, indorsers who indorse as joint payees, or anomalous indorsers are jointly and severally liable in the capacity in which they sign.

(b) Except as provided in Section 3–419(e) or by agreement of the affected parties, a party having joint and several liability who pays the instrument is entitled to receive from any party having the same joint and several liability contribution in accordance with applicable law.

(c) Discharge of one party having joint and several liability by a person entitled to enforce the instrument does not affect the right under subsection (b) of a party having the same joint and several liability to receive contribution from the party discharged.

§ 3-117. Other Agreements Affecting Instrument.

Subject to applicable law regarding exclusion of proof of contemporaneous or previous agreements, the obligation of a party to an instrument to pay the instrument may be modified, supplemented, or nullified by a separate agreement of the obligor and a person entitled to enforce the instrument, if the instrument is issued or the obligation is incurred in reliance on the agreement or as part of the same transaction giving rise to the agreement. To the extent an obligation is modified, supplemented, or nullified by an agreement under this section, the agreement is a defense to the obligation.

§ 3-118. Statute of Limitations.

(a) Except as provided in subsection (e), an action to enforce the obligation of a party to pay a note payable at a definite time must be commenced within six years after the due date or dates stated in the note or, if a due date is accelerated, within six years after the accelerated due date.

(b) Except as provided in subsection (d) or (e), if demand for payment is made to the maker of a note payable on demand, an action to enforce the obligation of a party to pay the note must be commenced within six years after the demand. If no demand for payment is made to the maker, an action to enforce the note is barred if neither principal nor interest on the note has been paid for a continuous period of 10 years.

(c) Except as provided in subsection (d), an action to enforce the obligation of a party to an unaccepted draft to pay the draft must be commenced within three years after dishonor of the draft or 10 years after the date of the draft, whichever period expires first.

(d) An action to enforce the obligation of the acceptor of a certified check or the issuer of a teller's check, cashier's check, or traveler's check must be commenced within three years after demand for payment is made to the acceptor or issuer, as the case may be.

(e) An action to enforce the obligation of a party to a certificate of deposit to pay the instrument must be commenced within six years after demand for payment is made to the maker, but if the instrument states a due date and the maker is not required to pay before that date, the six-year period begins when a demand for payment is in effect and the due date has passed.

(f) An action to enforce the obligation of a party to pay an accepted draft, other than a certified check, must be commenced (i) within six years after the due date or dates stated in the draft or acceptance if the obligation of the acceptor is payable at a definite time, or (ii) within six years after the date of the acceptance if the obligation of the acceptor is payable on demand.

(g) Unless governed by other law regarding claims for indemnity or contribution, an action (i) for conversion of an instrument, for money had and received, or like action based on conversion, (ii) for breach of warranty, or (iii) to enforce an obligation, duty, or right arising under this Article and not governed by this section must be commenced within three years after the [cause of action] accrues.

§ 3-119. Notice of Right to Defend Action.

In an action for breach of an obligation for which a third person is answerable over pursuant to this Article or Article 4, the defendant may give the third person written notice of the litigation, and the person notified may then give similar notice to any other person who is answerable over. If the notice states (i) that the person notified may come in and defend and (ii) that failure to do so will bind the person notified in an action later brought by the person giving the notice as to any determination of fact common to the two litigations, the person notified is so bound unless after seasonable receipt of the notice the person notified does come in and defend.

PART 2: Negotiation, Transfer, and Indorsement

§ 3-201. Negotiation.

(a) "Negotiation" means a transfer of possession, whether voluntary or involuntary, of an instrument by a person other than the issuer to a person who thereby becomes its holder.

(b) Except for negotiation by a remitter, if an instrument is payable to an identified person, negotiation requires transfer of possession of the instrument and its indorsement by the holder. If an instrument is payable to bearer, it may be negotiated by transfer of possession alone.

§ 3-202. Negotiation Subject to Rescission.

(a) Negotiation is effective even if obtained (i) from an infant, a corporation exceeding its powers, or a person without capacity, (ii) by fraud, duress, or mistake, or (iii) in breach of duty or as part of an illegal transaction.

(b) To the extent permitted by other law, negotiation may be rescinded or may be subject to other remedies, but those remedies may not be asserted against a subsequent holder in due course or a person paying the instrument in good faith and without knowledge of facts that are a basis for rescission or other remedy.

§ 3-203. Transfer of Instrument; Rights Acquired by Transfer.

(a) An instrument is transferred when it is delivered by a person other than its issuer for the purpose of giving to the person receiving delivery the right to enforce the instrument.

(b) Transfer of an instrument, whether or not the transfer is a negotiation, vests in the transferee any right of the transferor to enforce the instrument, including any right as a holder in due course, but the transferee cannot acquire rights of a holder in due course by a transfer, directly or indirectly, from a holder in due course if the transferee engaged in fraud or illegality affecting the instrument.

(c) Unless otherwise agreed, if an instrument is transferred for value and the transferee does not become a holder because of lack of indorsement by the transferor, the transferee has a specifically enforceable right to the unqualified indorsement of the transferor, but negotiation of the instrument does not occur until the indorsement is made.

(d) If a transferor purports to transfer less than the entire instrument, negotiation of the instrument does not occur. The transferee obtains no rights under this Article and has only the rights of a partial assignee.

§ 3-204. Indorsement.

(a) "Indorsement" means a signature, other than that of a signer as maker, drawer, or acceptor, that alone or accompanied by other words is made on an instrument for the purpose of (i) negotiating the instrument, (ii) restricting payment of the instrument, or (iii) incurring indorser's liability on the instrument, but regardless of the intent of the signer, a signature and its accompanying words is an indorsement unless the accompanying words, terms of the instrument, place of the signature, or other circumstances unambiguously indicate that the signature was made for a purpose other than indorsement. For the purpose of determining whether a signature is made on an instrument, a paper affixed to the instrument is a part of the instrument.

(b) "Indorser" means a person who makes an indorsement.

(c) For the purpose of determining whether the transferee of an instrument is a holder, an indorsement that transfers a security interest in the instrument is effective as an unqualified indorsement of the instrument.

(d) If an instrument is payable to a holder under a name that is not the name of the holder, indorsement may be made by the holder in the name stated in the instrument or in the holder's name or both, but signature in both names may be required by a person paying or taking the instrument for value or collection.

§ 3-205. Special Indorsement; Blank Indorsement; Anomalous Indorsement.

(a) If an indorsement is made by the holder of an instrument, whether payable to an identified person or payable to bearer, and the indorsement identifies a person to whom it makes the instrument payable, it is a "special indorsement." When specially indorsed, an instrument becomes payable to the identified person and may be negotiated only by the indorsement of that person. The principles stated in Section 3–110 apply to special indorsements.

(b) If an indorsement is made by the holder of an instrument and it is not a special indorsement, it is a "blank indorsement." When indorsed in blank, an instrument becomes payable to bearer and may be negotiated by transfer of possession alone until specially indorsed.

(c) The holder may convert a blank indorsement that consists only of a signature into a special indorsement by writing, above the signature of the indorser, words identifying the person to whom the instrument is made payable.

(d) "Anomalous indorsement" means an indorsement made by a person who is not the holder of the instrument. An anomalous indorsement does not affect the manner in which the instrument may be negotiated.

§ 3-206. Restrictive Indorsement.

(a) An indorsement limiting payment to a particular person or otherwise prohibiting further transfer or negotiation of the instrument is not effective to prevent further transfer or negotiation of the instrument.

(b) An indorsement stating a condition to the right of the indorsee to receive payment does not affect the right of the indorsee to enforce the instrument. A person paying the instrument or taking it for value or collection may disregard the condition, and the rights and liabilities of that person are not affected by whether the condition has been fulfilled.

(c) If an instrument bears an indorsement (i) described in Section 4–201(b), or (ii) in blank or to a particular bank using the words "for deposit," "for collection," or other words indicating a purpose of having the instrument collected by a bank for the indorser or for a particular account, the following rules apply:

(1) A person, other than a bank, who purchases the instrument when so indorsed converts the instrument unless the amount paid for the instrument is received by the indorser or applied consistently with the indorsement.

(2) A depositary bank that purchases the instrument or takes it for collection when so indorsed converts the instrument unless the amount paid by the bank with respect to the instrument is received by the indorser or applied consistently with the indorsement.

(3) A payor bank that is also the depositary bank or that takes the instrument for immediate payment over the counter from a person other than a collecting bank converts the instrument unless the proceeds of the instrument are received by the indorser or applied consistently with the indorsement.

(4) Except as otherwise provided in paragraph (3), a payor bank or intermediary bank may disregard the indorsement and is not liable if the proceeds of the instrument are not received by the indorser or applied consistently with the indorsement.

(d) Except for an indorsement covered by subsection (c), if an instrument bears an indorsement using words to the effect that payment is to be made to the indorsee as agent, trustee, or other fiduciary for the benefit of the indorser or another person, the following rules apply:

(1) Unless there is notice of breach of fiduciary duty as provided in Section 3–307, a person who purchases the instrument from the indorsee or takes the instrument from the indorsee for collection or payment may pay the proceeds of payment or the value given for the instrument to the indorsee without regard to whether the indorsee violates a fiduciary duty to the indorser.

(2) A subsequent transferee of the instrument or person who pays the instrument is neither given notice nor otherwise affected by the restriction in the indorsement unless the transferee or payor knows that the fiduciary dealt with the instrument or its proceeds in breach of fiduciary duty.

(e) The presence on an instrument of an indorsement to which this section applies does not prevent a purchaser of the instrument from becoming a holder in due course of the instrument unless the purchaser is a converter under subsection (c) or has notice or knowledge of breach of fiduciary duty as stated in subsection (d).

(f) In an action to enforce the obligation of a party to pay the instrument, the obligor has a defense if payment would violate an indorsement to which this section applies and the payment is not permitted by this section.

§ 3-207. Reacquisition.

Reacquisition of an instrument occurs if it is transferred to a former holder, by negotiation or otherwise. A former holder who reacquires the instrument may cancel indorsements made after the reacquirer first became a holder of the instrument. If the cancellation causes the instrument to be payable to the reacquirer or to bearer, the reacquirer may negotiate the instrument. An indorser whose indorsement is canceled is discharged, and the discharge is effective against any subsequent holder.

PART 3: Enforcement of Instruments

§ 3-301. Person Entitled to Enforce Instrument.

"Person entitled to enforce" an instrument means (i) the holder of the instrument, (ii) a nonholder in possession of the instrument who has the rights of a holder, or (iii) a person not in possession of the instrument who is entitled to enforce the instrument pursuant to Section 3–309 or 3–418(d). A person may be a person entitled to enforce the instrument even though the person is not the owner of the instrument or is in wrongful possession of the instrument.

§ 3-302. Holder in Due Course.

(a) Subject to subsection (c) and Section 3–106(d), "holder in due course" means the holder of an instrument if:

(1) the instrument when issued or negotiated to the holder does not bear such apparent evidence of forgery or alteration or is not otherwise so irregular or incomplete as to call into question its authenticity; and

(2) the holder took the instrument (i) for value, (ii) in good faith, (iii) without notice that the instrument is overdue or has been dishonored or that there is an uncured default with respect to payment of another instrument issued as part of the same series, (iv) without notice that the instrument contains an unauthorized signature or has been altered, (v) without notice of any claim to the instrument described in Section 3–306, and (vi) without notice that any party has a defense or claim in recoupment described in Section 3–305(a).

(b) Notice of discharge of a party, other than discharge in an insolvency proceeding, is not notice of a defense under subsection (a), but discharge is effective against a person who became a holder in due course with notice of the discharge. Public filing or recording of a document does not of itself constitute notice of a defense, claim in recoupment, or claim to the instrument.

(c) Except to the extent a transferor or predecessor in interest has rights as a holder in due course, a person does not acquire rights of a holder in due course of an instrument taken (i) by legal process or by purchase in an execution, bankruptcy, or creditor's sale or similar proceeding, (ii) by purchase as part of a bulk transaction not in ordinary course of business of the transferor, or (iii) as the successor in interest to an estate or other organization.

(d) If, under Section 3–303(a)(1), the promise of performance that is the consideration for an instrument has been partially performed, the holder may assert rights as a holder in due course of the instrument only to the fraction of the amount payable under the instrument equal to the value of the partial performance divided by the value of the promised performance.

(e) If (i) the person entitled to enforce an instrument has only a security interest in the instrument and (ii) the person obliged to pay the instrument has a defense, claim in recoupment, or claim to the instrument that may be asserted against the person who granted the security interest, the person entitled to enforce the instrument may assert rights as a holder in due course only to an amount payable under the instrument which, at the time of enforcement of the instrument, does not exceed the amount of the unpaid obligation secured.

(f) To be effective, notice must be received at a time and in a manner that gives a reasonable opportunity to act on it.

(g) This section is subject to any law limiting status as a holder in due course in particular classes of transactions.

§ 3-303. Value and Consideration.

(a) An instrument is issued or transferred for value if:

(1) the instrument is issued or transferred for a promise of performance, to the extent the promise has been performed;

(2) the transferee acquires a security interest or other lien in the instrument other than a lien obtained by judicial proceeding;

(3) the instrument is issued or transferred as payment of, or as security for, an antecedent claim against any person, whether or not the claim is due;

(4) the instrument is issued or transferred in exchange for a negotiable instrument; or

(5) the instrument is issued or transferred in exchange for the incurring of an irrevocable obligation to a third party by the person taking the instrument.

(b) "Consideration" means any consideration sufficient to support a simple contract. The drawer or maker of an instrument has a defense if the instrument is issued without consideration. If an instrument is issued for a promise of performance, the issuer has a defense to the extent performance of the promise is due and the promise has not been performed. If an instrument is issued for value as stated in subsection (a), the instrument is also issued for consideration.

§ 3-304. Overdue Instrument.

(a) An instrument payable on demand becomes overdue at the earliest of the following times:

(1) on the day after the day demand for payment is duly made;

(2) if the instrument is a check, 90 days after its date; or

(3) if the instrument is not a check, when the instrument has been outstanding for a period of time after its date which is unreasonably long under the circumstances of the particular case in light of the nature of the instrument and usage of the trade.

(b) With respect to an instrument payable at a definite time the following rules apply:

(1) If the principal is payable in installments and a due date has not been accelerated, the instrument becomes overdue upon default under the instrument for nonpayment of an installment, and the instrument remains overdue until the default is cured.

(2) If the principal is not payable in installments and the due date has not been accelerated, the instrument becomes overdue on the day after the due date.

(3) If a due date with respect to principal has been accelerated, the instrument becomes overdue on the day after the accelerated due date.

(c) Unless the due date of principal has been accelerated, an instrument does not become overdue if there is default in payment of interest but no default in payment of principal.

§ 3-305. Defenses and Claims in Recoupment.

(a) Except as stated in subsection (b), the right to enforce the obligation of a party to pay an instrument is subject to the following:

(1) a defense of the obligor based on (i) infancy of the obligor to the

extent it is a defense to a simple contract, (ii) duress, lack of legal capacity, or illegality of the transaction which, under other law, nullifies the obligation of the obligor, (iii) fraud that induced the obligor to sign the instrument with neither knowledge nor reasonable opportunity to learn of its character or its essential terms, or (iv) discharge of the obligor in insolvency proceedings;

(2) a defense of the obligor stated in another section of this Article or a defense of the obligor that would be available if the person entitled to enforce the instrument were enforcing a right to payment under a simple contract; and

(3) a claim in recoupment of the obligor against the original payee of the instrument if the claim arose from the transaction that gave rise to the instrument; but the claim of the obligor may be asserted against a transferee of the instrument only to reduce the amount owing on the instrument at the time the action is brought.

(b) The right of a holder in due course to enforce the obligation of a party to pay the instrument is subject to defenses of the obligor stated in subsection (a)(1), but is not subject to defenses of the obligor stated in subsection (a)(2) or claims in recoupment stated in subsection (a)(3) against a person other than the holder.

(c) Except as stated in subsection (d), in an action to enforce the obligation of a party to pay the instrument, the obligor may not assert against the person entitled to enforce the instrument a defense, claim in recoupment, or claim to the instrument (Section 3–306) of another person, but the other person's claim to the instrument may be asserted by the obligor if the other person is joined in the action and personally asserts the claim against the person entitled to enforce the instrument. An obligor is not obliged to pay the instrument if the person seeking enforcement of the instrument does not have rights of a holder in due course and the obligor proves that the instrument is a lost or stolen instrument.

(d) In an action to enforce the obligation of an accommodation party to pay an instrument, the accommodation party may assert against the person entitled to enforce the instrument any defense or claim in recoupment under subsection (a) that the accommodated party could assert against the person entitled to enforce the instrument, except the defenses of discharge in insolvency proceedings, infancy, and lack of legal capacity.

§ 3-306. Claims to an Instrument.

A person taking an instrument, other than a person having rights of a holder in due course, is subject to a claim of a property or possessory right in the instrument or its proceeds, including a claim to rescind a negotiation and to recover the instrument or its proceeds. A person having rights of a holder in due course takes free of the claim to the instrument.

§ 3-307. Notice of Breach of Fiduciary Duty.

(a) In this section:

(1) "Fiduciary" means an agent, trustee, partner, corporate officer or director, or other representative owing a fiduciary duty with respect to an instrument.

(2) "Represented person" means the principal, beneficiary, partnership, corporation, or other person to whom the duty stated in paragraph (1) is owed.

(b) If (i) an instrument is taken from a fiduciary for payment or collection or for value, (ii) the taker has knowledge of the fiduciary status of the fiduciary, and (iii) the represented person makes a claim to the instrument or its proceeds on the basis that the transaction of the fiduciary is a breach of fiduciary duty, the following rules apply:

(1) Notice of breach of fiduciary duty by the fiduciary is notice of the claim of the represented person.

(2) In the case of an instrument payable to the represented person or the fiduciary as such, the taker has notice of the breach of fiduciary

duty if the instrument is (i) taken in payment of or as security for a debt known by the taker to be the personal debt of the fiduciary, (ii) taken in a transaction known by the taker to be for the personal benefit of the fiduciary, or (iii) deposited to an account other than an account of the fiduciary, as such, or an account of the represented person.

(3) If an instrument is issued by the represented person or the fiduciary as such, and made payable to the fiduciary personally, the taker does not have notice of the breach of fiduciary duty unless the taker knows of the breach of fiduciary duty.

(4) If an instrument is issued by the represented person or the fiduciary as such, to the taker as payee, the taker has notice of the breach of fiduciary duty if the instrument is (i) taken in payment of or as security for a debt known by the taker to be the personal debt of the fiduciary, (ii) taken in a transaction known by the taker to be for the personal benefit of the fiduciary, or (iii) deposited to an account other than an account of the fiduciary, as such, or an account of the represented person.

§ 3-308. Proof of Signatures and Status as Holder in Due Course.

(a) In an action with respect to an instrument, the authenticity of, and authority to make, each signature on the instrument is admitted unless specifically denied in the pleadings. If the validity of a signature is denied in the pleadings, the burden of establishing validity is on the person claiming validity, but the signature is presumed to be authentic and authorized unless the action is to enforce the liability of the purported signer and the signer is dead or incompetent at the time of trial of the issue of validity of the signature. If an action to enforce the instrument is brought against a person as the undisclosed principal of a person who signed the instrument as a party to the instrument, the plaintiff has the burden of establishing that the defendant is liable on the instrument as a represented person under Section 3–402(a).

(b) If the validity of signatures is admitted or proved and there is compliance with subsection (a), a plaintiff producing the instrument is entitled to payment if the plaintiff proves entitlement to enforce the instrument under Section 3–301, unless the defendant proves a defense or claim in recoupment. If a defense or claim in recoupment is proved, the right to payment of the plaintiff is subject to the defense or claim, except to the extent the plaintiff proves that the plaintiff has rights of a holder in due course which are not subject to the defense or claim.

§ 3-309. Enforcement of Lost, Destroyed, or Stolen Instrument.

(a) A person not in possession of an instrument is entitled to enforce the instrument if (i) the person was in possession of the instrument and entitled to enforce it when loss of possession occurred, (ii) the loss of possession was not the result of a transfer by the person or a lawful seizure, and (iii) the person cannot reasonably obtain possession of the instrument because the instrument was destroyed, its whereabouts cannot be determined, or it is in the wrongful possession of an unknown person or a person that cannot be found or is not amenable to service of process.

(b) A person seeking enforcement of an instrument under subsection (a) must prove the terms of the instrument and the person's right to enforce the instrument. If that proof is made, Section 3–308 applies to the case as if the person seeking enforcement had produced the instrument. The court may not enter judgment in favor of the person seeking enforcement unless it finds that the person required to pay the instrument is adequately protected against loss that might occur by reason of a claim by another person to enforce the instrument. Adequate protection may be provided by any reasonable means.

§ 3-310. Effect of Instrument on Obligation for Which Taken.

(a) Unless otherwise agreed, if a certified check, cashier's check, or teller's check is taken for an obligation, the obligation is discharged to the same extent discharge would result if an amount of money equal to the amount of the instrument were taken in payment of the obligation. Discharge of the obligation does not affect any liability that the obligor may have as an indorser of the instrument.

(b) Unless otherwise agreed and except as provided in subsection (a), if a note or an uncertified check is taken for an obligation, the obligation is suspended to the same extent the obligation would be discharged if an amount of money equal to the amount of the instrument were taken, and the following rules apply:

(1) In the case of an uncertified check, suspension of the obligation continues until dishonor of the check or until it is paid or certified. Payment or certification of the check results in discharge of the obligation to the extent of the amount of the check.

(2) In the case of a note, suspension of the obligation continues until dishonor of the note or until it is paid. Payment of the note results in discharge of the obligation to the extent of the payment.

(3) Except as provided in paragraph (4), if the check or note is dishonored and the obligee of the obligation for which the instrument was taken is the person entitled to enforce the instrument, the obligee may enforce either the instrument or the obligation. In the case of an instrument of a third person which is negotiated to the obligee by the obligor, discharge of the obligor on the instrument also discharges the obligation.

(4) If the person entitled to enforce the instrument taken for an obligation is a person other than the obligee, the obligee may not enforce the obligation to the extent the obligation is suspended. If the obligee is the person entitled to enforce the instrument but no longer has possession of it because it was lost, stolen, or destroyed, the obligation may not be enforced to the extent of the amount payable on the instrument, and to that extent the obligee's rights against the obligor are limited to enforcement of the instrument.

(c) If an instrument other than one described in subsection (a) or (b) is taken for an obligation, the effect is (i) that stated in subsection (a) if the instrument is one on which a bank is liable as maker or acceptor, or (ii) that stated in subsection (b) in any other case.

§ 3-311. Accord and Satisfaction by Use of Instrument.

(a) If a person against whom a claim is asserted proves that (i) that person in good faith tendered an instrument to the claimant as full satisfaction of the claim, (ii) the amount of the claim was unliquidated or subject to a bona fide dispute, and (iii) the claimant obtained payment of the instrument, the following subsections apply.

(b) Unless subsection (c) applies, the claim is discharged if the person against whom the claim is asserted proves that the instrument or an accompanying written communication contained a conspicuous statement to the effect that the instrument was tendered as full satisfaction of the claim.

(c) Subject to subsection (d), a claim is not discharged under subsection (b) if either of the following applies:

(1) The claimant, if an organization, proves that (i) within a reasonable time before the tender, the claimant sent a conspicuous statement to the person against whom the claim is asserted that communications concerning disputed debts, including an instrument tendered as full satisfaction of a debt, are to be sent to a designated person, office, or place, and (ii) the instrument or accompanying communication was not received by that designated person, office, or place.

(2) The claimant, whether or not an organization, proves that within

90 days after payment of the instrument, the claimant tendered repayment of the amount of the instrument to the person against whom the claim is asserted. This paragraph does not apply if the claimant is an organization that sent a statement complying with paragraph (1)(i).

(d) A claim is discharged if the person against whom the claim is asserted proves that within a reasonable time before collection of the instrument was initiated, the claimant, or an agent of the claimant having direct responsibility with respect to the disputed obligation, knew that the instrument was tendered in full satisfaction of the claim.

§ 3-312. Lost, Destroyed, or Stolen Cashier's Check, Teller's Check, or Certified Check.[2]

(a) In this section:

(1) "Check" means a cashier's check, teller's check, or certified check.

(2) "Claimant" means a person who claims the right to receive the amount of a cashier's check, teller's check, or certified check that was lost, destroyed, or stolen.

(3) "Declaration of loss" means a written statement, made under penalty of perjury, to the effect that (i) the declarer lost possession of a check, (ii) the declarer is the drawer or payee of the check, in the case of a certified check, or the remitter or payee of the check, in the case of a cashier's check or teller's check, (iii) the loss of possession was not the result of a transfer by the declarer or a lawful seizure, and (iv) the declarer cannot reasonably obtain possession of the check because the check was destroyed, its whereabouts cannot be determined, or it is in the wrongful possession of an unknown person or a person that cannot be found or is not amenable to service of process.

(4) "Obligated bank" means the issuer of a cashier's check or teller's check or the acceptor of a certified check.

(b) A claimant may assert a claim to the amount of a check by a communication to the obligated bank describing the check with reasonable certainty and requesting payment of the amount of the check, if (i) the claimant is the drawer or payee of a certified check or the remitter or payee of a cashier's check or teller's check, (ii) the communication contains or is accompanied by a declaration of loss of the claimant with respect to the check, (iii) the communication is received at a time and in a manner affording the bank a reasonable time to act on it before the check is paid, and (iv) the claimant provides reasonable identification if requested by the obligated bank. Delivery of a declaration of loss is a warranty of the truth of the statements made in the declaration. If a claim is asserted in compliance with this subsection, the following rules apply:

(1) The claim becomes enforceable at the later of (i) the time the claim is asserted, or (ii) the 90th day following the date of the check, in the case of a cashier's check or teller's check, or the 90th day following the date of the acceptance, in the case of a certified check.

(2) Until the claim becomes enforceable, it has no legal effect and the obligated bank may pay the check or, in the case of a teller's check, may permit the drawee to pay the check. Payment to a person entitled to enforce the check discharges all liability of the obligated bank with respect to the check.

(3) If the claim becomes enforceable before the check is presented for payment, the obligated bank is not obliged to pay the check.

(4) When the claim becomes enforceable, the obligated bank becomes obliged to pay the amount of the check to the claimant if payment of the check has not been made to a person entitled to enforce the check. Subject to Section 4–302(a)(1), payment to the claimant discharges all liability of the obligated bank with respect to the check.

(c) If the obligated bank pays the amount of a check to a claimant under subsection (b)(4) and the check is presented for payment by a person having rights of a holder in due course, the claimant is obliged to (i) refund the payment to the obligated bank if the check is paid, or (ii) pay the amount of the check to the person having rights of a holder in due course if the check is dishonored.

(d) If a claimant has the right to assert a claim under subsection (b) and is also a person entitled to enforce a cashier's check, teller's check, or certified check which is lost, destroyed, or stolen, the claimant may assert rights with respect to the check either under this section or Section 3–309. Added in 1991.

PART 4: Liability of Parties

§ 3-401. Signature.

(a) A person is not liable on an instrument unless (i) the person signed the instrument, or (ii) the person is represented by an agent or representative who signed the instrument and the signature is binding on the represented person under Section 3–402.

(b) A signature may be made (i) manually or by means of a device or machine, and (ii) by the use of any name, including a trade or assumed name, or by a word, mark, or symbol executed or adopted by a person with present intention to authenticate a writing.

§ 3-402. Signature by Representative.

(a) If a person acting, or purporting to act, as a representative signs an instrument by signing either the name of the represented person or the name of the signer, the represented person is bound by the signature to the same extent the represented person would be bound if the signature were on a simple contract. If the represented person is bound, the signature of the representative is the "authorized signature of the represented person" and the represented person is liable on the instrument, whether or not identified in the instrument.

(b) If a representative signs the name of the representative to an instrument and the signature is an authorized signature of the represented person, the following rules apply:

(1) If the form of the signature shows unambiguously that the signature is made on behalf of the represented person who is identified in the instrument, the representative is not liable on the instrument.

(2) Subject to subsection (c), if (i) the form of the signature does not show unambiguously that the signature is made in a representative capacity or (ii) the represented person is not identified in the instrument, the representative is liable on the instrument to a holder in due course that took the instrument without notice that the representative was not intended to be liable on the instrument. With respect to any other person, the representative is liable on the instrument unless the representative proves that the original parties did not intend the representative to be liable on the instrument.

(c) If a representative signs the name of the representative as drawer of a check without indication of the representative status and the check is payable from an account of the represented person who is identified on the check, the signer is not liable on the check if the signature is an authorized signature of the represented person.

§ 3-403. Unauthorized Signature.

(a) Unless otherwise provided in this Article or Article 4, an unauthorized signature is ineffective except as the signature of the unauthorized signer in favor of a person who in good faith pays the instrument or takes it for value. An unauthorized signature may be ratified for all purposes of this Article.

(b) If the signature of more than one person is required to constitute the authorized signature of an organization, the signature of the organization is unauthorized if one of the required signatures is lacking.

(c) The civil or criminal liability of a person who makes an unauthorized signature is not affected by any provision of this Article which makes the unauthorized signature effective for the purposes of this Article.

§ 3-404. Impostors; Fictitious Payees.

(a) If an impostor, by use of the mails or otherwise, induces the issuer of an instrument to issue the instrument to the impostor, or to a person acting in concert with the impostor, by impersonating the payee of the instrument or a person authorized to act for the payee, an indorsement of the instrument by any person in the name of the payee is effective as the indorsement of the payee in favor of a person who, in good faith, pays the instrument or takes it for value or for collection.

(b) If (i) a person whose intent determines to whom an instrument is payable (Section 3–110(a) or (b)) does not intend the person identified as payee to have any interest in the instrument, or (ii) the person identified as payee of an instrument is a fictitious person, the following rules apply until the instrument is negotiated by special indorsement:

(1) Any person in possession of the instrument is its holder.

(2) An indorsement by any person in the name of the payee stated in the instrument is effective as the indorsement of the payee in favor of a person who, in good faith, pays the instrument or takes it for value or for collection.

(c) Under subsection (a) or (b), an indorsement is made in the name of a payee if (i) it is made in a name substantially similar to that of the payee or (ii) the instrument, whether or not indorsed, is deposited in a depositary bank to an account in a name substantially similar to that of the payee.

(d) With respect to an instrument to which subsection (a) or (b) applies, if a person paying the instrument or taking it for value or for collection fails to exercise ordinary care in paying or taking the instrument and that failure substantially contributes to loss resulting from payment of the instrument, the person bearing the loss may recover from the person failing to exercise ordinary care to the extent the failure to exercise ordinary care contributed to the loss.

§ 3-405. Employer's Responsibility for Fraudulent Indorsement by Employee.

(a) In this section:

(1) "Employee" includes an independent contractor and employee of an independent contractor retained by the employer.

(2) "Fraudulent indorsement" means (i) in the case of an instrument payable to the employer, a forged indorsement purporting to be that of the employer, or (ii) in the case of an instrument with respect to which the employer is the issuer, a forged indorsement purporting to be that of the person identified as payee.

(3) "Responsibility" with respect to instruments means authority (i) to sign or indorse instruments on behalf of the employer, (ii) to process instruments received by the employer for bookkeeping purposes, for deposit to an account, or for other disposition, (iii) to prepare or process instruments for issue in the name of the employer, (iv) to supply information determining the names or addresses of payees of instruments to be issued in the name of the employer, (v) to control the disposition of instruments to be issued in the name of the employer, or (vi) to act otherwise with respect to instruments in a responsible capacity. "Responsibility" does not include authority that merely allows an employee to have access to instruments or blank or incomplete instrument forms that are being stored or transported or are part of incoming or outgoing mail, or similar access.

(b) For the purpose of determining the rights and liabilities of a person who, in good faith, pays an instrument or takes it for value or for collection, if an employer entrusted an employee with responsibility with respect to the instrument and the employee or a person acting in concert with the employee makes a fraudulent indorsement of the instrument, the indorsement is effective as the indorsement of the person to whom the instrument is payable if it is made in the name of that person. If the person paying the instrument or taking it for value or for collection fails to exercise ordinary

care in paying or taking the instrument and that failure substantially contributes to loss resulting from the fraud, the person bearing the loss may recover from the person failing to exercise ordinary care to the extent the failure to exercise ordinary care contributed to the loss.

(c) Under subsection (b), an indorsement is made in the name of the person to whom an instrument is payable if (i) it is made in a name substantially similar to the name of that person or (ii) the instrument, whether or not indorsed, is deposited in a depositary bank to an account in a name substantially similar to the name of that person.

§ 3-406. Negligence Contributing to Forged Signature or Alteration of Instrument.

(a) A person whose failure to exercise ordinary care substantially contributes to an alteration of an instrument or to the making of a forged signature on an instrument is precluded from asserting the alteration or the forgery against a person who, in good faith, pays the instrument or takes it for value or for collection.

(b) Under subsection (a), if the person asserting the preclusion fails to exercise ordinary care in paying or taking the instrument and that failure substantially contributes to loss, the loss is allocated between the person precluded and the person asserting the preclusion according to the extent to which the failure of each to exercise ordinary care contributed to the loss.

(c) Under subsection (a), the burden of proving failure to exercise ordinary care is on the person asserting the preclusion. Under subsection (b), the burden of proving failure to exercise ordinary care is on the person precluded.

§ 3-407. Alteration.

(a) "Alteration" means (i) an unauthorized change in an instrument that purports to modify in any respect the obligation of a party, or (ii) an unauthorized addition of words or numbers or other change to an incomplete instrument relating to the obligation of a party.

(b) Except as provided in subsection (c), an alteration fraudulently made discharges a party whose obligation is affected by the alteration unless that party assents or is precluded from asserting the alteration. No other alteration discharges a party, and the instrument may be enforced according to its original terms.

(c) A payor bank or drawee paying a fraudulently altered instrument or a person taking it for value, in good faith and without notice of the alteration, may enforce rights with respect to the instrument (i) according to its original terms, or (ii) in the case of an incomplete instrument altered by unauthorized completion, according to its terms as completed.

§ 3-408. Drawee Not Liable on Unaccepted Draft.

A check or other draft does not of itself operate as an assignment of funds in the hands of the drawee available for its payment, and the drawee is not liable on the instrument until the drawee accepts it.

§ 3-409. Acceptance of Draft; Certified Check.

(a) "Acceptance" means the drawee's signed agreement to pay a draft as presented. It must be written on the draft and may consist of the drawee's signature alone. Acceptance may be made at any time and becomes effective when notification pursuant to instructions is given or the accepted draft is delivered for the purpose of giving rights on the acceptance to any person.

(b) A draft may be accepted although it has not been signed by the drawer, is otherwise incomplete, is overdue, or has been dishonored.

(c) If a draft is payable at a fixed period after sight and the acceptor fails to date the acceptance, the holder may complete the acceptance by supplying a date in good faith.

(d) "Certified check" means a check accepted by the bank on which it is drawn. Acceptance may be made as stated in subsection (a) or by a writing on the check which indicates that the check is certified. The drawee of a check has no obligation to certify the check, and refusal to certify is not dishonor of the check.

§ 3-410. Acceptance Varying Draft.

(a) If the terms of a drawee's acceptance vary from the terms of the draft as presented, the holder may refuse the acceptance and treat the draft as dishonored. In that case, the drawee may cancel the acceptance.

(b) The terms of a draft are not varied by an acceptance to pay at a particular bank or place in the United States, unless the acceptance states that the draft is to be paid only at that bank or place.

(c) If the holder assents to an acceptance varying the terms of a draft, the obligation of each drawer and indorser that does not expressly assent to the acceptance is discharged.

§ 3-411. Refusal to Pay Cashier's Checks, Teller's Checks, and Certified Checks.

(a) In this section, "obligated bank" means the acceptor of a certified check or the issuer of a cashier's check or teller's check bought from the issuer.

(b) If the obligated bank wrongfully (i) refuses to pay a cashier's check or certified check, (ii) stops payment of a teller's check, or (iii) refuses to pay a dishonored teller's check, the person asserting the right to enforce the check is entitled to compensation for expenses and loss of interest resulting from the nonpayment and may recover consequential damages if the obligated bank refuses to pay after receiving notice of particular circumstances giving rise to the damages.

(c) Expenses or consequential damages under subsection (b) are not recoverable if the refusal of the obligated bank to pay occurs because (i) the bank suspends payments, (ii) the obligated bank asserts a claim or defense of the bank that it has reasonable grounds to believe is available against the person entitled to enforce the instrument, (iii) the obligated bank has a reasonable doubt whether the person demanding payment is the person entitled to enforce the instrument, or (iv) payment is prohibited by law.

§ 3-412. Obligation of Issuer of Note or Cashier's Check.

The issuer of a note or cashier's check or other draft drawn on the drawer is obliged to pay the instrument (i) according to its terms at the time it was issued or, if not issued, at the time it first came into possession of a holder, or (ii) if the issuer signed an incomplete instrument, according to its terms when completed, to the extent stated in Sections 3–115 and 3–407. The obligation is owed to a person entitled to enforce the instrument or to an indorser who paid the instrument under Section 3–415.

§ 3-413. Obligation of Acceptor.

(a) The acceptor of a draft is obliged to pay the draft (i) according to its terms at the time it was accepted, even though the acceptance states that the draft is payable "as originally drawn" or equivalent terms, (ii) if the acceptance varies the terms of the draft, according to the terms of the draft as varied, or (iii) if the acceptance is of a draft that is an incomplete instrument, according to its terms when completed, to the extent stated in Sections 3–115 and 3–407. The obligation is owed to a person entitled to enforce the draft or to the drawer or an indorser who paid the draft under Section 3–414 or 3–415.

(b) If the certification of a check or other acceptance of a draft states the amount certified or accepted, the obligation of the acceptor is that amount. If (i) the certification or acceptance does not state an amount, (ii) the amount of the instrument is subsequently raised, and (iii) the instrument is then negotiated to a holder in due course, the obligation of the acceptor is the amount of the instrument at the time it was taken by the holder in due course.

§ 3-414. Obligation of Drawer.

(a) This section does not apply to cashier's checks or other drafts drawn on the drawer.

(b) If an unaccepted draft is dishonored, the drawer is obliged to pay the draft (i) according to its terms at the time it was issued or, if not issued, at the time it first came into possession of a holder, or (ii) if the drawer signed an incomplete instrument, according to its terms when completed, to the extent stated in Sections 3–115 and 3–407. The obligation is owed to a person entitled to enforce the draft or to an indorser who paid the draft under Section 3–415.

(c) If a draft is accepted by a bank, the drawer is discharged, regardless of when or by whom acceptance was obtained.

(d) If a draft is accepted and the acceptor is not a bank, the obligation of the drawer to pay the draft if the draft is dishonored by the acceptor is the same as the obligation of an indorser under Section 3–415(a) and (c).

(e) If a draft states that it is drawn "without recourse" or otherwise disclaims liability of the drawer to pay the draft, the drawer is not liable under subsection (b) to pay the draft if the draft is not a check. A disclaimer of the liability stated in subsection (b) is not effective if the draft is a check.

(f) If (i) a check is not presented for payment or given to a depositary bank for collection within 30 days after its date, (ii) the drawee suspends payments after expiration of the 30-day period without paying the check, and (iii) because of the suspension of payments, the drawer is deprived of funds maintained with the drawee to cover payment of the check, the drawer to the extent deprived of funds may discharge its obligation to pay the check by assigning to the person entitled to enforce the check the rights of the drawer against the drawee with respect to the funds.

§ 3-415. Obligation of Indorser.

(a) Subject to subsections (b), (c), and (d) and to Section 3–419(d), if an instrument is dishonored, an indorser is obliged to pay the amount due on the instrument (i) according to the terms of the instrument at the time it was indorsed, or (ii) if the indorser indorsed an incomplete instrument, according to its terms when completed, to the extent stated in Sections 3–115 and 3–407. The obligation of the indorser is owed to a person entitled to enforce the instrument or to a subsequent indorser who paid the instrument under this section.

(b) If an indorsement states that it is made "without recourse" or otherwise disclaims liability of the indorser, the indorser is not liable under subsection (a) to pay the instrument.

(c) If notice of dishonor of an instrument is required by Section 3–503 and notice of dishonor complying with that section is not given to an indorser, the liability of the indorser under subsection (a) is discharged.

(d) If a draft is accepted by a bank after an indorsement is made, the liability of the indorser under subsection (a) is discharged.

(e) If an indorser of a check is liable under subsection (a) and the check is not presented for payment, or given to a depositary bank for collection, within 30 days after the day the indorsement was made, the liability of the indorser under subsection (a) is discharged.

As amended in 1993.

§ 3-416. Transfer Warranties.

(a) A person who transfers an instrument for consideration warrants to the transferee and, if the transfer is by indorsement, to any subsequent transferee that:

    (1) the warrantor is a person entitled to enforce the instrument;

    (2) all signatures on the instrument are authentic and authorized;

    (3) the instrument has not been altered;

    (4) the instrument is not subject to a defense or claim in recoupment of any party which can be asserted against the warrantor; and

(5) the warrantor has no knowledge of any insolvency proceeding commenced with respect to the maker or acceptor or, in the case of an unaccepted draft, the drawer.

(b) A person to whom the warranties under subsection (a) are made and who took the instrument in good faith may recover from the warrantor as damages for breach of warranty an amount equal to the loss suffered as a result of the breach, but not more than the amount of the instrument plus expenses and loss of interest incurred as a result of the breach.

(c) The warranties stated in subsection (a) cannot be disclaimed with respect to checks. Unless notice of a claim for breach of warranty is given to the warrantor within 30 days after the claimant has reason to know of the breach and the identity of the warrantor, the liability of the warrantor under subsection (b) is discharged to the extent of any loss caused by the delay in giving notice of the claim.

(d) A [cause of action] for breach of warranty under this section accrues when the claimant has reason to know of the breach.

§ 3-417. Presentment Warranties.

(a) If an unaccepted draft is presented to the drawee for payment or acceptance and the drawee pays or accepts the draft, (i) the person obtaining payment or acceptance, at the time of presentment, and (ii) a previous transferor of the draft, at the time of transfer, warrant to the drawee making payment or accepting the draft in good faith that:

(1) the warrantor is, or was, at the time the warrantor transferred the draft, a person entitled to enforce the draft or authorized to obtain payment or acceptance of the draft on behalf of a person entitled to enforce the draft;

(2) the draft has not been altered; and

(3) the warrantor has no knowledge that the signature of the drawer of the draft is unauthorized.

(b) A drawee making payment may recover from any warrantor damages for breach of warranty equal to the amount paid by the drawee less the amount the drawee received or is entitled to receive from the drawer because of the payment. In addition, the drawee is entitled to compensation for expenses and loss of interest resulting from the breach. The right of the drawee to recover damages under this subsection is not affected by any failure of the drawee to exercise ordinary care in making payment. If the drawee accepts the draft, breach of warranty is a defense to the obligation of the acceptor. If the acceptor makes payment with respect to the draft, the acceptor is entitled to recover from any warrantor for breach of warranty the amounts stated in this subsection.

(c) If a drawee asserts a claim for breach of warranty under subsection (a) based on an unauthorized indorsement of the draft or an alteration of the draft, the warrantor may defend by proving that the indorsement is effective under Section 3–404 or 3–405 or the drawer is precluded under Section 3–406 or 4–406 from asserting against the drawee the unauthorized indorsement or alteration.

(d) If (i) a dishonored draft is presented for payment to the drawer or an indorser or (ii) any other instrument is presented for payment to a party obliged to pay the instrument, and (iii) payment is received, the following rules apply:

(1) The person obtaining payment and a prior transferor of the instrument warrant to the person making payment in good faith that the warrantor is, or was, at the time the warrantor transferred the instrument, a person entitled to enforce the instrument or authorized to obtain payment on behalf of a person entitled to enforce the instrument.

(2) The person making payment may recover from any warrantor for breach of warranty an amount equal to the amount paid plus expenses and loss of interest resulting from the breach.

(e) The warranties stated in subsections (a) and (d) cannot be disclaimed with respect to checks. Unless notice of a claim for breach of warranty is given to the warrantor within 30 days after the claimant has reason to know of the breach and the identity of the warrantor, the liability of the warrantor under subsection (b) or (d) is discharged to the extent of any loss caused by the delay in giving notice of the claim.

(f) A [cause of action] for breach of warranty under this section accrues when the claimant has reason to know of the breach.

§ 3-418. Payment or Acceptance by Mistake.

(a) Except as provided in subsection (c), if the drawee of a draft pays or accepts the draft and the drawee acted on the mistaken belief that (i) payment of the draft had not been stopped pursuant to Section 4–403 or (ii) the signature of the drawer of the draft was authorized, the drawee may recover the amount of the draft from the person to whom or for whose benefit payment was made or, in the case of acceptance, may revoke the acceptance. Rights of the drawee under this subsection are not affected by failure of the drawee to exercise ordinary care in paying or accepting the draft.

(b) Except as provided in subsection (c), if an instrument has been paid or accepted by mistake and the case is not covered by subsection (a), the person paying or accepting may, to the extent permitted by the law governing mistake and restitution, (i) recover the payment from the person to whom or for whose benefit payment was made or (ii) in the case of acceptance, may revoke the acceptance.

(c) The remedies provided by subsection (a) or (b) may not be asserted against a person who took the instrument in good faith and for value or who in good faith changed position in reliance on the payment or acceptance. This subsection does not limit remedies provided by Section 3–417 or 4–407.

(d) Notwithstanding Section 4–215, if an instrument is paid or accepted by mistake and the payor or acceptor recovers payment or revokes acceptance under subsection (a) or (b), the instrument is deemed not to have been paid or accepted and is treated as dishonored, and the person from whom payment is recovered has rights as a person entitled to enforce the dishonored instrument.

§ 3-419. Instruments Signed for Accommodation.

(a) If an instrument is issued for value given for the benefit of a party to the instrument ("accommodated party") and another party to the instrument ("accommodation party") signs the instrument for the purpose of incurring liability on the instrument without being a direct beneficiary of the value given for the instrument, the instrument is signed by the accommodation party "for accommodation."

(b) An accommodation party may sign the instrument as maker, drawer, acceptor, or indorser and, subject to subsection (d), is obliged to pay the instrument in the capacity in which the accommodation party signs. The obligation of an accommodation party may be enforced notwithstanding any statute of frauds and whether or not the accommodation party receives consideration for the accommodation.

(c) A person signing an instrument is presumed to be an accommodation party and there is notice that the instrument is signed for accommodation if the signature is an anomalous indorsement or is accompanied by words indicating that the signer is acting as surety or guarantor with respect to the obligation of another party to the instrument. Except as provided in Section 3–605, the obligation of an accommodation party to pay the instrument is not affected by the fact that the person enforcing the obligation had notice when the instrument was taken by that person that the accommodation party signed the instrument for accommodation.

(d) If the signature of a party to an instrument is accompanied by words indicating unambiguously that the party is guaranteeing collection rather than payment of the obligation of another party to the instrument, the signer is obliged to pay the amount due on the instrument to a person entitled to enforce the instrument only if (i) execution of judgment against the other party has been returned unsatisfied, (ii) the other party is insolvent or in an insolvency proceeding, (iii) the other party cannot be served with process, or (iv) it is otherwise apparent that payment cannot be obtained from the other party.

(e) An accommodation party who pays the instrument is entitled to reimbursement from the accommodated party and is entitled to enforce the instrument against the accommodated party. An accommodated party who pays the instrument has no right of recourse against, and is not entitled to contribution from, an accommodation party.

§ 3-420. Conversion of Instrument.

(a) The law applicable to conversion of personal property applies to instruments. An instrument is also converted if it is taken by transfer, other than a negotiation, from a person not entitled to enforce the instrument or a bank makes or obtains payment with respect to the instrument for a person not entitled to enforce the instrument or receive payment. An action for conversion of an instrument may not be brought by (i) the issuer or acceptor of the instrument or (ii) a payee or indorsee who did not receive delivery of the instrument either directly or through delivery to an agent or a co-payee.

(b) In an action under subsection (a), the measure of liability is presumed to be the amount payable on the instrument, but recovery may not exceed the amount of the plaintiff's interest in the instrument.

(c) A representative, other than a depositary bank, who has in good faith dealt with an instrument or its proceeds on behalf of one who was not the person entitled to enforce the instrument is not liable in conversion to that person beyond the amount of any proceeds that it has not paid out.

PART :5 Dishonor

§ 3-501. Presentment.

(a) "Presentment" means a demand made by or on behalf of a person entitled to enforce an instrument (i) to pay the instrument made to the drawee or a party obliged to pay the instrument or, in the case of a note or accepted draft payable at a bank, to the bank, or (ii) to accept a draft made to the drawee.

(b) The following rules are subject to Article 4, agreement of the parties, and clearing-house rules and the like:

(1) Presentment may be made at the place of payment of the instrument and must be made at the place of payment if the instrument is payable at a bank in the United States; may be made by any commercially reasonable means, including an oral, written, or electronic communication; is effective when the demand for payment or acceptance is received by the person to whom presentment is made; and is effective if made to any one of two or more makers, acceptors, drawees, or other payors.

(2) Upon demand of the person to whom presentment is made, the person making presentment must (i) exhibit the instrument, (ii) give reasonable identification and, if presentment is made on behalf of another person, reasonable evidence of authority to do so, and (. . .) sign a receipt on the instrument for any payment made or surrender the instrument if full payment is made.

(3) Without dishonoring the instrument, the party to whom presentment is made may (i) return the instrument for lack of a necessary indorsement, or (ii) refuse payment or acceptance for failure of the presentment to comply with the terms of the instrument, an agreement of the parties, or other applicable law or rule.

(4) The party to whom presentment is made may treat presentment as occurring on the next business day after the day of presentment if the party to whom presentment is made has established a cut-off hour not earlier than 2 P.M. for the receipt and processing of instruments presented for payment or acceptance and presentment is made after the cut-off hour.

§ 3-502. Dishonor.

(a) Dishonor of a note is governed by the following rules:

(1) If the note is payable on demand, the note is dishonored if presentment is duly made to the maker and the note is not paid on the day of presentment.

(2) If the note is not payable on demand and is payable at or through a bank or the terms of the note require presentment, the note is dishonored if presentment is duly made and the note is not paid on the day it becomes payable or the day of presentment, whichever is later.

(3) If the note is not payable on demand and paragraph (2) does not apply, the note is dishonored if it is not paid on the day it becomes payable.

(b) Dishonor of an unaccepted draft other than a documentary draft is governed by the following rules:

(1) If a check is duly presented for payment to the payor bank otherwise than for immediate payment over the counter, the check is dishonored if the payor bank makes timely return of the check or sends timely notice of dishonor or nonpayment under Section 4–301 or 4–302, or becomes accountable for the amount of the check under Section 4–302.

(2) If a draft is payable on demand and paragraph (1) does not apply, the draft is dishonored if presentment for payment is duly made to the drawee and the draft is not paid on the day of presentment.

(3) If a draft is payable on a date stated in the draft, the draft is dishonored if (i) presentment for payment is duly made to the drawee and payment is not made on the day the draft becomes payable or the day of presentment, whichever is later, or (ii) presentment for acceptance is duly made before the day the draft becomes payable and the draft is not accepted on the day of presentment.

(4) If a draft is payable on elapse of a period of time after sight or acceptance, the draft is dishonored if presentment for acceptance is duly made and the draft is not accepted on the day of presentment.

(c) Dishonor of an unaccepted documentary draft occurs according to the rules stated in subsection (b)(2), (3), and (4), except that payment or acceptance may be delayed without dishonor until no later than the close of the third business day of the drawee following the day on which payment or acceptance is required by those paragraphs.

(d) Dishonor of an accepted draft is governed by the following rules:

(1) If the draft is payable on demand, the draft is dishonored if presentment for payment is duly made to the acceptor and the draft is not paid on the day of presentment.

(2) If the draft is not payable on demand, the draft is dishonored if presentment for payment is duly made to the acceptor and payment is not made on the day it becomes payable or the day of presentment, whichever is later.

(e) In any case in which presentment is otherwise required for dishonor under this section and presentment is excused under Section 3–504, dishonor occurs without presentment if the instrument is not duly accepted or paid.

(f) If a draft is dishonored because timely acceptance of the draft was not made and the person entitled to demand acceptance consents to a late acceptance, from the time of acceptance the draft is treated as never having been dishonored.

§ 3-503. Notice of Dishonor.

(a) The obligation of an indorser stated in Section 3–415(a) and the obligation of a drawer stated in Section 3–414(d) may not be enforced unless

(i) the indorser or drawer is given notice of dishonor of the instrument complying with this section or (ii) notice of dishonor is excused under Section 3–504(b).

(b) Notice of dishonor may be given by any person; may be given by any commercially reasonable means, including an oral, written, or electronic communication; and is sufficient if it reasonably identifies the instrument and indicates that the instrument has been dishonored or has not been paid or accepted. Return of an instrument given to a bank for collection is sufficient notice of dishonor.

(c) Subject to Section 3–504(c), with respect to an instrument taken for collection by a collecting bank, notice of dishonor must be given (i) by the bank before midnight of the next banking day following the banking day on which the bank receives notice of dishonor of the instrument, or (ii) by any other person within 30 days following the day on which the person receives notice of dishonor. With respect to any other instrument, notice of dishonor must be given within 30 days following the day on which dishonor occurs.

§ 3-504. Excused Presentment and Notice of Dishonor.

(a) Presentment for payment or acceptance of an instrument is excused if (i) the person entitled to present the instrument cannot with reasonable diligence make presentment, (ii) the maker or acceptor has repudiated an obligation to pay the instrument or is dead or in insolvency proceedings, (iii) by the terms of the instrument presentment is not necessary to enforce the obligation of indorsers or the drawer, (iv) the drawer or indorser whose obligation is being enforced has waived presentment or otherwise has no reason to expect or right to require that the instrument be paid or accepted, or (v) the drawer instructed the drawee not to pay or accept the draft or the drawee was not obligated to the drawer to pay the draft.

(b) Notice of dishonor is excused if (i) by the terms of the instrument notice of dishonor is not necessary to enforce the obligation of a party to pay the instrument, or (ii) the party whose obligation is being enforced waived notice of dishonor. A waiver of presentment is also a waiver of notice of dishonor.

(c) Delay in giving notice of dishonor is excused if the delay was caused by circumstances beyond the control of the person giving the notice and the person giving the notice exercised reasonable diligence after the cause of the delay ceased to operate.

§ 3-505. Evidence of Dishonor.

(a) The following are admissible as evidence and create a presumption of dishonor and of any notice of dishonor stated:

(1) a document regular in form as provided in subsection (b) which purports to be a protest;

(2) a purported stamp or writing of the drawee, payor bank, or presenting bank on or accompanying the instrument stating that acceptance or payment has been refused unless reasons for the refusal are stated and the reasons are not consistent with dishonor;

(3) a book or record of the drawee, payor bank, or collecting bank, kept in the usual course of business which shows dishonor, even if there is no evidence of who made the entry.

(b) A protest is a certificate of dishonor made by a United States consul or vice consul, or a notary public or other person authorized to administer oaths by the law of the place where dishonor occurs. It may be made upon information satisfactory to that person. The protest must identify the instrument and certify either that presentment has been made or, if not made, the reason why it was not made, and that the instrument has been dishonored by nonacceptance or nonpayment. The protest may also certify that notice of dishonor has been given to some or all parties.

PART 6: Discharge and Payment

§ 3-601. Discharge and Effect of Discharge.

(a) The obligation of a party to pay the instrument is discharged as stated in this Article or by an act or agreement with the party which would discharge an obligation to pay money under a simple contract.

(b) Discharge of the obligation of a party is not effective against a person acquiring rights of a holder in due course of the instrument without notice of the discharge.

§ 3-602. Payment.

(a) Subject to subsection (b), an instrument is paid to the extent payment is made (i) by or on behalf of a party obliged to pay the instrument, and (ii) to a person entitled to enforce the instrument. To the extent of the payment, the obligation of the party obliged to pay the instrument is discharged even though payment is made with knowledge of a claim to the instrument under Section 3–306 by another person.

(b) The obligation of a party to pay the instrument is not discharged under subsection (a) if:

(1) a claim to the instrument under Section 3–306 is enforceable against the party receiving payment and (i) payment is made with knowledge by the payor that payment is prohibited by injunction or similar process of a court of competent jurisdiction, or (ii) in the case of an instrument other than a cashier's check, teller's check, or certified check, the party making payment accepted, from the person having a claim to the instrument, indemnity against loss resulting from refusal to pay the person entitled to enforce the instrument; or

(2) the person making payment knows that the instrument is a stolen instrument and pays a person it knows is in wrongful possession of the instrument.

§ 3-603. Tender of Payment.

(a) If tender of payment of an obligation to pay an instrument is made to a person entitled to enforce the instrument, the effect of tender is governed by principles of law applicable to tender of payment under a simple contract.

(b) If tender of payment of an obligation to pay an instrument is made to a person entitled to enforce the instrument and the tender is refused, there is discharge, to the extent of the amount of the tender, of the obligation of an indorser or accommodation party having a right of recourse with respect to the obligation to which the tender relates.

(c) If tender of payment of an amount due on an instrument is made to a person entitled to enforce the instrument, the obligation of the obligor to pay interest after the due date on the amount tendered is discharged. If presentment is required with respect to an instrument and the obligor is able and ready to pay on the due date at every place of payment stated in the instrument, the obligor is deemed to have made tender of payment on the due date to the person entitled to enforce the instrument.

§ 3-604. Discharge by Cancellation or Renunciation.

(a) A person entitled to enforce an instrument, with or without consideration, may discharge the obligation of a party to pay the instrument (i) by an intentional voluntary act, such as surrender of the instrument to the party, destruction, mutilation, or cancellation of the instrument, cancellation or striking out of the party's signature, or the addition of words to the instrument indicating discharge, or (ii) by agreeing not to sue or otherwise renouncing rights against the party by a signed writing.

(b) Cancellation or striking out of an indorsement pursuant to subsection (a) does not affect the status and rights of a party derived from the indorsement.

§ 3-605. Discharge of Indorsers and Accommodation Parties.

(a) In this section, the term "indorser" includes a drawer having the obligation described in Section 3–414(d).

(b) Discharge, under Section 3–604, of the obligation of a party to pay an instrument does not discharge the obligation of an indorser or accommodation party having a right of recourse against the discharged party.

(c) If a person entitled to enforce an instrument agrees, with or without consideration, to an extension of the due date of the obligation of a party to pay the instrument, the extension discharges an indorser or accommodation party having a right of recourse against the party whose obligation is extended to the extent the indorser or accommodation party proves that the extension caused loss to the indorser or accommodation party with respect to the right of recourse.

(d) If a person entitled to enforce an instrument agrees, with or without consideration, to a material modification of the obligation of a party other than an extension of the due date, the modification discharges the obligation of an indorser or accommodation party having a right of recourse against the person whose obligation is modified to the extent the modification causes loss to the indorser or accommodation party with respect to the right of recourse. The loss suffered by the indorser or accommodation party as a result of the modification is equal to the amount of the right of recourse unless the person enforcing the instrument proves that no loss was caused by the modification or that the loss caused by the modification was an amount less than the amount of the right of recourse.

(e) If the obligation of a party to pay an instrument is secured by an interest in collateral and a person entitled to enforce the instrument impairs the value of the interest in collateral, the obligation of an indorser or accommodation party having a right of recourse against the obligor is discharged to the extent of the impairment. The value of an interest in collateral is impaired to the extent (i) the value of the interest is reduced to an amount less than the amount of the right of recourse of the party asserting discharge, or (ii) the reduction in value of the interest causes an increase in the amount by which the amount of the right of recourse exceeds the value of the interest. The burden of proving impairment is on the party asserting discharge.

(f) If the obligation of a party is secured by an interest in collateral not provided by an accommodation party and a person entitled to enforce the instrument impairs the value of the interest in collateral, the obligation of any party who is jointly and severally liable with respect to the secured obligation is discharged to the extent the impairment causes the party asserting discharge to pay more than that party would have been obliged to pay, taking into account rights of contribution, if impairment had not occurred. If the party asserting discharge is an accommodation party not entitled to discharge under subsection (e), the party is deemed to have a right to contribution based on joint and several liability rather than a right to reimbursement. The burden of proving impairment is on the party asserting discharge.

(g) Under subsection (e) or (f), impairing value of an interest in collateral includes (i) failure to obtain or maintain perfection or recordation of the interest in collateral, (ii) release of collateral without substitution of collateral of equal value, (iii) failure to perform a duty to preserve the value of collateral owed, under Article 9 or other law, to a debtor or surety or other person secondarily liable, or (iv) failure to comply with applicable law in disposing of collateral.

(h) An accommodation party is not discharged under subsection (c), (d), or (e) unless the person entitled to enforce the instrument knows of the accommodation or has notice under Section 3–419(c) that the instrument was signed for accommodation.

(i) A party is not discharged under this section if (i) the party asserting discharge consents to the event or conduct that is the basis of the discharge, or (ii) the instrument or a separate agreement of the party provides for waiver of discharge under this section either specifically or by general language indicating that parties waive defenses based on suretyship or impairment of collateral.

ADDENDUM TO REVISED ARTICLE 3

Notes to Legislative Counsel

1. If revised Article 3 is adopted in your state, the reference in Section 2–511 to Section 3–802 should be changed to Section 3–310.

2. If revised Article 3 is adopted in your state and the Uniform Fiduciaries Act is also in effect in your state, you may want to consider amending Uniform Fiduciaries Act § 9 to conform to Section 3–307(b)(2)(iii) and (4)(iii). See Official Comment 3 to Section 3–307.

REVISED ARTICLE 4: Bank Deposits and Collections

PART 1: General Provisions and Definitions

§ 4-101. Short Title.

This Article may be cited as Uniform Commercial Code—Bank Deposits and Collections.

As amended in 1990.

§ 4-102. Applicability.

(a) To the extent that items within this Article are also within Articles 3 and 8, they are subject to those Articles. If there is conflict, this Article governs Article 3, but Article 8 governs this Article.

(b) The liability of a bank for action or non-action with respect to an item handled by it for purposes of presentment, payment, or collection is governed by the law of the place where the bank is located. In the case of action or non-action by or at a branch or separate office of a bank, its liability is governed by the law of the place where the branch or separate office is located.

§ 4-103. Variation by Agreement; Measure of Damages; Action Constituting Ordinary Care.

(a) The effect of the provisions of this Article may be varied by agreement, but the parties to the agreement cannot disclaim a bank's responsibility for its lack of good faith or failure to exercise ordinary care or limit the measure of damages for the lack or failure. However, the parties may determine by agreement the standards by which the bank's responsibility is to be measured if those standards are not manifestly unreasonable.

(b) Federal Reserve regulations and operating circulars, clearing-house rules, and the like have the effect of agreements under subsection (a), whether or not specifically assented to by all parties interested in items handled.

(c) Action or non-action approved by this Article or pursuant to Federal Reserve regulations or operating circulars is the exercise of ordinary care and, in the absence of special instructions, action or non-action consistent with clearing-house rules and the like or with a general banking usage not disapproved by this Article, is prima facie the exercise of ordinary care.

(d) The specification or approval of certain procedures by this Article is not disapproval of other procedures that may be reasonable under the circumstances.

(e) The measure of damages for failure to exercise ordinary care in handling an item is the amount of the item reduced by an amount that could not have been realized by the exercise of ordinary care. If there is also bad faith it includes any other damages the party suffered as a proximate consequence.

As amended in 1990.

§ 4-104. Definitions and Index of Definitions.

(a) In this Article, unless the context otherwise requires:

(1) "Account" means any deposit or credit account with a bank, including a demand, time, savings, passbook, share draft, or like account, other than an account evidenced by a certificate of deposit;

(2) "Afternoon" means the period of a day between noon and midnight;

(3) "Banking day" means the part of a day on which a bank is open to the public for carrying on substantially all of its banking functions;

(4) "Clearing house" means an association of banks or other payors regularly clearing items;

(5) "Customer" means a person having an account with a bank or for whom a bank has agreed to collect items, including a bank that maintains an account at another bank;

(6) "Documentary draft" means a draft to be presented for acceptance or payment if specified documents, certificated securities (Section 8–102) or instructions for uncertificated securities (Section 8–102), or other certificates, statements, or the like are to be received by the drawee or other payor before acceptance or payment of the draft;

(7) "Draft" means a draft as defined in Section 3–104 or an item, other than an instrument, that is an order;

(8) "Drawee" means a person ordered in a draft to make payment;

(9) "Item" means an instrument or a promise or order to pay money handled by a bank for collection or payment. The term does not include a payment order governed by Article 4A or a credit or debit card slip;

(10) "Midnight deadline" with respect to a bank is midnight on its next banking day following the banking day on which it receives the relevant item or notice or from which the time for taking action commences to run, whichever is later;

(11) "Settle" means to pay in cash, by clearing-house settlement, in a charge or credit or by remittance, or otherwise as agreed. A settlement may be either provisional or final;

(12) "Suspends payments" with respect to a bank means that it has been closed by order of the supervisory authorities, that a public officer has been appointed to take it over, or that it ceases or refuses to make payments in the ordinary course of business.

(b) [Other definitions' section references deleted.]

(c) [Other definitions' section references deleted.]

(d) In addition, Article 1 contains general definitions and principles of construction and interpretation applicable throughout this Article.

§ 4-105. "Bank"; "Depository Bank"; "Payor Bank"; "Intermediary Bank"; "Collecting Bank"; "Presenting Bank".

In this Article:

(1) "Bank" means a person engaged in the business of banking, including a savings bank, savings and loan association, credit union, or trust company;

(2) "Depository bank" means the first bank to take an item even though it is also the payor bank, unless the item is presented for immediate payment over the counter;

(3) "Payor bank" means a bank that is the drawee of a draft;

(4) "Intermediary bank" means a bank to which an item is transferred in course of collection except the depositary or payor bank;

(5) "Collecting bank" means a bank handling an item for collection except the payor bank;

(6) "Presenting bank" means a bank presenting an item except a payor bank.

§ 4-106. Payable Through or Payable at Bank: Collecting Bank.

(a) If an item states that it is "payable through" a bank identified in the item, (i) the item designates the bank as a collecting bank and does not by itself authorize the bank to pay the item, and (ii) the item may be presented for payment only by or through the bank.

Alternative A

(b) If an item states that it is "payable at" a bank identified in the item, the item is equivalent to a draft drawn on the bank.

Alternative B

(b) If an item states that it is "payable at" a bank identified in the item, (i) the item designates the bank as a collecting bank and does not by itself authorize the bank to pay the item, and (ii) the item may be presented for payment only by or through the bank.

(c) If a draft names a nonbank drawee and it is unclear whether a bank named in the draft is a co-drawee or a collecting bank, the bank is a collecting bank.

As added in 1990.

§ 4-107. Separate Office of Bank.

A branch or separate office of a bank is a separate bank for the purpose of computing the time within which and determining the place at or to which action may be taken or notices or orders shall be given under this Article and under Article 3.

As amended in 1962 and 1990.

§ 4-108. Time of Receipt of Items.

(a) For the purpose of allowing time to process items, prove balances, and make the necessary entries on its books to determine its position for the day, a bank may fix an afternoon hour of 2 P.M. or later as a cutoff hour for the handling of money and items and the making of entries on its books.

(b) An item or deposit of money received on any day after a cutoff hour so fixed or after the close of the banking day may be treated as being received at the opening of the next banking day.

As amended in 1990.

§ 4-109. Delays.

(a) Unless otherwise instructed, a collecting bank in a good faith effort to secure payment of a specific item drawn on a payor other than a bank, and with or without the approval of any person involved, may waive, modify, or extend time limits imposed or permitted by this [act] for a period not exceeding two additional banking days without discharge of drawers or indorsers or liability to its transferor or a prior party.

(b) Delay by a collecting bank or payor bank beyond time limits prescribed or permitted by this [act] or by instructions is excused if (i) the delay is caused by interruption of communication or computer facilities, suspension of payments by another bank, war, emergency conditions, failure of equipment, or other circumstances beyond the control of the bank, and (ii) the bank exercises such diligence as the circumstances require.

§ 4-110. Electronic Presentment.

(a) "Agreement for electronic presentment" means an agreement, clearing-house rule, or Federal Reserve regulation or operating circular, providing that presentment of an item may be made by transmission of an image of an item or information describing the item ("presentment notice") rather than delivery of the item itself. The agreement may provide for procedures governing retention, presentment, payment, dishonor, and other matters concerning items subject to the agreement.

(b) Presentment of an item pursuant to an agreement for presentment is made when the presentment notice is received.

(c) If presentment is made by presentment notice, a reference to "item" or "check" in this Article means the presentment notice unless the context otherwise indicates.

As added in 1990.

§ 4-111. Statute of Limitations.

An action to enforce an obligation, duty, or right arising under this Article must be commenced within three years after the [cause of action] accrues. As added in 1990.

PART 2: Collection of Items: Depositary and Collecting Banks

§ 4-201. Status of Collecting Bank as Agent and Provisional Status of Credits; Applicability of Article; Item Indorsed "Pay Any Bank".

(a) Unless a contrary intent clearly appears and before the time that a settlement given by a collecting bank for an item is or becomes final, the bank, with respect to an item, is an agent or sub-agent of the owner of the item and any settlement given for the item is provisional. This provision applies regardless of the form of indorsement or lack of indorsement and even though credit given for the item is subject to immediate withdrawal as of right or is in fact withdrawn; but the continuance of ownership of an item by its owner and any rights of the owner to proceeds of the item are subject to rights of a collecting bank, such as those resulting from outstanding advances on the item and rights of recoupment or setoff. If an item is handled by banks for purposes of presentment, payment, collection, or return, the relevant provisions of this Article apply even though action of the parties clearly establishes that a particular bank has purchased the item and is the owner of it.

(b) After an item has been indorsed with the words "pay any bank" or the like, only a bank may acquire the rights of a holder until the item has been:

(1) returned to the customer initiating collection; or

(2) specially indorsed by a bank to a person who is not a bank.

As amended in 1990.

§ 4-202. Responsibility for Collection or Return; When Action Timely.

(a) A collecting bank must exercise ordinary care in:

(1) presenting an item or sending it for presentment;

(2) sending notice of dishonor or nonpayment or returning an item other than a documentary draft to the bank's transferor after learning that the item has not been paid or accepted, as the case may be;

(3) settling for an item when the bank receives final settlement; and

(4) notifying its transferor of any loss or delay in transit within a reasonable time after discovery thereof.

(b) A collecting bank exercises ordinary care under subsection (a) by taking proper action before its midnight deadline following receipt of an item, notice, or settlement. Taking proper action within a reasonably longer time may constitute the exercise of ordinary care, but the bank has the burden of establishing timeliness.

(c) Subject to subsection (a)(1), a bank is not liable for the insolvency, neglect, misconduct, mistake, or default of another bank or person or for loss or destruction of an item in the possession of others or in transit.

As amended in 1990.

§ 4-203. Effect of Instructions.

Subject to Article 3 concerning conversion of instruments (Section 3–420) and restrictive indorsements (Section 3–206), only a collecting bank's transferor can give instructions that affect the bank or constitute notice to it, and a collecting bank is not liable to prior parties for any action taken pursuant to the instructions or in accordance with any agreement with its transferor.

§ 4-204. Methods of Sending and Presenting; Sending Directly to Payor Bank.

(a) A collecting bank shall send items by a reasonably prompt method, taking into consideration relevant instructions, the nature of the item, the number of those items on hand, the cost of collection involved, and the method generally used by it or others to present those items.

(b) A collecting bank may send:

(1) an item directly to the payor bank;

(2) an item to a nonbank payor if authorized by its transferor; and

(3) an item other than documentary drafts to a nonbank payor, if authorized by Federal Reserve regulation or operating circular, clearing-house rule, or the like.

(c) Presentment may be made by a presenting bank at a place where the payor bank or other payor has requested that presentment be made.

As amended in 1990.

§ 4-205. Depositary Bank Holder of Unindorsed Item.

If a customer delivers an item to a depositary bank for collection:

(1) the depositary bank becomes a holder of the item at the time it receives the item for collection if the customer at the time of delivery was a holder of the item, whether or not the customer indorses the item, and, if the bank satisfies the other requirements of Section 3–302, it is a holder in due course; and

(2) the depositary bank warrants to collecting banks, the payor bank or other payor, and the drawer that the amount of the item was paid to the customer or deposited to the customer's account.

As amended in 1990.

§ 4-206. Transfer Between Banks.

Any agreed method that identifies the transferor bank is sufficient for the item's further transfer to another bank.

As amended in 1990.

§ 4-207. Transfer Warranties.

(a) A customer or collecting bank that transfers an item and receives a settlement or other consideration warrants to the transferee and to any subsequent collecting bank that:

(1) the warrantor is a person entitled to enforce the item;

(2) all signatures on the item are authentic and authorized;

(3) the item has not been altered;

(4) the item is not subject to a defense or claim in recoupment (Section 3–305(a)) of any party that can be asserted against the warrantor; and

(5) the warrantor has no knowledge of any insolvency proceeding commenced with respect to the maker or acceptor or, in the case of an unaccepted draft, the drawer.

(b) If an item is dishonored, a customer or collecting bank transferring the item and receiving settlement or other consideration is obliged to pay the amount due on the item (i) according to the terms of the item at the time it was transferred, or (ii) if the transfer was of an incomplete item, according to its terms when completed as stated in Sections 3–115 and 3–407. The obligation of a transferor is owed to the transferee and to any subsequent collecting bank that takes the item in good faith. A transferor cannot disclaim its obligation under this subsection by an indorsement stating that it is made "without recourse" or otherwise disclaiming liability.

(c) A person to whom the warranties under subsection (a) are made and who took the item in good faith may recover from the warrantor as damages for breach of warranty an amount equal to the loss suffered as a result of the breach, but not more than the amount of the item plus expenses and loss of interest incurred as a result of the breach.

(d) The warranties stated in subsection (a) cannot be disclaimed with respect to checks. Unless notice of a claim for breach of warranty is given to the warrantor within 30 days after the claimant has reason to know of the breach and the identity of the warrantor, the warrantor is discharged to the extent of any loss caused by the delay in giving notice of the claim.

(e) A cause of action for breach of warranty under this section accrues when the claimant has reason to know of the breach.
As amended in 1990.

§ 4-208. Presentment Warranties.

(a) If an unaccepted draft is presented to the drawee for payment or acceptance and the drawee pays or accepts the draft, (i) the person obtaining payment or acceptance, at the time of presentment, and (ii) a previous transferor of the draft, at the time of transfer, warrant to the drawee that pays or accepts the draft in good faith that:

(1) the warrantor is, or was, at the time the warrantor transferred the draft, a person entitled to enforce the draft or authorized to obtain payment or acceptance of the draft on behalf of a person entitled to enforce the draft;

(2) the draft has not been altered; and

(3) the warrantor has no knowledge that the signature of the purported drawer of the draft is unauthorized.

(b) A drawee making payment may recover from a warrantor damages for breach of warranty equal to the amount paid by the drawee less the amount the drawee received or is entitled to receive from the drawer because of the payment. In addition, the drawee is entitled to compensation for expenses and loss of interest resulting from the breach. The right of the drawee to recover damages under this subsection is not affected by any failure of the drawee to exercise ordinary care in making payment. If the drawee accepts the draft (i) breach of warranty is a defense to the obligation of the acceptor, and (ii) if the acceptor makes payment with respect to the draft, the acceptor is entitled to recover from a warrantor for breach of warranty the amounts stated in this subsection.

(c) If a drawee asserts a claim for breach of warranty under subsection (a) based on an unauthorized indorsement of the draft or an alteration of the draft, the warrantor may defend by proving that the indorsement is effective under Section 3–404 or 3–405 or the drawer is precluded under Section 3–406 or 4–406 from asserting against the drawee the unauthorized indorsement or alteration.

(d) If (i) a dishonored draft is presented for payment to the drawer or an indorser or (ii) any other item is presented for payment to a party obliged to pay the item, and the item is paid, the person obtaining payment and a prior transferor of the item warrant to the person making payment in good faith that the warrantor is, or was, at the time the warrantor transferred the item, a person entitled to enforce the item or authorized to obtain payment on behalf of a person entitled to enforce the item. The person making payment may recover from any warrantor for breach of warranty an amount equal to the amount paid plus expenses and loss of interest resulting from the breach.

(e) The warranties stated in subsections (a) and (d) cannot be disclaimed with respect to checks. Unless notice of a claim for breach of warranty is given to the warrantor within 30 days after the claimant has reason to know of the breach and the identity of the warrantor, the warrantor is discharged to the extent of any loss caused by the delay in giving notice of the claim.

(f) A cause of action for breach of warranty under this section accrues when the claimant has reason to know of the breach.
As amended in 1990.

§ 4-209. Encoding and Retention Warranties.

(a) A person who encodes information on or with respect to an item after issue warrants to any subsequent collecting bank and to the payor bank or other payor that the information is correctly encoded. If the customer of a depositary bank encodes, that bank also makes the warranty.

(b) A person who undertakes to retain an item pursuant to an agreement for electronic presentment warrants to any subsequent collecting bank and to the payor bank or other payor that retention and presentment of the item comply with the agreement. If a customer of a depositary bank undertakes to retain an item, that bank also makes this warranty.

(c) A person to whom warranties are made under this section and who took the item in good faith may recover from the warrantor as damages for breach of warranty an amount equal to the loss suffered as a result of the breach, plus expenses and loss of interest incurred as a result of the breach.
As added in 1990.

§ 4-210. Security Interest of Collecting Bank in Items, Accompanying Documents and Proceeds.

(a) A collecting bank has a security interest in an item and any accompanying documents or the proceeds of either:

(1) in case of an item deposited in an account, to the extent to which credit given for the item has been withdrawn or applied;

(2) in case of an item for which it has given credit available for withdrawal as of right, to the extent of the credit given, whether or not the credit is drawn upon or there is a right of charge-back; or

(3) if it makes an advance on or against the item.

(b) If credit given for several items received at one time or pursuant to a single agreement is withdrawn or applied in part, the security interest remains upon all the items, any accompanying documents or the proceeds of either. For the purpose of this section, credits first given are first withdrawn.

(c) Receipt by a collecting bank of a final settlement for an item is a realization on its security interest in the item, accompanying documents, and proceeds. So long as the bank does not receive final settlement for the item or give up possession of the item or accompanying documents for purposes other than collection, the security interest continues to that extent and is subject to Article 9, but:

(1) no security agreement is necessary to make the security interest enforceable (Section 9–203(1)(a));

(2) no filing is required to perfect the security interest; and

(3) the security interest has priority over conflicting perfected security interests in the item, accompanying documents, or proceeds.
As amended in 1990 and 1999.

§ 4-211. When Bank Gives Value for Purposes of Holder in Due Course.

For purposes of determining its status as a holder in due course, a bank has given value to the extent it has a security interest in an item, if the bank otherwise complies with the requirements of Section 3–302 on what constitutes a holder in due course.
As amended in 1990.

§ 4-212. Presentment by Notice of Item Not Payable by, Through, or at Bank; Liability of Drawer or Indorser.

(a) Unless otherwise instructed, a collecting bank may present an item not payable by, through, or at a bank by sending to the party to accept or pay a written notice that the bank holds the item for acceptance or payment. The notice must be sent in time to be received on or before the day when presentment is due and the bank must meet any requirement of the party to accept or pay under Section 3–501 by the close of the bank's next banking day after it knows of the requirement.

(b) If presentment is made by notice and payment, acceptance, or request for compliance with a requirement under Section 3–501 is not received by the close of business on the day after maturity or, in the case of demand items, by the close of business on the third banking day after notice was sent, the presenting bank may treat the item as dishonored and charge any drawer or indorser by sending it notice of the facts.
As amended in 1990.

§ 4-213. Medium and Time of Settlement by Bank.

(a) With respect to settlement by a bank, the medium and time of settlement may be prescribed by Federal Reserve regulations or circulars, clearing-house rules, and the like, or agreement. In the absence of such prescription:

(1) the medium of settlement is cash or credit to an account in a Federal Reserve bank of or specified by the person to receive settlement; and

(2) the time of settlement is:

(i) with respect to tender of settlement by cash, a cashier's check, or teller's check, when the cash or check is sent or delivered;

(ii) with respect to tender of settlement by credit in an account in a Federal Reserve Bank, when the credit is made;

(iii) with respect to tender of settlement by a credit or debit to an account in a bank, when the credit or debit is made or, in the case of tender of settlement by authority to charge an account, when the authority is sent or delivered; or

(iv) with respect to tender of settlement by a funds transfer, when payment is made pursuant to Section 4A–406(a) to the person receiving settlement.

(b) If the tender of settlement is not by a medium authorized by subsection (a) or the time of settlement is not fixed by subsection (a), no settlement occurs until the tender of settlement is accepted by the person receiving settlement.

(c) If settlement for an item is made by cashier's check or teller's check and the person receiving settlement, before its midnight deadline:

(1) presents or forwards the check for collection, settlement is final when the check is finally paid; or

(2) fails to present or forward the check for collection, settlement is final at the midnight deadline of the person receiving settlement.

(d) If settlement for an item is made by giving authority to charge the account of the bank giving settlement in the bank receiving settlement, settlement is final when the charge is made by the bank receiving settlement if there are funds available in the account for the amount of the item. As amended in 1990.

§ 4-214. Right of Charge-Back or Refund; Liability of Collecting Bank: Return of Item.

(a) If a collecting bank has made provisional settlement with its customer for an item and fails by reason of dishonor, suspension of payments by a bank, or otherwise to receive settlement for the item which is or becomes final, the bank may revoke the settlement given by it, charge back the amount of any credit given for the item to its customer's account, or obtain refund from its customer, whether or not it is able to return the item, if by its midnight deadline or within a longer reasonable time after it learns the facts it returns the item or sends notification of the facts. If the return or notice is delayed beyond the bank's midnight deadline or a longer reasonable time after it learns the facts, the bank may revoke the settlement, charge back the credit, or obtain refund from its customer, but it is liable for any loss resulting from the delay. These rights to revoke, charge back, and obtain refund terminate if and when a settlement for the item received by the bank is or becomes final.

(b) A collecting bank returns an item when it is sent or delivered to the bank's customer or transferor or pursuant to its instructions.

(c) A depositary bank that is also the payor may charge back the amount of an item to its customer's account or obtain refund in accordance with the section governing return of an item received by a payor bank for credit on its books (Section 4–301).

(d) The right to charge back is not affected by:

(1) previous use of a credit given for the item; or

(2) failure by any bank to exercise ordinary care with respect to the item, but a bank so failing remains liable.

(e) A failure to charge back or claim refund does not affect other rights of the bank against the customer or any other party.

(f) If credit is given in dollars as the equivalent of the value of an item payable in foreign money, the dollar amount of any charge-back or refund must be calculated on the basis of the bank-offered spot rate for the foreign money prevailing on the day when the person entitled to the charge-back or refund learns that it will not receive payment in ordinary course. As amended in 1990.

§ 4-215. Final Payment of Item by Payor Bank; When Provisional Debits and Credits Become Final; When Certain Credits Become Available for Withdrawal.

(a) An item is finally paid by a payor bank when the bank has first done any of the following:

(1) paid the item in cash;

(2) settled for the item without having a right to revoke the settlement under statute, clearing-house rule, or agreement; or

(3) made a provisional settlement for the item and failed to revoke the settlement in the time and manner permitted by statute, clearing-house rule, or agreement.

(b) If provisional settlement for an item does not become final, the item is not finally paid.

(c) If provisional settlement for an item between the presenting and payor banks is made through a clearing house or by debits or credits in an account between them, then to the extent that provisional debits or credits for the item are entered in accounts between the presenting and payor banks or between the presenting and successive prior collecting banks seriatim, they become final upon final payment of the item by the payor bank.

(d) If a collecting bank receives a settlement for an item which is or becomes final, the bank is accountable to its customer for the amount of the item and any provisional credit given for the item in an account with its customer becomes final.

(e) Subject to (i) applicable law stating a time for availability of funds and (ii) any right of the bank to apply the credit to an obligation of the customer, credit given by a bank for an item in a customer's account becomes available for withdrawal as of right:

(1) if the bank has received a provisional settlement for the item, when the settlement becomes final and the bank has had a reasonable time to receive return of the item and the item has not been received within that time;

(2) if the bank is both the depositary bank and the payor bank, and the item is finally paid, at the opening of the bank's second banking day following receipt of the item.

(f) Subject to applicable law stating a time for availability of funds and any right of a bank to apply a deposit to an obligation of the depositor, a deposit of money becomes available for withdrawal as of right at the opening of the bank's next banking day after receipt of the deposit. As amended in 1990.

§ 4-216. Insolvency and Preference.

(a) If an item is in or comes into the possession of a payor or collecting bank that suspends payment and the item has not been finally paid, the item must be returned by the receiver, trustee, or agent in charge of the closed bank to the presenting bank or the closed bank's customer.

(b) If a payor bank finally pays an item and suspends payments without making a settlement for the item with its customer or the presenting bank which settlement is or becomes final, the owner of the item has a preferred claim against the payor bank.

(c) If a payor bank gives or a collecting bank gives or receives a provisional settlement for an item and thereafter suspends payments, the suspension does not prevent or interfere with the settlement's becoming final if the finality occurs automatically upon the lapse of certain time or the happening of certain events.

(d) If a collecting bank receives from subsequent parties settlement for an item, which settlement is or becomes final and the bank suspends payments without making a settlement for the item with its customer which settlement is or becomes final, the owner of the item has a preferred claim against the collecting bank.

As amended in 1990.

PART 3: Collection of Items: Payor Banks

§ 4-301. Deferred Posting; Recovery of Payment by Return of Items; Time of Dishonor; Return of Items by Payor Bank.

(a) If a payor bank settles for a demand item other than a documentary draft presented otherwise than for immediate payment over the counter before midnight of the banking day of receipt, the payor bank may revoke the settlement and recover the settlement if, before it has made final payment and before its midnight deadline, it

(1) returns the item; or

(2) sends written notice of dishonor or nonpayment if the item is unavailable for return.

(b) If a demand item is received by a payor bank for credit on its books, it may return the item or send notice of dishonor and may revoke any credit given or recover the amount thereof withdrawn by its customer, if it acts within the time limit and in the manner specified in subsection (a).

(c) Unless previous notice of dishonor has been sent, an item is dishonored at the time when for purposes of dishonor it is returned or notice sent in accordance with this section.

(d) An item is returned:

(1) as to an item presented through a clearing house, when it is delivered to the presenting or last collecting bank or to the clearing house or is sent or delivered in accordance with clearing-house rules; or

(2) in all other cases, when it is sent or delivered to the bank's customer or transferor or pursuant to instructions.

As amended in 1990.

§ 4-302. Payor Bank's Responsibility for Late Return of Item.

(a) If an item is presented to and received by a payor bank, the bank is accountable for the amount of:

(1) a demand item, other than a documentary draft, whether properly payable or not, if the bank, in any case in which it is not also the depositary bank, retains the item beyond midnight of the banking day of receipt without settling for it or, whether or not it is also the depositary bank, does not pay or return the item or send notice of dishonor until after its midnight deadline; or

(2) any other properly payable item unless, within the time allowed for acceptance or payment of that item, the bank either accepts or pays the item or returns it and accompanying documents.

(b) The liability of a payor bank to pay an item pursuant to subsection (a) is subject to defenses based on breach of a presentment warranty (Section 4–208) or proof that the person seeking enforcement of the liability presented or transferred the item for the purpose of defrauding the payor bank.

As amended in 1990.

§ 4-303. When Items Subject to Notice, Stop-Payment Order, Legal Process, or Setoff; Order in Which Items May Be Charged or Certified.

(a) Any knowledge, notice, or stop-payment order received by, legal process served upon, or setoff exercised by a payor bank comes too late to terminate, suspend, or modify the bank's right or duty to pay an item or to charge its customer's account for the item if the knowledge, notice, stop-payment order, or legal process is received or served and a reasonable time for the bank to act thereon expires or the setoff is exercised after the earliest of the following:

(1) the bank accepts or certifies the item;

(2) the bank pays the item in cash;

(3) the bank settles for the item without having a right to revoke the settlement under statute, clearing-house rule, or agreement;

(4) the bank becomes accountable for the amount of the item under Section 4–302 dealing with the payor bank's responsibility for late return of items; or

(5) with respect to checks, a cutoff hour no earlier than one hour after the opening of the next banking day after the banking day on which the bank received the check and no later than the close of that next banking day or, if no cutoff hour is fixed, the close of the next banking day after the banking day on which the bank received the check.

(b) Subject to subsection (a), items may be accepted, paid, certified, or charged to the indicated account of its customer in any order.

As amended in 1990.

PART 4: Relationship Between Payor Bank and Its Customer

§ 4-401. When Bank May Charge Customer's Account.

(a) A bank may charge against the account of a customer an item that is properly payable from the account even though the charge creates an overdraft. An item is properly payable if it is authorized by the customer and is in accordance with any agreement between the customer and bank.

(b) A customer is not liable for the amount of an overdraft if the customer neither signed the item nor benefited from the proceeds of the item.

(c) A bank may charge against the account of a customer a check that is otherwise properly payable from the account, even though payment was made before the date of the check, unless the customer has given notice to the bank of the postdating describing the check with reasonable certainty. The notice is effective for the period stated in Section 4–403(b) for stop-payment orders, and must be received at such time and in such manner as to afford the bank a reasonable opportunity to act on it before the bank takes any action with respect to the check described in Section 4–303. If a bank charges against the account of a customer a check before the date stated in the notice of postdating, the bank is liable for damages for the loss resulting from its act. The loss may include damages for dishonor of subsequent items under Section 4–402.

(d) A bank that in good faith makes payment to a holder may charge the indicated account of its customer according to:

(1) the original terms of the altered item; or

(2) the terms of the completed item, even though the bank knows the item has been completed unless the bank has notice that the completion was improper.

As amended in 1990.

§ 4-402. Bank's Liability to Customer for Wrongful Dishonor; Time of Determining Insufficiency of Account.

(a) Except as otherwise provided in this Article, a payor bank wrongfully dishonors an item if it dishonors an item that is properly payable, but a bank may dishonor an item that would create an overdraft unless it has agreed to pay the overdraft.

(b) A payor bank is liable to its customer for damages proximately caused by the wrongful dishonor of an item. Liability is limited to actual damages proved and may include damages for an arrest or prosecution of the customer or other consequential damages. Whether any consequential damages are proximately caused by the wrongful dishonor is a question of fact to be determined in each case.

(c) A payor bank's determination of the customer's account balance on which a decision to dishonor for insufficiency of available funds is based may be made at any time between the time the item is received by the payor bank and the time that the payor bank returns the item or gives notice in lieu of return, and no more than one determination need be made. If, at the election of the payor bank, a subsequent balance determination is made for the purpose of reevaluating the bank's decision to dishonor the item, the account balance at that time is determinative of whether a dishonor for insufficiency of available funds is wrongful.

As amended in 1990.

§ 4-403. Customer's Right to Stop Payment; Burden of Proof of Loss.

(a) A customer or any person authorized to draw on the account if there is more than one person may stop payment of any item drawn on the customer's account or close the account by an order to the bank describing the item or account with reasonable certainty received at a time and in a manner that affords the bank a reasonable opportunity to act on it before any action by the bank with respect to the item described in Section 4–303. If the signature of more than one person is required to draw on an account, any of these persons may stop payment or close the account.

(b) A stop-payment order is effective for six months, but it lapses after 14 calendar days if the original order was oral and was not confirmed in writing within that period. A stop-payment order may be renewed for additional six-month periods by a writing given to the bank within a period during which the stop-payment order is effective.

(c) The burden of establishing the fact and amount of loss resulting from the payment of an item contrary to a stop-payment order or order to close an account is on the customer. The loss from payment of an item contrary to a stop-payment order may include damages for dishonor of subsequent items under Section 4–402.

As amended in 1990.

§ 4-404. Bank Not Obliged to Pay Check More Than Six Months Old.

A bank is under no obligation to a customer having a checking account to pay a check, other than a certified check, which is presented more than six months after its date, but it may charge its customer's account for a payment made thereafter in good faith.

§ 4-405. Death or Incompetence of Customer.

(a) A payor or collecting bank's authority to accept, pay, or collect an item or to account for proceeds of its collection, if otherwise effective, is not rendered ineffective by incompetence of a customer of either bank existing at the time the item is issued or its collection is undertaken if the bank does not know of an adjudication of incompetence. Neither death nor incompetence of a customer revokes the authority to accept, pay, collect, or account until the bank knows of the fact of death or of an adjudication of incompetence and has reasonable opportunity to act on it.

(b) Even with knowledge, a bank may for 10 days after the date of death pay or certify checks drawn on or before the date unless ordered to stop payment by a person claiming an interest in the account.

As amended in 1990.

§ 4-406. Customer's Duty to Discover and Report Unauthorized Signature or Alteration.

(a) A bank that sends or makes available to a customer a statement of account showing payment of items for the account shall either return or make available to the customer the items paid or provide information in the statement of account sufficient to allow the customer reasonably to identify the items paid. The statement of account provides sufficient information if the item is described by item number, amount, and date of payment.

(b) If the items are not returned to the customer, the person retaining the items shall either retain the items or, if the items are destroyed, maintain the capacity to furnish legible copies of the items until the expiration of seven years after receipt of the items. A customer may request an item from the bank that paid the item, and that bank must provide in a reasonable time either the item or, if the item has been destroyed or is not otherwise obtainable, a legible copy of the item.

(c) If a bank sends or makes available a statement of account or items pursuant to subsection (a), the customer must exercise reasonable promptness in examining the statement or the items to determine whether any payment was not authorized because of an alteration of an item or because a purported signature by or on behalf of the customer was not authorized. If, based on the statement or items provided, the customer should reasonably have discovered the unauthorized payment, the customer must promptly notify the bank of the relevant facts.

(d) If the bank proves that the customer failed, with respect to an item, to comply with the duties imposed on the customer by subsection (c), the customer is precluded from asserting against the bank:

(1) the customer's unauthorized signature or any alteration on the item, if the bank also proves that it suffered a loss by reason of the failure; and

(2) the customer's unauthorized signature or alteration by the same wrongdoer on any other item paid in good faith by the bank if the payment was made before the bank received notice from the customer of the unauthorized signature or alteration and after the customer had been afforded a reasonable period of time, not exceeding 30 days, in which to examine the item or statement of account and notify the bank.

(e) If subsection (d) applies and the customer proves that the bank failed to exercise ordinary care in paying the item and that the failure substantially contributed to loss, the loss is allocated between the customer precluded and the bank asserting the preclusion according to the extent to which the failure of the customer to comply with subsection (c) and the failure of the bank to exercise ordinary care contributed to the loss. If the customer proves that the bank did not pay the item in good faith, the preclusion under subsection (d) does not apply.

(f) Without regard to care or lack of care of either the customer or the bank, a customer who does not within one year after the statement or items are made available to the customer (subsection (a)) discover and report the customer's unauthorized signature on or any alteration on the item is precluded from asserting against the bank the unauthorized signature or alteration. If there is a preclusion under this subsection, the payor bank may not recover for breach or warranty under Section 4–208 with respect to the unauthorized signature or alteration to which the preclusion applies.

As amended in 1990.

§ 4-407. Payor Bank's Right to Subrogation on Improper Payment.

If a payor has paid an item over the order of the drawer or maker to stop payment, or after an account has been closed, or otherwise under circumstances giving a basis for objection by the drawer or maker, to prevent unjust enrichment and only to the extent necessary to prevent loss to the bank by reason of its payment of the item, the payor bank is subrogated to the rights

(1) of any holder in due course on the item against the drawer or maker;

(2) of the payee or any other holder of the item against the drawer or maker either on the item or under the transaction out of which the item arose; and

(3) of the drawer or maker against the payee or any other holder of the item with respect to the transaction out of which the item arose.

As amended in 1990.

PART 5: Collection of Documentary Drafts

§ 4-501. Handling of Documentary Drafts; Duty to Send for Presentment and to Notify Customer of Dishonor.

A bank that takes a documentary draft for collection shall present or send the draft and accompanying documents for presentment and, upon learning that the draft has not been paid or accepted in due course, shall seasonably notify its customer of the fact even though it may have discounted or bought the draft or extended credit available for withdrawal as of right.

As amended in 1990.

§ 4-502. Presentment of "On Arrival" Drafts.

If a draft or the relevant instructions require presentment "on arrival", "when goods arrive" or the like, the collecting bank need not present until in its judgment a reasonable time for arrival of the goods has expired. Refusal to pay or accept because the goods have not arrived is not dishonor; the bank must notify its transferor of the refusal but need not present the draft again until it is instructed to do so or learns of the arrival of the goods.

§ 4-503. Responsibility of Presenting Bank for Documents and Goods; Report of Reasons for Dishonor; Referee in Case of Need.

Unless otherwise instructed and except as provided in Article 5, a bank presenting a documentary draft:

(1) must deliver the documents to the drawee on acceptance of the draft if it is payable more than three days after presentment, otherwise, only on payment; and

(2) upon dishonor, either in the case of presentment for acceptance or presentment for payment, may seek and follow instructions from any referee in case of need designated in the draft or, if the presenting bank does not choose to utilize the referee's services, it must use diligence and good faith to ascertain the reason for dishonor, must notify its transferor of the dishonor and of the results of its effort to ascertain the reasons therefor, and must request instructions.

However, the presenting bank is under no obligation with respect to goods represented by the documents except to follow any reasonable instructions seasonably received; it has a right to reimbursement for any expense incurred in following instructions and to prepayment of or indemnity for those expenses.

As amended in 1990.

§ 4-504. Privilege of Presenting Bank to Deal With Goods; Security Interest for Expenses.

(a) A presenting bank that, following the dishonor of a documentary draft, has seasonably requested instructions but does not receive them within a reasonable time may store, sell, or otherwise deal with the goods in any reasonable manner.

(b) For its reasonable expenses incurred by action under subsection (a) the presenting bank has a lien upon the goods or their proceeds, which may be foreclosed in the same manner as an unpaid seller's lien.

As amended in 1990.

ARTICLE 4A: Funds Transfers

PART 1: Subject Matter and Definitions

§ 4A-101. Short Title.

This Article may be cited as Uniform Commercial Code—Funds Transfers.

§ 4A-102. Subject Matter.

Except as otherwise provided in Section 4A–108, this Article applies to funds transfers defined in Section 4A–104.

§ 4A-103. Payment Order-Definitions.

(a) In this Article:

(1) "Payment order" means an instruction of a sender to a receiving bank, transmitted orally, electronically, or in writing, to pay, or to cause another bank to pay, a fixed or determinable amount of money to a beneficiary if:

(i) the instruction does not state a condition to payment to the beneficiary other than time of payment,

(ii) the receiving bank is to be reimbursed by debiting an account of, or otherwise receiving payment from, the sender, and

(iii) the instruction is transmitted by the sender directly to the receiving bank or to an agent, funds-transfer system, or communication system for transmittal to the receiving bank.

(2) "Beneficiary" means the person to be paid by the beneficiary's bank.

(3) "Beneficiary's bank" means the bank identified in a payment order in which an account of the beneficiary is to be credited pursuant to the order or which otherwise is to make payment to the beneficiary if the order does not provide for payment to an account.

(4) "Receiving bank" means the bank to which the sender's instruction is addressed.

(5) "Sender" means the person giving the instruction to the receiving bank.

(b) If an instruction complying with subsection (a)(1) is to make more than one payment to a beneficiary, the instruction is a separate payment order with respect to each payment.

(c) A payment order is issued when it is sent to the receiving bank.

§ 4A-104. Funds Transfer-Definitions.

In this Article:

(a) "Funds transfer" means the series of transactions, beginning with the originator's payment order, made for the purpose of making payment to the beneficiary of the order. The term includes any payment order issued by the originator's bank or an intermediary bank intended to carry out the originator's payment order. A funds transfer is completed by acceptance by the beneficiary's bank of a payment order for the benefit of the beneficiary of the originator's payment order.

(b) "Intermediary bank" means a receiving bank other than the originator's bank or the beneficiary's bank.

(c) "Originator" means the sender of the first payment order in a funds transfer.

(d) "Originator's bank" means (i) the receiving bank to which the payment order of the originator is issued if the originator is not a bank, or (ii) the originator if the originator is a bank.

§ 4A-105. Other Definitions.

(a) In this Article:

(1) "Authorized account" means a deposit account of a customer in a bank designated by the customer as a source of payment of payment

orders issued by the customer to the bank. If a customer does not so designate an account, any account of the customer is an authorized account if payment of a payment order from that account is not inconsistent with a restriction on the use of that account.

(2) "Bank" means a person engaged in the business of banking and includes a savings bank, savings and loan association, credit union, and trust company. A branch or separate office of a bank is a separate bank for purposes of this Article.

(3) "Customer" means a person, including a bank, having an account with a bank or from whom a bank has agreed to receive payment orders.

(4) "Funds-transfer business day" of a receiving bank means the part of a day during which the receiving bank is open for the receipt, processing, and transmittal of payment orders and cancellations and amendments of payment orders.

(5) "Funds-transfer system" means a wire transfer network, automated clearing house, or other communication system of a clearing house or other association of banks through which a payment order by a bank may be transmitted to the bank to which the order is addressed.

(6) "Good faith" means honesty in fact and the observance of reasonable commercial standards of fair dealing.

(7) "Prove" with respect to a fact means to meet the burden of establishing the fact (Section 1–201(8)).

(b) Other definitions applying to this Article and the sections in which they appear are:

"Acceptance"	Section 4A–209
"Beneficiary"	Section 4A–103
"Beneficiary's bank"	Section 4A–103
"Executed"	Section 4A–301
"Execution date"	Section 4A–301
"Funds transfer"	Section 4A–104
"Funds-transfer system rule"	Section 4A–501
"Intermediary bank"	Section 4A–104
"Originator"	Section 4A–104
"Originator's bank"	Section 4A–104
"Payment by beneficiary's bank to	Section 4A–405 beneficiary"
"Payment by originator to	Section 4A–406 beneficiary"
"Payment by sender to receiving	Section 4A–403 bank"
"Payment date"	Section 4A–401
"Payment order"	Section 4A–103
"Receiving bank"	Section 4A–103
"Security procedure"	Section 4A–201
"Sender"	Section 4A–103

(c) The following definitions in Article 4 apply to this Article:

"Clearing house"	Section 4–104
"Item"	Section 4–104
"Suspends payments"	Section 4–104

(d) In addition, Article 1 contains general definitions and principles of construction and interpretation applicable throughout this Article.

§ 4A-106. Time Payment Order Is Received.

(a) The time of receipt of a payment order or communication cancelling or amending a payment order is determined by the rules applicable to receipt of a notice stated in Section 1–201(27). A receiving bank may fix a cut-off time or times on a funds-transfer business day for the receipt and processing of payment orders and communications cancelling or amending payment orders. Different cut-off times may apply to payment orders, cancellations, or amendments, or to different categories of payment orders, cancellations, or amendments. A cut-off time may apply to senders generally or different cut-off times may apply to different senders or categories of payment orders. If a payment order or communication cancelling or amending a payment order is received after the close of a funds-transfer

business day or after the appropriate cut-off time on a funds-transfer business day, the receiving bank may treat the payment order or communication as received at the opening of the next funds-transfer business day.

(b) If this Article refers to an execution date or payment date or states a day on which a receiving bank is required to take action, and the date or day does not fall on a funds-transfer business day, the next day that is a funds-transfer business day is treated as the date or day stated, unless the contrary is stated in this Article.

§ 4A-107. Federal Reserve Regulations and Operating Circulars.

Regulations of the Board of Governors of the Federal Reserve System and operating circulars of the Federal Reserve Banks supersede any inconsistent provision of this Article to the extent of the inconsistency.

§ 4A-108. Exclusion of Consumer Transactions Governed by Federal Law.

This Article does not apply to a funds transfer any part of which is governed by the Electronic Fund Transfer Act of 1978 (Title XX, Public Law 95–630, 92 Stat. 3728, 15 U.S.C. § 1693 et seq.) as amended from time to time.

PART 2: Issue and Acceptance of Payment Order

§ 4A-201. Security Procedure.

"Security procedure" means a procedure established by agreement of a customer and a receiving bank for the purpose of (i) verifying that a payment order or communication amending or cancelling a payment order is that of the customer, or (ii) detecting error in the transmission or the content of the payment order or communication. A security procedure may require the use of algorithms or other codes, identifying words or numbers, encryption, callback procedures, or similar security devices. Comparison of a signature on a payment order or communication with an authorized specimen signature of the customer is not by itself a security procedure.

§ 4A-202. Authorized and Verified Payment Orders.

(a) A payment order received by the receiving bank is the authorized order of the person identified as sender if that person authorized the order or is otherwise bound by it under the law of agency.

(b) If a bank and its customer have agreed that the authenticity of payment orders issued to the bank in the name of the customer as sender will be verified pursuant to a security procedure, a payment order received by the receiving bank is effective as the order of the customer, whether or not authorized, if (i) the security procedure is a commercially reasonable method of providing security against unauthorized payment orders, and (ii) the bank proves that it accepted the payment order in good faith and in compliance with the security procedure and any written agreement or instruction of the customer restricting acceptance of payment orders issued in the name of the customer. The bank is not required to follow an instruction that violates a written agreement with the customer or notice of which is not received at a time and in a manner affording the bank a reasonable opportunity to act on it before the payment order is accepted.

(c) Commercial reasonableness of a security procedure is a question of law to be determined by considering the wishes of the customer expressed to the bank, the circumstances of the customer known to the bank, including the size, type, and frequency of payment orders normally issued by the customer to the bank, alternative security procedures offered to the customer, and security procedures in general use by customers and receiving banks similarly situated. A security procedure is deemed to be commercially reasonable if (i) the security procedure was chosen by the customer after the bank offered, and the customer refused, a security procedure that was commercially reasonable for that customer, and (ii) the customer expressly agreed in writing to be bound by any payment order, whether or not authorized, issued in its name and accepted by the bank in compliance with the security procedure chosen by the customer.

(d) The term "sender" in this Article includes the customer in whose name a payment order is issued if the order is the authorized order of the customer under subsection (a), or it is effective as the order of the customer under subsection (b).

(e) This section applies to amendments and cancellations of payment orders to the same extent it applies to payment orders.

(f) Except as provided in this section and in Section 4A–203(a)(1), rights and obligations arising under this section or Section 4A–203 may not be varied by agreement.

§ 4A-203. Unenforceability of Certain Verified Payment Orders.

(a) If an accepted payment order is not, under Section 4A–202(a), an authorized order of a customer identified as sender, but is effective as an order of the customer pursuant to Section 4A–202(b), the following rules apply:

(1) By express written agreement, the receiving bank may limit the extent to which it is entitled to enforce or retain payment of the payment order.

(2) The receiving bank is not entitled to enforce or retain payment of the payment order if the customer proves that the order was not caused, directly or indirectly, by a person (i) entrusted at any time with duties to act for the customer with respect to payment orders or the security procedure, or (ii) who obtained access to transmitting facilities of the customer or who obtained, from a source controlled by the customer and without authority of the receiving bank, information facilitating breach of the security procedure, regardless of how the information was obtained or whether the customer was at fault. Information includes any access device, computer software, or the like.

(b) This section applies to amendments of payment orders to the same extent it applies to payment orders.

§ 4A-204. Refund of Payment and Duty of Customer to Report with Respect to Unauthorized Payment Order.

(a) If a receiving bank accepts a payment order issued in the name of its customer as sender which is (i) not authorized and not effective as the order of the customer under Section 4A–202, or (ii) not enforceable, in whole or in part, against the customer under Section 4A–203, the bank shall refund any payment of the payment order received from the customer to the extent the bank is not entitled to enforce payment and shall pay interest on the refundable amount calculated from the date the bank received payment to the date of the refund. However, the customer is not entitled to interest from the bank on the amount to be refunded if the customer fails to exercise ordinary care to determine that the order was not authorized by the customer and to notify the bank of the relevant facts within a reasonable time not exceeding 90 days after the date the customer received notification from the bank that the order was accepted or that the customer's account was debited with respect to the order. The bank is not entitled to any recovery from the customer on account of a failure by the customer to give notification as stated in this section.

(b) Reasonable time under subsection (a) may be fixed by agreement as stated in Section 1–204(1), but the obligation of a receiving bank to refund payment as stated in subsection (a) may not otherwise be varied by agreement.

§ 4A-205. Erroneous Payment Orders.

(a) If an accepted payment order was transmitted pursuant to a security procedure for the detection of error and the payment order (i) erroneously instructed payment to a beneficiary not intended by the sender, (ii) erroneously instructed payment in an amount greater than the amount intended by the sender, or (iii) was an erroneously transmitted duplicate of a payment order previously sent by the sender, the following rules apply:

(1) If the sender proves that the sender or a person acting on behalf of the sender pursuant to Section 4A–206 complied with the security procedure and that the error would have been detected if the receiving bank had also complied, the sender is not obliged to pay the order to the extent stated in paragraphs (2) and (3).

(2) If the funds transfer is completed on the basis of an erroneous payment order described in clause (i) or (iii) of subsection (a), the sender is not obliged to pay the order and the receiving bank is entitled to recover from the beneficiary any amount paid to the beneficiary to the extent allowed by the law governing mistake and restitution.

(3) If the funds transfer is completed on the basis of a payment order described in clause (ii) of subsection (a), the sender is not obliged to pay the order to the extent the amount received by the beneficiary is greater than the amount intended by the sender. In that case, the receiving bank is entitled to recover from the beneficiary the excess amount received to the extent allowed by the law governing mistake and restitution.

(b) If (i) the sender of an erroneous payment order described in subsection (a) is not obliged to pay all or part of the order, and (ii) the sender receives notification from the receiving bank that the order was accepted by the bank or that the sender's account was debited with respect to the order, the sender has a duty to exercise ordinary care, on the basis of information available to the sender, to discover the error with respect to the order and to advise the bank of the relevant facts within a reasonable time, not exceeding 90 days, after the bank's notification was received by the sender. If the bank proves that the sender failed to perform that duty, the sender is liable to the bank for the loss the bank proves it incurred as a result of the failure, but the liability of the sender may not exceed the amount of the sender's order.

(c) This section applies to amendments to payment orders to the same extent it applies to payment orders.

§ 4A-206. Transmission of Payment Order through Funds-Transfer or Other Communication System.

(a) If a payment order addressed to a receiving bank is transmitted to a funds-transfer system or other third party communication system for transmittal to the bank, the system is deemed to be an agent of the sender for the purpose of transmitting the payment order to the bank. If there is a discrepancy between the terms of the payment order transmitted to the system and the terms of the payment order transmitted by the system to the bank, the terms of the payment order of the sender are those transmitted by the system. This section does not apply to a funds-transfer system of the Federal Reserve Banks.

(b) This section applies to cancellations and amendments to payment orders to the same extent it applies to payment orders.

§ 4A-207. Misdescription of Beneficiary.

(a) Subject to subsection (b), if, in a payment order received by the beneficiary's bank, the name, bank account number, or other identification of the beneficiary refers to a nonexistent or unidentifiable person or account, no person has rights as a beneficiary of the order and acceptance of the order cannot occur.

(b) If a payment order received by the beneficiary's bank identifies the beneficiary both by name and by an identifying or bank account number and the name and number identify different persons, the following rules apply:

(1) Except as otherwise provided in subsection (c), if the beneficiary's bank does not know that the name and number refer to different persons, it may rely on the number as the proper identification of the beneficiary of the order. The beneficiary's bank need not determine whether the name and number refer to the same person.

(2) If the beneficiary's bank pays the person identified by name or knows that the name and number identify different persons, no person has rights as beneficiary except the person paid by the beneficiary's bank if that person was entitled to receive payment from the originator of the funds transfer. If no person has rights as beneficiary, acceptance of the order cannot occur.

(c) If (i) a payment order described in subsection (b) is accepted, (ii) the originator's payment order described the beneficiary inconsistently by name and number, and (iii) the beneficiary's bank pays the person identified by number as permitted by subsection (b)(1), the following rules apply:

(1) If the originator is a bank, the originator is obliged to pay its order.

(2) If the originator is not a bank and proves that the person identified by number was not entitled to receive payment from the originator, the originator is not obliged to pay its order unless the originator's bank proves that the originator, before acceptance of the originator's order, had notice that payment of a payment order issued by the originator might be made by the beneficiary's bank on the basis of an identifying or bank account number even if it identifies a person different from the named beneficiary. Proof of notice may be made by any admissible evidence. The originator's bank satisfies the burden of proof if it proves that the originator, before the payment order was accepted, signed a writing stating the information to which the notice relates.

(d) In a case governed by subsection (b)(1), if the beneficiary's bank rightfully pays the person identified by number and that person was not entitled to receive payment from the originator, the amount paid may be recovered from that person to the extent allowed by the law governing mistake and restitution as follows:

(1) If the originator is obliged to pay its payment order as stated in subsection (c), the originator has the right to recover.

(2) If the originator is not a bank and is not obliged to pay its payment order, the originator's bank has the right to recover.

§ 4A-208. Misdescription of Intermediary Bank or Beneficiary's Bank.

(a) This subsection applies to a payment order identifying an intermediary bank or the beneficiary's bank only by an identifying number.

(1) The receiving bank may rely on the number as the proper identification of the intermediary or beneficiary's bank and need not determine whether the number identifies a bank.

(2) The sender is obliged to compensate the receiving bank for any loss and expenses incurred by the receiving bank as a result of its reliance on the number in executing or attempting to execute the order.

(b) This subsection applies to a payment order identifying an intermediary bank or the beneficiary's bank both by name and an identifying number if the name and number identify different persons.

(1) If the sender is a bank, the receiving bank may rely on the number as the proper identification of the intermediary or beneficiary's bank if the receiving bank, when it executes the sender's order, does not know that the name and number identify different persons. The receiving bank need not determine whether the name and number refer to the same person or whether the number refers to a bank. The sender is obliged to compensate the receiving bank for any loss and expenses

incurred by the receiving bank as a result of its reliance on the number in executing or attempting to execute the order.

(2) If the sender is not a bank and the receiving bank proves that the sender, before the payment order was accepted, had notice that the receiving bank might rely on the number as the proper identification of the intermediary or beneficiary's bank even if it identifies a person different from the bank identified by name, the rights and obligations of the sender and the receiving bank are governed by subsection (b)(1), as though the sender were a bank. Proof of notice may be made by any admissible evidence. The receiving bank satisfies the burden of proof if it proves that the sender, before the payment order was accepted, signed a writing stating the information to which the notice relates.

(3) Regardless of whether the sender is a bank, the receiving bank may rely on the name as the proper identification of the intermediary or beneficiary's bank if the receiving bank, at the time it executes the sender's order, does not know that the name and number identify different persons. The receiving bank need not determine whether the name and number refer to the same person.

(4) If the receiving bank knows that the name and number identify different persons, reliance on either the name or the number in executing the sender's payment order is a breach of the obligation stated in Section 4A–302(a)(1).

§ 4A-209. Acceptance of Payment Order.

(a) Subject to subsection (d), a receiving bank other than the beneficiary's bank accepts a payment order when it executes the order.

(b) Subject to subsections (c) and (d), a beneficiary's bank accepts a payment order at the earliest of the following times:

(1) When the bank (i) pays the beneficiary as stated in Section 4A–405(a) or 4A–405(b), or (ii) notifies the beneficiary of receipt of the order or that the account of the beneficiary has been credited with respect to the order unless the notice indicates that the bank is rejecting the order or that funds with respect to the order may not be withdrawn or used until receipt of payment from the sender of the order;

(2) When the bank receives payment of the entire amount of the sender's order pursuant to Section 4A–403(a)(1) or 4A–403(a)(2); or

(3) The opening of the next funds-transfer business day of the bank following the payment date of the order if, at that time, the amount of the sender's order is fully covered by a withdrawable credit balance in an authorized account of the sender or the bank has otherwise received full payment from the sender, unless the order was rejected before that time or is rejected within (i) one hour after that time, or (ii) one hour after the opening of the next business day of the sender following the payment date if that time is later. If notice of rejection is received by the sender after the payment date and the authorized account of the sender does not bear interest, the bank is obliged to pay interest to the sender on the amount of the order for the number of days elapsing after the payment date to the day the sender receives notice or learns that the order was not accepted, counting that day as an elapsed day. If the withdrawable credit balance during that period falls below the amount of the order, the amount of interest payable is reduced accordingly.

(c) Acceptance of a payment order cannot occur before the order is received by the receiving bank. Acceptance does not occur under subsection (b)(2) or (b)(3) if the beneficiary of the payment order does not have an account with the receiving bank, the account has been closed, or the receiving bank is not permitted by law to receive credits for the beneficiary's account.

(d) A payment order issued to the originator's bank cannot be accepted until the payment date if the bank is the beneficiary's bank, or the execution date if the bank is not the beneficiary's bank. If the originator's bank executes the originator's payment order before the execution date or pays the beneficiary of the originator's payment order before the payment date and the payment order is subsequently cancelled pursuant to Section 4A–211(b), the bank may recover from the beneficiary any payment received to the extent allowed by the law governing mistake and restitution.

§ 4A-210. Rejection of Payment Order.

(a) A payment order is rejected by the receiving bank by a notice of rejection transmitted to the sender orally, electronically, or in writing. A notice of rejection need not use any particular words and is sufficient if it indicates that the receiving bank is rejecting the order or will not execute or pay the order. Rejection is effective when the notice is given if transmission is by a means that is reasonable in the circumstances. If notice of rejection is given by a means that is not reasonable, rejection is effective when the notice is received. If an agreement of the sender and receiving bank establishes the means to be used to reject a payment order, (i) any means complying with the agreement is reasonable and (ii) any means not complying is not reasonable unless no significant delay in receipt of the notice resulted from the use of the noncomplying means.

(b) This subsection applies if a receiving bank other than the beneficiary's bank fails to execute a payment order despite the existence on the execution date of a withdrawable credit balance in an authorized account of the sender sufficient to cover the order. If the sender does not receive notice of rejection of the order on the execution date and the authorized account of the sender does not bear interest, the bank is obliged to pay interest to the sender on the amount of the order for the number of days elapsing after the execution date to the earlier of the day the order is cancelled pursuant to Section 4A–211(d) or the day the sender receives notice or learns that the order was not executed, counting the final day of the period as an elapsed day. If the withdrawable credit balance during that period falls below the amount of the order, the amount of interest is reduced accordingly.

(c) If a receiving bank suspends payments, all unaccepted payment orders issued to it are are deemed rejected at the time the bank suspends payments.

(d) Acceptance of a payment order precludes a later rejection of the order. Rejection of a payment order precludes a later acceptance of the order.

§ 4A-211. Cancellation and Amendment of Payment Order.

(a) A communication of the sender of a payment order cancelling or amending the order may be transmitted to the receiving bank orally, electronically, or in writing. If a security procedure is in effect between the sender and the receiving bank, the communication is not effective to cancel or amend the order unless the communication is verified pursuant to the security procedure or the bank agrees to the cancellation or amendment.

(b) Subject to subsection (a), a communication by the sender cancelling or amending a payment order is effective to cancel or amend the order if notice of the communication is received at a time and in a manner affording the receiving bank a reasonable opportunity to act on the communication before the bank accepts the payment order.

(c) After a payment order has been accepted, cancellation or amendment of the order is not effective unless the receiving bank agrees or a funds-transfer system rule allows cancellation or amendment without agreement of the bank.

(1) With respect to a payment order accepted by a receiving bank other than the beneficiary's bank, cancellation or amendment is not effective unless a conforming cancellation or amendment of the payment order issued by the receiving bank is also made.

(2) With respect to a payment order accepted by the beneficiary's bank, cancellation or amendment is not effective unless the order was issued in execution of an unauthorized payment order, or because of a mistake by a sender in the funds transfer which resulted in the issuance of a payment order (i) that is a duplicate of a payment order previously issued by the sender, (ii) that orders payment to a beneficiary not entitled to receive payment from the originator, or (iii) that orders payment in an amount greater than the amount the beneficiary was entitled to receive from the originator. If the payment order is cancelled or amended, the beneficiary's bank is entitled to recover from the beneficiary any amount paid to the beneficiary to the extent allowed by the law governing mistake and restitution.

(d) An unaccepted payment order is cancelled by operation of law at the close of the fifth funds-transfer business day of the receiving bank after the execution date or payment date of the order.

(e) A cancelled payment order cannot be accepted. If an accepted payment order is cancelled, the acceptance is nullified and no person has any right or obligation based on the acceptance. Amendment of a payment order is deemed to be cancellation of the original order at the time of amendment and issue of a new payment order in the amended form at the same time.

(f) Unless otherwise provided in an agreement of the parties or in a funds-transfer system rule, if the receiving bank, after accepting a payment order, agrees to cancellation or amendment of the order by the sender or is bound by a funds-transfer system rule allowing cancellation or amendment without the bank's agreement, the sender, whether or not cancellation or amendment is effective, is liable to the bank for any loss and expenses, including reasonable attorney's fees, incurred by the bank as a result of the cancellation or amendment or attempted cancellation or amendment.

(g) A payment order is not revoked by the death or legal incapacity of the sender unless the receiving bank knows of the death or of an adjudication of incapacity by a court of competent jurisdiction and has reasonable opportunity to act before acceptance of the order.

(h) A funds-transfer system rule is not effective to the extent it conflicts with subsection (c)(2).

§ 4A-212. Liability and Duty of Receiving Bank Regarding Unaccepted Payment Order.

If a receiving bank fails to accept a payment order that it is obliged by express agreement to accept, the bank is liable for breach of the agreement to the extent provided in the agreement or in this Article, but does not otherwise have any duty to accept a payment order or, before acceptance, to take any action, or refrain from taking action, with respect to the order except as provided in this Article or by express agreement. Liability based on acceptance arises only when acceptance occurs as stated in Section 4A–209, and liability is limited to that provided in this Article. A receiving bank is not the agent of the sender or beneficiary of the payment order it accepts, or of any other party to the funds transfer, and the bank owes no duty to any party to the funds transfer except as provided in this Article or by express agreement.

PART 3: Execution of Sender's Payment Order by Receiving Bank

§ 4A-301. Execution and Execution Date.

(a) A payment order is "executed" by the receiving bank when it issues a payment order intended to carry out the payment order received by the bank. A payment order received by the beneficiary's bank can be accepted but cannot be executed.

(b) "Execution date" of a payment order means the day on which the receiving bank may properly issue a payment order in execution of the sender's order. The execution date may be determined by instruction of the sender but cannot be earlier than the day the order is received and, unless otherwise determined, is the day the order is received. If the sender's instruction states a payment date, the execution date is the payment date or an earlier date on which execution is reasonably necessary to allow payment to the beneficiary on the payment date.

§ 4A-302. Obligations of Receiving Bank in Execution of Payment Order.

(a) Except as provided in subsections (b) through (d), if the receiving bank accepts a payment order pursuant to Section 4A–209(a), the bank has the following obligations in executing the order:

(1) The receiving bank is obliged to issue, on the execution date, a payment order complying with the sender's order and to follow the sender's instructions concerning (i) any intermediary bank or funds-transfer system to be used in carrying out the funds transfer, or (ii) the means by which payment orders are to be transmitted in the funds transfer. If the originator's bank issues a payment order to an intermediary bank, the originator's bank is obliged to instruct the intermediary bank according to the instruction of the originator. An intermediary bank in the funds transfer is similarly bound by an instruction given to it by the sender of the payment order it accepts.

(2) If the sender's instruction states that the funds transfer is to be carried out telephonically or by wire transfer or otherwise indicates that the funds transfer is to be carried out by the most expeditious means, the receiving bank is obliged to transmit its payment order by the most expeditious available means, and to instruct any intermediary bank accordingly. If a sender's instruction states a payment date, the receiving bank is obliged to transmit its payment order at a time and by means reasonably necessary to allow payment to the beneficiary on the payment date or as soon thereafter as is feasible.

(b) Unless otherwise instructed, a receiving bank executing a payment order may (i) use any funds-transfer system if use of that system is reasonable in the circumstances, and (ii) issue a payment order to the beneficiary's bank or to an intermediary bank through which a payment order conforming to the sender's order can expeditiously be issued to the beneficiary's bank if the receiving bank exercises ordinary care in the selection of the intermediary bank. A receiving bank is not required to follow an instruction of the sender designating a funds-transfer system to be used in carrying out the funds transfer if the receiving bank, in good faith, determines that it is not feasible to follow the instruction or that following the instruction would unduly delay completion of the funds transfer.

(c) Unless subsection (a)(2) applies or the receiving bank is otherwise instructed, the bank may execute a payment order by transmitting its payment order by first class mail or by any means reasonable in the circumstances. If the receiving bank is instructed to execute the sender's order by transmitting its payment order by a particular means, the receiving bank may issue its payment order by the means stated or by any means as expeditious as the means stated.

(d) Unless instructed by the sender, (i) the receiving bank may not obtain payment of its charges for services and expenses in connection with the execution of the sender's order by issuing a payment order in an amount equal to the amount of the sender's order less the amount of the charges, and (ii) may not instruct a subsequent receiving bank to obtain payment of its charges in the same manner.

§ 4A-303. Erroneous Execution of Payment Order.

(a) A receiving bank that (i) executes the payment order of the sender by issuing a payment order in an amount greater than the amount of the sender's order, or (ii) issues a payment order in execution of the sender's order and then issues a duplicate order, is entitled to payment of the amount of the sender's order under Section 4A–402(c) if that subsection is otherwise satisfied. The bank is entitled to recover from the beneficiary of the erroneous order the excess payment received to the extent allowed by the law governing mistake and restitution.

(b) A receiving bank that executes the payment order of the sender by issuing a payment order in an amount less than the amount of the sender's order is entitled to payment of the amount of the sender's order under Section 4A–402(c) if (i) that subsection is otherwise satisfied and (ii) the bank corrects its mistake by issuing an additional payment order for the benefit of the beneficiary of the sender's order. If the error is not corrected, the issuer of the erroneous order is entitled to receive or retain payment from the sender of the order it accepted only to the extent of the amount of the erroneous order. This subsection does not apply if the receiving bank executes the sender's payment order by issuing a payment order in an amount less than the amount of the sender's order for the purpose of obtaining payment of its charges for services and expenses pursuant to instruction of the sender.

(c) If a receiving bank executes the payment order of the sender by issuing a payment order to a beneficiary different from the beneficiary of the sender's order and the funds transfer is completed on the basis of that error, the sender of the payment order that was erroneously executed and all previous senders in the funds transfer are not obliged to pay the payment orders they issued. The issuer of the erroneous order is entitled to recover from the beneficiary of the order the payment received to the extent allowed by the law governing mistake and restitution.

§ 4A-304. Duty of Sender to Report Erroneously Executed Payment Order.

If the sender of a payment order that is erroneously executed as stated in Section 4A–303 receives notification from the receiving bank that the order was executed or that the sender's account was debited with respect to the order, the sender has a duty to exercise ordinary care to determine, on the basis of information available to the sender, that the order was erroneously executed and to notify the bank of the relevant facts within a reasonable time not exceeding 90 days after the notification from the bank was received by the sender. If the sender fails to perform that duty, the bank is not obliged to pay interest on any amount refundable to the sender under Section 4A–402(d) for the period before the bank learns of the execution error. The bank is not entitled to any recovery from the sender on account of a failure by the sender to perform the duty stated in this section.

§ 4A-305. Liability for Late or Improper Execution or Failure to Execute Payment Order.

(a) If a funds transfer is completed but execution of a payment order by the receiving bank in breach of Section 4A–302 results in delay in payment to the beneficiary, the bank is obliged to pay interest to either the originator or the beneficiary of the funds transfer for the period of delay caused by the improper execution. Except as provided in subsection (c), additional damages are not recoverable.

(b) If execution of a payment order by a receiving bank in breach of Section 4A–302 results in (i) noncompletion of the funds transfer, (ii) failure to use an intermediary bank designated by the originator, or (iii) issuance of a payment order that does not comply with the terms of the payment order of the originator, the bank is liable to the originator for its expenses in the funds transfer and for incidental expenses and interest losses, to the extent not covered by subsection (a), resulting from the improper execution. Except as provided in subsection (c), additional damages are not recoverable.

(c) In addition to the amounts payable under subsections (a) and (b), damages, including consequential damages, are recoverable to the extent provided in an express written agreement of the receiving bank.

(d) If a receiving bank fails to execute a payment order it was obliged by express agreement to execute, the receiving bank is liable to the sender for its expenses in the transaction and for incidental expenses and interest losses resulting from the failure to execute. Additional damages, including consequential damages, are recoverable to the extent provided in an express written agreement of the receiving bank, but are not otherwise recoverable.

(e) Reasonable attorney's fees are recoverable if demand for compensation under subsection (a) or (b) is made and refused before an action is brought on the claim. If a claim is made for breach of an agreement under subsection (d) and the agreement does not provide for damages, reasonable attorney's fees are recoverable if demand for compensation under subsection (d) is made and refused before an action is brought on the claim.

(f) Except as stated in this section, the liability of a receiving bank under subsections (a) and (b) may not be varied by agreement.

PART 4: Payment

§ 4A-401. Payment Date.

"Payment date" of a payment order means the day on which the amount of the order is payable to the beneficiary by the beneficiary's bank. The payment date may be determined by instruction of the sender but cannot be earlier than the day the order is received by the beneficiary's bank and, unless otherwise determined, is the day the order is received by the beneficiary's bank.

§ 4A-402. Obligation of Sender to Pay Receiving Bank.

(a) This section is subject to Sections 4A–205 and 4A–207.

(b) With respect to a payment order issued to the beneficiary's bank, acceptance of the order by the bank obliges the sender to pay the bank the amount of the order, but payment is not due until the payment date of the order.

(c) This subsection is subject to subsection (e) and to Section 4A–303. With respect to a payment order issued to a receiving bank other than the beneficiary's bank, acceptance of the order by the receiving bank obliges the sender to pay the bank the amount of the sender's order. Payment by the sender is not due until the execution date of the sender's order. The obligation of that sender to pay its payment order is excused if the funds transfer is not completed by acceptance by the beneficiary's bank of a payment order instructing payment to the beneficiary of that sender's payment order.

(d) If the sender of a payment order pays the order and was not obliged to pay all or part of the amount paid, the bank receiving payment is obliged to refund payment to the extent the sender was not obliged to pay. Except as provided in Sections 4A–204 and 4A–304, interest is payable on the refundable amount from the date of payment.

(e) If a funds transfer is not completed as stated in subsection (c) and an intermediary bank is obliged to refund payment as stated in subsection (d) but is unable to do so because not permitted by applicable law or because the bank suspends payments, a sender in the funds transfer that executed a payment order in compliance with an instruction, as stated in Section 4A–302(a)(1), to route the funds transfer through that intermediary bank is entitled to receive or retain payment from the sender of the payment order that it accepted. The first sender in the funds transfer that issued an instruction requiring routing through that intermediary bank is subrogated to the right of the bank that paid the intermediary bank to refund as stated in subsection (d).

(f) The right of the sender of a payment order to be excused from the obligation to pay the order as stated in subsection (c) or to receive refund under subsection (d) may not be varied by agreement.

§ 4A-403. Payment by Sender to Receiving Bank.

(a) Payment of the sender's obligation under Section 4A–402 to pay the receiving bank occurs as follows:

(1) If the sender is a bank, payment occurs when the receiving bank receives final settlement of the obligation through a Federal Reserve Bank or through a funds-transfer system.

(2) If the sender is a bank and the sender (i) credited an account of the receiving bank with the sender, or (ii) caused an account of the receiving bank in another bank to be credited, payment occurs when the credit is withdrawn or, if not withdrawn, at midnight of the day on which the credit is withdrawable and the receiving bank learns of that fact.

(3) If the receiving bank debits an account of the sender with the receiving bank, payment occurs when the debit is made to the extent the debit is covered by a withdrawable credit balance in the account.

(b) If the sender and receiving bank are members of a funds-transfer system that nets obligations multilaterally among participants, the receiving bank receives final settlement when settlement is complete in accordance with the rules of the system. The obligation of the sender to pay the amount of a payment order transmitted through the funds-transfer system may be satisfied, to the extent permitted by the rules of the system, by setting off and applying against the sender's obligation the right of the sender to receive payment from the receiving bank of the amount of any other payment order transmitted to the sender by the receiving bank through the funds-transfer system. The aggregate balance of obligations owed by each sender to each receiving bank in the funds-transfer system may be satisfied, to the extent permitted by the rules of the system, by setting off and applying against that balance the aggregate balance of obligations owed to the sender by other members of the system. The aggregate balance is determined after the right of setoff stated in the second sentence of this subsection has been exercised.

(c) If two banks transmit payment orders to each other under an agreement that settlement of the obligations of each bank to the other under Section 4A–402 will be made at the end of the day or other period, the total amount owed with respect to all orders transmitted by one bank shall be set off against the total amount owed with respect to all orders transmitted by the other bank. To the extent of the setoff, each bank has made payment to the other.

(d) In a case not covered by subsection (a), the time when payment of the sender's obligation under Section 4A–402(b) or 4A–402(c) occurs is governed by applicable principles of law that determine when an obligation is satisfied.

§ 4A-404. Obligation of Beneficiary's Bank to Pay and Give Notice to Beneficiary.

(a) Subject to Sections 4A–211(e), 4A–405(d), and 4A–405(e), if a beneficiary's bank accepts a payment order, the bank is obliged to pay the amount of the order to the beneficiary of the order. Payment is due on the payment date of the order, but if acceptance occurs on the payment date after the close of the funds-transfer business day of the bank, payment is due on the next funds-transfer business day. If the bank refuses to pay after demand by the beneficiary and receipt of notice of particular circumstances that will give rise to consequential damages as a result of nonpayment, the beneficiary may recover damages resulting from the refusal to pay to the extent the bank had notice of the damages, unless the bank proves that it did not pay because of a reasonable doubt concerning the right of the beneficiary to payment.

(b) If a payment order accepted by the beneficiary's bank instructs payment to an account of the beneficiary, the bank is obliged to notify the beneficiary of receipt of the order before midnight of the next funds-transfer business day following the payment date. If the payment order does not instruct payment to an account of the beneficiary, the bank is required to notify the beneficiary only if notice is required by the order. Notice may be given by first class mail or any other means reasonable in the circumstances. If the bank fails to give the required notice, the bank is obliged to pay interest to the beneficiary on the amount of the payment order from the day notice should have been given until the day the beneficiary learned of receipt of the payment order by the bank. No other damages are recoverable. Reasonable attorney's fees are also recoverable if demand for interest is made and refused before an action is brought on the claim.

(c) The right of a beneficiary to receive payment and damages as stated in subsection (a) may not be varied by agreement or a funds-transfer system rule. The right of a beneficiary to be notified as stated in subsection (b) may be varied by agreement of the beneficiary or by a funds-transfer system rule if the beneficiary is notified of the rule before initiation of the funds transfer.

§ 4A-405. Payment by Beneficiary's Bank to Beneficiary.

(a) If the beneficiary's bank credits an account of the beneficiary of a payment order, payment of the bank's obligation under Section 4A–404(a) occurs when and to the extent (i) the beneficiary is notified of the right to withdraw the credit, (ii) the bank lawfully applies the credit to a debt of the beneficiary, or (iii) funds with respect to the order are otherwise made available to the beneficiary by the bank.

(b) If the beneficiary's bank does not credit an account of the beneficiary of a payment order, the time when payment of the bank's obligation under Section 4A–404(a) occurs is governed by principles of law that determine when an obligation is satisfied.

(c) Except as stated in subsections (d) and (e), if the beneficiary's bank pays the beneficiary of a payment order under a condition to payment or agreement of the beneficiary giving the bank the right to recover payment from the beneficiary if the bank does not receive payment of the order, the condition to payment or agreement is not enforceable.

(d) A funds-transfer system rule may provide that payments made to beneficiaries of funds transfers made through the system are provisional until receipt of payment by the beneficiary's bank of the payment order it accepted. A beneficiary's bank that makes a payment that is provisional under the rule is entitled to refund from the beneficiary if (i) the rule requires that both the beneficiary and the originator be given notice of the provisional nature of the payment before the funds transfer is initiated, (ii) the beneficiary, the beneficiary's bank, and the originator's bank agreed to be bound by the rule, and (iii) the beneficiary's bank did not receive payment of the payment order that it accepted. If the beneficiary is obliged to refund payment to the beneficiary's bank, acceptance of the payment order by the beneficiary's bank is nullified and no payment by the originator of the funds transfer to the beneficiary occurs under Section 4A–406.

(e) This subsection applies to a funds transfer that includes a payment order transmitted over a funds-transfer system that (i) nets obligations multilaterally among participants, and (ii) has in effect a loss-sharing agreement among participants for the purpose of providing funds necessary to complete settlement of the obligations of one or more participants that do not meet their settlement obligations. If the beneficiary's bank in the funds transfer accepts a payment order and the system fails to complete settlement pursuant to its rules with respect to any payment order in the funds transfer, (i) the acceptance by the beneficiary's bank is nullified and no person has any right or obligation based on the acceptance, (ii) the beneficiary's bank is entitled to recover payment from the beneficiary, (iii) no payment by the originator to the beneficiary occurs under Section 4A–406, and (iv) subject to Section 4A–402(e), each sender in the funds transfer is excused from its obligation to pay its payment order under Section 4A–402(c) because the funds transfer has not been completed.

§ 4A-406. Payment by Originator to Beneficiary; Discharge of Underlying Obligation.

(a) Subject to Sections 4A–211(e), 4A–405(d), and 4A–405(e), the originator of a funds transfer pays the beneficiary of the originator's payment order (i) at the time a payment order for the benefit of the beneficiary is accepted by the beneficiary's bank in the funds transfer and (ii) in an amount equal to the amount of the order accepted by the beneficiary's bank, but not more than the amount of the originator's order.

(b) If payment under subsection (a) is made to satisfy an obligation, the obligation is discharged to the same extent discharge would result from payment to the beneficiary of the same amount in money, unless (i) the payment under subsection (a) was made by a means prohibited by the contract of the beneficiary with respect to the obligation, (ii) the beneficiary, within a reasonable time after receiving notice of receipt of the order by the beneficiary's bank, notified the originator of the beneficiary's refusal of the payment, (iii) funds with respect to the order were not withdrawn by the beneficiary or applied to a debt of the beneficiary, and (iv) the beneficiary would suffer a loss that could reasonably have been avoided if payment had been made by a means complying with the contract. If payment by the originator does not result in discharge under this section, the originator is subrogated to the rights of the beneficiary to receive payment from the beneficiary's bank under Section 4A–404(a).

(c) For the purpose of determining whether discharge of an obligation occurs under subsection (b), if the beneficiary's bank accepts a payment order in an amount equal to the amount of the originator's payment order less charges of one or more receiving banks in the funds transfer, payment to the beneficiary is deemed to be in the amount of the originator's order unless upon demand by the beneficiary the originator does not pay the beneficiary the amount of the deducted charges.

(d) Rights of the originator or of the beneficiary of a funds transfer under this section may be varied only by agreement of the originator and the beneficiary.

PART 5: Miscellaneous Provisions

§ 4A-501. Variation by Agreement and Effect of Funds-Transfer System Rule.

(a) Except as otherwise provided in this Article, the rights and obligations of a party to a funds transfer may be varied by agreement of the affected party.

(b) "Funds-transfer system rule" means a rule of an association of banks (i) governing transmission of payment orders by means of a funds-transfer system of the association or rights and obligations with respect to those orders, or (ii) to the extent the rule governs rights and obligations between banks that are parties to a funds transfer in which a Federal Reserve Bank, acting as an intermediary bank, sends a payment order to the beneficiary's bank. Except as otherwise provided in this Article, a funds-transfer system rule governing rights and obligations between participating banks using the system may be effective even if the rule conflicts with this Article and indirectly affects another party to the funds transfer who does not consent to the rule. A funds-transfer system rule may also govern rights and obligations of parties other than participating banks using the system to the extent stated in Sections 4A–404(c), 4A–405(d), and 4A–507(c).

§ 4A-502. Creditor Process Served on Receiving Bank; Setoff by Beneficiary's Bank.

(a) As used in this section, "creditor process" means levy, attachment, garnishment, notice of lien, sequestration, or similar process issued by or on behalf of a creditor or other claimant with respect to an account.

(b) This subsection applies to creditor process with respect to an authorized account of the sender of a payment order if the creditor process is served on the receiving bank. For the purpose of determining rights with respect to the creditor process, if the receiving bank accepts the payment order the balance in the authorized account is deemed to be reduced by the amount of the payment order to the extent the bank did not otherwise receive payment of the order, unless the creditor process is served at a time and in a manner affording the bank a reasonable opportunity to act on it before the bank accepts the payment order.

(c) If a beneficiary's bank has received a payment order for payment to the beneficiary's account in the bank, the following rules apply:

(1) The bank may credit the beneficiary's account. The amount credited may be set off against an obligation owed by the beneficiary to the bank or may be applied to satisfy creditor process served on the bank with respect to the account.

(2) The bank may credit the beneficiary's account and allow withdrawal of the amount credited unless creditor process with respect to the account is served at a time and in a manner affording the bank a reasonable opportunity to act to prevent withdrawal.

(3) If creditor process with respect to the beneficiary's account has been served and the bank has had a reasonable opportunity to act on it, the bank may not reject the payment order except for a reason unrelated to the service of process.

(d) Creditor process with respect to a payment by the originator to the beneficiary pursuant to a funds transfer may be served only on the beneficiary's bank with respect to the debt owed by that bank to the beneficiary. Any other bank served with the creditor process is not obliged to act with respect to the process.

§ 4A-503. Injunction or Restraining Order with Respect to Funds Transfer.

For proper cause and in compliance with applicable law, a court may restrain (i) a person from issuing a payment order to initiate a funds transfer, (ii) an originator's bank from executing the payment order of the originator, or (iii) the beneficiary's bank from releasing funds to the beneficiary or the beneficiary from withdrawing the funds. A court may not otherwise restrain a person from issuing a payment order, paying or receiving payment of a payment order, or otherwise acting with respect to a funds transfer.

§ 4A-504. Order in Which Items and Payment Orders May Be Charged to Account; Order of Withdrawals from Account.

(a) If a receiving bank has received more than one payment order of the sender or one or more payment orders and other items that are payable from the sender's account, the bank may charge the sender's account with respect to the various orders and items in any sequence.

(b) In determining whether a credit to an account has been withdrawn by the holder of the account or applied to a debt of the holder of the account, credits first made to the account are first withdrawn or applied.

§ 4A-505. Preclusion of Objection to Debit of Customer's Account.

If a receiving bank has received payment from its customer with respect to a payment order issued in the name of the customer as sender and accepted by the bank, and the customer received notification reasonably identifying the order, the customer is precluded from asserting that the bank is not entitled to retain the payment unless the customer notifies the bank of the customer's objection to the payment within one year after the notification was received by the customer.

§ 4A-506. Rate of Interest.

(a) If, under this Article, a receiving bank is obliged to pay interest with respect to a payment order issued to the bank, the amount payable may be determined (i) by agreement of the sender and receiving bank, or (ii) by a funds-transfer system rule if the payment order is transmitted through a funds-transfer system.

(b) If the amount of interest is not determined by an agreement or rule as stated in subsection (a), the amount is calculated by multiplying the applicable Federal Funds rate by the amount on which interest is payable, and then multiplying the product by the number of days for which interest is payable. The applicable Federal Funds rate is the average of the Federal Funds rates published by the Federal Reserve Bank of New York for each of the days for which interest is payable divided by 360. The Federal Funds rate for any day on which a published rate is not available is the same as the published rate for the next preceding day for which there is a published rate. If a receiving bank that accepted a payment order is required to refund payment to the sender of the order because the funds transfer was not completed, but the failure to complete was not due to any fault by the bank, the interest payable is reduced by a percentage equal to the reserve requirement on deposits of the receiving bank.

§ 4A-507. Choice of Law.

(a) The following rules apply unless the affected parties otherwise agree or subsection (c) applies:

(1) The rights and obligations between the sender of a payment order and the receiving bank are governed by the law of the jurisdiction in which the receiving bank is located.

(2) The rights and obligations between the beneficiary's bank and the beneficiary are governed by the law of the jurisdiction in which the beneficiary's bank is located.

(3) The issue of when payment is made pursuant to a funds transfer by the originator to the beneficiary is governed by the law of the jurisdiction in which the beneficiary's bank is located.

(b) If the parties described in each paragraph of subsection (a) have made an agreement selecting the law of a particular jurisdiction to govern rights and obligations between each other, the law of that jurisdiction governs those rights and obligations, whether or not the payment order or the funds transfer bears a reasonable relation to that jurisdiction.

(c) A funds-transfer system rule may select the law of a particular jurisdiction to govern (i) rights and obligations between participating banks with respect to payment orders transmitted or processed through the system, or (ii) the rights and obligations of some or all parties to a funds transfer any part of which is carried out by means of the system. A choice of law made pursuant to clause (i) is binding on participating banks. A choice of law made pursuant to clause (ii) is binding on the originator, other sender, or a receiving bank having notice that the funds-transfer system might be used in the funds transfer and of the choice of law by the system when the originator, other sender, or receiving bank issued or accepted a payment order. The beneficiary of a funds transfer is bound by the choice of law if, when the funds transfer is initiated, the beneficiary has notice that the funds-transfer system might be used in the funds transfer and of the choice of law by the system. The law of a jurisdiction selected pursuant to this subsection may govern, whether or not that law bears a reasonable relation to the matter in issue.

(d) In the event of inconsistency between an agreement under subsection (b) and a choice-of-law rule under subsection (c), the agreement under subsection (b) prevails.

(e) If a funds transfer is made by use of more than one funds-transfer system and there is inconsistency between choice-of-law rules of the systems, the matter in issue is governed by the law of the selected jurisdiction that has the most significant relationship to the matter in issue.

REVISED ARTICLE 5: Letters of Credit

§ 5-101. Short Title.

This article may be cited as Uniform Commercial Code—Letters of Credit.

§ 5-102. Definitions.

(a) In this article:

(1) "Adviser" means a person who, at the request of the issuer, a confirmer, or another adviser, notifies or requests another adviser to notify the beneficiary that a letter of credit has been issued, confirmed, or amended.

(2) "Applicant" means a person at whose request or for whose account a letter of credit is issued. The term includes a person who requests an issuer to issue a letter of credit on behalf of another if the person making the request undertakes an obligation to reimburse the issuer.

(3) "Beneficiary" means a person who under the terms of a letter of credit is entitled to have its complying presentation honored. The term includes a person to whom drawing rights have been transferred under a transferable letter of credit.

(4) "Confirmer" means a nominated person who undertakes, at the request or with the consent of the issuer, to honor a presentation under a letter of credit issued by another.

(5) "Dishonor" of a letter of credit means failure timely to honor or to take an interim action, such as acceptance of a draft, that may be required by the letter of credit.

(6) "Document" means a draft or other demand, document of title, investment security, certificate, invoice, or other record, statement, or representation of fact, law, right, or opinion (i) which is presented in a written or other medium permitted by the letter of credit or, unless prohibited by the letter of credit, by the standard practice referred to in Section 5–108(e) and (ii) which is capable of being examined for compliance with the terms and conditions of the letter of credit. A document may not be oral.

(7) "Good faith" means honesty in fact in the conduct or transaction concerned.

(8) "Honor" of a letter of credit means performance of the issuer's undertaking in the letter of credit to pay or deliver an item of value. Unless the letter of credit otherwise provides, "honor" occurs

   (i) upon payment,

   (ii) if the letter of credit provides for acceptance, upon acceptance of a draft and, at maturity, its payment, or

   (iii) if the letter of credit provides for incurring a deferred obligation, upon incurring the obligation and, at maturity, its performance.

(9) "Issuer" means a bank or other person that issues a letter of credit, but does not include an individual who makes an engagement for personal, family, or household purposes.

(10) "Letter of credit" means a definite undertaking that satisfies the requirements of Section 5–104 by an issuer to a beneficiary at the request or for the account of an applicant or, in the case of a financial institution, to itself or for its own account, to honor a documentary presentation by payment or delivery of an item of value.

(11) "Nominated person" means a person whom the issuer (i) designates or authorizes to pay, accept, negotiate, or otherwise give value under a letter of credit and (ii) undertakes by agreement or custom and practice to reimburse.

(12) "Presentation" means delivery of a document to an issuer or nominated person for honor or giving of value under a letter of credit.

(13) "Presenter" means a person making a presentation as or on behalf of a beneficiary or nominated person.

(14) "Record" means information that is inscribed on a tangible medium, or that is stored in an electronic or other medium and is retrievable in perceivable form.

(15) "Successor of a beneficiary" means a person who succeeds to substantially all of the rights of a beneficiary by operation of law, including a corporation with or into which the beneficiary has been merged or consolidated, an administrator, executor, personal representative, trustee in bankruptcy, debtor in possession, liquidator, and receiver.

(b) Definitions in other Articles applying to this article and the sections in which they appear are:

   "Accept" or "Acceptance" Section 3–409

   "Value" Sections 3–303, 4–211

(c) Article 1 contains certain additional general definitions and principles of construction and interpretation applicable throughout this article.

§ 5-103. Scope.

(a) This article applies to letters of credit and to certain rights and obligations arising out of transactions involving letters of credit.

(b) The statement of a rule in this article does not by itself require, imply, or negate application of the same or a different rule to a situation not provided for, or to a person not specified, in this article.

(c) With the exception of this subsection, subsections (a) and (d), Sections 5–102(a)(9) and (10), 5–106(d), and 5–114(d), and except to the extent prohibited in Sections 1–102(3) and 5–117(d), the effect of this article may be varied by agreement or by a provision stated or incorporated by reference in an undertaking. A term in an agreement or undertaking generally excusing liability or generally limiting remedies for failure to perform obligations is not sufficient to vary obligations prescribed by this article.

(d) Rights and obligations of an issuer to a beneficiary or a nominated person under a letter of credit are independent of the existence, performance, or nonperformance of a contract or arrangement out of which the letter of credit arises or which underlies it, including contracts or arrangements between the issuer and the applicant and between the applicant and the beneficiary.

§ 5-104. Formal Requirements.

A letter of credit, confirmation, advice, transfer, amendment, or cancellation may be issued in any form that is a record and is authenticated (i) by a signature or (ii) in accordance with the agreement of the parties or the standard practice referred to in Section 5–108(e).

§ 5-105. Consideration.

Consideration is not required to issue, amend, transfer, or cancel a letter of credit, advice, or confirmation.

§ 5-106. Issuance, Amendment, Cancellation, and Duration.

(a) A letter of credit is issued and becomes enforceable according to its terms against the issuer when the issuer sends or otherwise transmits it to the person requested to advise or to the beneficiary. A letter of credit is revocable only if it so provides.

(b) After a letter of credit is issued, rights and obligations of a beneficiary, applicant, confirmer, and issuer are not affected by an amendment or cancellation to which that person has not consented except to the extent the letter of credit provides that it is revocable or that the issuer may amend or cancel the letter of credit without that consent.

(c) If there is no stated expiration date or other provision that determines its duration, a letter of credit expires one year after its stated date of issuance or, if none is stated, after the date on which it is issued.

(d) A letter of credit that states that it is perpetual expires five years after its stated date of issuance, or if none is stated, after the date on which it is issued.

§ 5-107. Confirmer, Nominated Person, and Adviser.

(a) A confirmer is directly obligated on a letter of credit and has the rights and obligations of an issuer to the extent of its confirmation. The confirmer also has rights against and obligations to the issuer as if the issuer were an applicant and the confirmer had issued the letter of credit at the request and for the account of the issuer.

(b) A nominated person who is not a confirmer is not obligated to honor or otherwise give value for a presentation.

(c) A person requested to advise may decline to act as an adviser. An adviser that is not a confirmer is not obligated to honor or give value for a presentation. An adviser undertakes to the issuer and to the beneficiary accurately to advise the terms of the letter of credit, confirmation, amendment, or advice received by that person and undertakes to the beneficiary to check the apparent authenticity of the request to advise. Even if the advice is inaccurate, the letter of credit, confirmation, or amendment is enforceable as issued.

(d) A person who notifies a transferee beneficiary of the terms of a letter of credit, confirmation, amendment, or advice has the rights and obligations of an adviser under subsection (c). The terms in the notice to the transferee beneficiary may differ from the terms in any notice to the transferor beneficiary to the extent permitted by the letter of credit, confirmation, amendment, or advice received by the person who so notifies.

§ 5-108. Issuer's Rights and Obligations.

(a) Except as otherwise provided in Section 5–109, an issuer shall honor a presentation that, as determined by the standard practice referred to in subsection (e), appears on its face strictly to comply with the terms and conditions of the letter of credit. Except as otherwise provided in Section 5–113 and unless otherwise agreed with the applicant, an issuer shall dishonor a presentation that does not appear so to comply.

(b) An issuer has a reasonable time after presentation, but not beyond the end of the seventh business day of the issuer after the day of its receipt of documents:

(1) to honor,

(2) if the letter of credit provides for honor to be completed more than seven business days after presentation, to accept a draft or incur a deferred obligation, or

(3) to give notice to the presenter of discrepancies in the presentation.

(c) Except as otherwise provided in subsection (d), an issuer is precluded from asserting as a basis for dishonor any discrepancy if timely notice is not given, or any discrepancy not stated in the notice if timely notice is given.

(d) Failure to give the notice specified in subsection (b) or to mention fraud, forgery, or expiration in the notice does not preclude the issuer from asserting as a basis for dishonor fraud or forgery as described in Section 5–109(a) or expiration of the letter of credit before presentation.

(e) An issuer shall observe standard practice of financial institutions that regularly issue letters of credit. Determination of the issuer's observance of the standard practice is a matter of interpretation for the court. The court shall offer the parties a reasonable opportunity to present evidence of the standard practice.

(f) An issuer is not responsible for:

(1) the performance or nonperformance of the underlying contract, arrangement, or transaction,

(2) an act or omission of others, or

(3) observance or knowledge of the usage of a particular trade other than the standard practice referred to in subsection (e).

(g) If an undertaking constituting a letter of credit under Section 5–102(a)(10) contains nondocumentary conditions, an issuer shall disregard the nondocumentary conditions and treat them as if they were not stated.

(h) An issuer that has dishonored a presentation shall return the documents or hold them at the disposal of, and send advice to that effect to, the presenter.

(i) An issuer that has honored a presentation as permitted or required by this article:

(1) is entitled to be reimbursed by the applicant in immediately available funds not later than the date of its payment of funds;

(2) takes the documents free of claims of the beneficiary or presenter;

(3) is precluded from asserting a right of recourse on a draft under Sections 3–414 and 3–415;

(4) except as otherwise provided in Sections 5–110 and 5–117, is precluded from restitution of money paid or other value given by mistake to the extent the mistake concerns discrepancies in the documents or tender which are apparent on the face of the presentation; and

(5) is discharged to the extent of its performance under the letter of credit unless the issuer honored a presentation in which a required signature of a beneficiary was forged.

§ 5-109. Fraud and Forgery.

(a) If a presentation is made that appears on its face strictly to comply with the terms and conditions of the letter of credit, but a required document is forged or materially fraudulent, or honor of the presentation would facilitate a material fraud by the beneficiary on the issuer or applicant:

(1) the issuer shall honor the presentation, if honor is demanded by (i) a nominated person who has given value in good faith and without notice of forgery or material fraud, (ii) a confirmer who has honored its confirmation in good faith, (iii) a holder in due course of a draft drawn under the letter of credit which was taken after acceptance by the issuer or nominated person, or (iv) an assignee of the issuer's or nominated person's deferred obligation that was taken for value and without notice of forgery or material fraud after the obligation was incurred by the issuer or nominated person; and

(2) the issuer, acting in good faith, may honor or dishonor the presentation in any other case.

(b) If an applicant claims that a required document is forged or materially fraudulent or that honor of the presentation would facilitate a material fraud by the beneficiary on the issuer or applicant, a court of competent jurisdiction may temporarily or permanently enjoin the issuer from honoring a presentation or grant similar relief against the issuer or other persons only if the court finds that:

(1) the relief is not prohibited under the law applicable to an accepted draft or deferred obligation incurred by the issuer;

(2) a beneficiary, issuer, or nominated person who may be adversely affected is adequately protected against loss that it may suffer because the relief is granted;

(3) all of the conditions to entitle a person to the relief under the law of this State have been met; and

(4) on the basis of the information submitted to the court, the applicant is more likely than not to succeed under its claim of forgery or material fraud and the person demanding honor does not qualify for protection under subsection (a)(1).

§ 5-110. Warranties.

(a) If its presentation is honored, the beneficiary warrants:

(1) to the issuer, any other person to whom presentation is made, and the applicant that there is no fraud or forgery of the kind described in Section 5–109(a); and

(2) to the applicant that the drawing does not violate any agreement between the applicant and beneficiary or any other agreement intended by them to be augmented by the letter of credit.

(b) The warranties in subsection (a) are in addition to warranties arising under Article 3, 4, 7, and 8 because of the presentation or transfer of documents covered by any of those articles.

§ 5-111. Remedies.

(a) If an issuer wrongfully dishonors or repudiates its obligation to pay money under a letter of credit before presentation, the beneficiary, successor, or nominated person presenting on its own behalf may recover from the issuer the amount that is the subject of the dishonor or repudiation. If the issuer's obligation under the letter of credit is not for the payment of money, the claimant may obtain specific performance or, at the claimant's election, recover an amount equal to the value of performance from the issuer. In either case, the claimant may also recover incidental but not consequential damages. The claimant is not obligated to take action to avoid damages that might be due from the issuer under this subsection. If, although not obligated to do so, the claimant avoids damages, the claimant's recovery from the issuer must be reduced by the amount of damages avoided. The issuer has the burden of proving the amount of damages avoided. In the case of repudiation the claimant need not present any document.

(b) If an issuer wrongfully dishonors a draft or demand presented under a letter of credit or honors a draft or demand in breach of its obligation to the applicant, the applicant may recover damages resulting from the breach, including incidental but not consequential damages, less any amount saved as a result of the breach.

(c) If an adviser or nominated person other than a confirmer breaches an obligation under this article or an issuer breaches an obligation not covered in subsection (a) or (b), a person to whom the obligation is owed may recover damages resulting from the breach, including incidental but not consequential damages, less any amount saved as a result of the breach. To the extent of the confirmation, a confirmer has the liability of an issuer specified in this subsection and subsections (a) and (b).

(d) An issuer, nominated person, or adviser who is found liable under subsection (a), (b), or (c) shall pay interest on the amount owed thereunder from the date of wrongful dishonor or other appropriate date.

(e) Reasonable attorney's fees and other expenses of litigation must be awarded to the prevailing party in an action in which a remedy is sought under this article.

(f) Damages that would otherwise be payable by a party for breach of an obligation under this article may be liquidated by agreement or undertaking, but only in an amount or by a formula that is reasonable in light of the harm anticipated.

§ 5-112. Transfer of Letter of Credit.

(a) Except as otherwise provided in Section 5–113, unless a letter of credit provides that it is transferable, the right of a beneficiary to draw or otherwise demand performance under a letter of credit may not be transferred.

(b) Even if a letter of credit provides that it is transferable, the issuer may refuse to recognize or carry out a transfer if:

(1) the transfer would violate applicable law; or

(2) the transferor or transferee has failed to comply with any requirement stated in the letter of credit or any other requirement relating to transfer imposed by the issuer which is within the standard practice referred to in Section 5–108(e) or is otherwise reasonable under the circumstances.

§ 5-113. Transfer by Operation of Law.

(a) A successor of a beneficiary may consent to amendments, sign and present documents, and receive payment or other items of value in the name of the beneficiary without disclosing its status as a successor.

(b) A successor of a beneficiary may consent to amendments, sign and present documents, and receive payment or other items of value in its own name as the disclosed successor of the beneficiary. Except as otherwise

provided in subsection (e), an issuer shall recognize a disclosed successor of a beneficiary as beneficiary in full substitution for its predecessor upon compliance with the requirements for recognition by the issuer of a transfer of drawing rights by operation of law under the standard practice referred to in Section 5–108(e) or, in the absence of such a practice, compliance with other reasonable procedures sufficient to protect the issuer.

(c) An issuer is not obliged to determine whether a purported successor is a successor of a beneficiary or whether the signature of a purported successor is genuine or authorized.

(d) Honor of a purported successor's apparently complying presentation under subsection (a) or (b) has the consequences specified in Section 5–108(i) even if the purported successor is not the successor of a beneficiary. Documents signed in the name of the beneficiary or of a disclosed successor by a person who is neither the beneficiary nor the successor of the beneficiary are forged documents for the purposes of Section 5–109.

(e) An issuer whose rights of reimbursement are not covered by subsection (d) or substantially similar law and any confirmer or nominated person may decline to recognize a presentation under subsection (b).

(f) A beneficiary whose name is changed after the issuance of a letter of credit has the same rights and obligations as a successor of a beneficiary under this section.

§ 5-114. Assignment of Proceeds.

(a) In this section, "proceeds of a letter of credit" means the cash, check, accepted draft, or other item of value paid or delivered upon honor or giving of value by the issuer or any nominated person under the letter of credit. The term does not include a beneficiary's drawing rights or documents presented by the beneficiary.

(b) A beneficiary may assign its right to part or all of the proceeds of a letter of credit. The beneficiary may do so before presentation as a present assignment of its right to receive proceeds contingent upon its compliance with the terms and conditions of the letter of credit.

(c) An issuer or nominated person need not recognize an assignment of proceeds of a letter of credit until it consents to the assignment.

(d) An issuer or nominated person has no obligation to give or withhold its consent to an assignment of proceeds of a letter of credit, but consent may not be unreasonably withheld if the assignee possesses and exhibits the letter of credit and presentation of the letter of credit is a condition to honor.

(e) Rights of a transferee beneficiary or nominated person are independent of the beneficiary's assignment of the proceeds of a letter of credit and are superior to the assignee's right to the proceeds.

(f) Neither the rights recognized by this section between an assignee and an issuer, transferee beneficiary, or nominated person nor the issuer's or nominated person's payment of proceeds to an assignee or a third person affect the rights between the assignee and any person other than the issuer, transferee beneficiary, or nominated person. The mode of creating and perfecting a security interest in or granting an assignment of a beneficiary's rights to proceeds is governed by Article 9 or other law. Against persons other than the issuer, transferee beneficiary, or nominated person, the rights and obligations arising upon the creation of a security interest or other assignment of a beneficiary's right to proceeds and its perfection are governed by Article 9 or other law.

§ 5-115. Statute of Limitations.

An action to enforce a right or obligation arising under this article must be commenced within one year after the expiration date of the relevant letter of credit or one year after the [claim for relief] [cause of action] accrues, whichever occurs later. A [claim for relief] [cause of action] accrues when the breach occurs, regardless of the aggrieved party's lack of knowledge of the breach.

§ 5-116. Choice of Law and Forum.

(a) The liability of an issuer, nominated person, or adviser for action or omission is governed by the law of the jurisdiction chosen by an agreement in the form of a record signed or otherwise authenticated by the affected parties in the manner provided in Section 5–104 or by a provision in the person's letter of credit, confirmation, or other undertaking. The jurisdiction whose law is chosen need not bear any relation to the transaction.

(b) Unless subsection (a) applies, the liability of an issuer, nominated person, or adviser for action or omission is governed by the law of the jurisdiction in which the person is located. The person is considered to be located at the address indicated in the person's undertaking. If more than one address is indicated, the person is considered to be located at the address from which the person's undertaking was issued. For the purpose of jurisdiction, choice of law, and recognition of interbranch letters of credit, but not enforcement of a judgment, all branches of a bank are considered separate juridical entities and a bank is considered to be located at the place where its relevant branch is considered to be located under this subsection.

(c) Except as otherwise provided in this subsection, the liability of an issuer, nominated person, or adviser is governed by any rules of custom or practice, such as the Uniform Customs and Practice for Documentary Credits, to which the letter of credit, confirmation, or other undertaking is expressly made subject. If (i) this article would govern the liability of an issuer, nominated person, or adviser under subsection (a) or (b), (ii) the relevant undertaking incorporates rules of custom or practice, and (iii) there is conflict between this article and those rules as applied to that undertaking, those rules govern except to the extent of any conflict with the nonvariable provisions specified in Section 5–103(c).

(d) If there is conflict between this article and Article 3, 4, 4A, or 9, this article governs.

(e) The forum for settling disputes arising out of an undertaking within this article may be chosen in the manner and with the binding effect that governing law may be chosen in accordance with subsection (a).

§ 5-117. Subrogation of Issuer, Applicant, and Nominated Person.

(a) An issuer that honors a beneficiary's presentation is subrogated to the rights of the beneficiary to the same extent as if the issuer were a secondary obligor of the underlying obligation owed to the beneficiary and of the applicant to the same extent as if the issuer were the secondary obligor of the underlying obligation owed to the applicant.

(b) An applicant that reimburses an issuer is subrogated to the rights of the issuer against any beneficiary, presenter, or nominated person to the same extent as if the applicant were the secondary obligor of the obligations owed to the issuer and has the rights of subrogation of the issuer to the rights of the beneficiary stated in subsection (a).

(c) A nominated person who pays or gives value against a draft or demand presented under a letter of credit is subrogated to the rights of:

    (1) the issuer against the applicant to the same extent as if the nominated person were a secondary obligor of the obligation owed to the issuer by the applicant;

    (2) the beneficiary to the same extent as if the nominated person were a secondary obligor of the underlying obligation owed to the beneficiary; and

    (3) the applicant to same extent as if the nominated person were a secondary obligor of the underlying obligation owed to the applicant.

(d) Notwithstanding any agreement or term to the contrary, the rights of subrogation stated in subsections (a) and (b) do not arise until the issuer honors the letter of credit or otherwise pays and the rights in subsection (c) do not arise until the nominated person pays or otherwise gives value. Until then, the issuer, nominated person, and the applicant do not derive under this section present or prospective rights forming the basis of a claim, defense, or excuse.

§ 5-118. Security Interest of Issuer or Nominated Person.

(a) An issuer or nominated person has a security interest in a document presented under a letter of credit to the extent that the issuer or nominated person honors or gives value for the presentation.

(b) So long as and to the extent that an issuer or nominated person has not been reimbursed or has not otherwise recovered the value given with respect to a security interest in a document under subsection (a), the security interest continues and is subject to Article 9, but:

    (1) a security agreement is not necessary to make the security interest enforceable under Section 9–203(b)(3);

    (2) if the document is presented in a medium other than a written or other tangible medium, the security interest is perfected; and

    (3) if the document is presented in a written or other tangible medium and is not a certificated security, chattel paper, a document of title, an instrument, or a letter of credit, the security interest is perfected and has priority over a conflicting security interest in the document so long as the debtor does not have possession of the document.

As added in 1999.

Transition Provisions

§ [   ]. Effective Date.

This [Act] shall become effective on _____, 20__.

§ [   ]. Repeal.

This [Act] [repeals] [amends] [insert citation to existing Article 5].

§ [   ]. Applicability.

This [Act] applies to a letter of credit that is issued on or after the effective date of this [Act]. This [Act] does not apply to a transaction, event, obligation, or duty arising out of or associated with a letter of credit that was issued before the effective date of this [Act].

§ [   ]. Savings Clause.

A transaction arising out of or associated with a letter of credit that was issued before the effective date of this [Act] and the rights, obligations, and interests flowing from that transaction are governed by any statute or other law amended or repealed by this [Act] as if repeal or amendment had not occurred and may be terminated, completed, consummated, or enforced under that statute or other law.

REPEALER OF ARTICLE 6 Bulk Transfers and [Revised] Article 6 Bulk Sales (States to Select One Alternative)

Alternative A

[§ 1. Repeal

Article 6 and Section 9–111 of the Uniform Commercial Code are hereby repealed, effective _____.

§ 2. Amendment

Section 1–105(2) of the Uniform Commercial Code is hereby amended to read as follows:

(2) Where one of the following provisions of this Act specifies the applicable law, that provision governs and a contrary agreement is effective

only to the extent permitted by the law (including the conflict of laws rules) so specified:

Rights of creditors against sold goods. Section 2–402.

Applicability of the Article on Leases. Section 2A–105 and 2A–106.

Applicability of the Article on Bank Deposits and Collections. Section 4–102.

Applicability of the Article on Investment Securities. Section 8–106.

Perfection provisions of the Article on Secured Transactions. Section 9–103.

§ 3. Amendment.

Section 2–403(4) of the Uniform Commercial Code is hereby amended to read as follows:

(4) The rights of other purchasers of goods and of lien creditors are governed by the Articles on Secured Transactions (Article 9) and Documents of Title (Article 7).

§ 4. Savings Clause.

Rights and obligations that arose under Article 6 and Section 9–111 of the Uniform Commercial Code before their repeal remain valid and may be enforced as though those statutes had not been repealed.]

§ 6-101. Short Title.

This Article shall be known and may be cited as Uniform Commercial Code—Bulk Sales.

§ 6-102. Definitions and Index of Definitions.

(1) In this Article, unless the context otherwise requires:

(a) "Assets" means the inventory that is the subject of a bulk sale and any tangible and intangible personal property used or held for use primarily in, or arising from, the seller's business and sold in connection with that inventory, but the term does not include:

(i) fixtures (Section 9–102(a)(41)) other than readily removable factory and office machines;

(ii) the lessee's interest in a lease of real property; or

(iii) property to the extent it is generally exempt from creditor process under nonbankruptcy law.

(b) "Auctioneer" means a person whom the seller engages to direct, conduct, control, or be responsible for a sale by auction.

(c) "Bulk sale" means:

(i) in the case of a sale by auction or a sale or series of sales conducted by a liquidator on the seller's behalf, a sale or series of sales not in the ordinary course of the seller's business of more than half of the seller's inventory, as measured by value on the date of the bulk-sale agreement, if on that date the auctioneer or liquidator has notice, or after reasonable inquiry would have had notice, that the seller will not continue to operate the same or a similar kind of business after the sale or series of sales; and

(ii) in all other cases, a sale not in the ordinary course of the seller's business of more than half the seller's inventory, as measured by value on the date of the bulk-sale agreement, if on that date the buyer has notice, or after reasonable inquiry would have had notice, that the seller will not continue to operate the same or a similar kind of business after the sale.

(d) "Claim" means a right to payment from the seller, whether or not the right is reduced to judgment, liquidated, fixed, matured, disputed, secured, legal, or equitable. The term includes costs of collection and attorney's fees only to the extent that the laws of this state permit the holder of the claim to recover them in an action against the obligor.

(e) "Claimant" means a person holding a claim incurred in the seller's business other than:

(i) an unsecured and unmatured claim for employment compensation and benefits, including commissions and vacation, severance, and sick-leave pay;

(ii) a claim for injury to an individual or to property, or for breach of warranty, unless:

(A) a right of action for the claim has accrued;

(B) the claim has been asserted against the seller; and

(C) the seller knows the identity of the person asserting the claim and the basis upon which the person has asserted it; and

(States to Select One Alternative)

Alternative A

[(iii) a claim for taxes owing to a governmental unit.]

Alternative B

[(iii) a claim for taxes owing to a governmental unit, if:

(A) a statute governing the enforcement of the claim permits or requires notice of the bulk sale to be given to the governmental unit in a manner other than by compliance with the requirements of this Article; and

(B) notice is given in accordance with the statute.]

(f) "Creditor" means a claimant or other person holding a claim.

(g) (i) "Date of the bulk sale" means:

(A) if the sale is by auction or is conducted by a liquidator on the seller's behalf, the date on which more than ten percent of the net proceeds is paid to or for the benefit of the seller; and

(B) in all other cases, the later of the date on which:

(I) more than ten percent of the net contract price is paid to or for the benefit of the seller; or

(II) more than ten percent of the assets, as measured by value, are transferred to the buyer.

(ii) For purposes of this subsection:

(A) delivery of a negotiable instrument (Section 3–104(1)) to or for the benefit of the seller in exchange for assets constitutes payment of the contract price pro tanto;

(B) to the extent that the contract price is deposited in an escrow, the contract price is paid to or for the benefit of the seller when the seller acquires the unconditional right to receive the deposit or when the deposit is delivered to the seller or for the benefit of the seller, whichever is earlier; and

(C) an asset is transferred when a person holding an unsecured claim can no longer obtain through judicial proceedings rights to the asset that are superior to those of the buyer arising as a result of the bulk sale. A person holding an unsecured claim can obtain those superior rights to a tangible asset at least until the buyer has an unconditional right, under the bulk-sale agreement, to possess the asset, and a person holding an unsecured claim can obtain those superior rights to an intangible asset at least until the buyer has an unconditional right, under the bulk-sale agreement, to use the asset.

(h) "Date of the bulk-sale agreement" means:

(i) in the case of a sale by auction or conducted by a liquidator (subsection (c)(i)), the date on which the seller engages the auctioneer or liquidator; and

(ii) in all other cases, the date on which a bulk-sale agreement becomes enforceable between the buyer and the seller.

(i) "Debt" means liability on a claim.

(j) "Liquidator" means a person who is regularly engaged in the business of disposing of assets for businesses contemplating liquidation or dissolution.

(k) "Net contract price" means the new consideration the buyer is obligated to pay for the assets less:

(i) the amount of any proceeds of the sale of an asset, to the extent the proceeds are applied in partial or total satisfaction of a debt secured by the asset; and

(ii) the amount of any debt to the extent it is secured by a security interest or lien that is enforceable against the asset before and after it has been sold to a buyer. If a debt is secured by an asset and other property of the seller, the amount of the debt secured by a security interest or lien that is enforceable against the asset is determined by multiplying the debt by a fraction, the numerator of which is the value of the new consideration for the asset on the date of the bulk sale and the denominator of which is the value of all property securing the debt on the date of the bulk sale.

(l) "Net proceeds" means the new consideration received for assets sold at a sale by auction or a sale conducted by a liquidator on the seller's behalf less:

(i) commissions and reasonable expenses of the sale;

(ii) the amount of any proceeds of the sale of an asset, to the extent the proceeds are applied in partial or total satisfaction of a debt secured by the asset; and

(iii) the amount of any debt to the extent it is secured by a security interest or lien that is enforceable against the asset before and after it has been sold to a buyer. If a debt is secured by an asset and other property of the seller, the amount of the debt secured by a security interest or lien that is enforceable against the asset is determined by multiplying the debt by a fraction, the numerator of which is the value of the new consideration for the asset on the date of the bulk sale and the denominator of which is the value of all property securing the debt on the date of the bulk sale.

(m) A sale is "in the ordinary course of the seller's business" if the sale comports with usual or customary practices in the kind of business in which the seller is engaged or with the seller's own usual or customary practices.

(n) "United States" includes its territories and possessions and the Commonwealth of Puerto Rico.

(o) "Value" means fair market value.

(p) "Verified" means signed and sworn to or affirmed.

(2) The following definitions in other Articles apply to this Article:

(a) "Buyer."   Section 2–103(1)(a).
(b) "Equipment."   Section 9–102(a)(33).
(c) "Inventory."   Section 9–102(a)(48).
(d) "Sale."   Section 2–106(1).
(e) "Seller."   Section 2–103(1)(d).

(3) In addition, Article 1 contains general definitions and principles of construction and interpretation applicable throughout this Article.
As amended in 1999.

§ 6-103. Applicability of Article.

(1) Except as otherwise provided in subsection (3), this Article applies to a bulk sale if:

(a) the seller's principal business is the sale of inventory from stock; and

(b) on the date of the bulk-sale agreement the seller is located in this state or, if the seller is located in a jurisdiction that is not a part of the United States, the seller's major executive office in the United States is in this state.

(2) A seller is deemed to be located at his [or her] place of business. If a seller has more than one place of business, the seller is deemed located at his [or her] chief executive office.

(3) This Article does not apply to:

(a) a transfer made to secure payment or performance of an obligation;

(b) a transfer of collateral to a secured party pursuant to Section 9–503;

(c) a disposition of collateral pursuant to Section 9–610;

(d) retention of collateral pursuant to Section 9–620;

(e) a sale of an asset encumbered by a security interest or lien if (i) all the proceeds of the sale are applied in partial or total satisfaction of the debt secured by the security interest or lien or (ii) the security interest or lien is enforceable against the asset after it has been sold to the buyer and the net contract price is zero;

(f) a general assignment for the benefit of creditors or to a subsequent transfer by the assignee;

(g) a sale by an executor, administrator, receiver, trustee in bankruptcy, or any public officer under judicial process;

(h) a sale made in the course of judicial or administrative proceedings for the dissolution or reorganization of an organization;

(i) a sale to a buyer whose principal place of business is in the United States and who:

(i) not earlier than 21 days before the date of the bulk sale, (A) obtains from the seller a verified and dated list of claimants of whom the seller has notice three days before the seller sends or delivers the list to the buyer or (B) conducts a reasonable inquiry to discover the claimants;

(ii) assumes in full the debts owed to claimants of whom the buyer has knowledge on the date the buyer receives the list of claimants from the seller or on the date the buyer completes the reasonable inquiry, as the case may be;

(iii) is not insolvent after the assumption; and

(iv) gives written notice of the assumption not later than 30 days after the date of the bulk sale by sending or delivering a notice to the claimants identified in subparagraph (ii) or by filing a notice in the office of the [Secretary of State];

(j) a sale to a buyer whose principal place of business is in the United States and who:

(i) assumes in full the debts that were incurred in the seller's business before the date of the bulk sale;

(ii) is not insolvent after the assumption; and

(iii) gives written notice of the assumption not later than 30 days after the date of the bulk sale by sending or delivering a notice to each creditor whose debt is assumed or by filing a notice in the office of the [Secretary of State];

(k) a sale to a new organization that is organized to take over and continue the business of the seller and that has its principal place of business in the United States if:

(i) the buyer assumes in full the debts that were incurred in the seller's business before the date of the bulk sale;

(ii) the seller receives nothing from the sale except an interest in the new organization that is subordinate to the claims against the organization arising from the assumption; and

(iii) the buyer gives written notice of the assumption not later than 30 days after the date of the bulk sale by sending or delivering a notice to each creditor whose debt is assumed or by filing a notice in the office of the [Secretary of State];

(l) a sale of assets having:

(i) a value, net of liens and security interests, of less than $10,000. If a debt is secured by assets and other property of the seller, the net value of the assets is determined by subtracting from their value an amount equal to the product of the debt multiplied by a fraction, the numerator of which is the value of the assets on the date of the bulk sale and the denominator of which is the value of all property securing the debt on the date of the bulk sale; or

(ii) a value of more than $25,000,000 on the date of the bulk-sale agreement; or

(m) a sale required by, and made pursuant to, statute.

(4) The notice under subsection (3)(i)(iv) must state:(i) that a sale that may constitute a bulk sale has been or will be made; (ii) the date or prospective date of the bulk sale; (iii) the individual, partnership, or corporate names and the addresses of the seller and buyer; (iv) the address to which inquiries about the sale may be made, if different from the seller's address; and (v) that the buyer has assumed or will assume in full the debts owed to claimants of whom the buyer has knowledge on the date the buyer receives the list of claimants from the seller or completes a reasonable inquiry to discover the claimants.

(5) The notice under subsections (3)(j)(iii) and (3)(k)(iii) must state: (i) that a sale that may constitute a bulk sale has been or will be made; (ii) the date or prospective date of the bulk sale; (iii) the individual, partnership, or corporate names and the addresses of the seller and buyer; (iv) the address to which inquiries about the sale may be made, if different from the seller's address; and (v) that the buyer has assumed or will assume the debts that were incurred in the seller's business before the date of the bulk sale.

(6) For purposes of subsection (3)(*l*), the value of assets is presumed to be equal to the price the buyer agrees to pay for the assets. However, in a sale by auction or a sale conducted by a liquidator on the seller's behalf, the value of assets is presumed to be the amount the auctioneer or liquidator reasonably estimates the assets will bring at auction or upon liquidation. As amended in 1999.

§ 6-104. Obligations of Buyer.

(1) In a bulk sale as defined in Section 6–102(1)(c)(ii) the buyer shall:

(a) obtain from the seller a list of all business names and addresses used by the seller within three years before the date the list is sent or delivered to the buyer;

(b) unless excused under subsection (2), obtain from the seller a verified and dated list of claimants of whom the seller has notice three days before the seller sends or delivers the list to the buyer and including, to the extent known by the seller, the address of and the amount claimed by each claimant;

(c) obtain from the seller or prepare a schedule of distribution (Section 6–106(1));

(d) give notice of the bulk sale in accordance with Section 6–105;

(e) unless excused under Section 6–106(4), distribute the net contract price in accordance with the undertakings of the buyer in the schedule of distribution; and

(f) unless excused under subsection (2), make available the list of claimants (subsection (1)(b)) by:

(i) promptly sending or delivering a copy of the list without charge to any claimant whose written request is received by the buyer no later than six months after the date of the bulk sale;

(ii) permitting any claimant to inspect and copy the list at any reasonable hour upon request received by the buyer no later than six months after the date of the bulk sale; or

(iii) filing a copy of the list in the office of the [Secretary of State] no later than the time for giving a notice of the bulk sale (Section 6–105(5)). A list filed in accordance with this subparagraph must state the individual, partnership, or corporate name and a mailing address of the seller.

(2) A buyer who gives notice in accordance with Section 6–105(2) is excused from complying with the requirements of subsections (1)(b) and (1)(f).

§ 6-105. Notice to Claimants.

(1) Except as otherwise provided in subsection (2), to comply with Section 6–104(1)(d) the buyer shall send or deliver a written notice of the bulk sale to each claimant on the list of claimants (Section 6–104(1)(b))

and to any other claimant of which the buyer has knowledge at the time the notice of the bulk sale is sent or delivered.

(2) A buyer may comply with Section 6–104(1)(d) by filing a written notice of the bulk sale in the office of the [Secretary of State] if:

(a) on the date of the bulk-sale agreement the seller has 200 or more claimants, exclusive of claimants holding secured or matured claims for employment compensation and benefits, including commissions and vacation, severance, and sick-leave pay; or

(b) the buyer has received a verified statement from the seller stating that, as of the date of the bulk-sale agreement, the number of claimants, exclusive of claimants holding secured or matured claims for employment compensation and benefits, including commissions and vacation, severance, and sick-leave pay, is 200 or more.

(3) The written notice of the bulk sale must be accompanied by a copy of the schedule of distribution (Section 6–106(1)) and state at least:

(a) that the seller and buyer have entered into an agreement for a sale that may constitute a bulk sale under the laws of the State of _____ ;

(b) the date of the agreement;

(c) the date on or after which more than ten percent of the assets were or will be transferred;

(d) the date on or after which more than ten percent of the net contract price was or will be paid, if the date is not stated in the schedule of distribution;

(e) the name and a mailing address of the seller;

(f) any other business name and address listed by the seller pursuant to Section 6–104(1)(a);

(g) the name of the buyer and an address of the buyer from which information concerning the sale can be obtained;

(h) a statement indicating the type of assets or describing the assets item by item;

(i) the manner in which the buyer will make available the list of claimants (Section 6–104(1)(f)), if applicable; and

(j) if the sale is in total or partial satisfaction of an antecedent debt owed by the seller, the amount of the debt to be satisfied and the name of the person to whom it is owed.

(4) For purposes of subsections (3)(e) and (3)(g), the name of a person is the person's individual, partnership, or corporate name.

(5) The buyer shall give notice of the bulk sale not less than 45 days before the date of the bulk sale and, if the buyer gives notice in accordance with subsection (1), not more than 30 days after obtaining the list of claimants.

(6) A written notice substantially complying with the requirements of subsection (3) is effective even though it contains minor errors that are not seriously misleading.

(7) A form substantially as follows is sufficient to comply with subsection (3):

Notice of Sale

(1) _____, whose address is _____, is described in this notice as the "seller."

(2) _____, whose address is _____, is described in this notice as the "buyer."

(3) The seller has disclosed to the buyer that within the past three years the seller has used other business names, operated at other addresses, or both, as follows: _____

_____ .

(4) The seller and the buyer have entered into an agreement dated _____, for a sale that may constitute a bulk sale under the laws of the state of _____.

(5) The date on or after which more than ten percent of the assets that are the subject of the sale were or will be transferred is _____, and [if not stated in the schedule of distribution] the date on or after which

more than ten percent of the net contract price was or will be paid is _____ .

(6) The following assets are the subject of the sale: _____
_____ .

(7) [If applicable] The buyer will make available to claimants of the seller a list of the seller's claimants in the following manner: _____
_____ .

(8) [If applicable] The sale is to satisfy $_____ of an antecedent debt owed by the seller to _____ .

(9) A copy of the schedule of distribution of the net contract price accompanies this notice.

[End of Notice]

§ 6-106. Schedule of Distribution.

(1) The seller and buyer shall agree on how the net contract price is to be distributed and set forth their agreement in a written schedule of distribution.

(2) The schedule of distribution may provide for distribution to any person at any time, including distribution of the entire net contract price to the seller.

(3) The buyer's undertakings in the schedule of distribution run only to the seller. However, a buyer who fails to distribute the net contract price in accordance with the buyer's undertakings in the schedule of distribution is liable to a creditor only as provided in Section 6–107(1).

(4) If the buyer undertakes in the schedule of distribution to distribute any part of the net contract price to a person other than the seller, and, after the buyer has given notice in accordance with Section 6–105, some or all of the anticipated net contract price is or becomes unavailable for distribution as a consequence of the buyer's or seller's having complied with an order of court, legal process, statute, or rule of law, the buyer is excused from any obligation arising under this Article or under any contract with the seller to distribute the net contract price in accordance with the buyer's undertakings in the schedule if the buyer:

(a) distributes the net contract price remaining available in accordance with any priorities for payment stated in the schedule of distribution and, to the extent that the price is insufficient to pay all the debts having a given priority, distributes the price pro rata among those debts shown in the schedule as having the same priority;

(b) distributes the net contract price remaining available in accordance with an order of court;

(c) commences a proceeding for interpleader in a court of competent jurisdiction and is discharged from the proceeding; or

(d) reaches a new agreement with the seller for the distribution of the net contract price remaining available, sets forth the new agreement in an amended schedule of distribution, gives notice of the amended schedule, and distributes the net contract price remaining available in accordance with the buyer's undertakings in the amended schedule.

(5) The notice under subsection (4)(d) must identify the buyer and the seller, state the filing number, if any, of the original notice, set forth the amended schedule, and be given in accordance with subsection (1) or (2) of Section 6–105, whichever is applicable, at least 14 days before the buyer distributes any part of the net contract price remaining available.

(6) If the seller undertakes in the schedule of distribution to distribute any part of the net contract price, and, after the buyer has given notice in accordance with Section 6–105, some or all of the anticipated net contract price is or becomes unavailable for distribution as a consequence of the buyer's or seller's having complied with an order of court, legal process, statute, or rule of law, the seller and any person in control of the seller are excused from any obligation arising under this Article or under any agreement with the buyer to distribute the net contract price in accordance with the seller's undertakings in the schedule if the seller:

(a) distributes the net contract price remaining available in accordance with any priorities for payment stated in the schedule of distribution and, to the extent that the price is insufficient to pay all the debts having a given priority, distributes the price pro rata among those debts shown in the schedule as having the same priority;

(b) distributes the net contract price remaining available in accordance with an order of court;

(c) commences a proceeding for interpleader in a court of competent jurisdiction and is discharged from the proceeding; or

(d) prepares a written amended schedule of distribution of the net contract price remaining available for distribution, gives notice of the amended schedule, and distributes the net contract price remaining available in accordance with the amended schedule.

(7) The notice under subsection (6)(d) must identify the buyer and the seller, state the filing number, if any, of the original notice, set forth the amended schedule, and be given in accordance with subsection (1) or (2) of Section 6–105, whichever is applicable, at least 14 days before the seller distributes any part of the net contract price remaining available.

§ 6-107. Liability for Noncompliance.

(1) Except as provided in subsection (3), and subject to the limitation in subsection (4):

(a) a buyer who fails to comply with the requirements of Section 6–104(1)(e) with respect to a creditor is liable to the creditor for damages in the amount of the claim, reduced by any amount that the creditor would not have realized if the buyer had complied; and

(b) a buyer who fails to comply with the requirements of any other subsection of Section 6–104 with respect to a claimant is liable to the claimant for damages in the amount of the claim, reduced by any amount that the claimant would not have realized if the buyer had complied.

(2) In an action under subsection (1), the creditor has the burden of establishing the validity and amount of the claim, and the buyer has the burden of establishing the amount that the creditor would not have realized if the buyer had complied.

(3) A buyer who:

(a) made a good faith and commercially reasonable effort to comply with the requirements of Section 6–104(1) or to exclude the sale from the application of this Article under Section 6–103(3); or

(b) on or after the date of the bulk-sale agreement, but before the date of the bulk sale, held a good faith and commercially reasonable belief that this Article does not apply to the particular sale is not liable to creditors for failure to comply with the requirements of Section 6–104. The buyer has the burden of establishing the good faith and commercial reasonableness of the effort or belief.

(4) In a single bulk sale the cumulative liability of the buyer for failure to comply with the requirements of Section 6–104(1) may not exceed an amount equal to:

(a) if the assets consist only of inventory and equipment, twice the net contract price, less the amount of any part of the net contract price paid to or applied for the benefit of the seller or a creditor; or

(b) if the assets include property other than inventory and equipment, twice the net value of the inventory and equipment less the amount of the portion of any part of the net contract price paid to or applied for the benefit of the seller or a creditor which is allocable to the inventory and equipment.

(5) For the purposes of subsection (4)(b), the "net value" of an asset is the value of the asset less (i) the amount of any proceeds of the sale of an asset, to the extent the proceeds are applied in partial or total satisfaction of a debt secured by the asset and (ii) the amount of any debt to the extent it is secured by a security interest or lien that is enforceable against the asset

before and after it has been sold to a buyer. If a debt is secured by an asset and other property of the seller, the amount of the debt secured by a security interest or lien that is enforceable against the asset is determined by multiplying the debt by a fraction, the numerator of which is the value of the asset on the date of the bulk sale and the denominator of which is the value of all property securing the debt on the date of the bulk sale. The portion of a part of the net contract price paid to or applied for the benefit of the seller or a creditor that is "allocable to the inventory and equipment" is the portion that bears the same ratio to that part of the net contract price as the net value of the inventory and equipment bears to the net value of all of the assets.

(6) A payment made by the buyer to a person to whom the buyer is, or believes he [or she] is, liable under subsection (1) reduces pro tanto the buyer's cumulative liability under subsection (4).

(7) No action may be brought under subsection (1)(b) by or on behalf of a claimant whose claim is unliquidated or contingent.

(8) A buyer's failure to comply with the requirements of Section 6–104(1) does not (i) impair the buyer's rights in or title to the assets, (ii) render the sale ineffective, void, or voidable, (iii) entitle a creditor to more than a single satisfaction of his [or her] claim, or (iv) create liability other than as provided in this Article.

(9) Payment of the buyer's liability under subsection (1) discharges pro tanto the seller's debt to the creditor.

(10) Unless otherwise agreed, a buyer has an immediate right of reimbursement from the seller for any amount paid to a creditor in partial or total satisfaction of the buyer's liability under subsection (1).

(11) If the seller is an organization, a person who is in direct or indirect control of the seller, and who knowingly, intentionally, and without legal justification fails, or causes the seller to fail, to distribute the net contract price in accordance with the schedule of distribution is liable to any creditor to whom the seller undertook to make payment under the schedule for damages caused by the failure.

§ 6-108. Bulk Sales by Auction; Bulk Sales Conducted by Liquidator.

(1) Sections 6–104, 6–105, 6–106, and 6–107 apply to a bulk sale by auction and a bulk sale conducted by a liquidator on the seller's behalf with the following modifications:

(a) "buyer" refers to auctioneer or liquidator, as the case may be;

(b) "net contract price" refers to net proceeds of the auction or net proceeds of the sale, as the case may be;

(c) the written notice required under Section 6–105(3) must be accompanied by a copy of the schedule of distribution (Section 6–106(1)) and state at least:

(i) that the seller and the auctioneer or liquidator have entered into an agreement for auction or liquidation services that may constitute an agreement to make a bulk sale under the laws of the State of _____;

(ii) the date of the agreement;

(iii) the date on or after which the auction began or will begin or the date on or after which the liquidator began or will begin to sell assets on the seller's behalf;

(iv) the date on or after which more than ten percent of the net proceeds of the sale were or will be paid, if the date is not stated in the schedule of distribution;

(v) the name and a mailing address of the seller;

(vi) any other business name and address listed by the seller pursuant to Section 6–104(1)(a);

(vii) the name of the auctioneer or liquidator and an address of the auctioneer or liquidator from which information concerning the sale can be obtained;

(viii) a statement indicating the type of assets or describing the assets item by item;

(ix) the manner in which the auctioneer or liquidator will make available the list of claimants (Section 6–104(1)(f)), if applicable; and

(x) if the sale is in total or partial satisfaction of an antecedent debt owed by the seller, the amount of the debt to be satisfied and the name of the person to whom it is owed; and

(d) in a single bulk sale the cumulative liability of the auctioneer or liquidator for failure to comply with the requirements of this section may not exceed the amount of the net proceeds of the sale allocable to inventory and equipment sold less the amount of the portion of any part of the net proceeds paid to or applied for the benefit of a creditor which is allocable to the inventory and equipment.

(2) A payment made by the auctioneer or liquidator to a person to whom the auctioneer or liquidator is, or believes he [or she] is, liable under this section reduces pro tanto the auctioneer's or liquidator's cumulative liability under subsection (1)(d).

(3) A form substantially as follows is sufficient to comply with subsection (1)(c):

Notice of Sale

(1) _____, whose address is _____, is described in this notice as the "seller."

(2) _____, whose address is _____, is described in this notice as the "auctioneer" or "liquidator."

(3) The seller has disclosed to the auctioneer or liquidator that within the past three years the seller has used other business names, operated at other addresses, or both, as follows: _____.

(4) The seller and the auctioneer or liquidator have entered into an agreement dated _____ for auction or liquidation services that may constitute an agreement to make a bulk sale under the laws of the State of _____.

(5) The date on or after which the auction began or will begin or the date on or after which the liquidator began or will begin to sell assets on the seller's behalf is _____, and [if not stated in the schedule of distribution] the date on or after which more than ten percent of the net proceeds of the sale were or will be paid is _____.

(6) The following assets are the subject of the sale: _____
_____.

(7) [If applicable] The auctioneer or liquidator will make available to claimants of the seller a list of the seller's claimants in the following manner: _____.

(8) [If applicable] The sale is to satisfy $ _____ of an antecedent debt owed by the seller to _____.

(9) A copy of the schedule of distribution of the net proceeds accompanies this notice.

[End of Notice]

(4) A person who buys at a bulk sale by auction or conducted by a liquidator need not comply with the requirements of Section 6–104(1) and is not liable for the failure of an auctioneer or liquidator to comply with the requirements of this section.

§ 6-109. What Constitutes Filing; Duties of Filing Officer; Information from Filing Officer.

(1) Presentation of a notice or list of claimants for filing and tender of the filing fee or acceptance of the notice or list by the filing officer constitutes filing under this Article.

(2) The filing officer shall:

(a) mark each notice or list with a file number and with the date and hour of filing;

(b) hold the notice or list or a copy for public inspection;

(c) index the notice or list according to each name given for the seller and for the buyer; and

(d) note in the index the file number and the addresses of the seller and buyer given in the notice or list.

(3) If the person filing a notice or list furnishes the filing officer with a copy, the filing officer upon request shall note upon the copy the file number and date and hour of the filing of the original and send or deliver the copy to the person.

(4) The fee for filing and indexing and for stamping a copy furnished by the person filing to show the date and place of filing is $ _____ for the first page and $ _____ for each additional page. The fee for indexing each name beyond the first two is $ _____.

(5) Upon request of any person, the filing officer shall issue a certificate showing whether any notice or list with respect to a particular seller or buyer is on file on the date and hour stated in the certificate. If a notice or list is on file, the certificate must give the date and hour of filing of each notice or list and the name and address of each seller, buyer, auctioneer, or liquidator. The fee for the certificate is $ _____ if the request for the certificate is in the standard form prescribed by the [Secretary of State] and otherwise is $ _____. Upon request of any person, the filing officer shall furnish a copy of any filed notice or list for a fee of $ _____.

(6) The filing officer shall keep each notice or list for two years after it is filed.

§ 6-110. Limitation of Actions.

(1) Except as provided in subsection (2), an action under this Article against a buyer, auctioneer, or liquidator must be commenced within one year after the date of the bulk sale.

(2) If the buyer, auctioneer, or liquidator conceals the fact that the sale has occurred, the limitation is tolled and an action under this Article may be commenced within the earlier of (i) one year after the person bringing the action discovers that the sale has occurred or (ii) one year after the person bringing the action should have discovered that the sale has occurred, but no later than two years after the date of the bulk sale. Complete noncompliance with the requirements of this Article does not of itself constitute concealment.

(3) An action under Section 6–107(11) must be commenced within one year after the alleged violation occurs.

Conforming Amendment to Section 2-403

States adopting Alternative B should amend Section 2–403(4) of the Uniform Commercial Code to read as follows:

(4) The rights of other purchasers of goods and of lien creditors are governed by the Articles on Secured Transactions (Article 9), Bulk Sales (Article 6) and Documents of Title (Article 7).

ARTICLE 7: Warehouse Receipts, Bills of Lading and Other Documents of Title

PART 1: General

§ 7-101. Short Title.

This Article shall be known and may be cited as Uniform Commercial Code–Documents of Title.

§ 7-102. Definitions and Index of Definitions.

(1) In this Article, unless the context otherwise requires:

(a) "Bailee" means the person who by a warehouse receipt, bill of lading or other document of title acknowledges possession of goods and contracts to deliver them.

(b) "Consignee" means the person named in a bill to whom or to whose order the bill promises delivery.

(c) "Consignor" means the person named in a bill as the person from whom the goods have been received for shipment.

(d) "Delivery order" means a written order to deliver goods directed to a warehouseman, carrier or other person who in the ordinary course of business issues warehouse receipts or bills of lading.

(e) "Document" means document of title as defined in the general definitions in Article 1 (Section 1–201).

(f) "Goods" means all things which are treated as movable for the purposes of a contract of storage or transportation.

(g) "Issuer" means a bailee who issues a document except that in relation to an unaccepted delivery order it means the person who orders the possessor of goods to deliver. Issuer includes any person for whom an agent or employee purports to act in issuing a document if the agent or employee has real or apparent authority to issue documents, notwithstanding that the issuer received no goods or that the goods were misdescribed or that in any other respect the agent or employee violated his instructions.

(h) "Warehouseman" is a person engaged in the business of storing goods for hire.

(2) Other definitions applying to this Article or to specified Parts thereof, and the sections in which they appear are:

"Duly negotiate". Section 7–501.

"Person entitled under the document". Section 7–403(4).

(3) Definitions in other Articles applying to this Article and the sections in which they appear are:

"Contract for sale". Section 2–106.

"Overseas". Section 2–323.

"Receipt" of goods. Section 2–103.

(4) In addition Article 1 contains general definitions and principles of construction and interpretation applicable throughout this Article.

§ 7-103. Relation of Article to Treaty, Statute, Tariff, Classification or Regulation.

To the extent that any treaty or statute of the United States, regulatory statute of this State or tariff, classification or regulation filed or issued pursuant thereto is applicable, the provisions of this Article are subject thereto.

§ 7-104. Negotiable and Non-Negotiable Warehouse Receipt, Bill of Lading or Other Document of Title.

(1) A warehouse receipt, bill of lading or other document of title is negotiable

(a) if by its terms the goods are to be delivered to bearer or to the order of a named person; or

(b) where recognized in overseas trade, if it runs to a named person or assigns.

(2) Any other document is nonnegotiable. A bill of lading in which it is stated that the goods are consigned to a named person is not made negotiable by a provision that the goods are to be delivered only against a written order signed by the same or another named person.

§ 7-105. Construction Against Negative Implication.

The omission from either Part 2 or Part 3 of this Article of a provision corresponding to a provision made in the other Part does not imply that a corresponding rule of law is not applicable.

PART 2: Warehouse Receipts: Special Provisions

§ 7-201. Who May Issue a Warehouse Receipt; Storage Under Government Bond.

(1) A warehouse receipt may be issued by any warehouseman.

(2) Where goods including distilled spirits and agricultural commodities are stored under a statute requiring a bond against withdrawal or a license for the issuance of receipts in the nature of warehouse receipts, a receipt issued for the goods has like effect as a warehouse receipt even though issued by a person who is the owner of the goods and is not a warehouseman.

§ 7-202. Form of Warehouse Receipt; Essential Terms; Optional Terms.

(1) A warehouse receipt need not be in any particular form.

(2) Unless a warehouse receipt embodies within its written or printed terms each of the following, the warehouseman is liable for damages caused by the omission to a person injured thereby:

(a) the location of the warehouse where the goods are stored;

(b) the date of issue of the receipt;

(c) the consecutive number of the receipt;

(d) a statement whether the goods received will be delivered to the bearer, to a specified person, or to a specified person or his order;

(e) the rate of storage and handling charges, except that where goods are stored under a field warehousing arrangement a statement of that fact is sufficient on a non-negotiable receipt;

(f) a description of the goods or of the packages containing them;

(g) the signature of the warehouseman, which may be made by his authorized agent;

(h) if the receipt is issued for goods of which the warehouseman is owner, either solely or jointly or in common with others, the fact of such ownership; and

(i) a statement of the amount of advances made and of liabilities incurred for which the warehouseman claims a lien or security interest (Section 7–209). If the precise amount of such advances made or of such liabilities incurred is, at the time of the issue of the receipt, unknown to the warehouseman or to his agent who issues it, a statement of the fact that advances have been made or liabilities incurred and the purpose thereof is sufficient.

(3) A warehouseman may insert in his receipt any other terms which are not contrary to the provisions of this Act and do not impair his obligation of delivery (Section 7–403) or his duty of care (Section 7–204). Any contrary provisions shall be ineffective.

§ 7-203. Liability for Non-Receipt or Misdescription.

A party to or purchaser for value in good faith of a document of title other than a bill of lading relying in either case upon the description therein of the goods may recover from the issuer damages caused by the nonreceipt or misdescription of the goods, except to the extent that the document conspicuously indicates that the issuer does not know whether any part or all of the goods in fact were received or conform to the description, as where the description is in terms of marks or labels or kind, quantity or condition, or the receipt or description is qualified by "contents, condition and quality unknown", "said to contain" or the like, if such indication be true, or the party or purchaser otherwise has notice.

§ 7-204. Duty of Care; Contractual Limitation of Warehouseman's Liability.

(1) A warehouseman is liable for damages for loss of or injury to the goods caused by his failure to exercise such care in regard to them as a reasonably careful man would exercise under like circumstances but unless otherwise agreed he is not liable for damages which could not have been avoided by the exercise of such care.

(2) Damages may be limited by a term in the warehouse receipt or storage agreement limiting the amount of liability in case of loss or damage, and setting forth a specific liability per article or item, or value per unit of weight, beyond which the warehouseman shall not be liable; provided, however, that such liability may on written request of the bailor at the time of signing such storage agreement or within a reasonable time after receipt of the warehouse receipt be increased on part or all of the goods thereunder, in which event increased rates may be charged based on such increased valuation, but that no such increase shall be permitted contrary to a lawful limitation of liability contained in the warehouseman's tariff, if any. No such limitation is effective with respect to the warehouseman's liability for conversion to his own use.

(3) Reasonable provisions as to the time and manner of presenting claims and instituting actions based on the bailment may be included in the warehouse receipt or tariff.

(4) This section does not impair or repeal . . .

Note: *Insert in subsection (4) a reference to any statute which imposes a higher responsibility upon the warehouseman or invalidates contractual limitations which would be permissible under this Article.*

§ 7-205. Title Under Warehouse Receipt Defeated in Certain Cases.

A buyer in the ordinary course of business of fungible goods sold and delivered by a warehouseman who is also in the business of buying and selling such goods takes free of any claim under a warehouse receipt even though it has been duly negotiated.

§ 7-206. Termination of Storage at Warehouseman's Option.

(1) A warehouseman may on notifying the person on whose account the goods are held and any other person known to claim an interest in the goods require payment of any charges and removal of the goods from the warehouse at the termination of the period of storage fixed by the document, or, if no period is fixed, within a stated period not less than thirty days after the notification. If the goods are not removed before the date specified in the notification, the warehouseman may sell them in accordance with the provisions of the section on enforcement of a warehouseman's lien (Section 7–210).

(2) If a warehouseman in good faith believes that the goods are about to deteriorate or decline in value to less than the amount of his lien within the time prescribed in subsection (1) for notification, advertisement and sale, the warehouseman may specify in the notification any reasonable shorter time for removal of the goods and in case the goods are not removed, may sell them at public sale held not less than one week after a single advertisement or posting.

(3) If as a result of a quality or condition of the goods of which the warehouseman had no notice at the time of deposit the goods are a hazard to other property or to the warehouse or to persons, the warehouseman may sell the goods at public or private sale without advertisement on reasonable notification to all persons known to claim an interest in the goods. If the warehouseman after a reasonable effort is unable to sell the goods he may dispose of them in any lawful manner and shall incur no liability by reason of such disposition.

(4) The warehouseman must deliver the goods to any person entitled to them under this Article upon due demand made at any time prior to sale or other disposition under this section.

(5) The warehouseman may satisfy his lien from the proceeds of any sale or disposition under this section but must hold the balance for delivery on the demand of any person to whom he would have been bound to deliver the goods.

§ 7-207. Goods Must Be Kept Separate; Fungible Goods.

(1) Unless the warehouse receipt otherwise provides, a warehouseman must keep separate the goods covered by each receipt so as to permit at all

times identification and delivery of those goods except that different lots of fungible goods may be commingled.

(2) Fungible goods so commingled are owned in common by the persons entitled thereto and the warehouseman is severally liable to each owner for that owner's share. Where because of overissue a mass of fungible goods is insufficient to meet all the receipts which the warehouseman has issued against it, the persons entitled include all holders to whom overissued receipts have been duly negotiated.

§ 7-208. Altered Warehouse Receipts.

Where a blank in a negotiable warehouse receipt has been filled in without authority, a purchaser for value and without notice of the want of authority may treat the insertion as authorized. Any other unauthorized alteration leaves any receipt enforceable against the issuer according to its original tenor.

§ 7-209. Lien of Warehouseman.

(1) A warehouseman has a lien against the bailor on the goods covered by a warehouse receipt or on the proceeds thereof in his possession for charges for storage or transportation (including demurrage and terminal charges), insurance, labor, or charges present or future in relation to the goods, and for expenses necessary for preservation of the goods or reasonably incurred in their sale pursuant to law. If the person on whose account the goods are held is liable for like charges or expenses in relation to other goods whenever deposited and it is stated in the receipt that a lien is claimed for charges and expenses in relation to other goods, the warehouseman also has a lien against him for such charges and expenses whether or not the other goods have been delivered by the warehouseman. But against a person to whom a negotiable warehouse receipt is duly negotiated a warehouseman's lien is limited to charges in an amount or at a rate specified on the receipt or if no charges are so specified then to a reasonable charge for storage of the goods covered by the receipt subsequent to the date of the receipt.

(2) The warehouseman may also reserve a security interest against the bailor for a maximum amount specified on the receipt for charges other than those specified in subsection (1), such as for money advanced and interest. Such a security interest is governed by the Article on Secured Transactions (Article 9).

(3) (a) A warehouseman's lien for charges and expenses under subsection (1) or a security interest under subsection (2) is also effective against any person who so entrusted the bailor with possession of the goods that a pledge of them by him to a good faith purchaser for value would have been valid but is not effective against a person as to whom the document confers no right in the goods covered by it under Section 7–503.

(b) A warehouseman's lien on household goods for charges and expenses in relation to the goods under subsection (1) is also effective against all persons if the depositor was the legal possessor of the goods at the time of deposit. "Household goods" means furniture, furnishings and personal effects used by the depositor in a dwelling.

(4) A warehouseman loses his lien on any goods which he voluntarily delivers or which he unjustifiably refuses to deliver.

§ 7-210. Enforcement of Warehouseman's Lien.

(1) Except as provided in subsection (2), a warehouseman's lien may be enforced by public or private sale of the goods in bloc or in parcels, at any time or place and on any terms which are commercially reasonable, after notifying all persons known to claim an interest in the goods. Such notification must include a statement of the amount due, the nature of the proposed sale and the time and place of any public sale. The fact that a better price could have been obtained by a sale at a different time or in a different method from that selected by the warehouseman is not of itself sufficient to establish that the sale was not made in a commercially reasonable manner. If

the warehouseman either sells the goods in the usual manner in any recognized market therefor, or if he sells at the price current in such market at the time of his sale, or if he has otherwise sold in conformity with commercially reasonable practices among dealers in the type of goods sold, he has sold in a commercially reasonable manner. A sale of more goods than apparently necessary to be offered to ensure satisfaction of the obligation is not commercially reasonable except in cases covered by the preceding sentence.

(2) A warehouseman's lien on goods other than goods stored by a merchant in the course of his business may be enforced only as follows:

(a) All persons known to claim an interest in the goods must be notified.

(b) The notification must be delivered in person or sent by registered or certified letter to the last known address of any person to be notified.

(c) The notification must include an itemized statement of the claim, a description of the goods subject to the lien, a demand for payment within a specified time not less than ten days after receipt of the notification, and a conspicuous statement that unless the claim is paid within the time the goods will be advertised for sale and sold by auction at a specified time and place.

(d) The sale must conform to the terms of the notification.

(e) The sale must be held at the nearest suitable place to that where the goods are held or stored.

(f) After the expiration of the time given in the notification, an advertisement of the sale must be published once a week for two weeks consecutively in a newspaper of general circulation where the sale is to be held. The advertisement must include a description of the goods, the name of the person on whose account they are being held, and the time and place of the sale. The sale must take place at least fifteen days after the first publication. If there is no newspaper of general circulation where the sale is to be held, the advertisement must be posted at least ten days before the sale in not less than six conspicuous places in the neighborhood of the proposed sale.

(3) Before any sale pursuant to this section any person claiming a right in the goods may pay the amount necessary to satisfy the lien and the reasonable expenses incurred under this section. In that event the goods must not be sold, but must be retained by the warehouseman subject to the terms of the receipt and this Article.

(4) The warehouseman may buy at any public sale pursuant to this section.

(5) A purchaser in good faith of goods sold to enforce a warehouseman's lien takes the goods free of any rights of persons against whom the lien was valid, despite noncompliance by the warehouseman with the requirements of this section.

(6) The warehouseman may satisfy his lien from the proceeds of any sale pursuant to this section but must hold the balance, if any, for delivery on demand to any person to whom he would have been bound to deliver the goods.

(7) The rights provided by this section shall be in addition to all other rights allowed by law to a creditor against his debtor.

(8) Where a lien is on goods stored by a merchant in the course of his business the lien may be enforced in accordance with either subsection (1) or (2).

(9) The warehouseman is liable for damages caused by failure to comply with the requirements for sale under this section and in case of willful violation is liable for conversion.

As amended in 1962.

PART 3: Bills of Lading: Special Provisions

§ 7-301. Liability for Non-Receipt or Misdescription; "Said to Contain"; "Shipper's Load and Count"; Improper Handling.

(1) A consignee of a non-negotiable bill who has given value in good faith or a holder to whom a negotiable bill has been duly negotiated relying in

either case upon the description therein of the goods, or upon the date therein shown, may recover from the issuer damages caused by the misdating of the bill or the nonreceipt or misdescription of the goods, except to the extent that the document indicates that the issuer does not know whether any part of all of the goods in fact were received or conform to the description, as where the description is in terms of marks or labels or kind, quantity, or condition or the receipt or description is qualified by "contents or condition of contents of packages unknown", "said to contain", "shipper's weight, load and count" or the like, if such indication be true.

(2) When goods are loaded by an issuer who is a common carrier, the issuer must count the packages of goods if package freight and ascertain the kind and quantity if bulk freight. In such cases "shipper's weight, load and count" or other words indicating that the description was made by the shipper are ineffective except as to freight concealed by packages.

(3) When bulk freight is loaded by a shipper who makes available to the issuer adequate facilities for weighing such freight, an issuer who is a common carrier must ascertain the kind and quantity within a reasonable time after receiving the written request of the shipper to do so. In such cases "shipper's weight" or other words of like purport are ineffective.

(4) The issuer may by inserting in the bill the words "shipper's weight, load and count" or other words of like purport indicate that the goods were loaded by the shipper; and if such statement be true the issuer shall not be liable for damages caused by the improper loading. But their omission does not imply liability for such damages.

(5) The shipper shall be deemed to have guaranteed to the issuer the accuracy at the time of shipment of the description, marks, labels, number, kind, quantity, condition and weight, as furnished by him; and the shipper shall indemnify the issuer against damage caused by inaccuracies in such particulars. The right of the issuer to such indemnity shall in no way limit his responsibility and liability under the contract of carriage to any person other than the shipper.

§ 7-302. Through Bills of Lading and Similar Documents.

(1) The issuer of a through bill of lading or other document embodying an undertaking to be performed in part by persons acting as its agents or by connecting carriers is liable to anyone entitled to recover on the document for any breach by such other persons or by a connecting carrier of its obligation under the document but to the extent that the bill covers an undertaking to be performed overseas or in territory not contiguous to the continental United States or an undertaking including matters other than transportation this liability may be varied by agreement of the parties.

(2) Where goods covered by a through bill of lading or other document embodying an undertaking to be performed in part by persons other than the issuer are received by any such person, he is subject with respect to his own performance while the goods are in his possession to the obligation of the issuer. His obligation is discharged by delivery of the goods to another such person pursuant to the document, and does not include liability for breach by any other such persons or by the issuer.

(3) The issuer of such through bill of lading or other document shall be entitled to recover from the connecting carrier or such other person in possession of the goods when the breach of the obligation under the document occurred, the amount it may be required to pay to anyone entitled to recover on the document therefor, as may be evidenced by any receipt, judgment, or transcript thereof, and the amount of any expense reasonably incurred by it in defending any action brought by anyone entitled to recover on the document therefor.

§ 7-303. Diversion; Reconsignment; Change of Instructions.

(1) Unless the bill of lading otherwise provides, the carrier may deliver the goods to a person or destination other than that stated in the bill or may otherwise dispose of the goods on instructions from

    (a) the holder of a negotiable bill; or

    (b) the consignor on a non-negotiable bill notwithstanding contrary instructions from the consignee; or

    (c) the consignee on a non-negotiable bill in the absence of contrary instructions from the consignor, if the goods have arrived at the billed destination or if the consignee is in possession of the bill; or

    (d) the consignee on a non-negotiable bill if he is entitled as against the consignor to dispose of them.

(2) Unless such instructions are noted on a negotiable bill of lading, a person to whom the bill is duly negotiated can hold the bailee according to the original terms.

§ 7-304. Bills of Lading in a Set.

(1) Except where customary in overseas transportation, a bill of lading must not be issued in a set of parts. The issuer is liable for damages caused by violation of this subsection.

(2) Where a bill of lading is lawfully drawn in a set of parts, each of which is numbered and expressed to be valid only if the goods have not been delivered against any other part, the whole of the parts constitute one bill.

(3) Where a bill of lading is lawfully issued in a set of parts and different parts are negotiated to different persons, the title of the holder to whom the first due negotiation is made prevails as to both the document and the goods even though any later holder may have received the goods from the carrier in good faith and discharged the carrier's obligation by surrender of his part.

(4) Any person who negotiates or transfers a single part of a bill of lading drawn in a set is liable to holders of that part as if it were the whole set.

(5) The bailee is obliged to deliver in accordance with Part 4 of this Article against the first presented part of a bill of lading lawfully drawn in a set. Such delivery discharges the bailee's obligation on the whole bill.

§ 7-305. Destination Bills.

(1) Instead of issuing a bill of lading to the consignor at the place of shipment a carrier may at the request of the consignor procure the bill to be issued at destination or at any other place designated in the request.

(2) Upon request of anyone entitled as against the carrier to control the goods while in transit and on surrender of any outstanding bill of lading or other receipt covering such goods, the issuer may procure a substitute bill to be issued at any place designated in the request.

§ 7-306. Altered Bills of Lading.

An unauthorized alteration or filling in of a blank in a bill of lading leaves the bill enforceable according to its original tenor.

§ 7-307. Lien of Carrier.

(1) A carrier has a lien on the goods covered by a bill of lading for charges subsequent to the date of its receipt of the goods for storage or transportation (including demurrage and terminal charges) and for expenses necessary for preservation of the goods incident to their transportation or reasonably incurred in their sale pursuant to law. But against a purchaser for value of a negotiable bill of lading a carrier's lien is limited to charges stated in the bill or the applicable tariffs, or if no charges are stated then to a reasonable charge.

(2) A lien for charges and expenses under subsection (1) on goods which the carrier was required by law to receive for transportation is effective against the consignor or any person entitled to the goods unless the carrier

had notice that the consignor lacked authority to subject the goods to such charges and expenses. Any other lien under subsection (1) is effective against the consignor and any person who permitted the bailor to have control or possession of the goods unless the carrier had notice that the bailor lacked such authority.

(3) A carrier loses his lien on any goods which he voluntarily delivers or which he unjustifiably refuses to deliver.

§ 7-308. Enforcement of Carrier's Lien.

(1) A carrier's lien may be enforced by public or private sale of the goods, in bloc or in parcels, at any time or place and on any terms which are commercially reasonable, after notifying all persons known to claim an interest in the goods. Such notification must include a statement of the amount due, the nature of the proposed sale and the time and place of any public sale. The fact that a better price could have been obtained by a sale at a different time or in a different method from that selected by the carrier is not of itself sufficient to establish that the sale was not made in a commercially reasonable manner. If the carrier either sells the goods in the usual manner in any recognized market therefor or if he sells at the price current in such market at the time of his sale or if he has otherwise sold in conformity with commercially reasonable practices among dealers in the type of goods sold he has sold in a commercially reasonable manner. A sale of more goods than apparently necessary to be offered to ensure satisfaction of the obligation is not commercially reasonable except in cases covered by the preceding sentence.

(2) Before any sale pursuant to this section any person claiming a right in the goods may pay the amount necessary to satisfy the lien and the reasonable expenses incurred under this section. In that event the goods must not be sold, but must be retained by the carrier subject to the terms of the bill and this Article.

(3) The carrier may buy at any public sale pursuant to this section.

(4) A purchaser in good faith of goods sold to enforce a carrier's lien takes the goods free of any rights of persons against whom the lien was valid, despite noncompliance by the carrier with the requirements of this section.

(5) The carrier may satisfy his lien from the proceeds of any sale pursuant to this section but must hold the balance, if any, for delivery on demand to any person to whom he would have been bound to deliver the goods.

(6) The rights provided by this section shall be in addition to all other rights allowed by law to a creditor against his debtor.

(7) A carrier's lien may be enforced in accordance with either subsection (1) or the procedure set forth in subsection (2) of Section 7–210.

(8) The carrier is liable for damages caused by failure to comply with the requirements for sale under this section and in case of willful violation is liable for conversion.

§ 7-309. Duty of Care; Contractual Limitation of Carrier's Liability.

(1) A carrier who issues a bill of lading whether negotiable or nonnegotiable must exercise the degree of care in relation to the goods which a reasonably careful man would exercise under like circumstances. This subsection does not repeal or change any law or rule of law which imposes liability upon a common carrier for damages not caused by its negligence.

(2) Damages may be limited by a provision that the carrier's liability shall not exceed a value stated in the document if the carrier's rates are dependent upon value and the consignor by the carrier's tariff is afforded an opportunity to declare a higher value or a value as lawfully provided in the tariff, or where no tariff is filed he is otherwise advised of such opportunity; but no such limitation is effective with respect to the carrier's liability for conversion to its own use.

(3) Reasonable provisions as to the time and manner of presenting claims

and instituting actions based on the shipment may be included in a bill of lading or tariff.

PART 4: Warehouse Receipts and Bills of Lading: General Obligations

§ 7-401. Irregularities in Issue of Receipt or Bill or Conduct of Issuer.

The obligations imposed by this Article on an issuer apply to a document of title regardless of the fact that

   (a) the document may not comply with the requirements of this Article or of any other law or regulation regarding its issue, form or content; or

   (b) the issuer may have violated laws regulating the conduct of his business; or

   (c) the goods covered by the document were owned by the bailee at the time the document was issued; or

   (d) the person issuing the document does not come within the definition of warehouseman if it purports to be a warehouse receipt.

§ 7-402. Duplicate Receipt or Bill; Overissue.

Neither a duplicate nor any other document of title purporting to cover goods already represented by an outstanding document of the same issuer confers any right in the goods, except as provided in the case of bills in a set, overissue of documents for fungible goods and substitutes for lost, stolen or destroyed documents. But the issuer is liable for damages caused by his overissue or failure to identify a duplicate document as such by conspicuous notation on its face.

§ 7-403. Obligation of Warehouseman or Carrier to Deliver; Excuse.

(1) The bailee must deliver the goods to a person entitled under the document who complies with subsections (2) and (3), unless and to the extent that the bailee establishes any of the following:

   (a) delivery of the goods to a person whose receipt was rightful as against the claimant;

   (b) damage to or delay, loss or destruction of the goods for which the bailee is not liable [, but the burden of establishing negligence in such cases is on the person entitled under the document];

Note: *The brackets in (1)(b) indicate that State enactments may differ on this point without serious damage to the principle of uniformity.*

   (c) previous sale or other disposition of the goods in lawful enforcement of a lien or on warehouseman's lawful termination of storage;

   (d) the exercise by a seller of his right to stop delivery pursuant to the provisions of the Article on Sales (Section 2–705);

   (e) a diversion, reconsignment or other disposition pursuant to the provisions of this Article (Section 7–303) or tariff regulating such right;

   (f) release, satisfaction or any other fact affording a personal defense against the claimant;

   (g) any other lawful excuse.

(2) A person claiming goods covered by a document of title must satisfy the bailee's lien where the bailee so requests or where the bailee is prohibited by law from delivering the goods until the charges are paid.

(3) Unless the person claiming is one against whom the document confers no right under Sec. 7–503(1), he must surrender for cancellation or notation of partial deliveries any outstanding negotiable document covering the goods, and the bailee must cancel the document or conspicuously note the partial delivery thereon or be liable to any person to whom the document is duly negotiated.

(4) "Person entitled under the document" means holder in the case of a negotiable document, or the person to whom delivery is to be made by the terms of or pursuant to written instructions under a non-negotiable document.

§ 7-404. No Liability for Good Faith Delivery Pursuant to Receipt or Bill.

A bailee who in good faith including observance of reasonable commercial standards has received goods and delivered or otherwise disposed of them according to the terms of the document of title or pursuant to this Article is not liable therefor. This rule applies even though the person from whom he received the goods had no authority to procure the document or to dispose of the goods and even though the person to whom he delivered the goods had no authority to receive them.

PART 5: Warehouse Receipts and Bills of Lading: Negotiation and Transfer

§ 7-501. Form of Negotiation and Requirements of "Due Negotiation".

(1) A negotiable document of title running to the order of a named person is negotiated by his indorsement and delivery. After his indorsement in blank or to bearer any person can negotiate it by delivery alone.

(2)(a) A negotiable document of title is also negotiated by delivery alone when by its original terms it runs to bearer.

(b) When a document running to the order of a named person is delivered to him the effect is the same as if the document had been negotiated.

(3) Negotiation of a negotiable document of title after it has been indorsed to a specified person requires indorsement by the special indorsee as well as delivery.

(4) A negotiable document of title is "duly negotiated" when it is negotiated in the manner stated in this section to a holder who purchases it in good faith without notice of any defense against or claim to it on the part of any person and for value, unless it is established that the negotiation is not in the regular course of business or financing or involves receiving the document in settlement or payment of a money obligation.

(5) Indorsement of a nonnegotiable document neither makes it negotiable nor adds to the transferee's rights.

(6) The naming in a negotiable bill of a person to be notified of the arrival of the goods does not limit the negotiability of the bill nor constitute notice to a purchaser thereof of any interest of such person in the goods.

§ 7-502. Rights Acquired by Due Negotiation.

(1) Subject to the following section and to the provisions of Section 7–205 on fungible goods, a holder to whom a negotiable document of title has been duly negotiated acquires thereby:

(a) title to the document;

(b) title to the goods;

(c) all rights accruing under the law of agency or estoppel, including rights to goods delivered to the bailee after the document was issued; and

(d) the direct obligation of the issuer to hold or deliver the goods according to the terms of the document free of any defense or claim by him except those arising under the terms of the document or under this Article. In the case of a delivery order the bailee's obligation accrues only upon acceptance and the obligation acquired by the holder is that the issuer and any indorser will procure the acceptance of the bailee.

(2) Subject to the following section, title and rights so acquired are not defeated by any stoppage of the goods represented by the document or by surrender of such goods by the bailee, and are not impaired even though the negotiation or any prior negotiation constituted a breach of duty or even though any person has been deprived of possession of the document by misrepresentation, fraud, accident, mistake, duress, loss, theft or conversion, or even though a previous sale or other transfer of the goods or document has been made to a third person.

§ 7-503. Document of Title to Goods Defeated in Certain Cases.

(1) A document of title confers no right in goods against a person who before issuance of the document had a legal interest or a perfected security interest in them and who neither

(a) delivered or entrusted them or any document of title covering them to the bailor or his nominee with actual or apparent authority to ship, store or sell or with power to obtain delivery under this Article (Section 7–403) or with power of disposition under this Act (Sections 2–403 and 9–307) or other statute or rule of law; nor

(b) acquiesced in the procurement by the bailor or his nominee of any document of title.

(2) Title to goods based upon an unaccepted delivery order is subject to the rights of anyone to whom a negotiable warehouse receipt or bill of lading covering the goods has been duly negotiated. Such a title may be defeated under the next section to the same extent as the rights of the issuer or a transferee from the issuer.

(3) Title to goods based upon a bill of lading issued to a freight forwarder is subject to the rights of anyone to whom a bill issued by the freight forwarder is duly negotiated; but delivery by the carrier in accordance with Part 4 of this Article pursuant to its own bill of lading discharges the carrier's obligation to deliver.

As amended in 1999.

§ 7-504. Rights Acquired in the Absence of Due Negotiation; Effect of Diversion; Seller's Stoppage of Delivery.

(1) A transferee of a document, whether negotiable or nonnegotiable, to whom the document has been delivered but not duly negotiated, acquires the title and rights which his transferor had or had actual authority to convey.

(2) In the case of a nonnegotiable document, until but not after the bailee receives notification of the transfer, the rights of the transferee may be defeated

(a) by those creditors of the transferor who could treat the sale as void under Section 2–402; or

(b) by a buyer from the transferor in ordinary course of business if the bailee has delivered the goods to the buyer or received notification of his rights; or

(c) as against the bailee by good faith dealings of the bailee with the transferor.

(3) A diversion or other change of shipping instructions by the consignor in a nonnegotiable bill of lading which causes the bailee not to deliver to the consignee defeats the consignee's title to the goods if they have been delivered to a buyer in ordinary course of business and in any event defeats the consignee's rights against the bailee.

(4) Delivery pursuant to a nonnegotiable document may be stopped by a seller under Section 2–705, and subject to the requirement of due notification there provided. A bailee honoring the seller's instructions is entitled to be indemnified by the seller against any resulting loss or expense.

§ 7-505. Indorser Not a Guarantor for Other Parties.

The indorsement of a document of title issued by a bailee does not make the indorser liable for any default by the bailee or by previous indorsers.

§ 7-506. Delivery Without Indorsement: Right to Compel Indorsement.

The transferee of a negotiable document of title has a specifically enforceable right to have his transferor supply any necessary indorsement but the transfer becomes a negotiation only as of the time the indorsement is supplied.

§ 7-507. Warranties on Negotiation or Transfer of Receipt or Bill.

Where a person negotiates or transfers a document of title for value otherwise than as a mere intermediary under the next following section, then unless otherwise agreed he warrants to his immediate purchaser only in addition to any warranty made in selling the goods

(a) that the document is genuine; and

(b) that he has no knowledge of any fact which would impair its validity or worth; and

(c) that his negotiation or transfer is rightful and fully effective with respect to the title to the document and the goods it represents.

§ 7-508. Warranties of Collecting Bank as to Documents.

A collecting bank or other intermediary known to be entrusted with documents on behalf of another or with collection of a draft or other claim against delivery of documents warrants by such delivery of the documents only its own good faith and authority. This rule applies even though the intermediary has purchased or made advances against the claim or draft to be collected.

§ 7-509. Receipt or Bill: When Adequate Compliance With Commercial Contract.

The question whether a document is adequate to fulfill the obligations of a contract for sale or the conditions of a credit is governed by the Articles on Sales (Article 2) and on Letters of Credit (Article 5).

PART 6: Warehouse Receipts and Bills of Lading: Miscellaneous Provisions

§ 7-601. Lost and Missing Documents.

(1) If a document has been lost, stolen or destroyed, a court may order delivery of the goods or issuance of a substitute document and the bailee may without liability to any person comply with such order. If the document was negotiable the claimant must post security approved by the court to indemnify any person who may suffer loss as a result of non-surrender of the document. If the document was not negotiable, such security may be required at the discretion of the court. The court may also in its discretion order payment of the bailee's reasonable costs and counsel fees.

(2) A bailee who without court order delivers goods to a person claiming under a missing negotiable document is liable to any person injured thereby, and if the delivery is not in good faith becomes liable for conversion. Delivery in good faith is not conversion if made in accordance with a filed classification or tariff or, where no classification or tariff is filed, if the claimant posts security with the bailee in an amount at least double the value of the goods at the time of posting to indemnify any person injured by the delivery who files a notice of claim within one year after the delivery.

§ 7-602. Attachment of Goods Covered by a Negotiable Document.

Except where the document was originally issued upon delivery of the goods by a person who had no power to dispose of them, no lien attaches by virtue of any judicial process to goods in the possession of a bailee for which a negotiable document of title is outstanding unless the document be first surrendered to the bailee or its negotiation enjoined, and the bailee shall not be compelled to deliver the goods pursuant to process until the document is surrendered to him or impounded by the court. One who purchases the document for value without notice of the process or injunction takes free of the lien imposed by judicial process.

§ 7-603. Conflicting Claims; Interpleader.

If more than one person claims title or possession of the goods, the bailee is excused from delivery until he has had a reasonable time to ascertain the validity of the adverse claims or to bring an action to compel all claimants to interplead and may compel such interpleader, either in defending an action for nondelivery of the goods, or by original action, whichever is appropriate.

REVISED (1994) ARTICLE 8: Investment Securities

PART 1: Short Title and General Matters

§ 8-101. Short Title.

This Article may be cited as Uniform Commercial Code—Investment Securities.

§ 8-102. Definitions.

(a) In this Article:

(1) "Adverse claim" means a claim that a claimant has a property interest in a financial asset and that it is a violation of the rights of the claimant for another person to hold, transfer, or deal with the financial asset.

(2) "Bearer form," as applied to a certificated security, means a form in which the security is payable to the bearer of the security certificate according to its terms but not by reason of an indorsement.

(3) "Broker" means a person defined as a broker or dealer under the federal securities laws, but without excluding a bank acting in that capacity.

(4) "Certificated security" means a security that is represented by a certificate.

(5) "Clearing corporation" means:

(i) a person that is registered as a "clearing agency" under the federal securities laws;

(ii) a federal reserve bank; or

(iii) any other person that provides clearance or settlement services with respect to financial assets that would require it to register as a clearing agency under the federal securities laws but for an exclusion or exemption from the registration requirement, if its activities as a clearing corporation, including promulgation of rules, are subject to regulation by a federal or state governmental authority.

(6) "Communicate" means to:

(i) send a signed writing; or

(ii) transmit information by any mechanism agreed upon by the persons transmitting and receiving the information.

(7) "Entitlement holder" means a person identified in the records of a securities intermediary as the person having a security entitlement against the securities intermediary. If a person acquires a security entitlement by virtue of Section 8–501(b)(2) or (3), that person is the entitlement holder.

(8) "Entitlement order" means a notification communicated to a securities intermediary directing transfer or redemption of a financial asset to which the entitlement holder has a security entitlement.

(9) "Financial asset," except as otherwise provided in Section 8–103, means:

> (i) a security;
>
> (ii) an obligation of a person or a share, participation, or other interest in a person or in property or an enterprise of a person, which is, or is of a type, dealt in or traded on financial markets, or which is recognized in any area in which it is issued or dealt in as a medium for investment; or
>
> (iii) any property that is held by a securities intermediary for another person in a securities account if the securities intermediary has expressly agreed with the other person that the property is to be treated as a financial asset under this Article.
>
> As context requires, the term means either the interest itself or the means by which a person's claim to it is evidenced, including a certificated or uncertificated security, a security certificate, or a security entitlement.

(10) "Good faith," for purposes of the obligation of good faith in the performance or enforcement of contracts or duties within this Article, means honesty in fact and the observance of reasonable commercial standards of fair dealing.

(11) "Indorsement" means a signature that alone or accompanied by other words is made on a security certificate in registered form or on a separate document for the purpose of assigning, transferring, or redeeming the security or granting a power to assign, transfer, or redeem it.

(12) "Instruction" means a notification communicated to the issuer of an uncertificated security which directs that the transfer of the security be registered or that the security be redeemed.

(13) "Registered form," as applied to a certificated security, means a form in which:

> (i) the security certificate specifies a person entitled to the security; and
>
> (ii) a transfer of the security may be registered upon books maintained for that purpose by or on behalf of the issuer, or the security certificate so states.

(14) "Securities intermediary" means:

> (i) a clearing corporation; or
>
> (ii) a person, including a bank or broker, that in the ordinary course of its business maintains securities accounts for others and is acting in that capacity.

(15) "Security," except as otherwise provided in Section 8–103, means an obligation of an issuer or a share, participation, or other interest in an issuer or in property or an enterprise of an issuer:

> (i) which is represented by a security certificate in bearer or registered form, or the transfer of which may be registered upon books maintained for that purpose by or on behalf of the issuer;
>
> (ii) which is one of a class or series or by its terms is divisible into a class or series of shares, participations, interests, or obligations; and
>
> (iii) which:
>
>> (A) is, or is of a type, dealt in or traded on securities exchanges or securities markets; or
>>
>> (B) is a medium for investment and by its terms expressly provides that it is a security governed by this Article.

(16) "Security certificate" means a certificate representing a security.

(17) "Security entitlement" means the rights and property interest of an entitlement holder with respect to a financial asset specified in Part 5.

(18) "Uncertificated security" means a security that is not represented by a certificate.

(b) Other definitions applying to this Article and the sections in which they appear are:

Appropriate person	Section 8–107
Control	Section 8–106
Delivery	Section 8–301
Investment company security	Section 8–103
Issuer	Section 8–201
Overissue	Section 8–210
Protected purchaser	Section 8–303
Securities account	Section 8–501

(c) In addition, Article 1 contains general definitions and principles of construction and interpretation applicable throughout this Article.

(d) The characterization of a person, business, or transaction for purposes of this Article does not determine the characterization of the person, business, or transaction for purposes of any other law, regulation, or rule.

§ 8-103. Rules for Determining Whether Certain Obligations and Interests Are Securities or Financial Assets.

(a) A share or similar equity interest issued by a corporation, business trust, joint stock company, or similar entity is a security.

(b) An "investment company security" is a security. "Investment company security" means a share or similar equity interest issued by an entity that is registered as an investment company under the federal investment company laws, an interest in a unit investment trust that is so registered, or a face-amount certificate issued by a face-amount certificate company that is so registered. Investment company security does not include an insurance policy or endowment policy or annuity contract issued by an insurance company.

(c) An interest in a partnership or limited liability company is not a security unless it is dealt in or traded on securities exchanges or in securities markets, its terms expressly provide that it is a security governed by this Article, or it is an investment company security. However, an interest in a partnership or limited liability company is a financial asset if it is held in a securities account.

(d) A writing that is a security certificate is governed by this Article and not by Article 3, even though it also meets the requirements of that Article. However, a negotiable instrument governed by Article 3 is a financial asset if it is held in a securities account.

(e) An option or similar obligation issued by a clearing corporation to its participants is not a security, but is a financial asset.

(f) A commodity contract, as defined in Section 9–102(a)(15), is not a security or a financial asset.

As amended in 1999.

§ 8-104. Acquisition of Security or Financial Asset or Interest Therein.

(a) A person acquires a security or an interest therein, under this Article, if:

> (1) the person is a purchaser to whom a security is delivered pursuant to Section 8–301; or
>
> (2) the person acquires a security entitlement to the security pursuant to Section 8–501.

(b) A person acquires a financial asset, other than a security, or an interest therein, under this Article, if the person acquires a security entitlement to the financial asset.

(c) A person who acquires a security entitlement to a security or other financial asset has the rights specified in Part 5, but is a purchaser of any security, security entitlement, or other financial asset held by the securities intermediary only to the extent provided in Section 8–503.

(d) Unless the context shows that a different meaning is intended, a person who is required by other law, regulation, rule, or agreement to transfer, deliver, present, surrender, exchange, or otherwise put in the possession of another person a security or financial asset satisfies that requirement by causing the other person to acquire an interest in the security or financial asset pursuant to subsection (a) or (b).

§ 8-105. Notice of Adverse Claim.

(a) A person has notice of an adverse claim if:

(1) the person knows of the adverse claim;

(2) the person is aware of facts sufficient to indicate that there is a significant probability that the adverse claim exists and deliberately avoids information that would establish the existence of the adverse claim; or

(3) the person has a duty, imposed by statute or regulation, to investigate whether an adverse claim exists, and the investigation so required would establish the existence of the adverse claim.

(b) Having knowledge that a financial asset or interest therein is or has been transferred by a representative imposes no duty of inquiry into the rightfulness of a transaction and is not notice of an adverse claim. However, a person who knows that a representative has transferred a financial asset or interest therein in a transaction that is, or whose proceeds are being used, for the individual benefit of the representative or otherwise in breach of duty has notice of an adverse claim.

(c) An act or event that creates a right to immediate performance of the principal obligation represented by a security certificate or sets a date on or after which the certificate is to be presented or surrendered for redemption or exchange does not itself constitute notice of an adverse claim except in the case of a transfer more than:

(1) one year after a date set for presentment or surrender for redemption or exchange; or

(2) six months after a date set for payment of money against presentation or surrender of the certificate, if money was available for payment on that date.

(d) A purchaser of a certificated security has notice of an adverse claim if the security certificate:

(1) whether in bearer or registered form, has been indorsed "for collection" or "for surrender" or for some other purpose not involving transfer; or

(2) is in bearer form and has on it an unambiguous statement that it is the property of a person other than the transferor, but the mere writing of a name on the certificate is not such a statement.

(e) Filing of a financing statement under Article 9 is not notice of an adverse claim to a financial asset.

§ 8-106. Control.

(a) A purchaser has "control" of a certificated security in bearer form if the certificated security is delivered to the purchaser.

(b) A purchaser has "control" of a certificated security in registered form if the certificated security is delivered to the purchaser, and:

(1) the certificate is indorsed to the purchaser or in blank by an effective indorsement; or

(2) the certificate is registered in the name of the purchaser, upon original issue or registration of transfer by the issuer.

(c) A purchaser has "control" of an uncertificated security if:

(1) the uncertificated security is delivered to the purchaser; or

(2) the issuer has agreed that it will comply with instructions originated by the purchaser without further consent by the registered owner.

(d) A purchaser has "control" of a security entitlement if:

(1) the purchaser becomes the entitlement holder;

(2) the securities intermediary has agreed that it will comply with entitlement orders originated by the purchaser without further consent by the entitlement holder; or

(3) another person has control of the security entitlement on behalf of

the purchaser or, having previously acquired control of the security entitlement, acknowledges that it has control on behalf of the purchaser.

(e) If an interest in a security entitlement is granted by the entitlement holder to the entitlement holder's own securities intermediary, the securities intermediary has control.

(f) A purchaser who has satisfied the requirements of subsection (c) or (d) has control, even if the registered owner in the case of subsection (c) or the entitlement holder in the case of subsection (d) retains the right to make substitutions for the uncertificated security or security entitlement, to originate instructions or entitlement orders to the issuer or securities intermediary, or otherwise to deal with the uncertificated security or security entitlement.

(g) An issuer or a securities intermediary may not enter into an agreement of the kind described in subsection (c)(2) or (d)(2) without the consent of the registered owner or entitlement holder, but an issuer or a securities intermediary is not required to enter into such an agreement even though the registered owner or entitlement holder so directs. An issuer or securities intermediary that has entered into such an agreement is not required to confirm the existence of the agreement to another party unless requested to do so by the registered owner or entitlement holder. As amended in 1999.

§ 8-107. Whether Indorsement, Instruction, or Entitlement Order Is Effective.

(a) "Appropriate person" means:

(1) with respect to an indorsement, the person specified by a security certificate or by an effective special indorsement to be entitled to the security;

(2) with respect to an instruction, the registered owner of an uncertificated security;

(3) with respect to an entitlement order, the entitlement holder;

(4) if the person designated in paragraph (1), (2), or (3) is deceased, the designated person's successor taking under other law or the designated person's personal representative acting for the estate of the decedent; or

(5) if the person designated in paragraph (1), (2), or (3) lacks capacity, the designated person's guardian, conservator, or other similar representative who has power under other law to transfer the security or financial asset.

(b) An indorsement, instruction, or entitlement order is effective if:

(1) it is made by the appropriate person;

(2) it is made by a person who has power under the law of agency to transfer the security or financial asset on behalf of the appropriate person, including, in the case of an instruction or entitlement order, a person who has control under Section 8–106(c)(2) or (d)(2); or

(3) the appropriate person has ratified it or is otherwise precluded from asserting its ineffectiveness.

(c) An indorsement, instruction, or entitlement order made by a representative is effective even if:

(1) the representative has failed to comply with a controlling instrument or with the law of the State having jurisdiction of the representative relationship, including any law requiring the representative to obtain court approval of the transaction; or

(2) the representative's action in making the indorsement, instruction, or entitlement order or using the proceeds of the transaction is otherwise a breach of duty.

(d) If a security is registered in the name of or specially indorsed to a person described as a representative, or if a securities account is maintained in the name of a person described as a representative, an indorsement, instruction, or entitlement order made by the person is effective even though the person is no longer serving in the described capacity.

(e) Effectiveness of an indorsement, instruction, or entitlement order is determined as of the date the indorsement, instruction, or entitlement order is made, and an indorsement, instruction, or entitlement order does not become ineffective by reason of any later change of circumstances.

§ 8-108. Warranties in Direct Holding.

(a) A person who transfers a certificated security to a purchaser for value warrants to the purchaser, and an indorser, if the transfer is by indorsement, warrants to any subsequent purchaser, that:

(1) the certificate is genuine and has not been materially altered;

(2) the transferor or indorser does not know of any fact that might impair the validity of the security;

(3) there is no adverse claim to the security;

(4) the transfer does not violate any restriction on transfer;

(5) if the transfer is by indorsement, the indorsement is made by an appropriate person, or if the indorsement is by an agent, the agent has actual authority to act on behalf of the appropriate person; and

(6) the transfer is otherwise effective and rightful.

(b) A person who originates an instruction for registration of transfer of an uncertificated security to a purchaser for value warrants to the purchaser that:

(1) the instruction is made by an appropriate person, or if the instruction is by an agent, the agent has actual authority to act on behalf of the appropriate person;

(2) the security is valid;

(3) there is no adverse claim to the security; and

(4) at the time the instruction is presented to the issuer:

(i) the purchaser will be entitled to the registration of transfer;

(ii) the transfer will be registered by the issuer free from all liens, security interests, restrictions, and claims other than those specified in the instruction;

(iii) the transfer will not violate any restriction on transfer; and

(iv) the requested transfer will otherwise be effective and rightful.

(c) A person who transfers an uncertificated security to a purchaser for value and does not originate an instruction in connection with the transfer warrants that:

(1) the uncertificated security is valid;

(2) there is no adverse claim to the security;

(3) the transfer does not violate any restriction on transfer; and

(4) the transfer is otherwise effective and rightful.

(d) A person who indorses a security certificate warrants to the issuer that:

(1) there is no adverse claim to the security; and

(2) the indorsement is effective.

(e) A person who originates an instruction for registration of transfer of an uncertificated security warrants to the issuer that:

(1) the instruction is effective; and

(2) at the time the instruction is presented to the issuer the purchaser will be entitled to the registration of transfer.

(f) A person who presents a certificated security for registration of transfer or for payment or exchange warrants to the issuer that the person is entitled to the registration, payment, or exchange, but a purchaser for value and without notice of adverse claims to whom transfer is registered warrants only that the person has no knowledge of any unauthorized signature in a necessary indorsement.

(g) If a person acts as agent of another in delivering a certificated security to a purchaser, the identity of the principal was known to the person to whom the certificate was delivered, and the certificate delivered by the agent was received by the agent from the principal or received by the agent from another person at the direction of the principal, the person delivering the security certificate warrants only that the delivering person has

authority to act for the principal and does not know of any adverse claim to the certificated security.

(h) A secured party who redelivers a security certificate received, or after payment and on order of the debtor delivers the security certificate to another person, makes only the warranties of an agent under subsection (g).

(i) Except as otherwise provided in subsection (g), a broker acting for a customer makes to the issuer and a purchaser the warranties provided in subsections (a) through (f). A broker that delivers a security certificate to its customer, or causes its customer to be registered as the owner of an uncertificated security, makes to the customer the warranties provided in subsection (a) or (b), and has the rights and privileges of a purchaser under this section. The warranties of and in favor of the broker acting as an agent are in addition to applicable warranties given by and in favor of the customer.

§ 8-109. Warranties in Indirect Holding.

(a) A person who originates an entitlement order to a securities intermediary warrants to the securities intermediary that:

(1) the entitlement order is made by an appropriate person, or if the entitlement order is by an agent, the agent has actual authority to act on behalf of the appropriate person; and

(2) there is no adverse claim to the security entitlement.

(b) A person who delivers a security certificate to a securities intermediary for credit to a securities account or originates an instruction with respect to an uncertificated security directing that the uncertificated security be credited to a securities account makes to the securities intermediary the warranties specified in Section 8–108(a) or (b).

(c) If a securities intermediary delivers a security certificate to its entitlement holder or causes its entitlement holder to be registered as the owner of an uncertificated security, the securities intermediary makes to the entitlement holder the warranties specified in Section 8–108(a) or (b).

§ 8-110. Applicability; Choice of Law.

(a) The local law of the issuer's jurisdiction, as specified in subsection (d), governs:

(1) the validity of a security;

(2) the rights and duties of the issuer with respect to registration of transfer;

(3) the effectiveness of registration of transfer by the issuer;

(4) whether the issuer owes any duties to an adverse claimant to a security; and

(5) whether an adverse claim can be asserted against a person to whom transfer of a certificated or uncertificated security is registered or a person who obtains control of an uncertificated security.

(b) The local law of the securities intermediary's jurisdiction, as specified in subsection (e), governs:

(1) acquisition of a security entitlement from the securities intermediary;

(2) the rights and duties of the securities intermediary and entitlement holder arising out of a security entitlement;

(3) whether the securities intermediary owes any duties to an adverse claimant to a security entitlement; and

(4) whether an adverse claim can be asserted against a person who acquires a security entitlement from the securities intermediary or a person who purchases a security entitlement or interest therein from an entitlement holder.

(c) The local law of the jurisdiction in which a security certificate is located at the time of delivery governs whether an adverse claim can be asserted against a person to whom the security certificate is delivered.

(d) "Issuer's jurisdiction" means the jurisdiction under which the issuer of the security is organized or, if permitted by the law of that jurisdiction, the law of another jurisdiction specified by the issuer. An issuer organized under the law of this State may specify the law of another jurisdiction as the law governing the matters specified in subsection (a)(2) through (5).

(e) The following rules determine a "securities intermediary's jurisdiction" for purposes of this section:

(1) If an agreement between the securities intermediary and its entitlement holder specifies that it is governed by the law of a particular jurisdiction, that jurisdiction is the securities intermediary's jurisdiction.

(2) If an agreement between the securities intermediary and its entitlement holder does not specify the governing law as provided in paragraph (1), but expressly specifies that the securities account is maintained at an office in a particular jurisdiction, that jurisdiction is the securities intermediary's jurisdiction.

(3) If neither paragraph (1) nor paragraph (2) applies and an agreement between the securities intermediary and its entitlement holder governing the securities account expressly provides that the securities account is maintained at an office in a particular jurisdiction, that jurisdiction is the securities intermediary's jurisdiction.

(4) If none of the preceding paragraph applies, the securities intermediary's jurisdiction is the jurisdiction in which the office identified in an account statement as the office serving the entitlement holder's account is located.

(5) If none of the preceding paragraphs applies, the securities intermediary's jurisdiction is the jurisdiction in which the chief executive office of the securities intermediary is located.

(f) A securities intermediary's jurisdiction is not determined by the physical location of certificates representing financial assets, or by the jurisdiction in which is organized the issuer of the financial asset with respect to which an entitlement holder has a security entitlement, or by the location of facilities for data processing or other record keeping concerning the account. As amended in 1999.

§ 8-111. Clearing Corporation Rules.

A rule adopted by a clearing corporation governing rights and obligations among the clearing corporation and its participants in the clearing corporation is effective even if the rule conflicts with this [Act] and affects another party who does not consent to the rule.

§ 8-112. Creditor's Legal Process.

(a) The interest of a debtor in a certificated security may be reached by a creditor only by actual seizure of the security certificate by the officer making the attachment or levy, except as otherwise provided in subsection (d). However, a certificated security for which the certificate has been surrendered to the issuer may be reached by a creditor by legal process upon the issuer.

(b) The interest of a debtor in an uncertificated security may be reached by a creditor only by legal process upon the issuer at its chief executive office in the United States, except as otherwise provided in subsection (d).

(c) The interest of a debtor in a security entitlement may be reached by a creditor only by legal process upon the securities intermediary with whom the debtor's securities account is maintained, except as otherwise provided in subsection (d).

(d) The interest of a debtor in a certificated security for which the certificate is in the possession of a secured party, or in an uncertificated security registered in the name of a secured party, or a security entitlement maintained in the name of a secured party, may be reached by a creditor by legal process upon the secured party.

(e) A creditor whose debtor is the owner of a certificated security, uncertificated security, or security entitlement is entitled to aid from a court of competent jurisdiction, by injunction or otherwise, in reaching the certifi-

cated security, uncertificated security, or security entitlement or in satisfying the claim by means allowed at law or in equity in regard to property that cannot readily be reached by other legal process.

§ 8-113. Statute of Frauds Inapplicable.

A contract or modification of a contract for the sale or purchase of a security is enforceable whether or not there is a writing signed or record authenticated by a party against whom enforcement is sought, even if the contract or modification is not capable of performance within one year of its making.

§ 8-114. Evidentiary Rules Concerning Certificated Securities.

The following rules apply in an action on a certificated security against the issuer:

(1) Unless specifically denied in the pleadings, each signature on a security certificate or in a necessary indorsement is admitted.

(2) If the effectiveness of a signature is put in issue, the burden of establishing effectiveness is on the party claiming under the signature, but the signature is presumed to be genuine or authorized.

(3) If signatures on a security certificate are admitted or established, production of the certificate entitles a holder to recover on it unless the defendant establishes a defense or a defect going to the validity of the security.

(4) If it is shown that a defense or defect exists, the plaintiff has the burden of establishing that the plaintiff or some person under whom the plaintiff claims is a person against whom the defense or defect cannot be asserted.

§ 8-115. Securities Intermediary and Others Not Liable to Adverse Claimant.

A securities intermediary that has transferred a financial asset pursuant to an effective entitlement order, or a broker or other agent or bailee that has dealt with a financial asset at the direction of its customer or principal, is not liable to a person having an adverse claim to the financial asset, unless the securities intermediary, or broker or other agent or bailee:

(1) took the action after it had been served with an injunction, restraining order, or other legal process enjoining it from doing so, issued by a court of competent jurisdiction, and had a reasonable opportunity to act on the injunction, restraining order, or other legal process; or

(2) acted in collusion with the wrongdoer in violating the rights of the adverse claimant; or

(3) in the case of a security certificate that has been stolen, acted with notice of the adverse claim.

§ 8-116. Securities Intermediary as Purchaser for Value.

A securities intermediary that receives a financial asset and establishes a security entitlement to the financial asset in favor of an entitlement holder is a purchaser for value of the financial asset. A securities intermediary that acquires a security entitlement to a financial asset from another securities intermediary acquires the security entitlement for value if the securities intermediary acquiring the security entitlement establishes a security entitlement to the financial asset in favor of an entitlement holder.

PART 2: Issue and Issuer

§ 8-201. Issuer.

(a) With respect to an obligation on or a defense to a security, an "issuer" includes a person that:

(1) places or authorizes the placing of its name on a security certificate, other than as authenticating trustee, registrar, transfer agent, or the like, to evidence a share, participation, or other interest in its property or in an enterprise, or to evidence its duty to perform an obligation represented by the certificate;

(2) creates a share, participation, or other interest in its property or in an enterprise, or undertakes an obligation, that is an uncertificated security;

(3) directly or indirectly creates a fractional interest in its rights or property, if the fractional interest is represented by a security certificate; or

(4) becomes responsible for, or in place of, another person described as an issuer in this section.

(b) With respect to an obligation on or defense to a security, a guarantor is an issuer to the extent of its guaranty, whether or not its obligation is noted on a security certificate.

(c) With respect to a registration of a transfer, issuer means a person on whose behalf transfer books are maintained.

§ 8-202. Issuer's Responsibility and Defenses; Notice of Defect or Defense.

(a) Even against a purchaser for value and without notice, the terms of a certificated security include terms stated on the certificate and terms made part of the security by reference on the certificate to another instrument, indenture, or document or to a constitution, statute, ordinance, rule, regulation, order, or the like, to the extent the terms referred to do not conflict with terms stated on the certificate. A reference under this subsection does not of itself charge a purchaser for value with notice of a defect going to the validity of the security, even if the certificate expressly states that a person accepting it admits notice. The terms of an uncertificated security include those stated in any instrument, indenture, or document or in a constitution, statute, ordinance, rule, regulation, order, or the like, pursuant to which the security is issued.

(b) The following rules apply if an issuer asserts that a security is not valid:

(1) A security other than one issued by a government or governmental subdivision, agency, or instrumentality, even though issued with a defect going to its validity, is valid in the hands of a purchaser for value and without notice of the particular defect unless the defect involves a violation of a constitutional provision. In that case, the security is valid in the hands of a purchaser for value and without notice of the defect, other than one who takes by original issue.

(2) Paragraph (1) applies to an issuer that is a government or governmental subdivision, agency, or instrumentality only if there has been substantial compliance with the legal requirements governing the issue or the issuer has received a substantial consideration for the issue as a whole or for the particular security and a stated purpose of the issue is one for which the issuer has power to borrow money or issue the security.

(c) Except as otherwise provided in Section 8–205, lack of genuineness of a certificated security is a complete defense, even against a purchaser for value and without notice.

(d) All other defenses of the issuer of a security, including nondelivery and conditional delivery of a certificated security, are ineffective against a purchaser for value who has taken the certificated security without notice of the particular defense.

(e) This section does not affect the right of a party to cancel a contract for a security "when, as and if issued" or "when distributed" in the event of a material change in the character of the security that is the subject of the contract or in the plan or arrangement pursuant to which the security is to be issued or distributed.

(f) If a security is held by a securities intermediary against whom an entitlement holder has a security entitlement with respect to the security, the issuer may not assert any defense that the issuer could not assert if the entitlement holder held the security directly.

§ 8-203. Staleness as Notice of Defect or Defense.

After an act or event, other than a call that has been revoked, creating a right to immediate performance of the principal obligation represented by a certificated security or setting a date on or after which the security is to be presented or surrendered for redemption or exchange, a purchaser is charged with notice of any defect in its issue or defense of the issuer, if the act or event:

(1) requires the payment of money, the delivery of a certificated security, the registration of transfer of an uncertificated security, or any of them on presentation or surrender of the security certificate, the money or security is available on the date set for payment or exchange, and the purchaser takes the security more than one year after that date; or

(2) is not covered by paragraph (1) and the purchaser takes the security more than two years after the date set for surrender or presentation or the date on which performance became due.

§ 8-204. Effect of Issuer's Restriction on Transfer.

A restriction on transfer of a security imposed by the issuer, even if otherwise lawful, is ineffective against a person without knowledge of the restriction unless:

(1) the security is certificated and the restriction is noted conspicuously on the security certificate; or

(2) the security is uncertificated and the registered owner has been notified of the restriction.

§ 8-205. Effect of Unauthorized Signature on Security Certificate.

An unauthorized signature placed on a security certificate before or in the course of issue is ineffective, but the signature is effective in favor of a purchaser for value of the certificated security if the purchaser is without notice of the lack of authority and the signing has been done by:

(1) an authenticating trustee, registrar, transfer agent, or other person entrusted by the issuer with the signing of the security certificate or of similar security certificates, or the immediate preparation for signing of any of them; or

(2) an employee of the issuer, or of any of the persons listed in paragraph (1), entrusted with responsible handling of the security certificate.

§ 8-206. Completion of Alteration of Security Certificate.

(a) If a security certificate contains the signatures necessary to its issue or transfer but is incomplete in any other respect:

(1) any person may complete it by filling in the blanks as authorized; and

(2) even if the blanks are incorrectly filled in, the security certificate as completed is enforceable by a purchaser who took it for value and without notice of the incorrectness.

(b) A complete security certificate that has been improperly altered, even if fraudulently, remains enforceable, but only according to its original terms.

§ 8-207. Rights and Duties of Issuer with Respect to Registered Owners.

(a) Before due presentment for registration of transfer of a certificated security in registered form or of an instruction requesting registration of transfer of an uncertificated security, the issuer or indenture trustee may treat the registered owner as the person exclusively entitled to vote, receive notifications, and otherwise exercise all the rights and powers of an owner.

(b) This Article does not affect the liability of the registered owner of a security for a call, assessment, or the like.

§ 8-208. Effect of Signature of Authenticating Trustee, Registrar, or Transfer Agent.

(a) A person signing a security certificate as authenticating trustee, registrar, transfer agent, or the like, warrants to a purchaser for value of the certificated security, if the purchaser is without notice of a particular defect, that:

    (1) the certificate is genuine;

    (2) the person's own participation in the issue of the security is within the person's capacity and within the scope of the authority received by the person from the issuer; and

    (3) the person has reasonable grounds to believe that the certificated security is in the form and within the amount the issuer is authorized to issue.

(b) Unless otherwise agreed, a person signing under subsection (a) does not assume responsibility for the validity of the security in other respects.

§ 8-209. Issuer's Lien.

A lien in favor of an issuer upon a certificated security is valid against a purchaser only if the right of the issuer to the lien is noted conspicuously on the security certificate.

§ 8-210. Overissue.

(a) In this section, "overissue" means the issue of securities in excess of the amount the issuer has corporate power to issue, but an overissue does not occur if appropriate action has cured the overissue.

(b) Except as otherwise provided in subsections (c) and (d), the provisions of this Article which validate a security or compel its issue or reissue do not apply to the extent that validation, issue, or reissue would result in overissue.

(c) If an identical security not constituting an overissue is reasonably available for purchase, a person entitled to issue or validation may compel the issuer to purchase the security and deliver it if certificated or register its transfer if uncertificated, against surrender of any security certificate the person holds.

(d) If a security is not reasonably available for purchase, a person entitled to issue or validation may recover from the issuer the price the person or the last purchaser for value paid for it with interest from the date of the person's demand.

PART 3: Transfer of Certificated and Uncertificated Securities

§ 8-301. Delivery.

(a) Delivery of a certificated security to a purchaser occurs when:

    (1) the purchaser acquires possession of the security certificate;

    (2) another person, other than a securities intermediary, either acquires possession of the security certificate on behalf of the purchaser or, having previously acquired possession of the certificate, acknowledges that it holds for the purchaser; or

    (3) a securities intermediary acting on behalf of the purchaser acquires possession of the security certificate, only if the certificate is in registered form and is (i) registered in the name of the purchaser, (ii) payable to the order of the purchaser, or (iii) specially indorsed to the purchaser by an effective indorsement and has not been indorsed to the securities intermediary or in blank.

(b) Delivery of an uncertificated security to a purchaser occurs when:

    (1) the issuer registers the purchaser as the registered owner, upon original issue or registration of transfer; or

    (2) another person, other than a securities intermediary, either becomes the registered owner of the uncertificated security on behalf of the purchaser or, having previously become the registered owner, acknowledges that it holds for the purchaser.

As amended in 1999.

§ 8-302. Rights of Purchaser.

(a) Except as otherwise provided in subsections (b) and (c), upon delivery of a certificated or uncertificated security to a purchaser, the purchaser acquires all rights in the security that the transferor had or had power to transfer.

(b) A purchaser of a limited interest acquires rights only to the extent of the interest purchased.

(c) A purchaser of a certificated security who as a previous holder had notice of an adverse claim does not improve its position by taking from a protected purchaser.

As amended in 1999.

§ 8-303. Protected Purchaser.

(a) "Protected purchaser" means a purchaser of a certificated or uncertificated security, or of an interest therein, who:

    (1) gives value;

    (2) does not have notice of any adverse claim to the security; and

    (3) obtains control of the certificated or uncertificated security.

(b) In addition to acquiring the rights of a purchaser, a protected purchaser also acquires its interest in the security free of any adverse claim.

§ 8-304. Indorsement.

(a) An indorsement may be in blank or special. An indorsement in blank includes an indorsement to bearer. A special indorsement specifies to whom a security is to be transferred or who has power to transfer it. A holder may convert a blank indorsement to a special indorsement.

(b) An indorsement purporting to be only of part of a security certificate representing units intended by the issuer to be separately transferable is effective to the extent of the indorsement.

(c) An indorsement, whether special or in blank, does not constitute a transfer until delivery of the certificate on which it appears or, if the indorsement is on a separate document, until delivery of both the document and the certificate.

(d) If a security certificate in registered form has been delivered to a purchaser without a necessary indorsement, the purchaser may become a protected purchaser only when the indorsement is supplied. However, against a transferor, a transfer is complete upon delivery and the purchaser has a specifically enforceable right to have any necessary indorsement supplied.

(e) An indorsement of a security certificate in bearer form may give notice of an adverse claim to the certificate, but it does not otherwise affect a right to registration that the holder possesses.

(f) Unless otherwise agreed, a person making an indorsement assumes only the obligations provided in Section 8–108 and not an obligation that the security will be honored by the issuer.

§ 8-305. Instruction.

(a) If an instruction has been originated by an appropriate person but is incomplete in any other respect, any person may complete it as authorized and the issuer may rely on it as completed, even though it has been completed incorrectly.

(b) Unless otherwise agreed, a person initiating an instruction assumes only the obligations imposed by Section 8–108 and not an obligation that the security will be honored by the issuer.

§ 8-306. Effect of Guaranteeing Signature, Indorsement, or Instruction.

(a) A person who guarantees a signature of an indorser of a security certificate warrants that at the time of signing:

(1) the signature was genuine;

(2) the signer was an appropriate person to indorse, or if the signature is by an agent, the agent had actual authority to act on behalf of the appropriate person; and

(3) the signer had legal capacity to sign.

(b) A person who guarantees a signature of the originator of an instruction warrants that at the time of signing:

(1) the signature was genuine;

(2) the signer was an appropriate person to originate the instruction, or if the signature is by an agent, the agent had actual authority to act on behalf of the appropriate person, if the person specified in the instruction as the registered owner was, in fact, the registered owner, as to which fact the signature guarantor does not make a warranty; and

(3) the signer had legal capacity to sign.

(c) A person who specially guarantees the signature of an originator of an instruction makes the warranties of a signature guarantor under subsection (b) and also warrants that at the time the instruction is presented to the issuer:

(1) the person specified in the instruction as the registered owner of the uncertificated security will be the registered owner; and

(2) the transfer of the uncertificated security requested in the instruction will be registered by the issuer free from all liens, security interests, restrictions, and claims other than those specified in the instruction.

(d) A guarantor under subsections (a) and (b) or a special guarantor under subsection (c) does not otherwise warrant the rightfulness of the transfer.

(e) A person who guarantees an indorsement of a security certificate makes the warranties of a signature guarantor under subsection (a) and also warrants the rightfulness of the transfer in all respects.

(f) A person who guarantees an instruction requesting the transfer of an uncertificated security makes the warranties of a special signature guarantor under subsection (c) and also warrants the rightfulness of the transfer in all respects.

(g) An issuer may not require a special guaranty of signature, a guaranty of indorsement, or a guaranty of instruction as a condition to registration of transfer.

(h) The warranties under this section are made to a person taking or dealing with the security in reliance on the guaranty, and the guarantor is liable to the person for loss resulting from their breach. An indorser or originator of an instruction whose signature, indorsement, or instruction has been guaranteed is liable to a guarantor for any loss suffered by the guarantor as a result of breach of the warranties of the guarantor.

§ 8-307. Purchaser's Right to Requisites for Registration of Transfer.

Unless otherwise agreed, the transferor of a security on due demand shall supply the purchaser with proof of authority to transfer or with any other requisite necessary to obtain registration of the transfer of the security, but if the transfer is not for value, a transferor need not comply unless the purchaser pays the necessary expenses. If the transferor fails within a reasonable time to comply with the demand, the purchaser may reject or rescind the transfer.

PART 4: Registration

§ 8-401. Duty of Issuer to Register Transfer.

(a) If a certificated security in registered form is presented to an issuer with a request to register transfer or an instruction is presented to an issuer with a request to register transfer of an uncertificated security, the issuer shall register the transfer as requested if:

(1) under the terms of the security the person seeking registration of transfer is eligible to have the security registered in its name;

(2) the indorsement or instruction is made by the appropriate person or by an agent who has actual authority to act on behalf of the appropriate person;

(3) reasonable assurance is given that the indorsement or instruction is genuine and authorized (Section 8–402);

(4) any applicable law relating to the collection of taxes has been complied with;

(5) the transfer does not violate any restriction on transfer imposed by the issuer in accordance with Section 8–204;

(6) a demand that the issuer not register transfer has not become effective under Section 8–403, or the issuer has complied with Section 8–403(b) but no legal process or indemnity bond is obtained as provided in Section 8–403(d); and

(7) the transfer is in fact rightful or is to a protected purchaser.

(b) If an issuer is under a duty to register a transfer of a security, the issuer is liable to a person presenting a certificated security or an instruction for registration or to the person's principal for loss resulting from unreasonable delay in registration or failure or refusal to register the transfer.

§ 8-402. Assurance That Indorsement or Instruction Is Effective.

(a) An issuer may require the following assurance that each necessary indorsement or each instruction is genuine and authorized:

(1) in all cases, a guaranty of the signature of the person making an indorsement or originating an instruction including, in the case of an instruction, reasonable assurance of identity;

(2) if the indorsement is made or the instruction is originated by an agent, appropriate assurance of actual authority to sign;

(3) if the indorsement is made or the instruction is originated by a fiduciary pursuant to Section 8–107(a)(4) or (a)(5), appropriate evidence of appointment or incumbency;

(4) if there is more than one fiduciary, reasonable assurance that all who are required to sign have done so; and

(5) if the indorsement is made or the instruction is originated by a person not covered by another provision of this subsection, assurance appropriate to the case corresponding as nearly as may be to the provisions of this subsection.

(b) An issuer may elect to require reasonable assurance beyond that specified in this section.

(c) In this section:

(1) "Guaranty of the signature" means a guaranty signed by or on behalf of a person reasonably believed by the issuer to be responsible. An issuer may adopt standards with respect to responsibility if they are not manifestly unreasonable.

(2) "Appropriate evidence of appointment or incumbency" means:

(i) in the case of a fiduciary appointed or qualified by a court, a certificate issued by or under the direction or supervision of the court or an officer thereof and dated within 60 days before the date of presentation for transfer; or

(ii) in any other case, a copy of a document showing the appointment or a certificate issued by or on behalf of a person reasonably believed by an issuer to be responsible or, in the absence of that document or certificate, other evidence the issuer reasonably considers appropriate.

§ 8-403. Demand That Issuer Not Register Transfer.

(a) A person who is an appropriate person to make an indorsement or originate an instruction may demand that the issuer not register transfer of a security by communicating to the issuer a notification that identifies the registered owner and the issue of which the security is a part and provides an address for communications directed to the person making the demand. The demand is effective only if it is received by the issuer at a time and in a manner affording the issuer reasonable opportunity to act on it.

(b) If a certificated security in registered form is presented to an issuer with a request to register transfer or an instruction is presented to an issuer with a request to register transfer of an uncertificated security after a demand that the issuer not register transfer has become effective, the issuer shall promptly communicate to (i) the person who initiated the demand at the address provided in the demand and (ii) the person who presented the security for registration of transfer or initiated the instruction requesting registration of transfer a notification stating that:

(1) the certificated security has been presented for registration of transfer or the instruction for registration of transfer of the uncertificated security has been received;

(2) a demand that the issuer not register transfer had previously been received; and

(3) the issuer will withhold registration of transfer for a period of time stated in the notification in order to provide the person who initiated the demand an opportunity to obtain legal process or an indemnity bond.

(c) The period described in subsection (b)(3) may not exceed 30 days after the date of communication of the notification. A shorter period may be specified by the issuer if it is not manifestly unreasonable.

(d) An issuer is not liable to a person who initiated a demand that the issuer not register transfer for any loss the person suffers as a result of registration of a transfer pursuant to an effective indorsement or instruction if the person who initiated the demand does not, within the time stated in the issuer's communication, either:

(1) obtain an appropriate restraining order, injunction, or other process from a court of competent jurisdiction enjoining the issuer from registering the transfer; or

(2) file with the issuer an indemnity bond, sufficient in the issuer's judgment to protect the issuer and any transfer agent, registrar, or other agent of the issuer involved from any loss it or they may suffer by refusing to register the transfer.

(e) This section does not relieve an issuer from liability for registering transfer pursuant to an indorsement or instruction that was not effective.

§ 8-404. Wrongful Registration.

(a) Except as otherwise provided in Section 8–406, an issuer is liable for wrongful registration of transfer if the issuer has registered a transfer of a security to a person not entitled to it, and the transfer was registered:

(1) pursuant to an ineffective indorsement or instruction;

(2) after a demand that the issuer not register transfer became effective under Section 8–403(a) and the issuer did not comply with Section 8–403(b);

(3) after the issuer had been served with an injunction, restraining order, or other legal process enjoining it from registering the transfer, issued by a court of competent jurisdiction, and the issuer had a reasonable opportunity to act on the injunction, restraining order, or other legal process; or

(4) by an issuer acting in collusion with the wrongdoer.

(b) An issuer that is liable for wrongful registration of transfer under subsection (a) on demand shall provide the person entitled to the security with a like certificated or uncertificated security, and any payments or distributions that the person did not receive as a result of the wrongful registration. If an overissue would result, the issuer's liability to provide the person with a like security is governed by Section 8–210.

(c) Except as otherwise provided in subsection (a) or in a law relating to

the collection of taxes, an issuer is not liable to an owner or other person suffering loss as a result of the registration of a transfer of a security if registration was made pursuant to an effective indorsement or instruction.

§ 8-405. Replacement of Lost, Destroyed, or Wrongfully Taken Security Certificate.

(a) If an owner of a certificated security, whether in registered or bearer form, claims that the certificate has been lost, destroyed, or wrongfully taken, the issuer shall issue a new certificate if the owner:

(1) so requests before the issuer has notice that the certificate has been acquired by a protected purchaser;

(2) files with the issuer a sufficient indemnity bond; and

(3) satisfies other reasonable requirements imposed by the issuer.

(b) If, after the issue of a new security certificate, a protected purchaser of the original certificate presents it for registration of transfer, the issuer shall register the transfer unless an overissue would result. In that case, the issuer's liability is governed by Section 8–210. In addition to any rights on the indemnity bond, an issuer may recover the new certificate from a person to whom it was issued or any person taking under that person, except a protected purchaser.

§ 8-406. Obligation to Notify Issuer of Lost, Destroyed, or Wrongfully Taken Security Certificate.

If a security certificate has been lost, apparently destroyed, or wrongfully taken, and the owner fails to notify the issuer of that fact within a reasonable time after the owner has notice of it and the issuer registers a transfer of the security before receiving notification, the owner may not assert against the issuer a claim for registering the transfer under Section 8–404 or a claim to a new security certificate under Section 8–405.

§ 8-407. Authenticating Trustee, Transfer Agent, and Registrar.

A person acting as authenticating trustee, transfer agent, registrar, or other agent for an issuer in the registration of a transfer of its securities, in the issue of new security certificates or uncertificated securities, or in the cancellation of surrendered security certificates has the same obligation to the holder or owner of a certificated or uncertificated security with regard to the particular functions performed as the issuer has in regard to those functions.

PART 5: Security Entitlements

§ 8-501. Securities Account; Acquisition of Security Entitlement from Securities Intermediary.

(a) "Securities account" means an account to which a financial asset is or may be credited in accordance with an agreement under which the person maintaining the account undertakes to treat the person for whom the account is maintained as entitled to exercise the rights that comprise the financial asset.

(b) Except as otherwise provided in subsections (d) and (e), a person acquires a security entitlement if a securities intermediary:

(1) indicates by book entry that a financial asset has been credited to the person's securities account;

(2) receives a financial asset from the person or acquires a financial asset for the person and, in either case, accepts it for credit to the person's securities account; or

(3) becomes obligated under other law, regulation, or rule to credit a financial asset to the person's securities account.

(c) If a condition of subsection (b) has been met, a person has a security entitlement even though the securities intermediary does not itself hold the financial asset.

(d) If a securities intermediary holds a financial asset for another person, and the financial asset is registered in the name of, payable to the order of, or specially indorsed to the other person, and has not been indorsed to the securities intermediary or in blank, the other person is treated as holding the financial asset directly rather than as having a security entitlement with respect to the financial asset.

(e) Issuance of a security is not establishment of a security entitlement.

§ 8-502. Assertion of Adverse Claim against Entitlement Holder.

An action based on an adverse claim to a financial asset, whether framed in conversion, replevin, constructive trust, equitable lien, or other theory, may not be asserted against a person who acquires a security entitlement under Section 8–501 for value and without notice of the adverse claim.

§ 8-503. Property Interest of Entitlement Holder in Financial Asset Held by Securities Intermediary.

(a) To the extent necessary for a securities intermediary to satisfy all security entitlements with respect to a particular financial asset, all interests in that financial asset held by the securities intermediary are held by the securities intermediary for the entitlement holders, are not property of the securities intermediary, and are not subject to claims of creditors of the securities intermediary, except as otherwise provided in Section 8–511.

(b) An entitlement holder's property interest with respect to a particular financial asset under subsection (a) is a pro rata property interest in all interests in that financial asset held by the securities intermediary, without regard to the time the entitlement holder acquired the security entitlement or the time the securities intermediary acquired the interest in that financial asset.

(c) An entitlement holder's property interest with respect to a particular financial asset under subsection (a) may be enforced against the securities intermediary only by exercise of the entitlement holder's rights under Sections 8–505 through 8–508.

(d) An entitlement holder's property interest with respect to a particular financial asset under subsection (a) may be enforced against a purchaser of the financial asset or interest therein only if:

    (1) insolvency proceedings have been initiated by or against the securities intermediary;

    (2) the securities intermediary does not have sufficient interests in the financial asset to satisfy the security entitlements of all of its entitlement holders to that financial asset;

    (3) the securities intermediary violated its obligations under Section 8–504 by transferring the financial asset or interest therein to the purchaser; and

    (4) the purchaser is not protected under subsection (e).

The trustee or other liquidator, acting on behalf of all entitlement holders having security entitlements with respect to a particular financial asset, may recover the financial asset, or interest therein, from the purchaser. If the trustee or other liquidator elects not to pursue that right, an entitlement holder whose security entitlement remains unsatisfied has the right to recover its interest in the financial asset from the purchaser.

(e) An action based on the entitlement holder's property interest with respect to a particular financial asset under subsection (a), whether framed in conversion, replevin, constructive trust, equitable lien, or other theory, may not be asserted against any purchaser of a financial asset or interest therein who gives value, obtains control, and does not act in collusion with the securities intermediary in violating the securities intermediary's obligations under Section 8–504.

§ 8-504. Duty of Securities Intermediary to Maintain Financial Asset.

(a) A securities intermediary shall promptly obtain and thereafter maintain a financial asset in a quantity corresponding to the aggregate of all security entitlements it has established in favor of its entitlement holders with respect to that financial asset. The securities intermediary may maintain those financial assets directly or through one or more other securities intermediaries.

(b) Except to the extent otherwise agreed by its entitlement holder, a securities intermediary may not grant any security interests in a financial asset it is obligated to maintain pursuant to subsection (a).

(c) A securities intermediary satisfies the duty in subsection (a) if:

    (1) the securities intermediary acts with respect to the duty as agreed upon by the entitlement holder and the securities intermediary; or

    (2) in the absence of agreement, the securities intermediary exercises due care in accordance with reasonable commercial standards to obtain and maintain the financial asset.

(d) This section does not apply to a clearing corporation that is itself the obligor of an option or similar obligation to which its entitlement holders have security entitlements.

§ 8-505. Duty of Securities Intermediary with Respect to Payments and Distributions.

(a) A securities intermediary shall take action to obtain a payment or distribution made by the issuer of a financial asset. A securities intermediary satisfies the duty if:

    (1) the securities intermediary acts with respect to the duty as agreed upon by the entitlement holder and the securities intermediary; or

    (2) in the absence of agreement, the securities intermediary exercises due care in accordance with reasonable commercial standards to attempt to obtain the payment or distribution.

(b) A securities intermediary is obligated to its entitlement holder for a payment or distribution made by the issuer of a financial asset if the payment or distribution is received by the securities intermediary.

§ 8-506. Duty of Securities Intermediary to Exercise Rights as Directed by Entitlement Holder.

A securities intermediary shall exercise rights with respect to a financial asset if directed to do so by an entitlement holder. A securities intermediary satisfies the duty if:

    (1) the securities intermediary acts with respect to the duty as agreed upon by the entitlement holder and the securities intermediary; or

    (2) in the absence of agreement, the securities intermediary either places the entitlement holder in a position to exercise the rights directly or exercises due care in accordance with reasonable commercial standards to follow the direction of the entitlement holder.

§ 8–507. Duty of Securities Intermediary to Comply with Entitlement Order.

(a) A securities intermediary shall comply with an entitlement order if the entitlement order is originated by the appropriate person, the securities intermediary has had reasonable opportunity to assure itself that the entitlement order is genuine and authorized, and the securities intermediary has had reasonable opportunity to comply with the entitlement order. A securities intermediary satisfies the duty if:

    (1) the securities intermediary acts with respect to the duty as agreed upon by the entitlement holder and the securities intermediary; or

    (2) in the absence of agreement, the securities intermediary exercises due care in accordance with reasonable commercial standards to comply with the entitlement order.

(b) If a securities intermediary transfers a financial asset pursuant to an ineffective entitlement order, the securities intermediary shall reestablish a security entitlement in favor of the person entitled to it, and pay or credit any payments or distributions that the person did not receive as a result of the wrongful transfer. If the securities intermediary does not reestablish a security entitlement, the securities intermediary is liable to the entitlement holder for damages.

§ 8—508. Duty of Securities Intermediary to Change Entitlement Holder's Position to Other Form of Security Holding.

A securities intermediary shall act at the direction of an entitlement holder to change a security entitlement into another available form of holding for which the entitlement holder is eligible, or to cause the financial asset to be transferred to a securities account of the entitlement holder with another securities intermediary. A securities intermediary satisfies the duty if:

(1) the securities intermediary acts as agreed upon by the entitlement holder and the securities intermediary; or

(2) in the absence of agreement, the securities intermediary exercises due care in accordance with reasonable commercial standards to follow the direction of the entitlement holder.

§ 8—509. Specification of Duties of Securities Intermediary by Other Statute or Regulation; Manner of Performance of Duties of Securities Intermediary and Exercise of Rights of Entitlement Holder.

(a) If the substance of a duty imposed upon a securities intermediary by Sections 8—504 through 8—508 is the subject of other statute, regulation, or rule, compliance with that statute, regulation, or rule satisfies the duty.

(b) To the extent that specific standards for the performance of the duties of a securities intermediary or the exercise of the rights of an entitlement holder are not specified by other statute, regulation, or rule or by agreement between the securities intermediary and entitlement holder, the securities intermediary shall perform its duties and the entitlement holder shall exercise its rights in a commercially reasonable manner.

(c) The obligation of a securities intermediary to perform the duties imposed by Sections 8—504 through 8—508 is subject to:

(1) rights of the securities intermediary arising out of a security interest under a security agreement with the entitlement holder or otherwise; and

(2) rights of the securities intermediary under other law, regulation, rule, or agreement to withhold performance of its duties as a result of unfulfilled obligations of the entitlement holder to the securities intermediary.

(d) Sections 8—504 through 8—508 do not require a securities intermediary to take any action that is prohibited by other statute, regulation, or rule.

§ 8—510. Rights of Purchaser of Security Entitlement from Entitlement Holder.

(a) An action based on an adverse claim to a financial asset or security entitlement, whether framed in conversion, replevin, constructive trust, equitable lien, or other theory, may not be asserted against a person who purchases a security entitlement, or an interest therein, from an entitlement holder if the purchaser gives value, does not have notice of the adverse claim, and obtains control.

(b) If an adverse claim could not have been asserted against an entitlement holder under Section 8—502, the adverse claim cannot be asserted against a person who purchases a security entitlement, or an interest therein, from the entitlement holder.

(c) In a case not covered by the priority rules in Article 9, a purchaser for value of a security entitlement, or an interest therein, who obtains control

has priority over a purchaser of a security entitlement, or an interest therein, who does not obtain control. Except as otherwise provided in subsection (d), purchasers who have control rank according to priority in time of:

(1) the purchaser's becoming the person for whom the securities account, in which the security entitlement is carried, is maintained, if the purchaser obtained control under Section 8—106(d)(1);

(2) the securities intermediary's agreement to comply with the purchaser's entitlement orders with respect to security entitlements carried or to be carried in the securities account in which the security entitlement is carried, if the purchaser obtained control under Section 8—106(d)(2); or

(3) if the purchaser obtained control through another person under Section 8—106(d)(3), the time on which priority would be based under this subsection if the other person were the secured party.

(d) A securities intermediary as purchaser has priority over a conflicting purchaser who has control unless otherwise agreed by the securities intermediary.

As amended in 1999.

§ 8—511. Priority among Security Interests and Entitlement Holders.

(a) Except as otherwise provided in subsections (b) and (c), if a securities intermediary does not have sufficient interests in a particular financial asset to satisfy both its obligations to entitlement holders who have security entitlements to that financial asset and its obligation to a creditor of the securities intermediary who has a security interest in that financial asset, the claims of entitlement holders, other than the creditor, have priority over the claim of the creditor.

(b) A claim of a creditor of a securities intermediary who has a security interest in a financial asset held by a securities intermediary has priority over claims of the securities intermediary's entitlement holders who have security entitlements with respect to that financial asset if the creditor has control over the financial asset.

(c) If a clearing corporation does not have sufficient financial assets to satisfy both its obligations to entitlement holders who have security entitlements with respect to a financial asset and its obligation to a creditor of the clearing corporation who has a security interest in that financial asset, the claim of the creditor has priority over the claims of entitlement holders.

PART 6: Transition Provisions for Revised Article 8

§ 8—601. Effective Date.
This [Act] takes effect . . . .

§ 8—602. Repeals.
This [Act] repeals . . . .

§ 8—603. Savings Clause.

(a) This [Act] does not affect an action or proceeding commenced before this [Act] takes effect.

(b) If a security interest in a security is perfected at the date this [Act] takes effect, and the action by which the security interest was perfected would suffice to perfect a security interest under this [Act], no further action is required to continue perfection. If a security interest in a security is perfected at the date this [Act] takes effect but the action by which the security interest was perfected would not suffice to perfect a security interest under this [Act], the security interest remains perfected for a period of four months after the effective date and continues perfected thereafter if appropriate action to perfect under this [Act] is taken within that period. If a security interest is perfected at the date this [Act] takes effect and the security interest can be perfected by filing under this [Act], a financing statement signed by the secured party instead of the debtor may be filed within that period to continue perfection or thereafter to perfect.

REVISED ARTICLE 9: Secured Transactions

PART 1: General Provisions

[Subpart 1. Short Title, Definitions, and General Concepts]

§ 9-101. Short Title.
This article may be cited as Uniform Commercial Code—Secured Transactions.

§ 9-102. Definitions and Index of Definitions.
(a) In this article:

(1) "Accession" means goods that are physically united with other goods in such a manner that the identity of the original goods is not lost.

(2) "Account", except as used in "account for", means a right to payment of a monetary obligation, whether or not earned by performance, (i) for property that has been or is to be sold, leased, licensed, assigned, or otherwise disposed of, (ii) for services rendered or to be rendered, (iii) for a policy of insurance issued or to be issued, (iv) for a secondary obligation incurred or to be incurred, (v) for energy provided or to be provided, (vi) for the use or hire of a vessel under a charter or other contract, (vii) arising out of the use of a credit or charge card or information contained on or for use with the card, or (viii) as winnings in a lottery or other game of chance operated or sponsored by a State, governmental unit of a State, or person licensed or authorized to operate the game by a State or governmental unit of a State. The term includes health-care insurance receivables. The term does not include (i) rights to payment evidenced by chattel paper or an instrument, (ii) commercial tort claims, (iii) deposit accounts, (iv) investment property, (v) letter-of-credit rights or letters of credit, or (vi) rights to payment for money or funds advanced or sold, other than rights arising out of the use of a credit or charge card or information contained on or for use with the card.

(3) "Account debtor" means a person obligated on an account, chattel paper, or general intangible. The term does not include persons obligated to pay a negotiable instrument, even if the instrument constitutes part of chattel paper.

(4) "Accounting", except as used in "accounting for", means a record:
   (A) authenticated by a secured party;
   (B) indicating the aggregate unpaid secured obligations as of a date not more than 35 days earlier or 35 days later than the date of the record; and
   (C) identifying the components of the obligations in reasonable detail.

(5) "Agricultural lien" means an interest, other than a security interest, in farm products:
   (A) which secures payment or performance of an obligation for:
      (i) goods or services furnished in connection with a debtor's farming operation; or
      (ii) rent on real property leased by a debtor in connection with its farming operation;
   (B) which is created by statute in favor of a person that:
      (i) in the ordinary course of its business furnished goods or services to a debtor in connection with a debtor's farming operation; or
      (ii) leased real property to a debtor in connection with the debtor's farming operation; and
   (C) whose effectiveness does not depend on the person's possession of the personal property.

(6) "As-extracted collateral" means:
   (A) oil, gas, or other minerals that are subject to a security interest that:
      (i) is created by a debtor having an interest in the minerals before extraction; and
      (ii) attaches to the minerals as extracted; or
   (B) accounts arising out of the sale at the wellhead or minehead of oil, gas, or other minerals in which the debtor had an interest before extraction.

(7) "Authenticate" means:
   (A) to sign; or
   (B) to execute or otherwise adopt a symbol, or encrypt or similarly process a record in whole or in part, with the present intent of the authenticating person to identify the person and adopt or accept a record.

(8) "Bank" means an organization that is engaged in the business of banking. The term includes savings banks, savings and loan associations, credit unions, and trust companies.

(9) "Cash proceeds" means proceeds that are money, checks, deposit accounts, or the like.

(10) "Certificate of title" means a certificate of title with respect to which a statute provides for the security interest in question to be indicated on the certificate as a condition or result of the security interest's obtaining priority over the rights of a lien creditor with respect to the collateral.

(11) "Chattel paper" means a record or records that evidence both a monetary obligation and a security interest in specific goods, a security interest in specific goods and software used in the goods, a security interest in specific goods and license of software used in the goods, a lease of specific goods, or a lease of specific goods and license of software used in the goods. In this paragraph, "monetary obligation" means a monetary obligation secured by the goods or owed under a lease of the goods and includes a monetary obligation with respect to software used in the goods. The term does not include (i) charters or other contracts involving the use or hire of a vessel or (ii) records that evidence a right to payment arising out of the use of a credit or charge card or information contained on or for use with the card. If a transaction is evidenced by records that include an instrument or series of instruments, the group of records taken together constitutes chattel paper.

(12) "Collateral" means the property subject to a security interest or agricultural lien. The term includes:
   (A) proceeds to which a security interest attaches;
   (B) accounts, chattel paper, payment intangibles, and promissory notes that have been sold; and
   (C) goods that are the subject of a consignment.

(13) "Commercial tort claim" means a claim arising in tort with respect to which:
   (A) the claimant is an organization; or
   (B) the claimant is an individual and the claim:
      (i) arose in the course of the claimant's business or profession; and
      (ii) does not include damages arising out of personal injury to or the death of an individual.

(14) "Commodity account" means an account maintained by a commodity intermediary in which a commodity contract is carried for a commodity customer.

(15) "Commodity contract" means a commodity futures contract, an option on a commodity futures contract, a commodity option, or another contract if the contract or option is:

(A) traded on or subject to the rules of a board of trade that has been designated as a contract market for such a contract pursuant to federal commodities laws; or

(B) traded on a foreign commodity board of trade, exchange, or market, and is carried on the books of a commodity intermediary for a commodity customer.

(16) "Commodity customer" means a person for which a commodity intermediary carries a commodity contract on its books.

(17) "Commodity intermediary" means a person that:

(A) is registered as a futures commission merchant under federal commodities law; or

(B) in the ordinary course of its business provides clearance or settlement services for a board of trade that has been designated as a contract market pursuant to federal commodities law.

(18) "Communicate" means:

(A) to send a written or other tangible record;

(B) to transmit a record by any means agreed upon by the persons sending and receiving the record; or

(C) in the case of transmission of a record to or by a filing office, to transmit a record by any means prescribed by filing-office rule.

(19) "Consignee" means a merchant to which goods are delivered in a consignment.

(20) "Consignment" means a transaction, regardless of its form, in which a person delivers goods to a merchant for the purpose of sale and:

(A) the merchant:

(i) deals in goods of that kind under a name other than the name of the person making delivery;

(ii) is not an auctioneer; and

(iii) is not generally known by its creditors to be substantially engaged in selling the goods of others;

(B) with respect to each delivery, the aggregate value of the goods is $1,000 or more at the time of delivery;

(C) the goods are not consumer goods immediately before delivery; and

(D) the transaction does not create a security interest that secures an obligation.

(21) "Consignor" means a person that delivers goods to a consignee in a consignment.

(22) "Consumer debtor" means a debtor in a consumer transaction.

(23) "Consumer goods" means goods that are used or bought for use primarily for personal, family, or household purposes.

(24) "Consumer-goods transaction" means a consumer transaction in which:

(A) an individual incurs an obligation primarily for personal, family, or household purposes; and

(B) a security interest in consumer goods secures the obligation.

(25) "Consumer obligor" means an obligor who is an individual and who incurred the obligation as part of a transaction entered into primarily for personal, family, or household purposes.

(26) "Consumer transaction" means a transaction in which (i) an individual incurs an obligation primarily for personal, family, or household purposes, (ii) a security interest secures the obligation, and (iii) the collateral is held or acquired primarily for personal, family, or household purposes. The term includes consumer-goods transactions.

(27) "Continuation statement" means an amendment of a financing statement which:

(A) identifies, by its file number, the initial financing statement to which it relates; and

(B) indicates that it is a continuation statement for, or that it is filed to continue the effectiveness of, the identified financing statement.

(28) "Debtor" means:

(A) a person having an interest, other than a security interest or other lien, in the collateral, whether or not the person is an obligor;

(B) a seller of accounts, chattel paper, payment intangibles, or promissory notes; or

(C) a consignee.

(29) "Deposit account" means a demand, time, savings, passbook, or similar account maintained with a bank. The term does not include investment property or accounts evidenced by an instrument.

(30) "Document" means a document of title or a receipt of the type described in Section 7–201(2).

(31) "Electronic chattel paper" means chattel paper evidenced by a record or records consisting of information stored in an electronic medium.

(32) "Encumbrance" means a right, other than an ownership interest, in real property. The term includes mortgages and other liens on real property.

(33) "Equipment" means goods other than inventory, farm products, or consumer goods.

(34) "Farm products" means goods, other than standing timber, with respect to which the debtor is engaged in a farming operation and which are:

(A) crops grown, growing, or to be grown, including:

(i) crops produced on trees, vines, and bushes; and

(ii) aquatic goods produced in aquacultural operations;

(B) livestock, born or unborn, including aquatic goods produced in aquacultural operations;

(C) supplies used or produced in a farming operation; or

(D) products of crops or livestock in their unmanufactured states.

(35) "Farming operation" means raising, cultivating, propagating, fattening, grazing, or any other farming, livestock, or aquacultural operation.

(36) "File number" means the number assigned to an initial financing statement pursuant to Section 9–519(a).

(37) "Filing office" means an office designated in Section 9–501 as the place to file a financing statement.

(38) "Filing-office rule" means a rule adopted pursuant to Section 9–526.

(39) "Financing statement" means a record or records composed of an initial financing statement and any filed record relating to the initial financing statement.

(40) "Fixture filing" means the filing of a financing statement covering goods that are or are to become fixtures and satisfying Section 9–502(a) and (b). The term includes the filing of a financing statement covering goods of a transmitting utility which are or are to become fixtures.

(41) "Fixtures" means goods that have become so related to particular real property that an interest in them arises under real property law.

(42) "General intangible" means any personal property, including things in action, other than accounts, chattel paper, commercial tort claims, deposit accounts, documents, goods, instruments, investment property, letter-of-credit rights, letters of credit, money, and oil, gas, or other minerals before extraction. The term includes payment intangibles and software.

(43) "Good faith" means honesty in fact and the observance of reasonable commercial standards of fair dealing.

(44) "Goods" means all things that are movable when a security interest attaches. The term includes (i) fixtures, (ii) standing timber that is to be cut and removed under a conveyance or contract for sale,

(iii) the unborn young of animals, (iv) crops grown, growing, or to be grown, even if the crops are produced on trees, vines, or bushes, and (v) manufactured homes. The term also includes a computer program embedded in goods and any supporting information provided in connection with a transaction relating to the program if (i) the program is associated with the goods in such a manner that it customarily is considered part of the goods, or (ii) by becoming the owner of the goods, a person acquires a right to use the program in connection with the goods. The term does not include a computer program embedded in goods that consist solely of the medium in which the program is embedded. The term also does not include accounts, chattel paper, commercial tort claims, deposit accounts, documents, general intangibles, instruments, investment property, letter-of-credit rights, letters of credit, money, or oil, gas, or other minerals before extraction.

(45) "Governmental unit" means a subdivision, agency, department, county, parish, municipality, or other unit of the government of the United States, a State, or a foreign country. The term includes an organization having a separate corporate existence if the organization is eligible to issue debt on which interest is exempt from income taxation under the laws of the United States.

(46) "Health-care-insurance receivable" means an interest in or claim under a policy of insurance which is a right to payment of a monetary obligation for health-care goods or services provided.

(47) "Instrument" means a negotiable instrument or any other writing that evidences a right to the payment of a monetary obligation, is not itself a security agreement or lease, and is of a type that in ordinary course of business is transferred by delivery with any necessary indorsement or assignment. The term does not include (i) investment property, (ii) letters of credit, or (iii) writings that evidence a right to payment arising out of the use of a credit or charge card or information contained on or for use with the card.

(48) "Inventory" means goods, other than farm products, which:
(A) are leased by a person as lessor;
(B) are held by a person for sale or lease or to be furnished under a contract of service;
(C) are furnished by a person under a contract of service; or
(D) consist of raw materials, work in process, or materials used or consumed in a business.

(49) "Investment property" means a security, whether certificated or uncertificated, security entitlement, securities account, commodity contract, or commodity account.

(50) "Jurisdiction of organization", with respect to a registered organization, means the jurisdiction under whose law the organization is organized.

(51) "Letter-of-credit right" means a right to payment or performance under a letter of credit, whether or not the beneficiary has demanded or is at the time entitled to demand payment or performance. The term does not include the right of a beneficiary to demand payment or performance under a letter of credit.

(52) "Lien creditor" means:
(A) a creditor that has acquired a lien on the property involved by attachment, levy, or the like;
(B) an assignee for benefit of creditors from the time of assignment;
(C) a trustee in bankruptcy from the date of the filing of the petition; or
(D) a receiver in equity from the time of appointment.

(53) "Manufactured home" means a structure, transportable in one or more sections, which, in the traveling mode, is eight body feet or more in width or 40 body feet or more in length, or, when erected on site, is 320 or more square feet, and which is built on a permanent chassis and designed to be used as a dwelling with or without a permanent foundation when connected to the required utilities, and includes the plumbing, heating, air-conditioning, and electrical systems contained therein. The term includes any structure that meets all of the requirements of this paragraph except the size requirements and with respect to which the manufacturer voluntarily files a certification required by the United States Secretary of Housing and Urban Development and complies with the standards established under Title 42 of the United States Code.

(54) "Manufactured-home transaction" means a secured transaction:
(A) that creates a purchase-money security interest in a manufactured home, other than a manufactured home held as inventory; or
(B) in which a manufactured home, other than a manufactured home held as inventory, is the primary collateral.

(55) "Mortgage" means a consensual interest in real property, including fixtures, which secures payment or performance of an obligation.

(56) "New debtor" means a person that becomes bound as debtor under Section 9–203(d) by a security agreement previously entered into by another person.

(57) "New value" means (i) money, (ii) money's worth in property, services, or new credit, or (iii) release by a transferee of an interest in property previously transferred to the transferee. The term does not include an obligation substituted for another obligation.

(58) "Noncash proceeds" means proceeds other than cash proceeds.

(59) "Obligor" means a person that, with respect to an obligation secured by a security interest in or an agricultural lien on the collateral, (i) owes payment or other performance of the obligation, (ii) has provided property other than the collateral to secure payment or other performance of the obligation, or (iii) is otherwise accountable in whole or in part for payment or other performance of the obligation. The term does not include issuers or nominated persons under a letter of credit.

(60) "Original debtor", except as used in Section 9–310(c), means a person that, as debtor, entered into a security agreement to which a new debtor has become bound under Section 9–203(d).

(61) "Payment intangible" means a general intangible under which the account debtor's principal obligation is a monetary obligation.

(62) "Person related to", with respect to an individual, means:
(A) the spouse of the individual;
(B) a brother, brother-in-law, sister, or sister-in-law of the individual;
(C) an ancestor or lineal descendant of the individual or the individual's spouse; or
(D) any other relative, by blood or marriage, of the individual or the individual's spouse who shares the same home with the individual.

(63) "Person related to", with respect to an organization, means:
(A) a person directly or indirectly controlling, controlled by, or under common control with the organization;
(B) an officer or director of, or a person performing similar functions with respect to, the organization;
(C) an officer or director of, or a person performing similar functions with respect to, a person described in subparagraph (A);
(D) the spouse of an individual described in subparagraph (A), (B), or (C); or
(E) an individual who is related by blood or marriage to an individual described in subparagraph (A), (B), (C), or (D) and shares the same home with the individual.

(64) "Proceeds", except as used in Section 9–609(b), means the following property:

(A) whatever is acquired upon the sale, lease, license, exchange, or other disposition of collateral;

(B) whatever is collected on, or distributed on account of, collateral;

(C) rights arising out of collateral;

(D) to the extent of the value of collateral, claims arising out of the loss, nonconformity, or interference with the use of, defects or infringement of rights in, or damage to, the collateral; or

(E) to the extent of the value of collateral and to the extent payable to the debtor or the secured party, insurance payable by reason of the loss or nonconformity of, defects or infringement of rights in, or damage to, the collateral.

(65) "Promissory note" means an instrument that evidences a promise to pay a monetary obligation, does not evidence an order to pay, and does not contain an acknowledgment by a bank that the bank has received for deposit a sum of money or funds.

(66) "Proposal" means a record authenticated by a secured party which includes the terms on which the secured party is willing to accept collateral in full or partial satisfaction of the obligation it secures pursuant to Sections 9–620, 9–621, and 9–622.

(67) "Public-finance transaction" means a secured transaction in connection with which:

(A) debt securities are issued;

(B) all or a portion of the securities issued have an initial stated maturity of at least 20 years; and

(C) the debtor, obligor, secured party, account debtor or other person obligated on collateral, assignor or assignee of a secured obligation, or assignor or assignee of a security interest is a State or a governmental unit of a State.

(68) "Pursuant to commitment", with respect to an advance made or other value given by a secured party, means pursuant to the secured party's obligation, whether or not a subsequent event of default or other event not within the secured party's control has relieved or may relieve the secured party from its obligation.

(69) "Record", except as used in "for record", "of record", "record or legal title", and "record owner", means information that is inscribed on a tangible medium or which is stored in an electronic or other medium and is retrievable in perceivable form.

(70) "Registered organization" means an organization organized solely under the law of a single State or the United States and as to which the State or the United States must maintain a public record showing the organization to have been organized.

(71) "Secondary obligor" means an obligor to the extent that:

(A) the obligor's obligation is secondary; or

(B) the obligor has a right of recourse with respect to an obligation secured by collateral against the debtor, another obligor, or property of either.

(72) "Secured party" means:

(A) a person in whose favor a security interest is created or provided for under a security agreement, whether or not any obligation to be secured is outstanding;

(B) a person that holds an agricultural lien;

(C) a consignor;

(D) a person to which accounts, chattel paper, payment intangibles, or promissory notes have been sold;

(E) a trustee, indenture trustee, agent, collateral agent, or other representative in whose favor a security interest or agricultural lien is created or provided for; or

(F) a person that holds a security interest arising under Section 2–401, 2–505, 2–711(3), 2A–508(5), 4–210, or 5–118.

(73) "Security agreement" means an agreement that creates or provides for a security interest.

(74) "Send", in connection with a record or notification, means:

(A) to deposit in the mail, deliver for transmission, or transmit by any other usual means of communication, with postage or cost of transmission provided for, addressed to any address reasonable under the circumstances; or

(B) to cause the record or notification to be received within the time that it would have been received if properly sent under subparagraph (A).

(75) "Software" means a computer program and any supporting information provided in connection with a transaction relating to the program. The term does not include a computer program that is included in the definition of goods.

(76) "State" means a State of the United States, the District of Columbia, Puerto Rico, the United States Virgin Islands, or any territory or insular possession subject to the jurisdiction of the United States.

(77) "Supporting obligation" means a letter-of-credit right or secondary obligation that supports the payment or performance of an account, chattel paper, a document, a general intangible, an instrument, or investment property.

(78) "Tangible chattel paper" means chattel paper evidenced by a record or records consisting of information that is inscribed on a tangible medium.

(79) "Termination statement" means an amendment of a financing statement which:

(A) identifies, by its file number, the initial financing statement to which it relates; and

(B) indicates either that it is a termination statement or that the identified financing statement is no longer effective.

(80) "Transmitting utility" means a person primarily engaged in the business of:

(A) operating a railroad, subway, street railway, or trolley bus;

(B) transmitting communications electrically, electromagnetically, or by light;

(C) transmitting goods by pipeline or sewer; or

(D) transmitting or producing and transmitting electricity, steam, gas, or water.

(b) The following definitions in other articles apply to this article:

"Applicant."	Section 5–102
"Beneficiary."	Section 5–102
"Broker."	Section 8–102
"Certificated security."	Section 8–102
"Check."	Section 3–104
"Clearing corporation."	Section 8–102
"Contract for sale."	Section 2–106
"Customer."	Section 4–104
"Entitlement holder."	Section 8–102
"Financial asset."	Section 8–102
"Holder in due course."	Section 3–302
"Issuer" (with respect to a letter of credit or letter-of-credit right). Section 5–102	
"Issuer" (with respect to a security).	Section 8–201
"Lease."	Section 2A–103
"Lease agreement."	Section 2A–103
"Lease contract."	Section 2A–103
"Leasehold interest."	Section 2A–103
"Lessee."	Section 2A–103
"Lessee in ordinary course of business."	Section 2A–103
"Lessor."	Section 2A–103
"Lessor's residual interest."	Section 2A–103
"Letter of credit."	Section 5–102

(c) Article 1 contains general definitions and principles of construction and interpretation applicable throughout this article.
Amended in 1999 and 2000.

§ 9-103. Purchase-Money Security Interest; Application of Payments; Burden of Establishing.

(a) In this section:

(1) "purchase-money collateral" means goods or software that secures a purchase-money obligation incurred with respect to that collateral; and

(2) "purchase-money obligation" means an obligation of an obligor incurred as all or part of the price of the collateral or for value given to enable the debtor to acquire rights in or the use of the collateral if the value is in fact so used.

(b) A security interest in goods is a purchase-money security interest:

(1) to the extent that the goods are purchase-money collateral with respect to that security interest;

(2) if the security interest is in inventory that is or was purchase-money collateral, also to the extent that the security interest secures a purchase-money obligation incurred with respect to other inventory in which the secured party holds or held a purchase-money security interest; and

(3) also to the extent that the security interest secures a purchase-money obligation incurred with respect to software in which the secured party holds or held a purchase-money security interest.

(c) A security interest in software is a purchase-money security interest to the extent that the security interest also secures a purchase-money obligation incurred with respect to goods in which the secured party holds or held a purchase-money security interest if:

(1) the debtor acquired its interest in the software in an integrated transaction in which it acquired an interest in the goods; and

(2) the debtor acquired its interest in the software for the principal purpose of using the software in the goods.

(d) The security interest of a consignor in goods that are the subject of a consignment is a purchase-money security interest in inventory.

(e) In a transaction other than a consumer-goods transaction, if the extent to which a security interest is a purchase-money security interest depends on the application of a payment to a particular obligation, the payment must be applied:

(1) in accordance with any reasonable method of application to which the parties agree;

(2) in the absence of the parties' agreement to a reasonable method, in accordance with any intention of the obligor manifested at or before the time of payment; or

(3) in the absence of an agreement to a reasonable method and a timely manifestation of the obligor's intention, in the following order:

(A) to obligations that are not secured; and

(B) if more than one obligation is secured, to obligations secured by purchase-money security interests in the order in which those obligations were incurred.

(f) In a transaction other than a consumer-goods transaction, a purchase-money security interest does not lose its status as such, even if:

(1) the purchase-money collateral also secures an obligation that is not a purchase-money obligation;

(2) collateral that is not purchase-money collateral also secures the purchase-money obligation; or

(3) the purchase-money obligation has been renewed, refinanced, consolidated, or restructured.

(g) In a transaction other than a consumer-goods transaction, a secured party claiming a purchase-money security interest has the burden of establishing the extent to which the security interest is a purchase-money security interest.

(h) The limitation of the rules in subsections (e), (f), and (g) to transactions other than consumer-goods transactions is intended to leave to the court the determination of the proper rules in consumer-goods transactions. The court may not infer from that limitation the nature of the proper rule in consumer-goods transactions and may continue to apply established approaches.

§ 9-104. Control of Deposit Account.

(a) A secured party has control of a deposit account if:

(1) the secured party is the bank with which the deposit account is maintained;

(2) the debtor, secured party, and bank have agreed in an authenticated record that the bank will comply with instructions originated by the secured party directing disposition of the funds in the deposit account without further consent by the debtor; or

(3) the secured party becomes the bank's customer with respect to the deposit account.

(b) A secured party that has satisfied subsection (a) has control, even if the debtor retains the right to direct the disposition of funds from the deposit account.

§ 9-105. Control of Electronic Chattel Paper.

A secured party has control of electronic chattel paper if the record or records comprising the chattel paper are created, stored, and assigned in such a manner that:

(1) a single authoritative copy of the record or records exists which is unique, identifiable and, except as otherwise provided in paragraphs (4), (5), and (6), unalterable;

(2) the authoritative copy identifies the secured party as the assignee of the record or records;

(3) the authoritative copy is communicated to and maintained by the secured party or its designated custodian;

(4) copies or revisions that add or change an identified assignee of the authoritative copy can be made only with the participation of the secured party;

(5) each copy of the authoritative copy and any copy of a copy is readily identifiable as a copy that is not the authoritative copy; and

(6) any revision of the authoritative copy is readily identifiable as an authorized or unauthorized revision.

§ 9-106. Control of Investment Property.

(a) A person has control of a certificated security, uncertificated security, or security entitlement as provided in Section 8–106.

(b) A secured party has control of a commodity contract if:

(1) the secured party is the commodity intermediary with which the commodity contract is carried; or

(2) the commodity customer, secured party, and commodity inter-

mediary have agreed that the commodity intermediary will apply any value distributed on account of the commodity contract as directed by the secured party without further consent by the commodity customer.

(c) A secured party having control of all security entitlements or commodity contracts carried in a securities account or commodity account has control over the securities account or commodity account.

§ 9-107. Control of Letter-of-Credit Right.

A secured party has control of a letter-of-credit right to the extent of any right to payment or performance by the issuer or any nominated person if the issuer or nominated person has consented to an assignment of proceeds of the letter of credit under Section 5–114(c) or otherwise applicable law or practice.

§ 9-108. Sufficiency of Description.

(a) Except as otherwise provided in subsections (c), (d), and (e), a description of personal or real property is sufficient, whether or not it is specific, if it reasonably identifies what is described.

(b) Except as otherwise provided in subsection (d), a description of collateral reasonably identifies the collateral if it identifies the collateral by:

    (1) specific listing;

    (2) category;

    (3) except as otherwise provided in subsection (e), a type of collateral defined in [the Uniform Commercial Code];

    (4) quantity;

    (5) computational or allocational formula or procedure; or

    (6) except as otherwise provided in subsection (c), any other method, if the identity of the collateral is objectively determinable.

(c) A description of collateral as "all the debtor's assets" or "all the debtor's personal property" or using words of similar import does not reasonably identify the collateral.

(d) Except as otherwise provided in subsection (e), a description of a security entitlement, securities account, or commodity account is sufficient if it describes:

    (1) the collateral by those terms or as investment property; or

    (2) the underlying financial asset or commodity contract.

(e) A description only by type of collateral defined in [the Uniform Commercial Code] is an insufficient description of:

    (1) a commercial tort claim; or

    (2) in a consumer transaction, consumer goods, a security entitlement, a securities account, or a commodity account.

[Subpart 2. Applicability of Article]

§ 9-109. Scope.

(a) Except as otherwise provided in subsections (c) and (d), this article applies to:

    (1) a transaction, regardless of its form, that creates a security interest in personal property or fixtures by contract;

    (2) an agricultural lien;

    (3) a sale of accounts, chattel paper, payment intangibles, or promissory notes;

    (4) a consignment;

    (5) a security interest arising under Section 2–401, 2–505, 2–711(3), or 2A–508(5), as provided in Section 9–110; and

    (6) a security interest arising under Section 4–210 or 5–118.

(b) The application of this article to a security interest in a secured obligation is not affected by the fact that the obligation is itself secured by a transaction or interest to which this article does not apply.

(c) This article does not apply to the extent that:

    (1) a statute, regulation, or treaty of the United States preempts this article;

    (2) another statute of this State expressly governs the creation, perfection, priority, or enforcement of a security interest created by this State or a governmental unit of this State;

    (3) a statute of another State, a foreign country, or a governmental unit of another State or a foreign country, other than a statute generally applicable to security interests, expressly governs creation, perfection, priority, or enforcement of a security interest created by the State, country, or governmental unit; or

    (4) the rights of a transferee beneficiary or nominated person under a letter of credit are independent and superior under Section 5–114.

(d) This article does not apply to:

    (1) a landlord's lien, other than an agricultural lien;

    (2) a lien, other than an agricultural lien, given by statute or other rule of law for services or materials, but Section 9–333 applies with respect to priority of the lien;

    (3) an assignment of a claim for wages, salary, or other compensation of an employee;

    (4) a sale of accounts, chattel paper, payment intangibles, or promissory notes as part of a sale of the business out of which they arose;

    (5) an assignment of accounts, chattel paper, payment intangibles, or promissory notes which is for the purpose of collection only;

    (6) an assignment of a right to payment under a contract to an assignee that is also obligated to perform under the contract;

    (7) an assignment of a single account, payment intangible, or promissory note to an assignee in full or partial satisfaction of a preexisting indebtedness;

    (8) a transfer of an interest in or an assignment of a claim under a policy of insurance, other than an assignment by or to a health-care provider of a health-care-insurance receivable and any subsequent assignment of the right to payment, but Sections 9–315 and 9–322 apply with respect to proceeds and priorities in proceeds;

    (9) an assignment of a right represented by a judgment, other than a judgment taken on a right to payment that was collateral;

    (10) a right of recoupment or set-off, but:

        (A) Section 9–340 applies with respect to the effectiveness of rights of recoupment or set-off against deposit accounts; and

        (B) Section 9–404 applies with respect to defenses or claims of an account debtor;

    (11) the creation or transfer of an interest in or lien on real property, including a lease or rents thereunder, except to the extent that provision is made for:

        (A) liens on real property in Sections 9–203 and 9–308;

        (B) fixtures in Section 9–334;

        (C) fixture filings in Sections 9–501, 9–502, 9–512, 9–516, and 9–519; and

        (D) security agreements covering personal and real property in Section 9–604;

    (12) an assignment of a claim arising in tort, other than a commercial tort claim, but Sections 9–315 and 9–322 apply with respect to proceeds and priorities in proceeds; or

    (13) an assignment of a deposit account in a consumer transaction, but Sections 9–315 and 9–322 apply with respect to proceeds and priorities in proceeds.

§ 9-110. Security Interests Arising under Article 2 or 2A.

A security interest arising under Section 2–401, 2–505, 2–711(3), or 2A–508(5) is subject to this article. However, until the debtor obtains possession of the goods:

(1) the security interest is enforceable, even if Section 9–203(b)(3) has not been satisfied;

(2) filing is not required to perfect the security interest;

(3) the rights of the secured party after default by the debtor are governed by Article 2 or 2A; and

(4) the security interest has priority over a conflicting security interest created by the debtor.

PART 2: Effectiveness of Security Agreement; Attachment of Security Interest; Rights of Parties to Security Agreement

[Subpart 1. Effectiveness and Attachment]

§ 9-201. General Effectiveness of Security Agreement.

(a) Except as otherwise provided in [the Uniform Commercial Code], a security agreement is effective according to its terms between the parties, against purchasers of the collateral, and against creditors.

(b) A transaction subject to this article is subject to any applicable rule of law which establishes a different rule for consumers and [insert reference to (i) any other statute or regulation that regulates the rates, charges, agreements, and practices for loans, credit sales, or other extensions of credit and (ii) any consumer-protection statute or regulation].

(c) In case of conflict between this article and a rule of law, statute, or regulation described in subsection (b), the rule of law, statute, or regulation controls. Failure to comply with a statute or regulation described in subsection (b) has only the effect the statute or regulation specifies.

(d) This article does not:

(1) validate any rate, charge, agreement, or practice that violates a rule of law, statute, or regulation described in subsection (b); or

(2) extend the application of the rule of law, statute, or regulation to a transaction not otherwise subject to it.

§ 9-202. Title to Collateral Immaterial.

Except as otherwise provided with respect to consignments or sales of accounts, chattel paper, payment intangibles, or promissory notes, the provisions of this article with regard to rights and obligations apply whether title to collateral is in the secured party or the debtor.

§ 9-203. Attachment and Enforceability of Security Interest; Proceeds; Supporting Obligations; Formal Requisites.

(a) A security interest attaches to collateral when it becomes enforceable against the debtor with respect to the collateral, unless an agreement expressly postpones the time of attachment.

(b) Except as otherwise provided in subsections (c) through (i), a security interest is enforceable against the debtor and third parties with respect to the collateral only if:

(1) value has been given;

(2) the debtor has rights in the collateral or the power to transfer rights in the collateral to a secured party; and

(3) one of the following conditions is met:

(A) the debtor has authenticated a security agreement that provides a description of the collateral and, if the security interest covers timber to be cut, a description of the land concerned;

(B) the collateral is not a certificated security and is in the possession of the secured party under Section 9–313 pursuant to the debtor's security agreement;

(C) the collateral is a certificated security in registered form and the security certificate has been delivered to the secured party

under Section 8–301 pursuant to the debtor's security agreement; or

(D) the collateral is deposit accounts, electronic chattel paper, investment property, or letter-of-credit rights, and the secured party has control under Section 9–104, 9–105, 9–106, or 9–107 pursuant to the debtor's security agreement.

(c) Subsection (b) is subject to Section 4–210 on the security interest of a collecting bank, Section 5–118 on the security interest of a letter-of-credit issuer or nominated person, Section 9–110 on a security interest arising under Article 2 or 2A, and Section 9–206 on security interests in investment property.

(d) A person becomes bound as debtor by a security agreement entered into by another person if, by operation of law other than this article or by contract:

(1) the security agreement becomes effective to create a security interest in the person's property; or

(2) the person becomes generally obligated for the obligations of the other person, including the obligation secured under the security agreement, and acquires or succeeds to all or substantially all of the assets of the other person.

(e) If a new debtor becomes bound as debtor by a security agreement entered into by another person:

(1) the agreement satisfies subsection (b)(3) with respect to existing or after-acquired property of the new debtor to the extent the property is described in the agreement; and

(2) another agreement is not necessary to make a security interest in the property enforceable.

(f) The attachment of a security interest in collateral gives the secured party the rights to proceeds provided by Section 9–315 and is also attachment of a security interest in a supporting obligation for the collateral.

(g) The attachment of a security interest in a right to payment or performance secured by a security interest or other lien on personal or real property is also attachment of a security interest in the security interest, mortgage, or other lien.

(h) The attachment of a security interest in a securities account is also attachment of a security interest in the security entitlements carried in the securities account.

(i) The attachment of a security interest in a commodity account is also attachment of a security interest in the commodity contracts carried in the commodity account.

§ 9-204. After-Acquired Property; Future Advances.

(a) Except as otherwise provided in subsection (b), a security agreement may create or provide for a security interest in after-acquired collateral.

(b) A security interest does not attach under a term constituting an after-acquired property clause to:

(1) consumer goods, other than an accession when given as additional security, unless the debtor acquires rights in them within 10 days after the secured party gives value; or

(2) a commercial tort claim.

(c) A security agreement may provide that collateral secures, or that accounts, chattel paper, payment intangibles, or promissory notes are sold in connection with, future advances or other value, whether or not the advances or value are given pursuant to commitment.

§ 9-205. Use or Disposition of Collateral Permissible.

(a) A security interest is not invalid or fraudulent against creditors solely because:

(1) the debtor has the right or ability to:

(A) use, commingle, or dispose of all or part of the collateral, including returned or repossessed goods;

(B) collect, compromise, enforce, or otherwise deal with collateral;

(C) accept the return of collateral or make repossessions; or

(D) use, commingle, or dispose of proceeds; or

(2) the secured party fails to require the debtor to account for proceeds or replace collateral.

(b) This section does not relax the requirements of possession if attachment, perfection, or enforcement of a security interest depends upon possession of the collateral by the secured party.

§ 9-206. Security Interest Arising in Purchase or Delivery of Financial Asset.

(a) A security interest in favor of a securities intermediary attaches to a person's security entitlement if:

(1) the person buys a financial asset through the securities intermediary in a transaction in which the person is obligated to pay the purchase price to the securities intermediary at the time of the purchase; and

(2) the securities intermediary credits the financial asset to the buyer's securities account before the buyer pays the securities intermediary.

(b) The security interest described in subsection (a) secures the person's obligation to pay for the financial asset.

(c) A security interest in favor of a person that delivers a certificated security or other financial asset represented by a writing attaches to the security or other financial asset if:

(1) the security or other financial asset:

(A) in the ordinary course of business is transferred by delivery with any necessary indorsement or assignment; and

(B) is delivered under an agreement between persons in the business of dealing with such securities or financial assets; and

(2) the agreement calls for delivery against payment.

(d) The security interest described in subsection (c) secures the obligation to make payment for the delivery.

[Subpart 2. Rights and Duties]

§ 9-207. Rights and Duties of Secured Party Having Possession or Control of Collateral.

(a) Except as otherwise provided in subsection (d), a secured party shall use reasonable care in the custody and preservation of collateral in the secured party's possession. In the case of chattel paper or an instrument, reasonable care includes taking necessary steps to preserve rights against prior parties unless otherwise agreed.

(b) Except as otherwise provided in subsection (d), if a secured party has possession of collateral:

(1) reasonable expenses, including the cost of insurance and payment of taxes or other charges, incurred in the custody, preservation, use, or operation of the collateral are chargeable to the debtor and are secured by the collateral;

(2) the risk of accidental loss or damage is on the debtor to the extent of a deficiency in any effective insurance coverage;

(3) the secured party shall keep the collateral identifiable, but fungible collateral may be commingled; and

(4) the secured party may use or operate the collateral:

(A) for the purpose of preserving the collateral or its value;

(B) as permitted by an order of a court having competent jurisdiction; or

(C) except in the case of consumer goods, in the manner and to the extent agreed by the debtor.

(c) Except as otherwise provided in subsection (d), a secured party having possession of collateral or control of collateral under Section 9–104, 9–105, 9–106, or 9–107:

(1) may hold as additional security any proceeds, except money or funds, received from the collateral;

(2) shall apply money or funds received from the collateral to reduce the secured obligation, unless remitted to the debtor; and

(3) may create a security interest in the collateral.

(d) If the secured party is a buyer of accounts, chattel paper, payment intangibles, or promissory notes or a consignor:

(1) subsection (a) does not apply unless the secured party is entitled under an agreement:

(A) to charge back uncollected collateral; or

(B) otherwise to full or limited recourse against the debtor or a secondary obligor based on the nonpayment or other default of an account debtor or other obligor on the collateral; and

(2) subsections (b) and (c) do not apply.

§ 9-208. Additional Duties of Secured Party Having Control of Collateral.

(a) This section applies to cases in which there is no outstanding secured obligation and the secured party is not committed to make advances, incur obligations, or otherwise give value.

(b) Within 10 days after receiving an authenticated demand by the debtor:

(1) a secured party having control of a deposit account under Section 9–104(a)(2) shall send to the bank with which the deposit account is maintained an authenticated statement that releases the bank from any further obligation to comply with instructions originated by the secured party;

(2) a secured party having control of a deposit account under Section 9–104(a)(3) shall:

(A) pay the debtor the balance on deposit in the deposit account; or

(B) transfer the balance on deposit into a deposit account in the debtor's name;

(3) a secured party, other than a buyer, having control of electronic chattel paper under Section 9–105 shall:

(A) communicate the authoritative copy of the electronic chattel paper to the debtor or its designated custodian;

(B) if the debtor designates a custodian that is the designated custodian with which the authoritative copy of the electronic chattel paper is maintained for the secured party, communicate to the custodian an authenticated record releasing the designated custodian from any further obligation to comply with instructions originated by the secured party and instructing the custodian to comply with instructions originated by the debtor; and

(C) take appropriate action to enable the debtor or its designated custodian to make copies of or revisions to the authoritative copy which add or change an identified assignee of the authoritative copy without the consent of the secured party;

(4) a secured party having control of investment property under Section 8–106(d)(2) or 9–106(b) shall send to the securities intermediary or commodity intermediary with which the security entitlement or commodity contract is maintained an authenticated record that releases the securities intermediary or commodity intermediary from any further obligation to comply with entitlement orders or directions originated by the secured party; and

(5) a secured party having control of a letter-of-credit right under Section 9–107 shall send to each person having an unfulfilled obligation to pay or deliver proceeds of the letter of credit to the secured party an authenticated release from any further obligation to pay or deliver proceeds of the letter of credit to the secured party.

§ 9-209. Duties of Secured Party If Account Debtor Has Been Notified of Assignment.

(a) Except as otherwise provided in subsection (c), this section applies if:

(1) there is no outstanding secured obligation; and

(2) the secured party is not committed to make advances, incur obligations, or otherwise give value.

(b) Within 10 days after receiving an authenticated demand by the debtor, a secured party shall send to an account debtor that has received notification of an assignment to the secured party as assignee under Section 9–406(a) an authenticated record that releases the account debtor from any further obligation to the secured party.

(c) This section does not apply to an assignment constituting the sale of an account, chattel paper, or payment intangible.

§ 9-210. Request for Accounting; Request Regarding List of Collateral or Statement of Account.

(a) In this section:

(1) "Request" means a record of a type described in paragraph (2), (3), or (4).

(2) "Request for an accounting" means a record authenticated by a debtor requesting that the recipient provide an accounting of the unpaid obligations secured by collateral and reasonably identifying the transaction or relationship that is the subject of the request.

(3) "Request regarding a list of collateral" means a record authenticated by a debtor requesting that the recipient approve or correct a list of what the debtor believes to be the collateral securing an obligation and reasonably identifying the transaction or relationship that is the subject of the request.

(4) "Request regarding a statement of account" means a record authenticated by a debtor requesting that the recipient approve or correct a statement indicating what the debtor believes to be the aggregate amount of unpaid obligations secured by collateral as of a specified date and reasonably identifying the transaction or relationship that is the subject of the request.

(b) Subject to subsections (c), (d), (e), and (f), a secured party, other than a buyer of accounts, chattel paper, payment intangibles, or promissory notes or a consignor, shall comply with a request within 14 days after receipt:

(1) in the case of a request for an accounting, by authenticating and sending to the debtor an accounting; and

(2) in the case of a request regarding a list of collateral or a request regarding a statement of account, by authenticating and sending to the debtor an approval or correction.

(c) A secured party that claims a security interest in all of a particular type of collateral owned by the debtor may comply with a request regarding a list of collateral by sending to the debtor an authenticated record including a statement to that effect within 14 days after receipt.

(d) A person that receives a request regarding a list of collateral, claims no interest in the collateral when it receives the request, and claimed an interest in the collateral at an earlier time shall comply with the request within 14 days after receipt by sending to the debtor an authenticated record:

(1) disclaiming any interest in the collateral; and

(2) if known to the recipient, providing the name and mailing address of any assignee of or successor to the recipient's interest in the collateral.

(e) A person that receives a request for an accounting or a request regarding a statement of account, claims no interest in the obligations when it receives the request, and claimed an interest in the obligations at an earlier time shall comply with the request within 14 days after receipt by sending to the debtor an authenticated record:

(1) disclaiming any interest in the obligations; and

(2) if known to the recipient, providing the name and mailing address of any assignee of or successor to the recipient's interest in the obligations.

(f) A debtor is entitled without charge to one response to a request under this section during any six-month period. The secured party may require payment of a charge not exceeding $25 for each additional response.

As amended in 1999.

PART 3: Perfection and Priority

[Subpart 1. Law Governing Perfection and Priority]

§ 9-301. Law Governing Perfection and Priority of Security Interests.

Except as otherwise provided in Sections 9–303 through 9–306, the following rules determine the law governing perfection, the effect of perfection or nonperfection, and the priority of a security interest in collateral:

(1) Except as otherwise provided in this section, while a debtor is located in a jurisdiction, the local law of that jurisdiction governs perfection, the effect of perfection or nonperfection, and the priority of a security interest in collateral.

(2) While collateral is located in a jurisdiction, the local law of that jurisdiction governs perfection, the effect of perfection or nonperfection, and the priority of a possessory security interest in that collateral.

(3) Except as otherwise provided in paragraph (4), while negotiable documents, goods, instruments, money, or tangible chattel paper is located in a jurisdiction, the local law of that jurisdiction governs:

(A) perfection of a security interest in the goods by filing a fixture filing;

(B) perfection of a security interest in timber to be cut; and

(C) the effect of perfection or nonperfection and the priority of a nonpossessory security interest in the collateral.

(4) The local law of the jurisdiction in which the wellhead or minehead is located governs perfection, the effect of perfection or nonperfection, and the priority of a security interest in as-extracted collateral.

§ 9-302. Law Governing Perfection and Priority of Agricultural Liens.

While farm products are located in a jurisdiction, the local law of that jurisdiction governs perfection, the effect of perfection or nonperfection, and the priority of an agricultural lien on the farm products.

§ 9-303. Law Governing Perfection and Priority of Security Interests in Goods Covered by a Certificate of Title.

(a) This section applies to goods covered by a certificate of title, even if there is no other relationship between the jurisdiction under whose certificate of title the goods are covered and the goods or the debtor.

(b) Goods become covered by a certificate of title when a valid application for the certificate of title and the applicable fee are delivered to the appropriate authority. Goods cease to be covered by a certificate of title at the earlier of the time the certificate of title ceases to be effective under the law of the issuing jurisdiction or the time the goods become covered subsequently by a certificate of title issued by another jurisdiction.

(c) The local law of the jurisdiction under whose certificate of title the goods are covered governs perfection, the effect of perfection or nonperfection, and the priority of a security interest in goods covered by a certificate of title from the time the goods become covered by the certificate of title until the goods cease to be covered by the certificate of title.

§ 9-304. Law Governing Perfection and Priority of Security Interests in Deposit Accounts.

(a) The local law of a bank's jurisdiction governs perfection, the effect of perfection or nonperfection, and the priority of a security interest in a deposit account maintained with that bank.

(b) The following rules determine a bank's jurisdiction for purposes of this part:

(1) If an agreement between the bank and the debtor governing the deposit account expressly provides that a particular jurisdiction is the bank's jurisdiction for purposes of this part, this article, or [the Uniform Commercial Code], that jurisdiction is the bank's jurisdiction.

(2) If paragraph (1) does not apply and an agreement between the bank and its customer governing the deposit account expressly provides that the agreement is governed by the law of a particular jurisdiction, that jurisdiction is the bank's jurisdiction.

(3) If neither paragraph (1) nor paragraph (2) applies and an agreement between the bank and its customer governing the deposit account expressly provides that the deposit account is maintained at an office in a particular jurisdiction, that jurisdiction is the bank's jurisdiction.

(4) If none of the preceding paragraphs applies, the bank's jurisdiction is the jurisdiction in which the office identified in an account statement as the office serving the customer's account is located.

(5) If none of the preceding paragraphs applies, the bank's jurisdiction is the jurisdiction in which the chief executive office of the bank is located.

§ 9-305. Law Governing Perfection and Priority of Security Interests in Investment Property.

(a) Except as otherwise provided in subsection (c), the following rules apply:

(1) While a security certificate is located in a jurisdiction, the local law of that jurisdiction governs perfection, the effect of perfection or nonperfection, and the priority of a security interest in the certificated security represented thereby.

(2) The local law of the issuer's jurisdiction as specified in Section 8–110(d) governs perfection, the effect of perfection or nonperfection, and the priority of a security interest in an uncertificated security.

(3) The local law of the securities intermediary's jurisdiction as specified in Section 8–110(e) governs perfection, the effect of perfection or nonperfection, and the priority of a security interest in a security entitlement or securities account.

(4) The local law of the commodity intermediary's jurisdiction governs perfection, the effect of perfection or nonperfection, and the priority of a security interest in a commodity contract or commodity account.

(b) The following rules determine a commodity intermediary's jurisdiction for purposes of this part:

(1) If an agreement between the commodity intermediary and commodity customer governing the commodity account expressly provides that a particular jurisdiction is the commodity intermediary's jurisdiction for purposes of this part, this article, or [the Uniform Commercial Code], that jurisdiction is the commodity intermediary's jurisdiction.

(2) If paragraph (1) does not apply and an agreement between the commodity intermediary and commodity customer governing the commodity account expressly provides that the agreement is governed by the law of a particular jurisdiction, that jurisdiction is the commodity intermediary's jurisdiction.

(3) If neither paragraph (1) nor paragraph (2) applies and an agreement between the commodity intermediary and commodity customer

governing the commodity account expressly provides that the commodity account is maintained at an office in a particular jurisdiction, that jurisdiction is the commodity intermediary's jurisdiction.

(4) If none of the preceding paragraphs applies, the commodity intermediary's jurisdiction is the jurisdiction in which the office identified in an account statement as the office serving the commodity customer's account is located.

(5) If none of the preceding paragraphs applies, the commodity intermediary's jurisdiction is the jurisdiction in which the chief executive office of the commodity intermediary is located.

(c) The local law of the jurisdiction in which the debtor is located governs:

(1) perfection of a security interest in investment property by filing;

(2) automatic perfection of a security interest in investment property created by a broker or securities intermediary; and

(3) automatic perfection of a security interest in a commodity contract or commodity account created by a commodity intermediary.

§ 9-306. Law Governing Perfection and Priority of Security Interests in Letter-of-Credit Rights.

(a) Subject to subsection (c), the local law of the issuer's jurisdiction or a nominated person's jurisdiction governs perfection, the effect of perfection or nonperfection, and the priority of a security interest in a letter-of-credit right if the issuer's jurisdiction or nominated person's jurisdiction is a State.

(b) For purposes of this part, an issuer's jurisdiction or nominated person's jurisdiction is the jurisdiction whose law governs the liability of the issuer or nominated person with respect to the letter-of-credit right as provided in Section 5–116.

(c) This section does not apply to a security interest that is perfected only under Section 9–308(d).

§ 9-307. Location of Debtor.

(a) In this section, "place of business" means a place where a debtor conducts its affairs.

(b) Except as otherwise provided in this section, the following rules determine a debtor's location:

(1) A debtor who is an individual is located at the individual's principal residence.

(2) A debtor that is an organization and has only one place of business is located at its place of business.

(3) A debtor that is an organization and has more than one place of business is located at its chief executive office.

(c) Subsection (b) applies only if a debtor's residence, place of business, or chief executive office, as applicable, is located in a jurisdiction whose law generally requires information concerning the existence of a nonpossessory security interest to be made generally available in a filing, recording, or registration system as a condition or result of the security interest's obtaining priority over the rights of a lien creditor with respect to the collateral. If subsection (b) does not apply, the debtor is located in the District of Columbia.

(d) A person that ceases to exist, have a residence, or have a place of business continues to be located in the jurisdiction specified by subsections (b) and (c).

(e) A registered organization that is organized under the law of a State is located in that State.

(f) Except as otherwise provided in subsection (i), a registered organization that is organized under the law of the United States and a branch or agency of a bank that is not organized under the law of the United States or a State are located:

(1) in the State that the law of the United States designates, if the law designates a State of location;

(2) in the State that the registered organization, branch, or agency designates, if the law of the United States authorizes the registered organization, branch, or agency to designate its State of location; or

(3) in the District of Columbia, if neither paragraph (1) nor paragraph (2) applies.

(g) A registered organization continues to be located in the jurisdiction specified by subsection (e) or (f) notwithstanding:

(1) the suspension, revocation, forfeiture, or lapse of the registered organization's status as such in its jurisdiction of organization; or

(2) the dissolution, winding up, or cancellation of the existence of the registered organization.

(h) The United States is located in the District of Columbia.

(i) A branch or agency of a bank that is not organized under the law of the United States or a State is located in the State in which the branch or agency is licensed, if all branches and agencies of the bank are licensed in only one State.

(j) A foreign air carrier under the Federal Aviation Act of 1958, as amended, is located at the designated office of the agent upon which service of process may be made on behalf of the carrier.

(k) This section applies only for purposes of this part.

[Subpart 2. Perfection]

§ 9-308. When Security Interest or Agricultural Lien Is Perfected; Continuity of Perfection.

(a) Except as otherwise provided in this section and Section 9–309, a security interest is perfected if it has attached and all of the applicable requirements for perfection in Sections 9–310 through 9–316 have been satisfied. A security interest is perfected when it attaches if the applicable requirements are satisfied before the security interest attaches.

(b) An agricultural lien is perfected if it has become effective and all of the applicable requirements for perfection in Section 9–310 have been satisfied. An agricultural lien is perfected when it becomes effective if the applicable requirements are satisfied before the agricultural lien becomes effective.

(c) A security interest or agricultural lien is perfected continuously if it is originally perfected by one method under this article and is later perfected by another method under this article, without an intermediate period when it was unperfected.

(d) Perfection of a security interest in collateral also perfects a security interest in a supporting obligation for the collateral.

(e) Perfection of a security interest in a right to payment or performance also perfects a security interest in a security interest, mortgage, or other lien on personal or real property securing the right.

(f) Perfection of a security interest in a securities account also perfects a security interest in the security entitlements carried in the securities account.

(g) Perfection of a security interest in a commodity account also perfects a security interest in the commodity contracts carried in the commodity account.

Legislative Note: Any statute conflicting with subsection (e) must be made expressly subject to that subsection.

§ 9-309. Security Interest Perfected upon Attachment.

The following security interests are perfected when they attach:

(1) a purchase-money security interest in consumer goods, except as otherwise provided in Section 9–311(b) with respect to consumer goods that are subject to a statute or treaty described in Section 9–311(a);

(2) an assignment of accounts or payment intangibles which does not by itself or in conjunction with other assignments to the same assignee

transfer a significant part of the assignor's outstanding accounts or payment intangibles;

(3) a sale of a payment intangible;

(4) a sale of a promissory note;

(5) a security interest created by the assignment of a health-care-insurance receivable to the provider of the health-care goods or services;

(6) a security interest arising under Section 2–401, 2–505, 2–711(3), or 2A–508(5), until the debtor obtains possession of the collateral;

(7) a security interest of a collecting bank arising under Section 4–210;

(8) a security interest of an issuer or nominated person arising under Section 5–118;

(9) a security interest arising in the delivery of a financial asset under Section 9–206(c);

(10) a security interest in investment property created by a broker or securities intermediary;

(11) a security interest in a commodity contract or a commodity account created by a commodity intermediary;

(12) an assignment for the benefit of all creditors of the transferor and subsequent transfers by the assignee thereunder; and

(13) a security interest created by an assignment of a beneficial interest in a decedent's estate; and

(14) a sale by an individual of an account that is a right to payment of winnings in a lottery or other game of chance.

§ 9-310. When Filing Required to Perfect Security Interest or Agricultural Lien; Security Interests and Agricultural Liens to Which Filing Provisions Do Not Apply.

(a) Except as otherwise provided in subsection (b) and Section 9–312(b), a financing statement must be filed to perfect all security interests and agricultural liens.

(b) The filing of a financing statement is not necessary to perfect a security interest:

(1) that is perfected under Section 9–308(d), (e), (f), or (g);

(2) that is perfected under Section 9–309 when it attaches;

(3) in property subject to a statute, regulation, or treaty described in Section 9–311(a);

(4) in goods in possession of a bailee which is perfected under Section 9–312(d)(1) or (2);

(5) in certificated securities, documents, goods, or instruments which is perfected without filing or possession under Section 9–312(e), (f), or (g);

(6) in collateral in the secured party's possession under Section 9–313;

(7) in a certificated security which is perfected by delivery of the security certificate to the secured party under Section 9–313;

(8) in deposit accounts, electronic chattel paper, investment property, or letter-of-credit rights which is perfected by control under Section 9–314;

(9) in proceeds which is perfected under Section 9–315; or

(10) that is perfected under Section 9–316.

(c) If a secured party assigns a perfected security interest or agricultural lien, a filing under this article is not required to continue the perfected status of the security interest against creditors of and transferees from the original debtor.

§ 9-311. Perfection of Security Interests in Property Subject to Certain Statutes, Regulations, and Treaties.

(a) Except as otherwise provided in subsection (d), the filing of a financing statement is not necessary or effective to perfect a security interest in property subject to:

(1) a statute, regulation, or treaty of the United States whose requirements for a security interest's obtaining priority over the rights of a lien creditor with respect to the property preempt Section 9–310(a);

(2) [list any certificate-of-title statute covering automobiles, trailers, mobile homes, boats, farm tractors, or the like, which provides for a security interest to be indicated on the certificate as a condition or result of perfection, and any non-Uniform Commercial Code central filing statute]; or

(3) a certificate-of-title statute of another jurisdiction which provides for a security interest to be indicated on the certificate as a condition or result of the security interest's obtaining priority over the rights of a lien creditor with respect to the property.

(b) Compliance with the requirements of a statute, regulation, or treaty described in subsection (a) for obtaining priority over the rights of a lien creditor is equivalent to the filing of a financing statement under this article. Except as otherwise provided in subsection (d) and Sections 9–313 and 9–316(d) and (e) for goods covered by a certificate of title, a security interest in property subject to a statute, regulation, or treaty described in subsection (a) may be perfected only by compliance with those requirements, and a security interest so perfected remains perfected notwithstanding a change in the use or transfer of possession of the collateral.

(c) Except as otherwise provided in subsection (d) and Section 9–316(d) and (e), duration and renewal of perfection of a security interest perfected by compliance with the requirements prescribed by a statute, regulation, or treaty described in subsection (a) are governed by the statute, regulation, or treaty. In other respects, the security interest is subject to this article.

(d) During any period in which collateral subject to a statute specified in subsection (a)(2) is inventory held for sale or lease by a person or leased by that person as lessor and that person is in the business of selling goods of that kind, this section does not apply to a security interest in that collateral created by that person.

Legislative Note: This Article contemplates that perfection of a security interest in goods covered by a certificate of title occurs upon receipt by appropriate State officials of a properly tendered application for a certificate of title on which the security interest is to be indicated, without a relation back to an earlier time. States whose certificate-of-title statutes provide for perfection at a different time or contain a relation-back provision should amend the statutes accordingly.

§ 9-312. Perfection of Security Interests in Chattel Paper, Deposit Accounts, Documents, Goods Covered by Documents, Instruments, Investment Property, Letter-of-Credit Rights, and Money; Perfection by Permissive Filing; Temporary Perfection without Filing or Transfer of Possession.

(a) A security interest in chattel paper, negotiable documents, instruments, or investment property may be perfected by filing.

(b) Except as otherwise provided in Section 9–315(c) and (d) for proceeds:

(1) a security interest in a deposit account may be perfected only by control under Section 9–314;

(2) and except as otherwise provided in Section 9–308(d), a security interest in a letter-of-credit right may be perfected only by control under Section 9–314; and

(3) a security interest in money may be perfected only by the secured party's taking possession under Section 9–313.

(c) While goods are in the possession of a bailee that has issued a negotiable document covering the goods:

(1) a security interest in the goods may be perfected by perfecting a security interest in the document; and

(2) a security interest perfected in the document has priority over any security interest that becomes perfected in the goods by another method during that time.

(d) While goods are in the possession of a bailee that has issued a non-negotiable document covering the goods, a security interest in the goods may be perfected by:

(1) issuance of a document in the name of the secured party;

(2) the bailee's receipt of notification of the secured party's interest; or

(3) filing as to the goods.

(e) A security interest in certificated securities, negotiable documents, or instruments is perfected without filing or the taking of possession for a period of 20 days from the time it attaches to the extent that it arises for new value given under an authenticated security agreement.

(f) A perfected security interest in a negotiable document or goods in possession of a bailee, other than one that has issued a negotiable document for the goods, remains perfected for 20 days without filing if the secured party makes available to the debtor the goods or documents representing the goods for the purpose of:

(1) ultimate sale or exchange; or

(2) loading, unloading, storing, shipping, transshipping, manufacturing, processing, or otherwise dealing with them in a manner preliminary to their sale or exchange.

(g) A perfected security interest in a certificated security or instrument remains perfected for 20 days without filing if the secured party delivers the security certificate or instrument to the debtor for the purpose of:

(1) ultimate sale or exchange; or

(2) presentation, collection, enforcement, renewal, or registration of transfer.

(h) After the 20-day period specified in subsection (e), (f), or (g) expires, perfection depends upon compliance with this article.

§ 9-313. When Possession by or Delivery to Secured Party Perfects Security Interest without Filing.

(a) Except as otherwise provided in subsection (b), a secured party may perfect a security interest in negotiable documents, goods, instruments, money, or tangible chattel paper by taking possession of the collateral. A secured party may perfect a security interest in certificated securities by taking delivery of the certificated securities under Section 8–301.

(b) With respect to goods covered by a certificate of title issued by this State, a secured party may perfect a security interest in the goods by taking possession of the goods only in the circumstances described in Section 9–316(d).

(c) With respect to collateral other than certificated securities and goods covered by a document, a secured party takes possession of collateral in the possession of a person other than the debtor, the secured party, or a lessee of the collateral from the debtor in the ordinary course of the debtor's business, when:

(1) the person in possession authenticates a record acknowledging that it holds possession of the collateral for the secured party's benefit; or

(2) the person takes possession of the collateral after having authenticated a record acknowledging that it will hold possession of collateral for the secured party's benefit.

(d) If perfection of a security interest depends upon possession of the collateral by a secured party, perfection occurs no earlier than the time the secured party takes possession and continues only while the secured party retains possession.

(e) A security interest in a certificated security in registered form is perfected by delivery when delivery of the certificated security occurs under Section 8–301 and remains perfected by delivery until the debtor obtains possession of the security certificate.

(f) A person in possession of collateral is not required to acknowledge that it holds possession for a secured party's benefit.

(g) If a person acknowledges that it holds possession for the secured party's benefit:

(1) the acknowledgment is effective under subsection (c) or Section 8–301(a), even if the acknowledgment violates the rights of a debtor; and

(2) unless the person otherwise agrees or law other than this article otherwise provides, the person does not owe any duty to the secured party and is not required to confirm the acknowledgment to another person.

(h) A secured party having possession of collateral does not relinquish possession by delivering the collateral to a person other than the debtor or a lessee of the collateral from the debtor in the ordinary course of the debtor's business if the person was instructed before the delivery or is instructed contemporaneously with the delivery:

(1) to hold possession of the collateral for the secured party's benefit; or

(2) to redeliver the collateral to the secured party.

(i) A secured party does not relinquish possession, even if a delivery under subsection (h) violates the rights of a debtor. A person to which collateral is delivered under subsection (h) does not owe any duty to the secured party and is not required to confirm the delivery to another person unless the person otherwise agrees or law other than this article otherwise provides.

§ 9-314. Perfection by Control.

(a) A security interest in investment property, deposit accounts, letter-of-credit rights, or electronic chattel paper may be perfected by control of the collateral under Section 9–104, 9–105, 9–106, or 9–107.

(b) A security interest in deposit accounts, electronic chattel paper, or letter-of-credit rights is perfected by control under Section 9–104, 9–105, or 9–107 when the secured party obtains control and remains perfected by control only while the secured party retains control.

(c) A security interest in investment property is perfected by control under Section 9–106 from the time the secured party obtains control and remains perfected by control until:

(1) the secured party does not have control; and

(2) one of the following occurs:

(A) if the collateral is a certificated security, the debtor has or acquires possession of the security certificate;

(B) if the collateral is an uncertificated security, the issuer has registered or registers the debtor as the registered owner; or

(C) if the collateral is a security entitlement, the debtor is or becomes the entitlement holder.

§ 9-315. Secured Party's Rights on Disposition of Collateral and in Proceeds.

(a) Except as otherwise provided in this article and in Section 2–403(2):

(1) a security interest or agricultural lien continues in collateral notwithstanding sale, lease, license, exchange, or other disposition thereof unless the secured party authorized the disposition free of the security interest or agricultural lien; and

(2) a security interest attaches to any identifiable proceeds of collateral.

(b) Proceeds that are commingled with other property are identifiable proceeds:

(1) if the proceeds are goods, to the extent provided by Section 9–336; and

(2) if the proceeds are not goods, to the extent that the secured party identifies the proceeds by a method of tracing, including application of equitable principles, that is permitted under law other than this article with respect to commingled property of the type involved.

(c) A security interest in proceeds is a perfected security interest if the security interest in the original collateral was perfected.

(d) A perfected security interest in proceeds becomes unperfected on the 21st day after the security interest attaches to the proceeds unless:

(1) the following conditions are satisfied:

(A) a filed financing statement covers the original collateral;

(B) the proceeds are collateral in which a security interest may be perfected by filing in the office in which the financing statement has been filed; and

(C) the proceeds are not acquired with cash proceeds;

(2) the proceeds are identifiable cash proceeds; or

(3) the security interest in the proceeds is perfected other than under subsection (c) when the security interest attaches to the proceeds or within 20 days thereafter.

(e) If a filed financing statement covers the original collateral, a security interest in proceeds which remains perfected under subsection (d)(1) becomes unperfected at the later of:

(1) when the effectiveness of the filed financing statement lapses under Section 9–515 or is terminated under Section 9–513; or

(2) the 21st day after the security interest attaches to the proceeds.

§ 9-316. Continued Perfection of Security Interest Following Change in Governing Law.

(a) A security interest perfected pursuant to the law of the jurisdiction designated in Section 9–301(1) or 9–305(c) remains perfected until the earliest of:

(1) the time perfection would have ceased under the law of that jurisdiction;

(2) the expiration of four months after a change of the debtor's location to another jurisdiction; or

(3) the expiration of one year after a transfer of collateral to a person that thereby becomes a debtor and is located in another jurisdiction.

(b) If a security interest described in subsection (a) becomes perfected under the law of the other jurisdiction before the earliest time or event described in that subsection, it remains perfected thereafter. If the security interest does not become perfected under the law of the other jurisdiction before the earliest time or event, it becomes unperfected and is deemed never to have been perfected as against a purchaser of the collateral for value.

(c) A possessory security interest in collateral, other than goods covered by a certificate of title and as-extracted collateral consisting of goods, remains continuously perfected if:

(1) the collateral is located in one jurisdiction and subject to a security interest perfected under the law of that jurisdiction;

(2) thereafter the collateral is brought into another jurisdiction; and

(3) upon entry into the other jurisdiction, the security interest is perfected under the law of the other jurisdiction.

(d) Except as otherwise provided in subsection (e), a security interest in goods covered by a certificate of title which is perfected by any method under the law of another jurisdiction when the goods become covered by a certificate of title from this State remains perfected until the security interest would have become unperfected under the law of the other jurisdiction had the goods not become so covered.

(e) A security interest described in subsection (d) becomes unperfected as against a purchaser of the goods for value and is deemed never to have been perfected as against a purchaser of the goods for value if the applicable requirements for perfection under Section 9–311(b) or 9–313 are not satisfied before the earlier of:

(1) the time the security interest would have become unperfected under the law of the other jurisdiction had the goods not become covered by a certificate of title from this State; or

(2) the expiration of four months after the goods had become so covered.

(f) A security interest in deposit accounts, letter-of-credit rights, or investment property which is perfected under the law of the bank's jurisdiction, the issuer's jurisdiction, a nominated person's jurisdiction, the securities intermediary's jurisdiction, or the commodity intermediary's jurisdiction, as applicable, remains perfected until the earlier of:

(1) the time the security interest would have become unperfected under the law of that jurisdiction; or

(2) the expiration of four months after a change of the applicable jurisdiction to another jurisdiction.

(g) If a security interest described in subsection (f) becomes perfected under the law of the other jurisdiction before the earlier of the time or the end of the period described in that subsection, it remains perfected thereafter. If the security interest does not become perfected under the law of the other jurisdiction before the earlier of that time or the end of that period, it becomes unperfected and is deemed never to have been perfected as against a purchaser of the collateral for value.

[Subpart 3. Priority]

§ 9-317. Interests That Take Priority over or Take Free of Security Interest or Agricultural Lien.

(a) A security interest or agricultural lien is subordinate to the rights of:

(1) a person entitled to priority under Section 9–322; and

(2) except as otherwise provided in subsection (e), a person that becomes a lien creditor before the earlier of the time:

(A) the security interest or agricultural lien is perfected; or

(B) one of the conditions specified in Section 9–203(b)(3) is met and a financing statement covering the collateral is filed.

(b) Except as otherwise provided in subsection (e), a buyer, other than a secured party, of tangible chattel paper, documents, goods, instruments, or a security certificate takes free of a security interest or agricultural lien if the buyer gives value and receives delivery of the collateral without knowledge of the security interest or agricultural lien and before it is perfected.

(c) Except as otherwise provided in subsection (e), a lessee of goods takes free of a security interest or agricultural lien if the lessee gives value and receives delivery of the collateral without knowledge of the security interest or agricultural lien and before it is perfected.

(d) A licensee of a general intangible or a buyer, other than a secured party, of accounts, electronic chattel paper, general intangibles, or investment property other than a certificated security takes free of a security interest if the licensee or buyer gives value without knowledge of the security interest and before it is perfected.

(e) Except as otherwise provided in Sections 9–320 and 9–321, if a person files a financing statement with respect to a purchase-money security interest before or within 20 days after the debtor receives delivery of the collateral, the security interest takes priority over the rights of a buyer, lessee, or lien creditor which arise between the time the security interest attaches and the time of filing.

As amended in 2000.

§ 9-318. No Interest Retained in Right to Payment That Is Sold; Rights and Title of Seller of Account or Chattel Paper with Respect to Creditors and Purchasers.

(a) A debtor that has sold an account, chattel paper, payment intangible, or promissory note does not retain a legal or equitable interest in the collateral sold.

(b) For purposes of determining the rights of creditors of, and purchasers for value of an account or chattel paper from, a debtor that has sold an account or chattel paper, while the buyer's security interest is unperfected, the debtor is deemed to have rights and title to the account or chattel paper identical to those the debtor sold.

§ 9-319. Rights and Title of Consignee with Respect to Creditors and Purchasers.

(a) Except as otherwise provided in subsection (b), for purposes of determining the rights of creditors of, and purchasers for value of goods from, a consignee, while the goods are in the possession of the consignee, the consignee is deemed to have rights and title to the goods identical to those the consignor had or had power to transfer.

(b) For purposes of determining the rights of a creditor of a consignee, law other than this article determines the rights and title of a consignee while goods are in the consignee's possession if, under this part, a perfected security interest held by the consignor would have priority over the rights of the creditor.

§ 9-320. Buyer of Goods.

(a) Except as otherwise provided in subsection (e), a buyer in ordinary course of business, other than a person buying farm products from a person engaged in farming operations, takes free of a security interest created by the buyer's seller, even if the security interest is perfected and the buyer knows of its existence.

(b) Except as otherwise provided in subsection (e), a buyer of goods from a person who used or bought the goods for use primarily for personal, family, or household purposes takes free of a security interest, even if perfected, if the buyer buys:

(1) without knowledge of the security interest;

(2) for value;

(3) primarily for the buyer's personal, family, or household purposes; and

(4) before the filing of a financing statement covering the goods.

(c) To the extent that it affects the priority of a security interest over a buyer of goods under subsection (b), the period of effectiveness of a filing made in the jurisdiction in which the seller is located is governed by Section 9–316(a) and (b).

(d) A buyer in ordinary course of business buying oil, gas, or other minerals at the wellhead or minehead or after extraction takes free of an interest arising out of an encumbrance.

(e) Subsections (a) and (b) do not affect a security interest in goods in the possession of the secured party under Section 9–313.

§ 9-321. Licensee of General Intangible and Lessee of Goods in Ordinary Course of Business.

(a) In this section, "licensee in ordinary course of business" means a person that becomes a licensee of a general intangible in good faith, without knowledge that the license violates the rights of another person in the general intangible, and in the ordinary course from a person in the business of licensing general intangibles of that kind. A person becomes a licensee in the ordinary course if the license to the person comports with the usual or customary practices in the kind of business in which the licensor is engaged or with the licensor's own usual or customary practices.

(b) A licensee in ordinary course of business takes its rights under a nonexclusive license free of a security interest in the general intangible created by the licensor, even if the security interest is perfected and the licensee knows of its existence.

(c) A lessee in ordinary course of business takes its leasehold interest free of a security interest in the goods created by the lessor, even if the security interest is perfected and the lessee knows of its existence.

§ 9-322. Priorities among Conflicting Security Interests in and Agricultural Liens on Same Collateral.

(a) Except as otherwise provided in this section, priority among conflicting security interests and agricultural liens in the same collateral is determined according to the following rules:

(1) Conflicting perfected security interests and agricultural liens rank according to priority in time of filing or perfection. Priority dates from the earlier of the time a filing covering the collateral is first made or the security interest or agricultural lien is first perfected, if there is no period thereafter when there is neither filing nor perfection.

(2) A perfected security interest or agricultural lien has priority over a conflicting unperfected security interest or agricultural lien.

(3) The first security interest or agricultural lien to attach or become effective has priority if conflicting security interests and agricultural liens are unperfected.

(b) For the purposes of subsection (a)(1):

(1) the time of filing or perfection as to a security interest in collateral is also the time of filing or perfection as to a security interest in proceeds; and

(2) the time of filing or perfection as to a security interest in collateral supported by a supporting obligation is also the time of filing or perfection as to a security interest in the supporting obligation.

(c) Except as otherwise provided in subsection (f), a security interest in collateral which qualifies for priority over a conflicting security interest under Section 9–327, 9–328, 9–329, 9–330, or 9–331 also has priority over a conflicting security interest in:

(1) any supporting obligation for the collateral; and

(2) proceeds of the collateral if:

(A) the security interest in proceeds is perfected;

(B) the proceeds are cash proceeds or of the same type as the collateral; and

(C) in the case of proceeds that are proceeds of proceeds, all intervening proceeds are cash proceeds, proceeds of the same type as the collateral, or an account relating to the collateral.

(d) Subject to subsection (e) and except as otherwise provided in subsection (f), if a security interest in chattel paper, deposit accounts, negotiable documents, instruments, investment property, or letter-of-credit rights is perfected by a method other than filing, conflicting perfected security interests in proceeds of the collateral rank according to priority in time of filing.

(e) Subsection (d) applies only if the proceeds of the collateral are not cash proceeds, chattel paper, negotiable documents, instruments, investment property, or letter-of-credit rights.

(f) Subsections (a) through (e) are subject to:

(1) subsection (g) and the other provisions of this part;

(2) Section 4–210 with respect to a security interest of a collecting bank;

(3) Section 5–118 with respect to a security interest of an issuer or nominated person; and

(4) Section 9–110 with respect to a security interest arising under Article 2 or 2A.

(g) A perfected agricultural lien on collateral has priority over a conflicting security interest in or agricultural lien on the same collateral if the statute creating the agricultural lien so provides.

§ 9-323. Future Advances.

(a) Except as otherwise provided in subsection (c), for purposes of determining the priority of a perfected security interest under Section 9–322(a)(1), perfection of the security interest dates from the time an advance is made to the extent that the security interest secures an advance that:

(1) is made while the security interest is perfected only:

(A) under Section 9–309 when it attaches; or

(B) temporarily under Section 9–312(e), (f), or (g); and

(2) is not made pursuant to a commitment entered into before or while the security interest is perfected by a method other than under Section 9–309 or 9–312(e), (f), or (g).

(b) Except as otherwise provided in subsection (c), a security interest is subordinate to the rights of a person that becomes a lien creditor to the extent that the security interest secures an advance made more than 45 days after the person becomes a lien creditor unless the advance is made:

(1) without knowledge of the lien; or

(2) pursuant to a commitment entered into without knowledge of the lien.

(c) Subsections (a) and (b) do not apply to a security interest held by a secured party that is a buyer of accounts, chattel paper, payment intangibles, or promissory notes or a consignor.

(d) Except as otherwise provided in subsection (e), a buyer of goods other than a buyer in ordinary course of business takes free of a security interest to the extent that it secures advances made after the earlier of:

(1) the time the secured party acquires knowledge of the buyer's purchase; or

(2) 45 days after the purchase.

(e) Subsection (d) does not apply if the advance is made pursuant to a commitment entered into without knowledge of the buyer's purchase and before the expiration of the 45-day period.

(f) Except as otherwise provided in subsection (g), a lessee of goods, other than a lessee in ordinary course of business, takes the leasehold interest free of a security interest to the extent that it secures advances made after the earlier of:

(1) the time the secured party acquires knowledge of the lease; or

(2) 45 days after the lease contract becomes enforceable.

(g) Subsection (f) does not apply if the advance is made pursuant to a commitment entered into without knowledge of the lease and before the expiration of the 45-day period.

As amended in 1999.

§ 9-324. Priority of Purchase-Money Security Interests.

(a) Except as otherwise provided in subsection (g), a perfected purchase-money security interest in goods other than inventory or livestock has priority over a conflicting security interest in the same goods, and, except as otherwise provided in Section 9–327, a perfected security interest in its identifiable proceeds also has priority, if the purchase-money security interest is perfected when the debtor receives possession of the collateral or within 20 days thereafter.

(b) Subject to subsection (c) and except as otherwise provided in subsection (g), a perfected purchase-money security interest in inventory has priority over a conflicting security interest in the same inventory, has priority over a conflicting security interest in chattel paper or an instrument constituting proceeds of the inventory and in proceeds of the chattel paper, if so provided in Section 9–330, and, except as otherwise provided in Section 9–327, also has priority in identifiable cash proceeds of the inventory to the extent the identifiable cash proceeds are received on or before the delivery of the inventory to a buyer, if:

(1) the purchase-money security interest is perfected when the debtor receives possession of the inventory;

(2) the purchase-money secured party sends an authenticated notification to the holder of the conflicting security interest;

(3) the holder of the conflicting security interest receives the notification within five years before the debtor receives possession of the inventory; and

(4) the notification states that the person sending the notification has

or expects to acquire a purchase-money security interest in inventory of the debtor and describes the inventory.

(c) Subsections (b)(2) through (4) apply only if the holder of the conflicting security interest had filed a financing statement covering the same types of inventory:

(1) if the purchase-money security interest is perfected by filing, before the date of the filing; or

(2) if the purchase-money security interest is temporarily perfected without filing or possession under Section 9–312(f), before the beginning of the 20-day period thereunder.

(d) Subject to subsection (e) and except as otherwise provided in subsection (g), a perfected purchase-money security interest in livestock that are farm products has priority over a conflicting security interest in the same livestock, and, except as otherwise provided in Section 9–327, a perfected security interest in their identifiable proceeds and identifiable products in their unmanufactured states also has priority, if:

(1) the purchase-money security interest is perfected when the debtor receives possession of the livestock;

(2) the purchase-money secured party sends an authenticated notification to the holder of the conflicting security interest;

(3) the holder of the conflicting security interest receives the notification within six months before the debtor receives possession of the livestock; and

(4) the notification states that the person sending the notification has or expects to acquire a purchase-money security interest in livestock of the debtor and describes the livestock.

(e) Subsections (d)(2) through (4) apply only if the holder of the conflicting security interest had filed a financing statement covering the same types of livestock:

(1) if the purchase-money security interest is perfected by filing, before the date of the filing; or

(2) if the purchase-money security interest is temporarily perfected without filing or possession under Section 9–312(f), before the beginning of the 20-day period thereunder.

(f) Except as otherwise provided in subsection (g), a perfected purchase-money security interest in software has priority over a conflicting security interest in the same collateral, and, except as otherwise provided in Section 9–327, a perfected security interest in its identifiable proceeds also has priority, to the extent that the purchase-money security interest in the goods in which the software was acquired for use has priority in the goods and proceeds of the goods under this section.

(g) If more than one security interest qualifies for priority in the same collateral under subsection (a), (b), (d), or (f):

(1) a security interest securing an obligation incurred as all or part of the price of the collateral has priority over a security interest securing an obligation incurred for value given to enable the debtor to acquire rights in or the use of collateral; and

(2) in all other cases, Section 9–322(a) applies to the qualifying security interests.

§ 9-325. Priority of Security Interests in Transferred Collateral.

(a) Except as otherwise provided in subsection (b), a security interest created by a debtor is subordinate to a security interest in the same collateral created by another person if:

(1) the debtor acquired the collateral subject to the security interest created by the other person;

(2) the security interest created by the other person was perfected when the debtor acquired the collateral; and

(3) there is no period thereafter when the security interest is unperfected.

(b) Subsection (a) subordinates a security interest only if the security interest:

(1) otherwise would have priority solely under Section 9–322(a) or 9–324; or

(2) arose solely under Section 2–711(3) or 2A–508(5).

§ 9-326. Priority of Security Interests Created by New Debtor.

(a) Subject to subsection (b), a security interest created by a new debtor which is perfected by a filed financing statement that is effective solely under Section 9–508 in collateral in which a new debtor has or acquires rights is subordinate to a security interest in the same collateral which is perfected other than by a filed financing statement that is effective solely under Section 9–508.

(b) The other provisions of this part determine the priority among conflicting security interests in the same collateral perfected by filed financing statements that are effective solely under Section 9–508. However, if the security agreements to which a new debtor became bound as debtor were not entered into by the same original debtor, the conflicting security interests rank according to priority in time of the new debtor's having become bound.

§ 9-327. Priority of Security Interests in Deposit Account.

The following rules govern priority among conflicting security interests in the same deposit account:

(1) A security interest held by a secured party having control of the deposit account under Section 9–104 has priority over a conflicting security interest held by a secured party that does not have control.

(2) Except as otherwise provided in paragraphs (3) and (4), security interests perfected by control under Section 9–314 rank according to priority in time of obtaining control.

(3) Except as otherwise provided in paragraph (4), a security interest held by the bank with which the deposit account is maintained has priority over a conflicting security interest held by another secured party.

(4) A security interest perfected by control under Section 9–104(a)(3) has priority over a security interest held by the bank with which the deposit account is maintained.

§ 9-328. Priority of Security Interests in Investment Property.

The following rules govern priority among conflicting security interests in the same investment property:

(1) A security interest held by a secured party having control of investment property under Section 9–106 has priority over a security interest held by a secured party that does not have control of the investment property.

(2) Except as otherwise provided in paragraphs (3) and (4), conflicting security interests held by secured parties each of which has control under Section 9–106 rank according to priority in time of:

(A) if the collateral is a security, obtaining control;

(B) if the collateral is a security entitlement carried in a securities account and:

(i) if the secured party obtained control under Section 8–106(d)(1), the secured party's becoming the person for which the securities account is maintained;

(ii) if the secured party obtained control under Section 8–106(d)(2), the securities intermediary's agreement to comply with the secured party's entitlement orders with respect to security entitlements carried or to be carried in the securities account; or

(iii) if the secured party obtained control through another person under Section 8–106(d)(3), the time on which priority would be based under this paragraph if the other person were the secured party; or

(C) if the collateral is a commodity contract carried with a commodity intermediary, the satisfaction of the requirement for control specified in Section 9–106(b)(2) with respect to commodity contracts carried or to be carried with the commodity intermediary.

(3) A security interest held by a securities intermediary in a security entitlement or a securities account maintained with the securities intermediary has priority over a conflicting security interest held by another secured party.

(4) A security interest held by a commodity intermediary in a commodity contract or a commodity account maintained with the commodity intermediary has priority over a conflicting security interest held by another secured party.

(5) A security interest in a certificated security in registered form which is perfected by taking delivery under Section 9–313(a) and not by control under Section 9–314 has priority over a conflicting security interest perfected by a method other than control.

(6) Conflicting security interests created by a broker, securities intermediary, or commodity intermediary which are perfected without control under Section 9–106 rank equally.

(7) In all other cases, priority among conflicting security interests in investment property is governed by Sections 9–322 and 9–323.

§ 9-329. Priority of Security Interests in Letter-of-Credit Right.

The following rules govern priority among conflicting security interests in the same letter-of-credit right:

(1) A security interest held by a secured party having control of the letter-of-credit right under Section 9–107 has priority to the extent of its control over a conflicting security interest held by a secured party that does not have control.

(2) Security interests perfected by control under Section 9–314 rank according to priority in time of obtaining control.

§ 9-330. Priority of Purchaser of Chattel Paper or Instrument.

(a) A purchaser of chattel paper has priority over a security interest in the chattel paper which is claimed merely as proceeds of inventory subject to a security interest if:

(1) in good faith and in the ordinary course of the purchaser's business, the purchaser gives new value and takes possession of the chattel paper or obtains control of the chattel paper under Section 9–105; and

(2) the chattel paper does not indicate that it has been assigned to an identified assignee other than the purchaser.

(b) A purchaser of chattel paper has priority over a security interest in the chattel paper which is claimed other than merely as proceeds of inventory subject to a security interest if the purchaser gives new value and takes possession of the chattel paper or obtains control of the chattel paper under Section 9–105 in good faith, in the ordinary course of the purchaser's business, and without knowledge that the purchase violates the rights of the secured party.

(c) Except as otherwise provided in Section 9–327, a purchaser having priority in chattel paper under subsection (a) or (b) also has priority in proceeds of the chattel paper to the extent that:

(1) Section 9–322 provides for priority in the proceeds; or

(2) the proceeds consist of the specific goods covered by the chattel paper or cash proceeds of the specific goods, even if the purchaser's security interest in the proceeds is unperfected.

(d) Except as otherwise provided in Section 9–331(a), a purchaser of an

instrument has priority over a security interest in the instrument perfected by a method other than possession if the purchaser gives value and takes possession of the instrument in good faith and without knowledge that the purchase violates the rights of the secured party.

(e) For purposes of subsections (a) and (b), the holder of a purchase-money security interest in inventory gives new value for chattel paper constituting proceeds of the inventory.

(f) For purposes of subsections (b) and (d), if chattel paper or an instrument indicates that it has been assigned to an identified secured party other than the purchaser, a purchaser of the chattel paper or instrument has knowledge that the purchase violates the rights of the secured party.

§ 9-331. Priority of Rights of Purchasers of Instruments, Documents, and Securities under Other Articles; Priority of Interests in Financial Assets and Security Entitlements under Article 8.

(a) This article does not limit the rights of a holder in due course of a negotiable instrument, a holder to which a negotiable document of title has been duly negotiated, or a protected purchaser of a security. These holders or purchasers take priority over an earlier security interest, even if perfected, to the extent provided in Articles 3, 7, and 8.

(b) This article does not limit the rights of or impose liability on a person to the extent that the person is protected against the assertion of a claim under Article 8.

(c) Filing under this article does not constitute notice of a claim or defense to the holders, or purchasers, or persons described in subsections (a) and (b).

§ 9-332. Transfer of Money; Transfer of Funds from Deposit Account.

(a) A transferee of money takes the money free of a security interest unless the transferee acts in collusion with the debtor in violating the rights of the secured party.

(b) A transferee of funds from a deposit account takes the funds free of a security interest in the deposit account unless the transferee acts in collusion with the debtor in violating the rights of the secured party.

§ 9-333. Priority of Certain Liens Arising by Operation of Law.

(a) In this section, "possessory lien" means an interest, other than a security interest or an agricultural lien:

(1) which secures payment or performance of an obligation for services or materials furnished with respect to goods by a person in the ordinary course of the person's business;

(2) which is created by statute or rule of law in favor of the person; and

(3) whose effectiveness depends on the person's possession of the goods.

(b) A possessory lien on goods has priority over a security interest in the goods unless the lien is created by a statute that expressly provides otherwise.

§ 9-334. Priority of Security Interests in Fixtures and Crops.

(a) A security interest under this article may be created in goods that are fixtures or may continue in goods that become fixtures. A security interest does not exist under this article in ordinary building materials incorporated into an improvement on land.

(b) This article does not prevent creation of an encumbrance upon fixtures under real property law.

(c) In cases not governed by subsections (d) through (h), a security interest in fixtures is subordinate to a conflicting interest of an encumbrancer or owner of the related real property other than the debtor.

(d) Except as otherwise provided in subsection (h), a perfected security interest in fixtures has priority over a conflicting interest of an encumbrancer or owner of the real property if the debtor has an interest of record in or is in possession of the real property and:

(1) the security interest is a purchase-money security interest;

(2) the interest of the encumbrancer or owner arises before the goods become fixtures; and

(3) the security interest is perfected by a fixture filing before the goods become fixtures or within 20 days thereafter.

(e) A perfected security interest in fixtures has priority over a conflicting interest of an encumbrancer or owner of the real property if:

(1) the debtor has an interest of record in the real property or is in possession of the real property and the security interest:

(A) is perfected by a fixture filing before the interest of the encumbrancer or owner is of record; and

(B) has priority over any conflicting interest of a predecessor in title of the encumbrancer or owner;

(2) before the goods become fixtures, the security interest is perfected by any method permitted by this article and the fixtures are readily removable:

(A) factory or office machines;

(B) equipment that is not primarily used or leased for use in the operation of the real property; or

(C) replacements of domestic appliances that are consumer goods;

(3) the conflicting interest is a lien on the real property obtained by legal or equitable proceedings after the security interest was perfected by any method permitted by this article; or

(4) the security interest is:

(A) created in a manufactured home in a manufactured-home transaction; and

(B) perfected pursuant to a statute described in Section 9–311(a)(2).

(f) A security interest in fixtures, whether or not perfected, has priority over a conflicting interest of an encumbrancer or owner of the real property if:

(1) the encumbrancer or owner has, in an authenticated record, consented to the security interest or disclaimed an interest in the goods as fixtures; or

(2) the debtor has a right to remove the goods as against the encumbrancer or owner.

(g) The priority of the security interest under paragraph (f)(2) continues for a reasonable time if the debtor's right to remove the goods as against the encumbrancer or owner terminates.

(h) A mortgage is a construction mortgage to the extent that it secures an obligation incurred for the construction of an improvement on land, including the acquisition cost of the land, if a recorded record of the mortgage so indicates. Except as otherwise provided in subsections (e) and (f), a security interest in fixtures is subordinate to a construction mortgage if a record of the mortgage is recorded before the goods become fixtures and the goods become fixtures before the completion of the construction. A mortgage has this priority to the same extent as a construction mortgage to the extent that it is given to refinance a construction mortgage.

(i) A perfected security interest in crops growing on real property has priority over a conflicting interest of an encumbrancer or owner of the real property if the debtor has an interest of record in or is in possession of the real property.

(j) Subsection (i) prevails over any inconsistent provisions of the following statutes:

[List here any statutes containing provisions inconsistent with subsection (i).]

Legislative Note: States that amend statutes to remove provisions inconsistent with subsection (i) need not enact subsection (j).

§ 9-335. Accessions.

(a) A security interest may be created in an accession and continues in collateral that becomes an accession.

(b) If a security interest is perfected when the collateral becomes an accession, the security interest remains perfected in the collateral.

(c) Except as otherwise provided in subsection (d), the other provisions of this part determine the priority of a security interest in an accession.

(d) A security interest in an accession is subordinate to a security interest in the whole which is perfected by compliance with the requirements of a certificate-of-title statute under Section 9–311(b).

(e) After default, subject to Part 6, a secured party may remove an accession from other goods if the security interest in the accession has priority over the claims of every person having an interest in the whole.

(f) A secured party that removes an accession from other goods under subsection (e) shall promptly reimburse any holder of a security interest or other lien on, or owner of, the whole or of the other goods, other than the debtor, for the cost of repair of any physical injury to the whole or the other goods. The secured party need not reimburse the holder or owner for any diminution in value of the whole or the other goods caused by the absence of the accession removed or by any necessity for replacing it. A person entitled to reimbursement may refuse permission to remove until the secured party gives adequate assurance for the performance of the obligation to reimburse.

§ 9-336. Commingled Goods.

(a) In this section, "commingled goods" means goods that are physically united with other goods in such a manner that their identity is lost in a product or mass.

(b) A security interest does not exist in commingled goods as such. However, a security interest may attach to a product or mass that results when goods become commingled goods.

(c) If collateral becomes commingled goods, a security interest attaches to the product or mass.

(d) If a security interest in collateral is perfected before the collateral becomes commingled goods, the security interest that attaches to the product or mass under subsection (c) is perfected.

(e) Except as otherwise provided in subsection (f), the other provisions of this part determine the priority of a security interest that attaches to the product or mass under subsection (c).

(f) If more than one security interest attaches to the product or mass under subsection (c), the following rules determine priority:

(1) A security interest that is perfected under subsection (d) has priority over a security interest that is unperfected at the time the collateral becomes commingled goods.

(2) If more than one security interest is perfected under subsection (d), the security interests rank equally in proportion to the value of the collateral at the time it became commingled goods.

§ 9-337. Priority of Security Interests in Goods Covered by Certificate of Title.

If, while a security interest in goods is perfected by any method under the law of another jurisdiction, this State issues a certificate of title that does not show that the goods are subject to the security interest or contain a statement that they may be subject to security interests not shown on the certificate:

(1) a buyer of the goods, other than a person in the business of selling goods of that kind, takes free of the security interest if the buyer gives value and receives delivery of the goods after issuance of the certificate and without knowledge of the security interest; and

(2) the security interest is subordinate to a conflicting security interest in the goods that attaches, and is perfected under Section 9–311(b), after issuance of the certificate and without the conflicting secured party's knowledge of the security interest.

§ 9-338. Priority of Security Interest or Agricultural Lien Perfected by Filed Financing Statement Providing Certain Incorrect Information.

If a security interest or agricultural lien is perfected by a filed financing statement providing information described in Section 9–516(b)(5) which is incorrect at the time the financing statement is filed:

(1) the security interest or agricultural lien is subordinate to a conflicting perfected security interest in the collateral to the extent that the holder of the conflicting security interest gives value in reasonable reliance upon the incorrect information; and

(2) a purchaser, other than a secured party, of the collateral takes free of the security interest or agricultural lien to the extent that, in reasonable reliance upon the incorrect information, the purchaser gives value and, in the case of chattel paper, documents, goods, instruments, or a security certificate, receives delivery of the collateral.

§ 9-339. Priority Subject to Subordination.

This article does not preclude subordination by agreement by a person entitled to priority.

[Subpart 4. Rights of Bank]

§ 9-340. Effectiveness of Right of Recoupment or Set-Off against Deposit Account.

(a) Except as otherwise provided in subsection (c), a bank with which a deposit account is maintained may exercise any right of recoupment or set-off against a secured party that holds a security interest in the deposit account.

(b) Except as otherwise provided in subsection (c), the application of this article to a security interest in a deposit account does not affect a right of recoupment or set-off of the secured party as to a deposit account maintained with the secured party.

(c) The exercise by a bank of a set-off against a deposit account is ineffective against a secured party that holds a security interest in the deposit account which is perfected by control under Section 9–104(a)(3), if the set-off is based on a claim against the debtor.

§ 9-341. Bank's Rights and Duties with Respect to Deposit Account.

Except as otherwise provided in Section 9–340(c), and unless the bank otherwise agrees in an authenticated record, a bank's rights and duties with respect to a deposit account maintained with the bank are not terminated, suspended, or modified by:

(1) the creation, attachment, or perfection of a security interest in the deposit account;

(2) the bank's knowledge of the security interest; or

(3) the bank's receipt of instructions from the secured party.

§ 9-342. Bank's Right to Refuse to Enter into or Disclose Existence of Control Agreement.

This article does not require a bank to enter into an agreement of the kind described in Section 9–104(a)(2), even if its customer so requests or directs. A bank that has entered into such an agreement is not required to confirm the existence of the agreement to another person unless requested to do so by its customer.

PART 4: Rights of Third Parties

§ 9-401. Alienability of Debtor's Rights.

(a) Except as otherwise provided in subsection (b) and Sections 9–406, 9–407, 9–408, and 9–409, whether a debtor's rights in collateral may be voluntarily or involuntarily transferred is governed by law other than this article.

(b) An agreement between the debtor and secured party which prohibits a transfer of the debtor's rights in collateral or makes the transfer a default does not prevent the transfer from taking effect.

§ 9-402. Secured Party Not Obligated on Contract of Debtor or in Tort.

The existence of a security interest, agricultural lien, or authority given to a debtor to dispose of or use collateral, without more, does not subject a secured party to liability in contract or tort for the debtor's acts or omissions.

§ 9-403. Agreement Not to Assert Defenses against Assignee.

(a) In this section, "value" has the meaning provided in Section 3–303(a).

(b) Except as otherwise provided in this section, an agreement between an account debtor and an assignor not to assert against an assignee any claim or defense that the account debtor may have against the assignor is enforceable by an assignee that takes an assignment:

(1) for value;

(2) in good faith;

(3) without notice of a claim of a property or possessory right to the property assigned; and

(4) without notice of a defense or claim in recoupment of the type that may be asserted against a person entitled to enforce a negotiable instrument under Section 3–305(a).

(c) Subsection (b) does not apply to defenses of a type that may be asserted against a holder in due course of a negotiable instrument under Section 3–305(b).

(d) In a consumer transaction, if a record evidences the account debtor's obligation, law other than this article requires that the record include a statement to the effect that the rights of an assignee are subject to claims or defenses that the account debtor could assert against the original obligee, and the record does not include such a statement:

(1) the record has the same effect as if the record included such a statement; and

(2) the account debtor may assert against an assignee those claims and defenses that would have been available if the record included such a statement.

(e) This section is subject to law other than this article which establishes a different rule for an account debtor who is an individual and who incurred the obligation primarily for personal, family, or household purposes.

(f) Except as otherwise provided in subsection (d), this section does not displace law other than this article which gives effect to an agreement by an account debtor not to assert a claim or defense against an assignee.

§ 9-404. Rights Acquired by Assignee; Claims and Defenses against Assignee.

(a) Unless an account debtor has made an enforceable agreement not to assert defenses or claims, and subject to subsections (b) through (e), the rights of an assignee are subject to:

(1) all terms of the agreement between the account debtor and assignor and any defense or claim in recoupment arising from the transaction that gave rise to the contract; and

(2) any other defense or claim of the account debtor against the assignor which accrues before the account debtor receives a notification of the assignment authenticated by the assignor or the assignee.

(b) Subject to subsection (c) and except as otherwise provided in subsection (d), the claim of an account debtor against an assignor may be asserted against an assignee under subsection (a) only to reduce the amount the account debtor owes.

(c) This section is subject to law other than this article which establishes a different rule for an account debtor who is an individual and who incurred the obligation primarily for personal, family, or household purposes.

(d) In a consumer transaction, if a record evidences the account debtor's obligation, law other than this article requires that the record include a statement to the effect that the account debtor's recovery against an assignee with respect to claims and defenses against the assignor may not exceed amounts paid by the account debtor under the record, and the record does not include such a statement, the extent to which a claim of an account debtor against the assignor may be asserted against an assignee is determined as if the record included such a statement.

(e) This section does not apply to an assignment of a health-care-insurance receivable.

§ 9-405. Modification of Assigned Contract.

(a) A modification of or substitution for an assigned contract is effective against an assignee if made in good faith. The assignee acquires corresponding rights under the modified or substituted contract. The assignment may provide that the modification or substitution is a breach of contract by the assignor. This subsection is subject to subsections (b) through (d).

(b) Subsection (a) applies to the extent that:

(1) the right to payment or a part thereof under an assigned contract has not been fully earned by performance; or

(2) the right to payment or a part thereof has been fully earned by performance and the account debtor has not received notification of the assignment under Section 9–406(a).

(c) This section is subject to law other than this article which establishes a different rule for an account debtor who is an individual and who incurred the obligation primarily for personal, family, or household purposes.

(d) This section does not apply to an assignment of a health-care-insurance receivable.

§ 9-406. Discharge of Account Debtor; Notification of Assignment; Identification and Proof of Assignment; Restrictions on Assignment of Accounts, Chattel Paper, Payment Intangibles, and Promissory Notes Ineffective.

(a) Subject to subsections (b) through (i), an account debtor on an account, chattel paper, or a payment intangible may discharge its obligation by paying the assignor until, but not after, the account debtor receives a notification, authenticated by the assignor or the assignee, that the amount due or to become due has been assigned and that payment is to be made to the assignee. After receipt of the notification, the account debtor may discharge its obligation by paying the assignee and may not discharge the obligation by paying the assignor.

(b) Subject to subsection (h), notification is ineffective under subsection (a):

(1) if it does not reasonably identify the rights assigned;

(2) to the extent that an agreement between an account debtor and a seller of a payment intangible limits the account debtor's duty to pay a person other than the seller and the limitation is effective under law other than this article; or

(3) at the option of an account debtor, if the notification notifies the account debtor to make less than the full amount of any installment or other periodic payment to the assignee, even if:

(A) only a portion of the account, chattel paper, or payment intangible has been assigned to that assignee;

(B) a portion has been assigned to another assignee; or

(C) the account debtor knows that the assignment to that assignee is limited.

(c) Subject to subsection (h), if requested by the account debtor, an assignee shall seasonably furnish reasonable proof that the assignment has been made. Unless the assignee complies, the account debtor may discharge its obligation by paying the assignor, even if the account debtor has received a notification under subsection (a).

(d) Except as otherwise provided in subsection (e) and Sections 2A–303 and 9–407, and subject to subsection (h), a term in an agreement between an account debtor and an assignor or in a promissory note is ineffective to the extent that it:

(1) prohibits, restricts, or requires the consent of the account debtor or person obligated on the promissory note to the assignment or transfer of, or the creation, attachment, perfection, or enforcement of a security interest in, the account, chattel paper, payment intangible, or promissory note; or

(2) provides that the assignment or transfer or the creation, attachment, perfection, or enforcement of the security interest may give rise to a default, breach, right of recoupment, claim, defense, termination, right of termination, or remedy under the account, chattel paper, payment intangible, or promissory note.

(e) Subsection (d) does not apply to the sale of a payment intangible or promissory note.

(f) Except as otherwise provided in Sections 2A–303 and 9–407 and subject to subsections (h) and (i), a rule of law, statute, or regulation that prohibits, restricts, or requires the consent of a government, governmental body or official, or account debtor to the assignment or transfer of, or creation of a security interest in, an account or chattel paper is ineffective to the extent that the rule of law, statute, or regulation:

(1) prohibits, restricts, or requires the consent of the government, governmental body or official, or account debtor to the assignment or transfer of, or the creation, attachment, perfection, or enforcement of a security interest in the account or chattel paper; or

(2) provides that the assignment or transfer or the creation, attachment, perfection, or enforcement of the security interest may give rise to a default, breach, right of recoupment, claim, defense, termination, right of termination, or remedy under the account or chattel paper.

(g) Subject to subsection (h), an account debtor may not waive or vary its option under subsection (b)(3).

(h) This section is subject to law other than this article which establishes a different rule for an account debtor who is an individual and who incurred the obligation primarily for personal, family, or household purposes.

(i) This section does not apply to an assignment of a health-care-insurance receivable.

(j) This section prevails over any inconsistent provisions of the following statutes, rules, and regulations:

[List here any statutes, rules, and regulations containing provisions inconsistent with this section.]

Legislative Note: States that amend statutes, rules, and regulations to remove provisions inconsistent with this section need not enact subsection (j).

As amended in 1999 and 2000.

§ 9-407. Restrictions on Creation or Enforcement of Security Interest in Leasehold Interest or in Lessor's Residual Interest.

(a) Except as otherwise provided in subsection (b), a term in a lease agreement is ineffective to the extent that it:

(1) prohibits, restricts, or requires the consent of a party to the lease to the assignment or transfer of, or the creation, attachment, perfection, or enforcement of a security interest in an interest of a party under the lease contract or in the lessor's residual interest in the goods; or

(2) provides that the assignment or transfer or the creation, attachment, perfection, or enforcement of the security interest may give rise to a default, breach, right of recoupment, claim, defense, termination, right of termination, or remedy under the lease.

(b) Except as otherwise provided in Section 2A–303(7), a term described in subsection (a)(2) is effective to the extent that there is:

(1) a transfer by the lessee of the lessee's right of possession or use of the goods in violation of the term; or

(2) a delegation of a material performance of either party to the lease contract in violation of the term.

(c) The creation, attachment, perfection, or enforcement of a security interest in the lessor's interest under the lease contract or the lessor's residual interest in the goods is not a transfer that materially impairs the lessee's prospect of obtaining return performance or materially changes the duty of or materially increases the burden or risk imposed on the lessee within the purview of Section 2A–303(4) unless, and then only to the extent that, enforcement actually results in a delegation of material performance of the lessor.

As amended in 1999.

§ 9-408. Restrictions on Assignment of Promissory Notes, Health-Care-Insurance Receivables, and Certain General Intangibles Ineffective.

(a) Except as otherwise provided in subsection (b), a term in a promissory note or in an agreement between an account debtor and a debtor which relates to a health-care-insurance receivable or a general intangible, including a contract, permit, license, or franchise, and which term prohibits, restricts, or requires the consent of the person obligated on the promissory note or the account debtor to, the assignment or transfer of, or creation, attachment, or perfection of a security interest in, the promissory note, health-care-insurance receivable, or general intangible, is ineffective to the extent that the term:

(1) would impair the creation, attachment, or perfection of a security interest; or

(2) provides that the assignment or transfer or the creation, attachment, or perfection of the security interest may give rise to a default, breach, right of recoupment, claim, defense, termination, right of termination, or remedy under the promissory note, health-care-insurance receivable, or general intangible.

(b) Subsection (a) applies to a security interest in a payment intangible or promissory note only if the security interest arises out of a sale of the payment intangible or promissory note.

(c) A rule of law, statute, or regulation that prohibits, restricts, or requires the consent of a government, governmental body or official, person obligated on a promissory note, or account debtor to the assignment or transfer of, or creation of a security interest in, a promissory note, health-care-insurance receivable, or general intangible, including a contract, permit, license, or franchise between an account debtor and a debtor, is ineffective to the extent that the rule of law, statute, or regulation:

(1) would impair the creation, attachment, or perfection of a security interest; or

(2) provides that the assignment or transfer or the creation, attachment, or perfection of the security interest may give rise to a default, breach, right of recoupment, claim, defense, termination, right of termination, or remedy under the promissory note, health-care-insurance receivable, or general intangible.

(d) To the extent that a term in a promissory note or in an agreement between an account debtor and a debtor which relates to a health-care-insurance receivable or general intangible or a rule of law, statute, or regulation described in subsection (c) would be effective under law other than this article but is ineffective under subsection (a) or (c), the creation, attachment, or perfection of a security interest in the promissory note, health-care-insurance receivable, or general intangible:

(1) is not enforceable against the person obligated on the promissory note or the account debtor;

(2) does not impose a duty or obligation on the person obligated on the promissory note or the account debtor;

(3) does not require the person obligated on the promissory note or the account debtor to recognize the security interest, pay or render performance to the secured party, or accept payment or performance from the secured party;

(4) does not entitle the secured party to use or assign the debtor's rights under the promissory note, health-care-insurance receivable, or general intangible, including any related information or materials furnished to the debtor in the transaction giving rise to the promissory note, health-care-insurance receivable, or general intangible;

(5) does not entitle the secured party to use, assign, possess, or have access to any trade secrets or confidential information of the person obligated on the promissory note or the account debtor; and

(6) does not entitle the secured party to enforce the security interest in the promissory note, health-care-insurance receivable, or general intangible.

(e) This section prevails over any inconsistent provisions of the following statutes, rules, and regulations:

[List here any statutes, rules, and regulations containing provisions inconsistent with this section.]

Legislative Note: States that amend statutes, rules, and regulations to remove provisions inconsistent with this section need not enact subsection (e).

As amended in 1999.

§ 9-409. Restrictions on Assignment of Letter-of-Credit Rights Ineffective.

(a) A term in a letter of credit or a rule of law, statute, regulation, custom, or practice applicable to the letter of credit which prohibits, restricts, or requires the consent of an applicant, issuer, or nominated person to a beneficiary's assignment of or creation of a security interest in a letter-of-credit right is ineffective to the extent that the term or rule of law, statute, regulation, custom, or practice:

(1) would impair the creation, attachment, or perfection of a security interest in the letter-of-credit right; or

(2) provides that the assignment or the creation, attachment, or perfection of the security interest may give rise to a default, breach, right of recoupment, claim, defense, termination, right of termination, or remedy under the letter-of-credit right.

(b) To the extent that a term in a letter of credit is ineffective under subsection (a) but would be effective under law other than this article or a custom or practice applicable to the letter of credit, to the transfer of a right to draw or otherwise demand performance under the letter of credit, or to the assignment of a right to proceeds of the letter of credit, the creation, attachment, or perfection of a security interest in the letter-of-credit right:

(1) is not enforceable against the applicant, issuer, nominated person, or transferee beneficiary;

(2) imposes no duties or obligations on the applicant, issuer, nominated person, or transferee beneficiary; and

(3) does not require the applicant, issuer, nominated person, or transferee beneficiary to recognize the security interest, pay or render performance to the secured party, or accept payment or other performance from the secured party.

As amended in 1999.

PART 5: Filing

[Subpart 1. Filing Office; Contents and Effectiveness of Financing Statement]

§ 9-501. Filing Office.

(a) Except as otherwise provided in subsection (b), if the local law of this State governs perfection of a security interest or agricultural lien, the office in which to file a financing statement to perfect the security interest or agricultural lien is:

(1) the office designated for the filing or recording of a record of a mortgage on the related real property, if:

(A) the collateral is as-extracted collateral or timber to be cut; or

(B) the financing statement is filed as a fixture filing and the collateral is goods that are or are to become fixtures; or

(2) the office of [ ] [or any office duly authorized by [ ]], in all other cases, including a case in which the collateral is goods that are or are to become fixtures and the financing statement is not filed as a fixture filing.

(b) The office in which to file a financing statement to perfect a security interest in collateral, including fixtures, of a transmitting utility is the office of [ ]. The financing statement also constitutes a fixture filing as to the collateral indicated in the financing statement which is or is to become fixtures.

Legislative Note: The State should designate the filing office where the brackets appear. The filing office may be that of a governmental official (e.g., the Secretary of State) or a private party that maintains the State's filing system.

§ 9-502. Contents of Financing Statement; Record of Mortgage as Financing Statement; Time of Filing Financing Statement.

(a) Subject to subsection (b), a financing statement is sufficient only if it:

(1) provides the name of the debtor;

(2) provides the name of the secured party or a representative of the secured party; and

(3) indicates the collateral covered by the financing statement.

(b) Except as otherwise provided in Section 9–501(b), to be sufficient, a financing statement that covers as-extracted collateral or timber to be cut, or which is filed as a fixture filing and covers goods that are or are to become fixtures, must satisfy subsection (a) and also:

(1) indicate that it covers this type of collateral;

(2) indicate that it is to be filed [for record] in the real property records;

(3) provide a description of the real property to which the collateral is related [sufficient to give constructive notice of a mortgage under the law of this State if the description were contained in a record of the mortgage of the real property]; and

(4) if the debtor does not have an interest of record in the real property, provide the name of a record owner.

(c) A record of a mortgage is effective, from the date of recording, as a financing statement filed as a fixture filing or as a financing statement covering as-extracted collateral or timber to be cut only if:

(1) the record indicates the goods or accounts that it covers;

(2) the goods are or are to become fixtures related to the real property described in the record or the collateral is related to the real property described in the record and is as-extracted collateral or timber to be cut;

(3) the record satisfies the requirements for a financing statement in this section other than an indication that it is to be filed in the real property records; and

(4) the record is [duly] recorded.

(d) A financing statement may be filed before a security agreement is made or a security interest otherwise attaches.

Legislative Note: Language in brackets is optional. Where the State has any special recording system for real property other than the usual grantor-grantee index (as, for instance, a tract system or a title registration or Torrens system) local adaptations of subsection (b) and Section 9–519(d) and (e) may be necessary. See, e.g., Mass. Gen. Laws Chapter 106, Section 9–410.

§ 9-503. Name of Debtor and Secured Party.

(a) A financing statement sufficiently provides the name of the debtor:

(1) if the debtor is a registered organization, only if the financing statement provides the name of the debtor indicated on the public record of the debtor's jurisdiction of organization which shows the debtor to have been organized;

(2) if the debtor is a decedent's estate, only if the financing statement provides the name of the decedent and indicates that the debtor is an estate;

(3) if the debtor is a trust or a trustee acting with respect to property held in trust, only if the financing statement:

(A) provides the name specified for the trust in its organic documents or, if no name is specified, provides the name of the settlor and additional information sufficient to distinguish the debtor from other trusts having one or more of the same settlors; and

(B) indicates, in the debtor's name or otherwise, that the debtor is a trust or is a trustee acting with respect to property held in trust; and

(4) in other cases:

(A) if the debtor has a name, only if it provides the individual or organizational name of the debtor; and

(B) if the debtor does not have a name, only if it provides the names of the partners, members, associates, or other persons comprising the debtor.

(b) A financing statement that provides the name of the debtor in accordance with subsection (a) is not rendered ineffective by the absence of:

(1) a trade name or other name of the debtor; or

(2) unless required under subsection (a)(4)(B), names of partners, members, associates, or other persons comprising the debtor.

(c) A financing statement that provides only the debtor's trade name does not sufficiently provide the name of the debtor.

(d) Failure to indicate the representative capacity of a secured party or representative of a secured party does not affect the sufficiency of a financing statement.

(e) A financing statement may provide the name of more than one debtor and the name of more than one secured party.

§ 9-504. Indication of Collateral.

A financing statement sufficiently indicates the collateral that it covers if the financing statement provides:

(1) a description of the collateral pursuant to Section 9–108; or

(2) an indication that the financing statement covers all assets or all personal property.

As amended in 1999.

§ 9-505. Filing and Compliance with Other Statutes and Treaties for Consignments, Leases, Other Bailments, and Other Transactions.

(a) A consignor, lessor, or other bailor of goods, a licensor, or a buyer of a payment intangible or promissory note may file a financing statement, or may comply with a statute or treaty described in Section 9–311(a), using the terms "consignor", "consignee", "lessor", "lessee", "bailor", "bailee", "licensor", "licensee", "owner", "registered owner", "buyer", "seller", or words of similar import, instead of the terms "secured party" and "debtor".

(b) This part applies to the filing of a financing statement under subsection (a) and, as appropriate, to compliance that is equivalent to filing a financing statement under Section 9–311(b), but the filing or compliance is not of itself a factor in determining whether the collateral secures an obligation. If it is determined for another reason that the collateral secures an obligation, a security interest held by the consignor, lessor, bailor, licensor, owner, or buyer which attaches to the collateral is perfected by the filing or compliance.

§ 9-506. Effect of Errors or Omissions.

(a) A financing statement substantially satisfying the requirements of this part is effective, even if it has minor errors or omissions, unless the errors or omissions make the financing statement seriously misleading.

(b) Except as otherwise provided in subsection (c), a financing statement that fails sufficiently to provide the name of the debtor in accordance with Section 9–503(a) is seriously misleading.

(c) If a search of the records of the filing office under the debtor's correct name, using the filing office's standard search logic, if any, would disclose a financing statement that fails sufficiently to provide the name of the debtor in accordance with Section 9–503(a), the name provided does not make the financing statement seriously misleading.

(d) For purposes of Section 9–508(b), the "debtor's correct name" in subsection (c) means the correct name of the new debtor.

§ 9-507. Effect of Certain Events on Effectiveness of Financing Statement.

(a) A filed financing statement remains effective with respect to collateral that is sold, exchanged, leased, licensed, or otherwise disposed of and in which a security interest or agricultural lien continues, even if the secured party knows of or consents to the disposition.

(b) Except as otherwise provided in subsection (c) and Section 9–508, a financing statement is not rendered ineffective if, after the financing statement is filed, the information provided in the financing statement becomes seriously misleading under Section 9–506.

(c) If a debtor so changes its name that a filed financing statement becomes seriously misleading under Section 9–506:

(1) the financing statement is effective to perfect a security interest in collateral acquired by the debtor before, or within four months after, the change; and

(2) the financing statement is not effective to perfect a security interest in collateral acquired by the debtor more than four months after the change, unless an amendment to the financing statement which renders the financing statement not seriously misleading is filed within four months after the change.

§ 9-508. Effectiveness of Financing Statement If New Debtor Becomes Bound by Security Agreement.

(a) Except as otherwise provided in this section, a filed financing statement naming an original debtor is effective to perfect a security interest in collateral in which a new debtor has or acquires rights to the extent that the financing statement would have been effective had the original debtor acquired rights in the collateral.

(b) If the difference between the name of the original debtor and that of the new debtor causes a filed financing statement that is effective under subsection (a) to be seriously misleading under Section 9–506:

(1) the financing statement is effective to perfect a security interest in collateral acquired by the new debtor before, and within four months after, the new debtor becomes bound under Section 9B–203(d); and

(2) the financing statement is not effective to perfect a security

interest in collateral acquired by the new debtor more than four months after the new debtor becomes bound under Section 9–203(d) unless an initial financing statement providing the name of the new debtor is filed before the expiration of that time.

(c) This section does not apply to collateral as to which a filed financing statement remains effective against the new debtor under Section 9–507(a).

§ 9-509. Persons Entitled to File a Record.

(a) A person may file an initial financing statement, amendment that adds collateral covered by a financing statement, or amendment that adds a debtor to a financing statement only if:

(1) the debtor authorizes the filing in an authenticated record or pursuant to subsection (b) or (c); or

(2) the person holds an agricultural lien that has become effective at the time of filing and the financing statement covers only collateral in which the person holds an agricultural lien.

(b) By authenticating or becoming bound as debtor by a security agreement, a debtor or new debtor authorizes the filing of an initial financing statement, and an amendment, covering:

(1) the collateral described in the security agreement; and

(2) property that becomes collateral under Section 9–315(a)(2), whether or not the security agreement expressly covers proceeds.

(c) By acquiring collateral in which a security interest or agricultural lien continues under Section 9–315(a)(1), a debtor authorizes the filing of an initial financing statement, and an amendment, covering the collateral and property that becomes collateral under Section 9–315(a)(2).

(d) A person may file an amendment other than an amendment that adds collateral covered by a financing statement or an amendment that adds a debtor to a financing statement only if:

(1) the secured party of record authorizes the filing; or

(2) the amendment is a termination statement for a financing statement as to which the secured party of record has failed to file or send a termination statement as required by Section 9–513(a) or (c), the debtor authorizes the filing, and the termination statement indicates that the debtor authorized it to be filed.

(e) If there is more than one secured party of record for a financing statement, each secured party of record may authorize the filing of an amendment under subsection (d).
As amended in 2000.

§ 9-510. Effectiveness of Filed Record.

(a) A filed record is effective only to the extent that it was filed by a person that may file it under Section 9–509.

(b) A record authorized by one secured party of record does not affect the financing statement with respect to another secured party of record.

(c) A continuation statement that is not filed within the six-month period prescribed by Section 9–515(d) is ineffective.

§ 9-511. Secured Party of Record.

(a) A secured party of record with respect to a financing statement is a person whose name is provided as the name of the secured party or a representative of the secured party in an initial financing statement that has been filed. If an initial financing statement is filed under Section 9–514(a), the assignee named in the initial financing statement is the secured party of record with respect to the financing statement.

(b) If an amendment of a financing statement which provides the name of a person as a secured party or a representative of a secured party is filed, the person named in the amendment is a secured party of record. If an amendment is filed under Section 9–514(b), the assignee named in the amendment is a secured party of record.

(c) A person remains a secured party of record until the filing of an amendment of the financing statement which deletes the person.

§ 9-512. Amendment of Financing Statement.
[Alternative A]
(a) Subject to Section 9–509, a person may add or delete collateral covered by, continue or terminate the effectiveness of, or, subject to subsection (e), otherwise amend the information provided in, a financing statement by filing an amendment that:

(1) identifies, by its file number, the initial financing statement to which the amendment relates; and

(2) if the amendment relates to an initial financing statement filed [or recorded] in a filing office described in Section 9–501(a)(1), provides the information specified in Section 9–502(b).

[Alternative B]
(a) Subject to Section 9–509, a person may add or delete collateral covered by, continue or terminate the effectiveness of, or, subject to subsection (e), otherwise amend the information provided in, a financing statement by filing an amendment that:

(1) identifies, by its file number, the initial financing statement to which the amendment relates; and

(2) if the amendment relates to an initial financing statement filed [or recorded] in a filing office described in Section 9–501(a)(1), provides the date [and time] that the initial financing statement was filed [or recorded] and the information specified in Section 9–502(b).

[End of Alternatives]
(b) Except as otherwise provided in Section 9–515, the filing of an amendment does not extend the period of effectiveness of the financing statement.

(c) A financing statement that is amended by an amendment that adds collateral is effective as to the added collateral only from the date of the filing of the amendment.

(d) A financing statement that is amended by an amendment that adds a debtor is effective as to the added debtor only from the date of the filing of the amendment.

(e) An amendment is ineffective to the extent it:

(1) purports to delete all debtors and fails to provide the name of a debtor to be covered by the financing statement; or

(2) purports to delete all secured parties of record and fails to provide the name of a new secured party of record.

Legislative Note: States whose real-estate filing offices require additional information in amendments and cannot search their records by both the name of the debtor and the file number should enact Alternative B to Sections 9–512(a), 9–518(b), 9–519(f), and 9–522(a).

§ 9-513. Termination Statement.
(a) A secured party shall cause the secured party of record for a financing statement to file a termination statement for the financing statement if the financing statement covers consumer goods and:

(1) there is no obligation secured by the collateral covered by the financing statement and no commitment to make an advance, incur an obligation, or otherwise give value; or

(2) the debtor did not authorize the filing of the initial financing statement.

(b) To comply with subsection (a), a secured party shall cause the secured party of record to file the termination statement:

(1) within one month after there is no obligation secured by the collateral covered by the financing statement and no commitment to make an advance, incur an obligation, or otherwise give value; or

(2) if earlier, within 20 days after the secured party receives an authenticated demand from a debtor.

(c) In cases not governed by subsection (a), within 20 days after a secured party receives an authenticated demand from a debtor, the secured party shall cause the secured party of record for a financing statement to send to the debtor a termination statement for the financing statement or file the termination statement in the filing office if:

(1) except in the case of a financing statement covering accounts or chattel paper that has been sold or goods that are the subject of a consignment, there is no obligation secured by the collateral covered by the financing statement and no commitment to make an advance, incur an obligation, or otherwise give value;

(2) the financing statement covers accounts or chattel paper that has been sold but as to which the account debtor or other person obligated has discharged its obligation;

(3) the financing statement covers goods that were the subject of a consignment to the debtor but are not in the debtor's possession; or

(4) the debtor did not authorize the filing of the initial financing statement.

(d) Except as otherwise provided in Section 9–510, upon the filing of a termination statement with the filing office, the financing statement to which the termination statement relates ceases to be effective. Except as otherwise provided in Section 9–510, for purposes of Sections 9–519(g), 9–522(a), and 9–523(c), the filing with the filing office of a termination statement relating to a financing statement that indicates that the debtor is a transmitting utility also causes the effectiveness of the financing statement to lapse.
As amended in 2000.

§ 9-514. Assignment of Powers of Secured Party of Record.
(a) Except as otherwise provided in subsection (c), an initial financing statement may reflect an assignment of all of the secured party's power to authorize an amendment to the financing statement by providing the name and mailing address of the assignee as the name and address of the secured party.

(b) Except as otherwise provided in subsection (c), a secured party of record may assign of record all or part of its power to authorize an amendment to a financing statement by filing in the filing office an amendment of the financing statement which:

(1) identifies, by its file number, the initial financing statement to which it relates;

(2) provides the name of the assignor; and

(3) provides the name and mailing address of the assignee.

(c) An assignment of record of a security interest in a fixture covered by a record of a mortgage which is effective as a financing statement filed as a fixture filing under Section 9–502(c) may be made only by an assignment of record of the mortgage in the manner provided by law of this State other than [the Uniform Commercial Code].

§ 9-515. Duration and Effectiveness of Financing Statement; Effect of Lapsed Financing Statement.
(a) Except as otherwise provided in subsections (b), (e), (f), and (g), a filed financing statement is effective for a period of five years after the date of filing.

(b) Except as otherwise provided in subsections (e), (f), and (g), an initial financing statement filed in connection with a public-finance transaction or manufactured-home transaction is effective for a period of 30 years after the date of filing if it indicates that it is filed in connection with a public-finance transaction or manufactured-home transaction.

(c) The effectiveness of a filed financing statement lapses on the expiration of the period of its effectiveness unless before the lapse a continuation statement is filed pursuant to subsection (d). Upon lapse, a financing statement ceases to be effective and any security interest or agricultural lien that was perfected by the financing statement becomes unperfected, unless the security interest is perfected otherwise. If the security interest or agricultural lien becomes unperfected upon lapse, it is deemed never to have been perfected as against a purchaser of the collateral for value.

(d) A continuation statement may be filed only within six months before the expiration of the five-year period specified in subsection (a) or the 30-year period specified in subsection (b), whichever is applicable.

(e) Except as otherwise provided in Section 9–510, upon timely filing of a continuation statement, the effectiveness of the initial financing statement continues for a period of five years commencing on the day on which the financing statement would have become ineffective in the absence of the filing. Upon the expiration of the five-year period, the financing statement lapses in the same manner as provided in subsection (c), unless, before the lapse, another continuation statement is filed pursuant to subsection (d). Succeeding continuation statements may be filed in the same manner to continue the effectiveness of the initial financing statement.

(f) If a debtor is a transmitting utility and a filed financing statement so indicates, the financing statement is effective until a termination statement is filed.

(g) A record of a mortgage that is effective as a financing statement filed as a fixture filing under Section 9–502(c) remains effective as a financing statement filed as a fixture filing until the mortgage is released or satisfied of record or its effectiveness otherwise terminates as to the real property.

§ 9-516. What Constitutes Filing; Effectiveness of Filing.

(a) Except as otherwise provided in subsection (b), communication of a record to a filing office and tender of the filing fee or acceptance of the record by the filing office constitutes filing.

(b) Filing does not occur with respect to a record that a filing office refuses to accept because:

(1) the record is not communicated by a method or medium of communication authorized by the filing office;

(2) an amount equal to or greater than the applicable filing fee is not tendered;

(3) the filing office is unable to index the record because:

(A) in the case of an initial financing statement, the record does not provide a name for the debtor;

(B) in the case of an amendment or correction statement, the record:

(i) does not identify the initial financing statement as required by Section 9–512 or 9–518, as applicable; or

(ii) identifies an initial financing statement whose effectiveness has lapsed under Section 9–515;

(C) in the case of an initial financing statement that provides the name of a debtor identified as an individual or an amendment that provides a name of a debtor identified as an individual which was not previously provided in the financing statement to which the record relates, the record does not identify the debtor's last name; or

(D) in the case of a record filed [or recorded] in the filing office described in Section 9–501(a)(1), the record does not provide a sufficient description of the real property to which it relates;

(4) in the case of an initial financing statement or an amendment that adds a secured party of record, the record does not provide a name and mailing address for the secured party of record;

(5) in the case of an initial financing statement or an amendment that provides a name of a debtor which was not previously provided in the financing statement to which the amendment relates, the record does not:

(A) provide a mailing address for the debtor;

(B) indicate whether the debtor is an individual or an organization; or

(C) if the financing statement indicates that the debtor is an organization, provide:

(i) a type of organization for the debtor;

(ii) a jurisdiction of organization for the debtor; or

(iii) an organizational identification number for the debtor or indicate that the debtor has none;

(6) in the case of an assignment reflected in an initial financing statement under Section 9–514(a) or an amendment filed under Section 9–514(b), the record does not provide a name and mailing address for the assignee; or

(7) in the case of a continuation statement, the record is not filed within the six-month period prescribed by Section 9–515(d).

(c) For purposes of subsection (b):

(1) a record does not provide information if the filing office is unable to read or decipher the information; and

(2) a record that does not indicate that it is an amendment or identify an initial financing statement to which it relates, as required by Section 9–512, 9–514, or 9–518, is an initial financing statement.

(d) A record that is communicated to the filing office with tender of the filing fee, but which the filing office refuses to accept for a reason other than one set forth in subsection (b), is effective as a filed record except as against a purchaser of the collateral which gives value in reasonable reliance upon the absence of the record from the files.

§ 9-517. Effect of Indexing Errors.

The failure of the filing office to index a record correctly does not affect the effectiveness of the filed record.

§ 9-518. Claim Concerning Inaccurate or Wrongfully Filed Record.

(a) A person may file in the filing office a correction statement with respect to a record indexed there under the person's name if the person believes that the record is inaccurate or was wrongfully filed.

[Alternative A]

(b) A correction statement must:

(1) identify the record to which it relates by the file number assigned to the initial financing statement to which the record relates;

(2) indicate that it is a correction statement; and

(3) provide the basis for the person's belief that the record is inaccurate and indicate the manner in which the person believes the record should be amended to cure any inaccuracy or provide the basis for the person's belief that the record was wrongfully filed.

[Alternative B]

(b) A correction statement must:

(1) identify the record to which it relates by:

(A) the file number assigned to the initial financing statement to which the record relates; and

(B) if the correction statement relates to a record filed [or recorded] in a filing office described in Section 9–501(a)(1), the date [and time] that the initial financing statement was filed [or recorded] and the information specified in Section 9–502(b);

(2) indicate that it is a correction statement; and

(3) provide the basis for the person's belief that the record is inaccurate and indicate the manner in which the person believes the record should be amended to cure any inaccuracy or provide the basis for the person's belief that the record was wrongfully filed.

[End of Alternatives]

(c) The filing of a correction statement does not affect the effectiveness of an initial financing statement or other filed record.

Legislative Note: States whose real-estate filing offices require additional information in amendments and cannot search their records by both the name of the debtor and the file number should enact Alternative B to Sections 9–512(a), 9–518(b), 9–519(f), and 9–522(a).

[Subpart 2. Duties and Operation of Filing Office]

§ 9-519. Numbering, Maintaining, and Indexing Records; Communicating Information Provided in Records.

(a) For each record filed in a filing office, the filing office shall:
  (1) assign a unique number to the filed record;
  (2) create a record that bears the number assigned to the filed record and the date and time of filing;
  (3) maintain the filed record for public inspection; and
  (4) index the filed record in accordance with subsections (c), (d), and (e).

(b) A file number [assigned after January 1, 2002,] must include a digit that:
  (1) is mathematically derived from or related to the other digits of the file number; and
  (2) aids the filing office in determining whether a number communicated as the file number includes a single-digit or transpositional error.

(c) Except as otherwise provided in subsections (d) and (e), the filing office shall:
  (1) index an initial financing statement according to the name of the debtor and index all filed records relating to the initial financing statement in a manner that associates with one another an initial financing statement and all filed records relating to the initial financing statement; and
  (2) index a record that provides a name of a debtor which was not previously provided in the financing statement to which the record relates also according to the name that was not previously provided.

(d) If a financing statement is filed as a fixture filing or covers as-extracted collateral or timber to be cut, [it must be filed for record and] the filing office shall index it:
  (1) under the names of the debtor and of each owner of record shown on the financing statement as if they were the mortgagors under a mortgage of the real property described; and
  (2) to the extent that the law of this State provides for indexing of records of mortgages under the name of the mortgagee, under the name of the secured party as if the secured party were the mortgagee thereunder, or, if indexing is by description, as if the financing statement were a record of a mortgage of the real property described.

(e) If a financing statement is filed as a fixture filing or covers as-extracted collateral or timber to be cut, the filing office shall index an assignment filed under Section 9–514(a) or an amendment filed under Section 9–514(b):
  (1) under the name of the assignor as grantor; and
  (2) to the extent that the law of this State provides for indexing a record of the assignment of a mortgage under the name of the assignee, under the name of the assignee.

[Alternative A]

(f) The filing office shall maintain a capability:
  (1) to retrieve a record by the name of the debtor and by the file number assigned to the initial financing statement to which the record relates; and
  (2) to associate and retrieve with one another an initial financing statement and each filed record relating to the initial financing statement.

[Alternative B]

(f) The filing office shall maintain a capability:
  (1) to retrieve a record by the name of the debtor and:
    (A) if the filing office is described in Section 9–501(a)(1), by the file number assigned to the initial financing statement to which the record relates and the date [and time] that the record was filed [or recorded]; or
    (B) if the filing office is described in Section 9–501(a)(2), by the file number assigned to the initial financing statement to which the record relates; and
  (2) to associate and retrieve with one another an initial financing statement and each filed record relating to the initial financing statement.

[End of Alternatives]

(g) The filing office may not remove a debtor's name from the index until one year after the effectiveness of a financing statement naming the debtor lapses under Section 9–515 with respect to all secured parties of record.

(h) The filing office shall perform the acts required by subsections (a) through (e) at the time and in the manner prescribed by filing-office rule, but not later than two business days after the filing office receives the record in question.

[(i) Subsection[s] [(b)] [and] [(h)] do[es] not apply to a filing office described in Section 9–501(a)(1).]

Legislative Notes:

1. States whose filing offices currently assign file numbers that include a verification number, commonly known as a "check digit," or can implement this requirement before the effective date of this Article should omit the bracketed language in subsection (b).

2. In States in which writings will not appear in the real property records and indices unless actually recorded the bracketed language in subsection (d) should be used.

3. States whose real-estate filing offices require additional information in amendments and cannot search their records by both the name of the debtor and the file number should enact Alternative B to Sections 9–512(a), 9–518(b), 9–519(f), and 9–522(a).

4. A State that elects not to require real-estate filing offices to comply with either or both of subsections (b) and (h) may adopt an applicable variation of subsection (i) and add "Except as otherwise provided in subsection (i)," to the appropriate subsection or subsections.

§ 9-520. Acceptance and Refusal to Accept Record.

(a) A filing office shall refuse to accept a record for filing for a reason set forth in Section 9–516(b) and may refuse to accept a record for filing only for a reason set forth in Section 9–516(b).

(b) If a filing office refuses to accept a record for filing, it shall communicate to the person that presented the record the fact of and reason for the refusal and the date and time the record would have been filed had the filing office accepted it. The communication must be made at the time and in the manner prescribed by filing-office rule but [, in the case of a filing office described in Section 9–501(a)(2),] in no event more than two business days after the filing office receives the record.

(c) A filed financing statement satisfying Section 9–502(a) and (b) is effective, even if the filing office is required to refuse to accept it for filing under subsection (a). However, Section 9–338 applies to a filed financing statement providing information described in Section 9–516(b)(5) which is incorrect at the time the financing statement is filed.

(d) If a record communicated to a filing office provides information that relates to more than one debtor, this part applies as to each debtor separately.

Legislative Note: A State that elects not to require real-property filing offices to comply with subsection (b) should include the bracketed language.

§ 9-521. Uniform Form of Written Financing Statement and Amendment.

(a) A filing office that accepts written records may not refuse to accept a written initial financing statement in the following form and format except for a reason set forth in Section 9–516(b):

[NATIONAL UCC FINANCING STATEMENT (FORM UCC1)(REV. 7/29/98)]

[NATIONAL UCC FINANCING STATEMENT ADDENDUM (FORM UCC1Ad)(REV. 07/29/98)]

(b) A filing office that accepts written records may not refuse to accept a written record in the following form and format except for a reason set forth in Section 9–516(b):

[NATIONAL UCC FINANCING STATEMENT AMENDMENT (FORM UCC3)(REV. 07/29/98)]

[NATIONAL UCC FINANCING STATEMENT AMENDMENT ADDENDUM (FORM UCC3Ad)(REV. 07/29/98)]

§ 9-522. Maintenance and Destruction of Records.

[Alternative A]

(a) The filing office shall maintain a record of the information provided in a filed financing statement for at least one year after the effectiveness of the financing statement has lapsed under Section 9–515 with respect to all secured parties of record. The record must be retrievable by using the name of the debtor and by using the file number assigned to the initial financing statement to which the record relates.

[Alternative B]

(a) The filing office shall maintain a record of the information provided in a filed financing statement for at least one year after the effectiveness of the financing statement has lapsed under Section 9–515 with respect to all secured parties of record. The record must be retrievable by using the name of the debtor and:

(1) if the record was filed [or recorded] in the filing office described in Section 9–501(a)(1), by using the file number assigned to the initial financing statement to which the record relates and the date [and time] that the record was filed [or recorded]; or

(2) if the record was filed in the filing office described in Section 9–501(a)(2), by using the file number assigned to the initial financing statement to which the record relates.

[End of Alternatives]

(b) Except to the extent that a statute governing disposition of public records provides otherwise, the filing office immediately may destroy any written record evidencing a financing statement. However, if the filing office destroys a written record, it shall maintain another record of the financing statement which complies with subsection (a).

Legislative Note: States whose real-estate filing offices require additional information in amendments and cannot search their records by both the name of the debtor and the file number should enact Alternative B to Sections 9–512(a), 9–518(b), 9–519(f), and 9–522(a).

§ 9-523. Information from Filing Office; Sale or License of Records.

(a) If a person that files a written record requests an acknowledgment of the filing, the filing office shall send to the person an image of the record showing the number assigned to the record pursuant to Section 9–519(a)(1) and the date and time of the filing of the record. However, if the person furnishes a copy of the record to the filing office, the filing office may instead:

(1) note upon the copy the number assigned to the record pursuant to Section 9–519(a)(1) and the date and time of the filing of the record; and

(2) send the copy to the person.

(b) If a person files a record other than a written record, the filing office shall communicate to the person an acknowledgment that provides:

(1) the information in the record;

(2) the number assigned to the record pursuant to Section 9–519(a)(1); and

(3) the date and time of the filing of the record.

(c) The filing office shall communicate or otherwise make available in a record the following information to any person that requests it:

(1) whether there is on file on a date and time specified by the filing office, but not a date earlier than three business days before the filing office receives the request, any financing statement that:

(A) designates a particular debtor [or, if the request so states, designates a particular debtor at the address specified in the request];

(B) has not lapsed under Section 9–515 with respect to all secured parties of record; and

(C) if the request so states, has lapsed under Section 9–515 and a record of which is maintained by the filing office under Section 9–522(a);

(2) the date and time of filing of each financing statement; and

(3) the information provided in each financing statement.

(d) In complying with its duty under subsection (c), the filing office may communicate information in any medium. However, if requested, the filing office shall communicate information by issuing [its written certificate] [a record that can be admitted into evidence in the courts of this State without extrinsic evidence of its authenticity].

(e) The filing office shall perform the acts required by subsections (a) through (d) at the time and in the manner prescribed by filing-office rule, but not later than two business days after the filing office receives the request.

(f) At least weekly, the [insert appropriate official or governmental agency] [filing office] shall offer to sell or license to the public on a nonexclusive basis, in bulk, copies of all records filed in it under this part, in every medium from time to time available to the filing office.

Legislative Notes:

1. States whose filing office does not offer the additional service of responding to search requests limited to a particular address should omit the bracketed language in subsection (c)(1)(A).

2. A State that elects not to require real-estate filing offices to comply with either or both of subsections (e) and (f) should specify in the appropriate subsection(s) only the filing office described in Section 9–501(a)(2).

§ 9-524. Delay by Filing Office.

Delay by the filing office beyond a time limit prescribed by this part is excused if:

(1) the delay is caused by interruption of communication or computer facilities, war, emergency conditions, failure of equipment, or other circumstances beyond control of the filing office; and

(2) the filing office exercises reasonable diligence under the circumstances.

§ 9-525. Fees.

(a) Except as otherwise provided in subsection (e), the fee for filing and indexing a record under this part, other than an initial financing statement of the kind described in subsection (b), is [the amount specified in subsection (c), if applicable, plus]:

(1) $[X] if the record is communicated in writing and consists of one or two pages;

(2) $[2X] if the record is communicated in writing and consists of more than two pages; and

(3) $[1/2X] if the record is communicated by another medium authorized by filing-office rule.

(b) Except as otherwise provided in subsection (e), the fee for filing and indexing an initial financing statement of the following kind is [the amount specified in subsection (c), if applicable, plus]:

(1) $——— if the financing statement indicates that it is filed in connection with a public-finance transaction;

(2) $——— if the financing statement indicates that it is filed in connection with a manufactured-home transaction.

[Alternative A]

(c) The number of names required to be indexed does not affect the amount of the fee in subsections (a) and (b).

[Alternative B]

(c) Except as otherwise provided in subsection (e), if a record is communicated in writing, the fee for each name more than two required to be indexed is $———.

[End of Alternatives]

(d) The fee for responding to a request for information from the filing office, including for [issuing a certificate showing] [communicating] whether there is on file any financing statement naming a particular debtor, is:

(1) $——— if the request is communicated in writing; and

(2) $——— if the request is communicated by another medium authorized by filing-office rule.

(e) This section does not require a fee with respect to a record of a mortgage which is effective as a financing statement filed as a fixture filing or as a financing statement covering as-extracted collateral or timber to be cut under Section 9–502(c). However, the recording and satisfaction fees that otherwise would be applicable to the record of the mortgage apply.

Legislative Notes:

1. To preserve uniformity, a State that places the provisions of this section together with statutes setting fees for other services should do so without modification.

2. A State should enact subsection (c), Alternative A, and omit the bracketed language in subsections (a) and (b) unless its indexing system entails a substantial additional cost when indexing additional names.

As amended in 2000.

§ 9-526. Filing-Office Rules.

(a) The [insert appropriate governmental official or agency] shall adopt and publish rules to implement this article. The filing-office rules must be[:

(1)] consistent with this article[; and

(2) adopted and published in accordance with the [insert any applicable state administrative procedure act]].

(b) To keep the filing-office rules and practices of the filing office in harmony with the rules and practices of filing offices in other jurisdictions that enact substantially this part, and to keep the technology used by the filing office compatible with the technology used by filing offices in other jurisdictions that enact substantially this part, the [insert appropriate governmental official or agency], so far as is consistent with the purposes, policies, and provisions of this article, in adopting, amending, and repealing filing-office rules, shall:

(1) consult with filing offices in other jurisdictions that enact substantially this part; and

(2) consult the most recent version of the Model Rules promulgated by the International Association of Corporate Administrators or any successor organization; and

(3) take into consideration the rules and practices of, and the technology used by, filing offices in other jurisdictions that enact substantially this part.

§ 9-527. Duty to Report.

The [insert appropriate governmental official or agency] shall report [annually on or before ———] to the [Governor and Legislature] on the operation of the filing office. The report must contain a statement of the extent to which:

(1) the filing-office rules are not in harmony with the rules of filing offices in other jurisdictions that enact substantially this part and the reasons for these variations; and

(2) the filing-office rules are not in harmony with the most recent version of the Model Rules promulgated by the International Association of Corporate Administrators, or any successor organization, and the reasons for these variations.

PART 6: Default

[Subpart 1. Default and Enforcement of Security Interest]

§ 9-601. Rights after Default; Judicial Enforcement; Consignor or Buyer of Accounts, Chattel Paper, Payment Intangibles, or Promissory Notes.

(a) After default, a secured party has the rights provided in this part and, except as otherwise provided in Section 9–602, those provided by agreement of the parties. A secured party:

(1) may reduce a claim to judgment, foreclose, or otherwise enforce the claim, security interest, or agricultural lien by any available judicial procedure; and

(2) if the collateral is documents, may proceed either as to the documents or as to the goods they cover.

(b) A secured party in possession of collateral or control of collateral under Section 9–104, 9–105, 9–106, or 9–107 has the rights and duties provided in Section 9–207.

(c) The rights under subsections (a) and (b) are cumulative and may be exercised simultaneously.

(d) Except as otherwise provided in subsection (g) and Section 9–605, after default, a debtor and an obligor have the rights provided in this part and by agreement of the parties.

(e) If a secured party has reduced its claim to judgment, the lien of any levy that may be made upon the collateral by virtue of an execution based upon the judgment relates back to the earliest of:

(1) the date of perfection of the security interest or agricultural lien in the collateral;

(2) the date of filing a financing statement covering the collateral; or

(3) any date specified in a statute under which the agricultural lien was created.

(f) A sale pursuant to an execution is a foreclosure of the security interest or agricultural lien by judicial procedure within the meaning of this section. A secured party may purchase at the sale and thereafter hold the collateral free of any other requirements of this article.

(g) Except as otherwise provided in Section 9–607(c), this part imposes no duties upon a secured party that is a consignor or is a buyer of accounts, chattel paper, payment intangibles, or promissory notes.

§ 9-602. Waiver and Variance of Rights and Duties.

Except as otherwise provided in Section 9–624, to the extent that they give rights to a debtor or obligor and impose duties on a secured party, the debtor or obligor may not waive or vary the rules stated in the following listed sections:

(1) Section 9–207(b)(4)(C), which deals with use and operation of the collateral by the secured party;

(2) Section 9–210, which deals with requests for an accounting and requests concerning a list of collateral and statement of account;

(3) Section 9–607(c), which deals with collection and enforcement of collateral;

(4) Sections 9–608(a) and 9–615(c) to the extent that they deal with application or payment of noncash proceeds of collection, enforcement, or disposition;

(5) Sections 9–608(a) and 9–615(d) to the extent that they require accounting for or payment of surplus proceeds of collateral;

(6) Section 9–609 to the extent that it imposes upon a secured party that takes possession of collateral without judicial process the duty to do so without breach of the peace;

(7) Sections 9–610(b), 9–611, 9–613, and 9–614, which deal with disposition of collateral;

(8) Section 9–615(f), which deals with calculation of a deficiency or surplus when a disposition is made to the secured party, a person related to the secured party, or a secondary obligor;

(9) Section 9–616, which deals with explanation of the calculation of a surplus or deficiency;

(10) Sections 9–620, 9–621, and 9–622, which deal with acceptance of collateral in satisfaction of obligation;

(11) Section 9–623, which deals with redemption of collateral;

(12) Section 9–624, which deals with permissible waivers; and

(13) Sections 9–625 and 9–626, which deal with the secured party's liability for failure to comply with this article.

§ 9-603. Agreement on Standards Concerning Rights and Duties.

(a) The parties may determine by agreement the standards measuring the fulfillment of the rights of a debtor or obligor and the duties of a secured party under a rule stated in Section 9–602 if the standards are not manifestly unreasonable.

(b) Subsection (a) does not apply to the duty under Section 9–609 to refrain from breaching the peace.

§ 9-604. Procedure If Security Agreement Covers Real Property or Fixtures.

(a) If a security agreement covers both personal and real property, a secured party may proceed:

(1) under this part as to the personal property without prejudicing any rights with respect to the real property; or

(2) as to both the personal property and the real property in accordance with the rights with respect to the real property, in which case the other provisions of this part do not apply.

(b) Subject to subsection (c), if a security agreement covers goods that are or become fixtures, a secured party may proceed:

(1) under this part; or

(2) in accordance with the rights with respect to real property, in which case the other provisions of this part do not apply.

(c) Subject to the other provisions of this part, if a secured party holding a security interest in fixtures has priority over all owners and encumbrancers of the real property, the secured party, after default, may remove the collateral from the real property.

(d) A secured party that removes collateral shall promptly reimburse any encumbrancer or owner of the real property, other than the debtor, for the cost of repair of any physical injury caused by the removal. The secured party need not reimburse the encumbrancer or owner for any diminution in value of the real property caused by the absence of the goods removed or by any necessity of replacing them. A person entitled to reimbursement may refuse permission to remove until the secured party gives adequate assurance for the performance of the obligation to reimburse.

§ 9-605. Unknown Debtor or Secondary Obligor.

A secured party does not owe a duty based on its status as secured party:

(1) to a person that is a debtor or obligor, unless the secured party knows:

(A) that the person is a debtor or obligor;

(B) the identity of the person; and

(C) how to communicate with the person; or

(2) to a secured party or lienholder that has filed a financing statement against a person, unless the secured party knows:

(A) that the person is a debtor; and

(B) the identity of the person.

§ 9-606. Time of Default for Agricultural Lien.

For purposes of this part, a default occurs in connection with an agricultural lien at the time the secured party becomes entitled to enforce the lien in accordance with the statute under which it was created.

§ 9-607. Collection and Enforcement by Secured Party.

(a) If so agreed, and in any event after default, a secured party:

(1) may notify an account debtor or other person obligated on collateral to make payment or otherwise render performance to or for the benefit of the secured party;

(2) may take any proceeds to which the secured party is entitled under Section 9–315;

(3) may enforce the obligations of an account debtor or other person obligated on collateral and exercise the rights of the debtor with respect to the obligation of the account debtor or other person obligated on collateral to make payment or otherwise render performance to the debtor, and with respect to any property that secures the obligations of the account debtor or other person obligated on the collateral;

(4) if it holds a security interest in a deposit account perfected by control under Section 9–104(a)(1), may apply the balance of the deposit account to the obligation secured by the deposit account; and

(5) if it holds a security interest in a deposit account perfected by control under Section 9–104(a)(2) or (3), may instruct the bank to pay the balance of the deposit account to or for the benefit of the secured party.

(b) If necessary to enable a secured party to exercise under subsection (a)(3) the right of a debtor to enforce a mortgage nonjudicially, the secured party may record in the office in which a record of the mortgage is recorded:

(1) a copy of the security agreement that creates or provides for a security interest in the obligation secured by the mortgage; and

(2) the secured party's sworn affidavit in recordable form stating that:

(A) a default has occurred; and

(B) the secured party is entitled to enforce the mortgage nonjudicially.

(c) A secured party shall proceed in a commercially reasonable manner if the secured party:

(1) undertakes to collect from or enforce an obligation of an account debtor or other person obligated on collateral; and

(2) is entitled to charge back uncollected collateral or otherwise to full or limited recourse against the debtor or a secondary obligor.

(d) A secured party may deduct from the collections made pursuant to subsection (c) reasonable expenses of collection and enforcement, including reasonable attorney's fees and legal expenses incurred by the secured party.

(e) This section does not determine whether an account debtor, bank, or other person obligated on collateral owes a duty to a secured party.
As amended in 2000.

§ 9-608. Application of Proceeds of Collection or Enforcement; Liability for Deficiency and Right to Surplus.

(a) If a security interest or agricultural lien secures payment or performance of an obligation, the following rules apply:

(1) A secured party shall apply or pay over for application the cash proceeds of collection or enforcement under Section 9–607 in the following order to:

(A) the reasonable expenses of collection and enforcement and, to the extent provided for by agreement and not prohibited by law, reasonable attorney's fees and legal expenses incurred by the secured party;

(B) the satisfaction of obligations secured by the security interest or agricultural lien under which the collection or enforcement is made; and

(C) the satisfaction of obligations secured by any subordinate security interest in or other lien on the collateral subject to the security interest or agricultural lien under which the collection or enforcement is made if the secured party receives an authenticated demand for proceeds before distribution of the proceeds is completed.

(2) If requested by a secured party, a holder of a subordinate security interest or other lien shall furnish reasonable proof of the interest or lien within a reasonable time. Unless the holder complies, the secured party need not comply with the holder's demand under paragraph (1)(C).

(3) A secured party need not apply or pay over for application noncash proceeds of collection and enforcement under Section 9–607 unless the failure to do so would be commercially unreasonable. A secured party that applies or pays over for application noncash proceeds shall do so in a commercially reasonable manner.

(4) A secured party shall account to and pay a debtor for any surplus, and the obligor is liable for any deficiency.

(b) If the underlying transaction is a sale of accounts, chattel paper, payment intangibles, or promissory notes, the debtor is not entitled to any surplus, and the obligor is not liable for any deficiency.

As amended in 2000.

§ 9-609. Secured Party's Right to Take Possession after Default.

(a) After default, a secured party:

(1) may take possession of the collateral; and

(2) without removal, may render equipment unusable and dispose of collateral on a debtor's premises under Section 9–610.

(b) A secured party may proceed under subsection (a):

(1) pursuant to judicial process; or

(2) without judicial process, if it proceeds without breach of the peace.

(c) If so agreed, and in any event after default, a secured party may require the debtor to assemble the collateral and make it available to the secured party at a place to be designated by the secured party which is reasonably convenient to both parties.

§ 9-610. Disposition of Collateral after Default.

(a) After default, a secured party may sell, lease, license, or otherwise dispose of any or all of the collateral in its present condition or following any commercially reasonable preparation or processing.

(b) Every aspect of a disposition of collateral, including the method, manner, time, place, and other terms, must be commercially reasonable. If commercially reasonable, a secured party may dispose of collateral by public or private proceedings, by one or more contracts, as a unit or in parcels, and at any time and place and on any terms.

(c) A secured party may purchase collateral:

(1) at a public disposition; or

(2) at a private disposition only if the collateral is of a kind that is customarily sold on a recognized market or the subject of widely distributed standard price quotations.

(d) A contract for sale, lease, license, or other disposition includes the warranties relating to title, possession, quiet enjoyment, and the like which by operation of law accompany a voluntary disposition of property of the kind subject to the contract.

(e) A secured party may disclaim or modify warranties under subsection (d):

(1) in a manner that would be effective to disclaim or modify the warranties in a voluntary disposition of property of the kind subject to the contract of disposition; or

(2) by communicating to the purchaser a record evidencing the contract for disposition and including an express disclaimer or modification of the warranties.

(f) A record is sufficient to disclaim warranties under subsection (e) if it indicates "There is no warranty relating to title, possession, quiet enjoyment, or the like in this disposition" or uses words of similar import.

§ 9-611. Notification before Disposition of Collateral.

(a) In this section, "notification date" means the earlier of the date on which:

(1) a secured party sends to the debtor and any secondary obligor an authenticated notification of disposition; or

(2) the debtor and any secondary obligor waive the right to notification.

(b) Except as otherwise provided in subsection (d), a secured party that disposes of collateral under Section 9–610 shall send to the persons specified in subsection (c) a reasonable authenticated notification of disposition.

(c) To comply with subsection (b), the secured party shall send an authenticated notification of disposition to:

(1) the debtor;

(2) any secondary obligor; and

(3) if the collateral is other than consumer goods:

(A) any other person from which the secured party has received, before the notification date, an authenticated notification of a claim of an interest in the collateral;

(B) any other secured party or lienholder that, 10 days before the notification date, held a security interest in or other lien on the collateral perfected by the filing of a financing statement that:

(i) identified the collateral;

(ii) was indexed under the debtor's name as of that date; and

(iii) was filed in the office in which to file a financing statement against the debtor covering the collateral as of that date; and

(C) any other secured party that, 10 days before the notification date, held a security interest in the collateral perfected by compliance with a statute, regulation, or treaty described in Section 9–311(a).

(d) Subsection (b) does not apply if the collateral is perishable or threatens to decline speedily in value or is of a type customarily sold on a recognized market.

(e) A secured party complies with the requirement for notification prescribed by subsection (c)(3)(B) if:

(1) not later than 20 days or earlier than 30 days before the notification date, the secured party requests, in a commercially reasonable manner, information concerning financing statements indexed under the debtor's name in the office indicated in subsection (c)(3)(B); and

(2) before the notification date, the secured party:

(A) did not receive a response to the request for information; or

(B) received a response to the request for information and sent an authenticated notification of disposition to each secured party or other lienholder named in that response whose financing statement covered the collateral.

§ 9-612. Timeliness of Notification before Disposition of Collateral.

(a) Except as otherwise provided in subsection (b), whether a notification is sent within a reasonable time is a question of fact.

(b) In a transaction other than a consumer transaction, a notification of disposition sent after default and 10 days or more before the earliest time of disposition set forth in the notification is sent within a reasonable time before the disposition.

§ 9-613. Contents and Form of Notification before Disposition of Collateral: General.

Except in a consumer-goods transaction, the following rules apply:

(1) The contents of a notification of disposition are sufficient if the notification:

    (A) describes the debtor and the secured party;

    (B) describes the collateral that is the subject of the intended disposition;

    (C) states the method of intended disposition;

    (D) states that the debtor is entitled to an accounting of the unpaid indebtedness and states the charge, if any, for an accounting; and

    (E) states the time and place of a public disposition or the time after which any other disposition is to be made.

(2) Whether the contents of a notification that lacks any of the information specified in paragraph (1) are nevertheless sufficient is a question of fact.

(3) The contents of a notification providing substantially the information specified in paragraph (1) are sufficient, even if the notification includes:

    (A) information not specified by that paragraph; or

    (B) minor errors that are not seriously misleading.

(4) A particular phrasing of the notification is not required.

(5) The following form of notification and the form appearing in Section 9–614(3), when completed, each provides sufficient information:

NOTIFICATION OF DISPOSITION OF COLLATERAL

To: [*Name of debtor, obligor, or other person to which the notification is sent*]

From: [*Name, address, and telephone number of secured party*]

Name of Debtor(s): [*Include only if debtor(s) are not an addressee*]

    [*For a public disposition:*]

We will sell [or lease or license, *as applicable*] the [*describe collateral*] [to the highest qualified bidder] in public as follows:

    Day and Date: ———

    Time: ———

    Place: ———

    [*For a private disposition:*]

We will sell [or lease or license, *as applicable*] the [*describe collateral*] privately sometime after [*day and date*].

You are entitled to an accounting of the unpaid indebtedness secured by the property that we intend to sell [or lease or license, *as applicable*] [for a charge of $———]. You may request an accounting by calling us at [*telephone number*].

[End of Form]

As amended in 2000.

§ 9-614. Contents and Form of Notification before Disposition of Collateral: Consumer-Goods Transaction.

In a consumer-goods transaction, the following rules apply:

(1) A notification of disposition must provide the following information:

    (A) the information specified in Section 9–613(1);

    (B) a description of any liability for a deficiency of the person to which the notification is sent;

    (C) a telephone number from which the amount that must be paid to the secured party to redeem the collateral under Section 9–623 is available; and

    (D) a telephone number or mailing address from which additional information concerning the disposition and the obligation secured is available.

(2) A particular phrasing of the notification is not required.

(3) The following form of notification, when completed, provides sufficient information:

    [*Name and address of secured party*]

    [*Date*]

NOTICE OF OUR PLAN TO SELL PROPERTY

[*Name and address of any obligor who is also a debtor*]

Subject: [*Identification of Transaction*]

We have your [*describe collateral*], because you broke promises in our agreement.

    [*For a public disposition:*]

We will sell [*describe collateral*] at public sale. A sale could include a lease or license. The sale will be held as follows:

    Date: ———

    Time: ———

    Place: ———

You may attend the sale and bring bidders if you want.

    [*For a private disposition:*]

We will sell [*describe collateral*] at private sale sometime after [*date*]. A sale could include a lease or license.

The money that we get from the sale (after paying our costs) will reduce the amount you owe. If we get less money than you owe, you [*will or will not, as applicable*] still owe us the difference. If we get more money than you owe, you will get the extra money, unless we must pay it to someone else.

You can get the property back at any time before we sell it by paying us the full amount you owe (not just the past due payments), including our expenses. To learn the exact amount you must pay, call us at [*telephone number*].

If you want us to explain to you in writing how we have figured the amount that you owe us, you may call us at [*telephone number*] [or write us at [*secured party's address*]] and request a written explanation. [We will charge you $——— for the explanation if we sent you another written explanation of the amount you owe us within the last six months.]

If you need more information about the sale call us at [*telephone number*] [or write us at [*secured party's address*]].

We are sending this notice to the following other people who have an interest in [*describe collateral*] or who owe money under your agreement:

    [*Names of all other debtors and obligors, if any*]

[End of Form]

(4) A notification in the form of paragraph (3) is sufficient, even if additional information appears at the end of the form.

(5) A notification in the form of paragraph (3) is sufficient, even if it includes errors in information not required by paragraph (1), unless the error is misleading with respect to rights arising under this article.

(6) If a notification under this section is not in the form of paragraph (3), law other than this article determines the effect of including information not required by paragraph (1).

§ 9-615. Application of Proceeds of Disposition; Liability for Deficiency and Right to Surplus.

(a) A secured party shall apply or pay over for application the cash proceeds of disposition under Section 9–610 in the following order to:

(1) the reasonable expenses of retaking, holding, preparing for disposition, processing, and disposing, and, to the extent provided for by agreement and not prohibited by law, reasonable attorney's fees and legal expenses incurred by the secured party;

(2) the satisfaction of obligations secured by the security interest or agricultural lien under which the disposition is made;

(3) the satisfaction of obligations secured by any subordinate security interest in or other subordinate lien on the collateral if:

    (A) the secured party receives from the holder of the subordinate security interest or other lien an authenticated demand for proceeds before distribution of the proceeds is completed; and

    (B) in a case in which a consignor has an interest in the collateral, the subordinate security interest or other lien is senior to the interest of the consignor; and

(4) a secured party that is a consignor of the collateral if the secured party receives from the consignor an authenticated demand for proceeds before distribution of the proceeds is completed.

(b) If requested by a secured party, a holder of a subordinate security interest or other lien shall furnish reasonable proof of the interest or lien within a reasonable time. Unless the holder does so, the secured party need not comply with the holder's demand under subsection (a)(3).

(c) A secured party need not apply or pay over for application noncash proceeds of disposition under Section 9–610 unless the failure to do so would be commercially unreasonable. A secured party that applies or pays over for application noncash proceeds shall do so in a commercially reasonable manner.

(d) If the security interest under which a disposition is made secures payment or performance of an obligation, after making the payments and applications required by subsection (a) and permitted by subsection (c):

(1) unless subsection (a)(4) requires the secured party to apply or pay over cash proceeds to a consignor, the secured party shall account to and pay a debtor for any surplus; and

(2) the obligor is liable for any deficiency.

(e) If the underlying transaction is a sale of accounts, chattel paper, payment intangibles, or promissory notes:

(1) the debtor is not entitled to any surplus; and

(2) the obligor is not liable for any deficiency.

(f) The surplus or deficiency following a disposition is calculated based on the amount of proceeds that would have been realized in a disposition complying with this part to a transferee other than the secured party, a person related to the secured party, or a secondary obligor if:

(1) the transferee in the disposition is the secured party, a person related to the secured party, or a secondary obligor; and

(2) the amount of proceeds of the disposition is significantly below the range of proceeds that a complying disposition to a person other than the secured party, a person related to the secured party, or a secondary obligor would have brought.

(g) A secured party that receives cash proceeds of a disposition in good faith and without knowledge that the receipt violates the rights of the holder of a security interest or other lien that is not subordinate to the security interest or agricultural lien under which the disposition is made:

(1) takes the cash proceeds free of the security interest or other lien;

(2) is not obligated to apply the proceeds of the disposition to the satisfaction of obligations secured by the security interest or other lien; and

(3) is not obligated to account to or pay the holder of the security interest or other lien for any surplus.

As amended in 2000.

§ 9-616. Explanation of Calculation of Surplus or Deficiency.

(a) In this section:

(1) "Explanation" means a writing that:

    (A) states the amount of the surplus or deficiency;

    (B) provides an explanation in accordance with subsection (c) of how the secured party calculated the surplus or deficiency;

    (C) states, if applicable, that future debits, credits, charges, including additional credit service charges or interest, rebates, and expenses may affect the amount of the surplus or deficiency; and

    (D) provides a telephone number or mailing address from which additional information concerning the transaction is available.

(2) "Request" means a record:

    (A) authenticated by a debtor or consumer obligor;

    (B) requesting that the recipient provide an explanation; and

    (C) sent after disposition of the collateral under Section 9–610.

(b) In a consumer-goods transaction in which the debtor is entitled to a surplus or a consumer obligor is liable for a deficiency under Section 9–615, the secured party shall:

(1) send an explanation to the debtor or consumer obligor, as applicable, after the disposition and:

    (A) before or when the secured party accounts to the debtor and pays any surplus or first makes written demand on the consumer obligor after the disposition for payment of the deficiency; and

    (B) within 14 days after receipt of a request; or

(2) in the case of a consumer obligor who is liable for a deficiency, within 14 days after receipt of a request, send to the consumer obligor a record waiving the secured party's right to a deficiency.

(c) To comply with subsection (a)(1)(B), a writing must provide the following information in the following order:

(1) the aggregate amount of obligations secured by the security interest under which the disposition was made, and, if the amount reflects a rebate of unearned interest or credit service charge, an indication of that fact, calculated as of a specified date:

    (A) if the secured party takes or receives possession of the collateral after default, not more than 35 days before the secured party takes or receives possession; or

    (B) if the secured party takes or receives possession of the collateral before default or does not take possession of the collateral, not more than 35 days before the disposition;

(2) the amount of proceeds of the disposition;

(3) the aggregate amount of the obligations after deducting the amount of proceeds;

(4) the amount, in the aggregate or by type, and types of expenses, including expenses of retaking, holding, preparing for disposition, processing, and disposing of the collateral, and attorney's fees secured by the collateral which are known to the secured party and relate to the current disposition;

(5) the amount, in the aggregate or by type, and types of credits, including rebates of interest or credit service charges, to which the obligor is known to be entitled and which are not reflected in the amount in paragraph (1); and

(6) the amount of the surplus or deficiency.

(d) A particular phrasing of the explanation is not required. An explanation complying substantially with the requirements of subsection (a) is sufficient, even if it includes minor errors that are not seriously misleading.

(e) A debtor or consumer obligor is entitled without charge to one response to a request under this section during any six-month period in which the secured party did not send to the debtor or consumer obligor an explanation pursuant to subsection (b)(1). The secured party may require payment of a charge not exceeding $25 for each additional response.

§ 9-617. Rights of Transferee of Collateral.

(a) A secured party's disposition of collateral after default:

(1) transfers to a transferee for value all of the debtor's rights in the collateral;

(2) discharges the security interest under which the disposition is made; and

(3) discharges any subordinate security interest or other subordinate lien [other than liens created under [cite acts or statutes providing for liens, if any, that are not to be discharged]].

(b) A transferee that acts in good faith takes free of the rights and interests described in subsection (a), even if the secured party fails to comply with this article or the requirements of any judicial proceeding.

(c) If a transferee does not take free of the rights and interests described in subsection (a), the transferee takes the collateral subject to:

(1) the debtor's rights in the collateral;

(2) the security interest or agricultural lien under which the disposition is made; and

(3) any other security interest or other lien.

§ 9-618. Rights and Duties of Certain Secondary Obligors.

(a) A secondary obligor acquires the rights and becomes obligated to perform the duties of the secured party after the secondary obligor:

(1) receives an assignment of a secured obligation from the secured party;

(2) receives a transfer of collateral from the secured party and agrees to accept the rights and assume the duties of the secured party; or

(3) is subrogated to the rights of a secured party with respect to collateral.

(b) An assignment, transfer, or subrogation described in subsection (a):

(1) is not a disposition of collateral under Section 9–610; and

(2) relieves the secured party of further duties under this article.

§ 9-619. Transfer of Record or Legal Title.

(a) In this section, "transfer statement" means a record authenticated by a secured party stating:

(1) that the debtor has defaulted in connection with an obligation secured by specified collateral;

(2) that the secured party has exercised its post-default remedies with respect to the collateral;

(3) that, by reason of the exercise, a transferee has acquired the rights of the debtor in the collateral; and

(4) the name and mailing address of the secured party, debtor, and transferee.

(b) A transfer statement entitles the transferee to the transfer of record of all rights of the debtor in the collateral specified in the statement in any official filing, recording, registration, or certificate-of-title system covering the collateral. If a transfer statement is presented with the applicable fee and request form to the official or office responsible for maintaining the system, the official or office shall:

(1) accept the transfer statement;

(2) promptly amend its records to reflect the transfer; and

(3) if applicable, issue a new appropriate certificate of title in the name of the transferee.

(c) A transfer of the record or legal title to collateral to a secured party under subsection (b) or otherwise is not of itself a disposition of collateral under this article and does not of itself relieve the secured party of its duties under this article.

§ 9-620. Acceptance of Collateral in Full or Partial Satisfaction of Obligation; Compulsory Disposition of Collateral.

(a) Except as otherwise provided in subsection (g), a secured party may accept collateral in full or partial satisfaction of the obligation it secures only if:

(1) the debtor consents to the acceptance under subsection (c);

(2) the secured party does not receive, within the time set forth in subsection (d), a notification of objection to the proposal authenticated by:

(A) a person to which the secured party was required to send a proposal under Section 9–621; or

(B) any other person, other than the debtor, holding an interest in the collateral subordinate to the security interest that is the subject of the proposal;

(3) if the collateral is consumer goods, the collateral is not in the possession of the debtor when the debtor consents to the acceptance; and

(4) subsection (e) does not require the secured party to dispose of the collateral or the debtor waives the requirement pursuant to Section 9–624.

(b) A purported or apparent acceptance of collateral under this section is ineffective unless:

(1) the secured party consents to the acceptance in an authenticated record or sends a proposal to the debtor; and

(2) the conditions of subsection (a) are met.

(c) For purposes of this section:

(1) a debtor consents to an acceptance of collateral in partial satisfaction of the obligation it secures only if the debtor agrees to the terms of the acceptance in a record authenticated after default; and

(2) a debtor consents to an acceptance of collateral in full satisfaction of the obligation it secures only if the debtor agrees to the terms of the acceptance in a record authenticated after default or the secured party:

(A) sends to the debtor after default a proposal that is unconditional or subject only to a condition that collateral not in the possession of the secured party be preserved or maintained;

(B) in the proposal, proposes to accept collateral in full satisfaction of the obligation it secures; and

(C) does not receive a notification of objection authenticated by the debtor within 20 days after the proposal is sent.

(d) To be effective under subsection (a)(2), a notification of objection must be received by the secured party:

(1) in the case of a person to which the proposal was sent pursuant to Section 9–621, within 20 days after notification was sent to that person; and

(2) in other cases:

(A) within 20 days after the last notification was sent pursuant to Section 9–621; or

(B) if a notification was not sent, before the debtor consents to the acceptance under subsection (c).

(e) A secured party that has taken possession of collateral shall dispose of the collateral pursuant to Section 9–610 within the time specified in subsection (f) if:

(1) 60 percent of the cash price has been paid in the case of a purchase-money security interest in consumer goods; or

(2) 60 percent of the principal amount of the obligation secured has been paid in the case of a non-purchase-money security interest in consumer goods.

(f) To comply with subsection (e), the secured party shall dispose of the collateral:

(1) within 90 days after taking possession; or

(2) within any longer period to which the debtor and all secondary obligors have agreed in an agreement to that effect entered into and authenticated after default.

(g) In a consumer transaction, a secured party may not accept collateral in partial satisfaction of the obligation it secures.

§ 9-621. Notification of Proposal to Accept Collateral.

(a) A secured party that desires to accept collateral in full or partial satisfaction of the obligation it secures shall send its proposal to:

(1) any person from which the secured party has received, before the debtor consented to the acceptance, an authenticated notification of a claim of an interest in the collateral;

(2) any other secured party or lienholder that, 10 days before the debtor consented to the acceptance, held a security interest in or other lien on the collateral perfected by the filing of a financing statement that:

(A) identified the collateral;

(B) was indexed under the debtor's name as of that date; and

(C) was filed in the office or offices in which to file a financing statement against the debtor covering the collateral as of that date; and

(3) any other secured party that, 10 days before the debtor consented to the acceptance, held a security interest in the collateral perfected by compliance with a statute, regulation, or treaty described in Section 9–311(a).

(b) A secured party that desires to accept collateral in partial satisfaction of the obligation it secures shall send its proposal to any secondary obligor in addition to the persons described in subsection (a).

§ 9-622. Effect of Acceptance of Collateral.

(a) A secured party's acceptance of collateral in full or partial satisfaction of the obligation it secures:

(1) discharges the obligation to the extent consented to by the debtor;

(2) transfers to the secured party all of a debtor's rights in the collateral;

(3) discharges the security interest or agricultural lien that is the subject of the debtor's consent and any subordinate security interest or other subordinate lien; and

(4) terminates any other subordinate interest.

(b) A subordinate interest is discharged or terminated under subsection (a), even if the secured party fails to comply with this article.

§ 9-623. Right to Redeem Collateral.

(a) A debtor, any secondary obligor, or any other secured party or lienholder may redeem collateral.

(b) To redeem collateral, a person shall tender:

(1) fulfillment of all obligations secured by the collateral; and

(2) the reasonable expenses and attorney's fees described in Section 9–615(a)(1).

(c) A redemption may occur at any time before a secured party:

(1) has collected collateral under Section 9–607;

(2) has disposed of collateral or entered into a contract for its disposition under Section 9–610; or

(3) has accepted collateral in full or partial satisfaction of the obligation it secures under Section 9–622.

§ 9-624. Waiver.

(a) A debtor or secondary obligor may waive the right to notification of disposition of collateral under Section 9–611 only by an agreement to that effect entered into and authenticated after default.

(b) A debtor may waive the right to require disposition of collateral under Section 9–620(e) only by an agreement to that effect entered into and authenticated after default.

(c) Except in a consumer-goods transaction, a debtor or secondary obligor may waive the right to redeem collateral under Section 9–62 only by an agreement to that effect entered into and authenticated after default.

[Subpart 2. Noncompliance with Article]

§ 9-625. Remedies for Secured Party's Failure to Comply with Article.

(a) If it is established that a secured party is not proceeding in accordance with this article, a court may order or restrain collection, enforcement, or disposition of collateral on appropriate terms and conditions.

(b) Subject to subsections (c), (d), and (f), a person is liable for damages in the amount of any loss caused by a failure to comply with this article. Loss caused by a failure to comply may include loss resulting from the debtor's inability to obtain, or increased costs of, alternative financing.

(c) Except as otherwise provided in Section 9–628:

(1) a person that, at the time of the failure, was a debtor, was an obligor, or held a security interest in or other lien on the collateral may recover damages under subsection (b) for its loss; and

(2) if the collateral is consumer goods, a person that was a debtor or a secondary obligor at the time a secured party failed to comply with this part may recover for that failure in any event an amount not less than the credit service charge plus 10 percent of the principal amount of the obligation or the time-price differential plus 10 percent of the cash price.

(d) A debtor whose deficiency is eliminated under Section 9–626 may recover damages for the loss of any surplus. However, a debtor or secondary obligor whose deficiency is eliminated or reduced under Section 9–626 may not otherwise recover under subsection (b) for noncompliance with the provisions of this part relating to collection, enforcement, disposition, or acceptance.

(e) In addition to any damages recoverable under subsection (b), the debtor, consumer obligor, or person named as a debtor in a filed record, as applicable, may recover $500 in each case from a person that:

(1) fails to comply with Section 9–208;

(2) fails to comply with Section 9–209;

(3) files a record that the person is not entitled to file under Section 9–509(a);

(4) fails to cause the secured party of record to file or send a termination statement as required by Section 9–513(a) or (c);

(5) fails to comply with Section 9–616(b)(1) and whose failure is part of a pattern, or consistent with a practice, of noncompliance; or

(6) fails to comply with Section 9–616(b)(2).

(f) A debtor or consumer obligor may recover damages under subsection (b) and, in addition, $500 in each case from a person that, without reasonable cause, fails to comply with a request under Section 9–210. A recipient of a request under Section 9–210 which never claimed an interest in the collateral or obligations that are the subject of a request under that section has a reasonable excuse for failure to comply with the request within the meaning of this subsection.

(g) If a secured party fails to comply with a request regarding a list of collateral or a statement of account under Section 9–210, the secured party may claim a security interest only as shown in the list or statement included in the request as against a person that is reasonably misled by the failure.

As amended in 2000.

§ 9-626. Action in Which Deficiency or Surplus Is in Issue.

(a) In an action arising from a transaction, other than a consumer transaction, in which the amount of a deficiency or surplus is in issue, the following rules apply:

(1) A secured party need not prove compliance with the provisions of this part relating to collection, enforcement, disposition, or acceptance unless the debtor or a secondary obligor places the secured party's compliance in issue.

(2) If the secured party's compliance is placed in issue, the secured party has the burden of establishing that the collection, enforcement, disposition, or acceptance was conducted in accordance with this part.

(3) Except as otherwise provided in Section 9–628, if a secured party fails to prove that the collection, enforcement, disposition, or acceptance was conducted in accordance with the provisions of this part relating to collection, enforcement, disposition, or acceptance, the liability of a debtor or a secondary obligor for a deficiency is limited to an amount by which the sum of the secured obligation, expenses, and attorney's fees exceeds the greater of:

(A) the proceeds of the collection, enforcement, disposition, or acceptance; or

(B) the amount of proceeds that would have been realized had the noncomplying secured party proceeded in accordance with the provisions of this part relating to collection, enforcement, disposition, or acceptance.

(4) For purposes of paragraph (3)(B), the amount of proceeds that would have been realized is equal to the sum of the secured obligation, expenses, and attorney's fees unless the secured party proves that the amount is less than that sum.

(5) If a deficiency or surplus is calculated under Section 9–615(f), the debtor or obligor has the burden of establishing that the amount of proceeds of the disposition is significantly below the range of prices that a complying disposition to a person other than the secured party, a person related to the secured party, or a secondary obligor would have brought.

(b) The limitation of the rules in subsection (a) to transactions other than consumer transactions is intended to leave to the court the determination of the proper rules in consumer transactions. The court may not infer from that limitation the nature of the proper rule in consumer transactions and may continue to apply established approaches.

§ 9-627. Determination of Whether Conduct Was Commercially Reasonable.

(a) The fact that a greater amount could have been obtained by a collection, enforcement, disposition, or acceptance at a different time or in a different method from that selected by the secured party is not of itself sufficient to preclude the secured party from establishing that the collection, enforcement, disposition, or acceptance was made in a commercially reasonable manner.

(b) A disposition of collateral is made in a commercially reasonable manner if the disposition is made:

(1) in the usual manner on any recognized market;

(2) at the price current in any recognized market at the time of the disposition; or

(3) otherwise in conformity with reasonable commercial practices among dealers in the type of property that was the subject of the disposition.

(c) A collection, enforcement, disposition, or acceptance is commercially reasonable if it has been approved:

(1) in a judicial proceeding;

(2) by a bona fide creditors' committee;

(3) by a representative of creditors; or

(4) by an assignee for the benefit of creditors.

(d) Approval under subsection (c) need not be obtained, and lack of approval does not mean that the collection, enforcement, disposition, or acceptance is not commercially reasonable.

§ 9-628. Nonliability and Limitation on Liability of Secured Party; Liability of Secondary Obligor.

(a) Unless a secured party knows that a person is a debtor or obligor, knows the identity of the person, and knows how to communicate with the person:

(1) the secured party is not liable to the person, or to a secured party or lienholder that has filed a financing statement against the person, for failure to comply with this article; and

(2) the secured party's failure to comply with this article does not affect the liability of the person for a deficiency.

(b) A secured party is not liable because of its status as secured party:

(1) to a person that is a debtor or obligor, unless the secured party knows:

(A) that the person is a debtor or obligor;

(B) the identity of the person; and

(C) how to communicate with the person; or

(2) to a secured party or lienholder that has filed a financing statement against a person, unless the secured party knows:

(A) that the person is a debtor; and

(B) the identity of the person.

(c) A secured party is not liable to any person, and a person's liability for a deficiency is not affected, because of any act or omission arising out of the secured party's reasonable belief that a transaction is not a consumer-goods transaction or a consumer transaction or that goods are not consumer goods, if the secured party's belief is based on its reasonable reliance on:

(1) a debtor's representation concerning the purpose for which collateral was to be used, acquired, or held; or

(2) an obligor's representation concerning the purpose for which a secured obligation was incurred.

(d) A secured party is not liable to any person under Section 9–625(c)(2) for its failure to comply with Section 9–616.

(e) A secured party is not liable under Section 9–625(c)(2) more than once with respect to any one secured obligation.

PART 7: Transition

§ 9-701. Effective Date.
This [Act] takes effect on July 1, 2001.

§ 9-702. Savings Clause.

(a) Except as otherwise provided in this part, this [Act] applies to a transaction or lien within its scope, even if the transaction or lien was entered into or created before this [Act] takes effect.

(b) Except as otherwise provided in subsection (c) and Sections 9–703 through 9–709:

(1) transactions and liens that were not governed by [former Article 9], were validly entered into or created before this [Act] takes effect, and would be subject to this [Act] if they had been entered into or created after this [Act] takes effect, and the rights, duties, and interests flowing from those transactions and liens remain valid after this [Act] takes effect; and

(2) the transactions and liens may be terminated, completed, consummated, and enforced as required or permitted by this [Act] or by the law that otherwise would apply if this [Act] had not taken effect.

(c) This [Act] does not affect an action, case, or proceeding commenced before this [Act] takes effect.

As amended in 2000.

§ 9-703. Security Interest Perfected before Effective Date.

(a) A security interest that is enforceable immediately before this [Act] takes effect and would have priority over the rights of a person that becomes a lien creditor at that time is a perfected security interest under this [Act] if, when this [Act] takes effect, the applicable requirements for enforceability and perfection under this [Act] are satisfied without further action.

(b) Except as otherwise provided in Section 9–705, if, immediately before this [Act] takes effect, a security interest is enforceable and would have priority over the rights of a person that becomes a lien creditor at that time, but the applicable requirements for enforceability or perfection under this [Act] are not satisfied when this [Act] takes effect, the security interest:

(1) is a perfected security interest for one year after this [Act] takes effect;

(2) remains enforceable thereafter only if the security interest becomes enforceable under Section 9–203 before the year expires; and

(3) remains perfected thereafter only if the applicable requirements for perfection under this [Act] are satisfied before the year expires.

§ 9-704. Security Interest Unperfected before Effective Date.

A security interest that is enforceable immediately before this [Act] takes effect but which would be subordinate to the rights of a person that becomes a lien creditor at that time:

(1) remains an enforceable security interest for one year after this [Act] takes effect;

(2) remains enforceable thereafter if the security interest becomes enforceable under Section 9–203 when this [Act] takes effect or within one year thereafter; and

(3) becomes perfected:

(A) without further action, when this [Act] takes effect if the applicable requirements for perfection under this [Act] are satisfied before or at that time; or

(B) when the applicable requirements for perfection are satisfied if the requirements are satisfied after that time.

§ 9-705. Effectiveness of Action Taken before Effective Date.

(a) If action, other than the filing of a financing statement, is taken before this [Act] takes effect and the action would have resulted in priority of a security interest over the rights of a person that becomes a lien creditor had the security interest become enforceable before this [Act] takes effect, the action is effective to perfect a security interest that attaches under this [Act] within one year after this [Act] takes effect. An attached security interest becomes unperfected one year after this [Act] takes effect unless the security interest becomes a perfected security interest under this [Act] before the expiration of that period.

(b) The filing of a financing statement before this [Act] takes effect is effective to perfect a security interest to the extent the filing would satisfy the applicable requirements for perfection under this [Act].

(c) This [Act] does not render ineffective an effective financing statement that, before this [Act] takes effect, is filed and satisfies the applicable requirements for perfection under the law of the jurisdiction governing perfection as provided in [former Section 9–103]. However, except as otherwise provided in subsections (d) and (e) and Section 9–706, the financing statement ceases to be effective at the earlier of:

(1) the time the financing statement would have ceased to be effective under the law of the jurisdiction in which it is filed; or

(2) June 30, 2006.

(d) The filing of a continuation statement after this [Act] takes effect does not continue the effectiveness of the financing statement filed before this [Act] takes effect. However, upon the timely filing of a continuation statement after this [Act] takes effect and in accordance with the law of the jurisdiction governing perfection as provided in Part 3, the effectiveness of a financing statement filed in the same office in that jurisdiction before this [Act] takes effect continues for the period provided by the law of that jurisdiction.

(e) Subsection (c)(2) applies to a financing statement that, before this [Act] takes effect, is filed against a transmitting utility and satisfies the applicable requirements for perfection under the law of the jurisdiction governing perfection as provided in [former Section 9–103] only to the extent that Part 3 provides that the law of a jurisdiction other than the jurisdiction in which the financing statement is filed governs perfection of a security interest in collateral covered by the financing statement.

(f) A financing statement that includes a financing statement filed before this [Act] takes effect and a continuation statement filed after this [Act] takes effect is effective only to the extent that it satisfies the requirements of Part 5 for an initial financing statement.

§ 9-706. When Initial Financing Statement Suffices to Continue Effectiveness of Financing Statement.

(a) The filing of an initial financing statement in the office specified in Section 9–501 continues the effectiveness of a financing statement filed before this [Act] takes effect if:

(1) the filing of an initial financing statement in that office would be effective to perfect a security interest under this [Act];

(2) the pre-effective-date financing statement was filed in an office in another State or another office in this State; and

(3) the initial financing statement satisfies subsection (c).

(b) The filing of an initial financing statement under subsection (a) continues the effectiveness of the pre-effective-date financing statement:

(1) if the initial financing statement is filed before this [Act] takes effect, for the period provided in [former Section 9–403] with respect to a financing statement; and

(2) if the initial financing statement is filed after this [Act] takes effect, for the period provided in Section 9–515 with respect to an initial financing statement.

(c) To be effective for purposes of subsection (a), an initial financing statement must:

(1) satisfy the requirements of Part 5 for an initial financing statement;

(2) identify the pre-effective-date financing statement by indicating the office in which the financing statement was filed and providing the dates of filing and file numbers, if any, of the financing statement and of the most recent continuation statement filed with respect to the financing statement; and

(3) indicate that the pre-effective-date financing statement remains effective.

§ 9-707. Amendment of Pre-Effective-Date Financing Statement.

(a) In this section, "Pre-effective-date financing statement" means a financing statement filed before this [Act] takes effect.

(b) After this [Act] takes effect, a person may add or delete collateral covered by, continue or terminate the effectiveness of, or otherwise amend the information provided in, a pre-effective-date financing statement only in accordance with the law of the jurisdiction governing perfection as provided in Part 3. However, the effectiveness of a pre-effective-date financing statement also may be terminated in accordance with the law of the jurisdiction in which the financing statement is filed.

(c) Except as otherwise provided in subsection (d), if the law of this State governs perfection of a security interest, the information in a pre-effective-date financing statement may be amended after this [Act] takes effect only if:

(1) the pre-effective-date financing statement and an amendment are filed in the office specified in Section 9–501;

(2) an amendment is filed in the office specified in Section 9–501 concurrently with, or after the filing in that office of, an initial financing statement that satisfies Section 9–706(c); or

(3) an initial financing statement that provides the information as amended and satisfies Section 9–706(c) is filed in the office specified in Section 9–501.

(d) If the law of this State governs perfection of a security interest, the effectiveness of a pre-effective-date financing statement may be continued only under Section 9–705(d) and (f) or 9–706.

(e) Whether or not the law of this State governs perfection of a security interest, the effectiveness of a pre-effective-date financing statement filed in this State may be terminated after this [Act] takes effect by filing a termination statement in the office in which the pre-effective-date financing statement is filed, unless an initial financing statement that satisfies Section 9–706(c) has been filed in the office specified by the law of the jurisdiction governing perfection as provided in Part 3 as the office in which to file a financing statement.

As amended in 2000.

§ 9-708. Persons Entitled to File Initial Financing Statement or Continuation Statement.

A person may file an initial financing statement or a continuation statement under this part if:

(1) the secured party of record authorizes the filing; and

(2) the filing is necessary under this part:

(A) to continue the effectiveness of a financing statement filed before this [Act] takes effect; or

(B) to perfect or continue the perfection of a security interest.

As amended in 2000.

§ 9-709. Priority.

(a) This [Act] determines the priority of conflicting claims to collateral. However, if the relative priorities of the claims were established before this [Act] takes effect, [former Article 9] determines priority.

(b) For purposes of Section 9–322(a), the priority of a security interest that becomes enforceable under Section 9–203 of this [Act] dates from the time this [Act] takes effect if the security interest is perfected under this [Act] by the filing of a financing statement before this [Act] takes effect which would not have been effective to perfect the security interest under [former Article 9]. This subsection does not apply to conflicting security interests each of which is perfected by the filing of such a financing statement.

As amended in 2000.

ENDNOTES

1. Additions and new wording are underlined. What follows represents only selected changes made by the proposed amendments. Although the National Conference of Commissioners on Uniform State Laws approved the amendments on August 2, 2002, as of this writing, they have not as yet been approved by the American Law Institute or by any state.

2. Section 3–312 was not adopted as part of the 1990 Official Text of Revised Article 3. It was officially approved and recommended for enactment in all states in August 1991 by the National Conference of Commissioners on Uniform State Laws.

Legal Dictionary

Acceleration clauses Clauses in contracts that advance the date for payment based on the occurrence of a condition or the breach of a duty.

Acceptance The agreement by the maker or the drawee to accept and/or pay a negotiable instrument upon presentment.

Accessory to the crime A person who assists another in the commission of a crime, without being the primary actor.

Accommodation Something supplied for a convenience or to satisfy a need.

Accounts Rights to payments for goods sold or leased or for services rendered that are not evidenced by an instrument or chattel paper.

Actionable Furnishing legal grounds for an action.

Adduced Given as proof.

Administrators The persons who have been empowered by an appropriate court to handle the estate of a deceased person.

Admission A statement acknowledging the truth of an allegation, and accepted in court as evidence against the party making the admission.

Advisory opinion A formal opinion by a judge, court, or law officer on a question of law but not presented in an actual case.

Affidavit Written statement made under oath.

Affirmative defense A defense to a cause of action that the defendant must raise.

Aid and abet To help, assist, or facilitate the commission of a crime; to promote the accomplishment of a crime.

Alien A person or corporation belonging to another country.

Alienage The status of being a foreign-born resident who has not yet become a naturalized citizen.

Alienation The transfer of ownership to another.

Alternate dispute resolution (ADR) Methods of resolving disputes other than traditional litigation.

Ambient Pertaining to the surrounding atmosphere or the environment.

Ambiguities Uncertainties regarding the meanings of expressions used in contractual agreements.

Amicus brief Court brief filed by individual or group that does not have standing in the dispute.

Amoral Being neither moral nor immoral; lying outside the sphere to which moral judgments apply.

Apparent authority A situation in which a principal gives the appearance that the agent acts with authority.

Appellate court A court that has the power to review the decisions of lower courts.

Appellee Party who "defends" the decision of the lower court.

Aquifers Water-bearing strata of permeable rock, sand, or gravel.

Arbitration The determination of a disputed matter by private unofficial persons selected in a manner provided by law or agreement, with the substitution of their award or decision for the judgment of a court.

Arbitrator An independent person chosen by the parties or appointed by statute and to whom the issues are submitted for settlement outside of court.

Arraigned Called before a court to enter a plea on an indictment or criminal complaint.

Assault A threat to touch someone in an undesired manner.

Assignable Legally capable of being transferred from one person to another.

Assignment for the benefit of creditors An assignment in trust made by debtors for the payment of their debts.

Attachment Seizure of the defendant's property.

At will Having no specific date or circumstance to bring about a dissolution.

Aural privacy A privacy right for normal conversations; the right to privacy from eavesdropping.

Autonomous The right of the individual to govern him- or herself according to his or her own reason.

Bail The posting of money or property for the release of a person charged with a crime while ensuring his or her presence in the court at future hearings.

Bailee One to whom goods are delivered with the understanding that they will be returned at a future time.

Bankruptcy An area of law designed to give an "honest debtor" a fresh start; the proceedings undertaken against a person or a firm under the bankruptcy laws.

Bar In the legal sense, to prevent or to stop.

Battery Unauthorized touching of another person without legal justification or that person's consent.

Beyond a reasonable doubt The degree of proof required in a criminal trial, which is proof to a moral certainty; there is no other reasonable interpretation.

Bona fide In good faith; honest; without deceit; innocent.

Bona fide occupational qualification (BFOQ) A defense to charges of discrimination based on religion, sex, or national origin but not to charges of racial discrimination; a situation in which one of these categories is essential to the performance of the job.

Bona fide purchaser A person who purchases in good faith, for value, and without notice of any defects or defenses affecting the sale or transaction.

Boycotts Concerted refusals to deal with firms so as to disrupt their business.

Cancellation Any action shown on the face of a contract that indicates an intent to destroy the obligation of the contract.

Capital contribution Money or assets invested by the business owners for commencing and/or promoting an enterprise.

Carriage The transportation of goods or people from one location to another.

Carrier A third party hired to deliver the goods from the seller to the buyer.

Cartage The act of carrying by truck, usually within a city; hauling by truck.

Cases and controversies Claims brought before the court in regular proceedings to protect or enforce rights or to prevent or punish wrongs.

Caucusing Mediation technique in which the mediator meets with each party separately.

Caveat emptor Let the buyer beware.

Censured Formally reprimanded for specific conduct.

Certiorari A writ used by a superior court to direct a lower court to send it the records and proceedings in a case for review.

Charging order A court order permitting a creditor to receive profits from the operation of a business; especially common in partnership situations.

Chattel paper A writing that evidences both a monetary obligation and a security interest in specific goods.

Chattels Articles of personal (as opposed to real) property.

Choses in action A personal right not reduced to possession, but recoverable in a suit at law.

Circumscribe To limit the range of activity associated with something.

Civil rights The rights in the first 10 amendments to the U.S. Constitution (the Bill of Rights) and due process and equal protection under the Fourteenth Amendment.

Class action suit Lawsuit involving a group of plaintiffs or defendants who are substantially in the same position as each other.

Clearinghouse An association of banks and financial institutions that "clears" items between banks.

Codicil A separate written document that modifies an existing will.

Common carrier A company in the business of transporting goods or people for a fee and holding itself out as serving the general public.

Common law Unwritten law, which is based on custom, usage, and court decisions; distinct from statute law, which consists of laws passed by legislatures.

Common law states States in which married couples cannot create community property.

Community property A special form of joint ownership between husband and wife permitted in certain states called community property states.

Community property states States in which married couples generally create community property.

Commutative justice The attempt to give all persons identical treatment based on the assumption that equal treatment is appropriate. Individual differences are not considered.

Compiler program One that converts a high-level programming language into binary or machine code.

Complaint In civil practice, the plaintiff's first pleading. It informs the defendant that he or she is being sued.

Concessionaires Operators of refreshment centers.

Condemnation proceeding Court proceeding to take property for public use or declare property forfeited.

Conditional sales contracts Sales contracts in which the transfer of title is subject to a condition, most commonly the payment of the full purchase price by the buyer.

Confirmation A written memorandum of the agreement; a notation that provides written evidence that an agreement was made.

Conglomerate mergers Mergers between noncompeting firms in different industries.

Consequential damages Damages or losses that occur as a result of the initial wrong but that are not direct and immediate.

Conservator A person appointed by a court to manage the affairs of one who is incompetent.

Consignee A person to whom goods are shipped by another party. Also a person to whom goods are shipped for sale and who generally can return all unsold goods to the consignor.

Consignor A person who ships goods to another party.

Conspicuous Easy to see or perceive; obvious.

Conspiracy An unlawful situation in which two or more people plan to engage in criminal behavior.

Constructive discharge A termination of employment that results from an employer's making the employee's working conditions so intolerable that the employee feels compelled to leave.

Constructive trust A trust imposed by law to prevent the unjust enrichment of the person in possession of the property (the purported owner).

Consumer price index Measurement at a particular time of the change in price of a group of consumer goods.

Contingency fee A fee stipulated to be paid to an attorney only if the case is settled or won, or is based on some other contingency or event.

Contracts of adhesion Contracts in which the terms are not open to negotiation; so-called take-it-or-leave-it contracts.

Convention An agreement between nations; a treaty.

Convert To change.

Cooperatives Groups of individuals, commonly laborers or farmers, who unite in a common enterprise and share the profits proportionately.

Corporation An artificial person or legal entity created by or under the authority of a state or nation, composed of a group of persons known as stockholders or shareholders.

Counterclaimed Presented a cause of action in opposition to the plaintiff's.

Court of Common Pleas Title used in some states for trial courts of general jurisdiction.

Creditor beneficiary A third party who is entitled to performance because the promisee has a contractual obligation with him or her.

Criminal forfeiture Government confiscation of property as a punishment for criminal activity.

Criminal law The body of law dealing with public wrongs called crimes.

Currency transaction report (CTR) A report businesses must file if a customer brings $10,000 or more in cash to the business.

Cy pres doctrine Doctrine permitting the court to modify a trust in order to follow the creator's charitable intention as closely as possible.

Debit card Card that transfers funds from customer's bank account to merchant's bank account.

Decedent A person who has died.

Default A failure to do what should be done, especially in the performance of a

contractual obligation, without legal excuse or justification for the nonperformance.

Defendant A person who answers a lawsuit; the person whose behavior is the subject of the complaint.

Defraud To deprive a person of property or of any interest, estate, or right by fraud, deceit, or artifice.

Delegated Assigned responsibility and/or authority by the person or group normally empowered to exercise the responsibility or authority.

Delivered Intentionally transferred physical possession of some thing or right to another person.

De novo A situation in which the court will hear the case or issue anew.

Deposition The process of asking a potential witness questions under oath before a court reporter.

Descriptive theory Theory that describes how things are. It reports what is observed.

Deterrent A danger, difficulty, or other consideration that stops or prevents a person from acting.

Dictum An observation or remark by a judge that is not necessarily involved in the case or essential to its resolution. An aside written by the judge.

Discharge Release from obligation or liability.

Discretion The right to use one's own judgment in selecting between alternatives.

Discretionary Involving the freedom to make certain decisions.

Disenfranchised Restricted from enjoying certain constitutional or statutory rights; burdened by systemic prejudice or bigotry.

Disgorge To give up ill-gotten or illicit gains.

Dishonor To refuse to accept or to pay a negotiable instrument upon proper presentment.

Distributive justice The attempt to allocate justice in a way that considers individual differences.

District court Trial court in the federal court system.

Diversity of citizenship A situation in which the parties are citizens of different states.

Document of title Written evidence of ownership or of rights to something.

Domicile One's permanent home and principal residence. It is the place to which a person will return after traveling.

Double jeopardy A rule of criminal law that states that a person will not be tried in court more than once by the same government for the same criminal offense.

Draft An order for a third person to pay a sum certain in money without conditions, either at a preset time in the future or "on demand."

Draw An arrangement by which an employee receives a predetermined amount each pay period.

Due process The proper exercise of judicial authority as established by general concepts of law and morality.

Duress A situation in which one party enters into a contract due to a wrongful threat of force. Wrongful use of force to obtain a gift or contract.

Easements Limited rights to use and enjoy the land of another.

Effluent An outflow of materials or an emanation.

Emancipation Freedom from the control or power of another; release from parental care; or the attainment of legal independence.

Eminent domain A state's or municipality's power to take private property for public use.

Employment at will An employment relationship in which, owing to the absence of any contractual obligation to remain in the relationship, either party can terminate the relationship at any time and for any reason not prohibited by law.

Encrypted code Code typed in one set of symbols and interpreted by the machine as another; used for security.

Encumbrancer The holder of a claim relating to real or personal property.

Entrustment The delivery of goods to a merchant who regularly deals in goods of the type delivered.

Equal protection The assurance that any person before the court will be treated the same as every other person before the court.

Equitable Arising from the branch of the legal system designed to provide a remedy where no remedy existed at common law; a system designed to provide fairness when there was no suitable remedy "at law."

ERISA Federal statute regulating employee retirement programs.

Escrow Process of preparing for the exchange of real estate, deed, and money. It is managed by a third party.

Estate tax A tax assessed on the total net (taxable) value of the estate.

Estoppel A legal bar or impediment that prevents a person from claiming or denying certain facts as a result of his or her previous conduct.

European Union (EU) The EU, formerly called the Common Market, creates a free-trade zone among the member nations of Europe.

Exculpatory clauses Parts of agreements in which a prospective plaintiff agrees in advance not to seek to hold the prospective defendant liable for certain losses for which the prospective defendant otherwise would be liable.

Executors The persons named and appointed in a will by the testator to carry out the administration of the estate as established by the will.

Exemplary damages Punitive damages; damages imposed in a case to punish the defendant.

Expert A person with a high degree of skill or with a specialized knowledge.

Ex post facto law A law passed after an occurrence or act, which retrospectively changes the legal consequences of such act.

Express Actually stated; communicated from one party to another.

Extinguished Destroyed, wiped out.

Facial/facially On its face, apparent.

Fact-finding A process where an arbitrator investigates a dispute and issues findings of fact and a nonbinding report.

Fair market value The current price for selling an asset between informed willing buyers and informed willing sellers.

Fee interest Broadest form of real estate ownership; an absolute interest in which the owner is entitled to the entire property and can transfer it during life and at death. Also called a fee or a fee simple.

Fiat An order issued by legal authority.

Fiduciary One who holds a special position of trust or confidence and who thereby is expected to act with the utmost good faith and loyalty.

Fiduciary duty The legal duty to exercise the highest degree of loyalty and good faith in handling the affairs of the person to whom the duty is owed.

Field warehousing A method of perfection in a secured transaction in which the creditor takes "possession" of a portion of the debtor's storage area.

First impression Case that is presented to the court for an initial decision; the case presents an entirely novel question of law for the court's decision. It is not governed by any existing precedent.

Forcible entry and detainer A summary proceeding to recover possession of premises unlawfully or forcibly detained.

Foreclose Cut off an existing ownership right in property.

Foreign corporation A corporation that had its articles of incorporation approved in another state.

Foreseeability The knowledge or notice that a result is likely to occur if a certain act occurs.

Forfeiture The loss of a right or privilege as a penalty for certain conduct.

Forum The court conducting the trial.

Franchising Special privileges granted by a corporation that allow the franchisee to conduct business under the corporate name of the franchisor.

Fraud The intentional misrepresentation of a material fact. Use of a false statement of material fact to obtain a gift or contract.

Free enterprise The carrying on of free, legitimate business for profit.

Fungible Virtually identical; interchangeable; descriptive of things that belong to a class and that are not identifiable individually.

Gag order Order by judge to be silent about a pending case.

Garnish To receive the debtor's assets that are in the hands of a third party; a remedy given to satisfy a debt owed.

Garnishment A legal proceeding in which assets of a debtor that are in the hands of a third person are ordered held by the third person or turned over to the creditor in full or partial satisfaction of the debt. Procedure to obtain possession of the defendant's property when it is in the custody of another person.

General intangibles Personal property other than goods, accounts, chattel paper, instruments, documents, or money; for example, goodwill, literary rights, patents, or copyrights.

Goods Movable, identifiable items of personal property.

Goodwill An intangible asset based on a firm's good reputation and ability to attract customers.

Grand jury A jury that receives complaints of criminal conduct and returns a bill of indictment if the jury is convinced that a trial should be held.

Greenmail The process by which a firm threatens a corporate takeover by buying a significant portion of a corporation's stock and then selling it back to the corporation at a premium when the corporation's directors and executives, fearing for their positions, agree to buy out the firm.

Guarantor One who promises to answer for the payment of a debt or the performance of an obligation if the person liable in the first instance fails to make payment or to perform.

Guardian A person legally responsible for taking care of another who lacks the legal capacity to do so.

Habeas corpus
The name given to a variety of writs issued to bring a party before a court or judge.

Hacker An outsider who gains unauthorized access to a computer or computer network.

Heirs People who actually inherit property from the decedent.

Holder A person who receives possession of a negotiable instrument by means of a negotiation.

Honorary trust An arrangement that does not meet trust requirements and thus is not enforceable, although it may be carried out voluntarily.

Illusory
Fallacious; nominal as opposed to substantial; of false appearance.

Impeach To question the truthfulness of a witness by means of some evidence.

Implied Presumed to be present under the circumstances; tacit.

Implied consent A concurrence of wills manifested by signs, actions, or facts, or by inaction or silence, that raises a presumption that agreement has been given.

Income beneficiaries Persons with an income interest in a trust.

Indemnify To reimburse a party for a loss suffered by that party for the benefit of another.

Independent contractor A person hired to perform a task but not subject to the specific control of the hiring party.

Indictment A written accusation of criminal conduct issued to a court by a grand jury.

Informational picketing Picketing for the purpose of truthfully advising the public that an employer does not employ members of, or have a contract with, a labor organization.

Inheritance tax A tax assessed on transfers of estate assets at the owner's death. The rates vary depending on the owner's relationship to the recipient.

Injunction A court order prohibiting a person from doing a certain thing or ordering that some particular thing be done.

Injunctive actions Lawsuits asking a court of equity to order a person to do or to refrain from doing some specified act.

Innately dangerous Dangerous as an existing characteristic; dangerous from the beginning.

In personam jurisdiction Authority over a specific person or corporation within the control of the court.

In rem jurisdiction Authority over property or status within the control of the court.

Insolvency Inability to pay one's debts as they become due.

Institutional shareholders A purchaser of shares acting for an institution, such as a pension fund, trust fund, mutual fund, insurance company, or bank.

Insular Isolated from others.

Insured Person or entity covered under an insurance policy.

Intangible asset Property that cannot be touched or felt.

Intended beneficiary A third-party beneficiary who is intended to receive goods or services.

Interested party A party with an interest in the estate, such as a beneficiary, heir, or creditor.

Interstate Between two or more states; between a point in one state and a point in another state.

Intestate share Portion of the estate that a person is entitled to inherit if there is no valid will.

Intestate statutes State statutes that specify who receives property when the decedent does not leave a valid will.

Intestate succession statute Statute that determines who will receive assets if a decedent does not have a valid will disposing of them.

Intrastate Begun, carried on, and completed wholly within the boundaries of a single state.

Intra vires Acts within the scope of the power of a corporation.

Inverse condemnation An action brought by a property owner against a governmental entity that has the power of eminent domain; the property owner typically seeks just compensation for land taken for public use in situations in which the governmental entity does not intend to initiate eminent domain proceedings.

Investment securities Bonds, notes, certificates, and other instruments or contracts from which one expects to receive a return primarily from the efforts of others.

Invidious Repugnant; discrimination stemming from bigotry or prejudice.

Issue Lineal descendants, such as children, grandchildren, and great-grandchildren.

Issuer One who officially distributes an item or document.

Joint venture
A commercial or maritime enterprise undertaken by several persons jointly; an association of two or more persons to carry out a single business enterprise for profit.

Judgment as a matter of law A decision by the court to remove the issue from the jury because there is only one possible answer to the issue.

Judgment debtor A person against whom a judgment has been entered.

Judicial questions Questions that are proper for a court to decide.

Judicial restraint A judicial policy of refusing to hear and decide certain types of cases.

Judicial review The power of the courts to say what the law is.

Junior secured parties Any secured parties whose security interests are subordinate to that of the foreclosing secured party.

Justiciability Capable of a court decision; decidable by a court.

Knocking down The acceptance of a bid by an auctioneer, signified by the falling of the gavel after the announcement that the goods are "Going, going, gone."

Laissez-faire Let (the people) do as they choose; a doctrine opposing governmental interference in economic affairs beyond the minimum necessary for the maintenance of peace and property rights.

Landlocked Surrounded by land owned by others.

Land use regulation Laws that regulate the possession, ownership, and use of real property.

Lapse The expiration or the loss of an opportunity because of the passage of a time limit within which the opportunity had to be exercised.

Law merchant The system of rules, customs, and usages generally recognized and adopted by merchants and traders, which constituted the law for their transactions.

Leachings Oozing of water that contains soil, sediments, chemicals, and other impurities.

Leases Contracts that grant the right to use and occupy realty.

Lessor Individual or company owner who rents out property.

Letters of credit Agreements made at the request of a customer that, upon another party's compliance with the conditions specified in the documents, the bank will honor drafts or other demands for payment.

Libel Any written or printed statement that tends to expose a person to public ridicule or injures a person's reputation.

License A permission granted by a competent authority to do some act that, without such authorization, would be illegal or a trespass or a tort.

Lien creditor One whose debt is secured by a claim on specific property.

Limited partner A limited-partnership member who furnishes certain funds to the partnership and whose liability is restricted to the funds provided.

Limited partnership A partnership where some partners' liability is limited to their contribution.

Liquidate To settle with creditors and debtors and apportion any remaining assets.

Liquidation preferences Priorities given to creditors and owners when the enterprise is terminated and the assets are distributed.

Lockout A plant closing or any other refusal by an employer to furnish work to employees during labor disputes.

Logotypes Identifying symbols.

Mala prohibita Wrong because it is prohibited.

Manifest A list or invoice.

Market value The current price the stock will sell for on a stock exchange.

Marshal To arrange assets or claims in such a way as to secure the proper application of the assets to the claims.

Mechanic's lien Given to certain builders, artisans, and providers of material, a statutory protection that grants a lien on the building and the land improved by such persons.

Mercantile Having to do with business, commerce, or trade.

Merchant A person who regularly deals in goods of this kind, or otherwise, through his or her occupation, holds him- or herself out as having knowledge or skill peculiar to the practice or goods involved in the transaction.

Midnight deadline Midnight of the next business day after the day on which an item is received.

Mining partnership An association of several owners of a mine for cooperation in working the mine.

Money A legally recognized medium of exchange authorized or adopted by a government.

Monopoly The power of a firm to carry on a business or a trade to the exclusion of all competitors.

Moot Abstract; a point not properly submitted to the court for a resolution. A point not capable of resolution.

Moot case A case not properly submitted to a court for resolution because it seeks to determine an abstract question that does not arise upon the existing fact pattern.

Mortgage insurance Insurance that will provide funds to pay the mortgage balance on a home if the insured dies.

Mortgages Conditional transfers of property as security for a debt.

Motion Request to a judge to take certain action. These requests are often in writing.

Mutual assent Agreement by the parties to be bound by exactly the same terms.

Negative clearance Permission given by the EU Commission to a firm to act in a manner that appears to violate EU competition laws.

Negligence Failure to do something a reasonable person would do, or doing something a reasonable and prudent person would not do.

Negligence per se Inherent negligence; negligence without a need for further proof.

Negotiable A document that is transferable either by endorsement and delivery or by delivery alone.

Negotiable instruments Checks, drafts, notes, and certificates of deposit; governed by Article 3 of the UCC, negotiable instruments are used for credit and/or as substitutes for money.

Nolo contendere A plea in a criminal proceeding that has the same effect as a plea of guilty but that cannot be used as evidence of guilt.

North American Free Trade Agreement (NAFTA) A treaty between the United States, Canada, and Mexico designed to create a free-trade zone within North America.

Novations By mutual agreement, substitutions of new contracts in place of preexisting ones, whether between the same parties or with new parties replacing one or more of the original parties.

Nuisance Unlawful use of one's own property so as to injure the rights of another. Wrongs that arise from the unreasonable or unlawful use of a person's own property.

Object code Translation of source code into lower-level language, consisting of numbers and symbols that the computer converts into electronic impulses (machine language).

Objective Capable of being observed and verified without being distorted by personal feelings and prejudices.

Obviousness of hazard A situation in which the hazard in the product is obvious, such as a sharp knife.

Oligopoly An economic condition in which a small number of firms dominates a market, but no one firm controls it.

Operating system computer programs Collections of systems software programs designed to help someone else program or use a computer and that allow the computer to execute programs and manage programming tasks.

Operation of law Certain automatic results that must occur following certain actions or facts because of established legal principles and not as the result of any voluntary choice by the parties involved.

Option A privilege existing in one person, for the giving of consideration, which allows him or her to accept an offer at any time during a specified period.

Output contract A contract that calls for the buyer to purchase all the seller's production during the term of the contract.

Outsiders Directors who are not shareholders or officers.

Overdraft A check or draft written by the drawer for an amount in excess of the amount on account, and accepted by the drawee.

Parol evidence Oral statements.

Parol evidence rule A rule stating that when contracts are in writing, only the writing can be used to show the terms of the contract.

Party Plaintiff or defendant in a lawsuit.

Par value The face value assigned to a stock and printed on the stock certificate.

Perjuries False statements made under oath during court proceedings.

Personal property Property that is not real estate.

Personal representative A person who manages the financial affairs of another or an estate.

Petit jurors Ordinary jurors composing the panel for the trial of a civil or criminal action.

Picketing Union activity in which persons stand near a place of work affected by an organizational drive or a strike so as to influence workers regarding union causes.

Plaintiff A person who files a lawsuit; the person who complains to the court.

Pleadings Statements filed in court specifying the claims of the parties.

Pledge A debtor's delivery of collateral to a creditor, who will possess the collateral until the debt is paid.

Plenary Full; complete; absolute.

Poison pill Any strategy adopted by the directors of a target firm in order to decrease the firm's attractiveness to an acquiring firm during an attempted hostile takeover.

Political questions Questions that would encroach on executive or legislative powers, concerning government, the state, or politics.

Postdeprivation After a deprivation or taking away.

Post-loss Obligations of insurance companies after a covered loss has actually occurred.

Precedents Decided cases that establish legal authority for later cases.

Preempt To seize upon to the exclusion of others. Taken over by the federal government to the exclusion of the state government.

Prejudicial Causing harm, injurious, disadvantageous, or detrimental.

Prepayment clauses Contract clauses that allow the debtor to pay the debt before it is due without penalty.

Prescriptive theory Theory that reports what people should do or what should occur.

Presentment A demand by a holder for the maker or the drawee of a negotiable instrument to accept and/or pay the instrument.

Presumed Assumed.

Preventive law Law designed to prevent harm or wrongdoing before it occurs.

Prima facie At first sight; on its face; something presumed to be true because of its appearance unless disproved by evidence to the contrary.

Privatization The process of going from government ownership of business and other property to private individual ownership.

Privilege A particular benefit or advantage beyond the common advantages of other citizens; an exceptional right, power, franchise, or immunity held by a person, class, or company.

Privity of contract Direct contractual relationship with another party.

Proactive Identifying potential problem areas and participating in resolving them.

Probate The procedure for verifying that a will is authentic and should be implemented.

Probate codes State statutes that deal with the estates of incompetents and people who have died with or without a valid will.

Procedural law The methods of enforcing rights or obtaining redress for the violation of rights.

Professional In the sense used here, a member of a "learned profession," such as a doctor, a lawyer, or an accountant.

Professional corporation A corporation providing professional services by licensed professionals.

Profits The gain made in the enterprise, after deducting the costs incurred for labor, materials, rents, and all other expenses.

Promisee One to whom a promise or commitment has been made.

Promisors Those who make a promise or commitment.

Promissory estoppel A doctrine that prohibits a promisor from denying the making of a promise or from escaping the liability for that promise because of the justifiable reliance of the promisee that the promise would be kept.

Promissory note A written promise to pay a sum certain in money without conditions, either at a preset time in the future or "on demand."

Proprietary Characterized by private, exclusive ownership.

Proprietorship A business with legal rights or exclusive title vested in one individual; a solely owned business.

Pro se Prepared by an individual appearing in his or her own behalf without hiring an attorney.

Prothonotary Title used in some states to designate the chief clerk of courts.

Proximate cause An act that naturally and foreseeably leads to harm or injury to another.

Proxy A person appointed and designated to act for another, especially at a public meeting.

Public domain Lands that are open to public use.

Purported Gave the impression that authority was present.

Quantifiable Capable of exact statement; measurable, normally in numbers.

Quasi in rem jurisdiction Authority obtained through property under the control of the court.

Quasi-judicial Partly judicial; empowered to hold hearings but not trials.

Quasi-legislative Partly legislative; empowered to enact rules and regulations but not statutes.

Quiet title Proceeding to establish that the petitioner is the owner of property.

Ratification Accepting an act that was unauthorized when committed and becoming bound to that act upon its acceptance.

Reactive Permitting others to act first and waiting to see what develops.

Real property Real estate and property permanently attached to real estate.

Rebuttable presumption A legal assumption that will be followed until a stronger proof or presumption is presented.

Receiver An unbiased person appointed by a court to receive, preserve, and manage the funds and property of a party.

Recognitional picketing Prohibited picketing in which a union attempts to force recognition of a union different from the currently certified bargaining representative.

Reformation Equitable remedy whereby a court corrects a written instrument in order to remove a mistake and to make the agreement conform to the terms to which the parties originally had agreed.

Registered agent Person designated by a corporation to receive service of process within the state.

Rejection A refusal to accept what is offered.

Rejects Refuses to accept something when it is offered.

Relative Not capable of exact statement or measurable; comparative.

Remainder beneficiaries Persons with an interest in what remains in the trust corpus after use by the income beneficiaries.

Remand The return of a case to the lower court for additional hearings.

Remanded Sent back; sending a case back to the court from which it came for purposes of having some action taken on it there.

Remedies Methods for enforcing rights or preventing the violation of rights.

Removed A request to have the case moved to another court.

Replevin Action brought to recover possession of goods unlawfully taken. Similar to specific performance, but the object of the contract is not unique; it must be currently unavailable.

Replevy To acquire possession of goods unlawfully held by another.

Repudiation Rejection of an offered or available right or privilege, or of a duty or relation.

Requirements contract A contract in which the seller agrees to provide as much of a product or service as the buyer needs during the contract term.

Residuary clause A clause that disposes of the remainder (the residual) of an estate.

Res judicata A rule of civil law that states that a person will not be sued more than once by the same party for the same civil wrong.

Restitutionary An equitable basis by which the law restores an injured party to the position he or she would have enjoyed had a loss not occurred.

Reverse discrimination Claims by whites that they have been subjected to adverse employment decisions because of their race and the application of employment discrimination statutes designed to protect minorities.

Revests Vests again; is acquired a second time.

Revocation The cancellation, rescission, or annulment of something previously done or offered.

Rhetoric The art or science of using words effectively.

Right of representation Right of children to inherit in their parent's place, if the parent is deceased.

ROM chips (read-only memory chips) Computer chips on which the data and information used to run computer operating systems are affixed; chips that can be "read" by a computer program but generally cannot be changed or altered.

Royalty fee Payment made in exchange for the granting of a right or a license.

RPAPL Abbreviation for New York statute on real estate entitled Real Property Actions and Proceedings Law.

Scienter Guilty knowledge; specifically, one party's prior knowledge of the cause of a subsequent injury to another person.

Seasonably Timely; something occurring in a prompt or timely manner.

Secondary boycotts Union activities meant to pressure parties not involved in the labor dispute and to influence the affected employer.

Secondary liability Conditional responsibility; liability following denial of primary liability.

Secured transactions Credit arrangements, covered by Article 9 of the UCC, in which the creditor retains a security interest in certain assets of the debtor.

Securities exchanges Organized secondary markets in which investors buy and sell securities at central locations.

Security interest Collateral interest taken in the property of another to secure payment of a debt or contract performance.

Separate property states States in which married couples cannot create community property.

Service marks Distinctive symbols designating the services offered by a particular business or individual.

Service of process Delivery of a notice to the person named to inform that person of the nature of the legal dispute.

Severance pay Wages paid upon the termination of one's job.

Shuttle mediation Mediation technique in which the mediator physically separates the parties during the session and then runs messages between them.

Slander Any oral statement that tends to expose a person to public ridicule or injures a person's reputation.

Solicitation A situation in which one person convinces another to engage in a criminal activity.

Source code Human-readable version of the program that gives instructions to the computer.

Sovereign Above or superior to all others; that from which all authority flows.

Specific performance A court order that the breaching party perform the contract as agreed; the object of the contract must be unique.

Stale checks Checks that a bank may dishonor due to their age (over six months old) without regard to the drawer's account balance.

Standing Legal involvement; the right to sue.

Stare decisis To abide by, or adhere to, decided cases; policy of courts to stand by decided cases and not to disturb a settled point of law.

Stated capital The amount of consideration received by the corporation for all shares of the corporation.

Statute of Frauds A statute requiring that specified types of contracts be in writing in order to be enforceable.

Statutory Created by statute; imposed by law.

Strict liability Liability for an action simply because it occurred and caused damage, and not because it is the fault of the person who must pay.

Sua sponte Voluntarily, without prompting or suggestion, of his or her own will or motion.

Subjective Capable of being observed and verified through individual feelings and emotions.

Subject matter jurisdiction The power of a court to hear certain kinds of legal questions.

Subpoena duces tecum A court order to produce evidence at a trial.

Substantially impair Make worth a great deal less, seriously harm or injure, or reduce in value.

Substantive law The portion of law that creates and defines legal rights. It is distinct from the law that defines how laws should be enforced in court.

Suit Lawsuit; the formal legal proceeding used to resolve a legal dispute.

Summons A writ requiring the sheriff to notify the person named that he or she must appear in court to answer a complaint.

Supervening Coming or happening as something additional or unexpected.

Surcharged Assessed a fee by the court for failure to follow fiduciary duties.

Surety A person who promises to pay or to perform in the event the principal debtor fails to do so.

Tenancy in partnership A special form of ownership of property, found only in partnerships, that gives each partner an equal right to possess and to use partnership assets for partnership purposes and that carries a right of survivorship.

Tender An offer to perform; an offer to satisfy an obligation.

Test A case brought to ascertain an important legal principle or right.

Testamentary Pertaining to a will.

Testamentary capacity Sufficient mental capability or sanity to execute a valid will.

Testator A man who makes a will.

Testatrix A woman who makes a will.

Things in action A personal right; an intangible claim not yet reduced to possession, but recoverable in a suit at law.

Time-price differential sales contracts Contracts with a difference in price based on the date of payment, with one price for an immediate payment and another for a payment at a later date.

Title Legal ownership of property; also, evidence of ownership.

Tortfeasor A wrongdoer; one who commits a tort.

Tortious Relating to private or civil wrongs or injuries.

Trademarks Distinctive marks or symbols used to identify a particular company as the source of its products.

Transfer tax Tax on the ability to transfer assets.

Transportation Carrying or conveying from one place to another; the removal of goods or persons from one place to another.

Treble damages A statutory remedy that allows the successful plaintiff to recover three times the damages suffered as a result of the injury.

Trust An arrangement in which legal title, indicated on the deed or other evidence of ownership, is separated from the equitable or beneficial ownership. An arrangement in which one person or business holds property and invests it for another.

Trust deed A legal document that specifies the recipients of a trust, their interests, and how the trust should be managed; also called a deed of trust.

Trustee in bankruptcy The person appointed by the bankruptcy court to act as trustee of the debtor's property for the benefit and protection of the creditors.

Trustees Persons in whom a power is vested under an express or implied agreement in order to exercise the power for the benefit of another.

Ultra vires Acts beyond the scope of the power of a corporation.

Uncollateralized Having no underlying security to guarantee performance.

Unconscionability Condition of being so unreasonably favorable to one party, or so one-sided, as to shock the conscience.

Unconscionable Blatantly unfair and one-sided; so unfair as to shock the conscience.

Underwriters Persons or institutions that, by agreeing to sell securities to the public and to buy those not sold, ensure the sale of corporate securities.

Undue influence Wrongful use of trust and confidence to obtain a gift or contract.

Unfair labor practices Employment or union activities that are prohibited by law as injurious to labor policies.

Uniform Commercial Code (UCC) State statutory provisions covering various aspects of commercial law in the United States.

United Nations Convention on Contracts for the International Sale of Goods (CISG) A treaty developed by the United Nations and intended to provide uniform treatment for contracts involving the international sales of goods.

Unsecured creditor A general creditor; a creditor whose claim is not secured by collateral.

U.S.C. Abbreviation for the United States Code (statutes).

Vested interest A fixed interest or right to something, even though actual possession may be postponed until later.

Vicarious liability Legal responsibility for the wrong committed by another person.

Viruses Computer programs that destroy, damage, rearrange, or replace computer data.

Voir dire The examination of potential jurors to determine their competence to serve on the jury.

Waiver The voluntary surrender of a legal right; the intentional surrender of a right.

Warehousemen Persons engaged in the business of receiving and storing the goods of others for a fee.

Warranties Representations that become part of the contract and that are made by a seller of goods at the time of the sale and that concern the character, quality, or nature of the goods.

Warranty of authority Implied warranties that the agent is an agent for the principal and is permitted to act in this manner.

Wildcat strikes Unauthorized withholding of services or labor during the term of a contract.

Winding up Paying the accounts and liquidating the assets of a business for the purpose of making distributions and dissolving the concern.

With prejudice A dismissal of a lawsuit that also prohibits reinitiating the lawsuit.

Workers' compensation Payments to injured workers based on the provisions in the state workers' compensation statute.

Writ A writing issued by a court in the form of a letter ordering some designated activity.

Writ of execution A court-issued writing that enforces a judgment or decree.

Wrongful death Unlawful death. It does not necessarily involve a crime.

Index

Italics indicate principal cases. Alphabetization is letter-by-letter (e.g., "Bankers" precedes "Bank One").

Index

Alphabetization is letter-by-letter (e.g., "Landlord" precedes "Land pollution").

Frustration of purpose, 352–353
FTAIA. *See* Foreign Trade Antitrust Improvement Act (FTAIA), 1982
FTC. *See* Federal Trade Commission
Fundamental right, 116
Funds transfers. *See* Electronic funds transfers EFTs)
Fungible property, 1039–1040
FUTA (Federal Unemployment Tax Act), 999–1000
FWPCA (Federal Water Pollution Control Amendments), 948

Gag order, 145
Gambling. *See* Wagering
Game theory of business, 37
Garnishment, 93, 640
GATT. *See* General Agreements on Tariffs and Trade
Gender-based discrimination, 983, 1001
    protection, 115
General Agreements on Tariffs and Trade (GATT), 65–66
    copyrights, 1064
    patents, 1071
    trademarks, 1077
General jurisdiction, courts of, 100
General usage standard, 324
Generation-skipping transfer tax, 1111
Genuine assent, 221
Germany's legal system, 20
Gifts, 1035–1038
    causa mortis, 1036, 1038
    executed, 1036
    future gifts, 1036
    inter vivos, 1036
    revocable, 1036
    testamentary, 1098
    transfer of, 1036
    unlawful, 887–888
    validity requirements, 1035–1036
Gift tax, 1104
Glass Ceiling Act of 1991, 994
GLB (Gramm-Leach-Bliley Act), 928
Global business, 54–57
    benefits of, 54–55
    cross-cultural negotiations, 56–57
    methods for entering, 56
Global market, 56
Golden parachutes, 806
Golden rule, 29, 32
Good faith, 523–524, 810
    bargaining, 979
Goods, 309. *See also* Consumer goods
    as collateral, 592–593
    conformity of, 424
    contracts for leasing, 385–387
    contracts for sale of. *See* Sales contracts
    definition, 375, 590
    types of, 592
Goodwill, 728, 790
Gramm-Leach-Bliley Act (GLB), 928
Grand jury, 207
Grant deed, 1012
Grease payment, 59
Great Britain. *See* England
Greenmail, 813
Guarantors, 310
Guardians, 280, 1094

Guayaquil Consensus, 65
Guilty plea, 207

Habeas corpus, 87
Habitability, warranty of, 1022
Hackers, 200
Handbooks, employment, 703–704
Handwritten wills, 1095
Harassment
    hostile environment, 983, 1001
    sexual, 983–986
Harm due to negligence, 180
Health. *See also* Disability
    AIDS/HIV discrimination, 990
    durable power of attorney for health care, 1105
    living wills, 1106
    Medicare, 999
    serious health condition, 996
Heirs
    definition, 1099
    no-contest clauses and, 1099
    pretermitted, 1099
Hindu legal system, 20
Historical theory, 13
Historic overview of corporations, 669–770
HIV discrimination, 990
Holders
    definition, 494, 522
    drawbacks of, 525
    function of, 521
Holders by due negotiation, 425, 532–533
Holders in due course, 522–531
    definition, 494, 523
    effects of status, 525–531
    FTC rule. *See* Federal Trade Commission Holder in Due Course Rule
    requirements to qualify as, 523–525
    statutory limitations, 532
Holographic wills, 1095, 1101
Homestead entry laws, 1013
Homicide, 197
Honorary trust, 1099
Hostile environment harassment, 983, 1001
Housing discrimination, 1012, 1024
HUD (Department of Housing and Urban Development), 1024
Hung jury, 210
Husband and wife. *See* Married couples
Hydrocarbons, 946

ICC (Interstate Commerce Commission), 109
ICJ (International Court of Justice), 73
Identity
    protection, 125–127, 928
    theft, 200, 928
Illegal agreements
    components of, 300
    mala in se, 300–301, 309
    mala prohibita, 300–301, 309
    not *in pari delicto*, 308
    partial illegality and, 308–309
    repentance for, 308
    upholding of, 308–309
    violating public policy, 300, 310
Illegal aliens, 281, 282
Illegality as defense, 531

Illness. *See* Health
Illusory promises, 258, 264
Immediate relinquishment, 351
Immigration Reform Act of 1986, 987
Immunity, sovereign, 11, 71–73
Impeachment, 139–141
Implied-agency rule. *See* Mailbox rule
Implied consent, 90, 177
Implied contracts, 226
Implied-in-fact contract, 228–232
Implied trusts, 1113–1114
Implied warranties, 338, 452–456
Imports, 67–68
    comparison with exports in United States, 54
    customs, passing, 67–68
Impossibility, 352, 353–354
Imputing knowledge, 721
Incapacity, 276
    as defense, 531
Incidental beneficiary, 328, 329
Income beneficiaries, 1108
Incoterms, 414–416
Indemnification, 746–747
Indemnification agreement, 826
Independent contractors, 695–698, 1001
    as agent, 695, 697–698
    responsibility for, 698
Indictment, bill of, 207
Indignity, serious, 173
Indirect infringement, 1067
Indorsees, 520
Indorsements, 516–521
    blank, 517–518
    definition, 516–517
    liability, 548–549
    qualified, 520–521
    restrictive, 518–521
    special, 517
    unqualified, 520
Indorsers, 541–542
Industrial Revolution, 222
Infancy as defense, 530–531
Informal contracts, 222–223
Informational picketing, 976
Infractions, 195
Inherent power, 798
Inheritance, 1036
Inheritance tax, 1103
Initial public offerings (IPOs), 866
Injunctions, 4, 100, 359, 364, 774
Injury
    in fraud, 284
    on job, liability for, 749–751
    Occupational Safety and Health Act, 997–998
    workers' compensation, 1000–1002
Innately dangerous, 460
Innocent misrepresentation, 286
Innocent trespasser, 1039
In pari delicto, 308
In personam jurisdiction, 90–91, 95
In rem jurisdiction, 91–92
Insane persons, 276, 280, 282
Insanity as defense, 204
Insider trading, 876–881
    Sarbanes-Oxley Act, 884–885
Insider Trading and Securities Fraud Enforcement Act of 1988, 881–882
Insider Trading Sanctions Act of 1984, 881